Handbook of
**Social Work in
Health and Aging**

Handbook of
Social Work in
Health and Aging

Barbara Berkman

EDITOR

Sarah D'Ambruoso

ASSOCIATE EDITOR

UNIVERSITY PRESS

2006

Oxford University Press, Inc., publishes works that further
Oxford University's objective of excellence
in research, scholarship, and education.

Oxford   New York
Auckland   Cape Town   Dar es Salaam   Hong Kong   Karachi
Kuala Lumpur   Madrid   Melbourne   Mexico City   Nairobi
New Delhi   Shanghai   Taipei   Toronto

With offices in
Argentina   Austria   Brazil   Chile   Czech Republic   France   Greece
Guatemala   Hungary   Italy   Japan   Poland   Portugal   Singapore
South Korea   Switzerland   Thailand   Turkey   Ukraine   Vietnam

Published by Oxford University Press, Inc.
198 Madison Avenue, New York, New York 10016

www.oup.com

Oxford is a registered trademark of Oxford University Press

Library of Congress Cataloging-in-Publication Data
Handbook of social work in health and aging / Barbara Berkman, editor;
    Sarah D'Ambruoso, associate editor.
        p. cm.
    Includes bibliographical references and index.
    ISBN-13 978-0-19-517372-7
    ISBN 0-19-517372-4
    1. Social work with older people—Handbooks, manuals, etc. 2. Medical social work—
Handbooks, manuals, etc.   I. Berkman, Barbara. II. D'Ambruoso, Sarah.
    HV1451.H34   2006
    362.1'0425—dc22   2005014223

9 8 7 6 5 4 3 2 1

Printed in the United States of America
on acid-free paper

We dedicate this book to older adults and their families worldwide who deserve only the best of social and health care services, and to those social workers who strive every day to help them manage their health with quality of life.

Preface

The leading causes of morbidity and mortality are almost all related to chronic diseases, resulting in acute episodes of illness over many years. The growing number of elderly with chronic disabling illnesses and the increasing need for rehabilitative services to support independent functioning means that patients and families will require more psychological and social assistance in order to address their problems effectively. Therefore, the goal of health care for the older adult is not only to provide state-of-the-art medicine and nursing, but must also focus on how the older person can manage his or her health with quality of life. Thus, we require state-of-the-art social work. Social workers and other health professionals with knowledge in aging will become even more essential to address the complex needs of older people and their families. Elderly people with chronic diseases and activity limitation will represent an increasing percentage of all persons helped by social workers.

Historically, the social work profession has separated the issues of aging from the fields of health and mental health. This has been most evident in social work education where we have developed specializations and concentrations in aging as distinct from those in health, mental health, and disability. However, a growing body of research has shown that social work practice with older adults and their families—once virtually the exclusive concern of social workers in geriatric sites—is increasingly becoming a major focus of care in a range of health and community-based services. For example, we know that in hospitals at least 40% of patients served by social workers are older adults and their caregivers. Given the dramatic growth in the numbers and proportion of older adults in our society, it is time to bring the concepts of aging and health care together in our educational programs, in our practice, in our policy considerations, and in our research.

The *Handbook of Social Work in Health and Aging* is the first reference text to combine the fields of health care, aging, and social work in one concise volume. The *Handbook* was developed to address a critical gap in reference literature among these areas, which are too often treated as discrete entities. The reality is that all social workers deal with issues in health and aging on a daily basis, regardless of practice specialization. And, as the baby boomers age, the impact on practice in health and aging will be dramatic with social workers needed to meet the increasing demands of a growing aging population. Social workers who consider themselves generalists may find their clientele "graying" in the next decade. All social workers need more specialized knowledge about aging, health care, and the resources available to best serve older adults and their families.

The *Handbook of Social Work in Health and Aging* was specifically planned and designed as an all-inclusive and practical reference. It contains 100 original chapters and 13 overviews written by the most experienced and prominent gerontological health care scholars in the United States and across the world. The *Handbook* was designed to provide social work practitioners and educators with up-to-date knowledge of evidence-based best practice guidelines for effectively assessing and treating older adults and their families; new models for intervention in both community-based practice and institutional care; and knowledge of significant policy and research issues in health and aging.

PLANNING AND DEVELOPMENT OF THE *HANDBOOK OF SOCIAL WORK IN HEALTH AND AGING*

Planning for the *Handbook of Social Work in Health and Aging* began in May 2003 and took its lead from the *Social Workers' Desk Reference* (Roberts, 2003). For further guidance, the editors relied on a ten-person editorial board composed of nationally known social work scholars in gerontology and health care. This board was formed in November 2003 to provide oversight and perform editorial support functions for each section of the *Handbook*. In addition, in order to ascertain which topics would be relevant to social workers in practice with older adults, Berkman and D'Ambruoso administered a national survey to over 150 gerontological social work educators

and practitioners from a database that exists thanks to the generosity of the John A. Hartford Foundation in its funding of the Hartford Geriatric Social Work Initiative, a multi-million dollar undertaking to strengthen research, teaching, and practice in gerontology and social work. The survey was inspired by a similar national survey done by Al Roberts, editor of the *Social Workers' Desk Reference* and generated a list of substantive topics for inclusion in the *Handbook*, as well as a list of known experts in the field. Based on the findings of the survey, the editors collaborated with the editorial board to finalize the topical areas, the chapter entries, and the contributor invitations. Contributors to the *Handbook* were selected for their established breadth and depth of knowledge in a given area. We are proud that the *Handbook* includes authors of various ethnic, racial, gender, and sexual identities, reflecting the diversity of the very populations with which we work.

ORGANIZATION OF THE *HANDBOOK*

Following a comprehensive chapter on aging by Nancy Hooyman, the *Handbook of Social Work in Health and Aging* is organized around seven unifying parts: part A, the populations social workers serve; part B, where social workers practice; part C, how social workers practice; part D, local, state, and federal policies affecting social work practice with older adults; part E, international social work and the care of older adults; part F, social work research in aging; and part G, social work education and careers in aging.

Parts A, B, and C are subdivided into sections each of which contain chapters that focus on similar domains. Each subsection has a section editor who has written an overview of the chapters in the section. Parts D, E, F, and G are not subdivided, as we believe the chapters contained in each of these parts relate to a similar domain. Each part has an editor who has written an overview of its chapters.

This *Handbook* is planned as a comprehensive reference text that covers the major areas of social work in health and aging in one volume. The chapters in the *Handbook* present a balanced mix of current research-based knowledge and current key policy decisions, issues, and trends, as well as research needs. Each chapter has been concisely written, synthesized, and integrated in order to create an overview of the topic. In addition, heuristics are used throughout the

Handbook to engage the reader and generate quickly and easily consumed knowledge. The references contained in each chapter are invaluable and can lead the reader to locate even more in-depth knowledge. The ideal way to begin reading this text is to peruse the table of contents, which, we believe, will give the reader a clear, comprehensive view of the field of health and aging. We hope you will be impressed and gratified as you review the depth and wealth of knowledge presented.

Acknowledgments

We must begin by thanking our editorial board, Amanda Smith Barusch, David E. Biegel, Iris Carlton-LaNey, Namkee G. Choi, Linda Harootyan, Nancy Hooyman, Amy Horowitz, Rosalie A. Kane, James E. Lubben, Deborah D. Padgett, Marsha Mailick Seltzer, and Patricia Volland. These brilliant scholars provided the guidance and support for what at times seemed like a monumental endeavor. Without their support, we doubt this book would ever have been undertaken. And, we could not have created this volume without the dedication and skills of our section editors. They worked beyond our expectations (and sometimes their own) to create this single volume knowledge base of social work in health and aging, a feat never before achieved. We also thank our contributors who wrote exceptional chapters that met our stringent guidelines for conciseness while thoroughly covering their subjects. And finally, we cannot begin to offer the appreciation we owe to the board and staff of the John A. Hartford Foundation of New York City. Their support for the Hartford Geriatric Social Work Initiative has created a rebirth of interest in social work in health and aging and generated a growing network of social work specialists in aging who, with other health professionals, will be available to meet the needs of our aging population.

Contents

**Part B
Where Social
Workers Practice**

**Part C
How Social
Workers Practice**

**Part D
Local, State, and Federal
Policies/Regulations
Affecting Older Adults**

Contributors

Margaret E. Adamek, PhD
Professor
School of Social Work
Indiana University

Ronald H. Aday, PhD
Director of Aging Studies
Middle Tennessee State University

Amy L. Ai, PhD, MS, MA, MSW
Associate Professor
University of Washington

Sheila H. Akabas, PhD
Professor and Director
Columbia University School of Social

Gretchen E. Alkema, MSW, LCSW
Doctoral Candidate
Leonard Davis School of Gerontology
University of Southern California

María P. Aranda, PhD, MSW
Associate Professor
School of Social Work
University of Southern California

Amanda Smith Barusch, MSW, PhD
Associate Dean for Research and Doctoral Studies
College of Social Work
University of Utah

A. E. Benjamin, MSW, PhD
Professor
Department of Social Welfare
School of Public Affairs
University of California—Los Angeles

David E. Biegel, PhD
Henry Zucker Professor of Social Work Practice
Mandel School of Applied Social Sciences
Case Western Reserve University

Angela R. Bommarito, MSW
School of Social Work
University of Michigan

Kevin W. Borders, PhD, MSSW, MDiv
Assistant Professor of Research
Kent School of Social Work
University of Louisville

Eva Brewer, MSW
Doctoral Candidate
School of Social Work
University of Wisconsin

Edna Brown, PhD
Research Fellow
Institute for Social Research
University of Michigan

Colette V. Browne, DrPH, MSW
Professor
School of Social Work
University of Hawai'i

Patricia Brownell, PhD, LMSW
Associate Professor
Graduate School of Social Service
Fordham University

Denise Burnette, PhD, MSSW
Professor & Associate Dean
Columbia University

Sandra S. Butler, PhD, MSW
Associate Professor and Interim Director
School of Social Work
University of Maine

Edward R. Canda, PhD, MA, MSW
Professor and Chair
Doctoral Program
The School of Social Welfare
The University of Kansas

Iris Carlton-LaNey, PhD
Professor
School of Social Work
University of North Carolina at Chapel Hill

Lynn Carrigan, MSW, LICSW
Lecturer
School of Social Work
University of Washington

Kimberly M. Cassie, MSSW, MA
Doctoral Student
College of Social Work
University of Tennessee

Letha A. Chadiha, PhD, MSW
Associate Professor
School of Social Work
University of Michigan

Rosemary Kennedy Chapin, PhD
Professor & Director of the Office of Aging and
    Long Term Care
University of Kansas School of Social Welfare

Li-Mei Chen, MSW, PhD
Assistant Professor
George Warren Brown School of Social Work
Washington University in St. Louis

Iris Chi, DSW
Golden Age Association
Francis Wu Chair Professor for Chinese Elders
School of Social Work
University of Southern California

Sandra Stukes Chipungu, PhD, MSW
Associate Professor
School of Social Work
Howard University

Namkee G. Choi, PhD
Professor
School of Social Work
University of Texas at Austin

Wesley T. Church II, PhD
Assistant Professor
School of Social Work
University of Alabama

Sandra Edmonds Crewe, PhD, MSW
Associate Professor
School of Social Work
Howard University

Denis Cronin, MSW, PhD
Educational Psychologist
School of Social Work
Columbia University

Sherry M. Cummings, PhD
Associate Professor
University of Tennessee

JoAnn Damron-Rodriguez, LCSW, PhD
Adjunct Professor
University of California

Louisa Daratsos, LCSW, ACSW
Psychosocial Coordinator for Oncology/Palliative Care
Veterans Affairs New York Harbor Health Care System
Brooklyn Campus

Osei Kofi Darkwa, PhD
Principal
Ghana Telecom University College

Joan K. Davitt, PhD, MSS, MLSP
Assistant Professor
School of Social Policy and Practice
University of Pennsylvania

Ruth E. Dunkle, PhD, MSW
Professor
Wilbur J. Cohen Collegiate Chair
University of Michigan

Burton D. Dunlop, PhD
Director of Research
The Center on Aging
Stempel School of Public Health
Florida International University

Jennifer Elkins, MSSW
Doctoral Candidate
School of Social Work
Columbia University

Charles A. Emlet, PhD, ACSW
Associate Professor of Social Work
University of Washington

Susan M. Enguidanos, MPH, PhD
Director, Research Center
Partners In Care Foundation

Elizabeth Lehr Essex, MSS, PhD
Hartford Faculty Scholar
Department of Social Work
College of Health Professions
Governors State University

Richard Benoit Francoeur, PhD, MSW, MS
Assistant Professor
School of Social Work
Columbia University

Judith G. Gonyea, PhD
Associate Professor
School of Social Work
Boston University

Lisa P. Gwyther, MSW
Associate Professor
Department of Psychiatry
Duke University Center for Aging
Duke University

Sharon M. Keigher, AM, PhD, ACSW
Professor
Helen Bader School of Social Welfare
University of Wisconsin-Milwaukee

Colleen Galambos, DSW, MSW
Professor and Director
School of Social Work
University of Missouri-Columbia

Lauren B. Gates, PhD
Research Director
Workplace Center
School of Social Work
Columbia University

Zvi D. Gellis, PhD
Associate Professor & Director
Center for Mental Health and Aging
State University of New York at Albany

Scott Miyake Geron, MSW, PhD
Associate Professor of Social Welfare and Policy
Director and PI, Institute for Geriatric Social Work
Boston University School of Social Work

Robyn Golden, MSW, LCSW
Director, Older Adult Programs
Rush University Medical Center

Gladys González-Ramos, Ph.D.
Associate Professor of Social Work
Ehrenkranz School of Social Work
New York University

Muriel Gray, MSW, PhD
Associate Professor
School of Social Work
University of Maryland-Baltimore

Irene A. Gutheil, DSW
Henry C. Ravazzin Professor of Gerontology
Graduate School of Social Service
Fordham University

Nancy R. Hooyman, PhD
Hooyman Endowed Professor in Gerontology
School of Social Work
University of Washington

Amy Horowitz, DSW/PhD
Senior Vice President for Research
Lighthouse International

Chang-ming Hsieh, PhD
Associate Professor
Jane Addams College of Social Work
University of Illinois at Chicago

Ruth Huber, PhD
Professor, Director
Doctoral Program
Kent School of Social Work
University of Louisville

Robert B. Hudson, PhD
Professor of Social Policy
School of Social Work
Boston University

Hae-Sook Jeon, MSW
Doctoral Candidate
University of Michigan

Rosalie A. Kane
Division for Health Services Research and Policy
School of Public Health
University of Minnesota

Lenard W. Kaye, DSW/PhD
Director & Professor
Center on Aging and School of Social Work
University of Maine

David M. Keepnews, PhD
Director, Office of Policy Development
New York Academy of Medicine

Waldo C. Klein, Ph.D., M.S.W.
Professor
School of Social Work
University of Connecticut

Terry L. Koenig, LSCSW, PhD
Assistant Professor
School of Social Welfare
University of Kansas

Jordan I. Kosberg, PhD, ACSW
Endowed Chair
School of Social Work
The University of Alabama

Ji Seon Lee, PhD, MSW, MPA
Assistant Professor
Graduate School of Social Service
Fordham University

Jonghyun Lee, MSW, M.Ed.
PhD candidate and adjunct lecturer
Simmons College Graduate School of Social Work

Sylvia Leibbrandt, MSW
Doctoral Candidate
Mandel School of Applied Social Science
Case Western Reserve University

Lydia W. Li, PhD, MSW
Assistant Professor
School of Social Work
University of Michigan

Elizabeth Lightfoot, PhD
Assistant Professor
School of Social Work
University of Minnesota

Wendy Lustbader
Affiliate Assistant Professor
School of Social Work
University of Washington

Kelley R. Macmillan, PhD, MSW
Project Coordinator
Office of Aging and Long Term Care
School of Social Welfare
The University of Kansas

Sandra Magaña, PhD, MSW
Assistant Professor
School of Social Work and Waisman Center
University of Wisconsin-Madison

Kathleen McInnis-Dittrich, MSW, PhD
Associate Professor
Graduate School of Social Work
Boston College

M. Joanna Mellor, DSW
Assistant Professor
Wurzweiler School of Social Work
Yeshiva University

Helen Miltiades, PhD
Department of Health Science
Gerontology Program
Fresno, California

Robert L. Mollica, EdD
Senior Program Director
National Academy for State Health Policy

Ailee Moon, PhD
Associate Professor
Department of Social Welfare
University of California—Los Angeles

Barbara Morano, LCSW-C, MSW, CMC
Geriatric Care Manager
Morano Consultants

Carmen Morano, PhD, LCSW-C
Associate Professor and Chair
Aging Specialization
School of Social Work
University of Maryland

Nancy Morrow-Howell, PhD
Ralph & Muriel Pumphrey Professor of Social Work
George Warren Brown School of Social Work
Washington University in St. Louis

Jean Correll Munn, MSW
Doctoral Candidate
University of North Carolina at Chapel Hill

Edna Naito-Chan, PhD, MSW, LCSW
Staff Research Associate
University of California

Mitsuko Nakashima, PhD, MSW
Assistant Professor
School of Social Work
University of Maryland

Shingo Nakayama, PhD
Associate Professor
Department of Social Work
Kagoshima International University
Kagoshima City, Japan

Matthias J. Naleppa, PhD
Associate Professor
Virginia Commonwealth University

Holly B. Nelson-Becker, PhD, LCSW
Assistant Professor & Hartford Faculty Scholar
The School of Social Welfare
The University of Kansas

F. Ellen Netting, PhD
Professor
School of Social Work
Virginia Commonwealth University

Greg O'Neill, PhD
Director, National Academy on an Aging Society
The Gerontological Society of America
Washington, DC

Elizabeth Ozanne, PhD, MSW, MA
Associate Professor
Head of Aging and Long Term Care Research Unit
School of Social Work
The University of Melbourne

Martha N. Ozawa, PhD
Bettie Bofinger Brown Distinguished Professor of
   Social Policy
George Warren Brown School of Social Work
Washington University in St. Louis

Deborah K. Padgett, PhD
Professor
School of Social Work
New York University

Michael W. Parker, DSW, LCSW, LTC
(U.S. Army Retired)
Assistant Professor
Department of Geriatrics and Gerontology
University of Alabama Birmingham
Associate Professor
School of Social Work
University of Alabama

Judith Phillips, MSc, CQSW, PhD
 Professor of Social Work and Gerontology
Department of Applied Social Sciences
University of Wales Swansea

Cynthia Cannon Poindexter, MSW, Ph.D.
Associate Professor
School of Social Service
Fordham University

Vera Prosper, MSW, Ph.D.
Senior Policy Analyst; Principal
New York State Office for the Aging
Adjunct Instructor
Gerontology and Public Policy
University at Albany
State University of New York

Michelle Putnam, PhD
Assistant Professor
George Warren Brown School of Social Work
Washington University in St. Louis

Jane A. Rafferty, MA
Doctoral Candidate
Department of Sociology
University of Michigan

Victoria H. Raveis, PhD
Associate Professor of Clinical Sociomedical Sciences
Mailman School of Public Health
Center for the Psychosocial Study of Health and
  Illness
Columbia University

James R. Reinardy, MA, MSW, PhD
Associate Professor
University of Minnesota-Twin Cities

Siyon Rhee, MSW, PhD
Professor
School of Social Work
California State University at Los Angeles

Virginia E. Richardson, PhD
Professor
College of Social Work
The Ohio State University

Joyce Grahl Riley BSN, MA
Associate Director
Health Administration and Policy Program
University of Maryland Baltimore County

Max B. Rothman, JD, LLM
Executive Director
The Center for Aging
Stempel School of Public Health

Philip A. Rozario, PhD, MSW
Assistant Professor
School of Social Work
Adelphi University

Leah A. Ruffin, MSW
Senior Research Associate
Center on Aging
University of Maine

Marsha Mailick Seltzer, PhD
Professor
Waisman Center
University of Wisconsin

Nancy W. Sheehan, PhD
Associate Professor
School of Family Studies
University of Connecticut

Tazuko Shibusawa, PhD
Associate Professor
School of Social Work
Columbia University

W. June Simmons, MSW
President/CEO
Partners in Care Foundation

Kelsey Simons, MSW, PhD
Post-Doctoral Fellow
Institute of Gerontology
Wayne State University

Margaret Souza, PhD, LCSW
Assistant Professor
SUNY/Empire State College

Susan Stark, PhD, OTR/L
Instructor
School of Medicine
Program in Occupational Therapy
Washington University in St. Louis

Cynthia Stuen, PhD/DSW
Senior Vice President for Education
Lighthouse International

Susan K. Tomita, MSW, PhD
Division of Gerontology and Geriatric Medicine
Harborview Medical Center
University of Washington-Seattle

Ronald W. Toseland, PhD
Professor & Director
Institute of Gerontology
University at Albany
State University of New York

Fredda Vladeck, LMSW
Director
Aging in Place Initiative
United Hospital Fund

Betsy Vourlekis, PhD
Professor Emeritis
School of Social Work
University of Maryland

Deborah P. Waldrop, MSW, PhD
Assistant Professor
School of Social Work
University at Buffalo

Kathleen Wilber, MSW, PhD
Mary Pickford Foundation Professor of
    Gerontology
Professor of Health Services Administration
Leonard Davis School of Gerontology
University of Southern California

Carter Catlett Williams, MSW
Pioneer Convener/Consultant
Pioneer Network
Rochester, New York

Cindy C. Wilson, PhD, CHES
Professor and Faculty Development Director
Uniformed Services University of the Health Sciences

Nancy L. Wilson, MA
Associate Professor of Medicine—Geriatrics
Huffington Center on Aging
Baylor College of Medicine

Monika White, PhD
CEO/President
Center for Healthy Aging
Adjunct Professor of Gerontology
University of Southern California

Jong Won Min, PhD, MSW
Assistant Professor
School of Social Work
San Diego State University

Richard Yakimo, PhD, APRN, BC
Assistant Professor
School of Nursing
Southern Illinois University

Greta Yoder-Slater, PhD
Assistant Professor
Ball State University

Eunkyung Yoon, PhD, MSW
School of Social Work
University of Georgia

Karen Zgoda, MSW
Doctoral Candidate
Graduate School of Social Work
Boston College

Sheryl Zimmerman, PhD
Professor
University of North Carolina at Chapel Hill

Bradley D. Zodikoff, PhD
Assistant Professor
School of Social Work
Adelphi University

Sara M. Zoff, MSW
A. H. Wilder Foundation

Introduction
Our Aging Society

DEMOGRAPHY OF AGING

The dramatic growth of the older population is the most compelling factor underlying the importance of this *Handbook of Social Work in Health and Aging*. Given such growth, social workers in all practice arenas and with all age groups increasingly encounter older adults and their families in the child welfare system, family services, schools, mental health centers, AIDS treatment clinics, and among the homeless. In 1900, older adults formed approximately 4% of the U.S. population, less than 1 in 25. In the past hundred years, the older population increased twelve-fold, compared with a threefold increase in those under age 65; older adults now comprise approximately 35 million or 13% of the total population. Moreover, the number of people over age 65 is projected to double to more than 70 million by the year 2030, approximately 21% of the U.S. population (Administration on Aging, 2002).

With a 300% increase from 1960 to 2000 among the "oldest old," those aged 85 and over now comprise more than 12% of the aging population. Although the young old (ages 65–74) currently form 53% of the older population, these proportions will shift to 44% young-old and 23% oldest-old by 2050. Among the oldest-old there was a 35% growth in "centenarians" from 1990 to 2000 (Administration on Aging, 2002; U.S. Bureau of the Census, 2001a). Because the oldest-old tend to have multiple physical and cognitive impairments and declining levels of functional disability, they are disproportionately represented in long-term care settings and publicly funded social and health services, where they and their families interact with social workers (U.S. Bureau of the Census, 2002).

Baby Boomers

The most striking increase in size of any age group in the 2000 census was the 49% jump in those 45 to 54 years old, prefiguring the baby boomer's entry into the 65-plus cohort, which begins in 2010. One in 26 baby boomers is expected to live to be 100 by 2025. By the year 2050, the older population (age 65 plus) is projected to comprise 20% of the U.S. population (U.S. Bureau of the Census, 2001, 2002). This significant percent increase in older adults will profoundly affect the demand for social, health, and long-term care services. With less than a ten-year window to prepare for the coming "Age Boom," the unprecedented jump in the number of older adults through the first half of this century has created a sense of a "demographic crisis" (Alliance for Aging Research, 2002).

Life Expectancy

These generational shifts are occurring because of increases in life expectancy (average length of time that one can expect to live based on the year born). Life expectancy in America has gone from 47 years in 1900 to 76.9 years currently, and is projected to reach 77.6 years in 2005 and 82.6 years in 2050. Approximately four out of five individuals can now expect to reach age 65, at which point there is a better than 50% chance of living past age 80. A five- to six-year gender difference in life expectancy is projected, with females born in 2000 expected to live to age 79.5 and men to age 74.1 (National Center for Health Statistics, 2000b; Population Reference Bureau, 2003). These projections do not, however, take into account potentially new diseases that could differentially affect mortality risks for men and women. If AIDS continues to infect younger men, the gender differential in life expectancy could increase. On the other hand, women's growing death rates due to heart attacks and stroke could narrow such gender differences over time. Most gains in life expectancy are not the result of medical advances in old age, but rather are due to better medical care and eradication of diseases at early ages (e.g., influenza, TB).

Worldwide Trends

All regions of the world are experiencing an increase in the absolute and relative size of their older populations. The number of elders in the world is expected to grow from approximately 420 million in 2000 to 761 million in 2025. In fact, one out of every seven people in the world will be 65 years or older by 2025 (U.S. Bureau of the Census, 2001b; 2002). Differences between industrialized and developing countries are dramatic. In 2000, the population age 65 and older for most Western European countries was estimated to be greater than 15%. With the highest life expectancy in the world, Japan is experiencing the world's most rapid rate increase of the older population—from 7% in 1970 to 17% in 2000. In contrast, only 3% of the population of South Asia and Sub-Saharan Africa are elders, largely because of high fertility and mortality rates. Nevertheless, as a result of improved sanitation, nutrition, and medical care, the less-developed regions of the world expect to show a nearly fivefold increase in their oldest citizens, from 3.8% in 1975 to 17% in 2075, with the most rapid growth among the oldest old. By the year 2025, only 30% of older adults are projected to live in industrialized nations, while 70% will be in developing countries (U.S. Bureau of the Census, 2001b; Population Reference Bureau, 2003; United Nations, 2001).

Normal Aging and Disease-Related Processes

Social workers need to understand the differences between normal aging and disease-related processes. As a universal biological phenomenon that begins with birth, aging refers to changes—good, bad, and neutral—that occur throughout the lifespan. After age 30, however, all physiological systems—sensory, organ, respiratory, and cardiovascular—tend to reflect normal decline and increased vulnerability to disease. Individuals cope in different ways with this gradual accumulation of irreversible functional losses. Even with 50% deterioration in many of these systems, an older person can still function adequately by modifying their environment (International Longevity Center, 1999). Wide variation in the aging process within and across individuals results from differences in heredity, diet, exercise, socioeconomic status, and living conditions.

Health status encompasses (1) the presence or absence of disease and (2) the degree of disability in level of functioning. More than 80% of older adults have at least one chronic condition, but this does not necessarily interfere with their activities of daily living or ADLs (e.g., cooking, getting dressed, bathing, toileting). Approximately 20% of elders have a mild degree of disability that alters daily routines, with only about 4% severely disabled and 2% confined to bed by chronic conditions (Merck Institute, 2002; NCHS, 2000a). The extent of disability, the need for help with daily activities, and the type of supports available typically determine whether older adults can remain in their own homes, or may need to move to an assisted living facility, adult family home, or nursing home (Lubben & Gironda, 2003). Because of inequities experienced across the life span, older women and ethnic minorities are most likely to experience disabling illness along with poverty and inadequate housing— problems that social workers must address.

Although normal aging does not result in significant declines in intelligence, learning, and memory, the prevalence of mental disorders ranges from 5 to 45% of the older population, depending on whether samples include older residents in institutional settings (Gatz & Smyer, 2001). In some instances, these represent mental illnesses that have occurred across the life span. Depression is the most common mental disorder in late life (Blazer, Hybels, & Pieper, 2001). The likelihood of dementia, particularly Alzheimer's, increases with advancing age, with some estimates as high as 50% for those age 85 and over (Institute of Medicine, 2001). Social workers are committed to enhancing the quality of life, sense of competence, and independence of older adults, regardless of elders' extent of disability or functional health.

HETEROGENEITY OF THE OLDER POPULATION

Ethnicity and Race

The older population is becoming more ethnically and racially diverse. Currently, a smaller proportion of ethnic minorities are over 65 and a larger percent are younger adults when compared to the white population. Those 65 and older comprise 8% of African Americans, 5.6% of Latinos, 2.4% of Asians/Pacific Islanders, and less than 1% of American Indians, compared to 14.4% of Caucasians. These differences result primarily from both the higher fertility and mortality rates among the nonwhite population under age 65. However, these proportions will shift dramatically when the large percent of ethnic minority children who, unlike their parents and grandparents, reach old age. The percent of people of color over age 65 is projected to increase from approximately 16% in 2002 to 34% by 2050, faster than the rate of growth among the Caucasian population (NCHS, 2000; U.S. Bureau of the Census, 2002). Given these demographics, it is imperative that gerontological social workers be culturally competent.

Gender

Women form the fastest-growing segment of the older population, especially among the oldest old, making the aging society both in the United States and globally primarily a female one. Because of women's longer life expectancy, they represent 55% of the population aged 65 to 74 and 71% of those over age 85 (U.S. Bureau of the Census, 2000). However, men who survive beyond age 85 are likely to be in better health and have a similar life expectancy—or even more remaining years than women (Calasanti & Slevin, 2002; Moen, 2001).

Sexual Orientation

Estimates of the number of older gay men and lesbians range from as low as 3% to as high as 18 to 20%. This translates into at least two million older lesbians and gay men, which will likely increase to over six million by the year 2030 (Cahill et al., 2001; Wojciechowski, 1998). As a result of their history of disadvantage, marginalization, and invisibility, lesbians and gay elders may encounter obstacles in both receiving and providing care, including discrimination from providers, limited access to supportive services, and lack of legal protection for their partners and other loved ones (Barranti & Cohen, 2001; Brotman, Cornier, & Ryan, 2001; Brotman, Ryan, & Cormier, 2003; Cahill et al., 2001; Clunis, Fredriksen-Goldsen, Freeman, & Nystrom, in press, Gabbay & Wahler, 2002).

Geographic Location

With regard to geographic diversity, about 52% of all adults age 65 and over live in nine states, with the greatest proportions in Florida (17.6%) and Pennsylvania (16%) and lowest in Alaska (5.7%) and Utah (8.5%). In some states, such as Florida, migration of older adults explains the increase, while in others, such as West Virginia and South Dakota, migration of young people out of the state leaves a greater proportion (15%) of older people. Residential relocation is relatively rare for older adults. In a typical year, less than 5% of older persons move compared with 18% of people under age 65 (Administration on Aging, 2000; 2002). Approximately 23% of elders live in rural areas, 21% in cities, and the largest cohort (56%) in suburbs, reflecting the "graying of the suburbs" (AARP, 2002).

Education

Today's older population is better educated, with 70% of those over age 65 being high school graduates compared with less than 20% in 1960. Nevertheless, racial and gender differences in education and socioeconomic status are striking. Among Caucasians age 65 and older in 2000, 74% had completed high school, compared with 51% of African American and 35% of Latino counterparts. Because educational level is closely associated with economic well-being, these differences impact poverty levels of persons of color across the life span, and particularly in old age (Elder & Liker, 2000; Stoller & Gibson, 2000).

Socioeconomic Status

Older adults comprise only 3% of the U.S. labor force, with 17% of men and 9.7% of women over age 65 reporting that they work full time outside the home, although many older adults prefer and seek part-time work (U.S. Bureau of the Census, 2002). Social Security is the primary source of income for most retired Americans; of the 90% of older adults who receive Social Security; approximately 66% rely on it for at least 50% of their income. In 2000, only 22% of elders identified earnings and 41% private pensions as primary income. In fact, Social Security benefits underlie the improved economic status of older adults. Currently, over 10.1% of elders are poor, compared to 35% in the late 1950s; another 6.3% of older adults are classified as "near poor" (Administration on Aging, 2002; Kingson & Williamson, 2001; National Center for Policy Analysis, 2003). This improved economic status as a whole, however, overlooks the growing poverty rates among older women, elders of color, the oldest old, and those living alone. Older women are nearly twice as likely to be poor as their male counterparts (13% vs. 7%), and older African American and Latino women are the poorest and most functionally disabled groups in our society. Poverty is highest among elders in central cities and rural communities (U.S. Bureau of the Census, 2002; Women's Institute for a Secure Retirement, 2003).

LIFE COURSE PERSPECTIVE

Since the meaning of chronological age varies by culture and social class, "people as they age" may be a more useful concept than older adults. A life course perspective, rather than a focus only on elders, recognizes (1) the reciprocity or interdependence across multiple generations; (2) the presence of older adults in settings that typically serve "younger populations"; and (3) the interplay among generational influences, the larger social and historical contexts, and economic and health inequalities, which results in cumulative disadvantage across the life span for historically disadvantaged populations (Elder & Johnson, 2001).

Given social work's mission of social justice, social workers are pivotal in addressing economic inequities and health disparities across the life span. While the likelihood of chronic illness grows with age, the origins of risk for chronic health conditions begin in early childhood or earlier (World Health Organization, 2002). Regardless of age, chronic disability magnifies the risk of poverty throughout the life course. Furthermore, this risk continues to be impacted by socioeconomic status and associated life experiences across the life cycle (Burton & Whitfield, 2003; Whitfield & Hayward, 2003). Similarly, childhood conditions explain a substantial portion of the race gap in men's mortality, operating indirectly through adult socioeconomic achievement, not lifestyle factors (Warner & Hayward, 2002). Alternatively, gains in socioeconomic status are related to people living longer and healthier lives (Lynch, Smith, Kaplan, & House, 2000). Life course research aims to uncover the patterns of relationship among resources or "social capital" earlier in the life span and their effects on different groups within the aging population (O'Rand, 2001, 2003). The importance of interventions early in the life course to enhance quality of life in old age was articulated by the 2003 Gerontological Society of America conference theme, *Our Future Selves: Research, Education, and Service for Early Development and Childhood in an Aging Society.*

Families as They Age

About 66% of older adults live with a partner, child, or sibling, although not necessarily in a multigenerational household, and nearly 94% have living relatives (Administration on Aging, 2002; Connidis, 2001). The 6% without family ties, particularly women and elders of color, typically turn to support from friends, neighbors, acquaintances, and community gatekeepers (Moen, Erickson, & Dempster-McClain, 2000). Nearly 60% of the young old are married and live with a spouse in an independent household, although the percent living with a spouse declines with age. Given the higher rates of widowhood among women than men, older men (83%) are more likely to live in a family setting, generally with a partner, than are women (59%). Accordingly, women represent 80% of the individuals who live alone. Although the majority of older parents do not live (and prefer not to) with adult children, they typically have at least one child nearby whom they regularly see (Administration on Aging, 2002). However, declining health, loss of a former caregiver or partner, desire for companionship, and lower income often precipitate a move to an adult child's home (Wilmouth, 2000).

With increased life expectancy, the multigenerational family has also grown. Among Americans over age 35, 80% are members of a three-generation family, and 16% of four generations (Bengtson, 2001, Bengtson, Putney, & Wakeman, 2004). Parents and children may now share five decades of life, siblings eight, and grandparents and grandchildren three or more decades that tend to be characterized by emotional closeness (Bengtson, Biblarz, & Roberts, 2002; Gonyea, forthcoming, 2006). This modified extended family, which appears to be stronger now than ever before, is characterized by moderate face-to-face contact and greater geographic distances between family members, yet high rates of communication (often electronically) and strong norms of filial obligation (Bengtson, Biblarz, & Roberts, 2002; Bengtson, Putney, & Wakeman, 2004; Navaie-Waliser, Feldman, Gould, Levine, Kuerbis, & Doneland, 2001).

Generally, families experience a pattern of reciprocal support between older and younger members, with older adults providing support to children and grandchildren as long as they are able (Silverstein, Conroy, Wang, Giarrusso, & Bengtson, 2002). Yet increased longevity also means extended years of caring for community-residing older relatives with chronic illness or disability (Bengtson, 2001; Bengtson, Biblarz, & Roberts, 2004). Families, who provide approximately 80% of such care, are a significant factor influencing whether an older adult will live in a nursing home. Paradoxically, because of reduced fertility, fewer people within each generation may be available in the future to provide care for older relatives. Caregiving is not only from younger to older generations. For example, with the increased life expectancy of adult children with developmental disabilities or mental illness,

more elders are providing care for their adult children while faced with their own declining health.

Women—daughters, daughters in law, and wives—form 80% of family caregivers of elders. In fact, nearly 40% of baby boomers are part of the "sandwich generation," facing demands from employment, dependent children, and older relatives (Brody, 2004; Ingersoll-Dayton, Neal, & Hammer, 2001). The financial, physical, and emotional burdens (Beach, Schulz, Yee, & Jackson, 2000; Connell, Janevic, & Gallant, 2001; Polen & Green, 2001; Tennstedt, 1999) and, more recently, gains of caring for older family members are extensively documented (Kramer, 1997; Beach et al., 2000; Narayn, Lewis, Tornatore, Hepburn, & Corcoran-Perry, 2001; Sherrell, Buckwalter, & Morhardt, 2001). Children and spouses typically turn to institutionalization as a "last resort" when faced with their own illness, severe family strain, or exhaustion of resources (Seltzer & Li, 2000). Although most family caregivers do not utilize formal services, psychoeducational programs, support groups, and respite care are found to be relatively effective interventions in reducing caregiver stress, all of which have implications for social work roles (Burgio, Stevens, Guy, Roth, & Haley, 2003; Gartska, McCallion, & Toseland, 2001; Mittelman, 2002; Morano, 2000; National Respite Network and Resource Center, 2002; Schulz et al., 2002; Toseland, Peak, & Smith, 1990).

The heterogeneity of American families, within the context of greater economic uncertainties, is also increasing with the growth in divorce and blended families, numbers of people living alone, single-parent households, and never-married individuals living together in other nontraditional family arrangements (e.g., grandparents raising grandchildren, gay and lesbian families, and single parents choosing to raise children on their own). Given this diversity, it is imperative to broadly define family by interactional quality, not necessarily by members' living together or blood ties. Kinship, a matter of social definition, varies by culture and socioeconomic class. This voluntary intergenerational latent kin matrix is typically activated in times of need (Bengtson, Putney, & Wakeman, 2004). For example, grandparents as primary caregivers to grandchildren, and the extended network of fictive kin—"play relatives," godparents, and friends—are defined as family among many ethnic minorities, and chosen or "friendship" families are a source of support for many gay men and lesbians.

The growth of the multigenerational family is illustrated by the fact that among the 80% of older parents currently, 94% are grandparents and nearly 50%

great grandparents. Similarly, approximately 96% of all persons have at least one grandparent alive when they reach age 20 (Uhlenberg & Kirby, 1998). Women may experience grandparenthood for more than 40 years, since the transition to grandparenting typically occurs in middle age, not old age (Giarrusso, Silverstein, & Bengtson, 1996; Szinovacz, 1998). Most grandparents derive satisfaction from their role and interaction with grandchildren (Davies & Williams, 2002). Grandparents have traditionally provided care for grandchildren, especially across families of color and immigrant families (Cox, 2002; Pruchno, 1999). What has changed in the past two decades is the rapid growth of grandparents (or great grandparents) who are the primary or sole caregivers for grandchildren (Fuller-Thompson & Minkler, 2001). In fact, such skipped generation households (e.g., the absence of the parental generation) are the fastest growing type (Wallace, 2001). Similarly, the number of children living in a home with both a parent and grandparent present has declined (Casper and Bianchi, 2002).

In 2000, 4.5 million children under the age of 18 lived in grandparent-headed households, and about 2.1 million were being raised solely by their grandparents with no parents present. These grandparent caregivers have been called the "silent saviors" of the family (Goodman & Silverstein, 2001), and face considerable stress and numerous obstacles when dealing with child welfare, health care, TANF (Temporary Assistance for Needy Families), and school systems (Giarrusso, Silverstein, & Feng, 2000; Green & Berrick, 2002; Minkler, 1999; Minkler, Berrick, & Needell, 1999).

AGING POLICY ISSUES

The Older Americans Act, Social Security, Medicare, and Medicaid are the primary federal policies and programs responding to these demographic, health, and familial changes. The Older Americans Act (OAA), passed in 1965, funds a wide range of programs that can help older adults remain in their homes. Services encompass access (information and referral, transportation, case management); in-home (homemaker, chore, respite, home health care); community (senior centers, meals on wheels, adult day care, elder abuse prevention, advocacy); and supports for family caregivers (respite, counseling, education) through the National Family Caregiver Support Program. Assistive technology, such as Lifeline and Life Safety Systems, voice-activated phones, and com-

puter reminders, is also a growing resource to enable elders to remain in their own homes, although available primarily to those with the ability to cover technology-associated costs. When older adults need a higher level of care, planned housing options other than nursing home care are available: congregate housing, continuing care communities, assisted living, and adult foster care/homes. Only about 5% of older adults live in a nursing home at a given point in time, although approximately 50% require such care during their lives. Because older adults and their families typically turn first to the growing number of non-nursing home options, nursing home residents are generally sicker, older, suffering from dementia, and require more intensive services than their counterparts 20 to 30 years ago. Nearly 50% of all nursing home residents are single women or widows without close family (NCHS, 2000).

While the Older Americans Act funds primarily social services for elders, Medicare and Medicare are the primary funding sources for health and long-term care. Medicare, however, covers less than 50% of the total health expenditures of older adults, since it does not pay for long-term care and only partially for prescription drugs (Schoen & Cooper, 2003). Medicaid does pay for nursing home care, but only for those who fall below a certain income level. In recent years, most states have petitioned the federal health care authority for Medicaid waivers to provide community-based options, such as adult day care and home health aids. Ongoing cuts in Medicaid, however, are limiting services at the state level. As noted above, the crisis facing our society is not the growth of the older population per se, but increased economic and racial inequities across the life span and into old age. Inadequate public policies and programs for elders and other historically disadvantaged populations have created such life course inequities, which are now exacerbated by trends of privatization, individualization of risk, and current economic difficulties in the United States and worldwide (Parrott, Mills, & Bengtson, 2000; O'Rand, 2003).

LOOKING TOWARD THE FUTURE

Senior boomers are projected to be healthier and of higher economic status than current cohorts of elders. If the trend toward early retirement continues, they may experience up to one third of their lives outside full-time employment. Senior boomers are likely to remain productive, not necessarily in the traditional sense of paid work, but by engaging in activities that contribute to society, whether through child care, volunteer work, leadership in organizations, and assistance to family, friends, and community members (Hinterlong, Morrow-Howell, & Sheraden, 2001). With older adults as our most underutilized societal resource, social workers can provide leadership in developing strategies to build upon elders' knowledge, wisdom, and time. Cross-generational coalitions addressing societal needs, such as Generations United and new intergenerational program models, may serve to reduce competition among age groups for limited resources. However, the increasing policy emphasis on the concepts of successful, active, vital, or productive aging can overlook ethnic minority elders and older women who lack the financial resources to sustain activities such as exercise or voluntarism in old age (Estes & Mahakian, 2001; Holstein & Minkler, 2003). Resilience may be more useful for conceptualizing elders' strengths (e.g., internal, family, community, and cultural capacities) when faced with adversity. In fact, many older adults find purpose and meaning in their lives because of adversity, not despite it, and may—even when impaired—contribute to society in diverse ways (Ryff, Keyes, & Hughes, 2003). The opportunity and challenge for the social work profession is to address both increased longevity for the majority of older adults along with life span inequities for historically disadvantaged populations. Social work, with its person-in-environment perspective and strengths-based values, is pivotally placed to foster innovative, multicultural, and cross-generational partnerships to enhance the well-being of adults and their families as they age.

REFERENCES

Administration on Aging. (2000; 2002). *A profile of older Americans*. Washington, DC: Department of Health and Human Services.

Alliance for Aging Research. (2002). *Medical never-land: Ten reasons why America is not ready for the coming age boom*. Washington, DC: Alliance for Aging Research.

American Association of Retired Persons. (2002). *Transportation: The older person's interest*. Washington, DC: Author.

Barranti, C., & Cohen, H. (2001). Lesbian and gay elders: An invisible minority. In R. Schneider, N. Kropf, & A. Kisor. *Gerontological social work: Knowledge, service settings and special populations* (pp. 343–368). Belmont, CA: Brooks/Cole.

Beach, S., Schulz, R., Yee, J., & Jackson, S. (2000). Negative and positive health effects of caring for a disabled spouse: Longitudinal findings from the Caregiver Health Effects Study. *Psychology and Aging, 15*(2), 259–271.

Bengtson, V. L. (2001). Beyond the nuclear family: The increasing importance of multigenerational relationships in American society. The 1998 Burgess Award Lecture. *Journal of Marriage and the Family, 63*, 1–16

Bengtson, V. L., Biblarz, T. J., & Roberts, R. E. L (2002). *How families still matter: A longitudinal study of youth in two generations*. New York: Cambridge University Press.

Bengtson, V. L., Putney, N. M., & Wakeman, M. A. (March 15, 2004). *The family and the future: Challenges, prospects, and resilience*. Paper presented at the Conference on Public Policy and Responsibility across the Generations. Boston College.

Blazer, D. G., Hybels, C. F., & Pieper, C. F. (2001). The association of depression and mortality in elderly persons: A case for multiple independent pathways. *Journals of Gerontology, 56A*, M505–509.

Brody, E. (2004). *Women in the middle: Their parent care years* (2nd ed). New York: Springer Publishing.

Brotman, S., Cormier, R., & Ryan, B. (2001). The marginalization of gay and lesbian seniors in eldercare services. *Vital Aging, 7*(3), 2.

Brotman, S., Ryan, B., & Cormier, R. (2003). The health and social service needs of gay and lesbian elders and their families in Canada. *The Gerontologist, 43*(2), 192–202.

Burgio, L., Stevens, A., Guy, D., Roth, D., & Haley, W. (2003). Impact of two psychosocial interventions on white and African American family caregivers of individuals with dementia. *The Gerontologist, 43*(4), 568.

Burton, L. M., & Whitfield, K. E. (2003). "Weathering" toward poor health in later life: Co-morbidity in urban low-income families. *Public Policy and Aging Report, 13*(3), 13–18.

Cahill, S., South, K., & Spade, J. (2001). *Outing age: Public policy issues affecting gay, lesbian, bisexual, and transgender elders*. New York: The Policy Institute of the National Gay and Lesbian Task Force.

Calasanti, T. M., & Slevin, K. F. (2002). *Gender, social inequalities, and aging*. Walnut Creek, CA: Altamira Press.

Casper, L. M., & Bianchi, S. M. (2002). *Continuity and change in the American family*. Thousand Oaks, CA: Sage Publishing.

Clunis, D. M., Fredriksen-Goldsen, K., Freeman, & Nystrom, N. (in press). *Looking back, looking forward:*

An insightful look at the realities of growing older as a gay woman. New York: Haworth Press.

Connell, C. M., Janevic, M. R., & Gallant, M. P. (2001). The costs of caring: Impact of dementia on family caregivers. *Journal of Geriatric Psychiatry and Neurology, 14*, 179–187.

Connidis, I. A. (2001). *Family Ties and Aging.* Thousand Oaks, CA: Sage Publications.

Cox, C. (2002). Empowering African American custodial grandparents. *Social Work, 47*(1), 262–267.

Davies, C., & Williams, D. (2002). *Grandparent study.* Washington, DC: American Association of Retired Persons.

Elder, G. H., & Johnson, M. K. (2001). The life course and aging: Challenges, lessons, and new directions. In R. A. Settersen, Jr. (Ed.), *Invitation to the life course: Toward new understandings of later life* (pp. 49–81). Amityville, NY: Baywood.

Elder, G. H., & Liker, J. (2000). Hard times in women's lives: Historical influences across forty years. In E. P. Stoller & R. Gibson (Eds.), *Worlds of difference: Inequality in the aging experience* (pp. 19–33). Thousand Oaks, CA: Pine Forge Press.

Estes, C., & Mahakian, J. L. (2001). The political economy of productive aging. In N. Morrow-Howell, J. Hinterlong, & M. Sherraden (Eds.), *Productive aging: Concepts and challenges* (pp. 197–213). Baltimore: Johns Hopkins University Press.

Fuller-Thompson, E., & Minkler, M. (2001). American grandparents providing extensive childcare to their grandchildren: Prevalence and profile. *The Gerontologist, 41*, 201–210.

Gabbay, S., & Wahler, J. (2002). Lesbian aging: Review of a growing literature. *Journal of Gay and Lesbian Social Services, 14*(3), 1–21.

Gartska, T., McCallion, P, & Toseland, R. (2001). Using support groups to improve caregiver health. In M. L. Hummert & J. F. Nussbaum (Eds.), *Aging, communication, and health* (pp. 75–98). Mahwah, NJ: Lawrence Erlbaum Associates.

Gatz, M., & Smyer, M. A. (2001). Mental health and aging at the outset of the 21st century. In J. E. Birren and K. W. Schaie (Eds.), *Handbook of the psychology of aging* (5th edition, pp. 523–544). San Diego: Academic Press.

Giarrusso, R., Silverstein, M., & Feng, D. (2000). Psychological costs and benefits of raising grandchildren: Evidence from a National Survey of Grandparents. In C. B. Cox (Ed.), *To grandmother's house we go and stay: Perspectives on custodial grand parenting* (pp. 71–90). New York: Springer.

Gonyea, J. (forthcoming 2006). Midlife, multigenerational bonds, and caregiving. In R. Talley & R. Montgomery (Eds.), *Caregiving: Science to practice.* New York: Oxford University Press.

Goodman, C. C., & Silverstein, M. (2001). Grandmothers who parent their grandchildren: An exploratory study of close relationships across three generations. *Journal of Family Issues, 22*(5), 557–578.

Green, R., & Berrick, J. (2002). Kinship care: An evolving service delivery option. *Children and Youth Services Review, 24*, 1–14.

Hinterlong, J., Morrow-Howell, N., & Sheraden, M. (2001). Productive aging: Principles and perspectives. In N. Morrow-Howell, J. Hinterlong, & M. Sherraden (Eds.), *Productive aging: Concepts and challenges* (pp. 3–18). Baltimore: Johns Hopkins University Press.

Holstein, M. B., & Minkler, M. (2003). Self, society, and the "New Gerontology." *The Gerontologist, 43*, 787–796.

Ingersoll-Dayton, B., Neal, M. B., & Hammer, L. B. (2001). Aging parents helping adult children: The experience of the sandwiched generation. *Family Relations*, 262–271.

Institute of Medicine. (2001). *Crossing the quality chasm.* Washington, DC: Author.

International Longevity Center. (1999). *Maintaining healthy lifestyles: A lifetime of choices.* New York: Author.

Kingston, E. R., & Williamson, J. B. (2001). Economic security policies. In H. R. Binstock & L. K. George (Ed.), *Handbook of aging and the social sciences* (5th ed.). San Diego: Academic Press.

Kramer, B. J. (1997). Gain in the caregiver experience: Where are we? What next? *The Gerontologist, 37*(2), 218–232.

Lubben, J. E., & Gironda, M. W. (2003). *Centrality of social ties to the health and well-being of older adults.* New York: Springer.

Lynch, J. W., Davey Smith, G., Kaplan, G. A., & House, J. S. (2000). Income inequality and mortality: Importance to health of individual income, psychosocial environment, or material conditions. *British Medical Journal 320*: 1200–1204.

Merck Institute and the Gerontological Society of America. (2002). *The state of aging and health.* Rahway, New Jersey: Author.

Minkler, M. (1999). Intergenerational households headed by grandparents: Context, realities, and implications for policy. *Journal of Aging Studies, 13*(2), 199–218.

Minkler, M., Berrick, J. D., & Needell, B. (1999). Impacts of welfare reform on California grandparents raising grandchildren: Reflections from the field. *Journal of Aging and Social Policy, 10,* 45–63.

Mittelman, M. S. (2002). Family caregiving for people with Alzheimer's disease: Results of the NYU Spouse Caregiver Intervention Study. *Generations, 3,* 104–106.

Moen, P. (2001). The gendered life course. In R. H. Binstock & L. K. George (Eds.), *Handbook of aging and the social sciences* (pp. 179–196). San Diego, CA: Academic Press.

Moen, P., Erickson, M. A., & Dempster-McClain, D. (2000). Social role identities among older adults in a continuing care retirement community. *Research on Aging, 22,* 559–579.

Morano, C. (2000). A psycho-educational model for Hispanic Alzheimer's disease caregivers. *The Gerontologist, 42.*

Narayn, S., Lewis, M., Tornatore, J., Hepburn, K., & Corcoran-Perry, S. (2001). Subjective responses to caregiving for spouses with dementia. *Journal of Gerontological Nursing, 27*(3), 19–28.

National Center for Health Statistics (NCHS). (2000a). *Deaths: Final data for 1998. National Vital and Health Statistics Reports.* Washington, DC: Author.

National Center for Health Statistics. (NCHS). (2000b). *Life expectancy at birth: 1940–1998.* Washington, DC: National Vital and Health Statistics Reports.

National Center for Health Statistics. (NCHS). (2003). *Trends in health and aging.* http://www.cdc.gov/nchs/about/otheract/aging/trendsoverview.htm.

National Center for Policy Analysis. (2003). 2003 Annual report of the Board of Trustees for the Federal Old-age and Survivors Insurance Trust Funds. Washington, DC: Author.

National Respite Network and Resource Center. (2002). *Adult day care: One form of respite for older adults, Fact Sheet #54.* Chapel Hill, NC: Author.

Navaie-Waliser, M., Feldman, P. H., Gould, D. A. Levine, C., Kuerbis, A. N., & Doneland, K. (2001). The experiences and challenges of informal caregivers: Common themes and differences among whites, blacks, and Hispanics. *The Gerontologist, 41,* 733–741.

O'Rand, A. M. (2001). Stratification and the life course: The forms of life course capital and their interrelationships. In R. Binstock & L. K. George (Eds.), *Handbook of Aging and the Social Sciences* (pp. 197–211). San Diego, CA: Academic Press.

O'Rand, A. M. (2003). The future of the life course: Late modernity and life course risks. In J. T. Mortimer & M. J. Shanahan (Eds.), *Handbook of the life course* (pp. 693–701). New York: Kluwer Academic/Plenum.

Parrott, T. M., Mills, T. L., & Bengtston, V. L. (2000). The United States: Population demographics, changes in the family, and social policy challenges. In K-D. Kim, V. L. Bengtson, G. D. Meyers, & K-S. Eun (Eds.), *Aging in east and west: Families, state, and the elderly* (pp. 191–224). New York: Springer.

Polen, M. R., & Green, C. A. (2001). Caregiving, alcohol use, and mental health symptoms among HMO members. *Journal of Community Health, 26*(4), 285–301.

Population Reference Bureau. (2003). 2003 World Population Date Sheet. Washington, DC: The Bureau. Retrieved February 2004 from *http://www.prb.org/pdf/WorldPopulatoinDS03_Eng.pdf.*

Pruchno, R. (1999). Raising grandchildren: The experiences of black and white grandmothers. *The Gerontologist, 39,* 209–21.

Ryff, C. D., Keyes, C. L. M., & Hughes, D. C. (2003). Status inequalities, perceived discrimination, and eudemonic well being: Do the challenges of minority life hone purpose and growth? *Journal of Health and Social Behavior, 44*(3), 275–291.

Schoen, C., & Cooper, B. S. (2003). *Medicare's future: Current picture, trends, and prescription drug policy debate.* New York: The Commonwealth Fund.

Schulz, R., & Beach, S. R. (1999). Caregiving as a risk factor for mortality: The caregiver Health Effects Study. *Journal of the American Medical Association, 282,* 2215–2219.

Schulz, R., O'Brien, A., Cazja, S., Ory, M., Norris, R., Martire, L. M., Belle, S. H., Burgio, L., Gitlin, L., Coon, D., Burns, R., Gallagher-Thompson, D., & Stevens, A. (2002). Dementia caregiver intervention research: In search of clinical significance. *The Gerontologist, 42,* 589–682.

Seltzer, M. M., & Li, L. W. (2000). The dynamics of caregiving: Transitions during a three-year prospective study. *The Gerontologist, 40,* 165–178.

Sherrel, K., Buckwalter, K., & Morhardt, D. (2001). Negotiating family relationships: Dementia care as a midlife developmental task. *Families in society, 82*(4), 383–392.

Silverstein, M., Conroy, S. J., Wang, H., Giarrusso, R., & Bengtson, V. (2002). Reciprocity in parent-child relations over the adult life course. *Journals of Gerontology, 57*(1), S3–13.

Silverstein, M., & Marenco, A. (2001). How Americans enact the grandparent role across the family life course. *Journal of Family Issues, 22*(4), 493.

Stoller, E. P., & Gibson, R. (2000) Advantages of using the life course framework in studying aging. In E. P. Stoller & R. Gibson (Eds.), *Worlds of difference: In-*

equality in the aging experience (pp. 19–33). Thousand Oaks, CA: Pine Forge Press.

Szinovacz, M (1998). Grandparents today: A demographic profile. *The Gerontologist, 38*(1), 37–52

Tennstedt, S. (1999). Family caregiving in an aging society. Washington, DC: Administration on Aging.

Toseland, R. R., C. Peak, T., & Smith, G. (1990). The comparative effectiveness of individual and group interventions to support family caregivers. *Social Work, 35*, 256–263.

Uhlenberg, P., & Kirby, J. B. (1998). Grandparenthood over time: Historical and demopgrahic trends. In M. E. Szinovacz (Ed.), *Handbook on grandparenthood* (pp. 23–30). Westport, CT: Greenwood Press.

United Nations. (2001). *World population prospects: The 2000 revision*. New York: United Nations Publications.

U.S. Bureau of the Census. (2002). *International database*. Washington, DC: U.S. Government Printing Office.

U.S. Bureau of the Census. (October, 2001a). *The 65 years and over population: 2000*. CSKBR/01-10.

U.S. Bureau of the Census. (2001b). *An Aging World: 2001. www.census.gov/prod/2001 pubs/p95-01-1.pdf.*

U.S. Bureau of the Census. (2000). *Statistical abstract of the United States*. Washington, DC: U.S. Government Printing Office.

Wallace, G. (2001). Grandparent caregivers: Emerging issues in elder law and social work practice. *Journal of Gerontological Social Work, 34*(3), 127–134.

Warner, D. F., & Hayward, M. D. (2002). *Race disparities in men's mortality: The role of childhood social conditions in a process of cumulative disadvantage*. Manuscript, University of Pennsylvania, Philadelphia, PA.

Whitfield, K. E., & Hayward, M. (2003). The landscape of health disparities among older adults. *Public Policy and Aging Report, 13*(3), 1–7.

Wilmouth, J. M. (2000). Unbalanced social exchanges and living arrangement transitions among older adults. *The Gerontologist, 40*(1), 64–74.

Wojciechowski, W. C. (1998). Issues in caring for older lesbians. *Journal of Gerontological Nursing, 24*, 28–33.

Women's Institute for a Secure Retirement. (2003). Minority women and retirement income. *Pension Benefits, 12*, 1–2.

World Health Organization. (2002). *Active aging: A policy framework*. Paper presented at the Second United Nations World Assembly on Aging, Madrid, Spain.

Populations Social Workers Serve

AMY HOROWITZ,
SECTION EDITOR

SECTION

Social Work Practice and Older Adults With Chronic Physical and Health Conditions

OVERVIEW

Social work practice with older adults, whether or not specifically focused on health issues, requires knowledge of the range of age-related health conditions and physical disabilities, as well as an appreciation of the impact of these conditions on the well-being of both the older adult and their family members. This section contains eight chapters that address the major health conditions experienced in later life that affect significant subgroups of older adults. Each chapter addresses the empirical and clinical evidence base in terms of prevalence, risk factors, characteristics of the condition, treatment options, psychosocial impact on older adults and their families, considerations for social work practice, and future research needs.

Peter Maramaldi and Jonghyun Lee focus on cancer and aging and emphasize that trends in prevalence and treatment are changing the perception of cancer from an inevitable terminal condition to a chronic disease that is largely age-related. Amy L. Ai and Lynn Carrigan examine age-related cardiovascular disease, one of the most prevalent conditions of later life and a major cause of mortality in older cohorts. One of the major themes in this chapter is the close relationship between the emotional status of the older individual and the morbidity and mortality associated with cardiovascular conditions. Diabetes is also an extremely prevalent and potentially life-threatening condition in later life and, as the chapter authors Richard Francoeur and Jennifer Elkins stress, can lead to significant systemic complications, including cardiovascular problems, vision disorders, neuropathy, and cognitive impairment. Helen Miltiades and Lenard W. Kaye review the major orthopedic diseases and associated conditions, including the predictors and consequences of both falls and fear of falling among older adults. They highlight the important role that social workers can play in encouraging active lifestyles among older adults, as both a preventive approach and one that can minimize the disability associated with orthopedic problems. Cynthia Stuen clearly highlights that, though often overlooked and/or misinterpreted as involving normal aging *changes,* sensory *impairments* in later life, especially those resulting from age-related vision and hearing disorders, can have profound functional and psychological consequences for older adults. Developmental disabilities, as discussed by Elizabeth Lightfoot, and HIV/AIDS, covered by Cynthia Poindexter and Charles Emlet, are conditions not typically associated with aging. However, each has increasing relevance for gerontological social workers as increased

life expectancy in both groups has resulted in emerging populations of older adults who are aging with these health conditions. Michelle Putnam and Susan Stark look at disability in later life across conditions. They argue for the social model of disability as a situation that is as much a function of environmental conditions as it is of individual characteristics.

There are several themes that emerge from these thoughtful reviews that have implications for social work practice with older adults. First, it is clear that physical and mental health have strong, reciprocal relationships. That is, age-related health conditions and impairments place the older adult at greater risk of mental health problems, especially depression. Depression, in turn, is a major risk factor for increased disability, further morbidity, and increased mortality rates in life-threatening illnesses. Evidence is mounting that, regardless of the particular condition, attention to the psychological consequences of age-related disease and disability is a critical component of overall care.

Second, health conditions of older adults affect the entire family system. Family members sometimes suddenly find themselves in caregiving relationships with their older relatives and, as other chapters in this volume also underscore, often experience extensive stress as a result of the physical and psychological demands of caregiving. Further, families often need information and education about the nature of the condition affecting their older relative, as well as help negotiating the typically fragmented systems of acute, rehabilitative, and long-term community and/or institutional care. Social work practice with older adults with health problems is clearly a family affair.

Third, it is evident that risk is not evenly distributed and that there are significant health disparities among older adults. Although not universal, African Americans, Latinos, and other ethnic groups often have higher rates of disease and disability when compared to Caucasians. Some differences apparently have a physiological base (e.g., higher rates of glaucoma among African Americans); others are clearly a function of societal inequities in access to care, as well as socioeconomic characteristics associated with poor health behaviors (e.g., obesity, smoking) that increase risk of conditions such as cardiovascular disease and diabetes. Advocacy on the individual and policy level is a critical component of social work practice with this population.

Fourth, social work practice with older adults with chronic health conditions increasingly means working with multidisciplinary health teams and across both systems of care and service networks. That is, older adults with health conditions often move in and out of the different sectors of the health care system—acute care, rehabilitative care, home care systems, and long-term care facilities—and not necessarily in linear fashion. Furthermore, providing care for particular subgroups often means coordinating aging network services with, for example, services available from mental health, disability and rehabilitation, and developmental disability networks.

Finally, the authors have identified directions for future research. Especially highlighted is the need for well-designed, controlled intervention studies that test service models (e.g., mental health interventions in health care settings, models to enhance self-care, family support programs) targeted to improving the care and enhancing the quality of life for older adults with chronic health conditions and impairments.

Following heart disease, cancer is the second leading cause of death in the United States (American Cancer Society [ACS], 2004a). The annual cancer projections published by the ACS indicate that more than 560,000 people will die of cancer in 2004; that is, approximately 1,500 people in the United States are expected to die from some form of cancer every day. During the same year, more than 1.4 million people are projected to be newly diagnosed with cancer (ACS, 2004b). Once diagnosed, an individual is considered to be a "survivor" for the remainder of her or his life (National Cancer Institute [NCI], 2005b). In 2001 (the most recent year for which data are available), it was estimated that 9.8 million people, or 3.5% of the U.S. population, were survivors of cancer. Of the almost 10 million survivors, 14% had been alive 20 years or longer (NCI, 2005a). For many people, especially older people, cancer has taken on dimensions of a chronic disease.

CANCER AS A CHRONIC CONDITION

Sustained public health efforts have resulted in increased participation in community-based cancer screening, improved diagnostic technology, and advances in treatment modalities. As a result, the number of cancer survivors will continue to increase, many of whom will be living with multiple chronic conditions. Although a malignant tumor can be resected and cancer cells can be destroyed through radiation therapy and chemotherapy, cancer can recur to the same site or other parts of the survivor's body. An individual with a past cancer history is considered at risk for a recurrence of the original cancer at the same site or other parts of the body. Therefore, regardless of age, an individual with a cancer history must be diligently monitored for recurrence of a previous cancer or the occurrence of a new form of cancer. With survivors living longer, often with more than one chronic condition, some types of treatable cancer can be seen less as a terminal disease and more as a manageable chronic condition. This is especially relevant for older populations who may have perceived a cancer diagnosis as a death sentence given their early life experiences prior to the current advances in cancer control. Yet, despite advances, cancer remains a deadly and debilitating disease.

CANCER MORTALITY

National data on cancer mortality in the United States were first collected in the 1930s. These data indicated

PETER MARAMALDI
JONGHYUN LEE

Older Adults With Cancer

that death rates from cancer continued to rise steadily for more than 50 years, until epidemiological surveillance revealed something astounding in the 1990s: a decline in cancer deaths. Extensive interdisciplinary efforts to control cancer appear to have had a cumulative effect on cancer incidence and mortality. Despite these gains, however, the aging of the population will result in greater numbers of people being diagnosed with cancer because of the association between cancer and aging, even if the current cancer rates remain constant. If cancer rates follow current patterns, cancer incidence will double over the next half-century, with 2.6 million newly diagnosed cases in the year 2050. This estimate is according to a 2002 interagency report by the major institutions in cancer research and population control: the NCI, the ACS, the North American Association of Central Cancer Registries, the National Institute on Aging, and the Centers for Disease Control and Prevention, which comprises the National Center for Health Statistics and the National Center for Chronic Disease Prevention and Health Promotion (Edwards et al., 2002).

AGING AND CANCER

Older people bear a disproportionate cancer burden in the United States. As a result, cancer is now classified as a disease of older adults (Cohen, 2003; Deimling, Kahana, Bowmon, & Schaefer, 2002; Ershler, 2003; Goodwin & Coleman, 2003; Kurtz, Kurtz, Stommel, Given, & Given, 1999; Nussbaum, Baringer, & Kundart, 2003; Overcash, 2004; Sacks & Abrahm, 2003; Wallace, 2001). Although older individuals have the highest incidence rates of almost all cancers, they have the lowest rates of screening procedures of proven efficiency. Data from Surveillance, Epidemiology, and End Results (the SEER Program of NCI) indicate that between 1994 and 1998, 60% of all newly diagnosed malignant tumors and 70% of cancer deaths occurred in people age 65 and older. Compared with younger segments of the population, cancer incidence rates are 10 times higher for people age 65 and older (Perlich, 2002). Considering that 75 million baby boomers born in the United States between 1946 and 1964 will age into higher risk groups for various forms of cancer, incidence rates are likely to reach all-time highs.

Although increasing age is a risk factor for almost every type of cancer, little is known about the nexus between aging and cancer. The dearth of knowledge in this area is best reflected by the multidisciplinary workshop convened by the National Institute on Aging

and the NCI in June 2001 to explore the integration of aging and cancer research. As a result of this workgroup's proceedings, the National Institutes of Health (NIH) acknowledged how little is really known in this area. Geriatric and cancer research have until this point moved in separate orbits—developing significant bodies of knowledge—with little or no intersection. As a result, NIH set a cross-institute priority to bring aging and cancer research together with research programs that will span the scientific continuum from biomedical research to behavioral aspects of population control. These coordinated efforts are likely to have a favorable impact on cancer control and the quality of life for survivors.

CANCER DEFINED

Cancer is a disease characterized by uncontrolled and abnormal cell growth that often invades nearby tissue. Cancer cells can spread through the lymphatic system and the bloodstream. There are four main types of cancer: Carcinoma begins in the skin or tissues that line or cover the internal organs; sarcoma begins in the bone, cartilage, fat, muscle, blood vessels, or other connective tissue; leukemia starts in blood-forming tissue, such as bone marrow, and floods the blood system with abnormal blood cells; and lymphoma is a type of cancer that begins in the cells of the immune system (NCI, 2005b). Cancer is not a single disease but any of more than 100 diseases that can occur in almost all of the organs and anatomic sites of the human body. Certain types of cancer are more lethal than others, and each one has its own unique profile (Cohen, 2003; Hess, 1991; Roy & Russell, 1992; Wallace, 2001).

COMMON TYPES OF CANCER

The five most commonly diagnosed cancers in women age 65 and older are cancer of the lung, breast, colon, rectum, and pancreas. In older men, the five most common cancer sites are lungs, prostate, colon, rectum, and pancreas (Sacks & Abrahm, 2003). Each of these cancers will be reviewed briefly, acknowledging that an entire volume could be dedicated to each.

Lung Cancer

Lung cancer is the leading cause of cancer deaths for both men and women over 60 years old (Jemal et al.,

2003), accounting for 30% of all cancer deaths in this age group (Ershler, 2003, p. 6). The incidence rate of lung cancer increases dramatically with age. Lung cancer incidence rates are 600 per 100,000 for men and 400 per 100,000 for women between ages 60 and 79.

Cigarette smoking is known to be a major risk factor for lung cancer, and the risk is significantly increased based on the duration, quantity, and age at onset of smoking. Content of nicotine and tar and the inhalation level are also significant risk factors to consider. For smokers age 75, mortality rates for lung cancer are estimated to be 1 per 100 for men and 1 per 200 for women. Although smoking cessation is beneficial at any age, the risk of lung cancer is greatly reduced by cessation at an earlier age (Haura, Blackwell, & Crawford, 2003; Oddone, Heflin, & Feussner, 2003). Environmental factors such as asbestos, radon gas, chromate, nickel, polyhydrocarbons, and alkylating compounds are also known to increase the risk of lung cancer (Haura et al., 2003; Oddone et al., 2003).

Diagnosing the stage of lung (and other types of cancer) is a highly technical procedure that is often complicated by multiple or overlapping classification systems and conflicting clinical approaches to staging at diagnosis. Although staging at diagnosis is beyond the scope of this chapter, it is important to note that survival rates are directly linked to stage at diagnosis. Advanced stage leads to lower survival rates.

Lung cancer is commonly known for its high incidence rate and poor prognosis. The 5-year survival rates for distant metastasis of advanced stage at diagnosis are only 2%, compared to earlier-stage diagnosis with 48% survival rates for those with localized tumors that have not spread (Haura et al., 2003; Oddone et al., 2003). Lung cancer is generally divided into two groups: small cell and non–small cell. Small cell lung cancer is a type of lung cancer in which the cells appear small and round when viewed under the microscope. This type of lung cancer metastasizes slowly and can be treated effectively at early-stage diagnosis. Non–small cell is a group of lung cancers that includes squamous cell carcinoma, adenocarcinoma, and large cell carcinoma. Current treatments do not cure non–small cell lung cancers. They are often found at an advanced stage due to rapid growth. They metastasize quickly, in contrast to small cell lung cancer, which tends to grow and spread slowly. Approximately 75% to 80% of all lung cancers are non–small cell cancers (Haura et al., 2003).

Early detection leads to higher survival rates. Screening tests for lung cancer are chest radiography, sputum, and low-dose spiral computed tomography,

although their effectiveness for the detection of lung cancer remains controversial. Diagnosis of lung cancer is made through sputum cytology, bronchoscopy, biopsy, and transthoracic needle therapy. Older adults appear to tolerate this diagnostic procedure well as long as they do not have a specific thyroid condition (Haura et al., 2003; Oddone et al., 2003).

Surgical resection offers the greatest chance of cure for many types of lung cancer, provided the disease has not metastasized to other parts of the body. Adjuvant chemotherapy or radiation therapy is offered to reduce reoccurrence of the disease. Preoperative chemotherapy is offered for those at more advanced stages before attempting to perform curative resection. At the inoperable stage, radiation therapy has been the most common form of treatment. It is a common treatment modality for older patients and has been recommended especially for those who display symptoms such as an intractable cough, hemoptysis, dyspnea, and chest pains. Common side effects due to radiation therapy are fatigue, loss of appetite, nausea, vomiting, and lowered numbers of blood cells. For people with a metastatic disease, platinum-based chemotherapy has been beneficial, although its benefit is often brief and has been accompanied by treatment-related toxicity (Haura et al., 2003; Krcmarik, Prendergast, Ely, & Runo, 2003).

Breast Cancer

Breast cancer is the second leading cause of cancer death in women age 65 and older, with approximately 50% of newly diagnosed cases occurring in this age group (Ershler, 2003). Less than 1% of all breast cancer is diagnosed in males. Women over 65 account for as much as 67% of breast cancer mortality. The highest incidence rates for breast cancer are seen in women around age 75 (Balducci & Phillips, 1998; Partridge & Winner, 2003; Sacks & Abrahm, 2003). Breast cancer incidence rates for women are 76 per 100,000 under age 65 and 441 per 100,000 age 65 and older. Breast cancer causes significant morbidity and disability, even in the case of survival (Balducci & Phillips, 1998; Oddone et al., 2003).

Risk factors for breast cancer among older women are advancing age, family history and genetic predisposition, higher estrogen levels, early age at menarche, late menopause, benign breast disease, alcohol use, number of or late pregnancies, hormone replacement therapy, and exposure to radiation. Other, less established risk factors include a high-fat diet, obesity, and use of oral contraceptives (Balducci & Phillips, 1998; Oddone et al., 2003; Partridge & Winner, 2003; Sacks & Abrahm, 2003).

Although older women are still less likely to receive mammograms or other tests for breast cancer than their younger counterparts (Eisner, Zook, Goodman, & Macario, 2002), the overall breast cancer screening rates among women 65 and over has increased from 48% in 1991 to 64% in 1998 (Oddone et al., 2003). Screening strategies for the early detection of breast cancer include self-examination, clinical breast examination performed by a health care professional without any special equipment, and mammography. When the clinical exam is combined with mammography, the accuracy of the detection rate is estimated at between 83% and 98.5%. Suspicious screening results are followed up by biopsy to confirm a positive diagnosis (Balducci & Phillips, 1998; Oddone et al., 2003; Roy & Russell, 1992).

For women age 50 and older, 5-year survival rates are 97.6% for localized breast cancer, 77.5% for metastases to regional lymph nodes, and 20.1% for distal metastases. The 5-year overall survival rate for women age 70 and older with early-stage breast cancer is about 54% (Sacks & Abrahm, 2003). Although older women have lower survival rates due to differences in tumor characteristics, individual factors, health care utilization, and the existence of comorbid conditions, screening should continue throughout the life span (Oddone et al., 2003; Partridge & Winner, 2003).

There are two general types of surgery to treat breast cancer: breast-sparing surgery (also known as breast-conserving surgery) and mastectomy. For women diagnosed at an early stage of breast cancer, breast-sparing surgery combined with radiation therapy results in the same survival rates as for those who have mastectomy. Breast-sparing surgery is a procedure intended to remove the breast cancer but not the breast itself. Types of breast-sparing surgery include lumpectomy (removal of the lump), quadrantectomy (removal of one quarter, or quadrant, of the breast), and segmental mastectomy (removal of the cancer as well as some of the breast tissue around the tumor and the lining over the chest muscles below the tumor). Mastectomy is a surgical procedure to remove as much of the breast as possible (NCI, 2005c). Additionally, radiation therapy, hormonal therapy, and chemotherapy are common treatment approaches for breast cancer. Depending on the stage of the disease, its characteristics, and the individual woman's life expectancy and comorbid conditions, these treatment modalities are used separately or in combination (Balducci & Phillips, 1998; Partridge & Winner, 2003). Older women are known to tolerate breast cancer surgery

fairly well compared to younger women. Unlike their younger counterparts, they are less likely to undergo breast-conserving surgery and generally receive less aggressive treatment (Partridge & Winner, 2003). The most common adjuvant chemotherapy is a combination of cytoxan, methotrexate, and 5-fluorouracil (CMF). Despite risks and more recent controversy associated with its use, tamoxifen has been known to be effective for older women who cannot tolerate surgery (Partridge & Winner, 2003; Sacks & Abrahm, 2003).

Prostate Cancer

Although the occurrence of prostate cancer is rare in men younger than 40 years, incidence rates double during each subsequent decade of life, and African American men are at the highest risk in all age groups (Hayes, 2004; SEER, 2004). Men 65 and older account for more than 80% of all prostate cancer, with those age 74 and older accounting for almost half of all prostate cancer mortality. Prostate cancer incidence rates are 50 per 100,000 for men younger than 65 years and 1,025 per 100,000 for men age 65 and older. Mortality rates are 2.6 per 100,000 for men younger than 65 years and 225 per 100,000 for men age 65 and older (Coleman, Hutchins, & Goodwin, 2004; Sacks & Abrahm, 2003).

Prostate cancer starts in the prostate gland, which is located at the base of the penis, just below the bladder and in front of the rectum, and which produces seminal fluid. At the beginning stage, it does not endanger life, as the disease remains localized in the gland. The 5-year survival rate of localized prostate cancer is 80%, compared to 8% for distant metastases. Without early detection and appropriate treatment, prostate cancer can spread to other organs and cause death (Hayes, 2004; National Education Association/Health Information Network, 2004; Oddone et al., 2003). Routine screening tests such as the serum prostate specific antigen and the digital rectal examination lead to early detection. If either of these tests are suspicious, follow-up tests include sonogram (also known as ultrasound) and biopsy. Biopsy is the most invasive but most effective means of detecting prostate cancer.

The exact etiology of prostate cancer is not known, making preventive behaviors difficult to recommend. Known risk factors linked to prostate cancer include advancing age, African American race/ethnicity, family history of the disease, and a high-fat diet (Illinois Department of Public Health, 2004; Matin & Trump, 2003; Oddone et al., 2003; SEER, 2004).

In general, prostate cancer treatment is divided into three categories based on the extent of the cancer

(Matin & Trump, 2003). The first, localized prostate cancer, is potentially curable through prostatectomy and various forms of irradiation therapy. However, these treatments carry significant risks of side effects, including acute cystitis, urinary retention, impotence, blood loss, and incontinence. The second category is an advanced state of the cancer. Although prostate cancer does not spread to other tissues or organs, local metastasis in the pelvic area makes prostatectomy or irradiation therapy less effective. The third category is metastatic prostate cancer. About 30% of prostate cancers are metastatic at the time of diagnosis. Metastatic prostate cancer afflicts patients with considerable morbidity and is associated with bone metastasis and spinal cord compression (Matin & Trump, 2003). Prognosis is poor, and hormonal therapy is considered one of the best treatment options (Matin & Trump, 2003; Roy & Russell, 1992).

Colon/Rectum Cancer

Although cancer of the colon and rectum are clinically differentiated, they are discussed under the rubric of colorectal cancer (CRC). CRC is the second most common cancer for older men and women, and its incidence and mortality rates increase with age. Incidence rates are 287.8 per 100,000 for women and men age 65 and older and 450 per 100,000 for those age 85 and older. Mortality rates are 5.7 per 100,000 for men and women under age 65 and 120 per 100,000 for those age 85 and older. Additionally, among women whose age is 80, CRC exceeds breast cancer as a cause of death (Enzinger & Mayer, 2003; Oddone et al., 2003; Sacks & Abrahm, 2003). Comorbid conditions such as hypertension, heart disease, and chronic obstructive pulmonary disease are found to increase with age and are associated with early CRC mortality (Enzinger & Mayer, 2003).

Eighty percent of CRC is known to develop from adenomatous polyps that take approximately 5 to 10 years to become malignant. As many as 1 in 3 people have adenomatous polyps by their mid-50s. The importance of targeting older populations for CRC screening is underscored by the incidence of adenomatous polyps reaching 50% by age 75 (Enzinger & Mayer, 2003; Oddone et al., 2003). Screening tests such as digital rectal examination, fecal occult blood testing (FOBT), sigmoidoscopy, and colonoscopy are, in ascending order, the current detection strategies of choice for colorectal cancer. FOBT is the most cost-effective and commonly used screening test for CRC. A positive FOBT should be followed by a colonoscopy.

Colonoscopy is the most expensive but the preferred screening procedure because it allows for the clinical examination of the entire colon and immediate biopsy of suspicious tissue. In addition, adenomatous polyps are removed during the screening procedure (Enzinger & Mayer, 2003; Oddone et al., 2003).

Risk factors for CRC include increased age, a personal history of CRC or ulcerative colitis (Crohn disease), a family history of CRC or familial adenomatous polyposis in a first-degree relative, and history of breast, ovarian, or uterine cancer. Approximately 75% of CRC patients had no known risk factors prior to diagnosis. Lack of physical activity, obesity, higher consumption of red meat and lower consumption of fruits and vegetables, in addition to the use of tobacco and alcohol are also risk factors that can increase the incidence (Enzinger & Mayer, 2003; Oddone et al., 2003). The best preventive strategy is to remove premalignant polyps. The 5-year survival rate is 90% for early diagnosis with localized malignancy. Survival drops to 64% for regional metastases and 8% for distal metastases (Enzinger & Mayer, 2003; Oddone et al., 2003).

Surgery and chemotherapy are common treatment approaches for CRC. Colorectal tumors are removed along with adjacent bowel, blood vessels, and lymphatics through en-bloc surgical resection. Adjuvant chemotherapy is offered after surgery. Postoperative chemotherapy is known to decrease reoccurrences and mortality by 40% and 33%, respectively. A 5-fluorouracil is offered in combination with leucovorin as the postchemotherapy for high-risk resected colorectal cancer. Although it is known that older adults receive adjuvant chemotherapy less often than younger people with the same disease, postoperative chemotherapy is as beneficial for individuals age 70 and over as it is to their younger counterparts (Enzinger & Mayer, 2003; Sacks & Abrahm, 2003). Finally, a colectomy and, in some cases, a partial colectomy, results in colostomy. Colostomy is an opening to the outside of the body that provides a new path for waste material to flow. In some cases, a colostomy can be temporary to allow a remaining section of the colon to heal. In all cases, colostomy maintenance requires patient training and, in some cases, regular assistance. In older populations, colostomy maintenance should be considered an additional activities of daily living (ADL) in all levels of assessment.

Pancreatic Cancer

The pancreas is located near the stomach and the small intestine. It produces several hormones used in regular digestion of food (Oncologychannel, 2004). Although pancreatic cancer accounts for only about 2% of new cancer cases, its high lethality accounts for about 5% to 6% of all cancer deaths in both men and women in the United States. It is the fifth most fatal of all cancer types (ACS, 2004a; Massachusetts Department of Public Health, 2002; Messinger-Rapport & Thacker, 2002). Because pancreatic cancer tends to be aggressive in nature, most cases are detected at an advanced stage, and the median survival period is approximately 5 months for individuals with the metastatic disease. As a result, the 5-year survival rate for pancreatic cancer is only 3% to 5% (Enzinger & Mayer, 2003; Messinger-Rapport & Thacker, 2002; Skinner et al., 2003).

Just as with other cancer cases, older adults account for a significant portion of pancreatic cancer patients. Most pancreatic cancer cases are detected in individuals between age 60 and 80 years, with the median age at diagnosis of 60 years (Enzinger & Mayer, 2003; Massachusetts Department of Public Health, 2002; Messinger-Rapport & Thacker, 2002). Although men show a higher prevalence rate compared to women, it is the fourth most fatal cancer for both men and women age 60 and older (Jemal et al., 2003). Despite its seriousness, little is known about this cancer.

The risk factors for pancreatic cancer are thought to be smoking, diet, medical conditions, family history, and environmental agents in addition to advancing age (Enzinger & Mayer, 2003; Massachusetts Department of Public Health, 2002; Messinger-Rapport & Thacker, 2002; Oncologychannel, 2004). African Americans show a higher rate of pancreatic cancer than other racial or ethnic groups. Although associations with the disease have not been tested, certain medical conditions, including chronic pancreatitis, diabetes, and cirrhosis, are considered to be risk factors. Higher intake of meat and fats in the diet are also associated with pancreatic cancer. Although the outcomes of various investigations have linked pancreatic cancer to environmental agents such as gasoline, asbestos, nickel and chromium compounds, and ionizing radiation, study findings are characterized as inconsistent and controversial. It is suggested that between 3% and 10% of pancreatic cancer cases are related to genetic predisposition (ACS, 2004b; Enzinger & Mayer, 2003; Massachusetts Department of Public Health, 2002; Messinger-Rapport & Thacker, 2002; Oncologychannel, 2004; Skinner et al., 2003).

Because the symptoms of pancreatic cancer are not specific, diagnostic tests are often delayed. Individuals with pancreatic cancer typically seek out medical attention due to jaundice, weight loss, epigastric and back pain, fatigue, loss of appetite, and glucose intolerance. Patients may report diarrhea, constipation, bloating, flatulence, chills, dizziness, or muscle pains (Enzinger & Mayer, 2003; Oncologychannel, 2004; Roy & Russell, 1992). Screening tests for pancreatic cancer are computerized axial tomography (CAT scan), endoscopic retrograde cholangiopancreatography (ERCP), ultrasound, magnetic resonance imaging, and biopsy. The ERCP procedure can be performed to not only detect the cancer but also to treat jaundice (Enzinger & Mayer, 2003; Oncologychannel, 2004).

Pancreatic cancer treatment includes surgery, chemotherapy, and radiation therapy. These treatment remedies are offered individually or in combination based on the degree of morbidity (Enzinger & Mayer, 2003; Oncologychannel, 2004). People with advanced pancreatic cancer usually undergo surgery to remove a small part of the pancreas. Another surgical approach is the pancreaticoduodenectomy, also called the Whipple procedure, to remove more extensive areas of the pancreas or, sometimes, the entire resection, including the distal duodenum, the proximal jejunum, the neck, head, and uncinate process of the pancreas, the gallbladder, and the distal bile duct. This is followed by postoperative adjuvant chemotherapy. This combined therapy has been considered to expand survival time. Patients with inoperable pancreatic cancer that has not spread to other organs often receive radiation therapy and chemotherapy. The most severe cases of distal metastatic pancreatic cancer are treated with chemotherapy or palliative care (Enzinger & Mayer, 2003; Roy & Russell, 1992).

PSYCHOSOCIAL CONSIDERATIONS

Understanding cancer, its treatment, posttreatment recovery, and maintenance are directly associated with an older individual's physical and cognitive ability. This is especially true for a person experiencing a cancer diagnosis for the first time. Comorbid conditions contribute to the physical and emotional impact of the cancer. If an individual is experiencing a condition with symptoms more severe than those accompanying the cancer, she or he may be less motivated to take treatment action. This is an especially important consideration in early-stage diagnosis, when relatively little or no discomfort may be experienced. Treatment delays and noncompliance with prevention, screening, and treatment regimens introduce the risk of metastases, which may result in less favorable prognosis for cure, survival, and quality of life after treatment. The delay or noncompliance phenomenon may be exacerbated by cognitive impairments.

Clinicians must consider symptom management and possible side effects or complications related to treatments. Pain management, possible physical impairments, effects on social relationships, psychological and emotional distress, nutritional issues, and financial burdens must all be considered in the context of the patient's age and resources (Haley, 2003; Ahmed, 2004; Jepson, 1999; Badura & Grohmann, 2002; Balducci, 2003; Sharp, Blum, & Aviv, 2003; Frongillo, Valois, & Wolfe, 2003; McCarthy, Phillips, Zhong, Drews, & Lynn, 2000; Hayman et al., 2001; Ingram, Seo, Martell, Clipp, Doyle, Montana, & Cohen, 2002). Older cancer patients require considerable support to achieve positive health outcomes from the treatment as well as to achieve an acceptable quality of life.

PHYSICAL/COGNITIVE FUNCTIONING

Impaired physical and cognitive capacities may complicate the treatment of older people with cancer. Some older people may experience chemotherapy as intolerable and require special medical attention (Ershler, 2003; Goodwin & Coleman, 2003). Cancer treatments must be established through careful individualized assessments that reflect comorbid and other physical conditions (Balducci, 2003; Yanick, Ganz, Varricchio, & Conley, 2001). Malnutrition, anemia, and neutropenia can result from the negative effects of chemotherapy and require careful attention and monitoring. Other types of chronic conditions, such as diabetes, arthritis, and respiratory problems, are also common conditions that may complicate treatment (Balducci, 2003; Cancer Care, 2003). Older patients' physical impairments, including of hearing, speech, and literacy, may influence their daily living activities, such as cooking, dressing, bathing, shopping, taking medications, and visiting hospitals for treatment, and therefore directly affect prognosis (Balducci, 2003).

Older patients with cognitive impairments may be unable to convey their needs and physical condition to health care providers: physicians, nurses, social workers, and other, informal caregivers. The inability to assess and/or convey one's own physical condition may have a direct outcome on diagnosis, treatment, and maintenance (Badura & Grohmann, 2002). Pain management is one of the great challenges for treating older patients because the cancer is often accompanied by acute and chronic pain (Balducci, 2003; Soscia, 2003). Cognitive impairments may interfere with the accurate assessment of older patients' experiences of pain. Pain assessment is a critical component of cancer care and quality of life. In addition to behavioral observations, clinicians should use pain assessment tools for people with cognitive impairments (Badura & Grohmann, 2002; Balducci, 2003; Ferrell, 2003; Soscia, 2003).

EMOTIONAL/PSYCHOLOGICAL RESPONSES

Cancer produces a range of emotional and psychological distress, often related to specific functional impairments. Fear, anxiety, sleep disturbance, depression, and avoidance often surface due not only to symptoms and side effects of treatment, such as surgery and chemotherapy, but to the looming fear of recurrence or death that is prevalent in older patients (Deimling et al., 2002; Ersher, 2003). Pain is a predictor of depression (Badura & Grohmann, 2002), and many cancer treatments, especially surgery, are extremely painful.

Lack of social support and restrictions on activity are other factors that cause emotional and psychological distress among older cancer patients. The disruption of social support is another consideration in treatment planning for older patients. It is not uncommon for patients to consider themselves disfigured or maimed by surgery. Older women are less likely to receive reconstructive surgery after breast cancer. A colostomy patient may live in horror of leakage, especially during the initial stages of adjustment. Cavalier attitudes about appearance or self-consciousness not mattering to an older person should be monitored and addressed by clinicians at every juncture of service provision in the medical setting and the patient's community.

Older cancer patients may be twice as old as their providers. It is important for providers to be sensitized to the vitality of older people. A younger provider approaching an older cancer patient as someone who has lived out her or his years is behaving inappropriately, unethically, and potentially detrimentally to a patient's prognosis. The despair of older women experiencing surgery for breast cancer should not be minimized because of their age. Neither should providers minimize an older man's concerns about side effects of prostate cancer treatment (Kurtz et al., 1999; Sharp, Blum, & Aviv, 2003). Emotional and psychological assessments and appropriate support must be offered to meet the emotional and psychological needs of older cancer patients.

SOCIAL/FINANCIAL RESOURCES

Limited social and financial resources may influence treatment decisions and outcomes among older people with cancer (Balducci, 2003). Financial burdens become a critical issue for older adults with cancer, due to their out-of-pocket medical expenses. Even a minimal copayment may present a real or perceived barrier for an older patient living on a fixed income. Visiting the treatment site, securing outpatient medications, receiving home care, and obtaining needed medical supplies are formidable tasks and additional worries for the older patient (Haley, 2003). Treatment planning must include accessible services, including a visiting nurse, community supports, and financial assistance; are all critical aspects of treatment for older cancer patients (Cancer Care, 2003).

Social support has a direct impact on the effectiveness of treatment (Koretz & Reuben, 2003; Kurtz et al., 1999). Without some form of social support, older adults may face very serious problems that interfere with their overall daily functions. Family members or caregivers are an important emotional resource that can offer various supports to older adults with cancer (Overcash, 2004). A caregiver is someone who has a personal connection and commitment to a cancer survivor. They provide care in activities of daily living, household chores, administering medication, visiting the treatment site, and managing side effects (Haley, 2003; Overcash, 2004).

Many of the services provided to cancer survivors by caregivers, 80% of whom are women, were once performed in hospitals or health facilities. Services now provided at no cost by caregivers are estimated to be worth over $300 million annually. Additionally, most people in this role do not identify themselves as caregivers. Caregivers of older cancer patients often have competing responsibilities and roles, such as partner, parent, and employee. Many experience high levels of stress as they face difficult end-of-life issues related to treatment decisions and procedures (Haley, 2003). Caregivers experience significant psychological, physical, and economic burdens in relation to the cancer patient (Haley, 2003; Hayman et al., 2001; Jepson, McCorkle, Adler, Nuamah, & Lusk, 1999; Query & Wright, 2003). Caregivers' own stress influences the quality of care that they can offer (Koretz & Reuben, 2003).

Clinicians should provide caregivers with information, emotional support, and case management advice. Focus should be on maintaining the well-being of both the cancer survivor and the caregiver (Haley, 2003).

An example of an important clinical intervention with caregivers is some form of respite service. The amount of respite can range from 1 or 2 hours to attend to personal matters or recreational activity such as a movie, to as much as days or weeks for other responsibilities or a vacation with family or friends. Caregivers should also be encouraged to request case management assistance from their insurance company to provide efficacious care for the cancer survivor. The cost benefit of effective case management provides social workers with strong leverage when advocating for services. Finally, when the caregiver is a family member, the Family and Medical Leave Act requires companies employing 50 or more people to allow up to 12 weeks of unpaid leave for an employee who must care for a family member. When considering this provision, the lack of income must be carefully weighed against the benefit of job protection.

SOCIAL WORK

Clinical social workers can provide older cancer survivors and caregivers comprehensive clinical case management designed to complement the medical, environmental, and economic conditions during initial diagnosis, treatment, and discharge into the community. At various stages of the cancer continuum, psychosocial treatment plans encompass patient and caregiver needs during diagnosis, treatment, survivorship, and, when the disease cannot be cured or controlled, palliative care. As members of interdisciplinary teams specializing in specific cancer types, clinical social workers' expertise in all aspects of the disease, including side effects of treatment, pain management, and assessment of self-care needs, helps patients navigate the complex medical terrain and bridge the gap between the biomedical and psychosocial aspects of the disease.

A comprehensive oncology social work approach will provide older cancer patients, families, and caregivers with an overview of services and resources available. Social workers are uniquely situated to help patients communicate with medical oncologists, to understand the disease and treatment options, and to explore emotional and social issues related to the specific cancer in the patients' psychosocial circumstances. Conversely, the social worker communicates the patient's situation, understanding of the disease, and treatment options back to the interdisciplinary team. Geriatric considerations, particularly as they relate to quality of life in survivorship, are particularly important. When appropriate, social workers help the patient and caregivers negotiate the complex medical, financial, and community health care systems introduced by the cancer diagnosis, treatment, and survivorship. In cases where the disease prognosis is poor, options for palliative care must be explored as well.

SUMMARY

During their youth, older individuals may have lived through a time in history when a cancer diagnosis was virtually a death sentence. Technological advances in cancer screening, diagnosis, and treatment have resulted in unprecedented cancer survivorship. So great are the numbers of survivors and the duration of survivorship, that cancer—in some cases—can be reframed as a chronic condition. This should not confuse the fact that a cancer diagnosis assaults every aspect of a person's being—especially older people. Unless a patient is significantly debilitated by a comorbid condition, other physical conditions must not interfere with continued cancer screening, treatment, and maintenance. The notion that the older individual has lived a full life and is ready to die is both false and potentially dangerous. Finally, older cancer patients require special consideration to help them understand the disease and its treatment, to remove barriers to treatment and maintenance, and to monitor not only the disease but also patients' physical and cognitive functioning during survivorship.

REFERENCES

Ahmed, S. M. (2004, October 10). Is ageism a factor in cancer screening? *Annals of Family Medicine* [Electronic letters]. Retrieved December 21, 2004, from *http://annfammed.org/cgi/eletters/2/5/481.*

American Cancer Society. (2004a). *Cancer statistics 2004: A presentation from the American Cancer Society.* Atlanta, GA: Author.

American Cancer Society. (2004b). *Cancer facts and figures 2004.* Atlanta, GA: Author.

Badura, A. S., & Grohmann, J. M. (2002). Psychological issues in pain perception and treatment in the elderly. *Annals of Long-Term Care, 10*(7), 29–34.

Balducci, L. (2003). New paradigms for treating elderly patients with cancer: The Comprehensive Geriatric Assessment and Guidelines for Supportive Care. *Journal of Supportive Oncology, 1*(4, Suppl. 2), 30–37.

Balducci, L., & Phillips, D. M. (1998, October 1). Breast cancer in older women. *American Family Physician.* Retrieved December 17, 2004, from *http://www.aafp.org/afp/981001ap/balducci.html.*

Cancer Care. (2003). *Working with an older person who has cancer.* Retrieved December 21, 2004, from *http://www.cancercare.org/FPEducationalPrograms/FPEducationalPrograms.cfm?ID=3553&c=394.*

Cohen, H. J. (2003). Cancer in the elderly: An overview. In C. K. Cassel, R. M. Leipzig, H. J. Cohen, E. B. Larson, & D. E. Meier (Eds.), *Geriatric medicine: An evidence based approach* (4th ed., pp. 361–373), New York: Springer.

Coleman, E. A., Hutchins, L., & Goodwin, J. (2004). An overview of cancer in the older adult. *MEDSURG Nursing, 13*(2), 75–109.

Deimling, G. T., Kahana, B., Bowmon, K. F., & Schaefer, M. L. (2002). Cancer survivorship and psychological distress in later life. *Psycho-Oncology, 11*(6), 479–494.

Edwards, B. K., Howe, H. L., Ries, L. A. G., Thun, M. J., Rosenberg, H. M., Yanick, R., et al. (2002). Annual report to the nation on the status of cancer, 1973–1999. *Cancer, 94*(10), 2766–2792.

Eisner, E. J., Zook, E. G., Goodman, N., & Macario, E. (2002). Knowledge, attitude, and behavior of women ages 65 and older on mammography screening and Medicare: Results of a national survey. *Women & Health, 36*(4), 1–18.

Enzinger, P. C., & Mayer, R. J. (2003). Colon cancer and other gastrointestinal malignancies. In C. K. Cassel, R. M. Leipzig, H. J. Cohen, E. B. Larson, & D. E. Meier (Eds.), *Geriatric medicine: An evidence based approach* (4th ed., pp. 417–440). New York: Springer.

Ershler, W. B. (2003). Cancer: A disease of the elderly. *Journal of Supportive Oncology, 1*(4, Suppl. 2), 5–10.

Ferrell, B. A. (2003). Acute and chronic pain. In C. K. Cassel, R. M. Leipzig, H. J. Cohen, E. B. Larson, & D. E. Meier (Eds.), *Geriatric medicine: An evidence based approach* (4th ed., pp. 323–342). New York: Springer.

Frongillo, E. A., Valois, P., & Wolfe, W. S. (2003). Using a concurrent events approach to understand social support and food insecurity among elders. *Family Economics and Nutrition Review, 15*(1), 25–32.

Goodwin, J. A., & Coleman, E. A. (2003). Exploring measures of functional dependence in the older adult with cancer. *MEDSURG Nursing, 12*(6), 359–366.

Haley, W. E. (2003). Family caregivers of elderly patients with cancer: Understanding and minimizing the burden of care. *Journal of Supportive Oncology, 1*(4, Suppl. 2), 25–29.

Haura, E. B., Blackwell, S. A., & Crawford, J. (2003). Lung cancer. In C. K. Cassel, R. M. Leipzig, H. J.

Cohen, E. B. Larson, & D. E. Meier (Eds.), *Geriatric medicine: An evidence based approach* (4th ed., pp. 441–454). New York: Springer.

Hayes, R. B. (2004). Risk factors: Prostate. Retrieved December 17, 2004, from Surveillance, Epidemiology, and End Result, National Cancer Institute, *http://seer.cancer.gov/publications/raterisk/risks185.html*.

Hayman, J. A., Langa, K. M., Kabeto, M. U., Katz, S. J., DeMonner, S. M., Chernew, M. E., et al. (2001). Estimating the cost of informal caregiving for elderly patients with cancer. *Journal of Clinical Oncology, 19*(13), 3219–3225.

Hess, J. W. (1991). Health promotion and risk reduction for later life. In R. F. Young & E. A. Olson (Eds.), *Health, illness, and disability in later life: Practice issues and interventions* (pp. 25–43). Newbury Park, CA: Sage.

Illinois Department of Public Health. (2004). Prostate cancer. *Health Beat.* Retrieved December 17, 2004, from *http://idph.state.il.us/public/hb/hbproscner.htm*.

Ingram, S. S., Seo, P. H., Martell, R. E., Clipp, E. C., Doyle, M. E., Montana, G. S., et al. (2002). Comprehensive assessment of the elderly cancer patient: The feasibility of self-report methodology. *Journal of Clinical Oncology, 20*(3), 770–775.

Jemal, A., Murray, T., Samuels, A., Ghafoor, A., Ward, E., & Thun, M. J. (2003). Cancer statistics, 2003. *CA: A Cancer Journal for Clinicians, 53*(1), 5–26.

Jepson, C., McCorkle, R., Adler, D., Nuamah, I., & Lusk, E. (1999). Effects of home care on caregivers' psychosocial status. *Journal of Nursing Scholarship, 31*(2), 115–120.

Koretz, B., & Reuben, D. B. (2003). Instruments to assess functional status, In C. K. Cassel, R. M. Leipzig, H. J. Cohen, E. B. Larson, & D. E. Meier (Eds.), *Geriatric medicine: An evidence based approach* (4th ed., pp. 185–194), New York: Springer.

Krcmarik, J. P., Prendergast, T. J., Ely, E. W., & Runo, J. R. (2003). Chronic lung disease and lung cancer. In R. S. Morrison & D. E. Meier (Eds.), *Geriatric palliative care* (pp. 173–191), New York: Oxford University Press.

Kurtz, M. E., Kurtz, J. C., Stommel, M., Given, C. W., & Given, B. (1999). The influence of symptoms, age, comorbidity and cancer site on physical functioning and mental health of geriatric women patients. *Women & Health, 29*(3), 1–12.

Massachusetts Department of Public Health. (2002, December). Pancreatic cancer. *Risk Factors, Information for Selected Cancer Types.* Community Assessment Unit, Bureau Environmental Health Assessment. Retrieved December 17, 2004, from *http://www.mass.gov/dph/beha/cau/reports/rodney_metals/pancreatic_cancer.pdf*.

Matin, K., & Trump, D. L. (2003). Prostate cancer. In C. K. Cassel, R. M. Leipzig, H. J. Cohen, E. B. Larson, & D. E. Meier (Eds.), *Geriatric medicine: An evidence based approach* (4th ed., pp. 455–468). New York: Springer.

McCarthy, E. P., Phillips, R. S., Zhong, Z., Drews, R. E., & Lynn, J. (2000). Dying with cancer: Patients' function, symptoms, and care preferences as death approaches. *Journal of the American Geriatric Society, 48*(5, Suppl.), 110–121.

Messinger-Rapport, B. J., & Thacker, H. L. (2002). Prevention for the older women: A practical guide to managing risk of malignancies. *Geriatrics, 57*(10), 42–49.

National Cancer Institute. (2005a). Facts about Office of Cancer Survivorship. Retrieved February 10, 2005, from *http://dccps.nci.nih.gov/ocs/ocs_factsheet.pdf*.

National Cancer Institute. (2005b). Glossary of statistical terms. Retrieved February 10, 2005, from *http://www.nci.nih.gov/statistics/glossary*.

National Cancer Institute. (2005c). Surgery choices for women with early-stage breast cancer. Retrieved February 10, 2005, from *http://www.nci.nih.gov/cancer topics/breast-cancer-surgery-choices*.

National Education Association/Health Information Network. (2004). *Male related cancer information.* Retrieved December 17, 2004, from *http://neahin.org/programs/cancerinfo/male.htm*.

Nussbaum, J. F., Baringer, D., & Kundart, A. (2003). Health, communication, and aging: Cancer and older adults. *Health Communication, 15*(2), 185–192.

Oddone, E. Z., Heflin, M. T., & Feussner, J. R. (2003). Screening for cancer. In C. K. Cassel, R. M. Leipzig, H. J. Cohen, E. B. Larson, & D. E. Meier (Eds.), *Geriatric medicine: An evidence based approach* (4th ed., pp. 375–394). New York: Springer.

Oncologychannel. (2004). *Pancreatic cancer.* Retrieved December 20, 2004, from *http://www.oncologychannel.com/pancreaticcancer/*.

Overcash, J. A. (2004). Using narrative research to understand the quality of life of older women with breast cancer. *Oncology Nursing Forum, 31*(6), 1153–1159.

Partridge, A., & Winner, E. (2003). Breast cancer. In C. K. Cassel, R. M. Leipzig, H. J. Cohen, E. B. Larson, & D. E. Meier (Eds.), *Geriatric medicine: An evidence based approach* (4th ed., pp. 393–416). New York: Springer.

Perlich, P. (2002, October). *Utah minorities: The story told by 150 years of census data.* Retrieved July 2, 2003, from Bureau of Economic and Business Research, David S. Eccles School of Business, University of Utah Web site, *http://www.business.utah.edu/bebr/onlinepublications/Utah_Minorities.pdf*.

Query, Jr., J. L., & Wright, K. (2003). Assessing communication competence in an online study: Toward informing subsequent interventions among older adults with cancer, their lay caregivers, and peers. *Health Communication, 15*(2), 203–218.

Roy, F. H., & Russell, C. R. (1992). *The encyclopedia of aging and the elderly care.* New York: Facts on File.

Sacks, N. R., & Abrahm, J. L. (2003). Cancer. In R. S. Morrison & D. E. Meier (Eds.), *Geriatric palliative care* (pp. 123–133). New York: Oxford University Press.

Sharp, J. W., Blum, D., & Aviv, L. (2004). Elderly men with cancer: Social work interventions with prostate cancer. *Cancer Care.* Retrieved December 21, 2004, from *http://www.cancercare.org/FPEducationalPro grams/FPEducationalPrograms.cfm?ID=3251&c=395.*

Skinner, H. G., Michaud, D. S., Colditz, G. A., Giovannucci, E. L., Stampfer, M. J., Willett, W. C., et al. (2003). Parity, reproductive factors, and the risk of pancreatic cancer in women. *Cancer: Epidemiology, Biomarkers & Prevention, 12*(5), 433–438.

Soscia, J. (2003). Assessing pain in cognitively impaired older adults with cancer. *Clinical Journal of Oncology Nursing, 7*(2), 174–177.

Surveillance, Epidemiology, and End Result. (2004). *Cancer incidence in the United States, 1973–91: Changing pattern for major cancers by sex among Whites and Blacks.* Retrieved December 17, 2004, from *http://seer.cancer.gov/publications/raterisk/rates14.html.*

Wallace, R. B. (2001). Prevention of cancer in elderly. In E. A. Swanson, T. Tripp-Reimer, & K. Buckwalter (Eds.), *Health promotion and disease prevention in the older adults: Interventions and recommendations* (pp. 146–155). New York: Springer.

Yanick, R., Ganz, P. A., Varricchio, C. G., & Conley, B. (2001). Perspectives on comorbidity and cancer in older patients: Approaches to expand the knowledge base. *Journal of Clinical Oncology, 19*(4), 1147–1151.

AMY L. AI

LYNN CARRIGAN

Older Adults With Age-Related Cardiovascular Disease

According to the U.S. Census Bureau, 40 million Americans will be age 65 or older in 2010 (cited in AHA, 2005). This population-aging trend will considerably increase the incidence of chronic diseases, especially age-related cardiovascular diseases (CVD). Social workers must enhance their knowledge of CVD to improve their practice with the elderly. This chapter describes the immense impact of age-related CVD on society, older persons, and the disadvantaged, its important mental health comorbidity, particularly depression, and related social work practice.

THE SIGNIFICANT IMPACT OF CVD ON SOCIETY AND AN AGING POPULATION

According to the World Health Organization (WHO), 16.7 million of the global population die of CVD each year; about one-half of all deaths (8.6 million) are women (cited in AHA, 2003). CVD has been the leading cause of death in Europe each year and in the United States since 1900. Incidence of CVD is now higher in India and China than in all developed countries combined. With the global population aging, CVD will become the leading cause of death in developing countries by 2010 (American Heart Association, 2003).

In the United States, the estimated cost of CVD and stroke was $393.5 billion in 2005, nearly $175 billion more than the estimated cost of all cancers and HIV infections (AHA, 2005). More than 1 of 4 Americans were affected by CVD in 2001 (AHA, 2003). It is the leading cause of premature death for men and women of all racial/ethnic groups. CVD claimed 1,400,000 lives, that is, 1 of every 12.6 deaths in 2002. Each year, CVD claims as many lives as the next five leading causes of death combined (i.e., cancer, chronic lower respiratory diseases, accidents, diabetes mellitus, and influenza/pneumonia). Over 83% of CHD deaths occur in people age 65 and older (AHA, 2005). Since 1984, more women have died of CVD than men, and this gap continues to increase dramatically (American Heart Association, 2003).

Regarding incidence, 1 in 3 individuals age 65 or older has suffered some form of heart disease or stroke (AHA, 2003). Studies have found that average annual rates of first major CVD event rose from 7 per 1,000 men at ages 35 to 44 to 68 per 1,000 at ages 85 to 94 (American Heart Association, 2005). The comparable rates occur 10 years later for women, but the gap between men and women narrows with advancing age. After age 75, the prevalence of CVD is greater in women than men (AHA, 2003). CVD such as coronary heart disease (CHD), ischemic attack in brain (stroke), high blood pressure (hypertension), irregular heart beat (arrhythmia), and congestive heart failure (CHF) are related to aging. Women after menopause are 2 to 3 times more likely to have CHD than are women of the same age who are premenopausal (AHA, 2005).

Regarding mortality, CHD is the single largest killer of Americans among all CVDs (National Academy on an Aging Society, 2000a). Of Americans who die of CHD, 83% are age 65 and older (AHA, 2005). After age 70, lifetime risk of CHD is 35% for men and 24% for women. CHD is the leading reason for short-stay hospitalization, of which 58% was for older persons (American Heart Association, 2003). Of people age 70 and older, those with heart disease are more likely to use prescription drugs and social services such as a social worker, adult day care, rehabilitation, transportation, and Meals on Wheels than their younger counterparts. CHD is the most debilitating type of CVD. Among adults with CHD, about 33% of those age 51 to 61 and about 50% of those age 70 and older have difficulty with one or more activities of daily living (ADL), and 40% require assistance. Family members provide 65% of their in-home help and 70% of their instrumental ADL needs. So, older persons with CHD are likely to experience early retirement and low satisfaction with retirement (National Academy on an Aging Society, 2000a).

Resulting from narrowing coronary arteries that causes insufficient blood and oxygen supply to the heart, CHD causes angina pectoris (chest pain), myocardial infarction (MI or heart attack), and sudden cardiac arrest. In the United States, the average age of a person experiencing a first MI is 65.8 for men and 70.4 for women. After suffering a recognized MI, 25% of men and 38% of women will die within a year. Because women tend to have MI in older age, they are more likely to die within a few weeks of the occurrence. After surviving an MI, the risk of another MI, sudden death, angina pectoris, heart failure, or stroke remarkably increases. In such survivors, within 6 years, nearly 22% of men and 46% of women will be disabled with heart failure. CHD is the leading cause of premature, permanent disability in the U.S. labor force and accounts for 19% of Social Security disability insurance payments (American Heart Association, 2003 (AHA, 2005); National Academy on an Aging Society, 2000a).

CVD, including CHD, strike many workers in the lower social strata, who are often served by social workers. In the United States, monthly earnings for workers with heart disease, especially older adults with ADL limitations, are considerably lower than for other workers (National Academy on an Aging Society, 2000a). The premature death rate from CHD for male manual workers (e.g., builders) is 58% higher than for nonmanual workers (e.g., lawyers). The comparable rate for female manual workers is more than twice as high than for their nonmanual counterparts (American Heart Association, 2003). In developed countries, people with lower socioeconomic status (SES) have a higher incidence and higher mortality of CVD, including CHD. The burden of CHD will shift to the low-SES group in developing countries as a CVD epidemic matures along with economic transition, urbanization, industrialization, and globalization that bring about lifestyle changes there.

DIFFERENTIAL RACE AND ETHNICITY IMPACTS OF CVD

Rates of CVD are higher in non-Hispanic Blacks than in non-Hispanic Whites in the United States (American Heart Association, 2005). In people age 65 and older, rates of new and recurrent MI are higher in non-Black men than in Black men, but lower in non-Black women than in Black women. This discrepancy seems not to be explained simply by genetic factors. Other socioeconomic contributors may also need to be taken into account. Blacks are more likely than Whites to die from heart disease. This gap between Blacks and Whites has widened since the 1980s (Centers for Disease Control and Prevention, 1998). The incidence of CHF approaches 1% of Americans age 65 and older (American Heart Association, 2005). CHF rates are higher in Black men than in other men only in the subgroup of ages 75 to 84, and higher in Black women than in other women in ages 65 to 84. Stroke is a leading cause of serious, long-term disability in the United States, and about 88% of stroke deaths occur in people age 65 and older. Rates of stroke in older persons increase with age, from 2.7% to 3.6% in men and 1.6% to 4.1% in women. In ages 65 to 85, racial and ethnic minority populations have a higher relative risk of stroke death (American Heart Association, 2003). This disparity can be understood only through more research on the SES of aging in conjunction with race factors in the United States.

Around the globe, 600 million people with hypertension are at risk of MI, stroke, and CHF, according to WHO (American Heart Association, 2003). Among people older than age 60, as many as 50% in some populations are hypertensive (AHA, 2003). Nearly one in three Americans has hypertension, but 30% of them are unaware of it because no symptoms are present (AHA, 2005). Of Americans diagnosed with hypertension, nearly 66% are age 55 and older, of whom 42% are covered by Medicare and 12% by Medicaid.

Among those age 70 and older, nearly all are publicly insured, and 63% are women (National Academy on an Aging Society, 2000b). Rates of hypertension are higher in Blacks (41.8%) and Mexicans (34.5%) than in Whites (32.2%). In Blacks, especially women, hypertension is a particularly powerful risk factor for CHD. Blacks with hypertension are more than twice as likely to suffer health-related work limitations than are other Blacks (American Heart Association, 2003).

Black and Mexican American women have more CVD risk factors than do White women with comparable SES. Most CVD risk factors that tend to increase with lower SES are preventable. Rates of tobacco smoking are exceptionally higher in American Indian and Alaska Native men (32.0%) and women (36.9%) than in White men (25.2%) and women (20.7%). The prevalence of high total cholesterol levels is greater in Mexican American men (54%) than in other racial and gender groups, except in White men (51%). Yet, the rate of total cholesterol levels higher than 240 mg/dL is even greater in Asian American, Pacific Islanders, American Indians, Alaska Native, and Hispanics (25.6%–28.6%) than White and Black populations (10.6%–19.9%). Black and Hispanic men and women, as well as Asian American women, have higher physical inactivity rates. Defined as a body mass index of 25.0 Kg/m and higher, overweight and obesity in people age 60 and older is much more common in Black women (77.2%) and Mexican American men (73.1%) and women (71.7%) than in non-Hispanic White men (69.4%) and women (57.2%). Finally, another CVD risk factor, diabetes mellitus, is almost twice as common in Mexican Americans and non-Hispanic Blacks than it is in non-Hispanic Whites (American Heart Association, 2005).

THE MENTAL HEALTH COMORBIDITY OF AGE-RELATED CVD

According to the National Institute of Mental Health (2005), depression affects more than 18.8 million adults in the United States. However, depressive symptoms are often missed by health care professionals. Depression is one of the most common complications of every chronic condition, including CHD, MI, and stroke (National Academy on an Aging Society, 2000c). Particularly in the past decade, numerous studies have shown depression and anxiety as major CVD comorbidities (Hemingway, Malik, & Marmot, 2001; Pignay-Demaria, Lesperance, Demaria, Frasure-Smith, & Perrault, 2003; Rozanski, Blumenthal, & Kaplan, 1999).

Over the past 10 years, mounting evidence has shown depression to be an important predictor of CHD morbidity and prognosis. Research finds an increasing prevalence of depression in various CHD conditions, including unstable angina, CHF, MI, and coronary catheterization or angioplasty (Burg & Abrams, 2001; Frasure-Smith, Lespérance, Juneau, & Talajic, 1999; Krantz, Sheps, Carney, & Natelson, 2000; Lane, Carrol, & Lip, 2003; Scheidt, 2000; Severus, Littman, & Stoll, 2001; Smith, 2001). Depending on the sample and instrument used, the prevalence of major depression is estimated to be 16% to 23%, and that of clinically significant depressive symptoms 31.5% to 60% (Musselman, Evans, & Nemeroff, 1998). Current meta-analyses have linked depression with CHD-related mortality, especially 3 years after an initial assessment (Barth, Schumacher, & Herrmann-Lingen, 2004), and with post-MI mortality and CV events (van Melle et al., 2004). Anxiety also was shown to influence CHD prognosis and mortality (Kubzansky, Kawachi, Weiss, & Sparrow, 1998; Rozanski et al., 1999) and to be an independent predictor for post-MI cardiac events and health care consumption (Strik, Denollet, Lousberg, & Honig, 2003).

Mental health symptoms manifest in the process of and affect the outcomes of advanced cardiac surgery treatments for heart disease. From 1979 to 2002, the number of cardiac procedures (e.g., diagnostic cardiac catheterization, percutaneous transluminal coronary angioplasty or PTCA procedures, cardiac pacemaker procedures, endarterectomy procedures, coronary artery bypass graft procedure or CABG, and heart valve procedures) increased 470% in the United States (American Heart Association, 2005). Through vasculization of coronary arteries, CABG surgery has achieved impressive long-term clinical efficacy in terms of symptom relief. Although coronary bypass graft and valve replacement can save life and improve cardiac function, all patients must be fully informed before the operation about related side effects and risks (Ai, Peterson, Tice, Bolling, & Koenig, 2004). Research has shown that distress in the waiting time prior to surgery may account for the variance in recovery indices (Pirraglia, Peterson, Williams-Russo, Gorkin, & Charlson, 1999). The majority of CABG patients experience psychosocial effects before the surgery, from psychological complications to impaired social functioning.

The cost of cardiac surgery strains some social factors (e.g., financial resources and other support) that may intensify the stressful situation preoperatively (Ai, Peterson, & Bolling, 1997). However, studies have found that age is inversely related to preoperative distress in cardiac surgery patients (Plach, Napholz, & Kelber, 2003). Among patients undergoing cardiac surgery, the incidence of depression varies among studies between 7.5% and 47% preoperatively and 19%

and 61% postoperatively, depending on instruments used (Pignay-Demaria et al., 2003). Depression symptom levels remained stable before and after surgery (Andrew, Baker, Kneebone, & Knight, 2000; Pignay-Demaria et al., 2003) and even predicted mental status 1 year after operation (Boudrez & DeBacker, 2001). Several follow-up studies have indicated that depression is a major risk factor for readmission, new cardiac events, poorer quality of life, and especially cardiac mortality in patients undergoing cardiac surgery (Baker, Andrew, Schrader, & Knight, 2001; Ben-Zur, Rappaport, Ammar, & Uretzky, 2000; Pignay-Demaria et al., 2003).

Until recently, however, no major attempt has been made to influence routine screening, prevention, or treatment of depression among patients with MI or CHF or undergoing cardiac surgery (Richardson, 2003; Scheidt, 2000). Yet, even if symptoms were identified in these patients, pharmacological treatment of depression under a surgical or MI circumstance would be difficult, given the complex pathophysiology involved (Pignay-Demaria et al., 2003). For instance, selective serotonin reuptake inhibitors (SSRIs) are currently the most widely prescribed antidepressant drugs because of their good safety profile, but some SSRIs may interact with cardiovascular drugs.

Researchers have recommended the combination of SSRIs with cognitive-behavior therapy as the most effective treatments of depression in CHF (Guck, Elsasser, Kavan, & Barone, 2003). A review of available research, however, reveals that current treatment for depression has not necessarily improved cardiac event-free survival in post-acute-MI patients (Carney, Freedland, Veith, & Jaffe, 1999; Louis, Manousos, Coletta, Clark, & Cleland, 2002).

One large-sample clinical trial, Enhancing Recovery in Coronary Heart Disease, compared the cognitive-behavioral intervention for depression and social isolation to usual care. Despite reduced depression, the treatment showed no effect on post-MI reinfarction or mortality. One explanation was that depression was not related to increased post-MI mortality, a finding inconsistent with other studies (The ENRICHD Investigators, 2001). In another large clinical trial, the Sertraline Antidepressant Heart Attack Trial (Shapiro, Lesperance, & Frasure-Smith, 1999), although antidepressant use reduced depression, it did not affect left ventricular ejection fraction and ventricular arrhythmia. In addition to these two clinical trials, inconsistency has been noted in the association between post-MI prognosis and negative emotions from various observational studies (Lane et al., 2003). Therefore,

interdisciplinary research is now focusing on multiple psychophysiological pathways between mental and cardiac health and mechanisms in these associations. These include health-related behaviors, negative emotions, acute stress, autonomic nervous system regulation, platelet activation, hypothalamo-pituitary-adrenal axis activity, and inflammatory processes.

Without a singled-out "cure," the key to the prognosis and the quality of life in CVD patients with depression or anxiety may lie in the appropriate multidisciplinary management. To play a significant role in this team approach, social workers need to understand psychosocial protectors in CVD patients in current research. Lower SES contributed to greater depression, whereas social support, adaptive coping, and exercise may improve symptomatology and well-being (Ai, Dunkle, Peterson, & Bolling, 1998; Ai et al., 1997; Pirraglia et al., 1999; Sykes, Hanley, Boyle, & Higginson, 2000; van-Elderen, Maes, & Dusseldorp, 1999). In middle-aged and older cardiac surgery patients, social involvement and lack of finding comfort in religion were significant predictors of mortality (Oxman, Freeman, & Mannheimer, 1995). Using prayer for coping contributed to better mental health postoperatively (Ai et al., 1998).

There is also evidence that positive attitudes predicted better outcomes in CVD patients. Following a first MI, optimism was related to fewer hospital readmissions, whereas pessimism predicated subsequent death. Among patients undergoing CABG, optimism was associated with better quality of life, a faster rate of physical recovery during the period of hospitalization, a faster rate of return to normal life activities subsequent to discharge, and better postoperative quality of life at 6 months. Within 6 months following the first PTCA procedure, patients at lower risk for a new cardiac event (e.g., CABG, PTCA, MI, or disease progression) were those who responded to their illness by perceiving control over their future, having positive expectations about their future, and having a positive view of themselves, as measured in a previous study (Helgeson & Fritz, 1999). A study of larger samples has linked hope with the survival advantage of stroke patients (Lewis, Dennis, O'Rourke, & Sharpe, 2001).

IMPLICATIONS FOR SOCIAL WORK ASSESSMENT AND INTERVENTION

Given the importance of mental health and sociocultural factors in CVDs, gerontological social work can play a significant role in future cardiac care. Social workers may contribute to the outcome of CVD in the aging society through policy analysis, advocacy, community intervention, and psychosocial care. For example, in the policy arena, the lack of sufficient health insurance coverage results in the failure of nearly 1 in 5 Medicare beneficiaries with hypertension to purchase the recommended prescription drugs (National Academy on an Aging Society, 2000b). The national debate about health care reform and funding for prescription drug coverage, Medicare, and Social Security is an opportunity for social workers to pursue policies that will provide needed assistance for their clients. Social workers in geriatric and community care should voice the needs of these older CVD patients and help them obtain comprehensive and supplemental health insurance, other state or federal health program benefits, discounted drugs direct from pharmaceutical companies, or other resources to prevent the worst outcomes, such as MI, stroke, and sudden cardiac arrest. These consequences are mostly likely to increase the expensive use of emergency care and the chance of disability, resulting in great socioeconomic burden for individuals, their family members, and the society.

Because of the complexity of CVD impact on individuals and families, care of older cardiac patients must be interdisciplinary. New research suggests that their mental health and social needs remain largely unmet (Anderson et al., 2001). Social workers should assume various responsibilities in preventive and clinical cardiac care (Anderson et al, 2001; Proctor, Morrow-Howell, Li, & Dore, 1999–2000; Sulman & Verhaeghe, 1994; Thurlow, 1995). Because most types of CVD are both treatable and preventable, gerontological social workers should in general promote the awareness of and prevention strategies for CVDs among older clients. These should include both the promotion of health behaviors that can prevent the CVD-related functional declination and the treatment of mental health symptoms that can contribute to poor prognosis of CVDs.

To assist older patients and families to cope with acute and chronic cardiac conditions, gerontological social workers must first engage in an in-depth exploration of responses to cardiac events in hospital and community-oriented care. Assessment involves multiple elements and their interrelationships: socioeconomic factors, access to health care services, prescription drug coverage, mental health symptoms, coping behaviors, daily activity level, functional abilities, adjustment to illness, social support, family dynamics, financial resources, sexual concerns, and legal issues of competency, advanced directives, and durable

power of attorney for health care. Risks such as obesity, physical inactivity, smoking, chemical dependency, and abuse or neglect must also be explored. Family members should be interviewed to determine their understanding of care needs and their ability to support the patient in constructive and concrete ways. Assessing existing involvement with community agencies and the need for additional support to meet basic living and medical requirements is a key aspect of developing a treatment plan, as is the readiness, willingness, and ability of the patient and family to accept new services.

Using standardized measurements can enhance comprehensive biopsychosocial assessment and help practitioners gauge patients' perceptions of their health status in the treatment process. The MacNew Heart Disease Health-Related Quality of Life questionnaires (Hofer, Lim, Guyatt, & Oldridge, 2004) assess three primary domains—physical limitations, emotional function, and social function—as well as physical symptoms (chest pains, shortness of breath, fatigue, dizziness, aching legs). Such tools allow social workers to be aware of the multilevel impacts of heart disease from the patient's perspective. With an in-depth assessment, the social worker can develop effective action plans with patients to address their needs, including the complex interplay of depression symptoms in all three domains. Social workers are then prepared to contribute as an effective team member for multidisciplinary intervention.

Social workers assisting CVD patients must include families in treatment planning, not only as therapeutic allies, but also in regard to the multiple stresses that caregivers experience (Lim & Zebrack, 2004). In addition to evaluating the patient's coping methods, gerontological social workers need to assess the impact of shifting roles and responsibilities on family members, who often suffer great disruptions in their daily routine and quality of life as they are called on for help in care coordination. Stressors include the degree of caregiving demands, patient impairment, the duration and intensity of care, ADL dependency, caregiver overload, recurrence of illness and problem behavior in the patient, and lack of assistance in caregiving. Family members who are older, isolated, or with prior health or disability problems have been found to have more difficulty in their attempts to assist with care. Loss of physical strength and its impact on the caregiver's self-esteem is associated with lower quality of life, as is lower income and a distressed relationship with the patient.

CVD, especially MI and stroke, can occur in seemingly healthy persons in their most productive years, causing sudden death and permanent disability that leave unprepared families in devastation. Assistance with family communications and decision making around critical events is a very important part of the social work service. Support for acceptance of limitations, personal self-care, and the possible need for additional help can reduce conflict around the potential burden of caregiving. Family members also need ongoing education to aid them in formulating realistic perceptions of caregiving in relations to the dynamic processes of disease, treatment, and recovery or decline. Because hospitalization from CVDs creates major social and individual costs, in their assessment social workers should pay special attention to identify older cardiac patients at risk for readmission. Advanced age increased risk of readmission within 3 months after discharge, as did living alone and coping difficulties (Berkman, Millar, Holmes, & Bonander, 1991). Social and environmental factors, such as the adequacy of home care, have been found to be critical for preventing hospital readmission. One study attributed 40% to 50% of CHF readmissions to social problems and lack of community services (Proctor et al., 1999–2000). Risk factors for readmission included sicker conditions during the first 2 weeks postdischarge, inadequate compliance with prescribed medication regimens, and insufficient home care. The key to preventing readmission thus lies in the quantity and quality of home care supports. Gerontological social workers in hospital and home care must take an integrative approach to the posthospital care assessment and discharge planning. Central to this plan is to identify a helper or programs for assisting with specific ADLs: preparing meals, helping with toilet functions, managing medications, and encouraging or supervising appropriate levels of exercise for rehabilitation.

For effective psychosocial intervention with CVD patients, geriatric social workers can provide individual and family support, treatment for depression and anxiety, crisis intervention, prevention and health promotion workshops, and psychosocial cardiac education. They can also facilitate interdisciplinary teamwork, offer grief counseling, and make referrals and community connections to address needs of patients and families. In addition, social workers may need to help patients and families navigate systems of insurance and drug coverage, disability income, and subsidized housing, assisted living, or nursing home care. Advance planning for expected further deterioration or a terminal event is recommended if the patient or family is amenable. A discussion about health care directives or funeral planning can be linked to the value of self-determination and decision making, which is most effective when not crisis-driven.

The role of gerontological social workers in assisting patients and families with durable powers of attorney for health care, living wills, and decisions regarding resuscitation and its various components cannot be overstated. Families need help understanding the difference between these documents, when each go into effect, and how to ensure that all health care providers, family members, and emergency personnel know the wishes of the CVD patient.

As noted, disease burden associated with CVD falls disproportionately on several racial/ethnic minority populations (American Heart Association, 2003; 2005). Other than their disadvantaged SES, the high prevalence of risk factors, such as higher cholesterol levels, obesity, inactive lifestyles, unhealthy food, smoking, and diabetes mellitus are major contributors to this disparity. Medical professionals, however, tend neither to be aware of cultural-related problems, nor to pay attention to health disparity issues.

Geriatric social workers can become valuable team members by incorporating culture-sensitive assessment and interventions into health care for minority CVD patients (Galambos, 2003; Panos & Panos, 2000). They should obtain the cardiac and self-care information about diverse populations and understand the particular socioeconomic and political environment that directly affects the incidence of comorbidity in minority CVD patients. Medical and community social workers must develop awareness of institutionalized oppression and their own cultural values, biases, and beliefs that may influence clinical practice. Culturally competent practice may improve compliance with medical care. It is thus critical to develop communication skills that adequately demonstrate respect for and address cultural orientation, primary language, level of acculturation, historical trauma, and community involvement in care for minority, older cardiac patients.

In the development of treatment plans, geriatric social workers must be prepared to challenge prevailing medical models that may pathologize culturally based behavior. They should consider and incorporate patients' beliefs about health, disease, service utilization, and culture-bound healing systems. Community-based collective experience and values may preempt cardiac patients' decision making regarding roles and relationships, expectations of functioning, and determinants of quality of life. Illustratively, traditional risk factors in the disproportionately high incidence of CHD among native Hawaiians were found to be compounded by barriers in the health care system.

The high costs of medications and care, isolated communities, and lack of culturally compatible practitioners and indigenous healing practices reduced the acceptability of Western health services. Culturally responsive strategies (e.g., lower-cost nutrition programs, outreach to *traditional* clubs, health education involving traditional foods, sliding fee scales, and encouragement of family involvement in decision making) appeared to enhance disease management in this population (Mokuau, Hughes, & Tsark, 1995).

Finally, the heart is related to mind and spirit in many cultural legacies. In Oriental medicine, the heart is highly sensitive to abrupt emotional stress; it was believed to be "an organ of the mind." In the West, French philosopher Blaise Pascal in his famous *Pensées* stated: "The heart has its reasons which reason does not know." (An American poet, Henry Wadsworth Longfellow, wrote, "The heart hath its own memory like the mind, And in it are enshrined the precious keepsake, into which is wrought the giver's loving thought"(cited in Ai, 1996). Given the positive role of spirituality and expectations in cardiac care, social workers should be keenly attentive to the spirituality of older patients. They should help them to identify and mobilize such resources as faith strength, deepest values, disciplines, and positive attitudes (hope and optimism) in their coping with difficulties in the cardiac disease process (Anandarajah & Hight, 2001; Fallot, 1998). As team members, gerontological social workers may need to educate older patients and other health care professionals about the importance of a contextual biopsychosocial-spiritual approach to cardiac care. The integration of culturally sensitive clinical models of care, with awareness of structural, political, and economic disparities and advocacy for equal access to care, is a challenge to which we must rise in conventional medical care to promote the quality of life for cardiac patients.

NOTE

The cardiac study of Amy L. Ai was supported by National Institute on Aging Grant 1 RO3 AGO 15686-01, National Center for Complementary and Alternative Medicine Grant P50 AT00011, a grant from the John Templeton Foundation, and the Hartford Geriatric Faculty Scholars Program. The opinions expressed in this chapter are those of the authors and do not necessarily reflect the views of these organizations.

REFERENCES

Ai, A. L. (1996). Psychosocial adjustment and health care practices following coronary artery bypass surgery (CABG). Dissertation Abstracts International: Section B: The Sciences and Engineering, 57 (6-B), 4078.

Ai, A. L., Dunkle, R. E., Peterson, C., & Bolling, S. F. (1998). The role of private prayer in psychosocial recovery among midlife and aged patients following cardiac surgery. The Gerontologist, 38, 591–601.

Ai, A. L., Peterson, C., & Bolling, S. F. (1997). Psychological recovery following coronary artery bypass graft surgery: The use of complementary therapy. The Journal of Alternative and Complementary Medicine, 3, 343–353.

Ai, A. L., Peterson, C., Bolling, S. F., & Koenig, H. (2002). Private prayer and the optimism of middle-age and older patients awaiting cardiac surgery. The Gerontologist, 42, 70–81.

Ai, A. L., Peterson, C., Tice, T. N., Bolling, S. F., & Koenig, H. (2004). Faith-based and secular pathways to hope and optimism subconstructs in middle-aged and older cardiac patients. Journal of Health Psychology, 9, 435–450.

American Heart Association (2003). Heart disease and stroke statistics 2003 update. Dallas, TX: American Heart Association.

American Heart Association. (2005). Heart disease and stroke statistics 2005 update. Retrieved July 19, 2005, from http://www.americanheart.org/downloadable/heart/1105390918119HDSStats2005Update.pdf.

Anandarajah, G., & Hight, E. (2001). Spirituality and medical practice: Using the HOPE questions as a practical tool for spiritual assessment. American Academy of Family Physicians, 63, 81–89.

Anderson, H., Ward, C., Eardley, A., Gomm, S. A., Connolly, M., Coppinger, T., et al. (2001). The concerns of patients under palliative care and a heart failure clinic are not being met. Palliative Medicine, 15, 279–286.

Andrew, M. J., Baker, R. A., Kneebone, A. C., & Knight, J. L. (2000). Mood state as a predictor of neuropsychological deficits following cardiac surgery. Journal of Psychosomatic Research, 48, 537–546.

Baker, R. A., Andrew, M. J., Schrader, G., & Knight, J. L. (2001). Preoperative depression and mortality in coronary artery bypass surgery: Preliminary findings. Australia and New Zealand Journal of Surgery, 71, 139–142.

Barth, J., Schumacher, M., & Herrmann-Lingen, C. (2004). Depression as a risk factor for mortality in patients with coronary heart disease: A meta-analysis. Psychosomatic Medicine, 66(6), 802–813.

Ben-Zur, H., Rappaport, B., Ammar, R., & Uretzky, G. (2000). Coping strategy, life style changes, and pessimism after open-heart surgery. *Health Social Work, 25*, 201–209.

Berkman, B., Millar, S., Holmes, W., & Bonander, E. (1991). Predicting elderly cardiac patients at risk for readmission. *Social Work Health Care, 16*, 21–38.

Boudrez, H., & DeBacker, G. (2001). Psychological status and the role of coping style after coronary artery bypass graft surgery. Results of a prospective study. *Quality of Life Research, 10*(1), 37–47.

Burg, M. M., & Abrams, D. (2001). Depression in chronic medical illness: The case of coronary heart disease. *Journal of Clinical Psychology, 57*, 1323–1237.

Carney, R. M., Freedland, K. E., Veith, R. C., & Jaffe, A. S. (1999). Can treating depression reduce mortality after an acute myocardial infarction? *Psychosomatic Medicine, 61*, 666–675.

Centers for Disease Control and Prevention. (1998). Trends in ischemic heart disease death rates for Blacks and Whites: United States, 1981–1995. *Mortality and Morbidity Weekly Report, 47*, 945–949.

Duits, A. A., Boeke, S., Taamms, M. A., Passchier, J., & Erdman, R. A. M. (1997). Prediction of quality of life after coronary artery bypass graft surgery: A review and evaluation of multiple, recent studies. *Psychosomatic Medicine, 59*, 257–268.

The ENRICHD Investigators. (2003). Enhancing Recovery in Coronary Heart Disease (ENRICHD): Baseline characteristics. *American Journal of Cardiology, 88*, 316–322.

Fallot, R. D. (1998). Recommendations for integrating spirituality in mental health services. *New Directions in Mental Health Services, 80*, 3–12.

Frasure-Smith, N., Lesperance, F., Junean, M., Talajic, M., & Bourassa, M. G. (1999). Gender, depression, and one-year prognosis after myocardial infarction. *Psychosomatic Medicine, 61*, 26–37.

Galambos, C. M. (2003). Moving cultural diversity toward cultural competence in health care. *Health and Social Work, 28*, 3–7.

Guck, T. P., Elsasser, G. N., Kavan, M. G., & Barone, E. J. (2003). Depression and congestive heart failure. *Congestive Heart Failure, 9*, 1–8.

Helgeson, V. S., & Fritz, H. L. (1999). Cognitive adaptation as a predictor of new coronary events after percutaneous transluminal coronary angioplasty. *Psychosomatic Medicine, 61*, 488–495.

Hemingway, H., Malik, M., & Marmot, M. (2001). Social and psychosocial influences on sudden cardiac death, ventricular arrhythmia and cardiac autonomic function. *European Heart Journal, 22*, 1082–1101.

Hofer, S., Lim, L. Guyatt, G., & Oldridge, N. (2004). The MacNew heart disease health-related quality of life instrument: A summary. *Health and Quality of Life Outcomes, 2*(3), January 8, 2004. Retrieved from *www.hqlo.com/content/2/1/3*.

Krantz, D. S., Sheps, D. S., Carney, R. M., & Natelson, B. H. (2000). Effects of mental stress in patients with coronary artery disease: Evidence and clinical implications. *Journal of the American Medical Association, 283*, 1800–1802.

Kubzansky, L. D., Kawachi, I., Weiss, S. T., & Sparrow, D. (1998). Anxiety and coronary heart disease: A synthesis of epidemiological, psychological, and experimental evidence. *Annals of Behavioral Medicine, 20*, 47–58.

Lane, D., Carrol, D., & Lip, G. Y. H. (2003). Anxiety, depression, and prognosis after myocardial infarction: Is there a causal association? *Journal of the American College of Cardiology, 42*, 1808–1810.

Lewis, S. C., Dennis, M. S., O'Rourke, S. J., & Sharpe, M. (2001). Negative attitudes among short-term stroke survivors predict worse long-term survival. *Stroke, 32*, 1640–1645.

Lim, J., & Zebrack, B. (2004). Caring for family members with chronic physical illness: A critical review of caregiver literature. *Health and Quality of Life Outcomes, 2*, 50.

Louis, A. A., Manousos, I. R., Coletta, A. P., Clark, A. L., & Cleland, J. G. F. (2002). Clinical trials update: The Heart Protection Study, IONA, ACUTE, ALIVE, MADIT II and REMATCH. *European Journal of Heart Failure, 4*, 111–116.

Mokuau, N., Hughes, C. K., & Tsark, J. U. (1995). Heart disease and associated risk factors among Hawaiians: Culturally responsive strategies. *Health and Social Work, 20*, 46–59.

Musselman, D. L., Evans, D. L., & Nemeroff, C. B. (1998). The relationship of depression to cardiovascular disease. *Archives of General Psychiatry, 55*, 580–592.

National Academy on an Aging Society. (2000a, January). *Heart disease: A disabling yet preventable condition.* No. 3. Washington, DC: Author. Available at *www.agingsociety.org*.

National Academy on an Aging Society. (2000b, October). *Hypertension.* No. 12. Washington, DC: Author. Available at *www.agingsociety.org*.

National Academy on an Aging Society. (2000c, July). *Depression: A treatable disease.* No. 9. Washington, DC: Author. Available at *www.agingsociety.org*.

National Institute of Mental Health. (2005). *Depression* Available at http://www.nimh.nik.gov./publication/depression.cfn.

Oxman, T. E., Freeman, D. H., Manheimer, E. D., (1995). Lack of social participation or religious strength and comfort as risk factors for death after cardiac surgery in the elderly. *Psychosomatic Medicine, 57,* 5–15.

Panos, P. T., & Panos, A. J. (2000). A model for a culture-sensitive assessment of patients in health care settings. *Social Work in Health Care, 31,* 49–62.

Pignay-Demaria, V., Lesperance, F., Demaria, R. G., Frasure-Smith, N., & Perrault, L. P. (2003). Depression and anxiety and outcomes of coronary artery bypass surgery. *Annals of Thoracic Surgery, 75,* 314–321.

Pirraglia, P. A., Peterson, J. C., Williams-Russo, P., Gorkin, L., & Charlson, M. E. (1999). Depressive symptomatology in coronary artery bypass graft surgery patients. *International Journal of Geriatric Psychiatry, 14,* 668–680.

Plach, S. K., Napholz, L., & Kelber, S. T. (2003). Depression during early recovery from heart surgery among early middle-age, midlife, and elderly women. *Health Care for Women International, 24,* 327–339.

Proctor, E., Morrow-Howell, N., Li, H., & Dore, P. (1999–2000). Adequacy of home care and hospital readmission for elderly congestive heart failure patients. *Health and Social Work, 24–25,* 87–96.

Richardson, L. G. (2003). Psychosocial issues in patients with congestive heart failure. *Progressive Cardiovascular Nursing, 18,* 19–23.

Rozanski, A., Blumenthal, J. A., & Kaplan, J. (1999). Impact of psychological factors on the pathogenesis of cardiovascular disease and implications for therapy. *Circulation, 99,* 2192–2217.

Scheidt, S. (2000). The current status of heart-mind relationships. *Journal of Psychosomatic Research, 48* (4–5), 317–320.

Severus, W. E., Littman, A. B., & Stoll, A. L. (2001). Omega-3 fatty acids, homocysteine, and the increased risk of cardiovascular mortality in major depressive disorder. *Harvard Review of Psychiatry, 6,* 280–293.

Shapiro, P. A., Lesperance, F., & Frasure-Smith, N. (1999). An open-label preliminary trial of sertraline for treatment of major depression after acute myocardial infarction (the SADHAT trial): Sertraline Antidepressant Heart Attack Trial. *American Heart Journal, 137,* 1100–1106.

Smith, D. F. (2001). Negative emotions and coronary heart disease: Causally related or merely coexistent? A review. *Scandinavian Journal of Psychology, 42,* 57–69.

Strik, J. J. M. H., Denollet, J., Lousberg, R., & Honig, A. (2003). Comparing symptoms of depression and anxiety as predictors of cardiac events and increased health care consumption after myocardial infarction. *Journal of the American College of Cardiology, 42*(10), 1801–1807.

Sulman, J., & Verhaeghe, G. (1994). Social work practice with myocardial infarction patients in an acute care hospital. In M. J. Holosko & P. A. Taylor (Eds.), *Social work practice in health care settings* (pp. 45–61). Toronto: Canadian Scholar's Press.

Sykes, D. H., Hanley, M., Boyle, D. M., & Higginson, J. D. (2000). Work strain and the post-discharge adjustment of patients following a heart attack. *Psychology and Health, 15,* 609–623.

Thurlow, T. J. (1995). The role of the cardiovascular social worker. *Nursing Clinics of North America, 30,* 211–219.

van-Elderen, T., Maes, S., & Dusseldorp, E. (1999). Coping with coronary heart disease: A longitudinal study. *Journal of Psychosomatic Research, 47,* 175–183.

van Melle, J. P., de Jonge, P., Spijkerman, T. A., Tijssen, J. G., Ormel, J., van Veldhuisen, D. J., et al. (2004). Prognostic association of depression following myocardial infarction with mortality and cardiovascular events: A meta-analysis. *Psychosomatic Medicine, 66,* 814–822.

The American Diabetes Association (ADA; 2004a, pg. S5) defines diabetes mellitus as "a group of metabolic diseases characterized by hyperglycemia resulting from defects in insulin secretion, insulin action, or both." Type 1 diabetes mellitus (T1DM) accounts for approximately 5% to 10% of all diagnosed cases of diabetes; it is also referred to as insulin-dependent diabetes or juvenile-onset diabetes. Type 2 diabetes mellitus (T2DM) is the most common form of diabetes, accounting for approximately 90% to 95% of all diagnosed cases, and is frequently referred to as non-insulin-dependent diabetes or adult-onset diabetes. Whereas individuals with T1DM need insulin injections to survive, this is not true for individuals with T2DM, who can control hyperglycemia through a careful diet and exercise regimen and oral medication (ADA, 2003) Older age, obesity, and minority race/ethnicity are among the most significant risk factors for T2DM (ADA, 2004b).

According to the ADA (2003), approximately 8.6 million adults age 60 years or older were affected with diabetes in 2002. By 2050, the largest increase (336%) in prevalence of diagnosed diabetes will be in individuals 75 years or older (Boyle, Honeycutt, Narayan, Hoerger & Geiss, et al., 2001). Older adults with diabetes are at especially high risk for developing cardiovascular complications, kidney damage, vision problems, neuropathy, foot problems, and cognitive impairment (Croxson & Jagger, 1995; Fletcher & Dolben, 1996; Gregg, Engelgau, & Narayan, 2002; Howard, Cowan, Go, Welty, & Robbins, et al., 1998; Nilsson, Fastbom & Wahlin, 2002; Sinclair, Bayer, & Girling, 2000; Smith, Savage, Heckbert, Barzilay, & Bittner et al., 2002). Diabetes can exact a devastating toll on an older adult's biopsychosocial functioning and, if left undetected or untreated, can have life-threatening consequences (DeCoster, 2001).

Social workers frequently provide services to older populations and as a result, will regularly encounter individuals coping with diabetes. Social workers in health care settings, hospitals, nursing homes, assisted living communities, home health care agencies, and senior centers are most likely to work on a regular basis with older adults with diabetes. Social workers in other settings may be less likely to work with older adults, or with older adults diagnosed with diabetes; even so, they are likely to provide services to individuals in social support networks involving older adults, such as friends, relatives, and caregivers.

It is essential that every social worker become more knowledgeable about the impact of diabetes and its complications in older populations, as this will allow social workers to provide more appropriate and

RICHARD FRANCOEUR
JENNIFER ELKINS

Older Adults With Diabetes and Complications

3

effective services not only directly with older adults, but indirectly through family and friends. This chapter discusses complications associated with diabetes, including the medical, psychological, and social risk factors. Treatment and intervention approaches relevant to social work practice are reviewed, and implications for social work practice are highlighted at the conclusion of the chapter.

COMPLICATIONS AND RISK FACTORS ASSOCIATED WITH DIABETES

Medical Factors

Cardiovascular disease (CVD) represents perhaps the most life-threatening complication for individuals with diabetes. An adult diagnosed with diabetes carries the same cardiovascular risk as someone who already has had a heart attack. Statistics show that approximately 2 out of every 3 people with diabetes die from heart disease or stroke (Centers for Disease Control and Prevention [CDC], 2003). Erlinger, Pollack, and Appel (2000) found in a nationally representative general population of older adults that almost 90% of individuals over age 65 had one or more nutrition-related cardiovascular risk factors. Not only are women with diabetes at a higher overall risk for CVD, but diabetes also appears to have a greater negative impact across individual risk factors for CVD in women (Howard et al., 1998).

Treatment and control of cardiovascular risk factors tends to be less than ideal in a general population of older adults, and this is much more the case for older adults with diabetes (Smith et al., 2002). Unfortunately, despite being at highest risk for stroke, older adults are the least likely to be able to identify even one risk factor or warning sign (Pancioli et al., 1998). Therefore, it is particularly important for social workers, along with other members of the multidisciplinary treatment team, to focus on recognizing and educating older adults in general and older adults with diabetes about the early warning signs and risk factors for CVD.

Microvascular complications of the smallest blood vessels constitute the second category of medical complications prevalent in older adults with diabetes. Microvascular complications include retinopathy (damage to the small blood vessels in the retina resulting in vision loss), nephropathy (kidney disease, preventing removal of waste and excess fluid from the bloodstream), and peripheral neuropathy (painful nerves in the feet, legs, and hands). Most microvascular complications can be prevented, delayed, or even reversed with appropriate glycemic control (Beers & Berkow, 2004).

The strongest predictor for development and progression of retinopathy is the duration of diabetes (Fong et al., 2004). Up to 21% of individuals with T2DM have retinopathy on initial diagnosis, and most will develop some degree of nonproliferative retinopathy (NPR). And although T1DM is less common than T2DM, nearly all individuals who have T1DM for over 20 years will develop NPR (CDC, 2003). Similar to younger and middle-aged adults, control of diabetes is as important in older adults and one of the most important factors in preventing progression of retinopathy (Morisaki, Watanabe, Kobayashi, Kanzaki, & Takahaski, et al., 1994). Diabetic retinopathy progresses from mild NPR, also known as background retinopathy, which does not significantly alter vision, to moderate to severe NPR, and finally to proliferative retinopathy (PR), which can result in blindness. Other eye complications with disproportionately high prevalence in individuals with diabetes include glaucoma and cataracts.

Due in large part to the growing trends in obesity, a significant risk factor for diabetes, T2DM is increasingly diagnosed at younger ages (Maahs & Zeitler, 2004). As part of a larger 25-year longitudinal study on health in Pima Indians, the risk for retinopathy and nephropathy in individuals diagnosed with T2DM at younger ages (before 20 years) and individuals diagnosed at older ages was examined while accounting for duration of the disease (Krakoff, Lindsay, Looker, Nelson, & Hanson, et al., 2003). The investigators found that the incidence of nephropathy increased with duration and was equal in all age groups, whereas incidence of retinopathy was significantly lower in the young-onset group and in all duration categories compared to older-onset groups. Although development of retinopathy was somewhat lower in the young-onset group, a significant percentage still went on to develop complications. By an average age of 30 years, 57% of individuals with young-onset diabetes were diagnosed with nephropathy and 45% with retinopathy (Krakoff et al., 2003).

Diabetic nephropathy (DN), which is associated with kidney disease, is less common, with 10% to 21% of all people with diabetes developing kidney disease (CDC, 2003). Older adults with diabetes are twice as likely to be hospitalized for kidney infections compared to their healthy counterparts. The most severe form of DN is end-stage renal disease, which requires kidney dialysis and even transplant. Following ADA (2004d) treatment guidelines for detection of DN at an early stage by testing annually for microalbuminura is critical to preventing more severe kidney damage. End-stage renal disease is much more common in African Americans, Native Americans, and Mexican Americans than in non-Hispanic Whites (CDC, 2003).

Social workers and other health professionals can look to the promising research of the Diabetes Control and Complications Trial (DCCT) and the Epidemiology of Diabetes Interventions and Complications (EDIC) study, which demonstrated that early intensive treatment of individuals with T1DM reduces the risk of microvascular complications over a long-term period (DCCT/EDIC Research Group, 2003; EDIC Research Group, 1999). Early intensive treatment and prevention of T2DM and its complications is particularly important if we consider the growing trend toward T2DM diagnosis in children and adolescents.

About 60% to 70% of individuals with diabetes will develop mild to severe forms of DN (CDC, 2003). Severe forms of neuropathy affecting the nerves in the spinal cord and brain are much less common than milder forms of neuropathy affecting the feet, legs, and hands, which can still be very painful. Symptoms of neuropathy include loss of feeling, numbness, prickling, tingling, burning, aching, and sharp jabs of needlelike pain (ADA, 2003). Diabetes is the most common cause of neuropathy, yet at least one study found that neuropathy caused by diabetes was more common in young-old (65–79 years) patients than it was in old-old (over 80 years) patients (Verghese, Bieri, Gellido, Schaumburg, & Herskovitz, 2001). If true, social work practice and research needs to be more careful in accounting for age differences among older adults.

Plummer and Albert (1996), in a retrospective review of all charts for patients referred to a foot care service over a 2-year period, found that 56% of those with diabetes had peripheral neuropathy. Foot problems are another consequence of complications from DN. A significant number of older adults with diabetes, even those with risk factors for foot complications, do not have the recommended annual foot exams (Fletcher & Dolben, 1996). Older adults also can have difficulty completing simple and/or routine foot care advice (Plummer & Albert, 1996; Thompson & Masson, 1992). Medical complications can also interact with and exacerbate this problem. For example, an older adult with vision problems will have greater difficulty recognizing foot ulcers. Although we might initially dismiss foot problems as minor in comparison to other problems, when left untreated, they could result in more severe consequences, such as lower limb amputations. Therefore, it is critical that both the providers and the patient receive education regarding preventive foot care.

Psychological Factors

Because the number of severe and sometimes fatal complications associated with diabetes can be overwhelming to individuals living with the disease, it should come as no surprise that, like other chronic diseases, diabetes is associated with disproportionately high risk for psychological disorders. One of the consequences of comorbid diabetes and psychological disorders, such as depression, is that it can complicate an individual's ability to self-manage diabetes, which can, in turn, result in even more medical complications associated with diabetes (Araki, Murotani, Kamimiya, & Ito, 2004; Black, 1999; Kinder, Kamarck, & Baum, 2002; Rubin & Peyrot, 2001; Williams et al., 2002). The physical limitations associated with the medical complications described earlier can exact a devastating psychosocial toll on the lives of older adults. But is this always the case?

In a nationally representative sample, Blaum, Ofstedal, Langa, and Wray (2003) found that 25% of individuals 70 years or older with diabetes reported high functional status and fewer comorbid conditions. At least one study suggests that depressive symptoms are related more to the degree to which diabetes intrudes in an individual's life than the number of complications an individual might have (Talbot, Nouwen, & Gingras, 1999). Assessment of quality of life is an important aspect of the management of chronic diseases in general, and diabetes specifically (Ragonesi, Ragonesi, Merati, & Taddei, 1998). But what exactly does the term "quality of life" encompass? Frequently, it is measured in terms of functional disabilities and role limitations. A recent study (Egede, 2004) found that individuals with both diabetes and depression have more functional disabilities in comparison to individuals with diabetes or depression alone. Other studies have likewise found that the effect on functional disabilities of both diabetes and depression is greater than the effect of having only one condition or neither condition, suggesting that detecting and ameliorating mental health symptoms may offset the risk of developing functional limitations (Fultz, Ofstedal, Herzog, & Wallace, 2003).

In a study comparing older and younger adults with diabetes, Treif, Wade, Pine, and Weinstock (2003) found that, although older adults report more physical problems leading to greater role limitations, they also report less diabetes-specific emotional distress and are better at coping with and more readily accept diabetes-related lifestyle changes. The authors suggest that "coping skills, social relationships or other factors may act as buffers and prevent high levels of distress that often accompany diabetes" (p. 617). This study contradicts some others by suggesting that, although quality of life factors can lead to depression, they do not always do so. Understanding the psychological impact of diabetes in older adults can be complicated, and as such, social workers need to be careful in their assessment process to guard against making too many generalizations or assumptions. At the same time, however, it is important to be aware that the psychological and social problems associated with diabetes have the potential to adversely affect the quality of life of older adults with the disease (Ragonesi et al., 1998).

Many studies have confirmed the relationship between diabetes and depression, anxiety, eating disorders, loneliness, distress, and use of antipsychotic medications (Adamis & Ball, 2000; Araki et al., 2004; Black, 1998, 1999; Feldman, Hay, Deberdt, Kennedy, & Hutchins, et al., 2004; Peterson et al., 1998; Rubin & Peyrot, 2001). Rubin & Peyrot and DeCoster (2001) are excellent sources for social work professionals interested in a more detailed review of psychological issues. Yet, despite this link, we cannot determine definitively the causal pathways between diabetes and depression. However, at least two recent longitudinal studies have demonstrated that individuals with depression are significantly more likely to develop diabetes (Golden, Williams, Ford, Yeh, et al., 2004; Williams & Paton Sanford, et al., 2002). Golden et al. found that individuals with the most severe depressive symptoms were more likely to develop T2DM 6 years later. However these findings are far from conclusive, and the authors point out that these findings might be partially confounded by low socioeconomic status and obesity.

All this being so, psychological disorders are so common in individuals with diabetes that screening for depression is a standard component for all older adults during a diabetes evaluation (ADA, 2004c; California Healthcare Foundation/American Geriatrics Society, 2004). Why is living with diabetes so often linked to psychological complications? One explanation may be that

the regimen for diabetes is probably the most complex and demanding of any common disease . . . [including] complex nutritional practices, weight management, frequent monitoring of blood or urine glucose, foot care, special procedures in the event of common maladies such as cold or flu, and, in many cases insulin injections. (Fisher, Delamater, Bertelson & Kirkley, 1982, p. 993)

Rood (1996, p. 730) reports that "even with meticulous attention to detail, things may go wrong and wrong things often lead to blindness, nerve damage, kidney failure, and amputation." Common emotional reactions to diabetes include denial, stress, fear, sadness, anger, guilt, frustration, being fed up, and feeling overwhelmed (DeCoster, 2001, 2003; Fisher et al., 1982; and Rubin & Peyrot, 2001). It is important that social workers do not overlook these common emotional reactions when working with older adults with diabetes.

Social Factors

It is important to understand factors representing barriers to prevention of complications and integration of optimal self-care recommendations. Examples of barriers include lack of financial resources, lack of access to affordable health care, lack of education about diabetes, improperly treated pain, and discontinuity in care (Bazargan, Bazargan, & Baker, 1998; Piette, Heisler & Wagner, 2004; Roubideaux, Buchwald, Beals, Middlebrook, et al., 2004; Schoenberg & Drungle, 2001). Frequently, barriers to optimal self-care and prevention of complications are influenced by factors such as race/ethnicity, education, income, and social support. Several studies have suggested that the barriers in diabetes care for individuals living in rural areas are more difficult to overcome than for those in urban areas (Andrus, Kelly, Murphey, & Herndon, 2004; Zoorob & Mainous, 1996). Barriers specific to preventive care in rural areas include lack of adequate insurance coverage, lower income, lack of transportation or greater travel distance to a primary care provider, inadequate screening and preventive services, and poorer compliance with standards of care of the ADA (Andrus et al., 2004; Zoorob & Mainous, 1996).

Schoenberg and Drungle (2001) examined barriers to optimal self-care in older women with T2DM, focusing primarily on three areas: financial challenges, lack of access to quality self-care, and pain and disability. They found that 35% of participants had difficulty obtaining medical appointments, 20% experienced logistical barriers, and impaired vision represented a major problem for many (25% of the entire sample) along with the inability to check their feet on a regular basis. Generally, the authors found that being African American, less educated, and poor was associated with increased barriers to optimal self-care. Although this study focused exclusively on non-Hispanic Whites and African Americans, there has been increasing focus on the impact of diabetes across different racial/ethnic groups.

On average, African Americans, Hispanic/Latino Americans, and Native Americans are 1.6, 1.5, and 2.2 times more likely, respectively, to have diabetes than non-Hispanic Whites; native Hawaiians and Japanese and Filipino residents of Hawaii are approximately 2 times more likely to have diabetes than White residents of Hawaii (CDC, 2003). How do we interpret these numbers? If we consider the fact that diabetes prevalence increases with age and that African Americans, Hispanic/Latino Americans, Native Americans, and some Asian Americans are also at particularly high risk for diabetes, it demonstrates the need to prioritize social work assessment and interventions tailored to working with older adults in minority populations.

One way this can be accomplished is by gaining a better understanding of culturally specific knowledge regarding diabetes. For example, the literature informs us that African American and Native American women tend to report significantly greater concern with developing diseases, such as diabetes, compared to their non-Hispanic White counterparts (Wilcox, Ainsworth, LaMonte, & DuBose, 2002); older minority individuals, particularly African Americans, persistently underutilize medical/health services (Bazargan et al., 1998); the cultural definition of an "elder" in the Native American community typically refers to individuals at ages much younger than 65 years (Roubideaux et al., 2004); and Mexican Americans are more likely to be active in self-care if they perceive their own behaviors as causes of diabetes (Hunt, Valenzuela, & Pugh, 1998). The ADA Web site is an excellent resource for culturally specific resources, education, interventions, and materials written in different languages.

Perhaps the most comprehensive example of culturally competent research in this area, however, is the Diabetes Prevention Marketing Study (CDC, 1997). In this study, a total of 27 focus groups were conducted in populations disproportionately affected by diabetes. One of the goals of the study was to com-

municate how Native Americans (from various tribes), African Americans, Hispanics/Latinos (from Mexico, Central America, and the Dominican Republic), and Asian Americans (Korean, Filipino, Chinese, and Vietnamese) live with diabetes in various communities. Key focus group findings are summarized in Table 3.1. A literature review across these populations was also conducted. The literature review, focus group findings, and references (CDC, 1997) may be downloaded at *http://www.cdc.gov/diabetes/pubs/focus/index.htm#contents*.

Among the findings from the literature review, notions of attribution, though similar in some respects, pose important differences regarding whether diabetes is considered a cause or a result of bodily disturbance, or whether preventive care or behavior modification is likely to be considered. For instance, Native Americans consider diabetes to be a disease imposed by a social environment altered by contact with Whites and loss of traditional lifestyles. Hispanic/Latino populations consider illnesses such as diabetes to be a punishment by God that requires stoic endurance. A strong present orientation among many African Americans may not be compatible with preventive care, and Asian Americans may be receptive to modifying behaviors because cultural beliefs about food and illness relationships are based on principles of bodily energy balance involving polarities of hot and cold, male and female, or yin and yang. The summary of key findings from this literature review, together with the findings from the focus groups, provide an excellent start to realizing culturally sensitive social work practice with older adults.

TREATMENT APPROACHES AND INTERVENTIONS

Rood (1996, p. 739) points out that the frequent frustration on the part of the medical community when working with patients with diabetes is related to how difficult it is for the patient to change, and that education frequently leads to "knowledgeable noncompliant patients." Social workers have the opportunity to play a prominent role in the lives of older adults coping with diabetes, particularly in addressing some of the gaps in treatment that can lead to professional frustration and generalizations or stereotypes about older adults diagnosed with diabetes. DeCoster (2001, p. 30) does an excellent job of explaining how the unique contribution of social workers' "behavioral science background; ability to work with individuals,

TABLE 3.1. CDC Diabetes Prevention Marketing Study Focus Group Findings

Native American Populations

- Many participants expressed intense feelings of shame about having diabetes. They felt that they would be stigmatized in their communities if other people found out. This perception seemed quite prevalent among the men.

- Some of the women who lived on a reservation bemoaned the fact that although one of the best ways for them to exercise is walking, they fear attack from stray dogs.

- Although participants want to follow a diet regimen that will help them control their diabetes, they said that foods such as fresh fruits and vegetables and leaner cuts of meat are not affordable. Government commodities—often high in fat and sugars—constitute a significant portion of their diet.

- Some participants expressed a longing for continuity in their health care. They said that through the Indian Health Service, they may see a particular doctor only once or twice and are unable to establish a longer-term relationship.

- Some participants who use nontraditional treatment methods for diabetes said that they rarely tell their doctors for fear of being ridiculed. Others do not share the information with doctors because the methods are considered sacred.

- Most participants felt that the ethnicity of the treating physician did not need to be the same as the patient with diabetes. However, they did feel that a Native American doctor would put a Native American patient at ease, would take more time with the examination, and would be more patient and thorough in answering questions.

African American Populations

- No one felt prepared for the life changes that followed the diagnosis of diabetes.

- Participants attributed high incidence of diabetes to stress in the community, lack of information, a preponderance of other serious illnesses, and dietary preferences. Some participants described a perception of stress related to social ills, citing crime, work layoff, lack of transportation, lack of resources, AIDS, racism, and lack of communication between family members.

- Many said that because African Americans tend to put off seeking health care, diabetes may be discovered late.

- Participants in all groups expressed concerns about the financial burden of diabetes. Many participants voiced appreciation for health care providers who were flexible about payment for services.

- Many sources of information were mentioned, including print material from health care providers; workshops, classes, other presentations at hospitals and clinics; and the American Diabetes Association. In general, participants were satisfied with the information they receive but said that it needs to be disseminated more widely among young adults.

- Participants did not express a strong preference for African American health care providers, but some said that providers' knowledge of the cultural significance of diet would be useful.

- Several participants said that diabetes does not get the same attention in the African American community as do cancer, high blood pressure, and stroke.

Hispanic/Latino Populations

- Several participants said they typically forgo buying needed medication, glucose-testing strips, or both until they can afford them or a family member buys them.

- Among male participants' concerns about the complications of diabetes, one of the most important is the fear of sexual dysfunction. Many admitted that their experience with impotence negatively affected their self-esteem.

- Some participants said they believe that the onset of diabetes results from a strong emotional reaction to a good or bad event (e.g., winning the lottery, being robbed, witnessing a suicide).

- Some participants said they feel inhibited about asking their physicians diabetes-related questions because they feel ashamed of taking up too much of the doctors' time and are afraid that the doctors will become angry.

- Most participants said that their community offers them little support in managing their diabetes.

- When discussing why some Hispanics/Latinos might not manage their diabetes well, participants pointed to a lifestyle that emphasizes the joys and pleasures of eating.

Asian American Populations

- Women were concerned about injections.

- Many Chinese participants stated that both Western doctors and Chinese herbal doctors participate in their health care. The herbal doctors were valued by participants in part because they speak the same language and understand their culture and eating habits.

- Some believed that doctors try to control patients by doling out information a little at a time and discounting the value of non-Western treatment.

(continued)

TABLE 3.1. CDC Diabetes Prevention Marketing Study Focus Group Findings (*continued*)

- Participants said that diabetes is caused by a combination of factors, including intense emotional stress, consumption of sweets, and hereditary disposition.
- Participants said that illness is more manageable if the mind is peaceful and positive.
- Chinese participants felt that their diet did not lend itself to developing diabetes, stating that they consumed foods low in fat and low in sugar. However, the Korean participants believed that there is a high incidence of diabetes among their cohorts. They spoke of the Korean diet, pointing to an emphasis on meat and spicy foods.
- Family support was particularly important among the Asian participants.
- Several worried about the impact that diabetes could have on their interactions with others. They explained that among Asian people, there is a strong focus on the group's harmony and well-being, as opposed to an individual's well-being. Thus, Asians do not want to stand out from the crowd. To do so would create embarrassment, said participants. They also pointed out that they do not want to embarrass their hosts by not eating what is served at social gatherings.

Source: Centers for Disease Control and Prevention (1997).

groups or families; cultural competence; and ecological approach can be useful to patients and diabetes programs."

Ideally, treatment is team-based, and professionals should have expertise in the field of diabetes and/or gerontology. Members of this team can include primary care doctors, diabetes educators, registered dietitians, eye doctors, podiatrists, dentists, exercise physiologists, and mental health professionals. Continuity of care is one of the most critical components for successful diabetes care. Going beyond this team-based approach to diabetes care, Jack, Airhihenbuwa, Namageyo-Funa, Owens, and Vinicor (2004) describe a collaborative care management approach, which involves the patient as a member of the team, and a transdisciplinary approach, which further involves the community as a member of the team. Although their work is geared to an audience of primary care providers, the authors convey the importance of approaching diabetes care from a strengths-based, empowerment, and ecological approach, making it a valuable tool for social workers collaborating with health care professionals who may not specialize in gerontology or diabetes or be familiar with social work concepts.

Social workers are integral to the case management and brokerage between all the providers and the patient. Consequently, they must be familiar with the current standards and components of diabetes care. The ADA Web site has a link to these recommendations. Another recent publication, "Guidelines for Improving the Care of the Older Person with Diabetes" (California Healthcare Foundation/American Geriatrics Society, 2003), containing evidence-based guidelines specific to older adults, is also an excellent resource. The basic goals in treatment of diabetes are not much different for older than for younger adults (e.g., glycemic control, weight and exercise management, medical nutritional therapy, treatment of macrovascular and microvascular complications, self-management), but some modifications are necessary. It is also important that social workers tailor their interventions to the setting they are in and whether they have the opportunity to provide short- or longer-term treatment.

Effective treatment of diabetes and its associated macrovascular and microvascular complications is critical, but not to the exclusion of the numerous psychosocial complications, many of which may precede or exacerbate these vascular complications. As discussed earlier, psychological complications associated with diabetes can be considerable. Likewise, there is mounting evidence that social and emotional support can have a positive effect on diabetes care, prevention of complications, and well-being in older adults (Bertera, 2003; Seeman & Chen, 2002; Treif, Grant, Elbert, & Weinstock, 1998). For example, in a sample of older Chinese adults with T2DM, Cheng and Boey (2000) found that support outside the family played a more important role than family support in adaptation to the disease.

Group interventions are one method of enhancing social and emotional support. They have the benefit of being cost-effective and provide older adults with needed socialization and support. Robison (1993) describes a 12-week training and support group for older adults with diabetes. Not only did participants successfully meet the goals (to improve compliance with diet plans and lower their weekly peak glucose levels) in comparison to a control group, but these results were maintained at 12- and 24-month follow-ups. Although this study had several significant limitations, the intervention is well described and could easily be replicated by social workers in the field. A second example is a year-long group intervention with the goal of solving psychosocial problems associated with diabetes (Alley & Brown, 2002). It is based on a task-centered model. The results were mixed, but it is important to note that the setting for this study was an HMO, and the study describes how some of the barriers and politics of starting a group were addressed.

Social workers should take into consideration any factors that might impede an older adult's ability to learn or to attend a group that might be associated with aging and/or diabetic complications (Beers & Berkow, 2004). Telephone-, Internet-, and home-based interventions are several recent approaches to circumvent some of these complications (Barrera, Glasgow, McKay, Boles, & Feil, 2002; Huang, Wu, Jeng, & Ling, 2004; Sacco, Morrison, & Malone, 2004). One study is particularly promising. Barrera et al. (2004) focused on enhancing social support through Internet-based interventions focused on diabetes. Participants receiving the social support interventions had significant improvements in their perceptions of social support in comparison to those receiving information-only interventions. Considering the growing number of adults familiar with and comfortable using computers and the Internet, this intervention has a lot of potential in the diabetes field.

The participatory action research (PAR) model is an excellent example of a culturally sensitive, evidenced-based approach to community intervention. People are seen as experts in their own lives, and the strengths of local people are used to plan action for change. Giachello et al. (2003, p. 311) define PAR as pursuing "research objectives (knowledge, understanding) with the meaningful involvement of community members (stakeholders) and an ultimate focus on social action leading to improvements in social conditions." The authors outline the community-based PAR approach they used to reduce the impact of diabetes in an underserved minority neighborhood and describe how that process led to increased awareness of the complexities of diabetes and readiness for system reform.

These approaches also tend to be more effective in minority racial/ethnic communities. Samuel-Hodge et al. (2000) examined culturally based psychosocial issues and other factors influencing behaviors of African American women with diabetes. Spirituality, general life stress, multiple caregiving responsibilities, and psychological impact emerged as important factors in adjustment, coping, and management of the disease. Likewise, these authors recommend family-centered and church-based approaches to diabetes care interventions in this population. McNair and Smith (1998) stress the importance of engaging natural supportive networks within the community, particularly in churches. Finally, two very important components of diabetes education, exercise and diet/nutrition, provide an excellent example of how interventions can be tailored to the community in which a social worker practices. Providing dance classes or adapting recipes in cooking classes to accommodate working in Asian American, African American, Hispanic/Latino, or Native American populations is as important for social workers as educating and preparing older adults and their family members for the myriad complications associated with diabetes.

CONCLUSION

Social work practice with older adults who have diabetes will vary depending on the setting. Social workers in health care settings are more likely to focus on enhancing psychosocial factors that can affect compliance with diabetes care; social workers in community-based settings are more likely to focus on education, prevention, and screening for diabetes in high-risk groups (Bertera, 2003). Due to the growing epidemic of obesity and increases in T2DM in the United States, family- and community-centered interventions arguably have the most potential for preventing diabetic complications in older adults, in the delay or even reversal of complications with T2DM in younger adults, children, and adolescents, and in creating large-scale change.

Social work research should focus on addressing knowledge gaps that hinder social workers from capitalizing most effectively on their unique role on the health care team and in the community. We highlight two critical areas here. First, there is a need to test whether earlier screening and intervention with at-risk adults could prevent or reduce depressive symptoms that can lead to poor glycemic control, diabetic complications, stroke, and dementia. Arguably, interventions for depression, such as cognitive-behavioral treatment, should begin *before* depressive symptoms escalate to major depression ("Diabetes and Depression," 1999). Social work research on psychosocial and physical symptoms in diabetes should make better use of ongoing support groups and the Internet to conduct these screenings and interventions. Second, there are important research gaps about specific cultural beliefs, illness attributions, behaviors, and practices in various older, ethnic populations. How widely held are the cultural beliefs, attributions, behaviors, and practices that we assume to be common? Which are the most strongly held, amenable to change, or diffuse within underserved, ethnic elder populations?

As the population ages and lives longer, the so-called baby boom generation has placed particular demands on our society and brought dramatic changes as they pass through the various changes in the life cycle. As this generation approaches the age when T2DM becomes a serious risk, and if the statistics for onset of T2DM remain the same or even decrease somewhat, the numbers of people needing treatment for T2DM will dramatically increase, putting extreme pressure on those who provide services to older T2DM patients. It is essential that the infrastructure to deal with this likely increase be in place before the problem becomes a crisis. In addressing this issue, of all the professionals working in the area of diabetes, social workers are perhaps the most uniquely suited to lead the effort to provide education, prevention, and screening for diabetes and to implement effective interventions across multiple systems with the individual, the family, the treatment team, in local communities, and statewide.

NOTE

1. The ADA Web site provides a dictionary of diabetes-related terms. See *www.diabetes.org/diabetesdictionary.jsp?WTLPromo=FOOTER_dictionary.*

REFERENCES

Adamis, D., & Ball, C. (2000). Physical morbidity in elderly psychiatric inpatients: Prevalence and possible relations between the major mental disorders and physical illness. *International Journal of Geriatric Psychiatry, 15*(3), 248–253.

Alley, G. R., & Brown, L. B. (2002). A diabetes problem solving support group: Issues, process and preliminary outcomes. *Social Work in Health Care, 36*(1), 1–9.

American Diabetes Association. (2003). *National diabetes fact sheet: General information and national estimates on diabetes in the United States, 2002.* Retrieved June 10, 2004, from the American Diabetes Association Web site: *http://www.diabetes.org/diabetes-statistics/national-diabetes-fact-sheet.jsp.*

American Diabetes Association. (2004a). Diagnosis and classification of diabetes mellitus. *Diabetes Care, 27* (Suppl. 1), S5–S10.

American Diabetes Association. (2004b). Screening for Type 2 diabetes. *Diabetes Care, 27* (Suppl. 1), S11–S13.

American Diabetes Association. (2004c). Standards of medical care in diabetes. *Diabetes Care, 27* (Suppl. 1), S15–S35.

American Diabetes Association. (2004d). Nephropathy in diabetes. *Diabetes Care, 27* (Suppl. 1), S79–S83.

Andrus, M. R., Kelley, K. W., & Murphey, L. M., & Herndon, K. C. (2004). A comparison of diabetes care in rural and urban medical clinics in Alabama. *Journal of Community Health, 29*(1), 29–44.

Araki, A., Murotani, Y., Kamimiya, F., & lto, H. (2004). Low well-being is an independent predictor for stroke in elderly patients with diabetes mellitus. *Journal of the American Geriatrics Society, 52*(2), 205–210.

Barrera, M., Jr., Glasgow, R. E., McKay, H. G., Boles, S. M., & Feil, E. G. (2002). Do Internet-based support interventions change perceptions of social support? *American Journal of Community Psychology, 30*(5), 637–654.

Bazargan, M., Bazargan, S., & Baker, R. S. (1998). Emergency department utilization, hospital admissions, and physician visits among elderly African American persons. *The Gerontologist, 38*, 25–36.

Beers, M., & Berkow, R. (2004). Disorders of carbohydrate metabolism. In *The Merck manual of geriatrics* (ch 64). Retrieved June 10, 2004, from *http://www.merck.com/mrkshared/mm_geriatrics/sec8/ch64.jsp.*

Bertera, E. M. (2003). Psychosocial factors and ethnic disparities in diabetes diagnosis and treatment among older adults. *Health & Social Work, 28*(1), 33–42.

Black, S. A. (1999). Increased health burden associated with comorbid depression in older diabetic Mexican Americans: Results from the Hispanic Established Population for the Epidemiologic Study of the Elderly Survey. *Diabetes Care, 22*, 56–64.

Black, S. A., Goodwin, J. S., & Markides, K. S. (1988). The association between chronic diseases and depressive symptomatology in older Mexican Americans. *Journals of Gerontology Series A. Biological Sciences & Medical Sciences, 53A*(3), M188–M194.

Blaum, C. S., Ofstedal, M. B., Langa, K. M., & Wray, L. A. (2003). Functional status and health outcomes in older Americans with diabetes mellitus. *Journal of the American Geriatrics Society, 51*, 745–753.

Boyle, J., Honeycutt, A., Narayan, K., Hoerger, T., et al. (2001). Projection of diabetes burden through 2050: Impact of changing demography and disease prevalence in the U.S. *Diabetes Care, 24*(11), 1936–1940.

California Healthcare Foundation/American Geriatric Society. (2003). Guidelines for improving the care of the older person with diabetes mellitus. *Journal of the American Geriatrics Society, 51*(5), S265–S280.

Centers for Disease Control and Prevention. (1997). Seeing the faces, hearing the stories, learning from our communities: Using focus groups to gain an understanding of living with diabetes in various communities. D. Satterfield & P. Mitchell (Eds.). Atlanta: U.S. Department of Health and Human Services, CDC, Division of Diabetes Translation. Retrieved January 5, 2005, from *http://www.cdc.gov/diabetes/pubs/focus/index.htm#contents*.

Centers for Disease Control and Prevention. (2003). *National diabetes fact sheet: General information and national estimates on diabetes in the United States, 2002*. Atlanta, GA: U.S. Department of Health and Human Services, CDC. Retrieved June 10, 2004, from *http://www.diabetes.org/diabetes-statistics/national-diabetes-fact-sheet.jsp*.

Cheng, T. Y. L., & Boey, K. W. (2000). Coping, social support, and depressive symptoms of older adults with Type II diabetes mellitus. *Clinical Gerontologist, 22*(1), 15–30.

Croxson, S. C. M., & Jagger, C. (1995). Diabetes and cognitive impairment: A community-based study of elderly subjects. *Age and Ageing, 24,* 421–424.

DCCT/EDIC Research Group. (2003). Sustained effect of intensive treatment of Type 1 diabetes mellitus on development and progression of diabetic neuropathy. *Journal of the American Medical Association, 290*(16), 2159.

DeCoster, V. A. (2001). Challenges of Type 2 diabetes and role of health care social work: A neglected area of practice. *Health and Social Work, 26*(1), 26–37.

DeCoster, V. A. (2003). The emotions of adults with diabetes: A comparison across race. *Social Work in Health Care, 36*(4), 79–99.

Diabetes and depression: Consequences of comorbidity? (1999, April). *Medical Crossfire: Debates, Peer Exchange, and Insights in Medicine*. Retrieved January 5, 2005, from *www.medicalcrossfire.com/debate_archive/1999/Apr99/diabetesAPR99.html*.

EDIC Research Group. (1999). Epidemiology of diabetes interventions and complications. *Diabetes Care, 22*(1), 99–111.

Egede, L. (2004). Diabetes, major depression and functional disability among U.S. adults. *Diabetes Care, 27*(2), 421–428.

Erlinger, T. P., Pollack, H., & Appel, L. J. (2000). Nutrition-related cardiovascular risk factors in older people: Results from the Third National Health and Nutrition Examination Survey. *Journal of the American Geriatrics Society, 48*(11), 1486–1489.

Fisher, E. B., Jr., Delamater, A. M., Bertelson, A. D., & Kirkley, B. G. (1982). Psychological factors in diabetes and its treatment. *Journal of Consulting and Clinical Psychology, 50,* 993–1003.

Fletcher, A. K., & Dolben, J. (1996). A hospital survey of the care of elderly patients with diabetes mellitus. *Age and Ageing, 25,* 349–352.

Fong, D., Aiello, L., Gardner, T., King, G., Blankenship, G., & Cavallerano, J. (2004). Retinopathy in diabetes. *Diabetes Care, 27*(1), S84–S87.

Fultz, N., Ofstedal, M., Herzog, A., & Wallace, R. (2003). Additive and interactive effects of comorbid physical and mental conditions on functional health. *Journal of Aging and Health, 15*(3), 465–481.

Giachello, A., Arrom, J., Davis, M., Savad, J., Ramirez, D., et al. (2003). Reducing diabetes health disparities through community-based participatory action research: The Chicago Southeast Diabetes Community Action Coalition. *Public Health Reports, 118,* 309–323.

Golden, S., Williams, J., Ford, D., Yeh, H., Paton Sanford, C., & Nieto, F. J., et al. (2004). Depressive symptoms and the risk of Type 2 diabetes: The Atherosclerosis Risk in Communities Study. *Diabetes Care, 27*(2)k, 419.

Gregg, E. W., Engelgau, M. M., & Narayan, V. (2002). Complications of diabetes in elderly people. *British Medical Journal, 325*(7370), 916–917.

Howard, B., Cowan, L., Go, O., Welty, T., et al. (1998). Adverse effects of diabetes on multiple cardiovascular disease risk factors in women. *Diabetes Care, 21*(8).

Huang, C., Wu, S., Jeng, C., & Lin, L. (2004). The efficacy of a home-based nursing program in diabetic control of elderly people with diabetes mellitus living alone. *Public Health Nursing, 21*(1), 49–56.

Hunt, L. M., Valenzuela, M. A., & Pugh, J. A. (1998). Porque me tocó a mi? Mexican American diabetes patients' causal stories and their relationship to treatment behaviors. *Social Science & Medicine, 46*(8), 959–969.

Jack, L., Airhihenbuwa, C., Namageyo-Funa, A., Owens, M. & Vinicor, F. (2004). The psychosocial aspects of diabetes care. *Geriatrics, 59*(5), 26.

Kinder, L., Karmarck, T., & Baum, A. (2002). Depressive symptomatology and coronary heart disease in Type I diabetes mellitus: A study of possible mechanisms. *Health Psychology, 21*(6), 542–552.

Krakoff, J., Lindsay, R., Looker, H., Nelson, R., et al. (2003). Incidence of retinopathy and nephropathy in youth-onset compared with adult-onset Type 2 diabetes. *Diabetes Care, 26*(1), 76.

Langa, K. M., Vijan, S, Hayward, R., Chernew, M., Kabeto, M., Weir, D., et al. (2002). Informal caregiving for diabetes and diabetic complications among elderly

Americans. *Journals of Gerontology, Series B: Psychological Sciences and Social Sciences, 57B*(3), S177–S186.

Maahs, D., & Zeitler, P. (2004). Type 2 diabetes in children: A growing epidemic. *Current Opinions in Epidemiology, 11*, 60–64.

McNair, J., & Smith, H. K. (1998). Community based natural support through local churches. *Mental Retardation, 36*(3), 237–241.

Nilsson, E., Fastbom, J., & Wahlin, A. (2002). Cognitive functioning in a population-based sample of very old non-demented and non-depressed persons: The impact of diabetes. *Archives of Gerontology & Geriatrics, 35*(2), 95–105.

Pancioli, A. M., Broderick, J., Kothari, R., Brott, T., Tuchfarber, A., Miller, R., et al. (1998). Public perception of stroke warning signs and knowledge of potential risk factors. *Journal of the American Medical Association, 279*(16), 1288–1292.

Peterson, T., Lee, P., Hollis, S., Young, B., Newton, P., & Dornan, T. (1998). Well being and treatment satisfaction in older people with diabetes. *Diabetes Care, 21*(6), 930–935.

Piette, J., Heisler, M., & Wagner, T. (2004). Problems paying out-of-pocket medication costs among older adults with diabetes. *Diabetes Care, 27*(2), 384.

Plummer, E. S., & Albert, S. G. (1996). Focused assessment of foot care in older adults. *Journal of the American Geriatrics Society, 44*, 310–313.

Ragonesi, P., Ragonesi, G., Merati, L., & Taddei, M. (1998). The impact of diabetes mellitus on quality of life in elderly patients. *Archives of Gerontology & Geriatrics, 6*, (Suppl.), 417–422.

Robison, F. F. (1993). A training and support group for elderly diabetics: Description and evaluation. *Journal for Specialists in Group Work, 18*(3), 127–136.

Rood, R. P. (1996). Patient and physician responsibility in the treatment of chronic illness: The case of diabetes. *American Behavioral Scientist, 39*, 729–751.

Roubideaux, Y., Buchwald, D., & Beals, J., Middlebrook, D., Manson, S., et al. (2004). Measuring the quality of diabetes care for older American Indians and Alaska Natives. *American Journal of Public Health, 94*(1), 60–65.

Rubin, R. R., & Peyrot, M. (2001). Psychological issues and treatments for people with diabetes. *Journal of Clinical Psychology, 57*(4), 457–478.

Samuel-Hodge, C. D., Headen, S. W., Skelly, A. H., Ingram, A. F., Keyserling, T. C., Jackson, E. J. (2000). Influences on day-to-day self-management of type 2 diabetes among African-American women: Spirituality, the multi-caregiver role, and other social context factors. *Diabetes Care, 23*(7), 928–933.

Schoenberg, N., & Drungle (2001). Barriers to non-insulin dependent diabetes mellitus self-care practices among older women. *Journal of Aging and Health, 13*(4), 443–466.

Seeman, T., & Chen, X. (2002). Risk and protective factors for physical functioning in older adults with and without chronic conditions: MacArthur Studies of Successful Aging. *Journals of Gerontology, Series B: Psychological Sciences and Social Sciences, 57B*(3), S135–S144.

Sinclair, A. J., Bayer, A. J., & Girling, A. J. (2000). Older adults, diabetes mellitus and visual acuity: A community-based case-control study. *Age and Ageing, 29*(4), 335–339.

Smith, N. L., Savage, P. J., Heckbert, S. R., Barzilay, J. I., Bittner, V., & Kuller, L. H. et al. (2002). Glucose, blood pressure, and lipid control in older people with and without diabetes mellitus: The Cardiovascular Health Study. *Journal of the American Geriatrics Society, 50*(3), 416–423.

Talbot, F., Nouwen, A., Gingras, J., Belanger, A., & Audet, J. (1999). Relations of diabetes intrusiveness and personal control to symptoms of depression among adults with diabetes. *Health Psychology, 18*(5), 537–542.

Treif, P., Grant, W., Elbert, K., & Weinstock, R. (1998). Family environment, glycemic control, and the psychosocial adaptation of adults with diabetes. *Diabetes Care, 21*(2), 241–245.

Treif, P., Wade, M., Pine, D., & Weinstock, R., (2003). A comparison of health-related quality of life of elderly and younger insulin-treated adults with diabetes. *Age and Ageing, 32*, 613.

Verghese, J., Bieri, P. L., Gellido, C., Schaumburg, H. H., & Herskovitz, S. (2001). Peripheral neuropathy in young-old and old-old patients. *Muscle & Nerve, 24*(11), 1476–1481.

Wilcox, S., Ainsworth, B. E., LaMonte, M. J., & DuBose, K. D. (2002). Worry regarding major diseases among older African-American, Native-American, and Caucasian women. *Women & Health, 36*(3), 83–99.

Williams, S. A., Kasi, S. V., Heiat, A., Abramson, J. L., Krumholz, H. M., & Vaccarino, V. (2002). Depression and risk of heart failure among the elderly: A prospective community-based study. *Psychosomatic Medicine, 64*(1), 6–12.

Zoorob, R. J., & Mainous, A. G., III. (1996). Practice patterns of rural family physicians based on the American Diabetes Association standards of care. *Journal of Community Health, 21*, 175–182.

HELEN MILTIADES
LENARD W. KAYE

Older Adults With Orthopedic and Mobility Limitations

This chapter considers the major orthopedic diseases and associated conditions that older adults face and the challenges they pose for them, their families, and the social workers and other health care professionals that work with them. Recommendations are offered for social work practitioners who are likely to work with older adults with orthopedic diseases and who are at risk for falls, fractures, and joint replacements.

OSTEOPOROSIS

Osteoporosis is a systemic skeletal disease characterized by low bone mass and deterioration of bone tissue, with a consequent increase of bone fragility and susceptibility to fracture. It is estimated that between 13% and 18% of older women (Looker et al., 1995; "Osteoporosis among Estrogen-Deficient Women," 1998) and between 3% and 6% of older men (Bilezikian, 1999) have osteoporosis. Osteoporosis has been historically associated with menopause and hence thought of as a "women's" disease. The prevalence of osteoporosis is higher in Caucasian women, women 65 or older, and women with a low body mass index ("Osteoporosis among Estrogen-Deficient Women," 1998). Women with lower socioeconomic status and limited access to health care are less likely than women with resources to report a diagnosis of osteoporosis ("Osteoporosis among Estrogen-Deficient Women," 1998). This is most likely due to lack of knowledge regarding osteoporosis, not a lower incidence of osteoporosis.

Several risk factors have been linked to osteoporosis. Age, low calcium intake (Bauer et al., 1993; Marcus, Feldman, & Kelsey, 2001), family history (Bauer et al., 1993), vitamin D deficiency (Marcus et al., 2001), hypogonadism in men, steroid use for inflammatory conditions, alcoholism, smoking (Orwoll & Klein, 1995), and diabetes (Nicodemus & Folsom, 2001) all increase the risk of developing osteoporosis. The consequences of osteoporosis are severe. More than 1.5 million osteoporotic fractures occur each year (Riggs & Melton, 1992). Loss of height and curvature of the spine (Hofman, Grobbee, de Jong, & van den Ouseland, 1991) lead to limited mobility and pain (Roberto & Reynolds, 2001).

Osteoporosis is often undiagnosed and undertreated. Missed diagnosis and undertreatment may be due to poor physician-to-physician communication, a lack of awareness that osteoporosis is prevalent in older men and premenopausal women, and adverse reactions to prescription osteoporosis medication

(Neuner, Zimmer, & Hamel, 2003). Older adults and their caregivers need to be encouraged to advocate for osteoporosis testing. Unfortunately, many men and women are unaware of their risk of developing osteoporosis (B. Williams, Cullen, & Barlow, 2002).

Older women with osteoporosis report changing their daily life and social interactions due to mobility restrictions caused by osteoporosis (Roberto & Reynolds, 2001). These changes include slowing daily activities, such as cooking, and restricting social engagements. A special issue to be addressed in working with women with osteoporosis is their fear of becoming increasingly dependent, falling, and losing the ability to maintain their own home (Roberto & Reynolds, 2001).

It is important to be aware of the fact that osteoporosis is preventable (McCoy, 2001). Calcium and vitamin D supplements are the first line of defense (McCoy, 2001). Weight-bearing exercise and resistance training have been shown to be effective in maintaining and/or increasing bone mass (Klesges et al., 1996). The importance of social support to encourage proper exercise and nutrition is vital to healthy aging. Encouraging women to join an osteoporosis prevention program can help them maintain healthy levels of bone density. Treatment of the condition is crucial. The hallmark of osteoporosis treatment for postmenopausal women is hormone replacement therapy (HRT; McCoy, 2001). HRT has been shown to increase bone mineral density and reduce the risk of fractures. Even so, the risks and benefits of HRT should be weighed by patients considering this treatment.

For further information, the National Osteoporosis Foundation (1998) has published guidelines on osteoporosis prevention, diagnosis, and treatment (see Table 4.1).

ARTHRITIS

Arthritis refers to 100 different diseases that affect the joints. Arthritis and rheumatoid arthritis are characterized by joint inflammation; the latter is considered an autoimmune disorder. Both are associated with joint stiffness, swelling, and pain. Arthritis is the most common self-reported condition among older persons today. The prevalence of arthritis increases with age. The prevalence rate of arthritis in the United States is projected to range between 43 and 60 million in 2020, with activity limitations associated with this condition projected to affect 11.6 million people (Cen-

ters for Disease Control and Prevention [CDC], 1999). Higher prevalence rates for arthritis are associated with lower educational levels (Dunlop, Manheim, Song, & Chang, 2001), lower socioeconomic status (Hill, Parsons, Taylor, & Leach, 1999), female gender, and obesity (CDC, 2002).

Arthritis is the leading cause of disability for middle-aged and older persons. People with arthritis can have varying degrees of difficulty in walking, lifting and carrying items, climbing stairs, and generally maintaining their household. In a study using Medicare data pooled over 6 years, Porell and Miltiades (2001) found that arthritis was consistently associated with increased risk of functional decline and reduced the chances of functional improvement in older adults with activities of daily living (ADL) and instrumental activities of daily living (IADL) disability. The odds of disability are higher with age, for women, for non-Whites, and for those with comorbid conditions (Peek & Coward, 1999).

Even though activity limitations associated with arthritis have been reported to be higher for African Americans, the use of medical services remains higher for Whites than for Blacks (Mikuls, Mudano, Pulley, & Saag, 2003). Mayer-Oakes and all (1992) found that Whites with arthritic-like conditions were more likely to see a physical or occupational therapist than were Blacks. Ibrahim et al. (2003) discovered that African Americans and Whites report perception of pain associated with osteoarthritis differently; they posit that this may lead to undertreatment of rheumatoid conditions for African Americans.

Due to the pain associated with arthritis, many older adults withdraw from social and physical activity. Persons who experience severe arthritis are most likely to cease social participation. Persons with an active social network are more likely to remain engaged (Kaplan, Huguet, Newsom, & McFarland, 2003). Inactivity has serious physical and psychological consequences. Depression appears to be quite prevalent among persons with arthritis (DeVillis, 1995). Other health risks include increased dependence, poor health, loss of joint motion, and diminished quality of life (Hill et al., 1999; Kaplan et al., 2003; Penninx et al. 2001; G. Wang, Helmick, Macera, Zhang, & Pratt, 2001;). Comorbid conditions are also known to be associated with arthritis. Most important, the risk of institutionalization has been shown to increase with arthritis, most likely due to decreased functioning of the lower extremities (Hughes & Dunlop, 1995). It is unfortunate that half of arthritis sufferers associate the disease with normal aging and do not believe that their symptoms can be alleviated.

TABLE 4.1. Where to Turn for More Information

The Arthritis Foundation is the only national not-for-profit organization that supports the more than 100 types of arthritis and related conditions with advocacy, programs, services, and research. http://www.arthritis.ca/custom%20home/default.asp?s=1

The Arthritis Society is Canada's only not-for-profit organization devoted solely to funding and promoting arthritis research, programs, and patient care. http://www.niams.nih.gov/

The mission of the National Institute of Arthritis and Musculoskeletal and Skin Diseases is to support research into the causes, treatment, and prevention of arthritis and musculoskeletal and skin diseases, the training of basic and clinical scientists to carry out this research, and the dissemination of information on research progress in these diseases. Their Web site on osteoarthritis is. http://www.niams.nih.gov/hi/topics/arthritis/oahandout.htm

The Arthritis Research Campaign, founded in 1936, raises funds to promote medical research into the causes, treatments, and cures of arthritic conditions. This site also provides over 80 downloadable publications on arthritis and related conditions. http://www.aoa.gov/eldfam/Healthy_Lifestyles/Art_Ost/art_ost.asp

The U.S. Administration on Aging's Web site has links to information on arthritis and osteoporosis. http://www.nlm.nih.gov/medlineplus/osteoarthritis.htm

Medline Plus provides news, research, and consumer information on osteoarthritis. http://www.oarsi.org/

OsteoArthritis Research Society International is a nonprofit, scientific organization promoting and encouraging fundamental and applied research to permit better knowledge of osteoarthritis and its treatment. http://www.rheumatology.org/index.asp?and=mem

The American College of Rheumatology is the professional organization of rheumatologists and associated health professionals. http://www. fallprevent.com/Index.htm

The goal of fallPREVENT is to provide community- and institutional-based health professions with a one-stop-shopping Web site, a place where individuals can learn about falls in older people and what strategies are available to prevent falls. http://www.nof.org/

Established in 1984, the National Osteoporosis Foundation is solely dedicated to osteoporosis and bone health.

It is generally recognized that an exercise regimen is an important vehicle for maintaining physical functioning among elders with arthritis. Tai Chi (Gallagher, 2003), aerobic and resistance training (Penninx et al., 2001), and fitness walking (Hughes et al., 2004) all show promise in decreasing the pain and stiffness associated with arthritis. In fact, women who believe they can control their exercise behavior do have higher levels of functional performance (Gaines, Talbot, & Metter, 2002). An effective treatment for pain in the later stages of osteoarthritis is joint replacement (discussed further in this chapter).

FALLS

Falls are a frequent occurrence among older adults. Thirty percent of community-dwelling elders fall once a year (O'Laughlin, Robitaille, Boivin, & Suissa, 1993); the rate is 3 times higher for hospitalized and/or institutionalized older adults (American Geriatrics Society, British Geriatrics Society, and the American Academy of Orthopaedic Surgeons Panel of Falls Prevention [AGS], 2001). Women are more likely than men to experience a fall (Baker, 1992; Tromp, 1998). Over 130 risk factors for falls have been identified

(Myers, Young, & Langlois, 1996). A combination of environmental, physical, and psychological factors increases the likelihood that an elder will fall. The AGA identified 11 of the most common risk factors. Lack of balance control significantly increases risk of falling (Lord, Sherrington, & Menz, 2003), as does impaired gait (Tideiksaar, 2002). Other risk factors include increased age (Samelson, 2002), arthritis (Huang, Gau, Lin, & Kernohan, 2003), cognitive impairment (Tromp, 2001; van Doorn et al. 2003), history of falls (Nevitt, Cummings, & Hudes, 1991), muscle weakness (Moreland, Richardson, Goldsmith, & Clase, 2004), use of assistive device (Kiely, Kiel, Burrows, & Lipsitz, 1998), visual impairment (Legood, Scuffham, & Cryer, 2002), ADL impairment (Kiely et al., 1998), and depression (Lipsitz, Jonsson, Kelley, & Koestner, 1991). Diabetes (Hanlon et al., 2002) and polypharmacy (Flaherty, Perry, Lynchard, & Morley, 2003) also increase the risk of falls.

Falls have serious health consequences. Between 10% and 30% of falls are injurious to the extent of requiring hospitalization, decreasing mobility, and increasing chances of mortality (King, & Tinetti, 1995; Sterling, 2001). Falls are the leading cause of accident mortality among older adults (Murphy, 2000). Approximately 3% to 5% of falls result in fractures (Stalenhoef,

Crebolder, Knottnerus, & Van der Horst, 1997; Wilkins, 1999); 95% of hip fractures are caused by falls (Nyberg, Gustafson, Berggren, Brannstrom, & Bucht, 1996).

A major health concern, even among older adults who have never fallen, is the fear of falling. Between 33% and 50% of community-dwelling adults fear falling (Cumming, Salkeld, Thomas, & Szonyi, 2000; Yardley & Smith, 2002), and 46% of nursing home residents fear falling (Frazoni, Rozzini, Boffelli, Frisoni, & Trabucchi, 1994). In addition to the health risks of falling, many older adults fear the social embarrassment of falling and the loss of functional capacity. Dependence on others is another fear; in 50% of nonfatal fall cases, fallers require assistance to rise (Tinetti, Lui, & Claus, 1993). Falling and fear of falling lead many older adults to restrict their activities (Fletcher, & Hirdes, 2004). Consequences include increased social isolation, depression, development of physical limitations, and increased dependence on caregivers (Stel, Smit, Pluijm, & Lips, 2004). Fear of falling has been shown to predict institutionalization, even among older adults who have never fallen (Cumming et al., 2000).

Caregivers play an important role in reducing an older adult's chances of falling and providing emotional support. Older adults who have emotional and instrumental support are less likely to fear falling and restrict their activities (Fletcher & Hirdes, 2004). Family members are likely to provide the majority of beneficial social support. Faulkner, Cauley, Zmuda, Griffin, and Nevitt (2003) found that family networks are more likely than friendship networks to offer a protective effect against falls. They hypothesize that family members are more likely than friends to offer physical help and emergency care and to express concern about an older adult's safety. Caregivers may help with tasks such as grocery shopping and housekeeping, thus limiting fall-producing circumstances (Andrew, 1993).

It is important to note that caregiver responsibilities and anxiety may increase after a fall. The majority of older adults who experience fall-related fractures and other injuries have yet to recover their prefall functional levels 1 year later (Kempen et al., 2003). This can be expected to increase dependence on caregivers and consequently increase caregiver stress.

Although a single best preventive method may not yet have been identified, most falls are preventable. Various comprehensive checklists and measures of physical ability exist to assess the risk of falls (Tideiksaar, 2002). The Get-Up and Go test is the simplest measure of balance and is recommended as an initial screening tool (AGS, 2001). Older adults are asked to get up from a chair, walk 10 meters, return, and sit down in the chair (Mathias, Nayak, & Isaacs, 1986). The Home Fall Hazard Assessment Tool (Clemson, Fitzgerald, Heard, & Cumming, 1999) is used to assess environmental conditions inside and outside the home that potentially contribute to falls. Tinetti, Richman, and Powell (1990) developed a 10-item scale to assess confidence in performing ADLs without falling. This scale is beneficial in understanding the anxiety associated with completing daily life tasks.

A multifaceted approach to interventions is the most effective method of fall prevention. The American Geriatrics Society has established guidelines for fall prevention (AGS, 2001). Tai Chi, an exercise that emphasizes balance stability and postural control, has been shown to increase self-efficacy and reduce the risk of falling and fear of falling (Wolf et al., 2003). Up to one-half of falls occur around the home environment (Wilkins, 1999). Creating a slip-free and clutter-free environment is essential to reducing falls. Interventions that include home hazard assessment and environmental modifications have been shown to be effective in reducing falls (Nikolaus & Bach, 2003). A review of medications to identify side effects such as dizziness and, if possible, to reduce the number of medications taken could also prevent falls (Ray & Griffin, 1990). Regular visits by volunteers to assess general health have also been shown to be effective in reducing falls (Carpenter & Demopoulos, 1990). Use of health and social services, such as home health care and Meals on Wheels, provides social support and help with daily living. Unmet need for personal assistance services has been associated with falls (LePlante, Kaye, Kang, & Harrington, 2004). It is important to encourage older adults to see a health care provider for disease management, particularly health conditions related to falls. Older adults should also be encouraged to supplement their diet with calcium and Vitamin D to maintain healthy bones.

FRACTURES

More than 500,000 hospitalizations occur each year from fractures (NHDS, 1998); by 2040, the number of hip fractures alone is expected to be 500,000 (Cummings, 1990). Hip fractures and vertebral fractures lead to mobility restrictions, increased dependence, and a lower quality of life. In a study that examined recovery from various fracture types, hip and wrist fractures had the greatest impact on IADL and ADL disability a year later (Scaf-Klomp, van Sonderen, Sanderman, Ormel, and Kempen (2001)). Mortality rates are highest for hip fractures (Woolf & Akesson, 2003). Among older adults, fracture rates are 3 times higher for women than men (Praemer, Furner, & Rice, 1999).

One out of six women will experience a hip fracture (Melton, 1995). Men are less likely than women to experience a hip fracture because they possess fewer risk factors (Walter, Lui, Eng, & Covinsky, 2003). Risk factors for hip fracture include age, White ethnicity, cognitive decline, difficulty transferring, and ADL and lower body limitations (Walter et al., 2003; Wolinsky, Fitzgerald, & Stump, 1997). Nursing home residents who are able to transfer independently are more likely to experience hip fractures (Gregg, Pereira, & Caspersen, 2000). Similarly, studies have shown that older adults who wander are more likely to fall (Cesari et al., 2002). This creates a challenge for caregivers, who must balance an older adult's right to autonomy with the need to create a safe environment. Overprotective caregivers may foster learned helplessness. Additionally, restricting movement causes muscle atrophy and increased dependence (Campanelli, 1996).

The average length of hospitalization for a hip fracture is a week. Forty percent of hip fracture patients are discharged to a residential facility; estimates show that a year later, 25% to 33% are still in a nursing home (Magaziner, 2000). After an approximately 8-week rehabilitation period, older adults who are not in residential facilities are discharged home. However, the majority of hip fracture patients do not regain their prefracture levels of mobility (Kempen, Scaf-Klomp, Ranchor, Sanderman, & Ormel, 2001). Another complication of hip fracture is incontinence (Palmer, Baumgarten, Langenberg, & Carson, 2002), a distressing condition that limits an older adult's social engagement.

Caregivers of older female hip fracture patients underestimate caregiving activities related to continence, length of mobility impairment, and the pain levels associated with hip fracture recovery (M. A. Williams, Oberst, Bjorklund, & Hughes, 1996). Nonspousal caregivers report the greatest difficulty with caregiving tasks (M. A. Williams et al., 1996). Social support through an older adult's primary network has been shown to positively influence long-term recovery (Kempen et al., 2001). Even phone contact appears to have a positive benefit on 1-year recovery rates (Magaziner, Simonsick, Kashner, Hebel, & Kenzora, 1990). Instrumental support, such as help with gro-

cery shopping and transportation, also has a positive impact on recovery (Oh & Feldt, 2000). These studies indicate that caregivers' emotional and physical assistance are most instrumental in assisting an older adult's recovery from hip fracture.

A hip fracture is more likely than other medical conditions to cause long-term functional impairment. Impairment in ADLs, IADLs, and lower and upper body limitations are common and long-lasting (Wolinsky et al., 1997). Various factors influence recovery from a hip fracture. Factors that positively influence recovery include good overall physical health, younger age (Parker & Palmer, 1995), and higher levels of functional ability prior to fracture (Roberto, 1992b). There is evidence that positive mental outlook speeds recovery (Parker & Palmer, 1995). Older adults who expect to recover experience greater gains in ambulating than older adults who do not have recovery expectations (Borkan & Quirk, 1992). Depression and anxiety are negatively correlated with recovery (Oh & Feldt, 2000). Older adults who have cognitive impairment (X. Wang & Emery, 2002) or comorbidity (Roberto, 1992a) experience limited functional recovery. Pain is another barrier to recovery (Oh & Feldt, 2000). Rehabilitation efforts may be thwarted if an older adult feels excessive pain.

Multiple interventions exist to prevent hip fractures. Use of hip protectors in nursing homes has been shown to reduce the incidence of hip fractures (Meyer, Warnke, Bender, & Muhlhauser, 2003). Fall prevention is crucial to reducing hip fractures (Woolf & Akesson, 2003). Exercise that strengthens muscles and improves balance and gait stability reduces falls and subsequently hip fractures (Wolf et al., 2003). Increasing bone mineral density through calcium supplementation, Vitamin D, and nutrition also reduces hip fractures (Woolf & Akesson, 2003). HRT for menopausal women has been encouraged to promote bone density (Reginster, 2004); however, recent findings from the Women's Health Initiative point to the need to weigh the risks and benefits of HRT.

JOINT REPLACEMENT: HIP AND KNEE

Joint replacement is the treatment of choice for end-stage arthritis for the hip or knee (Fortin et al., 1999). Pain and disability are the leading reasons to elect primary arthroplasty (Holtzman, Saleh, & Kane, 2002). In contrast, revision arthroplasty is a procedure done to replace a failing joint implant, and thus is not an elective procedure. One of the few epidemiological population-based studies of Medicare beneficiaries found that 61,568 patients had a primary hip replacement and 13,483 had a revision hip replacement in one year (Mahomed et al., 2003). Medicare patients most likely to undergo a primary hip replacement are older, female, and Caucasian and have higher incomes (Mahomed et al., 2003). A nationally representative sample of community hospitals revealed that 254,370 primary and 23,180 revision knee replacements occurred among Medicare beneficiaries in 1997 (Hervey et al., 2003). The Medicare beneficiaries were primarily Caucasian (70%) with an average age of 69; 63% of persons undergoing primary arthroplasty were female, but only 58% of Medicare beneficiaries undergoing revision arthroplasty were female. Beneficiaries undergoing revision arthroplasty had higher levels of comorbidity. The average length of hospital stay was 4 to 5 days. Discharge dispositions were similar for both groups: Almost 50% were discharged to a short-term hospital or other facility, 30% were discharged home, and 20% were discharged home with home health care.

Various factors influence recovery. Older adults in poor preoperative health who have functional ability impairments, such as walking and IADL limitations, and moderate to severe pain do not reach the same postoperative level of functional ability as older adults who are less severely impaired (Holtzman et al., 2002; Fortin et al., 1999); however, the gains in improvement surpass the gains made by older adults in good preoperative health (Holtzman et al., 2002). Mahomed et al. (2003) found that increased age, revision hip arthroplasty, male gender, low income, Black ethnicity, comorbidity, and a diagnosis of rheumatoid arthritis were all associated with adverse outcomes and/or mortality. In a recent comprehensive review of the literature, Ethgen, Bruyere, Richy, Dardennes, and Reginster (2004) concluded that hip and knee arthroplasty improves health and physical functioning. Older age was not a barrier to functional improvement.

Spousal caregivers of older adults who undergo joint replacement require assistance with the changes in social roles and the health care complexities of recovery (Showalter, Burger, & Salyer, 2000). Increased dependence and the need for ADL and IADL assistance are common immediately after knee or hip replacement, but often abate after rehabilitation. Because individual healing trajectories vary, older adults who undergo knee or hip replacement often underestimate the pain and length of recovery time. Older adults express insecurity and impatience with the healing process; their caregivers express difficulty balancing increased household and personal assistance tasks (Showalter et al., 2000). The social worker will want to be aware that the dynamics of caregiving under these circumstances may be different from many other situations where the presence of chronic conditions, by definition, precludes full recovery and a return to independent functioning by the older adult.

Education on postoperative functional abilities and explanation of the rehabilitation process has been shown to reduce length of stay and decrease medication use and anxiety (Daltroy, Morlino, Eaton, Poss, & Liang, 1998). Adaptive and assistive devices that allow older adults to manipulate the environment and regain independence ease the recovery transition period (Showalter et al., 2000). Participating in rehabilitation programs and exercise has been shown to hasten functional recovery and decrease stiffness and pain (Moffet et al., 2004). Self-efficacy, the belief that one can perform the rehabilitation exercises, increases compliance and speeds rehabilitation (Moon, 2000).

IMPLICATIONS FOR GERONTOLOGICAL SOCIAL WORK PRACTICE AND RESEARCH

Social workers can and should play a significant role in addressing the social, psychological, emotional, and environmental consequences of the physical diseases and conditions discussed in this chapter during the course of their work with older adults and their caregivers. A basic knowledge of the symptoms, risk factors, treatment approaches, and information and referral sources available can improve your practice and benefit your clients significantly. The special challenges and responsibilities associated with orthopedic diseases and conditions for social workers who work with older adults and their families have been highlighted throughout this chapter. In summary, the following are recommended:

1. Gerontological social workers should have a basic understanding of orthopedic diseases, injuries, and procedures, including accompanying symptoms, available procedures and treatments, and their role as a member of the health care team. Social workers should maintain or have access to others who have the necessary health care resources, referral sources, and specialist contacts that their older clients and caregivers can turn to in times of need.

2. Older adults need to be encouraged to take responsibility for maintaining their own health and well-being, staying active, and being in touch with their own bodies. Older adults must be encouraged to see their primary care practitioners on a regular basis and to feel more comfortable expressing their concerns about health issues with medical professionals and engaging generally in open exchange during patient-physician encounters.

3. It is important that both social workers and family members not be overprotective in their helping and caregiving efforts. Overprotectiveness has the potential to foster excessive dependency or learned helplessness among older adults, whereas undue restriction of movement can contribute to muscle atrophy.

4. Helping older adults and their caregivers minimize the socially isolating and emotionally demoralizing effects of orthopedic infirmities and procedures is critical. Strategies for helping older adults maintain a positive spirit, deal with depressive reactions, stay active, and maintain their opportunities for social contact and interactions even in the face of significant functional impairment is a high priority of your work.

5. Older adults need to be helped to understand that they are at risk but that many orthopedic conditions are preventable. Safe mobility practices, smart home design, healthy lifestyles, regular testing, and prompt treatment can make enormous differences in preventing, reversing, or alleviating the negative impact of orthopedic diseases and injuries.

6. Family, friends, and neighbors of elders with orthopedic-related impairment or at risk for such conditions should be kept informed of the risk factors and issues surrounding the disease so that they may serve effectively as an additional line of defense and support. Family members suddenly thrust into the role of caregiver may need crisis counseling and intense support when they are called on to respond unexpectedly to an older relative who has suffered an accident, fallen, or otherwise experienced an unexpected and disabling fracture.

Practice research is needed to help us reach a better understanding of the unique challenges and needs of spouses and other family members called on to assist relatives with orthopedic conditions, especially those who need to transition to the role of caregiver unexpectedly or engage in such functions for time-limited periods during the older adult's recovery period. Social workers would also benefit from research that seeks to better understand the emotional and psychological dimensions of living with orthopedic disease and related conditions and the implications such knowledge has for more informed practice.

REFERENCES

American Geriatrics Society, British Geriatrics Society, and the American Academy of Orthopaedic Surgeons Panel of Falls Prevention. (2001). Guideline for the prevention of falls in older persons. *Journal of the American Geriatrics Society, 49,* 664–672.

Andrew, G. (1993). *Geriatric physical therapy.* St. Louis, MO: Mosby-Year Book.

Baker, S. P., O'Neill, B., Ginsburg, M. J., & Guohua, L. (1992). *The injury fact book.* New York: Oxford University Press.

Bauer, D. C., Browner, W. S., Cauley, J. A., Orwoll, E. S., Scott, J. C., Black, D. M., et al. (1993). Factors associated with appendicular bone mass in older women: The Study of Osteoporotic Fractures Research Group. *Annals of Internal Medicine, 118,* 657–665.

Bilezikian, J. P. (1999). Osteoporosis in men. *Journal of Clinical Endocrinology and Metabolism, 84,* 3431–3434.

Borkan, J. M., & Quirk, M. (1992). Expectations and outcomes after hip fracture among the elderly. *International Journal of Aging and Human Development, 34*(4), 339–350.

Campanelli, L. C. (1996). Mobility changes in older adults: Implications for practitioners. *Journal of Aging and Physical Activity, 4*(2), 105–118.

Carpenter, G. I., & Demopoulos, G. R. (1990). Screening the elderly in the community: Controlled trial of dependency surveillance using a questionnaire administered by volunteers. *British Medical Journal, 12,* 1253–1256.

Centers for Disease Control and Prevention. (1999). *National arthritis action plan: A public health strategy.* Atlanta, GA: Author.

Centers for Disease Control and Prevention. (2002). Prevalence of self-reported arthritis or chronic joint symptoms among adults: United States, 2001. *Morbidity and Mortality Weekly Report, 51*(42), 948–950.

Centers for Disease Control and Prevention, National Center for Health Statistics. (1998). *Public use data tape documentation compressed mortality file, 1989–1998.* Hyattsville, MD: U.S. Department of Health and Human Services.

Cesari, M., Landi, F., Torre, S., Onder, G., Lattanzio, F., & Bernabei, R. (2002). Prevalence and risk factors for falls in an older community-dwelling population. *Journals of Gerontology: Medical Sciences, 57A*(11), M722–M726.

Clemson, L., Fitzgerald, M. H., Heard, R., & Cumming, R. G. (1999). Inter-rater reliability of a home fall hazards assessment tool. *Occupational Therapy Journal of Research, 19*(2), 8–100.

Cumming, R. G., Salkeld, G., Thomas, M., & Szonyi, G. (2000). Prospective study of the impact of fear of falling on activities of daily living, SF-36 scores, and nursing home admission. *Journal of Gerontology: Medical Sciences, 55A*(5), M299–M305.

Cummings, S. R., Rubin, S. M., & Black, D. (1990). The future of hip fractures in the United States: Numbers, costs, and the potential effects of postmenopausal estrogen. *Clinical Orthopaedics and Related Research, 252,* 163–166.

Daltroy, L. H., Morlino, C. I., Eaton, H. M., Poss, R., & Liang, M. H. (1998). Preoperative education for total hip and knee replacement patients. *Arthritis Care and Research, 11*(6), 469–478.

DeVellis, B. M. (1995). The psychological impact of arthritis: Prevalence of depression. *Arthritis Care Research, 8*(4), 284–293.

Dunlop, D. D., Manheim, L. M., Song, J., & Chang, R. W. (2001). Arthritis prevalence and activity limitations in older adults. *Arthritis and Rheumatism, 44*(1), 212–221.

Ethgen, O., Bruyere, O., Richy, F., Dardennes, C., & Reginster, J. Y. (2004). Health-related quality of life in total hip and total knee arthroplasty: A qualitative and systematic review of the literature. *Journal of Bone and Joint Surgery, 86A*(5), 963–974.

Faulkner, K., Cauley, J., Zmuda, J. M., Griffin, J. M., & Nevitt, M. C. (2003). Is social integration associated with the risk of falling in older community dwelling women? *Journals of Gerontology: Medical Sciences, 58,* M954–M959.

Flaherty, J. H., Perry, H. M., Lynchard, G. S., & Morley, J. E. (2000). Polypharmacy and hospitalization among older home care patients. *Journals of Gerontology: Medical Sciences, 55A,* M554–M559.

Fletcher, P. C., & Hirdes, J. P. (2004). Restriction in activity associated with fear of falling among community-based seniors using home care services. *Age and Ageing, 33*(3), 273–279.

Fortin, P. R., Clarke, A. E., Joseph, L., Liang, M. H., Tanzer, M., Ferland, D., et al. (1999). Outcomes of total hip and knee replacement: Preoperative functional status predicts outcomes at six months after surgery. *Arthritis and Rheumatism, 42*(8), 1722–1728.

Frazoni, S., Rozzini, R., Boffelli, S., Frisoni, G. B., & Trabucchi, M. (1994). Fear of falling in nursing home patients. *Gerontology, 40*(1), 38–44.

Gaines, J. M., Talbot, L. A., & Metter, E. J. (2002). The relationship of arthritis self-efficacy to functional performance in older men and women with osteoarthritis of the knee. *Geriatric Nursing, 23*(3), 167–170.

Gallagher, B. (2003). Tai Chi Chuan and Qigong: Physical and mental practice for functional mobility. *Topics in Geriatric Rehabilitation, 19*(3), 172–182.

Gregg, E. W., Pereira, M. A., & Caspersen, C. J. (2000). Physical activity, falls and fracture among older adults: A review of the epidemiologic evidence. *Journal of the American Geriatric Society, 48,* 883–893.

Hanlon, J. T., Landerman, L. R., Fillenbaum, G. G., & Studenski, S. (2002). Falls in African American and white community-dwelling elderly residents. *The Journals of Gerontology, Series A: Biological Sciences and Medical Sciences 57,* M473–M478.

Hervey, S. L., Purves, H. R., Guller, U., Toth, A. P., Vail, T. P., & Pietrobon, R. (2003). Provider volume of total knee arthroplasties and patient outcomes in the HCUP-Nationwide Inpatient Sample. *Journal of Bone and Joint Surgery, 85A,* 1775–1783.

Hill, C. L., Parsons, J., Taylor, A., & Leach, G. (1999). Health related quality of life in a population sample of arthritis. *Journal of Rheumatology, 26*(9), 2029–2035.

Hofman, A., Grobbee, D. E., de Jong, P. T., & van den Ouseland, F. A. (1991). Determinants of disease and disability in the elderly: The Rotterdam Elderly Study. *European Journal of Epidemiology, 7,* 403–422.

Holtzman, J., Khal Saleh, M. S., & Kane, R. (2002). Effect of baseline functional status and pain on outcomes of total hip arthroplasty. *Journal of Bone and Joint Surgery, (84),* 1942–1948.

Huang, H., Gau, M., Lin, W., & Kernoham, G. (2003). Assessing risk of falling in older adults. *Public Health Nursing, 20*(5), 399–411.

Hughes, S. L., & Dunlop, D. D. (1995). The prevalence and impact of arthritis in older persons. *Arthritis Care Research, 8*(4), 257–264.

Hughes, S. L., Seymour, R. B., Campbell, R., Pollak, N., Huber, G., & Sharma, L. (2004). Impact of the fit and strong intervention on older adults with osteoarthritis. *The Gerontologist, 44*(2), 217–228.

Ibrahim, S. A., Whittle, J., Bean-Mayberry, B., Kelley, M. E., Good, C., & Conigliaro, J. (2003). Racial/ethnic variations in physician recommendations for cardiac revascularization. *American Journal of Public Health, 93*(10), 1689–1693.

Kaplan, M. S., Huguet, N., Newsom, J. T., & McFarland, B. H. (2003). Characteristics of physically inactive older adults with arthritis: Results of a population based study. *Preventive Medicine, 37*, 61–67.

Kempen, G., Ormel, J., Scaf-Klomp, W., van Sonderen, E., Ranchor, A., & Sanderman, R. (2003). The role of perceived control in the process of older people's recovery of physical functions after fall-related injuries: A prospective study. *Journal of Gerontology: Psychological Sciences, 58B*(1), P35–P41.

Kempen, G., Scaf-Klomp, W., Ranchor, A., Sanderman, R., Ormel, J. (2001). Social predictors of recovery in late middle-aged and older persons after injury to the extremities: A prospective study. *Journal of Gerontology: Social Sciences, 56B*(4), S229–S236.

Kiely, D. K., Kiel, D. P., Burrows, A. B., & Lipsitz, L. A. (1998). Identifying nursing home residents at risk for falling. *Journal of the American Geriatrics Society, 46*(5), 551–556.

King, M. B., & Tinetti, M. E. (1995). Falls in community-dwelling older persons. (1995). *Journal of the American Geriatrics Society, 43*, 1146–1154.

Klesges, R. C., Ward, K. D., Shelton, M. L., Applegate, W. B., Cantler, E. D., Palmieri, et al. (1996). Changes in bone mineral content in male athletes: Mechanisms of action and intervention effects. *Journal of the American Medical Association, 276*, 226–230.

Legood, R., Scuffham, P., & Cryer, C. (2002). Are we blind to injuries in the visually impaired? A review of the literature. *Injury Prevention, 8*(2), 155–160.

LePlante, M. P., Kaye, H. S., Kang, T., & Harrington, C. (2004). Unmet need for personal assistance services: Estimating the shortfall in hours of help and adverse consequences. *Journal of Gerontology: Social Sciences, 59*(2), S98–S108.

Lipsitz, L. A., Jonsson, P. V., Kelley, M. M., & Koestner, J. S. (1991). Causes and correlates of recurrent falls in ambulatory frail elderly. *Journals of Gerontology: Medical Sciences, 46*(4), M114–M122.

Looker, A. C., Johnston, C. C., Wahner, H. W., Dunn, W. L., Calvo, M. S., Harris, T. B., et al. (1995). Prevalence of low femoral bone density in older U.S. women from NHANES III. *Journal of Bone and Mineral Research, 10*, 796–802.

Lord, S. R., Sherrington, C., & Menz, H. B. (2001). *Falls in older people: Risk factors and strategies for prevention.* New York: Cambridge University Press.

Magaziner, J., Hawkes, W. J., Hebel, R., Zimmerman, S. I., Fox, K. M., Dolan, M., Felsenthal, G., & Kenzora, J. (2000). Recovery from hip fracture in eight areas of function. *The Journals of Gerontology, Series A: Biological Sciences and Medical Science, 55*, M498–M507.

Magaziner, J., Simonsick, E. M., Kashner, M., Hebel, J. R., & Kenzora, J. E. (1990). Predictors of functional recovery one year following hospital discharge for hip fracture: A prospective study. *Journal of Gerontology: Medical Sciences, 45*, M101–M107.

Mahomed, N. N., Barrett, J. A., Katz, J. N., Phillips, C. B., Losina, E. L., Robert, A., et al. (2003). Rates and outcomes of primary and revision total hip replacement in the United States Medicare population. *Journal of Bone and Joint Surgery, 85*, 27–32.

Marcus, R., Feldman, D., & Kelsey, J. (Eds.). (2001). *Osteoporosis* (2nd ed.). San Diego: Academic Press.

Mathias, S., Nayak, U., & Isaacs, B. (1986). Balance in elderly patients: The "Get-up and Go" test. *Archives of Physical Medicine and Rehabilitation, 67*, 387–389.

Mayer-Oakes, S. A., Hoenig, H., Atchison, K. A., Lubben, J. E., De Jong, F., & Schweitzer, S. O. (1992). Patient-related predictors of rehabilitation use for community-dwelling older Americans. *Journal of the American Geriatrics Society, 40*(4), 336–342.

McCoy, P. W. (2001). Pharmacologic management of osteoporosis. *Topics in Geriatric Rehabilitation, 17*, 38–51.

Melton, L. (1995). How many women have osteoporosis now? *Journal of Bone and Mineral Research, 10*, 175–177.

Meyer, G., Warnke, A., Bender, R., & Muhlhauser, I. (2003). Effect of hip fractures of increased use of hip protectors in nursing homes: Cluster randomised controlled trial. *British Medical Journal, 326*, 76.

Mikuls, T. R., Mudano, A. S., Pulley, L. V., & Saag, K. G. (2003). Association of race/ethnicity with the receipt of traditional and alternative arthritis-specific health care. *Medical Care, 41*(11), 1233–1239.

Moffet, H., Collet, J. P., Shapiro, S. H., Paradis, G., Marquis, F., & Roy, L. (2004). Effectiveness of intensive rehabilitation on functional ability and quality of life after first total knee arthroplasty: A single-blind randomized controlled trial. *Archives of Physical Medicine and Rehabilitation, 85*(4), 546–556.

Moon, J. B. (2000). Relationships among self-efficacy, outcome expectancy, and postoperative behaviors in total joint replacement patients. *Orthopaedic Nursing, 19*(2), 77–85.

Moreland, J. D., Richardson, J. A., Goldsmith, C. H., & Clase, C. M. (2004). Muscle weakness and falls in older adults: A systematic review of the literature. *Journal of the American Geriatric Society, 52*(7), 1121–1129.

Moreland, J. D., Richardson, J. A., Goldsmith, C. H., & Clase, C. M. (2004). Muscle weakness and falls in older adults: A systematic review of the literature.

Journal of the American Geriatric Society, 52(7), 1121–1129.

Murphy, S. L. (2000). Deaths: Final data for 1998. National vital statistics reports from the Centers for Disease Control and Prevention, National Center for Health Statistics, *National Vital Statistics System, 48*(11), 1–105.

Myers, A. H., Young, Y., & Langlois, J. A. (1996). Prevention of falls in the elderly. *Bone, 18,* 87S–01S.

National Osteoporosis Foundation. (1996). *Gallup survey on men's knowledge of osteoporosis.* Washington, DC: Author.

National Osteoporosis Foundation. (1998). *Physician's guide to prevention and treatment of osteoporosis.* Washington, DC: Author.

Neuner, J. M., Zimmer, J. K., & Hamel, M. B. (2003). Diagnosis and treatment of osteoporosis in patients with vertebral compression fractures. *Journal of the American Geriatrics Society, 51,* 483–491.

Nevitt, M. C., Cummings, S. R., & Hudes, E. S. (1991). Risk factors for injurious falls: A prospective study. *Journals of Gerontology, 46*(5), M164–170.

Nicodemus, K. K., & Folsom, A. R. (2001). Type 1 and Type 2 diabetes and incident hip fractures in postmenopausal women. *Diabetes Care, 24,* 1192–1197.

Nikolaus, T., & Bach, M. (2003). Preventing falls in community-dwelling frail older people using a home intervention team (HIT): Results from the randomized Falls-HIT trial. *Journal of the American Geriatrics Society, 51*(3), 300–305.

Nyberg, L., Gustafson, Y., Berggren, D., Brannstrom, B., & Bucht, G. (1996). Falls leading to femoral neck fractures in lucid older people. *Journal of the American Geriatrics Society, 44*(2), 156–160.

Oh, H., & Feldt, K. (2000). The prognostic factors for functional recovery in elders with hip fracture. *Nursing and Health Sciences, 2,* 237–242.

O'Laughlin, J. L., Robitaille, Y., Boivin, J., & Suissa, S. (1993). Incidence of and risk factors for falls and injurious falls among the community-dwelling elderly. *American Journal of Epidemiology, 137,* 342–354.

Orwoll, E. S., & Klein, R. F. (1995). Osteoporosis in men. *Endocrine Reviews, 16,* 87–116.

Osteoporosis among estrogen-deficient women: United States, 1988–1994. (1998). *Morbidity and Mortality Weekly Report, 47,* 969–973.

Palmer, M. H., Baumgarten, M., Langenberg, P., & Carson, J. L. (2002). Risk factors for hospital-aquired incontinence in elderly female hip fracture patients. *Journals of Gerontology: Medical Sciences, 57,* M672–M677.

Parker, M. J., & Palmer, C. R. (1995). Prediction of rehabilitation after hip fracture. *Age and Ageing, 24*(2), 96–98.

Peek, M. K., & Coward, R. T. (1999). Gender differences in the risk of developing disability among older adults with arthritis. *Journal of Aging and Health, 11*(2), 131–150.

Penninx, B. W., Messier, S. P., Rejeski, W. J. K., Williamson, J. D., DiBari, M., Cavazzini, C., et al. (2001). Physical exercise and the prevention of disability in activities of daily living in older persons with osteoarthritis. *Archives of Internal Medicine, 161*(19), 2309–2324.

Porell, F. W., & Miltiades, H. B. (2001). Access to care and functional status change among aged Medicare beneficiaries, *Journal of Gerontology: Social Sciences, 56B*(2), S69–S83.

Praemer, A., Furner, S., & Rice, D. P. (1999). *Musculoskeletal conditions in the U.S.* Rosemont: American Academy of Orthopaedic Surgeons.

Ray, W., & Griffin, M. R. (1990). Prescribed medications and the risk of falling. *Topics in Geriatric Rehabilitation, 5,* 12–20.

Reginster, J. Y. (2004). Prevention of postmenopausal osteoporosis with pharmacological therapy: Practice and possibilities. *Journal of Internal Medicine, 255*(6), 615–628.

Riggs, B. L., & Melton, L. J. (1992). The prevention and treatment of osteoporosis. *New England Journal of Medicine, 327,* 620–627.

Roberto, K. A. (1992a). Elderly women with hip fractures: Functional and psychosocial correlates of recovery. *Journal of Women and Aging, 4*(2), 3–20.

Roberto, K. A. (1992b). Role of social supports in older women's recovery from hip fracture. *Journal of Applied Gerontology, 11*(3), 314–325.

Roberto, K. A., & Reynolds, S. G. (2001). The meaning of osteoporosis in the lives of rural older women. *Health Care for Women International, 22,* 599–611.

Samelson, E. J., Zhang, Y., Kiel, D. P., Hannan, M. T., & Felson, D. T. (2002). Effect of birth cohort on risk of hip fracture: Age-specific incidence rates in the Framingham Study. *American Journal of Public Health, 92*(5), 858–862.

Scaf-Klomp, W., van Sonderen, E., Sanderman, R., Ormel, J., & Kempen, G. I. J. M. (2001). Recovery of physical function after limb injuries in independent older people living at home. *Age and Ageing, 30*(3), 213–219.

Showalter, A., Burger, S., & Salyer, J. (2000). Patient's and their spouses' needs after total joint arthroplasty: A pilot study. *Orthopaedic Nursing, 19,* 49–57.

Stalenhoef, P. A., Crebolder, H. F. J. M., Knottnerus, J. A., & Van der Horst, F. G. E. M. (1997). Incidence, risk factors and consequences of falls among elderly subjects living in the community: A criteria-based analysis. *European Journal of Public Health, 7,* 328–334.

Stel, V. S., Smit, J. H., Pluijm, S. M., & Lips, P. (2004). Consequences of falling in older men and women and risk factors for health service use and functional decline. *Age and Ageing, 33*(1), 58–65.

Tideiksaar, R. (2002). *Falls in older people: Prevention and management* (3rd ed.). Baltimore: Health Professions Press.

Tinetti, M. E., Lui, W. L., & Claus, E. (1993). Predictors and prognosis of instability to get up after falls among elderly persons. *Journal of the American Medical Association, 269,* 65–70.

Tinetti, M. E., Lui, W. L., & Claus, E. (1993). Predictors and prognosis of instability to get up after falls among elderly persons. *Journal of the American Medical Association, 269,* 65–70.

Tinetti, M. E., Richman, D., & Powell, L. (1990). Falls efficacy as a measure of fear of falling. *Journal of Gerontology: Psychological Sciences, 45*(6), 239–243.

Tromp, A. M., Smit, J. H., Deeg, D. J. H., Bouter, L. M., & Lips, P. (1998). Predictors for falls and fractures in the Longitudinal Aging Study Amsterdam. *Journal of Bone Mineral Research, 13,* 1932–1941.

van Doorn, C., Gruber-Baldini, A. L., Zimmerman, S., Hebel, J. R., Port, C. L., Baumgarten, M., et al. (2003). Dementia as a risk factor for falls and fall injuries among nursing home residents. *Journal of the American Geriatrics Society, 51*(9), 1213–1220.

Walter, L. C., Lui, L., Eng, C., & Covinsky, K. E. (2003). Risk of hip fracture in disabled community-living older adults. *Journal of the American Geriatrics Society, 51,* 50–55.

Wang, G., Helmick, C. G., Macera, C., Zhang, P., & Pratt, M. (2001). Inactivity associated medical costs among U.S. adults with arthritis. *Arthritis Care Research, 45,* 430–435.

Wang, X., & Emery, L. J. (2002). Cognitive status after hip replacement. *Physical and Occupational Therapy in Geriatrics, 21*(1), 51–64.

Wilkins, K. (1999). Health care consequences of falls for seniors. *Health Reports, 10*(4), 47–55.

Williams, B., Cullen, L., & Barlow, J. H. (2002). "I never realised how little I knew!": A pilot study of osteoporosis knowledge, beliefs, and behaviors. *Health Care for Women International, 23,* 344–350.

Williams, M. A., Oberst, M. T., Bjorklund, B. C., & Hughes, S. H. (1996). Family caregiving in cases of hip fracture. *Rehabilitation Nursing, 21*(3), 124–131, 138.

Wolf, S. L., Barnhart, H. X., Kutner, N. G., McNeely, E., Coogler, C., Xu, T., et al. (2003). Reducing frailty and falls in older persons: An investigation of Tai Chi and computerized balance training. *Journal of the American Geriatric Society, 51*(12), 1794–1803.

Wolinsky, F. D., Fitzgerald, J. F., & Stump, T. E. (1997). The effect of hip fracture on mortality, hospitalization, and functional status: A prospective study. *American Journal of Public Health, 87*(3), 398–403.

Woolf, A., & Akesson, K. (2003). Preventing fractures in elderly people. *British Medical Journal, 327,* 89–95.

Yardley, L., & Smith, H. (2002). A prospective study of the relationship between feared consequences of falling and avoidance of activity in community-living older people. *The Gerontologist, 42*(1), 17–23.

ELIZABETH LIGHTFOOT

Older Adults With Developmental Disabilities

5

Developmental disabilities are a diverse group of physical and/or mental impairments that begin anytime up until 22 years of age and are usually life-long. Development disabilities limit a person's capacity to engage in major life activities, such as independent living, mobility, language, learning, working, decision making, and self-care. In the United States, there is a precise federal definition of a developmental disability (Table 5.1). Common diagnoses that often fall under the definition of developmental disabilities include intellectual disability (Table 5.2), autism, cerebral palsy, hearing impairment, vision impairment, and attention-deficit/hyperactivity disorder (ADHD). There are currently about 4 million people in the United States with a developmental disability. Although the definition of developmental disability is broad, this chapter primarily focuses on issues faced by older people with intellectual disabilities.

The issues surrounding aging with a developmental disability have received more attention in the past decade due to both the increased longevity of people with developmental disabilities and an increased focus on the rights and quality of life issues of people with disabilities overall. In 2000, there were approximately 641,000 adults with developmental disabilities over the age of 60 in the United States (Heller, Janicki, Hammel, & Factor, 2002). By the year 2030, it is estimated that the number of older people with developmental disabilities in the United States will almost double to approximately 1,242,800 (Heller et al., 2002). The size of the baby boom cohort partially explains this growing figure, but as important is the growing life expectancy of people with developmental disabilities. In 1930, the average life span for a person with an intellectual disability in the United States was only about 20 years (Carter & Jancar, 1983). However, by the late 1990s, the life expectancy for people with developmental disabilities had risen dramatically. People with Down syndrome now have an average life expectancy of around 60 years, and people with other types of developmental disabilities now have a life expectancy approaching 70 years (Janicki, Dalton, Henderson, & Davidson, 1999; Warren, 1998).

In the late 20th century a major paradigm shift commenced in service provisions for people with developmental disabilities. Services used to be provided primarily in institutions, with professionals making the primary decisions on where and how a person would live. Now services are becoming more consumer-driven and community-based. Growing numbers of people with developmental disabilities are living in the community in their own homes, working

TABLE 5.1. U.S. Federal Definition of Developmental Disabilities

The term "developmental disability" means a severe, chronic disability of an individual 5 years of age or older that:[1]

1) Is attributable to a mental or physical impairment or combination of mental and physical impairments

2) Is manifested before the individual attains age 22

3) Is likely to continue indefinitely

4) Results in substantial functional limitations in three or more of the following areas of major life activity:

   (i) Self-care

   (ii) Receptive and expressive language

   (iii) Learning

   (iv) Mobility

   (v) Self-direction

   (vi) Capacity for independent living

   (vii) Economic self-sufficiency

5) Reflects the individual's need for a combination and sequence of special, interdisciplinary, or generic services, supports, or other assistance that is of lifelong or extended duration and is individually planned and coordinated.

in real jobs for real wages, and participating in leisure activities of their choice. The concept of *person-centered planning,* which involves supporting people with developmental disabilities to make choices about how they live their lives, has increased their self-determination. Although supports for community living have not developed at the same rate as the desire for community living, there are now greatly expanded community-based options for people with developmental disabilities.

Likewise, the roles of social workers and social service organizations have changed dramatically in the field of developmental disabilities. Social workers are moving away from their previous role of primary assessor of needs and decision maker for services and are now becoming more involved in supporting individuals with developmental disabilities to make their own choices, helping to coordinate or broker services,

and assisting in individual and systems advocacy for appropriate services. Social service organizations providing services to people with developmental disabilities are moving away from being primarily institution-based service providers and are becoming more likely to be community support organizations—providing supports to individuals with developmental disabilities to live, work, and interact in the community (Lightfoot, Hewitt, & Sauer, 2004). This trend toward community-based supports and person-centered planning fits with the social work values of self-determination and respect for the dignity of all people (National Association of Social Workers, 1996).

The new paradigm in developmental disabilities has not lessened the complexity of the developmental disabilities field. Effective social workers need to be knowledgeable about the various federal and state

TABLE 5.2. Language Matters

Intellectual Disability

The terminology in the field of developmental disabilities has been continuously changing in an attempt to increase both respect and preciseness. The term "intellectual disability," used internationally, has recently been adopted by many U.S. advocacy, research, and governmental agencies as a more appropriate and respectful synonym for "mental retardation." However, many federal and state programs in the United States are still currently using the older term. Developmental disability and intellectual disability, though similar, have slightly different definitions.

People-First Language

The most important aspect in the use of language is to try to avoid labeling individuals (e.g., "He is blind") or using words with negative connotations (e.g., "stroke victim") or words regarded as slurs (e.g., "handicapped"). In the United States, many people with disabilities advocate using "people-first language." People-first language puts the person before the disability, and it describes what a person has or uses, not what a person is (e.g., "person with an intellectual disability" rather than "mentally retarded person"; "he uses a wheelchair" rather than "he is confined to a wheelchair"; "people with disabilities" rather than "the disabled").

laws and policies that protect the rights of people with developmental disabilities and provide funding for services (Table 5.3), the various program options that allow people with developmental disabilities to receive adequate supports, and the organizations that work to enact progressive legislation and to provide information and support to individuals and families (Table 5.4).

SOCIAL WORK PRACTICE WITH OLDER PERSONS WITH DEVELOPMENTAL DISABILITIES

The underlying social work issues surrounding *aging* with a developmental disability are not dissimilar from social work practice in the general area of aging. Social workers support older people to age with dignity, maintain a good quality of life, meet their basic needs, have their rights respected, access appropriate health care, and deal with the physical and emotional changes associated with aging. Until recently, there have not been strong linkages between the aging service network and the developmental disabilities service network as they relate to addressing the needs of persons aging with a developmental disability. However, in the past decade there has been a growing collaboration between the fields of aging and disability.

The general issues surrounding aging are similar for people of all abilities, but there are some different areas of emphasis that social workers need to be aware of when supporting older people with developmental disabilities. This chapter discusses some of the important issues that social workers will encounter when supporting older people with developmental disabilities. In particular, to practice effectively and ethically with older persons and their families, social workers need to know about:

- Health concerns
- Community participation and retirement
- Residential options
- Family caregiving issues
- Later-life planning
- Loss and grief
- Assistive technology and environmental interventions
- Rights and advocacy

HEALTH CONCERNS

Social workers in the area of developmental disabilities need to be aware of health concerns associated with aging with a developmental disability. These include not only the normal health trajectory of older people with developmental disabilities, but also access to health care and the promotion of a healthy lifestyle. One of the reasons for increased life expectancy for people with developmental disabilities is the vastly improved medical care available to them in childhood and early adult years. As people with developmental disabilities are living much longer, they are now experiencing age-related health conditions similar to other older people. Our medical knowledge is still limited about many of the particularities of these age-related health concerns (Evenhuis, Henderson, Beange, Lennox, & Chicoine, 2000), though there are

TABLE 5.3. Major U.S. Federal Disability Laws

Americans with Disabilities Act of 1990 (ADA)

Prohibits discrimination on the basis of disability in employment, state and local government, public accommodations, commercial facilities, transportation, and telecommunications.

Section 504 of the Rehabilitation Act of 1973

Prohibits discrimination on the basis of disability in programs that receive federal funds.

Developmental Disabilities Assistance and Bill of Rights Act

Provides federal funding to developmental disabilities councils, protection and advocacy agencies, and university centers on excellence in developmental disabilities.

The Fair Housing Act Amendments of 1988

Prohibits discrimination in housing on the basis of disability.

The Civil Rights of Institutionalized Persons Act (CRIPA)

Authorizes the U.S. attorney general to investigate conditions of confinement at state and local government institutions, including institutions for people with developmental disabilities.

TABLE 5.4. Organizations Serving Older People With Developmental Disabilities

---

Administration on Developmental Disabilities

The federal organization responsible for implementation of the Developmental Disabilities Assistance and Bill of Rights Act.

  http://www.acf.hhs.gov/programs/add/

American Association on Mental Retardation (AAMR)

Promotes progressive policies, sound research, effective practices, and universal human rights for people with intellectual disabilities.

  http://www.aamr.org/

The ARC

A national organization providing information, support, advocacy, and research for people with developmental disabilities and their families, including older people.

  www.thearc.org

Canadian Association for Community Living

National Canadian organization for people with intellectual disabilities and their families.

  www.cacl.org

Foundation for People with Learning Disabilities (UK)

Provides research, develops projects, and provides information on people with intellectual disabilities (called learning disabilities in the United Kingdom).

  http://www.learningdisabilities.org.uk

International Association for the Scientific Study of Intellectual Disabilities

An international scientific organization that promotes worldwide research and exchange of information on intellectual disabilities and has a special interest group on aging.

  http://www.iassid.org/

Rehabilitation Research and Training Center on Aging with Developmental Disabilities, University of Illinois at Chicago

Conducts research and provides technical assistance and information on aging with developmental disabilities.

  http://www.uic.edu/orgs/rrtcamr/index.html

Self-Advocates Empowering Ourselves

A national organization of self-advocates that provides training, information, and support for individuals and self-advocacy organizations.

  http://www.sabeusa.org/

United Cerebral Palsy

A national organization dedicated to improving independence, productivity, and full citizenship of people with cerebral palsy.

  http://www.ucp.org/

---

numerous medical studies under way that will aid in our knowledge (Seltzer, 2004)

One area in which aging-related health knowledge has progressed is dementia and people with Down syndrome. People with Down syndrome appear to have more significant age-related health concerns, particularly with the high prevalence and early onset of dementia (Janicki & Dalton, 2000), as well as other age-related health issues such as adult-onset epilepsy, sensory losses, hip disease, and thyroid disorders (Dinani & Carpenter, 1990; Janicki, Heller, Seltzer, & Hogg, 1996; Puri, Ho, & Singh, 2001; Van Allen, Fung, & Jurenka, 1999). For other people with developmental disabilities, there are some early indicators that prevalence rates of dementia, one of the most serious age-related health concerns, are roughly equal for adults with and without developmental disabilities (Zigman et al., 2004).

Social workers need to advocate for access to appropriate health care for older people with developmental disabilities. There are a number of barriers these individuals face in the health arena that may limit their access, including bureaucratic barriers, such as extraordinarily complicated health care financial reimbursements, which can limit medical professionals' desire to take on such patients. Further, few medical professionals have received training on working with older people with developmental disabilities, and thus many are not familiar with their typical health and functioning issues (Messinger-Rapport & Rapport,

1997). There are few valid health assessment tools that can assist medical professionals in diagnosing some age-related conditions in this population, which may be difficult to diagnose because of their cognitive ability (Shultz et al., 2004). People with developmental disabilities may also be resistant to receiving medical care due to poor previous experiences with untrained medical staff (Seltzer & Luchterhand, 1994). A final barrier is health rationing, which sometimes negatively affects older people with developmental disabilities. Due to limited resources, there is often a need to ration or prioritize medical treatment. Many people with developmental disabilities have been denied access to some forms of medical care, most notably access to organ transplants, because of their disability (National Work Group on Disability & Transplantation, 2004).

Social workers also have a role in promoting a healthy lifestyle for older people with developmental disabilities. Along with improved medical care, a healthier lifestyle associated with living in the community has helped to improve life expectancy for these individuals. However, people with developmental disabilities are still more likely to have sedentary lifestyles and poor nutrition (Braunschweig et al., 2004; Heller et al., 2002). Health promotion activities can help them avoid age-related conditions related to poor fitness and nutrition, such as Type II diabetes, osteoporosis, and coronary heart disease. Studies are showing that people involved in fitness and health education training programs have improved attitudes toward exercise (Heller, Hsieh, & Rimmer, 2004).

COMMUNITY PARTICIPATION AND RETIREMENT

Adults with developmental disabilities are becoming increasingly involved in their communities, including working and participating in leisure activities. As these individuals age, they vary on how they wish to continue their community involvement, whether through continued work, retirement, or volunteer activities. The concept of retirement is relatively new for older persons with developmental disabilities. As many are still not working at jobs with competitive wages, retirement may signify a shift in activities that allows more leisure time, rather than finishing their careers and receiving retirement benefits (Heller, 1999).

Many older people with developmental disabilities simply continue to work past the typical retirement age (Sutton, Sterns, & Schwartz-Park, 1993) or stay in their current day activity programs. Often, they like

the structure of their current programs (Mahon & Mactavish, 2000) and worry that changing to a new activity or program would result in the loss of friends and/or income (Janicki, 1992).

Older persons and their families may not be aware that retirement options exist. When planning for retirement does occur, it has usually not included asking individuals with developmental disabilities themselves what their own desires are for changing their daily plans as their health or energy levels change (Sutton et al., 1993). For those who do wish to retire from work, vocational programs, or day activity centers, there have been few retirement options available until recently. Some of the larger developmental disability support providers are starting to provide retirement options, such as supported volunteering or recreational opportunities. There are also attempts to encourage existing senior programs, such as senior centers or senior parks and recreation programs, to be more inclusive of older people with developmental disabilities. Despite the advent of new retirement options, these options are still limited and are altogether unavailable in many areas. Further, the lack of knowledge about these options persists.

Another issue surrounding retirement is the different health trajectories that some people with developmental disabilities may have. Like all people, people with developmental disabilities experience age-related health conditions at different ages. For example, the majority of people with Down syndrome begin to experience health declines at an earlier age than average and may need to consider shifting to retirement at an earlier age, such as in their 50s or even 40s. Other people with developmental disabilities may not experience an earlier onset of age-related health changes. Social workers need to be aware of these different health trajectories, both to allow their clients a chance to experience retirement and to advocate for changing programmatic age requirements that effectively bar some people with developmental disabilities from retiring.

RESIDENTIAL OPTIONS

The types of formal residential options for people with developmental disabilities have expanded dramatically in the past 25 years. For people living in the formal care system, the overall trend is to live outside of large institutions, and the majority of large institutions have been closed across the United States. The U.S. Supreme Court has recently affirmed this trend with its *Olmstead* decision, which guarantees the rights of individuals with disabilities to live in the community or in the most integrated setting feasible (*Olmstead et al. v. L.C. et al.,* 1999).

Formal living options that have become more common are medium and small group homes and shared homes and apartments with paid staff providing more flexible support. Community-based living arrangements have expanded rapidly in the past several decades. However, the formal system of residential living options for older people with disabilities is currently well beyond capacity. As of 1997, there were more than 80,000 people with developmental disabilities on formal state waiting lists for residential services (Prouty & Lakin, 1998). We can expect the number of individuals on waiting lists to grow dramatically as the number of older people with developmental disabilities increases, with the accompanying need to transfer from their elderly parents' homes.

The most common living arrangement for adults with developmental disabilities is living with their families, rather than in formal or informal arrangements in the community. It has been estimated that about 60% of adults with developmental disabilities live with their families (Braddock, 1999; Fujiura, 1998). For these adults, the types of residential supports available include respite care, personal care assistance, and in-home health care. However, the needs for these services are much greater than their availability, and the waiting lists for these community-based supports are long. Only a small portion of federal and state residential funding is spent on community and family supports for community-based living (Stancliffe & Lakin, 2004).

The growing waiting lists for all types of residential services and supports place stress on aging parent caregivers who are unsure where their adult children will reside when they are no longer able to care for them. It also suggests a need for a coordinated effort to address the lack of community housing options for adults with developmental disabilities.

The concept of "aging in place," which means growing older without having to move as one becomes more functionally limited, is becoming more prominent in the area of developmental disabilities. There is a shift away from expecting people with developmental disabilities to move to an institution or a residential setting, such as a group home, as their first option when they are no longer able to live with their parents. The concept of aging in place becomes more difficult when an older person with a developmental disability suffers an age-related functional disability, such as dementia. For those older people already in formal care, aging in place requires myriad support services, including early detection, clinical supports to help staff provide appropriate care, program adaptations that fit an individual's changing functional level, specialized programs such as hospice, and environmental adaptations such as ramps, adapting restrooms, or installing alarm systems (Janicki, McCallion, & Dalton, 2002). Despite many advocates' preference for the aging in place model, many group homes do not have the training, finances, or other resources available to offer this option. Alternatives to aging in place for people with dementia include transferring to specialized group homes or to a nursing home (Janicki et al., 2002).

FAMILY CAREGIVER ISSUES

For families, issues surrounding caregiving for adult children with developmental disabilities are some of the greatest concerns associated with aging. As parent-caregivers grow older, they are concerned about caring for their adult children as long as possible and what will happen to their adult children when they die or become unable to provide care. Aging caregivers often find both rewards and stressors in caring for their aging children (Essex, Seltzer, & Krauss, 1999).

Families with both aging parents and an aging adult child with a developmental disability, sometimes called "two-generation elderly families" (Davis & Berkobien, 1994), often have had little or no involvement with the formal disability service network (Smith, Fullmer, & Tobin, 1994). Many don't receive any support services, such as respite care. Some are distrustful of the social service system, especially as the philosophy of the social service system at the time when their children were born was one of customary institutionalization of children. Others simply feel they do not need supportive services (Smith, 1997). Some report a need for support groups, family counseling, or individual counseling, but report that these services are not available (Smith, Majeski, & McClenny, 1996). For some ethnic groups, such as Puerto Ricans, the natural social support system present in their families and communities has taken the place of a formal support system (Magana, 1999). However, the use and availability of respite care and other support services have been increasing, as such services are more and more seen as a support for caregiving rather than only for crisis situations (Freedman, Griffiths, Krauss, & Seltzer, 1999). Further, studies are showing that younger caregivers are more likely to seek supportive services and have higher expectations of the social service system (Hayden & Heller, 1997), which suggests that the next cohort of aging caregivers may make more use of support services.

As parents of adult children with developmental disabilities begin facing their own health concerns, one of the greatest is planning for the transfer of caregiving. Families often have to make the decision of whether to transfer care to another family member, such as a sibling of the adult with a developmental disability, or to a formal residential option. Those who have not been involved in the formal service system are contemplating entering the system for the first time after having been the primary or only caregiver, sometimes for more than 50 years.

Many parents simply do not make plans for their adult children's future care (Heller & Factor, 1991; Kaufman, Adams, & Campbell, 1991). This can be due to a lack of information about their options, as well as the stress and worry related to facing the reality that their children will outlive them. Parents tend to feel fewer worries when planning a transfer to a sibling (Griffiths & Unger, 1994). Social workers have a primary role in supporting families emotionally as they deal with this stressful life stage, as well as helping them learn about and access resources and plan for their adult child's future. Social workers can also be involved in the building of coalitions of aging, developmental disabilities, and other social service agencies that can work together to support the needs of elderly families (Davis & Berkobien, 1994).

LATER-LIFE PLANNING

A key role for social workers supporting older people with developmental disabilities and their families is to assist them in the area of later-life planning. As mentioned, the stresses involved in older-age transition can lead some families to avoid planning for the future. And when planning does occur, people with developmental disabilities themselves are often not included in the planning process or even informed of the changes that will take place in the future (Heller, Miller, Hsieh, & Sterns, 2000).

Person-centered planning is an approach to planning that assists individuals with disabilities to make decisions about how they would like to live their lives, with support from individuals in the community who know them well, such as family members, friends, neighbors, and support staff (Abery & McBride, 1998). This is in contrast to provider-based planning, in which providers or professionals make plans for individuals based on their professional assessments and service availability, without necessarily asking the individual and his or her family what they envision for their later years. The person-centered planning approach fits well with the social work values of empowerment and self-determination. The social worker's role becomes one of facilitating the process of planning based on an individual's desires and helping the individual to realize his or her vision (Abery & McBride, 1998).

Key areas that are covered in later-life planning include where a person will reside, future work and leisure activities, financial matters, and guardianship concerns. As detailed earlier, residential planning can be one of the most stressful issues for families, as many have never lived away from their parents, and there will at some point be a need for either bringing supports into the home, moving to live with a relative or friend, or entering into formal care. Person-centered planning can help families make the best choice of residence based on the individual's and family's own desires, along with making choices for future retirement and leisure activities.

Individuals and families also have to plan future finances for their adult children, such as determining to what extent an individual can manage his or her own financial matters, planning who might be involved in assisting with this chore, estimating the future costs of different types of support, and assuring that transference of estates do not jeopardize an individual's eligibility for government benefits (Davis & Berkobien, 1994). Social workers can help families understand the wide array of often confusing financial planning options, ranging from informal options to complicated trusts, and help them coordinate the planning process to include financial advisors who are aware of the family's needs. Financial planning is obviously intricately intertwined with residential planning, as the amount of money available to individuals relates directly to the choices they have for living. As Medicaid pays for most publicly funded residential services, directly transferring income on a parent's death to the child or child's proxy may actually limit the adult child's residential options.

The issue of planning for guardianship is also an important consideration in later-life planning. Basically, a guardian has the legal authority to manage the affairs of another person. A family member or state guardianship used to be the norm for people with developmental disabilities; it is now used more specifically to protect individual rights as much as possible.

The decision for guardianship is made by the court, based on an individual's ability to make decisions, not based on diagnosis (Davis & Berkobien, 1994). There are important reasons why an individual may need either a full, partial, or temporary guardian, such as his or her need for help in managing finances or need for medical care.

Planning for guardianship is often discussed in the context of future health care planning. Just as doctors cannot perform medical procedures without informed consent, an individual with a developmental disability who cannot express an understanding of a complicated medical issue cannot demonstrate consent. This necessitates some arrangement of surrogate medical decision making, depending on an individual's ability to understand and make complicated medical choices. Although guardianship protects individuals with developmental disabilities, allowing them to access medical care, for example, it also limits self-determination. Other complicated issues that individuals and parents might want to plan for include advanced directives, such as a living will. Social workers need to help families with these important planning issues.

LOSS AND GRIEF

As is true for all older people, older people with developmental disabilities experience both age-related joys and age-related losses. Some of the losses may be unique or more profound for people with developmental disabilities, but the underlying issues of loss and grief are similar. Social workers need to be aware of these unique losses and help their clients with their grief.

Because so many of these individuals have lived with their parents for so long, the loss of a parent can be extremely traumatic. Not only may they be grieving their parents, but their parents' death may also result in their having to move from the family home that they have been residing in for many years to a formal service system. This change of location and the accompanying change in routines can compound the loss they are already feeling. Further, they may feel a loss of self-worth or self-esteem, as they may have had a valuable role in the family that no longer exists or is disregarded with their parents' death (Ludlow, 1999). People with developmental disabilities may also experience a greater sense of loneliness as they age, as they are often more isolated from the community, whether living in a group home or their parents'

home. If they have not been involved in any later-life planning, they may not understand exactly what is happening to them. Participating in bereavement rituals according to their culture or religion can help people with disabilities cope with their grief (Ludlow, 1999).

Social workers practicing with this population need to be aware of the grief and sense of loss they experience and help them mourn the passing of their family and friends. Involving them in later-life planning may help them anticipate some of the changes they may experience before a major change occurs.

ASSISTIVE TECHNOLOGY AND ENVIRONMENTAL INTERVENTIONS

There is a growing focus on the use of assistive technology and environmental interventions to help older people with developmental disabilities maintain their functioning and independence. Assistive technology includes any products, devices, or equipment that are used to maintain or improve one's functioning. Examples of assistive technology are low-tech devices such as an adapted door handle, a walker, a telephone amplifier, or a grab-bar near the bathtub, and high-tech equipment such as a voice synthesizer or an electronic scooter. Environmental interventions are changes in an individual's environment that help maintain or improve functioning, such as building a fence, painting walls different colors, or adding ramps. Very high-tech environmental interventions are on the horizon, such as "smart homes," which electronically monitor older people's movement in their home, their health status, and even their self-care needs in a perhaps inobtrusive way (Rehabilitation Engineering Research Center on Technology for Successful Aging, 1999).

There is some evidence that the use of assistive technology and environmental interventions do result in better functioning for older people with developmental disabilities (Hammel, Lai, & Heller, 2002). However, there are currently limited resources to pay for such technology and interventions, and little knowledge available about the types and appropriateness of such interventions for older persons with developmental disabilities. Further, social workers need to be sure to keep the issue of protecting privacy and autonomy of the individual in the forefront when using such equipment, especially with some of the new monitoring techniques. There is also a danger that some people will be left behind in benefiting from these new advances due to a lack of resources, with a resulting digital divide in technological supports for people with disabilities.

RIGHTS AND ADVOCACY

The push for rights for people with developmental disabilities has come from national advocacy groups, such as the ARC and TASH; self-advocacy groups, such as People First; and many individuals and relatives of people with developmental disabilities. The social work profession has not been in the forefront of the disability rights movement (Mackelprang & Salsgiver, 1996), though many social work professionals are now involved in supporting systems-level changes.

Partially as a direct result of such advocacy, the later years of the 20th century brought increased federal and state protections for the rights of people with developmental disabilities. Federal laws, such as the Americans with Disabilities Act of 1990, now protect people with disabilities from discrimination in employment, state and local government, public accommodations, and transportation. State and federal lawsuits have closed down many institutions and required services to be provided in the least restrictive environments.

Of particular importance for older people with developmental disabilities is the worldwide self-advocacy movement, a movement *of* mostly younger people with developmental disabilities *for* people with developmental disabilities. Participation in self-advocacy has generally not been encouraged among older adults in this population, though self-advocacy organizations are beginning to look more closely into issues of aging (Levitz, 1999). As individuals' degree of community inclusion and self-determination is linked with their ability to advocate for what they want and need (Herr & Weber, 1999), social workers should encourage older people with developmental disabilities to become or continue to be involved in self-advocacy.

NEW DIRECTIONS FOR SOCIAL WORK PRACTICE

Social workers who embrace the paradigm shift that has occurred in the field of developmental disabilities will find themselves well situated to support older persons with developmental disabilities to live quality lives. Social workers can assist these clients to have more control of their lives, participate in the community, receive appropriate health care, access appropriate assistive technology, and cope with grief and loss associated with aging. Social workers can assist older people with developmental disabilities and their family members to plan together regarding the future. And social workers can be involved in building collations among providers for more effective services and in advocating for civil rights, adequate funding, and a more consumer-directed, community-based service system. Social work researchers can help design and evaluate new models for providing services and supports to older people with developmental disabilities in the 21st century. This will be particularly important, as the next cohort of older people will have grown up with more involvement in the community, and issues such as retirement and community residential options will be more in demand. The values and skills of social workers are ideal for supporting the new paradigm of service provision and supports for older people with developmental disabilities.

REFERENCES

Abery, B., & McBride, M. (1998). Look and understand before you leap. *Impact, 11*, 2–3.

Braddock, D. (1999). Aging and developmental disabilities: Demographic and policy issues affecting American families. *Mental Retardation, 37*(2), 155–161.

Braunschweig, C., Gomez, S., Sheean, P., Tomey, K., Rimmer, J., & Heller, T. (2004). Nutritional status and risk factors for chronic disease in urban-dwelling adults with Down syndrome. *American Journal on Mental Retardation, 109*(2), 186–193.

Carter, G., & Jancar, J. (1983). Mortality in the mentally handicapped: A fifty year survey at State Park Group Hospitals (1930–1980). *Journal of Mental Deficiency Research, 27*, 143–156.

Davis, S., & Berkobien, R. (1994). *Meeting the needs and challenges of at-risk, two-generation, elderly families.* Silver Spring, MD: The Arc.

Dinani, S., & Carpenter, S. (1990). Down's syndrome and thyroid disorder. *Journal of Mental Deficiency Research, 34*, 187–193.

Essex, E., Seltzer, M. M., & Krauss, M. (1999). Differences in coping effectiveness and well-being among aging mothers and fathers of adults with mental retardation. *American Journal on Mental Retardation, 104*(6), 545–563.

Evenhuis, H., Henderson, C., Beange, H., Lennox, N., & Chicoine, B. (2000). *Healthy ageing—Adults with intellectual disabilities: Physical health issues.* Geneva, Switzerland: World Health Organization.

Freedman, R., Griffiths, D., Krauss, M., & Seltzer, M. M. (1999). Patterns of respite use by aging mothers of adults with mental retardation. *Mental Retardation, 37*(2), 93–103.

Fujiura, G. T. (1998). The demography of family households. *American Journal on Mental Retardation, 103,* 225–235.

Griffiths, D., & Unger, D. (1994). Views about planning for the future among parents and siblings of adults with mental retardation. *Family Relations, 43,* 221–227.

Hammel, J., Lai, J., & Heller, T. (2002). The impact of assistive technology and environmental interventions on function and living situation status with people who are ageing with developmental disabilities. *Disability & Rehabilitation, 24*(1–3), 93–105.

Hayden, M., & Heller, T. (1997). Support, problem-solving/coping ability, and personal burden of younger and older caregivers with mental retardation. *Mental Retardation, 35,* 364–372.

Heller, T. (1999). Emerging models. In S. S. Herr & G. Weber (Eds.), *Aging, rights and quality of life: Prospects for older people with developmental disabilities* (pp. 149–166). Baltimore, MD: Brookes.

Heller, T., & Factor, A. (1991). Permanency planning for adults with mental retardation living with family members. *American Journal on Mental Retardation, 96*(2), 163–176.

Heller, T., Hsieh, K., & Rimmer, J. (2004). Attitudinal and psychological outcomes of a fitness and health education program on adults with Down syndrome. *American Journal on Mental Retardation, 109*(2), 175–185.

Heller, T., Janicki, M., Hammel, J., & Factor, A. (2002). *Promoting healthy aging, family support and age-friendly communities for persons aging with developmental disabilities: Report of the 2001 Invitational Research Symposium on Aging with Developmental Disabilities.* Chicago: Rehabilitation Research and Training Center on Aging with Developmental Disabilities, Department of Disability and Human Development, University of Illinois at Chicago.

Heller, T., Miller, A., Hsieh, K., & Sterns, H. (2000). Later-life planning: Promoting knowledge of options and choice-making. *Mental Retardation, 85*(5), 395–406.

Herr, S. S., & Weber, G. (1999). Prospects for ensuring rights, quality supports and a good old age. In S. S. Herr & G. Weber (Eds.), *Aging, rights and quality of life: Prospects for older people with developmental disabilities* (pp. 343–370). Baltimore, MD: Brookes.

Janicki, M. (1992). Lifelong disability and aging. In L. Rowitz (Ed.), *Mental retardation in the year 2000* (pp. 115–127). New York: Springer-Verlag.

Janicki, M., & Dalton, J. (2000). Prevalence of dementia and impact on intellectual disability services. *Mental Retardation, 38*(3), 276–288.

Janicki, M., Dalton, A., Henderson, C., & Davidson, P. (1999). Mortality and morbidity among older adults with intellectual disability: Health services considerations. *Disability and Rehabilitation, 21,* 284–294.

Janicki, M., Heller, T., Seltzer, M. M., & Hogg, J. (1996). Practice guidelines for the clinical assessment and care management of Alzheimer's disease and other dementias among adults with intellectual disabilities. *Journal of Intellectual Disability Research, 40,* 374–382.

Janicki, M., McCallion, P., & Dalton, A. (2002). Dementia-related care decision-making in group homes for persons with intellectual disabilities. *Journal of Gerontological Social Work, 38*(1/2), 179–195.

Kaufman, A., Adams, J., & Campbell, V. (1991). Permanency planning by older parents who care for adult children with mental retardation. *Mental Retardation, 5,* 293–300.

Levitz, M. (1999). Self-advocacy for a good life in our older years. In S. S. Herr & G. Weber (Eds.), *Aging, rights and quality of life: Prospects for older people with developmental disabilities* (pp. 279–287). Baltimore, MD: Brookes.

Lightfoot, E., Hewitt, A., & Sauer, J. (2004). Organizational change and restructuring to provide consumer directed supports. In S. Larson & A. Hewitt (Eds.), *Effective recruitment, retention and training: Strategies for human services organizations* (pp. 271–285). Baltimore, MD: Brookes.

Ludlow, B. (1999). Life after loss: Legal, ethical and practical issues. In S. S. Herr & G. Weber (Eds.), *Aging, rights and quality of life* (pp. 189–221). Baltimore, MD: Brookes.

Mackelprang, R., & Salsgiver, R. (1996). People with disabilities and social work: Historical and contemporary issues. *Social Work, 41*(1), 7–14.

Magana, S. (1999). Puerto Rican families caring for an adult with mental retardation: Role of familism. *American Journal on Mental Retardation, 104*(5), 466–482.

Mahon, M., & Mactavish, J. (2000). A sense of belonging: Older adults' perspectives on social integration. In M. Janicki & E. Ansello (Eds.), *Community supports for aging adults with lifelong disabilities* (pp. 41–53). Baltimore, MD: Brookes,

Messinger-Rapport, B., & Rapport, D. (1997). Primary care for the developmentally disabled adult. *Journal of General Internal Medicine, 12*(10), 629–636.

National Association of Social Workers. (1996). *NASW code of ethics.* Washington DC: Author.

National Work Group on Disability & Transplantation. (2004). *Summary report of individual and family disability survey.* Washington, DC: National Work Group on Disability & Transplantation, American Association on Mental Retardation.

Olmstead et al. v. L.C. et al., 527 U.S. 581 (1999).

Prouty, R. W., & Lakin, K. C. (Eds.) (1998). *Residential services for persons with developmental disabilities: Status and trends through 1997.* Minneapolis: University of Minnesota, Research and Training Center on Community Living/Institute on Community Integration.

Puri, B., Ho, K., & Singh, I. (2001). Age of seizure onset in adults with Down syndrome. *International Journal of Clinical Practice, 55,* 442–444.

Rehabilitation Engineering Research Center on Technology for Successful Aging. (1999). *Executive summary.* Gainesville, FL: Rehabilitation Engineering Research Center on Technology for Successful Aging, University of Florida.

Seltzer, M. M. (2004). Introduction to the special issue on aging. *American Journal on Mental Retardation, 109*(2), 81–82.

Shultz, J., Aman, M., Kelbley, T., Wallace, C., Burt, D., Primeaux-Hart, S., et al. (2004). Evaluation of screening tools for dementia in older adults with mental retardation. *American Journal on Mental Retardation, 109*(2), 98–110.

Smith, G. (1997). Aging families of adults with mental retardation: Patterns and correlates of service use, need, and knowledge. *American Journal on Mental Retardation, 102,* 13–26.

Smith, G. C., Fullmer, E. M., & Tobin, S. S. (1994). Living outside the system: An exploration of families who do not use day programs. In M. M. Seltzer, M. W. Krauss, & M. P. Janicki (Eds.), *Life course perspectives on adulthood and old age* (pp. 1–38). Washington, DC: American Association on Mental Retardation.

Smith, G., Majeski, R., & McClenny, B. (1996). Psychoeducational support groups for aging parents: Development and preliminary outcomes. *Mental Retardation, 34,* 172–181.

Stancliffe, R., & Lakin, C. (2004). *Costs and outcomes of community services for persons with intellectual and developmental disabilities.* Minneapolis, MN: Research and Training Center on Community Living, Institute on Community Integration, University of Minnesota.

Sutton, E., Sterns, A., & Schwartz-Park, L. (1993). Realities of retirement and preretirement planning. In E. Sutton, A. Factor, B. Hawkins, T. Heller, & G. Geltzer (Eds.), *Older adults with developmental disabilities: Optimizing choice and change* (pp. 95–106). Baltimore, MD: Brookes.

Van Allen, M., Fung, J., & Jurenka, S. (1999). Health care concerns and guidelines for adults with Down syndrome. *American Journal of Medical Genetics, 89,* 100–110.

Warren, D. (May, 1998). *The health care needs of the aging person with mental retardation.* Paper presented at the 122nd annual meeting of the American Association of Mental Retardation, Washington, DC.

Zigman, W., Schupf, N., Devenny, D., Miezejeski, C., Ryan, R., & Urv, T. (2004). Incidence and prevalence of dementia in elderly adults with mental retardation without Down syndrome. *American Journal on Mental Retardation, 109*(2), 126–141.

The emotional effects of macular degeneration often seem more troublesome than the physical ones. Anger? Depression? Yes. Several fellow sufferers told me that they had sought help from therapists but found that few, if any were expert at dealing with our problems.

Henry Grunwald, former editor of *Time* (2003, p. 103)

Most of us who lose hearing in adulthood, of whom I am one, do experience diminished hearing as impairment, as disability, as lost competence. Few of us have sign language fluency and, even if we do, most of our family and friends are "culturally hearing" and cannot use a manual language for communication. We too were raised "culturally hearing," but now are no longer able to use sound to interact freely and comfortably with others. Relationships that once were effortless are no longer easy.

The late Laurel Glass, professor emerita (2003, p. 106)

Groups of people at dinners, meetings, cocktail parties . . . groups turn into faceless blurs. Worse is I can't see who is speaking and my longstanding hearing impairment becomes a greater handicap. Talk about sensory deprivation! I've been dealt a double whammy.

Helen Kandel Hyman, freelance writer (2003, p. 109)

CYNTHIA STUEN

Older Adults With Age-Related Sensory Loss

6

Sensory impairment has a profound impact on older persons, effecting their health, mental health, and quality of life status. Recognition of and attention to age-related sensory loss, particularly vision and hearing, are important in providing social work services to older adults. Knowing the difference between the normal changes in sensory systems and those that are caused by age-related disorders should be basic knowledge for gerontological social workers. It is also important to recognize that for many older adults, sensory losses occur in the context of other comorbid health conditions. Although sensory losses may not be life-threatening in comparison to cancer or heart disease, it may be the condition that has the most impact on the older person's quality of life.

This chapter focuses mainly on the continuum of sensory loss of vision and hearing, although some brief attention will be given to the chemosensory areas of taste and smell. The focus is on older adults who acquire an age-related sensory loss in later life, not on the population of older persons who are aging with an early-onset sensory loss. Large numbers of older persons experience varying degrees of vision loss and/or hearing loss, which can have a profound impact on their quality of life as well as access to information and health and human services.

I first discuss normal changes and disease-related sensory impairments and their prevalence. An overview of the specialized service systems of vision rehabilitation and aural rehabilitation and the functional and psychosocial consequences of sensory losses are then presented, followed by the implications for social work practice and policy issues. How social work has dealt with people with disabilities concludes the chapter.

DEFINITIONS AND PREVALENCE

Vision

All people experience normal changes in vision, usually beginning in their 40s. The most common normal age-related vision change is presbyopia. The lens of the eye becomes denser, less elastic, and more yellow, making it harder to focus on near-vision tasks such as reading. It is correctable with reading glasses or bifocal, trifocal, or progressive lenses. Another normal age-related change is that one's pupil becomes smaller. As a result, older adults need more light than younger cohorts. There is a slower reaction time in adjusting to changing illumination levels. Generally, older adults have diminished contrast sensitivity and colors appear less vivid, more faded. All of these normal changes generally occur gradually and can either be accommodated to or corrected with regular prescription glasses or contacts.

Vision impairments, on the other hand, typically result from eye disease and are not part of normal age-related vision changes. *The Lighthouse National Survey on Vision Loss: The Experience, Attitudes and Knowledge of Middle-Aged and Older Americans* (The Lighthouse, Inc., 1995), a telephone survey conducted by Louis Harris and Associates, documented that 17% among those aged 65 to 74 and 26% of adults age 75 years and older self-reported a vision impairment.

There is evidence of health disparities by race. The prevalence of age-related vision impairment is higher for African and Hispanic Americans than it is for their white counterparts (Prevent Blindness America, 2002). Glaucoma and diabetic retinopathy are particularly more prevalent for non-White older persons. Given the dramatic projected growth of the minority population of older persons over the next few decades, this disparity needs urgent attention in terms of early identification and treatment. There are no consistent differences by gender, but higher rates of vision impairment are related to lower socioeconomic status (The Lighthouse, Inc., 1995).

The most common age-related eye disorders are macular degeneration, glaucoma, diabetic retinopathy, and cataract. The functional impact of each of these conditions, which can occur independently or in combination, is of concern for social workers interacting with older adults.

Cataract, which is the most prevalent of age-related eye diseases, affects nearly 20.5 million people in the United States age 40 and over. A cataract causes a clouding of the normally clear lens of the eye; this clouding reduces the passage of light to the eye. Things look hazy and blurred, and there is increased sensitivity to glare (Figure 6.1a shows normal vision and Figure 6.1b simulates overall blur). Removal of the cataract is a very successful surgical procedure. However, some older persons are not candidates for surgery; in these cases, a person has very reduced visual function.

Diabetic retinopathy affects more than 5 million adults in the United States. In addition to overall blur, one may have very hazy, distorted, or splotchy vision caused by leaking blood vessels resulting from diabetes (Figure 6.1c). Laser treatment to seal the leaking blood vessels in the eye may arrest the leakage, but wherever the laser seals a blood vessel, scar tissue results, and one is unable to see through the scar tissue. Fluctuation in visual ability, sometimes by the hour, is not uncommon because vision is affected by one's blood sugar level. There is no cure for diabetes, and uncontrolled diabetes can lead to total loss of vision; hence, early and prompt intervention is critical.

Age-related macular degeneration (AMD) affects 6 million people in the United States, with another 13 to 15 million with presymptomatic signs of the disease (AMD Alliance International, 2003). One's central field of view is obliterated so that reading, performing any near-distance task, and recognizing faces is very challenging (Figure 6.1d). There are two forms of the disorder. Dry AMD is the most common form (estimated to be 85% to 90% of cases) and usually progresses slowly. The less common form is wet AMD; it is more threatening to vision because at the early stages, tiny new blood vessels grow under the retina

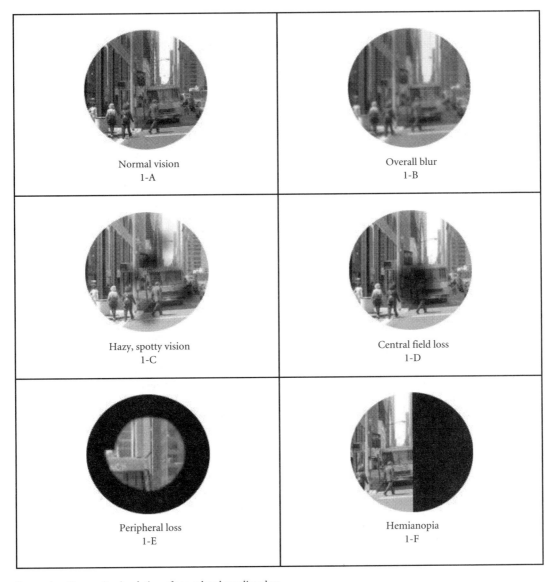

FIGURE 6.1. Composite simulation of age-related eye disorders.

and leak fluid that causes distorted central vision. Two FDA-approved treatments are being used to stabilize the condition, and clinical trials are also under way for other new treatments for the disease. There is no cure for macular degeneration at this time.

Glaucoma has the opposite functional impact of AMD; it takes away the peripheral or side field of vision but leaves the central vision intact. The cause of glaucoma is unknown, but it gradually destroys the cells of the optic nerve that carry information from the eye to the brain. As the nerve cells die, vision is slowly lost at the periphery of one's visual field (Figure 6.1e). Glau-

coma is often referred to as the "silent thief of sight" because the loss happens so gradually that it may take years for a person to realize the loss of peripheral vision.

In most cases, medications, laser treatments, and/or surgery can be used to slow or arrest the loss of vision, but the disease cannot be prevented. Glaucoma affects more than 2.2 million people age 40 and over in the United States and is strongly related to age and race. It is most prevalent among aging adults and among Black and Hispanic Americans. The loss of peripheral vision affects safe mobility in the home and community.

There is one other type of field loss, hemianopia, that gerontological social workers need to understand. This is the loss of half of one's visual field in both eyes; it may be the upper half, lower half, right or left half, and is most common for persons who have experienced a stroke, tumor, or trauma to the head. The most frequent defect is right homonymous hemianopia, which occurs in corresponding halves of the right field of vision (Figure 6.1f). It is often overlooked and not diagnosed among persons who had a stroke. This type of loss affects reading; the person does not realize there is still a half-page or line remaining and wonders why nothing is making sense. Movement and safe mobility are also impacted.

Hearing

Just as there are normal and disease-related changes in vision, the same is true for hearing loss. The auditory system experiences degenerative changes as the individual ages. The organ of Corti houses the sense organ of hearing; it is a structure within the snail-shaped cochlea, and it is most susceptible to age-related hearing changes (Schuknecht, 1993). Age-related atrophy interferes with the reception of high-frequency sounds, which makes it difficult to understand speech even in a quiet environment.

Data from the 1994 National Health Interview Survey (National Center for Health Statistics, 1998) indicate that hearing impairment, defined as deafness in one or both ears, or any other trouble hearing, was reported by 33% of adults age 70 and over, representing approximately 6.7 million persons (Crews & Campbell 2004). It was also noted that only 11.6% of these persons report using a hearing aid.

Hearing loss can be classified as a conducive central auditory processing or sensorineural disorder. A conducive disorder is an impairment in the transmission of sound to the inner ear, which can be caused by a buildup of cerumen (wax) or otosclerosis (a growth). Central auditory processing disorders are problems at the level of the brain, which can be caused by any head trauma or other systemic problem affecting the brain (Strawbridge, Wallhagen, Shema, & Kaplan, 2000).

Older adults are most susceptible to age-related atrophy that diminishes the reception of high-frequency sounds, especially for men; low-frequency sounds are more diminished for women. Both compromise the understanding of speech. This sensorineural loss that accompanies aging is called presbycusis. The sensory structures within the balance mechanism of the inner ear also undergo degenerative change with age and this contributes in part to the dizziness, instability, and falls so common among older adults (Weinstein, 2003).

Hearing loss can also be caused by a number of other factors. Exposure over long periods to work or recreational noise, genetic factors, trauma, metabolic disease in organs such as the kidney, vascular disease, and infections may cause hearing loss. Another high risk for older persons is ingestion of medications, such as some diuretics, and chemotherapy treatments that have an ototoxic effect, one that is damaging to hearing and balance (Weinstein, 2003).

Dual Sensory Impairment

Having a concurrent hearing impairment and vision impairment, referred to as dual sensory impairment, is quite prevalent and creates a very special challenge for social workers, particularly in the area of communication. Analyses of the Longitudinal Study of Aging Version found that 35% of adults age 70 and older reported some degree of vision impairment, and 42% reported some hearing impairment, with 21% having both a visual and a hearing impairment. African and Hispanic Americans were found to be at greater risk than Whites for both single and dual sensory impairments (Brennan, 2003; Horowitz, Brennan, & Su, 2001). Considered by age cohorts, 13% of those age 70 to 74, 20% of those age 75 to 79, 27% of those age 80 to 84, and 40% of those over age 85 have a dual sensory loss.

Negative outcomes in several domains related to sensory impairment have been documented also. Older persons who have a vision impairment only are more likely to report their health as poor than those with no sensory problems (15.3% vs. 6.7%). Those older persons with dual sensory impairment report higher rates of poor health (18.5% vs. 6.7%; Crews & Campbell, 2004). In this study, older persons with dual sensory impairments were 3 times more likely to have fallen in the past year than people without vision or hearing problems and 2 times more likely to fracture a hip, which often has a cascading set of negative consequences.

For persons with vision impairment and, to a somewhat lesser extent, for those with hearing impairment, the literature also documents greater functional disability, more informal help received in instrumental activities of daily living (IADL) and personal activities of daily living (PADL) tasks, dissatisfaction with social interactions, and more health care utilization (Brennan, 2003; Brennan, Horowitz, & Su, 2002; Burmedi, Becker, Heyl, Wahl, & Himmelsbach, 2002; Crews & Campbell, 2004). These data are very significant as the population of older persons increases, with the baby boom cohorts nearing retirement age, and the increases in longevity.

Vision and Hearing Loss in the Nursing Home Setting

The rates of vision and hearing impairments are especially high in nursing home populations. Chafee (1967) estimated that 90% of nursing home residents had hearing impairments. A moderate or severe vision impairment among nursing home residents was reported to be over 50% in a study by Horowitz and Balistreri (1994). An earlier study by Horowitz (1994) showed that even in the context of multiple chronic impairments, vision impairment significantly contributed to functional disability among older persons living in an institutional health care environment. A study of nursing home residents found that those with impaired vision and hearing independently predicted lower levels of social engagement and less time spent in leisure activities (Resnick, Fries, & Verbrugge, 1997).

Recognizing vision and hearing impairments in the nursing home setting is very important to ensure that older persons maintain their maximum independence. Because vision and hearing provide critical information for communication and wayfinding, older persons may be mislabeled as confused when in fact they have a vision and/or hearing impairment. Stuen (1994) documented a successful three-part strategy to introduce nursing home personnel to the field of vision rehabilitation. First, facilitywide staff training is an essential strategy to ensure knowledge and sensitivity about vision loss. A second strategy is an environmental assessment and modification to maximize functional independence of residents with normal age-related and abnormal vision loss. The third strategy is the on-site provision of low vision and other vision rehabilitation services. The project resulted in the preparation of a training manual and video to teach and disseminate the strategies.

CHEMOSENSORY IMPAIRMENT

Chemosensation is the term used to describe the sensory systems responsible for taste, smell, and chemical irritation. Rawson (2003) describes several features that make these systems susceptible to age- and disease-associated changes. Long-term exposure to harsh external environments and exposure to pharmacological agents can induce chemosensory side effects. A reduction in saliva that might be caused by denture use can create a physical barrier to membranes where receptors lie and/or where receptors are exposed to denture adhesives that can have a negative impact on taste. Sometimes, sensory dysfunction is the result of a chronic disease such as diabetes.

Taste sensitivity diminishes with age for some, but not all flavors and odors are affected (Mojet, Christ-Hazelhor, & Heidema, 2001). Older adults often complain that things no longer taste right; however, this is generally due to changes in olfaction (smell). Decreases in smell sensitivity begin sooner for men than women and may be related to the protective role of estrogen for women (Doty, 1984). There is also literature showing that chemosensory deficits may be early indications of neurological disorders, such as Parkinson's disease (Busenbark, Huber, Greer, Pahwa, & Koller, 1992) and Alzheimer's disease (Morgan, Nordin, & Murphy, 1995).

Changes in taste and smell, regardless of the cause, can have consequences for the older person in terms of safety issues, such as not being able to detect an odor when food has spoiled or a gas leak. Of course, the health and social implications of good dietary food selection and the pleasure of eating have tremendous significance for the health and well-being of older adults.

One-third of all older people report dissatisfaction with their sense of taste or smell, and the actual incidence of chemosensory loss among older adults is probably higher (Pelchat & Schaefer, 2000). According to Rawson (2003), the most common complaint among older adults coming to her chemosensory research center is the frustration they experience at not being taken seriously by their health care professionals. She advises that the best approach for health care workers is to make appropriate referrals for medical evaluation and to help older persons develop strategies to compensate for their losses to promote nutritional health and safety in their environment. Some of the strategies involved labeling food stored in the refrigerator with a date to discard and using different spices to enhance the taste areas that are compromised. Supplemental flavorings in food have been shown to improve food intake and the degree of satisfaction among older adults with diminished smell (Mathey, Siebelink, de Graaf, & Van Staveren, 2001).

VISION AND AURAL REHABILITATION

Most of the age-related eye disorders previously described result in partial sight or low vision, although some disorders, if untreated, can lead to total blindness. When there is no treatment, medicine, or surgery to correct vision to the normal range, one is said to have *low vision*. A person needs to be evaluated by a low vision specialist, an ophthalmologist or optometrist with specialized training, who can prescribe appropriate optical and nonoptical aids.

Optical devices include a wide variety of magnifiers, ranging from a small hand-held model to a video magnification system such as a closed-circuit television or portable video magnifier. There are microscopic spectacles and telescopes that can be prescribed, depending on the task to be accomplished and the type of vision loss. Computer hardware and software also provide screen magnification, synthesized speech, and tactile display, and a combination of these can also be useful to persons with vision loss. There are many other assistive devices that can enhance independent daily living for persons with impaired vision, such as voice-output clocks, thermometers, large dial appliances, and specialized telephones.

Members of the vision rehabilitation team include the vision rehabilitation therapist, who helps an individual learn techniques to remain independent at home, at work, and in the community. Techniques range from adapting everyday items, such as a stove or microwave, to labeling medications and adapting a social activity. An orientation and mobility specialist teaches people with vision loss to move safely indoors and outdoors using any residual vision, auditory cues, or other techniques, such as a white cane or dog guide.

Once hearing impairment is recognized and the medical factors explored, usually by an otolaryngologist, to make sure there is no medical or surgical treatment that can restore the hearing to a normal range, an older adult should have an audiological assessment by an audiologist. The goal of the assessment is to identify the areas in which the hearing loss has an impact and to find appropriate hearing technologies and referrals for counseling to help the person overcome the hearing handicap.

Fortunately, hearing aids, which come in many types, are not the only resources available to older persons. Other hearing assistance technologies include hardwired, infrared, and FM systems. A simple hardwired assistive listening device can be very useful for social workers to utilize when interviewing/counseling an older adult with a hearing loss. Theaters often have infrared assistive listening systems available to patrons upon request.

It is very important that persons with a hearing impairment have an audiologic exam to determine if a hearing aid or other amplification systems will be helpful. The audiologist takes into account the communication needs of the individual, communication partners, and communication environments in which the person functions and makes the best recommendations for aural enhancement. The great majority of older adults with hearing loss could benefit from hearing aids but never acquire them (McCarthy & Sapp, 2000). Some of the reasons cited are cost, cosmetic, and older persons not feeling the need even though those around them may disagree (Montano, 2003).

Counseling by social workers in individual, family, and/or group sessions is an important therapeutic intervention for older adults who experience hearing and/or vision loss. Involvement of the older person's family, friends, and formal and informal caregivers can also be useful to provide information on the nature of the sensory loss and its impact on daily functioning.

Every state in the United States has an office or commission that addresses rehabilitation for people who are visually impaired. There are also not-for-profit vision rehabilitation agencies throughout the country. A Web site that identifies services in local areas is *www.visionconnection.org*. Until very recently, the vision rehabilitation field itself has not embraced the growing population of older adults who are in need of their services. Historically, the field focused its service delivery on children and vocationally bound adults.

Access to audiologists can be found through the American Speech, Language and Hearing Association at *www.asha.org*. Gerontological social workers should familiarize themselves with the resources in their locale that serve older adults with vision and/or hearing loss.

SOCIAL WORK AND PSYCHOSOCIAL ADJUSTMENT TO SENSORY LOSS

Empowerment of the individual and the right to self-determination are central values of both social work and independent living; however, social work approaches empowerment from the professional's involvement in the client's or patient's care. Weick, Rapp, Sullivan, and Kisthardt (1989) propose a strengths-based practice approach that is useful for older adults who experience sensory loss. This approach focuses on the strengths and positive capacities people have, rather than their deficits. It encourages the already recognized positive capacities of individuals so that they will be more likely to continue to build on and develop those capacities as they cope with sensory change. This practice approach holds promise as the social worker seeks to provide services to the very diverse population of persons who are experiencing sensory loss as a disability later in life.

Hearing impairment affects one's ability to communicate with others and can have a serious impact on interpersonal relationships. Research has shown that hearing loss is associated with less satisfaction with life, the loss of independence, isolation, depression, and anxiety (Mehta, 2003; National Academy on an Aging Society, 1999; Smith & Kampfe, 1997). Weinstein (2003) reports that hearing loss in older adults restricts multiple dimensions of quality of life, including functional status and cognitive, emotional, and social function. She states that hearing impairment interferes with face-to-face and long-distance communication, strains family relations, compromises independence, and interferes with therapeutic interventions across all disciplines, including social work.

Similarly, research on the impact that vision impairment has on older persons documents that it may significantly disrupt patterns of behavior and social interaction in a broad range of psychological domains, such as self-concept, self awareness, and social domains of communication, mobility, work, and recreation (Brennan & Cardinali, 2000; Horowitz, 2004).

Depression is a major problem among older adults who experience a functional disability (Blazer, 2003; Bruce, 2001). Horowitz (2003) draws attention to the unique situation of an older person who has functioned a lifetime as fully sighted and hearing and then loses vision and hearing later in life; it can have a profound impact on the older person's well-being. Disability is a key risk factor for the onset of depressive symptoms, and depression in turn creates a risk for both physical illness and functional disability. There is a strong relationship between age-related vision impairment and, to a somewhat lesser extent, hearing impairment and later-life depression. Among community-dwelling elderly, rates of depression range from 8% to 16%, and between 25% and 33% of all visually impaired persons have been found to report clinically significant depressive symptoms (Blazer, 2003). Older adults who experience one or more of the age-related eye disorders are at higher risk for depression and excess disability, especially if not referred for vision rehabilitation (Horowitz, 2003).

Horowitz and Reinhardt (2000) proposed two primary explanations for this particularly strong relationship between sensory impairment and depression. One is that even a moderate vision impairment impacts daily task accomplishment, and, as noted earlier, this increased disability increases the risk of depression. Furthermore, far too few older persons with vision impairment are aware of or receive vision rehabilitation services to learn new ways of accomplishing daily tasks independently. The second explanation posited by Horowitz and Reinhardt involves the subjective experience of a visual disability. Public opinion polls have found that people fear blindness almost more than any other impairment, ranking fourth after AIDS, cancer, and Alzheimer's disease (National Society to Prevent Blindness, 1984). They report that this fear seems to stem primarily from fear of dependency as a concomitant of vision loss and one that threatens the very identity of older people.

Information loss is another major factor associated with both vision and hearing impairments and has been identified as a major trauma for older persons (Herschberger, 1992). Hearing loss makes communication and social interaction more difficult, and the loss of reading and driving abilities become very traumatic for older persons with vision loss. Losing the ability to drive, in particular, is one of the most feared aspects of vision loss (Horowitz & Higgins, 2000).

PRACTICE IMPLICATIONS

Social workers need to educate themselves about the normal age-related vision and hearing changes and how to identify and screen older persons for referral for specialized vision and aural assessment/rehabilitation. The Functional Vision Screening Questionnaire is a 15-item (yes/no) questionnaire; a large-print version is available, or it can be administered in an interview format. It is available for social workers to help determine if a client has probable vision impairment and needs referral for a clinical evaluation by an eye care specialist (Horowitz, 1998). The 10-item Hearing Handicap Inventory can be useful to assess whether the older person has a hearing impairment and needs referral for an audiological assessment (Ventry and Weinstein, 1982). Both instruments are presented in appendixes to this chapter.

As noted, hearing loss can have a profound impact on quality of life for older adults as well as their cognitive, emotional, and social functioning. Hearing loss alters psychosocial behavior, strains family relations, limits the enjoyment of daily activities, jeopardizes physical well-being, and interferes with communication/understanding across the spectrum of health diagnosis, treatment, and management (Weinstein, 2003). Of course, aural rehabilitation is essential, but a social worker needs to address the hearing impairment at the outset of interactions with the client. The best approach is for the social worker to ask the individual in any initial assessment about difficulties hearing and what causes problems and to determine what can be done to reduce the stress the hearing loss creates.

The environment where the older person is seen can be critical for the social worker dealing with an older adult with hearing impairment. In the office setting, it is important to control the ambient noise and to provide privacy at the front desk when registering private information. Asking the hearing impaired person to repeat back information, such as time of next appointment, is a good strategy to ensure understanding.

As mentioned earlier, one of the simplest and least costly assistive listening devices is a hand-held, battery-operated amplification device. A social worker may keep one of these in the office or a briefcase and find it very useful when an older person is having difficulty hearing.

Family Involvement

Involvement of family in the rehabilitation process has historically been relatively minimal, as the traditional model of rehabilitation focused on the individual. Research has documented the importance of family in providing emotional and instrumental support to older adults with physical and cognitive disabilities; there is also a growing literature to support the importance of the involvement of family and friends in the rehabilitation process to maximize both functional and psychosocial rehabilitation outcomes (McIlvane & Reinhardt, 2001; Reinhardt, Boerner, & Benn, 2003).

A family-focused model is a fundamental shift that takes place whereby family members are involved in the rehabilitation process without diminishing the autonomy of the older person with a sensory impairment. In some cases, helping the older adult deal with his or her relatives is the most important intervention (Stuen, 1999). Social workers should assess the family and friend networks of their clients and determine if they will be potential supporters or detractors of the rehabilitation process. The key is to recognize the family dynamics, the cultural differences, and the dynamics of the larger social network to enable supportive

behaviors that will contribute to maximizing the independent functioning of the older adult and promoting the general well-being of the entire family system.

Sighted spouses or partners of older people with impaired vision may find themselves feeling anger or guilt that are difficult to admit, especially if they feel they have to take on added responsibilities. Support groups for sighted spouses and partners were demonstrated to be very effective in improving their communication with the visually impaired partner and enhancing their functioning in everyday life (Sussman-Skalka, 2003). It is also important for couples to address the balance of giving and receiving in their relationships, to ensure that both feel they are contributing and receiving.

Policy Concerns

Awareness of vision rehabilitation is woefully lacking among the aging network of service providers (Stuen, 1991). Part of this problem may be that this area has been neglected by public policy and ignored by publicly supported programs and by third-party payers (Lidoff, 2003). Lidoff argues that the problem goes beyond the aging and the rehabilitation systems. Sensory impairments are a physical health problem. Medicare reimburses an ophthalmologist or optometrist for diagnosing eye diseases, and otolaryngologists are reimbursed for diagnosing hearing and balance disorders. Audiologists are reimbursed for evaluating hearing loss, and clinical social workers for providing counseling for mental health issues related to the sensory loss.

When an older adult has a stroke, the need for physical, occupational, and/or speech rehabilitation immediately comes to mind; however, this is not the case when someone loses vision. This may be directly attributable to the lack of Medicare funding for vision rehabilitation professionals. The recent Medicare Modernization Act of 2004 carried a provision that calls for a mandated one-year study to look at Medicare reimbursement for vision rehabilitation services provided by certified vision rehabilitation therapists, low vision therapists, and orientation and mobility specialists. This is a very hopeful sign.

SOCIAL WORK WITH PEOPLE WITH DISABILITIES

Blindness and deafness are associated with a lot of myths and stereotypes, and social workers are not exempt from their impact. Judeo-Christian tradition in the Middle Ages taught that people with disabilities were expressions of God's displeasure, and they were generally ostracized. Literature and drama are also filled with blind people portrayed as evil, as in Robert Louis Stevenson's Blind Pew in *Treasure Island,* or as better off dead, as in Kipling's *The Light That Failed.* Blindness has also been portrayed as punishment, as in Shakespeare's *King Lear* with the blinding of Gloucester. In more modern times, blinding and castration are ultimate forms of punishment and humiliation, as depicted in the early 1990s Gulf War.

Equally damaging can be the media accounts of the "super-disabled," such as a blind person ski jumping or a bilateral amputee completing a marathon. The public is filled with admiration for such feats, but behind them lurks the negative stereotype that people with a disability cannot or should not be expected to achieve.

The Americans with Disabilities Act (ADA) was passed in 1990 (P.L. 101-336) as a civil rights landmark case for the 43 million Americans with disabilities. Although social work professes to be a profession with primary responsibility toward people who are subjected to discrimination and oppression, Mackelprang and Salsgiver (1996) claim that it has not embraced the causes of people with disabilities as it has other oppressed groups. As a result, there are few social workers working with people with disabilities and few people with disabilities entering the profession. And the profession has done little to promote disability rights.

The disability movement grew out of the turbulent era of the 1960s but was led by independent living proponents such as Judy Heumann, who advocated for civil rights for people with disabilities. The independent living movement rejects the medical model of treatment approaches and views individuals not as patients or clients but as active and responsible consumers, people in charge of their own lives and care (Berkowitz, 1987). This movement was occurring at a time when there was tremendous growth in the aging network of health and human service delivery. Beginning with the historic passage of Medicare and Medicaid in 1965 and the Older Americans Act, the field of aging came of age quite apart from the disability rights/independent living movement.

The independent living movement and the proliferation of the aging network were occurring simultaneously. Social work philosophy shares much with the independent living movement, but it has had a much greater role in the aging network, especially as the role of case management for the older person emerged. "As social work matured from a person-in-environment to an ecological systems approach, a major method of practice evolved from casework to case management" (Mackelprang & Salsgiver, 1996, p. 11). The proliferation of private geriatric care managers and agencies that utilize a case or care management approach is evident in practice settings. As the baby boomers and the middle-aged cohorts of the independent living movement begin to join the ranks of older adulthood, we will likely see a greater shift to a stronger empowerment model. Evidence for this shift is apparent in the *Olmstead* decision of the U.S. Supreme Court on June 22, 1999, that requires states to administer their services, programs, and activities in the most integrated, least restrictive setting appropriate to the needs of qualified individuals with disabilities. This marks a historic trend to end the institutional bias that prevents many from living in their own homes and communities.

"The lack of social work involvement in the independent living movement is disturbing because both have much to offer each other" (Mackelprang & Salsgiver, 1996, p. 12). Both approaches can benefit from each other: Social work can move from case/care management to a more consumer-driven model of practice that is more empowering for the older person, and the independent living movement can recognize that many persons need social work assistance to develop the knowledge and abilities to function more independently.

CONCLUSION

Sensory loss affects a large number of older persons. It is incumbent on social workers to become familiar with normal and age-related disorders and help older people access appropriate interventions and remain socially engaged. The goals are to maximize functional independence, prevent excess or unnecessary disability, and enhance the quality of life for older persons with sensory loss. There is a tremendous need for social workers to be knowledgeable about sensory loss and the interventions available to ameliorate its effect. No area of a social worker's practice is unaffected by sensory impairment in clients.

APPENDIX 6.1

Screening Version of the Hearing Handicap Inventory for the Elderly (HHIE-S)

INSTRUCTIONS: Answer Yes (4 points), Sometimes (2 points), or No (0 points) for each question. If you are a hearing aid user answer questions according to how you hear with the hearing aid. If the question does not apply merely enter no as your response.

E-1. Does a hearing problem cause you to feel embarrassed when meeting new people?

E-2. Does a hearing problem cause you to feel frustrated when talking to members of your family?

S-1. Do you have difficulty hearing when someone speaks in a whisper?

E-3. Do you feel handicapped by a hearing problem?

S-2. Does a hearing problem cause you difficulty when visiting friends, relatives, or neighbors?

S-3. Does a hearing problem cause you to attend religious services less often than you would like?

E-4. Does a hearing problem cause you to have arguments with family members?

S-4. Does a hearing problem cause you difficulty when listening to TV or radio?

E-5. Do you feel that any difficulty with your hearing limits or hampers your personal or social life?

S-5. Does a hearing problem cause you difficulty when in a restaurant with relatives or friends?

Abbreviations: S items probe social/situational consequences of hearing loss; E items probe emotional consequences of hearing loss.

Total Score: (Refer if score > 8)

Source: Ventry and Weinstein, 1982.

APPENDIX 6.2

Functional Vision Screening Questionnaire (FV)

Purpose

The Functional Vision Screening Questionnaire (FV) is a screening tool to identify functional indicators of vision problems in older adults. The questionnaire is not a clinical or diagnostic assessment and should not be used to replace one. It identifies older people who may be experiencing a vision problem and who would benefit from seeing an optometrist or ophthalmologist.

Administration

The questionnaire may be filled out by the older adult independently or administered by an interviewer. The questionnaire should be read to the subject, if there are concerns about reading ability or literacy.

Be sure to tell the older adult that all questions should be answered in terms of their best vision; that is, how they see when they are wearing their glasses or contact lenses, if they typically use glasses or contact lenses. This does not include the use of any special low vision devices such as magnifiers or telescopes.

There are 15 questions, all of which can be answered by a simple "yes" or "no." If the subject answers with some qualifier, e.g., "sometimes," "in bad light," this should be noted on the questionnaire and scored as a problem.

Scoring

A score of "1" is given for each item where a vision problem is reported and "0" if it is not. Scores are indicated next to the answer for each item. Simply add up the scores. Total scores range from 0 to 15.

1. Do you ever feel that problems with your vision make it difficult for you to do the things you would like to do?
   1. Yes 0. No

2. Can you see the large print headlines in the newspaper?
   0. Yes 1. No

3. Can you see the regular print in newspapers, magazines or books?
   0. Yes 1. No

4. Can you see the numbers and names in a telephone directory?
   0. Yes 1. No

5. When you are walking in the street, can you see the "walk" sign and street name signs?
   0. Yes 1. No

6. When crossing the street, do cars seem to appear very suddenly?
   1. Yes 0. No

7. Does trouble with your vision make it difficult for you to watch TV, play cards, do sewing, or any similar type of activity?
   1. Yes 0. No

8. Does trouble with your vision make it difficult for you to see labels on medicine bottles?
   1. Yes 0. No

9. Does trouble with your vision make it difficult for you to read prices when you shop?
   1. Yes 0. No

10. Does trouble with your vision make it difficult for you to read your own mail?
    1. Yes 0. No

11. Does trouble with your vision make it difficult for you to read your own handwriting?
    1. Yes 0. No

12. Can you recognize the faces of family or friends when they are across an average size room?
    0. Yes 1. No

13. Do you have any particular difficulty seeing in dim light?
    1. Yes 0. No

14. Do you tend to sit very close to the television?
    1. Yes 0. No

15. Has a doctor ever told you that nothing more can be done for your vision?
    1. Yes 0. No

Scores are indicated next to the answer for each item. A total score of nine (9) or more indicates the need for a vision examination conducted by an optometrist or ophthalmologist.

Sources: Horowitz, 1998; Horowitz, Teresi, & Cassels, 1991.

REFERENCES

AMD Alliance International. (2003). Facts about AMD. Retrieved from *http://amdalliance.org/AMD_Information/facts_about_amd.html*.

Berkowitz, E. D. (1987). *Disabled policy: America's programs for handicapped.* London: Cambridge University Press.

Blazer, D. G. (2003). Depression in late life: Review and commentary. *Journals of Gerontology: Medical Sciences, 58A,* 249–265.

Brennan, M. (2003). Impairment of both vision and hearing among older adults: Prevalence and impact on quality of life. *Generations, 27*(1), 52–56.

Brennan, M., & Cardinali, G. (2000). The use of preexisting and novel coping strategies in adapting to age-related vision loss. *The Gerontologist, 40*(3), 327–334.

Brennan, M., Horowitz, A., & Su, Y. (November, 2002). *The widespread consequences of dual sensory loss among older U.S. adults.* Paper presented at the 55th annual scientific meeting of the Gerontological Society of America, Boston.

Bruce, M. L. (2001). Depression and disability in late life: Directions for future research. *American Journal of Geriatric Psychiatry, 9,* 102–112.

Burmedi, D., Becker S., Heyl V., Wahl, H., & Himmelsbach, I. (2002). Behavioral consequences of age-related low vision. *Visual Impairment Research, 4*(1), 15–45.

Busenbark, K. L., Huber, S. J., Greer, G., Pahwa, R., & Koller, W. C. (1992). Olfactory function in essential tremor. *Neurology, 42*(8), 1631–1632.

Chafee, C. E. (1967). Rehabilitation needs of nursing home patients. *Rehabilitation Literature, 28,* 377–382.

Crews, J. E., & Campbell, V. A. (2004). Vision impairment and hearing loss among community-dwelling older Americans: Implications for health and functioning. *American Journal of Public Health, 94*(5), 823–829.

Doty, R. L. (1984). Smell identification ability: Changes with age. *Science, 22,* 1441–1443.

Glass, L. (2003). Entendre fr: To hear, to understand. A personal perspective on hearing loss. *Generations, 27*(1), 105–107.

Grunwald, H. (2003). Twilight: Losing light, gaining insight. *Generations, 27*(1), 102–104.

Herschberger, P. J. (1992). Information loss: The primary psychological trauma of the loss of vision. *Perceptual and Motor Skills, 74,* 509–510.

Horowitz, A. (1994). Vision impairment and functional disability among nursing home residents. *The Gerontologist, 34*(3), 316–323.

Horowitz, A. (1998). Validation of a functional vision screening questionnaire for older people. In *Vision '96: Proceedings of the International Low Vision Conference* (pp. 492–494). Madrid, Spain: Organizacion Nacional de Ciegos Españoles.

Horowitz, A. (2003). Depression and vision and hearing impairments in later life. *Generations, 27*(1), 32–38.

Horowitz, A. (2004). The prevalence and consequences of vision impairment in later life. *Topics in Geriatric Rehabilitation, 20*(3), 185–195.

Horowitz, A., & Balistreri, E. (1994). *Field initiated research to evaluate methods for the identification and treatment of visually impaired nursing home residents. Final report: Part II, Research methods and results.* New York: The Lighthouse Inc.

Horowitz, A., Brennan, M., & Su, Y. (2001). *Dual sensory impairment among the elderly: Final report to the*

AARP Andrus Foundation. New York: Lighthouse International.

Horowitz, A., & Higgins, K. E. (2000). Older drivers and failing vision: Time to surrender the keys! *Consultant 40*(7), 1310–1316.

Horowitz, A., & Reinhardt, J. P. (2000). Mental health issues in visual impairment: Research in depression, disability and rehabilitation. In B. M. Silverstone, M. Lang, B. Rosenthal, & E. E. Faye (Eds.), *The Lighthouse handbook on vision impairment and vision rehabilitation* (Vol. 2, pp. 1089–1109). New York: Oxford University Press.

Horowitz, A., Teresi, J. E., & Cassels, L. A. (1991). Development of a vision screening questionnaire for older people. *Journal of Gerontological Social Work, 17*(3/4), 37–56.

Hyman, H. K. (2003). Out of sight: A personal journey through ten months of blindness. *Generations, 27*(1), 108–110.

Lidoff, L. (2003). Public policy and age-related sensory loss. *Generations 27*(1), 78–82.

The Lighthouse, Inc., (1995). *The Lighthouse National Survey on Vision Loss: The experience, attitudes and knowledge of middle-aged and older Americans.* New York: The Lighthouse, Inc.

Mackelprang, R. W., & Salsgiver, R. O. (1996). People with disabilities and social work: Historical and contemporary issues. *Social Work, 41*(1), 7–14.

Mathey, M. F., Siebelink, E., de Graaf, C., & Van Staveren, W. A. (2001). Flavor enhancement of food improves dietary intake and nutritional status of elderly nursing home residents. *Journals of Gerontology: Biological Sciences and Medical Sciences, 56*(4), M200–M205.

McCarthy, P., & Sapp, J. V. (2000). Rehabilitative needs of the aging population. In J. Alpern & P. McCarthy (Eds.), *Rehabilitation audiology: Children and adults* (pp. 88–101). Baltimore: Lippincott Williams & Wilkins.

McIlvane, J. M., & Reinhardt, J. P. (2001). Interactive effect of support from family and friends in visually impaired elders. *Journal of Gerontology: Psychological Sciences, 56B*,(6), P374–P382.

Mehta, K. M. (2003). Prevalence and correlates of anxiety symptoms in well-functioning older adults: Findings from the Healthy Aging and Body Composition Study. *Journal of the American Geriatrics Society, 51*(4), 499–504.

Mojet, J., Christ-Hazelhor, E., & Heidema, J. (2001). Taste perception with age: Generic or specific losses in threshold sensitivity to the five basic tastes. *Chemical Senses, 26,* 845.

Montano, J. J. (2003). Available and emerging technologies on hearing loss: An ecological approach. *Generations, 27* (1), 71–77.

Morgan, C. D., Nordin, S., & Murphy, C. (1995). Odor identification as an early marker for Alzheimer's disease: Impact of lexical functioning and detection sensitivity. *Journal of Clinical and Experimental Neuropsychology, 17*(5), 793–803.

National Academy on an Aging Society. (1999). Hearing loss: A growing problem that effects quality of life. In *Challenges for the 21st century: Chronic and disabling conditions* [online]. Available: *http://www.agingsociety.org/agingsociety/pdf/hearing.pdf.*

National Society for the Prevention of Blindness. (1984). Survey '84: Attitudes towards blindness prevention. *Sight-Saving, 53,* 14–17.

Olmstead, v. L. C., 527 U.S. 581, U.S. Supreme Court decision, June 22, 1999.

Pelchat, J. L., & Schaefer, S. (2000). Dietary monotony and food cravings in young and elderly adults. *Physiology & Behavior, 68,* 353–359.

Prevent Blindness America. (2003). Vision problems in the U.S. Schaumberg, Il.: Prevent Blindness America.

Rawson, N. E. (2003). Age-related changes in perception of flavor and aroma. *Generations, 27*(1), 20–26.

Reinhardt, J. P., Boerner, K., & Benn, D. (2003). Predicting individual change in support over time among chronically impaired older adults. *Psychology and Aging, 18*(4), 770–779.

Resnick, H. E., Fries, B. E., & Verbrugge, L. M. (1997). Windows to their world: The effect of sensory impairments on social engagement and activity time in nursing home residents. *Journals of Gerontology: Social Sciences 52B*(3), S135–S144.

Schuknecht, H. (1993). *Pathology of the ear* (2nd ed.). Philadelphia: Lea & Febinger.

Smith, S. M., & Kampfe, C. M. (1997). Interpersonal relationship implications of hearing loss in persons who are older. *Journal of Rehabilitation, 63,* 15–21.

Strawbridge, W. J., Wallhagen, M. I., Shema, S. J., & Kaplan, G. A. (2000). Negative consequences of hearing impairment in old age: A longitudinal analysis. *The Gerontologist, 40,* 320–326.

Stuen, C. (1991). Awareness of resources for visually impaired older adults among the aging network. In N. Weber (Ed.), *Vision and aging: Issues in social work practice* (pp. 165–179). New York: Haworth Press.

Stuen, C. (1994). *Field initiated research to evaluate methods for the identification and treatment of visually impaired nursing home residents. Final report: Part I.* New York: The Lighthouse, Inc.

Stuen, C. (1999). *Family involvement: Maximizing reha-bilitation outcomes for older adults with a disability.* New York: Lighthouse International.

Sussman-Skalka, C. (2003). Support group programs for partners with vision loss. *Generations, 27*(3), 98–101.

Ventry, I., & Weinstein, B. (1982). The Hearing Handi-cap Inventory for the Elderly: A new tool. *Ear Hear-ing, 3*, 128–134.

Weick, A., Rapp, C., Sullivan, W. P., & Kisthardt, W. (1989). A strengths perspective for social work prac-tice. *Social Work, 34*, 350–354.

Weinstein, B. E. (2003). A primer on hearing loss in the elderly. *Generations, 27*(1), 15–19.

MICHELLE PUTNAM
SUSAN STARK

Aging and Functional Disability

7

One of the most significant demographic changes during the 20th century was the increase in average life expectancy. During the period from 1900 to 2000, average life expectancy nearly doubled, from 48 to 73 years for men and 51 to 80 years for women (U.S. Census Bureau, 2004). In 2001, people age 65 can expect to live on average another 18 years—double the length of time most of their parents and grandparents lived from that age (Arias, 2004). Accompanying these gains in life expectancy are declining trends in mortality and a compression of morbidity, or shortened period of time adults live with chronic conditions (Fries, 2003). Overall disability incidence rates among older adults are declining, suggesting that the proportion of older adults experiencing functional impairment as an outcome of having a chronic disease or physical condition is decreasing (Crimmins, 2004; Freedman, Martin, & Schoeni, 2002). Together, these trends have yielded on average a longer and healthier life span for most people.

Despite these improvements, the prevalence of diseases and chronic conditions among the older population is increasing as the duration of time people are able to live with these conditions has increased. Just under 36% of adults age 55 to 64 have a disability. This rate increases to approximately 45% for adults 65 to 75 years. For adults age 70 to 74, 58% experience some kind of disability, and among adults 80 and older this percentage rises to nearly three-quarters (74%) of the population in that age range (U.S. Census Bureau, 2001). Thus, functional impairment remains a common occurrence among older adults, and the absolute number of older adults experiencing functional impairment is expected to increase with the growth of the older adult population (Crimmins, 2004).

For most older adults, being able to do the things they want to do at home and in the community is a significant component of healthy aging (Menec, 2003; Phelan, Anderson, LaCroix, & Larson, 2004). This is true for older adults with and without functional impairments. In this chapter, we highlight individual factors, programs, and policies that contribute to achieving goals of healthy aging for adults experiencing functional impairment. Our primary goal is to present a range of elements that influence opportunities older adults have to meet their individual healthy aging objectives and remain active members of their communities. Our secondary goal is to encourage professional social workers to learn more about these elements by providing brief examples of interventions, including theoretical models, assessment tools, model programs, and policy initiatives, throughout the chapter.

FUNCTIONAL DISABILITY AND HEALTHY AGING

"Healthy aging" is a somewhat trendy term that generally attempts to counter negative stereotypes portraying old age as a period when physical decline and illness are the most prevalent characteristics in an elder's life. Although for some individuals, it may be true that their physical health greatly reduces their capacity to participate in home and community life, for the vast majority of people withdrawal from prior activities is related more to lack of appropriate personal and environmental supports. Often, our own personal biases about disability influence our professional assessments of people with disabilities and intervention strategies we may employ to help them meet their healthy aging goals. Thus, before we proceed, it is important to briefly discuss theories and conceptualizations of disability.

Viewing Disability as a Contextual Situation, Not a Personal Health Limitation

Definitions and theories of what disability is and how it occurs differ. The medical model of disability focuses mainly on the person who is experiencing disability, seeking to identify biological and physiological factors contributing to limitations in physical function (Bickenbach, 1993). Social models of disability move beyond a person-centered view to include social and physical environmental factors in the determination of disability (Brandt & Pope, 1997; Lawton & Nahemow, 1973; Nagi, 1965; Pope & Tarlov, 1991; Verbrugge & Jette, 1994; World Health Organization, 2001). Political models of disability examine assumptions and motivations of cultural, social, and physical factors within the disability equation (Hahn, 1994). All of these frameworks influence how persons with disability are categorized and counted, as well as what types of programs and services are designed to meet their needs. Over the past decade, social models of disability have gained wider acceptance in the United States and around the world as necessary for understanding factors that contribute to disability.

The core premise of social models of disability is that disability is a situation, not a characteristic. That is, individuals have a certain set of (in this case) physical capabilities, and their environments have a specific set of demands or requirements. If an individual's capabilities and the environment's demands are not in sync, then it is likely that the person will experience some level of disability. For example, if an older woman needs to reach the second floor of a building that does not have an elevator, and she is unable to climb the stairs, the woman will experience disability. If, however, there is an elevator that the woman can take to the second floor, then there is no disability. In this situation, the woman may have a physical impairment that limits her mobility, but that limitation does not create disability in and of itself. Fundamentally, the issue is this: Can the person do what she needs to do? In some cases, the environment provides supports that help to limit disability. In other cases, assistive technology such as wheelchairs, reaching devices, and even levered door handles serve to eliminate potential disabling situations. Additionally, individuals themselves can modify their physical capabilities through physical and/or occupational therapy and health and wellness practices like maintaining a healthy diet, engaging in regular exercise, and reducing smoking to help limit the amount of disability they experience. Social workers can be of assistance to people with disabilities in both improving environments and facilitating greater physical capacity by helping to identify individual needs and community resources, assess and evaluate individuals and environments, and advocate for any changes required to address unmet needs.

Using this framework, we begin our discussion of healthy aging by looking at a range of factors that influence both the existence and experience of disability for older adults. In this discussion, we recognize two significant populations of older adults with disabilities. The first is the population traditionally considered to constitute older adults with disabilities: those persons who "age into" disability, individuals who experience substantial functional impairment for the first time in later life. The second population comprises those individuals who are "aging with" disability; included in this group are people who first began to experience disability during childhood, youth, or sometime in early or middle adulthood, having diagnostic conditions such as polio, multiple sclerosis, spinal cord injury, cerebral palsy, rheumatoid arthritis, or spina bifida, to name a few. The difference between these populations occurs mainly with regard to when, how, and for how long they have experienced disability and what the impact of disability has been on their lives. For many adults aging with disability, the experience of disability has shaped their life course by influencing their ability to work, to engage with others in their communities, and to live independently. Access to health care and philosophical orientations of health service models have a corollary role to these activities as well.

Having a long-term functional limitation can have a significant influence on an individual's health and wellness, as well as that of their family. Over their lifetime, persons experiencing disability in early and mid-life generally have higher rates of unemployment (National Organization on Disability & Harris Interactive, 2004), poverty (U.S. Census Bureau, 2001), and health care expenditures (Blanchard & Hosek, 2003; Chan et al., 2002). In addition, they have lower rates of home ownership (O'Hara & Miller, 2001), smaller social networks (Hilari, Wiggins, Roy, Byng, & Smith, 2003; Litwin, 2003; Reinhardt, Boerner, & Benn, 2003), and lower levels of community engagement (National Organization on Disability & Harris Interactive, 2000, 2004). These factors alone are significant. However, when viewed in combination with institutional biases in health care service delivery that have limited home- and community-based care for persons with disabilities, limitations in opportunities of an individual and his or her family members to develop economic and social resources are highlighted further.

Historically, health care services for people with disabilities have been based on a medical model, preferring institutional settings for long-term service provision (e.g., nursing homes) and service delivery by certified health care professionals. Arising from the independent living movement, led by disability rights activists, consumer-directed care options in home health services seek to shift this balance by affording consumers more choice and control over which services they receive, when the services are provided, and by whom. Additionally, in many instances, home care services such as chore work and personal attendant services are "de-medicalized," allowing for nonmedical personal to perform these tasks. This shift in perspective on service delivery is part of a growing national trend in health care services that moves away from institutional settings of care toward more home- and community-based settings. In the consumer-directed model, services can become less restrictive and more integrative, allowing persons with disabilities to continue to be active and productive members of their communities.

Many of these trends have the potential to be reversed, and social workers are often in key roles where they can provide assistance and act as allies to people with disabilities. For example, people with disabilities often face significant barriers to employment due to inaccessible environments, inflexible work schedules, and prejudicial attitudes of both employers and coworkers. The underemployment of people with disabilities combined with the high costs of health care often produce a direct path to poverty for many individuals. Many have smaller social networks and are less engaged in their communities for similar reasons. Social workers engaged in work across these areas (e.g., with low-income populations, in labor relations or employment equity, community development, health care and mental health, and diversity awareness) have the opportunity to become allies to people with disabilities and help promote opportunities for their greater inclusion and advocate for change, whether or not the specific focus of their work is with people with disabilities.

For adults aging with disability, many challenges they encounter at older ages are familiar, as they have occurred previously during their lifetime. Other challenges, such as the development of secondary health conditions and health care needs related to aging, are less familiar and constitute new experiences. However, for older adults for whom disability is recent and previously not experienced, disability represents a new, and often unknown, experience. We attempt to recognize these variations in our discussions when possible. The net effect of functional impairment and disability in old age is generally the same: reduced opportunities to achieve healthy aging objectives and participate fully as community members when appropriate supports, accommodations, and/or accessible environments are not available. We now turn to some specific factors that influence healthy aging and community participation and provide examples of potential interventions.

FACTORS INFLUENCING HEALTHY AGING AND COMMUNITY PARTICIPATION

Health and Wellness

Health and wellness is defined by persons with disabilities as including a range of factors, such as health behaviors, social contribution, and access to health care (Putnam et al., 2003). Levels of health and wellness among adults aging with and aging into disability are significantly lower than their nondisabled same-age counterparts when measured by prevalence of depression (Kemp, 1999), self-rated health status (Patrick, Kinne, Engelberg, & Pearlman, 2000), engagement in physical activity (DiPietro, 2001), and participation in community activities (National Organization on Disability & Harris Interactive, 2000, 2004). Health and wellness are sometimes believed to be unachievable goals for adults aging with and aging into disability. This is primarily the case when disability is viewed as a medical condition indicative of illness or loss of function. However, new models (Hughes, Nosek, Howland, Groff, & Mullen, 2003; Reynolds & Silverstein, 2003; R. Seeman & Chen, 2002) are being developed that point to the significance of diet, exercise, and social engagement in maintaining health and wellness for persons experiencing functional limitations. Additionally, new research is producing encouraging evidence that engagement in health and wellness behaviors such as regular exercise (King, 2001), diet and nutrition programs (Amarantos, Martinez, & Dwyer, 2001), reduction in smoking and alcohol consumption (Burke et. al., 2001), and productive engagement such as volunteering (Musick, Herzog, & House, 1999) may reduce the impact of a variety of chronic diseases and health conditions.

Across the country, health and wellness as an issue for older adults has become more visible and helped to facilitate specific evaluation measures of and programs for health and wellness for older adults. At the individual level, measurement instruments of physical activity among older adults, such as the Community Health Activities Questionnaire (CHAMPS; A. Stewart et al., 2001), the Physical Activity Scale for the Elderly (PASE; Dinger, Oman, Taylor, Vesley, & Able, 2004), and the Yale Physical Activity Survey (YPAS; Harada, Chiu, King, & Stewart, 2001) have all been shown to be robust. Model program interventions within communities include the Escalante Health Partnership and the OASIS program. The Escalante Health Partnership is a community-based health and wellness program in Arizona that develops individual wellness plans for older adults through local senior centers. The program's offerings include prevention screenings, nurse consultations, educational courses, and medical referrals. Initial postprogram evaluations of clients indicate higher levels of health and wellness compared to national averages (Nunez, Armbruster, Phillips & Gale, 2003). Focused more broadly on wellness, OASIS, a national nonprofit educational organization, provides physical activity programs, educational courses, and volunteer activities for adults 50 and older; the program has had positive effects on older adults' perceived levels of well-being (Morrow-Howell, Kinnevy, & Mann, 1999). The OASIS Friends Program in St. Louis, Missouri, provides opportunities for persons aging with developmental disabilities to partner with OASIS members and receive mentorship and support across OASIS courses and programs.

At each of these levels of intervention, it is important for professionals to engage older adults in determining and evaluating their own health and wellness needs. All of the interventions described are consumer-focused, allowing for individuals' behaviors and preferences to be addressed and appropriate personal and environmental modifications to be made.

Social Support

The use of social supports both formal (programs and services) and informal (family and friends) is a common strategy to mediate the potential consequences of functional impairment and disability. There are many definitions of social support. From a therapeutic perspective, social support for individuals with disabilities is often defined by determining whether they are cared for, loved, and able to count on others should the need arise (McColl & Friedland, 1993; McColl & Skinner, 1995). Social support can include practical support, informational support, and emotional support (McColl, Lei, & Skinner, 1995). Practical support is generally considered tangible, physical support. Assistance with transfers between seating or laying positions, preparation of meals, and driving to a doctor's appointment are examples of practical support. This support can be informal (provided by a family member or loved one) or formal (provided by a paid caregiver or personal care attendant). Informational support is generally considered to be advice or guidance. Social workers often serve in this role, offering assistance across a range of activities, from case management to referrals. Peers (individuals with the same or similar disability) often provide this type of information also. Emotional support is generally the provision of a sense of belonging or esteem. Although professionals such as social workers and occupational therapists may provide this type of support, it is generally the role of family members and peer groups to provide everyday opportunities to be a member of a group or to provide moral support during difficult times.

Although practical problems can be solved by providing any of these types of support to older adults, the outcome results are often negative when practical support has been offered as the only solution (McColl

& Rosenthal, 1994; Weinberger, Tierney, Booher, & Hiner, 1990). Informational support has been perceived as helpful when provided by professionals (Kondo, Mann, Tomita, & Ottenbacher, 1997), and emotional support has consistently been shown to demonstrate positive outcomes (Holicky & Charlifue, 1999), pointing out the importance of interventions that allow caregivers the opportunity to provide more emotional support and less instrumental (practical) assistance. In some cases, the care of family members with disabilities in the home has contributed to increased caregiver stress or burden (Banks, 2003; Schulz & Beach, 1999; Tolson, Swan, & Knussen, 2002), so that the intervention plan may also include social support provided directly to the caregiver through peer support programs (Goldstein et al., 2004; Peacock & Forbes, 2003).

There is both anecdotal and empirical evidence that social support interventions can improve the overall well-being of older adults experiencing disability as well as their family members who may provide them support. Social workers are often engaged in the development and implementation of social support programs, including peer support and training for families and caregivers. Peer support programs are frequently cited as being important contributors to successful rehabilitation and aftercare treatment models for chronic conditions ranging from heart disease (Winder, Hiltunen, Sethares, & Butzlaff, 2004) to stroke (Fink & Schwartz, 2000) and spinal cord injury (Sable, Craig, & Lee, 2000). In addition, such programs have been found to have both short- and long-term positive effects in areas such as coping (Stewart, M. et al., 2001), life satisfaction (Sherman, DeVinney, & Sperling, 2004), and maintaining functional ability (Avlund, Rikke, Holstein, & Due, 2003). Being providers of social support has also been shown to have positive effects on the well-being of older adults with functional impairments (Boerner & Reinhardt, 2003; Brown, Nesse, Vinokur, & Smith, 2003). For family members, peer support programs for family members, including those sponsored through local nonprofit organizations such as the Alzheimer's Association and the National Multiple Sclerosis Society, have been significant in bringing education, information, and support to families.

Social and Productive Engagement

There is a growing body of evidence suggesting that active social engagement may provide significant health benefits for older adults with functional limitations. Broadly defined, social engagement includes interacting with friends and family, participation in community organizations and events, and engaging in leisure activities. Productive engagement can be thought of broadly as meaningfully contributing to community life in a socially and/or economically valued way (Hinterlong, Morrow-Howell, & Sherraden, 2001). Positive outcomes related to greater social activity engagement include increased quality and length of life for older adults (Avlund, Rikke, Holstein, & Due, 2003; T. Seeman, Lugisngolo, Albert & Berkman, 2001) and enhanced well-being among older adults serving as volunteers (Morrow-Howell, Hinterlong, Rozario, & Tang, 2003). However, older adults with functional impairments may encounter various personal, social, and physical barriers that reduce their levels of participation.

For adults aging with and aging into disability, personal barriers to social engagement and productive contribution may include mental or physical health issues related to living with disability, such as chronic depression, pain, fatigue, or ill health (Strain, Grabusic, Searle & Dunn, 2002; G. Williamson & Shaffer, 2000). In addition, individuals may lack social support that encourages continuous engagement (Duke, Leventhal, Brownlee, & Leventhal, 2002; Eyler et al., 1999). Common social and physical barriers include lack of accessible environments and accommodations in social settings. Such issues as accessible parking, appropriate walking surfaces, and the provision of seating may influence whether or not a person with functional limitation attempts to participate in an activity. Regarding productive engagement, flexible work schedules, ergonomic workspaces, easily accessed buildings, and sensitive colleagues all have the potential to impact engagement.

Strategies to assess interest in social activities include the Activity Card Sort (Baum & Edwards, 2001; Katz, Karpin, Lak, Furman, & Hartman-Maeir, 2003), an assessment tool evaluating individual participation in activities both at home and in the community. Activity Cards have pictures of adults performing a host of tasks that clients sort into piles according to the frequency with which they engage in them. Scores are derived by dividing the total of current activities engaged in by the total of activities previously engaged in. This provides a guide to understanding how activity levels have changed and provides possible activities to target for increased participation. At the community level, tools are being developed to evaluate the receptivity of communities in an attempt to quantify how open an entire community is to persons with functional impairments and make specific recommendations on how opportunities for access and participation by persons with disabilities can be improved (Bricout, Stark, Gray, & Hollingsworth, 2004).

Housing

"Aging in place" is a term describing aging adults living in familiar home environments. It is in the home that individuals perform some of their most important activities of daily living (ADLs) and instrumental activities of daily living (IADLs), such as bathing, dressing, and preparing meals, leisure activities such as hobbies, and productive pursuits such as managing a household. The home is also the context of many activities related to valued roles, such as preparing and sharing holiday meals and caring for children. As the setting of these important activities, home is frequently one of the most cherished environments in people's lives. Home has been described as a reflection of individual values and has been associated with personal identity (Smith, 1994). Although there is significant growth in senior communities, including independent apartment complexes for older adults, continuing care communities, and assisted living facilities, most older adults say that they prefer to live out their later years in their own home (AARP, 2003).

The goal of maintaining a home is often threatened by the high number of environmental barriers present in the homes of individuals who experience functional limitations. Mismatches between the home environment and the physical capacity of community-dwelling older adults is estimated to be as high as 80% (Gill, Williams, Robison, & Tinetti, 1999). Common barriers in the home include items located out of reach, stairs, controls that are difficult to manage, and safety issues such as slippery floors (Mann, Hurren, Tomita, & Bengali, 1994; Stark, 2004). Estimates of the presence of barriers in the homes of older adults range from approximately 4 per household (Mann et al., 1994; Stark, 2004), when individual homeowners rate their current accessibility barriers, to an extreme of 75 per household during professional audits to identify safety, home maintenance, and accessibility problems (Steinfeld & Shea, 1993).

Given that most older adults prefer to age in place, many intervention strategies target modifying home environments to make them more accessible or accommodating. Through individual assessments, occupational therapists and other trained professionals are able to evaluate homes and determine appropriate changes to make. Widening doorways, installing shower grab bars, and changing door handles are frequent suggestions. Changes such as these have shown environmental modification to be an important intervention strategy to help manage chronic health care conditions, maintain or improve functioning, increase independence, ensure safety, reduce the need to relocate to institutional facilities, and even reduce the costs of personal care services (Connell & Sanford, 2001; Gitlin, Levine, & Geiger, 1993; Gitlin, Mann, Tomit, & Marcus, 2001).

Another important way to change the environment is by providing specialized products or assistive technology (AT). Such products include adaptive hardware and modifications to environmental controls. AT is defined as any product or system that is used to improve the functional capacity of persons who have disabilities (U.S. Congress, 1988). This technology is designed to make best use of an individual's abilities in order to overcome environmental barriers that may prevent the person from achieving maximal occupational performance (Seelman, 1993). There are numerous types of assistive devices and systems, including seating and mobility devices that can influence community access, computer access systems, augmentative communication devices, adapted driving devices, and environmental control units, as well as adaptive equipment that make it possible to accomplish tasks such as dressing. When providing AT, the costs must be considered, as much AT available today is still costly and may not be funded by a health insurance program. Additionally, the possibility of disuse or abandonment of AT by individuals for various reasons, such as complexity of use or embarrassment related to using something different, may occur (Gitlin, Corcoran, & Leinmiller-Eckhardt, 1995). However, despite these barriers, our knowledge of people's use of AT to help maintain independence is growing, as is our recognition of the significant role it plays in moderating the disability experience.

Removing environmental barriers and increasing use of AT have been shown to significantly improve occupational performance and satisfaction with performance of everyday activities (Stark, 2004). Many evaluation tools are available to determine home modification and AT needs, including the Gerontological Environmental Modifications assessment (Bakker, n.d.) and the Americans with Disabilities Act accessibility guidelines (U.S. Department of Justice, 1994). Commonly, occupational therapists or other health science professionals conduct individualized evaluations to determine the particular needs of older adults and their homes. Home modification services are often provided through area agencies on aging. At the national level, programs working to further these initiatives include the National Resource Center on Supportive Housing and Home Modification at the University of Southern California and AARP's Livable Communities initiative (Pollack, 1999). Social workers working with older adults with functional limitations are in key positions to help initiate home assessments and advocate for home modification and AT resources as part of any care management and healthy aging plan.

Transportation

Older adults who are unable to drive often rely on family members, friends, public transportation, and Paratransit programs to get to community destinations. Although there appear to be multiple transportation options, community surveys indicate that unmet need for transportation services is high (Coughlin, 2001). Many older adults with functional limitations experience difficulty using public bus or metro systems given the duration of waiting, limitations in seating, and distance to transportation stops (Straight, 1997). In particular, low-cost services available to transport adults with functional impairments to social engagements, community activities, and during evening hours are extremely limited in most communities. Transportation is often the crucial difference between participating in community activities and becoming isolated and home-bound (Glasgow, 2000). Given the importance of engagement in activities on life satisfaction, health, and depression (Everard, Lach, Fisher & Baum, 2000), transportation becomes a critical link to health and wellness.

Despite extensive reviews regarding the problems of and potential solutions for unmet transportation needs, there is a significant shortage of research to inform policy and program development. Much available evidence suggests that the majority of older adults prefer driving themselves or using a car to reach their destination (Straight, 2001). Losing one's driver's license is a significant life event (Sandeen, 1997), as automobiles are a means of facilitating community participation for older adults. Transportation solutions range from helping older adults prioritize transportation needs (Cvitkovich & Wister, 2001) to creating supplemental transportation services that fill the gaps between private and public transportation (Freund, 2003; Kerschner, 2003).

Discrimination: Physical, Social, and Cultural Barriers

Adults of all ages with disabilities are subject to prejudice and discrimination. Experiences with prejudice and discrimination among persons aging with disability may be different from experiences among persons aging into disability; primarily, the duration of bias may be longer, and it may affect or have affected aspects of their lives differently, for example limiting opportunities in employment, selection of housing, and ability to engage in community activities. In some cases, it may be difficult to distinguish bias against disability from ageism, as ageist beliefs tend to incorporate prejudice against physical and mental impairments commonly found among older adults (Wilkinson & Ferarro, 2002). In addition, many older adults themselves do not distinguish between disability and age, subscribing to a medical model that traditionally views disability as representing a decline of physical function related to old age (J. Williamson & Fried, 1996). There is also a cultural history of older adults with disabilities and younger adults with disabilities having negative perceptions of each other, older adults not wanting to be labeled as disabled and younger adults not wanting to be thought of as having the same characteristics as the elderly (Campbell, 1997; Torres-Gil & Putnam, 1999).

Despite these differences in experience and perception, adults aging with and aging into disability face many of the same physical, social, and cultural barriers, including inaccessible environments, pervasive stereotypes and discriminatory actions, and general lack of education about and respect for physiological difference. Interventions to reduce discrimination include educational training for professionals (Alford, Lawler, Talamantes, & Espino, 2002; Madan, Aliabadi-Wahle, & Beech, 2001), age-related diversity awareness trainings for the broader public (Braithwaite, 2002; Ragan & Bowen 2001), and increasing opportunities for community participation and community integration for persons aging with and aging into disability.

Broader Program and Policy Issues

There is a web of social welfare policies that broadly supports healthy aging and community participation for older adults with functional impairments. Although distinct in their origins and scope, taken together they form a foundation for developing, implementing, and evaluating programs and services for adults aging with and aging into disability. Key policies in this web include the Older Americans Act, Medicare, Medicaid, the Rehabilitation Act, and the Americans with Disabilities Act.

Historically, there have been different service networks and programs for adults based on age and/or life stage. For persons experiencing disability at younger ages, certain types of rehabilitation services, including employment training, counseling, and personal attendant assistance, were provided in conjunction with Centers for Independent Living, established through the Rehabilitation Act of 1973. Although there is no upper age limit for these services, they have traditionally been targeted to working-age persons, typically 64 and younger. Adults age 60 and older are eligible for a wide variety of programs and services provided through the Older Americans Act, such as transportation assistance, low-cost meals or meal delivery, health and wellness screenings, and assistance with some home health care needs and home repairs. Although there is some overlap in age eligibility for these programs and services, traditionally there has been little crossover, due in part to the limited number of adults aging with disability who lived long enough to enter old age, a lack of awareness about program offerings, and the capacity of traditional aging and/or disability service networks to meet the needs of the respective nontraditional consumers.

Over the past few years, the lines separating aging and disability service networks are beginning to fade somewhat as program innovations in Medicaid emphasizing home- and community-based care have grown in significance. Following the U.S. Supreme Court's ruling in the 1999 *Olmstead* case (*Olmstead v. LC*, 1999), President Bush issued two executive orders in 2001, *Olmstead* and the Freedom Initiative. Both have furthered initiatives to ensure that persons experiencing disability remain integrated in their communities. Of particular significance is the elevation of consumer control and direction as a program feature in home- and community-based services. We believe these steps help to move forward broader goals of healthy aging by providing greater opportunities for older adults with functional limitations to participate in home and community life.

THE ROLE OF THE SOCIAL WORKER

When working with older adults experiencing disability, one of our challenges as professionals is to under-

stand the range of factors that influence healthy aging and determine what types of interventions are needed for persons who are not reaching their own healthy aging goals. Social workers bring much knowledge and skill to this endeavor. However, the wide array of issues that factor into fostering healthy aging and community participation often requires partnering with professionals such as occupational therapists, psychologists, physicians, recreational counselors, public administrators, and policymakers to further interventions at the individual, community, and policy levels. In this area, we have many research and practice gaps. As noted earlier, there are often substantial differences in how disability is viewed and understood based on which field of knowledge scholars and professionals are trained in. Only recently have we begun to view people with disabilities and older adults as having similar interests and needs. Much of the research on interventions and strategies to improve quality of life has not been conducted across populations, but either for older adults or for persons with disability alone. As policies change and demographics shift, developing partnerships and building bridges across service agencies and organizations will become increasingly important for understanding the needs of older adults aging with and aging into disability and the programs that are available to help meet these needs. To do so effectively, scholars and practitioners need to work together to identify both successful models of collaboration and areas where further research is required. There is a substantial role for social workers to play in fostering cross-population and cross-network connections, and we strongly encourage those working with older adults experiencing disability to do so.

REFERENCES

AARP. (2003, May). *These four walls: Americans 45+ talk about home and community*. Washington, DC: Author.

Alford, C., Lawler, W., Talamantes, M., & Espino, D. (2002). A geriatrics curriculum for first year medical students: Community volunteers become "senior professors." *Gerontology & Geriatrics Education, 23*(1), 13–29.

Amarantos, E., Martinez, A., & Dwyer, J. (2001). Nutrition and quality of life in older adults [Special issue II]. *Journals of Gerontology, Series A, 56A*, 54–64.

Arias, E. (2004). United States life tables, 2001. In *National Vital Statistics Reports, 52*(14). Hyattsville, MD: National Center for Health Statistics, 21.

Avlund, K., Rikke, L., Holstein, B., & Due, P. (2003). So-cial relations as determinant of onset of disability in aging. *Archives of Gerontology and Geriatrics, 38,* 85–99.

Bakker, R. (n.d.) *GEM: Gerontological environmental modifications. Environmental assessment, apartment safety and design.* Ithaca, NY: Weill Medical College of Cornell University.

Banks, M. (2003). Disability in the family: A life span per-spective. *Cultural Diversity & Ethnic Minority Psy-chology, 9*(4), 367–384.

Baum, C., & Edwards, D. (2001). *Activity Card Sort.* Un-published manuscript, Washington University, St. Louis, MO.

Bickenbach, J. (1993). *Physical disability and social policy.* Toronto: University of Toronto Press.

Blanchard, J., & Hosek, S. (2003). *Financing health care for women with disabilities.* Santa Monica, CA: RAND.

Boerner, K., & Reinhardt, J. (2003). Giving while in need: Support provided by disabled older adults. *Journals of Gerontology: Series B: Psychological Sciences & So-cial Sciences, 58B*(5), S297–S304.

Brandt, E., & Pope, A. (1997). Models of disability and re-habilitation. In E. Brandt & A. Pope (Eds.), *Enabling America: Assessing the role of rehabilitation science and engineering* (pp. 62–80). Washington, DC: National Academy Press.

Braithwaite, V. (2002). Reducing ageism. In T. Nelson (Ed.), *Ageism: Stereotyping and prejudice against older persons* (pp. 311–337). Cambridge, MA: MIT Press.

Bricout, J., Stark, S., Gray, D., & Hollingsworth, H. (2004). *Community receptivity: The ecology of public participation for people with a disability.* Manuscript submitted for publication. Available from JBricout @wush.edu

Brown, S., Nesse, R., Vinokur, A., & Smith, D. (2003). Providing social support may be more beneficial than receiving it: Results from a prospective study of mor-tality. *Psychological Science, 14*(4), 320–327.

Burke, G., Arnold, A., Bild, D., Cushman, M., Fried, L., Newman, A., et al. (2001). Factors associated with healthy aging: The Cardiovascular Health Study. *Journal of the American Geriatrics Society, 49*(3), 254–262.

Campbell, M. (1997). Two worlds of disability: Bridging the gaps between the aging network and the disabil-ity community. *Southwest Journal on Aging, 13*(2), 3–11.

Chan, L., Beaver, S. Maclehose, R., Jha, A. Maciejewski, M., & Doctor, J. (2002). Disability and health care costs in the Medicare population. *Archives of Physical & Medical Rehabilitation, 83*(9), 1196–1201.

Connell, B., & Sanford, J. (2001). Difficulty, dependence, and housing accessibility for people aging with a dis-ability. *Journal of Architectural & Planning Research, 18*(3), 34–42.

Coughlin, J. (2001). *Transportation and older persons: Perceptions and preferences.* Washington, DC: AARP Public Policy Institute.

Crimmins, E. (2004). Trends in the health of the elderly. *Annual Review of Public Health, 25,* 79–98.

Cvitkovich, Y., & Wister, A. (2001). The importance of transportation and prioritization of environmental needs to sustain well-being among older adults. *En-vironment and Behavior, 33*(6), 809–829.

Dinger, M., Oman, R., Taylor, E., Vesely, S. & Able, J. (2004). Stability and convergent validity of the Phys-ical Activity Scale for the Elderly (PASE). *Journal of Sports Medicine and Physical Fitness, 44*(2):186–192.

DiPietro, L. (2001). Physical activity in aging: Changes in patterns and their relationship to health and func-tion. *Journals of Gerontology: Series A: Biological Sci-ences & Medical Sciences, 56*(Special issue 2), 13–22.

Duke, J., Leventhal, H., Brownlee, S., & Leventhal, E. (2002). Giving up and replacing activities in response to illness. *Journals of Gerontology: Series B: Psycholog-ical Sciences & Social Sciences, 57B*(4), P367–P376.

Everard, K., Lach, H., Fisher, E., & Baum, M. (2000). Re-lationship of activity and social support to the func-tional health of older adults. *Journal of Gerontology: Social Sciences, 55B*(4), S208–S212.

Eyler, A, Brownson, R, & Donatelle, R., King, A., Brown, D., & Sallis, J. (1999). Physical activity, social support, and middle-and older-aged minority women: Results from a U.S. survey. *Social Science & Medicine, 49*(6), 781–789.

Fink, R., & Schwartz, M. (2000). MossRehab Aphasia Center: A collaborative model for long-term rehabil-itation. *Topics in Stroke Rehabilitation, 7*(2), 32–43.

Freedman, V., Martin, L., & Schoeni, R. (2002). Recent trends in disability and functioning among older adults in the United States. *Journal of the American Medical Association, 228*(24), 3137–3146.

Freund, K. (2003). Independent transportation network: The next best thing to driving. *Generations, 27*(2), 70–71.

Fries, J. (2003). Measuring and monitoring success in compressing morbidity. *Annals of Internal Medicine, 139*(5), Pt. 2, 455–459.

Gill, T., Williams, C., Robinson, J., & Tinetti, M. (1999). A population-based study of environmental hazards in the homes of older persons. *American Journal of Public Health, 89*(4), 553–557.

Gitlin, L., Corcoran, M., & Leinmiller-Eckhardt, S. (1995). Understanding the family perspective: An ethnographic framework for providing occupational therapy in the home. *American Journal of Occupational Therapy, 49*(8), 802–809.

Gitlin, L., Levine, R., & Geiger, C. (1993). Adaptive device use by older adults with mixed disabilities. *Archives of Physical Medicine and Rehabilitation, 74*(2), 149.

Gitlin, L., Mann, W., Tomit, M., & Marcus, S. (2001). Factors associated with home environmental problems among community-living older people. *Disability and Rehabilitation, 23*(17), 777–787.

Glasgow, N. (2000). Transportation transitions and social integration in the second half of life. In K. Pillemer & P. Moen (Eds.), *Social integration in the second half of life* (pp. 108–131). Baltimore, MD: Johns Hopkins University Press.

Goldstein, N., Concato, J., Fried, T., Kast, S., Johnson-Hurzeler, R., & Bradley, E. (2004). Factors associated with caregiver burden among caregivers of terminally ill patients with cancer. *Journal of Palliative Care, 20*(1), 38–43.

Hahn, H. (1994). The minority group model of disability: Implications for medical sociology. *Research in Sociology of Health Care, 11*, 3–24.

Harada, N., Chiu, V., King, A., & Stewart, A. (2001). An evaluation of three self-report physical activity instruments for older adults. *Medicine & Sciences in Sports & Exercise, 33*(6), 962–970.

Hilari, K., Wiggins, R., Roy, P., Byng, S., & Smith, S. (2003). Predictors of health-related quality of life (HRQL) in people with chronic aphasia. *Aphasiology, 17*(4), 365–381.

Hinterlong, J., Morrow-Howell, N., & Sherraden, M. (2001). Productive aging: Principles and perspectives. In J. Hinterlong, N. Morrow-Howell, & M. Sherraden (Eds.), *Productive aging: Concepts and challenges* (pp. 3–18). Baltimore, MD: Johns Hopkins University Press.

Holicky, R., & Charlifue, S. (1999). Ageing with spinal cord injury: The impact of spousal support. *Disability & Rehabilitation, 21*(5–6), 250–257.

Hughes, R., Nosek, M., Howland, C., Groff, J., & Mullen, P. (2003). Health promotion for women with physical disabilities: A pilot study. *Rehabilitation Psychology, 48*(3), 182–188.

Katz, N., Karpin, H., Lak, A., Furman, T., & Hartman-Maeir, A. (2003). Participation in occupational performance: Reliability and validity of the Activity Card Sort. *OTJR: Occupation, Participation and Health, 23*(1), 10–17.

Kemp, B. (1999). Quality of life while aging with disability. *Assistive Technology, 11*(2), 158–163.

Kerschner, H. (2003). A low-cost, low-maintenance approach: The Pasadena PasRide pilot. *Generations, 27*(2), 63–67.

King, A. (2001). Interventions to promote physical activity by older adults. *Journals of Gerontology, Series A, 56A*(Special issue 2), 36–46.

Kondo, T., Mann, W., Tomita, M., & Ottenbacher, K. (1997). The use of microwave ovens by elderly persons with disabilities. *American Journal of Occupational Therapy, 51*(9), 739–747.

Lawton, M. P., & Nahemow, L. (1973). Ecology and the aging process. In C. Eisdorfer & M. P. Lawton (Eds.), *Psychology of adult development and aging* (pp. 619–674). Washington, DC: American Psychological Association.

Litwin, H. (2003). The association of disability, socio-demographic background, and social network type in later life. *Journal of Aging and Health, 15*(2), 391–408.

Madan, A., Aliabadi-Wahle, S., & Beech, D. (2001). Ageism in medical students' treatment recommendations: The example of breast-conserving procedures. *Academic Medicine, 76*(3), 282–284.

Mann, W., Hurren, D., Tomita, M., & Bengali, M. (1994). Environmental problems in home of elders with disabilities. *Occupational Therapy Journal of Research, 14*(3), 191.

McColl, M. A., & Friedland, J. (1993). Depression among people with physical disabilities. In P. Cappeliez & R. Flynn (Eds.), *Depression and the social environment: Research and interventions with neglected populations* (pp. 257–288). Montreal, Canada: McGill-Queen's University Press.

McColl, M., Lei, J., & Skinner, H. (1995). Structural relationships between social support and coping. *Social Science & Medicine, 41*(3), 395–407.

McColl, M. A., & Rosenthal, C. (1994). A model of resource needs of aging spinal cord injured men. *Paraplegia, 32*(4), 261–270.

McColl, M. A., & Skinner, H. (1995). Assessing inter- and intrapersonal resources: Social support and coping among adults with a disability. *Disability & Rehabilitation, 17*(1), 24–34.

Menec, V. (2003). The relation between everyday activities and successful aging: A 6-year longitudinal study. *Journal of Gerontology: Social Sciences, 58B*(2), S74–S82.

Morrow-Howell, N., Hinterlong, J., Rozario, P., & Tang, F. (2003). Effects of volunteering on the well-being of older adults. *Journals of Gerontology: Series B: Psychological Sciences & Social Sciences, 58B*(3), S137–S145.

Morrow-Howell, N., Kinnevy, S., & Mann, M. (1999). The perceived benefits of participating in volunteer and educational activities. *Journal of Gerontological Social Work, 32*(2), 65–80.

Musick, M., Herzog, R., & House, J. (1999). Volunteering and mortality among older adults: Findings from a national sample. *Journals of Gerontology, Series B: Psychological Sciences and Social Sciences, 54B*(3), S173–S180.

Nagi, S. (1965). Some conceptual issues in disability and rehabilitation. In M. Sussman (Ed.), *Sociology and rehabilitation* (pp. 100–113). Washington, DC: American Sociological Association.

National Organization on Disability & Harris Interactive. (2000). *Executive summary: 2000 NOD/Harris survey of community participation.* New York: Harris Interactive.

National Organization on Disability & Harris Interactive. (2004). *2004 NOD/Harris Interactive Survey of Americans with Disabilities.* New York: Harris Interactive.

Nunez, D., Armbruster, C., Phillips, W., & Gale, B. (2003). Community-based senior health promotion program using a collaborative practice model: The Escalante Health Partnerships. *Public Health Nursing 20*(1), 25–32.

O'Hara, A., & Miller, E. (2001). *Priced out in 2000: The crisis continues.* Boston: Technical Assistance Collaborative, Inc.

Olmstead v. LC, 1999.

Patrick, D., Kinne, S., Engelberg, R., & Pearlman, R. (2000). Functional status and perceived quality of life in adults with and without chronic conditions. *Journal of Clinical Epidemiology, 53,* 779–785.

Peacock, S., & Forbes, D. (2003). Interventions for caregivers of persons with dementia: A systematic review. *Canadian Journal of Nursing Research, 35*(4), 88–107.

Phelan, E., Anderson, L., LaCroix, A., & Larson, E. (2004). Older adults' views of "successful aging": How do they compare with researchers' definitions? *Journal of the American Geriatrics Society, 52,* 211–216.

Pollack, P. (1999). *Liveable communities: An evaluation guide.* Washington, DC: AARP Public Policy Institute.

Pope, A., & Tarlov, A. (1991). *Disability in America: Toward a national agenda for prevention.* Report of Committee on a National Agenda for Prevention of Disabilities, Division of Health Promotion and Disease Prevention, Institute of Medicine. Washington, DC: National Academy Press.

Putnam, M., Geenen, S., Powers, L., Saxton, M., Finney, S., & Dautel, P. (2003). Health and wellness: People with disabilities discuss barriers and facilitators to well being. *Journal of Rehabilitation, 69*(1), 37–45.

Ragan, A., & Bowen, A. (2001). Improving attitudes regarding the elderly population: The effects of information and reinforcement for change. *Gerontologist, 41*(4), 511–515.

Reinhardt, J., Boerner, K., & Benn, D. (2003). Predicting individual change in social support over time among chronically impaired older adults. *Psychology and Aging, 18*(4), 770–779.

Reynolds, S., & Silverstein, M. (2003). Observing the onset of disability in older adults. *Social Science & Medicine, 57,* 1875–1889.

Sable, J., Craig, P., & Lee, D. (2000). Promoting health and wellness: A research-based case report. *Therapeutic Recreation Journal, 34*(4), 348–361.

Sandeen, B. (1997, September). Transportation experiences of suburban older adults: Implications of the loss of driver's license for psychological well-being, health, and mobility. *Dissertation Abstracts International Section A: Humanities & Social Sciences, 58*(3-A), 1031.

Schulz, R., & Beach, S. (1999). Caregiving as a risk for mortality: The Caregiver Health Effects Study. *Journal of the American Medical Association, 282*(23), 2215–2219.

Seelman, K. (1993). Assistive technology policy: A road to independence for individuals with disabilities. *Journal of Social Issues, 49*(2), 115.

Seeman, R., & Chen, X. (2002). Risk and protective factors for physical functioning in older adults with and without chronic conditions: MacArthur Studies of Successful Aging. *Journals of Gerontology: Series B: Psychological Sciences & Social Sciences, 57B*(3), S135–S144.

Seeman, T., Lusingnolo, T., Albert, M., & Berkman, L. (2001). Social relationships, social support, and patterns of cognitive aging in healthy, high-functioning older adults: MacArthur Studies of Successful Aging. *Health Psychology, 20*(4), 243–255.

Sherman, J., DeVinney, D., & Sperling, K. (2004). Social support and adjustment after spinal cord injury: Influence of past peer-mentoring experiences and current live-in partner. *Rehabilitation Psychology, 49*(2), 140–149.

Smith, S. (1994). The essential qualities of a home. *Journal of Environmental Psychology, 14*(1), 31–46.

Stark, S. (2004). Removing environmental barriers in the homes of older adults with disabilities improves occupational performance. *OTJR: Occupation, Participation & Health, 24*(1), 32–39.

Steinfeld, E., & Shea, S. (1993). *Enabling home environments: Identifying barriers to independence, technology and disability.* Stoneham, MA: Butterworth-Heinemann.

Stewart, A., Mills, K., King, A., Haskell, W., Gillis, D., & Ritter, P. (2001). CHAMPS physical activity questionnaire for older adults: Outcomes for interventions. *Medicine & Science in Sports & Exercise, 33*(7), 1126–1141.

Stewart, M., Mann, K., Jackson, S., Downe-Wamboldt, B., Bayers, L., Slater, M., et al. (2001). Telephone support groups for seniors with disabilities. *Canadian Journal on Aging, 20*(1), 47–72.

Straight, A. (1997). *Community transportation survey.* Washington, DC: AARP.

Straight, A. (2001, March). *In brief. Transportation and older persons: Perceptions and preferences.* Washington, DC: AARP.

Strain, L., Grabusic, C., Searle, M., & Dunn, N. (2002). Continuing and ceasing leisure activities in later life: A longitudinal study. *The Gerontologist, 42*(2), 217–223.

Tolson, D., Swan, I., & Knussen, C. (2002). Hearing disability: A source of distress for older people and carers. *British Journal of Nursing, 11*(15), 1021–1025.

Torres-Gil, F., & Putnam, M. (1999). The growing pains of aging: Disability, aging and baby boomers. In K. Dychtwald (Ed.), *Healthy aging* (pp. 261–283). Gaithersburg, MD: Aspen.

U.S. Census Bureau. (2001). Americans with disabilities. In *Household economic studies: 2001* [online]. Washington, DC: Author.

U.S. Census Bureau. (2004). Keeping up with older adults: Older adults, 2000. In U.S. Census Bureau, International Programs Center, International Data Base, *Population profile of the United States: 2000* [online]. Washington, DC: Author.

U.S. Congress. (1988). Technology-Related Assistance for Individuals with Disabilities Act. Public Laws 100-407, 103–218.

U.S. Department of Justice. (1994). *ADA standards for accessible design* (28 CFR Part 36). Washington, DC: U.S. Government Printing Office.

Verbrugge, L., & Jette, A. (1994). The disablement process. *Social Science and Medicine, 38*(1), 1–14.

Weinberger, M., Tierny, W., Booher, P., & Hiner, S. (1990). Social support, stress and functional status in patients with osteoarthritis. *Social Science & Medicine, 30*(4), 503–508.

Wilkinson, J., & Ferraro, K. (2002). Thirty years of ageism research. In T. Nelso (Ed.), *Ageism: Stereotyping and prejudice against older people* (pp. 339–358). Cambridge, MA: MIT Press.

Williamson, G., & Shaffer, D. (2000). The activity restriction model of depressed affect: Antecedents and consequences of restricted normal activities. In G. Williamson, D. Shaffer, & P. Parmelee (Eds.), *Physical illness and depression in older adults: A handbook of theory, research, and practice* (pp. 173–200). Dordrecht, Netherlands: Kluwer Academic.

Williamson, J., & Fried, L. (1996). Characterization of older adults who attribute functional decrements to "old age." *Journal of the American Geriatrics Society, 44*(12), 1429–1434.

Winder, P., Hiltunen, E., Sethares, K., & Butzlaff, A. (2004). Partnerships in mending hearts: A nurse and peer intervention for recovering cardiac elders. *Journal of Cardiovascular Nursing, 19*(3), 184–191.

World Health Organization. (2001). *International classification of functioning, disability and health: Final draft, full version* [electronic version]. Report of the Classification, Assessment, Surveys and Terminology Team. Geneva, Switzerland: World Health Organization.

CYNTHIA POINDEXTER
CHARLES EMLET

HIV-Infected and HIV-Affected Older Adults

This chapter presents an overview of social work practice implications that can arise when the experience of HIV[1] and aging intersect. It is important to consider HIV and aging together for two reasons. First, medical and/or social service practitioners still frequently fail to identify and serve HIV-infected midlife and older adults; thus, HIV-infected persons over the age of 50 often remain hidden and their needs unaddressed. Second, the caregivers of HIV-infected younger adults or children with HIV are often midlife and older persons, who may be grieving, unprepared, unsupported, hidden, and frail. While there is no certainty regarding the number of HIV-positive adults being cared for by older adults, it has been estimated that half of the persons with AIDS are being cared for by older relatives (Allers, 1990; Joslin, 1995).

HIV-related advocacy, service provision, and policy analysis are highly compatible with social work because the profession is focused on forming productive partnerships with disenfranchised, oppressed, and marginalized individuals, couples, families, and groups (Shernoff, 1990). However, examining and addressing the intersection of HIV and aging has not been a strength of social work. HIV service systems have tended to underserve midlife and older persons, and social service workers in the HIV field need to know more about and attend to aging-related issues. At the same time, local service systems for older Americans have rarely sought out older persons with HIV, and gerontological social workers sometimes seem to be uncomfortable or unknowledgeable about HIV disease (Emlet, 1996, 1997; Emlet & Poindexter, 2004).

However, after initially neglecting this population, both HIV and aging researchers and advocates are more recently attending to the special needs of HIV-infected and HIV-affected midlife and older persons (Zablotsky & Kennedy, 2004). The task at hand is to distribute this knowledge and awareness to social work practitioners in both micro and macro practice, no matter their setting or specialty. (For a discussion of service delivery specific to these populations, see Emlet and Poindexter, this volume).

MIDLIFE AND OLDER PERSONS WITH HIV

When HIV was first identified, it was typically considered a young person's disease. However, from the beginning of the pandemic, the Centers for Disease Control (CDC, 1998) were documenting that 10% to 12% of the persons with AIDS were over age 50.[2] By 1998, there was a greater increase in the incidence of

AIDS in adults over 50 than among young adults. By 2001, 11% of all persons in the United States diagnosed with AIDS were over age 50 (CDC, 2002). Mack and Ory (2003) recently reported that 18.9% of persons living with AIDS were 50 years of age or older. As is the case in all age groups, females, Blacks, and Latinos are overrepresented in midlife and older persons with HIV (CDC, 2003). As people are now living longer with HIV due to more effective and accessible medical and pharmaceutical treatments, the numbers of older people with HIV are increasing. At the end of 2001, 1.4% of all reported cases of AIDS were in persons 65 and older (CDC, 2003). At the end of 2002, nearly 2% of all persons living with AIDS in the United States were 65 years and older (CDC, 2003). Advances in treatments have improved longevity for persons with HIV, thus increasing the likelihood that persons diagnosed in late life will live into older age. These individuals, like older adults in the general population, will face a myriad of issues, including concurrent medical conditions and chronic illnesses, decreasing social networks, and increased risk of needing care.

Persons who are living with HIV disease tend to face some of the same emotional and interpersonal concerns, regardless of their demographic characteristics (Poindexter, 2000). Older persons face exactly the same issues as younger persons, with the added strain of physical, familial, and existential concerns that arrive with middle and older age (Lavick, 1994). Older people who have HIV tend to be isolated and afraid to disclose their diagnosis to family members and friends and may be even more reluctant than are younger persons to seek social services and mental health support (Emlet, 1997). Older HIV-positive persons are more likely to live alone than their younger counterparts (Crystal & Sambamoorthi, 1998; Emlet & Farkas, 2002); therefore, it is important to recognize that decreased social support can be a complicating and serious issue.

MIDLIFE AND OLDER HIV-AFFECTED CAREGIVERS

It is common for older family members to serve as caregivers for their adult children and/or their grandchildren living with HIV (Joslin, Mevi-Triano, & Berman, 1997). When children (whether HIV-negative or -positive) are orphaned by HIV, their care often falls to grandparents or great-grandparents (Levine, 1993). Older adults with HIV are frequently cared for by friends, partners, or parents who are also old. Older gay men are especially likely to serve as caregivers to friends or partners with symptomatic HIV (Grossman, 1995). The lived experienced of HIV-affected midlife and older caregivers has been inadequately explored by researchers (Brabant, 1994) and by service providers and advocates in both the aging and the HIV fields (Linsk, 1994); social service practitioners should better understand and address the needs of this population (Mellins & Ehrhardt, 1994).

Midlife and older caregivers are often providing HIV care as they are struggling with difficult family dynamics, grieving deaths or illnesses, becoming socially isolated, lacking information about HIV, fearing the effects of HIV stigma, managing their own physical or emotional difficulties, and feeling unequipped to be involved in caregiving or child rearing at this stage of their lives. Often out of necessity, they tend to neglect their own health and become more vulnerable to burnout or illness. Older people who lose their adult children to HIV are robbed of the informal caregivers on whom they would have been able to count when they are ill or dying (Emlet, 1996; MacLean & Clapp, 2001; Poindexter, 2001).

▨ For example, Bea, a divorced African American woman in her mid-50s, was looking forward to some time to herself after her children had grown. She then learned that an adult son, Kevin, from whom she had been estranged for several years, had tested positive for HIV while he was serving prison time for drug possession. The mother of his children had died from AIDS. Bea is now taking care of Kevin, who lives with her, and helping to raise his 3 children, the youngest of whom has HIV. She feels burdened at times by having to start over with childrearing, but she would never consider turning them away. She has told none of her friends or fellow churchgoers that Kevin has HIV because she wants to protect her family from stigma and judgment. Because she is not talking with anyone honestly about the extent of her caregiving responsibilities or the fact that she is worried that Kevin will die, sometimes she feels very isolated and sad. She does not know much about the trajectory of HIV disease, which leads her to wonder about how sick Kevin might get and what she might be facing. She is so busy managing the household, attending to Kevin's medical needs, and getting everyone to appointments, that she has not seen her own doctor in 2 years. She worries sometimes about how little she sleeps and eats, but keeps pushing on through the days, thinking, "What choice do I have?" ▨

SPECIFIC CONCERNS AND RESPONSES

It is almost impossible to generalize about the experiences, feelings, and concerns of HIV-infected and HIV-affected midlife and older persons, because both aging and HIV cause different reactions in each human body, individual personality, and family unit. However, there are certain emotional and social realities that are common for many persons given the nature of HIV. In this section, we discuss several of these commonalities and suggest basic social work considerations. The issues are living with a chronic and dangerous disease; dealing with increased crises, grief, and stress; managing HIV stigma and disclosure; making decisions about safer behavior; and deriving spiritual meaning from their struggles.

Disease Management

AIDS is a collection of cancers, opportunistic infections, and symptoms related to a suppressed immune system. AIDS is so variable that there is no normal illness trajectory. Not only is HIV disease frightening and unpredictable, but the medication protocols are quite complex and often lead to debilitating side effects. Persons with HIV must work hard to adhere to complicated regimens, monitor and medicate side effects, and manage health and stress through nutrition, exercise, and complementary therapies. Older persons living with HIV tend more than younger people to report other ongoing medical difficulties and limitations in physical functioning (Nokes et al., 2000). An older person with HIV as well as other aging-related chronic illnesses may have to juggle many complex medication protocols that may result in confusion about which cognitive or physical symptoms are caused by which conditions (Linsk, 1997). As a 51-year-old woman living with HIV recently asked, "Is it HIV or A-G-E? That's my question all the time" (Cafazzo, 2004, D4).

Midlife and older caregivers are often heavily involved in the monitoring and maintenance of the infected person's health status. Often, these caregivers are struggling with reading labels, managing schedules, learning about drug and food interactions, watching for side effects, and supporting infected persons in taking medications that may make them feel sick. If a caregiver is taking care of more than one person with HIV, such as a daughter and grandchildren, the management of HIV, infections, medication, and side effects becomes a full-time job.

HIV-positive persons tend to be able to adhere to their complex medication protocols better when they have professional support to do so, such as good case management or social workers and involved medical professionals. (Powell-Cope et al., 1998). Social workers should be familiar with the importance of medical and pharmaceutical adherence and should work in partnership with older persons with HIV and older caregivers to maximize housing stability, respectful medical care, culturally competent services, and accepting social support (Ka'opua, 2001; Linsk & Bonk, 2000).

Crises, Grief, and Heightened Stress

Because HIV disease has a wildly uncertain trajectory, it can lead to a physical and emotional roller coaster, a life filled with episodes of crisis (Poindexter, 1997). Even in a stable life, HIV can wreak havoc. For those who are in a marginal financial position, are underinsured, have immigrant status, abuse substances, and/or have mental health concerns, HIV can be overwhelming. People who receive an HIV diagnosis usually enter into a world characterized by fear, regret, panic, sadness, anxiety, isolation, existential despair, hopelessness, and helplessness. It is inescapable that difficult decisions lie ahead, that illnesses, disability, and dying are likely (Dworkin & Pincu, 1993; Forstein, 1994; Jue, 1994). Existing data suggest that mental health issues may be a prominent problem for older adults living with HIV. Heckman and colleagues (2002) found in a study of 83 older HIV-infected adults that 25% suffered from moderate or severe depression as determined by the Beck Depression Inventory Scores. Emlet (2005) reported that 36% of study respondents had CES-D scores above the clinical cut-off for depression.

Midlife and older caregivers can experience much stress as they work to balance complex medical, financial, emotional, physical, and logistical needs. Their own emotional, financial, and physical stability can be at risk (Leblanc, London, & Aneshensel, 1997; Wardlaw, 1994). Many older persons are overburdened with multiple care responsibilities. Caregivers also experience sorrow as they witness the struggles and deterioration of the person with HIV. They feel the loss of their old relationship with the sick person and the HIV-positive person's functioning, health, dreams, and future (Jankowski, Videka-Sherman, & Laquidara-Dickinson, 1996). In addition, many HIV-affected families have experienced or are anticipating multiple deaths, which increases grief (Wardlaw, 1994).

Social workers should be observant for serial and serious HIV-related crises in the lives of those they serve and respond with immediacy, creativity, sensitivity, and flexibility when someone is especially troubled. In a crisis, HIV-affected or infected elders may not be best served by having to wait for an appointment or being limited to a formal visit in an office. The social worker may need to adjust hours, settings, or timeframes to respond to someone in a crisis, such as visiting someone in a hospital during the evening. In addition, depression and anxiety may be problems for elders who are HIV-infected or HIV-affected, so social workers may work with medical and mental health professionals on comprehensive assessments, differential diagnoses, and appropriate social and pharmaceutical interventions to support the person. Sadness is not the same as depression; social workers should incorporate that differentiation into their assessments and interventions, offering bereavement counseling and support groups if appropriate rather than immediately assuming pathology and referring to psychiatrists.

Concern With Stigma

HIV is probably the most intensely stigmatized physical condition (Crawford, 1996). Although HIV stigma has decreased in the United States over the course of the pandemic, it is still an impediment to disclosure and requests for support or services (Herek & Capitanio, 1993; Powell-Cope & Brown, 1992). HIV stigma can hold persons with HIV and their loved ones hostage behind a wall of silence and social isolation, hiding their experiences, needs, emotions, and health status (Crandall & Coleman, 1992; Laryea & Gien, 1993). Feelings of isolation and depression may result from the fact that social networks tend to shrink for HIV-infected (Shippy & Karpiak, 2005) and HIV-affected midlife and older adults (Poindexter & Linsk, 1999) because of stigma and fear of disclosure. Older caregivers may feel associative stigma acutely; a disclosure of HIV infection may trigger a disclosure of sexual activity, sexual orientation, or drug use, which can cause feelings of judgment or shame (McKinlay, Skinner, Riley, & Zablotsky, 1993).

HIV stigma may be the cause of persons not seeking, delaying, or refusing social services and information. Midlife and older persons who are living with HIV and/or caring for someone with HIV are highly sensitized to the threat of ostracism, judgment, and censure and will carefully manage disclosure of diagnosis and help seeking as a result (Poindexter, 2002; Poindexter & Linsk, 1999; Solomon, 1996). Emlet (2003) found in a sample of 88 individuals with HIV/AIDS that 51% of the older adults in the sample stated they felt ashamed of their illness sometimes or often, and 46% felt people were uncomfortable being with them. Thus, they may seek services, information, and medical care outside of their home neighborhood or town out of this concern for protecting privacy.

A social worker cannot work with HIV-infected or HIV-affected midlife and older persons without being constantly aware of the context of virulent stigma. When an older person discloses that he or she is dealing with HIV, that person is honoring and trusting you. A practitioner may need to repeatedly assure the person of confidentiality measures, normalize concerns about information management, and help with problem solving about disclosure decisions.

Need for Safe Behavior Assessment and Education

Because of deeply ingrained ageist attitudes and misinformation, social service and health care providers are often blind to the possibility that an older person is at risk for or has HIV or even wants information about transmission and safety. Stereotypes about older persons include that they do not inject drugs, have sex with opposite- or same-gender partners, or employ sex workers. Gott (2001) found that 80% of persons over age 50 surveyed at a genital-urinary clinic in the UK were at possible risk of contracting HIV, and 25% reported that they desired more information on HIV and sexually transmitted diseases than they had been offered.

While conducting assessments and throughout the case management or counseling relationship, social workers should strive to forge a climate conducive to discussing health concerns, including HIV status and risk. The practitioner should periodically ask if the service recipient has any concerns about safe sex or drug behavior, and be prepared with answers to questions. Older persons who are taking care of children or grandchildren with HIV may be uninformed about how the retrovirus is and is not transmitted, and social workers should be prepared to teach them. If professionals treat condom use and syringe cleaning as taboo subjects, where can service consumers turn for this life-saving information?

Concern for Relationships and Communication

Knowing that you or a loved one has HIV throws you into a complex, frightening communication arena. An HIV-infected or HIV-affected older person will likely have to decide when and to whom to disclose the diagnosis, decide whether and from whom to ask for help, learn to be appropriately assertive with health care providers and case managers, negotiate with loved ones around caregiving boundaries, and learn about HIV transmission and safety.

Social workers can help older persons practice approaching others about painful topics and being assertive with physicians, caregivers, and sexual partners, perhaps using various forms of rehearsal or coaching. Older persons may need assistance with decision making about HIV disclosure as well; in this case, social workers can review family history and behavior regarding difficult disclosures to facilitate realistic problem solving and putting safeguards and supports into place.

Spiritual Concerns

HIV brings myriad challenges, but the literature is also very clear that HIV-infected and HIV-affected caregivers frequently take the opportunity to forge better relationships, increased spirituality and meaning, and personal growth in the wake of their crises (Ayres, 2000; Jankowski et al., 1996; Wardlaw, 1994). Social workers in the HIV field have consistently marveled at the level of resilience, fortitude, and strength they find in HIV-infected and HIV-affected persons. Although HIV-infected and -affected older persons are at times quite vulnerable and fragile, practitioners are often surprised by their energy, optimism, hope, ability to laugh and love, and adaptation. Social workers should do everything possible to support these positive outlooks, not labeling the fortitude and optimism as denial or resistance.

In contrast, older persons often report that because of HIV stigma and judgment about infection routes, they feel unable to turn to formal religious organizations for comfort regarding their HIV challenges and losses (Poindexter, Linsk, & Warner, 1999). Social workers may need to help older persons find more accepting faith communities or clergy when their clients desire spiritual community or pastoral counseling.

GENERAL PRACTICE IMPLICATIONS

In addition to the social work responses to the concerns discussed above, the following general practice considerations may help in designing services for HIV-infected and HIV-affected midlife and older persons.

Offering Specific Outreach and Services

Ageism interacts with HIV stigma to render HIV-infected and HIV-affected midlife and older persons invisible and neglected. Older people can feel out of place in AIDS service organizations, which they perceive to be geared to younger people, and in the aging network, which has historically been unwelcoming to persons with HIV. Although specialized AIDS service organizations are vital, it is also important that HIV be mainstreamed into every social service agency so that older persons with HIV concerns are not marginalized. No matter the organization in which or level at which they work, social workers can help improve access to information, services, benefits, and social networks for older persons with HIV concerns.

Practitioners in the aging network, hospitals and clinics, and AIDS service organizations should strive to identify older persons with HIV concerns so that they can be steered to HIV education, relevant support groups, benefits advocacy, legal services, individual and group counseling, and case management. AIDS service organizations should not just wait for older persons to arrive at their doorsteps, but rather should develop and advertise programs with this population in mind, train workers in aging concerns, strive to make agencies more welcoming to older persons, and form interagency partnerships with aging network organizations. Likewise, gerontological social workers should ask older people, in a way that is nonjudgmental and normalizing, if they have any HIV-related concerns they wish to discuss, make sure that staff are adequately trained regarding HIV, and reach out to AIDS service organizations to make sure that case management programs are intersecting successfully for this population.

Inviting Individual Participation

In addition to formulating systemic ways in which to serve older persons with HIV concerns, social workers in individual practice must gently open the door so that older persons can discuss their sexual and drug histories, HIV status, and caregiving realities. It helps to ask people about their knowledge and experience with HIV as a matter of course, just as you would approach any other health concern. Gerontological social workers can begin by identifying those service applicants and recipients who have HIV concerns. Practitioners in the aging network can offer educational programs about HIV and the number of older persons infected and affected, and offer support groups geared specifically to midlife and older men and women with HIV or to grandparents caring for AIDS orphans. HIV practitioners can ask HIV-positive persons about their networks and thus identify midlife and older persons' caregivers who may need information and support.

Assessment

A social worker who is working with an HIV-affected or HIV-infected midlife or older person should first acknowledge the intense struggle inherent in the situation and create a safe and confidential working contract. It is then necessary to conduct a mutual, comprehensive, culturally competent, and HIV-knowledgeable assessment, including both assets and needs. Assessments should include HIV as well as aging concerns. Emlet, Gusz, and Dumont (2002) have suggested eight domains that should be included in the assessment process: physical functioning, cognitive issues, social support, sexual and drug health, spirituality, immune function, disclosure, and caregiver well-being. Additional discussion of each domain in provided in Table 8.1.

Services

Depending on the HIV-positive older person's perceptions of his or her needs, the social worker can offer information on HIV transmission, safety, pathogenesis, treatment, and adherence; care management, crisis intervention, and referrals; supportive individual, dyadic, family, or group counseling; legal services; concrete services and logistical help; and benefits advocacy. HIV-affected midlife and older caregivers may require competent child care, respite services, home health and hospice, homemaker or chore services, transportation, individual or group supportive counseling, education about HIV transmission and safety, and financial assistance. Support-

ive counseling for HIV-infected or HIV-affected midlife and older persons can be for an individual, couple, family, or group and can take place in person or over the telephone. Nokes, Chew, and Altman (2003) report on time-limited psychoeducational support groups for HIV-infected persons over age 50 that occurred weekly over the telephone through conference calling. They found that it worked well for persons who were not too hearing-impaired or cognitively impaired to participate fully found the support group helpful. A similar model would work well for older HIV-affected caregivers who cannot leave children or ill adults at home.

▨ It might be useful to return to the earlier example of Bea and Kevin to illustrate how social work might help. A social worker in Kevin's medical clinic asked him to get his mother an appointment. Over a series of meetings, both at the clinic and at Bea's home, the social worker talked to her about HIV transmission, trajectory, and medications and left written material for her; referred the HIV-positive grandchild to a special day care for children living with HIV; referred Bea and Kevin to a legal clinic to discuss permanency planning and guardianship for the grandchildren in the event of his death; arranged for weekly help with housecleaning; helped her complete an application for food stamps; and arranged for her to join a support group of other older HIV-affected caregivers.   ▨

SUMMARY

When working with HIV-infected and HIV-affected midlife and older persons, social workers will likely need to be creative and flexible. For example, regardless of the organization's norms, it might be necessary to incorporate home visits for all stages of helping: assessment, arranging for services, ongoing case management, benefits advocacy, legal and estate planning, and supportive counseling. Although a good social worker treats everyone with respect and honors all individuals' experience, dignity, privacy, and right to choose, this may be doubly important when in a helping relationship with an older person with HIV. HIV-positive persons, as well as older persons, often do not fare well in the vast machinery of human service and health care provision. Social workers must monitor

TABLE 8.1. Assessment Domains for Specific and Combined Populations

Domain	Older Adults	Persons Living With HIV/AIDS	Older Persons With HIV/AIDS
Physical Functioning	✓	✓	Comorbidity may result in decline in functioning from various sources. Functioning may decline more rapidly and more sporadically with HIV disease than with chronic diseases typically associated with aging.
Cognitive/ Affective	✓	✓	Cognitive decline in older adults may be due to a variety of factors, including dementias normally associated with aging in addition to HIV dementia. Initial symptoms of HIV-related cognitive decline may not be found using traditional mental status exams often used with older adults.
Social Support	✓	✓	Depending on their history, older adults with HIV/AIDS may have limited contact with biological family. Additionally, social supports common to younger persons with HIV, such as parents and even siblings, may be unavailable to older adults due to death or frailty of family members.
Sexual and Drug Health	✓	✓	Taking sexual and drug histories with older adults requires an understanding of cohort terminology and may require altering language typically used with younger clients. Ageist attitudes among professionals about sexuality and drug use must be recognized and avoided.
Spirituality	✓	✓	Older adults may need assistance with disclosing diagnosis to clergy or may need to locate spiritual resources that are HIV-sensitive. Individuals may have broken past ties with religious organizations that engaged in blaming behaviors.
Immune Function		✓	Senescence of the immune system (aging process) may serve to accelerate the decline of CD4 t-cells that are diminished through HIV. Older adults will need to be educated about the importance of CD4 and viral load and may need to be assisted with regular and ongoing testing.
Disclosure		✓	Determine to whom clients have disclosed their HIV status. This should include various family members, friends, health care providers, clergy, as well as individuals from the client's job (if working).
Caregiver Well-being	✓	✓	Caregivers of individuals with HIV may suffer from many of the same physical, emotional, financial, and social burdens as other caregivers. In addition, associative stigma may exist, depending on the disclosure of the care receiver's HIV status.

their own attitudes and behaviors for ageism and HIV stigma, along with other prejudgments, so that the helping relationship does not become yet another place where people suffer from maltreatment and misunderstanding.

NOTES

1. The human immunodeficiency virus (HIV) is an infectious retrovirus leading to an incurable life-threatening condition known as HIV disease or AIDS (Ac-

quired Immune Deficiency Syndrome). Persons living with HIV are also called "HIV-positive" or "HIV-infected"; those who are significant to them are called "HIV-affected." HIV diminishes and then destroys the human immune system so that the infected person is more susceptible to cancers and bacterial, viral, parasitic, fungal, and other opportunistic infections. Despite effective and promising pharmaceutical developments, HIV remains highly life-threatening, and to date there is no vaccine or cure.

2. When CDC began monitoring reported incidence and prevalence of AIDS in 1982, age was reported by the

following categories: under 25, 25 to 44, 44 to 49, and over 49. For that reason, "aging" in the HIV field was initially defined as over 50. CDC now includes HIV and AIDS reporting by these age groups: 45 to 54, 55 to 64, and 65-plus (CDC, 2003, p. 14).

REFERENCES

Allers, C. T. (1990). AIDS and the older adult. *The Gerontologist, 30*(33), 405–407.

Ayres, L. (2000). Narratives of family caregiving: The process of making meaning. *Research in Nursing and Health, 23,* 424–434.

Brabant, S. (1994). An overlooked AIDS affected population: The elderly parent as caregiver. *Journal of Gerontological Social Work, 22*(1/2), 131–145.

Cafazzo, D. (2004, June 7). Aging with AIDS. *News Tribune* (Tacoma, WA), pp. D1, D4.

Centers for Disease Control. (1998). AIDS among persons aged greater than or equal to 50 years, United States, 1991–1996. *Morbidity and Mortality Weekly, 47*(2), 21–27.

Centers for Disease Control. (2002). *HIV/AIDS Surveillance Report, 13*(2), 1–44.

Centers for Disease Control. (2003). AIDS cases in adolescents and adults, by age, United States, 1994–2000. *HIV/AIDS Surveillance Supplemental Report, 9*(1), 1–25.

Crandall, C. S., & Coleman, R. (1992). AIDS-related stigmatization and the disruption of social relationships. *Journal of Social and Personal Relationships, 9*(2), 163–177.

Crawford, A. M. (1996, March). Stigma associated with AIDS: A meta-analysis. *Journal of Applied Social Psychology, 26,* 398–416.

Crystal, S., & Sambamoorthi, U. (1998). Health care needs and service delivery for older persons with HIV/AIDS: Issues and research challenges. *Research on Aging, 20,* 739–759.

Dworkin, S. H., & Pincu, L. (1993). Counseling in the era of AIDS. *Journal of Counseling and Development, 71,* 275–281.

Emlet, C. A. (1996). Case managing older people with AIDS: Bridging systems, recognizing diversity. *Journal of Gerontological Social Work, 27*(1/2), 55–71.

Emlet, C. A. (1997). HIV/AIDS in the elderly: A hidden population. *Home Care Provider, 2*(2), 69–75.

Emlet, C. A. (2003, November). *Social support and stigma in the lives of older adults living with HIV/AIDS.* Paper presented at the 56th annual scientific meeting of the Gerontological Society of America. San Diego, CA.

Emlet, C. A. (2005). Unpublished raw data.

Emlet, C. A., & Farkas, K. J. (2002). Correlates of service utilization among midlife and older adults with HIV/AIDS: The role of age in the equation. *Journal of Aging and Health, 14,* 315–335.

Emlet, C. A., Gusz, S. S., & Dumont, J. (2002). Older adults with HIV disease: Challenges for integrated assessment. *Journal of Gerontological Social Work, 40* (1/2), 41–62.

Emlet, C. A., & Poindexter, C. (2004). The unserved, unseen, and unheard: Integrating programs for HIV-infected and affected elders. *Health and Social Work, 29*(2), 86–96.

Forstein, M. (1994). Testing for HIV: Psychological and psychotherapeutic considerations. In S. A. Cadwell, R. Burnham, & M. Forstein (Eds.), *Therapists on the front line: Psychotherapy with gay men in the age of AIDS* (pp. 185–204). Washington, DC: American Psychiatric Press.

Gott, C. M. (2001). Sexual activity and risk-taking in later life. *Health and Social Care in the Community, 9*(2), 72–78.

Grossman, A. H. (1995). At risk, infected, and invisible: Older gay men and HIV/AIDS. *JANAC, 6*(6), 13–19.

Heckman, T. G., Kochman, A., & Sikkema, K. J. (2002). Depressive symptoms in older adults living with HIV disease: Application of the chronic illness quality of life model. *Journal of Mental Health and Aging, 8*(4), 267–280.

Herek, G. M., & Capitanio, J. P. (1993). Public reactions to AIDS in the United States: A second decade of stigma. *American Journal of Public Health, 83*(4), 574–577.

Jankowski, S., Videka-Sherman, L., & Laquidara-Dickinson, K. (1996). Social support networks of confidants of people with AIDS. *Social Work, 41*(2), 206–312.

Joslin, D. (1995). Older adults as caregivers in the HIV/AIDS epidemic. *Coalition on AIDS in Passaic County Winter newsletter.* N.J.: Coalition on AIDS in Passaic County.

Joslin, D., Mevi-Triano, C., & Berman, J. (1997, November). *Grandparents raising children orphaned by HIV/AIDS: Health risks and service needs.* Paper presented at the 50th annual scientific meeting of the Gerontological Society of America, Cincinnati, OH.

Jue, S. (1994). Psychosocial issues of AIDS long-term survivors. *Families in Society, 75,* 324–332.

Ka'opua, L. S. (2001). Treatment adherence to an antiretroviral regime: The lived experience of Native Hawaiians and kokua. *Pacific Health Dialog, 8*(2), 290–334.

Laryea, M., & Gien, L. (1993). The impact of HIV-positive diagnosis on the individual, Part 1: Stigma, rejection, and loneliness. *Clinical Nursing Residency, 2*(3), 245–266.

Lavick, J. (1994, June). Psychosocial considerations of HIV infection in the older adult. *AIDS Patient Care,* 127–129.

LeBlanc, A. J., London, A. S., & Aneshensel, C. S. (1997). The physical costs of AIDS caregiving. *Social Science Medicine, 45*(6), 915–923.

Levine, C. (Ed.) (1993). *Orphans of the HIV epidemic.* New York: United Hospital Fund.

Linsk, N. L. (1994). HIV and the elderly. *Families in Society, 75,* 362–372.

Linsk, N. L. (1997). Experience of older gay and bisexual men living with HIV/AIDS. *Journal of Gay, Lesbian, and Bisexual Identity, 2*(3/4), 285–307.

Linsk, N., & Bonk, N. (2000). Adherence to treatment as social work challenges. In V. Lynch (Ed.), *HIV/AIDS at year 2000: A sourcebook for social workers* (pp. 211–227). Boston: Allyn & Bacon.

Mack, K. A., & Ory, M. G. (2003). AIDS and older Americans at the end of the twentieth century. *Journal of Acquired Immune Deficiency Syndromes, 33*(Suppl. 2), S68–S75.

MacLean, M. J., & Clapp, C. (2001). HIV/AIDS and aging: Implications for social work with older caregivers. *Canadian Social Work, 3*(1), 67–74.

McKinlay, J. B., Skinner, K., Riley, J. W., & Zablotsky, D. (1993). On the relevance of social science concepts and perspectives. In M. W. Riley, M. G. Ory, & D. Zablotsky (Eds.), *AIDS in an aging society* (pp. 125–146). New York: Springer.

Mellins, C. A., & Ehrhardt, A. A. (1994). Families affected by pediatric Acquired Immunodeficiency Syndrome: Sources of stress and coping. *Journal of Developmental and Behavioral Pediatrics, 15*(3), S54–S60.

Nokes, K. M., Chew, L., & Altman, C. (2003). Using a telephone support group for HIV-positive persons aged 50+ to increase social support and health-related knowledge. *AIDS Patient Care and STD's, 17*(7), 345–351.

Nokes, K. M., Holzemer, W. L., Corless, I. B., Bakken, S., Brown, M. A., Powell-Cope, G. M., et al. (2000). Health-related quality of life in persons younger and older than 50 who are living with HIV/AIDS. *Research on Aging, 22*(3), 290–310.

Poindexter, C. (1997). In the aftermath: Serial crisis intervention with persons with HIV. *Health and Social Work, 22*(2), 125–132.

Poindexter, C. (2000). Common concerns: Social and psychological issues for persons with HIV. In V. Lynch (Ed.), *HIV/AIDS at the year 2000: A sourcebook for social workers* (pp. 178–187). Boston: Allyn & Bacon.

Poindexter, C. (2001). "I'm still blessed": The assets and needs of HIV-affected caregivers over fifty. *Families in Society, 82*(5), 525–536.

Poindexter, C. (2002). "It don't matter what people say as long as I love you": The stigma of raising HIV-affected or HIV-infected grandchildren. *Journal of Mental Health and Aging, 8*(Special issue 4), 1–18.

Poindexter, C., & Linsk, N. (1999). HIV-related stigma in a sample of HIV-affected older female African-American caregivers. *Social Work, 44*(1), 46–61.

Poindexter, C., Linsk, N., & Warner, S. (1999). "He listens . . . and never gossips": Spiritual coping without church support among older, predominantly African-American caregivers of persons with HIV. *Review of Religious Research, 40*(3), 230–243.

Powell-Cope, G. M., & Brown, M. A. (1992). Going public as an AIDS family caregiver. *Social Science Medicine, 34*(5), 571–580.

Powell-Cope, G. M., Turner, J. G., Brown, M. A., Holzemer, W. L., Corless, I. B., Inouye, J., et al. (1998). Perceived health care providers' support and HIV adherence. Abstract no. 32354. *International Conference on AIDS, 12,* 592.

Shernoff, M. J. (1990). Why every social worker should be challenged by AIDS. *Social Work, 35*(1), 5–8.

Shippy, A., & Karpiak, S. E. (2005, May). The aging HIV/AIDS population: Fragile social networks. *Aging and Mental Health, 9*(3), 246–254.

Solomon, K. (1996). Psychosocial issues. In K. M. Nokes (Ed.), *HIV/AIDS and the older adult* (pp. 33–46). Washington, DC: Taylor & Francis.

Wardlaw, L. A. (1994). Sustaining informal caregivers for persons with AIDS. *Families in Society: The Journal of Contemporary Human Services, 75*(6), 373–384.

Zablotsky, D., & Kennedy, M. (2004). Assessing the progress and promise of research on midlife and older adults and HIV/AIDS. In C. A. Emlet (Ed.), *HIV/AIDS and older adults: Challenges for individuals, families, and communities* (pp. 1–35). New York: Springer.

DEBORAH PADGETT,
SECTION EDITOR

SECTION II

Social Work Practice With Older Adults With Mental Health Problems

OVERVIEW

The chapters in this section cover a range of neurological and mental disorders having cognitive, affective, and behavioral components that present challenges for those suffering from the disorder as well as their providers and caregivers. Some of these disorders are biological in origin, others are rooted in psychosocial causes. Yet all share a degree of diagnostic uncertainty and unpredictable trajectories dependent on a number of factors beyond the efficacy of biomedical treatment. It is here that social work practice can make an important difference.

Diagnostic confusion refers to the need to rule out alternative conditions when symptoms are variable and overlapping—a situation exacerbated by stereotypic assumptions that older adults should be expected to be depressed, fatigued, or confused. On the other hand, conditions older people are not expected to manifest, such as substance abuse, may go unaddressed. Thus, depression may be considered a normal reaction to aging, and alcoholism might be overlooked entirely.

Although reversing the course of degeneration is usually not possible for progressive neurological diseases, careful assessment and intervention can reduce disability and significantly enhance quality of life. Emotional problems—depression, anxiety, substance abuse, and suicidality—may be comorbid with physical illness (or coexist in some combination).

Taken together, these disorders usually involve pharmacological treatment; recent advances in medications for Parkinson's disease and multiple sclerosis along with new generations of psychotropic drugs have brought significant advances in symptom reduction and improved functioning. Though often necessary, medication for these conditions is never sufficient. Even pharmacologic management has a psychosocial context that must be taken into consideration to be effective.

Gladys González-Ramos describes growing public concern around Parkinson's disease and multiple sclerosis, two neurological diseases that bring uncertain but almost inevitable decline and disability to afflicted patients. The age of onset is earlier for persons with multiple sclerosis and fewer live to old age, whereas Parkinson's disease is associated with the aging process. Both cause significant motor problems and neurological impairment resulting in reduced mobility and an increased risk of psychological comorbidity for patients and their burdened caregivers.

Practitioners with dementia patients confront cognitive rather than motor deficits. In the chapter by Ronald W. Toseland and Michael Parker, dementia is described as an insidious disease whose course is marked by subtle, then more pronounced impairments in memory, executive functioning, and speech. As caregivers' responsibilities increase, practitioners assist in linking dementia patients and their families to support services (including home care and caregiver respite).

As noted by Zvi D. Gellis in his contribution to this section, depression and anxiety are widely prevalent in aging populations as in younger groups. Typically overlooked by primary care physicians, who are focused more on physical than psychological states, depression and anxiety take a toll on older adults, who are themselves less likely to recognize it as a problem in need of formal treatment. This phenomenon, in which younger generations are more likely to seek specialty mental health services, means that the gap between mental health needs and service use is greatest for older adults. The aging baby boom generation may reduce this gap, as this cohort matured during the post–World War II era of expanded attention to mental health and less stigma associated with seeing a therapist or counselor.

The enormous demographic impact of aging baby boomers can be seen in the increased prevalence of the relatively invisible problem of substance abuse among elders. Tazuko Shibusawa's chapter on this topic is a thorough portrayal of how alcohol abuse and misuse of prescription and over-the-counter medications constitute a growing problem often neglected by providers insensitive to their presence and ill-prepared to assess or treat them. Though far less common, illicit drug abuse among elders is not unknown and poses a serious threat in terms of exposure to HIV. Poor oversight of multiple drug prescriptions with lack of attention to side effects and drug interactions as well as stereotypic assumptions that older adults are less likely to abuse alcohol increase the likelihood that substance abuse will be overlooked as a problem among elders.

Margaret E. Adamek and Greta M. Yoder-Slater address what is perhaps the most urgent need a social work practitioner can face with an aging adult: suicidality. Although the causes of elder suicide are as poorly understood as in younger populations, patterns differ in terms of fewer warning signs in older adults as well as lower likelihood of completion in younger adults. Notwithstanding the faulty assumption that aging brings inevitable health declines and a sense of futility, it is true that social isolation, easy access to firearms, and poor mental status place elders at risk. Promising interventions such as cognitive-behavioral treatment are available to provide help.

Taken together, these chapters provide comprehensive coverage of the scope of each problem as well as practice-relevant guidelines. Common themes include the following:

- Comorbidity: The possible co-occurrence of poor mental health, chronic physical illness, and one or more forms of substance abuse should underlie assessments and treatment plans.
- Greater attention to these disorders among older adults of non-European descent: Persons of African American, Hispanic, and Asian backgrounds—to name only a few broad categories— are too often overlooked in research and practice among geriatric populations.

- The multidisciplinary nature of practice: Best practices employ a team approach that includes medicine (psychiatry, neurology, and primary care), nursing, and social work. The role of clergy and attention to spirituality are additional components.
- Importance of balancing medication regimens with psychosocial support for patients and caregivers: Caring for older adults with neurological and/or mental health problems can too easily be confined to medications without adequate attention to psychosocial context.
- The unique and complementary role of social work: Social workers are ideally prepared to address physical and mental health problems among elders and the needs of their caregivers. Working alongside health providers, they fill important roles in linking clients to formal support systems and counseling patients and families.

This chapter covers two of the most prevalent neurological disorders, Parkinson's disease (PD) and multiple sclerosis (MS). Although both diseases typically can be quite debilitating and impact a person's entire life, social workers have been largely absent from involvement in the care of persons and families living with these diseases. In fact, because so few social workers have specialized in the understanding of PD and MS, social work–based best practices with these populations are virtually nonexistent. This absence of attention starts in social work education, where most curricula do not cover material about these disease entities, despite their prevalence and the fact that persons living with PD and MS have high rates of comorbid mental health problems and need multiple social work services. As the number of older persons in the United States continues to grow, the prevalence of these diseases (particularly PD) is likely to continue to rise.

This chapter aims to provide readers with a beginning understanding of both PD and MS as they impact individuals and families so that informed care and referrals can be provided. Social workers have an opportunity to make a true contribution to practice with and research about persons and caregivers affected by neurological disorders such as PD and MS.

PARKINSON'S DISEASE

It was Dr. James Parkinson in 1817 who first described this disease in "An Essay on the Shaking Palsy." In recent years, celebrities such as Michael J. Fox, Muhammad Ali, and Janet Reno have publicly acknowledged their diagnosis of this disease. *Parkinsonism* is a clinical entity with multiple pathologic processes and various causes. It is divided into four categories:

- *Primary or idiopathic Parkinson's* (PD), which accounts for 80% of the cases of Parkinsonism.
- *Secondary parkinsonism,* which is associated with infectious agents, drugs, toxins, vascular disease, brain trauma, and tumor. Drugs that can produce secondary parkinsonism includes neuroleptics such as Thorazine, Haldol, Prolixin, Zyprexa, and Risperdal (Parkinson's Disease Foundation, 2004).
- *Parkinson's-plus syndromes* (such as progressive supranuclear palsy, dementia with Lewy body, multiple system atrophy). This group of disorders progresses rapidly and is often not as responsive to the usual antiparkinsonian medications.

GLADYS GONZÁLEZ-RAMOS

Older Adults With Neurological Problems Without Significant Dementia

- *Heredodegenerative diseases,* which include inherited degenerative disorders such as Huntington's disease and Wilson's disease. (Waters, 1999)

Parkinson's disease (PD), the most well-known and prevalent among the group of disorders known as parkinsonism, is a chronic, progressive, neurological movement disorder thought to affect approximately 1 million persons in the United States (Waters, 1999). The exact number of persons with PD (PWP) is not known, as many are undiagnosed or misdiagnosed. PD is the second most prevalent neurodegenerative disorder, following Alzheimer's disease. Typically, the first and most prominent symptom noticed is one of impaired movement, but PD can also present with symptoms of depression and may be misdiagnosed by a clinician unfamiliar with this phenomenon. Although the disease is nonfatal, its progression brings increasing functional limitations and disability. Medications for treatment of PD provide symptomatic relief but can have debilitating side effects, with persons coming to rely heavily on their caregivers.

Because primary or idiopathic Parkinson's disease is the most prevalent in parkinsonism, this chapter focuses on this form of the disease.

Etiology

Although there is extensive research on PD, there is still no clear understanding of its etiology; at present, it is thought to be multifactorial. Environmental and genetic factors appear to play a role in the development of the disease, but their exact role is still unclear. It is known that about 15% to 25% of PD patients have a relative with Parkinson's. Although the majority of PD cases are not inherited, research has found that in a small number of families, several genes have been shown to cause the disease (Parkinson's Disease Foundation, 2004).

The pathological features include:

- Loss of cells in the substantia nigra, a section in the midbrain residing in a motor control area located above the brain stem. These cells are responsible for manufacturing the chemical dopamine, a neurotransmitter that helps to regulate movement. The result is a significant depletion of dopamine in this part of the brain, which leads to the cardinal motor symptoms found in PD (tremor, slowness of movement, rigidity, and postural instability).

- The presence of Lewy bodies (pink-staining spheres found in nerve cells), thought to be a marker for PD. Lewy bodies can only be found at autopsy.

Epidemiology and the Challenge of Getting Accurate Numbers

Typically, PD begins between the ages of 40 and 70; the average age of onset is 60 years. It is not unusual to have PD for several years before the actual diagnosis is made, as symptoms may be attributed to other health problems or thought to be signs of normal aging. Diagnosis is also complicated by the scarcity of specialty PD services, such as movement disorder neurologists, who can best diagnose PD. Household prevalence surveys have found that 35% to 42% of cases in the general population remain undiagnosed (Hagestuen, 2002). About 5% to 10% have young-onset Parkinson's, a diagnosis given to those under the age of 40. Parkinson's before the age of 20, called juvenile PD, is extremely rare and thought to have a stronger genetic link than other forms of the disease.

PD is more common in men, with a male:female ratio of 3:2 (Waters, 1999). Although previously thought to be most prevalent among non-Hispanic Whites, researchers are finding the same if not higher incidence of PD within Hispanic and other ethnically diverse populations (Chaudhuri, Hu, & Brooks, 2000; Nicoletti, Sofia, & Bartoloni, 2003).

Diagnosing Parkinson's Disease

PD is diagnosed by a physician's clinical exam; there are no definitive diagnostic tests, though a person may be sent for neurological imaging evaluations to rule out other possible diseases. PD begins on one side of the body and progresses to involve the other side as well. The symptoms may not be of equal severity on both sides. Symptom severity can fluctuate within and across individuals; this high rate of unpredictability causes much stress and anxiety.

Typically, a physician makes the diagnosis of Parkinson's if the person has two or more of these four cardinal signs:

- *Resting tremor:* where the limb, usually an arm or leg, shakes at rest, but the tremor might also be in the jaw or the face. This is the most easily recognized symptom, initially seen in about 75% of

PWP. This symptom typically starts unilaterally and distally (arm or leg) and may progress to the opposite side and involve the chin and tongue. The tremor usually disappears during sleep, is temporarily suppressed with voluntary movement, and is accentuated by anxiety or stress. Although in the long run it may be the least disabling symptom, it is often the most embarrassing for patients, with many trying to hide the tremor if they can.

- *Rigidity:* stiffness; the involuntary increase in muscle tone that results in resistance to passive movement of muscles. This symptom contributes to the characteristic stooped posture, forward-flexed head, flexed knees, and elbows seen in PWP.
- *Bradykinesia:* slowness of movement. This is a central feature of PD, which impacts most daily activities such as writing, eating, and dressing. It also has secondary effects such as decreased eyeblink, facial masking, slowed chewing and swallowing, and drooling. A slowed shuffling gait with decreased arm swing is common in the early stage.
- *Postural instability:* usually the last of the cardinal signs to appear. Impairment of postural reflexes accompanied by gait disorder is a major contributing factor in the progression from being ambulatory to being wheelchair-bound. The loss of postural reflexes and associated inability to make rapid postural corrections to compensate for any imbalance leads to falls and loss of independent gait. (Hagestuen, 2002)

Other symptoms of PD are listed in Table 9.1. PWP may come to experience any or all of these. Many of these functions will become significantly impaired as the disease progresses.

Parkinson's Disease and Comorbidity With Mental Disorders

Depression is the most frequently reported psychiatric comorbidity in PD, yet it is usually underdiagnosed and/or undertreated. Depending on the study criteria and patient population, depression has been reported in between 4% and 75% of PWP. The National Institute of Mental Health (NIMH, 2002) places the prevalence at about 50%. Depression may predate the diagnosis of PD and, in certain cases, may be the first symptom and may be a biological risk factor for those later diagnosed with PD (Leentjens, Van den Akker, Metsemakers, Lousberg, &Verhey, 2003).

Certain symptoms of depression in PWP are the same as in dysthymia or major depression (using *Diagnostic and Statistical Manual of Mental Disorders IV-TR* criteria); however, sadness, apathy, and anxiety are more prevalent than self-blame, suicidal tendencies, or feelings of guilt (NIMH, 2002). There are no standardized assessment tools to evaluate depressive symptoms in the context of PD; many studies use the Beck or Hamilton scales to assess depression, though they all have limitations. These scales may overdiagnose depression, as they include features such as motor slowing, fatigue, and trouble concentrating (symptoms that are present in PD).

Although the causes of depression in PD are not known, current theories link it to specific neurochemical changes and/or the psychological responses of having PD. Some researchers have observed that depression is associated with advancing severity, recent deterioration, and falls. It also seems to be more influenced by the person's perception of disability rather than actual disability. The PWP's own perception of disease is important to consider in treatment (Schrag, Jahanshahi, & Quinn, 2001). Psychotropic medications used currently are typically the selective serotonin reuptake inhibitors (SSRIs), though there are few studies showing the effectiveness of these drugs with this population. There are also potentially dangerous interactions of the SSRIs with antiparkinsonian medications, with some patients reporting an exacerbation of PD symptoms. Research on nonmedical treatments of depression in PWP is lacking.

Adding to the development or worsening of depression is the fact that many PWP tend to isolate themselves from their social networks because of the loss and/or unpredictability of their motor movements and other complicating symptoms. In addition to unpredictability of movement are communication difficulties; in many PWP, speech becomes slurred or the volume becomes too low to be heard. Such symptoms make it very difficult for many to continue to interact socially. This isolation can contribute to depression (Cote, 1999).

Table 9.2 lists other neuropsychological problems in this population.

Treatment of Parkinson's Disease

The National Parkinson Foundation, Inc. (NPF), with over 40 Centers of Excellence across the United States and internationally, along with other Parkinson organizations strongly recommends the use of inter-

TABLE 9.1. Other Symptoms of Parkinson's

- *Speech changes*—low voice volume; monotone; slurred speech; hoarse or breathy quality
- *Swallowing problems* (dysphasia)—may occur in up to 40% of PWP, usually in advanced stages; can lead to development of aspiration pneumonia
- *Cognitive changes*—problems with memory and executive functions
- *Visual changes*—loss of contrast sensitivity and/or poor or blurred vision
- *Handwriting changes* (micrographia)—handwriting becomes small or illegible
- *Seborrhea—excessive oiliness and scaling of skin*
- *Sialorrhea—drooling, from loss of autonomic swallow reflex*
- *Decreased olfactory function—loss of sense of smell*
- *Autonomic disturbances*—orthostatic hypotension (drop in blood pressure upon standing); causes dizziness, lightheadedness, fatigue
- *Bladder, bowel, and/or sexual dysfunction*
- *Neuropsychiatric symptoms* (see table 9.2)

---

disciplinary teams for the assessment and treatment of PD. There is growing recognition in the field that, given the complexity of this disease and its impact on the person and family, an integrated team consisting of movement disorder neurologists, nurses, physical therapists, occupational therapists, speech-language pathologists, and social workers is essential for good care. Best practices for the nonmedical treatment of PD have not yet been developed in the United States, although teams have been used in Australia and Israel for years, and the use of teams and their effectiveness is currently under investigation in the United States (Hagestuen, 2002).

The medications most often used to treat PD either replenish or enhance dopamine levels in the brain, with carbidopa/levodopa (Sinemet) being the cornerstone of pharmacologic treatment, taken by approximately 70% to 80% percent of PWP. Because

medications do not stop the progression of the disease, most patients require more medication and a combination of medications as time passes. As Sinemet becomes less effective, several side effects become common, including dyskinesias (abnormal, involuntary, writhing movements), motor fluctuations, and neuropsychological complications, described earlier. Dyskinesias and sudden "freezing" can be severe; after 5 years of therapy, 50% of patients develop these problems.

Motor fluctuations caused as a side effect of PD medications are very different from the symptoms of PD, even though they are also motor problems. As Sinemet becomes less effective, it causes an "on-off" effect, so that in the "off" state, persons experience a sudden drop in mobility; that is, they freeze and are unable to move for moments of time. If they are in an "on" state, they might move well or have excessive

TABLE 9.2. Facts About Other Neuropsychiatric Problems in Persons With Parkinson's

---

- Dementia occurs in more than 20% of PWP, more frequently in persons older than 65 and rare in those with young-onset PD. It is associated with poorer prognosis. Early dementia is indicative of other dementias such as Alzheimer's and dementia with Lewy body (Hagestuen, 2002).

- Anxiety is common in PWP and can range from mild discomfort to panic attacks. It may be part of the disease or due to the medication wearing off (Hagestuen, 2002; see section on treatment).

- Sleep disorders, quite common in progressing PD, may be related to or independent of the depression and/or anxiety states. For many, this becomes one of the most difficult symptoms.

- Psychosis is most likely to occur if the person is older, has dementia, has a prior psychiatric history, or has been on antiparkinson medication for some time. Psychosis, including hallucinations, delusions, and paranoia, can be drug-induced by PD medications. Visual hallucinations are typically nonthreatening and more common than auditory hallucinations. Psychotic symptoms often can be treated by changing the medication regimen (Waters, 1999).

Reports are emerging from the field about compulsive behaviors that include excessive fixation and inappropriate sexual behavior and compulsive gambling and shopping. These behaviors are often exacerbated by medications or surgery for PD (Hagestuen, 2002).

---

movements, such as dyskinesias, where the PWP will be involuntarily writhing. This on-off effect is progressive and can cause much anxiety to the PWP and caregivers because of its unpredictability. In this situation, it is impossible to know how the person with PD will be functioning on any given day or time in the day; no two days are the same. The off times increase and become more pronounced as the disease progresses (Hagestuen, 2002; Parkinson's Disease Foundation, 2004).

Dopamine agonists such as Mirapex, Requip, Comtan, and Stalevo are also used as a way to stimulate dopamine receptors or to boost and prolong the effect of levodopa. Other classes of medications also exist, but all have side effects, which can become quite disabling and need to be closely monitored by a movement disorder neurologist. Most of these medications are not in generic form and can be very costly. In addition, surgical treatments, particularly deep brain stimulation (DBS), have recently become a viable and effective treatment for those persons who are carefully evaluated by specialists and found to be suitable candidates for surgical intervention. DBS can be very helpful to those with advanced PD as it can help to manage some symptoms or side effects such as disabling dyskinesias (Parkinson's Disease Foundation, 2004). Surgery is neither a cure for PD, nor does it always work well, and it can have serious side effects. Thus, it is important that patients and caregivers be well informed about the pros and cons of this treatment and the risks involved.

There is growing recognition of how traditionally underserved populations are affected by PD. There are various programs that are now specifically reaching out to diverse communities, particularly via the NPF network. One such NPF program is the Community Partners for Parkinson Care (see NPF's Web site, *www.parkinson.org*). The program is now in six regions of the United States and is expected to expand.

Specific Caregiver Considerations in Parkinson's Disease

Research is consistently finding that caregivers of PWP experience high levels of stress, and spousal caregivers are more severely depressed than adult children or other caregivers (Aarsland, Larsen, Karlsen, Lim, & Tandberg, 1999). Depression and cognitive impairment frequently contribute more to caregiver distress than motor problems; caregivers experience strain even when PWP have minimal motor problems

(Carter, Lyons, Stewart, & Archibald, 2002). These high levels of strain have been found even when comparing caregivers of PWP to other caregivers of persons with dementia but without PD (Parrish & Giunta, 2003). Speer (1993) found that the strongest predictor of later adjustment in the disease was based on the PWP's and caregiver's own earlier adjustment to the disease. There is often a lack of recognition as to the importance of family caregivers and their needs in caring for someone with PD. Research points to the importance of understanding the strain and burden experienced by caregivers from early on and being responsive to their needs (Hodgson, Garcia, & Tyndall, 2004). In 2003, a quality of life measure was validated for caregivers of PWP, making it possible to more accurately study caregiver strain (Calne et al., 2003).

MULTIPLE SCLEROSIS

Multiple sclerosis (MS) is a chronic, frequently progressive, neuroimmunologic disease of the central nervous system (brain, optic nerve, and spinal cord). Although it can start at any age, the onset of MS typically occurs in early to mid-adulthood, from ages 20 to 50. Three-quarters of persons with MS living in the United States are diagnosed by age 40 (Rumrill, 1996). The disease usually has been thought of as one affecting younger persons, but it is also associated with near-normal life expectancies (Hennessey & Rumrill, 2001). Thus, older persons diagnosed with MS and their caregivers often need and seek social work services.

MS was first described in detail by the physician Jean-Martin Charcot in 1868. Although extensive research continues, no cure has been found, though in recent years, great strides have been made in the treatment and management of MS. A particular characteristic is that the course of the disease is very unpredictable from person to person and within the diagnosed individual. This unpredictability, which can affect everything from getting the correct diagnosis to managing a life fraught with uncertainty, can make for high levels of stress and anxiety in persons with MS and their caregivers (Holland 2002; Minden & Frankel, 2002).

Epidemiology

MS is more common in women than in men by a ratio of about 2:1, with differences most noted in younger ages. The National Multiple Sclerosis Society (NMSS; Holland, 2002) reports that prevalence is inversely related to the person's proximity to the equator. In the United States, the estimated prevalence is 100–150/100,000 above the 37th parallel. Below this latitude, the rate is 57–78/100,000. This phenomenon is not well understood. It is estimated that perhaps there are 350,000 to 400,000 people in the United States diagnosed with MS. The latest estimates from NMSS are that approximately 90% of individuals diagnosed are non-Hispanic Whites. Non-White Hispanics, Blacks, and other races are thought to account for the remaining 10%. Whether these are accurate numbers, or whether the traditionally underserved populations have been undercounted because of lack of access to specialty diagnostic and treatment services, is unknown.

Etiology

MS is an autoimmune disease in which the body's own defense system attacks myelin, the fatty substance that surrounds and protects the nerve fibers of the brain, optic nerves, and spinal cord. The damaged myelin forms scar tissue (called lesions), and sometimes the nerve fiber is damaged. When either the myelin or the nerve fiber is damaged, nerve impulses, which coordinate all mental and physiological processes, are distorted and/or interrupted. This slowed or blocked conduction of information can disrupt every physical, sensory, mental, and emotional activity. The exact causes of MS are unknown, but current thinking is that it is due to a combination of immunologic, viral, and genetic factors. It is hypothesized that MS develops when a person has a genetic predisposition in combination with an environmental agent (including viruses) that trigger autoimmune responses (Hennessey & Rumrill, 2001).

Diagnosis, Symptoms, and Course of Multiple Sclerosis

There is no one definitive medical test for MS; the diagnosis is primarily based on clinical criteria established some years ago. In recent years, extensive use of magnetic resonance imaging (MRI) has helped to clarify the diagnosis. Most persons with MS show specific changes (white spots in the myelin) in the brain, which can be detected by an MRI. Tests of the spinal fluid can also show changes consistent with MS.

However, misdiagnosis does occur, especially by those who are not specialists in this area. The diagnostic process may take a long time as a neurologist will not make a diagnosis until there has been more than one episode of neurological impairment and more than one symptom. Because persons may have very mild symptoms or the symptoms may come and go, there can be long periods of uncertainty before a final diagnosis of MS can be made (Minden & Frankel, 2002; Schapiro, 2001).

A particular characteristic of MS is the presence of symptoms that affect several sensory or motor functions in the central nervous system (CNS; see Table 9.3). Symptoms may fluctuate or steadily progress in severity. MS can be marked by long periods of stability, even for those who progress to having a severe disability. However, even 20 years after diagnosis, two-thirds of persons are ambulatory, though many will require a cane or some other assistive walking device (Schapiro & Schneider, 2002).

There are several factors that can make MS symptoms worse. Aside from fatigue, body temperature is also an important issue. If body temperature rises for whatever reason (e.g., due to a hot day or because of fever), MS symptoms will often worsen (Schapiro, 2001). For more specific information about this aspect of the disease, see *www.nationalmssociety.org/Source book-Heat.asp.*

Multiple Sclerosis and Comorbidity With Mental Disorders

Approximately 50% of persons with MS are reported to experience at least one episode of major depression during the course of illness. It is unknown whether this is due to neurological changes in the brain or to a psychological response to living with a chronic illness. Risk for suicide is significantly higher than in the general population (Minden, Frumin & Erb, 2003).

Other mood disturbances have been reported. The second most prevalent psychiatric disorder found in persons with MS is anxiety and can exacerbate physical symptoms and bring on other secondary problems such as insomnia (McReynolds & Koch, 2001). Persons with MS also evidence higher rates of bipolar affective disorder than the general population; the cause is unknown. The incidence is estimated to be up to 13% (Hennessey & Rumrill, 2001). "Pathological laughing and weeping" with no provocation and mood incongruence can also be experienced by individuals with MS (Minden et al., 2003).

TABLE 9.3. Symptoms of Multiple Sclerosis

- *Fatigue* is reported by 75% to 95% of persons with MS. Fatigue is not a single, easily identifiable symptom, as it varies greatly and is experienced in very different ways by persons with MS. Fatigue can be felt as persistent and general tiredness, a "worn out" feeling, or as overwhelming exhaustion that comes suddenly and without warning. It can be a primary symptom due to depression or a side effect of medication. Fatigue is recognized as a significant cause of unemployment among persons with MS (NMSS, 2003a).

- *Motor problems* are often the first symptom and can include gait problems caused by muscle weakness, loss of balance, and severe numbness of the feet. Spasticity, a condition caused by abnormal increase in muscle tone, means muscles are resistant when stretched; this impacts motor function. Tremors manifest in the extremities and can range from small, barely noticeable tremors to those that are quite obvious.

- *Pain and other sensory symptoms,* such as numbness, tingling, and burning sensations, are very common. Pain can either be a primary symptom due to the loss of myelin, or it can be secondary symptom as a result of poor posture or balance problems for ambulating individuals or improper fit or use of a wheelchair.

- *Bladder and bowel dysfunction* can include urgency, frequency, constipation, or complete incontinence. These are very common problems early on and increase with disease progression.

- *Visual changes* usually manifest as blurred or double vision from inflammation of the optic nerve. For most, it is temporary; for others, it can lead to functional blindness. For many, optic neuritis is a first symptom of MS.

- *Diminished sexual function* and sexual dysfunction can include problems such as impotence, vaginal dryness, and decreased feelings in the genitals.

Cognitive loss may be experienced by approximately 50% of persons with MS and is considered a common symptom of all stages and disease types. Cognitive loss includes slowed information processing, impaired attention and concentration, impaired recent memory, and reduced executive functioning (Hennessey & Rumrill, 2001; Schiffer, 2002).

Clinical Course of Multiple Sclerosis

The clinical course of MS varies, but usually falls under one of the following four categories:

- *Relapsing-remitting MS:* Persons in this category experience clearly defined relapses, or episodes of acute worsening of neurological function, followed by periods of remission.
- *Secondary progressive MS:* Persons in this category experience relapsing-remitting course at the onset, followed by progression, minor remissions, and plateaus.
- *Progressive-relapsing MS:* Persons in this category experience progressive illness from the onset, with clear, acute relapses that may or may not resolve with full recovery. In this pattern, periods between relapse are characterized by continuing disease progression.
- *Primary progressive MS:* Persons in this category experience a nearly continuous worsening of the disease that is not typically interrupted by distinct relapses. Some do have occasional plateaus and temporary minor improvements.

Most persons start with a relapsing-remitting course and go on to develop a progressive course.

Treatment of Multiple Sclerosis

Due to the unpredictable and changing course of the illness, treatment needs to be individualized. Because this disease potentially affects every aspect of the person's life, a holistic approach is recommended. Symptom management is crucial and can make for better quality of life. The NMSS and many MS specialists recommend the use of an interdisciplinary team approach for the treatment of the person with MS as well as for the family affected by this disease. This includes not only rehabilitation specialists, but social workers and others who can attend to the mental and cognitive changes as well as the many other changes experienced by people living with MS. The use of support services, formal and informal, is essential in the management of MS.

There is no one medical treatment that has been found to work for everyone, prevent new lesions from forming, or stop the progression of existing CNS lesions. There is no medical procedure to change or eliminate existing lesions. There are various medications that can slow or moderate relapses, but none cures the disease. Avonex, Betaseron, Copaxone, and Rebif are self-injectable drugs for long-term use that have been shown to reduce the frequency of exacerbations and to reduce new or active lesions on MRI. The NMSS

(2003b) Medical Advisory Board's published opinion is that all four self-injectable drugs may reduce future disability for many who have MS. To learn more about these medications, refer to *www.nationalmssociety.org/Brochures-Comparing.asp.*

In addition, costly intravenous treatments are sometimes used, such as Novantrone, indicated for rapidly worsening relapsing-remitting MS or progressive-relapsing or secondary MS. It can only be given for a limited period of time to avoid possible side effects (NMSS, 2003b). Rehabilitation therapies (physical therapy, occupational therapy and speech-language pathology) are very helpful in maintaining functionality and are seen as part of the comprehensive care model. Exercise and learning different ways to manage and compensate for loss of function are essential aspects of living with MS.

Management of stress, which can precipitate and/or exacerbate symptoms, is an important part of living well with MS. Suggestions have been made about the positive use of meditation, Tai Chi, and relaxation exercises (McReynolds & Koch, 2001). Because a rise in the core body temperature can make symptoms worse, managing this situation is essential. Typically, regular cooling will be needed, which can be accomplished by drinking cold beverages and/or being in air-conditioned places (Schapiro, 2001). The NMSS has numerous booklets with recommendations for how to best manage the various symptoms. This information can be downloaded from their Web site (*www.nationalmssociety.org*).

The Family Experience and Caregiver Concerns

When someone develops MS, the lives of family members tend to be affected as well; who is affected and how will vary. Because most people with MS are diagnosed between 20 and 50 years of age, there may be life cycle issues to consider, such as pregnancy, parenting young children, and employment. Parents of young people with MS, who may be facing their own aging, will have specific caregiver issues and may feel strain in their role. The NMSS has a wealth of excellent resources for professionals and persons affected by the disease that can be downloaded from their Web site or ordered in hard copy (see appendix to this chapter).

Specific to MS, much like Parkinson's, is the unpredictability of the disease. This has been shown to add to the stress families feel. In addition, many of the symptoms of MS are invisible, such as the fatigue, visual problems, and pain, and family members may not recognize the symptoms or may misinterpret them, often adding to stress in the couple or family relationship (Crawford, 2001). Changes in role functioning are not uncommon, particularly with disease progression. This can disrupt the romantic-sexual bond, which is worsened if the couple has not learned how to cope together with the stressors and unpredictability of MS. Support groups have been helpful to couples and families in learning to understand MS and manage how best to live with the disease.

SUMMARY

The following are key points for social workers working with populations affected by PD or MS:

- Current trends in best practice recommendations call for care delivery in an interdisciplinary team. Social workers have been largely absent in such teams.
- The caregiver has specific stressors that need attention. Problem-solving approaches seem to be helpful with this population.
- Persons with MS and PD and their caregivers tend to experience a series of ongoing losses that need to be assessed.
- Depression and anxiety are common, yet are underdiagnosed and undertreated in populations with MS and PD. Support measures and clinical services might be helpful.
- It is likely that persons from diverse populations have been undercounted; outreach to the traditionally underserved is important as a way to serve whole communities. Most care reaches only the middle-class, educated population able to access existing services.

APPENDIX 9.1

Resources for Parkinson's Disease and Multiple Sclerosis

Parkinson's Disease

National Associations
National Parkinson Foundation (NPF)
1501 NW 9th Avenue
Miami, FL 33136
800-327-4545; Web site: *www.parkinson.org*
NPF has over 40 Centers of Excellence in the United States and internationally and chapters with support groups throughout the United States. NPF offers education, support, outreach, and information and funds research to find the cause and cure for PD. The user-friendly Web site is full of information. They have numerous publications in English and Spanish which can be ordered, free of charge, with many available on the Web. NPF also offers Allied Team Training for Parkinson (ATTP), a specialty PD training program for allied health professionals, including social workers.

American Parkinson Disease Association (APDA)
1250 Hyland Boulevard Suite 4B
Staten Island, NY 10305
800-223-2732; Web site: *www.apdaparkinson.org*
APDA offers information and referral centers, chapters, and support groups throughout the United States. They have numerous publications in English and other languages, which can be downloaded or requested free of charge.

Parkinson's Advocacy Network (PAN)
1000 Vermont Avenue, NW, Suite 900
Washington DC 20005
800-850-4726; Web site: *www.parkinsonsaction.org*
PAN, the leading advocacy organization, educates the community about pressing issues regarding PD to advocate for increased funding to find the cause and cure.

National Institute for Mental Health (NIMH)
Office of Communications and Public Liaison
Information Resources and Inquiries Branch
6001 Executive Blvd., Room 8184, MSC 9663
Bethesda, MD 20892-9663
301-443-4513; Web site: *www.nimh.nih.gov*
NIMH Depression Publications 800-421-4211

Worldwide Education and Awareness for Movement Disorders (WE MOVE)
204 West 84th Street
New York, NY 10024
800-437-MOV2; Web site: *www.wemove.org*
This Web-based resource offers information for both the lay population and professionals about many movement disorders, including Parkinson's. The Web site is constantly updated and monitored by physicians.

Melvin Weinstein Parkinson's Foundation
1340-1272 North Great Neck Road, #193
Virginia Beach, VA 23454
757-313-9729; Web site: www.mwpf.org
This foundation helps PWP who are financially challenged by helping to purchase equipment and supplies necessary to maintain a safe and healthy environment.

Books and Magazines

There are a growing number of paperback books readily available in popular bookstores about Parkinson's. A recent publication with an extensive resource list is *What Your Doctor May Not Tell You about Parkinson's Disease: A Holistic Program for Optimal Wellness* by Jill Marjama Lyons, MD, and Mary Shomon (New York: Time Warner Books, 2001).

A free magazine for PWD and families, which can also be helpful to professionals, is *Parkinson's Disease Living Well,* which can be obtained from:
c/o Clinicians Group
1515 Broad Street
Bloomfield, NJ 07003
973-954-9306

Multiple Sclerosis

National Multiple Sclerosis Society (NMSS)
733 Third Avenue
New York, NY 10017
800-344-4867; Web site: *www.nationalmssociety.org*
The NMSS provides education, emotional support, and a variety of programs and services for people with MS, their families, and the public. They have an extensive list of publications (many in Spanish) on a wide variety of topics, which can be downloaded from their Web site. They provide professional consulta-

tion via their Professional Resource Center at 800-MS-TREAT or *HealthProf_info@nmss.org*. They also offer a variety of continuing education programs.

Multiple Sclerosis Association of America
706 Haddonfield Road
Cherry Hill, NJ 08002
800-532-7667; Web site: www.msaa.com

United Spinal Association
75-20 Astoria Blvd.
Jackson Heights, NY 11370-1177
800-807-0192; Web site: *www.unitedspinal.org*
United Spinal assists all persons with spinal cord injury or disease. They publish a quarterly newsletter and have programs to assist members to improve home accessibility.

Books

There are a variety of books for persons with MS available at local bookstores. Two to consider are the following: *Meeting the Challenge of Progressive Multiple Sclerosis* by P. K. Coyle and J. Halper (New York: Demos Medical, 2001) and *Health Insurance Resource Manual: Options for People with a Chronic Illness or Disability* by D. E. Northrop and S. Cooper (New York: Demos Medical, 2003).

REFERENCES

Aarsland, D., Larsen, J. P., Karlsen, K., Lim, N. G., & Tandberg, E. (1999). Mental symptoms in Parkinson's disease are important contributors to caregiver distress. *International Journal of Geriatric Psychiatry, 14,* 866–874.

Calne, S., Mak, E., Hall, J., Fortin, M. J., King, K., McInnes, G., et al. (2003). Validating a quality of life scale in caregivers of patients with Parkinson's disease: Parkinson's Impact Scale (PIMS). In A. Gordin, S. Kaakkola, & H. Teravainen (Eds.), *Advances in neurology* (pp. 115–122). Philadelphia: Lippincott Williams & Wilkins.

Carter, J., Lyons, K., Stewart, B. J., & Archibald, P. (2004, April). *Do the clinical features of Parkinson's disease explain spouse caregiver strain?* Poster presented at annual meeting of the American Academy of Neurology, San Francisco, CA.

Charcot, J. M. (1868). Histologie de la sclérose en plaques. *Gazette des hospitaux* 41, 554–555.

Chaudhuri, K. R., Hu, M. T., & Brooks, D. J. (2000). Atypical parkinsonism in Afro-Caribbean and Indian origin immigrants to the U.K. *Movement Disorders, 15,* 18–23.

Cote, L. (1999). Depression: Impact and management by the patient and family. *Neurology, 52,* S7–S9.

Crawford, P. (2001). Family issues. In M. Hennessey & P. Rumrill (Eds.), *Multiple sclerosis: A guide for rehabilitation and health care professionals* (pp. 79–108). Springfield, IL: Charles C. Thomas.

Hagestuen, R. (2002). *Parkinson's disease: A curriculum for the Allied Team Training for Parkinson program.* Miami, FL: National Parkinson Foundation.

Hennessey, M., & Rumrill, P. (2001). Overview of multiple sclerosis. In M. Hennessey & P. Rumrill (Eds.), *Multiple sclerosis: A guide for rehabilitation and health care professionals* (pp. 3–22). Springfield, IL: Charles C. Thomas.

Hodgson, J., Garcia, K., & Tyndall, L. (2004). Parkinson's disease and the couple relationship: A qualitative analysis. *Families, Systems and Health, 22,* 101–118.

Holland, N. (2002). *Basic MS facts.* New York: National MS Society.

Leentjens, A., Van den Akker, M., Metsemakers, J., Lousberg, R., & Verhey, F. (2003). Higher incidence of depression preceding the onset of Parkinson's disease: A register study. *Movement Disorders, 18,* 414–418.

McReynolds, C., & Koch, L. (2001). Psychological issues. In M. Hennessey & P. Rumrill (Eds.), *Multiple sclerosis: A guide for rehabilitation and health care professionals* (pp. 44–78). Springfield, IL: Charles C. Thomas.

Minden, S., & Frankel, D. (2002). *Plaintalk: A booklet about MS for families.* New York: National MS Society.

Minden, S. L., Frumin, M., & Erb, J. L. (2003). Treatment of disorders of mood and affect in multiple sclerosis. In J. Cohen, R. A. Rudick, & H. McFarland, (Eds.), *Multiple sclerosis therapeutics* (pp. 651–688). New York: Martin Dunitz.

National Institute of Mental Health. (2002). *Depression and Parkinson's disease.* Bethesda, MD: Author.

National MS Society. (1998). *Gait.* New York: Author.

National MS Society. (2003a). *What is MS?* New York: Author.

National MS Society. (2003b). *Comparing the disease-modifying drugs.* New York: Author.

Nicoletti, A., Sofia, V., & Bartoloni, A. (2003). Prevalence of Parkinson's disease: A door-to-door survey in rural Bolivia. *Parkinsonism Related Disorders, 10,* 19–21.

Parkinson, J. (1817). *An essay on the shaking palsy.* London: Whittingham and Rowland.

Parkinson's Disease Foundation. (2004). *Parkinson's disease: Questions and answers.* New York: Author.

Parrish, M., & Giunta, N. (2003). Parkinson's disease caregiving: Implications for care management. *Care Management Journal, 4,* 53–60.

Rumrill, P. (1996). *Employment issues and multiple sclerosis.* New York: Demos Medical.

Schapiro, R. (2001). Disease and symptom management strategies. In M. Hennessey & P. Rumrill (Eds), *Multiple sclerosis: A guide for rehabilitation and health care professionals* (pp. 23–43). Springfield, IL: Charles C. Thomas.

Schapiro, R. & Schneider, D. (2002). Symptom management in multiple sclerosis. In J. Harper & N. Holland (Eds.), *Comprehensive nursing care in multiple sclerosis* (pp. 31–52). New York: Demos Medical.

Schiffer, R. (2002). *Cognitive loss in MS.* New York: National MS Society.

Schrag, A., Jahanshahi, M., & Quinn, N. P. (2001). What contributes to depression in Parkinson's disease? *Psychological Medicine, 31,* 65–73.

Speer, D. C. (1993). Predicting Parkinson's disease patient and caregiver adjustment: Preliminary findings. *Behavior, Health and Aging, 3,* 139–146.

Waters, C. (1999). *Diagnosis and management of Parkinson's disease.* Caddo, OK: Professional Communications, Inc.

RONALD W. TOSELAND
MICHAEL PARKER

Older Adults Suffering From Significant Dementia

Dementia is very difficult to cope with because it affects both mental and physical functioning progressively, until death. Dementing illnesses have been called "the most feared and devastating disorder of later life" (Zarit & Zarit, 1998, p. 32). The purpose of this chapter is to provide an overview of the social work role in the care of persons with dementia. The social work role is to provide services and support to persons with dementia to help them cope with the disease. These services also extend to family members and to those who care for persons with dementia.

BACKGROUND

Dementia comes from the Latin term *de mens* or "out of mind." It is used to describe a group of symptoms, a syndrome, characterized by multiple cognitive deficits of sufficient severity to interfere with daily activities and social relationships (American Psychiatric Association, 2000). Typically, the symptoms are insidious at onset, gradually progressing until death as an increasing number of brain cells become impaired. Although progressive, the course of dementia symptoms is variable depending on underlying disease processes.

Because dementia affects many areas of functioning, social workers' assessments and interventions must be broad, focusing on the whole person. Thus, assessment and intervention should include the emotional, physical, psychological, social, and spiritual aspects of the functioning of persons with dementia and their caregivers. Also, because of the progressive nature of the disease, advance planning is essential. Good social work intervention focuses both on current functioning and planning for the future.

Dementia in the elderly can be grouped into four broad categories by etiology and approximate incidence: (1) primary degenerative dementia (in 50% to 60% of dementia cases, e.g., Alzheimer's disease, Pick's disease); (2) multi-infarct dementias (stroke-related, 10% to 20%); (3) partially reversible dementias (20% to 30%, e.g., vascular diseases, infections, metabolic disorders); and (4) other neurological disorders (5% to 10%, Huntington's and Parkinson's diseases; Kane, Ouslander, & Abrass, 2004). Alzheimer's disease is by far the most common cause of dementia, with vascular-related diseases a distant second. Dementia can be caused by a variety of other diseases and conditions, including HIV/AIDS, alcoholism, traumatic brain injury (i.e., head trauma), Creutzfeldt-Jakob's disease, Down syndrome, and dementia due to other general medical conditions and etiologies (American Psychiatric Association, 2000; Gauthier, 2003; Kane et al., 2004; Weiner, 1991; Zarit & Zarit, 1998).

The prevalence of dementia increases rapidly with advancing age. For example, it has been estimated that at age 65, only about .06% of males and .8% of females have dementia, whereas by age 85, the rates rise to 21% for males and 25% for females. By age 95, 36% of males and 41% of females are affected with some form of dementia (American Psychiatric Association, 2000). Because of the aging of the population in the United States and other nations, the prevalence of dementia is expected to increase dramatically in the next several decades (e.g., Katzman, 2001). Therefore, social workers can be expected to encounter an increasing number of persons with dementia and their caregivers in future years.

Dementia causes profound changes in a person's functional abilities. The essential feature of dementia is memory impairment, but at least one of the following cognitive disturbances must also be present: (1) aphasia (vague or empty speech), (2) apraxia (impaired ability to execute motor functioning), (3) agnosia (failure to recognize or identify objects), and (4) disturbance in executive function (ability to think abstractly and to plan, initiate, sequence, monitor, and stop complex behavior; American Psychiatric Association, 2000).

As dementia progresses, memory, judgment, language, and abilities to engage in activities of daily living become increasingly impaired, and behavioral disturbances can arise. Psychiatric symptoms may also occur and cause personality changes, depression, anxiety, delusions, or hallucinations. Gerontological social workers need to be able to recognize and treat these symptoms. They also need to help persons with dementia and their caregivers to cope with the limitations and impairments that arise with continuing declines in physical and mental functioning.

ASSESSMENT

The first step in working with older persons with dementia and their caregivers is to conduct a thorough assessment of the situation. If a diagnosis of dementia has not already been established, the social worker's role is to help people with dementia and their caregivers get an accurate diagnosis. Dementia is diagnosed by ruling out other physical illnesses that may be causing the symptoms and by history taking, which establishes progressive memory loss. Because it affects many aspects of functioning, a good assessment of dementia is conducted most thoroughly by a multidisciplinary team (Mulligan, Linden, & Juillerat, 2003).

For example, social workers should encourage older persons with suspected dementia and their caregivers to get a comprehensive geriatric assessment that includes a social and medical history, a physical exam, appropriate laboratory work, a mental status exam, environmental assessment, and assessment of functional status (ADLs, IADLs; see Table 10.1; Kane et al., 2004; Toseland, Derico, & Owen, 1984). Such an assessment is necessary to rule out other illnesses and to track the trajectory of the illness and the effects of care. Therefore, it is important to have referral sources of physicians who specialize in dementia (Toseland et al., 1984). This includes geriatric-trained doctors who can lead a team of professionals in conducting and coordinating a comprehensive assessment (Fuller et al., 2003; Kane et al., 2004). Memory clinics and Alzheimer's disease assistance centers, now available in some communities, often employ multidisciplinary, geriatric teams that include the disciplines of medicine, nursing, and social work. If a dementia specialist or geriatric-trained internist or family practitioner is not available, the social worker may need to recommend to the family the involvement of other professionals (neurologists, psychiatrists, nurses, nutritionists, physical and occupational therapists) in the assessment process.

While making an assessment, social workers should consider using one of the instruments available to assess the level of cognitive impairment experienced by the person, such as the Mini Mental Status Exam (Folstein, Folstein, & McHugh, 1975). Social workers may also want to use other instruments, such as the Global Deterioration Scale, to determine the stage of disease progression (Reisberg, Ferris, & deLeon, 1982), or the Life Space Assessment (Parker, Baker, & Allman, 2002) to assess early changes in functional status and to monitor changes in mobility over time.

The assessment of dementia should include determining the current stage of the disease. Many resources are available to identify what stage of dementia a person is currently experiencing. For example, a CD-ROM is available that can be used by both professionals and laypersons to identify the stage of the disease and to address concerns arising during each stage (Health Care Interactive, 2001). There is still some controversy about whether to disclose the diagnosis of dementia to the person with the disease, and some have argued that the best approach is to ask the person at the outset whether he or she would like to know the result of the diagnos-

TABLE 10.1. A Comprehensive Geriatric Assessment

- Social and Medical History
- Physical Exam:
  - vital signs
  - behavior and appearance
  - sensory (ears/eyes)
  - dental
  - skin
  - chest/cardiovascular
  - abdomen/genitourinary
  - extremities
  - neurological
- Laboratory Assessment
- Mental Status Exam
- Spirituality Assessment
- Environmental Assessment
- Functional Assessment
  - ADLs
    - feeding
    - dressing
    - ambulation
    - toileting
    - bathing
    - continence
    - grooming
    - communication
  - IADLs
    - writing
    - reading
    - cooking, cleaning, shopping, climbing stairs, using telephone, managing medication, managing money
- Social Service Assessment
  - family dynamics
  - service needs
  - resource needs
  - benefits
  - legal issues (e.g., power of attorney, health care proxy)
  - advance care planning: functional needs
  - advance care planning: medical and end-of-life preferences

tic process (Downs, 1999). Although we respect the person's right not to know, in the overwhelming majority of situations, our clinical experience suggests that people want to know the diagnosis. Disclosing the diagnosis is also important because it affirms the person's right to know and because early diagnosis can lead to earlier and better treatment.

Part of the role of the social worker in the early stage of work with persons with dementia and their caregivers is to provide support as they go through the process of accepting the diagnosis and understanding its implications. Social workers provide information to help persons with dementia and their caregivers gradually understand the consequences of the diagnosis to functional abilities. According to Kaplan (1996), caregivers of dementia patients go through the following states of adjustment: (1) denial and making excuses for the person's behavior; (2) overinvolvement and overcompensation for the person's losses; (3) anger over the loss, frustration about the inability to halt the disease progression, and embarrassment caused by the person's behavior; (4) guilt about the inability to accommodate and fully meet the person's behavior and care needs; and (5) grieving and acceptance.

During the assessment process it is important to identify the primary caregiver. For persons with early-stage dementia, Kuhn (1999) suggests that at least one person who is close to the person with dementia should be helped to step into a leadership role. This person takes overall responsibility for ensuring the well-being of the person with dementia, while not undermining the remaining abilities of the person, and encouraging the active involvement of others interested in the person's well-being. However, because caregiving frequently involves a primary caregiver and secondary caregivers, an important role for social work is to help families define roles, to cooperate in care planning and decision making, and to negotiate and resolve conflicts as they occur.

Once a diagnosis of dementia has been confirmed, the social worker can proceed with the assessment process. A comprehensive assessment of persons with dementia should consider the physical, emotional, psychological, social, practical, and spiritual aspects of their functioning and that of their caregivers.

PHYSICAL FUNCTIONING AND DEMENTIA

Dementia has a profound impact on functional abilities, language and speech, motor ability, judgment and reasoning, and many other areas of functioning. Functional status measures can be used to measure basic activities of daily living skills such as bathing and toileting and also higher-level instrumental activities of daily living skills such as managing money and driving. In early stages of dementia, social workers' role is often to help the person with dementia and care-givers to make adaptations in their environment to help them compensate for memory loss. In the mid-dle stages of dementia, functional assessments can aid social workers in helping caregivers to learn commu-nication strategies that compensate for impairments in language and speech. Later in the disease process, social workers' role is often focused on assessing in-formal support services and providing information about formal community supports such as day care and home care. At a minimum, this information can help to reassure caregivers that help is available and that they are able to have some respite from caregiv-ing if needed. Social workers may also help caregivers to obtain needed home care, adult day care, or nurs-ing home services.

PSYCHOLOGICAL AND EMOTIONAL IMPACT OF DEMENTIA

Emotional lability and emotional problems are com-mon among both persons with dementia and their caregivers. Caregivers often struggle emotionally as they reflect on the continual cognitive decline. They face profound changes in their loved one. Social workers can help caregivers in many ways, including providing support and reassurance, developing long-term care plans that address medical care (e.g., locat-ing a geriatrician), addressing legal issues (e.g., completion of a durable power of attorney), under-standing family dynamics (coordination of a family meeting to determine who does what), and address-ing work and financial issues, spiritual concerns, grief and loss counseling, emotional support, and assis-tance with practical issues such as obtaining needed health and social services (Parker et al., 2004). Be-cause people cope in many different ways with emotional challenges, a careful assessment of the emotional concerns of persons with dementia and their caregivers can help to guide intervention efforts. Some persons with dementia and their caregivers may, for example, benefit from early-stage dementia support groups (Yale, 1995). Others may benefit from individual or family counseling to alleviate emotional problems.

Psychological impairments can occur in all stages of the disease. In early stages, depression is a common problem, and anxiety may also be present. In later stages of the disease, psychotic symptoms such as hal-lucinations and delusions may occur, and agitation is common. Pharmacologic treatment may help, but the use of psychotropic medications is complicated by the underlying disease processes, and some medications, such as the benzodiazepines, may make the dementia worse. Therefore, it is essential for social workers to work closely with psychiatrists who are familiar with the treatment of persons with dementia.

We have observed that behavioral symptoms are often the result of inappropriate environmental stim-ulation or poor pain management. Therefore, it is important to conduct a careful assessment of the en-vironment and the physical comfort of the person with dementia before assuming that behavioral symp-toms are due to psychiatric problems. Because of the adverse effects that psychotropic medications can have on persons with dementia, it is always preferable to use nonpharmacological approaches if these are effective. (For additional information, see Callaway, 1998; Galasko, 1996; Kennedy, 2000; Zarit & Zarit, 1998.)

THE SOCIAL IMPACT OF DEMENTIA

Socially, the person with dementia often becomes iso-lated. Dementia causes problems in word finding, in sentence structure, and in ability to communicate. As dementia progresses, it becomes increasingly difficult to understand what the person is trying to communi-cate. Even close family caregivers may become frus-trated, and some become angry and short-tempered. Because of these problems, caregivers often feel ashamed to take the person out in public or to have visitors. When visitors do come, they may find it dif-ficult to interact with the person with dementia.

Caregivers also often become socially isolated as they increasingly have to be available around the clock to make sure that the person with dementia is safe. Therefore, it is important for social workers to en-courage caregivers to take care of themselves. It is also important to make use of informal and formal ser-vices as part of the care plan. Social workers can teach caregivers communication skills and activities that can be used to continue engagement as skills deterio-rate and dementia progresses. Some of these skills and activities are briefly described later in this chapter.

PRACTICAL ASPECTS OF CARE

Another important social work assessment and inter-vention role is to help with the practical aspects of care planning and management. Social workers assess the capacity of persons with dementia and their caregivers to get practical needs met. As a result of this type of assessment, social workers, for example, frequently become involved in helping the person with dementia and family caregivers to understand the role of Medicaid and Medicare and other health and social service programs, such as home heating assistance and food stamps. This assistance may include helping them with questions about eligibility and with required application procedures. It also may include helping to coordinate or manage services once they are obtained.

Social workers frequently become involved in planning for future care needs. For example, social workers may help persons with mild dementia and their caregivers to develop health care proxies and advance directives regarding medical care wishes if they become incapacitated. They may also encourage caregivers and persons with dementia who are still capable to develop or update wills, powers of attorney, and other legal documents, to review financial arrangements, and to plan for the assistance and support that will be needed during later stages of the disease.

THE ROLE OF RELIGION AND SPIRITUALITY

Many families confronted with the effects of dementia find strength in their spiritual beliefs and the support they receive from their communities of faith (Myers, Roff, Klemmack, & Parker, 2004; Parker et al., 2004; Roff & Parker, 2003). Religious beliefs are particularly strong in North America among elderly women and members of some minority groups (Koenig, McCullough, & Larson, 2001; McInnis-Dittrich, 2002; Roff, Klemmack, Parker, Baker, & Allman, 2005; Tobin 1999).

The early stage of a dementing illness is a good time to help persons express what type of religious or spiritual support, if any, they would like as their symptoms progress. For some individuals, this may include continued or renewed contact with clerics or with formal religious organizations such as churches or synagogues. For others, it may mean help in coming to terms with the illness and its course, the meaning of their lives and making peace with family, friends, and those with whom they may have had conflictual relationships. Social workers can help older persons with mild dementia to incorporate spirituality and religion in life review, reminiscence, and legacy work that helps to make sense of and give

meaning to life (Roff & Parker, 2003). It can also mean helping persons with dementia to articulate and record preferences for medical care and funeral arrangements at the end of their life that reflect their religious and spiritual values.

ATTENDING TO THE NEEDS OF CAREGIVERS

Although we have already mentioned the importance of including the primary caregiver in the assessment process, a comprehensive biopsychosocial and environmental assessment should always consider the needs of all family members and other concerned persons who are involved with the person with dementia. In some families, for example, a diagnosis of dementia can rekindle or exacerbate long-standing family conflicts. In others, it can bring family members closer together. One or more family meetings are often helpful to assess the strengths and weaknesses of the family system in planning for the future, in problem solving, and in resolving conflicts and differences of option about care options and roles (Toseland, Smith, & McCallion, 1995).

Cummings (1996) points out that it is essential for social workers to recognize that understanding, accepting, and coming to terms with the dementing illnesses of a family member may be a long and slow process and that this process varies significantly by individual family member. Family caregivers are faced not only with the prospect of providing care over the long term, but also with the emotional challenge of coming to grips with the gradual loss of their loved one and changing expectations about the relationship they will have with the person as disease processes progress (Cummings, 1996). Social workers have an important role to play in helping individual family members and the entire family system to cope with these emotional adjustments and to work together to plan for and manage the care of the person with dementia as symptoms progress.

INTERVENTION ROLES

Social workers can be called on to play a variety of roles when working with persons with dementia. These roles can include consultant, coordinator, care manager, and interdisciplinary care team member (Toseland, Smith, & McCallion, 2001; Toseland, Smith, & Zinoman, 2004). In consulting roles, social workers utilize the competencies, expertise, and skills of persons with dementia and their family care systems to the maximum extent possible. They rely heavily on the input of persons with dementia and their caregivers during both assessment and care planning. Social workers assume that caregivers and persons with dementia will take primary responsibility for the day-to-day implementation and monitoring of the care plan.

After an intensive period of consultation during which the assessment is conducted and a care plan is made, social workers in the consulting role reduce contact, occasionally checking that the care plan is being implemented properly and responding to problems or issues as they arise. Frequently occurring problems often include emotional lability, agitation, and behavioral disturbances such as aggressiveness and apathy. They may also include adjustments in living status (such as when a person with dementia moves in with a caregiver or moves to supportive housing or a nursing home), resistance to some forms of care such as bathing, or safety issues arising from the declining judgment and reasoning of the person with dementia. The consultant role is often used by private social work care managers and agency-based social workers in outpatient memory clinics, housing projects, family service agencies, and senior centers in the early stages of dementing illnesses and when strong family supports are available.

In the care coordinator role, social workers take greater responsibility for implementing the care plan they have developed with family members and persons with dementia. Social workers help to link persons with dementia and their informal caregivers to needed community resources and services and help to ensure that these services are received in a timely and consistent fashion by resolving any ongoing care plan implementation issues. In the care coordinator role, social workers are frequently called on to help with applications for medical, social service, and housing assistance and may serve as an advocate to help obtain them. As care coordinators, they may also provide education about the disease and limited individual, family, or group counseling. The social worker plays a broker role linking the person with dementia and family members to more extensive counseling services if needed.

Once services are in place, the care coordinator's role is to ensure that services continue to meet ongoing needs and that they are responsive to changing circumstances as the dementia progresses. The care coordinator role is frequently used by social workers

who are called on to work with persons with moderate dementia. Care coordination is also frequently needed in situations where informal caregivers can't assume these responsibilities or where they are unable or unwilling to provide day-to-day monitoring of care plans.

The care management role is assumed by social workers when their comprehensive assessments reveal that persons with dementia are severely impaired or when informal caregivers are unavailable or unwilling to provide the type of around-the-clock monitoring of the situation and the extensive day-to-day care that is often needed. In this role, social workers involve informal caregivers in the care planning and implementation process. In general, however, care managers help caregivers by putting services in place that remove some or all of the responsibility for day-to-day care of persons with dementia.

Kaplan (1996) points out that there are several different forms of care management. Medical care management was originally developed by health maintenance organizations and insurance companies to contain medical costs. Typically, medical care management emphasizes the provision of quality care at the lowest possible cost, coordination of care between providers and informal caregivers, and the utilization of benefit coverage to provide preventive services, health care maintenance services, and the management of chronic diseases. Social care management services typically help persons with dementia and their caregivers obtain needed social services such as Meals on Wheels and day care. Social care management may also include limited or extensive medical care management. Kaplan also mentions that there are mental health care management services that provide supportive care or rehabilitation and private geriatric care management provided to persons with dementia and their family members on a fee-for-service basis. These latter services are particularly useful for long-distance caregivers who have sufficient resources to pay for these services but who are not in a position to relocate to provide the necessary ongoing monitoring and day-to-day assistance that may be needed by the person with dementia.

Typically, in the care management role the social worker (1) completes a comprehensive assessment of the situation, (2) develops a care plan, (3) implements the plan by coordinating health and social service delivery from different providers and by providing services directly to both the caregiver and informal caregivers, (4) maintains regular and frequent contact with the person with dementia and informal caregivers to ensure that appropriate care is delivered in a timely fashion and that adjustments to changing circumstances are made on an ongoing basis, and (5) advocates to close gaps and fill in needs that are not being fully met by the care plan. Overall, the focus of care management is to keep the person living at home for as long as possible in a safe and comfortable setting. When needs become too great, the care manager's role includes helping to place the person with dementia in a more sheltered environment such as assisted living or a special care unit in a nursing home that may better meet his or her needs.

Social workers' roles may include being members of interdisciplinary teams in outpatient and inpatient organizations designed to help persons with dementia. These include outpatient programs such as memory clinics designed to provide multidisciplinary assessment and care plans (often a geriatrician, nurse, and social worker team) to help caregivers maintain persons with dementia in community settings (see, e.g., Freed, Elder, Lauderdale, & Carter, 1999). These may also include social workers in home care agencies, adult day care centers, and other community agencies designed to support caregivers and persons with dementia. Social workers play vital roles in sheltered housing programs and nursing homes where they work with other team members to provide high-quality care to persons with advanced dementia. In their role as interdisciplinary team members, social workers frequently serve as care coordinators but may also take on consultation or care management roles.

INTERVENTION STRATEGIES

There are a wide variety of intervention strategies that can be used to help persons with dementia and their caregivers cope with the disease. These can be classified into strategies focused on prevention, remediation, and support. Although an extensive discussion of each of these types of intervention strategies is beyond the scope of this chapter, brief overviews are presented with references to more comprehensive resources for further reading.

The label "prevention" is not meant to imply that there are intervention strategies that can prevent or reverse the course of dementing illnesses. At this time, there are no such strategies. There are, however, intervention strategies that can slow the course of dementia and mitigate some of its harmful side effects.

There are now several drugs on the market that are helpful in slowing the course of the dementia in some

persons. For an overview of pharmacological treatment from a social work perspective, see Callaway (1998), but for up-to-date information about the latest medications to reach the market, a review of the results of recent clinical drug trials is necessary. Some reviews of the recent literature are written in language easily understood by practicing social workers and include medications not only to treat cognitive loss but also to treat depression, agitation, delusions, and hallucinations (e.g., Kawas, 2003). The social work role in pharmacology management is to help persons with dementia and their caregivers to obtain appointments with geriatricians, neurologists, and psychiatrists who can help them determine whether they are good candidates for medications useful in the treatment of symptoms of dementia. In general, it is thought that pharmacological agents to treat cognitive loss are most effective if they are administered in early dementia. Therefore, social workers can play an important role in urging persons with dementia and their caregivers to have medication reviews as early as possible. Social workers can also play an important role by helping persons with dementia to consistently take medications as prescribed.

Another type of preventive intervention consists of cognitive stimulation programs. Early attempts at cognitive stimulation include reality orientation, reminiscence, and remotivation therapy. The efficacy of these approaches for persons with dementia is limited (the evidence is discussed in several reviews; e.g., Beck, 1998; Kasl-Godley & Gatz, 2000; Miller & Morris, 1993; Spector, Davies, Woods & Orrell, 2000; Spector, Orrell, Davies, & Woods, 1998a, 1998b, & 2001; Van der Linden, Juillerat, & Adam, 2003; Zarit & Zarit, 1998). More recent cognitive stimulation and training programs that have focused on cognitive deficits in episodic memory, language, and numerical skills have also been attempted (for a review, see Van der Linden et al., 2003).

Although social workers sometimes become involved in cognitive training programs, most of their involvement has been limited to cognitive stimulation programs, such as reality orientation and reminiscence programs, and to efforts designed to structure the environment of persons with dementia by providing external cognitive aides to enhance memory. These interventions include suggesting specific places to store keys and other items used daily, medication organizers, the use of labels and color coding, and similar memory aides.

Apathy and lack of engagement are major problems for persons with dementia, particularly during middle and late stages of the disease, problems that can be vexing to family caregivers. Programs to maintain communication and to stimulate interaction have been developed (e.g., Toseland & McCallion, 1998). Table 10.2 presents some general strategies for maintaining communication. Other strategies for maintaining communication with persons with dementia at early, moderate, and severe stages of the disease can be found in Toseland and McCallion.

Memory albums and memory charts can be used to stimulate reminiscence and life review and to engage persons with dementia whose language abilities may be quite limited. Memory albums are small photo albums with pictures of important people, places, and events from the distant past that are particularly meaningful to the person with dementia. Simple words describing each picture are placed underneath the picture or on the opposite page of the photo album. Memory charts are larger boards that contain photographs and simple words in different panels that can be placed where a person with dementia spends a considerable amount of time. Memory albums and memory charts are particularly effective for engaging persons with moderate and severe dementia (for more information, see Toseland & McCallion, 1998).

Remedial intervention strategies include those that are focused on emotional and psychological problems and personality changes that are frequently observed in early- and middle-stage dementia as well as agitation and behavior problems that are commonly encountered in moderate to severe stages of dementia. Emotional and psychological problems such as depression, anxiety, delusions, and hallucinations (more common in later-stage dementia) can be treated effectively with psychotropic medications, but support and reassurance also play an important role.

A useful theoretical framework to reduce emotional and psychological problems is the Progressively Lowered Stress Threshold (PLST) model originally developed by Hall and Buckwalter (1987). Adapted from stress adaptation and coping models, the PLST model identifies clinical triggers such as fatigue, change in routine, inappropriate stimulation, and internal and external demands that exceed the capacities of the person with dementia. According to PLST, these triggers can lead to a sudden decline in functional ability. The PLST model recommends establishing daily routines, making environmental modifications, minimizing fatigue, managing inappropriate stimuli, minimizing affective responses, decreasing excessive demands, limiting physical triggers, and improving communication and behavior management strategies (Buckwalter et al., 1999; Gerdner, Hall, & Buckwalter, 1996; Hall & Laloudakis, 1999; Toseland & McCallion, 1998).

Most remedial approaches to agitation and behavior problems rely on some form of behavioral

TABLE 10.2. General Communication Guidelines

---

1. Begin all communications by first ensuring that you are relaxed and are conveying that you are relaxed.

   One technique to get rid of stress has been called deep breathing. This is a method of breathing for relaxation. This technique should not take more than approximately two minutes.

   • Concentrate on one spot in your stomach.

   • Concentrate on the flow of your breath as you inhale.

   • Concentrate on the flow of your breath as you exhale.

   • Focus on your breathing as you repeat this procedure several times slowly.

   • Visualize your breath going in through your nose, into the center of your body, and out again.

2. Reduce background noise and other distractions and stimuli.

3. Ensure that there is adequate lighting for the person with dementia or move to a brighter location.

4. If the person with dementia usually wears glasses or a hearing aid, try to have the person with dementia use them. However, do not argue if the person with dementia does not want to wear them.

5. Speak in a slow, calm, respectful manner and keep the pitch of your voice low.

6. Avoid speaking to the person with dementia as if he or she is a child.

7. Even when the person with dementia has severe language problems, never assume that he or she does not understand you. Always assume that he or she will understand at least some of the information you are attempting to convey.

8. Do not talk about the person with dementia with others as if the person with dementia is not there.

9. Sit at the same eye level as the person with dementia to show that your attention is focused on him or her.

---

analysis, with caregivers becoming behavior detectives identifying when problems occur and the antecedents and consequences of behavior. The idea is to find out precisely when behaviors occur and to try to determine the underlying needs that are not being met. Caregivers can be encouraged to identify antecedents that may stimulate the behavior and consequences that maintain the behavior. Based on these data, the environment can often be modified so that the comfort of the person with dementia is restored. Simple strategies such as making the room cooler or warmer, engaging the person in an activity, reducing noise or other stimulation, and reassurance and attention to positive behaviors often help reduce behavior problems.

Some agitated behaviors and behavior problems may be the result of poor pain management. Therefore, a careful review of physical causes (e.g., arthritis pain) for such behavior problems should be undertaken before behavioral intervention programs are initiated. A number of helpful books give directions for how to handle a variety of specific behavior problems, including but not limited to apathy, combativeness, food refusal, insomnia, resistance to care, and wandering (e.g., Hoffman & Platt; 1991; Mahoney, Volicer, & Hurley, 2000; Rau, 1993). There are also many excellent articles and book chapters that address apathy as well as behavioral and sleep problems (e.g., Cohen-Mansfield, 2000; Engelman, Altus, & Mathews, 1999; McCurry, Logsdon, Vitiello, & Teri, 1998). Recently, a CD has been created to help social workers and allied professionals to address problem behaviors and promote positive behaviors (McCallion, Lacey, & Toseland, 2003).

In our haste to address agitation and behavior problems and to prevent further declines in memory and communication, support strategies are sometimes neglected. Social workers, however, have a vital role to play in supporting persons with dementia and caregivers through the inevitable decline to death that is the ultimate result of dementia. In the early stages of dementia, support may take the form of affirming the coping abilities of persons with dementia and their caregivers. In later stages, reassurance and gentle touch can be used, and strategies to continue verbal and nonverbal engagement can be implemented by continuing to engage and stimulate whatever aspects of long-term memories and language abilities remain intact. Supportive interventions also include keeping caregivers and persons with dementia educated about the stages of the disorder new developments in care, helping caregivers and persons with dementia to obtain needed services and resources, and helping them plan for the future. For family members and other caregivers, supportive interventions may include family care planning and problem-solving meetings, supportive counseling and reassurance, and assistance with community and institutional options for care as dementia advances.

CONCLUSIONS

Because it affects many different aspects of emotional, physical, mental, social, and spiritual functioning, dementia is a very challenging disease to cope with both for the person afflicted and for family caregivers. Social workers are called on to play a vital role in supporting and assisting persons with dementia and their family caregivers in many different community and institutional settings. During assessment and intervention, it is essential for social workers to take a broad view of the whole person, considering the impact of dementia on the biopsychosocial and environmental functioning of the person with dementia and their informal caregivers. The social work profession is ideally suited for this role, working alone and in conjunction with other disciplines to help persons with dementia and their family caregivers cope with the devastating impact of this disease.

REFERENCES

American Psychiatric Association. (2000). *Diagnostic and statistical manual of medical disorders* (4th ed., text rev.). Washington, DC: Author.

Beck, C. K. (1998). Psychosocial and behavioral interventions for Alzheimer's disease patients and their families. *American Journal of Geriatric Psychiatry, 6*(2), S41–S48.

Buckwalter, K. C., Gerdner, L., Kohout, F., Hall, G. R., Kelly, A., Richards, B., et al. (1999). A nursing intervention to decrease depression in family caregivers of persons with dementia. *Archives of Psychiatric Nursing, 13*(2), 80–88.

Callaway, J. (1998). Psychopharmacological treatment of dementia. *Research on Social Work, 8*(4), 452–474.

Cohen-Mansfield, J. (2000). Nonpharmacological management of behavioral problems in persons with dementia: The TREA model. *Alzheimer's Care Quarterly, 1*(4), 22–33.

Cummings, S. (1996). Spousal caregivers of early stage Alzheimer's patients: A psychoeducational support group model. *Journal of Gerontological Social Work,* *26*(3/4), 83–98.

Downs, M. (1999). How to tell? Disclosing a diagnosis of dementia. *Journal of the American Society on Aging,* *23*(3), 30–34.

Engleman, K., Altus, D., & Mathews, R. M. (1999). Increasing engagement in daily activities by older adults with dementia. *Journal of Applied Behavior Analysis,* *32*, 107–110.

Folstein, M., Folstein, S., & McHugh, P. (1975). Mini-mental state: A practical method for grading the cognitive state of patients for the clinicians. *Journal of Psychiatric Research, 12*, 189.

Freed, D., Elder, W., Lauderdale, S., & Carter, S. (1999). An integrated program for dementia evaluation and care management. *The Gerontologist, 39*(3), 356–361.

Fuller, G., Baker, P., Larimore, W., Allman, R., Martin, J., & Parker, M. W. (2003). Helping military families establish a medical care plan for an elderly parent. *Geriatric Care Management, 13*(1), 16–22.

Galasko, D. (1996). Pharmacological approaches to behavioral symptoms in Alzheimer's disease. In Z. Khachaturian & T. Radebaugh (Eds.), *Alzheimer's disease cause(s), diagnosis, treatment, and care* (pp. 249–255). Boca Raton, FL: CRC Press.

Gauthier, S. (2003). Clinical aspects. In R. Mulligan, M. Van der Linden, & A. Juillerat (Eds.), *The clinical management of early Alzheimer's disease: A handbook* (pp. 21–34). Mahwah, NJ: Lawrence Erlbaum.

Gerdner, L. A., Hall, G. R., & Buckwalter, K. C. (1996). Caregiver training for people with Alzheimer's based on a stress threshold model. *IMAGE: Journal of Nursing Scholarship, 28*(3), 241–246.

Hall, G. R., & Buckwalter, K. C. (1987). Progressively lowered stress threshold: A conceptual model for care of adults with Alzheimer's disease. *Archives of Psychiatric Nursing, 1*(16), 399–406.

Hall, G. R., & Laloudakis, D. (1999). A behavioral approach to Alzheimer's disease: The progressively lowered stress threshold model. *Advance for Nurse Practitioners, 7*(7), 39–44, 81.

Health Care Interactive. (2001). *Alzheimer's caregiving strategies* [CD-ROM]. Washington, DC: Department of Veteran's Affairs. Global Multimedia.

Hoffman, S., & Platt, C. (1991). *Comforting the confused: Strategies for managing dementia.* New York: Springer.

Kane, R., Ouslander, J., & Abrass, I. (2004). *Essentials of clinical geriatrics* (5th ed.). New York: McGraw-Hill.

Kaplan, M. (1996). *Clinical practice with caregivers of dementia patients.* Washington, DC: Taylor & Francis.

Kasl-Godley, J., & Gatz, M. (2000). Psychosocial interventions for individuals with dementia: An integration of theory, therapy, and a clinical understanding of dementia. *Clinical Psychological Review, 20,* 755–782.

Katzman, R. (2001). Epidemiology of Alzheimer's disease and dementia: Advances and challenges. In K. Iqbal, S. Sisodia, & B. Winblad (Eds.), *Alzheimer's disease: Advances in etiology, pathogenesis and therapeutics* (pp. 11–21). Chichester, England: Wiley.

Kawas, C. (2003). Early Alzheimer's disease. *New England Journal of Medicine, 349*(11), 1056–1063.

Kennedy, G. (2000). *Geriatric mental health care: A treatment guide for health professionals.* New York: Guilford Press.

Koenig, H., McCullough, M., & Larson, D. (2001). *Handbook of religion and health.* New York: Oxford University Press.

Kuhn, D. (1999). *Alzheimer's early stages: First steps in caring and treatment.* Alameda, CA: Hunter House.

Mahoney, E., Volicer, L., & Hurley, A. (2000). *Management of challenging behaviors in dementia.* Baltimore, MD: Health Professions Press.

McCallion, P., Lacey, D., & Toseland, R. (2003). *Promoting positive behaviors. Excellence in Aging Services* [CD-ROM]. Albany: University at Albany, State University of New York.

McCurry, S., Logsdon, R., Vitiello, M., & Teri, L. (1998). Successful behavioral treatment for reported sleep problems in elderly caregivers of dementia patients: A controlled study. *Journal of Gerontology: Psychological Sciences, 53B*(2), 122–129.

McInnis-Dittrich, K. (2002). *Social work with elders: A biopsychosocial approach to assessment and intervention.* Boston: Allyn & Bacon.

Miller, E., & Morris, R. (1993). *The psychology of dementia.* Chichester, England: Wiley.

Mulligan, R., Van der Linden, M., & Juillerat, A.-C. (2003). *The clinical management of early Alzheimer's disease.* Mahwah, NJ: Lawrence Erlbaum.

Myers, D., Harris, H., Klemmack, D., & Parker, M. (2004). A feasibility study of a parent care planning model with two faith-based communities. *Journal of Religion, Spirituality, and Aging 17*(1/2), 39–53.

Parker, M. W., Baker, P., & Allman, R. (2002). A life space approach to the functional assessment of the elderly. *Journal of Gerontological Social Work, 35*(4), 35–55.

Parker, M. W., Roff, L., Myers, D., Martin, J., Toseland, R., Fine, C., et al. (2004). Parent care and religion: A faith-based intervention model for caregiving readiness of congregational members. *Journal of Family Ministry, 17*(4), 51–69.

Rau, M. (1993). *Coping with communication challenges in Alzheimer's disease.* San Diego: Singular.

Reisberg, B., Ferris, S., & deLeon, M. (1982). The global deterioration scale for assessment of primary degenerative dementia. *American Journal of Psychiatry, 139,* 1136.

Roff, L., Klemmack, D. L., Parker, M. W., Baker, P., & Allman, R. (2005). Spirituality and depression in African American and White elders. *Journal of Human Behavior and the Social Environment, 10*(1), 175–211.

Roff, L. L. & Parker, M. W. (2003). Spirituality and Alzheimer's disease care. *Alzheimer's Care Quarterly, 4*(4), 267–270.

Spector, A., Davies, S., Woods, B., & Orrell, M. (2000). Reality orientation for dementia: A systematic review of the evidence of effectiveness from randomized controlled trials. *The Gerontologist, 40,* 206–212.

Spector, A., Orrell, M., Davies, S., & Woods, B. (1998a). *Reality orientation for dementia: A review of the evidence for its effectiveness* [Cochrane Library 4]. Oxford: Update Software.

Spector, A., Orrell, M., Davies, S., & Woods, B. (1998b). *Reminiscence therapy for dementia: A review of the evidence for its effectiveness* [Cochrane Library 4]. Oxford: Update Software.

Spector, A., Orrell, M., Davies, S., & Woods, B. (2001). Can reality orientation be rehabilitated? Development and piloting of an evidence-based programme of cognition-based therapies for people with dementia. *Neuropsychological Rehabilitation, 11,* 377–397.

Tobin, S. (1999). *Preservation of the self in the oldest years.* New York: Springer.

Toseland, R., Derico, A., & Owen, M. (1984). Alzheimer's disease and related disorders: Assessment and intervention. *Health and Social Work, 9*(3), 212–228.

Toseland, R., & McCallion, P. (1998). *Maintaining communication with persons with dementia.* New York: Springer.

Toseland, R., Smith, G., & McCallion, P. (1995). Supporting the family in elder care. In G. C. Smith, S. S. Tobin, E. A. Robertson-Tchabo, & P. W. Power (Eds.), *Strengthening aging families: Diversity in practice and policy* (pp. 3–24). Newbury Park, CA: Sage.

Toseland, R., Smith, G., & McCallion, P. (2001). Helping family caregivers. In A. Gitterman (Ed.), *Handbook of social work practice with vulnerable and resilient populations* (2nd ed.; pp. 548–581). New York: Columbia University Press.

Toseland, R., Smith, T., & Zinoman, M. (in press). Social work practice with family caregivers for frail older persons. In M. J. Holosko & P. A. Taylor (Eds.), *Social work practice in health care settings* (2nd ed., pp. 229–252). Toronto: Canadian Scholars Press.

Van der Linden, M., Juillerat, A., & Adam, S. (2003). Cognitive intervention. In R. Mulligan, M. Van der Linden, & A. Juillerat (Eds.), *The clinical management of early Alzheimer's disease* (pp. 169–233). Mahwah, NJ: Lawrence Erlbaum.

Weiner, W. (1991). The dementias: Diagnosis and management. Washington, DC: American Psychiatric Press.

Yale, R. (1995). *Developing support groups for individuals with early-stage Alzheimer's disease: Planning, implementation, and evaluation.* Baltimore: Health Professions Press.

Zarit, S., & Zarit, J. (1998). *Mental disorders in older adults: Fundamentals of assessment and treatment.* New York: Guilford Press.

ZVI D. GELLIS

Older Adults With Mental and Emotional Problems

11

The changing demographics of American society have received a great deal of attention in recent years. As the population ages, the overall number of elderly persons with mental disorders, particularly anxiety and mood disorders, will increase. Older adults with mental health problems are likely to have relatively longer life spans in the future due to expected advances in treatments and healthier aging lifestyles. Mental health problems will demand more attention from providers to minimize their effects on disability, the use of health care services, and the quality of life for older adults and caregivers. This chapter presents the current state of knowledge on mental disorders of late life, focusing on prevalence, consequences, and effective evidence-based treatments.

Common mental disorders in late life include anxiety disorders and mood disorders such as depression. The development of schizophrenia in late life is less common, but a significant number of persons diagnosed with these disorders as young adults do age (Jeste & Nasrallah, 2003). Suicide among the elderly, particularly among men, is an epidemic in our society. Older men (80+) take their own lives 4 to 6 times the rate of women (Scocco & DeLeo, 2002). Depression, isolation, loneliness, lack of social supports, and declining physical disabilities are some of the probable factors.

Older adults are seriously underserved by mental health service systems across all care settings. Current estimates of the incidence of mental illness among older persons range from 15% to 25% (Gallo & Lebowitz, 1999), yet only 2.5% receive assistance from traditional mental health services and another 2% receive help for mental health problems from their primary care physician (Schulberg, Pilkonos, & Houck, 1998). Research suggests that the rate of emotional disorders among the baby boomers exceeds the rate among the current cohort of older persons (Koenig, George, & Schneider, 1994). The large anticipated growth in the number of older persons makes the provision of mental health services to older adults increasingly important. Combining this growth with an increased rate of emotional disorders magnifies the problem.

The provision of mental health care to older adults with severe mental disorders poses a unique set of challenges to service providers. Barriers to the provision of care exist at both the individual and system levels. Many older adults are reluctant to seek mental health services due to stigma, denial of problems, access barriers, language barriers, or a lack of culturally appropriate programs. Sometimes older adults do not receive appropriate care when they do seek help due to fragmented mental health services, or gaps in services. Moreover, there is a critical shortage of professional staff trained in the geriatric mental health field.

LATE-LIFE DEPRESSION

Depression is the most well-researched psychological problem of later life. Evidence is clear that late-life depression is one of the most common mental disorders to present in primary care settings (Lyness, King, Cox, Yoediono, & Caine, 1999; Reynolds & Kupfer, 1999). According to the Surgeon General's Mental Health Report, depression in older adults leads to physical, mental, and social dysfunction (U.S. Department of Health and Human Services [DHHS], 1999). Nearly 5 million of the 31 million Americans over 65 suffer from clinically significant depressive syndromes. The prevalence of major depression increases as one moves from community settings (1% to 3%) to primary care (5% to 9%), to institutional settings such as nursing homes (12% to 30%; Hendrie et al., 1995; Unützer et al., 1997; Unützer, Katon, Sullivan, & Miranda, 1999). Rates of depression among medically ill elderly range from 10% to 43% (Peterson, Williams-Russo, & Charlson, 1996; Steffens et al., 2000; Willams-Russo, Sharrock, & Mattis, 1995).

Primary care and home care services are essential to maintaining elders with disability in the community and reducing their hospitalization and nursing home use. Compared with the general elderly population, home care recipients are older, more socially isolated, more likely to be women, and more likely to have high rates of physical illness and disability and depression (Banerjee, 1993). The Cornell Institute of Geriatric Psychiatry at Weill Medical College estimated a prevalence of current *Diagnostic and Statistical Manual of Mental Disorders IV* (*DSM-IV*) major depression at 13.7% in a probability sample (N=539) of older (age ≥ 65) new patients from a home care agency (Bruce et al., 2002). These researchers found that depression was highly prevalent, characterized by symptoms and various conditions (functional disability, cognitive impairment, and comorbid vascular disease) associated with poor outcomes (Alexopoulos et al., 1996). Other researchers have estimated a prevalence of depressive symptoms at 27.5% in a probability sample (N=618) of older (age ≥ 65) community-dwelling persons (Gellis et al., 2004). However, few elderly receive appropriate treatment of depression. For instance, in two stud-

ies, only 21% (E, L. Brown, McAvay, Raue, Moses, & Bruce, 2003) and 16% (Banerjee, Shamash, Macdonald, & Mann, 1996) received treatment.

The older person, treating physician, and health care organizational factors interact to impede the detection and treatment of depression, particularly among older clients (Klinkman, 1997; Meyers, 1996; Schulberg, Magruder, & deGruy, 1996). From a biopsychosocial framework, the complexity of depression is reflected by variability in onset, presentation, and course, as well as functional disability, negative life events, and medical comorbidity. The heterogeneity of depression coupled with physical and cognitive impairment, social vulnerabilities, and various medical conditions prevalent in health care make it more difficult for accurate assessment, diagnosis, and treatment in the elderly population. Older patients are less likely to voluntarily report affective symptoms of depression (Lyness et al., 1995). They are more likely to ascribe symptoms of depression to a physical illness (Knauper & Wittchen, 1994). Depressed older adults of various ethnic backgrounds are less likely to use specialty care and more likely to use the general health care system (S. L. Brown et al., 1995; Unützer et al., 1997).

Comorbidity of Depression and Suicide in Older Adults

The consequences of depression in later life are potentially serious. Depressive disorders can be persistent (Unützer et al., 1997, 1999), intermittent, and/or recurrent (Little et al., 1998) and result in significant physical and psychological comorbidity and functional impairment (Katon, Lin, Von Korff, & Bush, 1994) that negatively influences the course of depression (Sherbourne & Wells, 1997).

Depression with physical illness increases levels of functional disability (Alexopoulos et al., 1996), use of health services (Beekman, Deeg, Braam, Smit, & Van-Tilburg, 1997; Saravay, Pollack, Steinberg, Weinsched, & Habert, 1996), and health care costs (Callahan, Kesterson, & Tierney, 1997; Simon, Von Korff, & Barlow, 1995), particularly among older adults (Unützer et al., 1997). It also delays or inhibits physical recovery (Covinsky, Fortinsky, Palmer, Kresevic, & Landefeld, 1997; Katz, 1996).

Late-onset, unipolar depression is characteristic of suicides in later life (Bruce et al., 2004; Conwell et al., 1996; Henriksson et al., 1995). Older suicide victims often have had late-onset undetected or untreated depressions, although typically they have had contact with their primary care provider prior to their death (Conwell, 1994; Van Casteren, Van der Veken, Tafforeau, & Van Oyen, 1993), presumably reflecting high rates of comorbid illness (Conwell, Rotenberg, & Caine, 1990) and/or fears of dependency or pain (Duberstein, 1995). Taken altogether, these findings support the importance of treatment of depression in late life. For further discussion of suicide in older adults, see the chapter by Adamek and Yoder-Slater in this section.

Evidence-Based Psychosocial Treatments

Psychosocial interventions have been demonstrated to be effective among the elderly, particularly those who reject medication or who are coping with low social support or stressful situations (Lebowitz et al., 1997). Evidence-based approaches, including structured cognitive-behavioral, interpersonal, and problem-solving treatments (PST), are effective alternatives or adjuncts to medication treatment (DeRubeis, Gelfand, Tang, & Simons, 1999; Gath & Mynors-Wallis, 1997; Hegel, Barrett, Cornell, & Oxman, 2002; Jacobson & Hollon, 1996; Schulberg, Katon, Simon, & Rush, 1998;). There is evidence that psychosocial interventions alone are effective with older populations, including members of ethnic minority groups (Coulehan, Schulberg, Block, Madonia, & Rodriguez, 1997; Mossey, Ying, Bernal, Perez-Stable, 1996; Munoz, Knott, Higgins, & Talerico, 1995). Cognitive therapies, including PST, are particularly promising (McCusker, Cole, Keller, Bellavance, & Berard, 1998; Nezu, 2004; Robinson et al., 1995) among older men and women of diverse ethnic backgrounds (Gil, Wilson, Edens, & Webster, 1996). Patient attitudes and preference for type of treatment has been shown to affect acceptance of and adherence to the prescribed treatment for depression (Schulberg et al., 1996), and the majority of primary care patients prefer counseling over medication (Brody, Khaliq, & Thompson, 1997; Landreville, Landry, Baillargeon, Guerette, & Matteau, 2001).

Brief psychosocial interventions by nonmedical mental health practitioners are effective for medically ill populations (Mynors-Wallis, Gath, Davies, Gray, & Barbour, 1997). Adjunct written educational materials for patients and family members have been shown to improve medication adherence and clinical outcomes (Robinson et al., 1997). P. A. Arean and colleagues (1993) found robust effects in treating elderly

depression using 12 sessions of PST. Some studies have found that 6 sessions of PST are as effective as pharmacotherapy among ambulatory primary care patients with minor and major depression (Hegel et al., 2002; Mynors-Wallis, Gath, Lloyd-Thomas, & Tomlinson, 1995), are modestly effective with older adults with minor depression, and lead to greater improvement in self-reported social adjustment (Mynors-Wallis, Gath, Lloyd-Thomas, & Tomlinson, 1995). PST can also be used by therapists of different theoretical orientations (P. A. Arean et al., 1993; Mynors-Wallis et al., 1997).

Pharmacologic Interventions

During the past two decades, there have been over 30 randomized placebo-controlled clinical trials as well as many comparative trials (das Gupta, 1998; Salzman, Wong, & Wright, 2002) documenting the efficacy and safety of antidepressant medications (tricyclics and selective serotonin reuptake inhibitors [SSRIs]) for older adults with depression. There has been one trial in relatively old medically ill patients randomizing nortriptyline and placebo (Katz, Parmelee, Beaston-Wimmer, & Smith, 1994). This trial generally showed efficacy of nortriptyline but with side effects including orthostatic hypotension. Nortriptyline is effective with older adults (Reynolds, Frank, & Perel, 1995), but it may have intolerable side effects for some. One large efficacy study of fluoxetine showed efficacy but a relatively low response rate (Tollefson, Rampey, Beasley, & Gregory, 1994). Another study demonstrated that fluoxetine was equivalently effective to nortriptyline but with fewer cardiovascular side effects among a sample of late middle-aged and older adults with coexisting cardiovascular disease (Roose et al., 1997). Because the SSRIs appear to be as effective as the older tricyclic antidepressants, their use in treatment in late-life depression may result in improved outcomes due to their lower side effect profile (Schneider, 1996).

Minor Depression

Recently, attention has been given to subthreshold or subsyndromal mental disorders. As a subthreshold disorder, minor depression is viewed as a set of symptoms that does not meet full criteria for a specific depressive disorder, yet the symptoms are associated with clinically significant impairment (Pincus, Davis, & McQueen, 1999). Minor depression is generally defined as the presence of at least two but fewer than five depressive symptoms, including depressed mood or anhedonia during the same 2-week period with no history of major depressive episode or dysthymia but with clinically significant impairment (American Psychiatric Association, 1994). Rates of minor depression range from 10% to 30% in older community-dwelling adults (Hybels, Blazer, & Pieper, 2001) and 5.2% to 8.5% in older primary care patients (Lyness et al., 1999). Minor depression has been found to be associated with an increased risk for mortality in older men and has a relatively high prevalence in some ethnic groups (Penninx, 1999). As many as 15% of older Latinos, 12% of older Asian Americans, and 10% of older African Americans meet criteria for minor depression (A. Arean & Alvadrez, 2001). Cognitive-behavioral, interpersonal and problem-solving practice models appear to be promising treatments for older adults with minor depression.

Importance of Depression Screening

Much effort has been expended trying to improve the psychiatric skills of primary care physicians but with only modest effects (Lin et al., 1997; Rihmer, Rutz, & Pihlgren, 1995). Integration of specialty mental health care within primary care and system of care enhancements are found to be more effective (Meyers, 1996). Flaherty and colleagues (1998) found that a collaborative management home care intervention for depression resulted in lower hospitalization rates (23.5%) compared to a historical control group (40.6%). A randomized controlled trial with blind follow-up 6 months after recruitment found that psychogeriatric team home care versus usual primary care improved depressive outcomes for 58% versus 25% of people 65 and over (Banerjee, et al., 1996).

Leading researchers cite the need for future studies to address critical questions about feasibility, generalizability, and cost of treatment for depression in home health and primary care systems (Bruce et al., 2002; Katon et al., 1997; Schulberg et al., 1996); use of brief intervention models by nonphysicians (Brown & Schulberg, 1995); the management of detected patients (Coyne, Schwenk, & Fechner-Bates, 1995); and ways to improve access to care among low-income populations (Miranda et al., 2003). See chapter by Adamek and Yoder-Slater (this volume) for information on depression assessment scales.

ANXIETY DISORDERS IN LATER LIFE

Anxiety is defined as a subjective state of internal discomfort reflecting autonomic nervous system arousal. Anxiety becomes constructed as an emotional problem in the following situations:

- It is experienced with great frequency and intensity.
- It interferes with psychosocial functioning.
- The response is out of proportion to the stimulus.

Psychological and physical symptoms may include reduced concentration, impaired attention, impaired memory, anxious thoughts, fears, cardiac palpitations, respiratory problems, and motor, muscular, and gastric problems. *DSM-IV-TR* anxiety disorders include general anxiety disorder, panic disorder, phobias, posttraumatic stress disorder, and obsessive-compulsive disorder.

Research suggests that clinically significant anxiety symptoms affect as many as 20% of older adults living in the community. The prevalence of anxiety disorders among older adults is a serious public health issue in the United States, yet they remain underdiagnosed and undertreated. Older adults with anxiety disorders are less likely than older adults with depression or any other mental disorder to receive treatment from a mental health specialist.

Anxiety disorders are often associated with common age-related medical and chronic conditions such as asthma, thyroid disease, coronary artery disease, dementia, and sensory loss. Unfortunately, anxiety in later life has been identified as a risk factor for greater disability among older adults in general and has also been associated with less successful recruitment into and outcomes of geriatric rehabilitation services. Researchers and practitioners are beginning to recognize that aging and anxiety are not mutually exclusive: Anxiety is as common in the old as in the young, although how and when it appears is distinctly different in older adults.

Recognizing Anxiety in Older Adults

Recognizing an anxiety disorder in an older person poses several challenges. Aging brings with it a higher prevalence of certain medical conditions, realistic concern about physical problems, and higher use of prescription medications. As a result, separating a medical condition from physical symptoms of an anxiety disorder is more complicated in the older adult. Diagnosing anxiety in individuals with dementia can be difficult, too: Agitation typical of dementia may be difficult to separate from anxiety; impaired memory may be interpreted as a sign of anxiety or dementia, and fears may be excessive or realistic depending on the person's situation.

Prevalence of Anxiety Disorders in Later Life

Anxiety disorders appear to be the most common class of psychiatric disorder among older people, more prevalent than depression or severe cognitive impairment (Beekman et al., 1998). Prevalence rates range from 0.7% to 18.6% for all anxiety disorders of individuals at least 65 years and older, with phobias and generalized anxiety disorder (GAD) most common (Flint, 1994). Other researchers summarized the prevalence of various anxiety disorders in older community-based epidemiological samples as follows: phobias, including agoraphobia and social phobia, 0.7% to 12.0%; GAD, 1.1% to 7.1%; obsessive-compulsive disorder, 0.1% to 1.5%; and panic disorder, 0.0% to 0.3% (Krasucki, Howard, & Mann, 1998).

The prevalence of clinically significant anxiety, including symptoms that do not meet criteria for a specific disorder (subthreshold anxiety syndrome), may be as high as 20% among older adults (Beekman et al., 1998). This includes anxiety symptoms associated with common medical conditions such as asthma, thyroid disease, coronary artery disease, and dementia, as well as adjustment disorders following significant late-life stressors such as bereavement or caregiving. There is also controversy over whether the prevalence of anxiety has been accurately determined in older adults, because *DSM-IV* criteria may not apply as well, and the clinical presentation of anxiety in late life may be more likely to include depressive symptoms (Fuentes & Cox, 1997).

Consequences of Anxiety in Later Life

Anxiety symptoms and disorders are associated with increased disability, lower levels of well-being, and inappropriate use of medical services among older adults (De Beurs et al., 1999). Primary care patients with untreated anxiety report functioning and well-being scores within ranges characteristic of patients with chronic physical diseases (Fifer et al., 1994). Comorbid medical conditions such as hypoglycemia, hypertension, and coronary heart disease can be worsened through chronic stress and anxiety (Hersen & Van Hasselt, 1992). Compared with men reporting no symptoms of anxiety, men in the Normative Aging Study reporting two or more anxiety symptoms had elevated risk of fatal coronary heart disease (Kawachi, Sparrow, Vokonas, & Weiss, 1994). Higher levels of anxiety have been associated with greater use of pain-relieving medications and more postoperative disability days for surgical patients (Taenzer, Melzack, & Jeans, 1986). Anxiety was also related to pain in a sample of nursing home residents (Casten, Parmelee, Kleban, Lawton, & Katz, 1995).

Pharmacological Treatment for Anxiety Disorders

Anxiolytic medications, including the benzodiazepines, are the most common treatment for late-life anxiety (Kennedy, 2000). Epidemiological data suggest that benzodiazepine use among the elderly is approximately 14%, higher than the rates for younger adults (Swartz et al., 1991). Benzodiazepines and tricyclic antidepressants have been associated with increased risk of hip fracture (Ray, Griffin, Schaffner, Baugh, & Melton, 1987). Benzodiazepines can impair memory and other cognitive functions and can also cause tolerance and withdrawal, interactions with other drugs, and toxicity (Krasucki, Howard, & Mann, 1999).

Other medications, such as SSRIs, are often used to treat anxiety in later life because they have a lower side effect profile. However, SSRIs have not completely replaced benzodiazepines as a treatment for anxiety in older people. Benzodiazepine use among older adults decreased somewhat over a 10-year period in one recent investigation, although approximately 10% of those over the age of 65 were still taking benzodiazepines in 1996 (Blazer, Hybels, Simonsick, & Hanlon, 2000).

Psychosocial Interventions for Anxiety Disorders in Later Life

Relatively few studies have explored the treatment of anxiety in older adults (Krasucki et al., 1999; Stanley & Beck, 2000). Most have used community or senior center volunteers. For example, DeBerry and colleagues (DeBerry, 1982; DeBerry, Davis, & Reinhard, 1989) found significant effects on subjective anxiety for relaxation and relaxation with meditation over cognitive restructuring and pseudo-relaxation conditions. These gains were maintained at 1-year follow-up. Scogin and his colleagues (Scogin, Rickard, Keith, Wilson, & McElreath, 1992) compared the efficacy of four sessions of individual progressive relaxation (involving tensing and releasing muscle groups) or imaginal relaxation (no tensing required) to a wait-list control condition among a group of older adult volunteers who reported subjective tension or anxiety. Both active conditions significantly reduced state, but not trait, anxiety and miscellaneous psychological symptomatology relative to the control condition; neither active condition was superior to the other.

Barrowclough and colleagues (2001) reported on a randomized trial of individual, home-delivered cognitive-behavioral treatment (CBT) versus supportive counseling. Most of the sample (51%) had panic disorder, whereas 2% had social phobia, 19% had GAD, and 28% had anxiety disorder not otherwise specified. The CBT for GAD consisted of 8 to 12 one-hour sessions over a 16-week period and included the following components: psychoeducation, challenging dysfunctional cognitions and maladaptive behaviors, addressing metabeliefs about the worry process (Wells, 1997), and relapse prevention. Results provided evidence for the superiority of CBT on self-ratings of anxiety and depression, with better performance for CBT on most measures across a 12-month follow-up period.

PSYCHOTIC DISORDERS IN LATER LIFE

Psychotic disorders such as schizophrenia are among the most costly medical disorders (Cuffel, Alford, Fischer, & Owen, 1996). The high cost of care in nursing homes, state hospitals, and general hospitals contributes to the greater economic burden associated with late-life psychotic disorders. Schizophrenia is generally thought of as an illness of young adulthood, yet it can both extend into and first appear in later life. Diagnostic criteria for schizophrenia are the same across the life span, and *DSM-IV* places no restrictions on age of onset for a diagnosis to be made. Symptoms include hallucinations, delusions, disorganized speech, disorganized or catatonic behavior ("positive" symptoms), as well as affective flattening and avolition ("negative" symptoms).

Prevalence of Psychotic Disorders in Late Life

Although it is estimated that 80% of older adults diagnosed with schizophrenia developed the disorders as young adults (early onset), about 20% developed schizophrenia in middle-age (late onset; Howard, Rabins, Seeman, & Jeste, 2000). Most older adults with schizophrenia (85%) are living in the community (Cohen et al., 2000). One-year prevalence of schizophrenia among those 65 years or older is estimated at around 0.6%, about half the 1-year prevalence of the 1.3% that is estimated for the population age 18 to 54 (Howard, Rabins, Seeman, & Jeste, 2000).

Studies have compared patients with late-onset (age at onset 45 years or older) schizophrenia and similarly aged patients with earlier onset of schizophrenia (Jeste et al., 1997); both were very similar in terms of genetic risk, clinical presentation, treatment response, and course. Patients with late-onset schizophrenia were more likely to be women in whom paranoia was a predominant feature of the illness. Patients with late-onset schizophrenia had less impairment in specific neurocognitive areas of learning and abstraction/cognitive flexibility and required lower doses of neuroleptic medications for management of their psychotic symptoms. These disparities between patients with early- and late-onset illness suggest that there might be neurobiological differences mediating the onset of symptoms (Jeste et al., 1997).

Treatment of Schizophrenia in Later Life

The primary treatment of schizophrenia in later life consists of long-term use of antipsychotic medications (neuroleptics) such as haloperidol, proven effective in managing the positive symptoms (such as delusions and hallucinations) of many older patients, but these medications have a high risk of potentially disabling and persistent side effects (Jeste, Dunn, & Lindamer, 2004). Studies with mostly younger schizophrenia patients suggest that the newer, atypical antipsychotics, such as clozapine, risperidone, olanzapine, and quetiapine, may be effective in treating those patients previously unresponsive to traditional neuroleptics. They also are associated with a lower risk of side effects (Jeste & Dolder, 2003). Two barriers to the widespread use of atypical antipsychotic medications in older adults are the lack of large-scale studies to demonstrate the effectiveness and safety of these medications in older patients with multiple medical conditions, and the higher cost of these medications relative to traditional neuroleptics (Thomas & Lewis, 1998).

SUMMARY

Mental health problems such as depression and anxiety disorders are associated with increased disability, lower levels of well-being, and increased use of medical services among older adults. Geriatric social work practitioners require specialized skill sets in assessing and managing mental disorders of late life. In examining the scientific evidence supporting routine screening for depression, for example, practitioners would be advised to review the following criteria: (1) The incidence is sufficiently high in the older adult population; (2) mental health problems have a significant impact on the older person's life; (3) effective treatments are available; (4) valid and cost-effective screening tests are available; and (5) adverse effects of screening should be acceptable to patients and clinicians. The goal of screening is early identification and thus prevention through early intervention to reduce costs and improve the quality for life for older adults. The implications of not detecting the possibility of mental disorders in the elderly are serious.

REFERENCES

Alexopoulos, G., Vrontou, C., Kakuma, T., Meyers, B. S., Young, R. C., Klausner, E., et al. (1996). Disability in geriatric depression. *American Journal of Psychiatry, 153*, 877–885.

Arean, A., & Alvarez, J. (2001). Prevalence of mental disorder, subsyndromal disorder and service use in older disadvantaged medical patients. *Interpersonal Journal of Psychiatry in Medicine, 31*(1), 9–24.

Arean, P. A., Perri, M. G., Nezu, A. M., Schein, R. L., Christopher, F., & Joseph, T. X. (1993). Comparative effectiveness of social problem-solving therapy and reminiscence therapy as treatments for depression in older adults. *Journal of Consulting and Clinical Psychology, 61*, 1003–1010.

Banerjee, S. (1993). Prevalence and recognition of psychiatric disorder in the elderly clients of a community care service. *International Journal of Geriatric Psychiatry, 8*, 125–131.

Banerjee, S., Shamash, K., Macdonald, A. J. D., & Mann, A. H. (1996). Randomised controlled trial of effect of intervention by psychogeriatric team on depression

in frail elderly people at home. *British Medical Journal, 313*, 1058–1061.

Barrowclough, C., King, P., Colville, J., Russell, E., Burns, A., & Tarrier, N. (2001). A randomized trial of the effectiveness of cognitive-behavioral therapy and supportive counseling for anxiety symptoms in older adults. *Journal of Consulting and Clinical Psychology, 69*, 756–762.

Beekman, A. T. F., Bremmer, M. A., Deeg, D. J. H., Van Balkom, A. J. L. M., Smit, J. H., De Beurs, E., et al. (1998). Anxiety disorders in later life: A report from the Longitudinal Aging Study Amsterdam. *International Journal of Geriatric Psychiatry, 13*, 717–726.

Beekman, A. T., Deeg, D. J., Braam, A. W., Smit, J. H., & VanTilburg, W. (1997). Consequences of major and minor depression in later life: A study of disability, well-being and service utilization. *Psychological Medicine, 27*, 1397–1409.

Blazer, D., George, L. K., & Hughes, D. (1991). The epidemiology of anxiety disorders: An age comparison. In C. Salzman & B. D. Lebowitz (Eds.), *Anxiety in the elderly: Treatment and research* (pp. 17–30). New York: Springer.

Blazer, D., Hybels, C., Simonsick, E., & Hanlon, J. T. (2000). Sedative, hypnotic, and antianxiety medication use in an aging cohort over ten years: A racial comparison. *Journal of the American Geriatrics Society, 48*, 1073–1079.

Brody, D. S., Khaliq, A., & Thompson, T. (1997). Patient's perspectives on the management of emotional distress in primary care settings. *Journal of General and Internal Medicine, 12*, 403–406.

Brown, C., & Schulberg, H. C. (1995). The efficacy of psychosocial treatments in primary care: A review of randomized clinical trials. *General Hospital Psychiatry, 17*(6), 414–424.

Brown E. L., McAvay, G. J., Raue, P. J., Moses, S., & Bruce, M. L. (2003). Recognition of depression in the elderly receiving homecare services. *Psychiatric Services, 54*(2), 208–213.

Brown, S. L., Salive, M. E., Guralnik, J. M., Pahor, M., Chapman, D. P., & Blazer, D. (1995). Antidepressant use in the elderly: Association with demographic characteristics, health-related factors, and health care utilization. *Journal of Clinical Epidemiology, 48*, 445–453.

Bruce, M. L., McAvay, G. J., Raue, P. J., Brown, E. L., Meyers, B. S., Keohane, D. J., et al. (2002). Major depression in elderly home health care patients. *American Journal of Psychiatry, 159*, 1367–1374.

Bruce, M. L., Ten-Have, T., Reynolds, C., Katz, I., Schulberg, H., Mulsant, B., et al. (2004). Reducing suicidal ideation and depressive symptoms in depressed older primary care patients: A randomized controlled trial. *Journal of the American Medical Association, 291*(9), 1081–1091.

Callahan, C. M., Kesterson, J. G., & Tierney, W. M. (1997). Association of symptoms of depression with diagnostic test charges among older adults. *Annals of Internal Medicine, 126,* 426–432.

Casten, R. J., Parmelee, P. A., Kleban, M. H., Lawton, M. P., & Katz, I. R. (1995). The relationships among anxiety, depression, and pain in a geriatric institutionalized sample. *Pain, 61,* 271–276.

Cohen, C., Gene, G., Blank, K., Gaitz, C., Katz, I., Leuchter, A., et al. (2000). Schizophrenia and older adults: An overview: Directions for research and policy. *American Journal of Geriatric Psychiatry, 8*(1), 19–28.

Conwell, Y. (1994). Suicide in elderly patients. In L. S. Schneider, C. F. Reynolds, B. D. Lebowitz, & A. J. Friedhoff (Eds.), *Diagnosis and treatment of depression in late life* (pp. 397–418). Washington, DC: American Psychiatric Press.

Conwell, Y., Duberstein, P. R., Cox, C., Herrmann, J. H., Forbes, N. T., & Caine, E. D. (1996). Relationships of age and Axis I diagnoses in victims of completed suicide: A psychological autopsy study. *American Journal of Psychiatry, 153,* 1001–1008.

Conwell, Y., Rotenberg, M., & Caine, E. D. (1990). Completed suicide at age 50 and over. *Journal of the American Geriatrics Society, 38,* 640–644.

Coulehan, J. L., Schulberg, H. C., Block, M. R., Madonia, M. J., & Rodriguez, E. (1997). Treating depressed primary care patients improves their physical, mental, and social functioning. *Archives of Internal Medicine, 157,* 1113–1120.

Covinsky, K. E., Fortinsky, R. H., Palmer, R. M., Kresevic, D. M., & Landefeld, C. S. (1997). Relation between symptoms of depression and health status outcomes in acutely ill hospitalized older persons. *Annals of Internal Medicine, 126,* 417–425.

Coyne, J. C., Schwenk, T. L., & Fechner-Bates, S. (1995). Nondetection of depression by primary care physicians reconsidered. *General Hospital Psychiatry, 17,* 3–12.

Cuffel, B., Alford, J., Fischer, E., & Owen, R. (1996). Awareness of illness in schizophrenia and outpatient treatment adherence. *Journal of Nervous and Mental Disease, 184*(11), 653–659.

Das Gupta, K. (1998). Treatment of depression in elderly patients: Recent advances. *Archives of Family Medicine, 7,* 274–280.

DeBerry, S. (1982). The effects of meditation-relaxation on anxiety and depression in a geriatric population.

Psychotherapy: Theory, Research, and Practice, 19, 512–521.

DeBerry, S., Davis, S., & Reinhard, K. E. (1989). A comparison of mediation-relaxation and cognitive behavioral techniques for reducing anxiety and depression in a geriatric population. *Journal of Geriatric Psychiatry, 22,* 231–247.

De Beurs, E., Beekman, A. T. F., van Balkom, A. J. L. M., Deeg, D. J. H., van Dyck, R., & van Tilburg, W. (1999). Consequences of anxiety in older persons: Its effect on disability, well-being and use of health services. *Psychological Medicine, 29,* 583–593.

DeRubeis, R. J., Gelfand, L. A., Tang, T. Z. & Simons, A. D. (1999). Medications versus cognitive behavior therapy for severely depressed outpatients: Mega-analysis of four randomized comparisons. *American Journal of Psychiatry, 156,* 1007–1013.

Duberstein, P. R. (1995). Openness to experience and completed suicide across the second half of life. *International Psychogeriatrics, 7,* 183–198.

Fifer, S. K., Mathias, S. D., Patrick, D. L., Mazonson, P. D., Lubeck, D. P., & Buesching, D. P. (1994). Untreated anxiety among adult primary care patients in a health maintenance organization. *Archives of General Psychiatry, 51,* 740–750.

Flaherty, J. H., McBride, M., Marzouk, S., Miller, D. K., Chien, N., Hanchett, M., et al. (1998). Decreasing hospitalization rates for older home care patients with symptoms of depression. *Journal of the American Geriatrics Society, 46,* 31–38.

Flint, A. J. (1994). Epidemiology and comorbidity of anxiety disorders in the elderly. *American Journal of Psychiatry, 151,* 640–649.

Fuentes, K., & Cox, B. J. (1997). Prevalence of anxiety disorders in elderly adults: A critical analysis. *Journal of Behavioural Therapy and Experimental Psychiatry, 28,* 269–279.

Gallo, J. J., & Lebowitz, B. D. (1999). The epidemiology of common late-life mental disorders in the community: Themes for the new century. *Psychiatric Services, 50,* 1158–1166.

Gath, D., & Mynors-Wallis, L. (1997). Problem-solving treatment in primary care. In D. Clark & C. Fairburn (Eds.), *Science and practice of cognitive behavior therapy* (pp. 415–431). London: Oxford University Press.

Gellis, Z. D., McGinty, J., Burton, J., Jordon, C., & Tierney, L. (2004). Depression in older adults: Screening, assessment, and treatment. Paper presented at the 1st annual Geriatric Mental Health Conference: Mental Health and Aging in Place, University of Albany, Albany, NY.

Gil, K., Wilson, J., Edens, J., & Webster, D. (1996). Effects of cognitive coping skills training on coping strategies and experimental pain sensitivity in African American adults with sickle cell disease. *Health-Psychology, 15*(1), 3–10.

Hegel, M., Barrett, J., Cornell, J., & Oxman, T. (2002). Predictors of response to problem-solving treatment of depression in primary care. *Behavior Therapy, 33*(4), 511–527.

Hendrie, H. C., Callahan, C. M., Levitt, E. E., Hui, S. L., Musick, B., Austrom, M. G., et al. (1995). Prevalence rates of major depressive disorders: The effects of varying the diagnostic criteria in an older primary care population. *American Journal of Geriatric Psychiatry, 5*, 119–131.

Henriksson, M. M., Marttunen, M. J., Isometsä, E. T., Heikkinen, M. E., Aro, H. M., Kuoppasalmi, K. I., et al. (1995). Mental disorders in elderly suicide. *International Psychogeriatrics, 7*, 275–286.

Hersen, M., & Van Hasselt, V. B. (1992). Behavioral assessment and treatment of anxiety in the elderly. *Clinical Psychology Review, 12*, 619–640.

Howard, R., Rabins, P., Seeman, M., & Jeste, D. (2000). Late onset schizophrenia and very late onset schizophrenia-like psychosis: An international consensus. *American Journal of Psychiatry, 157*(2), 172–178.

Hybels, C. Blazer, D., & Pieper, C. (2001). Toward a threshold for subthreshold depression: An analysis of correlates of depression by severity of symptoms using data from an elderly community sample. *Gerontologist, 41*(3), 357–365.

Jacobson, J. S., & Hollon, S. D. (1996). Cognitive-behavior therapy versus pharmacotherapy: Now that the jury's returned its verdict, it's time to present the rest of the evidence. *Journal of Consulting and Clinical Psychology, 64*, 74–80.

Jeste, D., & Dolder, C. (2003). Medication-induced movement disorders. In A. Tasman, J. Lieberman, & J. Kay (Eds.), *Psychiatry* (2nd ed., pp. 1657–1676). London: Wiley.

Jeste, D., Dunn, L., & Lindamer, L. (2004). Psychoses. In J. Sadavoy, L. F. Javik, G. T. Grossberg, & B. S. Meyers (Eds.), *Comprehensive textbook of geriatric psychiatry* (3rd ed., pp. 655–685). New York: American Association of Geriatric Psychiatry.

Jeste, D., & Nasrallah, H. (2003). Schizophrenia and aging: No more dearth of data? *American Journal of Geriatric Psychiatry, 11*(6), 584–587.

Jeste, D., Symonds, L., Harris, M., Paulson, J., Palmer, B., & Heaton, R. (1997). Nondementia nonpraecox de-

mentia praecox? Late-onset schizophrenia. *American Journal of Geriatric Psychiatry, 5*(4) 302–317.

Katon, W., Lin, E., von Korff, M., Bush, T. (1994). The predictors of persistence of depression in primary care. *Journal of Affective Disorders, 31*(20), 81–90.

Katon, W., Von Korff, M., Lin, E., Simon, G., Walker, E., Bush, T., et al. (1997). Collaborative management to achieve depression treatment guidelines. *Journal of Clinical Psychiatry, 58*(Suppl. 2), 20–23.

Katz, I. R. (1996). On the inseparability of mental and physical health in aged persons: Lessons from depression and medical comorbidity. *American Journal of Geriatric Psychiatry, 4*, 1–16.

Katz, I. R., Parmelee, P., Beaston-Wimmer, P., & Smith, B. (1994). Association of antidepressants and other medications with mortality in the residential-care elderly. *Journal of Geriatric Psychiatry and Neurology, 7*(4), 221–226.

Kawachi, I., Sparrow, D., Vokonas, P. S., & Weiss, S. T. (1994). Symptoms of anxiety and risk of coronary heart disease: The Normative Aging Study. *Circulation, 90*, 2225–2229.

Kennedy, G. (2000). *Geriatric mental health care.* New York: Guilford Press.

Klinkman, M. (1997). Competing demands in psychosocial care: A model for the identification and treatment of depressive disorders in primary care. *General Hospital Psychiatry, 19*, 98–111.

Knauper, B., & Wittchen, H. (1994). Diagnosing major depression in the elderly: Evidence for response bias in standardized diagnostic interviews? *Journal of Psychiatric Research, 28*, 147–164.

Koenig, H., George, L., & Schneider, R. (1994). Mental health care for older adults in the year 2020. *Gerontologist, 34*(5), 674–679.

Krasucki, C., Howard, R., & Mann, A. (1998). The relationship between anxiety disorders and age. *International Journal of Geriatric Psychiatry, 13*, 79–99.

Krasucki, C., Howard, R., & Mann, A. (1999). Anxiety and its treatment in the elderly. *International Psychogeriatrics, 11*, 25–45.

Landreville, P., Landry, J., Baillargeon, L., Guerette, A., & Matteau, E. (2001). Older adults' acceptance of psychological and pharmacological treatments for depression. *Journal of Gerontology, 56B*(5), 285–291.

Lebowitz, B. D., Pearson, J. L., Schneider, L. S., Reynolds, C. F., Alexopoulow, G. S., Bruce, M. L., et al. (1997). Diagnosis and treatment of depression in late life: Consensus statement update. *Journal of the American Medical Association, 278*, 1186–1190.

Lin, E., Katon, W., Simon, G., VonKorff, M., Bush, T., Rutter, C., et al. (1997). Achieving guidelines for the treatment of depression in primary care: Is physician education enough? *Medical Care, 35,* 831–842.

Little, J., Reynolds, C., Dew, M., Frank, E., Begley, A., Miller, M., et al. (1998). How common is resistance to treatment in recurrent, nonpsychotic geriatric depression? *American Journal of Psychiatry, 155,* 1035–1038.

Lyness, J. M., Cox, C., Curry, J., Conwell, Y., King, D. A., & Caine, E. (1995). Older age and the underreporting of depressive symptoms. *Journal of the American Geriatrics Society, 43,* 216–221.

Lyness, J. M., King, D., Cox, C., Yoediono, Z., & Caine, E. (1999). The importance of subsyndromal depression in older primary care patients: Prevalence and associated functional disability. *Journal of the American Geriatrics Society, 47,* 647–652.

McCusker, J., Cole, M., Keller, E., Bellavance, F., & Berard A. (1998). Effectiveness of treatments of depression in older ambulatory patients. *Archives of Internal Medicine, 158,* 705–712.

Menninger, J. A. (2002). Assessment and treatment of alcoholism and substance-related disorders in the elderly. *Bulletin of the Menninger Clinic, 66*(2), 166–184.

Meyers, B. (1996). Psychiatric interventions to improve primary care diagnosis and treatment of depression. *American Journal of Geriatric Psychiatry, 4*(Suppl. 1), S91–S95.

Miranda, J., Chung, J., Green, B., Krupnick, J., Siddique, J., & Revicki, D. (2003). Treating depression in predominantly low-income young minority women: A randomized control trial. *Journal of the American Medical Association, 290*(1), 57–65.

Moore, A. A., & Hays, R. D. (1999). Drinking habits among older persons: Findings from the NHANES I Epidemiologic Follow-up Study (1982–84). National Health and Nutrition Examination Survey. *Journal of the American Geriatrics Society, 47*(4), 412–416.

Moss, R. H., Mortens, M. A., & Brennan, P. L. (1993). Patterns of diagnosis and treatment among late-middle-aged and older substance abuse patients. *Journal of Studies in Alcohol, 54,* 479–487.

Mossey, J., Knott, K., Higgins, M., & Talerico, K. (1996). Effectiveness of a psychosocial intervention, interpersonal counseling for subdynamic depression in mentally ill elderly. *Journals of Gerontology, 51A*(4), M172–M178.

Munoz, R., Ying, Y., Bernal, G., Perez-Stable, E. (1995). Prevention of depression in primary care patients: A randomized control trial. *American Journal of Community Psychology, 23*(2), 199–222.

Mynors-Wallis, L. M., Gath, D., Davies, I., Gray, A., & Barbour, F. (1997). Randomised controlled trial and cost analysis of problem-solving treatment given by community nurses for emotional disorders in primary care. *British Journal of Psychiatry, 170,* 113–119.

Mynors-Wallis, L. M., Gath, D. H., Lloyd-Thomas, A. R., & Tomlinson, D. (1995). Randomised controlled trial comparing problem-solving treatment with amitriptyline and placebo for major depression in primary care. *British Medical Journal, 310,* 441–445.

Nezu, A. (2004). Problem solving and behavior therapy revisited. *Behavior Therapy, 35,* 1–33.

Penninx, B. (1999). Minor and major depression and the risk of death in older persons. *Archives of General Psychiatry, 56,* 889–895.

Peterson, J. C., Williams-Russo, P., Charlson, M., et al. (1996). Longitudinal course of new-onset depression after cardiac bypass surgery. *International, Journal of Psychiatry Medicine, 26,* 37–41.

Pincus, H., Davis, W., & McQueen, L. (1999). Subthreshold mental disorders: A review and synthesis of studies on minor depression and other brand names. *British Journal of Psychiatry, 174,* 288–296.

Ray, W. A., Griffin, M. R., Schaffner, W., Baugh, D. K., & Melton, L. J. (1987). Psychotropic drug use and the risk of hip fracture. *New England Journal of Medicine, 316,* 363–369.

Reynolds, C. F., Frank, E., Perel, J. (1995). Maintenance therapies for late life recurrent major depression: Research and review circa 1995. *International Psychogeriatrics, 7*(Suppl. 1), 27–40.

Reynolds, C. F., & Kupfer, D. (1999). Depression and aging: A look to the future. *Psychiatric Services, 50*(9), 1167–1172.

Rihmer, Z., Rutz, W., & Pihlgren, H. (1995). Depression and suicide on Gotland: An intensive study of all suicides before and after a depression-training programme for general practitioners. *Journal of Affective Disorders, 35,* 147–152.

Robinson, P., Bush, T., VonKorff, M., Katon, W., Lin, W., Simon, G., et al. (1995). Primary care physician use of cognitive behavioral techniques with depressed patients. *Journal of Family Practice, 40,* 352–357.

Robinson, P., Katon, W., vonKorff, M., Bush, T., Simon, G., Lin, E. et al. (1997). The education of depressed primary care patients: What do patients think of interactive booklets and a video? *Journal of Family Practice, 44,* 562–571.

Roose, S., Glassman, A., Attia, E., Woodring, S., Giardina, E., & Bigger, T. (1997). Cardiovascular effects of fluoxetine, in depressed patients with heart disease. *American Journal of Psychiatry, 155*(5), 660–665.

Salzman, C., Wong, E., & Wright, B. C. (2002). Drug and ECT treatment of depression in the elderly, 1996–

2001: A literature review. *Biological Psychiatry, 52*(3), 265–284.

Saravay, S. M., Pollack, S., Steinberg, M. D., Weinsched, B., & Habert, M. (1996). Four-year follow-up of the influence of psychological comorbidity on medical rehospitalization. *American Journal of Psychiatry, 153,* 397–403.

Schneider, L. (1996). Pharmacological considerations in the treatment of late-life depression. *American Journal of Geriatric Psychiatry, 4*(Suppl. 1), S51–S65.

Schulberg, H. C., Katon, W., Simon, G., & Rush, A. (1998). Treating major depression in primary care practice: An update of the Agency for Health Care Policy and Research practice guidelines. *Archives of General Psychiatry, 55*(2), 1121–1127.

Schulberg, H. C., Magruder, K., & deGruy, F. (1996). Major depression in primary medical care practice: Research trends and future priorities. *General Hospital Psychiatry, 18*(6), 395–406.

Schulberg, H., Pilkonis, P., & Houck, P. (1998). The severity of major depression and choice of treatment in primary care practice. *Journal of Consulting and Clinical Psychology, 66,* 932–938.

Scocco, P., & DeLeo, D. (2002). One year prevalence of death thoughts, suicide ideation and behaviors in the elderly population. *International Journal of Geriatric Psychiatry, 17*(9), 842–846.

Scogin, F., Rickard, H. C., Keith, S., Wilson, J., & McElreath, L. (1992). Progressive and imaginal relaxation training for elderly persons with subjective anxiety. *Psychology and Aging, 7,* 419–424.

Sherbourne, C., & Wells, K. (1997). Course of depression in patients with comorbid anxiety disorders. *Journal of Affective Disorders, 43*(3), 245–250.

Simon, G. E., VonKorff, M., & Barlow, W. (1995). Health care costs of primary care patients with recognized depression. *Archives of General Psychiatry, 52,* 850–856.

Stanley, M. A., & Beck, J. G. (2000). Anxiety disorders. *Clinical Psychology Review, 20,* 731–754.

Steffens, D., Skoog, I., Norton, M., Hart, A., Tschanz, J., Plassman, B., et al. (2000). Prevalence of depression and its treatment in an elderly population: The Cache County Study. *Archives of General Psychiatry, 57*(6), 601–607.

Swartz, M., Landerman, R., George, L. K., Melville, M. L., Blazer, D., & Smith, K. (1991). Benzodiazepine anti-anxiety agents: Prevalence and correlates of use in a southern community. *American Journal of Public Health, 81,* 592–596.

Taenzer, P., Melzack, R., & Jeans, M. E. (1986). Influence of psychological factors on postoperative pain, mood and analgesic requirements. *Pain, 24,* 331–342.

Thomas, C., & Lewis, S. (1998). Which atypical antipsychotic? *British Journal of Psychiatry, 172,* 106–109.

Tollefson, G., Rampey, A., Beasley, C., Gregory, G. (1994). Absence of a relationship between adverse events and suicidality during pharmacotherapy for depression. *Journal of Clinical Psychopharmacology, 14*(3), 163–169.

Unützer, J., Katon, W., Sullivan, M., & Miranda, J. (1999). Treating depressed older adults in primary care: Narrowing the gap between efficacy and effectiveness. *Millbank Quarterly, 77,* 225–256.

Unützer, J., Patrick, D. L., Simon, G., Grembowski, D., Walker, E., Rutter, C., et al. (1997). Depressive symptoms and the cost of health services in HMO patients age 65 years and older: A 4-year prospective study. *Journal of the American Medical Association, 277,* 1618–1623.

U.S. Department of Health and Human Services. (1999). Mental health: A report of the surgeon general. Rockville, MD: Author.

Van Casteren, V., Van der Veken, J., Tafforeau, J., & Van Oyen, H. (1993). Suicide and attempted suicide reported by general practitioners in Belgium, 1990–1991. *Acta Psychiatrica Scandinavica, 87,* 451–455.

Wells, A. (1997). *Cognitive therapy of anxiety disorders: A practice conceptual guide.* Whichester, Eng.: Wiley.

Williams-Russo, P., Sharrock, N. E., & Mattis, S. (1995). Cognitive effects after epidural vs. general anesthesia in older adults. *Journal of the American Medical Association, 274,* 44–50.

Alcohol and drug abuse and misuse among older adults are one of the fastest growing public health problems in the United States (U.S. Department of Health and Human Services [DHHS], 1999). The problems, however, remain underdiagnosed and undertreated and have been referred to as an invisible epidemic (Center for Substance Abuse Treatment [CSAT], 1998). With the aging of the baby boomers, a cohort with more liberal attitudes toward substance use than previous cohorts, the problem is expected to increase in the coming years (DHHS, 1999). As with the younger population, the three types of substance abuse among older adults are alcohol abuse, medication abuse and misuse, and illicit drug use.

ALCOHOL ABUSE

Although alcohol abuse declines with age, it is estimated that 4% to 20% of community-dwelling older adults abuse alcohol (Adams, Garry, Rhyne, Hunt, & Goodwin, 1990). According to some reports, 20% of the residents in retirement communities have two or more drinks per day (Gurnack, 1997). The National Institute of Alcohol Abuse and Addictions recommends that older adults consume no more than one drink per day because of age-related physical changes (Dufour, Archer, & Gordis, 1992).

In health care settings, 6% to 11% of older adults exhibit symptoms of alcoholism (Ondus, Hujer, Mann, & Mion, 1999). The rates for alcohol abuse among older adults in psychiatric settings and emergency rooms are 20% and 14%, respectively (CSAT, 1998). In acute care settings, just as many older adults are admitted for alcohol-related problems as for heart attacks (Adams, Yuan, & Barboriak, 1993).

As with younger populations, alcohol abuse and dependence are more common among older men than women. Approximately 4 times the number of older men than women abuse alcohol (CSAT, 1998). Although alcoholism rates are higher for Whites among younger men and women, the rates among older adults are higher among African American men and women and Latino men. Latinas, on the other hand, have much lower rates than Whites or African American women (Helzer, Burnam, & McEvoy, 1991).

Older adults who abuse alcohol can be categorized into early- and late-onset groups (Benshoff, Harrawood, & Koch, 2003). It is estimated that two-thirds of older adults are early-onset drinkers who developed alcohol problems while young (Rigler, 2000). These adults suffer from various physical and psy-

TAZUKO SHIBUSAWA

Older Adults With Substance/Alcohol Abuse Problems

12

chological consequences of long-term alcohol abuse, such as impaired cardiovascular, digestive, neurological, and skeletal functioning (Atkinson, Tolson, & Turner, 1990). Late-onset drinking is often precipitated by life events such as retirement, death of a spouse or partner, loss of status, and chronic health problems as well as loneliness and depression (Atkinson et al., 1990; Rigler, 2000). The prognosis for later-onset drinkers is better than that for early-onset drinkers because they have not suffered from the physical and psychological consequences of long-term abuse (Benshoff et al., 2003).

MISUSE OF PRESCRIPTION AND OVER-THE-COUNTER MEDICATION

Older adults consume large amounts of prescription drugs and over-the-counter (OTC) medications. They are estimated to spend $15 billion annually on prescription drugs, which is 4 times the amount spent by younger populations (DHHS, 1999). An average older patient takes 5.3 prescription medicines per day (Gurnack, Atkinson, & Osgood, 2002). OTCs that are commonly used by older adults include pain relievers, sleeping aids, cold remedies, antacids, laxatives, and vitamins (CSAT, 1998).

When discussing prescription and OTC medication abuse, it is important to distinguish between the terms *misuse* and *abuse*. Misuse refers to the inappropriate use of medications and includes underuse, overuse, and erratic use (DHHS, 1999). Misuse can be caused by difficulties with reading and following prescription labels, keeping track of medications, and taking inappropriate dosages. Vision and hearing loss can increase the misuse of prescription and OTC medication among older adults. Misuse can also be caused by inappropriate prescribing by physicians. Abuse, on the other hand, refers to the use of medication in a way that is nontherapeutic and not for its intended purposes (Ondus et al., 1999). A typical form of abuse occurs when older adults use prescription or OTC medications as a form of self-medication.

Psychoactive drugs tend to be more misused than other medications. Older adults use 2 to 3 times more psychoactive drugs than do younger groups (Sheahan et al., 1995). Benzodiazepines, which are prescribed for conditions such as insomnia, anxiety, and chronic pain, are prescribed widely among older adults. Studies report that 17% to 23% of drugs prescribed to older adults in North America are benzodiazepines (D'Archangelo, 1993). Older women are more likely than men to receive psychoactive drugs, and drug dependence is more common among older women than men (Adams et al., 1990).

ILLICIT DRUG ABUSE AND DEPENDENCE

Older adults use fewer illicit drugs such as marijuana, cocaine, and heroin than younger populations. Recent studies, however, cast doubt on the "maturing-out theory," which contends that people age out of illicit drug use or die prematurely from abuse (Levy, 1998). According to the 2000 National Household Survey on Drug Abuse (NHSDA), 568,000 adults age 55 or older (1% of all older adults in the United States) reported using illicit drugs in 2000 (SAMHSA, 2001). Methadone treatment and needle exchange have added to the longevity of heroin and injection drug users. In addition, there are a number of older adults who start to use crack cocaine for the first time after age 50 (Johnson & Sterk, 2003).

A major concern related to this phenomenon is HIV transmission because sexual risk behavior is a critical exposure category for HIV infection among older injection drug users (Kwiatkowski & Booth, 2003). As mentioned earlier, baby boomers as a cohort are more accepting of illicit drug use (DHHS, 1999) which could result in an increase in illicit drug use and HIV exposure.

EFFECTS OF ALCOHOL AND SUBSTANCE ABUSE ON OLDER ADULTS

Older adults have a decreased tolerance for alcohol and drugs. Their bodies do not absorb food and drugs as well as they did in their younger years. Because of reduced body mass and body water, slowed metabolism, and decreased absorption rate in the gastrointestinal system, alcohol and drugs remain in the body for longer periods of time and at higher rates of concentration (Benshoff et al., 2003). Alcohol, prescription drugs, and illicit drugs have stronger effects on older than younger adults, especially when they are used in combination.

Long-term alcohol use can result in malnutrition, osteoporosis, decreased red blood cell production, increased cancer risk, myopathy, hypertension, hepatitis, pancreatitis, stroke, dementia, and esophagitis/gastritis (Gurnack, 1997). Depression is often comorbid with alcohol and substance abuse; mood and anxiety disorders can be exacerbated by alcohol or drug use. Prescription or OTC medication misuse or combining drugs with alcohol can lead to decreased functional capacity and cognition, including impairment of memory and attention, excessive sedation, delirium, and greater risk for falling (Benshoff et al., 2003). Psychoactive medication when taken with alcohol can have serious consequences. For example, benzodiazepines when mixed with alcohol can result in decreased alertness, impaired judgment, respiratory failure, and falls and accidents (CSAT, 1998).

IDENTIFICATION OF ALCOHOL AND SUBSTANCE ABUSE

Although alcohol abuse by older adults is less prevalent than in younger populations, it is more difficult to detect, particularly because the workplace is where alcohol and drug problems are frequently detected. In particular, older adults who are White, female, or of upper-middle-class background are less likely to be identified by health care providers because they do not fit the stereotype of someone who has an alcohol or drug problem (CSAT, 1998). Other risk factors for alcohol and substance abuse are listed in Table 12.1.

Questions about alcohol and substance use are rarely included in routine intake sessions in health care and social service settings. Symptoms of alcohol and substance abuse often present as age-related problems such as insomnia, gastrointestinal problems, sexual dysfunction, forgetfulness, dementia, and depression, further deterring service providers from exploring the possibilities of alcohol and substance abuse (Ondus et al., 1999; see Table 12.2). The trend toward shorter medical visits and the shortage of providers with training in geriatric medicine also serve as barriers to the detection of alcohol and substance problems (CSAT, 1998).

Patient-related deterrents to identifying alcohol and drug problems in older adults include a lack of awareness or denial on the part of the elder. In addition, older adults in general are reluctant to seek nonmedical help such as counseling and mental health care because of stigma and shame. This reluctance de-

ters older adults with substance abuse problems from accepting referrals for treatment even when made by the provider.

Perhaps not surprisingly, caregivers and health care professionals often shy away from confronting the older adult or referring him or her for treatment. Some believe that older adults should not be forced to give up a life-long habit that is one of the few pleasures left for them to enjoy. They believe that forcing abstinence would be cruel. Another reason for inaction is a mistaken assumption that alcohol and substance abuse treatment is not effective for older adults. Research, however, indicates that older adults have better outcomes for treatment than younger adults (Curtis, Geller, Stokes, Levine, & Moore, 1989).

Screening Instruments

Screening instruments that have been utilized with older adults include the CAGE, the Michigan Alcohol Screening Test–Geriatric Version (MAST-G), and the Alcohol Use Disorders Identification Test (AUDIT; CSAT, 1998). The CAGE (Ewing, 1984) is used commonly in assessment and evaluations and has been used by physicians examining older patients (Fleming, 2001). However, the questions need to be modified when inquiring about prescription of OTC medicine misuse and abuse (CSAT, 1998; see Table 12.3).

The MAST-G includes items that address issues related to aging such as increased drinking following death and losses (Blow et al., 1992). AUDIT is a 10-item survey that measures negative alcohol-related consequences and descriptions of total alcohol consumption. According to research, MAST-G is more sensitive than AUDIT for identifying alcoholism in older adults (Menninger, 2002).

It is important to note that these screening instruments are limited in that they rely on client self-report. Screening questions need to be integrated into health assessments or other forms of assessments in a confidential setting. The questions should be asked in a nonjudgmental manner and as part of a health assessment to lessen the sense of stigma for older adults.

TABLE 12.1. Risk Factors for Alcohol and Substance Abuse Among Older Adults

Depression/anxiety	Homebound	Retirement
Loss and bereavement	Chronic pain	Loss of employment
Social isolation	Loss of physical mobility	New caregiving role
Living alone	Loss of spouse or partner	

TABLE 12.2. Signs of Possible Alcohol and Substance Abuse in Older Adults

Dementia	Depression/anxiety	Mood swings, irritability
Dulling of senses	Recent memory loss	Disorientation
Swelling	Inflammation of joints	Slowed thought process
Indigestion	Malnutrition	Heart disease
Changes in sleep patterns	Changes in eating habits	Lack of energy
Loss of short-term memory	General loss of interest	Social isolation
Unexplained accidents and falls	Self-neglect	Tremors

AGE-SPECIFIC TREATMENT FOR ALCOHOL AND SUBSTANCE ABUSE

Intervention and treatment for alcohol and substance abuse depends on the severity of the problem and includes educational sessions, outpatient care, residential care, and psychiatric hospitalization (DHHS, 1999). It is important that all levels of intervention are tailored to meet the physical, psychological, and social needs of older adults (Schonfeld & Dupree, 1995; Zimberg, 1996). Programs serving older adults should include the following:

1. Identify and address stressors that are related to the aging process, such as loss and bereavement.
2. Assess and understand alcohol and substance abuse problems in the context of the life stage of the older adult.
3. Focus on enhancing (or rebuilding) the client's social support network.
4. Assist clients in restoring a sense of self-worth by helping them to develop or maintain activities of interest.
5. Refer clients to services that are age-sensitive and age-appropriate, such as Alcoholics Anonymous for seniors.
6. Attend to aspects of the older adult's life such as nutrition, activities of daily living, and physical functioning.

7. Link clients with medical and social services such as housing, transportation, and senior programs.
8. Maintain a flexible treatment program that meets the changing physical, psychological, and social needs of the clients.

Practitioners and researchers note that alcohol and substance abuse treatment for older adults needs to be more supportive and less confrontational than interventions for younger populations (Schonfeld & Dupree, 1995). Because older adults are reluctant to receive help, especially important are developing a trusting relationship and a nonjudgmental attitude on the part of the service provider.

Barriers to treatment must also be addressed before referring older adults for services. Facilities where programs such as Alcoholics Anonymous (AA) meetings are offered must be able to accommodate functional disabilities such as ambulation problems. Transportation to programs must be secured and special accommodations need to be made for older adults with vision and hearing losses. Service providers must also attend to financial resources so that older adults can pay for treatment. Medicare requires a 50% copayment for the treatment of substance abuse problems (CSAT, 1998). This can be a challenge for service providers in finding affordable treatment for older adults.

TABLE 12.3. CAGE Questions

(a) Have you ever tried to cut down on your drinking?

(b) Do you become annoyed when others ask you about your drinking?

(c) Do you ever feel guilty about your drinking?

(d) Have you ever used alcohol in the morning, taking an "eye-opener"?

Service providers conduct a more thorough assessment of alcohol abuse if a client answers yes to any of the above questions.

Note. One drink equals 12 ounces of beer, 1.5 ounces of distilled spirits, or 5 ounces of wine.

INTERVENTIONS AND TREATMENT

Educational and Psychological Interventions

Single-session *educational interventions* have been effective for older adults who are not aware that they are consuming too much alcohol or misusing medications (CSAT, 1998). Some practitioners use the CAGE screening questions, then educate older adults about alcohol consumption while reviewing the results of the screening. Interventions for older adults who misuse prescription or OTC medications include medication checklists and home visits by care providers to remove unwanted pills from the home (CSAT, 1998).

Psychological intervention strategies include unstructured and structured counseling to motivate older adults to change their behaviors to reduce alcohol and substance use. Although traditional treatment emphasizes total abstinence, a harm-reduction approach, which focuses on clients' readiness to change, has been increasingly utilized in the field of substance abuse treatment. Research indicates that counseling that employs motivational interviewing, which helps clients develop a desire to change, has been effective for older adults (Fleming, 2001). Another therapy modality that has been found to be effective for this population is cognitive-behavioral therapy (CBT; Barrowclaugh et al., 2001; Schonfeld & Dupree, 1995). CBT has also been effective in working with older adults with chronic pain, depression, and anxiety.

CBT can be conducted in individual as well as group sessions. Group interventions that have been effective working with older adults with alcohol problems include psychoeducation and self-help groups such as AA. Couples and family interventions are also useful in resolving conflicts between the older adult and his/her spouse or partner and between the older adult and other family caregivers (CSAT, 1998).

Detoxification and Psychopharmacological Interventions

Withdrawal from alcohol can be a life-threatening medical emergency for older adults with significant physical dependency on alcohol. Compared to younger adults, withdrawal can take longer, and hospitalization is recommended for the detoxification of older adults because of potential medical complications (CSAT, 1998).

The use of medications to inhibit alcohol use among older adults has not been adequately studied (DHHS, 1999). Disulfiram (Antabuse), a medication that is used to deter patients from alcohol consumption, causes toxic reactions when a patient consumes even a small amount of alcohol. It can have side affects for older adults such as confusion and memory impairment. One medication that has been proven effective in reducing cravings for alcohol when used in conjunction with counseling is naltrexone (ReVia), and it has been reported to be safe for older adults (Oslin, Liberto, O'Brien, Krois, & Norbeck, 1997; DHHS, 1999).

Spirituality is receiving increasing attention as playing an important role in recovery from alcohol and substance abuse (CSAT, 1998). However, studies of programs that employ spirituality in assisting this population with alcohol and substance abuse problems are absent from the literature. Seeking help from clergy and being involved in spiritual communities, however, has been found to have positive outcomes among older adults (CSAT, 1998).

CONCLUSION

Alcohol and substance abuse problems in older adults are less likely to be recognized by health care providers than in younger populations because the symptoms are often mistaken for problems associated with aging such as dementia and depression. The high prevalence of older adults who receive prescription medication also exacerbates the risk of medication misuse and abuse. Furthermore, lack of awareness of this problem among family members and denial on the part of elders often deters them from receiving appropriate treatment.

Although it is difficult to identify and treat older adults with substance abuse problems, research indicates that once elders are in treatment they have better outcomes than younger adults. Evidenced-based treatments such as CBT, when tailored to the specific needs of older adults, have been proven effective in treating alcohol and drug abuse in this population. With demographic changes resulting in an increase in the number of older adults at risk for alcohol and substance abuse, it is important for social workers to be able to identify the symptoms and signs of abuse and provide age-appropriate treatment.

APPENDIX 12.1

Resources

Brochure

U.S. Department of Health and Human Services. Substance Abuse and Mental Health Services Administration. *As you age . . . A guide to aging, medicines, and alcohol.* Available at *www.samhsa.gov.*

Books

Barry, K. L., Oslin, D. W., & Blow, F. C. (2001). *Alcohol problems in older adults: Prevention and management.* New York: Springer.

Beecham, M. (2002). *Elderly alcoholism: Intervention strategies.* Springfield, IL: Charles C. Thomas.

Gurnack, A. M., Atkinson, R., & Osgood, N. (Eds.). (2001). *Treating alcohol and drug abuse in the elderly.* New York: Springer.

Web Sites

Alcohol and Substance Use Disorders in Older Adults: Older Adults and Mental Health. Mental Health: A Report of the Surgeon General. (1999).

Office of the Surgeon General, U.S. Department of Health and Human Services. *http://www.surgeon general.gov/library/mentalhealth/chapter4/sec5.html service_substance.*

At Any Age, It Does Matter: Substance Abuse and Older Adults (for Professionals). U.S. Substance Abuse and Mental Health Administration. *http://pathways courses.samhsa.gov/samhsa_pathways/courses/aaap_4 _pg1.htm.*

Alcohol, Medication and Older Adults: For Those Who Care About or Care for an Older Adult. U.S. Substance Abuse and Mental Health Administration. *http://pathwayscourses.samhsa.gov/samhsa_pathways /courses/aaac_intro.htm.*

Aging and Addiction: Helping Older Adults Overcome Alcohol or Medication Dependence. Hazelton. *http://agingandaddiction.net/.*

Alcohol Use Disorders In Older Adults: Resources and References. American Geriatrics Society. *http://www. americangeriatrics.org/products/alcohbib.pdf.*

Late-Onset Alcoholism: Gaining Understanding. Treatment Improvement Exchange. *http://www.treat ment.org/TAPS/TAP17/tap17late.onset.html.*

The Physician's Guide to Helping Patients with Alcohol Problems. National Institute on Alcohol Abuse and Alcoholism. *http://www.niaaa.nih.gov/publications/ physicn.htm.*

Substance Abuse Among Older Adults. Treatment Improvement Protocol [TIP] Series 26. Center for Substance Abuse Treatment. (1998). SAMHSA. *http://www.health.org/govpubs/BKD250/.*

REFERENCES

Adams, W. L., Garry, P. J., Rhyne, R., Hunt, W. C., & Goodwin, J. S. (1990). Alcohol intake in the healthy elderly: Changes with age in a cross-sectional and longitudinal study. *Journal of the American Geriatrics Society, 38,* 211–216.

Adams, W. L., Yuan, Z., & Barboriak, J. J. (1993). Alcohol-related hospitalizations of elderly people. *Journal of the American Medical Association, 270*(10), 1222–1225.

Atkinson, R., Tolson, R. L., & Turner, J. A. (1990). Late versus early onset problem drinking in older men. *Alcoholism: Clinical and Experimental Research, 14*(4), 574–579.

Barrowclaugh, C., King, P., Colville, J., Russell, E., Burns, A., & Tarrier, N. A. (2001). A randomized trial of the effectiveness of cognitive-behavioral therapy and symptoms in older adults. *Journal of Consulting and Clinical Psychology, 69*(5), 756–762.

Benshoff, J. J., Harrawood, L. K., & Koch, D. S. (2003). Substance abuse and the elderly: Unique issues and concerns. *Journal of Rehabilitation, 69*(2), 43–48.

Blow, F. C., Brower, K. J., Schulenberg, J. E., Demo-Dananberg, L. M., Young, J. P., & Beresford, T. P. (1992). The Michigan Alcoholism Screening Test–Geriatric version (MAST-G): A new elderly-specific screening instrument. *Alcoholism: Clinical and Experimental Research, 16,* 372.

Center for Substance Abuse Treatment. (1998). Substance abuse among older adults. (DHHS Publication No. SMA 98-3179, Treatment Improvement Protocol [TIP] Series 26). Rockville, MD: Department of Health and Human Services. Available at *http:// www.health.org/govpubs/BKD250/.*

Curtis, J. R., Geller, G., Stokes, E. J., Levine, D. M., & Moore, R. D. (1989). Characteristics, diagnosis, and treatment of alcoholism in elderly patients. *Journal of the American Geriatrics Society, 37,* 310–316.

D'Archangelo, E. (1993). Substance abuse in later life. *Canadian Family Physician, 39,* 1986–1993.

Dufour, M. C., Archer, L., & Gordis, E. (1992). Alcohol and the elderly. *Clinics in Geriatric Medicine, 8,* 127–141.

Ewing, J. A. (1984). Detecting alcoholism: The CAGE questionnaire. *Journal of the American Medical Association, 252*(14), 1905–1907.

Fleming, M. (2001). Identification and treatment of alcohol use disorders in older adults. In A. M. Gurnack, R. Atkinson, & N. Osgood (Eds.), *Treating alcohol and drug abuse in the elderly* (pp. 85–108). New York: Springer.

Gurnack, A. M. (1997). *Older adults' misuse of alcohol, medicines, and other drugs.* New York: Springer.

Gurnack, A. M., Atkinson, R., & Osgood, N. (Eds.). (2002). *Treating alcohol and drug abuse in the elderly.* New York: Springer.

Helzer, J. E., Burnam, A., & McEvoy, L. T. (1991). Alcohol abuse and dependence. In L. N. Robins & D. A. Regier (Eds.), *Psychiatric disorders in America: The Epidemiologic Catchment Area study* (pp. 81–115). New York: Free Press.

Johnson, W. (2000). *Late-onset crack cocaine use* [Abstract]. Paper presented at the 128th annual meeting of the American Public Health Association, Boston.

Johnson, W. A., & Sterk, C. E. (2003). Late-onset crack Users: An emergent HIV risk group. *Journal of Acquired Immune Deficiency Syndromes, 33,* S229–S232.

Kwiatkowski, C. & Booth, R. E. (2003). HIV risk behaviors among older American drug users. *Journal of Acquired Immune Deficiency Syndromes, 33,* S131–S137.

Levy, J. (1998). AIDS and injecting drug use in later life. *Research on Aging, 20*(6), 776–797.

Menninger, J. A. (2002). Assessment and treatment of alcoholism and substance-related disorders in the elderly. *Bulletin of the Menninger Clinic, 66,* 166–184.

Ondus, K. A., Hujer, M. E., Mann, A. E., & Mion, L. C. (1999). Substance abuse and the hospitalized elderly. *Orthopedic Nursing, 18*(4), 27–37.

Oslin, D., Liberto, J. G., O'Brien, J., Krois, S., & Norbeck, J. (1997). Naltresone as an adjunctive treatment for older patients with alcohol dependence. *American Journal of Geriatric Psychiatry, 5*(4), 324–332.

Rigler, S. K. (2000). Alcoholism in the elderly. *American Family Physician, 61,* 1710–1716.

SAMHSA. (2001). *Summary of the findings from the 2000 National Household Survey on Drug Abuse* (NHSDA Series: H-13, DHHS Publication No. SMA 01-3549). Rockville, MD: Author.

Schonfeld, L., & Dupree, L. W. (1995). Treatment approaches for older problem drinkers. *International Journal of the Addictions, 30*(13/14), 1819–1842.

Sheahan, R. I., Coons, S. J., Robbins, C. A., Martin, S. S., Hendricks, J., & Latimer, M. (1995). Psychoactive medication, alcohol use, and falls among older adults. *Journal of Behavioral Medicine, 15*(2), 127–140.

U.S. Department of Health and Human Services. (1999). Mental health: A report of the surgeon general. Rockville, MD: U.S. Department of Health and Human Services, Substance Abuse and Mental Health Services Administration, Center for Mental Health Services, National Institutes of Health, National Institute of Mental Health. Available at *http://www.surgeongeneral.gov/library/.*

Zimberg, S. (1996). Treating alcoholism: An age-specific intervention that works for older patients. *Geriatrics, 51*(10), 45–52.

MARGARET E. ADAMEK
GRETA YODER SLATER

Older Adults at Risk for Suicide

THE NATURE AND SCOPE OF ELDER SUICIDE

Adults age 65 and over have the highest suicide rate of any age group in the United States. In 2001 5,393 persons age 65 and older took their own lives—an average of 16 per day (Centers for Disease Control and Prevention [CDC], 2004a). That translates into approximately one older adult suicide in the United States every 90 minutes (Center for Elderly Suicide Prevention & Grief Counseling, 2004). Although they are 1 out of 8 (12.8%) individuals in the population, older adults accounted for nearly 1 in 5 (19%) suicides (American Association of Suicidology, 2003). Older adults' rate of suicide, 16.8 per 100,000 in 1997, was significantly higher than the rate for young adults (age 15 to 24), which mirrored the national rate of 11.4 per 100,000 (Murphy, 2000). Not surprisingly, the surgeon general's *Call to Action to Prevent Suicide* (U.S. Public Health Service, 1999) identified older adults as a priority group for research and intervention.

It is likely that official rates of elder suicide are undercounted. Clark (1992) estimates that 5% of suicides in the United States go unreported in mortality data. The stigma attached to suicide and the potential loss of insurance benefits are two factors that likely contribute to this phenomenon. In addition, deaths resulting from self-neglect or "intentional life-threatening behaviors (ILTB)" (Osgood, Brandt, & Lipman, 1991) are not typically labeled a suicide. Farberow (1980) used the term "subintentional suicide" to describe a collection of covert behaviors such as refusing to eat, drink, or take required medications, and other forms of self-neglect. This class of behaviors is also called "intentional self-destructive behaviors" and was the focus of Osgood's research in long-term care (LTC) facilities (Osgood, 1992; Osgood, Brandt, & Lipman, 1989, 1991). Estimates from probability-based national samples of LTC facilities have found overt rates of suicide of 15.8 deaths per 100,000 and deaths due to ILTB as high as 94.9 per 100,000 (Osgood et al., 1991). A study in New York found the overt rate of suicide in LTC was 19.7 per 100,000 (Abrams, Young, Holt, & Alexopoulos, 1988).

Despite documentation that thousands of older adults in the United States kill themselves each year, suicide remains a "relatively silent epidemic" (Dahl, 2004). As helping professionals we must be informed about the extent and nature of elder suicide.

Suicide among older adults is a complex phenomenon, with many risk factors and seemingly few protective factors. A variety of risk factors, including age, gender, race, physical and mental health, multiple losses (e.g., retirement, widowhood, functional ability), and access to lethal means, have been associated with increased suicide risk in late life. Older men have a suicide rate about 5.5 times that of older women (CDC, 2004a). In fact, males 75 and older have the highest rates of suicide in nearly all industrialized countries (Conwell et al., 2002; Pearson, Conwell, Lindesay, Takahashi, & Caine, 1997; World Health Organization [WHO], 2003). Although ethnic minority elders have often faced significant structural obstacles such as racism, oppression, and overt and covert discrimination throughout their lives, they are unlikely to commit suicide. African American older women have the lowest rates of suicide among their age cohort (CDC, 2002). In contrast, White men over 85 are at the greatest risk of suicide, with rates nearly 6 times the national rate (National Center for Health Statistics [NCHS], 2000).

Epidemiological studies have revealed several important differences between older and younger suicides. Duberstein and colleagues (1999) found that increased age was associated with significantly less suicidal ideation; older adults often do not give warnings about suicide and seldom seek mental health treatment. Not only are older adults less likely to seek treatment, but physicians are less likely to offer treatment for depression to older patients (Uncapher, 2000). There are also age differences with regard to substance abuse and suicide. Garlow (2002) found that older adults were the least likely group to have alcohol or inhalants in their body at autopsy following suicide. Adults over 65 have a much lower attempt-to-completion rate (4:1) than younger people, whose rate is estimated to be between 8:1 and 200:1 (McIntosh, Santos, Hubbard, & Overholser, 1994; Szanto et al., 2002). It is likely that these rate differentials reflect the fact that older adults frequently have more health problems, are more likely to live alone, tend to avoid interventions, are less likely to communicate suicidal ideation, take precautions to avoid discovery, and are less likely to be detected immediately after an attempt (Duberstein et al, 1999; Szanto et al., 2002). In addition, older adults are more likely than younger persons to use a firearm to end their lives (NCHS, 2000).

Physical illness is more prevalent with advancing age and has been widely identified as an issue in suicide completions among older adults (McIntosh et al., 1994). Nevertheless, it is estimated that only 2% to 4% of terminally ill older adults kill themselves (Szanto et al., 2002). The risk of suicide is significantly increased among older adults with certain illnesses. Using a population-based controlled study, Juurlink, Herrmann, Szalai, Kopp, and Redelmeier (2004) found an increased suicide risk for older adults with depression, bipolar disorder, severe pain, and several other chronic illnesses, including seizure disorder, congestive heart failure, and chronic lung disease. Furthermore, treatment for multiple illnesses was strongly associated with an increased suicide risk. Chronic physical illness has been associated with higher risk of completed suicide when accompanied by depression (Szanto et al., 2002). Researchers suggest it is actually the comorbid depression or mental illness that increases suicide risk (Harris & Barraclough, 1994).

Many older adults, as many as 20%, experience mental health problems that are not associated with normal aging (U.S. Department of Health and Human Services [DHHS], 1999). Depression has been well-established through several recent meta-analyses as a risk factor for suicide (Bartels et al., 2002; Kleepsies & Dettmer, 2000; Oei & Free, 1995; Szanto et al., 2002). Among older adults, depression is associated with suicide in approximately 90% of cases (DHHS, 1999). Many instrument development studies have documented the correlation between depression and suicidal ideation or suicide risk (Beck, Kovacs, & Weissman, 1979; Brown, n.d.; Szanto et al., 2002). Although there is a strong link between depression and suicide, not all depressed people kill themselves. Clinically, it is important to distinguish between those at high risk of suicide and those who are depressed.

The cumulative effect of multiple losses in late life—of roles, functional ability, relationships, and resources—has been associated with depression and suicidality. For example, studies have demonstrated higher rates of suicide among divorced and widowed elders (McIntosh et al., 1994; Stillion & McDowell, 1996). The greatest challenges and needs are among the oldest-old (ages 85+), who more often have significant health restrictions and require assistance with activities of daily living (ADL) and instrumental activities of daily living (IADL; McInnis-Dittrich, 2002; Quadagno, 1999). Although there are many exceptions to the frail-elder stereotype, many in this age group have significant needs that make them vulnerable to depression.

Perhaps the least understood risk factor for elder suicide is access to lethal means. Numerous studies link access to lethal means, primarily firearms, to higher rates of suicide (Conwell et al., 2002; Cutright & Fernquist, 2000; Kellerman et al., 1992; Killias, van Kesteren, & Rindlisbacher, 2001; Miller, Arazel, & Hemenway, 2002; Romero & Wintemute, 2002; Shenassa, Catlin, & Buka, 2003; Wiebe, 2003). International comparisons point to increased suicide death when a gun is available. For example, the UK has a low percentage of households with guns (4%) and a relatively low suicide rate (.03 per 100,000). By comparison, in Canada, 26% of households have a gun and the suicide rate is 3.35. In the United States, 41% of households have guns and the suicide rate is 7.23—nearly twice the rate of the UK and Canada combined (Cukier, 1998).

Firearms are the most common method of suicide for both men and women (see Table 13.1), including older adults. Between 1980 and 1992, firearm-related suicides increased from 60% to 69% among older adults (Adamek & Kaplan, 1996), and this upward trend has persisted. The firearm suicide rate for older women has increased 10% since 1979, replacing poisoning as the most commonly chosen method of suicide among older women (Adamek & Kaplan, 1996). Firearm-related suicides accounted for 70% of all suicides among older adults from 1990 through 1996: 77.3% of suicides among men and 34.4% among women (CDC, 2002). Whereas the rate of firearm suicide among youth has been decreasing (CDC, 2004b), it has increased over time for older adults (see Table 13.2). In 2000, 73% of older adults who killed themselves used a firearm (CDC, 2002).

Access to a firearm may be the aggravating factor differentiating attempts from completions among older adults when other high-risk factors are present, such as isolation, retirement stress, and depression. Using the psychological autopsy method, Conwell and colleagues (2002) examined the suicide deaths of 86 victims age 50 and older. They matched the victims with 86 community-dwelling residents on age, sex, race, and county of residence and found that, even after controlling for psychiatric illness, the presence of a handgun was associated with increased risk for suicide. Clearly, social workers need to be aware of the risk factors for suicide among older adults: age, race, gender, physical and mental health, cumulative loss, and access to lethal means. We need a better understanding of how multiple risk factors interact to increase the suicide risk among this population.

EVIDENCE-BASED PRACTICES WITH SUICIDAL ELDERS

Psychological risk factors found to be associated with elder suicide include chemical imbalances, learned helplessness, personality disorders, unmet needs, irrational thoughts, and attachment problems (McIntosh et al., 1994; Stillion & McDowell, 1996). It is beyond the scope of this chapter to discuss the theoretical context of elder suicide; instead, we offer several useful sources for more information. McIntosh et al. give a thorough summary of original sources examining various psychological approaches to understanding suicide: psychoanalytic (Achté, 1988; Adler, 1968; Kastenbaum & Aisenberg, 1972), behavioral (Beck, 1995; Jerger, 1979; Seligman, 1975), personal construct theory (Hughes & Neimeyer, 1990; Kelly, 1955; Neimeyer, 1983), and the cubic model of suicide (Schneidman, 1985). The common thread in the various psychological theories of suicide is a focus on the individual psyche and sense of agency.

When practicing with high-risk clients, clinicians must take time to conduct frequent, comprehensive suicide risk assessments to learn if the individual is experiencing suicidal ideation. Several treatment approaches have been empirically tested for intervention with suicidal elders, including cognitive-behavioral therapy (CBT), interpersonal therapy, psychopharmacology, and crisis intervention services.

TABLE 13.1. Cause of Death Among 1998 Suicide Victims (All)

Method of Suicide	Male (percentage)	Female (percentage)	Total Number
Firearm	61.6	38.4	17,424
Drugs, medicaments, and biologicals	6.4	26.1	3,138
Hanging, strangulation, or suffocation	19.2	16.8	5,726
Gases and vapors	5.4	6.7	1,726
Solid or liquid poisons	0.6	1.0	208
All other (fire, falling, cutting, drowning, and unspecified)	6.9	11.0	2,353
Total number of suicides in 1998	24,538	6,037	30,575

Source: Based on data from National Center for Health Statistics, 2000.

TABLE 13.2. Percentages of Suicides by Firearm, by Gender and Age (1980 and 1998)

	Males		Females		Combined	
	1980	*1998*	*1980*	*1998*	*1980*	*1998*
Age						
60–64	68.0	72.8	36.2	41.6	58.9	**66.2**
65–69	71.0	74.5	30.9	37.6	61.9	**67.8**
70–74	71.0	79.0	27.6	41.1	62.1	**73.1**
75	66.2	79.0	16.2	30.6	57.1	**72.0**
Elder Firearm suicide average	**68.8**	**77.1**	**28.3**	**36.1**	**59.7**	**70.4**

Source: Based on data from National Center for Health Statistics, 2000.

Cognitive Therapy/Cognitive-Behavioral Therapy

There are several variations of cognitive and cognitive-behavioral therapies, but all share the basic idea that thinking and behavior are learned and can be unlearned as well. Several prominent experts have written about CBT and the ways that thinking affects behavioral outcomes (Adler, 1963; Beck, 1995; Ellis, 1962). For example, when a person is depressed, thoughts like "I am worthless" come to mind. In reality, the person has worth, so the thinking is considered irrational and the person can work on replacing those negative thoughts with positive, more realistic ones like "I make mistakes sometimes." This process takes training and often requires exercises outside of the therapy setting to "cognitively restructure" the client's thinking process. McInnis-Dittrich (2002) provides a good overview of CBT as it is practiced with older adults. Bartels and colleagues (2002) summarized meta-analyses of psychosocial treatments for geriatric depression and reported significant evidence for using cognitive and cognitive-behavioral therapy with suicidal and depressed elders.

Interpersonal Therapy

Interpersonal therapy, or solution-focused therapy, is the process of identifying problems that cause interpersonal or personal distress. McIntosh and colleagues (1994) emphasize that interpersonal therapy emphasizes role transitions and conflict, social skills training, and complicated grief. This type of therapy is expected to be time-limited and focused on tangible, specific problems. Both individual and group

psychosocial interventions have been shown to be effective with depressed older adults (e.g., Husaini et al, 2004; Schwartz, 2004).

Psychopharmacology

Psychopharmacology is the use of psychotropic medications to alter mood. It is the most common intervention for depression in late life (Blazer, 2003). Clinical trials have demonstrated the effectiveness of selective serotonin reuptake inhibitors (SSRIs) for reducing suicidal ideation and behavior (Hawton et al., 1998). Bartels et al. (2002) summarized the extensive research on antidepressant medication and recommend the use of SSRIs (e.g., Prozac, Zoloft, Paxil, Celexa). These medications have highly effective treatment benefits and far fewer side effects than the older monoamine oxidase inhibitors and tricyclics (Bartels et al., 2002). These authors also note that despite the evidence supporting the use of antidepressants, organizational obstacles and poor service coordination often interfere with compliance and management of medications. It is interesting to note that none of the 26 studies reviewed by Bartels et al. mentioned strategies to reduce firearms or at least screen for them in the assessment or intervention process.

Combination Therapies

Although a combined psychosocial-pharmacologic approach for treating geriatric depression has been recommended for some time (National Institutes of Health Consensus Panel, 1992), too often psychotropic medication is the only intervention for depressed elders (Adamek, 2003). A comprehensive review of geriatric suicide and parasuicide literature by Szanto and colleagues (2002) confirmed the recommendation for combination therapies, specifically CBT with an SSRI protocol. These researchers are involved with a multisite collaborative research study funded by several National Institute of Mental Health grants, the Prevention of Suicide in the Primary Care Elderly Collaborative Trial (PROSPECT; Brown, Bruce, & Pearson, 2001; Luoma, Martin, & Pearson, 2002; Mulsant et al., 2001; Raue et al., 2001). The aim of the study is to evaluate the effectiveness of a multidisciplinary primary care intervention in preventing and reducing suicidal ideation and behavior, associated hopelessness, and depressive symptoms in a population-based sample of older adults. Preliminary results suggest that the intervention has been effective in reducing the number of suicides among older primary care patients (Mulsant et al., 2001). The PROSPECT studies provide strong support for routine screening for depression among older adults and for the use of combination, multidisciplinary approaches to preventing suicide. Callahan (2001) notes that the systems of care for late-life depression have not caught up with the latest research. He also suggests that older patients have a responsibility to be motivated and informed about their own treatment for depression.

Crisis Intervention Services

Although many studies assess suicidal ideation or a specific treatment regimen for particular diagnoses, few studies guide clinicians about evidence-based practice with acutely suicidal elders. Kleepsies and Dettmer (2000) conducted a meta-analysis of studies addressing strategies for managing acutely suicidal patients of all ages. They stress the importance of viewing risk factors within a framework of comprehensive suicide assessment. At the point of acute suicidal emergency, it is important to thoroughly assess for comorbid features. A high-risk profile includes depression with comorbid alcohol abuse, insomnia, decreased concentration, anxiety, obsessive-compulsive features, and previous history of suicide attempts. Despite the thoroughness of their review, Kleepsies and Dettmer (2000) do not discuss or explain the differences between older and younger adults in managing acute suicidal emergencies. At the time this chapter was written, no meta-analyses of interven-

tions for older adults in suicidal crisis or best practice guidelines for work with acutely suicidal elders had been published (Yoder, 2004).

BEST PRACTICE MODEL

Given the lack of evidence-based practices for acute suicidal emergencies with older adults, we recommend the following model as a *promising practice* for reducing older adult suicidal behavior. The CBT model of intervention with older adults has demonstrated effectiveness with depressed and suicidal elders (Bartels et al., 2002; Hawton et al., 1998; Wampold, Minami, Baskin, & Tierney, 2002). The premise of this therapeutic strategy is to identify *cognitive distortions* and formulate more realistic alternative thoughts, which then lead to changes in behavior. Because CBT is not recommended for those with cognitive disabilities or dementia, helping professionals may need to assess for cognitive deficiencies. This type of therapy is not recommended for people with mental illness of the psychotic or organic type, such as Alzheimer's disease.

Phase I: Orientation, Preparing, and Beginning

The clinician-client relationship is the most important part of the therapeutic endeavor. When meeting an older adult client for the first time, it is important to make good eye contact, unless that is not considered respectful by the client's culture. (Alemán, Fitzpatrick, Tran, & Gonzales, 2000 provide a useful review of cultural issues in working with ethnic elders.) If the older adult has been referred because of suicidal ideation or behavior, it is particularly important to maintain a calm, empathic presence during the interview. Brown et al. (2001) recommend being attentive and present for the person while interviewing. Although this seems simply basic advice, it is sometimes true that this initial level of empathy and intervention is successful in reducing the suicidal ideation. Many older adults are aging in place, which often means they do not have many contacts outside their home. Clients should be given time to talk and not have to rush through an assessment with a prescribed explicit agenda. It is necessary to use an assessment instrument, but it is damaging to the therapeutic relationship when a client feels like "just another case." Multidisciplinary, combination therapy is recommended for reducing suicidal behavior among older adults, and a thorough medical and mental health assessment is essential for developing a treatment plan with older adults at risk of suicide.

During the assessment phase, clinicians should use valid, reliable instruments designed for older adults. There are many well-developed instruments for assessing suicide risk and the often-associated diagnosis of depression (see Appendix 13.1). The Beck Depression Inventory (BDI), Center for Epidemiological Studies Depression Scale (CES-D), and Geriatric Depression Scale (GDS) are the most widely used and offer highly valid and reliable results in assessing depression. One particularly useful instrument, the Geriatric Depression Scale (Brink et al., 1982), is available in a long (30-item) or short (15-item) form and in several languages. A recent modification of the GDS is geared toward a residential population (Sutcliffe et al., 2000). An online version provides an automatically scored format, allowing older adults to screen themselves as an assignment for therapy, to assess their own progress, and to determine outcomes at the completion of therapy (Yesavage, 2003).

After forming an alliance, there are several good ways of addressing suicidal ideation and plans for suicidal behavior. Szanto et al. (2002) recommend asking the older adult the following questions:

Have you been feeling so sad lately that you were thinking about death or dying?
Have you had thoughts that life is not worth living?
Have you been thinking about harming yourself?

Given that 73% of older adults who committed suicide in 2000 used a gun, we want to emphasize the importance of asking specific questions about firearms, for example, "Do you have any guns at home?" If the client answers affirmatively, then it is crucial to follow up with the question, "Have you thought about using the gun to end your life?" or "Do you have plans to use the gun to end your life?" These questions may seem blunt, but it is important to ask clients about plans and means to end their life.

Sherman et al. (2001) demonstrated the efficacy of a multidisciplinary Firearms Risk Management (FRM) program with suicidal adults (N=46). In addition to tracking gun availability using a firearms flow sheet, the social worker took several steps to neutralize the risk of the patient's using a firearm to commit suicide upon discharge. These steps included contacting the patient's family and case manager as well as

law-enforcement officials. The social worker provided gun-risk education and worked with families to remove the gun from the home. The multidisciplinary team provided ongoing consultation and evaluation. Neutralization of the risk of firearm use was stable for 89% of the sample at 24 months. In other words, only 5 of 46 patients threatened the use of a gun or had access to a firearm following the intervention. Though not yet tested with older adults, this model offers a promising direction for the reduction of firearm suicide in late life.

Phase II: Contracting

No-harm contracts, as they are sometimes called, were initially designed to manage and document suicide risk (Miller, 1999). The American Psychiatric Association (APA; 2003, p. 41) states:

> Since the utility of the suicide prevention contract is based on subjective belief rather than objective evidence, it is over-valued as a clinical or risk management technique. Furthermore, the suicide prevention contract is not a legal document and cannot be used as exculpatory evidence in the event of litigation.

Thus, these contracts should not be used as the only accountability measure with suicidal older adults, but they are one way to demonstrate that the issues of safety and emergency contact procedures have been discussed and documented. Such contracts for safety have no demonstrated effectiveness and are *contraindicated* with clients who are new, in active psychosis, under the influence of substances, or agitated (APA, 2003). With older adults, this might include persons with dementia or who are heavily medicated.

Although suicide prevention contracts have limited effectiveness, they can be helpful as a means of communicating who, what, and how to contact professional help in a suicide crisis (APA, 2003). Miller, Jacobs, and Gutheil (1998) outline a model of suicide prevention treatment that uses informed consent to outline risks and benefits of treatment with clients in order to assess the client's willingness to form a therapeutic alliance with the clinician. When the suicide prevention contract is used alone, as an agreement that the client will not harm himself or herself, the real issue is the strength of the therapeutic alliance. If a client is unwilling to sign the contract, he or she is really putting the clinician on notice that the therapeutic alliance is in jeopardy and the suicide risk needs to be reassessed (APA, 2003). When practicing with high-risk clients, clinicians must conduct frequent, comprehensive suicide risk assessments and thoroughly document such procedures.

In the CBT model, establishing a plan (or contract) for therapeutic work with the client is as important as frequent, comprehensive risk assessments. A therapeutic contract—not to be confused with a no-harm, suicide prevention contract or a contract for safety—is an agreement between therapist and client on the scope, goals, and procedures for therapeutic change. Clients are expected to work at least 30 minutes each week on the assigned homework regarding their thinking patterns. Clients can be given assignments on a schedule or as they fit into the session.

Phase III: Working and Evaluation

Several useful tools are available for working long term with older clients who are at risk of suicide. Burns's *Feeling Good Handbook* (1999) and *Ten Days to Self-Esteem* (1993) are client-directed workbooks that come with evaluation instruments and tracking sheets to record data each week about the client's mood, thoughts, progress, and homework. Another useful resource is the *Therapist's Tool Kit* (Burns, 2003), which includes tools for keeping the client on track and for demonstrating effectiveness in the evaluation. One such example is a cost-benefit analysis. The client lists one particularly troubling thought and the outcomes that could come from this way of thinking. After listing pros and cons for these behavioral outcomes, the client then reevaluates the practical value of these thinking patterns. This analysis has demonstrated effectiveness with reducing problem behaviors and thoughts that lead to depression (Burns & Nolen-Hoeksema, 1991; Burns & Spangler, 2000).

Phase IV: Ending and Follow-up

The conclusion phase of treatment needs to include a summary of the goals and outcomes achieved with the client. This is helpful for both the client and the therapist in reviewing the progress made and lessons learned and for reaching agreement that the treatment process is coming to an end. The client must be given time to talk about the termination process and the feelings associated with ending the therapeutic relationship.

Clients often are reminded of other losses and transitions in life when the treatment process ends. It is crucial to assess for depressive symptoms and suicidal ideation again at termination. Follow-up procedures should include checking on the client's progress at 3-, 6-, and 9-month intervals. The clinician should carefully record and analyze the evaluation data to determine the overall effectiveness of the CBT course of treatment. The clinician should review with the client the emergency contacts for safety in case suicidal thoughts arise in the future.

Clearly, clinical social workers need to develop specific skills for work with depressed and suicidal older adults. Given the scope of elder suicide, it is also critical to work for prevention on a broader scale.

POLICY AND PREVENTION

Federal funding for mental health programs for older adults has been relatively meager. Funding through the Community Mental Health Services block grant has not required states to address the unique mental health needs of older adults separately from the general adult population, as they are required to do for children (Volkert, 2003). In 2002, Substance Abuse and Mental Health Administration (SAMHSA) received $5 million to increase evidence-based mental health services for older adults through a program called Mental Health Outreach and Treatment to the Elderly. Despite this promising start, the program was eliminated. The Older Adult Consumer Mental Health Alliance is leading the effort to raise public awareness and restore this funding (Volkert, 2004). Social workers can partner with such consumer groups to advocate for increased funding for mental health services for older adults.

Prevention programs specifically focused on elder suicide are few and far between, but there are some promising initiatives. At the national level, the National Strategy for Suicide Prevention (SAMHSA, 2004) provides a framework for action aimed at reducing and preventing suicide among all groups. According to the crafters of the National Strategy:

> A public health approach to suicide prevention represents a rational and organized way to marshal prevention efforts and ensure that they are effective. . . . The *National Strategy* requires a variety of organizations and individuals to become involved in suicide prevention and emphasizes coordination of resources and culturally appro-

priate services at all levels of government . . . and with the private sector. The NSSP represents the first attempt in the United States to prevent suicide through such a coordinated approach. . . . The *Goals and Objectives for Action* articulates a set of 11 goals and 68 objectives, and provides a blueprint for action.

A related national resource, the Suicide Prevention Resource Center (SPRC, 2004), helps states and communities increase their capacity to develop, implement, and evaluate suicide prevention efforts. The SPRC "supports suicide prevention with the best of science, skills and practice. The Center provides prevention support, training, and informational materials to strengthen suicide prevention networks and advance the National Strategy for Suicide Prevention." Although some states have suicide prevention plans in place (existing state-level suicide prevention plans can be accessed at the SPRC site) few statewide plans specifically target older adults.

In California, HHS Prevention 2010 block grants were awarded by the EMS Authority to local EMS agencies to support the Toolkit for Elderly Suicide Prevention project (Injury Prevention Network, 2002). The San Diego County EMS Agency distributed the funds to the 32 statewide local EMS agencies to assist providers in recognizing and intervening with potentially suicidal older adults. In San Francisco, the Center for Elderly Suicide Prevention and Grief Counseling (Institute on Aging, 2004) targets older adults suffering from life-threatening depression. Recognizing the importance of older adults being connected to the community, the Center offers a 24-hour Friendship Line, outreach calls, supportive home visits, grief support, and workshops on suicide intervention for volunteers and the community. In South Carolina, a collaborative effort involving the Institute of Psychiatry, State Office on Aging, Area Agency on Aging, South Carolina Center for the Study of Suicide, and the Charleston County Redevelopment Authority is offering a life review intervention to older adults with minor depression as a suicide prevention measure (National Center for Injury Prevention and Control, 2004). Dr. Barbara Haight, the study's principal investigator, explains:

> Since older people attach a stigma to mental illness and suicide, many do not seek help even if they suspect a problem. Accordingly, an intervention must be perceived as acceptable to older people in order to be effective. The life review is an intervention that is empirically based and conceptually grounded. . . . Because the life review is a seemingly natural storytelling process with no stigma attached, it engages older people with minor depression who often, otherwise, refuse mental health services.

A description of the intervention can be found at: *http://www.cdc.gov/ncipc/dvp/suianno.htm*. Risk of suicidal ideation was assessed at 8 weeks, 1 year, and 2 years following the life review intervention and compared to older adults receiving no life review intervention. The forthcoming findings are expected to show reduced suicide risk among program participants.

It seems counterintuitive that the group with the highest rate of suicide, older adults, and the means by which most who commit suicide take their lives, firearms, are persistently neglected in practice and policy-relevant research. Firearm access is a policy issue that social workers can help address. "Evidence from many countries and cultures shows that limiting access to lethal means of self-harm may be an effective strategy to prevent self-destructive behaviors" (National Mental Health Information Center, 2003, p. 3).

Although there are many programs aimed at preventing youth suicide, few programs are geared toward preventing suicide among the group with the highest rates (Jenkins & Kovess, 2002; McIntosh et al., 1994). Given the strong connection between depression and suicide among older adults, social workers interested in suicide prevention must advocate for better assessment and treatment of depression among older adults. Social workers can play a role in assessing for depression and educating older adults, their family members, and other health and mental health providers about the connections among physical illness, depression, and suicide among older adults (Csikai & Manetta, 2002).

CONCLUSION

The high rates of elder suicide should alarm every helping professional encountering older adults. The problem of elder suicide will likely be magnified with the demographic trends of the post–World War II generation steadily moving toward retirement and older adulthood (CDC, 2002). According to Pearson, Caine, Lindesay, Conwell, and Clark (1999, p. 203), "Suicide in later life represents a significant public health challenge that will rapidly grow during the early decades of the 21st century." One estimate projected a twofold increase in the number of elderly suicides by 2030 (Haas & Hendin, 1983).

The impending demographic shift underscores the urgent need for effective measures to reduce late-life suicide. The prevention of suicide among older adults has been identified as "a major opportunity and priority for research in geriatric depression" (Reynolds & Kupfer, 1999, p. 1170).

Even though firearms are the most likely and lethal method, there are significant gaps in the practice, policy, and epidemiologic research on this topic. Clinicians who work with older adults need to have more evidence about the relationship between guns and suicide. Practitioners need to know how, when, and in what way to ask about firearms with their older patients, especially when the elder is depressed or suicidal. Although the data suggest that suicide risk increases with access to lethal means, we need a clearer understanding of the connections between gun policy, firearm access, and elder suicide (Yoder, 2003).

Although research on elder suicide is relatively sparse, published work on protective factors that operate against suicide among older adults is rarer still. Good health, no or limited disability, a strong social support network, and spiritual beliefs are obvious protective factors for adults of all ages. The low rate of suicide among members of older ethnic minority groups, despite the many burdens brought on by structural inequalities, suggests the presence of a racial or cultural protective factor, perhaps related to social support and spirituality. Given the strong connection between depression and suicide in late life, much more research is needed to understand the dynamics of late-life depression and the protective factors that stave off depression among some older adults, even in the presence of chronic illness.

APPENDIX 13.1

Beck Depression Inventory*

Beck, A., Ward, C., Mendelson, M., Mock, J., & Erbarugh, J. (1961). An inventory for measuring depression. *Archives of General Psychiatry, 4,* 561–571.

Brief Symptom Inventory

Scocco, P., & Leo, D. (2002). One year prevalence of death thoughts, suicide ideation, and behaviors in an elderly population. *International Journal of Geriatric Psychiatry, 17,* 842–846.

Geriatric Depression Scale

Yesavage, A., Brink, T. L., Rose, T. L., Lum, O., Huang, V., Adey, M. B., et al. (1982). Development and validation of a geriatric depression screening scale: A preliminary report. *Journal of Psychiatric Research, 17,* 37–49.

Hamilton Rating Scale for Depression*

Hamilton, M. (1960). A rating scale for depression. *Journal of Neurology, Neurosurgery and Psychiatry, 33,* 56–62.

Hopelessness Scale

Beck, A., Weissman, A., Lester, D., & Trexler, L. (1974). The measurement of pessimism: The Hopelessness Scale. *Journal of Consulting and Clinical Psychology, 42,* 861–865.

Millon Clinical Multiaxial Inventory I and II

Millon, T. (1982). *Millon Clinical Multiaxial Inventory Manual* (3rd ed.). Minneapolis, MN: National Computer Systems.
Millon, T. (1987). *Millon Clinical Multiaxial Inventory II: Manual for the MCMI-II.* Minneapolis, MN: National Computer Systems.

Reasons for Living Inventory

Linehan, M., Goodstein, J., Nielsen, S., & Chiles, J. (1983). Reasons for staying alive when you are thinking of killing yourself: The Reasons for Living Inventory. *Journal of Consulting and Clinical Psychology, 51,* 276–286.

Risk of Suicide Questionnaire

Horowitz, L., Wang, P., Koocher, G., Burr, B., Fallon-Smith, M., Klavon, S., et al. (2001). Detecting suicide risk in a pediatric emergency department: Development of a brief screening tool. *Pediatrics, 107,* 1133–1137.

Scale for Suicide Ideation*

Beck, A., Kovacs, M., & Weissman, A. (1979). Assessment of suicidal intention: The Scale for Suicide Ideation. *Journal of Consulting Clinical Psychology, 47*, 343–352.

Semantic Differential Scale–Attitudes towards Suicidal Behavior

Jenner, J., & Niesing, J. (2000). The construction of the SEDAS: A new suicide-attitude questionnaire. *Acta Psychiatrica Scandinavica, 102*, 139–146.

Short Geriatric Depression Scale

Almeida, O., & Almeida, S. (1999). Short versions of the Geriatric Depression Scale: A study of their validity for the diagnosis of a major depressive episode according to the ICD-10 and DSM-IV. *International Journal of Geriatric Psychiatry, 14*, 858–865.

Suicide Assessment Checklist

Rogers, J., & Alexander, R. (1994). Development and psychometric analysis of the Suicide Assessment Checklist. *Journal of Mental Health Counseling, 16*, 352–369.

Suicidal Behaviors Questionnaire

Linehan, M. (1981). *Suicidal Behaviors Questionnaire (SBQ).* Unpublished Inventory, University of Washington, Seattle.

Suicidal Intent Scale

Beck, A., Schuyler, D., & Herman, I. (1974). Development of suicide intent scales. In A. Beck, H. Resnick, & D. Lettieri (Eds.), *The prediction of suicide* (pp. 45–56). Bowie, MD: Charles Press.

Suicide Ideation Questionnaire

Beck, A., Kovacs, M., & Weissman, A. (1979). Assessment of suicidal ideation: The scale for suicidal ideation. *Journal of Consulting and Clinical Psychology, 47*(2), 343–352.

Suicidal Ideation Screening Questionnaire

Cooper-Patrick, L., Crum, R., & Ford, D. (1994). Identifying suicidal ideation in general medical patients. *Journal of the American Medical Association, 272*(22), 1757–1762.

Suicide Opinion Questionnaire

Domino, G., Gibson, L., Poling, S., & Westlake, L. (1980). Students' attitudes toward suicide. *Social Psychiatry, 15*, 127–130.

Under development:

Reasons for Living Inventory–Older Adult

Edlestein, B., McKee, D., & Martin, R. (1999). *Reasons for Living Inventory–Older Adults.* Unpublished manuscript, Department of Psychology, West Virginia University, Morgantown, WV.

Notes: Those in italics are recommended for work with elders (valid and reliable with adults 65+).

*Predictive of suicide in adults.

REFERENCES

Abrams, R. C., Young, R. C., Holt, J. H., & Alexopoulos, G. S. (1988). Suicide in New York City nursing homes: 1980–1986. *American Journal of Psychiatry, 145*, 1487–1488.

Achté, K. (1988). Suicidal tendencies in the elderly. *Suicide and Life-Threatening Behavior, 18*, 55–64.

Adamek, M. (2003). Late-life depression in nursing home residents: Social work opportunities to prevent, educate, and alleviate. In B. Berkman & L. Harootyan (Eds.), *Social work and health care in an aging society: Education, policy, practice, and research* (pp. 15–47). New York: Springer.

Adamek, M., & Kaplan, M. (1996). The growing use of firearms by suicidal women, 1979–1992. *Suicide & Life-Threatening Behavior, 26*, 71–78.

Adler, A. (1963). *The practice and theory of individual psychology.* New York: Premier Books.

Adler, A. (1968). Suicide. In J. Gibbs (Ed.), *Suicide* (pp. 146–150). New York: Harper & Row.

Alemán, S., Fitzpatrick, T., Tran, T., & Gonzales, E. (2000). *Therapeutic interventions with ethnic elders: Health and social issues.* Binghamton, NY: Haworth.

American Association of Suicidology. (2003). *U.S.A. suicide: 2000 final official data.* Retrieved April 5, 2003, from *http://www.suicidology.org/associations/1045/files/2000datapg.pdf.*

American Psychiatric Association (APA). (2003). *Practice guidelines for the assessment and treatment of patients with suicidal behaviors.* Retrieved March 25, 2004, from the American Psychiatric Association Web site, *www.psych.org/cme.*

Bartels, S., Dums, A., Oxman, T., Schneider, L., Arean, P., Alexopoulos, G., et al. (2002). Evidence-based practices in geriatric mental health care. *Psychiatric Services, 53,* 1419–1431.

Beck, A. (1995). *Cognitive therapy: The basics and beyond.* New York: Guilford.

Beck, A., Kovacs, M., & Weissman, A. (1979). Assessment of suicidal intention: The scale for suicide ideation. *Journal of Consulting Clinical Psychology, 47,* 343–352.

Blazer, D. G. (2003). Depression in late life: Review and commentary. *Journals of Gerontology: Biological and Medical Sciences, 58,* M249–M265.

Brink, T. L., Yesavage, J. A., Lum, O., Heersema, P., Adey, M. B., & Rose, T. L. (1982). Screening tests for geriatric depression. *Clinical Gerontologist, 1,* 37–44.

Brown, G. (n.d.). *A review of suicide assessment measures for intervention research.* Retrieved March 1, 2004, from *www.nimh.nih.gov/suicideresearch/adultsuicide.pdf.*

Brown, G., Bruce, M., & Pearson, J. (2001). High risk management guidelines for elderly suicidal patients in primary care settings. *International Journal of Geriatric Psychiatry, 16,* 593–601.

Burns, D. (1993). *Ten days to self-esteem.* New York: William Morrow.

Burns, D. (1999). *Feeling good handbook.* New York: Plume.

Burns, D. (2003). *Therapist's tool kit.* Retrieved June 30, 2004, from *www.feelinggood.com.*

Burns, D., & Nolen-Hoeksema, S. (1991). Coping styles, homework compliance, and the effectiveness of cognitive behavioral therapy. *Journal of Consulting and Clinical Psychology, 59,* 305–311.

Burns, D., & Spangler, D. (2000). Does psychotherapy homework lead to improvements in depression in cognitive-behavioral therapy or does improvement lead to increased homework compliance? *Journal of Consulting and Clinical Psychology, 68,* 46–56.

Callahan, C. (2001). Quality improvement research on late life depression in primary care. *Medical Care, 39,* 756–759.

Center for Elderly Suicide Prevention & Grief Counseling. (2004). Retrieved June 18, 2004, from *www.ioaging.org/programs/cesp/cesp.html.*

Centers for Disease Control and Prevention. (2002). *National Vital Statistics Reports, 50*(15), 1–120.

Centers for Disease Control and Prevention, National Center for Injury Prevention and Control. (Producer). (2004a). *Web-Based Injury Statistics Query and Reporting System* (WISQUARS). [online]. Retrieved June 30, 2004, from *www.cdc.gov/ncipc/wisquars.*

Centers for Disease Control and Prevention. (2004b). Methods of suicide among persons aged 10–19 years: United States, 1992–2001. *Mortality & Morbidity Weekly Report, 53*(22), 471–474.

Clark, D. (1992). "Rational" suicide and people with terminal conditions or disabilities. *Issues in Law and Medicine, 8,* 147–166.

Conwell, Y., Duberstein, P., Connor, K., Eberly, S., Cox, C., & Caine, E. (2002). Access to firearms and risk for suicide in middle-aged and older adults. *American Journal of Geriatric Psychiatry, 10,* 407–416.

Csikai, E., & Manetta, A. (2002). Preventing unnecessary deaths among older adults: A call to action for social workers. *Journal of Gerontological Social Work, 38,* 85–97.

Cukier, W. (1998). Firearms regulation: Canada in the international context. *Chronic Diseases in Canada.* Retrieved April 5, 2003, from *http://www.hc-sc.gc.ca/pphb-dgspsp/publicat/cdic-mcc/19-1/d_e.html.*

Cutright, P., & Fernquist, R. (2000). Firearms and suicide: The American experience, 1926–1996. *Death Studies, 24,* 705–719.

Dahl, D. (2004, September). New suicide prevention plans seek broader involvement. Message posted to *www.jointogether.org.*

Duberstein, P., Conwell, Y., Seidlitz, L., Lyness, J., Cox, C., & Caine, E. (1999). Age and suicidal ideation in older depressed inpatients. *American Journal of Geriatric Psychiatry, 7,* 289–296.

Ellis, A. (1962). *Reason and emotion in psychotherapy.* New York: Stuart.

Farberow, N. (1980). *The many faces of suicide: Indirect self-destructive behavior.* New York: McGraw-Hill.

Garlow, S. J. (2002). Age, gender and ethnicity differences in patterns of cocaine and ethanol use preceding suicide. *American Journal of Psychiatry, 159,* 615–619.

Haas, A., & Hendin, H. (1983). Suicide among older people: Projection for the future. *Suicide & Life-Threatening Behavior, 13,* 147.

Harris, E., & Barraclough, B. (1994). Suicide as an outcome for medical disorders. *Medicine, 73,* 281–296.

Hawton, K., Arensman, E., Townsend, E., Bremner, S., Fledman, E., Goldney, R., et al. (1998). Deliberate self-harm: Systematic review of efficacy of psychosocial and pharmacological treatments in preventing repetition. *British Medical Journal, 317,* 441–447.

Hughes, S., & Neimeyer, R. (1990). Cognitive model of suicidal behavior. In D. Lester (Ed.), *Current concepts of suicide* (pp. 1–28). Philadelphia: Charles Press.

Husaini, B., Cummings, S., Kilbourne, B., Roback, H, Sherkat, D., Levine, R., et al. (2004). Group psychotherapy for depressed elderly women. *International Journal of Group Psychotherapy, 54*, 295–319.

Injury Prevention Network. (2002, Fall). Updates from California. *Region IX Newsletter, 7,* 1. Retrieved June 16, 2004, from *http://www.emsa.cahwnet.gov/ emsdivision/Newsletter_fall2002.doc.*

Jenkins, R., & Kovess, V. (2002). Evaluation of suicide prevention: A European approach. *International Review of Psychiatry, 14,* 34–41.

Jerger, A. (1979). Behavior theories and their application. In D. Hankoff & B. Einsidler (Eds.), *Suicide: Theory and clinical aspects* (pp. 179–199.) Littleton, MA: PSG Publishing.

Juurlink, D., Herrmann, N., Szalai, J., Kopp, A., & Redelmeier, D. (2004). Medical illness and the risk of suicide in the elderly. *Archives of Internal Medicine, 164,* 1179.

Kastenbaum, R., & Aisenberg, R. (1972). *The psychology of death.* New York: Springer.

Kellermann, A. L., Rivara, F. P., Somes, G., Reay, D. T., Francisco, J., Banton, J. G., et al. (1992). Suicide in the home in relation to gun ownership. *New England Journal of Medicine, 327,* 467–473.

Kelly, G. (1955). *The psychology of personal constructs.* New York: Norton.

Killias, M., van Kesteren, J., & Rindlisbacher, M. (2001). Guns, violent crime, and suicide in 21 countries. *Canadian Journal of Criminology, 43,* 429–448.

Kleepsies, P., & Dettmer, E. (2000). An evidence-based approach to evaluating and managing suicidal emergencies. *Journal of Clinical Psychology, 56,* 1109–1130.

Luoma, J., Martin, C., & Pearson, J. (2002). Contact with mental health and primary care providers before suicide: A review of the evidence. *American Journal of Psychiatry, 159,* 909–916.

McInnis-Dittrich, K. (2002). *Social work with elders: A biopsychosocial approach to assessment and intervention.* Boston: Allyn & Bacon.

McIntosh, J. L., Santos, J. F., Hubbard, R. W., & Overholser, J. C. (1994). *Elder suicide: Research, theory, and treatment.* Washington, DC: American Psychological Association.

Miller, M. (1999). Suicide prevention contracts: Advantages, disadvantages, and an alternative approach. In D. Jacobs (Ed.), *Harvard Medical School guide to suicide assessment and intervention* (pp. 463–481). San Francisco: Jossey-Bass.

Miller, M., Azarel, D., & Hemenway, D. (2002). Firearm availability and suicide, homicide, and unintentional death among women. *Journal of Urban Health: Bulletin of the New York Academy of Medicine, 79,* 26–38.

Miller, M., Jacobs, D., & Gutheil, T. (1998). Talisman or taboo: The controversy of the suicide prevention contract. *Harvard Review of Psychiatry, 6,* 78–87.

Mulsant, B., Alexopoulos, G., Reynolds, C., Katz, I., Abrams, R., Oslin, D., et al. (2001). Pharmacological treatment of depression in older primary care patients: The PROSPECT algorithm. *International Journal of Geriatric Psychiatry, 16,* 585–592.

Murphy, S. L. (2000). Deaths: Final deaths for 1998. *National Vital Statistics Report, 48*(11), 1–105.

National Center for Health Statistics. (2000). Deaths: Final data for 2000. *National Vital Statistics Report, 50*(15), 1–119.

National Center for Injury Prevention and Control. (2004). *The evaluation of interventions to prevent suicide.* Retrieved June 16, 2004, from *http://www.cdc.gov/ncipc/ dvp/suianno.htm.*

National Institutes of Health Consensus Development Panel on the Diagnosis and Treatment of Depression in Late Life. (1992). Diagnosis and treatment of depression in late life. *Journal of the American Medical Association, 286,* 1018–1024.

National Mental Health Information Center. (2003). *Challenging Stereotypes: An Action Guide.* Retrieved January 27, 2003, from *http://www.mentalhealth.org/ publications/allpubs/SMA01-3518/default.asp.*

Neimeyer, R. (1983). Toward a personal construct conceptualization of depression and suicide. *Death Studies, 7,* 127–173.

Oei, T., & Free, M. (1995). Do cognitive behavior therapies validate cognitive models of mood disorder? A review of the empirical evidence. *International Journal of Psychology, 30,* 145–179.

Osgood, N. (1992). *Suicide in later life: Recognizing the warning signs.* Lanham, MD: Lexington.

Osgood, N., Brandt, B., & Lipman, A. (1989). Patterns of suicidal behavior in long-term care facilities: A preliminary report of an ongoing study. *Omega, 19,* 69–78.

Osgood, N., Brandt, B., & Lipman, A. (1991). *Suicide among the elderly in long-term care facilities.* Westport, CT: Greenwood.

Pearson, J., Caine, E., Lindesay, D., Conwell, Y., & Clark, D. (1999). Studies of suicide in later life: Methodologic considerations and research directions. *American Journal of Geriatric Psychiatry, 7,* 203–210.

Pearson, J., Conwell, Y., Lindesay, J., Takahashi, Y., & Caine, E. (1997). Elderly suicide: A multi-national view. *Aging and Mental Health, 1,* 107–111.

Quadagno, J. (1999). *Aging and the life course: An introduction to social gerontology.* Boston: McGraw-Hill.

Raue, P., Alexopoulos, G., Bruce, M., Klimstra, S., Mulsant, B., & Gallo, J. (2001). The systematic assessment of depressed elderly primary care patients. *International Journal of Geriatric Psychiatry, 16,* 560–569.

Reynolds, C. F., & Kupfer, D. J. (1999). Depression and aging: A look to the future. *Psychiatric Services, 50,* 1167–1172.

Romero, M., & Wintemute, G. (2002). The epidemiology of firearm suicide in the United States. *Journal of Urban Health: Bulletin of the New York Academy of Medicine, 79,* 39–48.

SAMHSA. (2004). National Strategy for Suicide Prevention. Retrieved June 16, 2004, from *http://www.mentalhealth.samhsa.gov/suicideprevention/.*

Schneidman, E. (1985). *Definition of suicide.* New York: Wiley.

Schwartz, K. (2004). Concurrent group and individual psychotherapy in a psychiatric day hospital for depressed elderly. *International Journal of Group Psychotherapy, 54,* 177–201.

Seligman, M. (1975). *Helplessness: On depression, development, and death.* San Francisco: Freeman.

Shenassa, E., Catlin, S., & Buka, S. (2003). Lethality of firearms relative to other suicide methods: A population-based study. *Journal of Epidemiology, & Community Health, 57,* 120–125.

Sherman, M., Burns, K., Ignelzi, J., Raia, J., Lofton, V., Toland, D., et al. (2001). Firearms risk management in psychiatric care. *Psychiatric Services, 52,* 1057–1061.

Stillion, J., & McDowell, E. (1996). *Suicide across the lifespan.* Bristol, PA: Taylor & Francis.

Suicide Prevention Resource Center. (2004). Retrieved June 16, 2004, from *www.sprc.org.*

Sutcliffe, C., Cordingley, L., Burns, A., Mozley, C., Bagley, H., Huxley, P., et al. (2000). A new version of the Geriatric Depression Scale for nursing and residential home populations: The Geriatric Depression Scale (residential) (GDS-12R). *International Psychogeriatrics, 12,* 173–181.

Szanto, K., Gildengers, A., Mulsant, B., Brown, G., Alexopoulos, G., & Reynolds, C. (2002). Identification of suicidal ideation and prevention of suicidal behavior in the elderly. *Drugs & Aging, 19,* 11–24.

Uncapher, H. (2000). Physicians less likely to offer depression therapy to older suicidal patients than to younger ones. *Geriatrics, 55,* 82.

U.S. Department of Health and Human Services. (1999). *Mental health: A report of the surgeon general. Executive summary.* Rockville, MD: Author.

U.S. Public Health Service. (1999). *The surgeon general's call to action to prevent suicide.* Washington, DC: U.S. Government Printing Office.

Volkert, T. (2003). Message posted to mhaging@mailman.dca.net.

Volkert, T. (2004, June 18). Mental health for older adults. Message posted to mhaging@mailman.dca.net.

Wampold, B., Minami, T., Baskin, T., & Tierney, S. (2002). A meta-(re) analysis of the effects of cognitive therapy versus other therapies for depression. *Journal of Affective Disorders, 68,* 159–165.

Wiebe, D. (2003). Homicide and suicide risks associated with firearms in the home: A national case-control study. *Annals of Emergency Medicine, 41*(6), 771–782.

World Health Organization. (2003). Adherence to long-term therapies: Evidence for action. Retrieved June 10, 2003, from *http://www.who.int/chronic_conditions/adherencereport/en/.*

Yesavage, A. (2003). *Geriatric Depression Scale.* Retrieved April 28, 2003, from *http://www.stanford.edu/~yesavage/GDS.html.*

Yoder, G. (Nov. 2003). *Firearm suicide among older adults: A sociological autopsy.* Paper presented at the 56th annual meeting of the Gerontological Society of America, San Diego.

Yoder, G. (2004). *Best practice guidelines for treating acutely suicidal elders.* Unpublished manuscript, School of Social Work, Indiana University, Indianapolis.

SECTION III

Special Populations

OVERVIEW

The heterogeneity of the aging population is well recognized. This section of the handbook is intended to provide an understanding of the characteristics, needs, and practice issues of particular at-risk subpopulations of older persons. Specifically, the section focuses on the following issues: (1) an overview of the extent of poverty among at-risk subgroups of elderly persons; (2) the role of work among older adults; (3) characteristics and service needs of the oldest old; (4) the nature and extent of elder immigration and refugee status; (5) an overview of mistreatment of the elderly; and (6) the characteristics of older prisoners in state and federal prisons.

Chapter 14, by David E. Biegel and Sylvia Leibbrandt, demonstrates that although overall rates of poverty are lower for elderly than for nonelderly adults, there are large differences in the rates of poverty among subgroups of elderly persons. In particular, older elderly persons, elders living alone, and elders from minority racial and ethnic groups have higher rates of poverty than other elders. A framework for examining service delivery barriers on system, community, agency staff, and individual and family levels is presented. Recommendations are made for addressing identified barriers and strengthening practice and service delivery among women, racial and ethnic minorities, and rural elderly persons.

Chapter 15, by Sheila H. Akabas and Lauren B. Gates, discusses the nature of work, the types of different work statuses of the elderly, policies designed to protect older workers, factors affecting labor force participation by older adults, and implications for social work practice with working older adults. Today many older adults are working beyond the traditional retirement age, with almost one fifth of persons 65 and older still in the labor force. Factors identified by Akabas and Gates that can serve to keep older adults in the labor force include increasing recognition that aging doesn't inevitably lead to a decline in abilities or the obsolescence of skills, increased number of elderly and reduced numbers of younger people available for work, inadequate accumulation of wealth, economic insecurity, and an increase in numbers of women in the labor force who often come to their career peaks later than men. The authors discuss roles for social workers on micro, mezzo, and macro levels in assisting older adults to address their relationship to the labor force.

Chapter 16, by Ruth E. Dunkle and Hae-Sook Jeon, discusses the fastest-growing group of older adults, the oldest old, those elderly individuals who are 85 years old and older. This group is projected to compose 2% of the population in 2010, growing to 5% of the population by 2050. The authors provide a description of the demographic and socioeconomic characteristics of the oldest-old population, as well as their mental and physical health needs and need for social support. They note that the oldest old have more combined health and mental health problems, with fewer financial and social resources to address these problems, than do other older adults. Implications for mental health service delivery and caregiving are presented.

Chapter 17, by Ailee Moon and Siyon Rhee, discusses social work practice with immigrant and refugee elders. As Moon and Rhee point out, the elderly immigrant population in the United States is becoming increasingly diverse based on racial and ethnic background, reasons for immigration, age at time of immigration, length of residence in the United States, and English proficiency. The well-being and process of adjustment of immigrant elders is affected by their immigration histories, cultural norms and values, and socioeconomic backgrounds. The authors discuss the role of family and caregiving with immigrant elders, emphasizing both the importance of traditional family values and the impact on family issues of living in a different culture. The authors also discuss mental health issues and psychological distress, service utilization and barriers to service use, and implications for social work practice with immigrant and refugee elders. They stress the need for social workers to be culturally competent and to recognize both intragroup and intergroup differences within this population.

Chapter 18, by Susan Tomita, focuses on social work practice with elders who have been mistreated or neglected, a problem area that has been recognized only within the past two decades. A variety of types of elder mistreatment are discussed, including physical abuse, sexual abuse, psychological abuse, financial abuse, identity theft, undue influence, and neglect and self-neglect. Whether an act is considered abusive or neglectful is defined based on intentionality, severity, intensity, frequency, and consequences. Tomita reviews theories of causation of elder mistreatment, as well as the characteristics of perpetrators and victims. A major emphasis of the chapter is the presentation of specific assessment and counseling strategies for social workers to use in working with elders when maltreatment is suspected.

Chapter 19, by Ron Aday, addresses the issue of older adults who are in state and federal prisons. The number of such individuals has been steadily rising during the past decade. There are now 10,000 individuals in state and federal prisons ages 50 years and older (8.6% of all prisoners), the age that correctional officials usually consider to be an older adult. Given the overcrowding in these institutions and the increasing number of prisoners with mental illness, Aday points out the significant need for social and health services for older adults in state and federal prisons. He discusses the heterogeneity of the population of older prisoners, as well as their extensive mental health, medical, and social needs. Although about half of the states now provide geriatric facilities and programming for elderly inmates, these programs have limitations, such as restricting prisoner contact with outside communities, inadequate monitoring of inmate needs, and insufficient funding. Aday presents a variety of suggestions for social work services with this population, including educational and social programming and use of therapeutic groups.

DAVID E. BIEGEL

SYLVIA LEIBBRANDT

Elders Living in Poverty

14

Despite the advent of a variety of federal-level income support and social service programs that have had positive effects in reducing the extent of poverty among older adults, poverty among the elderly is still a significant problem. Given the heterogeneity of the elderly population, poverty is of particular concern among elderly women, elders who are 75 years and older, elders of color, and elderly persons living in rural communities. This chapter reviews the extent of poverty among the elderly and discusses the characteristics and needs of vulnerable older populations. Of significant concern to social workers is the underutilization of health, mental health, and social services by older people, especially by those at-risk populations most in need. A framework for conceptualizing service delivery barriers is presented, and the literature concerning the nature and extent of these barriers is reviewed. Practice and service delivery recommendations to address the identified barriers are then presented and discussed.

EXTENT OF POVERTY AMONG THE ELDERLY IN THE UNITED STATES

Poverty rates among adults ages 65 years old and over have been steadily falling since 1965, from about 30% of the overall elderly population below the poverty line to 10.2% of elderly persons below the poverty line in 2003 (U.S. Census Bureau, 2004a). This significant drop in poverty rates among the elderly is principally due to the increases in Social Security benefits and the advent of federal Medicare and other safety net programs (Bok, 1996; Hungerford, Rassette, Iams, & Koenig, 2001–2002). In fact, as Ozawa and Lum (1996) indicate, social insurance benefits (Social Security and unemployment insurance) and welfare payments (all means-tested cash payments and food stamps) for the elderly raised their median income status from 1% to 70% of poverty-line income. The rate of poverty among elderly persons in the United States is now lower than the poverty rates of both children under 18 years of age and nonelderly adults (U.S. Census Bureau, 2004a). It should be noted, however, that poverty rates for the elderly in the United States, especially for elderly men and elderly women who live alone, are considerably higher than for elderly citizens of European industrialized nations (Smeeding & Sandstrom, 2004).

The declining rates of overall elderly poverty in the United States have been interpreted by some to indicate that we no longer have to be concerned with elders in poverty and that, rather, our attention and

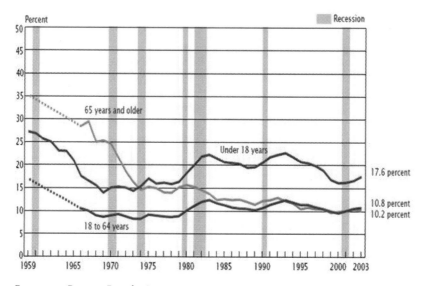

FIGURE 14.1. Property Rates by Age: 1959 to 2003.
Note: The data points are placed at the midpoints of the respective years. Data for people 18 to 64 and 65 and older are not available from 1960 to 1965.
Source: U.S. Census Bureau. Current Population Survey, 1960 to 2004 Annual Social and Economic Supplements.

resources should be spent primarily on other population groups with higher rates of poverty. However, examining only a cross-sectional view of overall poverty among elderly persons can be misleading for several reasons. First, the elderly population is very heterogeneous, with resultant higher poverty rates among vulnerable elderly subpopulations. Second, there is a failure to consider the "near poor," those individuals whose incomes are below 150% of the poverty line and who therefore still have significant income needs (Bogdon, Katsura, & Mikelsons, 2001; Villa, Wallace, & Markides, 1997). As will be seen, rates of elders who are "near poor" are considerably higher than the rates of near-poor nonelderly adults. Third, a cross-sectional analysis of elderly poverty does not provide any information about elders' cumulative chances of being poor during their elder years, the duration of their poverty, or their chances of escaping from poverty and thus does not provide an accurate picture of the degree to which elderly individuals experience poverty during their later years.

Heterogeneity of Poverty Rates Among the Elderly

As can be seen in Table 14.1, which is based on census data from 2003, there are large differences in the rates of poverty among subgroups of elderly persons. Thus

older elderly persons, women, elders living alone, and racial and ethnic elders have higher rates of poverty than other elders (U.S. Census Bureau, 2004b). For example, the poverty rate for elderly individuals who live alone is almost double the poverty rate for elders overall, whereas the poverty rate for Black elderly and elders of Hispanic origin is over twice as high as the poverty rate for White elders. In addition, the poverty rates for elderly Blacks, Asians, and individuals of Hispanic origin are all higher than the corresponding poverty rates for nonelderly adults in these racial and ethnic groups (U.S. Census Bureau, 2004b).

There are also differences in rates of poverty within elderly racial and ethnic groups, presented in Table 14.1. Thus in each group the poverty rates for women are higher than those for men and for older as compared with younger elderly individuals. The rates of poverty for elderly persons living alone are at least twice as high among Black, Asian, and elders of Hispanic origin as compared with White elders. The poverty rate for females living alone is higher than that of males for the three racial/ethnic groups for which data are available.

"Near Poor" Elders

The "near poor"—those with incomes less than 150% of the poverty rate—often have incomes too high to

TABLE 14.1. Income and Poverty Ratio for Persons 65 Years and Older by Race: 2003 (numbers in thousands)

Population Group	All Income Levels	Number & Percent Below 100% of Pov.	Below 150% of Pov.
65 and Over (All races)	34,659	3,552 (10.2)	8,512 (24.6)
65–74	18,238	1,647 (9.0)	3,720 (20.4)
75 and over	16,421	1,905 (11.6)	4,792 (29.2)
Males	14,797	1,079 (7.3)	2,721 (18.4)
65–74	8,356	597 (7.1)	1,380 (16.5)
75 and over	6,441	482 (7.5)	1,341 (20.8)
Females	19,862	2,473 (12.5)	5,791(29.2)
65–74	9,883	1,050 (10.6)	2,340 (23.7)
75 and over	9,980	1,423 (14.3)	3,451(34.6)
Living Alone (65 and over)	10,658	1,985 (18.6)	4,840 (45.4)
Male	2,785	379 (13.6)	1,024 (36.8)
Female	7,873	1,606 (20.4)	3,816 (48.5)
65 and Over (White)	30,514	2,686 (8.8)	6,847 (22.4)
65–74	15,845	1,212 (7.6)	2,884 (18.2)
75 and over	14,670	1,475 (10.1)	3,962 (27.0)
Males	13,121	810 (6.2)	2,163 (16.5)
65–74	7,325	444 (6.1)	1,070 (14.6)
75 and over	5,796	366 (6.3)	1,094 (18.9)
Females	17,394	1,877 (10.8)	4,683 (26.9)
65–74	8,520	768 (9.0)	1,815 (21.3)
75 and over	8,874	1,109 (12.5)	2,869 (32.3)
Living Alone (65 and over)	9,372	1,528 (16.3)	4,015 (42.8)
Males	2,425	283 (11.7)	820 (33.8)
Females	6,947	1,244 (17.9)	3,195 (46.0)
65 and Over (Black)	2,933	688 (23.5)	1,257 (42.9)
65–74	1,631	335 (20.6)	610 (37.4)
75 and over	1,302	353 (27.1)	647 (49.7)
Males	1,123	198 (17.7)	394 (35.1)
65–74	665	113 (17.0)	211 (31.7)
75 and over	459	86 (18.6)	184 (40.0)
Females	1,810	490 (27.1)	863 (47.7)
65–74	966	222 (23.0)	400 (41.4)
75 and over	843	267 (31.7)	463 (54.9)
Living Alone (65 and over)	1,049	378 (36.0)	662 (63.1)
Males	297	80 (27.0)	168 (56.6)
Females	752	298 (39.6)	494 (65.6)
65 and Over (Hispanic origin)	2,080	406 (19.5)	804 (38.7)
65–74	1,272	239 (18.8)	481 (37.8)
75 and over	808	167 (20.7)	323 (40.0)
Males	881	146 (16.6)	320 (36.3)

(*continued*)

TABLE 14.1. Income and Poverty Ratio for Persons 65 Years and Older by Race: 2003 (numbers in thousands) (*continued*)

Population Group	Number & Percent		
	All Income Levels	Below 100% of Pov.	Below 150% of Pov.
65–74	545	95 (17.3)	198 (36.4)
75 and over	336	52 (15.4)	122 (36.3)
Females	1,199	260 (21.7)	484 (40.4)
65–74	727	145 (19.9)	283 (38.9)
75 and over	473	115 (24.4)	201 (42.6)
Living Alone (65 and over)	436	160 (36.8)	290 (66.6)
Males	138	39 (28.2)	73 (53.0)
Females	298	121 (40.8)	217 (72.9)
65 and Over (Asian)	1,065	152 (14.2)	354 (33.2)
65–74	650	82 (12.7)	194 (29.9)
75 and over	416	69 (16.7)	160 (38.4)
Males	483	60 (12.3)	139 (28.8)
65–74	308	32 (10.4)	83 (26.9)
75 and over	175	28 (15.8)	56 (32.0)
Females	583	92 (15.8)	215 (36.8)
65–74	342	50 (14.7)	111 (32.5)
75 and over	241	42 (17.4)	104 (43.0)
Living Alone (65 and over)	204	67 (32.7)	135 (66.5)
Males	49	11 (B)	27 (B)
Females	155	55 (35.8)	109 (70.0)

Note: B: Percentages suppressed

Source: U.S. Census Bureau, Current Population Survey, *2004 Annual Social & Economic Supplement.*

qualify for public assistance, but yet too low to cover their housing, food, transportation, and health care needs. In addition, researchers have noted a shrinking of the elderly middle class, with a resultant drop of income among the bottom fifth of elderly households (Bogdon et al., 2001; Villa et al., 1997).

As can be seen in Table 14.1, overall more elders are living in "near poverty" than under the poverty level. Overall, one quarter of all elders live near the poverty line, a higher figure than that of nonelderly adults who live in near poverty. Table 14.1 also shows the same patterns for near poverty as for poverty, reported earlier, with higher near-poverty rates among elders who are 75 years and older, among female elders, among racial and ethnic elders, among elders living alone, and among combinations of these variables. The highest subgroups of elderly persons in near poverty are women living alone who are Black or of Asian or Hispanic origin; over two thirds of these individuals are living in near poverty (U.S. Census Bureau, 2004).

Long-Term Poverty Among the Elderly

Rank and Hirschl (1999) examined poverty among the elderly from 1968 to 1992 using data from the Panel Study of Income Dynamics in order to estimate the probabilities of poverty across the entire elderly life span. Major findings of this study showed the following: 4 out of 10 elders between the ages of 60 to 90 experienced at least 1 year living below the poverty line, with almost one half of elders having at least 1 year in which their income fell 125% below the poverty line. The likelihood of experiencing poverty was considerably higher for elderly individuals who were Black, who had lower educational levels, and who were not married. The combination of these variables produced extremely high rates of poverty. The study also pointed out that almost 9 out of 10 unmarried Black females with low levels of education fell below the poverty line at some period of time during the 60- to 85-year age period.

Several other studies using the same data source examined exits from poverty of elderly at-risk populations. Focusing on the period from 1981 to 1992, Wu (2003) found that older persons were less likely than younger persons to exit from poverty regardless of their length of time in poverty. Additionally, findings showed that almost one third of older persons remained in poverty for 10 years or more, as compared with only 1 of 10 for those under 65 years of age. Jensen and McLaughlin (1997) found that elderly persons in nonmetropolitan communities had a lower exit rate out of poverty than elderly persons living in metropolitan communities.

Future Rates of Poverty Among the Elderly

It is difficult to predict future rates of poverty for elderly individuals given the multiple variables that affect poverty levels. Nonetheless, Wentworth and Pattison (2001–2002) estimate that if benefit rules for Social Security and Supplemental Security Income (SSI) are not changed and if real earnings and other income of the elderly increase at 1% per year (the intermediate assumption cited in the *2000 Report of the Social Security Board of Trustees*), poverty among the elderly would decrease to an overall rate of about 7.2% in 2020 and to 4.1% in 2047. However, as the authors point out, future poverty rates of the elderly could be affected by changes in SSI levels, earnings and pensions, longevity, and marital patterns. One can add other variables to the equation that could affect future poverty rates of the elderly, including the fact that the population of vulnerable elderly with higher poverty rates—for example, older elders and elders of color—is anticipated to grow at a faster rate than the elderly population as a whole in the future (Administration on Aging, 2003; Gonyea, 1995; Sotomayor, 1997), as well as concern about rising health care expenditures of the elderly (Johnson & Penner, 2004; Manchester, 1997). Thus there are pessimistic as well as optimistic future projections about the rates of elderly poverty. Given the difficulty of predicting economic trends even over the short term, predictions made far into the future are often inaccurate and should therefore be examined with some caution.

AT-RISK ELDERLY POPULATIONS

Women

The poverty rate data presented in the previous section have demonstrated the higher poverty rates of elderly women as compared with elderly men; older women from racial and ethnic minority groups are at greatest risk for poverty and near poverty. A number of variables that influence the risk for women becoming poor have been identified in the literature, including divorce, widowhood, increased longevity, intermittent work histories, lower likelihood of receiving pension income, and lower wages (Anzick & Weaver, 2001; Kingson & Williamson, 2001; Rupp, Strand, & Davies, 2003).

Marital status in particular has a significant impact on the income of elderly women (Ozawa, 1997; Sevak, Weir, & Willis, 2004). Although there has been a large drop in the impact of widowhood on women's poverty, from 37% of new widows falling below the poverty line in the 1970s to 12–15% by the 1990s, widowhood nevertheless remains a significant risk factor for older women's transition into poverty (Sevak et al., 2004). Ozawa (1997) examined the income status of elderly women 10 years after retirement. She found that older women who were already widowed at retirement had only 59% of the income status of elderly women who were married throughout this 10-year period. Meanwhile, elderly women who became widowed after retirement had 68% of the income status of elderly women who were married throughout the 10-year postretirement period. Sevak et al. (2004) point out that given the strong relationship between mortality and wealth, Social Security policy needs to consider the particular situation of widows. Women widowed after their children have grown but before their retirement preparations have been completed are usually not eligible for Temporary Assistance for Needy Families (TANF), Supplemental Security Income (SSI), or Social Security and are therefore particularly vulnerable to poverty.

Racial and Ethnic Minorities

The higher levels of poverty among elders of color is of increasing concern given the fact that the non-White elderly population is growing at a faster rate than is the White elderly population. It is projected that one quarter of the elderly population will be non-White by the year 2025. This number will increase to a third within a decade of that (American Association of Retired Persons [AARP], 1993). Given the significantly higher rates of poverty among adults ages 45 to 54 years, the growing percentage of minority elderly in the future will mean growing numbers of elderly individuals without adequate financial assets (Binstock, 1999). Higher rates of poverty among racial and ethnic elderly individuals are also associated with greater deficits in education, lower self-reported health status, greater physical impairment, less access to health care, underutilization of health care services, and inadequate housing (Binstock, 1999; Greene, 2000; Harris, 1998; Reed, Hargraves, & Cassil, 2003; Tran & Williams, 1998). However, as Torres-Gil and Moga (2001) point out, racial and ethnic minority elder populations have developed considerable strengths and resiliencies from their physical and social survival in the face of poverty and, oftentimes, racial and ethnic discrimination.

Rural Elderly

Rates of poverty among elderly persons living in non-metropolitan areas are higher than those of elderly persons living in metropolitan communities. Using data from the 1990 Census, McLaughlin and Jensen (1993) reported that 15.4% of nonmetropolitan elders lived in poverty as compared with 10.0% of all metropolitan elders and 13.8% of central city elders. These differences were not explained by differences in the population by gender, age, race, education, marital status, or living arrangements (McLaughlin & Jensen, 1993). In addition, nonmetropolitan elders are more likely to be near poor (less than 150% of the poverty line) than metropolitan elders, with over one third of nonmetropolitan elders being near poor as compared with about one quarter of metropolitan elders (McLaughlin & Jensen, 1993). Finally, it has been reported that nonmetropolitan elderly individuals are more likely to become poor than metropolitan elders, even after controlling for other confounding variables such as race, education, marital status, and widowhood (McLaughlin & Jensen, 1995). Higher poverty rates among the elderly in nonmetropolitan areas are felt to be due to certain aspects of the rural economic and social structure that have negative effects on economic security. Elders in rural communities have lower lifetime earnings, fewer Social Security benefits, less pension coverage, and less likelihood of enrollment in the SSI program (Glasgow & Brown, 1998; McLaughlin & Jensen, 1993). Given the higher levels of elder poverty in rural areas, there would be an anticipated greater need for services. Yet a number of researchers point out that few services are available and used in rural communities due to lack of governmental resources, lower population densities, shortages of trained professionals, and high

levels of self-reliance in the rural elderly (Krout, 1998). There is also concern that the out-migration of younger populations from rural communities weakens the informal social networks of elderly persons (Glasgow, 1993).

SERVICE DELIVERY BARRIERS

A variety of barriers to the use of health, mental health, and social services by at-risk older people have been identified in the literature (Baker & Pallett-Hehn, 1995; Biegel, Farkas, & Song, 1997; Biegel, Petchers, Synder, & Beisgen, 1989; Jervis, Jackson, & Manson, 2002; Minear & Crose, 1996; Tran, Dhooper, & McInnis-Dittrich, 1997; Yeatts, Crow, & Folts, 1992). These barriers are often the greatest for subgroups of the most vulnerable elders in poverty that we have described earlier. Biegel and colleagues (Biegel & Farkas, 1989; Biegel, Johnsen, & Shafran, 1997) have categorized service delivery barriers on four different levels—system, community, agency staff, and individual and family (see Table 14.2). This framework highlights the places at which barriers occur in order to guide the development of interventions at the proper locations to address these barriers and thus improve practice and service delivery to elders in need. In addressing barriers to service delivery to older people, we believe that it is important to focus on all four levels.

Though the four levels of barriers are relevant and appropriate for any type of service, the specific barriers identified in Table 14.2 will vary to some degree depending on the type of service. In addition, some barriers pertain to a greater degree or in particular to vulnerable elderly subpopulations. For example, a barrier such as lack of services is a greater problem in rural than in urban communities, whereas past experiences with racial/ethnic discrimination and lack of culturally competent service providers pertain particularly to minority older populations.

Systems-level barriers refer to deficits at the service agency and at the agency network level that are affected by political, economic, and social forces that shape the development of agency services and funding for such services. The principal system-level barriers to elderly individuals' use of services that have been identified in the research literature include: lack of accessibility of services (cost, location, transportation); fragmentation of services as reflected by lack of linkages with other service systems and providers, both formal and informal; lack of supports provided

TABLE 14.2. Service Delivery Barriers for Elders in Poverty

System Level (Agency and agency network deficits)
• Lack of linkages with informal networks
• Lack of linkages with other service systems and providers
• Financial/cost of services
• Lack of services/lack of specialized services
• Inappropriately designed services
• Location of services/transportation issues

Staff Level (Knowledge, skills, attitudes, and behaviors of staff)
• Lack of non-English-speaking staff members
• Lack of cultural competency of agency staff members/insensitive service providers
• Lack of knowledge of problems/needs of elders in poverty
• Lack of training to address specific problems of the elderly
• Staff is not reflective of the racial and ethnic diversity of the population to be served
• Ageism

Community Level (Attitudes toward service use by lay helpers and organizations/relationships between lay helpers and professional services)
• Discouragement of formal help seeking
• Lack of knowledge of agency services
• Lack of relationships with service providers
• Unwillingness to recognize/define "problems" of elders in poverty

Individual/Family Level (Personal and family attitudes and behaviors toward service use)
• Language barriers/lack of proficiency in English
• Past/present experiences with racism, racial/ethnic or age discrimination
• Past negative experiences with service use/distrust of service providers
• Negative attitudes toward seeking help—stigma, fear, embarrassment, shame, confidentiality concerns
• Discouragement of service use by family members
• Belief that treatment/services will not be effective
• Preference for use of family care and other informal networks
• Lack of knowledge of services
• Accessibility issues—concern about transportation, location of services, cost of services
• Concern about acceptance by agency staff
• Unaware of need for services/denial of problems

to informal caregivers; lack of services or specialized services; and inappropriately designed services (Baker, 1994; Baker & Pallett-Hehn, 1995; Burggraf, 2000; Damron-Rodriguez, 1998; Ford & Hatchett, 2001; Greene, 2000; Jervis et al., 2002; Knight & Kaskie, 1995; Noelker & Bass, 1988; Rittner & Kirk, 1995; Yeatts et al., 1992). Given the importance of informal support networks in minority communities (Jackson & Wolford, 1992; Urdaneta, Saldana, & Winkler, 1995), the lack of supports provided to informal caregivers and the purported lack of linkages between professionals and informal caregivers is of particular concern.

Staff-level barriers are the levels of knowledge, skills, attitudes, and behaviors of agency staff. Staff-level barriers that have been identified in the literature include: lack of knowledge of specific problems and needs of subgroups of older people; lack of staff members who are specifically trained to handle the problems associated with these needs; negative attitudes by professionals about aging and/or particular problems of the elderly (e.g., mental health problems); lack of staff members who speak languages other than English; lack of culturally competent staff; and insufficient number of staff members that reflect the racial and ethnic makeup of the communities of elders they serve (Applewhite, 1998; Baker, 1994; Biegel et al., 1989; Browne & Broderick, 1994; Burggraf, 2000; Damron-Rodriguez, 1998; Jones, 1999; Yeatts et al., 1992). Lack of professional commitment and the tendency to treat minority elders without regard to differences of individuals within minority groups are two issues which present particular difficulties for the delivery of services to African American, Asian, and Hispanic elders. The failure of professionals to fully understand the unique life experiences of particular older minority individuals can be an important service barrier.

Community-level barriers refer to negative attitudes and behaviors toward professional service use by informal helpers and community-based organizations (neighborhood associations, self-help groups, ethnic and fraternal organizations, etc.; Biegel, Johnsen, & Shafran, 1997). Community-level barriers to service use by the elderly that have been identified in the literature include: unwillingness to recognize or define "problems" of elders in poverty; lack of knowledge of agency services by informal helpers; lack of relationships between informal and agency service providers; and discouragement of formal help-seeking by informal helpers.

Individual-level barriers refer to personal and family attitudes and behaviors toward service use. Individual and family-level barriers that have been identified in the research literature include: negative attitudes toward service use (stigma, fear, distrust, or lack of confidence in service providers, preference for self-reliance, confidentiality issues); denial of problems; accessibility issues (language barriers, transportation, concern about cost); lack of knowledge of services; negative experiences with previous attempts at professional help seeking; and preference for use of family care and other informal networks (Baker, 1994; Burggraf, 2000; Dancy & Ralston, 2002; Gordon, 1995; Jervis et al., 2002; Knight & Kaskie, 1995; Miller & Stull, 1999; Minear & Crose, 1996; Richardson, 1992; Yeatts et al., 1992). A number of the aforementioned barriers are especially relevant for African American, Asian, and Hispanic elders. There is considerable evidence of negative experiences by minority individuals with a variety of service delivery systems. These problems can be expected to influence elders' use of community services. For health services in particular, given the evidence that ethnicity plays an important role in the conceptualization of illness (Hall & Tucker, 1985; Urdaneta et al., 1995), how ethnic elders define illness and their knowledge of service delivery systems can also affect service utilization.

PRACTICE AND SERVICE DELIVERY RECOMMENDATIONS

In order to fully address and remedy the widespread health and psychosocial ramifications of economic hardship of at-risk elders in poverty, a multidimensional approach targeting all four barrier levels—system, staff, community, and individual/family—is required. Recommendations are, therefore, directed toward these levels as they pertain to the needs of poor elderly women, racial and ethnic minorities, and rural residents.

One of the greatest barriers to service delivery, affecting all at-risk elderly, is the lack of knowledge about the problems and needs of poor elders, both at the system and staff levels. This barrier is significant, as it contributes to the development and delivery of services that do not adequately meet the needs of this population. A second barrier at the staff level involves the provision of services by professionals who lack the specialized knowledge and skills needed to attend to older adults in poverty. In general, competent practice with these at-risk elders requires a specialized knowledge of gerontological social work and of the resources (both formal and informal) that are available to support older women, racial and ethnic minorities, and rural clients. Equally important is a thorough understanding of the experience of being poor in older adulthood, including a familiarity with the risk factors and implications of poverty, an awareness of the barriers these older adults face, and the cumulative effects of lifelong discrimination (e.g., racial, gender, and now age discrimination).

Elderly Women

As we have seen, one subgroup that is especially vulnerable to the risks of poverty is elderly women. The prevalence of poverty among elderly women, as compared with men, is significantly greater. Those who are particularly vulnerable to these effects are divorced, widowed, or single women over the age of 70 and living alone. Minority and rural women are the most vulnerable. Although a large majority of those in poverty rely on Social Security to survive, women and widows generally receive the fewest benefits because of their low-wage histories and major interruptions in their employment histories. At the staff level, social workers should be aware of the unique issues facing older women, including their financial constraints, and understand that, although many would prefer to continue working to support themselves, greater numbers of them are leaving the workforce prematurely due to health problems (Perkins, 1992). In addition to health and financial barriers, elderly women are subject to gender discrimination and social isolation. With this awareness, the social worker's primary role should be to assess the older woman's financial and health status, the social supports she has in place, and her ability to afford health care. If gender discrimination figured prominently in her life, she may have little faith in "the system" and be reluctant to accept services.

Recommendations at the individual level might involve resource counseling and provision to support women who are socially isolated (e.g., widows and childless older women) through enrollment at a senior center, a support group for widows, a volunteer home-visitor program, or some other social or religious organization that appeals to the client. Social work advocacy may be necessary to ensure that the client is not assuming any excess costs for enrollment or transportation. Following psychosocial and supportive counseling, the older woman might be more willing to reach out to family, friends, and neighbors to bolster her support system. Interventions at the individual level might also include referral to a health promotion program, financial counseling, or application to a more affordable housing facility. At the community level, social workers can disseminate information at churches, community centers, and social organizations about resources available to support socially isolated older adults, widows, or those who are frail. At the systems level, staff can learn about other services in the community and develop linkages by visiting other agencies, sharing the ways in which the two can work together to serve at-risk elders, and by becoming involved in a social worker exchange (in which two social workers exchange roles and spend a week at the other agency to become familiarized with staff, the agency's programs and services, and its clientele). Given the growing number of elderly women in poverty, creative interventions directed at all barrier levels will be necessary to ameliorate the living conditions of older women, especially those who are also ethnic minorities.

Racial and Ethnic Minority Elders

When the older woman's ethnicity differs from that of the provider, the helping process becomes even more complex. Intervention with ethnic minorities, regardless of their economic status, requires a specific set of skills and competencies in order to respond in a manner that is culturally sensitive, relevant, and empowering.

The National Association of Social Workers [NASW] Code of Ethics (1996) outlines key social work values and principles for working with ethnic minorities. Informed practice, for example, is characterized by a respect for the *inherent dignity and worth of the person* and a *cultural competence* that reflects an understanding of *social diversity*. A major barrier to service delivery with ethnic minorities, therefore, is the social worker's unwillingness or inability to respect differences in other individuals. Tripp-Reimer (1999) advocates three elements necessary for cultural competence: (1) awareness-oriented strategies, to use the process of self-examination to identify prejudice; (2) knowledge-oriented strategies, to promote learning about the elder's culture; and (3) skill-oriented strategies, to develop the skill sets of those working with ethnic minorities. A central feature of culturally sensitive social work is the provider's capacity for self-insight for the purpose of identifying early on any bias that might interfere with client assessment and treatment. Equally important is an acknowledgment of one's own values and conceptualization of health, illness, help seeking, treatment, and quality of life vis-à-vis the client's, because various ethnic groups use different paradigms to interpret these conditions (Sotomayor, 1997). Self-analysis is not complete without a fuller understanding of the older adult in his or her cultural context. For example, a determination of the elder's social boundaries, degree of acculturation and assimilation, approaches to problem solving, and perception of his or her life situation and presenting problem is necessary in order to provide culturally sensitive interventions. Language, both spoken and unspoken, is one aspect of the professional exchange that requires preliminary consideration given that fundamental concepts and terms used throughout the helping process may not exist in the primary language of the client or that the terms may simply have a different meaning. Therefore, careful preparation, ongoing assessment, and active listening are necessary to avoid conduct that may be perceived as offensive to the elder or, at the very least, irrelevant to the problem at hand (Applewhite, 1998).

Although it is important to acquire knowledge about the ethnic group in question, it is perhaps more important to understand that there is always within-group diversity. For example, a provider may believe that African Americans tend to use home remedies to treat illness. But without checking this preconception with the client, the social worker is apt to make inappropriate assumptions about the senior's attitude toward treatment. Therefore, a comprehensive evaluation of the older adult's values and attitudes is necessary, including the elder's self-perceptions regarding his or her affiliation to the racial/ethnic group.

These cultural competencies are essential when interacting with any minority client. One subgroup that is growing in numbers and is at high risk for poverty and its repercussions is that of grandparent caregivers. Although grandparents represent a wide variety of racial and ethnic groups, African American women account for the highest proportion of grandparents raising grandchildren. These elders living in poverty have unique challenges that require effective resourcing and support services. Social workers should be aware of the high prevalence of health problems in this special population, including physical impairment and depression, both of which could become exacerbated in the role of caregiving. Therefore, access to respite services to provide relief from caregiving or, at the very least, from the more strenuous tasks of child care should be facilitated. In addition, providing home health care to offer emotional and instrumental support, education, and information regarding effective coping strategies and alternative resources is recommended. Important too is the knowledge that grandparents with the most health problems and caregivers whose grandchildren have physical or behavioral problems tend not to seek help (Burnette, 1999; Fuller-Thomson & Minkler, 2000), yet these are the seniors at greatest risk.

To be truly effective, the social worker should be informed about the reasons that increasing numbers of African American grandparents are taking over the responsibility of raising their grandchildren. Research indicates that this move is often a result of parental substance abuse, incarceration of the mother, or HIV/AIDS. Given the stigma associated with each of these issues, it is not surprising that grandparent caregivers become socially isolated and fail to utilize the supports and services to which they are entitled (Fuller-Thomson & Minkler, 2000). Social workers should be involved in outreach efforts to connect with these individuals who, for whatever reasons, do not take advantage of available services.

Failed attempts at outreach might be the result of two barriers in particular: (1) the provider, whose ethnic identity does not match the client's, and (2) the service offered, which does not cater to members of the client's ethnic group. Recommendations at the staff level involve hiring a diverse group of staff members representing a variety of ethnic backgrounds, using multilingual staff members as resources to provide translation and interpretation when necessary, providing in-service staff training and education to nonminority agency consumers regarding minority groups and cultural sensitivity, incorporating activities and meals that also appeal to minority consumers, and including ethnic minority representatives on the advisory board of the agency (Yeatts et al., 1992). A community-level recommendation would involve providing services to ethnic minority elders in a location that is culturally sensitive and familiar to these seniors, such as a church or ethnic organization.

Jones (1999) developed two strategic approaches to addressing the barriers faced by older African Americans in poverty: administrative strategies and direct service strategies. The most relevant recommendations follow:

Administrative Strategies

- Community-based care must be viewed and administered via a social rather than a medical model. It should be organized under the county levels of government.
- Practitioners and researchers must educate health service staff, elected officials, and the community about the health status of the Black elderly population.
- Adequate financial resources must be provided for primary and preventive services.
- Valid and reliable health status needs assessments must be conducted. These can range from something as simple as focus groups to more sophisticated research designs.
- Legislation that may impact health status and minority elderly should be monitored by all.
- Structured coordination must be provided in order to reduce the fragmentation that currently exists within various health-promotion and disease-prevention services.

Direct Service Strategies

- Community partnership arrangements must be developed to meet the total community health needs of the Black older population (Jones, 1999, pp. 230–231).

Rural Elders

Whereas outreach with ethnic minority seniors presents enormous service delivery challenges, social work in rural regions presents a unique set of challenges in delivering services, especially to at-risk groups, including the oldest old, racial and ethnic minority elders, and older women. Older adults living in nonmetropolitan settings have fewer community resources, especially specialized services; therefore, they experience greater deprivation than do urban elderly (Coward, Duncan & Netzer, 1993; Glasgow, 1993; Krout, 1994). An awareness of the minimal services for older adults, the inadequate transportation available, and the social isolation of rural elders lends appreciation for the struggle of seniors and providers and an understanding of the creativity necessary to ameliorate conditions.

Krout (1998) identified some creative initiatives implemented by some rural Area Agencies on Aging (AAA). He cautioned, however, that consideration is needed when developing such initiatives so that recommendations are realistic yet without rural stereotypes, respectful of the local values and social systems in place, and mindful of the diversity that exists within and between rural regions. Interventions should incorporate the community's preference for services, using flexibility and multimethod approaches, and should build on the strengths and resources already present in these rural areas. The goal is to maximize these resources through efficient service coordination and coalition building, utilizing existing relationships with local leaders and the private sector to offer services that promote personal autonomy and dignity (Krout, 1998). Of particular relevance to these points is that a majority of care in rural communities is provided by family members and that these providers need to be supported, too (Stoller & Lee, 1994).

Given the preceding considerations, recommendations are directed at all barrier levels to overcome obstacles to access and utilization of services (including transportation issues), reluctance on the part of the older adult to access community resources, availability of specialized services and professionals, and the lack of variety in services that are offered. One recommendation in particular addresses a variety of obstacles, including the social isolation elders experience as rural residents. This initiative, implemented by several AAAs, establishes a network of satellite senior centers to provide outreach to socially isolated older persons. For those seniors who are reluctant to access formal services, this familiar site offers health promotion, information, screening, and referral, while providing them with social stimulation and nutrition. Employing another familiar location—local parishes—public health nurses are able to provide health screening and education to frail seniors. One AAA leveraged its relationship with area hospitals and nursing homes to increase the availability and array of home health services that could be offered to at-risk elders. Exploiting the linkages between rural AAAs enabled the development of housing coalitions, thereby increasing the housing resources for older adults (Krout, 1989).

Access to these services can be facilitated through the development of a transportation system, which for one AAA involved the use of local and federal funds and community volunteers to provide an alternative to the transportation resources already in place. The issue of access pervades any discussion of services for rural seniors. Aside from transportation resources, a common approach to improving access to services is through the use mobile health services, which offer screening, treatment, and referral (Bell, 1975). Another option to providing essential services involves a recommendation at the systems level and concerns the use of urban resources to meet rural needs. For example, a psychogeriatric social worker based in an urban center might be assigned to a county in which there are three rural communities. Providing assessment and treatment services to all these rural and urban communities means that elderly clients do not miss out on specialized care. Seniors who accept these services can then receive clinical intervention from other multidisciplinary members of the psychogeriatric team, such as the geriatric nurse, occupational therapist, and geriatric psychiatrist. Although access is important, equally important is the utilization of these services, which can be facilitated in rural areas by employing consumers to act as peer educators and mediators between formal and informal systems. This resource is especially relevant when designing interventions for ethnic minority elders.

In summary, despite reductions in overall poverty rates for the past four decades, very old individuals, women, racial and ethnic minorities, and rural elderly residents are at significantly greater risk for poverty, with the population of at-risk poor elderly individuals increasing at a faster rate than that of the elderly population as a whole. In addition, we have noted the significant barriers to the use of health, mental health, and social services by older adults and have presented strategies for social workers to help address these barriers on system, staff, community, and individual and family levels.

REFERENCES

Administration on Aging. (2003). *A profile of older Americans: 2003.* Washington, DC: U.S. Department of Health and Human Services, Administration on Aging.

American Association of Retired Persons. (1993). *A portrait of older Americans.* Washington, DC: Author.

Anzick, M. A., & Weaver, D. A. (2001). *Reducing poverty among elderly women* (ORES Working Paper Series No. 87). Washington, DC: Social Security Administration, Office of Policy.

Applewhite, S. L. (1998). Culturally competent practice with elderly Latinos. In M. Delgado (Ed.), *Latino elders and the 21st century: Issues and challenges for culturally competent research and practice* (pp. 1–15). New York: Haworth Press.

Baker, D. I., & Pallett-Hehn, P. (1995). Care or control: Barriers to service use by elderly people. *Journal of Applied Gerontology, 14*(3), 261–274.

Baker, F. M. (1994). Psychiatric treatment of older African Americans. *Hospital and Community Psychiatry, 45*(1), 32–37.

Bell, B. (1975). Mobile medical care to the elderly. *Gerontologist, 15,* 100–103.

Biegel, D., Farkas, K., & Song, L. (1997). Barriers to the use of mental health services by African-American and Hispanic elderly persons. *Journal of Gerontological Social Work, 29*(1), 23–44.

Biegel, D. E., & Farkas, K. (1989). *Mental health and the elderly: Service delivery issues* (Monograph Series). Cleveland, OH: Case Western Reserve University, Western Reserve Geriatric Education Center.

Biegel, D. E., Johnsen, J. A., & Shafran, R. (1997). Overcoming barriers faced by African-American families with a family member with mental illness. *Family Relations, 46*(2), 163–178.

Biegel, D. E., Petchers, M., Snyder, A., & Beisgen, B. (1989). Unmet needs and barriers to service delivery for the blind/visually impaired elderly. *Gerontologist, 29*(1), 86–91.

Binstock, R. H. (1999). Public policies and minority elders. In M. L. Wykle & A. B. Ford (Eds.), *Serving minority elders in the 21st century* (pp. 5–24). New York: Springer.

Board of Trustees of the Federal Old Age & Survivors Insurance & Disability Insurance Trust Funds (2000). Annual Report. Washington, DC: U.S. Government Printing Office.

Bogdon, A. S., Katsura, H., & Mikelsons, M. (2001). Exploring the housing assistance needs of elderly renters. *Journal of Housing for the Elderly, 15*(1/2), 111–130.

Bok, D. (1996). *The state of the nation: Government and the quest for a better society.* Cambridge, MA: Harvard University Press.

Browne, C., & Broderick, A. (1994). Asian and Pacific elders: Issues for social work practice and education. *Social Work, 39*(3), 252–259.

Burggraf, V. (2000). The older woman: Ethnicity and health. *Geriatric Nursing, 21*(4), 183–187.

Burnette, D. (1999). Custodial grandparents in Latino families: Patterns of service use and predictors of unmet needs. *Social Work, 44,* 22–34.

Coward, R. T., Duncan, R. P., & Netzer, J. K. (1993). The availability of health care resources for elders living in nonmetropolitan persistent low-income counties in the South. *Journal of Applied Gerontology, 12,* 368–387.

Damron-Rodriguez, J. A. (1998). Respecting ethnic elders: A perspective for care providers. *Journal of Gerontological Social Work, 29*(2/3), 53–72.

Dancy, J., Jr., & Ralston, P. (2002). Health promotion and Black elders. *Research on Aging, 24*(2), 218–242.

Ford, M. E., & Hatchett, B. (2001). Gerontological social work with older African-American adults. *Journal of Gerontological Social Work, 36*(3/4), 141–155.

Fuller-Thomson, E., & Minkler, M. (2000). African American grandparents raising grandchildren: A national profile of demographic and health characteristics. *Health and Social Work, 25*(2), 109–118.

Glasgow, N. (1993). Poverty among rural elders: Trends, context, and directions for policy. *Journal of Applied Gerontology, 12*(3), 302–319.

Glasgow, N., & Brown, D. L. (1998). Older, rural, and poor. In R. T. Coward & J. A. Krout (Eds.), *Aging in rural settings: Life circumstances and distinctive features* (pp. 187–207). New York: Springer.

Gonyea, J. (1995). Age-based policies and the oldest-old. *Generations,* 25–31.

Gordon, A. K. (1995). Deterrents to access and service for Blacks and Hispanics: The Medicare hospice benefit, healthcare utilization and cultural barriers. *Hospice Journal, 10*(2), 65–83.

Greene, R. A. (2000). *Social work with the aged and their families.* New York: Aldine de Gruyter.

Hall, L. E., & Tucker, C. M. (1985). Relationships between ethnicity, conceptions of mental illness, and attitudes associated with seeking psychological help. *Psychological Reports, 57,* 907–916.

Harris, H. L. (1998). Ethnic minority elders: Issues and interventions. *Educational Gerontology, 24,* 309–323.

Hungerford, T., Rassette, M., Iams, H., & Koenig, M. (2001–2002). Trends in the economic status of the elderly, 1976–2000. *Social Security Bulletin, 64*(3), 12–22.

Jackson, J. S., & Wolford, M. L. (1992). Changes from 1980 to 1987 in mental health status and help-seeking among African Americans. *Journal of Geriatric Psychiatry, 25*(1), 15–67.

Jensen, L., & McLaughlin, D. K. (1997). The escape from poverty among rural and urban elders. *Gerontologist, 37*(4), 462–468.

Jervis, L. I., Jackson, M. Y., & Manson, S. M. (2002). Need for, availability of, and barriers to the provision of long-term care services for older American Indians. *Journal of Cross-Cultural Gerontology, 17,* 295–311.

Johnson, R. W., & Penner, R. G. (2004). *Will health care costs erode retirement security? An issue brief.* Boston: Center for Retirement Research.

Jones, S. (1999). Bridging the gap: Community solutions for black-elder health care in the 21st century. In M. L. Wykle & A. B. Ford (Eds.), *Serving minority elders in the 21st century* (pp. 223–234). New York: Springer.

Kingson, E. R., & Williamson, J. B. (2001). Economic security policies. In R. H. Binstock & L. K. George (Eds.), *Handbook of aging and the social sciences* (pp. 369–386). New York: Academic Press.

Knight, B. G., & Kaskie, B. (1995). Models for mental health service delivery to older adults. In M. Gatz (Ed.), *Emerging issues in mental health and aging* (pp. 369–386). Washington, DC: American Psychological Association.

Krout, J. A. (1989). *Senior centers in America.* Westport, CT: Greenwood Press.

Krout, J. A. (1994). *Providing community-based services to the rural elderly.* Thousand Oaks, CA: Sage.

Krout, J. A. (1998). Services and service delivery in rural environments. In R. T. Coward & J. A. Krout (Eds.), *Aging in rural settings: Life circumstances and distinctive features* (pp. 247–266). New York: Springer.

Manchester, J. (1997). Aging boomers and retirement: Who is at risk? *Generations, 19–22.*

McLaughlin, D. K., & Jensen, L. (1993). Poverty among older Americans: The plight of nonmetropolitan elders. *Journals of Gerontology, 48*(2), S44–S54.

McLaughlin, D. K., & Jensen, L. (1995). Becoming poor: The experiences of elders. *Rural Sociology, 60*(2), 202–223.

Miller, B., & Stull, D. (1999). Perceptions of community services by African American and White older persons. In M. L. Wykle & A. B. Ford (Eds.), *Serving minority elders in the 21st century* (pp. 267–287). New York: Springer.

Minear, M., & Crose, R. (1996). Identifying barriers to services for low-income frail elders. *Journal of Gerontological Social Work, 26*(3/4), 57–64.

National Association of Social Workers. (1996). *Code of ethics of the National Association of Social Workers.* Silver Spring, MD: NASW Press.

Noelker, L. S., & Bass, D. M. (1989). Home care for the elderly persons: Linkages between formal and informal caregivers. *Gerontology, 44*(2), 563–570.

Ozawa, M. N. (1997). *Income and net worth of the elderly in the United States* (Report to the International Longevity Center, Japan). St. Louis: Washington University, George Warren Brown School of Social Work.

Ozawa, M. N., & Lumb, Y. S. (1996). How safe is the safety net for poor children? *Social Work Research, 20,* 238–254.

Perkins, K. (1992). Psychosocial implications of women and retirement. *Social Work, 37*(6), 526–532.

Queiro-Tajalli, I. (2000). Social work: Intervention with special populations. In R. R. Greene (Ed.), *Social work with the aged and their families.* New York: Aldine de Gruyter.

Rank, M. R., & Hirschl, T. A. (1999). Estimating the proportion of Americans ever experiencing poverty during their elderly years. *Journals of Gerontology: Series B. Psychological Sciences and Social Sciences, 54B*(4), S184–S193.

Reed, M., Hargraves, J. L., & Cassil, A. (2003). *Unequal access: African-American medicare beneficiaries and the prescription drug gap* (Issue Brief No. 64). Center for Studying Health System Change. Washington, DC.

Richardson, V. (1992). Service use among urban African American elderly people. *Social Work, 37*(1), 47–54.

Rittner, B., & Kirk, A. B. (1995). Health care and public transportation use by poor and frail elderly people. *Social Work, 40*(3), 365–373.

Rupp, K., Strand, A., & Davies, P. S. (2003). Poverty among elderly women: Assessing SSI options to strengthen social security reform. *Journals of Gerontology: Series B. Psychological Sciences and Social Sciences, 58*(6), S359–S368.

Sevak, P., Weir, D. R., & Willis, R. J. (2004). *The economic consequences of a husband's death: Evidence from the HRS and AHEAD.* Ann Arbor: University of Michigan.

Smeeding, T. M., & Sandstrom, S. (2004). *Poverty and income maintenance in old age: A cross-national view of low income older women.* Syracuse, NY: Syracuse University.

Sotomayor, M. (1997). Aging: Racial and ethnic groups. In Richard L. Edwards (Ed.), *Encyclopedia of Social Work* (Suppl., pp. 26–36). Washington, DC: NASW Press.

Stoller, E. P., & Lee, G. R. (1994). Informal care of rural elders. In R. T. Coward, C. N. Bull, G. Kukulka, &

J. M. Galliher (Eds.), *Health services for rural elders* (pp. 33–64). New York: Springer.

Torres-Gil, F., & Moga, K. B. (2001). Multiculturalism, social policy and the new aging. *Journal of Gerontological Social Work, 36*(3/4), 13–32.

Tran, T. V., Dhooper, S. S., & McInnis-Dittrich, K. (1997). Utilization of community-based social and health services among foreign born Hispanic American elderly. *Journal of Gerontological Social Work, 28*(4), 23–43.

Tran, T. V., & Williams, L. F. (1998). Poverty and impairment in activities of living among elderly Hispanics. *Social Work in Health Care, 26*(4), 59–78.

Tripp-Reimer, T. (1999). Culturally competent care. In M. L. Wykle & A. B. Ford (Eds.), *Serving minority elders in the 21st century* (pp. 235–247). New York: Springer.

U.S. Census Bureau. (2004a). *Income, poverty and health insurance coverage in the United States: 2003* (Publication No. P60-226). Washington, DC: U.S. Department of Commerce, U.S. Census Bureau.

U.S. Census Bureau. (2004b). *Current population survey, 2004: Annual social and economic supplement.* Washington, DC: U.S. Department of Commerce, U.S. Census Bureau.

Urdaneta, M. L., Saldana, D. H., & Winkler, A. (1995). Mexican-American perceptions of severe mental illness. *Human Organization, 54*(1), 70–77.

Villa, V. M., Wallace, S. P., & Markides, K. (1997). Economic diversity and an aging population: The impact of public policy and economic trends. *Generations,* 13–18.

Wentworth, S. G., & Pattison, D. (2001–2002). Income growth and future poverty rates of the aged. *Social Security Bulletin, 64*(3), 23–37.

Wu, K. B. (2003). *Poverty experience of older persons: A poverty study from a long-term perspective.* Washington, DC: American Association of Retired Persons, Public Policy Institute.

Yeatts, D. E., Crow, T., & Folts, E. (1992). Service use among low-income minority elderly: Strategies for overcoming barriers. *Gerontologist, 32*(1), 24–32.

SHEILA H. AKABAS
LAUREN B. GATES

Older Adults and Work in the 21st Century

THE MEANING OF WORK

What would you like to be when you grow up? What do you do? What did you do before you retired? These are probably the most frequently asked questions in our daily dialogues, and, not surprisingly, they all have to do with work. That is probably because work is the most universal phenomenon in society. We tend to define ourselves by the work we do. Our fantasies are about accomplishments at work and our sorrows are about the pain at work. When we are young, we prepare for work. When we are in our middle years we depend on it, hoping it will bring fulfillment economically, socially, and psychologically. When we are older we reminisce about work. Our social policy is directed at getting people to work. Where and how families live and grow is determined by work. How we live in old age has very much to do with our experiences when we were at work.

Work is so ingrained in the American spirit that it is almost seen as unpatriotic not to be employed. People may have more money than they can ever expect to spend in their or their children's lifetimes, yet they are often the most dedicated and committed workers. Lucky lottery winners, when asked their future plans now that they are millionaires, frequently indicate that they will buy a home, give to family members or charity, but they will continue to spend their daily hours at work. We are a nation that prioritizes work as others do religion or respect for the family (Akabas, 1995). As Akabas and Kurzman (2005) note, "Being in the world of work means that one is swimming with the prevailing current and therefore is likely to be part of the mainstream of America rather than on the margin."

We may ask why work is so significant in American society. Work offers us social status, helps structure our daily life, secures our financial rewards, gives us a sense of self-efficacy and accomplishment, and assures us of a context for social interactions (Akabas, 1995). For older adults, work may have particular meaning as an opportunity to transfer knowledge, skill, and experience to younger generations (Mor-Barak, 1995). Countless observers have commented on the importance of work. Jahoda (1988, p. 17) observes, "Whether one likes or hates one's job, it structures time for the day, the week, the years; it broadens the social horizon beyond family and friends, it enforces participation in collective purposes, it defines one's social status; it demands reality-oriented activities." "It's the economy, stupid!" (widely interpreted as the universal desire for jobs) was the winning motto of the first Clinton campaign. Camus observed, "Without work all life goes rotten." Freud identified the two hallmarks of adult functioning as the ability to love and to work—but he and the rest of the mental health professions have concentrated on love (Freud, 1930).

A distinct lack of attention has been paid to work not only by Freud but also by social work in general. Yet entering work, remaining at work, and leaving work are some of the main passages of life for most of us, including those who seek social work services. Being able to find meaningful, rewarding work is one of the greatest challenges facing individuals and society today, and older adults are not exempt from this challenge. Although some welcome the end of work demands and retire at the earliest possible moment, many people work long after retirement age (for example, the 2000 U.S. Census reported a labor force participation rate for persons 65 and older at 17.5%), and still others crave work after retirement (Fullerton & Toossi, 2001).

Policy makers in the world of work respond in varied ways to employment of older adults. Some encourage their participation because they value the older adults' experience, knowledge, and flexible availability, among other reasons, recognizing their significant contribution to the bottom line. Others discriminate against aging workers, believing them to be too expensive, unable to learn, or likely to become ill, among other myths (Moen, 1990). Many workplaces provide incentives for older workers to leave employment. Whatever the situation, the role of work in aging seems worthy of our attention for its importance to well-being throughout life and because the individual who is thinking about leaving work is usually facing a complex and often difficult transition point in the life cycle.

This chapter identifies who older working adults are by legislative definition, workplace policy, and life experience. We examine their contact with work in relation to the various statuses they may occupy, including transitional retirement, total retirement, and continuing employment, and how this varies with individual characteristics and other factors affecting withdrawal from the labor force due to age. We then suggest what social workers can do to help older workers achieve the connection to a work role that they may desire or to satisfy a successful termination of that role if that is their choice. We contend that it is not possible to serve the needs of older adults without understanding their work histories, what has influenced the status they now hold with regard to work, what their preferences are in relation to work, and how to help them achieve their desired state, as well as how the workplace culture and social policy act as an influential context for individual experience. There are clear indications that the issue of work warrants attention from social service personnel.

AGING AND WORK: A DEFINITION

One means of establishing a definition of aging is to base it on the way society behaves around age with relation to work. In a subsistence economy, everyone works except very young children and the infirm. In such an economy, not being able to work defines "aging," and falling into the category of "aging" can even be a death sentence from starvation—witness the Inuit culture that abandoned the aged to remain on the ice floe (McDonald, 2002). It is only as societies become more affluent that some members, among them the older adults, have an option to be financially supported by virtue of prior accumulation of wealth or by generous contribution of their family or the community. Thus retirement is a recent option historically. For many, retirement itself defines "aging" in relation to work.

Legislative Definition

Extensive studies have confirmed that, starting at age 40, individuals in the labor market encounter stigma attached to their aging. Bendick, Brown, and Wall (1999) found that when two candidates of exactly equal competence who are different in age, one being 32 and one 57, present themselves for hire, the younger will be preferred 42% of the time, and both candidates, regardless of age, will be equally treated only 58% of the time. Many others confirm that age discrimination in hiring continues to exist (Shen & Kleiner, 2001). Other data indicate that unemployed long-tenured workers (those employed 3 or more years at the time of displacement) ages 55 and over take longer to find jobs than their younger colleagues and tend to be reemployed in jobs that provide lower earnings than their lost jobs (U.S. Department of Labor, 2004; Brewington & Nassar-McMillan, 2000). The Age Discrimination in Employment Act of 1967 (ADEA), therefore, acknowledged that being over 40 places one in jeopardy of discrimination in the workplace when seeking employment. By designating age 40 as the limit of its protection, the Act defines the beginning of "aging" with regard to workplace participation. The congressional statement of findings and intent attached to the ADEA states:

(a) The Congress hereby finds and declares that—
    1) in the face of rising productivity and affluence, older workers find themselves disadvantaged in their efforts to retain employment, and especially to regain employment when displaced from jobs;
    2) the setting of arbitrary age limits regardless of potential for job performance has become a common practice, and certain otherwise desirable practices may work to the disadvantage of older persons;
    3) the incidence of unemployment, especially long-term unemployment with resultant deterioration of skill, morale, and employer acceptability is, relative to the younger ages, high among older workers; their numbers are great and growing; and their employment problems grave;
    4) the existence in industries affecting commerce, of arbitrary discrimination in employment because of age, burdens commerce and the free flow of good in commerce
(b) It is therefore the purpose of this chapter to promote employment of older persons based on their ability rather than age; to prohibit arbitrary age discrimination in employment; to help employers and workers find ways of meeting problems arising from the impact of age on employment.

Although the Act originally protected those ages 40–65, the protection coverage was raised to 70 in 1978, and a 1986 amendment prohibited mandatory retirement (Neumark, 2003). It applies to all employers of 20 or more workers, government agencies, and labor organizations. ADEA is administered (since 1979) by the U.S. Equal Employment Opportunity Commission, which is charged with enforcement of all affirmative action legislation.

Another influential piece of legislation is the Social Security Act of 1935. As a social invention, retirement is mostly confined to Western, highly advanced economies (Clark, York, & Anker, 1999). Legislation offering insured formal retirement, by which income continues beyond working years, started in the Bismarck era in Germany toward the end of the 19th century. The age of retirement was set at 65 largely because almost no one was expected to live that long, thereby keeping down the cost of this social benefit.

In the United States, the Social Security Act used the same cutoff age for eligibility for fully funded retirement. Recent amendments have moved the age of withdrawal from work with total pension, so that by 2027 it will be 67, but reduced payments remain available starting at age 62. Mandatory retirement has been eliminated, as has payment penalty for earned income after 65. Further, life expectancy has increased appreciably, and large numbers of persons live long years after reaching 65 (Hogan & Kerstein, 1999). Although life expectancy differs by gender, marital status, race, and income level, the average life expectancy for all Americans who reach age 65 was 17.6 more years in 1966, and this number was expected to increase by 0.05 annually for the following 75 years (Weller, 2000). The Social Security Act, therefore, though it is the single most influential force for defining age at work, has inherent contradictions as policy, both encouraging and discouraging a specific definition for exit from the labor force.

Workplace Policy

Although there are gender, race, ethnic, and many other categories of difference that correlate with labor force participation rates, at least until 1985 participation rates declined noticeably for all groups after the age of 55, encouraged by private pension plans (Hayward, Friedman, & Chen, 1996). Retirement in pension plans varies, from eligibility at any age with 20 years of service—the plan used by the armed forces and police and fire departments—to provisions of the Social Security Act that allow reduced-benefit retirement at 62, to private plans in which a combination of years of service and age allow the application of a floating retirement opportunity depending on circumstances. A 2003 survey by the Society of Human Resource Managers found that human resource professionals differ widely in defining the age of older workers, ranging from age 40 to age 70 (Lockwood, 2003). Thus we can conclude that the definition of age in relation to work is a condition based on personal circumstances and the particular policy applied by a specific work organization and that it may start at age 40, with upper boundaries limited only by individual mortality.

Individual Experience

Who are the aging workers? Thinking about those over 40, they are the baby boomers, their parents, and perhaps a few of their grandparents, that is, anyone born before 1964 who is still available and looking for work or is employed. In numbers they include more than 38 million individuals. They entered the workplace during the Great Depression, during World War II, or during the feminist movement. They include persons who started life believing that men were the breadwinners and the world of work was the domain of men to those who have been introduced to work at a time when the labor force is almost equally distributed between women and men. The aging include the first cohort of women who have had a significant labor force attachment, as well as those who have gone through the civil rights movement that made it a matter of public policy to provide equal opportunity in employment for racial and ethnic minorities, among other disadvantaged groups. They have experienced a period of non-European immigration, resulting in the most diverse labor force ever.

Aging workers also have lived through an evolution in the economy that has involved significant change in the industrial mix. This has resulted in a steady decline in manufacturing—the stronghold of male employment—to an economy dominated by service industries. This shift has tended to displace men and has pushed them out of the workplace as they saw their jobs disappear. It has pulled women into the workplace as such traditional female occupations as retail sales, clerical work, health care, and government employment have expanded and proven less vulnerable to global competition and its accompanying recession layoffs (Cotter, Hermsen, & Vanneman, 2002). The aging have lived through a period during which longevity has increased so significantly that the old model of school, work, and death has been replaced by a life course that includes more than a decade of leisure following formal retirement (Encel, 2000). Notably, each cohort of workers has a different experience, which leads to the many unique characteristics among this population in relation to the world of work.

OLDER ADULTS AND THEIR CONNECTION TO WORK

Favreault, Ratcliffe, and Toder (1999, p. 484) suggest that the forces that influence an older adult's decision concerning work are one's ability, economic resources, psychological condition and family situation: "The importance of each of these factors varies both across and within different birth cohorts."

Ability

Ability implies that one is physically able to do the job and has the skill required for job performance. Today, jobs are less physically demanding, and people reach older years in better health than ever before. Life expectancy has increased appreciably, and large numbers of persons live many years after reaching 65. There is scientific validation that aging *may* cause a decline in abilities (Johnson, 2003) and evidence that, in the absence of training, skills *may* become obsolescent (Schwartz & Kleiner, 1999). But Schwartz and Kleiner (1999) report finding great variations in the aging process such that "optimal agers" do as well as or better on aptitude tests than those in their prime of life. Other experts note that older workers tend to have more positive work attitudes and have valued traits such as loyalty, motivation, and a solid work ethic. As well, older workers are viewed as being willing to work different schedules, they have the ability to serve as mentors, and they bring invaluable experience to the workplace (Lockwood, 2003). It is largely the obsolescence of skills, therefore, which is the primary limiting factor in the ability of older workers to continue on the job. Skill obsolescence is compounded by negative attitudes of employers who believe that investing in training is not cost effective because older workers will not stay long enough to provide the employer with a sufficient return on investment (Encel, 2000). Researchers find that training can overcome lack of skill and that intellectual decline is far from universal. On balance, it is probable that aside from those who experience a severe decline in health, few are driven from the workplace by inability to perform.

Economic Resources

As workers reach the age and financial circumstances at which retirement is a serious option, the literature suggests that economic resources play a major role in the decision-making process concerning the relation of the older adult to work. Today's aging workers include the first generation of Americans that was covered by the Social Security Act of 1935 from the onset of their employment and that hence enjoys the individual right to the social invention of public financial support in retirement. This social policy has encouraged, through financial incentive, the exit of older workers, and older workers have responded in kind with sharp withdrawal at age 62, when reduced Social

Security payments become available, and another spike at age 65, when full payment is available (Moen, 1990; Ruhm, 1995). For example, the labor force participation rate for men at age 63 dropped from 80% in 1950 to less than 50% by the end of the century, showing precipitous decline starting when men became eligible for Social Security benefits at age 62 in 1961 (Woodbury, 1999). Similar patterns are observable for women, but because of the overall increase of women in the labor force during this period, they are less pronounced. Employers, too, have solicited the exit of workers, providing incentives in the form of pensions and liberal financial buyouts, often by age 55. Affluence has also increased so that many find themselves able to leave work at much earlier ages if they wish. This has caused a massive exit from the labor force by men, who previously worked until death or serious disablement. Thus retirement has taken over for many, and the average age of retirement seems to have grown younger and younger (Hardy, 2002).

Yet recent economic and other trends have also had a reverse influence. The increasing number of the elderly and the reduced numbers of young people available for work has fostered some reduction in the pressure for early retirement. This reflects both the desire to reduce the economic burden of early retirement and increased longevity and the concern about inadequate labor force replacement coming from the "baby bust" generation (Hirschman, 2001). As baby boomers reach the older years, furthermore, they are not expected to be as affluent as their parents. This is the result of the law of supply and demand. Their numbers have been so numerous that their earnings have tended to be lower than their parents' because of the competition of their excessive supply. The decline of stock market values has also influenced their savings situation. The longevity they face may be welcome, but it might be longer than the lasting power of their accumulated wealth or the impact of inflation on pension plans that do not include cost of living adjustment provisions (Herz, 1995). Fixed incomes are savaged by the passage of time. The rising cost of health care and medication, less and less likely to be covered by previous employers, constitutes an undefined but frightening future burden. For women, all these limitations on the level of earnings are magnified by the fact that they drop out of employment for periods to provide free and "invisible" labor in caring for children and elderly family members and friends (Cotter et al., 2002); also, fewer women can look forward to pensions from employers than men of the same age. Aged women are often victims of poverty as a result of these circumstances (U.S. Census Bureau, 1996). In short, potentially inadequate accumulation of wealth and economic uncertainty is a prevailing force in the lives of many aging baby boomers, causing them to consider remaining in the labor force for a longer period of time than originally planned (Fullerton & Toossi, 2001).

This trend is not entirely unwelcome, because other realities are reinforcing an interest in having older adults continue their labor force participation. As the baby boomers move toward retirement, there is an expected shortage of replacement workers (Hirschman, 2001; Herz, 1995). Given that women's labor force participation rates are almost equal to those of men, the largest single pool of additional labor is the older work force (Doeringer, Sum, & Terkla, 2002). There is also a growing concern about paying the retirement bill for the nonemployed elderly as their numbers expand (Hardy, 2002). Finally, the numbers of older adults in the population will grow at accelerated rates over the next decades. Whereas the number of workers 45 or younger is expected to grow slowly or actually to decline between 2002 and 2012, those 55 to 64 years of age will increase by 51%, and those over 65 are projected to increase by 43% as the baby boomers shift to older age groups ("Labor Force," 2003–2004). There is concern about who will care for them, given smaller families and higher labor force participation rates expected for their children, those in the "baby bust" generation (otherwise known as Generation X). Older adults themselves are viewed as a potential supply of paid caregivers (Rix, 2001).

Psychological Condition

The issue of economic uncertainty is not just an economic circumstance but is reflected in an individual's psychological condition as well. A primary consideration is one's feeling of physical well-being and perception of one's ability to meet the demands of formal employment. The issue of health has a complex relationship to continued employment. It is obvious that some work (think about the job of sanitation truck operators, for example) is too physically demanding to continue into later years. For those who are getting older, the view that one's personal health is at risk is the most likely influence in driving individuals from the labor force. But because most people gain health care insurance through work, even those who see work as a risk to their health are torn about leaving work and losing their health benefit (Blau & Gilleskie, 1997). Sorting this out differs depending on how this issue plays for a particular individual.

Gender becomes another determinant of one's reaction to continued employment. Research has identified that women as a specific group are increasingly interested in paid employment for later periods in their lives as compared with men. Because many women change their work roles to comply with the demands of the household (Zimmerman, Mitchell, Wister, & Gutman, 2000), they come to their career peaks at later ages than men, and they value work at that point in their lives because they are experiencing success. Thus women, instead of being tied to spouses' decisions, have become actors in their own right (Coile, 2003) and often maintain an impressive level of attachment to employment beyond their personal age of eligibility for retirement, even if their spouses decide to retire (Choi, 2000). Having to retire before one is emotionally ready can lead to depression and lack of personal satisfaction (Zimmerman et al., 2000).

Alternatively, the perception that older workers have of attitudes toward them influences their actions. When faced with unemployment, many withdraw from the labor force, believing that employers will not be interested in them as workers (Taylor & Walker, 1998). There is evidence to support the accuracy of older workers' perceptions. Findings show that some employers believe that older workers are fearful of new technology, slower to learn, less educated, and unwilling to change the way they do things (Doeringer et al., 2002; Shen & Kleiner, 2001) and that they are more costly and may resent taking orders from younger people or that younger workers may feel uncomfortable supervising them (Brewington & Nassar-McMillan, 2000). These beliefs are at odds with the experience of older workers, who find work to be mentally energizing and seek to maintain some active work roles, confirming researchers' findings that the quality of life is enhanced by continuing labor force involvement (Ruchlin & Morris, 1991; McMahan & Phillips, 2000; Francese, 2004).

Family Situations

Throughout their lives, family situations often determine the actions of individuals. American society offers limited child care or elder care resources, leaving these responsibilities to families, and particularly women (Akabas & Kurzman, 2005; Akabas & Gates,

in press). Those who care for more than one person, for a seriously ill person, or for a male spouse are most likely to withdraw from work permanently to fulfill these family needs (Dentinger & Clarkberg, 2002). This may differ by ethnic group as well as gender, with African American women more likely than others to respond to family crisis by withdrawal from work (Bullock, Crawford, & Tennstedt, 2003). Marital relationships also may influence personal behavior. Individuals in situations characterized by serious tensions are less likely to opt for joint retirement than those in more supportive relationships. Unquestionably, the decision of older adults to work or not is a complex one with many interrelated conditions that influence the process of disengagement from work (Blau, 1994).

OPTIONS AVAILABLE FOR OLDER WORKERS

Total retirement is not the only possible response. Although many forces are moving toward early retirement, a countertrend is in the making—people are living longer and longer. Instead of death at the heels of retirement, a life expectancy of 20 years of leisure emerges, an unwelcome and long time for some. If retirement is defined as a situation in which an individual draws a pension for severance from a particular job, abrupt retirement is on the decline. The most recent evidence reflects a pattern of alternative work arrangements (Ruhm, 1995). Researchers have noted retirement as a process rather than a single event. People engage in what is variously known as "bridge employment," "phased retirement," "revolving retirement," or "transitional retirement." All refer to a process by which individuals reduce their work schedules or responsibilities. They leave their career jobs to take on less demanding responsibilities with their customary employer; or they "reverse retire" by terminating employment with a particular employer and then gaining new employment on either a full- or part-time basis with a new employer; or they achieve self-employment; or they delay retirement altogether (Blau, 1994; Hirschman, 2001; Kim & Feldman, 2000; Ruhm, 1995; Quinn, 1999; Quinn & Kozy, 1996). It appears that only 13.2% of adults over 65 are employed or seeking employment (Administration on Aging, 2003), but observers view this figure as misleading. Because of the just described activity of these workers, moving in and out of the labor force and replacing each other, the percentage at any one time does not reflect the reality. Research confirms that the actual numbers are greater (Herz, 1995). Furthermore, these trends appear to be long term. Surveys of younger workers indicate that 80% expect to work after the age of 65 (Quinn, 1999).

Notably, patterns differ by age, race, ethnicity, gender, education, and type of work represented by career job (Ruhm, 1995; Quinn & Kozy, 1996). It is beyond the scope of this chapter to do anything more than indicate these differences, but, in general, total disengagement at an earlier age without subsequent work experience is characteristic of less educated, minority males who have done physical labor and find themselves in poor health. Some, particularly the white, older age group with economic security, utilize volunteer positions to fulfill their desire to achieve continuity and adjustment to retirement (Kim & Feldman, 2000). In their conclusion, Quinn and Kozy (1996, p. 373) sum up the situation:

> The retirement patterns of older Americans are far from simple. Although the majority do leave their career jobs and the labor market simultaneously, a significant minority use bridge jobs to retire more gradually. Second careers are a common phenomenon. As the nation ages and changes in federal policy, including Social Security, reduce the work disincentives facing older Americans, these rich and varied retirement routes are likely to become all the more prevalent and important.

THE PROFESSIONAL ROLE

Clearly, there is much to do on micro, mezzo, and macro levels for social workers interested in assisting older adults in their relationship to the labor market. Professionals who work with those who are aging need to know about the world of work, policies and practices in that world, the rights, benefits, and opportunities available, and the expectations that employers are likely to hold concerning those wishing to continue employment or presenting themselves for hire. To be uninformed or misinformed in this area is to rob clients of the help they need with regard to their work options.

Older adults need assistance in reviewing their present status and potential opportunities, in making decisions concerning choices, and in adjusting to the transitions involved in their choices. On the individual or micro level, the issue of work should enter into any assessment and counseling relationship so that individuals can receive help in sorting out the varied circumstances they face, causing work or retirement decisions to be made in a planned manner rather than by default. A social work professional needs to take a work history and to listen with the third ear concerning what is or was rewarding about the work experience, what are or were the difficulties with that experience, and how the person feels, now, about work, its demands, and its rewards. This will provide information on the meaning of work to the client. Is the individual employed at a physically or mentally overdemanding or unpleasant job from which retirement would come as a relief? Is the individual interested in continuing, reassuming, or being released from a work role? Does he or she have skills that will be valued in today's workplace, or is the person interested in training or pursuing educational opportunities to meet such demands? What are the motivations leading to work engagement or its termination? Are financial considerations significant? Is satisfaction in contributing to a work setting dominant? Is the individual pulled by a need for companionship and an activity around which to organize his or her time? Alternatively, is there a long desired activity that can be undertaken only at the end of a formal work connection or a volunteer opportunity the individual wishes to pursue? These questions will help identify what relationship to work is right for the particular individual and will offer guidance concerning what issues need attention if the person wishes to prepare for work.

Such an exploration will allow individuals to assess their ability (including health), economic resources, psychological needs, and family situations and the influence of each with regard to a work decision and may provide clues as to how to help the candidate for work communicate successfully at job interviews. Preretirement counseling and attention to financial management education can enrich these discussions. When offered significantly before an individual reaches the point of decision, they can be extremely helpful. Providing these services calls on the social worker's developmental understanding, and educational and therapeutic skills (Steun & Worden, 1993). Additionally, older workers need to be exposed to the skills of negotiation so that they are empowered to take an active role in determining their own work conditions and status. Social workers also can help guide the preparation of résumés and the identification of possible job openings. These interventions can be performed by a professional in private practice, by one offering services in a family or other community counseling agency, or directly through an Employee Assistance Program (EAP) or its union counterpart, a Membership Assistance Program (hereafter subsumed under the heading EAP) at a worksite (Kurzman, 1992; Kurzman, 1993; Akabas & Kurzman, 2005). Notably, EAPs are usually staffed by social workers who know the culture and personnel of a particular workplace. EAP staffers can and do advise on the best approaches for older adults seeking to maintain or gain access to jobs in an organization, including negotiating the accommodations necessary to make the employment successful from everyone's point of view. Because they often are interconnected with such workplace units as human resource services, social workers with EAP status can influence recruitment, hiring, and retention policy decisions within organizations. Although many EAP personnel are reluctant to extend their turf to encompass organizational policy, others view such activities as the natural outcome of a systems approach to service delivery and participate actively in preretirement counseling and other aspects of planning for older working adults (Akabas & Kurzman, 2005; Kurzman & Akabas, 1993). As the workforce ages, social workers in EAPs may find increasing pressure from both individuals and organizations to take an active role in planning with older workers for their future labor force participation.

But it is not only EAP social workers who can influence organizational behavior. On the mezzo level, social workers should be prepared to develop organizational programs, in work settings and in community agencies, that will meet the needs of those older adults who are seeking new careers, developing entrepreneurial initiatives, maintaining existing work roles in organizations, searching for training opportunities, looking for fulfilling volunteer activities, or needing help adjusting to their new status, including overcoming social isolation. Individual interactions can serve as the basis for a needs assessment to identify the kind of program development that is indicated. Workplaces and unions can establish retirees' clubs which provide social support in a familiar setting to those who have given long years of service to the organization. Such programs are usually run by occupational social workers who either are employed by the sponsoring organization or are employed by a service provider that is workplace focused and may have a contract with the retirees' former employer or union. These programs can be duplicated in community settings. Organized to help people through the transition from work to retirement or to explore alternative work options, such efforts require a different focus than is placed on the more typical older adult recreation groups offered by community social service providers. They need to be concerned with the coordination of services with the workplace itself.

Programs that would help older adults deal with employment and retirement issues need to build bridges to workplaces, bridges that develop trust among the parties on which job development can be based. The time is exceedingly propitious for such initiatives. The expected shortage of workers as baby boomers reach retirement age will make employers more desirous of maintaining older workers or recruiting from among the older adult pool than they have been in the recent past (Porter, 2004). Social workers can use this trend to establish ties with work organizations and educate them to the potential contribution of older workers independent of the interests or job placement needs of any particular client. The goal of such endeavors would be to build an employer network that is ready, willing, and able to provide employment to interested older adults, that is, to put the structure in place that can be responsive when the need arises. It is then possible to use such connections to follow the client/worker into the workplace and help create interrelationships that are supportive of successful employment through interventions such as psychoeducation with the work group (Gates, Akabas, & Oran-Sabia, 1998).

The advocacy such activities require has even more relevance on the macro level. Social workers need to be aware of current legislation and more general social policy dilemmas and use advocacy to encourage policy changes that would respond to the issues of social concern posed by the graying of the American labor force. Attention to the enforcement of the ADEA is another outlet for social work advocacy. Laws are only as effective as the strength of the effort invested in enforcement. There is need to overcome the present circumstances, identified by Neumark (2003, p. 315), who concluded that despite the ADEA there is "ample evidence consistent with hiring discrimination against older workers."

For the social worker who would take on these new but important responsibilities, there are many sources of help. The *O-Net Occupational Dictionary*, easily accessible on the Internet, provides information on different occupations in the United States economy and the demand for each. Local and state departments of labor tend to have information and knowledgeable staff ready to provide advice on labor market issues. The American Association of Retired Persons (AARP), the AFL-CIO, and many other organizations offer Web-based information that can be quite helpful. Research findings on related issues are increasingly available.

Certainly our society should not renege on the promise of basic economic security for older adults provided in the Social Security Act of 1938. Neither should society pressure, by stereotyping and stigmatizing, older adults who seek to maintain work past an age for labor force exit set when life expectancy was several decades shorter and when the physical demands of work were much greater. Social workers have an important role in helping to sort out this changing horizon and can offer significant services to aging adults and to our society by so doing.

REFERENCES

Administration on Aging. (2003). *A profile of older Americans: 2003.* Retrieved September 21, 2004, from *http://www.aoa.gov/prof/Statistics/profile/2003/2003profile.pdf.*

Akabas, S. H. (1995). Occupational social work. In R. L. Edwards et al. (Eds.), *Encyclopedia of social work* (19th ed., Vol. 2, pp. 1779–1786). Washington, DC: National Association of Social Work.

Akabas, S. H., & Gates, L. B. (in press). Employment and caregiving: Concerns and responses by employers, unions and social policy. In B. Berkman (Ed.), *Handbook on social work in aging.* New York: Oxford University Press.

Akabas, S. H., & Kurzman, P. A. (2005). *Work and the workplace: A resource for innovative policy and practice.* New York: Columbia University Press.

Bendick, M., Jr., Brown, L. E., & Wall, K. (1999). No foot in the door: An experimental study of employment discrimination against older workers. *Journal of Aging and Social Policy, 10*(4), 5–23.

Blau, D. M. (1994). Labor force dynamics of older men. *Econometrics, 62*(1), 117–156.

Blau, D. M., & Gilleskie, D. B. (1997). *Retiree health insurance and the labor force behavior of older men in the 1990's* (Working Paper No. 5948). Cambridge, MA: National Bureau of Economic Research.

Brewington, J. O., & Nassar-McMillan, S. (2000). Older adults: Work-related issues and implications for counseling. *Career Development Quarterly, 49*(1), 2–15.

Bullock, K., Crawford, S. L., & Tennstedt, S. L. (2003). Employment and caregiving: Exploration of African American caregivers. *Social Work, 48*(2), 150–162.

Choi, N. G. (2000). Determinants of engagement in paid work following Social Security benefit receipt among older women. *Journal of Women and Aging, 12*(3/4), 133–154.

Clark, R. L., York, E. A., & Anker, R. (1999). Economic development and labor force participation of older persons. *Population Research and Policy Review, 18*(5), 411–432.

Coile, C. C. (2003). *Retirement incentives and couples' retirement decisions* (Working Paper No. 9496). Cambridge, MA: National Bureau of Economic Research.

Cotter, D. A., Hermsen, J. M., & Vanneman, R. (2002). Gendered opportunities for work. *Research on Aging, 24*(6), 600–629.

Doeringer, P., Sum, A., & Terkla, D. (2002). Devolution of employment and training policy: The case of older workers. *Journal of Aging and Social Policy, 14*(3/4), 37–60.

Dentinger, E., & Clarkberg, M. (2002). Informal caregiving and retirement timing among men and women: Gender and caregiving relationships in midlife. *Journal of Family Issues, 23*(7), 857–879.

Encel, S. (2000). Later-life employment. *Journal of Aging and Social Policy, 11*(4), 7–13.

Favreault, M., Ratcliffe, C., & Toder, E. (1999). Labor force participation of older workers: Prospective changes and potential policy responses. *National Tax Journal, 52*(3), 483–503.

Francese, P. (2004). Labor of love. *American Demographics, 26*(92), 40–42.

Freud, S. (1930). *Civilization and its discontents.* London: Hogarth Press.

Fullerton, H. N., & Toossi, M. (2001, November). Labor force projection to 2010: Steady growth and changing composition. *Monthly Labor Review,* 21–38.

Gates, L. B., Akabas, S. H., & Oran-Sabia, V. (1998). Relationship accommodations involving the work group: Improving work prognosis for persons with mental health conditions. *Psychiatric Rehabilitation Journal, 21*(3), 264–272.

Hardy, M. A. (2002). The transformation of retirement in twentieth-century America: From discontent to satisfaction. *Generations Journal, 26*(2), 9–16.

Hayward, M. D., Friedman, S., & Chen, H. (1996). Race inequities in men's retirement. *Journals of Gerontology, Series B: Psychological Sciences and Social Sciences, 51B*(1), S1–S10.

Herz, D. E. (1995). Work after early retirement: An increasing trend among men. *Monthly Labor Review, 118*(4), 13–21.

Hirschman, C. (2001). Exit strategies. *HR Magazine, 46*(12), 52–58.

Hogan, R. G., & Kerstein, S. J. (1999). Employer retirement obligations in a changing world. *Journal of Financial Service Professionals, 53*(6), 62–67.

Jahoda, M. (1988). Economic recession and mental health: Some conceptual issues. *Journal of Social Issues, 44*(4), 13–23.

Johnson, C. (2003, April 4). Case of senior partners v. feeble, dodder & gray. *The Washington Post,* p. E01.

Kim, S., & Feldman, D. C. (2000). Working in retirement: The antecedents of bridge employment and its consequences for quality of life in retirement. *Academy of Management Journal, 43*(6), 1195–1216.

Kurzman, P. A. (1992). Employee Assistance Program staffing: Past, present and future. *Employee Assistance Quarterly, 8*(2), 79–88.

Kurzman, P. A. (1993). Employee Assistance Programs: Toward a comprehensive service model. In P. A. Kurzman & S. H. Akabas (Eds.), *Work and well-being: The occupational social work advantage* (pp. 26–45). Washington, DC: NASW Press.

Kurzman, P. A., & Akabas, S. H. (Eds.). (1993). *Work and well-being: The occupational social work advantage.* Washington, DC: NASW Press.

Labor force. (2003–2004, Winter). *Occupational Outlook Quarterly,* 42–48.

Lockwood, N. R. (2003). The aging workforce. *HR Magazine, 48*(12), 1–12.

McDonald, L. (2002). *The invisible retirement of women.* (Social and Economic Dimensions of an Aging Population, Research Papers 69). Hamilton, Ontario, Canada: McMaster University.

McMahan, S., & Phillips, K. (2000). Aging and employment: Characteristics of those working and retired in California. *Journal of Education for Business, 76*(1), 11–14.

Moen, J. R. (1990). Fewer older men in the U.S. work force: Technological, behavioral, and legislative contributions to the decline. *Economic Review—Federal Reserve Bank of Atlanta, 75*(6), 16–31.

Mor-Barak, M. E. (1995). The meaning of work for older adults seeking employment: The generativity factor. *International Journal of Aging and Human Development, 41*(4), 325–344.

Neumark, D. (2003). Age discrimination legislation in the United States. *Contemporary Economic Policy, 21*(3), 297–317.

Porter, E. (2004, August 29). Coming soon: The vanishing workforce. *The New York Times,* p. 3.1.

Quinn, J. F. (1999, May 20–21). *Has the early retirement trend reversed?* Paper presented at the first annual Joint Conference of the Retirement Research Consortia, Washington, DC.

Quinn, J. F., & Kozy, M. (1996). The role of bridge jobs in the retirement transition: Gender, race and ethnicity. *Gerontologist, 36*(3), 363–373.

Rix, S. E. (2001). The role of older workers in caring for older people in the future. *Generations, 25*(1), 29–34.

Ruchlin, H. S., & Morris, J. N. (1991). Impact of work on the quality of life of community-residing young elderly. *American Journal of Public Health, 81*(4), 498–500.

Ruhm, C. J. (1995). Secular changes in the work and retirement patterns of older men. *Journal of Human Resources, 30*(2), 362–385.

Schwartz, D. A., & Kleiner, B. H. (1999). The relationship between age and employment opportunities. *Equal Opportunities International, 18*(5/6), 105–110.

Shen, G. G.-Y., & Kleiner, B. H. (2001). Age discrimination in hiring. *Equal Opportunity International, 20*(8), 25–32.

Steun, C., & Worden, B. D. (1993). The older worker and service delivery at the workplace. In P. A. Kurzman & S. H. Akabas (Eds.), *Work and well-being: The occupational social work advantage* (pp. 256–275). Washington, DC: NASW Press.

Taylor, P., & Walker, A. (1998). Employer and older workers: Attitudes and employment practices. *Ageing and Society, 18,* 641–658.

U.S. Census Bureau. (1996). *65+ in the United States* (Current Population Reports, Special Studies, P23-190). Washington, DC: U.S. Government Printing Office.

U.S. Department of Labor. (2004). *Displaced workers summary: Worker displacement, 2001–03.* Retrieved September 21, 2004, from *http://www.bls.gov/news.release/disp.nro.htm*

Weller, C. E. (2000). *Raising the retirement age: The wrong direction for social security* (Briefing Papers, pp. 1–8). Washington, DC: Economic Policy Institute.

Woodbury, R. (Ed.). (1999, January). Retirement in the United States. (*Research Highlights in the Demography and Economics of Aging,* Issue 3). Washington, DC, National Institute.

Zimmerman, L., Mitchell, B., Wister, A., & Gutman, G. (2000). Unanticipated consequences: A comparison of expected and actual retirement timing among older women. *Journal of Women and Aging, 12*(1/2), 109–128.

As the demographic landscape of the world changes, people are curious about those who live well beyond their life expectancy; those people we call the oldest old. Their chronological age has been a fascination to researchers and practitioners. In this chapter, we report findings in the main areas of function and well-being, sociodemographic factors, mental health, social support, and health. Where possible, findings regarding the very old (85+) are compared and contrasted with those on the young old (65–75 years of age) and the old old (75–85 years of age). Racial and ethnic variations are addressed, as well as caregiving and service delivery issues and culturally competent care for the very old.

SOCIODEMOGRAPHICS

The increase in life expectancy and the decline in fertility have contributed to the aging society in developed countries. With the aging of the baby boomers, American society has grown old rapidly, resulting in a dramatic increase in the demographic projections for the oldest old. There will be 71 million people ages 65 years and over by 2030, representing 20% of the population in 2030 (U.S. Census Bureau, 2003). The oldest old, the fastest-growing age group, will constitute 2% of the population in 2010, and it is projected to be 5% of the population by 2050 (U.S. Census Bureau, 2003). Figure 16.1 graphically displays the population distribution by age over a 100-year period (1880–2080). It is clear that the coming decades bring many more people into the very old age groups and fewer into the younger age periods.

Race

As shown in Table 16.1, there were 4.6 million people age 85 and over in the United States, representing 1.6% of total population, in 2002 (U.S. Census Bureau, 2003). Among the oldest old, the majority of people were non-Hispanic Whites, compared with Blacks, those of Hispanic origin, and Asians (U.S. Census Bureau, 2003). Even though this racial composition reflected much less diversity than that of the U.S. population as a whole in 2002 (U.S. Census Bureau, 2003), the racial diversity among the oldest old is projected to increase somewhat during coming decades (U.S. Census Bureau, 2003).

Gender

Gender disparity becomes more remarkable with advancing age. As shown in Table 16.2, 70% of women

RUTH E. DUNKLE
HAE-SOOK JEON

The Oldest Old

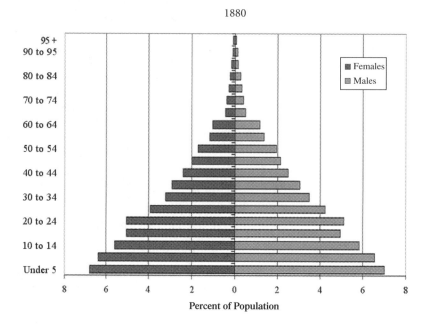

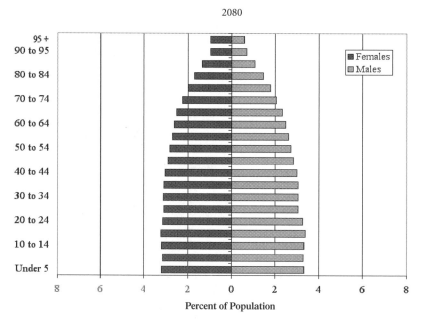

Source: U.S. Census Bureau. (1998). Reprinted from *http://www.bc.edu/centers/crr/issues/ib_ 16.pdf* with permission of A. H. Hunnell.

FIGURE 16.1. Population Distribution by Age and Sex in the United States, 1880 and 2080.

TABLE 16.1. Older Population by Race and Hispanic Origin Status in 2002*

	All Ages	*Young/Old*	*Old/Old*	*Oldest/Old*
White	232,647 (80.7%)	15,812 (86.5%)	11,368 (89.3%)	4,140 (90.1%)
Black	36,746 (12.7%)	1,669 (9.1%)	954 (7.5%)	332 (7.2%)
Asian	11,559 (4.0%)	561 (3.1%)	292 (2.3%)	81 (1.8%)
Others**	7,417 (2.6%)	232 (1.3%)	121 (0.9%)	39 (0.9%)
Total	288,369 (100.0%)	18,279 (100.0%)	12,734 (100.0%)	4,593 (100.0%)
Hispanic origin***	36,761 (12.7%)	1,181 (6.5%)	599 (4.7%)	180 (3.9%)
Non-Hispanic White	196,845 (68.3%)	14,701 (80.4%)	10,802 (84.8%)	3,969 (86.4%)

*Numbers in thousands

**Others include American Indian, Alaska Native, Native Hawaiian and other Pacific Islander, and two or more races.

***Persons of Hispanic origin may be of any race

Source: U.S. Census Bureau, Statistical Abstract of the United States 2003

and 30% of men are among the population age 85 and over, whereas there were 45% elderly women and 55% elderly men among the young old (U.S. Census Bureau, 2003). The extreme gender gap in advanced age poses more challenges for elderly women than for men. For instance, elderly women are more likely to be widowed, economically disadvantaged, physically frail, and institutionalized than their male counterparts (Taeuber & Rosenwaike, 1993).

Marital Status

The pattern of marital status is changing with advancing age. In addition to age, gender imbalance among the oldest old influences the shift in the pattern of marital status compared with other older age groups. As shown in Table 16.3, whereas 9% of women and 45% of men among the oldest old are married and living with their spouses, 72% and 35% are widowed, respectively. The oldest old men are five times as likely as women to be married (Kreider & Simmons, 2003).

Living Arrangements

Although most of the oldest old live in the community, people in this age group constitute the largest proportion of nursing home residents. In 1999, 47% of the nursing home residents were among the oldest old, compared with 32% for elders ages 75–84 and 12% for those ages 65–74 (Bernstein et al., 2003). Overall, though, the proportion of elders living in nursing homes is declining, and this is true for the oldest old as well. Eighteen percent of the oldest old lived in nursing homes in 2000, down from 25% in 1990 (Hetzel & Smith, 2001).

Socioeconomic Status

With advancing age, the poverty rate among older adults is increasing, indicating that the oldest old are more likely to be poor. In 1992, the poverty rate among community-dwelling elders ages 65 to 74 was 10.7%, which was not significantly different from other adult age groups, such as people ages 55 to 59 or those ages

TABLE 16.2. Older Population by Gender in 2002*

	All Ages	*Young/Old*	*Old/Old*	*Oldest/Old*
Men	141,661	8,301 (45.4%)	5,081 (39.9%)	1,390 (30.3%)
Women	146,708	9,973 (54.6%)	7,654 (60.1%)	3,203 (69.7%)
Total	288,369	18,274 (100.0%)	12,735 (100.0%)	4,593 (100.0%)

*Numbers in thousands

Source: U.S. Census Bureau, Statistical Abstract of the United States 2003

TABLE 16.3. Marital Status by Age Among Older Adults (2000)

	Elderly Men		
	Young/Old	Old/Old	Oldest/Old
Population	8,355,575	4,823,419	1,203,376
Married			
Spouse present	74.9%	67.3%	45.4%
Spouse absent	2.5%	4.6%	10.9%
Widowed	8.3%	18.2%	35.3%
Divorced	8.3%	4.9%	3.3%
Separated	1.4%	0.9%	0.8%
Never married	4.6%	4.1%	4.3%
Total	100.0%	100.0%	100.0%
	Elderly Women		
	Young/Old	Old/Old	Oldest/Old
Population	10,145,574	7,493,843	2,957,185
Married			
Spouse present	51.7%	30.5%	8.5%
Spouse absent	2.0%	4.3%	10.9%
Widowed	30.8%	54.6%	71.6%
Divorced	10.1%	5.8%	3.3%
Separated	1.3%	0.7%	0.5%
Never married	4.1%	4.3%	5.2%
Total	100.0%	100.0%	100.0%

Source: Kreider & Simmons (2003). Marital status: 2000, Census 2000 Brief

60 to 64. The poverty rate was 15.3% for elders ages 75 to 84 and 19.8% for the oldest old (Hobbs, 1996).

Educational attainment, one of the crucial determinants for socioeconomic status, was found to be lower among the oldest old than the young old. In 2002, 61% of oldest old men and 57% of oldest old women had had at least a high school education, whereas 73% of men and 74% of women 65–74 years of age had completed high school (Smith, 2003).

Mortality

Life expectancy increased significantly during the 20th century. According to *National Vital Statistics Reports* (Arias, 2004), from 1900 to 2001, overall life expectancy at birth increased from 49 years to 77. Specifically, for Whites, life expectancy increased from 49.6 in 1900 to 77.7 in 2001; for Blacks, life expectancy at birth was 72.2 in 2001, an increase more

than double that of 33.8 in 1900. Life expectancy for the oldest old increased as well. At age 85, the average number of years remaining in life was less than 4 years in 1900, but it increased to 6.5 in 2001 (Arias, 2004). In part, lower mortality is the reason that people are living longer (Preston, Himes, & Eggers, 1989). This is a particularly interesting issue among the oldest old of color. Recent examination of racial mortality highlights that racial crossover in mortality rates is one of the newly emerging issues among the oldest old. It has been a general notion that White Americans outlive African Americans, given that African Americans are more disadvantaged and face more discrimination than White Americans (Rogers, 1992). Empirical research reports mortality rates crossing over at age 80 years or so. Specifically, mortality rates for those younger than age 80 were higher for African Americans than for Whites but lower for African Americans than for Whites after age 80 (Corti et al., 1999; Manton & Stallard, 1981; Markides & Machalek,

1984). One explanation of the racial crossover effect is explained by "survival of the fittest" (Manton & Stallard, 1981). Specifically, because African Americans have experienced more disadvantages and unfavorable health conditions, it is likely that more vulnerable people died earlier (Preston, Elo, Rosenwaike, & Hill, 1996). On the other hand, some researchers indicate that crossover may be the result of misreporting of age on the death certificate (Crispell, 1996). Preston and colleagues (1996) showed that the reported age on the death certificate was lower than that in Social Security records, especially for African Americans. After adjusting for age at death, mortality rates in African Americans substantially increased above age 85, and racial crossover disappeared.

MENTAL HEALTH

Depression is one of the most common mental health problems among older populations. Five million older Americans age 65 and over suffer from serious and persistent symptoms of depression, and 1 million out of 5 million suffer from major depression (American Psychological Association, 1993). Among older populations, the oldest old are at high risk for mental disorders due to multiple functional disabilities, medical illness, and increasing vulnerabilities to various stressors with age, resulting from declining health and dwindling social relationships (Borson, Bartels, Colenda, Gottlieb, & Meyers, 2001). The oldest old reported higher levels of depressive symptoms than the young old dwelling in the community (Blazer, 2000; Blazer, Burchett, Service, & George, 1991; Stallones, Marx, & Garrity, 1990). In a longitudinal study of the oldest old, the participants reported increasing depressive symptoms over a 9-year period (Dunkle, Roberts, & Haug, 2001).

Although literature supports the notion that the oldest old present higher levels of depressive symptoms, the prevalence of clinically diagnosable depression among this population is not clear. Available literature, however, suggests that the amount of clinically diagnosable depression among the oldest old may be lower than that among younger populations. For example, in Haynie and colleagues' (Haynie, Berg, Johansson, Gatz, & Zarit, 2001) longitudinal study with Swedish twins over age 80, most participants had a depressive symptom level that was below the clinical cutoff for the Center for Epidemiologic Studies Depression Scale (CES-D), suggesting low rates of clinical depression among the oldest old.

Given that the oldest old survive longer than many of their age cohort, the low prevalence rate of depression among the oldest old may be explained by their physical and mental advantages, as well as their coping capacities (Kiljunen et al., 1997).

Suicide is strongly associated with depression among older adults (Katz, 1998). Recent research suggests that the oldest old are at higher risk of suicide (e.g., Erlangsen, Bille-Brahe, & Jeune, 2003; Turvey et al., 2002). The rate of suicide is the highest among people age 65 and over and continues to increase for those over age 80 (Turvey et al., 2002). Erlangsen and colleagues (2003) examined suicide trends among the young old, ages 65 to 79, and the oldest old in Denmark who committed suicide for the period 1972–1998. They found that the suicide level among the oldest old remained very high, whereas that of the young old declined. Their study also showed that the oldest old employed determined suicide methods, such as hanging or jumping, compared with the young old, indicating that suicide intention is stronger with advancing age. Similarly, Barnow and Linden (1997) found that 15% of the very old from the Berlin Aging Study (BASE) presented symptoms of tiredness of life, 5% had a wish to die, and 0.5–1% showed suicidal behavior. Age was significantly associated with suicidal ideation; 1.2% of those ages 70 to 80 reported having plans to commit suicide or wished to be dead, whereas 7.6% of the oldest old, ages 90 and over, had plans for suicide. Cook, Pearson, Thompson, Black, and Rabins (2002) examined suicidal ideation in a sample of 835 Black elderly residing in six urban public housing developments. They found that passive suicidal ideation was associated with depressive and anxiety symptoms, whereas social support and religiosity were protective factors of suicide ideation.

Worry is another significant factor influencing mental health. Examining worry in the sample of the very old, ages 85 and over, living in the community over a 9-year period, Dunkle et al. (2001) found that worry was low at the initial interview but significantly increased over the 9 years of the study. The oldest old reported that their greatest worries were associated with health and dependence in daily activities. Consistent with other studies including predominantly young old participants (Skarborn & Nicki, 1996), for the oldest old, worry was strongly associated with depressive symptoms and poor mental health (Dunkle et al., 2001; Robert, Dunkle, & Haug, 1994).

Dementia, in particular Alzheimer's disease, affects predominantly the oldest old and increases even in advanced ages. This is another major mental health issue among the elderly. A recent study reports a prevalence of dementia of 13% among elders ages 77 to 84 that increased to 48% in those age 95 and over (Strauss, Viitanen, Ronchi, Winblad, & Fratiglioni, 1999). In 2000, the number of people age 85 and over with Alzheimer's disease was 1.8 million, making up 40% of the 4.5 million people with Alzheimer's disease (Hebert, Scherr, Bienias, Bennett, & Evans, 2003). This number of the oldest old with Alzheimer's disease will increase to 8 million in 2050 (Hebert et al., 2003). In addition to the prevalence rate, the oldest old reported an 8.4% annual incidence of Alzheimer's disease. The incidence rate was 0.6% for the young old, ages 65 to 69, 1.0% for elders ages 70 to 74, 2.0% for elders ages 75 to 79, and 3.3% for elders ages 80 to 84 (Hebert et al., 1995).

HEALTH

The often-heard discussion of an increasing life span incurs thoughts of a longer and healthier life, but an increasing life span often comes at a price of increasing health problems. Evidence indicates that in the face of declining mortality, there is worsening health among those who survive (Olshansky, Rudberg, Carnes, Cassel, & Brody, 1991). Health is no longer regarded as an absence of disease because of the increasing number of diagnosable diseases in old age, especially among the very old (Steinhagen-Thiessen & Borchelt, 1999). After age 45, issues of disability and declining functional ability become a concern for many. With advancing age, these concerns escalate, with an increasing prevalence of activities of daily living (ADL) limitations (Guralnik & Simonsick, 1993). The greatest limitations are among those over the age of 85 (Parker, Thorslund, Lundberg, & Kareholt, 1996). During this age period, elders become more dependent, with greater reliance on social and health resources (Schneider & Guralnik, 1990; Thorslund, Norstrom, & Weinberg, 1991). About 88% of the very old have at least five diagnosable physical illnesses. Thirty percent are diagnosed as having at least five moderate to severe illnesses, and 21% have five illnesses that are treated with medications (Steinhagen-Thiessen & Borchelt, 1993). With the belief that health is no longer defined as "disease free" for the elderly, Steinhagen-Thiessen and Borchelt coined the term *rather healthy,* now being used to identify a reference category of healthy old people with the recognition that most very old people have some health problems. As Steinhagen-Thiessen and Borchelt (1993) note, this term describes "those having less than five somatic diagnoses, less than five prescription drugs, no diagnosis of dementia or depression, no severe loss of vision or hearing, who are mobile, continent, and not restricted in ADL" (p. 634).

Although diagnosis, medication issues, and other factors are very important in describing the health of the elderly, the most essential component of geriatric practice is the functional aspects of physical health (Steinhagen-Thiessen & Borchelt, 1993). Functional capacity includes the ability to do instrumental activities of daily living. It also includes sensory and sensorimotor capacity. The instruments used to evaluate these have recently been extended to include measurements of social activity and psychological state (Applegate, Blass, & Williams, 1990; Reuben & Siu, 1990), as well as mobility (Guralnik, Branch, Cummings, & Curb, 1989; Tinetti, 1986). The measures of ADL among very old adults produce heterogeneous results (Zarit, Johansson, & Malmberg, 1995). In addition, an inconsistent pattern of decline emerges from longitudinal studies of the oldest old (Dunkle et al., 2001; Femia, Zarit, & Johansson, 1997), indicating significant variability in function among the very old.

Even with the identification of functional problems among the very old and their increase with advancing age, disability is not always the result. Recent figures from the U.S. Census (McNeil, 2001) indicate that 34.9% of people over age 80 need personal assistance (57.6% indicating they have severe disability). Severe disabilities are greater for women than men overall (61.4% vs. 51.1%), with the gender difference holding for all racial groups and for all degrees of severity. Overall, the oldest old are not viewed as in a state of eventual decline but rather a state influenced by social, psychological, and physical factors (Femia et al., 1997).

Disability is usually defined using self-reported functional ability and includes the older person's ability to interact with his or her environment (Schoenfeld, Malmrose, Blazer, Gold, & Seeman, 1994). Taking this idea of environment into consideration, Verbrugge and Jette (1994) make the distinction of intrinsic versus actual disability. They describe *intrinsic disability* as the physiological hardship or medical problem that someone faces in attempting to accomplish a task. *Actual disability* is the case in which the physical demands placed on an individual are difficult or impossible to meet (Johnson, 2000). Having help in walking with the use of a cane or walker does not erase the intrinsic disability, but it does allow the individual to get around, thus diminishing the actual disability faced. Disability is conceived as a gap between personal and environmental factors. Therefore, the nature of disability involves the measure of both physical and psychological abilities.

Little research exists that identifies the factors associated with narrowing the gap between actual and intrinsic disability. Identification of these factors could promote independence and delay disability (Femia et al., 1997), thereby improving the quality of life of the elder, as well as decreasing the cost of treatment in the health care system (Johnson, 2000).

Identifying risk factors that accelerate the need for care, as well as determining the effectiveness of intervention strategies, would help in the development of prevention strategies. Some work has been designed to understand what socioeconomic and demographic factors are related to the use of an assistive device. Zimmer and Chappell (1994) found that age predicted the use of assistive devices. Verbrugge, Rennert, and Madans (1997) found that people over age 75 were more likely to accept assistance in managing a lower-extremity problem than were those under age 75. Hartke, Prohaska, and Furmer (1998) note that Whites were more likely than African Americans to use any assistive device. Gender plays a role. Older women were more likely than men to use personal assistance devices only, and men are more likely to use equipment such as motorized scooters than women (Verbrugge et al., 1997). Johnson (2000) explored the influence of living environments of elders (metro vs. nonmetro) on the use of assistive devices and personal helpers. No differences in intrinsic disability were found between people residing in the two types of environments, but the nonmetro elders were less likely to overcome the hardship of walking across the room due to having fewer architectural accommodations in their residences than those living in metropolitan areas. Overall, as long as the elders lived in the community and not in a sheltered environment such as an assisted-living facility or nursing home, they were more likely to be stable in functional ability (Femia et al., 1997).

In addition, psychological resources such as mastery and subjective evaluation of health also influence functional ability. Psychosocial resources influence need for help among older people (Mor et al., 1989). In numerous studies, subjective health is associated with stability in ADL functioning, at least in the short run (Femia et al., 1997). Others (Heckhausen & Krueger, 1993) suggest that subjective health is the result of social comparison, in which one's health is viewed in relationship to another person's. Mastery is

also a predictor of short-term changes in ADL (Femia et al., 1997), with lower mastery predicting more ADL problems. Although mastery diminishes over time (Mirowsky, 1995), the variability in mastery seems to increase with age (Rodin, 1989). Others have also found the importance of mastery in later life, suggesting that mastery can affect level of activity (Roberts, Anthony, Matejczyk, & Moore, 1994; Schoenfeld et al., 1994). All in all, research on the oldest old is expanding the evidence of an existing relationship between physical and psychological functioning.

Physical morbidity and disability often lead to decline in social and psychological functioning (Borchelt, Gilbert, Horgas, & Geiselmann, 1999). Functional problems can produce depression or even dementia (Katona, 1995) and lower subjective well-being (Smith, Fleeson, Geiselmann, Settersten, & Kunzmann, 1999). For example, Borchelt et al. (1999) suggest that immobility is a risk factor for depression. Vision and sensory limitations create problems for the older person in interacting with the environment, a strong detriment to limiting disability (Verbrugge & Jette, 1994). Conversely, poor social and psychological functioning can lead to poorer physical health through self-neglect, poor diet, and so forth (Maier, Watkins, & Fleshner, 1994; Marmot et al., 1991). Age alone does not explain the relationship between health and psychosocial factors.

Evidence of this relationship has important implications for intervention in this very old group of elders. Mastery, in particular, represents a sense of control over events confronted in life. Practitioners could help very old people by acknowledging the relationship between health and mental health and the importance of a sense of effectiveness in promoting better functioning over time. Femia et al. (1997) suggest that increasing physical frailty in very late life may be offset by these psychological resources that function as protective factors and that compensate for decline in health with increasing age.

SOCIAL SUPPORT

Extensive research on the importance of social support among the elderly has filled behavioral and social science journals over the past two decades (Antonucci, Sherman, & Vandewater, 1997; Biegel, 1984; Minkler, 1985; Wan, 1982).

Competing perspectives describe social support across the life span. The continuity perspective articulates the relative stability of social support (Palmore,

1981), whereas the social problems approach describes the constriction of social support with advancing age due to retirement, relocation, and death of friends and family (Hess, 1972; Morgan, Schuster, & Butler, 1991). Research, primarily involving the younger old, supports the continuity perspective, showing that these elders are embedded in kin and family contexts (Bengtson & Schutze, 1992; Troll, 1986). Among the very old, social isolation is more likely to exist than among the younger old (Knipscheer, 1986), more in line with the notion of constriction of support.

Age differences exist regarding who belongs to social networks. With personal social networks of elders, the young old name significantly more people in their social networks than the very old do (this was primarily among friends and acquaintances and not among intimates; Smith & Baltes, 1999). Field and Minkler (1988) examined social contacts among young old and very old people, as well. Although they found that involvement within the family and friendship patterns did not change over time for the young old or the very old, the picture was different when other facets of social support were examined. Their very old participants had less frequent contact with some children, were less likely to have a spouse in their social network, and had lessened involvement in church and social club activities. In part, these changes in social contacts resulted from death of family and friends and geographic dispersion among family members. Another longitudinal study (Dunkle et al., 2001) found similar results. Although many women were without spousal support, they had confidants, family, and friends who were available to provide support. One study (Dunkle et al., 2001) provides a longitudinal view of support among the very old over time. Their participants who completed all waves of the study most frequently identified a child as someone who could provide occasional assistance if needed (25%). This increased to 42% eighteen months later. Most had living children at the beginning of the study (78.3%), but this number declined to 21.7% after 9 years. With increasing age, elders relied less on family and more on neighbors and friends; this may be due to the health conditions of their children, as well as their children living farther away. Siblings were not identified as being able to provide even occasional help. In all likelihood, they were very old as well and in need of support themselves. Evidence suggests that the network size shrinks over time. At wave 1, about 95% of the sample knew someone to visit. Nine years later, 83% said they knew someone to visit. About 68% of the respondents in this study said

that they were lonely (Dunkle et al., 2001). This is significantly different from the 10% identified as lonely in the Georgia Centenarian Study (note that participants were all over 100 years of age; Martin, Poon, Kim, & Johnson, 1996). Even though worry seemed to be an issue among the very old, it does not necessarily jeopardize the well-being of these elders. Research supports the idea that well-being is associated with the feeling that there is at least one person on whom you can rely for emotional support (Thomae, 1994).

Unfortunately, most authors do not consider the influence of the health of the elder on social support. It seems clear that the relationship of the elder's health to social support is significant (Kaplan & Haan, 1989; Ory, Abeles, & Lipman, 1992); that is, as old people age, their health is likely to change in significant ways and thus influence the need for social support. The greater likelihood of change in social support among the very old suggests an ebb and flow that may be very dynamic for these elders.

Older people are more likely to need social support related to health care needs in particular. Roberts and colleagues (1994) found that men and women dwelling in the community mobilized social support differently when facing stressful circumstances. Women with better mobility had more tangible support and greater emotional support than men with similar mobility.

CULTURALLY COMPETENT CARE

Although little has been written about culturally competent care among the oldest old, nonetheless it is important to begin to think about its relevance for elders in this age group. They are more likely to be frail and in need of health and social services. Social service practitioners are increasingly aware of the need for culturally competent health care. There continue to be health disparities between racial/ethnic groups that need to be addressed (Lillie-Blanton, Parsons, Gayle, & Dievler, 1996; Williams, Lavizzo-Mourey, & Warren, 1994). One area is within the caregiving network. Research conducted on caregiver networks and race shows that the effect of race on expanding the caregiver network beyond the marital dyad is unclear. Feld, Dunkle, and Schroepfer (2004) found that Black couples were more likely than White ones to have instrumental activities of daily living (IADL) caregiver networks including helpers outside the dyad. On the other hand, Stoller and Cutler's (1992) results did not show racial differences in sole reliance on the spouse for either IADL or ADL caregiving. Unfortunately, race and gender were not considered simultaneously.

Community service is another area that has been examined. Work conducted with various minority groups sheds light on variations in service utilization by race as well. In work conducted by Miller and Stull (1999), they determined that African American elders were more likely to distrust the staff of community services than were Whites. As suggested by these authors, factors contributing to this distrust are probably lodged in heterogeneity of attitudes toward care. Service-providing individuals, as well as service contexts, influence service use and should be taken into account when designing services (Miller & Stull, 1999). One service context, the care system of Kaiser Permanente Health System, has designed diversity training programs that include handbooks for health care with specific minority populations (Gilbert, 1998).

Service providers need to master three elements of cultural competence: awareness-oriented strategies, knowledge-oriented strategies, and skill-oriented strategies. With awareness-oriented strategies, the practitioner engages in self-examination of personal biases and prejudices. Knowledge-oriented strategies aid the practitioner in learning about the culture of his or her clients; and with skill-oriented strategies, the practitioners learn behaviors that are culturally responsive. With the growing recognition that the elderly are better served with team-based care (Wadsworth & Fallcreek, 1999), individual practitioners are being organized into culturally competent care teams with educational programs designed for interdisciplinary teams of health care professionals who understand the elements of cultural competence (Wadsworth & Fallcreek, 1999). The oldest old are a heterogeneous group of people. More will be people of color; more will embrace their own cultures. Practitioners need to learn about these cultures and health beliefs if they hope to care successfully for these very old people.

IMPLICATIONS FOR SERVICE DELIVERY AND FUTURE RESEARCH

In many ways, those who are very old are not very different in their needs from other older people. What does make them different is their heterogeneity of needs. The very old experience more health and certain mental health problems simultaneously, and as a group they have fewer health, financial, and social resources to deal with the problems they face. Researchers have only begun to examine service needs of the very old and the resources that they bring to their health and mental health needs.

Mental Health Service Delivery

With increasing numbers of older adults with mental health problems, demand for mental health services is expected to increase. Interestingly, the utilization rate of mental health service among older adults is found to be lower than among younger adults with certain mental health problems. In part, this may be due to the lack of specialized mental health services for older adults (Koenig, George, & Schneider, 1994). Jin et al. (2003) found that community-dwelling elders with schizophrenia used fewer public mental health services, except case management, than young adults and middle-aged people. In addition to age, mental health problems such as depression seem to deter elders from seeking help. Whereas elders utilized fewer mental health services compared with other age groups, older adults with depression were more likely to use health care services. For example, Luber et al. (2001) examined the association between primary care provider's diagnosis of depression and health care utilization in the sample of elderly patients seen in a primary care practice. They found that older people diagnosed as depressed utilized more outpatient visits, underwent more laboratory tests, and had more consultations with medical, surgical, and other specialists than nondepressed counterparts.

Identifying resources that aid the very old in dealing with their mental health and health needs is important. Mastery is one resource that has been suggested as particularly helpful for the oldest old. Elders who feel some control over the events in their lives may be able to function at a higher level than those with a lower sense of mastery. Another resource is found in social support. Who provides social support to the very old is not clearly understood. It seems that their support networks shrink, and yet they report adequate help (Dunkle et al., 2001). Identifying the members of the support network and bolstering those people with formal support could aid in the development of a network that has enough depth to function not just in a crisis but over a prolonged period of time if needed.

Even though it is difficult to know the reason for age variations in mental health service utilization rates, it is important to identify barriers that may contribute to lower usage among elders in order to understand mental health service delivery issues among the oldest old. Older adults are less likely to seek help than younger adults, as they are more vulnerable to the stigmatization of mental illness and have more negative attitudes toward seeking help (Hastings, 1993; U.S. Department of Health and Human Services, 1999). Older adults tend to seek help from primary care physicians or clergy than from mental health specialists (Husaini, Moore, & Cain, 1994; Tiemans, Ormel, & Simon, 1996; Unutzer et al., 1997). The characteristic of late-life depression that is frequently comorbid with chronic illness seems to influence help-seeking patterns among elders. Given that the oldest old are at greater risk of frailty and comorbidity (Blazer, 2000), they may think depressive symptoms are a normal part of growing older and thus may consult with primary care physicians or religious persons. In spite of inconsistent findings in depression and age, depression among the very old is associated with comorbid physical conditions or chronic illness (Blazer, 2000), resulting in greater need for paid care, as well as informal care. Because older adults are more likely to have financial limitations, especially when they reach advanced ages, it might be difficult for the very old to obtain appropriate care. In particular, when the oldest old with depressive symptoms fail to get care, emotional distress, as well as physical dysfunction, might be exacerbated, causing higher dependence on others and increase in societal costs. Given that the prevalence of driving among the oldest old rapidly declines compared with that of the young old, causing the very old to be more transportation dependent (Foley, Heimovitz, Guralnik, & Brock, 2002), transportation may be a bigger issue in lower utilization of mental health services among older adults (Lasoki, 1986).

Caregiving Issues

The significant increase in the prevalence and incidence of dementia among the oldest old has imposed a great burden on informal caregivers, as well as on the public health care system. Dementia caregiving is more complicated and burdensome than nondementia caregiving, as dementia affects cognitive, behavioral, and affective functioning (e.g., Ory, Hoffman, Yee, Tennstedt, & Schulz, 1999). Dementia caregivers spend more time providing care and report more stressful situations related to work, family, and health than do nondementia caregivers (Ory et al., 1999). In addition, caregivers with higher stress levels are more likely to place elders with dementia in nursing homes (McFall & Miller, 1992; Montgomery & Kosloski, 1994).

Related to the issue of need for assistance is a focus on the availability of caregivers, those who can provide support. In large part, caregivers are children or age peers, with spouses making up the greatest percentage of caregivers (Rivlin & Wiener, 1989). This is particularly true with female caregivers (Feld, Dunkle, & Schroepfer, 2004). This situation has implications for caregiving. Recently published work on caregiving in marital dyads provides insight into who is involved in the caregiving network of older couples (not among the oldest old). Wives are especially likely to provide all the functional care their frail husbands receive, and husbands are more likely to share their caregiving with others. IADL and ADL caregiver networks were more likely to include helpers other than the spouse when the help recipient was the wife than when the husband was the help recipient. This gender difference has been found in a study of both IADL and ADL networks (Feld, Dunkle, & Schroepfer, 2004, under review; Stoller & Cutler, 1992).

When the care recipient is very old, the spouse and children are also likely to be old. Because of this, the caregivers often face similar problems to those of the older care recipient. Among these very old people, this may mean that the social support network shrinks due to death and illness of the caregivers themselves. With evidence of increasing health problems among the very old, coupled with the likelihood that social support systems shrink with age (Bould, Sanborn, & Reif, 1989; Soldo & Manton, 1985), research is needed that examines the relationship of health and social support among very old people.

CONCLUSION

The heterogeneity in health and functional ability among those who are very old is a critical feature that practitioners should remember. Inconsistent patterns of decline (Dunkle et al., 2001) suggest that a comprehensive evaluation of very old patients is in order to determine the strengths and weaknesses of each individual. In part, this evaluation consists of awareness-oriented strategies that require the practitioner to examine his or her own feelings and beliefs about aging. In addition, the practitioner should be educated in the intervention strategies that have been successfully used with older people and consider what adaptation may be helpful to meet the needs of the oldest old. Lastly, executing the intervention in a fashion that has been found to be helpful to older people is a necessity. Identifying risk factors that accelerate the need for care, as well as the effectiveness of intervention strategies, would help in the development of prevention strategies.

A growing body of literature exists regarding the oldest old. Unfortunately, little is known about successful intervention strategies to meet the health and mental health needs of these very old people. By learning who these very old people are, where they live, who they care about, and what health issues they face, practitioners can begin to develop relevant services to meet the health and care needs of the very old.

REFERENCES

American Psychological Association. (1993). *Vitality for life: Psychological research for productive aging: Research initiative concerning behavioral solutions for the maintenance of health and vitality in late adulthood.* Washington, DC: Author.

Antonucci, T. C., Sherman, E., & Vandewater, E. (1997). Measures of social support and caregiver burden. *Generations, 21,* 48–51.

Applegate, W. B., Blass, J. P., & Williams, T. F. (1990). Instruments for the functional assessment of older patients. *New England Journal of Medicine, 322,* 1207–1214.

Arias, E. (2004). United States life tables, 2001. *National Vital Statistics Reports, 52*(14). Hyattsville, MD: National Center for Health Statistics.

Barnow, S., & Linden, M. (1997). Suicidality and tiredness of life among very old persons: Results from the Berlin Aging Study (BASE). *Archives of Suicide Research, 3,* 171–182.

Bengtson, V. L., & Schütze, Y. (1992). Altern und Generationenbeziehungen: Aussichten für das kommende Jahrhundert. In P. B. Baltes & J. Mittelstrab (Eds.), *Zukunft des Alterns und gesellschaftliche Entwicklung* (pp. 492–517). Berlin, Germany: De Gruyter.

Bernstein, A. B., Hing, E., Moss, A. J., Allen, K. F., Siller, A. B., & Tiggle, R. B. (2003). *Health care in America: Trends in utilization.* Hyattsville, MD: National Center for Health Statistics.

Biegel, D. (1984). *Building support networks for the elderly: Theory and applications.* Beverly Hills, CA: Sage.

Blazer, D., Burchett, B., Service, C., & George, L. (1991). The association of age and depression among the elderly: An epidemiologic study. *Journals of Gerontology: Series A. Biological Sciences and Medical Sciences, 46,* M210–M215.

Blazer, D. G. (2000). Psychiatry and the oldest old. *American Journal of Psychiatry, 157,* 1915–1924.

Borchelt, M., Gilbert, R., Horgas, A., & Geiselmann, B. (1999). On the significance of morbidity and disability in old age. In P. Baltes & K. Mayer, *The Berlin Aging Study: Aging from 70–100* (pp. 403–430). Cambridge, UK: Cambridge University Press.

Borson, S., Bartels, S. J., Colenda, C. C., Gottlieb, G. L., & Meyers, B. (2001). Geriatric mental health services research: Strategic plan for an aging population. *American Journal of Geriatric Psychiatry, 9*(3), 191–204.

Bould, S., Sanborn, B., & Reif, L. (1989). *Eighty-five plus: The oldest-old.* Belmont, CA: Wadsworth.

Cook, J. M., Pearson, J. L., Thompson, R., Black, B. S., & Rabins, P. V. (2002). Suicidality in older African Americans: Findings from the EPOCH Study. *American Journal of Geriatric Psychiatry, 10*(4), 437–446.

Corti, M., Guralnik, J. M., Ferrucci, L., Izmirlian, G., Leveille, S. G., Pahor, M., et al. (1999). Evidence for a Black-White crossover in all-cause and coronary heart disease mortality in an older population: The North Carolina EPESE. *American Journal of Public Health, 89*(3), 308–314.

Crispell, D. (1996). The matching game. *American Demographics, 18*(9), 31–33.

Dunkle, R. E., Roberts, B., & Haug, M. (2001). *The oldest old in everyday life: Self perception, coping with change, and stress.* New York: Springer.

Erlangsen, A., Bille-Brahe, U., & Jeune, B. (2003). Differences in suicide between the old and the oldest old. *Journals of Gerontology: Series B. Psychological Sciences and Social Sciences, 58,* S314–S322.

Feld, S., Dunkle, R., & Schroepfer, T. (under review). Factors affecting the expansion of the IADL caregiver network beyond the marital dyad. *International Journal of Human Development and Aging.*

Feld, S., Dunkle, R., & Schroepfer, T. (2004). When do couples expand their ADL caregiver network beyond the marital dyad? *Marriage and Family Review.*

Femia, E., Zarit, S., & Johansson, B. (1997). Predicting change in activities of daily living: A longitudinal study of the oldest old in Sweden. *Journals of Gerontology: Series B. Psychological Sciences and Social Sciences, 52*(6), 294–302.

Field, D., & Minkler, M. (1988). Continuity and change in social support between young-old and old-old or very old age. *Journals of Gerontology: Series B. Psychological Sciences and Social Sciences, 43*(4), 100–106.

Foley, D. J., Heimovitz, H. K., Guralnik, J. M., & Brock, D. B. (2002). Driving life expectancy of persons aged 70 years and older in the United States. *American Journal of Public Health, 92*(8), 1284–1289.

Gilbert, M. J. (1998). Kaiser created multicultural model for eldercare. *Aging Today, 19,* 1–13.

Guralnik, J., Branch, L. G., Cummings, S. R., & Curb, J. D. (1989). Physical performance measures in aging research. *Journals of Gerontology: Series A. Biological Sciences and Medical Sciences, 44*, M141–M146.

Guralnik, J. M., & Simonsick, E. M. (1993). Physical disability in older Americans. *Journal of Gerontology: Series B. 48*, 3–10.

Hartke, R. J., Prohaska, T. R., & Fumer, S. E. (1998). Older adults and assistive devices. *Journal of Aging and Health, 10*, 99–116.

Hastings, M. M. (1993). Aging and mental health services: An introduction. *Journal of Mental Health Administration, 20*(3), 186–190.

Haynie, D. A., Berg, S., Johansson, B., Gatz, M., & Zarit, S. H. (2001). Symptoms of depression in the oldest old: A longitudinal study. *Journals of Gerontology: Series B. Psychological Sciences and Social Sciences, 56*, P111–P118.

Hebert, L. E., Scherr, P. A., Beckett, L. A., Albert, M. S., Pilgrim, D. M., Chown, M. J., et al. (1995). Age-specific incidence of Alzheimer's disease in a community population. *Journal of the American Medical Association, 273*(17), 1354–1359.

Hebert, L. E., Scherr, P. A., Bienias, J. L., Bennett, D. A., & Evans, D. A. (2003). Alzheimer disease in the U.S. population. *Archives of Neurology, 60*, 1119–1122.

Heckhausen, J., & Krueger, J. (1993). Developmental expectations for the self and most other people: Age-grading in three functions of social comparison. *Developmental Psychology, 25*, 539–548.

Hess, B. (1972). Friendship. *Aging and Society, 13*, 357–393.

Hetzel, L., & Smith, A. (2001). The 65 years and over population: 2000. *Census 2000 Brief.* Washington, DC: U.S. Census Bureau.

Hobbs, F. B. (with Damon, B. L.). (1996). 65+ in the United States. *Current Population Reports: Special Studies* (P23-190). Washington, DC: U.S. Census Bureau.

Husaini, B. A., Moore, S. T., & Cain, V. A. (1994). Psychiatric symptoms and help-seeking behavior among the elderly: An analysis of racial and gender differences. *Journal of Gerontological Social Work, 21*(3/4), 177–195.

Jin, H., Folsom, D. P., Lindamer, L., Bailey, A., Hawthorne, W., Garcia, P., et al. (2003). Patterns of public mental health service use by age in patients with Schizophrenia. *American Journal of Geriatric Psychiatry, 11*(5), 525–533.

Johnson, N. (2000). Attempts to resolve a disability in walking: Different strategies or different outcomes for nonmetro elderly Americans? *Journal of Family Issues, 21*(5), 587–610.

Kaplan, G., & Haan, M. (1989). Is there a role for prevention among the elderly?: Epidemiological evidence from the Alameda County Study. In M. Ory & K. Bond (Eds.), *Aging and health care: Social science and policy perspectives* (pp. 27–51). Florence, KY: Taylor & Frances/Routledge.

Katona, C. L. E. (1994). *Depression in old age.* Chichester, NY: Wiley.

Katz, I. R. (1998). Depression as a pivotal component in secondary aging: Opportunities for research, treatment and prevention. In J. Lomranz (Ed.), *Handbook of aging and mental health* (pp. 463–482). New York: Plenum Press.

Kiljunen, M., Sulkava, R., Niinisto, L., Polvikoski, T., Verkkoniemi, A., & Halonen, P. (1997). Depression measured by the Zung depression status inventory is very rare in Finnish population aged 85 years and over. *International Psychogeriatrics, 9*, 359–368.

Knipscheer, K. (1986). Anomie in der Mehrgenerationerfamilie: Kinder und die Versworgung ihrer altern Eltern. *Zeitschrift für Gerontologie, 19*, 40–46.

Koenig, H., George, L., & Schneider, R. (1994). Mental health care for older adults in the year 2020: A dangerous and avoided topic. *Gerontologist, 34*, 674–679.

Kreider, R., & Simmons, T. (2003). Marital status: 2000. *Census 2000 brief* (No. C2KBR-30). Washington, DC: U.S. Census Bureau.

Lasoki, M. (1986). Reasons for low utilization of mental health services by the elderly. *Hospital and Community Psychiatry, 39*(7), 721–722.

Lillie-Blanton, M., Parsons, P., Gayle, H., & Dievler, A. (1996). Racial differences in health: Not just black and white, but shades of gray. *Annual Review of Public Health, 17*, 411–448.

Luber, M. P., Meyers, B. S., Williams-Russo, P. G., Hollenberg, J. P., DiDomenico, T. N., Charlson, M. E., et al. (2001). Depression and service utilization in elderly primary care patients. *American Journal of Geriatric Psychiatry, 9*(2), 169–176.

Maier, S. F., Watkins, L. R., & Fleshner, M. (1994). Psychoneuroimmunology: The interface between behavior, brain, and immunity. *American Psychologist, 49*, 1004–1016.

Manton, K. G., & Stallard, E. (1981). Methods for evaluating the heterogeneity of aging processes in human populations using vital statistics data: Explaining the black/white mortality crossover by a model of mortality selection. *Human Biology, 53*, 47–67.

Markides, K. S., & Machalek, R. (1984). Selective survival, aging, and society. *Archives of Gerontology and Geriatrics, 3*, 207–229.

Marmot, M. B., Smith, G. D., Stansfeld, S., Patel, C., North, F., & Head, J. (1991). Health inequalities among British civil servants: The Whitehall II Study. *Lancet, 337*, 1387–1393.

Martin, P., Poon, L., Kim, E., & Johnson, M. A. (1996). Social and psychological resources in the oldest old. *Experimental Aging and Research, 22*, 121–139.

McFall, S., & Miller, B. H. (1992). Caregiver burden and nursing home admission of frail elderly persons. *Journals of Gerontology: Series B. Psychological Sciences and Social Sciences, 47*(2), S73–S79.

McNeil, J. (2001). Americans with disabilities: Household economic studies. *Current Population Reports* (Report No. P70-73). Washington, DC: U.S. Census Bureau.

Miller, B., & Stull, D. (1999). Perceptions of community services by African American and White older persons. In M. Wykle & A. Ford (Eds.), *Serving minority elders in the 21st century* (pp. 267–286). New York: Springer.

Minkler, M. (1985). Social support and health of the elderly. In S. Cohen & S. L. Syme (Eds.), *Social support and health* (pp. 199–216). New York: Academic Press.

Mirowsky, J. (1995). Age and sense of control. *Social Psychology Quarterly, 58*, 31–43.

Montgomery, R. J. V., & Kosloski, K. (1994). A longitudinal analysis of nursing home placement for dependent elders cared for by spouses vs. adult children. *Journals of Gerontology: Series B. Psychological Sciences and Social Sciences, 49*(2), S62–S74.

Mor, V., Murphy, J., Masterson-Allen, S., Willey, C., Razmpour, A., Jackson, M. E., et al. (1989). Risk of functional decline among well elders. *Journal of Clinical Epidemiology, 42*, 895–904.

Morgan, D., Schuster, T., & Butler, E. (1991). Role reversals in the exchange of social support. *Journals of Gerontology: Series B. Psychological Sciences and Social Sciences, 46*(5), S278–S287.

Olshansky, S. J., Rudberg, M. A., Carnes, B. A., Cassel, C., & Brody, J. (1991). Trading off longer life for worsening health. *Journal of Aging and Health, 3*, 194–216.

Ory, M., Abeles, R., & Lipman, P. (Eds.). (1992). *Aging, health and behavior.* New York: Sage.

Ory, M. G., Hoffman, R. R., III, Yee, J. L., Tennstedt, S., & Schulz, R. (1999). Prevalence and impact of caregiving: A detailed comparison between dementia and nondementia caregivers. *Gerontologist, 39*(2), 177–185.

Palmore, E. (1981). *Social patterns in normal aging: Findings from the Duke Longitudinal Study.* Durham, NC: Duke University Press.

Parker, M. G. Thorslund, M., Lundberg, O., & Kareholt, I. (1996). Predictors of physical education among the oldest old: A comparison of three outcome variables in a 24-year follow-up. *Journal of Aging and Health, 8*(3), 444–460.

Preston, D. B., Himes, C., & Eggers, M. (1989). Demographic conditions responsible for population aging. *Demography, 26*(4), 691–704.

Preston, S. H., Elo, I. T., Rosenwaike, I., & Hill, M. (1996). African-American mortality at older ages: Results of a matching study. *Demography, 33*(2), 193–209.

Reuben, D. B., & Siu, A. L. (1990). An objective measure of physical function of elderly outpatients: The physical performance test. *Journal of the American Geriatrics Society, 38*, 1105–1112.

Rivlin, A., & Wiener, J. (1989). Caring for the disabled elderly: Who will pay? *Gerontologist, 29*, 279–280.

Roberts, B. L., Anthony, M. K., Matejczyk, M., & Moore, D. (1994). The relationship of social support to functional limitations, pain, and well-being among men and women. *Journal of Women and Aging, 6*, 3–19.

Robert, B., Dunkle, R., & Haug, M. (1994). Physical, psychological, and social resources as moderators of the relationship of stress to mental health of the very old. *Journals of Gerontology: Series B. Psychological Sciences and Social Sciences, 49*, S35–S43.

Rodin, J. (1989). Sense of control: Potentials for intervention. *Annals of the New York Academy of Psychological and Social Sciences, 503*, 29–42.

Rogers, A. (1992). Living and dying in the USA: Sociodemographic determinants of death among blacks and whites. *Demography, 29*, 287–303.

Schneider, E. L., & Guralnik, J. M. (1990). The aging of America: Impact on health care costs. *Journal of the American Medical Association, 263*(17), 2335–2340.

Schoenfeld, D., Malmrose, L., Blazer, D., Gold, D., & Seeman, T. (1994). Self-rated health and mortality in the high functioning elderly: A close look at healthy individuals: MacArthur field study of successful aging. *Journals of Gerontology: Series A. Biological Sciences and Medical Sciences, 49*, M109–M115.

Skarborn, M., & Nicki, R. (1996). Worry among Canadian seniors. *International Journal of Aging and Human Development, 43*, 169–178.

Smith, D. (2003). *The older population in the United States: March 2002* (Report No. P20-546). Washington, DC: U.S. Census Bureau.

Smith, J., & Baltes, P. (1999). Trends and profiles of psychological functioning in very old age. In P. Baltes & K. Mayer (Eds.), *The Berlin Aging Study: Aging from 70–100* (pp. 197–226). Cambridge, UK: Cambridge University Press.

Smith, J., Fleeson, W., Geiselmann, B., Settersten, R., & Kunzmann, U. (1999). In P. Baltes & K. Mayer

(Eds.), *The Berlin Aging Study: Aging from 70–100* (pp. 450–471). Cambridge, UK: Cambridge University Press.

Soldo, B., & Manton, K. (1985). Changes in the health status and service needs of the oldest old: Current patterns and future trends. *Milbank Memorial Fund Quarterly, 63*, 286–319.

Stallones, L., Marx, M. B., & Garrity, T. F. (1990). Prevalence and correlates of depressive symptoms among older U.S. adults. *American Journal of Preventive Medicine, 6*, 295–303.

Steinhagen-Thiessen, E., & Borchelt, M. (1993). Health differences in advanced old age. *Aging and Society, 13*, 619–655.

Stoller, E. P., & Cutler, S. J. (1992). The impact of gender on configurations of care among elderly couples. *Research on Aging, 14*, 313–330.

Strauss, E. V., Viitanen, M., Ronchi, D. D., Winblad, B., & Fratiglioni, L. (1999). Aging and the occurrence of dementia. *Archives of Neurology, 56*, 587–592.

Taeuber, C. M., & Rosenwaike, I. (1993). A demographic portrait of America's oldest old. In R. M. Suzman, D. P. Willis, & K. G. Manton (Eds.), *The oldest old* (pp. 17–49). New York: Oxford University Press.

Thomae, H. (1994). Trust, social support, and relying on others: A contribution to the interface between behavioral and social gerontology. *Zeitschrift für Gerontologie, 27*, 103–109.

Thorslund, M., Norstrom, T., & Weinberg, K. (1991). The utilization of home help in Sweden: A multivariate analysis. *Gerontologist, 31*, 116–119.

Tiemans, B. G., Ormel, J., & Simon, G. E. (1996). Occurrence, recognition, and outcome of psychological disorders in primary care. *American Journal of Psychiatry, 153*, 636–644.

Tinetti, M. E. (1986). A performance oriented assessment of mobility problems in elderly patients. *Journal of the American Geriatrics Society, 34*, 119–126.

Troll, L. E. (1986). *Family issues in current gerontology.* New York: Springer.

Turvey, C. L., Conwell, Y., Jones, M. P., Phillips, C., Simonsick, E., Pearson, J. L., et al. (2002). Risk factors for late-life suicide: A prospective, community-based study. *American Journal of Geriatric Psychiatry, 10*(4), 398–406.

Unutzer, J., Patrick, D. L., Simon, G., Grembowski, D., Walker, E., Rutter, C., et al. (1997). Depressive symptoms and the cost of health services in HMO patients aged 65 and older. *Journal of the American Medical Association, 277*, 1618–1623.

U.S. Census Bureau (2003). *Statistical abstract of the United States: 2003* (123rd ed.). Washington, DC: Government Printing Office.

U.S. Department of Health and Human Services. (1999). *Mental health: A report of the Surgeon General.* Rockville, MD: U.S. Department of Health and Human Services, National Institutes of Health, National Institute of Mental Health.

Verbrugge, L., & Jette, A. M. (1994). The disablement process. *Social Science and Medicine, 38*, 1–14.

Verbrugge, L., Rennert, C., & Madans, J. H. (1997). The great efficacy of personal equipment assistance in reducing disability. *American Journal of Public Health, 87*, 384–392.

Wadsworth, N., & Fallcreek, S. (1999). Culturally competent care teams. In M. Wykle & A. Ford (Eds.). *Serving minority elders in the 21st century* (pp. 248–266). New York: Springer.

Wan, T. (1982). *Stressful life events, social support networks, and gerontological health.* Lexington, MA: Lexington Books.

Williams, D. R., Lavizzo-Mourey, R., & Warren, R. C. (1994). The concept of race and health status in America. *Public Health Reports, 109*(1), 26–41.

Zarit, S., Johansson, B., & Malmberg, B. (1995). Changes in functional competency in the oldest old: A longitudinal study. *Journal of Aging and Health, 1*, 3–23.

Zimmer, Z., & Chappell, N. L. (1994). Mobility restriction and the use of devices among seniors. *Journal of Aging and Health, 6*, 185–208.

AILEE MOON

SIYON RHEE

Immigrant and Refugee Elders

IMMIGRATION HISTORY AND PATTERNS

As a nation of immigrants, the United States has admitted more than 68 million immigrants, including refugees and asylum seekers, between 1820 and 2002 (U.S. Department of Homeland Security, 2003). Whereas immigrants in the late 19th century and early 20th century were mostly from European countries, the past five decades have seen rising numbers of immigrants from the Americas and Asia (U.S. Department of Homeland Security, 2003). Beginning with the Displaced Persons Act of 1948, more than 600,000 people came from Eastern Europe and what were then "Iron Curtain" countries, and the Immigration and Naturalization Act of 1965 opened the door to several million Asians. Following the fall of South Vietnam in 1975, more than 1.1 million Vietnamese, Hmong, Laotians, and Cambodians came to the United States as refugees between 1975 and 2002 (Niedzwiecki & Duong, 2004).

Of 9.1 million new immigrants from more than 200 countries between 1991 and 2000, almost one half (49%) were from the Americas, 31% from Asia, 15% from Europe, and 4% from Africa. The percentage of older adults age 65 years or older fell from 5.6% of all immigrants in the 1980s to 3.2% in the 1990s (U.S. Census Bureau, 2001). In 2002, however, 7.6% were 60 years or older, and 14.4% were 50 years or older. The vast majority of the 60 and older age group arrived in the United States under the category of "immediate relatives of U.S. citizens." Over 60% of immigrants live in six states: California, New York, Florida, Texas, New Jersey, and Illinois. In 2000, the median length of residence in the United States was 14.4 years.

The continued increase in the immigrant population, which has grown at a rate faster than that of the U.S. population, especially during the 1990s, has led to an increase in the proportion of the foreign born, from 6.2% (14.1 million) in 1980 to 10.4% (29 million) of the U.S. population in 2000 (U.S. Census Bureau, 2001). In 2000, Mexico, as the country of origin, accounted for over one fourth (7.8 million) of all foreign born in 2000, followed by China (1.4 million), the Philippines (1.2 million), India (1 million), Cuba (1 million), Vietnam (0.9 million), El Salvador (0.8 million), Korea (0.7 million), the Dominican Republic (0.7 million), Canada (0.7 million), and Germany (0.7 million). These numbers represent underestimates to the extent that foreign-born or illegal immigrants did not participate in the census.

GROWING DIVERSITY AND ITS IMPLICATIONS

The continued influx of older adult immigrants and refugees from more than 200 countries, together with the aging younger immigrants of past decades, has meant that the elderly immigrant and refugee population in the United States has become increasingly diverse. This diversity includes not only racial and ethnic background but also reasons for immigration (e.g., family reunification, economic opportunities, fleeing from war, fear of persecution, or political turmoil in the country of origin), age at the time of immigration, length of residence in the United States, and English proficiency. Besides historical and demographic diversity, one finds expanding diversity in cultural norms and values governing the family, its role as caregiver for the elderly, living arrangements, family relations, interpersonal behavior, health beliefs, the role of religion and spirituality, and attitudes toward health and social services.

The immigration history, cultural norms and values, and socioeconomic background of immigrants have significant effects on their well-being and on the process of adjustment in the new environment. These factors may vary not only among immigrant elderly groups from different regions or countries but also within the same ethnic group. For example, ethnic Chinese elders from the People's Republic of China, Hong Kong, Singapore, and Taiwan may have different values and ideologies, different educational and economic backgrounds, different levels of acculturation and English proficiency, and different service needs. Muslim war refugee elders who recently came from Kosovo and Bosnia may experience different levels and types of war-related trauma than Afghan elders who came in the 1970s, when they were in their 40s, fleeing the war with Russia. On the other hand, the importance of religious and spiritual coping and healing may be similar among predominantly Christian Korean, Buddhist Cambodian and Laotian, and Muslim Indonesian immigrant elderly people.

For many immigrant elders who escaped from persecution and poverty in their homeland, the United States is the land of relief and improved economic opportunities. For many of those who immigrated to join children who had already been living in the United States, arrival in America brings tremendous happiness. Some elders, however, may conclude that the losses involved in immigration to the United States outweigh perceived advantages of the move to the new country (Gelfand, 2003). Indeed, it is difficult to generalize the life experiences and issues of increasingly heterogeneous immigrant and refugee elderly populations, not only because they all have different backgrounds, but also because their experiences and expectations change in the process of adjustment and settlement in the United States.

Although immigration may have a varied impact on individuals, most elderly immigrants and refugees, especially during the early period of adjustment to their new environment, experience stresses associated with migratory grief, attachment to their home country, language, social isolation, unfamiliarity with health and social services, limited social support and mobility, increased dependency on children and their families, lowered status within the family and the society, and barriers to participating in mainstream social and political activities (Casado & Leung, 2001; Gelfand, 2003; Moon, Lubben, & Villa, 1998; Strumpf, Glicksman, Goldberg-Glen, Fox, & Logue, 2001; Wong, 2001). For example, a study of caregiver and elder experiences of Cambodian, Vietnamese, Soviet Jewish, and Ukrainian refugee elders in Philadelphia (Strumpf et al., 2001) found that, with few exceptions, the major impact of immigration on refugee elders was loneliness and isolation. As a result of increased vulnerability and lowered status in the family, some immigrant and refugee elders have become subject to various types of mistreatment by family members (Moon, 2000; Tatara, 1999).

FAMILY AND CAREGIVING

From a general perspective, the family, in all cultures, is the main source of support, and many of the issues and challenges faced by the elderly and their families may be more similar than different among different cultures and ethnic groups. However, the specific problems and needs of older people, and the perceptions of issues and approaches to problem solving, can vary substantially depending on the cultural norms, available economic and social resources, and special circumstances in which the family and the elderly person are situated.

Immigrant/refugee families from developing countries have often been characterized by a strong family tradition of parental authority, rigid sex roles and male dominance, mutual support, strong parent-child bond, and filial piety. For example, a study of caregiver and elder experiences of Cambodian, Vietnamese, Soviet Jewish, and Ukrainian refugees in Philadelphia found that in Asian populations, family harmony, negation of personal needs, and self-control were emphasized. For Cambodian caregivers, the "rightness" of parental care was understood as proper repayment of debts owed to elders and a way to show gratitude. Obligation, love, and respect were common themes as well among the Soviet Jewish and Ukrainian caregivers; and for the Ukrainian cohort, commitment to the Baptist faith was highly emphasized, and the focus on spiritual life appeared to mute the losses associated with relocation (Strumpf et al., 2001). In some cultures, an elderly woman who lives with her child's family, cares for her grandchildren, and helps with house chores typifies happy aging, as opposed to elder exploitation; whereas placing an elderly parent in an institutional facility, such as a nursing home, is considered an abandonment of filial responsibility.

Families have played a critical role in caring for and assisting with daily needs of their elderly members in most immigrant/refugee populations. As reflected in *familismo,* which can be defined as a "strong feeling of reciprocity and solidarity among family members," immigrant Latino families mobilize a large network of relatives and friends in order to provide needed care and support for their elderly relatives (Gelfand, 2003). Family is an even more important source of care for the elderly in rural areas, where supportive services in general and culturally and linguistically tailored services in particular may be less available than in urban areas. In a study of Vietnamese immigrant elders in Texas, the family was almost the exclusive source of help with language issues, loneliness, and internal family problems (Die & Seelbach, 1988). A study of South Asian caregivers composed of Hindus, Muslims, Sikhs, and Christians concluded that belief in filial piety norms among caregivers plays a significant role in lowering perceived levels of caregiver burden (Gupta & Pillai, 2002).

In examining living arrangement patterns, Wilmoth, DeJong, and Himes (1997) found that even after controlling for the differences in demographic characteristics, economic resources, functional limitations, and acculturation, elderly immigrants were significantly more likely to live in a household with extended family and nonfamily than were nonimmigrants. Another study further demonstrated that elderly immigrants from developing countries, as compared with those from developed countries, were significantly more likely to live with their children and/or others (Kritz, Gurak, & Chen, 2000). This study also indicated that reduced socioeconomic resources, lack of integration (measured by English-language skills), shorter durations of U.S. residence,

noncitizenship status, and demand for the elderly relative's assistance with domestic work significantly influenced the likelihood of immigrant elders' living with children and/or others. Thus practitioners must not automatically regard a multigenerational living arrangement as a sign of a strong family ties or practice of filial responsibility for care of the elderly client.

Similarly, living alone or with a spouse only may not necessarily mean isolation or a lack of family support. For example, in some locales, the majority of Asian immigrant elderly appear to live alone. This in part reflects suburbanization of younger Asian American families and the desire of the elderly parents to live near the center of their ethnic community, such as Chinatown, Koreatown, Little Saigon, and Little Tokyo (Cheung, 1989; Yoo & Sung, 1997). By living close to the ethnic community, they can socialize with people in their ethnic language and take advantage of various health, social, recreational, and other services offered by ethnic-specific agencies.

Thus the location of the residence, in terms of geographic proximity to their ethnic community, appears to be an important factor in influencing the ability to live independently and the quality of life among immigrant elders, although perceived good relationships and frequent contacts with their children still remain important for their life satisfaction (Moon, 1996). This also suggests that those who live alone in locations where there are few people like themselves or where access to health and social services for the elderly is severely limited due to language and cultural barriers are at higher risk for developing health and psychological problems associated with isolation and loneliness.

Although the centrality of the family and the norm of family care for the elderly prevail in many immigrant families, there has been a gradual shift in values and attitudes regarding traditional family structure, relations, and care arrangements for the elderly. Typically, younger immigrant women tend to experience these changes sooner and faster than their older relatives. This implies that to the extent to which American norms and values differ from those of the country of origin, elderly immigrants may face cultural conflicts and related problems with their children who have been assimilated or acculturated into the American culture.

For example, an elderly immigrant from a culture of extended, hierarchical family structure that emphasizes interdependence and collective well-being of the family may find it difficult to accept or adjust, initially at least, to the American norm of nuclear family arrangement and the values of independent living and individualism, as well as the principle of democracy in defining the status and relationships among family members. Tension, conflict, and distress can result from the differences between the elderly immigrant/refugee and the children in their expectations about where and how they should live, what and how much the children should do for the parents, and what the parents should do for the children in return.

Studies suggest that dissatisfaction and isolation of the elderly in immigrant families stem from the elderly's high expectations for family socialization and from constraints on kin interaction, limited mobility, inability to speak English, and heavy domestic responsibilities in their children's household (Balgopal, 1999; Jones, Zhang, Jaceldo-Siegl, & Meleis, 2002; Treas & Mazumdar, 2002). Overall, fear of dependence on children or others and uncertainty about whether children will care for them as they grow older and whether they would be placed in a nursing home are perhaps the most common concerns across the immigrant elderly population (Balgopal, 1999; Kropf, Nackerud, & Gorokhovski, 1999). Practitioners, however, must not underestimate the ability of immigrant elders to cope with and adapt to the new environment.

Issues and challenges faced by family caregivers of elderly immigrants may vary depending on the intensity of care needed, available economic and other resources, and quality of the relationship with the elder, as well as culturally expected roles of family caregivers. After moving to the United States, most elders, especially those from non-English-speaking countries, become dependent on their children and grandchildren for help with even the tasks of daily living, such as making doctor's appointments and going places. After some adjustment period, however, some elders find other sources of help and become independent in performing a variety of tasks.

Although this situation undermines elders' authority and their traditional status in the family and may cause distress and worry for the elderly, their family caregivers are also challenged to adjust not only their thinking back and forth between the traditional and Western values in the process of caregiving but also their ability to perform caregiver roles, as they have other competing demands for their time and resources (Chenoweth & Burdick, 2001; Jones et al., 2002). Prolonged dependence of the elderly can lead to the caregiver's feeling of overburden and frustration, causing intergenerational conflicts in families. This is especially true for women in immigrant/refugee families who are already overburdened

by dual or triple roles they perform in and outside the family: the traditional role as homemaker and a new role as participant in the labor force.

Performing filial responsibilities is especially challenging to those children who have their own adjustment problems and other family issues, such as unemployment, conflicts with their children, crowded housing, and pressure to succeed in the new homeland. Caring for immigrant/refugee elders may require a greater intensity of care than in the previous homeland, but family caregivers may be less able to provide adequate care due to decreased economic resources, limited knowledge of services, few appropriate coping resources, and little experience in resolving cultural conflicts with their elderly parents (Kropf et al., 1999). Studies have also shown that caregivers' ambivalence about the use of formal services, misperceptions about the legal and other eligibility requirements of government programs, and strong view of formal services as the last resort, as well as the elder's belief that children would provide full support and care, present additional barriers to use of social services among some immigrant/refugee elderly and their families (Chicago Department on Aging and Disability, 1988; Chenoweth & Burdick, 2001; Jones et al., 2002; Kropf et al., 1999; Strumpf et al., 2001).

Increased burden on family caregivers and limited coping resources, combined with lower social pressure to practice filial piety and declining status of the elderly, could result in neglect and abuse of elders in immigrant/refugee families. In fact, there is a growing concern that elder abuse and neglect in immigrant/refugee populations may be equal to or even more serious than in U.S.-born populations and that incidents in immigrant/refugee populations may be more likely to be kept hidden or secret within the family (Tatara, 1999). In two similar studies, 34% of Korean and 33% of Mexican immigrant elders reported awareness of at least one incident of elder abuse in their respective community (Chang & Moon, 1997; Sanchez, 1999).

MENTAL HEALTH PROBLEMS AND PSYCHOLOGICAL DISTRESS

Stressful life events have a significant impact on physical morbidity and mental health problems, and depression, both major and minor, has been reported to be the most prevalent affective disorder found in the elderly population in the United States (Blazer & Koening, 1996; Hendrie et al., 1995). Given the inherently stressful nature of the immigration experience and the concomitant stressors associated with living as an immigrant/refugee, these problems have been more pronounced in elderly immigrant/refugee populations (Black, Markides, & Miller, 1998; Brener, 1991; Casado & Leung, 2001; Ghaffarian, 1998; Min, Moon, & Lubben, 2005; Mui, 1996, 2001; Ngo, Tran, Gibbons, & Oliver, 2001). For example, one study found a high prevalence of depression among elderly Chinese immigrants and identified migratory grief as the most significant contributing factor (Casado & Leung, 2001). A similar significant relationship between psychological distress and migratory grief was found among Mexican, Haitian, and Hispanic immigrants (Brener, 1991; Prudent, 1988; Lakatos, 1992).

In another study (Black et al., 1998), 26% of the immigrant Mexican elderly showed high levels of depression. As found in other ethnic minority groups, gender (female), lack of health coverage, financial difficulty, and presence of chronic health conditions and disabilities were major predictors of depressive symptoms. Brener (1991) found low acculturation levels associated with high depression and high perceived losses among most of the Mexican immigrants. In a study of Iranian immigrants, a significant relationship was found between age and acculturation: The older Iranians had lower levels of cultural shift and cultural incorporation and higher levels of cultural resistance than the younger Iranians (Ghaffarian, 1998). These findings suggest that older immigrants may experience more difficulties in learning and adjusting to the new environment than younger immigrants, as reflected in low acculturation levels, thereby experiencing more mental and psychological difficulties than younger immigrants. Among older Soviet immigrants, unsatisfactory living arrangements, such as the stress of multiple generational households, could lead to the feeling of depression (Kropf et al., 1999), whereas lack of contact with children was a significant factor contributing to low morale and high depression among older Korean immigrants living alone or with spouse only (Lee, Crittenden, & Yu, 1996; Moon, 1996).

Depression is also one of the most significant risk factors associated with suicide in late life (Carney, Rich, Burke, & Fowler, 1994; U.S. Surgeon General, 1999). In addition, immigration, particularly during old age, and being female seem to be associated with high risk of suicide (Barron, 2000; Yu, 1986). For example, Yu (1986) found that the suicide rate for elderly Chinese immigrants was almost three times higher than the rate for U.S.-born Chinese elderly in 1980. The high prevalence of depression and suicide

among elderly Asian immigrant women may be attributed to a variety of adjustment difficulties and stressful life events, poverty, and low socioeconomic status (Bagley, 1993; Gelfand & Yee, 1991).

Refugees from war-torn countries are a high-risk population for mental health problems because of their extensive exposure to numerous premigration traumatic events and stressors, such as torture, extensive detention, starvation, battlefield experiences, massacre, separation and loss of significant others, and hardships during the flight and/or in the refugee camps (Abueg & Chun, 1996; Morioka-Douglas, Sacks, & Yeo, 2004; Ngo et al., 2001; Olness, 1998). The effect of traumatic life experiences among refugees is often a lifelong process that is likely to continue from the country of origin to the country of exile (Olness, 1998).

Studies also show that immigrants and refugees are more susceptible to a broad range of symptoms associated with culture-bound folk illnesses (Molina, Zambrana, & Aguirre-Molina, 1994; Pang, 1990). For example, Hwa-Byung (HB), literally anger syndrome, is a widely perceived folk illness among elderly immigrant Korean women who endured feelings of victimization within their oppressive patriarchal family structure and experienced suppressed anger for an extensive period of time in life. Many of those experiencing HB report a variety of somatic, as well as psychological, symptoms, such as headache, sensations of heat, oppressed sensations in the chest, presence of epigastric mass, diminished concentration, and anxiety (Lin et al., 1992; Park, Kim, Schwartz-Barcott, & Kim, 2002).

In fact, physical complaints or somatizations of psychological or emotional problems are relatively common among many immigrant and refugee elderly groups. According to Hong, Lee, and Lorenzo (1995), typical somatic symptoms commonly reported by immigrant Chinese clients, especially elderly Chinese, include difficulty falling asleep, loss of appetite, headaches, feeling weak, shortness of breath, and pain all over their bodies. Pang (2000) also found a significant relationship between somatization and symptom expression among elderly Korean immigrants: Those who met the criteria for depression on the Brief Symptom Inventory (BSI) had the highest mean score on the BSI somatization dimension.

As a result of their tendency to experience the body and mind as a unitary system and to communicate psychosocial distress arising from old age, immigration, cultural adjustment difficulties, and other stressful life events through somatic symptoms and complaints, these elderly are more likely to seek medical care for physical symptomatology than to seek mental health services (Brodsky, 1988; Trevino & Rendon, 1994). Among the Afghan immigrant elders, for example, the most frequently reported "health" complaint was mental health problems, particularly depression and physical symptoms related to stress from refugee trauma and loss, occupational and economic problems, cultural conflict, and social isolation (Lipson, Omidian, & Paul, 1995; Morioka-Douglas et al., 2004). Similarly, in the Russian culture, mental health and psychosocial problems are defined in somatic terms (Kropf et al., 1999), and it is a cultural norm among elderly immigrants from the former Soviet Union to use medical rather than psychiatric or social services for loneliness and depression (Aroian, Khatutsky, Tran, & Balsam, 2001).

In many of the cultures from which immigrant and refugee elders come, mental illness is a stigmatized condition, and cultural explanations of mental health problems often do not coincide with Western interpretations (Die & Seelbach, 1988; Gelfand, 2003). The non-Western traditional causes of mental or even physical illness may be strongly rooted in traditional spiritual and religious beliefs, such as punishment for sins committed in one's previous life among some Buddhist elders from Asian countries or failure to adhere to the principles of Islam and the will of God and possession by evil spirits among Muslim elders. Many elders from Asian cultures tend to view mental health problems as one's emotional weakness and failure to control one's own emotions and thereby internalize the problems.

It is generally found that acculturation—often measured by the length of residency in the United States and ability to speak English—economic well-being, and social support can reduce the negative impact of premigration traumatic experiences and postmigration adjustment difficulties on the psychological well-being among immigrant and refugee elders. For example, in a recent study of 261 adult Vietnamese Americans, premigration traumatic experiences had a stronger effect on depression among those with lower levels of acculturation than among those who were highly acculturated (Ngo et al., 2001). Research generally shows that family and social support or coping resources as potential mediators for stressful life events can help prevent the development of psychological pathologies, such as depression, anxiety, and posttraumatic stress disorder (PTSD), not only among the U.S.-born elderly population but also among the immigrant and refugee elderly (Husaini et al., 1990; Mui, 1996, 2001; Ngo et al., 2001).

HEALTH AND SOCIAL SERVICE UTILIZATION

Research shows that immigrant and refugee elders, especially among those recently arrived from non-English-speaking and less developed countries, tend to underutilize community-based health and social services, whereas a higher proportion of them receive government income support and have access to health care services through Medicare and/or Medicaid. For example, a study of foreign-born Hispanic elderly (707 Cubans, 369 Mexicans, and 295 Hispanics from other countries) found that Hispanic immigrants had a generally low use of both community-based health and social services (Tran, Dhooper, & McInnis-Dittrich, 1997). Age, activity of daily living (ADL) limitations, and living alone were common factors associated with use of health services in these groups, whereas living alone and being in poverty were common factors for social service use. The study also revealed that psychological factor variables had no significant relationship with the utilization of either health or social services among these Hispanic immigrant groups.

Choi (2001) also found that far fewer Asian Americans and Hispanics took advantage of elderly nutrition programs, especially home-delivered meal programs, than did African Americans and attributed the lower participation rates to different food habits and preferences, as well as the lack of English-language proficiency among many recent immigrant elders. Lai (2001) reported that although most of the elderly Chinese immigrants visited senior centers, they substantially underutilized support services; predictors of supportive services use were living arrangements (living alone), satisfaction with services, and fewer mental health symptoms. Korean immigrant elderly were found to have very low levels of awareness and utilization of most of the 15 community-based long-term-care health and social services used in the study (Moon et al., 1998). It was evident, however, that they did use the services that were known to them.

Many immigrant and refugee elderly seek both Western medical services and indigenous health care services, predominantly herbal and acupuncture treatment, in their ethnic communities. Chung and Lin (1994), in their study of almost 3,000 Southeast Asian refugee adults (ages 18–68) in California, found that traditional health care methods still continued to be important, whereas all five groups showed a significant increase in the usage of Western medicine after they migrated to the United States: The percentages of each group seeking Western medicine in the United States were 88% for Cambodians, 86% for Laotians, 76% for Vietnamese, 69% for Chinese Vietnamese, and 56% for Hmong. The study also reported that younger and more educated respondents and those with a high level of English proficiency were more likely to utilize Western medicine. In fact, studies have generally found that culture and levels of acculturation are related to health and mental health service utilization among immigrants and refugees, specifically suggesting a direct effect of acculturation on increased levels of service utilization (Calderon-Rosado, Morrill, Chang, & Tennstedt, 2002; Chesney, Chavira, Hall, & Gary, 1982).

Many immigrants and refugees, especially those from non-Western and less developed countries, do not seek help for their mental health problems. Recent immigrant Asians and Hispanics, regardless of age differences, are particularly more reluctant to utilize mental health services than Anglo Americans are (Trevino & Rendon, 1994; Wells, Golding, Hough, Burnam, & Karno, 1989). An analysis of national survey data indicates that the proportion of Asian Americans and Pacific Islanders utilizing mental health services at all types of public and private facilities was a third of the proportion for European Americans (Matsuoka, Breaus, & Ryujin, 1997). They may not seek help with mental health problems for several reasons in addition to the barriers to access mentioned earlier. Some of the major reasons include unfamiliarity with formal mental health services or the concept of professional psychosocial counseling, as these things often did not exist in their home countries; skepticism about the treatability of mental illness; institutional barriers such as lack of understanding regarding the nature of their problems among biomedically trained psychiatrists or other mental health professionals, especially when the service providers are not from the same culture or class (Trevino & Rendon, 1994); and fear of shame and stigma attached to mental illness.

Furthermore, in many of the cultures from which immigrants and refugee elderly come, religious and spiritual beliefs seem to influence their views of illness, methods of coping, and utilization of formal services (Die & Seelbach, 1988; Gelfand, 2003; Paulino, 1998). Those from Asian cultures prefer not to talk to anyone, including family members, about their emotional or mental health problems. Among them, it is still more common practice to seek advice and help from religious and spiritual leaders for their family problems and emotional support. This situation suggests that effective strategies to increase service use among immigrant and refugee elderly groups whose religion and spirituality have strong influences on them should include working with their religious and spiritual leaders as brokers to link the elderly to potentially beneficial services.

Service utilization among immigrant and refugee elders, regardless of the type of services and agency offering them, requires that services are available, accessible, and acceptable to them (Cox & Ephross, 1998). Although this general principle is also applicable to the U.S.-born elderly population, immigrant and refugee elderly groups face numerous challenges and barriers to service use, including lack of information about available services; language, transportation and financial barriers; negative attitudes toward formal services; culturally and religiously unacceptable perceptions of services; and culture-specific definitions of illness and healing that contrast with Western concepts and biomedical perspectives (Fetzpatrick & Freed, 2000; Marshall, Koenig, Grifhorst, & Ewijk, 1998; Moon et al., 1998; Tsai & Lopez, 1997; Weech-Maldonado et al., 2003).

The most fundamental barrier is the lack of knowledge about available services. Available but unknown services are meaningless and practically nonexistent to the intended population. In this regard, some research findings raise a serious concern. In a study on caregiver and elder experiences of Cambodian, Vietnamese, Soviet Jewish, and Ukrainian refugees, most elders and their caregivers across all groups reported that services for the elderly did not exist or were unknown to them (Strumpf et al., 2001). Across all groups, caregivers identified home health care, transportation, and social opportunities as the most urgent needs for their elders. Tsai and Lopez (1997) found the lack of knowledge of services, English skills, and transportation to be important barriers to Chinese immigrant elders' utilization of formal services. These and other similar findings on the lack of knowledge and understanding of health and social services reported by other immigrant and refugee groups suggest an urgent need for effective dissemination of information about available services to them (Fetzpatrick & Freed, 2000; Moon et al., 1998; Strumpf et al., 2001).

Even when immigrant and refugee elders are eligible for health care services through Medicare and/or Medicaid and are provided with access to other services, those with limited English skills still face barriers. Some services may not be culturally responsive or acceptable. For example, some ethnic immigrant elders who have strong preferences for their ethnic foods may not use day activity centers and residential facilities that serve typical American-style meals. Although ethnic-specific service facilities may more easily accommodate those who prefer ethnic food, multiethnic agencies or those in areas where ethnic food is not readily available face a challenge.

Similarly, health and social service providers' lack of knowledge about cultural norms of interpersonal behavior and patterns of relationship formation that are different from the American norms can result in dissatisfaction with the services and consequent underutilization of services by the immigrant and refugee elderly (Cox & Ephross, 1988). Cultural differences can create misunderstanding and tension between service providers and their elderly clients. For example, a handshake as a polite greeting gesture may be considered rude by most Asian cultures, especially if the service provider is much younger than the elderly individual and the two are meeting for the first time. Also, it is often a culturally desirable pattern to start a meeting with remarks about topics unrelated to the purpose of the meeting, such as weather, upcoming holidays, and even asking about personal and family well-being rather than "getting down to business" as quickly as possible. The latter can be viewed by some elderly clients as being uncaring and cold, creating a barrier to establishing rapport and trust with the client. In many cultures, respect, authority, and wisdom are closely tied to one's age: calling an elderly client by his or her first name is disrespectful, and an elder receiving services from a young professional may doubt the professional's expertise. Elderly men from the Muslim culture are particularly reluctant to be treated by female health and social service providers. Also, asking questions related to sexual behavior is a taboo in most cultures. Therefore, practitioners must be aware and sensitive to potentially different cultural norms and beliefs of their clients, although they must be cautioned not to overgeneralize or stereotype, as clients may be at different levels of acculturation or may be bicultural in both American and their own ethnic culture.

IMPLICATIONS FOR SOCIAL WORK PRACTICE

Consideration of the characteristics, major issues, and service needs of immigrant and refugee elders and their families suggests the following social work practice implications within an evidence-based generalist perspective:

1. Understand that there are intergroup and intragroup differences among immigrant and refugee elderly in their religious and spiritual beliefs and practice, in their attitudes toward health and social services, in the appropriateness of involving family caregivers in service planning, in cultural norms for effective interpersonal behavior and relationship formation processes, and in other cultural preferences, such as food and type of program activities, as they influence help-seeking decisions in general and utilization of formal services in particular.

2. Become familiar with and sensitive to the cultural norms of living arrangements and family caregiving practices while acknowledging the potential variability in the actual roles the elderly client's family is willing and able to perform in meeting the needs of the client.

3. Carefully consider whether and how involving family members in discussions regarding service needs and planning would help or hinder service delivery; family endorsement is essential for some elders, yet for others it is inappropriate to involve adult children and caregivers in an open discussion.

4. Become knowledgeable about legal and other eligibility requirements of financial, medical, and other benefit programs that are applicable to different immigrants and refugees. Even when the elderly client and the family seem to be aware of their entitlements, social workers should identify and address their reluctance to use services or their confusion with procedures, which can limit the client's utilization of the supposedly helpful benefits/services.

5. Address the need for concrete services, such as transportation, and for resources for learning English, for performing basic tasks of daily living, and for accessing the community health and social service systems. Provide opportunities for socialization, job skill development, and employment. All of these services and opportunities can contribute to lower dependence on the family and less isolation and loneliness while increasing self-esteem and life satisfaction of the elderly client.

6. Develop intergenerational programs to address cultural conflict between the elderly and their caregivers, to increase mutual understanding across generations, to reduce generation gaps and isolation, and to thereby restore respect and commitment to care for the elderly.

7. Considering the importance of interdependence rather than self-reliance among immediate and extended family members in ethnic minority cultures, mental health service programs targeting the immigrant/refugee elderly should employ treatment strategies designed to facilitate support from family members (Blair, 2000).

8. For optimal treatment effects, identify and respect the indigenous beliefs about the cause and healing practices of physical and mental health problems as an essential part of a holistic treatment plan while addressing the gap between traditional and Western methods of treatment. Mental health practitioners should consider and validate indigenous approaches, including comfort by spiritual leaders and the use of folk medicines, in addition to mainstream treatment methods such as cognitive-behavioral therapy and family intervention.

9. For an effective approach to relationship formation with an elderly client, practitioners must be aware that many immigrant and refugee elders, especially Asians and Latinos, respond better to a congenial, personal manner rather than to an impersonal, businesslike one (Lum, 2000; Molina et al., 1994). Because most immigrant and refugee elders are not familiar or comfortable with the existing service system, it is especially important for the practitioner to show a personal interest and empathy with the client's problems and to be warm, friendly, and reassuring.

10. Practitioners serving relatively recently arrived refugee groups must consider their premigration trauma as the immediate focus of assessment and treatment. The worker should be aware that those refugee clients who experienced the loss of immediate family might have a higher risk for developing both PTSD and major depression than those who were able to live with immediate family in refugee camps.

11. Practitioners must assess whether somatic complaints are indicators of some type of mental health problem or a real physical ailment in order to address the client's problems and service needs accurately and effectively. It is important to consider the cultural perspective that physical complaints, rather than psychological symptom manifestations, are regarded as more acceptable and are given more positive attention. A systematic collaboration among primary care physicians, mental health professionals, culturally accessible indigenous ethnic practitioners, and

spiritual/religious organizations can further promote wellness among immigrant/refugee elders.

12. Ensure that services are available, accessible, and acceptable to the intended immigrant and refugee elderly population. Consider three major types of potential barriers to service utilization: (1) institutional or structural barriers, such as unavailability of services, eligibility restrictions related to noncitizen and illegal immigrant status, cost of service, and racism; (2) instrumental or functional barriers, such as the lack of transportation and service information, and (3) cultural and linguistic barriers, such as health beliefs, lack of English skills, and insensitivity to cultural norms of interactive behavior.

13. Actively reach out to the intended ethnic immigrant elderly population and provide information about available services in culturally and linguistically sensitive ways. It is especially important to have outreach workers who speak their language and who are, preferably, from the same ethnic background. Obtain the support and participation of community and religious leaders in the outreach effort. Use ethnic media and organizations, which are often the most effective means of information dissemination in many ethnic communities. Finally, translate the informational materials into the ethnic language and design the materials using a culturally attractive and familiar format.

CONCLUSION

Social work practice with immigrant/refugee elderly populations requires cultural competence and the ability to understand the target population's special issues and needs in service delivery, as well as an understanding of their cultural and immigration/refugee background. Special service delivery arrangements to overcome the language and cultural barriers, acknowledgement of the traditional methods of coping and healing, and demonstration of culturally appropriate interpersonal skills, in both verbal communication and behavioral aspects of interaction, can significantly increase effectiveness in meeting the service needs and thereby improving the well-being of the immigrant elderly. For example, the practitioner's effort to show respect for the client's culture and special needs, such as expressing an interest in and appreciation of the client's cultural background during the initial stage of relation formation, and speaking clearly and slowly and sometimes repeatedly, with patience, to clients with limited English can make a difference in gaining the client's acceptance and trust of the practitioner.

In this regard, although matching a practitioner and an immigrant elderly client by ethnicity often has the advantages of meeting the language need and gaining early acceptance of the client, the practitioner's ethnicity alone is no guarantee of the desirable cultural competence or responsiveness. Considering the growing heterogeneity not only among different immigrant/refugee elderly populations but also within the same ethnic group, practitioners must be cautioned against overgeneralizing and stereotyping groups and individuals solely based on their immigrant/refugee and ethnic background. A study of social workers' interactions with Iu-Mien refugees from Laos found that those who did not exhibit cultural competency made assumptions about the clients with regard to stereotypes, lack of appropriate care for elders, and lack of English-language acquisition (Schuldberg, 2001).

Multiplicity and complexity of ethnicity and culture demand a multidimensional approach to social work practice with the immigrant and refugee populations, whose culture and immigration-related factors are only some of the numerous factors to be considered in practice. Nevertheless, cultural competency enables practitioners to better understand "where the client is" and how best to meet the client's needs. In this regard, Cox and Ephross (1998) state:

> Finally, it is imperative to recognize that all cultural patterns are based on a universal human need: to solve problems of human existence and find meaning in the face of physical, social, and technological ecologies. The framework for social work involvement must respect and legitimize the diverse ways in which ethnicity can influence the efforts to solve these problems. By working through a clear ethnic lens that recognizes the factors that can impede growth and functioning, while also recognizing cultural strengths and preferences, social services can enable ethnic persons and groups to obtain the benefits ascribed to others in society. (p. 118)

REFERENCES

Abueg, R. R., & Chun, K. M. (1996). Traumatization stress among Asians and Asian Americans. In A. J. Marsella, M. J. Friedman, E. T. Gerrity, & R. M. Scurfield (Eds.), *Ethnocultural aspects of posttraumatic stress disorder: Issues, research, and clinical applications* (pp. 285–299). Washington, DC: American Psychological Association.

Aroian, K. J., Khatutsky, G., Tran, T. V., & Balsam, A. L. (2001). Health and social service utilization among elderly immigrants from the former Soviet Union. *Journal of Nursing Scholarship, 33*(3), 265–271.

Bagley, C. R. (1993). Mental health and social adjustment of elderly Chinese immigrants in Canada. *Canada's Mental Health, 41*(3), 6–10.

Balgopal, P. (1999). Getting old in the U.S.: Dilemmas of Indo-Americans. *Journal of Sociology and Social Welfare, 24*(1), 51–68.

Barron, S. L. (2000). *Suicide in context: Elderly Chinese female suicide in San Francisco from 1987 through 1996* (Doctoral dissertation, Pacific Graduate School of Psychology, 2000). *Dissertation Abstract International, 61*(03B), 1624.

Black, S. A., Markides, K. S., & Miller, T. Q. (1998). Correlates of depressive symptomatology among older community-dwelling Mexican Americans: The Hispanic EPESE. *Journals of Gerontology: Series B. Psychological Sciences and Social Sciences, 53*(4), S198–S208.

Blair, R. (2000). Risk factors associated with PTSD and major depression among Cambodian refugees in Utah. *Health and Social Work, 25*(1), 23–30.

Blazer, D. G., & Koening, H. G. (1996). Mood disorders. In E. W. Busses & D. G. Blazer (Eds.), *Textbook of geriatric psychiatry* (pp. 235–263). Washington, DC: American Psychiatric Press.

Brener, E. (1991). *Losses, acculturation and depression in Mexican immigrants* (Doctoral dissertation, California School of Professional Psychology, San Diego, 1991). *Dissertation Abstracts International, 51*(12-B), 6148.

Brodsky, B. (1988). Mental health attitudes and practices of Soviet Jewish immigrants. *Health and Social Work, 13*, 130–136.

Calderon-Rosado, V., Morrill, A., Chang, B., & Tennstedt, S. (2002). Service utilization among disabled Puerto Rican elders and their caregivers: Does acculturation play a role? *Journal of Aging and Health, 14*(1), 3–24.

Carney, S. S., Rich, C. L., Burke, P. A., & Fowler, R. C. (1994). Suicide over 60: The San Diego study. *Journal of the American Geriatrics Society, 42*, 174–180.

Casado, B., & Leung, P. (2001). Migratory grief and depression among elderly Chinese American immigrants. *Journal of Gerontological Social Work, 36*(1/2), 5–26.

Chang, J., & Moon, A. (1997). Korean American elderly's knowledge and perceptions of elder abuse: A qualitative analysis of cultural factors. *Journal of Multicultural Social Work.* 11(1/2), 139–154.

Chenoweth, J., & Burdick, L. (2001). The path to integration: Meeting the special needs of refugee elders in resettlement. *Canada's Periodical on Refugees, 20*(1), 20–29.

Chesney, A. P., Chavira, J. A., Hall, R. P., & Gary, H. E. (1982). Barriers to medical care of Mexican-Americans: The role of social class, acculturation, and social isolation. *Medical Care, 20*(9), 883–891.

Cheung, M. (1989). Elderly Chinese living in the United States: Assimilation or adjustment. *Social Work, 34*(5), 457–461.

Chicago Department on Aging and Disability. (1988). *Ethnic elderly needs assessment.* Chicago: Author.

Choi, N. (2001). Frail older persons in nutrition supplement programs: A comparative study of African American, Asian American, and Hispanic participants. *Journal of Gerontological Social Work, 36*(1/2), 187–207.

Chung, R. C., & Lin, K. (1994). Help-seeking behavior among Southeast Asian refugees. *Journal of Community Psychology, 22,* 109–120.

Cox, C., & Ephross, P. (1998). *Ethnicity and social work practice.* New York: Oxford University Press.

Die, A. H., & Seelbach, W. C. (1988). Problems, sources of assistance, and knowledge of services among elderly Vietnamese immigrants. *Gerontologist, 28*(4), 448–452.

Fetzpatrick, T., & Freed, A. (2000). Older Russian immigrants to the USA: Their utilization of health services. *International Social Work, 43*(3), 305–323.

Gelfand, D., & Yee, B. W. (1991). Influence of immigration, migration, and acculturation on the fabric of aging in America. *Generations, 15*(4), 7–10.

Gelfand, D. E. (2003). *Aging and ethnicity: Knowledge and services* (2nd ed.). New York: Springer.

Ghaffarian, S. (1998). The acculturation of Iranian immigrants in the United States and the implications for mental health. *Journal of Social Psychology, 138*(5), 645–654.

Gupta, R., & Pillai, V. K. (2002). Elder care giving in South Asian families: Implications for social services. *Journal of Comparative Family Studies, 33*(4), 565–576.

Hendrie, H. C., Callahan, C. M., Levitt, E. E., Hui, S. L., Musick, B., Austrom, M. G., et al. (1995). Prevalence rates of major depressive disorders: The effects of varying the diagnostic criteria in an older primary care population. *American Journal of Geriatric Psychiatry, 3,* 119–131.

Hong, G. K., Lee, B. S., & Lorenzo, M. K. (1995). Somatization in Chinese American clients: Implications for psychotherapeutic services. *Journal of Contemporary Psychotherapy, 25*(2), 105–118.

Husaini, B. A., Castor, R. S., Linn, G., Moore, S. T., Warren, H. A., & Whitten-Stovall, R. (1990). Social support and depression among the black and white elderly. *Journal of Community Psychology, 18,* 12–18.

Jones, P. S., Zhang, X. E., Jaceldo-Siegl, K., & Meleis, A. I. (2002). Caregiving between two cultures: An integrative experience. *Journal of Transcultural Nursing, 13*(3), 202–209.

Kritz, M. M., Gurak, D. T., & Chen, L. (2000). Elderly immigrants: Their composition and living arrangements. *Journal of Sociology and Social Welfare, 27*(1), 85–114.

Kropf, N. P., Nackerud, L., & Gorokhovski, I. (1999). Social work practice with older Soviet immigrants. *Journal of Multicultural Social Work, 7*(2), 111–126.

Lai, D. (2001). Use of senior services of the elderly Chinese immigrants. *Journal of Gerontological Social Work, 35*(2), 59–79.

Lakatos, P. (1992). *The effects of migratory grief on the adjustment of the adult Hispanic immigrant* (Doctoral dissertation, California School of Professional Psychology, Los Angeles, 1992). *Dissertation Abstracts International, 53*(8-B), 4376.

Lee, M., Crittenden, K., & Yu, E. (1996). Social support and depression among elderly Korean immigrants in the United States. *International Journal of Aging and Development, 42*(4), 313–327.

Lin, K. M., Lau, J. K. C., Yamamoto, J., Zheng, Y., Kim, H., Cho, K., et al. (1992). Hwa-Byung: A community study of Korean Americans. *Journal of Nervous and Mental Disorder, 180*(6), 386–391.

Lipson, J., Omidian, P., & Paul, S. (1995). Afghan health education project: A community survey. *Public Health Nursing, 12,* 143–150.

Lum, D. (2000). *Social work practice and people of color* (4th ed.). Belmont, CA: Brooks/Cole.

Marshall, P. A., Koenig, B. A., Grifhorst, P., & Ewijk, M. V. (1998). Ethical issues in immigrant health care and clinical research. In S. Loue (Ed.), *Handbook of immigrant health* (pp. 203–226). New York: Plenum Press.

Matsuoka, J. K., Breaus, C., & Ryujin, D. H. (1997). National utilization of mental health services by Asian Americans/Pacific Islanders. *Journal of Community Psychology, 25*(2), 141–145.

Min, J., Moon, A., & Lubben, J. (2005). Determinants of psychological distress over time among older Korean Americans and non-Hispanic White elders: Evidence from a two-wave panel study. *Journal of Mental Health and Aging, 9*(3), 210–222.

Molina, C., Zambrana, R. E., & Aguirre-Molina, M. (1994). The influence of culture, class, and environment on health care. In C. W. Molina & M. Aguirre-Molina (Eds.), *Latino health in the U.S.: A growing challenge* (pp. 23–43). Washington, DC: American Public Health Association.

Moon, A. (1996). Predictors of morale among Korean immigrant elderly in the USA. *Journal of Cross-Cultural Gerontology, 11*(4), 351–367.

Moon, A. (2000). Perceptions of elder abuse among various cultural groups: Similarities and differences. *Generations, 24*(2), 75–80.

Moon, A., Lubben, J. E., & Villa, V. (1998). Awareness and utilization of community long-term care services by elderly Korean and non-Hispanic White Americans. *Gerontologist, 38*(3), 309–316.

Morioka-Douglas, N., Sacks, T., & Yeo, G. (2004). Issues in caring for Afghan American elders: Insights from literature and a focus group. *Journal of Cross-Cultural Gerontology, 19*, 27–40.

Mui, A. C. (1996). Depression among elderly Chinese immigrants: An exploratory study. *Social Work, 41*(6), 633–645.

Mui, A. C. (2001). Stress, coping, and depression among elderly Korean immigrants. *Journal of Human Behavior in the Social Environment, 3*(3/4), 281–299.

Ngo, D., Tran, T. V., Gibbons, J. L., & Oliver, J. M. (2001). Acculturation, premigration traumatic experiences, and depression among Vietnamese Americans. *Journal of Human Behavior in the Social Environment, 3*(3/4), 225–242.

Niedzwiecki, M., & Duong, T. C. (2004). *Southeast Asian American Statistical Profile.* Washington, DC: Southeast Asia Resource Action Center.

Olness, K. (1998). Refugee health. In S. Loue (Ed.), *Handbook of immigrant health* (pp. 227–241). New York: Plenum Press.

Pang, K. Y. C. (1990). Hwa-Byung: The construction of a Korean popular illness among Korean elderly immigrant women in the United States. *Culture, Medicine and Psychiatry, 14*, 495–512.

Pang, K. Y. C. (2000). Symptom expression and somatization among elderly Korean immigrants. *Journal of Clinical Geropsychology, 6*(3), 199–212.

Park, Y., Kim, H. S., Schwartz-Barcott, D., & Kim, J. (2002). The conceptual structure of Hwa-Byung in middle-aged Korean women. *Health Care for Women International, 23*(4), 389–398.

Paulino, A. (1998). Dominican immigrant elders: Social service needs, utilization patterns and challenges. *Journal of Gerontological Social Work, 30*(1/2), 61–74.

Prudent, S. (1988). *The grief associated with immigration: An examination of Haitian immigrants' psychological adjustment to the United States* (Doctoral dissertation, Pennsylvania State University, 1988). *Dissertation Abstracts International, 49*(10-B), 4555–4556.

Sanchez, Y. (1999). Elder mistreatment in Mexican American communities: The Nevada and Michigan experiences. In T. Tatara (Ed.), *Understanding elder abuse in minority populations* (pp. 67–78). Philadelphia: Brunner/Mazel.

Schuldberg, J. (2002). *Cultural competency of non-Iu-Mien social workers: Iu-Mien social workers' perspectives* (Doctoral dissertation, University of San Francisco, 2002). *Dissertation Abstracts International, 62*(10-A), 3575-A.

Strumpf, N. E., Glicksman, A., Goldberg-Glen, R. S., Fox, R. C., & Logue, E. H. (2001). Caregiver and elder experiences of Cambodian, Vietnamese, Soviet Jewish, and Ukrainian refugees. *International Journal of Aging and Human Development, 53*(3), 233–252.

Tatara, T. (1999). *Understanding elder abuse in minority populations.* Philadelphia: Brunner/Mazel.

Tran, T. V., Dhooper, S. S., & McInnis-Dittrich, K. (1997). Utilization of community-based social and health services among foreign born Hispanic American elderly. *Journal of Gerontological Social Work, 28*(4), 23–43.

Treas, J., & Mazumdar, S. (2002). Older people in America's immigrant families: Dilemmas of dependence, integration, and isolation. *Journal of Aging Studies, 16*(3), 243–258.

Trevino, F. M., & Rendon, M. I. (1994). Mental illness/mental health issues. In C. W. Molina & M. Aguirre-Molina (Eds.), *Latino health in the U.S.: A growing challenge* (pp. 447–475). Washington, DC: American Public Health Association.

Tsai, D., & Lopez, R. (1997). The use of social supports by elderly Chinese immigrants. *Journal of Gerontological Social Work, 29*(1), 77–94.

U.S. Census Bureau. (2001). *Profile of the foreign-born population in the United States.* Retrieved April 14, 2004, from *www.census.gov/prod/2002pubs/p23-206.pdf*

U.S. Department of Homeland Security. (2003). *Yearbook of immigration statistics, 2002.* Washington, DC: U.S. Government Printing Office.

U.S. Surgeon General. (1999). Mental health and aging. In *Mental health: A report of the Surgeon General.* Rockville, MD: U.S. Department of Health and Human Services, National Institutes of Health, National Institute of Mental Health.

Weech-Maldonado, R., Morales, L. S., Elliot, M., Spritzer, K., Marshall, G., & Hay, R. D. (2003). Race/ethnicity, language, and patients' assessment of care in Medicaid managed care. *Heath Services Research, 38*(3), 789–808.

Wells, K. B., Golding, J. M., Hough, R. L., Burnam, M. A., & Karno, M. (1989). Acculturation and the probability of use of health services by Mexican Americans. *Health Services Research, 24*(1), 237–257.

Wilmoth, J. M., De Jong, G. F., & Himes, C. L. (1997). Immigrant and non-immigrant living arrangements among America's White, Hispanic, and Asian elderly population. *International Journal of Sociology and Social Policy, 17*(9), 57–82.

Wong, M. (2001). The Chinese elderly: Values and issues in receiving adequate care. In I. Olson (Ed.), *Age through ethnic lenses: Caring for elderly in a multicultural society* (pp. 17–32). Lanham, MD: Rowman & Littlefield.

Yoo, S., & Sung, K. (1997). Elderly Koreans' tendency to live independently from their adult children: Adaptation to cultural differences in America. *Journal of Cross-Cultural Gerontology, 12*(3), 225–244.

Yu, E. S. (1986). Health of the Chinese elderly in America. *Research on Aging, 8*(1), 84–109.

CURRENT KNOWLEDGE

In the early 1980s, the phenomenon of elder mistreatment was introduced as a form of domestic violence—it was a latecomer to the field that had paid greater attention to child abuse, child sexual assault, woman battering, and rape. Many steps have been taken to deal with the problems: the passage of reporting laws in every state, education of practitioners, formation of multiagency consultation teams, and development of assessment tools and techniques for intervention, including criminal prosecution of some abusers. Conferences and forums devoted exclusively to elder mistreatment are held regularly, and research efforts have been made to understand the circumstances, profiles of victims and abusers, and extent of the problem.

Extent of a Hidden Problem

Estimates of elder mistreatment vary among studies due to differences in use of definitions, time frame, participant age, sampling and data collection methods, and objectives. Prevalence rates have been reported to be 3.2% by Pillemer and Finkelhor (1998), 4% by Podnicks (1992) in Canada, and 5.6% by Comijs, Smit, Pot, Bouter, and Jonker (1998) in Amsterdam. Pillemer and Finkelhor (1988) estimate that for every case known to a regulatory agency, an additional 14 cases are unreported. The National Elder Abuse Incidence Study derived an incidence rate of 1.2% (National Center on Elder Abuse, 1998; Thomas, 2000) and calculated that for every case reported to adult protective service agencies, five additional cases were known to community agencies. The actual rate of elder mistreatment is probably much higher than reported, because secrecy and isolation, common in all forms of intimate abuse, prevent an accurate count. The norms of American society make behavior inside the home a private affair, and even after mistreatment occurs, the rule of family privacy is so strong that it often works to prevent victims from seeking help.

Types of Elder Mistreatment

- *Physical abuse* includes physical force that results in bodily injury, pain, or impairment. It may include acts of assault, battery, and inappropriate use of restraints.

SUSAN TOMITA

Mistreated and Neglected Elders

- *Sexual abuse* includes any form of nonconsensual sexual contact. Sexual abuse should be considered when elders report being sexually victimized or when there are symptoms that are commonly associated with sexual victimization: genital or urinary irritation, injury, or scarring; intense fear in reaction to a particular individual or to procedures that might involve the pelvic area, such as bathing or cleansing after incontinence; and trauma in the pelvic region.
- *Emotional or psychological abuse* is the willful infliction of mental or emotional anguish by threat, humiliation, or other verbal or nonverbal conduct.
- *Financial abuse* includes the misuse of trust to steal money from bank accounts, obtain credit cards to make unauthorized purchases, and embezzle large sums of money through refinancing the elders' home. In addition, exploiters may steal jewelry and cash, forge or alter checks, and add their names to elders' bank accounts or deeds to the house. Notarized documents, powers of attorney, quit claim deeds, refinance documents, and wills are some of the common tools used by financial abuse perpetrators (Sklar, 2000).
- *Identity theft* has recently been recognized as a serious financial crime as well. This involves accessing the elders' identifiers, including Social Security number, credit card, driver's license, and bank account numbers, for financial gain.
- *Undue influence* occurs when some people, often in their capacity as caregivers, use their position to exploit the trust, dependency, or fear of elders. Over time, exploiters may use fraud, duress, threats, and isolation to gain control over the elders' finances and decision making. Over time, dependency develops, and a "siege mentality" is created, with exploiters saying, "It's only you and me against the world" or "No one cares for you as much as I do. . . . I know what is best for you." Eventually, elders become fearful and are an easy target for financial and material exploitation (Nievod, 1992; Singer, 1992; Quinn, 2000).
- *Neglect* is the failure of caregivers to fulfill their responsibilities. It includes withholding the basic necessities of life, such as personal care, nutrition, medical attention or medication, and a safe, well-maintained environment. Neglect may be active or passive: in active neglect, the withholding of basic necessities of life and physical care is willful; in passive neglect, the withholding is usually due to lack of experience or information. In either case, neglect can lead to death just as abuse can.
- *Self-neglect* is the failure to adequately provide oneself with the basic necessities of life, including food, clothing, shelter, medical care, and medication. The lack of such necessities can threaten the elders' health and safety.

In all of these categories, whether an act is considered abusive or neglectful may depend on its intentionality, severity, intensity, frequency, and consequences (Daly & Jogerst, 2001).

REVIEW OF RESEARCH

Theories of Causation

The main hypotheses regarding the causes of elder mistreatment that is inflicted by others are: (1) elder dependency; (2) learned violence; (3) individual problems of the perpetrator; and (4) societal attitudes, including ageism, sexism, destructive attitudes toward the disabled, and greed. Although some of these hypotheses are popular, they are not supported by the research done so far. For cases of self-neglect, one theoretical explanation is that it is a social-psychological process to maintain identity and control.

With regard to the dependent-elder concept, in the late 1970s and early 1980s, during the first phase of research on elder mistreatment, several researchers noted that the majority of elder mistreatment victims were impaired—physically, mentally, or both (Block & Sinnott, 1979; Douglass, Hickey, & Noel, 1980; Steinmetz, 1978; Steuer & Austin, 1980). However, in the mid-1980s and later, second-phase research found that the victims were not more ill nor functionally disabled (Pillemer & Finkelhor, 1989) and that dependency of *abusers* was a stronger explanation for the mistreatment (Hwalek, Sengstock, & Lawrence, 1984; Phillips, 1986; Pillemer, 1985a, 1985b; Wolf & Pillemer, 1984, 1989). Abusers had a history of mental illness, psychiatric hospitalizations, or substance abuse problems or a combination of these three factors. They were dependent on the elder for money and housing. With these newer findings, it is *not* accepted that victim impairment by itself causes elder mistreatment.

Next, the hypothesis of the stressed caregiver has received a great deal of attention from researchers and clinicians, not only because it is the most readily acceptable explanation but also because it fits with interventions that have been pioneered by those working in the field of domestic violence, particularly in child abuse and neglect. With the finding that abuser dependency, not elder dependency, is a significant factor in elder mistreatment cases, the stressed-caregiver concept has lost favor among those researching the problem. Also, the stressed-caregiver concept is not supported by empirical research (Phillips, Torres de Ardon, & Briones, 2000; Pillemer & Finkelhor, 1988, 1989; Reis & Nahmiash, 1997, 1998). Having emphasized this point, in very specific instances, caregiver stress may be a vulnerability, not a causal, factor. Homer and Gilleard (1990) found that physical abuse by caregivers was triggered by physical abuse or threats of violence by the patient, by incontinence, or both. The abusers identified elders' behaviors as the main problem, not physical impairment, financial problems, social isolation, or emotional strain. The abused patients were not more dependent but had more communication problems and were more socially disturbed than those who were not abused. The caregivers who admitted to physical and verbal abuse scored higher on the depression scale than the nonabusive caregivers.

Paveza and colleagues (1992), also recognizing that caring for persons with Alzheimer's disease and related disorders can be stressful enough to lead to violence, studied the frequency of violence and risk factors for violent behavior in the caregiver-patient dyad. Two variables were statistically associated with the violent patient-caregiver dyads: The caregiver was depressed and the patient was residing with relatives other than the spouse. As with Homer and Gilleard's study (1990), elder impairments were not predictive of violence among the dyads. Caregiver depression was related to violence: The caregivers who scored high on the depression scale were at three times greater risk for violence than caregivers who scored below the cutoff score.

Although still important, characteristics of the elder alone are insufficient explanations for the various forms of mistreatment. Characteristics of the abuser and the nature of the abuser-elder interaction, perhaps affected by elder behaviors, are emerging as primary theoretical explanations. Findings from these two studies compel social workers to ask caregivers about depression, lowered self-esteem, and fear of becoming violent, as well as assisting them in ways to alleviate their symptoms. Further studies will determine which factors will prevail as the strongest explanations. It may be that specific explanations apply to certain subgroups of the elderly but not to the general elderly population.

The concept of intergenerational transmission of violence is almost as popular as the concept of the stressed caregiver, but it is not supported by the research on elder mistreatment. At this time, a paucity of empirical data makes it impossible to form conclusions on the use of this concept; it is not known whether grown children harm elders for retaliatory or imitative reasons.

Thus far, one of the strongest explanations for elder mistreatment has been abuser impairment. Research has found that abusers are dependent on their victims financially, emotionally, and for housing (Pillemer, 1985a, 1985b; Podnieks, 1992; Wolf & Pillemer, 1984). Some exhibit psychopathological features, and others have substance abuse problems (Anetzberger, Korbin, & Austin, 1994; Bristowe & Collins, 1989; Wolf, Godkin, & Pillemer, 1986). For example, neighbors may assume that the grandson who has moved in to live with the 85-year-old woman next door is being helpful and performing caregiver tasks, while in reality, the grandson is a drug-addicted, unemployed male who threatens harm and cashes his grandmother's Social Security check. With time and further research, it is possible that among perpetrators of elder mistreatment, impaired abusers will make up a smaller percentage, because in other areas of domestic violence, all demographic categories are represented among the perpetrators: males and females, high- and low-income earners, and college and high-school graduates.

One last explanation for other-inflicted mistreatment is that societal attitudes create an atmosphere that paves the way for elder mistreatment. Ageism includes myths and stereotypes about the old and the aging process. Old age has become synonymous with loss of personal power, disability, and lack of control over one's own life. In addition, female elder mistreatment victims outnumber male victims by a ratio of 2:1, and sexism may play a part in their mistreatment. Some elderly widows, lonely and with no relative available to help them with financial affairs, fall prey to strangers who offer help. Human greed is another attitude implicated in elder mistreatment. Some relatives may rationalize that because elders would have given them the money later, it is justifiable to spend these elders' money now for what is claimed to be an emergency.

Self-neglect, the most prevalent type of mistreatment, is a complex process with varying scenarios. Bozinovski's (2000) theoretical explanation is that elders are "geared toward preserving identity, protecting and remaining in preferred environments, staying in control of their worlds, and presenting themselves as competent social beings" (p. 54). Maintaining continuity, or trying to hold on to one's longtime environments, relationships, and activities, is very important to self-neglecters. Using a set of behaviors that are comfortable and usual to them, they preserve their lifestyles and protect their identities while perceiving their present problems to be the result of situations such as abandonment by divorce or death of significant others and pets (Bozinovski, 2000). Ironically, those self-preservation behaviors often are not socially acceptable and precipitate referrals to protective service agencies and offers of help. Rathbone-McCuan & Bicker-Jones (1992) add that the neglecters' saying "no" to help is a means of exerting control.

By the time they reach old age, self-neglecters have minimal supports and few attachments; past betrayals, abandonment, and other negative experiences create mistrust and alienation in later life. Their families report that these clients have "burned their bridges" due to their personalities and unsociable behaviors. These clients have a "reality discrepancy," or different perceptions of what are appropriate community standards or socially acceptable behaviors. They also have difficulty at "role taking" or grasping others' perspectives that are required for appropriate social interactions. These difficulties are compounded by impairments in hearing and mental faculties (Bozinovski, 2000).

The preceding hypotheses about the causes of other-inflicted elder mistreatment and self-neglect are not mutually exclusive. Elder mistreatment may be the result of a multiplicity of factors. Further research will refine, confirm, or take issue with some of these hypotheses. But for now, they provide a logical framework that can help social workers understand the phenomenon of elder mistreatment.

Victims and Perpetrators

The majority of cases reported to adult protective services involve neglect and self-neglect (Bozinovski, 2000; Teaster, 2003). Most studies have consistently found a higher percentage of female victims than male, amounting to a 2:1 ratio (Dimah & Dimah, 2002; Dunlop, Rothman, Condon, Hebert, & Martinez, 2000; Greenberg, McKibben, & Raymond, 1990; Lachs, Williams, O'Brien, Hurst, & Horwitz, 1997; National Center on Elder Abuse, 1998; Otiniano, Herrera, & Teasdale, 1998; Teaster, Roberto, Duke, & Kim, 2000). Other than finding that victims are mainly female, studies have not established a clear profile of an elder mistreatment victim.

Family members are usually the perpetrators of other-inflicted elder mistreatment. Studies based on reports to adult protective services and other agencies (Brownell, Berman, & Salamone, 1999; Greenberg et al., 1990; Lachs et al., 1997; National Center on Elder Abuse, 1998; Otiniano et al., 1998; Vladescu, Eveleigh, Ploeg, & Patterson, 1999) have found that adult children are the most likely perpetrators, whereas random sample studies report spousal abuse in greater frequency (Pillemer & Finkelhor, 1989; Podnieks, 1992). These reports found that sons are more abusive than daughters, and in reports on elder sexual abuse, sons are most likely to be the abusers of their mothers (Ramsey-Klawsnik, 1991, 2003).

In general, there are many limitations in the studies from which information on victims and abusers has been obtained. Only a few studies have been large random sample studies; almost none used control groups; and some of the studies' conclusions were based on reported cases or a small number of victims.

Ethnic Group Information

Among professionals, it is generally agreed that elder mistreatment is not confined to a few countries or certain ethnic groups. Limited data based on reports to regulatory agencies in the United States indicate that African American and Hispanic elders are overrepresented and that reports are rarely made on Asians (except in Hawaii, where Asians make up a good portion of the population; Tatara, 1999; Teaster, 2003). Griffin (1999) found that African Americans were more susceptible to financial exploitation, and this finding is supported by Dimah and Dimah (2002), who found that among substantiated elder mistreatment cases at one agency in Illinois, older African Americans were more likely to be victims of financial exploitation and physical neglect. The majority of the perpetrators were daughters (75%) and sons (67%). It is not possible to make generalized statements with these data, because some minority elders may be referred preferentially and investigated due to their poverty status (Lachs, Berkman, Fulmer, & Horwitz, 1994), whereas others are not reported because individual wrongdoings are hidden within the community and victims are stereotyped as having caring families who would never abuse their elders (Tomita, 1999).

Research so far on minority elders indicate that some elders are not aware that others consider them to be victims (Moon & Williams, 1993), differ among themselves about the definitions of abusive behavior

(Anetzberger, Korbin, & Tomita, 1996; Hudson & Carlson, 1999; Moon & Benton, 2000), have varying levels of tolerance for abusive behaviors (Moon, Tomita, & Jung-Kamei, 2001), and also are unaware of sources of help (Moon & Evans-Campbell, 1999). Native Americans in one study reported that one incident of mistreatment was sufficient to warrant a label of elder abuse, in contrast to an expert panel's view that mistreatment was defined by repeated and frequent incidents. They also rated more vignettes as abusive than their European American and African American counterparts did (Hudson, Armachain, Beasley, & Carlson, 1998; Hudson & Carlson, 1999). In another study, Moon and Williams (1993) explored African American, European American, and Korean American elderly women's perceptions of elder mistreatment using 13 scenarios that involved a female elder as a victim and a family member as the perpetrator. Overall, a smaller percentage of Korean Americans (50%) than African Americans (73%) or European Americans (67%) perceived the scenarios as mistreatment, leading the authors to conclude that the Korean Americans were less sensitive to or more tolerant of abusive situations. Many in the Korean American group indicated that they would be reluctant to reveal the abuse or neglect to others, out of shame or fear of creating conflict. This corresponds with the greater cultural emphasis on community and family harmony than on individual needs or well-being within some cultures. The following sections provide social workers a guideline for assessment and intervention.

SOCIAL WORK ASSESSMENT AND INTERVENTION

Assessment Guide

The assessment of elder mistreatment begins when there is a suspicion that the elders' relationships are contributing to unnecessary suffering, or when elders hint at or directly report relationship problems. A variety of instruments are available to assess elder mistreatment, with shorter versions being more appropriate for such settings as an emergency room of a hospital (Fulmer, Guadagno, Dyer, & Connolly, 2004; Kahan & Paris, 2003; Quinn & Tomita, 1997).

Interview with the Elder Elders very rarely seek help for other-inflicted elder mistreatment; they often present themselves to an agency for resolution of other problems. If mistreatment is suspected, seize the op-portunity to assess the situation. Take precautions to maximize privacy and confidentiality, for it is not uncommon to discover during an assessment that those accompanying elders are the alleged abusers.

In general, assessments review the risk of abuse and the elders' cognitive ability and ability to function independently. They may require several contacts over a period of time and should be conducted in a nonjudgmental manner. Although having a high index of suspicion is important in ruling out elder mistreatment, elders should not be diagnosed prematurely as being victims. Work assessment questions into a conversation in a relaxed manner. It is more problematic to assess self-neglecters because they rarely initiate the request for help; they would rather be left alone. The main task is to assess their capacity to make decisions for themselves before an intervention plan can be implemented. For elders who willingly disclose mistreatment, some of the questions suggested that follow may be skipped.

Collect pertinent data. Ask what type of transportation elders use to get to the center, what services they obtain in the home, and with whom elders live.

Ask elder about a typical day as a way of assessing activities of daily living. Find out how elders spend a typical day to determine the degree of dependence on others and who are the most frequent and significant contacts (e.g., "Who helps you with the laundry? How often does he take you out?"). Abusers are often among this pool of people mentioned by elders.

Ask the elder about expectations regarding care (e.g., "Does she do everything you want? Does she come on time?").

Have the elder report any recent crises in family life (e.g., "Have you been worrying about anything in particular in your family lately? Is something in your family troubling you?").

Ask about alcohol problems, drug use, illnesses, and behavior problems among household or family members (e.g., "Are you worried about that son? How long has he been out of work? Are you comfortable with him being in your home for three months?").

Ask the elder about abuse, neglect, and exploitation incidents (e.g., "Do you eat together? Is he good to you? Tell me how you've suffered. Have you been yelled at . . . shoved, shaken, hit . . . ? Then what happened? Show me how she did that").

Record the description of the mistreatment. When possible, record the statements in quotes and document in detail the incidents of mistreatment.

Determine the elder's current mental status. The elder's mental status can be assessed quickly with such tools as the Mini–Mental State exam (Folstein, Folstein & McHugh, 1975). This adds credibility to elders' reports of elder mistreatment and can counter attempts by others to dismiss the allegations that the elders are senile or confabulating.

Address the elder's concerns about revealing the mistreatment. Fear of reprisals, loss of control over the elder's own environment, and ambivalent feelings toward abusers also may be expressed. Assure elders that their opinions and involvement in the strategy phase are of great importance and will guide the workers' actions.

In summary, because elder mistreatment is a hidden phenomenon, elders do not readily volunteer information about it. Warming up to the subject by first asking nonthreatening questions is helpful, followed by questions that focus on the elder's relationships, then questions about problems in the family, and finally questions about incidents of mistreatment. The term "abuse" is unfamiliar to many elders, so asking, "Is he good to you?" may elicit a response more easily than asking, "Did he abuse you?" Also paying attention to what is not said or someone who is not mentioned may provide clues about who the perpetrators are.

Interview the suspected perpetrators. Questions are less provocative if suspected perpetrators perceive them to be elder-centered and perceive workers as wanting to make a detailed assessment of the elder's situation rather than focus on the perpetrator's behavior or actions.

When possible, interview the suspected abuser immediately after the elder is interviewed in order to avoid collusion. First, assure elders that confidentiality will be maintained and that the perpetrators will not know what the elders have said. Use some of the following questions and statements:

> "I am doing an assessment of your mother's current functioning and situation, in order to determine what services are appropriate at this time. I would like to spend some time with you and have you tell me your perception of how things are here."
>
> "Tell me what you want me to know about your mother."
>
> "What do you expect her to do for herself?"
>
> "What does she expect you to do for her? Do you do those things? Are you able to do them? Have you had any difficulties? What kind?"

Assess the suspected perpetrator's degree of dependence on the elder's income, pensions, or assets:

> "If you help your mother pay her bills, how do you do it? Is your name on her account?"
>
> "Do you pay rent? Whose name is on the deed?"
>
> "Do you have power of attorney? Does it have a durable clause? When did you get it?"

Interview the family and others. If the elders consent, collateral contacts must be made promptly before the suspected perpetrators attempt to collude with others. Concerned people who possess important information may be reluctant to get involved, and workers may need to appeal to them as "good Samaritans."

Determine Capacity

Once the assessment is complete, determine the elder's willingness for intervention and capacity to make decisions. Protective interventions are based partly on the elder's ability to understand transactions and withstand undue influence. One of the first questions raised during an assessment is, Did the elders understand what they were doing, and were they able to withstand undue influence tactics, for example, when the deed was signed over to the nephew.

Determine Willingness for Intervention

After determining the elder's comprehension of the incident, a second common set of questions raised by workers is, Does the elder have sufficient mental capacity to accept or to refuse help? Does the elder want outside help? The dynamics of elder mistreatment as a form of family violence, in which power and control play a big part, differ from being harmed by strangers. Often victims prefer to maintain some form of a relationship in spite of being victimized and would like workers to help stop the abusive behavior, not end the relationship. In such instances, the focus of the intervention is on correcting the power imbalance and on victim safety and abuser accountability.

Reporting Suspected Mistreatment

All states have mandatory or voluntary reporting laws (St. James, 2001). A point of emphasis is that, although reporting by workers is often mandatory, the receipt of services by victims is voluntary. Adult protective services must assess the situation and offer services, but elders have the option to say, "Yes, I am being mistreated by my son, but I don't want your help—leave me alone." Often referring social workers and the public in general, due to confidentiality protocols, may not realize that the victims have been offered intervention options and that the cases have been closed due to their refusal of services.

This unwillingness to receive help is probably the most confusing and frustrating aspect of intervention. Instead of "giving up" on victims who seem to choose their relationship with perpetrators over others' interventions, workers should discuss with elders the factors influencing their choice of intervention options: fear, hope, love, low self-esteem, financial dependence, emotional dependence, isolation, duty, lack of proper help and support from outsiders, an assumption that the abuse is normal behavior, a tendency to be passive and avoidant in coping (Comijs, Penninx, Knipscheer, & van Tilburg, 1999), and the fact that the abuse is not severe enough to make them want to leave.

COUNSELING STRATEGIES

Other-Inflicted Mistreatment: Correct the Power Imbalance

Situations of other-inflicted elder mistreatment involve an unequal power distribution between elders and their abusers, often due to a lack of checks and balances in the relationship. Mistreatment continues when there are no consequences for the acts; when elders are unaware of their own power resources, blame themselves, and are selfless parents; when the elder-abuser dyad is isolated; and when there is support by a culture or community for the mistreatment behaviors.

In these contexts, victims may believe that the mistreatment is beyond their control and may stop trying to do anything about it. This "learned helplessness" (Seligman, 1975) creates fearfulness in victims, saps their motivation if they perceive that they are unable to influence events, and causes an inability for them to perceive success. Social workers have an important twofold role: to maximize the victim's potential power—replacing the symptoms of learned helplessness with a sense of mastery over the elder's own situation—and to minimize the abuser's use of power resources, which consist of affection, verbal promises, threats, physical strength, and mobility.

Often elders do not realize that their own power sources easily make up for comparatively less physical strength and mobility: housing, the ability to remove themselves from the abusive situation, alliances and friends, agencies, professionals, income, and public knowledge of the mistreatment.

Power Balancing via Victim Advocacy and Abuser Accountability

Provide education and prevention. It is easier to get elders to receive difficult information by turning statements into questions: "Have you ever heard of the term 'abuse'? When your son hits you, that is called domestic violence or elder abuse. . . . When he takes your money, that is financial abuse." Or, "Are you aware that others consider you to be a victim of abuse?"

Identify and correct maladaptive thinking. Workers can represent a different reality and combat self-blame, excessive fantasies, and magical thinking—the idea that the mistreatment will end by itself. For example, say, "Accidentally using his towel does not justify a slap. No matter what you did, it is wrong to be hurt like that. No one deserves to be abused." Remind elders of their *hardiness* and *powerfulness,* their ability to withstand adversity. Recount past events in which they survived and emphasize their ability to do so again.

Provide information and prepare for the next incident. Ask "What will you do when this happens again?" "Taking her name off your bank account is not difficult; we could go to your bank. . . ." "Let's pack a bag and copy your important papers just in case. . . ."

Practice the intervention. Help elders dial the phone and speak into it: "I live at 1234 Elm St. and need help right now."

Work on the expression and management of feeling. Help elders discuss their feelings instead of dismissing them as "hopeless." For example, when workers say, "I believe you when you say you love your son. Even when he hurts you, you don't want him to be arrested," elders may reply eventually, "Well, maybe love isn't worth this misery. . . . I should do something else."

Restructure the elder's environment and expand the social circle to maximize safety. Outside contacts and socialization diminish the chances of mistreatment. In approaching financial exploitation, acknowledge the strong bond between elders and perpetrators, but at the same time intervene to prevent elders from further harm. Say, "I know John is your grandson and you love each other and always will. But he has taken advantage of you with regard to your savings. It isn't your fault. He was clever and he was wrong. We must stop his taking advantage of you. That is why we must find someone else, perhaps your niece, to help you with your finances. This way, you can continue to have a relationship with John, and at the same time, be protected" (Quinn, 2000). A family conference mediated by the agency staff or an attorney may resolve financial issues quickly (Nerenberg, 2000). As with any intense relationship of a long duration, when the relationship is severed, elders often experience a severe sense of loss. It may be necessary to help elders 6 months or more to fill the void with activities and other, trustworthy relationships. If this phase is skipped, victims may very well return to the abusive relationship.

Suggest self-removal or disengagement for relief. The general rule of thumb is to provide services while maintaining elders in the least restrictive environment. Although domestic violence professionals advocate separation of victims from perpetrators, in elder mistreatment cases, most elders consider that to be a plan of last resort. Nevertheless, separation even for a few hours may defuse the situation and help elders have a sense of control. Ask, "Where can you go until you feel better?" With the elders' permission, solicit help from such third parties as neighbors, apartment managers, and supportive relatives to prevent isolation and unwitnessed mistreatment.

Promote abuser accountability. Provide information to abusers: "Are you aware that others consider this behavior to be a form of elder mistreatment?" "Did you know that blaming and accusing your mother daily is a form of emotional abuse?" In addition, be insistent and gather details about the relationship, and put abusers on notice that the relationship will be monitored: "Tell me again what you do for your mother . . . how you spent the $60 she gave you for groceries." "We will visit regularly. . . ." "Yes, I know she has a memory problem, but I'd still like to talk to her."

Educate possible victims and witnesses. Many elders do not realize that being forced to share their pension, food, and housing through power and control tactics (e.g., threatening to kill their pet) is a form of elder mistreatment. Encourage them to discuss such incidents with others and seek help. Also, educate families and elders about undue influence, as most people do not realize that it happens to people who are alert, competent, and capable. Surveys indicate that victims

are known to a good percentage of the general public. Neighbors and housing managers are in a position to overhear harsh words or elders crying or to notice that elders are seldom seen outside. If access is denied when a visit is attempted, or if persons answering the door or phone constantly say that the elders are sleeping or are not to be disturbed, a well-being check by relatives, law enforcement, or adult protective services may be necessary.

Create professional teams. Communities have benefited from the formation of multiprofessional and multiagency teams that meet regularly, discuss cases, and provide comprehensive services (see, for example, Aziz, 2000). A team may consist of representatives from law enforcement, the prosecutor's office, social and protective services agencies, long-term care facilities, hospitals, and emergency phone (e.g., 911) networks. A detective may present a case to find out if the bed sores of the elder resulted from caregiver neglect; or a social worker, presenting a case of a self-neglecting elder whose house has been condemned, may ask others for intervention ideas not yet considered.

Self-Neglecting Elders: Respecting Control While Avoiding Harm

Social workers take on the role of "social influencers" with self-neglecters, who respond in varying ways to this outside social influence. Some elders may feel threatened and controlled, whereas others may welcome the intervention (Bozinovski, 2000). The worker's job is made difficult by the conflict between society's wish to protect vulnerable adults from harm and respect for individual autonomy (Mixon, 1991). Self-neglecters have a right to refuse services, but workers have a duty to protect them. During the assessment, have a thorough understanding of the underlying factors that led to the reported behavior. Next, decide on the intervention, which may range from advocacy to persuasion to finding a surrogate decision maker. If elders are capable and understand the consequences of refusing help, they have a right to refuse services. Involuntary interventions such as conservatorships or guardianships are justified when incapable elders face imminent harm (Mixon, 1991).

The intervention process with self-neglecters consists of the following steps: (1) establish trust and ally with the elder, focusing more on rapport than on the problem (Dubin, Lelong, & Smith, 1988); (2) find out how the elder processes information so that the worker's messages are congruent with the elder's thinking and actions; (3) use exchange strategy—that is, state an expectation, find out the problem it poses, find ways to resolve the questions that the elder raises about the request, offer incentives to gain the elder's cooperation, and find mutually acceptable solutions that allow control by the elder; and (4) provide one concrete piece of assistance, regardless of the current presenting problem, which may evoke some feelings of trust (Mixon, 1991).

SUMMARY

In summary, when social workers fight their own denial and avoidance, they can effectively intervene in cases of elder mistreatment; they can be prepared to take advantage of teachable moments with elders, correct the power imbalance, and consider themselves to be a power component that can enable elders to work on the mistreatment successfully. With self-neglecters, the focus is on assessing their capacities and assisting with making decisions that prevent further self-harm.

The biggest challenge is to identify and help victims in communities who do not realize that they are victims (Wood & Stephens, 2003), while neighbors and friends do not realize that they are witnessing acts of elder mistreatment. Workers may reframe as unacceptable those acts to which everyone has become accustomed and also reach out to ethnic groups, as well as to older lesbians and gay men, and educate them about power and control tactics used on elders. Current counseling practices need to be modified to accommodate cultural differences (Kosberg, Lowenstein, Garcia, & Biggs, 2002; Moore, 2000; Tomita, 2000; Vazquez & Rosa, 1999). For example, in some cultures, individual counseling is not a familiar concept; instead, the entire family or a family representative must be consulted before an intervention can be carried out successfully. In addition, elders who immigrate from other countries are especially vulnerable due to language barriers and cultural norms that discourage seeking help.

There is a dearth of empirical studies that focus on the outcome of social work elder-mistreatment interventions. One suggestion is for clinicians to pair up with academicians to find out what the current best practices are. With regard to male victims, there are greater numbers of males among elder mistreatment victims than are seen in the younger domestic violence victim population. More research needs to be done to help practitioners identify elder male victims

and understand their needs (Mouton, Talamantes, Parker, Espino, & Miles, 2001; Pillemer & Finkelhor, 1989). Using gender-neutral language in materials written for older persons, such as safety planning tools and legal advocacy, may help professionals reach more victims (Brandl & Cook-Daniels, 2002).

On a policy development and implementation level, challenges include varying definitions, methodologically weak research, fragmented program policies and services, lack of standardized protective services laws and procedures, and underfunded and unenforced directives related to interventions (Anetzberger, 2001; Bonnie & Wallace, 2002; Roby & Sullivan, 2000; St. James, 2001).

RESOURCES

National Center on Elder Abuse: *http://www.elderabuse center.org*

National Committee for the Prevention of Elder Abuse: *www.preventelderabuse.org*

National Library of Medicine & the National Institutes of Health: *http://www.nlm.nih.gov/medlineplus/elder abuse.html*

REFERENCES

Anetzberger, G. (2001). Elder abuse identification and referral: The importance of screening tools and referral protocols. *Journal of Elder Abuse and Neglect, 13*(2), 3–22.

Anetzberger, G., Korbin, J., & Austin, C. (1994). Alcoholism and elder abuse. *Journal of Interpersonal Violence, 9*(2), 184–193.

Anetzberger, G., Korbin, J. & Tomita, S. (1996). Defining elder mistreatment in four ethnic groups across two generations. *Journal of Cross-Cultural Gerontology, 11*(2), 187–212.

Aziz, S. (2000). Los Angeles County Fiduciary Abuse Specialist Team: A model for collaboration. *Journal of Elder Abuse and Neglect, 12*(2), 79–83.

Block, M., & Sinnott, J. (1979). *The battered elder syndrome: An exploratory study.* College Park: University of Maryland Center on Aging.

Bonnie, R., & Wallace, R. (2002). *Elder mistreatment: Abuse, neglect and exploitation in an aging America.* Washington, DC: National Academies Press.

Bozinovski, S. (2000). Older self-neglecters: Interpersonal problems and the maintenance of self-continuity. *Journal of Elder Abuse and Neglect, 12*(1), 37–56.

Brandl, B., & Cook-Daniels, L. (2002, August). *Domestic abuse in later life: Victims.* Retrieved in 2000 from *http://www.elderabusecenter.org.*

Bristowe, E., & Collins, J. (1989). Family mediated abuse of noninstitutionalized frail elderly men and women living in British Columbia. *Journal of Elder Abuse and Neglect, 1*(1), 45–64.

Brownell, P., Berman, J., & Salamone, A. (1999). Mental health and criminal justice issues among perpetrators of elder abuse. *Journal of Elder Abuse and Neglect, 11*(4), 81–94.

Comijs, H., Penninx, B., Knipscheer, K., & van Tilburg, W. (1999). Psychological distress in victims of elder mistreatment: The effects of social support and coping. *Journals of Gerontology: Series B. Psychological Sciences and Social Sciences, 54*(4), P240–P245.

Comijs, H., Smit, J., Pot, A., Bouter, L., & Jonker, C. (1998). Risk indicators of elder mistreatment in the community. *Journal of Elder Abuse and Neglect, 9*(4), 67–76.

Daly, J., & Jogerst, G. (2001). Statute definitions of elder abuse. *Journal of Elder Abuse and Neglect, 12*(4), 39–57.

Dimah, A., & Dimah, K. (2002). Gender differences among abused older African Americans and African American abusers in an elder abuse provider agency. *Journal of Black Studies, 32*(5), 557–573.

Dubin, B., Lelong, J., & Smith, B. (1988). *Faces of neglect.* Austin: University of Texas, Hoff Foundation for Mental Health.

Douglass, R., Hickey, T., & Noel, C. (1980). *A study of maltreatment of the elderly and other vulnerable adults.* Ann Arbor: University of Michigan, Institute of Gerontology.

Dunlop, B., Rothman, M., Condon, K., Hebert, K., & Martinez, I. (2000). Elder abuse: Risk factors and use of case data to improve policy and practice. *Journal of Elder Abuse and Neglect, 12*(3/4), 95–122.

Folstein, M., Folstein, S., & McHugh, P. (1975). Mini-mental state. *Journal of Psychiatric Research, 12*(3), 189–198.

Fulmer, T., Guadagno, L., Dyer, C., & Connolly, M. (2004). Progress in elder abuse screening and assessment instruments. *Journal of the American Geriatrics Society, 52*(2), 297–304.

Greenberg, J., McKibben, M., & Raymond, J. (1990). Dependent adult children and elder abuse. *Journal of Elder Abuse and Neglect, 2*(1/2), 73–86.

Griffin, L. (1994). Elder maltreatment among rural African Americans. *Journal of Elder Abuse and Neglect, 6*(1), 1–27.

Griffin, L. (1999). Elder maltreatment in the African American community: You just don't hit your momma!!! In

T. Tatara (Ed.), *Understanding elder abuse in minority populations* (pp. 27–48). Philadelphia: Brunner/Mazel.

Homer, A., & Gilleard, C. (1990). Abuse of elderly people by their carers. *British Medical Journal, 301,* 1359–1362.

Hudson, M., Armachain, W., Beasley, C., & Carlson, J. (1998). Elder abuse: Two Native American views. *Gerontologist, 38*(5), 538–548.

Hudson, M., & Carlson, J. (1999). Elder abuse: Its meaning to Caucasians, African Americans, and Native Americans. In T. Tatara (Ed.), *Understanding elder abuse in minority populations* (pp. 187–204). Philadelphia: Brunner/Mazel.

Hwalek, M., Sengstock, M., & Lawrence, R. (1984, November). *Assessing the probability of abuse of the elderly.* Paper presented at the annual meeting of the Gerontological Society of America.

Kahan, F., & Paris, B. (2003). Why elder abuse continues to elude the health care system. *Mount Sinai Journal of Medicine, 70*(1), 62–68.

Kosberg, J., Lowenstein, A., Garcia, J., & Biggs, S. (2002). Challenges to the cross-cultural and cross-national study of elder abuse. *Journal of Social Work Research and Evaluation, 3*(1), 19–31.

Lachs, M., Berkman, L., Fulmer, T., & Horwitz, R. (1994). A prospective community-based pilot study of risk factors for the investigation of elder mistreatment. *Journal of the American Geriatrics Society, 42,* 169–173.

Lachs, M., Williams, C., O'Brien, S., Hurst, L., & Horwitz, R. (1997). Risk factors for reported elder abuse and neglect: A nine-year observational cohort study. *Gerontologist, 37*(4), 469–474.

Mixon, P. (1991). Self-neglect: A practitioner's perspective. *Journal of Elder Abuse and Neglect, 3*(1), 35–42.

Moon, A., & Benton, D. (2000). Tolerance of elder abuse and attitudes toward third-party intervention among African American, Korean American and White elderly. *Journal of Multicultural Social Work, 8*(3/4), 283–303.

Moon, A., & Evans-Campbell, T. (1999). Awareness of formal and informal sources of help for victims of elder abuse among Korean American and Caucasian elders in Los Angeles. *Journal of Elder Abuse and Neglect, 11*(3), 1–23.

Moon, A., Tomita, S., & Jung-Kamei, S. (2001). Elder mistreatment among four Asian American groups: An exploratory study on tolerance, victim blaming and attitudes toward third party intervention. *Journal of Gerontological Social Work, 36*(1/2), 153–169.

Moon, A., & Williams, O. (1993). Perceptions of elder abuse and help-seeking patterns among African-American, Caucasian American and Korean-American elderly women. *Gerontologist, 22,* 386–395.

Moore, W. (2000). Adult protective services and older lesbians and gay men. *Clinical Gerontologist, 21*(2), 61–64.

Mouton, C., Talamantes, M., Parker, R., Espino, D., & Miles, T. (2001). Abuse and neglect in older men. *Clinical Gerontologist, 24*(3/4), 15–26.

National Center on Elder Abuse. (1988). *NCEA National Elder Abuse Incidence Study.* Retrieved in 1998 from *http://www.elderabusecenter.org.*

Nerenberg, L. (2000). Forgotten victims of financial crime and abuse: Facing the challenge. *Journal of Elder Abuse and Neglect, 12*(2), 49–73.

Nievod, A. (1992). Undue influence in contract and probate law. *Journal of Questioned Documentation Examination, 1*(1), 14–26.

Otiniano, M., Herrera, C., & Teasdale, T. (1998). Hispanic elder abuse. In *Understanding and combating elder abuse in minority communities.* Long Beach, CA: Archstone Foundation.

Paveza, G., Cohen, D., Eisdorfer, C., Freels, S., Semla, T., Ashford, J., et al. (1992). Severe family violence and Alzheimer's disease: Prevalence and risk factors. *Gerontologist, 32*(4), 493–497.

Phillips, L. (1986). Theoretical explanations of elder abuse: Competing hypotheses and unresolved issues. In K. Pillemer & R. Wolf (Eds.), *Elder abuse: Conflict in the family* (pp. 197–217). Dover, MA: Auburn.

Phillips, L., Torres de Ardon, E., & Briones, G. (2000). Abuse of female caregivers by care recipients: Another form of elder abuse. *Journal of Elder Abuse and Neglect, 12*(3/4), 123–144.

Pillemer, K. (1985a). *Domestic violence against the elderly: A case-control study.* Unpublished doctoral dissertation, Brandeis University.

Pillemer, K. (1985b). The dangers of dependency: New findings on domestic violence against the elderly. *Social Problems, 33*(2), 146–157.

Pillemer, K., & Finkelhor, D. (1988). The prevalence of elder abuse: A random sample survey. *Gerontologist, 28*(1), 51–57.

Pillemer, K., & Finkelhor, D. (1989). Causes of elder abuse: Caregiver stress versus problem relatives. *American Journal of Orthopsychiatry, 59*(2), 179–187.

Podnieks, E. (1992). National survey on abuse of the elderly in Canada. *Journal of Elder Abuse and Neglect, 4*(1/2), 5–58.

Quinn, M. J. (2000). Undoing undue influence. *Journal of Elder Abuse and Neglect, 12*(2), 9–17.

Quinn, M. J., & Tomita, S. (1997). *Elder abuse and neglect: Causes, diagnosis, and intervention strategies.* New York: Springer.

Ramsey-Klawsnik, H. (1991). Elder sexual abuse: Preliminary findings. *Journal of Elder Abuse and Neglect, 3*(3), 73–90.

Ramsey-Klawsnik, H. (2003). Elder sexual abuse within the family. *Journal of Elder Abuse and Neglect, 15*(1), 43–58.

Rathbone-McCuan, E., & Bricker-Jenkins, M. (1992). Elder self-neglect: A blurred concept. In E. Rathbone-McCuan & D. Fabian (Eds.), *Self-neglecting elders: A clinical dilemma.* New York: Auburn House.

Reis, M., & Nahmiash, D. (1997). Abuse of seniors: Personality, stress, and other indicators. *Journal of Mental Health and Aging, 3*(3), 337–356.

Reis, M., & Nahmiash, D. (1998). Validation of the Indicators of Abuse (IOA) Screen. *Gerontologist, 38*(4), 471–480.

Roby, J., & Sullivan, R. (2000). Adult protection service laws: A comparison of state statutes from definition to case closure. *Journal of Elder Abuse and Neglect, 12*(3/4), 17–51.

Seligman, M. (1975). *Helplessness.* San Francisco: Freeman.

Singer, M. (1992). Undue influence and written documents: Psychological aspects. *Journal of Questioned Examination, 1*(1), 2–13.

Sklar, J. (2000). Elder and dependent adult fraud: A sampler of actual cases to profile the offenders and the crimes they perpetrate. *Journal of Elder Abuse and Neglect, 12*(2), 19–32.

Steinmetz, S. (1978). Battered parents. *Society, 15*(15), 54–55.

Steuer, J., & Austin, E. (1980). Family abuse of the elderly. *Journal of the American Geriatrics Society, 28,* 372–376.

St. James, P. (2001). Challenges in elder mistreatment programs and policy. *Journal of Gerontological Social Work, 36*(3/4), 127–140.

Tatara, T. (1999). *Understanding elder abuse in minority populations.* Philadelphia: Brunner/Mazel.

Teaster, P. (2003). *A response to the abuse of vulnerable adults: The 2000 survey of state adult protective services.* Retrieved in 2000 from *http://www.elderabusecenter.org.*

Teaster, P., Roberto, K., Duke, J., & Kim, M. (2000). Sexual abuse of older adults: Preliminary findings of cases in Virginia. *Journal of Elder Abuse and Neglect, 12*(3/4), 1–16.

Thomas, C. (2000). The first national study of elder abuse and neglect: Contrast with results from other studies. *Journal of Elder Abuse and Neglect, 12*(1), 1–14.

Tomita, S. (1999). Exploration of elder mistreatment among the Japanese. In T. Tatara (Ed.), *Understanding elder abuse in minority populations* (pp. 119–139). Philadelphia: Brunner/Mazel.

Tomita, S. (2000). Elder mistreatment: Practice modifications to accommodate cultural differences. *Journal of Multicultural Social Work, 8*(3/4), 305–326.

Vazquez, C., & Rosa, D. (1999). An understanding of abuse in the Hispanic older person: Assessment, treatment, and prevention. *Journal of Social Distress and the Homeless, 8*(3), 193–206.

Vladescu, D., Eveleigh, K., Ploeg, J., & Patterson, C. (1999). An evaluation of a client-centered case management program for elder abuse. *Journal of Elder Abuse and Neglect, 11*(4), 5–22.

Wolf, R., Godkin, M., & Pillemer, K. (1986). Maltreatment of the elderly: A comparative analysis. *Pride Institute Journal of Long Term Home Health Care, 5*(4), 10–17.

Wolf, R., & Pillemer, K. (1984). *Working with abused elders: Assessment, advocacy, and intervention.* Worcester: University of Massachusetts Medical Center.

Wolf, R., & Pillemer, K. (1989). *Helping elderly victims: The reality of elderly abuse.* New York: Columbia University.

Wood, S., & Stephens, M. (2003). Vulnerability to elder abuse and neglect in assisted living facilities. *Gerontologist, 43*(5), 753–757.

Older offenders committing violent crimes and being sentenced to lengthy periods of imprisonment has become an astonishing fact. The number of geriatric inmates in many state and federal prisons has been rising steadily since the early 1980s. Their numbers have jumped substantially over the past decade, both in absolute terms and as a proportion of states' entire prison populations. Of the 1.4 million inmates confined in state and federal prisons, 121,432 prisoners, or 8.6%, are over the age of 50 (*Corrections Yearbook,* 2003). With the graying of America, it appears that an increasing number of older adults will find their way into the criminal justice system as perpetrators. This dilemma, along with an increasing number of mentally ill inmates and an already overcrowded prison system, is creating a new challenge for our correctional system and those who must provide social and health services.

This chapter provides a greater understanding of the mental, physical, and social concerns facing aging inmates and those who must provide for their care. Also addressed are end-of-life issues resulting from mandatory sentencing practices that have produced policies to accommodate an increasing number of frail and dying inmates. Finally, a section on social work practice with this special population identifies useful approaches for practitioners as they develop specific case management strategies.

This comments in this chapter specifically focus on state and federal prison issues and avoid any discussion of jails. Whereas jails are utilized to house older offenders who commit minor offenses and as holding units for those who commit major crimes prior to sentencing, state and federal programs are more likely to experience the day-to-day challenges of providing appropriate housing for extended periods of time. As a result, greater attention has been given to the sentencing guidelines, health care delivery, end-of-life issues, and the economic impact that caring for the growing number of aging inmates can have on state and federal budgets.

DEFINING THE OLDER OFFENDER

The lack of consensus on what constitutes an "elderly" offender is one of the most bothersome aspects of comparing research outcomes (Fattah & Sacco, 1989; Forsyth & Gramling, 1988). A review of the literature finds that previous researchers have used a variety of age cutoffs when collecting and analyzing data. For example, Forsyth and Gramling (1988) de-

RONALD H. ADAY

Aging Prisoners

19

fined elder inmates as those 65 years of age or older; other researchers reported findings using age 60 (Aday, 2003; Douglass, 1991; Kratcoski, 1990); in yet other research projects, the ages of 50 and over were used (Aday & Nation, 1999; Falter, 1999; Colsher, Wallace, Loeffelholz, & Sales, 1992; Wahidin, 2004).

Whereas governmental programs typically recognize age 65 as the demarcation into old age, correctional officials usually consider "50 and over" as old (Aday, 1999). Correctional officials commonly agree that the typical inmate in his 50s has the physical appearance and accompanying health problems of someone at least 10 years older. House (1990, p. 398) supports this view of "early aging" when he states that "the lowest socioeconomic stratum manifests a prevalence of chronic conditions at ages 45–55 that is not seen in the highest socioeconomic stratum until after age 75." Morton (1992) also stresses that age 50 is the ideal age to initiate preventive health care and the taking of other appropriate measures to reduce long-term medical costs for older inmates. Of course, although the declining health of many inmates substantiates the phrase "old before their time," other inmates may remain in reasonably good health into their 60s and 70s. Although 50 and over are the ages used in this chapter, caution should be used when using chronological age exclusively to define the onset of old age.

OLDER OFFENDER CRIMES

The 50-and-older prison population is responsible for an assortment of crimes ranging from violent offenses, including homicides and assaults, to other crimes, such as forgery and crimes involving drugs. For example, 55% of Louisiana's 3,321 offenders over the age of 50 are incarcerated for violent crimes, 23% for drug-related crimes, 11% for property crimes, and 11% listed under an "all other crimes" category (Louisiana Department of Corrections, 2004). Older homicide offenders are generally serving time for impromptu first offenses committed against younger relatives who had formerly served as caretakers to the assailants but who had relinquished caregiving responsibilities. The events, often alcohol-related, generally occur after altercations in the homes of the victims or the assailants. The crime may be the first offenses for older men who could no longer cope with age-related health or social losses, or they may be serious outward manifestations of low frustration tolerances that perpetrators had had throughout the life course. Only a few are "mercy killings" against

spouses. Nearly two thirds of older female offenders are serving time for nonviolent, often drug-related, offenses. However, about one third have committed violent crimes such as aggravated assault, murder, or manslaughter of a spouse or male companion. Although nearly three quarters are serving time for first (often violent murder and manslaughter) offenses, the number of older women sentenced for drug offenses, forgery, and theft is increasing.

A significant number of older male inmates are incarcerated for committing sexual offenses such as rape, pedophilia, and exhibitionism (Clark & Mezey, 1997). Crime statistics show that those over age 50 accounted for 10% of all sexual offenses, excluding forcible rape (U.S. Department of Justice, 2001). States report that anywhere between 25 and 35% of offenders over age 50 are incarcerated for sexual offenses (Aday, 2003). Older sex offenders are typically white married males who target minor children who are relatives, and the perpetrators frequently attribute these acts to having poor health or living in close proximity to the victim. Research findings have yet to conclude whether sex offenses are first offenses or offenses that have gone undetected prior to the perpetrator's reaching old age.

HETEROGENEITY OF AGING PRISONERS

The majority of older offenders currently housed in state and federal prisons are non-Hispanic Whites. This population does, however, include a disproportionate number of African Americans (Krebs, 2000). Many of the southern states typically incarcerate a greater proportion of African Americans than states in other regions of the country. For example, of the 3,321 older inmates held in Louisiana prisons, 65% are African American, and the remaining 35% are European American. Similar to other prison population age groups, the older offender is also typically undereducated as a whole. Most older inmates come to prison having few coping skills and having made poor choices in structuring their lives on the outside. Many older prisoners are in poor health, have little support from family or friends, and have frequently abused drugs and alcohol. The following provides a summary of older offender attributes (Aday, 2003):

- The majority of older offenders age 50 and over are non-Hispanic Whites.
- The older-prisoner population includes a disproportionate number of Blacks.

- A substantial number of older inmates have sparse educational backgrounds.
- The average age of incarcerated inmates age 50 and over is 57 years.
- Males make up the overwhelming majority of the older prisoner population, with 95%.
- Only about one third of older offenders are married; the proportion is lower among females.
- A substantial number of older offenders are unskilled laborers or unemployed.
- A significant number of elderly prisoners have histories of poor health.
- About two thirds of older female prisoners have experienced some type of abuse.
- Approximately one half of 50-and-over inmates are serving time for a first offense.

Women represent approximately 5% of the 50-and-older prison population. Most women aging behind bars are unmarried Whites, have limited educational backgrounds, and have no prior employment history (Kratcoski & Babb, 1990). For example, Georgia, like many other states, reports that 77% have fewer than 9 years of formal education, and approximately 98% never completed high school. An overwhelming 66% have intelligence quotient scores below 70. Deficient in basic literary skills, a significant number have little ability to write letters home or pursue education programs without further training (Georgia Department of Corrections, 2003). In contrast, older females in Tennessee were more likely to be high school graduates, and one third had attended some college (Aday & Nation, 2001). However, nearly 60% were former victims of emotional, physical, or sexual abuse prior to incarceration.

MENTAL HEALTH NEEDS AND CHARACTERISTICS

The general population suffering from mental disorders is increasingly entering the prison system. Correctional facilities in the United States currently house more mentally ill individuals than hospitals and mental institutions (Ditton, 1999). A significant portion of the aged suffer from various mental or emotional disorders (Chaiklin, 1998). Whereas 15–25% of older adults in the general population have psychiatric disorders, the estimate of aging prisoners with mental health problems has been reported to be as high as 50%, depending on the populations considered and the diagnostic criteria used (Ditton, 1999; Douglass, 1991; Koenig, Johnson, Bellard, Denker, & Fenlon,

1995). Older white females housed in state prisons are more likely than other aging prisoners to suffer from mental illnesses (Ditton, 1999).

Disorders most prevalent among aging prisoners include organic brain syndrome, depression, anxiety, antisocial personality disorders, schizophrenia, and substance abuse. Although some of these issues result from declines in physical functioning, others can be attributed to the stressful nature of incarceration (Faiver, 1998; Vega & Silverman, 1988). Still others entered prison with psychiatric problems (e.g., organic brain syndrome) that contributed to the offenses committed (Clark & Mezey, 1997; Paradis, Broner, Maher, & O'Rourke, 2000). Although mental health problems are a growing concern among aging prisoners, a significant proportion (25–50%) do not receive appropriate treatment—a figure attributed to the stigma our society places on mental illnesses (Regan, Alderson, & Regan, 2002). Some of the more common mental health issues facing aging prisoners include (Aday, 2003; Tice & Perkins, 1996; Wahidin, 2004):

- Psychological stressors related to lack of privacy, inadequate prison structure
- Emotional problems and coping barriers related to drug/alcohol abuse
- Fears related to dying in prison, victimization, inadequate health care
- Grief reactions to losses such as physical health and life without parole
- Guilt and suicidal thoughts associated with crimes such as sexual offenses
- Symptoms related to prison shock and difficulties with late-life imprisonment
- Early states of dementia, Alzheimer's, and personality rigidity, anxiety disorders
- Loneliness, alienation, depression, and general low morale
- Coping with abusive histories, sleep disturbances, social withdrawal

Anxiety affects nearly one quarter of America's 65-and-older population, and the prevalence among older prisoners is expected to be much higher. Medical-related fears include seeing different physicians during each sick call, not receiving proper medical treatment, having heart attacks, and dying behind bars. Relatives who never visit; dwelling on the crimes committed; threats of financial exploitation, physical abuse, and ridicule by younger inmates; indeterminate sentences; noise; and lack of privacy may also heighten existing anxieties (Aday, 2003; Wahidin, 2004).

Depression affects 15–20% of older adults in the general population but as many as 70% of aging prisoners (Douglass, 1991; Eliopoulos, 1997). Missing outside friends and social life, not knowing when one will be released, and having limited opportunities to participate in age-appropriate recreational activities may lead many aging prisoners to feel bored and hopeless, to change their sleeping patterns, to lose interest in daily routines, to feel guilty about the behaviors that led to incarceration, and, in extreme circumstances, to contemplate suicide. Other symptoms of depression include feeling lonely and useless and describing life as dull. Older persons most often affected by this condition include those who have recently encountered declines in physical functioning or social losses, those who are under the influence of prescription medications, and those who are struggling with their own mortality.

MEDICAL NEEDS AND CHARACTERISTICS

Numerous studies have made valuable contributions to the understanding of the special health needs of the aging inmate (Aday, 2001; Colsher et al., 1992; Falter, 1999; Gallagher, 1990; Marquart, Merianos, Herbert, & Carroll, 1997; Smyer, Gragert, & LaMere, 1997). On average, these studies found a significant incidence of chronic illness for ailments such as arthritis (41%), heart disease (26%), menopause problems (33%), prostate problems (18%), emphysema (20%), stomach disorders (17%), diabetes (12%), cancer (6%), and stroke (8%). Previous studies have found that elderly prisoners suffer from three or more of these chronic illnesses (Aday, 2001; Douglass, 1991; Krebs, 2000) and consume an even greater number of medications. It has also been suggested that the health of the typical older prisoner tends to decline rapidly during incarceration (McCarthy, 1983; Rubenstein, 1984). This rapid decline or accelerated biological aging has been attributed to the following factors (Fabelo, 1999; Fattah & Sacco, 1989):

- Tendency to engage in high-risk behaviors (smoking, drugs, alcohol) prior to incarceration
- Lack of preventive health care prior to incarceration due to lack of access
- Unhealthy lifestyles fostered in prison, including poor diets and lack of exercise
- Greater rate of infectious disease than persons of the same age in the free world
- Harshness and stressors of prison life, especially in maximum security prisons

Other researchers see elderly inmates as experiencing a refuge from the traumas of life on the outside (Brogden & Nijhar, 2000). In this sense, the prison can serve as a haven and can potentially slow the aging process for vulnerable older offenders who experienced a destructive lifestyle and conditions of poverty prior to imprisonment (Fattah & Sacco, 1989).

Chronic illness has been reported to negatively affect a person's body image, psychological well-being, and social identity (Royer, 1995). At a minimum, for many persons, the diagnosis of a chronic illness forces an awareness of a permanent defect, however slight, that potentially reduces the accustomed level of functioning. As Table 19.1 illustrates, the ability of a group of 318 inmates over the age of 60 housed in Tennessee prisons to negotiate their environment is severely limited. When comparing the young-old (60–64) with the oldest (65–81) inmates, it was found that functional capabilities declined significantly for all indicators for persons in the latter age group. As they experience a more restricted life, chronically ill persons become cognizant of the fact that they cannot engage in many of the activities they valued and enjoyed in the past.

With some chronic illnesses, older adults first confront their own mortality, which may lead to greater uncertainty and profound fear. Inmates housed in correctional facilities at some institutions in remote areas may fear having a heart attack or some other sudden life-threatening symptom and worry about the response time for getting them to a medical facility where they could receive proper treatment. The presence of chronic illnesses can create a sense of vulnerability among aging inmates, who frequently have to rely on an unfamiliar or untrusting medical system for critical care. Of course, such chronic conditions also leave the aging inmate more vulnerable to victimization by younger inmates.

SOCIAL NEEDS AND CHARACTERISTICS

Understanding the social world experienced by older inmates requires a fundamental knowledge of Goffman's (1961) notion of "total institutions" and the extent to which prisons, as total institutions, strip inmates of former identities while placing them in settings with "undesirable" populations. Prison offers a new subculture, a new set of rules, and language that can be overwhelming for mentally fragile inmates. For the first time in their lives, older individuals are placed in a system in which they must submit to orderly rou-

TABLE 19.1. TDOC Inmates Over Age 60 With Special Health Care Needs

Special Needs	Percent
Requires ground-level housing	60.2
Requires lower bunk for easy access	68.9
Has difficulty walking long distances	48.6
Has difficulty standing up for 15 minutes	37.5
Independent but exhibits slow mobility	55.0
Requires special equipment for mobility	19.7
Incapable of ascending/descending stairs	51.4
Frail, brittle, unstable, or physically weak	43.3
High risk of victimization by other inmates	44.2
Possesses some vision problems	39.3
Possesses some hearing problems	72.9
Considered legally blind	12.9
Judged to have unstable chronic condition	33.0
Exhibits symptoms of confusion	10.5

$N = 318$

Note: From *A Comprehensive Health Assessment of Aged and Infirm Inmates,* by R. Aday, 2001, Nashville: Tennessee Department of Correction. Copyright. Reprinted with permission.

tine and exercise very little self-determination. When entering the institution, correctional personnel immediately replace the inmate's name with a number, require him or her to relinquish all personal possessions, and strictly control the times during which inmates may eat, work, or receive visitors.

Despite more liberal visiting and correspondence policies in recent times, inmates still must relinquish substantial contact with family and friends while serving their respective sentences. As a result, imprisonment contributes to the weakening of relationships between inmates and their respective families and friends (Aday & Nation, 2001; Kratcoski & Babb, 1990). The fact that many older inmates are unlikely to receive visitors on a regular basis can stem from a number of factors:

- Some aging inmates may outlive their family members on the outside.
- Strict visitation requirements found in some institutions may create significant barriers.
- Aging inmates may be placed in special needs facilities that make it geographically impossible to maintain close family ties.
- Most inmates come from poverty-stricken backgrounds and unstable families in which there is little support.

- Poor health of inmates or family members may inhibit regular family visits.
- Aging inmates who commit violent crimes (sexual offenders and murderers) on family members often become estranged from the family.
- The shame of imprisonment in old age may serve to reduce the desire for family members (i.e., grandchildren) to visit.

In particular, Kratcoski and Babb (1990) found that older women are less likely to receive visitors than their male counterparts. Being separated from family members can prove to be difficult. Not being able to fulfill the role of parent or grandparent on a day-to-day basis can be frustrating. It can be a tremendous stigma for a grandmother to know that her grandchildren have known her only as an imprisoned person. Based on these shameful feelings, some older inmates prefer not to have visitors but rather to rely on letters and phone calls (Aday & Nation, 2001).

The break in the link with the free community can be a traumatic experience for the older offender already attempting to adjust to certain physical and emotional changes associated with aging itself. If the social attachments outside the prison decrease, this broken relationship may serve to make the older prisoner more dependent on the institution, especially if he or she has no immediate family or friends on the outside. When accompanied by a shrinking social environment, the length of institutionalization, as does old age itself, may serve to decrease the number of significant others on the outside. As a result, a significant number of aging inmates may experience what has been termed "institutional dependency." In this sense, prison becomes their home, and they are fearful, or in some cases unwilling, to return to the free world.

END-OF-LIFE ISSUES

The aging prison population has created a new panoply of end-of-life issues. Over a 12-year period, inmate deaths in state prisons have doubled, increasing from 1,630 in 1989 to 3,203 in 2000 (*Corrections Yearbook,* 2002). The percentage of inmate deaths due to natural causes has steadily increased, from 58.8% in 1996 to 80.0% in 2001. Overall, more than 2,500 convicted criminals now die of natural causes in state and federal prison each year (*Corrections Yearbook,* 2002). The mortality rate is expected to continue to increase primarily because of the graying of the U.S. prison populations and because an increasing number of offenders are receiving sentences that will keep them imprisoned for the remainder of their lives.

Most inmates fear dying in prison, and these anxieties will become more commonplace as America's prison population continues to age (Byock, 2002). After anticipating and planning for release, terminally ill long-term inmates may fear dying in institutions that house aggressive inmates, hire uncaring staff, and restrict visits (Aday, 2003; Byock, 2002). Aging prisoners likely to fear death are those who report their health as poor, who have witnessed the deaths of their prison peers, and who rarely receive support from people other than uncaring paid prison staff (Aday, 2003). For those who have supportive friends and family, thoughts of leaving behind grief-stricken loved ones may also instill fears of death. Older prisoners cope with thoughts of dying in prison by gaining strength from religious beliefs, engaging in prison activities, and viewing death as the end of suffering endured while ill behind bars (Aday, 2003).

America's courts do not mandate prisons to release terminally ill older, infirm prisoners, but most federal and state prisons do provide compassionate release for inmates who have medical records and physicians' statements documenting their prognoses; low-risk security classifications; future economic security; and an established dwelling outside the institution (National Institute of Corrections, 1998). Sending minimal-risk, terminally ill inmates home to die reduces prison medical expenditures (Yates & Gillespie, 2000), but placing inmates in the care of others is not always possible. Aging relatives often do not have the strength, stamina, or time to adequately support the inmate, and many nursing homes do not want to assume the liability of caring for former prisoners (Aday, 2003). Therefore, correctional officials must provide in-house services for inmates who have no other option but to spend their final days behind bars.

SOCIAL WORK PRACTICE WITH OLDER OFFENDERS

About half of the states now provide geriatric facilities and programming for elderly inmates, ranging from separate facilities for the aged and infirm to selected clustering within a large prison setting (American Correctional Association, 2001). Numerous states are developing nursing home–like settings, which provide a greater degree of shelter and accommodation (Aday, 1999; Flynn, 1992). Grouping inmates with similar health care needs has been considered to be

more cost effective, as well as offering prison officials the opportunity to respond more efficiently to the unmet needs of elderly prisoners. Special facilities also provide aging inmates with a quieter living environment and one considered safer than living in the general prison population (Marquart, Merianos, & Doucet, 2000).

Geriatric facilities in Florida, Ohio, Pennsylvania, and North Carolina offer some of the more ambitious programs for older offenders. Among others, these states routinely provide inmates with geriatric walking programs, as well as other low-impact sports activities, including intramural basketball and softball for inmates 50 and over. Psychologists and social workers provide case management, counseling services, mercy parole recommendations, nursing home placement, and other special care. Services are offered so inmates can learn to deal with their reactions to health issues, problems with their spouses, adjusting to prison life, and strained relationships with children and grandchildren. Numerous states also provide hospice programs for the terminally ill and also arrange for appropriate aftercare to elderly inmates who are released.

There are, however, limitations in the implementation of new geriatric policies and programming efforts. Prison officials must be more imaginative in programming for this subgroup of inmates. In facilities designed solely for older, special-needs offenders, finding suitable work assignments for everyone may be difficult. Contacts with outside agencies can provide new opportunities for older, frail inmates. However, location of prisons in isolated areas can hinder such programming. On the other hand, many older inmates are incapable of successfully completing work assignments or training programs. Chronic health problems may prevent older offenders from participating in normal work assignments. Also, with the tremendous growth of the aging prison population, the number of beds dedicated to this population is far from adequate, and many aging inmates never have the opportunity to live in a special-needs environment. A system with a more careful monitoring process can allow inmates to be placed in an appropriate prison environment and prevent many of the negative outcomes associated with living in prison.

OLDER INMATE TYPES

Aging inmates are a diverse population, presenting a wide range of challenges for those providing services.

When developing strategies for working with older inmates, it is important to differentiate between three types. Approximately one half of older inmates housed in federal and state prisons are "new elderly" offenders who never intended to violate the law but committed first offenses (primarily murder and sex crimes) against younger relatives or close acquaintances after age 50. Formerly regarded as "model citizens," these prisoners frequently have difficulties adjusting to life in prison—abiding by prison policies, living with a potentially violent population, and being away from family and former friends. The pains of imprisonment can leave some feeling guilty for disappointing loved ones, lonely, apprehensive about the future, and anxious about surviving in a total institution. As a result, many begin to exhibit symptoms of depression, withdrawal from prison staff and inmates, change in sleep and eating patterns, and suicidal ideations. Remorseful for the crimes committed, other "new elderly" offenders are appreciative of the free food, shelter, and clothing they now have and adjust rather well to institutional living.

A second group, the recidivist or habitual criminals, generally began a life of crime at a rather early age. Over the years, they have found themselves in and out of the criminal justice system and are now reincarcerated in later life. This group of offenders is generally well adjusted to the prison system, having an active support group of other inmates. Unmarried or divorced and abusers of drugs and alcohols, they have lived through hard lives on the outside and are typically in poor health. More times than not, they have committed a crime that will keep them incarcerated for 10 or more years, and many in this group will face end-of-life issues in prison. Due to their crime history, obviously habitual offenders are not considered a good risk for parole.

Another, smaller group who require unique programming include long-term inmates (lifers) who first offended early in life and received 20-plus-year prison sentences. Often young, uneducated, poor black men who pleaded guilty to the charges against them and never requested release have grown old behind bars. Since imprisonment, many have severed any contact they once had with members of the free world, and they would have no home where they could return if set free. Long-term inmates require special consideration, as many will lose motivation to participate in prison activities, obsess over visible signs of deteriorating health, and contemplate dying in prison. If these inmates were to receive parole and could tomorrow return to the free world, they would first require extensive release preparation, including assistance obtaining financial support, affordable lodging, and inexpensive health care services, because many have become heavily dependent on the institution to meet all of their needs for basic survival.

HELPING AGING PRISONERS ADAPT

As suggested by Gewirtz (1984), the goals, values, attitudes, knowledge base, and practice skills of social work provide a useful framework for working with the older inmate population. Research has demonstrated that those providing services to the geriatric inmate population need specialized training if they are to be effective (Kratcoski, 2000). Understanding that older offenders have the same rights as other clients in the free world is important. As suggested by Kropf and Hutchison (2000, p. 3), any special group of "elderly clients have the right to sensitive and ethical practice that preserves the greatest autonomy." Although policies relating to medical care, social services, and parole planning for inmates have been hotly debated, there is a growing recognition that inmates should receive services consistent with prevailing community norms. Under the Eighth Amendment, not providing inmates programming conducive to their levels of cognitive, physical, and psychological functioning is considered "cruel and unusual punishment" (Krebs, 2000). According to Krebs, we must not merely permit older inmates permission to participate in existing programs but must also create new activities suitable to inmates with health limitations. Practitioners should be aware that they will likely encounter aging inmates requiring different types of intervention and assistance than other elderly clients.

For example, the entry into and adaptation to prison for late offenders can be a difficult transition, as can be the transition back out of society for long-termers after spending a considerable portion of life behind bars. To capture some of the unique problems facing aging prisoners, Kratcoski (2000) has suggested that special consideration be given to the following when working with older inmates in the prison context:

- Those who violate rules may not have understood the rules.
- Inmates may be forgetful, misinterpret instruction, or simply not understand the meaning of slang terms often used by correctional staff and officers.
- Older inmates will need more assistance and attention than younger inmates, as they may not be-

come involved in inmate subculture or be assisted by family members.

- Older inmates are more likely to have serious mental and physical problems.
- Some may be bed wetters, and others need to make constant trips to the bathroom.
- Many older inmates will need more encouragement to become involved in recreational, social, and education activities.
- Programming should be designed to elevate self-esteem rather than to prepare for a job.
- Lifers may be more fearful of being released back to the community.

In addition to prisoner characteristics, prison adaptation is also influenced by the prison environment in which they reside. The sheer physical condition and structure of the institution can create significant problems for older inmates. Few older men and women aging in prison report being satisfied with their living conditions (Aday, 2001; Kratcoski & Babb, 1990). Older, frail offenders often find the prison environment to be oppressive, with poor lighting and ventilation. Stale air from smokers, top bunking, and being housed too far away from the dining room and bathrooms have been viewed as significant environmental problems. Unlike people in the general population, who can generally adapt to oppressive housing arrangements, those aging in prison have no choice but to accept and find mechanisms to cope with the noise, limited recreational activities, lack of privacy, and potential victimization by other inmates.

Aging inmates typically benefit from involvement in some type of educational or social programming. As a broker (Kropf & Hutchison, 2000), a practitioner assesses both client needs and, in this case, environmental resources available in the prison and the community at large. To combat the many losses aging prisoners may experience, the empowerment model has been suggested as a way counselors and other mental health professionals can assist individuals in coping with their life changes and transitions (Waters & Goodman, 1990). Empowering older adults is practitioner oriented and includes establishing goals and supporting inmates in their efforts to adjust. In some instances the enabler role will serve to help aging inmates accept the fact that they will spend the remainder of their lives incarcerated. In other cases, emphasis may be placed on dealing with past abuses, offender behavior, or reentry back to the community. Life skills education programs are one way some correctional institutions have used to prepare older inmates for reentry to the community.

The program includes a number of referral activities and assistance in locating housing after release; in adjusting to having a criminal record; in reestablishing ties with family members; in obtaining financial resources such as food stamps, Medicaid, and Medicare; in developing social skills; and in taking care of personal hygiene. Preparation for reentry can be an onerous task for inmates who have spent 20 or more years separated from the outside world.

THE USE OF THERAPEUTIC GROUPS

As a planned programmed activity, working with the elderly in groups can serve as a valuable tool to help plan and implement effective intervention strategies in the prison environment. An important reason for conducting groups in correctional settings is that many inmates need socialization skills (Stojkovic & Lovell, 1997). Members learn from other members, and inmates feel reassured when they hear others sharing similar fears and concerns (Masters, 1994). According to Jacobs and Spadaro (2003), inmates are often distrustful of prison staff, but they may listen to their peers in a group counseling situation. The use of groups can be ideal in overcoming loneliness, dealing with guilt or grief issues, and, in general, facilitating positive personal changes. Toseland (1995, pp. 18–19) has identified numerous benefits of group participation:

- Groups provide feelings of belonging and affiliation that can help older adults to overcome the social isolation and loneliness.
- Group participation helps to validate and affirm the experiences of older adults.
- Groups provide members with an opportunity to share and to learn new information.
- Groups provide older adults with unique opportunities for interpersonal learning.
- Groups offer older adults the opportunity to resolve problems with the help and support of fellow members.

There are three basic categories of older adults for whom groups are particularly beneficial: (1) older adults who are socially isolated, (2) older adults who have interpersonal problems, and (3) older adults who need assistance in identifying and participating in new social roles. Older inmates transitioning into prison, as well as those coping with the effects of long-term imprisonment, can benefit greatly from effective group participation. Remotivation, reminiscing, support, recreational, and psychotherapy groups have all been used productively in working with aging inmates (Aday, 2003). Table 19.2 is a modified list of support group topics frequently used with older incarcerated females, and most would be equally relevant for males.

It is essential for prison practitioners who work with older inmates to become thoroughly familiar with the process of grieving. Loss is a theme that frequently reemerges when working with older inmates. Loss of freedom, health, work roles, identity, family members, marriage partners, or other prison acquaintances is quite common. Group therapy can provide the means for elderly inmates to accept and resolve long-standing attitudes and feelings related to their life in prison. Psychotherapy is also helpful, as it can expand older inmates' coping strategies.

TABLE 19.2. Support Group Topics for Aging Inmates

Topics Addressing Personal Growth
Loneliness

Mortality

How to make each moment count

Self-esteem

Future fears and desires

Life transitions

Ageism

Drug/alcohol abuse

How to maintain independence

Energy level changes

Anger management

Lack of mobility

Feelings of isolation

Weight gain

Topics Addressing Daily Life Issues
Work activities

Learning to live in prison

Getting along with others

Learning to live with chronic illness, etc.

Legal issues

Financial concerns

Environmental stress

Topics Addressing Family and Social Relationships
Desertion by families

Children and grandchildren

Sexuality and relationships

Making prison friends

Family visits

Social issues

Abusive relationships

Death of family/friends

Note: From L. W. Kaye, *Self-Help Support Groups for Older Women,* by L. W. Kaye, 1997, Washington, DC: Taylor & Francis, p. 97. Copyright 1997. Reprinted with permission.

EXPANDING THE ROLE OF PRACTITIONERS

The transition of the social work philosophy into the prison setting can be challenging. Although a significant number of states are providing special facilities to accommodate the needs of the aging prison population, numerous obstacles hinder service providers. For example, overcrowding and financial constraints frequently take first priority in states strapped for resources. The rising costs of health care inhibit some correctional systems from offering comprehensive services beyond the "medical model." Some facilities may have a small number of aging inmates, reducing the likelihood that special programming will be provided.

Some public sentiment remains against providing special therapeutic treatment or separate facilities for the older inmate. The public still disagrees about the ethical obligation to provide inmates with extensive services, such as palliative care or kidney transplants. Prison therapeutic programs may create high expectations that in a correctional setting cannot entirely be met. Identifying and meeting the special needs of aging inmates is a challenge filled with contradictions and pitfalls. Prisons as a rule have promoted conformity rather than individuality. Prison is a place where even simple platonic gestures are often discouraged. Simple human contact, such as touching a patient's hand or shoulder during assessment, is often frowned on. Some security and even medical personnel may have misperceptions about the mission and value of treatment programs.

Although researchers are beginning to address with more frequency the policy concerns associated with the aging prison population, the body of knowledge on elderly inmates is not extensive. Prison officials have stressed that indicators are needed to more clearly identify model programs to meet the needs of the elderly inmate (Edwards, 1998). For example, although a variety of programs and facilities have been introduced, a systematic way to evaluate them is sorely needed. Important questions remain about their effectiveness in meeting the special needs of the aging prisoner. Also, little research has been conducted on aging prisoners themselves and the nature of their family relationships, the coping strategies of those entering prison late in life, or the utility of social networks in prison adjustment.

Prison administrators have pointed out the need for better-qualified staff to work with aging prisoners (Caldwell, Jarvis, & Rosefield, 2001). Selecting and training staff to deal effectively with older offenders will be an increasingly important challenge. Special sensitivity training may be necessary to adequately prepare staff to work with the aging population. Practitioners with background and training in gerontology can take an active policy role in educating the public about the important issues associated with the graying of American prisons. In addition to providing direct care to an increasingly frail aging prison population, social workers can take a leadership role in training administrative personnel, line security staff, and other prison staff to be more sensitive to the social, emotional, and health needs of aging prisoners. In effectively meeting these challenges, social workers will provide a valuable service to the correctional field.

REFERENCES

Aday, R. H. (1999). *Golden years behind bars: A ten-year follow-up.* Paper presented at the annual meeting of the Academy of Criminal Justice Sciences, Orlando, FL.

Aday, R. H. (2001). *A comprehensive health assessment of aged and infirm inmates.* Nashville: Tennessee Department of Correction.

Aday, R. H. (2003). *Aging prisoners: Crisis in American corrections.* Westport, CT: Praeger.

Aday, R. H., & Nation, P. (2001). *A case study of older female offenders.* Nashville: Tennessee Department of Correction.

American Correctional Association. (2001). Elderly inmates: Survey summary. *Corrections Compendium, 26*(5), 7–21.

Brogden, M., & Nijhar, P. (2000). *Crime, abuse and the elderly.* Portland, OR: Willan.

Byock, I. R. (2002). Dying well in corrections: Why should we care? *Journal of Correctional Health Care, 9,* 21–29.

Caldwell, C., Jarvis, M., & Rosefield, H. (2001). Issues impacting today's geriatric female offenders. *Corrections Today, 65*(5), 110–113.

Chaiklin, H. (1998). The elderly disturbed prisoners. *Clinical Gerontologist, 20*(1), 47–62.

Clark, C., & Mezey, G. (1997). Elderly sex offenders against children: A descriptive study of child sex abusers over the age of 65. *Journal of Forensic Psychiatry, 8*(2), 357–369.

Colsher, P. L., Wallace, R. B., Loeffelholz, P. L., & Sales, M. (1992). Health status of older male prisoners: A comprehensive survey. *American Journal of Public Health, 83,* 881–884.

Corrections Yearbook. (2003). Middletown, CT: Criminal Justice Institute.

Ditton, P. M. (1999). *Mental health and treatment of inmates and probationers.* Washington, DC: Department of Justice Statistics.

Douglass, R. L. (1991). *Oldtimers: Michigan's elderly prisoners.* Lansing: Michigan Department of Corrections.

Edwards, T. (1998). *The aging inmate population: SLC special series report.* Atlanta, GA: Council of State Governments.

Eliopoulos, C. (1997). *Gerontological nursing.* Philadelphia: Lippincott.

Fabelo, T. (1999). *Elder offenders in Texas prisons.* Austin, TX: Criminal Justice Policy Council.

Faiver, K. L. (1998). Special issues of aging. In K. L. Faiver (Ed.), *Health care management issues in corrections* (pp. 123–132). Lanham, MD: American Correctional Association.

Falter, R. G. (1999). Selected predictors of health service needs of inmates over age 50. *Journal of Correctional Health Care, 6,* 149–175.

Fattah, E. A., & Sacco, V. F. (1989). *Crime and victimization of the elderly.* New York: Springer-Verlag.

Flynn, E. E. (1992). The graying of America's prison population. *Prison Journal, 72*(1–2), 77–98.

Forsyth, C. J., & Gramling, R. (1988). Elderly crime: Fact and artifact. In B. McCarthy & R. Langworthy (Eds.), *Older offenders: Perspectives in criminology and criminal justice* (pp. 3–13). New York: Praeger.

Gallagher, E. M. (1990). Emotional, social, and physical health characteristics of older men in prison. *International Journal of Aging and Human Development, 31,* 251–266.

Georgia Department of Corrections. (2003). *Georgia's aging inmate population.* Department of Corrections, Atlanta, GA.

Gewirtz, M. L. (1984). Social work practice with elderly offenders. In E. S. Newman, D. J. Newman, & M. L. Gewirtz (Eds.), *Elderly criminals* (pp. 193–208). Cambridge, MA. Oelgeschlager, Gunn, & Hain.

Goffman, I. (1961). *Asylums: Essays on the social situation of mental patients and other inmates.* Garden City, NY: Doubleday.

House, J. (1990). Age, socioeconomic status, and health. *Milbank Quarterly, 68,* 343–411.

Jacobs, E., & Spadaro, N. (2003). *Leading groups in corrections: Skills and techniques.* Lanham, MD: American Correctional Association.

Koenig, H. G., Johnson, S., Bellard, J., Denker, M., & Fenlon, R. (1995). Depression and anxiety disorder among older male inmates at a federal correctional facility. *Psychiatric Services, 46*(4), 399–401.

Kratcoski, P. C. (1990). Circumstances surrounding homicides by older offenders. *Criminal Justice and Behavior, 17,* 420–430.

Kratcoski, P. C. (2000). Older inmates: Special programming concerns. In P. C. Kratcoski (Ed.), *Correctional counseling and treatment* (pp. 648–662). Prospect Heights, IL: Waveland Press.

Kratcoski, P. C., & Babb, S. (1990). Adjustment of older inmates: An analysis by institutional structure and gender. *Journal of Contemporary Criminal Justice, 6,* 139–156.

Krebs, J. J. (2000). The older prisoner: Social, psychological, and medical considerations. In M. B. Rothman, B. D. Dunlop, & P. Entzel (Eds.), *Elderly, crime and the criminal justice system* (pp. 207–228). New York: Springer.

Kropf, N. P., & Hutchison, E. D. (2000). Effective practice with elderly clients. In R. L. Schneider, N. P. Kropf, & A. J. Kosor (Eds.), *Gerontological social work* (pp. 3–25). Belmont, CA: Wadsworth.

Marquart, J. W., Merianos, D. E., & Doucet, G. (2000). The health-related concerns of older prisoners: Implications for policy. *Aging and Society, 20,* 79–86.

Marquart, J. W., Merianos, D. E., Herbert, J. L., & Carroll, L. (1997). Health condition and prisoners: A review of research and emerging areas of inquiry. *Prison Journal, 77,* 184–208.

Masters, R. (1994). *Counseling and criminal justice offenders.* Thousand Oaks, CA: Sage.

McCarthy, M. (1983, February). The health status of elderly inmates. *Corrections Today, 64–65, 74.*

Morton, J. B. (1992). *An administrative overview of the older inmate.* Washington, DC: U.S. Department of Justice.

National Institute of Corrections (1998). Prison medical care: Special needs populations and cost control. Washington, D.C.: U.S. Department of Justice.

Paradis, C., Broner, N., Maher, L., & O'Rourke, T. (2000). Mentally ill elderly jail detainees: Psychiatric, psychological and legal factors. *Journal of Offender Rehabilitation, 31,* 77–86.

Regan, J. J., Alderson, A., & Regan, W. M. (2002). Psychiatric disorders in aging prisoners. *Clinical Gerontologist, 26*(1/2), 8–13.

Royer, A. (1995). Living with chronic illness. *Research in the Sociology of Health Care, 12,* 25–48.

Rubenstein, D. (1984). The elderly in prison: A review of the literature. In E. S. Newman, D. J. Newman, & M. L. Gewirtz (Eds.), *Elderly criminals* (pp. 153–168). Boston: Oelgeschlager, Gunn, & Hain.

Smyer, T., Gragert, M. D., & LaMere, S. H. (1997). Stay safe! Stay healthy! Surviving old age in prison. *Journal of Psychosocial Nursing, 35*(9), 10–17.

Special report on inmate population. Louisiana Department of Corrections. (2004). Baton Rouge, LA: Author.

Stojkovic, S., & Lovell, R. (1997). *Corrections: An introduction.* Cincinnati, OH: Anderson.

Tice, C. J., & Perkins, K. (1996). *Mental health issues and aging.* Boston: Brooks/Cole.

Toseland, R. W. (1995). *Group work with the elderly and family caregivers.* New York: Springer.

U.S. Department of Justice. (2001). *Sourcebook of criminal justice statistics.* Washington, DC: U.S. Government Printing Office.

Vega, M., & Silverman, M. (1988). Stress and the elderly convict. *International Journal of Offender Therapy and Comparative Criminology, 32,* 153–162.

Wahidin, A. (2004). *Older women in the criminal justice system.* Philadelphia: Kingsley.

Waters, E. B., & Goodman, J. (1990). *Empowering older adults.* San Francisco: Jossey-Bass.

Yates, J., & Gillespie, W. (2000). The elderly and prison policy. *Journal of Aging and Social Policy, 11*(2–3), 167–175.

LETHA A. CHADIHA,
SECTION EDITOR

Cultural Diversity and Social Work Practice With Older Adults

OVERVIEW

The concept of cultural diversity implies recognition by social workers of the differences in the life experiences of older adults. Differences may include but are not limited to cultural history, language, values, religion, ethnicity, nationality, regionality, immigration status, and sexual orientation. Both the National Association of Social Workers (NASW) and the Council on Social Work Education (CSWE) emphasize that social workers should be knowledgeable about the cultures of clients. These organizations of the social work profession also emphasize social workers' being trained to deliver culturally appropriate services to clients. To this end, this section addresses social work practice with diverse groups of U.S. older adults: African Americans and other Black populations; Asian Americans; gays, lesbians, bisexuals and transgender persons; religious and regional minorities; Native Hawaiian and Pacific Islanders; Latinos; and Native Americans.

In chapter 20, Chadiha, Brown, and Aranda focus on the largest group of U.S. elders of color—native and non-native Black Americans of African origin. Contrary to popular beliefs that the Black elderly population is monolithic, these authors note that the Black elderly population is a diverse group in ethnic composition and nationality. They also note variability within the Black elderly population and differences from other racial-ethnic elderly persons on social, demographic, economic, and health characteristics—factors that provide service providers with both challenges and opportunities when working with Black elderly persons. Further, Chadiha and colleagues identify three key informal sources of support—family, church, and religion—that help offset social, demographic, economic, and health challenges. They end with a discussion of different levels of interventions to address the special needs of elderly Blacks.

Min and Moon, in chapter 21, address the growth and diversity of Asian American elders—the fastest growing U.S. racial group. They cite 24 ethnic groups (excluding Pacific Islanders, information on which can be found in the last chapter in this section). Further, other elements of diversity and variability include language, immigration history (e.g., reason for immigration, age at time of immigration), length of stay and life experiences in the United States, religious affiliation, socioeconomic status, and level of acculturation—all factors that affect the well-being of Asian American elderly persons. These authors provide an illuminating discussion on issues of physical health status, psychological and mental health status,

and family and caregiving among Asian American elderly. They conclude from empirical studies that Asian American elderly persons underutilize services and end with recommendations aimed to help practitioners to practice culturally competent social work with these elderly persons.

In chapter 22, Butler profiles the diversity of one of the most invisible groups of elderly Americans—gay, lesbian, bisexual, and transgendered (GLBT) persons—in empirical research. She notes that precise numbers about the size of this population of elderly persons are unavailable, with figures ranging from 1 million to 2.8 million; however, the Administration on Aging estimates population growth to 6 million by 2030. Butler outlines GLBT elders' history of oppression and invisibility, as well as what is known about them on the basis of "few studies" and "small nonrepresentative samples." Butler ends with an informative discussion on the unique strengths and challenges of GLBT elders and the implications of these strengths and challenges for practitioners to consider when working with GLBT elders.

Chapter 23 by Aranda focuses on elders of Latino/Hispanic descent, another diverse group in "language, culture, sociopolitical history, acculturation, cumulative life experiences and opportunities." As do prior chapters in this section, Aranda also discusses social, demographic, and cultural characteristics, as well as physical health and disability among Latino elders. She anchors her discussion of these characteristics in issues of mental health, specifically late-life depression, for Latino elders. Through prior literature she clearly establishes the relatively high risk of depressive disorder and low service utilization among older Mexican Americans. The chapter ends with a case example that illustrates practice strategies for working with Latino elders.

Barusch, in chapter 24, addresses the history and demographics of the Native American elders, of their current living conditions, and of forced assimilation and colonization. She elucidates the negative impact that prior federal policies had on dislocating Native Americans and the extent to which such dislocation has meant that contemporary urban-dwelling Native elders lack access to services that are provided by Indian Health Services. Barusch ends this chapter with strategies to support and empower Native American elders. Further, she also addresses the need for increased numbers of trained Native American professionals to work with Native elders.

Whereas prior chapters focus on diverse groups based on race, ethnicity, and sexual orientation, the last chapter in this section, written by Browne and Richardson, focuses on elderly persons in "other minority groups"—groups that represent "marginal religions and regions." Specifically, these authors address the demographics, health (physical and mental), and cultural values of elderly persons of Jewish faith and elderly persons of Muslim faith. Correspondingly, they address the demographics, health (physi-

cal and mental), and cultural values of elderly persons residing in the Appalachian Mountain region and the Pacific Islands. Each discussion of a religious or regional group is followed by a set of innovative recommendations for social work interventions that take into consideration the unique characteristics of these "other minority groups."

The Black elderly population (i.e., African Americans, Caribbean and African immigrants) ages 65 years or older comprises the largest group of elders of color in the United States. Growth in population size, as well as in age and cultural diversity, of the Black elderly population presents both challenges and opportunities for effective service delivery by social workers to these Americans. The purpose of this chapter is to address the special concerns of social work practice with older Blacks while taking into account the ethnic diversity within the U.S. Black elderly population. In order to address such concerns, it is essential to preface them with a discussion on certain salient issues in empirical literature on the older Black population. These issues, which form major subheadings in this chapter, include the expansion and subsequent cultural heterogeneity of the older Black population; social, demographic, and economic characteristics; physical health and mental health status, as well as access to health care; and family, church, and religion as sources of informal support to older Blacks. Extant literature, including government documents and other empirical research, provided evidence for addressing these issues. We use the knowledge from this evidence to draw implications for social work practice with older Black adult populations living in the United States. Throughout this chapter, we use the terms Black and Black Americans to refer to native and non-native Americans of African descent.

GROWTH AND HETEROGENEITY OF THE ELDERLY BLACK POPULATION

A little over three decades ago 16.6 million elderly people lived in the United States. This figure had more than doubled by 2000 to 35 million elderly people (Angel & Hogan, 2004). Of these elderly persons, 16.4% were persons of color (i.e., Black, Asian, Native American, or Hispanic). Elderly Blacks (8.4%), persons of African, Caribbean, and European ancestry, composed the majority of these elderly persons of color living in the United States in 2000. The percent of older Blacks ages 65 years or older in the U.S. Black population is expected to almost double (16.1%) by 2030, reaching 20% by 2050 (Angel & Hogan, 2004).

The U.S. Black elderly population comprises primarily native-born persons of African descent, typically referred to as African Americans or Black Americans. Growth of the Black elderly population is attributed to the rising longevity that has come as a result of improved health status and medical care. The Black elderly population is a diverse group in ethnic

LETHA A. CHADIHA
EDNA BROWN
MARIA P. ARANDA

Older African Americans and Other Black Populations

20

makeup, nationality, language, and religious orientation (Sotomayor, 1997). Immigration trends during the 20th century, especially in the latter part of the century, portend that unprecedented numbers of non-native-born older Blacks will constitute the future population of older Black Americans. Since 1965, the year marking an increase in the number of persons of African descent migrating to the United States (Allen, 1997; Ross-Sheriff, 1997), millions of Black immigrants from the Caribbean and the continent of Africa have settled in the United States. For instance, by the turn of the last century, "1.4 million Blacks (3.9%) had at least 1 foreign-born parent" (Lucas, Barr-Anderson, & Kington, 2003, p. 1740). Although non-native Blacks share the same marginal social status of native-born Blacks, non-native Blacks possess higher levels of human capital (i.e., education; Djamba, 1999) and report better overall health than native-born Blacks (Lucas et al., 2003). However, non-native Black men are less likely to be insured than either native-born Black or White men (Lucas et al., 2003). These contrary findings suggest that the current population of non-native Blacks represents a changing landscape of aging among U.S. Black residents.

SOCIAL, DEMOGRAPHIC, AND ECONOMIC CHARACTERISTICS

The social, demographic and economic characteristics of elderly Black U.S. residents add another dimension of heterogeneity. Data for characteristics, including age, gender, marital status, living arrangements, and poverty, represent the general Black population because data are unavailable by origin of Black elderly people. The number of persons reaching 85 years of age and older is a distinguishing feature of the general U.S. elderly population, reflecting increased heterogeneity in population aging (Siegel, 1994). The number of Blacks 85 years old or more increased from 67,000 in 1960 to 322,000 in 2000, with an expected increase in this number to 2.1 million by 2050 (Angel & Hogan, 2004).

The gender composition of the elderly population is a consequence of differences in the survival rates of men and women across the life course (Angel & Hogan, 2004). As people age across the life span, the sex ratio (i.e., the number of males per 100 females) declines with increasing age. For Blacks ages 65–74 years old in 2000, the sex ratio was 70 males per 100 females (Angel & Hogan). Further, the number of males to females continues to decline with increasing

age in the elderly population. For instance, in 1995 the sex ratio for elderly Blacks was approximately 40 males per 100 females (Siegel, 1994). The two main reasons for the existence of more females than males in the elderly Black population are a higher male than female mortality rate over the life course and a lower number of male births to female births (Siegel, 1994). Regardless of the reasons for a gender imbalance in old age, it has consequences for marital status, living arrangements, and poverty among Blacks in old age.

Regarding marital status and living arrangements among elderly Blacks, a substantially greater number of females than males live outside a married household. Using data from the 2000 U.S. Census, Angel and Hogan (2004) report that 24.3% of Black women, 42.4% of White women, 41.3% of Asian women, and 36.9% of Hispanic women lived in married households. Similarly, among elderly men, Black men living in married households (53.5%) lagged behind White men (74.3%), Asian and Pacific Islander men (72.0%), and Hispanic men (66.8%). Paralleling patterns of living arrangements in the general older adult population, more older Black women than Black men lived alone. Still, substantially greater numbers of elderly Black men (25.9%) than elderly White men (17.0%) and elderly men of color (6.6% Asian and Pacific Islander; 14.0% Hispanic) lived alone (Angel & Hogan, 2004).

These demographic and social characteristics have consequences for the economic circumstances of Black elderly. According to Angel and Hogan (2004), older persons of color experience more severe poverty (i.e., being 100% below the poverty threshold) than older Whites. A greater percentage of women living alone (41.5%) are impoverished than either unmarried males (29.3%) or female heads of households living with other individuals (23.6%). The lowest percentage of impoverished persons in the older Black population is married couples (9.1% husbands; 9.3% wives; Angel & Hogan, 2004). These economic data reflect the relationship between demographic and social patterns such as age, gender, marital status, and living arrangements of elderly Blacks. They direct social workers to the relationship between various factors that affect the well-being of Blacks in later years of life.

HEALTH ISSUES

Physical Health

Health is a complex phenomenon that is more than a physical status; it also includes mental and social well-being (Johnson & Misra, 2001). A discussion of the physical and mental health of older Blacks is based on data for the general Black population because we have not found health data by ethnic origin for older Black adults. One can gain an understanding of the physical health status of older Blacks through an examination of such factors as life expectancy, mortality, and chronic health conditions.

Life Expectancy Despite the fact that people of all races and genders are living longer and healthier lives, longevity is not the same among all people. There is great variability in longevity by gender and by race: Women outlive men and Whites outlive Blacks (National Center for Health Statistics, cited in Rooks & Whitfield, 2004; Siegel, 1994). With regard to Black Americans, a Black female born in 1950 had a life expectancy of 62.9 years compared with her Black male counterpart, who had a life expectancy of 59.1 years, reflecting a gap of almost 4 years. A Black female born in 1999 could expect to live to almost 74.7 years of age, compared with 67.8 years for her Black male counterpart, reflecting a gap of 6.5 years. These figures show improvement in life expectancy of both Black females and males. Interestingly, the gender gap is wider in 1999 than in 1950, with Black males having a substantially lower life expectancy than Black females. A Black female born in 1950 could expect her White counterpart to live 9.3 years longer, reflecting a life expectancy of 72.2 years. A Black male born in 1950 could expect his White counterpart to live 7.4 years longer. By 1999, black females had a life expectancy of 74.7 years, compared with 79.9 years for White females. Black males had a life expectancy of 67.8 years, compared with 74.6 years for White females (Angel & Hogan, 2004). An exception to this pattern of longevity is the "Black-White mortality crossover" around ages 75–85 years, reflecting a reversal of the pattern of mortality pattern between races. After age 75, older Blacks have a chance of higher life expectancy than Whites. Explanations of the Black-White mortality crossover range from reporting inaccuracies of age to adaptation and selection processes that predispose heartier Blacks to longer lives (see Rooks & Whitfield, 2004, for explanations and debates on the Black-White mortality crossover).

Chronic Disease, Morbidity and Mortality The leading chronic diseases for Black elderly persons are hypertension, heart disease, stroke, and end-stage renal disease (Mouton, 1997; National Academy on an Aging Society, 2000c). More older Blacks contract and die from heart disease and stroke, particularly those in the age range of 65 to 84, than older Whites (Rooks & Whitfield, 2004). The risk of having heart disease and of dying from it for older Blacks must be considered along with other widespread risk factors of heart disease and stroke, such as hypertension, obesity, and high cholesterol—factors known to be influenced by social (e.g., socioeconomic status) and individual (e.g., sedentary lifestyle) factors (Federal Interagency Forum on Aging-Related Statistics, 2004; Rooks & Whitfield, 2004). Differences in heart disease rates between Blacks and Whites tend to reverse for Blacks ages 84 and over. Further, prostate cancer strikes disproportionate numbers of older African American men, and more of them die from prostate cancer than men of any other racial/ethnic group (see review by Pierce, Chadiha, Vargas, & Mosley, 2003).

Other Risk Factors and Access Issues Personal or individual factors such as lack of exercise, overeating, smoking, and alcohol consumption are part of the equation of risk factors that affect the health of older persons. Curtailing or eliminating these risks may mean that older Blacks reduce the risk of developing chronic conditions and mortality from disease complications and also enhance the quality of their lives. Further, people of low socioeconomic status (SES) are more vulnerable to risk of chronic conditions (National Academy on an Aging Society, 1999). Older Blacks generally have disproportionately low incomes, thus suggesting an association between health and SES among older Blacks (Sotomayor, 1997). Drawing on the work of House and colleagues, Williams and Wilson (2001) note a curvilinear relationship between SES and health that is "small in early adulthood, increases markedly in middle and early old age, and decreases in late old age" (p. 165). One explanation offered by House and colleagues (cited by Williams & Wilson, 2001) for a decreasing relationship between SES and health in late old age is entitlement programs that have helped ameliorate social circumstances and lower adverse affects of low SES on health. Although Williams and Wilson acknowledge this as a plausible explanation, they also contend that racial disparities in access and quality of medical care for older Blacks play a critical role in the continuing racial disparity in health. Research corroborates these contentions by documenting racial disparities in the quality of health care received by Medicare enrollees, as well as other elderly persons (Escarce, Epstein, Colby, & Schwartz, 1993; Schneider, Zaslavsky, & Epstein, 2002). Further, social explanations of racial disparities appear to outweigh genetic and biological explanations (LaVeist, 2004; Williams, 2004; Williams & Wilson, 2001).

Functional Status Concomitant with an aging U.S. population, a substantial number of elderly persons experience disability associated with a decline in functioning, including limitations in activities of daily living (ADLs; e.g., bathing and grooming) and instrumental activities of daily living (IADLs; e.g., traveling to the doctor and preparing meals). Besides these limitations, many elderly persons also experience a decline in social functioning. The Forum Report (Federal Interagency Forum on Aging-Related Statistics, 2004) on age-related statistics indicates a decline in disability rates for both males and females: From 27% of females and 20% of males in 1982 to 25% and 16%, respectively, in 1994. This report also notes Black-White differences in functional disability involving physical tasks. For instance, more older Blacks than older Whites are unable to perform physical activities such as walking up steps, lifting and carrying a heavy load, reaching overhead, and so on. Substantial numbers of older Blacks are also disproportionately affected by arthritis, a condition that does not lead to death but makes it challenging for older adults to lead active and productive lives (National Academy on an Aging Society, 2000a).

Cognitive Status With increasing longevity of older Blacks, more knowledge is accumulating on their experience with dementia. Although a high prevalence of hypertension and stroke among older Blacks would imply that they are susceptible to vascular dementia associated with these health conditions, many older Blacks with increased longevity now risk developing dementia of the Alzheimer's type, a degenerative disease of the brain (Alzheimer's Association of America, 2001). Whether or not African Americans have a greater likelihood than Whites of having Alzheimer's disease is equivocal. For instance, a recent prospective study of 1,079 African Americans, White, and Hispanic Medicare recipients in New York documented that the likelihood of African Americans and Hispanics developing Alzheimer's disease by age 90 years in the absence of an apolipoprotein allele increased significantly over the likelihood of Whites developing

the disease by a similar age (Tang et al., 1998). Further, these results were found independently of effects of sociodemographic variables such as age, education, income, marital status, and employment status. However, in the absence of this allele, all three groups had similar likelihood of developing Alzheimer's disease by age 90 years. These findings contrast with information reported by the National Academy on an Aging Society (2000b) that indicate that a disproportionate number of Whites (85%) relative to Blacks (9%) and persons of other races or ethnicities (6%) are affected by Alzheimer's disease. With the population aging among older Blacks in the 75–85 year old group and without a cure for this disease, we are likely to witness a substantial rise in Alzheimer's disease in the Black elderly population. The economic and psychosocial cost of the disease to elders and their caregivers can be staggering, requiring as much support as professionals can offer families who care for elders with Alzheimer's disease.

Besides the aforementioned objective health status evidence in the older Black population, self-rated health status is an essential piece in their health equation. Self-rated health has not been without criticism and controversy (see the review by Gibson, 1991). Yet researchers, policy makers, and practitioners recognize that older people's perceptions of their physical health are crucial to understanding their health and overall well-being. Data in a recent report indicate that positive self-rated health reports declined across age groups (i.e., 65–74; 75–84; 85 or older) for both Black and White elderly, as well as for males and females ("Older Americans 2000," 2000). However, older Black males and females of any age group were less likely to rate their health status as good than were Whites. The gradient of self-rated health for Blacks was more similar to that of Hispanics than to that of Whites. Black females and males reported nearly comparable levels of health status across age groups.

In sum, data on the life expectancy, mortality, chronic conditions, and physical and cognitive disabilities of older Blacks, principally for native Blacks, indicate both improvements and lack of improvements when Blacks are compared with older Whites of similar age. Comparative data for native-born older Blacks and non-native-born older Blacks for these health indicators are seriously lacking; however, studies on younger cohorts of native-born and non-native-born Blacks indicate within-race difference on physical health. For example, Lucas et al. (2003) report, after adjusting for age and controlling for SES, that non-native-born Black men were less likely to report fair or poor health and less likely to report a functional limitation than native-born Black men. Further, the health status of non-native-born Black men was more similar to or better than the health status of native-born White men. Non-native-born Black men were less likely to report risky health behaviors such as smoking. The likelihood of non-native-born Black men smoking, however, increased with longer stay in the United States. Native-born men were more likely to report health insurance coverage than non-native-born men. Findings from the study by Lucas et al. (2003) direct the attention of social work practitioners to the growing ethnic heterogeneity and potential health disparity within the black elderly population.

Mental Health

The mental health status of the older Black population is also an essential piece of the fabric of their health and overall life quality. Poussaint (1990) has proposed that the mental health of Blacks is less about mental disorders and more about their life situation in old age, such as their relatively poor physical health, poor functioning, and low socioeconomic status due largely to a lifetime of cumulative social and economic disadvantage.

A recent Report of the Surgeon General (U.S. Department of Health and Human Services [USDHHS], 2001) notes that most older people experience "good" mental health, with only about one in five adults ages 55 years old or older likely to experience mental disorders. Ranked by order of prevalence, anxiety disorders (e.g., phobias and obsessive-compulsive disorder) and mood disorders such as depression are the most common mental health conditions, whereas schizophrenia, as well as personality disorders, are least common in the elderly population 65 years or older. The effects of these common disorders on the overall health and function of older Blacks remains unclear. Baker (1994) notes that little is known about the prevalence rates of mental disorders in the older adult Black elderly population because of their underrepresentation in epidemiological studies.

Poor health, low socioeconomic status, social isolation, minority status, being unmarried, being female, and having low education are linked to depressive symptoms among elderly Blacks (Baker, 1994; Baker, Okwumabua, Philipose, & Wong, 1996; National Academy on an Aging Society, 2000d). However, research is mixed on the well-established

link between gender (i.e., being female) and depressive symptoms in old age (Baker et al., 1996; Brown, Milburn, & Gary, 1992). Additionally, Baker (1994) also notes that older Black people are at risk of being diagnosed with mental disorders related to taking prescribed medications for their physical health and from environmental stress such as living in unsafe neighborhoods. A high prevalence of chronic conditions such as diabetes, particularly among older Black women, and functional limitations in chronic illness in older Blacks may generally predispose individuals to depressive symptoms and depressive illness (National Academy on an Aging Society, 2000d). Older persons with impaired cognitive ability may be more susceptible to depression, dysphoria, and comorbid conditions (Baker, 1996).

In conclusion, it is reasonable to assume that older Black Americans, like older adults generally, enjoy relatively good mental health. Still, literature documents depressive symptoms as an important mental health issue for older Black Americans. Contributing factors to depressive symptoms among Black elderly include a high prevalence of specific chronic health conditions, comorbid and co-occurring in old age. They also include side effects of consuming multiple medications, psychosocial stressors (isolation and loss due to death of significant others), and environmental stressors. A caveat about the literature on mental disorders among elderly Blacks is the underreporting and misdiagnosis of mental conditions in the elderly population, as indicated in the 2001 Report of the Surgeon General on mental health of older persons (U.S. Department of Health and Human Services, 2001).

INFORMAL SOURCES OF SUPPORT— FAMILY, CHURCH, AND RELIGION

A discussion of the social, economic, physical, and mental health issues of older Black Americans has highlighted the many challenges they face in late life. To gain fuller understanding of the situation of older Blacks, one also needs to consider their sources of informal support from family, church, and religion.

Family members are an invaluable source of informal support to elderly Blacks. For instance, older Blacks are embedded in an informal network of multiple sources of support flowing from family, church, and friends (Taylor & Chatters, 1986). Family members, typically women, rank first in the line of unpaid helpers (Chatters, Taylor, & Jackson, 1986; Dilworth-Anderson, Williams, & Cooper, 1999), providing assistance to frail and severely ill Black elderly persons (Chadiha, Proctor, Morrow-Howell, Darkwa, & Dore, 1995; Stommel, Given, & Given, 1998).

Support from family members engages multiple caregivers—persons having most of the care responsibility for elderly persons and also persons having less care responsibility for elderly persons (Dilworth-Anderson et al., 1999). Further, Black family caregivers report high rewards and low burden in caring for their elderly relatives (Knight, Silverstein, McCallum, & Fox, 2000; Picot, 1995; Picot, Debanne, Namazi, & Wykle, 1997). However, a concern involving family caregiving is that it can be a demanding role contributing to negative well-being of Black caregivers—especially women (see Chadiha, Adams, Biegel, Auslander, & Gutiérrez, 2004). Many older Blacks, particularly grandmothers, are providing care to grandchildren (Fuller-Thomson, 2000; Minkler & Fuller-Thomson, 2000; Whitley, Kelley, & Sipe, 2001). Although there is evidence that custodial grandparenting may have negative outcomes for older Black women's physical health (Whitley et al., 2001), research on the consequences of custodial care to grandchildren is in its infancy stage, and it is inconclusive what such consequences are for older Black intergenerational caregivers.

Research shows that older persons who engage in religious activities report better physical and mental health than elderly people not engaged in religious activities (Levin, 1996). Historically, church and religion have been a source of inspiration and assistance to Blacks generally, providing invaluable resources to cope with problems of secular life, such as racial and economic discrimination. Not only does the church provide a base for the informal support networks among older Blacks, but it is also the source of much informal support from church members, along with family members and friends (Taylor, Chatters, & Levin, 2004). The importance of religion in the lives of older Blacks does not start in old age. Rather, it is a critical source of social support to Blacks over the life course (Williams & Wilson, 2001). Williams and Wilson argue that "religion may be especially salient in the lives of minority elderly," providing them with spiritual, social, and oftentimes financial resources that are not accessible through the formal service sector.

Researchers acknowledge that religious coping, like other informal sources of support, has its down side, such as promoting avoidance and acceptance of a negative condition rather than facilitating a proactive or problem-solving approach (Taylor et al.,

2004). Further, a heavier reliance on informal systems of social support such as the family and the church may place older Blacks at risk of poor health outcomes (Williams & Dilworth-Anderson, 2002), particularly if members of those systems lack the prerequisite health care skills and training needed to meet the health needs of impaired elderly Blacks. Acknowledging these contradictions does not negate the overwhelming evidence that the church and religion are strong, positive, and natural helping systems that have a significant impact on the lives of elderly Blacks.

CULTURAL DIVERSITY AND SOCIAL WORK PRACTICE WITH BLACK ELDERLY

A working definition of culture is that it includes language, values, religion, societal norms, and a person's worldview (Landrine & Klonoff, 1992). The growth and heterogeneity of the Black population due to the increase of immigration from various countries has augmented cultural diversity within the older Black population. Yee (2002) defines diversity as recognizing differences, including ones that are uncomfortable for us, and "recognizing barriers that prevent access to our social systems and building a broader community infrastructure" (p. 6). Irrespective of origin, older Blacks living in the United States share racial oppression and may face similar barriers to accessing services due to continuing societal biases directed at persons of African descent. Still, older native-born Blacks and non-native-born Blacks differ in language, nationality, and religious orientation—differences that direct attention of social work professionals to the ethnic and cultural diversity within older Black adults. Such differences suggest that social work professionals must consider the principles of diversity and cultural competence that have been directed toward older people with origins in Europe, Asia, South America, and Mexico. For instance, Capitman (2002) notes that the challenge for social work professionals is how to deliver culturally appropriate (i.e., competent) services to old people in one setting so that social work professionals do not offend old people in another setting. Unfortunately, neither the field of aging nor social work has developed an accurate measure of cultural competency that would allow social work professionals to assess it or evaluate the effectiveness of culturally competent social work practice (Geron, 2002).

Regarding issues of social and economic disadvantage, as well as issues of racial disparity, in access to mental and physical health care, prior works suggest directions for professionals to pursue when working with older Black adults. Ford and Hatchett (2001), for instance, in a treatise on social work practice with older Black adults, note three levels of intervention that are applicable to older Blacks. Primary intervention is necessary to promote the social, economic, and health-related well-being of older Blacks over the life course. A life-course perspective recognizes linkages between the present and past lives of people; it also recognizes that individual life histories are shaped and intertwined with social histories, such as passage of laws and social changes (Hatch, 2001). Viewed through the lens of a life-course perspective, it suggests that efforts on behalf of social workers to prevent social and economic disadvantages, as well as health inequalities, in the older Black population must be dealt with over the life course prior to old age. Underscoring this point are the words of Wallace, Enriquez-Haass, and Markides (1998): "The health and economic problems of older minorities are rooted in historic practices of discrimination" (p. 338). Therefore, in the absence of social work professionals' ability to correct the mistakes of the past, a special concern of contemporary social work practice with older adults will be to ensure that policy initiatives such as Medicare and Social Security that greatly benefit older Black adults are kept intact (Wallace et al., 1998). Social work practitioners will further benefit from considering a political economy of health care explanation for reducing racial disparities in health. Wallace (1990) and Williams (2004), for instance, note the role of structural factors involving residential segregation, racial discrimination, and a medical care system that values profit over patient care as contributing factors to Black-White health disparities.

A secondary level of intervention in social work practice with older Black adults would address social, economic, and health problems and issues (Ford & Hatchett, 2001). Here, an example from empirical literature is applicable. Many older Black Americans with chronic physical conditions and declining mental health may fail to seek care, even when services may be available (USDHHS, 2001). Social workers' knowledge of barriers to seeking help (e.g., stigma, denial, access barriers, financial barriers, and service fragmentation and gaps in health care) is an essential first step of the secondary level of intervention. Another essential practice step to take with older Black Americans is to assist them in managing their own health conditions through partnering with elders and their families to develop and implement suitable programs.

A third level of interventions focuses on mitigating the effects of chronic disease and disabling functioning on older Black adults and their family members (Ford & Hatchett, 2001). As others have suggested, the implementation of case management procedures such as linking older Black adults to community resources, matching their needs with resources, and advocating for them are appropriate for working with older adults at all levels (Ford & Hatchett, 2001; Yagoda, 2004). Such services may be useful at the tertiary level of intervention, particularly when the social, economic, and health care needs of older Blacks may be more challenging for the informal network to meet (Ford & Hatchett, 2001). Recognizing that older Blacks are not a monolithic group and taking this into consideration are crucial steps in the case management approach. Older Blacks experience within-race heterogeneity due to nativity status, gender, residential context, and age. When it comes to serving older Blacks, Dancy and Ralston (2002) report barriers to accessing health care in the older adult Black population due to rural residence and differences in attitudes between women and men, as well as between relatively old versus relatively young-old persons.

Evidence of social support from family, church, and religion for older Blacks directs attention of social work professionals to natural support systems that older Blacks trust and rely on for care. On the other hand, knowing the risks of long-term caregiving for Black women caregivers and the challenges they experience with social inequalities, as well as racial disparities in health and income, alerts social workers to these caregivers' vulnerability to powerlessness and the applicability of an empowerment approach to practice with them (Chadiha et al., 2004).

In conclusion, older Black Americans are living longer and healthier lives than ever. Unprecedented numbers of non-native Black elderly have come and will become of age in their adopted homeland, thus contributing to growing ethnic diversity within an aging Black population and the service delivery system that serves them. This ethnic and age diversity of the older Black population is expected to present the field of gerontological social work and workers with both opportunity and challenge to deliver services to an unprecedented number of elderly Blacks. Thus, as Ford and Hatchett (2001) have noted for the general population of older Black Americans: "Only by combining practice and research can gerontological social workers begin to address the multi-faceted needs of older [African Americans and other Black] adults" (p. 152).

Acknowledgments: We thank Jane Rafferty and Mimi Lee for editorial assistance with this chapter.

REFERENCES

Allen, J. A. (1997). African Americans: Caribbean. In R. L. Edwards et al. (Eds.), *Encyclopedia of social work* (19th ed., pp. 121–129). Washington, DC: National Association of Social Workers Press.

Alzheimer's Association of America. (2001). *A race against time: 2001 National Public Policy Program to conquer Alzheimer's disease.* Washington, DC: Author.

Angel, J. L., & Hogan, D. P. (2004). Population aging and diversity in a new era. In K. Whitfield (Ed.), *Closing the gap: Improving the health of minority elders in the new millennium* (pp. 1–12). Washington, DC: Gerontological Society of America.

Baker, F. M. (1994). Psychiatric treatment of older African Americans. *Hospital and Community Psychiatry, 45,* 32–37.

Baker, F. M. (1996). An overview of depression in the elderly: A U.S. perspective. *Journal of the National Medical Association, 88,* 178–184.

Baker, F. M., Okwumabua, J., Philipose, V., & Wong, S. (1996). Screening African-American elderly for the presence of depressive symptoms: A preliminary investigation. *Journal of Geriatric Psychiatry Neurology, 9,* 127–132.

Brown, D. R., Milburn, N. G., & Gary, L. E. (1992). Symptoms of depression among older African-Americans: An analysis of gender differences. *Journal of Gerontology, 32,* 789.

Capitman, J. (2002). Defining diversity: A primer and a review. *Generations, 26,* 8–14.

Chadiha, L., Proctor, E. K., Morrow-Howell, N., Darkwa, O., & Dore, P. (1995). Post-hospital home care for African-American and White elderly. *Gerontologist, 35,* 233–239.

Chadiha, L. A., Adams, P., Biegel, D. E., Auslander, W., & Gutierrez, L. (2004). Empowering urban African American women caregivers: A literature synthesis and practice strategies. *Social Work, 49*(1), 97–108.

Chatters, L. M., Raylor, R. J., & Jackson, J. S. (1986). Aged blacks' choice for an informal helper network. *Journal of Gerontology, 41*(1), 94–100.

Dancy, J., & Ralston, P. A. (2002). Health promotion and Black elders: Subgroups of greatest need. *Research on Aging, 24,* 218–242.

Dilworth-Anderson, P., Williams, S., & Cooper, T. (1999). Family caregiving to elderly African Americans: Caregiver types and structures. *Journal of Gerontology: 54B,* S237–S241.

Djamba, Y. K. (1999). African immigrants in the United States: A socio-demographic profile in comparison to native Blacks. *Journal of Asian and African Studies, 34,* 1–4.

Escarce, J. J., Epstein, K. R., Colby, D. C., & Schwartz, J. S. (1993). Racial differences in the elderly's use of medical procedures and diagnostic tests. *American Journal of Public Health, 83,* 948–954.

Federal Interagency Forum on Aging-Related Statistics. (2004, November). *Older Americans 2004: Key indicators of well-being.* Washington, DC: Government Printing Office.

Ford, M. E., & Hatchett, B. (2001). Gerontological social work with older African American adults. *Journal of Gerontological Social Work, 36,* 141–155.

Fuller-Thomson, E. (2000). African-American grandparents raising grandchildren: A national profile of demographic and health characteristics. *Health and Social Work, 25,* 109–118.

Geron, S. M. (2002). Cultural competency: How is it measured? Does it make a difference? *Generations, 26,* 39–45.

Gibson, R. C. (1991). Race and the self-reported health of elderly persons. *Journal of Gerontology, 46,* S235–S242.

Hatch, L. R. (2000). *Beyond gender differences: Adaptation to aging in life course perspective.* Amityville, NY: Baywood.

Johnson, C. D., & Misra, D. (2001). Mental health. In D. Misra (Ed.), *The women's health data book* (3rd ed., pp. 104–115). Menlo Park, CA: Jacobs Institute of Women's Health and the Henry J. Kaiser Family Foundation.

Knight, B. G., Silverstein, M., McCallum, T. J., & Fox, L. S. (2000). A psychological stress and coping model for mental health among African American caregivers in Southern California. *Journal of Gerontology: 55B,* 142–150.

Landrine, H., & Klonoff, E. A. (1992). Culture and health-related schemas: A review and proposal for interdisciplinary integration. *Health Psychology, 11*(4), 267–276.

LaVeist, T. A. (2004). Conceptualizing racial and ethnic disparities in access, utilization, and quality of care. In K. E. Whitfield (Ed.). *Closing the gap: Improving the health of minority elders in the new millennium* (pp. 87–93). Washington, DC: The Gerontological Society of America.

Lucas, J. W., Barr-Anderson, D. J., & Kington, R. S. (2003). Health status, health insurance, and health care utilization patterns of immigrant Black men. *American Journal of Public Health, 93*, 1740–1747.

Minkler, N., & Fuller-Thomson, E. (2000). Second time around parenting: Factors predictive of grandparents becoming caregivers for their grandchildren. *International Journal of Aging and Human Development, 50*(3), 185–200.

Mouton, C. P. (1997). Special health considerations in African-American elders. *American Family physician, 55*(4), 1243–1253.

National Academy on an Aging Society. (1999). *Chronic conditions: A challenge for the 21st century.* Washington, DC: Author.

National Academy on an Aging Society. (2000a). *Arthritis: A leading cause of disability in the United States.* Washington, DC: Author.

National Academy on an Aging Society. (2000b). *At risk: Developing chronic conditions later in life.* Washington, DC: Author.

National Academy on an Aging Society. (2000c). *Alzheimer's disease and dementia: A growing challenge.* Washington, DC: Author.

National Academy on an Aging Society. (2000d). *Depression: A treatable disease.* Washington, DC: Author.

Picot, S. (1995). Rewards, costs, and coping of African-American caregivers. *Nursing Research, 44*, 147–152.

Picot, S. J., Debanne, S. M., Namazi, K. H., & Wykle, M. L. (1997). Religiosity and perceived rewards of black and white caregivers. *Gerontologist, 37*, 89–101.

Pierce, R., Chadiha, L. A., Vargas, A., & Mosley, M. (2003). Prostate cancer and psychosocial concerns in African American men: Literature synthesis and recommendations. *Health and Social Work, 28*, 302–311.

Poussaint, A. F. (1990). The mental health status of black Americans, 1983. In D. S. Ruiz (Ed.), *Handbook of mental health and mental disorders among black Americans* (pp. 17–52). New York: Greenwood Press.

Rooks, R. N., & Whitfield, K. E. (2004). Health disparities among older African Americans: Past, present, and future perspectives. In K. E. Whitfield (Ed.). *Closing the gap: Improving the health of minority elders in the new millennium* (pp. 45–54). Washington, DC: The Gerontological Society of America.

Ross-Sheriff, F. (1997). African Americans: Immigrants. In R. L. Edwards, I. C. Colby, A. Garcia, R. G. McRoy, & L. Videka-Sherman (Eds.), *Encyclopedia of

social work* (19th ed., pp. 130–136). Washington, DC: National Association of Social Workers Press.

Siegel, J. S. (1994). Demographic introduction to racial/Hispanic elderly populations. In T. P. Miles (Ed.), *Full-color aging: Facts, goals, and recommendations for America's diverse elders* (pp. 1–20). Washington, DC: Gerontological Society of America.

Sotomayor, M. (1997). Aging: Racial and ethnic groups. In R. L. Edwards, I. C. Colby, R. G. McRoy, & L. Videka-Sherman (Eds.), *Encyclopedia of social work* (19th ed., pp. 26–36). Washington, DC: National Association of Social Workers Press.

Stommel, M., Given, W. C., & Given, B. A. (1998). Racial differences in the division of labor between primary and secondary caregivers. *Research on Aging, 20*, 199–219.

Tang, M., Stern, Y., Marder, K., Bell, K., Gurland, B., Lantigua, R., Andrews, H., et al. (1998). The APOE-(epsilon 4) allele and the risk of Alzheimer disease among African Americans, Whites, and Hispanics. *Journal of the American Medical Association, 279*, 751–755.

Taylor, R. J., & Chatters, L. M. (1986). Patterns of informal support to elderly Black adults: Family, friends, and church members. *Social Work, 31*, 432–438.

Taylor, R. T., Chatters, L. M., & Levin, J. (2004). *Religion in the lives of African Americans.* Thousand Oaks, CA: Sage.

U.S. Department of Health and Human Services. (2001). Older adults and mental health. In *Mental health: A report of the Surgeon General* (pp. 336–381). Rockville, MD: Author. Retrieved June 25, 2004, from *http://www.surgeongeneral.gov/library/mentalhealth/pdfs/C5.pdf.*

Wallace, S. P. (1990). The political economy of health care for elderly Blacks. *International Journal of Health Services, 20*, 665–680.

Wallace, S. P., Enriquez-Haass, V., & Markides, K. (1998). The consequences of color-blind health policy for older racial and ethnic minorities. *Stanford Law and Policy Review, 9*, 329–346.

Whitley, D. M., Kelley, S. J., & Sipe, T. A. (2001). Grandmothers raising grandchildren: Are they at increased risk of health problems? *Health and Social Work, 26*, 105–114.

Williams, D. R. (2004). Racism and health. In K. E. Whitfield (Ed.), *Closing the gap: Improving the health of minority elders in the new millennium* (pp. 69–80). Washington, DC: The Gerontological Society of America.

Williams, D. R., & Wilson, C. M. (2001). Race, ethnicity, and aging. In R. H. Binstock & L. K. George (Eds.),

Handbook of aging and the social sciences (5th ed., pp. 160–178). San Diego, CA: Academic Press.

Williams, S. W., & Dilworth-Anderson, P. (2002). Systems of social support in families who care for dependent African American elders. *Gerontologist, 42,* 224–226.

Yagoda, L. (2004). *Aging practice update case management with older adults: A social work perspective.* Washington, DC: National Association of Social Workers.

Yee, D. (2002). Introduction: Recognizing diversity, moving toward competence. *Generations, 26,* 5–7

The United States Census 2000 identified at least 24 Asian American groups, excluding Pacific Islanders. It included both nationally and ethnically defined groups: Asian Indian, Bangladeshi, Bhutanese, Burmese, Cambodian, Chinese, Filipino, Hmong, Indo-Chinese, Indonesian, Iwo Jiman, Japanese, Korean, Laotian, Malaysian, Maldivian, Nepalese, Okinawan, Pakistani, Singaporean, Sri Lankan, Taiwanese, Thai, and Vietnamese (U.S. Census Bureau, 2002).

Although the elderly among these Asian American groups may share some common background, values, and issues, considerable diversity prevails between and within the groups, as each individual has brought with him or her a distinct blend of culture, language, and history of the country of origin. Although most of the Asian American elderly came to the United States after the passage of the Immigration and Naturalization Act of 1965, considerable differences still exist among them in their immigration background (e.g., U.S. or foreign born, refugee or recent immigrant), reason for immigration (e.g., family reunification, fleeing from war, economic opportunity, educational opportunity for their children, or political turmoil in the country of origin), age at the time of immigration, and length of residence in the United States. Besides historical diversity, they also differ in religious affiliation (e.g., predominantly Christian Filipino and Korean, Hindu Asian Indian, Muslim Indonesian, and Buddhist Cambodian and Laotian American elders), socioeconomic status, acculturation, English proficiency, and life experience in the United States, all of which affect their well-being.

These variations make it difficult to generalize about relevant issues and their implications for social work practice with the 24 diverse groups of Asian American elders. Nevertheless, this chapter presents central cultural and social issues important to social work practice with Asian American elders and suggests a set of practice guidelines intended to enhance cross-cultural understanding and culturally sensitive social work practice with these populations. It begins with a review of the demographic and socioeconomic characteristics of selected Asian American elderly groups and is followed by discussion of major issues and challenges confronting them. Finally, practice guidelines for communication, assessment, and intervention with Asian American elders are presented.

JONG WON MIN
AILEE MOON

Older Asian Americans

GROWTH AND DIVERSITY OF OLDER ASIAN AMERICANS

For the third decade in a row, the Asian American population grew faster than any other racial group in the United States. The U.S. Census counted 11.9 million Asian Americans in 2000 (10.2 million "Asian alone" plus 1.7 million "Asian in combination with one or more other races"), an increase from 1990 by 48% (using the "Asian alone population") or 72% (using the "alone or in combination population"). These percentages are significantly higher than the 13% increase in the total population during the same period (U.S. Census Bureau, 2002).

The elderly Asian American population grew at a rate even faster than the total Asian American population and the overall elderly population ages 65 and older. As shown in Table 21.1, the U.S. Census 2000 counted 843,543 Asian Americans ages 65 and older (782,994 "Asian alone" plus 60,549 "in combination with other races"), a remarkable increase of 78% (Asian alone) or 92% (combination with other race), compared with a 12% increase in the total elderly population, between 1990 and 2000. Among 10 separate Asian ethnic groups with 1990 (U.S. Census Bureau, 1992) and 2000 (U.S. Census Bureau, 2002) census data, two groups more than doubled their elderly population: Vietnamese (205%) and Asian Indian (170%). As a result, the proportion of the elderly in each of these census-selected Asian American groups has increased from 1990 to 2000, except the Hmong elderly, whose share of the overall Hmong American population fell from 2.8% to 2.6%, reflecting an even faster growth of the nonelderly Hmong population.

Despite this rapid growth in the elderly Asian American population during the past decade, they represented only 2.3% of the 65-and-older age population in 2000, excluding Pacific Islanders. Furthermore, whereas individuals of age 65 or older constituted 12.4% of the total population, Asian American elders accounted for 7.7% of the total "Asian alone" population, or 7.1% of the "combination" population. Table 21.1 shows substantial variation among 16 Asian American subgroups in terms of the representation of older adults in the respective populations, ranging from lows of 1.5% and 2.0% for Malaysian and Bangladeshi Americans, respectively, to highs of 9.8% and 20.4%, respectively, for Chinese and Japanese Americans.

Using the Census 2000 "Asian alone" data, Chinese elderly constituted the largest group, representing almost 30% of all elderly Asian Americans,

followed by Filipino (20.8%), Japanese (20.8%), Korean (8.5%), and Asian Indian (7.9%) Americans. Whereas approximately 78% of the Asian American elderly were foreign born, the foreign-born percentage exceeded 90% for 14 of the 16 subgroups, excepting the Japanese (29.2%) and Chinese (86.7%) American elders. Among the foreign-born elderly, the average length of residence in the United States was 23 years as of 2000, ranging from 12 years for the Bangladeshi and Malaysian to 40 years for the Japanese Americans (Ruggles et al., 2004).

Table 21.2 presents English use/ability, educational attainment, and poverty status of the Asian American elderly. Focusing on the "Asian alone" data in 2000, an average of 18.6% spoke English "only" at home, and almost 60% spoke English "less than very well" or "linguistically isolated," a number almost nine times greater than that of 6.7% of the overall elderly population. The percentage of the Asian American elderly with English-language barriers varied substantially among subgroups: 28.8% for Japanese, 42.8% for Asian Indian, 52.8% for Filipino, 77.1% for Korean, 84.5% for Chinese, and over 90% for Cambodian and Laotian American elders.

A similar bimodal pattern is evident in the level of educational attainment: over three quarters of elders Hmong (93.9%), Cambodian (81.3%), and Laotian Americans (80.8%) had less than a high school education, whereas over 40% of Filipino (44.4%), Malaysian (46.6%), Indonesian (51.8%), Sri Lankan (50.5%), and Taiwanese (56.7%) American elders had some college or more education. As a group, 43.6% of Asian American elders had less than a high school education, 22.4% finished high school, and 34% had some college or more education.

As shown in Table 21.2, 12.3% of the older Asian American population lived in poverty in 1999, slightly higher than the 9.9% of the overall elderly population living in poverty. Among the 16 Asian American elders subgroups, 4 reported their poverty rate lower than the overall average: Filipino (6.3%), Malaysian (7.4%), Japanese (9.7%), and Asian Indian (9.8%). In sharp contrast, four subgroups exceeded a level of 20% of elders living in poverty: Hmong (37.8%), Bangladeshi (36.2%), Cambodian (28.6%), and Laotian (23.7%) American elders.

The diversity and variability in the demographic and socioeconomic characteristics among and within the 16 Asian American elders subgroups examined so far caution against the danger of overgeneralizing about "Asian American" group. Wide variability in these factors suggests diverse needs between groups

TABLE 21.1.   Demographic Characteristics of Asian American Elderly in the U.S., 1990 and 2000[1]

Group	Population Size (65+) 1990	Population Size (65+) 2000	% Increase	% of 65+ per Total Population 1990	% of 65+ per Total Population 2000	Age Subgroup (%) in 2000 65–74	Age Subgroup (%) in 2000 75–84	Age Subgroup (%) in 2000 85+	% of Foreign Born in 2000
U.S. Population	31,241,831	34,978,972	12.0	12.5	12.4	52.9	35.2	11.9	9.6
AA Self-identified	454,458	-	-	6.2	-	-	-	-	-
AA alone[2]	(454,458)	782,994	78.1	-	7.7	62.1	30.4	7.5	78.4
AA combination[3]	(454,458)	843,543	91.8	-	7.1	62.0	30.4	7.6	n/a
Asian Indian	23,004	62,089	169.9	2.8	3.8	70.7	24.2	5.0	96.0
Bangladeshi	n/a	838	n/a	n/a	2.0	73.9	15.6	10.5	100.0
Cambodian	3,724	6,764	81.6	2.5	3.8	64.0	30.3	5.8	96.6
Chinese/Taiwanese	133,977	231,903	73.1	8.1	9.6	60.2	31.4	8.4	n/a
(Chinese)	(n/a)	(225,486)	(n/a)	(n/a)	(9.8)	(59.9)	(31.7)	(8.4)	(86.7)
(Taiwanese)	(n/a)	(6,417)	(n/a)	(n/a)	(5.23)	(70.3)	(23.9)	(5.8)	(98.1)
Filipino	104,206	162,809	56.2	7.4	8.7	61.5	30.3	8.3	91.9
Hmong	2,535	4,395	73.4	2.8	2.6	54.7	36.1	9.2	97.0
Indonesian	n/a	1,378	n/a	n/a	3.7	65.7	28.4	5.9	97.1
Japanese	105,932	162,551	53.4	12.5	20.4	58.0	34.3	7.7	29.2
Korean	35,247	66,254	85.0	4.4	6.2	64.4	28.7	6.8	93.8
Laotian	3,697	5,757	55.7	2.5	3.4	63.3	29.9	6.7	98.1
Malaysian	n/a	163	n/a	n/a	1.5	74.8	21.5	3.7	100.0
Pakistani	n/a	4,717	n/a	n/a	3.0	77.1	19.8	3.1	99.4
Sri Lankan	n/a	1,058	n/a	n/a	5.6	66.2	30.9	2.9	100.0
Thai	1,416	2,755	94.6	1.6	2.5	71.4	24.5	4.1	97.9
Vietnamese	18,084	55,057	204.5	2.9	5.0	68.7	25.1	6.2	97.6
Other Asian	7,901	1,686	−300.7	2.6	6.3	66.3	30.6	3.1	82.6

Source: U.S. Bureau of Census, 1992, 2000; Compiled from PCT3 (Sex by Age), Summary File 4 (SF-4), Census 2000. Since information on foreign-born population for Asian subgroups aged 65 years and older was not available in Summary File 4, 5% iPUMS Census data (*http://www.ipums.org*) was used to obtain percent of foreign-born for Asian subgroups. Figures are based on SF-4 File and slightly different from those based on Summary File 1 (100% data), because SF-4 estimates are based on sampling. For example, SF-1 figure for the U.S. population of 65+ in 2000 is 34,991,753, Asian American alone 800,994, and Asian American combination 861,725. For detailed information, please refer to Technical Documentation at *http://www.census.gov/Press-Release/www/2003/SF4.html*.

Notes:

1. Census 2000 added a separate "Other Asian" response category with a write-in area for respondents to indicate specific Asian groups not included on the census questionnaire. Data on some Asian groups not included, as separate response categories in the earlier census questionnaires became available in 2000 census data. This, to large extent, explains the 300% decrease in the number for the "Other Asian" category in Table 21.1. It is important to note that unlike previous censuses, which obtained individuals' race information based on self-identification, the 2000 census collected race information using two broad categories, one race or more than one race ("Asian American alone" or "Asian American combination" in Tables 21.1 and 21.2), allowing individuals to indicate combination of races (e.g., Asian and White and American Indian). Because of these changes, the 2000 census data on race/ethnicity are not directly comparable with data from the 1990 census. Therefore, changes in the two censuses' data must be interpreted with caution.

2. Figures for each subgroup of Asian American elderly presented are based on Asian alone, excluding those reporting two or more races (combination).

3. AA subgroup's figures may not add up to a total number of AA alone, since info on one group, "Asian or Asiatic in general term" is not available.

TABLE 21.2. Linguistic Abilities and Socioeconomic Characteristics of Asian American Elderly in the U.S., 2000

Elderly Group (65+)	Language Spoken at Home (%)		Educational Attainment (%)				Poverty Status in 1999[a] (%)
	English Only	English Less Than "Very Well"	Less Than HS	HS Graduate	Some College, Bachelor's Degree	Graduate/ Professional Degree	
U.S. Population	87.4	6.7	34.5	32.0	27.1	6.4	9.9
AA alone	18.6	59.6	43.6	22.4	26.1	7.9	12.3
AA combination	20.5	57.7	43.5	22.5	26.0	8.0	12.5
Asian Indian	14.5	42.8	45.9	14.1	21.4	18.6	9.8
Bangladeshi	0.0	82.9	58.7	18.0	14.0	9.3	36.2
Cambodian	5.8	91.8	81.3	9.3	8.2	1.2	28.6
Chinese	11.8	84.5	50.6	16.5	24.9	8.0	19.4
Filipino	9.5	52.8	39.7	18.0	34.6	7.8	6.3
Hmong	7.9	87.6	93.9	3.0	1.8	1.2	37.8
Indonesian	7.9	57.7	21.3	27.0	40.1	11.7	12.9
Japanese	48.4	28.8	24.1	42.4	28.1	5.4	9.7
Korean	11.0	77.1	45.0	22.9	24.3	7.8	14.8
Laotian	7.5	92.7	80.8	11.8	6.5	0.8	23.7
Malaysian	28.8	76.8	30.7	22.7	29.4	17.2	7.4
Pakistani	4.4	61.5	46.3	14.9	24.7	14.1	15.0
Taiwanese	2.5	86.5	31.4	21.9	30.2	16.5	15.7
Sri Lankan	25.1	32.4	29.2	19.3	33.7	17.8	11.6
Thai	10.8	80.3	53.4	16.4	18.2	12.0	13.2
Vietnamese	5.1	86.8	67.6	15.2	14.0	3.1	16.0
Other Asian	27.0	64.4	44.7	20.3	26.0	9.0	9.4

Source: U.S. Bureau of Census, 2000; Information on racial groups presented is based on racial group alone. This does not include "combination."

Compiled from PCT38 (Age by Language Spoken at Home by Ability to Speak English for the Population 5 years and over), Summary File 4, Census 2000.

Compiled from PCT65 (Sex by Educational Attainment for the Population 18 years and Over), Summary File 4 (SF4) Sample Data, Census 2000.

Compiled from PCT142 (Poverty Status in 1999 by Sex by Age) for Population for whom poverty status is determined, Summary File 4 (SF4) Sample Data, Census 2000.

[a]Poverty Status in 1999: Whites (9.1%) and Black (24.9%)

and between individuals. It also suggests that many factors may affect provision of social services to Asian American elders and their families, including history of the country of origin, immigration background, socioeconomic status, language, cultural values and norms governing family roles and relations, health, and religious beliefs. Given the rapid increase of older people in these Asian American groups and in the population in general, social work practitioners must be prepared to assess a wide range of background factors and needs among older Asian American groups.

PHYSICAL HEATH STATUS AND ISSUES

Asian Americans are generally portrayed as a healthy minority, even healthier than White Americans (Tanjasiri, Wallace, & Shibata, 1995). A few studies conducted in the 1980s and the early 1990s documented that older Asian American groups tend to be healthier than other ethnic groups in terms of perceived health status, health-promoting behaviors, and exposure to health risk factors (Chen, 1993; Lubben, Weiler, & Chi, 1989). A study of California's Medicaid recipients found that low-income immigrant elderly Asians engaged in healthier habits related to physical health than did low-income non-Asian elderly. For example, Asian elders tend to avoid detrimental health habits such as smoking and drinking (Lubben et al., 1989). Another study shows that the prevalence of some cardiovascular risk factors is lower in several Asian American elderly groups compared with Whites (Chen, 1993). Additionally, some Asian American groups, particularly Chinese and Japanese, are known to have longer life expectancies than White Americans.

However, the notion that Asian American elders enjoy better heath than other elderly populations is largely based on lower health service utilization rates among elderly Asian Americans, along with some national health statistics that portray slightly lower rates of coronary heart disease and cancer-related deaths among selected groups of Asian American elders than in the population at large (Takata, Ford, & Lloyd, 1998; Zane, Takeuchi, & Young, 1994). The lower incidence of major diseases documented by a limited number of studies and longer life expectancies among some older Asian American groups have been generalized to all Asian American elderly populations regardless of the differences that exist between and within immigrant elderly Asian groups (Takata et al., 1998).

A reliable estimate of disease prevalence is hard to establish because of limited national-level health data for Asian American elders (LaVeist, 1995). Published findings from various sources (Kagawa-Singer, Hikoyeda, & Tanjasiri, 1997; Lum, 1995; Douglas & Fujimoto, 1995) indicate that, although they experienced a lower mortality rate than Whites, Asian Americans experienced significantly higher levels of chronic conditions than their White counterparts: diabetes among Japanese Americans (Lum, 1995), cardiovascular disease among elderly Korean Americans (Kim, Juon, Hill, Post, & Kim, 2001), and hypertension among elderly Chinese and Filipino immigrants (Kagawa-Singer et al., 1997). A study conducted in Los Angeles using a probability sampling method found that elderly Korean immigrants, compared with non-Hispanic Whites, perceived their health to be poorer and reported higher rates of hypertension, arthritis, kidney disease, and functional limitation (Villa, Wallace, Moon, & Lubben, 1997).

Identifying and reducing health disparities among racial groups in the United States has been one of many national agendas, as indicated in *Healthy People 2000 and 2010* (U.S. Department of Health and Human Services, 1995; 2000). Although many practice and policy efforts have been made to address such disparities, inequality still persists in health status and access to health care among racial/ethnic groups in the United States (U.S. Department of Health and Human Services, 2003). According to the *National Healthcare Disparities Report* (U.S. Department of Health and Human Services, 2003), Asian Pacific Islanders are more likely to be subject to physical restraints in nursing homes than are non-Hispanic Whites, and more Asian elders (55%) than White elders (47%) have difficulty in understanding health care information provided by their physicians.

Human health, as a complex system, is affected by multidimensional factors, including personal, sociopolitical, environmental, and cultural components, throughout life (Pender, 1996). Culture, in particular, influences people's perceptions of health and disease, as well as their health-care-seeking behavior. Many ethnic-cultural minority groups in the United States view health as a product of continuity and balance in life or a long-term and continuous manifestation of changing relationships in the family, in the community, and in nature (Emami, Benner, Lipson, & Ekman, 2000; Ell & Castaneda, 1998). Although it is difficult to generalize the multiplicity and varying degrees of health beliefs between and even within older Asian American populations, their traditional health beliefs include the Yin-Yang equilibrium or balance (Yee & Weaver, 1994) and a fatalistic worldview of the cause of health and illness (Kitano, Shibusawa & Kitano, 1997) that may contribute to suppressing the pursuit of services from health care professionals. Religion and spirituality also play an important role in that some Asian American elders, especially immigrants from Southeast Asia, tend to rely on spiritual leaders for healing of illnesses. Therefore, it is important for health care practitioners to be aware of, to respect, and to incorporate indigenous health beliefs and practice in treatment plans for Asian American elders.

Many immigrant Asian elders seek both Western medical services and indigenous health care services, predominantly herbal and acupuncture treatment in their ethnic communities. For example, a study showed that 42% of Korean American elders in Los Angeles reported using a traditional healer, including herbal and acupuncture treatment, in the past year (Pourat, Lubben, Wallace, & Moon, 1999). Another study of almost 3,000 Southeast Asian refugee adults (Cambodians, Hmongs, Laotians, Vietnamese, and Chinese Vietnamese) in California also found traditional health care methods to be an important part of overall health care services, although all five groups showed a significant increase in the use of Western medicine after they immigrated to the United States (Chung & Lin, 1994).

Individuals' autonomy and self-determination have been the major moral and legal tenet in the current U.S. health care system, as evidenced by the Patient Self-Determination Act (PSDA) and advance directives. However, there has been a growing concern that the dominant Western health practice based on individualistic decision-making styles may not be consistent with collectivistic values of Asian Pacific Islanders regarding health care decision making (i.e., shared or deferred decision making, filial piety, and silent communication; Blackhall, Murphy, Frank, Michel, & Azen, 1995; Kagawa-Singer & Blackhall, 2001; McLaughlin & Braun, 1998). When Asian American elders and their family face decisions regarding nursing home placement, end-of-life care, or communication and execution of advance directives, they are confronted with enormous challenges in dealing with the dilemma. According to Commonwealth Fund Health Care Quality Survey (McIntosh, 2001), Asians (41%) more frequently report underinvolvement in the decision-making process than Whites (22%). Furthermore, for some Asian American elders, patient autonomy is burdensome, rather than empowering (Blackhall et al., 1995), and they may feel disenfranchised in the health care decision-making process (U.S. Department of Health and Human Services, 2003).

In light of the cultural orientation of Asian American elders toward health care decision making, understanding their attitudes and preferences for health and long-term care services would be an important step in developing culturally sensitive services for them. Two studies, which examined attitude and preferences for long-term care services among Japanese (McCormick et al., 1996) and Korean American (Min, 2001; Min, 2005) elders, highlighted the importance of acculturation and adherence to traditional values in developing culturally appropriate long-term care arrangements and services for older Asian Americans.

FAMILY AND CAREGIVING ISSUES

Most Asian cultures are strongly influenced by Confucian teachings of filial piety and respect for older people: *oyakoko* among Japanese, *hyo* among Koreans, *utang na loob* among Filipinos (Browne & Broderick, 1994; Cheung, 1989; Kitano et al., 1997). In traditional Asian families, age is a symbol of authority and wisdom, and thus older adults are expected to make important family decisions, whereas younger adults and children are expected to respect, obey, and care for their elderly parents or grandparents in an extended living arrangement. In such cultures, the family is the dominant source of support for older adults.

Immigrants from Asian countries bring with them their cultures and family values to the new homeland. In the process of settlement in America, however, many Asian immigrants not only adjust to the American social and familial norms of individualism and independence, as opposed to collectivism and interdependence, but also see the new opportunities and resources the American society provides for the care of their older family members. Although it is difficult to generalize the adjustment experience of Asian American immigrants, as they represent a wide range of immigration and socioeconomic background, the pace of acculturation to the American values and ways of life is generally faster for younger and female immigrants. Those who came to America in old age, compared with long-time immigrant elders, may take longer and find it more difficult to adjust to their diminished status and role in the family; they may also face more adjustment issues, including loneliness, language barrier, and unfamiliarity with the new social and cultural environments.

Traditional cultures, American culture, and opportunities play roles in shaping Asian American family life and relations. The traditional norm and practice of filial piety, in terms of living with and caring for elderly parents and providing emotional and financial support, has weakened, as has the status and authority of the elders in the family (Kauh, 1997; Pang, Jordan-Marsh, Silverstein, & Cody, 2003). On the other hand, most Asian American elders do not want to be a burden to their children, and in fact, many low-income elderly live independently in government-subsidized housing and receive Supplemental Security Income (SSI) and health care services through Medicaid and Medicare. Nevertheless, the fact that many Asian American elders live alone or with only a spouse may not necessarily mean erosion of filial piety or a lack of family support. In certain locales with concentrated Asian ethnic communities, such as Chinatown, Koreatown, Little Saigon, and Little Tokyo, many Asian American elders, especially those foreign born, prefer to live near their own ethnic community rather than in suburbs with their children, in order to socialize with people in their ethnic language and to have more ready access to various social, cultural, recreational, and health care services provided by ethnic-specific agencies or professionals who speak their language and understand their culture (Cheung, 1989; Kim & Lauderdale, 2002; Yoo & Sung, 1997).

Although many Asian American families may not practice filial piety in a traditional sense, as there is reduced social pressure to do so and as alternative arrangements for care of their elderly relatives are available in the United States, family ties and family care are still strongly emphasized foundations of individual and family life among Asian Americans. A recent study of caregivers in the United States by the National Alliance for Caregiving and the American Association for Retired People (2004) estimated that although the proportion of older adults is significantly smaller among Asian Americans than Whites, 15% of Asian Americans, compared with 17% of Whites, provided unpaid care to someone 50 or older in the last 12 months, and the proportion of younger caregivers between the ages of 18 and 34 was 38% for Asian American caregivers, the highest among all subgroups (22% White, 35% African American, 33% Hispanic caregivers). The same study also found that Asian American caregivers were far more likely to indicate "old age" or "being old" as the main problem or illness of the person they care for (23%, as compared with 12% White, 10% African American, and 9% Hispanic caregivers) (National Alliance for Caregiving and American Association for Retired People, 2004).

Considering that over three quarters of Asian American elders are foreign born and that the majority of them are linguistically isolated, family caregivers of relatively recent immigrant elders, especially those from non-English-speaking countries, often face additional challenges. As older people become dependent on their children for many daily tasks, including going places and learning and adjusting to new places and systems, the prolonged dependence can create a sense of overburden and frustration, especially when the families have their own adjustment problems and other family issues, such as financial difficulty, crowded housing, and conflict with their children. Inability to provide adequate care for the elder due to a lack of time and family resources creates a feeling of guilt among family caregivers. Limited knowledge and accessibility of services, including supportive services available to family caregivers, and a lack of culturally appropriate coping skills and resources can result in the neglect of vulnerable immigrant elderly people.

Most research findings clearly suggest the importance and centrality of family in quality of life for many Asian American elders. A study of Laotian and Vietnamese refugees 55 years of age and older found that the family was the most critical factor for an elder person's satisfaction with life and living environment (Tran, 1991). In another study of Vietnamese elders in Texas, the family was almost the exclusive source of help with language, loneliness, and internal family problems (Die & Seelbach, 1988). A study of South Asian caregivers concluded that belief in filial piety norms among caregivers plays a significant role in lowering perceived levels of caregiver burden (Gupta & Pillai, 2002). Research on Korean immigrant elderly has found that a close family relationship improves the adjustment of elders to American society (Kiefer et al., 1985; Koh & Bell, 1987; Moon, 1996), increases level of morale (Moon, 1996), and mitigates the harmful impacts of life stress (Lee, Crittenden, & Yu, 1996). The family was also a critical factor for lower levels of depressive symptoms among Chinese and Korean immigrant elderly (Lee et al., 1996; Min, Moon, & Lubben, 2005; Mui, 1996).

PSYCHOLOGICAL/MENTAL HEALTH STATUS AND ISSUES

Unattended psychological/mental health issues can seriously and detrimentally affect mortality, morbidity, functional ability, and quality of life. Although there is no national estimate of prevalence data on mental health disorders for older Asian Americans and information on mental health care needs among Asian American elders remains limited and fragmented, growing evidence suggests that a higher proportion of Asian American elders suffer from mental health disorders than Whites and that most of them do not receive appropriate treatment (Browne, Fong, & Mokuau, 1994; Harada & Kim, 1995; Kang & Kang, 1995; Kuo, 1984).

Among many mental health issues, depression is the most studied among Asian American elders. An earlier depression study on Asian Americans, which examined 449 Asian Americans in Seattle, found that Chinese, Japanese, Filipino and Korean Americans were significantly more depressed than Whites based on the Center for Epidemiologic Scale of Depression (CES-D; Kuo, 1984). The study also revealed that among the four Asian American groups, Koreans, the most recent immigrant group, scored the highest rate of depression and that their depressive scores were higher among older than among younger respondents in their own ethnic group, whereas the scores were lower for older respondents in the three other ethnic groups. In a two-wave panel study of psychological distress measured by CES-D between 172 older Korean immigrants and 157 White elders, the Korean respondents on average reported significantly higher levels of depression at both of the two time points (Min et al., 2005).

Several other studies further investigated depression and its correlates and effects for Chinese American elders (Casado & Leung, 2001; Mui, 1996, 1998; Stokes, Thompson, Murphy, & Gallagher-Thompson, 2001), Japanese American elders (Shibusawa & Mui, 2001), and Korean American elders (Lee et al., 1996). Other psychological constructs, such as posttraumatic stress disorder among Indo-Chinese refugee elders (Abueg & Chun, 1996; Lin, Tazuma, & Masuda, 1979; Ngo, Tran, Gibbons, & Oliver, 2001), and alienation and morale among elderly Korean immigrants (J. H. Moon & Pearl, 1991; A. Moon, 1996) were also examined. Significant correlates of depression, alienation, or low morale include shorter length of residency in the United States for elderly Korean and Chinese Americans (Kuo, 1984: Moon & Pearl, 1991; Stokes et al., 2001), lower levels of acculturation as measured primarily by limited English proficiency (Casado & Leung, 2001; Kuo, 1984; Moon & Pearl, 1991), poor self-assessed health and functional limitation (Min et al., in press; Moon, 1996; Shibusawa & Mui, 2001), living alone (Mui, 1998), and lack of family support and quality relationships (Casado & Leung, 2001; Lee et al., 1996; Min et al., 2005; Moon, 1996; Moon & Pearl, 1991; Shibusawa & Mui, 2001).

Multiple traumas experienced before emigration among refugees—such as torture, battlefield experiences, and loss of significant others—and various postimmigration stress and adjustment problems experienced by immigrant and refugee elders suggest that recent refugee and immigrant elders from Asian countries are high-risk populations for mental health problems, while at the same time they are less familiar or willing to use mental health services compared to U.S.-born and long-time immigrant Asian American elderly. An earlier study of the mental health status of first-wave Vietnamese refugees indicated that over half of study participants manifested severe psychological problems (Lin et al., 1979). A more recent study, however, found that the Cambodian, Hmong, and Mien refugees who arrived in the United States more recently represent the three most traumatized subgroups among Southeast Asian refugee groups (Abueg & Chun, 1996). Another study of adult Vietnamese Americans points to the positive effect of ac-

culturation on depression: premigration traumatic experiences had a strong effect on depression among those with lower levels of acculturation than among those who were highly acculturated (Ngo et al., 2001).

Data on suicide rates for some Asian American elderly groups also suggest need for serious concern. According to Lester (1994) and Kitano et al. (1997), suicide rates for Chinese and Japanese Americans ages 65 and older were the highest; 25.9 and 18.9, respectively, per 100,000 per year, whereas those of White and African American elders were 19.1 and 5.5, respectively. Yu (1986) reported that the suicide rate for elderly Chinese immigrants was almost three times higher than the rate for U.S.-born Chinese elderly in 1980. A more recent study of suicide rates between 1987 and 1996 among several Asian and other ethnic minority female cohorts in San Francisco showed that immigrant Chinese elders accounted for 89% of all elderly Chinese suicides and that Chinese women had a higher suicide rate than women in all other racial/ethnic groups, including Japanese, Filipino, African, Latino, and Native Americans (Barron, 2000).

Mental illness in most Asian American communities, especially among immigrant elders, is a stigmatized, if not a taboo, issue. The perceptions that mental illness is caused by unexplainable superpower, by spiritual forces, or by one's predetermined fate and that it cannot be cured by Western or medical treatment are strongly rooted in traditional Asian cultures and still prevail among many elderly Asian Americans. In fact, studies have shown that culture influences Asian Americans' perceptions, expression, and coping with mental illness and emotional or psychological problems (Braun & Browne, 1998; Douglas & Fujimoto, 1995; Fugita, Ito, Abe, & Takeuchi, 1991; Kagawa-Singer et al., 1997; Kleinman, 1980). In Japanese culture, as well as in many other Asian cultures, emotional and psychological problems are perceived as "craziness" (Fugita et al., 1991). Asian Americans in a focus group study believed dementia was part of the natural aging process about which nothing could be done (Braun, Takamura, Forman, & Sasaki, 1995).

Somatic complaints and distress are the most common expression of depression for older Asian Americans, partly because of their belief in the inseparability of affective and somatic systems (Browne et al., 1994) and partly because of a lack of experience in labeling, describing, and communicating about affect (Douglas & Fujimoto, 1995). Depression in Chinese culture is expressed mainly by symptoms of fatigue, low energy, and sleep disturbance, with little sign of dysphoria (Douglas & Fujimoto, 1995). A culturally unique psychiatric symptom of *Hwa-Byung* among elderly Korean women refers to prolonged suppression of unbearable pain, suffering, loss, anger, or resentment, which develops into clinical depression, anxiety, and somatic symptoms (Lin et al., 1992; Pang, 1990). The most unique aspect of this *Hwa-Byung* is that Koreans label themselves as having this "illness" (or *byung* in Korean), and it is a commonly used and accepted expression of one's psychological and physiological status.

Internalization and denial of existing mental problems in most Asian American cultures tend to undermine utilization of mental health services, which means that many people with mental health disorders go unnoticed and untreated, resulting in further and perhaps unnecessary deterioration. Among Japanese American elders, for example, *Gaman* (the internalization and suppression of anger and emotion, avoiding confrontation, and accepting the results of negative social interaction) and *shikata ga nai* (whatever happened cannot be helped or nothing more can be done to improve the situation) are common coping mechanisms, which amount to denial of a problem and of the need to deal with it (Fugita et al., 1991). This observation also prevails in other elderly Asian American groups. Because it is a stigmatized condition, many Asian Americans prefer to keep mental illness problems within the family, failing to take advantage of various treatment options available to them. In many cases, Asian American elders maintain modesty in their expression, suppress extreme feelings, control their emotions, and exhibit an unwillingness to reveal emotions to others. In some instances, such emotional control may be unduly considered as dysfunction or as treatment resistance. Therefore, social work practitioners should be knowledgeable and capable of demonstrating their understanding of the wide array of culturally defined perceptions of mental health issues among Asian American elders, including expression and communication styles, skepticism regarding treatability of mental illness, and reluctance to use formal mental health services.

HEALTH, MENTAL HEALTH, AND LONG-TERM CARE SERVICE UTILIZATION: PATTERNS AND ISSUES

A major finding that emerges from most studies on service use among older Asian Americans is *underutilization*. Research on various Asian American elderly groups has generally found low rates of utilization of or participation in health services (Yee & Weaver, 1994; Shin, Kim, Juon, Kim, & Kim, 2000), mental health services (Browne et al., 1994; Harada & Kim, 1995; Matsuoka, Breaus, & Ryujin, 1997), and home, community, and institutional long-term care services (Choi, 2001; Lai, 2001; Moon, Lubben, & Villa, 1998; Tsai & Lopez, 1997).

For example, an analysis of national survey data found that the proportion of Asian American and Pacific Islanders who utilized mental health services at all types of public and private facilities was a third of the proportion of European Americans (Matsuoka et al., 1997). In addition, Asian American elders were significantly less likely to participate in home-delivered nutritional meal programs than White, African American, and Hispanic participants, primarily due to different food preferences and the lack of English proficiency among many recent immigrant elders (Choi, 2001). A comparative study of awareness and utilization of 15 community long-term care services (e.g., transportation; Meals on Wheels; congregate meals; visiting nurse, hospice, and mental health services) between Korean immigrant and White elders in Los Angeles clearly indicates that the lack of knowledge of existing services is the primary barrier to utilization of services. Korean elders were far less aware of all 15 services than Whites were. However, among those aware of services, the group disparities in service usage were much smaller, and in some cases, Koreans showed higher utilization rates than Whites (Moon et al., 1998).

Studies that examined service use in individual Asian American elderly subgroups showed that significant within-group variations exist (Kuo & Torres-Gil, 2001; Lai, 2001; Shin et al., 2000; Tsai & Lopez, 1997). In a study of Chinese immigrant elders, Lai (2001) found substantial underutilization of supportive services in general and identified three predictors of service use within the group: living alone, satisfaction with services, and fewer mental health symptoms. Another study of 240 elderly Taiwanese Americans found a higher number of doctor visits by those who used alternate medicine and preferred same-culture professionals (Kuo & Torres-Gil, 2001). The study also reported that a greater likelihood of using home- and community-based services was associated with living alone, longer years since immigration, preference for same-culture professionals, and higher functional limitations.

As mentioned earlier, culturally driven health beliefs, communication styles, coping mechanisms, and attitudes toward use of formal services, especially for family and mental health problems, among Asian American elders people influence service utilization. For example, seeking help for psychological distress and problems from outside the family and disclosure of emotions to a stranger, even a professional mental health specialist, is still considered an act of weakness, resulting in loss of face to the family by many Asian Americans, especially immigrant elders. Loss of face or shame, as one of the central Asian values, may hamper help seeking among Asian American elderly (Casado & Leung, 2001; Kitano et al., 1997; Tsai & Lopez, 1997). Furthermore, many elderly Asian Americans seem to have little understanding of or confidence in the rule of confidentiality; they often worry that health and social service practitioners might tell others about their personal and family problems. Also, some Asian American elders might find it difficult to adopt Western-style help-seeking behaviors that may require them to be more assertive and proactive in seeking professional help (Kagawa-Singer et al., 1997).

In addition to cultural issues (and language problems for recent immigrant elders from non-English-speaking countries), various institutional and socio-structural barriers to service utilization exist in the Asian American communities. They include benefit/service eligibility restrictions to legal immigrants who are non-American citizens, as well as to undocumented immigrants; lack of awareness of and unfamiliarity with various supportive home- and community-based services, as well as mental health services; lack of transportation services; the stereotype that Asian American elders are taken care of by their families; and lack of culturally appropriate services and bilingual staffs.

GUIDELINES FOR SOCIAL WORK PRACTICE

In this last section, we translate reviewed empirical findings into concrete and useful practice guidelines for social work practice with older Asian Americans. Vastly diverse characteristics of many Asian American elderly subgroups (e.g., history, language, culture, immigration history and experience, socioeconomic status, and acculturation levels) make it impossible to provide a uniform set of practice guidelines applicable to all subgroups. Nevertheless, the very "diversity" within the Asian American elderly group warrants more efforts to refine a much-discussed notion of

"culturally competent practice"* for the population. Kagawa-Singer and Blackhall (2001) argue that cultural competence is a law, not a choice, and it can be achieved. The following recommendations aim to help health and social service practitioners to conceptualize and practice cultural competence in their work with Asian American elders.

Communication and Assessment

Effective communication and accurate assessment of the needs of older adults are critical to effective social work intervention, regardless of the individual's cultural/ethnic background, language, and socioeconomic status. Needless to say, a comprehensive biopsychosocial assessment (McInnis-Dittrich, 2005) should be conducted for every older client on his or her physical health, functional capacity, and psychological and social functioning. A fundamental principle of social work practice with the Asian American elderly is to recognize the importance of respect for them and to understand their cultural orientations, devoid of stereotypes and misconceptions (Kitano et al., 1997; Takamura, 1991).

The following suggestions are put forth for more effective communication and assessment in social work practice with Asian American elders:

- Language barriers hinder social worker-client relationship and communications. A priority should be set on assuring accuracy in communication and cross-cultural understanding.
- When working with clients with limited English proficiency and a cultural/ethnic background different from that of the practitioner, the practitioner should consider using an ethnic consultant (Mokuau, 1987; Takamura, 1991) or cultural broker (Valle, 1998) to ensure the client's primacy and the sense of connectedness and effective communication between the client and the practitioner.
- Accurate assessment of individual Asian American elders should be made in the context of their historical experiences (e.g., internment experience for Japanese Americans), generational status, and immigration/refugee status (Fugita et al., 1991).
- Older Asian American clients often express their emotions in a nonverbal and indirect manner. Nonverbal communication and behavioral cues in some instances may be equally or even more important than verbal expressions (Moon, Tomita, & Jung-Kamei, 2001).

- Attitudes toward formal services and service preferences vary and need to be assessed (Moon et al., 2001; Shibusawa & Mui, 2001). Explain how formal services and professionals would be helpful to clients in concrete ways. Explain the confidentiality rule and its strict enforcement, assuring clients that violation of the rule is against the laws and professional code of ethics.
- Engage in cross-culturally informed nonjudgmental active listening (Valle, 1998) to identify Asian American elderly clients' culturally based meanings of dilemmas and of help. Incorporate clients' cultural perspectives in discussions of issues, problems, and service needs, as well as in intervention plans.
- Establish and demonstrate understanding of cultural and other aspects of clients' problems and needs, especially during the relation formation period, in order to gain credibility with, and increase the trust of, ethnic Asian American elders.
- Explore approaches to identifying and evaluating cultural influences in clients, such as the "attitudes, beliefs, context, decision making, and environment (ABCDE)" approach of Koenig and Gates-Williams (1995), later adapted by Kagawa-Singer and Blackhall (2001), or the "cultural mapping process" of Valle (1998).
- Adopt screening and assessment tools that are validated as culturally and linguistically appropriate for use with the target group (Stokes et al., 2001; Tran, Ngo & Conway, 2003).

Culturally Competent Intervention or Services

- Develop social work interventions and services that would have "cultural buy-ins" from the intended target elderly Asian American group. Start with the group's own understanding of issues, problems, needs, service goals, and preferred approaches to achieving the goals.
- Be aware of potential differences not only between different Asian American elderly groups but also within the same ethnic group in designing clinical and programmatic intervention services.
- Develop and expand community education and outreach programs that are linguistically and culturally effective in order to increase knowledge and usage of available services among Asian American elders. Such efforts should consider use

of (1) outreach workers who speak the language of the target group and who are preferably from the same ethnic background, (2) ethnic media and organizations, as well as respected community and religious leaders, to obtain support for the effort and cost-effective dissemination of information, and (3) informational materials written in the ethnic language, with pictures of elders from the target group, if necessary.

- In discussing and planning for intervention, terms and issues such as autonomy, self-determination, empowerment, and aggressiveness, especially as intervention goals, should be used with care with Asian American elders, because they may be interpreted as lacking concerns for harmony, interdependence, modesty, and consideration for significant others, values inherent in Asian cultures, thereby leading to miscommunication and misunderstanding between Asian American elders and professionals.
- Although no definite information is available as to whether nondirect counseling or directive and structured counseling style is more effective with or preferred by Asian American elders (Mokuau, 1987), flexible and eclectic practice approaches should be explored that consider an awareness of and sensitivity to a client's worldviews and values (Takamura, 1991).
- Social workers should be encouraged to participate in more cultural-sensitivity training on culture, values, acculturation, biopsychosocial aspect of the aging, and social work skills for working with elderly from different racial/ethnic backgrounds.

CONCLUSION

Older adults experience and adjust to a wide range of changes in biological, psychological, and social functioning (McInnis-Dittrich, 2005). They also cope with various kinds of losses in their physical and functional capacity, cognitive abilities, loved ones, work, and social status. In addition to these changes and challenges associated with the normal aging process, Asian American elders are at greater risk of experiencing multiple and compounding issues in their aging process due to their experiences of historical oppression, discrimination, and migration. Negative historical experiences resulting from discriminatory immigration laws, structural and cultural barriers, as well as lack of knowledge of available services, have meant that many

Asian American elders, especially monolingual recent immigrants and refugees, are underserved.

With a massive influx of immigrant and refugee elders from nearly all Asian countries during the past three decades, the growing number and increasing diversity between and within various Asian American elderly groups complicate our understanding of who they are, what they need, and how best to serve them, making it extremely difficult, if not impossible, to arrive at clear conclusions for effective social work practice with the population. Despite the complexity and limited knowledge of the rapidly growing older Asian American populations, however, this chapter attempted to describe some characteristics of growing diversity, influence of culture, research findings on major social work-related issues, and their implications for social work practice.

It is hoped that the growing diversity does not result in growing disparities in quality of life or access to services but instead contributes to a growing recognition of diversity and culture as an integral and natural part of consideration for service design and social work practice. Indeed, the "where the client is" principle as the most basic consideration for social work practice with any individuals or groups implies that acquisition of knowledge of, and culturally competent practice skills with, the intended ethnic group is not an option but a requirement for practitioners. This is impossible without reliable information. For this reason, the need for comprehensive, large-scale, and systematic research studies on older Asian American populations on the wide range of topics that affect older people and their families (e.g., dementia, end of life, family caregiving, service knowledge and utilization, effective assessment and intervention methods) is greater than ever before.

REFERENCES

Abueg, R. R., & Chun, K. M. (1996). Traumatization stress among Asian and Asian Americans. In A. J. Marsella, M. J. Friedman, E. T. Gerrity, & R. M. Scurfield (Eds.), *Ethnocultural aspects of posttraumatic stress disorder: Issues, research, and clinical applications* (pp. 285–299). Washington, DC: American Psychological Association.

Barron, S. L. (2000). Suicide in context: Elderly Chinese female suicide in San Francisco from 1987 through 1996 (Doctoral dissertation, Pacific Graduate School of Psychology, 2000). *Dissertation Abstracts International, 61*(03B), 1624.

Blackhall, L. J., Murphy, S. T., Frank, G., Michel, V., & Azen, S. (1995). Ethnicity and attitudes toward patient autonomy. *Journal of the American Medical Association, 274*, 820–825.

Braun, K. L., & Browne, C. V. (1998). Perceptions of dementia, caregiving, and help seeking among Asian and Pacific Islander Americans. *Health and Social Work, 23*(4), 262–274.

Braun, K. L., Takamura, J. C., Forman, S. M., & Sasaki, P. A. (1995). Developing and testing outreach materials on Alzheimer's disease for Asian and Pacific Islander Americans. *Gerontologist, 35*, 122–126.

Browne, C., & Broderick, A. (1994). Asian and Pacific Island elders: Issues for social work practice and education. *Social Work, 39*, 252–259.

Browne, C., Fong, R., & Mokuau, N. (1994). The mental health of Asian and Pacific Islander elders: Implications for mental health administrators. *Journal of Mental Health Administration, 21*(1), 52–59.

Casado, B. L., & Leung, P. (2001). Migratory grief and depression among elderly Chinese American immigrants. *Journal of Gerontological Social Work, 36*(1/2), 5–26.

Chen, M. S. (1993). Cardiovascular health among Asian Americans/Pacific Islanders: An examination of health status and intervention approaches. *American Journal of Health Promotion, 7*, 199–207.

Cheung, M. (1989). Elderly Chinese living in the United States: Assimilation or adjustment? *Social Work, 34*(5), 457–461.

Choi, N. G. (2001). Frail older persons in nutrition supplement programs: A comparative study of African American, Asian American, and Hispanic participants. *Journal of Gerontological Social Work, 36*(1/2), 187–207.

Chung, R. C., & Lin, K. (1994). Help-seeking behavior among Southeast Asian refugees. *Journal of Community Psychology, 22*, 109–120.

Cox, C. B., & Ephross, P. H. (1998). *Ethnicity and social work practice.* New York: Oxford University Press.

Die, A. H., & Seelbach, W. C. (1988). Problems, sources of assistance, and knowledge of services among elderly Vietnamese immigrants. *Gerontologist, 28*(4), 448–452.

Douglas, K. C., & Fujimoto, D. (1995). Asian Pacific Islanders: Implications for health care providers. *Clinics in Geriatric Medicine, 11*(1), 69–82.

Ell, K., & Castaneda, I. (1998). Health care seeking behavior. In S. Loue (Ed.), *Handbook of immigrant health* (pp. 125–143). New York: Plenum Press.

Emami, A., Benner, P. E., Lipson, J. G., & Ekman, S. L. (2000). Health as continuity and balance in life. *Western Journal of Nursing Research, 22*(7), 812–825.

Fong, R., & Furuto, S. (2001). *Culturally competent practice: Skills, interventions, and evaluations.* Boston: Allyn & Bacon.

Fugita, S., Ito, K. L., Abe, J., & Takeuchi, D. T. (1991). Japanese Americans. In N. Mokuau (Ed.), *Handbook of social services for Asian and Pacific Islanders* (pp. 61–78). New York: Greenwood Press.

Gupta, R., & Pillai, V. K. (2002). Elder care giving in South Asian families: Implications for social services. *Journal of Comparative Family Studies, 33*(4), 565–576.

Harada, N. D., & Kim, L. S. (1995). Use of mental health services by older Asian and Pacific Islander Americans. In D. K. Padgett (Ed.), *Handbook on ethnicity aging and mental health* (pp.185–202). Westport CT: Greenwood Press.

Kagawa-Singer, M., & Blackhall, L. J. (2001). Negotiating cross-cultural issues at the end of life: "You got to go where he lives." *Journal of the American Medical Association, 286*(23), 2993–3001.

Kagawa-Singer, M., Hikoyeda, N., & Tanjasiri, S. R. (1997). Aging, chronic conditions, and physical disabilities in Asian and Pacific Islander Americans. In K. S. Markides & M. R. Manuel (Eds.), *Minorities, aging, and health* (pp. 149–180). Thousand Oaks, CA: Sage.

Kang, T. S., & Kang, G. E. (1995). Mental health status and needs of the Asian American elderly. In D. K. Padgett (Ed.), *Handbook on ethnicity, aging, and mental health* (pp. 113–131). Westport CT: Greenwood.

Kauh, T.-O. (1997). Intergenerational relations: Older Korean-Americans' experiences. *Journal of Cross-Cultural Gerontology, 12,* 245–271.

Kiefer, C. W., Kim, S., Choi, K., Kim, L., Kim, B. L., Shon, S., & Kim, T. (1985). Adjustment problems of Korean American elderly. *Gerontologist, 25,* 477–482.

Kim, J., & Lauderdale, D. S. (2002). The role of community context in immigrant elderly living arrangements: Korean American elderly. *Research on Aging, 24,* 630–653.

Kim, M. T., Juon, H. S., Hill, M. N., Post, W., & Kim, K. B. (2001). Cardiovascular disease risk factors in Korean American elderly. *Western Journal of Nursing Research, 23,* 269–282.

Kitano, H., Shibusawa, T., & Kitano, K. J. (1997). Asian American elderly mental health. In K. S. Markides & M. R. Manuel (Eds.), *Minorities, aging, and health* (pp. 295–315). Thousand Oaks, CA: Sage.

Kleinman, A. (1980). *Patients and healers in the context of culture.* Berkeley: University of California Press.

Koenig, B. A., & Gates-Williams, J. (1995). Understanding cultural difference in caring for dying patients. *Western Journal of Medicine, 163,* 244–249.

Koh, J., & Bell, W. (1987). Korean elders in the United States: Intergenerational relations and living arrangements. *Gerontologist, 27,* 66–71.

Kuo, W. H. (1984). Prevalence of depression among Asian Americans. *Journal of Nervous and Mental Disease, 172,* 449–457.

Kuo, T., & Torres-Gil, F. (2001). Factors affecting utilization of health services and home- and community-based care programs by older Taiwanese in the United States. *Research on Aging, 23*(1), 14–37.

Lai, D. (2001). Use of senior services of the elderly Chinese immigrants. *Journal of Gerontological Social Work, 35*(2), 59–79.

LaVeist, T. A. (1995). Data sources for aging research on racial and ethnic groups. *Gerontologist, 35,* 328–339.

Lee, M. S., Crittenden, K. S., & Yu, E. (1996). Social support and depression among elderly Korean immigrants in the United States. *International Journal of Aging and Human Development, 42*(4), 313–327.

Lester, D. (1994). Differences in epidemiology of suicide in Asian Americans by national origin. *Omega, 29*(2), 89–93.

Lin, K. M., Tazuma, L., & Masuda, M. (1979). Adaptational problems of Vietnamese refugees: Part I. Health and mental health status. *Archives of General Psychiatry, 36,* 955–961.

Lin, K., Lau, J. K., Yamamoto, J., Zheng, Y., Kim, H., Cho, K., & Nakasaki, G. (1992). Hwa-Byung: A community study of Korean Americans. *Journal of Nervous and Mental Illness, 180,* 386–391.

Lubben, J. E., Weiler, P. G., & Chi, I. (1989). Gender and ethnic differences in the health practices of the elderly poor. *Journal of Clinical Epidemiology, 42,* 725–733.

Lum, D. (2000). *Social work practice and people of color: A process-stage approach* (4th ed.). Pacific Grove, CA: Brooks/Cole.

Lum, D. (2003). *Culturally competent practice: A framework for understanding diverse groups and justice issues* (2nd ed.). Pacific Grove, CA: Brooks/Cole.

Lum, O. M. (1995). Health status of Asians and Pacific Islanders. *Clinics in Geriatric Medicine, 11*(1), 53–67.

Matsuoka, J. K., Breaus, C., & Ryujin, D. H. (1997). National utilization of mental health services by Asian Americans/Pacific Islanders. *Journal of Community Psychology, 25*(2), 141–145.

McCormick, W. C., Uomoto, J., Young, H., Graves, A., Vitaliano, P., Mortimer, J., et al. (1996). Attitudes toward use of nursing homes and home care in older Japanese-Americans. *Journal of the American Geriatrics Society, 44,* 769–777.

McInnis-Dittrich, K. (2005). *Social work with elders: A biopsychosocial approach to assessment and intervention.* Boston: Allyn & Bacon.

McIntosh, M. (2001). *Survey on disparities in quality of health care.* Retrieved October 14, 2004, from the website of The Commonwealth Fund: *http://www.cmwf.org/grants/grants_show.htm?doc_id=223417.*

McLaughlin, L. A., & Braun, K. L. (1998). Asian and Pacific Islander cultural values: Considerations for health care decision making. *Health and Social Work, 23,* 116–126.

Min, J. W. (2001). *The process and outcomes of long-term care decision-making among Korean American elders.* Unpublished doctoral dissertation, University of California, Los Angeles.

Min, J. W. (2005). Preference for long-term care arrangement and its correlates for older Korean Americans. *Journal of Aging and Health, 17,* 363–395.

Min, J. W., Moon, A., & Lubben, J. E. (2005). Determinants of psychological distress over time among older Korean Americans and non-Hispanic White elders: Evidence from a two-wave panel study. *Aging and Mental Health, 9,* 210–222.

Mokuau, N. (1987). Social workers' perceptions for counseling effectiveness for Asian American clients. *Social Work, 32*(4), 331–335.

Moon, A. (1996). Predictors of morale among Korean immigrant elderly in the USA. *Journal of Cross-Cultural Gerontology, 11,* 351–367.

Moon, A., Lubben, J. E., & Villa, V. (1998). Awareness and utilization of community-long-term care services by elderly Korean and non-Hispanic white Americans. *Gerontologist, 38,* 309–316.

Moon, A., Tomita, S. K., & Jung-Kamei, S. (2001). Elder mistreatment among four Asian American groups: An exploratory study on tolerance, victim blaming and attitudes toward third-party intervention. *Journal of Gerontological Social Work, 36,* 153–169.

Moon, J. H., & Pearl, J. H. (1991). Alienation of elderly Korean American immigrants as related to place of residence, gender, age, years of education, time in the U.S., living with or without a spouse. *International Journal of Aging and Human Development, 32,* 115–124.

Mui, A. C. (1996). Depression among elderly Chinese immigrants: An exploratory study. *Social Work, 41,* 633–645.

Mui, A. C. (1998). Living along and depression among older Chinese immigrants. *Journal of Gerontological Social Work, 30*(3/4), 147–166.

National Alliance for Caregiving and American Association for Retired People. (2004). *Caregiving in the U.S.* Retrieved August 8, 2004, from AARP website: *http://research.aarp.org/il/us_caregiving.html.*

Ngo, D., Tran, T. V., Gibbons, J. L., & Oliver, J. M. (2001). Acculturation, premigration traumatic experiences, and depression among Vietnamese Americans. *Journal of Human Behavior in the Social Environment, 3*(3/4), 225–242.

Pang, E. C., Jordan-Marsh, M., Silverstein, M., & Cody, M. (2003). Health-seeking behaviors of elderly Chinese Americans: Shifts in expectations. *Gerontologist, 43,* 864–874.

Pang, K. Y. (1990). Hwabyung: The construction of a Korean popular illness among Korean elderly immigrant women in the United States. *Culture, Medicine, and Psychiatry, 14,* 495–512.

Pender, N. J. (1996). *Health promotion in nursing practice* (3rd ed.). Stanford, CT: Appleton & Lange.

Pourat, N., Lubben, J., Wallace, S. P., & Moon, A. (1999). Predictors of use of traditional Korean healers among elderly Koreans in Los Angeles. *Gerontologist, 39,* 711–719.

Ruggles, S., Sobek, M., Alexander, T., Fitch, C. A., Goeken, R., Hall, P. K., et al. (2004). *Integrated Public Use Microdata Series: Version 3.0* [Machine-readable database]. (Available from the Minnesota Population Center, *http://www.ipums.org*)

Shibusawa, T., & Mui, A. C (2001). Stress, coping, and depression among Japanese American elders. *Journal of Gerontological Social Work, 36*(1–2), 63–81.

Shin, H., Kim, M. T., Juon, H. S., Kim, J., & Kim, K. B. (2000). Patterns and factors associated with health care utilization among Korean American elderly. *Asian American Pacific Islander Journal of Health, 8*(2), 116–129.

Stokes, S. C., Thompson, L. W., Murphy, S., & Gallagher-Thompson, D. (2001). Screening for depression in immigrant Chinese-American elders: Results of a pilot study. *Journal of Gerontological Social Work, 36,* 27–44.

Takamura, J. C. (1991). Asian and Pacific Islander elderly. In N. Mokuau (Ed.), *Handbook of social services for Asian and Pacific Islanders* (pp. 185–202). New York: Greenwood Press.

Takata, E., Ford, J. M., & Lloyd, L. S. (1998). Asian Pacific Islander Health. In S. Loue (Ed.), *Handbook of immigrant health* (pp. 303–327). New York: Plenum Press.

Tanjasiri, S. P., Wallace, S. P., & Shibata, K. (1995). Picture imperfect: Hidden problems among Asian Pacific Islander elderly. *Gerontologist, 35,* 753–760.

Tran, T. V. (1991). Family living arrangement and social adjustment among three ethnic groups of elderly Indochinese refugees. *Intergenerational Journal of Aging and Human Development, 32,* 91–102.

Tran, T. V., Ngo, D., & Conway, K. (2003). A cross-cultural measure of depressive symptoms among Vietnamese Americans. *Social Work Research, 27*(1), 56–65.

Tsai, D. T., & Lopez, R. A. (1997). The use of social support by elderly Chinese immigrants. *Journal of Gerontological Social Work, 29*(1), 77–94.

U.S. Census Bureau. (1992). *Census of the population, 1990 (U.S.) General population characteristics (CP-1-1)*. Washington, DC: U.S. Department of Commerce, Bureau of the Census.

U.S. Census Bureau. (2002). *The Asian Population: 2000* [Census 2000 Brief]. Retrieved May 2, 2004, from *http://www.census.gov/prod/2002pubs/c2kbr01–16.pdf.*

U.S. Department of Health and Human Services. (2003). *National Healthcare Disparities Report.* Retrieved May 6, 2004, from *http://www.qualitytools.ahrq.gov/disparitiesreport/download_report.aspx.*

U.S. Department of Health and Human Services. (2000). *Healthy People 2010*, 2nd ed. *With understanding and improving health and objectives for improving health.* 2 vols. Washington, DC: U.S. Government Printing Office.

U.S. Department of Health and Human Services. (1995). *Healthy people 2000: Midcourse review and 1995 revisions.* Washington, DC: U.S. Government Printing Office.

Valle, R. (1998). *Caregiving across cultures: Working with dementing illness and ethnically diverse populations.* Washington, DC: Taylor & Francis.

Villa, V. M., Wallace, S. P., Moon, A., & Lubben, J. E. (1997). A comparative analysis of chronic disease prevalence among older Koreans and non-Hispanic Whites. *Family and Community Health, 20*(2), 1–12.

Yee, B., & Weaver, W. K. (1994). Ethnic minorities and health promotion: Developing a "culturally competent" agenda. *Generations, 18*(1), 39–45.

Yoo, S., & Sung, K. (1997). Elderly Koreans' tendency to live independently from their adult children: Adaptation to cultural differences in America. *Journal of Cross-Cultural Gerontology, 12*(3), 225–244.

Yu, E. S. (1986). Health of the Chinese elderly in America. *Research on Aging, 8*(1), 84–109.

Zane, N., Takeuchi, D. T., & Young, K. (1994). *Confronting critical health issues of Asian and Pacific Islander Americans.* Newbury Park, CA: Sage.

SANDRA S. BUTLER

Older Gays, Lesbians, Bisexuals, and Transgender Persons

Although the experience of aging for gay, lesbian, bisexual, and transgender (GLBT) individuals, in many regards, is indistinguishable from that of their non-GLBT counterparts, there are nonetheless special circumstances and a history of discrimination which bear noting when working with this population. There is considerable diversity within the GLBT community itself (e.g., Herdt, Beeler, & Rawles, 1997). Gay, lesbian, bisexual, and transgender elders vary in characteristics such as cultural, ethnic, or racial identity, physical ability, income, education, history of marriage and/or child rearing, and place of residence. They also vary in terms of the degree to which their GLBT identities are central to their own self-definition and their level of affiliation with other GLBT individuals and organizations (Meyer, 2001). Despite these differences, GLBT individuals of all ages share experiences related to stigma, rejection, discrimination, and, at times, violence. In most parts of the United States, it is legal to discriminate against GLBT persons in housing, employment, and basic civil rights, although selected cities, states, and businesses have nondiscrimination ordinances, laws, and clauses.

It is difficult to be precise when estimating the number of GLBT seniors. Conservative estimates of the prevalence of gay men, lesbians, and bisexuals in the U.S. population range from 3–8%; this is likely to be an undercount due to the ongoing taboo of identifying as gay, lesbian, or bisexual in an interview or survey (Cahill, South, & Spade, 2000). Using this estimated prevalence rate, Cahill, South, and Spade (2000) suggest that there are currently from 1 million to 2.8 million GLB individuals ages 65 or older, and, based on Administration on Aging estimates of elder population growth, they predict that this number will increase to 2 to 6 million by 2030. Only recently have there been preliminary efforts to estimate the number of transgender individuals in the United States—individuals who fall along the full range of sexual orientation from homosexual to bisexual to heterosexual and into many subcategories based on numerous factors (Witten, 2002); rough estimates suggest that at least 3% or more of the U.S. population is transgendered (National Association of Social Workers [NASW], 2003). The population of GLBT elders includes the same racial and class diversity as the larger U.S. population. Despite a widespread myth that gay men and lesbians are economically privileged, multiple studies have shown this not to be the case at all.

This chapter examines social work practice with GLBT older adults. The purpose of this chapter is to introduce practitioners to information and resources so that they might better serve older GLBT individuals. It begins by tracing some of the historical events and circumstances which have shaped the lives of the current cohort of GLBT elders. The invisibility of GLBT elders will be discussed next, a phenomenon that has resulted from a history of discrimination and oppression. What we know about GLBT elders is constrained by this invisibility and the scarcity of representative empirical research; nonetheless, some observations and estimations can be made to describe this population, and they are presented here. GLBT elders bring certain unique strengths to the aging process; they also face some particular challenges. These are outlined, along with suggested practice guidelines. Resources for further investigation of this topic conclude the chapter.

It has been well documented that health and social service systems are often perceived as unwelcoming by GLBT individuals. For example, Brotman, Ryan, and Cormier (2003) enumerate the types of negative reactions gay men and lesbians may encounter from service providers, including embarrassment, direct rejection, hostility, excessive curiosity, pity, avoidance of physical contact, and breaches of confidentiality. Furthermore, Brotman et al. (2003) submit that discrimination toward GLBT persons may be particularly pervasive in the elder care system, which has gone largely unchallenged with respect to its treatment of this group.

Just as old age, by itself, is not a reason for social work intervention, neither are sexual orientation and gender identity generally the cause of intervention. Older GLBT individuals, similarly to all elders, become involved with social workers because of illness, frailty, disability, or life crises (Langley, 2001). However, although presenting problems may be similar to those of non-GLBT elders, solutions for the GLBT client need to be seen in the context of the individual's life experience. Social workers are ideally suited to work with GLBT elders given the profession's dual focus on the individual and his or her environment and that the nature of the work involves both direct service and advocacy for social change (Appleby & Anastas, 1998). Unfortunately, although it is quite certain that all social service and mental health agencies serving older adults have GLBT clients, many of these clients hide their identities; thus social workers and social service agencies must foster environments that promote trust from these elders so that their needs can be more fully understood and addressed (Gallance & Warshaw, 2004).

Definition of Terms

Homosexual—has largely been dismissed by the gay community because of its link to pathological diagnosis.

Gay—came into favor after the 1969 Stonewall riots and refers to men whose primary emotional and sexual connections are with other men. Although gay is an overarching term for homosexuality, it is generally used to refer particularly to men.

Lesbian—came out of the feminist movement of the 1970s as a substitute for the word gay and refers to women whose primary emotional and sexual connections are with other women. Some elder lesbians may refer to themselves as gay rather than lesbian.

Bisexual—refers to men and women who have sexual attractions to both sexes.

Transgender—came into usage in the 1990s and applies to people who resist gender stereotypes or who transgress sex-gender norms. Transgender individuals may identify as either gay or "straight" (i.e., heterosexual; Hunter & Hickerson, 2003).

HISTORY OF OPPRESSION

The life experiences of older GLBT individuals differs quite markedly from those of younger cohorts (McDougall, 1993). Brotman et al. (2003) refer to this cohort as "preliberation" gays and lesbians, drawing attention to the context of their youth and early adulthood, which occurred prior to the gay liberation movement of the 1970s. The Stonewall rebellion of 1969 has been considered a watershed event initiating the movement for gay civil rights (Morrow, 2001; Kochman, 1997). The Stonewall Inn was a gay bar in New York City that was frequently raided by police in the 1960s. On June 27, 1969, the patrons did not acquiesce to the raid but rather fought back, resulting in three days of rioting; this pivotal event has been described as the point in gay culture at which active resistance replaced submission to antigay violence (Morrow, 2001).

Most of the current cohort of elder GLBT individuals grew up before this time of liberation, often in very hostile environments. *Homophobia* and *heterosexism* are the terms frequently used to describe the severe oppression that existed prior to gay liberation and which continues to permeate society today, though in a less blatant form.

Forms of Oppression That Affect GLBT Elders

Homophobia—the irrational fear of homosexuals and the hatred of GLB individuals based solely on their sexual orientation.

Heterosexism—an ideological system that denies, denigrates, and stigmatizes any nonheterosexual form of behavior, identity, relationship, or community; refers to beliefs and attitudes that favor opposite-sex over same-sex partnerships (Cahill et al.; Kochman, 1997; van Wormer, Wells, & Boes, 2000).

Transphobia—social prejudice against transgendered people; can be even more intense than homophobia (Cook-Daniels, 1997).

Liberal humanism—a concept which expresses tolerance or acceptance but denies the experience of GLBT individuals—a "sexually blind" approach (Langley, 2001).

Prior to the Stonewall riots, the first two editions of the *Diagnostic and Statistical Manual of Mental Disorders* (DSM-I, 1952 and DSM-II, 1968), published by the American Psychiatric Association (APA), labeled homosexuals as sexual deviants and classified them as child molesters, voyeurs, exhibitionists, and people who committed antisocial or destructive crimes (Hidalgo, Peterson, & Woodman, 1985). The societal impact of the gay liberation movement led to the APA's historic removal of homosexuality from its official list of disorders in 1973. This action rippled through the helping professions, including the profession of social work. Prior to the APA revision, social work had been guilty of defining homosexuality as an illness and subjecting gay clients to conversion (to heterosexuality) treatment (Kochman, 1997). Since the late 1970s, the policy statements of the National Association of Social Workers (NASW) have reflected increasingly affirmative approaches to practice with and advocacy for gay men and lesbians and, since 2000, bisexuals and transgender individuals, as well (Hidalgo et al., 1985; NASW, 2003).

INVISIBILITY OF THE POPULATION

Given this history of oppression, it is not surprising that elder GLBT have become very practiced at concealment. In their youth and young adulthood, they learned to hide their orientation from family, friends, and employers; some chose heterosexual marriage and having children as one way to conceal their sexual orientation from society—and perhaps themselves (D'Augelli, Grossman, Hershberger, & O'Connell, 2001; Sitter, 1997). Blando (2001) refers to elder lesbians and gay men as "twice hidden" and the most "invisible of an already invisible minority" (p. 87). Having grown up with the prevailing message that homosexuality is a sickness, sin, perversion, or arrested development, this cohort of elder GLBT individuals has been particularly vulnerable to "internalized homophobia," resulting in a reticence to reveal their sexuality or gender identity to service providers (Langley, 2001). Smith (2002) submits that, compared with gay men and lesbians, people with a bisexual orientation are even less visible because they fear rejection by both the gay and straight communities.

Although older GLBT adults are invisible in part because they seek anonymity to avoid discrimination, they are also invisible because the dominant heterosexual society generally seeks to ignore their existence (Connolly, 1996). This attitude, sometimes described as "heterosexual assumption" (Healy, 2002), presents barriers to full disclosure by elder GLBT who have learned—with good cause—to live their lives "passing" as straight (Wojciechowski, 1998). Quam (1997) recalls asking a group of 15 to 20 social workers, who were both sensitive to gay and lesbian issues and practicing in long-term care, to estimate the number of gay or lesbian clients they had had in their careers; only one practitioner could recall any GLBT clients, and this social worker could only think of one: "he never exactly came out to me . . . but then I never asked him about it" (p. xv). Clearly this invisibility can affect quality of care. For example, Cook-Daniels (1997) notes that GLBT elders have so routinely taken extraordinary measures to protect their privacy that they are frequently unwilling to allow persons who provide personal care into their homes.

It is important to emphasize again the diversity that exists in the population of GLBT elders, a diversity which also encompasses degree of identity concealment. For example, some of today's GLBT older adults have "come out" (i.e., assuming self-definition as gay, lesbian, bisexual, or transgender) in their middle age, and their experiences may be quite different from those who identified as GLBT in their youth, during the more oppressive preliberation years. Friend (1991) suggests that older gay men and lesbians fall along a continuum in terms of their cognitive/behavioral responses to heterosexism. One end of this continuum represents GLBT individuals who have internalized the negative societal messages, and the other end represents individuals who have formed affirmative self-perceptions.

In addition to the heterosexism, homophobia, and transphobia that affect GLBT individuals across their life spans, ageism is an added insult for the GLBT elder. The GLBT community has not been immune to the youth worship reflected in mainstream U.S. society (Boxer, 1997; Connolly, 1996; van Wormer et al., 2000). Gay culture has been guilty of being particularly youth focused; what is old has been seen as less attractive and less worthy than what is young (Auger, 1992; Brotman et al., 2003; Cahill et al., 2000). For example, in a study conducted by Jacobs, Rasmussen, and Hohman (1999), GLB respondents reported greater levels of ageism in the gay/lesbian community than in the society at large. This issue of ageism may be particularly prevalent among gay males, for whom the gay identity is often focused on sexualized physical attractiveness, which is frequently associated with youth (Jones, 2001). Moreover, ageism in the GLBT community may be an extension of internalized homophobia, which, at times, affects GLBT individuals' self-acceptance and acceptance of other GLBT persons.

WHAT IS KNOWN ABOUT GLBT ELDERS?

Although there has been increasing research on GLBT elders in recent years, what we know is gathered from relatively few studies, which are based on small nonrepresentative samples (Humphreys & Quam, 1998). The majority of these studies are of gay men, with a smaller number on lesbians, and very few include bisexual or transgender individuals. Furthermore, most investigations have utilized small samples that do not reflect the racial and economic diversity within the GLBT community (Cahill et al., 2000; Christian & Keefe, 1997). Meyer (2001) notes a range of obstacles that stand in the way of gathering knowledge about GLBT populations. Some of these obstacles are methodological, and "others are related to homophobia and heterosexism, which place GLBT studies outside the mainstream in terms of importance and allocation of resources" (p. 857).

In the seminal report, *Outing Age: Public Policy Issues Affecting Gay, Lesbian, Bisexual and Transgender Elders,* Cahill, South, and Spade (2000) synthesize current research. It appears that elder GLBT individuals are more likely to live alone than their heterosexual counterparts. They are also less likely to be living with life partners and less likely to have children than

heterosexual seniors (Cahill et al., 2000). For example, one New York City-based study found 65% of their sample of 253 gay and lesbian seniors to live alone; this was nearly twice the rate of living alone among the entire population of New Yorkers 65 and older (36%; Brookdale Center on Aging of Hunter College and Senior Action in a Gay Environment, 1999). Another study with a sample of gay and lesbian elders in the Los Angeles area found that 75% of their respondents reported living alone (Rosenfeld, 1999).

It is important to distinguish living alone from being lonely. There is a pervasive stereotype of GLBT elders as lonely and isolated. This caricature has been refuted repeatedly in the literature (Blando, 2001; Christian & Keefe, 1997; Dorfman et al., 1995; Whitford, 1997): GLBT elders are no more lonely than heterosexual elders or than GLBT younger adults (Cahill et al., 2000). Moreover, some have posited that GLBT elders may have a social advantage given their well-developed social networks of choice, which provide a broad base of support in times of loss and need (Barranti & Cohen, 2000; Butler & Hope, 1999; Healy, 2002). Committed partner relationships are important to many GLBT elders; surveys of gay and lesbian individuals have documented "a range of 40–60% of gay men and 45–80% of lesbians in a committed relationship at any given time" (Cahill et al., 2000, p. 10). Grossman, D'Augelli, and Hershberger (2000) found that partners provide the most support, as compared with friends and family, in GLB support networks.

PARTICULAR STRENGTHS OF GLBT ELDERS

Contrary to the myths of a pathetic and lonely old age, many gay men and lesbians approach their elder years with unique resiliency and particular strengths. Barranti and Cohen (2000) enumerate specific factors which may allow GLBT individuals to enter their elder years with greater ease than their non-GLBT peers:

- Coping skills developed through the process of accepting their sexual identity may help GLBT seniors in the acceptance of aging.
- Skills developed through the coming-out process and the management of the social perception of "difference" throughout life prepare GLBT individuals for society's perception of older people in a youth-oriented society.

- The stigma of being older is often experienced as less severe than the stigma of being "queer," which gay men and lesbians faced in their youth.
- In part due to rejections by families of origin and/or procreation, GLBT individuals often create "families of choice," which are able to provide extensive social support in times of need.
- Greater flexibility in gender roles exhibited by GLBT individuals can be helpful in the aging process.

These factors have been highlighted by numerous authors in the literature on GLBT elders (e.g., Butler & Hope, 1999; Healy, 2002; Humphreys & Quam, 1998; McDougall, 1993; Morrow, 2001: Quam & Whitford, 1992; Wojciechowski, 1998).

Despite these advantages, GLBT individuals do experience some obstacles in their latter years, some of which are not shared with their heterosexual counterparts. For example, GLBT older adults may face declining health, loss of partners and friends, ageism, and reduced income in their later years, just as many heterosexual older adults do. But they may also face barriers to services due to discrimination, reduced financial security when their partnerships are not recognized, and blatant homophobia from health and social service professionals, which may not be shared by their heterosexual counterparts. Although there is greater acceptance of gay and lesbian relationships and GLBT individuals in general in our society than existed 30 years ago, considerable discrimination, stigma, and overt hatred toward homosexuality remain (Brotman et al., 2003).

CHALLENGES FACED BY GLBT ELDERS

Heterosexism, homophobia, transphobia, legal discrimination, and the inability of GLBT partners to benefit from the advantages of being married spouses lead to many specific problems and barriers to service for GLBT seniors (Smith & Calvert, 2001). I enumerate a few of these challenges here, drawing largely from the work of Cahill, South, and Spade (2000).

Access to Services

There are very few organizations whose mission is specifically to meet the needs of GLBT elders. They exist in large cities with relatively visible GLBT communities. Nevertheless, the majority of GLBT elders in the country do not have access to such specialized services and must seek services in more mainstream aging organizations such as the Area Agencies on Aging (AAAs). Most mainstream aging organizations are not sensitive to the needs of GLBT elders (Behney, 1994).

Lack of Recognition of GLBT Families

Legal marriage affords certain rights and privileges that are unavailable to same-sex partners. People of the same sex are not allowed to marry, and domestic partnerships are neither widely available nor as comprehensive as the rights and responsibilities of marriage (Cahill et al., 2000). Some rights generally unavailable to GLBT partners include Social Security benefits for survivors, employee health benefits, inheritance, housing, and hospital visitation.

Social Security and Gay/Lesbian Couples

Cahill and his coauthors suggest that Social Security's treatment of same-sex couples may be the most blatant and costly example of institutionalized heterosexism in federal policy. Under the current Social Security system, married spouses, some divorced spouses, and children are eligible for survivor benefits; unmarried spouses (e.g., same-sex partners) are ineligible for these benefits no matter how many years they may have lived with and supported their partners. Similarly, minor children in unrecognized GLBT families are ineligible for benefits (Dubois, 1999). The Social Security Administration estimated that in 1998, 781,000 widows and widowers received an average of $442.00 a month in survivor benefits, costing the Social Security system $4.1 billion (Cahill et al., 2000). If only 3% of those individuals who survived their life partners were gay or lesbian, the failure to pay Social Security benefits to GLBT surviving partners would total about $124 million a year (Cahill et al., 2000).

Nursing Homes and Homophobia

Although less than 5% of older adults over 65 reside in nursing homes at any one time (Hooyman & Kiyak, 2002), the fear of ending one's life in a nursing facility is pervasive. This fear is particularly ubiquitous among GLBT elders who worry that their integrity and life choices will not be honored as they become physically frail and/or mentally vulnerable (Auger, 1992; Butler & Hope, 1999; Connolly, 1996; Quam, 1997). When GLBT elders enter mainstream assisted living, nursing facilities, or retirement communities, they are frequently presumed to be heterosexual; their long-term partnerships may not be recognized or valued.

Other challenges described in the literature on GLBT aging include accessing quality health care (Barranti & Cohen, 2000; Brotman et al., 2003; Humphreys & Quam, 1998; U.S. Administration on Aging [AoA], 2001)—particularly for transgender elders (Donovan, 2001; Niedermayer, 2002; Witten, 2002); obtaining adequate housing (Humphreys & Quam, 1998; Langley, 2001); securing social support (Grossman et al., 2000; Humphreys & Quam, 1998; Jacobs et al., 1999); bereavement issues (Gallance & Warshaw, 2004; Kochman, 1997; McDougall, 1993; Wojciechowski, 1998); loneliness (Boxer, 1997; D'Augelli et al., 2001; Kehoe, 1991; Kochman, 1997; Quam & Whitford, 1992); and poverty (Quam & Whitford, 1992; AoA, 2001).

PRACTICE GUIDELINES

Given the strengths that GLBT elders bring to the aging process, as well as the extra challenges they face in a heterosexist, homophobic, and transphobic society, there are implications for both culturally competent practice and proactive policy change. In order to lessen and eventually eliminate both the subtle and blatant discrimination and oppression faced by current and future GLBT seniors, attention must be paid to micro, mezzo, and macro level practice. Affirmative practice with GLBT elders involves a framework that is based on clients' strengths and that encompasses aspects of empowerment, ecological, and feminist approaches to practice (Hunter & Hickerson, 2003). Langley (2001) warns against the liberal humanist approach to tolerance, which fails to acknowledge the importance of understanding the life context of GLBT elders.

The following broad practice guidelines are a synthesis of suggestions offered by Berger (1985), Connolly (1996), Cook-Daniels (1997), Healy (2002), Humphreys and Quam (1998), and Morrow (2001):

- Engage in self-reflection and work through your own heterosexism and homophobia.
- Recognize diversity in the GLBT community.

- Protect privacy and confidentiality.
- Listen especially carefully and strive to connect with your client.
- Recognize that all presenting problems are not due to being old or being GLBT.
- Honor relationships and treat identified family as family.
- Assess your agency and combat heterosexist assumptions and homophobia.
- Utilize inclusive language and plan activities that are neutral with respect to sexual orientation.
- Educate yourself about special issues facing GLBT elders and resources in the community.
- Find respectful service providers to whom to make referrals.
- Assist the client in connecting with the GLBT community.
- Work to develop more GLBT-friendly resources.
- Include GLBT elders in program planning.
- Advocate to change heterosexist organizational, local, state, and federal policies.

Practitioners can look to the literature for ideas regarding affirmative activities and interventions with GLBT elders and training for culture change in organizations serving older adults. Examples include a program utilizing a buddy system for homebound elders (Jacobs et al., 1999); a community organizing approach to involving GLBT elders in program planning (Beeler, Rawles, Herdt, & Cohler, 1999); pet therapy with lonely GLBT elders (Kehoe, 1991); the use of support groups (Slusher, Mayer, & Dunkle, 1996); life-review workshops (Galassi, 1991); changing agency culture to be more GLBT friendly (Smith & Calvert, 2001); and providing staff training for more affirmative practice with GLBT clients (Metz, 1997; Senior Action in a Gay Environment [SAGE] and Brookdale Center on Aging, 2003).

Many challenges facing GLBT older adults will not be easily solved without policy change. As a profession, social work is committed to advancing policies that will improve the status and well-being of all GLBT persons (NASW, 2003). Cahill et al. (2000) provide a comprehensive list of recommendations for policy advocacy and activism with regard to GLBT elders. The reader is encouraged to access this sourcebook for detailed suggestions under the following broad categories: research; service, training, and caregiving; recognition of GLBT families; housing; health care; and discrimination and income support (Cahill et al., 2000, pp. 70–78).

Today's GLBT elders have lived through years of legalized oppression and discrimination. Although their numbers are significant, they are not always visible, having spent many years protecting their private lives, sexual orientation, and/or gender identity from public view. Social worker practitioners can be at the forefront of improving the quality of life for today's GLBT elders and for the elder generations to follow.

Listserv and Selected Web Resources Related to GLBT Elders

International listserv on GLBT aging issues—send e-mail to: *lgb-elder-studies-subscribe@yahoo groups.com*

Lesbian and Gay Aging Issues Network (LGAIN), Interest Group of the American Society on Aging: *http://www.asaging.org/lgain*

Senior Action in a Gay Environment (SAGE): *http://www.sageusa.org*

Transgender Aging Network: *http://www.forge-forwrd.org/TAN*

Gay and Lesbian Association for Retired Persons: *http://www.gaylesbianretiring.org*

Pride Senior Network: *http://www.preidesenior.org*

Old Lesbians Organizing for Change (OLOC): *http://www.oloc.org*

Classic Dykes: *http://classicdykes.com*

REFERENCES

Appleby, G. A., & Anastas, J. W. (1998). *Not just a passing phase: Social work with gay, lesbian and bisexual people.* New York: Columbia University Press.

Auger, J. A. (1992). Living in the margins: Lesbian aging. *Canadian Woman Studies, 12*(2), 80–84.

Barranti, C. C. R., & Cohen, H. L. (2000). Lesbian and gay elders: An invisible minority. In R. L. Schneider, N. P. Kropf, & A. J. Kisor (Eds.) *Gerontological social work: Knowledge, service settings, and special populations* (2nd ed., pp. 343–367). Pacific-Grove, CA: Brooks/Cole.

Beeler, J. A., Rawles, T. W., Herdt, G., & Cohler, B. (1999). The needs of older lesbians and gay men in Chicago. *Journal of Gay and Lesbian Social Services, 9*(1), 31–49.

Behney, R. (1994, Winter). The aging network's response to gay and lesbian issues. *Outword: Newsletter of the Lesbian and Gay Aging Issues Network, 1*(2), 2.

Berger, R. M. (1985). Rewriting a bad script: Older lesbians and gays. In H. Hidalgo, T. L. Peterson, & N. J. Woodman (Eds.), *Lesbian and gay issues: A resource manual for social workers* (pp. 53–59). Silver Spring, MD: National Association of Social Workers.

Blando, J. A. (2001). Twice hidden: Older gay and lesbian couples, friends, and intimacy. *Generations, 25*(2), 87–89.

Boxer, A. M. (1997). Gay, lesbian and bisexual aging into the twenty-first century: An overview and introduction. *Journal of Gay, Lesbian and Bisexual Identity, 2*(3/4), 187–197.

Brookdale Center on Aging of Hunter College and Senior Action in a Gay Environment. (1999). *Assistive housing for elderly gays and lesbians in New York City: Extent of need and the preferences of elderly gays and lesbians.* New York: Author.

Brotman, S., Ryan, B., & Cormier, R. (2003). The health and social service needs of gay and lesbian elders and their families in Canada. *Gerontologist, 43*(2), 192–202.

Butler, S. S., & Hope, B. (1999). Health and well-being for late middle-aged and old lesbians in a rural area. *Journal of Gay and Lesbian Social Services, 9*(4), 27–46.

Cahill, S., South, K., & Spade, J. (2000). *Outing age: Public policy issues affecting gay, lesbian, bisexual and transgender elders.* Washington, DC: Policy Institute, National Gay and Lesbian Task Force.

Christian, D. V., & Keefe, D. A. (1997). Maturing gay men: A framework for social service assessment and intervention. In J. K. Quam (Ed.) *Social services for senior gay men and lesbians* (pp. 47–78). New York: Harrington Park Press.

Connolly, L. (1996). Long-term care and hospice: The special needs of older gay men and lesbians. *Journal of Gay and Lesbian Social Services, 5*(1), 77–91.

Cook-Daniels, L. (1997). Lesbian, gay male, bisexual and transgendered elders: Elder abuse and neglect issues. *Journal of Elder Abuse and Neglect, 9*(2), 35–49.

D'Augelli, A. R., Grossman, A. H., Hershberger, S. L., & O'Connell, T. S. (2001). Aspects of mental health among older lesbian, gay and bisexual adults. *Aging and Mental Health, 5*(2), 149–158.

Donovan, T. (2001). Being transgender and older: A first person account. *Journal of Gay and Lesbian Social Services, 13*(4), 19–22.

Dorfman, R., Walters, K., Burke, P., Hardin, L., Karanik, T., Raphael, J., & Silverstein, E. (1995). Old, sad and alone: The myth of the aging homosexual. *Journal of Gerontological Social Work, 24*(1/2), 29–44.

Dubois, M. R. (1999). Legal planning for gay, lesbian, and non-traditional elders. *Albany Law Review, 63*(1), 263–332.

Friend, R. A. (1991). Older lesbian and gay people: A theory of successful aging. *Journal of Homosexuality, 20*(3/4), 99–118.

Galassi, F. S. (1991). A life-review workshop for gay and lesbian elders. *Journal of Gerontological Social Work, 16*(1/2), 75–86.

Gallance, R., & Warshaw, S. (2004, Spring). Working with lesbian, gay, bisexual and transgender seniors. *Aging Section Connection,* 10–13.

Grossman, A. H., D'Augelli, A. R., & Hershberger, S. L. (2000). Social support networks of lesbian, gay, and bisexual adults 60 years of age and older. *Journals of Gerontology: Series B. Psychological Sciences and Social Sciences, 55*(3), P171–P179.

Healy, T. (2002). Culturally competent practice with elderly lesbians. *Geriatric Care Management Journal, 12*(3), 9–13.

Herdt, G., Beeler, J., & Rawles, T. W. (1997). Life course diversity among older lesbians and gay men: A study in Chicago. *Journal of Gay, Lesbian, and Bisexual Identity, 2*(3/4), 231–246.

Hildago, H., Peterson, T. L., & Woodman, N. J. (1985). Introduction. In H. Hildago, T. L. Peterson, & N. J. Woodman (Eds.) *Lesbian and gay issues: A resource manual for social workers* (pp. 1–6). Silver Spring, MD: National Association of Social Workers.

Hooyman, N. R., & Kiyak, H. A. (2002). *Social gerontology: A multidisciplinary perspective* (6th ed.). Boston: Allyn & Bacon.

Humphreys, N. A., & Quam, J. K. (1998). Middle-aged and old gay, lesbian, and bisexual adults. In G. A. Appleby & J. W. Anastas (Eds.), *Not just a passing phase: Social work with gay, lesbian and bisexual people* (pp. 245–267). New York: Columbia University Press.

Hunter, S., & Hickerson, J. C. (2003). *Affirmative practice: Understanding and working with lesbian, gay, bisexual, and transgender persons.* Washington, DC: NASW Press.

Jacobs, R. J., Rasmussen, L. A., & Hohman, M. M. (1999). The social support needs of older lesbians, gay men, and bisexuals. *Journal of Gay and Lesbian Social Services, 9*(1), 1–30.

Jones, B. E. (2001). Is having the luck of growing old in the gay, lesbian, bisexual, transgender community good or bad luck? *Journal of Gay and Lesbian Social Services, 13*(4), 13–14.

Kehoe, M. (1991). Loneliness and the aging homosexual: Is pet therapy an answer? *Journal of Homosexuality, 20*(3/4), 137–142.

Kochman, A. (1997). Gay and lesbian elderly: Historical overview and implications for social work practice. In J. K. Quam (Ed.), *Social services for senior gay men and lesbians* (pp. 1–10). New York: Harrington Park Press.

Langley, J. (2001). Developing anti-oppressive empowering social work practice with older lesbian women and gay men. *British Journal of Social Work, 31,* 917–932.

McDougall, G. J. (1993). Therapeutic issues with gay and lesbian elders. In T. L. Brink (Ed.), *The forgotten aged: Ethnic, psychiatric, and societal minorities* (pp. 45–57). Binghamton, NY: Haworth Press.

Metz, P. (1997). Staff development for working with lesbian and gay elders. In J. K. Quam (Ed.), *Senior services for gay men and lesbians* (pp. 35–45). New York: Harrington Park Press.

Meyer, I. H. (2001). Why lesbian, gay, bisexual, transgender public health? *American Journal of Public Health, 91*(6), 856–859.

Morrow, D. F. (2001). Older gays and lesbians: Surviving a generation of hate and violence. *Journal of Gay and Lesbian Social Services, 13*(1/2), 151–169.

National Association of Social Workers. (2003). *Social work speaks: National Association of Social Workers policy statement 2003–2006* (6th ed.). Washington, DC: Author.

Niedermayer, G. (2002). A transgender elder's healthcare odyssey: "At age 60, I'm having to teach doctors. . . . ." *Outword: Newsletter of LGAIN, 8*(3), 3, 8.

Quam, J. K. (1997). Preface. In J. K. Quam (Ed.), *Social services for senior gay men and lesbians* (pp. xv–xvi). New York: Harrington Park Press.

Quam, J. K., & Whitford, G. S. (1992). Adaptation and age-related expectations of older gay and lesbian adults. *Gerontologist, 32*(3), 367–374.

Rosenfeld, D. (1999). Identity work among lesbian and gay elderly. *Journal of Aging Studies, 13*(2), 121–144.

Senior Action in a Gay Environment and Brookdale Center on Aging. (2003). *No need to fear, no need to hide: A training program for inclusion and understanding of lesbian, gay, bisexual and transgender (GLBT) elders in long term care facilities.* New York: Author.

Slusher, M. P., Mayer, C. J., & Dunkle, R. E. (1996). Gay and lesbians older and wiser (GLOW): A support group for older gay people. *Gerontologist, 36*(1), 118–123.

Sitter, K. (1997). Jim: Coming out at age sixty-two. In J. K. Quam (Ed.) *Social services for senior gay men and lesbians* (pp. 101–104). New York: Harrington Park Press.

Smith, P. R. (2002). Bisexuality: Reviewing the basics, debunking the stereotypes for professionals in aging. *Outword: Newsletter of LGAIN, 8*(4), 2, 8.

Smith, H., & Calvert, J. (2001). *Opening doors: Working with older lesbians and gay men.* London: Aging Concern England.

U.S. Administration on Aging. (2001). *Lesbian, gay, bisexual and transgender older persons* [Fact sheet for

Older Americans' Month, May 2001]. Washington, DC: Author.

van Wormer, K., Wells, J., & Boes, M. (2000). *Social work with lesbians, gays and bisexuals: A strengths perspective.* Boston: Allyn & Bacon.

Whitford, G. S. (1997). Realities and hopes for older gay men. In J. K. Quam (Ed.), *Social services for senior gay men and lesbians* (pp. 79–95). New York: Harrington Park Press.

Witten, T. M. (2002). Geriatric care and management issues for the transgender and intersex populations. *Geriatric Care Management Journal, 12*(3), 20–24.

Wojciechowski, C. (1998). Issues in caring for older lesbians. *Journal of Gerontological Nursing, 24*(7), 28–33.

The population ages 65 and older of Latino/Hispanic descent numbered 2 million in 2002 and is expected to grow to 13.4 million by the year 2050 (Administration on Aging, 2003). Older Latinos/Hispanics will comprise the largest racial/ethnic minority group in this age group by the year 2028 (Administration on Aging, 2003). According to the U.S. Census Bureau:

> [p]ersons of Hispanic origin are those who classified themselves in one of the specific Hispanic origin categories listed on the questionnaire—"Mexican," "Puerto Rican," or "Cuban"—as well as those who indicated that they were of "other Spanish/Hispanic/Latino" origin. Persons of "Other Spanish/Hispanic/Latino" origin are those whose origins are from Spain, the Spanish-speaking countries of Central or South America, or the Dominican Republic, or they are persons of Hispanic origin identifying themselves generally as Spanish, Spanish-American, Hispanic, Hispano, Latino, and so on.
> (*http://www.census.gov/acs/www/UseData/Def/Hispanic.htm*)

People of Latino/Hispanic origin may be of any race, thus adding to an already existing ethnic diversity. Among older Latinos/Hispanics in the United States, the majority (50%) is of Mexican descent, 17% are Cuban, 11% are Puerto Rican, and 24% are other Hispanic (Angel & Hogan, 2004). Moreover, older Latinos/Hispanics (hereinafter called older Latinos), are considered a diverse group of persons differentiated by a plethora of contextual experiences such as language, culture, sociopolitical history, acculturation, cumulative life experiences, and opportunities (Angel & Angel, 1998; Bean & Tienda, 1987).

The purpose of this chapter is to discuss a selected group of sociodemographic and cultural indicators in the service of showing how these indicators are relevant to social work practice in the mental health arena. Alternately stated, what role do income, education, living arrangements, physical illness and disability, culture and language play in the development of culturally competent mental health practice with older persons of Latino descent? Thus the information presented here goes beyond describing the contextual realities of older Latinos to offer a bridge to the next stage of developing mental health services related to older adults living with psychiatric disabilities. In order to provide a more tangible discussion, the material is applied to the case of late-life depressive illness. Although in the past more attention has focused on the health status of older Lati-

MARIA P. ARANDA

Older Latinos: A Mental Health Perspective

nos, this chapter attempts to narrow the serious gap in the mental health literature, specifically in terms of treatment of depressive disorders in communities of color. Such information has important implications for practice, because social workers are typically the "front-line" providers of mental health services in the United States (Miller, 2002). Focusing on depression is also a public health concern given that depression is associated with increased mortality, comorbidity, health service use and costs, and overall quality of life (Murphy, Smith, & Slatter, 1988; Murray & López, 1996; Wells et al., 1989; Katon et al., 1990; Koenig & Kuchibhatla, 1998; Unützer et al., 1997).

LATE-LIFE DEPRESSION

Clinically significant depression affects between 15 to 20% of older adults in the United States (Koenig & Blazer, 1996; Lebowitz, 1997) or 5.2 million of the 35 million Americans over the age of 65. A recent review by Blazer (2002) highlights the phenomenal growth in understanding the prevalence, etiology, nature, trajectory, and treatment of depressive illness in late life. Of particular interest to social workers are the promising treatments or care strategies—biological and psychological—available to practitioners in their commitment to prevent or mitigate the consumer- and society-related consequences of depressive illnesses. Still, key questions remain: Do older adults of color have at their disposal the same access to timely information, evaluation, and treatments as do mainstream older adults? What type of modifications in evidenced-based treatments are needed in order to make these treatments not only more linguistically and culturally congruent but acceptable to a wider range of older minorities who also experience structural disadvantages in terms of access to mental health care? The following section discusses several sociodemographic and cultural indicators relevant to the discussion of depression care in older Latinos.

SOCIODEMOGRAPHIC INDICATORS AND IMPLICATIONS FOR DEPRESSION AND DEPRESSION TREATMENT

Income, Wealth, and Retirement

Latinos, like other adults, look forward to living a healthy and productive life in their later years. To what degree this comes to fruition is in part dependent on the person's ability to accumulate sufficient wealth and income to sustain himself or herself during the retirement years. Conversely stated, to what degree has the older person developed a "three-pronged" income profile composed of Social Security benefits, private pensions, and savings and investment income?

Having confronted significant cumulative educational and employment disadvantages during their earlier years, many Hispanics have been unable to accumulate sufficient financial resources to sustain themselves during retirement (Villa & Aranda, 2000). Older Latinos are less likely to receive income from Social Security, yet typically Social Security benefits remain the *sole* source of income for Latinos (Villa & Aranda, 2000). Second, Latino elderly individuals are less likely than Blacks or Whites to report receiving income from pension benefits or supplemental Medigap health insurance than non-Hispanics (Angel & Angel, 1997). Third, older Latinos are as likely as Blacks and much less likely than Whites to receive income from interest on savings and investments. Thus it comes as no surprise that the poverty rate for Latino older adults over the age of 65 is about twice that of the total older adult population (21% compared to 10%, respectively; Federal Interagency Forum on Aging-Related Statistics, 2004).

The implications of poverty and low economic resources during the retirement years are significant and numerous. The following discussion addresses the implications related to Latinos' at-risk status for depression and low access to mental health services. First, the association between depression and lower income status (or financial strain) is well supported in population-based studies of preretirement and older adult populations (see Blazer, 2003; Cornoni-Huntley et al., 1990; Dunlop, Song, Lyons, Manheim, & Chang, 2003). This association has also been found in studies on depression in older Latinos. For example, using epidemiological data from the Hispanic Established Populations for Epidemiologic Studies of the Elderly (H-EPESE) study of more than 3,000 Mexican Americans in the southwestern United States, Black, Markides, and Miller (1998) found that both females and males have elevated rates of depressive symptomatology than those found among older adults in general (25.6% vs. 10%, respectively; Black et al., 1998; Blazer, Hughes, & George, 1987), as well in comparison with the 15.1% reporting the same symptom range in the primarily Anglo American New Haven EPESE (White, Kohout, Evans, Cornoni-Huntley, & Ostfeld, 1986). Similar results indicating higher rates of depressive symptomatology were found by Gonzalez and his associates in the Sacramento Area Latino Study on Aging (SALSA) study of older Latinos in the Sacramento area (Gonzalez, Haan, & Hinton, 2001). Moreover, higher levels of financial strain were found to be associated with twice the risk of clinically significant depressive symptomatology for both males and females (Black et al., 1998). Additional data from the H-EPESE (Angel, Frisco, Angel, & Chiriboga, 2003; Chiriboga, Black, Aranda, & Markides, 2002) suggest that a "cluster" of economic stressors and conditions may play an enhanced role in the etiology of depressive symptoms in older Mexican Americans, namely annual income, acute financial event, and chronic financial strains. Work with non-Latino populations has also underscored the especially noxious effects of chronic financial strains on mental health due to its persistent and unrelenting nature (Krause, 1997; Krause, Liang, & Gu, 1998; Lincoln, Chatters, & Taylor, 2003).

Disaggregating the data by gender and Latino subgroup reveals that the most economically vulnerable among this population are older Latinas: 25% of Latinas live in poverty compared to 18.1% of their male counterparts (Proctor & Dalakar, 2002) while close to 50% of older Latinas living alone live in poverty (Angel & Hogan, 2004). Although prevalence studies of psychiatric disorders of younger Latinos indicate more favorable mental health outcomes for immigrant versus U.S.-born Latinos (see review by USDHHS, 2001), older immigrant Latinos (especially females) tend to be at higher risk (Black et al., 1998; Kemp, Staples, & López-Aqueres, 1987; Mendes de Leon & Markides, 1988). Taken together, these findings show that older Latinos are overrepresented in terms of low income and high financial strain, with older Latinas and immigrants being most at risk of developing depressive symptomatology.

The second implication of low economic resources is that, although older Latinos may be at risk for depressive disorders, they also tend to be low utilizers of specialty mental health care (López-Aqueres, Kemp, Plopper, Staples, & Brummel-Smith, 1984; Vega, Kolody, Aguilar-Gaxiola, & Catalano, 1999). Significant barriers exist that lead to limited access to—and utilization of—mental health services by older Latinos. System-level barriers are often found to be the most important barriers to mental health service utilization—barriers such as insufficient mental health resources, unavailability of bilingual/bicultural staff, long waiting time, lack of outreach, lack of transportation, lack of publicity or information, service

fragmentation, and low level of Medicare reimbursement (Abramson, Trejo, & Lai, 2002; Aranda & Torres, 1997; Biegel, Farkas, & Song, 1997; Padgett, Burns, & Grau, 1998). In a depression treatment study of primary care consumers, Latinos (as well as African Americans) reported substantially lower rates of lifetime and recent depression care (Unützer et al., 2003). Although the majority of the participants (all racial/ethnic groups) indicated a preference for psychotherapy rather than antidepressant medications, only 8% actually received counseling or psychotherapy in the months before enrolling in the study.

Limited financial means also translates into less available capital for purchasing services or accessing clinical services. For example, one out of two Mexican Americans over the age of 65 reported not having enough money at the end of the month to make ends meet (Chiriboga et al., 2002). Access to care is compromised given the person's inability to pay for an adequate trial of depression treatment, such as pharmacological therapies, as well as sociobehavioral and psychosocial interventions. Drawing from the health services literature, racial and ethnic minority groups receive limited or inadequate mental health services (Cheung & Snowden, 1990; Hu et al., 1991) and are less satisfied with the quality of services they receive (Alegría et al., 2002; Smedley, Stith, & Nelson, 2003; Snowden et al., 2003). Although the first literature to address the disparity in Latino mental health service utilization appeared approximately 30 years ago (see Lopez, 2002), Latinos continue to utilize mental health services at lower rates than their non-Latino counterparts (USDHHS, 2001). As has been documented extensively, Latinos (35%) are more likely than Whites (14%) or African Americans (21%) to report being without insurance (Pew Hispanic Center & Kaiser Family Foundation, 2002).

Thus older Latinos may wait until their conditions worsen before seeking care or following up with their treatment regimens. Then what providers may be confronted with in terms of depression is dealing with consumers who have been affected by depression for a longer time without receiving services or with an episodic trajectory of services. This is unfortunate given the emerging work that indicates that low-income Latinos are able to respond favorably to depression care even with modest linguistic and cultural adaptations (Miranda et al., 2003) and, in some cases, supersede the effects found for their White counterparts (Unützer et al., 2003) Delaying appropriate treatment may have adverse effects in that low-income, older Latinos may accommodate to the symptoms of depressive illness and appear more fatalistic in their perceptions about being able to get better. Sometimes this sense of fatalism is misperceived as a cultural value, when in reality it is an accommodation and a survival strategy in the face of chronic strain (Aranda & Knight, 1997). Thus the social worker and other providers are typically faced with real-life situations that are at a crisis—or near crisis—level, that have gone unnoticed or ignored for many years. This increases the likelihood that the social work practitioner will be involved in providing therapeutic services, as well as case management and other forms of resource-enhancing, crisis-mitigating activities. The case management approach to depression care has received support in recent years as a viable component to a multimodal program of services (Dwight-Johnson, Ell, & Jiuan-Lee, 2005; Unützer et al., 2003).

Another issue is the complex interaction between depression, chronic illness, and medication adherence. For example, using multiple sources of longitudinal, population-based data on older adults, researchers (Heisler et al., 2004) found that patients with serious chronic illnesses experience adverse health events when they restrict their use of prescription drugs due to cost. Specifically, middle-aged and older Americans who cut back on their prescribed medications experienced a statistically significant decline in their self-reported health status, and among those with preexisting heart conditions, there was a 50% higher risk of subsequent heart attacks, strokes, and angina. For those older adults over the age of 72 who restricted the use of prescription drugs due to cost, there was a significant increase in the risk of more severe depressive symptomatology. Disparities in the ability to purchase medications has far-reaching implications for older racial and ethnic minorities, such that those who restricted buying medications were more likely to have lower annual income and educational levels and to have no insurance or insurance without full prescription medication coverage. Thus being uninsured or underinsured could result in not being able to initiate—or to continue—guideline-concordant pharmacological treatments, which in turn could have a deleterious effect on mental health outcomes for older individuals from ethnic and racial minorities who are at risk.

Perhaps having higher educational status in late life is important in order to be able to access the myriad opportunities and resources that can foster psychological well-being: ability to access tangible, emotional, and cognitive resources such as housing, transportation, medical care, self-esteem, self-effi-

cacy, cognitive flexibility, positive attributions, pleasant activities (religious, social, family, civic), and so forth.

Educational Level

Although the educational attainment among older Americans has increased in the last few decades, large educational differences exist among older Latinos and their non-Latino counterparts. Older Latinos represent one of the most structurally disadvantaged groups in the United States as a result of their low educational attainment. According to census reports (Federal Interagency Forum on Aging-Related Statistics, 2004), about 70% of older Hispanics fail to complete high school, compared with almost 30% of the overall older adult population. Only 5% of older Latinos have bachelor's degrees or higher, compared with 16% of the older adult population in general. Specific groups of older Latinos are disproportionately represented in terms of educational attainment, such that older Cubans, for example, have comparable high school completion rates to those of Whites (Villa & Aranda, 2000). Even when education levels are the same, Latinos often earn less than their non-Hispanic White counterparts (Council of Economic Advisers, 1998), evidence that occupational segregation and glass ceilings experienced by older Latinos and their family members are a stark reality.

Formal education is a key mechanism by which people develop more expansive cognitive strategies for learning and the acquisition of knowledge and vocabulary, as well as enlarge their repertoires of positive coping strategies and develop resources and increase access to a wider array of helping networks associated with adaptation and resiliency. This situation has implications for clinical social work practice and mental health. Lower education levels present a challenge to practitioners to the degree that many current evidence-based interventions were initially developed and refined based on certain types of peoples with certain sociodemographic characteristics.

Living Arrangements

Coresidence tends to be higher among older Latinos in comparison with the general older population. For example, living alone tends to be proportionately less common among both older Latino males and females, whereas older Latinos are twice as likely to live with a relative (nonspouse) as compared with the general older adult population. For example, 25% of older Latinas live with other relatives (mostly adult children) as compared with 7% of females in the total older adult population. Similarly, 15% of older Latino males live with other relatives, compared with 4% of the male non-Latino population (Federal Interagency Forum on Aging-Related Statistics, 2004).

Coresidence has implications for the assessment of the extent and nature of the older consumers' natural networks, including family and significant others. Although coresidence is only one aspect of the consumer's network, it is nonetheless a measure of proximity to help when help is needed, as well as the nature of reciprocity between individuals living in the same household. Second, coresidence provides some gauge of the potential participation of significant others in the care of older consumers. For instance, in a current qualitative study of depression treatment among home health patients over the age of 65, family members or significant others perform a key gatekeeper function for the older persons' participation in depression treatment; not only are they distillers of information, but they also function as protective agents in terms of the consent process and treatment regimens (Aranda, 2001; Aranda & Ell, 2004).

Similarly, lower rates of institutionalization (nursing home use) by older Latinos have been attributed to various demographic (higher fertility, larger families, multigenerational households), cultural (familism, filial obligation, low acculturation) and economic (low income, financial strain) factors (see discussion by Angel et al., 2004). Regardless of the reasons for low institutionalization rates, families tend to absorb a lion's share of the responsibility for the older person's long-term care needs. This notion was supported by Angel and her associates, who found that among older Mexican Americans (who make up 50% of the older Latino population in the United States), "even when they exhibit serious deficits in functional capacity, though, older individuals are more likely to remain in the community than to enter a nursing home. Indeed, our data indicate that death is a more likely outcome than institutionalization as the result of seriously compromised physical and cognitive status" (2004, p. 13).

Still, current profiles in terms of living arrangements and family structure may be changing, as evidenced by other work that points to the changing availability of family to provide assistance. Some studies have found that Latino caregivers have identified fewer networks for support (Phillips, Torres, de Ardon, Kommenich, Killen, & Rusinak, 2000), and others underscore the reality that for some Latinos, having a caregiver available to help them in the future may not be a consistently viable option (Talamantes, Cornell, Espino, Lichtenstein, & Hazuda, 1996). Thus, although previous generations of older Latinos have been described as surrounded by extensive and supportive networks, social workers are more likely to work with future cohorts of Latinos who have fewer caregiver supports available to them.

Physical Illness and Disability

There exists a consensus that depression coexists with physical illness and functional disability in older adults (Berkman et al., 1986; Gurland, Wilder, & Berkman, 1988; Hays, Wells, Sherbourne, Rogers, & Spitzer, 1995; NIH Consensus Development Panel on Depression in Late Life, 1992; Zeiss, Lewinsohn, Rohde, & Seeley, 1996). Moreover, depression is not only associated with the presence of disease but is also implicated in the development of disease and disability over time. Whereas mortality for certain conditions is equivalent to—and in some cases better than—that of non-Latino Whites, Latinos are disadvantaged for certain chronic conditions and have higher rates of disability than non-Latino Whites (Hazuda & Espino, 1997; Markides, Rudkin, Angel, & Espino, 1997). The evidence also suggests a higher prevalence of chronic medical conditions such as diabetes and its complications, obesity, certain cancers, Alzheimer's disease, and cardiovascular disease (especially in Latinas; Villa & Aranda, 2000; Espino, Burge, & Moreno, 1991; Perkowski et al., 1998). About 72% of Latinas and 42% of Latinos report a limitation in functional ability (Hazuda & Espino, 1997). This indicates a higher risk of functional impairment among Latinas over the age of 65. In developing depression care, it is important to address the role that physical illness and disability play in the etiology of depression, as well as in the ways that one approaches treatment.

Culture and Language

The goal of positive outcomes in mental health encounters is predicated to a substantial degree on the formulation of the consumer-provider relationship or alliance, regardless of the treatment orientation of the providers or service provided (Hepworth,

Rooney, & Larsen, 2002). A precursor to developing the therapeutic or care alliance is the ability of the consumer to express his or her situation in such a way that the provider can comprehend not only the spoken word but also culturally laden idioms, patterns of communication, and nonverbal gestures and cues (Aranda, 1999; Dyche & Zayas, 2001; Valle, 1998). Thus the language and ethnicity of both consumer and provider play a key role in the communication between both parties and the ability to formulate a helping relationship. In the mental health systems literature, one of the most studied hypotheses regarding the underutilization of services by Latinos is the lack of linguistically and culturally relevant mental health services (Lopez, 2002). These studies, mostly large-scale studies of mental health departments or centers in urban settings in large counties, have found that matching of consumers with same-language, same-ethnicity providers has for the most part resulted in more positive outcomes. What are less certain are the mechanisms and pathways that may account for the improved mental health of the consumers—for example, cultural expressions of mental health and illness, cultural explanatory models or notions of the etiology of psychological distress, personal and sociocentric beliefs regarding responsibility, help-seeking behaviors, the acceptance of and adherence to treatments, and so forth (Talamantes & Aranda, 2004; Lewis-Fernández & Díaz, 2002). Emerging work in clinical services research (Balsa, Seiler, McGuire, & Bloche, 2003; Cooper et al., 2000), especially more qualitatively driven efforts (Guarnaccia & Rodriguez, 1996), points to culturally laden beliefs and behaviors that may easily be misinterpreted by mainstream, professionally trained providers who make clinical judgments about who needs what type of treatment and the reasons why (Lewis-Fernàndez & Díaz, 2002).

CONCLUSION

Support for addressing the special mental health needs and strengths of older Latinos follows the principle of consumer- and family-centered services as set forth by the President's New Freedom Commission on Mental Health (2003). This chapter has addressed a selected set of sociodemographic indicators, along with cultural variables, and how these are related to the mental health needs and special circumstances of social work practice in the mental health arena. Older Latinos are at risk for depression, tend to underutilize

mental health services, and are least likely to be institutionalized even with higher levels of functional limitation. Although rates of coresidence are higher than for many other subgroups of older adults, the burden of caregiving may be more evident in subsequent generations of caregivers. With the aging of subsequent cohorts of U.S. Latinos, we can expect social workers to play a significant role in the delivery of mental health services to older Latinos and their families.

REFERENCES

Abramson, T. A., Trejo, L., & Lai, D. W. (2002). Culture and mental health: Providing appropriate services for a diverse older population. *Generations, 26,* 21–27.

Administration on Aging (2003). A statistical profile of Hispanic older Americans aged 65+. Washington, DC: U.S. Department of Health and Human Services. Author.

Alegría, M., Canino, G., Ríos, R., Vera, M., Calderón, J., Rusch, D., & Ortega, A. N. (2002). Inequalities in use of specialty mental health services among Latinos, African Americans, and Non-Latino Whites. *Psychiatric Services, 53,* 1547–1555.

Angel, J. L., & Angel, R. J. (1998). Aging trends: Mexican Americans in the Southwest. *Journal of Cross-Cultural Gerontology, 13,* 281–290.

Angel, R. J., & Angel, J. L. (1997). *Who will care for us? Aging and longterm care in multicultural America.* New York: New York University Press.

Angel, R. J., Frisco, M., Angel, J. L., & Chiriboga, D. (2003). Financial strain and health among elderly Mexican-origin individuals. *Journal of Health and Social Behavior, 44,* 536–551.

Angel, J. L., & Hogan, D. P. (2004). Population aging and diversity in a new era. In K. E. Whitfield (Ed.), *Closing the gap: Health of minority elders in the new millennium* (pp. 1–12). Washington, DC: The Gerontological Society on Aging.

Angel, R., Angel, J. Aranda, M. P., & Miles, T. P. (2004). Risk of nursing home use among elderly Mexican Americans. *Journal of Aging and Health, 15,* 1–13.

Aranda, M. P. (1999). Cultural issues and Alzheimer's disease: Lessons from the Latino community. *Geriatric Case Management Journal, 9,* 13–18.

Aranda, M. P. (2001). Racial and ethnic factors in dementia caregiving research in the United States. *Aging and Mental Health, 5,* S116–S123.

Aranda, M. P., & Ell, K. R. (2004, July). *Using in-depth interviews to understand the nature and course of depression in older adults with chronic illness.* Poster session presented at the annual Summer Institute, Family Research Consortium, Center on Culture and Health, University of California, Los Angeles, San Juan, Puerto Rico.

Aranda, M. P., & Knight, B. G. (1997). The influence of ethnicity and culture on the caregiver stress and coping process: A sociocultural review and analysis. *The Gerontologist, 37*(3), 342–354.

Aranda, M. P., & Torres, M. S. (1997). Self-reported barriers to the use of community-based, long-term care services: A comparative study of elderly and disadvantaged Mexican Americans and non-Latino whites. In M. Sotomayor & A. Garcia (Eds.), *La familia: Traditions and realities* (pp. 45–66). Washington, DC: National Hispanic Council on Aging.

Balsa, A. I., Seiler, N., McGuire, T. G., & Bloche, M. G. (2003). Clinical uncertainty and healthcare disparities. *American Journal of Law and Medicine, 29*, 203–219.

Bean, F. D., & Tienda, M. (1987). *The Hispanic population of the United States*. New York: Russell Sage Foundation.

Berkman, L. F., Berkman, C. S., Kasl, S., Freeman, D. H., Jr., Leo, L., Ostfeld, A. M., et al. (1986). Depressive symptoms in relation to physical health and functioning in the elderly. *American Journal of Epidemiology, 124*, 372–388.

Biegel, D. E., Farkas, K. J., & Song, L. (1997). Barriers to the use of mental health services by African-American and Hispanic elderly persons. *Journal of Gerontological Social Work, 29*, 23–44.

Black, S. A., Markides, K. S., & Miller, T. Q. (1998). Correlates of depressive symptomatology among older community-dwelling Mexican Americans: The Hispanic EPESE. *Journals of Gerontology: Series B. Psychological Sciences and Social Sciences, 53* (4), S198–S208.

Blazer, D. (2002). Depression in late life: Review and commentary. *Journals of Gerontology: Series A. Biological Sciences and Medical Sciences, 58*(3), m249–m265.

Blazer, D. (2003). *Depression in late life* (3rd ed.). New York: Springer.

Blazer, D., Hughes, D. C., & George, L. K. (1987). The epidemiology of depression in an elderly community population. *The Gerontologist, 16*, 118–124.

Blazer, D. G. (2003). *Depression in late life* (3rd ed.). New York: Springer.

Cheung, F. K., & Snowden, L. R. Community mental health and ethnic minority populations. *Community Mental Health Journal, 26*, 277–291.

Chiriboga, D. A., Black, S. A., Aranda, M. P., & Markides, K. S. (2002). Stress and depressive symptoms among Mexican American elderly. *Journals of Gerontology: Series B. Psychological Sciences and Social Sciences, 57*, P559–P568.

Cooper, L. A., Gonzalez, J. J., Gallo, J. J., Rost, K. M., Meredith, L. S., Rubenstein, L. L., Wang, N-Y., & Ford, D. E. (2003). The acceptability of treatment for depression among African-American, Hispanic, and white primary care patients. *Medical Care, 41*, 479–489.

Cornoni-Huntley, J., Blazer, D., Laffety, M., Everett, D., Brock, D., & Farmer, M. (Eds.). (1990). *Established populations for epidemiologic studies of the elderly.* Bethesda, MD: National Institute on Aging.

Council of Economic Advisers. (1998). *Changing America: Indicators of economic well-being by race and Hispanic origin.* Washington DC: The White House.

Dunlop, D. D., Song, J., Lyons, J. S., Manheim, L. M., & Chang, R. W. (2003). Racial/ethnic differences in rates of depression among preretirement adults. *American Journal of Public Health, 93*, 1945–1952.

Dwight-Johnson, M., Ell, K., & Jiuan-Lee, P. (2005). Can collaborative care address the needs of low-income Latinas with comorbid depression and cancer? Results from a randomized pilot study. *Psychosomatic Medicine, 46*, 224–232.

Dyche, L., & Zayas, L. (2001). Cross-cultural empathy and training the contemporary psychotherapist. *Clinical Social Work Journal, 29*(3), 245–258.

Espino, D. V., Burge, S. K., & Moreno, C. A. (1991). The prevalence of selected chronic disease among the Mexican-American elderly: Data from the 1982–84 Hispanic Health and Nutrition Examination Survey. *Journal of the American Board of Family Practice, 4*, 217–222.

Federal Interagency Forum on Aging-Related Statistics. (2004). *Older Americans 2004: Key indicators of well-being.* Washington, DC: U.S. Government Printing Office.

Gonzalez, H., Haan, M., & Hinton, L. (2001). Acculturation and the prevalence of depression in older Mexican Americans: Baseline results from the Sacramento Area Latino Study on Aging. *Journal of the American Geriatrics Society, 49*, 948–953.

Guarnaccia, P. J., & Rodriguez, O. (1996). Concepts of culture and their role in the development of culturally competent mental health services. *Hispanic Journal of Behavioral Sciences, 18*, 419–443.

Gurland, B. J., Wilder, D. E., & Berkman, C. (1988) Depression and disability in the elderly: Reciprocal relations and changes with age. *International Journal of Geriatric Psychiatry, 3*, 163–179.

Hays, R. D., Wells, K. B., Sherbourne, C. D., Rogers, W., & Spitzer, K. (1995). Functioning and well-being outcomes of patients with depression compared with chronic general medical illnesses. *Archives of General Psychiatry, 52*(1), 11–19.

Hazuda, H. P., & Espino, D. V. (1997). Aging, chronic disease, and physical disability in Hispanic elderly. In K. S. Markides & M. R. Miranda (Eds.), Minorities, aging, and health (pp. 127–148). Thousand Oaks, CA: Sage.

Heisler, M., Langa, K. M., Eby, E. L., Fendrick, A. M., Kabeto, M. U., & Piette, J. D. (2004). The health effects of restricting prescription medication use because of cost. *Medical Care 42,* 626–634.

Hepworth, D. H., Rooney, R. H., & Larsen, J. A. (2002). *Direct social work practice: Theory and skills* (6th ed.). 147–272. San Francisco: Brooks/Cole Publishing Co.

Hu, T. W., Snowden, L. R., Jerrell, J. M., & Nguyen, T. D. (1991). Ethnic populations in public mental health: Services choice and level of use. *American Journal of Public Health, 81,* 1429–1434.

Katon, W., Von Korff, M., Lin, E., Lipscomb, P., Russo, J., Wagner, E., & Polk, E. (1990). Distressed high utilizers of medical care: DSM-III-R diagnoses and treatment needs. *General Hospital Psychiatry, 12,* 355–362.

Kemp, B. J., Staples, F., & López-Aqueres, W. (1984). Epidemiology of depression and dysphoria in an elderly Hispanic population. *American Geriatrics Society, 35,* 920–926.

Koenig, H. G., & Blazer, D. G. (1996) Minor depression in late life. *American Journal of Geriatrics Psychiatry, 4*(Suppl. 1), S14–S21.

Koenig, H. G., & Kuchibhatla, M. (1998). Use of health services by hospitalized medically ill depressed elderly patients. *American Journal of Psychiatry, 155,* 871–877.

Krause, N. (1997). Anticipated support, received support, and economic stress among older adults. *Journals of Gerontology: Series B. Psychological Sciences and Social Sciences, 52,* P284–P293.

Krause, N., Liang, J., & Gu, S. (1998). Financial strain, received support, anticipated support, and depressive symptoms in the People's Republic of China. *Psychology and Aging, 13,* 58–68.

Lebowitz, B. D. (1996). Depression and treatment of depression in late life: An overview of the NIH Consensus Statement. *American Journal of Geriatrics Psychiatry, 4*(Suppl. 1), S3–S6.

Lewis-Fernàndez, R., & Díaz, N. (2002). The cultural formulation: A method for assessing cultural factors affecting the clinical encounter. *Psychiatric Quarterly, 73,* 271–295.

Lincoln, K., Chatters, L., & Taylor, R. J. (2003). Psychological distress among black and white Americans:

Differential effects of social support, negative interactions and personal control. *Journal of Health and Social Behavior, 44,* 390–407.

Lopez, S. R. (2002). Mental health care for Latinos: A research agenda to improve the accessibility and quality of mental health care for Latinos. *Psychiatric Services, 53,* 1569–1573.

López-Aqueres, W., Kemp, B. J., Plopper, M., Staples, F., & Brummel-Smith, K. (1984). Use of health care services by older Hispanics. *Journal of the American Geriatrics Society, 32,* 434–440.

Markides, K. S., Rudkin, R. L. H., Angel, R. J., & Espino, D. (1997). Health status of Hispanic elderly in the United States. In L. G. Martin & B. J. Soldo (Eds.), *Ethnic and racial differences in late life in the United States* (pp. 285–300). Washington, DC: National Academy of Sciences.

Mendes de Leon, C., & Markides, K. (1988). Depressive symptoms among Mexican Americans: A three-generation study. *Journal of Epidemiology, 127,* 150–160.

Miller, J. (2002). Social workers as diagnosticians. In K. J. Bentley (Ed.), *Social work practice in mental health: Contemporary roles, tasks and techniques* (pp. 43–72). Pacific Grove, CA: Brooks/Cole.

Miranda, J., Duan, N., Sherbourne, C., Schoenbaum, M., Lagomasino, I., Jackson-Triche, M., & Wells, K. B. (2003). Improving care for minorities: Can quality improvement interventions improve care and outcome for depressed minorities? Results of a randomized, controlled trial. *Health Services Research, 38,* 613–630.

Murphy, E., Smith, R., & Slatter, J. (1988). Increased mortality rates in late-life depression. *British Journal of Psychiatry, 152,* 347–353.

Murray, C. L., & López, A. D. (Eds.). (1996). *The global burden of disease: A comprehensive assessment of mortality and disability from diseases, injuries, and risk factors in 1990 and projected to 2020.* Cambridge, MA: Harvard University.

NIH Consensus Development Panel on Depression in Late Life. (1992). Diagnosis and treatment of depression in late life. *Journal of the American Medical Association, 268,* 1018–1024.

Padgett, D., Burns, B. J., & Grau, L. A. (1998). Risk factors and resilience: Mental health needs and service use of older women. In B. L. Levin, A. K. Blanch, & A. Jennings (Eds.), *Women's mental health services: A public health perspective* (pp. 390–413). Thousand Oaks, CA: Sage.

Perkowski, L. C., Stroup-Benham, C. A., Markides, K. S., Lichtenstein, M. J., Angel, R. J., Guralnik, J. M., et al. (1998). Lower extremity functioning in older Mexican Americans and its association with medical problems. *Journal of the American Geriatrics Society, 46,* 411–418.

Pew Hispanic Center & Kaiser Family Foundation. (2002). *2002 National Survey of Latinos.* Washington, DC: Henry J. Kaiser Family Foundation.

Phillips, L. R., Torres de Ardon, E., Kommenich, P., Killeen, M., & Rusinak, R. (2000). The Mexican American caregiving experience. *Hispanic Journal of Behavioral Sciences, 22*(3), 296–313.

President's New Freedom Commission on Mental Health. (2003). *Achieving the promise: Transforming mental health care in America: Final report* (DHHS Pub. No. SMA-03-3832). Rockville, MD: U.S. Department of Health and Human Services.

Proctor, D. B., & Dalakar, J. (2002). Poverty in the United States: 2001. *Current Population Reports* (Report No. P60-219). Washington, DC: U.S. Census Bureau. Retrieved June, 1, 2004, from *http://www. census.gov/prod/2002pubs/p60-219.pdf.*

Smedley, B. D., Stith, A. Y., & Nelson, A. R. (Eds.). (2003). *Unequal treatment: Confronting racial and ethnic disparities in health care.* Washington, DC: Institute of Medicine.

Snowden, L., Guerrero, R., Masland, M., Ma, Y., & Ciemens, E. (2003). *Ethnic access to public mental health services in California.* Technical research report to the California Policy Research Center, California Program on Access to Care. Berkeley, CA.

Talamantes, M., & Aranda, M. P. (2004). *Cultural competency in working with family caregivers* [Monograph]. San Francisco: Family Caregiver Alliance. Retrieved May 21, 2004, from *http://www.caregiver. org/caregiver/jsp/content_node.jsp?nodeid=*1095.

Talamantes, M., Cornell, J., Espino, D. V., Lichtenstein, M. J., & Hazuda, H. P. (1996). SES and ethnic difference in perceived caregiver availability among young-old Mexican Americans and non-Hispanic Whites. *The Gerontologist, 36,* 88–99.

Unützer, J., Katon, W., Callahan C. M., Williams, J. W., Hunkeler, E., Harpole, L., et al. (2003). Depression treatment in a sample of 1,801 depressed older adults in primary care. *Journal of American Geriatrics Society, 51,* 505–514.

Unützer, J., Patrick, D. L., Simon, G., Brembowski, D., Walker, E., Rutter, C., & Katon, W. (1997). Depres-

sive symptoms and the cost of health services in HMO patients aged 65 and older: A 4-year prospective study. *Journal of the American Medical Association, 277,* 1618–1623.

U.S. Census Bureau. (2000). *Population projections of the United States by age, sex, race, Hispanic origin, and nativity: 1999 to 2100.* Retrieved June 16, 2004, from www/census.gov/population/www/projections/natproj.html.

U.S. Department of Health and Human Services. (1999). *Mental health: A report of the Surgeon General.* Rockville, MD: Author.

U.S. Department of Health and Human Services. (2001). *Mental health: Culture, race, and ethnicity. A supplement to Mental health: A report of the Surgeon General* (pp. 127–155). Rockville, MD: Author.

Valle, R. (1998). *Caregiving across cultures: Working with dementing illness and ethnically diverse populations.* Washington, DC: Taylor and Francis.

Vega, W. A., Kolody, B., Aguilar-Gaxiola, S., & Catalano, R. (1999). Gaps in service utilization by Mexican Americans with mental health problems. *American Journal of Psychiatry, 156,* 928–934.

Villa, V. M., & Aranda, M. P. (2000). The demographic, economic, and health profile of older Latinos: Implications for health and long-term care policy and the family. *Journal of Health and Human Services Administration, 23*(2), 161–180.

Wells, K. B., Hays, R. D., Burnham, M. A., Rogers, W., Greenfield, S., & Ware, J. E. (1989). Detection of depressive disorder for patients receiving prepaid or fee-for-service care: Results of the Medical Outcomes Study. *Journal of the American Medical Association, 262,* 3298–3302.

White, L. R., Kohout, F., Evans, D. A., Cornoni-Huntley, J., & Ostfeld(?), A. M. (1986). Related health problems. In J. C. Cornoni-Huntley, D. B. Brock, A. M. Ostfeld, J. O. Taylor, & R. B. Wallace (Eds.). (1986). *Established populations for epidemiologic studies of the elderly: Resources data book* (NIH Publication No. 86-2443, pp. 129–165). Washington, DC: U.S. Department of Health and Human Services.

Zeiss, A. M., Lewinsohn, P. M., Rohde, P., & Seeley, J. R. (1996). Relationship of physical disease and functional impairment to depression in older people. *Psychology and Aging, 11,* 572–581.

Although they represent a tiny fraction of the U.S. population, Native American elders' history and culture lead to distinct opportunities and needs. This chapter uses figures from the most recent census to examine the status of Native American elders in the United States. Following a brief review of current living conditions, it examines the history of forced assimilation and colonization and the impact of that history on Native American elders. This is followed by a discussion of service approaches that empower elders and improve their quality of life—and a suggestion that the pursuit of culturally appropriate interventions should begin with the employment of Native American service providers (Barusch & Ten-Barge, 2003).

Because this chapter focuses on harsh living conditions and special needs of this population, it is important to acknowledge the diversity and the strengths among Native American elders. As Weaver (1999) reminded us, "each tribe is different." Many Native American traditions offer privileges and respect to their elders and assign them honorific titles and roles. Elders preserve heritage and wisdom, so can serve as healers, counselors, and leaders by virtue of their advanced age. Having lived through a violent and challenging history, some elders are the very embodiment of resilience (Weaver & White, 1997). These individuals present social work practitioners with opportunities, and they can serve as vital resources to strengthen and heal Native American families and communities. Other elders experience health and mental health limitations and may be victims of neglect or abuse. Given their distinctive history, these Native American elders have special needs that may (or may not) be met through social work intervention.

AMANDA BARUSCH

Native American Elders: Unique Histories and Special Needs

DEMOGRAPHICS

Prior to the 2000 census, the last careful count of the nation's Native American population was that mandated by the Dawes Act in 1887. Census counts during the interim undercounted the Native American population, and as a result much was written about the so-called "vanishing race" (Churchill, 1999; Johansen, 2002; Thornton, 1987, 1996). Using a strategy familiar to social work since the Settlement House days, the Census Bureau hired Native American people to collect data for the 2000 census. The need to cooperate with Census personnel was advertised, and Native Americans were encouraged to participate in the cen-

24

sus at powwows and other cultural events, urban Indian centers and clinics, schools and universities, and other settings. Images of famous Native American figures—Sitting Bull, Chief Joseph, Geronimo—were imposed on huge posters exhorting people to "stand up and be counted," and Census personnel offered gifts—key chains, flashlights, pens, notepads, mirrors, posters, and t-shirts—respecting a universal Native American tradition.

They did a better job than usual with the count. In the 2000 census, more than 4.1 million people said they were at least partially Native American, which is double the 2 million who reported Native ancestry in the 1990 census and 14 times the official figure of about 300,000 a century ago (Johansen, 2002; Thornton, 1987, 1996, U.S. Census Bureau, 2002). By comparison, the total U.S. population grew by 13% between the 1990 and 2000 censuses (U.S. Census Bureau, 2002).

Most of the growth in the Native American population was due to a change in the census procedures. Census 2000 was also the first in which respondents were allowed to choose more than one race. A total of 1.6 million Americans identified themselves as part American Indian/Alaska Native, which accounted for most of the increase. But even when those identifying as part American Indian/Alaska Native are not included, Census 2000 documented a 25% increase in the number of Americans identified as Native American peoples since the 1990 census. The 2000 census also indicated which states were home to most Native American elders. Nearly half of Native Americans ages 55 and older lived in just five states: Oklahoma, California, Arizona, New Mexico, and North Carolina (Ogunwole, 2002).

CURRENT LIVING CONDITIONS

Federal recognition is critical for tribes seeking to establish services and provide benefits to their people. There are 562 federally recognized tribes in the United States and about 148 groups seeking federal recognition. The process of attaining federal recognition is difficult and arbitrary. During the 1950s and 1960s the federal government pursued a policy of "termination," discontinuing recognition of several tribes (Churchill, 1998; Yellow Bird, 2001a). At the same time, a program of relocation dispatched Native American peoples from reservations to cities with the goal of forcing them to assimilate into mainstream society.

A direct result of this policy is seen today in the greater numbers of Native American peoples living off reservations. In 1900, over 99% of federally recognized Native Americans lived on reservations. By 1970, nearly half (44.5%) lived off reservations. Current estimates suggest that over half of Native Americans—between 55 and 70%—live off the reservation (Churchill, 1998; Walters, 1999).

Of course, elders are more likely than younger generations to live on reservations. Nonetheless, Native American elders live in diverse settings—in *hogans* in the deserts of Arizona, Utah, and Nevada, in concrete block houses on reservations, in urban apartments, and in suburban homes. Many Native American elders live in urban centers, such as New York and Los Angeles (Ogunwole, 2002). Urban elders generally enjoy greater income and better health than those living on reservations, although urban settings do not allow for access to Indian Health Service facilities. As Chapleski, Gelfand, and Pugh (1997) pointed out, this situation results in lower utilization of in-home care services among urban elders.

Native American elders are significantly more likely than Whites to live in rural settings. According to the 2000 census, only one in four non-Hispanic Whites lived in rural locations, whereas nearly half of Native American elders live in rural areas. These statistics led Share DeCroix Bane to observe that "Native American elderly are the most rural of the minorities . . ." (1991, p. 63). Reservation-based elders live on treaty-based, executive-ordered, and state-created reservations, as well as in bands not federally recognized. Although reservations offer greater access to tribal community and Indian Health Services, living conditions are extremely difficult. Many homes have no electricity, refrigeration, or indoor toilets. Transportation is also difficult on reservations, where many rely on poorly maintained dirt roads that become impassable in rain or snow. Finally, communication is a challenge, as most elders do not have telephones, receive newspapers, or have television sets (Bane, 1991).

Access to health care is problematic, even on reservations. As the National Indian Health Board (NIHB; 2004) noted, funding for the Indian Health Service has lagged behind need and even basic fairness. Indeed, the federal government spends nearly twice as much money for a federal prisoner's health care as it does on a per capita basis for Native Americans and Alaska Natives. Per-person HIS expenditures were approximately $1,900 last year, a figure that, when adjusted for inflation, represents a net decline compared with budgets of the mid-1970s (NIHB, 2004).

Harsh, impoverished living conditions and limited access to health care contribute to lower life expectancies for Native Americans. In 1980 John (1980) estimated the average life expectancy for Native Americans at 45 years, but this figure has improved. In the mid-1990s, life expectancy for American Indian/Alaska Native men was estimated at 66.1 years, and life expectancy for women was 74.4 years. This compares to life expectancies of 73.2 years for White men and 79.6 years for White women. Only African American men have shorter life expectancies (U.S. Department of Health and Human Services, 1998).

Despite this improvement, short life expectancy continues to limit the number of years that elders can access benefits widely available to older non-Native elders. A person with a shorter life has fewer years to collect Social Security and related benefits, even though he or she contributed to the system for as many years as someone who enjoys a longer life.

FORCED ASSIMILATION AND COLONIZATION

Any understanding of the lives of Native American elders must be informed by knowledge of the trauma imposed by forced assimilation and colonization. Assimilation refers to the process through which members of minority cultures give up their way of life and take on that of the dominant group. It is associated with the "melting pot" theory of cultural interaction. In the case of Native Americans, forced assimilation was the result of systematic policies designed to eradicate the Native American culture.

For example, the U.S. government set out to "kill the Indian in every child" by removing Native American children from their homes and placing them in government-run boarding schools (George, 1997; Churchill, 1998). These schools forced the children to wear the clothes, eat the food, speak the language, and practice the customs of the dominant culture. In the United States, this practice continued from the late 19th century until the middle years of the 20th century (George, 1997). Most boarding schools were closed by the 1960s and 1970s, although a number continue to operate.

Boarding schools were succeeded by perhaps a more insidious form of repression, the Indian Adoption Program. A joint venture of the Bureau of Indian Affairs and the Child Welfare League of America, this program placed Native American children in White adoptive homes located as far as geographically possible from their families of origin. Between the 1950s and the 1970s, an estimated 395 Native American children were adopted through this program (George, 1997). The general practice of placing Native American children in White homes was slowed about 25 years ago, with the passage of the Indian Child Welfare Act in 1978.

Religious sects were willing partners in government efforts to force Native American peoples to adopt the majority culture. Churches were given federal funds to establish and operate schools on reservations, and some engaged in aggressive proselytizing (Linn, Berardo & Yamamoto, 1998; McCarty, 1998). Religious conversion meant abdication not only of traditional religious practices but also of health practices, which in Native American cultures have a strong spiritual component.

Another policy designed to force assimilation was the Indian Relocation Act of 1953. Couched in the concept of "entitling [Native American peoples] to the same privileges and responsibilities as are applicable to other citizens of the United States," this act initiated a process commonly referred to as "termination policy." The purpose of the resolution was to end the protected trust status of Native American land and to withdraw the federal support of educational, health, and social programs promised in exchange for lands when treaties were signed. The resolution included plans for the immediate termination of tribes in California, Florida, New York, and Texas (Bonvillain, 2001).

Eradication of Native American languages is pivotal to the process of forced assimilation. As Fillmore (1994) pointed out, "the question of cultural identity is synonymous with the question of language" (p. 1; as cited in Linn et al., 1998). The U.S. government has long recognized the importance of language. In the boarding schools children were severely punished for using their native tongue. This policy was also pursued by the Kennedy administration during the Americanization of the western Pacific (Barusch & Spaulding, 1989). The result is what some linguists call "language extermination." Roughly half of the Native American languages of California have no fluent speakers left at all (Hinton, 1998). As Teresa McCarty explained:

Native American languages in the United States are under siege . . . of the 175 Native American languages still extant in the USA, only 20 are being transmitted as child languages. The remainder are spoken by parental or grandparental generations, and over a third are spoken only by the most elderly members of the community, often fewer than ten individuals. (McCarty, 1998, p. 27)

COLONIZATION

What assimilation does to culture, colonization does to political and economic power. Through the process of colonization, Native American people became second-class citizens and lost control of their land and other sources of wealth. The result of this process is seen in the financial poverty of Native American people. In 1999, for example, American Indian/Alaska Natives had the highest poverty rate of any ethnic group in the United States. Whereas 7% of non-Hispanic Whites lived with incomes below the federal poverty threshold, 25.9% of Native American people lived in poverty. Thus, in this country, Native American people have *over three times* the risk of poverty of the White majority (U.S. Census Bureau, 2000). Native American elders experience even higher rates of poverty. The Indian Health Service (IHS) reported that 31.6% of Native American elders had incomes below the poverty threshold, compared with 9.8% of Whites ages 60 or older (IHS, 1996).

The association between poverty and ill health is evident in the health and functional status of Native American elders. Assessments of functional status and need for long-term care consistently suggest that Native American elders suffer from more activity limitations than the general population (McFall, Solomon, & Smith, 2000). For example, Bane (1991) reported that "Native Americans experience the same limitations in their activities of daily living at age 45 as do non-Indian people at age 65" (p. 64).

In addition to greater functional impairments, Native American peoples experience high rates of many diseases. These include phenomenal rates of diabetes, with experts suggesting a prevalence of 40–50% among Native American adults (Roubideaux, 2002). Indeed, the Pima tribe in Arizona reports the highest recorded prevalence of diabetes in the world (Acton et al., 2002). This finding led one IHS doctor to remark, "I was often surprised to see a patient *without* diabetes" (italics added, Roubideaux, p. 1401). Native American peoples are more likely than others to die of tuberculosis, influenza, and pneumonia (Harris, 2002).

In addition to health problems, practitioners who work with Native American peoples see the legacy of forced assimilation and colonization in the behavioral and emotional problems they confront each day. In 1992, Maxwell and Maxwell conducted an ethnographic study of elder abuse on two reservations. The reservation with the highest rate of poverty and isolation also had the highest rate of elder abuse. Their findings underscored the role of social conditions in producing what some perceive as individual dysfunction. As they explained, "We attribute differences in prevalence of mistreatment of elders to variations in economic opportunities for younger residents" (1992, p. 3). Like the tribal respondents they interviewed, these researchers concluded that mistreatment of elders was the explosive result of perceived powerlessness, "a dysfunction in community health" (p. 3). As two leading Native American scholars write:

> Historical trauma refers to cumulative wounding across generations as well as during one's current life span. For Native people, the legacy of genocide includes distortions of Native American identity, self-concept and values. The process of colonization and varying degrees of assimilation into the dominant cultural value system have resulted in altered states of an Indian sense of self. (Weaver & Brave Heart, 1999, p. 22)

Similarly, Yellow Bird (2001b) argued that:

> Today, more than ever, I am convinced that the disproportionate amount of substance abuse, family violence, and suffering within First Nations communities is a result of the continuing effects of European American colonialism. First Nations Peoples are the survivors of a massive and prolonged campaign of racial and cultural terrorism perpetuated by the United States of America. (p. 2)

A young person's history is an old person's lived experience. Many of today's elders had direct experience in boarding schools and White foster homes. They carry the memory of having their mouths washed out with soap for speaking a language some considered "primitive." Many have had to relearn their cultural practices late in life because they were unable to do so as children. Still others have had to learn to parent, having spent years moving from foster home to foster home. So Native American elders are especially sensitive to the effects of historical trauma, and those who work with them must be, as well.

STRATEGIES TO SUPPORT AND EMPOWER NATIVE AMERICAN ELDERS

Observing that interventions designed to reduce elder abuse by treating individuals have proven ineffective, Maxwell and Maxwell (1992) argued for the potential efficacy of community-based interventions. They acknowledged that we tend to "slight trauma suffered by the community as a whole" and noted that "police do not arrest 'conditions,' they arrest someone naïve or unlucky enough to have drawn attention to himself by doing something disapproved of" (1992, p. 20). Further, interventions that target social conditions risk alienating those currently privileged as they inevitably require the reallocation of resources. Nonetheless, there are several promising community-based interventions.

Some interventions address the health needs of Native American peoples. The Indian Self-Determination and Educational Assistance Act of 1975 set the stage for tribes to manage health programs that had been under the Indian Health Service. Many tribes have taken advantage of this opportunity, and Yvette Roubideaux (2002) reported that "approximately half of the IHS budget is now managed by tribes" (p. 1402). Recognizing the growing need for long-term care, several tribes have, both in collaboration with the Indian Health Service and on their own, established nursing homes and home-health agencies on their reservations. Noting that "most elderly Indians who require nursing home care must leave the reservation and their families" (p. 181), Susan Mercer (1996) described the culturally sensitive care provided by a nursing home operated by the Navajo nation with primarily Navajo staff. Similar care is provided by the Navajo Area Home Health Agency (McCabe, 1988). The Alaska Native Women's Wellness Project has successfully increased cancer prevention screening rates among Native American elders in its catchment area through respect for the individual and her culture (Stillwater, 1999). Napoli & Gonzalez-Santin (2001) described an intensive home-based wellness service based on Native American values that was developed for families living on reservations.

To address the weakening of intergenerational bonds, activists in New York established ELDERS (Encouraging Leaders Dedicated to Enriching Respect and Spirituality), a week-long gathering at which elders teach youths the traditional ways of the Iroquois. Although primarily intended as a substance-abuse-prevention program for youths, this effort has the secondary benefit of offering meaningful activity and connection to local elders (Skye, 2002).

Language revival and restoration efforts have the dual benefits of salvaging language and empowering elders. The 1990 Native American Languages Act (PL 101-477) reflected the discovery that hundreds of native languages in this country were endangered. That is, they were spoken by only a handful of elders. Linguists have pointed out the importance of language diversity, not only for minority language speakers themselves but also for the nation as a whole, noting that "language loss is part of a much larger process of loss of cultural and intellectual diversity in which politically dominant languages and cultures simply overwhelm Native American local ones" (Linn et al., 1998, p. 63).

Several community-based interventions have been initiated to salvage the nation's Native American languages. Christine Sims (1998) described one such intervention, designed to preserve and restore the native language of the Karuk tribe in northern California. Using tribal funds, a language-immersion camp was offered in 1992 for children, parents, and fluent-speaking elders. Both overnight and day-camp experiences were offered in which children learned the language of their elders in highly structured sessions. Sims reported that "language support and interaction that elders provide is a key element" of the program, establishing "the crucial intergenerational linkages necessary for language vitality" (1998, pp. 103–104). The tribe also established "master-apprentice language teams," who devote at least 20 hours each week to language learning. Language interventions such as these not only help to restore cultural diversity to the United States but also add meaning and power to the lives of Native American elders.

THE NEED FOR NATIVE AMERICAN PRACTITIONERS

Although laudable, current efforts to develop cultural competency do not meet the needs of Native American elders in ways that are personally satisfying and culturally appropriate. Certainly, the White practitioner needs cultural knowledge and skills to even begin to provide support to a Native American elder, and certainly that support will be better than nothing.

But it would be more effective and more efficient to recruit and train Native American practitioners.

It is almost comic to consider advice that has been given to White practitioners (and researchers) seeking to work with Native American elders. For example, Ferraro (2001) identified "hurdles" faced by researchers seeking to collect information on elders in "Indian Country." The first such hurdle "is gaining the trust of the native elder to actually want to participate in your study" (p. 314). He suggests that a "gift of tobacco" might be offered and warns the potential researcher that "in some Native cultures it is considered disrespectful to look someone in the eyes." Similarly, McDonald, Morton, and Stewart (1992) offered suggestions for clinical practice with Native American peoples. The first piece of advice, "Begin and end each session with a handshake," will poorly serve a practitioner working with the Navajo, for example, for whom such physical contact can be uncomfortable.

Indeed, most tribal people do not use the handshake as a greeting. It was thought (and still is to some extent) that in a handshake the other person might be trying to steal your soul and your energies. One didn't know if that person was friend or foe, especially in the case of the White man. So physical contact involved risk of loss. The same thing applies, although to a lesser extent, to the reluctance to engage in eye contact with an unfamiliar person. That person could be an enemy or, as in Navajo stories, a witch capable of cursing you with her eyes.

CONCLUSION

Today's Native American elders experience the consequences of yesterday's efforts to eradicate Native American cultures (assimilation) and appropriate the resources of Native American peoples (colonization). They were victimized by policies that have since been abandoned: boarding schools, adoption by Whites, and language suppression. Many live in harsh and impoverished conditions—the direct result of colonization. A few are neglected and abused by family members.

Recognition of these devastating experiences yields a difficult conclusion: non-Native American practitioners working by themselves may not effectively meet the needs of Native American elders. Asking an elder to "trust" a White person who offers a gift of tobacco and a hearty handshake adds insult to injury. Native American elders deserve to receive care from someone who does not remind them of past humiliations.

There is a crying need for Native American practitioners from all professions (doctors, teachers, social workers, counselors, rehabilitation specialists, administrators) to serve elders in rural areas. The Census Bureau figured this out when in a masterful stroke it hired Native American staff to count the nation's Native American people. Non-Native American practitioners by themselves should be considered a second choice for direct service (on the dubious principle that "something is better than nothing"). First choice would be a well-trained, highly skilled Native American practitioner.

We also note the limited impact of interventions that punish individual perpetrators and recommend expansion of community-based programs designed to empower elders and enhance the quality of their lives. No doubt, the interested reader will add to our list of examples, which includes health services for Native American elders, as well as language restoration efforts in which the elders play a pivotal role. At the policy level, it is way past time for federal, state, and local governments to defer to tribal authority on matters affecting Native American peoples.

REFERENCES

Acton, K. J., Burrows, N. R., Moore, K., Querec, L., Geiss, L. S., & Engelgau, M. M. (2002). Trends in diabetes prevalence among American Indian and Alaska Native children, adolescents, and iyoung adults. *American Journal of Public Health, 92*(9), 1485–1490.

Bane, S. D. (1991, Fall/Winter). Rural minority populations. *Generations,* 63–65.

Barusch, A. S. & Spaulding, M. L. (1989). The impact of Americanization on intergenerational relations: An exploratory study on the US territory of Guam. *Journal of Sociology and Social Welfare, 16*(3), 61–79.

Barusch, A. S., & TenBarge, C. (2003). Indigenous elders in rural America. In L. Kaye & S. Butler (Eds.), *Aging in rural America* (pp. 121–136). Haworth Press.

Bernard, M. A., Lampley-Dallas, V., & Smith, L. (1997). Common health problems among minority elders. *Journal of the American Dietetic Association, 97*(7), 771–777.

Bonvillain, N. (2001). *Native nations: Cultures and histories of Native North America.* Upper Saddle River, NJ: Prentice-Hall.

Brugge, D., & Goble, R. (2002). The history of uranium mining and the Navajo people. *American Journal of Public Health, 92*(9), 1410–1419.

Chapelski, E., Gelfand, D., & Pugh, K. (1997). Great Lakes American Indian elders and service utilization: Does residence matter? *Journal of Applied Gerontology, 16*(3), 333–354.

Churchill, W. (1998). *A little matter of genocide: Holocaust and denial in the Americas, 1492 to the present.* San Francisco: City Lights Books.

Ferraro, F. R. (2001). Assessment and evaluation issues regarding Native American elderly adults. *Journal of Clinical Geropsychology, 7*(4), 311–318.

George, L. J. (1997). Why the need for the Indian Child Welfare Act? *Journal of Multicultural Social Work, 5*(3/4), 165–175.

Harris, C. (2002). Native American health: Fulfilling our obligation to future generations. *American Journal of Public Health, 92*(9), 1990.

Hinton, L. (1998). Language loss and revitalization in California: Overview. *International Journal of the Sociology of Language, 132,* 83–93.

Indian Health Service. (1996). *Regional differences in Indian health: 1996.* Rockville, MD: U.S. Department of Health and Human Services, Public Health Service.

Johansen, B. (2002). Native Americans in the 2000 census: Far from the "vanishing race." *Native Americas, 19*(1/2), 42–45.

John, R. (1980). The Older American Act and the elderly Native American. *Journal of Minority Aging, 5*(2–4), 293–298.

Kivett, V. R. (1993). Informal supports among rural minorities. In N. C. Bull (Ed.), *Aging in rural America* (pp. 204–215). Newbury Park, CA: Sage.

Linn, M., Berardo, M., & Yamamoto, A. Y. (1998). Creating language teams in Oklahoma Native American communities. *International Journal of the Sociology of Language, 132,* 61–78.

Maxwell, E. K., & Maxwell, R. J. (1992). Insults to the body civil: Mistreatment of elderly in two plains Indian tribes. *Journal of Cross-Cultural Gerontology, 7,* 3–23.

McCabe, M. L. (1988). Health care accessibility for the elderly on the Navajo Reservation. *Pride Institute Journal of Long Term Home Health Care, 7*(4), 22–26.

McCarty, T. L. (1998). Schooling, resistance, and American Indian languages. *International Journal of the Sociology of Language, 132,* 27–41.

McDonald, J. D., Morton, R., & Stewart, C. (1992). Clinical concerns with American Indian patients. *Innovations in Clinical Practice, 12,* 437–454.

McFall, S. I., Solomon, T. G. A., & Smith, D. W. (2000). Health-related quality of life of older Native American primary care patients. *Research on Aging, 22*(6), 692–714.

Mercer, S. O. (1996). Navajo elderly people in a reservation nursing home: Admission predictors and culture care practices. *Social Work, 41*(2), 181–189.

Napoli, M., & Gonzalez-Snatin, E. (2001). Intensive home-based and wellness services to Native American families living on reservations: A model. *Families in Society, 82*(3), 315–324.

National Indian Council on Aging. (2003). Retrieved February 24, 2003, from *http://www.nicoa.org/.*

National Indian Health Board. (2004). *Fiscal Year 2005 AI/AN National Budget Perspective.* Retrieved October 25, 2004, from *www.nihb.org.*

Ogunwole, S. U. (2002). *The American Indian and Alaska Native population: 2000. Census 2000 brief.* Washington, DC: U.S. Census Bureau. Retrieved from *http://www.census.gov/prod/2002pubs/c2kbr01–15.pdf.*

Roubideaux, Y. (2002). Perspectives on American Indian health. *American Journal of Public Health, 92*(9), 1401–1403.

Simmons, L. W. (1945). *The role of the aged in primitive societies.* New Haven, CT: Yale University Press.

Sims, C. P. (1998). Community-based efforts to preserve native languages: A descriptive study of the Karuk tribe of northern California. *International Journal of the Sociology of Language, 132,* 95–113.

Skye, W. (2002, March). ELDERS gathering for Native American youth: Continuing Native American traditions and curbing substance abuse in Native American youth. *Journal of Sociology and Social Welfare, 29*(1), 117–135.

Stillwater, B. (1999). The Alaska Native Women's Wellness Project. *Health Care for Women International, 20,* 487–492.

Thornton, R. (1987). *American Indian holocaust and survival: A population history since 1492.* Norman, OK: University of Oklahoma Press.

Thornton, R. (1996). Tribal membership requirements and the demography of "old" and "new" Native Americans. In G. D. Sandefur, R. R. Rindfuss, & B. Cohen (Eds.), *Changing numbers, changing needs: American Indian demography and public health* (pp. 103–112). Washington, DC: National Academy Press.

U.S. Census Bureau. (2000). *Poverty rate lowest in 20 years, household income at record high* [News release]. Retrieved from *http://www.census.gov/Press-Release/ www.2000/cb00-158.html.*

U.S. Census Bureau. (2002). *Statistical abstract of the United States* (1116th ed.). Retrieved from *www.census.gov/population/www/socdemo/race/indian.html.*

U.S. Department of Health and Human Services. (1998). *Women of Color Health Data Book.* Retrieved from *http://www.4woman.gov/owh/pub/woc/figure1.htm.*

U.S. Department of Health and Human Services. (2002). Grants awarded for Native American elders and caregivers. *Health Care Financing Review, 23*(4), 208–210.

Walters, K. L. (1999). Urban American Indian identity attitudes and acculturation styles. *Journal of Human Behavior and the Social Environment, 2*(1/2), 163–178.

Weaver, H. N. (1999). Indigenous people and the social work profession: Defining culturally competent services. *Social Work, 44*(3), 217–225.

Weaver, H. N., & Brave Heart, M. Y. (1999). Examining two facets of American Indian identity: Exposure to other cultures and the influence of historical trauma. *Journal of Human Behavior and the Social Environment, 2*(1/2), 19–33.

Weaver, H. N., & White, B. J. (1997). The Native American family circle: Roots of resiliency. *Journal of Family Social Work, 2*(1), 67–79.

Yellow Bird, M. J. (2001a). Critical values and First Nations Peoples. In R. Fong & S. Furuto (Eds.), *Culturally competent social work practice: Practice skills, interventions, and evaluation* (pp. 61–74). Boston: Allyn & Bacon.

Yellow Bird, M. J. (2001b, February). *Substance abuse and family violence affecting First Nations Peoples: The continuing effects of European American colonialism.* Paper presented at the Task Force Meeting of Cultural Competence in Child Welfare Practice,

Members of minority groups share a common identity and collectively experience subordination relative to the dominant culture. We typically define minority groups according to such criteria as race, gender, ethnicity, religion, and national origin in the United States. Previous chapters have addressed the most common minority groups based on race, gender, ethnicity, and sexual orientation. This chapter focuses on older adults from "other minority groups," specifically those from marginal religions and regions. Our intent is to raise social workers' awareness and understanding of these other older minority persons, highlight salient issues that social workers must address with these older adults, and introduce innovative interventions. First, we discuss older adults from Jewish and Muslim religions, and, second, we consider older Appalachians and Pacific Islanders.

RELIGION AND OLDER PERSONS

Religion is a central issue for many older persons (Kosmin & Mayer, 2001a). It provides people with meaning, support, and guidance in their daily lives, in their jobs, and in their relationships with family members, friends, and colleagues. Kosmin and Mayer (2001a) found that whereas 47% of adults over the age of 65 described themselves as religious, only 27% of younger adults described themselves this way. Although national census guidelines preclude gathering information on Americans' religious preferences and characteristics, other organizations and research centers have conducted surveys that shed light on people's religious affiliations. The American Religious Identification Survey (ARIS) included a random-digit-dialing telephone survey of more than 50,000 Americans in 2001. The survey revealed that although most Americans identify with the Christian religions, people represent diverse faiths in this country. In addition, people within these religious groups vary in their worldviews and religious beliefs. The Jewish and Muslim populations are especially diverse; they include individuals from different countries and various ethnic backgrounds.

COLETTE BROWNE
VIRGINIA RICHARDSON

Older Adults in Other Minority Groups

JEWISH OLDER ADULTS

Demographics

The American Jewish population numbers about 5.3 million adults, including Holocaust survivors, Jews

301

from the former Soviet Union who recently immigrated to the United States, and those unaffiliated with Jewish organizations (Harel, 2001). Most older Jewish persons are U.S.-born, whereas others are first- or second-generation immigrants (Harel, 2001). About one-half of the Jewish population identifies with Judaism as a religion, whereas about 20% associate with no religion, and another 20% affiliate with a religion other than Judaism (Kosmin & Mayer, 2001a; United Jewish Communities, 2004).

The American Jewish population is older than the non-Jewish population in the United States; between 19 and 25% of the Jewish population is over the age of 65 (Kosmin & Mayer, 2001a; United Jewish Communities, 2004). Whereas the median age of the U.S. population in 2000 was 35, the median age of the Jewish population was 42.

Physical and Mental Health

Most older Jewish persons are in good health, but they are more likely than younger Jewish persons to report poor or fair health, to have lower incomes, and to live alone. Compared with younger Jewish persons, older Jewish adults more often participate in their Jewish communities. They more closely identify with their Jewish heritage and tend to have more Jewish friends, to feel more emotionally attached to Israel, and to more frequently regard being Jewish as being important than their younger counterparts (United Jewish Communities, 2004).

Elderly Soviet Jews, many of whom are non-English speaking, minimally acculturated, and without adequate economic support, are especially vulnerable and in need of social work services (United Jewish Communities, 2004). In addition, depression is more common among Russian Jews than among those born in the United States (Harel, 2001; Fitzpatrick, 2000). Older Holocaust survivors also require special attention. They have experienced anti-Semitism throughout their lives and often have lingering trauma, resulting in intrusive thoughts, associated with their Holocaust experiences (Harel, 2001).

Cultural Values and Social Work Interventions

Many organizations provide counseling and support to older Jewish persons, although this varies by region. These organizations include the Jewish Association for Services for the Aged in New York (*http://www.jasa.org*), the Council for the Jewish Elderly in Chicago (*http://www.cje.net*), and the Jewish Council for the Aging in Washington, DC (*http://www.jcagw.org*), along with Jewish agencies in urban communities such as Jewish Family Services, Jewish Community Centers, and Jewish Homes for the Aged, which are excellent resources for these older adults. These programs offer adult day programs and other respite services for caregivers, congregate meal sites and meals-on-wheels programs (including hot kosher meals), various group programs, and home- and community-based services that can help older Jewish persons who want more support. Most agencies offer mental health services, including in-home assessments and interventions. Some, such as the Council for Jewish Elderly, provide Holocaust community services for aging survivors of Nazi persecution. Several national organizations, such as United Jewish Communities, actively advocate for national, state, and local aging policies and services.

As social workers increase their knowledge and appreciation of older Jewish adults and engage in culturally competent practice, they will more effectively help these older minority persons get the services they need. Cultural competence involves several components, including (1) knowledge and skills that are compatible with culturally diverse populations; (2) attitudes and values that honor diversity; and (3) a dual focus on the responsibilities of the provider and the institution to improve practice, policy, and research related to the culturally diverse (Lum, 1999; Mokuau, 1999). The Office of Minority Health (2001) has published standards for cultural and linguistic competence that emphasize culturally competent care (i.e., showing respectful care of diverse clients), language access services (i.e., providing bilingual staff) and organizational supports (i.e., maintaining demographic, cultural, and epidemiological profiles of the community; Office of Minority Health, 2001). Literature related to cultural competence and older populations, although severely limited, nonetheless supports these general concepts (Caplan, Wells & Haynes, 1992; Delgado & Tennstedt, 1997; Kosloski, Montgomery, & Karner, 1999).

The strengths perspective, as conceptualized by Saleebey (1997), is another useful approach that social workers can successfully use with older minority persons. This perspective emphasizes clients' assets, such as their talents, knowledge, capabilities, and strengths. When social workers combine the strengths perspective with culturally competent practice, they will be more successful in empowering and fostering the resiliency of these older clients.

MUSLIM OLDER ADULTS

Demographics

Less than 1% of adults (between 2 and 5 million adults) identify themselves with the Muslim/Islamic religion in the United States; however, it is likely that this fact may be underestimated due to older Muslims' reluctance to respond to questions about their religion (Bukhari, 2003; Kosmin & Mayer, 2001a). The majority of Arab Americans are not Muslims, and the majority of Muslims are not Arab Americans (Kosmin & Mayer, 2001b). The Muslim population is similarly ethnically diverse, including about 20% who are from African American backgrounds, 26% who are Arabs, and 32% who are South Asians (Bukhari, 2003). About 17% have emigrated from Pakistan (Bukhari, 2003). Muslims over the age of 65 represent about 7% of the U.S. Muslim population, although these estimates vary depending on the sample and the survey used (Bukhari, 2003). Older Muslim adults reside in many cities, but especially in New York, Chicago, Los Angeles, and Detroit.

Samana Siddiqui, a Muslim social worker from Canada, describes three groups of older Muslims. The first group includes individuals who immigrated to the United States at the turn of the century and lived with younger family members. Intergenerational differences sometimes arise in these families. The second group is the parents of younger family members who accompanied them to America during the 1960s and 1970s. The third and smallest group, the most socially isolated older Muslims, are persons who have converted to Islam. Most older persons reside with younger relatives, but some live alone (Siddiqui, 1999).

Physical and Mental Health

Although Sengstock (1996) found few complaints in her study of older Muslims, some did need help with transportation, caregiving, and medical assistance. Others needed assistance with cooking, grocery shopping, taking medications, and socializing with others, whereas a few required help with self-care. Following the events of September 11, 2001, Muslims have experienced increased apprehension from other Americans. Muslims who dress in their traditional garments or speak English with a foreign accent are harassed more often than older Muslim adults who conceal their cultural or ethnic identities (Salari, 2002). Social workers must advocate against such hostility and discriminatory practices and educate others about Muslims to eradicate stereotypical attitudes. Social workers should conduct needs assessments of older Muslims' physical and mental health to more effectively target services to these older adults.

Cultural Values and Social Work Interventions

Helping others is central to Muslim daily life. The help is usually informal and family based, but increasing numbers of social service agencies, such as Muslim Family Services, are emerging. According to Siddiqui (1999), many older Muslim families eschew formal help because of the stigma associated with seeking professional guidance, but social workers who practice culturally sensitive approaches with Muslim traditions and rituals will appeal more to older Muslims. In addition, many older Muslim persons feel more comfortable talking to social workers who share the same religious background. Social workers who partner with the natural, informal support systems in Muslim communities also will lessen the stigma many older Muslims associate with seeking formal help.

The oldest and largest Muslim social service agency is the Arab Community Center for Economic and Social Services, in Dearborn, Michigan, created in the mid-1970s, but smaller organizations are also emerging. These programs are usually organized around participants' ethnic and religious values and provide assistance to individuals in need of food, clothing, and/or money (Nimer, 2003). Social workers will more successfully consider older Muslims' ethnic and religious preferences when they collaborate with these agencies.

REGIONAL MINORITIES

Some older adults become members of other minority groups as a result of living in certain areas, such as in Appalachia or as indigenous peoples from the Pacific Islands. Older persons from Appalachia and the Pacific Islands maintain distinct social and economic characteristics and need support in various ways.

Appalachian Older Persons

Demographics

The Appalachian Mountains are a major mountain chain in the northeastern United States, covering 1,500 miles of land from the Canadian province of Quebec to northern Alabama. It includes several sub-regions: (1) northern Appalachia, which comprises areas in New York, Pennsylvania, Maryland, Ohio and parts of West Virginia; (2) central Appalachia, which incorporates nine southern counties in West Virginia, all of Appalachian Kentucky, and parts of Virginia and Tennessee; and (3) southern Appalachia, which encompasses areas in Virginia, Tennessee, the Carolinas, Georgia, Alabama, and Mississippi (Appalachian Regional Commission [ARC], 1974; see also *http://www.arc.gov*).

Although the Appalachian region is a diverse area, in 1964 the President's Appalachian Regional Commission concluded that the people who lived there demonstrated distinct social and economic characteristics (Pollard, 2003). The percentage of older persons in Appalachia, most of whom have resided in the region since birth, is higher and growing faster than in the rest of the country.

About 14.3%, or 3.3 million, older persons live in Appalachia, in contrast to 12.4%, or 35 million, in the rest of the country, and the highest percentage of older adults (16%) resides in the northern areas, in portions of Pennsylvania, eastern Ohio, and northern and eastern West Virginia. The percentage of older Appalachian adults will remain higher than that of the general population in the future (U.S. Census Bureau, 2000). Although the number of people over the age of 65 in the U.S. population is expected to reach 18.2%, or 63.5 million, in 2025, the percentage among similarly aged Appalachians should rise to 19.8%, or 5.1 million. The number of older persons over the age of 85 in this region will remain about the same as the rest of the population in 2025; about 1.7% and 1.5%, respectively (U.S. Census Bureau, 2003a).

The aging Appalachian population resembles national trends, but whereas many Americans' life expectancies have increased, they have remained the same in Appalachia. The demographic shifts in Appalachia are due mostly to emigration of young adults seeking jobs outside of Appalachia because of unemployment and other economic pressures. Few older persons, especially those in poor health, leave the area, in part because they maintain stronger attachments to the land and their communities than do younger persons (Dorfman, Murty, Evans, Ingram, & Power, 2004).

Despite these lifelong connections, many older persons, especially older women, live alone in Appalachia. About 40% of older Appalachian women maintained single households in 2000, compared with about 36% of women over the age of 65 in the total population. Only about 18% of older Appalachian men lived alone, which is only slightly higher (17%) than the percentage in the rest of the country.

Many older Appalachian women who live alone also struggle with poverty. Whereas the poverty rate for women over the age of 65 in the general population is 20%, among similarly aged Appalachian women, it is 27.5%. Among older men, the percentages are 15% and 24%, respectively. More than a quarter of older Appalachian persons living alone are economically impoverished, in contrast to about one-fifth of older women and about one-tenth of older men in the rest of the United States.

Physical and Mental Health

Older Appalachian persons, especially Appalachian women, have high disability rates, as measured by their abilities to perform activities of daily living and instrumental activities of daily living. For example, compared with non-Appalachian women and men over the age of 85, who had disability rates at about 78% and 67%, respectively, the rates for similarly aged Appalachian persons located in eastern Kentucky were 81% for women and 91% for men (Haaga, 2004).

Lack of access to preventative care is one reason these disability rates are so high (Wilcox, Bopp, Oberrecht, Kammermann, & McElmurray, 2003). Many older persons live at great distances from hospitals and other clinics, and transportation to these places is often difficult. Another problem results from the decline in informal supports as increasing numbers of younger persons relocate. Traditionally, older Appalachian adults have relied on friends and family members to assist them in their later years, but when family members leave, many older persons become socially isolated (McCulloch, 1995). Gerontological social workers will become increasingly needed as these trends continue.

Although many researchers have investigated the physical health problems of Appalachians, few have studied their mental health. Susan Keefe, who published *Appalachian Mental Health* in 1988, found that many women, especially older women, sought treatment for their "nerves" (Keefe, 1988), for which physicians frequently prescribed "nerve pills," that is, Valium and other tranquilizers. Keefe (1988) observed that many Appalachian women felt stressed from constantly struggling to make ends meet.

Cultural Values and Social Work Interventions

Older Appalachians share many common values and lifestyles despite some cultural variations across the subregions (Pollard, 2003). For example, most older Appalachians maintain strong religious beliefs and emphasize self-reliance and hard work (Dorfman et al., 2004). Older Appalachian women are remarkably resilient and thrive on their friendships, which they value and nurture. Mutual self-help groups are especially efficacious in these settings. For example, McInnis-Dittrich (1997) organized an innovative program, referred to as "The Women's Club," based on these older women's natural support systems.

The integration of social and medical services is especially crucial when assisting older clients, including Appalachian older persons, whose mental and physical conditions often interact (see Wilcox et al., 2003). Ritchie and colleagues (2002) found that case management teams composed of nurses and social workers that visited older persons in their homes, used state-of-the-art, standardized assessments, and implemented patient-specific care plans successfully enhanced older Appalachians' mental and physical functioning. Keefe (1988) offers several suggestions for mental health professionals working in Appalachia. They include: increasing public awareness of mental health services; locating mental health agencies in accessible areas; adopting flexible services to accommodate low-income persons; involving Appalachians in the mental health system; familiarizing professionals with Appalachian culture; incorporating a family perspective; and encouraging more mental health research in Appalachia that will reveal the most effective interventions for these individuals and their families.

Advocacy is also important when assisting older Appalachian persons. Social workers must advocate for older Appalachians in several areas, but the most important involve: (1) increasing their economic resources, given the high rate of poverty among older persons in Appalachia; (2) expanding their physical and mental health care, which is often fragmented and difficult for many older Appalachian adults to access; (3) strengthening their social resources, especially for the most socially isolated older adults; and

(4) improving their transportation and other community services assistance for those who live alone and at great distances from services.

The 2002 reauthorization of the Appalachian Regional Development Act of 1965, which created the ARC, mandates increased funds for partnerships committed to improving Appalachian persons' lives. These partnerships should include teams of social workers and other health professionals that reach out to the most impoverished and vulnerable older adults. Although older Appalachian elderly persons share a common region, they represent diverse cultural, racial, and religious perspectives. Social workers should tailor interventions by conducting comprehensive, holistic assessments that consider these older clients' biological, psychological, social, and environmental influences and by implementing treatments that are sensitive to older Appalachians' cultural and religious preferences and practices. Social workers will avoid stereotyping these older clients and more successfully address their concerns when they use culturally competent biopsychosocial interventions.

Older Native Hawaiian and Pacific Islanders

Demographics

The term *Pacific Islander* refers to those individuals whose origins are from the indigenous or original people of Hawai'i, Guam, Samoa, or other Pacific Islands (U.S. Census Bureau, 2003b). Native Hawaiian and Pacific Islanders (NHPI) make up 0.3% of the total population, which represents 874,414 persons, and only 5% of this population includes people over the age of 65, according to the 2000 U.S. Census reports. The NHPI are a relative young population, with a median age of 35.2 (U.S. Census Bureau, 2000). Nearly three-fourths of the NHPI residing in the United States and its territories live in the western states, and more than half live in two states—California and Hawai'i. Ten states—California, Hawai'i, Washington, Texas, New York, Florida, Utah, Nevada, Oregon, and Arizona—account for 80% of the nation's NHPI population.

Native Hawaiians are the largest NHPI group, including 401,000 persons, or 46% of the NHPI population. This group consists of 141,000 respondents who report being Native Hawaiian and another 261,000 who report being Native Hawaiian and at least one other race. Five percent of these persons are over the age of 65. The next two largest groups are Samoans (either alone or in combination with other races), comprising 133,000 people and making up 15% of the NHPI population, and Guamanian/Chamorro (either alone or in combination), consisting of 93,000 persons, or 11% of the population. Five percent of the Samoans and 2% of Guamanian/Chamorro include people over the age of 65. Twenty percent of NHPI did not report belonging to a cultural group but identified themselves as "Pacific Islander." For various historical reasons, these NHPI had a much higher proportion of respondents who reported two or more races (U.S. Census Bureau, 2001). Native Hawaiians, Samoans, and Guamanian/Chamorro Pacific Islanders accounted for 74% of all respondents who reported a single Pacific Islander group and 71% who identified as Pacific Islander with race combinations (U.S. Census Bureau, 2001).

Older NHPI differ from the overall older adult population in the United States in several other ways. For example, the median household income and the per capita incomes for older NHPI are significantly lower than the incomes of older U.S. residents in general, although nearly the same proportion (10%) of NHPI and U.S. elders lives in poverty. Nearly 30% of NHPI elders do not list English as their first language, and 28% of these older persons report not speaking English fluently or at all. In contrast, less than 1% of U.S. elders state that English is not their first language, with only 12.4% of this group reporting that they don't speak English fluently or at all. Additionally, NHPI elders rarely live alone compared with U.S. elders. The average household and family sizes are larger among NHPI than among Americans. In addition, contrary to popular opinion, NHPI families are less likely than the general population to live in rural areas (U.S. Census Bureau, 2004).

Older Pacific Islanders are composed of many cultures, including Polynesians (e.g., Hawaiians, Samoans, and Tongans), Micronesians (e.g., Chamorros, the indigenous people of Guam, and other groups), and Melanesians (e.g., Fijians). Each group represents a unique culture with distinct languages, values, lifestyles, histories, and patterns of adaptation to the United States (Srinivisan & Guillermo, 2000).

The heterogeneity among Asian Americans and Pacific Islanders in culture, language, and origin is one reason the U.S. Census separated Asian Americans (AA) from Native Hawaiians and other Pacific Islanders (NHPI) and created two distinctive racial categories (U.S. Census Bureau, 2001). The aggregated data tended to mask rather than illuminate the mental and physical health issues in the Pacific Islander population (Srinivisan & Guillermo, 2000).

Physical and Mental Health

Although the leading causes of death for NHPI mirror those of other Americans—heart disease, stroke, and cancer—Native Hawaiians have one of the nation's shortest life expectancies and have significantly higher death rates for these three diseases. A number of researchers have linked increased morbidity and mortality from chronic diseases among NHPI to the changes in lifestyle in the past century. Contrary to the traditional Pacific Islander diet of low-fat, high-fiber foods and active lifestyles, today's NHPI have adopted a Western diet high in fats and refined foods and a sedentary lifestyle (Englberger, Marks, & Fitzgerald, 2003; Hezel, 2001). Others have attributed their poorer health to forced colonization of Pacific Islanders that robbed them of their land and spirituality and left them with high rates of poverty (Bushnell, 1993; Mokuau, 1996).

Pacific Islanders also are at greater risk for mental health problems than Whites, due to stressors such as immigration, adjustment to living in an alien culture, discrimination and prejudice, language barriers, economics, and educational and occupational stresses and diseases (U.S. Department of Health and Human Services, 2001). Many NHPI feel socially alienated and disenfranchised as a result of internalizing discrimination and others' prejudiced attitudes toward them (Lee & Mokuau, 2002). NHPI also exhibit more psychological symptoms than the overall population, although few researchers have examined the mental health issues in this population (Prizzia & Mokuau, 1991).

Cultural Values and Social Work Interventions

Many social and historical factors have adversely affected NHPI mental and physical health (Braun, Yee, Browne, & Mokuau, 2004). These include international trade, military strategies, missionary influences, and the loss of sovereignty that were imposed on NHPIs and resulted in the replacement of local traditions and rituals with Western norms and practices (Bushnell, 1993; Braun et al., 1995; Mokuau, 1996). Other forces, such as diseases, migrations, economic ruins, and intermarriages between NHPI and non-NHPI have exacerbated these trends. Cultural values and social structures also contribute to many health disparities among NHPI and to problems they have accessing and participating in various social services (Brach & Fraser, 2000).

Older NHPI are, however, resilient, and like many older minority persons, they have much strength that has sustained them during difficult times. For example, the majority of NHPI maintain strong spiritual beliefs, believe in holism, and revere nature and spiritual realism. They tend to value mutuality in relationships and the collective over individual needs (Mokuau & Tauili'ili, 1998; Palafox & Warren, 1980). In addition, most NHPI, especially Native Hawaiians, Samoans, and Chamorros, believe in reciprocity and helpfulness (Alailima, 1996; Torsch & Ma, 2000; Mokuau & Tauili'ili, 1998). Similar to many traditional cultures, NHPI also respect and admire elders for their strength, wisdom, and courage. They appreciate their older adults' skills as arbitrators and the knowledge they share with younger generations (Harden, 1999; Mokuau & Browne, 1994; Mokuau, Browne, & Braun, 1998). Despite varying levels of acculturation, many older NHPI maintain leadership roles in their families, churches, and communities. However, elders' roles and status in their families are undermined when poverty, discrimination, and poor health persist in their communities.

Like most older persons, NHPI adults struggle with rising health care costs, but they must also confront many culturally specific issues and barriers in the medical system. For example, NHPI elders have one of the shorter life expectancies compared with all other ethnic minority populations, and many struggle with English as a second language (Braun et al., 2004; Braun, Takamura, Forman, Sasaki, & Meininger, 1995; Braun & Browne, 1998). Social workers will appeal to more older NHPI by learning more about these problems. In addition, social workers must educate themselves about the cultural values and history of various Pacific Islanders and the relevance of these values and history to their health and social service utilization. Social workers who understand the association between NHPI's own illness and health to spiritual balance might collaborate with spiritual and traditional healers and use more holistic interventions when working with these older persons (Braun et al., 2004). Equally important is the need for social workers to empower NHPI elders by teaching them coping strategies, interacting with their extended families, linking them to appropriate services that counter and alleviate the adverse effects of poverty and poor health, advocating on their behalf in various contexts and situations, and enforcing nonhierarchical interactions, which is especially important in creating an alliance with NHPI clients who have had long histories of oppression and unwelcomed interventions.

The anticipated growth rate of older persons from these and other minority populations underscores the need for more widespread social work training in the strengths perspective and in culturally competent practice that takes into account older minority persons' diverse resources and challenges. These demographic trends also support the need for more research about culturally competent interventions to guide practice and policy making. Social workers will encounter increasingly more older persons from various religions and residences, as older cohorts become increasingly heterogeneous. As social workers, our commitment must be steadfast in ensuring that all older persons receive quality care and services.

REFERENCES

Alailima, F. C. (1996). The Samoans in Hawai'i. In B. L. Hormann & A. W. Lind (Eds.), *Ethnic sources in Hawai'i* (pp. 88–94). New York: McGraw-Hill.

Appalachian Regional Commission. (1974). The new Appalachian subregions and their development strategies. *Appalachia: A Journal of the Appalachian Regional Commission, 8*(1), 11–27.

Brach, C., Fraser, I. (2000). Can cultural competency reduce racial and ethnic health disparities? A review and conceptual model. *Medical Care Research and Review, 57,* 181–217.

Braun, K., & Browne, C. (1998). Perceptions of dementia, caregiving, and help seeking among Asian and Pacific Islander Americans. *Health and Social Work, 23,* 262–274.

Braun, K., Takamura, J., Forman, S., Sasaki, P., & Meininger, L. (1995). Developing and testing outreach materials on Alzheimer's disease for Asian and Pacific Islander Americans. *The Gerontologist, 35,* 122–126.

Braun, K., Yee, B., Browne, C., & Mokuau, N. (2004). Native Hawaiian and Pacific Island elders: Health status, health disparities, and culturally competent services. In K. Whitfield (Ed.), *Closing the gap* (pp. 55–68). Washington, DC: Gerontological Society of America.

Bukhari, Z. H. (2003). Demography, identity, space: Defining American Muslims. In P. Strum & D. Tarantolo. (Eds.), *Muslims in the United States* (pp. 7–20). Washington, DC: Woodrow Wilson International Center for Scholars.

Bushnell, O. A. (1993). *The gifts of civilization: Germs and germicide in Hawaii.* Honolulu: University of Hawaii Press.

Caplan, L. S., Wells, B. L., & Haynes, S. (1992). Breast cancer screening among older racial/ethnic minorities and whites: Barriers to early detection. *Journal of Gerontology, Special Issue, 47,* 101–110.

Delgado, M., & Tennstedt, S. (1997). Making the case for culturally appropriate services: Puerto Rican elders and their caregivers. *Health and Social Work, 22*(4), 246–255.

Dorfman, L. T., Murty, S. A., Evans, R. J., Ingram, J. G., & Power, J. R. (2004). History and identity in the narratives of rural elders. *Journal of Aging Studies, 18,* 187–203.

Englberger, L., Marks, G. C., & Fitzgerald, M. H. (2003). Insights on food and nutrition in the Federated States of Micronesia: A review of the literature. *Public Health Nutrition, 6*(1), 5–17.

Fitzpatrick, T. (2000). Elderly Russian Jewish immigrants. In S. Alemán, T. Fitzpatrick, T. V. Tran, & E. W. Gonzalez (Eds.), *Therapeutic interventions with ethnic elders: Health and social issues* (pp. 55–78). Binghamton, NY: Haworth Press.

Haaga, J. (2004). *The aging of Appalachia.* Washington, DC: Appalachian Regional Commission, Population Reference Bureau.

Harden, M. J. (1999). *Voices of wisdom: Hawaiian elders speak.* Kula, HI: Aka Press.

Harel, Z. (2001). Jewish aged: Diversity in need and care solutions. In L. K. Olson (Ed.), *Age through the ethnic lenses* (pp. 145–159). Lanham, MD: Rowman & Littlefield.

Hezel, F. X. (2001). *The new shape of old island cultures.* Honolulu: University of Hawaii Press.

Keefe, S. (1988). *Appalachian mental health.* Lexington: The University Press of Kentucky.

Kosloski, K., Montgomery, R. J., & Karner, T. X. (1999). Differences in the perceived need for assistive services by culturally diverse caregivers of persons with dementia. *Journal of Applied Gerontology, 18*(2), 239–256.

Kosmin, B. A., & Mayer, E. (2001a). *American religious identification study.* New York: City University of New York Graduate Center. Retrieved June 21, 2004, from *http://www.gc.cuny.edu/studies/aris.pdf.*

Kosmin, B. A., & Mayer, E. (2001b). *Profile of the US Muslim population* (ARIS Report No. 2). New York: City University of New York Graduate Center, Retrieved June 21, 2004, from *http://www.gc.cuny.edu/studies/aris_part_two.htm.*

Lee, E., & Mokuau, N. (2002). *Cultural diversity series: Meeting the mental health needs of Asian and Pacific Islander Americans.* Alexandria, CA: National Technical Assistance Center for State Mental Health Planning.

Lum, D. (1999). *Culturally competent practice: A framework for growth and action.* Pacific Grove: Brooks/Cole.

McCulloch, B. J. (1995). The relationship of family proximity and social support to the mental health of older rural adults: The Appalachian context. *Journal of Aging Studies, 9,* 65–81.

McInnis-Dittrich, K. I. (1997). An empowerment-oriented mental health intervention with elderly Appalachian women: The women's club. *Journal of Women and Aging, 9,* 91–105.

Mokuau, N. (1999). Responding to Pacific Islanders: Culturally competent perspectives for substance abuse prevention. (DHHS Publication No. SMA 98–3195.) Washington, DC: U.S. Government Printing Office.

Mokuau, N. (1996). Health and well being for Pacific Islanders: Status, barriers, and resolutions. *Asian American and Pacific Islander Journal of Health, 41*(1–3), 55–67.

Mokuau, N., & Browne, C. (1994). Life themes of Native Hawaiian female elders: Resources for cultural preservation. *Social Work, 39*(1), 43–49.

Mokuau, N., Browne, C., & Braun, K. (1998). *Na kupuna* in Hawaii: Social and health status of Native Hawaiian elders. *Pacific Health Dialogue Journal of Community Health and Clinical Medicine for the Pacific, 52*(2), 282–289.

Mokuau, N., & Tauili'ili, P. (1998). Families with Native Hawaiian and Samoan roots. In E. W. Lynch & M. J. Hanson (Eds.), *Developing cross-cultural competence* (pp. 409–440). Baltimore: Brookes.

Nimer, M. (2003). Social and political institutions of American Muslims: Liberty and civic responsibility. In P. Strum & D. Tarantolo (Eds.), *Muslims in the United States* (pp. 45–61). Washington, DC: Woodrow Wilson International Center for Scholars.

Office of Minority Health. (2001, February–March). *Closing the gap.* Washington, DC: U.S. Department of Health and Human Services, Office of Minority Health.

Palafox, N., & Warren, A. (Eds.). (1980). *Cross-cultural caring: A handbook for health care professionals in Hawai'i.* Honolulu: University of Hawaii School of Medicine Transcultural Health Care Forum.

Pollard, K. M. (2003). *Appalachia at the millennium: An overview of results from census 2000.* Washington, DC: Population Reference Bureau.

Prizzia, R., & Mokuau, N. (1991). Mental health services for Native Hawaiians: The need for culturally relevant services. *Journal of Health and Human Service Administration, 14,* 44–61.

Ritchie, C., Wieland, D., Tully, C., Rowe, J., Sims, R., & Bodner, E. (2002). Coordination and advocacy for rural elders (CARE): A model of rural case management with veterans. *The Gerontologist, 42,* 399–405.

Salari, S. (2002). Invisible in aging research: Agram Americans, Middle Eastern immigrants, and Muslims in the United States. *The Gerontologist, 42,* 580–588.

Saleebey, D. (Eds.). (1997). *The strengths perspective in social work practice.* New York: Longman.

Sengstock, M. C. (1996). Care of the elderly among Muslim families. In B. C. Aswad & B. Bilge (Eds.), *Family and gender among American Muslims: Issues facing Middle Eastern immigrants and their descendants* (pp. 271–297). Philadelphia: Temple University Press.

Siddiqui, S. (1999). *The senior citizens of our Ummah.* Retrieved June 13, 2004, from *http://www.soundvision.com/info/misc/elderly/senior.asp.*

Srinivisan, S., & Guillermo, T. (2000). Toward improved health: Disaggregating Asian American and Native Hawaiian Pacific Islander data. *American Journal of Public Health, 90*(11), 1731.

Torsch, V. L., & Ma, G. X. (2000). Cross cultural comparison of health perceptions, concerns, and coping strategies among Asian and Pacific Islander American elders. *Qualitative Health Research, 10,* 471–489.

United Jewish Communities. (2004). *A United Jewish Communities report.* New York: Author.

U.S. Census Bureau. (2000). Redistricting data CPL 94–171. Summary File. American FactFinder. Retrieved August 5, 2004, from *http://factfinder.census.gov.*

U.S. Census Bureau. (2001). *The Native Hawaiian and other Pacific Islander population: 2000.* Washington, DC: Author.

U.S. Census Bureau. (2003a, July). *International Program Data Base: [Regional Economic Models, Inc.].* Amherst, MA.

U.S. Census Bureau. (2003b). *The Asian and Pacific Islander population in the United States: March 2002. Population Characteristics.* Washington, DC: Author.

U.S. Census Bureau (2004). American FactFinder Datasets. Retrieved March 20, 2004, from *http://factfinder.census.gov/servlet/datasetmainpageservlet?-program=DEC&_lang.*

U.S. Department of Health and Human Services. (2001). *Mental health: Culture, race, and ethnicity: A supplement to Mental Health: A report of the Surgeon General* (DHHS Publication No. SMA01-3613). Rockville, MD: U.S. Department of Health and Human Services, Substance Abuse and Mental Health Services Administration.

Wilcox, S., Bopp, M., Oberrecht, L., Kammermann, S., & McElmurray, C. (2003). Psychosocial and perceived environmental correlates of physical activity in rural and older African American and White women. *Journals of Gerontology: Series B. Psychological Sciences and Social Sciences, 58,* P329–P337.

JUDITH L. HOWE,
SECTION EDITOR

SECTION V

Social Work Practice in Palliative and End-of-Life Care

OVERVIEW

The importance of the social worker's role in providing palliative and end-of-life care is well established. Social workers are uniquely qualified to work with clients and their families and caregivers in this field because of the profession's focus on psychosocial issues, group and individual work, advocacy, and linkages with the community. The following chapters, by Gutheil and Souza and Howe and Daratsos, examine social work's expanding involvement in providing end-of-life care in terms of settings, roles, skills, assessment, resources, legal issues, and bereavement support.

A discussion of the social worker's role in end-of-life care for older adults is complex. Longer life expectancy has led to a widening age range for older persons, with increased diversity and more chronic and life-limiting illnesses. Greater use of technology in health care has resulted in persons living longer with more disabilities and illnesses, sometimes resulting in longer and more complicated death trajectories. Thus advance care planning takes on major importance, with an imperative for social workers to provide education and counseling about advance directives with clients and their families before a health crisis strikes.

Social workers carry out multiple roles in palliative and end-of-life care, optimally within the context of the interdisciplinary team. These roles include, but are not limited to, administration, liaison, advocacy, clinical assessment, counseling, education, and research. Psychosocial assessment is particularly complex and crucial for clients facing life-limiting illnesses. For the dying person, psychosocial and spiritual issues are as important as physiological ones, and the social worker, representing the personal and social concerns of the dying person and family, plays a critically important role at this time. The social worker serves as the patient advocate and is often the person on the team who can help facilitate the patient's wishes and articulate them to the team. Furthermore, social workers understand the cultural issues for dying persons and their families and can facilitate recognition and incorporation of customs and traditions surrounding death in the setting. The social worker is a resource to other members of the interdisciplinary health care team because of the profession's focus on the emotional and social aspects of care and human need. Finally, social workers are principal providers of bereavement and grief counseling, and we recognize that this is an area that needs further expansion.

In summary, the social work contribution to palliative and end-of-life care is a significant one and includes domains ranging from interdisciplinary team member to assessor to grief counselor to advocate to educator to administrator. As we look to the future, the role of social work in end-of-life and palliative care will be increasingly articulated and recognized, as has already occurred in the professions of nursing and medicine. The Social Work Summit on End-of-Life and Palliative Care held in 2002 helped to shape an agenda, and other professional activities are under way to develop competencies and information exchange among social workers in end-of-life care. For instance, the National Association of Social Workers recently issued *Standards for Social Work Practice in Palliative and End of Life Care,* based on the work of the Social Work Summit that brought together social work leaders and social work organizations in this field. These standards are geared to enhancing social workers' awareness of the skills, knowledge, methods, and attitudes necessary to effectively work with clients and their families (see the website *www.socialworkers.org*). Social work–based initiatives such as this are welcome and call for the inclusion of social workers in a range of practice settings given the broad impact and importance of palliative and end-of-life care. In addition, social workers must be included and must provide leadership in interdisciplinary training programs and initiatives. The Veterans Health Affairs Interprofessional Palliative Care Fellowship Program is one such example. It trains promising individuals during a 1-year fellowship in a range of disciplines, including master's-prepared social workers, to be future leaders in palliative and end-of-life care. Initiatives such as this put social work right in the middle of the interdisciplinary mix of palliative and end-of-life care, where it should be.

JUDITH L. HOWE
LOUISA DARATSOS

Roles of Social Workers in Palliative and End-of-Life Care

CONTEXT OF PALLIATIVE AND END-OF-LIFE CARE AND ROLE OF SOCIAL WORK PRACTICE

In recent years, there has been a movement to increase the availability of palliative and end-of-life care for patients and families. This is due in part to foundation and government support, media attention, and significantly increasing public and professional demand for more compassionate and appropriate care for those with life-limiting illnesses. Indicative of this groundswell was the Social Work Summit on End-of-Life and Palliative Care held in March 2002, aimed at developing a national consortium of social work leaders and organizations to shape an agenda for social work and end-of-life care and develop programs in practice, education, and research (Christ, 2002).

Social work is an essential and significant part of palliative and end-of-life practice. Whereas not all social workers practice in settings devoted to palliative or end-of-life care, all social workers will probably work with clients who are themselves experiencing or who have loved ones who are experiencing life-threatening illnesses, as well as people who are grieving (Kramer, 1998, 2002). Competent care for those facing life-threatening, serious illness is recognized to be multifaceted and holistic. By its nature, palliative care is an interdisciplinary area of practice, and hence the psychosocial domains of a client's well-being must be addressed in a comprehensive manner (National Consensus Project for Quality Palliative Care, 2004). As noted by Steinhauser and colleagues, "whereas physicians tend to focus on physical aspects, patients and families tend to view the end of life with a broader psychosocial and spiritual meaning, shaped by a lifetime of experiences" (Steinhauser et al., 2000). The social worker is often the key individual assisting patients, families, and caregivers in addressing the emotional, psychological, social, spiritual, cultural, financial, and environmental aspects of care.

The interdisciplinary team is the cornerstone of palliative care, and the social worker is a principal member of that team. For instance, the Veterans Health Administration (VHA; 2003) mandates that every VHA facility have a palliative care consult team (PCCT), at least 25% of whose members should be physicians, social workers, nurses, or chaplains, in addition to at least 25% administrative personnel (Veterans Health Administration, 2003). Social workers have specific roles and functions in working with clients, their families, and caregivers, requiring spe-

26

cific competencies in knowledge, skills, and attitudes. Palliative care social workers have a particularly important role in working with clients and families coping with impending loss of life, which is often experienced as yet another loss layered on a series of prior losses.

This chapter addresses the settings of care for social work practice in palliative care, the role of the social worker in delivering palliative care, the social worker's role in assessment and service provision, psychosocial and financial resources, cultural and spiritual issues, and bereavement support services.

SETTINGS OF CARE

Social workers practice in a range of settings in palliative and end-of-life care, including the hospital, nursing home, outpatient clinic or practice, hospice, and home. Although 90% of all individuals state their wish to die at home, in fact only about one in five individuals actually do. The National Mortality Follow-back Survey found that 56% die in the hospital, 19% in a nursing home, 21% at home, and 4% in other settings (National Center for Health Statistics, 2003).

Social workers are key individuals on the palliative care team in ensuring smooth transitions from setting to setting along the care continuum. Individuals with life-threatening illnesses may move frequently from setting to setting, and the social worker is often the team member who recognizes crisis points in the illness trajectory. These crisis points represent opportunities for effective social work intervention. Social workers are the team members with the expertise and training in community resources and referrals. They apply the tasks associated with discharge planning and merge that planning with their counseling skills to assist the individual and his support system in attaining the best available setting for palliative and end-of-life care.

Hospice may be defined as a model for quality and compassionate care for individuals facing a life-limiting illness. It involves a team approach to medical care, pain management, and emotional and spiritual support for patients, family, and caregivers. Hospice focuses on caring, not curing, and is usually provided in the patient's home, but it is also offered in other settings (see the National Hospice and Palliative Care website, *http://nhpco.org*). The holistic approach of hospice emphasizes social, psychological, and spiritual, as well as medical, needs. Medicare, which covers hospice care for those predicted to have less than 6

months to live, requires hospices to provide psychosocial and spiritual counseling services as a condition of participation. Many states have licensing or certification requirements as well, which reinforce this approach to hospice care. A recent study of state regulatory reports, however, found that often the role of social work was not adequately documented in assessment, care planning, bereavement, and interdisciplinary team meetings. The conclusion of this study was that social workers must improve their documentation to demonstrate their effectiveness as powerful team members in the hospice setting (Oliver, 2003).

Another recent study reports on the findings of a survey of members of the Association of Oncology Social Workers about the likelihood of social workers referring a terminally ill client to hospice. Although the social workers held very favorable attitudes toward hospice care, the average proportion of terminally ill clients whom they referred to hospice was just 49.5% (Becker, 2004). This finding suggests that social workers may need greater education about when a client is ready for hospice, better training to present the hospice option to patients and families, and the empowerment skills within the team setting to recommend that referral.

The recent *Clinical Practice Guidelines for Quality Palliative Care* note that palliative care is most effective when integrated into existing care settings, such as the hospital, nursing home, or home care. At the end of life, the proven model of care is hospice (National Consensus Project for Quality Palliative Care, 2004). The common organizational delivery models of palliative care, including hospice programs, are delineated in Table 26.1 (National Consensus Project for Quality Palliative Care, 2004).

Hospital

The hospital is frequently the host site for palliative and hospice care. There are a variety of models for care delivery, including freestanding hospice or supportive care units and palliative care consultation teams. Often, facilities have inpatient units, consultation teams, and outpatient clinics. These teams are charged with case-finding in the medical center to identify patients who require palliative and end-of-life care with the goal of making earlier referrals to hospices and decreasing the number of patients dying in the intensive care unit. The teams also facilitate development of goals for ongoing care. The social worker is an instrumental team member in ascertain-

TABLE 26.1. Palliative Care and Hospice Settings

Hospital (acute and rehabilitation)	Nursing Home	Home/Outpatient Practice or Clinic
Consultation team	Consultation team	Private-practice based
Inpatient unit	Inpatient unit	Home-based primary care
Combined w/ freestanding inpatient hospice	Combined w/ freestanding inpatient hospice	Hospice-based consultation team
Combined consultation team, inpatient unit, and outpatient clinic	Combined consultation team and inpatient unit	Hospice-based palliative care

ing when a transfer is appropriate for nonmedical reasons such as caregiver functioning and changes in the patient-family-caregiver triad.

Nursing Home

One in five Americans dies in a nursing home, with projections indicating that this number may increase to as much as 40% by the year 2030 ("Developing Quality Indicators," 2000). For nursing home social workers, end-of-life care is an integral and day-to-day part of practice. Increasingly, nursing homes have palliative care teams, which include social workers.

Home/Outpatient Practice or Clinic

The outpatient practice or clinic serves two purposes for palliative care patients. For patients whose palliative care needs are just beginning to be identified, the clinic functions as a transitional care setting in which symptoms can be managed and recommendations for more intensive interventions can be identified and arranged. In the second instance, the outpatient setting will function as the provider of record for patients receiving hospice care at home. In this case, the outpatient clinic team works collaboratively with the hospice team to care for patients with minimal travel to and from the clinic. This is an advantageous arrangement because it allows the patients to have their care managed by their providers of choice and, at the same time, it integrates the expertise of the hospice team.

THE ROLE OF THE SOCIAL WORKER AND SCOPE OF PRACTICE

Quality of care at the end of life is highly individual and should be achieved through a process of shared decision making and clear communication that acknowledges the values and preferences of patients, caregivers, and families. In an interdisciplinary team, social workers, chaplains, and others can aid with resolving psychosocial end-of-life issues (Steinhauser et al., 2000).

Social workers carry out multiple roles in palliative and end-of-life care, often in the context of the interdisciplinary team. These roles include:

- *Clinician.* The social worker provides the counseling to patients and families to help them cope with the changes in physical, cognitive, and emotional functioning and to cope with the anticipated death.
- *Educator.* The social worker, with an interdisciplinary educational foundation, can play a significant role in curriculum development and teaching in end-of-life and palliative care. There are increasing opportunities for leadership in this area with the emergence of advanced training programs. (See the websites http://www.smith.edu/ssw/index1.htm, http://www.nyu.edu/socialwork/, http://www.va.gov/oaa/fellowships/palliative.asp.)
- *Researcher.* The social worker can, and should, take the lead in palliative care and end-of-life research. As noted by the Social Work Summit on Palliative and End-of-Life Care (Christ, 2002), there is a pressing need for increased financial support for research in social work and end-of-life care, as well as the inclusion of social workers in research collaboratives. In particular, social work practitioners, with their unique, day-to-day perspectives, need to be included in the conceptualization and implementation of research in this area.
- *Team member.* The social worker, having advanced communication and facilitation skills, can play an important role on the interdisciplinary team in the areas of leadership, problem solving, and other team-building and maintenance tasks so critical to effective teamwork.

Skills Needed to Provide Services to Patients and Families

Comprehensive Assessment

Psychosocial assessment in palliative care appraises an individual's mental status, emotional stability, social resources, and ability to interact with others. Terminally ill patients often view their current experience as part of a broader life course trajectory. Measures used to assess end-of-life quality should account for a patient's emotional and spiritual growth in spite of the limited life expectancy. The work of Dr. Ira Byock, among others, has taught us that when biopsychosocial and spiritual needs are well satisfied, there are tremendous opportunities for healing and closure at the end of life for both the patient and the family (Byock, 1997).

Psychosocial assessment at the end of life is critically important for several reasons. The comprehensive assessment facilitates the development of a care plan specific to that patient and family (Blum, Clark, & Marcusen, 2001). The assessment also promotes the initiation of strong working relationships among the patient, family, and care team, facilitates articulation of goals of care and sets the tone by which these goals can be achieved (Cox & Stovall, 2001).

During the 20th century, the culture of death changed. With the location of death shifting to the hospital from the home, physicians assumed greater responsibility for interventions designed to postpone an individual's death. As a result, death is viewed as a physiological event. For the professionals and patients involved with care at the end of life, however, death carries a broader meaning. Psychosocial and spiritual issues are as important as physiological events. For most terminally ill older adults, two components are important in end-of-life events: generativity and the need to be treated as a whole person rather than a case or disease (Erikson, 1994). Caregivers and other members of the patient's support system have a need to feel that they have done whatever possible for the patient. The caregivers themselves also need emotional and practical support, as well as bereavement care.

The patient-family-caregiver unit rarely "speaks with one voice." Thus comprehensive assessment contains individualized assessments of the patient, the family as defined by the patient, and the informal caregivers involved, instead of a focus only on the patient. The multifaceted assessment provides important historical and developmental details about each person within the patient system. It documents financial, employment, and educational details. It notes cultural, ethnic, and spiritual backgrounds and compares and contrasts the differences among the involved parties. Because of this broad scope, the assessment detects the subtle range of coping styles, behaviors, beliefs, and opinions within each involved individual who is assessed. This kind of assessment reveals varying abilities to cope with the patient's needs at the end of life (see list below).

Components of Comprehensive Assessment

- Needs and goals as expressed by the patient and family
- Strengths, competencies, and coping resources of the patient and the support network
- Life history and developmental needs
- Emotional issues, including death anxiety
- Impact of illness on patient's body integrity and concerns about dependence
- History of prior losses
- Perceptions about illness and prognosis and cognitive and emotional integration of diagnosis by the patient and family members
- Present pain and symptom management
- Potential treatment barriers and risk factors that may impede success of the plan of care
- Family history, structure, roles, and dynamics of the family network
- Financial, social, emotional, spiritual, and psychological resources and supports available to the patient and family
- Expressed educational, practical, health care, advance care planning, discharge planning, and support needs
- Safety issues and functional and environmental issues
- Concerns about sexuality and intimacy
- Cultural expectations and preferences
- Spiritual and/or religious beliefs
- Bereavement risk assessment
- Legal and ethical principles

Performing the assessment in this fashion takes time—something that palliative care administrators must respect. With the details also comes a commitment by the palliative care social worker and the team to attend to the presenting issues to the best of their abilities. We believe that this devotion to detail from the initial contacts with the patient system will lead to a deeper understanding of the presenting issues, an appropriately detailed plan of care, and a more rapid response from the palliative care team to meet these needs and to help the patient system negotiate their differences.

Identification of Psychosocial Resources

The specific information gained from the psychosocial assessment will lead to an understanding of the patient system's strengths and areas for further address. Social work education's fundamental tenet is to view people in the contexts of their environment. The palliative care social worker's training integrates the practical considerations with the emotional reserves, which, when taken together, uncover the available psychosocial resources.

In the last stages of life, when patients are likely to be in health care settings, the psychosocial assessment and subsequent recommendations for intervention, executed by a competent social worker, can restore or maintain hope in both the patient and the survivors. Hope, in the context of palliative care, takes on a particular meaning. Early on, when news of any advanced disease is first learned, there is nearly always a hope for a restoration of health. Palliative care social work, with its emphases on continuity of care, competency-based practice, and smooth transitions from setting to setting, can allow the patient and family to develop a new definition of hope. Palliative care social work can lessen patient and family anxiety and thus "prove" to the patient system that they have the internal strength to sustain themselves during this phase of the life cycle. Social workers who specialize in palliative care can attest to receiving heartfelt thank-you notes from grateful patients and families for assistance given even though the social worker will feel as though she or he had done very little. It is that offering of active listening for which the families express thanks.

In addition to the psychosocial counseling that the palliative care social worker provides, there are several other sources of professional and peer counseling that patients and their caregivers can pursue. Some organizations provide individual and group counseling over the Internet and by telephone to people who, for whatever reason, cannot leave their homes. Among the most well known of these agencies is Cancer Care.

The use of technology to bring counseling to people in their homes has been an enormous advance toward reducing distress among the homebound. In many instances, caregivers are also homebound either because of their own physical issues or because the

terminally ill patient cannot be left alone. In underserved communities, whether urban, suburban, or rural, the telephone and the Internet provide specialized psychosocial counseling where this skill set might not exist. Consider, as well, a few of the many reasons why mobility within the community is reduced at the end of life for both the patient and the caregiver: self-perception about physical changes, lack of transportation, and medication side effects. Group counseling promotes formations of new relationships with similarly situated people under circumstances that would ordinarily isolate people. Some Internet formats are ideal for patients and families to access emotional support and social bonding according to their own scheduling needs. With some planning, the counseling can continue even as the patient moves from setting to setting. The success of these formats in providing counseling is based on reducing the social and emotional isolation that advanced illness fosters. Social workers who work with families who are facing terminal illness should recognize what value these two resources have and should encourage clients to use these referrals whenever appropriate.

Providing Linkages to Financial Resources

Regardless of the patient's income level and age, terminal illness can be a tremendous financial burden on a patient and family. Medical expenses may have mounted before the patient became designated as in need of palliative care. Besides hospital bills, all medical treatment, even hospice care, can include many direct and indirect expenses that public and private insurance do not cover, such as medications (hospice does not pay for medications not related to the terminal diagnosis), transportation (for the patient as well as the caregivers), some home care and nursing home costs, child care, and so forth. Fear of financial problems can also be related to physical symptoms, as is the case in which patients forgo needed services or treatments because of a perception that medical care will adversely affect the household (Francoeur, 2001). Among working-age patients and caregivers, consideration for lost wages, time away from work, the real or perceived threat of job loss, and the presence or lack of a financial safety net can cause a financial crisis for the family.

There can be no doubt that the threats of debt and impoverishment are sources of emotional distress. Social workers working in palliative care settings often encounter situations in which the patient had been the primary breadwinner and provisions had not previously been made to obtain access to checking and bank accounts so that critical monthly expenses such as rent and utilities can be paid. The oldest patients may be reluctant to use their savings to pay for care out of the false belief that government programs such as Medicare and the Veterans Health Administration cover all expenses related to illness. Distress related to financial issues is an area in which social work training, with its emphasis on counseling and accessing resources, can be of enormous assistance to the patient, his or her family, and the palliative care team. Palliative care social workers must know the available resources to assist patients and families in obtaining relief. They additionally need to use their counseling, negotiation, consumer, and advocacy skills in helping patients and families to access these resources in a timely and appropriate fashion.

Some patients and families might observe an initial barrier of privacy that prevents a social worker from obtaining a complete financial assessment. The resulting delay may prevent that aspect of the care plan from developing and going forward. Some patients and families, on hearing of the news that the illness is terminal, attempt to seek financial assistance from unrealistic sources, such as attempting to purchase life insurance when the patient is *in extremis*. As noted, some patients and families initially do not believe that the government resources will not pay for the total costs of care. For others, the crisis of the illness makes it difficult to mobilize their energies to follow through with gathering the necessary documentation or keeping required appointments. It may be necessary, for example, for the palliative care social worker to help the patient and family to review his or her health insurance policy and, when present, disability policies to better understand the available coverage. When the palliative care social worker facilitates this focused financial review, anxiety about the patient's needs can be reduced, even if the review does not yield a financial windfall. Instead, this work demonstrates a concern about how the family might continue to go on living in spite of the severity of the illness and the expected outcome. The following list presents some organizations and agencies that can be resources to the palliative care team and to the patient and family.

- Financial assistance and tips for meeting other practical needs are available through some disease organizations such as the American Cancer Society, Cancer Care and the Leukemia and Lymphoma Society.
- The Department of Veterans Affairs can provide a variety of financial, medical, and other assistance to qualified veterans. To find the local VA, contact 1-800-827-1000 or *www.va.gov*.
- Pharmaceutical companies have medication assistance programs to help patients obtain certain prescription drugs. Palliative care social workers can help to obtain the necessary information about access these programs and can help advocate to obtain this benefit.
- Palliative care social workers should be knowledgeable about sources of support in the community. They should be able to research religious, ethnic, and cultural communities that can help patients and their families. These organizations can assist with an array of supportive services.
- For patients over 60 and disabled, the local or state agency on aging can locate sources of assistance, such as Meals on Wheels, home repair, and local home care assistance programs. To find local Area Agency on Aging and other online elder resources, visit the Administration on Aging: Information for Older Persons and Their Families website at *www.aoa.gov*.
- For information regarding Social Security, disability, and Medicare benefits, see *www.ssa.gov*.
- For information about Medicaid, the state-administered health insurance program for those in need, visit *www.hcfa.gov/mcaicnsm.htm* or the local welfare agency. These sites provide information on local Medicaid eligibility.
- For information about food stamps, public assistance, or emergency cash grants, contact the local welfare office.
- To provide assistance with hospital expenses, the palliative care social worker can develop a working relationship with the financial counselor in the business office of the hospital to help develop a monthly payment plan. Such a working relationship also helps demonstrate the role of the social worker in promoting appropriate revenue collection.

If the family cannot meet its daily living expenses and has outstanding credit expenses, the palliative care social worker can assist the patient and family by directly contacting these creditors to work out a payment plan before these obligations become critical.

Identifying Cultural and Spiritual Resources

The need to recognize the role of both cultural and spiritual issues at the end of life is obvious to social workers involved with palliative care. At the same time, palliative care social work continues to deepen its understandings of these areas. Although it is often a challenge to incorporate spiritual care into health care, particularly within secular organizations, the relevance of spiritual care at the end of life has been increasingly recognized as critical (O'Connell, 1999).

Palliative care social workers recognize that the rewards for meeting the challenges posed by increasing awareness and understanding of spiritual and culturally appropriate care are great. The Joint Commission on Accreditation of Healthcare Organizations (JCAHO) and National Council of Hospice and Palliative Care Professionals (NHPCO) both support spiritual and cultural competence among staff members. There are many ways in which social workers can factually learn about spiritual and cultural practices of different religious and ethnic groups. In general, professionals can improve their ability to provide spiritual care by:

- Being open to multiple interpretations of reality and ways of believing and being
- Having a desire to learn about self and others
- Being aware of biases
- Becoming nonjudgmental
- Welcoming challenging experiences that allow for personal growth
- Being aware of one's limitations

To truly master these domains of palliative care, social workers must look inward to ascertain their cultural and spiritual identities. Along with this self-reflection comes self-care, as the social worker contemplates the effects of this work on all aspects of his or her life. Replenishing one's own vessel in culturally and spiritually renewing ways is important in supporting the health professional's caregiving potential to clients, team members, families, communities and ourselves. This enables the social worker to come to the bedside with a strong healing presence and true compassion, as well as sensitivity to the cultural and spiritual needs of patients and families. Regardless of what we practice, no doubt we will recognize the value of the therapeutic use of self and improve our listening, presence, and commitment to nonabandonment. We will be able to make referrals to pastoral care not as a way of passing along a task that we define as being "not our job" but rather with the level of understanding that the spiritual domain deserves.

Identifying Bereavement Support Resources

The palliative care movement has made a significant contribution to how people are cared for at the end of life. One area of needed expansion is bereavement support services. On intake and at critical points in the patient's care, hospice programs do assess how the caregivers and extended family are likely to cope with the patient's death. Hospices are also charged with continuing bereavement care for survivors 1 year after the patient's death. In general, the bereavement services of hospice programs are separate departments, reflecting that the delivery of bereavement care is a specialty. Unfortunately, that level of understanding of the impact of loss is evident only within the palliative care community.

Intrapersonal, cultural, ethnic, and spiritual needs are ignored by the community at large after the time just following the death. This could be viewed as an abrupt change from the spiritually and culturally competent care and practices provided by the palliative care team that supported and sustained the patient system during the illness. Cable (1998) notes that because social support networks are now not necessarily confined to a specific community or geographic region, the bereaved are very often isolated in their communities. In contrast, before there was great mobility and easy communication in the United States, families lived close to one another and communities mourned deaths as a shared experience (Cable, 1998). Currently, few employers offer designated time off for the death of a loved one, and when this benefit exists, it tends to be defined in terms of the familial relationship rather than by the significance of the deceased to the survivor. Most employees would be expected to use vacation days or leave without pay to attend funerals. Furthermore, there is a general expectation that when the person returns from time off for the death, the survivor will be able to resume his societal roles.

The generalized expectation that death should be attended to in a discreet manner runs counter to the experience of suffering a loss. According to Rando, grief is the personalized biopsychosocial reaction to the loss (Rando, 1993). This reaction takes place over a time frame unique to the individual. Rando defines mourning as the display of grief, which is expressed through the bereaved's behaviors. Over time, the bereaved adapts to the loss.

All social workers, regardless of their settings, will work with people who are bereaved. Thus all social workers should have a basic training in grief work appropriate to the age, culture, and spiritual backgrounds of the population served. This aspect of the work will model sensitivity to the issues presented in the workplace and will make referrals to grief specialists. Having and using the training will create a culture of caring and concern so needed by the bereaved, one that has become absent in the community at large. The atmosphere of understanding does not minimize the loss based on degree of kinship to the deceased or the time that has passed since the death or any other domain. It tolerates expressions of emotion and at the same time demonstrates concern for the person's well-being and conveys a sense of hope that the pain of the loss will lessen. By acknowledging the bereavement issues in the workplace and spearheading the facility's approach, the social worker will yet again exert valuable leadership and coordination skills and demonstrate her or his keen understanding of how the person fits into the environment.

CONCLUSION

As the World War II and baby boomer generations age, social work practice in the area of palliative and end-of-life care is becoming increasingly complex. Social workers are involved in palliative care no matter what setting or what population they find themselves in, because death and dying are universal experiences. The social work contribution to palliative care touches on many domains, from interdisciplinary team member to administrator to educator to therapist to researcher to peer support leader. Social workers who have an interest in this work are encouraged to share their experiences and lessons learned with their colleagues on their teams, within their practice settings and beyond, in regional and national venues. It is exactly this sharing that will continue to deepen the knowledge base, improve the level of practice, and promote the leadership role of the social worker.

USEFUL WEBSITES

www.aahpm.org
American Academy of Hospice and Palliative Medicine

www.abcd-caring.org
Americans for Better Care of the Dying
www.americanhospice.org
American Hospice Foundation
www.aoa.gov
Administration on Aging
www.aosw.org
Association of Oncology Social Work
www.beliefnet.org
An online community for religion and spirituality
www.cancer.org
American Cancer Society
www.cancercare.org
Help for patients with a diagnosis of cancer
www.capcmssm.org
Center to Advance Palliative Care
www.cms.hhs.gov/medicaid/consumer.asp
Centers for Medicaid and Medicare Services
www.eperc.mcw.edu
End of Life/Palliative Education Resource Center
www.growthhouse.org
An online community for End-of-Life Care
www.hospicefoundation.org
Hospice Foundation of America
www.hpna.org
Hospice and Palliative Care Nurses Association
www.lastacts.org
Last Acts Coalition
www.leukemia-lymphoma.org
The Leukemia and Lymphoma Society
www.mcw.edu/pallmed/
Medical College of Wisconsin, Palliative Care Center
www.medicaring.org
The Washington Home, Center for Palliative Care Studies
www.medsch.wisc.edu/painpolicy
University of Wisconsin Pain and Policy Studies Group
www.nasw.org
National Association of Social Workers
www.nationalcensusproject.org
Recent Clinical Practice Guidelines for Quality Palliative Care
www.nhpco.org
National Hospice and Palliative Care Organization
www.partnershipforcaring.org
America's Voices for the Dying
www.ssa.gov
U.S. Social Security Administration
www.stoppain.org
Beth Israel Medical Center, Department of Pain Medicine and Palliative Care

www.swlda.org
Project on Death in America, Social Work Leadership Development Award
http://www.smith.edu/ssw/index1.htm
Smith College School for Social Work
http://www.nyu.edu/socialwork/
New York University, Shirley M. Ehrenkranz School of Social Work
http://www.va.gov/oaa/fellowships/palliative.asp
Veterans Health Administration, Interprofessional Palliative Care Fellowship Program

REFERENCES

Becker, J. E. (2004). Oncology social workers' attitudes toward hospice care and referral behavior. *Health and Social Work, 29*(1), 36–46.

Blum, D., Clark, E. J., & Marcusen, C. P. (2001). Oncology social work in the 21st century. In *Social Work in Oncology* (pp. 45–71). Atlanta, GA: American Cancer Society Health Content Products.

Byock, I. (1997). *Dying well.* New York: Riverhead Books.

Cable, D. G. (1998). Grief in American culture. In K. J. Doka & J. D. Davidson (Eds.), *Living with grief: Who we are, how we grieve* (pp. 61–70). New York: Brunner/Mazel.

Christ, G. (2002, March). *Designing an agenda for social work and end-of-life and palliative care.* Report presented at the Social Work Summit on Palliative and End-of-Life Care, Durham, NC.

Cox, M. F., & Stovall, A. (2001). Social work interventions with children and adolescents. In *Social Work in Oncology* (pp. 143–167). Atlanta, GA: American Cancer Society Health Content Products.

Developing quality indicators for end-of-life care in nursing homes. (2000, April). *State Initiatives in Long Term Care, 8,* 1–2.

Erikson, E. (1994). *Vital involvement in old age.* New York: Norton. Francoeur, R. B. (2001). Reformulating financial problems and interventions to improve psychosocial and financial outcomes in cancer patients and their families. *Journal of Psychosocial Oncology, 19*(1), 1–20

Kramer, B. J. (1998). Preparing social workers for the inevitable: A preliminary investigation of a course on grief, death, and loss. *Journal of Social Work Education, 34*(2), 211–277.

Kramer, B. J. (2002) *End-of-life care content guidelines for social work.* Madison: University of Wisconsin School of Social Work.

National Center for Health Statistics. (1993). *National Mortality Followback Survey.* Hyattsville, MD: Author.

National Consensus Project for Quality Palliative Care. (2004). *Clinical practice guidelines for quality palliative care.* Retrieved August 9, 2004, from *www.national-consensusproject.org.*

O'Connell, L. (1999). Integrating spirituality into health care near the end of life. *Innovations in End-of-Life Care, 1*(6). Retrieved from *www.edc.org/lastacts.*

Oliver, D. P. (2003). Social work and spiritual counseling: Results of one state audit. *Journal of Palliative Medicine, 6*(6), 919–925.

Rando, T. A. (1993). *Treatment of complicated mourning.* New York: Research Press.

Steinhauser, K. E., Christakis, N. A., Clipp, E. C., McNeilly, M., McIntyre, L., & Tulsky, J. A. (2000). Factors considered important at the end of life by patients, family, physicians, and other care providers. *Journal of the American Medical Association, 284*(19), 2476–2482.

Veterans Health Administration. (2003). *Palliative care consult teams* (Directive No. 2003-008). Retrieved August 9, 2004, from *http://www1.va.gov/geriatric-sshg/.*

IRENE GUTHEIL

MARGARET SOUZA

Psychosocial Services at the End of Life

27

Although in many ways dying has become a medical and legal issue, it is and always has been a profoundly personal and social event. Because social workers focus on psychosocial issues and are trained to work with individuals and families, as well as with larger systems, they are uniquely situated to work in end-of-life care. Social workers view people from a holistic perspective and have expertise in helping facilitate communication, addressing taboo topics, and mediating between individuals and organizations. All of these skills are essential to effective end-of-life care. Social workers have been identified as critical to the health care team (Csikai, 2004), involved in patient education (Baker, 1995, Christ & Sormanti, 1999), and actively involved in working with family members in end-of-life planning (Werner & Carmel, 2001).

This chapter, which addresses dying and older adults, does not seek to develop universal principles. Although general guidelines are presented, the concept that dying is a personal event related to the choices and values of the persons involved, especially the dying person and his or her family, is paramount. The setting in which the social worker intersects with the dying person also affects the available roles and interventions. Within this context it is the responsibility of the clinician to listen for and to elicit the needs of the persons involved and to seek to respond to these needs as much as possible. The social work roles of broker, teacher, mediator, enabler, and advocate (Compton & Galaway, 1999) provide a direction for the actions of the worker in addressing goals based on the needs and wishes of the involved persons.

A critical first step for all social workers in end-of-life care is awareness of the losses in their own lives and the meaning that death has for them. Social workers must be aware of their beliefs, their values, and their own needs to ensure that these do not influence their work with the dying person and his or her family. Although self-reflection is an essential component of all work, dying raises particular problems because of the larger social and cultural environment that seeks to keep death at a distance. Despite the growing attention paid to dying in recent years, continuing limitations in our society's ability to comfortably address this topic (Moller, 1996) affect the scope of work for the social worker.

In addition to self-knowledge, social workers in end-of-life care have a responsibility to be knowledgeable about the stages of the dying process, illness-related issues, the manifestations of pain, advance directives, and the range of settings that provide care at the end of life (National Association of Social Workers [NASW], 2004).

DYING IN OLD AGE

The diversity and widening age range among older persons makes discussion of end of life and older adults a complex topic. A grandmother of 67 confronted with terminal illness, who is raising her grandchildren and still employed, has vastly different needs than a 90-year-old infirm and demented resident who has spent the last 5 years of her life in a nursing home. Both persons and their families may require professional but different types of assistance in dealing with and coming to terms with the finality of a terminal illness. Regardless of the age or condition of the older person, death represents a finality and loss to the person and to those who are connected to him or her.

Death in older adults may be poorly dealt with because, in the natural progression of the life cycle, it is inevitable. Care providers may minimize the intensity of the experience and its importance to the participants. This diminishes the centrality of lifelong relationships and neglects the importance of parental ties, however complicated, and of grandparent relationships. It also can diminish the loss of a spouse who has been a life companion for decades. Although death for some older persons is welcomed, for many older persons and their families, death is still a dreaded experience that they try to hold at bay for as long as possible.

Understanding death as simply the "natural" next step in old age may result in unrealistic expectations that persons be accepting of it. Often clients who are grieving reveal that other family members or friends try to soothe their grief by indicating they should be grateful that the person had a "long and good life." At a viewing for his recently deceased mother a physician stood by her coffin. In her mid-80s, she died after a difficult adjustment to dementia and nursing home placement. As the physician began to recite how she had had a good, long life and all the appropriate responses about what is best, he sat in a chair, put his head down, and said "So why do I feel so bad?"

ADVANCE DIRECTIVES

The increased use of technology in medicine has resulted in persons with increased disabilities and multiple illnesses living longer, at times resulting in long and difficult deaths. Although it is imperfect and often fraught with difficulties, advance care planning can help older persons discuss and plan for their own health care decisions in the event they are unable to speak for themselves. Consequently, the social work role in end-of-life care should begin long before major illness or crisis strikes.

The importance of providing individuals with information about end-of-life decision-making tools and advance directives has been well documented (Gutheil & Heyman, 2000; Meier et al., 1996). Advance directives are legal documents that individuals can use to name someone to make medical decisions for them (health care proxy) or specify instructions for care (living will) should they become unable to speak for themselves. Although, in the past, attention had focused on working to increase the completion rate and developing the best forms, more recently attention has turned to the process of end-of-life planning and decision making (Souza, 2004; Teno, 1998). Effective planning for end of life must be grounded in a process of communication. Older adults need to be provided with adequate information about advance planning and with opportunities to discuss their concerns and wishes with family, with the individual they will name as their agent, and with their health care providers. Because these discussions may be difficult for all parties involved, social workers can play important roles in helping individuals overcome resistance to discussing upsetting topics and fostering communication by serving as teachers, mediators, and enablers.

The health care proxy, the most widely recognized advance directive, is used to give one individual (the agent) the authority to speak for the incapacitated person. Even under the best of circumstances, when the older person has had extensive conversations with and carefully conveyed her wishes to the health care agent, problems may develop. Other family members may disagree with the agent's choice of actions, or health care providers may fail to act on the agent's decisions. Social workers may need to bear in mind that advance directives have also become a means to protect medical providers from litigious concerns (Souza, 2004). Acting as a mediator or advocate, the social worker can help the health care agent carry out awesome and, at times, overwhelming responsibilities.

Carefully thought-out advance care planning and in-depth communication about concerns and wishes can help older persons ensure that they are cared for as they wish during their dying. Careful planning can also help families more comfortably make difficult decisions and deal effectively with medical care providers. However, even the best advance planning communication between older adults and their family members does not guarantee that there will not be problems when illness or crisis occurs. Clinical support and empowerment are essential at this time.

Another difficulty is that practitioners may focus on the medical and legal language of advance directives. Consequently, they may fail to hear or listen to the ways in which persons talk about life choices. Focusing on issues of feeding tubes, resuscitation, and intubation and requesting that forms be completed may meet with resistance. At times, focusing on the legal aspects of directives and the tension associated with the completion of these documents in a timely manner may lead to discomfort for both the medical provider and the family.

Concern that participants will not sign the documents that medical practitioners deem appropriate is particularly troublesome when the participants are ambivalent about what is occurring. A mistaken notion often exists that because dying persons and their families remain hopeful in their communication and plan for the future, they have not accepted the terminal condition or the impending death. Most persons aware of impending death do maintain a hopeful demeanor despite their understanding of the proximity of death and the choices they have made regarding refusal of aggressive treatments.

Communication is a key factor in ensuring that end-of-life wishes are understood and respected. Practitioners need to be attentive to the ways in which older adults express their wishes for care. When older persons observe care being rendered to another in a debilitated condition and remark that they would not want that to happen to them, there is a need to follow up with open-ended and general questions to find out what they would and would not want. Social workers need not only to be alert to those types of communication as indications of a direction for care but also to instruct and support direct-care staff members in facilities to be alert for remarks that indicate a resident's thoughts about treatments and interventions.

Because an advance directive cannot spell out wishes for every potential situation, family members, often the decision makers, may have difficulty being certain what their older relative would want. As they struggle with the responsibility of making life-and-death decisions, the social worker can help with cues that may jog their memory concerning prior conver-

sations and utterances made about how people die. Questions such as "When family members died, did your mother remark on the type of death that occurred, and did she say how she felt about it or what she thought about it?" can be helpful. Another approach is to bring up nationally known figures; for instance, "When Karen Quinlan (or others) was in the news did your father say what his opinion was and what he felt should occur?" These conversations that people have informally may reveal end-of-life choices more directly than the formal language of an advance directive.

Because many older adults have multiple illnesses for which they have continued to receive treatment for a long period of time, the decision to discontinue, stop, or not pursue a particular treatment makes visible the reality that death is timed and a choice that is made. It is difficult to know when is the correct time to stop and prepare for death. The roles of enabler, mediator, and advocate are essential in this context, as social workers use their listening skills accompanied by supportive techniques to help older persons and their families reject or request interventions according to their needs. Advance care planning usually focuses on the elimination of treatment, but it is also meant to provide treatments that patients and families may need and want.

When health care agents hesitate to authorize a DNR (Do Not Resuscitate order) or to refuse treatment that staff members deem inappropriate as they carefully sort out the options and choices available, staff members may suggest that the family members "can't let go" or "make up their minds." Often the focus of social work intervention can be on enabling the family to complete the documentation for the discontinuation of treatment by helping them work through the struggle inherent in such painful decision making. Refocusing on where the older individual and family are in the process and being in that place with them are critical skills. Workers may come to recognize that the rationale for refusal has profound implications for the family at some point in time and may need to communicate to the staff the importance of family events and process. Social workers must also be alert to the changing decisions that dying persons make.

CARE AT THE END OF LIFE

Palliative care and hospice acknowledge and validate the holistic needs of dying persons. However, at times, these programs may tend to focus on nursing and medical needs, seeking to provide comfort and symptom control from what may be painful and difficult physical processes that occur in long-term illness. This approach to comfort is often essential to dying persons and their families, but it must not obscure other, less visible needs that at times may have greater significance. Addressing these needs will not take away the pain of loss experienced by all in the process of dying, but it can enable an acceptance or an accommodation that helps survivors eliminate needless and ongoing guilt after death has occurred. It can also empower a person who is dying to complete the last act of life on her or his own terms.

SOCIAL WORK ASSESSMENT

Although social work assessment is a generic skill, there are some aspects of work in end-of-life care that demand specific attention. Assessment in end-of-life care considers relevant biopsychosocial factors, as well as the needs of the dying person and the family (NASW, 2004). This section considers some specific assessment issues.

The first and foremost assessment task of social workers in end-of-life care is to identify the different clients. The social worker's primary clients are generally the dying person and the family. The assessment of the needs of the dying person and his or her family generally begins at a concrete level. These needs may include information, help with advance directive completion, or brokering arrangement of services. These needs often have emotional components. If assessment prematurely ends at the concrete level, critical needs may be overlooked. Often dying persons are unable to assert their needs or articulate them directly. Therefore, the needs of the family may take precedence over the dying person's, with an implicit assumption that they are coterminous. Although the needs of the dying person and family may be compatible, social workers must be attuned to the discrepancies that may exist. Discomfort about death and the difficulties involved in communicating with dying persons may result in work with the family inappropriately taking precedence over work with the person who is dying.

Death is usually the result of a deteriorating condition that may have either a continual and rapid downward spiral or continuing acute episodes that leave the individual in an increased debilitated condition after each episode. This disabled and dependent condition leaves the person at a disadvantage in relation to the ability to articulate needs. Being attuned to nonverbal communication and the responses and reactions of the dying person can assist the social worker in recognizing her or his needs.

Dying persons may become objectified as the process of disengagement is promoted by health care professionals. Consequently, it is essential that the social worker constantly be aware of the context of care for the dying person and family. The social worker must understand the functioning of the organization providing services and the impact it has on care to the individual and on attention to the concerns of family members. Too many times, family caregivers are seen as impediments to care rather than essential members of the care team (Levine, 1998).

Social workers are in the unique position of operating as part of both the health care team and the larger system, while at the same time needing to step back and evaluate how this larger system is affecting clients and how the client is affecting the team. Each member of the team operates from a different perspective. The social worker's viewpoint should be to represent the personal and social concerns of the dying person and family. Social workers may need to call on all of their skills to give other care providers the perspective of the dying person and, if it becomes necessary, to act as mediators between their clients and the health care team. Because of their focus on the emotional and social aspects of care and human need, social workers can also be a resource for the medical team, whose training and practice may limit their ability to recognize or validate their own personal responses to the dying process.

EMOTIONAL LOSS

Loss is a critical component of dying for all persons involved. The dying person faces the loss of a future and continued participation in the life cycle. The family is diminished. Even when the dying person is not a highly regarded member of the family, or when the person was lost long ago to dementia, the family members still face the physical absence of that person in their lives. When a family member provided care for the older adult, that member loses the caregiver role. The experience of loss, although universal, is experienced in each family and by each family member in a unique way. One of the challenges the social worker faces is assessing the meaning of the loss to all involved. A death reveals to all persons involved their own mortality. The worker must be accepting of all feelings and recognize that not everyone will be saddened by the loss of their family member or be able to communicate their sadness.

SOCIAL SUPPORT

Assessment of the social resources of the dying person is critical. Some older persons have no families or are estranged from their families. Unless they have others intimately involved in their lives, they may be bereft of social resources, facing the end of their lives alone.

When family is present, there may be strong interfamilial support or there may be discord. The discord may be long-standing, or it may be the result of differences in how to best deal with the current situation. A head of an intensive care unit commented that he often sees family members who were not actively involved in elder caregiving suddenly show up at the hospital with their own ideas of how end-of-life care should be handled.

Finally, it is important to understand the support available from outside the family. Many families have strong connections to individuals or organizations in the community, such as churches, that can serve as resources to them. Death is a time when families need to be encouraged to avail themselves of their informal resources so that they can meet the needs of the dying person, as well as their own needs.

FINANCIAL CONCERNS

Financial concerns are an unwelcome but powerful participant in health care provision. Funding sources and family finances often determine what care is available and where care is provided. Financial concerns may influence decision making by dying persons, families, or care providers. Social workers need to be attentive to the power of financial concerns, even when they are unspoken.

Social workers need to be attuned to the formal and informal resources available to participants and creatively help dying persons and their families make choices based on their needs whenever possible by finding ways to meet those needs. They can empower the dying person and family by having a well-developed list of resources, and they may need to use advocacy or their informal networks to help families access these resources.

RELIGIOUS AND SPIRITUAL NEEDS

As in any practice setting, social workers need to be aware of religious and spiritual needs. Although it is often a source of strength, the importance of religion differs among families. These differences must be recognized and respected. A belief that the future is "in God's hands" can limit an older individual or her or his family's involvement in end-of-life decision making. In such situations, it may be the state and not a higher power that will make the decisions if they relinquish their rights.

Death can cause a spiritual crisis for the dying person and family members. The social worker needs to evaluate whether religious assistance is needed. She or he can help broker the connection to enable spiritual help to be enlisted. However, social workers also need to be willing to discuss spiritual concerns and needs and to recognize when the spiritual aspect of an individual's life is a source of strength in the absence of religious beliefs. The dying person or family may want a safe place to talk about the meaning life has for them and how to find strength in the face of death. These essential conversations do not necessarily require the assistance of a spiritual person.

CULTURAL NEEDS

Social workers understand the importance of sensitivity to the cultural differences of dying persons and their families and the need to adhere to specific customs and traditions that bring meaning to the dying process. Equally important is the particular way the dying person culturally believes the world should work and the need for consistency with the values he or she holds concerning life. The way in which the dying process is assisted or inhibited as this process and individual beliefs intersect within the individual's and family's culture is something the social worker must keep in mind.

Expectations of dependence and independence may be major cultural issues. In the United States, where independence is a strong value, most older persons attempt to maintain their independence as long as possible. When they are no longer able to do so and become increasingly in need of assistance, they look to family and formal resources in the community to meet their needs. In contrast, Japanese adults, expecting as they grow older to become dependent, develop and maintain familial and other informal arrangements that they foster during their lives to assure reciprocity as they age and become dependent (Hashimoto, 1996). These expectations continue as death becomes imminent, and the way these expectations are met can influence the comfort or distress the dying person experiences. In other cultures social pressure can be placed on family members in an attempt to ensure that the expectations of care are provided to older adults and dying persons (Catedra, 1992).

In end-of-life literature, much research has focused on cultural variations in relation to issues of advance care planning and directives (Blackhall et al., 1999; Hofmann et al., 1997). Although the focus is on the completion of these documents, there is recognition that a variety of approaches are required to assist completion. This cultural sensitivity must be extended to the context of the dying process and to the larger issues of role expectation, dependency, and other areas in which dominant values are not shared.

Social workers cannot be expected to have expertise in all cultures and the diverse ways in which their clients incorporate cultural values into their lives. However, using skills of open-ended questioning, exploring in depth and clarifying, as well as curiosity and naivete (Dyche & Zayas, 1995), can ensure that these cultural dimensions will be expressed in an environment that is open to accepting diversity and not labeling it as pathological.

QUALITY OF LIFE AND DEATH

Every effort must be made to ensure that the quality of life of the dying person is maintained up to the end. Some dying persons choose to forgo optimal pain medication in order to be able to remain as alert and involved with life as possible. Others may make a different choice. The important task is to create an environment in which the choice can be heard and will be respected. For quality of life to be maintained, social death cannot occur before physical death. Seeing and dealing with the older individual as a person and responding in a manner that accepts physical and mental losses without having those losses diminish the person, who is still alive, provide a model of behavior and an approach to the dying person for family and staff members to emulate.

Symptom management provides comfort to the dying person and often comforts family and professional caregivers as well. They are assured that they are doing the correct thing. The social worker is challenged to listen to ways in which the dying person verbally and nonverbally expresses his or her needs, as well as the needs expressed by family and staff members. These can be put together with a focus on the dying person as the central client. The social worker may work with family members to help them accept the primacy of the dying person's needs. In addition, staff members may need help in letting go of their own wishes to manage the situation.

SOCIAL WORK INTERVENTIONS

The previous sections have illustrated ways in which social work interventions can be used in end-of-life work. Here we review those processes in a more systematic and chronological way, using as a framework the five interventive roles outlined by Compton and Galaway (1999; see Table 27.1).

Teaching and enabling are essential skills in assisting persons in the completion of advance care planning tools. In helping individuals complete the health care proxy, social workers need to evaluate an older person's ability to complete this document when dementia is present. The completion of this document does not require the same level of capacity as other documents with legal standing, and it is important to ensure that an individual who is capable of choosing an agent be given the opportunity to do so. Generally dementia is less evident in the early morning hours, so the social worker should investigate whether the individual has times when she or he is more lucid. The individual's behavior may illustrate choices. Resistance to an intervention may be a nonverbal way of communicating. If the person is in a facility, education for direct-care staff members is needed to help them understand how the words older persons use and their behavior when referring to interventions for themselves or others can provide insight into their choices.

Broker, mediator, and enabler roles are used to assist individuals with terminal illness and their families with concrete care needs. Connecting to the services that persons need; assisting them with acceptance of a deteriorated status, loss of appetite, loss of energy, and so forth; and assisting family members to accept increased care needs and to provide or supervise the care are essential social work tasks. Helping families deal with the losses they experience as their loved one's condition deteriorates enables them to provide their presence or respond to care needs. When death occurs, although it is still painful, guilt may be lessened.

TABLE 27.1. Social Work Interventions in End-of-Life Care

Broker
- Locating the services that meet the specific family's and dying person's needs
- Arranging concrete and other services both formally and informally as needed
- Negotiating with various systems to meet the person's and family's specifically expressed wishes
- Helping families to negotiate with their informal systems for emotional support and needed assistance
- Assisting in operationalizing advance directives
- Connecting dying persons and/or family to spiritual resources as requested or in times of spiritual crisis

Teacher
- Educating about advance care planning
- Educating about the illness
- Educating about persons' medical rights to pursue or reject medical interventions
- Providing information about the dying process
- Assisting persons to focus on their concerns regarding health issues
- Discussing ways in which to communicate with the health care team
- Helping clients to prepare written lists of questions for the health care team
- Modeling styles of communication and approach to different team members
- Informing others about the differences in resources and various referrals
- Providing information about cultural differences to the health care team
- Helping the team to understand the unique needs of a dying person and his or her family
- Modeling communication with family members for the help care team
- Helping families find ways to communicate and respond to the dying person

Mediator
- Negotiating the needs of the dying person with the available family members' resources
- Assisting both the dying person and health care providers to listen and respond to each other
- Facilitating communication between family members and health care providers
- Encouraging open communication between family members for mutual support and understanding
- Negotiating the provision of appropriate and necessary concrete services from formal providers and/or family members
- Assisting in the resolution of long-standing family difficulties as needed
- Assisting family members with diverse opinions to listen and hear each other and resolve the resulting tensions

Enabler
- Empowering dying persons
- Empowering family members
- Working with the health care team to understand and respond creatively to each unique situation
- Affirming staff members' emotional needs and responses to death
- Assisting dying persons to be socially alive and connected as long as possible
- Supporting the multiple and mixed emotional responses the person and family have to the dying process
- Supporting and encouraging family to respond to the person during the dying process with words or touch
- Encouraging social and medical services to be responsive to the diverse needs of dying elders and their family members
- Providing bereavement services that enable survivors to integrate the person who has died into their ongoing lives
- Normalizing the diverse feelings of survivors
- Assisting survivors to develop personal, meaningful rituals for memorialization of the deceased individual

Advocate
- Interceding for the dying person with the organizations providing services

(*continued*)

TABLE 27.1. Social Work Interventions in End-of-Life Care (*continued*)

- Interceding for the family with the organizations providing services
- Advocating for the dying person or family with members of the health care team as needed
- Providing voice to the dying person's needs and wishes
- Mobilizing services
- Encouraging medical practitioners to communicate clearly and directly with older persons who are in the terminal phrase of life
- Assisting the dying person to be recognized as a social person while she or he is actively dying
- Helping families ensure that the dying person's wishes are being carried out

At some point in the trajectory of long-term illness, decisions may need to be made about limiting treatment. At times, particularly when treatment has already continued for multiple medical issues and lessened physical functioning, persons may decide that comfort instead of continued pursuit of curative medicine is appropriate. Social workers need to evaluate whether depression is present and is causing an individual to give up, whether untreated pain is the cause of the depression, and whether the person understands the situation and chooses to focus on comfort, recognizing that these choices may hasten death. At times, medical practitioners pursue interventions based on assumptions of the hopefulness of the person. Social workers in these situations need to be cognizant of changes, help clients to think about their needs, and assist medical staff to understand these changing needs. If clients choose comfort over treatment, they may need a mediator and, in some cases, an advocate. On the other hand, if clients want to pursue treatment against the advice of medical personnel, they may also need an advocate.

PSYCHOLOGICAL NEEDS

To some extent, the aforementioned interventions address the mechanics of end-of-life care, although they also address psychosocial needs. Often, the essence of the social worker's contribution is addressing the psychosocial needs of dying persons as they approach the end of their lives. A comparison of Lawton's (1997) ethnography of a hospice in England with de Hennezel's (1997) work in France underscores how recognition and validation of the dying person's psychosocial needs avert a social death before the physical death and also provide a sense of completion of one's life. Notwithstanding that death is a time of loss and pain, the process of dying can complete one's life, if recognition and affirmation of that life are made.

In addressing the psychosocial needs of dying persons and their families, social workers may assume the teacher, mediator, enabler, or advocate roles. For example, helping participants understand the dying process and anticipate the feelings that may be engendered may help them normalize their reactions. Creating an environment in which the dying individual and his or her family can talk freely about concerns and fears may help ease angry interactions, hurt, and blame. Assisting the dying person and family to prepare for the death and burial arrangements together (Jenkins, 2002) can provide a sense of control to the dying person and relief to the family. Respecting the words that individuals and families use can limit the insistence that those personally involved discuss dying in the way the medical team does. Representing the dying individual's view at team conferences may ensure that care providers hear her or his voice.

Social work interventions may take a range of forms, including individual counseling, family counseling, group modalities, case management, and system advocacy (NASW, 2004). Because each individual and family is unique, the choice of intervention is based on the needs of the dying person and his or her family. The social worker may be challenged to be creative when the needs call for help that is not readily available. For example, it may be necessary to develop a support group specifically for health care agents who have made decisions to withdraw life-sustaining treatment and are struggling to deal with the awesome responsibility this decision entails.

BEREAVEMENT AND GRIEF COUNSELING

Family members may need help integrating the lost person into their ongoing life after the death (Klass, Silverman, & Nickman, 1996). Grief is normal when dealing with loss and needs to be validated and affirmed. Providing opportunities for its expression through rituals that have meaning for the family can help the process. For example, friends of a deceased person may go to a casino on her birthday to celebrate it annually in the way she would have if she were alive.

Because sadness for the loss of someone of extreme old age or who has been demented for many years is not widely sanctioned in our society (Moss & Moss, 1989), families may need help with their grief. Persons who have experienced grief often need an opportunity to talk about the deceased. Unfortunately, family members and friends who encourage someone to "move on" may limit this. Groups or individual sessions provide a place for remembering the deceased individual.

Family members may continue to cherish objects, talk to the deceased individual, identify with him or her, and continue to make decisions with him or her in mind (Klass et al., 1996). A mature couple, both widowed, made a toast at their marriage proclaiming that the four of them would now be "living" happily together (cf. Moss & Moss 1996).

CONCLUSION

The role of the social worker in end-of-life care starts before illness or crisis strikes and continues after death occurs. Social workers may enter this continuum at various points, depending on the practice setting. This chapter has provided an overview of social work practice in end-of-life care. In highlighting psychosocial components, as well as the concrete needs, it underscores the valuable and diverse roles that social workers perform in working with dying persons and their families.

REFERENCES

Baker, M. E. (1995). *Advance directives: An examination of the knowledge, attitudes and behavior of health care social workers toward end-of-life decision making.* Unpublished doctoral dissertation, Ohio State University.

Blackhall, L. J., Frank, G., Murphy, S. T., Michel, V., Palmer, J. M., & Azen, S. P. (1999). Ethnicity and attitudes towards life sustaining technology. *Social Science and Medicine 48*(12), 1779–1789.

Catedra, M. (1992). *This world, other world: Sickness, suicide, death, and the afterlife among the Vaqueriros de Alzada of Spain.* Chicago: University of Chicago.

Christ, G., & Sormanti, M. (1999). Advancing social work practice in end-of-life care. *Social Work in Health Care, 30*(2), 81–99.

Compton, B. R., & Galaway, B. (1999). *Social work processes* (6th ed.) Belmont, CA: Wadsworth.

Csikai, E. L. (2004). Social workers' participation in the resolution of ethical dilemmas in hospice care. *Health and Social Work, 29*(1), 67–76.

de Hennezel, M. (1997). *Intimate death.* New York: Knopf.

Dyche, L., & Zayas, L. H. (1995). The value of curiosity and naivete for the cross-cultural psychotherapist. *Family Process, 34*(4), 389–399.

Gutheil, I. A., & Heyman, J. C. (2000). *Strengthening the role of the healthcare agent: Knowledge, attitude, comfort and communication* [Report to the Fan Fox and Leslie R. Samuels Foundation]. New York: Fordham University, Ravazzin Center for Social Work Research in Aging.

Hashimoto, A. (1996). *The gift of generations: Japanese and American perspectives on aging and the social contract.* New York: Cambridge University Press.

Hofmann, J., Wenger, N. S., Davis, R. B., Teno, J., Connors, A. F., Desbiens, N., et al. (1997). Patients' preferences for communication with physicians about end-of-life decisions. *Annals of Internal Medicine, 127*(1), 1–12.

Jenkins, M. (2002). *You only die once: Preparing for the end of life with grace and gusto.* Nashville, TN: Integrity.

Klass, D., Silverman, P. R., & Nickman, S. L. (Eds.). (1996). *Continuing bonds: New understandings of grief.* Philadelphia: Taylor & Francis.

Lawton, J. (1997). *The dying process: Patients' experiences of palliative care.* London: Routledge.

Levine, C. (1998). *Rough crossings: Family caregivers' odysseys through the health care system.* New York: United Hospital Fund.

Meier, D. E., Fuss, B. R., O'Rourke, M., Baskin, S. A., Lewis, M., & Morrison, R. S. (1996). Marked improvement in recognition and completion of health care proxies: A randomized controlled trial of counseling by hospital patient representatives. *Archives of Internal Medicine, 156*(11), 1227–1232.

Moller, D. W. (1996). *Confronting death: Values, institutions and human mortality.* New York: Oxford University Press.

Moss, M. S., & Moss, S. Z. (1989). Death of the very old. In K. J. Doka (Ed.), *Disenfranchised grief* (pp. 213–227). New York: Lexington Books.

Moss, M. S., & Moss, S. Z. (1996). Remarriage of widowed persons: A triadic relationship. In D. Klass,

P. R. Silverman, & S. L. Nickman (Eds.), *Continuing bonds: New understandings of grief* (pp. 163–178). Philadelphia: Taylor & Francis.

National Association of Social Workers. (2004). *NASW standards for social work practice in palliative and end-of-life care.* Retrieved May 29, 2004, from *http://www.socialworkers.org/practice/bereavement/standards/default/asp.*

Souza, M. (2004). *Multiple voices in the new medicalization of dying: The case for palliative care. Dissertation Abstracts International, 65(1),* 197. (UMI Number 3118796).

Teno, J. M. (1998). Looking beyond the "Form" to complex interventions needed to improve end-of-life care. *Journal of the American Geriatrics Society, 46(9),* 1170–1171.

Werner, P., & Carmel, S. (2001). End-of-life decision making: Practices, beliefs and knowledge of social workers in health care settings. *Educational Gerontology, 27(5),* 387–398.

MARSHA SELTZER,
SECTION EDITOR

SECTION VI

Family and Intergenerational Social Work
Practice in Special Caregiving Situations

OVERVIEW

This section includes six chapters that address special caregiving situations. It is well recognized that caregiving is a heterogeneous phenomenon, with some caregivers experiencing significant physical and mental health difficulties, whereas others seem to thrive and derive considerable gratification from similar circumstances. In this section, we consider the context of family caregiving to attempt to understand the sources of the heterogeneity of outcomes experienced by family caregivers.

Specifically, the section focuses on the following six key issues: (1) caregivers to older adults in general, (2) grandparents who are raising their grandchildren, (3) older adults who provide care to a family member with developmental disabilities, (4) aging Latino family caregivers, (5) rural African American caregivers, and (6) caregivers who are at a distance from their family care recipients. The landscape covered by these six chapters is overlapping, as well as distinct, due to the commonalities and unique qualities of the caregiving experience.

The first chapter, by Greenberg, Seltzer, and Brewer, is a general overview of caregiving to older adults. Fully 12.1 million Americans need long-term care, and thus caregiving is a major public health issue. It is well documented that caregivers have poorer mental and physical health than their age peers who are not in caregiving roles, but many also experience the rewards and gratifications of caregiving. Thus caregiving is a role with heterogeneous outcomes. Many factors can explain this degree of heterogeneity, including the context of caregiving, the level of caregiving stress, and the social and psychological resources available to caregivers. Among these, the type of illness or disability is a prominent source of heterogeneity of outcome, with disabilities that are characterized by cognitive impairments and behavior problems leading to the poorest outcomes in caregivers. In addition, women experience more difficulties with the caregiving role than men do. The evidence suggests that caregiving effects are not static over time but rather unfold over the course of the caregiving career.

The second chapter, by Kropf and Yoon, addresses the phenomenon of grandparent caregiving. Fully 2.4 million grandparents in the United States have primary responsibility for taking care of their grandchildren, and 6 million children in the United States live in grandparent-headed households. This rate has doubled over the past 30 years. Grandparent care-

givers have elevated rates of physical and mental health problems as compared with their age peers, and there is evidence that these difficulties get worse after the entry into the caregiving role. Grandparent caregivers also experience elevated rates of financial and legal difficulties. The circumstances leading to grandparent caregiving derive from challenges experienced by the adult children of the grandparents—death, drug abuse, incarceration, and HIV/AIDS are among the most prominent. The chapter also includes suggestions for social work interventions and policy considerations relevant to grandparent caregiving.

The third chapter, by McCallion, focuses on older adults who are caregivers for persons with developmental disabilities. Because individuals with developmental disabilities now have nearly average life expectancies, the period of family caregiving is currently much longer than it was in the past. Important issues pertinent to this type of family caregiving include sources of stress and gratification, sources of heterogeneity in caregiving well-being, planning for the future, and dealing with grief and bereavement.

The fourth chapter, by Magaña, deals with aging Latino family caregivers. Latinos are currently the largest minority group in the United States. Therefore, the unique caregiving challenges and resources of this group warrant investigation. The chapter explores five themes: (1) the well-being of Latino family caregivers, including the high rates of depression that they experience; (2) stress and coping processes, including the role of religion and spirituality in this group; (3) family support and the cultural value of familism, as the individual is strongly influenced by family well-being; (4) service utilization patterns, as Latinos underutilize services possibly because of culturally insensitive services; and (5) interventions, which must be adapted for Latino family caregivers.

The fifth chapter, by Carlton-LaNey, examines rural African American caregivers. These individuals face critical and potentially life threatening problems, including poverty, lack of transportation, inadequate child care, substandard housing, inadequate heath care, and insufficient child care. Although these challenges are formidable, rural African American caregivers can also draw on unique cultural resources, including the mutual-aid system that permeates African American culture, the importance of extended family, including fictive kin, religion, and the value of neighbors and the local geographic community. In this population, social support and caregiving are overlapping concepts. Implications for social work practice are discussed.

The last chapter in this section, by Parker, Church, and Toseland, examines caregiving at a distance. As many as 7 million family members provide distant care for an elderly relative. These numbers are expected to double in the next 15 years. Distance complicates the quality and quantity of care provided, as care recipients prefer to live near but not with their adult children. "Near" is defined as within one hour's drive, but many caregivers live quite a bit further away. Military personnel represent a case in point of distant caregivers and are a focus of this chapter. Interventions for distant caregiving within faith-based communities are offered in this chapter, as are lists of national and state resources for distant caregivers.

The sum total of these chapters reveals the heterogeneity of the caregiving experience in later life. Social workers may be faced with the full range of these special circumstances, and they must recognize the unique needs of each. Commonalities, as well as unique needs, are highlighted within this section.

Rapidly growing numbers of individuals in society are in need of care due to Alzheimer's disease, severe mental illness, long-term disability, chronic illness, terminal illness, other age-related diseases, or social dislocation. It has been estimated that 12.1 million Americans need long-term care from others to carry out everyday activities (Henry J. Kaiser Foundation, 1999). Most but not all of these persons are ages 65 and older. Family members provide the vast majority of this care. Almost two-thirds of older persons living in the community and in need of long-term care depend on family and friends as their only source of help, and another 28% receive a combination of informal and formal care. Indeed, were it not for the efforts of families, formal systems of care would be overwhelmed by service requests (Biegel, Sales, & Schulz, 1991). Thus family members provide a significant service to society by sustaining vulnerable members. However, these contributions do not come without cost, as family caregivers are at risk for mental health problems, physical illness, and social isolation (Schulz, O'Brien, Bookwala, & Fleissner, 1995; Schulz, Tompkins, Wood, & Decker, 1987; Seltzer, Greenberg, & Krauss, 1995). The resultant health and mental health problems of family caregivers, which may impede the capacity for continuation in the caregiving role, have become a major public health concern (Lebowitz & Light, 1996).

Over the past two decades, considerable effort has been devoted to documenting the experiences of family caregivers of frail elders, in particular those with Alzheimer's disease. Researchers have more recently begun to focus on special populations of caregivers. The first section of this chapter reviews the general research on caregivers to older adults using Pearlin and his colleagues' (Pearlin, Mullan, Semple, & Skaff, 1990) stress process model as a framework for organizing this literature. The second section of the chapter explores special populations of caregivers, specifically male caregivers, end-of-life caregivers, and aging parents as caregivers to adults with disabilities.

JAN GREENBERG
MARSHA SELTZER
EVA BREWER

Caregivers to Older Adults

28

CAREGIVERS TO OLDER ADULTS

Caregiver Outcomes

Researchers have consistently found evidence for the toll that caregiving takes on the mental health of family members. A growing number of cross-sectional studies comparing caregivers with age peers who do not have caregiving responsibilities have found that caregivers report poorer mental health than noncaregivers (e.g., Baumgarten et al., 1992; Dura, Stukenberg, & Kiecolt-Glaser, 1991; Kiecolt-Glaser, Dura, Speicher, Trask, & Glaser, 1991; Russo, Vitaliano, Brewer, Katon, & Becker, 1995; Schulz & Beach, 1999; Schulz et al., 1995). For example, in a comparison of caregivers and noncaregivers, Baumgarten et al. (1992) found that 38.8% of the caregivers had Center for Epidemiologic Studies of Depression (CES-D) scores above the cutoff for clinical depression (a score above 15) compared with 16.5% of noncaregivers. Dura et al. (1991) administered the Structured Clinical Interview for *DSM-III-R* (SCID), the gold standard in psychiatric research for making a research diagnosis, to a group of caregiving adult children and a noncaregiving comparison group matched on key sociodemographic variables. Among caregivers, 18% met the criteria for a current depressive disorder and 9% suffered from an anxiety disorder compared with no cases of depression or anxiety disorders in the comparison group. In addition, researchers have established that caregivers are more likely than noncaregivers to be using psychotropic medications (Baumgarten et al., 1992; Grafstrom, Fratiglioni, Sandman, & Winblad, 1992). Thus the body of cross-sectional research comparing caregivers of older adults to noncaregivers provides compelling evidence of the considerable toll that caregiving takes on the psychological well-being of those providing care.

However, longitudinal research suggests that over time few caregivers experience further declines in their mental health, and, in fact, some report improved psychological well-being. In a study of daughter caregivers, Li, Seltzer, and Greenberg (1999) found that 65.2% of the caregivers' CES-D scores remained stable over an 18-month period and that another 21% showed a clinically significant (defined as 5 or more points) decrease in depressive symptoms. Townsend, Noelker, Deimling, and Bass (1989) reported that 58% of the adult children caregivers had a decrease of at least one point in depressive symptomatology over a 14-month period and that 8% showed no change. Schulz, Williamson, Morycz, and Biegel (1992) reported that 74% of the caregivers showed little change in depression over an 18-month period, with change defined as a difference of one standard deviation or more. Thus, although caregivers have greater psychiatric morbidity than noncaregivers, they appear to adapt to the new challenges that they confront as the caregiving career unfolds over time, at least during the short run.

Research on the effects of caregiving on the physical health of care providers is less conclusive. On one hand, caregivers rate their health as significantly worse than noncaregivers do (Baumgarten et al., 1992; Grafstrom et al., 1992). Kiecolt-Glaser and colleagues (1987) found caregivers had weaker immune responses than noncaregivers. Also, Schulz and Beach (1999) found higher rates of death in caregivers than among noncaregivers. On the other hand, Kiecolt-Glaser et al. (1991) did not find differences between caregivers and noncaregivers in the number of illness episodes, alcohol consumption, smoking, caffeine use, or nutrition. Baumgarten et al. (1992) found that the number of chronic health conditions experienced by caregivers was comparable to that of noncaregivers and that caregivers actually consumed less alcohol and smoked less than noncaregivers. Thus the current research suggests that the effects of caregiving on physical health are much weaker than on mental health and not consistent across different health domains.

Although research has primarily focused on the deleterious effects of caregiving on the mental and physical health of care providers, there is a rapidly expanding body of research on the rewards and gratifications of caregiving. A number of studies have identified these rewards of caregiving; they are many and include a sense of satisfaction or pleasure in fulfilling the caregiving role, feelings of personal growth, a renewed sense of purpose in life, closer relationships with family and friends, political advocacy, and greater insight into the struggles of persons with disabilities (Harris, 2002; Kramer, 1997; Lawton, Moss, Kleban, Glicksman, & Rovine, 1991; Miller, 1989; Motenko, 1989; Worcester & Quayhagen, 1983). Estimates of the percentage of caregivers who experience rewards in enacting the caregiving role have varied widely, ranging from approximately 50–90% of the caregivers sampled (Farran, Keane-Hagerty, Salloway, Kupferer, & Wilken, 1991; Hinrichsen, Hernandez, & Pollack, 1992).

Predictors of Caregiving Outcomes

There is great individual heterogeneity in the experience of caregivers. Whereas some caregivers appear overwhelmed by the challenge, others are able to maintain or show gains in their well-being (Kramer, 1997). A major goal of caregiving research is to understand the factors that help to explain why some cope well with the daily stress of caregiving whereas others do not. A stress and coping model, based on the work of Pearlin and his colleagues (1990), provides a useful framework for understanding the reasons for individual differences in the caregiving experience. Pearlin et al.'s (1990) model focuses attention on the caregiving context in which the caregiving role is enacted. The caregiving context, defined by characteristics of the caregiver and care recipient, affects each step of the stress process, including the individual's exposure to stress, the resources available to mitigate the effects of stress, and ultimately how distress is expressed. The stressors of caregiving are conceptualized as sources of chronic strain that have the potential to cause distress. However, whether stress produces distress or results in positive adaptation and outcomes depends on the capacity of the individual to mobilize social or psychological resources that may counteract, moderate, or mediate the effects of caregiving stressors on well-being.

Caregiving Context

Factors that define the context of caregiving include the relationship of the caregiver to the care recipient (e.g., spouse, adult child, in-law); the caregiver's age, gender, race, and socioeconomic status; whether the caregiver and care recipient live in the same household; and the nature of the care recipient's diagnosis. In the section of this chapter on special populations, we discuss, in the context of male caregivers, how gender influences the caregiving experience. The impact of race and ethnicity in shaping the caregiving experience is the topic of several other chapters in this volume and thus will not be reviewed here.

The provision of assistance usually begins with the individual closest in proximity to the elder; thus spouses are natural primary caregivers (Zarit, Birkel, & Beach, 1989). If the elder is widowed, separated, or divorced, the elder typically turns first to an adult daughter, and then to an adult son, and finally to other family members (Cantor, 1983). Adult children as caregivers are more likely to receive assistance in the provision of care from another family member than are spousal caregivers. Stone, Cafferata, and Sangl (1987) found that whereas 60.4% of wives and 55.4% of husbands were the sole caregivers, only 23.0% of daughters and 10.8% of sons reported being the sole caregiver. Tennstedt, McKinlay, and Sullivan (1988) reported that spousal caregivers render up to four times the amount of care provided by nonspousal family caregivers. Spouses are involved in a broader range of caregiving tasks and activities than

are filial caregivers, and they provide this care in the face of their own declining health and increased frailty. They are more likely than other caregivers to report a lack of alternative roles and social activities outside the home that might function as a buffer against caregiving stress (Barber & Pasley, 1995; Hong & Seltzer, 1995).

Generally, spouses report greater burden and distress than other groups of family caregivers (Brodaty & Hadzi-Pavlovic, 1990; Deimling, Bass, Townsend, & Noelker, 1989; Fengler & Goodrich, 1979; George & Gwyther, 1986; Neal, Ingersoll-Dayton, & Starrels, 1997; Strawbridge, Wallhagen, Shema, & Kaplan, 1997; Zarit, Todd, & Zarit, 1986). McFall and Miller (1992) studied 940 spouse and adult child caregivers. Spouses reported higher levels of caregiver involvement, personal burden, and problems in personal activities related to caregiving than did adult children. However, adult children reported higher levels of interpersonal burden and problems in the relationship between themselves and the ill family member. Also, Hoyert and Seltzer (1992) found that the well-being of daughter caregivers declined over time, whereas the well-being of wife caregivers remained constant.

There has been a growing appreciation of the different challenges faced by caregivers depending on the nature of their loved one's diagnosis and the trajectory of the illness (Clipp & George, 1993). Some illnesses, such as Alzheimer's disease, have insidious onsets and progressively deteriorating courses, whereas other illnesses, such as heart disease and stroke, have abrupt onsets but relatively stable courses following the initial insult (Clipp & George, 1993). Biegel et al. (1991) pointed out that medical illnesses also differ in the degree to which they impair the mind and body. Whereas Alzheimer's disease attacks the mind but leaves the body intact until the end, other conditions, such as cancer and stroke, often destroy the physical being while leaving cognitive abilities intact. In an effort to understand how the nature of the care recipient's illness affects the caregiver's experience, researchers have conducted studies comparing different populations of caregivers for older adults, typically caregivers of persons with dementia, with caregivers of persons who are functionally but not cognitively impaired. In a study comparing 272 caregivers of persons with dementia to 30 caregivers of patients with cancer, Clipp and George (1993) found that Alzheimer's caregivers were more adversely affected, as indicated by more doctor visits in the previous three months, poorer self-rated health, lower positive affect, and higher negative affect. In another study of 25 caregivers of adults with Alzheimer's disease, 25 caregivers of stroke patients, and 25 noncaregiving individuals, both groups of caregivers showed elevated levels of stress, with the health of caregivers of those with Alzheimer's disease being even more compromised than that of caregivers of those with a stroke (Reese, Gross, Smalley, & Messer, 1994). Also, caregivers of persons with Alzheimer's disease had fewer social contacts and reported more loneliness and higher levels of burden than stroke caregivers. Similarly, Karlin and Bell (1992) compared caregivers of persons with dementia with caregivers of persons with terminal illnesses such as cancer and emphysema but who did not suffer from dementia. They found that caregivers of persons with dementia reported higher levels of burden than caregivers of persons with chronic but nondementing illnesses. In a large, national sample of 1,500 dementia and nondementia caregivers, Ory, Hoffman, Yee, Tennstedt, and Schulz (1999) also found that persons caring for an individual with dementia experienced more physical and mental problems and more family conflict and had less time available for family and leisure. Li (2000) compared daughter caregivers of parents with a cognitive impairment, daughter caregivers caring for a parent with a functional but no cognitive impairment, and daughters whose parent had no impairment. Daughters who provided care to a parent with a cognitive impairment had a poorer quality of relationship with the parent than daughters caring for a parent with a functional impairment or daughters whose parent had no impairment.

However, other studies report no differences between caregivers of elders with dementia and other caregiving groups. Liptzin, Grob, and Eisen (1988) found no differences in burden between caregivers of patients with dementia admitted to a geriatric psychiatric inpatient unit and caregivers of depressed patients. Dura, Haywood-Niler, and Kiecolt-Glaser (1990) compared spousal caregivers of persons with Alzheimer's disease and spousal caregivers of persons with Parkinson's disease with dementia with a group of married control participants matched for sex, age, and education. Both groups of caregivers showed greater distress than the comparison group, but the two groups of caregivers did not differ from each other in levels of distress. Cattanach and Tebes (1991) compared three groups of daughter and daughter-in-law caregivers: 39 caregivers to elders with cognitive impairments, 30 caregivers to elders with functional impairments, and 33 caregivers to elders with no significant cognitive or functional impairment. They found no significant differences between the groups in levels of depressive symptoms, perceived stress, social support, self-esteem, and perceived control. In a study comparing spousal caregivers of hospice patients with lung cancer or dementia with a group of their age peers without caregiving responsibilities, Haley and his colleagues (Haley, LaMonde, Han, Narramore, & Schonwetter, 2001) found that the two caregiver groups showed higher depression, lower life satisfaction, and poorer physical health compared with noncaregivers, but the two groups were not significantly different from one another. Finally, Rabins, Fitting, Eatham, and Fetting (1990) also contrasted caregivers of patients with dementia and cancer. Although a significant number of caregivers reported high levels of emotional distress, the nature of the patient's illness did not affect the presence or severity of caregiver symptoms.

What might explain the conflicting nature of the findings in studies comparing caregivers of those with Alzheimer's with other groups of caregivers? The Dura et al. (1990), Rabins et al. (1990), and Haley et al. (2001) studies all sampled caregivers late in the caregiving career. It is possible that initial differences between caregiving contexts decrease as caregiving approaches the final stages of the role because both functional and cognitive impairments are likely to be present as the end of life nears. In addition, Liptzin et al. (1988) sampled persons whose depression was sufficiently severe to require hospitalization. Older adults with severe major depression often experience cognitive and behavioral symptoms that mimic Alzheimer's disease. Thus inconsistencies in the findings from studies comparing caregivers of persons with Alzheimer's disease to other groups of caregivers may be explained, in part, by whether the selection of the comparison group provided a sufficiently distinct contrast to those with Alzheimer's disease. In general, the available research indicates that up until the last stages of the illness, caring for an individual with a cognitive impairment is more distressing than caring for a frail elder who is functionally but not cognitively impaired. As will be discussed, however, the stress may be due to behavior problems associated with the cognitive impairment rather than the cognitive impairment itself. End-of-life care appears highly distressing regardless of the nature of the care recipient's diagnosis.

The research on the effect of other characteristics of the caregiving context on caregiver distress is inconclusive. Older age of caregiver has been shown to be related to lower levels of distress in several studies

(Baumgarten et al. 1992; Clipp & George, 1990; Hoyert & Seltzer, 1992; Nijboer et al., 2000; Parks & Pilisuk, 1991; Russo et al., 1995) but unrelated to caregiver burden in other studies (Draper, Poulos, Cole, Poulos, & Ehrlich, 1992; Dura et al., 1991; Neundorfer, 1991; Schulz & Williamson, 1991; Semple, 1992). Most studies report that lower socioeconomic status (SES) is associated with higher levels of depression or distress (Barusch & Spaid, 1989; Dura et al., 1991; Morrissey, Becker, & Rubert, 1990; Robinson, 1989; Schulz & Williamson, 1991; Semple, 1992). Yet some researchers find either no relationship or a positive relationship between SES and caregiver burden (Nijboer et al., 2000; Russo et al., 1995). Hoyert and Seltzer (1992) found that daughter caregivers were more distressed the longer the duration of caregiving but that duration had no effect on the well-being of wife caregivers. Some researchers have found higher burden when the caregiver and care recipient live in the same household (Aneshensel, Pearlin, & Schuler, 1993; Brodaty & Hadzi-Pavlovic, 1990; Grafstrom et al., 1992; Zarit & Whitlatch, 1992), whereas others have not found any relationship between coresidence and burden (Cohen et al., 1990; Dura et al., 1991; Kiecolt-Glaser et al., 1991; Russo et al., 1995). Thus there is little consistency in the findings across studies on the relationship between how background characteristics of the caregiver affect levels of caregiving distress.

Stressors of Caregiving

The stressors of caregiving have most often been defined in terms of the functional and cognitive impairments of the care recipient and related behavioral problems that may be difficult to manage. Although many demands of caregiving arise when an individual has limitations in activities of daily living, most studies have not found that the amount of caregiving assistance is related to the caregiver's level of depression (e.g., Clipp & George, 1990; Russo et al., 1995). As noted previously, whereas researchers generally find that caring for an individual with a cognitive impairment takes a greater toll than caring for an elder who has a functional but no cognitive impairment, the relationship between the severity of cognitive impairment and levels of caregiver depression is less clear (Baumgarten et al., 1992; Boss, Caron, Horbal, & Mortimer, 1990; Brodaty & Hadzi-Pavlovic, 1990; Kiecolt-Glaser et al., 1991). However, researchers have consistently found that caregivers are at greater risk for depression and burden when they are faced regu-

larly with the challenge of managing their relative's problem behaviors (e.g., Baumgarten et al., 1992; Hoyert & Seltzer, 1992; Pruchno & Resch, 1989a; Schulz & Williamson, 1991). Variations from diagnosis to diagnosis in the type, severity, and frequency of behavior problems might better explain diagnostic-group differences in caregiver well-being than differences in severity of cognitive impairments.

It has been long recognized that the primary stressors of caregiving produce additional stressors in the lives of caregivers, such as financial stress, work-family strains, and family conflicts, a process that Pearlin et al. (1990) refer to as stress proliferation. Although caregivers typically spend an average of $200 in a typical month on the recipient's care, the great majority of caregivers say they feel little or no financial hardship as a result of providing care (National Alliance for Caregiving and American Association of Retired Persons [AARP], 1997). Most caregivers are employed at some time during their caregiving career (National Alliance for Caregiving and AARP, 1997). Approximately 60% of employed caregivers report making work-related adjustments as a result of caregiving responsibilities. Caregivers who are working report more stress than employees without caregiving responsibilities (Marks, 1998; Neal, Chapman, Ingersoll-Dayton, Emlen, & Boise, 1990; Scharlach & Boyd, 1989). However, several studies have found that occupying multiple roles, including the work role, has positive consequences for the psychological well-being of caregivers (Hong & Seltzer, 1995; Scharlach, 1994; Stoller & Pugliesi, 1989).

It is not surprising that family conflicts often arise in the process of caregiving. The source of these conflicts may be disagreements over the equitable distribution of caregiving tasks or differences in perception of the needs of the care recipient (Semple, 1992). Family conflict is related to an increased risk for depression among caregivers (Ory et al., 1999; Semple, 1992; Strawbridge & Wallhagen, 1991). Other secondary strains, including role captivity and role overload, are related to greater levels of caregiver distress (Aneshensel, Pearlin, Mullan, Zarit, & Whitlatch, 1995). Thus the available research indicates that the full impact of caregiving cannot be understood without taking into account the proliferation and pileup of other life stressors.

Social and Psychological Resources

Intervening between primary stressors and secondary strains on the one hand and the outcomes of stress on the other are psychological and social resources. Social resources may take the form of informal support from friends and family or of services and programs from the formal service sector. The receipt of emotional support from family and friends is generally associated with lower feelings of depression or burden (e.g., Aneshensel et al. 1995; Franks & Stephens, 1996; Haley, Levine, Brown, & Bartolucci, 1987; Suitor & Pillemer, 1992; Wilson, Moore, Rubin, & Bartels, 1990). Aneshensel and her colleagues (1995) suggested that different kinds of support are related to different outcomes. When caregivers receive help with care tasks from family and friends, they are less likely to experience feelings of overload. Aneshensel et al. (1995), however, did not find that this type of help was related to improved psychological well-being. In contrast, they found that emotional support was associated with improved psychological well-being but had no effect on role overload. Li, Seltzer, and Greenberg (1997) found that social support had different patterns of effects on depression for wife and daughter caregivers. For both groups, emotional support buffered the effects of stress emanating from the behavior problems of the care recipient. However, social participation had a main effect on depressive symptoms for daughters but not for wives. Thus the relationship of social support to caregiving outcomes is complex and likely depends on the goodness of fit between the type of stressor, the type of support, and nature of the outcome of interest. Li et al.'s (1997) research suggests that whether the fit is optimal or not may further depend on the relationship of the caregiver to the care recipient.

Research on the relationship between the use of formal services and caregiver burden has been quite limited. The continuous stress of caring for a relative with dementia suggests that respite services would be a priority for caregivers and should contribute to improved well-being. However, studies examining the effects of respite services, including adult day care, have found very modest effects on caregiver well-being as measured by burden and depressive symptoms (Bourgeois, Schulz, & Burgio, 1996). Lundervold and Lewin (1987) found that respite care decreased caregivers' feelings of isolation and enhanced their feelings of control but did not affect feelings of burden, depression, or stress. Lawton, Brody, and Saperstein (1989) found that respite services allowed caregivers to maintain the care recipient in the community about one month longer than those who did not receive respite care but that they had no effect on caregiver well-being. Montgomery

and Borgatta (1989) speculated that family caregivers often delay seeking help from the service system until a crisis is looming, which may explain the modest effects of respite services in reducing caregiver burden.

In addition to respite services, caregivers are often thought to benefit from support groups, which may be peer or professionally led and typically involve both an educational and support dimension (Toseland, Rossiter, & Labrecque, 1989). The majority of studies find that caregivers are highly satisfied with support groups. In a mailed survey of 301 members of 47 different Alzheimer support groups, Gonyea (1989) found that caregivers valued the information gained from the peer support. Also, Gonyea and Silverstein (1991) found that caregivers participating in support groups were more likely to use community services. However, as Toseland and Rossiter (1989) concluded, based on the meta-analysis of 19 support-group interventions, support groups have only modest effects in reducing feelings of burden. In a more recent review of effective interventions with caregivers, Sörensen, Pinquart, and Duberstein (2002) concluded that support groups have significant but moderate effects in reducing caregivers' burden and increasing caregivers' knowledge but have no impact on caregivers' depression or well-being. Programs that combine a psychoeducational approach or a psychotherapeutic cognitive-behavioral approach appear more effective than support groups or respite care alone (Sörensen et al., 2002). The most effective approach is likely a combination of different strategies (e.g., psychoeducational, respite care, support group) that complement one another to produce beneficial effects across a range of caregiver outcomes (Sörensen et al., 2002).

Psychological resources are individual characteristics that increase the person's resilience or capacity to cope with stress. In the search for psychological resources that enhance caregiver functioning, attention has focused on coping strategies and an individual's sense of mastery. When people are faced with stressful situations, they are sometimes able to avoid psychological distress by using effective coping strategies. Lazarus and Folkman (1984) defined two major types of coping strategies: problem-focused coping and emotion-focused coping. Problem-focused coping involves cognitive and behavioral problem-solving strategies aimed at altering or managing the stressful situation. Emotion-focused coping, on the other hand, involves cognitive and behavioral efforts to reduce or manage emotional distress that are not focused directly on solving the problem. Cross-sectional studies find that caregivers who use emotion-focused coping strategies in fact have higher levels of depression and distress (Haley et al., 1987; Patrick & Hayden, 1999; Seltzer et al., 1995). In contrast, the evidence from studies on the effectiveness of problem-focused coping is less conclusive. The preponderance of evidence suggests that the use of problem-focused strategies results in improved well-being (Aldwin, 1991; Essex, 1998; Haley et al., 1987; Kling, Seltzer, & Ryff, 1997; Seltzer et al., 1995). However, Pruchno and Kleban (1993) found that problem-focused coping was unrelated to levels of distress.

Mastery refers to "the extent to which people see themselves as being in control of the forces that importantly affect their lives" (Pearlin, Lieberman, Menaghan, & Mullan, 1981, p. 340). Higher levels of mastery are related to lower levels of depression in caregivers (Boss et al., 1990; Parks & Pilisuk, 1991). In a longitudinal study of daughter caregivers, Li et al. (1999) found that mastery had no direct effect on changes in depression over time but had an indirect effect by influencing how individuals coped in stressful situations. Daughters who had high levels of mastery were more likely to use problem-focused coping strategies, which led to decreases in depressive symptoms over time. In addition, daughters with high levels of mastery were less likely to rely on the use of emotion-focused coping strategies, a type of coping related to increasing levels of depression. These findings are consistent with the general literature on the relationship between mastery and coping (Aldwin, 1991; Elliot, Trief, & Stein, 1986; Folkman, Chesney, Pollack, & Coates, 1993) and suggest the importance of mastery in understanding the conditions under which different types of coping strategies are effective in reducing the negative effects of caregiver stress.

In summary, the care of older adults brings both gratifications and frustrations. The gratifications are many and include a sense of personal growth, a deeper appreciation of the struggles of persons with disabilities, and the satisfaction of performing a role well (Kramer, 1997). But there are many costs or strains associated with caregiving. Rather than the stress resulting from the physical demands of care, it is the stress of managing behavior problems associated with dementia that take the greatest toll on the caregiver's well-being. In addition, Aneshensel and her colleagues (1995) suggest that these caregiving strains have rippling effects, producing new stressors and strains such as financial strain, family-work strains, and family conflicts. If left unchecked, these strains of caregiving have a wear-and-tear effect on the caregiver's mental health and, to a lesser extent, on the caregiver's physical health. But it is clear that many, if not most, caregivers make a highly successful adaptation to the role. What distinguishes these caregivers from those who are less successful in adapting to the demands of caregiving? Research suggests that caregivers who show a pattern of resiliency receive higher levels of emotional support, maintain a strong sense of mastery, and use problem-focused coping and avoid the use of emotion-focused coping strategies. Also, there is some evidence that caregivers who are struggling can be helped, albeit modestly, by participating in psychoeducational programs and, to a lesser extent, by using respite services and by joining support groups.

SPECIAL POPULATIONS OF CAREGIVERS

Male Caregivers

Approximately 40% of all caregivers are men, typically the husband or son of a female care recipient (National Alliance for Caregiving and AARP, 1997). Many have speculated on the unique ways that men approach the challenges of caregiving. Fitting, Rabins, Lucas, and Eastham (1986) suggested that men utilize a "work" paradigm in approaching caregiving and focus on the task at hand. In addressing sons as caregivers, Pleck (1993) argues that sons are more likely to segment their lives to take on a caregiving role by clearly separating boundaries of work and caregiving (Thompson, 2002). In fact, the data suggest that there are few observable differences between male and female caregivers. Although sons may be more hesitant to take on the caregiving role, once involved they commit to it with the same intensity as women. Men and women seem to provide care for the same reasons and experience similar difficulties (Fisher, 1994). They perform similar numbers of caregiving tasks, although there may be slight differences in the nature of the tasks men and women perform (Barusch & Spaid, 1989).

Researchers, for the most part, have focused on how male caregivers of frail elders differ from female caregivers and not on understanding the natural variation existing among the experiences of men as caregivers (Kramer & Thompson, 2002). In comparison with male caregivers, female caregivers report higher levels of burden and depression (Fitting et al., 1986; Parks & Pilisuk, 1991; Pruchno & Resch, 1989b; Rose-

Rego, Strauss, & Smyth, 1998; Tennstedt, Cafferata, & Sullivan, 1992; Wallsten, 1998). In one of the first studies of gender differences, Barusch and Spaid (1989) found that women reported higher levels of burden than men but that the two groups did not differ on measures of physical health. In a meta-analysis of 14 studies of gender differences in caregiving, Miller and Cafasso (1992) reported that women were more likely to report greater caregiver burden than men. In a more recent meta-analysis, Yee and Schulz (2000) concluded that there is overwhelming evidence that women caregivers experience more psychiatric morbidity than male caregivers. However, one must be cautious in interpreting these results, as almost all of these studies are cross-sectional. In a longitudinal study, Zarit et al. (1986) found that even though women initially reported greater burden, they reported less burden over time, so that by the second wave of interviews there were no differences between women and men. Longitudinal studies are needed to investigate whether gender differences found in cross-sectional studies persist over the course of the caregiving career.

In their meta-analysis, Miller and Cafasso (1992) concluded that gender differences explain approximately 4% of the variance in caregiver burden. Several researchers have searched for explanations of why women appear more distressed by caregiving than men do. In addition to gender differences in depression in the general (i.e., noncaregiving) population, with women showing higher rates of depression than men, the available evidence suggests that caregiving may be more disruptive to the lives of women than it is to men. Kramer and Kipnis (1995) found that women were more likely than men to be distracted at work and forced to use sick days to fulfill their caregiving responsibilities. A higher proportion of women than men reported that caregiving limited their time with family and interfered with leisure activities. Thus men may experience less distress because caregiving demands may be less likely to spill over into other areas of their lives.

Several other hypotheses have been offered to explain lower levels of distress in male caregivers. There is some evidence that male caregivers may be more tolerant than female caregivers of the care recipient's behavior problems. Zarit et al. (1986) found that husband caregivers expressed greater tolerance and were less distressed by the behaviors of their wives with dementia than did wife caregivers of husbands with dementia. Others point to differences between men and women in their style of coping, with men more likely

to employ problem-focused coping and women more likely to use emotion-focused coping strategies (Pruchno & Resch, 1989a). Another theory is that men are more likely to receive assistance with caregiving than women (Stoller, 1990, 1992; Stoller & Cutler, 1992). Others often come to the aid of male caregivers because men in our culture are not expected to take on a caregiving role. In support of this hypothesis, researchers have found that men receive more informal support than women from friends and family with caregiving (Ingersoll-Dayton, Starrels, & Dowler, 1996; Stoller & Cutler, 1992). Horowitz (1985) found that married sons who were caregivers had more support from their spouses than did married daughters who took on the caregiving role. There is some evidence that male caregivers receive more formal support than female caregivers (Stoller & Cutler, 1992). These studies suggest that the caregiving networks of men and women are quite different. Whereas male caregivers may be supported by a network of secondary caregivers, female caregivers are often the sole providers of care, which may explain, in part, why men report less distress than women caregivers.

In summary, it is well documented that, on general psychological measures of well-being, male caregivers fare more favorably than female caregivers. But within the male caregiving population, there is considerable heterogeneity, which goes uninvestigated in studies comparing male and female caregivers. The next generation of research on male caregivers should focus on understanding the heterogeneity within the population of caregiving men, which will shed light on their unique caregiving challenges, as well as encourage the design of new psychosocial interventions targeting those men who provide care at great personal cost (DeVries, Hamilton, Lovett, & Gallagher-Thompson, 1997).

End-of-Life Care

Biomedical and technological advances in recent years have prolonged the lives of millions of Americans, while at the same time extending the dying process. The care of the dying is emerging as a major public health concern (Field & Cassel, 1997; Haley et al., 2002). Emanuel et al. (1999) found that 96% of primary caregivers of the terminally ill are family members and 72% are women. Caregiving at the end of life poses unique challenges because of the intensity of care often needed. The specific caregiving demands relate to the nature of the patient's disease and functional ability but often include controlling pain, coordinating the multiple formal and informal systems of care likely to be involved at the end of life, and coping both with the patient's grief and the anticipatory grief of family and friends (Schulz et al., 2003).

Although family caregiving has been widely studied over the past two decades, only a few studies have been conducted on end-of-life caregivers. Emanuel and colleagues (Emanuel et al., 1999; Emanuel & Fairclough, 2000) documented the high level of assistance provided by family members of terminally ill patients and the very high levels of burden and depression they experience. In the most comprehensive study to date, Schulz and his colleagues (2003) followed 217 family caregivers of persons with dementia during the year before the patients' deaths and also for an average of 15 weeks after the patients' deaths. Prior to the patients' deaths, caregivers spent an average of 46 hours per week assisting the patients with activities of daily living (ADL) and instrumental activities of daily living (IADL) tasks, a number that is almost three times the average number of hours caregivers typically spend weekly in the caregiving role (National Alliance for Caregiving and AARP, 1997). Of the 56 caregivers who were employed outside the home, 27 (48.2%) had to reduce their work hours because of the demands of caregiving. Schulz et al. (2003) found elevated levels of depression within the 3 months prior to the death and around the time of the death, but within one year after the death, the levels of depression were substantially lower. The researchers concluded that end-of-life caregiver interventions might have their greatest benefit during the period immediately preceding the patient's death, not after it. The majority of caregivers were able to make a satisfactory adjustment to the death of the patient but struggled with the complex and multiple caregiving demands associated with the last few months of life.

Aging Parents as Caregivers to Adults With Disabilities

A less common but increasingly recognized type of family care is provided by aging parents who have continuing caregiving responsibilities for a son or daughter with disabilities (Greenberg, Seltzer, & Greenley, 1993; Seltzer & Krauss, 1989). The emergence of this type of caregiving has resulted from several trends, including the increased longevity of persons with disabilities (Eyman, Grossman, Tarjan, & Miller, 1987), the aging of the baby-boom generation (Greenley, 1990; Janicki & Wisniewski, 1985), and

social policies of deinstitutionalization (Fisher, Benson, & Tessler, 1990; Fujiura & Braddock, 1992). It has become the norm for parents of adults with developmental disabilities and mental illness to be providing or overseeing the care of their adult children.

In an effort to understand the long-term toll of lifelong caregiving on aging parental caregivers, researchers have compared the experience of parents caring for a child with mental retardation with that of parents caring for a child with mental illness. Parental caregivers of adults with these two disabilities face overlapping yet distinct sets of stressors. Their experiences are similar with respect to feelings of grief and a sense of loss that their child may never achieve normal developmental milestones. Both mental illness and mental retardation are chronic conditions requiring long-term parental support and involvement. Finally, for both groups, parents are most concerned about what the future holds for their son or daughter after the parents' deaths.

Yet there are distinct differences. First, whereas mental retardation is ordinarily diagnosed at birth or in the first few years of life, mental illness generally occurs during adolescence or early adulthood. Therefore, the onset of the caregiving role comes at different points in the lives of these two groups of parent caregivers. Second, there is less predictability in the life of a parent whose child has mental illness because of the cyclical nature of the disorder compared with the relative stability of mental retardation. Third, whereas in recent years parents of adults with mental retardation have been welcomed as collaborators in the process of coordinating services for their sons or daughters, parents of adults with mental illness are still often kept at arm's length by mental health providers. Thus comparisons of family caregivers of adults with mental retardation with parental caregivers of adults with mental illness provide an opportunity to explore whether the effects of caregiving are generalizable across different caregiving environments or whether they depend on the specific context in which caregiving takes place.

The available evidence suggests that, whereas aging mothers caring for a child with mental retardation appear to adapt to the demands of lifelong caregiving, aging mothers caring for an adult child with mental illness show a wear-and-tear pattern. In a study based on a nonprobability sample of 107 maternal caregivers of adults with mental illness and 461 maternal caregivers of adults with mental retardation, Greenberg, Seltzer, and colleagues found that maternal caregivers of adults with mental illness reported significantly higher levels of caregiver burden and depression, were more pessimistic about the future, and felt less close to their child than similarly aged mothers caring for an adult child with mental retardation (Greenberg et al., 1993; Seltzer et al., 1995). Using data from the Wisconsin Longitudinal Study (WLS), which is a probability sample of approximately 15,000 participants who were interviewed when the respondents were 18, 36, and 53 or 54 years old on average, Seltzer, Greenberg, Floyd, Pettee, and Hong (2001) compared 165 parents who had adult children with developmental disabilities and 53 parents who had adult children with mental health problems with a comparison group of 218 parents who had nondisabled and healthy children. Whereas there were no differences in well-being between parents of adults with developmental disabilities and parents in the comparison group, parents of children with mental health problems had elevated rates of depression and alcohol use and more physical health problems than parents in the comparison group. Pruchno and her colleagues (1996a, 1996b) similarly found that mothers of adults with schizophrenia reported greater levels of distress and poorer quality of relationships with their sons or daughters than mothers of adults with mental retardation.

The findings from this body of comparative research on aging parents of adults with mental illness and aging parents of adults with developmental disabilities has some parallels with findings reported earlier in the chapter, suggesting that caregivers of persons with Alzheimer's disease appear to fare less well than aging caregivers of adults with other types of disabilities. Although Alzheimer's disease and mental illness present quite different sets of challenges to caregivers, they are similar with respect to the high degree of uncertainty arising in part from the unpredictable nature of symptoms and behavior problems associated with these disorders. Both groups of caregivers must cope with cyclic periods when symptoms are relatively quiescent and other periods of increased symptoms requiring constant vigilance. This body of comparative caregiving research suggests that the very uncertainty or unpredictability of the caregiving context may help explain why caring for certain populations appears to take a greater toll on the caregiver than others.

An emerging research literature is examining differences between aging mothers and fathers caring for adult sons or daughters with disabilities. In a study comparing 251 aging mothers and fathers of adults with disabilities, the majority of whom had developmental disabilities, Pruchno and Patrick (1999) found that mothers felt closer to their children with disabilities than fathers did. Mothers reported both higher levels of burden and greater satisfaction from the caregiving role than fathers. In contrast, Essex, Seltzer, and Krauss (1999) found that mothers and fathers of adults with mental retardation experienced similar levels of subjective burden and depressive symptoms. However, mothers reported feeling closer to their adult children with mental retardation than fathers did (Essex, 2002). Studies comparing mothers and fathers caring for adults with mental illness have found that mothers reported higher mean levels of subjective burden and depression than fathers (Cook, 1988; Greenberg, 2002).

In addition, researchers have begun to identify which characteristics of the caregiving context have similar effects and which characteristics of the caregiving context have differential effects on the well-being of mothers and fathers. Many of the same characteristics of the caregiving context are significant predictors of stress for mother and father caregivers of adults with disabilities. For instance, Pruchno and Patrick (1999) found that the child's living arrangements, emotional stability, functional ability, and parent health similarly predicted caregiver burden in mothers and fathers. The behavior problems of the adult with disabilities was a predictor of subjective burden for both mothers and fathers in studies of aging parental caregivers of adults with mental illness (Greenberg, 2002) and aging parental caregivers of adults with mental retardation (Essex, 1998).

However, several studies reveal that mothers and fathers are affected by different aspects of the caregiving context. For instance, Tessler and Gamache (2000) defined two modes of caregiving stress within objective burden: care and control. Care was operationalized as providing assistance for problems with self-care, and control was operationalized in terms of providing supervision. Their findings indicated that fathers were more distressed by the need to provide care and mothers were more distressed by the need to provide control. The authors argued that because the fathers were less likely to assist with these "care"-related tasks during the years of typical development, they might experience more distress when faced with these tasks later in life (Tessler & Gamache, 2000). Pruchno and Patrick (1999) found that the quality of the parent-child relationship was a predictor of burden for mothers, but not for fathers. Investigating whether different coping strategies had differential effects on parental caregivers of adults with mental retardation, Essex et al. (1999) found that whereas problem-focused coping buffered the impact of the child's functional status on the mothers' depressive symptoms, there were no significant buffering effects for fathers. These studies suggest that fathers might be more vulnerable than mothers of adults with disabilities to the stressors of caregiving because, for fathers, social and psychological resources appear to have fewer beneficial effects in counteracting or buffering stress.

CONCLUSION

In conclusion, the research literature on the effects of caregiving on the caregiver leads to three overall conclusions. First, caregiving effects are generally not static. They vary over time, either resulting in the adaptation or the further depletion and wear and tear of the caregiver. Second, a great deal of evidence suggests that the heterogeneity in caregiving effects can be explained by the severity of the care recipient's behavior problems and by the extent of symptom unpredictability. A related point is that differences in adaptation versus distress among caregivers of individuals with different diagnoses may similarly be accounted for by distinct profiles of behavior problems and degree of behavior unpredictability. Third, although it may be useful from a policy perspective to separate out special populations of caregivers (such as male caregivers, or parents of adults with lifelong disabilities), the factors that affect their well-being and patterns of adaptation and distress are very similar to the factors that affect women as caregivers and caregivers of persons with more prevalent age-related disorders, such as Alzheimer's disease, cancer, and stroke.

We have a fairly clear understanding of how personal resources, such as mastery, coping, or social support, can alter the impact of caregiving and how the caregiving context influences outcomes. Missing from the available literature are insights into what *external* resources can ameliorate the distress of caregiving. We need to investigate and determine what formal supports and services have the potential to substantively reduce caregiving distress. With the aging of the baby-boom generation, the aggregated financial, social, and psychological toll of caregiving will increase dramatically. Our efforts to develop strategies to counteract these negative effects therefore warrant high priority.

REFERENCES

Aldwin, C. M. (1991). Does age affect the stress and coping process? Implications of age differences in perceived control. *Journals of Gerontology, 46*, P174–P180.

Aneshensel, C. S., Pearlin, L. I., Mullan, J. T., Zarit, S. H., & Whitlatch, C. J. (1995). *Profiles in caregiving: The unexpected career.* San Diego, CA: Academic Press.

Aneshensel, C. S., Pearlin, L. I., & Schuler, R. H. (1993). Stress, role captivity, and the cessation of caregiving. *Journal of Health and Social Behavior, 34*, 54–70.

Barber, C. E., & Pasley, B. K. (1995). Family care of Alzheimer's patients: The role of gender and generational relationship on caregiver outcomes. *Journal of Applied Gerontology, 14*, 172–192.

Barusch, A. S., & Spaid, W. M. (1989). Gender differences in caregiving: Why do wives report greater burden? *The Gerontologist, 29*, 667–676.

Baumgarten, M., Battista, R. N., Infante-Rivard, C., Hanley, J. A., Becker, R., & Gauthier, S. (1992). The physiological and physical health of family members caring for an elderly person with dementia. *Journal of Clinical Epidemiology, 45*, 61–70.

Biegel, D. E., Sales, E., & Schulz, R. (1991). *Family caregiving in chronic illness: Alzheimer's disease, cancer, heart disease, mental illness, and stroke.* Thousand Oaks, CA: Sage.

Boss, P., Caron, W., Horbal, J., & Mortimer, J. (1990). Predictors of depression in caregivers of dementia patients: Boundary ambiguity and mastery. *Family Process, 29*, 245–254.

Bourgeois, M. S., Schulz, R., & Burgio, L. (1996). Interventions for caregivers of patients with Alzheimer's disease: A review and analysis of content, process, and outcomes. *International Journal of Aging and Human Development, 43*(1), 35–92.

Brodaty, H., & Hadzi-Pavlovic, D. (1990). Psychosocial effects on careers of living with persons with dementia. *Australian and New Zealand Journal of Psychiatry, 24*, 351–361.

Cantor, M. H. (1983). Strain among caregivers: A study of experience in the United States. *The Gerontologist, 23*, 597–604.

Cattanach, L., & Tebes, J. K. (1991). The nature of elder impairment and its impact on family caregivers' health and psychosocial functioning. *The Gerontologist, 31*, 246–255.

Clipp, E. C., & George, L. K. (1990). Psychotropic drug use among caregivers of patients with dementia. *Journal of the American Geriatrics Society, 38*, 227–235.

Clipp, E. C., & George, L. K. (1993). Dementia and cancer: A comparison of spouse caregivers. *The Gerontologist, 33*, 534–541.

Cohen, D., Luchins, D., Eidorfer, C., Paveza, G., Ashford, J. W., Gorelick, P., et al. (1990). Caring for relatives with Alzheimer's disease: The mental health risks to spouses, adult children, and other family caregivers. *Behavior, Health, and Aging, 1,* 171–182.

Cook, J. A. (1988). Who "mothers" the chronically mentally ill? *Family Relations, 37,* 42–49.

Deimling, G. T., Bass, D. M., Townsend, A. L., & Noelker, L. S. (1989). Care-related stress: A comparison of spouse and adult-child caregivers in shared and separate households. *Journal of Aging and Health, 1,* 67–82.

DeVries, H. M., Hamilton, D. W., Lovett, S., & Gallagher-Thompson, D. (1997). Patterns of coping preferences for male and female caregivers of frail older adults. *Psychology and Aging, 12,* 263–267.

Draper, B. M., Poulos, C. J., Cole, A. D., Poulos, R. G., & Ehrlich, F. (1992). A comparison of caregivers for elderly stroke and dementia victims. *Journal of the American Geriatrics Society, 40,* 896–901.

Dura, J. R., Haywood-Niler, E., & Kiecolt-Glaser, J. K. (1990). Spousal caregivers of persons with Alzheimer's and Parkinson's disease dementia: A preliminary comparison. *The Gerontologist, 30,* 332–336.

Dura, J. R., Stukenberg, K. W., & Kiecolt-Glaser, J. K. (1991). Anxiety and depressive disorders in adult children caring for demented parents. *Psychology and Aging, 6,* 467–473.

Elliot, D. J., Trief, P. M., & Stein, N. (1986). Mastery, stress, and coping in marriage among chronic pain patients. *Journal of Behavioral Medicine, 9,* 549–558.

Emanuel, E. J., & Fairclough, D. L. (2000). Understanding economic and other burdens of terminal illness: The experience of patients and their caregivers. *Annals of Internal Medicine, 21,* 451–459.

Emanuel, E. J., Fairclough, D. I., Slutsman, J., Alpert, H., Baldwin, D., & Emanuel, L. I. (1999). Assistance from family members, friends, paid caregivers, and volunteers in the care of terminally ill patients. *New England Journal of Medicine, 341,* 956–963.

Essex, E. L. (1998). Parental caregivers of adults with mental retardation: The experience of older mothers and fathers (Doctoral dissertation, University of Wisconsin, Madison, 1998). *Dissertation Abstracts International, 59*(8), 3208A.

Essex, E. L. (2002). Mothers and fathers with mental retardation: Feelings of intergenerational closeness. *Family Relations, 51,* 156–165.

Essex, E. L., Seltzer, M. M., & Krauss, M. W. (1999). Differences in coping effectiveness and well-being among mothers and fathers of adults with mental retardation. *American Journal of Mental Retardation, 104,* 545–563.

Eyman, R. K., Grossman, H. J., Tarjan, G., & Miller, C. R. (1987). *Life expectancy and mental retardation: A longitudinal study in a state residential facility.* Washington, DC: American Association on Mental Deficiency.

Farran, C. J., Keane-Hagerty, E., Salloway, S., Kupferer, S., & Wilken, C. S. (1991). Finding meaning: An alternative paradigm for Alzheimer's disease family caregivers. *Gerontologist, 31,* 483–489.

Fengler, A. P., & Goodrich, N. (1979). Wives of elderly disabled men: The hidden patients. *Gerontologist, 19,* 175–183.

Field, M. J., & Cassel, C. K. (Eds.). (1997). *Approaching death: Improving care at the end of life.* Washington, DC: National Academy Press.

Fisher, G. A., Benson, P. R., & Tessler, R. C. (1990). Family response to mental illness: Developments since deinstitutionalization. In J. R. Greenley (Ed.), *Mental illness as a social problem* (pp. 203–236). Greenwich, CT: JAI Press.

Fisher, M. (1994). Man-made care: Community care and older male carers. *British Journal of Social Work, 24,* 659–680.

Fitting, M., Rabins, P., Lucas, M. J., & Eastham, J. (1986). Caregivers for dementia patients: A comparison of husbands and wives. *The Gerontologist, 26,* 248–252.

Folkman, S., Chesney, M., Pollack, L., & Coates, T. (1993). Stress, control, coping, and depressive mood in human immunodeficiency virus-positive and -negative gay men in San Francisco. *Journal of Nervous and Mental Disease, 181,* 409–416.

Franks, M. M., & Stephens, M. A. P. (1996). Social support in the context of caregiving: Husbands' provision of support to wives involved in parent care. *Journals of Gerontology: Psychological Sciences and Social Sciences, 51,* 43–52.

Fujiura, G. T., & Braddock, D. (1992). Fiscal and demographic trends in mental retardation services: The emergence of the family. In L. Rowitz (Ed.), *Mental retardation in the year 2000* (pp. 316–338). New York: Springer-Verlag.

George, L. K., & Gwyther, L. P. (1986). Caregiver well-being: A multidimensional examination of family caregivers of demented adults. *The Gerontologist, 26,* 253–259.

Gonyea, J. G. (1989). Alzheimer's disease support groups: An analysis of their structure, format and perceived benefits. *Social Work in Health Care, 14,* 61–72.

Gonyea, J. G., & Silverstein, N. M. (1991). The role of Alzheimer's disease support groups in families' utilization of community services. *Journal of Gerontological Social Work, 16,* 43–55.

Grafstrom, M., Fratiglioni, L., Sandman, P. O., & Winblad, B. (1992). Health and social consequences for relatives of demented and nondemented elderly: A population-based study. *Journal of Clinical Epidemiology, 45,* 861–870.

Greenberg, J. S. (2002). Differences between fathers and mothers in the care of their children with mental illness. In B. J. Kramer & E. H. Thompson, Jr., (Eds.), *Men as caregivers: Theory, research, and service implications* (pp. 269–293). New York: Springer.

Greenberg, J. S., Seltzer, M. M., & Greenley, J. S. (1993). Aging parents of adults with disabilities: The gratifications and frustrations of later-life caregiving. *Gerontologist, 33,* 542–550.

Greenley, J. R. (1990). Mental illness as a social problem. In J. R. Greenley (Ed.), *Mental disorder in social context* (pp. 7–40). Greenwich, CT: JAI Press.

Haley, W. E., Allen, R. S., Reynolds, S., Chen, H., Burton, A., & Gallagher-Thompson, D. (2002). Family issues in end-of-life decision making and end-of-life care. *American Behavioral Scientist, 46,* 284–298.

Haley, W. E., LaMonde, L. A., Han, B., Narramore, S., & Schonwetter, R. (2001). Family caregiving in hospice: Effects on psychological health functioning among spousal caregivers of hospice patients with lung cancer or dementia. *Hospice Journal, 15,* 1–18.

Haley, W. E., Levine, E. G., Brown, S. L., & Bartolucci, A. A. (1987). Stress, appraisal, coping and social support as predictors of adaptational outcome among dementia caregivers. *Psychology and Aging, 2,* 323–330.

Harris, P. B. (2002). The voices of husbands and sons caring for a family member with dementia. In B. J. Kramer & E. H. Thompson, Jr., (Eds.), *Men as caregivers: Theory, research, and service implications* (pp. 213–233). New York: Springer.

Henry J. Kaiser Foundation. (1999, November). *Long-term care: Medicaid's role and challenges* (Publication No. 2172). Washington, DC: Author.

Hinrichsen, G. A., Hernandez, N. A., & Pollock, S. (1992). Difficulties and rewards in family care of the depressed older adult. *Gerontologist, 32,* 486–492.

Hong, J., & Seltzer, M. M. (1995). The psychological consequences of multiple roles: The nonnormative case. *Journal of Health and Social Behavior, 36,* 386–398.

Horowitz, A. (1985). Sons and daughters as caregivers to older parent: Differences in role performance and consequences. *The Gerontologist, 25,* 612–617.

Hoyert, D. L., & Seltzer, M. M. (1992). Factors related to the well-being and life activities of family caregivers. *Family Relations, 41,* 74–81.

Ingersoll-Dayton, B., Starrels, M. E., & Dowler, D. (1996). Caregiving for parents and parents-in-law: Is gender important? *The Gerontologist, 36,* 483–491.

Janicki, M. P., & Wisniewski, H. M. (Eds.). (1985). *Aging and developmental disabilities: Issues and approaches.* Baltimore: Brookes.

Karlin, N., & Bell, P. A. (1992). Self-efficacy, affect, and seeking support between caregivers of dementia and non-dementia patients. *Journal of Women and Aging, 4,* 59–77.

Kiecolt-Glaser, J. K., Dura, J. R., Speicher, C. E., Trask, J., & Glaser, R. (1991). Spousal caregivers of dementia victims: Longitudinal changes in immunity and health. *Psychosomatic Medicine, 53,* 345–362.

Kiecolt-Glaser, J. K., Glaser, R., Shuttleworth, E. C., Dyer, C. S., Ogrocki, P., & Speicher, C. E. (1987). Chronic stress and immunity in family caregivers of Alzheimer's disease victims. *Psychosomatic Medicine, 49,* 523–535.

Kling, K. C., Seltzer, M. M., & Ryff, C. D. (1997). Distinctive late life challenges: Implications for coping and well-being. *Psychology and Aging, 12,* 288–295.

Kramer, B. J. (1997). Gain in the caregiving experience: Where are we? What next? *Gerontologist, 37,* 218–232.

Kramer, B. J., & Kipnis, S. (1995). Eldercare and work-role conflict: Toward an understanding of gender differences in caregiver burden. *Gerontologist, 35,* 340–358.

Kramer, B. J., & Thompson, E. H. (2002). *Men as caregivers: Theory, research, and service implications.* New York: Springer.

Lawton, M. P., Brody, E. M., & Saperstein, A. R. (1989). A controlled study of respite service for caregivers of Alzheimer's patients. *The Gerontologist, 29,* 8–16.

Lawton, M. P., Moss, M., Kleban, M. H., Glicksman, A., & Rovine, M. (1991). A two-factor model of caregiving appraisal and psychological well-being. *Journals of Gerontology, 46,* P181–P189.

Lazarus, R. S., & Folkman, S. (1984). *Stress, appraisal, and coping.* New York: Springer.

Lebowitz, B. D., & Light, E. (1996). The aging caregivers of psychiatric patients: Healthcare perspectives. *Psychiatric Annals, 26,* 785–791.

Li, L. W. (2000). Intergenerational relationships and psychological well-being of midlife daughters. (Doctoral dissertation, University of Wisconsin, Madison, 2000). *Dissertation Abstracts International, 61*(8), 3353A.

Li, L. W., Seltzer, M. M., & Greenberg, J. S. (1997). Social support and depressive symptoms: Differential patterns in wife and daughter caregivers. *Journals of Gerontology: Psychological Sciences and Social Sciences, 52B,* S200–S211.

Li, L. W., Seltzer, M. M., & Greenberg, J. S. (1999). Change in depressive symptoms among daughter caregivers: An 18-month longitudinal study. *Psychology and Aging, 14,* 206–219.

Liptzin, B., Grob, M. C., & Eisen, S. V. (1988). Family burden of demented and depressed elderly psychiatric inpatients. *Gerontologist, 28,* 397–401.

Lundervold, D., & Lewin, M. (1987). Effects of in-home respite care on caregivers of family members with Alzheimer's disease. *Journal of Clinical Experimental Gerontology, 9,* 201–214.

Marks, N. F. (1998). Does it hurt to care? Caregiving, work-family conflict, and midlife well-being. *Journal of Marriage and the Family, 60,* 951–966.

McFall, S., & Miller, B. H. (1992). Caregiver burden and nursing home admission of frail elderly persons. *Journals of Gerontology, 47,* S73–S79.

Miller, B. (1989). Adult children's perceptions of caregiver stress and satisfaction. *Journal of Applied Gerontology, 8,* 275–293.

Miller, B., & Cafasso, L. (1992). Gender differences in caregiving: Fact or artifact? *The Gerontologist, 32,* 498–507.

Montgomery, R. J. V., & Borgatta, E. F. (1989). The effects of alternative support strategies on family caregiving. *Gerontologist, 29,* 457–464.

Morrissey, E., Becker, J., & Rubert, M. P. (1990). Coping resources and depression in the caregiving spouses of Alzheimer patients. *British Journal of Medical Psychology, 63,* 161–171.

Motenko, A. K. (1989). The frustrations, gratifications, and well-being of dementia caregivers. *The Gerontologist, 29,* 798–803.

National Alliance for Caregiving and the American Association of Retired Persons. (1997). *Family caregiving in the US: Findings from a national survey* [Final report]. Bethesda, MD: National Alliance for Caregiving.

Neal, M. B., Chapman, N., Ingersoll-Dayton, B., Emlen, A., & Boise, L. (1990). Absenteeism and stress among employed caregivers of the elderly, disabled adults, and children. In D. E. Biegel & A. Blum (Eds.), *Aging and caregiving: Theory, research, and policy* (pp. 160–183). Newbury Park, CA: Sage.

Neal, M. B., Ingersoll-Dayton, B., & Starrels, M. E. (1997). Gender and relationship differences in caregiving patterns and consequences among employed caregivers. *The Gerontologist, 37,* 804–816.

Neundorfer, M. M. (1991). Coping and health outcomes in spouse caregivers of persons with dementia. *Nursing Research, 40,* 260–265.

Nijboer, C., Triemstra, M., Tempelaar, R., Mulder, M., Sanderman, R., & van den Bos, G. A. (2000). Patterns of caregiving experiences among partners of cancer patients. *The Gerontologist, 40,* 738–746.

Ory, M., Hoffman, R. R., Yee, J. L., Tennstedt, S., & Schulz, R. (1999). Prevalence and impact of caregiving: A detailed comparison between dementia and nondementia caregivers. *The Gerontologist, 39,* 177–185.

Parks, S. H., & Pilisuk, M. (1991). Caregiver burden: Gender and the psychological costs of caregiving. *American Journal of Orthopsychiatry, 61,* 501–509.

Patrick, J. H., & Hayden, J. M. (1999). Neuroticism, coping strategies, and negative well-being among caregivers. *Psychology and Aging, 14,* 273–283.

Pearlin, L. I., Lieberman, M. A., Menaghan, E. G., & Mullan, J. T. (1981). The stress process. *Journal of Health and Social Behavior, 22,* 337–356.

Pearlin, L. I., Mullan, J. T., Semple, S. J., & Skaff, M. M. (1990). Caregiving and the stress process: An overview of concepts and their measures. *The Gerontologist, 30,* 583–594.

Pleck, J. H. (1993). Are "family-supportive" employer policies relevant to men? In J. C. Hood (Ed.), *Men, work, and family* (pp. 217–237). Newbury, CA: Sage.

Pruchno, R. A., & Kleban, M. H. (1993). Caring for an institutionalized parent: The role of coping strategies. *Psychology and Aging, 8,* 18–25.

Pruchno, R. A., & Patrick, J. H. (1999). Mothers and fathers of adults with chronic disabilities: Caregiving appraisals and well-being. *Research on Aging, 21,* 682–713.

Pruchno, R. A., Patrick, J. H., & Burant, C. (1996a). Aging women and their children with chronic disabilities. *Family Relations, 45,* 318–326.

Pruchno, R. A., Patrick, J. H., & Burant, C. (1996b). Mental health of aging women with children who are chronically disabled: Examination of a two-factor model. *Journals of Gerontology Psychological Sciences and Social Sciences, 51B,* S284–S296.

Pruchno, R. A., & Resch, N. L. (1989a). Mental health caregiving spouses: Coping as mediator, moderator, or main effect? *Psychology and Aging, 4,* 454–463.

Pruchno, R. A., & Resch, N. L. (1989b). Husbands and wives as caregivers: Antecedents of depression and burden. *The Gerontologist, 29,* 159–165.

Rabins, P. V., Fitting, M. D., Eatham, J., & Fetting, J. (1990). The emotional impact of caring for the chronically ill. *Psychosomatics, 31,* 331–336.

Reese, D. R., Gross, A. M., Smalley, D. L., & Messer, S. C. (1994). Caregivers of Alzheimer's disease and stroke patients: Immunological and psychological considerations. *The Gerontologist, 34,* 534–540.

Robinson, K. M. (1989). Predictors of depression among wife caregivers. *Nursing Research, 38,* 359–363.

Rose-Rego, S. K., Strauss, M. E., & Smyth, K. A. (1998). Differences in the perceived well-being of wives and husbands caring for persons with Alzheimer's disease. *The Gerontologist, 38,* 224–230.

Russo, J., Vitaliano, P. P., Brewer, D. D., Katon, W., & Becker, J. (1995). Psychiatric disorders in spouse caregivers of care recipients with Alzheimer's disease and match controls: A diathesis-stress model of psychopathology. *Journal of Abnormal Psychology, 104,* 197–204.

Scharlach, A. E. (1994). Caregiving and employment: Competing or complementary roles? *Gerontologist, 34,* 378–385.

Scharlach, A. E., & Boyd, S. (1989). Caregiving and employment: Results of an employee survey. *The Gerontologist, 29,* 382–387.

Schulz, R., & Beach, S. R. (1999). Caregiving as a risk factor for mortality: The caregiver health effects study. *Journal of the American Medical Association, 282,* 2215–2219.

Schulz, R., Mendelsohn, A. B., Haley, W. E., Mahoney, D., Allen, R. S., Zhang, S., et al. (2003). End-of-life care and the effects of bereavement on family caregivers of persons with dementia. *New England Journal of Medicine, 349,* 1936–1942.

Schulz, R., O'Brien, A. T., Bookwala, J., & Fleissner, K. (1995). Psychiatric and physical morbidity effects of dementia caregiving: Prevalence, correlates, and causes. *The Gerontologist, 35,* 771–791.

Schulz, R., Tompkins, C. A., Wood, D., & Decker, S. (1987). The social psychology of caregiving: Physical and psychological costs of providing support to the disabled. *Journal of Applied Social Psychology, 17,* 401–428.

Schulz, R., & Williamson, G. M. (1991). A 2-year longitudinal study of depression among Alzheimer's caregivers. *Psychology and Aging, 6,* 569–578.

Schulz, R., Williamson, G. M., Morycz, R. K., & Biegel, D. E. (1992). Costs and benefits of providing care to Alzheimer's patients. In S. Oskamp & S. Spacapan (Eds.), *Helping and being helped: Naturalistic studies* (pp. 153–181). Newbury Park, CA: Sage.

Seltzer, M. M., Greenberg, J. S., Floyd, F., Pettee, Y., & Hong, J. (2001). Life course impacts of parenting a child with a disability. *American Journal on Mental Retardation, 106,* 265–286.

Seltzer, M. M., Greenberg, J. S., & Krauss, M. W. (1995). A comparison of coping strategies of aging mothers of adults with mental illness or mental retardation. *Psychology and Aging, 10,* 64–75.

Seltzer, M. M., & Krauss, M. W. (1989). Aging parents with mentally retarded children: Family risk factors and sources of support. *American Journal of Mental Retardation, 94,* 303–312.

Semple, S. J. (1992). Conflict in Alzheimer's families: Its dimensions and consequences. *The Gerontologist, 32,* 648–655.

Sörensen, S., Pinquart, M., & Duberstein, P. (2002). How effective are interventions with caregivers? An updated meta-analysis. *The Gerontologist, 42,* 356–372.

Stoller, E. P. (1990) Males as helpers: The role of sons, relatives, and friends. *The Gerontologist, 30,* 228–235.

Stoller, E. P. (1992). Gender differences in the experiences of caregiving spouses. In J. W. Dwyer & R. T. Coward (Eds.), *Gender, families, and elder care* (pp. 49–64). Newbury Park, CA: Sage.

Stoller, E. P., & Cutler, S. J. (1992). The impact of gender on configurations of care among married elderly couples. *Research and Aging, 14,* 313–330.

Stoller, E. P., & Pugliesi, K. L. (1989). Other roles of caregivers: Competing responsibilities or supportive resources? *Journals of Gerontology: Psychological Sciences and Social Sciences, 44,* S231–239.

Stone, R., Cafferata, G. L., & Sangl, J. (1987). Caregivers of the frail elderly: A national profile. *The Gerontologist, 27,* 616–626.

Strawbridge, W. J., & Wallhagen, M. I. (1991). Impact of family conflict on adult child caregivers. *The Gerontologist, 31,* 770–777.

Strawbridge, W. J., Wallhagen, M. I., Shema, S. J., & Kaplan, G. A. (1997). New burdens or more of the same? Comparing grandparent, spouse, and adult-child caregivers. *The Gerontologist, 37,* 505–510.

Suitor, J. J., & Pillemer, K. (1992). Status transitions and marital satisfaction: The case of adult children caring for elderly parents suffering from dementia. *Journal of Social and Personal Relationships, 9,* 549–562.

Tennstedt, S. L., Cafferata, G. L., & Sullivan, L. (1992). Depression among caregivers of impaired elders. *Journal of Aging and Health, 4,* 58–76.

Tennstedt, S. L., McKinlay, J. B., & Sullivan, L. M. (1988, November). *Informal care for frail elders: The role of secondary characteristics.* Paper presented at the meeting of the Gerontological Society of America, San Francisco, CA.

Tessler, R., & Gamache, G. (2000). *Family experiences with mental illness.* Westport, CT: Greenwood Press.

Thompson, E. (2002). What's unique about men's caregiving. In B. J. Kramer & E. H. Thompson, Jr. (Eds.),

Men as caregivers: Theory, research, and service implications (pp. 20–47). New York: Springer.

Toseland, R. W., & Rossiter, C. M. (1989). Group interventions to support family caregivers: A review and analysis. *The Gerontologist, 29,* 438–448.

Toseland, R. W., Rossiter, C. M., & Labrecque, M. S. (1989). The effectiveness of peer-led and professionally led groups to support family caregivers. *The Gerontologist, 29,* 465–471.

Townsend, A., Noelker, L., Deimling, G., & Bass, D. (1989). Longitudinal impact of interhousehold caregiving in adult children's mental health. *Psychology and Aging, 4,* 393–401.

Wallsten, S. M. (November, 1998). *Subtly similar race and gender effects in elderly caregiver spouses.* Paper presented at the meeting of the Gerontological Society of America, Philadelphia, PA.

Wilson, P. A., Moore, S. T., Rubin, D. S., & Bartels, P. K. (1990). Informal caregivers of the chronically ill and their social support: A pilot study. *Journal of Gerontological Social Work, 15,* 155–170.

Worcester, M. I., & Quayhagen, M. P. (1983). Correlates of caregiving satisfaction: Prerequisites to elder home care. *Research in Nursing and Health, 6,* 61–67.

Yee, J. L., & Schulz, R. (2000). Gender differences in psychiatric morbidity among family caregivers: A review and analysis. *The Gerontologist, 40,* 147–164.

Zarit, S. H., Birkel, R. C., & Beach, M. E. (1989). Spouses as caregivers: Stresses and interventions. In M. Z. Goldstein (Ed.), *Family involvement in the treatment of the frail elderly* (pp. 23–62). Washington, DC: American Psychiatric Association.

Zarit, S. H., Todd, P. A., & Zarit, J. M. (1986). Subjective burden of hubands and wives as caregivers: A longitudinal study. *The Gerontologist, 26,* 260–266.

Zarit, S. H., & Whitlatch, C. J. (1992). Institutional placement: Phases of the transition. *Gerontologist, 32,* 665–672.

NANCY P. KROPF

EUNKYUNG YOON

Grandparents Raising Grandchildren: Who Are They?

WHO ARE GRANDPARENTS WHO RAISE GRANDCHILDREN?

As a hidden segment of America's caregiver population (Fuller-Thomson & Minkler, 2003), the number of grandparents raising grandchildren has dramatically increased. Several sources provide information about the incidence and prevalence of these caregivers and families (American Association of Retired Persons [AARP], 2004; Fuller-Thomson & Minkler, 2001; Lugaila, 1998; U.S. Census Bureau, 2001), including:

- An estimated 60 million grandparents currently live in the United States, with 2.4 million taking primary responsibility for their grandchildren.
- More than 1 in 10 of them have raised a grandchild for six months or longer.
- More than 6 million children under 18 live in grandparent-headed households (or with other relatives).

The number of children raised in grandparent-headed families has more than doubled over the past 30 years, from 2.2 million in 1970 (3.2% of all children) to more than 4.5 million in 2000 (6.3% of all children) (Bryson & Casper, 1999; U.S. Census Bureau, 2001). All data indicate that this family form has increased dramatically and includes significant portions of children and adults.

A profile of caregiving grandparents has been produced from a number of large data sets (Chalfie, 1994; Cox, 2000; Fuller-Thomson, Minkler, & Driver, 1997; Pebley & Rudkin, 1999; Szinovacz, 1998). These studies demonstrated that the characteristics of grandparents raising grandchildren transcend socioeconomic groups, geographic areas, and ethnicities:

- Grandparents come from all racial and ethnic groups. Although most grandparent caregivers are White (between 50 and 60%), a higher proportion (29%) than in the general population are African American. In addition, about 10% of the grandparents are Hispanic (any race), and 1–2% represent other groups (Chalfie, 1994; Fuller-Thomson et al., 1997).
- Geographically, grandparents predominantly live in urban areas, especially inner cities (Burnette, 1997; Minkler & Fuller-Thomson, 1999). However, the South is disproportionately represented, and significant numbers (approximately 25%) live in rural communities (Bryson & Casper, 1999; Robinson, Kropf, & Myers, 2000).

- The ages of grandparents range from mid-adulthood to old age. The average age of grandparent caregivers is 55 to 57 years (Burton, 1992; Dowdell, 1995). About one-fifth (21%) are older than 65, and 15% are younger than 45 (Bryson & Casper, 1999).

These characteristics indicate that grandparents who are raising grandchildren represent a varied segment of the population. As public recognition of intergenerational caregiving has increased, grandparents raising grandchildren should be highlighted as a critical social phenomenon in social work and aging (Kropf & Kolomer, 2004). The remaining sections provide an overview of the consequences of caregiving for the grandparent, the pathways and context of caregiving, and interventions to promote stable and effective functioning within these families.

OUTCOMES AND CONSEQUENCES OF CAREGIVING FOR GRANDPARENTS

A body of empirical literature has consistently demonstrated that many grandparent caregivers experience a multiplicity of social, physical, emotional, financial, and legal problems (Burton, 1992; Caputo, 2001; Dowdell, 1995; Emick & Hayslip, 1999; Minkler & Fuller-Thomson, 1999; Whitley, Kelley, & Sipe, 2001; Woodworth, 1996). Grandparents who are faced with the need to raise their grandchildren have health risks that could jeopardize a stable family environment established for their grandchildren. Both qualitative and quantitative research indicates that caregiving grandparents are vulnerable to a host of health and social challenges, including depression, social isolation, and poverty.

Physical Health

Taken collectively, the research on grandparents who are in caregiving roles indicates that their health status is compromised. Specific conditions include poorer self-assessed health status, considerable comorbidity, delayed help seeking, and a frequent tendency to "play down" the severity of personal health problems (Dowdell, 1995; Minkler & Fuller-Thomson, 1999; Minkler & Roe, 1993; Whitley et al., 2001). In addition, negative health practices, such as smoking and alcohol consumption, exacerbate preexisting physical illnesses (Whitley et al., 2001).

Specific health conditions are especially problematic for custodial grandparents. Minkler and Roe (1993) found that 28% of the caregivers reported that their health had deteriorated during the previous year, and, more important, 38% reported that their health had worsened since assuming full-time parenting responsibilities for grandchildren. While custodial grandparents often experience deteriorating health, they also tend to ignore their health problems to appear "up to task" (Pinson-Millburn, Fabian, Schlossberg, & Pyle, 1996). In spite of physical limitations or symptoms, many of the grandparents caring for their grandchildren evidenced a high sense of perseverance and determination to continue their responsibilities (Minkler & Fuller-Thomson, 1999).

Mental Health

Research on the mental health status of grandparent caregivers also indicates negative outcomes as a result of undertaking care of grandchildren. Custodial grandparents express feelings of personal losses, which include loss of their freedom, loss of their own child, and loss of a peer group. Furthermore, social isolation from their own families, friends, and communities may lead to higher levels of depression and anxiety (Hayslip, Shore, Henderson, & Lambert, 1998; Kolomer, McCallion & Janicki, 2002; Minkler, Fuller-Thomson, Miller, & Driver, 1997; Minkler, Roe, & Robertson-Beckley, 1994). In fact, psychological indicators suggest that a substantial portion of these grandparents suffer from mental health issues that are clinically significant (Burton, 1992; Kelley, Whitley, Sipe, & Yorker, 2000; Minkler, Fuller-Thomson, Miller, & Driver, 1997). In a study of different caregiver roles, grandparents who were providing care for grandchildren reported higher rates of depression than either spousal or adult-child caregivers (Strawbridge, Wallhagen, Shema, & Kaplan, 1997).

Financial Difficulties

Financial problems have been commonly documented in studies with grandparents raising grandchildren (Burnette, 1999; Flint & Perez-Porter, 1997). Overall, about one-fourth (26%) of custodial grandparents have income below the poverty level (Fuller-Thomson et al., 1997). However, poverty rates differ among various types of households in which grandparents are raising grandchildren (Bryson & Casper, 1999). If a grandfather is present, there is less probability that the household is classified as poor. In families in which both grandparents are present, about 14% of households are poor, with a household average income of $41,709. Twenty percent of grandfather-only households are poor, with an average income of $43,476. Single grandmothers, however, have a higher poverty risk. In grandmother-only households, 43% are classified as poor, with an average household income of $19,750.

Grandparents experience financial strains from expenses assumed as a consequence of care provision. Added costs are a result of expenses, poverty, and underemployment (Jendrek, 1994). Custodial grandparents assume added costs for educational, medical, dental, housing, food, and clothing expenses for grandchildren. Underemployment often occurs when grandparents are unable to earn sufficient income because of age-related discrimination in the labor force, competing demands of work and child care (e.g., taking part-time vs. full-time employment), or health consequences that compromise their ability to work (Sands & Goldberg-Glen, 1998). In addition, grandparents without full legal authority over grandchildren are not automatically entitled to receive financial benefits and may have difficulty establishing eligibility for assistance (Flint & Perez-Porter, 1997).

Legal Problems

Grandparents may encounter numerous types of legal problems in raising grandchildren, chiefly due to the informal arrangements of caregiving. Voluntary legal custody requires permission from a custodial parent, and such permission can be difficult for grandparents to obtain from an already troubled adult child who refuses to consent, such as the case of a parent with an addiction (Flint & Perez-Porter, 1997; Jendrek, 1994). Discussions about grandparental custody may intensify ongoing conflict with an adult child and erode familial relationships. Further, temporary guardianships make the relationship between grandparent caregivers and their grandchildren tenuous and insecure for both generations (Waldrop & Weber, 2001). Custody battles, court appearances, and legal fees are the cause of extra financial burdens for many families.

CIRCUMSTANCES OF CAREGIVING

The circumstances under which grandparents assume the primary caregiving responsibility for their grandchildren are often very complex. Several reasons have been cited as etiological factors, including substance abuse (Burton, 1992; Fuller-Thomson et al., 1997; Minkler & Roe, 1993; Minkler et al., 1994), HIV/AIDS (Linsk & Mason, 2004; Schable, Diaz, Chu, Caldwell, & Conti, 1995), incarceration (Dressel & Barnhill, 1994), mental illness (Dowdell, 1995), and teen pregnancy (Kropf & Robinson, 2004). The three most prevalent—addiction, HIV/AIDS, and incarceration—are explored more fully in terms of family situations and consequences.

Drug Addiction

An initial factor in the increase in grandparent caregivers was the crack cocaine epidemic, especially in major metropolitan areas. When a parent's life is ravaged or ended by involvement in crack, caregiving for the children is most often assumed by the grandmother (Roe, Minkler, Saunders, & Thomson, 1996). The highly addictive nature of this drug, the lack of available treatment programs, and the social context of crack addiction often leave the drug user and the family in a prolonged cycle of violence, desperation, and fear (Minkler & Roe, 1993).

Although crack cocaine is a dangerous substance, other types of addiction are also involved in this family situation. Rural communities in particular face a dramatic increase in methamphetamine use. "Crystal meth," "crank," or "ice" is a substance that is easily manufactured with over-the-counter ingredients, and remote locations are a perfect context for "meth labs." In California, a major production site, 3,900 pounds of methamphetamine were seized in 2003, which represents a 50% increase over the previous 3 years (Jewett, 2004). In another high-manufacturing state, Missouri, state troopers reported that 200 labs had been shut down in one county alone during the first half of 2004 (Hathaway, 2004). Methamphetamine is an especially popular choice for women, many of whom are involved with the manufacturing and distribution of the drug as well (Gorman et al., 2003; Strauss & Falkin, 2001). As greater numbers of families experience the negative aftermaths of this potent addiction, greater numbers of grandparents in rural communities are expected to be in caregiving roles for their grandchildren.

The intermittent cycle of substance abuse can create problems within the family system beyond the addiction. When parents are in periods of sobriety, they may initiate contact with their children. This experience may lead to problems such as confusion over familial lines of authority or the experience of reabandonment when the parent leaves again. These issues create caregiving and intergenerational challenges within the family system (Ehrle & Day, 1994; Goldberg-Glen, Sands, Cole, & Cristofalo, 1998).

Incarcerated Parents

Maternal incarceration increasingly contributes to the number of children placed in kinship care arrangements (Dressel & Barnhill, 1994; Young & Smith, 2000). Recent laws to fight drug-related crime have further contributed to the sharp increase in the number of incarcerated women (Gentry, 1998). At midyear of 1998, roughly 83,000 women were estimated to be in federal and state prisons, which translates to 6.4% of all prisoners (U.S. Department of Justice, 1999). Although the exact number of children affected by maternal incarceration is not well established, estimates indicate that female inmates in state prisons had an average of 2.18 children younger than age 18 (U.S. Department of Justice, 1994). Approximately 195,000 children younger than age 18 are affected by their mothers' incarceration (Young & Smith, 2000).

Women in prison, their children, and the children's caregivers present a special population with unique life experiences that warrant the attention of practitioners from several fields. Particular issues related to grandparents who are raising grandchildren of incarcerated parents include the emotional challenges of fostering the parent-child bond during the period of separation. In addition, some grandparents report emotional difficulties of managing attachment to their grandchildren, knowing that the parent will regain custody upon release from prison.

HIV/AIDS

The HIV/AIDS epidemic has also increased the number of grandparent caregivers as infected parents become incapacitated or succumb to the disease. Caregiving by older family members to HIV-infected adults and children has been common in this country

from the beginning of the epidemic (Joslin, 2000; Linsk & Mason, 2004; Poindexter, 2001). At least half of informal caregivers for adults with advanced HIV disease are older relatives (Joslin & Brouard, 1995). At this point, grandparents are typically the care providers who assume responsibility for these "AIDS orphans," many of whom may also have health problems related to their own HIV + status (Calliandro & Hughes, 1998; Poindexter & Linsk, 1999).

As with other pathways into caregiving, the emotional toll for the grandparents is high. Several studies report that older caregivers suffer from HIV stigma themselves. In addition, these caregivers experience grief reactions from anticipating or experiencing the death of an adult child from AIDS (Calliandro & Hughes, 1998; Joslin, 1995; Poindexter, 2001). In spite of the high levels of resilience that are documented in this group, HIV-affected grandparent caregivers report that HIV-related stigma leads to increased social isolation (Poindexter, 2002), and they fear rejection, practice secrecy, lack trust, and report reduced social supports (Joslin, 2000; Linsk & Mason, 2004).

SOCIAL WORK INTERVENTIONS

With the increases in grandparents who are raising grandchildren, social workers in a variety of service settings will work with members of this family form. Therefore, a great need exists for awareness among professionals about the unique problems that grandparents encounter when raising their grandchildren. Most program and service goals are to decrease the grandparents' psychological stress and improve their physical and mental health, social support, and family and legal resources. The following section addresses services and social policies that specifically relate to grandparents who are raising their grandchildren.

Direct Practice Interventions

The most pervasive type of intervention for grandparents who raise grandchildren is a group format. Groups, led by both professionals and nonprofessionals under the auspices of churches, schools, voluntary, and public agencies, have been widely available. Some groups have a more psychoeducational framework and deliver a set "curriculum" with the participants (Burnette, 1998; Cox, 2002, 2003). Others, however, function as support groups and provide a safe environment for grandparents to discuss the issues that are most important. More than 500 such groups are registered by the Grandparent Caregiver Information Center (AARP, 2004).

Groups are a useful, cost-effective way to meet the educational and support needs of caregiving grandparents. Support groups can help to reduce feelings of isolation, as well as play instrumental roles in providing information. The impact of these groups is underscored by the finding that grandparents have described them as their most valuable resources (Kolomer, McCallion, & Overendyer, 2003; Minkler & Roe, 1993). Support groups provide a safe environment for grandparents to increase their knowledge about child care and augment their social support network with others (McCallion, Janicki, Grant-Griffin, & Kolomer, 2000).

Another direct practice intervention is case management. Using a case management approach, social workers can help caregiving families to mobilize both internal and external resources. For grandparents in more remote locations—for example, those who reside in rural areas—the new experiences of having a child again can be overwhelming, as limited assistance may be available within their communities. Grandparents may lack understanding of how to connect with community programs and may benefit from supportive assistance in learning these skills (Myers, Kropf, & Robinson, 2002). In addition, case managers can help the family identify and develop those resources that exist within the family, such as strong, supportive sibling relationships or good coping resources. An example of a community-based intervention program, Project Healthy Grandparents (PHG), has been implemented in one state as a way to promote strength-based services to these care providers (Kelley, Whitley, Sipe, & Yorker, 2000; Whitley, White, Kelley, & Yorker, 1999). In addition to a primary case manager, a multidisciplinary team (social workers, nurses, lawyers, and others) partners to improve the social, psychological, physical, economic, and legal status among grandparent caregivers.

Social Policy Issues

Changes in social policy are required to make programs more accessible and responsive to the needs of grandparent caregivers. Within public welfare, a growing number of TANF (Temporary Assistance to Needy Families) recipients are grandparents and other relatives (Larrison, Nackerud, & Risler, 2001). TANF has had a particularly onerous impact on grandparents, with confusion over their benefit eligibility and the work requirements (Fuller-Thomson & Minkler, 2000; Mullen, 1998).

Secondly, the Older Americans Act (OAA; Public Law 106-501) was amended in 2001 to include the National Family Caregiver Support Program (NFCSP). NFCSP distributes funding to the states to work on developing partnerships with Area Agencies on Aging (AAA) and community service providers to develop five basic services for family caregivers: information, assistance in gaining access to support services, counseling, respite care, and supplemental services (Administration on Aging [AoA], 2004). States may use up to 10% of these funds to support services for relative caregivers ages 60 and over who have children in their care.

Several key policy components have been put forth by Generations United (GU), a national coalition that promotes intergenerational programs and policies, especially relative caregivers (Generations United, 2001). In particular, GU has advocated for additional residential options, given the low-income status of a substantial number of grandparents. One program that could alleviate these difficulties is the designation of intergenerational housing that is specifically designed for custodial grandparents (U.S. Department of Housing and Urban Development, 2000). These programs eradicate some of the existing barriers in public housing, such as maximum occupancy rates and space limitations (Kauffman & Goldberg-Glen, 2000).

In summary, the number of grandparents who have responsibility for raising grandchildren has increased dramatically. Various reasons account for this growing number, including increased addiction rates, incarceration of women, and the number of families affected by HIV/AIDS. Grandparents within caregiving roles experience physical, emotional, social, and economic stress. Various interventions, especially support groups and case management, provide grandparents with information, social support, and access to needed resources. However, policies need to be modified to sufficiently address more macro level issues associated with these caregivers.

Future research on grandparents who are raising grandchildren can add to the existing literature about this family form. In particular, the following areas are logical "next steps" in developing the knowledge base:

- *Additional outcome studies about effectiveness of interventions.* Currently, research outcomes have been limited to certain types of interventions, as well as particular groups of grandparents. What interventions are effective with grandparents who reside in rural areas? Besides group interventions and case management, what services or programs can provide education and support to custodial grandparents? What interventions are effective in reducing psychosocial stress in grandchildren who live with grandparents?

- *Longitudinal research designs.* To date, most research has been descriptive or cross-sectional. As grandparents age, how does the caregiving role affect their own aging process? How do children raised by grandparents perform in adult roles, such as intimate relationships, or as parents themselves?

- *Construction of theoretical models of family development.* Are there particular "risk junctures" in the family life course for intergenerational families? How do divergent pathways into caregiving affect family dynamics and functioning? How do grandparents enact their grandparent role with noncustodial grandchildren?

Although knowledge about grandparents raising grandchildren has increased, these additional areas of research will provide information that will be helpful in both understanding and intervening with intergenerational families.

REFERENCES

Administration on Aging. (2004). *The National Family Caregiver Support Program (NFCSP): An executive summary.* Retrieved June 3, 2004, from *http://www.aoa.gov/prof/aoaprog/caregiver/caregiver.asp.*

American Association of Retired Persons. (2004). *Census 2000 data about grandparent-headed households.* Retrieved June 2, 2004, from *http://www.aarp.org/life/grandparents/*

Bryson, K., & Casper, L. (1999, May). Coresident grandparents and grandchildren: Grandparent maintained families. *Current Population Reports* (No. P23-198, pp. 1–11). Washington, DC: U.S. Census Bureau.

Burnette, D. (1997). Grandparents raising grandchildren in the inner city. *Families in Society, 78,* 489–499.

Burnette, D. (1998). Grandparents raising grandchildren: A small-group, school-based intervention. *Research on Social Work Practice, 8*(1), 10–18

Burnette, D. (1999). Custodial grandparents in Latino families: Patterns of service use and predictors of unmet needs. *Social Work, 44,* 22–34.

Burton, L. M. (1992). Black grandparents rearing children of drug-addicted parents: Stressors, outcomes, and social services. *Gerontologist, 32,* 744–751.

Calliandro, G., & Hughes, C. (1998). The experience of being a grandmother who is the primary caregiver for her HIV-positive grandchild. *Nursing Research, 47*(2), 107–113.

Caputo, R. K. (2001). Depression and health among grandmothers co-residing with grandchildren in two cohorts of women. *Families in Society, 82,* 473–483.

Chalfie, D. (1994). *Going it alone: A close look at grandparents parenting grandchildren.* Washington, DC: American Association of Retired Persons.

Cox, C. B. (Ed.). (2000). *To grandmother's house we go and stay: Perspectives on custodial grandparents.* New York: Springer.

Cox, C. B. (2002). Empowering African American custodial grandparents. *Social Work, 47,* 45–54.

Cox, C. B. (2003). Designing interventions for grandparent caregivers: The need for an ecological perspective for practice. *Families in Society, 84*(1), 127–134.

Dowdell, E. B. (1995). Caregiver burden: Grandmothers raising their high risk grandchildren. *Journal of Psychosocial Nursing, 33,* 27–30.

Dressel, P. L., & Barnhill, S. K. (1994). Reframing gerontological thought and practice: The case of grandmothers with daughters in prison. *Gerontologist, 34,* 685–691.

Ehrle, G. M., & Day, H. D. (1994). Adjustment and family functioning of grandmothers rearing their grandchildren. *Contemporary Family Therapy, 16,* 67–82.

Emick, M. A., & Hayslip, B. (1999). Custodial grandparenting: Stresses, coping skills, and relationships with grandchildren. *International Journal of Aging and Human Development, 48*(1), 35–61.

Flint, M. M., & Perez-Porter, M. (1997). Grandparent caregivers: Legal and economic issues. *Journal of Gerontological Social Work, 28,* 1–2.

Fuller-Thomson, E., & Minkler, M. (2000). African American grandparents raising grandchildren: A national profile of demographic and health characteristics. *Health and Social Work, 25*(2), 109–118.

Fuller-Thomson, E., & Minkler, M. (2001). American grandparents providing extensive child care to their grandchildren: Prevalence and profile. *Gerontologist, 41,* 201–209.

Fuller-Thomson, E., & Minkler, M. (2003). Housing issues and realities facing grandparent caregivers who are renters. *Gerontologist, 43,* 92–98.

Fuller-Thomson, E., Minkler, M., & Driver, D. (1997). A profile of grandparents raising grandchildren in the United States. *Gerontologist, 37,* 406–411.

Generations United. (2001). *Public policy agenda for the 107th Congress.* Washington, DC: Author.

Gentry, P. M. (1998). Permanency planning in the context of parental incarceration: Legal issues and recommendation. *Child Welfare, 8,* 543–559.

Goldberg-Glen, R., Sands, R. G., Cole, R. D., & Cristofalo, C. (1998). Multigenerational patterns and internal structures in families in which grandparents raise grandchildren. *Families in Society: The Journal of Contemporary Human Services, 79,* 477–489.

Gorman, E. M., Clark, C. W., Nelson, K. R., Applegate, T., Amato, E., & Scrol, A. (2003). A community social work study of methamphetamine use among women: Implications for social work practice, education, and research. *Journal of Social Work Practice in Addictions, 3*(3), 41–62.

Hathaway, M. (2004, August 26). Jefferson County remains meth hotbed. *St. Louis Post-Dispatch,* B01.

Hayslip, B., Shore, R. J., Henderson, C. E., & Lambert, P. L. (1998). Custodial grandparenting and the impact of grandchildren with problems on role satisfaction and role meaning. *Journals of Gerontology: Psychological Sciences and Social Sciences, 53,* S164–173.

Jendrek, M. P. (1994). Grandparents who parent their children: Circumstances and decisions. *Gerontologist, 34,* 206–216.

Jewett, C. (2004, October 17). Meth labs spread to Mexico, California's rural north. *Sacramento Bee.* Retrieved on October 25, 2004, from www.shns.com.

Joslin, D. (2000). Grandparents raising grandchildren orphaned and affected by HIV/AIDS. In C. Cox (Ed.), *To grandmother's house we go and stay: Perspectives on custodial grandparents* (pp. 167–183). New York: Springer.

Joslin, D., & Brouard, A. (1995). The prevalence of grandmothers as primary caregivers in a poor pediatric population. *Journal of Community Health, 20,* 383–401.

Kauffman, S., & Goldberg-Glen, R. (2000). A comparison of low income caregivers in public housing: Differences in grandparent and nongrandparent needs and problems. In B. Hayslip & R. Goldberg-Glen (Eds.), *Grandparents raising grandchildren: Theoretical, empirical and clinical perspectives* (pp. 369–382). New York: Springer.

Kelley, S. J., Whitley, D. M., Sipe, T. A., & Yorker, B. C. (2000). Psychological distress in grandmother kinship care providers: The role of resources, social support and physical health. *Child Abuse and Neglect, 24,* 311–321.

Kelley, S. J., Yorker, B. C., Whitley, D. M., & Sipe, T. A. (2001). A multimodal intervention for grandparents raising grandchildren: Results of an exploratory study. *Child Welfare, 80,* 27–50.

Kolomer, S., McCallion, P., & Janicki, M. (2002). African-American grandmother carers of children with disabilities: Predictors of depressive symptoms. *Journal of Gerontological Social Work, 37*(3/4), 45–64.

Kolomer, S., McCallion, P., & Overendyer, J. (2003). Why support groups help: Successful interventions for grandparent caregivers. In B. Hayslip & J. H. Patrick (Eds.), *Working with custodial grandparents* (pp. 111–126). New York: Springer.

Kropf, N., & Kolomer, S. (2004). Grandparents raising grandchildren: A diverse population. *Journal of Human Behavior in the Social Environment, 9*(4), 65–83.

Kropf, N. P., & Robinson, M. M. (2004). Pathways into caregiving for rural custodial grandparents. *Journal of Intergenerational Relationships, 2*(1), 63–77.

Larrison, C. R., Nackerud, L., & Risler, E. (2001). A new perspective on families that receive Temporary Assistance for Needy Families (TANF). *Journal of Sociology and Social Welfare, 28*(3), 49–69.

Linsk, N. L., & Mason, S. (2004). Stresses on grandparents and other relatives caring for children affected by HIV/AIDS. *Health and Social Work, 29*(2), 127–136.

Lugaila, T. (1998, December). Marital status and living arrangements. *Current population reports* (Series P. 20-514). Washington, DC: U.S. Government Printing Office.

McCallion, P., Janicki, M. P., Grant-Griffin, L., & Kolomer, S. (2000). Grandparent carers: II. Service needs and services provision issues. *Journal of Gerontological Social Work, 33*(3), 57–84.

Minkler, M., & Fuller-Thomson, E. (1999). The health of grandparents raising grandchildren: Results of a national study. *American Journal of Public Health, 89,* 1384–1390.

Minkler, M., Fuller-Thomson, E., Miller, D., & Driver, D. (1997, September-October). Depression in grandparents raising grandchildren. *Archives on Family Medicine, 6,* 445–452.

Minkler, M., & Roe, K. M. (1993). *Grandmothers as caregivers: Raising children of the crack cocaine epidemic.* Newbury Park, CA: Sage.

Minkler, M., Roe, K. M., & Robertson-Beckley, M. (1994). Raising grandchildren from crack-cocaine households: Effects on family and friendship ties of

African-American women. *American Journal of Orthopsychiatry, 64,* 20–29.

Mullen, F. (1998). Grandparents raising grandchildren: Public benefits and programs. In Generations United (Ed.), *Grandparents and other relatives raising children: Background papers from Generations United's expert symposium* (pp. 19–25). Washington, DC: Generations United.

Myers, L., Kropf, N. P., & Robinson, M. M. (2002). Grandparents raising grandchildren: Case management in a rural setting. *Journal of Human Behavior in the Social Environment, 5*(1), 53–71.

Pebley, A. R., & Rudkin, L. L. (1999). Grandparents caring for grandchildren: What do we know? *Journal of Family Issues, 20,* 218–242.

Pinson-Millburn, N. M., Fabian, E. S., Schlossberg, N. K., & Pyle, M. (1996). Grandparents raising grandchildren. *Journal of Counseling and Development, 74,* 548–554.

Poindexter, C. (2001). I am still blessed: The assets and needs of HIV-affected caregivers over 50. *Families in Society, 82,* 525–536.

Poindexter, C. (2002). "It don't matter what people say as long as I love you": Experiencing stigma when raising an HIV-infected grandchild. *Journal of Mental Health and Aging, 4*(4), 331–348.

Poindexter, C. P., & Linsk, N. L. (1999). "I'm just glad that I'm here": Stories of seven African American HIV-affected grandmothers. *Journal of Gerontological Social Work, 32,* 63–81.

Robinson, M., Kropf, N., & Myers, L. (2000). Grandparents raising grandchildren in rural communities. *Journal of Mental Health and Aging, 6,* 353–365.

Roe, K. M., Minkler, M., Saunders, F., & Thomson, G. E. (1996). Health of grandmothers raising children of the crack cocaine epidemic. *Medical Care, 34,* 1072–1084.

Sands, R. G., & Goldberg-Glen, R. S. (1998). The impact of employment and serious illness on grandmothers who are raising their grandchildren. *Journal of Women and Aging, 10*(3), 41–58.

Schable, B., Diaz, T., Chu, S. Y., Caldwell, M. B., & Conti, L. (1995). Who are the primary caretakers of children born to HIV-infected mothers?: Results from a multistate surveillance project. *Pediatrics, 95,* 511–515.

Strauss, S. M., & Falkin, G. P. (2001). Women offenders who use and deal methamphetamine: Implications for mandated drug treatment. *Women and Criminal Justice, 12*(4), 77–97.

Strawbridge, W. J., Wallhagen, M. I., Shema, S. J., & Kaplan, G. A. (1997). New burdens or more of the same? Comparing grandparent, spouse, and adult-child caregivers. *Gerontologist, 37,* 505–510.

Szinovacz, M. E. (1998). Grandparents today: A demographic profile. *Gerontologist, 38,* 37–52.

Young, D. S., & Smith, C. J. (2000). When moms are incarcerated: The needs of children, mothers, and caregivers. *Families in Society, 81*(2), 130–141.

U.S. Census Bureau. (2001). *Grandchildren living in the home of their grandparents: 1970 to present* [Historical time series table CH-7]. Retrieved June 2, 2004, from *http://www.census.gov/population/socdemo/hh-fam/tabCH-7.pdf.*

U.S. Department of Housing and Urban Development. (2000). *Fair housing initiatives program (FHIP).* Retrieved June 2, 2004, from *http://www.hud.gov/progdesc/fhip.html.*

U.S. Department of Justice. (1994). *Bureau of Justice Statistics special report: Women in prison* (Publication No. NCJ-145321). Washington, DC: U.S. Government Printing Office.

U.S. Department of Justice. (1999). *Prison and jail inmates at midyear 1998* (Publication No. NCJ-173414). Washington, DC: U.S. Government Printing Office.

Waldrop, D. P., & Weber, J. A. (2001). From grandparent to caregiver: The stress and satisfaction of raising grandchildren. *Families in Society, 82,* 461–472.

Whitley, D. M., Kelley, S. J., & Sipe, T. A. (2001). Grandmothers raising grandchildren: Are they at increased risk of health problems? *Health and Social Work, 26,* 105–114.

Whitley, D. M., White, K. R., Kelley, S. J., & Yorker, B. (1999). Strengths-based case management: The application to grandparents raising grandchildren. *Families in Society, 80,* 110–119.

Woodworth, R. S. (1996). You're not alone . . . you're one in a million. *Child Welfare, 75,* 619–635.

The success that the aging of persons with developmental disabilities (DD) represents also means challenges for families who must provide longer term and new forms of care. In addition, traditional views of family caregivers, particularly older parents as caregivers, must be expanded to include other relatives, such as siblings and grandparents. The aging of persons with DD and their caregivers requires all social workers to renew perspectives, tools, and approaches. The increasing complexity of life history and experiences, health needs, and life transitions also require that a holistic and multidisciplinary perspective be embraced. Drawing on the related research and practice literatures, this chapter outlines key demographic issues for adults with DD and their families and describes changing family caregiving constellations. Suggestions are offered for the assessment and management of life transitions and of grief and bereavement issues that are increasingly a feature of the older years of both caregivers and persons with DD.

THE DEMOGRAPHICS OF AGING

Adults with DD are experiencing increased longevity, and concerns have been raised that this means increased needs for family caregivers and a demand for services and special attention that many jurisdictions are ill prepared to address (Seltzer & Krauss, 1994; Braddock, 1999). When persons with DD were not expected to live into old age, there was a reasonable expectation that parents would outlive their offspring and offer a lifetime of care. The reality that most care was provided in the home also meant that services for persons with DD in their older years were not developed or provided (Ludlow, 2002). For the first time we have sizeable groups of individuals with DD aging and needing related services. Also, the caregiving life of families is now spanning multiple decades and is increasingly a feature of advanced old age for parents and grandparents and of old age for siblings (McCarron & McCallion, in press).

In the United States, it is acknowledged that there are no mechanisms for complete counts of people with DD; reliance is only on estimates. Life expectancy for persons with DD is estimated to have increased from an average of 18.5 years in 1930 to 59.1 years in 1970 to an estimated 66.2 years in 1993 (Braddock, 1999). Based on analyses of New York State data generalized to the United States, Janicki and colleagues go further, projecting continued growth to match life expectancy of the general population (Jan-

PHILIP McCALLION

Older Adults as Caregivers to Persons With Developmental Disabilities

icki, Dalton, Henderson, & Davidson, 1999); by 2020 the number of persons with DD ages over 65 is expected to have doubled (Janicki & Dalton, 2000). There are reports of similar growth in the United Kingdom, in other European countries, and in Australia (Hogg, Lucchino, Wang, & Janicki, 2001).

For all of us, aging is a time of transitions, and although it may be compromised by ill health, successful aging may be sustained. However, it will require a different set of services and supports than was true in our younger years. This is also true for people with DD. As much as the aging of persons with DD is a credit to the sustained efforts of families, providers, communities, and professionals to improve their lives, aging also presents its own challenges. Looking at U.K. trends, Holland (2000) speculated that those who survived into old age were probably healthier and hardier than those who did not, but he expressed concern about their potential to develop additional aging-related disabilities, such as those associated with strokes, arthritis, and the consequences of chronic illness, and about the lack of preparedness of service networks to address these concerns (Holland, 2000). This is a concern echoed by Cooper (1997) and one that should also be raised for the families who are frequently continuing to provide care (McCarron & McCallion, in press).

DEMOGRAPHICS OF OLDER CAREGIVERS

For all the attention paid to out-of-home care, the majority of people with DD are cared for at home. Estimates from the United States are that 61% of persons with DD are cared for by families and that only 10% live in out-of-home placements. An additional 14% live in their own households, and 15% live with a spouse (Braddock, 1999; Fujiura, 1998). There are aging trends among the caregivers to which attention must be paid; already over 26% of family caregivers are themselves reported to be over age 60 (Braddock, 1999; Fujiura, 1998). Given demographic trends, there is every expectation that a majority of those with DD who are currently being cared for by older caregivers will themselves be over 60 by 2020, that they will likely be cared for by the same but much older caregiver, and that those currently being cared for by caregivers in their 40s and 50s will by 2020 still be cared for by these individuals, who will then be in their 60s and 70s. Finally, even when care has transferred from parents to siblings, they too are likely to be older care-

givers as the persons with DD they are caring for also age (McCallion & Kolomer, 2003).

REWARDS OF CAREGIVING

Effective social work with family caregivers of aging adults with DD requires an understanding of the experiences of those families. Social workers and other professionals face the danger of seeing caregiving families and aging only in terms of needs and deficits (McCallion & Toseland, 1993). Often this occurs because service providers may have limited contact with families, and professional staff members are only brought in when problems are being experienced (McCallion & Tobin, 1995). It is important for social workers to recognize that despite or maybe because of the demands of caring for an adult with DD, there are also rewards associated with being a caregiver. For example, older mothers caring for adults with mental retardation have been reported as having high morale and as rating their health as good or excellent (Seltzer, Greenberg, Krauss, & Hong, 1997). Also, in contrast to mothers caring for an adult child with a mental illness, mothers caring for an adult child with DD tended to report more social support, less subjective burden, and more effective coping strategies (Greenberg, Seltzer, Krauss, & Kim, 1997; Seltzer, Greenberg, & Krauss, 1995; Seltzer et al., 1997). It appears that a history of addressing DD-related concerns builds strengths and confidence in many families (Seltzer et al., 1997).

The research reported on families caring for adults with mental illnesses does suggest that, for mental illness and for care of persons with other disabilities that are not of lifelong duration, the protective effect of a lifelong caregiving experience may not be present. The differences found may also reflect that mental illness brings behaviors that are more difficult to manage and more unpredictable, increasing caregiver strain. Even with caring that has been lifelong, rewards are likely but should not be assumed. One way for social workers and other professionals to anchor their work with families, then, is to begin with an understanding of caregiving strengths by measuring the extent to which families feel in control of their caregiving situation (McCarron & McCallion, in press).

CAREGIVING STRESS

Families with members who have DD are also reported to endure stresses that other families do not experience. In a review of the available research and clinical literatures, McCallion and Toseland (1993) found that these stresses result from or are expressed in emotional strain, marital discord, sibling conflicts, difficult developmental transitions, unresponsive service delivery systems, and permanency planning concerns.

Although caregivers generally work through initial feelings of stress and strain over giving birth to and caring for a child with disabilities to a stage of adaptation and reorganization, for different members of the family this grieving can reoccur, especially when particular events—for example, increased infirmity and loss of previously learned independence in older age—remind family members of the individual's disability and the changes and sacrifices they have had to make (Ellis, 1989; Gilson & Levitas, 1987).

The presence of a child with DD has been found in some families to exacerbate both conflicts and joys and can place great stress on a marriage; this is often a major reason for caregivers requesting out-of-home placement (Sherman & Cocozza, 1984). Their own old age may be a time of retirement for one or both of the parents, that is, a time anticipated to be one of reduced responsibilities. This expected scenario may not be the case when there is an adult with DD in the home, increasing the potential for discord (McCallion & Toseland, 1993).

The needs of the person with DD may have monopolized the family's resources. Other siblings may have resented the expectation that they should spend large amounts of time caring for a sibling with a disability. These feelings and concerns may reoccur as increasing age of the parents requires that decisions be made as to whether a sibling will now assume caregiving responsibilities (Bigby, 1996).

Job loss, career changes, divorce, retirement, aging, relocation, deaths, and similar transitions in the family's life cycle can also be particularly stressful when a member with DD is present (Gilson & Levitas, 1987). In addition, if caregivers found that the people (including social workers) they turned to for help when their child with DD was born (or experienced other transitions) were unsupportive and that they had to work things through alone, they are more likely both to rely on their own resources during later transitions and to relive earlier stresses (Cook, 1990).

Families of persons with DD have often experienced service delivery systems as unresponsive, fragmented, and dehumanizing. When caregivers face difficulties in obtaining needed information and services, their relationships with professionals become an additional source of stress. That stress will reoccur when, in the older years of the family, they must reengage with professionals (McCallion & Toseland, 1993). The increasing longevity of people with DD has raised issues of permanency, futures, or long-term planning for persons with DD who outlive parents and even siblings (McCallion & Kolomer, 2003).

DIFFERENT CAREGIVERS, DIFFERENT NEEDS

Traditional caregiving of persons with DD is affected by several important trends: the dramatic increase in single-parent families and lowered birth rates, which reduce the size of caregiving networks; greater participation by women in the workforce, which increases the potential for conflict between work and caregiving responsibilities (Doty, Jackson, & Crown, 1998); and delayed childbearing by siblings and increased age of parents, together increasing the likelihood of multiple coincident caregiving demands on siblings. Caregiving demands are increasingly being placed on all available family members, and family caregivers are increasingly likely to be stressed by their multiple responsibilities (Kaye & Applegate, 1990; Sanborn & Bould, 1991; Toseland, Smith, & McCallion, 1995).

However, responsibility for the care of an adult with DD is rarely shared equally by all family members. It is primarily, but not exclusively, a female responsibility—usually that of the mother—and generally there is one primary caregiver. The identification of a primary caregiver has led many social workers to focus attention solely on this family member. However, there is increasing evidence of the importance of the additional secondary support provided by grandparents (McCallion et al., 2004); fathers (McCallion & Kolomer, 2003); siblings (Connidis, 1997), including brothers and brothers-in-law (Archer & MacLean, 1993; Harris, 1998); and by nephews and nieces (Beach, 1997). When a mother or father is no longer able or available to provide care, persons with DD generally do not have spouses or children to assume care, as do many other aging persons, so the responsibility falls to siblings, if not to out-of-home placements.

Research to date suggests that support by siblings is expressed in a variety of ways. Most often siblings provide emotional, affective support—for example, through telephone calls and visits to an adult with DD (Seltzer, Begun, Seltzer, & Krauss, 1991). Siblings are less likely to provide hands-on or instrumental care.

Indeed, parents are reported to be more likely to expect their other children to take on the role of overseer rather than hands-on care provider to their sibling (Seltzer, Begun, Magan, & Luchterhand, 1993). As social workers engage with siblings as older caregivers, therefore, the workers must be careful not to assume that the siblings will simply continue traditional family care.

Although disabilities occur in all cultural groups, persons of diverse cultures with DD and their caregivers have been found to be underrepresented among those enrolled for and receiving publicly funded services (Grant-Griffin, 1995). The cultural background of a family contributes to decisions about caregiving. Culture, that is, the values, beliefs, customs, behaviors, structures, and identity by which a group of people define themselves (Axelson, 1993), has been found to have an impact on caregiving and on the use of services, but its effects may be difficult to discern and may vary across families. One series of focus groups held with families of persons with DD and culturally based service provider organizations (McCallion, Janicki, & Grant-Griffin, 1997) offered recommendations that culture be assessed family by family if culturally competent interventions are to be initiated. The participants agreed that families often attribute conflict they experience to workers' insensitivity toward cultural concerns and to a lack of recognition of the need to build up trust sufficiently so that families feel comfortable discussing cultural and family issues with them. Some concerns offered were that workers are rarely open to family structures and ways of caring that are different from their own, that they need to avoid stereotyping family members by virtue of their gender or by society's or even their own culture's expectations, and that they must also be open to recognizing that different values and structures may mean that different services are called for. These findings emphasize the critical need for culturally competent practice in work with caregivers of persons with DD (McCallion & Grant-Griffin, 2000).

LIFE CHANGES

Reviews of studies of the self-identified needs of caregivers of persons with DD report that fears about future care when the family caregiver is no longer able to provide it was the highest rated need (Bradley, 1991; McCallion & Kolomer, 2003). Permanency, long-term, or future planning in the DD field, for both the family member with DD and the family caregiver, is related to such management-of-life transitions in later stages of life as establishing future arrangements for the person with DD in the areas of residential living, legal protection, and financial well-being (Smith & Tobin, 1989). Examples of residential-living permanency planning would be consideration of independent living; of shared households with siblings, with other relatives, or with family friends; and of transitions into supervised apartments, adult foster care, or group-home programs. Legal protection issues include consideration of legal guardianship and conservatorship of person and property issues, including the drafting of wills and other documents. Financial issues include developing arrangements that will ensure continued financial eligibility for needed services for the person with DD while providing for a safety net of resources if those services are not available or are insufficient (McCallion, 1993).

Developing a future-care plan requires effort and collaboration by workers from many disciplines. Social workers play a key role in ensuring that recommendations for care are consistent with the need for a plan, that they merge in a joint rather than a discipline-specific approach, and that they help engage and support families and the person with DD through a difficult process. Despite the potential for traumatic transitions on the death of a caregiver, parents and other aging caregivers are often averse to creating detailed future care plans for their adult children with DD, and many do not involve the person with DD himself or herself in such planning (Heller & Factor, 1991; McCallion & Tobin, 1995). Stress, concerns for safety, and anxiety all contribute to caregivers' reluctance to make concrete plans, and their concern about how the person with DD will feel and his or her ability to understand is used to justify not involving the person with DD in any planning that does occur (Bigby, 1996, 1997; Freedman, Krauss, & Seltzer, 1997). For example, Heller and Factor (1991) found that almost 75% of family care providers for persons over 30 years of age with DD did not make future living arrangements for their family member. Often, too, there is a reluctance to speak of future living arrangements with other family members. Therefore, the expectations that other family members will assume care responsibilities were often implied rather than formally documented (Bigby, 1996). This is the reality, then, in which social workers must address future planning.

However, families who successfully utilize respite and other services have been found to be more likely to consider residential placement (Caldwell & Heller, 2003). Therefore, one role for social workers may be to encourage and facilitate such related service use. Key services for social workers to be familiar with include: in-home respite care, out-of-home respite or vacation programs, home health aide services, transportation assistance, and day and recreation/leisure programs.

Several manualized approaches to future planning are available that social workers may access for more information and as a basis for developing formal programs:

- The Family Futures Planning Project offers a 10-session curriculum addressing housing options, estate planning, home and community-based services, and caregivers' emotional, physical, and recreational health.
- The Planned Lifetime Advocacy Network (PLAN) offers a six-step approach to guide the development of a personal future plan: clarifying the vision, building relationships, controlling the home environment, preparing for decision making, developing wills and estate plans, and deciding steps to secure the plan.
- In the Family-to-Family Project, family support centers offer presentations on financial arrangements and wills, home ownership and consumer-controlled housing, and developing circles of support. A resource manual is available with information concerning funding sources, housing options, and legal issues (translated into several different languages) and suggestions on outreach to hard-to-reach families.
- The RRTC Family Future Planning Project uses paid facilitators and mentor families to provide information on available supports to both the family caregivers and the person with DD so that they can make informed choices. Information on all these programs, including references and contact information, are summarized in Heller (2000).

GRIEF, BEREAVEMENT, AND FAMILY CAREGIVERS

The increasing age of persons with DD and of their caregivers increases the likelihood of losing family members and other support. Some authors argue that families have been in a perpetual state of bereavement since the birth of an individual with DD (for a discussion, see Todd, 2002). Others suggest that, as the

person with DD ages, many families gain strength and are well adjusted (see, for example, Seltzer et al., 1997). It may be, however, that family members reexperience past senses of loss at major life transitions, such as the death of caregivers (McCallion & Toseland, 1993). Regardless, in work with families, social workers must recognize that there will often be considerable sensitivities and that many family members will resist informing the persons with DD about a death, particularly that of a caregiving parent.

There is both a long-standing belief that persons with DD do not experience the range of emotions that others do—including feelings of grief at the loss of family members and close friends or neighbors—and, conversely, the concern that they will not be able to "handle" the associated feelings (Yanok & Beifus, 1993). These beliefs and concerns are often used by family members to justify not informing persons with DD of the death of parents and for not involving them in funerals and other death and mourning rituals. Yet as they age persons with DD are likely to experience losses through death. The implications of such losses may be greater for persons with DD, as the loss may also mean they will have to move to a sibling's home or to an out-of-home placement (McHale & Carey, 2002). Furthermore, if they have not experienced death and mourning, they will be poorly prepared to understand death and for their own deaths (Clegg & Lansdall-Welfare, 2003).

Although death and bereavement have been poorly researched (Todd, 2002), there is evidence that persons with DD do indeed understand the finality of death and that they have often formed bonds with family members and others such that they feel personal loss and grief. What they do not often have experience in is how to express that grief (Yanok & Beifus, 1993).

Yet grief does surface. Symptoms of normal grief, as defined in the *International Classification of Diseases* (ICD-10), usually occur within 1 month of the bereavement and do not exceed 6 months' duration. For persons with DD, later onset and longer duration of grief symptoms are more likely (for a review of the research literature, see McCarron & McCallion, in press). Also, grief reactions in persons with DD are often manifested in behavioral difficulties. These are more likely to be viewed by family members and others as psychosocial concerns than as the expression of grief (Hollins & Esterhuyzen, 1997; McHale & Carey, 2002).

In many ways, too, the point at which the primary caregiver or another significant family member dies is too late to be addressing issues of death and bereavement. Yanok and Beifus (1993) argue that, to help a person with DD understand death and the appropriate expression of grief, he or she should be prepared in advance. Such preparation may involve visiting funeral homes, cemeteries, and churches; helping the person to understand community standards regarding the expression of grief in public places; and teaching the person that death is inevitable and irreversible, as well as pertinent vocabulary words. Fauri and Grimes (1994) argue that, when possible, the person with DD should be prepared for death rather than simply left to react to it. An important role, then, for social workers is helping older caregivers develop an openness to dealing with grief and bereavement issues.

A number of formal programs offer suggested approaches and resource materials (see, for example, Blackman, 2002, Botsford, 2000; Cathcart, 1995; James, 1995). Also, the Scottish Down Syndrome Society offers booklets on explaining death and on dementia for persons with DD (available at *www.dsscotland.org.uk*).

CONCLUSIONS

Older family caregivers continue to provide the majority of care and support for community participation for persons with DD. They deserve the support of social workers in their own right, and the sustaining of family caregiving is an important societal outcome for social work services. This chapter has outlined critical issues involved in working with persons with DD and their aging families, with particular emphasis on those issues most likely to affect and involve social workers. The number of adults with DD is expected to grow further. Family caregivers are also likely to be older, and family care will most probably involve multiple supporters rather than traditional primary caregivers working alone, thus challenging preset notions about caregiving support. Also, social workers who previously saw themselves as working with children or young adults or focused on specific care populations such as the mentally ill or the elderly will find that older caregiver issues and the needs of persons with DD will be increasingly a feature of the families, clients, and systems they work with. For many social workers (and other professionals), this will be a cultural shift and may require that they renew their training to be effective. Future planning

and grief and bereavement are two areas that social workers must be equipped to address.

REFERENCES

Archer, C., & MacLean, M. (1993). Husbands and sons as caregivers of chronically ill women. *Journal of Gerontological Social Work, 21*(1/2), 5–23.

Axelson, J. A. (1993). *Counseling and development in a multicultural society* (2nd ed.). Pacific Grove, CA: Brooks/Cole Publishing Co.

Beach, D. (1997). Family caregiving: The positive impact on adolescent relationships. *Gerontologist, 37,* 233–238.

Bigby, C. (1996). Transferring responsibility: The nature and effectiveness of parental planning for the future of adults with intellectual disability who remain at home until mid-life. *Australian Society for the Study of Intellectual Disability, 21*(4), 295–312.

Bigby, C. (1997). Parental substitutes? The role of siblings in the lives of older people with intellectual disability. *Journal of Gerontological Social Work, 29*(1), 3–21.

Blackman, N. (2002). Grief and intellectual disability: A systemic approach. *Journal of Gerontological Social Work, 38*(1/2), 253–263.

Botsford, A. (2000). Integrating end of life care into services for people with an intellectual disability. *Social Work in Health Care, 31*(1), 35–48.

Braddock, D. (1999). Aging and developmental disabilities: Demographic and policy issues affecting American families. *Mental Retardation, 37,* 155–161.

Braddock, D., Emerson, E., Felce, D., & Stanliffe, R. J. (2001). Living with circumstances of children and adults with mental retardation and developmental disabilities in the United States, Canada, England, and Wales. *Mental Retardation and Developmental Disabilities Research Reviews, 7*(2), 115–121.

Bradley, V. (1991). AAMR testifies on family support. *AAMR News and Notes, 4*(4), 1,5.

Caldwell, J., & Heller, T. (2003). Management of respite and personal assistance services in a consumer-directed family support programme. *Journal of Intellectual Disability Research, 47*(4–5), 352–367.

Cathcart, C. (1995). Death and people with learning disabilities: Interventions to support clients and carers. *British Journal of Clinical Psychology, 34*(2), 165–175.

Clegg, J., & Lansdall-Welfare, R. (2003). Death, disability and dogma. *Philosophy, Psychiatry, and Psychology, 10*(1), 67–79.

Connidis, I. (1997). Sibling support in older age. *Journals of Gerontology, Series B: 49*(6), S309–317.

Cook, R. S. (1990). *Counseling families of children with disabilities.* Dallas: Word.

Cooper, S. A. (1997). Epidemiology of psychiatric disorders in elderly compared to younger adults with learning disabilities. *British Journal of Psychiatry, 170,* 375–380.

Doty, P., Jackson, M., & Crown, W. (1998). The impact of female caregivers' employment status on patterns of formal and informal elder care. *Gerontologist, 38*(3), 331–335.

Ellis, J. B. (1989). Grieving for the loss of the perfect child. *Child and Adolescent Social Work, 6,* 259–269.

Fauri, D. P., & Grimes, D. R. (1994). Bereavement services for families and peers of deceased residents of psychiatric institutions. *Social Work, 39*(2), 185–190.

Freedman, R. I., Krauss, M. W., & Seltzer, M. M. (1997) Aging parents' residential plans for adult children with mental retardation. *Mental Retardation, 35*(2), 114–123.

Fujiura, G. T. (1998). Demography of family households. *American Journal of Mental Retardation, 103,* 225–235.

Gilson, S. E., & Levitas, A. S. (1987). Psychological crisis in the lives of mentally retarded people. *Psychiatric Aspects of Mental Retardation, 6*(6), 27–31.

Grant-Griffin, L. (1995). *Best practices: Outreach strategies in multicultural communities.* Albany: New York State Office of Mental Retardation and Developmental Disabilities.

Greenberg, J. S., Seltzer, M. M., Krauss, M. W., & Kim, H. (1997). The differential effects of social support on the psychological well-being of aging mothers of adults with mental illness or mental retardation. *Family Relations, 46,* 383–394.

Harris, P. B. (1998). Listening to caregiving sons: Misunderstood realities. *Gerontologist, 38*(3), 342–352.

Heller, T. (2000, March). *Assisting older family caregivers of adults with intellectual disabilities.* Paper presented at the 12th IASSID Aging and Intellectual Disabilities Roundtable, Osaka, Japan.

Heller, T., & Factor, A. (1991). Permanency planning for adults with mental retardation living with family caregivers. *American Journal on Mental Retardation, 96,* 163–176.

Hogg, J., Lucchino, R., Wang, K., & Janicki, M. P. (2001). Healthy aging: Adults with intellectual disabilities: Ageing and social policy. *Journal of Applied Research in Intellectual Disabilities, 14*(3), 229–235.

Holland, A. J. (2000). Ageing and learning disability. *British Journal of Psychiatry, 176,* 26–31.

Hollins, S., & Esterhuyzen, A. (1997). Bereavement and grief in adults with learning disabilities. *British Journal Psychiatry, 170,* 497–501.

James, I. A. (1995). Helping people with learning disability to cope with bereavement. *Mental Handicap, 23,* 74–78.

Janicki, M. P., & Dalton, A. J. (2000). Prevalence of dementia and impact on intellectual disability services. *Mental Retardation, 38,* 277–289.

Janicki, M. P., Dalton, A. J., Henderson, C. M., & Davidson, P. W. (1999). Mortality and morbidity among older adults with intellectual disability: Health services considerations. *Disability and Rehabilitation, 21*(5/6), 284–294.

Kaye, L. W., & Applegate, J. S. (1990). Men as elder caregivers: A response to changing families. *American Journal of Orthopsychiatry, 60,* 86–95.

Ludlow, B. L. (2002). Life after loss: Legal, ethical and practical issues. In S. S. Herr & G. Weber (Eds.), *Aging, rights and quality of life* (pp. 189–222). Baltimore: Brookes.

McCallion, P. (1993). *Social worker orientations to permanency planning with older parents caring at home for family members with developmental disabilities.* Unpublished doctoral dissertation, State University of New York, Albany.

McCallion, P., & Grant-Griffin, L. (2000). Redesigning services to meet the needs of multi-cultural families. In M. P. Janicki, & E. Ansello (Eds.), *Community supports for older adults with lifelong disabilities* (pp. 97–108). Baltimore: Brookes.

McCallion, P., Janicki, M. P., & Grant-Griffin, L. (1997). Exploring the impact of culture and acculturation on older families caregiving for persons with developmental disabilities. *Family Relations, 46,* 347–357.

McCallion, P., Janicki, M. P., & Kolomer, S. R. (2004). Controlled evaluation of support groups for grandparent caregivers of children with developmental disabilities and delays. *American Journal on Mental Retardation, 109*(4), 352–361.

McCallion, P., & Kolomer, S. R. (2003). Aging persons with developmental disabilities and their aging caregivers. In B. Berkman & L Harootyan (Eds.), *Social work and health care in an aging world* (pp. 201–225). New York: Springer.

McCallion, P., & Tobin, S. (1995). Social worker orientations to permanency planning by older parents caring at home for sons and daughters with developmental disabilities. *Mental Retardation, 33*(3), 153–162.

McCallion, P., & Toseland, R. W. (1993). An empowered model for social work services to families of adolescents and adults with developmental disabilities. *Families in Society, 74,* 579–589.

McCarron, M., & McCallion, P. (in press). Supporting families who have aging members with disabilities. In P. N. Walsh, A. Carr, G. O'Reilly, & J. McEvoy (Eds.), *Handbook of intellectual disability and clinical psychology practice.* London: Routledge.

McHale, R., & Carey, S. (2002). An investigation of the effects of bereavement on mental health and challenging behaviour in adults with learning disability. *British Journal of Learning Disabilities, 30,* 113–117.

Sanborn, B., & Bould, S. (1991). Intergenerational caregivers of the oldest old. In S. K. Pfiefer & M. B. Sussman (Eds.), *Families: Intergenerational and generational connections* (pp. 125–142). Binghamton, NY: Haworth.

Seltzer, G., Begun, A., Magan, R., & Luchterhand, C. (1993). Social supports and expectations of family involvement after out-of-home placement. In E. Hutton, T. Heller, A. Factor, B. Seltzer, & G. Hawkins (Eds.), *Older adults with developmental disabilities* (pp. 123–140). Baltimore: Brookes.

Seltzer, G., Begun, A., Seltzer, M. M., & Krauss, M. W. (1991). The impacts of siblings on adults with mental retardation and their aging mothers. *Family Relations, 40,* 310–317.

Seltzer, M. M., Greenberg, J. S., & Krauss, M. W. (1995). A comparison of coping strategies of aging mothers of adults with mental illness or mental retardation. *Psychology and Aging, 10,* 64–75.

Seltzer, M. M., Greenberg, J. S., Krauss, M. W., & Hong, J. (1997). Predictors and outcomes of the end of co-resident caregiving in aging families of adults with mental retardation or mental illness. *Family Relations, 46,* 13–22.

Seltzer, M. M., & Krauss, M. W. (1994). Aging parents with coresident adult children: The impact of lifelong caregiving. In M. M. Seltzer, M. W. Krauss, & M. P. Janicki (Eds.), *Lifecourse perspectives on adulthood and old age* (pp. 3–18). Washington, DC: American Association on Mental Retardation.

Sherman, B. R., & Cocozza, J. J. (1984). Stress in the families of the developmentally disabled: A literature review of factors affecting the decision to seek out of home placements. *Family Relations, 33,* 95–103.

Smith, G. C., & Tobin, S. S. (1989). Permanency planning among older parents of adults with lifelong disabilities. *Journal of Gerontological Social Work, 14,* 35–39.

Todd, S. (2002). Death does not become us: The absence of death and dying in intellectual disability research. *Journal of Gerontological Social Work, 38*(1/2), 225–240.

Toseland, R., Smith, G., & McCallion, P. (1995). Supporting the family in elder care. In G. Smith, S. Tobin, E. Robertson-Tchabo, & P. Power (Eds.)., *Strengthening aging families: Diversity in practice and policy* (pp. 3–24). Newbury Park, CA: Sage.

Yanok, J., & Beifus, J. A. (1993). Communicating about loss and mourning: Death education for individuals with mental retardation. *Mental Retardation, 31*(3), 144–147.

SANDRA MAGAÑA

Older Latino Family Caregivers

31

Aging family caregivers face unique challenges. These challenges include managing the demands of taking care of someone with a disability at a time in their lives when their own health care needs, responsibilities, roles, and abilities are changing. How these caregivers cope with and adapt to the caregiving process may depend on the caregiving context, including the relationship the caregiver has to the person with the disability, the type of disability the person being cared for has, socioeconomic status (SES), and the ethnicity and cultural characteristics of the family.

It is particularly important and timely to examine aging Latino family caregivers and the racial, ethnic, and cultural context that they provide. The reason is not only that Latinos have become the largest minority group in the United States (Cohn, 2003) but also that Latino families, and especially women, are very likely to be intimately involved with caring for family members who have disabilities across the life span. Many Latino caregivers are faced with challenges associated with low SES, such as poor housing, poor health, and limited access to health insurance and resources. In addition, although "Latinos" come from different countries of origin, with distinct political histories, practices, and customs, some evidence shows that cultural values and practices related to the family may provide a common experience for many Latino caregivers.

Other aspects of the caregiving context that are important to explore among Latino caregivers involve persons who care for family members with different types of disabilities and those who have different relationships to the care recipient. Although these caregivers may have much in common with each other, to what extent do these contexts lead to different adaptations? Caregivers who are parents or relatives of adults with mental disabilities, spouses or children of persons with dementia or Alzheimer's, and grandparent caregivers of children with disabilities all have distinct and similar caregiving challenges. Those caring for adult children with developmental disabilities have been providing care for a disability that has been manifested since childhood, whereas parents caring for an adult child with mental illness are faced with a later and unexpected onset of mental illness. Caregivers who are spouses or children of persons with dementia, Alzheimer's, and other aging-related disabilities are similar to the mental illness caregivers in that they are faced with a more recent and often more intense caregiving challenge, but the relationship to the caregiving recipient is distinctly different. On the other hand, grandparents who are caring for grandchildren are often left to care for young children because the parent, for whatever reason, is unable to meet this challenge. They are different from the other caregivers and also deal with different systems, services, and needs related to children.

The terms *Latino* and *Hispanic* are often used interchangeably as a panethnic label. However, different Latino/Hispanic groups and individuals often prefer one term to the other. For the purposes of this chapter, I use the term *Latino* in general discussions, but when referring to specific studies, I use the terms chosen by the authors of those studies.

Based on the literature about Latino caregivers in these different caregiving contexts, five themes are addressed in this chapter:

1. The well-being of the Latino caregiver
2. Stress and coping among Latino caregivers
3. Family social support and the cultural value of familism
4. Service utilization by caregivers and their family members
5. Interventions with Latino caregivers

The majority of studies of Latino caregivers are of those who are caring for older adults with dementia and Alzheimer's disease. However, studies of older caregivers of persons with mental illness, developmental disabilities, and grandchildren are emerging and are included in this chapter. Because most studies refer to the primary caregiver, we first must explore who primary caregivers are in Latino families.

WHO ARE THE PRIMARY CAREGIVERS IN LATINO FAMILIES?

Similar to non-Latino caregivers, Latino primary caregivers are predominantly women. Studies of caregivers of persons with mental retardation have focused on mothers who tend to be the main caregiver (Magaña, Seltzer, Krauss, Rubert, & Szapocznik, 2002). With respect to family caregivers of persons with mental illness, mothers accounted for most of the primary caregivers, but sisters, spouses, and adult children were also primary caregivers in many cases (Milstein, Guarnaccia, & Midlarsky, 1995; Saldaña, Dassori, & Miller, 1999; Stueve, Vine, & Struening, 1997). In research on caregivers of persons with dementia and Alzheimer's disease, between 74 and 94% of the caregivers are women, with the largest proportion being daughters, and then spouses (Aranda,

Villa, Trejo, Ramirez, & Ranney, 2003; Cox & Monk, 1996; Gallagher-Thompson, Arean, Rivera, & Thompson, 2001; Ho, Weitzman, Cui, & Levkoff, 2000; Morano, 2003; Ranney & Aranda, 2001). A study of Latino grandparent caregivers found that more than 90% of grandparent caregivers are grandmothers (Burnette, 1999a).

Many of the Latino caregivers tend to be younger than caregivers in other ethnic groups, with study averages ranging from 48 to 70 years old (Cox & Monk, 1996; Guarnaccia & Parra, 1996; Ho et al., 2000; Magaña, Seltzer, & Krauss, 2004; Morano, 2003). This finding is partially due to the greater likelihood that middle-aged daughters are caregivers for Latinos with Alzheimer's and dementia. For Latinos with mental illness, many middle-aged sisters, spouses, and adult children provide care. Additionally, Latinos are more likely to be parents and grandparents at earlier ages than the non-Latino population.

With respect to SES, ethnicity matters. Studies of Cuban American caregivers find that they have similar levels of education and income to non-Latino White caregivers (Harwood et al., 2000; Morano, 2003), whereas studies that have included Mexican Americans, Puerto Ricans, Central Americans, and Dominicans show that they have significantly lower levels of income and education in comparison with either Cuban Americans or non-Latino Whites (Aranda et al., 2003; Burnette, 1999a; Ho et al., 2000; Magaña et al., 2002; Ranney & Aranda, 2001). The latter studies report that the majority of their Latino participants have less than a high school education.

Many studies that include Latino caregivers do not report language preference, immigrant status, or acculturation level. Five studies that reported whether caregivers were immigrants or born in the United States showed a range of 53 to 100% who reported having been born in a Latin American country (Aranda et al., 2003; Burnette, 1999a; Gallagher-Thompson et al., 2001; Magaña et al., 2004; Milstein et al., 1995; Ranney & Aranda, 2001). Six studies that reported language of preference of caregivers reported a range of 34 to 98% who preferred Spanish, with an average of 64% across the six studies (Aranda et al., 2003; Burnette, 1999a; Gallagher-Thompson et al., 2001; Magaña et al., 2004; Milstein et al., 1995).

In summary, Latino primary caregivers are more likely to be women across all caregiving contexts (similar to the general caregiving population). Latino caregivers of persons with dementia and Alzheimer's disease are most often daughters, and then spouses, and Latino caregivers of adults with mental and developmental disabilities are most often mothers, but sometimes siblings and spouses. Latino caregivers tend to be younger than caregivers from other ethnicities. They tend to have lower income and education than non-Latino White caregivers (with the exception of Cuban Americans). Finally, more than half of Latino caregivers (in studies that report this information) are primarily Spanish speaking and born in Latin American countries.

CAREGIVER WELL-BEING

Across all caregiving contexts and Latino ethnicities, research on aging Latino caregivers show that they suffer from high rates of depressive symptoms. This has been found for Mexican American caregivers of persons with dementia (Adams, Aranda, Kemp, Takagi, 2002; Ranney & Aranda, 2001), for Puerto Rican and Cuban American mothers of adults with mental retardation (Magaña et al., 2002), for family caregivers of persons with mental illness (Struening et al., 1995), and for grandparents caring for grandchildren with disabilities (Burnette, 2000).

Furthermore, compared with other groups, Latino caregivers appear to have higher rates of depression or distress. A study that compared well-being of spousal caregivers of persons with dementia from four ethnic groups (Mexican Americans, non-Latino Whites, African Americans, and Japanese Americans) found that the Mexican American caregivers were significantly more depressed and displayed more psychiatric distress than non-Latino White and African American caregivers (Adams et al., 2002). Although the mean number of depressive symptoms was higher for the Mexican American caregivers than for the Japanese American caregivers, this difference was not significant (Adams et al., 2002). Magaña et al. (2004) found that, compared with non-Latina White caregivers of adults with mental retardation, Puerto Rican caregivers reported significantly more depressive symptoms. A study of Hispanic and African American caregivers of persons with Alzheimer's disease found that Hispanic caregivers had significantly more personal and role strains than African American caregivers (Cox & Monk, 1996).

Findings are mixed regarding whether Cuban American caregivers exhibit more depressive symptoms than non-Latino Whites. In a recent study that included a fairly large sample of primarily Cuban Americans ($N = 184$), Harwood et al. (1998) found that the Cuban Americans were more depressed than non-Hispanic Whites, whereas a study with a smaller sample of Cuban American daughter caregivers ($N = 13$) found that there were no differences in depressive symptoms between Cuban American and non-Hispanic White caregivers (Mintzer et al., 1992). However, given the small sample size of the latter study, it may have been underpowered. Studies also show that Latino caregivers tend to be in poor health compared with other groups (Adams et al., 2002; Aranda et al., 2003; Magaña, et al., 2004).

Only one study examined whether poor psychological well-being among Latino caregivers might be a function of caring for a person with a disability. Burnette (2000) compared grandparents who care for a grandchild with special needs with those who care for grandchildren without special needs and found that those who are caring for grandchildren with special needs had significantly more depressive symptoms. Because distress may be expressed differently across different ethnic groups, more studies are needed that compare caregivers with noncaregivers within the same ethnic group.

Whether cultural or other environmental factors interact with caregiving and lead to higher depressive symptoms among Latinos or whether high rates of depression are the result of some combination of cultural and environmental factors independent of caregiving is a question that needs further exploration. Magaña et al. (2004) found that, although differences in health status explained most of the differences in depression between Puerto Rican and non-Latino White caregivers of adults with mental retardation, an interaction between family problems and ethnicity explained some of the additional variance. Although the presence of more family problems predicted higher depression for both groups, the relationship was significantly stronger for Puerto Rican mothers than for non-Latino Whites. This finding suggests a cultural and environmental explanation: that a greater number of family problems brought about by the caregiving situation affect Latina mothers more than they do non-Latino Whites, possibly due to the cultural value of familism and a more collectivist mindset. Familism includes strong feelings of loyalty, reciprocity, and solidarity among family members (Marín & Marín, 1991). Collectivist cultures emphasize the needs of the group over the needs of the individual (Marín & Marín, 1991). The collectivist nature of familism implies that individuals who are from a familistic culture may be more likely to consider the well-being of the family before considering their own well-being. The combination of this cultural factor and the poor health of the caregivers (which is highly related to low SES) compound the negative impact on emotional well-being. Other factors that could help explain ethnic differences in depression are the cumulative effects of environmental stressors that so many Latino caregivers face, particularly those who are immigrants. Immigrants face not only problems associated with poverty and low education but also many challenges dealing with immigrant status, language barriers, and lack of knowledge about North American service systems and culture.

To summarize this section on caregiver well-being, an important finding is that many Latino caregivers are at risk for depression across different caregiving contexts and Latino ethnicities. Additionally, Latino caregivers tend to show higher rates of distress than other ethnic groups. More research is needed to determine why. Because poor health is frequently reported for Latino caregivers, more research is needed on physical health as an outcome. Studies are needed that compare the health and well-being of Latino caregivers to those of noncaregivers in order to understand the impact that caregiving has on well-being.

STRESS AND COPING

Many studies on caregiving use stress process models, which examine the impact of environmental, caregiving, and cognitive factors on caregiver stress and which often include appraisals of stress, coping strategies, and resources that may mediate or moderate the effects of caregiving on the caregiver's well-being (Lawton, Kleban, Moss, Rovine, & Glicksman, 1989; Pearlin, Mullan, Semple, & Skaff, 1990). A few studies of Latino caregivers have used a stress-and-coping framework in their analyses (Adams et al., 2002; Cox & Monk, 1993; Cox & Monk, 1996; Magaña et al., 2004; Morano, 2003; Ranney & Aranda, 2001). However, even fewer studies have actually tested for mediation or moderation in their analyses (Magaña et al., 2004; Morano, 2003). Mediation refers to a factor or variable that helps to explain the pathway by which another factor affects the outcome. For example, if we were to say that more maladaptive behaviors of the person being cared for lead to depression in caregivers, we might wish to explain the mechanisms by which this happens. High levels of maladaptive behaviors might lead to an appraisal by the caregiver that he or she is very burdened, which would then lead to depression. We would say that the appraisal of

burden is a mediator between maladaptive behaviors and depression. Moderation often refers to a buffering or protective effect that a factor or variable might have. For example, if caregivers who are caring for someone with high levels of maladaptive behaviors also have high levels of social support, they might be expected to be less depressed than caregivers caring for someone with equally high levels of maladaptive behaviors who have low levels of social support. Social support would be considered a moderator of stress in this instance. Another way in which moderation can be conceptualized is as a variable that, when present at certain levels, actually exacerbates stress. Finally, moderation can also be used to test differences in the relationship of two variables for two groups of caregivers. For example, to test whether two racial or ethnic groups differ on the relationship of social support and depression, a moderation model can be used.

Magaña et al. (2004) hypothesized that family problems that result from caring for a son or daughter with mental retardation would function as a mediator in the caregiving process. They found, consistent with their hypothesis, that family problems mediated the effects of maladaptive behaviors on depression for Puerto Rican and non-Latino White maternal caregivers. This finding suggests that more maladaptive behaviors may lead to more problems in the family, which is then related to higher rates of maternal depression. They further found that there were no ethnic differences in this mediation pattern; however, as reported earlier, family problems were more strongly related to depression for the Puerto Rican mothers than for non-Latino White mothers (Magaña et al., 2004).

Morano (2003) examined appraisals of burden and satisfaction with caregiving and coping styles (e.g., emotion and problem-focused coping) as potential mediators or moderators of stress for Hispanic (primarily Cuban American) and non-Hispanic White caregivers. He found that for the pooled sample, appraisals of burden mediated the effects of caregiving stress on somatic complaints and burden, whereas appraisals of satisfaction moderated the effects of caregiving stress on personal gain and life satisfaction. This suggests a buffering effect in which the relationship of stress on outcomes was reduced for those with high levels of caregiver satisfaction. Research suggests that the presence of high levels of emotion-focused coping might exacerbate stress (Fingerman, Gallagher-Thompson, Lovett, & Rose, 1996; Lutzky & Knight, 1994). However, Morano

(2003) found that emotion-focused coping moderated caregiving effects on depression and life satisfaction in the opposite direction suggesting a buffering effect. Higher levels of emotion-focused coping reduced the relationship between stress and depression and stress and life satisfaction. Morano (2003) did not find mediating or moderating effects for problem-focused coping. Morano (2003) did not test for ethnic differences in the relationship of coping and appraisals to outcomes, so it is difficult to say whether non-Hispanic White and Hispanic caregivers in this study show the same patterns of stress and coping. Adams et al. (2002) found differential use of coping styles between Mexican Americans and other ethnic groups: Mexican American spousal caregivers of persons with dementia were more likely to use escape-avoidance coping than non-Latino White or African American spousal caregivers (Adams et al., 2002). The mediating or moderating effects of escape-avoidance coping were not examined in this study.

Other studies have examined aspects of a stress-coping framework, such as specific stressors, coping strategies and styles, and resources. In addition to coping styles, Adams et al. (2002) examined ethnic differences in different aspects of appraisal and found that Mexican Americans were more likely than non-Latino Whites to show positive appraisal and more likely than non-Latino Whites and African Americans to show pessimistic appraisal. This finding suggests that for Mexican Americans, positive and pessimistic appraisals are not necessarily on opposite poles from one another but represent different constructs. Mexican American caregivers also scored higher on spiritual appraisal than non-Latino White and Japanese American caregivers.

Spirituality has been found to be an important resource for Latino caregivers (Calderón & Tennstedt, 1998; Magilvy, Congdon, Martinez, Davis, & Averill, 2000; Milstein et al., 1995; Stueve et al., 1997; Thompson et al., 2002). Calderón and Tennstedt (1998) reported that Puerto Rican caregivers coped with the burden of caregiving by leaving the outcome in God's hands. Milstein et al. (1995) found that Hispanic caregivers of relatives with mental illness often had hope for a cure, which was linked to their faith in God. Magilvy et al. (2000) identified spirituality as a major theme with respect to health and healing in an ethnographic study of rural Hispanic elders and their caregivers. Stueve et al. (1997) found that Hispanic caregivers of relatives with mental illness were more likely than White caregivers to perceive religion as important in their lives. In a study of pleasureable activities and mood among dementia caregivers, Thompson et al. (2002) found that Latina caregivers reported obtaining more pleasure from spiritual activities than non-Latina White caregivers. Similarly, a representative study of informal caregivers (Navaie-Waliser et al., 2001) found that Hispanic caregivers were more likely to have experienced increased religiosity since becoming caregivers than non-Hispanic White caregivers.

To summarize this section on stress and coping, religion and spirituality has been found to be an important support factor for Latino caregivers. Some evidence suggests that coping strategies may manifest differently for Latinos than for other groups. The relationship between positive appraisal and burden needs to be explored, as they seem to coexist simultaneously for many caregivers. More research is needed that explores how coping styles and resources mediate or moderate stress and how these relationships are similar to or different from those of other groups. Finally, family variables as key constructs in stress and coping models need to be explored further for Latino caregivers.

SOCIAL SUPPORT AND THE FAMILY

The Latino family has been identified as central in social science literature on Latinos and is sometimes referred to in the context of the cultural value of familism (Aranda & Knight, 1997; Keefe, Padilla, & Carlos, 1979), which was briefly defined earlier. Behaviorally, familism is manifested through three mechanisms, each of which is reviewed in this chapter: support provided by the family, the individual's obligations to the family, and the use of relatives as referents (Sabogal et al., 1987). In the caregiving context, one might expect that support from the family for the caregiver and care recipient would be an important protective resource. Regarding obligations to the family, the obligation to care for a family member preferably in the home may be considered a cultural preference among Latinos. For many Latinas, the role of the caregiver as a cultural obligation becomes a primary role, which may conflict with other roles women play in modern U.S. society; but at the same time it may provide purpose and meaning to caregivers. Another aspect of familism, family members as referents, may be manifested by caregivers consulting with family members for advice on the care provided. This aspect of familism touches on the underlying value of collectivism, in which the good of the entire family is considered, not just the good of the individual. In this context, the caregiver's perceptions of her or his own well-being may be based partially on the well-being of the family. If other family members' needs are being ignored because of the caregiver's required attention to the care recipient, or if the family is in conflict over some aspects of the caregiving process, the caregiver's own well-being may be jeopardized.

With respect to the first aspect of familism, support from the family for the caregiver or care recipient, some research has examined the extent to which other family members provide direct help in caregiving. In her study of Puerto Rican mothers of adults with mental retardation, Magaña (1999) found that, although the mother performed most of the caregiving tasks, a range of different family members also helped with these tasks, including siblings, fathers, cousins, nieces, and nephews. Similarly, in a qualitative study of caregivers across three ethnic groups, Calderón & Tennstedt (1998) found that the majority of Puerto Rican caregivers had other family members who helped with different caregiving tasks.

Other research has examined social support networks of Latinos and how they compare with other ethnic groups. Studies that compare Latino older adults with non-Latino White older adults report that the Latinos rely more on informal helpers and support than the non-Latino Whites (Mui & Burnette, 1994; Tennstedt & Chang, 1998). In her study of grandparent caregivers, Burnette (1999b) found that many of these older adults had large family networks and other adult family members who helped them in raising their grandchildren. In their study of caregivers of relatives with mental illness, Guarnaccia and Parra (1996) found that Hispanic caregivers had larger social support networks than African American and non-Hispanic White caregivers in the study. However, a similar study of family caregivers of persons with mental illness found comparable levels of support from informal networks across the same three ethnic groups (Stueve et al., 1997), and a study of African American and Hispanic caregivers of dementia patients found similar levels of social support between these two groups (Cox & Monk, 1996). A study of spousal caregivers found that Mexican American, Japanese American, and European American caregivers had similar levels of social support, whereas African American caregivers had higher levels (Adams et al., 2002). These researchers theorized that because the Mexican American caregivers had lower service utilization rates than other groups, those that come to the attention of service providers may be those who have exhausted or have received minimal support from their social networks (Adams et al., 2002). Similarly, Mexican American caregivers of older adults reported having smaller social networks and using less of their social networks than non-Hispanic White caregivers (Phillips, Torres de Ardon, Komnenich, Killeen, & Rusinak, 2000). The authors theorized that because the Mexican American caregivers were more likely to be recent immigrants, fewer of their family members resided in proximity to them (Phillips et al., 2000).

How family and social support networks relate to caregiver well-being has been the focus of other studies. In the study of Puerto Rican mothers of adults with mental retardation, Magaña (1999) found that close to 90% of the mothers' social support networks were made up of family members and that larger networks and greater satisfaction with the network were related to lower depression among these mothers. Polich & Gallagher-Thompson (1997) similarly found that dissatisfaction with family support was related to higher depression among Hispanic caregivers of relatives with cognitive impairments. However, this was found only among bicultural caregivers, not caregivers who adhered to more traditional Hispanic culture. Cox and Monk (1996) found that the frequency of speaking with and seeking social support from relatives and friends was related to lower role strain among caregivers of relatives with dementia.

With respect to the second aspect of familism, obligation to the family, some research has focused on the commitment to caregiving among Latino caregivers. Calderón & Tennstedt (1998) found that the Puerto Rican women caregivers in their qualitative study felt a strong sense of responsibility and had a tendency to be self-sacrificing, fulfilling a cultural expectation for women. In a qualitative study of rural Hispanic elders and their caregivers, Magilvy et al. (2000) reported that one of the statements heard most frequently was "we take care of our own." These researchers reported that the importance of family and obligation was evident in interviews, observations, and photographic data (Magilvy et al., 2000). In her study of grandparent caregivers, Burnette (1999b) reported that many of the grandparents sacrificed their own well-being to care for family members over the course of their lives. Whether or not the care recipient lives with the caregiver can also be seen as an indication of obligation to caregiving. Some research has found that in comparison with non-Latino Whites, Latino caregivers are more likely to live with the care recipient (Ho et al., 2000; Mintzer, Rubert, & Herman, 1994). Interestingly, one study found that more non-Hispanic whites caring for elders lived with their care recipient than did Mexican American caregivers (Phillips et al., 2000). This finding may partially be explained by the fact that the majority of Mexican American caregivers in this particular study were adult children, whereas the majority of non-Hispanic White caregivers were spouses. Most research, however, did not report on the coresidency of the caregiver and care recipient.

Little research has focused on the collectivist aspect of familism in caregiving, that of families as referents. This aspect has been examined with respect to advice and decision making by the family on behalf of the individuals and with respect to the fact that caregivers' identity and well-being are strongly linked to that of the group or family. Guarnaccia and Parra (1996) found that caregivers of relatives with mental illness were more likely to go to the family for advice and concerns than to other sources. As cited previously, Magaña et al. (2004) found that there was a stronger relationship between family problems and maternal depression for Puerto Rican mothers of adults with mental retardation than for non-Latino White mothers. These authors theorize that because of a familistic orientation among Puerto Rican mothers in which family needs are emphasized over personal needs, the well-being of the family is closely linked with the personal well-being of the mother. In other words, if the mother perceives that the family is suffering, her own well-being suffers as well.

In summary, research on different aspects of familism shows many similarities across caregiving contexts. With respect to support from the family, caregivers tend to rely on family members for advice, in addition to support. Informal social support networks of caregivers tend to consist primarily of family members. Research is mixed about whether Latino families have larger or smaller informal support networks than other groups. Some reasons for small networks among some Latino families may include the fact that recent immigrants often have left a large part of their family in their country of origin and that caregivers who seek out services may have exhausted many of their natural supports. Size of and satisfaction with social support networks is significantly related to caregiver well-being.

With respect to obligation to the family, some studies have emphasized the exceptional commitment of the Latino caregiver to her role. Some aspects of obligation and role fulfillment may differ based on the relationship of the caregiver to the care recipient. Caregivers who are spouses or parents may be more likely to live with the recipient and provide direct care than caregivers who are adult children and siblings with their own family responsibilities. Although the primary caregiver performs most caregiving tasks, a range of family members help with these tasks.

With respect to family as referents, findings suggest that Latino families are more likely than other groups to seek advice from family members. In addition, research suggests that the well-being of the Latino caregiver's family is strongly linked to the individual well-being of the caregiver.

SERVICE UTILIZATION

Representative studies that compare formal service utilization of Latino older adults to that of non-Latino White older adults have found that Latinos report lower use of in-home services and nursing home care than non-Latino Whites do (Mui & Burnette, 1994; Tennstedt & Chang, 1998). Dementia-specific care services have also been reported to be underused by Latino caregivers (Aranda & Knight, 1997; Gallagher-Thompson et al., 1997). Because low service utilization often coexists with more reliance on informal family support, the phrase "we take care of our own" is often interpreted to mean that culturally Latino families prefer not to seek services and do not feel they need help. However, caregiver studies that have examined unmet service needs among caregivers have found that this assumption is not supported by the evidence.

In her study of grandparent caregivers, Burnette (1999a) found that although there was a high level of family support, grandparents reported many unmet service needs. Services they reported needing were support services such as toll-free hotlines, support groups, respite services, parent education, and legal services.

A similar analysis of unmet needs of adults with mental retardation and their caregivers was conducted by Magaña, Seltzer, and Krauss (2002). These researchers found that in comparison with non-Latino Whites, Puerto Ricans with mental retardation in the service system had more severe disabilities and lower functional skills. Despite more severe disabilities among the Puerto Rican adults, the number of services used was similar between the two groups. However, the Puerto Rican mother/caregivers reported significantly more unmet service needs. The types of services that Puerto Rican caregivers reported they most needed but had not received were occupational, physical, and speech therapy, respite services, and social and recreational services.

A study comparing service utilization of caregivers of older adults from different ethnicities (European American, African American, Chinese, and Latino) found that there were no differences in the total number of services received between groups. However, Latino caregivers reported more unmet service needs than both European American and African American caregivers (Ho et al., 2000). Latino caregivers reported a greater need for medical, social, and behavioral health services.

In a project that provides dementia-specific outreach and services targeting Latino caregivers, researchers found that by using culturally relevant outreach efforts the agency was able to increase calls to the program by 50% over the pre-outreach project period (Aranda et al., 2003). These efforts included Spanish and English language help lines, bilingual print and electronic media advertising, presentation to consumer and provider groups, community fairs, and consumer-to-consumer referrals. In addition, a bilingual outreach coordinator was hired who conducted face-to-face outreach in nontraditional outreach locations such as laundromats, beauty parlors, and botánicas. Caregivers in this project reported needing support groups, adult day care, respite, transportation services, legal services, and case management (Aranda et al., 2003). The fact that Latino caregivers in these studies are reporting a greater need for services contradicts previous assumptions that culture is somehow a barrier to service utilization.

With respect to barriers to receiving services, Aranda et al. (2003), Magaña, Seltzer, and Krauss (2002), and Burnette (1999a) all found that lack of knowledge about services was the greatest barrier reported by caregivers. Lack of knowledge about services may be linked to lack of culturally and linguistically appropriate outreach in the community, unfamiliarity with how or where to access services, and language barriers between potential recipients and service providers. Magaña, Seltzer, and Krauss (2002) found that an important predictor of fewer unmet service needs and higher use of services was participation in a Spanish-speaking support group. These authors suggest that this may be a culturally appropriate way to educate families about services and how to obtain them.

To summarize, research shows that Latino older adults and caregivers underutilize services. The main barrier to utilization as reported by caregivers is lack of knowledge about services and how to access them. Latino caregivers value services that help them provide better care to their family member, such as case management, respite care, information and education, support groups, and day care programs. Culturally specific support groups may be an effective way to provide information about services and access, and outreach tailored to the Latino community can be effective in increasing service utilization.

INTERVENTIONS WITH LATINO CAREGIVERS

Only two published studies were found that test the effectiveness of interventions designed to reduce stress or burden for Latino caregivers (Gallagher-Thompson et al., 2001; Morano & Bravo, 2002).

Gallagher-Thompson et al. (2001) compared Latino caregivers of family members with dementia who received a psychoeducational intervention to reduce stress with Latino caregivers who did not and found that fewer depressive symptoms were reported for the intervention group. Although this intervention program was initially developed for non-Latino White caregivers, adaptations were made, such as translation of materials by a bilingual-bicultural panel, increased use of visual aids, and oral presentation of lessons with the written materials as backup.

Morano and Bravo (1993) conducted a study of Hispanic caregivers of persons with Alzheimer's disease using a psychoeducational model and found that the caregivers improved significantly on a survey of caregiver knowledge. Although no conclusions can be drawn due to the lack of a comparison group, the researcher learned about adaptations that were needed to make the group more effective. These adaptations included the need to be more flexible about strict starting and ending times, the need to include time for caregivers to socialize with and provide support to one another, and the importance of allowing caregivers to bring home-cooked treats.

Clearly, more intervention studies are needed with Latino caregivers, but the aforementioned studies suggest that with culturally relevant adaptations, already developed interventions can be effective.

CONCLUSION

Older Latinos are one of the fastest growing groups in the nation and will have increased by 300% between the years 1990 and 2020 (Administration on Aging). The Administration on Aging (AoA) reports that 27% of Latino households provide informal caregiving to a friend or relative (AoA,). Latino caregivers are diverse with respect to countries of origin, language, culture, and religion and with respect to the persons they are providing care to. Not only is the number of older Latinos with chronic conditions expected to increase, but the number of Latinos with mental illnesses and developmental disabilities who need care will also increase with growth of the Latino population.

In this chapter, I examined caregiving across Latino ethnicities and across chronic conditions of the care recipients. I found more similarities than differences. Although the majority of studies were cross-sectional and used convenience samples, many of the results are consistent with one another across studies. Some of the most consistent findings are that Latino caregivers are often in poor health, face high rates of depressive symptoms, and report high levels of unmet service needs. Although informal support may be a strength for many Latino families, the extent to which it is available varies greatly, and caregivers who have large family networks still express the need for services. Emerging evidence shows that culturally adapted service outreach and interventions can be effective with Latino caregivers. More research is needed that uses representative samples, examines issues over time, compares caregivers with noncaregivers, and examines differences across type of care recipient and within Latino ethnicities. However, the evidence that there are pronounced needs among this group of caregivers is compelling. There should be no delay in expanding resources to provide services and interventions to Latino caregivers.

Support for the preparation of this chapter was provided by the Hartford Foundation and the Waisman Center at the University of Wisconsin-Madison.

REFERENCES

Adams, B., Aranda, M., Kemp, B., & Takagi, K. (2002). Ethnic and gender differences in distress among Anglo-American, African-American, Japanese-American and Mexican-American spousal caregivers of persons with dementia. *Journal of Clinical Geropsychology, 8,* 279–301.

Aranda, M., & Knight, B. (1997). The influence of ethnicity and culture on the caregiver stress and coping process: A sociocultural review and analysis. *Gerontologist, 37,* 342–354.

Aranda, M., Villa, V., Trejo, L., Ramirez, R., & Ranney, M. (2003). El Portal Latino Alzheimer's Project: Model program for Latino caregivers of Alzheimer's disease-affected people. *Social Work, 48,* 259–271.

Burnette, D. (1999a). Custodial grandparents in Latino families: Patterns of service use and predictors of unmet needs. *Social Work, 44,* 22–34.

Burnette, D. (1999b). Social relationships of Latino grandparent caregivers: A role theory perspective. *Gerontologist, 39,* 49–58.

Burnette, D. (2000). Latino grandparents rearing grandchildren with special needs: Effects of depressive symptomology. *Journal of Gerontological Social Work, 33,* 1–16.

Calderón, V., & Tennstedt, S. (1998). Ethnic differences in the expression of caregiver burden: Results of a qualitative study. *Journal of Gerontological Social Work, 30,* 159–178.

Cohn, D. (2003, June 19). Hispanics declared largest minority. *The Washington Post,* p. A01.

Cox, C., & Monk, A. (1993). Hispanic culture and family care of Alzheimer's patients. *Health and Social Work, 18,* 92–100.

Cox, C., & Monk, A. (1996). Strain among caregivers: Comparing the experiences of African American and Hispanic caregivers of Alzheimer's relatives. *International Journal of Aging and Human Development, 43,* 93–105.

Fingerman, K., Gallagher-Thompson, D., Lovett, S., & Rose, J. (1996). Internal resourcefulness, task demands, coping, and dysphoric affect among caregivers of the frail elderly. *International Journal of Aging and Human Development, 42,* 229–248.

Gallagher-Thompson, D., Arean, P., Rivera, P., & Thompson, L. (2001). A psychoeducational intervention to reduce distress in Hispanic family caregivers: Results of a pilot study. *Clinical Gerontologist, 23,* 17–32.

Guarnaccia, P., & Parra, P. (1996). Ethnicity, social status, and families' experiences of caring for a mentally ill family member. *Community Mental Health Journal, 32,* 243–260.

Harwood, D., Barker, W., Ownby, R., Bravo, M., Aguero, H., & Duara, R. (2000). Predictors of positive and negative appraisal among Cuban American caregivers of Alzheimer's disease patients. *Women and Health, 30,* 61–76.

Ho, C., Weitzman, P., Cui, X., & Levkoff, S. (2000). Stress and service use among minority caregivers to elders with dementia. *Journal of Gerontological Social Work, 33,* 67–88.

Keefe, S., Padilla, A., & Carlos, M. (1979). The Mexican-American extended family as an emotional support system. *Human Organization, 38,* 144–152.

Lawton, M., Kleban, M., Moss, M., Rovine, M., & Glicksman, A. (1989). Measuring caregiving appraisal. *Jour-*

nals of Gerontology: Series B. Psychological Sciences and Social Sciences, 44, P61–70.

Lutzky, S., & Knight, B. (1994). Explaining gender differences in caregiving distress: The role of emotional attentiveness and coping styles. *Psychology and Aging, 9,* 513–519.

Magaña, S. (1999). Puerto Rican families caring for an adult with mental retardation: The role of familism. *American Journal on Mental Retardation, 104,* 466–482.

Magaña, S., Seltzer, M., & Krauss, W. (2002). Service utilization patterns of adults with intellectual disabilities: A comparison of Puerto Rican and non-Latino white families. *Journal of Gerontological Social Work, 37,* 65–86.

Magaña, S., Seltzer, M., & Krauss, W. (2004). The cultural context of caregiving: Differences in depression between Puerto Rican and non-Latina White mothers of adults with mental retardation. *Mental Retardation, 42,* 1–11.

Magaña, S., Seltzer, M., Krauss, M., Rubert, M., & Szapocznik, J. (2002). Well-being and family role strain among Cuban American and Puerto Rican mothers of adults with mental retardation. *Journal of Human Behavior in the Social Environment 5,* 31–55.

Magilvy, J., Congdon, J., Martinez, R., Davis, R., & Averill, J. (2000). Caring for our own: Health care experiences of rural Hispanic elders. *Journal of Aging Studies, 14,* 171–191.

Marín, G., & Marín, B. (1991). *Research with Hispanic populations.* Newbury Park, CA: Sage.

Milstein, G., Guarnaccia, P., & Midlarsky, E. (1995). Ethnic differences in the interpretation of mental illness: Perspectives of caregivers. *Research in Community and Mental Health, 8,* 155–178.

Mintzer, J., Rubert, M., & Herman, K. (1994). Caregiving for Hispanic Alzheimer's disease patients. *American Journal of Geriatric Psychiatry, 2,* 32–38.

Mintzer, J., Rubert, M., Loewenstein, D., Gamez, E., Millor, A., Quinteros, R., et al. (1992). Daughters caregiving for Hispanic and non-Hispanic Alzheimer patients: Does ethnicity make a difference? *Community Mental Health Journal, 23,* 293–301.

Morano, C. (2003). Appraisal and coping: Moderators or mediators of stress in Alzheimer's disease caregivers? *Social Work Research, 27,* 116–128.

Morano, C., & Bravo, M. (2002). A psychoeducational model for Hispanic Alzheimer's disease caregivers. *Gerontologist, 42,* 122–126.

Mui, A., & Burnette, D. (1994). Long-term care service use by frail elders: Is ethnicity a factor? *Gerontologist, 34,* 190–198.

Navaie-Waliser, M., Feldman, P., Gould, D., Levine, C., Kuerbis, A., & Donelan, K. (2001). The experiences and challenges of informal caregivers: Common themes and differences among Whites, Blacks, and Hispanics. *Gerontologist, 41,* 733–741.

Pearlin, L., Mullan, J., Semple, S., & Skaff, M. (1990). Caregiving and the stress process: An overview of concepts and their measures. *Gerontologist, 30,* 583–594.

Phillips, L., Torres de Ardon, E., Komnenich, P., Killeen, M., & Rusinak, R. (2000). *Hispanic Journal of Behavioral Sciences, 22,* 296–313.

Polich, T., & Gallagher-Thompson, D. (1997). Results of a preliminary study investigating psychological distress among female Hispanic caregivers. *Journal of Clinical Geropsychology, 3,* 1–15.

Ranney, M., & Aranda, M. (2001). Factors associated with depressive symptoms among Latino family dementia caregivers. *Journal of Ethnic and Cultural Diversity in Social Work, 10,* 1–21.

Sabogal, F., Marin, G., Otero-Sabogal, R., Marin, B., & Perez-Stable, E. (1987). Hispanic familism and acculturation: What changes and what doesn't. *Hispanic Journal of Behavioral Sciences, 9,* 397–412.

Saldaña, D., Dassori, A., & Miller, A. (1999). When is caregiving a burden? Listening to Mexican American women. *Hispanic Journal of Behavioral Sciences, 21,* 283–301.

Struening, E., Stueve, A., Vine, P., Kreisman, D., Link, B., & Herman, D. (1995). Factors associated with grief and depressive symptoms in caregivers of people with serious mental illness. *Research in Community Mental Health, 8,* 91–124.

Stueve, A., Vine, P., & Struening, E. (1997). Perceived burden among caregivers of adults with serious mental illness: Comparisons of Black, Hispanic and White families. *American Journal of Orthopsychiatry, 67,* 199–209.

Talamentes, M., & Aranda, M. (2004). *Cultural competency in working with Latino family caregivers.* San Francisco: Family Caregiver Alliance.

Tennstedt, S., & Chang, B. (1998). The relative contribution of ethnicity versus socioeconomic status in explaining differences in disability and receipt of informal care. *Journal of Gerontology: Series B. Psychological Sciences and Social Sciences, 53,* S61–S70.

Thompson, L., Solano, N., Kinoshita, L., Coon, D., Mausbach, B., & Gallagher-Thompson, D. (2002). Pleasurable activities and mood: Differences between Latina and Caucasian dementia family caregivers. *Journal of Mental Health and Aging, 8,* 211–224.

IRIS CARLTON-LANEY

Rural African American Caregiving

In general there is a dearth of information about the rural elderly, particularly African Americans (Bullock, 2004; Carlton-LaNey, 1992; Ralston, 1993). Yet a sizable number of African American elders live in rural or nonmetropolitan communities. According to Coward, Netzer, and Peek (1998), 16.2% percent of African American elders live in rural areas, primarily in the southeastern region of the United States. Because of the small number of studies conducted on rural elder African Americans, the data are fragmented, leaving our pool of knowledge somewhat shallow. We do, nonetheless, know that elder African Americans who live in rural communities must cope with an array of critical and often life-threatening problems, including poverty, lack of transportation, inadequate child care, unemployment, substandard housing, inadequate health care, and insufficient elder care. Given these problems, images of spacious, safe, comfortable, relaxed rural communities ring hollow for many African American elders (Carlton-LaNey, Edwards, & Reid, 1999).

According to Arcury, Bell, and Carlton-LaNey (1998), much of the research on rural minority elders in the southeast has been conducted in North Carolina. Several reasons may account for this fact. First, many of the social scientists engaged in research on rural elder African Americans are housed in North Carolina universities. And, further, the state is home to a large population of elders, many of whom are poor, have aged in place, or have returned to the state as "return migrants," providing a rich participant pool for these scientists. Based on their examination of research, Arcury and his colleagues conclude that future research on minority elders, who are overwhelmingly African American, must take history into account. Ergo, in discussing rural elder African Americans, the impact of blatant and overt racism within a historical context of rural community life is an essential factor that must be considered (Trotman, 2002). This historical backdrop, along with both physical and social isolation, has created barriers to formal services (Arcury, Quandt, Bell, McDonald, & Vitolins, 1998), causing people to avoid the uncertainty of requesting formal services and to instead create their own unique strategy for help seeking, care receiving, and caregiving.

Historically, caregiving among African Americans has existed as part of the fabric of life in those communities. In an article titled "Sitting with the Sick: African American Women's Philanthropy," Carlton-LaNey, Hamilton, Ruiz, and Alexander (2001) discuss the history of caregiving from U.S. African enslavement and the slave doctor woman to the racially seg- regated old folks' homes to Marcus Garvey's Black Cross Nurses through the Great Depression and the Alpha Kappa Alpha Sorority's Mississippi Health Project of the mid-1930s and early 1940s. These au- thors discuss "sitting with the sick" as a metaphor for myriad caregiving services, including preparing meals for, housekeeping for, feeding, bathing, and gener- ally visiting with individuals who are mentally or physically ill, injured, or grieving. Elders have par- ticipated as both givers and receivers of help, and African American women have been intimately in- volved in all aspects of the caregiving process (Chadiha, Adams, Biegel, Auslander, & Gutierrez, 2004; Trotman, 2002).

Caregiving among African Americans is part of the mutual-aid system that permeates the culture and is a fundamental part of the West African tradition that was replicated in this country (Blassingame, 1979). It was through this system that the slave com- munity and later the community of freedmen and women were able to survive and thrive (Carlton- LaNey, 1999; Hamilton & Sandelowski, 2003).

Groger (1992) emphasized the importance of land ownership in the perpetuation of the mutual aid sys- tem. Groger's study of 35 African American infor- mants in rural North Carolina described a series of six informal poverty-coping strategies, including (1) cre- ating a compound, (2) joining a compound, (3) pool- ing resources in extended households, (4) sharing poverty/making do, (5) drawing on a lifetime of banked favors, and (6) educating one's children (p. 210). Creating a compound with others living on or near the land to which the elder holds sole ownership seemed to set the stage for developing a pool of helpers and for creating long-standing reciprocal ex- changes. Scholars agree that this mutual-aid orienta- tion has served African American elders very well by creating an available pool of people who have learned the art of self-help and can offer social support (Dil- worth-Anderson, 1992; Hamilton & Sandelowski, 2003). Others note that the mutual-aid system has created a heavy reliance on informal assistance from family, friends, and neighbors and that that reliance, coupled with low income, has tied rural elders to ge- ographic areas, cutting off their options to relocate and limiting their mobility (Koff, 1992; Skinner, 1992). Yet Griffin (1994) found that many rural African American elders acknowledge a commitment to the "homestead" as their primary rationale for preferring to live in their traditional hometowns. This commit-

ment reflects a strong family and community orien- tation and questions the desirability of relocating.

Within African American communities, family is defined relationally. It includes kin by blood line and marriage, as well as fictive kin. Fictive kin often be- come vital and important family members who are incorporated into the mutual-aid system. Further- more, Dilworth-Anderson (1992) notes that within these families, boundaries are permeable and flexible, which fosters caregiving and social debt or a sense of obligation to the family group. The flexible bound- aries mean that families are both temporal and stable and are, therefore, poised to meet members' needs as they arise. Elements of the African American world- view help to explain this family structure. This world- view, according to Exum and Moore's (1993) adaptation from Hilliard's work, emphasized the whole, not the parts; focused on acceptance and inte- gration with the environment; favored approxima- tions over accuracy; and valued people over things. This worldview has contributed to African American elders' resilience and has helped to structure their caregiving strategies.

Caregiving is an essential part of African American mutual aid and self-help that has historically perme- ated the community, providing much-needed service where gaps existed. There are several sources of care- giving for rural elderly African Americans. Table 32.1 identifies many of the major types of caregivers and their positions in the help-seeking journey that rural elder African Americans take. It is important to note that rural elder African Americans utilize a manifold informal helper system, as the table demonstrates. Es- sentially, they rely on a multifaceted network of in- formal unpaid helpers who share an array of responsibilities for the elders' care (Chadiha et al., 2004; Li, Edwards, & Morrow-Howell, 2004; Porter, Ganong, & Armer, 2000). These elders, however, are not simply passive recipients of care (Bullock, Craw- ford, & Tennstedt, 2003). Rather, they are active givers of care, as well. Hamilton and Sandelowski's re- search (2003) describes an intricate system of recipro- cal mutual aid within the African American community that has helped generations to survive racial oppression and economic hardship. Their re- search findings suggest that there is a need to redefine social support as caregiving and caregiving as social support. They also concluded that the complex and dense nature of social networks function to link peo- ple with shared experiences, creating supportive rela- tionships.

TABLE 32.1 Rural Elderly African American Caregiver Paradigm

Personal Resources	Informal/Communal Resources	Formal/Professional Resources
Self	Church (elders, stewards, deacons, church mothers)	Social workers
Nuclear family (spouse & children)	Church auxiliaries (Pastors' Aid committees, sick & shut-in ministries)	Physicians
Fictive kin	Secret orders (Masons & Eastern Star)	Other health care providers
Extended family	Folk healers	Agriculture & home economics extension agents
Friends	General stores (feed stores, seed stores, rural diners)	Social welfare services
Neighbors		Nursing homes

PERSONAL RESOURCES

Caregiving for African American elders begins with personal resources, including themselves, their families—nuclear, extended, and fictive—their friends, and their neighbors (Armstrong, 2000; Barnes, Given, & Given, 1992; Griffin, 1994; Jett, 2002; Porter et al., 2000). Rural elderly African Americans are notoriously self-reliant (Carlton-LaNey, 1993; Carlton-LaNey, 2003; Coogle, 2002). Their reliance on God for support and strength fortifies them and provides the impetus that they need to sustain themselves. Their tendency to call on God as they perform their daily tasks reflects their belief in God's omnipotence and omnipresence. Jett (2002, p. 373) found that it is not uncommon for elders to be heard uttering prayers such as "Oh Lordy Jesus make a way." Similarly, as an elderly African American North Carolina woman caring for her sick husband struggled to get herself out of bed, she invoked the Almighty, saying, "In the name of Jesus, I shall rise" (Kelley, 2004, p. 1E). Through God, these elders believe that they are able to care for themselves. Evoking God's name may also reflect a belief that illness is God's will and that God possesses the power to cure, not people (Reese, Ahern, Nair, O'Faire, & Warren, 1999; Wilson-Ford, 1992).

As mentioned earlier, the family, whether nuclear, extended, or fictive, is one of the rural African American elder's most important sources for care (Dancy & Ralston, 2002; Porter et al., 2000). Living in communities of kin extends the family network. Sengstock, Thibault, and Zaranek (1999) discuss two types of communities that reflect the lives of rural elderly African Americans. They include the "emotionally close communities" and the "geographic communi-

ties" (Sengstock et al., 1999, p. 83). The emotionally close community

> continues to be found in the family, which ideally shares a sense of personal closeness, regardless of geographic distance that separates them or how infrequently they see each other. (Sengstock et al., 1999, p. 83)

For rural African American elders, the emotionally close community overlaps with the geographic community, which is the community in which the individual lives. Sengstock et al. (1999) and others note that people must interact, to some extent, with this community due to their common living arrangement. Yet residents may minimize their identity or extent of belonging with the others who live in that community. For rural elderly African Americans, many of whom are aging in place, the community, whether it is an emotionally close community or a geographic community, is a lifeline that professional helpers, including social workers, should learn to nurture.

Skinner (1992) recognizes that aging in place is not a racially or ethnically neutral phenomenon. He notes that African Americans and other minorities experience a unique form of aging in place. He identifies low income, racial segregation, and ageism as three interrelated variables that combine "to create formidable barriers to housing and the free choice or movement" (p. 50). In conclusion, Skinner notes that the aging in place phenomenon creates intense reliance on personal resources, as identified in Table 32.1. The family, friends, and neighbors are important to the survival of the elders in the community and are an essential part of the personal resources system.

Koff (1992) criticizes governmental policy for perpetuating a system of neglect to those elders who age in place in rural communities. He notes that governmental policies reflect a lack of interest in enabling rural elders to age in their residence of choice, in fact negating the provisions of the Older Americans Act of 1965 (amended in 1988), which proposes an array of services and programs to sustain people appropriately in their communities and homes. Koff concludes that a denial of funds has resulted in a de facto policy of differential services for rural and urban elders. As Koff explains it, the four service areas, transportation, health care, housing, and family support are all adversely affected by inadequate governmental funding. The transportation problem, for example, stems from the high cost of providing door-to-door services and of maintaining a bus route for elder passengers, whereas responsive health care is negatively affected by the relatively fewer number of physicians, specialists, and ancillary services in rural areas, along with a maldistribution of these providers. Adequate housing is an especially critical issue for elders in rural communities. Koff (1992) noted that 80% of rural elders own their homes but that the housing is substandard and federal funding to support these individuals has been cut. Further, family support has been affected by the aging of neighbors, along with the continued outmigration of younger family members, making informal help less viable and begging the need for culturally sensitive formal services.

It is important to note that the rural African American population is diverse and becoming more so each day. One group that is adding to the diversity is the return-migrant population. Return migrants are those individuals who migrated to cities in the northeast and midwest during their youth for employment and better opportunities and who, on retirement, are returning to their states and communities of birth (Waites & Carlton-LaNey, 1999). Return migrants present a special complication, as they are viewed as family members retuning home after living away for many years. However, this perspective ignores the fact that they are very different from their counterparts who have aged in place. Moreover, we know very little about them, because they are an invisible segment of the community. Hence we are unable to plan for them as they stream into our small towns and rural communities. Waites and Carlton-LaNey (1999) found, however, that they are active in their communities and that they make good neighbors and strong community advocates. They promise to be a good resource for social workers and for the rural community overall. Yet they are an unmined neighborhood resource.

Jayakody (1993) has used the term "neighboring" to refer to the relationships and interactions occurring between people living in spatial proximity of one another." She identifies neighboring as "perceptual and behavioral neighboring" (p. 22). Perceptual neighboring is the sense of caring and good will that is established between neighbors irrespective of contact. Behavioral neighboring involves contact such as visiting and is likely to occur among people who live in rural communities, as well as in mobile home parks, row houses, or ethnically homogeneous communities. Both perceptual and behavioral neighboring influence the type of caregiving that has evolved within the rural community.

Jett (2002) describes an intricate system of caregiving and care-receiving rules that she observed in her research with rural African American elders. The rules essentially state that the person must:

(a) deserve help, that is, be sure to have lived a good life; (b) have needs that are both essential and genuine; (c) seek help only from those known to be capable of helping; (d) seek help from biological children first; (e) seek help along female bloodlines if biological children are not available or capable and willing; (f) maintain a proper attitude, that is, be humble and not make demands; (g) use the correct language, that is, asking without asking; and (h) trust and wait for people to do without asking (p. 378).

Researchers (Coogle, 2002; Hamilton & Sandelowski, 2003; Li et al., 2004) find that African American elders prefer to get help from those in their personal resource system. When these resources have been exhausted, elders may move to other systems of support, albeit with some reluctance. Behavioral patterns suggest that rural African American elders may use caregivers in the personal and communal system simultaneously or move back and forth between the systems as need arises (Jett, 2002).

INFORMAL/COMMUNAL RESOURCES

The informal/communal resources that are available to rural elderly African Americans include the church, church auxiliaries, secret orders, folk healers, and a network of people who congregate at local gathering places such as the general stores at many crossroads in rural America (Dancy & Ralston, 2002; Parks, 1988.)

The church is an important part of African American life. It has traditionally served multiple functions, which include providing spiritual sustenance, a community gathering place, a political forum, a social service agency, and an emergency refuge. It continues to hold its place as the most important social institution in the African American community, second only to the family. In rural communities, the church may be small with limited concrete resources, yet it serves as a significant social support for elders. Through the church, elders, who often make up a majority of the congregation, receive compassion, respect, and social support that closely resemble those given by family (Boyd-Franklin, 1989).

Boyd-Franklin describes the church family as another extended family in which the minister is the central figure. The church family provides a support network for rural elders. Through the church family a number of informal social services may be provided. Using the Baptist church as an example, the church family includes the various church auxiliaries, from the deacon board to the Mothers of the Church to the usher board to the various choirs that make up the music ministry. Breakfast or dinner is often served at church—breakfast after the early morning service and dinner after the mid-morning service. If elders are not able to attend church services, church members who visit them may take a meal when they visit on Sunday afternoons. The visitation is also part of the church's outreach to the "sick and shut-in." Members of the church family also provide transportation for elders who are in need. Individuals may routinely take responsibility for taking elders to their doctors' visits or other regular appointments and errands, such as to supermarkets (Watson, 1990). Churches also sometimes have van services that provide transportation for elders who cannot get to church on their own. These vans are also used to transport elders to congregate meal sites that are sometimes located at the church or other governmental facilities.

Porter and her colleagues (Porter et al., 2000) identify two types of church families—the church family in the collective and the church family in the singular. The church family in the collective includes extended family members, friends, the pastor and his or her family, and a host of others. The church family in the singular identifies specific individuals who provide supportive services to an elderly person when needed. The personal assistance that the church family provides may also refer to services provided by a specific individual who sees the provision of this particular service as part of his or her personal ministry. When the church and various auxiliaries cannot provide care, they are often able to direct the elder to the appropriate formal care system (Walls, 1992).

Secret fraternal orders are also an important supportive service to elders in rural areas. These groups are a significant part of the life of rural communities and have a long, rich history of service to their members. Secret orders include groups such as the Masons, the Order of the Eastern Star, the Grand United Order of Salem, the Sisters of the Tent, the Daughters of Rebeccah, the Daughters of Zion, and so forth. These groups have traditionally allowed people to hold leadership positions and to rise to an unprecedented level of community prominence. Ergo, they have given people the opportunity to develop leadership skills that are important in other aspects of community life. Part of the raison d'etre of these organizations is to provide service to the members and their families. They are secret in ritual but benevolent in purpose. Historically, many of these groups provided burial insurance policies for members who were not allowed to purchase this type of insurance in the open market because of racial discrimination. The sisterhood and brotherhood that these groups create and perpetuate provides another type of extended or fictive kin system, expanding the elders' network of caregivers.

Folk medicine and folk healers provide a source of informal help for rural African American elders. These individuals provide care when people are ill or injured and cannot or will not seek health care from the formal system. African American elders in rural communities suffer from chronic conditions such as diabetes and hypertension more often than their urban counterparts and more often than Whites (Dancy & Ralston, 2002). They are also at higher nutritional risk, and women have a higher breast cancer mortality rate than their White counterparts (Altpeter, Earp, & Schopler, 1998). Yet they seek health care irregularly and may find it more difficult to secure because of poverty, lack of transportation, and a shortage of physicians within their communities (Dancy & Ralston, 2002).

In addition to the lack of available health care providers and a tradition of racial discrimination, health beliefs also influence rural African American elders' help-seeking choices. Reliance on folk healers, folk remedies, and home remedies often replaces a doctor's care (Taylor, Boyd, & Shrimp, 1998). Because physicians are more available to African Americans and discrimination is not as blatant today as it once was, African Americans are less likely now to seek folk healers or to use home remedies. Dancy and Ralston (2002) note, however, that rural elders in isolated areas may continue to rely on folk medicine. Similarly, Wilson-Ford (1992) contends that rural elderly African American women continue to use home remedies and self-medication, including over-the-counter drugs, in lieu of physician care.

Caregiving is also provided in commercial community gathering places. Like the urban barber shop or beauty shop, the grocery store-service station equipped with a grill or diner at the rural crossroads (Petrow, 1982), the feed or seed store, or the feed mill are all places where European American and African American elders (usually men) gather on early spring and summer mornings or more frequently during winter months. These were at one time bustling places of business in small towns and rural communities, but as large corporate farming has grown and become more widespread and as the small family farms have died out and many rural elderly African American farmers and landowners have retired or sharecroppers have turned to day labor, these places are sometimes simply places to make small purchases, but mostly places to "sit and talk." Talk, gossip, news sharing, and general caring for each other have replaced discussions of farming strategies and market information sharing. A cohort of men routinely gathers at these places to simply be together. These environments can become therapeutic settings worthy of note. Social workers and other helping professionals might find these settings strategic places to intervene.

The preceding discussion may appear to demonstrate social support rather than caregiving; however, as noted, Hamilton and Sandelowski (2003) contend that social support is a form of caregiving and caregiving is a form of social support. Social support literature, they contend, presents the typical elderly patient as a passive recipient of care given by one whose only function is that of provider. Their research with cancer patients showed, however, that these persons are in a variety of reciprocal relationships before they become ill and throughout their illness trajectory. They describe a reciprocal exchange that they liken to a "support bank." They believe that individuals make regular deposits in this bank and "consciously or unconsciously keep mental records of what they have given and received from this bank over the years," acknowledging the help that they receive as "withdrawing only from previously made deposits" (p. 670). This support bank is a version of the mutual-aid system of support that has historically characterized the African American community's response to need. It is critical to the provision of adequate service that professionals are aware of the community's response to need and its structure, complexity, size, history, and effectiveness.

IMPLICATIONS FOR SOCIAL WORK PRACTICE

Social workers, physicians, agriculture and home economics extension agents, social service agencies, nursing homes, and other health care providers are all part of the formal, professional system of care. They constitute the last line of help that rural African American elders seek. All of these service providers have a professional obligation to meet the needs of this population. Some speculate that the underuse of formal services may result from feelings of vulnerability and powerlessness over resources in the service sector (Chadiha et al., 2004). Griffin (1994) notes that rural African American elders vividly remember the "double standards associated with racial segregation" and the humiliation suffered at the hands of White people that makes them avoid approaching public social institutions for help. Seeking help formally may also suggest family unwillingness to help.

Social workers cannot wait for these elders to seek our services. We must recognize that by the time we see these elders, they have probably exhausted their personal and communal resources. We must, therefore, be especially adept at serving this group, and we are uniquely positioned to do so. Because of the practice breadth, social workers are able to make multiple contributions to this group's well-being. Social work's person-in-environment focus, its client-centeredness, and its strengths-based perspective place the profession in a strategic position, beyond that of other professions, to empower and assist rural African American elders (Chadiha et al., 2004).

Social workers must understand the social context of caregiving for this group and engage in planned interventions at all three resource levels—personal, communal, and formal. Intervention at the personal resource level requires that social workers develop meaningful, trusting relationships with their elderly consumers in order to understand and support their caregiving system. Bullock (2004) notes that social workers must become aware of issues associated with preserving resources in African American families and communities. This includes observing and documenting changes in community dynamics, politically, socially, and economically. It also means noting breakdowns in the personal and communal caregiving systems, such as the death of a caregiver, which can be observed simply by keeping one's finger on the pulse of the community through involvement in community life.

In order to keep our fingers on the pulse of the community, social workers must take time to listen to the members of the target community. This is the best way to learn the types of interventions that are needed and wanted and to develop them with cultural sensitivity and applicability.

Coogle (2002) notes that successful interventions for African American and rural caregivers must "reinforce the basic family infrastructure" (p. 60). She described the Families Who Care Project, which had the following four objectives:

(1) to form a partnership of the most relevant and significant organizations that might address the continuing needs of African Americans and rural caregivers of elders with dementia, to be called Regional Needs and Resources Teams (RNRTs); (2) to develop a comprehensive, culturally sensitive training package, targeted to caregivers of elders with dementia and organized according to the progression of cognitive, social, and behavioral impairments; (3) to implement and test the train-the-trainer model as a mechanism for caregiver education; and (4) to evaluate the project and disseminate findings for replicability beyond the project period and beyond the geographical regions. (2002, p. 62)

Coogle (2002) found that the use of trusted community leaders as trainers of caregivers was one of the most notable aspects of the project. Through the project, individuals in the community were afforded the opportunity to develop competencies and to become known experts capable of helping families to deal with dementia.

Chadiha and her colleagues (2004) support Coogle (2002) and indicate that social workers should help caregivers to increase their capacity to acquire concrete problem-solving skills. Furthermore, they suggest that social workers aid caregivers to develop the needed political power to influence change at the macro level. Chadiha et al. (2004) also recommend that, when working with African American women

caregivers, social workers build on these individuals' natural strengths and resilience, help them to become empowered, share common ground with them, encourage them to use their own words when speaking, and help them to stay focused on social change.

As professional change agents, social workers must also stay focused on social change. For example, inadequate Medicare policies that do not reimburse for needed services such as patient care coordination, counseling, and education need to be examined, along with other federal, state, and local policies that do not function in the best interests of this population.

In addition to addressing varied social policy issues, social workers also need to examine their profession and to focus on ways to increase social work interest in aging, with special attention to a very vulnerable and neglected segment of that population, rural elderly African Americans.

Furthermore, social scientists need to focus more of their attention on issues that affect the quality of these individuals' lives by evaluating and validating strategies for problem solving. Avenues for further research with rural elderly African Americans include developing and evaluating interventions within a rural context to assist families in mobilizing their informal and community support. They also include utilizing and evaluating Chadiha and her colleagues' (2004) three-layered empowerment model that focuses on (1) raising critical group consciousness through storytelling, (2) teaching concrete problem-solving skills, and (3) teaching advocacy skills and mobilizing resources. And finally, social scientists must identify barriers to formal and informal services and present strategies for overcoming these barriers.

REFERENCES

Altpeter, M., Earp, J., & Schopler, J. (1998). Promoting breast cancer screening in rural, African American communities: The "science and art" of community health promotion. *Health and Social Work, 23*, 104–115.

Arcury, T., Bell, R., & Carlton-LaNey, I. (1998). Research in rural minority aging in the southeast U.S.: Results and directions. In W. Gesler, D. Rabiner, & G. De-Friese (Eds.), *Rural health and aging research theory, methods and practical application* (pp. 151–176). Amityville, NY: Baywood.

Arcury, T., Quandt, S., Bel, R., McDonald, J., & Vitolins, M. (1998). Barriers to nutritional well-being for rural elders: Community experts' perceptions. *Gerontologist, 38,* 490–498.

Armstrong, M. (2000). Older women's organization of friendship support networks: An African American–White American comparison. *Journal of Women and Aging, 12,* 93–108.

Barnes, C., Given, B., & Given, C. (1992). Caregivers of elderly relatives: Spouses and adult children. *Health and Social Work, 17,* 282–289.

Blassingame, J. (1979). *The slave community: Plantation life in the ante-bellum South.* New York: Oxford University Press.

Boyd-Franklin, N. (1989). *Black families in therapy: A multisystems approach.* New York: Guilford Press.

Bullock, K. (2004). The changing role of grandparents in rural families: The results of an exploratory study in Southeastern North Carolina. *Families in Society: The Journal of Contemporary Social Services, 85,* 45–54.

Bullock, K., Crawford, S., & Tennstedt, S. (2003). Employment and caregiving: Exploration of African American caregivers. *Social Work, 48,* 150–162.

Carlton-LaNey, I. (1992). Elderly Black farm women: A population at-risk. *Social Work, 37,* 517–523.

Carlton-LaNey, I. (1993). The last quilting bee: Social truths from aging African American women in the rural south. *Generations: Journal of the American Society on Aging, 17,* 55–58.

Carlton-LaNey, I. (1999). African American social work pioneers' response to need. *Social Work, 44,* 311–322.

Carlton-LaNey, I. (2003). Stories from rural elderly African Americans lessons in strength. *Generations: Journal of the American Society on Aging, 27,* 34–38.

Carlton-LaNey, I., Edwards, R., & Reid, N. (1999). Small towns and rural communities: From romantic notions to harsh realities. In I. Carlton-LaNey, R. Edwards, & N. Reid (Eds.), *Preserving and strengthening small towns and rural communities* (pp. 5–12). Washington, DC: NASW Press.

Carlton-LaNey, I., Hamilton, J., Ruiz, D., & Alexander, S. (2001). "Sitting with the sick": African American women's philanthropy. *Affilia, 16,* 447–466.

Chadiha, L., Adams, P., Biegel, D., Auslander, W., & Gutierrez, L. (2004). Empowering African American women informal caregivers: A literature synthesis and practice strategies. *Social Work, 49,* 97–108.

Coogle, C. (2002). The Families Who Care Project: Meeting the educational needs of African American and rural family caregivers dealing with dementia. *Educational Gerontology, 28,* 59–71.

Coward, R., Netzer, J., & Peek, C. (1998). Older rural African Americans. In R. Coward & J. Krout (Eds.), *Aging in rural settings, life circumstances and distinctive themes* (pp. 167–185). New York: Springer.

Dancy, J., & Ralston, P. (2002). Health promotion and Black elders. *Research on Aging, 24,* 218–242.

Dilworth-Anderson, P. (1992). Extended kin networks in Black families. *Generations, 17,* 29–32.

Exum, H., & Moore, Q. (1993). Transcultural counseling from African-American perspectives. In J. McFadden (Ed.), *Transcultural counseling: Bilateral and international perspectives* (pp. 193–212). Alexandria, VA: American Counseling Association.

Griffin, L. (1994). Elder maltreatment among rural African Americans. *Journal of Elder Abuse and Neglect, 6,* 1–27.

Groger, L. (1992). Tied to each other through ties to the land: Informal support of Black elders in a Southeast U.S. community. *Journal of Cross-Cultural Gerontology, 7,* 205–220.

Hamilton, J., & Sandelowski, M. (2003). Living the golden rule: Reciprocal exchanges among African Americans with cancer. *Qualitative Health Research, 13,* 656–675.

Jayakody, R. (1993). Neighborhoods and neighbor relations. In J. Jackson, L. Chatters, & R. Taylor (Eds.), *Aging in Black America* (pp. 21–37). New bury Park, CA: Sage.

Jett K. (2002). Making the connection: Seeking and receiving help by elderly African Americans. *Qualitative Health Research, 12,* 373–387.

Kelley, P. (2004, May 16). In a son's care. *The Charlotte Observer,* pp. 1E, 6A.

Koff, T. (1992). Aging in place: Rural issues. *Generations, 16,* 53–55.

Li, H., Edwards, D., & Morrow-Howard, N. (2004). Informal caregiving networks and use of formal services by inner-city African American elderly with dementia. *Families in Society: The Journal of Contemporary Social Services, 85,* 55–62.

Parks, A. (1988). *Black elderly in rural America: A comprehensive study.* Bristol, IN: Wyndham Hall.

Petrow, S. (1982). The last of the tenant farmers in the old new South: A case study in Franklin County, North Carolina. In R. Hall & C. Stack (Eds.), *Holding on to the land and the Lord* (pp. 131–145). Athens: University of Georgia Press.

Porter, E., Ganong, L., & Armer, J. (2000). The church family and kin: An older rural Black woman's support network and preferences for care providers. *Qualitative Health Research, 10,* 452–470.

Ralston, P. (1993). Health promotions for the rural Black elderly: A comprehensive review. *Journal of Gerontological Social Work, 20,* 53–78.

Reese, D., Ahern, R., Nair, S., O'Faire, J., & Warren, C. (1999). Hospice access and use by African Americans: Addressing cultural and participatory action research. *Social Work, 44,* 549–559.

Sengstock, M., Thibault, J., & Zaranek, R. (1999). Community dimensions of elder self-neglect. *Journal of Elder Abuse and Neglect, 11,* 77–93.

Skinner, J. (1992). Aging in place: The experiences of African Americans and other minority elders. *Generations, 16,* 49–51.

Taylor, S., Boyd, E., & Shrimp, L. (1998). A review of home remedy use among African Americans. *African American Research Perspectives, 4,* 126–134.

Trotman, F. (2002). Historical, economic, and political contexts of aging in African America. *Journal of Women and Aging, 14,* 121–138.

Waites, C., & Carlton-LaNey, I. (1999). Returning to rural roots: African American return migrants' use of senior centers. In I. Carlton-LaNey, R. Edwards, & N. Reid (Eds.), *Preserving and strengthening small towns and rural communities* (pp. 236–248). Washington, DC: NASW Press.

Walls, C. (1992). The role of church and family support in the lives of older African Americans. *Generations: Journal of the American Society on Aging, 17,* 33–36.

Watson, W. (1990). Family care, economic, and health. In Z. Harel, E. McKinney, & M. Williams (Eds.), *Black aged: Understanding diversity and service needs* (pp. 50–68). Newbury Park, CA: Sage.

Wilson-Ford, V. (1992). Health-protective behaviors of rural Black elderly women. *Health and Social Work, 17,* 28–36.

Within one month of Desert Storm and the deployment of American troops, a general assigned to a key position in Europe received a long-distance telephone call from his family priest in Middle America. During the priest's visit to the home of the general's mother, he noticed that she seemed oblivious to the smell of gas in her home and to the fact that the gas valve on her stove was open and not lighted. The general had made no plans for such a contingency and was greatly worried about the welfare of his mother while facing incredible responsibilities at work. (Parker, Call, & Barko, 1999)

Recent research by the National Council on the Aging and the Pew Charitable Trusts (1997), the Metropolitan Life Insurance Company (2004), and the National Alliance for Caregivers and the American Association of Retired Persons (AARP; 2004) suggests that maintaining contact with elderly parents and providing care for them from a long distance represent major challenges for a burgeoning number of families in the United States. According to the National Council on Aging (NCOA), approximately 7 million family members currently provide long distance care, and the NCOA estimates that these numbers will double in 15 years. Other estimates put the number of long-distance caregivers at more than 5 million (Metropolitan Life, 2004). Like the military officer in the opening story, many distant caregivers face an initial crisis with an elderly relative that brings them into contact with America's badly fragmented long-term care system. Such a crisis can signify the transition from "family member" to "caregiver" and the onset of a series of long-term care commitments for which distant caregivers (CGs) are unprepared. We define a *distant caregiver* as anyone (1) who provides informal, unpaid care to a person experiencing some degree of physical, mental, emotional, or economic impairment that limits independence and necessitates assistance; and (2) who experiences caregiving complications because of geographic distance from the care recipient, as determined by distance, travel time, travel costs, personal mobility problems, limited transportation, and other related factors that affect the caregiver's access to the care recipient.

The primary purpose of this chapter is to equip social workers and other human service providers with information that can be used to prepare and empower families who are geographically separated from their

MICHAEL PARKER
WESLEY CHURCH
RONALD TOSELAND

Caregiving at a Distance

care recipients. First, we examine research on distant caregiving to provide an evidence-based context for interventions and an overview of key issues faced by distant caregivers. Second, we identify general guidelines, resources, and related issues and questions inherent in the practice literature. Next, we describe an intervention program designed for distant caregivers that has shown promising results in a clinical trial with military families and in a feasibility study with two faith-based communities. We supply important techniques and non-Web-based and Web-based resources from this program that can be used by practitioners in their work with this population, and we conclude with a focus on how professionals can help caregivers assess the merits of the growing number of Web-based resources.

GEOGRAPHIC DISTANCE

To the practitioner, "distant caregiving" may seem antithetical. How can someone provide "care" from a distance? Yet a growing body of research confirms that care is often provided by a growing number of caregivers from a distance. For example, a recent Metropolitan Life study (2004) indicates that nearly half of all long-distance caregivers spend time arranging for needed services or checking that care is being received and that almost three quarters spend time managing finances or providing or arranging for help with other instrumental activities of daily living, such as managing medications, transportation, cooking, or house cleaning. This and other studies indicate that distance complicates the quality and quantity of care provided. Given these considerations, what evidence-based measures of distance are best for practitioners to use in designing an intervention strategy?

Though research on elder caregiving has focused primarily on caregivers who live close to or with care recipients, a few studies have explored the impact of distance on patterns of intergenerational contact and care among current cohorts of caregivers (Wolf, Breslau, Ford, Ziegler, & Ward, 1983). Researchers have assessed whether caregiver contact is affected by the distance of a commute and whether it has a linear relationship with access to the recipient (e.g., Kwan, 1999). These researchers have often used distance and zone-based measures. Researchers using these measures assume equal accessibility within the same zone or distance. Yet this may be, in actuality, a poor indi-

cator of accessibility (Pirie, 1979). For longer distances, numerous other factors—such as the characteristics of the location, personal time budgets for travel, and "travel velocities" allowed by the transportation system—have all been found to affect accessibility (Miller, 1999). As a result, we do not have a clear understanding of the trajectories of contact and care among distant caregivers and their recipients. Furthermore, effective intervention strategies that target distant caregivers are only beginning to be tested (Myers, Roff, Klemmack, & Parker, 2004; Parker, Roff, Toseland, & Klemmack, 2003; Steffen & Mangum, 2003).

In the most recent national study of caregivers in the United States, the National Alliance for Caregivers (NAC) and the American Association of Retired Persons (AARP; 2004) utilized three primary distance categorizations: caregivers who live with the care recipient, caregivers who live less than one hour away from the care recipient, and caregivers who live more than one hour away from the care recipient. Although these measures were effective in discovering patterns of care, a practitioner might ask about a caregiver who lives 500 miles from the care recipient rather than more than one hour away from the care recipient. More than one hour away may not reflect the more typical, distant caregiver's experience. For example, the National Council on Aging (NCOA) and Pew Charitable Trust's study (1997) that found distant caregivers average 4 hours' travel time to reach their care recipient, and the MetLife (2004) study reported that travel distance averaged 450 miles and 7.23 hours of travel one way. Also, if only the measure of *miles away* from the care recipient is used, this may not reflect the experience of someone living within a large city who may have a long commute to go a relatively short distance. Such a caregiver might live only 10 miles from the care recipient, but it might take considerable money (cab fare) and travel time (traffic problems) to respond to a care recipient's crisis. Other care recipients might live in remote areas with limited accessibility by air or auto. Thus a threshold of more than one hour away from the care recipient seems a poor reflection of reality when considering the disadvantages a caregiver who lives 500 miles away would have in responding to a crisis.

Kart (1997) and Atchley (2000) concluded that almost all studies show that parents prefer to live near, but not with, their adult children. They defined "near" in functional terms as one hour's travel time rather than geographic distance. In keeping with a life course perspective, we posit that most caregivers and care recipients will move closer as issues of late life (e.g., chronic disease and disability, death of a spouse, retirement) begin to affect their trajectories of residence and patterns of migration. Future research should attempt to use cluster analysis and other methods to portray more accurately meaningful categories of distant caregivers for practitioners; however, the previously presented research clearly reveals that distance is a complicating factor that should be considered in some manner by the practitioner. Therefore, we recommend that practitioners be *aware* of the thresholds discussed but that they also *collect* the caregiver's actual miles from the care recipient, caregiver's travel time to the care recipient, the caregiver's primary mode of transportation to the care recipient, and caregiver's financial capacity to travel.

CAREGIVING AND WORK

Parent care is becoming an increasingly important personnel issue because it affects worker productivity, retention, and health (e.g., Neal, Chapman, Ingersoll-Dayton, & Emler, 1993). In the latest national survey, distant caregivers who live one hour or more from the care recipient are more likely to have completed a college degree or graduate work and to be working full time. Therefore, it was not surprising that 68% of distant caregivers report making more job-related adjustments than those who lived within one hour's travel from their care recipient (57%; NAC & AARP, 2004). In view of these findings, it is important to note that a review of 15 organization-based programs designed to assist employed caregivers found no evidence of specific assistance for employed, distant caregivers (Coberly & Hunt, 1995).

For many families, residential proximity of adult children to their aging parents is a complicating factor in decisions regarding career advancement. For example, some military personnel elect to retire or resign because of parent care responsibilities (Parker, Call, Dunkle, & Vaitkus, 2002). Those who choose to pursue career advancement options are often required to move farther away from their aging parents for extended periods, thereby decreasing their availability to maintain direct contact with aging parents (Parker, Call, & Barko, 1999). Conditions of distant caregiving add elements of complexity to the potential triple bind of work, child, and elder responsibilities, particularly for working women. More women with children work full time in the United States than in any other nation in the world (Wisensale, 2002). As the full impact of this demographic and cultural change is experienced, the life course theme of elder care will be shared by a growing number of working women and men during midlife. However, competing commitments to parents, to nuclear and other extended family members, and to work make women who care for aging parents particularly vulnerable to stress and career disruption (Moen, Robison, & Fields, 2000).

In assessing the work-related issues for an employed, distant caregiver, the practitioner should gather information through pertinent questions that would explain a caregiver's personal availability and capacity to travel, remembering that an employed woman is more likely to be at higher risk than a man for role conflict and work spillover associated with caregiving responsibilities. For example, the practitioner might want to ask: Is the caregiver fully employed? Does the caregiver have more than one job? Does the caregiver have a work history of issues related to her distant caregiving responsibilities (e.g., being late to work, losing or giving up other positions or promotions, considering early retirement)? Is continued employment considered essential to the caregiver's family's well-being? The answers to these and other questions should help shape a distant caregiver's plan.

DISTANCE CAREGIVING AND FAMILY

The distance factor in family caregiving heavily influences who provides care and the nature and frequency of the care provided (Joseph & Hallman, 1998). In investigating this influence, researchers have defined frequency of interaction between distant caregivers and their care recipients in two ways. Some investigators view various forms of contact (i.e., telephoning, in-person visits) with parents as additive (e.g., Hogan, Eggebeen, & Clogg, 1993). These researchers have assumed that forms of contact are somewhat interchangeable, so that children who are likely to visit are also as likely to call when they cannot visit their parents (Bumpass, 1994). Others have suggested that the frequency and form of contact with parents depend, in part, on the geographic distance between parents and children (Climo, 1992; Baldock, 2000). These later researchers have suggested that distance alters the nature of the contact with parents by reducing the frequency of personal visits while increasing other types of contact with parents. Call, Parker, Roff, and Toseland (2002) studied the effects of geographic separation from parents on adult children's relationships with their parents and on the nature and extent of parent-child contacts in American families using secondary analysis of data from the National Survey of Families and Households ($N = 3,352$). This research indicates that parent care opportunities are substantially affected by distance, again pointing to the importance of planning.

A major life-course transition, such as a parent's serious illness, may also require adult children to alter their relationship with their parent and to make emotional adjustments. As children perceive that their parents' health is deteriorating, a sense of duty may overtake affections (Abel, 1991); daughters, in particular, are reported to feel less close to parents experiencing poor health (Rossi & Rossi, 1990). Koerin and Harrigan (2002) reported that caregivers had great difficulty watching the deterioration of their parents and found that the greater the distance from parents was, the greater was the challenge to caregivers. Yamamoto-Mitani, Aneshensel, and Levy-Storms (2002) found that parental health status influences the nature and frequency of caregiver contact and support. A national Canadian study of 1,149 caregivers revealed significant, distance-decay effects in the average (weekly) number of hours devoted to elder care and that women were willing to travel farther more often than male caregivers (Joseph & Hallman, 1998). Kaufman and Uhlenberg (1998) postulated that critical life-course transitions affected family relationships, and Szinovacz and Davey (2001) found that retirement was associated with a complex pattern of change in parent-child contact that varied by geographic distance. Kart (1997), Rossi and Rossi (1990), and Logan and Spitze (1996) found that distance was a strong determinant of the frequency of contact between adult children and their parents. Because caregivers want to be there for the care recipient but need to balance that desire with the demands of their employers and their own immediate family members' needs, Baldock (2000) reported that children who live great distances from parents experience considerable emotional conflict and suggested that adult children cope by increasing their telephone and mail contact with their parents. Other researchers (e.g., Dewitt, Wister, & Burch, 1988) found that as distance increases and visits become more problematic, caregivers substitute other forms of contact to bridge the miles and maintain strong intergenerational ties. Logan and Spitze (1996) found sizeable drops in numbers of visits and telephone calls if the child lived more than 5, 15, and 30 minutes away from parents.

The NAC and AARP (2004) found that distance measured by time-travel thresholds clearly affected caregivers' visits with care recipients. Only 16% of those who lived more than an hour away visited once a week or more, compared with 65% of those who lived less than an hour away. Distant caregivers (one hour away or more) were far more likely to hire a housekeeper to help with caring for their care recipient (50% vs. 36% who coreside), and they were more likely to make family adjustments, such as spending less time with their own families or giving up vacations (56%), to meet caregiving responsibilities than were those who lived less than one hour away from the care recipient (44%). Perhaps the most striking finding from this study was that more distant caregivers reported emotional stress (47%) than any other type of caregivers—that is, those coresiding (43%) or living less than one hour away (28%).

Overall, practitioners working with distant caregivers should consider the following familial issues in developing a long-term care plan: (1) the number of siblings and other relatives able to provide or currently providing assistance to the care recipient; (2) the nature of the caregiver's relationship with the care recipient and with her or his siblings, (3) the personality of the caregiver, (4) care recipient's and caregiver's awareness and satisfaction with current caregiving plans, (5) the caregiver's current pattern of visitation and communication with the care recipient, and (6) the care recipient's medical and functional status.

PRACTICE GUIDELINES, RESOURCES, AND PROGRAMS

When reviewing the practice literature for standard guidelines on work with distant caregivers, we identified some resources that might prove beneficial in such work. In 2003, a comprehensive review of the literature by a panel of national experts representing Caring from a Distance (CFAD), which is a nonprofit organization formed to assist distant caregivers, located over 1,000 books on the subject of caregiving, but only one, by Heath (1993), addressed the topic of distant caregiving. This book includes some potentially useful planning and organizing worksheets for distant caregivers, but it does not contain newly created Web-based resources. Myers (2003) provides a critique of eleven contemporary books and four videos on the general subject of caregiving, and he includes excellent "encyclopedia-like" resource books for caregivers developed by interdisciplinary teams. We reviewed a variety of documentaries on the subject of caregiving that could be used by practitioners and educators and located only one on distant caregiving, by Patton (2004). Regarding resources under development, CFAD (2003) contacted the U.S. Census Bureau, the Administration on Aging, and the Department of Health and Human Services and concluded that distant caregivers were not on the "federal radar screen"; however, the National Institute of Aging is currently working on the development of a resource and information guide for distant caregivers.

Accepted practice wisdom with distant caregivers typically includes utilization of national elder care locator services, of local Area Agencies on Aging (AAA), of experienced hospital discharge planners and geriatric social workers, of worksheets that assist with the planning and organizing of caregiving tasks, and of geriatric care managers when not cost prohibitive (e.g., Franklin, 2000; Heath, 1993). With respect to geriatric care managers, states have not set comprehensive, uniform standards of conduct (e.g., codes of ethics) and competency (certification and licensure) for geriatric care managers. There are no systematic methods of monitoring geriatric care management for fraud and abuse at the state level, although more than 40 different certification designations related to geriatric care management have been identified (Stone, Reinhard, Machemer, & Rudin, 2002). Although these and other guidelines are well intentioned, the evidence-based benefit of these directives remains in question. For example, we were unable to locate studies that examined the caliber of services available to distant caregivers with AAAs and the merits of the locator services in searching out the full range of services and resources needed for distant caregivers and their care recipients.

Our review of the overall, evidence-based literature located only four published studies and one conference presentation that evaluated the efficacy of a specific intervention program for distant caregivers (Myers et al., 2004; Parker et al., 2002; Parker, Call, Toseland, Vaitkus, & Roff, 2003; Parker, Roff, Toseland, & Klemmack, 2003; Steffen & Mangum, 2003). Preliminary research with distant caregivers suggests that those with a parent care plan are at reduced risk for stress-related problems and that employed women, adult children without siblings, and caregivers providing care to parents with cognitive disorders are particularly vulnerable to stress from these responsibilities (Martin & Parker, 2003; Parker et al., 2002; Parker, Roff, et al., 2003; Steffen & Mangum, 2003).

In an effort to address the need for an empirically based comprehensive assessment and intervention program that simplifies the parent care planning process, Parker and an interdisciplinary team of geriatric professionals conducted, over a 5-year period, a series of cross-sectional, prospective, qualitative, feasibility, and clinical trial studies aimed first at military caregivers and their parents and later expanding to academic and faith-based groups (e.g., Jennings, Roff, & Parker, 2004; Myers et al., 2004; Parker et al., 1999; Parker et al., 2002; Parker, Call, et al., 1999; Parker et al., 2001; Parker, Roff, et al., 2003). In one study, Parker, Call, Dunkle, and Vaitkus (2002) explored variables that influenced the mental health of 277 officers at midlife. A structural equation model of mental health and parent care variables provided quantitative support to previous qualitative findings that satisfaction with a realistic parent care plan enhances the mental health of caregivers. In an ongoing effort, Parker (2002) compiled a comprehensive, geographically sensitive state of science and practice resource directory that can be linked conceptually to caregiving tasks. These results and other studies (Parker et al., 2001) provided the impetus for the development of the Parent Care Readiness (PCR) Program.

Parker (2002) and colleagues (Parker, Roff, et al., 2003) identified a total of 50 parent care tasks representing four domains (legal, medical, familial, and spiritual) by systematically surveying adult distant caregivers and a sample of interdisciplinary experts in gerontology and geriatrics (elder law attorneys, geriatricians, geriatric care managers, social workers, psychologists, registered nurses, etc.). Parker (2002) constructed a Parent Care Readiness (PCR) Assessment, the first element of the PCR Program, by combining these tasks psychometrically and using a unique set of scoring algorithms based on the transtheoretical model of change (TMC; e.g., Prochaska & DiClemente, 1983) to score and to assess caregiver readiness to provide care. This assessment strategy, combined with other program elements (workshop, website, resource directory, expert consultation), was subjected to (1) a randomized clinical trial at the U.S. Air War College using a 2 × 2 partial rollover research design with military families and (2) feasibility studies conducted in Alabama and Texas with faith-based organizations (Myers et al., 2004; Parker, Roff, et al., 2003).

Caregiving Model

The distant caregiving program we propose is illustrated in Figure 33.1. The program consists of a comprehensive evidence-based assessment, computerized scoring and interpretation, and programmed linkage of assessment outcomes to state of science, practice information (prescriptions), and resources to aid caregivers in accomplishing high priority tasks. In short, the PCR Program provides an assessment that leads to a tailored intervention. Practitioners can use the PCR Program during family and individual counseling, and it can be easily augmented for didactic use

in workshops that address primary caregiving themes (medical, legal, spiritual, familial) associated with the task domains. We also recommend using Hollywood motion picture and television program clips taken from movies such as *Dad* or television series such as *JAG* that illustrate the importance of specific tasks and help to activate caregivers.

We view the development of a caregiving plan as a dynamic, ongoing process that involves the initial assessment of the landscape of possible tasks and the completion of specific tasks, followed by a reappraisal process as circumstances change. Using this approach, the caregiving plan consists of specific tasks that have been completed or are in the process of being completed. As the model illustrates, many of the tasks are complex and professionally intensive. For example, if the caregiver needs to find qualified geriatricians who live near her parent, the PCR Program provides a list of qualified geriatricians based on an extensive national and state resource directory that reliably captures this information and geographically

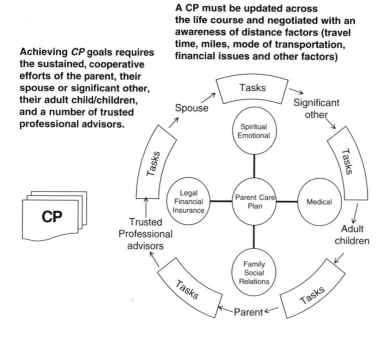

Parker & Martin, 2003

FIGURE 33.1. Model for Developing and Sustaining a Comprehensive Care Plan.

tailors the informational needs for the caregiver and her family. This information helps practitioners locate accurate distant information for their clients, and it may be particularly useful in assisting and directing underserved and disadvantaged caregivers who do not have access to as many resources.

In keeping with this model, the practitioner should emphasize that caring for a parent or elder represents a normal, age-graded (midlife) developmental responsibility that requires preparation. When caregivers are prepared for these tasks, they are likely to experience less anxiety and depression and more of the positive aspects of caregiving, such as the development of closer kinship ties (Kramer & Lambert, 1999; Parker et al., 2002; Parker, Roff, et al., 2003; Steffen & Mangum, 2003). Further, early and thoughtful parent care planning can minimize future barriers (e.g., onset of dementia) to task completion (e.g., durable power of attorney with a health care proxy).

The creation of a caregiving plan begins with a review of the full landscape of caregiving tasks. This is accomplished when the caregiver completes the PCR Assessment consisting of 50 tasks. The PCR Assessment is based on a systematic survey of distant caregivers and national gerontological experts in different disciplines (geriatricians, elder law attorneys, geriatric care managers, gerontological social workers, psychologists, nurses, and psychiatrists). The instrument was subjected to psychometric analysis, and it is scored using algorithms based on the TMC, a viable health intervention framework (Parker, Roff, et al., 2003; Prochaska & DiClemente, 1983). These tasks are listed in an abbreviated manner by domain in Table 33.1. It should be noted that not all tasks apply to all persons. For example, although spirituality and religion are very important to the current generation of older Americans, parent care tasks such as encouraging your parents' faith will not apply to all caregivers or care recipients (see Crowther, Parker, Koenig, Larimore, & Achenbaum, 2002; Crowther, Baker, Larimore, Koenig, & Parker, 2003; Tobin, 1999).

Each domain reflects a set of real-life challenges (specific parent care tasks) that potentially makes up an important aspect of a parent's care plan. For example, the newly automated version of the program has the capacity to identify qualified elder law attorneys who live in close proximity to the care recipient and thereby to facilitate the completion of high-

priority legal tasks (e.g., durable power of attorney). For example, care recipients and caregivers may need a health care power of attorney and advance directives for health care, a power of attorney to conduct business transactions for an incapacitated care recipient, or a "durable" power of attorney directive that endures through the parent's potential incapacity. If the parent has signed a power of attorney and later becomes incompetent by way of dementia, Alzheimer's, illness, or accident, the power of attorney is automatically terminated. In these same circumstances, a *durable* power of attorney would still be in effect.

If practitioners are working with caregivers without the care recipient, caregivers should discuss the outcomes of the PCR Assessment with their care recipients if possible, along with other family members and professionals with expertise in specific areas (geriatric-trained physician, elder law attorney, geriatric care manager). A preliminary feasibility study using this approach suggests that such a joint review fosters consensual forms of communication, minimizes redundancy, and clarifies tasks that require immediate attention (Myers et al., 2004). Examples of tasks listed on the assessment include "Determine the full extent of your parent's health/life insurance coverage as well as Medicare and Medicaid entitlement" and "Evaluate the safety of your parent's home situation (e.g., falls, isolation) and employ appropriate strategies to increase safety." The value of reviewing the full landscape of tasks minimizes the risk of leaving important tasks (e.g., durable power of attorney with a health care proxy) unattended or incomplete. Leaving important tasks unattended or incomplete may result in caregiver burden and depression and inadequate health care, family conflict, and financial exploitation or unintentional dissipation of assets for the care recipient (Campisi, Parker, Marson, Cook, & Moore, 2003; Parker et al., 2002; Steffen & Mangum, 2003).

The PCR Assessment helps caregivers prioritize caregiving tasks. After this process, practitioners can turn their attention to assisting caregivers with the completion of high-priority tasks. Outcomes from the PCR Assessment are linked to *prescriptions* (state of science guidance and resources) to help caregivers complete high priority tasks. As suggested, this process may involve contact with geriatricians and other providers (geriatric care managers) who live in close proximity to the care recipient.

When initially approached by family caregivers, some care recipients may be reluctant to engage in

TABLE 33.1. Domains of Parent Care and Associated Tasks

Legal-Financial Tasks	Medical Tasks	Social-Familial Tasks	Spiritual-Emotional Tasks
Discuss with your parents the advantages of completing and the consequences of neglecting to complete each of the following documents related to estate dispersion and management, advance directives, etc.	Discuss with your parents how involved or knowledgeable he or she would like you to be about their health conditions, diagnoses, medications, and functional status.	Together with your spouse, clarify your own values about where parents' care fits with your other life responsibilities.	Make peace with your parents.
Estate dispersion: • Will • Joint Ownership & Tenancy • Trust/Revocable living trust • Durable Power of Attorney • Preferred possession list	Obtain access to results of comprehensive geriatric assessment.	Assess your relationships with your parents, siblings, and other relatives who would realistically be an acceptable resource for your parent's care.	Secure a video or oral history from your parents.
Advance Directives • Health care proxy • Do Not Resuscitate orders • Living Will	Log information acquired from medical appointments.	Convene a family conference to formulate plans. Address who can and will do what, when, and how for your parents.	Investigate the nature of religious programs for seniors. available for your parents in their home community.
Secure accessible location for legal documents.	Compile a list of parents' health care providers and telephone numbers.	Make sure that you know the name, address, e-mail, and phone number of at least three people who live near your parents and who you could telephone if you could not reach your parents.	Consider active prayer with your parents, and cultivate prayer time with them by phone.
Rule out legal dependency of parents as a way to secure medical and treatment options.	Compile a list of current medications and obtain a copy of current medical records.	Develop a plan that would allow your parent to remain safely in his or her home and a plan that includes a move to another location if this becomes necessary.	Identify your parents' wishes for funeral and burial or cremation. If plans have been made, locate the documentation.
Assist parents in identifying assets, liabilities, income, and expenses.	Verify that primary care doctor or pharmacist is monitoring medications.	Discuss with your parent the possibility of a "panic button" service.	Establish a reliable point of contact of at least one member of your parents' church, synagogue, mosque, or religious organization.
Check parent's social security care for accuracy and review parents' credit history. If applicable, make sure mother has access to joint or separate credit.	Maintain a list of local emergency service providers (addresses, telephone numbers).	Understand the long-term care options available in your parent's home community (living options, in and out of home services).	Encourage your parents to complete a codicil to the will that represents what he or she would like to say to the next generation.

(continued)

TABLE 33.1. Domains of Parent Care and Associated Tasks (*continued*)

Legal-Financial Tasks	Medical Tasks	Social-Familial Tasks	Spiritual-Emotional Tasks
Investigate the costs of long-term care scenarios (e.g., long-term care insurance, savings).	Compile a list of services and programs that encourage successful aging practices and suggest appropriate parental involvement.	Evaluate the safety of your parent's home situation (falls, isolation, scams) and employ appropriate strategies to increase safety.	Understand hospice and palliative care so as to assist your parents in the death and dying process if it becomes necessary.
Determine the full extent of your parent's health and life insurance coverage, as well as Medicare and Medicaid entitlements.	Identify signs that indicate that your parent can not live independently.	Discuss the feasibility of a driving assessment.	Encourage your parents' faith.

Source: Parker, Roff, Myers, Martin, Larimore, Klemmack, Allman, Toseland, Fine, Campasi, Koenig, Cook and Moore, 2003. (Permission granted from D. Myers.)

planning activities. Many of the strategies for formulating a family meeting are addressed in the PCR Program prescriptions located in the domain of family tasks. Caregivers should be aware that care recipients might see their attempts at planning as a transgression of their privacy or traditional parent-child boundaries. Care recipients may also view attempts at initiating planning as implying that they cannot plan for themselves or as a way for their caregivers to limit their independence and autonomy, especially with respect to control of their finances. Therefore, it is important for clinicians to help caregivers think through the nature of their relationships with their parents and their parents' likely reactions to engaging in the planning process. This will help caregivers to be sensitive to the likely reaction of care recipients and to think about how to approach the issue with care recipients and about what strategies are needed to prepare for different reactions from the care recipients. There is some preliminary evidence to suggest that a workshop format using the PCR Program provides a useful strategy for addressing these issues, particularly with faith-based groups (e.g., Myers et al., 2004).

The PCR Program model was applied in a 1-day, 5-hour workshop on parent care planning. Unlike a similar feasibility study conducted in Alabama, the Texas intervention was aimed at both adult children and their parents and thus provided an opportunity for members of both generations to address caregiving issues in the same setting. A PCR Assessment was developed for the parents, and the outcomes of the caregivers' and care recipients' assessments provided a valuable avenue for discussion. Whereas church assistance with child care is normative, parallel programs with older adults may be met with resistance, particularly when there is a cultural perception that finances, health concerns, and legal matters are private family matters. The favorable response and reactions of the older adults and their adult children appeared to be an indicator that open discussion of parent care can be effectively managed. Following a feasibility study, Myers et al. (2004, p. 51) described the PCR program as "a comprehensive map for developing an effective ministry innovation to congregational leaders who want to strengthen the family in later life and promote case readiness." The cultural taboo is that those matters are not spoken of publicly. The PCR Program and workshop for both parents and their adult children intentionally placed the generations together to address care readiness and offered an opportunity for the beginning of conversation about difficult topics introduced by the presenters and activated by mutual completion of PCR Assessments.

During workshops or during work with an individual family, the practitioner can approach reluctant care recipients by focusing on issues such as long-term care or by preparing a health care proxy, concerns that many care recipients may welcome addressing. Once these tasks have been successfully addressed, other, more controversial issues may be introduced as a way to complete the planning process that has been going along well up to that point. Another way to approach the situation is to talk with care recipients about their need for planning and to encourage care recipients to talk about their reactions to the planning process. Care recipients can be encouraged to choose only the types of tasks on which they would like to work. The PCR Assessment facilitates this process because it reflects those tasks viewed as most important. When PCR Assessment information is available from the care recipient and caregiver, caregivers may also find that care recipients have some plans in place of which caregivers are unaware. This can be very helpful because then caregivers know where to look for documents or other evidence if the care recipients are incapacitated. Caregivers can also discuss with care recipients other tasks that have not been completed and how care recipients plan to address these tasks. Over the long term, this type of gradual approach can help care recipients get used to the idea that they need to plan and that caregivers are available to help them if needed.

In Tables 33.2 and 33.3, we present short lists of valuable national and state resources from this program. Table 33.2 gives important generic sites by task domain (e.g., legal links), and Table 33.3 contains a list of state commissions on aging and related Web addresses through which important links to local services within a state can be reliably identified. Both tables contain sites that address a broad range of caregiving tasks, such as the hiring of a caregiver or the locations of assisted living facilities or geriatric-trained physicians.

The PCR Program was standardized and tested with middle-class caregivers from military, academic, and faith-based communities. Though the efficacy of the PCR Program with underserved populations needs to be evaluated, focus groups and clinical trials are planned for residents of Alabama's Black Belt region, one of the poorest regions in the United States. Despite the preliminary nature of this research with caregivers from military and faith-based communities, the initial outcomes of these studies suggest that caregivers can be helped to prepare *proactively* for the tasks of caregiving using the PCR Program (Parker et al., 2002; Parker, Roff, et al., 2003; Myers, et al., 2004). Though this program has been described in some detail in this section, more explicit information is available (email: mwparker@sw.ua.edu).

The Internet and the World Wide Web

According to the most recent national survey (NAC & AARP, 2004), caregivers turn *first* to the Internet for health information (29%), followed by consultation with doctors (28%), family or friends (15%), and other health professionals (10%). Of those who use the Internet, nearly 90% search for information about

the care recipient's condition or treatment; more than half seek information about services available for care recipients; and 40% look for support or advice from other caregivers. More than 33% of respondents indicate that they need help with information about balancing work and caregiving responsibilities, and minorities are far more likely to request assistance and to experience financial stress related to caregiving.

Other research suggests that distant caregivers, particularly those in crisis, find it difficult to assess and digest the smorgasbord of largely untested informational sources available on the Internet (Parker & Martin, 2003; Setting Priorities for Retirement Years Foundation [SPRY], 2003). Further, those seeking help from local professionals often experience frustration because a paucity of trained professionals are available to assist them in the overall planning process (Martin & Parker, 2003; Parker, Roff, Myers, Martin, Toseland, et al., 2004). Finally, much of the caregiving information on the Internet and in lay-oriented books has not been subjected to scientific scrutiny (SPRY, 2003), and this process is further convoluted because caregivers must tailor the accessible information to the particular needs of their families (e.g., proximate vs. distance care) without the direct guidance of geriatric experts (Martin & Parker, 2003).

It is easy to see why many caregivers are experiencing an "information overload" when consideration is given to the sheer quantity of Internet resources. A recent review of caregiving and health information on three of the most widely used search engines revealed approximately 20,000,000 citations from Excite (www.excite.com), 32,000,000 citations from Alta Vista (www.altavista.com), and 1,346,966,000 citations from Google (www.google.com; SPRY, 2003). Although SPRY (2001) has developed a guide for older adults and caregivers to use in evaluating health information on websites, given these figures, it seems unlikely that caregivers will be able to systematically apply these criteria to potentially relevant sites. It is more reasonable for practitioners to assume this role. In this regard, practitioners should find the PCRP and the SPRY-generated guidelines (e.g., Can you tell who created the content? Are you given enough information to judge if the author is reliable? Can you tell if the content is current?) helpful in evaluating caregiving sites before recommending them to caregivers. Eventually, we would like to see a SPRY stamp of approval or grade on all caregiving sites, but for now the

TABLE 33.2. National Resources by Task Domain

Domain	Web Address
Universal	
AARP	*www.aarp.org/*
Administration on Aging	*www.aoa.gov/*
AgeNet Eldercare Network	*www.agenet.com/*
Alliance for Aging Research	*www.agingresearch.org/*
American Society on Aging	*www.asaging.org/*
Eldercare Locator	*www.eldercare.gov/*
Elderweb	*www.elderweb.com/*
Family Caregiver Alliance	*www.caregiver.org/*
Gerontological Society of America	*www.geron.org/*
National Association of Area Agencies on Aging	*www.n4a.org/*
National Association of State Units on Aging	*www.nasua.org/*
National Council on the Aging	*www.ncoa.org/*
National Institute on Aging (NIA)	*www.nia.nih.gov/*
SPRY Foundation	*www.spry.org*
Medical	
Alzheimer's Association	*www.alz.org/*
American Cancer Society	*www.cancer.org/*
American Geriatrics Society	*www.americangeriatrics.org/*
American Health Assistance Foundation	*www.ahaf.org/*
American Heart Association	*www.americanheart.org/*
Families USA	*www.familiesUSA.org*
InfoAging.org	*www.infoaging.org/*
Living Strategies	*www.livingstrategies.com/*
Medline Plus	*www.nlm.nih.gov/medlineplus/*
National Association of Professional Geriatric Care Managers	*www.caremanager.org/*
National Policy and Resource Center on Nutrition and Aging	*www.fiu.edu/~nutreldr/*
National Stroke Association	*www.stroke.org/*
Senior Health Care	*www.seniorhealthcare.org/*
WebMD	*webmd.com/*
Legal/Financial	
American Bar Association Commission on Law and Aging	*www.abanet.org/aging/*
Centers for Medicare and Medicaid Services	*www.cms.hhs.gov/*
FirstGov.gov for Seniors	*www.firstgov.gov/Topics/Seniors.shtml*
National Academy of Elder Law Attorneys	*www.naela.com/*
National Senior Citizens Law Center	*www.nsclc.org*
NOLO: Law for All	*www.nolo.com/*
Senior Resource	*www.seniorresource.com/*
Social Security Online	*www.ssa.gov/*
Family/Social	
American Association of Homes and Services for the Aging	*www.aahsa.org*
Assisted Living Federation of America	*www.alfa.org/*

(continued)

TABLE 33.2. National Resources by Task Domain (*continued*)

Domain	Web Address
Caregiving.com	*www.caregiving.com/*
Generations Together	*www.gt.pitt.edu/*
Homecare Online	*www.nahc.org/*
Homemods.org	*www.homemods.org/*
How to Care	*www.howtocare.com/*
Meals on Wheels	*www.mowaa.org/*
MemberoftheFamily.net	*www.memberofthefamily.net/*
National Adult Day Services Association	*www.nadsa.org/*
National Center on Elder Abuse	*www.elderabusecenter.org/*
National Family Caregivers Association	*www.nfcacares.org/*
Nursing Homes Facts	*www.nursing-homes-ratings.com/*
Senior Citizens at HUD	*www.hud.gov/groups/seniors.cfm*
Senior Corps	*www.seniorcorps.org/*
Senior Net	*www.seniornet.org/*
Senior Resource	*www.seniorresource.com/*
Senior Service America	*www.seniorserviceamerica.org/*
Total Life and End of Life Planning	*www.deni.net/*
Spiritual/Emotional	
American Hospice Foundation	*www.americanhospice.org/*
Beliefnet	*www.beliefnet.com/*
Center for Aging, Religion, and Spirituality	*www.aging-religion-spirituality.com/*
Growth House	*www.growthhouse.org/*
National Hospice and Palliative Care Organization	*www.nhpco.org/*
Partnership for Caring	*www.partnershipforcaring.org/*
Shepherd's Centers of America	*www.shepherdcenters.org*

wise practitioner will use the latest SPRY criteria in assessing information on the World Wide Web.

CONCLUSION

Although we are beginning to understand how distance complicates the provision of care to elderly relatives for some populations, we do not have a wealth of evidence-based programs that have been tested with different populations of distant caregivers. Rather than implementing carefully constructed plans that have been formulated on the best possible information and in consultation with the parent and trusted professionals, it would appear that most distant caregivers are not ready to provide care to their parents. Current and future research initiatives should be aimed at automating assessment and intervention techniques, such as those described in this chapter, and testing the merits of these technological advances in a series of clinical trial studies with various groups, including underserved populations. Until these and other products are broadly available, informed social workers and other practitioners can help distant caregivers by facilitating early and thoughtful parent care planning using some of the resources reviewed in this chapter.

The views expressed in this chapter are the exclusive opinions of its authors, who gratefully acknowledge the assistance of the Gerontological Society of America and the John A. Hartford Foundation's Geriatric Social Work Faculty Scholars' Program, the Center for Mental Health & Aging at the University of

TABLE 33.3 Current U.S. State Commissions (Agencies) on Aging

State	Website	E-mail Address	Phone
Alabama	www.adss.state.al.us	agelinc@adss.state.al.us	334-242-3250
Alaska	www.alaskaaging.org/	N/A	907-465-4716
Arizona	www.azdes.gov/aaa/	N/A	602-542-4446
Arkansas	www.state.ar.us/dhs/aging/index.html	N/A	501-682-2441
California	www.aging.state.ca.ua/	N/A	916-322-1903
Colorado	www.state.co.us/seniors/index.html	N/A	303-866-2696
Connecticut	www.dss.state.ct.us/divs/eldsvc.htm	N/A	860-424-4966
Delaware	www.state.de.us/dhss	dhssinfo@state.de.us	302-577-4791
District of Columbia	www.dcoa.dc.gov/dcoa/site/default.asp	dcoa@dc.gov	202-724-5322
Florida	www.elderaffairs.state.fl.us/	information@elderaffairs.org	850-414-2000
Georgia	www2.state.ga.us/Departments/DHR/ aging.html		404-657-5258
Hawaii	www2.state.hi.us/eoa	N/A	808-586-0100
Idaho	www.idahoaging.com/abouticoa/index.htm	N/A	208-334-3833
Illinois	www.state.il.us/aging/	N/A	217-758-3356
Indiana	www.state.in.us/fssa/elderly	N/A	317-232-7020
Iowa	www.state.ia.us/elderaffairs/	Sherry.James@iowa.gov	515-242-3333
Kansas	www.agingkansas.org/kdoa/	N/A	785-296-4986
Kentucky	www.chs.state.ky.us	N/A	502-564-6930
Louisiana	www.gov.state.la.us/depts/elderly.htm	N/A	225-342-7100
Maine	www.state.me.us/dhs/beas/	N/A	207-624-5335
Maryland	www.mdoa.state.md.us/	N/A	410-767-1100
Massachusetts	www.mass.gov/portal/index.jsp?pageID= eldershomepage&L=1&10+ Home&sid-elders	N/A	617-727-7750
Michigan	www.mdch.state.mi.us/mass/ masshome.html	N/A	517-373-8230
Minnesota	www.mdoa.state.md.us/	mba@state.mn.us	651-2962770 800-882-6262
Mississippi	www.mdhs.state.ms.us/	N/A	601-359-4929 800-948-3090
Missouri	www.health.state.mo.us	info@dhss.mo.gov	573-751-3082
Montana	www.dphhs.state.mt.us/	N/A	406-444-4077
Nebraska	www.hhs.state.ne.us/ags/agsindex.htm	N/A	402-471-2307
Nevada	www.aging.state.nv.us/	N/A	702-486-3545
New Hampshire	www.dhhs.state.nh.us/DHHS/DEAS/ default.htm	N/A	603-271-4680
New Jersey	www.state.nj.us/health/	N/A	609-943-3433 609-943-3436
New Mexico	www.nmaging.state.nm.us/	N/A	505-827-7640
New York	aging.state.ny.us/index.htm	N/A	518-474-5731
North Carolina	www.dhhs.state.nc.us/aging/	N/A	919-733-3983

(continued)

TABLE 33.3. Current U.S. State Commissions (Agencies) on Aging (*continued*)

State	Website	E-mail Address	Phone
North Dakota	*www.state.nd.us/humanservices/services/ adultsaging/*	*dhseo@state.nd.us*	701-328-8910
Ohio	*www.goldenbuckeye.com/*	N/A	614-466-5500
Oklahoma	*www.okdhs.org/aging/*	*Roy.keen@okdhs.org*	405-521-2281
Oregon	*www.dhs.state.or.us/seniors/*	*dhs.info@state.or.us*	503-945-5811
Pennsylvania	*www.aging.state.pa.us/*	N/A	717-783-1550
Rhode Island	*www.dea.state.ri.us/*	N/A	401-222-2858
South Carolina	*www.dhhs.state.sc.us/ServiceRecipients/ seniors.htm*	*info@dhhs.state.sc.us*	803-898-2501
South Dakota	*www.state.sc.us/social/ASA/index.htm*	*ASA@state.sc.us*	605-773-3656
Tennessee	*www.state.tn.us/comaging/*	*tnaging.tnaging@state.tn.us*	615-741-2056
Texas	*www.tdoa.state.tx.us/*	N/A	512-424-6840
Utah	*www.hsdaas.state.ut.us/default.htm*	N/A	801-538-3910
Vermont	*www.dad.state.vt.us/*	N/A	802-241-2400
Virginia	*www.aging.state.va.us/*	*aging@vda.virginia.gov*	804-662-9333
			800-552-3402
Washington	*www.aasa.dshs.wa.gov/*	N/A	360-725-2300
			800-422-3263
West Virginia	*www.state.wv.us/seniorservices/*	N/A	304-558-3317
Wisconsin	*www.dhfs.state.wi.us/aging/index.htm*	N/A	608-266-2536
Wyoming	*www.wdhfs.state.wy.us.aging/*	*cnoon@state.wy.us*	307-777-5340

Alabama, and the U.S. Air War College. We are particularly grateful for the research assistance provided by Brian Ford, MSW, and Daniel Durkien, MSW.

REFERENCES

Abel, E. (1991). *Who cares for the elderly? Public policy and the experience of adult daughters.* Philadelphia: Temple University Press.

Atchley, R. C. (2000). *Social forces and aging: An introduction to social gerontology* (9th ed.). Belmont, CA: Wadsworth.

Baldock, C. V. (2000). Migrants and their parents: Caregiving from a distance. *Journal of Family Issues, 21,* 205–224.

Bumpass, L. L. (1994). A comparative analysis of co-residence and contact with parents in Japan and the United States. In L. Cho & M. Yada (Eds.), *Tradition and change in the Asian family.* Honolulu, HI: East-West Center.

Call, V. R., Parker, M. W., Roff, C., & Toseland, R. (2002, November). *Geographic distance and associational sol-idarity between generations: The impacts of parental health.* Paper presented at the meeting of the Gerontological Society of America, Boston, MA.

Campisi, L., Parker, M., Marson, D., Cook, S., & Moore, F. (2003). Legal-insurance-financial tasks associated with parent care in military families. *Geriatric Care Management, 13,* 8–14.

Caring from a Distance. (2003). *February 9, 2003 final proposal.* Brookline, MA: Author.

Climo, J. (1992). *Distant parents.* New Brunswick, NJ: Rutgers University Press.

Coberly, S., & Hunt, G. (1995). *The MetLife study of employer costs for working caregivers.* Washington, DC: Washington Business Group on Health.

Crowther, M., Baker, P., Larimore, W., Koenig, H., & Parker, M. W. (2003) Military families: Spiritual and emotional tasks associated with elder care. *Geriatric Care Manager, 13*(1), 15–22.

Crowther, M., Parker, M. W., Koenig, H., Larimore, W., & Achenbaum, A. (2002). Row and Kahn's model of successful aging revisited: Spirituality, the forgotten factor. *Gerontologist, 42*(5), 1–8.

Dewitt, D. J., Wister, A., & Burch, T. K. (1988). Physical distance and social contact between elders and their adult children. *Research on Aging, 10*(1), 56–80.

Franklin, M. B. (2000). Caring across the miles. *Kiplinger's Personal Finance Magazine 54*(11), 86–90.

Heath, A. (1993). *Long distance caregiving: A survival guide for far away caregivers.* New York: American Source Books.

Hogan, D. J., Eggebeen, D. J., & Clogg, C. C. (1993). The structure of intergenerational exchanges in American families. *American Journal of Sociology, 98*(6), 1428–1458.

Jennings, L. K., Roff, L. L., & Parker, M. W. (2004, February). *Duty, obligation or responsibility? An exploration of the adult child's caregiving experience.* Paper presented at the National Gerontological Social Work Conference, Anaheim, CA.

Joseph, A. E., & Hallman, B. C. (1998). Over the hill and far away: Distance as a barrier to the provision of assistance to elderly relatives. *Social Science and Medicine, 46*(6), 631–639.

Kart, C. S. (1997). Aging and family life. In C. S. Kart & J. M. Kinney (Eds.), *The realities of aging* (5th ed., pp. 232–264). London: Allyn & Bacon.

Kaufman, G., & Uhlenberg, P. (1998). Effects of life course transitions on the quality of relationships between adult children and their parents. *Journal of Marriage and the Family, 60*, 924–938.

Koerin, B. B., & Harrigan, M. P. (2002). P.S. I love you: Long-distance caregiving. *Journal of Gerontological Social Work, 40*(1/2), 63–81.

Kramer, B. J., & Lambert, J. D. (1999). Caregiving as a life course transition among older husbands: A prospective study. *Gerontologist, 39*(6), 658–667.

Kwan, M. (1999). Gender and individual access to urban opportunities: A study of space-time measures. *Professional Geographer, 51*(2), 370–394.

Logan, J. R., & Spitze, G. D. (1996). *Family ties: Enduring relations between parents and their grown children.* Philadelphia: Temple University Press.

Martin, J., & Parker, M. W. (2003). Understanding the importance of elder care preparations in the context of 21st century military service. *Geriatric Care Management, 13*, 3–7.

Metropolitan Life Insurance Company. (2004). *Miles away: The MetLife study of long-distance caregiving.* Westport, CT: MetLife Mature Market Institute.

Miller, H. J. (1999). Measuring space-time accessibility benefits within transportation networks: Basic theory and computational procedures. *Geographical Analysis, 31*(2), 187–213.

Moen, P., Robison, J., & Fields, V. (2000). Women's work and caregiving roles: A life course approach. In E. P. Stoller & R. C. Gibson (Eds.), *Worlds of difference: Inequality in the aging experience* (3rd ed., pp. 165–175). Thousand Oaks, CA: Pine Forge Press.

Myers, D. (1993). Transformational parent care ministry: A resource guide for congregations. *Family Ministry, 17*(4), 11–34.

Myers, D., Roff, L. L., Harris, H. W., Klemmack, D. C., & Parker, M. W. (2004). A feasibility study of parent care planning model with two faith-based communities. *Journal of Religion, Spirituality, and Aging, 17*,(1/2), 41–57.

National Council on the Aging & Pew Charitable Trusts. (1997). *Caring across the miles: Findings of a survey of long-distance caregivers.* Washington, DC: National Council on the Aging.

National Alliance for Caregivers & American Association for Retired Persons. (2004). Caregiving in the US. *Gerontology News, 32*(5), 4. Retrieved December 18, 2004, from research.aarp.org/il/us_caregiving.pdf.

Neal, M., Chapman, M., Ingersoll-Dayton, B., & Emler, A. (1993). *Balancing work and caregiving for children, adults, and elders.* Newbury Park: CA: Sage.

Parker, M. W. (2002). Web and resource directory. In N. P. Kropt & C. J. Tompkins (Eds.), Teaching aging: Syllabis, resources, and infusion materials for the social work curriculum (pp. 192–215). New York: CSWE.

Parker, M. W., Call, V., & Barko, W. (1999). Officer and family wellness across the life course: A growing role for social workers. In J. Daley (Ed.), *Social work practice in the military* (pp. 255–274). New York: Haworth Press.

Parker, M. W., Call, V. R., Dunkle, R., & Vaitkus, M. (2002). "Out of sight" but not "out of mind": Parent care contact and worry among military officers who live long distances from parents. *Military Psychology, 14*(4), 257–277.

Parker, M. W., Call, V. R., Toseland, R., Vaitkus, M., & Roff, L. (2003). Employed women and their aging family convoys: A life course model of parent care assessment and intervention. *Journal of Gerontological Social Work, 40*(1), 101–122.

Parker, M. W., Fuller, G., Koenig, H., Bellis, J., Vaitkus, M., & Eitzen, J. (2001). Soldier and family wellness across the life course: A developmental model of successful aging, spirituality and health promotion: Part II. *Military Medicine, 166*, 561–570.

Parker, M. W., & Martin, J. (2003). Introduction to special edition. *Geriatric Care Management, 13*, 1–2.

Parker, M. W., Roff, L. L., Myers, D., Martin, J., Toseland, R., et al. (2004). Parent care and religion: A faith-based intervention model for caregiving readiness of congregational members. *Journal of Family Ministry, 17*(4), 51–69.

Parker, M. W., Roff, L. L., Toseland, R., & Klemmack, D. (2003, March). *The Hartford military parent care project: A psycho-social educational intervention with long distance parent care providers.* Poster presented at First National Gerontological Social Work Conference, held in conjunction with Council of Social Work Education Annual Conference, Atlanta, GA.

Patton, E. (2004). *Caring from a distance.* Video.

Pirie, G. H. (1979). Measuring accessibility: A review and proposal. *Environment and Planning, 11,* 299–312.

Prochaske, J. O., & DiClemente, C. C. (1983). Stages and processes and self-change of smoking: Toward an integrative model of change. *Journal of Consulting Clinical Psychology, 51,* 390–395.

Rossi, A. S., & Rossi, P. H. (1990). *Of human bonding: Parent-child relations across the life course.* New York: Aldine de Gruyter.

Setting Priorities for Retirement Years Foundation. (2003). *Evaluating health information on the World Wide Web: A hands-on guide for older adults and caregivers* [Reference manual]. Retrieved *www.spry.org.*

Steffen, A., & Mangum, K. (2003). Distance-based skills training for depressed dementia family caregivers. *Clinical Psychologist, 7*(1), 1–10.

Stone, R., Reinhard, S., Machemer, J., & Rudin, D. (2002). Geriatric care managers: A profile of an emerging profession. *Data Digest, 82,* 1–6. Washington, DC: AARP Policy Insititute.

Szinovacz, M. E., & Davey, A. (2001). Retirement effects on parent-adult child contacts. *Gerontologist, 41*(2), 191–200.

Tobin, S. (1999). *Preservation of the self in the oldest years.* New York: Springer.

Wolf, J. H., Breslau, N., Ford, A. B., Ziegler, H. D., & Ward, A. (1983). Distance and contacts: Interactions of black urban elderly adults with family and friends. *Journal of Gerontology, 38*(4), 465–471.

Wisensale, S. (2002). The inescapable balancing act: Work, family, and caregiving. *Gerontologist, 42*(3), 421–424.

Yamamoto-Mitani, N., Aneshensel, C. S., & Levy-Storms, L. (2002). Patterns of family visiting with institutionalized elders: The case of dementia. *Journals of Gerontology: Series B. Psychological Sciences and Social Sciences, 57*(4), S234–S246.

Where Social Workers Practice

B

AMANDA BARUSCH,
SECTION EDITOR

SECTION

Practice in the Community: Settings for Practice

OVERVIEW

Unique to the profession of social work is our focus on the interface between an individual and his or her social environment or community. So most professional social workers who serve the elderly and their families practice in the community. These practice settings are varied, and the chapters in this section reflect that diversity. Each chapter considers the legal basis of social work practice in the setting under consideration, as well as the population served and the roles filled by social work professionals. This section offers a wealth of information about the broad-ranging functions that are filled by professional social workers.

Patricia Volland offers a description of social work practice in hospital settings, noting a shortage of professionals qualified to fill these important roles. This shortage is especially important for older Americans, themselves the highest users of hospital services. In an inpatient setting, social work professionals play key roles, not only through direct practice but also as advocates for patient safety and quality of life.

Ted Benjamin and Edna Naito-Chan examine the role of social workers in the development and delivery of home-based care. They note that home based-care is preferred over out-of-home care by most older adults and their families but bemoan the lack of outcome studies on the effectiveness of social workers in these settings. Benjamin and Naito-Chan argue social workers can enhance their status in home-based care through research, improved training, and redefinition of the social work role in this setting.

Pat Brownell tackles the practice of social work in public welfare and social services—settings from which the profession has retreated. She notes a survey by NASW that indicated less than 1% of membership worked in these public sector settings. Then Brownell goes on to describe historic and contemporary roles of professional social workers in public welfare and social services, including work in income maintenance, adult protective services, special housing programs, HIV/AIDS services, kinship care, and domestic violence programs. She offers an insightful description of the dilemmas and tensions inherent in these roles.

Carmen and Barbara Morano offer a description of social work practice in geriatric care management settings. They consider contemporary challenges that arise in these settings, including definitional issues around what constitutes "care management" as opposed to "case management," the need for culturally relevant services, and developing professional credentials and identification in a relatively new area of practice.

Deborah Waldrop addresses the complex roles played by professional social workers in hospice settings. This chapter considers the history of hospice care, as well as recent trends that have improved care for people who are dying and their families. It includes detailed information about the availability and structure of hospices, as well as the Medicare and Medicaid regulations governing hospice care.

Traditionally underutilized by seniors, community mental health centers (CMHCs) are the focus of a chapter prepared by Sherry Cummings. Tracing the background of social work practice in community mental health centers, she notes the impact of deinstitutionalization and devolution. She notes an emerging focus on "behavioral health care," and a role for CMHCs in managed care. Indeed, recent studies cited in this chapter suggest that nearly all CMHCs provide services to older adults, and a majority of centers now offer specialized geriatric services. Nonetheless, mental illness among older adults continues to be undertreated, and seniors continue to be underrepresented in these care settings. Cummings projects increased CMHC use by seniors in coming years and outlines the challenges this will pose for the setting itself and the professionals involved.

Philip Rozario presents a call to arms for underfunded and understaffed senior centers. This chapter presents senior centers as vital resources for improving the quality of life for older adults, and facilitating independence. He outlines the important contributions social work professionals have made in this venue and argues that senior centers have untapped potential to serve the aging population.

June Simmons and Susan Enguidanos have prepared a look at social work practice in managed care settings. This chapter offers an overview of managed care in this country, before outlining major debates about the impact of this care model on clients and professionals. Simmons and Enguidanos outline important ethical dilemmas that confront social workers in managed care, with a focus on retaining the core values of the profession while developing "the business acumen" necessary to communicate our effectiveness in this industry.

In a carefully crafted chapter, Robert Hudson examines the role of planning agencies at state and substate levels in improving the quality of life for older adults. He outlines the history of the aging network, with careful focus on the planning challenges professionals have confronted in these settings. Hudson emphasizes the emerging role of these agencies in the planning and delivery of long-term care, predicting that this will define the identity of the network in coming decades.

Sheila Akabas and Lauren Gates examine the tensions of job and caregiving in their chapter on social work professionals in employment settings. This chapter outlines the cost to employers of failure to address the caregiving needs of their employees, as well as demographic trends that predict these costs will increase in coming years. Akabas and Gates outline the provisions of the Family and Medical Leave Act of 1993, as well as measures taken by individual companies to support family caregivers. They emphasize the potential roles social workers can play in making workplaces more supportive for employees who must care for disabled and dependent elders.

As with CMHCs, substance abuse settings have not traditionally focused their services on older adults. In their chapter, Connie Corley, M. Gray, and R. Yakimo summarize epidemiological studies on the prevalence of alcoholism in older adults, as well as the diagnostic challenges presented by this population. They describe the service delivery network, and consider the role of Employee Assistance Programs (EAPs). Corley and her colleagues argue that the service delivery system is ill equipped to meet the needs of older adults who suffer from substance use disorders and calls for professional education to alert social workers in all settings to the signs of these problems.

Taken together, these chapters present the array of roles—from direct care to program development and advocacy—filled by social work professionals in our communities. They highlight some of the challenges involved in this work and offer suggestions for future practitioners.

PATRICIA J. VOLLAND
DAVID M. KEEPNEWS

Generalized and Specialized Hospitals

34

The purpose of this chapter is to inform readers about the health care delivery landscape, with a specific focus on inpatient hospital settings. The chapter briefly describes older adults' use of acute care settings and the types of hospitals providing acute care, examines the payment mechanisms that older adults use to pay for this care, and outlines what special concerns older adults and their families have about acute hospital care. The chapter also includes an overview of the organization and delivery of social worker services in these hospitals.

OLDER ADULTS AND ACUTE HOSPITAL CARE

As Americans live longer, they require more health and social services to address the onset of acute and chronic medical conditions. Aging itself is associated with increased vulnerability to a variety of chronic physical and mental health conditions. Historically, health care in the United States developed around acute inpatient care in hospitals. However, advances in medical technology and increases in life expectancy have expanded care to community, home, and ambulatory settings.

Older adults are disproportionately high users of hospitals. Older people represent 13% of the population (Federal Interagency Forum on Aging-Related Statistics, 2000). Yet, they account for 35% of hospital discharges (Healthcare Cost and Utilization Project [HCUP], 2002). Older people have four times the number of days of hospitalization as those under 65 years of age (Administration on Aging [AoA], 2001).

Chronic illnesses such as hypertension, diabetes, heart disease, arthritis, and cancer are some of the more frequently reported medical conditions of the elderly (AoA, 2001). These conditions are episodic in nature and often require hospitalization to treat the acute episodes. As older patients move in and out of health care systems more rapidly than in the past, their interaction with all health care professionals, including social workers, is likely to be time limited and episodic (Shortell, Gilles, & Devers, 1995).

People age 75 and older experience an average of three chronic health problems at any one time (Gonyea, Hudson, & Curley, 2004). In addition to being at greater risk for chronic physical conditions, a significant proportion of older adults experience mental health problems. For example, older Americans with moderate or severe memory impairment range from about 4% among persons ages 65 to 69 to about 36% among persons ages 85 or older; 23% of persons ages 85 or older report severe symptoms of depression (Federal Interagency Forum on Aging-Related Statistics, 2000). In short, older adults are hospitalized for both physical and mental health episodes. Hospitalization itself can complicate recovery due to iatrogenic events such as infection and other adverse effects of being in a hospital.

TYPES OF INPATIENT HOSPITALS AND HOSPITAL SERVICES

Number and Types of Hospitals

The American Hospital Association (AHA) reported that, in 2002, there were 5,794 hospitals in the United States. The majority were community hospitals (4,927): Of these, 3,025 were nongovernmental not-for-profits, 766 were investor-owned for-profits, and 1,136 were state and local government community hospitals. In addition, there were 240 federal government hospitals, 477 nonfederal psychiatric hospitals, and 128 nonfederal long-term care hospitals (American Hospital Association, 2004).

The AHA defines *community hospitals* as all nonfederal, short-term general, and other special hospitals. Special hospitals include psychiatric, obstetrics and gynecology, rehabilitation, and orthopedic hospitals. Community hospitals also include academic medical centers or teaching hospitals. Many hospitals are part of health care systems such as multihospital or diversified single-hospital systems; 2,261 community hospitals are in such a system. Hospitals are also part of *networks*—these are groups of hospitals, physicians, other providers, insurers, and/or community agencies working together to coordinate and deliver care to their community; 1,343 community hospitals are in such a network (American Hospital Association, 2004).

There are four types of hospitals: general, special, rehabilitation, and chronic disease or psychiatric. A hospital's primary function determines how it is classified by the AHA (see list below).

Types of Hospitals

- *General Hospitals* are institutions whose basic function is to provide patient, diagnostic, and therapeutic services for a variety of medical conditions.

- *Special Hospitals* are institutions that provide diagnostic and treatment services for patients with specified medical conditions, both surgical and nonsurgical.
- *Rehabilitation and Chronic Disease Hospitals* are institutions that provide diagnostic and treatment services to handicapped or disabled individuals requiring restorative and adjustive services.
- *Psychiatric Hospitals* are institutions that provide diagnostic and treatment services for patients who have psychiatric-related illnesses.

The bulk of federal government hospitals are those operated by the Veterans Health Administration (VHA). The VHA provides services to 6 million Veterans; 45% are ages 65 and older. The VHA is a community-based model of more than 1,300 sites of care that include 162 hospitals and 21 health care networks (Department of Veteran Affairs, Veterans Health Administration, 2002). The VHA provides care in all categories of hospitals and a wide array of community and ambulatory services.

Collectively, all U.S. hospitals have 983,628 beds; the majority of beds—848,565—are in general hospitals. Hospitals employ 97,931 physicians and dentists; 1,039,994 registered nurses; 151,684 licensed practical nurses; and 3,164,498 other salaried personnel, including social workers. These hospitals train over 90,000 medical, dental, and other trainees. Hospitals range from as few as 6 to well over 500 beds; 39% of hospitals have between 100 and 300 beds (American Hospital Association, 2002). Hospital utilization is projected to increase an additional 7% by 2013, due largely to the aging baby boomer population (Rodgers & Leutz, 2003).

Hospital Services

Services provided are generally similar in acute care hospitals, although the emphasis may be different based on hospital type, location, and governing auspice. For instance, rural hospitals generally provide fewer specialized services; public hospitals may serve larger numbers of underserved and/or uninsured patients. Every hospitalized patient has a physician and receives nursing care. Hospital care is generally focused on diagnosis and treatment of the acute circumstance that led to the hospitalization. Some older patients will require attention for more than one medical condition. Rehabilitation and psychiatric hospitals provide assessment and longer term, intensive therapy services for patients recovering from disabling medical and psychiatric conditions.

Finally, specialized units in some hospitals provide specific types of services to patients, often including older patients. Both acute care hospitals and psychiatric hospitals might have separate geropsychiatric units for older patients with psychiatric disorders and/or behavioral problems. These units include evaluation and treatment from staff specialized in working with patients with dementia, Alzheimer's disease, and other mental disorders that are associated with advanced aging. The existence of specialized units changes based on the needs of the population served by the hospital, the expertise of the staff, and the financing available for specific diseases and treatments.

PAYMENT

The organization and financing of medical care services in the United States is complex; private enterprise and all levels of government are involved (Rice, 1995). Payment for the hospitalization of older adults is usually provided, at least in part, by Medicare and Medicaid or some form of private insurance. Of the total hospital discharges in 2002 (37,804,021), Medicare paid for 34.06%, Medicaid paid for 21.86%, commercial insurers paid for 36.33%, 4.8% were uninsured, and 2.85% were paid by other means (HCUP, 2002).

Medicare

Medicare is a federal health insurance program established by the U.S. Congress in 1965 as Title 18 of the Social Security Act. Medicare is designed to assist individuals ages 65 and older, some disabled individuals under 65, and patients with end-stage renal (kidney) disease. Medicare coverage is tied to Social Security Eligibility or Railroad Retirement Benefits. Individuals who retire before age 65 are not eligible for Medicare until age 65 (Centers for Medicare and Medicaid Services, 2004). There are two major types of Medicare coverage. *Part A* is mandatory and is called Hospital Insurance; it covers services received in hospitals. Thirty-four million older adults were covered by Medicare A in 1999 (Perloff, 2003); 40% of all hospital revenues come from Medicare (Beers & Berkow, 2000); 25% of all Medicare expenditures for a given year are spent during the last year of life of enrollees (Beers & Berkow, 2000). *Part B,* also called

Supplemental Medical Insurance, covers services of physicians and several other practitioners, including clinical social workers, under specific conditions. Part B is available on a voluntary basis to those who are covered by part A. Most Medicare beneficiaries accept part B coverage; over 96% of older adults covered by part A were also covered by part B in 1994 (Moon, 1996). Beneficiaries pay a monthly premium to Medicare for part B coverage (in 2004, the monthly premium was $66.60).

Medicare pays only 53% of elderly Americans' healthcare costs (Davis & Raetzman, 1999). Beneficiaries face considerable out-of-pocket expenses for uncovered services, copayments, deductibles, and part B premiums. Some of these expenses are associated with outpatient rather than inpatient services (e.g., Medicare covers the cost of prescription drugs provided during an inpatient hospital stay). But there are also significant out-of-pocket costs associated with hospitalization. For instance, beneficiaries are responsible for a deductible for the first day of their hospital stay (in 2004, the amount was $876) and for copayments for hospital stays beyond 60 days.

Many beneficiaries utilize one or another form of additional coverage to pay for or offset some of these expenses. These include employee health benefits (for both retirees and older adults who are still active members of the workforce), Medicare supplemental ("Medi-gap") plans, and Medicaid (described following; Goldman & Zissimopoulus, 2003). In many states, assistance with Medicare out-of-pocket expenses is available for low-income Medicare beneficiaries who do not qualify for Medicaid coverage through Qualified Medicare Beneficiary and Specified Low-Income Medicare Beneficiary programs (Centers for Medicare and Medicaid Services, 2004).

In most inpatient hospitals, Medicare part A pays for services on a prospectively determined rate—Prospective Payment System (PPS). As a result of the 1997 Balanced Budget Act, PPSs have also been developed for rehabilitation hospitals and psychiatric hospitals (Medicare Payment Advisory Commission, 2003).

Medicare uses different factors in determining payment rates for each type of setting. For inpatient hospital care, payment amounts are based primarily on the patient's diagnosis using a system of Diagnostic Related Groups. Payment is based on an estimate of the intensity of the patient's care needs, combined with factors that vary by geographic region (e.g., wages and the costs of goods and services) and some degree of risk adjustment (e.g., for age). Payment reflects an approximation of costs for the "average" patient with similar needs rather than reflecting the actual hospital costs. Services are bundled; the hospital is paid a "global" rate that includes all the services the "average" patient needs. Thus, variations in the types of services that individual patients receive usually makes no difference in payment (see example below).

Medicare Practicum Partnership Program— Case Example

▓ Flora is an 83-year-old woman who is hospitalized with pneumonia. She spends 4 days in an acute care hospital. She is given a course of intravenous antibiotics and receives "routine" nursing care. She complains about stiffness in her left leg and is evaluated by a physical therapist. She is discharged soon thereafter. Sylvia, her best friend and next-door neighbor, also 83 years old, is admitted the following week with a similar diagnosis. She receives similar treatment, but she responds more slowly. She appears frail and weak and has substantial difficulty walking without assistance. Her son, who lives in a distant state, mentions that he has grown increasingly worried about her ability to take care of herself living alone. He has invited her to move to live with him and his family, but she has refused. A social worker is called in to assess her needs, talk to her family, and arrange for follow up and evaluation of her home situation. Together, the social worker, Sylvia, and her family, in conversation with the physician, agree that Sylvia will return home with follow-up home nursing care and that her ability to remain at home will be assessed periodically.

Flora and Sylvia received different services, but the hospital will most likely be paid the same amount for the care it provided to each of them. Medicare will pay for care based on the diagnosis, factoring in overall differences in labor and other costs for the area in which the hospital is located. That payment will not specifically reflect Flora's physical therapy services and Sylvia's social work services. However, without the social work services, Sylvia would probably have to remain in the hospital for several days more.

This payment system has important implications for all health care professionals involved in hospital care. Most physician services are paid separately and are not reflected in the hospital's Medicare payment. The other professional services that the hospital provides, including social work services, are not specifically associated with the Medicare payment that the hospital will receive. However, even though specific services such as social work services may not generate additional revenue, they may save the hospital money. Because the hospital receives the same level of reimbursement regardless of a patient's length of stay, services that can facilitate earlier discharge can represent a cost savings. ▓

Medicaid

Medicaid is a state/federal program that provides medical coverage for many poor patients. About 11% of Medicaid recipients are low-income elderly people (Perloff, 2003). In 2002, Medicaid paid for 21.86% of hospital discharges; 12.99% of those discharges were individuals ages 65 years and older (HCUP, 2002). Medicaid operates with a combination of federal and state funding and is administered by the states. As a condition of receiving federal Medicaid funding, states must provide the following basic services: inpatient and outpatient hospital care, physician services, nursing facility care for persons ages 21 and over, and home health services for persons eligible for nursing facility services. State Medicaid programs can offer many additional services; several state Medicaid programs include the services of clinical social workers and case management services, which, of course, are often provided by social workers. States also vary widely in how (and how much) they pay hospitals and individual practitioners. Some have PPSs, whereas other states pay based on costs and/or a negotiated rate (National Council of State Legislatures, 2005).

SPECIAL CONCERNS OF OLDER ADULTS WHO ARE HOSPITALIZED

No matter what type of hospital an older adult may need to use, many of the same concerns will arise. Paramount is having access to appropriate care and being able to pay for the care. Medicare beneficiaries with low incomes are at greater risk for experiencing difficulties in gaining access to care (Davis & Raetzman, 1999). Older adults and their families will be concerned about being able to successfully recuperate from the hospitalization and, while in the hospital, are concerned about being treated with respect and dignity by the health care team. It is important that all patients, including older adults, are able to count on confidentiality and privacy. A number of regulations have been put in place to protect patient rights, as well as to protect confidentiality (Health Insurance Portability & Accountability Act, 1996; Knee & Vourlekis, 1995). In addition, older adults want to be active participants in decisions about their treatment in the hospital and their care after discharge (Zuniga, 1995). All decisions that will impact their independence need to include the preferences of the older adult patient. Frequently, end-of-life care decisions are necessary; older adults and their families seek guidance, compassion, and understanding to make the best decision. These decisions will focus on issues such as palliative care, do not resuscitate orders, and electing health care proxies—all decisions with serious ethical implications that require careful and thoughtful deliberation. Americans often view older adults negatively and as less useful because they do not work; this "ageism" is often subtle, but it can impact how health care providers consider alternative treatment choices for older adults. Older adults and their families should be able to expect all health care professionals to present treatment options without this ageism bias.

The percentage of older adults who are non-White or Hispanic is projected to increase to about 31% by 2040 from 11% in 1994 (Beers & Berkow, 2000). This increase in cultural diversity can create language barriers and can lead to misunderstanding if health care professionals, including social workers, do not understand language and religious and cultural beliefs of older adults. Older adults want to stay in charge of their own lives and want to remain independent for as long as it is feasible. Social workers are often the health care professionals most qualified to advocate for, and on behalf of, older adults and their families.

SOCIAL WORK PRACTICE

Social work practice has been an important component of health care since the early 1900s. Initially conceived as a service for poor and needy dispensary patients, social work services are now required by a diversity of individuals, both culturally and in terms of health status (Berkman & Volland, 1997). Social work with older adults in health care settings is the fastest growing segment of social work (Beers & Berkow, 2000). Employment of social workers is expected to increase more than 36% by 2012. Reduced length of stay in hospitals may limit the demand for

social workers in hospitals, but it will result in increased demand for social workers in home health services (*S. Rep. No. 108–81 at 219*, 2004). Social work practice with older adults in health care settings is focused on adapting to chronic illness, adjusting to disability and physical limitations, decisions about end of life, compliance with medical regimens, wellness, long-term care, and quality of life. Mental health social work practice focuses on the treatment of depression, substance abuse, chronic mental illness, cognitive deficits, suicide prevention, and adjusting to the changes that these conditions will require of the older adult patient and family (Clark, 2003). The broad scope of gerontological social work services is available in a National Association of Social Workers (NASW) document, "The Gerontological Social Work Spectrum" (NASW, 2004).

Social workers serve as part of the interdisciplinary team to evaluate the patient's cognitive, behavioral, and emotional status, as well as his or her social support network. Interdisciplinary collaboration is recognized as an essential element to providing effective patient care and facilitating successful social work services (Mizrahi & Abramson, 2000). Working directly with geriatric patients and their families, social workers deal with social support factors that create or exacerbate problems in living (Beers & Berkow, 2000; Mizrahi & Abramson, 2000). Social workers are viewed as helping older patients and their families navigate systems of care and provide case management services that are designed to help older adults stay in charge of their lives.

Because of fiscal constraints and the advent of managed care, length of stay in all hospitals has been decreasing; this leaves less time for social workers to provide needed services. As a result, social work services in hospitals are often short-term crisis-based interventions (Aviram, 2002). Recognizing the hospital's need to control costs, social workers have adopted strategies to provide care to older adults and, at the same time, help the hospital meet this goal. Such strategies include development of care maps and care management strategies (Berger, Robbins, et al., 2003). An expectation of these strategies is that social workers will be effective in helping patients manage the utilization of resources in a cost-effective way.

The functions of social work practice in health care vary by level of care and type of health and mental health setting. Social workers employed in acute hospital settings place the emphasis of their work on high-risk screening, brief counseling, bereavement services, discharge planning, collaboration, information, referral, follow up, and emergency services on-call programs (Poole, 1997; Ross, 1997).

Social workers are usually assigned to specific medical or psychiatric services or specialty units in hospitals. Social work services are not routinely provided to hospitalized patients (whether they should be is another question). A number of methods for identifying patients who need social work services have been developed; these include high-risk screening (Berkman, 1996), attendance on rounds and in discharge planning conferences, referrals from other health care professionals—usually nurses or physicians, or patient or family referral. In one study of over 1,000 patients in 5 acute hospitals, 18% received social work services. Patients most likely to receive social work services were older, single women who lived alone, had physical limitations, and experienced long lengths of stay (Oktay & Steinwachs, 1992).

On specialty units, such as geropsychiatry and geriatric evaluation units, social workers usually provide at least an initial psychosocial assessment to determine the need for ongoing social work services. A study by Oktay and Steinwachs (1992) revealed that social work services (discharge planning) with older adults in hospitals is increasingly important; their study confirmed that older adults do benefit from social work services, but many older adults did not see a social worker during hospitalization, even though they reported needing this service.

Hospitalized older adults often need evaluation of psychosocial factors that determine where the patient will go following discharge. Factors such as caregiving needs and availability, family support, home and community environment, and financial supports need to be assessed and understood so that an older adult has the best chance of the fullest recovery possible. Often, social workers address financial/payment issues—including insurance coverage and arrangements for postdischarge services. This often requires case management to determine which postdischarge option best meets the patient's needs—home health care or longer term treatment in a skilled nursing facility, a rehabilitation facility, or other setting.

In the VHA system, social work services provided include evaluation and crisis intervention, as well as psychosocial case management and discharge planning (Becerra & Damron-Rodriguez, 1995). The VHA—one of the largest employers of social workers in the nation (employing over 4,000 graduate social workers)—defines *psychosocial case management* as including family relationships, community integration, and financial/legal/housing issues that impact health

and functioning and need for support (J. Manske, personal communication, 2004).

With the pressure on hospitals to reduce length of stay and control costs, social work services, like all professional services, have been impacted. Reduction in supervisory and management staff (Berger, Cayner, et al., 1996; Mizrahi & Berger, 2001), increased case loads, and a perceived lack of support from other staff (Kadushin & Kulys, 1995) have been the result of these pressures on hospitals. Organizational changes have also been reported; the traditional departments of social work are usually maintained with some departments being combined with other professions, such as nursing, as part of case management and discharge planning units (Mizrahi & Berger, 2001). Leaders in hospital-based social work are developing methods to support social workers in this challenging environment, including promoting professional staff (Blumenfield & Epstein, 2001).

There is a reported shortage of social workers trained to work with older adults in all settings; the U.S. Congress has directed the Department of Health & Human Services to prepare a report about this shortage (Department of Labor, Health & Human Services & Education & Related Agencies Appropriation Bill, 2004). The workforce shortage is not the only challenge facing social work leaders. The shifts in social work practice in health care settings have also led to recognition that recent graduates are not well prepared to help patients and families who need health and mental health services. One study has identified the need for increased synergy between the two components of graduate social work education—the field experience and the didactic instruction in the classroom as a method to increase the pool of skilled social workers to work in health care settings (Volland, Berkman, Phillips, & Stein, 2003). One such model—The Practicum Partnership Program (PPP)—is a part of the $26.3 million Geriatric Social Work Initiative (GSWI, available at *www.gswi.org/programs_services/index.html*) funded by the John A. Hartford Foundation. The PPPs have already produced over 300 graduates competent to work with older adults in all settings (Damron-Rodriguez, Lawrance, & Lee, 2000–2003). The combined efforts of the GSWI—faculty scholars, PPP, doctoral fellows, faculty development, and geriatric enrichment programs—are having a positive effect on increasing the number of social work students being trained to work with older adults (GSWI, 2004; John A. Hartford Foundation, 2003).

Social workers who work with older adults in all hospital settings will be required to meet challenges that result from (a) the increased number of older adults, (b) the increase in chronic illness, (c) the changing systems of service delivery, (d) the increased diversity of the aging population, (e) the increased expectations for family responsibility in care, and (f) the lack of capacity in gerontological social work (Volland & Berkman, 2004).

The community of social work practitioners and educators is already preparing to meet this challenge. The GSWI is one example. Social work researchers have established priorities for research in gerontological social work that includes the development of evidence to support the positive outcomes associated with good social work practice (Burnette, Morrow-Howell, & Chen, 2003). This is compatible with development of evidence-based practice that has emerged as a part of hospital service delivery.

Quality-of-Care Issues

During the early part of the 1990s, significant concern arose in the health care system about the ability of providers and institutions to maintain quality of care in the face of growing pressure from managed care and in an environment of fiscal constraint. As a result, evidence-based practice emerged, and a literature has emerged on the "quality chasm" (Institute of Medicine Committee on Quality of Health Care in America, 2001; Rizzo & Rowe, 2003). The value of evidence-based practice rests on its systematic examination and appraisal of professional practices and outcomes, whether clinical, fiscal, organizational, or educational (Rosenfeld, 2003).

One method for ensuring the quality of social work services is through the establishment of standards. NASW has developed standards for social work practice in health care settings and for social work case management. Credentialing and specialty certifications are available for individuals as evidence that social workers have met these standards (National Association of Social Workers Credentialing Center, 2004). As older adults and their families become informed consumers, such credentials will be more important as evidence of quality practice.

The profession of social work is in the formative stages of developing evidence-based practices. Although there are studies that report high patient satisfaction with the care that social workers provide (Boult, Boult, Murphy, Ebbitt, Luptak, & Kane, 1994;

McNeill & Nicholas, 1998; Toseland, O'Donnell, Engelhardt, Hendler, Richie, & Jue, 1996; Toseland, O'Donnell, Engelhardt, Richie, Jue, & Banks, 1997; Williams, Williams, Zimmer, Hall, & Podgorski, 1987), there is also some evidence that older adults and their caregivers perceive the discharge planning process as negative and somewhat coercive (Clemens, 1995).

Evidence does articulate the effectiveness of social work with older adults in hospital settings. There is evidence that social work interventions result in positive care management; as a result of social work services, caregivers report decreased feelings of stress (Peak, Toseland, & Banks, 1995; Toseland, Labrecque, Goebel, & Whitney, 1992; Toseland, McCallion, Smith, Huck, Bourgeois, & Garstka, 2001), communications between patient/family and health care providers are improved (McCallion, Toseland, & Freeman, 1999), care coordination is improved, quality of social and health care is improved (Toseland et al., 1996; Toseland et al., 1997; Williams et al., 1987), knowledge of community resources is increased (Peak et al., 1995; Toesland et al., 1992; Toseland et al., 2001), and cost savings for hospitals can result (Rizzo & Rowe, 2003). The social work profession will need to continue to build evidence of effectiveness of practice and demonstrate the importance of its role in providing high quality and safe patient care to older adults who use inpatient hospital service.

SUMMARY

Social work practice in hospital settings is linked with social work practice with older adults (Berkman, 2004). The aging of the baby boomers will further stress hospitals and health care professionals who work in hospitals. Evidence of effective practice will be required to address the shortage of trained social workers to work with older adults in all hospital settings. Quality of care and patient safety will remain key focuses for professionals in hospital settings for the foreseeable future. Social workers will be essential as advocates for older adults who will require hospital care.

REFERENCES

Administration on Aging. (2001). *A profile of older Americans: 2001.* Washington, DC: AOA.

American Hospital Association. (2002). *Hospital Statistics. 2002.* Chicago: Health Forum.

American Hospital Association. (2004). *Fast facts on US hospitals from hospital statistics.* Available: *www.aha.org/aha/resource_center/fastfacts/fast_facts_US_hospitals.html.*

American Hospital Association and Federation of American Hospitals. (2003). *Cost of caring: Key drivers of growth in spending on hospital care.:* Price Waterhouse Coopers.

American Hospital Association Medicare. (2004). Available: *www.aha.org/aha/key_issues/medicare/index.html.*

Aviram, U. (2002). The changing role of the social worker in the mental health system. *Social Work in Health Care, 35*(1/2), 615–632.

Becerra, R. M., & Damron-Rodriguez, J. A. (1995). Veterans and veterans services. In R. L. Edwards & J. G. Hopps (Eds.), *Encyclopedia of Social Work* (19th ed., Vol. 3, pp. 2431–2439). Washington, DC: NASW Press.

Berger, C. S., Cayner, J., Jensen, G., Mizrahi, T., Scesny A., & Trachtenberg, J. (1996). The changing scene of social work in hospitals: A report of a national study by the society for social work administrators in health care and the National Association of Social Workers (NASW). *Health & Social Work 21*(3), 167–177.

Berger, C. S., Robbins, C., Lewis, M., Mizrahi, T., & Fleit, S. (2003). The Impact of organizational change on social work staffing in a hospital setting: A national, longitudinal study of social work in hospitals. *Social Work in Health Care, 37*(1), 1–18.

Berkman, B. (1996). The emerging healthcare world: Implications for social work practice and education. *Journal of Social Work, 41*(5), 541–551.

Berkman, B. (2004, March 24). *The changing face of health and aging: Implications for health care practice with older adults.* Presented at Social Work Month Celebration, Columbia Presbyterian Medical Center, New York.

Berkman, B., & Volland, P. (1997). Health care practice overview. In R. L. Edwards & J. G. Happs (Eds.), *Encyclopedia of Social Work* (19th ed., supp., pp. 143–149). Washington, DC: NASW Press.

Blumenfield, S., & Epstein, I. (2001). Introduction: Promoting and maintaining a reflective professional staff in a hospital-based social work department. Copublished simultaneously in *Social Work in Health Care, 33*(3/4), 1–13; and in Blumenfield, S., & Epstein, I. (2001). *Clinical data-mining in practice-based research: Social work in hospital settings* (pp. 1–13). New York: Haworth Social Work Practice Press.

Boult, C., Boult, L., Murphy, C., Ebbitt, B., Luptak, M., & Kane, R. L. (1994). A controlled trial of outpatient geriatric evaluation and management. *Journal of the American Geriatrics Society, 42*(5), 465–470.

Burnette, D., Morrow-Howell, N., & Chen, L. (2003). Setting priorities for gerontological social work research: A national Delphi study. *Gerontologist, 43,* 828–838.

Centers for Medicare and Medicaid Services. (2004a). *Enrolling in Medicare.* Balitmore, MD: CMS. Available: *www.medicare.gov/Publications/Pubs/pdf/11036.pdf.*

Centers for Medicare and Medicaid Services. (2004b). *Medicaid Eligibility.* Available: *www.cms.hhs.gov/medicaid/eligibility/criteria.asp?,.*

Clark, E. J. (2003). The future of social work practice. In R. L. Edwards & J. G. Hopps (Eds.), *Encyclopedia of Social Work* (19th ed., supp., pp. 61–70). Washington, DC: NASW Press.

Clemens, E. L. (1995). Multiple perceptions of discharge planning in one urban hospital. *Health & Social Work, 20*(4), 254–262.

Damron-Rodriguez, J., Lawrance, P., & Lee, S. (2000–2003). *Practicum Partnership Program (PPP) collaborative evaluation report II: Outcomes 2000–2003.* Unpublished manuscript.

Davis, K., & Raetzman, S. (1999). Meeting future health and long term care needs of an aging population. New York: Commonwealth Fund. Available: *www.cmwf.org/programs/eldersdavis_ltc_aging_ib_350.asp.*

Department of Veteran Affairs, Veterans Health Administration. (2002). *VHA at your fingertips.* Washington, DC: Veterans Health Administration Office of Communications.

Federal Interagency Forum on Aging-Related Statistics. (2000, August). *Older Americans 2000: Key indicators of well-being.* Washington, DC: Government Printing Office.

Goldman, D. P., & Zissimopoulus, J. M. (2003). High out-of-pocket health care spending by the elderly. *Health Affairs, 22*(3), 194–202.

Gonyea, J. G., Hudson, R. B., & Curley, A. (2004). *The geriatric social work labor force: Challenges and opportunities in responding to an aging society.* Institute for Geriatric Social Work, Boston University School of Social Work.

Healthcare Cost and Utilization Project. (2002). *2002 National Statistics.* Available: http://hcup.ahrq.gov/HCUPnet.asp.

Health Insurance Portability and Accountability Act of 1996, 42 U.S.C. section 201 et seq.

Institute of Medicine Committee on Quality of Health Care in America. (2001). *Crossing the quality chasm:*

A new health system for the twenty-first century. Washington, DC: National Academies Press.

John A. Hartford Foundation. (2003). *Annual report: Strengthening geriatric social work*. New York: JAHF.

Kadushin, G., & Kulys, R. (1995). Job satisfaction among social work discharge planners. *Health & Social Work, 20*(3), 174–187.

Knee, R. I., & Vourlekis, B. S. (1995). Patient rights. In R. L. Edwards & J. G. Hopps (Eds.), *Encyclopedia of Social Work* (19th ed., Vol. 3, pp. 1802–1810). Washington, DC: NASW Press.

McCallion, P., Toseland, R., & Freeman, K. (1999). An evaluation of a family visit education program. *Journal of the American Geriatrics Society, 47*(2), 203–214.

McNeill, T., & Nicholas, D. (1998). Perceived outcomes of social work intervention: Beyond consumer satisfaction. *Social Work in Health Care, 26*(3), 1–19.

Medicare Payment Advisory Commission. (2003). *Report to Congress: Medicare Payment Policy*. Washington, DC: MedPAC.

Mizrahi, T., & Abramson, J. S. (2000). Collaboration between social workers and physicians: Perspectives on a shared case. *Social Work in Health Care, 31*(3), 1–24.

Mizrahi, T., & Berger, C. (2001). The impact of a changing health care environment on social work leaders: Obstacles and opportunities in hospital social work. *Social Work, 46*(2), 170–182.

Moon, M. (1996). *Medicare now and in the future*. Washington, DC: Urban Institute Press.

Moon, M. (2004). *The gerontological social work spectrum*. Washington, DC: NASW Press.

National Association of Social Workers. (2004a). *Certified Social Work Case Manager (C-SWCM)*. Available: *www.naswdc.org/credentials/casemgmt.asp.*

National Association of Social Workers. (2004b). *The gerontological social work spectrum*. Available: *www.socialworkers.org.*

Oktay, J., & Steinwachs, D. (1992). Evaluating social work discharge planning services for elderly people: Access, complexity and outcome. *Health and Social Work, 17*(4), 290–298.

Peak, T., Toseland, R. W., & Banks, S. M. (1995). The impact of a spouse-caregiver support group on care recipient health care costs. *Journal of Aging and Health, 7*(3), 427–449.

Perloff, J. D. (2003). Medicare and Medicaid: Health policy. In R. L. Edwards & J. G. Hopps (Eds.), *Encyclopedia of Social Work* (19th ed., supp., pp. 107–113). Washington, DC: NASW Press.

Poole, D. L. (1997). Health care: Direct practice. In R. L. Edwards & J. G. Hopps (Eds.), *Encyclopedia of Social*

Work (19th ed., supp., pp. 1156–1167). Washington, DC: NASW Press.

Rice, D. P. (1995). Health care: Financing. In R. L. Edwards & J. G. Hopps (Eds.), *Encyclopedia of Social Work* (19th ed., Vol. 2, pp. 1161–1174). Washington, DC: NASW Press.

Rizzo, V. M., & Rowe, J. (2003). *Studies of the efficacy and cost-effectiveness of social work services in aging: A report commissioned by the National Leadership Coalition*. New York: NY Academy of Medicine. Available: *http://socialwork.org.*

Rodgers, J., & Leutz, S. (2003). *Cost of caring: key drivers of growth in spending on hospital care*. Washington, DC: Price Waterhouse Coopers.

Rosenfeld, P. (2003). *Exploring the current status and future direction for professional social workers along the long term care continuum: A concept paper with research and policy implications*. New York: Office of Special Populations, New York Academy of Medicine.

Ross, J. W. (1997). Hospital social work. In R. L. Edwards & J. G. Hopps (Eds.), *Encyclopedia of Social Work* (19th ed., Vol. 2, pp. 1365–1377). Washington, DC: NASW Press.

Shortell, S., Gilles, R., & Devers, K. (1995). Reinventing the American hospital. *Milbank Quarterly, 73*(2), 131–159.

Toseland, R. W., O'Donnell, J. C., Engelhardt, J. B., Hendler, S. A., Richie, J. T., & Jue, D. (1996). Outpatient geriatric evaluation and management: Results of a randomized trial. *Medical Care, 34* (6), 624–640.

Toseland, R. W., O'Donnell, J. C., Engelhardt, J. B., Richie, J. T., Jue, D., & Banks, S. M. (1997). Outpatient geriatric evaluation and management: Is there an investment effect? *Gerontologist, 37*(3), 324–332.

Toseland, R. W., Labrecque, M. S., Goebel, S. T., & Whitney, M. H. (1992). An evaluation of a group program for spouses of frail elderly veterans. *Gerontologist, 32*(3), 382–390.

Toseland, R. W., McCallion, P., Smith, T., Huck, S., Bourgeois, P., Garstka, & T. A. (2001). Health education groups for caregivers in an HMO. *Journal of Clinical Psychology, 57*(4), 551–570.

U.S. Department of Labor, Bureau of Labor Statistics. (2004). *Occupational outlook handbook: Social workers*. Available: *www.bls.gov/oco/ocos060.htm.*

Volland, P., & Berkman, B. (2004). Educating social workers for emerging urban problems with an aging population: The need to integrate field experience with didactic training. *Journal of Academic Medicine 79*(12): 1192–1197.

Volland, P., Berkman, B., Phillips, M., & Stein, G. (2003). Social work education for health care: Addressing practice competencies. *Journal of Social Work in Health Care, 37*(4), 1–18.

Williams, M., Williams, T. F., Zimmer, J. G., Hall, W. J., & Podgorski, C. A. (1987). How does the team approach to outpatient geriatric evaluation compare with the traditional care: A report of a randomized controlled trial. *Journal of the American Geriatrics Society, 35*(12), 1071–1078.

Zuniga, M. (1995). Aging: Social work practice. In R. L. Edwards & J. G. Hopps (Eds.), *Encyclopedia of Social Work* (19th ed., Vol. 1, pp. 173–183). Washington, DC: NASW Press.

Social work plays an important role in the development and implementation of home care, which has become the preferred care option for growing numbers of disabled and chronically ill older adults. While professional social work knowledge, skills, and values are well suited to address the needs of home care clients and their caregivers, social work is often viewed as a professional service secondary to physician and nursing care, which are considered the primary home care services (Berger, 1988; Kane, 1987). Moreover, the lack of outcome studies on the effectiveness of social work services has contributed to this perception of social work as an ancillary service, and thus to the underutilization of social workers in home care (Lee & Gutheil, 2003). Nonetheless, the emerging field of home care provides opportunities for social work that can significantly expand its role and contribute to the health and well-being of older adults and their families. This chapter provides an overview of social work practice in home care, including a historical perspective on this practice arena, social work's current role and functions, and government policies and funding mechanisms for home care that have both shaped and constrained social work practice. We conclude with a brief discussion of some challenges involved in enhancing the visibility and role of social workers in home care and suggest some possible solutions.

DEFINITIONS

"Home care" refers to services provided by home care organizations, which include home health agencies, hospices, homemaker and home care aide agencies, staffing and private-duty agencies, and companies specializing in medical equipment and supplies, pharmaceuticals, and drug infusion therapy (National Association for Home Care & Hospice [NAHC], n.d.). Several types of home care organizations may merge to provide a wide variety of services through an integrated system. For example, a home health agency might also provide hospice care and homemaker services. This chapter will focus on home health care and homemaker service agencies, which are the most frequent users of social work services among home care organizations. Hospice care, in which social work plays an integral role, is addressed at length in chapter 38 in this book.

Home health care (HHC) is often associated with the type of care provided under the Medicare home health benefit. Medicare characterizes HHC as en-

A. E. BENJAMIN
EDNA NAITO-CHAN

Home Care Settings

compassing "a wide range of health and social services . . . delivered at home to recovering, disabled, chronically or terminally ill individuals in need of medical, nursing, social, or therapeutic treatment and/or assistance with activities of daily living" (Centers for Medicare & Medicaid Services [CMS], 2003a). Activities of daily living (ADLs) are self-care activities that include bathing, dressing, feeding, toileting, and transferring. Assistance with ADLs is known as personal assistance or care. Despite Medicare's rather broad characterization of HHC, older persons actually qualify for home health care because of medical conditions and related assistance needs, and supportive care needs are considered secondary. *Homemaker service agencies,* on the other hand, employ workers who provide personal assistance, that is, help with ADLs, as well as homemaker and chore services, which include assistance with meal preparation, housekeeping, laundry, shopping, and transportation, termed instrumental activities of daily living (IADLs). The needs of older adults requiring these services tend to be ongoing and primarily related to functional impairment more than medical need; hence they are supportive rather than medically oriented services.

HOME CARE FOR AN AGING SOCIETY

The growth of the home care industry in the United States has been both dramatic and dynamic. The National Association for Home Care and Hospice (NAHC) reported that there were about 1,100 home care agencies in 1963. By 2001, this number had grown to more than 20,000 providers delivering home care services to about 7.6 million persons with acute or chronic health conditions, permanent disability, or terminal illness (NAHC, 2001). While the 1965 enactment of Medicare and Medicaid legislation accelerated the growth of the home care industry, the high risk of disability and chronic illness that are hallmarks of an aging society has made home care an increasingly attractive option for older adults and their caregivers. In 2000, about 26.1% of those 65–74 years old and 45.1% of those 75 years and over reported a limitation caused by a chronic condition. Moreover, the majority of older people have at least one chronic condition, and many have multiple conditions. The most frequently occurring conditions per 100 elderly in 1996 were (in descending order) arthritis, hypertension, hearing impairments, heart disease, cataracts, orthopedic impairments, sinusitis, and diabetes (Administration on Aging, 2002).

Disability is also experienced by a significant proportion of older adults. In 2000, approximately 42% (14 million) of the noninstitutionalized older population 65 years and over reported having at least one disability: 14.2% had a severe visual or hearing impairment; 28.6% had a physical disability that limits walking, climbing stairs, reaching, lifting or carrying; 10.8% reported a mental disability that impedes learning, memory, and concentration; 9.5% had difficulties in doing ADLs; and 20.4% reported having difficulties in leaving their homes to shop or visit the doctor's office (Administration on Aging, 2002).

As the risk for chronic illness and disability increases with age, so does the need for assistance with ADLs. Data from the 2003 National Health Interview Survey (NHIS; National Center for Health Statistics [NCHS], 2004a) indicate that adults aged 85 years and over were more than seven times as likely as adults aged 65–74 years old to need help with personal care from other people (22.6% versus 3.2%). Moreover, the NHIS data also show that the proportions of older women and minorities who needed personal care assistance were higher than for older white men. For those 85 years old and over, 25.3% of women versus 17.3% of men reported needing ADL assistance; and the proportion of those needing assistance aged 65 and over was higher for Hispanic (10.1%) and non-Hispanic black (9.9%) elders than for non-Hispanic white elders (6.0%).

HISTORICAL PERSPECTIVE

A century ago, virtually all medical care was provided in the home, first by family members and other "natural" caregivers, and later by physicians making house calls and by visiting nurses (Benjamin, 1993; Cowles, 2003). The provision of services in the homes of clients is also not new to social work practice. Social work practice in home care is steeped in two relevant traditions—community-based "friendly visitor" services and hospital social work. Indeed, contemporary social work practice had its beginnings in the nineteenth century with "friendly visitor" services provided by charitable organizations on behalf of the ill and the indigent (Brieland, 1995; Romaine-Davis, Boondas, & Lenihan, 1995). Friendly visitations were part of "outdoor relief"—assistance to people who resided in their homes and outside of an almshouse, orphanage, or other residential facility (Barker, 2003). Friendly visitors, usually middle- and upper-class women, began as volunteers, then became paid employees of charity organization societies (COSs), and eventually became known as social workers. In general, the main duties of the friendly visitors were not very different from those of social workers in home care today: to investigate homes of indigent families; determine the causes of problems; provide guidance for solving problems; and, in some cases, provide material aid. The latter was rarely granted, since COSs stressed the morality of giving material assistance to only the "worthy" and not those who were considered able-bodied and thus employable, such as the "sturdy beggar," alcoholic, or prostitute. As a result, "support went to the smallest number, at the least cost, and for the shortest time" (Brieland, 1995, p. 2247)—an approach to administering public assistance that continues to this day. Eventually, friendly visiting was replaced by the practice of professional social casework, currently referred to as "clinical social work," as the friendly visitors developed greater professionalism, received better training, and improved understanding of the causes of health and social ills (Barker, 2003).

The other progenitor of social work in home care is hospital or medical social work. The role of the hospital social worker was initially modeled after that of the "friendly visitor" in its sympathetic and paternalistic attempt to alleviate social problems (Nacman, 1977). Richard Cabot, a physician at Massachusetts General Hospital in Boston, recognized the importance of psychological and social conditions that lead to illness and recovery. He is credited with introducing social work practice in a medical setting by adding social workers to his staff in 1905 for the purpose of "augment[ing] the physician's treatment of patients by studying, reporting, and alleviating, to the extent possible, the patients' social problems that interfered with the plan for medical care" (Cabot, 1915, as cited in Caputi, 1978). Cabot's delineation of social work as an ancillary function to medical care continues to resonate to this day in most entitlement programs and health care settings. As a result of the efforts of Cabot and Ida Cannon, a nurse with social work training who was charged by Cabot to establish the nation's first medical social work department at Massachusetts General in 1906, the American Hospital Association developed the first formal description of medical social work in the mid-1920s (Caputi, 1978; Nacman, 1977; Ross, 1995). It includes the augmentation role suggested by Cabot, along with other practice roles: liaison between the physician and patient; liaison between the physician and community resources necessary for continuing patient care; and educator serving as an agent of the physician to promote pa-

tient compliance in the medical treatment plan (Caputi, 1978).

During the decades prior to 1965, the importance of home care waned as the delivery of medical care and social services shifted from the home to hospitals and physicians' offices in response to scientific advances and major socioeconomic changes like urbanization, industrialization, and immigration. But interest in home care reemerged as concern increased for the growing numbers of persons with chronic illnesses who began to occupy large numbers of hospital beds. Consequently, efforts to find suitable alternatives to institutional care would motivate federal home care policy development and reform for years to come (Benjamin, 1993).

By the mid-1950s, a commission of the U.S. Public Health Services called for organized home care programs to provide medical and social services to patients in their homes following hospitalization. Care was to be provided by a team of health care professionals through a range of services under a physician's plan of care, including medical, nursing, social work, housekeeping, transportation, medication, and other benefits. The commission's home care model was largely based on the first hospital-based home care service at New York City's Montefiore Hospital, which was established in 1947 as a response to the limited home services then provided by visiting nurse organizations (Benjamin, 1993; Cowles, 2003; Goode, 2000). Some private health insurance companies—specifically Blue Cross-Blue Shield—were convinced that home care following hospitalization for certain patients could, under institutional and physician oversight, deliver high-quality and cost-effective care. As a result, the introduction of home care coverage by the "Blues" significantly enhanced the visibility and respectability of organized home care programs (Benjamin, 1993). The passage of Medicare (Title 18) and Medicaid (Title 19) legislation in 1965, which established federally funded health care for older adults and the medically needy, conclusively established the role of home care in mainstream health care. Moreover, the role of social work was formally established as an important professional service in organized home care programs.

HOME CARE POLICY AND FUNDING

In developing home care policy, federal planners embraced the range of services offered through the Montefiore home care model, but limited them to the kind of coverage provided by the Blue Cross plans (Benjamin, 1993). Although nursing visits, home therapies (physical, occupational, and speech), medical social services, home health aide care, and medical supplies and equipment are included, the physician (who rarely makes home visits) is charged with establishing a care plan and providing the medical supervision consistent with postacute medical care. Various observers have conceptualized current home care policy and funding in terms of two models: the predominant medical or post-acute model represented by HHC, which is largely financed by Medicare; and the social-supportive model, which involves personal assistance and homemaker services typically covered by Medicaid and out-of-pocket payment (Benjamin, 1993; Dhooper, 1997).

Medicare and the Medical Model

Established as an age-based entitlement program to provide medical care for those 65 years and over, Medicare has played a significant role in the rapid growth of the home care industry. Medicare beneficiaries are the largest consumers of HHC. In 2000, over 70% of the 1.36 million patients receiving home health care were Medicare beneficiaries aged 65 and older (NCHS, 2004b, table 7). Medicare coverage of home health services is based fundamentally on the medical model, which approaches the beneficiary as a postacute patient with an illness that needs to be treated with medically oriented interventions (termed "skilled care"). Medicare's home health benefit is not designed to address environmental factors that may influence illness and recovery or long-term care needs (Komisar, 2002). Thus, home care services are initiated by a physician's order and are usually reserved for those who have been recently hospitalized and whose care needs are short-term and intermittent. A Medicare beneficiary can qualify for HHC if he or she meets all of the following conditions.

- Physician decides that beneficiary needs medical care at home, and makes a plan for care at home
- Beneficiary must need at least one of the following: intermittent (fewer than seven days each week or less than eight hours each day over a period of 21 days or less) skilled nursing care, or physical therapy or speech-language therapy, or continue to need occupational therapy
- Beneficiary must be homebound (unable to leave home unassisted)

- Home health agency providing care is Medicare-certified (CMS, 2003c)

An "episode of care" (i.e., length of benefit coverage) lasts 60 days. Because it is based on the medical model, Medicare home health coverage allows beneficiaries to receive medical social work services, home health aide services, and occupational therapy *only* when they are also receiving skilled nursing, physical therapy or speech therapy. Therefore, nonprimary services such as social work are not provided to all HHC patients, but are only required when ordered by the physician (Dhooper, 1997). In addition to skilled services, Medicare also covers medical supplies like wound dressings and equipment such as wheelchairs or walkers. However, Medicare coverage of HHC does *not* include 24 hour-a-day care at home, home-delivered meals, and homemaker services such as cooking, cleaning, and shopping. Prescription drug coverage, previously not provided under Medicare, is now available as a result of the passage of the Medicare Prescription Drug, Improvement and Modernization Act (MMA) of 2003.

Despite its status as an optional home health service, medical social work is characterized by Medicare as a service that is "necessary to resolve social or emotional problems that are or are expected to be an impediment to the effective treatment of the patient's medical condition or his or her rate of recovery" (CMS, 2003a, chap. 2, para. 206.3). The services provided by HHC social workers can include assessment, community resource planning, counseling services (which includes discharge planning), short-term therapy (i.e., two or three visits) for the patient's family member or caregiver to address problems that hinder effective patient treatment, and "other" services approved by physician's orders, such as interventions related to suspected abuse/neglect and suicide risk.

Medicaid and Social-Supportive Care

Medicaid—the jointly financed federal and state health care program for low-income people—represents a small but growing portion of total payments for home care. In some states, Medicaid may also pay all or a portion of Medicare premiums, deductibles, and coinsurance payments for qualified low-income Medicare beneficiaries (CMS, 2003c). Medicaid payments for home care are divided into three main categories: the traditional home health benefit, which is required in all state plans and reimburses basic home health care and medical equipment; and two optional programs—the personal care option and home and community-based waivers (NAHC, 2001). The availability of these two options varies from state to state and reflects the social-supportive model of home care. Both personal care and waiver programs involve "unskilled" care that assists clients with ADL, IADL, or homemaker tasks necessary to remain in their homes. Under this model, the need for home care services is determined by limitations in functioning due to chronic conditions rather than an acute medical episode. Supportive home care, therefore, involves longer-term services for individuals with chronic care needs and is heavily utilized by eligible older adults and younger people with disabilities (NCHS, 2004b).

In Medicaid-funded home care programs, social workers generally are less well-represented than in Medicare-funded programs, since Medicaid does not pay for social work services provided by home health care and homemaker service agencies unless the client is enrolled in a waiver program to reduce nursing home stays. Under Medicaid, clients deemed at high risk for nursing home placement may be provided personal assistance, homemaker services, meals-on-wheels, respite care, transportation, adult daycare, and numerous other services (Goode, 2000). Clients in waiver programs can also receive case management by social workers.

Funding Sources

Medicare is the largest single payer of home care services. In 1999, Medicare spending accounted for about 26.3% of total estimated home health expenditures, while Medicaid accounted for 9.7% (NAHC, 2001). Other public funding sources—the Older Americans Act, Title 20 Social Services Block Grants, the Veterans Administration, and the Civilian Health and Medical Program of the Uniformed Services (CHAMPUS)—funded 12.7% of home health care spending. Private sources accounted for 46.2%: 19% was paid by private insurance companies, while 27.2% was paid out-of-pocket. (About 5% comes from other sources, including philanthropy.) By 2010, Medicare and private payments for home health care are expected to grow to 28% and 53%, respectively (NAHC, 2001). Despite the increasing need for home care services among older people, this projected growth has been slowed considerably as a consequence of the Balanced Budget Act (BBA) of 1997, which marked a major policy change in home care financing.

Policy Changes: Prospective Payment System

Home care expenditures rose steadily during the 1980s and 1990s, and the number of Medicare-certified home health agencies peaked at over 10,000 in 1997 (NAHC, 2001). Total Medicare home health expenditures increased at an annual rate of 21% between 1987 and 1997, accounting for 9% of total Medicare spending in 1997, up from 2% in 1987 (Health Care Financing Administration [HCFA], 1999). To curb rising costs and increase efficiency, the BBA of 1997 introduced a prospective payment system (PPS) for home care organizations that changed reimbursement from fee-for-service to a flat rate based on classification of patient condition and associated needs (Cowles, 2003). As a result, Medicare spending between fiscal years 1998 and 2000 decreased by 34%, the number of Medicare-certified home health providers declined by 31.5% (NAHC, 2001), and visits per user were cut nearly in half (Liu, Long, & Dowling, 2003). Between 1997 and 1998, the reduction in home health care utilization was heavily concentrated among lower income Medicare beneficiaries (Zhu, 2004). Of great concern has been the impact on minority older populations, who already experience poverty in greater numbers and have lower utilization rates of community-based services (including home care), despite having higher service needs in terms of medical problems and functional limitations (Damron-Rodriguez, Wallace, & Kingston, 1994; Wallace, Levy-Storms, Kingston, & Andersen, 1998). Added to existing structural and cultural barriers to utilization, the PPS may result in lower home care utilization rates among ethnic elders.

Assuring Quality of Care

Several organizations are involved in addressing issues of quality in home care. In most cases, an agency must be certified in order to receive public funding. For example, HHC agencies must be certified by Medicare or Medicaid in order to receive reimbursement. Other efforts to assure quality include accreditation provided by nonprofit advocacy groups, which depend on industry-wide acceptance and the weight of public opinion to exercise influence (Romaine-Davis, Boondas, & Lenihan, 1995). The nation's predominant accrediting body in health care is the Joint Commission on Accreditation of Healthcare Organizations (JCAHO), which evaluates more than 17,000

organizations, including hospitals, health maintenance organizations (HMOs), home health agencies,
long-term care facilities, behavioral health care organizations, and ambulatory care providers. Other
home care accreditation bodies include the Accreditation Commission for Home Care, Inc. (ACHC), the
Community Health Accreditation Program (CHAP),
and Homecare University.

Despite the presence of formal accrediting bodies,
assessing the quality of home care services is complicated by the following factors: diversity of programs
and services, goals, and clientele; the lack of provider
controls in multiple home care settings; and the lack
of valid patient outcome measures (Kane, Kane, Illston, & Eustis, 1994; Institute of Medicine, 2001). In
home health care, these challenges are being addressed by introduction of the Outcome and Assessment Information Set (OASIS), an instrument
utilized by Medicare-certified home health agencies
to measure patient medical, functional, emotional,
behavioral, and cognitive outcomes for purposes of
outcome-based quality improvement (Hittle et al.,
2003; Shaughnessy, Crisler, Schlenker, & Arnold,
1997). While critics have called for more information
on the reliability of OASIS (Berg & Mor, 2001), the
widespread dissemination and utilization of OASIS
seems to be yielding an impressive set of outcomes
data based on well-tested measures.

SOCIAL WORK ROLE AND FUNCTIONS

Constraints

The roles of social work in home care have been limited in two important ways by the design of health insurance, both public and private. First, predominance
of the medical model limits the range of tasks that insurers will cover to those associated directly with
acute episodes. Second, funding constraints perenni-
ally confronting the Medicare and Medicaid programs have pressured provider agencies to control
costs, often by minimizing or eliminating services (like
social work) not considered "core" in home care. For
example, Medicare does not require social workers to
see all home health patients or to participate in the
planning of their care; it only requires that social work
services be made available to patients (Dhooper, 1997).
Consequently, within Medicare-certified home health
agencies, social workers comprise only 2% of personnel,
compared with 45% for nurses (see Table 35.1).

TABLE 35.1. HHC Personnel Mix, 2003

Service	Percent
Home health aides	38
Professional nurses	33
Vocational nurses	12
Physical therapists	5
Occupational therapists	2
Social workers	2
Other	8

Note: From *Health Care Industry Market Update—Home
Health.* Baltimore: Centers for Medicare and Medicaid Services, September 22, 2003.

Similarly, in 1999, social workers accounted for 1% of
Medicare home health visits, compared with 48% for
nurses and just under 10% for therapists (Komisar,
2002).

Another barrier to the wider use of social work
services in home care is the lack of evidence-based research on the effectiveness of social work services.
This gap likely reflects the preponderance of medically oriented outcomes, the secondary status of social work in health care, and the lack of meaningful
measurement of social work outcomes in home care
(Lee & Gutheil, 2003). Moreover, results from the few
studies on the impact of social work efficacy in home
care are inconclusive (Braun & Rose, 1994; Cloonan,
Phillips, Irvine, & Fisher, 1991; Lee & Gutheil, 2003).
The literature on social work in home care is mostly
descriptive and exploratory and typically addresses
two themes: (1) the roles of social work (Davitt &
Kaye, 1996; Kerson & Michelsen, 1995; Reese &
Brown, 1997); and (2) the obstacles to effective social
work practice, including poor coordination with hospital discharge planners (Proctor, Morrow-Howell, &
Kaplan, 1996), geographic factors (Naleppa & Hash,
2001), and ethical dilemmas concerning advance directives, assessment of mental competence, and access
to services (Egan & Kadushin, 1998; Healy, 1998, 2003;
Kadushin & Egan, 2001).

Theoretical Model of Practice

Despite the lack of empirical evidence, the knowledge
base, skills, and values of the social work profession
would seem to position social workers to be an effective member of the home care team. There are several

theoretical models from psychology, sociology, and gerontology that inform and organize the knowledge base of social work practice with home care clients, such as continuity theory, exchange theory, social constructionism, and Erikson's theory of ego development (i.e., the stages of psychosocial development). Moreover, social work's biopsychosocial approach provides a broader, multidimensional perspective on the client's situation, and is intended to replace the "sickness" model that too frequently influences both medically based and psychodynamically based practitioners (Berkman & Volland, 1997). While in the past, psychological and interpersonal elements of social functioning have been emphasized in social work practice, there is increasing support for integrating biomedical, social, cultural, and environmental knowledge into social work practice (Berkman & Volland, 1997). Taking into account the biomedical, psychological, and social dimensions of the personal environment is useful to social workers in screening and assessing the needs of home care clients and their families, and in identifying effective interventions and needed resources.

Social Work Functions and Case Management

The problems commonly faced by home care clients and their families (detailed in Table 35.2) are diverse and fall into several categories: adjustment to illness, end of life, dementia and behavior management, caregiver issues, suspected abuse or neglect, family conflict, housing arrangements/placement, financial problems, discharge planning, inadequate living arrangements/safety and level of care issues, inadequate social support, mental health, legal issues, nonadherence to treatment, and access problems (CMS, 2003a; Cowles, 2003; Goode, 2000).

In addressing these problems, social workers in home care have assumed case management roles and have designed interventions appropriate for clients in both HHC and homemaker service agencies.

Social workers have been increasingly involved in case management activities—particularly in community-based, long-term care settings for older adults—and the National Association of Social Workers (NASW) has established both practice standards and professional certification as an "Advanced Social Work Case Manager" (National Association of Social

Workers [NASW], 2002; Yagoda, 2004). Although the role of case manager in HHC is not reimbursable and probably engenders conflicts with nursing regarding care coordination responsibilities, some case management activities (such as counseling and resource brokering) are reimbursable services under Medicare.

Although not well documented, Medicaid waiver programs may offer more opportunities for social workers to function as case managers than HHC programs. One such opportunity is provided by the Program of All-Inclusive Care for the Elderly (PACE), a capitated benefit authorized by the BBA of 1997, featuring a comprehensive medical and social service delivery system and integrated Medicare and Medicaid funding for the purposes of helping older adults at risk for institutionalization to continue living at home. In principle, capitated payment allows providers to deliver all services participants need, including social services, rather than limiting them to those reimbursable under the Medicare and Medicaid fee-for-service systems. San Francisco's On-Lok project is the first and best known of the PACE models. Currently there are 14 states with 26 approved demonstration sites, and eight states have included PACE as an option in their state plans (CMS, 2000).

There is no single, widely accepted definition of case management. Yagoda (2004, p. 1) characterizes case management (sometimes referred to as care management or care coordination) as "a highly individualized approach that considers the unique aspects of the person and at the same time provides a holistic orientation that views all aspects of the client system, including the client family, friends, their situation, and their environment." White (2001, p. 162) conceptualizes it as a set of activities "directed at locating and coordinating care from a variety of resources in response to identified need." The National Association of Social Workers (1992, Definition section, para. 2) distinguishes social work case management from other forms of case management, in that it addresses "both the individual client's biopsychosocial status [micro] as well as the state of the social system in which case management operates [macro]." In reviewing various models, we have identified several core functions for social work case management in home care (see Table 35.3): engagement, biopsychosocial assessment/reassessment, service planning, implementation of service plan, coordination and monitoring of service delivery, advocacy, and termination (Cowles, 2003; NASW, 1992; Raiff & Shore, 1993; Yagoda, 2004).

TABLE 35.2. Client Problems in Home Care Addressed by Social Workers

Problem Category	Description
Adjustment to illness	Reaction to new diagnosis, treatment, and/or changes in physical functioning
End of life issues	Grief, loss, impending death, concerns about death and dying
Dementia and behavior management	Cognitive impairment and/or behavior that negatively impacts client's treatment, quality of life, and safety
Caregiver issues	Caregiver burden, caregiver stress, and crises experienced by caregivers such as illness, hospitalization, relocation, and death
Suspected abuse/neglect	Suspected physical or sexual abuse, psychological abuse, financial exploitation, neglect by abuser, or self-neglect
Family conflict	Behavior of family members that obstructs, contravenes, or prevents client's medical treatment or rate of recovery
Housing arrangements/placement	Need for alternate placement for long-term care, such as assisted living or nursing home
Financial problems	Financial issues that create stress, anxiety, and interfere with client's ability to adhere to treatment plan, e.g., inadequate financial resources to pay for medications or medical equipment
Discharge planning	Need for assistance to make transition when home care services end and to ensure client's needs are met through linkages to community resources
Inadequate living arrangements/safety and level of care issues	Physical, emotional, social, or home environment issues that negatively affect client's safety; need for increased care/supervision
Inadequate social support	Lack of informal support, social isolation
Mental health	Emotional and psychological aspects of illness that negatively impact the plan of care, such as depression, anxiety, substance abuse, suicidal ideation; need to determine client's decision-making capacity
Legal issues	Need for education and resource linkage to legal services on issues such as advance health care planning, financial power of attorney, representative payer, guardianship, conservatorship, adult protective services
Nonadherence to treatment	Client does not follow health care treatment plan
Access problems	Barriers in access to needed medical care (including transportation) often caused by home care policy or program constraints

Note: Adapted from *Social work practice in home health care*, by R. A. Goode, 2000, New York: Haworth Press.

CHALLENGES AND OPPORTUNITIES FOR SOCIAL WORK PRACTICE

The future of social work practice in home care remains fluid and uncertain. It is constrained by increasingly restrictive reimbursement policies—particularly since 1997—and prospective payment system for HHC, as well as by a growing interest in adopting a consumer-directed approach to home care services for older people, which may limit the need for case managers (Benjamin, 2001; Simon-Rusinowitz & Hofland, 1993). The utilization of case management services is further hindered by the lack of screening instruments that help identify those in home- and community-based services programs who need social work case management (Diwan, Ivy, Merino, & Brower, 2001).

Models

Although these challenges suggest that social workers may be "losing ground" (Dhooper, 1997), models of home care are in place or being proposed that could expand the role of social workers. For example, tele-health programs and psychiatric home care have been discussed as areas where social workers can establish an important clinical role (Berkman, Heinik, Rosenthal, & Burke, 1999; Black & Mindell, 1996; Byrne, 1999). The Veterans Health Administration (VHA), the nation's single largest employer of social workers, has traditionally approached home care as an interdisciplinary program in which social work plays an integral role. Unlike Medicare-certified HHC, the provision of social work services at the VHA does not

TABLE 35.3. Social Work Case Management Functions in Home Care

Core Function	*Description*
Engagement	Through outreach and screening, identify and engage individual who would qualify for and benefit from case management services.
Biopsychosocial assessment/ reassessment	Assess interplay of physical, environmental, behavioral, psychological, economic, and social factors addressing, but not limited to:
	• Physical and mental health status
	• Functioning status (ADL/IADL)
	• Risk (including lethality, safety)
	• Client's needs and availability of resources in client's social support system (e.g., family, friends, organizational memberships)
	• Client's customary coping style
	• Economic status and needs
	• Equipment and home environment needs
	• Relevant cultural and religious factors
	• Input of relevant specialists, including home care team members and client's self-assessment
	Client's needs and progress should be periodically reassessed as prescribed by the program and/or case manager, or when there is a change in the client's situation.
Service planning	Development of service plan that includes:
	• Client preferences and feedback
	• Short- and long-term goals consistent with client's values, strengths, and preferences
	• Achievable, measurable goals with time lines for objectives and plan review
	• Criteria for success
	• Emergency plan in advance
	• With client's input, timely updates based on changes in conditions
	• Input from home care team
	• Identification of discipline or individual responsible for specific functions
Implementation of service plan	Provide psychosocial services, including:
	• Counseling and support to empower clients to participate in services
	• Link clients to resources to strengthen/build client autonomy and self-sufficiency
	• Service brokering
	• Crisis management if needed
Coordination/monitoring of service delivery	Coordinate and monitor service delivery to ensure continuity and complementarity of the interventions by:
	• Monitoring service provision for appropriateness, intensity, quantity, quality, and efficacy
	• Systematically documenting unmet needs and gaps in services/resources
	• Developing mechanisms to monitor outcomes (e.g., client satisfaction)
Advocacy	Advocate for clients and their families to receive entitlements or obtain needed services, including those provided by social worker's own agency. Tasks include:
	• Helping client to collect evidence of need and qualify for benefits
	• Explaining client's perspective to others
	• "Marketing" client to program(s)
	• Ensuring client's services are not prematurely terminated, and are terminated when appropriate
	• Encouraging client through role play and support to self-advocate

(*continued*)

TABLE 35.3.   Social Work Case Management Functions in Home Care (*continued*)

Core Function	Description
Termination	Termination can be planned or unplanned, and involve any of the following activities: • Discharge planning • Case transfer • Helping client assess need for continued services and make appropriate arrangements • Counseling and support to allow ventilation of client's feelings about termination • Mutual review and assessment of client's progress and goal achievement • Providing follow-up services to ensure quality and continuity of care

Note: From *Social work in the health field: A care perspective* (2nd ed.), by L. A. F. Cowles, 2003, New York: Haworth Social Work Practice Press; *NASW Standards for social work case management*, Washington, DC, National Association of Social Workers, 1992; *Advanced case management*, by N. R. Raiff and B. Shore, 1993, Newbury Park, CA: Sage; and "Case management with older adults: A social work perspective," by L. Yagoda, May 2004, *NASW Aging Practice Update*, pp. 1–3.

require a physician's order. Instead, social work is considered a primary service by the VHA's Hospital-Based Primary Care Program (the VHA's hospital-based home health program), and the team social worker is required to visit the home in order "to assess the patient's and the home caregiver's psychosocial strengths and weaknesses as well as the adequacy of the formal and informal social support system" (Veterans Health Administration [VHA], 1992, chap. 2.11).

Possible Solutions

Geriatric social work leaders in the areas of health care policy, practice, research, and education have begun to address some of the challenges confronting social work in home care. For example, two studies have been funded by the John A. Hartford Foundation—one on the relationship between social work education and practice in health care (Volland, Berkman, Stein, & Vaghy, 2000) and the other on the impact of the prospective payment system on social work in home health care (Lee & Gutheil, 2003; Lee & Rock, 2001). These studies have produced several recommendations, including (1) enhancing social work curriculum content through a greater focus on health care practice (including case management), outcomes research, and data management; (2) establishing independent case finding for social work services to replace the current system of dependence on physicians and nurses; (3) developing a clearer definition of social work roles in HHC that is understood by other health care professionals; (4) fostering evidence-based research on the effectiveness of social work services; and (5) developing screening instruments for social work services for use in HHC.

In light of current constraints, there is enormous potential for expanding the role of social work in home care and for demonstrating the impact of social interventions on health. Without the evidence on impact, however, it has been difficult to make the case for expanded resources to support social work services. To address this dilemma, advocates need to identify a small number of demonstration programs to test the impact of selected social work interventions with home care clients and to build support for funding both the demonstrations and their evaluation. While a solid evidence base will probably not be sufficient to garner the political support required to enlarge the role of social work in home care, it is certainly necessary if the profession is to expand the service options available to vulnerable populations at home.

REFERENCES

Administration on Aging. (2002). *A profile of older Americans 2002*. Washington, DC: Administration on Aging. Available: *www.aoa.gov/prof/Statistics/profile/12_pf.asp*.

Barker, R. L. (2003). *The social work dictionary* (5th ed.). Washington, DC: NASW Press.

Benjamin, A. E. (1993). An historical perspective on home care policy. *Home Health Care Services Quarterly, 71*(1), 129–166.

Benjamin, A. E. (2001). Consumer-direction services at home: A new model for persons with disabilities. *Health Affairs, 20*(6), 80–95.

Berg, K., & Mor, V. (2001). Long-term care assessment. In G. L. Maddox (Ed.), *Encyclopedia of aging* (3rd ed., Vol. 1, pp. 631–633). New York: Springer.

Berger, R. M. (1988). Making home health social work more effective. *Home Health Care Services Quarterly, 9*(1), 63–75.

Berkman, P., Heinik, J., Rosenthal, M., & Burke, M. (1999). Supportive telephone outreach as an interventional strategy for elderly patients in a period of crisis. *Social Work in Health Care, 28*(4), 63–76.

Berkman, B., & Volland, P. (1997). Health care practice overview. In R. L. Edwards (Ed.), *Encyclopedia of social work: 1997 supplement* (pp. 143–149). Washington, DC: NASW Press.

Black, J., & Mindell, M. (1996). A model for community-based mental health services for older adults: Innovative social work practice. *Journal of Gerontological Social Work, 26*(3–4), 113–127.

Braun, K. L., & Rose, C. L. (1994). Testing the impact of a case management program on caregiver appraisal. *Journal of Gerontological Social Work, 21*(3–4), 51–69.

Brieland, D. (1995). Social work practice: History and evolution. In R. L. Edwards & J. G. Hopps (Eds.), *Encyclopedia of social work* (19th ed., Vol. 3, pp. 2247–2257). Washington, DC: NASW Press.

Byrne, J. (1999). Social work in psychiatric home care: Regulations, roles, and realities. *Health & Social Work, 24*(1), 65–71.

Caputi, M. A. (1978). Social work in health care: Past and future. *Health & Social Work, 3*(1), 9–29.

Centers for Medicare and Medicaid Services. (2000). *A profile of Medicaid: Chart book 2000.* Baltimore: Centers for Medicare and Medicaid Services. Available: *www.cms.hhs.gov/charts/medicaid/2Tchartbk.pdf.*

Centers for Medicare and Medicaid Services. (2003a). Coverage of services. In *Home health agency manual* (chap. 2). Baltimore: Centers for Medicare and Medicaid Services. Available: *www.cms.hhs.gov/manuals/ 11_hha/hh205–2.asp.*

Centers for Medicare and Medicaid Services. (2003b, September 22). *Health care industry market update— Home health.* Baltimore: Centers for Medicare and Medicaid Services. Available: *www.cms.hhs.gov/reports/ hcimu/hcimu_09222003.pdf.*

Centers for Medicare and Medicaid Services. (2003c). *Medicare and home health care.* Baltimore: Centers for Medicare and Medicaid Services. Available: *www.medicare.gov/Publications/Pubs/pdf/10969.pdf.*

Centers for Medicare and Medicaid Services. (n.d.). *OASIS overview.* Baltimore: Centers for Medicare and Medicaid Services. Available: *www.cms.hhs.gov/oasis/ hhoview.asp.*

Cloonan, P. A., Phillips, E. K., Irvine, A., & Fisher, M. E. (1991). A study of patients receiving no billed nursing care. *Home Health Care Services Quarterly, 12*(1), 37–45.

Cowles, L. A. F. (2003). *Social work in the health field: A care perspective* (2nd ed.). New York: Haworth Social Work Practice Press.

Damron-Rodriguez, J., Wallace, S., & Kingston, R. (1994). Service utilization and minority elderly: Appropriateness, accessibility, and acceptability. *Gerontology & Geriatrics Education, 15*(1), 45–63.

Davitt, J. K., & Kaye, L. W. (1996). Supporting patient autonomy: Decision making in home health care. *Social Work, 41*(1), 41–50.

Dhooper, S. S. (1997). *Social work in health care in the twenty-first century.* Thousand Oaks, CA: Sage.

Diwan, S., Ivy, C., Merino, D. A., & Brower, T. (2001). Assessing need for intensive case management in long-term care. *Gerontologist, 41*(5), 680–686.

Egan, M., & Kadushin, G. (1998). The social worker in the emerging field of home care. *Health & Social Work, 24*(1), 43–55.

Goode, R. A. (2000). *Social work practice in home health care.* New York: Haworth Press.

Health Care Financing Administration. (1999). *A profile of Medicare home health: Chart book* (Publication No. HCFA-10138). Washington, DC: U.S. Government Printing Office.

Healy, T. C. (1998). The complexity of everyday ethics in home health care: An analysis of social workers' decisions regarding frail elders' autonomy. *Social Work in Health Care, 27*(4), 19–37.

Healy, T. C. (2003). Ethical decision making: Pressure and uncertainty as complicating factors. *Health & Social Work, 28*(4), 293–301.

Hittle, D. F., Shaughnessy, P. W., Crisler, K. S., Powell, M. C., Richard, A. A., Conway, K. S., Stearns, P. M., & Engle, K. (2003). A study of reliability and burden of home health assessment using OASIS. *Home Health Care Services Quarterly, 22*(4), 43–63.

Institute of Medicine. (2001). *Improving the quality of long-term care.* Washington, DC: National Academy of Sciences.

Kadushin, G., & Egan, M. (2001). Ethical dilemmas in home health care. *Health & Social Work, 26*(3), 136–149.

Kane, R. A. (1987). Long-term care. In A. Minahan (Ed.), *Encyclopedia of Social Work* (18th ed., Vol. 2, pp. 59–72). Silver Spring, MD: National Association of Social Workers.

Kane, R. A., Kane, R. L., Illston, L. H., & Eustis, N. N. (1994). Perspectives on home care quality. *Health Care Financing Review, 16*(1), 69–89.

Kerson, T. S., & Michelsen, R. W. (1995). Counseling homebound clients and their families. *Journal of Gerontological Social Work, 24*(3–4), 159–190.

Komisar, H. L. (2002). Rolling back Medicare home health. *Health Care Financing Review, 24*(2), 33–55.

Lee, J. S., & Gutheil, I. A. (2003). The older patient at home: Social work services and home health care. In B. Berkman & L. Harootyan (Eds.), *Social work and health care in an aging society* (pp. 73–95). New York: Springer.

Lee, J. S., & Rock, B. D. (2001). *Social work in home health care (HHC): Challenges in the new prospective payment system (PPS).* Policy Action Paper. New York: Fordham University Ravazzin Center for Social Work Research in Aging.

Liu, K., Long, S. K., & Dowling, K. (2003). Medicare interim payment system's impact on Medicare home health utilization. *Health Care Financing Review, 25*(1), 81–97.

Nacman, M. (1977). Social work in health settings. *Social Work in Health Care, 2*(4), 407–418.

Naleppa, M. J., & Hash, K. M. (2001). Home-based practice with older adults: Challenges and opportunities in the home environment. *Journal of Gerontological Social Work, 35*(1), 71–89.

National Association for Home Care and Hospice. (2001). *Basic statistics about home care.* Washington, DC: National Association for Home Care and Hospice. Available: *www.nahc.org/Consumer/hcstats.htm.*

National Association for Home Care and Hospice. (n.d.). *Who provides home care?* Washington, DC: National Association for Home Care and Hospice. Available: *www.nahc.org/NAHC/NewsInfo/who.html.*

National Association of Social Workers. (1992). *NASW standards for social work case management.* Washington, DC: National Association of Social Workers. Available: *www.socialworkers.org/practice/standards/sw_case_mgmt.asp.*

National Center for Health Statistics. (2004a). *Early release of selected estimates based on data from the 2003 National Health Interview Survey.* Washington, DC: Centers for Disease Control and Prevention. Available: *www.cdc.gov/nchs/data/nhis/earlyrelease/200406_12.pdf.*

National Center for Health Statistics. (2004b). *National home and hospice care survey.* Washington, DC: Cen-

ters for Disease Control and Prevention. Available: *www.cdc.gov/nchs/data/nhhcsd/curhomecare.pdf.*

Proctor, E. K., Morrow-Howell, N., & Kaplan, S. J. (1996). Implementation of discharge plans for chronically-ill elders discharged home. *Health & Social Work, 21*(1), 30–40.

Raiff, N. R., & Shore, B. (1993). *Advanced case management.* Newbury Park, CA: Sage.

Reese, D. J., & Brown, D. R. (1997). Psychosocial and spiritual care in hospice: Differences between nursing, social work, and clergy. *Hospice Journal, 12*(1), 29–41.

Romaine-Davis, A., Boondas, J., & Lenihan, A. (Eds.). (1995). *Encyclopedia of home care for the elderly.* Westport, CT: Greenwood Press.

Ross, J. W. (1995). Hospital social work. In R. L. Edwards & J. G. Hopps (Eds.), *Encyclopedia of social work* (19th ed., Vol. 2, pp. 1365–1377). Washington, DC: NASW Press.

Shaughnessy, P. W., Crisler, K. S., Schlenker, R. E., & Arnold, A. G. (1997). Outcomes across the care continuum: Home health care. *Medical Care, 35*(Suppl. 11), NS115–NS123, and 35(12), 1225–1226.

Simon-Rusinowitz, L., & Hofland, B. F. (1993). Adopting a disability approach to home care services for older adults. *Gerontologist, 33*(2), 159–167.

Veterans Health Administration. (1992). HBPC (Hospital Based Home Care) program. In *VHA manual* (Vol. M-5, Pt. 5, pp. 1–55). Washington, DC: Department of Veterans Affairs.

Volland, P. J., Berkman, B., Stein, G., & Vaghy, A. (2000). *Social work education for practice in health care: Final report.* New York: New York Academy of Medicine.

Wallace, S. P., Levy-Storms, L., Kingston, R., & Andersen, R. M. (1998). The persistence of race and ethnicity in the use of long-term care. *Journal of Gerontology: Social Sciences, 53B*(2), S104–S112.

White, M. (2001). Case management. In G. L. Maddox (Ed.), *The encyclopedia of aging* (3rd ed., Vol. 1, pp. 162–166). New York: Springer.

Yagoda, L. (2004, May). Case management with older adults: A social work perspective. *NASW Aging Practice Update,* 1–3.

Zhu, C. W. (2004). Effects of the Balance Budget Act on Medicare home health utilization. *Journal of the American Geriatrics Society, 52*(6), 989–994.

Gerontological social work practice aims to address environmental, psychosocial, health and mental, organizational, and societal barriers to physical and emotional well-being of older adults. Gerontological social workers promote responsiveness and effectiveness of social institutions to the needs and social problems of an elderly clientele (Mellor & Lindeman, 1998). Gerontological social workers employed in the public sector serve older adult clients under laws and regulations promulgated at federal, state, and local levels.

Public welfare and social service agencies provide safety net benefits to the truly needy based on the principle of "less eligibility," a poor law concept made explicit in early nineteenth-century social welfare legislation in both England and America (Axinn & Levin, 1997). Social workers in these public service systems deliver, plan, and administer social welfare services of last resort in the domains of income support, medical care, housing, personal social services, and employment. These services are available to older adult clients living in the community who qualify under law because they are destitute, have no one willing or able to provide for them, or are at risk of harm and lack the capacity to make informed decisions on their own behalf (U.S. House of Representatives, 1999).

SERVICES AVAILABLE

Service programs for older adults in government departments of public welfare and social services include adult protective services (Otto, 2000; Wolf, 1995); emergency cash grant assistance; food stamps and home energy assistance program; Medicaid eligibility determination; home attendant or personal care case management and medical review services; adult foster care (Sherman, 1995; U.S. House of Representatives, 1999); and AIDS case management services (Emlet, 1996).

Indirectly, county departments of public welfare serve older adults raising grandchildren with Temporary Assistance to Needy Families (TANF) and through public child welfare kinship foster care programs (Burnette, 1999). Some counties administer employment programs for older adults. In New York City, the county department of public welfare provides employment services and transitional benefits for older adult receiving general assistance who require up to a year of work credits to qualify for Old Age Survivors and Disability Insurance (OASDI) benefits when they turn 65. Professional social workers

PATRICIA BROWNELL

Departments of Public Welfare or Social Services

staff this innovative program, called Senior Works (K. Lee, personal communication, May 21, 2004).

LEGAL AUTHORITY (ROLES OF FEDERAL AND STATE GOVERNMENTS), REGULATIONS, OVERSIGHT

State and county public welfare and social service departments are unique settings for professional social work practice. Public sector social work practice is defined by laws enacted at the federal, state, and local levels. The county departments of social services operate under state regulatory oversight. For those state- and county-based public welfare and social service programs funded with federal tax dollars, the federal government is also responsible for oversight activities.

While most states had programs to assist the elderly before the passage of the Social Security Act of 1935 (P.L. 74–271, H.R. 7260, August 14, 1935), public sector social work practice came into its own with the passage and implementation of the Social Security Act of 1935 and the emergency assistance provisions of the New Deal (DiNitto & Dye, 1983). Social workers like Frances Perkins and Harry Hopkins were key players in the development of this federal legislation and its implementation (Axinn & Levin, 1997).

Although public assistance is often associated with aid to families and children, in fact, assistance to the indigent elderly and blind, including social casework and cash assistance, were core components of country welfare programs from their inception. Old Age Assistance (Title 1 of the 1935 Social Security Act) stipulated that state cash grant programs also include services to applicants and recipients to protect them from exploitation or harm, help them attain self-care, and ensure maximum utilization of other agencies providing similar services (U.S. House of Representatives, 1999).

Adult services provided by state and county public welfare agencies are defined by the Social Services Block Grant, enacted in 1981, in Section 2001, as

> services directed at the goals of 1) achieving or maintaining economic self-support to prevent, reduce, or eliminate dependency; 2) achieving or maintaining self-sufficiency, including reduction or prevention of dependency; 3) preventing or remedying neglect, abuse, or exploitation of . . . adults unable to protect their own interests . . . ; 4) preventing or reducing inappropriate institu-

tional care by providing for community-based care, home-based care, or other forms of less intensive care; and 5) securing referral or admission for institutional care when other forms of care are not appropriate, or providing services to individuals in institutions. (U.S. House of Representatives, 1999, pp. 1531–1532)

Section 2002, 42 U.S.C. 1397a (2) (1) (A), further defines services as

> protective services for adults, services for . . . adults in foster care; services related to the management and maintenance of the home, daycare services for adults; transportation services; information, referral and counseling services . . . health support services and appropriate combinations of services designed to meet the special needs of . . . the aged. (U.S. House of Representatives, 1999, p. 1532)

Low-income home energy assistance is also identified as a service that can be funded through the Social Services Block Grant. While the legislation does not specify that these services must be delivered or managed by professional social workers, in fact, many state and county jurisdictions have determined that professional social workers are well suited for these functions.

PREVALENCE, STRUCTURE (INCLUDING STAFFING), PROCESS

According to a 1991 survey by the National Association of Social Workers (NASW), less than 1% of its membership responded that they worked in the public sector (Gibelman, 1995). There are several reasons for this. One is that across the country, there is a trend toward downsizing state and local government, so that many services formerly provided to the elderly through the public sector are now contracted out to the voluntary or private sector. Another, however, is that many public sector social workers do not work within designated social work titles, and may not appreciate the value of affiliating with other professional social workers through membership within a professional organization. County and state governments often do not keep track of employees who have professional social work degrees but are not working in social work titles. For example, a professional social worker may work under a civil service title of planner, administrator, commissioner, analyst, or caseworker. It may not be apparent from a professional social worker's civil service title that he or she earned a Master of Social Work degree.

Many county and state departments of social service hire both bachelor's level social service workers and bachelor's and master's level social workers to provide casework and other direct services to public sector clients. The direct service workers are supervised by both preprofessionals and professional social workers. However, social workers also serve in management, planning, and research capacities in the public sector, with job titles ranging from agency commissioner to director of research or budget to senior planner. These positions may not fall under civil service law, and social workers may be appointed to them by mayors, governors, and appointed commissioners.

Not all public sector social services for older adults are provided by professional social workers, however. A survey conducted in California of personnel serving older adults in county adult and aging departments found that only 42% of adult protective services workers, 36% case managers, and less than 10% of other staff had master's degrees in social work (Scharlack, Simon, & Dal Santo, 2002). While the services and competencies needed to service older adults in the public sector, as identified in state laws and regulations, suggest the value of professional social work, there has been greater emphasis on professionalizing public child welfare than adult services.

SPECIAL CONCERNS OF THE POPULATION SERVED

The populations served by departments of public welfare and social services are those defined by law and regulation as indigent and/or requiring the services of the state in the form of *parens patriae*, or "father of the land" (Karp, 1999, p. 8). The state and county welfare departments have their roots in the public charity system begun with English poor law that was brought to colonial America by English settlers. The indigent elderly, and those elderly who lack the capacity to manage their affairs or protect themselves from harm, comprise the geriatric client population of public social welfare programs. These elderly clients are among the nation's most vulnerable residents, and the problems they bring to the service arena can challenge the most experienced workers.

SOCIAL WORK ROLES: CURRENT

The roles of social workers in public sector programs for the elderly are broadly defined. These roles include delivering direct services such as case management and counseling; designing, implementing, evaluating, and monitoring programs; administering programs and projects; conducting outreach; and advocacy (Yankley, 1987). Because the public sector is an interdisciplinary service setting, professional social workers may assume a diverse array of roles, with job titles that may not identify them as social workers (Yankley, 1987).

When professional social workers practice in government settings, they are carrying out legislative and regulatory mandates to serve people with identified characteristics through defined programs with proscribed services. This may appear to limit the autonomy of the professional social workers to engage in independent practice and exercise professional judgment. However, the need for public sector social service workers to identify emergent needs among target populations, design and implement creative ways to meet these needs within the defined structure of legislative mandates, and advocate for systems and legislative change are all part of a public sector social workers' responsibility within government social service departments. This is also consistent with professional social work practice.

Professional social work differs from some other professions, in that the scope of practice is very broad. Lawyers engaging in administrative practice within agencies are not considered to be lawyering, or practicing law. Professional social workers practice social work using many methods, with multiple units of concern, to address diverse and often emergent social problems, in a number of fields of practice (Popple & Leighninger, 2002).

Within public welfare and social service departments, methods practiced by professional social workers include administration, supervision, planning and program development, group work, individual work, and social case work. Units of concern include states and communities, groups, families, and individuals. Social problems addressed by professional social workers serving older adults in state and county public welfare and social service systems include poverty (income assistance and employment services), homelessness (special housing), substance abuse (counseling and case management, domestic violence (residential and nonresidential services), ill health (home care and Medicaid coverage), abuse and neglect, including self-neglect (protective services), dependent grandchildren (elderly grandparents raising grandchildren in child-only Temporary Assistance for Needy Families cases), and AIDS.

SOCIAL WORK ROLES: HISTORICAL

Public welfare departments evolved out of local social service programs enacted by localities under colonial poor law, and eventually local and state legislative authority. In 1935, with the passage of the Social Security Act of 1935, the federal government assumed a role in supporting the development of social services on local, state, and federal levels.

Elizabethan poor law defined the indigent and impaired elderly as a category of worthy poor entitled to public assistance from local parishes. When America was colonized by English settlers, they brought the concept of local responsibility for the indigent elderly, widows, and children and implemented it in the colonies and eventually the United States of America. This included programs of both indoor and outdoor relief. The indigent homeless elderly without family to provide care or protection often lived in almshouses, a form of indoor relief (Trattner, 1999).

With the industrialization of cities in the nineteenth century, the urban elderly were vulnerable to poverty and homelessness. Pensions and benefits for the indigent elderly were concerns promoted by the settlement house workers in the Progressive era. Some states and counties enacted old age pensions in the early twentieth century. However, it was not until the passage of Title 1 of the 1935 Social Security Act (Old Age Assistance) that federal matching funding was made available to states choosing to provide cash grants and social services to the indigent elderly as part of their county welfare programs.

The importance of social work and social services in public welfare was recognized by the passage of the Title 20 amendment of the Social Security Act in 1975 (Social Security Amendments of 1974, Pub. L. No. 93–647, H.R. 17045, January 4, 2005, title xx, Grants to States for Services, 42 USC 1397), legislated as the Social Services Block Grant (SSBG) in 1981, which provided federal funding for state- and county-based social service programs. In the early days of the public welfare movement, public sector social workers did not identify themselves as specializing in serving specific client populations. However, this began to change when the county welfare departments began to expand and develop specialized social service programs operated by government. These included services to the community-based elderly.

DEPARTMENT OF SOCIAL WELFARE AND SOCIAL SERVICES PROGRAMS IN WHICH PROFESSIONAL SOCIAL WORKERS SERVE THE ELDERLY

County welfare caseloads did not become specialized in serving the elderly, disabled, and blind until 1962, with the enactment of the 1962 Public Welfare Amendments to the Social Security Act (Wolf, 1995). Included in the Act were provisions for states to receive 75% matching funds for training and a defined list of social services for the needy, blind and disabled. Federal regulations defined persons in need of protective services as those who are unable to act on their own behalf because of limitations in their ability to manage their own affairs, or are living in unsafe conditions, or are exploited or neglected (Wolf, 1995).

The counties' implementation of these regulations included the creation of a special division within the county welfare departments, the Disabled, Aged and Blind (DAB) units, with social workers and case workers assigned to work specifically with the elderly and disabled indigent populations. This included not only ensuring receipt of cash grants but also assisting with the housing, health care, and safety needs of the clientele. According to Burr (1982), Title 1 of the Social Security Act of 1935 mandated county welfare departments to provide protective case work services to indigent elderly in receipt of cash grant Old Age Assistance (OAA).

In 1974, the DAB caseloads were federalized with the implementation of Title 16 of the Social Security Act, Supplemental Security Income (Social Security Amendments of 1972, Pub. L. 92–6031, H.R. 1, October 30, 1972, Title xvi—Supplemental Security Income for the Aged, Blind and Disabled [DAB], or SSI). The Social Security Administration (SSA) assumed centralized responsibility for the eligibility determination and cash assistance for the DAB cases. However, the service needs of this population became the responsibility of country and state public welfare departments (Meller & Mudrick, 1987. Public welfare departments still serve older adults, however, to provide emergency cash assistance, prevent homelessness, or intervene in a crisis situation to enable an older adult to remain in the community, and indirectly through the TANF Program, serving the increasing number of grandparents raising grandchildren on TANF.

Adult Protective Services

The most visible of the adult service programs operated by state and county public welfare departments is Adult Protective Services (APS). While there is controversy about the beginning of APS, an early study was conducted by the National Council on the Aging in 1960, and the White House Conference on Aging in 1961 recommended that there be a coordinated model developed by social agencies, the medical profession, bar associations, and legal aid to improve protective services for the elderly (Otto, 2000). The passage of Title 20 of the Social Security Act in 1974 provided funding for a number of programs that served the elderly, including APS (Mixson, 1995).

Without overarching federal authority, states developed diverse approaches to service delivery for vulnerable older adults through APS service program models. Some APS programs provide case management and other services to vulnerable adults age 18 and above, and others serve only those 60 years of age and older (S. Somers, personal communication, June 28, 2004). Most programs are administered by county departments of social service under state oversight, and provide case management and interdisciplinary crisis intervention services to older adults in need of protection.

In states like New York, state social service and mental hygiene laws and regulations enable APS workers to gain access to households, seek court approval for hospitalization for observation, and apply for guardianships on an involuntary basis if necessary to ensure necessary protection and treatment of incapacitated older adults (Sachs, 1993). Adult Protection Services programs serve vulnerable older adults in crisis situations that require workers to solve complex problems and demonstrate a sophisticated knowledge of risk factors and service interventions (Choi & Mayer, 2000).

Special Housing Programs

In urban areas, single room occupancy (SRO) hotels house many indigent elderly and disabled adults, including those with AIDS. County departments of social services provided case work services to occupants in SRO hotels, in order to stabilize their housing situations. Social workers also administer and provide case work services and program oversight to indigent elderly who are mentally ill or have developmental disabilities served by adult foster care programs.

Adult foster care (AFC) is a housing program operated by the county departments of social services since the 1960s, although its early development may be traced back to the English poor laws in the colonies when unrelated families provided lodging, food, and care to the indigent elderly and were reimbursed with public funds. Its description varies among jurisdictions; however, foster boarding homes are usually residences that house up to six unrelated individuals in private houses. In 1975, AFC was listed as a Title 20 service. Currently these programs are likely to be funded through the SSI institutional rate (Sherman, 1995), and AFC clients must qualify for SSI, a means-tested cash benefits program, as a condition of eligibility. Placement and follow-up are responsibilities of local department of social services, and are carried out by multidisciplinary teams that include social workers, who provide case planning and case management services.

AIDS Services

When AIDS began to affect older adults, either because people were beginning to live longer with the virus or because older people engaged in behaviors that made them at risk of HIV, county welfare departments began to serve them through existing case management programs (Emlett, 1996). Planning for the needs of the indigent elderly with AIDS and serving them in county DSS programs designed for younger clients with AIDS who may have dependent children, or are IV drug users, require professional social workers with gerontological competencies to serve as caseworkers, planners, and administrators to draw on professional gerontology competencies. In large counties, or in New York City, AIDS case management programs may be provided in a separate division of the department of social services. In smaller counties, services to clients with AIDS are provided through county APS programs (S. B. Somers, assistant commissioner, Adult Protective Services, New York State Office of Child and Family Services, personal communication, June 28, 2004).

Means-Tested Entitlements

The indigent elderly utilize food stamps, emergency cash grant assistance, Medicaid, and Medicaid-funded home care. Public sector social workers in APS, Medicaid-funded home care, AIDS, and domestic violence programs may provide access to these public welfare entitlements through case management programs (Sonnag, 1995). Professional social workers operate county food stamp programs, oversee Medicaid eligibility determination processes, and make medical determinations of the need for Medicaid-funded home case services.

Grandparents Raising Grandchildren in TANF and Kinship Foster Care Households

Grandparents raising grandchildren in child-only TANF households have experienced difficulties across the country in accessing needed benefits for their grandchildren through departments of public welfare. Professional social workers have been helpful in assisting them negotiate these systems on behalf of their grandchildren from within the public welfare bureaucracies. Innovative programs like the portal projects implemented in county welfare offices in Tennessee, or in El Paso, Colorado, have provided programmatic supports and special access for custodial grandparents who depend on TANF benefits to raise their grandchildren. The public child welfare programs are experiencing greater numbers of grandparents raising grandchildren as foster parents. The challenges of working with older adults in the child-centered world of public child welfare have prompted interest in gerontological social work education and training for professional social workers in public child welfare (Brownell, Berman, Nelson, & Colon Fofana, 2003).

Domestic Violence Programs

Adult Protective Services provides case management services to the elderly living in the community who are in need of protection, including many who are victims of self-neglect. However, those elderly who are victims of abuse or exploitation and are not candidates for APS, adult homes, or nursing homes can be served by domestic violence shelters operated by the county department of social services, initially through Title 20 funding. Currently many shelters are funded through TANF, with state and local supplementation for elderly victims of abuse who do not qualify for TANF. Complex issues involving informed consent, and need to ensure congruence of service

needs and program fit for older victims of abuse, can require professional social work skills and gerontological competencies (Bergeron, 2001). Special service needs of older domestic violence victims suggest the importance of gerontological social workers in the county domestic violence service systems (Osgood & Manetta, 2002).

FUNDING MECHANISMS

Professional social worker positions in departments of public welfare and social services are generally funded through the same legislative appropriations that fund programs enacted by social welfare legislation in which they work. Most common sources of funding for public welfare social work salaries include Title 19 Medicaid administrative funds, state AIDS funding, and Title 20 Social Services Block Grant funding. For example, Medicaid administrative funds (Title 19) may fund medical social workers and disability review team members in Medicaid-funded home care and Medicaid eligibility; Social Services Block Grant funds are often used to fund social workers' salaries in adult protective services and foster care programs; and food stamp administrative funding pays salaries for social workers in food stamp programs.

Some funding streams, such as Medicaid administrative funding, provide enhanced reimbursement for professional social work services in job categories such as medical or disability review for home care levels of care or Medicaid eligibility determinations. These are recognized by the federal government as requiring social work competencies such as assessment and diagnosis of disabilities.

QUALITY OF LIFE AND QUALITY OF CARE

Professional social workers in departments of public welfare and social services are concerned about meeting basic living and safety needs of elderly clientele. Quality-of-life and quality-of-care issues are significant for professional social workers providing case management and service oversight in programs like Medicaid-funded home care and adult boarding homes. Social workers in adult protective services, AIDS, and domestic violence where victims are elderly are often primarily concerned with addressing crisis situations and ensuring that elderly clients are safe and have access to basic entitlements and health care.

Professional social workers in these public programs interface with law enforcement and the courts, to ensure safety for their elderly clients, and health and mental health systems, to ensure that emergency needs are met. While clients in Medicaid-funded home care receive care for chronic conditions, and may be served by the department of public welfare for extended periods of time, often the goal of adult protective or domestic violence social workers is to address the client's crisis, stabilize the client's living situation, and refer the client for ongoing services in other service systems before closing the case. Quality-of-life issues are very much in the forefront when an APS social worker provides crisis services to a self-neglecting elder, and quality-of-care issues are of paramount concern for a social worker overseeing an adult foster care household.

CULTURALLY RELEVANT SERVICES

Public sector social workers practice in a highly politicized environment. The public sector faces political pressure from the communities served to provide culturally relevant services to clients and constituents. Most county departments of social services are required to offer translation services to applicants who do not speak English and have no one to translate on their behalf. Professional social work education emphasizes that ethical practice requires the provision of culturally relevant services. This is reinforced through training on culturally competent practice provided by most departments of social service (New York State Department of Social Services, 1997).

Affirmative action requirements in government services have ensured a diverse work force; this includes front line and supervisory social workers in programs that serve older adults. Some counties experience difficulties in ensuring culturally relevant services because workers from other countries are hired through the civil service process. In programs like adult protective services, where elderly clients may lack the capacity to protect themselves from harm, there is a legal obligation for government to provide the needed protection if there are no family members willing and able to do so. However, a growing number of immigrants have joined public agency staff. Some immigrants come from countries and cultures that do not see governement as having a role in

life quality enhancement and protective service provision for elders. Those workers coming from such cultures care deeply about service to the community, but may have internalized value systems that conflict with the values of the American social welfare system, reflected in laws and regulations governing public sector programs serving older adults and their families. These differences may create barriers for new immigrant staff in connecting with and effectively serving vulnerable older clients and their families. Professional education and training is critical to address these workforce issues that affect client services.

AGEISM

Any assumption that impairments of older adults are an inevitable part of the aging process can be defined as ageist. It is particularly important that these assumptions are not applied to vulnerable older adults served by protective service or home care programs. This is understood by gerontological social workers responsible for ensuring that clients receive appropriate health and mental health treatment for what may be a treatable and reversible condition. Ageist assumptions that older adults are not capable of making informed judgments about their lives can lead to inappropriate and intrusive interventions that are not made in the best interest of the client.

PRIVILEGE AND OPPRESSION

Public sector social workers often wield enormous power over their clients and their families, particularly if they are providing mandated services through adult protective services or are in a position to approve or deny access to benefits like cash grants and health care. Older adults may be socialized to respect and not question government authority, or conversely to refuse needed services out of a concern about accepting charity. Among the most serious decisions a social worker can make about an elderly client is that of removing them to a nursing home or requesting a legal guardianship.

RURAL/URBAN DIFFERENCES

While elderly clients in urban areas may face crime, isolation, rising housing expenses, and a daunting pace of life outside their homes, they also are more likely than their rural counterparts to have access to community-based services, public transportation, and accessible health care facilities. The rural social worker working for a department of public welfare or social services must serve elderly clients who live long distances from social service offices, may experience a higher than average level of poverty, may be more dependent than their urban counterparts on family members or significant others who may be abusive or neglectful, and may have a narrower range of available support services (Butler, 2004).

ETHICAL DILEMMAS

Ethical dilemmas are a challenge for geriatric social workers in public welfare and social services. Laws and regulations can mandate overriding the autonomy and judgment of older adults deemed to be at risk of harm. This places professional social workers in conflict with the provision of the NASW code of ethics to respect the autonomy and self-determination of clients. Public sector social workers must also follow laws, regulations, and procedures that limit access to needed services, such as Medicaid-funded home care, for an older client who needs the service but refuses to spend down assets to the legal limit. Public sector social workers may be limited in their ability to directly advocate for serving the needs of elderly clients if legislative decisions or bureaucratic procedures preclude this.

While public social workers can sometimes influence policy decisions or find creative ways of providing service to their older clients, they may also have less flexibility than professional social workers in some not-for-profit organizations because of lack of access to purely discretionary funding. Confidentiality, an important value in client–social work relationships, may be compromised with public sector clients in rural areas, where a visit from a social worker from a public agency can signal to neighbors that the client is experiencing problems with poverty, family members, or health.

Competing values are inherent in social work practice in public welfare settings. Diminished capacity of clients may make informed consent problematic and even impractical. Professional social workers in departments of public welfare and social services face an ongoing dilemma in ensuring a client's safety and well-being while respecting autonomy and freedom of choice (Mixon, 1995).

CONCLUSION

Gerontological social work is not often associated with departments of public welfare and social services. Even in the public sector, gerontological social work is often associated with the state and Area Agencies on Aging funded through the Older Americans Act of 1965 (Older Americans Act, Pub. L. No. 89–73, 89th Congress, H.R. 3708, July 14, 1965) and its subsequent amendments. However, departments of public welfare and social services have served the most vulnerable elderly since the early twentieth century, and professional social workers continue to provide vital services in these practice settings today.

REFERENCES

Axinn, J. & Levin, H. (1997). *Social welfare: A history of the American response to need* (4th ed.). New York: Longman.

Bergeron, L. R. (2001). An elder abuse case study: Caregiver stress or domestic violence? You decide. *Journal of Gerontological Social Work, 34*(4), 47–63.

Brownell, P., Berman, J., Nelson, A., & Colon Fofana, R. (2003). Grandparents raising grandchildren: The risks of caregiving. *Journal of Elder Abuse and Neglect, 15*(3/4), 5–31.

Burnette, D. (1999). Custodial grandparents in Latina families: Patterns of service utilization and predictors of unmet need. *Social Work, 44*(1), 22–34.

Burr, J. J. (1982). Protective services for adults. (Publication No. 82-20505). Washington, DC: U.S. Department of Health and Human Services.

Butler, S. S. (2004). *Gerontological social work in small towns and rural communities.* Binghamton, NY: Haworth Press.

Choi, N. G., & Mayer, J. (2000). Elder abuse, neglect, and exploitation: Risk factors and prevention strategies. *Journal of Gerontological Social Work, 33*(2), 5–25.

DiNitto, D. M., & Dye, T. R. (1983). *Social welfare: Politics and public policy.* Englewood Cliffs, NJ: Prentice Hall.

Emlet, C. A. (1990). Case managing older people with AIDS: Bridging systems; recognizing diversity. *Journal of Gerontological Social Work, 27*(1/2), 55–71.

Gibelman, M. (1995). *What social workers do.* Washington, DC: NASW Press.

Karp, M. B. (1999). *Geriatrics and the law.* New York: Springer.

Meller, Y., & Mudrick, N. (1987). The impact of program centralization on the utilization of social services: The case of the SSI Program. *Journal of Sociology and Social Welfare, 14*(1), 85–93.

Mellor, M. J., & Lindeman, D. (1998). The role of the social worker in interdisciplinary teams. *Journal of Gerontological Social Work, 30*(3/4), 3–7.

Mixson, P. M. (1995). An adult protective services perspective. *Journal of Elder Abuse and Neglect, 7*(2/3), 69–87.

New York State Department of Social Services (1997). *Protective services for adults competency-based training.* New York: Office of Children and Family Services.

Osgood, N. J., & Manetta, A. A. (2002). Physical and sexual abuse, battering and substance abuse: Three clinical studies of older women. *Journal of Gerontological Social Work, 38*(3), 99–112.

Otto, J. M. (2000). The role of adult protective services in addressing abuse. *Generations, 24*(13), 33–38.

Popple, P. R., & Leighninger, L. (2002). *Social work, social welfare, and American society* (5th ed.). Boston: Allyn and Bacon.

Sachs, D. (1993). *A guide to adult guardianship.* New York: Brookdale Center on Aging and the New York State Law Revision Commission.

Scharlach, A., Simon, J., & Dal Santo, T. (2002). Who is providing social services to today's older adults? Implications of a survey of aging service personnel. *Journal of Gerontological Social Work, 38*(4), 5–18.

Sherman, S. R. (1995). Adult foster care. In G. L. Maddox, (Ed.), *The Encyclopedia of Aging* (2nd ed., pp. 19–22). New York: Springer.

Social Services Block Grant, 42 U.S.C. § 1397 (1981).

Sonnag, J. (1995). A case manager's perspective. *Journal of Elder Abuse and Neglect, 7*(2/3), 115–130.

Trattner, W. (1999). *From poor law to welfare state: A history of social welfare in America* (6th ed.). New York: Free Press.

U.S. House of Representatives. (1999). *Compilation of the Social Security laws* (Vol. 1). Washington, DC: Government Printing Office.

Wolf, R. S. (1995). Adult protective services. In G. L. Maddox (Ed.), *The Encyclopedia of Aging* (2nd ed., pp. 22–24). New York: Springer.

Yankley, J. (1987). Public social services. In A. Minahan (Ed.), *Encyclopedia of Social Work* (18th ed., Vol. 2, pp. 417–426). Silver Spring, MD: NASW Press.

CARMEN MORANO
BARBARA MORANO

Geriatric Care Management Settings

37

Defining Geriatric Care Management (GCM), let alone social work practice in a geriatric care management setting, requires significantly more space than any single chapter could provide. Just as our profession has struggled throughout its history to define social work and/or social work practice (Bartlett, 2000, 1970; Gordon, 1962; Holosko, 2003), there is no one single definition that can be applied to the practice of GCM. In fact, until recently (McInnis-Dittrich, 2004), there was little, if any, discussion about GCM in any social work practice texts. And while the National Association of Social Workers (NASW) does offer a definition for case management, as well as two levels of certification for case management, they do not offer a specific definition for GCM.

The NASW definition of case management does, however, provide a good foundation upon which to build a working definition of GCM. "Case management is a mechanism for ensuring a comprehensive program that will meet an individual's need for care by coordinating and linking components of a service delivery system" and, as such, serves as a link between the client and the service delivery system (NASW, 1992). While case management can and does serve as a process that coordinates and links clients with services, it is also "a principle that guides the provision of a full range of services" (Frankel & Gellman, 2004, p. 5). And while other professions (for example nursing, psychology) also have their own definitions for case management, the assessing, coordinating, and linking functions (Robinson, 2000) are common to each.

Until recently, there was little mention of care management and specifically GCM in American social work literature, so the lack of a clear definition is understandable. Interestingly, the British social services adopted the use of the term "care management" as a strengths-based, consumer-driven model of care that includes the same core functions of case management (assessment, care planning, and service coordination; Burns, 1997). And while many support the use of case and care management interchangeably (see, for example, Bodie-Gross & Holt, 1998), some distinctions between the two are noteworthy.

For example, while case and care management are similar, in terms of their shared focus on client assessment, the care management assessment also focuses on how the current situation of the identified client impacts the well-being of all the individuals who make up the identified client's support system. The current situation is viewed as an opportunity to assess the impact of the presenting situation on the short- and long-term physical, emotional, financial, and social functioning of the older adult, as well as his or her informal caregiving system (i.e., spouse, life partner, adult child, etc.). "The overall goal is to enable the individual to maintain the greatest amount of independence and dignity, while assisting the client and family with problem-solving and access" (Aronson & Kennedy, 1998, p. 11).

The consumer-driven philosophy of care management also results in a significantly more comprehensive set of tasks and activities for both the client system and the care manager (McInnis-Dittrich, 2004; Parker, 1998). Care management services frequently include supportive crisis intervention, patient and family advocacy, family mediation, and conflict resolution (McInnis-Dittrich, 2004). In addition, unlike most case management models that provide services from 9 to 5 on weekdays, care management services are usually provided in a 24-hours-a-day, 7-days-a-week model. Consequently, because of the expanded roles of the geriatric care manager, another difference between case and care management is that the caseloads of care managers are significantly smaller.

Thus, given some of the differences between case and care management, the authors suggest that care management is as much a philosophical approach as a skill set that is applied in a consumer-driven model. There is a clear emphasis on the risks and strengths of the larger client system, with three guiding principles: (1) emphasizing the relationship between the client system and (care) manager (Brun & Rapp, 2001); (2) the active and efficient involvement of appropriate informal and formal helping networks; and (3) maximizing client self-determination and involvement (National Association of Professional Geriatric Care Managers, 2003).

LEGAL REGULATORY AUTHORITY

Although the practice of care management is not regulated or licensed by any federal or state authority, there have been some recent developments that indicate this will change in the near future. For example, the National Association of Professional Geriatric Care Managers (NAPGCM), incorporated in 1989, has provided consistent leadership that resulted in standards for practice that were adopted in 1992 (see the NAPGCM Web site listed at the end of this chapter), as well as supporting the initial credentialing of care managers. In 1994, NAPGCM joined with the Case Management Institute of Connecticut Commu-

nity Care, Inc., to form the National Academy of Certified Case Managers. This independent organization, which included representatives from a number of aging and disability organizations, then developed and administered the first geriatric care management credential (Parker & McNattin, 2002). The care manager certified (CMC) credential was first offered in 1995, and to date there are approximately (550) care managers who hold this credential. This entry-level credential remains the first and only attempt to develop a care manager credential based on a standardized and validated exam.

Interestingly, at approximately the same time that these efforts were taking place, the much larger Individual Case Management Association (ICMA) was engaged in a similar effort. Following the recommendation of the Certification of Insurance Rehabilitation Specialists, an independent organization called the Commission for Case Manager Certification, consisting of 29 allied organizations, formed to develop and administer the certified case manager (CCM) credential (Parker & McNattin, 2002). Just as there are operational differences in the definitions of care and case management, there is also a significant difference in the two credentials. While individuals with a high school diploma and 12 years of supervised work in the field of care management were eligible to be certified as a care manager, the more medically driven certified case manager credential required all applicants to hold a master's degree in their profession (i.e., social work, nursing). Table 37.1 provides a listing of the more common credentials held by members of NAPGCM.

Another factor that will contribute to the development of licensing and regulation is the recent increase in the number of programs and certificates in GCM. As academic institutions become more involved with developing curricula for care management, there will also be a growing focus on conducting methodologically sound research to evaluate the effectiveness of GCM. An expanded knowledge base and an increasing number of practitioners, combined with more consumers utilizing GCM services, will highlight the need for licensing and/or regulation.

OVERSIGHT

Although there is no current state or federal policy that provides oversight or regulation for GCM, there is some limited informal oversight for care management provided by NAPGCM, in addition to the indirect oversight that is provided by the regulation and

TABLE 37.1.   Certification of NAPGCM Membership*

Credential	Abbreviation	Percent*
Care manager certified	CMC	21
Licensed clinical social worker	LCSW, LCSW-C	19
Certified case manager	CCM	13
Geriatric clinical specialist nurse practitioner	GCS/GNP	9
Registered nurse	RN	7

Note: Adapted from "Geriatric care managers: A survey on long-term chronic care," by K. Knutson and S. Langer, 1998, *Geriatric Care Management Journal*, 8(3), pp. 9–13.

*Represents approximately 14% response rate to member survey.

licensing of social workers or nurses who practice GCM. The oversight provided by NAPGCM is through a formal policy and procedure for addressing client or collegial grievances. Unfortunately, this oversight only applies to members, and is limited to sanctioning or loss of membership, with no legal authority.

The indirect, and stronger, level of oversight does occur through the care manager's primary professional licensing authority. For example, a care manger licensed as a clinical social worker will be subject to the state's oversight of a professional social worker. However, other than the professional (social work, nursing, etc.) oversight from these professions, care managers who are not educated or licensed in an allied profession are not subject to any oversight. In addition to licensing oversight of the various professions, there is also a form of sanctioning or oversight that occurs through membership in a number of professional associations (i.e., NASW, American Nurses Association, American Psychological Association). Again, however, this oversight would be limited to only members of the associations, with little legal authority.

PREVALENCE

There is no single source that provides specific information on the number of GCM agencies or individuals providing care management. The NAPGCM currently lists 1,650 members. However, there are a number of other health-related associations that also have members who practice a model of GCM. In that many continue to use the terms of case and care management interchangeably, and given the number of professional care/case management associations, and the lack of a single regulatory oversight authority, it is impossible to estimate the actual number of GCMs.

STRUCTURE

In that GCM is a developing area of practice, GCM agencies can range from loosely structured individual solo practitioners who work out of home offices to large private, for-profit companies employing a number of care managers. There are also a number of public and private, not-for-profit agencies, hospitals, and allied health care agencies that are now providing GCM services. And while there has been significant growth in both of these areas, the majority of GCM agencies remain the smaller solo-practitioner type or partnership.

Data from NAPGCM suggest that approximately 62% of members are full-time care managers working as either a solo practitioner or with one other care manager and approximately 27% are affiliated with agencies employing three to five full-time care managers (Knutson & Langer, 1998). The membership consists of approximately 83% who indicate they are structured as a private, for-profit agency.

More recently, a number of for-profit and not-for-profit agencies and institutional settings (hospitals, retirement communities, faith-based, and long-term care insurance providers) have also been offering GCM services. There is currently no way to calculate the number of agencies that fall into this category. Certainly, how GCM fits in the organizational structure of each existing setting, as well as the specific model of care management being practiced, varies greatly. What does appear to be clear is that the model of GCM practiced in these types of setting more closely resembles traditional case management.

As corporate culture becomes more dominant in the care management landscape, the focus has moved from providing only GCM services to a model of care management that is structured to provide a more comprehensive array of eldercare services. Consequently, the structure of these larger entities has become significantly more complex than that of the smaller traditional agencies.

PROCESS

A survey of the membership of NAPGCM identified 10 core services that are provided in the traditional care management agency. In order of their indicated importance, they are: assessment, care management, information and referral, advocacy, placement, caregiver support, education, crisis intervention, counseling, and entitlements (Knutson & Langer, 1998). However, how each of these are operationalized, as well as how the service is delivered, varies from agency to agency. Although a number of core functions (i.e., inquiry, intake, assessment, and care plan development) are considered basic to case management (see table 37.2), there is no one uniform process for how geriatric care managers provide these services. Most care managers will provide basic core functions such as managing inquiries, assessing clients, developing care plans, and providing referrals, although not all care managers will provide advocacy, ongoing monitoring, clinical or crisis intervention, or reassessment functions.

Inquiry. The basic core function of initial inquiry can vary greatly. For example, with the private fee-for-service model, it is not unusual for the care manager to spend a great deal of time listening to the caller's problems (with an elderly relative), explaining what care management is, how it is customized according to the needs of the client, and why it may be an appropriate alternative. It is also during the inquiry phase that the care manager provides information about the fees associated with the services. In the public, not-for-profit model, one might spend less time explaining why care management is the right service and more time explaining the menu of services available.

Assessment. "Underlying good care management is good assessment" (Aronson & Kennedy, 1998, p. 11).

Some care managers begin the assessment by visiting with the identified client, while others will begin the assessment process with the person who initiated the contact (usually, but not always, a family member). This empowers the care manager to initiate the process of developing a more complete assessment of the entire client system. It also provides the care manager with important information about family dynamics. We would like to emphasize the importance of the family/caregiver consultation as a part of the GCM assessment. This is one of the features that distinguishes care from case management. In order to empower the client system with the most appropriate resources, a good understanding of the risks and strengths of the family/caregiver system is vital. A comprehensive genogram of the entire family system helps to identify important points of support as well as identify potential areas of concern. This is then used to develop a more proactive care plan.

A strengths-based assessment of the client must include a functional assessment (Green, 2002) of the client system. Functional assessment is the key to understanding the impact of medical illness on the older adult (Gallo, 2000) and those involved with the older adult. Care managers can use scales measuring the status of activities of daily living (ADLs) such as bathing, grooming, dressing, walking, and so on, and scales measuring Instrumental activities of daily living (IADLs) such as shopping, driving, money management, and so on. (A more complete discussion of geriatric assessment can be found in part D of this handbook.)

The assessment should also include a mental status assessment that includes both cognitive function-

TABLE 37.2. Case Management Functions Identified by Four

Rose & Moore (1995)	*Rothman (2002)*	*Naleppa & Reid (2003)*	*Knutson & Langer (1998)**
Outreach; assessment of needs; services or treatment planning; linking and referring; monitoring	Access; intake; assessment; goal setting; intervention planning; resource identification; indexing; formal linkage; informal linkage; monitoring; reassessment; outcome evaluation; interagency coordination; counseling; therapy; advocacy	Identify target problems; set goals; develop task alternatives; evaluate potential obstacles; select and contract tasks; implement tasks; evaluate tasks	Assessment; care management; information and referral; advocacy; placement; caregiver support education; crisis intervention; counseling; entitlements/public benefits

Note: Adapted from "Geriatric care managers: A survey on long-term chronic care," by K. Knutson and S. Langer, 1998, *Geriatric Care Management Journal, 8*(3), pp. 9–13.

*Identified by more than 70% of respondents to NAPGCM membership survey as the top 10 services.

ing and psychiatric evaluation. Again, there are a number of scales that can be used to determine cognitive impairment, but it is the experience of the authors that the Mini Mental Status Examination (MMSE) is one of the most widely used. Social work care managers will also assess for level of depression and anxiety, as well as caregiver-related stress and burden. A complete assessment also includes an evaluation of environmental (home or current residence), financial (for current and future planning), legal, and social needs. Because there is no universal GCM tool that addresses all areas of the assessment process (Aronson & Kennedy, 1998), the depth and quality of the assessment significantly varies among care mangers.

Care plan. Although there has been some effort to develop GCM protocols for specific types of presenting situations (diabetes, dementia, etc.), there are as many differences in the development of the care plan as there are in the assessment process. The challenge is often balancing the wishes of the client with issues of safety, affordability, and practicality. The care manager must also develop a plan that has a high probability of working (Jackson, 2000). It is incumbent upon the care manager to be knowledgeable about resources and to be clinically astute, creative, persistent, flexible, and nonjudgmental when developing a plan of care.

The use of written care plans with clearly articulated problems, goals, and interventions is important to successful outcomes. Verbal care plans that are not clarified in writing can frequently lead to confusion and misunderstanding that eventually sabotage the care management process. Given the consumer-driven approach of care management, both the problems identified, as well as the intervention proposed, may not always appear to be traditional social work practice. For example, an intervention to decrease the client's level of depression and increase his socialization may require a more social atmosphere, such as going to lunch, hitting golf balls, or shopping. A non-threatening, more social venue can be used to overcome resistance and lead to productive relationship building. Each of these opportunities is used to develop a working alliance with the client in order to accomplish some of the more difficult tasks that will follow.

Brokering versus providing services. As discussed earlier, there are various models of GCM. While some care management agencies only provide a comprehensive list of potential referrals, others make the contact and arrange for the services. There are other models of care management, especially in the larger corporate models, that provide the client with all the services. While there is no agreement on which model is better, each has advantages and disadvantages. Care managers who "outsource" every service can shop and select from multiple providers. The in-house, one-stop shopping type of model provides for a seamless and integrated network of services (home care, equipment, medical, etc.).

Care management. Perhaps no single process or function will vary as much as the care management process. Care management, used in this context, refers to the ongoing process whereby the care manager engages the older adult in a process of building a relationship to work on specific areas of concern. Just as in the example given earlier, a private, fee-for-service model can provide the care manager with the time to use a variety of techniques to build this pivotal relationship with the client, without the pressure of time limitation.

Throughout the care management process, the geriatric care manager will simultaneously reassess the situation and make appropriate adjustments in the care plan. When the situation does allow for this ongoing care management, the role of the care manager is to anticipate future needs and provide the family with proactive approaches to maintain the client's health, well-being, and quality of life.

HISTORY OF CARE MANAGEMENT

Although the roots of case management can be traced as far back as the early writings of Mary Richmond (1917), the settlement houses of New York and Chicago (Frankel & Gelman, 2004), and the early work of the board of charities established in 1883 by the state of Massachusetts to coordinate programs and services for the poor and infirm (Weil & Karls, 1985), the history of GCM is not as long or as illustrious. A relatively recent practice model, GCM was initially adopted by a private entrepreneurial group of social workers in the early 1980s.

The history of GCM can in part be connected to the growing number of aging persons with complex physical, emotional, financial, and psychosocial needs who are living longer, institutional changes in the role of social work in acute health care settings, and family support systems (i.e., spouse, adult children, grandchildren) that have lacked the knowledge, time, and resources to advocate and navigate through the increasingly complex network of aging services. As

GCM has been a consumer-driven response to the needs of older adults and their family members, this consumer-driven philosophy remains a cornerstone of GCM.

The complicated and complex network of services and programs provided by the policies of the Older Americans Act (1965, 1992, 2000), while well intended, lacked both accessibility and adaptability to meet the diverse needs of the aging population. Thus it was in this context that a small group of social workers from a variety of private practice settings came together to form what eventually became the National Association of Private Geriatric Care Managers (Cress, 2001). From its early inception, this association struggled to separate and distinguish its practice from case management and to establish practice guidelines, codes of conduct, and ethical standards, many of which were rooted in the standards of practice in social work and nursing. In an attempt to reach out and include practitioners who were mostly associated with community-based case management practice, the organization changed its name to the National Association of Professional Geriatric Care Managers. While today this organization has grown to more than 1,600 members from both private and public agencies, the vast majority of its members are private practitioners.

The authors have frequently been asked how and why they started in the field of GCM. Geriatric care management is one of the few opportunities where a social worker can use all of his or her social work education and training without the limited resources faced by our colleagues in many of the other social work settings. To quote some of the original founders of NAPGCM, "I got frustrated with paper instead of people," or "I wanted to be able to customize services for older people and their families and provide quality services" (White, 2004, p. 4).

POPULATIONS SERVED

GCM agencies, especially the private fee-for-service agencies, serve a relatively small niche segment of the population. Given that the fee structure of the private agency can range from $75 to $150 per hour, the population served is for the most part upper-middle-class or wealthy professional adult children of older adults. The adult children are typically seeking services on behalf of a parent(s) who frequently has some degree of physical and/or cognitive impairment. Perhaps it is an age cohort perspective of a social work type of ser-

vice, but the older adults seldom seek GCM services on their own. However, it has been projected that as the baby boomers age, a growing number of informed and sophisticated consumers will seek out GCM services. Certainly, given this cohort's youth-oriented consumerism (Gilleard & Higgs, 2001), there will be a growing need for professionally delivered and consumer-directed care to help navigate the increasingly fragmented and complicated health care system.

While the adult children currently contracting for GCM services are primarily well-educated professionals, their parents are more heterogeneous. It is not uncommon for a care manager to work with older adults who range from those with limited education who worked in a wide range of unskilled, government, and semiskilled professions to those who are well-educated, accomplished professionals. Historically, it is common for the person making the initial call to be an adult daughter or daughter-in-law on behalf of an older relative. More recently, a growing number of men are initiating contact for GCM services, as well as receiving GCM services (Kosberg & Morano, 2000).

SOCIAL WORK ROLES

Historically, many of the roles for social workers in the GCM setting are similar to those in traditional case management settings. The roles for social workers in the private, for-profit settings, however, also include the constant need to educate providers and consumers about GCM and how it fits into the continuum of care. When asked what the biggest challenge in starting a GCM business was, a former president of NAPGCM stated: "Marketing, marketing, marketing." No one knew what care management was, and few were interested in care of elders unless they had a personal experience" (White, 2004, p. 4).

Depending on state licensing regulations, the BSW practitioner can practice independently as a geriatric care manager; however, state licensing regulations can restrict the use of the title "social worker." The BSW can also work with, or be employed by, a GCM agency to perform a variety of other functions, such as care manager assistant, care coordinator, or administrative assistant. Care manager assistants and care coordinators can be responsible for working with the care manager to implement the prescribed care plan. Depending on the size and scope of the agency, this can involve accompanying clients to medical appointments, negotiating with service providers, coordinating care, and reconciling insurance-related issues. Agencies that charge lower fees for the services of a care manager assistant indicate that this is more cost effective to the consumer and therefore assists in selling the product.

Social workers with an advanced degree, such as MSW or LCSW (LCSW, LCSW-C, etc.), also function in a variety of roles. As solo practitioners, they will usually have to perform all functions, including clinical and administrative. The ultimate responsibility for the well-being of clients and the business is that of the geriatric care manager alone (Modigliani, 2004). It is not an exaggeration to say that in the consumer-driven, fee-for-service model, the geriatric care manager will fill whatever role is needed to accomplish the stated goals while always practicing within accepted ethical standards. Descriptions of some of the common roles for social workers in the field of GCM follow.

Interdisciplinary team member. Given the fragmentation of health care services (Hoenig, Nusbaum, & Brummel-Smith, 1997), the role of team member is frequently one of the most important roles for the social work care manager. With a grounded understanding of systems theory, this practitioner is uniquely qualified to represent the needs of both the identified patient and his or her caregivers on interdisciplinary care teams in a number of different health care settings (i.e., hospital, acute or long-term care settings, etc.). Interdisciplinary practice is a way of thinking as well as an approach to working with others (Netting, 1998).

This role becomes even more important in that they are frequently the only professionals that can connect the multiple interdisciplinary teams as the client progresses throughout the continuum of care. For example, the cognitively impaired person with a hip fracture will experience different interdisciplinary teams in the hospital, acute care, rehabilitative care, and home care settings. As was recently highlighted in a report from The National Consensus Conference on Improving the Continuum of Care for Patients With Hip Fracture (2002), "the pathogenesis of hip fracture is multi-factorial, and there is an increasing disconnect along the hip-fracture continuum of care which results in patients receiving fragmented post-acute care. As a result, patients often receive fragmented care" (p. 671).

Advocate. A significant part of effective care management involves advocating with multiple health care systems (hospitals, insurance, public agencies on aging, etc.) and providers (physicians, therapists,

medical equipment providers, etc.). Certainly this role is not unique to GCM, but the social work geriatric care manager uses a systemic orientation and an ecological approach that provide an excellent foundation for understanding the importance of advocacy that frequently goes beyond just advocating for the patient. Since the family is employing the geriatric care manger, it is therefore incumbent upon the care manager to advocate for and represent the needs of the entire client system (identified patient and caregivers).

Family mediator. Another role for the social work care manager is that of family mediator. Given the ecological approach to GCM and the competing demands of caring for an older adult, family mediation is critical. Again, while some GCM agencies might refer the client and family to a family therapist or psychologist, some GCM agencies employ clinical social workers so that they can fulfill this role. The social worker's education and training in systems, group work, and family therapy provides the skills to facilitate healthier family dynamics that have both short- and long-term implications.

Supervisor. A licensed clinical social worker can provide supervision for other MSW or BSW geriatric care managers. The size and scope of the agency will determine the amount of time spent with direct client contact versus other supervisory functions. In the model of care management we practice, every care manager participated in both individual supervision, as well as weekly care planning team conferences. Geriatric care managers who are sole proprietors are strongly encouraged to contract for clinical supervision or meet regularly with colleagues to discuss cases and issues.

Administrator. Finally, the administrative role is another crucial role for social workers in a GCM setting. As was discussed earlier, many of the original GCM practices were solo MSW practitioners who came from either the health care arena or private psychotherapy practices. Consequently, the administrative roles included everything that needed to be done to remain in operation. Developing budgets and business and marketing plans, hiring and supervision of staff, developing the care management protocol (clinical forms, fee structure, etc.), handling all inquiries, as well as developing relationships with other providers and referral sources, are just some of the administrative roles that can be filled by the MSW.

While each of these roles could occur in either the private, fee-for-service model or the public agency that is doing GCM, another role specific to the public sector is that of fund-raiser and/or grant writer. Because the majority of public settings are more closely associated with a case management model, where services are significantly more restricted by the source of reimbursement, it is important that the funding of the agency keeps up with the demand. Consequently, the MSW can frequently be the individual who is responsible for updating potential funding sources, as well as actually preparing the necessary applications.

As the profession of GCM continues to grow, and as the regulation of GCM develops, many of the roles discussed in this chapter will remain in place. The more the public sector moves from the current case management model to a more consumer-driven GCM model, the more the roles for social workers will continue to expand. However, it is unlikely that GCM in the public sector will ever be able to provide the 24/7 model of GCM that currently exists in the private, fee-for-service models.

REIMBURSEMENT

Family members who are contracting for services most often pay for GCM services. Although there has been an increase in long-term care insurance providers who do offer a care management benefit (see table 37.3), this provides minimal reimbursement. While a fee-for-service model of reimbursement does provide for the ability to be completely consumer driven, it also presents a number of difficult ethical dilemmas for the practitioner, the most reoccurring one being "Who is the client?"

QUALITY OF LIFE AND QUALITY OF CARE

Perhaps one of the hallmarks of professionally sound GCM is the focus on developing care plans that maximize the quality of life and the quality of care. In that quality of life is directly impacted by the quality of care, the ecological approach of GCM is particularly focused on how the care manager is able to develop a seamless aging network in a fragmented system of care. Given the increasing rate of health care specialization, which unfortunately further complicates an already complex, fragmented system of care, the coordinating focus of GCM cannot be overstated.

Quality of life is also directly and indirectly impacted by GCM. As the care manager assesses both the short- and long-term needs of the client system, there is an opportunity for a proactive approach to improving the quality of life of the identified client and his or her larger caregiving system. In that there can often times be competing demands on the part of the identified client and his or her caregiving system, this focus on quality of life does not come without a number of ethical conflicts. For example, when the client asks to remain at home, the strain (financial, physical, or emotional) on his or her family needs to be considered. Consequently, balancing quality-of-life issues is not always a simple or clear decision and can frequently result in ethical dilemmas for both the care manager and the family members involved.

CULTURALLY RELEVANT SERVICES

Perhaps one of the least discussed or understood areas of GCM services is that of providing culturally relevant services. In that care management is for the most part a private, fee-for-service model of social work practice, there could be an assumption of homogeneity for those with adequate financial resources. And while there is limited socioeconomic heterogeneity among the users of care management services, the cultural values of both identified clients and the familial caregivers could influence both the reporting of and response to impairment and disability (McGahan, 2000). While those from a white American background might be comfortable with the concept of hiring caregivers and a professional consultant, such as a care manager, those from an African American or Hispanic background are more inclined to manage the responsibility of caregiving within the family system.

However, given the projected growth of the minority populations, the projected growth in the number of more affluent from diverse cultural backgrounds, and the growing number of older adults who have emigrated to be closer to their adult children, culturally sensitive services will be required. In addition to this more obvious description of culture, another important aspect of culture refers to the culture of the different age cohorts (Gilleard & Higs, 2001). The perceptions held by today's "oldest old" about using any type of clinical social work service will be significantly different from the perceptions of the aging baby boomers.

In addition to cultural factors related to age cohort, race, and ethnicity, there has also been some discussion about issues related to GCM practice with men (Kosberg & Morano, 2000), as well as with gay, lesbian, bisexual, and transgender older adults

TABLE 37.3. Example of Long-Term Care Insurance Coverage of Care Management Services

Insurance Company	Type of Coverage	Authorized Providers	Coverage
John A Hancock	Optional benefit service to assist with determining care and treatment plan	Not specified	Up to 10 times the daily benefit, or 1/3 of monthly benefit per year; can be paid before elimination period; does not reduce maximum benefit
GE Capital	Optional benefit; privilegedcare coordinator assesses need, develops care plan, helps choose and monitor care; benefits are enhanced if care coordinator is used	Privileged care coordinator (not specified)	Does not reduce maximum benefits; elimination period reduced
Massachusetts Mutual	Optional benefit; personal care advisor is available through company to assist with eligibility for benefits, appropriate level of care availability of facilities	Personal care advisor	Does not reduce maximum benefit
	Care coordination by R.N. to assess and coordinate appropriate care, assist with claims documentation	Care coordinator, R.N. specified	
Met Life	Needs assessment; one free needs assessment by a care management organization selected by insurance company of independent care management organization	Selected by company or by insured	Up to lifetime maximum of $250; can reduce daily care benefit
Prudential	Optional; toll-free referral and process services; can be used during elimination period; home visits; coordinate care; advise about options	Private care consultant licensed not associated with Prudential	Does not reduce daily benefit; 20 times nursing home daily benefit can be used during elimination period

Note: All information was obtained from the promotional materials of the listed providers.

(Cahill, 2002; Healy, 2002; Sullivan, 2002). Suffice it to say that, given the expected demographic changes, as well as the diverse lifestyles of those elders of the future, there is a need for further research with culturally diverse older adults and their familial caregivers.

SUGGESTED CARE MANAGEMENT WEB SITES

http://caremanagement.dce.ufl.edu
The University of Florida Division of Continuing Education and Center for Gerontological Studies offer a certificate in GCM. The certificate is designed to enhance the ability of health and social service profes-

sionals to manage the care of the elderly in a variety of settings, including the home. The certificate is also designed to develop the ability of recent graduates in health-related fields to manage the comprehensive care of our aging population. The program is currently offered to geriatric care professionals, care and case managers, registered nurses, social workers, and members of other health-related professions who are involved in care of the elderly.

www.acmaweb.org
The American Case Management Association, Inc. (ACMA) is a nonprofit organization that was established as the professional association that offers solutions to support the evolving collaborative practice of

hospital/health system case management. The ACMA endeavors to provide a forum for interdisciplinary collaboration. Full and associate memberships are available for individuals who are responsible for and functionally providing case management services. Student memberships are also available for individuals in the process of learning case management services.

www.cmsa.org

The Case Management Society of America is an international, nonprofit organization founded in 1990; it is dedicated to the support and development of the profession of case management through educational forums, networking opportunities, and legislative involvement. The mission of this organization is to promote the growth and value of case management and to support the evolving needs of the case management professional.

www.caremanager.org

The National Association of Professional Geriatric Care Managers (NAPGCM) is a nonprofit, professional organization of practitioners whose goal is the advancement of dignified care for the elderly and their families. With more than 1,600 members, NAPGCM is committed to maximizing the independence and autonomy of elders, while striving to ensure that the highest quality and most cost-effective health and human services are used when and where appropriate.

www.naccm.net

The National Academy of Certified Care Managers (NACCM) is "Committed to quality and competent care management practice. This association works to meet this commitment by assuring individual competence to perform the full range of care management tasks through a validated, standardized examination that tests the skills, knowledge, and practice ethics needed to serve consumers.

www.ctcommunitycare.org

Connecticut Community Care, Inc. (CCCI), is a nonprofit agency that The mission of CCCI is to provide care management services to older individuals, and other persons with similar chronic care needs and their caregivers, and to assist them in remaining as independent as possible in the most cost-effective manner. This agency will continue to be the premier provider of long-term care management to low-income elderly in Connecticut. In addition to the direct service component, CCCI has been a leader in the field

of geriatric care management through the organization's educational division, Care Management Institute (CMI), which is a founding member of the National Academy of Certified Care Managers (NACCM), an accreditation organization that offers the designation of certified care manager to care managers throughout the country. The institute's faculty has extensive experience in areas associated with care management and geriatric program design, from service provision to benefit administration and data analysis to research. These skilled practitioners and experienced administrators understand the needs of the older population and the role of effective management in the conservation of limited resources.

REFERENCES

Aronson, M. K., & Kennedy, J. (1998) Assessment: The linchpin of geriatric care management. *Geriatric Care Management Journal, 8*(1), 11–14.

Bartlett, H. M. (1970). *The common base of social work practice.* New York: National Association of Social Work.

Bartlett, H. M. (2003). Working definition of social work practice. *Social Work, 3*(2), 5–8.

Bodie-Gross, E., & Holt, E. (1998). Care and case management summit: The white paper. *Geriatric Care Management Journal, 8*(3), 22–24.

Borland, A., McRae, J., & Lycan, C. (1989). Outcomes of five years of continuous intensive case management. *Hospital and Community Psychiatry, 40,* 376–396.

Brun, C., & Rapp, R. C. (2001). Strengths-based case management: Individuals' perspectives on strengths and the case manager relationship. *Social Work, 46,* 278–288.

Burns, L. R., Lamb, G. S., & Wholey, D. R. (1996). Impact of integrated community nursing services on hospital utilization and cost in a Medicare risk plan. *Inquiry, 33,* 30–41.

Burns, T. (1997). Case management, care management and care programming. *British Journal of Psychiatry, 170,* 393–406.

Cahill, S. (2002). Long-term care issues affecting gay, lesbian, bisexual and transgender elders. *Geriatric Care Management Journal, 12*(3), 4–6.

Capitman, J. A., Haskins, B., & Bernstein, J. (1986). Case management approaches on coordinated community-oriented long-term care demonstrations. *Gerontologist, 4,* 398–404.

Cress, C. (2001). *Handbook of geriatric care management.* Gaithersburg, MD: Aspen.

Cudney, A. E. (2002). Case management: A serious solution for serious issues. *Journal of Healthcare Management, 47,* 149–152.

Diwan, S. (1999). Allocation of case management resources in long-term care: Predicting high use of case management time. *Gerontologist, 39,* 580–590.

Folstein, M. F., Folstein, S. E., & McHugh, P. R. (1975). "Mini-mental state": A practical method for grading the cognitive state of patients for the clinician. *Journal of Psychiatric Resources, 12,* 189–198.

Frankel, A. J., & Gelman, S. R. (2004). *Case management.* Chicago: Lyceum.

Gallo, J. J., Fulmer, T., Paveza, G. J., & Reichel, W. (2000). *Handbook of geriatric assessment* (3rd ed.). Gaithersburg, MD: Aspen.

Gilleard, C., & Higgs, P. (2001). *Cultures of Aging: Self, Citizen, and the Body.* Harlow, Eng.: Prentice Hall.

Gordon, W. E. (1962). A critique of the working definition. *Social Work, 7*(4), 3–13.

Green, R. (2002). *Social work with the aged and their families.* New York: de Gruyter.

Healy, T. (2002). Culturally competent practice with lesbian elders. *Geriatric Care Management Journal, 12* (3), 9–13.

Hip fracture in seniors: A call for health system reform. (1999). (Position Statement). Rosemont, IL: American Academy of Orthopedic Surgeons.

Hoenig, H., Nusbaum, N., & Brummel-Smith, K. (1997). Geriatric rehabilitation: State of the art. *Journal of the American Geriatric Society, 45*(11), 1371–1381.

Holosko, M. J. (2003). The history of the working definition of social work practice. *Research on Social Work Practice,* 271–283.

Jackson, J. A. (2000). *Health care without Medicare.* Lenox, MA: Solarian Press.

Knutson, K., & Langer, S. (1998). Geriatric care managers: A survey on long-term chronic care. *Geriatric Care Management Journal, 8*(3), 9–13.

Kosberg, J. I., & Morano, C. (2000). Cultural considerations in care management with older adults. *Geriatric Care Management Journal.*

McGahan, K. (2000). Seven tools for culturally aware care management. *Care Management Journal, 10*(2), 14–18.

McInnis-Dittrich, K. (2004). *Social work with elders: A biopsychosocial approach.* Boston: Allyn and Bacon.

Modigliani, S. (2004). Starting and maintaining a solo practice. *Geriatric Care Management Journal, 14*(2), 11–13.

Naleppa, M. J., & Reid, W. J. (2003). *Gerontological social work.* New York: Columbia University Press.

NASW. (1992). *NAS standards for social work case management.* Washington, DC: NASW Press.

National Association of Professional Geriatric Care Managers (2003). *Membership Directory.* Tucson, Az.

Netting, F. E. (1998). Interdisciplinary practice and the geriatric care manager. *Geriatric Care Management Journal, 8*(1), 20–24.

Older Americans Act of 1965. Pub L. No, 89–23, 42 §3001 et seq; as amended or reauthorized 1967, 1968, 1972, 1973, 1974, 1975, 1977, 1978, 1984, 1987, 1992, 1997, 2000.

Parker, M. (1998). Positioning care management for future health care trends. *Geriatric Care Management Journal, 8*(3), 4–8.

Parker, M., & McNattin, S. P. (2002). *Past, present and future trends in care management.* Available: *www.caremanager.org.*

Robinson, M. M. (2000). Case management for social workers: A gerontological approach. In N. P. Kropf, R. L. Schneider, & A. J. Kisor (Eds.), *Gerontological social work.* Belmont, CA: Brooks/Cole.

Rose, S., & Moore, V. L. (1995). Case management. In R. L. Edwards & J. G. Hopps (Eds.), *Encyclopedia of social work* (19th ed., pp. 335–340). Washington, DC: NASW Press.

Rothman, J. (1994). *Practice with highly vulnerable clients: Case management and community-based practice.* Englewood Cliffs: Prentice Hall.

Sullivan, J. D. (2002). Notes from the field: Care management with GLBT elderly. *Geriatric Care Management Journal, 12*(3), 14–15.

Weil, M., & Karls, J. (1985). *Case management in human services practice.* San Francisco: Jossey Bass.

White, M. (2004). The business of care management: Reflections from experts. *Geriatric Care Management Journal, 14*(2), 3–6.

DEBORAH P. WALDROP

Hospices

38

This chapter discusses social work practice in hospice settings with older people and their families. The chapter's introduction sets the context by providing both historical and current perspectives on hospice care, including a differentiation between of end-of-life, palliative, and hospice care, and it integrates current utilization and length-of-stay information from the National Hospice and Palliative Care Organization (NHPCO). The chapter's three main sections discuss (1) regulations and policies that guide hospice social work, (2) hospice care environments, and (3) hospice social work with older adults and their families. Although people of all ages enroll in hospice, this chapter focuses on older patients and their families. The chapter was guided by focus group discussions and in-depth interviews with 21 hospice social workers, whose expertise made these regulatory, care environment, and practice issues come to life.

Historically, "hospice" comes from the same linguistic root as "hospitality" and can be traced back to medieval times, when it referred to a place of shelter and rest for weary or ill travelers on a long journey (Saunders, 2000). Currently, hospice has many meanings; it is a philosophy, a type of care, a benefit, and a health care program that is offered in different settings. The *hospice philosophy* affirms life, neither hastening nor postponing death. *Hospice care* focuses on the patient and family as a unit, recognizing death as the final stage of life, and enabling terminally ill people to continue an alert, pain-free life so that their last days may be spent with dignity and quality, surrounded by their loved ones. The *Medicare Hospice Benefit* (MHB) establishes coverage of comprehensive care for people with a prognosis of six months or less and who decide to stop treatments that are aimed at curing the illness. *Hospice programs* provide care in patients' homes, hospitals, nursing homes, assisted living facilities, free-standing inpatient units, and hospice houses within some communities (National Hospice and Palliative Care Organization [NHCPO], 2004).

The first hospice, St. Christopher's in London, was founded in 1967 by Cicely Saunders, who had been trained as a social worker, nurse, and physician. Hospice care began in the United States during the 1970s and was signed into law as a health care benefit in 1982. Since that time, the hospice movement has grown and changed, being influenced by demographics, advancing medical technology, and healthcare financing. Presently, more than 70% of those who die each year are over age 65 and have experienced an extended dying process from gradually progressive conditions such as heart disease, kidney failure, and cancer (Field & Cassel, 1997). Health care cost containment efforts have shortened hospital stays and encouraged the utilization of less acute environments for care. In combination, these changes have influenced care for people who are terminally ill (Bern-Klug, Gessert, & Forbes, 2002; Luptak, 2004).

Recent trends have stimulated the development of new approaches that are aimed at improving care for people who are dying. The terms "end-of-life care," "palliative care," and "hospice care" are sometimes used interchangeably; for the purpose of conceptual clarity, definitions are critical. *End-of-life care* refers broadly to the physical, psychological, spiritual, and practical dimensions of care that is provided for people who are dying in all settings, including ICUs or emergency departments (IOM, 1997). *Palliative care* seeks to prevent, relieve, reduce, or soothe the symptoms of disease or a disorder without effecting a cure. Although this term is most often used within the end-of-life context, palliative care is not restricted to those who are dying, and is also important to people with chronic pain. Palliative care is delivered by interdisciplinary teams and consultation services in hospitals, nursing homes, and outpatient settings and sometimes in conjunction with hospice services. As a model for the delivery of end-of-life care, *hospice programs* provide palliative care for people whose illness is expected to end in death within six months.

Social work practice in palliative and end-of-life care settings has become a specialty field of practice (National Association of Social Workers [NASW], 2003). Hospice social work is a subspecialty of this field, sharing common features with practice in other end-of-life care settings, but also encompassing features that are unique and distinct. Further, distinctions can be drawn between the issues that characterize social work practice in different hospice settings, (e.g., home, nursing home, or residential unit).

AN OVERVIEW OF HOSPICE CARE

Current estimates by the National Hospice and Palliative Care Organization indicate that 3,200 operational hospice programs provided care to more than 885,000 terminally ill people and their families in 2002 (NHPCO, 2004). Hospices operate in all regions of the country; about one quarter (24%) are located in urban areas, a larger number can be found in rural areas (38%), and some cover both urban and rural

areas (38%). Some hospice organizations have only one office, while others have multiple delivery locations; half are free-standing entities (50%), about one-third are affiliated with hospitals (31.5%), some are connected with home health agencies (18%), and a smaller number were affiliated with nursing facilities (<1%). Hospices also have varying financial structures; a majority are nonprofit (69%), a smaller number were for-profit organizations (27%), and a small number are run by the government (3%) (NHPCO, 2004).

Hospice patients die in a variety of settings: at home (57.9%), in a nursing facility (21.5%), in a hospice unit (4.8%), in a hospital (9%), in free-standing inpatient hospice units (4.1%), and in residential care settings (2.7%) (NHPCO, 2004). More patients died from cancer (50.5%) than other terminal conditions. The top five noncancerous causes of death in hospice include end-stage heart disease (10.7%), dementia (8.3%), lung disease (6.7%), end-stage kidney disease (3%), and end-stage liver disease (1.6%). Although growing numbers of hospice patients demonstrate the increasing societal awareness of hospice, the average length of stay (LOS) continues to be about 51 days (less than 2 months); the median LOS is 21 days. Considered together with the fact that 34% of all hospice patients die within 7 days of admission, these statistics indicate a large number of short stays (NHPCO, 2004).

REGULATIONS AND POLICIES THAT GUIDE HOSPICE CARE

Federal, state, and organizational policies shape the experience of people who are dying and their family members, as well as social work practice in hospice settings. This section briefly addresses the major regulations that influence hospice care: MHB, Medicaid, the Patient Self-Determination Act, and organizational policies about resuscitation and rehospitalization.

Medicare. The MHB pays for a majority (80%) of hospice care in the United States (NHPCO, 2004). To utilize Medicare hospice benefits, an individual must: (1) have been certified by two physicians as having a life expectancy of six months or less if the disease runs its normal course, (2) have chosen to forgo curative treatment, and (3) be enrolled in a Medicare-approved program (Social Security Act, 42 C.F.R. 418, 2000). Medicare part A covers noncurative medical and support services for terminal care, which include physician services, nursing care, medical appliances and supplies, drugs for symptom management and pain relief, short-term inpatient and respite care, homemaker and home health aide services, counseling, social work services, spiritual care, volunteer assistance, and bereavement counseling (NHPCO, 2004).

Medicare hospice rates vary according to the type of care that is provided. *Routine home care* covers care in a home setting (e.g., own home, family members' home, assisted living facility or nursing home). *Continuous home care* covers skilled services for a period of at least 8 hours within a 24-hour period for brief periods of crisis and only as necessary to maintain the terminally ill individual at home. *General inpatient care* involves interventions for pain control or symptom that cannot feasibly be managed at home and is delivered in hospitals, nursing homes, or inpatient hospice facilities. *Inpatient respite care* is covered for no more than 5 days at a time, when caregivers become ill or need a break. The variable fee structure of the MHB has made it possible for hospice organizations to develop new ways of providing care, consequently also meeting individual patient and family needs and preferences (Code of Federal Regulations, 2000).

The MHB "6-month rule" initially required beneficiaries to be within 6 months of their death to be eligible for hospice. However, because many people experience a long, slow decline from a terminal illness, the 6-month rule became a barrier to hospice utilization (Code of Federal Regulations, 418.22, 2000; Lynn, 2002). The Balanced Budget Act of 1997 amended the MHB and established differential benefit periods: an initial 90-day period; a subsequent 90-day period; an unlimited number of subsequent 60-day benefit periods for as long as the patient remains terminally ill (Hospice Association of America [HAA], 2002).

Increasingly, all health care services in the United States, including Medicare benefits, are financed through managed care organizations (MCOs). When a person who has both Medicare and a managed care plan elects hospice, the services must be provided through a Medicare-approved hospice, and the individual must meet the eligibility requirement. The patient does not need a referral and is not required to disenroll from the MCO. Medicare pays for attending physician charges and for services that are not related to the patient's terminal illness (Centers for Medicare and Medicaid [CMS], 2003; Yagoda, 2002).

Medicaid. Medicaid hospice benefits vary dramatically between states because broad federal guidelines provide wide latitude in eligibility, benefits, and payment mechanisms (Kaiser Family Foundation, 2004; Tilly & Wiener, 2001). Hospices that are Medicare certified must offer all services required to relieve the symptoms of a terminal illness, even if the patient is not covered by Medicare and does not have the ability to pay (NHPCO, 2004). However, to participate in Medicaid, hospices must meet Medicare's conditions of participation, which require that an interdisciplinary team supervise or deliver a defined set of services that are based on a written plan of care (Code of Federal Regulations, 418.22, 2000). Although Medicaid accounts for only about 7% of total hospice revenue, it is a significant source of funding for the 35% of older people who use nursing home care during the last year of life (Spillman & Lubitz, 2000).

The Patient Self-Determination Act requires that all health care agencies ask about advance directives, recognize patients' written wishes, and provide educational materials about end-of-life decision-making (Caring Connections, 2001). As a result, in many settings, social workers introduce, discuss, and help people complete one or both types of advance directives: (1) living will and (2) medical power of attorney (POA). A medical POA is sometimes called a health care proxy, durable power of attorney, or health care agent. Particularly when end-of-life decisions have not been made before admission, social workers assist patients and families in identifying options and articulating their preferences during the early stages of hospice care. Finally, discussions of *Do Not Resuscitate* (DNR) or *Do Not Re-hospitalize* (DNH) orders are part of the hospice admission process and social work assessment. (Additional sources of information on hospice regulations can be found at the Web sites listed below.)

- *CMS Hospice Information Resource for Medicare* *www.cms.hhs.gov/providers/hospiceps/default.asp*
- *Code of Federal Regulations* (Title 42, vol. 2, revised as of October 1, 2003): http://frwebgate5.access.gpo.gov/cgi-bin/waisgate.cgi?WAISdocID=234290164362+1+0+0&WAISaction=retrieve
- *Hospice Manual:* Centers for Medicare and Medicaid www.cms.hhs.gov/manuals/21_hospice/hs200.asp?
- *Managed Care and Medicare* www.cms.hhs.gov/healthplans/systems/hospice.asp
- *Medicaid Benefits:* www.kff.org/medicaidbenefits/hospice.cfm
- *Medicare Hospice Benefits:* www.ssa.gov
- *Partnership for Caring:* Advance directives www.partnershipforcaring.org/HomePage/index.html

HOSPICE CARE ENVIRONMENTS

Certified hospice programs provide the same core services in all settings. The development of different care environments has made it possible and sometimes desirable for hospice patients to move between different environments as the illness progresses. Each care environment is briefly described in this section.

In-home care is provided in a patient's or caregiver's house, apartment, or trailer, as well as in assisted living facilities, senior apartment complexes, or retirement facilities. Comprehensive home care includes durable medical equipment, prescription delivery, and visits from each team member. An on-call system is available for crises that occur at any time. Most hospice care is provided in home settings (NHPCO, 2004).

Hospital-based hospice care is usually short-term care and is provided in different arrangements. Beds may be located within a designated hospice unit, scattered throughout the institution, or located within a limited area of the hospital, such as an oncology floor. Care is reimbursed at the general inpatient rate.

Free-standing hospice inpatient units are facilities that provide only inpatient hospice care. Established by a parent hospice organization that also provides care in other environments, these facilities offer short-term inpatient stays for one of three reasons: (1) acute symptom management is needed (e.g., pain, seizures, or nausea are intractable), (2) there is a caregiving system breakdown and respite is needed, or (3) the final hours and days of a person's life are unmanageable at home.

Residential hospice units are home-like and nonmedical settings where terminally ill people can relocate to receive care for weeks to months before death when there is no able caregiver at home. Presently, the number of residential hospice facilities is small but increasing. Hospice programs with residential units (a "hospice house") have been developed in response to the growing need for inpatient care and utilize a variety of funding sources, often combining MHB routine home care payments, Medicaid benefits, managed care and other commercial insurance arrangements, sliding fee scales, and charitable giving (NHPCO, 2004).

Nursing home–based hospice care is delivered in one of two situations: either (1) a resident of a nursing home is determined to be terminally ill and a hospice is called to assist with end of life care, or (2) a hospice patient is admitted to a nursing home because care needs have exceeded what can be provided in a less acute setting such as a home or an assisted living facility.

Bereavement counseling. Bereavement counseling is provided under the MHB for the family members of people who died in hospice care, for 13 months after the death. Although the MHB does not stipulate the educational background of bereavement counselors, many hospice organizations employ social workers in these positions. Bereavement counseling is offered by telephone, in an agency setting, or in the relative's home.

HOSPICE SOCIAL WORK WITH OLDER ADULTS AND THEIR FAMILIES

Social work practice in end-of-life and palliative care settings has "come of age" (Beresford, 2003). Recently, new energy and attention have been focused on developing guidelines for social work practice in end-of-life care. Collaborative efforts have involved the Project on Death in America's Social Work Leadership Development Program, the Social Work Section of the National Council of Hospice and Palliative Professionals (NCHPP), and the National Association of Social Workers (NASW). Some of the sources of additional information that can be used to guide social work practice in hospice settings are presented below.

- *Bibliography on Social Work in Palliative Care/End of Life Care:* NHPCO www.nhpco.org/files/public/PallCareSWbiblio.pdf
- *Guidelines for Social Work in Hospice:* Published by the Social Worker Section, National Council of Hospice and Palliative Professionals (NCHPP)/ NHPCO. Available from NHPCO Marketplace. 800-646-6460.
- *NASW Practice Update:* End-of-life care: Social workers in hospice and palliative care settings. www.socialworkers.org/practice/bereavement/updates/EndOfLifeCare-PU0204.pdf
- *NASW Specialty Practice Section:* www.socialworkers.org/practice/bereavement/
- *NASW Standards for Palliative and End of Life Care:* www.naswdc.org
- *Social Work Assessment Tool:* A tool for assessing patient/caregiver at each visit; Social Work Outcomes Task Force of the Social Worker Section, NCHPP/NHPCO www.nhpco.org/files/public/SWAT3–1-04.doc

- *Social Work Leadership Development Awards, Project on Death in America:* Updates available www.swlda.org/
- *Social Worker Competencies:* Published in *How to Establish a Palliative Care Program,* the online manual of the Center to Advance Palliative Care www.64.85.16.230/educate/content/elements/social work

As a subspecialty of social work in end-of-life care, hospice social work is guided by policies that regulate the MHB, influenced by the environments in which care is rendered and reflective of the specific needs of individual terminally ill people and their families. The work of a hospice social worker includes meeting Medicare guidelines and completing required paperwork, working closely and meeting regularly with interdisciplinary team members, making home and facility visits, and fulfilling on-call responsibilities. Hospice social workers weave together their knowledge of regulations, organizations, and programs, as well as the interpersonal and family dynamics that occur at the end of life. Hospice social work is about helping people deal with the changes and losses that accompany the end stage of a terminal illness within a program that aims to ease suffering and prepare the individual for death and help the family in bereavement. Two types of hospice social work are described in this section: (1) components of social work practice that are common to all hospice settings, and (2) components of social work practice that are specific to each hospice environment. Conceptualization of the overall features of hospice social work with older people and the differences found across settings was guided by focus group discussions with social work practitioners from two hospice organizations.

OVERALL FEATURES OF HOSPICE SOCIAL WORK

Organized by concepts from the ecological framework, the overall features of hospice social work can be viewed as an integration of macro, mezzo, and micro practice (see Table 38.1).

The *macro* practice elements of hospice social work include knowledge of regulations about: financing and eligibility, transitions between different environments of care, and the end-of-life decision-making. Hospice social workers are interpreters; they explain policies to patients and families, while simul-

taneously analyzing and describing the patient's social context to the interdisciplinary team. For example, to be eligible for hospice, doctors must certify that a patient is in the final 6 months of life, and the patient must acknowledge that the condition is terminal and agree to forego curative treatment (Becker, 2004; Stein, 2004). When people resist or struggle with these guidelines, social workers interpret the policies for them and work through the issues to attain a mutually beneficial outcome. Complex ethical issues can emerge during the course of hospice care that involve the patient's medical condition, involvement (or lack) of family, or the avoidance of discussing terminality; thus, social workers are often required to incorporate medical and social work ethics in problem resolution (Csikai, 2004).

Macro elements of hospice social work also involve contributions to volunteer training, public education, and community outreach. While working with community agencies, social workers educate others about hospice guidelines and services, they determine eligibility, and they help dispel myths about hospice. Finally, social workers assist their employing hospice organization in balancing fiscal realities with patients' needs. Through the process of problem resolution, social workers help maintain the continuity of patient care (measured as nights in continuous care), manage the average cost per patient, and enhance patient/family satisfaction (Reese, Raymer & Richardson, 2000; Yagoda, 2002).

The *mezzo* practice components of hospice social work involve interdisciplinary teamwork and the integration of knowledge about organizational, team and group dynamics, team roles and boundaries, and varied environments of care. Social workers conduct family conferences (e.g., about disposition, transfer, or death), advocate for the patient/family with team members, and negotiate referrals and services with community agencies.

Teamwork can involve both role "overlap" and "blur" with other disciplines and calls for professionals to be simultaneously flexible and assertive (Christ & Sormanti, 1999; Reese & Sontag, 2001; Wesley, Tunney, & Duncan, 2004). Hospice social workers work closely with each member of the team, often making joint visits to a home or facility and combining expertise to help a patient/family. True interdisciplinary teamwork emerges when professionals are both "understanding of" and "understood by" each other. It is as important for the other professionals to grasp the integrated macro, mezzo, and micro components of the social work role as it is for social workers to un-

TABLE 38.1. Hospice Social Work With Older People

Macro Practice

Knowledge of:

- Hospice financing regulations: Medicare, Medicaid, MCO
- Advance directives: health care proxies, living wills
- Do Not Resuscitate or Rehospitalize orders; Family Medical Leave Act

Skills to:

- Assess eligibility determination (e.g., Medicaid LTC)
- Interpret regulations for people who are making end-of-life decisions
- Clearly articulate social work values, ethics
- Communicate patient's financial concerns effectively to hospice organization
- Negotiate resources with the community agencies; educate about hospice

Mezzo Practice

Knowledge of:

- Organizational, team, and group dynamics
- Interdisciplinary team roles and boundaries
- Different environments in which hospice care is provided

Skills to:

- Be flexible and assertive with overlapping roles
- Interpret psychosocial dynamics and social context to team members
- Conduct family conferences (e.g., disposition, transfer, death)
- Advocate for patient/family with team members, community agencies
- Arrange transitions between hospice units (e.g., hospital to nursing home)

Micro Practice

Knowledge of:

- Biological and psychological processes of dying
- Religious and faith-based practices at the end of life
- Pain and symptom exacerbations and management (e.g., when to call for help)
- Grief; physical, emotional, social responses to loss
- Grief vs. depression in patient and caregiver

Skills to:

- Conduct a rapid, biopsychosocial assessment; build rapport quickly
- Be present during difficult, painful, emotional times; deal with tears and anger
- Use direct and sensitive language to discuss and educate about death and dying
- Assess symptoms of exacerbated substance use and mental illness with loss
- Provide patient/family intervention (e.g., conflict resolution, crisis intervention)
- Anticipate/plan with families about needs following death

Note: This list is representative but not exhaustive; it was compiled with the assistance of hospice social workers from Hospice Buffalo and Niagara Hospice.

derstand the parameters and potential conflicts that their colleagues face. For example, social workers who understand the stressors faced by nurses who work to manage uncontrolled pain when the family does not want the person to have morphine, or the dilemmas that chaplains face when asked to perform a funeral service for a patient they met once, can foster stronger relationships. A well-functioning hospice team is a model of interdisciplinary collaboration.

Social workers also utilize their skills to provide conflict resolution and emotional support for their team members (Christ & Sormanti, 1999; Reese et al., 2003). Examples of the conflicts that social workers have helped their teams resolve include: professional-personal boundary issues, differences in approach to self-determination, interdisciplinary "turf" issues, differences in perspectives on confidentiality, possible interventions, and possible approaches to diversity issues (Reese et al., 2000).

The micro, or direct practice, elements of hospice social work include but are not limited to: the psychosocial issues that accompany the physical and functional losses of terminal illness; the social, spiritual, religious, and cultural responses to dying; end-of-life preferences and decision-making; facilitation of transitions between environments of care (e.g., hospital to home hospice care); and grief work. Also particularly germane to a chapter on hospice social work with older people is that social work practitioners must differentiate between three processes of decline—(1) physical and cognitive decline accompanying a terminal illness, (2) comorbid conditions, and (3) normal aging—and help families understand the differences.

Clinical work with people who are dying requires the ability to conduct a rapid biopsychosocial assessment and to build rapport quickly, because sometimes only one visit occurs before death (Stein, 2004). The individual experience of terminal illness and the process of caring for someone who is dying are perhaps two of the most intimate, personal, and emotional times in life. Hospice social workers bring the "gift of presence"; sometimes just listening can help a family through the ravages of a death experience. Hospice social workers use direct and sensitive language to discuss death and become comfortable dealing with tears, anger, and emotional intensity. Social workers are the team members who are called on to assess and intervene when a patient or caregiver is demonstrating symptoms of exacerbated substance use and mental illness as a way of coping. Social workers provide family interventions, which include conflict resolution and crisis intervention. Because most people provide care for a dying relative infrequently, family members often benefit from situation-specific support and information. Finally, social workers anticipate and help families plan for their needs after death (e.g., social support, financial concerns, grief counseling)

HOSPICE SOCIAL WORK IN VARIED ENVIRONMENTS

Not all terminal illnesses are the same; thus many paths lead to hospice. Some patients and their loved ones may have been dealing with the terminal diagnosis for months or years and have expected that hospice admission would eventually occur. Other patients may receive a definitive diagnosis late in the course of a disease and feel that discussion of hospice occurred abruptly and without warning. Admission to hospice is also influenced by the series of decisions that patients and their families make during earlier stages of the illness, the care environments that are available, the ill person's needs, and how the family can meet them. Subsequently, after admission, patients may move between different hospice environments of care. Each care environment creates a different end-of-life context and patient/family experience. Practice in each environment is briefly described here.

In-home hospice. Home or facility visits present unique opportunities to know and understand the individual within the environmental, social, and family contexts. Home environments vary widely from stark to lavish, clean to unkempt, and rural to urban. Pets may or may not be present, and if they are, there may be one or many who range from friendly to frightening. Home visits make it possible to incorporate visual assessment of items such as family photos or memorabilia, and these help the social work assessment come to life. Home visits also offer the opportunity to assess the environment for needs that the person may have as the disease progresses (e.g., the presence of stairs, proximity of the bathroom). Consequently, hospice social work assessment in the home environment requires the use of active observation and inquiry.

Hospice home care can involve being present when the terminally ill person is having intense pain or symptom exacerbations. A general understanding of symptom management is important, as well as knowledge about when to call for assistance. Establishing a caregiving system is a priority for home care social workers; learning who will stay with the person and if caregiving is the responsibility of one person or shared by many, together with an assessment of the caregivers' knowledge of dying and physical abilities, is essential. People who live alone may require assistance with placement or a discussion about how to manage physical needs as the disease progresses. Social work practice in the home setting always requires flexible thinking and adaptability to develop a plan that is well grounded within the social context.

Home care that occurs in assisted living, senior, or retirement facilities is accompanied by some additional challenges. Understanding the facility's policy

TABLE 38.2. Hospice Social Work in Varied Environments

Environment	Environmental Issues	Practice Issues	Salient Knowledge/Skills
In-home care: inividual residence	Homes range from: trailers & apartments to large houses; rural to urban locations; clean/tidy to dirty/odorous; Pets: friendly or frightening Photos, memorabilia help assessment come to life	Assess social context & environmental needs Understand caregiving system, assess abilities & knowledge Assist people who live alone	Adaptability & flexible thinking Community networking Use home environment for a "living" psychosocial assessment Quickly assess family dynamics; build rapport
In-home care: assisted living, retirement, senior housing	Facilities range from: communal living/dining (all apartments open on core area) to individual apartments with kitchens; & no structured contact with others Staff can be very comfortable or uncomfortable with dying	Rapport with facility Educate staff about EOL Collaborate with the staff Understand facility policies	Increased acuity may require transfer Evaluate safety: an alarm system? Family conferencing/planning (re: transfer, loss)
Free-standing inpatient units	Nonhospital setting Children, pets allowed Family can stay; open visiting hours Comfortable surroundings 24-hour nursing care	First contact may be in the final hours/days of life High intensity, urgency of work; frequent death Ongoing observation of pain, symptoms of dying, and death	Crisis intervention; support families about death; plan and prepare for bereavement Boundary concerns (emotions, burnout, transference)
Nursing home (NH)-based hospice care	Resident becomes terminally ill and hospice called in (long-term placement) *or* Hospice patient is admitted to the nursing home (new placement)	Assess nursing home culture (is hospice welcome or a threat?) Help patient accommodate to NH living	Advocate for the resident Support and educate family Clarify lines of communication (when to contact NH, hospice) Facilitate eligibility for Medicaid
Residential hospice facilities	Home-like, non-acute care Lives alone, no caregiver Family/friends are unable to manage EOL care	Longer term stay may allow for reminiscence, planning, family meetings Transitional plans needed; will the person stay here until death	Patient hasn't entered functional decline Loss of home, social support, routine, independence Anticipate approaching death
Hospital-based hospice	Acute care facility Designated hospice beds, floor *or* Beds scattered throughout hospital	Team within a team (hospice plus hospital staff) Balancing the fiscal realities faced by hospice and hospital care (discharge planning may be a priority)	Discharge planning Describe and explore options with people at very difficult times
Bereavement counseling	Telephone contact In-home counseling In-agency counseling	Hospice social worker following the person in bereavement *or* separate bereavement counselors	Being comfortable with tears, anger, intense emotions; readiness for bereavement counseling is individual/unique

Note: This list is representative but not exhaustive; it was compiled with the assistance of hospice social workers from Hospice Buffalo and Niagara Hospice.

on having residents who are becoming dependent remain in the facility is important. Some facilities will allow dying residents to remain as long as additional caregivers are available; others require that residents who need increasing care must transfer out. In addition, social workers may enlist the help of friends or neighbors in the facility, or they may reach out to help them with the loss.

Free-standing inpatient units. Social work practice with people who are temporarily admitted for symptom management or respite requires an assessment of the patient/family plan for disposition and of whether the person will return to the home setting or need placement in a nursing home. The inpatient unit social worker may conduct a family conference and initiate discharge planning immediately after admission. If the hospice patient is admitted because the terminal decline becomes unmanageable in the home setting, the social work role involves assessment of the family's understanding of the approaching death, death education, anticipation of needs, and support through the dying process.

Residential hospice facilities. Social work practice with people who have moved into a "hospice house" involves assessing the person's previous lifestyle, illness trajectory, and end-of-life preferences. Residents of a hospice house may be able to manage some of their own personal care and thus "live with dying" over a period of months. This affords the opportunity to develop a longer term relationship with residents.

Hospital-based hospice units. Because hospital-based hospice care is generally very temporary, social work practice in hospital-based hospice units is disposition-focused. Social workers discuss options for transfer with family members, and planning may focus on what Medicare and other insurance policies cover (Stein, 2004). In some situations, even while patients are actively dying, there is ongoing pressure to place the patient elsewhere. Balancing the discharge planning pressures with patient and family needs in this setting presents unique and distinct pressures.

Nursing home–based hospice care involves additional medical, nursing, social work, and pastoral care services that are provided on top of the routine nursing home regimen. The focus of social work practice with nursing home residents who are hospice patients depends on whether the nursing home resident became terminally ill and hospice was called in or the hospice patient was relocated to the nursing home. If the patient was a long-term nursing home resident, the social work assessment attends to the existing re-lationships that the resident has with others (staff and patients) as well as the quality of the ongoing relationship between family members and the nursing home. If a hospice patient relocates to a nursing home, social work can assist the person/family in adapting to nursing home life and facing an approaching death.

"Team within a team" phenomenon. Hospice care that is provided in any facility setting (assisted living, nursing home, or hospital-based care) generates a "team within a team" phenomenon. The hospice team enters an environment in which there are previously existing relationships between the patient, family, and staff and existing structures for service delivery and communication. The hospice team brings a specific, focused approach to end-of-life care, which can be welcomed or seen as a threat. The potentially complex three-way relationship requires the hospice team to create a partnership with the facility. Hospice social workers who work in this type of host setting may become involved in problem resolution with the facility's administration or in death and hospice education, which aims to help both the staff and residents deal with the person's decline and approaching death.

Bereavement counseling. It is important to emphasize that grief and loss issues are pervasive in hospice social work; thus social work practitioners in all settings encounter and work with patient and family grief responses. Bereavement counseling is a specifically focused intervention that is provided to help family members integrate the losses they have experienced after the person has died. Two different models of bereavement counseling exist: (1) the social worker who has followed the patient/family before death remains available to them afterward, and (2) following the death, a new person invites their participation in individual or group counseling.

CONTINUING CHANGE— FUTURE CHALLENGES

Three converging trends are precipitating both ongoing change and future challenges for hospice and for social workers in all areas of aging and end-of-life care, as follows.

Demographic imperatives. Presently, more than 80% of the people who utilize hospice services are over age 65, and indicators suggest that this trend will continue. The growth in numbers of hospice organizations and people who use this program indicate increasing recognition of the importance of care that is patient and family focused and is delivered within a variety of environments.

Healthcare financing. Reimbursement cuts, mergers, more stringent benefit management, and focused medical review have forced many hospices to closely examine their business practices (Reese et al., 2000). In addition, costly new drugs and treatments such as palliative radiation have increased the average cost to hospices faster than the reimbursement rates. The fixed Medicare per diem rate that is paid to hospice providers often is insufficient to cover daily services, particularly when patients have short hospice stays and extraordinary expenses. Medicaid benefit limitations are too low to allow hospices in some states to provide the most advanced types of pain relief (Tilly & Wiener, 2001).

Hospice utilization. Clear patterns of utilization have emerged, indicating that hospice is used by some groups more than others and in ways that diverge from program expectations. Remarkably, the majority (82%) of hospice patients are white. A significant number of people have short stays; 35% die within 7 days of admission; and the median LOS hovers at around 21 days (NHPCO, 2004). These statistics suggest that the hospice program as it is presently structured does not appeal to people in some racial and ethnic groups (Reese, Ahern, Nair, O'Faire, & Warren, 1999). In addition, despite increased knowledge about the program, many people do not wish to enter the program until the very final stage of life. Deeper understanding about individual racial and cultural differences, as well as ideologies and preferences about care at the end of life, is needed; the outcomes will influence future program evolution.

Hospice has developed many meanings since its inception, and these trends demonstrate that the progression will continue. As a core component of the hospice program, gerontological social workers have significant opportunities to advocate for patient/family needs and to be a voice for the issues and concerns of terminally ill older adults and their families in the midst of ongoing policy and program change.

Grateful acknowledgment is made of the knowledge, wisdom and experiences shared by 21 social workers from Hospice Buffalo and Niagara Hospice who participated in focus group discussions about hospice social work to guide the development of this chapter.

APPENDIX 38.1

Additional Information: Reports Available for Downloading

Center to Advance Palliative Care (CAPC): offers an online manual of tools and assistance to start palliative care programs; addresses social work competencies *www.capcmssm.org/*

Center for the Advancement of Health (2003): *Report on bereavement and grief research* *www.cfah.org/pdfs/griefreport.pdf (182 p)*

National Consensus Project for Quality Palliative Care (2004): offers guidelines developed by five palliative care organizations *www.nationalconsensusproject.org/*

Means to a better end: A report on dying in America today (2002): *www.wjf.org/files/publications/other/ meansbetterend.pdf.*

Living well at the end of life: Adapting health care to serious illness in old age, by L. Lynn and D. M. Adamson (2003): synthesizes literature about chronic illness in the last phase of life *www.rand.org/publications/WP/WP137/WP137.pdf*

Web Sites for Additional Information

www.eperc.mcw.edu/.

End-of-Life/Palliative Resource Center (EPERC). A database of peer reviewed educational materials. *www.growthhouse.org/hospice.html.*

Growth House: An international gateway to resources for life-threatening illness and end of life care. *www.hospicefoundation.org/.*

Hospice Foundation of America. Information for patients and professionals.

REFERENCES

Becker, J. E. (2004). Oncology social workers' attitudes toward hospice care and referral behavior. *Health and Social Work, 29*(1), 36–45.

Beresford, L. (2003). EOL social work: A coming of age. New Hampshire Hospice and Palliative Care Organization, Vol. 4. Available: *www.nhho.org.*

Bern-Klug, M., Gessert, C., & Forbes, S. (2001). The need to revise assumptions about the end of life: Implications for social work practice. *Health and Social Work, 26*(1), 38–46.

Burnette, D., Morrow-Howell, N., & Chen, L. (2003) Setting priorities for gerontological social work research: A national Delphi study. *Gerontologist, 43*(6), 828–838.

Caring Connections. (2001). *Advocating quality end-of-life care: What are advance directives?* Available: *www.partnershipforcaring.org/HomePage/.*

Centers for Medicare and Medicaid. (2001, November 1). *Medicare hospice manual. Reimbursement for hospice care.* Available: *www.cms.hhs.gov/manuals/21_hospice.hs100.asp.*

Centers for Medicare and Medicaid. (2003). Hospice information resource for Medicare. Available: http://*www.cms.hhs.gov/providers/hospiceps.*

Christ, G. H., & Sormanti, M. (1999). Advancing social work practice in end-of-life care. *Social Work in Health Care, 30*(2), 81–99.

Code of Federal Regulations 42, 418.22 (2000). Available: *www.gpoaccess.gov/cfr/index.html.*

Csikai, E. L. (2004). Social workers' participation in the resolution of ethical dilemmas in hospice care. *Health & Social Work, 29*(1), 67–76.

Hospice Association of America. (2002, November). *Hospice facts and statistics.* Available: *www.nahc.org/Consumer/hpcstats.html.*

Institute of Medicine. (1997). *Approaching death: Improving care at the end of life.* Washington, DC: National Academy Press.

Field, M. J., & Cassel, C. (Eds). (1997) *Approaching death: Improving care at the end of life.* Institute on Medicine, Committee on Care at the End of Life. Washington, DC: National Academy of Sciences.

Kaiser Family Foundation, Kaiser Commission on Medicaid and the Uninsured. (2004). *Medicaid benefits and hospice.* Available: *www.kff.org/medicaidbenefits/hospice.cfm*

Luptak, M. (2004). Social work and end-of-life care for older people: A historical perspective. *Health and Social Work, 29*(1), 7–15.

Lynn, J. (2002).Where to live while dying. *Gerontologist, 42,* 68–71.

Medicare hospice benefits. (2003, July). Available: *www.medicare.gov/Publications/Pubs/pdf/02154.pdf.*

National Association of Social Workers. (2005). NASW standards of social work practice in palliative care and end of life care. Available: *www.socialworkers.org/practice/bereavement/standards.*

National Hospice and Palliative Care Organization. (2005). *Caring connections: Advance directives.* Available: *www.caringinfo.org/i4a/forms/form.cfm?id=16&pageid=3462.*

National Hospice and Palliative Care Organization. (2004). *Alternatives to in-home care.* Available: *www.hhpco.org/i4a/pages/index.cfm?pageid=3344.*

Partnership for Caring (2001). *Advance directives.* Available: *www.partnershipforcaring.org/HomePage/index.html.*

Reese, D. J., Ahern, R. E., Nair S., O'Faire, J. D., & Warren, C. (1999). Hospice access and use by African Americans: Addressing cultural and institutional barriers through participatory action research. *Social Work, 44*(6), 549–559.

Reese, D. J., & Brown, D. R. (1997). Psychosocial and spiritual care in hospice: Differences between nursing, social work, and clergy. *Hospice Journal, 12*(1), 29–41.

Reese, D. J., Raymer, M., & Richardson, J. (2000, March). *National Hospice Social Work Survey: Summary of final results.* Available: *www.nhpco.org/files/public/social-work-finaladminreport.pdf.*

Reese, D., & Sontag, M. (2001). Successful interprofessional collaboration on the hospice team. *Health & Social Work, 26*(3), 167–176.

Saunders, C. (2000). The evolution of palliative care. *Patient Education and Counseling, 41,* 7–13.

Sheldon, F. M. (2000). Dimensions of the role of the social worker in palliative care. *Palliative Medicine, 14*(6), 491–498.

Social Security Act of 1965 (Title xviii). C42CFR418.1 Pub. L. No. 100–93.

Social Security Act of 1965 (Title xix). C42CFR431 Pub. L. No. 100–93.

Spillman, B. C., & Lubitz, J. (2000). The effect of longevity on spending for acute and long-term care. *New England Journal of Medicine, 342*(19), 1409–1415.

Stein, G. (2004). Improving our care at life's end: Making a difference. *Health & Social Work, 29*(1), 77–79.

Tilly, J., & Wiener, J. M. (2001, April 1). *Medicaid and end-of-life care.* Available: *www.urban.org/Uploadedpdf/410409_Medicaid.pdf.*

Walsh, K. (2003, December). *Social workers in hospice and palliative care settings: End of life care.* NASW Practice Update. Available: *www.socialworkers.org/practice/bereavement/updates/EndOfLifeCare-PU0204.pdf.*

Wesley, C., Tunney, K., & Duncan, E. (2004). Educational needs of hospice social workers: Spiritual assessment and interventions with diverse populations. *American Journal of Hospice and Palliative Care, 21*(1), 40–46.

Yagoda, L. (2002). End of life care for older clients: What social workers should know about the Medicare Hospice Benefit. Available: *www.socialworkers.org/practice/aging/.*

Although the majority of the elderly population has sound mental health, studies indicate that almost 20% of this age group experience mental health disorders (U.S. Department of Health and Human Services, 1999). The correlation between elder mental disorders and physical illness, poor social support, and disability presents unique challenges for the mental health care system. The vast majority of older persons suffering from mental health disorders (69.2%) reside in the community (Rowland, Burns, Schafft, Randolph, & McAninch, 1997). Therefore, it is imperative that effective community-based options for mental health treatment be available for older adults. Over the past several decades one community-based option has been Community Mental Health Centers (CMHCs). These centers, which gained prominence in the 1960s and 1970s through the support of direct federal funding, received federal funds to provide comprehensive, community-based mental health services to all citizens residing within established catchment areas. Federal mandates directed CMHCs to provide culturally sensitive mental health and substance abuse services, and to address the needs of high-priority clients, including the severely mentally ill, older adults, and children. Over time, however, CMHCs have been barraged by changing political, social, and economic realities. These realities have brought about an evolution in the CMHC system. Today, community-based mental health care agencies are sustained by a variety of funding mechanisms, provide a diversified array of services, and target various client populations.

EARLY HISTORY (1963–1980)

After World War II, a growing consensus among psychiatrists and others in the mental health community held that psychosocial and psychoanalytic therapy within community settings offered greater treatment efficacy than did mental health treatment within institutionalized settings (Grob, 1991). The discovery of psychotropic medications to treat schizophrenia and other mental health disorders decreased the need to house the severely mentally ill in state institutions and heightened professionals' and mental health advocates' interest in community-based treatment. *Action for Mental Health,* a summary report of the Joint Commission on Mental Illness and Health (Appel & Bartemeier, 1961), reflected this sentiment and highlighted the need for community-based mental health services. The newly elected president, John F.

SHERRY M. CUMMINGS
KIMBERLY M. CASSIE

Community Mental Health Centers

Kennedy, read this report and came to believe in the need for a federal mental health policy that would foster the movement from institution-based to community-based mental health services. In 1963, Present Kennedy called for a "bold new approach" in the treatment of the mentally ill and recommended that Congress authorize grants to the states for the development of comprehensive community mental health centers (Cutler, 1992). President Kennedy's address marked the beginning of the community mental health center movement in the United States (National Council for Community Behavioral Healthcare, 2003). Later in 1963, the Mental Retardation Facilities and Community Mental Health Centers Construction Act (1963) was signed into law. Because of lobbying from the American Medical Association and congressional opposition, staffing for these centers was omitted from the Act, and only allocation for construction of buildings was included. However, in 1965, under President Johnson, funding amendments for staff were passed. From 1965 though 1970, designated mental health catchment areas all across the country began to apply for federal funding to build and develop CMHCs.

The original centers were mandated to provide five services: inpatient, outpatient, day treatment, crisis services, and education and consultation. In addition, each center was to serve 75,000 to 200,000 persons in a defined catchment area, and continuity of care was to be provided to all clients served (Naierman, Haskins, Robinson, Zook, & Wilson, 1978). The CMHCs Construction Act stipulated that local communities appoint boards that were composed of mental health professionals, consumers, and family members and were reflective of the community racial, ethnic, and demographic profile, to help guide the development of needed services. In 1975, Congress passed a series of amendments to the CMHCs Construction Act. A new CMHC definition mandated the comprehensiveness and accessibility of mental health services for all clients regardless of ability to pay. The amendments also served to further increase the spectrum of services offered by federally funded CMHCs. Services to older adults and children were required, as were drug abuse services and follow-up services such as halfway houses. As a result of the original Act and the subsequent amendments, 445 CMHCs were funded between 1968 and 1975 (Smith, 1984). By 1981, when direct federal funding was eliminated, 754 catchment areas nationwide had applied for and received funds for the development of CMHCs (Cutler, 1992).

As the result of the new federal mental health policy and the passage of Medicaid and Medicare, the population of state mental hospitals began to decline rapidly. "Deinstitutionalization," the movement of persons with severe mental health disorders from state hospitals to the community, occurred rapidly throughout the 1960s and 1970s. The intent behind the deinstitutionalization movement was for persons with mental health disorders to receive needed treatment and services in community-based settings. The CMHCs were designed to play a vital role in meeting the needs of and maintaining the severally mentally ill in the community.

Although the new centers were set up as an alternative to state hospitals, in reality, they did not serve the same clientele. Persons with severe mental illness continued to receive services in state hospitals or from state hospital aftercare programs. The CMHCs focused more on a new group of clients and provided insight-oriented therapy to those with less serve illnesses who, in the past, did not have access to services. Thus, while those with severe mental illness were leaving institutionalized care, adequate support mechanisms to provide needed care within the community were not readily available (Grob, 1991). In 1977, President Carter appointed his wife, Rosalyn, to head the President's Commission on Mental Health, which held public hearings to examine the status of persons with mental health disorders. The commission found a lack of services to meet the needs of deinstitutionalized persons with severe mental illness. As a result, the National Mental Health Systems Act (1980) authorized an additional $800 million and gave priority to vulnerable groups, including the severely mentally ill, children, and older adults.

However, in 1981 President Reagan signed the Omnibus Budget Reconciliation Act (1981), which cut 25% of all CMHC funding and eliminated direct federal funding of CMHCs. The additional monies authorized through the National Mental Health Systems Act (1980) were written off. Federal funds were converted into block grants to be distributed by the states, according the states' estimations of the mental health needs of their own citizens. The CMHCs were stripped of their federally qualified status, and the previous mental health service requirements established by the CMHCs Construction Act and its subsequent amendments were eliminated. Thus, the new legislation dramatically reduced the federal government's involvement in shaping mental health programs and services and shifted this responsibility to states and local communities (Pardes, 1990). Following OBRA 1981, the financial status of CMHCs became precarious. In an effort to cope with this reality, CMHCs changed their staffing patterns to include less highly paid personnel, focused their services more on the severely mentally ill, and began to experiment with alternate sources of funding (Cutler, 1992).

CURRENT SITUATION (SINCE 1981)

Currently, the structure of the mental health care system is intergovernmental, involving federal, state, and local entities (Coddington, 2001). The federal government, through the Community Mental Health Services Block Program, awards grants to states to provide community-based mental health services to their citizens and thereby reduce psychiatric hospitalizations. The Community Mental Health Services Block Program works closely with each state to develop a state mental health plan, and states may use block grant monies to fund CMHCs. The assumption underlying the block grant program is that mental health needs vary from state to state, as do effective mental health treatment approaches. The block grant supports the grassroots involvement of key stakeholders in mental health services at the local, state, and federal levels. For this reason, each state is required to have a mental health planning council to review and provide input for the state's mental health plan (Substance Abuse Mental Health Services Administration [SAMHSA], 2004). Each state, therefore, establishes its own approach to the structure and funding of community-based mental health treatment. Because of diversity within states' geographic regions, some states have given those at the local level the ability to customize mental health service offerings and organizational structures. Thus, although at one point in time, federally funded CMHCs shared a common mandate and offered a required set of services, CMHC programs have increasingly diversified, since "the organization, structure and funding of CMHCs varies from state to state as does the per capita funding of mental health programs from state sources" (Callicutt, 1997, p. 12).

Decreased federal and state funding over the past several decades coupled with soaring health care costs have challenged the stability of centers offering mental health services to the public. In order to respond to changing governmental priorities and evolving market forces, mental health centers have had to put together an increasingly complex array of funding streams, including Medicare, Medicaid, fee-for-service, employee assistance contracts, local funding, managed care contracts, and block grant money (Broskowski & Eaddy, 1994). Because each of these funding mechanisms may cover varying services and offer differential reimbursement levels, the type and amount of mental health services offered may vary greatly from center to center. One study that analyzed payer sources for and type of services offered by CMHCs found that those centers that rely more heavily on public funds target their services more strongly to clients with severe mental illness, while centers supported primarily by private funds focus on those with less serious mental disorders (Hadley, Culhane, Mazade, & Manderscheid, 1994). Because of increasing financial challenges, many CMHCs are no longer able to offer comprehensive services. Their boards of directors must decide which population(s) will best benefit from the center's services and then develop a business plan and marketing strategy to ensure adequate funding for services offered (Dyer & Williams, 1994).

In response to the forces just outlined, states and CMHCs have begun to experiment with managed behavioral health care. States have focused on publicly funded managed care systems for state employees, Medicaid beneficiaries, and the indigent. In 1988, Massachusetts was the first state to employ managed care for its behavioral health care needs. Many states now have Medicaid managed care, in which mental health services for those receiving public assistance are capitated. Utah's managed Medicaid plan, for example, involves contracts between the state and CMHCs that serve regional catchment areas. Reports on the impact of managed care on services provided by CMHCs vary. In Massachusetts, CMHC providers surveyed after the establishment of Medicaid managed care indicated that the service continuum of mental health services provided expanded as the result of managed care (Cohen & Bloom, 2000). A study done in New York state, however, revealed that managed care resulted in significant changes in the types of mental health service provided, with decreases in open-ended psychotherapy and psychological testing and increases in medication management, brief therapy, and crisis intervention (Cypres, Landsberg, & Spellman, 1997).

In summary, over the last 40 years CMHCs have undergone multiple evolutions. The CMHC Construction Act of 1963 and its amendments brought about a common definition and mandated service offerings for federally funded CMHCs and highlighted the role of CMHCs as providers of a wide array of mental health services for community-based populations. The deevolution of mental health policy to the state and local levels, however, coupled with decreased government funding of mental health services and the rise of managed behavioral health care, has led to greater diversification in the structure and organization of community mental health service agencies and in the services they provide.

STAFFING

Community mental health centers are staffed by a variety of mental health professionals, including social workers, nurses, psychologists, and psychiatrists. It has been estimated that 50% of all mental health treatments in the United States are provided by social workers (Rosen & Persky, 1997). In 1977, Blank defined the role of social workers in community mental health centers as that of advocates and community liaisons. According to Blank (1977), social workers bring the individual mental health client, groups of clients, and communities together. Social workers are responsible for assessing the social strengths and weaknesses of clients and coordinating services with community resources to meet the client's needs and maintain the client in the community at his or her highest practicable level of functioning (Blank, 1977). In a survey of 200 licensed mental health organizations in New York, Cypres et al. (1997) found that 45% of the employees were social workers. Cypres et al. noted that the number of social workers in mental health organizations had increased over the past four years, but due to the managed care movement, the number of social workers in mental health is expected to decrease in the future. Among the many services provided by social workers are psychosocial assessments, information and referral services, therapeutic interventions, skills training, and crisis intervention. Specialized gerontological education and experience serve to better equip social workers to address the unique mental health needs of older adults.

CMHCS AND OLDER ADULTS

The goal of community mental health centers is to encourage maximum independence as clients receive mental health care in the community to prevent the need for institutionalization (Kent, 1990). Clients participate in the therapeutic relationship by assisting with the creation of goals and objectives, and by executing action plans that are designed to enhance their level of functioning and continue their independent lifestyles. In 1988, Light, Lebowitz, and Bailey surveyed 290 CMHCs nationally to assess the number of older adults receiving services and the types of services rendered to this special population. Light et al. found that 281 of the 290 community mental health centers surveyed provided services to older adults. On average, almost 11% of the clients served were aged 60 and over. Approximately 52% of the centers identified themselves as offering *specialized* services for older adults. Centers with specialized older adult programs employed staff with increased gerontological knowledge, training, and skills, and as a result, these centers served a greater proportion of clients aged 60 and over (almost 16%, compared to 11%). In order to reach older adults, most CMHCs surveyed partnered with other agencies in the aging network to leverage resources, coordinate planning and training, and increase mental health service usage by older adults (Kent, 1990; Light et al., 1988; Lebowitz, 1988). Facilities that partnered with other senior service agencies reported serving a greater proportion of clients aged 60 and over than those that did not seek out partnerships in the aging network (Light et al., 1988).

Mental health disorders among older adults are undertreated, and older adults are underrepresented in CMHCs. Several reasons for the undertreatment of older adults in community-based mental health care settings have been proposed. Lebowitz (1988) suggested that most mental health professionals have limited training and experience in differentiating normal age-associated changes from changes requiring clinical or medical attention. The lack of adequate gerontological training has created a workforce of practitioners who are not prepared to work with this special population. In addition, practitioners may be unable to assess mental health problems and intervene to assist older adults in resolving their mental health issues. Second, many older adults, their families, and other potential referral sources for mental health services do not recognize the signs and symptoms of mental health problems (Lebowitz, 1988). Many community mental health centers lack an aggressive outreach program to raise awareness of mental health issues among older adults within the community and generate increased referrals (Lebowitz, 1988). Third, ageism among staff of CMHCs and other referring professionals can lead to the mistaken belief that mental health problems among older adults are neither preventable nor treatable. Therefore, no action is taken to assist older adults exhibiting mental health changes. In addition, many older adults and their families have ageist beliefs that negatively influence their perceptions of the usefulness of mental health care for older adults and their decisions to access community mental health services (Lebowitz, 1988; Rosen & Persky, 1997). Finally, a social stigma inhibits older adults' use of mental health services due to embarrassment or fear (Kent, 1990; Light et al., 1988). These issues pose barriers that mental health centers must address in order to increase the accessibility of mental health services to older persons within their communities.

REFERRALS

Older adults make the decision to use CMHCs or are referred for mental health services for a variety of reasons. Unfortunately, many wait until their mental health condition is exacerbated before seeking services. Kent (1990) revealed that most individuals do not use mental health services until their situation reaches a crisis level. Situations that result in referral for older adults to community mental health services include depression, memory problems, personality changes, inappropriate behavior, family conflicts, communication problems, chronic illnesses, loss of a spouse or friends, decreased income, and contraindicated drug interactions (Swan, Fox, & Estes, 1986; Kent, 1990; Mosher-Ashley, 1993). In a study of 298 clients over the age of 59 receiving mental health services at CMHCs in Massachusetts, Mosher-Ashley (1993) found that most community-dwelling clients were referred for depression or family conflicts. Residents of long-term care facilities were most commonly referred for the management of behavior problems or emotional problems.

In a random probability sample of 532 adults aged 70 and over in Arkansas, Chumbler, Cody, and Beck (2001) found three factors that increased utilization of community mental health services among older persons. To begin with, Chumbler and his associates found that individuals with impairments in activities of daily living or impairments in instrumental activities of daily living were more likely to use mental health services than those with no impairments. Second, researchers found that as age increased, mental health service use also increased. Finally, those receiving informal care were more likely to use CMHCs than those who were not receiving informal care.

Referrals to CMHCs come from a variety of sources. Families, social workers, hospitals, information and referral centers, physicians, court systems, churches, long-term care facilities, and other agencies are among the many referral sources (Kent, 1990; Mosher-Ashley, 1993). According to Mosher-Ashley (1993), most referrals are made by social workers at other agencies, while the fewest referrals come from self-initiated contact. For this reason, education outreach efforts by CMHCs that serve to increase referral sources' understanding of recognizable warning signs of unmet mental health needs among older adults are critical.

SERVICES PROVIDED

Community mental health centers provide a variety of direct and indirect services for older adults. Direct services include assessments, case management, comprehensive medical exams, support groups, information on community resources and referral to other agencies, medication monitoring, and a variety of therapeutic interventions, including psychotherapy, cognitive restructuring, behavior modification, grief therapy, and skill development in the areas of stress management, assertiveness, and self-esteem (Kent, 1990; Light et al., 1988; Swan, Fox, & Estes, 1986). Indirect services include case consultations with long-term care facilities and community education and training (Kent, 1990; Light et al., 1988; Swan et al., 1986). Other services that are available at some CMHCs include transportation to and from appointments, recreational activities, respite, adult daycare, and partial day treatment programs (Light et al., 1988; Swan et al., 1986). Notably, CMHCs do not limit the provision of services to the confines of their center. Services are also provided in long-term care facilities, senior centers, in congregate nutrition sites, and in the clients' homes (Kent, 1990; Light et al., 1988).

Dementia-related conditions and accompanying behavior problems can be particularly challenging for caregivers and mental health professionals. Family caregivers and staff of long-term care facilities turn to mental health professionals in CMHCs for assistance in learning to better manage the symptoms of dementia. Individuals in the early stages of dementia also benefit from therapeutic interventions that help to maintain their present level of functioning and help them adjust to the changes they encounter as the disease progresses. Mosher-Ashley and Witkowski (1999) surveyed 36 community mental health centers in Massachusetts that provide services to older adults. Of these 36 agencies, 75% provided services to people with dementia. These CMHCs provided services to families, long-term care facilities, and individuals with dementia. Services commonly provided to families included counseling, family therapy, and support groups. Families also commonly received case consultations to assist them in managing behavior problems in people with dementia. In long-term care facilities, staff of CMHCs provided case consultations, staff training, counseling to residents with dementia, and assessments. People with dementia received individual counseling, assessments, and group treatments, as appropriate. In some cases, additional services, including psychological/psychiatric evaluations, medication monitoring, case management, adult daycare, outreach efforts, and education for other agencies were also provided. Reported benefits for caregivers and people with dementia included decreased anxiety, decreased depression, increased understanding of the disease process and behavior problems, increased adjustment, and decreased stress. However, treatment efforts were not always productive because of the cognitive impairments of clients with dementia.

Termination of services. Dropout rates are high among clients at CMHCs. According to a study of dropout from community mental health services (Lerner, Zilber, Barasch, & Wittman, 1993), 50% of clients drop out during the first 3 months. Common reasons for dropout include transportation difficulties, low socioeconomic status, and decreased motivation (Fraps, McReynolds, Beck, & Heisler, 1982; Trepka, 1986; Vaslamatzis & Verveniotis, 1986). The therapeutic relationship between the older adult client and the therapist can be dissolved under a variety of circumstances. Mosher-Ashley (1994) conducted research on 298 adults over the age of 59 receiving mental health services from CMHCs in two Massachusetts counties between 1980 and 1986 to determine the reasons for termination of services and factors associated with client persistence in therapy. Of these 298 clients, 180 were no longer receiving mental health services from the CMHC at the end of 1986. The client terminated in 59% of the cases, the therapist terminated in 32%, and 9% were terminated on the basis of mutual agreement of the therapist and the client. In addition, 37.5% dropped out by the fourth visit. One-third of the self-terminated clients cited no need for therapy as their reason for termination. Fifteen percent terminated because they no longer wanted to participate, 10% felt as though therapy wouldn't help, 6% were concerned the therapeutic process would be too painful, 4% moved, and 19%

just didn't return for the remainder of their appointments.

Mosher-Ashley (1994) found a statistically significant difference between the dropout rates of clients residing in the community and those residing in long-term care facilities. Therapists terminated approximately half of the cases of individuals in long-term care facilities, compared to one-fifth of those residing in the community. The most common reason for therapist-terminated cases was the presence of an organic brain syndrome that interfered with the therapeutic relationship. On average, community-residing clients dropped out more often than those in long-term care facilities (70% compared to 26%). According to the therapists' assessment of client dropout rates, only 10% of clients residing in the community and 8.4% of clients residing in long-term care facilities terminated with improvement. In assessing the factors associated with persistence, Mosher-Ashley (1994) concluded that self-referral was not related to persistence.

FUTURE DIRECTIONS

As the aging population continues to grow, CMHCs will be faced with the challenge of providing mental health services to an increasing number of older clients. In order to meet the needs of older adults more effectively, it is necessary that CMHCs equip themselves with knowledgeable and skilled staff. Currently, most staff in CMHCs have no specialized geriatric training (Weitzman et al., 1998). Lebowitz (1988) found that increased staff training in gerontological issues resulted in a broader range of services being offered to older adults and a 50% increase in utilization of mental health services by older adults. Comprehensive training initiatives are necessary to better enable existing staff to meet the needs of older adults. To begin with, staff must be able to recognize the difference between the normal aging process and mental health problems (Kent, 1990). Without a basic understanding of normal age-associated changes, therapists cannot effectively assess and intervene in mental health problems that older adults may experience. It is also important for therapists to be able to recognize the relationship between mental health problems and physical illnesses (Rosen & Persky, 1997). Other specific areas where CMHC staff require increased gerontological training include depression, dementia, clinical assessment, pharmacological issues, case management, and barriers to accessing services

(Rosen & Persky, 1997; Weitzman et al., 1998). Experts also contend that due to the growing managed care movement, CMHC staff must enhance their knowledge of brief therapy, and of emergency and crisis interventions for older adults (Cypres et al., 1997). In conclusion, addressing the mental health needs of community-based older adults will require increased attention to policy, gerontological training of mental health service providers, service accessibility, and collaboration between community mental health centers and providers within the aging network (Rosen & Persky, 1997; Lebowitz, 1988).

REFERENCES

Appel, K. E., & Bartemeier, L. H. (1961). *Action for mental health: Final report of the Joint Commission on Mental Illness and Health.* New York: Basic Books.

Blank, M. L. (1977). Meeting the needs of the aged: The social worker in the community health center. *Public Health Reports, 92*(1), 39–42.

Broskowski, A., & Eaddy, M. (1994). Community mental health centers in a managed care environment. *Administration and Policy in Mental Health, 21,* 335–352.

Callicutt, J. W. (1997). Overview of the field of mental health. In T. R. Watkins & J. W. Callicutt (Eds.), *Mental health policy and practice today* (pp. 3–16). Thousand Oaks, CA: Sage.

Chumbler, N. R., Cody, M., & Beck, C. (2001). Mental health service use by cognitively impaired older adults. *Clinical Gerontologist, 22*(3/4), 118–122.

Coddington, D. G. (2001). Impact of political, societal, and local influences on mental health. *Administration and Policy in Mental Health, 29,* 81–87.

Cohen, E., & Bloom, J. R. (2000). Managed care and service capacity development in a public mental health system. *Administration and Policy in Mental Health, 28,* 63–74.

Cutler, D. L. (1992). A historical overview of community mental health centers in the United States. In S. Cooper & T. H. Lenter (Eds.), *Innovations in community mental health* (pp. 1–22). Sarasota, FL: Professional Resource Press.

Cypres, A., Landsberg, G., & Speilmann, M. (1997). The impact of managed care on community mental health outpatient services in New York state. *Administration and Policy in Mental Health, 24*(5), 509–521.

Dyer, R. L., & Williams, R. (1994). CMHC survival: Adapting to the community mission. *Administration and Policy in Mental Health, 21,* 309–317.

Fraps, C. L., McReynolds, W. T., Beck, N. C., & Heisler, G. H. (1982). Predicting client attrition from psychotherapy through behavioral assessment procedures and a critical response approach. *Journal of clinical Psychology, 38,* 759–764.

Grob, G. N. (1991). From hospital to community: Mental health policy in modern America. *Psychiatric Quarterly, 62,* 187–212.

Hadley, T. R., Culhane, D. P., Mazade, N., & Manderscheid, R. W. (1994). What is a CMHC? A comparative analysis by varying definitional criteria. *Administration and Policy in Mental Health, 21,* 295–308.

Kent, K. L. (1990). Community mental health centers. *Generations Counseling & Therapy, 14*(1), 19–21.

Lebowitz, B. D. (1988). Correlates of success in community mental health programs for the elderly. *Hospital and Community Psychiatry, 39*(7), 721–722.

Lerner, Y., Zilber, N., Barasch, M., & Wittman, L. (1993). Utilization patterns of community mental health services by newly referred patients. *Social Psychiatry Psychiatric Epidemiology, 28,* 17–22.

Light, E., Lebowitz, H. D., & Bailey, F. (1988). CMHCs and elderly services: An analysis of direct and indirect services and service delivery sites. *Community Mental Health Journal, 22*(4), 294–302.

Mosher-Ashley, P. M. (1993). Referral patterns of elderly clients to a community mental health center. *Journal of Gerontological Social Work, 20*(3/4), 5–23.

Mosher-Ashley, P. M. (1994). Therapy termination and persistence patterns of elderly clients in a community mental health center. *Gerontologist, 34*(2), 180–189.

Mosher-Ashley, P. M., & Witkowski, J. (1999). Counseling older adults with dementia: A survey of therapists in Massachusetts. *Journal of Clinical Geropsychology, 5*(4), 265–279.

Naierman, N., Haskins, B., Robinson, G., Zook, C., & Wilson, D. (1978). *Community mental health: A decade later.* Cambridge, MA: Abt Books.

National Council for Community Behavioral Healthcare. (2003). *Mental healthcare in America: A history of caring.* Available at: *www.nccbh.org/40th/timeline.pdf.*

Pardes, H. (1990). The demise of a major innovation: Carter's 1980 Community Mental Health Systems Act in Reagan's hands. In I. M. Marks & R. A. Scott (Eds.), *Mental health care delivery: Innovations, impediments, and implementation* (pp. 189–203). New York: Cambridge University Press.

Rosen, A. L., & Persky, T. (1997). Meeting mental health needs of older people: Policy and practice issues for social work. In C. Corley (Ed.), *Social work response to the White House Conference on Aging: From issues to actions* (pp. 45–54). New York: Haworth Press.

Rowland, M. D., Burns, B. J., Schafft, G. E., Randolph, F. L., & McAninch, C. B. (1997). Innovative services for elderly populations. In S. W. Henggeler & A. Santos (Eds.), *Innovative approaches for difficult to treat populations* (pp. 289–310). Washington, DC: American Psychiatric Press.

Smith, C. J. (1984). Geographic patterns of funding for community mental health centers. *Hospital and Community Psychiatry, 35,* 1133–1141.

Substance Abuse and Mental Health Services Administration. (2004). *Community mental health services block grant program.* Available at: *www.mental health.samhsa.gov/publications/allpubs/KEN95–0022.*

Swan, J. H., Fox, P. J., & Estes, C. L. (1986). Community mental health services and the elderly: Retrenchment or expansion? *Community Mental Health Journal, 22*(4), 275–285.

Trepka, C. (1986). Attrition from an out-patient psychology clinic. *British Journal of Medical Psychology, 59,* 181–186.

U.S. Department of Health and Human Services. (1999). *Mental health: A report from the Surgeon General.* Rockville, MD: National Institute of Mental Health.

Vaslamatzis, G., & Verveniotis, S. (1986). Early dropouts in brief dynamic psychotherapy. *Psychotherapy and Psychosomatics, 44,* 205–210.

Weitzman, P. F., Papsidero, J. A., Yonker, J. D., Black, E. E., Lindeman, D., & Levkoff, S. E. (1998). Survey of community health center geriatric care training needs: Massachusetts and Michigan. *Gerontology and Geriatrics Education, 19*(2), 47–56.

Senior centers, or multipurpose senior centers, serve many important social and recreational functions in the continuum of community-based services for older adults. According to the National Council on the Aging (NCOA), senior centers embody the beliefs of human growth and humanism, in that their underlying philosophy espouses the continued growth and development of older individuals with ambitions, capabilities, and creative capacities (in Lowy, 1985). These principles are in line with the promotion of successful and productive aging that has gained salience in contemporary gerontology (Moody, 2001). Further, as community-based services for older people, senior centers are well suited to promote the values of the Older Americans Act, which seeks to maximize independence, support individual preferences, and empower consumers to assume meaningful roles in program governance (Justice, 1997).

OVERVIEW

Definition. Notwithstanding the lack of agreement on the definitions of senior centers with regard to their programmatic content and delivery (Krout, 1989), the National Institute of Senior Centers (1990) defines a *senior center* as "a community focal point . . . where older adults come together for services and activities that reflect their experience and skills, respond to their diverse needs and interests, enhance their dignity, support their independence, and encourage their involvement in and with the center and the community" (cited in Wagner, 1995a, p. 4). This definition emphasizes the role the senior center plays in the serving the total needs of the older person within his or her community.

The 1973 amendments to the 1965 Older Americans Act officially introduced the term *multipurpose senior center,* "as a community facility for the organization and provision of a broad spectrum of services for older persons (Gelfand, 1999, p. 139). However, the term *multipurpose senior center* remains vague, as it could refer to the goals or content of programming, or the types of individuals served by these centers (Krout, 1989). In an online publication on exemplary senior center programs, the NCOA (n.d.) described senior centers as vital community-based social and nutritional supports that help older adults remain independent in their respective communities. Lowy (1985) defines senior centers as "community (facilities) in which older people come together to fulfill many of their social, physical, and intellectual needs" (p. 274).

PHILIP A. ROZARIO

Senior Centers

Smiley (1995) contends that senior centers traditionally offer a wide range of protective care services and a place to socialize and find a sense of community and are located in a place convenient for the people they serve.

The difficulty in defining senior centers lies partially in the differences in their models of delivery. Some use a social agency model, and others employ a voluntary organization model. According to Sabin (1993), senior centers employing the social agency model are more likely to have programs and services that are geared to the survival needs of their members, while senior centers employing the voluntary organization model are more likely to create opportunities for the recreation and self-expression of their members. To better define senior centers, Krout (1993) offers several criteria that should include the minimum numbers of days and hours of operation and the minimum number of paid staff, as well as the minimum number and types of activities that a center has to have in order to qualify as a senior center.

Legal authority. Senior centers existed long before the legislation that authorized them. However, the Older Americans Act (OAA) of 1965—and the subsequent amendments—is considered to be one of the main impetuses for their expansion (Krout, 1989; Lowy, 1985). Unfortunately, the absence of separate funding authorization under the OAA for senior centers and the discretionary nature of funding for senior centers have forced senior centers to compete with other community-based social services for relatively meager federal funding under Title 3 of the OAA (Council of Senior Centers and Services of New York City [CSCS], 2002; Gelfand, 1999; Justice, 1997; Krout, 1989; Lowy, 1985).

Currently, there is no separate provision for the acquisition, alteration, or renovation of existing facilities to serve as senior centers under the OAA (Gelfand, 1999; Krout, 1989). Along with other public social programs, senior centers face cost-cutting and cost-containment trends that have become a part of the social welfare landscape since the 1980s. Indeed, the percentage of support for senior centers from the OAA has "consistently dwindled," despite the acknowledgment of their important role in the continuum of community-based services for older adults (Wagner, 1995b). Low levels of funding have forced senior centers to "accomplish extraordinary work on extremely frugal budgets" (Smiley, 1995, p. 29). Further, Justice (1997) argues that there has been a serious mismatch between the lofty goals of the OAA and the meager resources that are set aside by the federal government. In their national survey of health and supportive services in the aging network, the NCOA (2001) reported that high-quality programming does not necessarily require large funding.

Senior centers rarely receive funding from a single funding source (Krout, 1989). Gelfand (1999) identifies various federal government funding sources. Although public funding is an important source of funding, few senior centers rely exclusively on private funding. Many centers combine public and private dollars. Senior centers that receive OAA funding are encouraged to develop a "contribution schedule" that provides senior center participants with the opportunity to contribute to defray the cost of services (Title 3 of OAA, 2004). In addition, "in-kind contributions," in the form of free space and staffing support, while difficult to quantify, are another important funding source (Gelfand, 1999).

Interestingly, senior centers are not licensed by any state or federal agency. Through the self-assessment instrument, the NCOA provides guidelines to senior centers for the improvement and maintenance of quality services. These guidelines help centers assess the extent to which they adhere to the standards of good practice, plan for growth, and identify areas for training and need for technical assistance (Lowy, 1985). The lack of licensing, thus, has contributed to a lack of consistency in the type, amount, and quality of services that are offered at senior centers nationwide. However, Title 3 of the OAA (2004) states that the facility that houses the senior center should comply with existing "health, fire, safety, building, zoning, and sanitation laws, ordinances, or codes." Because of the lack of registration and licensing standards, there is no exact census of senior centers in the United States (Lowy, 1985).

Structure. A number of researchers have argued that the choice of a facility plays a role in making the senior center attractive and accessible to older people (Gelfand, 1999; Krout, 1989). Depending on their history and funding source, senior centers can either be free-standing facilities or part of community-based social agency. It is not uncommon to find senior centers housed in a variety of facilities that can include old schools, community centers, churches, housing projects, and purpose-built centers (Krout, 1989).

The accessibility of senior centers remains an important issue for service providers. Transportation continues to be a major concern for many older adults, especially for those who are not able to drive on their own. In a small study in Maine, the National Eldercare Institute on Multipurpose Senior Centers and Community Focal Points (1995) found that inadequate transportation was one of the major problems faced by older adults in Knox County. The issue of inadequate transportation is especially salient for older adults in living in suburban and rural areas, where public transportation is inadequate or nonexistent. In addition, rural centers are more likely to have less space, fewer paid staff (Wagner, 1995a), and fewer activities and services (Krout, 1994) than their nonrural counterparts. Over half of all senior centers are located in cities (Lowy, 1985).

In his national study of senior centers, Krout (1989) found that more than a quarter of senior centers did not have full-time paid staff, while half of the centers had less than three full-time paid staff. Agencies that run centers at multiple sites might have staff working at different sites on different days. As such, most senior centers rely overwhelmingly on part-time volunteers to meet their staffing needs (Krout, 1989). For this reason, Smiley (1995) argues that centers have not been able to attract better-qualified professionals to fill key positions and may not be well positioned to compete with other service providers for human resources in the evolving aging network.

Services available. Senior centers are seen as an essential source of "vital community-based social and nutrition supports that help older Americans to remain independent in their communities" (NCOA, n.d.). The guidelines provided by the NCOA specify that "a senior center shall provide a broad range of group and individual activities and services designed to respond to the interrelated needs and interests of older people in its service area" (cited in Lowy, 1985, p. 291). However, the type and number of services that are available are constrained by the funding and staffing levels of the senior centers (Krout, 1989). In some centers, educational programs are peer-led, which has the added benefit of tapping on the expertise of the older person.

Most senior centers provide a combination of services, education, and recreation programs; information and referral that include printed materials on community services and government programs for older adults, volunteer opportunities, nutrition programs, and health promotion programs (Gelfand, 1999; Lowy, 1985; Krout, 1989). Senior center programming can be broadly divided into two categories: recreation-education programs and services (Gelfand, 1999; Krout, 1989). Lowy (1985), on the other hand, specifies four types of services: direct services, which include recreation-education programs as well as social and nutritional services; services that

are offered by other institutions or organizations in the community; community action, which includes transportation and advocacy services; and training and consultation services. Well-planned programs can promote "healthy aging," which "encompasses . . . intellectual, emotional, social, vocational, and spiritual health," thus enabling older adults to successfully age in place (NCOA, n.d.).

Further, the type and amount of services offered influences the attractiveness of a particular senior center to a certain kind of client or consumer group. Cutler and Danigelis (1993) found that senior center participants were more likely to be older, women, better educated, lower income, and in better subjective health. In a case study of one senior center in Allegheny County in Pennsylvania, 81% of men attributed their attendance to the social-recreational activities, such as shooting pool, playing cards, and socializing with their friends at the center; while more than 50% of them listed the noontime meals as the reason for their attendance (National Eldercare Institute on Multipurpose Senior Centers and Community Focal Points, 1995).

According to Sabin (1993), the type of programming offered at a senior center reflects one of two models: the social agency model and the voluntary organization model. In testing the relevance of the delivery models, Sabin (1993) found support for both the social agency model, in that senior center participants were older, less educated, and nonwhite, as well as the voluntary organization model, in that participants tended to be socially active rather than isolated.

In their aim to be the focal point in the community for older adults, senior centers need to plan programs that are culturally sensitive for an increasingly diverse older population (Urbach, 1995). Cultural sensitivity includes offering culturally appropriate meals and programming. With an increasing number of foreign-born older adults, it is also important that centers employ staff who are effectively bilingual, so as to reduce the miscommunication that might occur. Further, Wagner (1995a) proposed that service providers stay committed to the inclusion of community representatives in their program planning.

Sagy, Antonovsky, and Adler (1990) posit that the tension between disengagement and continued involvement (as operationalized by activities) is a core crisis of later adulthood and a given cultural context of Western societies. They argue that Western culture places a premium on active involvement in life. Indeed, much of the programming at senior centers may reflect this cultural bias, leading some critics to wonder if we are promoting a busy-ethic in later life, especially since we have not developed any significant roles for older adults who are retired from their work roles (Ekerdt, 1986). Thus, service providers should seek the input of older adults on planning meaningful activities, so that center participants are not merely killing time at senior centers.

POPULATION SERVED

According to Wagner (1995a), senior center participants reflect the diversity of the communities that these centers serve. In his examination of the changes in senior center participants, Krout (1994) found support for aging in place among participants, but found no support for the argument that centers were serving a significantly better off population. In his study of eight senior centers, Krout (1989) found that more than two-thirds of the participants were women, and the median age of participants was 72 years. However, people of color remain underrepresented in senior participation (Krout, 1989; Wagner, 1995a), resulting in the policy emphasis on serving older people of color. Under the OAA Title 3 regulations, area agencies have to specify how they intend to increase "low-income minority" participation as a condition for the receipt of OAA funds (2004).

SOCIAL WORK ROLES (HISTORICAL AND CURRENT)

Social workers have been instrumental in the development and growth of senior centers (Lowy, 1985). Because of funding limitations, most centers do not have specific social work positions, though social workers do function as center administrators. Of the seven exemplary senior centers highlighted by the NCOA (n.d.), none of them specifically mentioned a social worker on staff. Social workers who espouse values of self-determination and social justice can infuse these values into the program planning and delivery processes. In terms of programming, social workers can help older adults deal with issues on life transitions, run group and individual counseling sessions for people with mental health problems, plan socialization opportunities, organize advocacy and action groups, and provide case management services.

CRITICAL ISSUES AFFECTING SENIOR CENTERS

It is important to note that senior centers serve an important function in an age-segregated society, where leisure is considered the reserve of older adults and society has yet to develop meaningful roles for later adulthood. In such a context, society might continue to view older adults as drains on societal resources. In response to the public debates on generational equity in the 1980s, the aging movement responded by promoting productive aging, which recognizes the current contributions of older adults to the well-being of the community and nation (Moody, 2001). Thus, it becomes increasingly important that senior centers move beyond serving the leisured needs of older adults and expand their programming to promote other needs-such as increasing opportunities for volunteering, employment, and caregiving, according to the wishes of older adults. For example, intergenerational programming that meets the needs of grandparents who care for their grandchildren may be a concrete way for senior centers to respond to the changing realities of later adulthood.

Most older adults prefer to remain in their homes for as long as possible, and senior centers serving as community focal points are well placed to address the needs of older adults who are aging in place. The opportunity to age in place is not only beneficial to the older individual but also to his or her community. The Council of Senior Centers and Services (CSCS) of New York City (2002) stated that senior centers are an integral component of the community, enabling the older person to successfully age in place. With the expected increases in the numbers of older adults with frailty, there is a need for senior centers to respond to this burgeoning group of older adults (Krout, 1995; Wagner, 1995b). However, Cox and Monk (1990) found that center directors are less inclined to work with older adults with mental impairments than those with physical and sensory impairments. Although senior centers are not recognized as key components of the long-term care system for older adults who are at risk for institutionalization (Krout, 1996), some current participants have serious chronic illness and disabling physical conditions, and live alone. According to Krout (1996), programming for frail older adults could include health promotion, health assessment and referral, and special services for people with sensory impairments, as well as group work for older adults with mental health problems. Another future challenge facing senior centers is the aging baby boomer generation. This group of older adults is expected to have higher levels of education. Wagner (1995b) argues that senior centers should face the challenge of making themselves relevant for the baby boom generation, whose members are likely to have higher expectations with regard to types and quality of programming. However, to better respond to the diverse needs of an aging population, senior centers need to adopt new methods and make creative use of their limited space (Urbach, 1995).

Interestingly, we have to question the adequacy of institutional arrangements of senior centers in their provision of opportunities for socialization for older adults (Hagestad & Dannefer, 2001). Senior centers play an important role in providing a structure for socialization needs of older adults, as people meet and make friends while participating in social-recreational activities (Adams, 1993). Further, social relations have long been recognized as protective to the well-being of older people (Avlund et al., 2004). However, it is unclear that senior centers are successful in providing opportunities for positive social relations that enhance the well-being of their participants. In a study on formal and informal network factors on morale, Litwin (1999) found that higher levels of activity at the senior centers were positively related with higher levels of morale among older participants. Conversely, respondents who reported higher levels of fellow senior center participants in their network were more likely to report lower morale (Litwin, 1999). In another study by Mui (1998), about a third of the respondents who were participants of senior centers and congregate meal programs reported that they had not had contact with friends in the past week. Although the frequency of their attendance at these centers is unknown, it is still interesting to note that a larger number of respondents may not have considered fellow participants at senior centers and congregate meal sites as part of their friendship network.

CONCLUSION

Senior centers have served the social-recreational needs of many older adults, despite their low funding and staffing levels. Social work has made and can continue to make important contributions to the senior center movement. Many agree that as community focal points, senior centers are well placed to serve the growing numbers of older adults who age in place with the necessary input of human and financial re-

sources. Further, senior centers will have the added challenge of making themselves relevant to the aging baby boomers.

REFERENCES

Adams, R. G. (1993). Activity as structure and process: Friendships of older adults. In J. R. Kelly (Ed.), *Activity and aging: Staying involved* (pp. 73–85). Newbury Park, CA: Sage.

Avlund, K., Lund, R., Holstein, B. E., Due, P., Sakari-Rantala, R., & Heikkinen, R.-L. (2004). The impact of structural and functional characteristics of social relations as determinants of functional decline. *Journal of Gerontology: Social Sciences, 59B*(1), S44-S51.

Council of Senior Centers and Services of New York City, Inc. (2002). *Growing old in New York: A changing environment issues in the age revolution.* New York: Author. Available at: *www.cscs-ny.org.*

Cox, C. & Monk, A. (1990). Integrating the frail and well elderly: The experience of senior centers. *Journal of Gerontological Social Work, 15*(3/4), 131–147.

Cutler, S. J., & Danigelis, N. L. (1993). Organized contexts of activity. In J. R. Kelly (Ed.), *Activity and aging: Staying involved in later life* (pp. 146–163). Newbury Park, CA: Sage.

Ekerdt, D. J. (1986). The busy ethic: Moral continuity between work and retirement. *Gerontologist, 26* (3), 239–244.

Gelfand, D. E. (1999). *The aging network: Programs and services* (5th ed.). New York: Springer.

Hagestad, G. O., & Dannefer, D. (2001). Concepts and theories of aging: Beyond microfication in social science approaches. In R. H. Binstock & L. K. George (Eds.), *Handbook of aging and the social sciences* (5th ed., pp. 3–21). San Diego: Academic Press.

Justice, D. E. (1997). The aging network: A balancing act between universal coverage and defined eligibility. In R. B. Hudson (Ed.), *The future of age based public policy* (pp. 168–177). Baltimore: Johns Hopkins University Press.

Krout, J. A. (1989). *Senior centers in America.* New York: Greenwood Press.

Krout, J. A. (1993). *Senior centers and at-risk older persons: A national research agenda.* Washington, DC: National Eldercare Institute on Multipurpose Senior Centers and Community Focal Points.

Krout, J. A. (1994). Community size differences in senior center resources, programming, and participation: A longitudinal analysis. *Research on Aging, 16* (4), 440–462.

Krout, J. A. (1995). Senior centers in the future: A demographic overview. In National Eldercare Institute on Multipurpose Senior Centers and Community Focal Points, *Senior centers in America: A blueprint for the future* (pp. 11–15). Washington, DC: National Council on Aging.

Krout, J. A. (1996). Senior center programming and frailty among older persons. *Journal of Gerontological Social Work, 26* (3/4), 19–34.

Litwin, H. (1999). Formal and informal network factors as sources of morale in senior center population. *International Journal of Aging and Human Development, 48* (3), 241–256.

Lowy, L. (1985). Multipurpose senior centers. In A. Monk (Ed.), *Handbook of gerontological services* (pp. 274–301). New York: Van Nostrand Reinhold.

Moody, H. R. (2001). Productive aging and the ideology of age. In N. Morrow-Howell, J. Hinterlong, & M. Sherraden (Eds.), *Productive aging: Concepts and challenges* (pp. 175–196). Baltimore: Johns Hopkins University Press.

Mui, A. C. (1998). Living alone and depression among older Chinese immigrants. *Journal of Gerontological Social Work, 30* (3/4), 147–166.

National Council on the Aging. (2001). *A national survey of health and supportive services in the aging network.* Washington, DC: Author.

National Council on the Aging. (n.d.). *Healthy aging: A good investment—Exemplary programs for senior centers and other facilities.* Washington, DC: Author. Available at: *www.ncoa.org.*

National Eldercare Institute on Multipurpose Senior Centers and Community Focal Points. (1995). *Senior center studies and program evaluations: Outcomes of the challenge grants initiative of the National Eldercare Institute on Multipurpose Senior Centers and Community Focal Points.* Washington, DC: Author.

Sabin, E. P. (1993). Frequency of senior center use: A preliminary test of two models of senior center participation. *Journal of Gerontological Social Work, 20*(1/2), 97–114.

Sagy, S., Antonovsky, A., & Adler, I. (1990). Explaining life satisfaction in later life: The sense of coherence model and activity theory. *Behavior, Health, and Aging, 1*(1), 11–25.

Smiley, E. (1995). Senior centers and the traditional model. In National Eldercare Institute on Multipurpose Senior Centers and Community Focal Points, *Senior centers in America: A blueprint for the future* (pp. 28–34). Washington, DC: National Council on Aging.

Title 3 of Older Americans Act, 45 CFR1321 (2004).

Urbach, N. (1995). Senior centers and issues of heterogeneity. In National Eldercare Institute on Multipurpose Senior Centers and Community Focal Points, *Senior centers in America: A blueprint for the future* (pp. 22–27). Washington, DC: National Council on Aging.

Wagner, D. L. (1995a). Senior center research in America: An overview of what we know. In National Eldercare Institute on Multipurpose Senior Centers and Community Focal Points, *Senior centers in America: A blueprint for the future* (pp. 3–10). Washington, DC: National Council on Aging.

Wagner, D. L. (1995b). Senior centers and the "new" elderly cohorts of tomorrow. In National Eldercare Institute on Multipurpose Senior Centers and Community Focal Points, *Senior centers in America: A blueprint for the future* (pp. 16–21). Washington, DC: National Council on Aging.

Historically health social work practice developed in response to the social, environmental, and social-context needs of individuals with health problems. Working with individuals on the issues resulting from and impinging on their medical conditions is a constant theme through the 100-plus years of the history of health social work practice. This has become more essential in our increasingly complex society. To this end, social workers have extensive experience in assisting individuals and families in navigating complicated organizational structures and safety net systems, serving as advocates and sources of essential comfort and support. As medicine has evolved, social work has also become an intermediary between competing interests. The growth of managed care presents yet another opportunity for social workers to apply their skills in negotiating disparate needs, following their core values in achieving their desired goals. Managed care has significantly impacted the social work profession through its demand for limited services, cost containment, and evidence-based practices. With the growth of managed care use, particularly among older adults, social workers must be prepared to adapt their practices to meet these new demands while continuing to advocate for quality improvement and social justice.

W. JUNE SIMMONS
SUSAN ENGUIDANOS

Health Maintenance Organizations and Managed Care Companies

41

DEFINITION OF MANAGED CARE

Since its inception in 1929, managed care, defined as a system that integrates financing and delivery of medical care through contracts with physicians and hospitals that provide comprehensive health services to enrolled members in exchange for a monthly premium, has continued to grow across the United States. The primary aim of managed care organizations is to control costs, quality, and access to health care services for enrolled members. This is achieved by serving as a third party that bridges payers, providers, and patients together to provide cost-effective medical care by organizing the coordination and provision of care among doctors, hospitals, and other providers.

Funding mechanisms. The term *managed care* is an umbrella under which several financing and organizing models exist, such as health maintenance organizations (HMOs), preferred provider organizations (PPOs), and point-of-service financing and delivery of services. Managed care organizations operate under a capitated fiscal structure. This means that the providers, whether they be hospitals, physicians, or medical groups, agree to accept a preset payment in exchange for provision of health care services for a group of people. The medical care provider receives a payment for each member in exchange for a comprehensive set of medical services. The rate of service use by the member does not affect the payment given to the provider. In some cases there may be a monthly premium per enrolled member, in others a case rate with a maximum payment amount for an episode of care. In all cases, the reimbursement has a cap and is designed to reward prudence on the part of the provider.

Health maintenance organization. These organizations offer prepaid, comprehensive health coverage for both hospital and physician services. The HMO is paid monthly premiums or capitated rates by the payers, which include employers, insurance companies, government agencies, and other groups representing covered lives.

Preferred provider organization. This is a partnership of providers, such as a hospital and physician group, that agree to render particular services to a group of people for discounted rates under contract with a private insurer. A PPO can also be a legal entity, or it may be a function of an already formed health plan, HMO, or PPO. The entity may have a health benefit plan that is also referred to as a PPO. Preferred provider organizations are a common method of managing care while still paying for services through an indemnity plan. Most PPO plans are point-of-service plans, in that they will pay a higher percentage for care provided by providers in the network. However, the insured population may incur out-of-pocket expenses for covered services received outside the PPO if the charge exceeds the PPO payment rate.

PREVALENCE OF MANAGED CARE

Since its inception, the rate of enrollment of managed care members has continued to rise, with the largest enrollment following the initiation of the Medicaid and Medicare managed care plans. Overall, more than 71 million people nationwide are enrolled in managed care, and an additional 113 million have PPO plans. Currently, 57% of Medicaid, 14% of Medicare recipients, and 91% of those commercially insured are enrolled in a managed care plan plans (see Figure 41.1). Projected to continue to rapidly increase, enrollment in managed care plans has actually plateaued and somewhat declined in recent years as skyrocketing health care costs have resulted in reduction of benefits offered by managed care organizations. According to the Kaiser Family Foundation (2004), these declines are due to plan withdrawals from some areas because of shrinking Medicare rates, reduced benefits, and higher premiums.

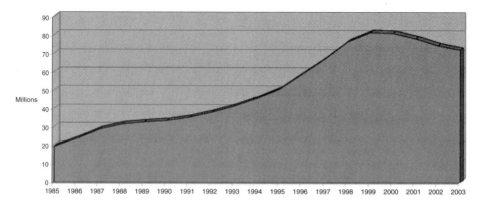

FIGURE 41.1. National HMO Enrollment. *Note: From* Managed care fact sheet managed care national statistics, *Available: http://insurance.about.com/gi/dynamic/offsite.htm?site=http%3a%2f%2fwww.mcareol. com%2ffactsht%%2ffactnati.htm.*

THE MANAGED CARE DEBATE

Managed care has been the target of both censure and praise among health care practitioners, advocates, and policy pundits.

> Critics of managed care . . . contend that managed care potentially compromises quality by withholding needed services and that the intensity of these services can be guaranteed only by a fee-for-service system of payment that protects patients from underutilization. (Lachs & Ruchlin, 1997, p. 24)

Yet under fee-for-service medicine, other special hazards exist: care is not coordinated, resulting in overutilization of services, as well as some needs falling through the cracks, and dramatic levels of medication errors (the fifth leading cause of death).

Some geriatricians and researchers have asserted that the purpose of medicine with older populations is to keep people well/functional through coordination, follow-up, and preventive/lifestyle care. A reimbursement system that would pay for promoting and preserving health and function is desirable instead of waiting for advanced decline, injury, or illness to rush expensive rescue to the patient. The search is for the right care in the right place at the right time. The essential focus is on health and prevention, versus allocating most payments for late stage, expensive preventable conditions. Ideally, managed care is designed to permit pursuit of this clinical philosophy, although it often falls short.

Fee-for-service medicine, however, also suffered from misalignment of incentives, as it lacks proper balances to contain costs. This dilemma is derived from two central causes: (1) reimbursement with minimal incentive to focus on early detection and prevention of injury and functional decline that typically precedes a medical crisis, but rather generous reimbursement for managing the medical crisis once it occurs, and (2) multiple payers, providers, and systems, with no single entity with global clinical or fiscal responsibility. This system doesn't maximize functional status and quality for older adults, the central goal of modern geriatric medicine.

The case can swing the other way in quality and value-based managed care arrangements, as demonstrated by some of the major nonprofit integrated HMOs like Kaiser Permanente and Group Health Puget Sound. In these instances, where the system has aligned financial incentives through co-ownership by the payer, the medical group, and the insurance program, the high potential of managed care can be reached. In these systems, there are serious efforts to identify the best investments in health through prevention and early intervention. Some managed care systems have created a reputation for withholding essential and timely care, but the great nonprofit integrated managed care systems have actively pursued the promise of this health care financing system.

REGULATORY AGENCIES

Throughout the past two decades, all health care providers, including managed care organizations (MCOs), have had increasing regulations imposed, largely due to public displeasure with rising costs, coupled with increasing allegations of misconduct. Although more than 100 bills have been introduced in Congress in an effort to regulate MCOs, the primary health care oversight mechanism continues to remain enforcement of accreditation standards by federal and state agencies. Key governing bodies include the Joint Commission on Accreditation of Healthcare Organizations (JCAHO), the National Committee on Quality of Care (NCQA), and judicial rulings. Although accreditation is voluntary, more and more health care purchasers (such as employers) are requiring accreditation. Although accreditation does not provide legal jurisdiction over providers, including the MCO, it does provide a mechanism for ensuring standard levels of quality through the development of practice guidelines, performance standards, and expected clinical outcomes. Further, data publicly reported by regulatory agencies such as NCQA and Health Plan Data and Information Sets (HEDIS) provides an additional source of oversight and quality marker for health plan purchasers and consumers.

Although these regulatory agencies are necessary in order to assure that health care providers are delivering high-quality care, serious consequences have resulted from the policies they created. Increasing regulatory review by public entities has pushed providers to provide an exacting search for the right amount of the right care—to not exceed care needed but to assure timely access to essential care. This is a difficult task, considering the great amount of diversity in health care needs that exists among the population. Controversies have raged about what insurers should pay for, which care is experimental and excluded, what care is essential, and when access to special care and medications is appropriate.

SOCIAL WORK ROLES IN HEALTH CARE

Although the history of health and mental health social work practice is rooted in public and teaching hospitals, centering around acute episodes that require hospitalization, current fiscal pressures on our health care system have encouraged the shift of social work from the hospital to the community setting. Social work practice in the hospital setting has largely been advanced through advocacy or prescribed by regulatory agencies. In the 1970s, Medicare conditions of participation for hospitals were developed, requiring health care organizations to participate in the Medicare and Medicaid programs. These standards are used to improve quality and protect the health and safety of beneficiaries. A new requirement imposed by these standards was to have trained social workers (MSWs) available to patients in all hospitals, preferably through organized departments, which transformed social work practice in these settings. Similar requirements for skilled nursing homes and home health services led to the emergence of social work practice within these care settings, although the social work role in these settings never developed as dramatically as in hospitals. With the establishment of the Medicare Hospice benefit in the late 1980s, the role of the social worker was further expanded through the mandate of social services in this organized and "capitated" program that brought comprehensive end stage care to terminally ill patients.

Also, in 1970 the JCAHO adopted standards that included the availability of social services to patients admitted to the hospital and their families. As a result, hospitals across the nation began to support organized social work departments that provided a range of services centered around the hospital setting, including emotional support, referral and resource mobilization, health education and transition/discharge planning services. These services gradually grew into fields of specialization around specific medical scenarios such as rehabilitation, cancer, neonatal units, and discharge planning for other common conditions. This was especially new in the western states, where the history and traditions of health care and hospitals were not as well established as in the East and Midwest.

When diagnostically related groups (DRGs), an early version of managed care, were introduced in 1984, lengths of stay in hospitals shortened dramatically, and patients were moved to community care much earlier. Before this, patients remained in hospitals for longer periods of time, permitting the social work intervention to include crisis intervention, counseling, and health education. In many instances, social work staffs grew substantially in these settings. Following the introduction of DRGs, the hospital social work role shifted dramatically, as hospital lengths of stay were limited, reducing time for counseling and increasing pressures to focus on safe and rapid discharge plans. In addition, the role of nursing was evolving, leading to competition from nurses for the traditional social work roles of discharge planning.

The 1980s and 1990s were also a time of rapid growth for managed care. Managed care had been primarily confined to the West Coast due to legislative actions that restricted insurance companies from contracting with select providers. Following the introduction of prospective payment into Medicare, states began to repeal this legislation, and the growth of managed care rapidly escalated. This growth in managed care brought dramatic redesign to the health care system, emphasizing cost-containment strategies, including utilization review, outcomes-based practices, and preventive medicine aimed at transferring the site of care from acute care facilities to outpatient settings.

This shift in focus significantly influenced the roles of all, including the social worker. Social workers no longer had the luxury of providing care without evidence of the effectiveness of that care. Effectiveness could not be limited to simply measuring client satisfaction, or even improvement in patient level health outcomes. Social workers are now charged with showing effectiveness in terms of

> concrete and identifiable therapeutic gain . . . achieved, in the quickest amount of time, and with the least amount of financial and professional support. This means that not only must the treatment that social workers provide be therapeutically necessary and effective, it must also be professionally competitive with other disciplines that claim similar treatment strategies and techniques. (Dziegielewski, 1998, p. 261)

Thus social workers must now consider the cost-benefit of their practice and how it is uniquely different from other professional disciplines. Within the inpatient setting, management of departments was consolidated and layers of leadership reduced, to lower costs as managed care continuously forced contract rates for hospital stays downward. Studies have documented that many social work department directors either lost their administrative roles or had to assume a broader scope of services in addition to social work. More recently, the value of social work and of interdisciplinary practice, as well as the nursing shortage, has led to restoration of social work in many settings. The shift to capped payments initially led to cuts in social work, but over time, research has begun to suggest that overall cost per case is lower with interdisciplinary care, with social work playing a key role.

The growing need for case management to care for increasing rates of chronic conditions also contributed to the social work role shift. Chronic illness has become the dominant focus of health services in recent years, and the key role of self-care in outcomes has become clear through research. The role of social work in addressing patient empowerment and identifying and treating high risks, such as depression, has helped to advance the role of social work in managed care in recent years, laying ground for developing the social work contribution and expanding the social work presence based on this new evidence.

Noting the impact of policy changes that resulted in reduced length of hospital stay and the growing role of primary care in the community, social work leaders pioneered and began to evolve new programs. The changing complexity brought by increasing numbers of individuals with multiple chronic conditions called for a continuum of care included social work components within various care settings. For example, observing that Medicare patients averaged almost one visit per month to their physician, social workers at Huntington Hospital, with funding from the John A. Hartford Foundation, developed social work models of service for the physician office. Great interest in this model led to multiple replications across the nation.

The rise of managed care has also impacted the role of the social worker in mental health. Throughout the past several decades, psychiatrists, psychologists, and social workers have been trained to address the needs of the mentally ill; however, social workers remained in a lower professional category, with lower pay, lesser respect, and more limited roles. As managed care companies have taken over the management of mental health services through their payer influence, social workers have emerged as the provider of choice, delivering 65% of all psychotherapy and mental health services, partly due to generally lower fees and similar skill sets. Psychiatrists have been moved to specialization in medications management. Recent research has demonstrated that placing social workers in primary care offices to address mental health issues helps capture patients for mental health services at an earlier and more appropriate stage and permits many to use and benefit from ser-

vices they would avoid if labeled mental health and requiring going to a new setting.

On the downside, however, are the parallel limitations on types of mental health care and numbers of visits. Long-term ongoing therapies have been replaced with limited, short-term, behaviorally oriented interventions. Moreover, practitioners report that managed care constraints have increased the need for use of medication as an adjunct therapy.

QUALITY OF LIFE, QUALITY OF CARE, AND ETHICAL DILEMMAS

For the last two decades, the ethics of managed care has been under fire. Simply defining managed care as a cost-controlling agent lends fuel to the growing barrage of criticism and questions about the ethics involved in caring for individuals under a cost-containment system. Critics of the managed care system are quick to point to traditional social work values (service, social justice, dignity and worth of the person, importance of human relationships, integrity, and competence) and the inconsistency of these values with care provided in the controversial end of the managed care continuum. These values are compromised when social work care focuses on economics and cost containment in exchange for quality professional care. Within the medical managed care environment, social workers work with increasingly diverse issues in health care, such as declining hospital admissions, reduced lengths of stay, increased restrictions, and increased cost containment methods. The disparate goals of the organization and the social worker create role conflict, placing the social worker in the uncomfortable position of choosing between job security and quality of care for the client.

Several professional ethical challenges of managed care have been identified. In some instances, reduced access to medical services has been shown to be associated with poorer outcomes. If social workers are being asked to inappropriately decrease length of services or circumvent service use, it places them in an ethical dilemma of having to choose between adequate quality of care and conforming to their employers' demands. Perhaps most important, these limitations reflect a higher level of payer control over clinical practice, threatening the integrity of the physician and the social worker.

Further, within immature managed care environments, the social work role often is viewed as an expendable and nonessential service, easily seen as obsolete within this streamlined, cost-efficient environment. Social work roles are frequently viewed as adjunct to medical services and not "required," or professional social workers may be replaced with untrained paraprofessionals who are not trained to perform social work roles. This can swing both ways, however, as we see the replacement of doctorate-level professionals within the mental health arena, where master's level and licensed social workers are replacing doctoral-educated mental health professionals such as psychiatrists and psychologists. The following list (from Scanlon, 1997, as cited in Camunas, 1998, p. 8) delineates the issues and challenges of managed care.

1. Tension between cost containment and quality of care
2. Threats to the patient/professional relationship
3. Policies that constrain professional judgment
4. Safeguarding patients from harm
5. Allocation of decision-making authority
6. Financial incentives
7. Abandonment of patient

Managed care advocates remind us that cost containment is not inherently evil. In fact, some discipline in health care allocation was needed, and managed care was brought in as a reform effort. That is why some suggest that managed care actually eliminates moral problems often encountered in fee-for-service systems, where financial incentives exist to provide unnecessary care. Managed care offers a balance to these allocation dilemmas. Further, it provides an environment and fiscal structure that can allow for much greater flexibility and innovation in medical models of care and special services.

In a monograph on organizational interventions to improve health outcomes of older individuals, Reuben (2002) classifies these organizational interventions into two groups: (1) component models, models that can be integrated into the existing model of care but do not fundamentally change the health care system, and (2) systems changes, which includes models that require significant changes in the delivery of health care. While the results of these interventions are mixed, several studies have found that these innovations can improve care. Effective component models include new services such as disease management programs that have been found to be effective in improving patient health while decreasing costs of care.

Kaiser Permanente Southern California offers an illustration of a systems change in their modification of the hospice benefit to develop a new program aimed at providing palliative care and pain relief for patients in the last year of life. The In-Home Palliative Care Program reduced ICU deaths, expanded home care, and thus improved patient satisfaction with care and increased the likelihood of patients' dying in their preferred environment, as well as reducing acute care service use and associated costs. This model demonstrates the flexibility of the managed care environment to develop and test new models of care aimed at improving both patient and system-level outcomes.

SPECIAL CONCERNS OF POPULATION SERVED

In the 1980s, Medicare introduced a prospective payment system for Medicare beneficiaries that allowed HMOs to enroll Medicare beneficiaries. This change in the Medicare benefit contributed to an increased growth in managed care, largely through the enrollment of older adults. Thus older adults, in particular, have been affected by the rise in managed care and impacted by the evolving role of the social worker. Concerns of older adults vary considerably, as does the population itself. Healthy older adults require much the same care as younger populations, plus special models to address their added care needs, as issues particular to aging encroach. Multiple chronic conditions, such as arthritis, diabetes, respiratory and cardiac problems, and Alzheimer's, emerge. Treatment of these diseases not only requires the use of preventative medicine and techniques aimed at slowing the progression of the conditions but also extended self-care, which requires investment in education and lifestyle change support.

Older adults and their families fear there will be a lack of access to the receipt of the right services when needed in a managed care setting. In a study comparing older adults' access to care, differential access to specialists was noted under managed care. Of greatest concern was that older HMO members had inadequate identification and treatment of pain, although this is a widespread medical problem outside of managed care as well. Older adults anticipate developing multiple chronic conditions and experiencing threats to their functional abilities and want help optimizing their health as they age. At the same time, they want protection from high premiums and out-of-pocket costs, low copays, and other essential financial protections.

Studies have also found that poor and minority patients often fare less well under managed care policies, as compared to traditional fee for service. These disparities range from issues of access to timely and appropriate levels of treatment.

END-OF-LIFE CARE: AN OPPORTUNITY TO ADVOCATE

Social work has played an integral part in representing the concerns of the elderly at the end of life, especially in hospice care. Hospice care demonstrates an ideal model of integrating key elements of social work practice into the management of health, mentally and physically. Alternatives to hospice, such as palliative care programs, to facilitate access to quality end-of-life care are being developed across the country. In an integrated managed care system or HMO, successful reallocation of health dollars to improve end-of-life care is possible, while traditional fee-for-service structures lack the fiscal incentives and face regulatory barriers to this helpful reorganization of the funding mechanism for this kind of care model. A major study at Kaiser in California demonstrated a 45% cost reduction under an innovative palliative home care model, but traditional reimbursement outside that contained system makes it very difficult to implement the same model in non-managed-care settings. Models like this tend to incorporate social work, as it is a discipline that helps to integrate care and improve the effectiveness of other disciplines.

TODAY'S SOCIAL WORK CHALLENGES

Social workers in managed care environments must seek to optimize the opportunities for health care reform in managed care and also engage in a battle between quality-of-care issues and cost-containment strategies, fighting to identify a middle ground where both social work ethics and organizational forces can effectively cohabitate. Two primary challenges faced by social workers in managed care have been identified:

First, we want to retain the core values of the profession—advocacy, self-determination, and client focus—often considered at odds with corporate for-profit health care. Second, we need to develop the business acumen to demonstrate so-cial work's effectiveness in a service industry where demonstrated outcomes predominate. (Schneider, Hyer, & Luptak, 2000, p. 276)

Yet in some managed care settings, social work is a perfect fit with the ideal goals of the nonprofit managed care system that focuses on early intervention, improved self-care, prevention, health maximization, and the right care in the right place at the right time. Here social work's contribution is valued and has a key role to play.

To maintain the delicate balance between core values of the profession and the evolving needs of the service industry, social workers must be prepared to expand their roles and change practice in response to new research and evidence of effective practice models. Further, in meeting the challenges in any host practice setting, the health and mental health social workers must address the following.

- Marketing social work services and linking them to cost-benefit measures
- Presenting social work as an essential role of the interdisciplinary team
- Anticipating and addressing the environment and roles that political and social forces have on service delivery
- Moving beyond traditional roles and developing new and innovative strategies to optimize health and assure the social work contribution is properly designed
- Taking an active role in macro issues to advocate for better patient quality
- Being "flexible, open, and ready to embrace the future," while staying focused on the ethics of clinical social work
- Engaging in time-limited brief interventions that produce outcomes valuable to patients, families, and the organization
- Changing from a curative focus to a patient-centered focus. Social work does not cure patients but provides training and education for patients to support them in changes
- Attaching cost-benefit analysis to all care provided—services must be linked with health care dollar savings

These components will not only strengthen the impact of social work practice, but also substantiate and validate the role of the social worker within managed care settings.

REFERENCES

Aubert, R. E., Herman, W. H., Waters, J., Moore, W., Sutton, D., Peterson, B. L., Bailey, C. M., & Koplan, J. P. (1998). Nurse case management to improve glycemic control in diabetic patients in a health maintenance organization. A randomized, controlled trial. *Annals of Internal Medicine, 129*(8), 605–612.

Berkman, B. (1996). The emerging health care world: Implications for social work practice and education. *Social Work, 41*(5), 541–551.

Brenner, B., Beallor, G., Mizrahi, T., & Kaufer, S. (1998). *Social work and managed care: The impact of social risk on health care delivery and the need for social services.* Available: *www.naswnyc.org/1.html.* NASW, New York City Chapter Report. New York, NY.

Brumley, R. D., Enguidanos, S., & Cherin, D. (2003). Effectiveness of a home-based palliative care program for end-of-life. *Journal of Palliative Medicine, 6*(5), 715–724.

Brummel-Smith, K. V. (1998). Alzheimer's disease and managed care: How much will it cost? *Journal of the American Geriatrics Society, 46*(6), 780–781.

Camunas, C. (1998). Managed care, professional integrity, and ethics. *Journal of Nursing Administration, 28*(3), 7–9.

Cherin, D. A., Huba, G. J., Brief, D. E., & Melchoir, L. A. (1998). Evaluation of the transprofessional model of home health care for HIV/AIDS. *Home Health Care Services Quarterly, 17*(1), 55–72.

Chodosh, J., Solomon, D. H., Roth, C. P., Chang, J. T., MacLean, C. H., Ferrell, B. A., Shekelle, P. G., & Wenger, N. S. (2004). The quality of medical care provided to vulnerable older patients with chronic pain. *Journal of the American Geriatrics Society, 52*(5), 756–761.

Clement, D. G., Retchin, S. M., Brown, R. S., & Stegall, M. H. (1994). Access and outcomes of elderly patients enrolled in managed care. *Journal of the American Medical Association, 271*(19), 1487–1492.

Dranove, D. (2000). *The economic evolution of American health care.* Princeton, NJ: Princeton University Press.

Dziegielewski, S. (1998). *The changing face of healthcare social work: Professional practice in the era of managed care.* New York: Springer.

Gibelman, M., & Mason, S. E. (2002). Treatment choices in a managed care environment: A multi-disciplinary exploration. *Clinical Social Work Journal, 30*(2), 199–214.

Gibelman, M., & Schervish, P. (1997). *Who we are: A second look.* Washington DC: NASW Press.

Gorin, S. (2003). The unraveling of managed care: Recent trends and implications. *Health & Social Work, 28*(3), 241–246.

Holleman, W. L., Holleman, M. C., & Graves, J. (1997). Are ethics and managed care strange bedfellows or a marriage made in heaven? *Lancet, 349*(9048), 350–351.

Iglehart, J. K. (1994). Physicians and the growth of managed care. *New England Journal of Medicine, 331*(17), 1167–1171.

Jecker, N. S., & Braddock, C. (1998). *Ethics in Medicine.* Available: *http://eduserv.hscer.washington.edu/bioethics/topics/manag.html.* University of Washington School of Medicine, Seattle.

Kaiser Family Foundation. (2004). *Enrollment in Medicare managed care and traditional Medicare.* Available: *www.kff.org/insurance/7031/ti2004-2-17.cfm.* Health Care Marketplace Project.

Lachs, M. S., & Ruchlin, H. S. (1997). Is managed care good or bad for geriatric medicine? *Journal of the American Geriatrics Society, 45*(9), 1123–1127.

Lynn, J., Wilkinson, A., Cohn, F., & Jones, S. B. (1998). Capitated risk-bearing managed care systems could improve end-of-life care. *Journal of the American Geriatrics Society, 46*(3), 322–330.

Managed Care National Statistics. (2004). Available: *www.mcareol.com/factshts/factnati.htm.* Managed Care On-Line, Modesto, CA.

Mitchell, C. G. (1998). Perceptions of empathy and client satisfaction with managed behavioral health care. *Social Work, 43*(5), 404–411.

Mizrahi, T., & Berger, C. S. (2001). Effect of a changing health care environment on social work leaders: Obstacles and opportunities in hospital social work. *Social Work, 46*(2), 170–182.

Neuman, K. M., & Ptak, M. (2003). Managing managed care through accreditation standards. *Social Work, 48*(3), 384–391.

Patel, K., & Rushefsky, M. E. (1999). Health care politics and policy in America. In (2nd ed., Vol. 25, p. 452). Armonk, NY: M. E. Sharpe.

Reuben, D. B. (2002). Organizational interventions to improve health outcomes of older persons. *Medical Care, 40*(5), 416–428.

Rich, M. W., Beckham, V., Wittenberg, C., Leven, C. L., Freedland, K. E., & Carney, R. M. (1995). A multidisciplinary intervention to prevent the readmission of elderly patients with congestive heart failure. *New England Journal of Medicine, 333*(18), 1190–1195.

Rodwin, M. A. (1998). Conflicts of interest and accountability in managed care: The aging of medical ethics. *Journal of the American Geriatrics Society, 46*(3), 338–341.

Scanlon, C. (1997). *Integrity and health care professionals under managed care.* Washington DC: Kennedy Institute of Ethics. In Camunas, 1998, p. 8.

Scheid, T. L. (2002). Managed care, managed dollars, managed providers: Ethical dilemmas in mental healthcare. *Hospital Ethics Committee Forum, 14*(2), 99–118.

Schneider, A. W., Hyer, K., & Luptak, M. (2000). Suggestions to social workers for surviving in managed care. *Health & Social Work, 25*(4), 276–279.

Shearer, S., Simmons, W. J., White, M., & Berkman, B. (1995). Physician Partnership Project: Social work case managers in primary care. *Continuum, 15*(4), 1, 3–7.

To err is human: Building a safer health system. (1999). Washington, DC: National Academy Press.

Tufts Health Care Institute. (1998). *A brief history of managed care.* Boston, MA.

More than many other social policy constituencies, older Americans have long benefited from the presence of planning agencies at both the state and substate levels. Passage of the Older Americans Act (OAA) in 1965, in addition to creating the Administration on Aging (AoA) in the federal government, authorized creation of State Units on Aging (SUAs). Amendments to the OAA in 1972 mandated creation throughout the country of substate regional planning bodies: Area Agencies on Aging (AAAs). Initially using OAA funds (and, later, Medicaid and state-level appropriations), these agencies contracted with local service providers to fund social, nutritional, transportation, legal, and other direct services to residents of their planning and service areas. Since the late 1970s, this array of agencies has constituted what has since become known as "the aging network."

DEVELOPMENT OF AREA AGENCIES AND THE AGING NETWORK

In its roughly 30-year existence, this network has evolved in important ways. In its nascent stage, the aging network engaged in basic start-up and capacity-building activities. By the 1980s, the network was well established and widely recognized, and had come to represent a substate and local political presence unique among population-based human services constituencies. Beginning in the late 1980s and continuing to this day, the network has been increasingly drawn into the large and challenging world of community-based long-term care.

Early Developments

Both rational and political elements lay behind the creation of area agencies (Hudson, 1974). Passed with considerable fanfare in 1965, the OAA was also better understood as symbolic rather than substantive legislation. The initial appropriation for FY 1966 was $7.5 million, and the fledgling SUAs could use no more than $15,000 each for state-level administration. By 1969, total funding had risen to $23 million, with the amount available for their own operations having risen to $25,000 (Hudson, 1973). States were encouraged to appropriate additional funds, but, as Congressman John Brademas noted in hearings in 1969, Nebraska was typical in contributing no more than 16 cents per older resident to augment the federal funds. By the early 1970s, criticism of the OAA, the AoA, and

ROBERT B. HUDSON

Social Service and Health Planning Agencies

the SUAs was widespread; one report spoke of "rampant tokenism" (Greenblatt & Ernst, 1972), and another was entitled "The Administration on Aging—Or a Successor?" (Sheppard, 1971).

Against this backdrop, a White House Conference on Aging was convened in 1971, bringing some 4,500 older Americans to Washington to press for additional federal programming across a range of aging-related arenas, including social services. In a moment of high political theater, President Nixon—as a means of deflecting attention from his opposition to a proposed 20% increase in Social Security benefits—seized on the OAA as a vehicle for showing his commitment to the well-being of senior citizens. To the surprise of nearly everyone in the auditorium, Nixon announced:

> We want to begin by increasing the present budget of the Administration on Aging nearly five-fold—to 100 million dollars. Now, you may wonder where I got that number because . . . it was 80 million dollars last night, and I decided why not 100 million dollars! (White House Conference on Aging, 1971)

In light of this surprise announcement, there immediately arose a need to address the planning and administrative problems that were seen as endemic among both the AoA and the SUAs. The answer lay in drawing on a "substate planning strategy" then in vogue within the Department of Health, Education, and Welfare. This led to creation of the AAAs through the 1972 amendments to the Act. Being "closer to the people," these agencies were seen as better positioned to set priorities and engage in a meaningful planning process. Beyond creation of the AAAs, amendments in 1972 and 1973 also created a new elderly nutrition program (centrally involving the AAAs) and a new older Americans community service employment program (involving a delicate distribution of contracts between the SUAs and "federal contractors," including such aging-based interest groups as the American Association of Retired Persons, Green Thumb, the National Council of Senior Citizens, and the National Council on Aging). While many SUA directors and Democrats had objected to creation of AAAs—fearing they would further weaken the SUAs—enactment of the employment program and dramatic appropriations increases swept away the opposition. Ultimately, overall appropriations for the OAA rose to $227 million in 1974, $324 million in 1976, $749 million in 1978, and $919 million by 1980.

Recent Developments

By the late 1970s, the aging network was firmly in place. In addition to the 57 SUAs (including territories, and the District of Columbia), 655 AAAs had come into being, funding thousands of direct service providers. The 1980s represented a period of consolidation for the network. While funding under the OAA essentially leveled off at roughly $1 billion (not counting Department of Agriculture commodity contributions associated with the nutrition program), the National Association of State Units on Aging (2004) reports that these expenditures now annually fund:

- 145 million home-delivered meals
- 115 million congregate meals
- 40 million rides
- 30 million hours of combined personal care, homemaker, and adult day services
- 3.8 million hours of case management
- Over 13 million information and assistance contacts and other supportive services to elders and their caregivers

Additional legislative changes over this time period included new authorizations for in-home services for frail elders, a long-term care ombudsman program, health education and illness prevention programs, programs for preventing elder abuse and neglect, and a heightened emphasis on the needs of older people with the greatest economic and social needs. New attention was also brought to bear on intergenerational concerns and the needs of those providing care to the frail elderly. The latter effort was institutionalized in 2000 with the passage of the Family Caregivers Support Act, the most significant legislative addition to the OAA in 30 years. Organizationally, the biggest change was the elevation of the commissioner on aging—charged with administering the OAA—to the rank of assistant secretary for aging within the Department of Health and Human Services.

PLANNING CHALLENGES

Social and health planning for the nation's aging population has long been a complicated endeavor. Questions about the planning function tap into different dimensions. The first centers on comprehensiveness, the most basic question being whether the public sector should take on the task of "planning" for the well-being of millions of older people. Or if not all older people, whom among them should it plan for? And if such planning is to be undertaken, at what level(s) of government should it take place? Second, should planning in aging be organized by population or by function, that is, should it be conducted centrally by an "aging planning agency" or should planning be organized along functional lines such as health, transportation, income, or housing, with the needs of older persons being addressed in conjunction with those of the larger population? Finally, should planning be a separate, quasi-abstract activity, or should it be integrated with the provision of the services that concretize the planning function?

Planning for Whom: Eligibility

Because the very notion of "planning" is marginally suspect in the American political culture, no one has called for policy-relevant blueprint planning for the future of the older population. Symbolically, Title 1 of the OAA resolves to improve most aspects of older people's lives, but it is little more than a wish-statement. Social Security and Medicare are larger and more concrete programs, directing over $600 billion annually in federal funding to senior citizens, but they have no formal planning component to them.

Formal planning for the aged has been left largely to the network of aging agencies operating under the OAA. Although these programs are neither purely symbolic nor especially large, thorny questions around planning have long arisen here as well (Justice, 1997). Because there is no formal means-testing under the OAA, a nominal case can be made that all older people are eligible for planning services. Resource constraints preclude such broad-based efforts, but in selected areas, such as the nursing home ombudsman program and elder abuse and neglect services, SUAs and AAAs have assumed population-wide intervention roles.

What has transpired for the most part, however, has been administrators of the OAA at all levels of government struggling with the how to best target their limited resources. Much debate during bouts of OAA reauthorization has centered on this question. Early guidelines that centered on "those with greatest economic and social need" later evolved into an enumeration centered on older populations of color, those living in rural areas, and those who were frail or disabled (Hasler, 1990). Apart from these often being overlapping categories, important selection questions remained: Is being over age 70 or 75 "to be disadvantaged"? What proportion of services should be directed to older populations of color? What is an adequate measure of "social need"? And so on.

Beyond these relatively nuanced distinctions, the energies and resources of the aging services network, beginning in the 1980s, have clearly gravitated toward those elders who could be deemed especially vulnerable by one measure or another. And this is a far different emphasis from that found in the planning and services network's early years. In global terms, this transition was largely about moving away from early efforts under the OAA, directed at providing socialization and educational opportunities for older people living in the community (including, for example, funds for senior center construction and operation) toward concerted efforts centered on allowing frail older people to remain at home or in other community settings rather than being relegated to nursing homes or other institutional placements.

The most recent and equally important chapter in eligibility standards for these agencies began largely during the late 1980s. Having lessened emphasis on service provision to relatively well elders in the community, many states now extended the coverage of the vulnerable from the frail old to younger adults with disabilities. In this way, the "eligibility axis" began to swing from elders in various circumstances to frail and disabled adults of all ages. Thus, in 21 states today, the SUA is charged with serving both elderly and adult disabled clients (National Association of State Units on Aging [NASUA], 2004).

Planning for What: Program Benefits

The substance, as well as the targets, of planning efforts has also been subject to controversy and evolution in the three decades of the aging planning and services network. One subject of debate has long been the degree to which the network should concentrate its efforts on services delivery and coordination or on broader advocacy efforts directed at the so-called functional arenas not under its purview. Major efforts were made in the late 1960s and 1970s to undertake advocacy or "leadership planning," wherein SUAs and AAAs would press health, transportation, and other agencies to direct more of their efforts (and comparatively larger budgets) to better serving older people (Binstock, Cherington, & Woll, 1974). Activities of this kind were undertaken with limited success, but the odds were long that new, small, and constituency-based agencies could meaningfully move the agendas of these larger bureaucratic entities (Hudson & Veley, 1974).

In the years before the advent of the AAAs, services planning was rudimentary at best, with the nascent SUAs seeking to distribute small community grants across their states in ways that were both programmatically and politically defensible. With the coming of the AAAs and the very significant increase in OAA funding, new efforts were made to coordinate as well as fund service provision. Toward this end, the AAAs themselves were forbidden to engage in direct service delivery. As with the question of client eligibility, efforts were made to prioritize services, moving from an original list of 18 discrete services found in the 1973 amendments to a later three-part listing of access, in-home, and legal services and the requirement that at least 50% of the AAAs' Title 3 funds be used for these purposes. Pressures from the network later led to this provision being softened, so that an "adequate proportion" of their funds were used for these purposes (Hudson, 1994).

During the 1970s and early 1980s, these debates centered almost exclusively on social services alone. By the mid-1980s, however, pressures increased to add more health-related services to the mix. In this way, the larger reality of the aging of the population and, in particular, the aging of the older population began to impact directly the aging planning and services network. The programmatic mandate of the aging network agencies began shifting toward developing home and community-based services (HCBS) to maximize the possibilities for older residents' "independent living." The political mandate came from officials who wanted to please constituents, save money, or, if possible, both.

The principal impetus to network involvement in HCBS has been implementation of Medicaid waiver programs, beginning in 1981. These state-based waivers typically allow states to bypass statewide income eligibility requirements in order to develop regionally specific or site-specific community service alternatives. Services such as home health, case management, personal care, and adult day health care, which traditional Medicaid cannot offer in noninstitutional settings and which OAA funds alone are not sufficient to support, are now offered nationwide. In 21 states, such programs for the elderly and disabled are administered under the auspices of the SUA; in an additional 12 states, these programs serve elderly persons alone; in 25 of these state efforts, the AAAs participate in the Medicaid waiver program (NASUA, 2004).

Planning by Whom: Organization of the Delivery System

From both a planning and a political perspective, what has made the aging services delivery system nearly unique among the social services is the vertically integrated network represented by AoA, the SUAs, the AAAs, and the host of direct service agencies with whom the state and area agencies contract. The creation of this network is the lasting legacy of Arthur S. Flemming, who served as AoA commissioner under Richard Nixon and who saw in the newly formed AAAs a political as well as a services infrastructure for the old. Political and programmatic advantage was seen in the "vertical" protection afforded regional and local agencies by federal and state-level legislative, regulatory, and accountability language requiring that monies be spent for the old (and later the disabled) in specified ways. Planners and providers in other service domains are in many respects envious of this aging-based services system and have sought at times to emulate it (Grason & Guyer, 1995).

Even in this earlier period, however, there were drawbacks to this organization of aging services. As noted, the larger functionally oriented systems, such as health, mental health, and transportation, operated outside of this network. Two particular problems arose. Much as the aging network might lobby these agencies to do more for its older client base, the network has had little leverage to move them in that direction. Moreover, these larger agencies, having seen that there was aging services network in place, were induced to do less rather than more for older consumers. Transportation provides one example, where a regional bus service may not have felt it necessary to tailor its routes and schedules to older riders because the aging network might have been providing specialized bus or van services to older people (e.g., the Older Americans Transportation Service [OATS] program in rural Missouri).

Public health provides a second example. A recent study by the Chronic Disease Directors and National Association of State Units on Aging (2003) finds coordination between the two networks quite limited. The SUA respondents identified several issues that are critical to health promotion among the aged that they felt were not sufficiently recognized by state health departments (SHDs). Even more to the point, the report finds that "there appears to be widespread confusion about which agency in a state has lead responsibility for health promotion and disease prevention for older adults" (Chronic Disease Directors [CDD] and NASUA, 2003, p. 24). As the authors note as well, there is some irony in health departments' limited role in aging-related activities, in that decades of public health successes may have more to do with the numerical rise of the old than any other single factor.

State and local officials have long struggled with how to integrate these "vertical functional autocracies" (Wright, 1972) into broader service agendas such as those in transportation or health. Because more particularistic agencies, such as those in aging, may be constrained (or protected, depending on one's vantage point) by federal law and regulation, it has often been difficult for general-purpose government officials (mayors, county commissioners, governors) to coordinate otherwise interrelated services agendas. Thus in the case of health, federal funding, usually from the Centers for Disease Control, is often disease specific rather than population specific. Only in a time of crisis—as in the case of the flu vaccination shortage of fall 2004—do agendas and agencies come together; thus, the assistant secretary on aging was in Florida one week before the 2004 election, reassuring seniors that more vaccine would soon be on the way (Harris, 2004).

PRESSING ISSUES IN SOCIAL AND HEALTH SERVICES PLANNING

The aging planning and services network has gone through growth, consolidation, and, most recently, redefinition phases. For many network agencies, it is hard to exaggerate the shift in their organizational environments between the period of around 1970–85 and the period since then. The earlier period was marked by a role of symbolic affirmation, a limited programmatic mandate, and resources adequate to the relatively modest tasks at hand. The more recent period finds SUAs and AAAs increasingly drawn into larger policy-relevant issues associated with the "aging of America." The foremost of these centers on HCBS, but governors, county commissioners, and mayors could increasingly point to SUAs and AAAs to be "point agencies" around larger health care, housing, transportation, and legal issues.

Concern with long-term care is clearly now very much in play within the erstwhile aging network. In most jurisdictions, earlier organizational issues have been shunted aside by the emergence of community-based, long-term care as a pressing state-level issue. The rise of the "old old," earlier hospital discharges under Medicare, and cost-containment efforts in institutional long-term care services under Medicaid have brought HCBS issues increasingly to center stage. In addition to the Medicaid waiver programs, many states allocated so-called state only funds toward HCBS services. Demonstration projects, such as "Channeling" in the 1980s and the Program of All Inclusive Care for the Elderly (PACE) adult day health services programs, have attempted to develop truly integrated services packages for community-based frail residents in many parts of the country. In these efforts, health, housing, social, respite, and other services are brought together to maximize elders' independence in community settings.

Without question, pressure to extend these services and devise ways to pay for them will continue to build. The aging of the population and vigorous advocacy efforts on the part of the impaired elders and the disabled are "expanding the scope of conflict" around these traditional bureaucratic divisions. With expenditures for the old and disabled already accounting for two-thirds of spiraling Medicaid budgets (which themselves account for nearly one fifth of all state-level expenditures), long-term care has risen to the top of gubernatorial agendas. In the words of Governor Bob Taft of Ohio, a Republican, "this is a huge national issue both because of the aging population and with regards to the costs of caring for this population" (Tanner, 2004).

The SUAs and AAAs have increasingly assumed major roles in these efforts, and such efforts have become central to their mission. Thus, National Association of Area Agencies on Aging (N4A), the AAAs' national trade association, lists as its top policy priority in 2004 "the development of a home and community-based services system which provides consumers access to the most appropriate services in the least restrictive environment" ([N4A], 2004). Because the Medicaid and state-only dollars are substantially greater than those available through the OAA, the AAAs are widely assuming the role of facilitators and guides for elders wishing to access the services system. Thus, N4A (2004) sees AAAs as "the front door" into aging services, and Massachusetts, for example, has renamed its substate service and planning agencies Elder Services Access Points.

In conclusion, there is a dynamic at work among "social and health services planning agencies," and that dynamic is in the direction of health-related services on behalf of frail elders and away from social services for elders able to live in relative comfort in the community. To be sure, traditional services such as nutrition and transportation continue to be offered, and non-health-related services such as adult protective services have been developed. But the historical and rather insular service set associated with the vertical "aging network" metaphor has been notably supplanted by a more involving and challenging role in the arena of community-based long-term care.

REFERENCES

Binstock, R. H., Cherington, C. M., & Woll, P. (1974). Federalism and leadership-planning: Predictions of variance in state behavior. *Gerontologist, 14*(2): 114–21.

Chronic Disease Directors and the National Association of State Units on Aging. (2003). *The Aging States Project: Promoting opportunities for collaboration between the public health and aging networks.* Atlanta, GA: Centers for Disease Control and Prevention.

Grason, H., & Gruyer, B. (1995). Rethinking the organization of children's programs: Lessons from the elderly. *Milbank Quarterly, 73*(4): 565–598.

Greenblatt, E., & Ernst, T. (1972). The Title III Program: Field impressions and policy options. *Gerontologist, 12*, 189–94.

Harris, G. (2004, October 31). In American health care, drug shortages are chronic. *New York Times,* Retrieved October 31, 2004, from: *www.nytimes.com/2004/10/31/weekinreview/31harri.html.*

Hasler, B. S. (1990). *Reporting of minority participation under Title III of the Older Americans Act.* Washington, DC: American Association of Retired Persons.

Hudson, R. B. (1973, September). Client politics and federalism: The case of the Older Americans Act. Paper presented at the annual meeting of the American Political Science Association, New Orleans.

Hudson, R. B. (1974). Rational planning and organizational imperatives: Prospects for area planning in aging. *Annals of the American Academy of Social and Political Science, 413,* 41–54.

Hudson, R. B. (1994). The Older Americans Act and the defederalization of community-based care. In P. Kim (Ed.), *Services to the aging and aged* (pp. 45–76). New York: Garland.

Hudson, R. B., & Veley, M. (1974). Federal funding and state planning: The case of the State Units on Aging. *Gerontologist, 14*(2): 122–128.

Justice, D. (1997). The aging network: A balancing act between universal coverage and defined eligibility. In R. B. Hudson (Ed.), *The future of age-based public policy* (pp. 168–177). Baltimore: Johns Hopkins University Press.

National Association of Area Agencies on Aging. (2004). *Policy priorities 2004.* Available: *www.n4a.org/policypriorities2004.cfm.*

National Association of State Units on Aging. (2004). *Forty years of leadership: The dynamic role of State Units on Aging.* Washington, DC.

Older Americans Act, 42 U.S.C. 3001. (1965).

Sheppard, H. (1971). *The administration on aging—Or a successor?* Report to the Special Committee on Aging, U.S. Senate. Special Committee on Aging. 92nd Congress, 1st Session. Committee Print. Washington, DC: Government Printing Office.

Tanner, R. (2004, July 19). Governors grapple with boosting care for elderly: Urge greater role of state governments. *Boston Globe.* Retrieved July 19, 2004, from: *www.boston.com/news/nation/articles/governors_grapple.*

White House Conference on Aging. (1972). *Toward a national policy on aging.* Washington, DC: White House Conference on Aging.

Wright, D. (1972). The states and intergovernmental relations. *Publius, 1,* 19–28.

Jan has been a highly productive food preparer at the local hospital. She is the one the supervisor could always count on to be there, to have trays ready on time, filled with the foods ordered by each specific patient, and properly labeled. But in the last month, Jan has been absent frequently, is making errors in her tray preparation, and always seems behind in the work. Her supervisor does not know that Jan, a worker whose employment is possible because she holds a green card, is experiencing serious family problems that interfere with her concentration and, indeed, frequently keep her at home.

Jan's mother came for a visit from China. While here, she was diagnosed with cancer and operated on successfully at the hospital. She is still receiving aftercare treatment. Now, however, her visitor's visa is up. Jan wants her to stay, but Jan's husband is afraid that keeping her mother, whom he now perceives as being here illegally, will jeopardize their own hope to become citizens. They quarrel incessantly, and he has threatened to turn Jan's mother in to the authorities if she does not leave within the month.

Thus, Jan, a good worker, has become a problem worker.

SHEILA H. AKABAS
LAUREN B. GATES

The Workplace

43

Juanita, an accounts supervisor at a branch bank, is a divorced mother with two daughters, aged 8 and 11. She has been with the bank for 6 years and has had two promotions during that time. She is highly regarded by her peers, customers, and supervisors, and there is general agreement that she will be a branch manager before long. Juanita has a "secret weapon," in that her mother has been the primary caregiver for the two girls, allowing Juanita to work without concern.

Two months ago, all this changed. Juanita's mother experienced a severe cardiovascular incident and now requires almost constant care. Since then, Juanita has used up all her accrued vacation time, and she has been on unpaid leave under the provision of the Family and Medical Leave Act for several weeks. Now she has visited human resources, indicating that she will have to resign since she does not believe she can manage her new caregiving responsibilities, for both her mother and her daughters, and the demands of her job.

Thus, Juanita, a worker featured significantly in the firm's succession planning, is about to leave the firm's employ. ▪

These two scenarios are matched in workplaces all over the country every day, sharing many of the same ingredients. A competent, valued worker confronts a serious problem involving an aging family member or is sandwiched between the needs of an aged person and children. The problem disrupts the family's situation and relationships and is reflected in poor job performance. A valued worker turns into a problem worker whose continued performance and employment are in jeopardy because of absenteeism, late arrival, early departure, work interruption, and even resignation from work (Dautzenberg et al., 2000).

Research has confirmed that caregiving needs of the aging and other family members may have a severe negative impact on the work connections and performance of members of the labor force, and thereby on the employers' organizational efficiency, productivity, and profits (Akabas & Kurzman, 2005; Dunham & Dietz, 2003; Lyon, Hallier, & Glover, 1998; Zimmerman, Mitchell, Wister, & Gutman, 2000). Few people work alone in the workplace. One person's poor performance can disrupt the usual functional processes and may impede a whole work group. The special demands resulting from the crisis an individual worker faces may be resented by coworkers, compromising work group morale and productivity (Fischel-Wolovick et al., 1988; McNeely, 1988). Furthermore, just as good performance sets a model for other workers, poor performance can be contagious in a workplace. Even if these significant costs are borne by the employer in the hope that they are a passing glitch in a fine performance record, there is no guarantee that the individual will maintain his or her work connection. The key asset of most organizations is its employees. Employers make significant investments in developing their labor force, recognizing such action as vital to long-term organizational effectiveness (Lyon et al., 1998). For the employer, therefore, the scenario of deteriorating performance or losing key workers as a result of the demands of their caregiving roles is potentially significant.

The cost of caregiving is not only levied against the employer. It becomes an important issue as well for women, in particular, and society in general. Whereas marriage used to be the road to economic security for women, their economic well-being now is intimately tied to their work experience (Carmichael & Charles, 2003; Morgan, 2000; Wilson & Hardy, 2002). Soci-

ety's expectation that caregiving is primarily a private, personal, and female responsibility makes caregiving a problem for working women and their economic well-being and, lacking their availability, an issue for employers and society (Sands & Goldberg-Glen, 1998).

The purpose of this chapter is to review the demographics and trends that are making the role of caregiver to the aged central to the lives of many, with consequences for the well-being of workers and their families and for the effectiveness of their employing organizations. We will then explore what workplaces and society have done in response and suggest additional possibilities for both prevention and intervention and the role social workers can play in achieving their implementation.

DEMOGRAPHICS AND TRENDS IN CAREGIVING AFFECTING EMPLOYMENT

Dentinger and Clarkberg (2002, p. 857) note that "an estimated one quarter of the entire American wage and salaried workforce provided informal care to their elders during 1996." Innes (2001, p. 12) reports that "before 2010, almost half the workforce will be parent-caring!" The impact of this demographic tidal wave can influence employers to develop greater interest in making it feasible for women to combine caregiving and employment—to keep them at work and productive. But several other trends emerge to feed employer interest in responding to caregiving demands. First, as baby boomers age, they will leave the labor force in large numbers (Kinsella & Velkoff, 2001). A labor shortage is expected because the smaller generational cohort that follows (often referred to as the baby bust generation because of the reduced birth rate from 1964 to 1980) will not meet the replacement demand for workers in an expanding economy (Doeringer, Sum, & Terkla, 2002; Faught, 1998). In addition, the baby boomers, now primarily caregivers, can be expected to develop their own massive needs for care in the not-too-distant future, requiring care that will distract the already depleted replacement pool from full-time work.

Second, the demand for women in the labor force is increasing, attributable to the change in occupational mix that favors women's jobs over traditionally male employment (Cotter, Hermsen, & Vanneman, 2002). Keeping men in the labor force longer or encouraging higher rates of immigration of young adults may help to meet employers' labor demand. The largest potential pool of workers to draw on, however, is women whose labor force participation rate, though increasing, still does not equal men's participation rate at any age grouping.

Third, at the same time that the demand for their labor force participation is increasing, women's caregiving responsibilities are expanding. Women are postponing childbearing (Anonymous, 2001). Simultaneously, longevity has increased. As a result, many working women have family members in their late eighties and nineties. It is likely that, while still caring for a child, a worker will be confronted with the responsibility to care for a parent (Robinson, Barbee, Martin, Singer, & Yegidis, 2003). In fact, today's "typical" couple has more living parents than children (Perkins, 1993).

IMPACT OF DUAL ROLE AS WORKER AND CAREGIVER

As mentioned, caregiving can have an impact on a woman's economic well-being. Caregiving often requires women to leave work or to accept part-time and/or low-paying jobs that maximize their flexibility, with negative impact on their economic well-being (Evandrou & Glaser, 2003; Pohl, Collins, & Given, 1998). In a British study, for example, "One-in-five mid-life women who have ever had caring responsibilities reported that, upon starting caring they stopped work altogether, and another one-in-five reported that they worked fewer hours, earned less money or could only work restricted hours" (Evandrou & Glaser, 2003, p. 583).

Research indicates, furthermore, that economically poor caregivers are more likely to reduce employment than those who are well off, reflecting realistic decision-making in light of the immediate opportunity costs of caregiving (White-Means, 1992). Thus, not only are present earnings likely to be reduced but also eventual retirement income is affected for women who leave work to provide care, because by leaving work they reduce the base upon which their eventual Social Security benefit is calculated (Dunham & Dietz, 2003).

Concepts of role strain, role conflict, and role overload are the usual context for studying the experience of employed providers of eldercare (Dentinger & Clarkberg, 2002). Researchers report findings of stress when the role of caregiver is added to the role of employee (role overload), particularly when one faces psychological uncertainty in defining priorities (role conflict) and difficulty finding sufficient time to meet all responsibilities (role strain) (Akabas, 1988; Mark, 1988). The result of these influences is usually reduced

labor force participation. Caregiving also influences the continued participation of women in the workforce through its impact on the transition to retirement. Caregiving causes women to retire and make caregiving primary, while it motivates men to continue to work to secure financial resources to afford care (Dentinger & Clarkberg, 2002). Evidence shows that wives caring for husbands are more likely to retire than caregivers in other relationships. Also influential is how sick the person getting the care is, as well as the number of persons to whom the caregiver must give care, each having an impact in the expected direction.

Not all caregiving has negative consequences. Younger cohorts of caregivers who are more accustomed to work may be more adept at balancing the multiple responsibilities of work and care than older ones (Laditka & Laditka, 2000). Further, participation in outside work may mitigate the stress associated with caregiving and improve the balance in life (Dunham & Dietz, 2003; Mark, 1998). Differences also may be offset by ability to purchase some care (Laditka & Laditka, 2000). Full-time workers acknowledge the significance of work as a support and positive component of their complex lives and try to balance their multiple roles without time off in any significant amount (Pohl, Collins, & Given, 1998). Evidence indicates that employed daughters provide less instrumental help to their mothers than unemployed daughters, but employed daughters arrange for additional support by purchased help. Research confirms that employment reduces the chances of being a helper and that employed caregivers tend to reduce caregiving hours rather than work hours (Dautzenberg et al., 2000). From a policy point of view, this is desirable behavior, since maintaining work results in improved earnings throughout the life cycle, and having a better economic position is associated with improved well-being (Zimmerman et al., 2000). The National Long-Term Care Survey and National Survey of Informal Caregivers study of almost 2,000 caregivers of impaired elderly found that although one-third of caregivers made significant adjustments to their employment by quitting their jobs, "the higher the caregiver's family income (opportunity cost of employment time), the less likely are hours to be allocated away from the labor market" (White-Means, 1992, p. 82). Also on a positive note, the alternative concepts of role accumulation and role expansion suggest that the individual can expand role sets, even under circumstances of increasing role strain. If the worker feels committed to each role, the strain of multiple roles is less severe (Dautzenberg et al., 2000).

The intersection among later-in-life child-bearing, the increasing numbers of persons who are aging, the expanding labor force participation of women, and their dependence on work for economic well-being poses a serious dilemma for women, to wit: How should they prioritize the demands of work and family and the competing demands among family members? The dilemma facing individual women can, in concert, create a social and world-of-work problem of crisis proportions, in view of the fact that there will be fewer younger caregivers to employ to meet the caregiving responsibilities of those women who might opt to continue work because of their high earning capacity, necessary income, and/or their own personal preferences (Hochschild, 1997). It is clearly in the self-interest of employers, unions, and society in general to mitigate the burden of caregiving. Not surprisingly, therefore, the parties have taken some action, and these are described here.

RESPONSES TO THE DEMANDS OF CAREGIVING

There are few public social policies that support the function of caregiving, though it is widely recognized that growing poverty is related to this domestic role for women (Bullock, Crawford, & Tennstedt, 2003; Dunham & Dietz, 2003; Zimmerman et al., 2000). Furthermore, employer dependence on women to fill the gap in replacement workers while their role as caregivers is increasing magnifies the need for a responsive workplace policy dealing with caregiving (Akabas, 1990; Spillman & Pezzin, 2000). Currently, however, workplace responses are relatively new, and their effectiveness, for the most part, is unknown.

Social policy. The social policy of a society is expressed in its legislation. In the case of caregiving, the response in the United States has been minimal. Despite the obvious need for assistance to families who provide extensive informal care to adults who are aging, there are no financial supports unless the individual receiving care is a dependent of the caregiver, in which case the usual personal tax exemption applies. The only federal law that assists those who provide informal care is the Family and Medical Leave Act of 1993 (FMLA). The first legislation passed by the Clinton administration, it had been rejected during the earlier Bush administration as too demanding of business. The law provides that full-time workers may take up to 12 weeks of unpaid leave in any calendar year to meet their own "serious" health condition

needs or those of an immediate family member (spouse, parent, or child under 18). Worksites with 50 or more workers located within a 75-mile radius are covered. Health benefits for their employees are continued during leave, and their job return to the same or a similar position is guaranteed. Advance warning, when possible, is required, but leave may be taken without notice and in increments of less than a full day, depending on circumstances. Employees may have to liquidate any accrued leave against the allowed 12-week leave period. Employees may be asked to provide medical evidence of the need for leave. Employers may request that employees submit to a medical examination. Employers' top 10% of earners may be excluded from the Act's protection at the discretion of the employer. Claimed denial of any right covered by the law can be filed for review at the nearest office of the Employment Standards Administration of the Wage and Hour Division of the U.S. Department of Labor (U.S. Department of Labor, 1995).

The Act publicly recognizes the impact of caring and is a great stride forward in social policy. Its requirements put employers on notice that society expects them to adopt reasonable policies to support employees in caregiving roles. Continuing health benefit coverage and a guaranteed right of job return certainly help reduce the stress that an employed caregiver is likely to experience in a crisis medical situation. The right to leave on an intermittent basis recognizes caregiving realities and the need to balance work and the demands of aged family members.

These are all-important protections and are among the conditions necessary to promote the well-being of employed persons, but they are not sufficient conditions to assure employee/caregiver well-being. The fact that the law's requirements apply only to employers of 50 or more employees eliminates almost half the workers in the United States, who work for smaller employers. Noteworthy is the fact that smaller employers tend to pay less and offer less extensive benefit structures, so that employees of small employers experience double jeopardy. They have less money to purchase care than their counterparts who work for larger employers, and they have no job protection if they take time to provide the care themselves. In addition, specified relationships do not include in-laws or friends, both groups who receive a great deal of actual attention from working caregivers (Medjuck, Keffe, & Fancey, 1998).

The fact that the leave is unpaid, however, is the legislation's greatest deficit. Those who cannot afford to purchase formal caregiving are probably the most in need of leave for family medical emergencies. Most can ill afford to miss even a day's pay, let alone lose income for an extended period. Thus, they have a right that they cannot afford to exercise. There have been suggestions that unemployment funds should be used to cover associated leaves or that other provision be made for paid leave, but none of these recommendations have been adopted. Several states and municipalities have laws with more generous protections, but these are far from universal. New York, New Jersey, Rhode Island, California, and Hawaii have state laws providing financial coverage when the employed person requires personal disability–related leave. Nowhere can one find paid leave to provide care to a family member who is aged.

There is also a more subtle problem in assuring the benefits promised by the law. Anecdotal evidence suggests that workplaces can have a culture that, while it does not deny the benefits of the Act to those who seek to use them, discourages access to those benefits in both clear messages and suggestive behavior. Most employees in such settings understand and abide by these suggestive statements and give up their right to the benefit supposedly guaranteed by law (Akabas & Kurzman, 2005; Medjuck et al., 1998). Other workplaces have established policies that require employees to use any leave to which they are entitled before they utilize unpaid leave, with all leave counting toward the 12 weeks allowable under FMLA. The law permits employers to exercise this policy, although it seems to abrogate the intent of the legislation, and effectively deny employees the right to vacation, since for most workers the only accrued leave they have is vacation time. These problems have been identified in research studies and anecdotal evidence (Akabas & Kurzman, 2005). The law has not been the subject of amendment in the 12 years since its passage, suggesting a lack of society's commitment to recognize the contribution of the informal care provided by those who work.

Employers' responses. Employers are concerned about the bottom line. They are aware that well-motivated employees are instrumental to profitability. Maslow (1943/1974) suggests that motivation is related to a hierarchy of levels of satisfaction in which self-actualization is the pinnacle. Enlightened management that addresses and meets the needs of workers that are lower on the hierarchy will be rewarded with workers who reach the top hierarchial level, that is, self-actualizing workers who are motivated to do their best work without prodding. Herzberg (1987) points out that there are hygiene factors, such as pay, that are required to keep employees working, but it is neces-

sary to offer other forces to motivate employees to maximize productivity. Conditions that promote feelings of being valued are positive motivators. The successful workplace is one that achieves full motivation from all its employees. Distractions from employees' focus on productivity become employers' concerns.

As trends indicate, since those most likely to take on caregiving responsibilities are women, the general demographics of the company become important. An employer with a majority of female employees over 40 years of age will have greater need to respond than one with a largely male, and/or younger workforce (Grensing-Pophal, 2003). If the employees are largely baby boomers, the expectation is that caregiving for their older parents will increase, causing absenteeism to rise and job performance and satisfaction to diminish. For example, a study among deans of schools of social work found that caregiving affected organizational effectiveness. Deans who participated in the survey identified that caregivers missed obligations for covering classes, attending meetings, and carrying out scholarly research. There was evidence of chronic stress through requests for leaves and delays toward tenure and search for support from other colleagues (Robinson et al., 2003).

There is enough basis for concern to cause employers to deal with eldercare issues, that is, to provide a benefit structure that removes or mitigates obstacles to employees' ability to concentrate on work schedules and productivity (Lambert, 1993). The ambiguity of outcome in the face of caregiving demands, that is, the fact that caregiving is stressful but satisfying, clarifies the potential value to employers for acting to neutralize the negative impact of caregiving on the employed caregiver's behavior. Although they may feel that it is an employee's responsibility to solve caregiving problems, employers would rather help with these problems than be ordered to do so by government, or lose a valuable employee's services to these problems.

The challenge faced by workplaces is to develop the mechanisms of support. Employee assistance programs (EAPs), membership assistance programs (MAPs), and family/work programs constitute the structure for providing policy and service in the workplace to respond to the consequences of caregiving on employment. Offering these programs confirms employers' awareness of this reality. Employee assistance programs exist in most medium- and large-scale workplaces and are often available to employees in relatively small companies. A 1995 survey found that 82.3% of all companies with over 1,000 workers had an EAP (Cohen, Gard, & Hefferman, 1998). Employee assistance programs, and related MAPs in unions, were first established in a few very large corporations in the 1940s in order to deal humanely with workers with alcoholism problems. It became clear that the mechanisms for helping employees resolve issues related to substance abuse could be applied to other presenting problems as well (Caldwell, 1993). Employee assistance programs have become widespread as the first line of defense in meeting the varied needs that employees may present that threaten to interfere with their ability to maintain job performance. As services expanded to respond to a more varied menu of needs, trained professionals were introduced to the staffing pattern. Increasingly the programs were staffed by mental health professionals, with social workers in the majority (Akabas & Kurzman, 2005; Kurzman, 1993).

With the rise of dual earner and single parent families, employers discerned that caring for family and work were frequently in conflict, resulting in stress and burnout of the employee, followed by lowered production, increased absenteeism, and high job turnover (Spillman & Pezzin, 2000). Although EAP/MAP initiatives remain dominant, some solely work/family initiatives have emerged, to apply a policy analysis to the problems that arise, and to implement responsive practices. Today these programs take many forms. Some employing organizations have in-house staff who, through EAPs, cover the gamut of needs, including work/family situations that employees may present, and offer information, referral, and even counseling on-site to resolve the problem that endangers productivity (Anonymous, 1994). At the other extreme, corporations may contract with two separate outside service providers. A general EAP acts as gatekeeper to carved-out managed care mental health benefits to deal with generic problems, while a work/family referral service offers intake interviews that identify need, and then assigns a care manager to suggest resources in the community to assist with the identified need or to offer advice on how to manage the complex situation that presents itself. Between these two extremes, there are varied patterns for providing coverage, but almost all initiatives include a response to the competing demands of employment and the care of parent or spouse that may interfere with full attention to work. Many unions, through MAPs and other collectively bargained contract provisions, have mirrored the structures established by employers, though their motivation is membership loyalty rather than productivity.

The employers' interest in minimizing, or eliminating, if possible, any disruption in the employees' job performance suggests the value of prevention (Robinson et al., 2003). Caregiving often occurs as an unexpected, crisis event that is transitory in the work life of an employee, although it may not necessarily be short-term (Faught, 1998; Lefkovich, 1992). Through educational seminars, eldercare fairs, and distribution of informative written material that provide information on public benefits, the availability of care management services, help with household tasks, home health care resources, how to secure Meals on Wheels and other in-home care, and selection of nursing home and other long-term care facilities (Grensing-Pophal, 2003; Parus, 2004; Scott, 2002), the EAP/MAP or the specialized work/family initiative can prepare the labor force to identify the signs of a potential need. The expectation is that once alerted, an employee will recognize the need at the onset of a problem and act to assure his or her own continuous and seamless maintenance of productive employment. Notably, these services become extremely important when an employer hopes to relocate a caregiver, or when the concerned employee lives at a distance from the older adult in need of care (Sunoo, 1997).

Add-on services can include continuing support groups for caregivers. Increasingly, work organizations offer policies that allow for reduced quantity of work, hoping that thereby the quality of performance will be sustained. Arrangements for flex-time, telecommuting, job sharing, and other work schedule adjustments are the most valued (Dunham & Dietz, 2003; Lefkovich, 1992). In organized settings, these services may be offered by labor/management partnerships ("Labor/Management Partnerships," 1992). The gamut of services is based on a realistic understanding by cost-conscious corporate financial officers of the costs of loss from work, attrition, displaced careers, and other negative factors (Faught, 1998).

Union responses. Unions are concerned about the well-being of members and build membership loyalty by attending to their needs (Dunn, 2000). The AFL-CIO Web site notes that "workers who care for elderly relatives have an average loss over a lifetime of more than $600,000 in wage, pension, and Social Security benefits." Not surprisingly, the AFL-CIO has defined eldercare as a significant issue ([AFL-CIO], 2001). They advise unions to bargain for eldercare during contract negotiations. As a result, many organized workers are covered by benefits that relate to the issue of employment while caring for older adults. For example, by contract the United Auto Workers at

General Motors are provided with a 24/7 Elder Care Response Line, where 24 qualified care managers provide personal consultation, educational materials, and individualized referrals and are also available for home assessment of eldercare needs. The International Union of Electricians, in their contract with General Electric, secured a flexible spending account that allows all employees to set aside up to $5,000 per annum, tax free, to pay for eldercare-related expenses. The San Francisco Multiemployer Hotel Group has agreed with the Hotel Employees and Restaurant Employees Union, Local 2, that the group will deposit 15 cents per worker per hour to a fund from which members can draw up to $150 per month for nonreimbursable expenses related to health needs of spouses, parents, in-laws, grandparents, or the members themselves. Finally, the California State Employees Association, the Service Employees International Union, and the State of California have contractually provided that employees may make donations of their own leave to be drawn on by fellow employees facing financial hardship due to illness of self or a family member, with the employer bearing the cost of administration of the provision.

SOCIAL WORK ROLES

The need to resolve the conflict between employment and the demands of caring for an aged adult is important now and can be expected to grow more so in the near future. Social workers can find many significant roles in promoting this agenda at the individual, organizational, and community level, both within workplace settings and in their own practice as self-employed therapists, in agency settings, and in government policy positions. A good starting point would be for social workers themselves to become more aware of the significance of work in people's lives and the importance of support systems that can help those who work maintain their work role, regardless of the other roles they carry.

Individuals need information on resources and entitlements, help thinking through how they wish to manage their multiple demands, encouragement to engage in self-advocacy at the workplace to negotiate the conditions necessary to succeed at both roles, referral to community resources that can fill any gap between the care they can offer and the care that is needed, and ongoing support from case managers who know local facilities. Social workers can incorporate financial and health education in their counseling activities, so that people are better prepared to deal with their own old age, as well as the aging of those who are dependent on them for care.

Work organizations need assistance in becoming more sensitive to the problems involved in managing eldercare and work. Social workers can help business and union settings develop policies that maximize flexibility, train supervisors to be empathetic and structure a supportive workplace culture, build communication systems that assure the flow of information necessary for workers to know their rights and entitlements, and then exercise them, and utilize corporate philanthropy to make contributions to community services that help caregivers. Social workers can also encourage community social services to be more responsive to the needs of women.

Ultimately, there is a need for a public redefinition of responsibility, so that care is not an informal effort, with women as the assumed providers. Government must act to provide and finance formal institutions that can share the caregivers' burdens. Social workers can do the analysis needed to inform public policy decisions and use community organizing skills to lobby for policies that might revise Medicaid requirements of indigence, support Social Security credits during periods when women "drop out" to provide care, so they are not penalized for their unpaid contribution to society; offer tax incentives to businesses to support caregiving employees; and do so in a gender-neutral manner, so that men and women can begin to share, more equally, the demands of giving care to their parents and other aging relatives.

In a telling remark, an IBM communications director summed up the importance to employers of initiatives that assist employees with meeting the care needs of older adults: "such policies are not merely altruistic, but an 'absolute business imperative.' . . . If we do not build flexibility into the way we work then we are going to turn our back on half of the workforce" (Centaur Communications Limited, 2003, p. 8). That seems to say it all.

REFERENCES

Akabas, S. H. (1988). Women, work and mental health: Room for improvement. *Journal of Primary Prevention, 9*(1–2), 130–140.

Akabas, S. H. (1990). Reconciling the demands of work with the needs of families. *Families in Society, 71*(6), 366–371.

Akabas, S. H., & Kurzman, P. A. (2005). *Work and the workplace: A resource for innovative policy and practice.* New York: Columbia University Press.

AFL-CIO. (2001). *Bargaining factsheet: Eldercare.* Available at: *www.aflcio.org/issuespolitics/worknfamily/up load/elder.pdf.*

Anonymous. (1994). Changed workplace expands role of EAPs. *Employee Benefit Plan Review, 49*(6), 38–39.

Anonymous. (2001). In the middle: A report on multi-cultural boomers coping with family and aging issues. *Migration World Magazine, 29*(4), 25–29.

Bullock, K., Crawford, S. L., & Tennstedt, S. L. (2003). Employment and caregiving: Exploration of African American caregivers. *Social Work, 48*(2), 150–162.

Caldwell, B. (1993). EAPs broadens their focus, evolve from substance abuse genesis. *Employee Benefit Plan Review, 48*(5), 26–27.

Carmichael, F., & Charles, S. (2003). The opportunity costs of informal care: Does gender matter? *Journal of Health Economics, 22*(5), 781–786.

Centaur Communications. (2003, October 6). IBM's £31m care bonanza. *Employee Benefits Magazine,* 8.

Cohen, G. S., Gard, L. H., & Hefferman, W. R. (1998). Employee assistance programs: A preventive, cost-effective benefit. *Journal of Health Care Finance, 24*(3), 45–54.

Cotter, D. A., Hermsen, J. M., & Vanneman, R. (2002). Gendered opportunities for work. *Research on Aging, 24*(6), 600–629.

Dautzenberg, M. G. H., Diederiks, J. P. M., Philipsen, H., Stevens, F. C. J., Tan, F. E. S., & Vernooij-Dassen, M. J. F. J. (2000). The competing demands of paid work and parent care. *Research on Aging, 22*(2), 165–187.

Dentinger, E., & Clarkberg, M. (2002). Informal caregiving and retirement timing among men and women. *Journal of Family Issues, 23*(7), 857–879.

Doeringer, P., Sum, A., & Terkla, D. (2002). Devolution of employment and training policy: The case of older workers. *Journal of Aging & Social Policy, 14*(3/4), 37–60.

Dunham, C. C., & Dietz, B. E. (2003). "If I'm not allowed to put my family first": Challenges experienced by women who are caregiving for family members with dementia. *Journal of Women & Aging, 15*(1), 55–69.

Dunn, K. (2000). Member-assistance program earns its wings. *Workforce, 79*(1), 76–79.

Evandrou, M., & Glaser, K. (2003). Combining work and family life: The pension penalty of caring. *Ageing and Society, 23*(5), 593–612.

Family and Medical Leave Act, Pub. L. No. 103–3 (1993). Pub. L. No. 103–3, 107 Stat. 6.

Faught, L. (1998). Corporate eldercare: The final frontier. *ACA Journal, 7*(4), 81–84.

Fischel-Wolovick, L., Cotter, C., Masser, I., Kelman-Bravo, E., Jaffe, S., Rosenberg, G., & Wittenberg, B. (1998). Alternative work scheduling for professional social workers. *Administration in Social Work, 12*(4), 93–101.

Grensing-Pophal, L. (2003) Aging America. *Credit Union Management, 26*(1), 40–44.

Herzberg, F. (1987). One more time: How do you motivate employees? *Harvard Business Review, 65*(5), 27–37.

Hochschild, A. R. (1997). *The time bind: When work becomes home and home becomes work.* New York: Holt.

Innes, B. (2001). Offer next-gen eldercare benefits to your corporate clients. *National Underwriter, 105*(3), 12.

Kinsella, K., & Velkoff, V. A. (2001). *An aging world: 2001.* Washington, DC: U.S. Department of Health and Human Services and U.S. Department of Commerce.

Kurzman, P. A. (1993). Employee assistance programs: Toward a comprehensive service model. In P. A. Kurzman & S. H. Akabas (Eds.), *Work and well-being: The occupational social work advantage* (pp. 26–45). Washington, DC: NASW Press.

Labor/management partnerships foster better employee relationships. (1992). *Business and Health, 10*(4), 73–77.

Laditka, J. N., & Laditka, S. B. (2000). Aging children and their older parents: The coming generation of caregiving. *Journal of Women & Aging, 12*(1/2), 189.

Lambert, S. (1993, June). Workplace policies as social policies. *Social Service Review, 67*(2), 237–260.

Lefkovich, J. L. (1992). Business responds to elder-care needs. *HR Magazine, 37*(6), 103–107.

Lyon, P., Hallier, J., & Glover, I. (1998). Divestment of investment? The contradictions of HRM in relation to older employees. *Human Resource Management Journal, 8*(1), 56–66.

Mark, N. F. (1998) Does it hurt to care? Caregiving, work-family conflict, and midlife well-being. *Journal of Marriage and the Family, 60*(4), 951–966.

Maslow, A. H. (1973). A theory of human motivation. In R. J. Lowry (Ed.), *Dominance, self-esteem, self-actualization: Germinal papers of A. H. Maslow* (pp. 153–173). Monterey, CA: Brooks/Cole. (Original work published 1943.)

McNeely, R. (1988, April). Five morale-enhancing innovations for human service settings. *Social Casework, 69*(4), 204–213.

Medjuck, S., Keffe, J. M., & Fancey, P. J. (1998). Available but not accessible: An examination of the use of workplace policies for caregivers of elderly kin. *Journal of Family Issues, 19*(3), 274–298.

Morgan, L. A. (2000). The continuing gender gap in later life economic security. *Journal of Aging and Social Policy, 11*(2/3), 157–165.

Parus, B. (2004). Who's watching grandma? Addressing the eldercare dilemma. *Workspan, 47*(1), 40–44.

Perkins, A. (1993). Eldercare: The employee benefit of the '90s? *Tribune Business Weekly, 4*(27), 1.

Pohl, J. M., Collins, C. E., & Given, C. W. (1998). Longitudinal employment decisions of daughters and daughters-in-law after assuming parent care. *Journal of Women & Aging, 10*(1), 59–74.

Robinson, M. M., Barbee, A. P., Martin, M., Singer, T. I., & Yegidis, B. (2003). The organizational costs of caregiving: A call to action. *Administration in Social Work, 27*(1), 83–102.

Sands, R. G., & Goldberg-Glen, R. S. (1998). The impact of employment and serious illness on grandmothers who are raising their grandchildren. *Journal of Women and Aging, 10*(3), 41–58.

Scott, M. B. (2002). FleetBoston Financial, Pearson Education help employees address eldercare needs. *Employee Benefit Plan Review, 56*(8), 33–36.

Spillman, R. C., & Pezzin, L. E. (2000). Potential and active family caregivers: Changing networks and the "sandwich generation." *Milbank Quarterly, 78*(3), 347–374.

Sunoo, B. P. (1997). Relocating caregivers: Handle with care. *Workforce, 76*(3), 46–52.

U.S. Department of Labor, Employment Standards Administration, Wage and Hour Division. (1995). *Fact sheet no. 28: The Family and Medical Leave Act of 1993.* Available: *www.dol.gov/esa/regs/compliance/whd/whdfs28.htm.*

White-Means, S. I. (1992). Allocation of labor to informal home health production: Health care for frail elderly, if time permits. *Journal of Consumer Affairs, 26*(1), 69–91.

Wilson, A. E., & Hardy, M. A. (2002). Racial disparities in income security for a cohort of aging America women. *Social Forces, 80*(4), 1283–1306.

Zimmerman, L., Mitchell, B., Wister, A., & Gutman, G. (2000). Unanticipated consequences: A comparison of expected and actual retirement timing among older women. *Journal of Women & Aging, 12*(1/2), 109–128.

Older adults are the fastest growing segment of the U.S. population and, in health and social services settings, are frequently characterized by the nature of their more prevalent acute and chronic conditions and higher utilization of health care services than the population at large (see Gonyea, Hudson, & Curley, 2004). A significant proportion of older adults experience mental health disorders as well, for example, they have the highest suicide rate of all age groups (U.S. Centers for Disease Control, 1999). In the case of suicide, alcohol and other drugs may be a precursor of suicide and even the cause of the death. Yet older Americans continue to be among the lowest utilizers of mental health and substance abuse/dependence services.

While services targeted to this population are limited (Cummings & Bride, in press), there is a pressing need to address new cohorts of older adults, whose patterns of substance use and abuse are more intense than those of previous generations (e.g., the baby boomers who will turn 65 in 2011). In addition, differentiating early-onset alcoholism and late-onset alcoholism and its impact (McGinnis-Dittrich, 2002) is critical (e.g., late-onset alcoholics are less likely to see their alcohol use as a problem). Further, defining what constitutes "problem drinking" is controversial, since older adults may not demonstrate the more prominent impairments seen in younger populations, such as financial and/or occupational challenges. Instead, the health impacts (e.g., increased falls; high blood pressure; memory loss) may be masked and only treated symptomatically (McGinniss-Dittrich, 2002).

This chapter addresses the epidemiology of substance abuse in older adults, including discussion of the accompanying challenges of diagnostic validity and assessment issues, and an overview of treatment settings.

EPIDEMIOLOGY AND DIAGNOSTIC VALIDITY

The treatment of alcohol and substance use disorders in the older adult is inherently tied to the assessment procedures used to diagnose these disorders and the segments of the population found to manifest these problems. In other words, *how* and *where* these disorders are identified influence the *ways* they are treated. The next section presents the prevalent characteristics of substance use disorders among the subpopulation of older adults, and the challenges of identifying older

CONNIE CORLEY
MURIEL GRAY
RICHARD YAKIMO

Substance Abuse Networks

adults with these disorders are discussed in the section thereafter.

Epidemiological Studies

Epidemiological studies to date have largely ignored issues of mental disorders in the elderly by excluding older people from the sampling frame, presumably because of the difficulty of separating psychiatric problems from the physical disorders that become more common with age (Hybels & Blazer, 2002; Lynskey, Day, & Hall, 2003). Other studies report sweeping age ranges (e.g., "over the age of 35") that make conclusions about specific periods of adult development difficult to determine. Findings across studies are often difficult to compare, due to inconsistent definitions of alcoholism (Fingerhood, 2000; Lakhani, 1997). Related to exclusion from study, age reporting, and inconsistent definitions are issues of diagnostic validity that will be discussed later in this chapter.

With regard to specific substance abuse disorders listed in the *Diagnostic and Statistical Manual of Mental Disorders* (DSM-IV; American Psychiatric Association, 1980), the Epidemiological Catchment Area Study (ECA) stands as the landmark survey for addressing mental disorders among community- and institutional-dwelling older adults in the United States (Hybels & Blazer, 2002; Robins & Regier, 1991). When 12-month prevalence for alcoholism was examined, 3.1% of men over the age of 65 and 0.46% of women met criteria for diagnosis of alcoholism in the past month. Rates steadily decreased among all age categories, with men reporting higher rates than women. Among ethnic groups, Hispanic men over the age of 65 showed the highest alcoholism rates (6.57%), while Hispanic women reported no alcoholism. Whites reported rates of 2.85% and 0.47% for men and women, respectively. Comparable rates were found for older black men and women at 2.93% and 0.60% (Helzer, Burnam, & McEvoy, 1991). Lifetime illicit drug use for this cohort in the ECA was remarkably low, with men reporting 2.88% and women 0.66%. (Anthony & Helzer, 1991).

Although there is scant information on prescription drug abuse among older adults, there is evidence that it often accompanies alcohol disorders and is more common among women (Finlayson & Davis, 1994). The use of benzodiazepines (e.g., Librium, Valium, Xanax) has been associated with automobile accidents, falls, and lower functional status (Hem-

melgarn, Suissa, Huang, Boivin, & Pinard; Neutel, Hirdes, Maxwell, & Patten, 1996; Ried, Johnson, & Gettman, 1998).

Recent studies comparing the National Institute on Alcohol Abuse and Alcoholism's (NIAAA) surveys in 1991–1992 and 2001–2002 confirmed the trends discussed here (Grant et al., 2004). Within the two surveys, successively older age groups reported decreasing rates of DSM-IV abuse and dependence compared to the younger groups. However, comparisons of the 65-plus age across the 10-year period showed significant increases in alcohol abuse, from 0.25% to 1.21%. This increment was shown for men as well as women, with men showing steeper increases. However, the prevalence of alcohol dependence for the older age group decreased during the 10-year period (from 0.39% to 0.24%), but the decrease was not significant.

While higher prevalence of alcoholism is typically observed in younger adults within the community, this does not mean that drinking in older adults is insignificant. An analysis of Medicare records revealed that hospitalizations for disorders related to alcohol use were as prevalent as those for heart attacks and carried significant costs (Adams, Yuan, Barboriak, & Rimm, 1993). In addition, clinical literature dating from the 1980s suggests that some individuals actually increase their consumption as they age. Within this group, increased consumption may be reactive to age-related stresses such as retirement, widowhood, disability, and other types of losses (Atkinson, Turner, Kofoed, & Tolson, 1983).

Diagnostic Validity and Difficulties in Assessing Substance Abuse in Older Adults

The defining characteristics for alcoholism may not be consistently meaningful or significant across age groups. In other words, *diagnostic validity* may not be congruent: the presence or absence of certain symptoms may not uniformly predict the presence, course, or outcome of substance use disorders across the lifespan. General criteria from the *Diagnostic and Statistical Manual of Mental Disorders* (American Psychiatric Association, 1994), for substance abuse and dependence were formulated with a younger adult population in mind, presumably those most likely to seek help from mental health professionals. For example, *DSM-IV* (1994) criteria for substance abuse that rely heavily on disruption of role function, financial stability, and social networks may not be obvious or appropriate for those older people with limited family and work responsibilities and fewer social connections. Further, many professionals are unfamiliar with existing screening instruments outside of specialized treatment settings (see chapter here for more on specific instruments).

Clinical guidelines, such as the standard for excessive drinking of more than two drinks a day for men or one for women, may also not be valid for an older population with limited discretionary income, increased sensitivity to alcohol, and reduced efficiency in metabolism due to cooccurring physical problems (McCracken, 1998; Moore et al., 1999). While alternative diagnostic schemes have been proposed based upon the interaction of alcohol with cooccurring disease, associated medications, and altered ability to function in daily life (Fingerhood, 2000; Moore et al., 1999; Scott & Popovich, 2001), *DSM-IV* (1994) criteria remain predominant in determining how alcohol problems are identified and subsequently how routes for treatment are opened.

Recognition of substance abuse disorders are also hindered by ageist assumptions held by clinicians and the larger society. While older people tend to visit primary care providers regularly, they do not actively seek or receive treatment for their mental health concerns (Bartels, 2003; Whelan, 2003). This lack of attention to mental health is compounded with substance abuse concerns because of clinicians' assumptions that long-term substance users do not survive into old age (Atkinson, Ryan, & Turner, 2001), that such disorders do not arise in later adulthood, and that older adults show the same symptoms and patterns of abuse and dependence as younger people.

In addition, many older adults prompt the attention of family members and ultimately the health care system for issues that do not immediately suggest problematic substance use. For example, falls, injuries, confusion, neglect, depression, memory loss, emotional lability, sleep disturbances, and adverse drug interactions may be attributed to chronic medical conditions, dementia, or the consequences of aging rather than alcohol use (Egbert, 1993; Eliason & Skinstad, 2001; Graham & Schmidt, 1998; Klein & Iber, 1991). Beginning solutions to these problems include education, both for the older adults who are typically interested in health promotion (Fink, Beck, & Wittrock, 2001) and for providers to increase their sensitivity to older individuals' substance abuse issues (Coogle, Osgood, & Parham, 2000). Careful and consistent screening of the older individual's intake of substances, consideration of chronic health conditions and medications that may have negative interactions with substance intake, and investigation of falls, memory difficulties, and other functional problems that may suggest substance abuse will point the way to more efficient problem formulation and referral to treatment resources.

SUBSTANCE ABUSE NETWORKS

The screening, assessment, and treatment of substance use disorders may take place in a variety of settings. The screening typically occurs in settings not commonly considered the "substance abuse service network" (such as the workplace and medical-related settings), while the assessment and treatment are part of the mission of the "substance abuse service network." In actuality, all of these services comprise the "substance abuse service network," because *screening and identification* (addressed in the first part of this section) must precede *assessment and treatment* (the second part of this section). However, treatment of substance abuse disorders is the focus of what is commonly referred to as the "substance abuse service network." This network of services consists of various types of settings that utilize various interventions and approaches.

Accessing treatment through these settings is typically congruent with the life stage, health and mental status, and economic status of the older adult. For instance, many older persons who are employed may have their behavioral health needs addressed through an employee assistance program or an occupational health service. On the other hand, those who are unemployed or retired may access behavioral health services (e.g., as comorbid conditions) through primary care facilities or specialty treatment physicians. Still others may access services for substance use disorders through community faith-based programs. Older veterans have traditionally accessed the substance abuse service network designed specifically for veterans, and other older persons might utilize community-based public health, mental health, or substance abuse treatment programs. An overview of primary treatment settings follows.

Screening and Identification

Because older adults are less likely to be involved in the traditional substance abuse service network, screening needs to take place in the settings in which they interact regularly—the workplace and the offices of health care/social service providers.

Employee assistance programs and occupational health programs. Employee Assistance Programs (EAPs) are designed to assist workers who may have personal concerns that may impact job performance or, conversely, to assist workers whose job performance has deteriorated. In this setting an assessment is conducted to determine the nature of the problems and make referrals for appropriate treatment. Especially with older workers, social workers in this setting need to be sophisticated in their understanding of the presentation of substance use disorders, age-related cognitive deficiencies, psychiatric disabilities, drug interactions, and the interrelationship between all of these comorbid conditions.

In conjunction with the EAP, another initiative of today's workplace is the maintenance of a drug-free workplace. It is estimated (Center for Substance Abuse Treatment [CSAT], 1998) that about 17% of adults age 60 and older abuse alcohol and/or legal drugs, prescribed and over-the-counter, and that approximately 50% of older adults use these drugs in combination with alcohol (CSAT, 1998). Many of these older adults are employed and work in environments that utilize routine, random, or for-cause toxicology screens. Depending on the substances used or misused, and their impact on the behavioral and cognitive functioning, older workers may find it difficult to continue working in a drug-free environment (CSAT, 1998). It may be this dynamic that will identify them as having a substance use disorder worthy of treatment.

The workplace, via the EAP or occupational health medical unit, typically refers a worker to treatment. Therefore, the EAP may serve as a gatekeeper or point of entry into the substance abuse service network for workers. Referral decisions are typically made based on individual client needs. However, despite the fact that studies have shown that older adults are more likely to respond to and complete treatment for substance abuse disorders when such treatment is designed specifically to address their needs, either as a separate treatment track in a mainstream setting or in an entirely separate program (CSAT, 1998), most treatment programs are not designed with the needs of older adults in mind. The reality is that very few of these types of programs exist. Since it is expected that in the next few decades a growing percentage of the workforce will be comprised of older workers, it will be necessary for the workplace, along with its influ-

ence on the managed care health delivery system, to address the treatment needs of older workers if it wants to maximize the efficiency of health care costs spending, and if it wants to retain older workers as employees.

Primary care and specialty care health providers. Older persons have more contact with primary care physicians than any other health care providers ("Treating Elderly Patients: Primary vs. Specialized Care," 2000). Because many older adults are concerned about their health and receive health care regularly, this setting is ideal for such screening—especially since many of their health problems may be substance related. For instance, a study by Adams (2002) found that Medicare is billed for alcohol-related hospitalizations among elderly patients as commonly as for acute myocardial infarction. On the other hand, mental health and substance abuse problems are not likely to be identified during routine office visits because the focus is typically on the presenting medical issue, not necessarily issues of substance use that may have caused or exacerbate those medical conditions. Furthermore, office visits have become increasingly short, and many providers are not trained to screen for such disorders ("Treating Elderly Patients: Primary vs. Specialized Care," 2000).

On the horizon is the growth of programs such as the Older Adult Substance Abuse Program of the Broward County (Florida) Elderly and Veterans Services Division. Multiple levels of care are targeted to persons age 55 and older, including a substance abuse prevention curriculum, outpatient services (both individual and group), and aftercare (S. Ferrante, personal communication, June 6, 2004). Brief screening, intervention, and treatment for a variety of conditions (alcohol abuse, medication misuse, illicit drug use, depression, anxiety, and suicide risk) was initiated in 2004 in collaboration with aging and health care providers. In addition, a pilot project on compulsive gambling among older adults is in process, in partnership with the Florida Council on Compulsive Gambling; gambling as an addiction among older adults is a growing concern and can be linked with alcoholism.

Assessment and Treatment

Assessment of the elderly presents special challenges because of their life stage circumstances, which may put them at risk of developing depression, anxiety, and substance abuse problems. While transitions such as retirement and widowhood may offer explanations for abusing substances, this should not minimize the need for treatment. Quite the contrary, they need to be considered in developing a treatment plan.

The treatment for substance use disorders for the elderly depends on a variety of variables. For instance, studies of managed care organizations (MCOs) (Garnick et al., 2002; Lish et al., 1995) found that few MCOs require alcohol, other drug, or mental health screening by primary care physicians, and that despite the availability of effective treatments, most individuals who had cooccurring mental health and substance use disorders were not receiving effective treatment. These studies noted the need for more systematic screening and more of a focus on strategies that increase the delivery of effective treatment. This is especially important, since treatment is no longer a monolithic modality that takes place in a substance abuse–specific setting.

A nationwide study funded by the Substance Abuse and Mental Health Services Administration (SAMHSA) (2000) that started in 1998 was designed to answer the question: Do older people with mental health and substance abuse problems do better when they receive treatment for these disorders within a primary care setting or when they receive referrals for specialized treatment? This study found that minor mental health problems and patients with mobility problems may be more responsive in a primary care setting. On the other hand, the study found that some patients require the more intensive services of specialized settings.

In recent years, treatment modalities attempt to address the needs of and differences among subgroups. For instance, gender-specific treatment takes into account the unique needs of women. Similarly, there are attempts to identify and address the needs of "elder-specific" or "age-specific" treatment (CSAT, 1998). In these programs, older patients as a group are in a specialized treatment setting that is entirely age specific, or they may be involved in age-specific treatment groups within a mixed-age mainstream treatment program. The results of effectiveness are mixed. In general, it has been found that older patients do just as well as younger patients in age-integrated programs (Blow, 2000).

It appears that as with all patients, treatment outcomes are most effective when the multiple and unique needs of patients are considered. However, substance abuse treatment providers must have knowledge of the age-specific needs of older adult patients and their circumstances, in general, as well as an assessment and understanding of the unique needs

and circumstances of each patient. Such treatment must also include building support for persons at risk using community-based treatment and referral, with long-term follow-up and services to pertinent family members and significant others. Although they are beyond the scope of this chapter, there are additional considerations in working with persons who abuse or are addicted to multiple substances and in addressing those persons who may also have a psychiatric history. Access to care and follow-up for those with multiple treatment needs is often inadequate and sometimes inappropriately provided.

While it is beyond the scope of this chapter, there are several components in the continuum of approaches that are essential in addressing the growing issues related to substance use disorders in older adults. First, *prevention* is key. Throughout the various networks where older adults are involved (see Corley, Takamura, & Siegel, 2004), there are opportunities to highlight some of the important problems that can arise from misuse/abuse of alcohol and other drugs. *Intervention* is critical in breaking through the denial when an older adult is identified by family members, coworkers, and/or others who are compelled to find pathways to help, yet this is understudied and often ends up happening as a result of an emergency room visit or other crisis. *Relapse prevention* is an additional element of the continuum receiving continued attention (e.g., Barrick & Connors, 2002; Corley, Lawton, & Gray, in press) and is important in promoting the overall well-being impaired older adults.

CONCLUSION

In spite of the growing numbers of older adults in the United States, and a more prominent history of substance use disorders in their incoming cohorts, service delivery systems and their providers are not well equipped to address the needs of older adults with substance dependence disorders. On the national level, SAMHSA has made available a comprehensive "Toolkit" (Michaud, 2004), and older adults with substance use disorders are considered to be a priority population. The National Association of Social Workers' special section Alcohol, Tobacco and Other Drugs (ATOD) was initiated by a group of SAMSHA-funded faculty fellows in the 1990s, some of whom addressed issues of older adults in bringing more substance abuse content into the social work curriculum. The American Society on Aging (2005) offers a series of seven modules that are user friendly and informative, in a free Web-based training, *Alcohol, Medication and Other Drugs*. These are promising approaches to broaden awareness and increase knowledge of substance abuse/dependence among social workers serving older adults.

Although most health education programs focus on younger drinkers, older adults are receptive to health promotion programs that present alcohol information tailored to their social contexts and specific health issues (Fink, Beck, & Wittrock, 2001). An approach that incorporates motivational strategies "that draw on motivational interviewing principles and a client's motivational readiness to change" (Hanson & Gutheil, 2004, p. 364) is an example of how social workers can incorporate essential skills in identification of older adults with substance abuse/dependence and help them to get into, and stay in, treatment.

Networks and services for older adults with substance dependency reflect the larger challenges of the lack of continuity of care in the field of aging at large (Corley, Takamura, & Siegel, 2004). In the case of substance abuse, the flow of services is complex, including: screening, assessment, intervention, treatment, relapse prevention, and support for long-term recovery (see Corley et al., in press). Since older adults in any kind of treatment setting are most likely to present with medical issues, the social, financial, legal, and spiritual challenges that bring younger persons into treatment settings for substance abuse are less likely to be recognized. It is often family members who bring their older relatives into treatment, again, more typically when a health crisis is the precipitating event, and family members may not recognize or want to admit the role that alcohol and other drugs (prescription or otherwise) may play in the larger picture. Social workers are well poised to serve as liaisons with other health care providers, particularly as they are noted for their expertise on the interdisciplinary team in assisting older adults and their families when transitioning across levels of care (Damron-Rodriguez & Corley, 2002).

It is imperative for social workers in all settings to be familiar with the signs and symptoms of substance use disorders, the complexities of assessment and diagnosis given the variations of presentation in older adults, and the critical need to provide appropriate services to older adults and their families across the continuum of care. Promoting research on the prevalence and cooccurring disorders among the nation's older adults who are increasing in number and diversity is imperative. In the larger picture, social workers must be part of research teams where gaps in data on the prevalence of substance use disorders can be examined, and where evidence-based practice can be identified to increase the availability and accessibility of services along the continuum of care tailored to the growing and diverse needs of older adults.

REFERENCES

Adams, W. L. (2002). The effects of alcohol on medical illnesses and medication interactions. In A. M. Gurnack, R. Atkinson, & N. J. Osgood, (Eds.), *Treating alcohol and drug abuse in the elderly* (pp. 32–49). New York: Springer.

Adams, W. L., Yuan, Z., Barboriak, J. J., & Rimm, A. A. (1993). Alcohol-related hospitalizations of elderly people: Prevalence and geographic variations in the United States. *Journal of the American Medical Association, 270*, 1222–1225.

American Psychiatric Association. (1980). *Diagnostic and statistical manual of mental disorders* (3rd ed.). Washington, DC: Author.

American Psychiatric Association, (1994). *Diagnostic and statistical manual of mental disorders.* (4th ed.). Washington, DC: Author.

American Society on Aging. (2005). *Alcohol, Medication and Other Drugs.* Available: *www.asaging.org/aod/webtraining.cfm.*

Anthony, J. C., & Helzer, J. E. (1991). Syndromes of drug abuse and dependence. In L. N. Robins & D. A. Regier (Eds.), *Psychiatric disorders in America: The Epidemiological Catchment Area Study* (pp. 116–154). New York: Free Press.

Atkinson, R. M., Ryan, S. C., & Turner, J. A. (2001). Variation among aging alcoholic patients in treatment. *American Journal of Geriatric Psychiatry, 9*(3), 275–282.

Atkinson, R. M., Turner, J. A., Kofoed, L. L., & Tolson, R. L. (1985). Early versus late onset alcoholism in older persons: Preliminary findings. *Alcoholism: Clinical & Experimental Research, 9*, 513–515.

Barrick, C., & Connors, G. (2002). Relapse prevention and maintaining abstinence in older adults with alcohol-use disorders. *Drugs and Aging, 19*(8), 583–594.

Bartels, S. J. (2003). Improving the system of care for older adults with mental illness in the United States: Findings and recommendations for the President's New Freedom Commission on Mental Health. *American Journal of Geriatric Psychiatry, 11*, 486–497.

Blow, F. C. (1998). *Substance abuse among older adults* (Treatment Improvement Protocol [TIP] Series 26).

Rockville, MD: Substance Abuse and Mental Health Services Administration.

Center for Substance Abuse Treatment. (1998). *Substance abuse among older adults.* (DHHS Publication No. SMA 98-3179, Treatment Improvement Protocal [TIP] Series 26). Rockville, MD.

Coogle, C. L., Osgood, N. J., & Parham, I. A. (2000). A statewide model detection and prevention program for geriatric alcoholism and alcohol abuse: Increased knowledge among service providers. *Community Mental Health Journal, 36,* 137–148.

Corley, C. S., Lawton, M., & Gray, M. (in press). Substance use disorders. In M. Eisenberg, R. Glueckauf, & H. Zaretsky (Eds.). *Medical aspects of disability: A handbook for the rehabilitation professionals* (3rd ed., pp. 675–693). New York: Springer.

Corley, C. S., Takamura, J., & Siegel, E. (2004). Supervision in older adult services. In Austin, M. J., & Hopkins, K. M. (Eds.). *Supervisory practice in the human services: The learning organization perspective* (pp. 283–293). Thousand Oaks, CA: Sage.

Cummings, S., & Bride, B. (in press). Alcohol abuse treatment for older adults: A review of recent empirical research. *Journal of Evidence-Based Social Work Practice.*

Damron-Rodriguez, J., & Corley, C. (2002). Social work education for interdisciplinary practice with older adults and their families. *Journal of Gerontological Social Work, 39,* 37–55.

Egbert, A. M. (1993). The older alcoholic: Recognizing the subtle clinical cues. *Geriatrics, 48*(7), 63–66, 69.

Eliason, M. J., & Skinstad, A. H. (2001). Drug and alcohol intervention for older women: A pilot study. *Journal of Gerontological Nursing, 27*(12), 18–24.

Fingerhood, M. (2000). Substance abuse in older people. *Journal of the American Geriatrics Society, 48,* 985–995.

Fink, A., Beck, J. C., & Wittrock, M. C. (2001). Informing older adults about nonhazardous, hazardous, and harmful alcohol use. *Patient Education and Counseling, 45,* 133–141.

Fink, A., Hays, R., Moore, A., & Beck, J. (1996). Alcohol-related problems in older persons: Determinants, consequences and screening. *Archives of Internal Medicine, 156,* 1150–1156.

Finlayson, R. E., & Davis, L. J. (1994). Prescription drug dependence in the elderly population: Demographic and clinical features of 100 inpatients. *Mayo Clinic Proceedings, 69,* 1137–1145.

Finlayson, R. E., Hurt, R. D., Davis, L. J., & Morse, R. M. (1988). Alcoholism in elderly persons: A study of the psychiatric and psychosocial features of 216 inpatients. *Mayo Clinic Proceedings, 63,* 761–768.

Garnick, D. W., Horgan, C. M., Merrick, E. L., Hodgkin, D., Faulkner, D., & Bryson, S. (2002). Managed care plans requirements for screening for alcohol, drug, and mental health problems in primary care. *American Journal of Managed Care, 8*(10), 879–888.

Gonyea, J., Hudson, R., & Curley, A. (2004, Spring). The geriatric social work labor force: Challenges and opportunities in responding to an aging society. *Institute for Geriatric Social Work Issue Brief,* 1–8.

Graham, K., & Schmidt, G. (1998). The effects of drinking on the health of older adults. *American Journal of Drug and Alcohol Abuse, 24*(3), 465–481.

Grant, B. F., Dawson, D. A., Stinson, F. S., Chou, S. P., Dufour, M. C., & Pickering, R. P. (2004). The 12-month prevalence and trends in DSM-IV alcohol abuse and dependence: United States, 1991–1992 and 2001–2002. *Drug and Alcohol Dependence, 74,* 223–234.

Hansen, M., & Gutheil, I. (2004). Motivational strategies with alcohol-involved older adults: Implications for social work practice. *Social Work, 49,* 364–372.

Helzer, J. E., Burnam, A., & McEvoy, L. T. (1991). Alcohol abuse and dependence. In L. N. Robins & J. E. Helzer (Eds.), *Psychiatric disorders in America: The Epidemiological Catchment Area Study* (pp. 81–115). New York: Free Press.

Hemmelgarn, B., Suissa, S., Huang, A., Boivin, J. F., & Pinard, G. Benzodiazepine use and the risk of motor vehicle crash in the elderly. *Journal of the American Medical Association, 278,* 27–31.

Hybels, C. F., & Blazer, D. G. (2002). Epidemiology and geriatric psychiatry. In M. T. Tsuang & M. Tohen (Eds.), *Textbook in psychiatric epidemiology* (2nd ed., pp. 603–628). New York: Wiley.

Klein, S., & Iber, F. L. (1991). Alcoholism and associated malnutrition in the elderly. *Nutrition, 7*(2), 75–79.

Lakhani, N. (1997). Alcohol use amongst community-dwelling elderly people: A review of the literature. *Journal of Advanced Nursing, 25,* 1227–1232.

Lish, J. D., Zimmerma, M., Farber, N. J., Lush, D., Kuzma, M. A., & Plescia, G. (1995). Psychiatric screening in geriatric primary care: Should it be for depression alone? *Journal of Geriatric Psychiatry and Neurology, 3,* 141–153.

Lynskey, M. T., Day, C., & Hall, W. (2003). Alcohol and other drug use disorders among older-aged people. *Drug and Alcohol Review, 22,* 125–133.

McCracken, A. L. (1998). Aging and alcohol. *Journal of Gerontological Nursing, 24*(4), 37–43.

McGinnis-Dittrich, K. (2002). *Social work with elders: A biopsychosocial approach to assessment and intervention.* Boston: Allyn and Bacon.

Michaud, S. (2004, May/June). Kit links service providers to resources for older adults. *SAMHSA News, 12*(3), 1.

Moore, A., Morton, S. C., Beck, J. C., Hays, R. D., Oishi, S. M., & Partridge, J. M. (1999). A new paradigm for alcohol use in older persons. *Medical Care, 37,* 165–179.

Neutel, C. I., Hirdes, J. P., Maxwell, C. J., & Patten, S. B. (1996). New evidence on benzodiazepine use and falls: The time factor. *Age and Ageing, 25,* 273–278.

Ried, L. D., Johnson, R. E., & Gettman, D. A. (1998). Benzodiazepine exposure and functional status in older people. *Journal of the American Geriatrics Society, 46,* 71–76.

Robins, L. N., & Regier, D. A. (Eds.). (1991). *Psychiatric disorders in America: The Epidemiological Catchment Area Study.* New York: Free Press.

Scott, C. M., & Popovich, D. J. (2001). Undiagnosed alcoholism and prescription drug misuse among the elderly: Special considerations for home assessment. *Caring, 20*(1), 20–23.

Substance Abuse and Mental Health Services Administration. (2001). *Summary of findings from the 2000 National Household Survey on Drug Abuse.* Available: *www.DrugAbuseStatistics.samhsa.gov.*

Toolkit. (2004, May/June). *SAMHSA News, 12*(3), Treating elderly patients: Primary vs. specialized care. (2000, Summer). *SAMHSA News, 8*(3), 1.

U.S. Centers for Disease Control and Prevention. (1999). Suicide deaths and rates per 100,000. Available: *www/cpc.gov/ncipc/data/us9794/suic.html.*

Whelan, G. (2003). A much neglected risk factor in elderly mental disorders. *Current Opinion in Psychiatry, 16*(6), 609–614.

AMANDA BARUSCH,
SECTION EDITOR

SECTION

Social Service Resources Available Through Community Settings

OVERVIEW

In this section, our focus shifts from community settings to the services provided in those settings. As in the previous section, each chapter examines the legal basis of social work practice, as well as the population served and the roles filled by social work professionals. Culturally relevant practice is a recurring theme.

With the growth of the older population has come increased demand for case management or care management services. Matthias Naleppa offers a detailed look at case management as a venue for social work practice. He discusses the national demonstration projects that have served as the proving grounds for case managers and then highlights the tension over who "owns" case management. The chapter then turns to a description of this practice modality and the services typically accessed by a professional care manager.

Leah Ruffin and Lenard Kaye examine the role of counseling services and support groups in helping the elderly maintain active and engaged lives. This chapter offers a careful description of both treatment groups and support groups, highlighting the positive philosophy that is reflected in these interventions.

Sandra Crewe and Sandra Cipungu describe services designed to support those who care for older adults. Their chapter reviews the social and demographic trends affecting caregiving, which is described primarily as a family matter. It then offers a profile of family caregivers and examines the special concerns of minority and immigrant groups in the United States. It closes with a valuable discussion of the programmatic resources now in place to support family caregivers.

Jordan Kosberg, Max Rothman, and Burton Dunlop consider services that provide advocacy and protection to older adults, including the ombudsman program, adult protective services, and services provided in legal settings. Their chapter highlights the numerous opportunities for social workers to serve as advocates for older adults, both within and outside their formal job responsibilities, and argues that these opportunities will increase in coming decades.

Judith Gonyea describes housing services available for older adults, noting that shelter is a basic need and describing the programs designed to meet that need. The chapter notes the role of income disparities in determining the housing options available to seniors and uses the concept of "environmental press" to argue that "goodness of fit" is an appropriate yardstick for determining the quality of a housing setting for adults with disabilities. She places the profession of social work squarely in the middle of housing decisions, arguing that our assessment skills and commitment to serving vulnerable populations leave us well positioned to improve the way the nation's seniors are housed.

Bradley Zodikoff offers an overview of services for lesbian, gay, bisexual, and transgender (LGBT) older adults. He examines broad considerations, such as the difficulty in providing an accurate description of this population and the special concerns of LGBT older adults. The chapter then describes available services throughout the country and offers practice guidelines for social workers serving this group.

Charles Emlet and Cynthia Poindexter consider social work practice in settings that serve HIV-infected "or affected" older adults. In an eye-opening discussion, these authors describe the growing number of older Americans who are experiencing HIV/AIDS and the system of care that minimally addresses their needs. This system is authorized under the Ryan White CARE Act, the Older Americans Act, and home- and community-based Medicaid waivers. These authors call for improved coordination between the aging and HIV service organizations, even while noting that it is unclear how this is to be achieved.

Once again, these chapters reflect the diversity of social work roles and emerging opportunities for our profession. As our nation prepares to meet the challenge of an aging population, the traditional tools of social work practice should serve us in good stead. Social work professionals bring a unique perspective to assessment of human needs and a commitment to social justice that is sorely needed in today's market-driven environment.

Case management, also referred to as care coordination or service management, is a process commonly characterized by a series of activities undertaken to address a client's lack of resources and required services. This section will provide some basic information on case management, primarily focusing on services frequently accessed and coordinated by geriatric case managers working with older adults in community settings.

MODELS OF CASE MANAGEMENT

Case management can be defined as a

> method of providing services whereby a professional . . . assesses the needs of the client and the client's family, when appropriate, and arranges, coordinates, monitors, evaluates and advocates for a package of multiple services to meet the client's complex needs. . . . Case management is both micro and macro in nature; intervention occurs at both the client and system level. (National Association of Social Workers [NASW], 1992, p. 5)

Case management consists of a series of activities that a case manager undertakes together with clients and, in many cases, their caregivers. Core functions of geriatric case management typically include access to the case management program, screening, a thorough multidimensional needs assessment, the development and coordination of a care plan, access and linkage to the required resources, monitoring of the services coordinated, and a regular reassessment (Austin, 2001; Austin & McClelland, 1996; Rothman, 1994). Additional case management tasks often include resource indexing, interagency coordination, advocacy, and collection of data on practice outcomes (Naleppa & Reid, 2003; Rothman, 1994). Clinical case management should be considered a key intervention approach in gerontological social work (Morrow-Howell, 1992).

An extensive range of geriatric case management models exists and has been tested and evaluated during the last three decades. In her comparative analysis of community-based case management models, Hyduk (2002) classifies programs into service provider–initiated models and demonstration models. Examples of service provider–initiated models include health maintenance organization (HMO) case management, community-based long-term care (CBLTC), outpatient geriatric evaluation and man-

MATTHIAS J. NALEPPA

Case Management Services

agement (GEM), postacute case management, and physician practice case management (Hyduk, 2002).

Demonstration projects were created as a response to problems in the service delivery system that included structural fragmentation, duplication and discontinuity of services, and lack of integrating mechanisms. Single-service responses (e.g., acute medical care, skilled nursing facilities, or home health services) alone could not solve the growing problem, which led to the development of several system alternatives of structural integration (merging funding and services into a single system) and service integration (referral systems, care coordination, and case management). A waiver program established through the Omnibus Budget Reconciliation Act of 1981 made it possible to combine health care, personal care, and case management costs (Quinn, 1993). Examples of waiver demonstration projects include the On Lok project in San Francisco and its successor projects (i.e., the Program of All Inclusive Care for the Elderly [PACE]), the Multi-purpose Senior Services Project (MSSP) in California, and the Nursing Home Without Walls project in New York state. Another set of demonstration projects, the National Long-Term Care "Channeling" Demonstrations, were started in 1980 by the federal government in an effort to direct services to elderly persons who were considered at high risk for entering a nursing home. Two types of channeling projects were implemented. In the basic channeling model, case managers were considered brokers of services, that is, their primary responsibility was to assist elderly clients to access and coordinate services. The financial channeling model, on the other hand, applied pooled funding and financial caps (Applebaum & Austin, 1990).

Another demonstration project, called the Social Health Maintenance Organization (S/HMO), began in the mid-1980s. These organizations were created through the Deficit Reduction Act of 1984 (Applebaum & Austin, 1990; Quinn, 1993). Differing from many other demonstration projects, the S/HMOs incorporated acute and long-term care and covered elderly clients with all levels of functioning (Abrahams, Capitman, Leutz, & Macko, 1989). All of the demonstration projects incorporated some form of case management (Applebaum & Austin, 1990; Zawadski, 1984).

PROFESSIONAL ORIENTATION AND ROLES OF CASE MANAGERS

While there has been some debate between the social work and nursing professions in the past over the "ownership" of case management, social work, nursing, and other health care workers are the primary professional reference groups of case managers. Most geriatric case managers today are either licensed social workers or nurses; however, licenses are currently not required in all states (American Association of Retired Persons [AARP], 2005). The educational level of geriatric case managers ranges from no degree to doctoral degree. This variation has an impact of the array and quality of tasks that are performed. For example, nonprofessionals are not suitable to carry out certain case management activities, such as clinical counseling or direct care tasks, and concern exists whether even bachelor's level education is adequate to carry out the range of responsibilities with sufficient expertise (Schmid & Hasenfeld, 1993). Research by the American Association of Retired Persons (AARP, 2005) found that the professional reference group can impact on the types of tasks performed by a case manager. The social work case managers were found to be more likely than nurse case managers to include family counseling (84% vs. 58%), while they were less likely to assess clients' health status (62% vs. 94%).

A survey of the members of the National Association of Professional Geriatric Care Managers (NAPGCM) indicates that approximately two-thirds of geriatric case managers hold a master's degree (AARP, 2005). The two largest professional groups providing geriatric case management were licensed social workers (37%) and licensed nurses (30%). Several credentials and certifications are available for geriatric case managers (AARP, 2005). The National Academy of Certified Case Managers (NACCM) confers the care manager certified (CMC) credential, and the Commission of Case Management Certification (CCMC) offers the certified case manager (CCM) credential. Both require a postsecondary degree in a field related to the practice requirements, as well as certain additional prerequisites. The National Association of Social Workers (NASW) offers two case management credentials. A certified social work case manager (C-SWCM) credential requires a BSW degree, a minimum of 1 year and 1,500 hours of supervised practice experience, and a state-level BSW-level license, or passing of the Association of Social Work Boards (ASWB) basic exam (NASW, 2005b). The certified advanced social work case manager (C-ASWCM) credential calls for, among other requirements, an MSW degree from an accredited social work program, 1 year and 1,500 hours of supervised post-MSW practice experience, a state social work license, or the NASW credentials of the Academy of

Certified Social Workers (ACSW) or a Diplomate in Clinical Social Work (DCSW) (NASW, 2005b).

The roles of case managers and the models of staffing can vary considerably. The most basic case management staffing option is the individual generalist case manager, that is, the same professional carrying out the complete set of functions from intake through service coordination and monitoring, with a high degree of authority. The benefit is that the client has one practitioner to relate to. A second common approach is the multidisciplinary case management team approach, which combines professional expertise from various disciplines. Frequently the multidisciplinary team takes over some case management functions, such as assessment, while linkage and coordination is carried out by one team member. Comprehensive service centers that provide and coordinate a range of services under one roof could be considered a third approach. Examples of this approach can be found in the On Lok program and its PACE replication sites (Kane, Illston, & Miller, 1992).

The survey by the AARP assessed the services that geriatric care managers directly provide to their clients. The most common services include: finding services for clients (95%), arranging services (94%), family and social support assessment (94%), functional assessment (90%), health status assessment (73%) development of care plans (93%), and management of care plan (90%). Family counseling services were included in the service mix of 70% of the respondents (AARP, 2005).

FINDING A CASE MANAGER

Case managers typically work for nonprofit service providers, private case management agencies, or as self-employed private geriatric case managers. Common nonprofit agencies providing case management include local Area Agencies on Aging, home health care providers, hospitals, senior or family service agencies, and other human services providers such as the Veterans Administration. Private case management agencies and private geriatric case managers provide their services for a fee, while fees for nonprofit providers range from free to integrated with other service delivery costs and fee-for-service.

Case mangers and referrals for case management or care coordination programs can be found through local Area Agencies on Aging, hospitals and health care providers, senior centers, HMOs, and Medicaid offices. Several online services are available to assist in locating case managers and case management resources, for example, the Web sites of the eldercare locator (*www.eldercare.gov*), Family Care America (*www.familycareamerica*), the Area Agencies on Aging (AAAs; *www.n4a.org*), and the National Association of Professional Geriatric Care Managers (NAPGCM; *www.caremanager.org*). The NAPGCM Web site also includes a useful guide for elderly clients and their caregivers on how to select and interview geriatric case managers.

COMMON SERVICES IN CASE MANAGEMENT

Many services available to elderly clients residing in the community are created, authorized, and funded through the Older Americans Act (OAA). First enacted in 1965 and signed into law by President Lyndon B. Johnson, the OAA has been amended several times since, most recently in 2000. Some, but not all, of the services coordinated by case managers and presented in this chapter are funded directly or indirectly through the mandates of the OAA. The remainder of this chapter will focus on such services, addressing the areas of personal care, homemaker and chore services, transportation, personal emergency response systems, information and referral programs, financial assistance, and nutrition programs.

PERSONAL CARE SERVICES

According to the U.S. Census Bureau (2000), approximately 14% of the elderly population living in the community have problems with performing activities of daily living (ADLs), and 21% have difficulties with instrumental activities of daily living (IADLs). Moreover, approximately every third person above 75 years and every second person above 85 years of age has one or more disabilities. Consequently, a great need exists for services that assist elderly individuals who are residing in the community with home and personal care tasks.

An older adult's need for assistance with personal care can range from light household chores to specialized personal care. Professional and trained nonprofessional workers are involved in the delivery of personal care. *Homemakers* assist with household chores, cleaning, laundry, errands, and shopping (see also the following section). They do not provide any health care–related services. A *personal care aide (companion)* will assist with household chores, personal care, and ambulating. The *home health aide* may assist with household chores but can also provide personal care, medication management, and monitoring of medical status. *Licensed practitioner nurses* (LPNs) *and registered nurses* (RNs) monitor vital signs, dispense medication, and provide wound care and other skilled nursing services.

CHORE SERVICES AND HOMEMAKER SERVICES

It is common for elderly clients to need home maintenance, particularly light and heavy housecleaning. Problems with heavy housecleaning, especially, are frequently encountered with clients who are otherwise independent enough to continue living on their own. Several approaches can be taken to address this need. Informal support systems, such as family members or local community groups, are often available and willing to help with both light and heavy housecleaning. Professional cleaning services, some specializing in housecleaning for elderly persons, may also be available. Case manager tasks include reviewing informal support systems for possible help with housecleaning, trying to enlist help from family, friends, or members of the local community, and educating clients about formal service options for housecleaning.

Chore and *homemaker services* are generally offered by religious groups, nonprofit agencies, and private agencies and usually require a fee for service, but on a sliding scale. Chore services typically provide assistance with heavy housework, such as snow shoveling, lawn mowing, and small home repairs, while homemaker services help with light housework, such as laundry, cleaning, and sometimes cooking.

Elderly clients are often unable to carry out parts of regular maintenance or required repairs, which can lead to safety problems and deteriorating conditions that may lead to the condemnation of the house. Common reasons for not undertaking needed maintenance include high costs, inability to repair due to poor health, and not knowing how to undertake repairs. Not only low-income but also middle-income elderly often require assistance. Types of formal assistance with repairs include neighborhood conservation programs, emergency repair programs, repair and maintenance programs, and weatherization. However, many smaller repair and maintenance jobs may be undertaken by local private businesses.

TRANSPORTATION AND ESCORT SERVICES

Transportation and *escort services* encompass a wide variety of service options that aim at increasing the mobility of older adults living in the community. Transit services range from the regular bus or train system to specialized senior transportation. The most common transportation service options include regular bus service (fixed-route system), deviated route systems, paratransit or demand-responsive systems, incidental transit, and escort services (U.S. Department of Transportation, 1997).

Funding and legal authority for transportation services are provided through the mechanisms of a wide variety of laws and regulations. The Social Security Act, Title 19 (Medicaid) regulates the transportation of low-income elderly persons to and from medical appointments. The OAA, Title 3, provides funding for transportation to senior centers, congregate meals sites, and medical appointments. Title 3 of the Intermodal Surface Transportation Efficiency Act of 1991, also called the Federal Transit Act, mandates reduced off-peak fares for elderly riders and provides capital purchase assistance for operators transporting elderly and disabled riders. The most important legislation impacting the transportation of older adults, however, is probably the Americans with Disability Act of 1990 (ADA), providing protection from discrimination against persons with disabilities, including elderly persons with a disability. The ADA mandates, for example, that all new buses must be wheelchair accessible. Fixed route systems are must be offered to persons with disabilities who are unable to use the regular bus system by providing a comparable paratransit system.

In a *fixed-route system,* public transportation or traditional transit services follow a predetermined route and schedule. The *deviated-route system* describes a transit system that generally follows a fixed route but will deviate from this route if a qualified rider requests it.

Paratransit describes transportation services that use smaller buses and vans and provide transportation to older adults and persons with disabilities. Usually they follow a *demand-responsive* approach, that is, a rider makes a request for transportation by phone and is either picked up in front of the home (curbside or at the door) or, in some cases, inside the home. Some demand-responsive systems require an advance request up to a day ahead of time, while others respond in an immediate time frame.

Incidental transit describes the transportation services provided by social service agencies to their clients, such as an adult daycare center that operates a van to transport its clients to and from the program site.

Escort and errand services are usually offered through private and nonprofit providers. In addition to personal transportation, they often provide other services as well, such as accompanied walks, companionship, and light housekeeping.

PERSONAL EMERGENCY RESPONSE SYSTEMS

Personal emergency response systems (PERSs) are devices that can be activated and send a signal to an emergency contact if a person is in distress. A trained professional answers the distress call immediately, usually over a speaker system integrated into the transponder unit in the home. The responder assesses the situation and activates the appropriate emergency response. If there is no response by the elderly person, an emergency response team is dispatched to the person's home. Two types of PERS are common, a push button worn around the neck or wrist or a push-button or pull-cord device placed on the wall, usually in the bedroom or bathroom. A variety of private providers offer PERSs. Some providers integrate the service with medication management.

Two additional procedures can provide added security to older adults living at home or in assisted living. Telephone reassurance is a procedure in which a volunteer makes a daily phone call at a predetermined time to ensure that the elderly person is well. In case the person does not respond, a call is made to an emergency contact. A so-called vial-of-life can provide vital information about the person to the emergency responders. A sticker is positioned at a place that will be seen by an emergency response professional when entering the home, alerting him or her to the fact that a small vial with vital information such as blood type, chronic health problems, and medications used can be found inside the refrigerator.

INFORMATION AND REFERRAL

In 1965, in an effort to improve the knowledge of resources available to older adults living in the community, a mandate by the OAA, funded through OAA, Title 3-B, created information and referral (I & R) services. The goals of these services can be summarized as follows: offering up-to-date information on local services for older adults; providing information on assistive technology; assessment and linkage to appropriate services; monitoring service delivery; and a focus on all older persons living in the community (Wacker, Roberto, & Piper, 2002).

Local AAAs implement and coordinate I & R services in different ways, with some offering the services themselves and others contracting with outside providers. Some communities house their I & R efforts in public libraries or government institutions. In other communities, I & R services are provided through private or nonprofit organizations.

Two I & R efforts on the national level are the 2-1-1 Initiative and the Eldercare Locator. The 2-1-1 initiative, modeled after the 9-1-1 emergency phone number, is a program with the goal of making information and referral data on health and human services available to callers on an around-the-clock basis (Wacker et al., 2002). The Eldercare Locator is a program jointly sponsored by the Administration on Aging, the Area Agencies on Aging, and the State Units on Aging. Using the Eldercare Locator, a caller can easily obtain information about services in his or her community by providing the ZIP code and type of need for which services are requested.

FINANCIAL MANAGEMENT AND LEGAL ASSISTANCE

Daily money management is a service that assists older persons in managing their finances and coordinating other paperwork. Daily money managers (DMMs) help with balancing checkbooks, paying bills, reconciling medical statements, and organizing personal records and files. They ensure that bills are paid in a timely fashion and intervene on their client's behalf in Medicare and health insurance matters. Some DMMs also provide accounting and income tax preparation, as well as relocation management. These managers charge on a fee-for-service basis, usually $40–80 per hour, and should be bonded and insured.

Eldercare attorneys are licensed attorneys who specialize in legal services for older adults. On a fee-for-service basis, they assist elderly clients and their families with estate planning, preparing wills and trusts, establishing a durable power of attorney and advance health care directives, long-term care planning, guardianship, and Medicare and Medicaid issues. The American Bar Association provides several useful programs for elderly persons, such as lawyer referral and information services and volunteer lawyer panels (see also chapter 48 here).

NUTRITION PROGRAMS

Nutrition programs for older adults include nutritional screening, home-delivered meals and meals-on-wheels, food stamps, congregate meals, emergency food services, and food banks, as well as shopping assistance programs and grocery delivery. The goal of these nutrition programs is to provide older adults with a healthy diet and to prevent malnutrition and inadequate food intake. Several of the nutrition programs are administered through the OAA (originally OAA, Title 4, and now OAA, Title 3).

Wacker, Roberto, and Piper (2002) summarize factors that affect the nutritional status in elderly persons as physical (e.g., cognitive status, chronic and acute illness, oral and dental health problems, medication usage, digestive system) and psychosocial (economic status, ethnicity, social supports, access to nutrition programs, advanced age). Moreover, age-related changes to taste and smell may impact food intake.

The *National Nutrition Screening Initiative* is a program offered by organizations such as the American Academy of Family Physicians, the American Dietetic Association, and the National Council on the Aging to improve the nutritional status of older adults (Wacker et al., 2002). A key element of this initiative is the development of a 10-item screening tool called DETERMINE, that assesses the risk of nutritional deficiencies. The screening instrument is widely used by nutritional programs and by health care professionals working with older adults. Nutrition programs that receive funding through the OAA require a nutritional screening, and certain nutritional standards apply. For example, hot meals offered at congregate meals sites and through home-delivered meals programs should provide at least one-third of the recommended daily nutritional allowance for adults.

The OAA, Title III, established the *Elderly Nutrition Program,* and it provides funding for congregate nutrition services and home-delivered meals. *Congregate meals* programs funded through the OAA provide one hot meal per day for at least 5 days a week. Only a few congregate meals sites offer breakfast or dinner. Congregate meals programs can be found in a range of community settings such as senior centers and churches. Many congregate meals sites provide nutritional screening, information, and education, and other community-based long-term care services.

They also serve an important social function for their visitors.

Meals-on-wheels and *home-delivered meals programs* are offered by community, county, and nonprofit providers. They are targeted at older adults who cannot prepare meals themselves and are not able to visit a congregate meals site. Home-delivered meals programs receiving funding through the OAA; they must provide the delivery of at least one meal per day to the person's home for at least 5 days a week. According to Wacker, Roberto, and Piper (2002), the costs of these meals are covered by a little over one-third through OAA funding and about two-thirds through other funding such as local, state, and federal sources and private donations. Volunteers deliver meals to the elderly person's home. Home-delivered meals programs usually ask for a donation and have a sliding fee scale.

Food stamps are an income-based nutrition program available to low-income older adults. The aim of food stamps is to reduce malnutrition among all low-income populations. Any person receiving Supplemental Security Income benefits also qualifies for food stamps. Food stamps can be used in regular grocery stores, and, with the exception of some items, the person can decide what to purchase with them.

Emergency food services and *food banks* are also targeted toward low-income populations. Food banks receive food donations from a variety of sources and distribute them to those in need, including older adults. The Emergency Food Assistance Program (TEFAP) and the Commodity Supplemental Food Program (CSFP) are administered by the Department of Agriculture's Food and Nutrition Service. Both programs provide low-income persons with basic food items such as butter, flour, cereal, rice, and vegetables at no cost.

Shopping assistance programs and *grocery delivery* aim to help older adults who are living independently but lack transportation or have mobility problems. A variety of shopping assistance programs have been established by communities, volunteer organizations, and similar groups. In most programs, a volunteer escorts the older adult to the store, assists with shopping, and then accompanies his or her home. A growing number of grocery stores also provide grocery delivery. Usually the elderly person calls in hir or her order or orders online, and the groceries are delivered the same day by a volunteer. Some grocery stores offer grocery delivery to all customers for a fee.

This chapter focused on a brief overview of some of the primary services coordinated through geriatric case management. Additional information on some of these programs can be found in chapters in this section.

REFERENCES

Abrahams, R., Capitman, J., Leutz, W., & Macko, P. (1989). Variations in care planning practice in the Social/HMO: An exploratory study. *Gerontologist, 29,* 725–736.

American Association of Retired Persons. (2005). *Geriatric care managers: A profile of an emerging profession.* Washington, DC: Author. Available: *http://research.aarp.org/il/ dd82_care.html.*

Americans with Disability Act of 1990, 42 U.S.C. §12101 et seq.

Applebaum, R. A., & Austin, C. D. (1990). *Long-term care case management: Design and evaluation.* New York: Springer.

Austin, C. D. (2001). Case management. In Mezey, M. E. (Ed.), *The encyclopedia of elder care: The comprehensive resource on geriatric and social care* (pp. 121–123). New York: Springer.

Austin, C. D., & McClelland, R. W. (Eds.). (1996). *Perspectives on case management practice.* Milwaukee, WI: Families International.

Deficit Reduction Act of 1984, P.L. 98-369 (98 Stat. 494).

Hyduk, C. A. (2002). Community-based long-term care case management models for older adults. *Journal of Gerontological Social Work, 37,* 19–47.

Intermodal Surface Transportation Efficiency Act of 1991, Pub. L. No. 102-240, 105 Stat. 1914.

Kane, R., Illston, L., & Miller, N. (1992). Qualitative analysis of the Program of All-inclusive Care for the Elderly (PACE). *Gerontologist, 32,* 771–780.

Morrow-Howell, N. (1992). Clinical case management: The hallmark of gerontological social work. *Journal of Gerontological Social Work, 18,* 119–131.

Naleppa, M. J., & Reid, W. J. (2003). *Gerontological social work: A task-centered approach.* New York: Columbia University Press.

National Association of Social Workers (1992). *NASW standards for social work case management.* Washington, DC: Author.

National Association of Social Workers. (2005a). *NASW credentials and specialty certifications: Certified Advanced Social Work Case Manager (C-ASWCM).* Washington, DC: Author. Available: *www.naswdc.org/credentials/specialty/c-aswcm.asp.*

National Association of Social Workers. (2005b). *NASW credentials and specialty certifications: Certified Social Work Case Manager (C-SWCM).* Washington, DC: Author. Available: *www.naswdc.org/credentials/specialty/c-swcm.asp.*

Older Americans Act of 1965, Pub. L. No. 89-73, 42 U.S.C. §3001 et seq., as amended or reauthorized.

Omnibus Budget Reconciliation Act of 1981, Pub. L. No. 97-35, 95 Stat. 357, 5 U.S.C. §8340 et seq., as amended.

Rothman, J. (1994). *Practice with highly vulnerable clients: Case management and community-based service.* Englewood Cliffs, NJ: Prentice Hall.

Schmid, H., & Hasenfeld, Y. (1993). Organizational dilemmas in the provision of home-care services. *Social Service Review, 67,* 40–54.

Social Security Act of 1935, 42 U.S.C. §301 et seq., as amended.

U.S. Census Bureau. (2000). *The Census 2000 Brief Series: Population change and distribution: 1990–2000* (C2KBR/01-2). Washington, DC: U.S. Government Printing Office. Available: *www.census.gov/prod/2001pubs/c2kbr01-2.pdf.*

U.S. Department of Transportation. (1997). *Improving transportation for a maturing society.* Washington, DC: Author. Available: *http://ntl.bts.gov/DOCS/index2/index2.htm.* (Report No. DOT-P10-97-01).

Quinn, J. (1993). *Successful case management in long-term care.* New York: Springer.

Wacker, R. R., Roberto, K. A., & Piper, L. E. (2002). *Community resources for older adults: Programs and services in an era of change* (2nd ed.). Thousand Oaks, CA: Pine Forge.

Zawadski, R. T. (1984). Research in the demonstrations: Findings and issues. *Home Health Care Services Quarterly, 4,* 209–228.

LEAH RUFFIN
LENARD W. KAYE

Counseling Services and Support Groups

HISTORICAL AND PHILOSOPHICAL CONTEXT

Counseling and support services for older adults have reflected changing philosophies over time. For much of the 1900s, especially prior to 1945, older adults were conceived largely as a dependent population for which the charitable efforts of social workers and other human service professionals were needed. Arguably, the prominent interventive philosophy at that time emphasized inevitable decline, incapacity, and impairment in the older adult. Elders, according to this perspective, were viewed as having entered an extended period of loss, experienced across multiple domains of living, including the physical, social, emotional, and economic. The older individual was likely to be experiencing not only loss of physical strength but also diminished social networks and financial resources. In other words, the older person's physical, social, and psychological environment was shrinking or contracting. In response, human services professionals sought to both help the older person prepare or adjust to such losses and, to the degree possible, slow the process of decline by buttressing remaining personal resources.

The 1960s saw the passage of the Older Americans Act of 1965 (OAA, 1965), which, for the first time, legislated an extensive range of social services as rights for older adults. Since then, albeit gradually, an increasingly optimistic or positive orientation to service intervention has been evidenced. In large part because of the changing profile of the aging population, human service professionals in the last 10 to 15 years have been increasingly working with a more active, educated, and vocal older adult population. These individuals often bring to the professional-client relationship higher expectations, including the desire to maintain active and engaged lives. Rather than accepting or passively adjusting to shrinkage or contraction in their social and psychological lives, they seek opportunities to continue to live active lives even in the face of physical challenges. It is in the context of these shifting population profiles and philosophies of what it means to grow old that we consider the range of clinical counseling and support services available to older adults.

COUNSELING SERVICES

Kirst-Ashman & Hull (1999) describe the generalist role of social work counselor as a useful one in providing guidance to clients while assisting in planned change or the problem-solving process, while Naleppa & Reid (2003) note a more traditional view of counseling as providing psychotherapy and family therapy. Because social work skill levels and practice abilities vary from practitioner to practitioner, depending on training, education, and experience, for the purposes of this chapter, *counseling services* is used as an encompassing term to describe a variety of direct services ranging from traditional psychotherapy to consumer and financial counseling services.

Counseling Service Locations

Older adults access counseling and support services through a combination of public and private, community-based, and institutional organizations. The counseling services system consists of private providers funded by third-party insurers and private-pay consumers, and publicly mandated, not-for-profit, and privately owned providers funded by the federal government, as well as states, counties, and municipalities. Institutional or facility-based counseling services include those provided by acute and long-term providers, residential treatment centers, and foster, boarding, or group homes (U.S. Department of Health and Human Services [USDHHS], 2001).

Community-based mental health services may include outpatient psychotherapy, partial hospitalization/day treatment, crisis services, case management, and home-based and "wraparound" services. Many community-based organizations, especially those operating under public or governmental auspices, provide services regardless of the elder's ability to pay (USDHHS, 2001).

Other community social service organizations, including Area Agencies on Aging (AAAs), health care facilities, community action programs (CAPs), and senior citizen centers provide non–mental health counseling services. Services may be offered directly at an agency or delivered in the elder's home. Over time, there appears to have been a tendency to offer services more centrally at the agency site. At the same time, increasing use of video, telehealth, and internet technology has figured in making such services more available remotely.

Classic techniques of counseling intervention include: supportive counseling, where the worker uses supportive listening techniques to help the client feel understood; financial counseling, in which the worker or agency helps the client set a budget or plan for fu-ture expenses; and eligibility or entitlements counseling, where the worker helps the client understand which social service programs, benefits, and services he or she may be eligible for. Typically, a person with an undergraduate degree in social work provides these services.

The foregoing counseling programs are often paired with other services, including assessment, case management, referral, and case coordination (National Council on the Aging [NCOA], 2001). Sometimes peers or volunteers may provide these services, through retired and senior volunteer programs, senior companion programs, or community telephone reassurance and friendly visitor programs. Local community treatment centers may also team up with substance abuse programs or homeless shelters to provide care for those programs' older clientele.

Many agencies provide counseling and support services via telephone hotlines. The Alzheimer's Association, with local offices situated throughout the United States, staffs a 24-hour support and referral service for persons with Alzheimer's disease and their caregivers (call 800-272-3900). The Alzheimer's Association also employs clinical professionals to provide more in-depth counseling support.

Special geriatric care managers may also provide counseling services, depending on the qualifications of the worker. These are commonly master's level professionals in social work, nursing, and other helping professions who have demonstrated competencies in geriatric case management and are affiliated with a professional care management association. Geriatric care managers are often self-employed or employed by a private fee-for-service organization. You can visit the Web site of the National Association of Professional Geriatric Care Managers, Inc. (*www.caremanager.org*) to find a professional care manager in a particular region of the country (Parker & McNattin, 2002).

Faith-based counseling programs are also an option for many elders. Faith communities, with long histories of social and spiritual support, are beginning to consider their formal role in the health and well-being of their members. Buijs & Olsen (2001) describe faith communities as ideal settings for a focus on health and health promotion, citing traditional values of support, personal skills, and social justice. Pastoral counselors and ministers provide counseling services, often on a sliding fee scale, or make such service available at no cost to members of their faith communities. Some faith communities employ social workers or nurses as a unique method of delivering health and social service information and referral services to their congregants.

SUPPORT GROUPS

The Social Work Dictionary (Barker, 2003, p. 185) defines a group as "a collection of people, brought together by mutual interests, who are capable of consistent and uniform action." Perhaps this definition best helps the practitioner understand the beginnings of social work group practice in the settlement houses of the late nineteenth and early twentieth centuries, where the focus was on mutual aid and democratic process to change the social environment and address the needs of tenement dwellers (Garvin, 1997).

During those early days of social work practice, social groups for older adults flourished in the settlement houses, community centers, homes for the aged, and state mental institutions. Crowded conditions and limited staffing made groups an effective and efficient vehicle to meet the needs of elderly residents (Toseland, 1995). It was not until the early 1950s, however, that social work publications began focusing on group therapy in a variety of settings. Today, group work with older adults is informed by a well-established theory base, structure, range of services provided, and roles that social workers can assume (Garvin, 1997).

There are many different types of groups used in social work practice. Most groups fall into one of two categories in terms of purpose: groups that provide direct treatment or service to their members and those that do not. Groups that meet for purposes other than direct service, sometimes called task-centered groups, are created to do just what their name implies—complete a specific task or set of objectives. The purpose of these groups is not to focus on the individual needs of their members (Henry, 1992).

The membership of these groups is likely to be based on individual skills, roles, and/or knowledge of members. Work goals are often determined outside the group, perhaps by the governing agency, on the basis of a stated purpose or task, or by means of group mandate. Depending on the nature of the group, member roles may be more structured and decision-making processes organized through democratic tradition (Henry, 1992). Committees, boards of directors, legislative bodies, supervision, staff development, consultation, interdisciplinary teams, and social action groups are all examples of social work task-centered groups (Henry, 1992; Kirst-Ashman & Hull, 1999) in which older adults certainly may play a valuable role.

In contrast, social work treatment-centered groups meet to focus on the individual needs of the members.

Examples of treatment-centered groups include therapy groups, education groups, socialization groups, and support groups (Hartford, 1985; Kirst-Ashman & Hull, 2002). Treatment-centered groups may have an open or closed membership, depending on the needs and intent of the group. Referral to the group may or may not be required, depending on program philosophy, participant eligibility, and funding.

Some treatment groups tend to be time limited, such as therapy or education groups, while others are more likely to be ongoing, open to new participants as long as members express interest in continuing the program. Often socialization groups have open admission policies, as do some support groups. Social work roles in these groups will vary depending on the needs and structure of each group. Possible social work roles include facilitator, leader, and consultant.

The following list (Kirst-Ashman & Hull, 2005, p. 261) outlines social work roles with groups.

Social Work Leadership Roles

Broker: Social workers use the role of broker to help clients obtain resources by connecting them to community services.

Mediator: The social work mediator helps the group resolve conflicts by helping each side voice their concerns, recognize the opposing argument's validity, and come to negotiated agreement.

Educator: Social work educators provide clients with new information and skills.

Facilitator: The social work facilitator helps the group stay on task, encourages participation, and open discussion.

TYPES OF SOCIAL WORK TREATMENT GROUPS

Therapy groups focus on changing participant behaviors. Membership may be determined on the basis of a particular treatment issue, age group, or location, or the profile of a given agency's client base. Membership may be open or closed. Members will often participate in determining the group's structure, goals, and decision-making processes. Treatment theory rationale will also vary on the basis of group need, outcome-based indicators, social worker training, and agency orientation. Typically, the social worker may assume more of a leadership role in treatment groups, particularly in the early stages of group formation. Therapy groups with elders may focus on such topics as coping with loss, depression, substance abuse, or a particular mental health diagnosis (McInnis-Dittrich, 2002).

Education groups are formed to provide education to the membership concerning a particular issue or topic. These groups do not focus on changing behavior, but rather provide information. In education groups, the social worker commonly assumes the role of teacher or trainer, often utilizing a formal curriculum or plan of presentation (Kirst-Ashman & Hull, 2005). Examples of education groups for older adults include those teaching new computer skills at the library media lab, healthy cooking for one at the local community meal site, managing diabetes skills at the health clinic, and parenting skills for older relatives providing care to younger relatives, at the university daycare.

Sometimes groups exist to serve the social and recreational needs of their members. These socialization groups usually draw together members who are from different backgrounds and with different talents but have similar interests in companionship, sharing interests, or learning something new. In these groups, the social worker's role is that of facilitator, encouraging participation and active communication between members, assisting in planning activities, and gathering needed information and resources. Many older adults join travel or interest-based groups held at senior centers and nursing facilities sponsored by social work agencies, or hosted by informal older adult networks (Toseland, 1995).

Support groups meet to provide encouragement and a safe environment for members to share their experiences. Support groups for older adults may address a particular type of loss, difficult life experience, or health issue, such as widowhood, employment transition, or chronic illness. They may also provide opportunities for particular subgroups of older adults, such as older women, to strengthen their informal networks and experience a sense of personal empowerment (Kaye, 1997b). Elements of therapeutic growth, socialization, and educational learning may be used separately or combined at different points in time in support group facilitation (McInnis-Dittrich, 2002). Support groups may have an open or closed membership. Typically little formal referral is required. The term *support group* is also used to describe self-help groups, which differ in their formal structure, likely having member facilitators, and may or may not follow a social work theoretical orienta-

tion. In any case, the term *support group* usually indicates a group that is attentive to the emotional needs of the membership as they pertain to a particular life event or challenge.

Regardless of the structure and intent of the group, certain dynamics will surely play a part in the life of the group. Special considerations in terms of designing and marketing support groups to appeal to particular subgroups of older adults may need to be considered as well (Kaye & Applegate, 1993). While not all groups will undergo exactly the same process, social work group theory has outlined typical stages of group development, as follows (Henry, 1992; Kirst-Ashman & Hull, 1999; McInnis-Dittrich, 2002; Toseland, 1995).

Group Formation Stages

Before the Group: The social worker or group leader begins to outline the basic structure of the proposed group. Location, time requirements, general purpose, and membership are all considered. The worker will need to review expectations with potential members.

Beginning Phase: The group meets for the first few times. It is important, when working with older adults, to make sure the group purpose is clearly defined. Initially, the leader takes a strong role while members establish individual roles, group norms, and group identity. As the group gains a cohesive identity, the worker assists this transition by promoting group decision-making and support-seeking among the membership.

Middle Phase: Conflict is not always a negative factor during group development. Most groups experience a stage of conflict or disequilibrium that serves to reexamine group ownership, goals, and objectives. Individuals may vie for power within the group or try to sway the group to serve their own personal needs. Many times, group members, particularly older adults, will not be comfortable addressing conflict and will shy away from direct expressions of tension, perhaps even dropping out of the group. It is important for the leader to address the conflict with the members and encourage the group to deal openly with the problem and possible solutions.

Once the group has confronted conflict, the members enter a period of productiveness. This is when the bulk of the work of the group is completed. This stage is a time of cohesion, bonding, and growth. Group members take on responsibility for both completion of tasks and attendance to the needs of members. In this stage, the worker's role is typically that of consultant or advisor.

Ending Phase: Groups cannot continue indefinitely. As the group completes its work and nears the time of termination, members begin to disengage themselves from the group. It is important that the leader address the termination before the event to allow members time to express their feelings. Often members feel sadness or engage in mourning. The leader can help members recap the skills and growth they have achieved through group affiliation.

FUNDING FOR COUNSELING SERVICES AND SUPPORT GROUPS

Counseling services and group work with older adults are funded in a variety of ways. Private agencies provide services through private insurance and participant copayments. Many community social service agencies provide counseling treatment as part of billable social work practice, depending on state and federal regulations, through private insurance, Medicaid, and Medicare programs. Agencies may also incorporate funds for treatment groups in federal and state grant requests, or charge clients fees to participate.

The OAA, most recently amended in 2000, also provides a source of funding for certain counseling and support services (Older Americans Act as Amended in 2000). Under Title 3 (Grants for State and Community Programs about Aging), part B (Supportive Services and Senior Centers), the OAA authorizes funding for health services (including mental health) and information and assistance services, as well as other services, including transportation, housing, long-term care, and legal assistance (Langer & Tirrito, 2004).

Title 3, part D (Disease Prevention and Health Promotion Services), provides for health risk assessments, routine health screening, nutritional counseling and education, health promotion programs, exercise and fitness programs, home injury control services, screening for prevention of depression, educational programs on medication management, information concerning diagnosis, prevention, treatment, and rehabilitation of age-related diseases and conditions, gerontological counseling, and counseling regarding social services (Langer & Tirrito, 2004).

Medicare, the federal health insurance program for people 65 and over, as well as people with certain disabilities or end-stage renal disease, has undergone many changes with the recent passage of the Medicare Prescription Drug, Improvement and Modernization Act (MMA) of 2003. For older adults who decide to stay with the original Medicare plan, or the fee-for service option, mental health and counseling treatment is available on a limited basis. Through Medicare part A, the insured pays the same deductibles and copayment as for non–mental health hospitalization. For participants who purchase the Medicare part B insurance, community mental health treatment is covered at about 50% of the Medicare-approved amount. The older adult is responsible for the remainder, as well as certain copayments and deductibles (USDHHS, 2004).

Coverage for older adults choosing Medicare Advantage Plans, a program that gives participants choices and, in some cases, extra benefits, by letting private companies offer Medicare benefits, is likely to vary from plan to plan. Medicare Advantage Plans must offer at least the basic coverage of the original Medicare plan (USDHHS, 2004), although insurance options will vary from region to region.

Similarly, Medicaid is another federal health insurance program that covers people with low incomes, pregnant women, children, teenagers, and people who are aging, blind, or disabled. Funds are distributed to states, which then set eligibility and service provision levels. In order to receive federal funds, Title 19 of the Social Security Act (Grants to States for Medical Assistance Programs, 1965) requires that certain basic services be offered to eligible recipients, including hospitalization, physician services, and nursing services. States may also provide home- and community-based care waiver services to eligible individuals through the Medicaid program, including case management, personal care services, respite care services, adult day health services, homemaker/home health aide services, rehabilitation, and so on.

Often self-help groups or support groups will find an organizational sponsor that is willing to make an in-kind donation of space, while members take turns bringing snacks and sharing material costs (if any). Faith communities may regularly hold groups as part of their community outreach, relying on laity donation for support. While some self-help groups are affiliated with national parent organizations, for many member-driven groups, fund raising is the sole responsibility of the group (Beigel, Farkas, & Wadsworth, 1994).

Community centers and YM/YWCAs may charge a fee to join the organization; afterward, participants pay minimal amounts per event or may only need to cover the cost of supplies for particular groups. Typically, senior discounts or scholarships are available. These types of community organizations may also hold capital campaigns in the local business community, as well as receiving support from charitable organizations such as the United Way.

COUNSELING SERVICES AND SUPPORT GROUPS FOR OLDER ADULTS TYPICAL OF MANY COMMUNITIES

Disease-Specific Supports

For many communities, support groups and self-help groups are commonly available for people seeking disease-specific supports. Such groups are sometimes offered in affiliation with a local hospital or rehabilitation center, as well as through community faith-based organizations and consumer-driven advocacy groups; support group locations and schedules are often published in the local newspaper. The regional Area Agency on Aging should also have a good listing of local resources.

According to the National Center for the Aging's 2001 nationwide survey of health and support services in the aging network, approximately 35% of programs surveyed used a nationally recognized treatment model when designing their programs. Nationally recognized, disease-specific models that exist in many communities may include, but are certainly not limited to, Arthritis Foundation programs, Ohio State University's Body Recall, an exercise program for those recovering from an operation or facing chronic illness, Tuft University's Strong Living Program, an exercise program to improve overall health, and the YWCA's ENCOREplus, designed to help women diagnosed with cancer (NCOA, 2001).

Many skilled nursing facilities or day treatment programs also provide disease-specific counseling services, particularly addressing dementia. For older adults with mild to moderate dementia, social work reality orientation groups may be helpful. Often used in nursing facilities and day treatment programs, reality orientation groups focus on helping the older adult maintain or relearn current information such as names, time, place, and current events. Leaders use verbal repetition, visual cues, and sensory stimulation to engage clients (McInnis-Dittrich, 2002). Care must

be taken when assessing the elder's functioning level at the time of reality orientation group assignment, so as not to lump persons who have less confusion or memory loss with those who have greater needs (Greene, 2000).

Health Education

In the past, older adults were often not seen as appropriate candidates for health promotion and education programs because goals invariably included long-term change. As the focus of health education for older adults has shifted to prevention of illness and injury, the maintenance of present functioning, and enhancement of health, this treatment bias has lessened (Wacker, Roberto, & Piper, 1998).

Health education programs promote healthy choices. Education may be provided through organized groups and health fairs or incorporated into existing programming. Groups may be disease specific, such as those targeting a reduction in high blood pressure or building bone density, or encompass a whole body perspective. A general health promotion group may include sessions on healthy lifestyles and health promotion, chronic disease prevention, nutrition, exercise, and medication education (Huang, Chen, Yu, Chen, & Lin, 2002). Health education groups are found at hospitals, health centers, skilled nursing facilities, senior centers, and elsewhere in the community. Participants should always consult with their physician before beginning any diet and exercise change. Education programming is most likely to succeed if it adheres to the following fundamentals.

Fundamentals of Successful Education Programming

- Focus on positive and healthy aging
- Ensure community presence and outreach
- Use peer support networks
- Develop age-appropriate materials
- Promote family involvement
- Emphasize active roles for participants
- Use respected experts
- Focus on improvement of health habits
- Provide health screening

Mental Health

For many older adults, particularly in rural areas, mental health treatment is underutilized (Bane &

Bull, 2001; Wacker et al., 1998). Unutzer et al. (2003) reported depression rates of 5–10% in older adults visiting a primary care provider, while the 1999 report of the Surgeon General estimated 19.8% of the older adult population has a diagnosable mental disorder during any 1-year period. Of these, anxiety disorders, cognitive disorders, and mood disorders were most prevalent (USDHHS, 1999).

Although stigma and embarrassment may prevent elders from seeking treatment, many elders simply do not have access to specialized mental health services, the resources available to pay for such services, or the appropriate types of services available in the community. Service providers themselves face deficits in needed funding, lack of interagency collaboration, and chronic worker shortages (USDHHS, 2001).

Outreach on the part of the social worker in the form of mental health education groups or informational sessions can be helpful (Bane & Bull, 2001) when seeking to inform the community of treatment availability. The use of "gatekeepers," that is, nontraditional supports like local businesses, hairdressers, and utility service persons, can provide useful referral information to older adults they come in contact with (Wacker et al., 1998). Primary care physician offices can also be partners in the care of an older adult with mental illness, screening for depression and making referrals as needed.

There are many different types of clinical social work therapeutic approaches to working with older adults. Historically, many felt that elders would not benefit from individual counseling, operating on the premise that learning in later life was difficult to achieve; however, research has shown this to be inaccurate (Davis & Collerton, 1997). Some authors suggest that elders feel less stigmatization when treatment is brief, although a particular treatment strategy will likely best be determined by the specific training of the clinician, the clinician's assessment of client need, and the relative comfort level of the client (Davis & Collerton, 1997). Today's clinicians may employ traditional psychotherapy, cognitive behavioral therapy, family therapy, brief therapy, or crisis intervention methods (Corwin, 2002).

Reminiscence may also be a helpful tool in the social work counselors' practice with older adults. Reminiscence group work has been used to cope with grief, reinforce sense of life meaning, and improve social relationships (Adamak, 2003; Westcott, 1983). Theorists see reminiscence addressing Erickson's final stage of development, integrity versus despair (Greene, 2000; Toseland, 1995). Reminiscence can be used to help

group members share experiences and weave a sense of mutual understanding among members.

Substance Abuse

Although in the past most social work research was focused on the substance abuse of younger and middle-aged adults, older adult substance abuse, including problem drinking, is now recognized as a growing area of concern. In general, the number of people in the general population who drink is known to decline with age (USDHHS, 2000). However, older adults are certainly not immune to alcohol- and drinking-related problems. As the nation's population ages, the number of older adults with alcohol problems and alcohol related problems is expected to rise.

Although numbers vary, a recent survey showed a prevalence of older adults with alcohol-related problems ranging from 20% to 22% nationwide (Fink et al., 2002). Others report alcohol abuse and dependence rates of 5–10% in older primary care outpatients (Kraemer et al., 1999) and up to 50% of older patients utilizing psychiatric hospitalizations (Hinkin et al., 2001). Between 25% and 50% of nursing home residents display active symptoms of problem drinking (Klein & Jess, 2002).

For many adults, even continuing moderate alcohol use may cause significant health related problems as they age (USDHHS, 2000). Alcohol-related hospitalizations are reported to rival the rates of hospitalization for myocardial infarction among older adults (Fink et al., 2002) and the National Highway Traffic Safety Administration reports that 11% of all drivers aged 65–74 involved in fatal automobile crashes in 1994 were positive for alcohol use (USDHHS, 2000). Other health risks linked to alcohol abuse include hypertension, congestive heart failure, liver disease, stroke, and alcohol-induced dementia.

Ruffin and Kaye (2004) note that many older adults may respond to treatment practices that are nonconfrontational, focus on coping and skill building, and offer health links. In this respect, group therapies may be particularly helpful for many older adult drinkers. Several self-help groups also offer substance abuse meetings specifically for older adults.

CONCLUSION

Counseling and support services can be expected to be used by increased proportions and numbers of older adults in the years ahead. Leading-edge baby boomers entering retirement will represent a generation quite familiar and comfortable with using counseling and support group services. There will be less stigma attached to their use. A positive, strengths-based, productive aging philosophy should be reflected in such interventions, with the focus on active community engagement and personal growth. It can be expected that certain subgroups of older adults will exhibit greater resistance to participation in programming than others (e.g., minority ethnic groups, older men) (Kaye, 1997a). As the older adult population becomes increasingly diverse culturally, racially and ethnically in the years to come, such services will need to be increasingly sensitive to the myriad of needs expressed and issues faced by a heterogeneous older adult population.

APPENDIX 46.1

Selected Counseling and Support Groups

Education and Prevention
Health Enhancement Program, Seattle/King County, Washington
www.seniorservices.org

Operating as one of three complementary programs of the Senior Wellness Program, the Health Enhancement Program centers around helping seniors adopt healthy behaviors. The Health Enhancement Program's client-driven practice also helps seniors to recognize and take advantage of health improvement opportunities. Participants initiate their involvement by completing a self-evaluation. Once completed, the participants partake in a comprehensive health and social assessment, which identifies improvement opportunities. Nurse feedback is offered for each area of concern. After the assessment is completed, participants formulate goals to be addressed through self-management programs, counseling, and support groups.

Screening, Referral, Intervention, and Treatment
Over 60 Health Center, Berkeley, California
www.lifelongmedical.org

By combining primary care and mental health services, Over 60 Health Center offers health promotion, disease prevention, screening, diagnosis, and treatment, as well as substance abuse services. Drawing older members of the community, Over 60 Health Center offers primary care provided by physicians, informal screenings, and referrals to mental health, so-

cial, and substance abuse service clinical staff as appropriate. By using an interdisciplinary team of a clinical social worker, a clinical psychologist, a primary care physician, and a nurse, Over 60 Health Center is able to address and treat many key concerns in the aging community.

Service Improvement through Coalitions and Teams
Elders Wrap-Around Team, Concord, New Hampshire
www.riverbendcmhc.org

Serving adults over 60, the Elders Wrap-Around Team, at the Riverbend Community Mental Health Center, joins with community agencies to coordinate services to make certain that no elders slip through service-delivery cracks. The Elders Wrap-Around Team consists of representatives from 12 core agencies, and an additional 40 community agencies who lend support and participate when necessary, to review specific cases and discuss community implications. Clients and their families may also attend a Wrap-Around meeting to participate in the discussion of their needs and services.

Education and Prevention
Positive Aging Theater, Madison, Wisconsin
www.madstage.com/companies/PATG.html

The Positive Aging Theater provides an environment where local older adults can connect and energetically create an entertainment revue. The traveling theater performs at local senior centers, adult daycare centers, and low-income housing developments. Even though the performance changes every year, the themes, which focus on issues such as living life to the fullest, debunking myths of aging, and alcohol and drug abuse prevention, stay the same.

Financial Counseling Service
Money Minders, Scarborough, Maine
www.smaaa.org

The Money Minders Program is sponsored by the Southern Maine Agency on Aging in collaboration with the American Association of Retired Persons (AARP). The Money Minders Program provides bonded, carefully screened, trained volunteers who offer in-home support with financial matters to older adults wishing to live independently and worry free. Volunteers provide help with budget development and implementation, checkbook balancing, check writing, and organizing and sending out mail and provide support to the client who is dealing with creditors. Help is confidential, and all financial decisions about the handling of a participant's money are made by the participant.

Support Groups
National Alliance for the Mentally Ill
www.nami.org

A nonprofit, self-help, support, and advocacy group for persons with severe mental illness and their families, NAMI has chapters in all 50 states, the District of Columbia, Puerto Rico, the Virgin Islands, and Canada. NAMI hosts support groups, education for consumers and families, and advocacy at the state and federal level. Visit NAMI's Web site to find local chapters and contact information.

The Alzheimer's Association
www.alz.org

The Alzheimer's Association is the world leader in Alzheimer's research and support. The nationwide network of chapters offers support to individuals affected by Alzheimer's disease. Services include information and referral, education, and support groups. The Alzheimer's Association also sponsors Safe Return, a nationwide program that assists in the identification and reunification of persons with Alzheimer's who have become lost. Since 1993, the program has assisted in the recovery of 8,000 people. Visit the Web site to find information about Safe Return and local support services.

REFERENCES

Adamek, M. E. (2003). Late-life depression in nursing home residents: Social work opportunities to prevent, educate, and alleviate. In B. Berkman & L. Harootyan (Eds.), *Social work and health care in an aging society: Education, policy, practice and research* (pp. 15–47). New York: Springer.

Bane, S. D., & Null, C. N. (2001). Innovative rural mental health service delivery for rural elders. *Journal of Applied Gerontology, 20*(2), 230–240.

Barker, R. L. (2003). *The social work dictionary* (5th ed.). Washington, DC: NASW Press.

Barlam, S., & Soares, H. H. (1997). Clinical practice with the elderly. In J. R. Brandell (Ed.), *Theory and practice in clinical social work* (pp. 471–500). New York: Free Press.

Biegel, D. E., Farkas, K. J., & Wadsworth, N. (1994). Social service programs for older adults and their families: Service use and barriers. In D. K. Harris (Series Ed.) & P. K. H. Kim (Vol. Ed.), *Issues in aging: Vol. 3. Services to the aging and aged* (pp. 141–178). New York: Garland.

Buijs, R., & Olson, J. (2001). Parish nurses influencing determinants of health. *Journal of Community Health Nursing, 18,* 13–23.

Corwin, M. (2002). *Brief treatment in clinical social work practice.* Pacific Grove, CA: Brooks/Cole.

Davis, C., & Collerton, D. (1997). Psychological therapies for depression with older adults: A qualitative review. *Journal of Mental Health, 6*(4), 335–345.

Fink, A., Morton, S. C., Beck, J. C., Hayes, R. D., Spritzer, K., & Sabine, O. (2002). The alcohol-related problems survey: Identifying hazardous and harmful drinking in older primary care patients. *Journal of the American Geriatrics Society, 50,* 1717–1722.

Garvin, C. D. (1997). Group treatment with adults. In J. R. Brandell (Ed.), *Theory and practice in clinical social work* (pp. 315–342). New York: Simon and Schuster.

Greene, R. R. (2000). *Social work with the aged and their families* (2nd ed.). New York: de Gruyter.

Hartford, M. E. (1985). Group work with older adults. In A. Monk (Ed.), *Handbook of gerontological services* (pp. 169–183). New York: Van Nostrand Reinhold.

Henry, S. (1992). *Group skills in social work: A four-dimensional approach* (2nd ed.). Pacific Grove, CA: Brooks/Cole.

Hinkin, C. H., Castellon, S. A., Dickson-Fuhrman, E., Daum, G., Jaffe, J., & Jarvik, L. (2001). Screening for drug and alcohol abuse among older adults using a modified version of the CAGE. *American Journal on Addictions, 10,* 319–326.

Huang, L. H., Chen, S. W., Yu, Y. P., Chen, P. R., & Lin, Y. C. (2002). The effectiveness of health promotion education programs for community elderly. *Journal of Nursing Research, 10,* 261–269.

Kaye, L. W. (1997a). Informal caregiving by older men. In J. I. Kosberg & L. W. Kaye (Eds.), *Elderly men: Special problems and professional challenges* (pp. 231–249). New York: Springer.

Kaye, L. W. (1997b). *Self-help support groups for older women.* Washington, DC: Taylor and Francis.

Kaye, L. W., & Applegate, J. S. (1993). Family support groups for male caregivers: Benefits of participation. *Journal of Gerontological Social Work, 20,* 167–185.

Kirst-Ashman, K. K., & Hull, G. H., Jr. (2002). *Understanding generalist practice* (5th ed.). Pacific Grove, CA: Brooks/Cole.

Klein, W. C., & Jess, C. (2002). One last pleasure: Alcohol use among elderly people in nursing homes. *Health & Social Work, 27,* 193–202.

Kraemer, K. L., Conigliaro, J., & Saitz, R. (1999). Managing withdrawal in the elderly. *Drugs & Alcohol, 14,* 409–425.

Langer, N., & Tirrito, T. (Eds.). (2004). *Aging education: Teaching and practice strategies.* Lanham, MD: University Press of America.

Lewis, M. L. (2001). Spirituality, counseling, and elderly: An introduction to the spiritual life review. *Journal of Adult Development, 8,* 231–239.

McInnis-Dittrich, K. (2002). *Social work with elders: A biopsychosocial approach to assessment and intervention.* Boston: Allyn and Bacon.

Naleppa, M. J., & Reid, W. J. (2003). *Gerontological social work: A task-centered approach.* New York: Columbia University Press.

National Council on the Aging. (2001, Summer). *A national survey of health and supportive services in the aging network.* Washington, DC: Author. Available: *www.ncoa.org/content.cfm?sectionID=91&detail=98.*

Older Americans Act as Amended in 2000. PL-106-501. Formerly H.R. 782.

Older Americans Act of 1965. (1965, July 14). Public Law 89-73. 89th Congress, H.R. 3708.

Parker, M., & McNattin, S. P. (2002, August 6). *Past, present and future trends in care management.* Tucson, AZ: Author. Available: *www.caremanager.org/gcm/newsevents.htm.*

Ruffin, L., & Kaye, L. W. (2004, May/June). Alcohol and aging: Do ask, do tell. *Social Work Today, 4,* 24–27.

Schneider, R. L., Kropf, N. P., & Kisor, A. J. (Eds.). (2000). *Gerontological social work: Knowledge, service settings, and special populations* (2nd ed.). Belmont, CA: Brooks/Cole.

Tirrito, T. (2004). Program and services for older adults: A national and international focus. In N. Langer & T. Tirrito (Eds.), *Aging education: Teaching and practice strategies* (pp. 1–36). Lanham, MD: University Press of America.

Title XIX of the Social Security Act. (1965). United States Code as §1396–1396v, subchapter xix, chapter 7, Title 42.

Toseland, R. W. (1995). *Group work with the elderly and family caregivers.* New York: Springer.

Unutzer, J., Katon, W., Callahan, C. W., Williams, J. W., Hunkeler, E., & Harpole, L. (2003). Depression treatment in a sample of 1,801 depressed older adults in primary care. *Journal of American Geriatrics Society, 51,* 505–514.

U.S. Department of Health and Human Services. (1999). *Mental health: A report of the surgeon general.* Washington, DC: Author. Available: *www.surgeongeneral.gov/library/mentalhealth/home.html.*

U.S. Department of Health and Human Services. (2000). *Tenth special report to the U.S. Congress on alcohol and health: Highlights from current research.* Washington, DC: Author. Available: *www.niaaa.nih.gov/publications/publications.htm.*

U.S. Department of Health and Human Services. (2001, January). *Older adults and mental health: Issues and opportunities.* Washington, DC: Author. Available: *www.openminds.com/indres/seniormh.pdf.*

U.S. Department of Health and Human Services. (2004). *Your Medicare benefits.* (CMS Publication No. 10116). Baltimore, MD: Author.

Wacker, R. R., Roberto, K. A., & Piper, L. E. (1998). *Community resources for older adults: Programs and services in an era of change.* Thousand Oaks, CA: Pine Forge Press.

Westcott, N. A. (1983). Application of the structured life-review technique in counseling elders. *Personnel and Guidance Journal, 62,* 180–181.

Among the things most hoped for and treasured is a long life. People are living longer, and with their increased longevity, it is likely that at some point they will either require the assistance of a family caregiver or become a family caregiver. Parent care has become a normative experience in American families (Brody, 1990, as cited by Martire, 2003). In 1988, the U.S. Administration on Aging reported that for the first time in history, couples had more parents than children to care for (Hooyman & Gonyea, 1995). In addition, the report indicated that women would spend 18 years caring for aging parents, as compared to 17 years caring for children. By the year 2040, the older population is expected to more than double, and the number of people age 85 and older will triple (Kramer, 2000), and one half of them are likely to require assistance with one or more activities of daily living (Kart & Kinney, 2001; Siegel, 1999). The unprecedented growth of older persons, and in particular the projected increase in the 85-and-older population to 8.5 million by 2030 (American Association of Retired Persons [AARP], 2004), make it urgent for the nation to aggressively plan and develop caregiving resources.

These realities summon social workers to respond to the nation's growing caregiving responsibilities. Today's realities also point to the need to examine and plan for the diversity of needs of caregivers. Among the new realities are the changing role of women (more in the outside-of-home workplace), growing minority elders with cultural expectations, more male caregivers, the "sandwich" and "club sandwich" generation, and technological advances that prolong independence and care-receiver freedom (Stowe, 2004). The sandwich generation refers to those sandwiched between aging parents needing help and their own children while the club sandwich generation is responsible for three generations, including parents, grandparents, children, or grandchildren.

This chapter discusses the background and prevalence of family caregivers, the definition and profile of family caregivers, the legal authority for services to family caregivers, social work roles and practices with family caregivers, support services available to family caregivers, and the next generation of family caregiver resources.

SANDRA EDMONDS CREWE
SANDRA STUKES CHIPUNGU

Services to Support Caregivers of Older Adults

DEFINITION, BACKGROUND, AND PREVALENCE

The *Encyclopedia of Social Work* defines caregiving as the "custodial or maintenance help or services rendered for the well-being of individuals who cannot perform such activities themselves" (Hooyman & Gonyea, 1995, p. 953). The authors note the multidimensionality of caregiving by stressing the emotional ties associated with caring for and about older relatives. Caregiving is primarily a family matter. Historically, families have been responsible for the needs of their older relatives. This has been especially true in the case of minority elders, where kinship and informal community arrangements have been dictated by inequality of resources and cultural traditions. This family caregiving tradition is further documented by a 1997 study by the National Alliance of Caregivers and the AARP that reported over 22.4 million U.S. households provide unpaid help to elders, giving an average of 18 hours a week of assistance. Consistently, a 1991 U.S. Senate Special Committee on Aging reported that 4.9 million seniors with some type of impairment in activities of daily living (ADLs) live in the community, and 70% of them rely exclusively on the unpaid assistance of family and friends (Garner, 2000). Nearly 90% of disabled older persons who were not in nursing homes received assistance from relatives and friends. This is another compelling indicator of the vital role of the family in caring for elder members.

The *Compendium of HHS Caregiver Support Activities* (U.S. Department of Health and Human Services [USDHHS], 2003, p. 1) indicates that

> informal caregiver and family caregiver are terms that refer to unpaid individuals such as family members, friends, neighbors and volunteers who provide help or arrange for help. These individuals can be primary or secondary caregivers, full time or part time, and can live with the person being cared for or live separately.

Some family caregivers receive pay as a part of a family arrangement; however, they are usually considered as unpaid caregivers because they are not associated with paid care providers. In addition, some receive benefits, such as public housing, that exempt their income from rent determination because of their caregiver status.

LEGAL AUTHORITY: THE OLDER AMERICANS ACT AND THE AGING NETWORK

The Older Americans Act of 1965 (OAA) created the "aging network" to address concerns and provide services to older Americans (Administration on Aging

[AoA], 2004; DiNitto & McNeece, 1997; Gelfand, 1999; Hooyman & Kiyak, 2002). The OAA has 10 goals that are carried out through the federal, regional, state, and local levels of the aging network. The aging network includes governmental and private resources as noted in Table 47.1.

The aging network. The National Family Caregiver Support Program (NFCSP), was established by Older Americans Act Amendments of 2000 (Public Law 106-501) and was based in large part on felt and expressed needs of caregivers across the country (AARP, 2004; AoA, 2004; Guthiel & Chernesky, 2001). Authorized for 5 years, it is the first federal legislation specifically addressing the needs of the millions of Americans caring for older relatives (Guthiel & Chernesky, 2001). The NFCSP was funded for $125 million in its first year and offered grant flexibility to allow states to provide a continuum of caregiver services that best meet caregivers and individual needs. These may include information, assistance, and other services. Services support family caregivers of persons age 60 and older and grandparent and relative caregivers of children not more than 18 years of age.

The NFCSP program was developed in recognition of the fact that over 70% of older persons are cared for in home by family caregivers "and are an important component of any home and community-based care system" (p. 1). As noted by DiNitto and McNeece (1997), most diagrams of the aging network fail to include the family that provides the bulk of services for this population. Despite the extraordinary service of caregivers, many older people who receive assistance from family members also receive assistance from other sources. A typical source of support is provided through OAA-funded home- and community-based services such as home-delivered meals, personal care, transportation, and chore services. These services help lessen the burden on family caregivers and help them maintain their caregiving role in a healthy way.

Findings from a survey of a random sample of 413 individuals who provided caregiver support to older people who also used OAA-funded services in 2004 showed that caregivers find OAA services to be vital in helping them support the older people they care for, and 86% reported that OAA services helped them provide care longer than they would have been able to without the services. In addition, a majority of the states (86%) reported a need for additional caregiver support, the greatest of which is for additional respite and supplemental service support (AoA, 2004).

Family caregiver profile. Family caregivers are made up of spouses, children, parents, and other relatives

TABLE 47.1. Aging Network

Service and Funding Entities	Major Functions
Federal government Administration on Aging (AoA), U.S. Department of Health and Human Services	• Funds programs • Coordinates federally operated programs for older persons (i.e., nutrition programs) in the 10 regional offices of the United States • Conducts evaluation of programs and research on aging, including a clearinghouse on aging-related information • Provides advocacy function for older persons and their caregivers
State government Usually a part of the human services department	• Assists in implementing federal policies • Acts as advocate for older persons and their caregivers
Local government Area Agencies on Aging (AAAs); approximately 700 AAAs are located in communities throughout the country, and each is guided by an advisory council	• Provides advocacy functions • Conducts community-based needs assessments • Distributes funding to community agencies • Provides services such as information and referral, respite, legal council, daycare, telephone assurance
Private agencies Public and private nonprofit and for-profit agencies; churches and faith-based affiliated social services	• Provide direct services through OAA programs such as daycare, respite care, and case or care management • Provide assistance at market rates for those who can afford to pay • Provide support groups for caregivers
Families Unpaid caregivers, including primarily daughters, spouses (wives)	• Provide wide range of instrumental and emotional support to older person to assist with ADLs and IADLs

who have loved ones who are ill or have disabilities that require care ranging from minimal to 24-hour assistance. The 1997 National Alliance for Caregiving and the AARP collaborated on a report on family caregiving in the United States that provides the following profile of a family caregiver (National Alliance for Caregiving and the AARP, 1997).

- Average age is 45
- 12% are 65 years and older
- 73% are female
- Two thirds are married
- 41% have children under the age of 18 living in the home
- 64% are working
- 52% work full-time

A second study in 2003, *Caregiving in the United States*, co-authored by National Alliance for Caregiving and AARP, shows an increase in caregivers to 22.9 million (21% of U.S. households) as compared to 22.4 million in 1997 (National Alliance for Caregiving and

the AARP, 2005). This updated nationwide sample estimated 44.4 million caregivers age 18 and older who provide unpaid care for an adult. Demographics were similar to those in the 1997 study with the notable exception of more male caregivers in the sample (39% as compared to 25% in 1997). The 2003 study also emphasized that most caregivers were working with over 62% having to make adjustments to their work schedules to accommodate their caregiving roles. Although the study found that males were more likely to be working than females, females were providing more hours of care and higher levels of care (burden). The 2003 study listed the top unmet needs as finding time for self, managing emotional stress, and balancing work responsibilities. Also, cultural differences in the caregiving experience emerged in this report—there were specific differences related to methods of coping with stress and levels of caregiver burdens. For example, African Americans were more likely than Whites to report praying as a way of coping as well as caregiving being a financial burden. They also report performing more IADLS. The study findings report Asians as least likely to be stressed by caregiving and having the highest incomes. The cultural differences seen in caregiving reflect other inequities in society such as health problems and income disparities. These disparities result in cumulative disadvantage (Crewe, 2005) that increases caregiver burdens especially for economically disadvantaged groups.

A 2004 survey of caregivers receiving services under the Older Americans Act (OAA) offers additional information about caregivers. It reported that 24% report difficulty providing care because of their own physical limitation; 37% also care for someone else; 33% are over 65 years old themselves; 74% of the elders cared for are at least 75 years old; and 32% of the elders cared for are 85 or older. These caregivers provide a variety of services for the elders they care for, including 88% who provide transportation assistance, 79% who provide help with meals, laundry, and household chores, and 73% who provide help with financial matters (AoA, 2004).

As individuals age, caregiver support will become more and more critical to keeping them at home or in a noninstitutionalized setting. According to the National Alliance or Caregiving and the AARP study (1997), 52% of caregivers are employed full-time, and more than 50% report tension between work and caregiver needs that has resulted in work-related changes, including reduction in hours, rearranged work schedules, or taking unpaid leave. They also reported caregiving as taking a toll on their physical health. Thus support is needed to meet the interdependent emotional, economic, health, and social needs (Hooyman & Kiyak, 2002) of the caregiver. When one of these needs is neglected, the caregiver-receiver dyad is placed at risk, and the quality of the relationship is compromised. Thus, programs and services that focus on keeping harmony and balance in the caregiver-receiver relationship serve as protective factors related to financial, physical, and emotional caregiver stress.

SOCIAL WORK ROLES

As noted by McInnis-Dittrich (2002), the caregiver serves as a vital member of the caregiving team not only to the older person but also to the gerontological social worker. Social work has historically provided services that embraced the entire family system, using a range of micro and macro interventions. In addition, strength-based assessment skills and the ecological perspective acknowledge a dual caregiving network: an internal one that includes the family and an external network that includes the community and mezzo structures. Using the professional mantra of "starting where the client is," social work uses frameworks such as the "life-course perspective" and the "convoy model" and integrates them into practice. The life-course perspective is a framework (Hooyman & Kiyak, 2002) that concentrates on age-related transitions through recognizing that aging is a lifelong process that influences and is influenced by social processes and is experienced differently by different age, ethnic, racial, economic, and geographical cohorts (Hooyman & Kiyak, 2002; Kart & Kinney, 2001; Stoller & Gibson, 1994).

All of the traditional social work functions and roles are needed to help family caregivers navigate through a system that is sometimes not "user oriented." Drawing upon the work of Miley, Omelia, and DuBois (2001), social work has three major functions: (1) consultancy; (2) resource management; and (3) education. Through consultancy, social work seeks to find solutions, drawing upon knowledge, skills, and values. The resource management function fosters or stimulates exchanges with existing and undeveloped or unrecognized resources, and the education function focuses on information exchange and is grounded in understanding that dialogue is essential to problem solving. Within these three functions, social workers can assume various roles such as facilitator, planner, broker, and educator. Table 47.2 provides an example of social work roles in working with caregivers, showing that social workers have multiple ways of connecting with caregivers and multiple points of contact. This indicates the numerous opportunities afforded to social workers to access caregivers and offer needed instrumental, emotional, appraisal, and informational support as decisions are made about older relatives.

As employees of departments of social services agencies that are charged with adult and protective services, social workers have the opportunity and responsibility to work with caregivers. In addition, private social service agencies employ social workers to make decisions about placing children in homes where the caregiver of the child is also the caregiver of an older adult. This arrangement also creates the opportunity for social workers in the school system to intervene with caregivers of older adults (Crewe, 2004). Similarly, social workers employed by housing agencies interact with caregivers as they seek to meet the housing needs of families with older members.

TABLE 47.2. Social Work Roles

| Social Work Roles | Micro Level | Midlevel | Macro Level | Social Work Profession |
	Individuals, Families, Small Groups	Organizations and Formal Groups	Communities and Societies	The System of the Social Work Profession
Consultancy • enabler • facilitator • planner • mentor	Counseling with caregivers and family members, i.e., facilitating support groups	Facilitating change in organizational culture to understand and act upon needs of caregivers	Participating in community planning process for aging community	Support of programs and public policy aimed at providing direct support to caregivers (NCFSP, FMLA)
Resource management • broker/advocate • convener/mediator • activist • catalyst	Linking caregivers with additional community resources	Coordinating service delivery planning among multiple community-based resources	Identifying potential funding sources that are flexible enough to serve caregivers—critically assessing silo funding	Spearheading national alliances and partnerships that bring attention to the needs of caregivers and the lack of funding
Education • teacher • trainer • outreach • research/scholar	Providing educational resources that lead to better understanding of illness or disabling condition	Conducting staff development training that focuses on the caregivers as the primary target of intervention	Informing the public of the role of the family caregiver and involving them in advocacy for a continuum of service in their communities	Publicizing through qualitative and quantitative research the "hidden public costs" of family caregiving, especially for populations at risk

Note: Adapted from *Generalist Social Work Practice,* by K. K. Miley, M. Omelia, and B. DuBois, 2001. Boston: Allyn and Bacon.

Social workers are also employed in a range of roles in offices on aging, employee assistance programs (EAPs), and mental health delivery systems. Faith communities also use social workers to provide services for their congregations. Finally, social workers are sometimes assigned to constituent services in congressional offices where they hear about the needs of caregivers and care receivers. This list is not exhaustive. By expanding their knowledge about community-based caregiver resources (Family Caregiver Alliance, 2004) and working outside of their networks, social workers can maximize their sphere of influence.

SUPPORT SERVICES AVAILABLE FOR FAMILY CAREGIVERS

A healthy caregiver-receiver dyad consists of support services that meet the needs of the caregiver and older person in a manner that is sensitive to their distinct lifestyles and culture. Antonucci (as cited by Tirrito,

Nathanson, & Langer, 1996, p. 128) defines social support as "interpersonal transactions involving key elements such as aid, affect and affirmation." While a myriad of services and programs are emerging to address caregiver needs, the social work profession must be in the forefront in advocating for programs that respond to shared needs yet distinctive family characteristics and circumstances. For example, social workers can advocate for families to get needed time to make caregiver arrangements. Equally important is the professions' advocacy for direct rather than indirect services to caregivers and historical emphasis on self-determination and promoting programs and services that maximize family choice. Similarly, social workers can become more involved in raising public awareness of the need for family members to begin care dialogues before crises erupt and truncate planning time.

A review of the literature shows a cadre of support services that are currently available to support caregivers of older persons. These services include both formal and informal resources, in-home and community based, and traditional and innovative services. They include respite care, adult daycare, support groups, technological resources, and EAPs aimed at enhancing quality of life.

Respite services. Respite care is the use of short-term temporary services that use trained sitters to provide relief for caregivers (Kart & Kinney, 2001; Kropf, 2000; Montgomery, 2002; Staicovici, 2003). This is extremely important, considering the evidence that the stress of providing long-term care is associated with compromised mental and physical health (Feinberg & Whitlach, 1998). Kart and Kinney (2001) describe four models of respite care: (1) home-based; (2) group daycare; (3) group residential care; and (4) residential programs providing respite care as an adjunct service. The Government Accountability Office, formerly the General Accounting Office (GAO), states that "respite care offers support to caregivers so that they can continue to provide care for the frail elderly" (Kart & Kinney, 2001, p. 464). Numerous studies have shown that respite care benefits both caregivers and care receivers. There is evidence that respite care results in improved emotional and physical health for care providers and has resulted in the decline of institutionalization of the elder family member (Staicovici, 2003). There is also research that documents that respite care does not offer rest and relaxation but rather freedom to perform other required tasks (Bedini, 2002). This suggests the need for models that include information, education, and support in addition to respite care (Gutheil & Chernesky, 2001). Ethnicity is also an important predictor of levels of respite care use, and different ethnic groups have distinct trajectories of service use over time (Cox, 1998; Montgomery, 2002). In addition, some of the services have a limited number of days available, and this may also limit the use of the services.

Adult daycare. Another form of respite for caregivers, adult daycare (ADC) provides a community-based, supervised environment for the elderly who are unable to stay at home (Kropf, 2000). Respite services are scheduled around certain events and times, while ADC centers require regular attendance; they include a wide range of tailor-made therapeutic services for older persons who have mental or physical impairments (Kart & Kinney, 2001). Adult daycare centers allow the older person to remain at home while receiving some health and social services (Hooyman & Kiyak, 2002). Some ADC centers are based on a health-rehabilitative model sometimes referred to as adult day health care (ADHC), while others have a focus more social-psychological. Both

models may provide recreation, meals, and transportation and are governed by individualized treatment plans that are jointly developed by the care receiver, the caregiver, and the center staff (McInnis-Dittrich, 2002). Adult daycare centers allow the primary caregiver to continue to work and perform other responsibilities with the assurance that their older relative is being properly cared for. *The Encyclopedia of Social Work* (Gordon, 1995) lists providing respite, support, and education for family caregivers as one of the seven goals of ADC. Recent studies have found that the use of ADC centers by the care recipient reduces caregiver stress and, when coupled with counseling, can delay institutionalization (Takamura, 2000). Increasingly, ADC centers are developing or adapting to providing services to clientele with special needs such as dementia, AIDS, mental illness, visual impairment, hearing loss, or communication disorders (Gordon, 1995). In addition, intergenerational centers are available where older adults and children are brought together in the same program (Kropf, 2000) to increase interactions between older and younger generations and offer older persons meaningful roles.

Support and educational groups. One of the 10 tips for caregivers offered by National Family Caregivers Association is to "seek support from other caregivers" (McInnis-Dittrich, 2002, p. 322). This advice is grounded in the belief that there is great value and strength to caregivers' knowing that they are not alone. There is general agreement that support groups foster caregivers' taking care of themselves (Monahan, 1994). Caregivers can benefit from support and education groups for themselves and their elder care receivers. Support groups are intended to offer emotional support to protect the caregiver-receiver dyad from stress buildup, as well as serve as a source of information and referral. Participating in support and educational groups is a way to relieve stress, because they focus on caregiving and provide information on the specifics of the care receiver's disease or chronic condition (Hooyman & Kiyak, 2002). Caregiver support groups provide resources and techniques that ameliorate caregiver stress and offer a safe haven for caregivers to voice their concerns and frustrations. Caregiver support groups are particularly helpful for new caregivers and assist in sifting through the myriad new demands on their time and help them better control their lives (McInnis-Dittrich, 2002; Monahan, 1994; Williams & Barton, 2003/2004).

Available technological resources. Increases in the older adult population are accompanied by an increase in technology that can be used to enhance quality of life for both the caregiver and receiver (Chambers & Connor, 2002; Cortes et al., 2003; Meadows, 2001; Shellenbarger, 2002b). Zarit and Edwards (1996) relate that the provision of information to caregivers is key in managing stressors. Older persons and their caregivers now have greater access to online resources that offer them the advantage of up-to-date information on health care, support groups, community-based resources, and family members (close by as well as far away). For example, the AoA has a Web site for caregivers with links to the National Family Caregiver Support Program and other federal, state, and local resources (Meadows, 2001). The resulting partnership between caregivers and health organizations can result in greater efficiencies in the health care system and ultimately assist caregivers with some of the financial burden.

Advances in technology have been helpful in the following ways:

1. Increasing access between caregiver and care received (Shellenbarger, 2002a)
2. Facilitating communication with physician, resulting in reduced in-office visits (Hooyman & Kiyak, 2002)
3. Maintaining or improving the functional capacity of individuals (Gilson, 2000)
4. Enhancing clinical support capabilities by giving caregivers remote access to client data and clinical alerts (Meadows, 2001)

Internet-based social support is primarily used to expand one's social network of status-similar others. Participants report they use it because of psychological distress, including isolation, loneliness, and desperation (Colvin, 2003). However, this technology is also used to address the desire of caregivers to keep relatives in the least restrictive environment. This desire often raises concerns about the safety of their relative in the home. Low-tech tools such as door alarms and intercoms are being supplemented by Internet-based monitoring systems.

Kinney, Kart, Murdoch, and Ziemba (2003) found that affordable technologies such as computers, Web cams, mobile telephones, and wireless devices have great potential to reduce caregiver burden and distress. They conclude that electronic technologies will be critical components of caregiving, and caregivers' voices will be needed to inform those who design, develop, and implement them. Assisted technology is being designed to be used by not only professional

caregivers but also family caregivers (Cortes et al., 2003). For example, the Link2Care resource has as a goal increasing caregiver well-being and coping skills through convenient access to information, connection to caregivers, and other services provided in the home via electronic delivery (Kelly, 2003/2004). These assisted-technology devices are defined as mechanical devices and instruments used to communicate, see, hear, or maneuver (Gilson, 2000). These and other forms of technology can help increase the autonomy of caregivers, free them from some of the caregiving roles, and offer greater ease when they have to be away from the home or are remote or distance caregivers. Because of these potential benefits, Bradley and Poppen (2003) advocate for social policy that increases the use of assisted technology. Some examples follow of technological innovations that are being used to support caregivers.

> *Web-based radio broadcast: Coping with Caregiving* is a weekly broadcast that features guests and speakers of a range of caregiving topics. It also airs via Internet. Caregivers need no appointment to discuss the topic or offer advice for other listeners (*www.wsradio.com/copingwithcaregiving*).
> *Interactive voice response (IVR)* offers caregivers support through stress monitoring, counseling information, personal voicemail linkage, and telephone support groups (Mahooney, Tarlow, & Jones, 2003).
> *Transponders (E-gear)* are electronic monitors, placed around the neck, that communicate the activities of the care receiver to the caregiver by way of an electronic device that can be accessed by the remote caregiver's computer. They also function as alarms, room keys, and location monitors. The equipment allows remote/distance caregivers to have a more active role with elder and reduces some of the stress associated with not seeing their elder on a regular basis. The equipment serves as their eyes and ears and helps to monitor the elder for signals of worsening health such as loss of weight and so on. (Shellenbarger, 2002a, 2002b)

Similarly, technology is also used to assist the professional social worker in meeting caregiver needs. Although a broad range of instruments are used by professionals to assess caregiver stress and burden, Chambers and Connor (2002) advance the concept of a computer-based, systematic self-assessment and conclude that the software was helpful by providing reassurance and emotional support that enabled caregivers to assess their coping capacity and information to enhance their skills. In summary, technological advances can offer assistance to the caregiver, care receiver, and professional staff.

Employment assistance programs (EAPs). These programs provide a variety of assistance to employees in the public and private sector. An increasing number of people in the workforce are actively involved in caregiving for an older relative or friend (Metlife, 2003). Family Caregiver Alliance (2003) indicates that a majority of the 25 million family caregivers are employed and forced to make work-related changes to accommodate caregiving. Employment assistance program services are offered to offset the loss in employee productivity and increased absenteeism and interrole conflict, which results in estimated costs of $29 billion yearly to employers in terms of lost productivity (Franklin, 2001; Martire, 2003) and $659,000 in wages, pensions, and Social Security for the caregiver (Family Caregiver Alliance, 2003). Workers also miss promotion opportunities because of caregiving responsibilities. Caregiver services, including counseling and eldercare search, are increasingly sought by caregivers (Franklin, 2001; Metlife, 2003). A 2000 survey of Hewitt Associates found that nearly half of large employers (over 1,000 employees) offer some type of eldercare assistance, with information and referral being the most common (Franklin, 2001). Franklin (2001) reports that Fannie Mae and companies like the Federal Deposit Insurance Corporation (FDIC) offer services, through social workers, to guide workers, bring in speakers, and offer resources.

THE NEXT GENERATION OF SERVICES AND SUPPORT FOR CAREGIVERS

Toseland and Rivas (2001) state that a major role of social workers is to "facilitate hope for the future and motivate members to improve coping skills through self-help and mutual aid" (p. 24). Rieske, Holstege, and Faber (2000) describe the need for "coordinated information distilled from gerontological research" (p. 759) to maximize the quality of life of both the care recipient and the caregiver. The resource list at the end of the chapter shows selected online resources that are available to both caregivers and social workers as they work cooperatively to maximize the quality of the caregiving experience for both the caregiver and the care receiver. The new generation of caregivers will need services that allow maximum flexibility and deemphasize governmental control of the caregiving process.

Old mindsets and conventional wisdom about caregiving must be addressed. To respond to current realities, traditional programs and caregiving roles must be "unlearned" and replaced by new resources. For example, the assumption that caregiving is exclusively the domain of women must be reexamined, on

TABLE 47.3. Selected Caregiver Resources Web Sites

Web Site	Brief Description
www.AoA.gov/caregivers	Administration on Aging
www.alzinfor.org	Alzchat: chatroom for patients and caregivers for up-to-date information on Alzheimer's
www.benefitscheckup.org	Preliminary eligibility information for federal programs
www.caregivers-usa.org	Directory of caregiving resources
www.caregiving.com	Various caregiving resources
www.caregivers.org	National Family Caregiver Alliance
	Handbook for Long-Distance Caregivers
www.eldercare.gov	Eldercare locator
www.geriatric-resources.com	Alzheimer's geriatric resources
www.hospicefoundation.org/caregiving	Hospice Foundation of America
www.nahc.org	National Association of Home Care
www.nfca.org	National Family Caregivers Association
www.nia.nih.gov	National Institute on Aging
www.womensissues.about.com	Caregiving resources guide

the basis of evidence such as the Metlife Study of Sons at Work, which reported that one in three caregivers are men. Findings of the survey of 1,400 employed caregivers at three Fortune 500 companies found men caregivers increasingly in the workplace. They reported feeling uncomfortable discussing their responsibilities and therefore not seeking to receive support from colleagues and supervisors (Metlife, 2003). In addition, cultural and ethnic differences must be addressed (AARP, 2001) to maximize subjective and objective quality of life for caregivers. Considering that many members of the new generation of caregivers are likely to serve as caregivers for longer periods, the social work profession must be a leader in providing "emotional insurance," through informed social work practice that offers a myriad of caregiver-centered services and programs at both micro and macro levels that are responsive to the diversity of caregivers and caregiving experiences.

Society gives family caregivers a dual message. On the one hand, they are praised for assuming the responsibility of their relative, and on the other hand, they are marginalized by the full burden being placed on their shoulders. Caregivers who find themselves enmeshed in the multiple roles of caregiver are likely to look for professional and formal interventions that are responsive to their lifestyles. Through understanding the complexity of the caregiving relationships and becoming familiar with the various programs and services available in the community, social workers can maximize the quality of life of family caregivers by connecting families with needed resources that are affordable, accessible, and culturally appropriate. Today's families are managing multiple tasks, and unplanned changes in their internal or external environments can interrupt established routines. Caregiving of older persons is an example of unplanned change that can impact a family's equilibrium. The success of caregiving for older persons can be maximized by social work professionals recognizing and helping families to plan for the changes that are needed for successful caregiving and can result in mutual benefits and protect families from experiencing unnecessary stress. Without proper support, the caregiving experience can be stressful and end with final memories that are painful and overshadow the positives of the relationship.

The needs of caregivers are going to increase as the population requiring care increases. Addressing the increased needs will require changes in policies and the coordination and collaboration of social workers, doctors, nurses, families, and other community-based organizations to meet these needs. Finally, informed social workers can ensure that the tradition of family caregiving is embraced by families and supported by policy and practice initiatives that make the caregiving experience one that is positive and causes minimal disruption to the family system. When you think about it, caregiving is the anchor of the beginning and end of life. Often the last memory of a loved one is experienced in a caregiver-receiver relationship. Social workers must continue to make a concerted effort to make this a positive experience that completes the life cycle with the same optimism it began with. In the words of a caregiver:

> Taking care of my mother was a lasting memory that I cherish because I received the support from my family, friends, church, and social services programs that helped me to make the needed changes in my lifestyle to really get to know her and enjoy spending time with her.

REFERENCES

Administration on Aging (AoA). (2004). Older Americans Act services support the role of family caregivers. Available: *http://www.aoa.dhhs.gov/prof/aoaprog/caregiver/overview/esec_summary.asp.*

American Association of Retired Persons. (1997). *Family caregiving and long-term care.* Factsheet. FS Number 91. Available: *www.research.aarp.org/il/fs91_ltc.pdf.*

American Association of Retired Persons. (2001). In the middle: A report on multicultural boomers coping with family and aging issues. Washington, DC: Author.

American Association of Retired Persons. (2004). Policy Book: AARP public policies 2004. Washington, DC: Author. Available: *http://aarp.org.*

Bedini, L. A. (2002). Family caregivers and leisure: An oxymoron? *Parks & Recreation, 37*(1), 25.

Bradley, N., & Poppen, W. (2003). Assistive technology, computers and Internet may decrease sense of isolation for homebound elderly and disabled persons. *Technology and Disability, 15,* 19–25.

Chambers, M., & Connor, S. (2002). User-friendly technology to help family caregivers cope. *Journal of Advanced Nursing, 40*(5), 569–577.

Colvin, J. (2003). Caregivers of older adults on line: Perceptions of Internet-based social support. (Doctoral dissertation, Texas Women's University, 2003). *Dissertation Abstracts International, 63,* 2708A.

Cortes, U., Annicchiarico, R., Vazquez-Salceda, J., Urdiales, C., Canamero, L., Lopez, M., Sanchez-Marre, M., & Caltigirone, C. (2003). Assistive technologies for the disabled and for the new generation of senior citizens: The e-tools architecture. *AI Communications, 16*, 193–207.

Cox, C. (1998). The experience of respite: Meeting the needs of African American and White caregivers in a statewide program. *Journal of Gerontological Social Work, 30*(3/4), 59–72.

Crewe, S. E. (2004). Ethnogerontology: Preparing culturally competent social workers for the diverse faces of aging. *Journal of Gerontological Social Work, 43*(4), 45–58.

Crewe, S. E., & Stowell-Ritter, A. (2003). *Grandparents raising grandchildren in the District of Columbia: Focus group report.* Washington, DC: AARP.

DiNitto, D. M., & McNeece, C. A. (1997). Social work: Issues and opportunities in a challenging profession. Boston: Allyn and Bacon.

Family Caregiver Alliance. (2003). *Family caregiving and public policy: Principles of change.* National Center on Caregiving. San Francisco, CA: Author.

Family Caregiver Alliance. (2004). *Navigating the care system: A guide for providers to help family caregivers.* National Center on Caregiving. San Francisco, CA: Author. Available: *www.caregiver.org.*

Feinberg, L. F., & Whitlatch, C. J. (1998). Family caregivers and in-home respite options: The consumer-directed versus agency-based experience. *Journal of Gerontological Social Work 30*(3/4), 9–27.

Franklin, M. B. (2001, August). On-the-job aid for caregivers. *Kiplinger's Personal Finance Magazine.* Available: *http://www.findarticles.com/p/articles/mi_m1318/is_8_55/ai_76577547.*

Garner, J. D. (2000). Long-term care. In Sharon M. Keigher, Anne E. Fortune, & Stanley L. Witkin (Eds.), *Aging and social work: The changing landscapes* (pp. 1625–1634). Washington, DC: NASW Press.

Gelfand, D. E. (1999). *The aging network: Programs and services* (5th ed.). New York: Springer Press.

Gilson, S. F. (2000). Disability and aging. In R. Schneider, N. Kropf, & A. Kisor (Eds.), *Gerontological social work: Knowledge, service settings and special populations* (2nd ed., pp. 368–395). Belmont, CA: Wadsworth.

Gordon, N. (1995). Adult day care. In R. L. Edwards & J. G. Hopps (Eds.), *Encyclopedia of Social Work* (19th ed., Vol. 2, pp. 74–82). Washington, DC: NASW Press.

Gutheil, I., & Chernesky, R. H. (2001). Grantmaker support to caregivers of family members with Alzheimer's disease. *Journal of Gerontological Social Work, 35*(3), 17–31.

Hooyman, N. R., & Gonyea, J. G. (1995). Family caregiving. In R. L. Edwards & J. G. Hopps (Eds.), *Encyclopedia of Social Work* (19th ed., Vol. 2, pp. 951–959). Washington, DC: NASW Press.

Hooyman, N. R., & Kiyak, H. A. (2002). *Social gerontology: A multidisciplinary perspective* (6th ed.) Boston: Allyn and Bacon.

Kart, C. S., & Kinney, J. M. (2001). *The realities of aging: An introduction to gerontology* (6th ed.). Boston: Allyn and Bacon.

Kelly, K. (2003/2004). Link2Care: Internet-based information and support for caregivers. *Generations, 27*(4), 87–88.

Kinney, J. M., Kart, C. S., Murdoch, L.D., & Ziemba, T. F. (2003). Challenges in caregiving and creative solutions: Using technology to facilitate caring for a relative with dementia. *Aging International, 3,* 295–314.

Kramer, B. J. (2000). Husbands caring for wives with dementia. In Sharon M. Keigher, Anne E. Fortune, & Stanley L. Witkin (Eds.), *Aging and social work: The changing landscapes* (pp. 335–349). Washington, DC: NASW Press.

Kropf, N. P. (2000). Home health and community services. In R. L. Schneider, N. P. Kropf, & A. Kisor (Eds.), *Gerontological social work: Knowledge, service settings and special populations* (2nd ed., pp. 167–190). Belmont, CA: Wadsworth.

Mahoney, D. F., Tarlow, B. J., & Jones, R. N. (2003). Effects of automated telephone support systems on caregiver burden and anxiety: Findings from REACH for TLC intervention study. *The Gerontologist, 43*(4), 556–567.

Martire, L. M. (2003). Juggling parent care and employment responsibilities: The dilemmas of adult daughter caregivers in the workforce. *Sex Roles: A Journal of Research, 48*(3/4), p. 167.

McInnis-Dittrich, K. (2002). *Social work with elders: A biopsychosocial approach to assessment and intervention.* Boston: Allyn and Bacon.

Meadows, G. (2001). The Internet promise: A new look at e-health opportunities. *Nursing Economics 19*(6), 294–295.

Metlife. (2003). *Sons at work: Balancing employment and eldercare.* Findings from a National Study by the National Alliance for Caregiving and the Center for Productive Aging at Towson State University. Westport, CT: Mature Market Institute. Available: *www.maturemarketinstitute.com.*

Miley, K. K., Omelia, M., & DuBois, B. (2001). *Generalist social work practice.* Boston: Allyn and Bacon.

Monahan, D. J. (1994). Caregiver support groups: Efficacy issues for educators. *Education in Gerontology, 20,* 699–714.

Montgomery, R. J. (2002). A new look at community-based respite programs: Utilization, satisfaction, and development. *Home Health Care Services Quarterly, 21*(3/4), 1–4.

National Alliance for Caregiving and the American Association of Retired Persons. (1997). Family caregiving in the U.S.: Findings from national survey. (Final Report). Washington, DC: Author.

National Alliance for Caregiving and the American Association of Retired Persons. (2005). Caregiving in the U.S.: Findings from national survey. (Final Report.) Washington, DC: Author.

Older Americans Act of 1965. P.L. 89-73, 79 Stat. 218.

Rieske, R. J., Holstege, H., & Faber, M. (2000). Using interactive television technology to disseminate applied gerontological information. *Educational Gerontology 26*, 751–760.

Shellenbarger, S. (2002a, July 18). The Brave New World of elder care: Gadgets track loved ones' every move. *Wall Street Journal*, p. D1.

Shellenbarger, S. (2002b, July 25). *Technology holds promise for easing families' worries over the elderly. Wall Street Journal*, p. D1.

Siegel, J. S. (1999). Demographic introduction to racial/Hispanic elderly populations. In Toni P. Miles (Ed.), *Full-color aging: Facts, goals, and recommendation for America's diverse elders* (pp. 1–19). Washington, DC: Gerontological Society of America.

Staicovici, S. (2003). Respite care for all family caregivers: The LifeSpan Respite Care Act. *Journal of Contemporary Health Law and Policy, 20*, 243–271.

Stoller, E. P., & Gibson, R. C. (1994). *Worlds of difference: inequality in the aging experience*. Thousand Oaks, CA: Pine Forge Press.

Stowe, H. D. (2004). The invisible journey: An ethnographic study of African American female caregivers. Unpublished doctoral dissertation. Howard University, Washington, DC.

Takamura, J. C. (2000). The aging of America and the Older Americans Act. In Sharon M. Keigher, Anne E. Fortune, & Stanley L. Witkin (Eds.), *Aging and social work: The changing landscapes* (pp. 127–135). Washington, DC: NASW Press.

Tirrito, T., Nathanson, I., & Langer, N. (1996). *Elder practice: A multidisciplinary approach to working with older adults in the community*. Columbia: University of South Carolina Press.

Toseland, R. W., & Rivas, R. F. (2001). *An introduction to group work practice* (4th ed.). Boston: Allyn and Bacon.

U.S. Department of Health and Human Services. *A compendium of HHS caregiver support activities*. Washington, DC: Author. Available: *http://www.aoa.gov/prof/ aoaprog/caregiver/careprof/progguidance/resources/ CAREGIVER%20COMPENDIUM%201.3.02.pdf.*

Williams, E., & Barton, P. (2003/2004). Successful support groups for African American caregivers. *Generations, 27*(4), 81–83.

Zarit, S., & Edwards, A. (1996). Family caregiving research: Research and clinical intervention. In R. Woods (Ed.), *Handbook of the clinical psychology of aging*, pp. 333–368. London: Wiley.

We focus in this chapter on those who are vulnerable to possible adversity and the mechanisms by which social workers can be engaged in the surveillance and protection of such persons. Specifically, this chapter will provide an overview of the ombudsman program, concerned with the quality of care within long-term care facilities; adult protective service (APS) programs, created to intervene in cases of community-based abuse, neglect, and maltreatment; and legal efforts designed to safeguard the elderly and their resources.

THE OMBUDSMAN PROGRAM

Over the years, ombudsman programs have played an important role in seeking to ensure the quality of care given to institutionalized older populations through different activities. Social workers have been intricately involved in programs as paid staff members or as volunteer participants. Although the quality of institutional care has improved over the years, institutionalized persons can be the victims of abusive acts of omission and commission.

Legislative History and Authority

To counter potential problems, the long-term care ombudsman program is the major mechanism having responsibility for advocacy and protection of residents within nursing homes, board and care facilities, assisted living units, and similar adult care settings. *Ombudsman,* as both a word and a concept, comes from Sweden. The Swedish Parliament established the office of Justiticombudsman in 1809, and this person received complaints and protected citizens from injustice, no matter where that injustice might have arisen (Lowy, 1980). (Inasmuch as the term *ombudsman* is of Swedish origin, without gender specificity, it is customary to continue the use of the term.)

In the early 1970s, several states passed patients' rights legislation in response to the belief that the personal rights and liberties of patients were being lost following institutionalization (Gelfand, 1999). In 1974, the federal government developed regulations that established a set of patients' rights for individuals in skilled and intermediate care facilities. These rights, which relate to individual liberties, were to be readily displayed, explained to the patients, and assigned to nursing home personnel for enforcement. Programs were to identify, investigate, and resolve

JORDAN I. KOSBERG
MAX B. ROTHMAN
BURTON D. DUNLOP

Advocacy and Protection of Older Adults

complaints regarding the care given within long-term care facilities.

In 1978, the ombudsman program, with statutory definition of ombudsman functions and responsibilities, was incorporated into the Older Americans Act (OAA), to be administered by the Administration on Aging (AoA) and state laws (Administration on Aging [AoA], 2004). Under the act, every state is required to have an ombudsman program that addresses complaints and advocates for improvements in the long-term care system.

Significant amendments to the OAA were enacted by the Ombudsmen Budget Reconciliation Act (1987), which required states to provide for ombudsman access to residents and residents' records, immunity to ombudsmen for the good-faith performance of their duties, and prohibitions against willful interference with the official duties of an ombudsman and/or retaliation against an ombudsman, resident, or other individual assisting representatives of the program in the performance of their duties. In 1992, the program was strengthened and transferred to a new title in the OAA, Title 7, Vulnerable Elder Rights Protection Activities, which also includes Programs for Prevention of Elder Abuse, Neglect and Exploitation and Elder Rights and Legal Assistance Development.

Program Design

The program is federally mandated in the OAA, but it is managed on the state level, resulting in a multitude of program designs. Huber, Borders, Badrak, Netting, and Nelson (2001) indicate that local ombudsmen exist in all 50 states to identify, investigate, and work to resolve complaints initiated by, or on behalf of, residents in nursing homes, board and care homes, or similar adult care facilities. In 1999, there were 587 local and regional ombudsman programs (AoA, 1999). In 1995, the Institute on Medicine (IoM) published a report (Harris-Wehling, Feasley, & Estes, 1995) that was based upon their study of ombudsmen programs. The study, commissioned by AoA, concluded: Given variability in organizational location, funding sources, and staffing characteristics of ombudsmen programs, each state has a different model (Harris-Wehling et al., 1995).

Currently, most ombudsman programs are affiliated with the State Units on Aging and work through the Area Agencies on Aging (Gelfand, 1999). Each state has a different configuration for its ombudsman

program, in part dependent upon the size of the population, government, and budget. Some states rely primarily on paid staff, while others make extensive use of trained volunteers. While programs are administered by state governments, federal sources (mainly from the OAA) provide about 60% of the funding, supplemented by state and local support and from Area Agencies on Aging, the United Way, and foundations.

Volunteer involvement can be considered the "backbone" of ombudsman programs. According to the Administration on Aging Resources (2004), there are about 1,000 paid and 14,000 volunteer staff investigating over 260,000 complaints and providing information, referrals, and consultation on a myriad of topics (such as how to select and pay for long-term care) to more than 280,000 people each year.

Social Work Roles and Responsibilities

As mandated in the OAA, there are many responsibilities for ombudsmen, who may be either paid members of the staff or volunteers. First and foremost is the need to identify, investigate, and resolve complaints made by or on behalf of residents (Netting, Paton, & Huber, 1992). The identification of possible problems (such as abuse, maltreatment, neglect, infringements of resident rights) can result from visits to long-term care facilities by ombudsmen or from calls made to the ombudsmen program office. Complaints can come from residents, members of their families or friends, and staff members of a facility, among others. Investigation by an ombudsman necessitates the collection of information from individuals, reports, records, and so on, so as to verify the alleged complaint that can pertain to the acts of omission (i.e., neglectful behavior, failure to provide needed care) or commission (i.e., inappropriate use of restraints, theft of possessions) by a staff member (including administrators) from an institution. The need to document and verify the complaint is vital.

Social workers are well suited for the performance of these diverse responsibilities in conflict resolution, mediation, and information gathering, as well as advocacy efforts and knowledge of community resources. Netting, Huber, Paton, and Kautz (1995) have written about social workers' roles as reporters of abuse, advocates for change, educators, and coordinators of community efforts on behalf of institutionalized older persons. The ombudsman can act proactively in visiting nursing homes, board and care or assisted living facilities, or other settings within his or her sphere of responsibility. The ombudsman often reacts to (and investigates) complaints about care, and to proposed policies and practices that are believed to be contrary to the best interest of long-term care residents. Each ombudsman program, although retaining the important role of being the focal point for complaints regarding nursing home care, also acts as a nursing home referral service and organizes friendly visiting programs.

Resolution Efforts

The tactics of an ombudsman to resolve a documented and confirmed adversity against a resident or patient within a long-term care facility exist on a continuum from collaboration to confrontation. Gelfand (1999) suggests that the ultimate enforcement of standards and principles for good care is difficult to undertake, inasmuch as "the only disciplinary tool available is decertification of the facility" (p. 219), a recourse that is perceived to be too severe for individual violations. Indeed, it has not been uncommon for long-term care facilities to respond to violations in standards or practices by threatening to close the doors of their facilities and "putting the residents on the street." When and where the need for long-term care beds exceeds supply, there are often lengthy "periods of grace" before compliances are required to occur.

Gutheil (1990) suggests that grievances are resolved within the nursing home in collaboration with the administrator and staff, and that when appropriate outcome cannot be reached at the facility level, the ombudsman will make use of outside resources (such as the state health department). Adversarial tactics, including nonviolent protest, confrontations, boycotts, and litigation, are chosen by a very few advocacy organizations, although a case could be made for an approach that, while accenting cooperation, includes the possibility of confrontation. In discussing the collaborative model, Atchley and Barusch (2004) state:

> This approach works when the nursing home is open to this kind of participation. But in many cases, the nursing home is defensive about criticism, and regulatory agencies may be reluctant to investigate complaints. In these cases, a more assertive ombudsman process may be needed. (p. 414)

The National Long Term Care Ombudsman Resource Center provides support, technical assistance, and training to state ombudsman programs and statewide networks of almost 600 regional (local) programs (*www.ltcombudsman.org*). Representing ombudsman and private nursing home resident advocacy organizations is the National Citizens' Coalition for Nursing Home Reform (available online at: *www.nccnhr.or*g).

ADULT PROTECTIVE SERVICES

The term *adult protective services* refers to "publicly funded programs that investigate and intervene in reports of abuse, neglect, and exploitation of adults who are physically or mentally impaired and unable to protect themselves from harm" (Mixson, 1995, p. 69). Most APS workers (also referred to as practitioners and case managers) function within agencies that are covered by state statutes to receive reports, conduct investigations, evaluate client risk, assess clients' capacity to agree to services, develop and implement case plans, and monitor ongoing service delivery (Otto, 2000).

Legislative and Program Background

"The history of adult protective services [APS] in the United States is difficult to trace" (Elder Justice, 107th Cong., 1st Sess., 2002). Teaster (2001) suggests that it emerged from the government's concern for adults who were vulnerable and dependent, and Mixson (1995) indicates that the idea of such services originated in 1958, when the National Council of Aging created an ad hoc committee of social workers to discuss the potential need for some type of protective service for older people. In 1961 the White House Conference on Aging recommended that social agencies be created and that legal associations and medical professionals cooperate in some manner to facilitate the provision of protective services to older persons. The Administration on Aging (AoA) funded a number of demonstration projects in the 1960s, but "by 1968, there were still less than twenty community protective services programs in the country" (Mixson 1995, p. 70). In 1974, the Title 20 amendment to the Social Security Act gave permission for states to utilize Social Services Block Grant funds for the protection of adults (as well as children) (Older Americans Act, 1974). By 1981, "all the states, in one way or another, noted that they had an office with responsibility to provide protective services to some segment of the population" (H.R. Doc. No. 97–277, 1981). The focus of APS has expanded and evolved from treating the impaired, low-income elderly to treating all adults over 18 years of age without regard to income, and more recently to treating elder abuse and neglect victims as a special population (Quinn & Tomita, 1986).

By the early 1990s, many states had mandatory elder-abuse reporting laws that mandated the reporting of suspected cases of abuse, maltreatment, exploitation, and neglect to APS agencies. Those required to report suspected abuse vary between states. Quinn and Tomita (1986) state:

> Clients are referred often by practitioners from other agencies such as utility companies, meals on wheels, senior center programs, and law enforcement. Concerned citizens are becoming more aware of the needs of frail elders and the agencies that serve them. Reports of endangered elders are made increasingly by friends, neighbors, apartment managers, and relatives. (p. 236)

In fact, generally, those required to report suspected cases of abuse include employees of departments of social and heath services, law enforcement agents, social workers, professional school personnel, employees of social services, and social welfare and mental health agencies, as well as home care, hospice, home health, and adult daycare services workers, or employees of nursing homes, boarding homes, or adult family homes, and health care providers (nurses and doctors).

Funding and Administrative Issues

With the origin of APS in the 1960s, Otto (2002a) notes:

> Nearly forty years later, there are still no federal statutes regulating the delivery of Adult Protective Services (APS), no federal agency charged with responsibility to collect data and issue reports, and no discrete funds provided to states to support and enhance service delivery. (p. 1)

Thus, some programs provide protection to all those 18 and older, and others focus upon those persons considered old.

Some programs operate out of the state offices on aging, state human service agencies, or private contracting agencies, and the funding of state programs may be based upon Social Services Block Grants or state general funds. While APS always conducts investigations in independent domestic settings within communities, in some states APS agencies also have responsibility for abuse investigations within congregate settings (i.e., board and care facilities) and within long-term care institutions.

APS Activities

APS programs are the principal public source of response to reports and cases of vulnerable adult abuse, neglect, and exploitation. Social workers have been very prominent in APS programs and services, in general, as well as in the study of elder abuse and maltreatment, in particular. Adult protective services programs are empowered by states and local communities to accept and investigate reports of abuse, neglect, and financial exploitation of the elderly and younger persons with disabilities (Otto, 2002a). Some protective services may be provided without cost, and some are provided on a sliding-fee basis.

Adult protective services workers are trained to investigate allegations of physical, sexual, mental, or emotional abuse, neglect or self-neglect, financial exploitation, or abandonment. The report of suspected elder abuse is often made by telephone, either to a local elder abuse agency or through an "800" line of the state APS agency, and is transferred to the local elder abuse agency. An APS worker is then required to investigate the case by a deadline that is determined by the severity of the case (Hwalek, Goodrich, & Quinn, 1996).

Following an investigation, and in consultation with others, a determination is made whether there is evidence to substantiate the claim of alleged abuse. It should be noted that some competent older persons, suffering abuse, may refuse the assistance of APS workers; given the right of self-determination for a cognitively competent adult, the worker cannot ignore the older person's wishes. The mentally competent individual, although living within an abusive situation, should not be subject to involuntary relocation or interventions. As Hwalek, Goodrich, and Quinn (1996) state: "Unlike abused children, elderly victims have the right to refuse interventions, even if this means their lives are in danger" (p. 126).

For those victims who seek assistance, once the report of abuse is substantiated, the APS intervention process begins. A care plan is developed for the victim that includes needed services and resources. The client-specific plan is typically multidisciplinary in nature and intended to ensure the safety, while maximizing the autonomy, of the older adult. The service plan may involve informal care provision by family or friends, or formal social, health, or mental health services offered by public, private, and/or voluntary agencies. Interventions may include home care, referrals, pursuit of guardianship, or institutionalization (if the abused victim is frail and impaired).

Challenges to Program Effectiveness

The recent down-turn in the economy has resulted in freezes and reductions of APS staff, cutbacks on travel and training, as well as the adoption of waiting lists for abuse investigations. These reductions put victims in increased danger of additional and more serious abuse. (Otto, 2002a)

Given this forewarning, APS case managers and administrators, many of them social workers, face very real challenges for the future.

State budgetary limitations, priorities given to the needs of children, and general ageism in society often result in insufficient training for APS workers involved in protecting and focusing upon the needs of older persons and their relationships with others. In part, this is a result of a lack of leadership by the federal government. Although most states require training for new workers, strained budgets might preclude complete training for some newly hired APS workers. In this regard, the only national group advocating for changes on behalf of APS is the National Association of Adult Protective Services Administrators (NAAPSA), a nonprofit volunteer organization made up of state and local APS administrators. The association is in partnership with the National Center on Elder Abuse (available online at: *www.elderabusecenter.org*) and is funded in part by AoA.

SOCIAL WORK ROLES IN LEGAL SETTINGS

Legal resources can play an important role in protecting the rights and resources of older persons. The role of social workers within the legal system has been slow to be recognized and slower to be utilized. Overall, the placement of social workers in private law practices is rather uncommon (Arnason, Fish, & Rosenweig, 2001).

Current Exceptions

Perhaps the most notable exceptions to this pattern occur in elder law offices specializing in family, probate, and estate planning law. Public or quasi-public agencies such as prosecutor, public defender, and Legal Aid offices, on the other hand, more frequently have employed social workers to deal with the psychosocial and extralegal needs of their older clients. Brownell and Roberts (2002) argue that the roles of forensic social workers have been substantial and growing but largely unrecognized by the profession. Bassuk and Lessem (2001) point out that it is not uncommon in geriatric community-based organizations for geriatric case managers (mainly social workers) and attorneys to work collaboratively.

Trial courts increasingly include social workers and psychologists on their staffs. This growing trend is enhanced within specialized, problem-solving courts, which are likely to follow one or both of the relatively recent judicial developments: therapeutic jurisprudence and, to a lesser extent, trial court performance standards (TCPS). These developments have come, in part, as a reaction to widespread dissatisfaction and even distrust of the courts. In response, trial courts have sought ways to improve their responsiveness to the public, to streamline dockets and other court processes, and to improve outcomes and reduce recidivism by linking with community-based services. In the country's two elder justice centers, both of which have emerged in Florida, social work has a significant function (Rothman & Dunlop, 2004).

Roles for Social Workers

In a recent study of the elder justice centers and six other trial court systems scattered throughout the country, Rothman and Dunlop uncovered numerous ways in which social workers fill roles in the courts. Their study was designed to examine the implications of the growing number of elderly persons in America on the courts and judicial administration, access to the courts, and resolution of the underlying issues that often precipitate court involvement by older adults (Rothman & Dunlop, 2004). Because of the demographics of older persons, and their increasingly complex physiological, psychological, and social profiles, there will be an increasing number of older persons who come into regular contact with court systems having more varied and complex circumstances. Thus, courts need to have the capacity to identify problem areas, as well as the practical ability to intervene and mobilize appropriate services. Social workers can play significant advocacy roles for such older persons.

The philosophy of therapeutic jurisprudence looks at the law and courts as social forces that produce consequences that may be therapeutic or antitherapeutic (Wexler & Winnick, 1996). Thus, for example, in addressing criminal areas involving substance abuse, mental problems, or domestic violence, courts have to make decisions that promote the health of all parties concerned, including the offender, while still ensuring justice for the victim (Rottman & Casey, 1999). Inevitably, this process involves establishing linkages with the community's health and social services systems.

In Florida, two "elder justice centers," in Tampa and West Palm Beach, represent approaches that courts have developed to address issues presented by the increase of older people. The purpose of these centers is to remove access barriers and to enhance linkages between elders and the courts, as well as with the legal, health, and social service systems (Rothman & Dunlop, 2004). The Tampa center, directed by an attorney, focuses on assistance to the probate court on guardianship cases, as well as serving victims of abuse and other crimes and providing general assistance to elders with other issues. The Palm Beach center, with a director having a master's degree in social work, assists older persons who are arrested for criminal activity, including those jailed, as well as older persons with a variety of other legal issues who need assistance or referrals. Staff members also assist the probate court. Both centers employ staff members with social work backgrounds and appropriate experiences for providing assistance and counseling. In both jurisdictions, these centers are offices of the judicial systems, and staff members are not independent case managers or advocates for individual elders. Rather, they assist the older person as appropriate, while advising the court of specific needs for services. It is a sophisticated role for social work professionals that will continue to increase with the aging of the population.

Rothman and Dunlop (2004) found additional roles and responsibilities carried out by social workers employed by, or working in collaboration with, court systems. For example, a social worker may be employed as the Americans with Disabilities Act coordinator responsible for compliance. Social workers will be needed to educate judges and staff about issues of older people and how to address them effectively. Drug and mental health courts provide models for how other courts can utilize social workers to help provide assessments and obtain services. Social workers can also manage self-help centers, which courts have established to educate potential litigants about their rights under the law, including the ability to file certain legal documents without having to employ an attorney. Court social workers also are needed to educate law enforcement and health, mental health, and social services organizations about issues and barriers affecting the participation of older people in the court system. They are also needed to educate older adults and the general community about issues of access to the courts and typical legal issues that may affect them. Finally, social workers can be utilized to help identify funding opportunities and to prepare grant proposals to obtain additional funding.

Special Concerns Regarding Guardianships

One of the more obvious ways social work involvement is necessary is in a court or legal context, with regard to guardianships. In fact, guardianship is the single largest area of judicial activity involving older persons (Rothman & Dunlop, 2004). Social workers may be involved, first of all, in assessments to determine the competency of potential wards in guardianship applications before the court. In doing this, social workers presumably will conduct a multidimensional evaluation of potential wards and their circumstances (Hull, Holmes, & Karst, 1990). Bassuk and Lessem (2001) indicate the following potential roles for social workers in the area of guardianships: (1) identifying the need for guardianship services, (2) initiating or supporting guardianship appointments, (3) providing expert testimony at hearings, (4) investigating guardianship applications for the court, (5) offering guardians professional assistance, and (6) serving as a private or public guardian.

Whatever the role for the social worker, the prospects of guardianship for the potential ward are very serious, indeed. In a plenary guardianship, wards lose all of their liberties, from the right to vote to deciding where they will live. Rarely are these rights returned. Thus, in this context, social workers may at times see the need to assume the role of advocate for older persons, to protect them.

Many states allow limited or partial guardianships that apply to only one or a limited number of life's activities. In the area of financial decisions, for example, a conservatorship preserves freedoms in other areas as well (Nolan, 1990). The only potential detriment of the option of limited guardianships is that it may be more appealing and, thus, more likely that a guardianship is ordered by the court in borderline cases. This presents a situation in which social workers may become involved in advocacy efforts for those older persons facing such possibilities.

To avoid the prospect of guardianship, a number of experts (see Alexander, 1990; Armstrong, 2000) have proposed the alternative of advance directives, especially the durable power of attorney and the living will, and even representative payee services that are sometimes used for Social Security and Supplementary Security Income beneficiaries (Dejowski, 1990). The extent to which older persons have advance directives is not known. Yet it is abundantly clear that many older adults are unaware of the need for such measures, especially those with few assets, and many persons cannot (or perceive that they cannot) pay a lawyer to draw up these documents, even in the face of increasing efforts by social workers and others who educate the public on such matters. Despite the growing number of older persons who will eventually adopt advance directives, it appears there will be a need in the foreseeable future for guardianships/conservatorships among a significant segment of the older population, especially the oldest old, who are most likely to suffer from dementias. The role for social workers in this context can be very substantial.

Social Work in Legal Settings

While there have been, at least, limited roles for social workers in legal settings for quite some time, opportunities for the practice of social work within these venues are clearly on the increase. First of all, this is due to the growing use of guardianships for (allegedly) incapacitated older adults. Within the past 15 years, the emergence of both the philosophy of therapeutic jurisprudence and problem-solving courts, in particular, has added significantly to the value of social workers functioning on behalf of vulnerable older persons. This results from the need to foster linkages between the legal community and social service community in order to deal with underlying issues that

cause individuals to come before the courts in the first place. With the rapid aging of the population, courts seem destined to be the locus of more and more social work practice.

CONCLUSION

Whether or not they function within APS, ombudsman, or legal programs, there are many opportunities for social workers to advocate for vulnerable older persons. "Social workers have always been engaged in advocacy roles, and their participation in consumer-patient rights movement has blended well with the values of the profession" (Netting et al., 1995, p. 355). Many social workers have played important roles in local, state, and national ombudsman programs, as social science researchers, and as observers and advocates (see Netting et al., 1995). Indeed, Arcus (1999) has indicated that with increased attention to the quality of care for those within long-term care facilities, social work "methodologies" become increasing important. Many APS workers, and their administrators, are social workers, and their professional skills are greatly needed by their vulnerable or abused clients. Although the legal system has only recently, and possibly cautiously, added social workers into its programs, it is quite evident that they are needed to protect and represent the best interests of older persons.

Given the increasing number and proportion of older persons, especially among the oldest of the old, the need for advocacy and protection will increase. A "demographic imperative," resulting from the aging of the population, is confronting the profession of social work, and there will be increasing roles for social workers in a variety of settings, especially within ombudsman programs, APS, and the legal field.

REFERENCES

Administration on Aging Resources. (2004). LTC Ombudsman. Available: *www.aoa.gov/prof/aoaprog/elder_rights/LTCombudsman/ltc_ombudsman.asp*.

Alexander, G. J. (1990). Avoiding guardianships. In E. F. Dejowski (Ed.), *Protecting judgment-impaired adults: Issues, interventions and policies* (pp. 163–175). New York: Haworth Press.

Arcus, S. G. (1999). The long-term care ombudsman program: A social work perspective. *Journal of Gerontological Social Work, 31*(1–2), 195–205.

Armstrong, D. G. (2000). *The retirement nightmare: How to save yourself from your heirs and protectors.* Amherst, NY: Prometheus Books.

Arnason, S., Fish, D. G., & Rosenweig, E. P. (2001). Elder law and elder care: A team response to the needs of elderly clients. *Journal of Gerontological Social Work, 34*(3), 3–11.

Atchley, R. C., & Barusch, A. S. (2004). *Social forces and aging: An introduction to social gerontology* (10th ed.). Belmont, CA: Thomson–Wadsworth.

Bassuk, K., & Lessem, J. (2001). Collaboration of social workers and attorneys in geriatric community based organizations. *Journal of Gerontological Social Work, 34*(3), 93–108.

Brownell, P., & Roberts, A. R. (2002). A century of social work in criminal justice and correctional settings. *Journal of Offender Rehabilitation, 35*(2), 1–17.

Casey, P. M., & Rottman, D. B. (2003). *Problem-solving courts: Models and trends.* Williamsburg, VA: National Center for State Courts.

Dejowski, E. F. (1990). Introduction. In E. F. Dejowski (Ed.), *Protecting judgment-impaired adults: Issues, interventions, and policies* (pp. 1–14). New York: Haworth Press.

Gelfand, D. E. (1999). *The aging network: Programs and services* (5th ed.). New York: Springer.

Gutheil, I. A. (1990). Long-term care institutions. In A. Monk (Ed.), *Handbook of gerontological services* (pp. 527–545). New York: Columbia University Press.

Harris-Wehling, J., Feasley, J. C., & Estes, C. L. (1995). *Real people, real problems: An evaluation of the Long Term Care Ombudsman Programs of the Older Americans Act.* Washington, DC: Institute of Medicine, Division of Health Care Services, National Academy of Sciences.

Huber, R., Borders, K. W., Badrak, K., Netting, F. E., & Nelson, H. W. (2001). National standards for the long-term care ombudsman program and a tool to assess compliance: The Huber Badrak Borders scales. *Gerontologist, 41*(2), 264–271.

Hull, L., Holmes, G. E., & Karst, R. H. (1990). Managing Guardianships of the Elderly: Protection and Advocacy as Public Policy. In E. F. Dejowski (Ed.), *Protecting judgment-impaired adults: Issues, interventions, and policies* (pp. 145–162). New York: Haworth Press.

Hwalek, M., Goodrich, C. S., & Quinn, K. (1996). The role of risk factors in health care and adult protective services. In L. A. Baumhover & S. C. Beall (Eds.), *Abuse, neglect, and exploitation of older persons: Strategies for assessment and intervention* (pp. 123–141). Baltimore: Health Professions Press.

Lowy, L. (1980). *Social policies and programs on aging.* Lexington, MA: Lexington Books.

Mixson, P. M. (1995). An adult protective services perspective. *Journal of Elder Abuse and Neglect 7*(2/3), 69–87.

Netting, F. E., Huber, R., Paton, R. N., & Kautz, J. R., III. (1995). Elder rights and the long-term care ombudsman program. *Social Work, 40*(3), 351–357.

Netting, F. E., Paton, R. N., & Huber, R. (1992). The long-term care ombudsman program: What does the complaint reporting system tell us? *Gerontologist, 32*(6), 843–848.

Nolan, B. S. (1990). A judicial menu: selecting remedies for the incapacitated elder. In E. F. Dejowski (Ed.), *Protecting judgment-impaired adults: Issues, interventions, and policies* (pp. 73–88). New York: Haworth Press.

Otto, J. M. (2000). The role of adult protective services in addressing abuse. *Generations 24*(11), 33–38.

Otto, J. M. (2002a, July 18). *Elder justice: Protecting seniors from abuse and neglect.* Hearings before the Senate Finance Committee. 107th Cong., 1st Sess. (testimony of Joanne Otto. Ref.) Available: *www.finance.senate.gov/ hearings/testimony/061802jotest.pdf.*

Otto, J. M. (2002b). *Program and administration issues affecting adult protective services.* (Public policy and aging report, No. 12). Washington, DC: National Academy on an Aging Society. Available: *www.globalaging. org/elderrights/us/aps.htm.*

Quinn, M. J., & Tomita, S. K. (1986). *Elder abuse and neglect: Causes, diagnosis, and intervention strategies.* New York: Springer.

Rothman, M. B., & Dunlop, B. D. (2004). *Judicial responses to an aging America. Final report to the Borchard Foundation on Law and Aging and the Quantum Foundation.* North Miami, FL: Center on Aging of Florida International University.

Rottman, D. B., & Casey, P. M. (1999, July). Therapeutic jurisprudence and the emergence of problem-solving courts. *National Institute of Justice Journal,* 12–19.

Teaster, B. P. (2001). A response to the abuse of vulnerable adults: The 2000 survey of state adult protective services. Available: *www.elderabusecenter.org/pdf/ research/apsreport030703.pdf.*

Senate Subcommittee on Aging. (1981). *Elder abuse: An examination of a hidden problem.* (Publication No. 97-277). H.R. Doc. No. 97-277, 97th Cong., 1st Sess., Washington, DC.

Wexler, D. E., & Winnick, B. J. (1996). *Law in a therapeutic key: Developments in therapeutic jurisprudence.* Durham, NC: Carolina Academic Press.

Housing, or the need for shelter, is one of our most basic human needs. For most people, however, housing is about much more than a physical space or structure. Rather, a home serves multiple functions and has a deeper meaning. A home offers individuals a safe haven and protection from the intrusion of the outside world. One's home and neighborhood are a crucial piece of one's self-identity and evoke a sense of belonging. For many older adults, a home is a highly cherished symbol of their independence and dignity (Brown & Perkins, 1992).

Achieving a "secure old age" for most Americans depends upon three pillars: an adequate retirement income, quality health care, and appropriate and affordable housing. However, many of our nation's housing policies and programs for older Americans have been developed and implemented with little reference to this population's health care or supportive service needs. This disconnect between the two fields of health care and housing, particularly the failure of our nation to develop an affordable and effective community-based, long-term care system, has placed some older citizens at risk of losing their homes and, for others, led to premature institutionalization. A key theme emphasized throughout this chapter is that the diversity of America's senior population requires a wide range of dwelling types and assistive supports that meet or match seniors' household sizes, budgets, and physical or mobility limitations. Despite the historical disconnect between the two fields—health care and housing—several recent trends suggest grounds for optimism. There does appear to be growing recognition that our nation must pursue a more comprehensive or holistic approach to protecting older citizens' health and housing security if we are to ensure America's seniors a safe, secure, and dignified old age. Social workers can play a pivotal role through advocacy on both the clinical and macro levels in promoting affordable and appropriate housing options that maximize all older Americans' ability to age successfully.

JUDITH G. GONYEA

Housing, Health, and Quality of Life

49

DEMOGRAPHIC TRENDS, HOUSING, AND "AGING IN PLACE"

Most older Americans express a strong desire to maintain their independence, to stay in control of their life decisions, and to age with dignity. Central to "successful aging" is having appropriate and affordable housing. The dramatic growth in America's older population has increasingly drawn attention to the challenges our nation will confront in meeting seniors' housing needs both now and in the near-term future. According to demographers, the number of Americans over 65 years of age will double between 1990 and 2025; and by 2030, the ranks of the elderly population will swell to 70 million, with one out of every five Americans being 65 and older. Much of this predicted surge in the senior population is the result of the baby boom cohort's arrival at old age (U.S. Census Bureau, 2002).

Equally important to the growth in our nation's older population are the longevity gains experienced by older Americans. The older population is itself aging, as more persons are surviving to their eighties and nineties. Indeed, the 85-and-over population is currently the fastest-growing segment of the older population. In 2000, approximately 2% of the U.S. population, or about 4 million Americans, were age 85 and older; by 2050, the ranks of the oldest old is projected to increase to almost 5% of the U.S. population, or almost 19 million Americans. Based on increasing life expectancies, the Census Bureau's population projections suggest that by the middle of this century, over 40% of adults age 65 and older can expect to live to at least age 90 (U.S. Census Bureau, 2000). These longevity gains will profoundly affect America's housing market. Chronic health conditions, which lead to a loss of function and mobility, increase with age. Whereas only about 3% of community-based Americans ages 65 to 74 reported problems performing activities of daily living (ADLs) such as dressing, bathing, and eating, this figure rises to almost 10% of community-based Americans age 75 and older. Similarly, while only slightly more than 6% of community-based Americans ages 65 to 74 cited having limitations in the instrumental activities of daily living (IADLs) such as meal preparation and house cleaning, almost one in every five (19.3%) Americans age 75 and older reported such restrictions (National Center for Health Statistics, 2002). Thus, for a significant number of older Americans, particularly the very old, the aging process will bring changing realities in personal health, functional abilities, and necessary home accommodations.

Income disparities present among today's older population will unfortunately continue to exist as the baby boom generation ages. Currently 9.2% of adults ages 65 to 74 and 11.2% of adults age 75 and older are among the ranks of the poor. However, older women and persons of color face a much greater risk of poverty in old age than white men. The interactive effects of gender, race, and age on the experience of poverty are underscored by the fact that the poorest group of older individuals is black or African American women, followed by Hispanic women. For example, African American women are four times more likely than older white men to experience poverty in later life (28% versus 7%) (U.S. Census Bureau, 2002). The disparity in economic well-being in later life will be increasingly important as America's older population becomes more racially diverse. By 2050, the percentage of the older population that is non-Hispanic white is expected to decline from 84% to 64%. Hispanic persons are projected to represent 16% of the older population; 12% of seniors will be non-Hispanic black; and 7% of adults over 65 will be non-Hispanic Asian and Pacific Islanders (U.S. Census Bureau, 2000). Whereas seniors of all income strata face the risks of institutionalization, isolation, and neglect due to declining health and diminished social supports, these risks are greatest for older Americans with low incomes, who are disproportionately women and persons of color.

Recognizing the diversity of America's graying population is important, as seniors' housing choices vary by characteristics such as age, income, race/ethnicity, marital status, availability of children, and need for assistance. Yet, despite the heterogeneity of America's older population, research has consistently shown that our nation's seniors overwhelmingly prefer to remain in their longtime homes and never move. The American Association of Retired Persons (AARP), which has conducted surveys of midlife and older Americans on a regular basis over the last decade, has consistently found that over 80% of respondents age 55 and older prefer to remain in their current residences as they age (84% in 1992; 89% in 2000) (AARP, 2000, 2003). This aspiration to "age in place" is now viewed as an important objective in the design and implementation of formal support services.

HOW AMERICAN SENIORS ARE HOUSED

Much of our understanding of how Americans are housed comes from the American Housing Survey (AHS). This survey, conducted by the U.S. Bureau of the Census for the Department of Housing and Urban Development (HUD), collects data nationally every two years on a wide range of housing characteristics, including apartments, single-family homes, mobile homes, vacant housing units, household characteristics, income, housing and neighborhood quality, housing costs, equipment and fuels, size of housing unit, and recent movers. Using the AHS data, in 1999 HUD published a seminal report, *Housing Our Elders,* which highlighted the current housing status and challenges confronting vulnerable elders living in our nation's communities (U.S. Department of Housing and Urban Development [HUD], 1999). In addition to HUD, a second helpful resource for obtaining information on national trends in America's housing, including seniors' living arrangements, is the Joint Center for Housing Studies (JCHS) of Harvard University (available online at: *www.jchs.harvard.edu/publications/ seniors/index.html*). Finally, the AARP, which has identified community living as one of the organization's priority research and policy areas, periodically conducts national surveys focused on assessing America's seniors' shifting housing preferences and needs (available online at: *www.aarp.org/research*). Together, these three resources—HUD, JCHS, and the AARP—offer social workers up-to-date information and analysis on the housing status of our nation's older population.

In fact, national data underscore that the vast majority of older Americans—82%—reside in conventional housing in the community. Approximately three out of four households over age 62 live in single-family homes, about one in five older households lives in a multiunit structure, and approximately 6% live in mobile homes. Social workers are therefore most likely to encounter seniors who are aging in place in their long-term communities (HUD, 1999).

The JCHS's analysis of the 1993 Assets and Health Dynamics of the Oldest-Old (AHEAD) survey offers further information on the living arrangements of Americans who are age 70 and older (Schafer, 1999). As reflected in Figure 49.1, the JCHS also found that three-quarters of over-age-70 households are living in conventional housing. Not surprisingly, married couples were the most likely to reside in conventional housing types. In addition, the AHEAD data revealed that about 10% of the 70-and-older population live in a "shared housing" arrangement, in which a nonolder member of the household provides assistance to the elder, and another 5% reside in "supported housing," which involves a non–family member living outside the home who provides supportive services. These supportive home environments—"shared housing" and "supported housing"—were more likely to be used by older adults who were separated, divorced, widowed, or never married. Shared housing was also an option that was chosen more often by older persons of color. Only a small percentage—1 out of every 10 individuals age 70 or older—lives in an age-

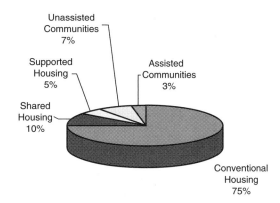

FIGURE 49.1.   Living Arrangements of Persons Age 70 and Older. Reprinted from *Housing America's Seniors,* with permission from the Joint Center for Housing Studies of Harvard University. All rights reserved.

restricted community. Of this 10%, approximately 7% live in unassisted, 60-plus communities, and just 3% reside in assisted living communities, a term used for multifamily housing with congregate and personal care services (Schafer, 1999).

This chapter focuses primarily on the approximately 80% of American seniors who reside as homeowners or renters in conventional housing. As previously noted, very few seniors currently reside in assisted living, although this figure does rise with advanced old age. Similarly, only a very small percentage of the young-old—approximately 1% of persons ages 65 to 74 and 4.7% of persons ages 75 to 84—reside in nursing homes. This figure does rise dramatically, however, with advanced old age; slightly more than one in five (22.2%) persons age 85 and older are nursing home residents (National Center for Health Statistics, 2002).

Older Americans have a very high rate of homeownership. Of the almost 22 million households headed by older persons in 2001, 80% were owners, and 20% were renters (Administration on Aging [AoA], 2002). Yet again, there are significant race disparities in homeownership. The homeownership rate is 81% for older non-Hispanic whites, whereas this rate declines to 65% for older African Americans and 60% for older Hispanics (HUD, 1999). Among older renters, approximately 70% live in private market-rate housing rather than government-subsidized or rent-assisted housing. The 1995 AHS database lists 6.2 million rent-assisted units in the United States, of which 1.4 million (or 22%) were occupied by individuals over the age of 62 (HUD, 1999). The AHS survey also revealed a high level of unmet housing need; there are almost six times as many seniors in need of rent-assisted housing, compared to those that are currently served by these programs. In 1999, approximately nine older applicants were on the waiting lists for each Section 202 rental unit that became vacant within a year (HUD, 1999).

Compared to their homeowner counterparts, the approximately 5 million older householders who are renters tend to be poorer, more often women and persons of color, and more likely to be living alone and in urban communities. Public housing residents are among the most vulnerable of our nation's seniors. Faced with few housing options, most older public housing residents are aging in place. Fifteen percent of senior public housing households are headed by someone age 85 or older, compared to 9% of older households nationwide. It is estimated that over one-quarter of seniors living in public housing have a disabling condition. Finally, the median annual income of older public housing residents is only $7,451, versus $20,761 for the older U.S. population (HUD, 1999).

In fact, residential mobility declines throughout our lives (see Figure 49.2). Only about 5% of persons

between the ages of 65 to 85 change residences in a given year. Almost half of all older homeowners have lived in the same home for more than 25 years. Aging in place means that the housing stock in which seniors live is also aging. For homes occupied by older householders in 2001, the median year of construction was 1963 (AoA, 2002). Despite the age of their housing stock, the vast majority of seniors live in dwellings that are in good condition. The 1995 AHS survey does, however, identify a segment of the 65-and-older households who are "at risk" in terms of their housing costs and quality. Almost 3.9 million senior households—owners and renters—are defined by HUD as having "priority problems," as determined by paying more than 50% of their monthly income on their housing costs or occupying dwellings with severe physical problems. An almost equal amount, another 3.9 million senior households are labeled as having "less serious problems," defined as a housing cost burden of 30% to 49% of their monthly income or occupying dwellings with moderate physical problems (Seniors Commission, 2002). The strongest predictor of physical housing problems is race or ethnicity. Confronted by discrimination in the housing market, along with lower lifetime earnings, elders

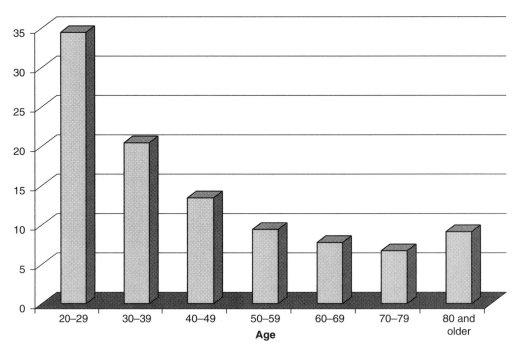

FIGURE 49.2 Residential Moves Annually by Age Group. Moves per 100 persons, 1996–1997. Tabulations of 1997 Current Population Survey. Reprinted from *Housing America's Seniors*, with permission from the Joint Center for Housing Studies of Harvard University. All rights reserved.

of color often live in the least desirable dwellings and neighborhoods. For example, although African Americans represent less than 10% of America's older population, they reside in 23% of all the housing units with severe housing problems and 30% of housing with moderate problems (HUD, 1999).

The interrelationship between the aging individual and his or her aging dwelling can create or exacerbate health problems. As Lawler (2001) notes, a circular relationship exists between health and housing:

> When a living environment is affordable and appropriate, an aging individual is more likely to remain healthy and independent. When an individual maintains good health, he or she is more able to keep up with the maintenance of his or her living environment. As the population ages in an aging housing stock, it becomes difficult to distinguish a health concern from a housing concern. (p. 1)

An aging body and an aging home may simultaneously demand attention and resources from an individual. Poor health and a fixed income may result in an older homeowner or renter being unable to perform and/or purchase home repairs, while substandard housing conditions may further compromise an individual's health. For example, confronted with diminished strength and/or energy and escalating prescription drug expenses, a senior may neglect replacing a broken or malfunctioning stove or refrigerator. However, having a broken stove or refrigerator may result in a poor diet and exacerbate existing health problems, such as diabetes or hypertension.

ENVIRONMENTAL CHALLENGES AND HOUSING DECISIONS

Individuals—across all age groups—choose living arrangements to meet their physical and social needs based on the resources available to them. Relocation or migration *triggers* are often characterized in terms of *push factors* and *pull factors*. Push factors are life events or circumstances that loosen an individuals' attachment to his or her current residence and lead him or her to consider relocation. Pull factors are life events or circumstances that occur at another location and draw an individual toward a new residence (Wiseman, 1980). The specific push and pull factors that influence housing decisions vary across the life

course. Although the primary push or reason older households seek alternative housing arrangements is escalating health problems and the need for assistance with the activities of daily living, these difficulties may be further compounded by declining economic and/or social resources. For example, the death of a spouse is often a push factor, particularly if the frail elder lives alone and does not have caring family members nearby. Loss of a spouse may also reduce or end some sources of income, thus creating greater financial burden for the widow(er) in meeting household expenses (e.g., utility bills, property taxes) and forcing a relocation or move. It is important to remember, however, that there is a great deal of diversity in the disablement process or the pathway to disability. While some seniors may experience a gradual and prolonged period of functional decline, for others it is a sudden event, such as a stroke or a fall, that abruptly changes their ability to function independently and/or safely in their current home. Pull factors might be the opportunity to relocate closer to one's adult children, the availability of a lower-rent apartment in a safer neighborhood, or the chance to move into a single-story dwelling closer to public transportation. Again, many of the triggers for older adults center on health concerns, either current or anticipated. It is important to remember that individuals' environments include not only their homes but also their neighborhoods. Neighborhoods present both opportunities and constraints to older residents as they age, including access to resources such as public transportation, parks, senior centers, doctors, groceries, and pharmacies.

Although most seniors do age in place, persons age 65 and older represent 10% of new homebuyers. As Schafer (2000) notes, the vast majority—approximately 80%—are local moves; only about 1% of seniors move across state lines. Those seniors who do migrate longer distances (e.g., Florida, Arizona) are typically younger, healthier, and wealthier. The slight rise in relocation after the age of 85 (see Figure 49.2) typically reflects the growing mismatch between an individual's assistance needs and his or her physical space.

The environmental press paradigm articulated by Lawton and Nahemow (1973) focuses on the "fit" of the older person with his or her home environments. A leader in the fields of environmental gerontology and environmental psychology, much of Lawton's lifelong work, underscores that an individual's ability to function may be either enhanced or impeded by one's immediate environment. Verbugge and Jette

(1994) note that disability has two aspects: *intrinsic ability* and *actual ability*. Intrinsic ability refers to an individual's abilities regardless of the environment, whereas actual ability focuses on how a person's intrinsic abilities interact with one's social and physical environment. In fact, a growing body of literature suggests that environmental interventions or physical manipulations of the home environment (e.g., home modifications, home repairs, assistive technologies) can postpone or prevent functional decline in older adults (Day, Carreon, & Stump, 2000; Gitlin, 1998; Mann, Ottenbecker, Frass, Tomita, & Granger, 1999).

Yet despite evidence that older individuals with disabilities could benefit from environmental supports, over 1 million senior households, particularly the households headed by the very old, report needing home modifications, such as ramps, and kitchen and bathroom access (Pynoos, 2001). The 1995 AHS survey, for example, revealed that 12% of households headed by a person age 85 and older have unmet household modification needs, as compared with 3% of households headed by a person ages 62 to 74 (HUD, 1999). Similarly, analysis of 1984 data from the Longitudinal Study of Aging (LSOA), a large panel study of Americans 70 years and older, revealed that although almost one third of seniors reported needing a bedroom, bathroom, and kitchen on the same floor, 11% lived in homes in which these rooms were on different floors (Tabbarah, Mihelic, & Crimmins, 2001). As dwellings age and incomes dwindle, seniors' out-of-pocket home modification expenses are more typically for replacing worn-out systems and critical repairs (e.g., furnaces, siding) rather than for adding, enlarging, or modifying rooms (Schafer, 2000). Given the existing level of unmet home modification need, coupled with the reality that the United States adds less than 2% yearly to the new housing stock, Pynoos (2001) stresses that it is critical we make home modifications more available and work to retrofit existing multiunit housing to meet seniors' needs.

LINKING HEALTH CARE AND HOUSING

Addressing the *suitability of fit* between seniors' assistance needs and their environments to maximize their competence also requires that the older adults be able to access the informal and formal services they require. Despite the fact that the health and housing concerns of seniors are highly interrelated, our current systems of health and housing delivery are typically independent and separate services. This lack of integration or coordination between these two systems—that is, the failure of the United States to develop an integrated approach to community-based long-term care—creates significant challenges for frail seniors who are seeking to remain in the community as they age. Lawler (2001) notes that because of this disconnect between health care and housing, seniors are often faced with two equally undesirable choices as they become frailer—*overcare* or *undercare:*

> They are often forced to choose between entering an expensive, restrictive elderly institution before the need arises, or remaining in their homes alone, to face the pressures of rising medical expenses and a deteriorating shelter while on a fixed income. (p. 5)

Recent social trends and policy directions suggest, however, some grounds for optimism. There is a growing convergence between the government's focus on cost containment and its encouragement of self- and community-based care and seniors' desire to age in place within their own homes. Indeed, it is increasingly being recognized that for most older Americans, the home is the primary setting in which long-term care occurs. In 1999, Congress, under the mandates of Public Law 106-7-4, established the Commission on Affordable Housing and Health Facilities Needs for Seniors in the 21st Century. The commission was empowered to study and report back to the Congress on the health and housing facility needs for America's seniors, both now and in the future. The commission was charged with developing specific policy and legislation recommendations to increase the range of options available to current and future generations of seniors. In June 2002, the commission issued a report to Congress, *A Quiet Crisis in America* (Seniors Commission, 2002), in which it states a vision for America:

> The Seniors Commission believes that all older Americans should have an opportunity to live as independently as possible in safe and affordable housing and in their communities of choice. No older person should have to sacrifice his or her home or an opportunity for independence to secure necessary health care and supportive services. (p. 6)

The extensive testimony and research that comprises this report, however, underscores that achieving this vision will not be easy. Barriers identified in

the report include a long history of policy discon-
nects between the health and housing fields, poor
communication, differing vocabulary, limited opportunities to interact between health care and housing
professionals, and different financing and regulatory
structures for the two domains. To develop public
and private sector housing programs that are "flexible," in order to maximize the choices of seniors of all
income strata, the commission recognized that it
would be necessary for the Medicare, Medicaid, and
HUD programs to move beyond a silo approach and
develop broad-base solutions. Ultimately, the commission developed five principles to guide its policy
recommendations:

> *Preserve* the existing housing stock
> *Expand* successful housing projection, rental as-
> sistance programs, home- and community-
> based services, and supportive housing models
> *Link* shelter and services to promote and encour-
> age aging in place
> *Reform* existing federal financial programs to
> maximize flexibility and increase housing pro-
> duction and health and service coverage
> *Create and explore* new housing and service pro-
> grams, models, and demonstrations (p. 62)

HUD, too, has begun to initiate several more comprehensive programs focused on integrating health
and housing services since the release of its 1999 report, *Housing Our Elders*. For example, the HUD Service Coordinator Program, in which the coordinator
acts as a broker of community services for seniors,
was expanded in 2001 to allow these professionals to
work with seniors in the surrounding communities as
well as residents of the HUD multifamily developments. Recognizing that low-income seniors might
also benefit from assisted living environments, in 2001
HUD made available funds for the conversion of
some of its multifamily developments to assisted living facilities (ALFs) to promote vulnerable elders'
ability to age in place. The U.S. Supreme Court decision in *Olmstead v. L.C.* (1999), affirming the right of
persons of all ages with disabilities to live and receive
services in the least restrictive setting they desire if at
all possible, gives further impetus to government coordination to create a more holistic system of care.
Despite these advances, overcoming the existing regulatory, structural, financing, and implementation
barriers to develop a comprehensive approach to the
health and housing needs of older Americans continues to be a significant challenge.

IMPLICATIONS FOR SOCIAL WORK PRACTICE

In addition to their aspiration to age in place, the importance of home to seniors is evident by the fact that,
particularly for the very old, it is the physical space in
which they spend the vast majority of their time and
most of their daily activities occur (Horgas, Wilms, &
Baltes, 1998; Moss & Lawton, 1982). For older people
who may be coping with multiple personal losses
(e.g., death of a spouse, declines in physical health),
one's home can offer a sense of normalcy and coherence about one's personhood (Rubenstein, 1989). The
social work profession's emphasis of strengths-based
and empowerment-oriented paradigms suggests a
commitment to honor seniors' desires to age in place.

Currently, older adults experience a number of
difficulties as they attempt to negotiate the separate
systems of health and housing services to maintain a
quality of care as they age. As noted in the Seniors
Commission (2002) report,

> the ultimate consumer—the senior citizen—
> faces the daunting task of obtaining care from
> these two disconnected sources. Confronted with
> complex entry requirements, insurance coverage
> limitations, and high costs, many seniors become
> overwhelmed just when they need help the most.
> (p. 19)

Social workers, positioned in community agencies, can play a critical role in accessing and coordinating services that allow older persons to live in their
own residences and communities as long as possible,
despite frailty and/or debilitating health conditions.
Moreover, social workers can identify those older individuals who are at risk for housing instability.
Within public housing, social workers often play a
sensitive but critical role in facilitating the needs of
the older residents and the housing management.
One of the primary reasons for older adults' eviction
from public housing is behavioral problems. Eviction
is often a tragic outcome for these vulnerable older
adults who have few alternative housing options.

The social work profession's *person-in-the-environ-
ment* perspective fits well with understanding the *importance of place* in older persons' lives. Through their
professional orientation and clinical training, social
workers are both attuned to and skilled in assessing the
environment-behavior interaction—that is, the interaction between the senior's home environment and his
or her well-being and daily life functioning. Social

workers' clinical assessments of the suitability of fit, however, must extend beyond a focus strictly on how the home and neighborhood environments enhance or impede the senior's *functionality* and *security* to examine their impact on the older adult's level of *comfort* and *social connection,* as well as *personhood.*

It is evident that clinical assessments must incorporate both objective and subjective aspects of the environment to understand seniors' perceived quality of life. Is it is critical to gain an understanding of how the older adults themselves assess the suitability of fit between their homes and neighborhood environments and needs and their preferences and expectations for future living arrangements. Moreover, social workers must strive to understand how older persons' assessments of their current environment, as well as future housing choices, are influenced by the context and meaning of their past environments, life-course changes, and the disablement process (Golant, 2003; Robison & Moen, 2000). Also key is a sensitivity to how an individual's assessment of suitability of fit and housing expectations may be shaped by one's cultural values and norms. Although these distal experiences are not typically included in clinical assessments, failure to frame seniors' housing choices as a process may seriously jeopardize treatment plans.

Attention has generally been focused on how environment supports or impinges upon seniors' physical health. It is also important to understand the impact of the home environment on mental health. The degree to which an older adult with a disabling condition is able to use the home environment to assert some control over the circumstances of daily life may affect his or her sense of self-efficacy and lead to higher morale (Gitlin, 2003; Schulz, Heckhausen, & O'Brien, 1994). In addition, the extent to which the home environment supports opportunities for social interaction or engagement may positively impact the older person's quality of life.

Older adults express confusion about the meaning of many of the types of housing options such as assisted living, supportive housing, adult care facilities, life care communities, continuing care facilities, and reverse mortgages. Social workers can play a valuable role in educating seniors about housing options so that they are able to exercise informed choices.

As a profession that has historically engaged in interdisciplinary practice, social workers can also contribute to community-based efforts to forge stronger linkages between health care and housing programs. For example, as highlighted in the Seniors Commission Report, the two worlds of health care and housing are even separated by language and vocabulary. Aging in place and community living for health care professionals is about beds, lengths of stay, and insurance, as well as the seniors' ADL skills and ability to access and pay for community services. In contrast, housing professionals typically speak about these issues in terms of dwelling units, turnovers, and subsidies, as well as the seniors' income as a percentage of area median income (AMI) (Seniors Commission, 2002).

Finally, on the state and federal level, social workers can actively advocate for policies that promote a more comprehensive and holistic approach to community-based long-term care. Central to this advocacy are the issues of affordability and accessibility, if we as a nation are to create a system of care that works effectively for *all* older citizens. A secure retirement for both current and future generations of older Americans requires all three pillars to be in place—appropriate and affordable housing, adequate income, and quality health care.

REFERENCES

American Association of Retired Persons. (2000). *Fixing to stay: A national survey of housing and home modification issues.* Washington, DC: Author.

American Association of Retired Persons. (2003). *These four walls . . . Americans forty-five-plus talk about home and community.* Washington, DC: Author.

Brown, B., & Perkins, D. (1992). Disruptions in place attachment. In I. Altman & S. Low (Eds.), *Place attachment* (pp. 119–132). New York: Plenum.

Day, K., Carreon, D., & Stump, C. (2000). The therapeutic design of environments for people with dementia: A review of the empirical research. *Gerontologist, 40,* 397–416.

Gitlin, L. N. (2003). Conducting research on home environments: Lessons learned and new directions. *Gerontologist, 43,* 628–637.

Gitlin, L. N. (1998). Testing home modification interventions: Issues of theory, measurement, design, and implementation. In R. Shulz, G. Maddox, & M. P. Lawton (Eds.), *Annual review of gerontology and geriatrics: Focus on interventions research with older adults* (Vol. 18, pp. 190–246). New York: Springer.

Golant, S. M. (2003). Conceptualizing time and behavior in environmental gerontology: A pair of old issues deserving new thought. *Gerontologist, 43,* 638–638.

Horgas, M. A., Wilms, H.-U., & Baltes, M. M. (1998). Daily life in very old age: Daily life as expression of successful aging. *Gerontologist, 43,* 556–568.

Lawler, K. (2001). *Aging in place: Coordinating housing and health care provision for America's growing elderly population* (Working Paper W01-03). Cambridge, MA: Joint Center for Housing Studies of Harvard University.

Lawton, M. P., & Nahemow, L. (1973). Ecology and the aging process. In C. Eisdorfer & M. P. Lawton (Eds.), *The psychology of adult development and aging* (pp. 619–674). Washington, DC: American Psychological Association.

Mann, W. C., Ottenbacher, K. J., Frass, L., Tomita, M., & Granger, C. V. (1999). Effectiveness of assistive technology and environmental interventions in maintaining independence and reducing home care costs for the frail elderly. *Archives of Family Medicine, 8,* 210–217.

Moss, M., & Lawton, M. P. (1982). Time budgets of older people: A window on four life styles. *Journal of Gerontology, 37,* 115–123.

National Center for Health Statistics. (2002). *Health, United States, 2002* (PHS 2002-1232). Washington, DC: Government Printing Office.

Pynoos, J. (2001, November 7). Meeting the needs of older persons to age in place: Findings and recommendations for action. Testimony submitted to the Commission on Affordable Housing and Health Facilities for Seniors in the Twenty-first Century, San Diego, CA. Retrieved June 1, 2004. *http://www.seniorscommission. gov/pages/hearings/011107/pynoos.html.*

Robison, J. T., & Moen, P. (2000). A life-course perspective on housing expectations and fits in late midlife. *Research on Aging, 22,* 499–532.

Rubenstein, R. L. (1989). The home environments of older people: A description of the psychosocial processes linking person to place. *Journal of Gerontology: Social Sciences, 44,* S45–S53.

Schafer, R. (1999). *Housing America's elderly population* (Working Paper 99-4). Cambridge, MA: Joint Center for Housing Studies at Harvard University.

Schafer, R. (2000). *Housing America's seniors* (Report 00-01). Cambridge, MA: Joint Center for Housing Studies at Harvard University.

Schulz, R., Heckhausen, J., & O'Brien, T. (1994). Control and the disablement process in the elderly. *Journal of Social Behavior and Personality, 9,* 130–152.

Seniors Commission. (2002, June). *A quiet crisis in America: A report to Congress by the Commission on Affordable Housing and Health Facility Needs for Seniors in the 21st Century.* Washington, DC: Government Printing Office. Available: *www.seniorscommission.gov.*

Tabbarah, M., Mihelic, A., & Crimmins, E. M. (2001). Disability: The demographics of physical functioning and home environments of older Americans. *Journal of Architectural and Planning Research, 18,* 183–193.

U.S. Administration on Aging. (2002). A profile of older Americans 2002–Housing. Retrieved June 1, 2004. *http://www.aoa.gov/prof/statistics/profile/9.asp.*

U.S. Census Bureau. (2002). *Current population survey: Annual social, and economic supplement.* Washington, DC: Author.

U.S. Census Bureau. (2000). *Population projections of the United States by age, sex, race, Hispanic origin, and nativity: 1999 to 2100.* Washington, DC: Author.

U.S. Department of Housing and Urban Development. (1999, November). *Housing our elders.* Washington, DC: Author. Retrieved May 1, 2004. *http://www.hud. gov/library/bookshelf18/pressrel/elderlyfull.pdf.*

Verbrugge, L., & Jette, A. (1994). The disablement process. *Social Science and Medicine, 38,* 11–24.

Wiseman, R. F. (1980). Why older people move: Theoretical issues. *Research on Aging, 2,* 141–154.

BRADLEY D. ZODIKOFF

Services for Lesbian, Gay, Bisexual, and Transgender Older Adults

50

The purpose of this chapter is to present an overview of community-based social services for lesbian, gay, bisexual, and transgender (LGBT) older adults. Specialized programs for LGBT older adults exist in several communities in the United States. However, nationwide, there is a severe shortage of specialized services for LGBT older adults (Cahill, South, & Spade, 2000; Senior Action in a Gay Environment [SAGE], in press). Most LGBT older adults requiring social work intervention obtain services from mainstream (rather than LGBT-specific) health and/or social service programs. Many of these LGBT older adults encounter obstacles in accessing services sensitive to their specific needs in mainstream settings (Cahill et al., 2000; SAGE, in press). With few exceptions, aging services organizations continue to design programs that presume the heterosexuality of their prospective clients, creating a barrier for LGBT older persons who present to these agencies for social work assistance. At the same time, LGBT older adults are often reluctant to disclose their sexual orientation to mainstream service providers, fearful that by doing so, they may subject themselves to potential stigmatization, hostility, and discrimination (Barranti & Cohen, 2000; Brotman, Ryan, & Cormier, 2003; Kochman, 1997). For the current cohort of LGBT older adults, the fear of stigmatization is grounded in a long historical experience of structural heterosexism, homophobia, and oppression (Kochman, 1997; Rosenfeld, 1999). Though cultural attitudes toward LGBT persons have evolved considerably and dramatically since the birth of the modern gay liberation movement (dating back to the Stonewall rebellion of 1969), there is evidence that LGBT older adults today continue to encounter heterosexism, homophobia, and discrimination in health and mental health settings (Brotman et al., 2003; Cahill et al., 2000). Negative reactions documented toward gay and lesbian patients (across the age spectrum) have included embarrassment, anxiety, direct rejection, refusal of treatment, hostility, excessive curiosity, avoidance of physical contact, and breach of confidentiality, among others (Brotman et al., 2003).

Demographically, the proportion of LGBT older persons in the United States remains difficult to estimate accurately, largely because national surveys asking respondents their sexual orientation or gender identity are very scarce (Cantor, Brennan, & Shippy, 2004). One recent report estimates that at least 1 to 2.8 million persons over the age of 65 living in the United States are gay, lesbian, or bisexual (Cahill et al., 2000). By 2030, the number of gay, lesbian, and bisexual persons age 65 and over is expected to increase to the range of 2 to 6 million seniors (Cahill et al., 2000). Given the unique challenges of estimating population parameters for lesbian and gay persons from available national data sources (Black, Gates, Sanders, & Taylor, 2000), these figures most likely undercount the total lesbian, gay, bisexual and transgender older population (Cahill et al., 2000).

In terms of race, ethnicity, socioeconomic status, health status, geographical location, and availability of social support from partners, children, family, friends, and neighbors, the LGBT older adult population is as diverse and heterogeneous a group as the older population as a whole (see chapter 22 here). It must be emphasized that LGBT older adults and their family members encounter the same range of problems in aging as heterosexual older adults. For this reason, LGBT older adults seek services in *all* types of geriatric settings, just as heterosexual older adults do. However, LGBT older adults face additional challenges in accessing health and social service programs that are sensitive and responsive to their individual needs. Culturally competent social work practitioners, administrators, policy makers, advocates, and researchers must understand LGBT older adult clients as consumers of the *full* spectrum of aging services and must work to develop sensitive and inclusive approaches to address the needs of this persistently underserved population.

Toward this goal, this chapter will focus specifically on service delivery issues with respect to LGBT older adults. (For a comprehensive literature review describing the LGBT older population in detail, please refer to chapter here.) Beginning with a discussion of the specific service concerns of the LGBT older adult population, drawing from current research, this chapter will then describe the availability of services for LGBT older adults across the country, including information to assist providers in locating existing services in their own communities. Key practice principles for working with LGBT older adults and for promoting LGBT-sensitive services within mainstream organizations will also be highlighted. Finally, this chapter will identify selected policy issues that directly affect the health and well-being of LGBT older adults and their families.

SPECIAL CONCERNS OF LGBT OLDER ADULTS

Barranti and Cohen (2000, p. 343) aptly refer to LGBT older adults as "an invisible minority." Many LGBT older adults, though certainly not all, have learned to cope with discrimination throughout their lifetimes by choosing to hide their sexual orientation in specific settings as a means of survival (Barranti & Cohen, 2000; Brotman, 2003; Kochman, 1997). Brotman et al. (2003) emphasize that LGBT older adults' strategy of "hiding" may be understood as an adaptive, long-term coping mechanism for dealing with ongoing discrimination. Many individuals from the current cohort of LGBT older adults came to terms with their sexual orientation long before the modern gay liberation movement began in the 1970s or before the American Psychiatric Association decided in 1973 to remove "homosexuality" from its list of mental disorders in its *Diagnostic and Statistical Manual* (Barranti & Cohen, 2000). Such individuals were faced with the extraordinary challenge of sustaining adult lives during whole decades in which familial, social, and cultural institutions remained intensely homophobic and repressive. "This cohort when they were young was labeled sick by doctors, immoral by clergy, unfit by the military, and a menace by the police" (Kochman, 1997, p. 2). Some LGBT older persons were subjected to treatments that attempted to "cure" their homosexuality using electroshock therapy, aversion therapy, or other means now scientifically discredited (Brotman et al., 2003). A deep sense of shame and stigma, particularly with respect to interacting with health professionals and institutions, remains very acute for some LGBT older adults today (Brotman et al., 2003). Yet at the same time, professionals must recognize the remarkable resilience of this diverse population, as many LGBT older adults have reached old age with affirmative self-identities, and armed with effective coping skills honed from surviving years of discrimination and oppression (Barranti & Cohen, 2000).

A number of research studies have appeared in the literature describing health and social service needs of LGBT older adults. Brotman et al. (2003) provide a highly recommended up-to-date literature review on this topic, in conjunction with their qualitative exploratory study on the service needs of LGBT older adults in Canada. Other research studies include the social service needs of older lesbians and gay men in Chicago (Beeler, Rawls, Herdt, & Cohler, 1999); the health care needs of older lesbians in rural Maine (Butler & Hope, 1999); the social support needs of older lesbians, gay men, and bisexual persons in San Diego County, California (Jacobs, Rasmussen, & Hohman, 1999); elder abuse and neglect issues in lesbian, gay male, bisexual, and transgender elders (Cook-Daniels, 1997); housing issues of LGBT older adults (Hamburger, 1997); long-term care and hospice needs of older lesbians and gay men in California (Connolly, 1996); and the long-term care plans of older lesbians and gay men in three mid-Atlantic states (McFarland & Sanders, 2003). These studies have contributed to the emerging knowledge base regarding the needs of a historically overlooked and neglected research population. Most of these studies have relied on relatively small convenience samples of predominantly white, middle-class, self-identified LGBT older adults recruited from LGBT-identified organizations in various regions of the United States. Therefore, the generalizability of these studies is limited. Notably, there is a dearth of empirical research literature on the characteristics and social service needs of LGBT older adults of color.

The following brief case vignettes, derived from my social work practice, describe the presenting concerns of two older gay male clients referred to an LGBT-identified social service program. These vignettes illustrate the relationship between the *uniquely experienced* aspects of an individual client's sexual orientation and the use of mainstream community-based aging services.

W., an 82-year-old gay white German Jewish male, lost his life partner to illness after they had been together in a committed partnership for over 40 years. W., a Holocaust survivor, has no living family and no gay friends and has been an active member of his local senior center, where virtually all his acquaintances are heterosexual contemporaries. Senior center members and staff knew W.'s "friend," as W. had always referred to his partner in public. However, after W.'s partner died, no one at the senior center acknowledged the magnitude and significance of his personal loss. During his bereavement, W. became severely depressed and socially isolated. He stopped attending the senior center completely, even after multiple attempts by senior center staff to reach out to him. In actuality, W. had never had a conversation with any staff or center members that acknowledged that the "friend" he had lived with for over 40 years was indeed his beloved life partner. "These are not the kind of things you discuss over there," he said about the senior center in the first interview

with a social worker from an LGBT-identified social service agency.

Z., a 69-year-old single gay African American male with end-stage renal disease, lives alone in an apartment in the city and goes to dialysis three times per week. Due to declining health and increasing frailty, the dialysis treatment team has recommended home care to assist Z. with activities of daily living. Z. repeatedly refuses the home care help, even though his insurance and financial resources cover the expense. Z. will not disclose to any health care staff the "real" reason why he does not want a home care worker in his home. Finally, a social worker from an LGBT-identified organization (whom Z. contacted independently) learned during the first home visit that Z. is extremely afraid to hire an unknown home care worker. He fears that upon entering his home and seeing his personal collection of art, books, and photography on the walls of his apartment, the home care worker would learn he is gay. He fears the home care worker might say or do something harmful to him because he is a gay man. Z. said he did not want to feel vulnerable and self-conscious within the comfort of his own home, especially in such weak physical condition. The social worker from an LGBT organization, in coordination with Z. and his dialysis team, helped arrange the hiring of a home care worker from an agency that had undergone sensitivity training working with LGBT older clients. Z found this to be an acceptable plan and then agreed to hire the home care.

LGBT-SPECIFIC PROGRAMS FOR OLDER ADULTS

In categorizing services to LGBT older adults, it is useful to distinguish between *LGBT-specific* versus *generic* services (Humphreys & Quam, 1998). *LGBT-specific* services are programs designed uniquely for LGBT older adult clients. Most LGBT-specific services for older adults are located within LGBT-identified community-based agencies, mental health centers, community centers, and social activity groups (SAGE, in press). However, a program does not need to be located within an LBGT organization to be considered LGBT specific. For example, there is at least one program cited in the literature describing an LGBT-specific, professionally moderated support group delivered within a mainstream outpatient geriatric medical clinic (Slusher, Mayer, & Dunkle, 1996).

Are the service needs of LGBT older adults "best" met in LGBT-specific or mainstream LGBT-sensitive programs? To meet the complete range of service needs, there is clearly a need for both approaches, ideally offering clients choices. There is also diversity within the LGBT older adult population regarding the degree to which LGBT older adults self-identify as LGBT persons and the degree to which they may choose to seek services from LGBT-identified organizations (Slusher, Mayer, & Dunkle, 1996). Many LGBT older adults prefer the services of LGBT-specific agencies. Jacobs et al. (1999) found that gay and lesbian community-based programs were considered more adequate in meeting needs in times of emotional crisis, compared to nongay and lesbian programs.

The oldest and perhaps most widely recognized LGBT-specific agency for older adults is SAGE New York. Founded as "Senior Action in a Gay Environment" in 1977, the organization recently changed its official name (while retaining its acronym) to "Services and Advocacy for Gay, Lesbian, and Transgender Elders" in order to more clearly articulate the organization's current professional mission (Hamilton, 2004). A community-based social service agency, SAGE New York provides a comprehensive range of social work, mental health, community organizing, advocacy, and education programs exclusively focused on the LGBT older adult population. It has been successful in securing both private philanthropic and public governmental funding to support many of its programs. Notably, SAGE New York has worked actively with other communities in the United States and Canada to develop similar service programs for LGBT older adults. As an organization, SAGE occupies a unique leadership role by organizing national conferences on LGBT aging issues. The organization also developed a training curriculum to sensitize long-term care providers to the needs of LGBT elders (SAGE & Brookdale Center on Aging [BCOA], 2003) and conducted the first national needs assessment report on the availability of services for LGBT older adults (SAGE, in press).

Other LGBT-specific programs for older adults operate across the country; however, most are located in large urban centers. In San Francisco, a well-known LGBT-specific program for older adults is "Gay and Lesbian Outreach to Elders" (GLOE). In the 1990s, GLOE transformed into New Leaf Outreach to Elders (NLOE). Funded by grants from the California Endowment, San Francisco Foundation, and Horizons Foundation, NLOE provides geriatric mental health services to LGBT seniors. The organization funds a mobile mental health team, consisting of a psychiatrist, psychiatric nurse, and social worker, that conducts home visits for isolated LGBT elders in need of mental health services, substance abuse treatment, and medication monitoring (White, 2004).

These organizations are but two examples of LGBT-specific service organizations/programs that provide professional social work and mental health services to LGBT older adults. They are frequently referred to in the research literature as model programs (Humphreys & Quam, 1998). There are other LGBT-specific organizations focused primarily on advocacy and policy, rather than the provision of direct service, that address the issues of LGBT older adults as well. Cahill et al. (2000) describe the activities of many of these service, advocacy, and political organizations focused on the critical issues affecting the health and welfare of LGBT older adults. Examples of advocacy organizations working on issues affecting LGBT older adults include the National Gay and Lesbian Task Force Policy Institute, Human Rights Campaign, Old Lesbians Organizing for Change (OLOC), and Pride Senior Network. Space does not permit a full listing of LGBT organizations here; therefore, the reader is encouraged to access Cahill et al.'s (2000) report and additional sources discussed hereafter.

Fortunately, for social workers seeking further information about LGBT-specific organizations/programs in their own communities, a number of excellent Web-based resources are available. The Lesbian Gay Aging Issues Network (LGAIN), a constituent group of the American Society on Aging, maintains a comprehensive Web site notable for not only its national list of LGBT organizations but also its useful annotated bibliography of LGBT aging-related topics, including sections on AIDS/HIV, caregiving, health, housing, and issues of older lesbians, older gay men, and older transgender persons (*www.asaging.org/lgain*). LGAIN also publishes *Outword*, a newsletter focused on the concerns and service needs of LGBT elders. SAGE posts an LGBT Senior Service Directory, listing programs for LGBT older adults throughout the United States (*www.sageusa.org*). The Policy Institute of the National Gay and Lesbian Task Force (NGLTF) is another excellent resource (*www.thetaskforce.org*); it offers several publicly available reports on the health and welfare of LGBT older adults and their families. On the NGLTF Web site, readers will find Cahill, South and Spade's (2000) report, providing a comprehensive listing of organizations working on LGBT aging issues, an extensive bibliography of research literature on LGBT aging, and national policy recommendations to address the needs of LGBT elders. In addition, Cantor, Brennan, and Shippy's (2004) report presents a comprehensive survey on LGBT caregivers over the age of 50 living in New York City, as well as a thorough analysis of policy issues affecting the lives of LGBT older adult caregivers and the members of their families of origin and choice for whom they provide care.

AVAILABILITY OF LGBT-SPECIFIC SERVICES FOR OLDER ADULTS

Until recently, there has been a dearth of national data to assess the availability and scope of programs for LGBT older adults across the country. To obtain much-needed data on this issue, SAGE recently completed the first national needs assessment study of services for LGBT older adults (SAGE, in press). This landmark study utilized snowball sampling to identify service providers from LGBT-specific and mainstream aging service organizations in diverse urban, suburban, and rural areas. The study collected data via key informant interviews, an online survey, five regional "town hall" meetings (held in Bangor, Maine, Boston, Seattle, Chicago, and Fort Lauderdale, Florida), and one transgender focus group. Study respondents reported on the availability, quality, and sensitivity level of existing services for LGBT older adults nationwide.

The report found that there is a severe national shortage of specialized and sensitive services for LGBT older adults. LGBT agencies providing a broad range of formal services to LGBT older adults exist in only a few large urban settings. In smaller cities and towns, often the only services currently available for LGBT older adults, if any, are social activities. While socialization activities are important to enhance social support and reduce social isolation of LGBT older adults, the SAGE national needs assessment study concluded that nationwide, LGBT older adults seeking LGBT-specific comprehensive services have very few options in most communities (SAGE, in press).

The SAGE report further documented a consistent concern among providers that LGBT elders do not believe they are welcome in mainstream aging services programs, or that existing mainstream service programs would be sensitive to their specific concerns and life experiences. In addition, the report found

that LGBT older persons of color and transgender older persons did not feel welcome within existing LGBT senior programs. Unfortunately, the SAGE findings provide further support to the contention of Cahill et al. (2000) that the aging services network remains ill prepared to meet the specific needs of this vulnerable population. Readers are strongly encouraged to refer to the full SAGE report for a comprehensive discussion of service availability issues, including policy and advocacy strategies that address the report's key findings (SAGE, in press).

WORKING WITH LGBT OLDER ADULTS: PRACTICE CONSIDERATIONS

To develop cultural competence practice skills for working with LGBT older adults, social workers must begin by examining their own values, attitudes, and assumptions about gay, lesbian, bisexual, and transgender persons (Bergh & Crisp, 2004; Berkman & Zinberg, 1997; Brotman et al., 2003; Metz, 1997). Bergh and Crisp (2004) propose a framework for defining cultural competence with sexual minorities (of all ages) in the domains of attitudes, knowledge, and skills, drawing on the gay affirmative practice model described by Appleby and Anastas (1998). Bergh and Crisp (2004) encourage practitioners to develop self-awareness regarding their own potentially negative attitudes about LGBT clients and to actively pursue practice knowledge relevant to LGBT populations through continuing education, in-service trainings, and clinical supervision. They also suggest practical ideas for communicating a safe, gay-affirmative agency environment, such as making literature or events on LGBT-related topics publicly available to *all* clients or placing a rainbow flag (a widely recognized symbol of LGBT community diversity) in a noticeable place in the agency setting (Bergh & Crisp, 2004).

Community-based agencies communicate a great deal about their attitudes toward LGBT older clients through the psychosocial assessment process. Several authors highlight the critical need for agencies to review outreach and intake procedures (Brotman et al., 2003; Humphreys & Quam, 1998; Metz, 1997). Prospective older LGBT clients, by virtue of their life-course experience, are highly attuned to subtle and overt forms of heterosexism in agency settings and therefore may interpret heterosexist attitudes as an indication that they are not welcome as clients (Metz, 1997). At intake, social workers should *assess* (rather than *assume*) a client's sexual orientation (Bergh & Crisp, 2004). Consider one of the most common intake questions: "What is your marital status?" or "Are you married?" Social workers might consider phrasing this question in a more neutral way. For example: "Please describe those relationships that are or have been most important to you" (Metz, 1997, p. 37). The alternative wording of this question demonstrates sensitivity to a prospective LGBT older client who may now feel more comfortable describing to the worker the significant same-sex relationships (past and present) in his or her life.

Humphreys and Quam (1998) highlight several important practice principles that agencies may consider in order to increase sensitivity and cultural competence regarding working with older LGBT clients, as follows.

- *Respect a client's right to privacy/confidentiality.* A client who "comes out" to a worker may not feel equally comfortable disclosing his or her sexual orientation to other agency staff and/or to other clients. Clients' wishes about privacy and confidentiality must be explored and respected.
- *Recognize diversity within LGBT communities.* Clients may differ significantly in their level of comfort with respect to discussing and/or accepting their own sexual orientation. In addition, the level of acceptance older LGBT clients experience from family members, friends, neighbors, and colleagues may also differ dramatically, depending on a client's unique life experience.
- *Not all problems a person has are associated with being gay or lesbian or with being old.* Like all seniors, older LGBT clients present to social workers with complex, multidimensional problems, many of which may have little or no relationship to "sexual orientation" or "old age."
- *Treat a client's identified family as family.* Social service agencies must recognize, validate, and support members of older LGBT clients' *chosen* families. Many older LGBT clients have committed partners and close friends whom they consider to be members of their chosen families, in addition to members of their families of origin. Agencies should honor LGBT older clients' decisions as to whom they choose to include regarding their treatment and other decisions about care.

POLICY ISSUES

Cantor et al. (2004), in a research survey documenting the caregiving experiences of LGBT older adults in New York City, identify several critical national policy issues that affect the lives of LGBT older adult caregivers, care recipients, and their families of origin and choice. They point out, for example, that language in the National Family Caregiver Support (NFCS) program (passed by the U.S. Congress in 2000) employs a definition of "caregiver" that is inclusive of individuals providing informal care to a same-sex partner, close friend, or family member. They strongly encourage LGBT-specific community-based agencies to apply for Area Agency on Aging funding to provide caregiver services through the NFCS program. They further emphasize the need to build awareness among LGBT older adults and their caregivers that they are currently eligible for existing services under the NFCS program and may access these services in their local communities (Cantor et al., 2004).

Another critical U.S. policy issue concerns the lack of legal same-sex partner recognition and its negative effects on gay and lesbian older adults in committed same-sex relationships. Legal marriage between same-sex partners is not, as yet, recognized across the United States. Though domestic partnership policies exist in a number of state and local jurisdictions, these policies do not assign all the rights and protections specifically afforded to legally married heterosexual couples. Bennett and Gates (2004) provide a detailed analysis of this issue with respect to LGBT seniors. Surviving partners in gay and lesbian partnerships are denied Social Security survivor benefits, are charged an estate tax on the inheritance of a jointly owned home, and are taxed on retirement plans inherited from a deceased partner. Among same-sex couples in which one member must enter a nursing home, the community-dwelling partner is at serious risk of losing his or her home because federal Medicaid spend-down regulations (while protecting heterosexual married spouses, who are allowed to keep their homes) do not protect community-dwelling partners of same-sex relationships (Bennett & Gates, 2004). These inequities in U.S. Social Security law, tax law, property law, and Medicaid law pose serious economic and social consequences for LGBT older Americans. As professionals committed to social justice for all oppressed groups, gerontological social workers need to understand how the lives of LGBT older adults are profoundly negatively affected by current government policies. As a profession, we must continue to work to effect policy reform at the local, state, and federal levels to address the negative consequences of discrimination against LGBT older adults and their families.

REFERENCES

Appleby, G. A., & Anastas, J. W. (1998). *Not just a passing phase: Social work with gay, lesbian, and bisexual people.* New York: Columbia University Press.

Barranti, C., & Cohen, H. (2000). Lesbian and gay elders: An invisible minority. In R. Schneider, N. Kropf, & A. Kisor (Eds.), *Gerontological social work: Knowledge, service settings and special populations* (2nd ed., pp. 343–367). Belmont, CA: Wadsworth.

Beeler, J., Rawls, T., Herdt, G., & Cohler, B. (1999). The needs of older lesbians and gay men in Chicago. *Journal of Lesbian and Gay Social Services, 9*(1), 31–49.

Bennett, L., & Gates, G. (2004). *The cost of marriage inequality to gay, lesbian and bisexual seniors: A Human Rights Campaign Foundation Report.* Washington, DC: Human Rights Campaign Foundation.

Bergh, N. V. D., & Crisp, C. (2004). Defining culturally competent practice with sexual minorities: Implications for social work education and practice. *Journal of Social Work Education, 40*(2), 221–238.

Berkman, C., & Zinberg, G. (1997). Homophobia and heterosexism in social workers. *Social Work, 42*(4), 319–332.

Black, D., Gates, G., Sanders, S., & Taylor, L. (2000). Demographics of the gay and lesbian population in the United States: Evidence from available systematic data sources. *Demography, 37*(2), 139–154.

Brotman, S., Ryan, B., & Cormier, R. (2003). The health and social service needs of gay and lesbian elders and their families in Canada. *Gerontologist, 43*(2), 192–202.

Butler, S. & Hope, B. (1999). Health and well-being for late middle-aged and old lesbians in rural areas. *Journal of Gay and Lesbian Social Services, 9*(4), 27–46.

Cahill, S., South, K., & Spade, J. (2000). *Outing age: Public policy issues affecting gay, lesbian, bisexual, and transgender elders.* New York: National Gay and Lesbian Task Force Policy Institute.

Cantor, M. H., Brennan, M., & Shippy, R. A. (2004). *Caregiving among older lesbian, gay, bisexual, and transgender New Yorkers.* New York: National Gay and Lesbian Task Force Policy Institute.

Connolly, L. (1996). Long-term care and hospice: The special needs of older gay men and lesbians. *Journal of Gay and Lesbian Social Services, 5*(1), 77–91.

Cook-Daniels, L. (1997). Lesbian, gay male, bisexual, and transgendered elders: Elder abuse and neglect issues. *Journal of Elder Abuse and Neglect, 9*, 35–49.

Hamburger, L. (1997). The wisdom of non-heterosexually based senior housing and related services. *Journal of Gay and Lesbian Social Services, 6*(1), 11–25.

Hamilton, S. (2004, Summer). New logo, name better reflect SAGE's mission. *SAGE Matters Newsletter*, p. 2.

Humphreys, N., & Quam, J. (1998). Middle-aged and old gay, lesbian, and bisexual adults. In G. A. Appleby & J. W. Anastas (Eds.), *Not just a passing phase: Social work with gay, lesbian, and bisexual people* (pp. 245–267). New York: Columbia University Press.

Jacobs, R., Rasmussen, L., & Hohman, M. (1999). The social support needs of older lesbians, gay men, and bisexuals. *Journal of Gay and Lesbian Social Services, 9*(1), 1–30.

Kochman, A. (1997). Gay and lesbian elderly: Historical overview and implications for social work practice. *Journal of Gay and Lesbian Social Services, 6*(1), 1–10.

McFarland, P., & Sanders, S. (2003). A pilot study about the needs of older gays and lesbians: What social workers need to know. *Journal of Gerontological Social Work, 40*(3), 67–80.

Metz, P. (1997). Staff development for working with lesbians and gay elders. *Journal of Gay and Lesbian Social Services, 6*(1), 35–45.

Rosenfeld, D. (1999). Identity work among lesbian and gay elderly. *Journal of Aging Studies, 13*(2), 121–144.

Senior Action in a Gay Environment and Brookdale Center on Aging. (2003). *No need to fear, no need to hide: A training program for inclusion and understanding of lesbian, gay, bisexual, and transgender (LGBT) elders in long-term care facilities.* New York: Authors.

Senior Action in a Gay Environment. (in press). *SAGE National Needs Assessment and Technical Assistance Audit.* Prepared for Senior Action in a Gay Environment by Marj Plumb and Associates. New York: Author.

Slusher, M., Mayer, C., & Dunkle, R. (1996). Gays and Lesbians Older and Wiser (GLOW): A support group for older gay people. *Gerontologist, 36*(1), 118–123.

White, M. (2004, Spring). Gay and Lesbian Outreach to Elders pioneers West Coast service provision. *Outword*, p. 1.

CHARLES EMLET
CYNTHIA POINDEXTER

Services for HIV-Infected or HIV-Affected Older Adults

Adults age 50 and over who are living with HIV[1] or AIDS have been called hidden (Emlet, 1997) or invisible (Genke, 2000) because they are not readily acknowledged by gerontologists and service providers, although they have always comprised at least 10% of the incidences of AIDS in the United States (Centers for Disease Control [CDC], 1998). HIV disease has often been regarded as affecting primarily younger persons, but HIV researchers and advocates have increasingly recognized midlife and older adults as being at risk for HIV infection. Recent data point to a graying of the HIV epidemic. As Levy, Ory, and Crystal (2003) point out, the cumulative number of AIDS cases reported to the Centers for Disease Control in adults age 50 and over quintupled between 1990 and 2001. By the end of 2001, 18.9% of persons living with AIDS were 50 years of age or older (Mack & Ory, 2003).

In addition to an increasing number of HIV-infected older adults, a growing number of older adults are *HIV-affected*, referring to "those family members who have responsibilities of caregiving for an adult or child who has HIV disease" (Poindexter, 2001, p. 525). Estimates suggest that one-third to one-half of persons living with AIDS are dependent upon older relatives (often parents or grandparents) for financial, emotional, and physical support (Allers, 1990; Joslin, 2000).

This chapter provides human service practitioners with information related to service delivery systems and their legislative underpinnings so that they can be more prepared to provide case management and referrals to older adults affected by HIV and AIDS. Commonly available services will be outlined, as well as the roles that social work can play in these organizations. The ways in which such services can enhance quality of life and be culturally relevant will be discussed.

SYSTEMS OF CARE AND FEDERAL PUBLIC POLICY

Historically, systems of care, influenced by public policy, have centered on particular needs or populations. Such foci have tended to separate issues that may be connected, such as aging and HIV (Emlet & Poindexter, 2004). While we may need to view pieces of legislation separately (by necessity), we must at the same time direct our attention to how, at the local level, we can improve care and services through coordination and collaboration. We discuss here three of the most vital federal programs for this population.

Ryan White Comprehensive AIDS Resources Emergency (CARE) Act

The CARE Act of 1990 was the first federal service delivery mechanism to aid persons with HIV. The act addresses the unmet health needs of persons living with HIV disease by funding primary health care and social support services. Enacted in 1990, it was amended and reauthorized in 1996 and 2000. The act services benefit 533,000 individuals each year, making it the federal government's largest program specifically for people living with HIV disease (U.S. Health Resources and Services Administration [USHRSA], 2002–2003). (See Poindexter, 1998, and Emlet & Poindexter, 2004, for details on the provisions of the Act.)

While it is not the purpose of this chapter to provide an extensive overview of relevant public policy, many social workers employed in settings serving older adults may be unfamiliar with the CARE Act. We have therefore included an overview of the various titles and their purposes in Table 51.1. Worthy of note are the AIDS Drugs Assistance Programs (ADAPs), which can provide HIV-related medications to those who do not have insurance coverage for drugs. The graying of the HIV epidemic is reflected in services provided through this program. According to a recently released study, 29% of the people served through Title 1 and 26% of the people served through Title 2 were age 45 or older in 2000, compared to 20% in 1998 (USHRSA, 2002–2003).

Service Delivery

Services for persons of all ages living with HIV may be provided through numerous mechanisms, including public health and social services, university medical centers and clinics, and AIDS service organizations (ASOs). ASOs are community-based agencies that developed to ensure the delivery of health-related and social services to HIV-affected individuals and families (Burrage & Porche, 2003). Historically, most ASOs were small grassroots organizations founded and operated by members of the gay community who raised funds in order to provide services (Lewis & Crook, 2001). Many of these organizations continued to grow and now provide a majority of services to HIV-positive individuals.

AIDS service organizations and other providers of services may not specifically target midlife and older adults through the CARE Act; however, CARE Act programs can easily be used to serve older persons with HIV, as well as offer support to older persons who are taking care of HIV-infected adult or child family members. The CARE Act requires consumer participation at the local level by stipulating that one third of local Title 1 planning councils or Title 2 consortia members be HIV infected. In this way the needs of older HIV-infected individuals and HIV-affected older caregivers can be taken into account when funding is discussed at the local level, and midlife and older persons can be given opportunities to participate on consortia and planning councils. The act also targets women, children, and families through set-asides and demonstration projects, which can include older caregivers.

Social Work Roles

Social workers should keep the following tasks in mind regarding the CARE Act.

- Being familiar with services and eligibility requirements of local ASOs and other organizations funded by the CARE Act
- Engaging in advocacy for older adults through participating in Title 1 planning councils or Title 2 consortia
- Encouraging and empowering older infected or affected persons to participate in educational and advocacy activities
- Working directly with ASOs to provide support groups or other services for serving midlife and older adults

Older Americans Act (OAA)

The OAA of 1965 was one of several major federal initiatives of President Lyndon B. Johnson's Great Society programs designed to benefit older persons (Estes, 1979). The act created the Administration on Aging (AoA) and authorized grants to states for community planning and services programs, as well as for research, demonstration, and training projects in the field of aging. The OAA calls for specific attention to those elders who are in the greatest social and economic need; anyone who is over 60 or the legal spouse of someone over 60 can access OAA services. Today the OAA has firmly established the aging network, which includes 57 State Units on Aging (SUAs), approximately 650 Area Agencies on Aging (AAAs), and 220 tribal organizations representing 300 native tribes (Takamura, 2001).

TABLE 51.1. Overview of CARE Act Titles and Subparts

Title or Program	Purpose	Types of Services Funded
Title 1	Provides emergency assistance to eligible metropolitan areas (EMAs) that are most severely affected by the HIV/AIDS epidemic.	• Outpatient and ambulatory health services, including substance abuse and mental health treatment • Early intervention that includes outreach, counseling, and testing, and referral services designed to identify HIV-positive individuals who know their HIV status • Outpatient and ambulatory support services, including case management • Inpatient case management services that expedite discharge and prevent unnecessary hospitalization
Title 2	Provides grants to all 50 states, the District of Columbia, and U.S. territories; grants are used to provide a variety of services, as listed here. Unlike Title 1, grants may include nonprofit as well as public entities.	• Ambulatory health care • Home-based health care • Insurance coverage • Medications • Support services • Outreach to HIV-positive individuals who know their HIV status • Early intervention services • HIV Care Consortia, which assess needs and contracts for services
Title 3	Early Intervention Services (EIS) program; funds comprehensive primary health care for individuals living with HIV disease.	• Risk-reduction counseling on prevention, antibody testing, medical evaluation, and clinical care • Antiretroviral therapies; ongoing medical, oral health, nutritional, psychosocial, and other services for HIV-infected clients • Case management to ensure access to services and continuity of care • Attention to other health problems that occur frequently with HIV infection, including tuberculosis and substance abuse
Title 4	These programs specifically serve women, infants, children, and youth living with HIV disease.	• Primary and specialty medical care • Psychosocial services • Logistical support and coordination • Outreach and case management
AIDS Drug Assistance Programs (ADAP)	A specific program under Title 2; these programs provide medications for the treatment of HIV disease. Program funds may also be used to purchase health insurance for eligible clients.	Congress "earmarks" funds that must be used for the ADAP, an important distinction, since other Title 2 spending decisions are made locally
Special Project of National Significance (SPNS)	This program advances knowledge and skills in the delivery of health and support services to underserved populations diagnosed with HIV infection. SPNS is considered the research and development arm of the CARE Act and provides the mechanisms for the services listed here.	• Assess the effectiveness of particular models of care • Support innovative program design • Promote replication of effective model

Note: From *Ryan White CARE Act Programs*, by U.S. Department of Health and Human Services, Health Resources and Services Administration, HIV/AIDS Bureau, 2002. Available: *http://hab.hrsa.gov/programs.htm*.

Titles 3, 5, 6, and 7 provide a wide array of services that may be relevant to older adults who are living with HIV disease, as well as HIV-affected caregivers. As shown in Table 51.2, Title 3 authorizes funds to states and AAAs for a variety of in-home and supportive services (Administration on Aging [AoA], 2001). Part C focuses on the provision of nutrition services, nutrition education, and counseling, while part D provides disease prevention and health promotion services to older adults (AoA, n.d.). Title 5 provides a means to increase individual economic self-sufficiency to those age 55 and over. Title 6 provides grants to Native Americans, and Title 7 focuses on the protection of vulnerable older adults and the prevention of elder abuse.

Service Delivery

The hallmark of the OAA at the local level is the development and maintenance of the AAA network. The act requires coordination and planning of aging services at the state as well as local and regional levels. Each state is divided into one or more planning service areas (PSAs) operated under the auspices of an AAA. The AAAs are important resources for gerontological social workers or those working with HIV-infected or -affected elders, as they not only provide social services directly but often contract with other agencies and organizations for the provision of services. These agencies are therefore a clearinghouse for information and resources available to older adults and their families (Kisor, McSweeney, & Jackson, 2000). The AoA provides a listing of each SUA and AAA at its Web site (*www.aoa.gov/eldfam/ How_To_Find/Agencies/Agencies.asp*).

Social Work Roles

The following tasks may be useful for social workers as they utilize the OAA's services.

- Identifying venues to educate social workers employed in the local aging network (including Area Agencies on Aging) about HIV disease
- Participating in AAA activities such as public hearings or annual plan developments
- Seeking a seat on the AAA advisory council and advocate for the inclusion of HIV education and services
- Helping forge partnerships or task forces among AAA providers and the HIV network

Home and Community-Based Waiver Programs

Medicaid is typically viewed as a payment source for institutional long-term care or medical care for low-income populations. In recent years, however, Medicaid has made substantial contributions to transform the long-term care system from institutionally based into community-based care through the home and community-based waiver (Miller, Ramsland, & Harrington, 1999).

The home and community-based waiver, added to the Social Security Act by the Omnibus Reconciliation Act of 1981, authorized the waiver of certain Medicaid limitations to allow states to cover home and community-based services to individuals as an alternative to institutional care in hospitals, nursing homes, or other facilities such as intermediate care facilities for persons with developmental disabilities (U.S. General Accounting Office [USGAO], 2003; Miller et al., 1999). The Omnibus Reconciliation Act was amended in 1985 to allow the creation of waiver programs specific to persons living with AIDS (Buchanan & Chakravorty, 1997). These home and community-based waiver programs provide a wide range of services to targeted subgroups of individuals. The original focus was on frail older adults and those with developmental disabilities; the targeted populations have been expanded to include individuals with AIDS, working-age individuals with physical disabilities, and children with a variety of conditions. Waiver programs are developed on a state-by-state basis and may provide nonmedical services such as case management, homemaker services, personal care services, and adult daycare, as well as medical care such as nursing services in the home (Miller et al., 1999).

A recent report from the U.S. General Accounting Office (2003) documented a substantial rise in the number of Medicaid waiver programs throughout the United States. Home and community-based waiver programs increased in number from 155 in 1991 to 263 in 2001 (USGAO, 2003). According to this report, every state except Arizona (which operates a different type of waiver program) operates at least one waiver for the elderly as of June 2002.

Service Delivery

An older adult with HIV could, depending upon age, disability status, and diagnosis, be eligible for services through a variety of waiver program categories. Waiver programs may target frail elderly specifically

TABLE 51.2. Overview of the Older Americans Act

OAA Title and Part	Purpose	Services
Title 3B	To improve the lives of older people, in particular the rural elderly, those with greatest economic and social need, including specific objectives for low-income minority older persons	• Access services, i.e., information and assistance, transportation and outreach • In-home services, including homemaker, visiting, and telephone reassurance; chore and supportive services; case management and supportive services for families of older individuals with Alzheimer's disease and related disorders • Legal services, including financial, insurance, and tax counseling
Title 3C	Provides for the establishment and operation of congregate and home-delivered nutrition programs	• Congregate meal program • Home-delivered meal program • Nutrition education, counseling, and screening
Title 3D	Provides disease prevention and health promotion services and information at senior centers, meal sites, and other appropriate locations	• Health risk assessments and screening • Health promotion, exercise, and fitness programs • Home injury control services • Screening for prevention of depression • Medication management & education programs • Information concerning diagnosis, prevention, treatment, and rehabilitation of age-related diseases and conditions • Gerontological counseling • Counseling regarding social services
Title 3E	The National Family Caregiver Support Program: provides services to family caregivers, grandparents, or other older individuals who are relative caregivers of a child under age 18	• Information to caregivers about available services • Assistance to caregivers in gaining access to supportive services • Individual counseling, organization of support groups, and caregiver training in making decisions and solving problems relating to their caregiving roles • Respite care • Supplemental services
Title 5	The Senior Community Service Employment Program:* fosters and promotes useful part-time opportunities in community service activities for unemployed low-income persons.	• Part-time employment training • Job placement at community and government agencies • Available to individuals age 55 and over
Title 6	Serves older individuals who are Indians, Alaskan Natives, and Native Hawaiians; services are provided to 241 Tribal and Native organizations and two organizations serving Native Hawaiians in a manner that preserves and restores their dignity, self-respect, and cultural identities	• Supportive and nutrition services that are comparable to services provided under Title 3 • The Native American Caregiver Support Program assists caregivers of Native American elders who are chronically ill or disabled
Title 7	To protect and enhance the basic rights and benefits of vulnerable older people who may need advocacy on their behalf because of physical or mental disabilities, social isolation, limited educational attainment, or limited financial resources	• Long-term care ombudsman services • Programs for the prevention of elder abuse • State legal assistance development programs

Note: From U.S. Department of Health and Human Services, Administration on Aging. Available at: *www.aoa.gov/*.

and combine frail older adults with disabled adults over 18 years of age, as well as specifically targeting those disabled from AIDS. According to Buchanan and Chakravorty (1997), most states do not have separate waiver programs differentiating disabled adults and the frail elderly. Buchanan and Chakravorty's analysis of home and community-based waiver programs identifies 35 states with waivers for combined aged/disabled individuals. Sixteen states operated separate waiver programs for persons living with HIV disease. In five instances, AIDS waiver programs existed in states without waiver programs for younger disabled (non-HIV-related) individuals, suggesting the availability of waiver services in a minimum of 40 states.

While the existence of home and community-based waiver programs provides another important source of help for older adults with HIV, some important limitations exist. First, services are limited to certain individuals based on types of disability and may be limited to specific geographical regions within states (Miller et al., 1999). Second, waiver programs targeting those with AIDS are obviously more severely limited to 16 states (those with AIDS waiver programs). Finally, income and functional status criteria limit an individual's eligibility for waiver services. The individual must meet the state's criteria for needing a level of care provided in an institution, must be able to receive care in the community at a cost not exceeding that of institutional care (USGAO, 2003), and must be Medicaid eligible in his or her state. For older adults living with HIV, particularly those who are seriously disabled from HIV disease or other age-related disabilities, these programs can provide a substantial amount of home and community-based help and support. The availability of home and community-based waiver programs will vary from state to state, but local Area Agencies on Aging, senior information and assistance programs, ASOs, and local public health departments are good sources of information.

Social Work Roles

Social workers can use waivers in the following ways.

- Maintaining an up-to-date awareness of Medicaid waiver services, eligibility criteria, and limitations
- Advocating for the development of expanded or additional waiver services in one's local area
- Seeking out and collaborating with health care agencies who offer Medicaid waivers to ensure cross-training, appropriate referrals, and coordinated case management

IMPROVING CARE FOR HIV-INFECTED AND HIV-AFFECTED ELDERS AT THE LOCAL LEVEL

This brief overview of several important federally sponsored or funded programs suggests a wide array of services that can assist HIV-infected or HIV-affected midlife and older persons. Joslin and Nazon (1996) suggest that older HIV-positive persons present themselves to service providers with needs that can only be partially met within one service system. For social workers working in the area of case management, the benefits of integrating services across systems can be easily seen from the following examples.

- A 63-year-old low-income Latina who is impaired by AIDS, in addition to multiple age-related chronic conditions, could benefit from an OAA-sponsored nutrition program and senior transportation while receiving homemaker services and nursing care from a locally administered Medicaid waiver program. She can receive medical care from a CARE Act–funded medical clinic and help with her HIV medications from the AIDS Drug Assistance Program.
- A 56-year-old HIV-infected gay man whose health has improved dramatically with the advent of highly active antiretroviral therapy might seek assistance through reemployment opportunities through Title 5 of the OAA (Community Service Employment for Older Americans), while maintaining needed support through the local AIDS service organization.
- A 74-year-old African American grandmother providing care to her 12-year-old HIV-infected grandson could be helped by the National Family Caregiver Support Program, as well as Title 4 of the CARE Act, providing services to women, children, and families.

While it seems obvious that HIV-infected or HIV-affected older adults could benefit from improved coordination and collaboration between aging and HIV service sectors, the best method for achieving this goal is less clear. Is service integration necessary in order to improve care, and if so, what do we mean by integration? Recently, Messeri, Kim, and Whetten (2003) presented a taxonomy for the integration of HIV services. They suggest that service integration may be accomplished on a continuum from minimal (client-centered) to maximum (government/funding-centered) integration. They suggest that "the former are efforts that work directly with clients without altering the delivery of services . . . the latter involve major reorganization and consolidation in the way state and federal government funds and administer health and human services" (p. 25). Once service providers recognize that older adults are infected with and affected by HIV, discussion about methods for improving service delivery across systems could take on a variety of approaches. In what follows, we supply examples that outline various ways services have been approached for older adults affected by HIV disease; these examples fall at various points on the continuum suggested by Messeri and colleagues.

Emlet (2004) studied 41 adults age 50 and over diagnosed with HIV or AIDS who were primarily clients of an ASO. Respondents were surveyed as to what services from the AIDS network they were familiar with and which services they had personally used. They were asked to respond to a similar list of services from the aging network. Respondents used a significantly greater number of HIV services compared to those from the aging network. Nearly 20%, however, did use in-home or chore services provided through the local AAA, and approximately 10% had used home-delivered meals and adult day health care programs. Integration of services, for these individuals, appeared to be effectively accomplished at the client level (with the help of case managers) with little or no need for more formalized mechanisms of service delivery (client-centered integration).

In 1997, the Senior HIV Intervention Project (SHIP) was created through a model of shared resources between the Florida Department of Elder Affairs and the Florida Department of Health (Nichols et al., 2002). Initial funding from OAA sources was organizationally housed in the Florida Department of Health, Bureau of HIV/AIDS (J. Mullins, personal communication, June 8, 2004). Focusing on three counties, and administered through the Broward County Health Department, SHIP trains volunteers as peer educators and provides educational seminars and workshops in a variety of venues. While changes in funding have over time diminished the OAA role in the project, SHIP has gained support from a Center for Disease Control and Prevention grant. Collaboration continues to exist between the local health departments of Broward, Miami-Dade, and Palm Beach Counties and local senior centers, community centers, and senior housing complexes. This collaboration is an exemplar of a continued relationship between the AAAs and their providers and the public health sector. Staff from the SHIP estimate the project reaches between 30,000 and 40,000 seniors each year. Recent funding from a local community foundation (private) will allow a focused prevention effort targeting older gay men of color (J. Mullins, personal communication, June 8, 2004) (program-centered integration).

An example of systems coordination overseen by shared governance can be found in the New York Association on HIV Over Fifty. The New York City HIV/AIDS and Aging Task Force was created in 1991 to "bring professionals from AIDS and aging networks together to address the impact of the HIV/AIDS epidemic on older adults" (Nokes, 2004, p. 182). The association currently has approximately 80 members, including health and social service professionals and consumers who are living with HIV and are over 50 years of age. The association was formally incorporated in January 2003 and allows both individual and organizational membership. Once a loosely structured coalition, this body has evolved and become more formal, taking on additional structure (policy-centered as well as program-centered integration).

SUGGESTED RESOURCES

If social workers are to improve their knowledge of issues related to older adults and HIV disease, they will need to become familiar with tools and resources to improve their understanding of these issues. In addition, they may then serve as resources themselves to improve the knowledge and understanding of other players in the community. It is through such a "ripple effect" that we can begin to increase society's understanding of the myriad of issues that affect this often overlooked and hidden population. A brief list follows of Internet and other resources social workers can use to begin this process.

> *National Association on HIV Over Fifty (NAHOF)* was founded at the National Conference on AIDS and Aging in October 1995 in New York City. Its mission is to promote the availability of a full range of educational, prevention, service, and health care programs for persons over age 50 affected by HIV (available at: *www.hivoverfifty.org*).
>
> *HIV Wisdom for Older Women* is an organization dedicated to prevention and care. Recognizing a need for awareness and support for older women affected by HIV, the group was formed

in 2002 to serve this underrepresented community and to educate older women about HIV (available at: *www.hivwisdom.org/*).

Senior Action in a Gay Environment (SAGE) is the nation's oldest and largest social service and advocacy organization dedicated to lesbian, gay, bisexual, and transgender (LGBT) seniors. This organization provides education and advocacy on LGBT aging issues nationwide (available at: *www.sageusa.org/*).

SUMMARY

We have provided an overview of three important sources of federal funding for services to HIV-infected and HIV-affected midlife and older adults. Social workers, as case managers, counselors, and advocates, have always strived to coordinate diverse human services programs for the benefit of those who are in need of support. An integrated continuum of care is vital for adults who are dealing with both aging and HIV. It is hoped that this chapter "primes the pump" and encourages practitioners and managers to offer outreach and targeted services to those who may be falling through the cracks.

NOTE

1. The human immunodeficiency virus (HIV) is an infectious retrovirus leading to an incurable, life-threatening condition known as HIV disease or AIDS (acquired immune deficiency syndrome). Persons living with HIV are also called "HIV-positive" or "HIV-infected"; those who are significant to them are called "HIV-affected." HIV diminishes and then destroys the human immune system, so that the infected person is more susceptible to cancers and bacterial, viral, parasitic, fungal, and other opportunistic infections. Despite effective and promising pharmaceutical developments, HIV remains highly life-threatening, and to date there is no vaccine or cure.

REFERENCES

Administration on Aging (AoA). (2001). *Selected highlights: Side by side comparison of OAA as amended in 1992 with OAA as amended in 2000*. Available: *www.aoa.gov/about/legbudg/oaa/side-by-side.pdf*. Washington, DC: Author.

Administration on Aging. (n.d.). *A layman's guide to the Older Americans Act*. Available: *www.aoa.gov/about/legbudg/oaa/laymans_guide/laymans_guide.asp#TitleIII*. Washington, DC: Author.

Allers, C. T. (1990). AIDS and the older adult. *Gerontologist, 30*, 405–407.

Buchanan, R. J., & Chakravorty, B. J. (1997). Medicaid home and community-based waiver programs: Providing services to people with AIDS. *Health Care Financing Review, 18*(4), 83–103.

Burrage, J., & Porche, D. (2003). AIDS service organization partnerships: A method to assess outcomes of community service organizations for vulnerable populations. *Journal of Multicultural Nursing and Health, 9*(1), 7–12.

Centers for Disease Control. (1998). AIDS among persons aged greater than or equal to 50 years, United States, 1991–1996. *Morbidity and Mortality Weekly, 47*(02), 21–27.

Emlet, C. A. (2004). Knowledge and use of AIDS and aging services by older, HIV infected adults. *Journal of HIV/AIDS and Social Services, 3*(1), 9–24.

Emlet, C. A. (1997). HIV/AIDS in the elderly: A hidden population. *Home Care Provider, 2*, 69–75.

Emlet, C. A., & Poindexter, C. C. (2004). The unserved, unseen and unheard: Integrating program for HIV-infected and affected elders. *Health and Social Work, 29*(2), 86–96.

Estes, C. L. (1979). *The aging enterprise*. San Francisco: Jossey-Bass.

Genke, J. (2000). HIV/AIDS and older adults: The invisible ten percent. *Care Management Journals, 2*(3), 196–205.

Joslin, D. (2000). Grandparents raising grandchildren orphaned and affected by HIV/AIDS. In C. Cox (Ed.), *To Grandmother's house we go and stay: Perspectives on custodial grandparents* (pp. 167–183). New York: Springer.

Joslin, D., & Nazon, M. (1996). HIV/AIDS and aging networks. In K. Nokes (Ed.), *HIV/AIDS and the older adult* (pp. 129–141). Bristol, PA: Taylor and Francis.

Kisor, A. J., McSweeney, E. A., & Jackson, D. R. (2000). Social problems and policies and the elderly. In R. L. Schneider & N. P. Kropf (Eds.), *Gerontological social work: Knowledge, service settings, and special populations* (2nd ed., pp. 65–95). Belmont, CA: Wadsworth.

Levy, J. A., Ory, M. G., & Crystal, S. (2003). HIV/AIDS interventions for midlife and older adults: Current status and challenges. *Journal of Acquired Immune Deficiency Syndromes, 33*(Suppl. 2), S59–S67.

Lewis, S., & Crook, W. P. (2001). Shifting sands: An AIDS service organization adapts to a changing environment. *Administration in Social Work, 25*(2), 1–20.

Mack, K. A., & Ory, M. G. (2003). AIDS and older Americans at the end of the twentieth century. *Journal of Acquired Immune Deficiency Syndromes, 33*(Suppl. 2), S68–S75.

Messeri, P., Kim, S., & Whetten, K. (2003). Measuring HIV services integration activities. *Journal of HIV/AIDS and Social Services, 2(1),* 19–44.

Miller, N. A., Ramsland, S., & Harrington, C. (1999). Trends and issues in the Medicaid 1915(c) waiver. *Health Care Financing Review, 20*(4), 139–160.

Nichols, J. E., Speer, D. C., Watson, B. J., Watson, M. R., Vergon, T. L., Valee, C. M., & Meah, J. M. (2002). *Aging with HIV: Psychological, social, and health issues.* San Diego: Academic Press.

Nokes, K. M. (2004). Sustaining a coalition: A case study of the New York Association on HIV Over Fifty. In C. A. Emlet (Ed.), *HIV/AIDS and older adults: Challenges for individuals, families, and communities* (pp. 181–190). New York: Springer.

Older Americans Act of 1965, Public Law 89-73, §101, 79 Stat. 218.

Poindexter, C. (1998). Promises in the plague: The Ryan White CARE Act as a case study for legislative action. *Health and Social Work, 24* (1), 35–41.

Poindexter, C. C. (2001). "I'm still blessed": The assets and needs of HIV-affected caregivers over fifty. *Families in Society, 82*(5), 525–536.

Ryan White Comprehensive AIDS Resource Emergency Act of 1990, Public Law No. 101-381, §2240, 104 Stat. 576.

Takamura, J. C. (2001). Older Americans Act. In M. D. Mezey (Ed.), *The Encyclopedia of Elder Care: The comprehensive resource on geriatric and social care* (pp. 468–471). New York: Springer.

U.S. General Accounting Office (2003, June). *Federal oversight of growing Medicaid home and community-based waivers should be strengthened* (Publication No. GAO-03-576). Washington, DC: Author.

U.S. Health Resources and Services Administration. (2002–2003). *The AIDS epidemic and the Ryan White CARE Act: Past progress and future challenges 2002–2003.* Available: *http://hab.hrsa.gov/tools/progressreport/.* Rockville, MD: Author.

ROSALIE A. KANE,
SECTION EDITOR

Social Work Practice With Older Adults and
Their Families in Long-Term Residential Care

OVERVIEW

Social work as a profession has a long history of working within residential settings for older people and a record of concern for the well-being of the residents of such settings. As a practice field for social work, residential care is dominated by nursing homes because of half a century of federal rules that require a social work presence in nursing homes. But as the chapters in this section testify, the residential settings where older people live and receive care have always been more varied than nursing homes alone, and they continue to evolve and change. Regardless of where social workers who practice with older people are employed, they must be keenly aware of the residential options available to older people who need care and the typical stresses involved with life in residential care settings. Such settings form a backdrop within the family life of older people with whom social workers might work as case managers or as clinicians in many health and social service settings.

This section discusses a range of group residential settings that constitute home to older people who also need help with health care and daily living. My beginning chapter ruminates on a century or so of developments related to older people receiving care in settings other than their own homes and presents a somewhat idiosyncratic view of our current challenges and opportunities. In keeping with the domination of the nursing homes in the residential sector, the setting-specific chapters begin there. Betsy Vourlekis and Kelsey Simons provide an incisive discussion of the context and roles for social work practice in nursing homes, taking into account trends and changes in the characteristics of nursing home residents. Next, Marylou Guihan discusses residential care within the Veterans Administration (VA), a setting where social workers are very much in evidence; her chapter treats the nursing homes on the campuses of VA medical centers, the contract program for veterans in community care, and some new residential settings under consideration by the VA. Then, Ruth Huber, Ellen Netting, Kevin Borders, and H. W. Nelson describe the nursing home ombudsman program, an area of practice that also primarily deals with nursing homes but does not entail employment in them. For those social workers who become nursing home ombudsmen, the role utilizes the full range of social work skills, including casework around individual complaints, group work and the formation of resident and family councils, and legislative and other advocacy. Jeanette Semke describes residential settings

for older people with severe and persistent mental illness. Wendy Lustbader and Carter Catlett Williams describe the Pioneer Network and culture change efforts, a movement that Williams herself inspired in a magnificent example of social worker as change agent. Following that, Lisa Gwyther and I discuss specialized dementia care units, largely as they have emerged in nursing homes but also in some programs licensed as assisted living.

Moving away from nursing homes, literally, Robert Mollica's chapter describes efforts to help nursing home residents return to the community; some of these efforts have been fostered by specific grants from the Centers for Medicare and Medicaid Services (CMS) beginning in 1999 under the federal New Freedom Initiative to help states affect transitions from reliance on nursing homes for care of people with disability of all ages. Nursing home social workers have a responsibility to help residents leave nursing homes just as much as they are responsible for facilitating their adjustment on admission and promote their well-being during their stay. The discharge-planning role in nursing homes is a rather awkward role for nursing home social workers to play, especially if they are expected to maintain the nursing home census. Perhaps for this reason, the efforts described in Mollica's chapter often are conducted by persons coming into the nursing home from outside, some of whom are social workers employed as community care managers.

The next chapters consider other group residential settings. F. Ellen Netting and Cindy Wilson describe continuing care retirement communities, which typically offer escalating levels of care on a single campus, from independent housing, through residential care facilities, to nursing homes. In writing about assisted living, Sheryl Zimmerman, Jean Munn, and Terry Koenig describe the full range of entities that go by that name. Vera Prosper's chapter discusses small family homes, sometimes called adult foster homes, which serve just a few residents, perhaps two or three, certainly no more than six, in an ordinary residential house. Such small homes are important in rural areas, and they have often been the setting of choice for minority people of color. Both apartment-style assisted living and small family homes, discussed, respectively, in the Zimmerman et al. and Prosper chapters, offer the possibility of a more normal life within a group residential setting. The challenge is to be sure that the settings are affordable and that they provide sufficient health care without altering their basic residential character or threatening resident autonomy.

The last two chapters bring us to the boundaries where residential care and home care are truly blurred. Nancy Sheehan and Waldo Klein discuss congregate housing programs, which in both public housing and subsidized low-income housing is characterized by private apartment, but which provide an opportunity for services for those aging in place. Social workers with an official social work title are unlikely to be on the scene, but the inclusion of care coordinators or case managers in the units has provided some roles for social workers, especially at the bachelor's level. Moreover, community social workers enter these settings in other capacities, particularly as case managers for Medicaid waiver programs, and they need to understand how to help their clientele age in place and remain in those settings as long as possible. Finally, Fredda Vladeck describes programs developed in naturally occurring retirement communities (NORCs), which are buildings or neighborhoods where older people cannot be "discharged" because their NORC is simply where they live. Those who work to overlay a service structure on such NORCs draw on a wide range of social work skills, as Vladeck shows.

The choices people make about where to live in their later years may affect the amount, type, and costs of support available to them at a crucial period of need. An older person's home should surely be a place of comfort and an expression of personal identity, and the environs of that home should help define that older person's community. It is in this spirit that social workers and others are coming to consider the wide range of group living settings where older people receive care, including nursing homes, with the aim that they be not only "homelike" but actually home. The chapters in this section illustrate many different ways that social workers might converge on that task.

ROSALIE A. KANE

A Social Worker's Historical and Future Perspective on Residential Care

52

GOALS FOR THE GROUP RESIDENTIAL SECTOR

When older people contemplate their lives after age 70, 80, or 90, their most basic list of needs includes a home to shelter them from the elements, food to sustain their bodies, and health care as needed. Realists may anticipate that their needs for medical care could increase dramatically in the decades before their deaths and that they might need ongoing nursing help and personal assistance. Using the evocative title "Survival of the Unfittest," scholars from the United Kingdom predicted in 1972 that a large number of old people would need labor-intensive care in their last years (Isaacs, Livingstone, & Neville, 1972). When care needs become too difficult or expensive to arrange and coordinate in one's own home, and especially when the older person lacks family members able to assist with the arrangements, a move to a residential setting where the care is provided seems sensible and perhaps even inevitable. A nursing home brings together housing, room and board, health care, and personal care in a package deal. Other group residential settings, such as assisted living, to some extent also package care and housing.

Social workers concerned about the well-being of old people in group residential care must note the nature of both the care and the housing. At some points in our history, and in some circumstances right up to the present, both the housing and care components of typical residential service provisions fell far short of the ideal. One's home carries powerful social images: a sanctuary; an expression of personal history and interests; a gathering place for family and friends; a repository of memories, some of which adhere to cherished possessions; a place that one controls, as in "my home is my castle." The cliché that a nursing home aims to be home to residents is transparent and fails to reassure, nor do all other residential care settings carry the image of home to their residents.

Older people have other goals beyond the basic need for security and shelter. They seek enjoyment, friendship and companionship, and interests to stimulate their minds. Despite physical frailty, they often retain a wish to contribute to their families and communities. Well-being in later years also includes experiencing a sense that their lives have meaning and also retaining control and choice in their lives. Unfortunately, many of the residential care settings that have evolved for seniors compromise the quality-of-life outcomes defined in a federal project, which include security, comfort, relationships, meaningful activity,

591

enjoyment, dignity, individuality, and autonomy (R. A. Kane, 2003). Sometimes even the basic sense of identity of the older person is compromised by moving to a residential care setting (Tobin, 1999). Social workers who practice in such settings must engage in the struggle to help their clients meet their basic needs for a viable home where they feel secure and safe and receive excellent technical care in an atmosphere that promotes other quality-of-life outcomes.

HISTORICAL PERSPECTIVES ON NURSING HOMES

Prior to the industrial revolution and on through the 19th and the first half of the 20th century, older people made few residential choices. They tended to remain in the geographic areas where they lived and worked most of their lives, perhaps moving to smaller homes or apartments as family size shrank. If they needed constant or very frequent nursing care and the help of others to manage their households, their options were few: Singly or in combination, they could rely on family to help, hire paid help, or move to a place where more care was available. In the earliest years of organized philanthropy in the United States, beginning at the end of the 19th century, the places where seniors moved were variously called homes for the aged or nursing homes. The nursing home, like the orphanage and the mental hospital, claims as its common ancestor the poorhouse—a stigma-ridden last refuge for indoor relief for the bereft of all ages who lacked the financial wherewithal or family support to keep them at home (Holstein & Cole, 1995). Social work as a profession also has roots in poor laws, poorhouses, and parish relief. A pleasant "homelike" atmosphere was not a goal for indoor relief.

With the gradual differentiation of social welfare programs and facilities in the late 19th and early 20th centuries, elderly people with health needs became construed as a population deserving of respect and care. Charitable (usually sectarian) organizations established the first homes for the aged early in the century. In many states, counties also maintained a system of county homes, which largely became old age homes as other populations (children, mentally ill, blind people) were cared for in more differentiated programs. In the 1930s, older people began using private boarding homes for care, partly stimulated by the fact that they could not receive payments from the new Social Security program in public institutions like county homes. Over time, with the increase of available health

care technology and the rising acuity of seniors, all of these settings became more medically oriented. Also, the post–World War II period saw a boom in proprietary nursing homes, particularly as a result of construction payments for nursing homes in the 1950s and Medical Assistance payments to support poor people in nursing homes under the Kerr-Mills provisions.

Elias Cohen (1974) identified six periods in the development of nursing homes from Colonial times to 1974, ending with the post-1965 period. With the advantage of hindsight, I would carry his last period forward to about 1986, when another period begins. In the post-Medicare years, nursing homes were expanding even more rapidly, with increased regulation and reaction against regulation, punctuated by frequent quality scandals (Mendelson, 1974; Moss & Halamandaris, 1977; Smith, 1981; Vladeck, 1980). The National Citizens' Coalition for Nursing Home Reform emerged during this period as a citizens' group advocating better nursing home care. The period culminated in the work of an Institute of Medicine committee, which between 1983 and 1985 examined the relationship between regulation and quality in nursing homes (Institute of Medicine, 1986).

The Nursing Home Reform Act of 1987, also known as OBRA 87, marked a period of major reforms related to the quality standards used (emphasizing quality of life, residents' rights, and accurate assessment) as new conditions for nursing homes to receive federal funds, the quality assessment used (adding components of direct interview and observation of residents, changing the inspection intervals to introduce a modicum of surprise, and calling for a two-phase inspection for facilities showing problems at screening), and the enforcement procedures (encouraging states to use intermediate sanctions short of license removal and developing scope and severity modifiers for deficiencies). The practice of physical restraints in nursing homes was circumscribed in this period, partly because of the leadership of social worker Carter Catlett Williams. The analogous practice of using medications to control resident behavior (so-called chemical restraints) was also curbed, with new guidelines for appropriate medication use.

The period from 1987 to 2005 could be considered a new period for nursing homes, characterized by efforts to apply the OBRA 87 stipulations, including reduction of physical and chemical restraints in nursing homes, the development and testing of the minimum data set (MDS) as a fulfillment of the assessment tool, and the development of the new enforcement procedures. This period also saw the rise of dementia special care units in nursing homes, the development of Medicare-funded postacute care units (which were encouraged by incentives to shorten hospitalizations because of prospective payment of hospitals), the refinement of nursing home payment systems based on resident characteristics at admission (i.e., case-mix adjusted payment systems), the use of data generated from the MDS to create quality indicators and comparative quality reports, and the federal quality initiative of the late 1990s that promoted comparative Web-based quality reports that could be used by consumers. These reports emphasize comparative rates of negative outcomes, such as development of new bedsores and infections, prevalence of untreated depression, incidence of deterioration in late-loss activities of daily living, and physical restraints use.

The last several decades have been a heady time for nursing homes in the United States. The OBRA implementation was a long process, lasting more than 10 years. The market also changed in a variety of ways, responding to new pressures on hospitals for early discharge, more differentiated approaches for people with dementia, and opportunities for wealthier and healthier old people with care needs to choose a place other than a nursing home. Unfortunately, however, another Institute of Medicine report (Wunderlich & Kohler, 2001), completed at the turn of the century, found that although nursing home quality of care had markedly improved since OBRA 1987, quality problems remained; just a little dent had been made in improving the quality of life in nursing homes.

OTHER GROUP RESIDENTIAL SETTINGS: ENTER ASSISTED LIVING

Nursing homes were never the sole residential care setting in the modern era for older people with care needs. The boarding home is an old tradition in American life, and in many such boarding homes and retirement hotels, older people "aged in place" and manifested a range of care needs. Low-income and public housing for seniors, often built in the 1970s, also came to house many individuals who have aged in place and demonstrate care needs. Purpose-built apartment-type assisted living expanded rapidly in the 1990s, with loans readily available and publicly traded companies emerging and building rapidly.

The residential care market, apart from nursing homes, in the United States is largely regulated by states, if regulated at all. In the last quarter of the 20th century, the residential care market outside nursing homes became quite differentiated. Older people with care needs live in small family homes (sometimes called adult foster homes), in social-model residential care facilities that ranged from institutional-style dormitories with shared rooms to upscale residential hotels with private rooms and restaurant-type dining, and in new-style assisted living apartments. Those with mental health needs may live in specialized therapeutic settings, but they also may be found in single-room-only residential hotels. As noted, purpose-built assisted living expanded, and at the same time, many states renamed their residential care facilities "assisted living facilities." Some states developed a licensure that allowed for multiple types of assisted living, such as adult family homes, traditional board and care homes with rooms that were often shared, and new-style apartment-type assisted living (Mollica & Lamarche, 2005). In some states, notably Florida, the number of assisted living settings exceeds the number of nursing homes.

Idealists who first envisaged assisted living sought a setting where residents experienced autonomy, privacy, and dignity in single-occupied apartments, while receiving a high level of care and service. The model that evolved in Oregon required that assisted living settings offer privately occupied private apartments with locking doors, kitchenettes, and full bathroom and that they also offer three meals a day and ongoing assistance with personal care and routine nursing. The term *tenant* was encouraged to suggest a philosophy of resident control over their space and care (K. B. Wilson, 1990). Those with greater financial resources were most able to select the new assisted living, however, and often states developed admission and retention rules for the setting that prohibited assisted living from becoming a true option in lieu of nursing homes. In a large national probability sample of assisted living settings serving more than 12 people, researchers found that only 11% offered both high privacy and high service levels, that substantial numbers offered neither, and that there was a trade-off between privacy and quality of life features and care capacity, with the highest level of care available in settings that were most institutional in nature (Hawes, Phillips, & Rose, 2000).

Gradually, under Medicaid or Medicaid waivers, states began to cover some of the costs of care in residential care settings other than nursing homes, leaving room and board to be covered out of income. This uncoupling of room and board from care could be seen as a positive development, rendering care in group residential settings more like home care and affording more control to consumers (R. A. Kane, 1995). But if people eligible for Medicaid and other low-income people cannot afford the rent component, their care subsidies will be utilized, if at all, in the least appealing settings.

Assisted living now occupies an unsettled and controversial place in public policy. Historian David Barton Smith referred to the growth of assisted living as a "killer application," alluding to a computer term for a new application that throws all others out of kilter (Smith, 2003). As neither an institution like a nursing home nor a private home, assisted living is a confusing program, raising issues about who should be in assisted living settings, what care they should receive, and what responsibility governments should have for both payment and quality oversight. Combining housing and services carries its complexities. For example, if the housing is truly seen as separate from the services, then Fair Housing Act and Americans with Disabilities Act standards should apply before residents are evicted. If the housing is a "facility," then discharges can be made because disabilities exceed the perceived capability of the program. Further, services detached from housing may be provided exclusively by the facility or by a contracted service provider, or the resident-tenant may have a choice of provider. If the model allows for choice of provider, the facility is unlikely to achieve economies of scale, and its prices may rise. To further illustrate the difficulties of the new model, depending on the assisted living program and the state in which it is licensed, the residents may be able to receive services from any combination of facility staff, outside home care agencies, private duty personnel hired by the consumer, and family. Those who would regulate the settings by proposing a staff-to-resident ratio may be stymied by the difficulty in counting the arrangements that are pieced together on an individual basis.

CRITIQUES OF RESIDENTIAL CARE FOR SENIORS

The very phrase "nursing home" evokes fear and dread in older people and many of their family members. Very soon after Medicare was enacted, nursing homes were likened to Goffman's "total institution" (Goffman, 1961), where inmates are processed in batches and subject to rules designed for the benefit of the organization, not the residents (R. G. Bennett, 1968).

The importance of privacy to seniors and their family members has received growing recognition, although old ideas still linger, and some commentators may still believe that companionship is fostered by forced sharing. For the most part, however, commentators are coming to recognize that loneliness occurs in the midst of group settings and that true friendships rarely flourish in crowded spaces. During the same years that some reformers sought to improve nursing home care, a raft of anthropologists and ethnographic researchers filed studies of nursing home life (Agich, 1993; Lidz, Fischer, & Arnold, 1992; Shield, 1988); one such writer was an enlightened nursing home administrator who could not tolerate even two weeks in the facility where he had checked himself in as a pseudo-patient (C. Bennett, 1980). Others concentrated on the difficulties this environment put in the way of staff workers who wished to develop primary relationships with residents, exercise judgment, and nurture residents' quality of life (Diamond, 1992; Henderson & Vesperi, 1995; Vesperi, 1995). Sociologist Jaber Gubrium coined the phrase "bed and body work" to encapsulate the focus expected of nurse's aides (Gubrium, 1975).

The Nursing Home Pioneers, now known as the Pioneer Network in Long-Term Care, a social movement to change the culture of nursing homes, largely sprang from a realization that the status quo was antithetical to the well-being of both residents and staff (see chapter 57 by Lustbader and Williams in this section). Thus, in the 1990s, more basic reforms were advocated, falling under the rubric of culture change and proposing changes in the power structure and operating practices and developing a caring community of residents and direct care staff to improve quality of life for both (Fagan, Williams, & Burger, 1997; Weiner & Ronch, 2003). Innovations suggested by the Pioneer Network tend to fall into three categories of change: changing physical environments to make them smaller and more normal, for example, creating neighborhoods in nursing homes and advocating private spaces; empowering and developing more capacity for caring among line caregivers; and instituting a philosophy that individualizes the approach to residents. One of the pioneer examples is the Eden Alternative, an approach developed by William Thomas to combat boredom, loneliness, and lack of meaning, which to him are "the three scourges" of nursing home life (Thomas, 1999). Although it is widely associated with advocating animals and plants in nursing homes, the Eden Alternative's more difficult changes are flattened hierarchies and individualized care. More recently, William Thomas articulated another model, known as Green Houses, which further deinstitutionalizes nursing homes into small houses where certified nurse's aide–level elder assistants provide a fuller range of care for 7 to 10 elders, preparing and serving meals, doing household laundry, and providing personal care. A group of Green Houses are linked administratively as a licensed, certified nursing home, and all professionals, including the social worker but also the nurses and medical director, form a clinical support team to assist the elders and the elder assistants (Thomas, 2003).

The culture change movement brings to a head some tensions between quality of care and quality of life. Although the two pursuits should be compatible, the quality of care emphasis typically centers on further regulation, including mandating higher staffing ratios of direct nursing staff to residents and enforcing "zero tolerance" policies for outcomes associated with poor quality of care, such as dehydration, falls with injuries, and bedsores. In contrast, some advocates for culture change prefer not to reify current staffing patterns by mandating higher ratios of staff in the nursing department, nor do they want to perpetuate the view that someone must be blamed and punished for all bad outcomes in nursing homes (Kapp, 1997).

Further, the culture change movement needs to come to grips with assisted living. To the extent that residents with the same disability levels as nursing home residents live in normalized assisted living settings, this is the biggest culture change of all. Authorities disagree about the extent to which it is appropriate for residents with true nursing home levels of need to experience the lack of oversight associated with assisted living. Government watchdog organizations and the media have both highlighted quality problems in assisted living. However, if assisted living settings adopt the rules, routines, and conventions of nursing homes, some commentators fear that they will lose the very characteristics that have made them popular to seniors. Meanwhile, some of the proposed changes in the culture of nursing homes and in the physical plans would accentuate the blurring of the lines between nursing homes and assisted living, whereas some of the proposed changes in assisted living would accentuate the blurring between assisted living and home care.

One helpful formulation envisages desirable residential care services for seniors as a three-legged stool, each leg having two prongs (see Figure 52.1). The first leg on which reform depends is a residential environment in both the private space and the public or shared spaces. The building and the materials influence whether the setting is homelike, or even whether one gets beyond "homelike" to home itself. The second leg is a residential capacity; one prong is the capacity for routine services (some of which can be scheduled in advance, and some of which cannot), such as personal care and medication management, and the other prong is specialized services that may be needed from time to time for particular residents. The routine services must be managed in-house, whereas consultants could be brought in for specialized services: psychiatric care, speech therapy, pharmacological review, ordering of prosthetic equipment, and the like. What is considered routine may expand if the general acuity and frailty of the population increases. The final leg of the stool is a philosophy that emphasizes consumer control; one prong is control over the amount, type, and timing of care, and the other is control over what happens in one's private space—who enters, how furnishings are arranged, what is done there, and at what times of day. Though the model was first developed for assisted living, all residential care, including nursing homes, could be examined and compared in terms of success in all three arenas.

SOCIAL WORK AND RESIDENTIAL CARE

Relevance of Social Work Skills

Although social workers have historically had periods when they considered work in residential care settings to require less skill than presumably more psychodynamic treatment settings, a consummate level of skill is needed to help nursing home residents deal with the psychic insult and social changes attendant on moving to a residential care setting. Social work skills are also required to help an older person make decisions about whether to enter residential care outside their own home, what sort of residential setting to seek, and how to choose a particular setting within a type of setting. Typically, this painful decision is a family matter, and many of the family members will be elderly, not just the people contemplating the move. Although such advice and consultation sometimes gets dismissed in the unfortunate phrase "nursing home placement," the importance of the task and the skill and knowledge needed to help are both high. Moreover, the nursing home calls forth the need for the full range of social work skills, including direct counseling of individual and family members, social group work and group therapy, community organization, systems management, and system change.

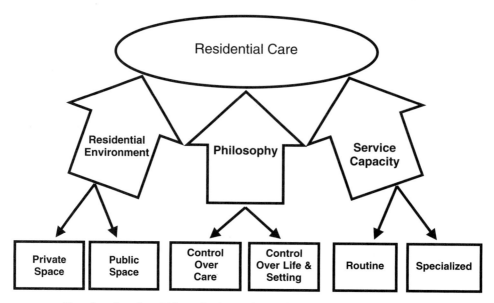

FIGURE 52.1 Three-legged stool model for evaluating attributes of any residential care setting. Source: This model was developed by Keren Brown Wilson, Portland, Oregon, and is described in *The Heart of Long-Term Care* by R. A. Kane, R. L. Kane, and R. C. Ladd, 1998, New York: Oxford University Press.

The challenges to social work to help meet the needs of older people who live in group residential settings and to help older people in the community decide about moving to group residential settings are legion. Part of the solution is to have enough social workers in the settings (either working directly in them or coming to them under other auspices), and part is for social workers to develop creative approaches for when they get there. Only the nursing home is a regulated entity requiring social work presence. Social workers are less likely to practice in assisted living or residential care facilities, unless those settings are part of a community with a nursing home attached. In some states, social workers may fill care management roles, through which they oversee the experience of older people in adult foster homes, residential care, and assisted living. In most of the roles just mentioned, social workers with bachelor's-level training are more frequently found than those with master's degrees. Further, in most of these settings qualified social workers, be they MSWs or BSWs, are likely to be somewhat alone in their practice, needing to determine their own roles and interpret what they can do under administrators from other disciplines. Unfortunately, the profession has not as yet provided much practice guidance for direct practice in residential settings where seniors are served, nor has research reached the stage where evidence-based advice can reach any depth.

Historical Leadership

Towering figures in the social work profession have addressed the urgency of the social work tasks in nursing homes and other residential settings. In her early guide to social work in nursing homes, Elaine Brody (Brody & Contributors, 1974) recognized the trauma of moving to an institution and the folly of considering the social component of care "a luxury to be avoided" (p. 66). She called even then for an emphasis on strengths, not deficits. An early model of practice-based researcher, during her career at the Philadelphia Geriatric Center, she brought to light important concepts that remain pivotal, including the need to avoid excess disability and the likelihood that aggression among nursing home residents, including those with dementia, was a life-prolonging strength rather than a behavior problem to be adjusted or medicated away.

Similarly, Herbert Shore, nursing home administrator and social worker, tirelessly pointed to the need to individualize and humanize the nursing home environment and to recognize that first and foremost a nursing home resident is a person with the same aspirations, hopes, fears, pleasures, and displeasures as any other human being. In an edited book in which he wrote many chapters (Leeds & Shore, 1964), his contributions suggested approaches to transforming dining, to developing a more intellectual and learning-oriented approach to activities, and to eliciting resident feedback and opinions about the programs. In a report to his board of directors in 1970, he wrote in terms that anticipated the culture change movement:

> Older people *need* security—economically (in terms of shelter, housing, and spending money), physically (in terms of medical care and adequate diet), and socially (in terms of status, friendship, and belonging). Older people *want* recognition—for what they can do mentally and manually, for their capacity to make a contribution to their community, country, and world, for social and political consciousness, and their ability to plan for themselves. Older people want response: to be liked for what they are, to hold friends and make new acquaintances; and older people want new experiences and adventures: to continue to learn and grow and develop, to enjoy the new and different, to extend interests, expand horizons, satisfy curiosity, to create for expression in artistic and aesthetic areas. . . . Like every other human being, they need social contact.

In that 30-year-old report, Shore also suggested that if staff are to give, "they need to be secure in self, gain satisfaction in giving, and must receive recognition, love, and compensation." He deplored "cultural hangups on who does what"—a precursor of the universal worker ideas of today. He concluded that "the major challenge is to provide for a continuity of life experience (no showcase for public relations, not tokenism but meaningful life—with freedom of choice, when and if to participate, a program of social health, personal identity, independence, privacy, stability, self-direction, re-engagement, discovery and re-institution of normal elements of daily social living)." These principles are almost identical to those enunciated by the Pioneer Network, discussed previously.

Social workers were instrumental in the formation and leadership of the National Citizens' Coalition for Nursing Home Reform, an advocacy organization that fought for the nursing home reforms of 1987 and that provides public information about nursing homes (Burger, Fraser, Hunt, & Frank, 1996). Social workers are often found in the ranks of the nursing home ombudsman program, a nationwide complaint resolution program initiated by the Older Americans' Act in 1975. In each major movement to improve the options for older people in residential care, social workers can be found, for example, leading the charge

against physical restraints (Williams, 1991), developing specialized dementia care (Gwyther, 2001), suggesting structural ways to identify and resolve ethical issues (R. A. Kane & Caplan, 1990), and testing approaches to combat learned helplessness (Mercer & Kane, 1979).

Trends and Challenges

Several trends already mentioned have implications for social work practice and research related to residential care for older people. First, the growing emphasis on quality of life as an outcome and the effort to measure quality of life give attention to social work issues and offer tools to examine practice (R. A. Kane et al., 2003). In the same vein, a new study from the United Kingdom provides evidence that entertainment and enjoyable, meaningful activity are crucial to a good-quality home (Mozley et al., 2004); these are outcomes that social workers could influence. Opportunities abound to test both the therapeutic interventions, and even more important, the environmental prerequisites that promote quality of life. Social workers should also examine the effects of various kinds of residential care arrangements on residents' involvement with their own families and on outcomes for family members per se.

Second, the culture change movement in long-term care, discussed previously, is offering hope for a new way of doing things, new scope for skills related to team building and leadership for organizational change, and new opportunities for leadership. Indeed, some social workers are joining leaders in other disciplines as culture change agents and have developed stage models to help organizations with which they consult move through the steps of culture change.

A third trend is the proliferation of a confusing array of residential settings, the overlap in resident functioning across settings, and the end of the quest to slot residents into the "most appropriate setting" based on functioning. Possibly, such judgments were never wise, but at present, such hubris is certainly contraindicated. Older people can have their care needs met in a wide range of settings, including their own homes and a diverse array of other group settings. Social workers who act as advisers can no longer seek refuge in the idea that there is an "appropriate" residential setting for the individual that matches his or her needs. At the same time, the recognition of overlap in resident characteristics in a wide array of settings challenges social workers and colleagues from other professions to consider how some of the most challenging situations can be handled in any group residential care setting. These include care of people with Alzheimer's disease and other dementias, care of people with severe mental health problems, provision of physical rehabilitation for those whose functioning can improve, and care of people who are dying. Any of these situations could occur in any of the care settings. The differentiation described for nursing homes in chapters 56 on mental health and 58 on dementia care can now be seen in other settings. Small family homes and larger assisted living settings have been known to specialize in conditions as various as ventilator dependency, multiple sclerosis, and deafness.

Fourth, we see growing recognition that older people often do and should be able to continue to take risks in their daily lives, just as any people do. Bioethical treatments of long-term care emphasize this right. Negotiated risk contracting was developed as both a process and a product to enable older people to live in ways that health professionals see as risky (R. A. Kane & Levin, 1998; K. Wilson, Burgess, & Hernandez, 2001). Determining what safety should mean in operational terms in the light of the human right to take risks is an important challenge for practitioners. Falls, for example, do not always imply that care is poor. Beyond enhancing the autonomy and individual goals of each resident, ethical challenges in residential settings entail balancing the needs and interests of the individual with that of the collective. As privacy is enhanced in group residential care settings, this challenge is easier but by no means resolved.

Fifth, the Supreme Court Olmstead decision and the New Freedom Initiative of the federal government have clarified the duty to offer older people care in the setting that is least restrictive and most integrated in the community. Much energy now is devoted to keeping people out of institutions, and those who practice in residential care settings must work in the spirit of that injunction. It means that social workers in nursing homes will be more engaged in assisting those who come into the nursing home for rehabilitation so that they make a smooth transition back to the community. It also means being open to the idea that former long-stay residents can move to less restrictive settings.

Taking all these trends together, social workers may find a need to reinvent themselves in residential care for older people. In direct practice, one would expect to see social workers utilize a fuller array of skills in individual, family, and group interventions, and one would expect to see social workers in the forefront of evolving the practices that render the setting a pleasant place to live—a place where the older person may develop to the fullest. In the future, we will expect a continuation of social workers occupying roles beyond the job title "social worker." In nursing homes, they may be administrators, program developers, or unit coordinators. They may be responsible for a wide range of efforts beyond social work, including spiritual programming, activities, and volunteer coordination. In assisted living, they may be administrators, community liaisons, or marketers. They may be involved in the design of regulations. They are likely to be in the forefront of the struggles for innovation and reform. Because of the wide variety of job titles and roles social workers hold, they may not easily be able to find each other or a reference group from their own profession to help sharpen their skills and guide their work.

Social workers are likely to keep their professional compass properly set if they adhere to social work's historical mission as they interact with older people in group residential settings—assisting the individual in the environment—and if they perceive the adjustment of the environment as a goal as important as the adjustment of the individual. They will also be well guided if they remember, along with Herbert Shore, Elaine Brody, Carter Williams, and others, that older people in group residential settings wish for and deserve to live lives as normal and as rich as the disabilities that brought them into care permit. Like those earlier leaders, they should never gloss over the shock and losses involved in moving to a group residential setting, a move that is rarely wholly voluntary or without ambivalence. Moreover, in the midst of facilitating therapy, including health care and also mental health therapies where social workers may play a direct provider role, we social workers need to recall that the individual's meaning in life will not be realized through adherence to a therapeutic regimen. In the place where they live to receive care, social workers can be a force that helps each individual make the connections inside and outside the residential setting that will make life worthwhile. In that pursuit, no policy or practice that might affect the way the senior perceives the world of the residential setting should be beneath the dignity of the social worker's attention. Although difficult to achieve, one overriding goal should be to help as many people as possible perceive the place where they live as their home in the true sense of what home means.

REFERENCES

Agich, G. J. (1993). *Autonomy and long-term care*. New York: Oxford University Press.

Bennett, C. (1980). *Nursing home life: What it is and what it could be*. New York: Tiresias Press.

Bennett, R. G. (1968). The meaning of institutional life. In N. Leeds & H. Shore (Eds.), *Geriatric institutional management* (pp. 68–90). New York: Putnam.

Brody, E. M., & Contributors. (1974). *A social work guide for long-term care facilities*. Washington, DC: Government Printing Office.

Burger, S. G., Fraser, V., Hunt, S., & Frank, B. (1996). *Nursing homes: Getting good care there*. San Luis Obispo, CA: Impact.

Cohen, E. (1974). An overview of long-term care facilities. In E. M. Brody & Contributors (Eds.), *Social work guide for long-term care facilities*. Washington, DC: Government Printing Office.

Diamond, T. (1992). *Making gold gray: Narratives of nursing home care*. Chicago: University of Chicago Press.

Fagan, R. M., Williams, C. C., & Burger, S. G. (1997). *Meeting of pioneers in nursing home culture change*. Rochester, NY: Lifespan of Greater Rochester.

Goffman, E. (1961). *Asylums: Essays on the social situation of mental patients and other inmates*. Garden City, NY: Anchor Books.

Gubrium, J. F. (1975). *Living and dying at Murray Manor*. New York: St. Martin's.

Gwyther, L. (2001). *Caring for people with Alzheimer's disease: A manual for facility staff*. Washington, DC: American Health Care Association and Alzheimer's Association.

Hawes, C., Phillips, C. D., & Rose, M. (2000). *High service or high privacy assisted living facilities, their residents and staff: Results from a national survey*. College Station: Texas A&M University System Health Science Center and Myers Research Institute.

Henderson, J., & Vesperi, M. (Eds.). (1995). *The culture of long-term care: Nursing home ethnography*. Westport, CT: Bergin & Garvey.

Holstein, M. B., & Cole, T. R. (1995). Long-term care: A historical reflection. In L. B. McCullough & N. L. Wilson (Eds.), *Long-term care decisions: Ethical and conceptual dimensions* (pp. 2–15). Baltimore, MD: Johns Hopkins University Press.

Institute of Medicine. (1986). *Improving the quality of care in nursing homes*. Washington, DC: National Academy Press.

Isaacs, B., Livingstone, M., & Neville, Y. (1972). *Survival of the unfittest*. London: Routledge and K. Paul.

Kane, R. A. (1995). Expanding the home care concept: Blurring distinctions among home care, institutional care, and other long term-care services. *Milbank Quarterly, 73*(2), 161–186.

Kane, R. A. (2003). Definition, measurement, and correlates of quality of life in nursing homes: Towards a reasonable practice, research, and policy agenda. *The Gerontologist, 43*(2), 28–36.

Kane, R. A., & Caplan, A. L. (Eds.). (1990). *Everyday ethics: Solving dilemmas in nursing home life*. New York: Springer.

Kane, R. A., Kling, K. C., Bershadsky, B., Kane, R. L., Giles, K., Degenholtz, H. B., et al. (2003). Quality of life measures for nursing home residents. *Journal of Gerontology: Medical Sciences, 58A*(3), 240–248.

Kane, R. A., & Levin, C. A. (1998, Fall). Who's safe? Who's sorry? The duty to protect the safety of clients in home- and community-based care. *Generations,* pp. 76–81.

Kapp, M. B. (1997). Who is responsible for this? Assigning rights and consequences in elder care. *Journal of Aging and Social Policy, 9*(2), 51–66.

Leeds, N., & Shore, H. (Eds.). (1964). *Geriatric institutional management*. New York: Putnam.

Lidz, C. W., Fischer, L., & Arnold, R. M. (1992). *The erosion of autonomy in long-term care*. New York: Oxford University Press.

Mendelson, M. A. (1974). *Tender loving greed*. New York: Alfred A. Knopf.

Mercer, S., & Kane, R. (1979). Helplessness and hopelessness in the institutionalized elderly. *Health and Social Work, 4,* 90–116.

Mollica, R., & Lamarche, H. (2005). *State residential care and assisted living policy: 2004*. (Report to HHS/ASPE/DALTCP under contract from Research Triangle Institute, March 31, 2005.) Portland, ME: National Academy for State Health Policy. At *http://aspe.hhs.gov/daltcp/report/04a/com.htm*.

Moss, F. E., & Halamandaris, V. J. (1977). *Too old, too sick, too bad: Nursing homes in America*. Germantown, MD: Aspen.

Mozley, C., Sutcliffe, C., Bagley, H., Cordingley, L., Challis, D., Huxley, P., et al. (2004). *Towards quality care: Outcomes for older people in care homes*. Hants, England, & Burlington, VT: Ashgate.

Shield, R. R. (1988). *Uneasy endings*. Ithaca, NY: Cornell University Press.

Smith, D. B. (1981). *Long-term care in transition: The regulation of nursing homes*. Washington, DC: Beard Books.

Smith, D. B. (2003). *Reinventing care: Assisted living in New York*. Nashville, TN: Vanderbilt University Press.

Thomas, W. H. (1999). *The Eden Alternative handbook: The art of building human habitats*. Sherburne, NY: Summer Hill.

Thomas, W. H. (2003). Evolution of Eden. In A. S. Weiner & J. L. Ronch (Eds.), *Culture change in long-term care* (pp. 141–158). New York: Haworth.

Tobin, S. S. (1999). *Preservation of self in the oldest years.* New York: Springer.

Vesperi, M. (1995). Nursing home research comes of age: Toward an ethnological perspective on long term care. In J. Henderson & M. Vesperi (Eds.), *The culture of long term care: Nursing home ethnography* (pp. 7–21). Westport, CT: Bergin & Garvey.

Vladeck, B. G. (1980). *Unloving care: The nursing home tragedy.* New York: Basic Books.

Weiner, A. S., & Ronch, J. L. (Ed.). (2003). *Culture change in long-term care.* New York: Haworth.

Williams, C. C. (1991). *Daily life of residents in restraint free nursing homes in Scotland and Sweden.* Paper presented at the meeting of the Gerontological Society of America, San Francisco.

Wilson, K., Burgess, K. L., & Hernandez, M. (2001). Negotiated risk: Opportunity or exploitation? *Journal of Ethics, Law, & Aging Review, 7.*

Wilson, K. B. (1990). *Assisted living: The merger of housing and long term care services, Vol. 4, Long term care advances.* Durham, NC: Duke University Long Term Care Center.

Wunderlich, G. S., & Kohler, P. O. (2001). *Improving the quality of long-term care.* Washington, DC: National Academy Press.

The nursing home provides an ideal opportunity to implement social work's unique person-in-environment perspective and skills. The complex psychosocial needs of residents and their families during a period of major life transition interact with an institutional environment that is both comprehensive in care and highly controlled, offering pervasive opportunities to craft a more adaptive fit. With average lengths of stay ranging from 272 days for discharged residents to 892 days for current residents (Jones, 2002), nursing home social work practice frequently can be conducted within the framework of longer-term helping relationships, a quality increasingly hard to come by in today's health care environment.

More than 3 million people are cared for in nursing homes each year (Centers for Medicare & Medicaid Services [CMS], 2003). They are among the most vulnerable members of our society. Nursing homes often are the least preferred alternative of older Americans and their loved ones and, unfortunately, more frequently make news and headlines because of poor care and concerns about quality than for their exemplary service. Nonetheless, nursing homes are an essential component of the health care continuum and an important arena for social work practice. Social work's focus on overall quality of life and its professional obligation to advocate for those who may lack capacity to defend themselves are especially relevant to the nursing home setting. To introduce the practice domain, this chapter (a) briefly examines the nursing home context and regulatory environment; (b) discusses the needs and strengths of nursing home "clients" and the home as a system in its own right; (c) describes key features of the social work role and functions, including the monitoring and quality improvement of social work services; and (d) identifies key research needs to support practice.

PRACTICE CONTEXT

Trends in Nursing Home Care

There are approximately 16,500 nursing facilities in the United States certified for Medicare, Medicaid, or, most commonly, both programs. Of this number, the vast majority are classified as skilled nursing facilities (SNFs), which provide "short-term, residentially-based skilled nursing and therapy care" (CMS, 2003, p. 5). The typical SNF is large, ranging from 104 beds among nonprofit SNFs to 120 among government-owned facilities. Most facilities are freestanding

BETSY VOURLEKIS
KELSEY SIMONS

Nursing Homes

(85%), and the rest are located in hospitals (15%). The majority of homes have for-profit status (65.4%), more than a quarter are nonprofit (28.4%), and a small number are government (city or county) owned (6.1%) (CMS, 2003). Chain ownership characterizes two thirds of all for-profit facilities but only 40% of nonprofits and 8% of publicly owned facilities (CMS, 2003; Harrington, Woolhandler, Mullan, Carrillo, & Himmelstein, 2001). Research suggests that greater quality of care and quality of life concerns exist within for-profit, chain facilities (Harrington et al., 2001).

The number of nursing home residents has been declining in recent years. Between 1985 and 1995, the percentage of those age 65 and over residing in nursing homes fell from 46.2 to 42.4 per thousand, a decline of 8.2%. Likewise, the average occupancy rate dropped from 92% to 87% during this time period (Bishop, 1999) and was 84.3% as recently as 2001 (CMS, 2001). Researchers cite a decline in disability among older adults (Lakdawalla et al., 2003), increased use of home health services, and competition from the assisted living industry (Bishop, 1999) as a few of the factors contributing to this decrease. However, future cohorts of older adults are predicted to have greater disability because of the rise in chronic health conditions such as obesity and asthma, which could reverse this trend and create an increased need for nursing home care (Lakdawalla et al., 2003).

Despite the apparent gains made in reducing the nursing home population, there has been an accompanying increase in nursing home resident acuity, as well as rapidly escalating costs for their care. Harrington and Carrillo (1999) reviewed federal nursing home data (the Online Survey and Certification Reporting [OSCAR] dataset) for the years 1991–1997 and identified statistically significant increases in the numbers of bedfast residents (from 3.5 to 7.2% of all residents) and residents with dementia (from 34.7 to 41.7%) and depression (9.3 to 12.4%). Meanwhile, total annual expenditures for U.S. nursing homes increased from $28 billion in 1987 to $70 billion by 1996, or 150% (Rhoades & Sommers, 2003). Among freestanding nursing homes with Medicare certification, the rise in expenditures has been most dramatic: from $307 million in 1980 to $9.6 billion by 1997, an annual increase of 30% (CMS, 2003). The prospective payment system (PPS) put into effect July 1, 1998, following the passage of the 1997 Balanced Budget Act (BBA), attempts to control the escalating costs of postacute care, paid through Medicare Part A, by setting fixed, predetermined payment rates that are adjusted for case mix and geographic variations in wages. Prior to PPS, nursing facilities were reimbursed retrospectively, according to their reported actual costs of care (CMS, 2003). Researchers have cited quality of care concerns as a result of cost-cutting measures under the PPS system, including shorter stays for rehabilitation (Yip, Wilber, & Myrtle, 2002), decreases in professional staffing, and greater regulatory deficiencies (Konetzka, Yi, Norton, & Kilpatrick, 2004).

Regulation, Licensing, and Financing

By definition (Jones, 2002), nursing homes today are settings providing nursing care that are certified by the federal government through the Medicare/Medicaid (M/M) program (and therefore entitled to receive reimbursement) and/or licensed by state departments of health. As assisted living facilities proliferate and tend to accommodate more affluent seniors who can pay for services (Hawes, Phillips, Rose, Holan, & Sherman, 2003), one critical distinction between nursing homes and assisted living facilities is the highly regulated nature of the nursing home industry. Approximately 80% of nursing homes are M/M certified (Jones, 2002), and the remainder must meet state licensure requirements, even if all residents are paying privately. To operate as a licensed and certified nursing home, a facility must meet extensive mandated requirements, including those especially relevant to social work (discussed later), and undergo periodic inspections that establish the degree of compliance with specified regulations as outlined in the Conditions of Participation for Long Term Care Facilities (42 CFR Part 483, Subpart B). CMS, an agency within the Department of Health and Human Services, oversees the federal government's nursing home program. CMS recently established the Nursing Home Compare Web site (*http://www.cms.hhs.gov/quality/nhqi/*), where the public can contrast homes' performance across a set of quality indicators.

The financial stake for a home to maintain certification status means that federal nursing home regulations play a predominant role in shaping the structure, processes, and services of nursing home care. This reality has important implications for social work practice in this setting, and nursing home social workers must understand and keep themselves informed about the regulatory process, the content of certification and licensing standards, and the specific procedures maintained by the home to prepare for and demonstrate compliance with mandated standards. Federal reimbursement to homes is also controlled by regulation. Social work services are covered as part of the overall facility operating costs, in the same way as in hospitals. Homes are reimbursed on a per capita basis, according to a daily rate or a case-mix-adjusted formula. Social workers need to understand the cost of their service to the home and be aware of the inevitable fiscal "bottom line" of costs versus reimbursement that drives administrators' decisions. For example, certain mental health services and hospice services (which include social work care) are considered auxiliary to the daily rate. Homes can bill separately for eligible residents under their Medicare Part B coverage, contracting with providers (including social workers) external to the home (Beaulieu, 2002), with the facility social worker serving as a liaison through referrals and follow-up.

Social Service Regulation

Since the original Medicare regulations of 1966, which required a professional social worker available to every Medicare-certified home, the federal government has explicitly regulated the provision of social services in nursing homes. Regulations were significantly weakened in the 1970s (Kosberg, 1973). Homes could use a "social service designee" to provide direct services, with a social work "consultant" to provide oversight. There were no specified educational requirements for the designee, and no required minimum amount of time for the consultant. Nursing home reform legislation in 1987 (Omnibus Budget Reconciliation Act of 1987 [OBRA]) strengthened federal requirements for psychosocial care and social work services in nursing homes. Current regulations (implemented in 1990) require all facilities to identify the medically related social and emotional (psychosocial) needs of each resident and develop a plan to help each resident adjust to the social and emotional aspects of his or her illness, treatment, and stay in the nursing home. Homes of more than 120 beds must provide a full-time social worker (BSW, MSW, or "educational equivalent"). Although the regulations require use of licensed personnel in facilities, this obligation has not yet been applied in the case of social work. Federal guidelines to state surveyors (who do the inspections) with respect to judging the adequacy of social services focus on the sections of regulations pertaining to quality of life and residents' rights in addition to the "over 120 bed" rule for staffing.

The National Association of Social Workers (NASW, 2003) recently revised its standards for practice in long-term care settings, providing guidelines for nursing home social worker qualifications above and beyond federal regulations. The standards place greater emphasis on professionalization by recommending that all social work staff have either BSW or MSW degrees. Further, they advocate licensing all social work staff according to state requirements and encourage all nursing home social workers to belong to professional organizations, including the NASW, and to attend continuing education programs.

THE "CLIENT"

The nursing home social worker needs a general understanding of the needs and strengths of the people living in the home, their families, and their significant others and of the home itself as an organization, keeping in mind that each of these systems levels can be a target for intervention. Although familiarity with medical and rehabilitative diagnostics, typical symptoms, and therapeutic regimens is necessary for effective practice and communication with other health personnel in the home, here the focus is on aspects of the psychosocial reality of life and care in the nursing home.

Resident Characteristics

The typical nursing home resident is female (68%), White (84.8%), and over the age of 75 (75%), although 40% of all nursing home residents fall into the demographic category of "oldest old," those age 85 and over (CMS, 2001). More than a third of all residents receive extensive assistance with four of five activities of daily living (CMS, 2001), such as bathing (93.8%), dressing (86.5%), toileting (56%), eating (47%), and transfers (29%) (Jones, 2002). Likewise, only slightly more than a quarter of residents have no cognitive impairment (CMS, 2001). Although racial minority groups currently comprise only a small portion of the nursing home population, the numbers of racially diverse residents are likely to increase in accordance with the changing racial profile of the U.S. population, including increasing numbers of Asian and Hispanic Americans (U.S. Census Bureau, 2004). Meanwhile, disparities in the quality of nursing home care by race and socioeconomic status have been identified, creating a "two-tiered system" not unlike other sectors of the U.S. health care system (Mor, Zinn, Angelelli, Teno, & Miller, 2004).

Social workers need to recognize nursing homes as mirroring the socioeconomic and cultural circumstances of the local community and of society at large. In many sections of the country, significant numbers of direct care staff are members of recent immigrant groups, who are therefore serving elderly individuals from cultures very different from their own. Culturally sensitive and competent social work practice requires awareness and understanding of the culturally distinctive aspects of residents' and their families' attitudes, preferences, and behaviors throughout the course of the nursing home experience. For example, family members' underlying reasoning and feelings about the placement decision may vary culturally (Calderon & Tennstedt, 1998; Fitzgerald, Mullavey-O'Byrne, & Clemson, 2001), and resident preferences and subjective well-being, including end-of-life care, are likely to be influenced by culture (Ejaz, 2002; Field, Maher, & Webb, 2002; Ingersoll-Dayton, Saengtienchai, Kespichayawattana, & Aungsuroch, 2004; Shibusawa & Mui, 2001). Moreover, social workers can be helpful in recognizing and mediating cultural differences between staff and resident or family members and among culturally diverse staff members that may contribute to misunderstandings, conflicts, and insensitive care.

Quality of Life

Clients themselves provide a critical perspective for understanding needs and capabilities, all the more important to recognize and reach for when cognitive and physical diminishments erode the confidence and assertiveness to speak up. From this perspective, quality care in nursing homes is understood to involve not just medical and personal care and functional assistance but also resident quality of life. Quality of life (QOL) was an important focus of the influential Institute of Medicine report (1986) on nursing home quality that preceded nursing home reform legislation in 1987. Considerable effort has gone into better defining what is meant by the concept from the points of view of the individual resident and of the facility as a whole in an effort to more meaningfully promote and measure QOL outcomes. Kane and colleagues (Kane, 2003; Kane et al., 2003) delineated 11 domains for QOL: autonomy, functional competence, privacy, dignity, meaningful activity, individuality, enjoyment, security, relationships, spiritual well-being, and comfort.

Residents have stressed the importance of staff attitudes and continuity of staff, choice and variety of food, and opportunities for individualized activities (Holder, 1987). Their families describe poor care as the failure of the facility to help the resident maintain dignity, hope, control of the environment, and family ties, factors they also viewed as contributing to residents' depression (Bowers, 1988). Although all providers and staff in the home and many aspects of the home environment itself contribute to QOL, the overlap with social work's practice focus on meeting social and emotional needs is substantial, and high-quality psychosocial care should connect in meaningful ways to improved quality of life.

Psychosocial Needs

Whether for a short stay or a long one, the person entering a nursing home confronts the stress of adjusting to a drastically new social environment at a time of diminished personal capabilities and emotional vulnerability. For family members, the transition, both in terms of the scope and shape of their relationship to their loved one and the interjection of the new and complex caretaker system into that relationship, generates an array of needs as well. During the time in the home, both the resident and the family may sustain multiple losses, whether of relationships, roles, or independence, and may confront dying and death. Ideally, care and activities are reflective of each resident's unique preferences and capabilities, but many obstacles stand in the way. These include residents' physical and cognitive impairments that impede communication, staff members' lack of attention and/or recognition of social and emotional needs, and facility procedures and attitudes that preclude individualized options.

From a social work perspective, the realm of psychosocial care requires definition and classification, just as exists for medical and nursing care. The undertaking is important to transform general but diffuse and wide-ranging concerns into specific and distinguishable needs. Social workers encounter a formal classification and specification of certain psychosocial needs in the minimum dataset (MDS) that has been a mandated part of resident assessment in nursing homes since 1990. However, the MDS fails to capture many areas that are of central importance to social work practice, and nursing home social workers require a more comprehensive understanding of the needs that are the focus of their efforts. One such list, professionally generated by a diverse group of nursing home experts (Vourlekis, Gelfand, & Greene, 1992), is presented in Table 53.1.

TABLE 53.1. Nursing Home Residents' Psychosocial Needs: Social Work Perspective

- Emotional support and assistance in coping with transition of move to the nursing home
- Orientation to the home, its staff, policies, and procedures, including rights, responsibilities, and grievances
- Recognition of status and wholeness of one's life history
- Ongoing relatedness and intimacy with family and loved ones
- Choice concerning important daily routines
- Choice and control over decisions affecting care
- Recognition and opportunity for expression of religious/ethnic/cultural identity
- Independence in functioning and the opportunity to do for oneself whenever possible, whatever the level of functioning
- Contributing to the life and functioning of the nursing home community
- Structured social and group interaction opportunities inside and outside the home
- Maintaining contact with friends, associates, and community ties outside the home
- Help with feelings of loss that occur throughout the stay in the home
- Help with fears and anxieties that may occur throughout the stay in the home
- Specific help in preparing for and coping with death
- Recognition by staff that "difficult behavior," including aggressiveness and withdrawal/apathy, may signify emotional distress; interventions based on a specific understanding of that distress
- Help with financial planning and decision making prior to coming to the home and assistance in locating and accessing financial resources at any point during the stay in the home
- Opportunity and assistance as needed with access to activities and events within the home that are diverse enough to match each resident's capabilities and interests
- Informal social opportunities with other residents
- Opportunity and assistance as needed with access to activities and events outside the home
- Help with acquiring or replacing needed personal belongings or other practical transactions
- Emotional support to family members and significant others in response to their needs or reactions
- Family collaboration in care planning and decision making
- Family/resident input into survey/certification and accreditation processes
- Opportunity for formal feedback to home personnel on level of satisfaction with aspects of home care
- Opportunity for structured dialogue between families/residents and home personnel concerning care management
- Security that appropriate care will be in place at points of transition whether into, within, or out of the home
- Assurance that care and resources that are supposed to be provided/available, in fact, are

Facility

The nursing home as a system is at the same time an institution and a potential community. The difference lies in the meaning given and uses made of the structures, rules, roles, and routines that constitute the home's functioning.

Institutions run the risk of depersonalizing and suppressing uniqueness through standardized operations and routines that are viewed as central to efficiency and quality control. They can be dehumanizing when multifaceted, life-accumulated identity is reduced to the single status and role of "resident." Important improvements in medical care and nursing routines do not guarantee an improved quality of life when residents continue to spend almost half of their time in their rooms (Harper Ice, 2002) and continue to have little or no say over their lives (Kane, 2001).

The social worker focused on the "home-as-a-whole" will find no shortage of opportunities for influence. These may include, for example, providing or arranging additional structured resident group experiences, addressing barriers to family involvement (Peak, 2000; Port, 2004), or designing staff development to facilitate greater cultural sensitivity in the home (Mizio, 1998).

Culture Change

Within the last 10 years, a movement to supplant the institutional qualities of nursing homes with more humanistic or social models of care has taken hold. This effort, termed "culture change," seeks to improve the quality of life and the quality of care for nursing home residents through organizational and environmental changes. The principles of culture change include promotion of resident choice and decision making, supporting intergenerational relationships and relationships with the natural world, reshaping the physical environment to make it more homelike rather than institutional, and flattening the bureaucratic structures of traditional homes to empower frontline staff and residents (Fagan, Williams, & Burger, 1997). Perhaps most notable are the architectural differences between traditional nursing facilities and those that embrace the physical transformations of culture change. For example, the Green House Project introduces a model of care more closely resembling group homes, with residents housed in clusters of 8 to 10 private rooms, each with its own bath but sharing common areas, including a full kitchen (Green House Project, 2004). This brief introduction is meant to familiarize the reader with the concept of culture change.

Resident Rights

As with health care more generally, rights of nursing home residents as consumers have received considerable attention and are defined by law and supported by specific structures. Beginning in 1975, state agencies on aging that were established under the Older Americans Act of 1965 received federal funds to establish a nursing home ombudsman program to monitor the implementation of regulations protecting patients' rights in nursing homes and to receive and investigate complaints. State laws ensure the ombudsman access to facilities, residents, and records. Regulations promulgated in response to nursing home reform legislation (Omnibus Budget Reconciliation Act of 1987) detail facility responsibilities to ensure specific resident rights as a requirement of Medicare/Medicaid certification. Among the many rights are (a) nondiscrimination in admission and care regardless of source of payment; (b) freedom from unnecessary physical and chemical restraints; (c) the right to be informed about all care and to participate in care planning; (d) freedom from verbal, sexual, physical, and mental abuse, corporal punish-ment, and involuntary seclusion; and (e) the right to personal property, access to the telephone, and privacy of mail and the right to share a room with a spouse who is also a resident of the facility (Knee & Vourlekis, 1995).

SOCIAL WORK PRACTICE

Social Service Staffing

Nursing home social service departments are predominantly small, with 30 to 43% employing only one social worker (Simons, 2005; Vourlekis, Bakke-Friedland, & Zlotnik, 1995). As a result, the typical caseload of a nursing home social worker is 90 to 95 residents (Kruzich & Powell, 1995; Simons, 2005). In prior research, job tenure in this setting averaged between 2 years, among a general population of social service staff (Gleason-Wynn & Mindel, 1999), and 6 years, among professionals with social work degrees (Vourlekis, Greene, Gelfand, & Zlotnik, 1992). Salaries do appear to be competitive. A recent national survey of social service directors identified an average salary of $39,290 (SD = 11.612); however, directors earned significantly more when they had degrees in social work, especially master's degrees, and were employed in not-for-profit or government-owned facilities that were not part of multifacility chains (Simons, 2005). It is known anecdotally that social workers are hired in nursing homes for a variety of roles other than provision of social services, such as director of admissions, unit head, or volunteer coordinator. There are also social work home administrators and homeowners. However, the extent to which nursing facilities employ people with social work degrees in other facility functions is unknown and should be an area for further investigation.

A recent federal government investigation of psychosocial services at Medicare-certified nursing homes, conducted by the Office of Inspector General, found that nearly all of these facilities (98%) met the minimum regulatory staffing requirement (Department of Health and Human Services, Office of Inspector General, 2003). Yet prior and recent research reveals that only three fifths to two thirds of social service staff have degrees in social work (Kruzich & Powell, 1995; Quam & Whitford, 1992; Simons, 2005; Vinton, Mazza, & Kim, 1998; Vourlekis, Bakke-Friedland, & Zlotnik, 1995) and that most (52.6%) are not licensed (Simons, 2005).

Roles and Functions

National Association of Social Workers (NASW) Guidelines

Years of professional conceptual and empirical effort have led to a well-articulated model of social workers' roles and functions in the nursing home, as both staff members and consultants. Building from this body of work, in 1993, NASW developed an important consensus statement on the mission and roles of the nursing home social work practitioner. This practice guideline embraces a comprehensive intervention field to include the resident, the resident's family, facility staff, and the institutional environment—that is, direct services to promote psychosocial well-being and, as a member of the multidisciplinary team, efforts to "foster climate, policy, and routines" that respect residents' cultural diversity, individual uniqueness, dignity, independence, and choice (NASW, 1993). Services provided by social workers include assessment of psychosocial needs and development of a care plan, facilitating the admissions process, facilitating the social and psychological well-being of nursing home residents and their families, promoting resident empowerment and choice, crisis intervention, linkage to resources, discharge planning, and advocacy for psychosocial needs facility-wide (NASW, 1993).

In addition, NASW's *Standards for Social Work Services in Long-Term Care Facilities* (2003), although not exclusive to nursing home practice, provides further guidance regarding the necessary and appropriate functions for social workers in this setting: "advocacy, care planning, discharge planning and documentation; participation in policy and program planning; quality improvement; staff education pertaining to social services; liaison to the community; and consultation to other staff members" (p. 13). Specifically, the standards recommend social work's participation in several key areas of service provision including, but not limited to,

1. preadmission services for potential residents to determine the need and readiness for placement
2. interdisciplinary care planning
3. the medical and legal decision making of residents and/or their family members
4. room or facility transfers, as well as discharge planning and follow-up
5. helping residents create or maintain positive interpersonal relationships
6. advocacy for appropriate care and treatment
7. ensuring the availability of psychosocial services
8. policy planning and development at the facility level
9. orientation and in-service training of employees
10. serving as a staff resource in behavioral interventions
11. orientation and supervision of volunteers and/or social work field students
12. development and/or facilitation of resident and family councils
13. development and/or implementation of independent or collaborative research projects

Such responsibilities challenge the professional social worker in the nursing home to use a range of clinical, organizational, and research skills in working directly with residents and their families and indirectly with facility staff and policies to improve psychosocial outcomes and QOL for residents.

Psychosocial Services

The research and practice literature identifies and elaborates on critical tasks and strategies that social workers carry out in meeting residents' psychosocial needs. These include approaches to supporting resident empowerment and choice, such as discussions and decisions concerning advanced directives (Ingersol-Dayton, Schroepfer, Pryce, & Waarala, 2003; Mercer & Kane, 1979; Reinardy, 1999), and facilitating residents' adjustment to multiple losses and to a radically new environment (Brody, 1975; Brody & Spark, 1966; Hirsh, 1987; Silverstone & Burack-Weiss, 1982; Toseland & Newman, 1982). The social worker's ongoing involvement with family members centers on promoting maintenance of residents' family ties; mediating issues and conflicts that arise among residents, families, and staff; ameliorating family emotional distress; and involving the family in care planning (Dobrof & Letwak, 1979; Greene, 1982; Peterson, 1986; Vinton et al., 1998; York & Colsen, 1977). Other research has found that facilitation of the admissions process, development of individualized care plans, and discharge planning are typical tasks fulfilled by social workers in nursing facilities (Parker-Oliver & Kurzejeski, 2003).

Social workers are commonly the only nursing home staff designated specifically for the provision of psychosocial care; therefore, they may be best able to identify and address mental health conditions among residents. From a regulatory perspective, they are often responsible for completion of the cognitive, mood, behavioral, and psychosocial portions of the mandated assessment tools used in nursing homes, namely, the minimum dataset (MDS) and their accompanying resident assessment protocols (RAPs) and care plan sections (Beaulieu, 2002). The Department of Veterans Affairs further recommends that its nursing home social workers screen for mental disorders and provide, if appropriately credentialed, individual, group, and family counseling (Department of Veterans Affairs, 2001). Still, given the great need for mental health services in nursing homes and the typically high caseloads for the social worker, it is more likely that a nursing facility will refer to external providers for mental health services. Therefore, the social worker may more often be viewed as a member of a team of mental health providers, perhaps a first point of contact for the resident and his or her family, and tasked with recognition of need and making a referral, rather than as the provider of mental health treatment (Beaulieu, 2002).

Practice Realities and Issues

The nursing home social work research and practice literature has been invaluable in explaining and reinforcing the highly skilled nature of social work functions for administrators, policy makers, and consumers. Even so, nursing home social workers confronting the realities of practice circumstances are likely to encounter problems of role overload and misunderstanding about role expectations on the part of administrators and other providers in the home (Greene, Vourlekis, Gelfand, & Lewis, 1992). Preoccupation with case-by-case needs may cloud the practitioner's perception and inclination to address home-as-a-whole circumstances with an impact on all residents. Significant barriers to direct service exist, such as extensive paperwork and documentation and being assigned responsibilities in addition to provision of psychosocial care (Department of Health and Human Services, 2003). Time constraints resulting from minimal social service staffing require social workers to prioritize among functions, not provide them all (Kosberg, 1973; Vourlekis, Greene, et al., 1992). Social work consultants who are used when full-time qualified staff are not required or are unavailable often face severe time limitations, constraining their ability to adequately oversee, let alone directly provide, priority psychosocial care (Vourlekis, Greene, et al., 1992).

Despite these limitations, there is beginning to be evidence of consistency in implementation of the central elements of the staff social work role. Professionally prepared practitioners reported their highest frequency functions were (a) orientation to the facility for resident and family; (b) help in coping with the transition of the move to the nursing home; (c) crisis intervention; (d) mediating among resident, family, and staff; and (e) assessment, with assessment and care planning accounting for close to half of working hours, much of it in documentation (Brooks, 2003; Vourlekis, Greene, et al., 1992). Social workers and home administrators have expressed considerable consensus on priority resident psychosocial needs in the home, including transitional support, help with loss, and ongoing relatedness and intimacy. Furthermore, administrators shared social workers' view of most of their highest-frequency functions to meet these needs (Vourlekis, Gelfand, et al., 1992). Evidence of greater role clarity and consistent performance expectations in this limited number of high-priority care activities can provide a practical road map to connect high-quality practice with high-quality care outcomes.

The nursing home setting presents the practitioner with both ethical dilemmas and values conflicts. The potential for conflict of interest exists when discharge or supplementary service referrals are expected to be within an integrated health care system of which the nursing home is one part, or with certain precontracted providers. Ethical questions can arise in end-of-life decisions and care, particularly if mental competency is in question. Finding balance between resident self-determination and autonomy and legitimate staff or family concerns can be difficult throughout the stay in the home. Willingness to advocate for the resident and/or family when this pits the social worker against the home's administrators requires a high degree of professional sound judgment, self-confidence, and ability to clarify whose "good" is of paramount concern.

Practice Networks

Nursing home social workers will find that opportunities to network with colleagues are an important resource. Some states have independent organizations of professional nursing home social workers, and a number of NASW state chapters have long-term care committees with active continuing education and social action agendas. Practitioners with an interest in the consumer point of view and advocacy for overall quality improvement can find information, activities, and social work colleagues through the National Citizens' Coalition for Nursing Home Reform (*http://www.nccnhr.org*).

Accountability

Social work processes and interventions, while conceptually sound, rarely have been linked to empirically demonstrated clinical outcomes and measurable QOL, leaving them vulnerable in today's outcome-oriented and evidence-based practice environment. Social work practice needs to demonstrate the high quality of its services in the nursing home and the difference these services can make to resident well-being and the quality of facility care overall. This evidence is crucial for visibility, accountability, and credibility, especially in this setting, where the professionalization of social services remains uneven and incomplete, and budget-constrained administrators lack compelling reasons to hire more (or higher-cost) social service providers.

Federal conditions of participation for nursing homes assign responsibility for meeting psychosocial needs to the facility as a whole, not to a specific discipline. Therefore, in determining facility compliance, surveyors do focus on aspects of quality of life and psychosocial care to which social work directly contributes, but current outcome measures and surveyor questions and protocols do not provide direct evidence of social work service quality, quantity, or effectiveness. Therefore, conceptual and measurable links between social service care processes and surveyors' facility-specific assessment of quality of care and quality of life must be designed at the level of the home.

For example, surveyors focus on the emotional and behavioral conduct of the residents, especially evidence of distress such as crying out, disrobing, agitation, and pacing, with a particular interest in whether and how staff are responding. Social work crisis intervention activities frequently address stressful and disruptive resident reactions, both to respond to the resident's underlying social-emotional circumstances and to help other staff recognize the meaning of the "difficult behavior." Whether through chart documentation or through a more formal process of monitoring the incidence and outcomes following social work intervention in this type of "problem," the nursing home social worker can heighten his or her visibility and accountability with respect to this im-

portant area. In the area of resident assessment, surveyors look for identification of psychosocial needs, which is a frequently performed social work function. However, when surveyors examine quality of care, they may not focus attention on follow-through for these particular needs—or may not find evidence if they do. Federal investigators recently conducted a nursing home chart review of a sample of Medicare beneficiaries and found that 39% did not have assessed psychosocial needs addressed in their care plans and 41% were not receiving all of the psychosocial services that were in their plans (Department of Health and Human Services, 2003). Social workers, the only providers in the home with an exclusive psychosocial focus, can be proactive in designing simple tracking systems to document actions taken to address needs that could be part of the home's formal accountability system.

Working in the continuous quality improvement framework, the National Association of Social Workers developed a set of six clinical indicators for social work practice in nursing homes (NASW, 1993), including measures of both social work care processes and resident outcomes. The indicators are timely psychosocial assessment, comprehensive psychosocial assessment, resident and family involvement in care planning, resident satisfaction with choice, and psychosocial problem resolution. Developed through extensive field reviews, the indicators can serve as a specific and uniform approach to demonstrating the level of performance of key social work functions and to linking these functions to resident outcomes in domains typically surveyed by regulators (Vourlekis et al., 1995).

For example, evidence of resident choice as well as affirmation of a key resident right could be devised using "presence of advance directive" as the operational "choice" outcome and linking this to the social work process of explaining, discussing, and negotiating this important decision. Barriers to accomplishing this task could be documented, providing opportunities for facility-as-a-whole examination of care improvement efforts.

RESEARCH FOR NURSING HOME PRACTICE

Precedents for social work's contribution to research to improve nursing home quality of care and quality of life have been established. Two notable examples are the work of prominent social work researchers

Elaine Brody and Rosalie Kane. Beginning in the 1960s, Brody's body of work on social components of nursing home care and the needs of the mentally impaired elderly led to publication of her seminal book (Brody, 1974), which still remains a linchpin of practice. For 20 more years, her research on filial care, particularly care provided by daughters, and many aspects of the realities of the dependent elderly, whether living at home or in the nursing home, provided findings that have influenced both policy and social work practice. Kane's widely recognized research dealing with nursing home quality, ethics, and, currently, resident quality of life has provided guidance for federal policy. Her research provides direction and support for social work practice in areas such as interventions to enhance resident choice and control and in outcomes measurement.

Nevertheless, the research base for social work practice is a limited one. Systematic tests of the effectiveness of social work interventions in the nursing home comprise a critically needed agenda for social work's research establishment. Intervention research focused on the social worker's potential contribution to improving mental health care (identification, assessment, and treatment) that is more accurate and offers a greater variety of nonpharmacological and pharmacological interventions is an example of a promising avenue (American Geriatrics Society, 2003; Burnett, Morrow-Howell, & Chen, 2003; Simmons et al., 2004).

A range of research efforts, including randomized controlled studies, cost analyses, and evaluation research, is necessary to provide the evidence base for practice that is now an expectation for health care in all settings. It is also needed to demonstrate the value added by a costly practitioner in an increasingly cost-conscious and cost-constrained environment. Practical and applied tools to monitor quality of care and connect social work care processes to current accreditation and/or surveying processes that are central to home certification and licensing can and should be crafted, whether the oversight approach is one of compliance or one of continuous quality improvement.

To date, the necessary national statistical profile for the profession's presence and contribution in nursing home care is lacking. Current federal and state regulatory processes do not routinely or systematically assess more than the structural absence or presence of a social service provider, who may, as discussed previously, possess a variety of credentials. A feasible blueprint to guide the development of evidence for a set of consistently implemented social work roles and functions, guidelines for expected "best practice" in those roles, and demonstration of the link between practice and valued resident and home-as-a-whole outcomes must be crafted, with the social work profession taking the lead. The parameters, key issues, and potential resources for this critical enterprise were laid out in a recent national multidisciplinary working conference, sponsored by the Institute for the Advancement of Social Work Research (2004) and funded by the federal Agency for Health Care Research and Quality.

CONCLUSION

Nursing home social work practice today presents worthy challenges to the practitioner and to the profession. For the practitioner, managing the demands and expectations of a large caseload and an extensive practice mission and role requires an ability to initiate, not just react, prioritize, and teach others how to make the best use of social work skills and time. The potential of social work interventions that can have an impact on the facility as a whole appears to be underutilized, or at least not well documented or described in the professional literature. Obtaining a better "working picture" of macro social work practice in the home that targets organizational and environmental change would be beneficial for practitioners, educators, and policy makers.

Professional social workers, partnering with their research colleagues, need to demonstrate their impact in this setting, especially when those with degrees in other human service professions are considered adequate substitutes and command lower salaries. The profession as a whole has a critical advocacy agenda with state and federal policy makers. It must argue convincingly and well for continued improvement of conditions and life in the nursing home, for professionally qualified social workers in every home, and for progress in the quality and effectiveness of social work practice itself.

REFERENCES

American Geriatrics Society and American Association for Geriatric Psychiatry. (2003). Consensus statement on improving the quality of mental health care in US nursing homes: Management of depression and behavioral symptoms associated with dementia. *Journal of the American Geriatrics Society, 51,* 1287–1298.

Beaulieu, E. M. (2002). *A guide for nursing home social workers.* New York: Springer.

Bishop, C. E. (1999). Where are the missing elders? The decline in nursing home use, 1985–1995. *Health Affairs, 18*(4), 146–155.

Bowers, B. J. (1988). Family perception of care in a nursing home. *The Gerontologist, 28,* 361–368.

Brody, E. M. (1974). *A social work guide for long term care facilities* (DHEW Publication No. ADM 75-177). Washington, DC: Government Printing Office.

Brody, E., & Spark, G. (1966). Institutionalization of the aged: A family crisis. *Family Process, 5,* 76–90.

Brooks, L. (2003, April 17). *Best practice nursing home study.* Paper presented at the CMS Social Work Nursing Home Panel teleconference and WebEX, Baltimore.

Burnett, D., Morrow-Howell, N., & Chen, L. M. (2003). Setting priorities for gerontological social work research: A national Delphi study. *The Gerontologist, 43,* 828–838.

Calderon, V., & Tennstedt, S. L. (1998). Ethnic differences in the expression of caregiver burden: Results of a qualitative study. *Journal of Gerontological Social Work, 30,* 159–178.

Centers for Medicare & Medicaid Services. (1989). *Requirements for long term care facilities, 42 C.F.R. 483,* Subpart B.

Centers for Medicare & Medicaid Services (2001). *Nursing home data compendium 2001.* Retrieved June 2004 from *http://www.cms.hhs.gov/medicaid/survey-cert/datacomp.asp.*

Centers for Medicare & Medicaid Services (2003, May 20). *Health care industry market update: Nursing facilities.* Retrieved June 2004 from *http://www.cms.hhs.gov/reports/hcimu/hcimu_05202003.pdf.*

Department of Health and Human Services, Office of Inspector General. (2003). *Psychosocial services in skilled nursing facilities.* Retrieved April 17, 2003, from *http://oig.hhs.gov/oei/reports/oei-02-01-00610.pdf.*

Department of Veterans Affairs, Office of Social Work Service. (2001). *Social worker functions in long-term care settings.* (Available from the Department of Veterans Affairs, Office of Social Work Service, Washington, DC 20011.)

Dobrof, R., & Letwak, E. (1979). *Maintaining family ties of long-term care patients: Theory and guide to practice* (HEW Publication No. ADM 79-400). Washington, DC: Government Printing Office.

Ejaz, F. K. (2002). The influence of religious and personal values on nursing home residents' attitudes toward life-sustaining treatments. *Social Work in Health Care, 32,* 23–39.

Fagan, R. M., Williams, C. C., & Burger, S. G. (1997). *Meeting of pioneers in nursing home culture change.* Rochester, NY: Lifespan of Greater Rochester.

Field, A., Maher, P., & Webb, D. (2002). Cross-cultural research in palliative care. *Social Work and Health Care, 35,* 523–543.

Fitzgerald, M. H., Mullavey-O'Byrne, C., & Clemson, L. (2001). Families and nursing home placements: A cross-cultural study. *Journal of Cross-Cultural Gerontology, 16,* 333–351.

Gleason-Wynn, P., & Mindel, C. H. (1999). A proposed model for predicting job satisfaction among nursing home social workers. *Journal of Gerontological Social Work, 32*(3), 65–79.

Green House Project. (2004). *Fact sheet 2004.* Retrieved June 11, 2004, from *http://thegreenhouseproject.com/factsheet.pdf.*

Greene, R. R. (1982). Families and the nursing home social worker. *Social Work in Health Care, 7,* 57–67.

Greene, R. R., Vourlekis, B. S., Gelfand, D. E., & Lewis, J. S. (1992). Current realities: Practice and education needs of social workers in nursing homes. *Geriatric Social Work Education, 18*(3/4), 39–54.

Harper Ice, H. (2002). Daily life in a nursing home. Has it changed in 25 years? *Journal of Aging Studies, 16,* 345–359.

Harrington, C., & Carrillo, H. (1999). The regulation and enforcement of federal nursing home standards, 1991–1997. *Medical Care Research and Review, 56,* 471–494.

Harrington, C., Woolhandler, S., Mullan, J., Carrillo, H., & Himmelstein, D. U. (2001). Does investor ownership of nursing homes compromise the quality of care? *American Journal of Public Health, 91*(9), 1–5.

Hawes, C., Phillips, C. D., Rose, M., Holan, S., & Sherman, M. (2003). A national survey of assisted living facilities. *The Gerontologist, 43,* 875–882.

Hirsh, E. (1987). Easing the transition to the institution. *Danish Medical Bulletin, Special Supplement Series, 5,* 81–84.

Holder, E. (1987). A consumer perspective on quality care: The resident's point of view. *Danish Medical Bulletin, Special Supplement Series 5,* 84–89.

Ingersoll-Dayton, B., Saengtienchai, C., Kespichayawattana, J., & Aungsuroch, Y. (2004). Measuring psychological well-being: Insights from Thai elders. *The Gerontologist, 2004,* 596–605.

Ingersoll-Dayton, B., Schroepfer, T., Pryce, J., & Waarala, C. (2003). Enhancing relationships in nursing homes through empowerment. *Social Work, 48,* 420–424.

Institute for the Advancement of Social Work Research. (2004). *Evaluating social work services in nursing homes: Toward quality psychosocial care and its measurement.* Retrieved June 15, 2005, from *http://www.iaswresearch.org.*

Institute of Medicine. (1986). *Improving the quality of care in nursing homes.* Washington, DC: National Academy Press.

Jones, A. (2002). The national nursing home survey 1999 summary. *National Center for Health Statistics: Vital Health Statistics, 13*(152), 1–5.

Kane, R. A. (2001). Long-term care and a good quality of life: Bringing them closer. *The Gerontologist, 41*(3), 293–304.

Kane, R. A. (2003). Definition, measurement, and correlates of quality of life in nursing homes: Toward a reasonable practice, research, and policy agenda. *The Gerontologist, 43*(Special issue II), 28–36.

Kane, R. A., Kling, K. C., Bershadsky, B., Kane, R. L., Giles, K., Degenholtz, H. B., et al. (2003). Quality of life measures for nursing home residents. *Journal of Gerontology: Medical Sciences, 58A*(3), 240–248.

Knee, R. I., & Vourlekis, B. S. (1995). Patient rights. In *Encyclopedia of Social Work* (ed. 19, pp. 1802–1810). Washington, DC: NASW Press.

Konetzka, T. R., Yi, D., Norton, E. C., & Kilpatrick, K. E. (2004). Effects of Medicare payment changes on nursing home staffing and deficiencies. *Health Services Research, 39*, 463–487.

Kosberg, J. I. (1973). The nursing home: A social work paradox. *Social Work, 18*(2), 104–110.

Kruzich, J. M., & Powell, W. E. (1995). Decision-making influence: An empirical study of social workers in nursing homes. *Health & Social Work, 20*, 215–222.

Lakdawalla, D., Goldman, D. P., Bhattacharya, J., Hurd, M. D., Joyce, G. F., & Panis, C. W. A. (2003). Forecasting the nursing home population. *Medical Care, 41*, 8–20.

Mercer, S., & Kane, R. A. (1979). Helplessness and hopelessness among the institutionalized aged: An experiment. *Health and Social Work, 4*, 91–116.

Mizio, E. (1998). Staff development: An ethical imperative. *Journal of Gerontological Social Work, 30*, 17–32.

Mor, V., Zinn, J., Angelelli, J., Teno, J. M., & Miller, S. C. (2004). Driven to tiers: Socioeconomic and racial disparities in the quality of nursing home care. *Milbank Quarterly, 82*, 227–256.

National Association of Social Workers. (1993). *NASW clinical indicators for social work and psychosocial services in nursing homes.* Washington, DC: NASW.

National Association of Social Workers. (2003). *Standards for social work services in long-term care facilities.* Washington, DC: NASW.

Older Americans Act of 1965, Public Law No. 89-73, Stat. 218 (1965).

Omnibus Reconciliation Act of 1987, Public Law No. 100-203, Sec. 42, 101 Stat. 1330 (1987).

Parker-Oliver, D., & Kurzejewski, L. S. (2003). Nursing home social services: Policy and practice. *Journal of Gerontological Social Work, 42*(2), 37–50.

Peak, T. (2000). Families and the nursing home environment: Adaptation in a group context. *Journal of Gerontological Social Work, 33*, 51–66.

Peterson, K. J. (1986). Changing needs of patients and families in long-term care facilities: Implications for social work practice. *Social Work in Health Care, 12*, 37–49.

Port, C. (2004). Identifying changeable barriers to family involvement in the nursing home for cognitively impaired residents. *The Gerontologist, 44*, 770–779.

Quam, J. K., & Whitford, G. S. (1992). Educational needs of nursing home social workers at the baccalaureate level. *Geriatric Social Work Education, 18*(3/4), 143–156.

Reinardy, J. R. (1999). Autonomy, choice, and decision making: How nursing home social workers view their role. *Social Work in Health Care, 29*(3), 59–77.

Rhoades, J. A., & Sommers, J. P. (2003). Trends in nursing home expenses, 1987 and 1996. *Health Care Financing Review, 25*, 99–114.

Shibusawa, T., & Mui, A. (2001). Stress, coping, and depression among Japanese American elders. *Journal of Gerontological Social Work, 36*, 63–81.

Silverstone, B., & Burack-Weiss, A. (1982). The social work function in nursing homes and home care. *Journal of Gerontological Social Work, 5*, 7–33.

Simmons, S. F., Cadogan, M. P., Cabrera, G. R., Al-Samarrai, N. R., Jorge, J. S., Levy-Storms, L., Osterweil, D., & Schnelle, J. F. (2004). The minimum data set depression quality indicator: Does it reflect differences in care processes? *The Gerontologist, 44*, 554–555.

Simons, K. (2005). *Factors affecting nursing home social workers' quitting intentions.* Unpublished doctoral dissertation. University of Maryland, Baltimore.

Toseland, R. W., & Newman, E. (1982). Admitting applicants to skilled nursing facilities: Social workers' role. *Health and Social Work, 7*, 262–272.

U.S. Census Bureau. (2004, June 14). *Hispanic and Asian Americans increasing faster than overall population.* Retrieved June 25, 2004, from *http://www.census.gov/Press-Release/www/releases/archives/race/001839.html.*

Vinton, L., Mazza, N., & Kim, Y. (1998). Intervening in family-staff conflicts in nursing homes. *Clinical Gerontologist, 19*(3), 45–67.

Vourlekis, B. S., Bakke-Friedland, K., & Zlotnik, J. L. (1995). Clinical indicators to assess the quality of social work services in nursing homes. *Social Work in Health Care, 22,* 81–93.

Vourlekis, B. S., Gelfand, D. E., & Greene, R. R. (1992). Psychosocial needs and care in nursing homes: Comparison of views of social workers and home administrators. *The Gerontologist, 32,* 113–119.

Vourlekis, B. S., Greene, R. R., Gelfand, D. E., & Zlotnik, J. L. (1992). Searching for the doable in nursing home social work practice. *Social Work in Health Care, 17*(3), 45–70.

Yip, J. Y., Wilber, K. H., & Myrtle, R. C. (2002). The impact of the 1997 Balanced Budget Amendment's prospective payment system on patient case mix and rehabilitation utilization in skilled nursing. *The Gerontologist, 42,* 653–660.

York, J., & Colsen, R. (1977). Family involvement in nursing homes. *The Gerontologist, 17,* 500–505.

The role of social workers in the Veterans Administration (VA) began in 1926, with the establishment of the social work program in the Veterans Bureau. In its first year, the VA had 14 social workers in psychiatric hospitals and 22 in regional offices throughout the country. At present, the Veterans Health Administration (VHA) employs almost 4,000 master's-prepared social workers in VA medical centers (VAMCs) all over the country. From their original focus on veterans with tuberculosis and psychiatric problems, VHA social work staff have addressed the needs of many distinct veteran populations, including the homeless, the aged, HIV/AIDS patients, spinal cord injury, former prisoners of war, and veterans and their families from World Wars I and II, Korea, Vietnam, and the Persian Gulf.

The Department of Veterans Affairs (DVA) health care system has one of the most comprehensive programs focused on the needs of older disabled persons in the United States. VA long-term care programs have their roots in care provided by the federal government for soldiers who became disabled in the Civil War.

In fiscal year 2002, the VA provided long-term care services to almost 67,500 veterans at a cost of more than $3.3 billion. The VA provides for the health care of veterans of all ages across the entire continuum of care. Veterans may receive acute care, outpatient care, or community-based or institutional long-term care through a variety of services and programs provided directly by VA or contracted or arranged with agencies in the community. Long-term care (LTC) in VA refers to all postacute programs and services provided to individuals who are frail, chronically ill, disabled, mentally ill, and/or in need of postacute rehabilitation. Within VA, the term *LTC* is also sometimes used interchangeably with the terms *chronic care* and *extended care,* particularly with respect to nursing home and home health care services. Long-term care services may be provided by a VA medical center, through a VA contract with a community agency, or arranged by VA staff and provided in a non-VA setting.

MARYLOU GUIHAN

Residential Care Settings for Veterans

54

VA NATIONAL LEADERSHIP IN GERIATRICS AND GERONTOLOGY

In the mid-1970s, VA planners began to focus on the large number of World War II and Korean War veterans who were rapidly approaching or who had already reached age 65. In 1977 approximately 25% of adult males over age 65 were veterans; by 1995, this percentage exceeded 60%. It has been estimated that 1,000 WWII veterans are dying every day. As a result of these projections, VA made a significant commitment to dealing with the needs of its aging population. As a result of this commitment, VA has become widely known for its education and training, its research, and its contributions to clinical innovations.

Contributions to Education and Training

VA is the largest single provider of geriatric training in the United States. The American Geriatrics Society estimates that up to 80% of the nation's academic leaders in geriatrics today received some VA training. Special fellowship programs in geriatrics have been designated for psychiatrists, dentists, nurses, and psychologists. Beginning in 1994, additional positions were allocated to support training of medical residents in long-term care settings. Also, of the approximately 112,000 health professions students who receive clinical training experiences in VA facilities annually, many gain experience in care of the elderly by rotating through one or more of VA's geriatric and extended care clinical programs.

As part of its commitment to care for older veterans, VA also established centers of excellence in geriatrics called Geriatric Research, Education, and Clinical Centers (GRECCs) in 1975. The mission of the GRECCs is to improve the health and care of elderly veterans through research, education, and training and to develop improved clinical models of care. VA supports 16 GRECCs throughout the VA system, each with a distinct programmatic focus, including interdisciplinary approaches to treatment of prostate cancer; neurobiology, epidemiology, and management of dementia; falls and instability; geropharmacology; cost-effective delivery of health care services to the elderly; and bioethical aspects of medical decision making in aging.

Contributions to Research

VA's commitment to the health problems of aging veterans can also be seen in its intramural research program, which includes basic biomedical and clinical medicine research, as well as research in health services, rehabilitation, and large-scale clinical trials. VA funds a large number of studies related to health problems of the elderly, including cancer, stroke, degenerative bone and joint diseases, dementias, and diabetes.

Contributions to Clinical Innovation

VA also pioneered the Geriatric Evaluation and Management (GEM) program. GEMs provide both primary and specialized care services to a targeted group of elderly patients. On inpatient GEM units, an interdisciplinary team of geriatric experts performs comprehensive, multidimensional evaluations of frail, elderly patients to improve their functional status, stabilize their acute and chronic medical conditions and/or psychosocial problems, and discharge patients to home, residential care, or the least restrictive environment feasible. GEM clinics provide similar comprehensive care for geriatric patients on an outpatient basis in addition to providing primary care for frail, older patients to prevent unnecessary institutionalization. The geriatric staffs also are available for specialty consultation on elderly patients with complex problems who are being cared for by primary care and other specialty services. Currently, 110 VA medical centers have GEM programs that include inpatient units and/or outpatient clinics, as well as consultation services.

PEOPLE SERVED BY VA

As a result of its demographic imperative, VA realized that it was facing an unprecedented demand for its LTC services. Although the total number of veterans is expected to decline between 2004 and 2014, the number of older veterans, especially those age 85 and older, will more than double to a total of 1.3 million by 2012. This is expected to significantly strain existing resources and increase the need for VA's long-term care. Although disability may strike at any age, older individuals are considerably more likely to develop disabilities and to need LTC as a result. Data from the National Health Interview Survey (Department of Health and Human Services, 1994–1995) indicate that 4.8% of those 65 to 84 years old report a disability (defined as two or more activities of daily living [ADL] deficiencies) and that this proportion nearly quadruples to 18.1% among those 85 and older.

Although the overwhelming majority of older veterans are male, in 2002, the female veteran population of 1.7 million constituted 6.5% of all veterans. VA has seen a significant increase in the number of women veterans who receive benefits and health care services from the department. The number of women veterans enrolled in VA's health care system grew from 226,000 in 2000 to 420,000 in 2002, an increase of 86%.

Data from the National Survey of Veterans indicates that as a group, female veterans are younger than male veterans, which, in turn, may explain their better health. Almost 83% of women veterans are younger than 65 years old, compared with only about 63% of male respondents. When the functional limitations of male and female veterans are compared, a higher percentage of female veterans (70.8%) than male veterans (67.0%) also reported having no ADL or instrumental ADL (IADL) difficulties. A higher percentage of male veterans reported difficulties with three or more ADLs than did female veterans (9.4% vs. 7.6%, respectively).

DESCRIPTION OF LTC PROGRAMS AND SERVICES

Veterans may receive one or more of a number of LTC services, depending on eligibility and need. Social workers outside VA need to be aware of veterans' benefits for which their clientele might be eligible. Broadly speaking, VA uses two methods of determining eligibility and need for LTC services: (a) service-connected disability status and (b) functional need for LTC.

Service-Connected Disability

Service-connected disability status is attained by a veteran who incurred a disability from a disease or injury that was sustained or aggravated by military service. Individuals are compensated according to the severity of their disability. Individuals with a 30% or higher rating of disability receive additional monies for spouses and/or dependents. Special monthly pensions may be authorized for veterans whose service-connected disabilities are very severe and meet certain statutory requirements (e.g., spinal cord injury). Service connection for a disability may be granted for certain chronic and tropical diseases (even if the conditions were not manifest or diagnosed during the veteran's military service). Service connection may also be established for a secondary disability or disease that is proximately the result of a service-connected disease or injury. A service-connected disability may entitle a veteran to receive additional benefits, such as VA medical care, vocational rehabilitation, and/or adaptive equipment or homes. The Millennium Act (discussed later) describes VA's new priorities for LTC services provided to veterans.

Functional Assessment

As of this writing, VHA is in the process of rolling out a new assessment tool, the Geriatrics and Extended Care (GEC) referral tool, that assesses functional criteria. At this time, clinical staff assessing a veteran's need for nursing home care is not required to adhere to standard functional criteria to determine eligibility.[1] Instead, individuals are defined as needing VA LTC services when a chronic condition, trauma, or illness limits their ability to carry out basic self-care tasks (ADLs) or household chores, such as using the phone or preparing a meal (IADLs), or when care is required following acute care discharge that cannot be effectively managed in an outpatient setting (e.g., postoperative wound care/dressing changing, IV antibiotics, rehabilitation, or catheter care).

VA provides two general types of LTC programs to veterans: (a) institutional long-term care and (b) home- and community-based care.

VA Institutionally Based LTC Programs and Services

For veterans in need of postacute or institutional long-term care services, services may be provided through (a) VA nursing home care units, (b) VA's contract nursing home program, or (c) state veterans' homes. About 73% of VA's budget for fiscal year 2000 nursing home care was for care in VA nursing homes; the remainder was for veterans' care in the state-owned and operated veterans' nursing homes (15%) or in community nursing homes under contract to VA (12%).

Nursing Home Care Units (NHCUs)

Nursing home care in VA NHCUs is provided to veterans under the auspices of Title 38 U.S.C. 610. Veterans may receive postacute and long-term care in 134 VA NHCUs. Veterans cared for in NHCUs are cared for by VA physicians, nurses, and/or nursing assistants. Nursing home care may include dietetic services, social work, dental work, supplies, equipment, and medical and skilled nursing services, such as assessment, planning, intervention, and evaluation of nursing care. Veterans may be cared for in VA NHCUs over an extended period of time depending on eligibility and availability of resources. Services may be directed toward veterans demonstrating a potential for improvement or maintenance of existing function.

Community Nursing Home (CNH) Program

To improve access to geographic locations closer to veterans' homes, VA created the CNH program in 1964. VA currently contracts with more than 3,400 community facilities in 43 states. In fiscal year 2002, more than 28,800 veterans were treated in community nursing homes at VA expense. Veterans who require nursing home care for a service-connected disability can receive care from a community facility for an indefinite time at VA expense; others may be placed in a community facility at VA expense, with the expectation they may leave or convert to self-pay or Medicaid.

VA's Community Nursing Home program[2] is managed by VA social workers, who are responsible for placing veterans and overseeing quality assurance aspects of care for the homes VA contracts with. VA sends its social workers out to conduct the initial assessment of nursing homes it wishes to contract with and then visits contract facilities on a monthly basis to oversee all aspects of care for veterans placed in these homes.

State Veterans' Homes

Although this program dates back to the post–Civil War era, it has grown dramatically since 1990, by 2004 encompassing 103 nursing homes in 47 states. The state home program substantially augments VA's capacity to provide a continuous residence for veterans in need of long-term care, especially veterans in rural areas. State homes are owned and operated by the state, with VA contributing up to 65% of the cost of construction or acquisition of state nursing homes or domiciliaries or for renovations to an existing home. VA also provides per diem payments for eligible veterans in state homes. VA does not directly place veterans in state veterans' homes. Instead, veterans must apply for admission, and eligibility and admission requirements vary by state. VA assures Congress that state homes provide high-quality care through inspections, audits, and reconciliation of records conducted by the local VAMC.

VA Community-Based LTC Programs and Services

In fiscal year 2002, approximately 37% of VA's total long-term care population received care in noninstitutional settings, a marked departure from the historical dependence on hospital-based services. The list below describes the remainder of VA's community-based LTC programs and services.

Community-Based Long-Term Care Programs and Services Offered by VA

- **Adult day health care:** health maintenance and rehabilitative services provided to frail older veterans in an outpatient day setting.
- **Alzheimer's/dementia care:** specialized outpatient services such as behavioral and medical management provided to veterans with Alzheimer's disease or related dementias.
- **Community residential care:**[3] a service in which veterans who do not require hospital or nursing home care—but who (because of medical or psychosocial health conditions) are unable to live independently—live in VA-approved community residential care facilities; VA provides staff to coordinate services for veterans in the community residential programs as well as pay for costs of services for which the veteran is eligible.
- **Geriatric evaluation:** evaluation of veterans with particular geriatric needs, generally provided by VA through one of two services: (a) geriatric evaluation and management (GEM), in which interdisciplinary health care teams of geriatric specialists evaluate and manage frail older veterans, and (b) geriatric primary care, in which outpatient primary care, including medical and nursing services, preventive health care services, health education, and specialty referral, is provided to geriatric veterans.
- **Home-based primary care:** primary medical care provided in the home by VA physicians, nurses, social workers, and other VA health care professionals to severely disabled, chronically ill veterans whose conditions make them unsuitable for management in outpatient clinics.
- **Homemaker/home health aide:** home health aide and homemaker services, such as grooming, housekeeping, and meal preparation services.
- **Home/institutional-based respite care:**[4] home- and institutional-based services provided to veterans on a short-term basis to give veterans' caregivers a period of relief or respite.
- **Hospice care:**[5] home- and institutional-based palliative and supportive services for veterans in the last phases of incurable disease so that they may live as fully and as comfortably as possible.

- **Skilled home health care:** medical services provided to veterans at home by non-VA health care providers.

The availability of community-based LTC services varies by VAMC. A recent Government Accountability Office (GAO) report concluded: "Veterans' access to the [adult day health care, geriatric evaluation, respite care, home-based primary care, homemaker/home health aide, and skilled home health care] is limited by service gaps and facility restrictions" (GAO, 2003). Only 13 of the 134 VAMCs offer all six community-based services. Skilled home health care is most available ($N = 127$), and respite care is least available ($N = 28$ VAMCs). About half ($N = 64$) reported offering community residential care. Veterans' access may be further limited by waiting lists or restrictions that individual facilities set for use of the services they offer. Thus, considerable disparity exists in what community-based LTC services are offered by individual VAMCs.

THE CHANGING FACE OF VA

In 1997, VA established the Federal Advisory Committee on the Future of VA Long-Term Care, composed of national leaders in LTC. The committee was asked to evaluate VA long-term care services and develop a strategy for meeting future LTC needs. The committee's report found that VA long-term care was unevenly funded and recommended that VA expand its use of noninstitutional long-term care services and emphasize these services, when clinically appropriate, for veterans needing long-term care (Department of Veterans Affairs, 1998).

With congressional support, VA has taken a number of steps to address this challenge. Congress has allocated $413 million since 2000 to expand VA's own nursing home (NH) program, with another $105 million to follow. VA has also taken several steps to increase the availability of community-based LTC services and has seen some success: The proportion of VA's long-term care costs for noninstitutional care has doubled from 4% to 8% of its total budget over the past decade. This progress lags behind that of the Medicaid program. And it is clear that the demand for LTC over the coming years cannot possibly be met by using the current mix of care.

Historically, VA LTC was generally provided on a first-come, first-served basis within budget constraints. However, the passage of the Veterans Mil-

lennium Health Care and Benefits Act (PL106-117, 1999) sets priorities for who should receive nursing home care, defined as any veterans who (a) need such care for a disability connected to his or her military service and (b) who is at least 70% disabled by a service-connected condition (i.e., resulting from their military service) and who needs nursing home care, regardless of whether the care is required specifically for the disabling condition.

The Millennium Act also mandates VA to make significant changes in how LTC services are delivered to older veterans, agreeing to increase the allocation of overall spending to increase community-based LTC by 37% over the next three years. In particular, VA will be focusing on increasing the availability of adult day health care, geriatric evaluation, and respite care to veterans.

The Millennium Act mandated VA to examine innovative ways to provide community-based LTC to help families. The act funded two research demonstration and evaluation projects to assess private-sector models of care for veterans: (a) the all-inclusive care program and (b) the assisted living pilot program. These demonstrations are expected to be completed in 2005. Results are embargoed until released by Congress at the completion of the evaluation periods. The purpose and design of these projects are as follows.

All-Inclusive Care Program

The Millennium Act authorized VA to implement three pilot programs based on PACE (Program for All-Inclusive Care for the Elderly), a replication of the model of care developed by On Lok Senior Health Services in San Francisco, California. The goal of these projects is to assess the comparative effectiveness of three models of all-inclusive care (AIC) delivery in reducing the use of hospital and nursing home care by frail older veterans. The PACE program offers and manages all medical, social, and long-term care services their enrollees need to preserve or restore their independence, remain in their homes and communities, and maintain their quality of life. One of the program's most notable features is its use of an adult day health care center as the primary means of delivering the full range of medical and long-term care services to enrollees. At the heart of the model is the interdisciplinary team, with professional and paraprofessional staff, which assesses enrollees' needs, develops care plans, and delivers and arranges for services, which are integrated for a seamless provision of total care for the veterans and their families.

The three models VA is evaluating are (a) VA staffed, (b) community provided with VA care manager, and (c) VA partnership with community provider. The objectives of the evaluation are (a) describing the implementation and operation of each of the three models of AIC, including the organizational and structural characteristics of each model; (b) describing the characteristics of veterans enrolled in each of the three models to a comparison group; and (c) assessing the use of institutional care and other health and support care services, veterans' and caregiver satisfaction, and quality under each model of AIC and between comparison groups.

Assisted Living Pilot Program (ALPP)

The Millennium Act authorized VA to establish a pilot program to determine the "feasibility and practicability of enabling veterans to secure needed assisted living services as an alternative to nursing home care, to enter into contracts with appropriate facilities for the provision for a period of up to six months of assisted living services." Through a competitive process, a group of clinicians located at VAMCs in the Pacific Northwest (covering the states of Alaska, Idaho, Oregon, and Washington) was selected to conduct the demonstration. VA is contracting with all Medicaid-approved providers of assisted living, including adult family homes, assisted living, and residential care facilities. Evaluation goals are to (a) describe the veterans placed in assisted living settings; (b) describe the facilities that contract with ALPP and assess the satisfaction of veterans and their family caregivers, VA referring staff, and assisted living providers with the program; and (c) describe the costs and outcomes of care for ALPP participants and a comparison group.

ROLE OF SOCIAL WORKERS IN VA LTC RESIDENTIAL SETTINGS

The role of social workers in VA LTC programs varies by the program and by their position. Master's-prepared social workers provide psychosocial assessment and intervention, screening, family and caregiver support, individual and group therapy treatment and discharge planning, case management, advocacy, and education.

Community Residential Care Program

For example, VA's oldest extended care program, the community residential care (CRC) program, is coordinated through local VA social work departments or mental health service lines. To enable the CRC program to be cost-effective, basic room and board and limited personal care and supervision are provided to veterans who are not able to live independently and/or do not have family to provide the needed care but do not require nursing home or hospital care. Veterans enrolled in CRC use their VA pensions or Social Security payments to subsidize the placement costs. VA social workers provide supervision and ensure that they receive a level of care appropriate to their needs, without which they would require readmission or be among the homeless population.

Social Work Education

The Department of Veterans Affairs is affiliated with more than 100 graduate schools of social work and operates the largest and most comprehensive clinical training program for social work students—training 600 to 700 students per year. As a leader in this area, VA has a major impact on the health care social work curriculum, establishing and applying standards for social work clinical practice, and expanding the roles and functions of the clinical social worker in interdisciplinary teams practicing health care service delivery. VA social workers are also involved in developing policy and in developing and conducting research to inform social work practice.

Social Work Role in Coordinating Care

As health care in general continues to change, VA clinicians have had to adjust to factors inside and outside the VA health care system. As health care in VA moves from a traditional inpatient model to a primary care outpatient-based model, VA social workers play an increasingly critical role in the delivery of services and in integrating VA and non-VA services used by veterans. Social workers play an important role in making community planning, coordination, and integration of services become a reality on federal, state, county, and local levels. Decentralization, accessibility, relevancy, continuity, and effectiveness of service delivery are all concepts that continue to be improved through implementation. The leadership, flexibility, and commitment of VA social workers to "Putting Veterans First" enable social work to thrive as a profession in the current health care environment. VHA now has an Office of Care Coordination where social workers and nurses use a full range of tele-health equipment in order to monitor the health of veterans in their own homes.

Assessment, Screening, and Discharge Planning

Crises, such as illness, that result in hospitalization create anxiety, fears, and issues to be resolved for veterans and their families. Regardless of the setting, the goal of VA social workers is to help veterans and their families help themselves. They assist families who are coping with troubling situations such as traumatic and chronic illness, alcoholism and/or drug dependency, the financial and emotional strain of disability, marital difficulties due to illness, abuse, and bereavement.

As discharge planners, the social workers' role is varied and complex, but in all cases, he or she plays a vital part in maximizing wellness during the hospital stay and in easing the transition back home or to a health care facility. During a veteran's hospital stay, social workers assess the veteran's family situation, including their involvement with the entire treatment team, keep the family apprised of the veteran's progress, and explain how the family can help the veteran recover. Physicians, nurses, and others provide medical support, but it is the responsibility of the VA social worker to provide the emotional support to ensure a positive outcome. VA social workers have been specially trained to work with individuals and families in dealing with personal and interpersonal crises caused by illness and hospitalization.

In their role as discharge planners, social workers help the veteran, family, and medical team identify the veteran's needs and target appropriate resources for follow-up care. Whether a veteran is going home or transferring to another health care facility, social workers make the transition as smooth as possible by identifying the resources, within VA or in the community, that are best suited to the veteran's medical and financial situation. They also recommend alternative care if the individual cannot return home.

Social workers are specially trained to assist veterans with the myriad issues related to financial problems and eligibility for services they may need after leaving the hospital. They also assist in completing advance directives to enable veterans to communicate about their wishes to health care providers.

Case Managers

Historically, VA has collected information at the program level, with little ability to track veterans across a variety of inpatient, community, and special programs. Person-centered case management has the potential to change that. This is a new and challenging area in which social workers have great potential to help.

For social workers, functioning as case managers is a natural extension of the care that social workers typically provide as discharge planners; that is, they assist individuals across and within programs. As an example, in the VA's Assisted Living Pilot Program, social workers functioned as case managers for the veterans throughout their entire stay in assisted living (and, in many cases, beyond). They were responsible for assessing the veteran's appropriateness for assisted living and helping to educate the veterans and their families about what assisted living was and what different kinds of facilities were available. In many cases, they accompanied the veterans on their visits to the facilities.

They also worked with the assisted living providers to educate them about the VA contracting and inspection processes, how to work with VA providers, and how to obtain the necessary services for the veterans they were caring for. Once the veteran was placed, the case managers visited them monthly. In addition, they made weekly (or more frequent, as determined by veteran needs) phone contacts to both the veteran and the facility. They facilitated all paperwork and contacts required to obtain financial assistance, such as compensation and pension, Social Security, Medicaid, and other sources so that veterans can transition from VA funding to other form(s) of funding. They coordinated follow-up care (appointments, transportation, and other needs related to VA care) for the veteran at the local VA facility. They worked to develop positive relationships with a number of facilities to promote acceptance of veterans for placement. They coordinated all pharmacy, equipment, and other special needs. They developed relationships with other community-based agencies to build social support networks for the veteran, including services such as transportation for the disabled, adult day care, senior centers, and leisure activities. They also provided education about ALPP to their VA colleagues, including administrative staff and clinical staff, social work departments, discharge planners, clinic staff, domiciliary staff, and non-VA clinical staff in areas where veterans are admitted to community hospitals. Presentations were also done to veterans' service organizations and state governmental organizations.

Facility Inspections/Monitoring Quality

VA generally requires its staff to conduct annual inspections of VA-approved community residential care homes, state veterans' homes, and community nursing homes. Monthly staff visits to veterans in community residential care homes and community nursing homes are also required. VA social workers are required to conduct annual inspections of all community nursing homes with which they have local contracts and to visit veterans in those homes monthly. If VA finds problems in a community nursing home, it can (a) stop placing veterans in the home, (b) withdraw veterans from the home, (c) terminate the home's contract, or (d) allow the contract to expire without renewal.

CONCLUSION

Social workers play a critically important role in VA LTC programs. Social workers are important team members with key roles in assessment and screening and in providing crisis intervention, discharge planning, case management, advocacy, and education. They educate veterans and their families about options within VA and in the community. They educate others within the VA system about the needs of veterans and their families.

We anticipate that VA will continue to be in the forefront of developing geriatric technologies and hope that VA will exercise the same leadership and human capital development in community care as it did in hospitals, nursing homes, geriatrics, and the GEMs. If so, VA will continue to be an important employment setting for social workers, and it will also be important for all social workers in geriatrics to be aware of VA.

NOTES

1. VHA Directive 2004-059, October 21, 2004, Geriatrics and Extended Care Referral Tool.
2. VHA Directive 2004-019, May 2004, Eligibility for Community Nursing Home Care.
3. VHA Handbook 1140.1, March 2005, Community Residential Care Programs.
4. VHA Handbook 1140.2, March 2005, Respite Care.
5. VHA Handbook 1140.2, March 2005, Hospice Care.

REFERENCES

Department of Health and Human Services. (1994–1995). *National health interview survey on disability.* Washington, DC: Author.

Department of Veterans Affairs. (1998). *VA long-term care at the crossroads: Report of the Federal Advisory Committee on the Future of VA Long-Term Care.* Washington, DC: Author.

GAO. (2003). Veterans' access to non-institutional care is limited by service gaps and facility restrictions (GAO-03-815T). Washington, DC: Government Printing Office.

The individual in the nursing home is powerless. If the laws and regulations are not being applied to her or to him, they might just as well not have been passed or issued.

Arthur S. Flemming, MD, Former Commissioner on Aging, 1975. Quoted by Harris-Wehling, Feasley, & Estes, 1995

RUTH HUBER
F. ELLEN NETTING
KEVIN W. BORDERS
H. W. NELSON

The Long-Term Care Ombudsman Program

Long-term care (LTC) ombudsmen investigate complaints from, or filed on behalf of, residents of LTC facilities. In 2000, these consisted of 17,799 nursing homes and 43,102 board and care (and similar) facilities. In this chapter, we first provide a brief history of the National Long-Term Care Ombudsman Program, which is followed by an overview of the program's mission and how it functions. We then describe the various structures across states of this publicly mandated program, how complaints are handled, and the roles for social workers in this advocacy (and sometimes adversarial) program. The chapter closes with a discussion of the quality of care and life to which these most vulnerable seniors are entitled, noting that it can emerge only from a culture of care in the larger society.

The long-term care ombudsman program (LTCOP) is federally mandated to investigate complaints about the care that people receive in LTC facilities. Long-term care ombudsmen inherited the public watchdog and citizen defender tradition (Ziegenfuss, 1985) that ultimately derived from Sweden's 1809 creation of the ombudsman,[1] who investigated and resolved the people's complaints about government. Today, states have a good deal of freedom in designing and implementing their LTC ombudsman programs. Consequently, there are many models and differing philosophical approaches to this role. Major differences can be found, such as (a) where the program is housed and (b) whether and in what capacity local programs use volunteers. In addition to investigating and resolving complaints, ombudsmen educate professionals and the public on relevant issues and advocate for residents of long-term care facilities.

In this chapter, we provide (a) a brief history of the program's origins and legislative authority and (b) the program's mission and functions. We then describe (c) the structure of the LTCOP, (d) how complaints are handled, and (e) the roles that social workers play in and with the ombudsman program. We close with a brief discussion of (f) the quality of life and care that elders experience in the nation's long-term care facilities.

HISTORICAL OVERVIEW

The need for specific LTC ombudsmen arose from social and demographic changes that fundamentally altered the structure and role of the family in caring for its infirm older members. Shifts away from the extended family to the more attenuated nuclear family left many indigent and chronically ill or disabled elderly to fend for themselves or turn to almshouses to survive. Their plight found resonance in sea changes in public policy: the passage of the Social Security Act in 1935 and the adoption of Medicare and Medicaid in 1965, which fueled a rapid spread of today's highly medicalized LTC facilities. Unfortunately, these facilities were plagued by recurring scandals. In the 1970s, these problems mobilized a new era of grassroots reformers who were dedicated to improving the basic quality of care and life in these institutions.

National Citizens' Coalition for Nursing Home Reform

A strong and important mover and shaker in this sea change was the National Citizens' Coalition for Nursing Home Reform (NCCNHR), formed in 1975. At that time, the National Gray Panthers' Long-Term Care Action Project, along with 12 citizens' groups and a number of ombudsman programs, convened in Washington, DC, prior to a conference of the American Health Care Association. Public outcries about substandard care in the nation's nursing homes spurred the coalition into action under the leadership of Elma Holder, as NCCNHR's founder, who was working for the National Gray Panthers at the time. NCCNHR became the advocacy organization for the consumer's voice.

Since its founding, NCCNHR has issued information papers and reports on nursing home issues, held annual meetings, expanded its focus to include board and care home issues, conducted national surveys on long-term care issues, published consumer information, developed the Campaign for Quality Care to push for the 1987 Nursing Home Reform Act (commonly referred to as OBRA 87, from the Omnibus Budget Reconciliation Act), and has worked continuously for legislative change. Among other advances, OBRA 87 (a) severely restricted the circumstances under which LTC facilities can physically or chemically restrain residents (e.g., tie them in wheelchairs)

and (b) gave ombudsmen a role in the licensing agencies' site visits to evaluate LTC facilities.

In 1993, the Administration on Aging (AoA) awarded NCCNHR the first of a series of multiyear grants to operate the National Long-Term Care Ombudsman Resource Center in cooperation with the National Association of State Units on Aging. The resource center provides support, technical assistance, and training to the 53 state ombudsman programs and their statewide networks. Its objectives are to enhance the knowledge, skills, and capacity of ombudsman programs and to advocate for residents' interests. (For information on NCCNHR and the resource center, see *http://www.nccnhr.org.*)

The LTCOP and NCCNHR continue to work with local, regional, and state citizens' organizations created to advocate for residents in long-term care facilities. Depending on the state, these organizations vary in what they do, but their efforts are part of a nationwide advocacy network targeting issues faced by vulnerable elders and their families. For example, Citizens for Better Care is a nonprofit organization with five offices in lower Michigan. Begun in 1969, they take on long-term care discrimination, regulatory enforcement, elder abuse, and related concerns. Another example is the Center for Advocacy for the Rights and Interests of the Elderly (CARIE), another nonprofit advocacy group, located in Philadelphia. Founded in 1997, CARIE is a leader in providing assistance to elders, their families, and professionals in aging. Yet another example is the Minnesota Alliance for Health Consumers, which has organized resident and family councils through a set-aside from the licensure fee, for which the ombudsman program lobbied. Each state has its own story of how citizens' groups have worked with local and state ombudsman programs, some more formally and others more informally, to advocate for high-quality resident care and systemic change.

The sea change, however, did not end abuse and neglect in LTC facilities; they continue into the 21st century. A U.S. House of Representatives report commonly referred to as the Waxman Report (2001) reported that 5,283 nursing homes (almost 1 in 3) were cited for abuse violations from January 1, 1999, through January 1, 2001. All citations "had at least the potential to harm nursing home residents. In over 1,600 . . . the abuse violations were serious enough to cause actual harm . . . or place the residents in immediate jeopardy of death or serious injury" (p. i).

THE BIRTH AND DEVELOPMENT OF THE LONG-TERM CARE OMBUDSMAN PROGRAM (LTCOP)

One of President Nixon's eight initiatives to improve nursing home care in 1971 called for "state investigative ombudsman units" (Harris-Wehling, Feasley, & Estes, 1995, p. 43). Thus, the LTCOP was born in 1972, when five states (ID, MI, PA, SC, and WI) were awarded demonstration grants by the Department of Health, Education, and Welfare's Health Services and Mental Health Administration. Demonstration programs were added in Oregon and Massachusetts in 1973, when AoA became responsible for the LTCOP; it has retained implementation and oversight to this date (Harris-Wehling et al., 1995). In 1975, Commissioner on Aging Arthur Flemming invited proposals from all states to develop community LTC ombudsman programs, and all except Nebraska and Oklahoma were funded (Harris-Wehling et al., 1995).

Legislative Authority

Mandated by the Older Americans Act in 1978, three major reauthorizations (in 1987, 1992, and 2000) have slowly strengthened the program (Harris-Wehling et al., 1995; Sue Wheaton, personal communication, June 6, 2004). Today there are programs in all 50 states, the District of Columbia, and Puerto Rico. The most recent reauthorization was signed by President Clinton on November 13, 2000, following 6 years of congressional hearings, debates, and votes, and established the LTC Ombudsman Program through fiscal year (FY) 2005. There were seven key factors in the 2000 reauthorization: (a) guidelines for conflicts of interest, (b) the importance of coordinating services with local law enforcement officers, (c) funding allocation patterns, (d) current funding levels, (e) the continuation of the National Ombudsman Resource Center, (f) policies on accepting voluntary contributions, and (g) a new focus on family caregivers (Turnham, 2000). The changes in the four reauthorizations of the Older Americans Act that have directly affected the LTCOP since its birth in 1965 (Sue Wheaton, personal communication, June 6, 2004) are summarized in Table 55.1.

MISSION AND FUNCTIONS

The mission of the LTCOP is to investigate and resolve complaints lodged by, or on behalf of, residents of LTC facilities, to educate both the health professions and the public about the needs and rights of residents of LTC facilities, and to advocate for those needs and rights. Notice, however, that Harris-Wehling et al. (1995) included the notion of *identifying* problems, and the philosophies of state ombudsmen vary on this point.

LTC ombudsmen have been accused of *looking for* wrongdoing or harmful situations in long-term[2] and similar facilities (AoA, 2002a) so that they can lodge complaints, and this may actually occur in a few states. To avoid the troublemaker label, however, a few state ombudsmen have policies that the local ombudsmen will not lodge complaints themselves but investigate only those that are called to the attention of the ombudsman's office. Most state ombudsmen encourage their local ombudsmen to visit their assigned facilities at random times so that any practices or policies that are harmful to the residents' physical and socioemotional well-being can be seen, reported, and, hopefully, fundamentally resolved. Most state ombudsmen do not, however, encourage their local ombudsmen to look for problems, as they feel that they already receive more externally lodged complaints than they can optimally handle. They also wish to avoid alienating facility staff with whom ombudsmen must collaborate to promote the best care, all of the time.

Growing research suggests that volunteer ombudsmen (a) fill a service gap between professionals and clients (Monk & Kaye, 1982; Monk, Kaye, & Litwin, 1984), (b) produce a sentinel effect (Litwin & Monk, 1984), (c) heighten regulatory activity (Nelson, Huber & Walter, 1995), (d) improve nursing care (Cherry, 1991), (e) challenge corporate and government policies that are not in residents' best interests (Harris-Wehling et al., 1995), and (f) seem to be appreciated by residents (Monk & Kay, 1982; Nelson, Netting, Huber, & Borders, 2004).

Oversight and accountability requirements for ombudsmen emanate from national, state, and local entities. At the national level, Edwin L. Walker is AoA's director of the Office of the Long-Term Care Ombudsman Program, and Sue Wheaton implemented the program at the national level from 1974 to 1985 and again from 1991 to the present.

The actual legal authority of ombudsmen is quite limited. Their unique power lies in their abilities to informally persuade and advocate—a role that is distinct from the regulators' due process–bound inspection and punitive enforcement function. Officially, however, all ombudsmen, paid or volunteer, have the authority to enter any LTC facility and, with resi-

TABLE 55.1. Summary of Changes in the Four Reauthorizations of the Older Americans Act

1981	Expanded ombudsman coverage to include board and care homes. The name was changed from Nursing Home Ombudsman to Long-Term Care Ombudsman to reflect this change.
1987	Required states to provide for ombudsman access to residents and residents' records and immunity to ombudsmen for the good faith performance of their duties and prohibitions against willful interference with the official duties of an ombudsman and/or retaliation against an ombudsman, resident, or other individual for assisting representatives of the program in the performance of their duties.
1992	Strengthened the program and transferred it to a new title in the act, Title VII, Vulnerable Elder Rights Protection Activities, which also included programs for prevention of elder abuse, neglect, and exploitation; the state elder rights and legal assistance development program; and an outreach, counseling, and assistance program (which was subsequently deleted).
2000	Retained and updated ombudsman provisions in Titles II, III, and VII, including guidelines for conflicts of interest, the importance of coordinating services with local law enforcement officers, funding allocation patterns, current funding levels, the continuation of the National Ombudsman Resource Center, policies on accepting voluntary contributions, and a new focus on family caregivers (Turnham, 2000).

From: AoA, 2004.

dents' permission, access medical charts and other records. And although they are not enforcers, ombudsmen invariably use the LTC system's tight regulation to leverage their entreaties and arguments.

THE STRUCTURE OF THE LONG-TERM CARE OMBUDSMAN PROGRAM

At minimum, every state must have a full-time state ombudsman, and most states have one or two layers of offices below that, regardless of the organizational auspice of the state program. One state ombudsman reports directly to the governor, and others, as noted previously, are located in state units on aging. The first layer under the state ombudsmen might be regional if, for example, a state has discrete service regions, such as the western, central, and eastern parts of the state, or some other design for geographically delivering services by district or service area. Some states, however, including New Hampshire and Oregon, do not have local offices under the state programs.

The second organizational layer may be in place if there are local ombudsman offices, and these are found under various auspices. For example, 7 of the 15 local programs in Kentucky are located in service units that were historically called area development districts (ADDs), and 3 are located in legal aid agencies. A local program may monitor the LTC facilities in a town, a county, or several counties; in some large areas, for instance, Washington, DC, there are local offices throughout the district. Another difference be-

tween states is whether volunteers are used and, if so, in what capacities or roles.

If the office of the state ombudsman is situated in the state unit on aging (as are 38, or 73%), the state ombudsman reports to the director of the state unit on aging, as well as to the ombudsman program specialist on the national policies, guidelines, and reporting requirements of the National Ombudsman Reporting System (NORS). Sixty-one percent of local ombudsmen are organizationally located in Area Agencies on Aging (AAA) and report to the local AAA director, as well as to the state LTC ombudsman (AoA, 2002b).

Auspices of State Long-Term Care Ombudsman Programs

All but 14 (AK, CO, DC, KS, ME, MI, NH, OR, RI, VA, VT, WA, WI, & WY; AoA, 2003) state long-term care ombudsman programs are organizationally situated in the state units on aging, and there are opposing views on this structure. One perspective is that an ombudsman program should be overseen by the state units on aging, because it is an aging program that needs oversight. Advantages to programs being located in AAAs were thought to include faster access to information and funds (Huber, Netting, & Kautz, 1996). Among the concerns voiced by local ombudsmen whose programs are located in state units on aging are (a) budget cuts leading to less effective programs, (b) lack of sufficient independence within their organizational placements to advocate on behalf of residents, (c) conflicts of interest (e.g., LTC facility owners serving on AAA governing or advisory boards), and (d) less focus on the needs of the institutionalized elders than on those living at home in the community.

Given the differing views between ombudsmen and the managers of their sponsoring agencies, are there differences in the types of complaints and how they are resolved by local long-term care ombudsmen operating in or not in AAAs? This question was posed for Kentucky in 1996 by Huber, Netting, and Kautz, who found some evidence that AAA-based LTC ombudsman programs were less likely than non-AAA-based programs to focus on resident quality of life and care and less likely to file complaints against facilities. AAA-based programs were more likely to address rights and administrative issues. The percentage of local ombudsman programs located in AAAs dropped by about 10 percentage points between 1996 (71%) and 2002 (61%).

Staffing for Long-Term Care Ombudsman Programs

The 1995 Institute of Medicine (IoM) report recommended one full-time equivalent (1 FTE) ombudsman for every 2,000 licensed LTC beds (Harris-Wehling et al., 1995; Turnham, 2000). According to AoA data (2002c), the ombudsman program nationwide is short by 328 ombudsmen to meet the standard of 1 FTE ombudsman for every 2,000 licensed beds. Ombudsmen are also to include in their NORS reports the number of facilities that are "served by the program on a 'regular basis,' which means visited at least quarterly, not in response to complaints" (NORS Instructions and Sue Wheaton, personal communication, June 6, 2004).

The IoM report also recommended that every 20 to 40 volunteers should be supported by 1 FTE paid staff ombudsman (Harris-Wehling et al., 1995; Turnham, 2000), and AoA's statistics are not clear enough to determine how this compares with reality. According to AoA (2002d), there were 11,333 volunteers nationwide and 1,065 FTE paid program staff. This results in 1 FTE paid staff person for every 11 volunteers. There is nothing to indicate, however, whether any of those paid staff FTEs were available to manage the very large job of recruiting, training, and monitoring volunteers. Clearly more specific data are needed to address this issue.

In FY 2000, there were approximately 970 paid staff FTEs and 14,000 volunteers. From FY 1996 to FY 2000, the number of paid program staff increased by 12.6%. The program relies heavily on volunteers to carry out ombudsman responsibilities. However, only 60% (8,400) of those volunteers were trained and certified to investigate complaints (an increase of 1,034 from FY 1998; AoA, 2002d).

Some state ombudsmen encourage local programs to use volunteers and usually certify them at the state level for each level of training they complete. Local programs are sometimes free to decide whether to use volunteers, and some pay them stipends or mileage and a token payment for their volunteer services.

Oregon has an exemplary program of recruiting, training, and monitoring volunteers to be the eyes and ears of paid staff in one centralized state office (Nelson, Netting, Huber, & Borders, 2003, 2004). Nelson and his colleagues have written extensively about both the benefits and the challenges of using volunteers in LTC ombudsman programs (Nelson, 1995, 2000; Nelson et al., 1995, 2003, 2004; Netting, Huber, Borders, Kautz, & Nelson, 2000), including a study of complaints *against* volunteer ombudsmen (Nelson et al., 2003). Thirteen states (AR, HI, IA, ID, IN, MI, MD, NV, SC, SD, VA, WI, WV) do not report using certified volunteers (AoA, 2002e).

There is a wide range in salary levels for local ombudsman staff. A study by the National Long-Term Care Ombudsman Center (NCCNHR, 1999) found that yearly full-time salaries for local ombudsmen ranged from $12,480 to $24,960 (Montana) to $34,278 to $61,540 (Maryland) (Choi, nd; personal communication with Sue Wheaton, AoA, June 7, 2004). A directory of ombudsman programs by state is on AoA's Web site (AoA, 2002b).

Although national ombudsman demographics are scant, Netting et al. (2000) reported from a six-state database of complaints investigated by 285 ombudsmen, 75% of whom were volunteers, and 74% of whom were women (who investigated 84% of the complaints); the 26% who were men investigated 16% of the complaints. In addition to reporting the differences in the kinds of complaints investigated by paid staff and volunteers, these researchers also reported that nearly two-thirds of the complaints handled by volunteers, both men and women, concerned routine events. Paid male ombudsmen, on the other hand, investigated about one-third each of routine, moderate, and complex complaints, and paid female ombudsmen investigated a higher percentage of complex complaints than paid men or than both female and male volunteers (Netting et al., 2000).

Paid staff and certified volunteers (9,363) investigated 231,889 complaints in 2000 and provided information to more than 297,268 individuals on myriad topics, including how to select and pay for care in a long-term care facility (AoA, 2002g). Concerns that ombudsman volunteers do not have adequate training, supervision, or support have been voiced by numerous writers (Harris-Wehling et al., 1995; Litwin & Monk, 1984); however, ombudsmen have made giant strides in training since those reports. Nelson et al. (2004) studied the factors that affected volunteers' continuing their volunteer activities. The two strongest encouraging factors were that (a) the work was meaningful and (b) their work affected residents for the better. The stronger discouraging factors were role ambiguity, boredom, and role conflicts. Some programs have different levels of training and assigned duties—that is, from friendly visitors who are the eyes and ears of paid ombudsmen but who are not expected to investigate and take action on potentially contentious problems and policies to those who are academically and specifically trained in areas such as conflict resolution.

HANDLING COMPLAINTS

Complaint handling is the main function of the ombudsman program. As noted earlier, complaints about the care that elders receive may be reported to the LTC ombudsman's office by phone from a resident, family member, or health/mental health workers in the community or even in the facilities being monitored. Complaints may also be identified by the ombudsmen, both paid and volunteer, who visit LTC facilities. The goal for most ombudsman programs is to visit every facility at least once a month—some more often.

Ombudsmen then work to resolve complaints to the satisfaction of the resident or complainant. This is problematic for some ombudsmen because residents or family members sometimes withdraw their complaints for fear of retaliation against the resident if the ombudsman becomes involved. When this happens, ombudsmen can be faced with ethical dilemmas. On one hand, they must discontinue their investigation and resolution process. On the other hand, it is ethically difficult, and in some cases legally impossible, for ombudsmen to ignore abusive, neglectful, and other harmful behaviors. Furthermore, ombudsmen usu-

ally have in mind a higher standard of care, or resolution to the problem, than that of residents and/or family members and friends. Nelson and his colleagues conceptualized different approaches to resolving problems based on a taxonomy of the severity and scope of the problem and the degree of resistance from the target of change efforts, the LTC facilities (Nelson, Netting, Huber, & Borders, 2001).

NORS offers eight different resolution conditions, from the least to the most desired outcomes (AoA, 2002b).

1. Regulatory or legislative action was required (so satisfactory resolution was not possible)
2. Not resolved to the satisfaction of the resident or complainant (some problems just cannot be fixed)
3. Withdrawn by the resident or complainant
4. Referred to another agency that did not report back
5. Referred to another agency that failed to act
6. No action was needed or appropriate
7. Partially resolved but some problem remained
8. Resolved to the satisfaction of the resident or complainant

In 2002, 77% of the programs' 261,257 complaints nationwide were partially or fully resolved to the satisfaction of the resident or complainant.

Other Services and Activities of the LTC Ombudsman Program

The other services of the ombudsman program fall generally under prevention, intervention, and advocacy (Table 55.2). More specifically, Table 55.3 details some of the extant services provided by ombudsmen nationwide (AoA, 2002g). They also monitored and worked on laws, regulations, policies, and actions at all levels of government.

Although originally known as the nursing home ombudsman program, subsequent changes in the Older Americans Act have extended the program's purview to virtually any type of elder-oriented or long-stay facility, including board and care facilities, assisted living facilities, adult residential care facilities, subacute care facilities (if they are licensed as long-stay institutions), and other congregate care settings. Several states have enabled their ombudsman programs to provide services to settings outside the normal long-term care continuum, including home and hospice care settings, and at least one ombudsman

TABLE 55.2. Summary Chart of Long-Term Care Ombudsman Activities

Prevention

1 Education and consultation to both staff and individuals on issues affecting residents in long-term care facilities

2 Problem solving before a crisis occurs and making recommendations to facility administration and staff concerning needed changes in policy and procedures

3 Information and referral to help connect persons to the best available resources

4 Regular visitation services to residents by certified long-term care Ombudsman Volunteers to try and identify and resolve issues before they become complaints or serious problems

Intervention

5 Investigation of problems and complaints, negotiation, and intervention to help residents and their family members resolve conflicts or problems

Advocacy

6 Service gap assessment and recommendations for the development of programs and supports to meet the needs of elder long-term care residents

7 Representing the interests of residents before governmental agencies and seeking administrative, legal, and other remedies to protect the health, safety, welfare, and rights of the residents

From: AoA, 2004.

program has expanded its advocacy role to include case management services.

This service creep—asking ombudsmen to take on more and more responsibilities—rings true to the old adage, *if you really need something done, give it to the busiest person you know.* In other words, those who are already doing myriad things well will also do additional tasks well. However, the ombudsman program's ability to meet these unfunded responsibilities is questionable. Insufficient numbers of paid and volunteer staff, for example, have long been recognized as limiting the program's ability to routinely visit nursing homes, let alone board and care facilities and home-based settings. Nevertheless, the National Association of State Long-Term Care Ombudsman Programs recommends that ombudsmen visit community-based facilities "at least once per month" (Grant, 2002, p. 19). This is little more than an ideal, however, as many of the nation's nursing homes are visited by an ombudsmen no more than "once or twice a year and for no longer than 1 to 3 hours" (Brown, 1999, p. 12). The gap between nursing home visitation rates and community-based visitation rates might be crudely surmised from data showing that while ombudsmen visit 83% of

TABLE 55.3. Other Ombudsman Activities Nationwide for FY 2002

The Number of Times in FY 2002 That Long-Term Care Ombudsmen . . .	*Local*	*State*	*Total*
1 Participated in facility surveys	9,968	658	10,626
2 Met with resident councils	14,913	779	15,692
3 Met with family councils	5,310	199	5,509
4 Presented community educational sessions	8,999	1,110	10,109
5 Provided training sessions for staff and volunteers	8,195	1,390	9,585
6 Provided training sessions for facility staff	6,985	637	7,622
7 Consulted with facilities	99,991	10,648	110,639
8 Provided information and consulted with individuals	252,804	44,464	297,268
9 Participated in media discussions and interviews	1,509	667	2,176
10 Issued press releases	3,110	1,184	4,294
Totals	411,784	61,736	473,520

From: AoA, 2002g.

all nursing homes annually (from once a week to once a year), they annually visit only 47% of all community-based facilities (at probably even lower rates of "routine" visitation) (AoA, 1999).

SOCIAL WORK ROLES

Social workers and ombudsmen are "natural allies" (Arcus, 1999, p. 196), and many social workers are, or have been ombudsmen, such as Iris Freeman, Sarah Hunt, Ruth Morgan, and Sam Arcus. Ombudsmen have been called the "community presence" in LTC facilities (Cherry, 1993, p. 336), and one of the key guiding principles of social work is for social workers to encourage community individuals and agencies to become involved in LTC facilities (Arcus, 1999; National Association of Social Workers, 2003). All of the jobs to be done by LTC ombudsmen are jobs that fit the values of social work professionals: investigators, advocates, lobbyists, public speakers, fund-raisers, teacher/trainers, community organizers, managers, and mediators. In short, both LTC facility social workers and ombudsmen are change agents and advocates with an intended priority to promote residents' socioemotional health. But the LTC facility social worker's role can be beset with difficulties. First, they are often obvious by their absence. Smaller facilities are not required to have social workers, and the larger facilities that are required to have social workers may contract for social services rather than employ a licensed social worker on staff. Social workers, therefore, work in host facilities when it comes to long-term care facilities, and the mental health needs of residents may take a back seat to admissions and discharge paperwork, activities, and volunteer coordination. They may also be responsible for implementing and coordinating resident and family councils.

Second, the vast majority of long-term care facility social workers and their medical colleagues are just that—colleagues working together in the best interest of the residents. We would be less than honest, however, if we did not acknowledge that social workers' abilities to make pro-resident changes are sometimes limited by their ancillary status in medical host settings. Social workers can sometimes find themselves with conflicting interests between residents' wishes and their employers' interests, including, chiefly, the legitimate needs for risk management and efficiency (Nelson et al., 2001). In such situations, ombudsmen are advocates and supporters of facility social workers who could put their jobs at risk if they challenge certain facility policies, whereas the outside ombudsman can sometimes address issues more forcefully without that risk. The result is that residents receive assistance that they may not have otherwise realized (Nelson et al., 2001).

All advocates need expertise in conflict resolution, systems, and social interactions. The LTCOP offers many opportunities for social workers' specialized expertise in planning, social policy, and research; for general practitioners who can conceptualize and implement training curricula and evaluate the results; and for those who can create databases to capture the activities, work, and outcomes of the ombudsmen's work, which could provide powerful evidence for systemic change. Also needed are those who have contacts and influence with political forces and the media. All of these are jobs for social workers who care about the care that older people receive in LTC facilities and are committed to working in larger systems to improve the care being provided to residents of LTC facilities.

OMBUDSMEN'S CHALLENGES

In addition to the problems inherent in trying to solve elders' problems, ombudsmen face other professional and systemic challenges: inadequate funding, conflicts of interests, confidentiality dilemmas, and balancing reactionary and supportive stances. There are many more, but a brief review of these will give you the idea.

Inadequate Funding

Depending on organizational placement, local and state ombudsman programs may not be allowed to conduct fund-raising activities that would allow them to, for example, recruit, train, and capitalize on volunteers, develop educational programs and materials, and lobby for legislative actions that would benefit residents of LTC facilities. This may be more of a problem for AAA-affiliated programs in which agency directors are concerned that fund raising by the ombudsman program could distract from similar agency-wide activities.

Conflicts of Interest

Conflicts of interest can be lurking in many cases and at all levels of the system. For example, what would you have done in the situation in the following example?

▩ Confession of a Patients' Rights Advocate: Empowering Disaster—the Irony of Autonomy

I remember when Pete called me. He got right to the point: "I just want to know if I have the right to go home," he asked.

"Well, that's a big question. Tell me, where are you now and where's home?"

He shot back: "I'm in a home with a bunch of old people who don't do a thing but sit and stare at the TV. I own a home in town, on the river, and I want to go back. Can I?"

I questioned him enough to determine that he was unquestionably decisionally capable (de facto competent). So I gave him the short answer: "You're not a prisoner, and you have the right to return home. However, it is an entirely different matter as to whether or not you are actually *able* to go home." He was silent for a moment, then asked if I would come out to talk to him. I agreed.

Peter's adult foster home was prim and tidy, and as his caregiver led me past the blaring TV and the four residents riveted to it, I thought it was a very nice place. Peter was a wiry little man, but he couldn't walk without assistance, so it was immediately clear that he couldn't live independently. He recognized this but explained that he had some pension money and that he could pay someone to bring him groceries. "I think you'll need more help than that," I warned. He asked about the availability of home support programs. "They're out there," I replied, "but I doubt if you'd qualify, but we'll see." I discussed all the possible challenges he would face, but he was determined to go home.

After again confirming his right to return to his home, he asked me to drive him there directly. I explained that this was against agency policy but assured him that no one could block him from making his own arrangements. He could hire movers, for example, and if he had trouble making phone contacts, the caregiver would have to assist him in making connections.

Three weeks later he was home. Shortly thereafter, I received a pained phone call from his daughter. She was distraught, angry and in tears. She wanted to let me know what I had done to her father. "Daddy was doing so much better in the care home," she sobbed. "He'd gained weight and was settling in, then you came along to tell

him his rights. Don't I as a daughter have a right to my dad, to be involved in his life, to protect him from himself and from do-gooders like you?"

"Well, I hope you're happy," she continued, "he's back home now, drinking again. I hope you're real thrilled with yourself. He's drunk all the time," she sobbed, "just like before. He's been drinking for 20 years and that's the only reason he wanted to go home. His damn liver nearly killed him. He had osteomalacia [soft bones caused by a deficiency of vitamin D], and the falls—why do you think he can't walk!" she sobbed in grief and anger. "Why didn't you check his medical records? Why didn't you call me? What kind of advocate are you? I'm getting a lawyer and I'm getting your job. What gives bureaucrats like you the right to meddle into other people's lives!"

I offered some inane, soothing, apologetic answers. I felt both guilty and deeply sympathetic. I didn't want to get legalistic, but I told her that her dad had the legal right to make bad decisions, just like she does. After the call, I ruminated and reassessed the whole situation.

I went home that night thinking that I would not have done things any differently. I didn't ask detailed questions about his medical background because they weren't pertinent to the rights issue at hand. Even if he had told me he wanted to drink his life away, that would have been his right. Oh, I would have tried to further dissuade him by pointing out that his drinking would only make him more dependent in the future, that it kill him. But I doubt if it would have mattered. ▩

What would you have done if your client had been Pete's daughter? Further, if a doctor is insisting that Pete must not go home because of his physical condition, the social worker is swimming in an ethical conflict of interest. If you support the resident, you may lose the confidence of the resident physician and medical staff, which could easily diminish your voice in future situations. But if you support Pete and he goes home to inadequate care, the results could further deteriorate his condition and his ability to be in his own home—or worse.

Other conflicts can occur between ombudsmen's personal and professional ethics and their political and job realities, briefly discussed earlier in terms of whether the ombudsman is employed by a long-term care facility or as an outside professional under contract. Another possibility is that a nurse's aide tells you, the facility social worker, that another aide (related to the owner) routinely steals from elderly residents but fears being fired if you take any action on that information. What would you do?

Confidentiality Dilemmas

The patient advocate's confession in the box included the element of confidentiality in that the advocate had no right to discuss Pete's intentions with his daughter or anyone else. Dilemmas are not just hard decisions to be made but decisions that have some good on both sides and/or some potentially harmful elements, regardless of the choice made. Had the advocate not determined that Pete was decisionally capable, he might have felt obliged to contact Pete's daughter about his plans to return home to see that he would be going to a safe place, thereby violating the resident's right to confidentiality and, no doubt, thwarting his plans to return to his home regardless of his reasons.

In short, this dilemma is similar to the autonomy versus beneficence debate. *Autonomy* refers to the client or resident's self-determination, and *beneficence* means doing the right thing. The catch is in determining *doing the right thing*—according to whom? In this case, Pete? His daughter? The advocate? In practice, the social worker cannot live solely at either end of the autonomy-beneficence continuum, as two extreme scenarios will demonstrate. Although self-determination is one of the profession's core values, could social workers stand by and watch Pete walk out into traffic to try to go home without assistance? Of course not. At the other extreme, could the social worker stand by while facility staff physically restrain Pete to keep him from going home? Again, of course not.

Balancing Reactionary and Supportive Stances

Another kind of challenge can plague those who are trained in advocacy and comfortable with conflict yet must develop and nurture collegial relationships with facility staff (or the industry) if they hope to be able to work with them in the long run for better care for residents. The very nature of advocacy work attracts devoted, committed, assertive, and sometimes even aggressive individuals, which is good. Those with

fainter hearts need not apply. On the other hand, neither should ombudsmen come from the ranks of those who tend to be comfortable with the status quo, people who may not have the fortitude to effectively advocate against systemic odds.

QUALITY OF LIFE AND CARE

Most long-term care facilities attempt to provide excellent care most of the time. But when quality of care breaks down, the investigational, educational, and advocacy work of the LTCOP is vital to the commitment to care for the nation's most vulnerable citizens. By studying the frequencies of various complaints that can (or often) result in neglect, we see from AoA's statistics that neglect may be more prevalent than abuse (AoA, 2002g). Of the 208,762 complaints lodged against (only) nursing homes in 2002, 8,781 (4.2%) pertained to physical, sexual, or verbal/mental abuse. Complaints categorized as gross neglect totaled 2,610, or 1.3% of the total. However, when we add other types of complaints that we know often result in neglect, this percentage quickly becomes nearly 16% (Table 55.4).

Elders in residential facilities cannot enjoy a good quality of life unless they have high-quality physical, emotional, and social care, which, in turn, does not occur outside of a *culture* of care. Sometimes it is this culture of care that falls by the wayside in the space between elders being cared for at home and cared for by strangers who are generally the least skilled and lowest paid members of the workforce. It is not that these facility staff are uncaring but rather that they are overworked, understaffed, overstressed, and frequently overtaxed when facing behavioral emergencies or handling complex socioemotional problems.

Until these basic problems with formal caregivers are resolved, there will be a strong need for LTC ombudsmen to advocate on behalf of individuals and groups of residents, provide information to residents and their families about the long-term care system, and work to effect systemic changes at the local, state, and national levels. Ombudsmen must continue to monitor caregiver practices and facility conditions and to speak out for those who cannot speak for themselves; this sentinel work remains the essential bulwark against harmful practices for the foreseeable future.

TABLE 55.4. Selected Complaint Categories That Pertain to Abuse and Neglect from 208,762 Complaints Against Long-Term Care Facilities

NORS Complaint #	Abuse Complaints		Number	Percentage
1	Physical abuse		4,777	2.30
2	Sexual abuse		749	0.36
3	Verbal/mental abuse		3,256	1.56
		Total Abuse	**8,781**	**4.22**

Neglect Complaint

NORS Complaint #	Neglect Complaints		Number	Percentage
5	Gross neglect		2,610	1.30
33	Staff nonresponsive to complaints		1,379	1.00
41	Call lights/requests for assistance unanswered		9,885	4.70
45	Personal hygiene unattended		7,519	3.60
47	Pressure sores		1,928	0.92
48	Symptoms unattended		4,886	2.30
69	Not helping with eating/eating devices		1,952	0.94
70	Fluid not available/dehydration		2,442	1.20
75	Weight loss due to inadequate nutrition		759	0.36
		Total Neglect	**33,360**	**15.98**

A Culture of Care

A brief word on a culture of care seems to be a fitting way to close this chapter. All of the workers in America's LTC system, regardless of education, position, ethnicity, or gender, are products of an overall societal culture that does not, as a whole, value older people. When we cross the threshold into caring or advocating for elders, however, we must create a more caring culture than the one behind us.

Just as with a continuum of care, each person in each link in the LTC chain of events and services must work from a caring heart; then, perhaps, a larger *culture of care* can embrace this most vulnerable population. It is critical, therefore, that a culture of care prevail in every service, agency, and facility that serves our nation's elders. The long-term care ombudsman program is designed to advocate for that culture of care and to investigate instances in which it has not been realized.

NOTES

1. No gender was attached to the term, and most *ombudsmen* in the United States are women.

2. The term *long-term care (LTC) facility* is used throughout this chapter to refer to the nation's 17,999 nursing homes and 43,102 board and care (and similar) facilities (AoA, 2002a).

REFERENCES

AoA (Administration on Aging). (1999). *Long-term care ombudsman annual report: Fiscal year 1996.* Washington, DC: Author.

AoA (Administration on Aging). (2002a). *Table A-6: LTC facilities and beds by region for FY 2000.* Retrieved June 27, 2004, from *http://www.ltcombudsman.org/uploads/NORS2000regltableA6a.PDF.*

AoA (Administration on Aging). (2002b). *Table A-7: Designated local ombudsman entities for FY 2002.* Administration on Aging, National Ombudsman Reporting System (NORS). Retrieved May 31, 2004, from *http://www.aoa.gov/prof/aoaprog/elder%5Frights/ltcombudsmannational%5Fand%5Fstate%5Fdata/2002hors/a%2D7%20entities.xls.*

AoA (Administration on Aging). (2002c). *Table A-1: Selected information by state for FY 2002.* Retrieved May 31, 2004, from *http://www.aoa.dhhs.gov/prof/aoaprog/*

elder_rights/LTCombudsman/National_and_State_Da
ta/2002nors/A-1%20sel%20info%20by%20St.xls.

AoA (Administration on Aging). (2002d). *Table A-8: Staff and volunteers for fiscal year 2002.* Retrieved June 5, 2004, from *http://www.aoa.dhhs.gov/prof/aoaprog/elder_rights/LTCombudsman/National_and_State_Da ta/2002nors/B-2%20NF-comp%20full.xls.*

AoA (Administration on Aging). (2002e). *Table A-1: Selected information by state for fiscal year 2002.* Retrieved June 27, 2004, from *http://www.ltcombudsman.org/uploads/NORS12000regltableA1.PDF.*

AoA (Administration on Aging). (2002f). *Table A-10: Complaint verification and disposition for fiscal year 2002.* Retrieved June 5, 2004, from *http://www.aoa. dhhs.gov/prof/aoaprog/elder_rights/LTCombudsman/ National_and_State_Data/2002nors/B-2%20NF-comp %20full.xls.*

AoA (Administration on Aging). (2002g). *Table B-2: Complaints for fiscal year 2002.* Retrieved June 5, 2004, from *http://www.aoa.dhhs.gov/prof/aoaprog/elder_ rights/LTCombudsman/National_and_State_Data/20 02nors/B-2%20NF-comp%20full.xls.*

AoA (Administration on Aging). (2003). *Ombudsman programs operated outside of state units on aging.* Retrieved June 7, 2004, from *http://www.ltcombudsman.org//uploads/ProgramStructure0703.pdf.*

AoA (Administration on Aging). (2004, March 9). *Department of Health and Human Services, elder rights: LTC ombudsman, legislation & regulations.* Retrieved June 6, 2004, from *http://www.aoa.dhhs.gov/prof/ aoaprog/elder_rights/LTCombudsman/Legislation_Re g/legislation_reg.asp.*

Arcus, S. G. (1999). The Long-Term Care Ombudsman Program: A social work perspective. *Journal of Gerontological Social Work, 31*(1/2), 195–205.

Brown, J. G. (1999). *Long-term care ombudsman program: Overall capacity* (OEI Publication No. 02-98-00351). Washington, DC: Department of Health and Human Services.

Cherry, R. L. (1991). Agents of nursing home quality of care: Ombudsmen and staff ratios revisited. *The Gerontologist, 31*(3), 302–308.

Cherry, R. L. (1993). Community presence and nursing home quality of care: The ombudsman as a complimentary role. *Journal of Health and Social Behavior, 34,* 336–345.

Grant, R. (2002). *Long-term care ombudsman program effectiveness: Rethinking and retooling for the future.* Washington, DC: National Association for Long-Term Care Ombudsmen.

Harris-Wehling, J., Feasley, J. C., & Estes, C. L. (1995). *Real people, real problems: An evaluation of the long-*

term care ombudsman programs of the Older Americans Act. Washington, DC: Institute of Medicine, Division of Health Care Services.

Huber, R., Netting, F. E., & Kautz, J. R. (1996, March). Differences in types of complaints and how they were resolved by local long-term care ombudsmen operating in/not in Area Agencies on Aging. *Journal of Applied Gerontology, 15*(1), 87–101.

Litwin, H., & Monk, A. (1984). Volunteer ombudsman burnout in long-term care services: Some causes and solutions. *Administration of Social Work, 8,* 99–110.

Monk, A., & Kaye, L. W. (1982). Assessing the efficacy of ombudsman services for the aged in long-term care institutions. *Evaluation and Program Planning, 5,* 363–370.

Monk, A., Kaye, L. W., & Litwin, H. (1984). Resolving grievances in the nursing home: A study of the ombudsman program. New York: Columbia University Press.

National Association of Social Workers. (2003). *NASW standards for social work services in long-term care facilities.* Washington, DC: Author.

National Citizens Coalition for Nursing Home Reform (NCCNHR). (1999). *Long-term care ombudsman salary analysis.* Washington, DC: Author.

Nelson, H. W. (1995). Long-term care volunteer roles on trial: Ombudsman effectiveness revisited. *Journal of Gerontological Social Work, 23*(3/4), 25–46.

Nelson, H. W. (2000). Injustice and conflict in nursing homes: Toward advocacy and exchange. *Journal of Aging Studies, 14*(1), 39–62.

Nelson, H. W., Huber, R., & Walter, K. L. (1995). The relationship between volunteer long-term care ombudsmen and regulatory nursing home actions. *The Gerontologist, 35,* 509–514.

Nelson, H. W., Netting, F. E., Huber, R., & Borders, K. (2001). The social worker-ombudsman partnership: A resident-centered model of situational conflict tactics. *Journal of Gerontological Social Work, 35*(3), 65–82.

Nelson, H. W., Netting, F. E., Huber, R., & Borders, K. (2003). Managing external grievances against volunteer advocates. *Journal of Volunteer Administration, 21*(4), 10–16.

Nelson, H. W., Netting, F. E., Huber, R., & Borders, K. (2004). Factors affecting volunteer ombudsman efforts and service duration: Comparing active and resigned volunteers. *Journal of Applied Gerontology, 23*(3), 309–323.

Netting, F. E., Huber, R., Borders, K., Kautz, J. R., & Nelson, H. W. (2000). Volunteer and paid ombudsmen investigating complaints in six states: A natural triaging. *Nonprofit and Voluntary Sector Quarterly, 29*(3), 419–438.

Turnham, H. (2000). Older Americans Act amendments of 2000, H.R. 782 and S. 1536: Reauthorization of the Older Americans Act. Retrieved May 29, 2004, from *http://www.ltcombudsman.org//uploads/OAASummary.htm*.

Waxman, H. A. (2001, July 30). *Abuse of residents is a major problem in U.S. nursing homes.* Minority staff, Special Investigations Division, Committee on Government Reform, U.S. House of Representatives. Washington, DC: U.S. House of Representatives.

Ziegenfuss, J. (1985). *Patient/client/employee complaint programs: An organizational systems model.* Springfield, IL: Charles C. Thomas.

JEANETTE SEMKE

Long-Term Residential Settings for Older Persons With Severe and Persistent Mental Illness

The majority of the nation's long-term residential care population is made up of older persons with severe and persistent mental disease (SPMD). Mental illness in older persons includes

- dementia and related behavioral symptoms, including psychosis
- depression
- schizophrenia and paranoia
- behavioral and emotional consequences of brain disease and dysfunction other than dementia
- psychotoxicity of prescription drugs (American Psychiatric Association, 1994; Fogel, Gottlieb, & Furino, 1990)

Although most of this population receives care in private homes in the community, a sizable group resides in for-profit or nonprofit group residences. Typically, these clients have cognitive, mood, and behavioral problems that interfere with their ability to fully and independently perform personal activities involved in living from day to day. Difficulty in performing these activities of daily living (ADLs) can limit an individual's quality of life and lead to serious health problems. For example, individuals with memory and neurological problems can have difficulty in caring for themselves and experience an avoidable decline in physical health.

Long-term residential settings for older persons with mental illness provide a shared environment for people who are not able to live on their own. In many cases, this congregate form of care allows for long-term care that is more affordable than care provided in private residences (Kane, Kane, & Ladd, 1998). Facilities are varied in design and in the residential and personal care services that are provided. The quality of care may range from poor to excellent (Pynoos & Golant, 1995).

Some residential settings are institutional (e.g., nursing homes and state mental hospitals).[1] As of 1997, about 1.6 million Americans lived in nursing homes (Kane et al., 1998). The Administration on Aging reports a high prevalence of mental illness in nursing homes, with one study estimating that more than 88% of nursing home residents have symptoms of mental illness (Lombardo, Fogel, Robinson, & Weiss, 1996; Smyer, She, & Streit, 1994; U.S. Department of Health and Human Services, 2001).

As of the end of 1993, about 10,500 older persons lived in state mental hospitals, accounting for about 45% of the population of adult state mental hospital patients nationally (Semke, 1996). State mental hospitals provide both short-term and long-term services

637

to a varied population, including older persons with mental illness. In fact, individual states vary widely in the extent to which they rely on state mental hospitals for care of older persons with SPMD and the extent to which the institution becomes a long-term residence for older persons (Semke, Goldman, Fisher, & Hirad, 1998). The economics of scale in relatively large facilities make specialized medical treatment and personal care more affordable. Often, older mental hospital patients receive care on specialized geriatric units. Some nursing homes have specialized dementia care units. They tend to be hospital-like, with housing as a secondary concern.

Another type of residential setting has special design features not readily available in conventional housing settings yet tends to be more "homelike" than the institutional setting. It includes a range of group housing environments in which concerns about housing and homelike amenities are primary. Some of these supported housing options specialize in care for older persons with mental illness. However, many long-term residential settings in which older people with mental illness reside have a varied population, including younger disabled persons and older persons with physical disabilities who do not have a mental illness.

HISTORY

In the 1960s, federal and state policy led to deinstitutionalization of state mental hospitals and encouraged the use of nursing homes. However, by the mid-1980s, the shift to nursing home care as an alternative to mental hospitals came to be seen as a failed policy. A report by the Institute on Medicine revealed that care for those with mental illness was inadequate (Institute of Medicine, 1986). Also, excessive use of physical and chemical restraints was documented. In response to this, Congress passed the Nursing Home Reform Act of 1986 as part of the Omnibus Budget Reconciliation Act of 1987 (Public Law No. 100-203), restricting inappropriate use of restraints.

The act also required that all persons suspected of having a serious mental illness be screened prior to admission to a nursing home. The purpose of this screening, called the preadmission screening and annual resident review (PASARR), was to assure that persons with mental illness receive appropriate mental health treatment. Policy makers saw it as a way to triage persons with mental illness seeking nursing home services to acute psychiatric hospital treatment

or to long-term community care, when appropriate. Unfortunately, the tool does not screen for dementia, a mental health condition that is commonly experienced by nursing home patients.

Also, the act was seen as a means to encourage appropriate mental health treatment within nursing homes. Unfortunately, inadequate nursing home reimbursement policies have limited improvement of mental health services in nursing homes. Although federal financing of mental health services for older persons creates incentives to use nursing homes rather than state mental hospitals, it imposes limits on reimbursement for mental health services. For example, Medicaid does not pay for care in mental hospitals or nursing homes that specialize in mental health services, creating an additional disincentive to deliver mental health services in nursing homes (Taube, Goldman, & Salkever, 1990). Also, the increased role of managed care is influencing mental health services in residential facilities. Komisar, Reuter, and Feder (1997) estimate that 35% of all Medicare beneficiaries will be in managed care plans by 2007. A number of reports suggest that, under managed care, current services for older persons tend to be inadequate (Friedman & Kane, 1993; Kane et al., 1997).

During the period when the locus of care for older persons with mental illness shifted from mental hospitals to nursing homes, another development emerged. A growing emphasis on potentially less costly community-based care led to a shift in the locus of residential care for older persons with mental illness to board and care settings, sometimes referred to as assisted living, and to small group homes, also referred to as adult foster homes, personal care homes, domiciliary care homes, and adult family homes. In 1998, approximately 521,500 people resided in assisted living facilities. Data from the 1991 National Health Provider Inventory indicate that more than half a million people were served by personal care homes that year.

In the past, it was commonly accepted that community-based group residences were intended for residents who could no longer stay with their natural families but were not so disabled as to require nursing home care. More recently, however, they are seen as a substitute for nursing home care for a more disabled population, who in the past would have been placed in a nursing home (Bachrach, 1996; Barton, 1983; Goldman, 1982; Goldman, Adams, & Taube, 1993; Lutterman, 1994; Roybal, 1988; Semke & Jensen, 1996; Talbott, 1983). Thus, the boundaries between homelike community-based residential care and "institutional care" are blurring (Kane et al., 1998).

COMMUNITY-BASED GROUP CARE

Most people prefer to live in their own homes and, short of that, in a homelike environment. The preference for community alternatives to nursing home care is in keeping with a philosophy referred to as "aging in place" (Klein, 1994; Rowles, 1994), which refers to residential stability in one's home or a homelike milieu with minimal disruptions. Aging in place is made possible with the aid of a range of health and personal care services that maximize residential stability without compromising quality of life and health outcomes. The concept has great appeal for care recipients, families, providers, and funders because of its potential to provide cost-effective services in a homelike milieu while enhancing an individual's independence.

Typically, health and social services can be provided more flexibly in the community than in nursing homes and other institutional settings. Different types and amounts of services can be bundled or unbundled, depending on the differing and changing health circumstances of long-term care clients. Thus, there is the potential to maintain aging in place and to match services more closely to the needs of the client than is possible in institutional settings, where a "one size fits all" approach tends to dominate.

Although skilled nursing and nurse monitoring are sometimes provided as part of a package of services for board and care and small group home clients, the greatest amount of care is provided by personal care workers. Services include, for example, assistance with bathing, transferring, supervision of medications, shopping, meal preparation, and laundry. Other health services important for positive outcomes, yet not necessarily administered by the residential care provider, include hospital services and outpatient mental health services offered by a variety of health care professionals in a variety of settings.

SPECIAL NEEDS

Dementia

Many residential care clients have some form of dementia with accompanying memory problems, difficulty in perf.orming routine tasks, impairment in judgment, and disorientation. Personality change, difficulty in learning, and loss of language skills are typical for those with dementia.

The losses associated with dementia can cause the person to be unintentionally difficult, irrational, stubborn, and angry. People with dementia may feel out of control when they are unable to explain their needs and exhibit aggressive or unsafe behaviors. The anguish and burden experienced by the client and the caregiver can be reduced through interventions aimed at identifying and ameliorating triggers for acting-out behavior, environmental modifications, meeting concrete personal care needs, and assistance to caregivers with emotional reactions to the client's changed behavior. Because chapter 58 is a detailed discussion of dementia care, this chapter focuses on mental illness other than dementia.

Depression

An estimated 12 to 22.4% of long-term residential clients have a diagnosis of major depression and an additional 17 to 30% are diagnosed with minor depression (Burrows, Satlin, Salzman, Nobel, & Lipsitz, 1995; Katz, Parmelee, & Streim, 1995). Older persons with depression are at higher risk for death from suicide and from cardiovascular disease. Also, depression among older persons with physical illness or disability is associated with poor functioning (Gurland et al., 1986; Harris et al., 1988). Depression in older persons may be overlooked because symptoms such as withdrawal may not draw the attention of caregivers. Also, major depression symptoms that are physical rather than mental may escape the mental health system. Residential care providers need to be aware that life-threatening illnesses and losses of loved ones and independence may trigger a clinically significant depression or anxiety state.

There is general agreement on the effectiveness of antidepressant medications in treating depression in older persons. Research studies report that more than half of older persons treated with antidepressants experienced 50% or greater reduction in depressive symptoms. Among psychosocial treatments, cognitive therapy, behavioral therapy, and cognitive-behavioral therapy are shown to be most effective (Bartels et al., 2002).

Schizophrenia and Paranoia

Older persons with chronic schizophrenia are estimated to make up a third of the elderly in state hospitals and nursing homes (Katz, Curlik, & Nemetz, 1988). Symptoms include delusions, hallucinations, disorganized speech, disorganized or catatonic behavior, flattened affect, poverty of speech, and lack of goal-directed behavior (U.S. Department of Health and Human Services, 1999). Most individuals with schizophrenia experience the onset of the illness prior to middle age. Some individuals with chronic schizophrenia may show less dramatic symptoms than do younger individuals with schizophrenia. Often, their symptoms overlap with those of individuals with dementia (e.g., impaired abstract reasoning, memory, and diminished capacity to cope with life) (Harrow et al., 1987). A fraction of older persons with schizophrenia experience its onset in late life. Another small fraction of older persons with schizophrenia-like symptoms have persecutory ideation, or paranoia, but do not experience the full schizophrenia syndrome. About half of this group are cognitively intact, and half are cognitively impaired (Christenson & Blazer, 1984). All of the symptoms associated with schizophrenia and paranoia can be problematic and require skilled psychiatric care.

Reports and reviews generally suggest that atypical antipsychotic medications should be considered in treatment of schizophrenia in older persons. Atypical antipsychotics have been demonstrated to be safer for older persons because they tend to have few side effects. Unfortunately, there has been little research on the efficacy of psychosocial interventions for schizophrenia in older persons.

Behavioral Consequences of Brain Disease Other Than Dementia

This is a heterogeneous group of disorders that includes delirium (acute confusional state), Parkinson's disease, stroke, epilepsy, hypothyroidism, and vitamin B_{12} deficiency (Fogel et al., 1990). Most of the behavioral and emotional consequences of these conditions are treatable, if not reversible. They are important to include among mental health issues in residential care because they may be at greatest risk of misdiagnosis or lack of diagnosis.

Psychotoxicity of Prescription Drugs

Older persons are three to seven times more likely than other age groups to have adverse reactions to prescription drugs (Caird & Scott, 1986). Problematic prescription drugs include cardiac drugs, anti-inflammatory drugs, most psychotropic drugs, antidepressants, and sedatives (Besdine, 1988). Common adverse reactions include depression, anxiety, memory loss, insomnia, apathy, and confusional states. Awareness of these reactions is important in the residential care setting.

ACCESS TO MENTAL HEALTH TREATMENT

As addressed previously, a number of specialized interventions can address the mental health needs of residential care clients. However, these interventions may not be easily accessible by residents. The Institute of Medicine defines *accessibility* as "the ease with which a patient can initiate an interaction for any health problem with a clinician" (Donaldson & Vanselow, 1996). A key precursor to this interaction and a condition of efficacious mental health interventions is *access* to specialized mental health providers, primary medical care providers, and adult day services. The fact that these mental health interventions are often provided by an array of health care professionals in settings outside the residential care homes raises the concern that the mental health needs of residents may be neglected in nonspecialized residential care homes.

Also, there is evidence that many older persons with mental illness do not receive appropriate mental health services even when they do have contact with medical and mental health professionals (Bartels et al., 2002). For example, primary care providers, who may be diligent in treating physical ailments, may not recognize that a person with depression has symptoms that are treatable. Also, specialty mental health providers may not view dementia as a "true mental illness" for which they are charged to provide services (Bartels et al., 2002). This is problematic because dementia is often accompanied by psychosis and agitation.

In addition to specialized mental health services, other interventions can help the older adult function better and increase quality of life in the residence itself. Individual interventions include interpersonal skill training, psychotherapy, reality orientation, self-care training, and social interaction. Group interventions may include interpersonal skill training, education and discussion, group therapy, and socialization therapy. Any of these can be used to help residents gain orientation to their surroundings and encourage those who are withdrawn to join social activities.

Mental health interventions can be provided by facility staff, including psychiatrists, nurses, and social workers. For example, some nursing homes and assisted living facilities hire social workers trained as mental health professionals who screen residents for symptoms of mental illness, provide direct services, and consult with other staff on how to be supportive of specific clients. Another approach is a partnership or formal contractual arrangement between a residential facility and a specialty community mental health program or home health care agency in which staff trained in geriatric psychiatry are called in on an as-needed basis to provide mental health treatment. Regardless of whether the residential care mental health program approach is psychiatrist centered, nurse centered, or multidisciplinary team centered, strong lines of communication among the multiple residential staff who interact with the older resident is critical to good outcomes.

For many older persons with mental illness, the small-group, homelike setting, in and of itself, may be more therapeutic than the larger institutional setting. In addition, interventions in nursing homes and community group residences that focus on the environment of the residence can significantly improve the quality of life of residents, including those with mental illness. Also, family-based interventions can help family members understand the challenges of the resident and enhance their ability to support their loved one in the residential living situation.

To assure access to mental health care, residential care providers who frequently interact with clients must have a basic knowledge about mental health issues. They must be aware of signs of mental illness, able to assist the client in coping with symptoms of mental illness, and prepared to consult with and refer to skilled mental health professionals when appropriate. A concern is that staff in residences based on socially driven models may not recognize or understand the complex care needs of older residents with mental illness. Care providers in these less "medicalized" settings may not be trained or equipped to give the specialized care required for people with serious mental illness. Nonetheless, there is ample evidence for the potential of community-based group residences to provide a therapeutic, supportive, homelike environment for older persons with mental illness (Kane et al., 1998).

Roles of the Federal and State Government

Government intervention in long-term residential care is especially salient because it is traditionally charged with protecting the most vulnerable of our citizens and with providing a safety net for those who do not have the personal resources to get the care they need. Nursing homes are mainly under federal regulation. Community-based group residential care is mostly regulated by the states. Therefore, there is considerable variation in community residential services across the states. Federal and state governments play roles in defining long-term care services derived from public laws designed to

- prevent injurious behavior
- create and finance social programs
- control how public resources are used
- assure the quality of services provided to citizens
- establish and protect personal rights (Kapp, 1996)

Prevention of Injurious Behavior

An important piece of federal legislation designed to protect nursing home residents from injury falls under the Omnibus Budget Reconciliation Act (OBRA). It affects facility design, informed consent, types of interventions, staffing, and limits on physical and chemical restraints. State laws pertaining to the prevention of injurious behavior vary widely.

Funding of Social Programs

Federal and state funding for Medicaid, Medicare, and various services supported by the Older Americans' Act target the social and health needs of older persons.

Control of Use of Public Resources

Federal and state governments control the circumstances under which public funds can be used for social and health services. For example, mechanisms for that control include licensure statutes for particular businesses and professions and funding for educational programs.

Quality Assurance

Government is responsible for assuring that services provided to consumers achieve a certain level of quality. For example, the Nursing Home Quality Reform Act that is a part of OBRA provides standards for the structure and process of long-term nursing home facilities that serve residents supported by Medicare and Medicaid.

Establishing and Protecting Personal Rights While Protecting Public Safety

Rights to privacy, religious practice, and unwanted intrusions by nursing home staff are extensively covered in the Nursing Home Quality Reform Act. States vary in the extent to which protection of personal rights is monitored in community-based group residences. Also, through involuntary commitment laws, government bodies oversee legal processes for involuntary commitment to treatment in a psychiatric facility, some of which occurs for the long term.

SOCIAL WORK ROLES

Disability and frailty bring older persons with mental illness into long-term care systems. Typically, assessment of the need for services by medical professionals focuses on health problems. Too often, the whole person is forgotten when the focus of assessment and intervention is an unmet need. This circumstance offers an opportunity for social workers to intervene, because their involvement stresses the social and psychological aspects of a problem more than the medical. The value base of the social work profession supports a strengths-based, holistic approach to practice, emphasizing the positive aspect of life in a context of matching needs to social and health interventions.

Most professional social work programs offer training in multidisciplinary teamwork and team leadership. The skill set that results from this training is of special value in service provision within long-term residential settings, because a variety of professional disciplines are often involved in care for the older adult with mental illness. Skill in teamwork can be applied to a team within the residence. However, broadly defined, teamwork may involve social and health practitioners and family members outside the residence. Especially in community-based group residences, knowledge and awareness of how to enhance continuity of care is crucial in circumstances in which providers are based in different social and health organizations and across different sites.

CONCLUSION

If cost savings is the main driver of the trend toward housing older persons with severe mental illness in board and care and small group homes, a concern is that deprofessionalization of caregivers could put clients at risk of inadequate care. Assurance of well-paid, well-trained staff in long-term residential settings for older persons with severe and persistent mental illness will continue to be a key policy issue for the foreseeable future. Social work has a strong tradition of advocacy for the poor, vulnerable, and disenfranchised. Older persons with mental illness may be especially vulnerable to poor care, because they often do not have the ability or motivation to speak up on their own behalf. Social workers have an important role in advocating for quality of care for these individuals.

NOTE

1. Private psychiatric hospitals tend to specialize in short lengths of stay. No statistics are available for the number of long-stay patients residing in private psychiatric hospitals.

REFERENCES

American Psychiatric Association. (1994). *Diagnostic and statistical manual of mental disorders* (4th ed.). Washington, DC: Author.

Bachrach, L. (1996). The state of the state mental hospital in 1996. *Psychiatric Services, 47*, 1071–1078.

Bartels, S. J., Dums, A. R., Oxman, T. E., Schneider, L. S., Arean, P. A., Alexopoulos, G. S., et al. (2002). Evidence-based practices in geriatric mental health care. *Psychiatric Services, 53*, 1419–1431.

Barton, W. E. (1983). The place, if any, of the mental hospital in the community mental health care system. *Psychiatric Quarterly, 55*, 146–155.

Besdine, R. W. (1988). Dementia and delirium in geriatric medicine. In J. W. Rowe & R. W. Besdine (Eds.), *Dementia and Delirium in Geriatric Medicine.* Boston: Little, Brown.

Burrows, A. B., Satlin, A., Salzman, C., Nobel, K., & Lipsitz, L. (1995). Depression in a long-term care facility: Clinical features and discordance between nursing assessment and patient interviews. *Journal of the American Geriatrics Society, 43*, 1118–1122.

Caird, F. I., & Scott, P. J. W. (1986). *Drug-Induced Diseases in the Elderly.* Amsterdam: Elsevier.

Christenson, R., & Blazer, D. (1984). Epidemiology of persecutory ideation in an elderly population in the community. *American Journal of Psychiatry, 141,* 1088–1091.

Donaldson, M. S., & Vanselow, N. A. (1996). The nature of primary care. *Journal of Family Practice, 42,* 113–116.

Fogel, B. S., Gottlieb, G. L., & Furino, A. (1990). Minds at risk. In B. S. Fogel, G. L. Gottlieb, & A. Furino (Eds.), *Mental Health Policy for Older Americans: Protecting Minds at Risk.* Washington, DC: American Psychiatric Press.

Friedman, B., & Kane, R. L. (1993). *HMO medical directors' perceptions of geriatric practice in Medicare HMOs. Journal of the American Geriatrics Society, 41,* 1144–1149.

Goldman, H. H. (1982). Mental illness and family burden, a public health perspective. *Hospital and Community Psychiatry, 33,* 1169–1177.

Goldman, H. H., Adams, N. H., & Taube, C. A. (1993). Deinstitutionalization: The data demythologized. *Hospital and Community Psychiatry, 34,* 129–134.

Gurland, B. J., Golden, R., Lantigua, R., et al. (1986). The overlap between physical conditions and depression in the elderly: A key to improvement in service delivery. In D. Nayer (Ed.), *The patient and those who care: The mental health aspect of long-term physical illness.* Nantucket, MA: Watson.

Harris, R. E., Mion, L. C., Patterson, M. B., et al. (1988). Severe illness in older patients: The association between depressive disorders and function dependency during the recovery phase. *Journal of the American Geriatrics Society, 36,* 890–896.

Harrow, M., Marengo, J., Pogue-Geile, M., et al. (1987). Schizophrenic deficits in intelligence and abstract thinking: Influence of aging and long-term care institutionalization. In N. E. Miller & G. D. Cohen (Eds.), *Schizophrenia and Aging.* New York: Guilford.

Institute of Medicine. (1986). *Improving the quality of care in nursing homes.* Washington, DC: National Academy Press.

Kane, R. A., Kane, R. L., & Ladd, R. C. (1998). *The heart of long-term care.* New York: Oxford University Press.

Kane, R. L., Kane, R. A., Finch, M., Harrington, C., Newcomer, R., Miller, N., et al. (1997). S/HMOs, the second generation: Building on the experience of the first Social Health Maintenance Organization demonstrations. *Journal of the American Geriatrics Society, 45,* 101–107.

Kapp, M. B. (1996). Aging and the law. In R. H. Binstock & L. K. George (Eds.), *Handbook of aging and the social sciences.* San Diego: Academic Press.

Katz, I. R., Curlik, S., & Nemetz, P. (1988). Functional psychiatric disorders in the elderly. In L. W. Lazarus (Ed.), *Essentials of geriatric psychiatry.* New York: Springer.

Katz, I. R., Parmelee, P. A., & Streim, J. E. (1995). Depression in older patients in residential care: Significance of dysphoria and dimensional assessment. *American Journal of Geriatric Psychiatry, 3,* 161–169.

Klein, H. A. (1994). Aging in place: Adjusting to late life changes. Special issue: Psychosocial perspective on disability. *Journal of Social Behavior & Personality, 9*(5), 153–168.

Komisar, H., Reuter, J., & Feder, J. (1997). *Medicare chart book.* Menlo Park, CA: The Henry J. Kaiser Family Foundation.

Lombardo, N. B., Fogel, B. S., Robinson, G. K., & Weiss, H. P. (1996). *Overcoming barriers to mental health care.* Boston: Hebrew Rehabilitation Center for the Aged and HCRA Research Training Institute; Washington, DC: Mental Health Policy Resource Center.

Lutterman, T. (1994). The state mental health agency profile system. In R. W. Manderscheid & M. A. Sonnenschein (Eds.), *Mental health, United States, 1994* (DHHS Publication No. SMA 94-3000). Rockville, MD: National Institute of Mental Health.

Pynoos, J., & Golant, S. (1995). Housing and living arrangements for the elderly. In R. H. Binstock & L. K. George (Eds.), *Handbook of aging and the social sciences.* San Diego: Academic Press.

Rowles, G. D. (1994). Evolving images of place in aging and "aging in place." In D. Sheck, W. Achenbaum, et al. *Changing perceptions of aging and the aged* (pp. 115–125). New York: Springer.

Roybal, E. R. (1988). Mental health and aging. The need for an expanded federal response. *American Psychologist, 43,* 189–194.

Semke, J., Fisher, W. H., Goldman, H. H., & Hirad, A. (1996). The evolving role of the state hospital in the care and treatment of older adults: State trends, 1984–1993. *Psychiatric Services, 47,* 1082–1087.

Semke, J., Goldman, H. H., Fisher, W. H., & Hirad, A. (1998). Functions of state hospitals in the care and treatment of older adults. *Administration and Policy in Mental Health, 25,* 593–608.

Semke, J., & Jensen, J. (1996). High utilization of inpatient psychiatric services by older adults: Analyses of available data. *Psychiatric Services: A Journal of the American Psychiatric Association, 48*(2), 172–174.

Smyer, M. A., She, D. G., & Streit, A. (1994). The provision and use of mental health services in nursing homes. Results from the national medical expenditure survey. *American Journal of Public Health, 84,* 284–287.

Talbott, J. A. (1983). A special population: The elderly de-institutuionalized chronically mentally ill patient. *Psychiatric Quarterly, 55,* 90–105.

Taube, C. A., Goldman, H. H., & Salkever, D. (1990). Medicaid coverage for mental illness: Balancing access and costs. *Health Affairs, 9,* 5–18.

U.S. Department of Health and Human Services. (1999). *Mental health: A report of the Surgeon General.* Rockville, MD: National Institute of Mental Health.

U.S. Department of Health and Human Services. (2001). *Older adults and mental health: Issues and opportunities.* Rockville, MD: U.S. Department of Health and Human Services, Administration on Aging.

WENDY LUSTBADER
CARTER CATLETT WILLIAMS

Culture Change in Long-Term Care

57

In health care settings, the social worker's role has always been clear: to oppose the narrow scope of physical care, to reveal the person behind the patient or resident. Necessarily, other members of the health care team have focused on pathology. When the acute care hospital model was transposed onto nursing homes in the 1960s (Vladeck, 1980), social workers faced a further need to advocate for the nonphysical dimensions of life that impart wholeness, even when the overarching model of care pointed in narrower directions.

The restraint-free movement in nursing homes, which began in the 1980s, exemplified this approach. Research confirmed what many social workers already knew on a clinical basis: that physical restraint was destructive to both body and spirit. A social worker, Carter Williams, working closely with nurse researchers and others, was a leader in this change movement (Williams, 1989a,b, 1997).

As a direct outgrowth of this work, Williams and nurse Sarah Burger of the National Citizens' Coalition for Nursing Home Reform identified a small group of providers in long-term care who were practicing approaches radically different from those of the traditional nursing home. They were brought together in 1997 through the coordinating work of Rose Marie Fagan, a Rochester, New York, ombudsman (Fagan, Williams, & Burger, 1997). During this gathering, long-existing practices and those that had been newly initiated were probed to define the *culture* of the nursing home as "expressed in its traditions, style of leadership, social networks, patterns of interaction, relations with the outer community, degree of connectedness to the natural world, use of language, and ways in which the community celebrates and mourns" (Lustbader, 2001). These innovators were then challenged to identify a common set of values and principles to guide future change efforts. The values and principles were:

- Know each person
- Each person can and does make a difference
- Relationship is the fundamental building block of a transformed culture
- Respond to spirit, as well as mind and body
- Risk taking is a normal part of life
- Put person before task
- All elders are entitled to self-determination wherever they live
- Community is the antidote to institutionalization
- Do unto others as you would have them do unto you
- Promote the growth and development of all

- Shape and use the potential of the environment in all its aspects: physical, organizational, psychosocial/spiritual
- Practice self-examination, searching for new creativity and opportunities for doing better
- Recognize that culture change and transformation are not destinations but a journey, always a work in progress

Throughout the culture change process, these and other initiatives have been bolstered by the Nursing Home Reform Law of 1987 (often referred to as OBRA), which, in addition to establishing the resident's right to be free of physical restraint, requires nursing homes to "provide services and activities to attain or maintain the highest practicable physical, mental, and psychosocial well-being of each resident in accordance with a written plan of care which . . . is initially prepared, with participation to the extent practicable of the resident or the resident's family" (Nursing Home Reform Amendments of the Omnibus Budget Reconciliation Act of 1987, Public Law 100-203).

This chapter depicts how social workers continue to play a key role in changing the nursing home culture from one in which dignity has been forfeited for the sake of care into one in which dignity is affirmed and meaning can be restored.

THEORETICAL BACKGROUND

To abide being in a hospital, a patient must accept being seen primarily in terms of a problem list. Members of the health care team come to the bedside and address the specific problems that stand between the patient and going home. The goal, *going back home,* is shared by all, except—occasionally—visiting family members who may be exhausted from caregiving. The patient surrenders to the will of the body and tries to heed instructions from those who claim to be advocating for the body's best possible recovery from the insult of the illness.

Arthur Frank, a sociologist who has written extensively about illness, insists that to be fully human, "a person must be recognized *as* fully human by someone else" and that "recognition becomes a thing: something given, or extracted, and then held as one's own." He claims that medical settings that deprive us of such recognition are dangerous places on the level of the soul:

In a secular society we seek to evade asking what makes life meaningful in conditions of suffering, when intactness is permanently jeopardized and bodily integrity gone. When suffering no longer allows this question to be evaded, but when lack of spiritual resources do not allow it to be answered either, that is the existential crisis of illness. Because so few of us can answer what our lives are for, we fear those who pose this question, whether they pose it explicitly or through the implicit witness of their suffering bodies. This fear then leads to withholding recognition of the existential suffering of the ill. (Frank, 1991)

When someone ends up residing in a traditional nursing home, to be addressed repeatedly in terms of a medical problem list is to cease to exist as a person. There is no homecoming to anticipate that will bring relief from this nothingness. There are few objects in the environment that suggest meaning or affirm personal identity. This *is* home, yet it feels like the opposite. One researcher, striving to define *home,* found through interviews with nursing home residents that it is "a whole that cannot be broken down into parts without losing the sense of meaning of the whole" and that the experience of home "thus acts as a center to the individual's existence: it provides meaning in a chaotic world and lies at the core of human existence" (Carboni, 1990).

Maggie Kuhn, the founder of the Gray Panthers, was interviewed in the mid-1970s about the fragmented care her brother received in the last months of his life. Her observations about his hospital stay contain the elements of how health care roles could be made responsive to all dimensions of a person's experience, regardless of the setting.

My brother died after being hospitalized for three months. . . . There was a succession of six different nurses who saw him. Each spent a few seconds—a couple of minutes at the most—but nobody looked at him as a whole person. . . . There was no primary nursing care, where one nurse looks at the whole case. It was the nurse's aides who had more continuous contact with him and who saw to it that he was looked after. How accurate can the reports be when each primary nurse is responsible for an incredible number of patients, with very little time to spend with each? The charge nurse who was supervising never came to visit him. The one person who was the kindest and most loving was a priest. He came to visit every day and was a friend to everyone—Catholic and non-Catholic. . . . Pastoral skills should be transferable to other fields . . . (and) providers ought to be encouraged to function as teams, not pyramids of power topped by physicians. (Hessel, 1977)

Shifting these "pyramids of power" turns out to be the essence of a transformed culture of long-term care. Those who have the most contact with the ill person, the nurse's aides, must be given a primary voice on the health care team, and the locus of control must be returned to the individual, rather than retained by the institution and its staff. This shift requires a revision, at a deep systemic level, of organizational structures, professional roles, and practices for hiring, training, and supervising staff. Only then can someone in need of daily assistance receive such help without forfeiting the ordinary freedoms of which dignity is comprised.

FLATTENED HIERARCHIES

In any institutional structure, deep transformation of the status quo is almost always accompanied by heated disagreements and burgeoning resentments, especially at the beginning of the process. Social workers make a primary contribution to the change process at the outset by ensuring that such feelings and perceptions are voiced and resolved openly. Otherwise, negative feelings tend to go underground, where they exert a corrosive effect and bring change to a standstill. For instance, an administrator declaring in a facility-wide memo "all opinions are respected" differs greatly from instituting management practices that ensure a respectful reception for all points of view, including the negative, and guarantee that divergent opinions are heard from the bottom up.

Warning against a top-down approach, many culture change advocates emphasize that "everyone must be involved in the process" and that this can be achieved "only when management encourages the voices of residents and staff" (Fagan, 2003). Culture change tends to advance fundamentally as soon as certified nursing assistants (CNAs) are given multiple avenues for voicing their points of view and employing their intimate knowledge of the people they assist. To accomplish this, some nursing homes are implementing learning circles, an Eden Alternative concept introduced by Bill Thomas, one of the original leaders of the culture change movement.

Learning circles are small groups of people who meet regularly to learn about and discuss areas of concern with the purpose of planning ways to resolve issues. Learning circles can be initiated for neighborhood work teams, residents, residents and work teams, families, leadership/management, or any configuration of people who have a need to communicate regularly. . . . In a learning circle, participants take turns one-by-one expressing their thoughts, preferences and opinions. After everyone has spoken, the topic is opened for discussion. (Norris-Baker, Doll, Gray, & Kahl, 2003)

The Eden Alternative was one of the first culture change models to insist on placing decision making as close to residents as possible, ensuring that residents could determine their own daily schedules and make their own choices about eating, bathing, dressing, and mobility. CNAs were empowered to respond to spontaneous wishes and to carry residents' unmet desires back to the care team for further consideration, particularly when loneliness, boredom, or emptiness was at stake. Fostering specific changes that proceed from the point of view of residents and those who serve them so closely produces the right conditions for transforming a sterile monoculture into a warm, human habitat (Thomas, 1994). The Eden model further suggests providing anonymous ways for direct-care workers to give feedback to management, as a counter to common barriers such as shyness and shame about writing or speaking skills (Thomas, 1999).

Researchers have found that CNAs given an efficacious voice in how their own care teams are managed tend to stay longer, display more positive attitudes about their work, and treat residents with more kindness (Eaton, 1998). Brewster Place, a nursing home in Topeka, Kansas, began including a CNA in each of their interview teams, reasoning that this person would be working directly with the candidate selected for the job. They also established self-directed teams in which CNAs negotiate their own schedules and work out on-the-job conflicts through learning circles. As a result of these changes, Brewster Place's turnover rate "has gone from over 100% to 56%," and they "anticipate this rate will go even lower over time as their workforce becomes more and more stable" (Norris-Baker et al., 2003).

Staff turnover and the resulting need to fill staff shortages with agency help are some of the costliest burdens that nursing homes with traditional management practices must bear. Conversely, a changed management culture can lead to cost efficiencies because staff who are more satisfied with their work environment stay longer and become more adept at what they do. At the same time, those who receive assistance from these satisfied workers benefit hugely from the opportunity to know and be known by the people they depend on so intimately.

FLUID PROFESSIONAL ROLES

Striving to foster cross-training and a dynamic exchange of skills across disciplines is another major social work contribution to culture change. Kevin Bail, a social worker who contributed to the formative stages of culture change, served as a Neighborhood Coordinator at Providence Mt. St. Vincent in Seattle, one of the earliest pioneering facilities. Instead of traditional nurse-managed units, this facility established neighborhoods of 12 to 20 residents run by coordinators who did not have to be nurses. The idea was to use nursing expertise where it was essential, such as in wound care management, and to open up the role definition of *coordinator* to include those with special skills in community building among staff and residents (Bail, 1999).

All professions benefit from increased fluidity in role definition and flexible management structures that support the strengths that each discipline contributes to the team. Yeatts and Seward (2000) studied self-managed work teams in a midsize nursing home in Wisconsin. One of the teams in the study consisted of eight central people in the facility's management structure, "the nursing home administrator; the directors of nursing, social work, and mental health; the assistant directors of nursing and social work; and the managers of grounds and dietary." The other two teams in the study were each made up of three CNAs. Interestingly, the high-performing team was the one in which the CNAs made their own decisions about resident care, often in quick "stand-up" meetings in the hallway. Observers found that these team members "held a high level of respect for one another and one another's viewpoints." In the low-performing team, care decisions were being made by the RN in charge, with "almost no decision-making at the team level." The RN is quoted as saying, "The main difference between before and now is that now I provide explanations of what's happening, why decisions are being made."

The RN's perception of change in this example relates to the provision of explanations for her decisions to her CNA staff. In effect, she admits that previously she would not have taken the time to say why she had

chosen one course of action rather than another. The fact that supervisory structures had not been altered and staff still could not make their own decisions based on immediate knowledge of residents' needs demonstrates how a superficial change in practice is often enacted, rather than true culture change for which a change in systems is necessary. A deeper shift would have been to transform her RN role into one of supporting the decisions made by her staff and providing her expert guidance whenever the CNAs were grappling with an arena of care beyond their scope of practice.

A CARING ATMOSPHERE

Social workers often excel at group process, working hard to promote effective teamwork at staff meetings and during casual encounters between nursing home staff. Sandy Meyers, a social worker in an urban nursing home, attends as much to how a team meeting feels as to the content of the discussion. She writes, "The key is for caregivers to be in touch with feelings, vulnerabilities, and anxieties, and to use the resources of a supportive environment to transform these into positive experiences for our work" (Meyers, personal communication, 2002). Similarly, in his pioneering work on dementia care, Tom Kitwood observes:

> Care is much more than a matter of individuals attending to individuals. Ideally, it is the work of a team of people whose values are aligned, and whose talents are liberated in achieving a shared objective. It is unlikely that this will happen just by chance; if teambuilding is neglected it is probable that staff will form their own small cliques, and begin to collude in avoiding the less obvious parts of care. Some developmental group work may be necessary in order to facilitate self-disclosure and to lower interpersonal barriers. . . . A rough boundary should be drawn between issues that are genuinely work-related, and those of a more personal kind (which might need to be dealt with through counselling outside the workplace). However, it is appropriate for supervision to provide some kind of "containment" for painful feelings arising directly from work. (Kitwood, 1997)

Facilitating self-disclosure and lowering interpersonal barriers has long been a strength that social workers bring to the health care team. When the preservation of dignity is at stake, these social work skills become vital in prompting staff to identify ways that they may be inadvertently detracting from residents' lives. Just as important, social workers often help staff speak up about their own needs for recognition and affirmation, as well as the hurt that ensues when these needs are not met. Such discussions serve to lessen team sabotage, such as calling in sick unnecessarily, being overly critical of others' mistakes, and backbiting others on the team rather than speaking directly.

Supporting the well-being of nursing assistants becomes critical when they must minister to sorrowful junctures in residents' lives. While giving a bath, for example, a nursing assistant may wash a bereaved person's hair so tenderly that long-pent-up tears emerge and finally receive comfort. Because grief heals when it is received by a caring other, nursing assistants often become central to promoting the mental and emotional health of those they assist. Researchers have found that "proven methods for improving mental health treatment and the quality of life for nursing home residents exist, but they rely on the skill and adequacy of nursing assistants" (Beck, Doan, & Cody, 2002).

Social worker Cathy Unsino was one of the first to affirm and develop this role in the transformed culture, finding that improved communication between shifts helped nursing assistants convey important breakthroughs in residents' emotional lives and to exchange ideas on ways to best individualize the care they were providing (Unsino, 1998). Researchers have confirmed that when social workers and other professionals take the time to teach compassionate responses to residents and family in distress, they help direct-care workers empathize with those "who may be demanding as they deal with profound loss" and show them how not to "personalize these demands" (Beck et al., 2002).

PUTTING THE PERSON BEFORE THE TASK

Culture change becomes most telling in the personal aspects of residing in a nursing home. Joanne Rader, a nurse who is one of the leaders of the culture change movement, has long asserted that the goals in bathing and dressing "are to keep decision making very close to the resident and to help that person maintain the highest possible level of independence and function." When someone refuses to bathe, the caregiver "needs to determine what must be cleaned for compelling

health reasons and have the skills to identify and carry out the most pleasant, least invasive way to do it." In a changed culture of care, the nursing assistant would not simply walk away from someone who said "no" to a standardized bath but would work with other team members to devise an individualized solution in keeping with that person's dignity and lifelong habits. Thus, the experience becomes pleasant for both the giver and receiver.

> If the job is viewed strictly as a number of tasks to be completed on a group of bodies (washing, dressing, feeding, changing) day after day, there is little reward and caregiving will be seen as an unattractive field of work. If instead, the job is viewed and supported as an opportunity to enter into meaningful and caring relationships with people in need of assistance, it provides a way to be of service to others, and can be quite attractive. To recruit and retain good caregivers, the organizational system should be set up to support relationship and caring. (Rader, McKenzie, Hoeffer, & Barrick, 2002)

The transformed culture celebrates the uniqueness of each person as a fundamental principle, particularly the need to individualize care in its most minute details. It takes time to get to know someone's idiosyncratic preferences and habits, rather than imposing standardized practices that seem to make the institution run more efficiently. To respect someone's autonomy, personal knowledge and understanding must take the place of routine practices, or the care can quickly revert to a deprivation of basic human rights under the guise of "doing what's best."

Rosalie Kane, one of the first to study everyday life in nursing homes, cites the case of a woman in her 80s who preferred returning to prison to remaining in a nursing home. She had taken up residence there as a result of a fall while out on probation. Kane observes, "Unable to tolerate the shared room and the confused environment, she committed a technical parole violation and returned to prison where she had a room of her own. . . . [The fact that she] preferred a prison to a nursing home is a severe indictment of our national provisions for the frail elderly." Kane points out that infringements of personal autonomy "are so commonplace and efforts to protect agreed-upon areas of autonomy so unsuccessful that many observers have come to accept rather severe limits in personal autonomy as the *way things are*" (Kane, 1990).

A SENSE OF COMMUNITY

Relationships are at the heart of life and must also be central to a care setting that wishes to promote well-being for those who live and work there (Williams, 1999). This key principle in a transformed culture emphasizes the importance of establishing and maintaining a sense of community. Barry Barkan, one of the pioneers in culture change, insists on "the conscious and consistent cultivation of a community developed with the intention of connecting people to who they are, to one another and to a positive vision of what it means to be an elder in this culture" (Barkan, 2003).

To observe a community meeting at a Live Oak Regenerative Community is to witness staff, residents, and family members respecting and beholding each other's humanity. For instance, residents' spouses who still live at home are encouraged to attend community meetings at the nursing home, thus becoming active participants in the life lived there. They develop relationships with other residents and staff that expand their feeling of being welcomed and appreciated each time they visit. Staff attending such meetings and joining in the discussions gain knowledge of residents on dimensions of life far beyond the needs of the body, while the residents become acquainted with aspects of staff members' lives beyond the work that they do.

Bringing family members' input into care discussions is another component of transforming a care setting into a community. Advocating for families has been a long-standing social work practice in most care settings, but the transformed culture seeks to integrate the family's knowledge of the person into what happens for their relative on a daily basis. Relatives provide valuable life history information, as well as details about individual preferences, accelerating staff's capacity to know the people they assist. Lisa Gwyther, a social work pioneer in dementia care, points out that "families appreciate the opportunity to get to know the special staff over time, and to share observations and tricks with the hands-on staff." She emphasizes how family members understand the variability and unpredictability of people with dementia, because they tend to be aware from their own caregiving that "what works today may not work tonight or tomorrow" and that "the best teacher is often experience with each patient over time" (Gwyther, 1985).

The need to be embraced by a community is most urgent for people with Alzheimer's disease and the other forms of dementia. They are often unable to convey their habits and preferences, and it is imperative for their caregivers to communicate what is known with one another. How each person with dementia is best calmed, which kinds of touch yield comfort, and particular ways to bring good cheer must be passed among staff and visitors alike. Astrid Norberg, a researcher in Sweden, declares that people with dementia suffer when they come to feel "disconnected, disintegrated, and homeless" and urges researchers and practitioners to consider how dementia is being experienced by each individual and to see each person's behavior as a meaningful expression of this experience. This approach contrasts dramatically with the prevailing tendency to study and manage "behavioral disturbances." Eloquently, Norberg depicts an attitude toward people with dementia that affirms each person's value and uniqueness while interacting on the level of feelings (Norberg, 2001), another principle of culture change.

ETHICAL PROBLEM SOLVING

Social workers in health care settings are often called on when ethical dilemmas leave a care team stymied and unable to more forward. For instance, a nursing home may have someone they term a *problem resident* who gets along with no one. Each roommate placed with this person complains to family members, who in turn demand a room change for their relative. Finally, the nursing home social worker may be asked to find someone to put in that room who has no family to provide noisy advocacy and therefore will have no choice but to abide the situation. One researcher portrays a social worker often faced with these predicaments who "does not like to move people around like dominoes" and therefore "tries her best to match people well and to handle problems creatively" (Kane, 1990).

Such situations are rife with tough ethical issues. Should the needs of the institution ever supersede the needs of the individual? What about the rights of a resident who is unable to complain or has no advocates from outside the facility? Should a social worker obey an instruction from a supervisor that is unethical? Social work as a profession possesses an extensive code of ethics, yet to invoke inconvenient ethical issues to an administrator pressured by budgetary considerations can provoke conflict or imperil one's job standing in traditional settings. In a facility striving to transform its culture, however, a social worker would be able to bring the values and principles of culture change to the fore and function as part of a team whose philosophy and ethics accord with social work ethics.

Instead of seeking to impose a solution on the problem resident, a transformed culture calls for including this resident, direct-care staff, and family members in an open discussion of options. It is more respectful to inform someone of the difficulties others are experiencing than to assume that this person is incapable of change. Occasionally, such a person may seize on this opportunity to deal with problems that have beset other relationships, grateful for the chance to learn more compatible behaviors. In other instances, the social worker's creative problem solving may include input from direct care staff on other shifts who can identify concerns not apparent to daytime observers. Addressing these concerns may resuscitate the relationship between a current pair of roommates, making the upheaval of a room change unnecessary. In a transformed culture, solutions are sought under the principles that behavior has meaning and that each person can, and does, make a difference. The fact that it is often time-consuming to arrive at such individualized solutions is recognized and respected by administrators who perceive culture change as an ongoing process, rather than a firm set of protocols.

BARRIERS AND OPPORTUNITIES

In *Aging: The Fulfillment of Life,* Henri Nouwen and Walter Gaffney argue that "care is more than helping people to accept their fate." They claim that all aspects of personhood must be engaged, and that this process requires honest engagement between the generations on issues many prefer to avoid.

> Real care includes confrontation. Care for the aging, after all, means care for all ages, since all human beings—whether they are ten, thirty, fifty, seventy, or eighty years old—are participating in the same process of aging. Therefore, care for the aging means, more often than not, confronting all men and women with their illusion of immortality out of which the rejection of old age comes forth. (Nouwen & Gaffney, 1974)

Acknowledging this reality, leaders in the culture change movement recognize that long-term care evolves in a wider cultural context than that of the facilities where care takes place. Restoring meaning and life satisfaction to the lives of frail elders ultimately must have its basis in the lives elders led prior to the

constraints illness imposes. To this end, the Pioneer Network for Culture Change declares in its vision statement: "In-depth change in systems requires change in the individual's and society's attitudes toward aging and elders; change in elders' attitudes toward themselves and their aging; change in the attitudes and behavior of caregivers toward those for whom they care and change in governmental policy and regulation."

The immediate goal is to create warm, homelike environments, where sources of dignity can be renewed and individual identity can be expressed, despite losses mandated by illness or frailty. In American nursing homes, the change process has been steady, but slow. Staff still entrenched in the traditional culture of control over those receiving care frequently react as if they have a lot to lose as residents gain autonomy and jurisdiction over their own lives. Simultaneously, the prospect of more satisfying work roles and happier residents motivates many to abide the "subtle and difficult art" of the transformation process, remembering that "warmth demands persistence, patience, forgiveness, tolerance and respect," virtues that "flourish only when cultivated" (Thomas, 2003). Social workers will continue to be the chief cultivators of such warmth, charged as the profession always has been with honoring the individual as the starting place of service to others.

REFERENCES

Bail, K. (1999, March). Views presented at the Pioneer Network Retreat, San Francisco, CA.

Barkan, B. (2003). The Live Oak Regenerative Community: Championing a culture of hope and meaning. In A. Weiner & J. Ronch (Eds.), *Culture change in long term care* (pp. 197–229). Binghamton, NY: Haworth Social Work Practice Press.

Beck, C., Doan, R., & Cody, M. (2002, Spring). Nursing assistants as providers of mental health care in nursing homes. *Generations,* pp. 66–71.

Carboni, J. (1990). Homelessness among the institutionalized elderly. *Journal of Gerontological Nursing, 16*(7), 32–38.

Eaton, S. (1998). *Beyond unloving care: Linking work organization and patient care quality in nursing homes.* Presented at the Academy of Management Annual Meeting, San Diego, CA.

Fagan, R. (2003). Pioneer network: Changing the culture of aging in America. In A. Weiner & J. Ronch (Eds.). *Culture change in long term care* (pp. 125–140). Binghamton, NY: Haworth Social Work Practice Press.

Fagan, R., Williams, C., & Burger, S. (1997). *Meeting of pioneers in nursing home culture change: Final report.* Lifespan of Greater Rochester.

Frank, A. (1991, November 14–16). *The quality of recognition: Suffering and illness in the Hegelian aftermath.* Paper presented at the International Consensus Conference on Doctor-Patient Communication, Toronto, Ontario, Canada.

Gwyther, L. (1985). *Care of Alzheimer's patients: A manual for nursing home staff.* Washington, DC: American Health Care Association.

Hessel, D. (Ed.). (1977). *Maggie Kuhn on aging: A dialogue.* Philadelphia: Westminster.

Kane, R. (1990). Everyday life in nursing homes: The way things are. In R. Kane & A. Caplan (Eds.), *Everyday ethics: Resolving dilemmas in nursing home life* (pp. 3–20). New York: Springer.

Kitwood, T. (1997). *Dementia reconsidered: The person comes first.* Buckingham, UK: Open University Press.

Lesnoff-Caravaglia, G. (1985). The aesthetic attitude and common experience. In G. Lesnoff-Caravaglia (Ed.), *Values, ethics, and aging* (pp. 185–203). New York: Human Sciences Press.

Lustbader, W. (2001). The Pioneer challenge: A radical change in the culture of nursing homes. In L. Noelker & Z. Harel (Eds.), *Linking quality of long-term care and quality of life.* New York: Springer.

Norberg, A. (2001). Communication in the care of people with severe dementia. In M. L. Hummert & J. F. Nussbaum (Eds.), *Aging, communication, and health: Linking research and practice for successful aging* (pp. 157–173). Mahwah, NJ: Erlbaum.

Norris-Baker, L., Doll, G., Gray, L., & Kahl, J. (2003). *Pioneering change: An illustrative guide to changing the culture of care in nursing homes with examples from the PEAK initiative.* Manhattan, KS: The Galichia Center on Aging, Kansas State University.

Nouwen, H., & Gaffney, W. (1974). *Aging: The fulfillment of life.* New York: Image.

Rader, J., McKenzie, D., Hoeffer, B., & Barrick, A. (2002). Organizing care within the institution or home. In A. L. Barrick, J. Rader, B. Hoeffer, & P. Sloane, (Eds.) *Bathing without a battle: Personal care of individuals with dementia* (pp. 117–124). New York: Springer.

Richards, M., Hooyman, N., Hansen, M., Brandts, W., Smith-DiJulio, K., & Dahm, L. *Choosing a nursing home: A guidebook for families.* Seattle: University of Washington Press.

Thomas, W. (1994). *The Eden Alternative: Nature, hope, and nursing homes.* Columbia: University of Missouri.

Thomas, W. (1994). *The Eden Alternative handbook: The art of building human habitats.* Shelburne, NY: Summer Hill Co., Inc.

Thomas, W. (2003). Evolution of Eden. In A. Weiner & J. Ronch (Eds.), *Culture change in long term care.* Binghamton, NY: Haworth Social Work Practice Press.

Unsino, C. (1998). *Staff and organizational development: A process for changing the culture in long term care.* Paper presented at the annual meeting of the National Citizens' Coalition for Nursing Home Reform, Washington, DC.

Vladeck, B. (1980). *Unloving care: The nursing home tragedy.* New York: Basic Books.

Williams, C. (1989a). The experience of long term care in the future. *Journal of Gerontological Social Work, 14*(1/2), 3–18.

Williams, C. (1989b). Liberation: Alternative to physical restraint. *The Gerontologist, 29*(5), 5.

Williams, C., with Finch, C. (1997). Physical restraint: Not fit for woman, man or beast. *Journal of the American Geriatrics Society, 45,* 773–775.

Williams, C. (1999). *Relationships: The heart of life and long term care.* Paper presented at the American Society on Aging conference, Quality of care in nursing homes: The critical role of the nursing assistant, Philadelphia.

Yeatts, D., & Seward, R. (2000) Reducing turnover and improving health care in nursing homes. *The Gerontologist, 40,* 358–363.

LISA P. GWYTHER
ROSALIE A. KANE

Dementia Special Care
Units in Residential Care

58

A high proportion of nursing home residents have a primary or secondary diagnosis of Alzheimer's disease, other dementias, or significant cognitive impairment. The Alzheimer's Association estimates that proportion to be 60% of all nursing home residents. Estimates on the numbers of people with dementia in nursing homes fluctuate, depending on the definitions and measurements used, but it is generally assumed that at least half of nursing home residents experience significant cognitive disability.

Nursing homes are typically structured into nursing units. Nursing units vary in the number of residents residing in them, though typically a unit serves at least 40 residents. Nursing homes vary, too, in the number of units (obviously, correlated with overall size) and the extent to which units are autonomous in management, consistent in staff, and organized to offer dining, communal activities, and various amenities right on the unit. The more disabled the resident, the more likely he or she is to be dependent on the environment of his or her own room and the immediate nursing unit, in terms of both physical attributes and the mix of residents and staff who influence his or her daily life.

Special care units (SCUs) in nursing facilities developed in response to concerns expressed by families, advocates, and providers about the quality and adequacy of dementia long-term care. Although innovations in SCUs originated in the nonprofit sector, the majority of SCUs are part of for-profit chains (Gwyther, 2003). Dementia SCUs are functionally defined as specific geographical areas of a nursing home that are licensed by a state as SCUs or that market themselves as SCUs that serve residents with dementia. Depending on state policy, dementia SCUs may be locked units. Typically, each nursing home has criteria to determine which residents are eligible for or appropriate to receive care in an SCU. Depending on the nursing home, the dementia SCU may be targeted for ambulatory residents and/or residents who require close supervision of behavior that may disturb other residents; in such cases, the resident may be discharged from the SCU when skilled nursing needs and loss of mobility become more challenging than behavioral disruptions. SCUs may discharge residents with disruptive behavior as frequently as nonspecialized units. These residents are frequently discharged to inpatient psychiatric facilities. In some facilities, the SCU is designed as a care setting for a person with dementia through his or her entire nursing home stay, and a few SCUs specialize in late-stage or palliative dementia care.

The prevalence of SCUs expanded rapidly in the late 1980s and the 1990s. A 1992 survey funded by the American Association of Retired Persons of a national sample of nursing homes, with results weighted to all Medicare and Medicaid nursing homes, suggested that about 14% of facilities had an SCU (Morris & Emerson-Lombardo, 1994). During the same period, Leon conducted a national study of homes with more than 30 beds and identified 9% with SCUs and much state variation in the rate (Leon, 1994). A 1992 population study of all Minnesota nursing homes found that 15% (66 of 434) of the nursing homes had at least one SCU, and five had more than one SCU. Facilities with SCUs were similar to the statewide profile except that larger facilities and facilities in urban areas were more likely to have SCUs (Grant, Kane, & Stark, 1994). A national survey in 1995 reported that 19% of nursing homes had SCUs, with an average capacity of 34 beds (Leon, Cheng, & Alverez, 1997). Estimates of the prevalence of SCUs in nursing homes vary because of varying sample frames and varying operational definitions of SCU, but the phenomenon of specialized programs for dementia centered in a special living area seems increasingly common in nursing homes large enough to have three or more units, and the trend is international. Various Alzheimer's Association and industry Web sites in 2004 put the prevalence above 20% of nursing homes in the United States.

Given the preponderance of residents with dementia in nursing homes, it is obvious that many residents receive care in general units rather than in specialized SCUs. Even in facilities with SCUs, more people with dementia are likely to be cared for in conventional non-SCU units. An estimate from Ontario, Canada, suggested that in homes with SCUs, about 60% of residents with moderate or severe dementia were served in the traditional units rather than the SCUs (Flett & Davis, 1992), a figure that would be similar in the United States. Those admitted to SCUs tend to be younger males who are admitted from home earlier in the course of their dementia, when they are still independently mobile. Nursing facility SCU residents are also more likely to be private pay and have a clinical diagnosis of Alzheimer's disease and fewer other physical limitations. Nursing facilities with older SCUs are often forced to develop late-stage, palliative, or hospice model units for residents aging in units designed, programmed, and staffed for social-model, less intense nursing care. This is especially true when family members and staff resist returning residents to the general population because established relationships among staff, residents, and families have been forged.

WHAT IS SPECIAL ABOUT SPECIAL CARE?

Advocates for people with Alzheimer's disease have endeavored to understand the theoretical and actual implications of the rapid spread of segregated care units for dementia in order to decide on an appropriate policy position. For example, a contrasting strategy would be to develop dementia-capable programs in every unit in every nursing home and facility-wide staff training about dementia-specific care. Also feasible are dementia "pull-out" day programs within a nursing home, analogous to pull-out special educational programming in mainstream schools. These enriched day programs are more likely in nonprofit facilities. Thus, the Alzheimer's Association (1992) released *Guidelines for Dignity*, which discusses specialized care for Alzheimer's disease in nursing homes without reference to the resident being in an SCU.

STUDIES OF SPECIAL CARE UNITS

In 1992, the former Congressional Office of Technology Assessment convened a panel to explore what was known about SCUs to that time (U.S. Congress, 1992). Some panelists perceived that the development of segregated services for dementia would benefit the person with dementia by establishing more appropriate physical environments, making individualized therapeutic approaches and dementia-appropriate group activities more feasible, reducing pressure on the residents to conform to expected behaviors, and utilizing a specially trained staff or deploying a different mix of staff on a different schedule that might be more appropriate to dementia care. Skeptics worried that dementia special care might in reality be a marketing ploy, a chance to increase private-pay rates for special care without discernible added services, or an attempt to circumvent moratoriums on nursing home bed construction with waivers for specialized unmet needs. Under nursing home regulations, each resident is expected to receive individualized care according to an individually tailored care plan, so that alone should not be seen as a special feature. Advocates express concern that SCUs segregate but fail to provide for special needs. There is increasing consumer and professional consensus that SCUs are most appropriately used to develop and characterize dementia care models that can be adapted to all levels of residential and institutional care.

In the early 1990s, the National Institute on Aging funded 10 cooperative studies on dementia special care. The investigations varied in scope and scale. Some entailed an intervention, whereas others followed populations over time. All investigators agreed to use a common core of measures for the study, making some comparisons possible. Initially, the grantees spent much effort trying to identify the special features that normatively should define dementia SCUs. Special care was originally conceived to include a "special" philosophy of care; staff specification, selection, and training; activity programming to accommodate cognitive impairment; specialized personal care strategies; segregated and modified physical and social environments; and admission and discharge policies profiling which residents are appropriate or most likely to benefit. A 1997 consensus conference determined a core philosophy of SCU care that included promoting safety and security, enhancing connections to others, mitigating disruptive emotional and physical behaviors, supporting cognitive function, maximizing independent function, and regulating stimulation. Unfortunately, practice does not necessarily reflect philosophy.

MODELS FOR SPECIAL CARE UNITS

There are four primary models of specialized dementia care. Variations in size and target population probably preclude a single approach. The curative model is based on treating all medical conditions to reduce "excess disability." The habilitation model focuses on maintaining or enhancing function through specialized programming and personal care. Environmental models adapt or modify the physical and human environment to achieve an elusive "optimal" amount of stimulation and retreat over the degenerative course of dementia. Palliative models provide a safe, comfortable environment with aggressive treatment of physical and emotional pain (sometimes expressed in screaming or repetitive disruptive vocalizations) and attention to spiritual needs of residents and families at the end of life.

The desirable special features of SCUs as identified through the cooperative trials and other work tended to fall into three general categories: the physical environment features (Day, Carreon, & Stump, 2000), the programmatic features (including the way ordinary daily routines are managed), and the way staff are trained and deployed. However, no consistent philosophy or theory guides SCUs, and a wide variety of physical designs and program plans can be found in SCUs.

The marketing of SCUs has focused on physical design, despite the fact that most units are minimally retrofitted. The most common and frequently the only change may be the addition of a security system to limit egress without use of physical restraints. The ideal small, secure, dignified, and stable personalized environments were lost when the industry concluded that a cost-effective unit must have a minimum of 30 beds. Cost, access, and a relative lack of positive outcome data still limit SCU development.

RELEVANT HISTORY OF THE SPECIAL CARE INITIATIVES

One of the first SCUs established in the United States was developed in 1972 at the former Philadelphia Geriatric Center (PGC). The physical and program design was based on observations made by researchers working under M. Powell Lawton, who carefully noted the circumstances that seemed associated with less anxiety and greater engagement and social participation. PGC also engaged in planning over a period of many years, bringing in experts from many disciplines and conducting meetings with staff and with cognitively intact residents. The result of efforts to maximize stimulation that residents received from sitting in crowded corridors without the corresponding danger and barriers to function was a building comprised of small private rooms around the periphery of the unit and a huge central space where activity could take place or be observed. In this example, a clear effort was made to design the building and program according to theories of need-driven behavior. In 2000, Lawton and Elaine Brody, who was director of social work when the unit was built, were interviewed for a history project. Both commented on the efforts to maximize positive behavior and minimize "excess disability," though Lawton suggested that the scale and design in some ways led to overstimulation (Katzman & Bick, 2000).

In the proliferating SCUs of the 1980s and 1990s, some were designed to mimic normal household life as much as possible and to provide stimulation to residents, whereas others were designed to minimize anxiety by muting stimulation and providing serene, noise-free shared spaces and minimalist private space. Some dementia care units are eclectic, drawing pragmatically on a variety of sometimes opposing theories. Validation therapies (where the staff members respond to the feelings of the person with dementia) coexist with reality therapy (where efforts are made to orient the resident to time and place), and initiatives designed to stimulate residents coexist with those designed to soothe or reassure them. Still, some common principles seemed to emerge. The ideal model was expected to provide predictable familiarity, stable routines, and flexible stimulation without overload in "homelike" living units that were safe but enriched with redundant cues like signs, pictures, familiar items, and reminders. Experts urged the reduction of noise, glare (with an increase in natural light), and traffic with small units and a higher ratio of selectively deployed, nonrotating staff. The focus was discrete perimeters that facilitate unobstructed safe movements under staff surveillance between private areas and group, dining, and outdoor spaces. Ideally, activities are designed for short segments of time, meals and snacks are served and available on the unit, finger foods and other strategies are utilized to help residents maintain weight, and families are drawn deeply into the lives of the units.

CURRENT STATUS OF SPECIAL CARE UNITS

Some dementia units have 100% private rooms and many amenities in well-designed private and communal space that would be welcomed by all residents. Others show few efforts to change the physical space or to tailor programs and training to dementia. Hoffman and Platt (2000) are highly critical of many SCUs. Among the common problems they cite are lack of training for staff, inadequate staffing levels (especially at night, when many people with dementia are awake), inadequate admission criteria, poorly designed environments, and lack of anything for residents to do, which in turn increases agitation.

Dementia SCUs potentially benefit residents with and without dementia indirectly, in addition to the direct benefit they provide to participating residents and their families. In many instances, they provide a nucleus for learning more about dementia and training the entire staff. Sometimes, they draw away from the general census those residents who are most disruptive. Though more controversial, it is now widely believed that dementia care units offer benefits to residents who are cognitively intact because they are less likely to be in close contact with other residents whose behavior is disturbing to them or lowers the level of

discourse in the facility. By the same token, however, some advocates for people with dementia worry about their segregation into dementia-specific units, where their needs and care may not be subject to sufficient family and community monitoring.

Research findings to date are mixed and do not show differences in resident outcomes on SCUs compared with residents who have dementia in the rest of the nursing home, once baseline characteristics are controlled for (Sloane, Zimmerman, & Ory, 2001). For example, when controlling for baseline characteristics, Phillips et al. (1997) and colleagues found no difference in functional outcomes, and Leon and Ory (1999) found no differences in aggressive behavior between SCUs and units not designated as an SCU. A similar large Canadian study found SCUs were not homogeneous, nor did SCU status or the individual dimensions of "special care" relate to better outcomes (Chappell & Reid, 2000). Outcome studies often identify more benefits of SCUs in reduced staff turnover and increased staff and family satisfaction. Some studies found reduced aggressive behavior was related to increased use of psychotropics and decreased use of restraints rather than programmatic aspects. Even the addition of wandering areas failed to document use of these areas, and there were additional safety issues.

Much less research is available that compares dementia SCUs with each other, and this might be a fruitful line of endeavor. Zeisel et al. (2003) effectively used hierarchical analysis to show that variations in SCU environments in assisted living affect measurable resident quality of life. At the time of this writing, a number of controlled clinical trials are being conducted within programs in both nursing homes and assisted living facilities to identify effective program, staffing, and training approaches. Also, dementia SCUs with internal research capacity afford the opportunity to provide evidence-based guidance to practitioners on clinical matters, such as how to enhance social engagement and positive emotions, curb or manage aggression, build on individual biographies, or discourage wandering. Such research-rich dementia environments facilitate the development and use of observation tools for examining interventions, such as dementia-care mapping or systematic rating of facial expressions. For examples of positive interventions in dementia care along these lines, see the collection of research results edited by Lawton and Rubinstein (2000). In this way, SCUs could become laboratories for more effective approaches to dementia care that could be exported to the mainstream of residential long-term care.

SOCIAL WORK IN NURSING HOME SCUs

Social workers have played leadership roles in developing generally effective approaches to dementia care within nursing homes. For example, Lisa Gwyther's 1985 Alzheimer's Association manual for nursing home staff on care of Alzheimer's patients preceded the widespread advent of SCUs and is replete with practical examples. The latest edition of this Alzheimer's Association book is used by social workers in training and program development in both nursing home and assisted living SCUs (Gwyther, 2001a). An SCU environment offers a focused opportunity to expand a social work role in comprehensive dementia care. SCUs often emphasize a team approach with nursing, activities, therapy, and social work personnel that has some blurring of discipline responsibility so that residents' person-centered needs can be addressed consistently by all available staff. Social work communication skills in working with teams, individuals, families, family conflict, and groups are especially relevant to the SCU environment. Latest estimates suggest that 70% of nursing facility residents have involved family, and social workers are uniquely positioned to address staff-family conflict and family issues (Port et al., 2001; Yamamoto-Mitani, Aneshensel, & Levy-Storms, 2002). Social workers may be involved, too, in marshaling resources for the residents and their families and in taking and communicating the kind of social history that makes the resident and family become known to the staff.

Typically, social workers are involved with the initial selection of residents to enter the SCU and (depending on the model) with recommendations that some residents no longer need or receive benefit from the SCU. This latter recommendation is often received poorly by family and even SCU frontline staff. The frontline staff in SCUs ideally are selected and self-selected because of an interest and capacity to work well with residents with dementia. As certified nursing assistants (CNAs), they are ideally encouraged to contribute to and knowledgably support the overall care plan, not just the nursing plan. Social workers may well be involved in group and individual efforts to help staff understand the purposive nature of behavior and identify what it is that the individual is trying to communicate.

Social workers in the nursing home should act as members of the management team in suggesting strategies for the development of a dementia SCU or for refinement or expansion of dementia-capable programming throughout the facility. Nursing homes vary in the resources that they have available to develop and staff SCUs. The social worker's expertise should be helpful on a management team that establishes the philosophy of care; defines admission and discharge criteria; sets priorities for use of funds; suggests ways to tailor the human, physical, and social environment for person-centered care; designs staff and family education and support activities (McCallion, Toseland, & Freeman, 1999); and develops community partnership programs (Gwyther, 2001b; Murphy et al., 2000). Like many other leadership opportunities in nursing homes, the social worker may need to initiate activities and express interest, because administration may not be familiar with the social worker's skills and full arena of practice.

Opportunities also exist for social workers to be leaders on the SCUs. Although nursing is the most frequent background for coordinators of dementia SCUs, activity therapists and social workers have also filled the jobs. Social workers frequently direct development and monitoring of nursing home chain SCUs on a regional and national level. Both unit management and overall development and oversight roles are consistent with social work skills and training. The most likely effects of dementia SCUs will be found in improved quality of life for residents, improved family-staff communication, and greater family involvement and satisfaction, goals that are within the expertise of professional social work to assess and to measure the degree to which desired outcomes are attained.

DEMENTIA SPECIAL CARE IN OTHER RESIDENTIAL SETTINGS

A nursing home may not be the best setting for people in the early to moderate stages of dementia. It is argued that the 24-hour nursing supervision and high care levels may not be needed by the majority of residents with dementia until later in their illnesses and that they might thrive in a less institutional, more homelike, and perhaps smaller setting. Estimates of the proportion of older people in residential care who have some degree of cognitive impairment reach 44% in the most current studies (Gruber-Baldini, Boustani, Sloane, & Zimmerman, 2004; Rosenblatt et al., 2004). Thus, the adult foster homes and adult family homes described in chapters 61 and 62 serve substantial numbers of residents with dementia in their general populations.

Some individual residential care facilities and assisted living facilities also provide specialized dementia care (Sloane et al., 2001). One model is that an entire freestanding setting—whether a small family care home serving five or six people, or a larger setting—is designed to serve dementia exclusively. The small family home has proven particularly felicitous for dementia care because of the familiarity of the settings, and those homes that specialize in dementia can further build specific programs to meet those needs. Some entire chains of freestanding assisted living programs specialize in dementia care.

Some specialized dementia programs are operated by firms that also operate nursing homes and other long-term care programs on a single campus. Not uncommonly, some exemplary and nationally known programs were started by nursing homes, but the innovators sought a residential care license to enhance the flexibility of the physical design and service. Thus, the Corinne Dolan Center for Memory and Aging in the Cleveland area is licensed as residential care. The Dolan Center pioneered the use of behavioral mapping in individualized care plans. It is designed to serve people with early and moderate dementia, and the nursing home on campus also has a dementia SCU to serve residents with more advanced dementia. Similarly, Woodside Place, an exemplary assisted living setting on the campus of Presbyterian Homes in Pittsburgh and Copper Ridge in Maryland, chose an assisted living rather than a nursing home license to facilitate its unique pod design and its planned staffing model. In such instances, the specialized dementia assisted living unit is self-contained but within easy reach of an affiliated nursing home.

Larger assisted living or residential care settings may develop dementia SCUs in somewhat the same manner as do nursing homes. Some have done so as the program ages and residents with dementia are having difficulty integrating with others in the dining room or disturbing other residents by wandering. Typically, dementia units in assisted living are locked or secured units with specially tailored environments, programs, and staff. In some large assisted living settings comprised of private, singly occupied apartments, dementia SCUs were established by having residents share apartments and creating large public spaces in the areas thus freed up. (In Oregon, where licensure of assisted living requires private apartments and single occupancy unless by choice, the dementia SCUs in such cases needed to become relicensed as residential care facilities, which carry a different reimbursement rate.) On a corporate level, large, publicly traded assisted living centers such as Sunrise Senior Living have developed branded memory care programs. In the case of Sunrise, they are called Reminiscence Neighborhoods and are characterized by rich and stimulating physical environments that evoke memory and pleasure. The extent to which residents can expect to remain in dementia programs based in residential care depends in part on the aspirations of the programs and in part on the licensure rules of the states. Generally speaking, it seems that residents are more likely to be retained until their deaths in the small adult foster homes or adult family homes than in the more complex apartment units, even if they are in a specialized dementia care setting.

In another variant on the theme, some firms operate dementia-specific programs within existing assisted living programs that contract for their services. An example is Hearthstone Assisted Living, which designs and operates such dementia programs within other care settings. The Hearthstone trademark will be associated with a number of innovatively designed care programs tailored to disease stages, including a program for enhanced care for those who develop health care needs, an information and quality control system developed by the principals of Hearthstone, and a day care and respite program. The Hearthstone staff are responsible for operating their dementia-specific programs independently of any of the management in the rest of the host setting. Each assisted living program is operated by an executive director. The requirements for executive director listed on the Web site are as follows: "thorough knowledge of and experience with dementia population and appropriate therapeutic interventions for this population. Candidates must also possess interpersonal skills, energy and desire necessary to work cooperatively with other staff, volunteers, families and residents. They must also have a degree in Nursing, Social Work, Counseling or comparable experience." It is noteworthy that social work is explicitly viewed as an appropriate educational background to direct such a program, and even more significant that the knowledge, skills, and experiences listed are within the purview of the profession.

FUTURE DIRECTIONS

Many issues regarding dementia special care in nursing homes and assisted living remain unresolved. It is possible that as nursing homes begin organizing in self-contained households and provide all residents with private rooms to which they can retreat, segregated units for dementia may become less necessary. Furthermore, many of these households aspire to offer continuity of community to all residents, even if they experience cognitive or physical decline at different rates. The notion of transferring a resident from such a household to a dementia-specific household may go directly against a care philosophy that emphasizes community. The preferences and experiences of residents in heterogeneous versus homogeneous units and especially of those who are moved because their functioning no longer matches the predominant level of the other residents require further research.

The ideal staff-to-resident ratios and staff mix for dementia-specific care are not yet known. In all likelihood, a variety of models would work. For that reason, some policy analysts have resisted the call for legislated staff ratios and patterns as too inflexible for an evolving model. Social workers have contributed widely to the development and research of these models, and they frequently provide leadership within dementia care units and programs. Because improved quality of life and improved family outcomes are expected from dementia SCUs, these units seem to be a fertile place for social work leadership, especially as more social workers develop specific competence in dementia care.

REFERENCES

Alzheimer's Association. (1992). *Guidelines for dignity: Goals of specialized Alzheimer/dementia care in residential settings.* Chicago.

Chappell, N. L., & Reid, R. C. (2000). Dimensions of care for dementia sufferers in long-term care institutions: Are they related to outcomes? *Journals of Gerontology, Social Sciences, 55B* (4): S234–S244.

Day, K., Carreon, D., & Stump, C. (2000). The therapeutic design of environments for people with dementia. A review of empirical research. *The Gerontologist, 40*(4), 397–416.

Flett, D., & Davis, C. K. (1992). Comparison of care practices for persons with dementia living on and outside special care units in Ontario's homes for the aged. In G. M. Guttman (Ed.), *Shelter and care of persons with dementia* (pp. 41–72). Vancouver, British Columbia, Canada: Simon Fraser University.

Grant, L. A., Kane, R. A., & Stark, A. J. (1994). Dementia care in and out of special care units: Design of a comprehensive survey of all units in Minnesota's nursing homes. *Alzheimer's Disease and Associated Disorders, 8*(Suppl. 1): S106–S111.

Gruber-Baldini, A. L., Boustani, M., Sloane, P. D., & Zimmerman, S. (2004). Behavioral symptoms in residential care/assisted living facilities: Prevalence, risk factors and medication management. *Journal of the American Geriatrics Society, 52*, 1610–1617.

Gwyther, L. P. (1985). *Care of Alzheimer's patients: A manual for nursing home staff.* Washington, DC: American Health Care Association.

Gwyther, L. P. (2001a). *Caring for people with Alzheimer's disease: A manual for facility staff.* Washington, DC: American Health Care Association and Alzheimer's Association.

Gwyther, L. P. (2001b). Family caregivers and long-term care: Caring together. *Alzheimer's Care Quarterly, 2*(1), 64–72.

Gwyther, L. P. (2003). Alzheimer's disease: Special care units. In *Encyclopedia of aging* (3rd ed., pp. 65–69). New York: Springer.

Hoffman, F. B., & Platt, C. A. (2000). *Comforting confused minds: Strategies for managing dementia* (2nd ed.). New York: Springer.

Holmes, D., & Teresi, J. A. (1998). Relating personnel costs in special care units and in traditional care units to resident characteristics. *Journal of Mental Health Policy and Economics, 1*(1), 31–40.

Katzman, R., & Bick, K. (2000). *Alzheimer's disease: The changing view.* San Diego, CA: Academic Press.

Lawton, M. P., & Rubinstein, R. L. (Eds.). (2000). *Interventions in dementia care: Towards improving quality of life.* New York: Springer.

Leon, J. (1994). The 1990/1991 national survey of special care units in nursing homes. *Alzheimer's Disease and Associated Disorders, 8*(Suppl. 1), S72–S86.

Leon, J., Cheng, C. K., & Alvarez, R. J. (1997). Trends in special care: Changes in SCUs from 1991–1995. *Journal of Mental Health and Aging, 3*, 149–168.

Leon, J., & Ory, M. (1999). Effectiveness of special care unit (SCU) placements in reducing aggressive behaviors in recently admitted dementia nursing home residents. *American Journal of Alzheimer's Disease and Other Dementias, 14*(5), 270–277.

McCallion, P., Toseland, R. W., & Freeman, K. (1999). An evaluation of a family visit education program. *Journal of the American Geriatrics Society, 47*(2), 203–214.

Morris, J. N., & Emerson-Lombardo, N. (1994). A national perspective on SCU service richness: Findings from the AARP survey. *Alzheimer's Disease and Associated Disorders, 8* (Suppl. 1), S72–S86.

Murphy, K. M., Morris, S., Kiely, K. D., Morris, J. N., Belleville-Taylor, P., & Gwyther, L. (2000). Family involvement in special care units. *Research and Practice in Alzheimer's Disease, 4*, 229–240.

Phillips, C. D., Sloane, P. D., Hawes, C., Koch, G., Hanm, J., Spry, K., et al. (1997). Effects of residence in

Alzheimer's special care units on functional outcomes. *Journal of the American Medical Association, 278*(16), 1340–1344.

Port, C. L., Gruber-Baldini, A. L., Burton, L., Baumgartner, M., Hebel, J., & Zimmerman, S. (2001). Resident contact with family and friends following nursing home admission. *The Gerontologist, 41,* 589–596.

Rosenblatt, A., Samus, Q. M., Steele, C. D., Baker, A. S., Harper, M. G., & Brandt, J. (2004). The Maryland Assisted Living Study: Prevalence, recognition and treatment of dementia and other psychiatric disorders in the assisted living population of Central Maryland. *Journal of the American Geriatrics Society, 52,* 1618–1623.

Sloane, P. D., Zimmerman, S., & Ory, M. G. (2001). Care for persons with dementia. In S. Zimmerman, P. D. Sloane, & J. K. Eckert (Eds.), *Assisted living: Needs, practices, and policies in residential care for the elderly* (pp. 242–270). Baltimore, MD: The Johns Hopkins University Press.

U.S. Congress Office of Technology Assessment. (1992). *Special care units for people with Alzheimer's and other dementias: Consumer education, research, regulatory, and reimbursement issues* (Publication No. OTA-H-543). Washington, DC: Government Printing Office.

Yamamoto-Mitani, N., Aneshensel, C. S., & Levy-Storms, L. (2002). Patterns of family visiting with institutionalized elders: The case of dementia. *Journals of Gerontology: Social Sciences, 57B*(4), S234–S246.

Zeisel, J., Silverstein, N. M., Hyde, J., Levkoff, S., Lawton, M. P., & Holmes, W. (2003). Environmental correlates to behavioral outcomes in Alzheimer's dementia care units. *The Gerontologist, 43*(5), 697–711.

ROBERT L. MOLLICA

Transitions From Nursing Homes to Community Settings

59

Just under 1.4 million people live in nursing homes in the United States, and 90% of nursing home residents are over 65 years of age. Despite an aging population, nursing home utilization and occupancy rates remained relatively stable between 1999 and 2003. Though the percentage is shifting, 67% of all Medicaid long-term care expenditures were spent on institutional care in federal fiscal year (FFY) 2003 (Eiken & Burwell, 2004) compared with 84% in FFY 1993. Between FFY 1993 and 2003, spending for home- and community-based services (HCBS) waivers grew 565%, and personal care increased 155%. Nursing facility spending rose 71%, and spending on intermediate care facilities for persons with mental retardation (ICFs-MR) increased 38% over 10 years. However, progress has been uneven. States and advocacy groups have made real progress in serving people with mental retardation and developmental disabilities (MR/DD) in community settings. Thirty-six states spent more than half their long-term care expenditures for individuals with MR/DD care on HCBS services, and 13 states spent more than 80% on HCBS for this population. On the other hand, no state spends more than half its money on HCBS waiver services for elders and adults with disabilities. Institutional care is the primary source of care for elders and adults with physical disabilities.

State policy makers, even in states with mature home- and community-based service systems, contend that 10 to 20% of residents could live in a residential setting or their own homes with appropriate support services. States have increased their efforts to help nursing home residents move to community settings; however, they face opposition from nursing home operators, lack of available affordable housing, the need for funding to cover the costs of establishing a home in the community, and lack of financing for Medicaid home- and community-based services. State officials and case managers report that they are often able to work collaboratively with nursing home social workers because they have contact with residents and are more likely to support a person's interest in moving to the community than administrators, who tend to be more concerned with occupancy rates and operating margins. Establishing rapport with nursing home staff is a necessary component to identifying and working with residents.

During the early phases in the development of community care systems, case managers developed care plans and authorized services to support people in their own homes. When someone entered a nursing home, the home care system closed the file. As the cost of nursing home expenditures rose and policy makers recognized that many nursing home residents could return to the community if the necessary housing and support services were available, states began to design programs to work with residents interested in moving to the community. Disability advocates have also played an important role in educating policy makers about the preferences of nursing home residents and the policies that need to be changed to support community living. The U.S. Supreme Court (*L.C. v. Olmstead,* 1999) made community options an imperative by ruling that, under the Americans with Disabilities Act (ADA), people with disabilities had the right to receive services in the most integrated setting. The ADA requires that public entities must make reasonable modifications in policies, practices, or procedures when the modifications are necessary to avoid discrimination on the basis of disability (Rosenbaum, Burke, & Teitelbaum, 2003). States are not required to make alterations that fundamentally alter policies and programs. The decision has prompted states to develop a plan to implement the ADA and given advocates grounds to press for additional funding for home- and community-based services.

STATE INITIATIVES

Between 1998 and 2000, the U.S. Department of Health and Human Services, Office of the Assistant Secretary for Planning and Evaluation (ASPE), and the Centers for Medicare and Medicaid Services (CMS) jointly funded 12 states to develop and implement nursing home transition programs. Beginning in 2001, CMS initiated the first of four rounds of Real Choice Systems Change grants under the administration's New Freedom Initiative. Nursing home transition awards have been made to 23 state agencies and 10 independent living centers. A report on start-up activities in 17 projects (Anderson & O'Keeffe, 2003) found that 370 individuals were transferred by 14 grantees and 370 individuals were in process. Several projects were developing procedures, designing outreach plans, and preparing assessment tools and did not expect to relocate residents during the first year. Eleven grantees cited the lack of affordable, accessible housing as a major barrier to helping residents move to the community. Section 8 rental assistance vouchers are in short supply, and public housing agencies often have lengthy waiting lists. Home- and community-based services waiver programs may also have waiting lists. Case managers or nursing home transi-

tion specialists must work closely with housing agencies to coordinate policy development and implementation in order to leverage resources for people who are moving from nursing homes to community settings.

In 1998, the New Jersey Department of Health and Senior Services implemented a counseling program for Medicaid-eligible nursing home residents with the potential to move to the community. The Community Choice Counseling program was developed separately from its single-entry-point agencies. The state hired 40 registered nurses and social workers to work with residents. The counselors received referrals from area agencies on aging, nursing home staff, and the ombudsman program. Counselors offered residents information about housing and service options and assisted with transition to the community. Counselors received extensive training from state leaders about state and local programs and services available under Medicaid, the Older Americans Act, assisted living and other housing resources, and local service agencies. Counselors visited local service agencies and other organizations to learn about the resources available and to build relationships. During the first three years of the program, counselors helped 3,400 people move to the community.

The State of Washington's comprehensive long-term care system assimilated nursing home transition activities as an integral part of the system. In 1987, the Aging and Adult Services Administration prepared a strategic planning document that noted that nursing home spending was growing so rapidly that it prevented expansion of in-home services, despite consumer preferences for them. The document recommended policy and budget steps to expand in-home services and curtail institutional care. Ten years later, 63% of the agency's clients were served in residential and in-home settings. The State of Washington has shifted from a reliance on nursing homes to a more balanced service system. The number of Medicaid nursing home residents has declined from a peak of just under 18,000 in 1993 to 12,500 in January 2003.[1] The number of people receiving home- and community-based services grew from about 20,000 in 1993 to 33,000 in January 2003. Of Medicaid beneficiaries receiving long-term care services, 71% are served in community and residential settings. By continuing to rebalance its system, state officials expected that the number of people receiving care in nursing homes will drop to 12,181 by January 2004 (Mollica, 2003).

Washington implemented a single-entry system to administer an array of long-term care services. The initial assessment, functional eligibility determination, and care plan are completed by state-employed nurses and social workers. Ongoing case management is done by state staff for beneficiaries in nursing homes, adult family homes, and assisted living settings and by area agencies on aging for in-home participants.

To identify and assist nursing home residents who want to move to the community, the Aging and Disability Services Administration reassigned social workers and nurses from hospitals to nursing homes to work with residents. Case managers are required to contact residents within seven days of admission to the nursing facility to discuss their interests, preferences, plans, likely care needs, and the supports that are available in the community. State social workers work closely with nursing home social workers to understand the needs of residents and to prepare relocation plans. A full comprehensive assessment is completed when the consumer indicates a readiness to work with the social worker to relocate and the nurse/social worker develops a transition plan with the consumer. Social workers often need to find resources to cover transition needs to help residents establish a community residence. Transition needs include furnishing a home or apartment, buying cooking utensils, paying utility deposits, and modifying bathrooms, entryways, and other areas of an apartment. Discharge to the community is obviously more difficult after residents have lost their home or apartment. States can help residents keep their homes by allowing them to retain sufficient income to pay the rent or other costs. Using Medicaid rules, income that would normally be paid to the nursing home can be exempted for up to six months.

In a process developed before CMS allowed coverage of transition services, social workers in Washington can access several sources of support that include a medical institution income exemption fund (MIIE), a residential care discharge allowance, a civil penalty fund, and the assistive technology fund.

Federal Medicaid rules allow states to exempt income of beneficiaries who qualify for Medicaid under the special income level or medically needy program that would normally be paid to the nursing home. Medicaid posteligibility treatment of income rules (CFR435.832) permits states to exempt income so it can be used to maintain a home or to pay for costs related to moving to a residential or community setting. The state also allows up to $816 in state general revenues to help a beneficiary move from a nursing home, hospital, adult residential care facility, en-

hanced residential care facility, assisted living facility, or adult family home to a less restrictive setting. The grant may be used to cover the first month's rent, damage deposits, moving expenses, furniture, utilities, groceries, cleaning services, telephone, or the purchase of necessary equipment, including handrails, ramps, assistive devices, furniture, bedding, and household goods and supplies. Civil money penalties (fines collected from nursing homes with deficiencies) may also be used to help people residing in nursing facilities that have been listed by the licensing agency as deficient to move to another nursing facility or to an alternate residential setting. The grant is limited to $800 per resident, but exceptions may be allowed if the facility has been decertified or an emergency requires several or all residents to relocate. Requests that exceed the limit are reviewed by the regional administrator. Finally, state general revenues were used to create an assistive technology fund that can be used to pay for assistive, adaptive, or durable medical equipment; evaluations; training; or minor home modifications. Assistive technology funds are also available to cover intervention services, which are evaluations or consultations by professionals in occupational or physical therapy, independent living, nutrition, psychology, nursing, or rehabilitation. These services are available for people who are likely to gain improved functioning, health, or independence. Services must meet the consumer's need.

As a result of the early federal demonstrations, CMS established transition services as an allowable service under home- and community-based services waivers (Smith, 2002). The new policy allows states to pay the reasonable costs of community transition services, including security deposits that are required to obtain a lease on an apartment or home; essential furnishings and moving expenses required to occupy and use a community domicile; set-up fees or deposits for utility or service access (e.g., telephone, electricity, heating), and health and safety assurances, such as pest eradication, allergen control, or one-time cleaning prior to occupancy.

COVERING CASE MANAGEMENT

Social workers perform important roles as case managers in helping residents explore community options. However, finding funding to support their activities has been difficult during difficult economic periods. Medicaid is an important source of federal funds for nursing home transition activities. States have three primary options to cover case management activities for nursing home residents under Medicaid. First, case management may be a service under a section 1915 (c) home- and community-based waivers. Second, it can be designed as a targeted case management service. Case management may also be considered an administrative activity that is necessary for the proper and efficient administration of the state plan.

The Medicaid manual describes case management as an "activity which assists individuals in gaining access to needed waiver and other State plan services, as well as needed medical, social, educational, and other appropriate services, regardless of the funding source for the services to which access is gained." Case management services may be used to locate, coordinate, and monitor necessary and appropriate services, to encourage the use of cost-effective medical care by referrals to appropriate providers, and to discourage overutilization of costly services such as emergency room care for routine procedures. Case management services may also provide necessary coordination with providers of nonmedical services, such as local education agencies or the department of vocational rehabilitation, when the services provided by these entities are needed to enable the individual to function at the highest attainable level or to benefit from programs for which he or she might be eligible.

Case management services can be delivered to residents up to 180 consecutive days prior to discharge from a nursing home. The assessment, functional determination, and preliminary plan of care can be completed while the person is still in the nursing home. This flexibility avoids creating a gap between the person's move to the community and the initiation of services. Federal financial participation (FFP) may be claimed by the state Medicaid agency only on the date the person leaves the institution and is enrolled in the waiver.

Targeted case management (TCM) is defined as "services which will assist individuals, eligible under the plan, in gaining access to needed medical, social, educational and other services." TCM may be furnished to nursing home residents who are preparing to move to the community. Like the 1915 (c) waiver, TCM may be furnished during the last 180 consecutive days of a Medicaid-eligible person's institutional stay. States may specify a shorter time period or other conditions under which targeted case management may be provided.

States must identify a target group to receive services, such as nursing home residents planning to move to the community. States may include limitations in comparability, which means that the service is not available in the same amount, scope, and duration to all eligible recipients, and statewideness, which means that the service may be offered in specific geographic areas of a state. Medicaid recipients must be given a choice of TCM providers who meet the state's qualifications. However, with regard to target groups that consist entirely of persons with developmental disabilities or individuals with chronic mental illness, the state may limit the providers of TCM to ensure that case managers are capable of seeing that needed services are actually delivered to these vulnerable populations.

Case management may be reimbursed "as a function necessary for the proper and efficient operation of the Medicaid State plan." The payment rate is either the 50% matching rate or the 75% FFP rate for skilled professional medical personnel, who are employed in state or local agencies other than the Medicaid agency who perform duties that directly relate to the administration of the Medicaid program. As an administrative activity, case management must be related to covered Medicaid services and does not cover gaining access to housing, food stamps, or other non-Medicaid services.

FUNDING SERVICES

Social workers also need a funding source for the services needed to support people in community settings. A few states, Oregon and Washington, pool all long-term care funding in a single appropriation, making it easier to use appropriated funds for nursing home, personal care, or waiver services without requiring legislative approval to move funds from one program or service to another. States without this flexibility have adopted "money follows the person" strategies that allow funds appropriated for nursing home care to be used to pay for community services when an individual moves from the nursing home to the community. Texas was the first state to adopt this strategy under Rider 37, which became Rider 28 in a subsequent legislative session.

Under the Texas money follows the person program, nursing home residents call a hotline staffed by the Department of Human Services. The staff verifies Medicaid eligibility and codes the beneficiary as a Rider 28 individual. A case manager prepares a care plan and initiates services once the resident has relocated. Funds are transferred from the nursing home account to the waiver account periodically. The program allows up to $2,500 for transition services, and the costs have averaged $1,962. Since September 2001, 3,400 people have moved to community settings.

Just over 37% of the individuals moved in with family members, 32% moved to an assisted living facility, and 26% moved to their own homes. Of the individuals who moved, 23% had lived in a nursing home for one year or longer, and 17% had stayed in a nursing home between 6 and 12 months.

Helping nursing home residents move to a community setting can also be a priority for capitated programs. The Utah Department of Health Long-Term Care Managed Care Initiative serves Medicaid beneficiaries who live in a nursing home. Participation is voluntary, and residents receive an assessment to determine their preferred living situation and the services needed to support that choice.

Finally, nursing home social workers and discharge planning staff also have a role in helping residents move to the community. Social workers and direct care staff have referred residents to independent living centers and other organizations that work with residents. They work cooperatively with state nurses in Washington. Staff in other nursing home transition programs described the conflicts faced by nursing home staff. The first priorities may be working with hospitals, handling admissions, and preparing discharge plans for short-term stays covered by Medicare. They may have less time available to work with Medicaid beneficiaries, especially residents who need housing, and they do not control the resources that will be needed to support individuals in the community. Some observers note that the primary role of nursing home social workers is to maintain the census, and there is less time and incentive to work with longer-stay residents who express interest in moving.

CONCLUSION

Consumer demands for services that enable them to live in the most integrated setting, the U.S. Supreme Court decision upholding the rights of individuals with disabilities to live in the community, and the rising cost of institutional care to state Medicaid budgets have led to increased efforts to help nursing home residents move to community settings. State Medicaid, aging, and other agencies and independent living centers and other community-based organizations are increasingly developing programs to promote community transitions. Among the important components of programs to help low-income nursing home residents relocate are

- Funding for community services to enable individuals with disabilities to live independently
- Availability of social workers, case managers, or transition specialists to help residents identify needs and resources to support relocation
- Availability of affordable housing options (with relatives, residential settings, or apartment buildings)
- Dedicated staff assigned to nursing homes to work with residents
- Availability of funds to cover special transition needs

Medicaid provides states with a range of options to develop these components, but the extent to which they are available depends on policy and funding decisions at the state level. However, once the policy and funding decisions have been made, the critical factors in determining whether someone leaves a nursing home is the availability of a social worker or registered nurse to work with the residents who are interested in moving.

NOTE

1. Caseload and spending figures were provided by the Washington Aging and Disability Services Administration.

REFERENCES

Anderson, W., & O'Keeffe, J. (2003). *Real choice systems change grants: First year reports.* Report to the Centers for Medicare and Medicaid Services. Retrieved June 20, 2005, from *http://www.hcbs.org/files/2/69/Systems ChangeGrantProgram_FirstYearReport.pdf.*

Eiken, S., & Burwell, B. (2004). *Medicaid long-term care expenditures in FY 2003.* [Memorandum]. Cambridge, MA: Medstat.

Mollica, R. L. (2003). *Building nursing home transition into a balanced long-term care system: The Washington model.* National Community Living Exchange Collaborative. Rutgers University Center for State Health Policy. Brunswick, NJ.

Rosenbaum, S., Burke, T., & Teitelbaum, J. (2003). *The Americans With Disabilities Act and community integration: An update on fundamental alteration litigation.* Princeton, NJ: Center for Health Care Strategies.

Smith, D. G. (2002). *State Medicaid Directors Letter No. 02-008.* Baltimore: Centers for Medicare and Medicaid Services.

As the older population increases in the United States, more and more congregate living options are emerging, particularly for persons who may need some combination of housing with social support and health care services readily accessible. Continuing care retirement communities (CCRCs) are one such option.

An earlier term, *life care community*, is often used synonymously with CCRC. Conceptually, life care dates back to the convent tradition in which persons gave their worldly possessions to a religious order in exchange for being cared for throughout their lives (Somers, 1993). "Among the precursors of the CCRCs were the medieval guilds, which were the beginnings of the postmodern attempt by self-reliant people, through prior contributions, to insure themselves against losses arising from death, sickness, injury, or old age" (Sherwood, Ruchlin, Sherwood, & Morris, 1997, p. 4). Although this chapter focuses on CCRCs in the United States, the CCRC concept is not restricted to this country. Hall (1999) reports on Gelderhorst, a Dutch CCRC for older deaf people. Carmon's (1997) study of a 35-year-old CCRC in Israel provides insights into occupant needs. Moran, White, Eales, Fast, and Keating (2002) refer to providing "continuing care" in their work with assisted living facilities in Canada.

Between the 1980s and 1990s, the American Association of Homes and Services for the Aging (AAHSA) reported a dramatic increase (50%) in the numbers of U.S. CCRCs, with 40% located in five states (PA, CA, FL, IL, OH) (AAHSA, 2004, p. 1). Today, AAHSA estimates that 625,000 older persons currently reside in 2,030 CCRCs across the United States (AASHA, 2004, p. 2).

F. ELLEN NETTING
CINDY C. WILSON

Continuing Care Retirement Communities

60

DEFINING CCRCS

AAHSA defines a CCRC as "an organization that offers a full range of housing, residential services, and health care in order to serve its older residents as their needs change over time." CCRCs are typically structured as campus-like continuum of care environments, providing various levels of care. Typically, priority is given to residents in the CCRC when health care needs necessitate a change in level of care.

CCRCs offer different types of contracts that influence how residents will move between levels of care. AAHSA classifies these levels as (a) independent apartments or cottages, (b) assisted living, and (c) nursing care. It is estimated that 98% of CCRCs provide apartment-style living, 95% offer nursing care, and 81% provide assisted living or some other type of intermediate step between independent apartment living and nursing care (AAHSA, 2004, p. 2). Typically, nursing care is offered on campus, and CCRC residents are given priority admission over persons from outside the CCRC. Basic services such as meals, maintenance, transportation, and on-site laundry, hairdressing, and even limited shopping services may be provided (Sanders, 1997, p. 4).

CCRCs offer three types of agreements.

1. The Type A extensive agreement is a traditional life care contract based on paying a large up-front investment in exchange for lifelong care. Included without substantial increases in cost are housing, various residential services, and whatever long-term health care is needed. This agreement is similar to purchasing insurance in that the CCRC assumes financial risk for long-term care costs that are not covered by third-party payers.
2. The Type B modified agreement differs from Type A in that the CCRC does not assume full financial risk for long-term care costs. Still covered are housing and residential services, but only a limited amount of nursing care is covered without costs rising. Typically, a certain number of days in nursing care are allowed each year, but once those days are used, a daily charge occurs. For CCRC residents, there may be a discounted rate for the nursing facility that is not available to someone coming in from outside, but the CCRC assumes only partial risk beyond the costs reimbursed by third-party payers.
3. The Type C fee-for-services agreement also includes housing and residential services, but residents are guaranteed access to health care only if they pay prevailing rates. Thus, residents assume full risk for the costs of services they will need as they age in place.

Differences in types of agreements center around the high cost of health care. In Type A arrangements, residents may pay a substantial up-front entry fee because they are essentially buying a long-term care insurance policy and will receive whatever amount of health care they may need. In Type B agreements, the up-front fee may be less because access is guaranteed to only a certain amount of health care. Fee-for-service agreements have a much smaller entry fee because funds do not have to be put into escrow to cover the potential cost of health care for residents who need long-term care for lengthy periods (Sanders, 1997, p. 6).

CCRCs vary, some offering two or three types of contracts, depending on the plan a potential resident wants. Costs, therefore, can vary tremendously within communities, depending on the plan selected, as well as across communities. The American Association for Retired Persons indicates that entry fees can range from $20,000 to $400,000, with monthly payments from $200 to $2,500. In some CCRCs, residents own and others rent living space (AARP, 2004).

Some Web sites list cost information, and others do not. Three examples of fees give an idea of what an accredited CCRC might cost. The Web site of Westminster Village, located in Spanish Fort, Alabama, reveals the following financial options available: "Return-of-Capital Plan in which entrance fees start at $81,600 with monthly service fees beginning at $1,331; this plan allows for 80% of the entrance fee to be refunded to you or your estate; Traditional Plan—entrance fees start at $48,000 with monthly services fees also beginning at $1,331.00; entrance and monthly fees are partially tax-deductible." The Web site of Pennswood Village, in Bucks County, Pennsylvania, reveals entry fees that range from a 504-square-foot studio apartment for $78,700 with a $2,194 monthly fee to a 1,470-square-foot two bedroom with den that has a $265,500 entry fee and a $4,271 monthly fee. An "all inclusive life care contract" is offered. And as a third example, La Posada, located in Green Valley, Arizona, offers independent apartments with entry fees from $67,000 to $287,500 and monthly fees of $1,597 to $4,111. There are garden homes with entry fees ranging from $149,200 to $209,700 and monthly fees from $2,088 to $2,806. There are assisted living suites with a nonrefundable deposit of $3,500 and a monthly fee of $2,886 to $4,558.

Most CCRCs have a lump sum entry fee plus a monthly fee. Depending on the agreement, entry fees may or may not be refundable. If a refund is available, it may be on a declining scale, with less and less refunded as time passes. Full refunds are rare (Sanders, 1997, p. 7).

Winklevoss, Powell, Cohen, and Trueblood-Rapor (1984) in their landmark study of CCRCs found a great deal of confusion over the concepts of life care and continuing care. They carefully distinguished life care as those communities that offer Type A agreements (guaranteed health care) and continuing care as requiring residents to pay some or all of their own health care expenses. However, two decades later, the terms are still used somewhat interchangeably, making it important to clarify what is meant when one is talking about CCRCs and what services they provide.

REGULATION AND OVERSIGHT

Over the last 30 years, CCRCs have matured in their fiscal operations. In the late 1970s and early 1980s, there was a good deal of concern over CCRCs that were having financial troubles. Many of these communities were faith based and run with good intentions but limited financial or management savvy. The dilemma was that residents would purchase a Type A contract, move into the CCRC, enjoy all its amenities, and live a long time—longer than the actuarial tables might predict for a person aging in place in his or her home environment. As health care costs rose, residents were guaranteed long-term care by an agreement that put the CCRC at financial risk for rising costs. The CCRC, even if it had placed funds in escrow to cover health care costs, could conceivably have older residents who use long-term health care for many years without contributing more than a small monthly fee.

In addition, the life care concept was being embraced by real estate developers who saw the potential to target affluent elders as a market niche. As nonprofits were experiencing financial problems while their residents aged in place, requiring more and more costly services, for-profit developers were increasing. By the late 1980s, at least 20 states had enacted life care statutes, and another 10 were in the process of considering legislative action. As quickly as a statute was enacted, developers altered their terms and definitions to build communities outside the purview of legislative oversight. For example, statutes in the late 1980s began to use the terms "life lease" and "long-term lease" agreements (rather than "life care") for Type B agreements (Netting & Wilson, 1987).

Studies of CCRC legislative activity (e.g., Stearns, Netting, & Wilson, 1989; Stearns, Netting, Wilson, & Branch, 1990) continued into the 1990s. Model state statutes were introduced, and the industry itself created quality care mechanisms. Sponsored by AAHSA, the Continuing Care Accreditation Commission (CCAC) was created in 1985 as a nonprofit organization "based on the belief that accreditation promotes and maintains quality and integrity in the aging services profession" (CCAC, 2004). Beginning in January 2003, the CCAC merged with the Commission on Accreditation of Rehabilitation Facilities (CARF), thus becoming CARF-CCAC and creating "an independent resource that will help consumers identify high-quality care providers—from children's services to those for older adults" (CCAC, 2004). In 2004, there were 351 accredited CCRCs, with the following

five states having the largest numbers: Pennsylvania (67), California (49), Florida (29), Ohio (26), and North Carolina (16). Leadership from the Kendal-Crosslands communities in Pennsylvania, a group of Quaker facilities, was instrumental in establishing the accreditation process in its early days. Therefore, it is not surprising that Pennsylvania has the largest number of accredited CCRCs.

CCRC oversight is typically provided through state legislation and varies tremendously by state. Actual oversight may be typically delegated to departments of insurance and/or health and ranges from collecting basic disclosure information to more aggressive interaction. Simultaneously, the accreditation process is overseen by a nonprofit organization that has established standards and a review process that have been developed over the last 20 years. In addition, AAHSA annually publishes an industry profile, summaries of CCRC regulations by state, and consumer guides to CCRCs.

Much of the early research on CCRCs focused on their oversight and financial stability. However, over the last decade CCRCs seem to be becoming more financially stable. For example, by 1996, 86% of CCRCs were covering their debt service, up from 75% in 1993 (Pallarito, 1996, cited in Sanders, 1997). Oversight is still needed, especially for the few CCRCs that are poorly managed, but increasing financial stability has allowed CCRC researchers to turn their attention toward resident life, resident satisfaction, and quality of life, in additional to regulatory oversight.

RESIDENT POPULATION AND SPECIAL NEEDS

Residents who bought into early CCRCs had to have moderate to high levels of income, particularly in purchasing Type A extensive contracts, because entry fees can range into six figures. In the early days, when communities were focused on Type A contracts, there was concern that CCRCs were an attractive option but only for persons with means. In 1990, Bishop conducted an economic analysis to determine features of lower-cost CCRCs that might assist in targeting consumers with more moderate income and assets. She found that "CCRCs, especially those with lower costs, have the potential to make comfortable living environments and insured long-term care available to a wider segment of our elderly population, and to reduce Medicaid costs, insofar as they enroll people who would have spent down if they had entered nursing homes without the long-term care insurance provided by CCRC membership" (p. 75).

Somers (1993) and others see the CCRC as one of the most promising viable options for providing managed care for elderly persons. A 1997 study by the U.S. General Accounting Office (GAO) of 11 CCRCs in California, Maryland, Pennsylvania, and Virginia also views these types of communities as a form of managed care for elders. Nyman (2000) refers to CCRCs as representing "annuities that pay off in kind. . . . In addition to the annuity, CCRCs also provide long-term care insurance. Like an annuity, insurance enables an individual to make more efficient use of his or her resources" (p. 91).

Increasing studies on CCRC residents and their needs are appearing in the literature. For example, in 1990 Alperin and Richie surveyed CCRCs in Florida to determine just what services were provided in these communities. They found a good deal of variation, with some gaps in the continuum of care, particularly in the provision of more sheltered care. They advised elders who were considering moving to a CCRC to find out as much as possible about what is and isn't provided in any CCRC they are considering as a retirement option.

DECIDING TO MOVE TO A CCRC

A number of studies have examined why older persons decided to move to a CCRC, as well as the decision-making process. Sherwood and her colleagues (1997) conducted one of the most comprehensive longitudinal studies of CCRCs, with approximately 2,000 residents in 19 CCRCs in four states (AZ, CA, FL, PA) with high numbers of these types of communities. They selected CCRCs with different types of agreements. They found that CCRC residents tended to be less racially and socioeconomically diverse than their age cohort in the United States. They also tended to be more educated, to be living alone, and to be older than other community-dwelling older persons. CCRC residents tended to plan ahead to access formal services rather than become dependent on their family or on informal support systems.

Sheehan and Karasik (1995) examined a cohort of 814 residents and 246 persons on the waiting list for a newly opened CCRC in the northeastern United States. Reasons for deciding to move to a CCRC for the majority of residents and applicants were primarily guaranteed health care, freedom from home maintenance, and supportive services. Results indicated

that decision making to move to a CCRC is a complex process, and for persons who were leaving a single-family home the decision appeared to occur over a long time period. Women were more likely than men to give safety, social opportunities, independence from family, educational opportunities, convenience to family, and loneliness as reasons for moving. They concluded by saying that "obviously, the salient reasons for moving to a CCRC vary among older persons. Of all factors, marital status had the most pervasive influence" (p. 120).

Identifying a panel of 92 older adults before and after their move to a CCRC in upstate New York, Moen and Erickson (2001) examined how residents framed their decisions to move into the CCRC in light of their life course, revealing just how different the decision-making process is for each individual. Whereas some persons were long term in their planning, others made the decision much more quickly. Persons with lower incomes were more planful in their decision-making process. Planning was associated with subsequent satisfaction once one was in the CCRC. Others moved to avoid a forced move in the future to a nursing home, whereas still others simply wanted someone else to take care of the burdens of home upkeep and maintenance. Some saw the CCRC as a way to avoid being burdensome to their children. Overall, Moen and Erickson (2001) reported that it is important to consider the move as a process, and their evidence suggested "heterogeneity of this process" (p. 66), underscoring the complexity also revealed in Sheehan and Karasik's study of residents and applicants.

Moen, Erickson, and Dempster-McClain (2000) examined the same cohort that moved into the New York CCRC in terms of their social role identities. Because CCRC residents elected to enter age-segregated communities, the move was a change in which the realities of aging were present every waking hour and also meant downsizing from single-family homes and larger spaces. They examined how this move affected social role identities of residents and how they adjusted. Yet, "despite the similarity in socioeconomic status and residential environment, [there was] considerable variation in [residents'] social identities" (p. 575).

Krout, Moen, Holmes, Oggins, and Bowen (2002) examined why 91 residents moved to a CCRC in upstate New York. Residents were primarily concerned about what they would need in the future and how that future would be secure. In this particular CCRC, its location in a college town allowed younger occupants to participate in cultural activities in the larger community. Not wanting to be a burden on one's family was an influence as well. Some reasons for moving differed by sociodemographics such as age, marital status, and gender. One caution was that the residents of this CCRC were financially secure and could afford the CCRC lifestyle, a finding underscored by others who have studied the industry (e.g., Sherwood et al., 1997).

LIVING IN THE CCRC

Researchers have examined what happens once the move is complete. Out of concern about whether types of housing designed for elders actually addressed their needs, a group of studies emerged in the 1960s and expanded in the last few decades. Known as the postoccupancy evaluation (POE) school, three characteristics defined this approach: (a) It is important to know what occupants think about their environment, (b) it is necessary to examine the context in which residents live after they have had time to settle in, and (c) the purpose of evaluating postoccupancy is to solve problems rather than advance theory (Carmon, 1997, p. 65).

Falconer, Naughton, Hughes, Chang-Rowland, and Singer (1992) examined moves that occurred within a Chicago-based CCRC as residents aged in place. Using a two-year longitudinal design, the functional status of 152 residents was assessed at enrollment. They found that self-reported functional status may be helpful in predicting dependency that might require a move to a less independent level of care. Similarly, Newcomer, Preston, and Roderick (1995) studied residents in seven CCRCs in the western United States to find out how much assisted living and nursing home care might be needed during residents' tenure in the community. Using a retrospective resident history model, the authors found substantial variation among facilities in utilization potential, but that "between 50 and 70% of residents can be expected to use either (or both) during their tenure. These likelihoods increase the longer one lives in the facility, and they are lower in high-rise facilities" (p. 164). Long-term care products targeted to consumers of congregate settings and relationships among facility characteristics were also examined. They concluded that "facilities have different incentives to move residents to higher levels of care, depending on who and how much is paid for this care" (p. 166). An earlier study (Newcomer & Preston, 1994) revealed

that compared with other retirees, CCRC residents were less likely to use hospital services.

A 1996 ethnographic study by Perkinson and Rockemann focused on 20 older women living in a Pennsylvania CCRC. The voices of interviewees were featured in their thick description of the trajectory of friendship formation. Public spaces allowed residents to observe one another "from afar" as they assessed the potential for developing relationships, and congregate meals and informal groups provided initial interactions that were supplemented by more structured activities in which common interests could be shared (p. 174). It was observed that this younger CCRC (open only 20 months) changed in its interactions and friendship patterns as residents aged together in place. Strategies for developing friendships varied tremendously, and observations revealed that more private residents benefited from moving among tables to engage with different dining partners, for example, in order not to be socially "overwhelmed" by the communal lifestyle. Another observation was that informal caregiving supports for wives or widows did not always spontaneously emerge.

Krout, Oggins, and Holmes (2000) examined service use in the same CCRC reported previously (Krout et al., 2002). Most frequently, residents used services such as the onsite pharmacy, insurance billing, banking, and health and fitness. Not surprisingly, residents in poorer health were greater users of services within the CCRC. Sugihara and Evans (2000) looked at physical space in one CCRC in the Mid-Atlantic region of the United States to determine how social interaction and support networks might be facilitated or hampered. They surveyed 67 residents who had lived in this new CCRC for 18 months. Social support development appeared to be facilitated by having activity space close to residential units. Attachment to place appeared to be enhanced by having outdoor gardening available.

Spears (1992) described a Pennsylvania CCRC called Pennswood Village, a Quaker facility that opened in 1980. Spears's case study is written from the experience of a practitioner who has witnessed every phase of a CCRC's development. The detail in which she describes Pennswood, combined with the research reported previously, has implications for the social work role within these communities.

SOCIAL WORK ROLES WITHIN CCRCS

Early research focused heavily on the oversight of facilities that were developing under various auspices but had not gained a solid financial footing in the retirement community industry. Today those questions are still relevant, as social workers and others work with or in CCRCs. In advising older persons who may be considering a CCRC, it is important to ask specific questions about the types of agreements that are offered, as well as the levels of care provided on campus. Within the context of the state in which the CCRC is located, it will be necessary to investigate whether CCRCs are regulated and what regulation means within that particular state. It may simply be that a state agency files disclosure forms, or there could be a monitoring process. It is also important to recognize that there are other regulatory bodies responsible for components within CCRCs, because assisted living is regulated in some states and may be called by a number of terms. Nursing units will be overseen by state inspectors, and long-term care ombudsmen should be available to CCRC residents, families, and others who might have complaints or concerns. The social worker will want to know this information.

Screening and assessment is an important social work role to be performed within the context of a CCRC. Boustani, Watson, Fultz, Perkins, and Druckenbrod (2003) have looked at the acceptance of dementia screening in CCRCs. Wimberly and his colleagues (2003) conducted research in a Florida-based CCRC with the intent to examine what assessment tools might assist in determining who is eligible for independent living and who needs more sheltered care within the community. Screening instruments need be used so that residents receive the appropriate level of care and services "within independent, assisted, and skilled levels of care at the least cost and for the greatest period of time" (p. 78). CCRCs may have interdisciplinary teams that perform various entry screenings and baseline and ongoing assessments. Social workers would logically be members of such a team.

Making the decision to move from one level of care to another is probably one of the most difficult processes in CCRC life. Although persons who plan for the unexpected may move into CCRCs, this does not mean that they are ready to leave their independent living unit. The inevitability of a move may be met with a great deal of anguish, depending on the circumstances surrounding that decision. Social workers and other staff need to be sensitive to the symbolic nature of such moves. Even the term *independent living* is somewhat of a setup for the resident in that it reflects the larger societal image of what it means to be able to function on one's own. In actual-

ity, most people are interdependent throughout their lives, but the symbolism in admitting that one needs assisted living or even nursing care is rife with emotionality. Social workers and other team members (e.g., nurses, physicians) will want to recognize the delicate nature of what it means to move to a different level of care for the person, as well as for their social system within the CCRC, and be prepared to provide appropriate counseling and support. Including the older resident and his or her family members in these decisions is critically important.

Just as decision-making processes occur within CCRCs, there are times when residents are subject to the nuances of the larger environment beyond the campus. Spears's (1992) concerns at Pennswood are particularly relevant when she talks about how residents feel that CCRC staff should be able to help them navigate the larger health care system. CCRCs are not hospitals or rehabilitation facilities. Some have nursing units that are not skilled-level care. Thus, for residents who are thrust into the larger environment, CCRC staff may not have the authority or even the capacity to intervene. Social workers in CCRCs can play the connectional role between systems when this happens. Even if they cannot solve problems encountered in the larger environment, they can advocate for the resident and connect with the appropriate case manager, social worker, nurse, or physician who can address the resident's concerns.

And last, CCRC residents buy into their communities because they recognize that at some point they will need end-of-life care. Baker (2000) and Baker and Nussbaum (1997) focus on spiritual issues for CCRC residents. Hays, Galanos, Palmer, McQuoid, and Flint (2001) conducted a cross-sectional study of 219 CCRC residents to determine their preference for place of death. For 40% of occupants, death-related planning played a role in their decision to move to the CCRC. Most respondents preferred to die at the CCRC rather than in a hospital facility. Thus, social workers within CCRCs can ask residents about their preferences and have information on file so that when death or incapacity occurs, a person's wishes will be known. Social workers can work with hospice programs so that their team can visit residents in CCRCs.

In sum, we provide a list of questions for social workers and other professionals to consider when they are working for a CCRC or interacting with residents who reside there.

1. What types of agreements are offered (extensive, modified, fee for service)? What are the costs?

2. What levels of care are provided (independent, assisted living, nursing, other)?

3. Are Medicare and Medicaid accepted in the nursing facility?

4. In this state, what laws and regulations are in place that affect the CCRC?

5. How is this CCRC structured (e.g., nonprofit, for profit, chain, etc.)?

6. Who started this CCRC, and is it affiliated with a faith community?

7. What is the physical layout, and how does that help or hinder resident interaction?

8. How and by whom are residents screened for entering the CCRC? Are standardized tools and procedures used?

9. What are the resident demographics, and how are resident needs assessed?

10. Is there a team approach to care, and who are the members of the team?

11. How are residents oriented and welcomed into the community? Are there strategies or mechanisms that facilitate adjustment?

12. Do residents interact across levels of care, and how are transitions between levels of care made? Who makes the decision when a permanent change from one level to another level is needed?

13. Should they need it on permanent or long-term basis, are CCRC residents assured a place or given priority in the nursing unit?

14. How do residents participate in community decision making, and how is that facilitated? Is there an active residents' council?

15. What role do staff play when residents go outside the CCRC to receive medical services, acute care, or rehabilitation services? Who communicates with providers in the larger community?

16. What information is collected on end-of-life concerns, and how are decisions made about end-of-life and spiritual care?

17. What role does staff have in hospice care?

QUALITY OF LIFE AND QUALITY OF CARE IN CCRC CULTURE

Quality of life and quality of care have been concerns of researchers interested in CCRCs. Several studies have focused on the relationships that develop within the CCRC culture and how these relationships affect the lives of residents.

Stacey-Konnert and Pynoos (1992) examined friendship and social networks in one CCRC. "A CCRC may provide a milieu in which friendships can be maintained as an individual grows old. With age, however, residents may interact less frequently with friends outside the CCRC" (p. 299). They investigated the contraction of networks, using participant observation and structured interviews over a three-month period. Overall, residents appeared to have a sense of community; however, there were limits to types of assistance that might be provided. Persons who had more difficulty becoming integrated into the CCRC's culture were "residents with cognitive deficits, depression, physical health problems, or long-standing isolative patterns. . . . In addition, caregivers, widows, and the very old were also vulnerable to social isolation" (p. 309). Confidant ties to nonkin elsewhere stood the passage of time.

A qualitative study conducted by Williams and Guendouzi (2000) in a West Coast CCRC focused on residents' personal relationships and communication with one another, families, and younger people. Focusing on the lifestyle choice to move into a retirement community as one that involves "the dialectical tensions of autonomy versus connection associated with choosing and adjusting to this lifestyle" (p. 81), the authors interviewed 15 residents in relatively good health who had moved to a nonprofit CCRC designed for retired teachers. Residents had to cope with negative stereotypes about what a move to a retirement community meant to their self-identity and to their contacts with the outside community. Residents struggled with how to maintain their family life identity when they had opted to move in order to avoid being a burden to family members. A set of contradictions about peer relationships emerged in the process, as residents often made negative comments about peers who were not as able, distancing themselves from peers whose health had deteriorated, as though poor health and frailty were "catching." The increasing fragility of the peer network was reinforced by the proximity of the health care facility behind the dining room. "It may well be wise to prepare elders to confront these issues—a preparation that would aid adjustment—rather than shrouding them in a veil of marketing positivity" (p. 81).

Jenkins, Pienta, and Horgas (2002) studied two midwestern CCRCs to find out if residents remained involved in external community activities once they became CCRC residents. Self-administered surveys returned by 167 residents revealed that higher levels of activity were associated with better health-related quality of life. Not surprisingly, residents in independent living units within CCRCs participated more in activities beyond the immediate campus, whereas once occupants moved to assisted living units, involvement in outside activities dropped significantly. A major reason for this drop is that residents had given up driving.

These studies demonstrate just how complicated close community life is. Certainly there is the potential for CCRC living to be a culture of care in which residents feel more secure in their physical environment. However, it is also close community living, and with that come the strengths and limitations of close proximity. The primary message in these studies appears to be that adjustment and integration into the community is different for each person as they set boundaries, establish their network, and seek to maintain ties to the broader community. Thus there is no one CCRC culture, but each CCRC's culture will be distinctive.

Potential residents should not only assess the culture of a CCRC being considered but also try to assess the "goodness of fit" with their own values and expectations. Likewise, social workers and other health providers must respect the wants and needs of residents as much as possible within the constraints of existing operating procedures and policies.

CONCLUSION

CCRCs have been part of the long-term care industry for many years. Many developed out of community concerns that older people needed a place where they could be more secure and have access to various services. In trying to put together a continuum of care in one campus-like location, CCRCs essentially spawned the concept of assisted living as an option between independent living and nursing home care. Obviously, assisted living has taken off on its own as developers have realized the importance of this market niche with a rapidly aging population in the United States. Yet, the numbers of CCRCs also continue to grow, many with multiple types of financial arrangements, offering menus of options to older persons. The flexibility of their financing options, the move away from offering only life care types of contracts, the recognition of different markets, and the targeting of persons with more moderate incomes have made the industry much more flexible in addressing consumer demands. For persons who want to travel, know that their home is taken care of, reduce their responsibilities in terms of maintenance and oversight, and perhaps feel that they have gained

a little control over life's uncertainty, the CCRC is likely to remain a viable option.

REFERENCES

Alperin, D., & Richie, N. (1990). Continuing/life care facilities and the continuum of care. *Journal of Housing for the Elderly, 6,* 125–130.

American Association of Homes and Services for the Aging (AAHSA). (2004). *Continuing care retirement communities.* Retrieved October 10, 2004, from http://www.aahsa.org/consumer_info/homes_svcs_directory.

American Association of Retired Persons (AARP). (2004). *Continuing care retirement communities.* Retrieved June 20, 2005, from http://www.aarp.org/life/housingchoices/Articles/a2004-02-26-retirement-community.html.

Baker, D. C. (2000). Investigation of pastoral care interventions as a treatment for depression among continuing care retirement community residents. *Journal of Religious Gerontology, 12*(1), 63–85.

Baker, D. C., & Nussbaum, P. D. (1997). Religious practice and spirituality—then and now: A retrospective study of spiritual dimensions of residents residing at a continuing care retirement community. *Journal of Religious Gerontology, 19*(3), 33–51.

Bishop, C. (1990). Features of lower-cost continuing care retirement communities: Learning from cost analysis. *Journal of Housing for the Elderly, 7,* 55–77.

Boustani, M., Watson, L., Fultz, B., Perkins, A. J., & Druckenbrod, R. (2003). Acceptance of dementia screening in continuous care retirement communities: A mailed survey. *International Journal of Geriatric Psychiatry, 18*(9), 780–786.

Carmon, N. (1997). Post-occupancy evaluation of life-care community for the aged in Israel. *Journal of Housing for the Elderly, 12*(1–2), 63–81.

Continuing Care Accreditation Commission (CCAC). (2004). *Have confidence in your choice.* Retrieved June 20, 2005, from http://www.ccaconline.org/index.htm.

Falconer, J., Naughton, B. J., Hughes, S. L., Chang-Rowland, W., & Singer, R. H. (1992). Self-reported functional status predicts change in level of care in independent living residents of a continuing care retirement community. *Journal of the American Geriatrics Society, 40*(3), 255–258.

Hall, G. (1999). Gelderhorst: An innovative Dutch community provides continuing care for older deaf people. *Innovations in Aging, 28*(2), 9–12.

Hays, J. C., Galanos, A. N., Palmer, T. A., McQuoid, D. R., & Flint, E. P. (2001). Preference for place of death in a continuing care retirement community. *The Gerontologist, 41*(1), 123–128.

Jenkins, K. R., Pienta, A. M., & Horgas, A. L. (2002). Activity and health-related quality of life in continuing care retirement communities. *Research on Aging, 24*(1), 124–149.

Krout, J. A., Moen, P., Holmes, H. H., Oggins, J., & Bowen, N. (2002). Reasons for relocation to a continuing care retirement community. *Journal of Applied Gerontology, 21*(2), 236–256.

Krout, J. A., Oggins, J., & Holmes, H. H. (2000). Patterns of service use in a continuing care retirement community. *The Gerontologist, 40*(6), 698–705.

La Posada. (2004). *La Posada is Arizona's first nationally accredited, not-for-profit continuing care retirement community!* Retrieved October, 10, 2004, from *http://www.lapposadav.complansprograms.html.*

Moen, P., & Erickson, M. A. (2001). Decision-making and satisfaction with a continuing care retirement community. *Journal of Housing for the Elderly, 14*(1–2), 53–69.

Moen, P., Erickson, M. A., & Dempster-McClain, D. (2000). Social role identities among older adults in continuing care retirement community. *Research on Aging, 22*(5), 559–579.

Moran, L., White, E., Eales, J., Fast, J., & Keating, N. (2002). Evaluating consumer satisfaction in residential continuing care settings. *Journal of Aging and Social Policy, 14*(2), 85–109.

Netting, F. E., & Wilson, C. C. (1987). Current legislation concerning life care and continuing care. *The Gerontologist, 27*(5), 645–651.

Newcomer, R., & Preston, S. (1994). Relationships between acute care and nursing unit use in two continuing care retirement communities. *Research on Aging, 16*, 280–301.

Newcomer, R., Preston, S., & Roderick, S. S. (1995). Assisted-living and nursing unit use among continuing care retirement community residents. *Research on Aging, 17*(2), 149–167.

Nyman, J. A. (2000). Continuing care retirement communities and efficiency in the financing of long-term care. *Journal of Aging and Social Policy, 11*(2–3), 89–98.

Pennswood Village. (2004). *Welcome to Pennswood Village.* Retrieved June 20, 2005, from *http://www.pennswood.org/.*

Perkinson, M. A., & Rockemann, D. D. (1996). Older women living in a continuing care retirement community: Marital status and friendship. *Journal of Women and Aging, 8*(3–4), 159–177.

Sanders, J. (1997). Continuing care retirement communities: A background and summary of current issues. Washington, DC: U.S. Department of Health and Human Services. Retrieved June 20, 2005, from *http://aspe.os.dhhs.gov/daltcp/Reports/ccrcrpt.htm.*

Sheehan, N., & Karasik, R. (1995). The decision to move to a continuing care retirement community. *Journal of Housing for the Elderly, 11*(2), 107–122.

Sherwood, S., Ruchlin, H., Sherwood, C., & Morris, S. (1997). *Continuing care retirement communities.* Baltimore: Johns Hopkins University Press.

Somers, A. R. (1993). "Lifecare": A viable option in long-term care for the elderly. *Journal of the American Geriatrics Society, 41*, 188–191.

Spears, N. L. (1992). Promise of health care in continuing care retirement community. *Pride Institute Journal of Long Term Home Health Care, 11*(3), 20–36.

Stacey-Konnert, C., & Pynoos, J. (1992). Friendship and social networks in a continuing care retirement community. *Journal of Applied Gerontology, 11*(3), 298–313.

Stearns, L. R., Netting, F. E., & Wilson, C. C. (1989). Continuing care retirement communities: Issues for state regulation. *Saint Louis University Public Law Review, 8*(2), 245–274.

Stearns, L. R., Netting, F. E., Wilson, C. C., & Branch, L. G. (1990). Lessons learned from the implementation of CCRC regulation. *The Gerontologist, 30*(2), 154–161.

Sugihara, S., & Evans, G. W. (2000). Place attachment and social support at continuing care retirement communities. *Environment and Behavior, 32*(3), 400–409.

U.S. General Accounting Office. (1997). *Health care services: How continuing care retirement communities manage services for the elderly* (GAO/HEHS Publication No. 97-36). Washington, DC: Author.

Westminster Village. (2004). *A retirement community with distinctive Southern charm.* Retrieved June 20, 2005, from *http://www.westminstervillageal.com/.*

Williams, A., & Guendouzi, J. (2000). Adjusting to "the home": Dialectical dilemmas and personal relationships in a retirement community. *Journal of Communication, 50*(3), 65–82.

Wimberly, E. T., Herrara, A., Kidrowski, B., Brown, D., & L'Esperance, L. (2003). Cognititve and physical performance assessment of retirees entering a continuing care retirement community: The moorings Assessment Protocol. *American Journal of Alzheimer's Disease and Other Dementias, 18*(2), 73–78.

Winklevoss, H. E., Powell, A. V., Cohen, D. C., & Trueblood-Rapor, A. (1984). *Continuing care retirement communities: An empirical, financial, and legal analysis.* Homewood, IL: Richard D. Irwin.

Assisted living (AL) is a term applied to a wide array of residential facilities for older adults. In the broadest sense, AL includes all group residential programs not licensed as nursing homes that provide personal care in activities of daily living and can respond to unscheduled needs for assistance (Kane & Wilson, 1993). In a more restrictive sense, it refers to the values underlying the manner in which that care is provided. Thus, AL has come to refer to both a *setting* of long-term care that combines housing and supportive services in a homelike environment and a distinct *philosophy* of residential care provision. The field of AL is a complex one, because as a setting of care, AL embodies a diversity of facility types, and as a philosophy of care, it espouses principles that are inconsistently in practice (Zimmerman, Sloane, & Eckert, 2001). To understand the distinction between setting and philosophy, as well as the current state of AL and the needs of its residents, it is helpful to consider the evolution of AL within the long-term care industry.

ASSISTED LIVING AS A SETTING AND A PHILOSOPHY OF CARE

Nonnursing home residential care for older adults was first recognized in the United States in the 1940s, as small "mom-and-pop" homes and later as senior housing (Morgan, Eckert, & Lyon, 1995). Over time, there was a growing awareness of a gap in the "continuum" of long-term care between residential settings that catered to older adults who had no functional impairments and nursing facilities that catered to the chronically ill. This awareness reflected the combined impact of growing numbers of older adults, a shortage of nursing home beds, increasing costs of nursing home care, the better overall health of new generations of older adults, and dissatisfaction with nursing home care (Bishop, 1999; Borra, 1986; Korcok, 1987). Thus, the need for a new model of care was recognized, a model that would provide an "invisible support system" in a residential setting (Sullivan, 1998). The utility of this concept drew investment from nursing home chains that saw the opportunity to use AL as a feeder for their nursing level of care, into which residents could be transferred as impairment increased. At the same time, market pressure created a stand-alone AL industry, intended to provide increasingly higher levels of care to enable aging in place and avoid nursing home transfer if possible (Mollica, 2001a; Thompson & Marinaccio, 1997). Over time, a diversity of residential settings that pro-

SHERYL ZIMMERMAN

JEAN MUNN

TERRY KOENIG

Assisted Living Settings

vide or bring in supportive services, including facilities otherwise named adult foster care, senior group homes, personal care homes, sheltered housing, homes for adults, board and care, and domiciliary care (among others), have come to be known as AL.

On a more purist level, AL is those facilities that embrace a philosophy of care explicated by the Assisted Living Quality Coalition. This coalition, formed in 1996, includes representatives of the Alzheimer's Association, American Association of Homes and Services for the Aging, American Association of Retired Persons, American Health Care Association/National Center for Assisted Living, American Seniors Housing Association, and the Assisted Living Federation of America. It has set forth 17 philosophies related to the quality of care and resident quality of life that are meant to be reflected in an AL facility's mission statement, policies, and procedures (Table 61.1).

The challenge in conceptualizing AL is that while the industry promotes goals of providing a homelike environment, independence, autonomy, and privacy, the term is used by facilities that do not subscribe to this philosophy, and it is not always used by facilities that do (Hawes, Rose, & Phillips, 1999). The result is that there is no single accepted definition of AL or guidelines for how to operationally distinguish it from other forms of care. This controversy notwithstanding, there are an estimated 37,000 such facilities in the United States today, housing between 700,000 and a million residents (Golant, 2004). Given the history of AL, it is not surprising that AL facilities range from those in private, converted houses with fewer than 10 beds to those on multilevel campuses with more than 1,400 beds; that some AL facilities have private apartments, whereas others have four residents per room; and that rates range from less than $400 to more than $4,000 per month (Lewin-VHI, 1996). Further, between 38 and 49% of residents have a chronic heart condition (figures vary, depending on the type of facility in which they live), 15 to 37% are dependent in at least one activity of daily living, and 23 to 42% have moderate or more severe cognitive impairment (Zimmerman et al., 2003). This diversity in

TABLE 61.1. The Philosophy of Assisted Living

1. Offer personalized, cost-effective, quality supportive services in a safe residential environment.

2. Maximize the independence of each resident.

3. Treat each resident with dignity and respect.

4. Promote the individuality of each resident.

5. Protect each resident's right to privacy.

6. Provide each resident the choice of services and lifestyles and the right to negotiate risk associated with that choice.

7. Involve residents and include family and friends in service planning and implementation when requested by a competent resident or when appropriate for incompetent residents.

8. Provide opportunity for residents to develop and maintain relationships in the broader community.

9. Minimize the need to move.

10. Involve residents in policy decisions affecting resident life.

11. Make full consumer disclosure before move in.

12. Ensure that potential residents are fully informed regarding the setting's approach and capacity to serve individuals with cognitive and physical impairments.

13. Ensure that specialized programs (e.g., for residents with dementia) have a written statement of philosophy and mission reflecting how the setting can meet the specialized needs of the resident.

14. Ensure that residents can receive health services provided as they would be within their own home.

15. Ensure that assisted living, while health care–related, focuses primarily on a supportive environment designed to maintain an individual's ability to function independently for as long as possible.

16. Ensure that assisted living, with its residential emphasis, avoids the visual and procedural characteristics of an "institutional" setting.

17. Ensure that assisted living, with its focus on the customer, lends itself to personalized services emphasizing the particular needs of the individual and his/her choice of lifestyle. The watchwords should be "creativity," "variety," and "innovation."

Source: Assisted Living Quality Coalition (1998).

care and the increasing levels of resident need have raised concerns related to the quality of care and spurred activity to regulate AL (Kane & Wilson, 2001). It is to these regulatory activities that we now turn.

ASSISTED LIVING REGULATION

The regulatory environment in AL is dynamic, with regulations continuing to evolve as AL emerges as an alternative to other forms of long-term care. Unlike nursing homes, there is no overarching federal regulatory body for AL; instead, individual states are empowered to define, license, regulate, fund, and oversee AL. Between the years 2000 and 2002, virtually every state addressed issues of AL regulation, doing so with regulatory models ranging from those that are highly defined and prescriptive with detailed criteria, to those that are broad and general, using criteria as nonspecific as "meeting resident needs" (Mollica, 2002). To further complicate the issue, approximately one third of states do not even use the term *assisted living* in their licensing regulations. Further, only slightly more than half of the states describe their philosophy of care as part of their regulations, with the language of some (e.g., Oregon) going so far as to include terms such as autonomy, dignity, and choice.

Models of AL Licensure

Overall, there are four models of state AL licensure: board and care or institutional, new housing and services, service, and umbrella. *Institutional models* reflect a more traditional board-and-care philosophy of AL, with minimal attention paid to matters such as privacy (e.g., the proportion of shared rooms and baths). In some states, this model prohibits the provision of nursing services and the retention of residents requiring them; in other states, nursing services are allowed for limited or even longer periods of time. In general, admission and discharge requirements relate to the level of support needed for activities of daily living and medical care. In total, in 2002, 11 states embraced an institutional model (Mollica, 2002). The *new housing and services model* of licensure specifies services that are defined by law or regulation, as well as the need for apartment-type settings, thereby differentiating AL from traditional board-and-care homes. The regulations are more flexible than those in the institutional model, by allowing retention of residents who are eli-

gible for nursing home services. Twelve states embraced this model in 2002, including Hawaii, Kansas, Oregon, and Vermont. The *service model* of care focuses solely on the services provided by facilities rather than the structure of facilities themselves; in many of the 16 states espousing this model, building requirements are covered by other state or local agencies in the form of building codes. Connecticut and Texas use the service model. Finally, an *umbrella model* of licensing covers a variety of housing and services with names such as residential care, congregate care, and adult care homes, as well as AL. The commonality of these states is that they allow for two or more types of housing and services, and among the 12 states (plus the District of Columbia) that have adopted an umbrella model are Florida, Maryland, New Jersey, and North Carolina (Mollica, 2002).

Four areas that have received notable attention within the regulatory models are the living unit, the residents (admission and retention criteria), staffing requirements, and services.

The Living Unit

The living unit is perhaps the most controversial area under regulation, reflecting conflict in policy requirements. Board-and-care homes meet minimal requirements, allowing for shared bedrooms and bathrooms. Regulations more focused on the AL philosophy, however, emphasize privacy and a homelike atmosphere and specify single-occupancy and apartment-style living (Mollica, 1998). When the U.S. Senate Special Committee on Aging recently convened an AL workgroup of 49 national organizations to develop guidelines for policy, regulation, and operations, there was no agreement on the need for private rooms because restricting the living unit in this manner was seen to have the unfortunate consequence of reducing consumer choice—an antithesis to the cornerstone of AL (Assisted Living Workgroup, 2003).

The Residents

Admission and retention criteria have a profound effect on the practice of AL. These policies define the client population and the limits as to which, and the mechanisms whereby, AL residents are allowed to age in place. Across the states, they range from no specification (e.g., Alaska, Connecticut, and Hawaii) to very specific exclusionary criteria, such as number of activities of daily living with which a resident can need assistance (e.g., Illinois). The intent of these regulations is to restrict resident need to the services that the facility is able to provide or secure—although in some states (e.g., New Jersey), acceptable levels of need may be as high as those necessitating 24-hour nursing care. Discharge criteria may relate to general needs (e.g., for 24-hour nursing), health conditions (e.g., stage III or IV pressure ulcers), functional status (e.g., bedridden or nonambulatory), cognitive status, or behavior (Bentley, Sabo, & Waye, 2003; Mollica, 1998). One motivation behind function as a discharge criterion relates to resident safety, as residents must be able to evacuate the building on their own in case of emergency. The field of AL allows for variability across facilities, however, and Pennsylvania facilities, for example, can admit nonambulatory residents if the facility can meet additional staffing, fire, and safety regulations (Mollica, 2002).

In reference to cognitive status, approximately three quarters of the states specify requirements related to serving residents with Alzheimer's disease or other forms of dementia. Kansas requires that facilities that admit residents with dementia train staff to treat behavioral symptoms, Louisiana requires that they provide an enclosed area next to the facility for wandering, Washington requires that facilities make special safety provisions to prevent elopement, and Missouri requires that the residents be capable of self-evacuation. Tennessee is unique in stating that facilities cannot admit or permit the continued stay of any resident in the latter stages of Alzheimer's disease (Bentley et al., 2003). Many of the regulations address issues related to special care units for residents with Alzheimer's disease and other dementias, as well (Mollica, 2002).

Behavioral problems are almost universally acknowledged in state regulations as prohibitions to admission or reasons for discharge, and they are commonly referred to as those that pose a danger to self and/or others, such as wandering, or are socially inappropriate. Also, the need for restraints is frequently specified as a prohibition against admission or retention. However, once again, exceptions are allowed: Ohio, for example, instead of requiring discharge, allows staff to have training on intervening with residents who display behavioral symptoms (Bentley et al., 2003).

The Staff

Residents in more than two thirds of AL facilities contract with home health agencies to provide nursing care, and a similar number of facilities contract with hospice agencies (National Center for Assisted Living, 1998). Thus, considerations of AL staffing levels and qualifications reflect the expectation that nonfacility staff may be providing resident care. Similar to the variability in models of care and resident characteristics, staffing requirements vary across states. Of the 15 states that specify minimum staffing levels, requirements range from one staff person per 40 residents (Missouri) to one staff person per 6 residents (Alabama); instead of ratios, other states designate a minimum number of care hours (e.g., one hour per resident day in Pennsylvania). Most states have separate staffing requirements for waking and sleeping hours and do not differentiate among different types of direct care staff (National Center for Assisted Living, 2000). Among those states without minimum staffing levels or care hours, 15 require the presence or on-call availability of a direct-care staff person 24 hours a day, Connecticut and New Jersey require 24-hour registered nurse (RN) availability, and others require the presence of an RN when medicines are administered or other nursing tasks are performed. The majority of states require that staffing be "sufficient to meet the needs of residents in the facility," allowing facility managers to decide this level and the complaint and survey process to assure that it is adequate (Hodlewsky, 2001).

Many state regulations include requirements for administrator and direct care staff background and training, including minimum age, educational level, years of work experience, and licensure requirements. For administrators, the minimum age ranges from 18 to 21 years. Although several states require only a high school diploma or its equivalent, Connecticut requires that administrators have an RN, and New York requires a master's degree in social work (MSW). Half of the states require some form of licensure, certification, or competency. Training is variably specified, in terms of required topics or hours. For example, Missouri requires administrators to be trained in medication administration, and Ohio requires "100 credit hours of post-high school education in the field of gerontology, if the administrator is not a licensed administrator or does not hold a college degree." Fifteen states have requirements for experience, either in conjunction with or in lieu of education, and 31 require continuing education. Several states require criminal background checks. Requirements for direct care staff follow much the same organizational framework but are more modest (Bentley et al., 2003).

The Services

Services required or allowed under regulation include medical services (e.g., general physician, podiatry, dentistry, nursing), social services, and support services, such as barber or beauty services. In one study of more than 1,200 AL facilities across the United States that had at least 11 beds, 71% of facilities reported having a licensed nurse on staff (Hawes, Phillips, Rose, Holan, & Sherman, 2003); this number was lower (47%) in a study that defined AL facilities as those with as few as 4 beds (Zimmerman et al., 2005). In this more inclusive examination, on-site physician services were provided by between 43 and 72% of facilities, psychotherapy/counseling by between 25 and 78% of facilities, case management/social work by between 36 and 64% of facilities, and weekly exercise and social activities by 44 and 95% of facilities (Zimmerman, Eckert, & Wildfire, 2001).

In addition to services provided in the facility, third-party services (provided by entities other than the facility staff) are common. They may be contracted by the resident, the resident's family, or the facility itself. The two most common third-party services are home health care (e.g., skilled nursing, occupational and physical therapy, dietary consultation, wound care, medication management) and hospice. Both treat the AL facility as the resident's primary home and provide the same services they do to community-dwelling individuals. Regulations in 35 states specify that home health services be allowable, although there is again variability, such as whether services need to be of a time-limited nature (as is the case in Arkansas) or expressly not interfere with services provided to other residents (as is the case in Alaska and Delaware) (Bentley et al., 2003).

An Important Caveat

The existence of state-based regulation should not be taken to assume homogeneity within states with reference to the living unit, the residents, the staff, the services, or any other component of AL care. Instead, the criteria set forth by regulation set parameters for care, and providers have the latitude to structure and provide care as they see fit within those guidelines.

ASSISTED LIVING FUNDING

With the growth of AL and its provision of services to impaired older adults, there has been an increasing trend toward the public subsidy of AL. In 1998, 32 states provided funding for AL services, a number that increased to 41 by 2003 (Bentley et al., 2003; Mollica, 2002). Methods of payment are diverse, with states providing payment as a flat rate (32%) or tiered rate (27%) or in accordance with care plans (24%) or resident case mix (<1%). In addition, three states combine two payment methods, one varies rates by region, and another negotiates rates. Twelve states allow room and board to be covered, but doing so constitutes an ongoing controversy (Mollica, 2002): Because AL is a residential setting based on a social model rather than a medical model of care, the implication is that room and board is a primary service; however, room and board traditionally have been (and continue to be) excluded from Medicaid coverage.

Specific reimbursement strategies for AL have evolved as the industry has developed. Private sources (i.e., resident and family funds) continue to provide the majority of payments (75%), with trivial additional amounts from long-term care insurance (<2%) and managed care (<2%) (National Center for Assisted Living, 2001). The remaining costs are covered through a combination of Medicaid waivers, state funds, and supplemental security income (SSI). The most common source of Medicaid funding is the Medicaid 2176 Home- and Community-Based Care Waiver (1915[c]). This funding is available to beneficiaries who would qualify for skilled nursing home care and meet the eligibility criteria of income less than 300% of SSI. Approximately 35 states have waiver plans in place, with some setting limits on the number of recipients (Bentley et al., 2003; Mollica, 2001b, 2002). Ten state plans also use Medicaid funding but do not do so through the waiver and have more lenient enrollment criteria: Recipients need not require skilled medical services and can meet more conservative financial criteria, such receiving SSI or qualifying for Medicaid. The state plan is an entitlement, and the services must be provided to all beneficiaries who meet the criteria. States also may provide funds directly, often to supplement SSI beyond federal levels.

ISSUES IN ASSISTED LIVING

In a field as evolving and variable as AL, a multitude of issues are of interest to the social work community. The three addressed here relate to the quality of care: socioeconomic and racial disparity in access and quality; autonomy, negotiated risk, and aging in place; and recognizing and treating psychosocial needs.

Disparity in Access and Quality

Early board-and-care type AL primarily served low-income older adults who could not live independently and relied on Medicaid, SSI, or other state and federal government funds. As AL grew and the business community recognized it as a profit-making opportunity, a schism developed between modest facilities catering to residents of lesser means and more upscale AL serving residents able to afford substantial private-pay rates (Kane & Wilson, 2001). As a consequence, the AL industry is largely private pay and unaffordable for low- or moderate-income persons, and due to these economic and other social factors, the proportion of AL residents who are minorities is minimal (i.e., 46 to 71% of facilities have no African American residents). Most African Americans reside in smaller facilities in rural, nonpoor, African American communities, which score less well on some ratings of environmental quality. This separation may result from economic factors, exclusionary practices, or resident choice, and attention is needed as to whether there are inequities in the quality of care they receive (Howard et al., 2002).

Autonomy, Negotiated Risk, and Aging in Place

The philosophy of AL is to promote control and choice, yet doing so can be a liability to providers if control and choice impede resident safety. Negotiated risk agreements are signed agreements between residents and providers that expressly state that the resident chooses to accept certain risks associated with care in order to maximize preferences (e.g., the choice to not adhere to dietary restrictions or medication schedules). Although 19 states have incorporated negotiated risk as part of their regulation, they are met by objections from the nursing home industry because they reduce nursing home admissions (Mollica, 2001b, 2002). Indeed, when a resident chooses to accept that the AL facility is not able to meet his or her needs, negotiated risk agreements are a mechanism to promote aging in place. Balancing autonomy, safety, and quality of life in AL is an ongoing challenge, however, and one of definite interest to the social worker (Kissam, Gifford, More, & Patry, 2003).

Recognizing and Treating Psychosocial Needs

Between 23 and 42% of AL residents have moderate or more severe cognitive impairment, 13% are depressed, and although more than 90% of residents participate in at least one social activity per week, those who are cognitively or functionally impaired do so less often (Golant, 2004; Watson, Garrett, Sloane, Gruber-Baldini, & Zimmerman, 2003; Zimmerman, Gruber-Baldini, et al., 2003; Zimmerman, Scott, et al., 2003). In consideration of the limited staff training requirements noted earlier, there is cause to believe that AL providers are not expert in the care of these conditions and that there is room for social work services in AL.

THE SOCIAL WORKER IN ASSISTED LIVING

Despite earlier reference to psychotherapy and case management/social work services in AL, by and large these services are not provided by individuals with a social work degree. However, given the levels of resident need and staff training, roles similar to those filled by hospital and nursing home social workers might similarly benefit AL residents.

When older persons face increased care needs, hospital social workers assist them and their family members in considering whether long-term care placement is indicated. This decision is not an easy one, as it raises competing values such as autonomy and safety. That is, group living by design places some restrictions on choice but at the same time increases safety by providing ongoing oversight. In AL, as prospective residents and their families first tour the facility, social workers can encourage them to address these feelings and values through active participation, collaborative decision making, and problem solving (Spano & Koenig, 2003). At the same time, the social worker might function in a role similar to that in nursing homes, considering whether the placement is an appropriate one and later helping residents make the transition into the new environment. In this regard, their ability to assess mental health needs and foster communication among the resident, family members, and staff in the development and implementation of resident care plans could be especially helpful (Ingersoll-Dayton, Schroepfer, Pryce, & Waarala, 2003; Kruzich & Powell, 1995).

These hospital and nursing home social work roles must be adjusted to the AL environment, of course. Whereas older persons often experience a medical crisis as a precipitant to nursing home admission (Borrayo, Salmon, Polivka, & Dunlop, 2002), residents in AL typically are less ill and disabled than those in nursing homes (Zimmerman, Gruber-Baldini, et al., 2003). Thus, these admissions are more planned and less crisis-driven. They are likely to be motivated by a need for assistance with activities of daily living, general oversight, or increased social interaction or in anticipation of impending need among comparatively independent older adults. Also, the decision to seek AL placement is usually intended to be for an extended period of time, whereas nursing home placement may be transient during a period of convalescence. The skills that social workers possess that make them able to serve in hospital and nursing home settings position them well for AL work, and familiarity with the AL settings and the residents will enable them to provide services to facilitate decision making, transition, care, and ultimate quality of life.

In addition to recognizing this viable social work role within AL, note that some social workers who are not directly employed by AL settings already provide services to them and their residents and families, such as case managers for Medicaid waiver programs and hospital discharge planners who facilitate AL placement. However, these workers may not understand the variability of AL services and the overlap of these residents with those of nursing homes; as a result, they may not be as expert as necessary to provide optimal social work services. Consequently, there remains a need to consider the development of a true AL social worker. Unfortunately, the inherent challenge in this quest is to secure the financial buy-in of public entities and profit-making companies to support the work. Thus, a goal of AL research should be to determine the true utility of—and therefore have an impact on the future existence of—the currently fictional AL social worker.

REFERENCES

Assisted Living Quality Coalition. (1998). *Assisted living quality initiative. Building a structure that promotes quality.* Washington, DC: Public Policy Institute, American Association of Retired Persons.

Assisted Living Workgroup. (2003). *Assuring quality in assisted living: Guidelines for federal and state policy, state regulation, and operations. A report to the U.S. Senate Special Committee on Aging.* Washington, DC: Author.

Bentley, L., Sabo, S., & Waye, A. (2003). *Assisted living state regulatory review.* Retrieved June 10, 2004, from *http://www.ncal.org/about/2003_reg_review.pdf.*

Bishop, C. E. (1999). Where are the missing elders? The decline in nursing home use, 1985 and 1995. *Health Affairs, 18,* 146–155.

Borra, P. C. (1986). Assisted living a timely alternative. *Provider, 12,* 14, 16–17.

Borrayo, E. A., Salmon, J. R., Polivka, L., & Dunlop, B. D. (2002). Utilization across the continuum of long-term care services. *The Gerontologist, 42,* 603–612.

Golant, S. M. (2004). Do impaired older persons with health care needs occupy U.S. assisted living facilities? An analysis of six national studies. *Journal of Gerontology Social Sciences, 59*(2), S68–79.

Hawes, C., Phillips, C. D., Rose, M., Holan, S., & Sherman, M. (2003). A national survey of assisted living facilities, *The Gerontologist, 43,* 875–882.

Hawes, C., Rose, M., & Phillips, C. D. (1999). *A national study of assisted living for the frail elderly. Executive summary: Results of a national survey of facilities.* Beachwood, OH: Meyers Research Institute.

Hodlewsky, R. T. (2001). Staffing problems and strategies in assisted living. In S. Zimmerman, P. D. Sloane, & J. K. Eckert (Eds.), *Assisted living: Needs, policies and practices in residential care for the elderly.* Baltimore: Johns Hopkins University Press.

Howard, D. L., Sloane, P. D., Zimmerman, S., Eckert, J. K., Walsh, J., Buie, V. C., et al. (2002). Distribution of African Americans in residential care/assisted living: More evidence of racial disparity? *American Journal of Public Health, 92,* 1272–1277.

Ingersoll-Dayton, B., Schroepfer, T., Pryce, J., & Waarala, C. (2003). Enhancing relationships in nursing homes through empowerment. *Social Work, 48,* 420–424.

Kane, R., & Wilson, K. B. (Eds.). (1993). *Assisted living in the United States: A new paradigm for residential care for frail older persons?* Washington, DC: Public Policy Institute, American Association of Retired Persons.

Kane, R., & Wilson, K. B. (2001). *Assisted living at the crossroads: Principles for its future.* Portland: The Jessie F. Richardson Foundation.

Kissam, S., Gifford, D. R., More, V., & Patry, G. (2003). Admission and continued-stay criteria for assisted living facilities. *Journal of the American Geriatrics Society, 51,* 1651–1654.

Korcok, M. (1987). "Assisted living": Developing an alternative to nursing homes. *Canadian Medical Association Journal, 137,* 843–845.

Kruzich, J. M., & Powell, W. E. (1995). Decision-making influence: An empirical study of social workers in nursing homes. *Health and Social Work, 20,* 215–222.

Lewin-VHI, Inc. (1996). *National study of assisted living for the frail elderly. Literature review update.* Contract No. HHS-1-94-0024. Washington, DC: U.S. Department of Health and Human Services.

Mollica, R. (1998). *State assisted living policy, 1998.* Retrieved June 10, 2004, from *http://aspe.os.dhhs.gov/daltcp/reports/98state.htm.*

Mollica, R. (2001a). The evolution of assisted living: A view from the states. *Caring, 20,* 24–26.

Mollica, R. (2001b). State policy and regulations. In S. Zimmerman, P. D. Sloane, & J. K. Eckert (Eds.), *Assisted living: Needs, policies and practices in residential care for the elderly.* Baltimore: Johns Hopkins University Press.

Mollica, R. (2002). *State assisted living policy, 2002.* Retrieved August 18, 2005, from *http://www.nashp.org/Files/ltc_15_AL_2002.pdf.*

Morgan, L. A., Eckert, J. K., & Lyon, S. M. (Eds.). (1995). *Small board-and-care homes: Residential care in transition.* Baltimore: Johns Hopkins University Press.

National Center for Assisted Living. (1998). *Facts and trends: The assisted living sourcebook, 1998.* Washington, DC: American Health Care Association.

National Center for Assisted Living. (2000). *Assisted living state regulatory review, 2000.* Washington, DC: American Health Care Association.

National Center for Assisted Living. (2001). *Assisted living: Independence, choice and dignity.* Retrieved June 10, 2004, from *http://www.ncal.org/about/alicd.pdf.*

Spano, R., & Koenig, T. (2003). Moral dialogue: A worker-client interactional model. *Social Thought, 22,* 91–104.

Sullivan, J. G. (1998). Redefining long term care. *Contemporary Long Term Care, 21,* 60–64.

Thompson, J. M., & Marinaccio, L. (1997). Improve continuity of care through collaboration: The growth of assisted living provides opportunities for nursing homes. *Balance, 1,* 14–15.

Watson, L., Garrett, J. M., Sloane, P. D., Gruber-Baldini, A. L., & Zimmerman, S. (2003). Depression in assisted living: Results from a four-state study. *American Journal of Geriatric Psychiatry, 11,* 534–542.

Zimmerman, S., Eckert, J. K., & Wildfire, J. B. (2001). The process of care. In S. Zimmerman, P. D. Sloane, & J. K. Eckert (Eds.), *Assisted living: Needs, policies and practices in residential care for the elderly.* Baltimore: Johns Hopkins University Press.

Zimmerman, S., Gruber-Baldini, A. L., Sloane, P. D., Eckert, J. K., Hebel, J. R., Morgan, L. A., et al. (2003). Assisted living and nursing homes: Apples and oranges? *The Gerontologist, 43,* 107–117.

Zimmerman, S., Scott, A. C., Park, N. S., Hall, S. A., Wetherby, M. M., Gruber-Baldini, A. L., et al. (2003). Social engagement and its relationship to service provision in residential care/assisted living. *Social Work Research, 27,* 6–18.

Zimmerman, S., Sloane, P. D., Eckert, J. K., Gruber-Baldini, A. L., Morgan, L. A., Hebel, R., et al. (2005). How good is assisted living? Findings and implications from an outcomes study. *Journal of Gerontology Social Sciences, 60B,* 195–204.

Zimmerman, S. I., Sloane, P. D., & Eckert, J. K. (2001). The state and quality of assisted living. In L. S. Noelker & Z. Harel (Eds.), *Linking quality of long-term care and quality of life.* New York: Springer.

VERA PROSPER

Adult Foster Care and Adult Family Care

62

The terms "adult foster care" and "adult family care" are used interchangeably (Folkemer, Jensen, Lipson, Stauffer, & Fox-Grage, 1996; Sherman & Newman, 1988). Both generally refer to "a service characterized by small, family-run homes that provide room, board, and varying levels of supervision, oversight, and assistance to individuals who are unable to care for themselves alone" (Folkemer et al., 1996). In defining foster care and family care, Sherman and Newman (1988) refer to "a private host family (or a single person) taking into their home a small number of adults (usually one to three, but no more than about six)." In their research, the concept includes "the provision of support services, supervision, and/or personal care"; and residents' "participation in the life of the family (without infantilization of the foster resident) and in the community are encouraged." Blanchette (1997) states that "adult foster care does not have a clearly defined philosophy like assisted living, but almost all states with adult foster care programs share the goal of providing services and care to residents in a family-like environment . . ." and "place an emphasis on maintaining a family-like atmosphere for residents."

Providing housing, care, and supervision for adults in a foster family environment has a long history as an alternative to an institutionalized environment and was used as placement for dependent adults long before it was used for children (Sherman & Newman, 1992). "Opening one's home to unrelated, dependent adults has been in operation for centuries in Europe"; and while "adult foster home care specifically for the elderly is a relatively recent development . . . Massachusetts officially began to operate a foster family care program for mentally ill adults in 1885" (Sherman & Newman, 1988). Despite its long history and the prevalence of homes, Reinardy and Kane (1999) note that "policymakers' and practitioners' knowledge about adult foster care . . . is scant."

Elsie Fetterman, an advocate for adult foster care (AFC), called these homes an "invisible" option, suggesting that the variety of names given to this concept contributes to its low visibility as an identifiable alternative (Burns, 1996). Fetterman noted that the Veterans Administration calls the option "community residential care," while others bundle AFC programs under terms such as "county home," "board and care," "geriatric foster care," "shelter home," and "alternative home." In the Folkemer et al. (1996) national survey of AFC, 26 states reported having a fully developed AFC program, and an additional 8 reported having a limited program or an intent to develop an AFC program. Program names included adult foster care, family care rest home program, adult family care homes, adult residential care home, family-life home program, the CARE program, project home, homes plus, residential facilities for groups, family-type homes for adults, certified foster home, and domiciliary care services for adults. Other terminology for the concept includes rest homes, personal care homes, individual residence alternative, Homeshare program, sheltered care, and community residential care.

In recent years, the concept of AFC has expanded beyond those operated by families to include "nonfamily AFC homes," which are owned and operated by nonprofit agencies, businesses, and corporations and in which the operator does not live in the home and is not the primary caregiver. These versions are emerging in response to the growing number of elderly people, as well as younger persons with a variety of disabilities, who are living longer and with more extensive care needs. Folkemer et al. (1996) did not disaggregate their surveyed homes by ownership (except for Oregon) but reported that 12 states authorize the provision of AFC in non-family-run homes. The authors note that an increasing share of AFC homes in three states (Oregon, Washington, and Minnesota) are owned and operated by businesses.

Although names, regulatory oversight, and public funding for AFC vary among states, enough similarities exist to enable placing family-based AFC in an identifiable housing-and-care category: (a) placement is available for clients age 18 and over; (b) clients are not fully capable of living alone and include frail elderly persons and younger individuals with physical impairments, developmental disabilities, or mental illness; (c) placement is in the home of the operator; (d) clients are unrelated to the operator; (e) the operator is the primary caregiver; (f) the number of clients per home is limited (primarily, between one and four or six); (g) care provided by the operator includes room and board, socialization, supervision and oversight, assistance with instrumental activities of daily living (IADLs), and varying levels of personal care assistance with activities of daily living (ADLs) but does not include skilled nursing or medical care; (h) the philosophical intent is to allow the client to maintain as much independence as possible within a family setting; (i) both private pay and various public reimbursement options are used for payment; and (j) programs operate within a public regulatory framework.

ADULT FOSTER CARE HOMES VIS-À-VIS OTHER HOUSING OPTIONS

The term "board and care homes" is also often used interchangeably with AFC homes. The definitions, as well as the types of residents and the level of services and care provided in each, are often similar. However, board and care is often a generic term for both licensed and unlicensed options, covering "a wide range of residential environments, sometimes including life care communities, congregate housing for the elderly, and what is currently known as assisted living" (Hawes, Wildfire, & Lux, 1993). In general, several features of board and care homes distinguish them from AFC: (a) There is great diversity in the size of board and care homes, with the number of residents ranging from 2 to 200 (Blanchette, 1997; Phillips et al., 1995); (b) Blanchette (1997) states that no consistent philosophy or approach to care characterizes board and care homes; and (c) Phillips et al. (1995) report that unlicensed board and care homes may be as numerous as licensed facilities and that while some homes are family- or individual-operated, more than 80% are operated by for-profit entities, with 33% of operators owning and operating multiple board and care facilities.

Over time, trends in demographics, public policy, and consumer markets have led to a blurring of definitional lines among housing options. For example, (a) in response to the burgeoning numbers of older persons, the variety of housing options for elderly people has increased significantly. These, too, are known by many names, including:

- active adult communities
- senior housing
- supportive housing
- congregate housing
- enriched housing
- assisted living
- retirement homes
- adult homes
- residential care facilities
- continuing care retirement communities

Two major characteristics distinguish AFC homes from these alternatives: size and residents' functional status. Typically, these senior models house more than the four to six individuals seen in AFC homes, and a considerable portion of senior housing developments are meant for individuals who can live independently on their own. (b) As do AFC homes, shared living residences, Abbeyfield Houses, and apartment-based shared housing programs house both elderly and nonelderly persons. They share the small size and physical space characteristic of AFC homes, as well as the administrative involvement of a community agency, the provision of supportive services, and, sometimes, live-in staff. However, unlike family-based AFC, these models are owned and operated by a community agency. Unlike business-owned AFC homes, these models are primarily not licensed to provide assistance with activities of daily living. (c) Group homes for persons of all ages with developmental, physical, or mental disabilities have proliferated in response to public policy changes, which have evolved in response to court decrees and consumer-won legislation that focus on housing people in community-integrated living environments in place of institutionalized facilities. Group homes share the size, licensure, physical-space, and service characteristics of AFC but are not family-based. (d) There has been a recent movement to create nursing homes that house seven or eight residents and emphasize resident empowerment and "living as a family." They share the size, physical space, and regulatory oversight characteristics of AFC homes but provide the higher levels of care required of a nursing home, and the ownership is not family based. (e) Various states' public policy strategies to contain the costs of long-term care have led them to consolidate previously distinct levels of care and housing under a single name, licensure category, and funding mechanism. For example, "assisted living" is sometimes used to encompass several housing options and/or service programs, including AFC homes. Tied to consolidation, states are increasingly turning to Medicaid home- and community-based waivers as a funding mechanism to increase flexibility and efficiency in long-term care service delivery. The AFC program, traditionally funded primarily through the Supplemental Security Income program (SSI), is sometimes included as a covered option under a state's Medicaid waiver.

CHARACTERISTICS OF ADULT FOSTER CARE HOMES

Prevalence

The most recent national measure of AFC homes was conducted by Folkemer et al. in 1996. Sixteen states reported limited or no AFC programs, and eight states did not respond to the survey. Twenty-six states reported their number of AFC homes: One had fewer than 100 homes, nine had 128 to 494 homes, five had 570 to 969 homes, and five had 1,334 to 2,160 homes. Oregon had 2,242 commercial homes in addition to its 1,500 family-based homes. Twenty-two states reported a combined total of 34,386 residents living in AFC homes. For the 16 states that reported both the number of homes and the number of residents, the average number of residents per home was 3.1. In Oregon, 9,396 persons lived in 2,242 business-operated homes, for an average of 4.2 persons per home.

Providers

Folkemer et al.'s (1996) study showed that 14 of the 26 reporting states allow only family-run AFC homes and that, generally, states require providers to reside in the home and provide 24-hour supervision. Adult foster care homes are located in residential areas, with more than 50% in rural areas (Sherman & Newman, 1988). Often, housing developers do not construct and operate multiunit housing for seniors and younger people with disabilities in rural areas because they find it financially unfeasible to develop a facility that is small enough for the limited population base in these areas. Using the existing homes of AFC providers for the targeted client size of one to six people makes AFC an ideal long-term care model for rural areas.

The primary objective of AFC is placement in a "family" environment and "to provide the best opportunity for enjoyment of normal family and community life" (Sherman & Newman, 1988). The authors report that fewer than 30% of providers consisted of a husband, wife, and children; another 25% consisted of a husband and wife with no children; 11% were a single parent and children; and the remainder were single persons, primarily females. As they note, in about 20% of the homes, the provider had no other family members in the home and it was the addition of the foster care client(s) that created a family.

In the growing number of business-owned AFC homes, services and care are provided by hired staff and outside agencies. Business ownership models include nonprofit agencies and for-profit businesses, single-home and multiple-home owners, and community-based owners and those based farther away.

Resident Populations

Adult foster care residents range in age from 18 to over 90, and the majority are female. They are characterized by varying educational levels; varying physical and mental status, including dementia; and varying marital status, although the majority are widowed or never married (Sherman & Newman, 1988).

Residents of AFC homes are typically deemed unable to live independently on their own; however, the functional profile of these residents varies significantly. Some require the social, interactive environment of living with others, others are mildly to severely physically or cognitively impaired, others have chronic mental health issues, and yet others are physically well but have lifelong developmental disabilities. In all states, AFC operators can serve discrete (age or functional status) or heterogeneous populations. Sherman and Newman (1988) cite Mor, Sherwood, and Gutkin's 1986 national study, which showed that more than half of surveyed programs served a heterogeneous population and fewer than half served only one client group. Folkemer et al. (1996) found overall population heterogeneity: In 11 states, the majority of all AFC residents are elderly; in 6 states, the majority are nonelderly; and in one state, half are elderly and half are not. Sherman and Newman's 1988 study of homes in New York State found that segregation of residents by sex was more pronounced than segregation by age, with most homes housing either all women or all men.

Longevity and relocation patterns among the general elderly population have resulted in residents in the various senior housing models being characterized by increasing age, greater functional impairment levels, and increasing incidence of dementia. As there have been few recent studies focusing on AFC, there is little information to indicate whether, overall, elderly residents in AFC homes are following these same trends. Some evidence is provided by Folkemer et al.'s 1996 survey, which pointed to the growing trend in business-owner models as a response to residents' higher service needs. Reinardy and Kane's (1999) work in Oregon provides further insight: They found that although AFC residents had significantly less disability, on average, than nursing home residents, the populations overlapped. However, if reimbursed by Medicaid, AFC residents in Oregon must be eligible for nursing homes. The authors also reported that private-pay residents had more disabilities than the Medicaid clientele.

Services

In addition to the room and board, 24-hour supervision, and assistance with IADLs and ADLs provided by the operator, residents can utilize additional services from the wider community, such as day care, home health care, therapy, mental health services, transportation, medical equipment, temporary skilled nursing, and, in a limited number of states where nursing facility or Medicaid waivers are employed, intensive, ongoing medical and nursing care.

Folkemer et al.'s (1996) survey of the 26 states that license or certify AFC homes showed that (a) all applicants are assessed for eligibility, (b) 17 states require a care plan for each resident, and (c) 8 provide case management for all residents, 12 require this service only for publicly funded residents, 4 provide case management for some clients (for example, mental health clients, residents with intensive needs, residents with developmental disabilities), and 2 do not require case management.

Rules regarding medication administration vary considerably. In 6 of the 26 surveyed states, AFC providers are allowed to administer medications. Eighteen states prohibit administration of medication by providers but allow administration by appropriate community-based professionals such as a licensed or practical nurse, physician, physician's assistant, or a home health agency; will allow administration by the provider if the provider holds one of these licenses or employs a staff person with such a license; or will allow temporary administration by the operator, with a physician's approval, during a recuperation phase.

Some states specify conditions for resident discharge: for example, a provider may discharge a resident who has unmanageable behavior problems, is a danger to oneself or others, wanders, is unable to ambulate, is suicidal, is bedfast, refuses services, is unable to communicate meaningfully, has certain medical care needs; or needs skilled nursing or a higher level of care than the home can provide. Other states do not state specific discharge criteria but determine the need for discharge on a case basis by judging the capacity of the provider to continue meeting a client's evolving needs.

Staffing and Training

The majority of states with licensed or certified AFC homes require providers or a formally designated person to reside in the home and provide 24-hour supervision. Nighttime supervision need not be "awake"; however, a few states state that 24-hour awake supervision is required for residents in high-care categories.

Training required or given to AFC providers ranges from none to training to provide skilled nursing care (Sherman & Newman, 1988). Folkemer et al.'s 1996 survey confirms Sherman and Newman's conclusion, finding that while 21 of 26 states "indicated that some form of initial orientation or training was required for AFC providers and staff . . . no clear pattern on the scope and nature of the orientation and training emerges." Folkemer et al. (1996) cluster states by six approaches to training: Five states require an initial orientation and annual training, seven require initial orientation or training but no subsequent annual training, five require that the operator have experience in direct service and also require initial orientation and/or annual training, and two require no initial orientation but require annual training, two states allow training and experience requirements to be determined by local staff, and in five states, no training or experience is specified. When training is required, there is significant variation in the amount of training hours required, the training topics covered, whether training is formal or informal, and whether the provider's or staff's required training status must be a specific professional level, such as a certified nurse's aide, licensed practical nurse, registered nurse, and so on.

As more states bundle AFC into a home- and community-based waiver, training requirements and staff qualifications may increase. For example, in Oregon (Folkemer et al., 1996), which includes AFC in a waiver program, AFC can be a consumer's alternative choice to a nursing home. Foster home caregivers must attend 18 hours of preservice training plus 10 hours of training annually, and staff may perform nursing tasks if they are trained and certified by a nurse.

Regulatory Environment

There are no national standards for AFC (Folkemer et al., 1996). There are an unsubstantiated number of individuals, families, and entities who provide a living environment and care that are comparable to AFC, serving similar numbers and types of clients, but are not licensed or do not require licensure or certification. For licensed or certified AFC homes, regulatory oversight varies significantly among states. Amount and type of oversight continue to evolve, but no available data provide a current national picture. Folkemer et al.'s 1996 survey is the most recent national survey, but it includes information only from the 26 states that regulate programs that include *both* elderly and

nonelderly persons among the program's residents. States with programs that do not include elderly persons are not included.

A review of the 1996 survey shows that nine states used voluntary certification standards, which are applicable to homes that wish to be identified as AFC providers or be eligible for public reimbursement programs. Certification is typically provided by local social services or aging agencies in accordance with state-determined standards and rules. Homes that do not seek name recognition (as an AFC home) or public funding (instead, residents pay for care with private resources) can legally offer services comparable to AFC without certification, and state rules or standards do not apply to their operation.

In 1996, 14 states required that all homes must be licensed by the state, and 1 state drew a distinction between homes that served private-pay residents (no need for licensure until a home has two or more private-pay residents) and homes that serve public-pay residents (must be licensed if it serves one or more public-pay residents). In 3 states, larger AFC homes required licensure, but smaller ones required certification. Definitions of *large* and *small* differed among the 3 states.

Across the country, various county, regional, and state government agencies are responsible for licensure and oversight, including departments of aging, health, public health and environment, social services, welfare, human resources, human services, family services, mental health, developmental disabilities, veterans affairs, and division of medical assistance (Folkemer et al., 1996; Sherman, 2001). Required on-site inspections of homes vary, occurring every 2 months, 6 months, annually, 18 months, or 2 years. The oversight process varies considerably among states, as well as by the type of regulatory agency and the specific population group under that agency's jurisdiction (elderly persons, mental health clients, and persons with developmental disabilities).

Funding

Licensed and certified AFC homes serve both private-pay residents and publicly subsidized residents. The major source of public funds is the Supplemental Security Income program (SSI). Folkemer et al.'s (1996) 26-state survey shows that 12 states fund the program for income-eligible residents using only the SSI program together with a state supplement to SSI; 3 states combine SSI, an SSI state supplement, and Medicaid;

2 states combine SSI, an SSI supplement, Medicaid, and other state support; 3 use Medicaid and other state support; 2 use Medicaid only; 4 use various combinations of SSI and other state and local support resources; and 1 uses only the social services block grant. Use of Medicaid funds is through a Medicaid home- and community-based waiver or through a Medicaid state plan.

WHY CHOOSE AN ADULT FOSTER HOME?

The greater majority of older people prefer to remain living where they are, in their own longtime homes (AARP, 2000). The increasing age and frailty characteristics of older people who relocate into supportive housing environments, as well as the increasing role that adult children play in making relocation decisions for their elderly family members, provide evidence of that strong preference. In general, older people are adamant about not being a burden to family members, prefer an age-integrated living environment to an age-segregated one, desire maximized autonomy and personal choice during the later years, and strongly reject the rigid, impersonal environment typically associated with nursing homes (Prosper, 1990). An adult foster family home satisfies these strong preferences.

In a study of 260 elderly AFC residents in Oregon, more than 90% reported that supervision and safety and the homelike atmosphere were the most important reasons for choosing their current AFC home, more than 80% reported that privacy was an important reason, and more than 75% said the flexible routine of the home and the personal assistance provided were important reasons (Reinardy & Kane, 1999).

For individuals with mental illness who are being transitioned out of nursing homes and psychiatric facilities and hospitals, AFC homes are an option that can "facilitate the transition of dependent adults into neighborhoods and homes . . . reserving hospitals for the most ill and threatening patients and allowing patients to adjust to community living" (Rhoades, 2000). In describing South Carolina's Homeshare AFC program, Rhoades noted that this AFC option can allow mental health clients to assume roles within the operator's family structure, and community integration becomes the norm in place of the segregation and isolation characterizing institutional placements.

Professionals estimate that the majority of individuals with developmental disabilities never enter the formal services system but remain living at home, with their parents as primary caregivers. They are experienced neither with living on their own nor with living in a congregate housing environment. As with other population groups, there is increasing longevity among individuals with developmental disabilities. Increasingly, their elderly parents are dying or becoming too frail to care for them. Adult foster care homes provide an option that closely replicates their previous living-at-home arrangement, allowing them to age in place in a setting that is environmentally familiar and manageable.

Role for Social Workers

In contrast to other health care professionals, the knowledge, skills, roles, and functions of social workers can be generalized across a great variety of work venues, including AFC homes. While there is limited measurement of the utilization of social workers regarding AFC, the opportunities to take advantage of their expertise and skills are great.

Sherman (1990) describes Kahana's theory of person-environment congruence as a framework for understanding the extent to which a person's well-being will be maximized. A person can be characterized by the types and degrees of her or his various needs and capabilities, and a living environment can be characterized by its capacity to appropriately meet these needs vis-à-vis the person's capabilities. The personality, character, and ambience of AFC homes vary substantially because they are family-based. In reflecting the tenets of Kahana's theory, this presents a significant opportunity to use the talents and skills of social workers to maximize the well-being of AFC clients. As agency caseworkers, social workers can perform the crucial screening and placement task of matching a resident's "personality characteristics, social interests, personal habits, gender, race, religion, cultural factors, smoking, pets, children, location, mental health/psychiatric needs, rehabilitation needs, support service needs, medical needs, alcohol/drug problems, wheelchair accessibility" (Sherman & Newman, 1986) with the characteristics of the provider and the provider's home.

Following placement, social workers can help residents make a successful relocation transition, create individualized care plans, provide ongoing case management tasks, make regular client site visits, act as residents' advocates to assure needs are adequately met, act as liaisons between providers and social service and oversight agencies, and also act as liaisons between residents and their own family members. Social workers can assist both residents and providers during relocations from AFC into higher levels of care. In their academic training, social workers may specialize in a particular area, such as family dynamics, gerontology, substance abuse, mental health, or developmental disabilities. They are a valuable resource for educating and training AFC providers about the characteristics and needs of their resident populations and are an authoritative resource for providing specialized technical assistance when providers encounter a resident situation or circumstance they feel unprepared to address.

Social workers also perform regulatory oversight tasks, assessing the physical environment, the quality of staffing and care provided, and the well-being of residents. For AFC residents who are clients of the mental health and developmental disabilities systems, social workers are members of these systems' multidisciplinary care teams responsible for the placement and care of clients.

Older persons and younger persons with various special needs are living longer lives and, when impaired, living more years with those frailties. More of these individuals, and their caregiver family members, are seeking information and counsel about the various housing and care options available, as well as assistance in negotiating the relocation decision-making process and the actual relocation itself. In response, the field of "housing counseling" has grown and is primarily staffed by professional and paraprofessional social workers. The particular training and skills of social workers make them sensitive to the importance of facilitating the client's sense of control over relocation decisions.

CONCLUSION

AFC homes, as a community-integrated, small, family-based housing and care option, can satisfy the goals of several confluent happenings: (a) The U.S. federal court decision in *Olmstead v. L.C.* requires that people of all ages with disabilities be housed in the most appropriate integrated (into the community) setting possible; (b) the preference of most people is to live in noninstitutionalized, homelike living environments; and (c) public agencies are promoting the expansion of community-based housing and care options as a means of containing the growth in long-term care costs.

Sherman (2001) notes both strengths and weaknesses of AFC as a long-term care option. Strengths include this option's informality, sociability, spontaneity, and familism; the meaningful role AFC provides for the provider; and the greater level of integration of this option into the surrounding community because the provider's private home is less obtrusive than multiunit housing or institutions. Weaknesses include the difficulty of monitoring these small homes, which are dispersed throughout the community; the widely varying staff-to-resident ratios among homes; and the inconsistent level of professionalism of the providers.

This chapter is dedicated to the memory of Susan R. Sherman, who was an extraordinary mentor and inspiration to me. Her voluminous work covering many areas related to older people contributed immensely to the field of aging. Her extensive research and writing regarding living environments for older people, including significant work on adult foster care, made her an acknowledged expert in this subject.

REFERENCES

AARP. (2000). *Fixing to stay: A national survey of housing and home modification issues.* Washington, DC: Author.

Blanchette, K. (1997). *New directions for state long-term care systems, Vol. 3: Supportive housing.* Washington, DC: Public Policy Institute, American Association of Retired Persons.

Burns, R. (1996, February 20). *Adult foster care the best kept "secret," says nationally known expert.* Retrieved May 17, 2004, from *http://overton2.tamu.edu/news/foster2. html.*

Folkemer, D., Jensen, A., Lipson, L., Stauffer, M., & Fox-Grage, W. (1996). *Adult foster care for the elderly: A review of state regulatory and funding strategies* (2 vols.). Washington, DC: American Association of Retired Persons.

Hawes, C., Wildfire, J., & Lux, L. (1993). *The regulation of board and care homes: Results of a survey in the 50 states and the District of Columbia—national summary.* Washington, DC: Public Policy Institute, American Association of Retired Persons.

Phillips, C., Wildfire, J., Hawes, C., Iannacchione, V., Green, R., & Lux, L. (1995). *Report on the effects of regulation on quality of care: Analysis of the effect of regulation on the quality of care in board and care homes.* Research Triangle Park, NC: Research Triangle Institute and Brown University.

Prosper, V. (1990). *Preferences of older persons: Housing older New Yorkers*. Albany: New York State Office for the Aging.

Reinardy, J., & Kane, R. (1999). Choosing an adult foster home or a nursing home: Residents' perceptions about decision making and control. *Social Work, 44*(6), 571–585.

Rhoades, D. (2000). The homeshare model: Caring for individuals with serious mental illness. *Journal of Mental Health Counseling, 22*(1), 59–67.

Sherman, S. R. (1990). Housing. In A. Monk (Ed.), *Handbook of Gerontological Services* (2nd ed., pp. 477–507). New York: Columbia University Press.

Sherman, S. R. (2001). Adult foster care. In G. L. Maddox (Ed.), *Encyclopedia of Aging* (3rd ed., pp 19–22). New York: Springer.

Sherman, S. R., & Newman, E. S. (1988). *Foster families for adults: A community alternative in long-term care.* New York: Columbia University Press.

Sherman, S. R., & Newman, E. S. (1992). The New York state family care program for adult persons with mental retardation and developmental disabilities. *Community Alternatives: International Journal of Family Care, 4*(2), 223–237.

Congregate housing, broadly speaking, is a generic term that refers to a shared living environment in which a core set of services designed to enhance elderly residents' independent functioning is provided (Golant, 1992). As a generic housing type, it encompasses a broad range of supportive residential environments intended to fill the gap between traditional independent housing and institutional care (Monk & Kaye, 1991). Other terms used to describe congregate housing are "sheltered housing" and "enriched housing." Under this definition, there are many different models that reflect unique constellations of housing and services. Furthermore, these residential options have a variety of entry points through which older adults may receive supportive services (Golant, 1992; Heumann & Boldy, 1992). These different combinations of housing and services have many different names, including board and care homes, residential care facilities, adult foster homes, continuing care retirement communities (CCRCs), assisted living facilities (ALFs), and congregate housing. Congregate housing can also refer to traditional senior housing that has been transformed by (a) adding supportive services and/or a service coordinator (SC), (b) retrofitting existing housing, and (c) converting traditional senior housing to assisted living.

For the purpose of this chapter, we restrict the meaning of congregate housing to housing-service arrangements that combine an apartment-like independent living unit with services that do not fall under the medical model (Heumann & Boldy, 1992). This definition excludes residential care facilities, such as board and care homes, adult foster homes, adult group homes, personal care homes, and domiciliary care settings, which typically have more institution-like characteristics, such as either a private or shared bedroom and three meals a day. Using this definition, some states' assisted living models that follow a residential approach fit within these parameters, whereas others that follow a medical model do not (Schuetz, 2003). Table 63.1 provides a brief description of each of the housing-service arrangements addressed in this chapter. Although many options do not use the term "congregate housing," all fall within the parameters of our definition.

LEGAL AUTHORITY

Unlike federal or state programs that involve a single agency, congregate housing involves complex constellations of agencies and programs with responsibil-

NANCY W. SHEEHAN
WALDO C. KLEIN

Congregate Housing

63

TABLE 63.1. Congregate-Type Housing and Service Arrangements

Housing-Service Arrangement	Description
Federally assisted senior housing	
• Service coordinators (SCs)	Trained social service professionals working with elderly residents. Possible funding sources: HUD SC grants, project's residual receipts, rent increases, AAAs, foundations, and other sources.
• Assisted living conversion program (ALCP)	HUD grant program to pay for costs of converting housing to offer assisted living services. Targeted to converting individual apartments, common spaces, and other areas to accommodate providing assisted living services. No funding for services.
• Congregate housing services program (CHSP)	HUD and Rural Housing Services (RHS) grant program that provides funding for SCs and partial support for support services. Both residents and housing sponsor or other agency must contribute to the costs of services. No "new" grants since 1995.
State assisted senior housing	
• Service coordinators (SCs)	Trained social service professionals working with elderly residents in state-subsidized housing. Funding through state housing agency, PHAs, AAAs, or other sources.
• Congregate service programs	Several states (e.g., New Jersey) offer congregate grants to housing agencies, such as public housing authorities (PHAs), to offer services to residents. PHAs link with local service providers who provide services.
State-subsidized congregate housing	Some states fund the construction of purpose-built congregate housing facilities for low- to moderate-income elders that offer core services (e.g., meals, housekeeping, transportation).
State-subsidized assisted living	Group residential setting with multiple levels of support service (both instrumental and personal care). In most states, Medicaid reimbursement pays for services.
Continuing care retirement communities (CCRCs)	Market-rate multilevel group residential living offering independent through dependent care. Residency is based on contractual arrangements. Some offer comprehensive, modified, or fee-for-service contractual arrangements.
Private congregate facility • Freestanding	Separate apartment units with core services for all residents designed to maintain independence
• Part of CCRC	Congregate services available either in designated units or as added services to independent living units
Private assisted living	Upscale residential communities that offer personal care (such as bathing), instrumental care, and some nursing services. AL varies across states.
Other "affordable assisted living"	Coming Home Program, from the RW Johnson Foundation, provides funding and technical assistance to states to develop affordable AL

ity for financing, construction, rental subsidies, housing management, and services. Agencies that may be involved include HUD regional offices, the state housing finance agency, the state housing and economic development agency, the state unit on aging, area agencies on aging (AAAs), the state home care program, public housing authorities, public health, social service agencies, nonprofit community organizations, and private developers or management companies (Schuetz, 2003). Depending on the individual state, type of program, and funding stream, regulations governing different types of congregate housing may entail federal (U.S. Department of Housing and Urban Development [HUD], Rural Housing Services,

Federal Housing Administration) or state housing agencies (state housing agency or state housing finance agency), fair housing laws (Fair Housing Amendments Act and the Americans With Disabilities Act), federal congregate housing services program (CHSP) guidelines, Medicaid and the Medicaid waiver program, and, when appropriate, state agencies responsible for regulating or licensing either the housing or the service components. No single oversight body is responsible for regulating or monitoring different types of congregate options. Overall, because of the sheer number of agencies, distinct missions, and operational styles of the housing, social service, and health care components involved in congregate housing, the integration of housing and services is extremely difficult, particularly because no one is responsible for coordinating the housing and service components (Commission on Affordable Housing and Health Care Facility Needs for Seniors in the 21st Century, 2002; Evashwick, 2000; Golant, 2003; Natchison, 1994; Pynoos & Liebig, 1995; Schuetz, 2003; Sheehan, 1992).

Most states require some type of licensing or regulatory standards when congregate-type settings provide personal care and/or health-related services. However, the regulatory standards and agencies responsible for oversight (e.g., health, health and aging, elder affairs) vary across states. The oversight agency may, in part, influence whether the emphasis of the supportive service program entails a medical model or a residential approach (Schuetz, 2003). Some states require licensing the housing facility that provides personal care and other types of assistance; others license the service agency and specific levels of care (Mollica, 2002).

PREVALENCE

Although most elders (82% or slightly more than 21.4 million) live in their own homes, more and more elders live in some type of congregate setting. Of these, some have relocated from private homes in the community to reside in multiunit residential settings, such as congregate housing, CCRCs, and ALFs, and others reside in traditional senior housing complexes that have been adapted to provide services. Given the many different approaches to congregate housing, the complexity of funding mechanisms to provide services, and the overlap among many different types of senior housing, it is impossible to derive accurate statistics concerning the numbers of older adults who live in different congregate settings. One estimate is that slightly more than 4% of persons 65 years of age and over live in some type of purpose-built supportive housing (congregate care, CCRCs, ALFs, and board and care homes) (Commission on Affordable Housing and Health Care Facility Needs for Seniors in the 21st Century, 2002). Alternately, the Administration on Aging notes that approximately 5% of elders live in some type of senior housing, many of which offer services (Administration on Aging, 2003). For older adults, as age increases, the percentage living in some type of supportive housing increases. HUD estimates that 10% of seniors ages 70 to 74 live in some type of supported housing (shared housing, supportive housing, or government housing with services), and 60% by age 90 (U.S. Department of Housing and Urban Development, 2000b).

For many seniors, the number of supportive housing options has grown rapidly over the past several years (AARP, 2003). However, for low- and moderate-income elders, the number of options may be limited (U.S. Department of Housing and Urban Development, 1999). Current estimates suggest that 1.3 to 1.7 million older persons live in some type of government-subsidized housing (e.g., public housing, Section 202 housing, Section 515) (Commission on Affordable Housing and Health Care Facility Needs for Seniors in the 21st Century, 2002; U.S. Department of Housing and Urban Development, 1999) with no guarantee that supportive services will be available. In contrast, older adults living in CCRCs, assisted living, and congregate facilities have ready access to services. Available estimates suggest that about 350,000 older adults live in CCRCs and approximately 900,000 elders live in assisted living facilities (U.S. General Accounting Office, 2004). Finally, most recent figures indicate that there are about 240 subsidized housing sites offering service under the CHSP (U.S. Senate, Special Committee on Aging, 2004).

STRUCTURE

The structure associated with congregate housing living arrangements presents an extraordinarily complex array of domains that categorize this option.

1. Type of housing (congregate, government subsidized, CCRC, or assisted living)
2. Physical characteristics of the setting (purpose-built or retrofitted, layout, size, etc.)
3. Housing finance arrangements (federal and state low-income tax credit programs, CDBG program, mortgage revenue bonds, Section 8, Section 202, Section 515, state funding, etc.)
4. Payment source for services (private pay, CHSP, Medicaid, Medicaid waivers, Older Americans Act, SC funds, social service block grants)
5. Service package, levels of service, and state regulations governing service delivery
6. Nature of the formal and informal relationship between the housing and service components
7. Eligibility criteria for services (strict versus more general criteria)
8. Affordability (market rate or subsidized)
9. Staffing patterns

Consequently, a myriad of housing-service arrangements can be considered congregate housing.

Not surprisingly, there is a wide variety of staffing patterns among the different options. Although all congregate-type arrangements typically have a person responsible for the management of the housing (admission, rent, etc.), the availability of other staff varies as a function of several factors: (a) source of funding (e.g., CHSP, HUD SC grants, residual receipts, self-pay), (b) ingenuity of the housing manager, and (c) colocation of services. A significant number of housing options offer the services of a trained social service professional or services coordinator (SC) to work with residents, but many do not. For example, a national survey of Section 202 facilities conducted in 1999 reported that more than 37% of facilities employed SCs (Heumann, Winter-Nelson, & Anderson, 2001). In the absence of an SC, housing managers may act on behalf of residents to assist them in accessing services.

In addition to the services of an SC, other services that may be present include meals in a communal dining room, housekeeping, social and recreational programming, and 24-hour emergency coverage. Upscale, private-pay congregate facilities, including freestanding congregate facilities, CCRCs, and ALFs, provide a much more extensive array of support services and amenities. In many of these private facilities, multiple levels of services are available either as core services or as a fee-for-service arrangement. Affluent private-pay facilities may include an extensive array of services and amenities (health promotion and health screening, counseling, fitness programming, educational activities, wellness programming, escort services, transportation, shopping, cultural events, etc.), as well as on-site instrumental and personal care services. For government-subsidized housing, the service options vary widely from complex to complex. Some offer an SC to assist residents to access existing services, and others combine an SC with the provision of on-site or contracted services. For public housing, recent estimates suggest that 40% have on-site service staff (U.S. Senate, Special Committee on Aging, 2004). HUD has funded approximately 1,100 SC positions, but this number dramatically underestimates the number of SCs. According to testimony before the Commission on Affordable Housing and Health Facility Needs for Seniors in the 21st Century, an unofficial estimate puts the number of SCs in subsidized housing settings at more than 4,000 (testimony of Janice Monks, September 2001, cited in Golant, 2003). Finally, a small number of subsidized housing complexes have received grants from HUD's assisted living conversion program to retrofit traditional senior complexes to better assist frail elderly residents. However, no funding is provided for the cost of services.

RESIDENT POPULATION AND SPECIAL NEEDS

Over the past 10 years, the age and level of frailty among older adults moving into congregate settings have increased significantly. The average age of elderly residents in subsidized and market-rate senior housing developments is approximately 75 and 77 years of age, respectively (American Seniors Housing Association, 2001; Heumann et al., 2001). Moreover, substantial percentages of residents in both market-rate and subsidized housing are in their 80s and 90s. Among older Section 202 projects, 39% of residents are over 80 years of age. Similar statistics apply to market-rate supportive housing options for seniors. The average age of residents in purpose-built congregate facilities is 80 (Golant, 1992). For many, the move to congregate housing may be precipitated by a critical life event, such as declining health, increased loss of vision, or death of a loved one, which limits the person's ability to be self-sufficient (Doherty & DeWeaver, 2002).

In comparison with other community-living older adults, residents in congregate-type settings tend to be older, female, living alone, unmarried, and have a smaller support network, although residents in the independent units of CCRCs are more likely to be married than residents in other congregate settings (American Seniors Housing Association, 2001). Of all residents, low-income persons in subsidized housing are particularly vulnerable or at risk. According to Golant (2003), "This group is often comprised of seniors in their 70s and 80s who have decrements in their physical and cognitive functioning and chronic health problems. . . . They may feel especially vulnerable because they are women living alone without reliable family assistance" (Golant, 2003, p. 22). It follows that residents in federally subsidized housing are especially "at risk" for nursing home placement (Wilden & Redfoot, 2002). A significant percentage of residents in federally assisted housing confront difficulties in carrying out essential activities of daily living. Golant (2003) reports that about a third of residents in government-subsidized housing need assistance with at least one activity of daily living (either instrumental or basic) and 5% experience limitations with three or more ADLs. Figures reported by the Commission on Affordable Housing and Health Care Facility Needs for Seniors in the 21st Century (2002) for government-subsidized housing indicate that almost 470,000 elderly residents have difficulty in performing ADL or IADL activities and 163,000 have a mental disability.

SOCIAL WORK ROLES: HISTORICAL AND CURRENT

It is generally recognized the older adults prefer to age in place in their own homes. However, when that becomes impossible, the goal should be to age in an environment that is both homelike and provides necessary support. The fundamental roles of social workers in the congregate living environment address both of these needs. Social workers help to navigate the unclear territory between independent living in the community and the highly constrained lifestyle of the nursing home. The congregate housing model with its supportive services goes beyond the provision of basic shelter to smooth the continuum of housing options—from independent living without formal services in one's own home to more supportive (and restrictive) environments like skilled nursing facilities. In this middle ground, service management by social workers or other professionals familiar with both geriatric assessment and the wide array of available supportive services becomes important. Congregate housing commonly incorporates this role within the housing-service package where it may be performed by social workers. Although the need for services by residents of congregate housing varies widely, more than 75% of assisted living facilities report admitting residents who experience at least some memory or judgment impairment, have a short-term need for nursing support, or require oxygen supplementation (U.S. Senate, Special Committee on Aging, 1999). These residents of assisted living settings may represent a more dependent segment of the congregate housing continuum; however, across the entire range of congregate settings, the need for services is common and will become more so as current residents age. The ability to add supportive services within a given residential setting is fundamental in reducing the likelihood of an additional move. This capacity allows older adults to "move on" with life rather than "moving out" (U.S. Senate, Special Committee on Aging, 2001).

Although the availability of social workers in congregate living settings is far from universal (Heumann et al., 2001), the activities and roles that they perform when they are present are wide-ranging. In part, this reflects the equally broad array of forms that congregate housing might take—from those settings that offer a fairly minimal service set to those that are characterized by a very rich service environment coordinated by social workers or other professionals. Because residents are not required to utilize any particular service offered within a congregate housing environment, social workers clearly recognize that they are working with voluntary clients who (appropriately) must actively participate in shaping their own service package. This brings to the forefront traditional social work roles of service mobilization, client advocacy, education, and empowerment. Social workers commonly provide help with transportation needs for health care, personal needs, and even discretionary activities like shopping or leisure travel. Social workers enhance opportunities for socialization for congregate housing residents by organizing programs such as workshops or classes in which residents may choose to participate. A very specific and especially important instance of such socialization programming involves welcoming new residents into the congregate housing community. The sense of "feeling at home" has been associated with successful relocation to congregate living environments (Young, 1998), and the importance of facilitating that emotional reaction to a move cannot be overstated.

Beyond these opportunities for personal enrichment and engagement, social workers in congregate living settings often arrange for or directly provide physical health screenings and psychosocial assessments. The social worker may well be among the first to become aware of a resident's failing capacities or increased impairments, triggering the need for more comprehensive assessment to support clear care planning. In addition to the benefits of such assessment to the individual resident, regular and standardized assessment by a qualified social worker may also provide the basis for avoiding liability issues associated with failing to seek a higher level of care, should such become necessary for a particular resident (Hellman, 1990). When relocation from a congregate housing setting is required, it is often the social worker who works to develop an alternate care plan that is acceptable to the older adult and his or her family. Often, social workers are involved in communicating these needs to an older adult's family. A myriad of other social work functions may be undertaken to reflect the distinct characteristics of the particular congregate setting. For instance, in some, the community-organizing role may move to the fore as the worker seeks to organize and empower residents to achieve collective ends. In other settings, the worker may engage individual or group work skills to aid in achieving client goals. The common theme of these activities is to facilitate the older adult's adaptation to a complex and often demanding environment.

Inasmuch as these services may be offered by a professionally trained social worker, it is also true that services may be provided by a resident services coordinator. This is a position title that may or may not be filled by a trained social worker. Although some services like the coordination of transportation may be appropriately provided by staff trained at many different levels, others—such as a geriatric psychosocial assessment—should clearly be reserved for those with appropriate training. It has also been noted that an inherent tension or conflict may arise between housing managers and SCs (of whatever training) with respect to fulfilling the service roles for older adults (Sheehan, 1996). This conflict has been described as a clash between cultures reflecting the different service perspectives of the two roles. When social workers assume responsibility for service coordination, it is important that they bring their understanding of intraorganizational stresses to bear in developing supportive working relationships with housing management colleagues.

Unfortunately, there is little in the professional literature that speaks directly to the roles that social workers fill in congregate housing. Beyond the journal literature, a review of six texts that are commonly used to train social workers in social gerontology and practice with older adults indicates that while five of the six explicitly acknowledged congregate living programs—at least briefly—none provided significant guidance for the social work student or practitioner regarding specialized practice in that setting (Atchley & Barusch, 2004; Hooyman & Kiyak, 2002; Kart & Kinney, 2001; McInnis-Dittrich, 2002; Schneider, Kropf, & Kisor, 2000; Wacker, Roberto, & Piper, 1998) beyond acknowledging the beneficial effect of activity programming for most older adults. Generally, these training sources limited coverage to either a very short presentation of the policies supporting congregate living or an equally brief discussion of the importance of supportive services to the goal of "aging in place." While Wacker et al. (1998) advise that the "typical" staff includes the building manager, janitor, and social/activity organizer, McInnis-

Dittrich (2002) suggests that "low-or moderate-income housing frequently have social workers on staff to provide a variety of services" (pp. 11–12).

A partial explanation for this limited focus on service delivery in congregate housing may be the housing "culture" that has developed in the United States. Housing policy in this country developed following a "bricks and mortar" approach, with services segregated in separate bureaucratic programs—most commonly health-related ("Bricks and mortar," 1998). In addition, a societal emphasis on private homeownership has resulted in relatively modest attention by government or others to providing supportive services in congregate or other public housing environments (Schneider et al., 2000). Instead, the emphasis on providing long-term care services through highly institutionalized settings pulls service provision away from a more comprehensive housing policy that includes supportive services. As a result, public funding for services provided within congregate housing has been limited. For example, the CHSP provides some federal funding for services in subsidized housing; however, the program was never widespread, nor has it ever covered a substantial proportion of older adult residential settings.

Although there is limited empirical evidence describing the impact of successful social work practice with older adults who reside in congregate settings, there are a few studies of either SCs or social workers in congregate settings. One study examining the impact of SCs (who may be social workers) in subsidized elderly housing noted that SCs succeeded in developing new services for elderly residents (Feder, Scanlon, & Howard, 1992); a second study noted that SCs had a positive impact on frail residents' reported functional ability, social participation, and housing satisfaction (Sheehan, 1999a). Finally, an evaluation study of SCs in 20 Section 202/8 housing projects in 12 states concluded that the presence of SCs has resulted in earlier detection of frail or at-risk tenants (Schulman, 1996). Specific evidence of successful social work practice in a number of specialized practice applications with older adults who reside in congregate settings also exists. One of the earliest studies was conducted in public senior housing complexes in Boston (Lanspery, 1989). The research examined the impact of six social workers from the Boston Consortium for Health and Social Services deployed in 18 of the 35 public senior housing complexes to work with tenants and tenant organizations. Results demonstrated that after a relatively short time, the social workers "helped to empower tenants, change their attitudes, and increase their activity" (Lanspery, 1989, p. 8). A second study addressed the loss of support that residents encounter. After observing the diminution of strong support for residents in the weeks following the death of a loved one, loss support groups were developed in a four-building, 420-resident senior apartment community (Ryan & Crawford, 2002). Participants were recruited individually to join closed groups of approximately 12 members. In addition to achieving the primary goal of coming to better terms with the loss that had been experienced, these groups also developed new friendship relationships and furthered the sense of community within the living environment.

A group work approach was also used to develop a heightened sense of empowerment and interpersonal relationships among residents of two low-income independent living complexes and one low-income assisted living facility (Cox & Parsons, 1996). Although active sponsorship of this group continued for seven months, a follow-up study done three years later found that the group was still meeting monthly. Such longevity speaks to the apparent value that these services bring to the lives of older adults.

If we look to the future, we are likely to find that the need for social work services in congregate housing will increase substantially for two fundamental reasons. First, the demographic reality that will prevail for the next 50 years will result in dramatically increased numbers of older adults needing supportive housing environments. Second, and perhaps even more important, older adults who are already residing in congregate housing environments will tend to become increasingly frail and service dependent. To be sure, evidence already documents an increasing utilization of services paralleling the increase in older and frailer residents in Section 202 housing (Heumann et al., 2001). As this transition takes place, it will be coupled with the continued goal to age in place. For some, this goal will no longer remain attainable; however, in the interim the increased utilization of services and their coordination and management by a professional social worker can help to actualize this important goal for the resident for as long as is appropriate.

FUNDING

Because we have defined congregate living to include programs that range from subsidized housing to "residential" assisted living facilities and CCRCs that operate on a private-pay model, the discussion of funding must be equally broad. Funding for congregate-type housing options requires constructing a complex array of financing for the housing and services components. Previously, we noted some of the housing finance agencies and programs involved in creating housing with services arrangements. Funding for the service component involves a wide range of sources. In some instances, supportive services in subsidized housing result when the housing sponsor partners with local service agencies that provide discrete services (e.g., transportation, meals). This approach, however, entails a fairly low-level, uncoordinated approach. More formal service arrangements may include hiring an SC and/or providing supportive services, which may be paid for by different funding sources. For example, SCs may be funded through HUD grants, AAAs, CHSP grants, residual receipts from the housing complex, or rent increases.

Traditionally, HUD has been extremely reluctant to fund services in federally assisted housing (Sheehan, 1987). Although the Housing Act of 1970 authorized support for the construction of service spaces, such as dining rooms and kitchens, in public senior housing, no subsidies were provided to cover the cost of services (U.S. House, Select Committee on Aging, 1986; Sheehan, 1987). Subsequent legislation passed in 1974, while specifying the need for services in subsidized housing, provided no funds. Finally, by 1978, the situation was somewhat improved with the passage of the Congregate Housing Services Act, which authorized a small-scale demonstration project (CHSP) to test the cost-effectiveness of services in either public housing or Section 202 housing. The CHSP was made permanent under the National Affordable Housing Act of 1990; however, HUD has not solicited applications for this program since 1995. Although the funding formula for services has changed over the years, it currently is as follows: Federal grant funds pay 40%, housing sponsors or grantees pay 50%, and tenants pay 10%. Services include at least one meal a day, housekeeping, transportation, and limited health care. Throughout the United States, only 240 elderly housing complexes participate in this program (U.S. Senate, Special Committee on Aging, 2004). A long-term evaluation of HUD's new CHSP and HOPE for Elderly Independence Demonstration Project (HOPE IV) concluded that most participants expressed satisfaction with the services. Further, residents receiving the services credited the program with maintaining their independence despite high levels of frailty (U.S. Department of Housing and Urban Development, 2000a). However, over the two-year demonstration period, 25% of CHSP participants had relocated to a higher level of care.

In addition to modest federal support, different states have chosen to fund various congregate housing options (either congregate services or assisted living conversion programs) as alternatives to institutionally based long-term care. Although such involvement varies across states, these initiatives are designed to expand long-term care options (Wilden & Redfoot, 2002). For states that offer both programs, congregate service programs are easier to implement than assisted living conversion programs because, in most instances, they avoid the licensing requirements for assisted living (Shafer, 2001). As states struggle to constrain long-term care spending, more and more states are transforming different housing settings to offer assisted living with funding for services coming from state Medicaid waiver programs, and in some states, additional funding is provided by the state. Although early empirical evidence documented the feasibility of transitioning nursing home residents to congregate settings (Anderson, 1985), these "successes" may have reflected inappropriate placements of these people in overly restrictive environments rather than the actual legitimacy of congregate housing as a true alternative to skilled nursing facilities. In this case, funding for congregate housing might be better justified by the goal of enhancing the housing continuum explicitly, rather than as an alternative to any other vehicle for the delivery of long-term care. Future results from the nursing facilities transition projects funded by CMS, which are designed to move persons with disabilities out of nursing homes into the community, may be a better indicator of the viability of congregate settings as long-term care alternatives.

At the other extreme of program funding, a growing market has emerged for privately funded assisted living and CCRCs. Consistent with our definition; these programs offer individualized residential environments that are coupled with supportive services. Many assisted living facilities that had been developed in the last decade target an affluent market with prices that range to several thousand dollars a month for an apartment with a modest service package. Similarly, many CCRCs require a fairly substantial cash payment upon moving into the facility, coupled with ongoing monthly fees that are not insignificant. These housing options are important for more affluent older adults, but it is unrealistic to think of them as providing potential service options for the majority of seniors living at more modest levels. As a practical matter, the floor of the fee structure reflects capital costs for constructing these housing options and is relatively fixed. There is little that can be done to drop the capital costs below a reasonable economic base. Increased production of these high-end housing products results in a more attractive but less affordable housing option (Moore, 2003). This appears to be the direction that most private market assisted living has taken. At the same time, however, states are looking to assisted living options as a strategy for curbing nursing home expenditures. Schuetz (2003) presents examples of how five states are developing models of affordable supportive housing.

QUALITY OF CARE AND QUALITY OF LIFE

Given the early longitudinal research in subsidized elderly housing that documented significant declines in residents' well-being, social activity, quality of life, and morale over time (Lawton, Moss, & Grimes, 1985), housing advocates have called for planned interventions in senior housing to enhance older adults' quality of life by either adding services to existing housing or constructing congregate-type settings. These interventions may be understood by the application of the Lawton and Nahemow (1973) ecological model, which posits a relationship between environment and older adults' competence and well-being. More specifically, the model assumes that there is an ideal balance between an individual's personal competence and the environmental press that he or she experiences. As we age and are more likely to have decreased competence as the result of functional limitations, the level of the environmental press must also be decreased for us to perform at our maximum levels. This is precisely the environment that is provided by supportive congregate housing. When basic and routine services are provided, time and energy are freed to engage in more fulfilling activities. When activities such as socialization are facilitated through convenient scheduling and location, a resident's limited store of energy may again be focused on the enjoyment of such activities rather than the mundane coordination of them. However, at the same time, if too many services are provided, there is a risk of encouraging dependence (Lawton, 1976).

Empirical evidence explicitly connects one's residence in the congregate housing setting with quality of life. One of the earliest evaluations of congregate services found that the availability of on-site staff and services seemed "to allay residents' fears regarding emergencies, illnesses, and disability in the future" (U.S. Department of Housing and Urban Development, 1976, p. 246). The same study found that congregate housing had a positive role in fostering the maintenance of independent living for older adults.

Other early research, while documenting the positive impact of supportive services on quality of life, provides equivocal findings regarding its impact on social activity, particularly involvement in the broader community. On one hand, an eight-year longitudinal study of elderly residents in public senior housing with services noted that residents in housing with services tended to be more involved in various activities than older adults in noncongregate community settings (Carp, 1978–1979). This study also indicated a dramatic increase in club and hobby activity, as well as other independent activity levels. Continuity of previous friendships in the community and establishing new "close friends" within the CH environment have also been documented (U.S. Department of Housing and Urban Development, 1976). However, an early short-term longitudinal study comparing residents in congregate and traditional senior housing concluded that while congregate residents showed increased morale, housing satisfaction, and available social networks, their involvement in the broader community decreased (Lawton, 1976). More recent research examining the impact of adding assisted living services to congregate settings supports the benefits of increased services for the quality of life of residents who receive the services and also other residents, who feel a sense of relief knowing that the services are available if they need them (Sheehan, 1999b; Sheehan & Oakes, 2003).

In short, congregate housing settings offer an effective vehicle for the provision of the broad spectrum of supportive services that are commonly utilized by older adults seeking to maintain their maximum level of independent living. There is little doubt that the social work functions of assessment, service coordination, and service provision result in an enhanced quality of life for congregate housing residents. By having social work as an integral part of the congregate housing service package, the opportunity for early assessment and intervention is strengthened, and such early intervention may enhance the likelihood of living a full and satisfying life.

CULTURE OF CARE

As we have indicated throughout this chapter, the range of variation among congregate housing settings is wide; so, too, are the variations that must exist within the culture of care that is represented by these housing and service options. Further, because the role that congregate housing plays in supporting older adults is continuing to evolve, the culture of care is necessarily dynamic. In such a context, the culture is not clearly articulated, and social workers find that they must define their role within a housing context. Furthermore, unlike in other settings with a formally defined role for social workers, social workers may often find that they are negotiating their role in the context of a particular housing setting. As a result, the culture of care in a congregate setting may vary as a function of the type of housing, the needs of the residents, the negotiated roles between the social worker and housing director or manager, and expectations. Therefore, in the absence of clear guidelines addressing the operational linkage and coordination between housing and services, social workers (and housing personnel, too) may encounter many areas of confusion as supportive services are added to housing.

Still, however, there are important dimensions that establish parameters on the culture of care within congregate housing and shape social work practice within that setting. Moreover, each of these is consistent with social work practice. First, residents of congregate housing function with high levels of *autonomy*. As service consumers, these older adults are able to make autonomous decisions about receiving or refusing services. Beyond the foundational respect for autonomy, the service-housing package that is represented by congregate housing is designed to maintain and enhance residents' *independence*. Although independence is probably never complete at any point in human development, the desire to maintain one's independence at the highest possible levels is a common goal for most older adults. Even when independence is compromised, the culture of care in congregate housing emphasizes *empowerment/self-determination* of residents in order to design service and support packages in a way that is most meaningful and comfortable for individual residents. These three dimensions—autonomy, independence, and empowerment/self-determination—offer a concise statement regarding the congregate culture of care.

As clear as this culture may be, unresolved issues do emerge. A number of these have been identified in a recent study examining bringing assisted living services into congregate housing (Sheehan & Oakes, 2004). Unresolved questions included

1. How much information about residents can be shared between the housing staff and the social worker?

2. Who determines the limits of when a resident with moderate to severe disability is no longer appropriate for the housing environment?

3. What safeguards are in place for assuring the right of residents to refuse services?

4. What are the limits for the number of residents who can be assisted by the social worker?

As issues such as these are further explored and resolutions are reached, congregate housing will continue to develop as a residential and service option for older adults. As it does, the increasingly comprehensive integration of supportive services within the context of personal housing will continue to provide a rich opportunity for the further development of the role social workers can play in empowering older adults to maximize their fullest potential.

REFERENCES

AARP. (2003). Beyond 50.03: A report to the nation on independent living and disability Retrieved August 11, 2005, from *http://assest.aarp.org/rgcenter/il/beyond_50_il.pdf*.

Administration on Aging. (2003). *A profile of older Americans: 2003*. Retrieved June 21, 2005, from *http://www.aoa.gov/about/over/over_history_pf.asp*

American Seniors Housing Association. (2001). *The independent living report*. Washington, DC: Author.

Anderson, E. (1985). Congregate service programs. *Journal of Housing, 42*(3), 78.

Atchley, R., & Barusch, A. (2004). *Social forces and aging* (10th ed.). Belmont, CA: Wadsworth.

Bricks and mortar or helping hands? An H/CD debate. (1998). *Journal of Housing and Community Development, 55*, 15–24.

Carp, F. M. (1978–1979). Effects of the living environment on activity in the use of time. *International Journal of Aging and Human Development, 9*, 75–91.

Commission on Affordable Housing and Health Facility Needs for Seniors in the 21st Century. (2002). *A quiet crisis in America*. Washington, DC: Author.

Cox, E. O., & Parsons, R. (1996). Empowerment-oriented social work practice: Impact on late life relationships of women. *Journal of Women and Aging, 8*(3–4), 129–143.

Doherty, J., & DeWeaver, K. (2002). Critical incidents in the lives of elders with a disability: Factors leading to institutional placement. *Journal of Gerontological Social Work, 38*, 39–51.

Evashwick, C. (2000, May–June). Integrating housing and healthcare. *Health Progress*, pp. 40–43, 51.

Feder, J., Scanlon, W., & Howard, J. (1992). Supportive services in senior housing: Preliminary evidence on feasibility and impact. *Generations, 16*, 61–62.

Golant, S. (1992). *Housing America's elderly: Many possibilities/few choices*. Newbury Park, CA: Sage.

Golant, S. (2003). Political and organizational barriers to satisfying low-income seniors' need for affordable rental housing with services. *Journal of Aging and Social Policy, 15*, 21–48.

Hellman, L. (1990). Senior resident vs. senior high-rise: Liability for transferring elderly residents. *Journal of Housing for the Elderly, 6*(1/2), 101–105.

Heumann, L., & Boldy, D. (1992). Aging in place: The growing need for new solutions. In L. Heumann & D. Boldy (eds.), *Aging in place with dignity: International solutions relating to the low-income and frail elderly* (pp. 9–24). Westport, CT: Praeger.

Heumann, L., Winter-Nelson, K., & Anderson, J. (2001). 1999 national survey of Section 202 elderly housing. Washington, DC: AARP.

Hooyman, N., & Kiyak, H. A. (2002). *Social gerontology: A multidisciplinary perspective* (6th ed.). Boston: Allyn & Bacon.

Kart, C., & Kinney, J. (2001). *The realities of aging* (6th ed.). Boston: Allyn & Bacon.

Lanspery, S. (1989). *Aging in place phase II, building bridges and promoting participation: A study of social workers as enablers in senior public housing*. Boston: Charles H. Farnsworth Housing Corporation.

Lawton, M. P. (1976). The relative impact of congregate and traditional housing on elderly tenants. *The Gerontologist, 16*, 237.

Lawton, M. P., Moss, M., & Grimes, M. (1985). The changing service needs of older tenants in planned housing. *The Gerontologist, 25*, 258–264.

Lawton, M. P., & Nahemow, L. (1973). Ecology and the aging process. In C. Eisendorfer & M. P. Lawton (Eds.), *Psychology of adult development and aging* (pp. 619–674). Washington DC: American Psychological Association.

McInnis-Dittrich, K. (2002). *Social work with elders*. Boston: Allyn & Bacon.

Mollica, R. (2002). *State assisted living policy: 2002*. Portland, ME: National Academy for State Health Policy.

Monk, A., & Kaye, L. W. (1991). Congregate housing for the elderly: Its need, function, and perspectives. *Journal of Housing for the Elderly, 9*(1/2), 5–19.

Moore, J. (2003). Affordability: What it means for aging people and some ways to achieve it. *Elder's Advisor, 4*(3), 11–29.

Nachison, J. (1994). Housing programs of the Department of Housing and Urban Development: Description and issues. In W. Folts & D. Yeatts (Eds.), *Housing and the aging population: Options for the new century* (pp. 83–104). New York: Garland.

Pynoos, J., & Liebig, P. (1995). Housing policy for frail elders: Trends and implications for long-term care. In J. Pynoos & P. Liebig (Eds.), *Housing frail elders: International policies, perspectives, and prospects* (pp. 3–16). Baltimore: Johns Hopkins University Press.

Ryan, B., & Crawford, P. (2002). Creating loss support groups for the elderly. In S. Henry, J. East, & C. Schmitz (Eds.), *Social work with groups: Mining the gold* (pp. 151–162). New York: Haworth.

Schneider, R., Kropf, N., & Kisor, A. (Eds.). (2000). *Gerontological social work: Knowledge, service settings, and special populations* (2nd ed.). Belmont, CA: Brooks/Cole.

Schuetz, J. (2003). *Affordable assisted living: Surveying the possibilities.* Joint Center for Housing Studies, Harvard University, and Volunteers of America. Cambridge, MA.

Schulman, A. (1996). Service coordination: Program development and initial findings. *Journal of Long-Term Home Health Care, 12,* 5–12.

Shafer, D. (2001). Coming of aging. *Journal of Housing and Community Development, 58,* 33–38.

Sheehan, N. W. (1987). "Aging in place" in public senior housing: Past trends and future needs. *Home Health Care Services Quarterly, 8,* 55–77.

Sheehan, N. W. (1992). *Successful administration of senior housing: Working with elderly residents.* Newbury Park, CA: Sage.

Sheehan, N. W. (1996). Management issues in service coordination: The experience of the resident services coordinator program. *Journal of Gerontological Social Work, 26*(1/2), 71–86.

Sheehan, N. W. (1999a). The resident services coordinator program: Bringing service coordination to federally assisted senior housing. In L. Pastalan (Ed.), *Making aging in place work* (pp. 35–49). Binghamton, NY: Haworth.

Sheehan, N. W. (1999b). *Assisted living services in congregate housing: Final report from Assisted Living Pilot Program at St. Jude Common,* Storrs, CT: University of Connecticut.

Sheehan, N. W., & Oakes, C. E. (2003). Bringing assisted living services into congregate housing: Residents' perspectives. *The Gerontologist, 43,* 766–770.

Sheehan, N. W., & Oakes, C. E. (2004). *Bringing assisted living services into congregate housing: Housing directors' perspectives.* Unpublished manuscript. University of Connecticut.

U.S. Department of Housing and Urban Development, Office of Policy Development and Research. (1976). *Evaluation of the effectiveness of congregate housing for the elderly* (Publication No. HUD-PDR-198-2). Washington, DC: Government Printing Office.

U.S. Department of Housing and Urban Development. (1999). *Housing our elders: A report card on the housing conditions and needs of older Americans.* Washington, DC.

U.S. Department of Housing and Urban Development. (2000a). *Elderly independence programs evaluated.* Retrieved June 21, 2005, from *http://www.huduser.org/periodicals/rrr/rrr_10_2000/1000_5.html*.

U.S. Department of Housing and Urban Development. (2000b). *Urban Research Monitor, 5.* Retrieved June 21, 2005, from *http://www.huduser.org/periodicals/urm/urm_07_2000/urmintro.html*.

U.S. General Accounting Office. (2004). *Assisted living: Examples of state efforts to improve consumer protection* (Publication No. GAO-04-684). Retrieved June 21, 2005, from *www.gao.gov/cgi-bin/getrpt?GAO-04-684.*

U.S. House, Select Committee on Aging. (1986). *Maximizing supportive services for the elderly in assisted housing: Experiences from the Congregate Housing Services Program* (Comm. Publication No. 99-553). Washington, DC: Government Printing Office.

U.S. Senate, Special Committee on Aging. (1999). *Assisted living: Quality of care and consumer protection issues* (Publication No. GAO/T-HEHS-99-111). Washington, DC: GAO.

U.S. Senate, Special Committee on Aging. (2001). *Assisted living in the 21st century: Examining its role in the continuum of care* (Serial No. 107-3). Washington, DC: U.S. Government Printing Office.

U.S. Senate, Special Committee on Aging. (2004). *Developments in aging: 2001 and 2002.* From the Senate reports online via GPO access. Retrieved August 11, 2005, from *http://frwebgate.access.gpo.gov/cgi-bin/useftp.cgi?IPaddress=162.140.64.88&filename=sr265v1.pdf&directory=/diskb/wais/data/108_cong_reports].* Accessed on August 11, 2005.

Wacker, R., Roberto, K., & Piper, L. (1998). *Community resources for older adults: Programs and services in an era of change.* Thousand Oaks, CA: Pine Forge.

Wilden, R., & Redfoot, D. (2002). *Adding assisted living services to subsidized housing: Serving frail older persons with low incomes.* Washington, DC: AARP Public Policy Institute.

Young, H. (1998). Moving to congregate housing: The last chosen home. *Journal of Aging Studies, 12*(2), 149–216.

FREDDA VLADECK

Residential-Based Care: New York's NORC-Supportive Services Program Model

64

The demographic changes we are experiencing and will continue to experience for years to come are producing significant changes in the makeup of many American communities. Never before in this country's history have older people constituted so large a proportion of the residents of so many communities. With people over the age of 65 expected to reach 20% of the population by the year 2030, concentrations of seniors will be living in their homes of long standing in most age-integrated communities across the country. And yet most policy discussions about housing and supportive services for older people focus on the small segment of the population living in residential care—facilities created and dressed up to look homelike.

At the same time, we have been stuck in a service-delivery paradigm that may not fit today's older population and the communities in which they live. Instead, we have been piling one categorical program on top of another to address individual needs one hip fracture at a time. Social work has been complicit in this effort, trying to fit its practice into a medicalized, reimbursement-driven construct rather than drawing from a basic tenet of social work—"Start where the client is at"–which in most cases is in the communities where they raised their families.

Age-integrated neighborhoods that for whatever reason (aging in place, in-migration of older people, or out-migration of younger people) have a high proportion of residents over 60 have come to be called naturally occurring retirement communities (NORCs). These are distinguished from purposeful retirement communities to which older people move in search of care or even a different lifestyle, such as continuing care retirement communities (CCRCs) (chapter 60) and assisted living (chapter 61).

The opportunity presented by the graying of most of America's communities—to rethink how, when, to whom, and where older people are served—has to date been largely ignored. We keep doing more of the same when we need to start doing things differently. Common to many communities of mixed ages is the heterogeneity of their older residents themselves. Be they single-family homeownership communities, large private or public housing apartment developments, or garden apartment complexes, the older generation who live there—old and young, rich and poor—have constant back-and-forth changes in health status; possess a wide range of interests, skills, and talents; and have changing needs over time. Geographic concentrations of seniors give us the opportunity to reconfigure the service system in ways that fit better with our understanding of aging as a dynamic process and not a one-way downward spiral. Our current service-delivery system, focused on individual deficits, is not designed to incorporate this understanding into a more balanced practice. It is at the community level that we will need to build the supports and systems necessary to support "successful aging" and respond more quickly and effectively to the changes older people experience.

This chapter makes the argument that we need to build coherent services within the communities where older people live so that we can have a different policy discussion from the one we've been having for the last 25 years. I begin with a brief description of the prevailing paradigm that governs community-based services for older people and the role of social work within it, quickly cataloging some of the major deficiencies with the current approach. Then I suggest a new paradigm that reflects today's understanding of aging and move quickly to illustrating how this new paradigm is applied in practice in the 27 NORC-SSPs in New York City. I conclude by identifying some lessons and implications from this experience and its replicability to other kinds of communities.

SQUARE PEGS IN ROUND HOLES

Designed at a different time, Medicare, Medicaid, and the Older Americans Act are the foundations for the myriad programs and services that have developed since 1965 to meet the needs of a growing and changing older population. These public programs were enormously successful in addressing the problems of their era—providing health insurance to almost all seniors, health care and nursing home coverage for those unable to pay for it themselves, and a nutritious meal in a social setting for the numerous seniors who were malnourished. Over the years, we have reacted to each new issue or problem by looking to the structure of one of these three programs to legislate or construct a new coverage policy or service response with the limited dollars available. The most recent example is the family caregivers support program, the latest addition to the Older Americans Act. Each add-on has its own set of complex rules, target population, limits, and regulations that providers and consumers must learn to navigate.

Often, access to a service under these three programs is reactive, triggered by a medical event that brings the older person into contact with a health or social services professional after the fact. A case in point:

▨ Mrs. Smith is 77 years old, a widow who lives alone. Her two children live more than 800 miles away. She has a fall, breaks her hip, and is hospitalized. During her stay it is discovered that her thyroid level is dangerously low. She is discharged home with intermittent home care covered by Medicare and home-delivered Meals on Wheels from her local senior center so that she will have a hot meal on the days the home health aide does not come.

The prior year, Mrs. Smith had been a regular at her local senior center but 8 months earlier had stopped going. At the time, Mrs. Smith had no idea that she was having a thyroid problem. She just hoped nobody else saw that she was having a hard time keeping it together, and she did not want to go to a nursing home or have a stranger in her house taking care of her. The center staff had called her a few times to encourage her to return, and when they were not successful, they arranged for her to receive a weekly telephone reassurance call so that she would not feel isolated. Six weeks after she left the hospital, Mrs. Smith was discharged from Medicare home care, but the meals continued and telephone reassurance resumed. Her continued difficulty ambulating made it hard for her to get to the drug store to fill her thyroid prescription, leading to further confusion and decline. Six months later, after another fall and hospitalization, Mrs. Smith had become a daily Medicaid home attendant client. ▨

While in the hospital after the initial fall, Mrs. Smith was assessed by a discharge planner (in the current environment, probably a nurse) to qualify her for Medicare home care services based on functional deficits and skilled care needs. The senior center social worker assessed Mrs. Smith for nutritional deficits under the Older Americans Act and qualified her for home-delivered meals and telephone reassurance calls—thus maintaining Mrs. Smith's "connection to her community." After her second hospitalization, when she no longer qualified for Medicare home care and it was clear that Mrs. Smith could not manage on her own and was now a discharge problem, a social worker was called in to "help" Mrs. Smith accept the need to apply for Medicaid. The social worker assessed the level of service needed, helped complete the application, and got the home attendant services in place.

In this case, each provider acted as an autonomous entity providing the contracted services from their fixed and limited armamentarium. These services might not be what is needed, but they are what the agencies have available. From the definition of her problem, the responses by the providers, the determination of eligibility for services, and the actual provision of services, Mrs. Smith and all her providers could be living on Mars. Other than assessing her for what functional deficits could be handled by a caregiver (if one exists), there is no connectedness to the community or web of social networks in which Mrs. Smith lives. Even those providers that describe themselves as community based may be located in the community, but they aren't really connected to the life of the community. They wait for the older person to self-identify or come to their attention as a result of a triggering event. Then, rather than fully assessing the strengths of the client in the context of her environment and marshaling the resources within it to provide calibrated supports and help return her to the role of a member of the community, the social work role has been reduced to a series of administrative tasks designed to qualify the client for services based on functional level and categorical need, coordinate the services, and then "manage" the case.

Gradually we are understanding that communities play a critical role in how well people age. Mobilizing at least part of those networks is often essential to delivering the kinds of services the client needs, and yet this function has largely disappeared from the social work role. "Community and neighborhood are important. So is the level of positive integration, neighborliness, looking out for others . . . which is . . . associated with higher life expectancy and better health," says Richard M. Suzman, associate director of the Behavioral and Social Research Program and the National Institute on Aging (Kilgorn, 2003). With the exception of a relatively small number of seniors whose social isolation is extreme, most older people live within a web of community, family, and social networks and are supported and provide support to others within these networks. Understanding that context is often critical to a complete assessment of a client. The common eligibility requirement that an older person must be homebound to receive services runs contrary to this imperative, serving to keep older people isolated behind their front doors, disconnected from the social fabric of their community, and stuck in the only role we have been willing to assign them—the dependent individual with a mass of needs.

REDESIGNING THE SYSTEM BASED ON THE COMMUNITY

Continuing to grow and learn new things, maintaining social connectedness, and remaining a vital and involved person in the world and surrounding community are as important to an older person's health as the public programs designed to treat or react to specific diseases or events. Our current categorical, event-triggered service systems have no way of incorporating this into their existing needs-based framework. To do so, we need to start in a different place—the community—redefining who is to be "served," what services are needed, and when and how they will be delivered.

In the new paradigm,

- Eligibility is determined by age and residence, not income or functional status.
- Health and social service providers are located on site, embedded in and accountable to the community.
- Clients have multiple roles as constituents, leaders, and consumers of service.
- Clients enter the system before a crisis through their other roles in the community.
- Comprehensive biopsychosocial assessment is based on the strengths of the individual at the time additional supports are needed.
- Additional service supports, designed to complement the public programs, are organized, utilizing the resources within the community.

Redesigning our service-delivery system based on such a new paradigm is rapidly becoming an imperative as the graying of America is happening in communities large and small, from dense urban neighborhoods and developments to sprawling suburbs and remote rural towns. Increasingly, neighborhoods and communities are becoming naturally occurring retirement communities (NORCs). Michael E. Hunt, a professor of architecture and urban planning at the University of Wisconsin, coined the term *NORC* in the early 1980s to describe neighborhoods and apartment buildings originally built for young families in which 50% or more of the residents are at least 50 years old (Hunt & Hunt, 1985).

By definition, NORCs cannot be built or developed. They evolve over time as a result of various phenomena. NORCs can emerge as a result of in-migration when people at or near retirement relocate. A desire to live in warmer climates or closer to cultural activities and other supports can be the impetus for some older people to relocate. The southern border of Texas is dotted with trailer parks that have sprung up as retirees from Minnesota and Wisconsin seek more temperate weather in their older years. Apartment buildings in revitalized sections of old urban centers have become magnets for retirees in search of lifestyle changes, including reduced dependence on cars for transportation and easy access to cultural activities. In a small town just outside New York City, older people are moving back from Florida—returning to the community in which they raised their families—so they can be closer to their children, who are now raising their own families in the same community where they grew up.

NORCs can also emerge in communities that have experienced a large out-migration of its younger people, leaving behind the older residents, who, for a variety of circumstances, cannot leave their homes of many years. Whole counties in rural farming and mining areas of the country have become NORCs, as the land ceases to support these livelihoods and the young migrate in search of employment. Neighborhoods in older urban areas can become NORCS as small manufacturing dries up or drugs and violence force out younger families in search of work or safer communities in which to raise their children.

However, the predominant evolution of NORCs results from the residents of a community aging in place. It is expected that many U.S. communities will become NORCs as the number of people age 65 and older, aging in place, continues to grow. Although more recent analysis is not available, Lanspery and Callahan (1994) identified nearly 4,500 census block groups across the United States as potential NORCs by using data from the 1990 census. And as far back as 1989, NORCs were recognized as an emerging phenomenon when an AARP study found that 27% of this country's older population lived in NORCs, which the study defined as age-integrated communities with large concentrations of seniors (AARP, 1992).

In many NORCs resulting from an aging-in-place process, its older residents are the pioneers who made these communities livable and good places to raise young families. They helped build the schools, playgrounds, and libraries; organize the nursery schools, after-school programs, and clubs that ensured a stimulating and safe environment in which children could grow; and wove together the social fabric of their communities by developing the mutual aid groups and formal and informal support networks necessary to help people manage their everyday lives. Few, if any, comparable opportunities and roles exist for older people in these communities that they helped build.

All NORCs—whether a result of in-migration, out-migration, or aging in place—differ from purpose-built senior housing or retirement communities in some significant ways. It is the only living environment that maximizes choice. Residents are free to come and go as they choose and to move in or leave on their own terms. There is no external entity or owner determining who can or cannot live in a NORC because there are no entrance criteria based on functional deficits. Conversely, the absence of an external entity or owner means that there are no exit criteria either. Residents are not forced to leave when they can no longer get to the dining room on their own, forget to take their medicine, or need help managing their finances or negotiating the world around them.

In the existing service-delivery paradigm, we react to individual residents' changing needs one at a time, disconnected from the very environment in which they live. If we continue with this approach, over time—as the balance in NORCs shifts to increasingly older and frailer residents—the social fabric begins to fray as connections are severed when residents die, are placed in facilities, or become homebound and locked behind their front doors. We can do nothing and passively watch these communities become undesirable places to live, where it appears that people are waiting to die, or we can take advantage of the economies of scale possible by such large concentrations of older people and redesign a delivery system that is responsive to the heterogeneity of older people with constantly changing needs.

SERVICE PROGRAMS IN NEW YORK CITY'S NORCS

One promising effort to redesign the service-delivery system has been under way in New York to rebuild the infrastructure in communities to help support older people as they age in place. Drawing on population-based public health principles and social work's ecosystems approach to serving older people in their environment, the NORC Supportive Service Program (NORC-SSP) model shifts the prevailing paradigm of aging services by upending the functional deficit-based programs and services we have elaborately constructed over the years to transform communities into good places to grow old.

The NORC-SSP model developed as a programmatic response to the aging-in-place phenomenon occurring in many of the high-rise apartment buildings and dense communities across New York City. These are collaborative financial and programmatic partnerships between housing entities, the residents, health and social service providers, government, and philanthropy to organize and locate a range of coordinated health care and social services and group activities onsite in the housing complexes. The goal of these programs is to promote healthy and successful aging and provide calibrated supports as individual needs change.

Together, the partners assess the needs, interests, and resources in a community that help inform the design of the program. Eligibility for services and participation in activities is based on age and residence rather than on functional deficits or economic status. And, at the risk of stating the obvious, unlike in facility-based residential care, there are no exit criteria because these are people's own homes. Some of the tools that are utilized for individual service provision are the existing categorical and entitlement programs (Medicare, Medicaid, and services under the Older Americans Act), but, contrary to most service-delivery models, they are not the only ones. Additional supports and services are developed to support older people in actively managing and maintaining their health and well-being and to pick up where the public programs leave off, finding ways to reintegrate seniors into the life of their community once an acute episode has subsided.

The first NORC-SSP began in 1986 in a large 10-building moderate-income cooperative in the middle of Manhattan (Penn South Mutual Redevelopment Houses) built in 1962. Many of the building's original 6,200 residents were trying to remain active and busy, dreading the day when a fall or serious health problem might limit their ability to participate in community life. It also had its share of problems with confused residents wandering, losing keys, and forgetting to pay their monthly maintenance charge. Working with me, a social worker at a local hospital, the resident board of directors conducted a survey to determine the needs of its frailer residents and the aspirations of all its residents as they aged in place. This process led to the creation of the Penn South Program for Seniors, which was funded initially by philanthropy. Within several years, the program exceeded expectations, and the housing company became a financial partner, allocating funds from its operating budget for program support. The success of this model led to its replication in two other communities in 1992 and a growing recognition of its potential for other communities.

In 1995, New York State passed legislation creating the NORC Supportive Services Program Initiative with $1 million (increased to $1.2 million in 1996) granted annually to promote the development of 14 programs. Twelve are located in New York City. This was a pioneering effort by a state to create policy that would change how services for seniors are defined and organized, where they are delivered and to whom, and how they are financed. The legislation established thresholds for the senior population needed to achieve economies of scale in service delivery, defined the geographic boundaries of a naturally occurring retirement community, and established an ownership interest in the program through a public-private financing formula requiring a housing company's financial participation. In 1999, the city government allocated another $4 million annually to this effort, which resulted in additional grants to the existing 12 state-supported programs and the development of 16 new programs. Modeled after the state legislation, the city's Department for the Aging modified some of the definitions to reflect the density of large housing developments in close proximity to one another and to increase the government financing role in these public-private partnerships (Figure 64.1).

There are now 27 NORC Supportive Service Programs in four of the five boroughs that make up New York City. Almost 46,000 seniors live in a mix of age-integrated developments. Programs range in size from a single building with 275 of its more than 500 residents over the age of 60, to a large, sprawling 12,000-unit complex of 171 different high-rise buildings in which 4,300 of its residents are seniors. Two programs are in two-story garden apartment complexes, with the remaining 25 located in high-rise apartment developments. Seventeen programs are located in moderate-income cooperatives in which the residents have an ownership interest, seven are in the public housing developments of the New York City Housing Authority, and four are in privately owned developments (two rental and two cooperative) for moderate- and low-income individuals.

New York City's NORC-SSPs are financed through a combination of public and private sources of support. Operating budgets range from a $148,000 program to more than $700,000 for a mature and multidimensional program. Government dollars (close to $5 million in state and city funds) leverage matching funds from the participating housing entities (public housing is exempt), philanthropy, local fund-raising, and membership fees for activities. Specific in-kind supports provide much-needed resources for the

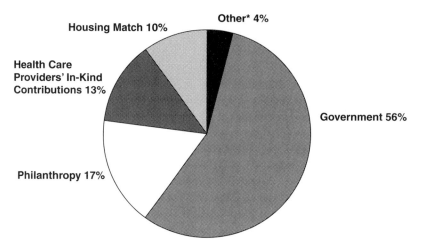

FIGURE 64.1. Funding for NORC-SSPs, New York City, Fiscal Year 2003–2004
"Other" includes income from group, program, and membership fees; fees for NORC-
program subsidized housekeeping, chore, and transportation services; local fund-raising
efforts; and annual legislative grants.

NORC-SSPs. From the housing corporation's provision of janitorial services and space for offices and activities, to the health provider's provision of dedicated nursing staff time, the partners provide a range of in-kind resources that extend program operations.

NORC-SSP SERVICES

The structure of a NORC-SSP is predicated on the axiom that the sum is greater than its parts. It brings the diverse partners together to create a shared mission and vision of the program, establish a governance structure (including resident representatives) with accountability to the whole, and set forth the range of activities and services to be delivered. A lead agency (in most instances the social service provider) coordinates the work of the partners and provides the day-to-day management at each site.

Staffed by social workers and nurses, the NORC-SSP service design framework integrates four core elements.

- **Social work services** include information and referral; benefits and entitlements advocacy; assistance negotiating the systems and services available from the wider community; biopsychosocial assessment and casework support, case management, service coordination, and monitoring for changing status of clinically complex or fragile individuals; and education and support for clients, family members, and paid and unpaid caregivers.

- **Health care–related services** include individual care management to help seniors live with and manage chronic conditions and address acute situations; the provision of nonreimbursable but necessary monitoring, care coordination, and support to maintain frail individuals at home; physical assessments, regular blood pressure monitoring, and individual instruction; advocacy in negotiating the myriad health care systems; coordination with the primary care physicians and the on-site social workers; and health promotion, prevention, and wellness programs.

- **Educational and recreational opportunities** are diverse and designed to engage the broadest mix of seniors living in a community. Lectures on a wide range of topics, an array of classes, discussion groups, support groups, health chats with health care professionals—the list is limitless and often defined by the seniors themselves. Although organized and managed by the professional staff, many of the classes and activities are identified and led by the program participants.

- **Volunteer opportunities** make it possible for seniors to take on new roles in their community as program ambassadors, leaders, and program extenders in addition to that of consumers of service. Volunteers' knowledge and understanding of their communities is instrumental in informing the planning process during a program's formative stages, setting program priorities as programs evolve, and identifying the resources, talents, and skills within each community. There are more than

800 resident volunteers in New York City's NORC-SSPs, performing more than 42 different functions, ranging from the individual support services (reader of mail, mender of clothes, translator, escort, friendly visitor, and the like), to the provision of programmatic activities (discussion leader, teacher, peer insurance counselor, etc.), to the provision of administrative and development support (fund-raiser, librarian, receptionist, events organizer, writer and designer of marketing and communication materials, and statistician for community assessments).

Often additional services need to be developed to respond to each community's specific characteristics and to needs that change over time. Beyond the core service design framework just described, programs have the flexibility to develop additional supports and services tailored to the uniqueness of each community. Successful programs draw on the social capital within the housing community itself, as well as the resources in the larger community surrounding it. Quite a range of solutions to local conditions and issues result from the process of professionals and residents working together: Younger residents volunteer to provide transportation services in car-dominated or remote areas of the city, residents who are retired accountants and bookkeepers provide program-supervised daily money-management assistance in those communities in which many seniors have little or no family close by, on-site geriatric psychiatry services are leveraged from a local hospital in a significantly aged-in community, and local fund-raising efforts help subsidize emergency home care in a community with limited resources or access to in-home services. The range of additional responses and supports that can be developed gets broader as understanding (by both the professionals and the residents) grows regarding what is needed and wanted to make life better for older people in a community.

The NORC-SSP model relies on partnerships with the residents that stretch the roles and boundaries of the traditional and formal helping professional–client relationship.

In the course of a single day, a resident can be a client, a volunteer, and a partner with an ownership interest in the success of the program. As a client, she is concerned about her fluctuating blood pressure and so comes to the program every Tuesday for the nurse to check her pressure and review her medications to make sure she is taking them correctly. While there, she meets with a social worker to discuss her growing concern about her husband's depression. Tuesday also happens to be the day that she volunteers by helping several legally blind older residents in the apartment building with their mail. When she comes back to the program office to report on her visits, she tells the director that the program needs to offer activities for those with low vision and that she intends to bring it up at the next advisory board meeting.

Building a partnership with the residents can be uncomfortable for professionals used to working in the traditional service-delivery paradigm. They must be willing to share power with the very individuals they are trying to help. In this model, the "helping" relationship takes on a new dimension in which residents are no longer clients who are acted upon but partners who have an active role in making their community a good place to grow old.

NECESSARY INGREDIENTS FOR SUCCESS

Based on the large number of programs in New York City and close to 20 years of programmatic experience, it is clear that successful development of a NORC-SSP requires different ways of working, at different levels, and in different roles than most social workers in the field of aging do today. At the macro level of community, social workers play a leadership role in assessing a community's assets (strengths) and gaps (vulnerabilities) on an ongoing basis; engaging a broad group of formal and informal leaders, constituents, health and social service providers, and other stakeholders in facilitating a community-wide discussion about their concerns and aspirations as people age in place; building consensus among the partners (each with their own objectives, language, and terminology) to define a shared mission with clear roles and responsibilities; and providing an environment that permits shared problem solving that encourages thinking outside the box, so each partner can contribute what it best has to offer. In essence, it is good old-fashioned community-organizing skills that are required to help a community pool its resources and work toward its vision of, or aspirations for, itself.

At the micro level of the older individual, social workers bring a multidimensional approach to addressing "problems arising out of disequilibrium between (*individuals*) and the environment." Moving beyond a deficits-based practice to plug the holes in functions that clients can no longer perform, social workers in NORC-SSPs utilize a strengths-based practice to help people at all functional levels remain engaged in and with the community, connect them to resources as needed, help negotiate systems and organizations, and "help people enlarge their competence and increase their problem solving and coping abilities" (Monk, 1986, p. 13). Professionals, skilled in biopsychosocial assessment and working in interdisciplinary social worker–nurse–volunteer teams, must be creative and flexible in this client-centered model.

DOES THIS KIND OF MODEL WORK?

The history of New York's NORC-SSPs and the very principles on which they are founded suggest that current approaches to evaluation are themselves mired in the old paradigm of service delivery. At the city level, efforts to measure performance have focused on counting units of services (referrals, case management hours, etc.) that build on the data system of the city's Department for the Aging, which has an entirely different agenda of formal accountability. At the state level, self-reporting efforts to measure outcomes have focused on the extent to which these programs have averted hospitalization and nursing home admissions to support the political desire to slow the growth of public expenditures on long-term care.

Neither of these efforts examines the extent to which the NORC-SSP model improves the quality of life for all kinds of older people living in a community. To do so, we will need to ask different questions that can measure the programs' success in transforming communities, providing a supportive environment for older people at all levels of health and functioning in a variety of circumstances, and engaging communities themselves as active partners in making NORCs good places to grow old. We will need to understand the extent to which NORC-SSPs

- Provide avenues for older people to take on positive roles (versus the stereotype of old people as a mass of needs)
- Empower older people and promote civic engagement (versus people who are acted upon)
- Promote social connectedness and a reweaving of the social fabric as earlier connections fray (versus home care policies that keep older people locked behind their front doors)
- Develop an array of flexible and calibrated supports as needs arise (versus providing services one hip fracture at a time)

- Help older people feel secure in their community (versus not knowing how to get help when they need it)

Although we don't yet have quantitative data on the assisted living and nursing home admissions of NORC clients to compare with residents of other communities, it is clear that many of the events that can trigger institutional admissions in other communities can, in most cases, be effectively addressed by well-functioning supportive service programs in NORCs. Such programs have developed the informal and intermittent networks of support needed to sustain frail older people at home and are skilled at mixing these supports with appropriate formal services to increase the sense of security people need to live out their days in the community.

If we are to more fully understand the potential of the NORC-SSP model, a systematic and comprehensive evaluation will need to be undertaken. Such an effort requires resources that are sufficient to develop appropriate tools and conduct the study. Absent such a commitment, descriptive information and anecdotes are the only sources for understanding the model. However, the AdvantAge Project of the Home Care Institute for Research and Policy of the Visiting Nurse Services of New York, while undertaken for different purposes, contains some useful approaches to evaluating the impact of NORC-SSPs. Seeking to measure the extent to which older people perceive their communities as "elder-friendly," using a broad range of indicators, the project asked a representative sample of older people in a national survey and in each of 10 different communities how well their communities addressed basic needs, optimized physical and mental well-being, promoted social and civic engagement, and maximized independence for the frail and disabled (http://www.vnsny.org/advantage).

One of the 10 participating communities was a New York City public housing development that has a NORC-SSP. This was the only low-income minority community in the study, and the overall findings about the effects of race and poverty across a wide range of indicators (and how the program and the community are using the data to address issues of safety, hunger, and health) are quite compelling. But the most surprising finding was the extent to which older people in the Amsterdam public houses feel secure in their community. When asked if they know where to go and whom to call if they need help, 93% of the respondents in this community said they did (they'd call their NORC program), compared with 76% of older people in the surrounding neighborhood.

LOOKING TOWARD THE FUTURE

Shifting paradigms is difficult. The system of services currently in place for America's older population, while highly variable from one place to another and frequently inadequate, is large, complex, and entrenched. The development and testing of new service-delivery models, based on the paradigm grounded in our richer understanding of the tasks in the later stages of life and the needs of older people, cannot proceed quickly enough. All sorts of efforts at developing new service models and elder-friendly communities are under way throughout the United States. In a number of retirement communities and "aged-in" neighborhoods in different parts of the country, residents are taking matters into their own hands, organizing, and developing programs and supports to make life better for themselves. Similarly, foundations and government are engaged with the professional and provider worlds in efforts to make communities more livable for older people.

New York's NORC-SSP model stands out for its scope, the number of different projects and communities involved in a single model, and the extent and duration of support from state and local governments. But what also sets the New York experience apart from all the others is the requirement that professionals and older people work together to design, develop, and maintain supportive communities, drawing on the expertise and resources each has to offer.

Communities come in all shapes and sizes. In New York City, the presence of a large number of moderate-income and public housing developments with large populations of older people who had aged in place presented a natural opportunity for the early development of the housing-based NORC-SSP model. The 27 programs currently in operation are predicated on the presence of housing management structures that define "community" and make it possible to organize a program and communalize part of the financing. Extending this model to other kinds of communities, such as those dominated by single-family homeownership, will require experimentation and systematic study to shed light on how to define the community and the elements it must possess in order to develop and support a successful program. Alternative vehicles or mechanisms (natural to communities or ones that can be developed) will be needed to replace the pivotal definitional and organizational functions that build off New York City's single housing management structure. We will need to understand the minimum thresholds of community size, population, and geographic practicality below which the development of successful programs will not be possible.

Moving from abstraction to real-world application, efforts are already under way in New York City's northeast section of Queens to address these issues and develop a neighborhood-based NORC-SSP prototype. Based on what has been learned so far, New York State's NORC legislation is being modified to support the neighborhood-based model replication in similar communities across the state. A sufficient critical mass of programs in place will permit us to better understand whether the NORC-SSP model can be generalized to the more spread-out communities and neighborhoods that dot America's landscape.

Looking toward the future, demographic changes that will intensify the graying of America's communities in the coming years provide the opportunity to rethink public policy and service delivery for an aging and increasingly heterogeneous older population. We can continue to have the same discussion we've been having for the last 25 years about how to build and pay for the components of a long-term care system that targets individuals with deficits—the one-hip-fracture-at-a-time approach—or we can update policy and practice to reflect the reality of who the older population is and the world in which older people live. The fact is that the overwhelming majority of older people will remain living in their homes of long standing, with no entrance or exit criteria automatically requiring them to move as their care needs change. The challenge is figuring out how to rebuild age-integrated communities that have large concentrations of older residents into good places to grow old.

REFERENCES

AARP. (1992). *Understanding senior housing for the 1990s: Survey of consumer preferences, concerns, and needs.* Washington, DC: Author.

Hunt, M. E., & Hunt, G. (1985). Naturally occurring retirement communities. *Journal of Housing for the Elderly, 3*(3/4).

Kilgorn, P. T. (2003, July 31). North Dakota town's payoff for hard lives is long life. *New York Times*, p. A22.

Lanspery, S., & Callahan, J. (1994). *Naturally occurring retirement communities: A report for the Pew Charitable Trust.*

Litwak, E. (1970). An approach to linkage in "grass roots" community organizing. In F. M. Cox, J. L. Erlich, J. Rothman, & J. E. Tropman (Eds.), *Strategies of community organizing: A book of readings.* Illinois: F. E. Peacock.

Monk, A. (1986). Social work with the aged: Principles of practice. In C. H. Meyer (Ed.), *Social work with the aging: Readings in social work.* Washington, DC: National Association of Social Workers.

Rowe, J. W., & Kahn, R. L. (1998). *Successful aging.* New York: Pantheon Books.

Vladeck, F. (2004). *A good place to grow old: New York's model for NORC Supportive Service Programs.* New York: United Hospital Fund.

How Social Workers Practice

KATHLEEN McINNIS-DITTRICH
JAMES LUBBEN,
SECTION EDITORS

SECTION

Assessment and Interventions With Older Adults and Their Families/Caregivers

OVERVIEW

This section of the *Handbook* is divided into three subsections. The first examines various facets of assessment; the second provides an overview of practice theories and models most relevant to work with individuals and families; the third takes a more macro perspective examining advocacy and empowerment models.

ASSESSMENT

In his chapter, Scott Miyake Geron examines the context of assessment, anchoring it in the heart and soul of social work practice. While talking about the process of assessment, Geron advises that geriatric social work consider the assessment phase as the commencement of a working relationship with a client and not an end in itself.

James Lubben makes a case for the development of valid and reliable short measures for geriatric social work practice. These abbreviated measures, which he defines as having no more than 10 items, can be practical screeners for risk factors as well as important tools for clarifying the relevance and importance of social health to the well-being of older adults. Rosalie A. Kane provides an overview of standardized measures used in geriatric assessment. Dr. Kane provides a critique of some of the traditional measures and offers suggestions for newer measures that should be considered.

THEORIES AND MODELS OF PRACTICE INTERVENTION

Kathleen McInnis-Dittrich describes a broad range of therapeutic interventions, ranging from the complicated process of cognitive restructuring to relatively simple behavior management techniques employed in some approaches to validation therapy. The interventions discussed in this chapter include cognitive-behavioral therapy, crisis intervention, and therapeutic validation interventions. The common denominator in these approaches is the focus on the older adult's thought process and how that process influences subsequent emotional and behavioral responses.

Therapeutic approaches to working with extended family and the power of the group process are the foci of Roberta R. Greene and Joyce Riley's chapter. The authors acknowledge the importance of supporting the well-being of caregivers as part of an ecological and systemic approach to providing services to older adults. Family-centered case management methods for recognizing and alleviating the stressors involved in caring for an aging family member are described in this chapter. The authors include an in-depth discussion of the use of group treatment models for both older adults and caregivers.

M. Joanna Mellor discusses interdisciplinary team practice and its importance in providing comprehensive services to older adults. This approach is valuable for its ability to attend to the wide range of needs of the older adult, utilizing the expertise of physical and mental health professionals. Mellor identifies both strengths and weaknesses of this approach and illustrates through the use of a case presentation how a multidisciplinary approach is superior to any specific profession's approach in identifying both problems and solutions.

A psychodynamic approach to treating the emotional problems of older adults remains a controversial issue, as is illustrated in Denis P. Cronin's chapter. Although clinical social work remains deeply influenced by Freud's early dismissal of older adults as inappropriate for a traditional psychodynamic approach, Cronin makes a passionate case for the importance of the richness of this time in the life cycle for gaining deep insight and working through emotional issues. He discusses the significance of an older adult's struggle with conflicts over death, the therapeutic nature of transference based on age-related issues, and the unique challenges to the therapist in this process.

Reminiscence and life review are significant natural coping mechanisms and as treatment modalities can help older adults find meaning through reflection on their life experiences, according to Berit Ingersoll-Dayton and Angela Bommarito. Therapeutic reminiscence and life review focus on the older adults' processing and acceptance of early life events to improve emotional health and revitalize previously used coping skills. The authors identify the personality characteristics of older adults and the specific emotional issues that have been most successfully treated using these approaches.

Rosemary Chapin, Holly Nelson-Becker, and Kelley Macmillan explore how strengths-based and solution-focused therapeutic approaches can be used with older adults. Rather than focusing on deficits in behavior, both of these approaches identify an individual's strengths as they can be applied to problem solving and in using the richness of the solution envisioned by the older adults. These approaches focus on a strong empowerment approach, identifying what is "strong rather than what is wrong," a positive and energizing approach to working with older adults.

One of the most recent and popular approaches to working with older adults is that of recognizing and mobilizing an older adult's spirituality, described in the chapter by Holly Nelson-Becker, Mitsuko Nakashima, and Edward Canda. They describe in detail the domains included in a spiritual assessment of the older adult and the use of spiritually oriented helping activities. The authors offer a thoughtful discussion of what clinician and client characteristics are most appropriate for spiritually based interventions.

ADVOCACY AND EMPOWERMENT

Kevin J. Mahoney and Karen Zgoda illustrate the practice modality of client empowerment. The authors first provide an overview of the history of empowerment models in social work, grounding this modality in the context of practice theories. They then use the Cash and Counseling project as a case study to illustrate various facets of empowerment. Linda Krogh Harootyan and Greg O'Neill examine the practice of advocacy with and for older populations. Harootyan and O'Neill identify a number of advocacy groups, both large and small. Some, such as AARP, are well-known and broad-based, whereas others are more targeted and less well-known. Harootyan and O'Neill make a case that all are important to furthering the cause of aging policy and programs.

A. Assessment

SCOTT MIYAKE GERON

Comprehensive and Multidimensional Geriatric Assessment

65

In the pantheon of social work accomplishments, assessment occupies a place of honor. Assessment can trace its pedigree to the earliest development of social work. As a distinct social work activity, assessment has its origins in the "scientific diagnosis" of the Charity Organization Society (Kunzel, 1995; Wenocur & Reisch, 1989). The lofty status of assessment in social work continues to this day. Any review of social work practice texts identifies assessment as a basic social work competency (e.g., Garthwait, 2004; Perlman, 1957; Pincus & Minahan, 1973; Sheafor, Horejsi, & Horejsi, 1988; Strean, 1978; Weissman, Epstein, & Savage, 1983). For example, in a recent study of social work competencies for working with older adults, conducted by the Council on Social Work Education, geriatric assessment is singled out as a core practice competency (Rosen, Zlotnik, Curl, & Green, 2000). High-touch and high-tech, with medical, psychosocial, financial, private, and public implications, assessment could also be called the quintessence of 21st-century social work. Indeed, it is somewhat ironic, at least to social workers, that other health care providers are now recognizing what social workers have long known: that patients should be assessed biopsychosocially.

What do social workers need to know about assessment with older adults? For many years, social workers had to rely on their general social work training, intuition, or practice experience in assessing older adults. Now a wide range of valid and reliable assessment tools are available. Social workers use comprehensive assessment forms, measures, instruments, and short screening tools to collect information about their clients. The use of assessment measures serves a basic clinical function for social workers working with older adults, which include helping the practitioner develop an adequate information base to understand the problems, needs, resources, and strengths in a client's situation. Results of these measures also assist the social worker, family, and agency to make decisions about the care plan. Social workers, but also many other professionals and paraprofessionals, engage in the use of such measures in the course of providing care.

Assessment is also a process done by social workers; it is a general problem-solving approach that is particularly characteristic of social work in all fields of practice. This approach can, of course, include the use of assessment measures, but it also relies on clinical judgment, the formalized problem-solving skills that practicing social workers develop and employ in every aspect of their professional work—when they are using specific assessment measures and when they are not.

The contemporary context of practice poses challenges to any type of assessment. Resources are shrinking, funding for services is rarely certain, agency staff are burdened, and social workers often lack a strong constituency or administrative support. Social work departments do not control the flow of clients, and the complexity of clients is changing and increasing. The generalized nature of social work interventions also poses challenges for assessment. Social work services are presumed to be customized, but they rarely are. As a result, geriatric social work intervention may not consist of a single service aimed at alleviating a specific problem, making the use of standardized assessment difficult. Moreover, although social workers may have a direct role in an intervention, often, especially in health settings, they play a supportive role. This type of "vertical complexity" limits the responsibilities of social workers and also their contact with clients and their families.

Nonetheless, geriatric assessment is in many ways a liminal social work activity. Viewed by many as the most basic of social work skills, geriatric assessment serves as the threshold between clients and needed services, and the skills needed to effectively complete geriatric social work assessments separate the untrained social worker from the advanced practitioner. Geriatric social work assessment has gained importance not only from the new models of assessment that are available, but also because social work roles and environments are changing, and hence the types of assessment skills needed are increasing. In this chapter, I describe the role that assessment plays in geriatric social work practice, provide basic information about geriatric assessment that practitioners need to know, and summarize some of the basic processes of conducting geriatric social work assessments.

ISSUES IN THE USE OF ASSESSMENT MEASURES

A wide variety of assessment tools are now available for geriatric social workers (e.g., Berkman, Maramaldi, Breon, & Howe, 2002; Geron, 1997; R. A. Kane & Kane, 1981). As Rosalie Kane describes in her chapter in this book, many of these are multidimensional assessment instruments that are designed to help social workers, case managers, and other health professionals develop an understanding of the problems, needs, resources, and strengths of an older client's situation and to guide the assessor and the client in making decisions about a care plan. Frequently used by

states and agencies to determine eligibility for community-based or residential long-term care services for adults, these type of assessments are designed to provide a holistic picture of the client and his or her family across a wide range of functioning. They address multiple dimensions or domains, providing, at a minimum, information about demographic characteristics, health status, functional performance, cognitive functioning, mental health status, social and informal supports, environment, and financial status (Geron & Chassler, 1994). Other common assessment tools are brief screening tools that social workers and others use to determine the presence of cognitive impairment or depression (e.g., Berkman et al., 1999). These types of screens may be embedded inside large assessments or stand alone.

Effective administration of any assessment instrument requires preparation. At a minimum, assessors must understand the purpose of the assessments they are asked to use. As a single assessment instrument may serve multiple purposes, this can be a difficult task. Different types of information, levels of detail, even seemingly duplicate types of information may be contained in the same assessment tool; for example, different types of information may be needed for clinical purposes as compared to establishing technical eligibility for programs and services. Ideally, the social worker will understand why an instrument is being used and will be prepared to reassure the client or caregivers of the purpose and value of the assessment.

Before using any instrument, geriatric social workers should thoroughly review the measure and each question in the instrument and be clear what information each question is designed to obtain. Social workers assigned to administer a new assessment measure should receive extensive training, which should include role-plays with colleagues, observing more experienced workers use the measure, reviewing FAQs (responses to frequently asked questions), and studying Q-by-Q (question-by-question) manuals that describe any administration or interpretation issues for any item in a measure. In the use of assessment measures in research projects, training in the use of a measure can take a week or more before actual assessments are conducted with clients, and this rule of thumb should apply to agencies as well. There are several purposes of such training, including to make the geriatric social worker comfortable using the measure, to understand the purpose and meaning of every item or question, to know whether and under what conditions proxy respondents are allowed, to learn how much latitude, if any, is tolerated in the use of probes, to become familiar with any skip patterns in the measure, and to gain experience in how to re-word questions to adapt to odd or difficult situations.

The use of an assessment measure is rarely designed to be an isolated event by an individual social worker; most are designed to serve as a common assessment protocol to be used by multiple workers in a particular agency, and some are designed to be used by all workers in a state, regardless of agency affiliation or funding stream. The goal of standardization is an important feature of most assessment tools. For geriatric social workers new to these types of assessments, it is important to understand the rationale and benefits that standardization provides. Standardization is a desirable feature in assessment because it allows for the reproducibility of findings and makes interpretation and sharing of results across workers possible. Uniformity in assessment provides a common language that permits communication across disciplines and agencies and provides a safety check to ensure that important elements of an assessment are not inadvertently omitted. A uniform approach makes it possible to develop meaningful information about the physical, psychological, and social well-being of clients over time and to learn which services are most effective in meeting needs. Standardization typically encompasses any of the following:

- Content (questions, responses to questions, instructions, and format).
- Data collection methods (e.g., face-to-face, telephone, self-administered).
- Scoring algorithm (how scores are calculated).
- Analytic methods used.
- Format for displaying results.

THE PROCESS OF GERIATRIC ASSESSMENT

Whatever the intended uses of geriatric assessment, the completion of assessment measures encompasses a number of clinical social work skills. Older adults may have multiple health problems with nonspecific origins or causes, may not have reliable proxy informants, and may have functional or cognitive limitations that make it difficult to provide accurate descriptions of symptoms. Depression is particularly common in older adults with poor physical health and can become a chronic or recurrent problem for up to 50% of older adults (Alexopoulos & Chester, 1992). Between 45% and 90% of mental illnesses are not detected by primary care physicians (Blanchard,

Waterreus, & Mann, 1995; Eisenberg, 1992; Orrell, Scurfield, Clarke, & Renshaw, 2000; Watts et al. 2002). Effective assessors draw on all of their experience, observations, judgment, and clinical expertise. The specialized skills needed to perform geriatric assessments include the ability to establish and maintain empathic relationships; experience in identifying symptoms of depression and cognitive impairment while conducting standardized social and health assessments; knowledge of human behavior, family and caregiver dynamics, aging, and disability; and awareness of community resources and services (Geron, 1997; Geron & Chassler, 1994).

The range and type of assessments available for older adults are now well documented (Geron, 1997; Kane & Kane, 1990, 2000; Lichtenberg, 1999; Osterwil, Brummel-Smith, & Beck, 2000), but the actual processes of conducting geriatric social work assessments with older adults are rarely addressed. To some extent, conducting a clinical interview in any social work setting is relevant experience (e.g., see Murphy & Dillon, 2003), but geriatric assessment with older adults also involves specialized concerns and expertise. Colleen King's (1997) and other, more recent texts in geriatric social work (e.g., McInnis-Dittrich, 2002) have identified some of the important idiosyncratic processes in conducting geriatric assessments, including the following:

- Establishing rapport with the respondent.
- Explaining the purpose of the assessment.
- Using observation and clinical judgment.
- Handling difficult situations.
- Maintaining confidentiality.

Establishing Rapport

Most social workers receive training in a number of clinical methods, and none is more basic than the therapeutic skill of engaging clients and establishing rapport with them. The engagement of older clients is an equally important part of the process of conducting geriatric assessments (Schneider, Kropf, & Kisor, 2000). Establishing trust with an older respondent, who may be more reluctant to participate in assessments than younger adults, is essential. To do so, social workers conducting assessments with older adults should spend as much time as necessary to reassure them and answer any questions they have. Establishing rapport involves listening sensitively and honestly to clients' concerns and problems, speaking in a conversational tone without the use of jargon, and showing enjoyment in talking and working with clients. The time it takes to establish this rapport varies from only a few minutes to 15 minutes or more, but failure to do so can doom an assessment.

Explaining the Purpose of the Assessment

Geriatric social workers should spend time talking to respondents about the assessment before beginning. This is necessary to explain the purpose of the assessment, reassuring clients that the procedure is important and worth their time, and, in some cases, to obtain informed consent. In research studies, for human subject protection, this step is mandatory and the language to be used is scripted. Even when consent has been obtained, the geriatric social worker should tell the client about the type of questions that will be asked and why.

An important function of this early disclosure is to anticipate questions that may be difficult or awkward for the respondent to answer, for example, asking questions about cognitive impairment of a cognitively intact respondent. Letting the respondent know that "we have to ask these questions of everyone" may help the respondent answer the questions without reticence. Geriatric social workers should not be afraid to answer any questions posed by respondents about the purpose, length, or implications of the assessment. This requires that the assessor understands and believes in the purposes for the questions, communicates those purposes to the client, and speaks to the client in a relaxed and interested way.

Using Observation and Clinical Judgment

Before, after, and during the administration of a formal assessment protocol, the geriatric social worker uses clinical judgment to assess the client and family. Clinical social work judgment is often referred to as a type of problem solving (McInnis-Dittrich, 2002; Murphy & Dillon, 2003; Perlman, 1957). If the assessment is completed at the client's home, the geriatric social worker uses clinical judgment to observe the client's behavior and interactions with others, to identify potential risks in the home environment, and to determine the level and type of caregiver support. From these observations, along with the results of a standardized assessment, the geriatric social worker identifies potential problems and unmet needs, formulates a care plan, and begins to implement problem-solving strategies.

For social workers working in interdisciplinary health teams, the opportunity to observe and interact with the client is precious, as few physicians or nurses have the opportunity to conduct home assessments. In recent focus groups we have conducted with primary care physicians and nurses in California to explore the potential of integrating social workers into primary care practice, health providers stated that they lacked basic information on the living conditions of patients, information that social workers can provide through their assessment (Geron & Keefe, in press).

Handling Difficult Situations

Social workers conducting assessments with older adults often encounter situations unlike those experienced with younger clients. Some of the most difficult situations facing assessors are when the older client is overcome with grief, loneliness, sadness, or anger (King, 1997) or when caregivers become similarly upset. Social workers unfamiliar with older adults may find these experiences uncomfortable at first, and their training should include how to respond to these types of client responses in a professional way while showing compassion and understanding. In trying to complete the assessment, the geriatric social worker needs to be direct, polite, and sensitive. In general, it is important not to ignore the client's concerns or pretend that the client is not upset. Social workers conducting formalized assessments should stop the assessment and listen to the client. They should try to reassure clients that it is safe to express their feelings and try to make them feel comfortable and at ease. Simple comments such as "I understand" and "I'm so sorry" can be reassuring and allow the social worker a way to acknowledge clients' feelings and demonstrate an understanding of their concerns.

Maintaining Confidentiality

A basic part of the process of conducting assessments is to respect the confidentiality of the information obtained. Confidentiality requires that interviewers not discuss the information obtained during the assessment with anyone not associated with the project. The geriatric social worker may need to reassure the client or the client's family about the confidentiality of the assessment. In agency-based assessment protocols, the client name and contact information is listed on the form, and, in these cases, it is imperative to keep the completed forms secure until they can be returned to the office. In most research studies involving geriatric assessments, client names are never associated with the completed assessments. Client names are usually listed on disposition sheets that provide directions to the client's home or telephone contact numbers, but not on the assessment form. When the completed interview forms are turned in to the office, the disposition sheet is separated from the survey. Identifying information never appears in reports, only aggregated information from a large number of clients.

Honoring the Person Assessed

I would add one other essential component of the geriatric assessment process. For many older adults who have entered the formal service system for help, the reality of their lives—their wishes, beliefs, history, likes, and dislikes—is reduced to whatever is revealed by the measurement tools used to assess them. The consequences of these assessments for the older person are enormous. The results often require coming to grips with a loss of or decline in functioning in one or more areas in which the person previously had been independent.

Because no assessment measure, however well-designed, can do justice to the person who is assessed, there is a risk that the client's beliefs, values, and preferences for care will be omitted. This is where the geriatric social worker can ensure that the client's voice is heard during the assessment process, whatever the intended purpose of the assessment. As agency workers or researchers, geriatric social workers are required to complete assessment protocols, even though most of these measures are designed to represent the interests of the agency or funder providing the services (e.g., determining whether this client is eligible for these services). Geriatric social workers can use their clinical skills to assess what is important in the lives of the clients they are assessing and to give voice to their clients' preferences and values, even if the measures they are using do not. Increasingly, assessing what is important to clients about the services they receive is becoming the focus of geriatric assessment measures (e.g., Applebaum, Straker, & Geron, 2000; R. A. Kane, 2003; R. A. Kane et al., 2004).

DISCUSSION

Geriatric social workers, like their social work colleagues in other practice settings, use assessment to guide their clinical judgments. With proper training, geriatric social workers can use assessment as a means to further the relationship they build with the client. Although not intuitively obvious, an important goal of assessment is to capture the full range of measurement for the concepts included in the assessment protocol; this is the research equivalent of the social worker's clinical objective of obtaining a holistic assessment of a client's functioning. Of course, geriatric social workers employ clinical judgment in their interactions with clients, whether formal assessment measures are used or not. Many of the most important clinical assessment skills involved in practice with older adults occur outside of the formal assessment process.

Although the science and art of geriatric assessment has come a long way, it is important for geriatric social work to move beyond assessment. There is a need to buttress this important practice competency with other interventions that social workers can implement to improve the lives of older adults. Completing assessments should never be an end in itself. Unfortunately, in some environments, there is a growing tendency to use geriatric social workers in that way. The current situation of social workers in Medicare-reimbursed nursing homes is a case in point. Current Medicare rules mandate that facilities have at least one social worker for every 120 residents, and, in facilities that hold to that minimum standard, social workers are sometimes reduced to conducting assessments of residents using the Minimum Data Set and have little time for anything else. The greatest threat to geriatric social work is that social workers will be restricted to conducting assessments, with no time to implement a care plan, no services in place to address identified problems, or, even worse, no authority to use proven interventions. Social work should not become a profession that only does assessments. Social workers should also act; they should intervene; they should conduct evidence-based interventions shown to make a difference in the lives of the clients they serve. No doubt, geriatric social workers can use the results of assessments to assist in their clinical judgment to identify and solve problems. Our challenge is to provide clients with the tools and authority to act once the assessment is completed.

REFERENCES

Alexopoulos, G. S., & Chester, J. G. (1992, May). Outcomes of geriatric depression. *Clinical Geriatric Medicine, 8*(2), 363–376.

Applebaum, R., Straker, J., & Geron, S. M. (2000). *Assessing satisfaction in health and long-term care: Practical approaches to hearing the voices of consumers.* New York: Springer Publishing Co.

Berkman, B., Chauncey, S., Holmes, W., Daniels, A., Bonander, E., Sampson, S., et al. (1999). Standardization screening of elderly patients' needs for social work assessment in primary care: Use of the SF-36. *Health & Social Work, 21*(1), 9–16.

Berkman, B. J., Maramaldi, P., Breon, E. A., & Howe, J. L. (2002). Social work gerontological assessment revisited. In J. L. Howe (Ed.), *Older people and their caregivers across the spectrum of care* (pp. 1–14). Binghamton, NY: Haworth Press.

Blanchard, M. R., Waterreus, A., & Mann, A. H. (1995). The effect of primary care nurse intervention upon older people screened as depressed. *International Journal of Geriatric Psychiatry, 10*(4), 289–298.

Eisenberg, L. (1992). Treating depression and anxiety in primary care: Closing the gap between knowledge and practice. *New England Journal of Medicine, 326*(16), 1080–1084.

Garthwait, C. (2005). *The social work practicum.* Boston: Pearson.

Geron, S. (1997). Taking the measure of assessment. *Generations, 21*(1), 5–9.

Geron, S. M. (1997). Multidimensional assessment measures. *Generations, 21*(1), 52–54.

Geron, S. M. & Chassler, D. (1994, November). *Guidelines for case management practice across the long-term care continuum. Report of the National Advisory Committee on Long-Term Care Case Management.* [Monograph prepared under a grant from the Robert Wood Johnson Foundation.] Bristol, CT: Connecticut Community Care, Inc.

Geron, S. M., & Keefe, B. (in press). Moving evidence-based interventions to populations: A case study using social workers in primary care. *Home Health Care Services Quarterly, 25*(1 and 2).

Kane, R. A. (2003). Definition, measurement, and correlates of quality of life in nursing homes: Toward a reasonable practice, research, and policy agenda. *The Gerontologist, 43*(2), 28–36.

Kane, R. A., & Kane, R. L. (1981). *Assessing the elderly: A practical guide to measurement.* Lexington, MA: Lexington Books.

Kane, R. L., Bershadsky, B., Kane, R. A., Degenholtz, H. H., Liu, J., Giles, K., et al. (2004). Using resident reports of quality of life to distinguish among nursing homes. *The Gerontologist, 44*(5), 624–632.

Kane, R. L., & Kane, R. A. (1990). The impact of long-term-care financing on personal autonomy. *Generations, 14*(Suppl. 1990), 86–89.

Kane, R. L., & Kane, R. A. (2000). Assessment in long-term care. *Annual Review of Public Health, 3,* 659–686.

Kane, R. L., & Kane, R. A. (2000). Assessment in long-term care. *Annual Review of Public Health, 21,* 659–686.

King, A. C. (1997). Intervention strategies and determinants of physical activity and exercise behavior in adult and older adult men and women. *World Review of Nutrition and Dietetics, 82,* 148–158.

Kunzel, R. (1995). *Fallen women, problem girls: Unmarried mothers and the professionalization of social work.* New Haven: Yale University Press.

Lichtenberg, P. A. (1999). *Handbook of assessment in clinical gerontology.* Toronto, Canada: Wiley.

McInnis-Dittrich, K. (2002). *Social work with elders: Biopsychological approach to assessment and intervention* (2nd ed.). Boston: Pearson Education.

Murphy, B. C., & Dillon, C. (2003). *Interviewing in action: Relationship, process, and change* (2nd ed.). Pacific Grove, CA: Brooks/Cole.

Orrell, M., Scurfield, P., Cloke, L., & Renshaw, J. (2000, November). The management of depression in older people in primary care: A survey of general practitioners. *Aging and Mental Health, 4*(4), 305–308.

Osterwil, D., Brummel-Smith, K., & Beck, J. C. (2000). *Comprehensive geriatric assessment.* New York: McGraw-Hill.

Perlman, H. (1957). *Social casework: A problem-solving process.* Chicago: University of Chicago Press.

Pincus, A., & Minahan, A. (1973). *Social work practice: Model and method.* Itasca, IL: F. E. Peacock.

Rosen, A. L., Zlotnik, J. L., Curl, A. L., & Green, R. G. (2000). *CSWE SAGE-SW National Aging Competencies Survey Report.* Washington, DC: Council on Social Work Education.

Schneider, R. L., Kropf, N. P., & Kisor, A. J. (Eds.). (2000). *Gerontological social work: Knowledge, service settings and special populations* (2nd ed.). Belmont, CA: Brooks/Cole.

Sheafor, B., Horejsi, C., & Horejsi, G. (1988). *Techniques and guidelines for social work practice.* Boston: Allyn and Bacon.

Strean, H. (1978). *Clinical social work: Theory and practice.* New York: Free Press.

Watts, S. C., Bhutani, G. E., Stout, I. H., Ducker, G. M., Cleator, P. J., McGarry, J., & Day, M. (2002). Mental health in older adult recipients of primary care services: Is depression the key issue? Identification, treatment and the general practitioner. *International Journal of Geriatric Psychiatry, 17*(5), 427–437.

Weissman, H., Epstein, I., & Savage, A. (1983). *Agency-based social work: Neglected aspects of clinical practice.* Philadelphia: Temple University Press.

Wenocur, S., & Reisch, M. (1989). *From charity to enterprise: The development of American social work in a market economy.* Urbana: University of Illinois Press.

The adoption of standardized abbreviated social health measures into social work practice and research holds much promise. Abbreviated geriatric measures that are highly reliable and valid for physical and mental health domains have existed for some time. However, a similar set of measures for the more social aspects of health and well-being in old age has only recently been developed.

Abbreviated and targeted geriatric assessment measures are those that, by definition, are very short, generally 10 items or fewer. Thus, they can be readily incorporated into clinical assessment protocols, used in wellness and health promotion clinics as quick screeners identifying groups for more intensive screening, or included in health surveys of large populations. Perhaps the most celebrated of these is the single-item measure for self-rated health that has been shown to be a powerful predictor of future health status and health care utilization. It has demonstrated so much salience to various facets of health status and service utilization that this single question has become a standard item in many geriatric assessment protocols and a normative item on health surveys.

SHORTAGE OF ABBREVIATED MEASURES FOR SOCIAL ASPECTS OF HEALTH

Whereas geriatric practitioners and health survey designers can readily identify a set of abbreviated measures for physical and mental health, there appears to be no consensus on what, if any, abbreviated and targeted social measures should be adopted. This deficiency was recently demonstrated in a federal report entitled *Older Americans 2004: Key Indicators of Well-Being* (Federal Interagency Forum on Aging-Related Statistics, 2004). This publication contains outstanding graphics and its audience is very broad, including the general public, service providers and planners, and top-level government policymakers. It contains numerous indicators of physical and mental health status with a clear message that these factors are significant aspects of well-being in old age. However, this otherwise excellent report does not contain a single indictor of social health status, such as social engagement, social support, or social isolation.

This is a serious omission. Had there been such measures included in this important overview of the state of health affairs among older persons, it would have communicated to the public in general and to older persons in particular that social health is just as important to well-being in old age as maintaining

JAMES LUBBEN

Abbreviated and Targeted Geriatric Assessment

physical and mental health. Further, data on such domains could have helped facilitate public understanding regarding the importance of geriatric social work for improving the well-being of older Americans.

The underdevelopment of abbreviated social health measures contrasts with the state of affairs in other domains. This can be illustrated by examining the domains of geriatric assessment protocols and national health status reports. Again, the *Older Americans 2004* report (Federal Interagency Forum on Aging-Related Statistics, 2004) provides a useful example to illustrate this point. It contains 16 tables that provide an abbreviated measure of the health status of older Americans and another 12 tables reporting an indicator of health behavior. For health status, the *Older Americans* report has a checklist of 9 common chronic health conditions: arthritis, asthma, bronchitis, cancer, diabetes, emphysema, heart disease, hypertension, and stroke. It also has abbreviated measures for sensory impairment (hearing and vision), oral health (number of missing teeth), memory impairment (20-word recall test), depression (Center for Epidemiological Studies Depression Scale), and functional disability (activities of daily living and instrumental activities of daily living). These are in addition to the standard single-item self-rated health question and charts indicating longitudinal trends on life expectancy and mortality. The following indicators were selected for health risks and behaviors: vaccinations, mammograms, diet, physical activity, obesity, smoking, and air quality.

There is no doubt about the importance of these health and mental health indicators to well-being in old age. However, the omission of social health measures is quite obvious. In fairness to the federal health researchers who assembled the set of health measures contained in the *Older Americans* report, a close look at other compendiums of health and well-being markers of older adults likely would have identified the same deficiency.

As a rule, the physical and mental health indicators are much better developed and accepted than those examining social health. It is true that social workers examine the biopsychosocial aspects of a client, and so all of the health status indicators mentioned for physical and mental health are considered relevant and even important to social work practice. However, the lack of readily agreed upon social health measures needs to be considered a serious deficiency for social work, if for no other reason than that the "social" is at the heart and soul of what social workers do. If federal and state health surveyors and similar

key researchers don't count what is central to social work, it sends a serious message to multiple audiences that the social is undervalued. The solution is to develop and adopt a set of valid and reliable abbreviated measures of social health.

SOCIAL WORK AND HEALTH PROMOTION

There are other reasons why considerably more work needs to be done to develop short assessment measures of social health domains. Fostering the development of abbreviated and targeted assessment tools for domains central to geriatric social work practice expands the potential for social workers to be engaged in the growing practice arena of prevention and health promotion (Institute on Medicine, 2000). Health promotion and disease prevention programs often involve screening large populations with brief assessment instruments with the goal of identifying an at-risk population who in turn are subjected to more intensive assessments. The adoption of standardized abbreviated social health measures could be integrated into these wellness-screening batteries to identify old adults perceived to be at risk. Those identified then could be referred to more traditional practitioners, including clinical social workers, for both more extensive assessment and possible treatment.

There are a number of case examples in the literature for social work involvement in health promotion for older adults. For example, Klein and Bloom (1997) provide an overview of strategies that geriatric social workers and other helping professions could employ to foster healthy living among older adults. Dorfman and associates (1995) report on the use of social workers to screen for depression among a Medicare population. Rubinstein and associates (R. L. Rubinstein, Lubben, & Mintzer, 1994) report on a program in which geriatric social workers screen for social isolation.

Besides identifying previously undetected health problems, health promotion includes a focus on preventive measures to decrease morbidity and improve quality of life in old age. To that end, health behavior and lifestyle have become increasingly important areas of concern in geriatric practice (R. L. Kane, Kane, & Arnold, 1985; Kaplan, Seeman, Cohen, Knudsen, & Guralnik, 1987; Schweitzer et al., 1994; Stuck et al., 2000; Weiler, Chi, & Lubben, 1989). At a more macro level, the burgeoning fields of building healthy aging communities (Damron-Rodriguez & Lubben, 2001; World Health Organization, 2002) and cultivating social capital (Klein & Bloom, 1997; Wallack,

2000) suggest additional opportunities for social work engagement in this growing field. Given that the major rationale for examining behaviors is fostering behavioral change, the potential for increased geriatric social work involvement in health promotion programs becomes quite apparent.

Regardless of whether the focus of health promotion and wellness is on the early detection of health problems or the changing of health behaviors among individuals, families, groups, or communities, appropriate abbreviated measures are needed. Such measures are required to document the need, mobilize action, and mark progress toward addressing those needs.

DESIRED PROPERTIES OF ABBREVIATED MEASURES

Good abbreviated measures are the result of good compromises. On the one hand, the measures must be relatively short and unobtrusive to gain wide acceptance. On the other hand, they must be reliable; as a rule, longer assessment instruments are more reliable. Reliability is a fundamental issue in psychological measurement (Nunnally, 1978). Thus, one of the first compromises in constructing good abbreviated measures is to create reliability without the redundancy of inquiry that is often employed to foster increased reliability. Cronbach's (1951) coefficient alpha is often used to measure reliability. An acceptable range of coefficient alpha values are 0.70 to 0.90 (DeVellis, 1991; Nunnally, 1978). Assessment instruments with reliability scores higher than 0.90 are likely to suffer from excessive redundancy, whereas those with alpha less than 0.70 are likely to be unreliable (Streiner & Norman, 2003).

Abbreviated measures must also withstand a test of validity (Streiner & Norman, 2003). Although there are many ways that validity can be measured, a common approach in the development of abbreviated measures is to ascertain *criterion validity,* usually divided into concurrent validity and predictive validity. *Concurrent validity* examines whether the new measure is highly correlated with some gold standard of the construct being measured. *Predictive validity* examines whether the measure can predict future events such as increased health service use, mortality, or other outcome measure.

These aspects of validity can be demonstrated by examining two measures of mental health among elderly populations: the Center for Epidemiological Studies Depression Scale (CES-D) and the Mental Health Inventory (MHI-5). The CES-D is a 20-item scale developed by the National Institute of Mental Health to measure symptoms of depression in community populations with emphasis on the affective component (Radloff, 1977). The CES-D has often been used in studies of elderly populations (Foelker & Shewchuk, 1992; Hertzog, Alstine, & Usala, 1990). The length of the CES-D has spawned a number of attempts to find a more abbreviated measure for mental health.

One such abbreviated measure that has been developed is the MHI-5. As the name implies, this newer measure contains 5 items and is a shortened version of the MHI developed by the RAND Corporation for the extensive RAND Health Insurance Experiment (Nelson & Berwick, 1989). The MHI-5 is indeed a valid and reliable abbreviated measure of mental health that can be used as an efficient screener for general mental health problems (Berwick et al., 1991). Correlating the MHI-5 with the longer and more established CES-D measure assesses the validity of the MHI-5. High correlations are indicative of concurrent validity. Similarly, using the MHI-5 to predict future events such as hospitalizations for mental health problems would illustrate predictive validity.

Another compromise that must be addressed in developing an abbreviated measure is the trade-off between *sensitivity* and *specificity* (Streiner & Norman, 2003). This dichotomy is also referred to as balancing false positives and false negatives. When administering any assessment test, some of the individuals classified as having a trait (e.g., depression, isolation) don't actually have that condition; thus, the assessment resulted in a false positive. On the other hand, there are individuals who indeed have the condition for which the population is being screened but the employed test reports that they do not have the condition; these results are considered false negatives. A desired trait of a good assessment measure is that it must be sensitive enough to actually identify individuals who have the condition for which screening is taking place. A sensitive measure minimizes the number of false negatives. Another desired trait for an assessment measure is that of specificity to minimize false positives, meaning that those who do not have the condition are ruled out. A special challenge in developing an abbreviated assessment measure is to find a good balance between the problems of false positives and negatives.

Another desired trait for abbreviated assessment instruments that is employed in practice settings is *open door* questions. These are questions that might be answered simply, or the response they elicit might prompt the geriatric social worker to probe for more information. For example, if a respondent answers that he or she has no friends or is sad, a health survey researcher is likely to move on to the next set of questions; however, a geriatric social worker or other health professional would likely explore the response for more detail before returning to the remaining structured questions in the assessment protocol. Thus, an abbreviated assessment measure might both record standard information on clients and also provide the opportunity to probe responses to specific questions.

TWO CASE EXAMPLES OF DEVELOPING ABBREVIATED SOCIAL HEALTH MEASURES

There are a number of outstanding handbooks on geriatric assessment that contain sections on social health (Gallo, Fulmer, Paveza, & Reichel, 2000; R. L. Kane & Kane, 2000; Osterweil, Brummel-Smith, & Beck, 2000). Few of the social health measures contained in these handbooks are ideal as abbreviated measures because most are much too long. Thus, they generally would require additional psychometric work to hone them into valid and reliable abbreviated measures of social health. Streiner and Norman (2003) provide a very useful practical guide on how to develop health measurement scales.

Lubben and Gironda (2000, 2003a, 2003b) provide two illustrative case examples of developing valid and reliable abbreviated measures of social health from existing scales. They took two commonly used measures that were relatively long and engaged in a deliberate process to identify shortened versions that would approximate the original scales in validity and reliability. One of the scales they abbreviated was the Medical Outcomes Study Social Support Scale (MOS-SSS; Sherbourne & Stewart, 1991) and the other was the Lubben Social Network Scale (LSNS; Lubben, 1988; Lubben & Gironda, 1997).

The MOS-SSS was developed for the RAND Medical Outcomes Study and is largely a measure of emotional support. Its current length (20 items) makes it especially cumbersome for clinical settings and a very unlikely candidate for inclusion in state or national health surveys. Because of a great deal of redundancy in items, there have been many suggestions made to abbreviate the MOS-SSS (e.g., Lubben & Gironda, 1997; Steiner et al., 1996).

Lubben and Gironda (2000) developed a 3-item abbreviated version of the MOS-SSS. These 3 items

show high internal consistency and are correlated with the total MOS-SSS score. The items are scored as a Likert-type response. The MOS-SSS 3-item abbreviated version is shown in Table 66.1.

The LSNS is a 10-item scale designed to measure social networks specifically for use among an elderly population. As evidence of the demand for abbreviated measures, even the 10-item LSNS has spawned shortened versions (e.g., Martire, Schulz, Mittelmark, & Newsom, 1999). The LSNS has become widely used in both research and clinical settings (e.g., Martire et al., 1999; Pourat, Lubben, Yu, & Wallace, 2000; Steiner et al., 1996; Stuck et al., 1999). It has demonstrated criterion validity through significant correlations with a wide array of health indicators. Low scores on the LSNS have been correlated with mortality (Ceria et al., 2001), all-cause hospitalization (Lubben, Weiler, & Chi, 1989; Mistry, Rosansky, McQuire, McDermott, & Jarvik, 2001), physical health problems (Hurwicz & Berkanovic, 1993; Mor-Borak, Miller, & Syme, 1991), depression and other mental health problems (Chou & Chi, 1999; Dorfman et al., 1995; Okwumabua, Baker, Wong, & Pilgrim, 1997), and lack of adherence to good health practices (Potts, Hurwicz, & Goldstein, 1992).

Lubben and Gironda (2000, 2003a) developed a 6-item abbreviated version of the LSNS and dubbed it the LSNS-6 to distinguish it from longer versions of the test (Table 66.2). The LSNS-6 assesses two critical domains of social networks: (1) family and (2) friends and neighbors. These 6 items can be combined to form a 3-item family subscale, a 3-item friends subscale, and the composite LSNS-6. All three measures have good reliability characteristics for such short scales.

An additional advantage of the three LSNS-6 measures is that in a clinical setting, it may be useful to determine particular strengths and weaknesses in family ties separate from those of an elderly person's relationships with friends and neighbors. For this purpose, the subscales can be used individually. The two subscales can also be combined to form a composite LSNS-6 score that in turn could be used as a marker for possible social isolation and suggestive of particular types of clinical interventions. The LSNS-6 and the

TABLE 66.1. MOS-SSS Abbreviated Version

1. How often do you have someone to love?
2. How often does someone show love and affection to you?
3. How often do you have someone to share worries?

TABLE 66.2. LSNS-6

1. How many of your *relatives* do you see or hear from at least once a month?

2. How many *relatives* do you feel at ease with that you can talk about private matters?

3. How many *relatives* do you feel close to that you can call on them for help?

4. How many of your *friends* do you see or hear from at least once a month?

5. How many *friends* do you feel at ease with that you can talk about private matters?

6. How many *friends* do you feel close to that you can call on them for help?

MOS-SSS-3 both illustrate the concept of open-door questions that allow a clinician to further probe particular responses.

SUMMARY

As R. A. Kane and Kane (1981) stated almost 25 years ago on the first page of the original version of their popular handbook on assessment, "Measurement is essential to good geriatric care." Good practice, whether in social work, nursing, or any other health profession, requires good measures to denote client need and record client progress. Valid and reliable abbreviated assessment measures are important to this process to fill the gaps when the use of longer measures is impractical. Similarly, health researchers and policymakers need good data. In this era of evidence-based practice, good health and social service programs may go unnoticed if they are not able to document their merits. Further, the critical shortage of abbreviated markers of social health status and behaviors in large population surveys sends the wrong message about the relative importance of the social health domain. Thus, the only course of action is to more deliberately engage in the process of developing a valid and reliable set of social health measures that will become more widely accepted for practice and research. The future of geriatric social work will be greatly enhanced if social workers accept this challenge.

REFERENCES

Berwick, D. M., Murphy, J. M., Goldman, P. A., Ware, J. E., Barsky, A. J., & Weinstein, M. C. (1991). Performance of a five-item mental health screening test. *Medical Care, 29*(2), 169–176.

Ceria, C. D., Masaki, K. H., Rodriguez, B. L., Chen, R., Yano, K., & Curb, J. D. (2001). The relationship of psychosocial factors to total mortality among older Japanese-American men: The Honolulu Heart Program. *Journal of American Geriatrics Society, 49,* 725–731.

Chou, K. L., & Chi, I. (1999). Determinants of life satisfaction in Hong Kong Chinese elderly: A longitudinal study. *Aging and Mental Health, 3,* 328–335.

Cronbach, L. J. (1951). Coefficient alpha and the internal structure of tests. *Psychometrika, 16,* 297–334.

Damron-Rodriguez, J., & Lubben, J. E. (2001). *A framework for understanding community health care in ageing societies.* Ageing and Health Technical Report Series, Report 2. Kobe, Japan: WHO Centre for Health Development. Available at *http://www.who. or.jp/ageing/index.html.*

DeVellis, R. F. (1991). *Scale development: Theory and applications.* Newbury Park, CA: Sage.

Dorfman, R., Lubben, J. E., Mayer-Oakes, A., Atchison, K. A., Schweitzer, S. O., DeJong, F., et al. (1995). Screening for depression among the well elderly. *Social Work, 40,* 295–304.

Federal Interagency Forum on Aging-Related Statistics. (2004). *Older Americans 2004: Key indicators of well-being.* Washington, DC: U.S. Government Printing Office.

Foelker, G. A., & Shewchuk, R. M. (1992). Somatic complaints and the CES-D. *Journal of the American Geriatric Society, 40,* 259–262.

Gallo, J. J., Fulmer, T., Paveza, G. J., & Reichel, W. (2000). *Handbook of geriatric assessment.* Gaithersberg, MD: Aspen.

Hertzog, C., Alstine, J. V., & Usala, P. D. (1990). Measurement properties of the Center for Epidemiological Studies Depression Scale (CES-D). *Journal of Consulting and Clinical Psychology, 1,* 64–72.

Hurwicz, M. L., & Berkanovic, E. (1993). The stress process of rheumatoid arthritis. *Journal of Rheumatology, 20,* 1836–1844.

Institute on Medicine. (2000). *Promoting health: Intervention strategies from social and behavioral research.* Washington, DC: National Academy Press.

Kane, R. A., &, Kane, R. L. (1981). *Assessing the elderly: A practical guide to measurement.* Lexington, MA: Lexington Books.

Kane, R. L., & Kane, R. A. (2000). *Assessing older persons.* New York: Oxford University Press.

Kane, R. L., Kane, R. A., & Arnold, S. B. (1985). Prevention and the elderly: Risk factors. *Health Services Research, 19,* 945–1006.

Kaplan, G. A., Seeman, T. E., Cohen, R. D., Knudsen, L. P., & Guralnik, J. (1987). Mortality among the elderly in the Alameda County study. *American Journal of Public Health, 77*, 307–312.

Klein, W. C., & Bloom, M. (1997). *Successful aging: Strategies for healthy living.* New York: Plenum Press.

Lubben, J. E. (1988). Assessing social networks among elderly populations. *Family and Community Health, 11,* 42–52.

Lubben, J. E., & Gironda, M. (1997). Social support networks among older people in the United States. In H. Litwin (Ed.), *The social networks of older people* (pp. 143–161). Westport, CT: Praeger.

Lubben, J. E., & Gironda, M. W. (2000). Social support networks. In D. Osterweil, K. Brummel-Smith, & J. Beck (Eds.), *Comprehensive geriatric assessment* (pp. 121–137). New York: McGraw-Hill.

Lubben, J. E., & Gironda, M. W. (2003a). Centrality of social ties to the health and well being of older adults. In B. Berkman & L. K. Harooytan (Eds.), *Social work and health care in an aging world.* New York: Springer.

Lubben, J. E., & Gironda, M. W. (2003b). Measuring social networks and assessing their benefits. In C. Phillipson, G. Allan, & D. Morgan (Eds.), *Social networks and social exclusion* (pp. 20–49). Hants, England: Ashgate.

Lubben, J. E., Weiler, P. G., & Chi, I. (1989). Health practices of the elderly poor. *American Journal of Public Health, 79,* 731–734.

Martire, L. M., Schulz, R., Mittelmark, M. B., & Newsom, J. T. (1999). Stability and change in older adults' social contact and social support: The Cardiovascular Health Study. *Journals of Gerontology: Series B: Psychological and Social Sciences, 54B,* S302–S311.

Mayer-Oakes, A., Atchison, K., Lubben, J., & Schweitzer, S. (1990). Targeting preventive health care for the elderly: The UCLA geriatric health risk appraisal. *Journal of American Geriatric Society, 38*(8).

Mistry, R., Rosansky, J., McQuire, J., McDermott, C., & Jarvik, L. (2001). Social isolation predicts re-hospitalization in a group of older American veterans enrolled in the UPBEAT Program. *International Journal of Geriatric Psychiatry, 16,* 950–959.

Mor-Barak, M. E., Miller, L. S., & Syme., L. S. (1991). Social networks, life events, and health of the poor, frail elderly: A longitudinal study of the buffering versus the direct effect. *Family Community Health, 14,* 1–13.

Nelson, E. C., & Berwick, D. M. (1989). The measurement of health status in clinical practice. *Medical Care, 27*(Suppl.), 77–90.

Nunnally, J. C. (1978). *Psychometric theory* (2nd ed.). New York: McGraw-Hill.

Okwumabua, J. O., Baker, F. M., Wong, S. P., & Pilgrim, B. O. (1997). Characteristics of depressive symptoms in elderly urban and rural African Americans. *Journals of Gerontology: Biological Sciences and Medical Sciences, 52A,* M241–M246.

Ossterweil, D., Brummel-Smith, K., & Beck, J. C. (2000). *Comprehensive geriatric assessment.* New York: McGraw-Hill.

Potts, M. K., Hurwicz, M. L., & Goldstein, M. S. (1992). Social support, health-promotive beliefs, and preventive health behaviors among the elderly. *Journal of Applied Gerontology, 11*(4), 425–440.

Pourat, N., Lubben, J., Yu, H., & Wallace, S. (2000). Perceptions of health and use of ambulatory care: Differences between Korean and White elderly. *Journal of Aging and Health, 12*(1), 112–134.

Radloff, L. (1977). The CES-D Scale: A self-report depression scale for research in the general population. *Applied Psychological Measurement, 1*(3), 385–401.

Rubenstein, L. Z., Josephson, K. R., Nichol-Seamons, M., & Robbins, A. S. (1986). Comprehensive health screening of well elderly adults: An analysis of a community program. *Journal of Gerontology, 41,* 342–352.

Rubinstein, R. L., Lubben, J. E., & Mintzer, J. E. (1994). Social isolation and social support: An applied perspective. *Journal of Applied Gerontology, 13*(1), 58–72.

Schweitzer, S. O., Atchison, K. A., Lubben, J. E., Mayer-Oakes, S. A., DeJong, F. J., & Matthias, R. E. (1994). Health promotion and disease prevention for older adults: Opportunity for change or preaching to the converted? *American Journal of Preventive Medicine, 10,* 223–229.

Sherbourne, C. D., & Stewart, A. L. (1991). The MOS Social Support Survey. *Social Science Medicine, 32,* 705–714.

Steiner, A., Raube, K., Stuck, A. E., Aronow, H. U., Draper, D., Rubenstein, L. Z., et al. (1996). Measuring psychosocial aspects of well-being in older community residents: Performance of four short scales. *The Gerontologist, 36*(1), 54–62.

Streiner, D. J., & Norman, G. R. (2003). *Health measurement scales: A practical guide to their development and use* (3rd ed.). New York: Oxford University Press.

Stuck, A. E., Minder, C., Peter-Woecz, I., Gillman, G., Egli, C., Kesserling, A., et al. (2000). A randomized trial of in-home visits for disability prevention in community dwelling older people at low and high risk for nursing home admissions. *Archives of Internal Medicine, 160*(7), 977–986.

Stuck, A. E., Walthert, J. M., Nikolaus, T., Bula, C. J., Hohmann, C., & Beck, J. (1999). Risk factors for the functional status decline in community-living elderly people: A systematic literature review. *Social Science and Medicine, 48,* 445–469.

Wallack, L. (2000). The role of the mass media in creating social capital: A new direction for public health. In *Promoting health: Intervention strategies from social and behavioral research.* Washington, DC: National Academy Press.

Weiler, P. G., Chi, I., & Lubben, J. E. (1989). A statewide preventive health care program for aged. *Public Health Reports, 104,* 215–221.

World Health Organization. (2002). Active ageing: A policy framework. Geneva, Switzerland: WHO Ageing and Life Course Programme. Available at *http://www.who.int/hpr/ageing/ActiveAgeingPolicyFrame.pdf.*

ROSALIE A. KANE

Standardized Measures Commonly Used in Geriatric Assessment

Standardized assessments are systematic protocols that are used to gather information using well-defined standard elements and procedures. This chapter is limited to noninvasive assessments that are composed of fixed questions posed to respondents or self-completed by respondents, or by ratings that are made by professionals after interviews and observations. (Assessments based on physical examinations, laboratory tests, and radiological tests are beyond the scope of this chapter.) In standardized assessments, questions are asked, observations made, and replies recorded according to fixed rules. Standardized measures go a step beyond assessment to yield scores to describe the attributes of the older person and the older person's world that are being assessed.

Standardized assessments and standardized measures are used extensively among health and human services professionals working with older people, and they are also widely used in research concerning older people. Some of the more commonly used assessments and measures have created their own language that is used within and across professional groups to reach common understanding about older people. The acronyms for types of measures and for specific widely used tools have become a short-hand in aging services. ADL status (i.e., the ability to perform activities of daily living) and MSQs (referring to mental status questionnaires, a class of measures used to screen for cognitive ability) are terms typically taken for granted in geriatric care teams, as are abbreviations for widely known instruments, such as the GDS (Geriatric Depression Scale; Yesavage & Brink, 1983), the MMSE (Mini-Mental Status Exam; Folstein, Folstein, & McHugh, 1975), the LSI (Life Satisfaction Index; Neugarten, Havighurst, & Tobin, 1961), and a host of others. The SF-36 (Ware & Sherbourne, 1992) is such a well-known multidimensional tool to measure general health status that the source of the acronym (short form) tends to be forgotten.

This chapter describes some of the more commonly used measures in the context of a discussion of why social workers need to be concerned about standardized assessment, the properties that should be considered in choosing and using assessment tools, and the domains or topics of assessment that are pertinent to social workers.

SOCIAL WORK AND STANDARDIZED ASSESSMENT

Social work practitioners have a variety of responsibilities related to assessment protocols and measures.

67

Often, social workers are part of a multidisciplinary team that uses a standardized tool to assess all clientele. Under these circumstances, social workers may be responsible for completing a portion of the tool related to psychological or social function; they may be responsible for completing an entire tool, which is then used by the entire team; or they may utilize data from an assessment tool that is completed by a team member who is not a social worker. Social workers may be designated to complete an entire tool, including components on physical health and other aspects not directly in social work's purview; because of the profession's expertise in establishing rapport and interviewing and because social workers often conduct intake for a variety of programs, such a role is natural. But regardless of the pattern for completion of an assessment protocol, social workers practicing in an environment using such tools are obliged to understand how to interpret the results. Social work practitioners may also be in a position to suggest a component to be added to a multidimensional assessment battery or to select an assessment tool to guide the work of a specific social work program. In those situations, social workers would be ill-advised to invent a new assessment tool unless a thorough search suggests that no extant instruments are appropriate for the measurements sought. Even to make such judgments, social workers need to understand something about how to judge an assessment tool. Indeed, social workers also need to be knowledgeable enough about assessment tools to recognize if the scales used by a practice team do a poor job of describing phenomena or outcomes of interest to their practice.

Assessment is employed for various purposes, and the criteria for choosing an assessment tool varies with that purpose. Assessment may be used diagnostically to characterize an older person, to decide on a therapy or plan of care, or to draw conclusions about the best place for care. Screening is a variant of diagnostic assessment where the goal is not to definitely categorize a phenomenon, but rather to narrow down the field of people or circumstances that need more detailed assessment. For example, one may screen for a disease or condition and then assess in more detail just those who are positive on the screen. Assessment may serve as the basis of eligibility for care or services, either type of care or amounts of care. It may be used as the basis for evaluating the effectiveness of a specific service or an entire program, and it may be used in quality assurance and quality improvement efforts.

In clinical research, assessments are used to establish baseline states, to measure outcomes of interventions, and to adjust results by differences at baseline (known as case-mix differences). In more basic research, assessments are used to study relationships among various phenomena and other attributes. Variants of commonly used assessments are embedded in standard publicly funded population surveys that social work researchers need to become familiar with to understand trends among older people. There is no particular added credibility for social workers to use only assessment tools developed by social workers, but at times social work researchers become engaged in developing instruments to fill voids in the tool kit available to examine outcomes of interest to them. Those attempting to develop assessment tools need to adhere to conventional approaches in identifying items, field-testing instruments, establishing their psychometric properties (such as reliability and scalability), testing validity, and establishing norms. Examples of different types of tools developed under social work leadership include Lubben's Social Network Scale (Lubben, 1988), Geron and colleagues' (2000) tools to measure home care satisfaction, and R. A. Kane and colleagues' (2003) measures of quality of life for nursing home residents.

ASSESSMENT DOMAINS: TOPICS FOR STANDARDIZED ASSESSMENT

Assessment domains or dimensions refer to the topics or areas to be assessed. In 1981, this writer coauthored a book that compared assessment tools used in long-term care and aging services, raising cautions about the choice and use of assessments (R. A. Kane & Kane, 1981). That volume considered assessments in five domains: physical functioning (referring to abilities to conduct basic and more complex activities of daily living); physical health; psychological well-being; cognitive functioning; and social functioning. We also considered multidimensional tools that cross domains to yield either a single score or subscores. Sometimes such multidimensional tools are called "quality of life measures." For that book, we sifted through many hundreds of assessment tools.

When we wrote a sequel to the 1981 volume about two decades later, the caveats on the use of assessments were unchanged, but the number of assessment tools available for use in gerontology and geriatrics had increased exponentially (R. L. Kane & Kane, 2000). Moreover, the number of domains for which serious measurement work was available had also multiplied. For the 2000 volume, the domains reviewed included function, health and physiological well-being, cognition, emotions, social functioning, quality of life, values and preferences, satisfaction, religiosity and spirituality, family caregivers, and physical environments. Many of the topics lent themselves to further division into subdimensions.

The remainder of this chapter summarizes the state of the art of gerontological assessment in each of the domains just listed and adds the domain of personality (an area of assessment of interest to social work). For each domain, a few tools that have achieved considerable prominence are suggested along with issues related to assessment of older people compared to the general population of adults. The summaries are necessarily cursory, and the listing of tools is illustrative rather than comprehensive. The goal is to present an overview of each area in a way that will help social workers take further steps to evaluate or select tools for that domain. First, however, the chapter presents some important distinctions and attributes related to standardized assessment tools and their use. This discussion is illustrated with reference to tools in the literature, many of them commonly used.

CHARACTERISTICS OF ASSESSMENTS AND MEASURES: USEFUL DISTINCTIONS

Sources of Information

Information for assessment may come directly from the older person, or it may come from various proxies for the older person, including family members and paid caregivers. Clearly, some older people will be incapable of providing direct information because of high levels of cognitive impairment, dire health conditions that prohibit communication, or advanced illness, such as hospice clients in the hours before death. In such instances, no alternative remains but to substitute information from proxies, based on their observations or their substituted judgments (in the case of quality of life measures, which depend on subjective appraisal). Assessments from proxy respondents are more reliable if the matters assessed are objective and the person responding is in a position to know; in the census, for example, one respondent speaks for the household, a strategy to minimize the already expensive costs of census data, and it appears that little is lost. Using data from the older person interchangeably with that from proxies (although often done) creates measurement problems, and some argue that

for some domains and subdomains that deal with subjective appraisal, such as satisfaction, perceived health, spiritual well-being, and pain, it is better to omit the measure for those who cannot respond rather than to use a proxy. Certainly, direct respondents should not be eliminated because they suffer from measurable cognitive impairment. Ample evidence exists in the literature to suggest that many older people with substantial cognitive impairment can reliably and meaningfully provide the information for assessment of their own status, particularly when the domains concern attitudes, opinions, and feelings rather than actual facts about recent activity (Brod, Stewart, Sands, & Walton, 1999; Logsdon, Gibbons, McCurry, & Terri, 1999).

Proxy data may be based on systematic or unsystematic observation or records (such as clinical records or diaries kept by family). Some well-established tools do exist to approximate mood among those who cannot describe it for themselves. The MOSES (Multidimensional Observation Scale for Elderly Subjects) is one good example; it yields measures of depression and anxiety as well as social dimensions like social involvement and relationships, based on ratings by someone who had observed the person for a week and who answers very specific questions (e.g., How often did X talk about being depressed, look depressed, sound depressed, respond to social contacts, initiate social contacts?). The MOSES uses specific response categories to arrive at the number of days the observation was made and the amount of time in the day the phenomenon was observed (Helmes, Csapo, & Short, 1987). Although rapidly completed, this tool engenders more confidence than a simple rating of whether the individual is anxious, depressed, or socially engaged. Another example is the AARS (Apparent Affect Rating Scale), which is completed by making multiple 5-minute observations of the older person's facial expression to gauge happiness, sadness, anger, anxiety, and engagement (Lawton, Van Haitsma, & Klapper, 1996; Lawton, Van Haitsma, Perkinson, & Ruckdeschel, 1999). Users of this tool can be trained to high interrater reliability through available videos and practice experience.

Time Dimension

Assessments must have a referent in time; for example, the questions may be posed in terms of "right now," in the past week, in the past month, in the past 6 months, or "ever in your life." The choice of time frame is important and should be based on the frequency of the measured phenomenon and its nature (if we used "past week" we might miss the intensity of family visits to a nursing home, and if we used "past year" to get information on the ability to dress oneself, we would lose focus on, say, the immediate poststroke period). To gather information about health conditions or history of health behavior of concern, such as alcohol consumption, the assessment may combine items cast as "ever in your life" with those related to a much more proximate time period. Also relevant is whether the information is needed to develop action plans for an individual or to gather research information on a population. If the latter, we might sacrifice utility for the individual to get the increased accuracy of recent experience. For example, we might ask about social activity or nutritional intake "yesterday" or family and paid help "this week" and achieve accuracy by taking the respondent through the hours or days. If the sample is large and unbiased and the time frame is not biasing (e.g., Christmas Day), a better approximation of eating habits, social activity, or help received in a population of interest can be gained from this approach than by asking each person to estimate over a year, which can cause recollection problems.

Recording Formats Versus Measures

Some systematic assessments widely used in gerontology are not measures, but systematic formats for recording data. The Minimum Data Set (MDS), now federally mandated for assessments at intervals for all residents in nursing homes that receive public funding, is such a recording tool (Morris et al., 1990). With few and recent exceptions, the many elements in the various iterations of the MDS were not intended to generate scores. However, after the fact, a number of approaches to scoring components of the recorded observations on the MDS have been developed, including various ADL and cognitive measures and measures of social engagement (Mor et al., 1995; Morris et al., 1994; Morris, Fries, & Morris, 1999). The assessment forms that many states use to guide their home- and community-based services also are typically recording formats not intended for scoring, though some states have incorporated specific standardized tools into their assessment formats that yield scores, and some have developed decision algorithms based on information in the assessment to establish eligibility for service and prioritize client needs. Other examples of a standardized approach to assessment developed to provide information for systematic reflection rather than scores include various assess-

ments of values and preferences, such as the Values Assessment Protocol (Degenholtz, Kane, & Kivnick, 1997), the Preferences for Everyday Life Inventory (PELI; Philadelphia Geriatric Center & Visiting Nurse Service of New York, 1999), and the Occupational Profile and the Strengths Inventory developed by Kivnick and colleagues (Kivnick & Murray, 2001; Kivnick, Stoffel, & Hanlan, 2001). The objective of such efforts is to discuss and record information about topics such as the older person's preferences, strengths, and usual interests and activities, and no particular property is being assessed that lends itself to scoring (in contrast, say, to measures of the intensity of any particular preference).

Scoring

Scores provide a convenient way of distilling information from assessments. Once scores come into common usage, however, they tend to be treated as though they have objective meaning; intelligence scores and grade point averages come to mind. Thus, care is needed to go beyond the name of a scale and the score in using scores to draw comparative conclusions about a person or situation; at a minimum, the items, response sets, and instructions used to achieve that score should be scrutinized.

Two competing drives relate to scoring assessment batteries: the urge to consolidate and the urge to differentiate, sometimes referred to as lumping and splitting. The lumpers may seek a single score to measure a complex, multidimensional construct such as quality of life or psychological well-being, whereas the splitters may prefer to consider a host of subscores. With any kind of scoring, whether lumping or splitting is the norm, it may be necessary to weight some items as more important than others (and, therefore, worthy of more points) to the construct being measured.

It is noteworthy that scores may be derived specifically from the assessment tools or may be derived from judgments made after collecting and considering all the information. For example, one of the most venerable measures in gerontology, the OARS instrument (named for the Older Americans Resources and Services Center at Duke University, where the instrument was developed), asked a number of questions across specific domains: health, functioning, mental health, and social functioning (Fillenbaum, 1988). After the assessors collected and reviewed that information, they were to make summary judgments about well-being on each domain.

Measurement Properties

A few basic concepts are usually employed to assess the usefulness of measures. These primarily center on reliability and validity. Measures that are used to detect differences in the outcomes of a treatment may be held to additional standards, such as whether they are responsive to meaningful changes in the intervention, capable of detecting treatment effects when those effects are present, and suited to the population being assessed.

Reliability

Reliability means that the tool is a consistent measurement over time and across assessors. *Intra-assessor* reliability is achieved if the same rater gets the same results in successive measurement efforts, assuming that the older persons did not change in the interim. *Interassessor* reliability means that several assessors get the same results when assessing the same individual or phenomenon. With physical settings or other observations, they can visit simultaneously and individually complete the protocols. With interviews, reliability may be compromised by the way the interviewer's manner and approach in interaction with the subject's characteristics and the interview situation affect what the subject says. Great pains are taken to standardize both the behavior of interviewers and the circumstances, but inevitably differences will occur.

For scales developed from discrete elements, *internal scale reliability* or *scale consistency* is another relevant form of reliability. The reliable scale in this instance is one where the items composing it contribute to overall coherence. This trait is usually measured by some type of item-scale correlation, often expressed in the form of a Cronbach's alpha statistic. The goal is achieve a high level of internal reliability but not total convergence, which would mean the item adds nothing to the scale or could simply be used instead of the scale.

Validity

Validity refers to the capacity of a measure to accurately reflect the attribute it was intended to measure. A measure may be reliable but not valid; an inaccurate bathroom scale may show high reliability, and so, too, may the judgments of social workers and nurses who think they know about the happiness of, say, nursing home residents. In such a case, the responses of staff may measure their consistent biases as they come up with the same answer consistently and similarly.

One form of validity is *face validity,* or the commonsense test. Essentially, this means that the measure appears to be measuring what it intends to measure, or reflects and covers the construct. *Concurrent validity* is achieved when the measure is highly correlated with another previous measure of the same construct. Unfortunately, we often lack a gold standard against which to test the new measure, and, for some domains (e.g., quality of life), using clinical judgment as the gold standard is likely to err by using a poorer standard than the new measure being validated. *Discriminant validity* is achieved if the measure correctly identifies those with the trait from those without; for example, a measure of depression applied to a mental health clinic population discriminates if it correctly identified those with a diagnosis of depression and fails to identify those without. *Predictive validity* refers to the measure's ability to predict the older person's future status. For example, the single item asking persons to rate their health on a 5-point scale has high predictive ability if those who rate their health as fair or poor have higher mortality 6 months later than the rest of the group.

OVERVIEW OF MEASUREMENT DOMAINS

Physiological and Health Domain

This general domain historically comprised lists of symptoms and active and past diagnoses, measures of health care utilization (e.g., hospital days, doctor visits), measures of time unable to perform usual activities because of health, use of common prosthetic and mobility devices, and self-rated health (the single item being extremely predictive of mortality, as stated earlier). In the past few years, the domain has become more differentiated. Tools are now available to objectively classify common clinical problems or risk factors, such as, among other examples, fall risk (Tinetti, 1986), nutritional status (Pendergast et al., 1989; Wolinsky, Coe, Chavez, Pendergast, & Miller, 1986), pressure sores (Goldstone, 1982), quality of sleep (Hays & Stewart, 1992), alcohol and drug problems, hearing and vision problems, and communication. Some of these paper-and-pencil measures are specific to a diagnosis.

Many tools are now available to measure the subdomain of pain and discomfort, though interpretation is still difficult because of the subjectivity of the topic (Herr & Mobily, 1993). Some type of adjectival rating is typically used to characterize the extent to which the pain has various attributes, along with some general measure of the frequency and intensity of pain. The field is divided between those who would never accept a proxy rating of someone else's pain and those who believe it is necessary and important to get some approximation of the pain experienced by those who are dying or those who cannot speak; the latter group accept the ratings of staff or relatives as the best we can do.

Functional Measures

Measures of functional status include measures of basic self-care activities, the so-called ADL measures, and measures of more complex activities in everyday life, which have come to be called IADL (instrumental activities of daily living).

ADL activities most usually include bathing, dressing, using the toilet, getting in and out of a chair or bed (called transferring), and eating. Sometimes ADL tools include other items (e.g., grooming, continence), and sometimes they further differentiate among items (dressing can be subdivided into upper and lower body dressing, and eating can be divided into drinking from a cup and eating with a fork and spoon). Some ADL tools tap a lower level of functioning and examine differential functioning among those confined to their bed. The most common ADL tool was developed by Katz as a 6-item dichotomous rating and later refined in various ways to drop continence and expand the response categories (Katz, Down, Cash, & Grotz, 1970; Katz, Ford, Moskowitz, Jackson, & Jaffee, 1963). More elaborate ADL assessments are used to guide rehabilitation programs. Notable among these are the Barthel Index (Mahoney & Barthel, 1965) and the newer Functional Independence Measure (Kidd et al., 1995).

IADL typically include functioning at tasks such as cooking, cleaning, laundry, using the telephone, taking medications, driving a car, and using a bus or other transportation. A large number of tasks could be used in an IADL measure. One of the more widely used IADL measures is the Multilevel Assessment Instrument developed at the Philadelphia Geriatric Center (Lawton, Moss, Fulcomer, & Kleban, 1982).

ADL and IADL measures and, to a lesser extent, mobility measures are among the most ubiquitous in the field. As a dependent variable or outcome sought, functional status assumes paramount importance because maintaining, improving, or slowing decline in functioning is what many services for older people are all about. As an independent variable—that is, something that might influence the outcomes being measured—functional status is almost as ubiquitous as the inevitable age, gender, marital status, and ethnicity as a case-mix adjustor. Baseline functional status is (and should be) taken into account when investigators examine other outcomes in the social and psychological spheres or when they examine changes in functional status itself.

With so many tools, the selection of a specific tool is less important than determining the definitions one is using, the time frame, and the decision rules. Functional measures can be directed at performance (what the person actually does) or at capability (what persons report they are capable of doing). They can use best performance or average performance. They can take into account pain, speed, or reported difficulty as criteria for judging that the person can perform the function, or they can ignore those modifiers. Some functional assessors may require that cleaning or dressing be performed to a certain standard of competence, and others may not build that into the protocol. Some tests of functioning involve actual demonstrated performance. The identical ADL items and response categories may be used, but the assumptions built into their use differ according to parameters, such as those discussed earlier. The best guide is to choose carefully based on the purpose of the measure and to take the trouble to describe in some detail the approach used to measure functioning.

Cognitive Functioning

As with functioning, the challenge of measuring cognitive abilities among older people has resulted in a huge number of instruments, some constituting brief screening tools and others more elaborate. Subdomains of cognition include recent memory, remote memory, attention, judgment, calculation, and problem solving. Tools to measure cognitive functioning have often been developed by and for the use of experimental psychologists. As such, they often entail demonstration of abilities, and their norms and psychometric properties are usually known. Instruments are less well developed to tap upper-level functioning, such as logic, creativity, and wisdom, but even here, some tools are available.

As with ADL measures, within limits, it probably does not matter which cognitive screening test is used;

many are interchangeable, though some seem less likely to alienate the older person being tested. Among the most commonly used tools are the Mini-Mental State Exam (Folstein et al., 1975), a 10-item Short Portable Mental Status Questionnaire derived from the OARS instrument (Pfeiffer, 1975), and versions of the Blessed Test (Blessed, Tomlinson, & Roth, 1968). As important as the choice is the interpretation of the results of a cognitive screening test. We may be too prone to use them to exclude direct input from older persons, deeming poor scorers unreliable. For example, it is typical to seek a proxy in a research study for anyone who falls below some preset MMSE score, despite the fact that persons scoring in the dementia range often can complete many assessments. Besides tests administered directly to the person whose cognition might be impaired, a variety of measures are available based on reports of informants (Langley, 2000). Finally, performance tests are available and are often used to develop stages for dementia. The Cognitive Performance Test is a particularly practical staging effort, used widely by occupational therapists because of its ability to suggest the need for care and support based on the demonstrated performance of common household tasks (Burns & Mortimer, 1994). For example, at early stages, a person can make buttered toast (one of the tasks), including assembling the items needed in the kitchen; at another stage, the person can perform the task if the toaster, bread, and butter are laid out in plain sight; and at a still later stage, the person may be able to make toast if asked to do each subtask separately.

Emotions and Mental Well-Being

Over the past 20 years there has been more acceptance of question-and-answer tests to gauge emotional well-being rather than exclusive reliance on a clinical interview by a qualified mental health professional. Many domains can be specified for assessment of affective or emotional functioning, including depression, anxiety, hopelessness, and anger, as well as positive domains such as hope, future orientation, and general psychological well-being. Depressive affect is the dimension most often measured, and numerous instruments are available; the best ones overcome the challenge of relying on somatic manifestations of depression that may be associated with illness in old people. Common instruments include the older Beck Depression Inventory (Beck, Ward, Mendelson, Mock, & Erbaugh, 1961) and Zung Self-

Rating Depression Scale (Zung, 1965), now overtaken in popularity by the Geriatric Depression Scale (Yesavage & Brink, 1983) and the CES-D tool used in multisite population studies (Radloff, 1977). Other instruments are available to assess anxiety and other negative emotional states. Some composite approaches attempt to tap a variety of emotions. The Affect Balance Scale (Bradburn, 1969), which counts both negative and positive emotions and generates two subscales, is widely used. Another self-report tool that includes positive and negative emotions has been well tested with people with poor cognitive functioning (Brod et al., 1999). In the general area of morale and life satisfaction, the two most commonly used tools are variants of the Life Satisfaction Index (Neugarten et al., 1961) and the Philadelphia Geriatric Center Morale Scale (Lawton, 1968). Also noteworthy to tap the positive end of psychological well-being are the scales developed by Ryff and colleagues (Ryff & Keyes, 1995), which use short scales to tap dimensions such as sense of purpose and self-esteem. For more examples and the actual items for many of these tools, see a recent review by Grann (2000).

A number of tools have been developed to assess behavioral disturbances of people with dementia. Among the more commonly used are Cohen-Mansfield's (1995) measures of agitation and several measures of disruptive behavior (Teri et al., 1992; Zarit, Reever, & Back-Peterson, 1980).

Social Functioning

Social functioning includes a wide range of phenomena. The available tools include measures of social network, of social support, and of social activity. Considerable agreement has now been reached about acceptable measures of social networks and of social support (variables that are often found as independent variables in research studies). Social well-being, which implies a value judgment, is much more difficult to measure as there is no unified body of theory that suggests the right blend of activity, stimulation, and relationships that constitutes social well-being. Moreover, this area is particularly sensitive to cultural and individual variation. The perception of meaningful relationships, of being loved by and loving others, of being trusted by and trusting others, seems pivotal to social well-being, which is probably why the questions about the reciprocal presence of a confidante (someone you trust and turn to, someone who trusts and turns to you) are a marker of the work that still remains to be done in this area. (For a review of measures, see Levin, 2000.)

The social functioning construct remains highly susceptible to societal values. Being busy and enjoying interaction with others is generally viewed as better than being alone, but many people enjoy solo tasks like reading and doing puzzles. Whereas there is growing evidence to suggest that having someone with whom to relate (even a pet) has some protective effect, it is unreasonable to argue that the level of protection increases with the number of friends. In general, despite the large number of measures in the literature, there has been little convergence on satisfactory measures to tap domains of great interest to social work, such as productive aging (sometimes conceptualized as a blend of activities in the labor force, volunteer activities, activities within family, and activities that involve creative expression). This is an area that requires more measurement development.

Religiousness and Spirituality

Although spiritual well-being has come to be considered a fourth dimension of well-being (along with the physical, psychological, and social spheres, identified by the World Health Organization), we have made only small steps toward determining how to measure it. As independent variables, religion, religious practices, and religiosity have been measured. In contrast, spiritual well-being is typically a dependent variable that may or may not be related to religious observances. The Fetzer Institute (1999) in Kalamazoo, Michigan, in conjunction with the National Institute on Aging, has provided the most authoritative compendium of short tools that can be used to measure aspects of religion and spirituality in studies of the health and well-being of older people.

Quality of Life

Quality of life (QOL) is a multidimensional construct that has been measured in a variety of ways. Most authorities agree that QOL is a summary of physical, psychological, social, and even spiritual well-being. Health-related quality of life (HRQOL) is contrasted to more general QOL. Further, QOL tools can be identified for specific diagnoses such as stroke, arthritis, and diabetes. Those exploring this topic are referred to three edited books on QOL for older people, which show the progression of thinking about this

topic over time and offer a wealth of examples (Abeles, Gift, & Ory, 1994; Birren, Lubben, Rowe, & Deutchman, 1991; Noelker & Harel, 2001), as well as a review by Frytak (2000).

Values and Preferences

Measures of values and preferences relevant to older people are underdeveloped, though it is encouraging that development of some of these tools is under way. The current practice climate that promotes consumer control and autonomy has enhanced the felt need for measures in this domain. Most of the instruments available, perhaps appropriately, are tools to systematically record information rather than to yield scores.

Satisfaction

Satisfaction is sometimes defined as experience compared to expectations. As such, it is hard to measure because human beings reduce their expectations in response to bad experiences. Satisfaction measures are often flawed by showing a bias toward the positive, though measurement experts have suggested ways to word items to achieve a greater distribution of responses. Specific tools have been developed to assess satisfaction with health care, living conditions, nursing homes, assisted living, and home care (Smith, 2000).

Personality

Personality traits are often difficult to distinguish from moods and attitudes; the former are relatively fixed, whereas the latter may change with circumstances and interventions. Personality batteries, the province of psychologists, have been well developed for self-completed tests in younger people. Typically, they tap dimensions such as neuroticism, conscientiousness, extroversion/introversion, openness, and agreeableness, known as the Big Five (John, 1990). The problem is that many of the items pertain poorly to older people outside of the workplace. Costa and McCrae (1988, 1990) have been associated with most work on personality measurement in elderly people. This writer and colleagues developed and tested a shortened version of the Big Five, capable of being administered in an interview to nursing home residents who would not be capable of using self-completed batteries. Items were simplified and the anchoring phrase "thinking about the kind of person you have been in your whole life" was used to avoid getting responses based on current energy levels and capabilities (R. A. Kane et al., 2004).

Family Caregiving

Until now, all the domains discussed entailed direct assessment of the older person. Family caregiver assessments pertain to people of all ages who are giving care to elderly family members. Assessment tools in this domain have proliferated. Initially, the main constructs measured were the burden of caregiving, itself a multidimensional construct including various types of burden. Among the most commonly used tools are the Montgomery Burden Scales (Montgomery, Ganyea, & Hooyman, 1985); the Zarit Burden Scale (Zarit et al., 1980), which is specific to the burden associated with care of a person with Alzheimer's disease; and the multiple short tools developed by Pearlin and colleagues (Pearlin, Mullan, Semple, & Skaff, 1990; Pearlin & Zarit, 1993) to make operational the stress process related to family caregiver outcomes. The Hassles Scale was developed to capture the small inconveniences and negative effects of caregiving on a daily basis (Kinney & Stephens, 1989a), and the Uplifts Scale was developed in response to an effort to identify more positive effects of family caregiving (Kinney & Stephens, 1989b).

Despite the enormous body of research available on this topic, assessment tools are still lacking for several aspects of family care. First, little attention has been given to measuring the actual activities of family care and their intensity and duration. Second, insufficient measures have been developed to assess the care recipient's perspective on the caregiving experience. Finally, as already hinted, the overwhelming emphasis on burden should be mitigated by work on a range of effects. One cannot assume that absence of burden is the upper range of reactions to family care; qualitative studies have suggested that psychological and tangible rewards can exist for family care.

Physical Environments

Finally, systematic assessment of physical environments for older people should be an important area for social work, given the profession's focus on the person and the environment. Elaborate approaches are available, the best known being Moos's (Moos & Lemke, 1996) Multiphasic Environmental Assessment Protocol, which in its entirety is often too difficult to apply even in research contexts. A number of environmental tools have been developed specifically for the assessment of care units in nursing homes, especially for dementia care units. These include the Therapeutic Environment Screening Scale (Sloane & Mathew, 1990) and the Professional Environment Screening Procedure (Lawton et al., 2000). More recently, Cutler and colleagues developed less subjective ways of assessing environments in assisted living and in nursing homes and derived measures of conceptual domains such as function-enhancing features, life-enriching features, controllability of environment, and privacy-enhancing attributes (Cutler, 2000; Cutler et al., in press). There remains a need to develop assessments for the home environment that go beyond the safety checklists that are widely used in home health and occupational therapy.

CONCLUSION

Standardized assessments in geriatrics and gerontology are extraordinarily plentiful and may be perceived as bewildering and confusing to neophyte practitioners and researchers. This chapter endeavored to offer an introduction to the many domains of assessment and dimensions within domains while providing some criteria for evaluating assessment tools either to choose an instrument or to interpret results of assessments given to clientele. The proliferation of assessment tools can be predicted to increase even further. Among the trends to watch are increasing automation of assessment tools and increasing mandates for specific assessment tools for publicly funded programs. Social workers should have little difficulty identifying assessment tools that assess many of the constructs of interest to them, though they should examine the qualities of any tool they decide to use in their practice or research.

REFERENCES

Abeles, R. P., Gift, H. C., & Ory, M. G. (Eds.). (1994). *Aging and quality of life*. New York: Springer.

Beck, A. T., Ward, C. H., Mendelson, M., Mock, J., & Erbaugh, J. (1961). An inventory for measuring depression. *Archives of General Psychiatry, 4,* 561–571.

Birren, J. E., Lubben, J. E., Rowe, J. C., & Deutchman, D. E. (Eds.). (1991). *The concept and measurement of quality of life in the frail elderly*. San Diego: Academic Press.

Blessed, G., Tomlinson, B. E., & Roth, M. (1968). The association between quantitative measures of dementia and senile change in cerebral gray matter of elderly subjects. *British Journal of Psychiatry, 114,* 797–811.

Bradburn, N. M. (1969). *The structure of psychological well-being.* Chicago: Aldine.

Brod, M., Stewart, A. L., Sands, L., & Walton, P. (1999). Conceptualization and measurement of quality of life in dementia: The Dementia Quality of Life Instrument (DQoL). *The Gerontologist, 39*(1), 25–35.

Burns, T., & Mortimer, J. A. (1994). The Cognitive Performance Test: A new approach to functional assessment in Alzheimer's disease. *Journal of Geriatric Psychiatry and Neurology, 7,* 46–54.

Cohen-Mansfield, J. (1995). The assessment of disruptive behavior/agitation in elderly persons: Function, methods, and difficulties. *Journal of Geriatric Psychiatry and Neurology, 8*(1), 52–60.

Costa, J. P. T., & McCrea, R. (1988). Personality in adulthood: A six-year longitudinal study of self-reports and spouse ratings on the NEO PTY Inventory. *Journal of Personality and Social Psychology, 54,* 853–863.

Costa, J. P. T., & McCrae, R. R. (1990). *Personality in adulthood.* New York: Guilford Press.

Cutler, L. J. (2000). Assessment of physical environments of older adults. In R. L. Kane & R. A. Kane (Eds.). *Assessing older persons: Measures, meanings, and practical applications* (pp. 360–379). New York: Oxford University Press.

Cutler, L. J., Kane, R. A., Hegenholtz, H. D., Miller, M. J., & Grant, L. (in press). Assessing and comparing physical environments for nursing home residents. *The Gerontologist.*

Degenholtz, H. D., Kane, R. A., & Kivnick, H. Q. (1997). Care-related preferences and values of elderly community-based LTC consumers: Can case managers learn what's important to clients? *The Gerontologist, 37*(6), 767–777.

Fetzer Institute. (1999). *Multidimensional measurement of religiousness/spirituality for use in health research.* Kalamazoo, MI: Author.

Fillenbaum, G. G. (1988). *Multidimensional functional assessment of older adults: The Duke Older Americans Resources and Services Procedures.* Hillsdale, NJ: Lawrence Erlbaum.

Folstein, M. F., Folstein, S., & McHugh, P. R. (1975). Mini-mental state: A practical method for grading the cognitive state of patients for the clinician. *Journal of Psychiatric Research, 12,* 189–198.

Frytak, J. R. (2000). Assessment of quality of life in older adults. In R. L. Kane & R. A. Kane (Eds.), *Assessing older persons: Measures, meaning, and practical applications* (pp. 200–236). New York: Oxford University Press.

Geron, S. M., Smith, K., Tennstedt, S., Jette, A., Chassler, D., Kasten, L., et al. (2000). The Home Care Satisfaction Measure: A client-centered approach to assessing the satisfaction of frail older adults with home care services. *Journal of Gerontology: Social Sciences, 55,* S259–S270.

Goldstone, L. A. (1982). The Norton score: An early warning of pressure sores? *Journal of Advanced Nursing, 7,* 419–426.

Grann, J. D. (2000). Assessment of emotions in older adults: Mood disorders, anxiety, psychological well-being, and hope. In R. L. Kane & R. A. Kane (Eds.), *Assessing older persons: Measures, meaning, and practical applications* (pp. 129–169). New York: Oxford University Press.

Hays, R. D., & Stewart, A. L. (1992). Sleep measures. In A. L. Stewart & J. E. Ware (Eds.), *Measuring functioning and well-being: The Medical Outcomes Study approach* (pp. 235–400). Durham, NC: Duke University Press.

Helmes, E., Csapo, K. G., & Short, J. A. (1987). Standardization and validation of the Multidimensional Observational Scale for Elderly Subjects (MOSES). *Journal of Gerontology, 42,* 395–405.

Herr, K. A., & Mobily, P. R. (1993). Comparison of selected pain assessment tools for use with the elderly. *Applied Nursing Research, 6*(1), 39–46.

John, O. P. (1999). The "big five" factor taxonomy: History measurement and theoretical perspectives. In L. A. Pervin (Ed.), *Handbook of personality: Theory and research, 2nd edition* (pp. 102–138). New York: Guilford Press.

Kane, R. A., & Kane, R. L. (1981). *Assessing the elderly: A practical guide to measurement.* Lexington, MA: D. C. Heath.

Kane, R. A., Kane, R. L., Bershadsky, B., Culter, L. J., Giles, K., Liu, J., et al. (2004). *Measures, indicators, and improvement of quality of life in nursing homes: Final report. Vol. 1: Methods and results.* Report to Centers for Medicare and Medicaid Services. Minneapolis, MN: Health Services Research and Policy, School of Public Health, University of Minnesota.

Kane, R. A., Kling, K. C., Bershadsky, B., Kane, R. L., Giles, K., Degenholtz, H. B., et al. (2003). Quality of life measures for nursing home residents. *Journal of Gerontology: Medical Sciences, 58A*(3), 240–248.

Kane, R. L., & Kane, R. A. (Eds.). (2000). *Assessing older persons: Measures, meaning, and practical applications.* New York: Oxford University Press.

Katz, S., Down, T., Cash, H., & Grotz, R. (1970). Progressive development of the Index of ADL. *The Gerontologist, 10,* 20–30.

Katz, S., Ford, A. B., Moskowitz, R. W., Jackson, B. A., & Jaffee, M. W. (1963). Studies of illness in the aged. The Index of ADL: A standardized measure of biological and psychosocial function. *Journal of the American Medical Association, 185*(12), 914–919.

Kidd, D., Stewart, G., Baldry, J., Johnson, J., Rossiter, D., Petruckevitch, A., et al. (1995). The Functional Independence Measure: A comparative validity and reliability study. *Disability and Rehabilitation, 17*(1), 10–14.

Kinney, J., & Stephens, M. A. P. (1989a). Caregiver Hassles Scale: Assessing the daily hassles of caring for a family member with dementia. *The Gerontologist, 28,* 328–332.

Kinney, J. M., & Stephens, M. A. P. (1989b). Hassles and uplifts of giving care to a family member with dementia. *Psychology and Aging, 4*(4), 402–408.

Kivnick, H. Q., & Murray, S. V. (2001). Life Strengths Interview Guide: Assessing elder clients' strengths. *Journal of Gerontological Social Work, 34*(4), 7–32.

Kivnick, H. Q., Stoffel, S. A., & Hanlan, D. (2001, November). *Occupational profile: An interdisciplinary tool for representing and reflecting on daily activities.* Poster presented at the 2001 meeting of the Gerontological Society of America, Chicago.

Langley, L. K. (2000). Cognitive assessment of older adults. In R. L. Kane & R. A. Kane (Eds.), *Assessing older persons: Measures, meaning, and practical applications* (pp. 65–128). New York: Oxford University Press.

Lawton, M. P. (1968). *The PGC Mental Status Questionnaire.* Unpublished manuscript, Philadelphia Geriatric Center.

Lawton, M. P., Moss, M., Fulcomer, M., & Kleban, M. H. (1982). A research and service oriented multilevel assessment instrument. *Journal of Gerontology, 37*(1), 91–99.

Lawton, M. P., Van Haitsma, K., & Klapper, J. (1996). Observed affect in nursing home residents with Alzheimer's disease. *Journal of Gerontology, 51B,* 3–14.

Lawton, M. P., Van Haitsa, K., Perkinson, M., & Ruckdeschel, K. (1999). Observed affect and quality of life: Further affirmations and problems. *Journal of Mental Health and Aging, 5*(1), 69–82.

Lawton, M. P., Weisman, G. D., Sloane, P. D., Norris-Baker, C., Caulkins, M., & Zimmerman, S. I. (2000).

Professional environment assessment procedure for special care units for elders with dementing illness and its relationship to the therapeutic environment schedule. *Alzheimer's Disease and Associated Disorders, 14*(1), 23–38.

Levin, C. A. (2000). Social functioning. In R. L. Kane & R. A. Kane (Eds.), *Assessing older persons: Measures, meaning, and practical applications* (pp. 170–199). New York: Oxford University Press.

Logsdon, R., Gibbons, L. E., McCurry, S. M., & Terri, L. (1999). Quality of life in Alzheimer's disease: Patient and caregiver reports. *Journal of Mental Health and Aging, 5*(1), 21–32.

Lubben, J. E. (1988). Assessing social networks among elderly populations. *Family Community Health, 11,* 45–52.

Mahoney, F. I., & Barthel, D. W. (1965). Functional evaluation: The Barthel Index. *Maryland State Medical Journal, 14,* 61–65.

Montgomery, R. J. V., Gonyea, J. G., & Hooyman, N. R. (1985). Caregiving and the experience of subjective and objective burden. *Family Relations, 34,* 19–26.

Moos, R. H., & Lemke, S. (1996). *Evaluating residential facilities.* Thousand Oaks, CA: Sage.

Mor, V., Branco, K., Fleishman, J., Hawes, C., Phillips, C., Morris, J., et al. (1995). The structure of social engagement among nursing home residents. *Journal of Gerontology: Psychological Sciences, 50B*(1), P1–P8.

Morris, J. N., Fries, B. E., Mehr, D. R., Hawes, C., Phillips, C., Mor, V., et al. (1994). MDS cognitive performance scale. *Journal of Gerontology: Medical Sciences, 49*(4), M174–M182.

Morris, J. N., Fries, B. E., & Morris, S. A. (1999). Scaling ADLs within the MDS. *Journals of Gerontology: Medical Sciences, 54A*(11), M546–M553.

Morris, J. N., Hawes, C., Fries, B. E., Phillips, C. D., Mor, V., Katz, S., et al. (1990). Designing the National Resident Assessment Instrument for nursing homes. *The Gerontologist, 3*(3), 293–307.

Neugarten, B. L., Havighurst, R. J., & Tobin, S. S. (1961). The measurement of life satisfaction. *Journal of Gerontology, 16,* 134–143.

Noelker, L. S., & Harel, Z. (Eds.). (2001). *Linking quality of long-term care and quality of life.* New York: Springer.

Pearlin, L. I., Mullan, J. T., Semple, S. J., & Skaff, M. M. (1990). Caregiving and the stress process: An overview of concepts and their measures. *The Gerontologist, 30*(5), 583–594.

Pearlin, L. I., & Zarit, S. H. (1993). Research into informal caregiving: Current perspectives and future directions. In S. H. Zarit, L. I. Pearlin, & K. W. Schaie (Eds.),

Caregiving systems: Informal and formal helpers (pp. 155–167). Hillsdale, NJ: Lawrence Erlbaum.

Pendergast, J. M., Coe, R. M., Chavez, M. N., Romeis, J. C., Miller, D. K., & Wolinsky, F. D. (1989). Clinical validation of a nutritional risk index. *Journal of Community Health, 14*(3), 125–135.

Pfeiffer, E. (1975). A short portable mental status questionnaire for the assessment of organic brain deficit in elderly patients. *Journal of the American Geriatrics Society, 23,* 433–441.

Philadelphia Geriatric Center & Visiting Nurse Service of New York. (1999). *Preferences for everyday living: A survey for the Visiting Nurse Service of New York.* New York: Author.

Radloff, L. L. (1977). The CES-D scale: A self-report depression scale for research in the general population. *Applied Psychological Measurement, 1,* 385–401.

Ryff, C. D., & Keyes, C. L. M. (1995). The structure of psychological well-being revisited. *Journal of Personality and Social Psychology, 69,* 719–727.

Sloane, P. D., & Mathew, L. J. (1990). Therapeutic environment screen scale. *American Journal of Alzheimer's Disease and Associated Disorders, 5,* 22–26.

Smith, M. (2000). Satisfaction. In R. L. Kane & R. A. Kane (Eds.), *Assessing older persons: Measures, meaning, and practical applications* (pp. 261–299). New York: Oxford University Press.

Teri, L., Truax, P., Logsdon, R., Uomoto, J., Zarit, S., & Vitaliano, P. P. (1992). Assessment of behavioral problems in dementia: The revised memory and behavior problems checklist. *Psychology and Aging, 7*(4), 622–631.

Tinetti, M. E. (1986). Performance-oriented assessment of mobility problems in elderly patients. *Journal of the American Geriatrics Society, 34,* 119–126.

Ware, J. E., Jr., & Sherbourne, C. D. (1992). The MOS 36-item short-form health survey (SF-36). I: Conceptual framework and item selection. *Medical Care, 30*(6), 473–483.

Wolinsky, F. D., Coe, R. M., Chavez, M. N., Pendergast, J. M., & Miller, D. K. (1986). Further assessment of the reliability and validity of a nutritional risk index: Analysis of a three-wave panel study of elderly adults. *Health Services Research, 20*(6 Pt. 2), 977–990.

Yesavage, J. A., & Brink, T. L. (1983). Development and validation of a geriatric depression screening scale: A preliminary report. *Journal of Psychiatric Research, 17*(1), 37–49.

Zarit, S. H., Reever, K. E., & Bach-Peterson, J. (1980). Relatives of the impaired elderly: Correlates of feelings of burden. *The Gerontologist, 20*(6), 649–655.

Zung, W. W. K. (1965). A self-rating depression scale. *Archives of General Psychiatry, 12,* 63–70.

The phrase "cognitive-behavioral" embraces a broad range of therapeutic interventions, ranging from the complicated process of cognitive restructuring to the relatively simple behavior management techniques employed in validation therapy. The common denominator of cognitive-behavioral interventions is the focus on the older adult's thought process and how that process influences subsequent emotional and behavioral responses. What an older adult thinks affects how he or she feels and behaves. With older adults, cognitive-behavioral approaches are most commonly used to treat mild to moderate forms of depression and anxiety. This chapter specifically examines cognitive-behavioral therapy (CBT), crisis intervention, and validation therapy.

B. Theories and Modes of Practice Intervention With Older Adults and Their Families/Caregivers

KATHLEEN McINNIS-DITTRICH

Cognitive-Behavioral Interventions

68

COGNITIVE-BEHAVIORAL THERAPY

CBT is based on the assumption that both cognitive and behavioral responses to events are learned (Adler, 1963; Beck, 1995; Ellis, 1962; Lantz, 1996; Malkinson, 2001). Once the older adult recognizes the triggers for automatic responses, new and more adaptive patterns of behavior can also be learned. CBT is perhaps underutilized in treating depression and anxiety in older adults. Depression sometimes is seen as a normal consequence of the aging process rather than as a treatable psychological condition (McInnis-Dittrich, 2005; O'Hara, 2000). There are also lingering Freudian perspectives suggesting that older adults' personality traits and behavior patterns are too rigid to respond to psychotherapy (Pinquart & Sorenson, 2001). More likely, however, the problem is the lack of training in the mental health community to address many of the emotional and behavioral problems that affect this age group.

Older Adults Who Respond Best to Cognitive-Behavioral Therapy

Accurate diagnosis of depression or anxiety in an older adult is the precursor of successful application of CBT to this population. Dementia, delirium, anxiety, and depression in older adults often mimic each other, and it may be difficult to clearly determine the cause of an older adult's depression or anxiety (Anderson, 2001; McInnis-Dittrich, 2005; Pinquart & Sorenson, 2001).

Even with an accurate diagnosis, CBT is not appropriate for use with all older adults. Late-onset maladaptive thinking and behavior appear to respond better to CBT than those patterns reinforced from childhood (O'Hara, 2000). It is most effective with elders who are verbal and have few, if any, cognitive impairments, even if such impairments are not due to dementia. The cognitive-behavioral process requires that an individual be able to identify thoughts and discuss feelings (McInnis-Dittrich, 2005). The ability to engage in abstract thinking and analyze behavior is the cornerstone of CBT. No matter how easily the social worker can see how cognitive distortions are causing the older adult to remain depressed or become anxious, it is the older adult's insight, not the worker's, that changes the person's feelings and behaviors.

The CBT approach has shown limited usefulness in work with older adults who are highly autonomous or have extreme difficulty asking for or receiving help (Mosher-Ashley & Barrett, 1997). This approach is also not appropriate for older adults who have exhibited suicidal ideations (Yost, Beutler, Corbishley, & Allender, 1986) or those who are actively abusing drugs or alcohol.

The Cognitive-Behavioral Process

The process of CBT, which has been adapted for use with older adults by Yost et al. (1986), Mosher-Ashley and Barrett (1997), and others, consists of four distinct stages: preparation, collaboration-identification, actual behavioral change, and consolidation. In the preparation phase, considerable time is devoted to developing the professional relationship between the older adult and the therapist. Older adults need to have a clear understanding of the cognitive-behavioral change process along with realistic expectations of how CBT can help them change emotional and behavioral responses. Individuals must be capable of, and interested in, committing to a process of intense introspection and trust the guidance and insight of the therapist.

In the collaboration-identification phase of CBT, the older adult is introduced to the process of identifying the relationship between events and feelings. The therapist explores those situations in which the older adult is acutely aware of being depressed or anxious, helping him or her see how certain situations elicit such feelings based on what the older adult was thinking. In the case of an older widow with mild to moderate depression, it is important for her to identify those times when she is acutely aware of her depressed feelings. For example, she may identify Sundays as particularly difficult times because she ex-

pects to receive a call from her son or she finds herself painfully alone on a day usually devoted to family activities. The lack of a phone call or being alone (the events) trigger sadness and feelings of being unloved (the emotions). She may have been thinking, "I am not important enough for my son to remember to call me. He must not care about me." She is learning to connect an event, the cognitive response, and the emotional response.

This degree of insight must be developed before entering the change phase of CBT. Once events, feelings, and thoughts are identified by the older adult, the therapist can explore the behavioral reaction to this change of events. For example, even though she welcomes the attention from her son when he does call later in the week, she is hypercritical and argumentative with him (the behavioral response). When she is able to see that she may be trying to punish her son for his neglect and that his unpleasant interaction with her may actually be exacerbating the problem of his not calling, she can begin to explore ways to change this chain of events. The change process occurs through the older adult's examination of distorted thinking. Cognitive distortions include globalizing, "awfulizing," mind reading, self-blaming, unrealistic demands on others, unrealistic expectations of self, and exaggeration of self-importance. It is easy to see how errors in thinking can lead this older woman to have a painful emotional reaction. If she believes that not receiving a phone call on Sunday from her son means he does not love her anymore, it is not surprising that she would be depressed. At this point in CBT, the therapist explores how she can employ corrective behavioral actions to prevent her depressed feelings from developing. Instead of brooding all day because her son has not called, she can decide to become proactive, empowering herself to do something positive to make herself feel better. Rather than fixating on the thought "He doesn't love me," she can substitute the thought "He must be very busy. I should call him and see how he is doing." Taking such positive steps empowers her to regain mastery over her environment and feel less depressed. This corrective action has the added advantage of making the interaction between mother and son more positive for both parties. If she is less difficult when he calls, perhaps he will call more.

The final phase of CBT is consolidation and termination. The therapist's job is to consolidate the changes observed during the treatment process. Reviewing with the older adult how far he or she has come, discussing what strengths have developed in identifying emotions and thoughts, and reinforcing the belief that he or she can handle future challenges is part of this process. An older adult needs to leave the therapeutic process confident that he or she has learned the skills to continue to fight depression or anxiety in the future.

A number of other techniques can be used in CBT to supplement traditional talk therapy. These include more traditional psychodynamic approaches, progressive muscle relaxation, reminiscence, increasing socialization, and stress inoculation (Puder, 1988). Other techniques employed specifically in using CBT to treat grief include guided imagery, exposure techniques, thought-stopping, breathing exercises, and skill acquisition (Malkinson, 2001).

The Effectiveness of CBT With Older Adults

The effectiveness of CBT in reducing both anxiety and depression in older adults is widely supported in the mental health research (Arean, 1993; Beck & Stanley, 1997; McCarthy, Katz, & Foa, 1991). O'Hara (2000) found CBT to be especially effective in reducing anxiety when it was combined with relaxation techniques. While working on correcting distortions in thinking, older adults benefited from the immediate anxiety-reducing influence of a variety of relaxation techniques.

Pinquart and Sorenson (2001) found that CBT was more effective in resolving issues in depression and anxiety among older adults than psychoeducational, activity promotion, and cognitive training approaches. They found that both CBT and psychodynamic approaches significantly improved an older adult's sense of well-being and the clinician's perception of the level of depression in the older adult. These researchers and others (Zarit & Zarit, 1998) attribute CBT's success to the concrete, problem-solving nature of the approach. Pinquart and Sorenson found CBT more effective in the context of individual therapy as opposed to use in the group setting.

CRISIS INTERVENTION

Crisis Versus Stressful Events

By the nature of life's challenges at this point in their lives, older adults are at high risk for myriad stressful events. However, stressful events do not always result in a *crisis,* as it is defined in the mental health field

(Duffy & Iscoe, 1990). The extent to which stressful events become a crisis lies in individuals' perceptions that they have reached an impasse in their ability to cope with the stressful event (Caplan, 1964; Duffy & Iscoe, 1990). Individuals may perceive that previously learned coping skills are no longer either effective or sufficient to face and manage a life event. The key to defining a crisis lies in the individual's *perception* of being overwhelmed.

An older adult's reaction to a crisis may be one of acute anxiety and a sense of panic and despair. He or she may become obsessed with "doing something," although what exactly will resolve the crisis may not be clear, and such behavior may seem irrational or counterproductive. On the contrary, the older adult may withdraw and retreat as a means of coping with an overwhelming challenge (Duffy & Iscoe, 1990; McInnis-Dittrich, 2005). This may include social isolation or a retreat to alcohol, drugs, or suicide as coping mechanisms. A sustained crisis response to an event may damage both physical and psychological health.

Are Older Adults at Higher Risk for Crisis Events?

Very little empirical research has been conducted on the incidence and treatment of crisis events in the lives of older adults, yet there is conflicting evidence as to whether older adults are at greater risk for responding to a stressful event as a crisis. Ebersole and Hess (1998) conclude that older adults are at higher risk for the development of a crisis in their lives and will need more time to resolve the crisis. Other studies have found that older adults are less likely to experience a crisis event; as a result of a lifetime of coping with stress and a larger repertoire of coping skills, they will resolve a crisis episode more quickly (Norris & Murrell, 1988). In one of the few studies of its kind, Winogrond and Mirassou (1983) found that although fewer older adults contacted crisis intervention services, when they or others in their support system did, the type of crisis they reported was much more severe and less amenable to traditional brief therapeutic interventions. Older adults are much more likely to come into the service system in a crisis situation identified by family, friends, or community members rather than through self-referral (Florio & Raschko, 1998).

There are a number of characteristics that place older adults as a group and specific individuals in particular at risk for a crisis event. A serious illness or sudden loss of one of the activities of daily living

(ADLs) were the most common events precipitating a crisis among older adults (Chima, 2002; Winogrond & Mirassou, 1983). Others included an unanticipated loss of financial resources due to illness or retirement, placement in a nursing home (Chima, 2002), domestic violence (Brandl & Horan, 2002), and loss of a life partner. Not all older adults respond to these events with a crisis reaction, but it appears the multiplicity of events may be the precipitating factor. Each stressful event exacerbates the influence of the others.

With an increased likelihood of illness, difficulties in maintaining adequate hydration and nutrition, asymptomatic infections, and complex medication regimens, older adults are at higher risk for the development of delirium, which often mimics a crisis reaction (McInnis-Dittrich, 2005; Rapp, 2001). Delirium is characterized by dementia-like symptoms, with a sudden onset and increased agitation, but can be linked to a physiological etiology, not a personal reaction to a stressful event. Delirium is a medical emergency, not a psychosocial crisis. In such cases, the older adult should receive immediate medical treatment. When an older adult presents in crisis, delirium should be ruled out before psychosocial intervention methods are employed.

Crisis Intervention Methods

Primary Intervention

Primary intervention occurs before a crisis actually develops and is aimed at developing coping skills prior to the demand for those skills. There are a number of events that commonly accompany one's later years that do not have to become a crisis if one is prepared. For example, a reduction in income is likely upon retirement. In anticipation, a couple could develop a sample budget before retirement, alerting them to the ways they will have to change existing spending patterns. Preparing older adults for the possibility of the reduced physical strength that often accompanies degenerative arthritis can be facilitated by helping them explore strength training and exercise programs aimed at maintaining abilities rather than seeking to recover them once the disease has progressed. Preparation through education can empower older adults to anticipate events (e.g., the loss of a partner) and plan before the event occurs. All of these events (retirement, chronic disease, and loss of a partner) may still be stressful, but the older adult has developed coping skills in anticipation of a likely stressful event.

Secondary Prevention

Secondary prevention occurs once an event or condition develops but is aimed at minimizing the growth of the stressful event into a crisis (Chima, 1996, 2002). Crisis intervention techniques at this level may include support groups for newly widowed older adults or social and recreation programs for older adults who find themselves depressed due to isolation from family and friends. Encouraging the transition to more supportive living arrangements such as independent or assistive community living rather than waiting until skilled nursing care is needed for a chronic health condition is another example of secondary prevention. The key to preventing an older adult's perception that a stressful event is beyond his or her coping skills, thus becoming a crisis, is helping the person to retain mastery and control of as much of his or her life as possible.

Tertiary Prevention

Once individuals perceive themselves at an impasse in their ability to rally the necessary coping skills to manage a stressful event, tertiary intervention is indicated. Steps in crisis intervention for older adults include the following:

1. Create a quiet, nonstimulating environment for the initial assessment of the individual. Visual and audio stimulation should be minimal. Make the older adult as comfortable as possible with comfortable seating or room to pace. Use a calm, soft voice to speak to the older adult.
2. As much as possible, and using collateral information from family and friends, quickly assess whether the psychosocial crisis is actually a delirious reaction to a physical illness, medication toxicity, dehydration, or malnutrition.
3. If delirium can be ruled out, encourage the older adult to tell you as much as possible about the events leading up to the crisis. Although the individual may be very anxious (or withdrawn), it is imperative to also assess at this point whether he or she has any cognitive limitations. Older adults in middle- and late-stage dementia are extremely difficult to engage in a rational conversation and may require hospitalization to stabilize them emotionally and cognitively. Let the older adult talk as much or as little as needed without interruption. Encourage the older adult to breathe deeply and "start at the beginning."

4. Provide a safe environment for the older adult. If it's chilly, provide a blanket. If the area is too warm, cool down the room. If the individual is afraid of being hurt by family or friends, separate the older adult from what he or she fears (Brandl & Horan, 2002). The perception of being safe and cared for is essential for reducing anxiety and drawing out the elder. The goal is to provide for the older adult's immediate needs, physical and psychological.

5. Identify at least one short-term goal that can be quickly accomplished and will provide immediate anxiety relief. For example, if the older adult is having a crisis reaction to recent widowhood, make sure he or she is not left alone. This not only is a safeguard against suicide but also meets an immediate need not to be alone. If an individual has been the victim of an assault, be sensitive to the need for some physical distance from strangers until he or she is ready to reach out. If the older adult has lost a home due to fire, identify an immediate short-term solution for a place to stay.

6. When the immediate crisis has passed and the older adult has regained some basic control over his or her emotional responses, begin the discussion of a long-term plan to resolve the crisis. However, discuss the long-term goal in terms of short-term steps (Jobes & Berman, 1996). "Emphasize the realistic positive" while not denying the perception of the overlying problem (Holkup, 2003, p. 13). Accomplishing small tasks successfully helps older adults to regain a sense of mastery and control over the environment. Small successes will build confidence for long-term goals.

7. Follow-up is necessary in treating any crisis reaction in an older adult. Identifying long-term supports or mobilizing resources that will prevent a future crisis reaction is an ongoing process. It will take some time for the older adult to return to emotional equilibrium.

VALIDATION THERAPY

Although a cognitive-behavioral approach works well with high-functioning older adults, it is not recommended for addressing troublesome affect or behavior in older adults with deficits in cognitive functioning, such as in Alzheimer's disease and other dementias. One alternative therapeutic approach for work with this population is known as validation therapy. Unlike the cognitive-behavioral approach, validation therapy does not try to change an older adult's thought patterns but rather tries to understand how the distorted thinking often associated with dementia is actually an older adult's attempt to communicate a need to those around him or her (Feil, 1996). Rather than attempt to reorient older adults with dementia to the correct time and space in their environment (the main focus of reality orientation), validation therapy communicates with older adults by validating and respecting their feelings in whatever time or place is real to them (Day, 1997).

Developed by Naomi Feil in the 1960s, validation therapy is based on the underlying belief that behavior in very old people is a complex interaction of physical, social, and biological changes that occur over the life span; failing to complete some earlier life tasks may lead to psychological problems later in life (Feil, 1967, 1984, 1993, 1996). When an older adult's memory begins to fail, he or she may attempt to restore balance to his or her life by retrieving earlier memories, which could include unresolved issues from early life experiences. Feil (1996) contends that when painful feelings are expressed, acknowledged, and validated by a trusted listener, they will diminish. If those feelings are ignored or suppressed, they will gain strength and contribute to difficulties in affective response or behavior.

Validation Therapy as a Long-Term Therapeutic Approach

Feil (1967, 1984, 1996) originally proposed validation therapy as an ongoing therapeutic approach that could be used by social workers, nurses, and nursing assistants with confused older adults over a sustained period of time. She identified four stages of confusion commonly observed in the progression of dementia: malorientation, time (and space) confusion, repetitive motion, and vegetation. She proposed specific therapeutic techniques for each of the stages coinciding with how severe confusion appeared and what seemed to work the best to calm an anxious and confused older adult in each stage. Her original work assumed that care would be provided consistently by the same group of mental health workers and staff. Working with the same older adult on a regular basis would allow these caregivers the opportunity to get to know the person, thus being capable of identifying the appropriate stage of confusion. An ongoing relationship would facilitate an accurate interpretation of the developmental challenges or problems the older adult was attempting to communicate (Babins, 1988).

The basic therapeutic techniques of validation therapy include the following:

- A conscious effort on the part of staff or family to first center themselves to dissipate the intense emotions often created by an older adult's agitated behavior.
- Using nonthreatening, factual words—such as who, what, when, where, and how—to build trust to explore what the older adult is trying to communicate.
- Rephrasing the older adult's words using the same rhythm and expression to minimize confrontation and validate what the older adult is saying.
- Using polarity, such as asking, "Is that the worst thing that happened?" The simple act of listening gives the person permission to talk.
- Reminiscing about former problem-solving skills the older adult has used in the past.
- Maintaining genuine, close eye contact to reduce anxiety on the part of the older adult.
- Using a clear, low, loving tone of voice to sooth agitation.
- Linking the observed behavior or affect to the unmet developmental need, especially the basic human needs for love, being needed, and the expression of emotion.
- Using music for those elders who are severely withdrawn to appeal to emotions and experiences from their past. (Feil, 1996)

Feil (1996) proposes that over time, the nature and extent of unresolved issues from the older adult's past will become apparent, allowing the professional helper or caregiver to help the person work through the issues. Even if the issues cannot be resolved, having the opportunity to express these feelings to a listener who validates the individual's feelings and responds with respect and empathy has its therapeutic benefits.

The Validation Approach as a Behavioral Management Technique

Ongoing relationship building between a confused older adult and a therapist or caregiver skilled in the use of therapeutic techniques may not be possible in most long-term care facilities serving this population. However, the validation approach may have its greatest usefulness in managing short-term behavior (McInnis-Dittrich, 2005; Pietro, 2002). Rather than attempt to constantly correct a confused older adult's

perception of reality, a validation approach accepts that any communication is attempting to express a need that may or may not be related to earlier unresolved conflicts.

For example, if a widow with dementia keeps asking "Where is my husband?" even though her husband has been dead for many years, the validation approach would contend that this statement reflects the woman's needs. Rather than correct the woman by reminding her that she is widowed and that her husband has been gone for many years, the response might be "You must miss your husband very much" or "I know it must be frightening to be alone right now." Rather than interpret the person's statement as a reflection of her confusion, a validation approach interprets the statement as her expression of loneliness or grief that her husband is not with her. The therapeutic benefits of such a statement come from the empathic, reassuring tone of the respondent and the lack of attempt to argue with or contradict the older adult. It can serve both as a distraction to the older adult to move him or her away from the troubling thought and as a way to minimize agitation. Not only does such an approach appear to de-escalate agitation in confused elders, but it does not allow caregivers and family members to become angry, resentful, and exhausted from constantly trying to bring a confused elder into their reality (Day, 1997).

The Pros and Cons of the Validation Approach

Feil (1993) observed improved speech, less regression, less crying, less wandering behavior, and improvements in gait, interaction, and eye contact among older adults who were treated using the validation approach rather than a reorientation approach. She also found less need for physical or chemical restraints due to the reduction in aggressive and violent behavior. Other observers found that older adults and their families were able to communicate more successfully during visits, resulting in less frustration on the part of both the older adult and caregivers (Babins, Dillion, & Merovitz, 1988; Fine & Rouse-Bane, 1995). Anecdotal evidence supports the contention that the approach can be effective in defusing potentially catastrophic behaviors by older adults who are agitated, confused, and potentially violent to self and others (Fine & Rouse-Bane, 1995). The primary advantage of the validation approach is that it is relatively safe; no medication or restraints are needed.

However, the use of validation therapy remains very controversial. Controlled studies have found no statistically significant connection between the use of a validation approach and improvements in behavior among older adults with dementia (Babins, Dillion & Merovitz, 1988; Morton & Bleathman, 1991, Robb, Stegman, & Wolanin, 1986; Scanland & Emershaw, 1993). In the studies that both supported and refuted the effectiveness of validation therapy, very small, nonrandomized samples were used without matched control groups or the establishment of credible preintervention behavior baselines. Other critics feel that validation techniques hasten confused older adults' difficulty orienting themselves to reality. That is, if confusion is not corrected, older adults will lose the ability to maintain whatever reality abilities they do have. These limitations make it impossible to discount the value of the validation approach as well as fail to support it as an effective alternative to reality orientation.

REFERENCES

Adler, A. (1963). *The practice and theory of individual psychology.* New York: Premier Books.

Anderson, D. N. (2001). Treating depression in old age: The reasons to be positive. *Age and Ageing, 30,* 13–17.

Arean, P. A. (1993). Cognitive behavioral therapy with older adults. *Behavior Therapist, 16,* 236–239.

Babins, L. (1988). Conceptual analysis of validation therapy. *International Journal of Aging and Human Development, 26*(3), 161–167.

Babins, L., Dillion, J., & Merovitz, S. (1988). The effects of validation therapy on disoriented elderly. *Activities, Adaptation & Aging, 12*(1/2), 73–86.

Beck, J. (1995). *Cognitive therapy: Basics and beyond.* New York: Guilford Press.

Beck, J. G., & Stanley, M. A. (1997). Anxiety disorders in the elderly: The emerging role of behavior therapy. *Behavior Therapy, 28,* 83–100.

Brandl, B., & Horan, D. L. (2002). Domestic violence in later life: An overview for health care providers. *Women & Health, 35*(2/3), 41–54.

Caplan, G. (1964). *Principles of preventive psychiatry.* New York: Basic Books.

Chima, F. O. (1996). Assessment in employee assistance: Integrating treatment and prevention objectives. *Employee Assistance Quarterly, 12*(2), 47–66.

Chima, F. O. (2002). Elder suicidality: Human behavior and social environment perspective. *Journal of Human Behavior in the Social Environment, 6*(4), 21–46.

Day, C. R. (1997). Validation therapy: A review of the literature. *Journal of Gerontological Nursing, 23*(4), 29–34.

Duffy, M., & Iscoe, I. (1990). Crisis theory and management: The case of the older person. *Journal of Mental Health Counseling, 12*(3), 303–313.

Ebersole, P., & Hess, P. (1998). *Toward healthy aging: Human needs and nursing response* (5th ed.). St. Louis, MO: Mosby.

Ellis, A. (1962). *Reason and emotion in psychotherapy.* New York: Stuart.

Feil, N. (1967). Group therapy in a home for the aged. *The Gerontologist, 7,* 192–195.

Feil, N. (1984). Communicating with the confused elderly patient. *Geriatrics, 39*(3), 131–132.

Feil, N. (1993). *The validation breakthrough.* Baltimore, MD: Health Professions Press.

Feil, N. (1996). Validation: Techniques for communicating with confused old-old persons and improving their quality of life. *Topics in Geriatric Rehabilitation, 11*(4), 34–42.

Fine, J. I., & Rouse-Bane, S. (1995). Using validation techniques to improve communication with cognitively impaired older adults. *Journal of Gerontological Nursing, 21*(6), 39–45.

Florio, E. R., & Raschko, R. (1998). The gatekeeper model: Implications for social policy. *Journal of Aging & Social Policy, 10*(1), 37–55.

Holkup, P. A. (2003). Evidence-based protocol: Elderly suicide—secondary prevention. *Journal of Gerontological Nursing, 29*(6), 6–17.

Jobes, D. A., & Berman, A. L. (1996). Crisis assessment and time-limited intervention with high-risk suicidal youth. In A. R. Roberts (Ed.), *Crisis management and brief treatment: Theory, technique and applications* (pp. 60–82). Chicago: Nelson-Hall.

Lantz, J. (1996). Cognitive theory and social work treatment. In F. J. Turner (Ed.), *Social work treatment: Interlocking theoretical approaches* (pp. 94–115). New York: Free Press.

Malkinson, R. (2001). Cognitive-behavioral therapy of grief: A review and application. *Research on Social Work Practice, 11*(6), 671–698.

McCarthy, P. R., Katz, I. R., & Foa, E. B. (1991). Cognitive-behavioral treatment of anxiety in the elderly: A proposed model. In C. Saltzman & B. D. Lebowitz (Eds.), *Anxiety in the elderly: Treatment and research* (pp. 197–214). New York: Springer.

McInnis-Dittrich, K. (2005). *Social work with elders: A biopsychosocial approach to assessment and intervention* (2nd ed.). Boston: Allyn and Bacon.

Morton, I., & Bleathman, C. (1991). The effectiveness of validation therapy in dementia: A pilot study. *International Journal of Geriatric Psychiatry, 6,* 327–330.

Mosher-Ashley, P. M., & Barrett, P. W. (1997). *A life worth living: Practical strategies for reducing depression in older adults.* Baltimore, MD: Health Professions Press.

Norris, F. H., & Murrell, S. A. (1988). Prior experience as a moderator of disaster impact on anxiety symptoms in older adult. *American Journal of Community Psychology, 16*(5), 655–683.

O'Hara, B. (2000). Cognitive-behavioral treatment of anxiety in late life from a schema-focused approach. *Clinical Gerontologist, 22*(3/4), 23–36.

Pietro, M. J. S. (2002). Training nursing assistants to communicate effectively with persons with Alzheimer's disease: A call to action. *Alzheimer's Care Quarterly 3*(2), 157–164.

Pinquart, M., & Sorenson, S. (2001). How effective are psychotherapeutic and other psychosocial interventions with older adults? A meta-analysis. *Journal of Mental Health and Aging, 7*(2), 207–243.

Puder, R. S. (1988). Age analysis of cognitive-behavioral group therapy for chronic pain outpatients. *Psychology and Aging, 3*(2), 204–207.

Rapp, C. G. (2001). Acute confusion/delirium protocol. *Journal of Gerontological Nursing, 27*(4), 21–33.

Robb, S. S., Stegman, C. E., & Wolanin, M. O. (1996). No research versus research with compromised results: A study of validation therapy. *Nursing Research, 35*(2), 113–118.

Scanland, S. G., & Emershaw, L. E. (1993). Reality orientation and validation therapy: Dementia, depression, and functional status. *Journal of Gerontological Nursing, 19*(6), 7–11.

Winogrond, I. R., & Mirassou, M. M. (1983). A crisis intervention service: Comparison of younger and older clients. *The Gerontologist, 23*(4), 370–376.

Yost, E. B., Beutler, L. E., Corsbishley, M. A., & Allender, J. R. (1986). *Group cognitive therapy: A treatment approach for depressed older adults.* New York: Pergamon.

Zarit, S. H., & Zarit, J. M. (1998). *Mental disorders in older adults: Fundamentals of assessment and treatment.* New York: Guilford Press.

ROBERTA R. GREENE
JOYCE RILEY

Family and Group Interventions

69

Despite the dramatic demographic changes known as the longevity revolution and the demonstrated need, older adults continue to receive inadequate mental health care. Mental health professions, including social workers, far too frequently ignore the grandparental generation, viewing aging as a time of decline. Practitioners also have tended to discount the utility of therapy with older adults, arguing that treatment is not efficacious (Newton, Brauer, Gutmann, & Grunes, 1986; Schneider & Kropf, 1992). Furthermore, professionals continue to debate how to overcome the lag existing in practice, research, education, policy, and planning (Council on Social Work Education [CSWE]/SAGE/SW, 2001; Gatz, 1996). Moreover, there is a dearth of research about what therapies work with older adults and their families (Orbach, 2003). At the same time, the allocation of resources to support caregiving families has always been routine among social work practitioners.

Ironically, research about the caregiving process has "flourished, [leading to] an intense concern about its economic, social, and psychological impact" (Pearlin, Mullen, Semple, & Skaff, 1990, p. 583). The information garnered has countered practice trends. The burgeoning of information about the impact of caregiving, and the increased recognition that informal caregiving is a typical family experience, has propelled practitioners and theorists alike to seek interventions that might alleviate caregiver stress (Toseland & Rossiter, 1989). Consequently, family therapy and group treatments have become more commonplace. That is, practitioners have gradually adopted or modified traditional family and group clinical social work approaches thought to be effective with the general population for use with frail older adults and their caregivers. By the mid-1980s, a growing interest in caregiver support began to close the gap between what is known about family functioning and clinical practice (Greene, 1989). This chapter discusses the development and nature of those social work family and group interventions.

CAREGIVING

Caregiving involves attending to the health, social, and personal care needs of people who are lacking some capacity for self-care. It encompasses the functional capacities of older adults, the caregiving patterns of families, and the use of community-based services (Greene, Dalin, & Lebow, 1991). Daatland (1983, p. 1) has proposed that family caregiving be seen as a form of social organization that includes the interpersonal relationships and the division of practical tasks: "a truly collective action, depending upon direct and indirect contributions from a number of actors, including the cared for himself."

It is a well-known fact that the majority of older adults who need assistance are cared for by a family member (AARP, 2003). The family transition to providing care for an older adult has become so widespread that Brody (1985, p. 25) called this phase of the life course "normative family stress." Caregiving tasks may include direct personal care, such as bathing and grooming, and indirect care, such as cooking, cleaning, and running errands. When an older adult has an acute or chronic illness, caregiving tasks may encompass simple forms of medical treatment such as injections.

Usually, a primary caregiver—often a wife, daughter, or daughter-in-law—assumes major responsibility. The generation of mostly women with direct caregiving responsibilities for two generations is called the sandwich generation; they juggle the responsibilities of mother-caregiver, daughter-caregiver, and worker (Marks, 1998; Stephens, Franks & Townsend, 1994). In addition, other family and friends, especially male relatives, may assume instrumental caregiving responsibilities, including bill paying (Hash, 2003).

Providing care for an older frail relative is complex and often involves rewards and risks. Rewards include feelings of being useful, appreciated, and satisfied with one's caregiving. Caregivers may also develop a sense of altruism and competence and have the opportunity to share feelings of love and empathy with the care recipient (Toseland & Smith, 2001). Risks thought to stem from the stress experienced by caregiving may include restrictions on the caregiver's activities, social isolation, reduced paid employment, and emotional difficulties such as depression and anxiety (Toseland & Smith, 2001).

Uncertainty about the older adult's illness or disability as well as the costs associated with such needs as special diets may also increase risks. Still another source of stress for caregivers is having to make end-of-life decisions for the care (Smerglia & Deimling, 1997).

INTERGENERATIONAL FAMILY INTERVENTIONS

Social work practice with older adults and their caregivers is based on knowledge that came to the fore in the 1970s and 1980s about intergenerational family functioning, filial relationships, and the biopsychosocial processes of aging. Theorists who defined intergenerational family dynamics contest the idea that there is a totally isolated nuclear family. Rather, they suggest that family dynamics involve the connecting link between generations based on loyalty, reciprocity, and indebtedness (Boszormenyi-Nagy & Spark, 1973). Research studies on the topic consistently reveal the financial, physical, and emotional reciprocity across generations, taking the form of telephoning, visiting, writing, and showing respect and concern. Care was also found to vary due to cultural factors associated with race/ethnicity. Diversity dimensions may also include size of household, intergenerational contacts and family support exchanges, gender, cohort group, and socioeconomic status (Tennstedt & Chang, 1998).

Following suit, family therapists suggested that therapy is indicated when a family experiences disagreements about autonomy issues or when the family experiences hidden and unresolved conflicts between generations (Greene, 1989). Autonomy issues encompass the balance between independence and dependence within the family; unresolved conflicts include unsettled scores or arguments. Moreover, it was noted that multigenerational conflicts often arise because of challenges to the family's longstanding interaction patterns, involving a shift in role transitions and family structure (Davey, Murphy, & Price, 2000; Newton & Lazarus, 1992).

Systems theory is frequently used to explore how people interact as a unit, particularly their structure and organization as a group. Systems theory assumes that a family is a functioning whole, with each person in constant interplay with another. Family dynamics is composed of these mutual influences and refocuses a practitioner's concerns on the here-and-now interactions that provoke difficulties. A family systems approach to family interventions offers the social worker a number of other useful guidelines:

- Assumes the family is a system with unique and discernible structure and communication patterns.
- Defines the boundaries of the family membership and cultural forms.
- Develops a picture of family structure, power relationships, and how roles are differentiated.
- Examines communication patterns to learn about the rules and cultural patterns.
- Determines how responsive the family is to stress as well as its ability to restructure to meet caregiving demands. (Based on Greene, 2001, p. 224)

The ecological perspective is also used to better understand how a family relates with other social systems. The perspective is based on Bronfenbrenner's (1979) conceptualization of person-environment fit. The ecological perspective lends itself to multisystemic analysis of how client families function and the consideration of what resources may support their endeavors. For example, practitioners work with small-scale microsystems (such as families and peer groups), the connection between systems known as mesosystems (such as the family and health care systems), exosystems (the connections between systems that do not directly involve the person, such as Social Security and Medicare), and macrosystems, or overarching large-scale systems, such as legal, political, and value systems.

Social work practice from an ecological perspective focuses on what Gitterman and Germain (1976) termed problems of daily living. It also underscores the need for social workers to promote everyday competence among older adults (Willis, 1991). Research on environmental press suggests that caregiving responsibilities have the potential to negatively affect the mental and physical well-being of the caregiver, be disruptive to marital and family relationships, and cause problems in meeting work and other social responsibilities (Pearlin, Aneshensel, & Leblanc, 1997). These research models make the distinction between primary and secondary stressors. Primary stressors are those associated with the necessities of the caregiving role, such as coping with the behaviors associated with dementia. Secondary stressors are more peripheral to or outside the caregiving role and may involve social or workplace issues of the sandwich generation. Such stressors in caregiving often precipitate families contacting social services agencies. From the ecological perspective, the social worker would determine how well the family fits with the environment, with a view toward ascertaining resource needs; choose intervention strategies congruent with a client's environmental and cultural context; direct interventions at any aspect of the ecosystem; and base interventions on client strengths and expertise (Greene & Barnes, 1998).

INTERVENTION MODELS

Models of geriatric health care are based on designs that promote optimal functioning among elders. At the core of this care process are comprehensive assessments used to gather a wide array of information about the quality of an older adult's biopsychosocial functioning (McInnis-Dittrich, 2002). The social worker evaluates the client's capacity to function effectively in his or her environment and to ascertain what resources are needed to improve interpersonal functioning (Greene & Sullivan, in press). The purpose of the biopsychosocial assessment is to assess functional capacity or everyday competence: the ability of older people to care for themselves, manage their affairs, and live independent, quality lives in their communities (Willis, 1991). The assessment may also include a diagnostic workup, which is an indepth medical and physical evaluation (McInnis-Dittrich, 2002).

MODELS OF FAMILY INTERVENTION

During the 1980s and 1990s, social workers developed models for working with older adults and their family caregivers. These included the family case management approach for Level I needs (Greene & Kropf, 2003), the auxiliary function model (Silverstone & Burack-Weiss, 1983), and the functional age model of intergenerational family treatment (Greene, 1986, 2001).

The family case management approach is a process of assisting families with multiple needs, helping them cope with stress and issues related to the use of multiple service providers (Table 69.1). "The goals of family case management are to mobilize a family's strengths, to marshal resources, and to maximize family functional capacity" (Greene & Kropf, 1995, p. 85). The social worker first engages the family in a helping relationship and then works with the family to develop and carry out a mutual care plan.

The auxiliary function model (Silverstone & Burack-Weiss, 1983) proposes that the major problems facing frail, impaired older adults are not disease or old age, but the effects these conditions may have on mental and physical functioning. The proponents of this model contended that therapy should be based on a supportive relationship and designed to counter the factors associated with depletion or loss. The major goal of the social worker in this model of intervention is to combat a family's feelings of helplessness in the face of its multiple losses, that is, to convey a sense of hope.

Another example of family-focused intervention is the functional age model of intergenerational family treatment (Greene, 1986, 2001). This model can be used to examine caregiving risk and well-being from

TABLE 69.1. Key Features of Family-Focused Social Work Case Management

Family-focused social work requires that the case manager

- Identify the family as the unit of attention.
- Assess the frail or impaired person's biopsychosocial functioning and needs within a culturally sound family context.
- Write a mutually agreed upon family care plan.
- Refer client systems to services and entitlements not available in the natural support system.
- Implement and coordinate the work that is done with the family.
- Determine what services need to be coordinated on behalf of the family.
- Intervene clinically to ameliorate family emotional problems and stress accompanying illness or loss of functioning.
- Determine how the impaired person and family will interact with formal care providers.
- Integrate formal and informal services provided by the family and other primary groups.
- Offer or advocate for particular services that the informal support network is not able to offer.
- Contact client networks and service providers to determine the quality of service provision.
- Mediate conflicts between family and service providers to empower the family when it is not successful.
- Collect information and data to augment the advocacy and evaluation efforts to ensure quality of care.

Source: Vourlekis and Greene (1992, p. 12).

a systems perspective; it is an approach used to promote a family's caregiving capacity. The model suggests that the social worker understand the "family as a mutually dependent unit with interdependent pasts and futures" (p. 20). As such, it employs a systems approach to intervene with families whose older relative is experiencing interference in performing activities of daily living—those skills that are called on to meet environmental demands. The model comprises assessment and intervention strategies in two domains: the functional age or biopsychosocial functioning of the older adult (Birren, 1969) and the role allocation and life course development of the family.

Functional Age

The central part of the functional age model is the social worker's assessment of the functional age or capacity of the older adult. Functional age is composed of three spheres related to adaptational capacity:

1. Biological age, referring to a client's health-related issues, such as chronic disease, medication effects, and physical concerns, such as energy levels. Decrements in memory, cognition, and judgment also are included in biological age.
2. Psychological age, encompassing affective and rational processes, such as mood, and thought processes, encompassing introspection and the meaning of events.

3. Social age, referring to the role one plays in the social structure, including norms, values, culture, and ethnicity.

Family

Along with the assessment of functional age, the social worker also develops an understanding of the family's adapting and coping capacity. The family is viewed as a social system with a high degree of interdependence and interrelatedness (however obscure) that is challenged when an older member has a crisis in functional capacity. The family is assessed from two perspectives:

1. The family as a set of reciprocal roles, including the expectations members share concerning behaviors in a certain situation, such as what a "good" older child does for his or her parent.
2. The family as a developmental unit, referring to the tasks expected of the family as a mutual aid system.

Family development emphasizes that family relationships are more than a combination of individual life cycles. Rather, family members' life stages are intertwined, with the effects of membership, including births, marriages, and deaths, introducing family change over time (Carter & McGoldrick, 1999).

Group Interventions

Because many older adults are more socially isolated than they were in their younger years, a group approach provides the therapeutic effect of group dynamics (McInnis-Dittrich, 2002). This reaffirmation of the human connection is based on the long-standing tradition of social group work with vulnerable older persons (Saul, 1983) and continues today in efforts of narrative gerontologists and others (Crimmens, 1998; Webster, 2001).

There are a variety of groups appropriate to work with older adults, using an array of theoretical frameworks, such as Yalom's (1985) existential perspective. According to McInnis-Dittrich (2002), group methods may have to be adjusted to account for elders' physical and sensory limitations. The group leader may have to take a more active role, and the pace may be slower. Group interventions may take several forms: group psychotherapy (Zarit & Knight, 1996), based on psychodynamic theory and intended to help clients gain insight; reality orientation groups (Greene, 2001), based on cognitive frameworks and designed to combat confusion and disorientation among elderly persons; support groups, based on the strengths perspective and intended to share solutions for common problems (Cox & Parsons, 1994); and reminiscing groups, based on Eriksonian life stages and aimed at recalling the past to settle past concerns.

Support Groups

Support groups are based on mutual aid and often provide information about a specific illness (Table 69.2). Support groups for caregivers take many forms and can reduce caregiver stress by providing a caregiver with respite; reducing loneliness; promoting ventilation of emotions; sharing feelings in a supportive environment; validating, universalizing, and normalizing thoughts, feelings, and experiences; instilling hope; affirming the significance of the caregiver role; educating caregivers about the aging process, resources, or health and disability topics; teaching problem-solving and coping strategies; and fostering the caregiver's capacity for problem solving (Hash, 2003, p. 223).

Reminiscing Groups

One of the most common theoretical frameworks used in group work with older adults and their caregivers is the reminiscing group format. Life review is based on Erikson's (1950) approach to the eighth stage of development, in which the developmental tasks involve resolving the crisis of integrity versus despair. Robert Butler (1963), one of the founding group of geriatric psychiatrists, believed that Erikson's approach provided the insight necessary to frame a life cycle psychiatry to guide psychotherapy with older adults. He contended that life review is "a progressive return to consciousness of past experiences in an attempt to resolve and integrate them" as well as a means of coming to terms with past conflicts and relationships (p. 65).

Based on his research at the National Institute of Mental Health and his private practice, Butler (1963, p. 237) came to believe that the "possibilities for intrapsychic change may be greater in old age than at any other period in life." He also thought that through therapies that define and seek opportunities, older adults come to terms with life, bear witness, find reconciliation, and achieve integration and transcendence.

Since the inception of Butler's life review therapy, the intervention has been applied with individuals, families, and groups. Its use with families can create a therapeutic milieu in which members can resolve conflict that may accompany various role changes in adulthood, such as shifts in responsibility involved in caregiving (Greene, 1983). There is some evidence that the use of reminiscence therapy can enhance family coping strategies (Comana & Brown, 1998).

Reminiscing groups with older adults can produce or enhance a cohort effect. That is, older adults find their historical connection and share accomplishments, tribulations, and viewpoints. The purpose may be to support social functioning, uncover and resolve unconscious conflicts, or ascribe new meaning to old events (Greene, 2001). Groups usually consist of no more than 10 people and may be run for a short period (10 weeks or less) or for as much as a year. Review content may be prompted by using visual or artistic devices such as videos, plays, or drama (Hargrave, 1994).

CONCLUSIONS

Although a number of group and family interventions are now seen as effective, the longevity revolution presses the profession to think about the aging process and caregiving in a broader context (Corman & Kingson, 1996; Kiyak & Hooyman, 1999; Silverstone, 2000). That expanded context embraces alterations in attitudes toward aging, an increasing empirically based gerontological knowledge base, as

TABLE 69.2. Forums for Educating and Training Caregivers

Community Workshops and Forums
Provides information about community services, usually single sessions lasting an hour to a day; often sponsored by health and human services organization.

Lecture Series and Discussion
Lectures given by clinical experts on topics of interest to specific groups of caregivers.

Support Groups
Allows for mutual sharing of information, usually unstructured, and encourages reciprocal and self-help among group members.

Psychoeducational and Skills Building Groups
Educates members usually in short-term, structured groups by teaching specific problem-solving and coping skills and sharing information about caregiving resources.

Individual Counseling and Training
Focuses on the individual caregivers' needs, helping them deal with the emotional and coping skills needed to be effective in the role and to handle the stresses of caregiving.

Family Counseling
Helps the family system deal with issues related to caregiving that will allow them to sustain the care recipient and maintain family balance and cohesiveness; often connects the family with other resources in the community.

Care Coordination and Management
Educates caregivers on how to perform caregiving roles more effectively and on how to connect with formal caregivers.

Technology-Based Interventions
Uses telephone-mediated groups, computer-mediated groups, and video conferencing to educate and train caregivers.

Source: Toseland and Smith (2001, pp. 10–12).

well as changing family forms (Bengtson, Giarrusso, Silverstein, & Wang, 2000; Greene, 2000).

From a research perspective, there have been numerous studies that emphasize the role of caregiving in reducing institutional placements. There have been few studies that examine the effects of programmatic interventions such as support groups. The strongest research efforts to date have focused on caregiver burden, stress, and strain. According to Cairl and Kosberg (1993, p. 86), this research has provided information on the (1) the nature and scope of burden or stress experienced by the caregiver; (2) the variance in the experience of burden relative to the type of relationship of the caregiver to the frail elderly or the involvement in external supports; and (3) the potential consequences of the experience of burden with regard to caregiver tolerance and, more specifically, the propensity to institutionalize. Cairl and Kosberg argue that although this tradition of research offers a clear picture of caregiver stress, it does not offer an understanding of whether burden results in decreased capacity. The baby boomer generation and information about successful aging compel practitioners to consider caregiving issues differently (Noonan & Tennstedt, 1997; Rowe & Kahn, 1998; Stull, Kosloski, & Kercher, 1994). The negative emphasis on caregiver burden has led some researchers to call for "a wholesale rethinking about caregiving experiences and outcomes to include positive aspects of caregiving and positive indicators of well-being" (Kramer, 1997, p. 218).

REFERENCES

AARP. (2003). *Beyond 50.03: A report to the nation on independent living and disability* [online]. Washington, DC: Author. Available at *www.aarp.org*.

Bengtson, V. L., Giarrusso, R., Silverstein, M., & Wang, H. (2000). Families and intergenerational relationships in aging societies. *Hallyn International Journal of Aging, 2*(1), 3–10.

Birren, J. E. (1969). Principles of research on aging. In J. E. Birren (Ed.), *The handbook of aging and the individual* (pp. 3–42). Chicago: University of Chicago Press.

Boszormenyi-Nagy, I., & Spark, G. (1973). *Invisible loyalties*. New York: Harper & Row.

Brody, E. (1985). Parent care as normative family stress. *Gerontologist, 25*, 19–29.

Bronfenbrenner, U. (1979). *The ecology of human development*. Cambridge, MA: Harvard University Press.

Butler, R. N. (1963). The life review: An interpretation of reminiscence in the aged. *Psychiatry 26*, 65–76.

Cairl, R. E., & Kosberg, J. I. (1993). The interface of burden and level of task performance of caregivers of Alzheimer's disease patients: Clinical profiles. *Journal of Gerontological Social Work, 19*(3/4), 133–151.

Carter, B., & McGoldrick, M. (1999). *The expanded family life cycle: Individual, family, and social perspectives.* Boston: Allyn & Bacon.

Comana, M. T., & Brown, V. M. (1998). The effect of reminiscence therapy on family coping. *Journal of Family Nursing, 4*(2), 182–198.

Corman, J. M., & Kingson, E. R. (1996). Trends, issues, perspectives, and values for the aging of the baby boom cohort. *The Gerontologist, 36*(1), 15–26.

Council on Social Work Education/SAGE-SW. (2001). *Strengthening the impact of social work to improve the quality of life for older adults and their families: A blueprint for the new millennium.* Alexandria, VA: Author.

Cox, E., & Parsons, R. (1994). *Empowerment-oriented social work practice with elderly.* Pacific Grove, CA: Brooks/Cole.

Daatland, S. O. (1983). Care systems. *Aging and Society, 3*(Pt. 1), 21–33.

Davey, A., Murphy, M., & Price, S. (2000). Aging and the family: Dynamics and therapeutic interventions. In W. C. Nichols (Ed.), *Handbook of family development and intervention* (pp. 235–252). New York: Wiley.

Erikson, E. (1950). *Child and society.* New York: Norton.

Gatz, M. (Ed.). (1995). *Emerging issues in mental health and aging.* Washington, DC: National Academy Press.

Gitterman, A., & Germain, C. B. (1976). Social work practice: A life model. *Social Service Review, 50*(4), 3–13.

Greene, R. R. (1983). Life review: A technique for clarifying family roles in adulthood. *Clinical Gerontologist, 1*(2), 59–67.

Greene, R. R. (1986). The functional-age model of intergenerational therapy: A social casework model. In T. L. Brink (Ed.), *Clinical gerontology: A guide to assessment and intervention* (pp. 335–346). New York: Haworth Press.

Greene, R. R. (1989). A life systems approach to understanding parent-child relationships in aging families. *Journal of Family Psychotherapy, 5*(1/2), 57–69.

Greene, R. R. (2001). *Social work with the aged and their families* (2nd ed.). New York: Aldine de Gruyter.

Greene, R. R., & Barnes, G. (1998). The ecological perspective, diversity, and culturally competent social work practice. In R. R. Greene & M. Watkins (Eds.), *Serving diverse constituencies: Applying the ecological perspective* (pp. 63–96). Hawthorne, NY: Aldine de Gruyter.

Greene, R. R., Dalin, H., & Lebow, G. (1991). A study of caregiving systems in one community: When and why elders enter a nursing home. *Journal of Jewish Communal Service, 67*(3), 244–250.

Greene, R. R., & Kropf, N. P. (2003). A family case management approach for level I functioning. In A. Kilpatrick & T. P. Holland (Eds.), *Working with families: An integrative model by level of functioning* (pp. 85–123). Needham Heights, MA: Allyn & Bacon.

Greene, R. R., & Sullivan, W. P. (in press). Putting social work values into action: Use of the ecological perspective with older adults in the managed care arena. *Journal of Gerontological Social Work.*

Hargrave, T. (1994). Using video life reviews with older adults. *Journal of Family Therapy, 16,* 259–268.

Hash, K. (2003). Practice with caregivers: Individuals and groups. In M. J. Naleppa & W. H. Reid (Eds.), *Gerontological social work: A task-centered approach* (pp. 203–234). New York: Columbia University Press.

Kiyak, N., & Hooyman, N. (1999). Aging in the twenty-first century. *Hallyn International Journal of Aging, 1,* 56–66.

Kramer, B. (1997). Gain in the caregiving experience: Where are we? What next? *The Gerontologist, 17*(2), 218–232.

Marks, N. (1998). Does it hurt to care? Caregiving, work-family conflict, and midlife well-being. *Journal of Marriage and the Family, 60,* 951–966.

McInnis-Dittrich, K. (2002). *Social work with elders: A biopsychosocial approach to assessment and intervention.* Boston: Allyn & Bacon.

Newton, N., Brauer, D., Gutmann, D. L., & Grunes, J. (1986). Psychodynamic therapy with the aged: A review. In T. L. Brink (Ed.), *Clinical gerontology: A guide to assessment and intervention* (pp. 205–243). New York: Haworth Press.

Newton, N., & Lazarus, L. W. (1992). Behavioral and psychotherapeutic interventions. In J. E. Birren, R. B. Sloane, & G. D. Cohen (Eds.), *Handbook of mental health and aging* (2nd ed., pp. 699–719). San Diego: Academic Press.

Noonan, A. E., & Tennstedt, S. L. (1997). Meaning in caregiving and its contribution to caregiver well-being. *The Gerontologist, 37,* 785–794.

Orbach, A. (2003). *Counseling older clients.* London: Sage.

Pearlin, L. I., Aneshensel, C. S., & A. J. Leblanc. (1997). The forms and mechanisms of stress proliferation: The case of AIDS caregivers. *Journal of Health and Social Behavior, 38*(3), 223–236.

Pearlin, L. I., Mullan, J. T., Semple, S. J., & Skaff, M. M. (1990). Caregiving and the stress process: An overview of concepts and their measures. *The Gerontologist, 30*(5), 583–594.

Rowe, J. W., & Kahn, R. L. (1998). *Successful aging.* New York: Pantheon.

Saul, S. (1983). *Groupwork with the frail elderly.* New York: Haworth Press.

Schneider, R. L., & Kropf, N. P. (1992). *Gerontological social work.* Chicago: Nelson-Hall.

Silverstone, B. (2000). The old and the new in aging: Implications for social work practice. *Journal of Gerontological Social Work, 33*(4), 35–50.

Silverstone, B., & Burack-Weiss, A. (1983). *Social work practice with the frail elderly and their families.* Springfield, IL: Charles C. Thomas.

Smerglia, V. L., & Deimling, G. T. (1997). Care-related decision-making satisfaction and caregiver well-being in families caring for older members. *The Gerontologist, 29*(5), 658–665.

Stephens, M., Franks, M., & Townsend, A. (1994). Stress and rewards in women's multiple roles: The case of women in the middle. *Psychology and Aging, 9*(1), 45–52.

Stull, D. E., Kosloski, K., & Kercher, K. (1994). Caregiver burden and generic well-being: Opposite sides of the same coin? *The Gerontologist, 34,* 88–94.

Tennstedt, S., & Chang, B. H. (1998). The relative contribution of ethnicity vs. socioeconomic status in explaining differences in disability and receipt of national care. *Journal of Gerontology: Social Sciences, 53B*(2), 861–870.

Toseland, R., & Rossiter, C. (1989). Group interventions to support family caregivers: A review and analysis. *The Gerontologist, 29,* 438–48.

Toseland, R., & Smith, T. (2001). *Supporting caregivers through education and training.* Prepared for U.S. Administration on Aging, National Family Caregiver Support Program (NFCSP): Selected Issue Briefs. Washington, DC: U.S. Department of Health and Human Services.

Vourlekis, B. S., & Greene, R. R. (1992). *Social work case management.* Hawthorne, NY: Aldine de Gruyter.

Webster, J. (2001). The future of the past: Continuing challenges for reminiscence research. In G. Kenyon, P. Clark, & B. de Vries (Eds.), *Narrative gerontology* (pp. 159–214). New York: Springer.

Willis, S. L. (1991). Cognition and everyday competence. In K. W. Schaie (Ed.), *Annual review of gerontology and geriatrics* (Vol. 11, pp. 80–109). New York: Springer.

Yalom, I. (1985). *The theory and practice of group psychotherapy.* New York: Basic Books.

Zarit, S., & Knight, B. G. (1996). *A guide to psychotherapy and aging.* Washington, DC: American Psychological Association.

Social work with older persons frequently includes interdisciplinary teamwork. An interdisciplinary team can be described variously as "a functioning unit, composed of individuals with varied and specialized training, who coordinate their activities to provide services to a client or group of clients" (Ducanis & Golin, 1979, p. 3), as "a group with a specific task or tasks, the accomplishment of which requires the interdependent and collaborative efforts of its members" (Beckhard, 1972, p. 287), and, more fully defined, as

> a group of persons who are trained in the use of different tools and concepts, among whom there is an organized division of labor around a common problem with each member using his own tools, with continuous intercommunication and reexamination of postulates in terms of the limitations provided by the work of the other members and often with group responsibility for the final product. (Luszki, 1958, as cited in Given & Simmons, 1977, p. 166)

RATIONALE FOR INTERDISCIPLINARY TEAM PRACTICE

The importance of an interdisciplinary team approach in the health care of older persons has been recognized and espoused in the literature for the past 30 years. As early as 1915, health educators, physicians, and social workers were working together in teams at Massachusetts General Hospital, but it was not until the 1950s when Drs. Cherasky and Silver advocated a team approach to the delivery of primary care service that attention began to be given to the interdisciplinary team modality. By the 1960s, interdisciplinary educational experiences were being developed for students in the health professions, and the federal government "advocated the use of health teams in its newly created Neighborhood Health Center Program" (Bernard et al., 1997, p. 155). The following decade witnessed funding of training for interdisciplinary teamwork in geriatrics by the Department of Veterans Affairs and the Bureau of Health Professions (Geriatric Education Centers) at the federal level and by the Robert Wood Johnson and W. K. Kellog Foundation in the private foundation arena. From the early 1970s through the 1980s there were numerous presentations at professional conferences and journal articles focused on interdisciplinary team care, nearly all of which were either descriptive, highlighting inter-

M. JOANNA MELLOR

Interdisciplinary Team Practices

70

disciplinary team development and activities, or prescriptive, encouraging the health care professions, including social work, to adopt such practices.

By the early 1980s, funding for interdisciplinary teams and training in interdisciplinary teamwork waned. Following this lull, interest in the team approach in the care of the older person once again came to the fore and was highlighted by the National Institutes of Health 1987 Consensus Development Conference, which issued the following statement:

> This process, comprehensive geriatric assessment, is defined as a multidisciplinary evaluation in which the multiple problems of older persons are uncovered, described and explained, if possible, and in which the resources and strengths of the person are catalogued, need for services assessed, and a coordinated care plan developed to focus interventions on the person's problems. . . . Comprehensive geriatric assessment involves clinicians from the many health care professions who are necessarily involved in good geriatric care. (Solomon et al., 1988, p. 342)

The concept that underlies interdisciplinary team health care is that the patient generally presents with a multitude of interlocking needs and issues and that no one discipline is equipped with the knowledge and skills to assess and develop appropriate care plans to meet these needs. Geriatric patients are frequently beset by many health, social, and environmental needs. The same is true of other populations, such as chronically ill children and the disabled. Complicating the care of these populations is not only that the patients/clients have several needs and issues but that these several needs may overlie each other or interact in such a manner that correct assessment is compromised and attention to any one need, in isolation, is ineffective.

In many situations involving older persons, a plethora of physical, psychological, social, environmental, and financial issues need to be addressed and holistic care provided. It is this holistic care that can be provided only by an interdisciplinary team. The following case studies provide examples of the need for a team approach to health care for the elderly.

Maria Harrod

▨ Maria Harrod is an 83-year-old widow who lives alone and is discovered by her daughter lying on the floor in her apartment in a weak-

ened state. Hospitalization follows, and Maria is diagnosed as suffering from malnutrition. After being stabilized and restored to health, she is discharged with the admonition to eat five small but nutritious meals each day. Maria's daughter works but manages to visit every evening and prepare a meal for her mother before returning home to care for her family. Six weeks later, Maria is again hospitalized. While in the hospital, she is visited by a social worker, who identifies Maria as depressed. Her previously undiagnosed depression and social isolation caused the initial incident and also resulted in noncompliance of the five-meals-a-day routine that the physician had recommended, contributing to ongoing malnutrition. ▨

George and Peggy Wylie

▨ Mr. and Mrs. Wylie are in their early 70s and recently celebrated their 50th wedding anniversary. They enjoy an active retirement which includes volunteering for several organizations, such as delivering meals to homebound neighbors once a week for the local Meals on Wheels program. Recently, the director of the Meals program, a social worker, received a complaint from one of the recipients, who declared that Mr. Wylie was unaccountably rude to her. The director, knowing George as a kind, friendly person, believed that the incident had been misinterpreted but decided to drop in on the Wylies on her way home from work. She found them drinking martinis before dinner and stayed for a brief chat. George seemed more outgoing than usual, but there seemed no cause for concern. The director wondered whether he might have a drinking problem but decided that she should watch for further signs of this before advising him to seek counseling. Two days later, both the Wylies turned up in the emergency room at their local hospital. Peggy had a deep gash on her leg and George was concussed. Apparently, Peggy discovered her husband about to leave the house wearing only shorts and a T-shirt, even though the temperature was below freezing. When she tried to stop him and told him to put on other clothing, he became violent and threw a pair of scissors at her. Peggy then pushed him and he fell to the floor, hitting his head and passing out. In the emergency room, Peggy receives stitches for the leg injury. Meanwhile, assessment of her husband's concussion results in the finding that he has suffered a stroke, which is probably the cause of his uncharacteristic behavior. ▨

Without the initial input of a social worker or psychiatrist, in the case of Maria, and the input of a physician or nurse, in the case of George Wylie, the complete pictures remained hidden. The correct diagnoses are relatively simple; even so, without the attention and teamwork of several disciplines, timely and effective care remained out of reach. For Maria, earlier involvement of a social worker or psychiatrist would have resulted in an initial assessment of depression, and for George, it was perhaps fortunate that his behavior caused him to be seen by a physician and nursing staff.

By the late 1980s, recognition of the value of interdisciplinary team care resulted in interdisciplinary team education becoming a mandatory requirement for the newly funded Geriatric Education Centers (GECs). Funded by the Bureau of Health Professions of the U.S. Health Resources and Services Administration, the GEC's goal is to increase the geriatric expertise of those who educate and train health care professionals. The inclusion of training in collaborative, interdisciplinary care remains a key element in the offerings of these centers. More recently, the John A. Hartford Foundation began funding the Geriatric Interdisciplinary Team Training (GITT) Program and its initiatives for promotion of geriatric education in the disciplines of medicine, nursing, and social work, further promoting interdisciplinary team care of older persons (Robbins & Rieder, 2002). The Institute of Medicine has issued a call for a "New Health System for the 21st Century," in which teams are identified as playing a central role in primary care (Grumbach & Bodenheimer, 2004).

INTERDISCIPLINARY TEAM MAKEUP

The core interdisciplinary team in geriatric care generally includes a physician, a nurse, and a social worker sharing their expertise in the assessment and treatment of older persons. Beyond these three core disciplines, it is recognized that many other professions may need to be included, depending on the individual circumstances. Clinic and hospital interdisciplinary teams may include representatives from

other disciplines on an ongoing basis or seek to include them as needed. Nursing facilities routinely include the disciplines of nutrition, psychiatry, and physical and occupational therapy and call on others as needed.

ADVANTAGES OF INTERDISCIPLINARY TEAM CARE

The understanding that geriatric interdisciplinary team care is beneficial to the older patient and the efforts of the Veterans Affairs Medical Centers, GECs, and the recent Hartford initiatives in training health care professionals in interdisciplinary team skills has created a growing interest in and practice of interdisciplinary team care. A number of research studies in the 1980s (Rubenstein et al., 1984; Rubenstein, Stuck, Siu, & Wieland, 1991; Williams, Williams, Zimmer, Hall, & Podgorski, 1987) reported on the beneficial impact of comprehensive geriatric assessment (i.e., team assessment) of hospitalized older patients. The more recent emphasis on evidence-based outcomes is underscoring the benefits of the interdisciplinary practice modality both for the older person in terms of improved care and quality of life and for health insurance companies in terms of cost savings. Grumbach and Bodenheimer (2004, p. 1246) conclude, "Medical settings in which physicians and nonphysician professionals work together as teams can demonstrate improved patient outcomes."

The holistic approach of the interdisciplinary geriatric health care team is more valuable than the sum of its parts. Representatives of a variety of health care professions working together promote the wellness of older persons, decrease acute care incidents, and are cost-effective.

BARRIERS TO TEAM CARE

In spite of the increasing support for interdisciplinary team care, the development of such teams is not without difficulties. Gathering together representatives of several disciplines to discuss older patients or ensuring that the various professionals communicate with each other in regard to assessment and treatment is insufficient in itself. The development of an effectively functioning interdisciplinary team, as opposed to a multidisciplinary group, itself requires interdisciplinary effort and the willingness of its members to overcome the following barriers.

Differences Between Disciplines

In developing a functioning team, as with any group developed for a purpose, one needs to overcome the differences in age, ethnicity and culture, gender, socioeconomic status, language, and personality of the members. But, beyond these factors, there are a number of differences related to the various disciplines that frequently create barriers to the formation of a smoothly functioning interdisciplinary team.

Communication Versus Jargon

Each discipline has its own professional language or jargon, enabling its members to communicate in a form of shorthand. The resulting alphabet soup and specific terminologies can be a source of confusion and give rise to charges of elitism by outsiders. Even more troubling, though frequently unrecognized, is the use of similar phrases or terms by members of different disciplines that hold different meanings for each discipline. For example, a patient's "support system" means one thing to a social worker and something altogether different to a nurse or physician. Lack of communication results, with accompanying damage to team functioning.

Culture and Philosophy

Philosophies and cultural milieus differ among the disciplines. For example, social workers are educated to value self-determination of the individual client/patient, whereas physicians are educated to cure and overcome illness. Social workers see the best interests of their clients as based on the clients' psychological and social needs; physicians view the best interests of their patients as lying in full restoration of health. This divergence in perspectives can create irreconcilable caring strategies when a patient or family is hesitant about or refusing treatment. Within the interdisciplinary team setting, these different perspectives can promote distrust between the disciplines.

Time Constraints and Schedules

Differing schedules and organization of practices result in concrete difficulties in finding time to meet or otherwise communicate between the disciplines. For instance, the availability of physicians on call or working in a community practice is often at odds with the schedules of nurses and social workers employed full time by a medical center or nursing facility. Other health care professionals, such as nutritionists, dentists, and therapists, may be available only on a part-time basis. Student education within the disciplines also tends to be structured differently: as semesters versus 4-week rotations, integrated class and field practice versus class followed by practice internships. All these differing schedules and time constraints become a programmatic barrier in fostering interdisciplinary teams.

Levels of Training

Health care disciplines vary in the level of knowledge and educational requirements for entry into the professions. Physicians are required to spend many years in gaining their medical credentials and expertise within their selected specialty. Nursing education can range from the minimal training of a nurse's aide to a licensed certificate or master's degree level. Similarly, social workers may hold master degrees but are also employed with undergraduate degrees, as are physical therapists. A functioning interdisciplinary team must overcome these differences in educational backgrounds and levels and the potential they afford to create superiority/inferiority complexes and consequent lack of respect for each other's contribution to the team.

Turf Issues

Health care professions are set apart from each other by the nature of their specific area of knowledge and expertise. It is this special knowledge and expertise that rightly give each profession its authority and credibility but also give rise to the universally recognized turf battles. Members of each profession naturally work to protect and enhance their own area of specialty. Participation in an interdisciplinary team both enhances the feeling that the boundaries of one's own discipline are being breached by another discipline and also provides a forum to react directly, in person, in asserting one's own turf. Overcoming this barrier is perhaps the hardest and yet most important task in the development of a functioning interdisciplinary team.

To be truly effective, all members of an interdisciplinary team have to be very clear about the specific knowledge and skill areas that they contribute to the team but also be willing to allow members of the other disciplines to talk their language and venture into their realm of knowledge. The term *transdisciplinary team* is increasingly used, especially in the field of palliative care, to identify a higher order of interdisciplinary team in which the members have earned each other's trust and learned each other's specialty so that they seamlessly carry out each other's discipline-specific tasks. However, an interesting dynamic is often experienced in interdisciplinary teams in their process of metamorphosing into transdisciplinary teams. Members of a discipline become open to other team members embracing their special knowledge, but when a member of a discipline reaches a point at which his or her use of adopted knowledge begins to equal that of members of that other discipline, the discipline-specific role is threatened, and there is a pulling back and reassertion of turf. In this sense, the task of overcoming the turf barrier may never completely be accomplished.

Administrative Issues

Leadership Support

Administrative support for interdisciplinary teamwork within a health care organization is crucial. Without such support, it is very unlikely that the various disciplines will buy in to the concept. Team participants require the support of the administration in order to justify the time that is spent in interdisciplinary teamwork at the expense of other tasks. In addition, putative teams wither away when support from the top is lacking, as a new team generally includes one or more less than enthusiastic participants. Without the acknowledged backing of the organization's leadership, there is no incentive for reluctant participants to remain involved, and the team will fail to thrive.

Financial Support

When state or federal regulations mandate interdisciplinary team assessments, as they may do in nursing facilities and Veterans Affairs medical centers, participation in an interdisciplinary team is one of the ongoing tasks of a salaried employee. For the vast majority of social and health care providers, however, whose earnings derive from fee for services or involve contractual arrangements between organizations and government or insurance companies, there is no third-party payment coverage for time spent in interdisciplinary teamwork. This lack of funding may be judged shortsighted in light of the cost effective-

ness of interdisciplinary team care, for it is clearly a barrier to the development and ongoing maintenance of teamwork.

Danger of Success

There is one final barrier to the making of the ideal interdisciplinary team, and this is peculiar in that it emerges only when a team is experiencing success. Generally this setback is found in stable teams that have been in existence for a lengthy period. The team members know each other well, respect each other's knowledge, and are comfortable with the team's decisions. The team may even be transdisciplinary in nature. The danger lies in the emergence of a "groupthink" mentality: The members know how each of them is thinking about a specific patient/client, there is little or no disagreement, and decisions regarding assessment and treatment plans are reached quickly. Therein lies the danger. The team members are no longer challenging each other, and although the group determinations may prove accurate, they are equally likely to be flawed. Either insufficient thought is given to the case under discussion and vital signs and symptoms are ignored, or the team moves unquestioningly to the acceptance of a multiplicity of overlapping variables and sees complications where simplicity is the reality. To outward appearances, the interdisciplinary team is functioning smoothly, but its outcomes may well be detrimental to the patient's/client's well-being.

CHARACTERISTICS OF A WELL-FUNCTIONING TEAM

Drinka and Clark (2000) note that interdisciplinary health care teams are "not just assemblages of individuals from different professions. They are complex and paradoxical entities that often seem to defy understanding." Most interdisciplinary geriatric care teams are neither a disaster nor the ideal. Interdisciplinary teams, like organizations, are evolving, changing systems and remain fluid.

A functioning interdisciplinary team is one in which its members:

- Recognize the knowledge and skills of each of the members.
- Understand and appreciate the differences between members, whether these are personal char-

acteristics, discipline-specific ideologies, or professional cultures.

- Trust and respect each other.
- Fulfill certain roles, such as leader, facilitator, recorder, or process evaluator. Leadership can be democratic, authoritarian, vested in one individual or shared.
- Convene on a regular basis. Interdisciplinary teams need not necessarily meet in person but can interact by phone or e-mail. The important criterion is a regular time schedule maintained for sharing assessments and developing/evaluating care plans.
- Are able to think "outside the box."
- Tolerate, and even welcome, conflict as an aid to problem solving.

SOCIAL WORKERS AS TEAM MEMBERS

Because of their relationship skills and professional training, social workers are ideally suited for interdisciplinary teamwork. Social workers' knowledge and specific training in biopsychosocial assessment, work with families, short-term treatment modalities, and identification and referral to community services are especially helpful to the work of the interdisciplinary team. Apart from these areas of expertise, social work training in working with individuals and groups and emphasis on relationship skills means that social workers tend to be good listeners, group facilitators, managers of interpersonal conflict, and focused on collaboration. As such, social workers are valuable not only as interdisciplinary team members but for the leadership they offer in the development and maintenance of fully functioning interdisciplinary teams.

The Role of Social Work in the Interdisciplinary Team

The geriatric health care interdisciplinary team has always counted social work as a core participating discipline, along with nursing and medicine, but it is only in the past few years that the specific role and contribution of the social worker to interdisciplinary team practice has been articulated. A national interest group, emerging from the Hartford Foundation's GITT program, spent several months in the late 1990s discussing and identifying social work's specific role and contributions to the geriatric health care team.[1] Mellor and Lindeman concluded that the role of the social worker as a member of an interdisciplinary team includes but is not limited to the following:

- Diagnosis/Assessment. The social work assessment takes into consideration how well the patient (and the family or caregiver) is functioning in six areas:

  Physical: a brief medical history, functional abilities, appearance, and observed behavior.

  Psychological: affect, mood, outlook, attitude, personality characteristics, cognitive functioning, self-image.

  Social: vocation, social roles, support networks, education, and financial status.

  Cultural: values, general rules of behavior, definition of the "sick role," beliefs about the root causes of illness and prescribed treatments, communication patterns that encompass varied language and speech patterns as well as bilingual issues.

  Environmental: living conditions and home surroundings, with focus on safety and maintaining functional independence.

  Spiritual: beliefs about people's roles and responsibilities, rules for living, belief system, diet, and acceptable medical treatments.

- Care Management. Also referred to as case management, this social work role includes problem identification (e.g., lack of financial resources, need for help with activities of daily living or mental health intervention) as well as linkages to and coordination of community resources to facilitate the highest practical level of functioning for the patient and family. It requires a knowledge of community resources and entitlements and skills in matching the patient/family with resources, linking resources, and serving as an interpreter and advocate for the patient/family.

- Individual Counseling. Psychosocial counseling includes treatment of mental health problems such as depression and anxiety through various techniques, including family therapy, relaxation, and stress management training for the patient and/or caregiver. This is intended to assist patients and families to adjust to major life stressors and transitions such as illness, disability, institutionalization, and loss as well as to empower the client. A patient's ability to adapt to an illness has a profound impact on his or her quality of life as well as the patient's willingness/ability to comply with the prescribed treatment and is paramount to recovery, physical and emotional healing, timely discharge from the hospital, risk management, and effective decision making. The social worker brings skills in listening, problem resolution, and negotiation with attention to community and environmental factors.

- Group Work. Group psychotherapy and supportive psychoeducational groups are designed to help patients and families/caregivers cope with a specific illness (e.g., depression, Alzheimer's disease, cancer, diabetes). The social worker brings skills in group development and facilitation.
- Liaison. The social worker can also serve as a liaison between the patient/family and the professional community, forming a vital link. This is particularly pertinent when the family lives out of the area and its input must be obtained via long-distance communication.
- Advocacy. Social workers' training, including a working knowledge of ethics, confidentiality, advance directives, cultural/ethnic factors, and patient/family rights, serves to help teams face the challenge of balancing patient needs with the system demands. Often, the most important service provided to patients and families by a geriatric/gerontological social worker is simply to assist in negotiating an overwhelmingly bureaucratic system, such as Medicaid, Social Security, disability, funeral arrangements, or dealing with insurance and hospital paperwork by acting on their behalf and/or teaching them to help themselves.
- Community Resource Expertise. Knowledge of community resources and how to access them is an invaluable piece of the social work profession. This involves high-level skill in negotiation and bargaining for appropriate resource allocation. A working knowledge of financial systems, including federal, state, and county programs, is part of this expertise. Serving as a resource referral coordinator requires negotiation and collaboration to assist patients and families in setting priorities, determining care goals, and balancing issues. (Mellor & Lindeman, 1998, pp. 5–7)

These areas are not necessarily exclusive to the discipline of social work, but they are knowledge and skill areas in which the social worker receives specific training and for which social work has particular expertise and responsibilities.

SUMMARY

Interdisciplinary health care teams are not yet universal, but the growing body of information from evidence-based studies underscores the value of this model of practice. Well-functioning interdisciplinary teams are understood to promote quality of life for the patient and family and to be cost-effective in terms of health dollars, through reduced hospital stays and more timely, holistic treatment interventions. Furthermore, baby boomers, the next cohort of older persons, identify access to interdisciplinary team care as a feature of the health care system they envisage for their future. Hence, social workers in the field of aging are increasingly likely to participate in interdisciplinary teamwork. Social work has a valuable and crucial role to fill in this growing practice model.

NOTE

1. Members of the Social Work Interest Group of the GITT program were Carole Ashendorf, Barbara Bacon, Judith Howe, Kathryn Hyer, Joann Ivry, David Lindeman, Marilyn Luptak, Marty Mandel, Russ Martineau, Joanna Mellor, James Reinardy, Barrie Robinson, Ann Schneider, Nancy Wadsworth, and Lisa West.

REFERENCES

Beckhard, R. (1972). Organizational issues in the team delivery of comprehensive health care. *Milbank Memorial Fund Quarterly, 50,* 287–316.

Bernard, M., Connelly, R., Kuder, L., Mellor, J., Norman, L., & Tsukuda, R. (1997). Interdisciplinary education. In S. Klein (Ed.), *A national agenda for geriatric education: White papers* (pp. 152–179). New York: Springer.

Drinka, T., & Clark, P. (2000). *Health care teamwork Interdisciplinary practice and teaching.* Westport, CT: Auburn House.

Ducanis, A. J., & Golin, A. K. (1979). *The interdisciplinary health care team: A handbook.* Rockville, MD: Aspen.

Given, B., & Simmons, S. (1977). The interdisciplinary health care team: Fact or fiction? *Nursing Forum, 16,* 165–184.

Grumbach, K., & Bodenheimer, T. (2004). Can health care teams improve primary care practice? *Journal of American Geriatric Society, 291,* 1246–1251.

Luszki, M. (1958). *Interdisciplinary team research methods and problems.* New York National Training Laboratories.

Mellor, J., & Lindeman, D. (1998). The role of the social worker in interdisciplinary geriatric teams. *Journal of Gerontological Social Work, 30*(3/4), 3–7. Available from The Haworth Document Delivery Service: 1-800-Haworth, docdelivery@haworthpress.com.

Robbins, L. A., & Rieder, C. H. (2002). The John A. Hartford Foundation Geriatric Social Initiative. In J. Mellor & J. Ivry (Eds.), *Advancing geriatric social work education* (pp. 71–89). New York: Haworth Press.

Rubenstein, L., Josephson, K., Wieland, G., English, P., Sayre, J., & Kane, R. (1984). Effectiveness of a geriatric evaluation unit: A randomized trial. *New England Journal of Medicine, 311,* 1664–1670.

Rubenstein, L., Stuck, A., Siu, A., & Wieland, D. (1991). Impacts of geriatric evaluation and management programs on defined outcomes: Overview of the evidence. *Journal of the American Geriatric Society, 398,* 88–168.

Solomon, D., Steel, K., Williams, T., Brown, A., Brummel-Smith, K., Buirgess, L., et al. (1988). National Institutes of Health consensus conference development statement: Geriatric assessment methods for clinical decision-making. *Journal of American Medical Association, 36*(4), 342–347.

Williams, M., Williams, T., Zimmer, J., Hall, W., & Podgorski, C. (1987). How does the team approach to outpatient geriatric evaluation compare with traditional care: A report of a randomized controlled trial. *Journal of the American Geriatric Society, 35,* 1071–1078.

Despite Freud's (1904/1950) dictum that older adults are not suitable for psychoanalysis because their mental processes are characterized by insufficient elasticity, psychodynamically oriented therapists now increasingly share the belief that the older adult is highly amenable to treatment. The myth that the older adult inevitably and irrevocably possesses rigid, inelastic personality structures has given way to clinical experience and empirical evidence stressing that it is the nature of the psychiatric disorder and not the age of the adult that is crucial in securing treatment (Lazarus, 1980, 1988; Muslin, 1984; Yalom, 1975, 1980a, 1980b, 1987).

Psychodynamically oriented therapists who treat the older adult all share a similar belief in the responsiveness of many older adults to psychodynamically oriented psychotherapy, along with the belief that the later part of the life cycle possesses considerable potential for self-understanding and the discovery or rediscovery of various aspects of the self (Cath, 1984; Lazarus, 1980, 1988; Muslin, 1984; Muslin & Epstein, 1980; Myers, 1984; Nemiroff & Colarusso, 1985; Sadavoy, 1994; Sadavoy, Jarvik, Grossberg, & Meyers, 2004). Older adults, in fact, are often keenly aware of their limited time left to live (Cath, 1984; Neugarten, 1979) and make productive use of psychotherapy.

IMPORTANCE OF PSYCHODYNAMIC TREATMENT OF THE ELDERLY

Psychodynamic therapy has a unique place in the treatment canon for the older adult because it is the form of treatment that is most suited to addressing the unique interplay among intrapsychic, personality, and developmental factors (Lazarus, 1984; Sadavoy, 1994; Sadavoy et al., 2004) that distinguishes an older person seeking psychotherapy from a younger adult. The older adult's formidable efforts to contend with the unique stressors of the aging process are often fraught with significant, often unprecedented tensions, challenges, and conflicts. These challenges call for an approach to treatment that will not be limited to mere alleviation of the symptoms of anxiety and depression, but one that will support the older adult in his or her efforts to reestablish a sense of inner cohesion and self-worth in the face of numerous narcissistic injuries in a culture that often denigrates the old.

According to Hyman Muslin (1984, p. 69), a psychoanalyst and practitioner of self-psychology:

> Intensive psychotherapy should be the treatment of choice in those older adults who possess the

DENIS P. CRONIN

Psychodynamic Psychotherapy

71

ordinary capacity for this work, depending on the nature and intensity of the problem, the psychological capacity to introspect, and the ability to form resolvable transferences.

Issues in Clinical Practice

There are many psychodynamic concerns that are especially relevant to the psychodynamic psychotherapy of the aged. Many therapists stress the critical importance of applying more psychodynamically oriented techniques systematically to the aged, both as therapy for depression and anxiety and to clarify the psychodynamic, developmental aspects of the later stages of the life cycle (Grunes, 1987).

Of all the age-specific dynamic themes, most prominent is the enormity of the sense of loss often endured by the older adult: loss of physical prowess, friends and family, and material wealth, among many others. However, the biggest losses that the older adult must endure are the profound sense of a loss of possibility (Yalom, 1975, 1980a, 1980b, 1987) and loss of a sense of self (Grunes, 1987; Guttman, Grunes, & Griffin, 1980). Some psychodynamic theorists see this lost sense of self as a process of disavowal of those aspects of the older person that he or she perceives as damaged or deteriorated in order to maintain the intactness of the personality in the face of decline. The loss accentuates the fact that a central function of the psychodynamic therapist's role with the aged adult is to "make the adult's past viable" (Grunes, 1987, p. 43).

> In the absence of external buttresses for the sense of self over time, the therapist becomes a replacement for . . . the adult's historical self. . . . The psychotherapist therefore acts as a stimulator of the adult's early identifying relationships which he brings alive through his empathic mirroring. (p. 43)

Older adults are also particularly vulnerable to survivor guilt. Many investigators have reported adults' disinterest in maintaining or enhancing their life after the demise or severe disability of a spouse (Cath, 1984; Silberschatz & Curtis, 1991). Many older adults express survival guilt more subtly, often denigrating any self-affirming, worthwhile aspirations as too unrealistic for "older people" like themselves. A psychodynamic approach is likely to be the most effective approach for helping the older adult deal with the self-deprecating feelings that often accompany survival guilt.

Important Characteristics of Older Adults for Successful Psychodynamic Therapy

As Kahana (1979, 1987) has argued, old age is best viewed on a continuum of functioning, from normative aging at one extreme to a state of significant mental and physical decline at the other extreme. Applying this functional perspective to an assessment of which older adults can benefit most from an insight-oriented form of psychotherapy, it is probably clear that such an approach would be most beneficial to older adults on the more functional, less debilitated end of the functional spectrum: those who have the capacity for introspection, insight, and who are motivated to pursue this form of therapy (Muslin, 1984; Pollock, 1987).

Crisis Situations

Neugarten (1979) and Lazarus (1984) stress that psychotherapy for the older adult is usually indicated when the individual is unable to master and adapt to the psychological impact of a crisis. As the older adult moves more and more to the debilitated end of the functional spectrum (Kahana, 1979, 1987), he or she becomes less suitable as a candidate for insight-oriented or psychodynamic therapy as the therapeutic vehicle most likely to help him or her overcome the adverse psychological effects of a crisis. More appropriate forms of treatment for this group include the less intrapsychic, more behaviorally and environmentally supportive techniques.

Long-term insight-oriented psychodynamic treatment can also be very beneficial for the older adult attempting to recover from a crisis. Because an integral component of the more ambitious, long-term clinical approach is the alteration of extant maladaptive defenses through ongoing interpretive efforts, Yesavage and Karasu (1982) stress that older adults embarking on such a challenging, albeit productive, clinical route have the resiliency to be able to replace long-standing maladaptive defenses with more adaptive ones that will support their efforts to regain self-esteem and cultivate healthy, productive self-object relationships (Kohut, 1971, 1977; Kohut & Wolf, 1978; Lazarus, 1980, 1988; Wolf, 1986).

PSYCHODYNAMIC APPROACHES TO TREATMENT

The most common forms in which psychodynamic therapy is practiced with the older adult include self-psychology (Kohut, 1971, 1977), short-term (brief) psychodynamic psychotherapy, and long-term intensive psychodynamic psychotherapy, including classical psychoanalysis. Although self psychology can be conducted either as short-term or long-term psychodynamic therapy, it is usually practiced in the long-term mode.

The cornerstone of all psychodynamic approaches is the therapeutic alliance that develops between therapist and client, with the therapist assuming responsibility for the environment in which the therapy takes place. In the context of psychodynamic treatment, this alliance, the associated transferences that emerge from it, and the insight attained by the client into the sources of his or her conflicts and distress all constitute the therapeutic medium through which the older adult experiences growth and change. The emphasis on unconscious mental life as both a contributing cause of the older adult's psychological difficulties and as a critical component of the treatment process distinguishes all forms of psychodynamic psychotherapy from the other, less insight-oriented approaches. In a psychodynamic formulation of a clinical problem, symptoms and behaviors are viewed as serving multiple functions that are determined by complex and often unconscious forces.

Long-Term Psychodynamic Therapy

A long-term psychodynamic assessment involves evaluating both the personality structure of the adult and the adult's disorder or clinical symptoms for their suitability for long-term psychodynamic therapy.

An older adult who is not interested in attaining in-depth understanding and for whom a brief course of psychotherapy and/or a particular medication can successfully treat his or her problem would not be an appropriate candidate for long-term psychodynamic psychotherapy. A long-term dynamic approach may be indicated when brief therapeutic approaches and pharmacology both fail to address the adult's problems, provided the adult has what Pollock (1987) and Muslin (1984) describe as the capacity (and probably penchant) for introspection; the stamina, motivation, and cognitive flexibility to undergo intensive, ongoing

self-scrutiny; and the capacity to experience the often unsettling affect that can accompany this process.

As Gabbard (2004) suggests, the focus of long-term psychodynamic therapy depends on the adult and on the theoretical perspective of the therapist. Therapeutic goals are shaped by the therapist's theory of how therapy works. Some practitioners of long-term therapy focus largely on symptom alleviation and removal. Others, depending on their theory of clinical practice, espouse loftier, more in-depth goals, such as a more cohesive, enhanced experience of self that is less subject to fragmentation and diminishment of self-esteem (Kohut & Wolf, 1978); improved reflective functioning; enhanced capacity to resolve interpersonal conflicts; and enhanced capacity to obtain effective self-object relationships (Gabbard, 2004).

Classical Psychoanalysis and Self Psychology

Classical psychoanalysis sees the root cause of psychological distress and dysfunction as lying in the conflict over basic drives and basic defenses. Resolution of these conflicts, the basis for psychological growth, occurs through the transference (labeled a transference neurosis) that develops between therapist and client and the insight attained into the source of these conflicts by the client. The emphasis placed on the vicissitudes resulting from the conflict between the press for basic drive gratification and the tendency of certain defenses to thwart this goal renders classical psychoanalysis less useful for the older adult than for the younger one.

Self psychology, a recent psychoanalytic paradigm of treatment, focuses on narcissistic injury to the functioning self, reflected in lack of cohesion and proneness to fragmentation and diminished self-esteem (Kohut, 1971, 1977; Kohut & Wolf, 1978; Wolf, 1986). This clinical approach has been employed successfully as an underlying model in psychodynamically based group psychotherapy and in both forms of individual (i.e., short-term and long-term) psychotherapy with the older adult (Lazarus, 1980, 1988; Muslin, 1984; Schwartzman, 1984). This approach is viewed by many theorists as generative of new psychodynamic-oriented insights that complement and supplement other theoretical models (Lazarus, 1980, 1984, 1988; Muslin, 1984). Self psychologists describe the self as a "developmental, psychological structure responsible for maintenance of one's self-image, self-esteem, feelings, and affects related to one's physical and psychological integrity and need for others to . . . help modulate one's self-esteem" (Muslin, 1984, p. 58). The potential for diminishment of the older adult's self-esteem and self-efficacy as he or she experiences the declines of aging renders the self psychologically oriented therapist's focus on rehabilitation of the fragmented self a felicitous theoretical model for treatment.

The focus on injury to the self undergoing fragmentation distinguishes self psychology from the conflict over drives and defenses that is central to traditional forms of psychoanalysis (Kohut, 1971, 1977; Kohut & Wolf, 1978; Wolf, 1986). In self psychology, both short term and long term, the adult is provided with an empathic, therapeutic atmosphere through which fixated aspects of the self reflected in maladaptive or inappropriate ways for maintaining self-esteem and sustenance from others can undergo rehabilitation. Progress is largely contingent on the therapist's use of empathy to facilitate the adult's resolution of a number of self-object transferences (Kohut & Wolf, 1978), each of which contributed to an impasse in the adult's healthy psychoemotional development, often reflected in lack of autonomous functioning and poor self-esteem regulation.

Brief Psychodynamic Psychotherapy

The most salient factors distinguishing brief psychodynamic treatment from the longer version are more restricted goals, the lessened intensity of therapist engagement, and the need to establish a therapeutic alliance quickly. According to Levinson, Butler, and Beitman (1997), the most critical criterion for an individual's suitability for brief as opposed to long-term dynamic therapy is the ability to rapidly attach and detach emotionally without an escalation in the severity of symptoms.

Lazarus (1980, 1988) recommends the use of brief psychodynamic therapy for the more resilient older adult whose problems, such as adjustment disorders, are both clearly defined and treatable over a manageable time frame. Lazarus stresses that by setting a time limit on therapy, brief psychodynamic therapy reinforces the older adult's confidence in his or her personal ability to resolve problems and master current stresses. Establishing a time limit not only accelerates the therapeutic process but also reduces the individual's anxiety over a prolonged therapeutic relationship and brings the prospect of termination into focus earlier in the treatment process. Malan (1963, 1976, 1979) was able to demonstrate that brief psychodynamic psychotherapy for older adults alleviates symptoms, resolves conflicts, and, equally important, helps bring about fundamental characterological change usually associated only with long-term psychodynamic treatment so long as the older adult is capable of insight and is able to forge a productive working relationship with the therapist.

Lazarus (1984) has suggested that developmental issues more specific to the older adult may be a major difference between brief psychotherapy with older adults when compared with younger ones. This author contends that narcissistic issues that continually threaten the older adult's self-esteem and sense of mastery may render the older adult more receptive and responsive to the therapist's empathy in brief psychodynamic therapy (Lazarus, 1984), resulting in the attainment of a productive therapeutic alliance more quickly for the older adult.

CRITICAL ISSUES IN PSYCHODYNAMIC TREATMENT

Transference Issues

The literature on geriatric psychotherapy supports the notion of the timelessness of the unconscious and the fact that transference processes are as vital and as much a phenomenon to be reckoned with in old age as in youth (Berezin, 1972; Meerloo, 1955; Newton & Jacobowitz, 1999). Little clinical evidence supports the concept of a highly age-specific transference, although the reactions of the older adult to the therapeutic process are likely to reflect the unique array of stressors that characterize this period of life.

Eroticized transferences are possible, with the client turning unconsciously to the therapist as a wished-for replacement for a lost partner or spouse, leading the client to identify with a much more youthful, sexually appealing self-image that he or she imagines to be potentially appropriate for the therapist (Crusey, 1985). Similarly, eroticized transferences may be mobilized as the older adult becomes aware of his or her sexual decline.

"Reverse" transferences often play a major role in the older adult's resistance to psychodynamic treatment. Many older adults who are in psychodynamic treatment develop a resistance to the treatment process (Myers, 1984, 1986) that takes the form of their challenging the therapist, for example, as being too young and inexperienced and therefore incapable of understanding an older adult. The crucial issue is that beneath the surface interaction between the older adult and therapist and at the root of all manifestations of the reverse transference, there often reside significant feelings of helplessness and inferiority on the part of the older adult for which the development of a reverse transference process can function as a defense against these painful feelings (Grotjahn, 1955; Myers, 1984, 1986).

Narcissistic Assaults

Narcissistic assaults resulting from the inevitable declines of old age (e.g., lost beauty, power, and physical prowess) often promote an idealizing or mirroring transference to the therapist on the part of the older adult (Kohut, 1971, 1977; Lazarus 1980, 1988). This transference involves older adults compensating for perceived narcissistic assaults accompanying the aging process by imagining themselves as the worthy recipient of a therapist who is unfaltering in his or her care and admiration and unrelenting in his or her approval of the adult. The tendency for older adults to develop an idealized type of transference can be extremely useful in securing their involvement in a cohesion-generating, self-esteem-enhancing (Kohut & Wolf, 1978) therapeutic process.

Conflicts Over Death

Conscious or unconscious conflicts over death and mortality may cause the older adult to view the therapist as an idealized, magical protector capable of warding off the inevitability of death. The realistic inability of the therapist to provide the much sought-after protection and reassurance may so alienate older adults that they may harbor significant angry feelings toward the therapist in his or her capacity as a disappointing transference figure.

Defense of Withdrawal From Treatment

Many older adults are inclined to use defenses of withdrawal and/or physical preoccupation to deal with intrapsychic conflicts and anxieties. They may also deploy these same defenses in their efforts to avoid therapy and resist the transferential process. Inordinate use of reminiscence, a highly useful therapeutic tool if

used appropriately, and overreliance on past accomplishments as a way of avoiding the present can also feature prominently in the resistance process of the older adult (Kahana, 1987; Myers, 1984, 1986; Nemiroff & Colarusso, 1985; Sadavoy & Leszcz, 1987).

Countertransference Issues

Older adults are more likely to mobilize the therapist's unresolved conflicts about aging, including unconscious fears of illness, decline, and death (Muslin, 1984; Nemiroff & Colarusso, 1985; Yesavage & Karasu, 1982). According to Muslin:

> In working with older adults . . . the analyst must be mindful of the self-needs of the adults and not to become unduly influenced by the adult's advanced age, superficial attitudes, or slowness of psychomotor functioning. These might mislead the analyst to dismiss the older adult as a potential candidate for psychoanalysis. For those analysts who work with the older adult, the self-transformations required to enable the analyst to empathize accurately with their older adults is of paramount importance. (p. 69)

Yalom (1987) suggests that the treatment of the older adult stimulates the therapist's memories of his or her relationships with parents and grandparents. Reinforcing his point, he asks, "To what extent does our sense of hopelessness or pessimism in treating the older patient reflect our personal dread of inexorable aging and death?" (p. xii).

The countertransference is a significant component of psychodynamic treatment. The therapist usually shares many psychoemotional, historical, and generational commonalities with his or her adult clients that the therapist eventually recognizes in the unique form in which his or her countertransference crystallizes. But for the younger therapist working with the older adult, lack of the experiential and affective breadth (e.g., continuous loss) that often characterizes the life of the older adult makes it more difficult to identify an appropriate range and number of parallel countertransference experiences in the treatment of the older adult. The result of this, in Grunes's (1987, p. 39) words, is that

> the therapist must struggle with re-experiencing his own early relationships both to his parents and to his grandparents. . . . A further living

counter transference experience derives from the often negative stereotypes and prejudices which the therapist may have adopted from society's attitude toward aging.

The goal of establishing adequate empathic rapport or attunement with the older adult always looms as a potential problem, given the range of respective life experiences between the usually younger therapist and older adult. This empathic breach often manifests itself in the form of reverse empathy on the part of the older adult to compensate for the empathic gap between the therapist and the older adult (Grunes, 1987). Through the process of reverse empathy, the aged adult attempts to strengthen the self-object relationship to facilitate the formation of a working alliance. This process of reverse empathy (Grunes, 1987) represents an attempt on the part of the aged adult to establish a bond with the therapist so that both therapist and client can become "mutual self objects" (p. 38). "A need to know significant details of the therapist's life may be viewed as manifestations of reverse empathy" (p. 38).

A therapist expressing countertransference in the guise of anxiety over an older adult's apparent helplessness and dependency can unwittingly so overwhelm the older adult that he or she withdraws from treatment and rejects the therapist. Conversely, in the face of the older adult's decline, a therapist may act on a grandiose need to conquer the forces of aging (Myers, 1984).

Overidentification with the older adult's problems, manifested in feelings of pity and sadness communicated inappropriately to the client, can appear inauthentic and disparaging when compared to the psychological oxygen of the therapist's accurate empathy, and can stymie the process of exploration of possible avenues for growth and change (Hiatt, 1971). Conversely, the therapist who unconsciously avoids the pain that accompanies the therapeutic process of accurately empathizing with the older adult's loneliness and loss may become so overwhelmed by the client's problems that he or she may attempt to keep the older adult alive by avoiding termination of therapy (King, 1980).

The thinking of many therapists, their training notwithstanding, reflects the unfortunate influence of the dominant lay culture in their persistent view of older adults as asexual individuals (Meerloo, 1955). Persistence in this erroneous view by the therapist often functions as a defense against unresolved conflicts associated with parental sexuality or Oedipal conflicts (Myers, 1984; Nemiroff & Colarusso, 1985; Zinberg & Kaufman, 1963). Revulsion over the adult's eroticized transference toward the therapist, or shock and disgust over the therapist's eroticized countertransference feelings, can be manifestations of deep-rooted sexual conflicts that can adversely impact the therapeutic relationship.

EMPIRICAL SUPPORT FOR THE PSYCHODYNAMIC APPROACH

Although numerous testimonials from many therapists attesting to the effectiveness of psychodynamic treatment with the older adult are encouraging, some researchers (e.g., Gallagher & Thompson, 1982, 1983; Lazarus, 1984) have expressed concern over the paucity of actual empirical research and the lack of systematic, methodologically sound studies of the effectiveness of psychodynamically oriented treatment of the older adult. Some empirical support for the effectiveness of psychodynamic therapy for the older adult exists, mostly in comparative studies comparing brief forms of psychodynamic treatment with other approaches in the treatment of older adult depression.

Thompson, Gallagher, and Breckenridge (1987), studying the differential effectiveness of behavioral, cognitive-behavioral, and insight-oriented brief therapy in the treatment of older adult depression, supported the efficacy of short-term psychodynamic therapy. They found the other modalities to be equally effective and concluded that psychotherapy, regardless of modality, can function as both a primary and an adjunctive method of treatment of the older adult, depending on the client and the presenting problem (Thompson et al., 1987).

Focusing on the maintenance of psychotherapeutic gains over a 2-year period among a sample of 91 older adults who were initially diagnosed as being in an episode of major depression, Gallagher-Thompson, Hanley-Peterson, and Thompson (1990) confirmed the earlier findings of the efficacy of short-term psychodynamic treatment of older adults by demonstrating the maintenance of therapeutic gains over time in the treatment of major depressive disorder. Gains were maintained over time for a substantial proportion of the sample who were depression-free following initial treatment. The highly significant improvement in symptoms and other measures of functioning by the older adults in these more recent studies reinforced earlier research findings highlighting the effectiveness of psychodynamic psychotherapy for older adults (Gallagher & Thompson, 1983).

Lazarus (1984) studied the process and outcome of brief psychodynamic psychotherapy in a sample of eight older outpatients (four men and four women) ranging in age from 63 to 77 years. These older adults upon entering therapy felt estranged from their historical image of themselves as competent adults. They also felt unable to cope with their current problems, and their self-esteem was diminished. Older adults treated with brief psychodynamic psychotherapy in this study tended to use the therapist to "reestablish a sense of continuity with their former, more positive self-image" (p. 27). Many older adults in this study improved in their interpersonal relationships and in their ability to resolve conflict.

After intensively studying the process and outcome of time-limited psychodynamic psychotherapy with older adults, Silberschatz and Curtis (1986, 1991) found that older outpatients entered treatment with specific conscious and unconscious goals. These same investigators also found that the most successful therapists were highly responsive to the therapeutic goals identified by the older adult and worked with the older adult to help him or her challenge and overcome distorted, maladaptive self-perceptions and beliefs.

CONCLUSION

There can be no doubt that psychodynamic psychotherapy is very suitable for the cognitively intact older adult who possesses the necessary personal qualities outlined by Pollock (1987) and Muslin (1984) for engagement in this more intense therapeutic process. This approach to therapy may well be the approach most likely to help the older adult whose therapeutic goals extend beyond alleviation of the painful feelings of depression and anxiety, to a focus on obtaining an enhanced capacity for dealing with issues of self-esteem and identity, pervasive loss and survival guilt in this "season of losses," the fear or reality of physical decline, and the painful feelings of isolation, loneliness, and narcissistic injury that the older person may experience.

REFERENCES

Berezin, M. (1972). Psychodynamic consideration of aging and the aged: An overview. *American Journal of Psychiatry, 128,*(12), 33–41.

Cath, S. (1984). A psychoanalytic hour: A late life awakening. In L. Lazarus (Ed.), *Clinical approaches to psychotherapy with the elderly* (pp. 2–14). Washington, DC: American Psychiatric Press.

Crusey, J. (1985). Short-term psychodynamic psychotherapy with a sixty-two year old man. In R. Nemiroff & C. Colarusso (Eds.), *The race against time* (pp. 147–170). New York: Plenum.

Freud, S. (1950). On psychotherapy. In *Collected papers* (Vol. 1, pp. 249–263). London: Hogarth Press. (Original work published 1904)

Gabbard, G. (2004). *Long-term psychodynamic psychotherapy: A basic text.* Washington, DC: American Psychiatric Publishing.

Gallagher, D., & Thompson, L. (1982). Differential effectiveness of psychotherapies for the treatment of major depressive disorders in older adult patients. *Psychotherapy Theory Research and Practice, 19,* 482–490.

Gallagher, D., & Thompson, L. (1983). Effectiveness of psychotherapy for both endogenous and non-endogenous depression in older adult outpatients. *Journal of Gerontology, 38,* 707–712.

Gallagher-Thompson, D., Hanley-Peterson, P., & Thompson, L. (1990). Maintenance of gains versus relapse following brief psychotherapy for depression. *Journal of Consulting and Clinical Psychology, 58*(3), 371–374.

Grotjahn, M. (1955). Analytic psychotherapy with the elderly. *Psychoanalytic Review, 42,* 419–427.

Grunes, J. (1987). The aged in psychotherapy: Psychodynamic contributions to the treatment process. In J. Sadavoy & M. Leszcz (Eds.), *Treating the elderly with psychotherapy: The scope of change in later life* (pp. 31–44). Madison, CT: International Universities Press.

Guttman, D., Grunes, J., & Griffin, B. (1980). The clinical psychology of later life. In N. Datan & N. Lohmann (Eds.), *The transitions of aging* (pp. 119–131). New York: Academic Press.

Hiatt, H. (1971). Dynamic psychotherapy with the aging patient. *American Journal of Psychotherapy, 25,* 591–600.

Kahana, R. (1979). Strategies of dynamic psychotherapy with the wide range of older individuals. *Journal of Geriatric Psychiatry, 12,* 71–100.

Kahana, R. (1987). Discussion: The Oedipus complex and rejuvenation fantasies in the analysis of a seventy-year-old woman. *Journal of Geriatric Psychiatry, 20,* 53–60.

King, P. (1980). The life cycle as indicated by the nature of the transference in the psychoanalysis of the middle-aged and elderly. *International Journal of Psychoanalysis, 61,* 153–159.

Kohut, H. (1971). *The analysis of the self.* New York: International Universities Press.

Kohut, H. (1977). *The restoration of the self.* New York: International Universities Press.

Kohut, H., & Wolfe, E. (1978). The disorders of the self and their treatment. *International Journal of Psycho-Analysis, 59,* 413–425.

Lazarus, L. (1980). Self-psychology and psychotherapy with the elderly: Theory and practice. *Journal of Geriatric Psychoatry, 18,* 402–406.

Lazarus, L. (Ed.). (1984). *Clinical approaches to psychotherapy with the elderly.* Washington, DC: American Psychiatric Press.

Lazarus, L. (1988). Self-psychology and its applications to brief psychotherapy with the elderly. *Journal of Geriatric Psychiatry, 21,* 109–125.

Levinson, H., Butler, S., & Beitman, B. (1997). *Concise guide to brief dynamic psychotherapy.* Washington, DC: American Psychiatric Press.

Malan, D. (1963). *A study of brief psychotherapy.* New York: Plenum Press.

Malan, D. (1976). *Toward the validation of dynamic psychotherapy.* New York: Plenum Press.

Malan, D. (1979). *Individual psychotherapy and the science of psychodynamics.* London: Butterworth.

Meerloo, J. (1955). Psychotherapy with elderly people. *Geriatrics, 10,* 538–587.

Muslin, H. (1984). Psychoanalysis in the elderly: A self psychological approach. In L. Lazarus (Ed.), *Clinical approaches to psychotherapy with the elderly* (pp. 55–71). Washington, DC: American Psychiatric Press.

Muslin, H., & Epstein, L. (1980). Preliminary remarks on the rationale for psychotherapy for the aged. *Comprehensive Psychiatry, 21,* 1–12.

Myers, W. (1984). *Dynamic therapy of the older patient.* New York: Jason Aronson.

Myers, W. (1986). Transference and counter-transference issues in treatments involving older patients and younger therapists. *Journal of Geriatric Psychiatry, 19,* 221–239.

Nemiroff, R., & Colarusso, C. (1985). The literature on psychotherapy and psychoanalysis in the second half of life. In R. Nemiroff & C. Colarusso (Eds.), *The race against time* (pp. 25–43). New York: Plenum.

Neugarten, B. (1979). Time, age, and the life-cycle. *American Journal of Psychiatry, 136,* 887–894.

Newton, N., & Jacobowitz, J. (1999). Transferential and countertransferential processes in therapy with older adults. In M. Duffy (Ed.), *Handbook of counseling and psychotherapy with older adults* (pp. 221–240). New York: Wiley.

Pollock, G. (1987). The mourning-liberation process: Ideas on the inner life of the older adult. In J. Sadavoy & M. Leszcz (Eds.), *Treating the elderly with psychotherapy: The scope of change in later life* (pp. 3–29). Madison, CT: International Universities Press.

Sadavoy, J. (1994). Integrated psychotherapy for the elderly. *Canadian Journal of Psychiatry, 39*(Suppl. 1), 519–526.

Sadavoy, J., Jarvik, L., Grossberg, G., & Meyers, B. (Eds.). (2004). *Comprehensive textbook of geriatric psychiatry.* New York: Norton.

Sadavoy, J., & Leszcz, M. (Eds.). (1987). *Treating the elderly with psychotherapy: The scope of change in later life.* Madison, CT: International Universities Press.

Schwartzman, G. (1984). The use of the group as a self-object. *International Journal of Group Psychotherapy, 34,* 229–242.

Silberschatz, G., & Curtis, J. (1986). Clinical implications of research on brief dynamic psychotherapy. II: How the therapist helps or hinders therapeutic progress. *Psychoanalytic Psychology, 3,* 27–37.

Silberschatz, G., & Curtis, J. (1991). Time-limited psychodynamic therapy with older adults. In W. Meyers (Ed.), *New techniques in the psychotherapy of older patients* (pp. 95–110). Washington, DC: American Psychiatric Press.

Thompson, L., Gallagher, D., & Breckenridge, J. (1987). Comparative effectiveness of psychotherapy for depressed elders. *Journal of Consulting and Clinical Psychology, 55,* 385–390.

Wolf, E. (1986). *Treating the self: Elements of clinical self psychology.* New York: Guilford.

Yalom, I. (1975). *The theory and practice of group psychotherapy.* New York: Basic Books.

Yalom, I. (1980a). *Existential psychotherapy.* New York: Basic Books.

Yalom, I. (1980b). *Inpatient group therapy.* New York: Basic Books.

Yalom, I. (1987). Introduction. In J. Sadavoy & M. Leszcz (Eds.), *Treating the elderly with psychotherapy: The scope of change in later life* (pp. ix–xiii). Madison, CT: International Universities Press.

Yesavage, J., & Karasu, T. (1982). Psychotherapy with elderly patients. *American Journal of Psychotherapy, 36,* 41–55.

Zinberg, N., & Kaufman, I. (1963). Cultural and personality factors associated with aging: An introduction. In N. Zinberg & I. Kaufman (Eds.), *Normal psychology of the aging process* (pp. 109–125). New York: International Universities Press.

Reminiscence and life review are significant natural coping mechanisms, and, as treatment modalities, both can help older adults find meaning through reflection on their life experiences (Butler, 1963; Coleman, 1986). The appeal of reminiscence and life review for geriatric social workers and other mental health professionals is that the interventions are nonjudgmental, nonstigmatizing, and easy to provide to older adults (Bohlmeijer, Smit, & Cuijpers, 2003; Jonsdottir, Jonsdottir, Steingrimsdottir, & Tryggvadottir, 2001).

This chapter is divided into four sections. The first section addresses the theoretical background of reminiscence and life review. The second examines the efficacy of life review and reminiscence interventions for different target groups. The third section describes successful intervention methods, and the fourth discusses implications for practice in relation to several emerging issues in reminiscence and life review research.

THEORETICAL BACKGROUND OF REMINISCENCE AND LIFE REVIEW

Reminiscence and life review as therapeutic interventions grew out of the intersection of Erik Erikson's (1964) conceptualization of later life and Robert Butler's (1963, 1974) interpretation of successful aging. For Erikson, the last stage of psychosocial development finds the older adult confronted with the crisis of ego identity versus despair. When successfully handled, ego integrity leads to a sense of dignity, fulfillment, and "emotional integration" of one's life (Erikson, 1964, p. 269). Without ego integrity, older adulthood brings a sense of disgust and despair, wherein the adult "expresses the feeling that time is now short, too short for the attempt to start another life and to try out alternate roads to integrity" (p. 269). According to this theoretical perspective, the key to successful older adulthood—and to feeling satisfied and complete as a human being—is the successful integration of all elements of one's life, both positive and negative.

Butler's (1963) conceptualization of the life review, in conjunction with Erikson's (1964) theoretical framework, normalized reminiscence during later life. Butler refuted the then common belief that reminiscence among older adults is symptomatic of an underlying pathology, asserting that it is a universal, normal occurrence in older adults who are reviewing their life experiences. Noting that life review could contribute to depression among some older adults, Butler argued

BERIT INGERSOLL-DAYTON
ANGELA BOMMARITO

Reminiscence and Life Review

72

that the life review was a form of reminiscence spanning the life of the individual that could actually facilitate the successful and adaptive integration of experiences, create meaning, and offer older adults the possibility of change. He also noted that reminiscence could be especially useful during stressful life transitions and events such as the death of loved ones and when facing one's own death.

The definitions and applications of both reminiscence and life review continue to evolve as their use as interventions is refined. More recent theoretical developments stress the importance of structuring reminiscence interventions to facilitate the integration, evaluation, reframing, and potential resolution of recalled experiences. For example, Coleman (1986) further conceptualized reminiscence and life review as treatment modalities, emphasizing that difficult memories should not be hidden but unearthed and treated therapeutically, potentially leading to empowerment rather than depression for the older adult. Haight and Burnside (1993) explored how life review and reminiscence, though often used interchangeably, can be considered separate interventions. Specifically, Haight and colleagues (2003) have argued that whereas reminiscence is unfocused and nonevaluative, life review, as a structured and evaluative process, is a more effective intervention for older adults.

REMINISCENCE AND LIFE REVIEW WITH DIFFERENT TARGET GROUPS

Social workers and other mental health professionals use reminiscence and life review to address a variety of mental health problems. This section describes evidence-based findings from life review and reminiscence interventions that pertain to four groups of older people that concern geriatric social workers: depressed older adults, cognitively impaired older adults, older adults undergoing life transitions, and older adults with their caregivers. The following criteria were used for selecting relevant journal articles and books: Participants were elderly (generally age 55 and over); the research design included control and/or comparison groups; and the study used pre- and posttest measures of change.

Depressed Older Adults

Though sparse, evidence-based research on this population comparing reminiscence and life review in-

terventions with no intervention is promising. For example, in a study of depressed or anxious nursing home residents (Hyer, Sohnle, Mehan, & Ragan, 2002), those participating in a group focusing on positive memories experienced a significant decrease in depressive symptoms as compared to a control group. In another study, community-dwelling depressed elderly participated in two kinds of individual reminiscing interventions (Fry, 1983), one structured around specific negative life event topical areas, and the other unstructured, covering any aspect of negative life events. When the two treatment groups were compared with a control group, participants in both reminiscence interventions displayed significant improvements with respect to depression and ego strength, with those in the structured reminiscence intervention experiencing the most improvement.

When compared to other kinds of psychotherapy, reminiscence and life review interventions are no more effective. For example, reminiscence group therapy was compared to goal-focused group therapy for older people with major depressive disorder (Klausner et al., 1998). Both groups experienced a decrease in depression and increase in functional ability; however, the goal-focused group also improved on several other psychological dimensions. In another study of those with major depressive disorder, three conditions were compared: reminiscence group therapy, problem-solving group therapy, and a wait-list control group (Arean et al., 1993). Both intervention groups experienced decreased depression and increased life integration as compared to the control group, but only the problem-solving group evidenced improved problem-solving skills. In a third study, depressed older people who attended a senior center were assigned to one of three interventions: reminiscence, current life events discussion, and no intervention (Perrotta & Meacham, 1981). When the three interventions were compared, there were no significant changes in depression or self-esteem among the groups.

Cognitively Impaired Older Adults

The limited amount of evidence-based research on reminiscence and life review with this population shows a mixed pattern of results. The most positive findings occurred in a life review program for nursing home residents with dementia or depression with cognitive impairments (Tabourne, 1995). At the end of the program, participants in the experimental group displayed a significant decrease in disorientation and increase in social interaction as compared to the control group.

Results from other studies are more ambiguous. One study of nursing home residents with dementia concluded that reminiscence group participants showed only short-term positive effects in depressive symptomatology when compared to a support group and a no-treatment group (Goldwasser, Auerbach, & Harkins, 1987). Another study of moderately confused nursing home residents found no significant differences between three reminiscence groups and three control groups (Orten, Allen, & Cook, 1989). Findings indicated that, based on improvements in one of the reminiscence groups, skilled group facilitator leadership may be a central ingredient to improved social behavior for participants with dementia. A third study, by Baines, Saxby, and Ehlert (1987) comparing reminiscence and reality orientation to control groups for confused nursing home residents, found that the group receiving reality orientation followed by reminiscence improved the most on cognitive ability, behavior, and communication. These findings suggest that reminiscence may be more effective for those who are more cognitively oriented and/or experiencing earlier phases of dementia (Spector, Orrell, Davies, & Woods, 2004).

One of the most sophisticated studies, conducted in Hong Kong on nursing home residents with Alzheimer's disease, also found no significant differences among reminiscence, socialization, and no-intervention control groups (Lai, Chi, & Kayser-Jones, 2004). However, when examining changes over time only for those in the reminiscence intervention, participants' social engagement and well-being improved. Lai and her colleagues summarize this research on reminiscence with cognitively impaired elderly as "promising but not definitive" (p. 45).

Older Adults Undergoing Life Transitions

One of the few evidence-based studies of reminiscence and life review interventions pertaining to this group has examined the efficacy of two reminiscing approaches (general reminiscence and life challenges reminiscence) for older people undergoing stressful procedures in the hospital (Rybarczyk & Bellg, 1997). When patients awaiting surgery participated in either of the two reminiscing approaches, they experienced a decrease in anxiety as compared to those who participated in a present-focus interview or no-treatment

control. When awaiting other medical procedures, the life challenges interview played an especially instrumental role in enhancing patients' feelings of self-efficacy. Another study examined life review with older people who were relocating (Haight, Michel, & Hendrix, 1998). This intervention was conducted on an individual basis with residents who had recently moved to a nursing home. When compared with a friendly-visit intervention, those who participated in the life review experienced significantly decreased depression and sense of hopelessness as well as increased life satisfaction and psychological well-being a year after the intervention.

Older Adults and Their Caregivers

One of the very few evidence-based studies examining the effectiveness of reminiscence and life review for this population was conducted in England for older people with dementia and their caregivers (Thorgrimsen, Schweitzer, & Orrell, 2002). When the reminiscence group was compared with a no-treatment control group, neither the older adults nor their caregivers experienced any significant improvements; however, positive trends occurred for the older adults (i.e., improved behaviors and activities of daily living) and the caregivers (i.e., reduced stress levels) who participated in the reminiscence group. In another study, older people with Alzheimer's disease and their caregivers received individual life review sessions with a practitioner that led to the development of a "life story book" (Haight et al., 2003). The older people with Alzheimer's disease who participated in these life review sessions experienced a significant improvement in their mood when compared with a life review intervention that was only caregiver-focused and a no-treatment control. Caregivers who participated in the life review intervention with their care recipient or in the caregiver-focused life review intervention experienced diminished burden in comparison to the no-treatment control.

REMINISCENCE AND LIFE REVIEW METHODS

Mental health professionals use a variety of approaches when conducting reminiscence and life review. In much of the literature on reminiscence and life review, the procedures have not been empirically evaluated, or, if tested, they are not described in sufficient detail to be useful for practitioners. Five interventions mentioned in the previous section are highlighted here based on their effectiveness and the clarity of their intervention methods.

The Life Story Book

This intervention is designed to facilitate life review with older participants and their caregivers (Haight et al., 2003). Two practitioners meet separately but simultaneously with the care receiver and caregiver to develop a book that portrays the life of the care receiver with dementia. The caregiver contributes to this effort by locating pictures and mementoes; the person with dementia selects from these options; and the practitioner asks the person with dementia to describe the pictures and mementoes. With the care receiver's permission, these sessions are tape-recorded and transcribed. Portions of these transcriptions are then used as captions for the book. Practitioners encourage the caregivers and care receivers to reminisce about the pictures between sessions as a way of increasing communication and enhancing pleasurable interactions. When the book is completed, the older person with dementia decides whether and how to share it with others.

Structured Reminiscence

This intervention is designed for depressed older people and consists of five weekly 90-minute sessions conducted on an individual basis (Fry, 1983). During each session, the practitioner helps the older participant to reminisce about one upsetting event from the past using a structured format that focuses on eight topical areas, each of which is discussed for 10 minutes. Fry (p. 23) lists these topical areas and provides illustrative questions, some of which are included here:

1. Strong negative and positive feelings associated with the events.
2. People, objects, or other experiences related to the event.
3. Images or ruminations about the event (e.g., "Were there thoughts you couldn't get rid of although you tried very hard?").
4. Fears, anxieties, or hopes related to the event (e.g., "Do you wish certain things would happen that would make you feel better?").

5. Dreams related to the event.
6. Preferences about interactions with others in relation to the event (e.g., "Did you wish people would let you alone?").
7. Unresolved feelings (e.g., "Were there people or situations that you tried very hard to avoid?").
8. How time was spent during the event.

As participants reminisce about the event in relation to each of these topical areas, the practitioner listens empathically but avoids giving advice or providing evaluative comments.

Positive Core Memories

This 12-week group approach is designed for nursing home residents who are experiencing depression or anxiety (Hyer et al., 2002). During the initial sessions, the practitioner works with the group members to identify two or three positive core memories (i.e., challenges and obstacles that were overcome). The practitioner encourages group interaction, thereby enhancing mutual identification with and appreciation for one another's positive core memories. Later sessions are devoted to applying the lessons learned from these memories to present-day experiences. In particular, the practitioner helps the participants to identify the coping methods they have used in the past and to apply these methods to problems in daily life.

Life Review and Experiencing

This 8-week intervention is used to help older people cope with relocation to a nursing home (Haight et al., 1998). Practitioners meet with older participants individually and use a Life Review and Experiencing Form to guide the intervention. The form consists of a series of questions which are organized around several phases of life (p. 128): childhood, adolescence, family and home, and adulthood. The final portion of this form focuses on summary questions (e.g., "What was the hardest thing you had to face in your life?"; "What was the proudest moment in your life?") that are intended to help older participants assess their lives so that they can acknowledge and integrate their mistakes as well as their contributions. Taken together, the questions provide a guide from which practitioners can selectively choose as they help older people chronologically review and evaluate their lives.

Life Challenges Interview

This intervention is a 1-hour individual interview designed to help older patients cope with anxiety prior to surgery or other invasive medical procedures (Rybarczyk & Bellg, 1997). The intervention begins by asking participants to recount early memories and follows themes that emerge in a chronological framework. A unique focus of this interview is on identifying specific challenges that were successfully met (e.g., obtaining good grades in school, learning to drive, finding a job). Practitioners ask questions that help older participants to reflect on how they met life challenges and highlight the strengths and resources of the older participants. Practitioners try to help older participants describe stressful situations that were "defining moments" (p. 90) because these events can serve as vivid reminders of their competence in the face of adversity. Finally, the session concludes with a summary of the two or three strengths and resources that emerge most consistently throughout these stressful situations. Practitioners provide this summary of the older participant's strengths or ask the participant to do so.

EMERGING ISSUES IN REMINISCENCE AND LIFE REVIEW

The literature on reminiscence and life review among the elderly has burgeoned over the past four decades since Butler's (1963) seminal work in this area. A number of research issues have emerged as particularly salient during this time. These issues are highlighted and their practice implications discussed.

Dosage

Reminiscence and life review interventions vary greatly in length, with no consensus about the ideal treatment dosage. Some interventions are a single session (Rybarczyk & Bellg, 1997); others last for many weeks (Thorgrimsen et al., 2002). Perhaps optimal treatment dosage varies in relation to presenting problems. For those undergoing a life transition such as nursing home placement, a 6-week intervention apparently "primes the pump of introspection," leading to a positive long-term outcome (Haight et al., 1998, p. 135). Older adults who are depressed may require higher intervention dosage; several interventions report successful outcomes after 10 to 12 sessions (Hseih & Wang, 2003).

Cognitively impaired older adults may need an even higher intervention dosage in which reminiscence and life review are part of a daily, ongoing treatment program (Spector et al., 2004).

Negative Outcomes

Both Butler (1963, 1974) and Coleman (1986) note that depression, obsession, and agitation are possible negative outcomes or concomitant factors with reminiscence and life review. Arguing that reminiscence per se is not necessarily adaptive, Watt and Wong (1991) suggest the need to identify those forms of reminiscence that may aid the older adult in adapting to aging (integrative, instrumental, transmissive, and narrative reminiscence), as well as those that may have a negative impact on the older adult (escapist and obsessive reminiscence). Interestingly, there are relatively few evidence-based approaches that address how to ameliorate the possible negative impact of reminiscing and life review. One exception is the work of Hyer and his colleagues (2002), who use a number of techniques to help reduce potential adverse effects of the reminiscence and life review process, such as providing time to experience sadness, empathizing with painful emotions, focusing on the meaning of hurtful memories, and highlighting personal strengths and resources that have resulted from painful life events.

Integrating Approaches

A number of treatment modalities are emerging that may naturally ally with reminiscence and life review because they offer tools to help older adults reinterpret and reevaluate events and experiences in a positive and functional way. For example, Watt and Cappeliez (1995) suggest that reminiscence can be integrated with cognitive approaches to address problems with depression. Similarly, Weiss (1995) asserts that the integration of life review and cognitive behavioral therapy allows older adults to first explore past events, inner strengths, and unresolved issues and conflicts, and then reexamine and reframe dysfunctional thought patterns and emotions to build a sense of positive control and self-efficacy.

Reminiscence can also be integrated with other treatment modalities. Klausner et al. (1998) outlined the treatment intervention of goal-focused group psychotherapy, which teaches older adults to reframe negative memories and use success stories rather than past failures to help individuals achieve their goals. Arean et al. (1993) found that problem-solving therapy, an intervention designed to help older adults find constructive ways of coping with current life stressors, alleviated depression significantly better than reminiscence therapy among older adults diagnosed with major depressive disorder, although reminiscence therapy was effective with individuals described as "good life integrators" (p. 1008). This study suggests that reminiscence therapy may not work as effectively with older adults characterized as "poor life integrators" (p. 1009) and that reminiscence therapy may be more effective if combined with problem-solving therapy.

Culture and Tailoring Interventions

Research on how contextual factors such as culture may influence the effectiveness of reminiscence and life review interventions is still preliminary. Atkinson, Kim, Ruelas, and Lin (1999) note that the life review of an older adult living in a collectivist culture such as those in Asia and Latin America may focus on life-long goals and achievements that subordinate individual achievements, and therefore may reminisce differently from those in Western culture, which is more individualistic and egocentric. An example of a culturally sensitive approach is described by Jonsdottir and colleagues (2001), who, when conducting a reminiscence group in an Icelandic nursing home, included stories from well-known Icelandic writers to stimulate the participants' storytelling.

Other factors such as intervention format may also play a key role in shaping the influence of reminiscence and life review. Haight and Dias (1992) found that reminiscence and life review conducted in individual versus group contexts were differentially effective for varying outcomes. They suggest that, if the purpose of the intervention is to promote psychological integration and healing, then individual life review sessions may be more appropriate because they permit greater privacy and more practitioner attention as older clients recount past hurts and fears. However, if the purpose is to enhance social relationships, then group sessions that encourage nonevaluative reminiscence may be more appropriate because such sessions promote enjoyable social interactions about pleasurable memories.

Other factors that impinge on intervention effectiveness are characteristics of the practitioner. Rybarczyk and Auerbach (1990) discovered that the effectiveness of different forms of reminiscence varied according to the age of the person providing the intervention. That is, participants in life challenge reminiscence interviews experienced more benefits, as compared to those in general reminiscence interviews, if they were interviewed by age peers rather than younger professionals. They reasoned that age peer interviewers shared knowledge about common cohort events (e.g., the Depression) that evoked greater trust and willingness to explore previous life challenges in greater depth. Taken together, these studies suggest that understanding the effectiveness of reminiscence and life review interventions in different cultural and social contexts enables practitioners to tailor their approaches to their clients' needs.

CONCLUSION

Reminiscence and life review interventions offer social workers and other mental health professionals creative ways to help older people find meaning in their lives. Though evidence-based research is limited, existing studies on reminiscence and life review interventions suggest that these approaches have promise for a variety of target groups. The challenge for practitioners is to contribute to the ongoing refinement of reminiscence and life review interventions as they tailor their approaches to address the specific needs of their older clients.

NOTE

We would like to thank Sally Haines Lawler who assisted us in the identification and retrieval of references for this chapter.

REFERENCES

Arean, P. A., Perri, M. G., Nezu, A. M., Schein, R. L., Christopher, F., & Joseph, T. X. (1993). Comparative effectiveness of social problem-solving therapy and reminiscence therapy as treatments for depression in older adults. *Journal of Counseling and Clinical Psychology, 61*(6), 1003–1010.

Atkinson, D. R., Kim, A. U., Ruelas, S. R., & Lin, T. A. (1999). Ethnicity and attitudes toward facilitated reminiscence. *Journal of Mental Health Counseling, 21*(1), 66–81.

Baines, S., Saxby, P., & Ehlert, K. (1987). Reality orientation and reminiscence therapy: A controlled cross-over study of elderly confused people. *British Journal of Psychiatry, 151,* 222–231.

Bohlmeijer, E., Smit, F., & Cuijpers, P. (2003). Effects of reminiscence and life review on late-life depression: A meta-analysis. *International Journal of Geriatric Psychiatry, 18,* 1088–1094.

Butler, R. N. (1963). The life review: An interpretation of reminiscence in the aged. *Psychiatry, 26,* 65–76.

Butler, R. N. (1974). Successful aging and the role of the life review. *Journal of the American Geriatrics Society, 22*(12), 529–535.

Coleman, P. G. (1986). *Ageing and reminiscence processes: Social and clinical implications.* New York: Wiley.

Erikson, E. (1964). *Childhood and society* (2nd ed.). New York: Norton.

Fry, P. S. (1983). Structured and unstructured reminiscence training and depression among the elderly. *Clinical Gerontologist, 1*(3), 15–37.

Goldwasser, A. N., Auerbach, S. M., & Harkins, S. W. (1987). Cognitive, affective, and behavioral effects of reminiscence group therapy on demented elderly. *International Journal of Aging and Human Development, 25*(3), 209–222.

Haight, B. K., Bachman, D. L., Hendrix, S., Wagner, M. T., Meeks, A., & Johnson, J. (2003). Life review: Treating the dyadic family unit with dementia. *Clinical Psychology and Psychotherapy, 10,* 165–174.

Haight, B. K., & Burnside, I. (1993). Reminiscence and life review: Explaining the differences. *Archives of Psychiatric Nursing, 7*(2), 91–98.

Haight, B. K., & Dias, J. K. (1992). Examining key variables in selected reminiscing modalities. *International Psychogeriatrics, 4*(2), 279–290.

Haight, B., Michel, Y., & Hendrix, S. (1998). Life review: Preventing despair in newly relocated nursing home residents short- and long-term effects. *International Journal of Aging and Human Development, 47*(2), 119–142.

Hseih, H., & Wang, J. (2003). Effect of reminiscence therapy on depression in older adults: A systematic review. *International Journal of Nursing Studies, 40,* 335–345.

Hyer, L., Sohnle, S., Mehan, D., & Ragan, A. (2002). Use of positive core memories in LTC: A review. In M. P. Norris, V. Molinari, & S. Ogland-Hand (Eds.), *Emerging trends in psychological practice in long-term care* (pp. 51–90). Binghamton, NY: Haworth Press.

Jonsdottir, H., Jonsdottir, G., Steingrimsdottir, E., & Tryggvadottir, B. (2001). Group reminiscence among people with end-stage chronic lung diseases. *Journal of Advanced Nursing, 35*(1), 79–87.

Klausner, E. J., Clarkin, J. F., Spielman, L., Pupo, C., Abrams, R., & Alexopoulos, G. S. (1998). Late-life depression and functional disability: The role of goal-focused group psychotherapy. *International Journal of Geriatric Psychiatry, 13,* 707–716.

Lai, C. K. Y., Chi, I., & Kayser-Jones, J. (2004). A randomized controlled trial of a specific reminiscence approach to promote the well-being of nursing home residents with dementia. *International Psychogeriatrics, 16*(1), 33–49.

Orten, J. D., Allen, M., & Cook, J. (1989). Reminiscence groups with confused nursing center residents: An experimental study. *Social Work in Health Care, 14*(1), 73–86.

Perrotta, P., & Meacham, J. A. (1981). Can a reminiscing intervention alter depression and self-esteem? *International Journal of Aging and Human Development, 14*(1), 23–30.

Rybarczyk, B. D., & Auerbach, S. M. (1990). Reminiscence interviews as stress management interventions for older patients undergoing surgery. *Gerontologist, 30*(4), 522–528.

Rybarczyk, B. D., & Bellg, A. (1997). *Listening to life stories: A new approach to stress intervention in health care.* New York: Springer.

Spector, A., Orrell, M., Davies, S., & Woods, R. T. (2004). Reminiscence therapy for dementia (Cochrane review). In *The Cochrane database of systematic reviews, 2.* New York: Wiley.

Tabourne, C. E. S. (1995). The effects of a life review program on disorientation, social interaction and self-esteem of nursing home residents. *International Journal of Aging and Human Development, 41*(3), 251–266.

Thorgrimsen, L., Schweitzer, P., & Orrell, M. (2002). Evaluating reminiscence for people with dementia: A pilot study. *Arts in Psychotherapy, 29*(2), 93–97.

Watt, L. M., & Cappeliez, P. (1995). Reminiscence interventions for the treatment of depression in older adults. In B. K. Haight & J. D. Webster (Eds.), *The art and science of reminiscing: Theory, research, methods, and applications* (pp. 221–232). Washington, DC: Taylor & Francis.

Watt, L. M., & Wong, P. T. P. (1991). A taxonomy of reminiscence and therapeutic implications. *Journal of Gerontological Social Work, 16*(1/2), 37–57.

Weiss, J. C. (1995). Cognitive therapy and life review therapy: Theoretical and therapeutic implications for mental health counselors. *Journal of Mental Health Counseling, 17*(12), 157–172.

ROSEMARY CHAPIN
HOLLY NELSON-BECKER
KELLEY MacMILLAN

Strengths-Based and Solutions-Focused Approaches to Practice

73

The strengths perspective is a philosophical standpoint that focuses on the inherent resilience in human nature that undergirds much of social work practice. This perspective is especially applicable to work with older adults, who have a lifetime of rich experience that can be used to address current difficulty. Strengths-based and solution-focused approaches are both rooted in the belief that capacity rather than pathology should be the primary focal point of the helping process. Both the strengths perspective and the strategic approaches are discussed in this chapter. The vignette that follows provides an example of an older client with whom the approaches were initiated.

▓ Celia Jones was referred to the home- and community-based services social worker by her daughter, who lived two states away and was very concerned about her mother's deteriorating mental and physical health. Celia was a 78-year-old African American woman. Her husband of 55 years, Emil, had died 2 months earlier after battling diabetes, hypertension, and heart disease. They had had a very stable marriage and loving relationship; Celia had been Emil's dedicated and sole caretaker after his leg had been amputated 5 years previously. Emil's heart condition worsened suddenly and resulted in a hospital admission. During this period, he sent Celia home one night, seeing her exhaustion from spending so much time with him. He died unexpectedly while she was at home resting. Her guilt at not being present with him when he died left her unable to work through her grief.

Emil's death compounded Celia's previous sense of loss and grief due to the death of their only son, David, 3 months earlier. David's death was attributed to the effects of Agent Orange used in the Vietnam War. David had publicly urged the military to conduct clinical treatment trials and offer compensation to veterans experiencing this syndrome after the war ended. He had received an award for his activism and had been invited to speak at congressional hearings, both of which provided affirmation for Celia of the contribution David had made in his life. David, who had never married, lived in the same town as his parents and had developed an especially strong bond with his mother.

The prolonged illnesses and subsequent loss of these two family members contributed to some of Celia's own health issues, and she experienced unremitting depression. In addition, Celia's caregiving responsibilities for her husband contributed to her becoming disconnected from her community and support systems such as friends and her church. Celia's reaction was to consider selling her small and cluttered house, move into an apartment, and withdraw from friends and family. She was refusing to answer phone calls and not eating or sleeping well.

The social worker, operating from strengths-based and solution-focused perspectives, did not assume that she understood Ms. Jones's viewpoint, even though she had encountered multiple issues of grief and loss in her prior practice experiences working with older adults. Rather, she listened carefully to her story of loss but also was alert to what had brought her joy: her strengths, her goals, her resources. She knew that only Ms. Jones was the expert on her situation and could develop the pathway for recovery and healing.

In the first visit, the social worker reinforced Ms. Jones's curiosity and willingness to let the social worker enter the house. After the social worker's visit, Ms. Jones felt more hopeful about her future than she had for the past 8 weeks and picked up the phone to call her daughter. ■

Strengths-based and solution-focused approaches to intervention with Celia Jones draw on similar assumptions about practice with older adults and form the basis for this chapter. These two approaches work well together and may serve to reinforce each other because they each contain complementary principles that constitute client-centered and holistic perspectives for social work practice.

This chapter first presents frameworks of strengths-based principles and solution-focused principles commonly used with older adult populations within a larger strengths perspective. Second, applications of these approaches in various settings are discussed to broaden comprehension of the uses of each approach. Strengths-based and solution-focused approaches can be used in community settings, such as senior centers and mental health centers, as well as support groups for caregivers and grief/loss support groups. In addition, social workers employed in home- and community-based services programs, assisted living facilities, and nursing facilities can use these approaches with older adults adjusting to decreases in

functioning, transitions to new settings, and efforts to deal with end-of-life issues. Benefits and cautionary notes about use of these perspectives are addressed, including how these perspectives contrast with a traditional problem focus in social work generalist practice. We include discussion of future research implications, focusing on the potential of the strengths-based and solution-focused approaches for improving social work practice for older adults.

STRENGTHS OVERVIEW

The strengths perspective, also referred to as the strengths-based perspective, is a philosophical view about how social workers can interact with clients to elicit positive outcomes (Cowger, 1994; Saleebey, 1997, 2002). When practiced fully, the strengths perspective is an operational stance that puts social work values into action; it is not just about providing support and motivation. It involves recognizing the inherent power that individuals can and must bring to bear on their own lives to achieve their potential and learn the life lessons that will facilitate their own distinctive journey toward aging well. It does not assume that clients are "other," but rather, in the classic stance developed by Martin Buber (1957/1970), addresses relationships as having I-Thou status, where the relationship is subject-to-subject rather than subject-to-object. Ageism is sometimes manifested in a paternalistic attitude that treats older adults as having lived past their ability to participate productively in society and acknowledges only limited options in their behavioral repertoires. By contrast, the strengths perspective engages individuals in a way that promotes the ongoing task of building a mindful and meaningful life. For instance, a social worker utilizing the strengths perspective reassures clients that he or she will not interfere with their independence and autonomy.

The strengths perspective seeks to empower people and communities. For example, as applied to an understanding of health care, the strengths perspective leads social workers to consider the multiple influences that shape health status. Social workers are urged to go beyond linear explanations for health and disease and to focus on the capacity of individuals and communities to take an active role in achieving and maintaining health (Weick, 1986). Emphasis is on removing barriers to access to formal health care, on more effective use of community resources, and on working to establish policies that support increased access. The strengths model is best understood in comparison to the traditional medical model that socializes the client to be a passive recipient of services largely determined through professional expertise. The strengths perspective serves as an antidote to victim blaming through its focus on dialogue, collaboration, resilience, empowerment, and, ultimately, wholeness as defined by the client (Saleebey, 2002).

The strengths perspective assumes that the key to opening up critical areas of dialogue is through sharpening the skill of listening deeply to client concerns, dreams, and visions of a desired future—a future that can fundamentally change behavior and thoughts in the present. Often, the simple power of language has the capacity to elevate or denigrate. The potential for social workers to engage clients in helpful ways may be influenced by the choice of words they employ and the way those words are understood or received by the client.

The strengths perspective also fosters a sense of belonging by recognizing the reciprocity between the client and the social environment even in the most extreme stages of coping with dementia or receiving full personal care. Although these relationships may appear one-sided, there are usually benefits for clients and caregivers as well as helping professionals. The communication between the client, family and friends, and professional helpers and advocates provides insights that improve direct care, empirical research, and policy.

The conceptual underpinnings of the strengths perspective reflect a social constructionist approach to reality, which posits that our explanations of all human interactions, including social problems, are based on views of reality that are socially and personally constructed (Berger & Luckmann, 1967; Geertz, 1973; Gergen, 1999). The phrase "socially and personally constructed" suggests that personal beliefs and group consensus shape what a group of people consider to be real at a given time. Hence, in the strengths perspective, understanding the beliefs and values of the older adult is the beginning point for all further work.

Principles of the strengths perspective (Saleebey, 2002) generally include the following:

- All individuals have strengths.
- All experiences, even negative ones, may present opportunities for growth.
- Practitioner diagnosis and the assessment process in direct practice often make assumptions that limit rather than expand capacity.
- Collaboration rather than coercion leads to highly motivated and engaged clients.

- All environments have resources.
- A civil society engages in care for all of its members.

Practice based on these principles always involves a delicate dance of interpretation as one applies them to the web of difficult work with clients and sometimes the people in their environments. However, incorporation of a focus that builds on individual and community strengths and resources and on forming a collaborative relationship with clients to help them achieve their goals opens new possibilities for effective practice. A parallel perspective has emerged with the development of the positive psychology movement. Peterson and Seligman (2004) have challenged psychologists to measure and describe what is right with people in lieu of what is wrong with them; Saleebey (1997) recommends avoidance of classifying people based on a *Diagnostic and Statistical Manual of Mental Disorders* diagnosis. The social worker's role is to skillfully create a helping relationship that empowers the client to resolve life struggles.

THE STRENGTHS-BASED APPROACH WITH OLDER ADULTS

The strengths-based approach was initially developed for use with adults served in mental health centers/agencies (Kisthardt, 1993; Rapp, 1998; Saleebey, 2002). A strengths-based perspective has also been successfully extended to social policy and direct practice with older adult populations (Chapin, 1995; Fast & Chapin, 2000, 2002; Tice & Perkins, 1996). These strengths-based approaches follow the general principles elicited by Saleebey and others, but they are particularly tailored for work with older adults:

- Discovering and building on strengths of older adults rather than problems will facilitate hope, self-reliance, and personal satisfaction.
- Acknowledging that older adults have the power to learn, grow, and change is fundamental.
- Developing the older adult–social worker relationship is essential to effectively assist the older adult.
- Participating in decisions, making choices, and determining the direction of the helping process is a primary role for the older adult.
- Acquiring resources based on active outreach to the community is a key role for the social worker.

Strengths-based social work practice with older adults requires assertively helping to acquire needed additional resources when necessary. However, naturally occurring helping systems in the community are first carefully explored and bolstered. For example, it may be possible to identify a neighbor who would be willing to take the older adult's trash to the curb in winter, or a fellow church member who may be willing to shovel snow from the driveway or provide rides to church, in return for mending or ironing. Fostering these kinds of reciprocal relationships also strengthens informal supports and chances for social interaction that are vital to aging well.

Although many social workers are now employing strengths perspective principles in their practice with older adults, work to further specify helping strategies and to develop a model that can be the basis for careful research is yet to be done. Staudt, Howard, and Drake (2001) reviewed nine research studies that examined the use of strengths-based case management in mental heath and substance abuse treatment. They recommended that future studies consider experimental designs where strengths-based case management approaches are treated as an independent variable. In addition, they recommended that research control for differences in case manager trainings and differences among case management styles. They also recommended that measurement of client outcomes be given increased attention.

PHILOSOPHICAL TENETS OF THE SOLUTION-FOCUSED APPROACH

Solution-focused therapy shares common roots with the strengths perspective. Solution-focused therapy traces its origins to work by de Shazer and colleagues (1986; for a more detailed development of theoretical underpinnings of solution-focused therapy, see Berg, 1994; de Shazer, 1988, 1991; Lipchik, 1993, 2002). Central to the solution-focused approach and all therapy models are certain assumptions, discussed below, about the nature of the person, how problems are formed and maintained, how change occurs, and the role of the individual and the social worker in the therapeutic/helping process (Bonjean, 2003; de Shazer et al., 1986).

First, the idiosyncratic nature of the person is affirmed because the solution-focused approach values the subjective experience and worldview of the individual (Bonjean, 2003). This is also an example of how the solution-focused approach shares its social constructionist epistemology with the strengths perspective. The social worker's role is to assist individuals to create their own solutions based on experiences when the difficulty is not present. The social worker draws on the strengths of the individual and resources available to him or her as a means to overcome challenges and attain the goals that will lead to a satisfactory life (de Shazer et al., 1986).

Second, the solution-focused approach makes clear how problems are formed and maintained. All individuals experience difficulties in life; however, the difficulty becomes a complaint when attempts to resolve the problem are ineffective despite recurring attempts to resolve it (de Shazer et al., 1986; Nelson-Becker, 2004). In some cases, the individual may perceive the situation as static or not changing despite behavior that was intended to resolve the complaint. The individual requests professional social work assistance when he or she has complaints about life that are no longer acceptable to the help seeker.

A solution-focused approach avoids identifying the cause and effect. Looking for a cause and effect maintains the focus of intervention on the problem or complaint. Just as the name suggests, the solution-focused intervention revolves around constructing or identifying solutions. The approach suggests that the solution to the complaint is found in exceptions to the complaint or those times when the complaint is absent (Bonjean, 2003; de Shazer et al., 1986). The social worker's role is to help the individual identify those exceptions. Hence, the interview questions or assessment focuses on those times when life is going well and attempts to find out what was happening that made life satisfactory. In this manner, the solution is separated from the problem and can build on the strengths and positive experiences of the individual.

Third, a solution-focused approach has a unique perspective on how change occurs. Constructing or identifying solutions creates an expectation of change. The expectation of change or actual change itself does not have to be great; in fact, any expectation of change is valuable because slight changes influence the interactional pattern between the client and other individuals (Bonjean, 2003; de Shazer et al., 1986). Part of the expectation of change is based on the fact that clients will do something different from what they did in the past to resolve the complaint.

Finally, the solution-focused approach defines the role of the individual and social worker as a collaboration to establish goals that are based on client values. Solution-focused interventions are client-centered: The individual decides what his or her goals are and when enough change has occurred to end therapy or the intervention. The client-centered approach to goal setting also de-emphasizes the social worker as the expert and develops a collaborative relationship that is respectful of the individual's life experience, worldview, and capacities (Bonjean, 2003; de Shazer et al., 1986).

Solution-focused approaches have been utilized in clinical work with older adults and their families; they illustrate how the approach can be used successfully as a clinical/psychosocial intervention in addition to case management or direct service intervention (Bonjean, 1997, 2003; Dahl, Bathel, & Carreon, 2000). A solution-focused approach includes principles that guide the social worker's action and are comparable to the strengths perspective principles (Bonjean, 2003). The focus is on the positive elements in one's life, on the solution, and on the future in order to facilitate change toward the older adult's goals:

- Goal attainment is accomplished in the older adult's own unique way, and he or she is able to resourcefully and creatively change.
- Both the older adult and the social worker are experts.
- Identifying exceptions to the problem enables the older adult and social worker to build or create solutions. An exception is any instance when the older adult does not experience the challenge.

The solution-focused approach emphasizes these principles as fundamental to intervention. Both solution-focused and strengths-based approaches have broad application to work with older adults. They may be easily utilized in many types of settings, and the fundamental principles, consistent with social work values, are quickly assimilated by social workers at any level of practice.

APPLICATIONS

In this section, we illustrate the application of strengths-based and solution-focused approaches in a variety of settings where social workers provide services to older adults. A challenge for social workers is that many settings use a traditional problem-solving model or a diagnosis is made as a basis for the intervention. The solution-focused and the strengths-based approaches avoid the traditional model's emphasis on diagnosis, pathology/deficits, or problems.

Regardless of the agency auspices or services, the strengths-based/solution-focused assessment lays the foundation for the social worker and older adult to develop goals important to the older adult and identify intrapersonal, interpersonal, and social-environmental resources to reach these goals. The social worker's role is to help the older adult define and articulate goals and the changes that will illustrate measurable achievement of the goals. This emphasizes and supports the self-efficacy, autonomy, and self-determination that are essential to client empowerment and a sense of hope.

In the case of Celia described earlier, the home- and community-based social worker has knowledge of human development and models of change, a wealth of information about community resources, and the professional skills to assist the older adult. Social work helping skills include assisting the older adult to focus her energy on solution identification as well as providing an alternative viewpoint about the challenges faced by the older adult. The expertise the older adult brings to the relationship is her own life experience, personal strengths, and viewpoints regarding her personal circumstances.

In addition, the older adult provides the definition of the challenges she faces, potential solutions to these challenges, and a preference about how she would like to overcome them (Bonjean, 2003). The social worker can use assessment and active listening skills as a means to elicit discussion with the older adult about how she conducted her life prior to the current circumstances and events as well as to review earlier life challenges and responses. After the home- and community-based social worker and older adult identify goals, they agree on the formal and informal resources to assist the older adult.

In this example, the social worker learned that Celia was a primary caregiver for more than 5 years. Prior to taking on the caregiving role, Celia was socially active and engaged with her church and other social groups and participated in activities to promote her health and well-being. Focusing on these positive dimensions and strengths, the social worker can work with Celia to reengage her with her support system and develop new support systems, for example, a grief and loss group through the local senior center. We primarily consider senior centers as a source of congregate meals and social activities; however, they can also provide services that support the health and well-being of older adults such as caregiver support and grief and loss groups. If such groups do not yet exist in the community, it is incumbent on the social worker practicing from a strengths perspective to work with community agencies to see that such services are made available. The senior center social worker using a strengths perspective approach would also work to expand such community support options and to enact policies to create those options.

Another resource available to address the depression experienced by Celia is the community mental health center. A mental health social worker could use a solution-focused approach to identify the exceptions to the problem (e.g., the depression) by concentrating on prior feelings when Celia felt life was going well. She could help Celia identify possible change opportunities to separate the problem from the solution (Bonjean, 1997). The social worker using the solution-focused approach will apply his or her assessment skills to find instances when the problem was not present or when feelings were less intense. This approach builds on the strengths and successes of the older adult instead of focusing on what is not working.

For instance, the mental health center social worker assessing Celia would learn about the small things that helped her feel better each day: taking walks in her garden, looking at the artwork her son had created for her, and thinking about the life her husband would want her to live. These exceptions could be used to help Celia recognize that there are brief lapses in her feelings of grief and loss when she reflects on the enjoyable times and rewarding life she had built with her husband and son. More important, Celia would recognize that there are moments and times when her grief and loss are not as painful. The mental health center social worker could encourage Celia to think about these exceptions to her emotional pain and use this process to take small, incremental steps to work through her grief and loss.

Long-term care institutions, such as assisted living and nursing care facilities, also offer many opportunities to apply the strengths and solution-focused perspectives. A social worker working in these locations may help to focus older adults' energy on those activities they found personally meaningful throughout their life and facilitate engagement in those same or similar activities in the new location. Initial anger in making the transition can also be a tool when the social worker helps direct it into building a significant future.

CAUTIONS AND BENEFITS

We believe the strengths-based and solution-focused approaches have great value particularly for older adults who encounter life challenges with diminished friendship networks, emerging health concerns, and other losses. However, there are three cautions in using these approaches. First, although there is much anecdotal evidence that these approaches offer benefit to older adults, there has been little formal research to provide empirical evidence of the specific mechanisms by which these approaches assist older adults in leading more fulfilling lives. There has been little discrimination of what type of older adult may benefit and who may not. Future research could include better delineation of how these approaches operate in comparison to other approaches and better evaluation of specific outcomes.

Second, when needs are minimized, a novice worker may lose the sense of urgency to address these needs. There are times when needs are of a critical nature and must be immediately addressed. A social worker does well to learn to discriminate when it is appropriate to engage a strengths-based or solution-focused approach and when emergent issues, such as domestic violence or other abuse, must be addressed first.

Third, although we believe the approaches discussed here have lasting value and can be used to some extent in nearly every context, it is important to understand that in specific situations other approaches might better meet certain needs. As with any social work approach, no one size fits all. It is important for social workers who work with older adults to become adept at incorporating many models of practice.

We believe there are many merits to integrating strengths and solution-focused perspectives into work with older adult clients. Foremost is that they sharpen the focus on the capacity of older individuals rather than on pathology and disability. The strengths-based and solution-focused approaches do not ignore biological components; the social worker conducts a biopsychosocial assessment and considers biological influences in the larger context of the older adult's social environment. Thus, these perspectives work to counter the dominant paradigm alive in many disciplines today that discounts the truth that the key to healing generally resides within the individual. The strengths and solution-focused perspectives require workers to assertively look for strengths and resources in their clients as well as the clients' families and environments. Such reframing can initially be a challenge, but social workers can train themselves to see in new ways, and this becomes a skill that develops over time.

The strengths perspective particularly gives voice to populations whose views previously were ignored. Listening to older adults, particularly older adults of oppressed groups, such as people of color, women, gays, lesbians, bisexual and transgender individuals, and people with disabilities, helps social workers understand more clearly how they managed to survive and even thrive in challenging environments. The emphasis on exploring strengths in the context of unique life experiences is beneficial across ethnic, cultural, and economic groups (Chapin, 2001).

Finally, using these perspectives can be energizing for the social worker who practices with older adults. Sometimes, when facing a long litany of challenges rehearsed by older adult clients who often find no redress in formal societal institutions, social workers can become overwhelmed and discouraged and experience compassion fatigue. The perspectives detailed in this chapter can keep social workers fully engaged as they encourage older individuals to explore their hopes, dreams, and goals and, in the process, replenish their own energy reserves.

CONCLUSION

The strengths perspective and the strengths-based and solution-focused approaches focus on client and community capacity, resilience, and goals. These distinct strategies offer social workers a practice framework that helps them put into action values such as self-determination and social justice. The strengths perspective draws on a long but sometimes neglected tradition in social work of starting where the client is and of honoring the insights into the capacity to identify their own solutions that clients possess. Because older adults bring a lifetime of experience in working out solutions, these approaches can be especially helpful for the gerontological social worker. The next step is for gerontological researchers and practitioners to further elucidate these approaches to determine how the strengths-based and solution-focused approaches can be most effectively implemented in specific settings and conditions.

REFERENCES

Berg, I. K. (1994). *Family-based services: A solution focused approach.* New York: Norton.

Berger, P., & Luckmann, T. (1967). *The social construction of reality.* Garden City, NY: Anchor/Doubleday.

Bonjean, M. J. (1997). Solution-focused brief therapy with aging families. In T. D. Hargrave & S. M. Hanna (Eds.), *The aging family: New visions in theory, practice and reality* (pp. 81–100). New York: Brunner/Mazel.

Bonjean, M. J. (2003). Solution-focused therapy: Elders enhancing exceptions. In J. L. Ronch & J. A. Goldfield (Eds.), *Mental wellness in aging: Strengths-based approaches* (pp. 201–236). Baltimore: Health Professions Press.

Buber, M. (1970). *Ich und Du.* New York: Scribner Press. (Original work published 1957)

Chapin, R. (1995). Social policy development: The strengths perspective. *Social Work, 40*(4), 506–514.

Chapin, R. (2001). Building on the strengths of older women. In K. J. Peterson & A. Lieberman (Eds.), *Building on women's strengths: An agenda for the 21st century* (rev. ed., pp. 169–195). Binghamton, NY: Haworth Press.

Cowger, C. D. (1994). Assessing client strengths: Clinical assessment for client empowerment. *Social Work, 39,* 262–268.

Dahl, R., Bathel, D., & Carreon, C. (2000). The use of solution-focused therapy with an elderly population. *Journal of Systemic Therapies, 19*(4), 45–55.

de Shazer, S. (1988). *Clues: Investigating solutions in brief therapy.* New York: Norton.

de Shazer, S. (1991). *Putting difference to work.* New York: Norton.

de Shazer, S., Berg, I. K., Lipchik, E., Nunnally, E., Molnar, A., Gingerich, W., et al. (1986, June). Brief therapy: Focused solution development. *Family Process, 25,* 207–221.

Fast, B., & Chapin, R. (2000). *Strengths-based care management for older adults.* Baltimore: Health Professions Press.

Fast, B., & Chapin, R. (2002). The strengths model with older adults. In D. Saleebey (Ed.), *The strengths perspective in social work practice* (3rd ed., pp. 143–162). Boston: Allyn & Bacon.

Geertz, C. (1973). *The interpretation of cultures.* New York: Basic Books.

Gergen, K. (1999). *An invitation to social construction.* Thousand Oaks, CA: Sage.

Kisthard, W. E. (1993). An empowerment agenda for case management research: Evaluating the strengths model from the consumer's perspective. In M. Harris & H. Bergman (Eds.), *Case management for mentally ill patients: Theory and practice* (pp. 165–182). Langhorn, PA: Harwood.

Lipchik, E. (1993). "Both/and" solutions. In S. Friedman (Ed.), *The new language of change: Constructive collaboration in psychotherapy* (pp. 25–49). New York: Guilford Press.

Lipchik, E. (2002). *Beyond technique in solution-focused therapy: Working with emotions and the therapeutic relationship.* New York: Guilford Press.

Nelson-Becker, H. (2004). Meeting life challenges: A hierarchy of coping styles in African-American and Jewish-American older adults. *Journal of Human Behavior in the Social Environment, 10*(1), 155–174.

Peterson, C., & Seligman, M. E. (2004). *Character strengths and virtues: A handbook and classification.* New York: Oxford University Press.

Rapp, C. A. (1998). *The strengths model: Case management with people suffering from severe and persistent mental illness.* New York: Oxford University Press.

Saleebey, D. (1997). The strengths approach to practice. In D. Saleebey (Ed.), *The strengths perspective in social work practice* (pp. 49–58). New York: Longman.

Saleebey, D. (2002). Introduction: Power in the people. In D. Saleebey (Ed.), *The strengths perspective in social work practice* (3rd ed., pp. 1–20). Boston: Allyn & Bacon.

Staudt, M., Howard, M. O., & Drake, B. (2001). The operationalization, implementation, and effectiveness of the strengths perspective: A review of empirical studies. *Journal of Social Service Research, 27*(3), 1–21.

Tice, C., & Perkins, K. (1996). *Mental health issues and aging: Building on the strengths of older persons.* Pacific Grove, CA: Brooks/Cole.

Weick, A. (1986). The philosophical contest of a health model of social work. *Social Casework, 76*(9), 551–559.

HOLLY NELSON-BECKER
MITSUKO NAKASHIMA
EDWARD CANDA

Spirituality in Professional Helping Interventions

74

Older adults typically value the importance of religion and spirituality in their lives. Fifty-eight percent of older Americans reported that religion is very important, the highest rating on a 4-point scale in a recent Gallup poll (Princeton Religious Research Center, 2001). As health and mobility decline in older ages, formal religious participation tends to decrease, but private spiritual expressions (use of prayer, the Bible, and religious radio/TV) tend to increase (Levin, 2001). Because religion and spirituality are often important aspects of their lives, older adults may welcome integration of a spiritual perspective when they interact with formal helpers.

Spirituality has recently begun to be a focal point for investigation in many gerontological disciplines. For example, in social work, recent studies about elders have explored connections between cultural diversity and religiousness (Ahearn, 2001), spirituality as an important resource for well-being (Ai, 2000), use of existential psychotherapy (Lantz, 1998), collaboration between social work and churches (Tirrito, 2000), and issues related to dying and hospice programs (Lloyd, 1997; Reese, 2001; Smith, 2001). Numerous empirical studies in other fields have examined the relationship between religion or spirituality and well-being, with about 80% reporting positive correlations between religiousness and greater happiness, life satisfaction, or other measures (H. G. Koenig, McCullough, & Larson, 2001). In particular, empirical studies of the effects of religion on the health and mental health of older adults, though having mixed outcomes, generally suggest that religious and spiritual practices have salubrious effects on social support, coping, and quality of life at the end of life (Krause, 1997; Levin & Chatters, 1998; Nakashima, 2003; Nelson-Becker, 2004). These findings imply that religious and spiritual interventions may be valuable resources for social workers in maintaining life satisfaction for some older adults.

Development of a spiritually sensitive practice requires a strengths-based approach that includes listening to the profound and diverse questions clients express and demonstrating openness to hear all expressions of grief, longing, confusion, and joy that emanate from the human experience. Spiritually sensitive practice involves the ability to recognize and respond to these expressions with clients, but it does not impose a viewpoint that is contrary to the perspective of the client. It is a hearing of the heart: an ability to hear the pain and the hope in the stories clients tell and an ability to highlight for clients important themes or subtexts of which they may not be fully aware.

SPIRITUALITY: WHAT IS IT?

Spirituality is the search for meaning, purpose, and morality. It develops through relationships with self, others, the universe, and/or ultimate reality or the ground of being, however a person or group understands this (Canda & Furman, 1999; James, 1909/1982; Tillich, 1962). Because spirituality has many aspects, attempts to define the term lead to at least three interrelated conceptualizations: an essential or irreducible core element of human nature; one aspect of many (biopsychosocial-spiritual) dimensions that constitute humans; and transpersonal experiences in which consciousness expands beyond the limits of ordinary ego and physical boundaries, for example, through a sense of connection with the divine (Carroll, 1998). Transpersonal experience includes the journey within to the deepest nature of oneself as well as the process of fulfilling and transcending the individual self in the context of our connections with others and the universe (Robbins, Chatterjee, & Canda, 1998). It may also include direct mystical experiences with the divine (James, 1908/1962). Individuals and groups may express their spirituality with or without involvement in religious organizations.

Spirituality is expressed through religious involvement somewhat more commonly among older adults compared to younger cohorts (Marler & Hadaway, 2002), although some older adults do not affiliate with a religion, that is, the beliefs, values, rituals, and institutions that are concerned with spirituality, shared by a community, and transmitted through traditions. Different disciplines view spirituality in varying ways (e.g., divinity schools often conceptualize spirituality as being one component of religion); social work generally views spirituality as the overarching dimension that may or may not include religious behaviors (Bullis, 1996; Canda & Furman, 1999; Joseph, 1988). Older adults, however, in contrast to their often younger social workers, are more likely to be able to define and discuss religion or their practical philosophy of living more easily than they define spirituality, a term they may find confusing (Nelson-Becker, 2003).

For a helping professional, spiritually sensitive practice involves a focus on the older adult client's distinctive and unique spiritual beliefs, values, practices, experiences, and community support systems. It also involves understanding general theories and ideas about spirituality that may be applicable across individuals and cultures. This parallels anthropological concepts of the emic or insider approach (considering the individual's unique perspective) and the etic or outsider approach (considering how other spiritual/religious traditions or theories would view this individual). These two points of view are complementary when trying to understand individual spiritual concerns.

AGING AND THE SPIRITUAL JOURNEY

A natural concomitant of the aging process seems to be a turn toward exploration of the meaning of existence in relation to the universe. This inner spiritual exploration coinciding with aging is an expected cultural norm across cultures and spiritual traditions (Atchley, 2001). Tornstam (1994) found that adults over 75 often exhibit an increase in transcendent attitudes, including delight in the inner world, less death anxiety, and greater sense of connection to the universe. Some older adults do seek satisfaction through humanistic philosophies by creating a life of service and altruism with a goal of generativity (Erikson & Erikson, 1997). Yet others find no appeal in religiosity or spiritual growth that are expressions of explicit spirituality, and maintain secular patterns that they established years earlier or developed in late life.

SPIRITUAL INTERVENTIONS OR SPIRITUAL HELPING ACTIVITIES

Although "interventions" is the term most often used in the social work literature to describe the activities conducted by social workers in collaboration with clients and is in fact part of the title of this chapter, the authors prefer the term "spiritually focused helping activities." This avoids the implication of the word "intervention" that helping should be imposed by professionals from an external or elite perspective. Instead, spiritually sensitive practice is a process of empathic and respectful person-centered engagement and dialogue. The remainder of this chapter identifies spiritual needs expressed by older adults and the clinical contexts where these needs may be addressed. Eleven domains of spirituality that may be addressed in the assessment process are considered, as well as sample questions that explore these domains. The need for self-reflection on the part of social workers who consider using spiritually focused activities with older adults is discussed and then types of spiritual activities that may be used under different circumstances are identified. Finally, ethical considerations for use of any type of spiritually focused helping activities are presented.

SPIRITUAL NEEDS AND CLINICAL CONTEXTS OF OLDER ADULTS

Spiritual Needs

Spiritual needs pertain to the universal desire to locate meaning and purpose in life. Among many types of spiritual needs, there are three commonly expressed by older adults: the need to create meaning and purpose, the need to become empowered through connection to a Higher Power/Transcendent Force or Nature, and the need to give and receive support through affiliation. Entering a later stage of the life course compels one to find meaning in one's life. This often includes looking beyond the immediate situation and refraining from defining oneself according to immediate circumstance. For example, one woman residing in a nursing care facility was overheard to describe herself as "wheelchair-bound with bad eyesight and a bad heart." Although that self-description was physically accurate, this individual was also proud to be a grandmother of 11 with an award-winning talent in writing children's literature.

Many older adults need to be able to find empowerment through their sense of connection to a Higher Sacred Power. A 66-year-old client of one of the authors had coped relatively well with Parkinson's disease and bipolar illness, but when she received a diagnosis of cancer in her nasal passage, her coping mechanisms were overwhelmed. A devout Catholic, she was very angry at God but felt her faith did not allow her to be angry, resulting in internal conflict that she was unable to resolve alone. The author helped her expand her view of God and, with her permission, contacted her chaplain for a visit.

Continuing old affiliations or making new ones is a way to remain connected to community and continue to make contributions. In older ages, adults typically receive many services; they need to know that they can still make significant contributions to others, whether through sharing wisdom-based stories or imparting knowledge gained as a by-product of lifelong vocational pursuits. They value the support they both receive and provide to others.

Clinical Contexts

There are numerous life challenges across settings where spirituality may be a resource for older adults who value this expression. For more information about social work practice in particular settings such as community-based services, long-term care, and hospice, see other chapters in this volume. There are four common contexts for spiritually focused helping activities: coping with chronic or terminal illnesses, bereavement, relocation, and caregiving.

When chronic illness leads to pain or life limitation, older adults often feel discouraged. One active response is to use emotion-focused coping (Lazarus & Folkman, 1986). "Religion helps me in a lot of ways. When I feel that I'm depressed about things, it just seems that I think about how the Lord is able and He rules the world. When I get that feeling, it helps," commented one older African American female study respondent (Nelson-Becker, 2004). Social workers may support clients by engaging with the spiritual support systems, language, and symbolism that appeal in accordance with clients' orientation on the spiritual/religious continuum.

Bereavement is difficult at any age, but losses are magnified in later life when one's life companion dies and friendship networks begin to thin. The loss of spouse, close siblings, friends, and pets can be very painful. Older adults' physical and mental well-being is often compromised during the bereavement process. One's spiritual beliefs and practices may bring comfort for those who suffer from the loss of important companions and grapple with the meaning of life and the deaths of their significant others. Spiritual mentors, such as clergy or wise friends and relatives, as well as religious or nonreligious spiritual support groups can provide guidance and social healing that help the bereaved individual build a life without the physical presence of the deceased.

Older adults who transition to greater levels of care, often in new locations, find it hard to maintain contact with their faith communities. In such cases, religious television and radio programs may take on new significance. Engagement with familiar religious activities, such as prayer, meditation, scripture reading, reciting a mantra or rosary, and attending religious ceremonies, can be facilitated for interested clients. Spirituality can thus be a special resource that aids in the transition process until the older adult is able to build new supports.

Caregiver burden is becoming an increasing concern as older adults live longer with chronic conditions (Centers for Disease Control, 2004). Researchers have begun to explore the role of caregivers' spirituality as well as the role of spirituality for the older adult. Spirituality has been viewed as a resource in dealing with multiple physical, emotional, and social demands that contribute to this burden. T. Koenig (in press) found that spirituality was used by caregivers to resolve ethical dilemmas. Overall, the clinical context of the problem an older adult encounters as well as the personal stance of the older adult may indicate whether spiritually based activities should be considered as potential resources.

SPIRITUAL ASSESSMENT

Many social work agencies now incorporate some questions on religion and spirituality as part of their formal intake process. Usually this takes the form of one or two brief questions surrounding religious affiliation and church/synagogue/spiritual group attendance. In social work and aging, Ortiz and Langer (2002) developed a short protocol for conducting spiritual assessments with older adults, and Ai and colleagues (in press) have developed a spiritual support scale. Olson and Kane (2000) conducted a broader review of ways to measure or assess spirituality in older adults, though this takes less of a clinical focus. In addition, social work has developed spiritual assessment tools to assist practitioners (Bullis, 1996; Canda & Furman, 1999; Hodge, 2001; Nelson-Becker, 2005), as have medicine and nursing (Anandarajah & Hight, 2001; Fitchett, 1993; H. G. Koenig, 2002; Puchalski & Romer, 2000; Sulmasy, 2002). The Fetzer Institute (1999) has an excellent resource for measurement of religious and spiritual dimensions that also has some possibilities for clinical application with older adults.

Spiritual assessment with older adults should form part of a comprehensive assessment that is ongoing. Some older adults consider religion and spirituality to be private matters, so they may not be forthcoming about these dimensions in the beginning. An essential starting point in spiritually sensitive practice is to create a supportive and collaborative space for older adults to freely reflect on their religious and spiritual views and experiences according to their own interests. For example, a social worker might initiate a conversation in a casual manner by mentioning the presence of a spiritual painting in the client's living room. Such an invitation creates an opportunity to make a smooth transition to conducting a spiritual assessment.

Spiritual assessment can help the social worker to determine whether the client would like to explore spirituality further by receiving counseling from the social worker or referrals to other resources. Before embarking on a detailed spiritual assessment, the social worker should ask four preliminary questions:

1. What helps you to experience a deep sense of meaning, purpose, and moral perspective in your life?
2. Are spirituality, religion, or faith important in your life? If so, please give examples. If not, please explain why they are not important.
3. If important to you, what terms for referring to spirituality, religion, or faith do you prefer?
4. Would you like to incorporate spirituality, religion, or faith in our work together? Please explain.

Posing these questions is crucial in setting an appropriate framework to customize the questions that are consistent with the client's orientation and needs. In Table 74.1, we present 11 domains of spiritual assessment that we developed from previously cited sources along with examples of questions for use as an assessment tool or guide. The goal of this guide is to obtain a comprehensive understanding of an older adult's relationship to spirituality.

In conducting an assessment, a worker needs to be ready to frame and present assessment questions in a manner that the client can easily understand and to which he or she can relate. Conducting a thorough spiritual assessment based on Table 74.1 is quite a formidable task to accomplish. We recommend that the extent of assessment and the selection and wording of questions should be determined by the issues at hand, the setting and nature of the client-worker relationship, and the social worker's clinical expertise. Spiritual assessment may be incorporated into ongoing work with the client if time allows. The simple act of asking these questions to explore the client's spiritual life together itself may generate a therapeutic effect, bringing some insights and clarification to issues that are important to the client. In some cases, simply asking the previous four preliminary questions will be sufficient.

SPIRITUALLY FOCUSED HELPING ACTIVITIES

All social work activities with older adults may be framed within a spiritually sensitive practice approach if the social worker is intentional about his or her own spiritual development and aware of the spiritual path. Thus, although the social worker may not use explicit spiritual activities with a client either because they are outside the area of focus or the older adult has no interest in spirituality or religion, the social worker may utilize implicit spiritual sensitivity in preparing for his or her own interactions throughout the day. Explicit spiritually focused helping activities are those activities that help older adults by promoting profound healing or spiritual development. These activities may be as-

TABLE 74.1. Eleven Domains to Explore During Spiritual Assessment

	Domains	*Definitions*	*Relevant Questions*
1	Spiritual Affiliation	The formal religious or nonreligious spiritual groups with which the client closely identifies his or her orientation.	✓ Do you belong to any spiritual/religious group? ✓ What does membership in this group signify to you? ✓ Do you express your spirituality outside of participation in a religious or spiritual support group?
2	Spiritual Beliefs	Perspectives and ideas related to existential issues, the divine, nature, meaning, or purpose in life.	✓ What religious or spiritual beliefs give you comfort or hope? Describe. ✓ What religious or spiritual beliefs upset you? Describe. ✓ Do you believe in God, a Transcendent Power, or Sacred Source of meaning? ✓ Describe your vision of who God or this Sacred or Higher Power is. ✓ How would your beliefs influence your medical decisions if you became very ill? Would your beliefs interfere with or enhance your medical care in any way? ✓ Do you believe in an afterlife? What does this mean for you now?
3	Spiritual Behavior	The spiritual practices or actions engaged in daily or special occasions such as prayer, meditation, or worship (including both private and public, organizational and nonorganizational).	✓ What religious or spiritual behaviors do you engage in? ✓ How often do you engage in these religious or spiritual behaviors? ✓ Do you engage in these privately, with family, or in spiritual groups? ✓ What about these behaviors do you find nourishing or undermining?
4	Emotional Qualities of Spirituality	Feelings associated with spiritual beliefs and/or experiences/activities (both positive and negative).	✓ Have you recently experienced an emotion such as anger, sadness, guilt, joy, love, or relief in the context of religious or spiritual experiences? ✓ What significance, if any, did this have for you? ✓ What feelings did you have in response to (a specific experience)?
5	Values	Moral principles and ethical guidelines derived from spiritual beliefs.	✓ What are the guiding moral principles and values in your life? ✓ How do these principles guide the way you live?
6	Spiritual Experiences	Private or shared profound transcendent experiences shaping sacred meanings, including both ordinary and altered states of consciousness.	✓ Have you had any spiritual experiences that communicate special meaning to you? If so, please describe. ✓ Do you experience a connection with spiritual forces such as God, angels, spirits, or deceased loved ones?
7	Spiritual History	Developmental trajectory of spiritual beliefs, values, practices, and experiences. Includes both gradual change and pivotal points involving crisis or life enhancement.	✓ Were you raised in a spiritual or religious tradition? Do you now practice in the tradition in which you were raised? Describe early experiences and parental involvement. *(continued)*

TABLE 74.1. Eleven Domains to Explore During Spiritual Assessment *(continued)*

	Domains	Definitions	Relevant Questions
			✓ In what decades of your life were you involved in spiritual practices? Would you rate your involvement as low, medium, or high for each? Were there any change points?
			✓ What events in your life were especially significant in shaping your spirituality?
			✓ Who encouraged your spiritual or religious practices?
			✓ Describe any spiritual breakthroughs that are relevant to you now.
8	Therapeutic Change Factors	Unique spiritually focused individual strengths and environmental resources available for healing, growth, and improvement of well-being.	✓ What might be an object or image that symbolizes/represents your spiritual strengths?
			✓ Could you tell me a story of how it helped you to cope with difficulties in the recent past?
			✓ How do you see that this particular spiritual strength may help your current problems?
			✓ What spiritually based strategies, rituals, or actions have helped you to cope with times of difficulty or to experience healing or growth?
9	Social Support	Assistance and support offered by other individuals and groups that promote client coping and spiritual well-being.	✓ When you have religious/spiritual concerns and problems, who do you talk to?
			✓ In the past, what types of supports have you received from these people?
10	Spiritual Well-Being	Client's subjective sense of happiness and satisfaction related to his or her spirituality.	✓ How worthwhile do you find living your current life? Can you tell me more about it? How does this relate to your spirituality?
			✓ How does your spirituality help you to find meaning in your life?
			✓ How strongly do you feel connected to God/Higher Power/Spiritual/Universe?
11	Extrinsic/ Intrinsic Spiritual Focus	Extrinsic focus: client's spiritual identity and orientation tied to a certain group membership and conformity.	✓ Do you find the teachings and values of your spiritual group similar to or different from your own? Please explain.
		Intrinsic focus: client's spiritual identity and orientation that may or may not be tied to a group membership, but is more flexible and relatively self-determined.	✓ How integrated are your spiritual practices with your daily life, apart from spiritual group participation?

Source: Developed from Nelson-Becker, Nakashima, & Canda (in press).

sociated with a religious organization or a nonreligious support group, or they may be private. A social worker may foster this type of helping indirectly through networking and/or collaboration with religious/spiritual organizations desired by the older adult or directly through exercise of spiritual activities during the session under specific conditions that are discussed below. Table 74.2 designates types of spiritually

focused practices and the conditions under which they may be considered for use.

Implicit Spiritual Activities

Spiritually sensitive practice with older adults develops when the social worker relates with the client

TABLE 74.2. Using Spiritually Focused Activities With Older Adults in Social Work

1. Client has not expressed interest in spirituality. (*Implicit Spiritual Sensitivity*)	A. Social worker uses other types of helping activities with client, for example:
	    1. Life review
	    2. Strengths-based interventions
	    3. Cognitive-behavioral techniques
	    4. Other therapeutic styles
	B. Social worker prepares self for therapeutic encounter through private spiritually based activities outside of session, for example:
	    1. Meditation
	    2. Relaxation
	    3. Visualization/imagery (e.g., seeing client surrounded by protective light)
	    4. Spiritual journaling
	    5. Engagement with a spiritual support group for grounding
	    6. Prayer for self-guidance
	C. Social worker engages with client in spiritually sensitive relationship, for example:
	    1. Relates with unconditional positive regard
	    2. Extends sense of hope to client until client can begin to build own
	    3. Listens with ears, mind, and heart to catch the meaning behind client verbalizations and nonverbalizations

2. Client has expressed interest, but social worker does not have relevant expertise or permission for direct use of spiritually focused activities; or social worker–older adult relationship has not yet been deeply established. (*Explicit Spirituality Focused Helping*)	D. Above activities plus (with caution): Social worker refers client to outside spiritual support systems, for example:
	    1. Ministers, rabbis, spiritual mentors with whom client already has relationship
	    2. Church/synagogue/mosque/temple leaders and spiritual teachers/healers congruent with client's expressed religious or spiritual affiliation
	    3. Other systems of potential spiritual support that are consistent with client interests

3. Client has expressed interest, *plus* a spiritually sensitive relationship and practice have been established. (*Explicit Spirituality Focused Helping*)	E. Social worker collaborates with outside spiritual support systems, for example:
	    1. Social worker works directly with outside supports chosen by client (e.g., chaplain or traditional healer) unless there is a concern
	    2. With client approval, social worker works with outside system members generally to build greater support for client or to assist in clarifying and mediating problems
	F. Above activities plus (with caution) direct use of spiritual helping activities by client request, for example:
	    1. Use of insights from spiritual/sacred writing
	    2. Exploration of personal sacred objects/symbols/stories
	    3. Use of art, music, poetry as therapy
	    4. Creation of spiritual map/time line including identification of significant mentors

(*continued*)

TABLE 74.2. Using Spiritually Focused Activities With Older Adults in Social Work *(continued)*

	5. Focused relaxation and breathing techniques
	6. Exploration of forgiveness issues
	7. Discussion of significant dreams
	8. Development of rituals/ceremonies
	9. Reading inspirational texts
	10. Discussion of attitudes toward death/dying/after-life
	11. Reflection on harmful/helpful aspects of spiritual group participation
4. Client has expressed interest, *plus* a spiritually sensitive practice has been established, *plus* social worker has credentials or qualifications for particular activities (*Explicit Spiritually Focused Helping*)	G. Above activities plus (with caution) direct use of technique/therapy/ritual for which social worker is formally sanctioned and client requests, for example:
	1. Use of prayer/religious ceremony with client when social worker is also a clergy person or recognized leader in the same religious group
	2. Biofeedback
	3. Jungian dreamwork
	4. Body-centered therapy
	5. Guided visualization
	6. Meditation with a spiritual focus (such as Zen mindfulness meditation or Christian centering prayer)
	7. Disciplines for healing and spiritual cultivation such as Reiki, Tai Chi, or hatha yoga
	8. Herbalism
	9. Acupuncture

Source: Adapted from Canda & Furman (1999, p. 254).

through genuine respect, unconditional positive regard, empathy, and openness to the client's distinctive spiritual perspective. These relational qualities should be the foundation of both implicit and explicit spiritually focused activities. Spiritual sensitivity requires explicit discussion of spirituality or use of overt spiritually focused activities only when appropriate for the client's goals and interests. Section 1 of Table 74.2 indicates some spiritually focused activities that may be appropriate when the client has not expressed interest in spirituality.

Establishing a personal intention to be fully and spiritually present helps center the social worker for whatever events or situations enter his or her physical, psychological, or emotional space. This type of preparation also is effective in countering compassion fatigue: It provides the ability to be fully connected to the present moment and manage the energy dissipation that often results from empathic engagement

with older adults who may experience many forms of pain. Building a work and/or home environment with inviting spaces, artwork, and beauty provides a place where one can release the accumulation of energy that may be absorbed in all facets of direct social work practice. Listening to calming sounds or relaxing music helps build a holding or safety zone. Creating supportive networks with other professionals, friends, and family and engaging in personal renewal strategies such as taking walks in a natural setting also provide a type of inoculation against burnout when work with older adults becomes very complex or sad.

Creativity is a principle that asks social workers to develop their imagination. Where the older adult can no longer see possibility, the task of the social worker is to help open up creative solutions in the context of the current difficulty. As Baltes and Baltes (1990) suggest, selective optimization with compensation encourages frail or disabled older adults to take full advantage of their ability level by choosing to focus on what they still can do, perhaps doing less of it or performing something differently and at a slower pace. An important task of the social worker is to reenvision the current situation and to assist older clients in reengaging their passions in innovative ways or to develop new ones.

Explicit Spiritual Activities

Spirituality can be engaged explicitly when the older adult has expressed interest in doing so. Sections 2, 3, and 4 of Table 74.2 indicate some explicitly spiritual activities that may be appropriate depending on the client's goals, the practice situation, and the qualifications of the social worker. Sections 2 to 4 represent increasingly direct levels of engaging spirituality. Greater caution to avoid inappropriate impositions of the social worker's own values and assumptions should be used as intrusiveness increases.

Basic explicit spiritually focused helping activities (section 2) are activities that do not necessarily require special training or supervision. On the first level, they may simply involve referral to outside spiritual support systems. For agents who are skilled at research and investigation, this may first involve locating the type of spiritual support system with which the older adult chooses to be affiliated and then facilitating the connection. At times, it may involve advocating for the older adult when the spiritual or religious system itself has been a source of misunderstanding, betrayal, or pain. It may involve collaboration when the older adult asks the social worker to share information or to remain in contact with the spiritual mentor or leader about some issue. As in all ethical social work practice, consents need to be signed for information sharing to occur.

If the older adult has expressed interest and a spiritually sensitive relationship is in place (Canda & Furman, 1999), the social worker may include activities directly in sessions, such as exploring personal sacred objects/stories or a spiritual time line (section 3). The activities described as possible choices should be used only if the social worker has competence or expertise in using them. Activities in section 4 require that the older adult expresses interest, a spiritually sensitive relationship has been established, and the social worker has credentials or qualifications to conduct the activity (e.g., assisting an older adult to interpret the contents of a dream through Jungian analysis).

Further Ethical Considerations

An important consideration in choosing to be engaged in any type of spiritually focused practice, whether implicit or explicit, involves thinking through ethical issues. Work with older adults involves a self-assessment process. In the context of practice, social workers often encounter situations that help them understand their own values better. They grow as they engage in self-reflection that assists in identifying limitations, biases, and negative attitudes. Achieving value clarity calls one to be open to explore personal understandings and to refine these understandings based on further evidence (Canda & Furman, 1999). Questions to ask oneself include: What types of experiences have I had that shaped my current reaction? What does this response suggest about my strengths and limits in regard to this helping situation and generally? Is there something here that I want to work on? If so, what is my plan?

Other principles that are important to consider from an ethical standpoint include respect, client-centeredness, and inclusivity (Canda & Furman, 1999; Canda, Nakashima, & Furman, 2004). Respect in work with older adults includes demonstrating respect for all secondary clients as well as the primary client. Sometimes family members have very different ideas from the older adult about what actions an older adult should take. Family members tend to privilege safety over independence and sometimes pressure their older relative to move to a more restricted environment where he or she will be safe. Respect involves recognition of the power of formal and informal support systems to provide important nurturance for clients and to listen to and address all viewpoints.

Client-centeredness involves honoring the older adult's aspirations, values, and dreams even when they are very different from our own. It means helping clients to achieve their goals, even when we might disagree that a goal is in their best interest. Related to this is the principle of inclusivity. Inclusivity concerns more than tolerance of an older adult's particular religious belief, for example, and includes honoring diverse spiritual expressions even when they are quite dissimilar from our own.

Before social workers engage in any type of spiritual helping activity with an older adult, they need to be clear that there is no motive aside from the welfare of the client. Even when the intent is only to help, the planned activity needs to be well considered. For example, if the social worker privately prays *for* a client with a petition for something that is contrary to the older adult's self-determined goal, this raises concerns about client self-determination and informed consent. Activities need to be performed in a way that honors the older adult and the traditions of the association or organization connected to the activity. Some activities are not permitted to be conducted outside of formal affiliation and authorization with the religious tradition, such as Christian sacraments and indigenous healing ceremonies. For example, unless a social worker is also an ordained or lay minister in a faith tradition that practices administration to the sick, also known as laying on of hands, and the older adult is a member of the same faith tradition or seeks out this ritual, it should not be practiced out of context. Not only should the social worker have competency and skill in the activity, but he or she also should have permission from the client and the culture or group that is associated with the activity to conduct it.

CONCLUSION

Spiritually focused assessment and helping activities should be included among the strategies social workers use with older adults, especially as spirituality tends to be important to older cohorts. Later life is a developmental time when spiritual questions often arise, even if they were not a concern at earlier life stages. If social workers are not comfortable addressing these issues themselves, more training should be sought or a referral network should be developed.

Older adults may be particularly aware of spiritual needs when they cope with challenges related to illness, death, relocation, and caregiving contexts. One of the resources this chapter presents is examples of questions that may be used to identify whether a client is interested in addressing spirituality and, if the client is interested, additional questions (Nelson-Becker, Nakashima, & Canda, in press). Implicit spiritual helping activities (those used to prepare for social work with older adults) and explicit spiritual helping activities (those that may be used directly with older adults) have been discussed, as well as ethical considerations on which to reflect when doing work in this area. A second resource included here identifies implicit and explicit types of spiritually focused helping activities and situations when they may be appropriate based on ethical considerations.

The resources contained in this chapter are intended to be very practical applications for social workers interested either in developing a spiritual component in their work with older adults or deepening and extending the spiritual foundation they already employ. Though there has recently been a surge of research in the areas of religion and spirituality, more specific research should be conducted related to aging studies. Gerontological social workers need to continue to explore spirituality through dialogue with other practitioners, researchers, educators, and older adults.

REFERENCES

Ai, A. (2000). Spiritual well-being, population aging, and a need for improving practice with the elderly: A psychosocial account. *Social Thought, 19*(3), 1–21.

Ai, A. L., Tice, T. N., Peterson, C., & Bu., H. B. (in press). Prayers, spiritual support, and positive attitudes in coping with the 9-11 national crisis. *Journal of Personality*.

Ahearn, F. L. (Ed.). (2001). Issues in global aging [Special issue]. *Social Thought, 20*(3/4).

Anandarajah, G., & Hight, E. (2001). Spirituality and medical practice: Using HOPE questions as a practical tool for spiritual assessment. *American Physician, 63*(1), 81–88.

Atchley, R. (2001). Spirituality. In G. L. Maddox (Ed.), *The encyclopedia of aging* (3rd ed., pp. 974–976). New York: Springer.

Baltes, P. B., & Baltes, M. M. (1990). Psychological perspectives on successful aging: The model of selective optimization with compensation. In P. B. Baltes & M. M. Baltes (Eds.), *Successful aging: Perspectives from the behavioral sciences* (pp. 1–34). New York: Cambridge University Press.

Bullis, R. K. (1996). *Spirituality in social work practice.* Washington, DC: Taylor & Francis.

Canda, E. R., & Furman, L. D. (1999). *Spiritual diversity in social work practice.* New York: Free Press.

Canda, E. R., Nakashima, M., & Furman, L. D. (2004). Ethical considerations about spirituality in social work: Insights from a national qualitative survey. *Families in Society, 85*(1), 27–35.

Carroll, M. (1998). Social works conceptualization of spirituality. *Social Thought, 18*(2), 1–13.

Centers for Disease Control. (2004). Chronic disease overview. Retrieved June 16, 2004, from *http://www.cdc.gov/nccdphp/overview.htm*.

Erikson, E. H., & Erikson, J. M. (1997). *The life cycle completed.* New York: Norton.

Fetzer Institute. (1999). *Multidimensional measurement of religiousness/spirituality for use in health research.* Kalamazoo, MI: Author.

Fitchett, G. (1993). *Assessing spiritual needs: A guide for caregivers.* Minneapolis: Augsburg Press.

Hodge, D. R. (2001). Spiritual assessment: A review of major qualitative methods and a new framework for assessing spirituality. *Social Work, 46*(3), 203–214.

James, W. (1961). *The varieties of religious experience.* New York: Collier Books. (Original work published 1902)

Joseph, M. V. (1988). Religion and social work practice. *Social Casework, 69*(7), 443–452.

Koenig, H. G. (2002). *Spirituality in patient care: Why, how, when, and what.* Philadelphia: Templeton Foundation Press.

Koenig, H. G., McCullough, M. E., & Larson, D. B. (2001). *Handbook of religion and health.* New York: Oxford University Press.

Koenig, T. (in press). Caregivers' use of spirituality in ethical decision making. *Journal of Gerontological Social Work.*

Krause, N. (1997). Religion, aging, and health: Current status and future prospects. *Journal of Gerontology, 52B,* S291–S293.

Lantz, J. (1998). Recollection in existential psychotherapy with older adults. *Journal of Clinical Geropsychology, 4*(1), 45–53.

Lazarus, R. S., & Folkman, S. (1984). *Stress, appraisal, and coping.* New York: Springer.

Levin, J. S. (2001). Religion. In G. L. Maddox (Ed.), *The encyclopedia of aging* (3rd ed., pp. 866–869). New York: Springer.

Levin, J. S., & Chatters, L. M. (1998). Research on religion and mental health: An overview of empirical findings and theoretical issues. In H. G. Koenig (Ed.), *Handbook of religion and mental health* (pp. 34–51). San Diego: Academic Press.

Lloyd, M. (1997). Dying and bereavement, spirituality, and social work in a market economy of welfare. *British Journal of Social Work, 27*(2), 175–190.

Marler, P. L., & Hadaway, C. K. (2002). Being religious or being spiritual in America: A zero-sum proposition? *Journal for the Scientific Study of Religion, 41*(2), 289–300.

Nakashima, M. (2003). Psychosocial and spiritual well-being among terminally ill older adults (Doctoral dissertation, University of Kansas, 2002). *Dissertation Abstracts International A: The Humanities and Social Sciences, 63,* 4095-A.

Nelson-Becker, H. B. (2003). Practical philosophies: Interpretations of religion and spirituality by African-American and Jewish elders. *Journal of Religious Gerontology, 14*(2/3), 85–99.

Nelson-Becker, H. B. (2004). Meeting life challenges: A hierarchy of coping styles in African-American and Jewish-American older adults. *Journal of Human Behavior in the Social Environment, 10*(1): 155–174.

Nelson-Becker, H. B. (2005). Development of a spiritual support scale for use with older adults. *Journal of Human Behavior in the Social Environment, 11*(3/4).

Nelson-Becker, H. B, Nakashima, M., & Canda, E. R. (in press). Spiritual assessment in aging: A framework for clinicians. *Journal of Gerontological Social Work.*

Olson, D. M., & Kane, R. A. (2000). Spiritual assessment. In R. L. Kane & R. A. Kane (Eds.), *Assessing older persons* (pp. 300–319). New York: Oxford University Press.

Ortiz, L. P., & Langer, N. (2002). Assessment of spirituality and religion in later life: Acknowledging clients' needs and personal resources. *Journal of Gerontological Social Work, 37*(2), 5–21.

Princeton Religious Research Center. (2001, March). Index of leading religious indicators remains at high level. *Emerging Trends, 23*(3), 1–5.

Puchalski, C. M., & Romer, A. L. (2000). Taking a spiritual history allows clinicians to understand patients more fully. *Journal of Palliative Medicine, 3,* 129–137.

Reese, D. J. (2001). Addressing spirituality in hospice: Current practices and a proposed role for transpersonal social work. In E. R. Canda & E. D. Smith (Eds.), *Transpersonal perspectives on spirituality in social work* (pp. 135–161). Binghamton, NY: Haworth Press.

Robbins, S. P., Chatterjee, P., & Canda, E. R. (1998). *Contemporary human behavior theory: A critical perspective for social work.* Boston: Allyn and Bacon.

Smith, E. D. (2001). Alleviating suffering in the face of death: Insights from constructivism and a transpersonal narrative approach. In E. R. Canda & E. D. Smith (Eds.), *Transpersonal perspectives on spirituality in social work* (pp. 45–61). Binghamton, NY: Haworth Press.

Sulmasy, D. P. (2002). A biopsychosocial-spiritual model of the care of patients at the end of life. *The Gerontologist, 42*(Special issue 3), 24–33.

Tillich, P. (1963). *The eternal now.* New York: Scribner.

Tirrito, T. (2000). The spirit of collaboration: Social work/the church/older adults. *Social Thought, 19*(3), 59–76.

Tornstam, L. (1994). Gero-transcendence: A theoretical and empirical exploration. In L. E. Thomas & S. A. Eisenhandler (Eds.), *Aging and the religious dimension* (pp. 203–229). Westport, CT: Auburn House.

C. Advocacy and Empowerment Models

KEVIN J. MAHONEY

KAREN ZGODA

Approaches to Empowering Individuals and Communities

75

Jane Addams, once described by FBI director J. Edgar Hoover as the most dangerous woman in America, was born in 1860 to an upper-class family and formally educated (Specht & Courtney, 1994). Abandoning her social class and the privilege it afforded, Addams dedicated her life to serving the poor. She worked hard to promote international peace and to improve the social conditions that caused poverty. Addams became internationally known for creating Hull House, a settlement house located in a poor, working-class neighborhood in Chicago. She strongly believed the poor were victims of social and economic conditions, so she lived and worked with these neighbors, in their cultural and community contexts, to help them help themselves (Addams, 1910).

Addams is credited with laying the groundwork for what is now called empowerment-based practice in social work. Building on the work of Addams, contemporary empowerment theory grew out of the progressive social movements of the 1960s and 1970s. These social movements, including the women's movement, the Black Power movement, and the welfare rights movement, were founded to change oppressive social conditions in the United States. Acting in accordance with the principle of self-determination, empowered communities and individuals fought for the right to determine their own fates. Micro- and macrolevel interventions of empowerment were designed to better the lives and communities of oppressed peoples and thus ultimately effect a progressive transformation in society (Gutiérrez, Parsons, & Cox, 1998).

Although specific definitions of empowerment abound, it is clear that many social workers are currently examining the significance of power for their clients (Gutiérrez, DeLois, & GlenMaye, 1995). Relying on a definition supplied by Solomon (1976), the National Association of Social Workers (NASW, 2001), as part of their National Committee on Racial and Ethnic Diversity, defines empowerment as essentially an individual's ability to do for himself or herself. This involves fostering a connection between an individual and his or her own power and reaching across cultural barriers to become further empowered. Lee (1994) adds to this definition by stating that the focus of empowerment should be on members of stigmatized groups. Askheim (2003), Boehm and Staples (2002), and Adams (2003) assert that empowerment deals with the transmission of power such that the disempowered take or receive power. In this case, individuals are the experts at using their skills, competencies, and self-determination to act in their best interest. The social worker facilitates this process. The World Bank (2002) defines empowerment in terms of poor people and their expansion of assets and capabilities such that they can assert power over the institutions that affect them.

Empowerment theory today is essentially a broad, yet fairly consistent, collection of concepts, methods, and models designed to develop power in individuals, families, groups, and communities (Gutiérrez et al., 1998). Empowerment theory asserts that there are numerous, perpetuating problems associated with an absence of power. Unequal access to resources, caused by an unequal distribution of power, prevents individuals and groups in oppressed communities from gaining the social goods they need. As a result, vulnerable persons are unable to shield themselves from the negative effects of oppression, including poor functioning in family and community systems.

The absence of power may produce intense feelings and behaviors. Pinderhughes (1994) asserts that individuals who are less powerful may feel less gratified, experience less pleasure and more pain, feel alone, fear their own anger and/or anger at the more powerful, fear abandonment, feel inferior, deprived, or incompetent, and have a strong tendency toward depression. Common behaviors among the less powerful include an inability to impact an external system or the self, projection of acceptable attributes (i.e., smart, attractive, competent) onto the power group, distrust, sensitivity to discrimination, paranoia, isolation, use of passive-aggressive behavior as a defense mechanism, rigidity in behavior to control feelings of powerlessness, striking out or becoming aggressive to avoid feeling powerless, and use of deception.

Major empowerment theorists recommend similar intervention strategies to achieve empowerment, most commonly beginning with an individual and expanding to include sociopolitical systems (Askheim, 2003; Cox & Parsons, 1993; Gutiérrez et al., 1998; Heumann, McCall, & Boldy, 2001; Lee, 1994). At an individual level, a relationship between the social worker and the client is established, linking families to needed services, raising consciousness, and empowering goals and outcomes. Individual goals may include increasing control over one's life, increasing self-confidence, and, as a result of increased knowledge and skills, better self-perception. If these elements are adequately addressed, individuals should be able to identify barriers to self-realization, increase power, and increase control over their life. At a structural level, the focus shifts to community and societal change. Social workers work with clients to gain knowledge about sociopolitical issues and power structures, develop advocacy skills, learn methods of sociopolitical change, and engage in social action. Fundamentally, work at this level deals with the social structures and power relations that construct barriers to individual and community empowerment. As a result of these interventions, people and communities resolve disempowering situations and thus rebuild and reclaim an empowered status in society. Outcomes of empowerment-based interventions may include changes in self-efficacy, self-awareness, feeling that one has rights, self-acceptance, critical thinking, knowledge, skills, assertiveness, asking for help, problem solving, accessing resources, practicing new skills, lobbying, community organization, collaboration, and political action.

It should be noted that, under the empowerment model, the relationship between social worker and client is based on collaboration and mutual responsibility, not the traditional professional-client relationship (Cox & Parsons, 1993; Guitérrez et al., 1998; Lee, 1994). Indeed, the success of the empowerment intervention depends heavily on the success of this relationship, also referred to as a balanced partnership or an egalitarian relationship. As problems of disempowerment are rooted in sociopolitical systems, social workers and clients should act as partners with a common interest in addressing the problem. Using dialogue and critical analysis, the social worker should both work with the client and facilitate the empowerment process of the client. Clients bring just as much valuable expertise to the problem situation as the social worker does.

EMPOWERING THE ELDERLY

The elderly face a unique set of factors that contribute to a loss of power (Cox & Parsons, 1993; Heumann et al., 2001; Thompson & Thompson, 2001; Waters & Goodman, 1990). At an individual level, the elderly cope with a decline in physical health, increase in mental stress (frequently as a result of depression, loss, and grief), and loss of social support systems, including peers and spouse. Elderly clients may view their problems as unique, personal, and theirs alone to solve. At a social level, many elderly individuals cope with economic loss from retirement, rising health care costs, poor housing, discrimination resulting from ageism, loss of status and contributory roles (i.e., from work and civic activities), political marginalization, continuing sociopolitical disadvantages for members of minority populations, and a disempowering social service model. These factors can interact to produce increased dependency, oppression, learned helplessness, internalization, and powerlessness and ultimately limit elders' independence and ability to actively participate in society. Indeed, due to ageism, an assumption may exist that the elderly need to be cared for and looked after, reducing unique needs to a focus on provision of care.

Elderly people in the United States value independence and privacy as the core of empowerment (Heumann et al., 2001; Waters & Goodman, 1990). Many seniors want to age in the home they have known their entire lives; to own that home and manage that household is empowerment. Many prefer not to depend on visiting service providers who gradually usurp more and more decisions for their own convenience.

Accordingly, when the elderly need care, they want efficient outcomes and concrete results (Boehm & Staples, 2002). In terms of empowerment, the elderly tend to focus on their financial situation and ability to maintain it. They also focus on improvements in health care, social networks, living conditions, and relations with family and friends. In contrast, social workers often focus on the process of empowerment, rather than the results of the process, thus reinforcing a professional-client relationship. To be considered worthwhile and effective by consumers, the empowerment process should be cost-effective in terms of time and effort and show tangible results.

THE CASH AND COUNSELING DEMONSTRATION AND EVALUATION

One approach for capturing and describing some of the ways social workers can work to empower individuals and families is through case example. The Cash and Counseling Demonstration and Evaluation (CCDE) shows how older adults and persons with disabilities who needed Medicaid-funded home- and community-based services were given the opportunity to direct and manage those services and the positive results that ensued. We begin by describing this intervention and its positive effects and then backtrack to examine the elements and techniques that empowered individuals and families and the roles that social workers can play.

Today, in most states, whether you are an elderly individual or a younger person with disabilities, if you need Medicaid assistance to perform major activities of daily living such as bathing, dressing, toileting,

transferring (walking), or eating, you will rarely have much say over who helps you or when they come, never mind what they actually do. But, for years, persons with disabilities have been saying, "If I had more control over my services, my quality of life would improve and I could meet my needs for the same amount of money or less." The Cash and Counseling Demonstration is, at its heart, a policy-driven evaluation of this basic belief.

The CCDE, funded by the Robert Wood Johnson Foundation and the Office of the Assistant Secretary for Planning and Evaluation in the U.S. Department of Health and Human Services, is a test of one of the most unfettered forms of consumer-directed care: offering elders and younger persons with disabilities a cash allowance in place of agency-delivered services. Operating under a research and demonstration waiver granted by the Centers for Medicare and Medicaid Services, 6,700 volunteers from across Arkansas, Florida, and New Jersey participated in this large-scale test, half of whom were randomly assigned to manage individualized budgets while the other half remained with traditional agency providers.

Consumers who meet project eligibility criteria and express interest in participating in CCDE are randomly assigned to participate in the program, managing a cash allowance to purchase services, or serve as a control group and receive services through the state's existing system. The evaluation compares outcomes for consumers receiving traditional service packages with those receiving cash allowances with respect to cost, quality, and satisfaction. The evaluation also examines impacts on informal caregivers and analyzes the experiences of paid workers.

In the Arkansas Cash and Counseling Demonstration, the first to get under way and therefore the first from which results are available, consumers had the opportunity to receive a monthly allowance, which they could use to hire their choice of caregivers (except spouses) and buy other services or goods (such as assistive devices and home modifications) to meet their personal care needs. Allowances were equal to the value of the number of hours of care consumers were expected to receive under the traditional Medicaid program, averaging about $350 per month. Consumers were required to develop written plans for managing the allowance and have them approved by counselors. In addition, virtually all consumers chose to have the program's fiscal agents write checks for their purchases and withhold payroll taxes for caregivers hired with the allowance. Consumers who were unable or unwilling to manage the allowance themselves could designate a representative, such as a family member, to do so for them.

The resulting analysis showed that when Arkansas Medicaid beneficiaries had the opportunity to direct their personal care services themselves, it significantly increased the proportion of consumers and (paid) caregivers who were very satisfied with their care, thinning the ranks of the dissatisfied in the process. Specifically, consumers were much more satisfied with the timing and reliability of their care, less likely to feel neglected or rudely treated by paid caregivers, and more satisfied with the way paid caregivers performed their tasks (Figure 75.1). The program also reduced some unmet needs for personal assistance services and substantially enhanced consumers' quality of life. Moreover, it produced these improvements without compromising consumer health or functioning (Foster, Brown, Phillips, Schore, & Carlson, 2003). There were no major incidents of fraud or abuse.

Both elderly and nonelderly adults had better experiences under Cash and Counseling than under agency-directed services, though impacts on most outcomes were larger for the nonelderly. In Arkansas, Cash and Counseling users of all ages were more likely than the agency-care group to receive paid care: 95%

of both elderly and working-age Cash and Counseling participants got paid care, compared with 79% of elderly and 68% of younger consumers who were supposed to get care from an agency. Even those who did receive agency care were provided only about two-thirds of the help they were eligible for, often because of agency staff shortages. In terms of Medicaid costs for their care, Cash and Counseling participants averaged about twice the cost of those assigned to agency care during the first year. However, by the second year, savings in nursing home and other long-term care costs offset nearly all of this extra cost (Dale, Brown, Phillips, Schore, & Carlson, 2003).

The effects on caregivers were equally dramatic. Caregivers for consumers managing the cash allowance experienced less financial, emotional, and physical strain. Furthermore, even though the workers hired by consumers frequently lacked formal training, they felt well-prepared for their jobs. Most were very satisfied with their pay and working conditions.

The results of the controlled experiment in Arkansas (and preliminary figures on the results in Florida and New Jersey) were so positive that the Robert Wood Johnson Foundation, the DHHS Office of the Assistant Secretary for Planning and Eval-

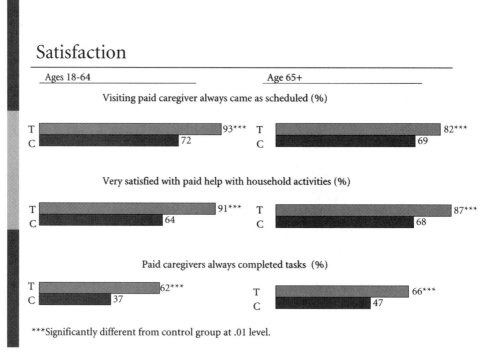

FIGURE 75.1.
Source: Mathematics Policy Research (2003).

uation, and the Administration on Aging have authorized funding to add 10 states to the demonstration in 2004.

HOW DOES CASH AND COUNSELING EMPOWER?

This case study gives us the opportunity to examine what the elements and activities are that empower or help to empower consumers. We can then draw lessons, on both the macro and the micro levels, suggesting ways social workers can work to enhance the power of older individuals, their families, and their communities.

We believe that the Cash and Counseling model itself empowered consumers. Some of the ways the model was operationalized formed empowerment tools in their own right, namely, providing information to facilitate informed decision making; designing the role of counselor/consultant to foster empowerment; building in opportunities for peer counseling and support; and introducing technological tools like Web-based programs for designing, approving, and revising cash plans and recording expenditures against those plans. We consider each in turn.

Consumers can be involved in directing their own home- and community-based services to varying degrees. Whereas our case example is drawn from the Medicaid world, parallel choices also exist in the private long-term care insurance arena. The levels of consumer empowerment in home- and community-based care can be characterized as in Table 75.1.

Under the original Cash and Counseling Demonstration, consumers could chose option C (and let the fiscal intermediary handle the paperwork of bookkeeping, check writing, tax paying, record keeping), or they could chose a modification of option D as long as they passed a skills test showing they understood their tax and labor law obligations and retained receipts showing they had spent the dollars to meet their personal care needs.

But remember: Cash and Counseling was a choice. The consumer could always choose to return to the traditional system. In this way, the design of the program was itself empowering. Consumers also played an active role in program design. Focus groups and surveys of representative samples of consumers provided valuable insights on who was interested in the Cash and Counseling choice and why, what features were attractive, what information consumers needed to make an informed choice, and what kind of supportive services they needed to manage their own cash allowances. Additional focus groups helped hone outreach messages and make sure program communications were understandable and efficient.

Cash and Counseling systematically involved consumers at three distinct levels: the state level, where the model was designed and monitored; the program operation level, where forms and training materials were pretested; and the individual level, where consumers were regularly asked for feedback on their sat-

TABLE 75.1. Levels of Consumer Empowerment in Home- and Community-Based Care

A. Enlightened Care Management	B. Consumer as Employer	C. Flexible Consumer Budget	D. Cash
Early forms of care management relied on a medical model where professionals made the key decisions as they were assumed to know what was best. But, under the best practice of care management, consumer preferences are elicited in the design of the care plan, and there is a regular feedback loop to ascertain consumer satisfaction.	At this level, we move from consumer involvement to consumer choice. Here the consumer is able to hire, manage, train, and even terminate his or her personal care worker.	At this level, the consumer has a choice over his or her whole service package. Instead of being limited to a personal care worker, the consumer has a budget that he or she can tailor to meet individual personal care needs. Consumers can purchase a variety of goods and services, including home modifications and assistive devices.	The ultimate form of consumer-directed care puts the dollars in the consumer's hands and does not restrict usage.

Less Empowerment ————————————————————————————→ *More Empowerment*

isfaction with all aspects of the program. Accessibility guidelines were developed (with separate funding) to make sure consumers with disabilities were truly able to take part in planning activities.

The model itself was empowering, but so, too, were some of the discrete ways the program was run. To put this another way, elements of the program design independently shifted power to the people.

Information: Knowledge Is Power

What information does a consumer need and want to make an informed decision? How much information is too much? What formats works best for which consumers? What reading level should be assumed? These questions were regularly revisited as the Cash and Counseling options were developed. Focus groups were used to get initial impressions about the program and to pretest program communications. Various approaches to training were tested on a small scale before going public. All materials were available in frequently used languages and in varied formats appropriate for persons with disabilities. The questions of who, to whom, what, when, where, why, and how to share information are critical in the health care and social service decisions.

The Consultant: Institutionalizing the Role of Power Broker

The job title for the counselor/consultant/support broker could well be "empowerment agent." Counselors interacted with consumers to (1) help consumers think expansively about their personal assistance needs and how best to meet them (this is often referred to as "person-centered planning"); (2) review initial and revised spending plans to ensure that they include only permissible goods and services; (3) assist consumers in linking up with necessary resources (e.g., how to find personal care workers or identify the best source of other goods and services); (4) help with employer functions; and (5) monitor the consumer's condition and the uses of the allowance. The consultant's role is described in ethnographic studies of Cash and Counseling participants in Arkansas and New Jersey (Cash and Counseling Library, available online at *http://www.cashand counseling.org/library*). For the counselors' own perceptions, one could also read *Consumer and Counselor Experiences in the Arkansas Independent Choices Program* (Mathematica Policy Research, 2004). Perhaps

the best hands-on guide to what counselors actually do can be found in the recently published "Guide to Quality in Consumer Directed Services" (Applebaum, Schneider, Kunkel, & Davis, 2004, pp. 35–44) in the pages devoted to consumer support strategies.

Peer Support

When the Cash and Counseling program held focus groups to secure consumer input, consumers stayed after every session and traded phone numbers and ideas on how to manage their personal assistance needs. Thus, the program's designers learned one quick lesson: Adults like to learn from people who have real-life experiences similar to their own. Drawing on this insight, the Cash and Counseling Demonstration devoted resources to encouraging peer interaction and support.

The Increasing Importance of Technology

Technology can empower. The flexibility to use the cash allowance for a wide range of goods and services paid dividends: Non-elderly treatment group members might have received fewer hours of total care because they reduced their need for human assistance. Treatment group members were more likely to obtain equipment to help with personal activities and communications, such as specialized telephones, lifts, or emergency response systems. (Dale et al., 2003).

As Cash and Counseling expands to additional states, one of the most promising activities is the development of a Web-based tool to assist in the development, approval, and revision of cash plans and the recording of expenditures made against those plans so consumers can have an up-to-the-minute picture of how much of their cash allowance is still on hand. Focus groups showed that a sizable proportion of consumers or their representatives had access to computers and favored such a Web-based tool to expedite communication between themselves and their counselors and fiscal management agencies.

WHY DID CASH AND COUNSELING HAVE SUCH SIGNIFICANT EFFECTS?

There may be a couple of reasons why the Cash and Counseling model has such dramatic effects on both consumers and their informal caregivers. The first centers on locus of control and the ability to affect one's environment. The second reason this model may have enjoyed such success is that the flexible budget often allowed and encouraged greater integration of the consumer into the family and the community. The flexible budget allows clients to hire family and friends (i.e., individuals with a personal caring relationship with the consumer) to be their personal care workers. It also releases the consumer from many of the restrictions typical of agency-delivered care. For example, agency workers, for liability reasons, are often not allowed to take consumers in their cars. With the flexible cash allowance, consumers could ask their worker to drive them to a grocery store so they could do their own shopping. Consumer-employed workers defined quality in terms of the relationship. Knowing that the consumer is in charge, and providing services according to his or her preferences, was a consistent theme.

Finally, the flexible cash allowance makes it possible for consumers to reciprocate and maintain some symmetry in their interpersonal relations. In line with exchange and equity theories, there is evidence to believe that individuals may be less depressed when relationships promote feelings of respect and value (Wolff & Agree, 2004).

EMPOWERING COMMUNITIES

We have seen how social workers, as program designers, can empower individuals and families, and we have seen how social work clinicians, taking on the role of counselor and consultant, can empower individuals and families. We also want to mention ways that social workers can empower communities. Again, we draw from home- and community-based services experiences. In a recent issue of *Community Living Briefs,* Lee Bezanson (2003, p. 5) describes "Beyond Incremental Change: The Challenge of Inclusion":

> In the model community approach, states' resources are being committed to engaging local communities to become fully accessible and inclusive. Medicaid and the social service network of providers and advocates are at the table, but so too are citizens with disabilities, the Town Selectmen, the Superintendent of Schools, the religious institutions, the Rotary Club, Kiwanis. The dialogue is inclusive of everyone. And from these new dialogues new local initiatives emerge: ac-

cessible meetings with accessible materials, accessible voting places, city councils and task forces with members who have disabilities, public education on the need for universal design in new buildings, a Hoyer lift at the town pool . . . the list is endless.

DISCUSSION AND CONCLUSION

The Cash and Counseling Demonstration is but one example of how social workers and the elderly can work together in partnership to actualize empowerment-based practice. This program was designed to build on the assets and capabilities of elderly clients by allowing them to choose their care providers and services. Elderly clients worked with program consultants to put their monetary allowances to good use, often saving money and markedly increasing satisfaction with care in the process. In fact, so powerful were these effects that caregivers of the elderly also felt significant positive effects as a result of program participation. Giving the elderly the power of choice and the resources to make choices about their care reduces feelings and behaviors associated with disempowerment. Having consultants on hand and the future development of a technology-based allowance management system also assist in developing client capabilities. In essence, the Cash and Counseling Demonstration respects the independence and dignity of the elderly while delivering tangible results.

This case study has allowed us to see many of the principles and attributes of empowerment described in the first sections of this chapter, but it has also put meat on the bones—giving examples of discrete practices social workers can engage in at both the micro and macro levels to return power to older persons.

Some, fueled by ageism, contend that older persons are not interested in consumer-directed care. Clearly, this is not true. The Cash and Counseling model is not an option for everyone, but it is important to note that in Arkansas fully 72% of those who volunteered to participate were over age 65.

Finally, what about social workers? Some had feared that an emphasis on empowerment might undermine the professionalization of social work. In this case study, we see evidence that the most empowering assistance social workers can offer the elderly is to work with them where they are, both mentally and physically, and to start with the client's goals and preferences. Consumers are usually the experts when it comes to their own lives and lifestyles. Our overarching goal as social workers is to help them maintain and improve their independence and dignity. In doing so, we revisit the very roots of social work. We work with the community, in their community, to help them help themselves, continuing a tradition that we hope Jane Addams would embrace today.

REFERENCES

Adams, R. (2003). *Social work and empowerment* (3rd ed.). Basingstoke, England: Palgrave Macmillan.

Applebaum, R. A., Schneider, B., Kunkel, S. R., & Davis, S. (2004). *A guide to quality in consumer directed services.* Unpublished manuscript. Scrips Gerontology Center, University of Miami, Ohio.

Askheim, O. P. (2003). Empowerment as guidance for professional social work: An act of balancing on a slack rope. *European Journal of Social Work, 6*(3), 229–240.

Bezanson, L. (2003). Beyond incremental change: The challenge of inclusion. *Community Living Briefs: ILRU Exchange, 1*(3), 1–7.

Boehm, A., & Staples, L. H. (2002, October). The functions of the social workers in empowering: The voices of consumers and professionals. *Social Work, 47*(4), 449–460.

Cox, E. O., & Parsons, R. J. (1993). *Empowerment-oriented social work practice with the elderly.* Pacific Grove, CA: Brooks/Cole.

Dale, S., Brown, R., Phillips, B., Schore, J., & Carlson, B. L. (2003, November 19). "The effects of cash and counseling on personal care services and Medicaid cost in Arkansas." *Health Affairs,* W3, 566–575.

Foster, L., Brown, R., Phillips, B., Schore, J., & Carlson, B. (2003, March 23). Improving the quality of Medicaid personal assistance through consumer direction. *Health Affairs,* W3, 162–175.

Gutiérrez, L., DeLois, K., & GlenMaye, L. (1995, November). Understanding empowerment practice: Building on practitioner-based knowledge. *Families in Society: The Journal of Contemporary Human Services, 76*(9), 534–542.

Gutiérrez, L., Parsons, R., & Cox, E. (1998). *Empowerment in social work practice: A sourcebook.* Pacific Grove, CA: Brooks/Cole.

Heumann, L. F., McCall, M. E., & Boldy, D. P. (2001). *Empowering frail elderly people: Opportunities and impediments in housing, health, and support service delivery.* Westport, CT: Praeger.

Lee, J. A. B. (1994). *The empowerment approach to social work practice.* New York: Columbia University Press.

Mathematica Policy Research. (2004, January). *Consumer and counselor experiences in the Arkansas Independent Choices Program* (MPR Reference No. 8349-108). Princeton, NJ: Author.

National Association of Social Workers, NASW National Committee on Racial and Ethnic Diversity. (2001, June 23). *NASW standards for cultural competence.* Retrieved August 17, 2004, from *http://www.socialworkers.org/sections/credentials/cultural_comp.asp.*

Pinderhughes, E. (1994). Empowerment as an intervention goal: Early ideas. In L. Gutiérrez & P. Nurius (Eds.), *Education and research for empowerment practice* (pp. 17–30). Seattle, WA: Center for Policy and Practice Research.

Solomon, B. (1976). *Black empowerment.* New York: Columbia University Press.

Specht, H., & Courtney, M. E. (1994). *Unfaithful angels: How social work has abandoned its mission.* New York: Free Press.

Thompson, N., & Thompson, S. (2001). Empowering older people: Beyond the care model. *Journal of Social Work, 1*(1), 61–76.

Wolff, J. L., & Agree, E. M. (2004). Depression among recipients of informal care: The effects of reciprocity, respect, and adequacy of support. *Journal of Gerontology, 59B*(3), S173–S180.

World Bank. (2002). *Empowerment and poverty reduction* (D. Narayan, Ed.). Washington, DC: Author.

Advocacy is defined as the "pursuit of influencing outcomes—including public policy and resource allocation decisions within political, economic, and social systems and institutions—that directly affect people's lives" (Advocacy Institute, 2004). It involves one party seeking to represent the interests of another, although it should be noted that those interests are not always congruent. The terms "advocacy" and "lobbying," often used interchangeably, are not synonymous. Advocacy refers to a range of activities, such as mass media campaigns, community organizing, formal legal proceedings, and public policy research, undertaken in an attempt to raise awareness and change government policy. Lobbying is a specific type of advocacy activity that is focused on influencing legislation (e.g., a mass media campaign undertaken to defeat or support a proposed piece of legislation). Lobbying efforts, therefore, are directed at a legislative body (Duitch, n.d.).

As part of their everyday work, social workers deal with people's immediate problems and concerns, often on a one-to-one basis. But individual problems are often related to larger social issues. Advocating to government agencies or lawmakers or appealing to the public for macrolevel change is essential to help communities of people and to address policy issues of importance to social workers. But change does not happen overnight. It is a long process involving research, discussions, compromise, and political maneuvering. At every stage, outside voices are making recommendations and applying pressure for particular changes (Duitch, n.d.).

This chapter focuses on national advocacy groups for older adults. Although individual advocacy in social work is important and necessary, organizational advocacy also is essential and has the advantage of potentially bringing greater and more sustained resources to advocacy efforts (McConnell, 2004). Organizational advocacy can be most powerful when combined with individual stories, thereby giving a personal face to the issues.

ORGANIZATIONAL ADVOCACY

Organizational advocacy can take a variety of forms. Steve McConnell (2004), senior vice president for policy and advocacy for the Alzheimer's Association, delineates five distinct types. Legislative advocacy, one of the most familiar types, involves attempts by an organization to influence legislation to the benefit of a group of individuals or a cause. There is also admin-

LINDA KROGH HAROOTYAN
GREG O'NEILL

National Advocacy Groups for Older Adults

76

istrative advocacy, in which the target of influence is government agencies. Government agencies should not be underestimated in terms of advocacy, for they largely determine how a law is carried out. Program advocacy, yet another type, is directed at improving services for a specific population by changing organizational practice. These efforts are typically focused either on service organizations or the trade organizations representing their interests. Issue advocacy, which frequently precedes legislative advocacy or lobbying, is designed to influence public opinion on a particular issue. A fifth type of organization advocacy, legal advocacy, relies on the courts to bring about social or policy change.

EARLY ADVOCACY EFFORTS

Early national efforts to advocate on behalf of older persons were largely undertaken by a small cadre of "policy elites located inside government itself" (Hudson, 2004, p. 18). The earliest advocacy efforts are thought to have occurred in the 1920s around pension issues (National Association of State Units on Aging [NASUA], 1985). The National Association of Retired Federal Employees, created in 1921, was one of the first advocacy organizations to appear on the national scene and sought to improve federal retirement benefits. In 1935, the Social Security Act was passed, the first piece of legislation to specifically address the needs of older persons. In 1950, the Federal Security Agency sponsored the first National Conference on Aging in Washington, DC. Shortly thereafter, advocate Ethel Percy Andrus founded the American Association of Retired Persons and the National Retired Teachers Association (AARP-NRTA) to assert the interests of retired teachers.

It was not until the 1960s that advocacy became more formalized. In 1961, the first White House Conference on Aging convened in Washington, DC, giving much-needed visibility to aging issues. Advocacy during these early years was largely rooted in activist movements: civil rights, women's rights, and disability rights (Stone, 2004). New organizations emerged in response to major enacted legislation: Medicare and the Older Americans Act. The Older Americans Act not only established new programs and services for older adults, but also created a national administrative network on aging, the Administration on Aging and the State Units and Area Agencies on Aging (National Association of State Units on Aging [NASUA], 1985). The incremental construction of an old-age welfare state through Social Security, Medicare, the Older Americans Act, and other measures created a latent constituency of older voters as well as a number of old-age interest groups (Binstock, 2004). "By the late 1970s," Hudson (2004, p. 19) observes, "an imposing, bureaucratic, mass-based advocacy and policy network was in place for the aged."

NATIONAL-LEVEL ADVOCACY

Nonprofit Organizations

Today, organizations advocating at the national level for the well-being of older persons are numerous and diverse (see Figure 76.1). They play a central role in articulating the special needs of older Americans on many important issues. Most of these groups are represented in the membership of the Leadership Council of Aging Organizations (LCAO), a coalition of national aging organizations established in 1978. The coalition was founded, in part, to defend existing benefit levels in old-age programs. At the time, President Nixon was trying to shift responsibility for the needs of older persons from the public to the private sector. Attempts were being made to abolish the Senate Special Committee on Aging. And significant cuts in human services and Social Security were being proposed in federal budgets.

The growth of the LCAO, both in terms of number of members (14 member organizations in 1978, 52 in 2004) and types of organizations represented, closely parallels the evolution of programs and services for older persons in this country over the second half of the 20th century. In 1980, LCAO had 23 member organizations; their key issues at the time included Social Security financing, universal national health insurance, senior housing, long-term care, and ageism. Over the next 20 years, LCAO more than doubled in size, encompassing many organizations representing broadly defined health-related interests (e.g., Catholic Health Association of the United States, American Public Health Association).

During this time, many organizations were creating special units or sections to address issues related to older persons. A fundamental shift in LCAO occurred when organizations that did not have the interests of older persons as their primary focus wanted to be included under the LCAO advocacy umbrella. For example, the National Association of Social Workers (NASW), the profession's largest membership organization, reports that fewer than 5% of its

OLDER PEOPLE
AARP
AFL-CIO
AFSCME Retiree Program
Alliance for Retired Americans
American Federation of Teachers, Program on Retirement & Retirees
Gray Panthers
National Committee to Preserve Social Security and Medicare
United Auto Workers Retired Workers Dept.
Military Officers Association of America
National Association of Retired Federal Employees

NATIONAL AGING NETWORK
National Association of Area Agencies on Aging
National Association of State Units on Aging

PROFESSIONALS AND SERVICE PROVIDERS
American Association of Homes and Services for the Aging
American Society of Consultant Pharmacists
Association of Jewish Aging Services of North America
B'nai B'rith International Center
Eldercare America, Inc.
National Academy of Elder Law Attorneys
National Association for Home Care and Hospice
National Association of Professional Geriatric Care Managers
National Association of Social Workers
National Senior Citizens Law Center
United Jewish Communities
Volunteers of America

SPECIAL POPULATIONS
Alzheimer's Association
American Foundation for the Blind
Asociacion Nacional Pro Personas Mayores
National Asian Pacific Center on Aging
National Caucus and Center on Black Aged
National Citizens' Coalition for Nursing Home Reform
National Hispanic Council on Aging
National Indian Council on Aging, Inc.
Older Women's League

RESEARCH, EDUCATION, and CLINICAL PRACTICE
Alliance for Aging Research
American Association for International Aging
American Geriatrics Society
American Society on Aging
Association for Gerontology and Human Development in Historically Black Colleges
The Gerontological Society of America
National Council on the Aging, Inc.

AGING PROGRAMS
Experience Works
Meals on Wheels Association of America
National Association of Foster Grandparent Program Directors
National Association of Nutrition and Aging Services Programs
National Association of Retired and Senior Volunteer Program Directors
National Association of Senior Companion Project Directors
National Association of State LTC Ombudsman Programs

HEALTH
American Public Health Association
Catholic Health Association
Families USA
National Osteoporosis Foundation

FIGURE 76.1. Leadership Council of Aging Organizations (2004), types of constituencies served.

members identify aging as their primary practice area (Barth, 2003). However, growing awareness of the aging of their client population has led NASW to become more involved and active in aging issues, as evidenced by their joining the LCAO in 2004.

Today, LCAO includes professional organizations representing a wide range of interests and constituencies in the field of aging, including retired union members (e.g., National Council of Senior Citizens,

United Auto Workers Retired Workers Department); the aging network (e.g., National Association of Area Agencies on Aging, National Association of State Units on Aging); aging service programs (e.g., National Association of Nutrition and Aging Service Programs); providers of aging services (e.g., American Association of Homes and Services for the Aging, National Academy of Elder Law Attorneys); special segments of the older population (e.g., National Center and Caucus on Black Aged, Asociacion Nacional Pro Personas Mayores, Older Women's League, Alzheimer's Association); professionals working in the field (e.g., NASW, National Association of Professional Geriatric Care Managers); and gerontological researchers and educators (e.g., Gerontological Society of America, American Geriatrics Society).

LCAO also includes mass membership organizations of older persons that have been particularly effective in gaining the attention of policymakers and decision makers (e.g., AARP, National Committee to Preserve Social Security and Medicare). The unique political power that these groups hold over policymakers and members of Congress stems from the perception that they can influence the voting behavior of their members (Binstock, 2004). With more than 35 million members, AARP is considered the most influential old-age interest group. AARP's annual expenditures on lobbying and public policy research easily exceed those of all other old-age interest groups combined. As Robert Binstock remarks, "It is probably not too much to say that if AARP took an advocacy position that all the other members of the LCAO coalition opposed, members of Congress and their staffs would be much more influenced by AARP's stance" (p. 51). Indeed, in 2003, AARP's expenditures on lobbying and lobbying-related activities—most of which was devoted to efforts to persuade Congress to pass a Medicare prescription drug benefit—exceeded those of all interest groups in Washington, including General Electric, Microsoft, Boeing, and General Motors (Gettlin & Vaida, 2004).

As LCAO, like the older population, has grown in size and diversity of interests represented, it has faced the challenge of speaking with a unified voice. The increasing number of LCAO member organizations with narrowly focused interests limits the coalition's ability to take positions on more broadly defined issues, particularly those relating to income security and health care issues. There is also the growing problem of competing interests among organizations representing providers, professionals, and older persons, especially as resources dwindle.

Federal Agencies

In addition to the network of private nonprofit organizations who advocate on behalf of older persons, there also is an important advocate for older persons in the federal structure. The Older Americans Act (OAA) of 1965 established the Administration on Aging (AoA), the federal focal point and advocate agency for older persons and their concerns (see Figure 76.2). In this role, it is AoA's responsibility to heighten awareness among other federal agencies, organizations, groups, and the public about the valuable contributions that older Americans make to the nation and alert them to the needs of vulnerable older people. In addition, the OAA created a national network of state units and area agencies on aging with broad responsibilities to serve as advocates on behalf of older persons and to plan for the effective development of state- and areawide service systems to best address their needs (NASUA, 1985).

CHALLENGES FOR FUTURE ADVOCACY

Advocacy efforts for older persons may face less popular support as the aging segment of the population changes. Today's older persons are no longer viewed as universally poor, frail, and socially dependent. Furthermore, knowing who is elderly is more difficult because programs for older persons created over the past century use eligibility ages ranging from 50 to 70 years. In addition, the elderly do not identify as a political group except on Social Security issues (Campbell, 2003). The emerging generation of older Americans is more diverse, is better educated, has a greater interest in personal choice and control, and is more skeptical of government than previous generations of older Americans (Rother, 2004). Future advocacy strategies will need to reflect these complexities and be open to a variety of options instead of focusing on a single solution (Rother, 2004).

Leadership is another challenge facing aging advocates. In the past decade, there has been a notable shortage of high-profile champions for aging issues. Advocates lack leaders inside government, people like statesman Arthur Flemming, who helped create the AoA and the White House Conference on Aging; Congressman and Senator Claude Pepper, who pushed health and long-term care policies for older persons and opposed mandatory retirement; and Senator John Heinz, who was an influential and effective leader in the Senate on aging issues. Leadership is lacking not only at the individual level but also at the aggregate level. There are no longer powerful advocates in Congress. The House Select Committee on Aging was abolished in 1993, and the Senate Special Committee on Aging has seen its sphere of influence diminished in recent years.

The future success of national advocacy groups, therefore, will depend on their collective ability to (1) clearly articulate the needs of America's aging

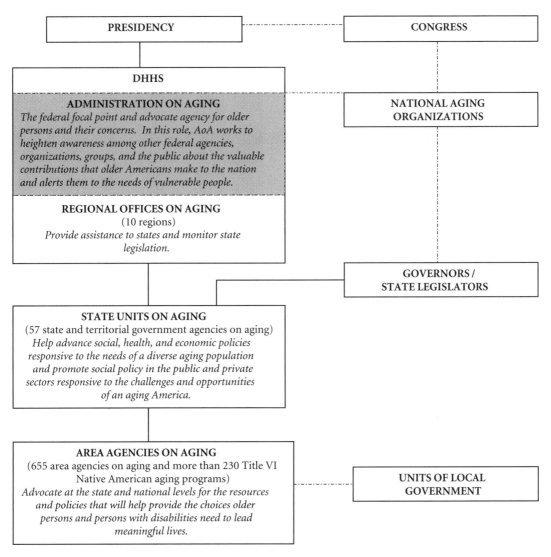

FIGURE 76.2. The National Aging Service Network.

population, (2) determine where shared interests lie on specific issues, (3) reach consensus on the most pressing issues, (4) identify a leader to champion their issues, and (5) sustain open channels of communication between the public and national leaders (NASUA, 1985).

Successfully meeting these challenges is critical to the future of aging programs. Although advocates can no longer expect to wield the influence of earlier days, their efforts are more important, and more difficult, than ever. The victories of earlier efforts resulted in programs on aging so large and successful that they have become a major focal point of national policy debates. Ironically, their very success makes them extremely vul-

nerable, as deficits continue to grow and Congress looks for ways to cut federal spending. Much is at stake. Developing new advocacy strategies and partnerships is essential if advocates are going to protect the programs so essential to the well-being of older people.

REFERENCES

Advocacy Institute. (2004). *What is advocacy?* Washington, DC. Retrieved June 17, 2004, from *http://www. advocacy.org.*

Barth, M. C. (2003). Social work labor force: A first look. *Social Work, 48,* 9–19.

Binstock, R. (2004). Advocacy in an era of neoconservatism: Responses of national aging organizations. *Generations, 28,* 49–54.

Campbell, A. (2003). *How policies make citizens: Senior political activism and the American welfare state.* Princeton, NJ: Princeton University Press.

Duitch, S. (n.d.). *Speak up: Tips on advocacy for publicly funded nonprofits.* New York: The Center for an Urban Future. Retrieved on June 17, 2004, from *http://www.nycfuture.org.*

Gettlin, R., & Vaida, B. (2004). K Street spending hit $2 billion in 2003. *National Journal, 24,* 1864–1865.

Hudson, R. (2004). Advocacy and policy success in aging. *Generations, 28,* 17–24.

McConnell, S. (2004). Advocacy in organizations: The elements of success. *Generations, 28,* 25–30.

National Association of State Units on Aging. (1985). *An orientation to the Older Americans Act.* Washington, DC: National Association of State Units on Aging.

Rother, J. (2004). Why haven't we been more successful advocates for elders? *Generations, 28,* 55–58.

Stone, R. (2004). Where have all the advocates gone? *Generations, 28,* 59–64.

Local, State, and Federal Policies/ Regulations Affecting Older Adults

OVERVIEW

This part of the Handbook discusses federal, state, and local policies and regulations that most directly affect older adults and their families. Effective social work practice with diverse groups of older adults and their families requires not only extensive knowledge of policies and regulations at multiple system levels but also expert skills for evaluating their impact and policy advocacy. This part is intended to provide students and practitioners with a critical overview of various policies, regulations, and attendant programs, with the hope that it will serve as a foundation for advanced policy analysis and advocacy skills.

Specifically, the part focuses on the following 10 key areas: (a) federal income maintenance policies and programs; (b) policies related to private retirement benefits; (c) health and mental health care policies—Medicare; (d) health and mental health care policies—Medicaid; (e) policies affecting long-term care in institutions and other long-term care issues; (f) policies affecting social services, housing, and transportation; (g) policies related to competency and proxy issues; (h) end-of-life policies; (i) policies affecting families of dependent older persons; and (j) policies to protect the rights of older adults. Each chapter provides a brief history of policy development; a critical evaluation of current status, gaps, and effectiveness; and future directions and recommendations. Implications for social work practice and policy advocacy are also discussed in the concluding section of each chapter.

In chapter 77, Choi discusses three important federal income maintenance programs for older persons: the Old-Age, Survivors, and Disability Insurance (OASDI) Program, or Social Security; the Supplemental Security Income (SSI) Program; and the Senior Community Service Employment Program (SCSEP). For each program, beneficiaries/participants, eligibility criteria, financing mechanisms and issues, and reform proposals or need for improvement are described and critically evaluated, with special attention to the program's effect on and implications for people of color, women, and/or low-income older persons.

Hudson begins chapter 78 with an overview of the development of private pensions and regulations governing private pensions in the United States. He then proceeds to discuss the types, roles, and functions of private pensions in the overall retirement income picture, recent trends in pension coverage, and the adequacy of private pensions in helping to meet the retirement needs of vulnerable populations.

In chapter 79, Lee describes Medicare program components, coverage, and eligibility. Recent changes, expansions, and additions to Medicare (such as Part D, outpatient prescription drug program) are described, and comparative advantages and disadvantages of the original Medicare provisions and those of changes are briefly illustrated. The chapter also covers issues related to projected Medicare financing difficulties, Medicare long-term care coverage and funding, and lack of mental health parity.

In chapter 80, Galambos provides a brief description of the historical context for the establishment of Medicaid and illustrates the program's basic standards and guidelines with respect to federal regulations, state responsibilities, and the impact of the Personal Responsibility and Work Opportunity Reconciliation Act of 1996. The author then examines programs and services available under Medicaid for older adults. In particular, dual eligibility, managed care, the freedom of choice and home- and community-based waiver programs, and Medicaid long-term care financing issues are discussed.

Given the looming issue of long-term care for the graying population, the content of chapter 81 is a timely topic. In this chapter, Chen examines the development of federal and state policies affecting institutional long-term care, especially nursing home care. She also discusses how the political, social, and economic changes have brought forth diversification in long-term care service settings where new issues of regulations, quality of care, service delivery, and financing have emerged. Future directions for this complicated and costly service are also discussed.

Chapter 82, written by Keigher, deals with a wide range of policies and programs that are designed to meet social services, housing, and transportation needs of community-dwelling older adults. Keigher provides a good overview of the provisions and/or mandates of the Older Americans Act, the *Olmstead* decision, and the Social Services Block Grant (Title XX of the Social Security Act). With respect to housing policies and programs, the author not only discusses different types of rental subsidy programs but also provides a description of other housing assistance programs, including property tax relief, home modification and home mortgage conversion programs, and home-energy assistance programs. The chapter concludes with the discussion and critical evaluation of the problems of transportation for an aging society and the discussion of special needs transportation programs.

Issues of older persons' competency and proxy determination are intertwined with many ethical, legal, economic, and civil rights issues. In chapter 83, Wilber and Alkema discuss the complicated but fragmented legal policies governing protective services and supportive and surrogate decision-making interventions for vulnerable older adults. Using a case example, the authors illustrate the ethics and realities of guardianship and guardianship alternatives, legal procedures, and the role of social workers in surrogate decision making.

In chapter 84, Raveis provides a detailed review of issues and policies related to end-of-life care. Discussion of the Medicare, out-of-pocket, and other costs of care at the end of life is followed by discussion of trends in hospice use and the gaps and limitations in end-of-life care with respect to coverage, service delivery, and geographic and socioeconomic disparities in care. Cultural factors impacting elders' care decisions are discussed. Ethical and legal issues related to end-of-life care for the elderly are also addressed, including advanced directives and assisted suicide. The chapter concludes with policy recommendations to improve end-of-life care.

In chapter 85, Li and Rafferty focus on two federal programs that are intended to support families of dependent older persons: the Family and Medical Leave Act (FMLA) and the National Family Caregiver Support Program (NFCSP). The authors present the history, provision, and implementation of each program and then discuss the deficits and inadequacies of each program in addressing the financial, respite care, and other needs of family caregivers.

In chapter 86, Davitt discusses legislation and policies in place to protect the rights of older adults. Specifically, the author focuses on those that prohibit discrimination due to age in employment, those that promote the civil rights of older adults by making discrimination based on disability illegal, grandparents' rights, the patient's bill of rights, and legislation to protect older adults from abuse, neglect, and exploitation. Along with the description of the intent and provisions of relevant laws, their loopholes and implementation and enforcement issues are also discussed.

NAMKEE CHOI

Federal Income Maintenance Policies and Programs

77

This chapter provides a brief description and discussion of three important income maintenance programs for older persons: Old-Age, Survivors, and Disability Insurance (OASDI), or Social Security; Supplemental Security Income (SSI); and the Senior Community Service Employment Program (SCSEP). For each program, beneficiaries/participants, eligibility criteria, financing mechanisms and issues, and reform proposals or need for improvement are discussed. Special attention is paid to the program's effect on and implications for people of color, women, and/or low-income older persons.

It is often said that economic security in old age is supposed to rest on a three-legged stool: savings, a public or private pension, and Social Security (Villa, Wallace, & Markides, 1997). For a large proportion of older persons, combined incomes from these three sources indeed constitute their retirement economic security. However, for many low-income older persons who have accumulated few assets and earned no or only a small amount of pension benefits, Social Security is their most important source of income, and it needs to be supplemented by SSI and/or earnings. For low-income or disabled older persons who have not accumulated enough earnings history to receive Social Security benefits, SSI may be the only source of income. Older persons who are dislocated workers and/or have a low level of education, skills, training, and work experience are likely to face difficulty finding a job or continuing to work in the rapidly changing labor market. Older job seekers may participate in a few federal employment assistance programs that serve all age groups; however, SCSEP is the only federal program specifically designed to provide employment training and education for low-income older persons.

The OASDI program, Title II of the Social Security Act, is an employment-, earnings-, and payroll-tax-contribution-based social insurance program that provides a partial replacement of lost earnings for retired and disabled workers and their dependents and survivors. SSI, Title XVI of the Social Security Act, is a public assistance safety-net program for low-income older and/or disabled persons whose eligibility is determined by strict income and resource tests and, in the case of those under age 65, by a disability determination process. The SSI program, which began disbursing benefits in January 1974, originates in the Old Age Assistance (OAA; Title I of the Social Security Act), Aid to the Blind (AB; Title X of the Social Security Act), and Aid to the (Totally and Permanently) Disabled (AD; Title XIV of the Social Security

Act) programs. Unlike its predecessors, which were state programs, SSI is the first and only federal public assistance program that applies uniform standards of eligibility and benefit calculation throughout the country. Both OASDI and SSI are administered by the Social Security Administration (SSA).

As an employment assistance program for low-income older persons, SCSEP is authorized by Title V of the Older Americans Act and funded and administered by the U.S. Department of Labor. It is the only such program that focuses on older persons; nevertheless, the level of funding is low and the number of program participants relatively small. Older job seekers also participate in programs funded by the Workforce Investment Act, which replaced the Job Training Partnership Act in 2000, and the Trade Adjustment Assistance Reform Act of 2002, which provides employment and training assistance for individuals who have lost their jobs due to the adverse effects of international trade. However, in most states these workforce development programs do not have a special allotment of positions or funds for older persons, and, as a result, the number of older job seekers enrolled in them is even smaller than that enrolled in SCSEP. Thus, only SCSEP is described in this chapter.

SOCIAL SECURITY

Who Receives Benefits?

Since the disbursement of its first retired worker benefits in January 1940, the Old Age and Survivors Insurance Program (OASI) has become the most important income maintenance program for older persons and their dependents in the United States. The Social Security program is almost universal, covering more than 95% of the working population, or 156 million workers, and paying out benefits to 47.4 million people in 2004 (Social Security Administration [SSA], 2004a). For a majority of people, old age is marked by retirement from their job(s) and receipt of Social Security benefits, which replace part of their lost earnings.

In addition to serving as a partial replacement of lost earnings for retired workers, Social Security benefits are also paid to spouses of retired workers, divorced and/or surviving spouses, dependent children and parents, and surviving dependent children and parents. Since the Disability Insurance (DI) program was added to the OASI in 1954, benefits have also become available to disabled workers under age 65 and

to their spouses and children. Of the 47.4 million Social Security beneficiaries in 2004, 63% were retired workers, 12% were disabled workers, 6% were spouses of retired or disabled workers, 11% were surviving spouses, and 8% were dependent or surviving children. In May 2004, the average monthly benefit for retired workers was $922, and those benefits for older couples and older widow(ers) or parents alone were $1,523 and $740, respectively (SSA, 2004a).

Since 1975, Social Security benefits have been automatically adjusted yearly to reflect the increase in the Consumer Price Index (CPI). These cost-of-living adjustments (COLAs) have been essential for protecting the real purchasing power of the Social Security benefits. Although those who worked in low-paid jobs receive a smaller Social Security benefit in absolute dollars than those who worked in high-paid jobs, the earnings-replacement rates are higher for the low earners (about 50%) than for the high earners (about 30%) because of Social Security's progressive benefit computation formula and the program's provisions for disabled workers, spouses, children, and survivors (Gist, 1998; U.S. General Accounting Office [U.S. GAO], 2004).

Eligibility Criteria

To be eligible for Social Security retired worker benefits, most people need 40 work credits (4 credits per year, with $900 in earnings constituting one credit in 2004). The full retirement age at which covered workers can receive full Social Security benefits (or primary insurance amount [PIA]) is 65 years for those born in 1937 or earlier, but it will be 66 years for those born between 1943 and 1954, and 67 years for those born in 1960 and later. For those born between 1938 and 1942 and those born between 1955 and 1959, the full retirement age will increase by 2 months for every successive birth year. For example, for those who were born in 1938, it will be 65 years and 2 months; for those who were born in 1939, it will be 65 years and 4 months. People can retire at any time between age 62 and the full retirement age, but the benefits of those who opt for early retirement are reduced by 5/9 of 1% per month for the first 36 months and 5/12 of 1% per month subsequently. People can also delay retirement beyond the full retirement age and receive delayed retirement credits added to their Social Security benefits. The delayed retirement credit for those born in 1943 and later will be 8% yearly.

Social Security retired beneficiaries are allowed to work, but the earnings of those between ages 62 and 64 are subjected to the Social Security earnings test. In 2004, for example, for every $2 earned over the limit of $11,640 annually ($970 a month), $1 in SSA benefits is withheld. (Disability Insurance beneficiaries can earn up to $810 [for nonblind] or $1,350 [for blind] per month in 2004 without having their benefits reduced. These earnings ceilings are adjusted yearly.) Attempting to remove perceived work disincentives of the earnings test among Social Security beneficiaries, the Senior Citizens Freedom to Work Act of 2000 eliminated the earnings test for beneficiaries aged 65 and older. However, a study showed no clear early evidence of increased employment among this age-group, although it found that higher earners had increased their earnings further (Song, 2003/2004).

An older spouse of a retired worker is eligible for 50% of the retired worker's benefits. Spouses who have their own earnings history and retired worker benefits can receive the higher benefit of the two—the spouse benefit or the retired worker benefit—but not both. A divorced spouse is treated the same as the current spouse if the marriage lasted 10 years or longer. Survivors benefits are paid to surviving spouses and dependent children and to dependent parents of covered workers or beneficiaries. A surviving spouse is entitled to full benefits at age 65 (if born before January 2, 1940) or to reduced benefits as early as age 60 (age 50 if disabled or earlier if taking care of a surviving dependent child). Divorced surviving spouses are treated the same as married surviving spouses if the marriage lasted 10 years or longer. Thus, Social Security survivors' benefits function as long-term life insurance.

Social Security and Low-Income Persons and Persons of Color

The poverty rates among older persons in general have been declining steadily since the mid-1970s, owing primarily to Social Security benefits. In 2000, Social Security, on average, accounted for 38.4% of income for those aged 65 and older, as compared with 17.9% of income from pensions, 17.5% from assets, and 23.1% from earnings (McDonnell, 2003; SSA, n.d.). Especially for a large proportion of older women and persons of color, Social Security benefits constitute the most significant source of retirement income, because these individuals are significantly less likely than older white men to receive income

from pensions and assets. Without Social Security benefits, the poverty rate among older women and persons of color would be more than 50% (Beedon & Wu, 2003; Rix & Beedon, 2003). In 2000, 34% of African American older married couples and 45% of Hispanic older married couples, compared with 25% of their white counterparts, received at least 80% of their income from Social Security. Among unmarried older women, 61% of African Americans and 62% of Hispanics, compared with 48% of whites, received at least 80% of their income from Social Security. Comparable figures for unmarried older men are 50% of African Americans and 62% of Hispanics, compared with 38% of whites. For 75% of all married and unmarried elderly units in the bottom quintile of income distribution, Social Security was the essential source of income, providing at least 90% (SSA, n.d.).

Despite the significance of Social Security as retirement income for women and persons of color, many low-income female workers and workers of color face some serious challenges in achieving equitable Social Security coverage. One such challenge is related to the fact that Social Security benefits are determined not only by the number of work credits but also by the amount of earnings actually reported by employers. This is particularly notable when considering the situation of domestic service workers, a career in which a disproportionate share of workers are women, especially women of color. These workers may not get full credits for all their wages because an employer is not required to report a household worker's wages less than a certain amount ($1,400 in 2004). Thus, if a domestic service worker were employed by three employers and paid less than $1,400 by each, there is a strong possibility that none of her (or his) wages would be reported. As a result, her (or his) Social Security benefits would be lower than they should be. Social Security wage-reporting rules need to be reconsidered to rectify this inequity for low-income household workers (Flippen & Tienda, 2002; Kijakazi, 2002).

Financing of Social Security

Social Security works as an intergenerational transfer program based on a pay-as-you-go system, under which payroll tax revenues from current workers (6.2% each from employees and employers or 12.4% from the self-employed up to a maximum taxable ceiling of $87,900 in 2004) are used to pay the benefits of current beneficiaries. In addition, proceeds from taxing part of the Social Security benefits of middle- and high-income recipients are added to the OASDI trust funds, but they constitute only a very small portion of the annual income of the trust funds.

The fiscal health of the pay-as-you-go system depends on a high worker-to-beneficiary ratio. In 1960, the ratio was 5 to 1, and in 2004, it was about 3 to 1. Because a majority of the baby boomers are currently in their prime working years, we have more payroll tax revenues than benefit outlays; as a result, the OASDI trust funds have been accumulating a surplus that is projected to reach $1.1 trillion between now and 2018 (Concord Coalition, 2003). (In reality, the surplus payroll tax revenues are not deposited in the trust funds, however, because the trust funds are simply bookkeeping devices, with the special-issue U.S. Treasury bonds they contain representing promissory notes from the Treasury Department to the Social Security Administration.)

As the boomers begin receiving Social Security checks in 2010 (or earlier for those opting for early retirement), the worker-to-beneficiary ratios will decline further (to 2 to 1 in 2035), and the benefit outlays will exceed the payroll tax revenues beginning in 2019. According to the OASDI Trustees Report of 2004, despite the yearly income-to-outlay deficits that are expected to begin in 2019, the redemption of the accumulated assets of the trust funds will be sufficient to pay the full cost of benefit outlays until 2041. However, after 2041 this cumulative amount will become negative, indicating a net unfunded obligation. Through the end of 2078, the combined funds have a present-value unfunded obligation of $3.7 trillion (Board of Trustees of the Federal OASDI Trust Funds, 2004). Another gauge of the increased burden of Social Security outlays is their share of the gross domestic product (GDP); in 2003, Social Security expenditures were about 4.4% of GDP, but in 2030, they are expected to be 6% of GDP, while the federal revenues dedicated to Social Security will remain at 5% of GDP (U.S. Congressional Budget Office [U.S. CBO], 2004).

Reform Proposals

Special presidential commissions under the Clinton and George W. Bush administrations, as well as many think-tank groups, have proposed reforms to improve Social Security's long-term fiscal health. Of these reform proposals, those that have suggested partial privatization of Social Security, which would allow voluntary individual carve-out accounts, have received the most attention because of their potentially radical departure from the social insurance ideal of Social Security. Proponents of individual carve-out accounts have touted the possibly higher return rates individuals could realize by investing part of the money now going into payroll taxes in private securities markets; however, Wall Street's slump and the increasing budget deficit in recent years have dampened the public's support for this plan. Other serious issues could arise if voluntary individual carve-out accounts were allowed (Orszag & Greenstein, 2001; Shelton & Beedon, 2002):

- High earners are more likely to select the carve-out option, leading to reduced revenue for the Social Security Trust Funds and reducing the redistributive effect of the Social Security system;
- Complicated administrative issues (e.g., transition cost at the macro level and property issues at the micro level in situations such as a couple's divorce, survivors benefits, etc.);
- High administrative or transaction costs for individual account holders; and
- Risk of misinformation and inability of less-educated individuals to manage their own investment strategies.

In addition to the partial privatization ideas, the following Social Security reform options have been proposed. First, it would be possible to increase the payroll tax revenue through the following measures:

- Increase payroll tax rates to draw additional resources;
- Eliminate the maximum taxable ceiling so that entire earnings can be subjected to Social Security payroll taxes;
- Tax all, rather than part of, the benefits for middle- and high-income recipients.

The potential problems of these measures are as follows:

- Given the flat rate, and therefore the regressive nature, of the payroll tax system, low-income workers may be disproportionately negatively affected by increased payroll tax rates;
- Elimination of the maximum taxable ceiling and taxation of all Social Security benefits for middle- and high-income recipients, though long overdue, will not generate enough revenue to significantly shore up Social Security's long-term deficit.

A second option would be to decrease the benefit outlay by doing the following:

- Cut the benefits for future beneficiaries;
- Reduce incentives for early retirement;
- Increase the Social Security early and/or full retirement age.

These options have a number of drawbacks:

- Negative impact on low-income older persons for whom Social Security is the most significant or sole source of their retirement income;
- Negative impact on blue-collar workers and workers in physically demanding jobs who are unable to find continuing employment or extend their working careers;
- Negative impact on low-income persons of color who are unable to extend their working careers, with the resulting possibility that SSDI and the SSI costs will increase (Choi, 2004; Munnell, Meme, Jivan, & Cahill, 2004);
- Negative impact on low lifetime earners in general and persons of color in particular, given the strong relationship between lifetime incomes and life expectancy, and resulting problems of inequity for low earners who tend to have shorter life expectancies and, thus, shorter benefit-receipt periods than their well-off counterparts (see Duggan, Gillingham, & Greenlees, 1995; Gist, 1998).

A third option would be to subsidize the OASDI program with general revenues, increase federal borrowing, make Social Security coverage of state and local employees mandatory, and restructure family benefits:

- Decrease consumption of resources by other federal programs to make up the shortfall in Social Security and divert the resources to shore up Social Security;
- Increase federal borrowing to fund deficits in benefit outlays;
- Extend coverage to the approximately 30% of state and local employees (4 million workers) who are not covered under Social Security to pull resources (i.e., payroll tax revenues) from this relatively stable group of workers (Munnell, 2000);
- Restructure the current benefit formula for spouses, as well as benefits for other dependents and survivors to increase the program's efficiency and social adequacy (higher earnings replacement rates for lower earners as an antipoverty measure) for low-income people (refer to Favreault, Sammartino, & Steuerle, 2002).

The problems with these measures are as follows:

- Given the projected fiscal problems of Medicare and Medicaid, which are even more serious than the ones just discussed, decreases in spending for these public programs are not likely;
- Increased federal borrowing will certainly burden the future generations that will have to repay the debt with interest;
- Inclusion of uncovered employees of state and local governments may incur short-term costs;
- The economic impact of restructuring family benefits will be small and will not solve the long-term fiscal crisis of Social Security.

A fourth possibility would be to combine the aforementioned options. Considering the strengths and weaknesses of the reform proposals described here, a combination of these options appears to be an ideal approach that will be able to close Social Security's long-term deficit and preserve the program's many strengths as the nation's most significant retirement income source, especially for low-income people (see Diamond & Orszag, 2004). Social Security has been one of the most efficient federal entitlement programs, if not the most, for more than 60 years, providing financial security to millions of older persons, their dependents, and their survivors. The long-term fiscal health of Social Security must be saved with careful deliberation of the micro- and macroeconomic impacts of all possible options.

SUPPLEMENTAL SECURITY INCOME

Who Receives Benefits?

Since SSI became the nation's first and only federal public assistance program in 1974, the number of its recipients has grown many times over. According to the SSA's annual report for 2004 (SSA, 2004b), an average of 6.6 million individuals received federally administered SSI benefits on a monthly basis in 2003. Of these, 1.8 million people were aged 65 years or older (1.1 million in the low-income aged category and 0.7 million in the disabled category), and 4.8 million were disabled or blind individuals under age 65. In 2004, the maximum federal benefit was $564 and $846 per month for individual and couple recipients, respectively. Like Social Security benefits, SSI benefits are automatically adjusted yearly to reflect the increase in the CPI. A majority of states also provide state supplementation to the federal SSI benefits. In January 2004, the average federal SSI payment averaged $393 for 6.9 million recipients, and 2.5 million of these also received monthly state supplementation averaging $138.

Of the recipients who were aged 65 or older in 2003, 45.4% received both federal SSI benefits and state supplementation, 57.4% were dual beneficiaries of both SSI and Social Security, and 2.5% received both SSI and Veterans Affairs disability cash benefits (SSA, 2004b). About 85% of older recipients were aged 70 or older, and 71% and 29% were women and men, respectively, reflecting the lower income status of those aged 70 or older and of women. A majority of these older recipients were unmarried (SSA, 2003, 2004b).

Eligibility Criteria

Supplemental Security Income is a means-tested public assistance program for low-income persons aged 65 or older, persons who are blind, and persons with other disabilities, and provides assistance of last resort. A person's or a couple's resources and income are used to determine eligibility and the amount of SSI benefits available. Resources, such as the applicant's home and a car (valued $4,500 or less), household goods and personal effects with equity not exceeding $2,000, life insurance with total face value of $1,500 or less, and burial funds not exceeding $1,500 per person, are exempt from the eligibility determination process. With respect to income, earned and unearned (or general) income exclusions/disregards apply when determining an individual's benefit. Earned income exclusions include the first $65 earned per month plus one half of the remainder plus impairment-related work expenses for the disabled or the blind and infrequently or irregularly received income of $30 or less per quarter. Also allowed is an income set-aside under special programs (e.g., the Plan for Achieving Self-Support program, or PASS) that are aimed at promoting self-support among SSI beneficiaries. Unearned income exclusions include the first $20 per month (e.g., Social Security benefits, pensions, and interest and dividends), food stamps, rent subsidies under the U.S. Department of Housing and Urban Development (HUD), other state or local as-

sistance based on need, and $60 or less per quarter of infrequently or irregularly received income.

When a married individual who lives with an ineligible spouse applies for SSI, part of the spouse's income and resources are considered in determining the applicant's benefits. If an individual lives in someone else's household and receives support and maintenance from the householder, his or her SSI benefits are reduced by one third. When an individual is a resident of a medical facility (e.g., skilled nursing facilities) in which Medicaid pays half of the bill, the federal SSI payment is reduced to a $30 personal allowance. Eligibility for SSI is also limited to U.S. citizens, noncitizens who were receiving SSI benefits on August 22, 1996, and others in certain categories of qualified noncitizens, including certain blind and other disabled persons who were lawfully residing in the United States on August 22, 1996, refugees, asylees, Cubans and Haitians with refugee-like status, and those with 40 qualified quarters of earnings and their spouses. Refugees and asylees may receive SSI benefits for only 7 years, but a proposal to extend the period has been considered in the Congress since 2004.

Underutilization of SSI Among Older Persons

Although the number of SSI recipients has grown since 1974, SSI participation rates are low, especially among eligible low-income older persons. Previous studies estimated that only 40% to 60% of SSI-eligible older persons participated in SSI and found that, compared with SSI participants, eligible nonparticipants had relatively higher incomes and a smaller amount of potential SSI benefits, higher rates of home and car ownership, and better health (Choi, 1992, 1998; Davies, 2001; McGarry, 1995). In addition, the analyses of self-reported reasons for SSI nonapplication among eligible Social Security beneficiaries show that a large proportion of eligible nonapplicants lacked accurate information on the program and believed that they did not need the benefit because they had managed to get by without the extra income (Choi, 1998). A study of underutilization of SSI among Mexican American older persons also found that the most commonly reported reasons for their nonparticipation were lack of knowledge about the program (especially among those with no or a low level of formal education) and previous feelings of discrimination or mistreatment by SSI representatives or other formal providers (Dietz, 2001).

Because of SSI's strict eligibility criteria, means test, and disability determination process, poor older persons (who are likely to have low levels of education) can be easily misinformed of and intimidated by the application process. Moreover, with the initial disqualification of noncitizens from SSI eligibility in the 1996 Personal Responsibility and Work Opportunity Reconciliation Act (PRWORA), many poor lawful permanent residents may still be confused about their eligibility. This is true even though, in 1997, Congress restored the eligibility of those who were receiving SSI benefits on August 22, 1996. Because SSI eligibility is grounded in old age and disability, the applicants and recipients are considered "deserving." Nevertheless, there have been periods of retrenchment when SSI eligibility determination and recertification processes became overly strict, and as a result, many recipients and applicants were denied the benefits. Although an appeals process is in place for those denied the benefit, the daunting task of appealing discourages many older persons and the disabled from applying for or reclaiming their benefits.

Coordinated Benefits

In addition to the federal SSI benefits, 45 states provide some form of optional supplementation administered by state government, federal government, or both. Eligibility criteria and the amount of supplementation vary by state. In general, SSI recipients are also eligible for Medicaid; 40 states use SSI eligibility criteria to determine Medicaid eligibility, and 11 states use their own Medicaid eligibility criteria. Applicants for SSI may be eligible for food stamps (except in California, where the cash value of food stamps is included in state supplementation), and a person can apply for food stamps at the time of the SSI application. The Ticket to Work and Work Incentives Improvement Act of 1999 also helps disabled SSI beneficiaries (and Social Security Disability Insurance beneficiaries) obtain vocational rehabilitation, employment, or other support services from an approved provider of their choice to help them go to work and achieve their employment goals.

Representative Payee System

When adult SSI (and/or Social Security) recipients are incapable of managing or directing the management of their benefits and are declared legally incompetent,

the SSA appoints representative payees for them and sends their SSI benefits to the representative payees. In many cases, the representative payee is a spouse, a parent, or other close relative who will act in the recipient's best interest. In some cases, an SSA-approved organization (such as a nursing home where a beneficiary is a resident or another qualified organization) may be appointed, and SSA has authorized some organizations to collect a fee from the benefit for acting as payee. The fee may not exceed the lesser of 10 percent of the benefit amount or a specified amount ($31 a month in 2004; SSA, 2004b). Individual representative payees may not collect a fee for their service. A representative payee should use the funds only for the current and foreseeable needs of the beneficiary and must account for all benefits received. Representative payees are also required to report to the SSA any changes that may affect SSI recipients' eligibility and payment amount (SSA, 2001).

Financing of SSI

The SSI federal benefits are financed by the federal general revenues. In fiscal year 2003, federal expenditures for SSI cash payments totaled $32.9 billion (of that amount, a little less than $4.0 billion went to those aged 65 and older). The SSA's administrative cost for the program was $2.7 billion, or 7% of the total federal SSI cash payments. The cost of state supplementation payment in the same year was about $5.0 billion. The federal SSI payments constituted 0.3% of GDP in 2003, but they are projected to decrease to 0.24% of GDP in 2028 due to the slow increase in SSI participation and SSI benefits (SSA, 2004b).

Improvements Needed to Increase the SSI's Income Security Function

The SSI program has significantly helped older and/or disabled persons with no other source of income or with limited income. However, as shown by the low utilization rate, only about half of eligible older persons participate in SSI. Since all SSI-eligible nonparticipants have low incomes and would be able to benefit not only from the federal cash benefit but also from the other benefits, such as state supplementation and Medicaid, effective outreach efforts must be implemented to help them apply for SSI benefits.

The SSI eligibility rules related to resource and income limits, as well as exclusions/disregards, should also be made less strict. The resource limits of $2,000 for an individual and $3,000 for a couple and the face value of life insurance and a burial fund not exceeding $1,500 each often disqualify otherwise-eligible older persons (Choi, 1998). Moreover, the unearned (or general) income exclusion of $20 also discourages many low-income Social Security recipients or other public or private pensioners from applying for SSI because the entire Social Security and pension benefits minus $20 will be counted against their prospective SSI benefits. The earned income exclusion ($65 plus one half of the remainder) should also be increased to encourage low-income older working persons to apply for SSI. The application and appeal processes per se, including the proof of income (or, rather, lack of it) and disability determination, should also be streamlined to be less complicated, demeaning, and intimidating for older persons with limited education and resources to assist their application.

Especially given that poor older unmarried women and people of color, who constitute the largest proportion of SSI aged recipients, are the ones who were poor prior to reaching age 65 (Kijakazi, 2001), they are likely to have very little, if any, income from other sources. Even a modest increase in SSI benefits will provide these and other most vulnerable older persons with extra cash to buy the basic necessities of food, clothing, and shelter and have a greater sense of security. Moreover, any future Social Security reforms that may have negative effects on low-income workers, retirees, dependents, and survivors must be accompanied by significant improvements in SSI's income subsidy and security function (Davies & Favreault, 2004).

SENIOR COMMUNITY SERVICE EMPLOYMENT PROGRAM

The SCSEP, authorized under Title V of the Older Americans Act, is the only federal employment training and educational program focusing on low-income persons aged 55 or older. The SCSEP aims at promoting part-time community service activities and fostering economic self-sufficiency through unsubsidized employment following a period of subsidized work experience and training at nonprofit and public sector agencies (U.S. GAO, 2003). The program is funded by the U.S. Department of Labor (DOL) and administered by the Employment and Training Administration, which awards grants to 10 national organizations—the AARP Foundation; Experience Works (EW; formerly Green Thumb); the National Asian Pacific Center on Aging (NAPCA); Asociación Nacional Pro Personas Mayores (ANPPM; National Association for Hispanic Elderly); the National Caucus and Center on Black Aged (NCCBA); the National Council on the Aging (NCOA); the National Indian Council on Aging (NICOA); Senior Service America; the National Urban League (NUL); and the U.S. Forest Service (USFS)—and to units of state and territorial governments. These grantees are responsible for recruiting and collaborating with the host agencies where SCSEP participants receive employment training (U.S. Department of Labor [U.S. DOL], 2004).

Participants, Eligibility Criteria, and Nature of Training

For the 2000–2001 grant year, 106,000 SCSEP participants worked in part-time subsidized community service jobs provided by nonprofit and governmental host agencies (U.S. GAO, 2003). During the grant year ending June 30, 2002, the SCSEP enrollees had the following characteristics (AARP, 2004):

- 30% male and 70% female
- 27% with less than a high school diploma
- 12% veterans and 13% disabled
- 51% white and 49% minorities
- 78% aged 60 and older

Program participants must have a family income at or below 125% of the federal poverty level, and enrollment priority is given to persons over age 60, veterans, and qualified spouses of veterans. Program participants are placed in a wide variety of community service positions at nonprofit and government agencies, but they most frequently hold positions in education and social service organizations as teacher aides, librarians/library aides, day care assistants, receptionists, and nurse's aides (U.S. DOL, 2004; U.S. GAO, 2004).

On average, participants work 20 hours a week in the assigned positions and are paid the highest of federal minimum wage, state minimum wage, or prevailing wage. The positions are assigned to provide participants with skills and experience that will enable them to obtain unsubsidized jobs. Other training may include classroom, lectures, seminars, individual instruction, and training through other employment and training programs or through community colleges. Specific kinds of training include the following (AARP, 2004):

- Skills assessment;
- Formal program orientation;
- Creation of an individual employment plan that will identify barriers to employment and will recommend assignments, training, and services to overcome these barriers;
- Assistance with setting employment goals;
- Résumé preparation;
- Referrals to employment opportunities; and
- Follow-up meetings, evaluations, and reviews to determine the participant's progress and "next steps."

Funding and Effectiveness of SCSEP

In 2001, SCSEP was funded at $440.2 million to support 61,762 job slots nationwide. (The number of actual participants surpassed the planned number, owing to enrollees who transitioned from the program into full- or part-time jobs and other program attrition.) The DOL allotted 78% of the funds to 10 national grantees and the remaining 22% to each of the 50 states, the District of Columbia, Puerto Rico, and the other territories. The SCSEP program is required to use at least 75% of its funds to subsidize participants' wages, with the remainder available for such activities as assessments, counseling, training, and job placement assistance (U.S. GAO, 2003).

In 2001, the proportion of the SCSEP enrollees who found unsubsidized full- or part-time jobs following their unsubsidized community service exceeded the DOL's goal of 20% (AARP, 2004). The SCSEP is cost effective, returning $1.50 for every dollar invested in empowering older adults to be productive, taxpaying citizens who provide value-added service to their communities (National Council on the Aging, 2001). Studies have also shown that employers who hired workers who had gone through the SCSEP program reported generally positive attitudes toward these older workers because of their low absenteeism, low turnover rates, and willingness to take on demanding or difficult tasks (Wagner, 1998).

Strengthening SCSEP for Development of an Older Workforce

The U.S. GAO (2003) estimated that only about 12% of 1.3 million older people who were not working and wanted a job participated in federal employment and training programs and that the majority of them

(68%) were enrolled in SCSEP. Considering its high success rates in transitioning older persons into unsubsidized employment, its cost-effectiveness, and the positive reception its clients have received by employers, SCSEP needs to be expanded to serve more low-income older persons. The funding level can be gradually increased to serve more people in years to come. As the baby boomers retire, it is projected, there may be a labor shortage of 35 million workers by 2030 (U.S. GAO, 2003). Especially because people aged 55 or older will constitute nearly a third of the population in 2030, it is imperative for low-income unemployed people in this age-group to have access to employment training and job placement programs. In addition to the badly needed additional income, a sense of involvement in the community and in society in general will greatly improve the quality of life among these low-income older persons. Investment in development of the older workforce also needs to be considered in the context of Medicare and Social Security's financing problems. By helping older persons extend their productive years, we can decrease the burden on the Medicare and Social Security systems.

CONCLUSION

Income security in old age, along with affordable and accessible health care, is a basic human right that must be met regardless of an individual's prior economic status or earnings history. The employment- and earnings-based Social Security, means-tested SSI, and SCESP providing employment assistance to older low-income job seekers constitute a reasonably sound system of income security for older persons, but, as discussed in this chapter, they also contain many deficits and limitations affecting those who are the most vulnerable. Along with careful strategies to solve the projected long-term fiscal problems of Social Security, increased funding levels, relaxation of overly strict eligibility criteria, and expanded outreach efforts for SSI and SCESP are needed to improve the effectiveness of these programs. Social workers should actively participate not only in ongoing debates of Social Security reforms to help preserve the program's social adequacy function but also in advocacy to make SSI and SCESP and other employment-assistance programs more accessible and adequate for low-income older persons. Social workers should continue to work to inform low-income older persons and their families of their entitlement to SSI and SCESP and help reduce the stigma attached to these programs.

REFERENCES

AARP. (2004). *What is SCSEP?* Washington, DC: Author. Retrieved from *http://www.aarp.org/scsep-what/Articles/a2003-02-26-nationalstats.html*

Beedon, L., & Wu, K. B. (2003). *Social Security and African Americans: Some facts.* Washington, DC: AARP Public Policy Institute. Retrieved from *http://research.aarp.org/econ/fs94_ss.html*

Board of Trustees of the Federal Old-Age and Survivors Insurance and Disability Insurance Trust Funds. (2004, March). *The 2004 annual report of the Board of Trustees of the Federal Old-Age and Survivors Insurance and Disability Insurance Trust Funds.* Washington, DC: Author.

Choi, N. G. (1992). Correlates of the elderly's participation and nonparticipation in the Supplemental Security Income (SSI) program: A new evaluation. *Journal of Sociology and Social Welfare, 19*(3), 85–104.

Choi, N. G. (1998). A comparative study of elderly SSI recipients, denied applicants, and eligible nonapplicants. *Journal of Aging and Social Policy, 10*(2), 7–28.

Choi, N. G. (2004). Social Security reform and people of color: Implications of barriers to continuous employment and reentry into the labor force. In K. E. Davis & T. B. Bent-Goodley (Eds.), *The color of social policy* (pp. 81–100). Alexandria, VA: Council on Social Work Education.

Concord Coalition. (2003, May). *Lessons from the 2003 Social Security Trustees report: Issue brief.* Retrieved from *http://www.concordcoalition.org/socialsecurity/030520issuebrief.htm*

Davies, P. S. (2001). SSI eligibility and participation among the oldest old: Evidence from the AHEAD. *Social Security Bulletin, 64*(3), 38–63.

Davies, P. S., & Favreault, M. M. (2004). *Interactions between Social Security reform and the Supplemental Security Income program for the aged* (Center for Retirement Research Working Paper No. 2004–02). Chestnut Hill, MA: Center for Retirement Research at Boston College.

Diamond, P. A., & Orszag, P. R. (2004). *Saving Social Security: A balanced approach.* Washington, DC: Brookings Institution Press.

Dietz, T. L. (2001). Mexican American elderly and Supplemental Security Income: Reasons and characteristics associated with nonuse. *Journal of Applied Gerontology, 20,* 292–306.

Duggan, J. E., Gillingham, R., & Greenlees, J. (1995). *Progressive returns to Social Security? An answer from Social Security records* (U.S. Department of Treasury Research Paper No. 9501, Office of the Assistant Secretary, Economic Policy). Retrieved from *http://www.treas.gov/offices/economicpolicy/papers/rp9501/pdf*

Favreault, M. M., Sammartino, F. J., & Steuerle, C. E. (2002). *Social Security and the family.* Washington, DC: Urban Institute.

Flippen, C., & Tienda, M. (2002). Workers of color and pathways to retirement. *Public Policy and Aging Report, 12*(3), 3–8.

Gist, J. R. (1998). *Social Security reform: How do minorities fare under Social Security/A response to two Heritage Foundation reports.* AARP Public Policy Institute. Retrieved from *http://research.aarp.org/econ/ib34_ssmindd_1.html*

Kijakazi, K. (2001). *Women's retirement income: The case for improving Supplemental Security Income.* Paper presented at the annual conference of the Institute for Women's Policy Research Annual Conference, Washington, DC.

Kijakazi, K. (2002). Impact of unreported Social Security earnings on people of color and women. *Public Policy and Aging Report, 12*(3), 9–11.

McDonnell, K. (2003, November). Income of the elderly population: 2002. *Employee Benefit Research Institute (EBRI) Notes, 24*(11), 7–10.

McGarry, K. (1995). *Factors determining participation of the elderly in SSI* (Working Paper No. 5250). Cambridge, MA: National Bureau of Economic Research.

Munnell, A. H. (2000). *The impact of mandatory Social Security coverage of state and local workers: A multistate review.* Washington, DC: AARP Public Policy Institute. Retrieved from *http://research.aarp.org/econ/2000_11_security.html*

Munnell, A. H., Meme, K. B., Jivan, N. A., & Cahill, K. E. (2004). *Should we raise Social Security's earliest eligibility age?* (Issue Brief No. 18). Chestnut Hill, MA: Center for Retirement Research at Boston College. Retrieved from *http://www.bc.edu/crr*

National Council on the Aging. (2001). *The nine "best practices" of highly effective SCSEP projects: Lessons in what makes these projects a success.* Washington, DC: Author.

Orszag, P. R., & Greenstein, R. (2001, August). *Voluntary individual accounts for Social Security: What are the costs?* Washington, DC: Center on Budget and Policy Priorities. Retrieved from *www.cbpp.org/8-21-01soc-sec.htm*

Rix, S., & Beedon, L. (2003). *Social Security and women: Some facts.* Washington, DC: AARP Public Policy Institute. Retrieved from *http://research.aarp.org/econ/fs96_sswom.html*

Shelton, A., & Beedon, L. (2002, October). *Ten points concerning carve-out Social Security individual ac-*

counts. Washington, DC: AARP Public Policy Institute. Retrieved from *http://research.aarp.org/econ/dd80_carve.html*

Social Security Administration. (2001). *A guide for representative payee* (SSA Publication No. 05-10076). Retrieved from *http://www.socialsecurity.gov/pubs/10076.html*

Social Security Administration. (2003). *Fast facts and figures about Social Security.* Retrieved from *http://www.ssa.gov/policy/docs/chartbooks/fast_facts/2003/ff2003.pdf*

Social Security Administration. (2004a). *OASDI Monthly Statistics, May 2004.* Retrieved from *http://www.ssa.gov/policy/docs/statcomps/oasdi_monthly/2004-05/index.html*

Social Security Administration. (2004b). *2004 annual report of the SSI program.* Retrieved from *http://www.ssa.gov/OACT/SSIR/SSI04*

Social Security Administration. (n.d.). *Income of the population 55 or older, 2000: Importance of income sources relative to total income.* Retrieved from *http://www.ssa.gov/policy/docs/statcomps/income_pop55/2000/sect6.html.*

Song, J. G. (2003/2004). Evaluating the initial impact of eliminating the retirement earnings test. *Social Security Bulletin, 65*(1), 1–15.

U.S. Congressional Budget Office. (2004, June). *The outlook for Social Security.* Congress of the United States. Retrieved from *ftp://ftp.cbo.gov/55xx/doc5530/06-14-SocialSecurity.pdf.*

U.S. Department of Labor. (2004). *Program overview of the Senior Community Service Employment Program.* Retrieved from *http://www.doleta.gov/Seniors/html_docs/overview.cfm.*

U.S. General Accounting Office. (2003, January). *Older workers* (Report to the ranking minority member, Subcommittee on Employer-Employee Relations, Committee on Education and the Workforce, House of Representatives, GAO-03-350). Retrieved from www.gao.gov/cgi-bin/getrpt?GAO-03-350.

U.S. General Accounting Office. (2004, June). *Social Security: Distribution of benefits and taxes relative to earnings level* (Report to Congressional Requests, GAO-04-747). Retrieved from *www.gao.gov/cgi-bin/getrpt?GAO-04-747.*

Villa, V. M., Wallace, S. P., & Markides, K. M. (1997). Economic diversity and an aging population: The impact of public policy and economic trends. *Generations, 21*(2), 13–18.

Wagner, D. L. (1998). *Factors influencing the use of older workers: A survey of U.S. employers.* Washington, DC: National Council on the Aging.

ROBERT B. HUDSON

Private Retirement Benefits

78

The "fear of outliving one's income" has long stood as the principal economic concern facing people in old age. From the time that "modern aging" was recognized in the middle to late 19th century, there was a protracted period in which both private and public sectors worked to augment the limited savings individuals might have amassed to cushion their later years. Yet, more recently, the growth and security of the private pension sector have faltered, just as increases in societal aging are putting new pressures on Social Security, the nation's principal public pension system.

This chapter reviews the place of private pensions in the overall retirement income picture, recent trends in private pension coverage, and the adequacy of private pensions in helping to meet the retirement needs of vulnerable populations. The last issue is of special importance to geriatric social workers, who must be aware of and knowledgeable about the income adequacy and security challenges that their clients are facing.

PRIVATE PENSION DEVELOPMENT

The American Express Company established the first private pension plan in the United States in 1875, although most of the initial plans were concentrated in the railroad industry (Sass, 1997). The number of workers covered grew slowly over the next several decades (roughly 3 million workers covered by the time of Social Security's enactment in 1935); grew dramatically in the years during and after World War II (coverage growing from roughly 4 million in the late 1930s to 10 million by 1950); and climbed to 31 million workers by 1975. Although in the ensuing years the number of workers covered under all types of employer-sponsored pension plans has continued to increase (reaching 52 million by 1998), the number of workers covered under so-called traditional plans (formally known as *defined benefit plans* and discussed later in this chapter) has declined from 27 million in 1975 to 23 million in 1998 (Employee Benefit Research Institute [EBRI], 2002).

The early plans, especially in the railroad industry, were justified (to shareholders) as a way of increasing workers' loyalty and reducing strikes and high turnover, which plagued the industry in those years. Pensions proved ineffective in meeting these objectives, but they did play a role in supporting mandatory retirement provisions directed at older workers who were deemed less productive. A number of factors led to the rapid growth of plans during and immediately after World War II:

- Wage freezes during World War II and the Korean War encouraged fringe benefit growth in lieu of wages;
- In 1949, the Supreme Court supported a National Labor Relations Board ruling that pensions were a proper issue for collective bargaining;
- There was growing recognition by unions of the inadequacy of Social Security benefits and the need for their supplementation; and
- Multiemployer pension plans were introduced in construction, transportation, and other industries (Schulz, 1988).

In addition to strong economic growth during the period, Sass (1997) argues that the last two items were critical to private pension plan growth in the postwar era; the United Mine Workers and the Congress of Industrial Organizations (CIO) pushed for industry-wide standards, pressures that led to coverage expanding from 19% to 45% of the labor force between 1949 and 1960.

Despite this growth in private pensions, by the late 1960s a number of problems had emerged involving both worker protection and plan solvency. When companies went bankrupt (e.g., Studebaker automobile company in 1963) or fraud was rampant (Teamsters union pension fund in 1964), workers were left unprotected. Long vesting periods also left many workers at risk should they be laid off or fired after years of service. These concerns led in 1974 to the passage of the nation's principal private pension legislation—the Employee Retirement Income Security Act (ERISA). Among other provisions, ERISA

- Established pension plan termination insurance through the newly created Pension Benefit Guarantee Corporation;
- Set minimum vesting standards (number of years required for pension benefits);
- Strengthened funding and fiduciary standards within plans;
- Required plans to report to participants their accrued benefits and vesting status;
- Permitted employees, upon job separation, to transfer their pension rights on a tax-free basis from one plan to another; and
- Created tax-deferred individual retirement accounts.

As Schulz (1988) points out, however, ERISA did not address all private pension problems. Employers were not required to offer a plan, only to adhere to these regulations if they did offer one. In addition, state and local government plans were excluded from coverage, survivors' provisions were weak, and—unlike Social Security—pension benefits were not indexed to increases in the cost of living.

The post-1970s period has been marked by a leveling off in the expansion of private pension coverage among workers and by a dramatic shift in the *type* of private pension coverage being offered to workers. Well into the 1970s, there was hope that coverage, which had tripled between the early 1950s and the mid-1970s, would continue to expand. Yet economic stagnation, changes in the domestic and international competitive marketplace, and employers' perceived needs for more flexible labor force policies precluded this further expansion in coverage. The growth in the number of "traditional" pension plans (defined benefit plans [DBPs]) essentially halted, and later began to decline notably, and the newly introduced defined contribution plans (DCPs), made possible by ERISA provisions, began to greatly expand. The consequences of these two trends are that roughly one half of workers continue to lack any private pension coverage, and the move in the direction of DCPs has shifted much of the risk associated with pension performance from the employer to the employee.

In a popular metaphor applied to sources of retirement income, private pensions have long been seen as one leg of a "three-legged stool," the other two being Social Security and individual savings. Yet liberalizations in Social Security over the past 30 years, the inability of many individuals to accumulate significant retirement savings, and the leveling off in the expansion of private pension coverage have meant that the Social Security "leg" is longer than the other two, especially among moderate- and low-income retirees. Thus, whereas employer-provided pensions provided about 20% of the total wealth of individuals aged 51 to 61 in 1992, this was considerably less than the proportion provided by Social Security, and it was very unevenly distributed, with roughly one half of workers having any such coverage.

THE ROLES AND FUNCTIONS OF PRIVATE PENSIONS

The role of pensions in assuring economic well-being in old age can be viewed from a number of perspectives. Most basically, pensions are tied to the advent of capitalism, wherein "family enterprises" were slowly supplanted by capitalized industry and paid labor (Sass, 1997). Well-functioning families—at least those involved in small business or family-owned farming—saved either for old age or for bestowing bequests. The supplanting of those traditional family and economic forms by the urbanized and bureaucratized world of modern industry dramatically undermined the viability of that level of economic planning.

As they have evolved, private pensions occasionally met competing and occasionally consonant needs of employers and employees. In the early years, private pension plans helped "firms get diligent service out of blue-collar workers, secure career commitments from white-collar workers, and facilitate retirement at a specific age" (Sass, 1997, p. 227). Organized labor recognized the need to protect older workers but was suspicious of companies using pension promises as a way to unjustly tie workers to a given company. Over time, unions sought both expansion of Social Security and development of union-based rather than employer-based plans. The third actor to get seriously involved in pension development and reform was the federal government. Social Security was expressly designed to be a floor, not a ceiling, for retirement income, and there have long been pressures to maintain its "adequacy" function (disproportionately of benefit to low-income workers) over its "equity" function (a private sector–type "money's worth" approach of benefit to higher-income workers).

By the 1970s, however, the piecemeal expansion of private pensions had created problems for each of the stakeholders. Businesses worried about the long-term burdens they were saddled with in the form of DBP obligations. Workers were being repeatedly victimized by the inadequate safeguards of functioning pension plans and by the dire consequences of both company plan bankruptcies and union plan scandals and poor management. For its part, the federal government—whose role in management of the economy and of public social benefits had dramatically expanded in the wake of the Great Depression and World War II—realized that pensions had emerged as an institutional leg of old-age policy in America. It was this confluence of concerns that led to the passage of ERISA in 1974.

Changes in the economy (relative decline of old-line manufacturing firms, rise of service and technology industries) and in both labor supply and demand (need for flexible labor market policies, decline of unions, rise of contingent workers) have led to the stagnation and decline of DBPs and their partial supplementation by DCPs. ERISA regulations helped stabilize the workings of existing DBPs, but these very regulations have dissuaded most new businesses from adopting these traditional pensions. At the same time, ERISA and the Omnibus Budget and Reconciliation Act of 1982 have provided major tax incentives for both workers and employers to switch employer-based pensions to the DCP model. Finally, today's younger workers find DCPs appealing because of their greater portability, an attribute that outweighs the security associated with DBPs in an era where career-long work with a single employer is dramatically declining (Munnell, Sunden, & Lidstone, 2002).

In short, the historical role of pensions to provide labor force stability to the employer and retirement security to the worker has shifted to a model that increases pension portability for the worker, reduces the employer's obligation to the worker, and places the risks of pension plan performance upon the worker.

TYPES OF PRIVATE PENSIONS

Currently, DBPs and DCPs constitute the two principal types of employer-sponsored pension plans available in the United States. These do not include two other well-known retirement vehicles: individual retirement accounts (IRAs; available generally to workers with no employer-sponsored plan) and Keogh plans (available to the self-employed or small-business owners). Public sector plans may also be categorized as DBPs (Social Security is the world's largest DBP) or DCPs (employees of the federal government now contribute to such plans), but the discussion here is confined to private sector plans only.

In a DBP, employers promise employees a given benefit amount upon retirement in accordance with a benefit formula stated in the plan. The following are the three principal types of DBPs:

1. Flat-benefit formula. A flat dollar amount is paid for each year of service recognized under the plan.
2. Career-average formulas. Under these plans, employees earn a percentage of the pay recognized for each year they are plan participants, or the formula averages the participant's earnings over the period of plan participation. At retirement, the benefit equals a percentage of the career-

average pay, multiplied by the participant's number of years of service.

3. Final-pay formulas. These plans base benefits on average earnings during a specified number of years at the end of a participant's career; this is presumably the period when earnings are the highest. This plan has the effect of providing pre-retirement inflation protection to the employee, but it can represent a higher cost to the employer (EBRI, 1997c).

In the case of DCPs, employers make provision for contributions to an account established for each participating employee. The final retirement benefit equals the total of employer contributions, employee contributions (if any), and investment gains and losses. Employer contributions are often based on a specific formula, such as a percentage of employee salary or company profits. Because of these features, a major difference between the DBP and the DCP is that, unlike those of the DBP, future benefits of the DCP cannot be calculated in advance (EBRI, 1997c). Indeed, there is a fundamental conceptual distinction between the two types of plan. Strictly speaking, only DBPs are "pensions" by virtue of their paying a monthly benefit that is based on a formula tied to length of service and earnings; DCPs should be understood as tax-deferred savings plans providing benefits that are based on underlying assets, interest, dividends, and capital appreciation (Friedland, 1996). There are several types of DCPs, the most common being money-purchase plans (mandatory employer contributions as a percentage of worker salary), profit-sharing plans (amount derived from company profits), a thrift or savings plan (essentially an employee savings account, often with matching contri-

butions by the employer), and 401(k) plans (a qualified deferral arrangement under this section of the tax code, which allows an employee to have a portion of compensation—otherwise payable in cash—contributed to a plan such as those described here; these contributions are most commonly treated as a pretax reduction in salary; EBRI, 1997b, 1997c).

Data from the EBRI, shown in Table 78.1, document the trend in the direction of DCPs. The number of DBPs has declined notably since the mid-1980s; the number of DCP plans has risen significantly; the number of individuals covered under DBPs has stagnated; and the number of participants covered under DCPs has grown enormously.

Within the DCP category, especially spectacular growth took place in the 401(k) plans, with assets growing by 16 times, contributions by 9 times, and benefit payments by 12 times. By 1998, assets in 401(k) plans had risen to 38% of all private retirement plan assets and 78% of all DCP plan assets. Finally, the move toward DCPs grew to the point where by 1997, DCP assets exceeded DBP assets for the first time (EBRI, 2002).

ERISA of 1974 also established IRAs to give workers who did not have employer-based pensions an opportunity to save for retirement on a tax-deferred basis. Legislation in 1981 dramatically liberalized IRA eligibility to include workers who also had employer-based coverage. In 1986, restrictions for the latter group were again imposed, limiting the tax-deferral provision to those families with relatively low incomes. Although considerable assets are held in IRA accounts (VanDerhei, 2001), much of this results from contributions made by middle- and upper-income workers in the early 1980s, when deductibility extended across both income and pension-covered

TABLE 78.1 Private Pension Plans and Participants

	1975	1980	1985	1990	1995	1998
Number of private plans						
DBP (thousands)	103	148	170	113	69	56
DCP (thousands)	208	341	462	599	624	674
DCP (as % of total)	67%	70%	73%	84%	90%	92%
Number of private plan participants						
DBP (millions)	33	38	40	39	40	42
DCP (millions)	12	20	35	38	48	58
DCP as % of total	26%	34%	47%	50%	55%	58%

From Employee Benefit Research Institute, *EBRI Issue Brief* (September 22).

groups. In the 1990s, however, the number of active IRA participants dropped, with only 9.2% of those with employee-based coverage and, more important, only 6.3% of workers without such coverage contributing (EBRI, 1997a).

Finally, the federal tax code now encourages the self-employed to establish retirement savings vehicles. So-called Keogh plans, also known as H.R. 10 plans, were authorized in 1962 and allow "unincorporated small business owners, farmers, and those in professional practice to establish and participate in tax-qualified plans similar to those of corporate employers" (EBRI, 1997c, chap. 17, p. 1). Quite restrictive until ERISA's passage in 1974, Keogh plans have been liberalized over the years, now allowing contributions that are the lesser of 25% of the worker's compensation or $30,000 per year. More than other retirement savings vehicles, Keogh plans remain the province of higher-income individuals. Table 78.2 shows the participation rates and amount of contributions into IRAs and Keoghs by adjusted gross income.

PRIVATE PENSION COVERAGE

Over more than a century, private pensions have developed unevenly, reflecting the divergent interests of many parties who might have a stake in their existence. As indicated earlier, the business community has been actively involved, although changes in the marketplace have generated new approaches to employer-based pensions. Organized labor has had a major role in pension development, but declines in union membership and changes in both labor force demand and supply have reduced its influence. The federal government has stepped in to bring some regulatory clarity and tax advantages to the industry, but in the absence of any government mandating of the provision of pensions by employers, that role must be considered highly truncated.

Yet enormous numbers of individuals and families have had little or no involvement in the development of private pension, nor have they had any or sufficient coverage under those pension schemes. For these groups, the "second leg" of the retirement income stool is either too short or nonexistent. Not surprisingly, many of these same individuals are those toward whom social workers direct many of their service efforts: low-income individuals, women, populations of color, part-time workers, employees of small firms, and many—to use Barbara Ehrenreich's (2001) term—in sectors where workers are "nickel and dimed." Within these categories of vulnerability, there is some variability in pension coverage; however, in contrast to workers who are White, male, full-time, highly educated, and working in traditional mainline or emerging high-technology fields, the contrasts are stark.

Since the late 1970s, the percentage of private sector workers ages 25 to 64 who are participating in employer-based plans has remained essentially constant at about 50%. There are, however, important internal dynamics within this overall pattern of constancy. There has been a slight reduction in male pension plan participation, dropping from 55% in 1979 to 51% in 2000. This decline has held for all male income groups except the highest earnings quintile, where participation rose from 70% to 72%. At the other end of the earnings spectrum, participation by men in the bottom income quintile dropped from 21% to 19% (Munnell et al., 2002).

TABLE 78.2   Workers' Participation in and Average Contributions to IRAs and Keogh Plans, 1997

Adjusted gross income	Keogh plans		IRAs	
	% Workers participating	Average contribution ($)	% Workers participating	Average contribution ($)
Under $20,000	—	2,245	2	630
$20,000 to $40,000	—	2,665	7	1,504
$40,000 to $80,000	1	4,098	7	2,621
$80,000 to $120,000	3	6,360	9	4,148
$120,000 to $160,000	5	9,433	14	5,451
$160,000 and over	9	14,578	17	7,015
All income groups	1	1,159	6	2,772

From Congressional Budget Office, *Utilization of tax incentives for retirement saving.* Retrieved June 7, 2004, from *www.cbo.gov/showdoc.cfm?index=4490&sequence=1.*

Participation for women has risen over the same period, although it still remains lower than for men. Women's private plan participation increased from 38% to 42% between 1979 and 2000, with participation increases being seen in all five income quintiles. However, as with men, participation rates fall as one goes down the income quintiles, the participation rate for the highest-income women in 2000 being 71%, and the rate for the lowest-income women being 11%. Interestingly, across all worker status categories—full-year/full-time, full-year/part-time, part-time/full-year, part-year/part-time—women's participation rates exceed men's. This seeming disparity from the aggregate figures appears to result from women workers' overall lower earnings and/or lower rates of full-time work in comparison to men, categories in which participation rates are disproportionately low (EBRI, 2003b).

Despite these relative improvements in private pension coverage for women, the income women receive from these pensions remains decidedly lower than that received by men. The upper portion of Table 78.3, using constant 2001 dollars, shows (a) how the growth in pension incomes for both men and women is growing only slowly, and (b) that women's benefits continue to hover at roughly one half of men's. Because these data are for current retirees (aged 50 and older in these calculations), they reflect the earnings experience of cohorts of women older than the majority of those included in data on pension plan participation among current workers.

Data from the Survey of Income and Program Participation (SIPP), based on pension income data from 1996 for individuals aged 65 and over, also show this "50% phenomenon," with men reporting pension income of $700 and women income of $346. These and other data also show differential patterns by education, race, and employer characteristics. Table 78.2 reveals the expected monotonic relationship between pension income and education, ranging from no high school diploma to graduate degree. SIPP data, organized slightly differently, show an essentially identical pattern (EBRI 2003a, Fig. 3). Private pension participation rates among Black and Hispanic workers are shown in data from the Current Population Survey (CPS; EBRI, 2003b) to be lower than those for White workers, although the gap narrowed somewhat at higher income levels, as shown in Table 78.4.

The more dramatic picture painted by these data shows the critical place of income and employment status in determining pension coverage. There are much greater similarities by income across race and ethnic groups than there are by race and ethnicity within income groups. Consistent with these findings is a trend reported by Snyder (1993) showing a 66% increase in the number of retired Black men receiving pension income between 1982 and 1990, and a 250% increase between 1970 and 1990. However, as with the comparison between men and women, pension incomes by race and ethnicity have not improved as much as has pension plan coverage. Thus, among retirees aged 65 or over receiving pension income, Whites receive $560, Blacks $507, Hispanics $375, and "Other" $416 (EBRI, 2003a).

Overall, there have been notable improvements in recent years in the numbers of women and people of color covered by private pension plans. The more sobering finding is that coverage declines markedly with decreasing income, and there are notably higher proportions of women and people of color earning

TABLE 78.3 Median Annual Income From Pensions and Annuities in Constant 2000 Dollars for the Population Over Age 50, 1988–2001

	1988	1990	1995	2001
Gender				
Male	$9,826	$9,485	$11,156	$12,000
Female	4,970	5,147	5,578	6,000
Educational level				
No high school diploma	4,114	4,280	4,978	5,220
High school to associate degree	7,485	7,058	8,130	8,436
Bachelor's degree	12,979	13,008	13,429	14,500
Graduate degree	17,636	16,049	21,466	21,600

From Employee Benefit Research Institute, *EBRI Notes* (January 2003). Estimates from Current Population Survey, U.S. Bureau of the Census (March 2002).

TABLE 78.4 Percentage of Wage and Salary Workers Ages 21–64 Who Participated in an Employment-Based Retirement Plan, by Earnings and Race/Ethnicity, 2002

	<5,000	*$10–$15K*	*$20–25K*	*$30–35K*	*$40–45K*	*>50K*
White	9%	26%	50%	63%	70%	74%
Black	8	23	47	64	69	73
Other	6	18	40	48	63	70
Hispanic	5	11	31	45	59	64

From Employee Benefit Research Institute, *EBRI Issue Brief* (October 2003). Estimates from Current Population Survey (March 2003).

low wages who thus remain disproportionately underprotected. In addition, the improvements seen in pension coverage and income among the Black population for the most part have not occurred among Hispanic workers and retirees.

THE RELATIVE CONTRIBUTIONS OF PRIVATE PENSIONS

The shortcomings of America's private pension system in meeting the income needs of vulnerable populations can be seen in both relative and absolute terms. The U.S. Bureau of the Census (2002) calculates the percentage of income derived from different sources for households ranked by income quintile. Table 78.5 shows that private pensions constitute a higher proportion of income as overall income rises, thereby showing that such income is both absolutely and relatively distributed very much toward the better-off.

Other quintile breakdowns of retirement income by source show that (a) among the older population,

private pensions constitute roughly 10% of retirement income for all groups except those aged 85 and over, among whom they make up only 6.8% of such income; (b) private pensions constitute 11.3% of retirement income among older unmarried men compared with 7.5% for older unmarried women; and (c) private pension income makes up 10.5% of retirement income among Black household units, compared with 9.9% among White units, and only 6.5% among Hispanic units (U.S. Bureau of the Census, 2002).

CONCLUSION

The workings of the private pension system in the United States and the patterns of participation in these plans have significant implications for geriatric social workers. Not surprisingly, these private sector vehicles—sweetened with inversely redistributive tax benefits—work to the advantage of relatively privileged groups in American society. Whether by gender, race, income, or education, the privileged tend to prevail.

TABLE 78.5 Shares of Aggregate Income of Aged Units 65 or Older From Particular Sources by Quintiles of Total Money Income, 2000

Income quintile	1st	2nd	3rd	4th	5th
Social Security	82.3	81.6	64.1	46.0	19.4
Private pensions	1.7	4.3	9.5	13.0	9.1
Earnings	1.3	2.6	6.7	14.2	35.3
Income from assets	3.3	5.1	9.4	12.8	24.2
Public assistance	8.4	1.7	.9	.2	.1
Government employee pensions	.7	2.4	6.2	10.2	9.4
Other	2.3	2.3	3.2	3.6	2.5
TOTAL	100%	100%	100%	100%	100%

Quintile limits are $9,295 (1st), $14,980 (2nd), $23,631 (3rd), $39,719 (4th), and >$39,719 (5th).

From U.S. Bureau of the Census, Current Population Survey (March 2002), retrieved June 7, 2004, from *www.ssa.gov/policy/docs/statcomps/income_pop55/2000.*

Two implications in particular emerge for geriatric social work. The first is to be cognizant of the ways in which the workings of the system—notably, which employers offer plans—work to the advantage of the better-off. It is imperative that social workers involved with low-income individuals and communities work to modify seeming inequities and, more immediately, to encourage clients—where they are able—to participate in plans to prepare for their retirement years.

The second implication is for geriatric social workers themselves. A growing body of literature is predicting that alarming numbers of Americans will be forced to rely too heavily on Social Security benefits in their retirement years. Since the maximum retirement benefit available under Social Security is about $20,000 (and most workers will receive far less), large numbers of workers approaching retirement will find their standard of living in serious jeopardy. And, as research by Martha Ozawa (1993) has documented, social workers are less financially prepared for retirement than professionals in either nursing or education. Not only is the personal professional; here, the professional is personal.

REFERENCES

Ehrenreich, B. (2001). *Nickel and dimed: On (not) getting by in America.* New York: Metropolitan Books.

Employee Benefit Research Institute. (1997a). *Data book on employee benefits.* Washington, DC: Author.

Employee Benefit Research Institute. (1997b). Defined benefit and defined contribution plans: Understanding the differences. In *Fundamentals of employee benefit programs* (5th ed.). Washington, DC: Author.

Employee Benefit Research Institute. (1997c). Pension plans. In *Fundamentals of employee benefit programs* (5th ed). Washington, DC: Author.

Employee Benefit Research Institute. (1997d). Retirement plans for the self-employed. In *Fundamentals of employee benefit programs* (5th ed.). Washington, DC: Author.

Employee Benefit Research Institute. (2002, September). *EBRI Issue Brief.* Washington, DC: Author.

Employee Benefit Research Institute. (2003a, February). *EBRI Notes.* Washington, DC: Author.

Employee Benefit Research Institute. (2003b, October). *EBRI Issue Brief.* Washington, DC: Author.

Friedland, R. (1996). Privatizing social insurance. *Public Policy and Aging Report, 7*(4), 11–15.

Munnell, A., Sunden, A., & Lidstone, E. (2002). *How important are private pensions?* Chestnut Hill, MA: Center for Retirement Research, Boston College.

Ozawa, M. N. (1993). Earnings history of social workers: A comparison to other professional groups. *Social Work, 38,* 542–551.

Sass, S. A. (1997). *The promise of private pensions.* Cambridge, MA: Harvard University Press.

Schulz, J. A. (1988). *The economics of aging* (4th ed.). New York: Auburn House.

Snyder, D. C. (1993). The economic well-being of retired workers by race and Hispanic origin. In R. V. Burkhauser & D. L. Salisbury (Eds.), *Pensions in a changing economy* (pp. 67–78). Washington, DC: National Academy on Aging.

U.S. Bureau of the Census. (2002). *Income of the population 55 or older, 2000.* Retrieved June 7, 2004, from *www.ssa.gov/policy/docs/statcomps/income_pop55/ 2000*

VanDerhei, J. (2001). *The changing face of retirement* (Issue Brief No. 232). Washington, DC: EBRI.

This chapter provides an overview of Medicare, a program that was enacted as part of Title XVIII of the Social Security Act of 1965. It also discusses Medicare's new policy developments, projected fiscal problems, limited long-term care coverage, and lack of mental health parity. The chapter concludes with a review of social work's role in Medicare.

OVERVIEW

What Is Medicare?

Medicare is a federal health insurance program for older persons and persons with disabilities enacted under Title XVIII of the Social Security Act of 1965. It is an entitlement program that covers persons regardless of income or prior health condition. The program currently covers more than 41 million Americans, of which 35 million are older persons and 6 million are nonelderly persons with disabilities (Kaiser Family Foundation, 2004). The total program outlays were $256.8 billion in fiscal year 2003 (Kaiser Family Foundation, 2004).

What Is the Structure of Medicare?

Medicare consists of four parts: Part A, the hospital insurance program; Part B, supplementary medical insurance; Part C, Medicare Advantage; Part D, outpatient prescription drug program (Table 79.1).

JI SEON LEE

Policies Affecting Health, Mental Health, and Caregiving: Medicare

Who Is Covered Under Medicare?

Almost all persons aged 65 and over are entitled to Part A if they or their spouse is eligible for Social Security payments. Persons who are 65 and under who receive Social Security Disability Insurance payments are also generally covered after a 2-year waiting period. All persons regardless of age who have end-stage renal disease (ESRD) are entitled to Part A. Persons who are not automatically entitled to enroll in Part A can voluntarily obtain coverage by paying full actuarial cost.

Participation in Medicare Part B is voluntary. All persons aged 65 and over who are enrolled in Part A are eligible to enroll in Part B by paying a monthly premium. About 95% of Part A beneficiaries voluntarily enroll in Part B.

In general, Medicare covers a diverse population, although the distribution of beneficiaries by race/

TABLE 79.1 Summary of Medicare Parts A Through D

	Description	Coverage (as of 2004)	Financing
Part A	Hospital insurance program	Inpatient hospital (first 60 days of hospital stay for each benefit period with a deductible of $876 in 2004; for 61–90 days in the same benefit period there is daily coinsurance; after 90 days in the same benefit period, one must draw upon their lifetime reserve; for anything over 150 days in the same benefit period there is no coverage; there is a lifetime reserve of 60 days), inpatient mental health/substance abuse care (for up to 190 days, lifetime limit), skilled nursing facility (up to 100 days following a hospital stay with a co-pay of $109.50 per day for the 21st through the 100th day of care), hospice (up to 210 days of care with a co-pay of 5% of the cost for inpatient respite care up to the cost of the inpatient hospital deduction), and home health care (postinstitutional home health care for 100 visits per episode, except for those persons with Part A coverage only).	1.45% of payroll tax paid by employees and employers. The self-employed pay a single tax of 2.9% on earnings.
Part B	Supplementary medical insurance	Physician and outpatient hospital care, lab tests, medical supplies, and home health, with a deductible of $100 in 2004.	Beneficiary premiums (25%) and federal general revenues (75%). Monthly Part B premium is $66.60 in 2004.
Part C	Medicare Advantage, managed care plans (formerly called Medicare + Choice)	Part A and Part B benefits depending on the plan, additional benefits that are not covered by traditional Medicare (e.g., eye and foot care).	Medicare pays plans to provide Parts A and B totaling $36.3 billion in 2003; 62% of enrollees on the basic plan pay a monthly premium in addition to the Part B premium.
Part D	Outpatient prescription drug program. Enacted under the Medicare Prescription Drug, Improvement and Modernization Act of 2003, to be implemented in 2006.	Beneficiaries pay a deductible for the first $250 in drug costs; pay 25% of total drug costs between $250 and $2,250; pay 100% of total drug costs between $2,250 and $5,100; and pay the greater of $2 for generics, $5 for brand drugs, or 5% co-insurance after reaching the $3,600 out-of-pocket limit. Medicare will provide additional assistance to beneficiaries who qualify based on low incomes and limited assets.	Beneficiary premiums (25.5%) and general revenues (74.5%). Congressional Budget Office estimates the monthly premium to be $35 in 2006.

From Kaiser Family Foundation (2004). State Health Facts Online. Distribution of Medicare Beneficiaries by Race/Ethnicity, State data 2000-2001, U.S. 2001.

ethnicity shows that a majority are White (84%). Blacks represent 8%, Hispanics 5%, and other groups 3% (Kaiser Family Foundation, 2004). Thirty-seven percent of the beneficiaries have incomes below 150% of the federal poverty line, and about 35% report needing assistance with at least one activity of daily living. About one quarter of recipients live in rural areas (Kaiser Family Foundation, 2004).

What Types of Medicare Plans Are Available for Beneficiaries?

There are two major types of Medicare plans: original Medicare and private Medicare plans. Regardless of which type of plan a person is enrolled in, as long as one has Medicare Part A and Part B, that person has a right to the same basic benefits.

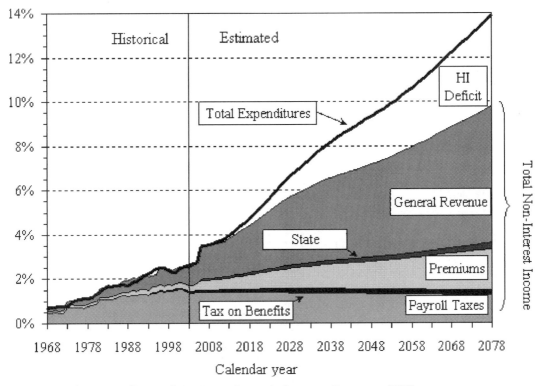

FIGURE 79.1 Medicare Expenditures and Non-Interest Income by Source as a Percentage of GDP
From Annual Report of the Trustees of Medicare HI and SMI funds (2004).

Original Medicare Plans

The Original Medicare plan is structured as a traditional fee-for-service plan offered by the federal government. A person who is eligible for Medicare will be automatically enrolled in this plan. One advantage of this plan is that the enrollee is able to choose to go to any doctor or hospital. The drawbacks include large out-of-pocket cost stemming from high hospital deductibles, annual deductible for doctor's visit, and co-payments for most outpatient medical care. In addition, there is no or limited coverage for routine dental care, hearing aids, vision care, routine foot care, or long-term care.

Private Medicare Plans

Medicare Advantage (formerly called Medicare + Choice), is offered by managed care companies, primarily health maintenance organizations (HMOs). To participate, one must have both Medicare Part A and Part B. HMOs have been an option under Medicare since the 1970s, but the role of these private plans expanded greatly under the Balanced Budget Act (BBA)

of 1997 by including other plans such as preferred provider organizations (PPOs), private fee-for-service plans (PFFS), provider-sponsored organizations (PSOs), and medical savings accounts. The Medicare Prescription Drug, Improvement and Moderation Act of 2003 created another option called regional PPOs.

The appeal of these private plans is relatively low out-of-pocket cost, which averaged from $429 in 1999 to $1,260 in 2003. However, these plans do not always offer savings for beneficiaries. About 31% of enrollees in Medicare Advantage programs do not have a plan that offers prescription drug benefits, which is usually a large out-of-pocket cost item. Plan participation and enrollment have varied over the years. In 2004, 11% of Medicare beneficiaries participated in these plans, down from 16% in 2000 (Kaiser Family Foundation, 2004). Enrollees are allowed to enroll in and disenroll from these plans only once, during a 6-month period beginning 2006. These plans offer a number of advantages. For example, they may be more affordable than traditional Medicare plans for persons on a fixed budget. They cover all benefits provided by traditional Medicare plans. In addition, they may provide benefits not covered by traditional

Medicare, such as limited prescription drugs, vision care, and foot care. However, the enrollee's choice of doctor and hospital may be limited to participating providers, and access to specialists and services usually is predetermined.

Supplemental Coverage

A majority of Medicare beneficiaries rely on some form of public or private supplemental insurance to fill in the gaps in Medicare's coverage. According to the Kaiser Family Foundation (2004), 34% had employer-sponsored benefits, 23% owned Medigap policies, 12% had Medicaid, and 2% had other public insurance.

- Employer-sponsored benefits: The pressures of rising health care costs have led to reductions in many employer-sponsored benefits. A survey by Kaiser and Health Research and Educational trust (2003) showed that between 1998 and 2003, a large percentage of employers dropped coverage to retirees from 66% to 38%. Furthermore, a 2002 survey by Kaiser Family Foundation and Hewitt Associates showed that large firms (1,000 or more employees) made changes in how they offer their benefits to retirees. About 44% increased contributions to premiums, 36% increased cost sharing for retirees, and 13% terminated benefits.
- Medigap policies: This form of insurance typically covers Medicare's deductible and coinsurance. It may also cover some benefits that Medicare typically does not cover. Enrollees after 1992 have a choice of 10 plans, Plans A through J. Plan A offers the most basic benefits, and the other plans offer the basic package with a combination of other benefits. Plans H through J offer prescription drug plans, all three having a $250 deductible (Committee on Ways and Means, 2004). Three recent laws (Balanced Budget Act of 1997; Balanced Budget Refinement Act of 1999; and Medicare, Medicaid, SCHIP Benefits Improvement and Protection Act of 2000) expanded guarantee issues for enrollees. They are 6-month open enrollment and guarantee issuances of Medigap policyholders whose coverage was previously terminated. This also extends to enrollees who were trying out Medicare + Choice.
- Medicaid: Some low-income and disabled Medicare beneficiaries are entitled to partial or full coverage under Medicaid as dual beneficiaries. Medicare is typically the payer of first choice when both Medicare and Medicaid provide the benefits; Medicaid then picks up the portion not covered by Medicare (typically the long-term care benefits). Prescription drugs are covered under Medicaid. In addition, certain low-income groups, called Qualified Medicare Beneficiaries, Specified Low Income Medicare Beneficiaries, and Qualified Individuals, qualify for limited Medicaid benefits. For these groups, Medicaid typically pays for Medicare Part A deductibles and coinsurance and/or Part B premiums. However, these groups do not qualify for prescription drug benefits under Medicaid.

What Is the Projected Financial Crisis of Medicare?

Medicare's financial crisis has long been predicted. Between 1994 and 1996, the trustees of Medicare projected that the Hospital Insurance (HI) fund would become insolvent by 2001 (Kaiser Family Foundation, 2004). By 2001, however, the trustees projected a 28-year solvency for the HI fund, the longest period of solvency in Medicare's history.

Why is there such fluctuation in projecting the health of Medicare funds? There are three main factors, the first relating to how the HI fund is financed—mainly through payroll taxes. Like Social Security's OASDI fund, the HI fund is a pay-as-you-go system in which current employees pay for the HI fund for current Medicare beneficiaries. As a result, the aging of the country's population and the smaller number of workers supporting beneficiaries through their payrolls directly affect the health of the HI fund. The number of beneficiaries is expected to rise from 40 million in 2001 to 77 million in 2030 due to the graying of the baby boomers. Furthermore, the number of workers per beneficiary will fall from 4.0 in 1999 to 2.3 in 2030 (Kaiser Family Foundation, 2004). Given these parameters, theoretically, the HI fund could become insolvent. In contrast, the Supplementary Medical Insurance (SMI) fund cannot be insolvent because its revenues come from premiums paid by beneficiaries and general tax revenues. Furthermore, Medicare requires general revenues and beneficiary premiums to be automatically adjusted to cover the cost of Medicare Part B. However, SMI costs are growing faster than those of the HI fund. To keep up with rising costs, beneficiaries' premiums must be raised, and more contributions from general revenues will be needed. Therefore, the insolvency of the HI fund has become a proxy for the overall financial health of Medicare.

The second factor is the rising cost of medical care. Medicare's spending is projected to grow at a faster

TABLE 79.2 Major Legislative History of Medicare

Date	Legislative milestones
July 30, 1965	Medicare was enacted under Title XVIII of the Social Security Act.
1972	Coverage was extended to disabled and those with permanent kidney failure.
1980	Medicare supplemental insurance (Medigap) was brought under federal oversight. Coverage of home health services was broadened.
1982	Tax Equity and Fiscal Responsibility Act of 1982 made it easier and more attractive for health maintenance organizations to contract with Medicare.
1983	Prospective payment system was implemented for hospitals—developed diagnostic related groups (DRGs).
1988	Medicare Catastrophic Coverage Act was enacted to include outpatient prescription drug benefits and a cap on patient liability.
1989	Medicare Catastrophic Coverage Act was repealed.
1996	The Health Insurance Portability and Accountability Act of 1996 (HIPAA) was enacted to provide improved continuity or "portability" of group health plan coverage and group health insurance provided through employment or through individual insurance market.
1997	The Balanced Budget Act of 1997 established Part C (Medicare + Choice), developed and implemented prospective payment system for home health care, skilled nursing, rehabilitation hospitals, and ambulatory outpatient care.
2003	Medicare Prescription Drug, Improvement and Modernization Act of 2003. Provides seniors and individuals with disabilities with a prescription drug benefit, more choices under Medicare.

From U.S. Department of Health and Human Services (1999) Mental Health: A Report of the Surgeon General. p. 412.

rate than that of the overall economy. The health care costs per enrollee are projected to rise faster than the wages per worker on which the payroll tax is paid (Kaiser Family Foundation, 2004). In 2002, health care costs rose 5.7 percentage points faster than the overall economy, measured by the growth of the gross domestic product (GDP; Centers for Medicare and Medicaid Services [CMS], 2004). As a result, whereas Medicare's annual costs are currently 2.7% of GDP, they will reach almost 14% of GDP by 2078 (Social Security Administration, 2004).

The third factor is related to the economy. With an improved economy, the availability of general tax revenues also improves. This potentially gives Medicare more funds to add to its trust fund.

In 2004, there were continued projections that the HI funds were headed for both near-term and longer term financial insolvency. Each year, Medicare's trustees (the secretaries of treasury, labor, and health and human services; and two public trustees of different political parties selected by the president and confirmed by the Senate) issue a report on the current state and outlook of the HI fund and SMI fund. According to the trustees' report (2004), the projected date of HI fund depletion has moved forward significantly to 2019, from 2026 in the previous year's report, mainly as a result of a lower projected payroll tax in-

come and higher projected expenditures for inpatient hospital care. Annual expenditures are expected to exceed noninterest income beginning this year, and tax income deficits will grow until HI fund reserves are exhausted in 2019.

The financial outlook for SMI has changed even more dramatically since the enactment of Medicare Part D (prescription drug plan). The cost of this new plan, combined with a higher projected cost for Part B, greatly steps up the overall projected rate of growth of the SMI fund. Given these projections, the sustainability of Medicare will be difficult without greatly altering how the program is financed.

Four options are available to potentially combat the financial crisis of Medicare (Philips, 2000):

1. Reduce the number of people enrolled in the program by increasing the eligibility age. (The Old Age Insurance program under Social Security has already adopted this option.)
2. Increase beneficiary cost sharing. The current out-of-pocket cost for beneficiaries is already high, and with this option the burden will become even greater.
3. Reduce the total per-beneficiary program cost. Holding down the cost per beneficiary will be the key (e.g., reducing how much Medicare reim-

burses providers), but it will be important to consider if these reductions in program costs will be helpful in the long run and how they would affect beneficiaries and the quality of their care.

4. Find an additional source of revenue. Doing so, however, would require some kind of taxation, and with any new taxes, there are key questions that must be answered. How much can the government tax for it to be adequate? Who will pay the tax (equity)? What effects will the new tax have on the economy? Would the new tax be efficient to administer?

NEW POLICY DEVELOPMENTS

Changes in Medicare Payments: Prospective Payment System for Home Health Care and the Integration of Managed Care

The BBA of 1997 made sweeping changes in Medicare payments to postacute care (PAC) services. Since 1984, acute short hospital stays had been paid based on the prospective payment system (PPS), which provided incentives for hospitals to reduce the length of stay and discharge patients either to the patient's home or to PAC earlier than in the past. Furthermore, hospitals that provided PAC services had opportunities to earn more revenues from Medicare. These payment incentives facilitated the shift from inpatient to outpatient services, leading to massive growth in Medicare payments for PAC services. Between 1990 and 1995, home health care services grew from $3.9 billion to $18.3 billion (U.S. Department of Health and Human Services, 1999). The proportion of Medicare beneficiaries using home health increased from 5.8% in 1990 to 10.8% in 1997. Between 1987 and 1991, the annual average number of home health visits per patient doubled, from 23 visits to 45 visits per user. By 1997, the number of visits had risen to 73, and patients who received more than 200 visits represented about 10% of all home health users (Health Care Financing Administration [HCFA], 1999). Medicare spending also grew rapidly, reflecting the growth in utilization. Medicare home health expenditures increased at an annual rate of 21% between 1987 and 1997, with these costs representing 2% of total Medicare spending in 1987 and 9% in 1997 (HCFA, 1999).

The BBA of 1997 was introduced to curb Medicare payments to PAC services, particularly in home health care. PPS in home health care and skilled nurs-

ing facilities is Medicare's latest attempt to control costs. The idea behind PPS is not new to Medicare, whose policies reflect its integration of the principles of managed care. However, managed care has never been a vital part of providing care for Medicare beneficiaries, for two principal reasons. Competition among health plans has been an issue for Medicare. Medicare is a government program, and many private health plans do not wish to negotiate rates and benefits or accept lower rates from the government. This has led to some private managed care plans dropping out of the program and/or dropping benefits under Medicare + Choice. The other issue is related to consumer information and how consumers use these private managed care plans. Many Medicare beneficiaries saw managed care plans as limiting choice and services. Others, however, saw them as an option for reducing their out-of-pocket costs and took advantage of the liberal enrollment policies by switching between the traditional Medicare plans and managed care plans when doing so was more financially attractive to the beneficiaries.

Although managed care has not taken a strong hold of Medicare, the process and structure of managed care have continuously evolved and will continue to evolve. Medicare, the largest health insurance provider, has also followed the evolution of managed care and has changed its policies to reflect the process of managing illness and cost. According to Fairfield, Mechanic, and Rosleff (1997), there have been five generations of managed care. The first generation focused on retrospective utilization reviews and mainly contracted with preferred providers. The second generation used more proactive utilization reviews, increased the use of capitation and gatekeeping, and paid hospitals through prospective payments. The third generation used sophisticated utilization management, full capitation of risk, and clinical practice guidelines and managed high-cost cases. The fourth generation is what the United States is currently working toward achieving. The managed care system is increasingly interested in health outcomes, more health systems integration, and improved information systems. The fifth generation is the future goal of managed care, which will use anticipatory case management, targeted disease management, and outcome-based reimbursement. These generations are apparent in Medicare's history starting in the 1970s, when HMOs were first introduced to Medicare. Beginning in 1983, hospitals were reimbursed for Medicare patients on a flat-rate basis, determined by the patient's diagnosis, known as the diagnostic related groups (DRGs). Whatever the payment was for a particular condition, hospitals were expected to treat patients within the limits of that flat payment. The question of case mix became crucial regarding the types of patients that were admitted, and discharge planning conducted by social workers became central to the survival of hospitals. The concept was further expanded to nursing homes using resource utilization groups (RUGs).

Under PPS for home health care, Medicare pays home health agencies a predetermined base payment. There are six main characteristics of home health PPS. First, the unit of payment under home health PPS will be for a 60-day episode of care. Second, there will be case-mix adjustment to the payment, which adjusts payment for a beneficiary's health condition and needs. Third, outlier payments will be made for care of the costliest beneficiaries. Fourth, adjustments to payment will be made for beneficiaries whose episodes consist of four or fewer visits. These episodes will be paid by a standardized, service-specific per-visit amount multiplied by the number of visits during an episode. Fifth, adjustments to payments will be made for beneficiaries who experience a significant change in their condition. Sixth, adjustments to payments will be made for beneficiaries who change home health agencies (HCFA, 1999).

Based on these six factors, payment to home health agencies will be adjusted for the health condition, the care needs of the beneficiary, and the geographic differences in wages for home health agencies across the country. Adjustments for health conditions, clinical characteristics, and service needs are referred to as case-mix adjustment. The home health PPS will provide home health agencies with payments for each 60-day episode of care for each beneficiary. There is no limit to the number of episodes per beneficiary as long as the person remains eligible for home health benefits. Although payment for each episode is adjusted to reflect the beneficiary's health condition and needs, a special outlier provision exists to ensure appropriate payment to reflect the home health agency's cost in caring for the sickest beneficiary and to ensure access to home health services for which they are eligible (HCFA, 1999)

Today, Medicare is focusing more on health outcomes and is investing in information systems that can provide critical data to help target specific high-cost diseases and track health outcomes. Furthermore, Medicare is looking toward various managed care structures (e.g., HMO and PPOs) to provide health care for older persons and the disabled. Part C

(formerly Medicare + Choice) was created to further integrate managed care structures (providers) as a primary alternative to the traditional fee-for-service Medicare. This has been seen as a move to privatize Medicare and control its ever-increasing costs.

Prescription Drug Benefits

On December 8, 2003, the Medicare Prescription Drug, Improvement and Modernization Act of 2003 (P.L. 108-173) was enacted. This created a new drug benefit as Part D of Medicare, which will begin in January 2006. Until that new benefit begins, an interim Medicare-endorsed drug discount card and transitional assistance programs will be available.

Medicare beneficiaries have access to a transitional discount card program (from June 2004 through January 2006) that will provide them with an estimated 10% to 15% savings. For beneficiaries whose incomes are below 135% of the federal poverty level and who do not have private or Medicaid drug coverage, the federal government will provide $600/per year for drug expenses in 2004 and 2005 and also will pay the annual enrollment fee.

In 2006, Medicare will begin to pay for outpatient prescription drugs through private plans. Under this arrangement, beneficiaries can remain on the traditional fee-for-service Medicare plan and enroll separately in a private prescription drug plan or enroll in Medicare Advantage plans for all Medicare-covered benefits plus the prescription drug coverage. Under this basic plan, in 2006 beneficiaries will be accountable for the following:

- A deductible for the first $250 in drug costs;
- 25% of total drug costs between $250 and $2,250;
- 100% of total drug costs between $2,250 and $5,100;
- The greater of $2 for generics, $5 for brand-name drugs, or 5% coinsurance after reaching the $3,600 out-of-pocket limit; and
- An estimated $35 per month in premiums for basic drug coverage in 2006.

Medicare will provide additional assistance to beneficiaries who qualify based on low incomes and limited assets. Beneficiaries for the first time will have to meet income and asset tests to receive assistance. The Congressional Budget Office estimates that 14.1 million beneficiaries will be eligible for this type of assistance, within the following categories:

- *Dually eligible beneficiaries for Medicare and Medicaid:* Beginning in 2006, the drug benefits traditionally received under Medicaid will be provided under Medicare. These beneficiaries will pay no premiums or deductibles, and no drug costs above the out-of-pocket threshold. Below the threshold, those with incomes under 100% of poverty will pay $1 to $3 co-pays; those above the poverty line will pay $2 to $5 co-pays.
- *Beneficiaries with incomes below 135% of the poverty level and assets under $6,000 for singles and $9,000 for couples:* A subsidy will be provided to cover the premium for basic coverage in their region. These beneficiaries will pay $2 to $5 co-pays with no deductible and no cost sharing above the out-of-pocket threshold.
- *Beneficiaries with incomes below 150% of poverty level and assets under $10,000 for singles and $20,000 for couples:* A subsidy will be provided to pay for premiums on a sliding-scale fee. These beneficiaries will pay a $50 deductible and 15% coinsurance up to the out-of-pocket threshold and $2 to $5 co-pays above the threshold.

This new prescription drug benefit will interact with other coverage, in particular, those programs that currently supplement Medicare. Medicare Advantage will have to provide prescription drug coverage beginning in 2006. Employer-sponsored plans that elect to provide prescription drug benefits comparable to Part D will receive subsidies from Medicare, which will pay 28% of the costs. In 2006, Medigap insurers will not be allowed to issue new policies that include drug coverage or supplement Part D coverage. Beneficiaries who already have Medigap policies may keep their policies (but a penalty may be faced when they choose to enroll in Part D at a later date).

According to the CMS (2004), about 7.4 million beneficiaries are expected to enroll. Savings from the discount card program are estimated to range from $1.4 to $1.8 billion, and savings from the transitional assistance program are projected at $2.4 billion.

Medicare needs to consider the following issues as it manages an outpatient prescription drug benefit (Fox, 2004):

1. What should be the role of the pharmacy benefits manager who will process the claims and administer the program?
2. What drugs will be covered? (Generic drugs, brand-name drugs, quality-of-life drugs, drugs that are expensive but have marginal effectiveness, new drugs first released to the public with limited information, over-the-counter drugs and equivalents?)
3. How broad should the pharmacy network be for the transitional discount card program when having broader networks means paying the pharmacies higher dispensing fees?
4. How can generic brands be promoted rather than more expensive brand-name drugs?
5. How can drug utilization be managed? This is an issue of quality of care and cost. Utilization reviews need to reflect the needs of older beneficiaries. Fox (2004) suggests three points for utilization reviews—prior authorization, at the time the prescription is filled, and after it is filled (retrospective review). Retrospective review can help target educational efforts for patients, physicians, and intensive disease management or case management programs.

LONG-TERM CARE AND MEDICARE

Relationship Between Medicare and Long-Term Care

Long-term care constitutes a variety of services that include medical and nonmedical care to people who have a chronic illness or a disability. Many people who need long-term care often receive support services such as help with activities of daily living (e.g., bathing, dressing, and toileting). Long-term care is provided in various settings, including but not limited to the home, the community, assisted-living facilities, and nursing homes. It is estimated that by 2005 about 9 million people aged 65 and over will need long-term care services (CMS, 2004). This number will increase to 12 million by the year 2020. It is estimated that about 40% of persons who are 65 and older have a chance of entering a nursing home and that those who enter nursing homes will remain there for 5 years or more (CMS, 2004).

Medicare was originally conceived not to provide long-term care services but to provide basic health care services to seniors. Medicare pays only for medically necessary services in skilled nursing facilities and home health care, and only on a short-term or "intermittent" basis. Most people who need long-term care, however, need more support services (nonskilled care), which help with activities of daily living. Medicare will not pay for this type of service.

Furthermore, Medicare's approach to health care is medically oriented and does not fully incorporate the psychosocial aspect of health care that can influence a patient's treatment outcomes. As a result, social work services, which can provide vital psychological and social services to older patients, have played a minimal role in providing care in skilled nursing facilities and home health care.

Given the large number of older persons potentially needing long-term care services and the high cost of care, many older persons are left financially vulnerable. They may have to pay out of pocket for long-term care services directly or through long-term care insurance. Ultimately, many older persons needing long-term care services may use up all their financial resources and qualify for Medicaid, which pays for support services and nursing home care.

Currently, there are about 7 million dually enrolled beneficiaries in Medicare and Medicaid. Of these 7 million, about 6 million receive full Medicaid benefits, and about 1 million receive Medicaid assistance with Medicare cost sharing (Kaiser Family Foundation, 2004). Dually eligible beneficiaries differ in many ways from other Medicare beneficiaries. They are the poorest, the sickest, and high users of health care services among Medicare beneficiaries. Almost 75% of dual enrollees have incomes under $10,000 (just above the poverty level), compared with 13% of other Medicare beneficiaries (Kaiser Family Foundation, 2004). Approximately 25% of dual enrollees reside in nursing homes, compared with only 2% of other Medicare beneficiaries (Kaiser Family Foundation, 2004). They are twice as likely to have significant limitations in activities of daily living and are more likely to have chronic illnesses such as diabetes and stroke (Kaiser Family Foundation, 2004).

For these dual enrollees, coverage of services is the key to their health care. Whereas Medicare covers basic health care services, Medicaid will pay for Medicare's premiums and cost sharing and cover other benefits not covered by Medicare, such as nonskilled long-term care services. For dually eligible beneficiaries, coverage of nonskilled long-term care services such as home care and nursing home care is critical. For many older persons in the United States, being dually eligible is the only way to receive coverage for long-term care.

Lack of Parity in Mental Health

Currently in the United States, coverage for mental health is much more limited than that for physical ill-

ness. Mental health coverage can be obtained through private health insurance, Medicare, Medicaid, or private payment. However, there is a disparity between mental and physical coverage under insurance plans. Many have argued that this inequality results from a lack of knowledge about treatment options and interventions for mental illness. This policy also stigmatizes persons with a mental disorder. For the business community, parity for mental and physical health coverage has been provided through a 1996 law, which required businesses with 50 or more employees to have an annual or lifetime limit on spending that does not differentiate among types of illness. This parity law, however, does not stop companies from charging higher deductibles or co-payments for mental health benefits or not providing mental health coverage altogether. The law also permits restrictions on the number of visits to a therapist or days of hospitalization (Alliance for Health Reform, 2004).

For Medicare, the issue of parity is important, given that mental disorders such as dementia, depression, and schizophrenia all increase as the population ages. According to the National Institute of Mental Health (2004), among 35 million older persons, an estimated 2 million have depressive illness, and another 5 million may have depressive symptoms that fall short of meeting the full diagnostic criteria. But Medicare has no parity for mental and physical health. Medicare pays for a lifetime benefit of 190 days of inpatient psychiatric treatment. Although HI payment is limited to 60 days per episode for general hospital care, it does not have a lifetime limit on the number of days for such care. For outpatient mental health services, there is a 50% cost sharing rather than the 20% for other outpatient services. With the growing number of older persons with mental disorders, it is critical for policymakers to ensure parity for Medicare.

SOCIAL WORK AND MEDICARE

Social work services have been a vital part of patient care for Medicare beneficiaries, who are often in need of mental health services and other social services. Historically, before PPS was introduced in skilled nursing facilities and home health care, social work had been reimbursed independently. The BBA of 1997 changed this to include social work services under a consolidated bill. This change has unintentionally discouraged the use of social workers in these settings. Although social workers have been the primary mental health care providers in skilled nursing facilities, psychologist and psychiatrist payments were not included in the consolidated billing and still maintain direct billing. The Clinical Social Work Medicare Equity Act of 2003 changed the reimbursement for clinical social work services and excluded these services from the consolidated billing under PPS. These changes mark an important point in Medicare, creating equity among mental health providers in direct Medicare payments.

Provisions of medical social service have been a part of Medicare home health since the beginning of the program. Medicare requires that social work services be available to patients (HCFA, 1992), but there is no requirement that social workers see patients or participate in the planning of their care (Dhooper, 1997). Under Medicare, social work services are not considered a primary service such as skilled nursing care or physical and speech therapy. Therefore, social work services cannot be the only services provided to a patient in home health care. For that reason, the traditional pathway for a patient to receive social work services under Medicare is to receive a referral from a nurse or a physical or speech therapist.

For home health agencies to get reimbursed for social work visits, Medicare requires that the visits be justified by "a clear and specific link between the social and emotional needs of the beneficiary and the beneficiary's medical condition or rate of recovery" (HCFA, HIM 11). Medicare mostly does not limit the number of social work visits provided to a patient as long as the visits are justified (Abel-Vacula, Nathans, Phillips, & Robbins, 2000). Direct patient contact is an important aspect of reimbursement for social work services. Therefore, Medicare does not reimburse social work services that are limited to assistance with Medicaid applications, arranging transportation for dialysis patients, and assisting with advance directives and living wills (Abel-Vacula et al., 2000).

As Medicare looks toward managing care and controlling costs, reimbursement will be increasingly tied to health outcomes. To improve outcomes, providers must look toward providing care for the whole person, including the patient's need for physical and mental health care and social services. As an individual's social and mental health are increasingly linked to improving physical health, social work services will become vital in managing the care of the older persons. As agencies look at ways to efficiently and effectively deliver services under a set rate, they must carefully weigh the cost and benefit of each profession, including social work. Under PPS, it is critical that social workers demonstrate their efficiency and effectiveness in improving patient outcomes that contribute to revenue for an agency.

REFERENCES

Abel-Vacula, C., Nathans, D., Phillips, K., & Robbins, J. (2000). *Home health care social work: Guidelines for practitioners and agencies.* IL: American Network of Home Health Care Social Workers.

Alliance for Health Reform. (2003). *A source book for journalists: Mental health coverage.* Retrieved July 19, 2004, from *http://www.allhealth.org/sourcebook2002/ch13_5.html*

Centers for Medicare and Medicaid Services. (2004a). Fact sheet: Medicare prescription drug discount card and transitional assistance program. Retrieved August 30, 2004, from *http://www.cms.hhs.gov/media/press/release.asp?Counter=990*

Centers for Medicaid and Medicare Services. (2004b). *Highlights: National health expenditures.* Retrieved August 30, 2004, from *http://www.cms.hhs.gov/statistics/nhe/historical/highlights.asp*

Centers for Medicare and Medicaid Services. (2004c). *Long term care.* Retrieved August 30, 2004, from *http://www.medicare.gov/LongTermCare/Static/Home.asp*

Committee on Ways and Means, U.S. House of Representatives. (2004) *The green book: Background data on programs within the jurisdiction of the Committee on Ways and Means.* Washington, DC: U.S. Government Printing Office.

Dhooper, S. S. (1997). *Social work in health care in the 21st century.* Thousand Oaks, CA: Sage.

Fox, P. D. (2003). Prescription drug benefits: Cost management issues for Medicare. *Health Care Financing Review, 25*(2), 7–21.

Health Care Financing Administration. (1992). *Medicare home health agency manual.* Washington, DC: U.S. Government Printing Office.

Health Care Financing Administration. (1999). *Medicare fact sheet: The home health prospective payment system.* Retrieved March 7, 2001, from *http://www.hcfa.gov/medicare/hhfact.htm*

Kaiser Family Foundation. (2004a). *Fact sheet: Medicare Advantage.* Retrieved August 30, 2004, from *http://www.kff.org/medicare/2052-07.cfm*

Kaiser Family Foundation. (2004b). *Fact sheet: Medicare at a glance.* Retrieved August 30, 2004, from *http://www.kff.org/medicare/1066-07.cfm*

Kaiser Family Foundation. (2004c). *Fact sheet: Medicare prescription drug law.* Retrieved August 30, 2004, from *http://www.kff.org/medicare/7044.cfm*

Kaiser Family Foundation. (2004d). *Kaiser Commission on Key Facts: Dual eligibles: Enrollment and spending, by state, 2002.*

Kaiser Family Foundation. (2004e). *Kaiser Commission on Medicaid Facts: Dual eligibles: Medicaid's role for low income Medicare beneficiaries.*

Kaiser Family Foundation. (2004f). *Medicare chartbook: Financing Medicare.* Retrieved August 21, 2004, from *http://www.kff.org/medicare/loader.cfm?url=/commonspot/security/getfile.cfm&PageID=13598*

Kaiser Family Foundation & Health Research Educational Trust. (2003). *Employer health benefits 2003. Summary of findings.*

Kaiser Family Foundation & Hewitt Associates. (2002). *Current state of retirees health survey.*

National Institute of Health. (2003). *Older adults: Depression and suicide facts.* Retrieved August 1, 2004, from *http://www.nimh.nih.gov/publicat/elderlydep-suicide.cfm*

Philips, M. H. (2000). *A primer for Medicare.* Washington, DC: Concord Coalition.

Social Security Administration. (2004). *A summary of the 2004 annual reports. Social Security and Medicare Boards of Trustees.* Retrieved August 30, 2004, from *http://www.ssa.gov/OACT/TRSUM/trsummary.html*

U.S. Department of Health and Human Services. (1999). Assistant Secretary of Planning and Evaluation: *Medicare's Post Acute Care Benefit: Background, trends and issues to be faced.* Washington, DC: U.S. Government Printing Office.

Title XIX of the Social Security Act, commonly referred to as Medicaid, became law in 1965. Prior to its enactment, health care services for persons with low incomes and assets were provided piecemeal through an arrangement of services offered by state and local programs, charities, and hospitals (Provost & Hughes, 2000). Modeled on the Kerr-Mills Act of 1960, Medical Assistance for the Aged, and the Social Security amendments of 1950, it was designed as a cooperative program, funded jointly by the federal and state governments, including the District of Columbia and the territories (Grogan & Patashnik, 2003; Provost & Hughes, 2000). Medicaid is an entitlement program that pays for medical care for certain individuals and families who demonstrate low income and limited resources (Hoffman, Klees, & Curtis, 2000; Rowland & Garfield, 2000). Originally established as a program to subsidize medical care for persons with low incomes and assets, its particular emphasis is on dependent children and their mothers, persons with disabilities, and older persons.

This chapter provides a description of the historical context for the establishment of Medicaid and explains basic standards and guidelines. It then examines programs and services available under Medicaid for older adults. In particular, dual eligibility, managed care, the freedom of choice and home and community-based waiver programs, and long-term care financing issues are discussed.

COLLEEN GALAMBOS

Policies Affecting Health, Mental Health, and Caregiving: Medicaid

MEDICAID: STANDARDS AND GUIDELINES

Using broad national guidelines that are established by federal regulations, each state shapes and administers its own Medicaid program and develops its own standards. These standards include eligibility requirements; type, amount, duration, and scope of services; and rate of payment for services. Due to state-developed standards, there is great variability in Medicaid policies throughout the country.

Medicaid is not designed to provide medical assistance for all persons with low incomes. Low income is only one test for Medicaid eligibility. In addition, resources and assets are tested against threshold levels. These threshold levels are determined by each state, using federal guidelines. States have discretion in determining the financial criteria for Medicaid eligibility and which groups of individuals their Medicaid program will cover. States may also develop a type of program called a state-only program that provides medical assistance for designated poor persons who do not qualify for Medicaid. These state-only programs are optional, and the amount and type of assistance vary from one state to another (Hoffman et al., 2000).

As part of the cooperative venture with the federal government, states are required to provide Medicaid coverage for particular individuals who receive federally assisted income-maintenance payments and for related groups who are not receiving cash payments. Table 80.1 outlines the mandatory Medicaid categorically needy eligibility groups for which the federal government provides matching funds. In addition to these mandatory related groups, states have the option of providing Medicaid coverage for other categorically related groups. These groups fall within defined categories, but the eligibility criteria are circumscribed more liberally.

Certain provisions of these optional and mandatory categorically related groups, such as the medically needy option, have particular relevance for older people in the United States. The medically needy option contains provisions that broaden eligibility requirements to persons who are eligible for Medicaid under one of the mandatory or optional groups with the exception that their income and/or resources exceed the eligibility level set by the state in which they reside. Under these circumstances, persons may qualify immediately or may be required to spend down their resources through incurring medical expenses that reduce their income below the level set for medically needy persons as outlined by individual state requirements. Using these spend-down procedures, individuals become eligible for Medicaid coverage after their medical expenditures exceed their assets.

TABLE 80.1 Mandatory Eligibility Groups and State Options

Medically categorically needy eligibility groups: Federal matching funds are provided

Individuals are generally eligible if they meet the requirement for the Aid to Families with Dependent Children (AFDC) program in effect in their state on July 16, 1996, or, at state option, more liberal criteria.

Children under age 6 whose family income is at or below 133% of the federal poverty level (FPL).

Pregnant women whose family income is below 133% of the FPL (services limited to those related to pregnancy, complications of pregnancy, delivery, and postpartum care).

Recipients of adoption or foster care assistance under Title IV of the Social Security Act.

All children born after September 30, 1983, who are under age 19, in families with incomes at or below the FPL (this process phases in coverage, so that by the year 2002 all such poor children under age 19 will be covered).

Supplemental Security Income (SSI) recipients in most states (some use more restrictive Medicaid eligibility requirements that predate SSI).

Special protected groups (typically individuals who lose their cash assistance due to earnings from work or from increased Social Security benefits, but who may keep Medicaid for a period of time).

Certain Medicare beneficiaries.

State options: Medicaid coverage for other categorically related groups
(The broadest optional groups for which states will receive federal matching funds for coverage under the Medicaid program include those listed below.)

Infants up to age 1 and pregnant women not covered under the mandatory rules whose family income is no more than 185% of the FPL (the percentage amount is set by each state).

Children under age 21 who meet the AFDC income and resources requirements in effect in their state on July 16, 1996.

Institutionalized individuals eligible under a special income level (states set the amount—up to 300% of the SSI federal benefit rate).

Certain aged, blind, or disabled adults who have incomes above those requiring mandatory coverage, but below the FPL.

Recipients of state supplementary income payments.

TB-infected persons financially eligible for Medicaid at the SSI income level if they were within a Medicaid-covered category (limited to TB-related ambulatory services and TB drugs).

Certain aged, blind, or disabled adults who have incomes above those requiring mandatory coverage, but below the FPL.

Certain working-and-disabled persons with family income less than 250% of the FPL who would qualify for SSI if they did not work.

Optional targeted low-income children included within the State Children's Health Insurance Program (SCHIP) established by the BBA of 1997.

Medically needy (MN) persons.

From Hoffman, E. D., Klees, B. S., & Curtis, C. A. (2000). Overview of the Medicare and Medicaid programs. *Health Care Financing Review, 22,* 1, 188.

Eligibility for Medicaid and benefit provisions for the medically needy are not required to be as extensive as for the categorically needy; in fact, regulations may be fairly restrictive. Although federal matching funds are available for medically needy programs, states are expected to follow certain federal requirements, including inclusion of certain groups and services under these guidelines. In addition to these mandated service requirements, states may elect to extend the medically needy eligibility to additional groups and to provide supplementary services. As of 2000, a total of 38 states had elected a medically needy program and were providing some services within this category. In 2002, the number of states offering medically needy programs dropped slightly to 36 (Centers for Medicare and Medicaid Services, 2003a). States that have not opted for a medically needy program may use the special income level option to extend Medicaid to the near poor in medical institutional settings (Hoffman et al., 2000).

Although Title XIX of the Social Security Act allows flexibility for states to craft their own Medicaid plan, some federal requirements are mandatory for states to receive federal matching funds. The federal government requires states to offer medical assistance for basic services to the categorically needy group as outlined by the federal guidelines. Mandated services particularly germane to older adults include nursing facility services for persons aged 21 and over, home health care for persons eligible for skilled nursing services (in addition to inpatient and outpatient hospital services), rural health clinic services, physician services, and laboratory and X-ray services. In addition to these mandatory services, states also may provide some optional services for which they receive a federal match. Examples of approved optional Medicaid services include diagnostic services, clinic services, intermediate care facilities for the mentally retarded, prescription drugs, prosthetic devices, optometrist services and eyeglasses, transportation services, rehabilitation and physical therapy services, and home and community-based care to certain persons with chronic impairments.

The Personal Responsibility and Work Opportunity Reconciliation Act of 1996 (P.L. 104-193) introduced restrictive changes to eligibility standards for Supplemental Security Income (SSI) coverage. This law had an impact on the Medicaid program, since one eligibility category is SSI recipients. The law imposed restrictions on SSI eligibility among legal resident aliens and other qualified aliens who entered the United States on or after August 22, 1996. The law requires a waiting period before these individuals can be eligible for SSI. Individual states can exercise the option to provide Medicaid coverage for aliens who entered before that date and to provide Medicaid for alien individuals after a waiting period. Emergency services continue to be mandatory for alien groups. For those aliens who lost SSI benefits due to the new restrictions imposed by P.L. 104-193, coverage can be provided only under another eligibility status outlined within Medicaid regulations (Hoffman et al., 2000).

HISTORICAL ANTECEDENTS IN COVERAGE OF OLDER ADULTS

Within its 40-year history, Medicaid has evolved as an assistance program for older adults with low income and assets and for persons with disabilities. A 1972 amendment to the Social Security Act established a federal program for cash assistance for the aged, blind, and disabled. This program, known as Supplemental Security Income, set uniform national minimum eligibility standards and benefits (Rowland & Garfield, 2000). Within this legislation, optional benefits eligible for federal matching funds included services provided by intermediate-care facilities and intermediate-care facilities for the mentally retarded. Further legislation in the 1980s assured Medicaid coverage to some Medicare beneficiaries who had not meet the eligibility requirements for any cash assistance program. Additionally, in the 1980s, changes to the Medicaid benefits package expanded within the options for home and community-based long-term care, increasing the role these programs have for low-income older adults. These legislative changes also emphasized increased access to care, quality of care, improved outreach programs, specific benefits, and fewer limits on services (Rowland & Garfield, 2000).

The proportion of older adults receiving Medicaid has declined over time. In 1973, 19% of Medicaid beneficiaries were 65 and over (Provost & Hughes, 2000). By 1998, persons 65 and over accounted for only 11% of the Medicaid population (Provost & Hughes, 2000). In 2000, it was estimated that older persons constituted 10% of all Medicaid beneficiaries (Centers for Medicare and Medicaid Services, 2003b). However, those Medicaid beneficiaries 65 and over account for an uneven share of total Medicaid expenditures. The same 11% in 1998, or 4 million aged participants, accounted for 31% of total Medicaid expenditures, or an average per-person expenditure of about $9,700 (Provost & Hughes, 2000; Hoffman et al., 2000). The same 10% in 2000, or 4.1 million older adults, had an average expenditure of about $11,345 per person (Centers for Medicare and Medicaid Services, 2003b). The number of older adult participants on Medicaid has declined, in part due to policy changes in both Medicaid and Medicare. These changes pertain to both eligibility requirements and service coverage requirements.

Additionally, Medicaid's total spending on long-term care accounted for approximately 40% of its total expenditures in 1998 (Rowland & Garfield, 2000). This amount was a result of its expansion of services for older adults and the disabled. In 2002, Medicaid's spending on long-term care accounted for 37.5% of total expenditures (Kaiser Commission on Medicaid and the Uninsured, 2003). Medicaid defines long-term care to include services provided in nursing facilities, intermediate-care facilities, intermediate-care facilities for the mentally retarded, mental health, home health services, and personal care support services.

THE RELATIONSHIP BETWEEN MEDICAID AND MEDICARE: STATE BUY-INS FOR "DUAL ELIGIBLES"

For individuals with low income and limited assets who receive Medicare, dual enrollment in Medicaid is an option. "Dual-eligible" beneficiaries are Medicare beneficiaries who also qualify for Medicaid benefits as a result of their low income. For eligible persons, Medicare health care coverage is supplemented by programs and services available through the state Medicaid program. Older adults with low income and assets may be eligible for Medicaid under the following categories:

• Recipients of the federal SSI program;
• Older adults with excessive medical or long-term care expenses in proportion to their income and assets;
• Older adults whose income levels are below the federal poverty threshold, and who have limited financial assets, referred to as Qualified Medicare Beneficiaries; and
• Older adults who have incomes between 100% and 120% of the federal poverty threshold and who have limited financial assets, referred to as Specified Low-Income Medicare Beneficiaries.

Services provided under the dual-enrollment program include such items as prescription drugs, eyeglasses, hearing aids, and nursing home care that extends beyond the 100-day limit allowed by Medicare. Assistance may also be provided in covering Medicare premiums and cost-sharing payments through the state Medicaid program. For all eligible services, Medicare is billed as the first payer, and Medicaid is considered the payer of last resort.

Since 1965, Medicaid has covered the Medicare premiums and the cost sharing of additional benefits not covered by Medicare for SSI recipients. Additionally, Medicaid's role in financing low-income Medicare beneficiaries was expanded through a series of incremental changes to the legislation. One such expansion is the development of Medicaid into a Medicare supplement.

In 1994, Medicaid covered approximately 20% of older people with incomes below 150% of the federal poverty threshold (Health Care Financing Administration, 1996a). Comparisons with recipients in other age-groups indicate that low-income older people have the highest per-user Medicaid payments. During 1997, 6.4 million dual-eligible persons represented just 19% of the Medicaid population but accounted for 35% of program expenditures (Provost & Hughes, 2000). It is estimated that Medicaid provides some level of supplemental health coverage for 6.5 million Medicare beneficiaries (Centers for Medicare and Medicaid Services, 2003b).

Another option available for dual-eligible older adults is a state option known as Programs of All-Inclusive Care for the Elderly (PACE). PACE started as a demonstration project, and Congress granted it program status in passing the Balanced Budget Act (BBA) of 1997 (Mollica, 2003). PACE is designed to provide an alternative to institutional care for persons aged 55 and older who are regarded as needing a nursing facility level of care (Mollica, 2003). This is a federal program option under both Medicare and Medicaid that allows for an integrated model of acute and long-term care services for individuals with dual eligibility (Mollica, 2003). PACE offers and manages the health, medical, and social services of participants enrolled in the program. In addition, PACE is responsible for coordinating the use of other services as indicated for rehabilitation, prevention, and psychosocial needs. Services may utilize day health centers, homes, hospitals, and nursing homes. The aim is to maintain independence, dignity, and quality of life. PACE providers receive payment for services through predeveloped PACE agreements. Providers must make available items and services covered under both Title XVIII and Title XIX. These services must be rendered without amount, duration, or scope limitations and without requiring deductibles, co-payments, or other forms of cost sharing. PACE is one option that allows for seniors to age in place (Mollica, 2003).

MEDICAID AND MANAGED CARE

There has been a movement to develop and utilize managed care systems as an alternative to the traditional fee-for-service system. In response to rising Medicaid costs and the national recession of the 1980s, state Medicaid programs turned to managed care, which aims to provide an accessible, cost-effective approach to health care service delivery. Under the managed care system, health maintenance organizations, prepaid health plans, and other forms of managed care contract with the state to provide an agreed-upon set of services to Medicaid enrollees. In return, the provider system receives a predetermined payment per enrollee for a specific period of time. The purpose of managed care is to provide an accessible, cost-effective approach to health care service delivery.

Since the 1980s, states have continued to experiment with various managed care approaches in an attempt to contain costs, reduce redundancy of services, and strive for better coordination and continuity of care. In 1997, Congress passed the BBA, which provides states with the option of setting up Medicaid managed care programs without the prior waivers required in the past (Klemm, 2000).

The change in law may have contributed to the rise in the proportion of Medicaid enrollees in some form of managed care, which increased from 14% of enrollees in 1993 to 58% in 2002 (Centers for Medicare and Medicaid Services, 2003b; Hoffman et al., 2000). The growth in Medicaid managed care has been rapid, but penetration rates vary widely among states. For example, two states (Alaska and Wyoming) have no managed care enrollment, and 12 states have penetration rates of between 76% and 100% (Provost & Hughes, 2000).

Most state Medicaid managed care enrollees consist of children and nondisabled adults. In the past, older adults and the disabled were considered high-risk population groups for managed care arrangements due to the need to deliver comprehensive services to a high-need group while controlling costs (Provost & Hughes, 2000). However, several states are moving this population group into managed care arrangements through managed care waivers. In 1997, a total of 24 states enrolled older adult Medicaid beneficiaries into managed care programs (Mollica, 2003). Overall, the number of Medicaid beneficiaries

enrolled in managed care programs increased from 14% of enrollees in 1993 to 58% in 2002 (Centers for Medicare and Medicaid Services, 2003b).

FREEDOM OF CHOICE AND HOME- AND COMMUNITY-BASED SERVICES WAIVERS

In response to a disproportionate amount of Medicaid expenditures that were being used for institutional care (Grannemann & Pauly, 1983; Provost & Hughes, 2000), Medicaid began shifting delivery of services to home and community-based settings. Part of the inappropriate use of nursing facilities was linked to an institutional bias in the Medicaid benefit and eligibility structure (Grannemann & Pauly, 1983; Holihan, 1975). In addition, studies indicated that some people who were residing in nursing homes and receiving Medicaid funding were capable of living in the community (Fox & Clauser, 1980; Kraus et al., 1976; Pegels, 1980). Furthermore, advocates and policymakers increasingly recognized that residents in nursing and intermediate-care facilities for the mentally retarded reported a poor quality of life (Gardner 1977; Scheerenberger, 1976). In response to all these factors, the Medicaid waiver program was born.

The legislative change that allowed for the development of Medicaid waiver programs was Section 2176 of the Omnibus Reconciliation Act of 1981. Since the waiver program was established, three mechanisms have allowed states to test Medicaid program innovations: (a) Section 1915(b), or freedom of choice waivers; (b) Section 1115, research and demonstration projects; and (c) Section 1915(c), home and community-based services (HCBS).

Section 1915(b) waivers refer to programs that enroll beneficiaries in managed care programs on a mandatory basis. Additional services are provided through savings produced from managed care, and carve-out systems are provided for specialty care such as mental health. There is the option to create programs that are available in certain regions or districts (Provost & Hughes, 2000).

Section 1115 Research and Demonstration Projects provide a mechanism for states to test new ideas. Under this initiative, states investigate program innovations, such as small-scale pilots of new benefits, various financing mechanisms, and major restructuring of state Medicaid funding (Provost & Hughes, 2000).

The HCBS waiver program, or Section 1915(c), allows states to develop and implement a network of health care and social services that makes it possible for individuals to remain in the community and avoid institutionalization (Hoffman et al., 2000; Provost & Hughes, 2000).

Under this waiver program, states may choose to provide a variety of services not otherwise covered under Medicaid as an alternative to institutionalization. Waiver services may be provided to individuals who are older and disabled, physically disabled, developmentally disabled, or mentally retarded or mentally ill. Waiver services may also be provided to persons with a specific illness or condition such as persons with AIDS.

Seven specific services outlined under the regulation may be offered as part of an HCBS waiver: case management services, homemaker services, home health aide services, personal care services, adult day health care services, habilitation services, and respite care services (Duckett & Guy, 2000; Health Care Financing Administration, 1996b). In addition, other services may be provided if they are requested by the state and approved by the Health Care Financing Administration. They must be cost effective and demonstrated to be necessary to avoid institutionalization. Examples of additional services include transportation, in-home support services, meal services, special communication services, minor home modifications, and adult day care (Duckett & Guy, 2000; Health Care Financing Administration, 1996b). In New York, for example, available services also include personal emergency response systems, housekeeping and chore services, and access to ancillary health services such as optometry, audiology, dentistry, and podiatry (Fisher & Raphael, 2003).

Under the HCBS waiver program, a capitation device allows plans to provide services that are not otherwise available through Medicaid. In capitation arrangements, providers receive from the state a monthly reimbursement rate for each Medicaid managed care enrollee. Within that reimbursement, the providers are at full risk to pay for all services covered by the managed care plan (Fisher & Raphael, 2003).

The HCBS program has experienced tremendous growth since its inception in 1981. In 1998, the estimated total Medicaid expenditures for this program reached over $9 billion for about 606,953 participants (Duckett & Guy, 2000). As of 2002, there were 263 approved waiver programs operating in 49 states (Centers for Medicare and Medicaid Services, 2003a). Community-based long-term care spending increased from 14.9% in 1992 to 25.3% in 1998 and to 27% in 2000 (Centers for Medicare and Medicaid Services, 2003a; Provost & Hughes, 2000).

LONG-TERM CARE FINANCING ISSUES

The high cost of nursing home care may be covered under Medicaid. Medicaid is the primary source of long-term care insurance for older adults and people with disabilities. National data indicate that Medicaid finances the nursing home care of about 60% to 70% of individuals in nursing facilities (Grogan & Patashnik, 2003). Medicaid covers skilled nursing facility care, intermediate facility nursing care, intermediate care for the mentally retarded and developmentally disabled, and HCBS (Provost & Hughes, 2000). Medicaid will finance nursing home care after an individual's savings and income are depleted or spent down. It is estimated that two thirds of individuals who enter long-term care facilities spend down their assets and become eligible for Medicaid (Grogan & Patashnik, 2003), and that nearly half of the nation's nursing home bill is covered by Medicaid (Min DeParle, 2000).

Historically, there has been tremendous growth in spending on nursing home care. For example, in 1966, it accounted for just 11% of Medicaid spending. By 1999, this amount had increased to 48% (Rowland & Garfield, 2000). A large percentage of expenditures for nursing facility care is spent on a relatively small number of individuals. In 1998, only 4% (1.6 million persons) of the individuals served by Medicaid received nursing facility services, but this accounted for about 25% of total Medicaid expenditures, or $44.1 billion (Provost & Hughes, 2000).

Recent data indicate some declines in nursing home care spending. In fiscal year 2002, a total of $93,219 billion was spent on nursing home care, or about 37.5% of total Medicaid expenditures for 1.7 million persons (Centers for Medicare and Medicaid Services, 2003b). These decreases may reflect the growing use of less costly service delivery systems such as HCBS waiver programs and managed care to deliver services that were traditionally provided by nursing homes.

Medicaid's expanded role in the financing of long-term care services has contributed to the development of quality standards for this industry (Rowland & Garfield, 2000). Key influences include implementation of comprehensive nursing home reform that raised standards for quality nursing home care and protections offered to spouses of nursing home residents outlined in the Spousal Impoverishment Act (Rowland & Garfield, 2000). Also, the HCBS initiatives for older adults provide less costly care options while allowing individuals to remain in the least restrictive setting.

CONCLUSIONS

President Lyndon Johnson signed the Medicaid legislation into law on July 30, 1965, at the Truman Library in Independence, Missouri. Wilbur Mills, chair of the House Ways and Means Committee, crafted the legislation as a federal matching program so that states would be able to provide additional health insurance to low-income parents and dependent children, older adults, and people with disabilities. This program established the principle that the government would take responsibility for the provision of health care to low-income individuals (Min DeParle, 2000). Challenges for the future of the financing of health care services for older Americans through Medicaid center around the question of how to provide comprehensive care to a growing population of persons in the most efficient and effective manner possible. This nation is confronted with larger numbers of older adults who are living longer. Utilization of health services will increase tremendously as the baby boomers age. This increase in utilization will challenge Medicaid's ability to provide needed services to older adults. Will the United States keep pace with the changes, or will a portion of the aging population go unserved? Only time will tell.

REFERENCES

Centers for Medicare and Medicaid Services. (2003a). *Home and community based services: From institutional care to self-directed supports and services.* Retrieved from *http://www.cms.hhs.gov/publications/overview-medicare-medicaid*

Centers for Medicare and Medicaid Services. (2003b). *Medicaid: A brief summary.* Retrieved from *http://www.cms.hhs.gov/publications/overview-medicare-medicaid/default4.asp*

Duckett, M. J., & Guy M. R. (2000). Home and community based services waivers. *Health Care Financing Review, 22,* 123–125.

Fisher, H. M., & Raphael, T. G. (2003). Managed long term care: Care integration through care coordination. *Journal of Aging and Health, 15,* 223–245.

Fox, P. D., & Clauser, S. B. (1980). Trends in nursing home expenditures: Implications for aging. *Health Care Financing Review, 2,* 65–70.

Gardner, J. M. (1977). Community residential alternatives for the developmentally disabled. *Mental Retardation, 15*(6), 3–8.

Grannemann, T. W., & Pauly, M. V. (1983). *Controlling Medicaid costs.* Washington, DC: American Enterprise Institute for Public Policy Research.

Grogan, C. M., & Patashnik, E. M. (2003, March). Universalism within targeting: Nursing home care, the middle class, and the politics of the Medicaid program. *Social Service Review,* 51–71.

Health Care Financing Administration. (1996a). Health care financing review: Medicare and Medicaid statistical supplement, 1996. Washington, DC: U.S. Government Printing Office.

Health Care Financing Administration. (1996b). *Home and community-based services waivers* (HCFA Fact Sheet). Baltimore: U.S. Government Printing Office.

Hoffman, E. D., Klees, B. S., & Curtis, C. A. (2000). Overview of the Medicare and Medicaid programs. *Health Care Financing Review, 22,* 175–183.

Holihan, J. (1975). *Financing health care to the poor.* Lexington, MA: Urban Institute.

Kaiser Commission on Medicaid and the Uninsured. (2003). *2002 State and national Medicaid spending data.* Retrieved from *http://www.kff.org/medicaid/kcmu031104apkg.cfm?*

Klemm, J. D. (2000). Medicaid spending: A brief history. *Health Care Financing Review, 22,* 105–112.

Kraus, A. S., et al. (1976). Elderly applications to long term care institutions: II. The application process: Placement and care needs. *Journal of the American Geriatric Society, 24,* 165–172.

Min DeParle, N. A. (2000). Celebrating 35 years of Medicare and Medicaid. *Health Care Financing Review, 22,* 1–7.

Mollica, R. (2003). Coordinating services across the continuum of health, housing, and supportive services. *Journal of Aging and Health, 15,* 165–188.

Pegels, C. C. (1980). Institutional versus noninstitutional care for the elderly. *Journal of Health Politics Policy Law, 5,* 205–212.

Provost, C., & Hughes, P. (2000). Medicaid: 35 years of service. *Health Care Financing Review, 22,* 141–174.

Rowland, D., & Garfield, R. (2000). Health care for the poor: Medicaid at 35. *Health Care Financing Review, 22,* 23–34.

Scheerenberger, R. C. (1976). Case study of public residential facilities. *Mental Retardation, 14*(1), 32–35.

LI-MEI CHEN

Policies Affecting Long-Term Care and Long-Term Care Institutions

In recent decades, the development of the long-term care (LTC) policies in the United States has lagged behind the growing care needs of older persons with chronic illnesses and mental or physical disabilities and their families. In most industrialized societies, the responsibilities for social policy and service delivery are seen as shared by the household, the state, and the marketplace. In these societies, an assurance of government involvement to protect an individual's minimum standard of living when the market fails to do so is an important policy principle. A policy based on a balanced and complementary system between the private (market and household) and public sectors is often sought by progressive reformers. However, in the United States, LTC polices are lopsided, with the responsibility for LTC provision primarily placed on the elder's household. As life expectancy lengthens and LTC becomes increasingly expensive and complex, this imbalance creates financial and social burdens for many families.

LTC policies for older persons have also been characterized as a political, incremental process with unpredictable outcomes (DiNitto, 1999). This incremental LTC public policy process has resulted in a gap in available, accessible, affordable, and acceptable LTC services. The outgrowth of this process is the failure to meet the changing needs of the current older adult population. Despite a decline in the utilization of institutional LTC, current public sector policy remains highly biased toward the nursing home industry, contributing further to the current LTC policy crisis.

This chapter examines the development of federal and state policies affecting LTC, namely, nursing homes and other providers of such care. It presents relevant issues surrounding LTC vis-à-vis the political, social, and economic changes in U.S. society.

THE DEVELOPMENT OF LTC POLICY IN THE UNITED STATES

Understanding the history of LTC policy, particularly in recent decades, provides an important perspective for understanding the forces that shaped the development of the institutional LTC sector and possible considerations for current and future policy reforms. The development of major policies affecting LTC institutions in the United States has indisputably paralleled the growth of the nursing home industry. The earliest federal legislation impacting the growth of nursing homes can be traced to the Social Security Act of 1935

(Institute of Medicine [IOM], 1986). This act created a federal-state public assistance program for older persons called Old Age Assistance (OAA). The act was drafted in opposition to the use of public poorhouses, which in those days housed older adults along with petty criminals, alcoholics, orphans, unwed mothers, and persons with mental illnesses (Vladek, 1980).

Growth of Nursing Homes

Although the abolition of poorhouses was a favorable policy decision, early policies offered few publicly funded alternatives for LTC. This pattern set the stage for the current policy problems and barriers to providing sound policy solutions. Similar to the development of other social and health care policies, LTC was not immune to the failure of the public sector to supply such care for older adults, hence allowing the private sector to provide the mainstay of the LTC services we see to this day. In 1954, the amendment of the 1946 Hill-Burton Act (which originally promoted the construction of hospitals in underserved rural areas) resulted in the state providing funding to market-based nonprofit organizations for the construction of skilled nursing facilities. The construction boom was fueled by successive legislation in 1958 and 1959 that authorized the Small Business Administration and the Federal Housing Administration to aid proprietary nursing home construction and operation.

Other forces also led to the growth of nursing homes. The 1950 amendment to the OAA changed the federal funding for nursing home care from paying the recipient to paying the nursing home providers and other medical suppliers directly. Also, under the OAA, the federal government gave public income assistance to older adults in need but excluded payments to older adults in public institutions. This was purposely implemented to move the institutionalized older adult population from poorhouses to nursing homes. Both strategies assisted the growth of both voluntary and proprietary nursing homes. More important, these ideas helped shape the current delivery and payment structure of the welfare state and supported the idea of distinguishing the "deserving" from the "undeserving" for public assistance, social care, and various health plans in the United States.

In the 1980s, the role of nursing homes in LTC continued to expand as a direct result of the acute hospital care cost containment policies on both federal and state levels. Until 1983, Medicare hospitals were reimbursed on a cost-plus basis, a method that encouraged long hospital stays. As Medicare moved to the prospective payment system (PPS) created under the Social Security amendment of 1983, hospitals were paid a flat fee for each admission based on either the admitting diagnosis or a specific surgical procedure code known as the diagnostic related group (DRG). The shift from cost-plus to flat-rate reimbursement for care motivated hospitals to reduce lengths of stay and to accelerate discharge of patients as soon as a discharge was medically feasible (Wood & Estes, 1988; Neu & Harrison, 1988). As a result, the average length of a Medicare hospital stay declined, and nursing homes took on another role as an important site for posthospital subacute care (Cohen & Dubay, 1990). Hospitals were also creating subacute care units to fill up their empty beds, for this emerging reimbursement opportunity added to the acute care reimbursements.

The phenomenon of "sicker and quicker" patients entering LTC facilities was actually a precursor to DRGs. Prior to PPS, the application of modern technology in older patients' care management resulted in people living longer with greater care needs. Treatments such as renal dialysis, complex surgical procedures, coronary artery bypass grafting, and cancer chemotherapy are examples of medical interventions that result in older patients surviving previously fatal diseases, and nursing homes providing longer periods of care and rehabilitation. The DRGs just added to this demand for institutional LTC, and the private sector market responded once again.

Diversification of LTC Services

In recent years, however, there has been an increasing array of services besides nursing home care to support older adults and adults with disabilities. Current trends do indicate the slowing growth of nursing homes as most LTC is now provided outside the nursing home in the community and increasingly in group residential care settings (Bishop, 1999; Quadagno & Stahl, 2003). According to the census report (Hetzel & Smith, 2001), the proportion of people 65 years and older living in nursing homes declined from 5.1% in 1990 to 4.5% in 2000. The public demand for a less medicalized model of LTC prompted growth of alternative types of institutional care such as assisted-living facilities and personal care homes, which were marketed as providing a more homelike environment for older adults who did not require serious medical attention. The National Academy for State Health

Policy reported 32,886 licensed assisted-living residences with 795,391 units or beds nationwide in 2000 (Mollica, 2000). The cohort of individuals aged 75 and older are the most likely to use assisted living. If current demand for assisted living were to increase solely according to the increase in the 75 and older population, ignoring all other market factors, the number of assisted-living beds would increase from 987,000 in 2000 to more than 1,900,000 in 2030 (National Center of Assisted Living, 2001). Unlike nursing homes, which are subjected to extensive federal regulations, these newer forms of institutional LTC generally have considerable flexibility to determine the resident populations that they serve and the services they provide. Also, unlike in nursing homes, payment for care, especially in assisted-living facilities, is borne to an even greater extent by the household as opposed to the state (see Zimmerman et al., 2003, for a recent comparative study between nursing homes and assisted-living facilities).

Recent advances of facilities with more homelike environments and community-based services were also assisted by the Medicaid-covered home and community-based services (HCBS), a program established in 1981 through section 1915(c) of the Social Security Act. These services have become a growing component of state LTC systems, with most of the growth accounted for by substantial increases in the number of HCBS waivers and the beneficiaries served through waivers. The 1915(c) HCBS waiver programs allow eligible individuals to either remain in their own homes or live in a community setting, rather than an institutional setting such as a hospital, nursing home, or intermediate-care facility for the developmentally disabled. In a few states, Medicaid use of preadmission screening along with these waivers is beginning to divert individuals away from nursing homes as the dominant means for providing LTC to older adults under Medicaid. Every state except Arizona operates at least one such waiver for older adults (see O'Brien & Elias, 2004, for further discussion on Medicaid HCBS programs).

An HCBS-like program provided under a unique capitated managed care environment is the Program of All-Inclusive Care for the Elderly, better known as the PACE program. Authorized under the Balanced Budget Act (BBA) of 1997, PACE is financed by both Medicare and Medicaid and is provided by not-for-profit or public entities. Currently, there are 25 approved PACE program sites modeled on the system of acute and long-term care services developed by On Lok Senior Health Services in San Francisco, California. PACE programs feature a comprehensive medical and social service delivery system, including all Medicare and Medicaid services provided by that state. At a minimum, a PACE program must provide an additional 16 services, including social work, drugs, and nursing facility care. Minimum services that must be provided in the PACE center include primary care services, social services, restorative therapies, personal care and supportive services, nutritional counseling, recreational therapy, and meals. When an enrollee is receiving adult day care services, these services also include meals and transportation. Participants must be at least 55 years old, live in the PACE service area, and be certified as eligible for nursing home care by the appropriate state agency.

Despite the noticeable presence of alternative forms of institutional and community-based LTC, the nursing home industry continues to hold back the growth of its competitors. This is largely due to the prominent role that the government has played in nursing home construction and continues to play as the principal payer for nursing home care (a topic covered in detail later in this chapter). Current policies impacting LTC institutions, including those affecting other formal LTC services, are significantly shaped by nursing home facility providers, who have become a strong political interest group in the United States. This political and legislative influence has resulted in a nursing home–dominated LTC system in the United States. The reason for this influence is twofold: (1) because LTC is too expensive to operate without federal help and (2) because the nursing home lobby has become a strong voice in nursing home funding and other policies (Kane, Kane, & Ladd, 1998). This influence overshadows the attempts of other LTC providers and elder care advocates to weaken the influence of the strong nursing home lobby. Hence, for many years, the nursing home industry continued to hinder the growth of other types of institutional care because federal laws and regulations have favored nursing facilities over others (see Kane et al., 1998, for further discussion).

KEY ISSUES SHAPING INSTITUTIONAL LTC POLICIES

Decreasing Use of Nursing Homes

There is a general consensus regarding the definition of LTC, as captured in the report prepared by the U.S.

Senate, Special Committee on Aging (2000), which describes LTC as follows:

> It [long-term care] differs from other types of health care in that the goal of long-term care is not to cure an illness, but to allow an individual to attain and maintain an optimal level of functioning. Long-term care encompasses a wide array of medical, social, personal, and supportive and specialized housing services needed by individuals who have lost some capacity for self-care because of a chronic illness or disabling condition.

The need for LTC is often measured in terms of the extent to which an older adult requires assistance or supervision in performing life tasks. These include basic *activities of daily living* (ADLs), such as bathing, dressing, toileting, or eating (Katz, Ford, Moskowitz, Jackson, & Jaffe, 1963), and *instrumental activities of daily living* (IADLs), which are activities related to independent living and include preparing meals, managing money, shopping for groceries or personal items, performing light or heavy housework, and using a telephone (Lawton & Brody, 1979). Currently, the majority (1.5 million, or 90 percent) of nursing home residents are older adults (65 years and over). The majority of these older persons are chronically ill and have difficulty in their physical and cognitive functioning, requiring dependence for an average 3.9 out of 5 ADLs (Jones, 2002; American Health Care Association, 2003).

Past studies have predicted increasing institutional LTC use by older adults as disability rates increased (Kemper & Murtaugh, 1991). Recent data, however, show that disability rates have decreased, overturning earlier predictions. Changes in the disability rates among older persons are certain to affect the demand for institutional LTC. Using data from the National Nursing Home Survey (NNHS), Redfoot and Pandya (2002) report that nursing home utilization among older persons, using age-standardized terms, declined by one fourth (26%) between the earliest wave of the NNHS (1973–1974) and 1999. In addition to the decline in disability rates, Redfoot and Pandya (2002) surmised that demographic and social changes may have influenced the substantial decline in utilization of institutional LTC among persons 75 years and older. These changes are as follows:

- Improved health and longevity outcomes due to better socioeconomic status (e.g., occupation, education, income, and wealth) and medical advances;

- Increased availability of informal caregiver support resulting when falling mortality rates narrowed the gender ratio of the number of older adults, leading to decreased widowhood and fewer older adults living alone;
- Increased ethnic diversity among older adults requiring LTC, reflecting changing patterns of LTC service utilization, since racial and ethnic minorities are more likely to use informal support than are non-Hispanic White elders; and
- Increased availability of other forms of LTC such as assisted-living facilities, personal care homes, and home health care.

Such recent trend data should not, however, decrease efforts to improve current institutional LTC policies. Institutional LTC continues to be a critical part of LTC services and serves approximately 5% of the older adult population. Many research reports surmise that in the coming decades there will be a significant increase in the demand for LTC services, particularly as the first baby boomers reach age 85 in 2030 (Applebaum & Kunkel, 1991; Knickman & Snell, 2002; U.S. Senate, Special Committee on Aging, 2002). It is projected that by 2040, growth in the over-85 population—the population most likely to need LTC services—will more than triple, from about 4 million to about 14 million (Walker, 2002). Furthermore, among the racial and ethnic minority population, data indicated that there has been a sharp increase in nursing home utilization rates among Black elders (28.2 per 1,000 in 1973–1974 to 55.6 per 1,000 in 1999; Redfoot & Pandya, 2002). Demographic trends indicate that policymakers will find themselves faced with both the traditional LTC problems and even more complex problems created by the increasingly diverse older adult population.

Cost and Financing of Institutional LTC

Despite the decrease in institutional LTC use, the costs of this form of care continue to rise. LTC expenditures (public and private) can be expected to grow significantly to meet this demand. Institutional LTC has become increasingly unaffordable for the majority of older adults without federal and/or state assistance. For example, in 2003, the average per diem rate at a nursing home was $181 for a private room, or about $66,000 annually (Congressional Budget Office, 2004).

It is often mistakenly believed that Medicare, the health insurance program for adults aged 65 and older and people with certain disabilities, covers all LTC costs. Medicare, enacted in 1965 as a component of the Social Security Act (SSA), was not originally intended to cover LTC costs. From the outset, Medicare coverage has focused on acute, episodic illness rather than chronic disease management and LTC. However, with the increased need for LTC, subsequent Medicare benefit amendments were made to cover some aspects of LTC. Currently, these LTC benefits are as follows:

- Medicare nursing home coverage: The beneficiary must spend at least 3 full days in a hospital and must have a physician's order providing the medical reason for needing skilled nursing care. The beneficiary's transfer from a hospital must occur within a certain period. Payment includes 20 days of care at a skilled nursing facility at full cost, and the difference between the amount above $109.50 per day (in 2004) and the actual cost for another 80 days.
- Medicare home health care: The beneficiary must require postacute care (such as recovery from joint replacement) and/or care for chronic conditions (such as congestive heart failure), be homebound, and require intermittent skilled nursing care, physical therapy, or speech therapy. In addition, the beneficiary must be under the care of a physician, and the home health services must be furnished under a plan of care ordered and periodically reviewed by a physician. Payment includes part-time or intermittent skilled nursing; physical, occupational, and speech therapy; medical social services; and home health aide visits. There are no annual or lifetime limits on home health care coverage as long as the beneficiary continues to meet the eligibility criteria. Under the Home Health Prospective Payment System (HHPPS), a national standardized home health episode payment, adjusted for case mix and wage index, is up to 60 days. Other types of payment adjustments are also available for episodes with four or fewer home health visits (low utilization payment adjustment, LUPA), certain intervening events that give rise to a partial episode (PEP adjustment), and significant change in condition (SCIC). In certain cases that exceed a specific cost threshold (an outlier), payment adjustment is available up to 5 percent of total home health payments (Center for Medicare and Medicaid Services [CMS], 2004).

Home health care coverage was introduced to prevent older adults needing LTC from entering costly nursing homes. The resultant boom in home health care visits and payments by Medicare has become a national concern. To contain these rising expenditures, Congress passed the Balanced Budget Act (BBA) of 1997 and the Health Insurance Portability and Accountability Act (HIPAA) of 1996, reasserting that Medicare coverage is available only for acute-care recovering patients. In 1997, Medicare adopted the interim payment system on the projected 1999 prospective payment system (PPS), further restricting home health care eligibility and reimbursements only for homebound patients. Although containing increasing Medicare expenditures remains a major concern, there has been a rise in complaints from the home health industry that the PPS rates are not covering the actual care given. Currently, Medicare continues to struggle as it tries to be the source of help for chronic, nonimproving, and homebound LTC recipients while containing the rising costs to the taxpayer of providing services.

Today, federal financing for LTC is more available for institutional LTC rather than home health care. The current financing of institutional LTC is dominated by Medicaid, the means-tested health coverage program for low-income persons. Low income, however, is only one test for Medicaid eligibility; assets and cash-redeemable resources are also tested against established thresholds (U.S. House of Representatives, 2004). Medicaid funding comes through a general tax revenue of federal and state funds. In addition to Medicaid, other federal and state programs also supplement LTC in the United States. These programs were created under federal legislations including the Social Security Act (Medicare), the Older Americans Act, the Rehabilitation Act, and Social Services block grant, as well as, state-legislated programs. Finally, private LTC insurance is available in the private sector for those who can afford it.

Combined with Medicare policy, Medicaid-related policies contribute to nursing homes' dominance of the U.S. LTC system (51.4%) over all other providers of Medicaid-funded LTC services. This is partly because eligibility requirements for Medicaid coverage of nursing home care are more generous than those for programs covering the medically indigent. These eligibility requirements are as follows:

- Medicaid nursing home care: The recipient must not have an income above 300% of the Supplementary Security Income (SSI) standard. (Note: A spouse of a nursing home resident living at home is also allowed to reserve a large portion of available income and assets, under the "spousal impoverishment laws.")

- Medically needy option in Medicaid: Many states allow even higher incomes for covering nursing home care under the medically needy option in Medicaid; if a person's income is above 300% of the SSI standard ($1,692 in 2004), but below the nursing home charges, Medicaid will pay the difference if a state has added this option to the medically needy program.

In 1997, more than half of U.S. nursing home residents were poor enough to qualify for Medicaid coverage (Congressional Budget Office, 2004), resulting in a substantial societal burden: The public share of payments rose to 64% of overall payments ($66.1 billion), with Medicaid paying 49.3% ($50.9 billion). Policymakers are faced with the challenge of how to reduce the public (i.e., taxpayer) burden as profound financial burden of LTC looms large with changing demographics.

Access to and Disparities in LTC Service Delivery

Existing policies fail to address the lack of coordination of LTC services, largely because of the strong presence of the nursing home industry in the policy-making process. The industry's influence prevents other similar services from replacing nursing home care or filling in gaps in the continuum of informal and formal LTC services. In recent years, LTC policies have evolved that do impact the distribution of different types of residential care, such as assisted-living facilities, intermediate nursing homes, and life care communities servicing older adults. The conception of LTC has steadily encompassed more types of services that, alone or combined, allow older adults to live in a noninstitutionalized setting or to remain in their own home. These services include 24-hour emergency call service, home health care, homemaker services, hospice programs, respite care, home-delivered meals, transportation, adult day care, home health aides or visitors, swing beds, family patient education, referral programs, and equipment rental. The boundaries between nursing homes and other types of care remain blurred as new and improved models of care are created and fragmented reimbursement mechanisms linger.

The majority of these services are extremely expensive, especially when the increase in longevity and morbidity in older adults render service need over a longer period of time. Insurance coverage and support toward payment for these needed services remain limited, with long-term financing and provision continuing to heavily rely on provision of care by the elders' households. Further, federal and state funding, largely through Medicaid, is available only to those who have impoverished themselves after spending down their cash assets. Because the majority of older adults and their primary caregivers eventually can no longer pay privately for LTC, Medicaid has inevitably become the largest payer.

The uneven distribution of service delivery and inequities in LTC public and private sector coverage both contribute to the lack of care coordination, which often divides the LTC population into haves and have-nots, resulting in large disparities in LTC service delivery. Low-income older adults tend to populate licensed nursing homes, since Medicaid reimburses skilled, intermediate, and custodial (basic) nursing care. The asset requirements of Medicaid eligibility often cause extreme financial strain on older adults and their families, who inevitably spend down to become eligible for Medicaid coverage of nursing home care. This is especially so for older women, racial and ethnic minorities, and middle-income households with few resources. In contrast, older adults who can afford to pay privately for LTC are more apt to populate assisted-living facilities, where residents pay out of pocket. Assisted living is largely not affordable for moderate- and low-income persons aged 75 or older, unless they disposed of their assets and spent them down to supplement their income (Hawes, Phillips, Rose, Holan, & Sherman, 2003). Few elderly persons had incomes sufficient to cover even the basic monthly charge in the average assisted-living facility (Hawes et al., 2003). This is true with the older female population, which is contributing to the higher than proportional use of health and LTC dollars due to a combination of higher life expectancy, lower economic status, higher incidence of chronic illness, and, often, lack of spousal caregivers (Blackburn & Chilman, 1987).

Quality of Care in Institutional LTC Settings

The issue of quality of care in LTC institutions has always been one of the important foci of LTC policy. In the 1950s, horrifying news of deaths of residents due to fire in out-of-date buildings and facilities with low standards made front-page news. This prompted many national studies, such as the 1955 study by the

Council of State Governments. The nation learned that the majority of nursing homes had low standards of service and relatively untrained personnel; the first attempt to create nursing home standards by several participating states took place shortly thereafter (IOM, 1986). These prompted further standards through increased federal financial involvement in nursing home services and new construction. However, early nursing home standards were vague as to what the minimum criteria of care provision or enforcement procedures should be. This led to great variability in standards of quality and enforcement approaches across states. It did, however, result in closure of a number of nursing homes that could not meet the new standards, and some other homes demolished their old facilities and built new ones.

By the 1960s, regulatory policy affecting nursing homes had evolved from a limited focus on safety to more elaborate state and federal health standards. This change, which was an outgrowth of the shift in service focus to residents with more complex medical needs and greater disability, resulted in increased regulatory standards focusing on competency in clinical care, as well as on safety and fire regulations. Current clinical problems that require close monitoring of care include malnutrition, incontinence, infection, overmedication, dehydration, decubitus ulcers, and depression, among others. Quality of life and residents' rights (lack of privacy, lack of preferred meal choices, and impolite staff members) are also critical components to be considered in nursing home care quality and standards.

Controversy over proposed changes in nursing home regulation led Congress to commission a study, to be performed by the Institute of Medicine (IOM) Committee on Nursing Home Regulation (IOM, 1986), on how to improve the quality of care in nursing homes. Many of the recommendations for changes in the quality regulation system made by the IOM committee were passed into law as part of the Omnibus Budget Reconciliation Act of 1987 (OBRA-87) and implemented in 1990 and 1991. One of the most important recommendations was to shift the focus of nursing home regulations from assessment of process and structure to a more resident-centered and outcome-oriented approach. The committee recommended the development of a national information system on residents that would allow development of outcome norms and integration into the quality assurance process. As a result of the law, the Resident Assessment Instrument (RAI), which includes a standard assessment instrument and the Minimum Data Set (MDS, with newer versions known as MDS 2.0) were developed (Feldman & Boulter, 1991). Completion of the MDS has been mandated for all Medicare- and Medicaid-certified nursing homes.

The federal government does not establish standards for new forms of institutional care such as assisted-living facilities. Most states license and regulate assisted-living residences, and an increasing number of states place Medicaid-eligible adults in assisted-living residences as an alternative to traditional placement in a nursing home. This trend has led many to speculate that the federal government will become increasingly involved in setting minimum standards of care in residences electing to participate in the federal-state Medicaid program. Motivated in part to delay federal oversight and regulation, national associations representing selective areas of the LTC industry have increased self-regulation efforts. According to the U.S. General Accounting Office (GAO) report (2004), assisted-living residents sometimes need help to pursue complaints against their providers, especially when faced with an involuntary discharge. LTC ombudsmen are available in all states, but nursing home residents claim most of their attention.

Although care has improved greatly from the era of poorhouses, quality of care continues to be a nursing home issue to this day (IOM, 1986, 2001; Kane, 2003; Quadagno & Stahl, 2003; Wiener, 2003). Poor care and elder abuse can result from understaffing, lack of proper training for staff members, and poor maintenance of the facilities. Consumer advocacy groups in California, Michigan, Illinois, Kansas, and other states are developing quality guides to help consumers choose nursing homes. These efforts generally rely on formal complaints and deficiency statements from the federal and state certification survey. The inclusion of outcome measures is rare, but staffing and ownership information is more common. In 1995, *Consumer Reports* ranked facilities in nursing home chains based on federal deficiency statements (Consumer Union, 2003). In addition, many state agencies publish consumer guides that include general information about nursing homes, but these do not usually include specific information about quality.

THE FUTURE OF FINANCING, ORGANIZING, AND DELIVERING INSTITUTIONAL LTC SERVICES

Current policy debates and research surrounding LTC have focused on issues related to its increasingly complex financing, organizing, and delivery of a spectrum of services and products over a longer period of time (Kemper, 2003; Quadagno & Stahl, 2003). Currently, both the public and private sectors play a role in financing LTC. Nursing homes are funded by private insurance, other private funds such as charitable or philanthropic funds, government (federal and state), and resident out-of-pocket payments (private pay). Financing LTC has progressively become a major policy issue as costs continue to rise; policy discussions continue on how to alleviate the burden on both public and private budgets.

Theoretically, states are required to provide LTC services to older adults. However, current economic growth rates are not likely to support public funding at the current percentage levels, much less the substantially increased ones that are projected. As the baby boomers reach old age, there will be greater fiscal pressure on the public programs (primarily Medicaid) that pay for most institutional LTC. To make matters worse, many private health insurance plans continue to have relatively limited LTC coverage, which keeps pressure on the public and household sectors to pay institutional LTC costs.

These pressures suggest that new ways of financing and delivering LTC services need to be considered today. Current debates focus on three major approaches:

- Reducing the number of people eligible for Medicaid coverage and limiting Medicare's home health care benefit.
- Altering the incentives that encourage people to substitute Medicaid for private LTC insurance. In recent years, private LTC insurance policies have become more comprehensive. Most private LTC insurers cover home health care, respite care, adult day services, assisted living, personal care, and hospice care. Some companies offer policy innovations that include reimbursement of family caregivers, payments for family caregiving training, and the option to receive a cash benefit that consumers can use for any purpose (AARP, 1999). The problem with private LTC insurance is that the majority of plans that provide meaningful coverage and appropriate consumer protections are relatively expensive and thus unaffordable for many people.
- Expanding publicly financed LTC insurance. This includes the expansion of Medicaid by broadening the eligibility criteria, creating more comprehensive LTC coverage under Medicare, or creating tax incentives.

The prospects of the first two policy changes being realized are bleak amid the current policy environment. As for the latter, the HIPAA of 1996, which amended the Internal Revenue Code, clarified the tax treatment of LTC insurance, out-of-pocket expenditures for LTC services, and "living benefits." Some of the major provisions of HIPAA include deductions for qualified LTC expenses, including LTC insurance premiums, as long as combined medical expenses and outlays for LTC services and supports exceed 7.5% of adjusted gross income. In addition, employers can offer LTC insurance as a tax-free employee benefit; qualified living benefits are no longer taxable. Additional public sector LTC incentives are found at the state level. As of 2002, a total of 24 states provide either a tax credit or a tax deduction more generous than that allowed at a federal level to purchasers of private LTC insurance (AARP, 1999). However, according to AARP (1999), almost half of older adults will not qualify for the federal tax deductibility provision because they have insufficient incomes to owe taxes. Many others may not have sufficient deductions to justify itemizing. These tax changes are, however, good examples of incremental policy change designed to redistribute the public, private, and household sector responsibilities for LTC payment.

Public-private partnerships have also sprung up in policies where Medicaid modifies its asset test for people who buy LTC insurance covering a specified amount of LTC services, such as 2 years of nursing facility coverage. People still in need of services and supports after using all their insurance benefits would be eligible for Medicaid without having to spend down a comparable amount of their assets. Some programs waive the asset requirement entirely for people who privately insure their care in a nursing home for a specified period.

Such efforts, however, often become engulfed in ideological debates about whether a social insurance or a private insurance approach is best (Meiners, 1996; Weiner & Rivlin, 1988). This debate centers on a conflict of values and beliefs about the appropriate role of the federal government in the financing and provision of social services. Documentation indicates that the baby boom generation is likely to be better educated and more financially secure than previous generations of older adults. Whether these individuals have factored financing for LTC into their retirement planning, however, is not clear. As Americans struggle to reconcile the paradoxical views of their welfare state, that is, self-sufficiency or group sufficiency, LTC will continue to be built on the basis of these cross-pressures (see Heclo, 1986, for a discussion on the two views of the U.S. welfare state).

THE ROLE OF SOCIAL WORK IN POLICIES AFFECTING INSTITUTIONALLY BASED LTC

The National Association of Social Workers (NASW) advocates the availability of services within a continuum that links all levels of LTC and addresses the physical, mental, cultural, and psychosocial health needs of the individual, family, and caregivers. The NASW (2004) continues to support the enactment of a universal, comprehensive health care system that provides affordable coverage for people of all ages and relieves individuals and families of burdensome out-of-pocket expenditures.

There is another challenge for social work. LTC policies have neglected the importance of social workers in institutional LTC settings vis-à-vis other health care professions. It is important to acknowledge and advocate for what social workers contribute to the functioning of older adults in LTC settings. Professional social work services are relevant for improving the functioning and quality of life of elders in nursing homes, assisted-living facilities, group homes, board and care homes, life care communities, hospice, and other types of institutional care.

REFERENCES

American Health Care Association. (2003, December). *CMS OSCAR Data Current Surveys: Nursing facility total, average and median number of patients per facility and ADL dependence.* Washington, DC: Author.

Applebaum, R., & Kunkel, S. (1991). *Long-term care for the boomers: A public policy challenge for the twenty-first century* (Contract No. 87ASPE1821). Washington, DC: Department of Health and Human Services.

AARP. (1999). *Long-term care insurance.* Washington, DC: Author.

Bishop, C. E. (1999). Where are the missing elders? The decline in nursing home use, 1985 and 1995. *Health Affairs, 18,* 146–155.

Blackburn, J., & Chilman, C. (1987). The probable impact of proposed legislative and budgetary changes on the lives of the elderly and their families. *Journal of Gerontological Social Work, 11*(3/4), 19–42.

Cohen, J. W., & Dubay, L. C. (1990). The effects of Medicaid reimbursement method and ownership on nursing home costs, case mix, and staffing. *Inquiry, 27,* 183–200.

Congressional Budget Office. (2004, April). *Financing long-term care for the elderly.* Washington, DC: Author.

Consumers Union. (2003, June). *How good are your state's nursing homes?* Yonkers, NY: Author.

DiNitto, D. M. (1999). *Social welfare: Politics and public policy* (5th ed.). Boston: Allyn and Bacon.

Feldman, J., & Boulter, C. (1991). *Minimum Data Set Plus training manual.* Natick, MA: Eliot Press.

Hawes, C., Phillips, C. D., Rose, M., Holan, S., & Sherman, M. (2003). A national survey of assisted living facilities. *Gerontologist, 43,* 875–882.

Heclo, H. (1986). General welfare and the two American traditions. *Political Science Quarterly, 101,* 179–196.

Hetzel, L., & Smith, A. (2001). *The 65 years and over population 2000* (Census brief C2KBR/01-10). Washington, DC: U.S. Census Bureau.

Institute of Medicine. (1986). *Improving the quality of care in nursing homes.* Washington, DC: National Academy Press.

Institute of Medicine. (2001). *Improving the quality of long-term care.* Washington, DC: National Academy Press.

Jones, A. (2002). The National Nursing Home Survey: 1999 summary. *Vital Health State, 152,* 1–116.

Kane, R. A. (2003). Definition, measurement and correlates of quality of life in nursing homes: Toward a reasonable practice, research, and policy agenda. *Gerontologist, 43,* 28–36.

Kane, R. A., Kane, R. L., & Ladd, R. C. (1998). *The heart of long-term care.* New York: Oxford University Press.

Katz, S., Ford, A. B., Moskowitz, R. W., Jackson, B. A., & Jaffe, M. W. (1963). Studies of illness in the aged. The index of ADL: A standardized measure of biological and psychosocial function. *Journal of American Medical Association, 185,* 914–919.

Kemper, P. (2003). Long-term care research and policy. *Gerontologist, 43,* 436–446.

Kemper, P., & Murtaugh, C. M. (1991). Lifetime use of nursing home care. *New England Journal of Medicine, 324,* 595–600.

Knickman, J. R., & Snell, E. K. (2002). The 2030 problem: Caring for aging baby boomers. *Health Services Research, 37,* 849–884.

Lawton, M. P., & Brody, E. M. (1979). Instrumental activities of daily living scale. In M. Stanhope & R. N. Knollmueller (2000), *Handbook of community and home health nursing: Tools for assessment intervention and education* (3rd ed., pp. 146–148). St. Louis, MO: Mosby.

Meiners, M. (1996). The financing and organizing of long-term care. In R. H. Binstock, L. E. Cluff, & O. Von Mering (Eds.), *The future of long-term care* (pp. 191–214). Baltimore: Johns Hopkins University Press.

Mollica, R. L. (2000). *State assisted living policy: 2000*. Portland, ME: National Academy for State Health Policy.

National Association of Social Workers. (2004). *Social work speaks* (6th ed.). Washington, DC: Author.

National Center of Assisted Living. (2001). *Facts and trends: The assisted living sourcebook 2001*. Washington, DC: Author.

Neu, C. R., & Harrison, S. (1988). *Posthospital care before and after the Medicare prospective payment system* (R-3590-HCFA). Santa Monica, CA: RAND.

O'Brien, E., & Elias, R. (2004). *Medicaid and long-term care* (The Kaiser Commission on Medicare and the Uninsured Publication No. 7089). Washington, DC: Kaiser Family Foundation.

Quadagno, J., & Stahl, S. M. (2003). Challenges in nursing home care: A research agenda. *Gerontologist, 43,* 4–6.

Redfoot, D. L., & Pandya, S. M. (2002). *Before the boom: Trends in long-term support services for older Americans with disabilities*. Washington, DC: AARP Public Policy Institute.

Rivlin, A., & Weiner, J. M. (1988). *Caring for the disabled elderly*. Washington, DC: Brookings Institution.

U.S. General Accounting Office. (2004). *Assisted living: Examples of state efforts to improve consumer protections. GAO-04-684*. Washington, DC: Author.

U.S. House of Representatives, Committee on Ways and Means. (2004). *2004 Green Book* (pp. 15:32–41). Washington, DC: U.S. Government Printing Office.

U.S. Senate, Special Committee on Aging. (2000, February). *Developments in aging: 1997 and 1998* (Vol.1, Report No. 106–229). Washington, DC: U.S. Government Printing Office.

U.S. Senate, Special Committee on Aging. (June, 2002). *Long-term care report* (Report No. 107–74). Washington, DC: U.S. Government Printing Office.

Vladek, B. C. (1980). *Unloving care: The nursing home tragedy*. New York: Basic Books.

Walker, David M. (2002). *Long-term care: Aging baby boom generation will increase demand and burden on federal and state budgets*. Washington, DC: U.S. General Accounting Office.

Wiener, J. M. (2003). An assessment of strategies for improving quality of care in nursing homes. *The Gerontologist, 43,* 19–27.

Wood, J. B., & Estes, C. L. (1988). The medicalization of community services for the elderly. *Health and Social Work, 13,* 35–43.

Zimmerman, S., Gruber-Baldini, A. L., Sloane, P. D., Eckert, J. K., Hebel, J. R., Morgan, L. A., et al. (2003). Assisted living and nursing homes: Apples and oranges? *Gerontologist, 43,* 107–117.

SHARON KEIGHER

Policies Affecting Community-Based Social Services, Housing, and Transportation

Created in a time of rising societal concern for the poor and disadvantaged, the Older Americans Act (P.L. 89-73), Medicare, and Medicaid (Titles XVIII and XIX of the Social Security Act) were all signed into law in 1965. Together their broad national principles are the bulwark of American "aging policy." As elders' capacities and limitations changed over the past four decades, the OAA has remained consistent with President Lyndon Johnson's assessment that it "affirms our Nation's sense of responsibility toward the well-being of all of our older citizens" (Administration on Aging, 2004c, p. 1).

Today, however, three strong and contesting forces threaten this bulwark. One is the subtle influence of the Americans with Disabilities Act (ADA) of 1990 (P.L. 101-336). "Aging advocates" tentatively embrace this law, while maintaining an uncertain alliance with "younger" disabled advocates in the independent living movement. As American institutions increasingly include persons with disabilities ("just another diversity group") and claim to provide appropriate inclusive accommodation, our judiciary is still parsing out governments' murky responsibilities for the care of persons in communities.

Juxtaposed against this commitment to appropriate care is the Bush administration's New Freedom Initiative, which, in the name of expanding civil rights and opportunities for persons with disabilities, is aggressively privatizing services and divesting government program responsibilities. As the Reagan administration did with New Federalism, this Bush administration is consolidating categorical programs into flexible but smaller state block grants. Federal "entitlements," implemented with fewer federal funds, now serve fewer and fewer low-income and disadvantaged people.

The third and most potent force shaping aging policy today is the fiscal and budget policy of George W. Bush's administration. States' budgets had increased by 5.2% in 1999, and received 4% increases from 2000 through 2002, but "beginning in fiscal 2001, states were confronted with a fiscal situation more severe than any they had dealt with during the past 60 years. State revenues . . . collapsed, declining in inflation-adjusted terms for eight straight quarters" (National Association of State Budget Officers, 2004). States were forced to make stark budget cuts, increase taxes, and drain their reserve funds. After the events of 9/11 and the subsequent recession, states' budgets dropped on average by 2.5% in 2003. The reserves were gone, and the IOUs had come due.

With the nation deep in a recession, in 2002 the Bush administration declared war in Afghanistan and

Iraq, spending some $200 billion by early 2005. It also granted $45 billion in tax cuts to benefit the wealthiest 1% of taxpayers. Together these actions dramatically reversed the federal budgetary surpluses accrued in the late 1990s and created a rationale for slashing federal discretionary assistance to states for human services. The progressive Center for Budget and Policy Priorities reported in 2004 that, "by 2009 the budget proposes to cut overall funding for domestic discretionary programs outside homeland security by $45.4 billion—or 10.4 percent—below today's level, adjusted for inflation. To lock in cuts of this magnitude, the Administration proposed five-year binding caps on discretionary spending" (Center for Budget and Policy Priorities [CBPP], 2004a).

These cuts will cause significant hardships for low-income persons who are older, are disabled, or have families and depend on this assistance. The fiscal year 2005 cuts to Section 8 housing vouchers could remove 250,000 households from the program. Yet the amount these cuts would save pales in comparison to the revenue losses in future years from the tax cuts. Over the next 5 years, savings from all the domestic discretionary cuts combined will be substantially less than the cost of the tax cuts just for the 1% of households with the highest incomes (CBPP, 2004b).

Within this dire political context, community services for older people may seem insignificant. Take, for example, a recent AARP housing survey, which found that 83% of older Americans express a desire to stay in their current homes for the rest of their lives. They find their homes comfortable and convenient and feel secure and independent there (AARP, 2004). However, as people age, and their health or physical abilities may decline, it is sometimes impossible to remain at home without changing living arrangements and the home itself. Social services and financial assistance to compensate for functional incapacities are essential to keeping elders "at home." Key among these since the 1960s are a range of federal programs, already heavily supplemented by state and local governments, and elders' own pockets, for community-based social services, housing, and transportation. And more, not less, will be needed in the future by some 76 million aging baby boomers.

Given the cost and budget pressures described here, the common theme underpinning U.S. aging policies since 2000 has been less about assisting older and disabled persons to stay in their own homes and communities and more about simply barring them from institutions (and becoming public charges) as long as (politically) possible. This chapter describes the essentials of "aging policy" in community services

for older, frail, and/or disabled adults living at home independently, and interdependently, in their communities with supportive social services, housing, and transportation. The first section highlights the broad mandates of the federal Older Americans Act (OAA), the foundation of our nation's "aging network" of state and local social services. The second section overviews federal housing policies that benefit low-income and disabled older Americans. The third section highlights federal transportation programs benefiting older adults and their local challenges. The discussion of the OAA is particularly timely, since July 14, 2005, will mark the 40th anniversary of this groundbreaking national legislation.

COMMUNITY-BASED SOCIAL SERVICES FOR OLDER PERSONS

In keeping with the traditional American concept of the inherent dignity of the individual in our democratic society, the older people of our Nation are entitled to, and it is the joint and several duty and responsibility of the governments of the United States, and of the several States and their political subdivisions *to assist our older people to secure equal opportunity to the full and free enjoyment of the following . . .* (Older Americans Act, 1965)

The goals and objectives of the OAA are global, idealistic, and sometimes contradictory. A product of the federal legislative process, the act embodies compromises negotiated every seven years when it is reauthorized. As is typical with most social services legislation under our federalist system, the federal government grants aid to the sovereign states, which further subcontract with local governments to administer programs. Despite the idealism of universal rights and flexible services articulated throughout the act, its $1.1 billion appropriation to the Administration on Aging (AoA) in 2001 paled in comparison with the $16 billion to Medicaid for home and community long-term care. By fiscal year 2005, the AoA's total discretionary budget has grown to $1.376 billion, a 9.9% increase over the previous 4 years.

The Older Americans Act

The OAA is the nation's primary vehicle for organizing, coordinating, and providing services, protections, and opportunities for older Americans and their families in local communities. The original act made its services universally available to persons aged 60 and over, while requiring states to target assistance to persons with the "greatest social or economic need." The subtle contradiction suggests the mission conflict that has dogged "the aging enterprise" ever since (Estes, 1980). Poverty among the elderly declined from 35% in 1959 to 11% in 2002 (Federal Interagency Forum on Aging-Related Statistics, 2000) due largely *not* to the OAA but to indexing Social Security's annual cost-of-living adjustments and to Medicare's covering most health care for virtually all elders.

The OAA is the cornerstone of our nation's state aging networks, facilitating the provision of home care, congregate and home-delivered meals, transportation, caregiver supports, information and assistance, health promotion and disease prevention, other community activities, and advocacy to persons aged 60 and over. The act requires elders' participation in policy making and provision of accessible, reliable information to elders and their families for making informed decisions. Every state has a comprehensive information, counseling, education, and assistance system linking consumers to resources and services needed to remain safe in their homes and communities. Thirty-six state units on aging (SUAs) administer the State Health Insurance Counseling and Assistance Program to advocate for, educate, and counsel older consumers regarding Medicare, Medicaid, Medigap supplemental insurance, long-term care insurance, and other choices.

The OAA's programs and services are administered and coordinated through a nationwide collaboration of federal, state, and local partners known as the Aging Service Network. This network includes the federal AoA in the Department of Health and Human Services (DHHS), 56 SUAs, 655 area agencies on aging (AAAs), 244 tribal organizations, about 30,000 local community-based service providers, and more than 500,000 volunteers across the nation. SUAs play significant policy, planning, and advocacy roles in leveraging other federal, state, and local public and private funds to support its programs.

The OAA today ensures home and community-based services (HCBS) for millions of older Americans, with 51 of the nation's 56 SUAs administering an array of state and federally funded programs that provide such services. Thirty-three SUAs are the operating agency for one or more Medicaid HCBS waivers for the elderly. Nationally, about a third of the fund-

ing provided by the states for HCBS is derived from the OAA, with the remainder from state, other federal, and private sources. In fact, today 51 SUAs administer state-funded HCBS programs for older persons and/or younger persons with physical disabilities. Some SUAs also administer waivers for traumatic brain injury, assisted living, adult foster care, medically fragile children, and other specific populations (National Association of State Units on Aging, 2004).

Reauthorized by Congress every seven years, most recently in 2000, the OAA establishes the administrative structure and funding for the federal AOA, SUAs, and local AAAs. The states, which have key planning responsibility, designate district planning and service areas (PSAs) within which AAAs coordinate and arrange for service delivery, typically through contracts with local governments and private agencies. Forty-six states have multiple substate planning areas; 10 states operate only a single PSA serving the entire state.

Each title of the OAA authorizes specific services. Title I defines the 10 objectives in the act regarding retirement, physical and mental health, suitable housing, community-based long-term care, employment, freedoms, and protections. Title II establishes administrative responsibilities for the AoA within the DHHS and mandates the duties of its chief executive, the assistant secretary for aging.

Title III, Grants for States and Community Programs on Aging, is the most extensive and important section for social workers. Through it, social and nutrition services reach 7 million citizens each year through senior centers, home-delivered meals, congregate meals, rides, case management, personal care, homemaker and adult day care services, information and referral contacts, and other supportive services. Since 2000, it has also provided respite and other services for family caregivers (Administration on Aging, 2004a).

Title IV, Training, Research, and Discretionary Projects, supports evidence-based research on program design, competency guidelines, and cooperative agreements. Alzheimer's demonstration grants, added in 1992, assist states in developing innovative models for serving individuals with Alzheimer's disease and their families.

Title V, the Senior Community Service Employment Program (SCSEP), provides part-time employment and training opportunities for low-income adults aged 55 and older. These programs, unlike those under the other titles, are administered by the

U.S. Department of Labor. Title VI provides grants for Native Americans (Indians, Alaska Natives, and Native Hawaiians) for supportive and nutrition services (comparable to Title III) to 241 tribal and Native organizations, and 2 organizations representing Native Hawaiians.

Title VII, created in 1992, established elder rights protection systems for the prevention of elder abuse, neglect, and exploitation. In 2000 this title incorporated the long-term care ombudsman programs and state legal assistance development, to strengthen all three legal advocacy programs. Most states have also used their own general revenue to expand these programs beyond the provisions of the OAA. For example, many states have also funded prescription drug assistance programs to offset the costs of purchasing medications. Thirty-eight have established some type of state program to provide pharmaceutical coverage or assistance to low-income elderly and disabled persons ineligible for the state's Medicaid waiver program. Most states provide information and assistance, and administer program funds and oversight. Most states are coordinating the new national pharmacy discount cards and have recently assumed additional duties for the Medicare prescription drug cards as well.

Home and Community-Based Services

In 2000 the OAA added provisions to strengthen its community-based aging programs. As part of the president's New Freedom Initiative, aging and disability resource centers have been jointly funded by the AOA and Centers for Medicare and Medicaid Systems as local collaboratives. By integrating information systems throughout different levels of government and enhancing access for individuals seeking long-term care services, these centers cross-reference information from local centers for independent living and AAAs. The AOA and the Centers for Disease Control and Prevention are also jointly funding state grants to link SUAs and state health departments in developing evidence-based state health promotion initiatives to improve the physical activity, health, and quality of life of older persons.

A new concept, consumer direction in care, evolved in the 1990s to describe programs of services offering maximum choice and control to persons needing help with daily activities, particularly those who qualify for public benefits, especially Medicaid. Offering a range of approaches permits users to choose their preferred services, when and how they will be delivered, and who, among professionals,

neighbors, friends, and family members, will provide them. A plethora of recent federal initiatives are seeking to eliminate barriers to community living by enhancing consumer choice in care planning. Since 1998, the cash and counseling demonstration projects (funded by DHHS and the Robert Wood Johnson Foundation) have been testing the use of a cash benefit for Medicaid consumers to purchase their own personal and attendant care. These quasi experiments have been successful in Arkansas, Florida, and New Jersey, and 10 new state demonstrations were being added in 2004 (Mahoney, Simone, & Simon-Rusinowitz, 2000).

Building on these agenda, the president's New Freedom Initiative is piloting a whole raft of Real Choice Systems Change demonstration grants, funding nursing home transition, personal assistance services, Money Follows the Person, quality assurance/ improvement, and broader systems change grants. More than 22 states are participating in these initiatives so far. A collaborative clearinghouse Web site (www.hcbs.org) provides up-to-date information on these activities in the states with federal agencies' support.

Together these various initiatives suggest an elder care system gearing up to serve the "age wave" of baby boomers expected to need long-term care in coming decades. More private market solutions are developing and being automatically incorporated throughout the aging network. On the one hand, this may be quite appropriate, given the improved level of private resources available to older people today. On the other hand, the entrepreneurial momentum stimulated by many aspects of the president's New Freedom Initiative is privatizing the decision-making processes even within publicly funded programs. Indeed, emerging hybrid programs (public-private partnerships) are giving middle- and high-income persons more choices, without much concern raised that means-tested government services for low-income elders—the 40% who are single, not homeowners, and have only Social Security for income—do not protect them sufficiently.

The Olmstead Decision: The Supreme Court's Landmark Ruling on Community Integration of People With Disabilities

A key impetus toward consumer direction was congressional passage of the Americans with Disability Act (ADA) of 1990. But implementation of that act remained moribund on the rights of the severely disabled until 1999, when the U.S. Supreme Court held in *Olmstead v. L.C.* that under the ADA, people with disabilities should be served in the most integrated settings possible—their own communities.

The case of *L.C. and E.W. v. Olmstead* was brought in 1995 by the Atlanta Legal Aid Society on behalf of two women with mental retardation and mental illness held in a state psychiatric hospital. The hospital's treating professionals all agreed that the women were appropriate for discharge into community programs, but slots were not available to them.

The state of Georgia asked the Supreme Court to decide "whether the public services portion of the federal ADA compelled the state to provide treatment and habilitation for mentally disabled persons in a community placement, when appropriate treatment and habilitation could also be provided to them in a State mental institution." The case was significant because it hinged on the meaning of a U.S. Justice Department regulation (28 C.F.R.§ 35.130(d)) enforcing Title II of the ADA that said: "A public entity shall administer services, programs, and activities in the most integrated setting appropriate to the needs of qualified individuals with disabilities." The Justice Department had interpreted this regulation as requiring community placement of institutional residents when the state's own treating professionals have recommended such placement.

In allowing the women's right to community placement, the 11th Circuit Court held that "by definition, where, as here, the State confines an individual with a disability in an institutional setting when a community placement is appropriate, the State has violated the core principle underlying the ADA's integration mandate." A final settlement of the case was reached on July 11, 2000. In upholding the circuit court's ruling, the Supreme Court set a very high standard for states to serve disabled persons in community and other integrated settings and made attainable a goal long sought by disability rights advocates.

Five years later, and 14 years since passage of the ADA, some believe our nation has made scant progress in this area. Ira Burnim, legal director at the Bazelon Center for Mental Health Law (one of the case's cosponsors), bemoans the meager progress made since then in mental health:

> Budget pressures have closed psychiatric hospitals across the country, but few appropriate community services have been adequately funded to help people with mental illnesses live successfully in the community. Instead, states have "trans-institutionalized" people with mental illnesses to settings as outmoded, isolating and inappropriate as the facilities they were meant to replace. Increasing numbers of people with psychiatric disabilities now find themselves in large board and care homes, "adult homes," nursing homes, and other institution-like settings. Thousands wind up in jail or prison because chronically underfunded community mental health systems fail to provide meaningful support.

Burnim believes individual lawsuits continue to be required to combat persistent segregation of people with mental illnesses (*www.bazelon.org/olmstead*).

Aging advocates across the country have been increasingly supportive of the goals and work of disability rights advocates. The directors of the SUAs are working with the Bush administration to develop a more definitive focus on older adults in the New Freedom Initiative, supporting the systems change grants and implementation of the *Olmstead* decision. Dozens of national organizations are encouraging the administration to issue a new executive order directing all federal agencies to review existing policies that create barriers to community living for older adults and recommend changes. Federal policy changes that enable states to incorporate consumer direction into their HCBS programs, including efforts to integrate Medicare- and Medicaid-funded services, will continue to generate controversy as long as true expansion requires public funds.

Social Services Block Grants (Title XX of the Social Security Act)

Title XX was added to the Social Security Act in 1975, in response to runaway federal spending under Title IV of the Social Security Act during the Nixon administration. A series of political deals had allowed Republican governors in major states to spend their Title IV grants, an open-ended source of federal funds, for social services provided in state institutions as varied as prisons and public schools (Derthick, 1975). Title XX put on the brakes, creating a new capped formula grant program. It was designed to complement the federal Community Development Block Grants to low-income communities with social services. Title XX allocated $1.8 billion to the states, enabling each to provide social services it found best suited to the needs of its residents. Services had to be directed to one of the following five goals:

1. Prevent, reduce, or eliminate dependency;
2. Achieve or maintain self-sufficiency;
3. Prevent neglect, abuse, or exploitation of children and adults;
4. Prevent or reduce inappropriate institutional care; and
5. Secure admission or referral for institutional care when other forms of care are not appropriate.

In 1981 the Reagan administration made Title XX one of the first block grants to states under its New Federalism reforms, capping the federal allocation. Congress soon tired of appropriating annual increments of general-purpose revenue for block grants that could not easily prove their national impacts.

Federal Title XX still funds states and five territories for "the proper and efficient operation of social service programs." Each state develops its own plan, details the type of activities and individuals to be served, and files the plan with DHHS. Federal funds are allocated to states according to population, and state matching funds are no longer required. In its 30 years, Title XX funding has declined relative to inflation, with total federal expenditures currently capped at $2.8 billion annually. While the extent to which older adults benefit from Title XX services is unknown, advocates need to monitor their state's planning process to assure that older adults receive their "fair share" of services.

Ultimately, the most critically important community-based social services for older Americans have distinct limitations. The most vital ones, medications and in-home personal care, are the most strictly means tested. Social workers are often faced with the challenge of using social services to fill gaps in critically needed personal income and community infrastructures (Lipsky & Smith, 1989). One of these, housing, will be discussed next.

HOUSING POLICIES FOR AGING COMMUNITIES

Community planning for older individuals and families requires consideration of a wide range of needs beyond the control of individuals. Adapting community infrastructures to the needs of older users involves consideration of income disparities, geography, zoning, housing stock, transportation patterns, availability of financing sources, and other public policy concerns. Demographic data on the personal living arrangements, household configurations, incomes, wealth, and trans-

portation needs of older persons are particularly important for community planning. New housing where it can sustain social support and "naturally occurring" relationships that are often the very reason older persons choose to remain in their communities.

Currently well over two thirds of the noninstitutionalized older population own their homes, the vast majority mortgage free (U.S. Bureau of the Census, 2001). For most of these individuals, the home is their primary and sometimes only asset. Unfortunately, single women and economically disadvantaged elders are frequently forced out of their homes by rising property taxes and their inability to make repairs, afford structural modifications, or even buy special adaptive equipment when they become disabled. And renters are even more challenged, since,

> the number of affordable rental units for the aged is steadily declining and has been at a crisis level for some time. Government-subsidized housing for the poor (section 202 and section 8: public housing and rental assistance, respectively) has conspicuously failed to meet growing demand. (Olson, 2003, p. 103)

The largest government housing program by far is the federal tax deduction allowed on mortgage interest and local property taxes. These "tax expenditures" allowed income deductions—taken almost entirely by middle- and upper-income homeowners—for mortgage interest of $43 billion and local property taxes of $42 billion in 2002, or $85 billion uncollected by the Internal Revenue Service (Citizens for Tax Justice, n.d.) After that, federal housing policy gives priority to low-income elderly who need assistance in paying rent and elderly homeowners who have difficulty paying property taxes or maintaining their property or who need to adapt their homes to remain there safely. For some of the latter, government-insured loans can help them use the equity in their homes to finance needed services and home modifications or to develop alternative options. Similarly essential to low-income renters and homeowners are government programs that help offset the costs of home energy use and weatherizing property. As we shall see, however, these subsidies are barely discernible in the federal budget.

This section describes the range of provisions that assist elders in finding, obtaining, and maintaining suitable, accessible, affordable, and safe housing, including (a) publicly funded subsidized housing, (b) property tax relief, (c) home equity conversion programs, (d) creative alternative housing, including home modifications and assisted living, and (e) home energy assistance programs.

Subsidized Housing

The federal government addresses the housing needs of the low-income elderly, primarily through the Department of Housing and Urban Development (HUD) and, in rural areas, the Farmers Home Administration (FmHA) of the Department of Agriculture. By the end of the 1980s, more than 1.9 million households containing persons aged 65 and older were living in low-rent housing subsidized in some way by the federal government. This represented 9.6% of all elderly households and 43% of all low-rent federal housing, although the elderly constituted only 22% of all households (U.S. Congressional Budget Office, 1988; U.S. Senate, 1991). Compared with the rest of the population, the elderly were quite overrepresented in subsidized housing (Golant, 1992, p. 117), and they continue to be today.

This "overrepresentation" occurred because elders traditionally have had lower incomes than other renters. From their very inception, several federal housing programs targeted assistance to older people and retirees. Residents who moved into subsidized housing when construction was at its peak in the 1970s have been "aging in place" since then, and the needs for assistance of today's longtime older residents of public housing have increased accordingly. This is the rationale for local demonstration partnerships between AAAs and housing authorities to upgrade facilities and create some services on-site for the first time.

The 1980s and 1990s saw a dramatic turnaround in federal housing priorities, however, away from increasing the stock of quality affordable housing through public construction toward the use of housing cost supplements in the form of certificates and Section 8 vouchers. Real expenditures resulted from the new Stewart McKinney Homelessness Assistance Act.

Low-Rent Public Housing

Established by the Housing Act of 1937, the first federal public housing program included construction for low-income elderly and nonelderly persons. Tenants must have very low incomes (50% or less of a locality's median income) and spend 30% of their net income on rent and utilities. This housing is owned, operated, and maintained by some 3,000 local nonprofit public housing authorities, typically governed by community members appointed by local governments.

In 1990, about 192,000 (of 482,209) public housing apartments were occupied by the elderly, or about 40% of the program's total inventory. Today openings typically occur only when a unit is vacated, since so few new projects are being built anymore. The cap on supply reflects the federal policy change from a "production-oriented, project-based" approach to rent subsidization for private market housing. The resultant decline in construction and rehabilitation of low-rent units has produced the growing gap between increasing demand for and declining supply of affordable housing, a gap that is growing wider every year. Current priorities are to sell off public housing stock, or to perform simple maintenance and limited remodeling, but with no new construction.

This shift to rent subsidization has made it more difficult to track the actual impact of federal housing expenditures. The number of households receiving aid and the federal outlays for traditional programs decreased in the mid-1980s, and the number of households assisted "may have declined" (U.S. House of Representatives, Ways and Means Committee, 2003, p. 15-Housing-1).

Section 202 Housing

First enacted as part of the Housing Act of 1959, Section 202 is one of the few programs (along with low-income tax credits and FmHA Section 515) that finances new construction of low-rent apartment projects specifically for the elderly and the nonelderly population. This program has had "a choppy legislative existence" and was actually phased out during the early 1970s (Golant, 1992, p. 127). The number of new units produced annually peaked at more than 20,000 in the late 1970s and then declined to under 10,000 a year in 1990. By then there were 218,000 units occupied by the elderly and about 12,000 nonelderly disabled. Today there are about 300,000 housing units.

Experts have long considered Section 202 one of the more successful federal housing programs serving low-income elders (U.S. House of Representatives, Select Committee on Aging, 1989), largely because of the dedicated efforts of its nonprofit sponsors. Default and vacancy rates have been very low. By 1990 about eight applicants over age 62 were on waiting lists for every unit that became vacant, and the demand for those units remains high.

Because residents were aging in place so rapidly, the 1990 Affordable Housing Act included provisions to begin including congregate dining rooms and other common spaces in Section 202 housing to accommodate the provision of services on site. It also dropped the requirement that every project include 25% efficiency apartments, which have been more difficult to lease.

Section 521 Rental Assistance Program

The Rural Rental Assistance program (Section 515) was initiated in 1962 in the FmHA to provide rental housing units or congregate housing for elderly populations (aged 62 and older) living in small towns and rural communities (towns under 10,000 and communities as large as 20,000 if not located within a Metropolitan Statistical Area). It was expanded in 1966 to serve all low- and moderate-income families, and in 1983 priority was restricted to low-income households and those in substandard housing.

Sponsors of developments may be individuals, state and local public agencies, profit-making corporations, and nonprofit organizations. Sponsors apply for insured low-interest loans (as low as 1% for up to 50 years) to construct, purchase, rehabilitate, and operate low-rent, multifamily housing projects. Approximately 200,000 (or half) of the more than 400,000 units in the program are occupied by the elderly.

Section 8 Vouchers

The Housing and Community Development Act of 1974 created the Section 8 rental program to serve all age-groups, including the elderly. Section 8 vouchers are used by individuals to supplement their renting a variety of new, already built, public and privately owned rental units. At the end of 1989 it was estimated that 48% (1,152,000) of the 2,400,000 apartments subsidized by Section 8 vouchers were occupied by the elderly (U.S. Senate, Special Committee on Aging, 1990). In 2004 the program supplemented the rents paid for about 2 million units occupied by low-income persons, and only about a quarter of eligible households received any housing assistance at all (CBPP, 2004b).

Unfortunately, one of the Bush administration's many housing policy changes on the horizon is a budget proposal to cut $1.6 billion from Section 8 vouchers in 2005, with larger cuts to follow annually. By 2009 the proposed budget would cut $4.6 billion below current utilization level by turning Section 8

and a whole series of other housing programs into a block grant program giving states greater discretion to set basic standards for tenants' rents. The perverse effect of this will be to favor use by more middle-income tenants, while shrinking the program by 250,000 households in fiscal year 2005, and by 600,000 in fiscal year 2009, or 30% of present support (CBPP, 2004b).

Property Tax Relief and Deferral Programs for Older Home Owners

Many states (and some counties) have property tax deferral programs, homestead tax credits, and other forms of property tax relief for persons on low, fixed incomes. Tax deferral programs basically provide a low-interest loan to cover the property tax owed in a given year, so that an individual's available income may be used for food, needed services, and medicine instead of taxes. Such assistance can make the difference in allowing elders to remain at home, especially in areas with rapidly rising property taxes.

A major problem, however, is the low benefit "take-up" rate by persons with very low incomes. Aware that the loan must be repaid, seniors are often reluctant to apply (*www.ncoa.org/content.cfm*). Consequently, an important role of AAA staff is outreach to and case advocacy with potentially eligible seniors, assisting them in applying for such benefits. AAAs also do class advocacy with local elected officials to establish such programs. Friendly local elected officials are sometimes amenable to waiving or deferring property taxes on an individual case-by-case basis.

Home Equity Conversion Mortgage Programs

One option available to individuals and couples who need cash for living expenses (and do not plan to leave their home to heirs) is to borrow against their home equity. Home equity conversion mortgages are offered by many private lenders, but the federally insured Home Equity Conversion Mortgage (HECM) program allows the largest loan advances and the greatest choice in how to receive the cash. Mortgages are insured by the Federal Housing Administration (FHA) of HUD. The FHA determines how much HECM lenders may loan, based on the borrower's age and the home's value. The HECM program limits loan costs, and the FHA guarantees that lenders will meet their obligations. The funds received from a HECM can be used for any purpose, and although they are costly, they are typically much less costly than other reverse mortgages. Generally, the only reverse mortgages that are less expensive than HECMs are those offered by state or local governments, which typically must be used for a specific purpose (to repair a home or pay property taxes) and generally are available only for homeowners with low to moderate incomes.

HECM loans are available in all 50 states, the District of Columbia, and Puerto Rico. (In Texas, HECM credit line options are not available.). Eligible, current homeowners must be aged 62 or over and must live in the home as a principal residence. The home must be a single-family residence, in a one- to four-unit dwelling, a condominium, or part of a planned unit development. (Some manufactured housing is eligible, but cooperatives and most mobile homes are not.) The home must be at least a year old and meet HUD's minimum property standards, but the HECM can be used to pay for needed repairs. The owner must discuss the program with a HUD-approved counselor.

HECM loans must be paid in full when the last surviving borrower dies or sells the home, but they may also become due if any of the following occurs:

- The property deteriorates and the problem is not corrected;
- All the borrowers permanently move to a new principal residence;
- The last surviving borrower fails to live in the home for 12 consecutive months because of physical or mental illness; or
- The owner(s) fails to pay property taxes or hazard insurance, or violates any other borrower obligation.

Options for Assisted Living and Day Care Services

Most older adults today have incomes "too high" to qualify for subsidized housing; consequently, the private housing market provides options for alternative housing and housing adaptation. There remains, however, a great need for more affordable, imaginative, attractive, and functional designs. Such housing and transportation alternatives are addressed by a panoply of consumer-oriented Web sites listed at the end of this chapter, which include user-friendly housing designs and adaptations. Topics include safety, lighting, universal design, and uses for specific areas of the home. Two of the most recognized long-term care settings include traditional continuing care retirement communities and the newer form, assisted-living facilities. An overview of the types and characteristics of various kinds of supportive housing options is shown in Table 82.1.

Assisted living and other forms of supportive housing are specifically designed for those who need extra help in their day-to-day lives but who do not require the 24-hour skilled nursing care found in traditional nursing homes.

Fortunately, the trend over the past two decades has been to create a wider variety of living options that are much more homelike than the institutional facilities of the past. The Los Angeles Caregiver Resource Center provides fact sheets that provide an overview of these options and guidance in finding information and referrals. Its goal is to help find facilities that are comfortable, safe, appropriate, and affordable.

What's in a Name?

Supportive housing options vary widely in terms of size, cost, services, and facilities. The terms used to describe these options vary from state to state. Table 82.1 outlines the most common terms and the differences among them.

The list in Table 82.1 is only a general guide, since the names of housing options available in different communities vary by state. Practitioners may familiarize themselves with their own state's options by contacting their state unit on aging.

Continuing Care Retirement Communities

Continuing care retirement communities (CCRCs) are sometimes called life care communities. Entering one is usually a onetime decision, and that is the appeal. Many have large campuses with separate housing for those who live very independently, assisted-living facilities that offer more support, and nursing homes for those needing skilled nursing care. With all these types of housing on the same grounds, people who are relatively active, as well as those who have serious physical and mental disabilities, all live nearby. Residents then move from one housing choice to another as their needs change.

TABLE 82.1 Between Home and Nursing Home

Names/types of facilities	Characteristics
Personal care homes Sheltered housing Homes for adults Board and care Domiciliary care Adult foster care Senior group home	Facilities using these names tend to be smaller (fewer than 10 individuals) and less expensive. Many are in traditional homes in residential neighborhoods. Shared bathrooms, bedrooms, and living spaces are the norm.
Residential care facilities Assisted-living facilities Adult congregate living	These facilities tend to be larger, more expensive, and specifically designed for the frail elderly or persons with disabilities, emphasizing independence and privacy. Most offer private rooms or apartments and large common areas for activities and meals.
Continuing care retirement communities Life care facilities	These are usually large complexes that offer a variety of options ranging from independent living to skilled-nursing home care. These facilities are specifically designed to provide lifetime care within one community. Facilities within this category tend to be the most expensive option.

From Los Angeles Caregiver Resource Center.

Although usually very expensive, CCRCs have traditionally guaranteed lifetime shelter and care with long-term contracts that detail the housing and care obligations of the CCRC, as well as its costs. A wide variety of independent living units may be available: large and small apartments, cottages, cluster homes, or single-family homes. In addition to usual features, they may provide grab bars, a monitored emergency call system, and other safety features. Residents of these units are usually active older people.

Assisted-living units may be small studio or one-bedroom apartments with scaled-down kitchens. These facilities may have group dining areas and common areas for social and recreational activities. Residents typically need some assistance in daily living activities but also want some independence. Nursing home accommodations are usually furnished one-room units for two or more persons with an attached bathroom. Residents require skilled nursing care (short- or long-term) and may benefit from rehabilitative therapy to maintain or improve their abilities.

Because CCRCs are expensive, they generally are beyond the means of low- or moderate-income seniors. Most communities require an entrance fee, which can range from $20,000 to $400,000, and monthly payments, which can range from $200 to $2,500. In some places, residents own their living space; in others, the space is rented. In some communities, the entrance fee may be partially refundable within the first year or two, if a resident moves out.

Typically three different fee schedules are available, depending on how much long-term nursing care is anticipated:

1. *Extensive contracts:* unlimited nursing care and little or no increase in the monthly fee;
2. *Modified contracts:* a specified amount of nursing care, with the user responsible for payments beyond that amount; or
3. *Fee-for-service contracts:* user pays full daily rates for long-term nursing care.

Some CCRCs have specific ethnic, religious, or fraternal order affiliations and may require membership. Most require potential residents to have a medical examination, and selected preexisting conditions may cause a CCRC to deny admission. Some CCRCs require residents to have both Medicare Part A and Part B. Residents must have the resources to meet the entrance fee and monthly payments (Los Angeles Caregiver Resource Center, 2004).

Assisted-Living Facilities

Assisted living is a relatively new residential care option for individuals needing long-term assistance. It and a plethora of care options are increasingly available as substitutes for traditional care in nursing homes for individuals needing assistance with activities of daily living. Currently about 33,000 assisted-living facilities operate in the United States, with more than 90% of the care privately funded. Although most states have Medicaid waivers that could pay for health care within assisted-living facilities, fewer than 60,000 Medicaid recipients currently reside in them. These facilities are regulated by and within states, and these regulations vary greatly (U.S. Senate, Special Committee on Aging, 2002, p. 14). Even definitions of "assisted living" vary significantly by state, sometimes including "board and care" homes or group homes (see Table 82.1).

In 2003 the Senate Special Committee on Aging asked the assisted-living industry, consumer advocates, providers, and others to work together to make recommendations about best ways to assure quality in assisted living. More than 30 organizations collaborated in producing a consensus report and recommendations (Assisted Living Work Group, 2003). Their report is now available through the American Association of Homes and Services for the Aging (Assisted Living Work Group, 2003, *http://www.aahsa store.org/Product/Display.asp*).

A good assisted-living facility helps residents be as independent as possible while providing assistance when needed. The AARP's checklist can assist consumers and families in selecting an appropriate assisted-living facility by facilitating comparisons among facilities. It urges consumers not to make visits and decisions alone but to talk with family and friends about this major life decision (AARP, 2004).

Adult Day Care and Services

Day care services for older adults are viable, cost-effective community-based programs that serve individuals throughout the day to help keep them living at home. There are 3,493 adult day centers in the United States serving individuals of all ages with a variety of chronic conditions such as dementia, mental retardation, developmental disabilities, mental illness, HIV/AIDS, brain injury, and physical disabilities. Twenty-one percent of these centers operate on a medical model, 37% on a social model, and 42% as a combination providing a vast array of services. Growth in the day services industry has been rapid, with 26% of current centers opened within the past 5 years. There remains a need for 5,444 new centers nationwide (U.S. Senate, Committee on Aging, 2002, p. 15).

Creative Alternative Housing, Home Modifications, and Other Resources

Frequently, widowed persons find themselves "house poor," owning a home that is too large and costly to maintain. Because of pressure to cover property taxes or a mortgage, or to modify the home to meet new needs, this may be the time to sell.

But if one has good reasons for staying put, a more desirable option might be creating an accessory apartment to rent out. Even without modification, when zoning permits, such housing may be ideal for either sharing a house, having boarders, or taking in older adults under foster care. AARP offers helpful guidelines for doing this, as does Jane Porcino's popular book (1991) on creating alternative community housing. Another option is creating an accessory apartment in the home of an adult child, or an ECHO cottage, a separate housing unit in the side or back yard of the relative's property, again if zoning allows. Either option facilitates provision of daily assistance. Home equity conversion loans can often make this arrangement quite affordable, and some ECHO cottage designs are actually portable (National Resource Center on Supportive Housing and Home Modification, 2004).

Low-Income Home Energy and Weatherization Assistance

The Low-Income Home Energy Assistance Program (LIHEAP, P.L. 105-185) allocates federal block grants to states, territories, and Indian tribal organizations to operate home energy assistance programs for low-income households. Established in 1981 and reauthorized and amended several times, the program will be reauthorized in 2005. It is administered by the Division of Energy Assistance in the Office of Community Services, Administration for Children and Families within DHHS and may be operated by any of several agencies within the states.

Funds are allocated to states according to a complex three-tier formula taking account of energy costs and state poverty levels; in fiscal year 2003 the federal appropriation was approximately $1.8 billion (U.S. House of Representatives, Ways and Means Committee, 2003, p. 15-LIHEAP-1). States may use the funds for assistance in paying heating and cooling bills, low-cost weatherization projects, services to reduce the need for energy assistance, assistance with energy-related emergencies, and developments to leverage the funds to attract matching funds from other sources. Administration/planning costs are limited to 10% of the state's total allotment. States may make payments directly to consumers or to home energy suppliers. Households with incomes up to 150% of the federal poverty level may be eligible, as are persons receiving SSI, TANF, food stamps, and other means-tested assistance. DHHS performance goals currently seek to increase the percentage of recipients aged 60 and over, as well as those in the lowest-income households. Because funding for this program may derive from several federal, as well as state, sources, the state agencies responsible for it may be human services, community development, and/or housing. States are required to hold public hearings and seek public participation in developing state plans, so advocates for older adults have a special role in monitoring its implementation.

TRANSPORTATION FOR AN AGING SOCIETY

Transportation availability is intimately tied to social welfare policy and is readily seen in the competition for government dollars between mass transit systems and highway construction. Expanding or improving mass transit favors city dwellers, individuals who do not own cars, and the less well-off, whereas highway construction benefits car owners, the auto industry (and rubber and steel industries), suburbanites, and more affluent communities (Blau, 2004, p. 27). This same competition heavily influences transportation policies and provisions for older adults in local communities, and, not surprisingly, automobiles are the undisputed winners.

A recent AARP telephone survey that interviewed a national, stratified sample of 2,422 adults aged 50 and older on their transportation preferences found that 4 out of 5 usually drive, but those aged 85 and older and those with poor health or disabling conditions were substantially less likely to drive. Thirteen percent of persons aged 50 and older rely on ride sharing most of the time, and fewer than 5% rely on walking, public transportation, taxis, and community or senior vans. Fewer than one in eight respondents felt that transportation problems interfered with their ability to do necessary errands, get to appointments, or engage with others, although 5% of those aged 75 and older said they often experienced such problems (AARP, 2002).

With older adults so reliant on automobiles, it is not surprising that the AOA's first priority is to ensure that older Americans can "drive as long and as safely as possible and that alternatives are available to individuals who no longer drive." As we anticipate the largest ever group of older drivers in U.S. history, the

AoA reports that research is showing that "older persons are successfully adjusting for these changes and are driving safely well into their 70s, 80s, and 90s" (Administration on Aging, 2004b, p. 1). One explanation for this is that state driving authorities have become more flexible, as well as vigilant, requiring more frequent driving exams after certain ages and issuing more licenses with restrictions to certain geographic areas, road types, or driving conditions.

When older individuals are no longer able to drive safely, families and sometimes physicians are needed to make alternative arrangements. Suburban areas may include senior van services, taxi vouchers, medical vans, and ride-share programs. In rural areas, individuals typically have little choice but to rely on relatives and friends for rides. Public mass transportation and paratransit are typically available only in urban areas.

Since 2001, the Bush administration's New Freedom Initiative has focused some attention on improving the coordination of transportation alternatives for all special-needs populations (children, elderly, and disabled persons) at the local level. A 2003 memorandum of understanding between AOA and the Federal Transit Administration (FTA) of the U.S. Department of Transportation commits each agency to assist its respective networks in coordinating transportation services and facilitating access to them by older adults. In 2004 the FTA issued grants to help localities assess their level of coordination and develop action plans, including leveraging local funding sources, technical assistance to enhance partnerships, enhancing technologies to improve scheduling and billing, and providing consumer education. A glimpse of the FTA's "road map" for "United We Ride" can be found online in the FTA administrator's presentation to the Community Transportation Association of America (Dorn, 2004).

Capital Assistance Programs (Section 5310)

Special-needs transportation is largely funded through the FTA Capital Assistance Program for Elderly Persons and Persons with Disabilities. This program provides financial assistance to states for meeting the transportations needs of special populations where public transportation is unavailable, insufficient, or inappropriate. The Section 5310 program supplements FTA's other capital assistance programs, funding transportation projects in urban, small urban, and rural areas. Only designated states may apply, and eligible subrecipients include private nonprofit organizations, public bodies approved by the state to coordinate services for elderly and disabled persons, and public bodies that certify to the governor that no nonprofit corporations or associations are available in an area to provide service. A typical project provides $1 million to a state to purchases 35 accessible vehicles for use by 30 local recipient organizations throughout the state. If states do not spend their allocation in the year it is given, funds are redistributed to other states in the subsequent year.

Funds are allocated to states by a formula based on the population of elderly and disabled persons, and may cover up to 80% of the eligible project costs. This special program assistance began in 1975, distributing $20 million to more than 1,000 private nonprofit organizations to purchase vehicles. In fiscal year 2004 the federal allocation of $98 million funded nearly 4,000 local subrecipients, enabling thousands of persons to achieve greater mobility and independence. Unfortunately the fiscal year 2005 allocation dropped to $88 million.

CONCLUSION

This chapter has used the federal funding framework to highlight the array of social service, housing, and transportation programs serving older adults in local communities. "Following the money" from the federal agencies through and within different levels of state and local government reveals where services come from and is essential to being an effective advocate for this age-group.

Following precedents set by Presidents Nixon and Reagan, the George W. Bush administration is striving to reduce the size of government by limiting and eliminating its responsibilities for basic human needs of disadvantaged persons. President Bush's New Freedom Initiative is hollow rhetoric compared with his administration's reductions in social services, housing benefits, and public infrastructure. In the name of "opportunity" and "free choice," the New Freedom Initiative is a proxy for what was once the security of basic subsistence provision for in-home services, adequate shelter, and transportation assistance. Privatization of services, increasing user co-payments, and preference for corporate welfare are the real policy goals. This, coupled with the recession of 2001–2004 and the continuing state fiscal crises, has made social

work advocacy for basic services for the aging an urgent imperative at all levels of government today.

REFERENCES

AARP. (2002). *Understanding senior transportation: Report and analysis of a survey of consumers 50+.* Washington, DC: Author. Retrieved from *http://research. aarp.org/il/2002)04_transport_1.html*

AARP. (2004). *Housing preferences.* Washington, DC: Author. Retrieved from *http://www.aarp.org/life/ housingchoices/*

Administration on Aging. (2004a). *The Older Americans Act National Caregiver Support Program (Title III-E and VI-C): Compassion in action.* Washington, DC: Author. Retrieved from *aoa.gov/prof/aoaprog/caregiver/careprof/progguidance/resources/*

Administration on Aging. (2004b). Transportation Web site. *http://www.aoa.gov/prof/transportation/transportation.asp*

Administration on Aging. (2004c). *Layman's guide to the Older Americans Act,* online at: *http://www.aoa.gov/ about/legbudg/oaa/laymans_guide_pf.asp*

Assisted Living Work Group. (2003). *Assuring quality in assisted living: Guidelines for federal and state policy, state regulations, and operations.* Washington, DC: American Association of Homes and Services for the Aging. Retrieved from *http://www.aahsastore.org/ Product/Display.asp*

Blau, J. (2004). *The dynamics of social welfare policy.* New York: Oxford University Press.

Center for Budget and Policy Priorities. (2004a, February 20). *Analysis of the President's budget.* Retrieved from *http://www.cbpp.org/2-2-04bud.htm*

Center for Budget and Policy Priorities. (2004b, March 8). *President's budget would slash major housing programs by 30% in 2009.* Retrieved from *http://www. cbpp.org*

Citizens for Tax Justice. (n.d.). *The hidden entitlements: Part III. Personal tax expenditures.* Retrieved from *www.ctj.org/hid_ent/part3/part3-1.htm*

Derthick, (1975). *Uncontrollable spending for social service grants.* Washington, DC: Brookings Institute.

Dorn, J. (2004, July 15). *Address by the Federal Transit Administrator to the Community Transportation Association of America conference.* Seattle, Washington. Retrieved from *http://www.fta.dot.gov/CCAM/www/ images/ctaa-slides-june-15-2004.ppt*

Estes, Caroll. (1980). *The aging enterprise.* San Francisco: Jossey-Bass.

Federal Interagency Forum on Aging-Related Statistics. (2000, August). *Older Americans 2000: Key indicators of well-being. Federal interagency forum on aging-related statistics.* Washington, DC: U.S. Government Printing Office. Retrieved from *http://agingstats.gov/ chartbook2000/economics.html#Indicator%206*

Golant, S. (1992). *Housing America's elderly: Many possibilities/few choices.* Newbury Park, CA: Sage.

Lipsky, M., & Smith, S. R. (1989). When social problems are treated as emergencies. *Social Service Review, 63,* 5–25.

Los Angeles Caregiver Resource Center. *Fact sheet: Assisted living and supportive housing.* Retrieved from *geroweb.usc.edu/lacrc/caregiverissues/FactSheets/as sisted_living.htm*

Mahoney, K., Simone, K., & Simon-Rusinowitz, L. (2000). Early lessons from the Cash and Counseling Demonstration and Evaluation. *Generations,* Fall, 41–46. Retrieved from *www.hcbs.org/files/*

National Association of State Budget Officers. (2004, April). *The Fiscal Survey of the States.* Washington, DC.

National Association of State Units on Aging. (2004, June). *40 years of leadership: The dynamic role of state units on aging.* 40th anniversary membership meeting, National Resource Center on Supportive Housing and Home Modification. Retrieved from *www. usc.edu/dept/gero/nrcshhm/*

National Council on the Aging. (2004). *Real estate tax deferral program.* Retrieved from *www.ncoa.org/con tent.cfm?sectionID=240&detail=241*

National Resource Center on Supportive Housing and Home Modification. (n.d.). *Fact sheet: Accessory units,* Andrus Center for Gerontology, University of Southern California, Los Angeles. Available at *www.homemods.org/folders/PDF/access.pdf.*

Older Americans Act of 1965 (42 U.S.C. 3001 note Enacted July 14, 1965, P.L. 89-73, sec 1, 79 Stat. 219) in Gelfand, D. E. *The aging network: Programs and services* (2nd ed., pp. 237–286) (New York: Springer Publishing Co., 1984).

Olson, L. Katz. (2003). *The not-so-golden years: Caregiving, the frail elderly, and the long-term care establishment.* New York: Rowman and Littlefield.

Porcino, J. (1991). *Living longer, living better: Adventures in community housing for those in the second half of life.* Continuum International.

U.S. Bureau of the Census. (2001, May). *Housing characteristics, 2000: Profiles of general characteristics.* Washington, DC: U.S. Government Printing Office.

U.S. Congressional Budget Office. (1988). *Current housing problems and possible federal responses.* Washington, DC: Superintendent of Documents.

U.S. House of Representatives, Select Committee on Aging. (1989). *The 1988 National Survey of Section 202*

Housing for the Elderly and Handicapped. Washington, DC: U.S. Government Printing Office.

U.S. House of Representatives, Ways and Means Committee. (2003). *The green book.* Retrieved from *http:// ways&means.house.gov*

U.S. Senate, Special Committee on Aging, (1990). *Developments on aging, 1989* (Vols. 1 and 2). Washington, DC: U.S. Government Printing Office.

U.S. Senate, Special Committee on Aging. (1991). *Developments on aging, 1990* (Vols. 1 and 2). Washington, DC: U.S. Government Printing Office.

U.S. Senate, Special Committee on Aging. (2002, January). *Long-term care report, 107th Congress.* Washington, DC: U.S. Government Printing Office.

SOME USEFUL RESOURCES

Gaddy, Karen. (2000). Special care environments: An overview of state laws for care of persons with Alzheimer's disease. *Bifocal: Newsletter of the ABA Commission on Legal Problems of the Elderly,* 21(2).

Hawes, Rose M., & Phillips, C. D. (1999). *A national study of assisted living for the frail elderly: Results of a national survey of facilities.* Beachwood, OH: Myers Research Institute.

Lieberman, T., & editors of Consumer Reports. (2000). *Consumer Reports complete guide to health services for seniors.* Three River Press/Random House.

Lieberman, T., & editors of Consumer Reports. (2001, January). Is assisted living the right choice? *Consumer Reports.*

Loverde, J. ( ) *The complete eldercare planner: Where to start, which questions to ask, and how to find help.* Time Books.

Mathews, J. L. *Beat the nursing home trap: A consumer's guide to assisted living and long-term care* (3rd ed.). Nolo Press.

Mollica, R. (2000). *State assisted living policy: 2000.* Portland, ME: National Academy for State Health Policy.

Stucki, B. R., & Mulvey, J. (2000). *Can aging baby boomers avoid the nursing home? Long-term care insurance for aging in place.* Washington, DC: American Council of Life Insurers.

Web Sites

American Association of Retired Persons (AARP), home, *www.aarp.org/life/homedesign/*

Elder Web, *http://www.elderweb.com*

Los Angeles Caregiver Resource Center, *www.usc.edu/ lacrc*

National Resource Center on Supportive Housing and Home Modification, *www.usc.edu/dept/gero/nrcshhm/*
Seniorresource.com, *http://www.seniorresource.com*

Organizations

American Association of Homes and Services for the Aging
901 E Street NW, Suite 500
Washington, DC 20004-2001
202-783-2242, Web site: *www.aahsa.org*

American Seniors Housing Association
5100 Wisconsin Avenue NW, Suite 307
Washington, DC 20016
202-237-0900, Web site: *www.seniorshousing.org*

Assisted Living Federation of America
10300 Eaton Place, Suite 400
Fairfax, VA 22030
703-691-8100, Web site: *www.alfa.org*, e-mail: *info@alfa.org*

Consumer Consortium on Assisted Living
P.O. Box 3375
Arlington, VA 22203
703-841-2333, Web site: *www.ccal.org*, e-mail: Membership@ccal.org

National Center for Assisted Living
1201 L Street, NW
Washington, DC 20005
202-842-4444, Web site: *www.ncal.org*

This chapter discusses a number of decision-making policies and proxy issues that affect the lives of older adults. The topic is a challenging one because there is little in the way of national policy on guardianship or the variety of related approaches sometimes referred to as guardianship alternatives. Each state develops its own protective service policies, and these policies are carried out by professionals at the local level, including probate judges, adult protective service workers, and health and social service providers. Given the lack of overarching national policy, we begin at the other end of the spectrum with an older adult who needs decision-making support. We use the following case example to discuss concepts that underlie protective services policies and to examine the various policy and program approaches available to social workers to meet the needs of vulnerable adults:

▓ Mrs. C. is a recent widow in her early 80s. In addition to being physically frail, she has been previously diagnosed with diabetes and congestive heart failure. A concerned neighbor calls the Area Agency on Aging, and an adult protective service worker is sent to the home. The home visit reveals that Mrs. C. is unable to accurately answer questions about her age, birth date, or where she lives. Since the death of her husband she has been unable to pay her bills, keep her apartment clean, or adequately prepare food. She appears to have little in the way of assets, but she reports that she is related to the king of England and had a grandfather in Montana who willed her money. She alleges that this money, which she kept in a suitcase, has been stolen from her by the building manager along with her furniture, dishes, and personal belongings. Mrs. C. does not have a working phone. Her refrigerator has been disconnected, there is no food in her house, and she remembers eating little in recent days. Her companions are two uncaged birds and a small dog. ▓

KATHLEEN WILBER
GRETCHEN E. ALKEMA

Policies Related to Competency and Proxy Issues

83

Mrs. C.'s situation illustrates a number of challenges that may involve social workers and other gerontological professionals. Given the present information, Mrs. C. appears to have little social support, few if any links to the formal service delivery system, and several complex medical and mental health problems that compromise her daily functioning and safety. It is unclear whether her apparent confusion stems from an immediately treatable condition such as dehydration, unstable blood sugar, or a urinary tract infection, or whether she has a progressive dementing illness. Regardless of the etiology, she appears to need urgent and probably long-term assistance. A social worker may be called upon to help Mrs. C. if she is hospitalized, at discharge, or after she has returned home.

CORE VALUES GUIDING SERVICE DELIVERY TO OLDER ADULTS

One of the major challenges of developing and applying policies that both protect Mrs. C. and safeguard her civil liberties is providing the appropriate level of support without inappropriately restricting her rights of autonomy and self-determination. A fundamental approach to keep the important goal of safety from incorrectly trumping individual freedom is to apply core values that guide how protective service policies are legislated and applied (Wilber, 2000). These core values include (a) striving to offer the least restrictive appropriate alternative, (b) marshaling services to support aging in place whenever possible, (c) centering decisions to the greatest extent possible around client preferences and expressed needs, (d) drawing from the repertoire of available interventions to develop an individualized plan of treatment, (e) supporting informal caregivers, and (f) interdisciplinary communication to clinically integrate medical, social, and housing services. Ideally these policies are operationalized in the context of self-determination and person-environment fit, offering social workers appropriate tools to balance respect for the client's personal freedom with legitimate concerns about personal safety.

Protective services and decision-making interventions are designed to assist people who are unable to manage their daily affairs (i.e., unable to provide for basic necessities such as food, shelter, and clothing) and/or for those who are at high risk of physical and/or fiduciary harm. Several approaches are available depending on the individual's needs, availability of a support system, and physical and mental capacity. Sometimes this range of services is referred to as *daily money management (DMM)*, a term coined by Jack McKay, a pioneer in the field who referred to financial and decision-making services offered by social service agencies for lower- and middle-income clients. Table 83.1 provides a general outline of these interventions based on capacity requirements, appro-

priateness for the service, and complexity of problems that each can address. Before describing these approaches, we briefly explore the legal and clinical definitions of capacity.

WHAT IS CAPACITY?

In the United States, those aged 18 and older are considered to be adults and, as such, are trusted to have independent decision-making capacity. This principle means they are allowed to engage in the world using their own cognitive power and accepting responsibility for their choices. Adult decision making includes "the right to folly," which is the right to make poor choices coupled with the responsibility to live with the consequences of those choices. Sometimes, however, poor choices stem from cognitive impairment, which affects the individual's ability to make a reasoned decision. When this is a concern, capacity can be challenged in court.

The legal determination of capacity is quite specific; a court of law determines whether or not someone has capacity or competence to make "reasoned decisions." Applebaum and Grisso (1988) identified four domains to evaluate capacity: (a) to communicate relatively consistent or stable choices, (b) to understand basic information about choices, (c) to evaluate reasonable implications or consequences of available choices, and (d) to use a reasoned process to rationally weigh risks and benefits of choices. As these domains suggest, examination of capacity should focus on the process of decision making, not the decisions themselves. For example, Mrs. C.'s decision making would be questionable if she did not seek help because she believed that her relationship to the "king of England" would protect her. She might have reached the same decision not to seek help because her neighbor threatened to harm her if she called anyone. In this instance, however, her decision shows evidence of a reasoned if not altogether appropriate approach.

In contrast to a legal determination, capacity is also a psychological construct. From this perspective, the term becomes much more ambiguous than its codified legal definition. Although an extensive body of research has developed to examine standards for determining capacity (e.g., Appelbaum & Grisso, 1988; Collopy, 1988; Kapp & Mossman, 1996; Sabatino, 1996), definitive guidelines remain elusive. The problem with developing a practical definition is that capacity may be fluctuating, intermittent, and deci-

TABLE 83.1 Characteristics of Financial and Health-Related Services Available to Older Persons

| Service | Capacity | | Appropriateness to address risk of older person | | | Complexity |
	Required for execution	Survives incapacity	Personal risk: high, medium, low	Financial risk: high, medium, low	Oversight / recourse	Ability to address complex financial / medical issues
Power of attorney	Yes	No	Low	Medium	Oversight by family; legal action	Medium
Bill-paying services	Yes	Not usually	Low	Medium	Agency audit; legal action	Low
Joint accounts/ joint tenancy	Yes	Yes	Low	Medium	Virtually none; legal action	Low
Durable power of attorney	Yes	Yes	Low	High	Oversight by family; legal action	Medium
Durable power of attorney for health care	Yes	Yes	Medium	Low	Oversight by family; legal action	Medium
Representative payee	No	Yes	Medium	Medium	Virtually none by federal governmental agency	Low
Personal trusts	Yes	Yes, if drawn properly	Medium	High	Internal audit, banking commissioner, legal action	High
Limited guardianship	No	Yes	High	High	Court; legal action	High
Plenary guardianship	No	Yes	High	High	Court; legal action	High

Note: *These criteria assume the availability of an appropriate social support network.*
From Wilber, K. H., & Reynolds, S. L. (1995). Rethinking alternatives to guardianship. *Gerontologist, 35,* 248–257.

sion specific (Buchanan & Brock, 1986). For example, Mrs. C. might be able to make decisions about her living arrangements but not her finances. She may be clear about her affairs one day yet confused the next.

Local courts determine capacity based on state statutes, focusing their capacity determinations on one of three areas: disabling condition tests, functional behavior tests linked to disability, or a risk model based on an "essential needs" test (Sabatino, 1996). The disabling conditions test indicates that a person could be deemed incapacitated by virtue of a specific diagnosis related to cognitive impairment, such as Alzheimer's disease. The problem with this definition alone is that it does not take into account the duration, extent, and/or severity of the illness or condition. Most states have moved away from this exclusive criterion and have added the functional behavior test to the measuring stick. The functional behavior test includes looking at a person's functional capacity related to self-care and the management of his or her own estate. Arkansas, for example, specifies

that the appointment of a guardian is appropriate when a person has a disabling condition (physical, mental, substance abuse) to the extent that he or she lacks sufficient understanding to make or communicate decisions to meet essential requirements for health, safety, or management of his or her estate (Social Security Administration, 2004a). However, the functional test could be interpreted broadly to include activities and responsibilities that may not be within the individual's purview (e.g., grocery shopping and meal preparation for a cognitively impaired older adult living in a retirement facility that includes these services). In this instance the third approach, the "essential needs" test, represents the most flexible interpretation of incapacity determination criteria. The essential needs test, which basically is a risk model tailored for a specific individual, focuses primarily on activities and behaviors that the individual will reasonably engage in and evaluating whether or not he or she can continue to make these decisions and/or execute these tasks. States laws in California,

Illinois, and Nebraska are based on this perspective. It is important to note, however, that the interpretation and execution of guardianship laws reside with the presiding judge, who typically serves in county probate court.

APPLYING SUPPORTIVE AND SURROGATE POLICIES AND PROGRAMS

Social workers and other professionals must understand the relevant policies in their states. They must also assess how these policies apply to each client's specific needs. Identification of Mrs. C.'s specific needs involves assessing what types of decisions she needs to make, what type of support is appropriate and available, and how and by whom decisions will be carried out. Collopy (1988) and Smyer (1993) distinguish between decisional capacity, the ability *to make* a reasoned choice, and executional capacity, the capacity *to act* on the choice. This distinction is important for choosing the appropriate level of intervention—supportive decision making or surrogate decision making. Individuals who retain decisional capacity but need support to act on their decisions can be served through *supportive decision-making* interventions. In contrast, *surrogate decision-making* support is most appropriate for those who have lost the capacity to make reasoned decision based on legal criteria and need a proxy to make decisions on their behalf.

Supportive Decision Making

Supportive decision-making services allow Mrs. C. to make decisions with help from another party to carry out her decisions through assistance with banking, bill paying, and budgeting. For example, after she is medically stable, Mrs. C. may be capable of making decisions about how to use her resources and where to live, but she may need help implementing these choices. She might not be able to organize her bills or understand medical claim forms, but she can agree on the amount she wants to pay for each item, sign checks, and mail paid bills. To illustrate, let us assume that Mrs. C. is treated in the hospital and her condition greatly improves so that she is able to return home. Hospital social workers link Mrs. C. to a community case management agency that offers DMM services to help her manage household finances. It becomes clear that Mrs. C.'s husband had managed the finances throughout their marriage, and Mrs. C. has

no experience or knowledge in financial matters. Within the realm of supportive decision-making services, DMM includes (a) offering education and advice to Mrs. C. so that she can learn how to manage her financial affairs; (b) ensuring that she receives benefits to which she is entitled, using tools such as the National Council on the Aging's Benefits Checkup (*http://www.benefitscheckup.org/*); and (c) providing hands-on assistance—helping her to create an overall budget, identify the bills that need to be paid, determine how much to pay, assist with making out checks, and enter transactions into her checkbook register. DMM services can also help Mrs. C. with setting up direct deposits for incoming funds, arranging for automatic deductions for bill payment, and identifying unknown assets such as retirement investments. Paperwork and processing forms after a hospital stay can be overwhelming, so DMM services can help Mrs. C. complete medical claim forms and follow up with insurance carriers. Finally, DMM services include future planning, such as help setting up a durable power of attorney (described later in this chapter) to name a decision maker if Mrs. C. should lose capacity and help with funeral planning. The process is *supportive* in that Mrs. C. herself makes the decisions about future plans, who to choose as surrogate decision makers, and under what conditions they would assist her.

DMM is the formal provider's response to supportive decision making in the event that Mrs. C. does not have a trusted family member or friend. Although some communities are fortunate enough to have DMM services, many do not. Another approach to providing services is for Mrs. C. to identify a loved one or trusted friend who can assist her, such as her niece Betty, who was located by the hospital chaplaincy service, to carry out these same tasks. In this circumstance, Mrs. C. could ask Betty to directly assist her as a DMM case manager would. She could also add Betty to her bank accounts, nonretirement investments, and property as a joint tenant. Using the services of an attorney, she could develop a trust to include all these assets and name Betty as a trustee so that she could act directly on Mrs. C.'s behalf (for more information on various financial planning transactions, see Quinn, 1997).

Social Worker's Role in Supportive Decision Making

Social workers and other gerontological professionals can function in a variety of roles through the supportive decision-making process. If Mrs. C. planned for future help from a family member by arranging for joint tenancy on her accounts, a social worker could facilitate communication between Mrs. C. and her niece Betty to explain Mrs. C.'s current physical and cognitive state, detail current and future needs upon discharge from the hospital, and help Betty assume responsibility of her aunt's financial matters. The social worker could also act as a community liaison by assisting Betty with locating needed services that would generally not be covered by insured services, such as attendant care or home modification equipment. Additionally, a social worker could provide psychosocial support to both Betty and Mrs. C. during this transition period. If Mrs. C. had not planned for incapacity, a social worker could assist her by a referral to a community agency for DMM or by providing DMM to her under the auspices of a community agency's defined protocols. Later we will describe how professionals can fulfill this role while maintaining appropriate boundaries for Mrs. C.'s safety and their own.

Surrogate Decision Making

Rather than recovering from a tractable health problem, Mrs. C. might be suffering from a progressive degenerative disease that has caused significant cognitive impairment such that she can no longer make necessary decisions about her care and her finances. In this case, activating surrogate decision-making tools on her behalf may be a social worker's most appropriate intervention. Surrogate decision-making tools include various powers of attorney that are preplanned and triggered by incapacity, as well as representative payeeship and legal guardianship, in which decisions facing Mrs. C. are formally transferred to another party.

Powers of Attorney

Powers of attorney (POAs) are mechanisms to delineate surrogate decision-making arrangements ahead of time so that if Mrs. C. loses capacity, her wishes about daily living and preferences for end-of-life care can be effectively carried out (Mrs. C. must still create a will to disperse her assets upon death, but testamentary decision making is beyond the scope of this chapter; see Quinn, 1997). A POA delegates authority to an "agent" to carry out specific or general tasks. Typically, because of this delegated authority, a POA

is in effect only as long as the person who is delegating the authority, the "principal," has capacity. However, durable powers of attorney (DPA) may be developed to allow the agent to make decisions for the principal (Mrs. C.) if she has lost decision-making capacity. The two important types of DPA are durable power of attorney for health care (DPAHC) and a DPA for finances. Using a DPAHC, Mrs. C. can make her health care wishes known in a "living will" and then designate an agent to carry out those wishes if she loses capacity. For example, she might specify that she wants to have a "do not resuscitate order" in the event that her heart stops. Likewise, Mrs. C. can spell out how she wants her finances managed through a DPA for finances if she is no longer able and designate an agent to administer her affairs. Although a DPA is a surrogate decision-making mechanism, it is developed by the principal to execute his or her wishes prior to an incapacitating event. In this way it offers a less restrictive alternative to other surrogate decision-making approaches. However, this method of decision making has been criticized because it is a private arrangement with little external oversight to protect against fraud and/or abuse (Dessin, 2003). Although the basic underlying principles are the same, advance directives are based on state policies, so again we stress the importance of understanding policies and regulations where one practices. Additionally, the service auspice is important in that different institutions have different requirements for managing POAs. Some banks may not honor a financial DPA unless coupled with the bank's own proxy forms. In health care, it is crucial to inform and involve physicians in the DPAHC process because they will have a critical role in carrying out decisions that the proxy makes if the DPAHC is activated.

Representative Payee

Representative payeeship, a tool targeted to manage public benefits such as Social Security, Social Security Disability Insurance (SSDI), and Supplemental Security Income (SSI), is the only nationally based surrogate decision-making policy. The Social Security Administration authorizes "rep payees" for beneficiaries who lack the capacity to manage their money based on physician certification reporting physical and/or mental impairment (Social Security Administration, 2004b). Rep payees are responsible for providing for basic necessities (food, clothing, and shelter) using the client's own money and maintaining separate accounting receipts for expenses incurred. Rep payees can be individuals or previously authorized organizations that agree to accept this responsibility. Beneficiaries can request this service on their own by naming a friend or family member to become the rep payee. The Social Security Administration may determine upon granting benefits that the beneficiary lacks capacity and will automatically require a rep payee before disbursement without his or her previously expressed consent.

The constraint of rep payee status is that the designee can manage only public benefits. Therefore, if Mrs. C. received Social Security and a pension, the rep payee would specifically oversee the Social Security payment, and Mrs. C. would still need to have completed a DPA for finances to manage her pension. To encourage family members, friends, or agencies to accept this limited financial responsibility, the Social Security Administration recently authorized the payee to receive up to $35 per month for their services. However, if Mrs. C. had few resources or received only SSI, even this small amount could significantly reduce the amount available to pay for her care.

Guardianship

If Mrs. C. lacks capacity, and alternatives are not in place or do not adequately meet her needs, guardianship may become the only option. Guardianship is intended to protect vulnerable, dependent persons who are at high risk of personal injury or financial loss, or those who require a legal decision maker to make treatment decisions and/or to authorize financial transactions. Considered the "court of last resort" (Schmidt, 1995), guardianship is best exercised in a judicious manner because it is a highly intrusive and restrictive intervention. Called conservatorship or committeeship in some states, guardianship is a legal arrangement in which a guardian—an individual or legal entity—is appointed by the court to manage the affairs of an adult who becomes a "ward." Sometimes there is confusion about adult guardianship in that guardianship is also used for placing children under the age of 18 with nonparental adults. If Mrs. C. was placed under legal guardianship, she would effectively lose *all* civil liberties, reducing her legal status to that of a minor (Alexander, 1990; Horstman, 1975; Kapp, 1999; Rein, 1992).

Guardianship is initiated when a petitioner makes a formal request to the court. Legal guardianship requires a court hearing involving a judge, the petitioner who requests the hearing, and the respondent—Mrs. C. in this case. The petitioner, who may or may not become the guardian, could be a family member or friend, a public guardian, or a private professional (a private agency or individual such as an attorney or accountant). Not all states have a public guardian program, but for those that do, this entity typically serves as the last alternative of protective care for wards who lack willing or qualified caregivers and do not have resources to pay for a private guardian (Schmidt, Miller, Bell, & New, 1981). Family members are most likely to act as petitioners and subsequent guardians, taking such action after a specific triggering event or critical incident in their loved one's life, such as physical health emergency, acute mental health problem, financial mismanagement, or the need for nursing home placement (Keith & Wacker, 1994). If the court finds that Mrs. C. lacks the capacity to manage her affairs, a guardian is appointed. Most hearings are brief, with the vast majority—more than 90%—resulting in guardianship (Lisi & Barinaga-Burch, 1995). Once guardianship is granted, the decision is essentially permanent because the ward, now having no legal rights, cannot contest its validity or appropriateness.

Although guardianships may be either full (plenary) or partial (limited), most are plenary. Under a plenary guardianship, the guardian is given responsibility for all aspects of the ward's life, including determining living arrangements, medical treatment, and financial expenditures and managing all assets (Keith & Wacker, 1994; Lisi & Barinaga-Burch, 1995). Sometimes this is referred to as guardianship of both the "person" and the "estate." In some instances, the court may limit the guardian's authority to specific areas. For example, if Mrs. C. has a rep payee and no other assets to be managed, she might need a guardian only for health care decisions. In this situation, the court might appoint a limited guardianship for health care decision making. Or if Mrs. C. had a complex estate but was able to make decisions about her personal affairs, the court may appoint a guardian of the estate to manage financial matters only.

Ethics and Realities of Guardianship

The guardian is expected to manage the ward's affairs with care and diligence based on the ward's best interests (Friedman & Savage, 1988). To effectively fulfill this mission, guardianship removes constitutionally guaranteed liberties and decision-making authority from wards, most of whom were previously autonomous and self-reliant. Guardianship operates under the state's *parens patriae* authority, which obligates government to safeguard individuals who lack the capacity to protect themselves even when they do not consent to the intervention. Although such paternalistic interventions are intended to be benevolent and ultimately to protect the individual's best interest (Hommel, 1996), guardianship has been criticized for a number of shortcomings, including inadequate supervision and monitoring of guardians by the court, lack of due process in guardianship proceedings, inappropriate use of guardianship when less restrictive approaches could be used, and inadequate care by guardians (Keith & Wacker, 1994; Wilber & Reynolds, 1995).

Currently, the entities responsible for creating and enforcing guardianship laws and regulations are states and U.S. territories, not the federal government. In the absence of a mandated national policy on guardianship, each state's laws and regulations determine the legal processes, the duties and responsibilities of the court and legal guardians, and the terminology used. In 1997, the National Conference of Commissioners on Uniform State Laws, a nonpartisan group of legal experts that develops uniform legislative templates for states to frame their own laws, adopted an updated version of the Uniform Guardianship and Protective Proceedings Act (UGPPA). Yet since the act's adoption, only 4 states (Alabama, Colorado, Minnesota, and Montana) have enacted statutes that are based on it. Additionally, only 26 states have a public guardianship program that provides low-income wards without available social support a court-appointed guardian. Public guardianship programs are generally implemented at the county level and are housed in a variety of administrative units, including aging, adult services, mental health, developmental disabilities, and district attorneys' offices. This lack of uniformity across the states and municipalities further contributes to a disjointed and fragmented service delivery system attempting to address the guardianship needs of vulnerable adults with limited resources.

Recently some states, including Colorado, Delaware, and New York, have stipulated that the appointment of a guardian does not necessarily constitute a finding of legal incompetence, which suggests a movement to a broader use of limited guardianships for specific tasks on behalf of the ward and a more nuanced definition of capacity. Although a number of states have built on the guardianship reform literature of the last several decades to enact more enlightened guardianship laws, the immediate impact of these reforms appears to be small (Keith & Wacker, 1994).

Although media exposés and government hearings have identified serious problems in guardianship, the few empirical studies on the quality of care and estate management have indicated that most guardians provide adequate services (AARP, 1990). In direct interviews with wards, Wilber, Reiser, and Harter (2001) found that the most frequently expressed problems were feelings of loneliness and isolation rather than concerns about guardianship. This research suggests the need to enhance quality of life by encouraging the ward's involvement in "everyday" decision making and opportunities for socialization. If Mrs. C. were placed under guardianship, she should still be encouraged to make and participate in all decisions that are practically possible. For example, the guardian should strive to honor her preference to live in her home with her pets if at all feasible.

The Role of Social Workers in Surrogate Decision Making

As interventions become more restrictive, so too does the importance of practitioners' clinical effectiveness in dealing with older adults with profoundly diminished capacity. Surrogate decision making is the most intrusive step toward the removal of personal liberties. Therefore, social workers possess two major responsibilities toward their older adult clients: to discuss planning tools for surrogate decision making such as the DPA, and/or to intervene cautiously and judiciously with older adults who need unplanned surrogate decision-making assistance via rep payee or guardianship. Both of these roles require fundamental social work skills of direct counseling, client education, and advocacy to ensure that a client's rights and best interests are appropriately safeguarded (National Association of Social Workers, 1999).

THE MISCHIEF FACTOR

Older adults engaged in any decision-making arrangements that transfer some level of authority to informal or formal service providers are vulnerable to mistreatment, malfeasance, and exploitation. Part of this dilemma is due to the limited external oversight for most alternatives to guardianship (Wilber & Reynolds, 1995). As with the areas discussed earlier, states rather than the federal government carry the responsibility of legislating and regulating policies related to elder abuse. This could change if Congress passes legislation such as the Elder Justice Act, which would establish a national Office of Adult Protective Services (*http://www.elderabusecenter.org/default.cfm?p=elderjustice.cfm*).

Currently all states have procedures in place to report elder abuse, and many states have mandatory reporting laws that require social workers and other professionals to report abuse. Because the range of behaviors constituting elder and/or dependent adult abuse vary from state to state (Wilber & McNeilly, 2001), social workers must know their state's elder abuse operational definitions and reporting guidelines. In applying state elder abuse statutes, social workers must carefully distinguish between family tensions or control issues involving a dependent older adult and his or her caregivers and legitimate complaints about financial mismanagement or abuse. This differential diagnosis of a challenging person-in-environment situation requires astute clinical judgment, patience, and often teamwork from other invested professionals.

Social workers are ethically bound to work in the best interests of their clients, and preventing role conflicts through appropriate professional boundaries is a key component of this principle. One potential conflict that might arise is when a social worker acting as the client's care provider is asked to assume either a supportive or a surrogate decision-making role. This is a common request given that many communities lack formal DMM services. For example, Mrs. C. might report "feeling comfortable" with her community social worker, John, and ask him to be her agent on a DPA for finance because "he's like the son I never had." This request may not be out of the question if John's community agency regularly provides DMM to older adults who have no other options. However, it is important that DMM services are performed as part of a formal program with written protocols and procedures and clearly defined limits of responsibility; it is fallacious to think that without a formal program, the agency holds no risk. John would furthermore have an ethical duty to inform Mrs. C. of how their therapeutic relationship would change in the event that the DPA was activated. Prior to this discussion, it is suggested that John garner the support of his supervisor and management on the appropriateness of this arrangement based on Mrs. C.'s current situation, her mental capacity to make this decision, and agency policies and protocols. Whatever the outcome, John and his agency must use appropriate and clear documentation of all transactions to shield against the potential for abuse or, perhaps equally important, the accusation of impropriety by Mrs. C., distant family members, or external regulatory agencies.

CONCLUSION

As this discussion has illustrated, social workers have a repertoire of decisional services to choose from when supporting older adults with diminished cognitive and/or execution capacity. These services are guided by state policies and operational definitions of capacity. Choosing the right blend of services may be difficult and may vary over time as circumstances change. A set of core values provides ethical tools to assist social workers when choices are not clear. In addition to understanding practice issues and applying these tools, it is imperative that social workers know and operate from the relevant state statutes and regulations where they practice.

REFERENCES

AARP. (1990). *National guardianship monitoring project.* Washington, DC: Author.

Alexander, G. J. (1990). Avoiding guardianship. In E. Dejowski (Ed.), *Protecting judgment-impaired adults: Issues, interventions, and policies* (pp. 163–175). New York: Haworth.

Appelbaum, P. S., &. Grisso, T. (1988). Assessing patients' capacities to consent to treatment. *New England Journal of Medicine, 319,* 1635–1638.

Buchanan, A., & Brock, D. (1986). Deciding for others. *Milbank Quarterly, 64*(Suppl.), 17–94.

Collopy, B. J. (1988). Autonomy in long term care: Some crucial distinctions. *The Gerontologist, 28*(Suppl.), 10–17.

Dessin, C. (2003). Financial abuse of the elderly: Is the solution a problem? *McGeorge Law Review, 34,* 267.

Friedman, L., &. Savage, M. (1988). Taking care: The law of conservatorship in California. *Southern California Law Review, 61,* 273–290.

Hommel, P. A. (1996). Guardianship reform in the 1980s: A decade of substantive and procedural change. In M. Smyer, K. W. Schaie, & M. B. Kapp (Eds.), *Older adults' decision-making and the law* (pp. 225–253). New York: Springer.

Horstman, P. M. (1975). Protective services for the elderly: The limits of parens patriae. *Missouri Law Review, 40,* 215–278.

Iris, M. A. (1988). Guardianship and the elderly: A multiperspective view of the decision-making process. *Gerontologist, 28*(Suppl.), 39–45.

Kapp, M. B. (1999). *Geriatrics and the law: Understanding patient rights and professional responsibilities* (3rd ed.). New York: Springer.

Kapp, M. B., & Mossman, D. (1996). Measuring decisional capacity: Cautions on the construction of a "capacimeter." *Psychology, Public Policy, and Law, 2,* 73–95.

Keith, P. M., & Wacker, R. R. (1994). *Older wards and their guardians.* Westport, CT: Praeger.

Lisi, L. B., & Barinaga-Burch, S. (1995, October). National study of guardianship systems: Summary of findings and recommendations. *Clearinghouse Review.*

National Association of Social Workers. (1999). *Code of ethics of the National Association of Social Workers.* Retrieved June 11, 2004, from *http://www.socialwork ers.org/pubs/code/code.asp*

Quinn, J. B. (1997). *Making the most of your money.* New York: Simon and Schuster.

Rein, J. E. (1992). Preserving dignity and self-determination of the elderly in the face of competing interests and grim alternatives: A proposal for statutory refocus and reform. *George Washington Law Review, 60,* 1818–1887.

Sabatino, C. P. (1996). Competency: Refining our legal fictions. In M. Smyer, K. W. Schaie, & M. B. Kapp (Eds.), *Older adults' decision-making and the law* (pp. 1–28). New York: Springer.

Schmidt, W. C. (1995). *Guardianship: The court of last resort.* Durham, NC: Carolina Academic Press.

Schmidt, W. C., Miller, W., Bell, K., & New, B. (1981). *Public guardianship and the elderly.* Cambridge, MA: Ballinger.

Smyer, M. (1993). Aging and decision-making capacity. *Generations, 17*(1), 51–56.

Social Security Administration. (2004a). *Digest of state guardianship laws.* Retrieved July 7, 2004, from *http:// policy.ssa.gov/poms.nsf/lnx/020050230/*

Social Security Administration. (2004b). *Representative payee program.* Retrieved June 9, 2004, from *http:// www.ssa.gov/payee/index.htm*

Wilber, K. H. (2000). Aging. In R. J. Patti (Ed.), *The handbook of social welfare management* (pp. 521–533). Thousand Oaks, CA: Sage.

Wilber, K. H., & McNeilly, D. P. (2001). Elder abuse and victimization. In J. E. Birren & K. W. Schaie (Eds.), *The handbook of the psychology of aging* (pp. 569–591). San Diego, CA: Academic Press.

Wilber, K. H., Reiser, T., & Harter, K. (2001). New perspectives on conservatorship: Views of older adult conservatees and their conservators. *Aging, Neuropsychology, and Cognition 8,* 225–240.

Wilber, K. H., & Reynolds, S. L. (1995). Rethinking alternatives to guardianship. *The Gerontologist, 35,* 248–257.

The elderly, those aged 65 or older, represented 74.2% of the deaths that occurred in the United States in 2002 (Kochanek & Smith, 2004). With the aging of the population, this percentage will continue to increase dramatically in the coming years. This basic fact underscores that the elderly are major stakeholders in policies affecting the dying. A number of key policy events over the last 20 years have shaped in important ways the current situation in end-of-life care for the elderly. These developments, detailed below, include Congress's 1982 act authorizing Medicare to provide end-of-life care to beneficiaries with a terminal illness. This led to the selection of hospice as the standard for end-of-life care in the United States. Another significant legislative event, the Patient Self-Determination Act of 1990, reaffirmed an individual's right to self-determination. The act has promoted the use of advance directives and sparked a still ongoing legal and ethical debate about euthanasia and physician-assisted suicide. Ultimately, this social movement led to Oregon's landmark policy legalizing physician-assisted suicide.

Legislative Events Impacting the End of Life

1982   Congress authorizes Medicare to provide end-of-life care to terminally ill beneficiaries. Medicare hospice benefit included in Part A in 1983.

1990   Congress passes the Patient Self-Determination Act (PSDA). Instituted in 1991, this act requires health care agencies receiving Medicare and Medicaid reimbursement to recognize the living will and power of attorney for health care as advance directives, inform patients about advance directives, and incorporate any advance directive into patients' medical records.

1994   Oregon voters approve the Oregon Death With Dignity Act. When this act goes into effect in October 1997, Oregon becomes the first state in the nation to legalize physician-assisted suicide (PAS).

2003   Congress approves the Medicare Prescription Drug, Improvement, and Modernization Act of 2003. This act authorizes the Part D prescription drug plan, providing prescription drug benefits to all enrollees by 2006, and covers consultation with hospice physicians to discuss hospice care options and referrals.

VICTORIA H. RAVEIS

Policies Related to End-of-Life Care

84

This chapter provides a detailed review of issues related to end-of-life care. Specific attention is focused on financing the care of dying elders, including information on how care is paid for, the gaps and limitations in coverage, and relevant regulations and policies impacting end-of-life care options. Disparities in care at the end of life are examined. Attention is also focused on cultural factors that influence elders' care decisions. Ethical and legal issues related to end-of-life care for the elderly are addressed, including advanced directives and assisted suicide. The chapter concludes with policy recommendations to improve care at the end of life.

COST OF CARE AT THE END OF LIFE

Medicare Expenditures

Health care expenditures are often high at the end of life. Analyses of Medicare spending patterns have found that, on average, health care costs are about six times higher in the last year of a beneficiary's life than they are for beneficiaries who did not die, a spending ratio that has remained unchanged over the last two decades (Hogan, Lunney, Gabel, & Lynn, 2001; Medicare Payment Advisory Committee [MedPAC], 2004e). In calendar year 2002, 18% of the total Medicare program payments were attributed to benefits provided to the 5% of program participants who died (MedPAC, 2004e; Hogan et al., 2001). The high costs of health care at the end of life are attributed to the increased number of multiple, significant medical problems elderly decedents typically experience in the last year of life (Hogan et al., 2001).

Medicare, as the primary source of health insurance for persons 65 and older in the United States, is the main payer of the costs of end-of-life health care for the elderly. From 1993 through 1998, Medicare covered 61% of the health care expenses of elderly decedents in the year before their death, with multiple payers bearing the remaining portion of these expenses. Out-of-pocket expenses represented 18% of these end-of-life care costs, other payers covered 12%, and Medicaid paid 10% (Hogan et al., 2001).

The end-of-life out-of-pocket expenses of Medicare beneficiaries are determined by the type of Medicare plan in which they are enrolled. Covered benefits, premium fees, deductibles, and co-pay expenses vary across plans. Supplemental insurance plans, such as Medigap (Medicare supplement insurance), offset some Medicare coverage gaps and reduce deductibles and co-pay fees, but beneficiaries must pay the additional premiums. Some beneficiaries also have access to employer-sponsored retirement health plans that provide assistance with Medicare's cost-sharing requirements, as well as offering additional benefits (Kaiser Family Foundation & Hewitt, 2004). Private long-term care policies provide expanded coverage for home care, skilled nursing, and institutional care at the end of life. However, these premiums tend to be expensive, and elders holding such policies tend to be wealthier and have significantly greater housing assets than those without this type of private insurance coverage (LifePlans, 1999).

For those Medicare beneficiaries whose income and financial assets are sufficiently low to qualify for Medicaid coverage, additional benefits are available. Medicaid covers Medicare beneficiaries' cost-sharing charges and provides a number of other assistance benefits, such as covering the costs of institutional residence. However, program eligibility requirements and service benefits vary by state.

Out-of-Pocket Expenses

The health-related out-of-pocket expenses the elderly can experience at the end of life may present a substantial economic challenge. The likelihood of being below the poverty level increases with age, with the highest rates found among those 85 and older (Kaiser Family Foundation, 2001). Medicare beneficiaries spend, on average, about 20% of their income on health care services (MedPAC, 2004d). Out-of-pocket spending levels for beneficiaries with supplemental coverage are similar to those for individuals without such coverage (MedPAC, 2004d). With declining health and advancing age, these expenses increase substantially. Medicare beneficiaries in poor health have 50% more out-of-pocket health expenses than those in good health (Kaiser Family Foundation, 2001). Similarly, those 85 and older have almost twice the out-of-pocket expenditures of those ages 65 to 74. Use of a residential facility increases with advancing age and adds substantially to the out-of-pocket expenses incurred by the oldest age-groups (Hoover, Crystal, Kumar, Sambamoorthi, & Cantor, 2002). It is estimated that about 90% of elderly nursing home residents spend down their assets sufficiently after one year in a nursing home to qualify for Medicaid (Zerzan, Stearns, & Hanson, 2000). Hoover et al. (2002) have estimated the mean out-of-pocket expenditures for persons 65 and older in the last year of life at $5,211 (in 1996 dollars). Recent Census Bureau estimates, adjusted for expected out-of-pocket medical expenses, classified 13.4% to 17.7% of persons 65 or older as below the poverty level in 2002 (MedPAC, 2004d).

Cost of Family Caregiving

Families are integral to care at the end of life. Most elderly persons prefer to age in place and express preference for dying at home (Burge, 2004; Higginson & Sen-Gupta, 2000; SUPPORT Principal Investigators, 1995). Families are intensively involved in the care and support of ill and dependent family members, and this commitment continues throughout the dying trajectory (Emanuel et al., 1999). Even with comprehensive end-of-life care programs, such as those available through Medicare's hospice benefit, family involvement is needed. The delivery of palliative services and comfort care is organized around family and friends being present to provide ongoing, routine care. For terminally ill elders residing in the community, the absence of readily available family caregivers can be a barrier to hospice. In some instances, it has necessitated a relocation at the end of life to an institutional setting (General Accounting Office [GAO], 2000; MedPAC, 20004e).

Estimates of the economic capital represented by families' role in informal care illustrate the substantial financial contribution that families provide in care at the end of life. Arno, Levine, and Memmott (1999) estimated the 1997 national market value of care provided by unpaid family members and friends to ill and disabled adults as $196 billion. This contribution eclipsed the $32 billion spent on formal home health care and $83 billion spent on nursing home care in 1997. Because this study did not include the expenses to the familial caregivers of unreimbursed health care fees and the loss of caregiver income and associated employment benefits, the total financial cost to families is likely to be even higher.

Cost of Hospice Versus Other Health Care

When the hospice benefit was added to the Medicare program, some proponents of the benefit argued that hospice would reduce program spending by eliminating unnecessary medical treatments and services. This predicted cost saving has not been realized. Current analysis of the costs in the last year of life has docu-

mented that mean expenditures for elderly Medicare beneficiaries were 4.0% higher overall among hospice enrollees than among non-enrollees (i.e., those with fee-for-service coverage; Campbell, Lynn, Louis, & Shugarman, 2004). This analysis revealed further that the higher hospice costs were incurred by enrollees with diagnoses other than cancer. Specifically, Medicare program expenditures were lower among cancer patients enrolled in hospice than among non-enrollees ($27,917 vs. $29,905). However, the reverse pattern occurred for enrollees with noncancer diagnoses. For them, hospice charges were higher ($26,751 vs. $22,879). Thus, although hospice may generate some savings by reducing curative treatment expenses, these expenditure reductions are somewhat offset by the cost of palliative services and the expanded supportive care the hospice benefit provides (MedPAC, 2004d; see Table 84.1 for a detailed description of the Medicare hospice benefit). Medicare reimburses hospice providers a per diem rate, adjusted for regional differences, for each day a beneficiary is enrolled in hospice. Payment levels are based on one of four levels of care: routine home care, continuous home care, inpatient respite care, and general inpatient care. Per diem payment is constant, even if no services are provided on a given day (MedPAC, 2004e). Ninety-five percent of the hospice care, across all service settings, is provided at the routine home care level (MedPAC, 2004a). The per diem rate for routine home care, on average, was $120 per day in 2004 (MedPAC, 20004b).

TRENDS IN HOSPICE USE

Growth in Hospice Care

Since the addition of the hospice benefit to the Medicare program in 1983, an increasing number of terminally ill elders have selected this care option. In 1998, 19% of those who died had used hospice in the year before their death. By 2002, this percentage had increased to 26% (MedPAC, 2004a). Medicare spending patterns reflect this growth. Hospice expenditures increased from $1.9 billion in 1995 to an estimated $5.9 billion in 2003 (MedPAC, 2004a).

Length of Stay

Changes have also occurred in the length of hospice stay. For the subset of hospice enrollees in the 90th

TABLE 84.1 Overview of Medicare's Hospice Benefit

Eligibility

- Beneficiary is eligible for Medicare Part A (hospital insurance)
- Beneficiary's physician and hospice medical director certify 6-month life expectancy
- Beneficiary agrees to forgo all Medicare-covered, nonhospice benefits for the terminal illness

Hospice care team

- Physician
- Nurse
- Mental health counselors (e.g., psychologists, pastoral counselors)
- Social worker
- Home health aides
- Volunteers

Services provided

- Physician services
- Nursing care
- Durable medical equipment (e.g., wheelchairs, walkers)
- Medical supplies
- Drugs and biologicals for symptom management and pain control
- Home health aide and homemaker services
- Physical and occupational therapy
- Speech therapy
- Social worker service
- Nutrition and dietary counseling
- Grief and loss counseling to beneficiary and family
- Inpatient respite care in a Medicare-approved hospital or nursing home, up to 5 days per episode
- Physician and nurse on call 24/7

Other key features

- Hospice care must be provided by a Medicare-approved hospice program
- Beneficiary can change hospice provider only once during each 90- or 60-day certification period
- Beneficiary can be recertified indefinitely, initially two 90-day periods, then every 60 days
- Beneficiary can elect to leave hospice, reselect prior Medicare health plan's nonhospice coverage for his/her condition, and at some future time reselect the hospice benefit
- Beneficiary can use Medicare health plan to receive care for unrelated conditions

Costs to beneficiary: Gaps and limitations in care

- Beneficiary pays part of the cost for outpatient drugs—$5 per prescription in 2004
- Beneficiary pays part of inpatient respite care—5% of the Medicare payment amount in 2004
- Medicare does not cover costs of room and board; exception is inpatient or respite care
- Hospice in the home requires informal/familial caregiving
- Hospice programs vary in range of palliative care services provided

For further information see Centers for Medicare and Medicaid Services, *Medicare hospice benefits,* retrieved August 2, 2004, from *http://www.medicare.gov/.*

percentile for length of stay, mean length of stay increased from 123 days in 1998 to 147 days in 2002 (MedPAC, 2002). This increase has been attributed to the expanded use in recent years of the hospice benefit among nursing home residents and a more diversified case mix. For the majority of hospice enrollees, though, length of stay is still relatively brief. The median length of stay remained at 16 days in 2002, with more than a quarter of the enrollees receiving hospice services for less than 1 week (MedPAC, 2004a). A disadvantage to having had a brief time in hospice is that it precludes beneficiaries and their family members from fully benefiting from hospice's special services, such as the respite care and grief counseling available to family members (Raveis, 2004). Brief hospice stays also represent a financial disadvantage to the hospice provider because there is a shorter time frame over which the costs associated with intake and setting up an individualized care plan, as well as the expenses associated with intense services that typically characterize the days preceding death, can be spread out (GAO, 2000; MedPAC, 2002). Hospice providers report that the hours a patient requires from social work, nursing, and administration in the first and last weeks of hospice enrollment are typically twice those required during the intervening period (GAO, 2000).

Trends in Use by Coverage Plan

There is evidence of beneficiaries' differential use of the hospice benefit by type of Medicare plan. There has been a consistently higher use of hospice by managed care enrollees than by fee-for-service enrollees (MedPAC, 2004e). In 2002, 34% of decedents in managed care used hospice, compared with 25% of those in fee-for-service (MedPAC, 2004a). Elderly cancer patients in managed care not only had higher rates of hospice use but also had significantly longer hospice stays than those enrolled in the fee-for-service plan (McCarthy, Burns, Ngo-Metzger, Davis, & Phillips, 2003).

The care setting where hospice is provided has also changed over time. Although the majority of hospice enrollees still dwell in the community, there has been an increase in the delivery of hospice to nursing home residents. Between 1992 and 2000, the percentage of hospice enrollees in nursing homes expanded from 11% to 36% (MedPAC, 2004a). For those enrollees in nursing homes, institutional staff are available to provide the routine care and monitoring that families are required in the home to provide, to complement hos-

pice's specialized support services (GAO, 2000; MedPAC, 2004c).

Geographic Differences

There have also been geographic differences in the growth of hospice use. The most rapid growth has been in the percentage of rural (as opposed to urban) beneficiaries electing hospice between 1992 and 2000 (MedPAC, 2002). Rates of hospice use, though, are still lower in rural areas than in urban environments. The lowest rates of hospice use are observed in rural areas not adjacent to urban areas (15.2% of all deaths), and the highest rates of use are in urban areas (22.2% of all deaths; Virnig, Moscovice, Durham, & Casey, 2004).

Case Mix

The case mix among hospice users has also changed and become more varied. Historically, elderly cancer patients have been the most common users. Although patients with a cancer diagnosis still represent the majority of hospice enrollees, the percentage has dropped from 75% in 1992 to 60% in 2002 (MedPAC, 2002, 2004a). The most common noncancer diagnoses among hospice decedents are congestive heart failure, dementia, and pulmonary disease (MedPAC, 2004a).

Sociodemographic Diversity

Recent growth in hospice use has been greatest among the oldest Medicare beneficiaries (MedPAC, 2004a). Consistent with the increased use of the hospice benefit among nursing home residents, the percentage of decedents 85 and older who used hospice has almost doubled between 1998 and 2002. Growth in hospice use has continued across all racial groups, but long-standing racial differences remain in who selects the hospice benefit. In 2002, hospice use was still highest among White Medicare decedents, with Asian American decedents having the lowest rates, followed by African Americans (MedPAC, 2004e). These patterns are consistent with the cultural precepts regarding end-of-life care and differential preferences for aggressive and life-sustaining treatments expressed by minority populations (Blackall et al., 1999; Yeo, 1995). Several investigations have documented White patients' tendency to select treatment options that limit or forgo care at the end of life, in contrast to decisions made by Black patients that focus on prolonging life by all possible treatment means (Berger, 1998; Caralis, Davis, Wright, & Marcial, 1993; Hopp & Duffy, 2000; McKinley, Garrett, Evans, & Danis, 1996; Steinhauser et al., 2001; Teno et al., 1990). Suspicions about the motives of health care institutions and clinicians, as well as the historical legacy of the Tuskegee Institute syphilis experiments and evidence of long-standing uneven access to care, may also account for the desire of minority patients to have all available treatment, especially at the end of life (Blackhall et al., 1999; Caralis et al., 1993; Dula, 1994; Garrett, Harris, Norburn, Patrick, & Danis, 1993; Grameslpacher, Zhou, Hanna, & Tierney, 1997; Hauser, Kleefield, Brennan, & Fischbach, 1997; McKinley et al., 1996; Siegel & Raveis, 1997; Steinhauser et al., 2001).

GAPS AND LIMITATIONS
IN END-OF-LIFE CARE

Features of the Hospice Benefit
Impact Usage

The incentive to select Medicare's hospice benefit may be impacted by the benefits covered and the savings in out-of-pocket expenses enrollees may realize with the hospice benefit. The prescription drug benefit for hospice enrollees is a compelling plan feature. Medication for symptom control can represent a considerable expense for beneficiaries, particularly the cost of pain medications. Outside of the hospice benefit, prescription drug coverage is a benefit that is primarily available through employer-sponsored health plans (Kaiser Family Foundation & Hewitt, 2004). However, by 2006, as a consequence of the Medicare Prescription Drug, Improvement, and Modernization Act of 2003, prescription drug coverage will become available to all Medicare beneficiaries who enroll in Medicare's Part D, a prescription drug plan (PDP) (MedPAC, 2004e). This coverage change will render the hospice benefit less significant. Policy analysts have expressed concern that PDP will adversely impact employer coverage of retiree health benefits (Kaiser Family Foundation & Hewitt, 2004). Dually eligible (Medicare and Medicaid) beneficiaries may also have less of a financial incentive to select the hospice benefit. Medicaid provides a range of assistive services and benefits that duplicate many of the features of hospice without the constraints that the Medicare hospice benefit imposes on coverage of services and forgoing of curative care (see list on p. 906).

Hospice Providers Control Delivery
of End-of-Life Care

Analysts and advocates for appropriate care at the end of life have expressed concern that Medicare's hospice payment schedule compels providers to use cost considerations in deciding who should be enrolled, when to initiate enrollment, and what services should be provided (Buntin & Huskamp, 2002; Huskamp, Buntin, Wang, & Newhouse, 2001; Gage et al., 2000). They cite the higher use of hospice (and longer stays) by managed care enrollees as an example of efforts to maximize revenue by managed care organizations and hospice providers. Hospice providers are not mandated to accept all enrollees. Some providers have not accepted enrollees who have high-cost needs or require services that are not routinely provided, such as chemotherapy for palliation. The difficulty these beneficiaries have in finding a hospice provider has been cited as further evidence of how cost considerations determine access to end-of-life care (Huskamp et al., 2001; Lorenz, Asch, Rosenfield, Liu, & Ettner, 2004; MedPAC, 2004b, 2004c).

Although hospice providers are mandated to offer a comprehensive package of palliative care services, they are not required to provide all possible palliative treatments. Changes in the practice of palliative medicine have led to the introduction of more higher cost services, such as the delivery of chemotherapy or radiation for pain and symptom management. Similarly, other advances in symptom control, such as transdermal administration of narcotic pain medication, are costlier than traditional pain management techniques (GAO, 2000). Hospices are not routinely making these treatments or medications available because of the expense involved, even though these services or approaches might better meet patients' needs. Providers have argued that such cost considerations are necessary, given the current Medicaid reimbursement system. However, hospices are not required to monitor quality of care or quality-of-life outcomes. In the absence of any evaluation effort, it remains uncertain to what extent, and/or for which patient groups, hospice providers are adhering to the precepts of palliative care, that is, delivering person-centered care that maximizes quality of life, reduces suffering, and respects patient rights (Task Force on Palliative Care, 1998).

Different Dying Trajectories Exist

A review of the causes of death among the elderly suggests that most deaths are likely to occur following a period of care and management. The four leading causes of death for persons 65 and older in 2002 were diseases of the heart, malignant neoplasms, cerebrovascular disease, and chronic lower respiratory disease. Alzheimer's disease, diabetes, and kidney disorders ranked among the top 10 (Kochanek & Smith, 2004). However, different fatal conditions present distinct dying trajectories (Lunney, Lynn, & Hogan, 2002). Some conditions, such as cancer, have a distinct terminal phase. Other conditions, such as congestive heart failure or chronic obstructive pulmonary disease, are characterized by gradual decline with periodic exacerbations of the illness and a survival period that is difficult to predict. Conditions associated with frailty or dementia have an even slower decline, and death may occur from complications associated with the condition. These variations in the dying process suggest that appropriate care for the elderly at the end of life is care that fits these different dying trajectories. An analysis of elderly Medicare decedents indicated that 47% met the criteria for frailty, 22% had a condition with a distinct terminal phase, and 16% had died of organ system failure (Lunney et al., 2002).

ETHICAL AND LEGAL ISSUES AT THE END OF LIFE

Advanced Directives

A national effort to promote the use of advanced directives was initiated in 1991 with the Patient Self-Determination Act (PSDA). However, the impact of advanced directives on end-of-life care has been mixed. The purpose of advance directives is to guide decision making after a patient has lost decision-making capacity. Many of the diseases and conditions the elderly are living with at the end of life may generate situations in which advanced directives would be helpful to guide the delivery of appropriate care. In the absence of clearly expressed preferences for care, investigations have shown that family, friends, and health care providers do not necessarily make an accurate judgment regarding a patient's care preference at the end of life (Sulmasy et al., 1998; Diamond, Jernigan, Moseley, Messina, & McKeown, 1989; Gerety, Chiodo, Kanten, Tuley, & Cornell, 1993; Seckler,

Meier, Mulvihill, & Paris, 1991; Steinhauser et al., 2001; Zweibel & Cassel, 1989). One investigation determined that the patient treatment options surrogate decision makers tended to select were ones they would choose for themselves (Covinsky et al., 2000).

An advance directive can include a "living will," specifying a patient's treatment preferences, including the conditions under which life-sustaining treatments (i.e., antibiotics, artificial feeding, ventilators, defibrillation, and cardiopulmonary resuscitation) would be withdrawn or withheld. It may also include a health care power of attorney, identifying a health care proxy authorized to act as the patient's agent. Advance directives can also include other instructions, such as organ donation and preferred care setting. Typically, advanced directives are written, but oral instructions are also possible. The PSDA requires health care institutions that receive Medicare and Medicaid funds to provide patients with a written summary of their health care decision-making rights (which vary somewhat by state) and the facility's policies regarding recognizing advanced directives. Institutions are also required to document in the patient's medical records that an advance directive exists, although patients are responsible for providing the copy of their advance directive to the institution (MedPAC, 1999).

Ideally, a patient's completion of an advance directive should be based on full understanding of his or her overall medical condition and probable illness course. Even though an advance directive would be a logical product of an advance care discussion with a physician, only 12% of patients completing an advance directive reported physician input (Teno et al., 1997). Although Medicare does reimburse physicians for advance care planning if it constitutes more than 50% of the visit (MedPAC, 1999), this finding suggests that this option is not widely exercised.

Advanced directives do not always ensure that family members (Ditto et al., 2001) or clinicians (Coppola, Ditto, Danks, & Smucker, 2001; Covinsky et al., 2000) will comply with the patient's end-of-life treatment preferences. Despite PSDA regulations, gaps in documentation also occur. One investigation documented that patient preferences for not receiving cardiopulmonary resuscitation were not reflected in do not resuscitate orders (Covinsky et al., 2000). It has also been found that discrepancies exist in perceptions by patients, family, and clinicians regarding whether discussions of end-of-life care preferences have been held (Curtis et al., 1999; SUPPORT Principal Investigators, 1995).

Racial and Cultural Prescriptions Impact End-of-Life Care Planning

End-of-life care needs to take into account culturally mandated patterns of communication and decision making. There are cultural preferences regarding whether a patient should be told of a terminal diagnosis or if this information should be provided only to the patient's family. As a matter of compassion and to permit a peaceful death, members of Pakistani families do not burden terminally ill patients with information about their diagnoses (Moazam, 2000). Korean Americans and Mexican Americans have been found less likely than European Americans and African Americans to support full disclosure to relatives of their diagnoses and prognoses (Blackhall et al., 1995).

Cultural and racial prescriptions also exist regarding the appropriateness of discussing and engaging in treatment decision making about end-of-life care. In the Navajo culture, for example, the very discussion of future illness or end-of-life care is considered harmful and, therefore, unacceptable, making it very difficult for health providers to determine patient care wishes or family understanding of them (Carrese & Rhodes, 1995, 2000). A similar prohibition has been found in some Chinese populations (Caralis et al., 1993). In many Hispanic groups, especially those of lower socioeconomic status and with limited education, discussions of death and planning for death are discouraged, for they are seen as tempting fate. African Americans are less likely to discuss and complete advance directives than are Whites (Shepardson, Gordon, Ibrahim, Harper, & Rosenthal, 1999). Decision making about life support is also considered the responsibility of Mexican American families as opposed to the patient autonomy model favored in European American cultures (Blackhall et al., 1995; Murphy et al., 1996).

Euthanasia and Physician-Assisted Suicide

Euthanasia and physician-assisted suicide (PAS) represent the ultimate option for the terminally ill. Oregon's legalization of PAS, with the passing of the Oregon Death With Dignity Act, permits terminally ill patients to receive lethal prescriptions from physicians to end their lives only after the physician fully informs the patient of any feasible alternatives to PAS, including comfort care, hospice, and pain control. Reports of assisted suicide cases indicate that this choice was exercised primarily by terminally ill patients who were in severe pain or physical discomfort and dependent on others for care (Roscoe, Malphurs, Dragovic, & Cohen, 2001; Back, Wallace, Starks, & Pearlman, 1996; Meier et al., 1998). Terminally ill African Americans and patients who were more religious were significantly less likely to regard euthanasia or PAS as an acceptable choice (Emanuel, Fairclough, & Emanuel, 2000; Emanuel et al., 1999). Although terminally ill patients who were feeling depressed or hopeless were found to be more likely to consider PAS or euthanasia, such considerations did not persist over time (Emanuel et al., 2000; Breitbart et al., 2000). These findings highlight the vulnerability of the dying individual and underscore the importance of ensuring that care at the end of life is person-centered care, organized to provide optimal support and medical management.

POLICY RECOMMENDATIONS TO IMPROVE CARE AT THE END OF LIFE

The introduction of the Medicare hospice benefit has initiated a transformation of end-of-life care for the elderly in the United States. Recent years have seen an expanded use of hospice in different delivery settings and among different groups, although notable service deficiencies and disparities remain. The addition of Medicare coverage for prescription drugs (Medicare Part D), which will be fully initiated in 2006, will continue to redefine end-of-life care options for the elderly. Access to low-cost drugs may enhance symptom management by reducing some of the economic burden the elderly now experience from the high cost of medications.

However, as summarized in Table 84.2, additional reform to policy and financing for end-of-life care is still merited. It is important to recognize that there are different dying trajectories. Although hospice is appropriate for some end-of-life conditions, more comprehensive benefits and flexible coverage regulations that would permit the integration of palliative care with active treatment would ensure care options that accommodate diversity at the end of life. Revisions to the Medicare hospice provider reimbursement schedule to address the higher program delivery costs at the initiation and end of stay and the expenses incurred by a broader case mix (e.g., patients requiring more expensive palliative therapies) would improve hospice access and enhance service options (MedPAC, 2004b).

TABLE 84.2 Policy and Finance Recommendations to Improve Care at the End of Life for the Elderly

- Revise Medicare's hospice provider reimbursement policy to address short stays and high costs of intake and last days of life
- Expand eligibility and benefits coverage to incorporate diversity in dying trajectories
- Recognize advances in palliative medicine and revise benefit coverage to include approaches that were previously used only for curative purposes
- Provide sufficient reimbursement to support access to the most appropriate and effective symptom management options
- Incorporate cultural sensitivity in the advance care planning, decision making, and service delivery at the end of life
- Institute monitoring and evaluation of hospice service delivery
- Support efforts to assess service needs at the end of life that incorporate patient and family perspectives, disease factors, and service settings treatment
- Provide sufficient reimbursement to support access to the most appropriate and effective symptom management

Medicare regulations do not require hospices to assess or monitor quality of care or services provided to program participants. Monitoring and evaluation efforts are needed to ensure that the elderly's care needs and preferences are appropriately met (MedPAC, 2004b). Practitioners and activists in the field are advocating for quality assurance efforts to be a part of the reimbursement procedures for hospice providers (MedPAC, 2004b).

Ensuring appropriate care for all individuals at the end of life needs to be informed by the evidence base. Gaps in knowledge exist. Comprehensive understanding of unmet needs and services required at the end of life across different service settings, disease conditions, and patient populations is lacking. Support for systematic efforts to inform these knowledge gaps is needed to ensure that services and programs are culturally sensitive and appropriately tailored to meet diverse patient groups.

REFERENCES

Arno, P. S., Levine, C., & Memmott, M. M. (1999). The economic value of caregiving. *Health Affairs, 18,* 182–188.

Back, A. L., Wallace, J. I., Starks, H. E., & Pearlman, R. A. (1996). Physician-assisted suicide and euthanasia in Washington state: Patient requests and physician responses. *Journal of the American Medical Association, 275,* 919–925.

Berger, J. T. (1998). Cultural discrimination in mechanisms for health decisions: A view from New York. *Journal of Clinical Ethics, 9,* 127–131.

Blackhall, L. J., Frank, G., Murphy, S. T., Michel, V., Palmer, J. M., & Azen, S. P. (1999). Ethnicity and attitudes towards life sustaining technology. *Social Science and Medicine, 48,* 1779–1789.

Blackhall, L. J., Murphy, S. T., Frank, G., Michel, V., & Azen, S. P. (1995). Ethnicity and attitudes toward patient autonomy. *Journal of the American Medical Association, 274,* 820–825.

Breitbart, W., Rosenfeld, B., Pessin, H., Kaim, M., Funesti-Esch, J., Galietta, M., et al. (2000). Depression, hopelessness, and desire for hastened death in terminally ill patients with cancer. *Journal of the American Medical Association, 284,* 2907–2911.

Buntin, M. B., & Huskamp, H. (2002). What is known about the economics of end-of-life care for Medicare beneficiaries? *Gerontologist, 42,* 40–48.

Burge, F. I. (2004). Hospice and home care. In R. Jones, N. Boritten, L. Culpepper, D. Gass, R. Grol, & D. Mant, et al. (Eds.), *Oxford textbook of primary medical care: Vol. 2. Clinical Management* (pp. 1292–1294). Oxford, England: Oxford University Press.

Campbell, D. E., Lynn, J., Louis, T. A., & Shugarman, L. R. (2004). Medicare program expenditures associated with hospice use. *Annals of Internal Medicine, 140,* 269–277.

Caralis, P. V., Davis, B., Wright, K., & Marcial, E. (1993). The influence of ethnicity and race on attitudes toward advance directives, life-prolonging treatments, and euthanasia. *Journal of Clinical Ethics, 4,* 155–156.

Carrese, J. A., & Rhodes, L. A. (1995). Western bioethics on the Navaho reservation: Benefit or harm? *Journal of the American Medical Association, 274,* 826–829.

Carrese, J. A., & Rhodes, L. A. (2000). Bridging cultural differences in medical practice: The case of discussing negative information with Navajo patients. *Journal of General Internal Medicine, 15,* 92–96.

Centers for Medicare and Medicaid Services. (n.d.-a). *Medicare and you, 2004.* Retrieved August 2, 2004, from *http://www.medicare.gov/*

Centers for Medicare and Medicaid Services. (n.d.-b). *Medicare hospice benefits.* Retrieved August 2, 2004, from *http://www.medicare.gov/*

Coppola, K. M., Ditto, P. H., Danks, J. H., & Smucker, W. D. (2001). Accuracy of primary care and hospital-based physicians' predictions of elderly outpatients' treatment preferences with and without advance directives. *Archives of Internal Medicine, 161*, 431–440.

Covinsky, K. E., Fuller, J. D., Yaffe, K., Johnston, C. B., Hamel, M. B., Lynn J., et al. (2000). Communication and decision-making in seriously ill patients: Findings of the SUPPORT project. *Journal of the American Geriatrics Society, 48*, S187–S193.

Curtis, J. R., Randall, P., Donald, L., Caldwell, E. S., Greenlee, H., & Collier, A. C. (1999). The quality of patient-doctor communication about end-of-life care: A study of patients with advanced AIDS and their primary care clinicians. *AIDS, 13*, 1123–1131.

Diamond, E. L., Jernigan, J. A., Moseley, R. A., Messina, V., & McKeown, R. A. (1989). Decision-making ability and advance directive preferences in nursing home patients and proxies. *Gerontologist, 29*, 622–626.

Ditto, P. H., Danks, J. H., Smucker, W. D., Bookwala, J., Coppola, K. M., Dresser, R., et al. (2001). Advance directives as acts of communication: A randomized controlled trial. *Archives of Internal Medicine, 161*, 421–430.

Dula, A. (1994). African American suspicion of the healthcare system is justified: What do we do about it? *Cambridge Quarterly of Healthcare Ethics, 3*, 347–357.

Emanuel, E. J., Fairclough, D. L., & Emanuel, L. L. (2000). Attitudes and desires related to euthanasia and physician-assisted suicide among terminally ill patients and their caregivers. *Journal of the American Medical Association, 284*, 2460–2468.

Emanuel, E. J., Fairclough, D. L., Slutsman, J., Albert, H., Baldwin, D. W., & Emanuel, L. L. (1999). Assistance from family members, friends, paid care givers, and volunteers in the care of terminally ill patients. *New England Journal of Medicine, 341*, 956–963.

Gage, B., Miller, S. C., Coppola, K., Harvell, J., Laliberte, L., Mor, V., et al. (2000). *Important questions for hospice in the next century* (Contract No. 100-97-0010). Retrieved August 2, 2004, from U.S. Department of Health and Human Services, Office of Disability, Aging and Long-Term Care Policy Web site: *http://www.aspe.hhs.gov/daltcp/*

Garrett, J. M., Harris, R. P., Norburn, J. K., Patrick, D. L., & Danis, M. (1993). Life-sustaining treatments during terminal illness: Who wants what? *Journal of General Internal Medicine, 8*, 361–368.

General Accounting Office. (2000). *MEDICARE: More beneficiaries use hospice but for fewer days of care. United States General Accounting Office Report to Congressional Requestors* (GAO/HEHHS-00-182). Washington, DC: U.S. General Accounting Office.

Gerety, M. B., Chiodo, L. K., Kanten, D. N., Tuley, M. R., & Cornell, J. E. (1993). Medical treatment preferences of nursing home residents: Relationship to function and concordance with surrogate decision-makers. *Journal of the American Geriatrics Society, 41*, 953–960.

Gramelspacher, G. P., Zhou, X. H., Hanna, M. P., & Tierney, W. M. (1997). Preferences of physicians and their patients for end-of-life care. *Journal of General Internal Medicine, 12*, 346–351.

Hauser, J. M., Kleefield, S. F., Brennan, T. A., & Fischbach, R. L. (1997). Minority populations and advance directives: Insights from a focus group methodology. *Cambridge Quarterly of Healthcare Ethics, 6*, 58–71.

Higginson, I. J., & Sen-Gupta, G. J. A. (2000). Place of care in advanced cancer: A qualitative systematic literature review of patient preferences. *Journal of Palliative Medicine, 3*, 287.

Hogan, C., Lunney, J., Gabel, J., & Lynn, J. (2001). Medicare beneficiaries' cost of care in the last year of life. *Health Affairs, 20*, 188–195.

Hoover, D. R., Crystal, S., Kumar, R., Sambamoorthi, U., & Cantor, J. C. (2002). Medical expenditures during the last year of life: Findings from the 1992–1996 Medicare current beneficiary survey. *Health Services Research, 37*, 1625–1642.

Hopp, F. P., & Duffy, S. A. (2000). Racial variations in end-of-life care. *Journal of the American Geriatrics Society, 48*, 658–663.

Huskamp, H. B., Buntin, M., Wang, V., & Newhouse, J. (2001). Providing care at the end of life: Do Medicare rules impede good care? *Health Affairs, 20*, 204–211.

Kaiser Family Foundation. (2001). *Medicare chartbook* (2nd ed.). Menlo Park, CA: Henry J. Kaiser Family Foundation.

Kaiser Family Foundation & Hewitt. (2004). *Retiree health benefits now and in the future: Findings from the Kaiser/Hewitt 2003 survey on retirees health benefits—January 2004*. Menlo Park, CA: Henry J. Kaiser Family Foundation.

Kochanek, D. D., & Smith, B. L. (2004). *Deaths: Preliminary data for 2002. National Vital Statistics Reports* (52(12)). Hyattsville, MD: National Center for Health Statistics.

LifePlans. (1999). *A descriptive analysis of patterns of informal and formal caregiving among privately insured and non–privately insured disabled elders living in the community*. Report prepared under contract from the U.S. Department of Health and Human Services (HHS), Office of Disability, Aging and Long-Term Care Policy (DALTCP). Retrieved August 2, 2004, from *http://www.aspe.hhs.gov/*

Lorenz, K. A., Asch, S. M., Rosenfeld, K. E., Liu, H., & Ettner, S. L. (2004). Where does hospice fit in the continuum of care? *Journal of the American Geriatrics Society, 52,* 725–730.

Lunney, J., Lynn, J., & Hogan, C. (2002). Profiles of older Medicare decedents. *Journal of American Geriatrics Society, 50,* 1108–1112.

McCarthy, E. P., Burns, R. B., Ngo-Metzger, Q., Davis, R. B., & Phillips, R. S. (2003). Hospice use among Medicare managed care and fee-for-service patients dying with cancer. *Journal of the American Medical Association, 289,* 2238–2245.

McKinley, E. D., Garrett, J. M., Evans, A. T., & Danis, M. (1996). Differences in end-of-life decision making among Black and White ambulatory cancer patients. *Journal of General Internal Medicine, 11,* 651–656.

Medicare Payment Advisory Commission. (1999). *Report to the Congress: Selected Medicare issues (June 1999).* Retrieved August 3, 2004, from *http://www.med pac.gov/*

Medicare Payment Advisory Commission. (2002). *Report to the Congress: Medicare beneficiaries' access to hospice (May 2002).* Retrieved August 3, 2004, from *http://www.medpac.gov/*

Medicare Payment Advisory Commission. (2004a). *A data book: Healthcare spending and the Medicare program (June 2004).* Retrieved August 3, 2004, from *http://www.medpac.gov/*

Medicare Payment Advisory Commission. (2004b). *Public meeting (March 19, 2004).* Retrieved August 3, 2004, from *http://www.medpac.gov/*

Medicare Payment Advisory Commission. (2004c). *Public meeting (April 22, 2004).* Retrieved August 3, 2004, from *http://www.medpac.gov/*

Medicare Payment Advisory Commission. (2004d). *Report to the Congress: Medicare payment policy (March 2004).* Retrieved August 4, 2004, from *http://www.medpac.gov/*

Medicare Payment Advisory Commission. (2004e). *Report to the Congress: New approaches in Medicare (June 2004).* Retrieved August 4, 2004, from *http://www.medpac.gov/*

Meier, D. F., Emmons, C. A., Wallenstein, S., Quill, T., Morrison, R. S., & Cassel, C. K. (1998). A national survey of physician-assisted suicide and euthanasia in the United States. *New England Journal of Medicine, 338,* 1193–1201.

Moazam, F. (2000). Families, patients, and physicians in medical decision making: A Pakistani perspective. *Hastings Center Report, 30,* 28–37.

Murphy, S. T., Palmer, J. M., Azen, S., Frank, G., Michel, V., & Blackhall, I. J. (1996). Ethnicity and advance directives. *Journal of Law, Medicine and Ethics, 24,* 108–117.

Raveis, V. H. (2004). Bereavement and grief. In R. Jones et al. (Eds.), *Oxford textbook of primary medical care: Vol. 2. Clinical management* (pp. 1283–1286). Oxford, England: Oxford University Press.

Roscoe, L. A., Malphurs, J. E., Dragovic, L. J., & Cohen, D. (2001). A comparison of characteristics of Kevorkian euthanasia cases and physician-assisted suicides in Oregon. *Gerontologist, 41,* 439–446.

Seckler, A. B., Meier, D. E., Mulvihill, M., & Paris, B. E. (1991). Substituted judgment: How accurate are proxy predictions? *Annals of Internal Medicine, 115,* 92–98.

Shepardson, L. B., Gordon, H. S., Ibrahim, S. A., Harper, D. L., & Rosenthal, G. E. (1999). Racial variation in the use of do-not-resuscitate orders. *Journal of the American Geriatrics Society, 45,* 528–530.

Siegel, K., & Raveis, V. H. (1997). Perceptions of access to HIV-related information, care and services among infected minority men. *Qualitative Health Research, 7,* 9–31.

Steinhauser, K. E., Christakis, N. A., Clipp, E. C., McNeilly, M., McIntyre, L., & Tulsky, J. A. (2001). Factors considered important at the end of life by patients, family members, physicians, and other care providers. *Journal of the American Medical Association, 284,* 2476–2482.

Sulmasy, D. P., Terry, P. B., Weisman, C. S., Miller, D. J., Stallings, R. Y., Vettese, M. A., et al. (1998). The accuracy of substituted judgments in patients with terminal diagnoses. *Annals of Internal Medicine, 128,* 621–629.

SUPPORT Principal Investigators. (1995). A controlled trial to improve care for seriously ill hospitalized patients: The study to understand prognoses and preferences of outcomes and risks of treatments (SUPPORT). *Journal of the American Medical Association, 274,* 1591–1598.

Task Force on Palliative Care LAST ACTS Campaign, Robert Wood Johnson Foundation. (1998). Precepts of palliative care. *Journal of Palliative Medicine, 1,* 109–112.

Teno, J. M., Lynn, J. U., Wenger, N. S., Phillips, R. S., Murphy, D. P., Connors, A. F., et al. (1997). Advance directives for seriously-ill hospitalized patients: Effectiveness with the patient self-determination act and the SUPPORT intervention. *Journal of the American Geriatric Society, 45,* 500–507.

Virnig, B. A., Moscovice, I. S., Durham, S. B., & Casey, M. M. (2004). Do rural elders have limited access to Medicare hospice services? *Journal of American Geriatrics Society, 52,* 731–735.

Yeo, G. (1995). Ethical considerations in Asian and Pacific Island elders. *Clinics in Geriatric Medicine, 11,* 139–152.

Zerzan, J., Stearn, S., & Hanson, L. (2000). Access to palliative care and hospice in nursing homes. *Journal of American Medical Association, 284,* 2489–2494.

Zweibel, N. R., & Cassel, C. K. (1989). Treatment choices at the end of life: A comparison of decisions by older patients and their physician-selected proxies. *Gerontologist, 29,* 615–621.

WEB SITES FOR INFORMATION ON POLICY, FINANCING, AND CARE AT THE END OF LIFE

Federal Agencies

Administration on Aging: *www.aoa.gov*

Agency for Healthcare Research and Quality: *www.ahrg.gov*

Centers for Medicare and Medicaid Services (CMS): *www.cms.hhs.gov*

Medicare Payment Advisory Commission (MedPAC): *www.medpac.gov*

National Organizations

American Association of Retired Persons (AARP): *www.aarp.org*

American Bar Association: *www.abanet.org/home.html/*

American Hospital Association: *www.ahd.com*

Advocacy Groups

Last Acts: *www.lastacts.org*

National Hospice and Palliative Care Organization: *www.nho.org*

Partnership for Caring: America's Voices for Dying: *www.partnershipforcaring.org/HomePage*

LYDIA LI
JANE A. RAFFERTY

Policies Affecting Families of Older Adults With Care Needs

85

The growth of the elderly population in the United States and the increased likelihood of chronic illness and disability with age have made elder care one of the major challenges faced by Americans and the U.S. government. As in the past, currently the bulk of elder care is unpaid assistance provided by families and friends of older persons, referred to as informal or family caregivers in the literature. It was estimated that approximately 66% of noninstitutionalized persons with limitations in activities of daily living (ADLs; e.g., bathing, dressing, eating) rely on informal caregivers exclusively for help; 25% supplement that with paid help; and only 5% rely solely on formal services (Liu, Manton, & Aragon, 2000). The unpaid assistance provided by family caregivers, if paid, would amount to $45 to $94 billion a year (Assistant Secretary for Planning and Evaluation & Administration on Aging, 1998).

Caregiving takes a toll on the physical, psychological, social, and financial well-being of caregivers. For instance, research has shown that wives who care for their husbands have higher levels of depressive symptoms and lower levels of social involvement than wives whose husbands do not need care (Seltzer & Li, 2000). About 21% of caregivers reported that caregiving has a negative effect on their health (Donelan et al., 2002). Employed caregivers often have to rearrange their work schedules, reduce work hours, or take unpaid leave, which, in the long term, can result in a substantial financial loss (Thompson, 2004).

In addition to the stress associated with caregiving, there is a growing concern about the availability of family caregivers, given the trend of women's labor force participation, marital dissolution due to separation and divorce, geographic mobility, and smaller family size (Tennstedt, Crawford, & McKinlay, 1993). Policymakers have begun to realize that family caregiving cannot be taken for granted and that informal caregivers play a vital role in our long-term care system. In this chapter, we describe two federal programs that aim to support families of elderly persons with care needs: the Family and Medical Leave Act and the National Family Caregiver Support Program. We first present the history, provision, and implementation of each program, then discuss their loopholes in addressing the needs of family caregivers and the implications for social work.

THE FAMILY AND MEDICAL LEAVE ACT

History

The Family and Medical Leave Act (FMLA) was signed into law by President Bill Clinton in February

1993, two weeks after he took office. The early version of the FMLA, called the Parental and Disability Leave Act, was introduced to the floor of the House of Representatives in 1985. This original leave bill did not include elder care because it was designed to address the issue of child care. In fact, during the formulation of a leave bill, the question of whether it should have a "parental" or "family" focus was a source of tension among its supporters (Wisensale, 2001). The latter, obviously, prevailed, and the FMLA was reintroduced to the House in 1987.

The FMLA passed both houses twice, first in 1990 and again in 1992. Both times it was vetoed by President George H. W. Bush. Wisensale (2003) argued that if Clinton had not been elected in 1992, we would not have the FMLA today.

Provision

The FMLA requires companies with 50 or more employees and all public sector employers regardless of the number of employees at a given work site to provide eligible employees with up to 12 weeks of unpaid leave per year, for the following reasons: care of a child, spouse, or parent with a serious health problem; care of a newborn, newly adopted, or foster child; or care for a serious health condition of the employee (Commission on Leave, 1996). Eligible employees are those who have worked for the company for at least 1 year and for 1,250 hours over the previous 12 months. The unpaid leave comes with two protections: job security and maintenance of health benefits. An employee is entitled to return to the same or an equivalent position after the leave and to receive the same health benefits as when working while on leave. Employees are required to notify their employers prior to taking leave, and employers can request medical certifications to justify the absence. A company can deny a leave request if the employee falls into the top 10% of the company's payroll and his or her absence would substantially hamper the functioning of the workplace.

Implementation

The FMLA took effect in August 1993; since then, the Department of Labor has commissioned two studies, one in 1995 and another in 2000, to evaluate its implementation (Commission on Leave, 1996; U.S. Department of Labor, 2000). Each study involved a survey of employers and a survey of employees. In the following we highlight the findings from the 2000 study that are relevant to families of dependent older persons, and note the difference between the 1995 and 2000 study findings, if any.

Coverage

About two thirds of the U.S. labor force work for employers covered by the FMLA. Among the covered companies, not all employees are eligible because of the act's requirement for length of employment and hours worked. Combining employees in both public and private sectors, about 54.9% are both covered and eligible. Workers who cannot benefit from the FMLA were more likely to be young (less than 25 years old) or old (more than 64 years old), never married, low-educated (less than a high school education), hourly paid, and have lower family income than covered and eligible workers.

Employees' Use of Leave

About 16.5% of all employees (regardless of whether their employers are covered by the act and their eligibility) took leave for a reason covered by the FMLA, but only a minority took the leave under the FMLA (1.9% of all employees, which was an increase from 1.2% in 1995; the majority of leave takers used other mechanisms such as sick leave and vacation days). Most of the leaves were short, with a median length of 10 days. The primary reason for taking leave was for one's own health, followed by caring for a newborn, adopted, or foster child. About 20% of all leaves were for reasons related to caring for a parent or spouse. There was a shift in the reason for taking leave between the 1995 and 2000 studies, with more employees taking leave for reasons related to caring for a parent or spouse, caring for a new child, or maternity-disability in 2000.

The 2000 study found that 2.4% of all employees needed but did not take leave, which was down from the 3.1% found in the 1995 study. Compared with other employees, these individuals were more likely to be separated, divorced, or widowed, to have children living at home, and to receive hourly pay.

About half of those needing a leave said that it was for their own health, and 22.6% reported caring for an ill parent as a reason for the needed leave. The majority (77.6%) did not take the leave they needed for financial reasons (could not afford to take the leave), and most (87.8%) said they would have taken the leave if it was paid.

Impact on Well-Being

Employees who have taken leave for an FMLA reason generally view the leave quite positively. For example, a majority indicated that taking the leave had a positive effect on their ability to care for a family member (78.7%), on the emotional well-being of their family members or themselves (70.1%), and on the physical health of their family members or themselves (63.0%).

Overall, the two reports issued by the Department of Labor (Commission on Leave, 1996; U.S. Department of Labor, 2000) depict a positive picture of the FMLA. Both reached the conclusion that the act had positive effects on employees, especially easing their conflict between family and work responsibilities. The two studies also found that the act was a minimal burden to employers. Studies by academic researchers concurred that the FMLA has had little negative impact, although academics are more critical of its limitations, including limited coverage and the leave being unpaid (Wisensale, 2001).

Since the passage of the FMLA in 1993, many initiatives have been put forth by members of Congress to expand the law. These initiatives included lowering company size to be covered by the act, expanding allowable reasons for taking leave, and inclusion of domestic partners, parents-in-law, and grandparents in the coverage (Wisensale, 2003). All expanding proposals, however, failed. In 1999, President Clinton issued an executive memorandum and ordered the secretary of labor to propose regulations that allow states to tap into unemployment insurance funds to provide paid leave. Many states responded to Clinton's initiative, and 26 states introduced legislation that involved some type of paid family leave in 2001 (Wisensale, 2003). But it was not until late 2002 that California—the first and only state to date (July 2004)—succeeded in passing a paid family leave law that allows workers to receive 55% to 60% of their salary (up to a cap of $728 per week) during 6 weeks of leave to care for a seriously ill child, spouse, domestic partner, or parent or to care for a new child by birth, adoption, or foster care (California Employment Development Department, 2004).

THE NATIONAL FAMILY CAREGIVER SUPPORT PROGRAM

History

The National Family Caregiver Support Program (NFCSP) was authorized under the Older Americans

Act (OAA) amendments of 2000. In operation, the program comprises both the NFCSP, authorized under Title III-E of the OAA, and the Native American Caregiver Support Program, authorized under Title VI-C. The NFCSP is administered by the Administration on Aging within the Department of Health and Human Services. It is the first national program for which the family caregiver rather than the older adult is the focus, and it is the first major initiative under the OAA since the 1970s.

Provision

The NFCSP calls for all states, in partnership with area agencies on aging (AAAs) and local community service providers, to provide direct support services to meet the range of family caregiver needs. Five categories of services are specified as basic (Administration on Aging, 2004):

1. Information to caregivers about available services;
2. Assistance to caregivers in gaining access to supportive services;
3. Individual counseling, support groups, and caregiver training to assist caregivers in making decisions and solving problems relating to their roles;
4. Respite care to temporarily relieve caregivers from their responsibilities; and
5. Supplemental services, on a limited basis, to complement the care provided by caregivers.

Federal grants are allocated to states, based on a proportionate rate of the population 70 years of age or older, to implement the program. Eligible service recipients include family caregivers, defined as an adult family member or an individual who provides informal care to an elderly person, and grandparents or other relative caregivers of children under 18. States are asked to give priority consideration to those with greatest social and economic needs, and those caring for persons with mental retardation or developmental disabilities.

Implementation

Congress appropriated $125 million in 2001, $141.5 million in 2002, and $155.2 million in 2003 for the NFCSP. In fiscal year 2001, $6 million of the $125 million was used to fund innovative programs, projects of national significance, and conferences and training to foster the development and testing of new approaches to sustain the efforts of family caregivers. An executive summary issued by the Administration on Aging in September 2003 reports that significant progress across the country has been made in implementing the NFCSP. For instance, the program has reached more than 3.8 million individuals with information about caregiver programs and services; provided assistance to 436,000 caregivers in accessing services; served almost 180,000 caregivers with counseling and training; provided respite to more than 70,000 caregivers; and provided supplemental services to more than 50,000 caregivers.

A report of 10 states' experience in implementing caregiver support services since the passage of the NFCSP identified two major challenges in implementing the NFCSP at the state and local levels (Family Caregiver Alliance, 2002). The first is insufficient funding. States varied greatly in the amount of funding received, ranging from $12.6 million in California to $639,540 in Hawaii in fiscal year 2002. But all states report that the funding level of the NFCSP is too low to meet the multifaceted needs of family caregivers. In particular, many states report a need for additional respite care and supplemental services (e.g., assistive devices, home modifications). A second challenge is a shortage of direct care workers. Many state representatives indicate that the labor shortage is a crisis that seriously hampers the delivery of quality services to caregiving families, especially those in rural areas.

In addition, the report notes that administrative fragmentation, balance between flexibility and standardization of service options, and quality assurance and evaluation are some of the issues to be addressed in further implementation of the NFCSP. First, administratively, coordinating and integrating caregiver support services and other community long-term care services (e.g., Medicaid waivers, state-funded home and community-based services) are essential but difficult, due to multiple funding sources, divergent eligibility criteria, and spreading of responsibility across numerous state agencies. Administrative fragmentation of long-term care services at the state and local levels makes it difficult for family caregivers and older persons to access the services they need. Second, the NFCSP's emphasis on local flexibility in designing and implementing its caregiver support services results in great variations in service options across and within states. Such variations, paradoxically, limit the choice for family caregivers and could be confusing and frustrating to those who attempt to access services. For instance, caregivers living in different parts of the same state may not be able to access the same package of caregiver support services under the NFCSP. Third, the lack of uniform assessment on caregivers across states, particularly with no standardized requirement on the collection of outcome data, makes it difficult to assess the impact of the services and to assure quality.

The experience of some states suggests that a consumer-directed approach has promise to deliver caregiver support services more effectively (Family Caregiver Alliance, 2002). The range of consumer-directed options is quite varied; for instance, some states (e.g., Pennsylvania) give cash to family caregivers, who then decide what services to use, when, and who provides the services; other states (e.g., Alabama) provide a menu of service options to family caregivers. The executive summary of Administration on Aging in 2003 identifies expanding consumer- and family-directed care as the next step in strengthening caregiver support services and a solution to the direct care workforce shortage.

The NFCSP represents a formal recognition of the importance to support family caregivers through direct services; however, resources devoted to this effort still lag, as indicated by the modest level of NFCSP funding. Thus far, no study has been conducted to evaluate the impact of the NFCSP on caregiver stress and burden, or whether the program helps to sustain family caregiving.

SUPPORT FOR CAREGIVING FAMILIES: IMPLICATIONS FOR SOCIAL WORK

Although the FMLA and the NFCSP both intend to support family caregivers, their current provisions have limitations. In the following we discuss who may be underserved, what needs may be unmet under the two programs, and the implications for social work.

Underserved Family Caregivers

Working caregivers are the potential beneficiary of the FMLA. Some working caregivers, however, cannot take advantage of the act, such as those working for smaller companies and those who are hired as part-time, seasonal, or temporary workers. Socioeconomically disadvantaged groups, such as ethnic minorities, women, and those with low education, are more likely to be in such employment conditions. These non-eligible workers are as likely as eligible workers to need leave for a health problem of their family members or themselves. Social workers, therefore, should push for expanding the FMLA to cover smaller companies, as well as part-time, seasonal, and temporary workers.

In addition, the definition of *family* under the current provision of the FMLA is too narrow. It should be expanded to include domestic partners, parents-in-law, grandparents, siblings, aunts, and uncles. Research has shown that a substantial proportion of informal caregivers are neither spouses nor adult children of the care recipients (Alecxih, Zeruld, & Olearczyk, 2002). Social workers may have to educate lawmakers about the diversity of family caregivers and urge them to recognize the function of family rather than its form.

It is difficult to assess who is underserved by the NFCSP, due to lack of data. However, the emphasis on integrating caregiver support services and other home and community-based services in many states may reduce the opportunity for vulnerable family caregivers to access caregiver support services. For instance, research has shown that older adults cared for by their wives only are less likely to use any home and community-based services (Li, in press). Consequently, these wife caregivers may be less likely to receive caregiver support services because they are not linked to the formal care system. Yet these caregivers may be quite isolated and in great need of support. To use the limited resources more effectively and to serve family caregivers who may need support services the most, it is necessary to find out who is using the NFCSP services and who is not. Collecting data about service users should be a requirement of the NFCSP funding and can be built into the current reporting system. Collecting data about the characteristics of family caregivers who do not use caregiver support services and the reasons for not using services is more challenging. However, such data will help to identify barriers for service use and to design targeted intervention for the hard-to-reach populations. Both social work researchers and practitioners should contribute to such data collection and outreach intervention efforts.

Unmet Needs

Some needs of family caregivers, including financial need, respite and supplemental services, and community-based long-term care services, are clearly unmet or undermet within the current provisions of the two federal programs.

Financial Need

The FMLA allows workers to take unpaid leave for health reasons of their family or themselves. Taking unpaid leave, however, can create financial hardship for some families, especially during the time when extra expenses for medication or hospital stays already may be causing a financial strain. Low-income families are more likely to be affected negatively by taking unpaid leave. The two studies by the Department of Labor (Commission on Leave, 1996; U.S. Department of Labor, 2000) consistently show that financial constraint is the primary reason for not taking leave among those eligible for leaves. The use rates of the FMLA have been low and are likely to remain so if paid leave is not available, which undermines the act's intention of promoting a healthier balance between employees' work and family responsibilities (Scharlach & Grosswald, 1997). Therefore, expanding the FMLA to paid leave should be a priority that not only offers substantive help to families of dependent older persons but also is a recognition of caregiving responsibility as work (Wisensale, 2001).

By the same token, the caregiving responsibility of family caregivers who are not or choose not to be in the labor force because of caregiving also should be recognized as work. Some states have allowed relatives and other informal caregivers to receive payment for performing homemaking, chores, and personal care services (Linsk, Keigher, Simon-Rusinowitz, & England, 1992). This may also be a way to deal with the shortage of direct care workers. Recent studies of consumer-directed programs involving payment to family caregivers, such as cash and counseling, show that these programs increase satisfaction, reduce unmet needs, and enhance quality of life of elderly persons (Phillips et al., 2003).

If family caregiving is recognized as work, then the time when the caregiver provides assistance should be included and accumulated in calculating Social Security benefits (Stone, 2000). Although not ideal, this is a way to protect the long-term financial well-being of informal caregivers, most of whom are women, and to ensure that those who assume caregiving roles are not penalized financially. Social workers should be in the forefront to advocate for paid leave, consumer-directed options, and Social Security benefits for family caregivers.

Respite Care and Supplemental Services

Respite care and supplemental services seem to be a demand of family caregivers that is far from being satisfied under the current funding level of the NFCSP (Family Caregiver Alliance, 2002). In addition, because states vary considerably in how they spend the funding in the five basic services (information, assistance, counseling and training, respite care, and supplemental services), it may be necessarily to make these services a standard provision under the OAA and to increase their funding. In this way, family caregivers, regardless of where they live, would have the opportunity to get respite care and supplemental services. Social workers' knowledge about the need of family caregivers puts them in a good position to advocate for these services.

Community-Based Long-Term Care

A more substantial support for family caregivers, nevertheless, is to provide a wide range of home and community-based services, such as adult day care, home health aides, and homemaking services, to support older persons with disability to live in the community. This would reduce the demand on family caregivers and enable older persons to choose who (e.g., family or formal agency) provides what type of care. The current funding for community-based long-term care is inadequate and severely circumscribed (Olson, 2003). For instance, only impoverished older persons who are "at risk" of institutionalization are eligible for publicly funded community-based long-term care programs through Medicaid waivers. The majority of disabled older adults are not eligible for publicly funded programs, and few can afford to purchase services to meet their long-term care needs.

Proponents of community-based long-term care often face two questions: Would formal services substitute for informal caregiving, and would community-based care save money compared with institutional care? Mounting evidence has shown that informal caregivers do not withdraw from caregiving even if formal services are available (Penning, 2002). Community-based long-term care, if provided on a limited scale, may not save money relative to institutional care. But there is evidence to suggest that a large-scale operation of community-based long-term care programs reduces overall care costs in the long run (Kane, Kane, & Ladd, 1998). Community-based care is also strongly preferred by older persons (Weissert & Hedrich, 1994). To truly support families of elderly persons, publicly funded home and community-based long-term care programs should be accessible to all persons with disability, and before their disability levels become severe. Research has shown that early home

and community-based service intervention improves subjective well-being and delays institutionalization for moderately impaired older adults (Shapiro & Taylor, 2002). Financing is an issue in any discussion of expanding social programs. Some developed countries, such as Germany and Japan, have implemented national long-term care insurance programs. Their models provide a reference for the United States to develop a long-term care system that provides options of care to disabled older persons and their families. Social workers should demand, and empower the current and future cohorts of older persons to demand, a better long-term care system for Americans.

CONCLUSION

The vast majority of older persons who require long-term care rely on family to meet their basic needs. Providing assistance to elderly relatives, however, engenders financial and personal costs for family caregivers. Policymakers thus far have taken modest actions to support families of older adults with care needs. The FMLA, while helping workers to deal with conflicts between work and caregiving responsibility, needs to expand to cover a broader workforce (e.g., workers in smaller companies and workers in part-time, seasonal, or temporary positions) and allowable reasons for taking leave (e.g., caring for domestic partners, parents-in-law, and grandparents). More important, paid leave has to be offered because most low-income families cannot afford to take unpaid leave. The NFCSP is important because it is the first national program that focuses on family caregivers. However, its low level of funding does not match its ambitious goal—to "develop multifaceted systems of support services for family caregivers" (Lewin Group, 2004, p. I-3). To prevent the NFCSP from being perceived as merely rhetoric, the funding level must be raised. In addition, caregiver support services need to reach vulnerable groups, such as more socially isolated caregivers. Finally, a more substantial support for families of disabled older persons would be to expand home and community-based long-term care. This would reduce the demand on family caregivers and provide options of care to older persons with disability.

Support for the preparation of this chapter was provided by an award to the first author from the Hartford Geriatric Social Work Faculty Scholars Program, which was funded by the John A. Hartford Foundation and administered by the Gerontological Society of America. Address correspondence to Lydia Li, School of Social Work, University of Michigan, 1080 S. University, Ann Arbor, MI 48109-1106. Phone: 734-936-4850; fax: 734-763-3372; e-mail: *lydiali@umich.edu*.

REFERENCES

Administration on Aging. (2003). *The National Family Caregiver Support Program: Compassion in action. Executive summary.* Retrieved April 20, 2004, from *http://www.aoa.gov/prof/aoaprog/caregiver/overview/exec_summary.asp*

Administration on Aging. (2004). *About the NFCSP.* Retrieved April 12, 2004, from *http://www.aoa.gov/prof/aoaprog/caregiver/overview/overview_caregiver.asp*

Alecxih, L., Zeruld, S., & Olearczyk, B. (2002). *Characteristics of caregivers based on survey of income and program participation.* Issue brief prepared for the Administration on Aging. Retrieved June 22, 2004, from *http://www.aoa.dhhs.gov/prof/aoaprog/caregiver/careprof/progguidance/background/program_issues/AlecxihMonograph.pdf*

Assistant Secretary for Planning and Evaluation & Administration on Aging. (1998). *Informal caregiving: Compassion in action.* Washington, DC: Author.

California Employment Development Department. (2004). *Paid family leave.* Retrieved June 29, 2004, from *http://www.edd.ca.gov/fleclaimpfl.htm*

Commission on Leave. (1996). *A workable balance: Report to Congress on family and medical leave policies.* Washington, DC: U.S. Department of Labor.

Donelan, K., Hill, C., Hoffman, C., Scoles, K., Feldman, P., Levin, E., et al. (2002). Challenged to care: Informal caregivers in a changing health system. *Health Affairs, 21,* 222–231.

Family Caregiver Alliance. (2002). *Family caregiver support: Policies, perceptions and practices in 10 states since passage of the National Family Caregiver Support Program.* San Francisco: Author.

Kane, R. A., Kane, R. L., & Ladd, R. C. (1998). *The heart of long-term care.* New York: Oxford University Press.

Lewin Group. (2004). NFCSP resource guide for the aging network. Retrieved June 10, 2004, from *http://www.aoa.dhhs.gov/prof/aoaprog/caregiver/careprof/progguidance/resources/nfscp_resources_guide.asp*

Li, L. W. (in press). Caregiving network compositions and use of supportive services by community-dwelling dependent elders. *Journal of Gerontological Social Work, 43(2/3).*

Liu, K., Manton, K. G., & Aragon, C. (2000). *Changes in home care use by older people with disabilities: 1982–1994.* Washington, DC: AARP Public Policy Institute.

Linsk, N., Keigher, S., Simon-Rusinowitz, L., & England, S. (1992). *Wages for caring: Compensating family care for the elderly.* New York: Praeger.

Olson, L. (2003). *The not-so-golden years: Caregiving, the frail elderly, and the long-term care establishment.* Lanham, MD: Rowman and Littlefield.

Penning, M. (2002). Hydra revisited: Substituting formal for self- and informal in-home care among older adults with disabilities. *Gerontologist, 42,* 4–16.

Phillips, B., Mahoney, K., Simon-Rusinowitz, L., Schore, J., Barrett, S., Ditto, W., et al. (2003). *Lessons from the implementation of cash and counseling in Arkansas, Florida, and New Jersey: Final report.* Princeton, NJ: Mathematica Policy Research. Retrieved July 2, 2004, from *http://www.cashandcounseling.org/downloads/grl/state_report.pdf*

Scharlach, A., & Grosswald, B. (1997). The Family and Medical Leave Act of 1993. *Social Service Review, 71,* 335–359.

Seltzer, M. M., & Li, L. W. (2000). The dynamics of caregiving: Transitions during a three-year prospective study. *Gerontologist, 40,* 165–178.

Shapiro, A., & Taylor, M. (2002). Effects of a community-based early intervention program on the subjective well-being, institutionalization, and mortality of low-income elders. *Gerontologist, 42,* 334–341.

Stone, R. (2000). *Long-term care for the elderly with disabilities: Current policy, emerging trends, and implications for the twenty-first century.* New York: Milbank Memorial Fund. Retrieved June 9, 2004, from *http://www.milbank.org/reports/oo8stone/*

Tennstedt, S., Crawford, S., & McKinlay, J. (1993). Is family care on the decline? A longitudinal investigation of the substitution of formal long-term care services for informal care. *Milbank Quarterly, 71,* 601–625.

Thompson, L. (2004). *Long-term care: Support for family caregivers* (Georgetown University Long-Term Care Financing Project: Issue brief). Retrieved June 10, 2004, from *http://ltc.georgetown.edu*

U.S. Department of Labor. (2000). *Balancing the needs of families and employers: Family and medical leave surveys.* Washington, DC: Author.

Weissert, W., & Hedrich, S. (1994). Lessons learned from research on efforts of community-based long-term care. *Journal of the American Geriatrics Society, 42,* 348–353.

Wisensale, S. (2001). *Family leave policy: The political economy of work and family in America.* Armonk, NY: Sharpe.

Wisensale, S. (2003). Two steps forward, one step back: The Family and Medical Leave Act as retrenchment policy. *Review for Policy Research, 20,* 135–151.

USEFUL WEB SITES

For the Family and Medical Leave Act

http://www.nationalpartnership.org (contains links to updated information regarding changes and implementation of the FMLA)

http://www.dol.gov (Department of Labor's Web site)

For the National Family Caregiver Support Program

http://www.aoa.gov/prof/aoaprog/caregiver/caregiver.asp (links to executive summaries, research reports, state and local agencies)

http://www.caregiver.org (Web page for Family Caregiver Alliance; contains research reports)

General

http://www.thomas.loc.gov (represents an official online source of U.S. federal legislative information)

The Older Americans Act provides a useful framework for reviewing policy to protect the rights of older adults. Under Title I the act lays out the duties of the federal, state, and local governments and of Native American tribes to "assist our older people to secure equal opportunity to the full and free enjoyment of the following objectives":

(1) An adequate income in retirement . . .
(2) The best possible physical and mental health which science can make available and without regard to economic status.
(3) Obtaining and maintaining suitable housing, independently selected, designed and located with reference to special needs and available at costs which older citizens can afford.
(4) Full restorative services for those who require institutional care, and a comprehensive array of community-based, long-term care services adequate to appropriately sustain older people in their communities and in their homes . . .
(5) Opportunity for employment with no discriminatory practices because of age.
(6) Retirement in health, honor, dignity . . .
(7) Participating in and contributing to meaningful activity within . . . civic, cultural, educational, training and recreational opportunities.
(8) Efficient community services . . . with emphasis on maintaining a continuum of care for vulnerable older individuals.
(9) Immediate benefit from proven research knowledge . . .
(10) Freedom, independence and the free exercise of individual initiative in . . . managing their own lives . . . and protection from abuse, neglect and exploitation. (Older Americans Act [OAA], P.L. 89-73, 42 U.S.C. § 3001 *et seq.;* Department of Health and Human Services, 1979, p. 2)

This chapter focuses on explicating select policies that protect the rights of older adults in relation to many of the above objectives. I begin by discussing those policies that prohibit employment discrimination due to age. I also address various policies that indirectly promote the civil rights of older adults by making discrimination based on disability illegal. In addition, the chapter addresses grandparents' rights, the patient's bill of rights, and the right to be free from abuse, neglect, or exploitation.

JOAN DAVITT

Policy to Protect the Rights of Older Adults

DISCRIMINATION BASED ON AGE: EMPLOYMENT

Age Discrimination in Employment Act: Purpose and Scope

Ageism is defined as "the process of systematic stereotyping of and discrimination against people because they are old" (Butler, 1969, p. 243). The key to ageism is that older adults are judged not as individuals but as members of a social category with certain traits (Quadagno, 2002). The secretary of labor reported in 1965 that there was widespread age discrimination in employment (U.S. Department of Labor, 1965). Such discrimination is based on negative stereotypes about older workers' productivity levels and abilities rather than on dislike of or intolerance toward older workers (Querry, 1995–1996). Congress thus enacted the Age Discrimination in Employment Act (ADEA, P.L. 90-202, 29 U.S.C. §§ 621–634, regulations at 29 C.F.R. § 1625), in 1967 to prohibit arbitrary age discrimination in hiring, termination, promotion, compensation, terms/conditions, and privileges (Querry, 1995–1996). The ADEA makes it illegal to discriminate in employment practices against employees aged 40 and older (Tichy, 1991). Private employers with more than 20 employees, employment agencies, and labor unions, as well as federal employers, are covered under this act (Kapp, 2001).

Employers can assert the following exemptions against an age discrimination claim: (a) where age is a bona fide occupational qualification (BFOQ) reasonably necessary to the normal operation of a particular business, (b) where the action is based on reasonable factors other than age (RFOA), (c) to observe the terms of a bona fide seniority system, (d) to observe the terms of a bona fide employee benefit plan, or (e) to discharge or otherwise discipline an individual for good cause (29 U.S.C. at 623 (f)) (Koff & Park 1999; Tichy, 1991). In some cases age may be a factor in one's ability to safely perform a job, such as police officer or firefighter, and can thus be used as a qualifying criterion for government employees (Kapp, 2001). In addition, employers can require medical exams for applicants over age 40 but only when they are directly related to the specific work to be performed and when exams are required for all applicants regardless of age (Tichy, 1991). Likewise, employers can promote a younger employee over an older employee due to greater seniority of the younger employee. Further, the employer cannot establish a mandatory retirement system but can legally offer a retirement incentive as long as it is voluntary (Kapp, 2001; Tichy, 1991). An employer is allowed to fire or refuse to hire or promote based on an individual's qualifications or actual job performance but cannot use chronological age as a proxy for job performance.

A plaintiff presents a prima facie case of age discrimination to the Equal Employment Opportunity Commission (EEOC) by showing that the plaintiff was a member of the protected group (e.g., over age 40), the plaintiff was qualified for the job, the plaintiff was adversely affected, and the employer hired or promoted someone else for the same position (Tichy, 1991). The alleged aggrieved employee does not have to provide direct evidence of the employer's unlawful intent; rather, he or she merely has to provide evidence to refute any legitimate reasons for rejecting an applicant (for hire, promotion, etc.) put forward by the employer (Kapp, 2001).[1,2]

Concerns With the Law

Problems with ADEA abound. First, the act does not clarify the term *arbitrary* (Querry, 1995–1996). Second, ADEA has had little effect on hiring decisions, because such discrimination can be very difficult to prove (Jolls, 1996). Third, Harper (1993) contends that ADEA and the Older Worker's Benefit Protection Act (OWBPA) do little to protect workers in relation to retirement incentives. Employers offer retirement incentives as a way to reduce the workforce through attrition rather than forced layoffs. Older workers in most cases cost employers more for a variety of reasons (service time, higher health care costs, etc.). Thus, it benefits the company more to reduce the number of older workers (regardless of productivity levels) than to reduce the number of younger workers (Frolik, 1999; Harper, 1993). "Conditional age-based exit incentives can be used to achieve precisely what the ADEA seeks to eradicate: the age-based elimination of productive older workers who would prefer continued employment to retirement" (Harper, p. 69).

Finally, recent case law in this area has made it difficult for older workers to win a claim around the use of age proxies (e.g., years of service; Bailey, 2001; see *Hazen Paper Co. v. Biggins*, 507 U.S. 604 (1993)). In the *Biggins* case the Supreme Court held that age and years of service are "analytically distinct" and thus years of service cannot necessarily be considered age based. This decision has also enabled employers to use reduction in force or downsizing strategies to eliminate older (and generally more costly) workers from their payrolls. According to Minda (1997), these strategies are largely immune to ADEA litigation because they are generally couched in economic necessity for the employer and thus are considered "reasonable factors other than age." Such case law developments have made it increasingly difficult for older adults to sustain an age discrimination complaint in the face of downsizing and cost-reduction strategies.[3]

AMERICANS WITH DISABILITIES ACT AND EMPLOYMENT DISCRIMINATION

Until 1990, older employees who had adverse action taken against them (firing, failure to promote, etc.) due to RFOAs had little recourse (Hood, 1998). In 1990, however, Congress passed the Americans With Disabilities Act (ADA, P.L. 101-336, 104 Stat. 327 (1990), 42 U.S.C. 12101–12213 (1994)), which may help those older workers who are terminated for health reasons (Kapp, 2001).

The ADA (specifically Title I) prohibits public and private employers with 25 or more employees from discriminating "against a qualified individual with a disability because of the disability of such individual in regard to job application procedures, the hiring, advancement or discharge of employees, employee compensation, job training, and other terms, conditions, and privileges of employment" (42 U.S.C. § 12112 (a)). A disabled person is defined under the act as one who either: "1) has an actual physical or mental impairment that substantially limits one or more major life activities; 2) has a record or past history of an impairment. . . ; 3) is regarded as having an impairment . . ." (42 U.S.C. § 12102(2)(A, B, C)). A qualified individual with a disability is defined as a person "who can perform the essential functions of the job with or without reasonable accommodations" (42 U.S.C. § 12111(8)). Such accommodations can include reassignment or restructuring of the job, providing special aids or training, and access to employer-provided facilities such as cafeterias, lounges, and fitness centers (42 U.S.C. § 12111(8)). The employer must provide these accommodations unless it can show that doing so would "impose an undue hardship on the employer" (Hood, 1998; Kapp, 2001).

According to Kapp (2001) and Hood (1998), prior to ADA, an older worker with arthritis could be terminated under the "reasonable factors other than age" exemption of the ADEA. "Now, however, that

same employer may be liable under the ADA if it could reasonably accommodate her arthritis on the job" (Hood, 1998, p. 8). (See *www.eeoc.gov/docs/accommodation* for further guidelines on the ADA.)

DISCRIMINATION IN PUBLIC SERVICES: THE ADA AND OLDER ADULTS

Title II of the ADA also protects individuals with disabilities in relation to discrimination by public services. Title II states that "no qualified individual with a disability shall by reason of such disability, be excluded from participation in or be denied the benefits of the services, programs, or activities of a public entity or be subjected to discrimination by such an entity" (42 U.S.C. § 12131(1)). A qualified individual is defined as

> an individual with a disability who, with or without reasonable modifications to rules, policies, or practices, the removal of architectural, communication, or transportation barriers, or the provision of auxiliary aids and services, meets the essential eligibility requirements for the receipt of services or the participation in programs or activities provided by a public entity. (42 U.S.C. § 12131 (2))

The Supreme Court decision in *Olmstead v. L.C.* (119 S. Ct. 2176 (1999)) further interpreted Title II of the ADA. The court held that "unjustified isolation . . . is properly regarded as discrimination based on disability." The court noted that

> institutional placement of persons who can handle and benefit from community settings perpetuates unwarranted assumptions that persons so isolated are incapable or unworthy of participating in community life [and] confinement in an institution severely diminishes the everyday life activities of individuals, including family relations, social contacts, work options, economic independence, educational advancement, and cultural enrichment. (*Olmstead v. L.C.,* 1999 at 2176)

Under this decision, states are now required to provide community-based services or less restrictive service settings when a professional determination indicates that such placement is appropriate, the affected person does not oppose the placement, and the placement can be reasonably accommodated (Fried, 2001; Kapp, 2001).

DISCRIMINATION IN HOUSING: THE ADA AND FAIR HOUSING AMENDMENTS

The housing rights of persons with disabilities are protected via the ADA (Title II, public services, and Title III, public accommodations); Section 504 of the Rehabilitation Act (29 U.S.C. § 794); and the Fair Housing Act Amendments of 1988 (FHAA, P.L. 100-430, 102 Stat.1619 (1988) 42 U.S.C. § 3601–3619).[4] The FHAA make it illegal to discriminate in the sale, rental, or terms, conditions, or privileges of sale/rental or in the provision of services or facilities because of a handicap of the buyer/renter, someone intending to live in the property, or someone connected with that buyer/renter (Kapp, 2001).[5]

Recent statistics show that 52.5% of the elderly have at least one disability as defined by the ADA (AARP, 1997). Of note is the fact that the act covers renters and buyers who live with or are associated with a person with a disability. Thus, families wishing to take in an elderly, disabled relative, or older adults caring for mentally or physically disabled adult children, or grandparents caring for a disabled grandchild would fall under these protections. The FHAA also may be applicable in cases where independent living complexes or communities refuse to rent to seniors in a wheelchair or with other disabilities (Ziaja, 2001). Providers may be exempt from this policy if they can show that the discriminatory policy is fundamental to the nature of the facility and such a change would instill an undue burden related to accommodation on the facility. Finally, the FHAA may prohibit certain state or local regulations (e.g., zoning and fire safety codes) that restrict certain types of housing operators from admitting residents with certain disabilities (*Cason v. Rochester Housing Authority*, 748 F. Supp. 1002 (W.D.N.Y. 1990)).

GRANDPARENT RIGHTS

Increasingly our society is seeing grandparents play a much larger role in the upbringing of children, in many cases as the sole caregiver. "More than three million children in the U.S. live with older relatives, and in at least one million homes a grandparent is the sole or primary caregiver" (American Bar Association [ABA], 1998b, p. 15). There are two key areas in relation to the rights of grandparents: visitation between grandparents and grandchildren who are still with their parents or other primary caregivers, and kinship care, when grandparents become the primary caregivers (ABA, 1998a).

Visitation Rights

Originally common law did not grant grandparents the right to see their grandchildren while in the custody of their biological or adoptive parents (ABA, 1998b). Since the mid-1960s, however, all 50 states and the District of Columbia have enacted legislation giving grandparents the right to petition the court for visitation. This results in two important problematics. First, grandparent visitation rights are governed by state law, which can make things confusing for both grandparents and advocates for older adults. Second, most state law simply grants the right to petition the courts for a visitation order (ABA, 1998b). This requires a detailed court process that can be adversarial, thus creating much disruption in the children's lives (ABA, 1998b).

In determining whether to grant visitation rights, most courts consider what would be in the "best interests of the child," but also they may look at any prior relationship with the person petitioning, the mental and physical health of those involved, and the child's preference (if the child is old enough to express such; ABA, 1998b). Most commonly, state laws allow for such petitions upon the death of a parent or in the case of divorce. Some states also include such situations as parental incarceration, out-of-wedlock birth, or "when the child previously lived with the grandparent" (ABA, 1998b, p. 13). In the case of adoption, most courts have found that the grandparents' rights are terminated, as are those of the biological parents. However, in cases where the child is adopted by a stepparent or other close relative, grandparent rights are not automatically terminated (ABA, 1998). Although some state statutes are broad enough to allow a grandparent to petition the court when the nuclear family is intact (the children reside with both parents), most courts frown upon granting visitation rights in these cases, deferring to the authority of the parents (ABA, 1998b). Finally, federal law requires states to honor visitation orders granted in another state (ABA, 1998b; see also Kapp, 2001, for a list of state statutes on visitation rights).

Kinship Care

Kinship care refers to a situation in which parents are unable to care for their children, and relatives (in many cases older relatives) step in to provide such care. Frequently, grandparents become kinship care providers on an informal basis. However, problems can arise if grandparents do not have legal custody or guardianship over the child. Thus they may have difficulty when enrolling the child in school, consenting to medical treatment, or applying for public benefits.

To formalize the arrangement, the grandparent must look to state law for guidance. However, there are generally three options available: custody, guardianship, or permanent adoption. Guardianships can be permanent or temporary (including standby) depending on the state law. In addition, some states allow for open adoption. Other states have enacted consent legislation to allow parents to grant authority for medical and other decisions to another adult without limiting the rights of the parents (ABA, 1998b; Kapp, 2001). Standby guardianship laws enable parents to designate a guardian in advance (similar to a springing power of attorney) if they have a chronic, debilitating, or terminal illness. In some cases, if the state has removed the child from the parent's custody, it may place the child with a grandparent while the state retains legal custody (generally referred to as foster care; ABA, 1998b).

One important reason for formalizing the kinship care arrangement is to obtain necessary financial support. In many cases grandparents may be on fixed incomes, not designed to support a family. Grandparents can become foster care parents and receive payment under Title IV-E of the Social Security Act. However, in this situation the state retains custody of the child, and the grandparent must be evaluated based on state licensing requirements. This may be difficult, especially if the older adult resides in subsidized housing or senior housing. A grandparent or grandchild may be eligible for several types of benefits, including TANF, Social Security Dependent Benefits, SSI, Medicaid, CHIP, food stamps, EITC, and guardianship subsidies. Many of these programs are administered at the state level; thus, eligibility would need to be determined case by case.

Another area of concern for grandparent caregivers involves their place of residence. Amendments to the Fair Housing Act[6] provided an exemption from FHAA rules regarding familial status for senior housing complexes. This exemption and the four-prong test to establish it may unintentionally reopen the door for "adult-only" apartment complexes (Panjwani, 1995). This may prove problematic for older adult grandparents who need to house their grandchildren while residing in such a complex. Unfortunately, this is more likely to affect African American and Hispanic older adults. Data from the U.S. Census show that 4.2% of White children under age 18 lived with a grandparent, whereas 13% of African American children and 7.5% of Hispanic children lived with a grandparent (U.S. Census, 2000, as cited in Nelson, 2003).

PROTECTION FROM ABUSE, NEGLECT, AND EXPLOITATION

The OAA defines abuse in the following way:

> Abuse is the willful infliction of injury, unreasonable confinement, intimidation, or cruel punishment with resulting physical harm, pain, or mental anguish; or deprivation by . . . a caregiver of goods or services . . . necessary to avoid physical harm, mental anguish, or mental illness. (42 U.S.C. § 3002(13)(A-B))
>
> Neglect is the failure to provide for oneself goods or services necessary to avoid physical harm, mental anguish or mental illness . . . [or] failure of a caretaker to provide such goods or services. (42 U.S.C. § 3002(37)(A-B))
>
> Exploitation means the illegal or improper act or process of an individual, including a caregiver, using the resources of an older individual for monetary or personal benefit, profit, or gain. (42 U.S.C. § 3002 (26))

These definitions provide guidelines for the states; however, the OAA does not stipulate penalties for the commission of abuse or neglect.

Every state has enacted elder abuse legislation that defines abuse. Most states have the equivalent of an adult protective services unit, which is responsible for investigating and substantiating cases of abuse or neglect, as well as providing protection from further mistreatment.[7] Most state statutes provide for criminal liability for willful acts or omissions which result in elder mistreatment (Kapp, 2001). Most statutes include both family and formal care providers under the definition of caregiver. Finally, some statutes mandate certain professionals to report elder abuse, and other statutes provide for voluntary reporting of abuse (Colorado, Illinois, New Jersey, New York, North Dakota, Pennsylvania, and South Dakota; see Kapp, 1999). All states protect individuals who report abuse; as long as they have made a report in good faith, they are immune from subsequent charges of harm or defamation (Kapp, 1999; see Exhibit C for other relevant legislation).

PATIENT'S BILL OF RIGHTS

In 1997 President Clinton appointed the Advisory Commission on Consumer Protection and Quality in the Health Care Industry to advise the president on issues related to changes in health care delivery, to assure quality health care, and to protect consumers and staff in health care systems. The commission was also asked to develop a bill of rights for health care consumers. The Consumer Bill of Rights and Responsibilities was intended to accomplish three major goals:

> First, to strengthen consumer confidence by assuring the health care system is fair and responsive to consumers' needs, provides consumers with credible and effective mechanisms to address their concerns, and encourages consumers to take an active role in improving and assuring their health.
>
> Second, to reaffirm the importance of a strong relationship between patients and their health care professionals.
>
> Third, to reaffirm the critical role consumers play in safeguarding their own health by establishing both rights and responsibilities for all participants in improving health status. (Office of Personnel Management, 2002, p. 10)

On February 20, 1998, President Clinton signed an executive order that extended the provisions of the patient's bill of rights to more than 85 million Americans with health care coverage under Medicare, Medicaid, and all other federally sponsored health care programs (U.S. Senate, 2001). The bill of rights specifies eight sets of rights and responsibilities for consumers of health care. These include the right to information, a choice of providers, access to emergency services, full participation in their medical care, respectful care, confidentiality, a fair and efficient process for filing appeals and complaints, and the responsibility to be active participants in their care (Department of Health and Human Services, 1999; for further details on the patient's bill of rights, see *www.opm.gov/insure/health/billrights.htm*, *www.democrats.senate.gov/pbr/history.html*, *www.os.dhhs.gov/news/press/1999press/990412.html*).

Congress has pursued passage of legislation in this area since 1997 to ensure similar protections for all health care consumers, particularly those in managed care systems. A recent Supreme Court decision in this area makes the need for a patient's bill of rights all the more crucial. *Cigna Healthcare of Texas, Inc. v. Calad*, No. 03-83 and *Aetna Health Inc. v. Davila*, No. 02-1845, 004 consolidated and were heard as one case. See also *Rush Prudential HMO, Inc. v. Moran*, 536 U.S. 355 (2002), which held that a state-level independent medical review statute was not preempted by ERISA. The holding in these two cases states that employer-sponsored health insurance plans are regulated by the Employee Retirement Income Security Act of 1974 (ERISA), which preempts any state law in this area. Thus, beneficiaries who are denied treatment coverage by an employer-sponsored health maintenance organization (HMO) can no longer sue for damages. Under ERISA rules, the beneficiary can sue only for reimbursement of the cost of providing the procedure. This virtually eliminates consumers' ability to pressure an HMO into providing essential, physician-prescribed care and opens the door for severe limits to be placed on access to care by managed care plans. "If a health plan makes a bad decision on coverage and you are harmed by it, you now have very little redress if the decision is negligent, in bad faith or even intentional" (*Christian Science Monitor*, 2004, p. 3). In response to this decision, Representative John Dingell has introduced a new version of the Patient Bill of Rights Act of 2004 (H.R. 4628, 108th Congress). The bill provides for utilization review, internal and external review of claims denials, consumer choice, access to emergency care and specialists, access to information, protection of the doctor-patient relationship, availability of civil remedies (amending ERISA), and tax incentives for small business.

CONCLUSION

The rights of older adults are protected by a hodge-podge of policies generated by case law, executive order, or legislative initiative. This chapter simply touches the tip of the proverbial iceberg in relation to these areas. The appendix provides several lists of related legislation or case law, as well as a list of organizations with expertise in many of these areas. Legislation is important, but equally important are court decisions interpreting these laws and the regulations that guide implementation. Thus older adults and their advocates not only need to be informed about new legislation but also must be aware of changes made in all areas of policy creation. The objectives of the OAA provide guidelines for those key areas that we, as a society, have identified as crucial to the health and well-being of older adults. However, as advocates we must go beyond these guidelines to continue to enhance and expand the rights of older adults.

Appendices

Exhibit A: Age Discrimination in Employment: Policy History

Policy	*Impact*
Social Security Act of 1935 (P.L. 271-74)	Decommodification of older workers from labor force, may have reinforced negative stereotypes regarding older workers. The original Social Security Act did not cover all workers (e.g., domestic workers, many professional groups were excluded at the beginning). Thus economic security in retirement in the early days of social insurance was not assured for all.
Executive Order No. 11,141, 3 C.F.R. 1811 (1964–1965), February 12, 1964, Lyndon B. Johnson	Established federal policy against age discrimination in employment for federal contractors and subcontractors. No enforcement provided or cause for action.
Civil Rights Act of 1964 (P.L. 88-352, 78 Stat. 265, 42 U.S.C. §§ 2000e–2000e-17 (1994))	Title VII of this act made it illegal to discriminate in employment decisions based on race, color, religion, national origin, or sex (Eglit, 1997; Koff & Park, 1999).
U.S. Department of Labor (1965) The Older American Worker: Age Discrimination in Employment	Reported to Congress widespread age discrimination in employment that was arbitrarily based on assumptions about older workers' productivity, etc.
ADEA of 1967, P.L. 90-202, 29 U.S.C. §§ 621–634, 29 C.F.R. § 1625	See full description in this chapter.
The Fair Labor Standards Act of 1974 (P.L. 93-259)	Expanded coverage of ADEA by including employers with 20 or more employees as well as federal, state, and local government employers.
ADEA amendments of 1978 (P.L. 95-256)	The original law set the age limit at 40–65. This was amended via the 1978 amendments to ADEA to age 70 for private sector, state and local governments, and removed age ceiling for federal employees. Raised compulsory retirement age for executives and tenured faculty to age 70.
Tax Equity and Fiscal Responsibility Act of 1982 (TEFRA, P.L. 97-248)	Required employers to keep the "working aged" on their health plans (offered to younger workers) rather than shifting them to Medicare (Koff & Park, 1999).
The Deficit Reduction Act of 1984 (DEFRA, P.L. 98-369)	Required employers to "offer employees under age sixty-five the same family group health coverage" (Koff & Park, 1999, p. 260). It also lifted the Medicare Part B premium penalty for workers who stayed on the private plan.
The 1984 Older Americans Act Reauthorization (P.L. 98-459)	Extended coverage of ADEA to U.S. citizens employed by U.S. employers in foreign countries (Koff & Park, 1999).
ADEA amendments of 1986 (P.L. 99-592)	Removed the upper age limit for all employers with 20 or more employees and eliminated mandatory retirement for both public and private sectors. Mandatory retirement for tenured faculty in institutes of higher education was allowed to expire in 1993. Also in 1986 employers were required to offer the same group health insurance to workers aged 69 and over as was provided to younger workers.
Older Workers Benefit Protection Act of 1990 (P.L. 101-433)	Clarified that ERISA benefit plans are subject to ADEA and created further protections to ensure that "older workers are not compelled or pressured into waiving their rights under the ADEA in relation to early retirement incentive plans" (Koff & Park, 1999, p. 263). These waivers of claims must be in writing, must specifically refer to claims under ADEA, must advise the employee to consult an attorney, must give the employee 21 days to consider the waiver, and 7 days to revoke after signed (29 U.S.C. § 626 (f)(1)(A)-(G)).

Exhibit B: ADEA Case Law History

Case	Holding
McDonnell Douglas Corp. v. Green, 411 U.S. 792 (1973)	"The fact that one person in the protected class has lost out to another person in the protected class is thus irrelevant, so long as he has lost out because of his age . . ." @ 802.
	Also found that if prima facie case established by plaintiff, then burden shifts to employer to present a legitimate nondiscriminatory reason for action taken.
Texas Dept. of Community Affairs v. Burdine, 450 U.S. 248 (1981)	"Burden of persuasion, proving discrimination, rests at all times with the plaintiff." @ 256. "Also discrimination can be proven by the plaintiff either directly by persuading a court that a discriminatory reason more likely motivated the employer or indirectly by showing that the employer's proffered explanation is unworthy of credence." @ 256.
Aikens, 460 U.S. at 7111 (1983)	Established the 4-point formula for presenting a prima facie case without direct evidence of employer's intent.
Griggs v. Duke Power Co., 401 U.S. 424 (1991)	In a race discrimination case, the court held that "Title VII proscribes not only overt discrimination but also practices that are fair in form, but discriminatory in operation." @ 431. Established the model of disparate impact discrimination, which relies on statistics to show disparate impact on protected class.
Hazen Paper Co. v. Biggins, 507 U.S. 604 (1993)	"Age and years of service are analytically distinct, [thus it is] incorrect to say that a decision based on years of service is necessarily age-based." @ 611 Case where employer fired a 62-year-old worker who was close to vesting in pension plan.
St. Mary's Honor Center v. Hicks, 509 U.S. 502 (1993)	Plaintiff must demonstrate both that the proffered reason was false and that discrimination was the real reason, commonly referred to as pretext only v. pretext-plus. @ 519.
Oubre v. Energy, Inc., 118 S. Ct. 838 (1998)	The Supreme Court found that employer's failure to comply with OWBPA on these waivers gives the aggrieved employee the right to sue under ADEA.
Reeves v. Sanderson Plumbing Products, Inc., 530 U.S 133 (2000)	A prima facie case of discrimination and sufficient evidence which allows the jury to reject the employer's explanation for the adverse employment action may permit a finding of liability. @ 147.
Kimel v. Florida Board of Regents, 120 S. Ct. 631 (2000)	Under judicial review, the Supreme Court ruled in 2000 that the ADEA does not apply to state or local governments as it "is not a valid exercise of Congress' power under § 5 of the Fourteenth Amendment. The ADEA's purported abrogation of the States' sovereign immunity is accordingly invalid."
Erie County Retirees Ass. v. County of Erie, 220 *F.3d* 193 *(3d Cir.* 2000*).*	Employer violated ADEA by providing Medicare-eligible retirees health benefits that were inferior to the benefits offered to retirees who were not eligible for Medicare; Medicare eligibility is a direct proxy for age. @ 211. Use of disparate impact theory.

Exhibit C: Legislation to Protect Older Adults From Abuse

Legislation	Impact
Title XX amendments to the Social Security Act of 1975 (42 U.S.C. §1397, Title XX, 45 C.F.R. 222.73)	Provided protective services for all adults aged 18 or over.
	Requires health care providers to report adverse actions involving medical staff, such as revocation of license or malpractice claims.
Health Care Quality Improvement Act of 1986 (P.L. 99-660)	Requires states to establish a registry of nurse aides and any finding of abuse, neglect, or exploitation by an aide.
Nursing Home Reform Act of 1987 (as part of OBRA 87, 100-203, 42 C.F.R. § 483.156)	Added prevention of abuse, neglect, and exploitation to OAA objectives.
Older Americans Act amendments of 1987 (P.L. 100-175)	Added definition of elder abuse, neglect, and exploitation to OAA.
OAA Amendments of 1992 (P.L. 102-375)	Ordered the attorney general to develop guidelines for protecting children, older adults, or persons with a disability from abuse; also to evaluate the effectiveness, availability, and cost of criminal background checks. Many states have enacted legislation to require criminal background checks.
Violent Crime Control and Law Enforcement Act of 1994 (P.L. 103-222)	
Safe Medical Devices Act (P.L. 101-629)	Required to report when a restraint may have caused or contributed to the death of a resident/patient or staff.

NOTES

1. Courts follow the precedent set in the *McDonnell Douglas v. Green* case (411 U.S 792 (1973)) establishing a three-part test of burdens and proof for cases lacking direct evidence (North, 1997). See also *Reeves v. Sandersen Plumbing Products, Inc.*, 120 S.Ct. 2097 (2000), and *Texas Dept. of Community Affairs v. Burdine*, 450 U.S. 248 (1981).

2. According to Kapp (2001) most states have their own version of the ADEA, some of which may provide broader protections. Thus older workers can also file suit in many state courts via the respective state statute. (See Kapp for a detailed list of state statutes (pp. 10–11) and Exhibit A for a policy history of age discrimination in employment.)

3. However, where the proxy has a direct connection to age, as in the case of Medicare eligibility, courts have found that this cannot be allowed as a reasonable factor other than age (RFOA). (See *Erie County Retirees Ass. V. County of Erie*, 220 F.3d 193 (3d Cir. 2000)). (See Exhibit C for ADEA case law history and Minda (1997) for a detailed discussion of reduction in force strategies and interpretation of case law in this area.)

4. The Fair Housing Act of 1968 was originally Title VIII of the Civil Rights Act of that year which prohibited discrimination in the sale, rental, or financing of housing on the basis of race, color, religion, or national origin. FAA was also amended in 1974 to include sex as a protected class (Nelson, 2003).

5. The FHAA also made it illegal to discriminate on the basis of family status, thereby invalidating the "adults only" restrictions of many housing complexes. "Congress included familial status as a protected class because of evidence that housing discrimination against families was pervasive and often affected minority families disproportionately" (Nelson, 2003, p. 4).

6. FHAA of 1988, P.L. 100-430, 102 Stat. 1619 (1988) 42 U.S.C. § 3601-3619 and Housing for Older Persons Act of 1995, P.L. 104-76.

7. Title XX amendments to the Social Security Act in 1975 provided protective services for all adults age 18 or over (42 U.S.C. §1397, Title XX, 45 C.F.R. 222.73). After these amendments states began passing laws to establish and implement their protective service plans.

REFERENCES

AARP. (1997). *A profile of older Americans.* Washington, DC: Author. Retrieved from *http://www.research.aarp.org/general/profile99.pdf*

American Bar Association. (1998a). *Facts about law and the elderly.* Chicago: Author.

American Bar Association. (1998b). *National handbook on law and programs affecting senior citizens.* Chicago: Author.

American Bar Association. (2004). *Legal guide for older Americans: The law every American over fifty needs to know.* Washington, DC: Author. Retrieved from *www.abanet.org/aging/chapter/home.html*

Bailey, J. C. (2001). Age discrimination models of proof after *Hazen Paper Co. v. Biggins. Elder Law Journal, 9,* 175–202.

Butler, R. (1969). Ageism: Another form of bigotry. *Gerontologist, 9,* 243–246.

Christian Science Monitor. (2004, June 23). *Why HMO angst is a hard issue for Congress; In wake of court ruling this week, some lawmakers renew push for patients' rights.*

Department of Health and Human Services. (1999). *Patient's Bill of Rights in Medicare and Medicaid.* Washington, DC: Author. Retrieved from *www.os.dhhs.gov/news/press/1999pres/990412.html*

Eglit, H. C. (1997). The Age Discrimination in Employment Act at thirty: Where it's been, where it is today, where it's going. *University of Richmond Law Review, 31*(3), 579–756.

Fried, L. B. (2001). *Olmstead:* Catalyst to expand services for the elderly. *Bifocal, 22*(3), 6, 8–9.

Frolik, L. A. (1999). *Aging and the law: An interdisciplinary reader.* Philadelphia: Temple University Press.

Harper, M. C. (1993). The effect of conditional age-based exit incentives, coercion, and the prospective waiver of ADEA rights: The failure of the Older Workers Benefit Protection Act. *Virginia Law Review, 79*(6), 1271–1344.

Hood, C. K. (1998). Age discrimination in employment and the Americans With Disabilities Act: A second bite at the apple. *Elder Law Journal, 6,* 1–28.

Jolls, C. (1996). Hands-tying and the Age Discrimination in Employment Act. *Texas Law Review, 74*(7), 1813–1847.

Kapp, M. B. (1999). *Geriatrics and the law* (3rd ed.). New York: Springer.

Kapp, M. B. (2001). *Lessons in law and aging.* New York: Springer.

Koff, T. H., & Park, R. W. (1999). *Aging public policy bonding the generations* (2nd ed.). Amityville, NY: Baywood.

Minda, G. (1997). Opportunistic downsizing of aging workers: The 1990s version of age and pension discrimination in employment. *Hastings Law Journal, 48*(3), 511–577.

Nelson, J. (2003). Notes and comments: The perpetuation of segregation. The Senior Housing Exemption in the 1988 amendments to the Fair Housing Act. *Thomas Jefferson Law Review, 26*, 103–125.

New York Times. (2004, June 22). *Justices limit ability to sue health plans.* June 22.

Office of Personnel Management. (2002). Patients' Bill of Rights and the Federal Employees Health Benefits Program. Washington, DC: Author. Retrieved from *www.opm.gov/insure/health/billrights.htm*

Panjwani, A. D. (1995). Beyond the Beltway: Housing for Older Persons Act of 1995. *Journal of Affordable Housing and Community Development Law, 5*(1), 197.

Quadagno, J. (2002). *Aging and the life course: An introduction to social gerontology.* Boston: McGraw-Hill.

Querry, T. J. (1995–1996). Note: A rose by any other name no longer smells sweet: Disparate treatment discrimination and the age proxy doctrine after *Hazen Paper Co. v. Biggins. Cornell Law Review, 81*(2), 530–582.

Reinhart, S. (2004). *Rush Prudential HMO, Inc. v. Moran:* 21 or bust! Does preemption give HMOs the power to gamble with our health? *Akron Tax Journal, 19,* 99–144.

Tichy, G. J. (1991). The Age Discrimination in Employment Act of 1967. *Catholic Lawyer, 34*(4), 373–385.

U.S. Department of Labor. (1965). *The older American worker: Age discrimination in employment.* Washington, DC: Author.

U.S. Senate. (2001). Patient's Bill of Rights: History. Washington, DC: Author. Retrieved from *www.democrats.senate.gov/pbr/history.html*

Ziaja, E. (2001). Do independent and assisted living communities violate the Fair Housing Amendments Act and the Americans With Disabilities Act? *Elder Law Journal, 9,* 313.

ORGANIZATION RESOURCE LIST

AARP
601 E Street NW
Washington, DC 20049
Phone: 888-OUR-AARP (888-687-2277)
http://www.aarp.org/

Administration on Aging
U.S. Department of Health and Human Services
200 Independence Avenue SW
Washington, DC 20201
Phone: 800-677-1116; 202-619-0724
Fax: 202-357-3555
http://www.aoa.gov

Alzheimer's Association National Office
225 N. Michigan Ave., Floor 17
Chicago, IL 60601
Phone: 800-272-3900
http://www.alz.org

American Association of Homes and Services
    for the Aging
2519 Connecticut Ave. NW
Washington, DC 20008
Phone: 202-783-2242
Fax: 202-783-2255
http://www2.aahsa.org/

American Bar Association
Service Center
321 North Clark Street
Chicago, IL 60610
312-988-5522
800-285-2221
http://www.abanet.org/aging/

American College of Legal Medicine
1111 North Plaza Drive, Suite 550
Schaumburg, IL 60173
Phone: 847-969-0283
Fax: 847-517-7229
http://www.aclm.org

American Geriatrics Society
The Empire State Building
350 Fifth Avenue, Suite 801
New York, NY 10118
Phone: 212-308-1414
Fax: 212-832-8646
http://www.americangeriatrics.org

American Health Care Association
1201 L Street, NW
Washington, DC 20005
Phone: 202-842-4444
Fax: 202-842-3860
http://www.ahca.org/

American Health Lawyers Association
1025 Connecticut Avenue NW, Suite 1025
Washington, DC 20036-5405
Phone: 202-833-1100
Fax: 202-833-1105
http://www.healthlawyers.org/

American Medical Association
515 North State Street
Chicago, IL 60610
Phone: 800-621-8335
http://www.ama-assn.org

American Society on Aging
833 Market Street, Suite 511
San Francisco, CA 94103
Phone: 800-537-9728; 415-974-9600
Fax: 415-974-0300
http://www.asaging.org/contact.cfm

American Society of Law, Medicine and Ethics
765 Commonwealth Avenue, Suite 1634
Boston, MA 02215
Phone: 617-262-4990
Fax: 617-437-7596
http://www.aslme.org/contact/index.php

Bazelon Center for Mental Health
1101 15th Street NW, Suite 1212
Washington, DC 20005
Phone: 202-467-5730
Fax: 202-223-0409
http://www.bazelon.org/

Center on Disability and Health
1522 K Street NW, Suite 800
Washington, DC 20005
Phone: 202-842-4408
Fax: 202-842-2402

Centers for Medicare and Medicaid Services
7500 Security Boulevard
Baltimore, MD 21244-1850
Phone: 877-267-2323
http://www.cms.hhs.gov/default.asp?

National Academy of Elder Law Attorneys, Inc.
1604 North Country Club Road
Tucson, AZ 85716
Phone: 520-881-4005
Fax: 520-325-7925
http://www.naela.org/contactus/index.htm

National Academy on an Aging Society
1030 15th Street NW, Suite 250
Washington, DC 20005
Phone: 202-408-3375
Fax: 202-842-1150
http://www.agingsociety.org/agingsociety/

National Association of Area Agencies on Aging
1730 Rhode Island Ave. NW, Suite 1200
Washington, DC 20036
Phone: 202-872-0888
Fax: 202-872-0057
http://www.n4a.org/

National Center on Elder Abuse
1201 15th Street NW, Suite 350
Washington, DC 20005
Phone: 202-898-2586
Fax: 202-898-2583
http://www.elderabusecenter.org

National Citizens' Coalition for Nursing Home Reform
    (NCCNHR)
1424 16th Street NW, Suite 202
Washington, DC 20036
Phone: 202-332-2276
Fax: 202-332-2949
http://www.nccnhr.org/public/50_541_2953.CFM

National Conference of Commissioners on Uniform
    State Laws
211 East Ontario Street, Suite 1300
Chicago, IL 60611
Phone: 312-915-0195
Fax: 312-915-0187
http://www.nccusl.org/Update/

National Council on the Aging
409 Third Street SW, Suite 200
Washington, DC 20024
Phone: 202-479-1200
http://www.ncoa.org/index.cfm

National Senior Citizens Law Center
Washington, DC, office
1101 14th Street NW, Suite 400
Washington, DC 20005
Phone: 202-289-6976
Fax: 202-289-7224

Los Angeles office
3435 Wilshire Boulevard, Suite 2860
Los Angeles, CA 90010-1938
Phone: 213-639-0930
Fax: 213-639-0934
http://www.nsclc.org/

U.S. Equal Employment Opportunity Commission
1801 L Street NW
Washington, DC 20507
Phone: 202-663-4900; 800-669-4000
TTY: 202-663-4494
Phone: 1-800-669-4000
http://www.eeoc.gov

U.S. National Institute on Aging
National Institutes of Health (NIH)
Building 31, Room 5C27
31 Center Drive, MSC 2292
Bethesda, MD 20892
Phone: 301-496-1752
http://www.nia.nih.gov/

U.S. Senate Special Committee on Aging
G31 Dirksen Senate Office Building
Washington, DC 20510
Phone: 202-224-5364
Fax: 202-224-8660
http://aging.senate.gov/

International Social Work and Care of Older Adults

OVERVIEW

Population aging was very much a blessing of the 20th century, and it has had major ramifications for the practice of social work throughout the world. This part of the Handbook examines social work with older adults and their families throughout the world. The part begins with an overview chapter by James Lubben and JoAnn Damron-Rodriguez that highlights the major demographic changes taking place in aging societies. A remarkable statistic quoted in that chapter is the tripling of the world's population 65 years of age and older over the next 50 years. As the authors state, the implications of this rapid aging will profoundly shape the 21st century.

The other chapters of this part feature social work practice in selected regions of the world. Both developing and developed nations are represented. Elizabeth Ozanne provides an extensive overview of some of the policies that have evolved as Australia has oscillated between conservative and liberal governments. Iris Chi provides an overview of social work in China, presenting both a historical and a political context for the tremendous aging of the world's most populous nation that is simultaneously experiencing rapid economic development. Japan is another country in the same region that has experienced rapid aging, although it had the benefit of securing economic development prior to the aging of its population. Thus, Japan was able to consider policies and programs that most countries could not. In particular, Japan has instituted one of the most comprehensive forms of long-term care insurance in the world. Judith Phillips offers an overview of social work practice with older adults and families in Europe. She compares and contrasts countries that share common cultural and political histories but have adopted slightly different forms of care. It would be useful to also compare this chapter with that offered by Ozanne, who writes about social work with older adults in Australia.

Osei Darkwa's chapter focuses on developing nations, with a special look at Africa. Sub-Saharan Africa has been hard hit with major health crises that have devastated large segments of its population. Darkwa discusses this crisis and considers ramifications for social work practice with older adults in such countries. Martha Ozawa and Shingo Nakayama provide an overview description of this novel system of care. They also provide an excellent description of the historical and political forces that lead to the adoption of this social program.

The paramount issue of economic security in old age is beyond the purview of this part, but it deserves some notice. Indeed, there is grave concern about the viability of public pensions in many developed countries. Political turmoil also has severe consequences for aging populations, as illustrated by the collapse of the Soviet Union. People who had built trust in one social system to care for them in old age were especially hard hit when those political and social systems suddenly changed. Whereas younger adults could readily adapt and build savings for eventual retirement in the new social system, older adults did not have that luxury and often were left impoverished.

A number of organizations can provide more information on income security in old age. One is the Foundation for International Studies on Social Security, a nonprofit organization that promotes international, multidisciplinary research on social security (its Web page is found at *http://web.inter.nl.net/users/fiss/*). Another international organization that facilitates sharing of information regarding social security is the International Social Security Association (ISSA; *www.issa.int*). The U.S. Social Security Administration also has useful data regarding social security programs in other countries (*www.ssa.gov/international/*). The Organization for Economic Cooperation and Development (OECD), which tracks the economic ramifications of aging societies, has a special Web site that provides access to numerous reports regarding the fiscal, financial, and labor market implications of aging. In addition, the OECD offers many special reports on pensions, social benefits, and systems of health and long-term care. Its Web site is found at *http://www.oecd.org/home/*.

JAMES LUBBEN
JOANN DAMRON-RODRIGUEZ

World Population Aging

87

Longevity was one of the great achievements of the 20th century, and its implications for the 21st century will be profound. From 1999 to 2050, the world population aged 65 and over is expected to triple (U.S. Bureau of the Census, 1996; U.S. National Institute on Aging, 1996). By the year 2030, more than 60 countries of the world will have 2 million or more people who are 65 years of age or older (Kinsella & Velkoff, 2001). Europe and North America presently have the oldest populations in the world and are expected to do so by the year 2030. What is remarkable is how rapidly other regions of the world are aging. As shown in Table 87.1, Oceania, Asia, and Latin America will double the percentage of older people in their populations. The only exception to this pattern of rapid aging societies is sub-Saharan Africa, where serious health problems, most notably the AIDS epidemic, are suppressing the progression toward an aged society.

Developing countries have smaller proportions and smaller absolute numbers of older persons in their societies, but the rate of growth in the aging population is vastly higher in developing countries. For instance, the number of Africans 60 years and older is expected to grow by 146% over the next 25 years. In the Muslim world, stretching from West Africa to Indonesia, the number of older people is expected to grow by an unprecedented 200% to 400% in this same time frame. Even in Nepal, where the elderly constitute only 4% of the population, their annual rate of growth is higher than for the overall population. The rapidity of these demographic shifts creates an extra social burden on developing nations.

An additional demographic shift is in the aging of the older population throughout the world. It is projected that 7% of Europe's population will be 80 years of age or older by the year 2030. The population 80 years and older in the United States was 25 times larger in 2000 than it was in 1900. By 2030, individuals who are octogenarians or older are projected to account for almost 5% of the total U.S. population and more than 25% of the total older adult (65+) population. Among all countries of the world, Japan stands out for the rapid aging of its aged population. In 1975, only 1.1% of Japan's population was 80 years or older. In 2000, almost 4% of its population was 80 years or older, and that percentage is expected to rise to more than 11% by 2030. Among other nations, only Italy and Sweden approach this figure; both of these European countries are expected to have around 9% of their population that is 80 years or older in 2030.

This remarkable population aging has generally taken place in two main stages (Rowe & Kahn, 1999).

TABLE 87.1 Percent Elderly by Age, 2000 and 2030

Region	Year	65 Years and Over	75 Years and Over	80 Years and Over
Europe	2000	15.5	6.6	3.3
	2030	24.3	11.8	7.1
North America	2000	12.6	6.0	3.3
	2030	20.3	9.4	5.4
Oceania	2000	10.2	4.4	2.3
	2030	16.3	7.5	4.4
Asia	2000	6.0	1.9	0.8
	2030	12.0	4.6	2.2
Latin America and Caribbean	2000	5.5	1.9	0.9
	2030	11.6	4.6	2.4
Near East and North Africa	2000	4.3	1.4	0.6
	2030	8.1	2.8	1.3
Sub-Saharan Africa	2000	2.9	0.8	0.3
	2030	3.7	1.3	0.6

From U.S. Bureau of the Census, *An Aging World 2001.*

The first stage was a dramatic reduction in infant mortality and early childhood death rates, accomplished largely through improved public health. As a result, more members of any given birth cohort have a chance to age. The second stage of population aging, which is more recent and ongoing, is characterized by a significant decrease in death rates among middle-aged and older people, attributable largely to improved self-care and medical science. These more recent developments enable more members of any given cohort of older adults to reach very old age.

The astonishing growth in the number of centenarians throughout the world provides an illustration of these phenomena. Kinsella and Velkoff (2001, p. 22) state, "Over the course of history, the odds of living from birth to age 100 may have risen from 1 in 20 million to 1 in 50 for females in low-mortality countries such as Japan and Sweden." The relatively small numbers of centenarians who are currently present in the population make future projections difficult, but it is highly likely that there may be well over 1 million centenarians in the United States citizens by 2050. Some demographers project that the United States might reach this plateau as early as 2030 (Krach & Velkoff, 1999).

North America, Europe, Japan, Australia, and New Zealand are regions or countries whose citizens gained 25 years of life expectancy during the last century alone. This gain in life expectancy was double

that in all of prior human history. Developing countries are also experiencing rapid growth in their older populations due in part to increased life expectancies. These countries continued to contend with significant threats to childhood survival and major public health challenges during much of the 20th century, and so there continues to be a gap in life expectancies between developed nations and developing nations. However, as shown in Table 87.2, this gap has narrowed, and life expectancies in most countries currently are projected to be over 70 years of age. This contrasts with the situation in the 1970s, when life expectancy in developing nations was less than 56 years.

At the same time that people are living longer, fertility rates are plummeting in most regions of the world, as a result of either deliberate public policy (e.g., China) or personal choice (e.g., Italy). Table 87.3

TABLE 87.2 Average Life Expectancies (in Years)

	1970–1975	1997	2025
More developed countries	71.0	74.5	79.2
Less developed countries	55.5	63.6	71.1
World	59.5	65.8	72.4

From WHO Kobe Centre for Health Development, *World Atlas of Ageing, 1998.*

TABLE 87.3 Total Fertility Rates (per Woman)

	1970–1975	*2000–2005*
More developed countries (OECD countries)	2.5	1.8
Less developed countries	5.4	2.8
World	4.5	2.7

From United Nations Human Population Report 2003, p. 253.

TABLE 87.4 Age Cohort Ratios, 2000 and 2030 (Number of Young and/or Older Persons per 100 People 20–64 Years of Age)

		Total (young+old)	*Youth (0–19)*	*Elderly (65+)*
Chile	2000	77	64	13
	2030	70	42	28
China	2000	67	56	12
	2030	65	39	26
Kenya	2000	139	133	7
	2030	70	61	9
Italy	2000	60	31	29
	2030	75	26	49
Malaysia	2000	96	88	8
	2030	79	62	17
Mexico	2000	95	87	8
	2030	67	50	17
United Kingdom	2000	69	43	27
	2030	80	37	42
United States	2000	70	48	21
	2030	87	49	37

From U.S. Bureau of the Census, *An Aging World 2001.*

illustrates this rapid transformation in both economically developed and less developed countries. Most of the more economically developed nations now have about equal numbers of children under 25 years of age and adults 55 years of age and older. Fertility declines in the future of developing countries are occurring over a much shorter period than what occurred in the more developed countries. Population aging is the direct result of moving from a demographic state in which both mortality and fertility are relatively high into a world in which both mortality and fertility rates become relatively low (Higuchi, 1997). An increasing number of Asian and Latin American countries have nearly completed the change from high to low mortality and fertility rates.

Many economic factors are related to these demographic shifts. The dynamics of intergenerational economic exchange may be measured in terms of age cohort ratios, which are a gross measure of dependency within a population and thus are sometimes referred to as *dependency ratios*. These ratios make the gross assumption that people 20 to 64 years of age, supposedly in their prime working years, provide the most essential support for those either too young or too old to be actively participating in the workforce. Obviously, there are some difficulties with such gross assumptions. However, such demographic indices do offer an opportunity to compare and contrast the dramatic age cohort shifts occurring throughout different regions of the world. To illustrate these trends, Table 87.4 provides data on eight countries. The proportional size of the youth cohort in most countries of the world will experience a significant decline. Although the youth cohort will continue to be larger than the aged cohort in most countries in the developing world, the aged cohort will soon surpass the youth cohort in size in most of the economically developed countries. The United States stands out as an exception to the other developed nations in this regard. In the United States, the youth dependency ratio

will be relatively stable over the next 30 years, and so the youth cohort will continue to be larger than the aged cohort. Kenya, typical of sub-Saharan Africa, is the exception to the overall tendency for most countries, whether economically developed or developing, to experience significant increases in aged dependency ratios. Again, this is a symptom of the seriousness of the AIDS epidemic in that part of the world.

Generations in the middle will have dual responsibilities for both younger and older dependent populations, with the number of elderly dependents increasing rapidly. Other factors include a diminution of the cascade of capital between generations. Although some have predicted vast transfers of wealth from one generation to the next, these projections may have failed to adequately account for all the consequences of extreme longevity. As older persons live considerably longer, they use up their assets in late life and have less left as inheritance or for support of younger generations (Lubben & Damron-Rodriguez, 2003; Damron-Rodriguez & Lubben, 2001).

Diversity must also be recognized as an important factor in aging societies. In terms of gender, for example, internationally, women can expect to live longer than men. Women make up 55% of all people over age 65. Although female life expectancy continued to rise into the new century, male life expectancy slowed down or stabilized (United Nations, 1999). The majority of the former Soviet Socialist Republics have a 12-year difference between the life expectancies of women and men. Less-developed countries have a smaller differential, of approximately 2 to 3 years. In developed countries, the gender gap in life expectancy is between 5 and 8 years. The female advantage in life expectancy is partially offset by the higher rates of disability in women. Women live proportionately fewer disability-free years. Internationally, women are more likely to be widowed, to live longer alone and with functional limitations, and to be poor. A major gender issue is the caregiving role of women in the intergenerational family and its subsequent costs physically and economically.

Urban and rural differences must also be considered. Urbanization is progressing rapidly. In 1975 just over one third of the world population was urban; by the year 2000, more than 60% of the population will be living in cities. The migration to cities predominantly involves a younger population, leaving more elderly in rural areas, though there are marked exceptions (Australia, New Zealand, and several Latin American countries). Elderly men are more likely than women to live in rural areas.

The majority of aging societies have groups of persons who have minority status and are marginalized or otherwise socially excluded. In 1990, ethnic minorities made up only 14% of the older U.S. population, with African Americans, Hispanics, and American Indians having markedly lower life expectancies. However, beginning in the early part of the 21st century, the percentage of growth of minority groups will be higher than for majority adults. U.S. ethnic minorities are at greater risk of economic insecurity, poorer health status, and social isolation in late life. Social exclusion due to gender and race over the life course is a major reason that older minority women who live alone are the poorest group in the United States (Wallace, Shneider, Walker, & Ingman, 1992; Wallace, Levy-Stroms, Kington, & Andersen, 1998; Quinn and Smeeding, 1994; Lubben, Weiler, & Chi, 1989). Though relative cultural homogeneity is found in some countries, many countries are multicultural and multiethnic and thus must consider this diversity in designing care systems.

The demographic revolution has a profound impact on the structure of the family. Longevity has created an unprecedented opportunity for inter-generational interaction and an unprecedented level of familial responsibility for elder care. The complex web of kin relationships in many countries creates ties with multiple elders (Bengtson, Rosenthal, & Burton, 1996). In 1900, in the United States, only 21% had a living grandparent, but by 2000, 76% will. Over this same period, the chance of a person over 60 having a parent alive increased from 18% to 44% (Quadagno, 1999). The divorce rate, now 50% of all marriages as compared with 10% at the end of the 19th century, adds to the complexity of the contemporary family.

The dramatic aging of the population, added to other social and demographic factors, has transformed the contemporary family (Pearlin, Aneshenel, & Whitlatch, 1996; Penrod, Kane, & Finch, 1995). As never before, families may contain four or five generations, with fewer members in each generation. This contrasts with the former more intense horizontal linkage with multiple members of a single generation. For example, in the United States only 21% of adults had a living grandparent in 1900, whereas 76% of adults currently do (Quadagno, 1999). Similarly, the chances of a 60-year-old adult having at least one parent still living increased from 8% in 1900 to 44% currently (Quadagno, 1999). Today, many families have multiple elders, parents, parents-in-law, stepparents, aunts, and uncles, for whom they may have some level of responsibility. Overall, families are smaller today but include more generations; this is referred to as the verticalization of the family system and is described as the beanpole family structure. Increasingly families have as many as five living generations (Bengston et al., 1996).

Because the proportion of adult children in relation to older persons is decreasing, the level of support required from adult children for aging parents is increasing. A measure of family dependency is indicated by the parent support ratio (PSR), which divides the population over age 80 by the population aged 50 to 64 years. In 1997, more than 40 countries had a PSR of more than 40, in comparison with only 3 countries in 1975. Table 87.5 illustrates the PSR trends in four representative regions of the world. These ratios clearly show an upward trend among all four regions but also wide variation in both the actual support ratios and the rate of increase. Western Europe will face the greatest increase in these PSRs.

Increased longevity and smaller family size have resulted in potential gaps in an older person's traditional social support network. In some extreme cases, older persons may face the prospect of aging without

TABLE 87.5 Parent Care Support Ratios (People 80+ Over 100 People 50–64 Years)

	1950	2000	2030
South America	4	10	15
Eastern Asia	3	9	17
Western Europe	7	20	37
Western Africa	3	4	7

From U.S. Bureau of the Census, *An Aging World 2001.*

having a son or daughter on whom they may depend for care. For example, Gironda, Lubben, and Atchison (1998) state that currently one fifth of elderly Americans do not have children, and that in the next cohort to reach 65 almost one third will be childless. Traditional norms in Korea call for oldest sons to provide for aging parents. However, approximately 15% of elderly women in Korea have no surviving son, and this figure is expected to rise to 30% by the year 2025 (Kinsella & Velkoff, 2001). Increasing structural gaps in the potential for kinship care will require more attention by policymakers and community health and welfare service providers.

Old-age pensions and health care are two areas that will be especially affected throughout the world as a result of rapid population aging. Widening public pension deficits could soon consume the economic savings of most developed countries (Peterson, 1999). Accordingly, economic security in old age must be an essential element in program and policy planning for aging societies around the world. Similarly, costs associated with providing health care in aging societies are expected to rise dramatically. A recent report from the Organization for Economic Cooperation and Development (OECD) countries indicated that the growth rate for the share of the gross national product (GDP) given over to publicly financed long-term care was likely to rise precipitously in most countries (Jacobzone, 1999). For example, the increase between 2000 and 2020 of Japan's GDP going to long-term care is estimated to be anywhere from 70% to 100%. Many other countries also expected to experience at least a 30% increase during this same 20-year period (World Health Organization Kobe Centre for Health Development, 1998).

There are also some interesting differences in disability rates around the world. In some countries, including Japan and Germany, the growth rate for the disabled is larger than the overall growth rate for older

persons. However, some developed countries are reporting drops in disability rates for the elderly. Disability rates for older persons in the United States have dropped by 1% to 2% annually since 1982. In Canada, the proportion of older persons who reported no disabilities rose from 60% in 1978 to 75% in 1991. In France, older men added 15 months to their disability-free expectancy between 1978 and 1991, and older women added 27 months (World Health Organization Kobe Centre for Health Development, 1999).

In summary, longevity was one of the great achievements of the 20th century, and with proper planning it will continue to be celebrated well into the 21st century. This can be realized if all levels of government work together to create a society for all ages as called for by the United Nations International Year of Older Persons in 1999. A society for all ages would embrace multigenerational equity and meaningful involvement at all life stages and would acknowledge the interdependence of the individual and society. The Active Ageing policy framework put forth by WHO Ageing and Life Course Programme (2002) provides policy strategies for achieving a society for all ages.

Another international beacon for health and welfare planning for aging societies has been the WHO Kobe Centre (WKC), a research center that has published numerous special reports on aging societies and held a number of international planning conferences. In typical public health care philosophy, the WKC approach has promoted older person's self-care capacity through enhanced home and community environments seeking to delay the onset of disability in older persons or prevent it from happening altogether. A unique aspect of the WKC has been its strong focus on the older person within the context of family and community.

Such approaches are likely to be more practical and less costly for economically developing nations than the large medical institution–based programs being promulgated in many economically developed nations (Lubben & Damron-Rodriguez, 2003; Damron-Rodriguez & Lubben, 2001; World Health Organization Kobe Centre for Health Development, 2002). It has been suggested that the nations of the developed world first experienced economic development and then the aging of their societies. In developing nations, these two phenomena are occurring simultaneously, which undoubtedly will alter the options available for health and welfare systems development appropriate for aging societies. Ironically, such community health care approaches may also become attractive models for more economically developed nations that are fast discovering that expensive institution-based programming is not sustainable within the context of rapid aging populations.

REFERENCES

Bengston, V., Rosenthal, C., & Benton, L. (1996). Paradoxes of families and aging. In R. Binstock & L. George (Eds.), *Handbook of aging and the social sciences* (pp. 253–282). San Diego, CA: Academic Press.

Damron-Rodriguez, J., & Lubben, J. E. (2001). *A framework for understanding community health care in ageing societies* (Ageing and Health Technical Series, Report No. 2). Kobe, Japan: WHO Centre for Health Development. Retrieved from *http://www.who.or.jp/ ageing/index.html.*

Gironda, M. W., Lubben, J. E., & Atchison, K. A. (1998). Social support networks of elders without children. *Journal of Gerontological Social Work, 27,* 63–84.

Higuchi, K. (1997). Towards a bright and cheerful aged society with fewer children. In *What is needed for a rapidly aging society* (pp. 45–53). Tokyo: Foreign Press Center.

Jacobzone, S. (1999). The health of older persons in OECD countries: Is it improving fast enough to compensate for population ageing? In *Ageing and health: A global challenge for the 21st century* (pp. 144–161). Proceedings of a WHO symposium in Kobe, Japan, November 10–13, 1998. Kobe, Japan: WHO Kobe Centre.

Kinsella, Kevin, and Victoria A. Velkoff. (2001). *An Aging World: 2001* (U.S. Census Bureau, Series P95/01-1). Washington, DC: U.S. Government Printing Office.

Krach, C. A. & V. A. Velkoff. (1999). *Centenarians in the United States* (U.S. Bureau of the Census, Current Population Reports, Series P23-199RV). Washington, DC: U.S. Government Printing Office.

Lubben, J. E. & Damron-Rodriguez. (2003). An international approach to community health care for older adults. *Family and Community Health, 26,* 338–349.

Lubben, J. E., & Gironda, M. (1997). Social support networks among older people in the United States. In H. Litwin (Ed.), *The social networks of older people* (pp. 143–161). Westport, CT: Praeger.

Lubben, J. E., Weiler, P. G., & Chi, I. (1989). Gender and ethnic differences in the health practices of the elderly poor. *Journal of Clinical Epidemiology, 42,* 725–733.

Pearlin, L., Aneshenel, J. M., & Whitlatch, C. (1996). Caregiving and its social support. In R. Binstock & L. George (Eds.), *Handbook of aging and the social sciences* (pp. 283–302). San Diego, CA: Academic Press.

Penrod, J., Kane, R., Kane, R., & Finch, M. (1995). Who cares? The size, scope, and composition of the caregiver support system. *Gerontologist,* 489–497.

Peterson, P. G. (1999). Gray dawn: The global aging crisis. *Foreign Affairs, 78,* 43–55.

Quadagno, J. (1999). *Aging and the life course.* Boston: McGraw-Hill College.

Quinn, J., & Smeeding, T. (1993). The present and future economic well being of the aged. In R. Burkhauser & D. Salibury (Eds.), *Pensions in a changing economy.* Washington, DC: Employee Benefit Research Institute.

Rowe, J. W., & Kahn, R. L. (1999). *Successful aging.* New York: Pantheon.

United Nations. (1999). *Towards a society for all ages: International year of older persons.* New York.

United Nations Development Programme. (2003). *Human Development Report 2003: Millennium Development Goals: A compact among nations to end human poverty.* New York: Oxford University Press.

U.S. Bureau of the Census. (1999). *World population at a glance: 1998 and beyond* (IB98-4). Washington, DC: U.S. Government Printing Office.

U.S. National Institute on Aging. (1996). *Global Aging in the 21st Century.* Washington, DC.

Wallace, S. P., Levy-Stroms, L., Kington, R. S., & Andersen, R. M. (1998). The persistence of race and ethnicity in the use of long-term care. *Journals of Gerontology. B Series, Psychological Sciences and Social Sciences, 53*(2), S104–12.

Wallace, S. P., Snyder, J. C., Walker, G. K., & Ingman, S. R. (1992). Racial differences among users of long-term care. *Research on Aging, 14,* 471B495.

World Health Organization. (2002). Active ageing: A policy framework. Geneva, WHO Ageing and Life Course Programme. Retrieved from *http://www.who. int/hpr/ageing/ActiveAgeingPolicyFrame.pdf*

World Health Organization Kobe Centre for Health Development. (1998). *World atlas of ageing.* Kobe, Japan: Centre for Health Development.

World Health Organization Kobe Centre for Health Development. (1999). *Aging and health: A global challenge for the 21st century.* Proceedings of a WHO symposium in Kobe, Japan, November 10–13, 1998. Kobe, Japan: WHO Kobe Centre.

World Health Organization Kobe Centre for Health Development. (2002). *Development of health and welfare systems: Adjusting to ageing.* Proceedings of a WHO Kobe Centre symposium in Valencia, Spain, April 1–4, 2002. Kobe, Japan: WHO Kobe Centre.

Gerontological social work is not well articulated and defined as a distinctive area of practice in Australia despite some centers of innovation around the country. This lack of definition relates to the small size of the professionally trained workforce in Australia, the absence of strong professional and educational leadership, and the failure to articulate social work's distinctive contribution relative to other professional groups. Opportunities for change in the current period come from recent proactive federal government policy initiatives in relation to population aging, the leadership of a relatively small group of professional gerontologists from a range of disciplines, and emergent pressures from a service system and frontline social work practitioners confronting increasing demands from aging baby boomers encountering the new challenges of parent care.

There have always been some notable individual pioneers in different areas of social work practice with the elderly. What is different in the current period is the need for a broader institutional approach. Responses from schools of social work and the organized profession to population aging have been slow to develop, but there have been, over the last decade, several major initiatives in teaching, research, and practice from individual schools and agencies, often in partnership with broader interdisciplinary gerontological consortia and coalitions.

THE DEMOGRAPHICS OF POPULATION AGING IN AUSTRALIA

The Australian population is aging numerically, in that the number of older people is increasing, and structurally, in that the proportion of people who are aged 65 and over is rising. At the date of the last census in 2002, people aged 65 years and over represented approximately 12.7% of Australia's total population, or 2.5 million people (Australian Institute of Health and Welfare [AIHW], 2002), with 54% aged 65–74 years, 35% aged 75–84, and 11% aged 85 and over. Thus, whereas half of all older people were aged between 65 and 74, there was a significant minority (more than 280,000) aged 85 and over. Fifty-six percent of older people (65+) were women. One in four people over 65 in Australia were born in a non-English-speaking country, and the ethnic diversity of the population is increasing with recent migration waves. Australian aboriginal life expectancy represent approximately 1% of the total population. The aborigines' life expectancy is, however, considerably lower than that of the gen-

ELIZABETH OZANNE

Older Adults in Australia

eral population, and by and large they have not participated in the demographic longevity revolution.

POLICY RESPONSES TO POPULATION AGING IN AUSTRALIA

Since the mid-1980s, Australia has taken a strategic and planned approach to population aging with a series of policy initiatives from successive governments of both social democratic and conservative persuasion (Gibson, 1998; Borowski, Encel, & Ozanne, 1997; Kendig & Duckett, 2001). Under the Labor (social democratic) government of Hawke/Keating, 1972–1996, services for the aged were reviewed and restructured with a major expansion of community care services and the introduction of new accreditation requirements to regulate quality in long-term residential care (Commonwealth Department of Health, Housing and Community Services, 1991; Ozanne, 2000, 2001).

Under the Howard Liberal (Conservative) government, 1996–2004, which has just won a fourth term with an increased majority, policy focus has shifted from an initial cost-cutting preoccupation (National Commission of Audit, 1996) to a more intergenerational and future social investment orientation (Costello, 2002; Bishop, 2004). This shift in thinking was first articulated by the commonwealth treasurer Peter Costello in his Intergenerational Report in 2002 and in a later paper delivered in 2004 in which he spelled out the key demographic challenges he perceived Australia to be confronting (Costello, 2004). Under the Howard government the service range has continued to expand, but there has also been more focus on fiscal efficiency and a much greater shift to consumers carrying more of the financial burden of their care. Several reviews of residential and community care have been undertaken, leading to the integration of high (nursing home) and low (hostel) care, the introduction of a new accreditation and certification system requiring three yearly audits, major expansion of home-based service delivery, and the continued exploration of new funding mechanisms (Hogan, 2004; Bishop, 2004a, 2004b).

THE SOCIAL WORK WORKFORCE IN AUSTRALIA: ITS SIZE AND DISTRIBUTION

The total social work workforce in Australia is relatively small, compared, say, with that of nursing, and is estimated to be approximately 12,000 persons (Australian Association of Social Workers, 2004). Australian social workers do not have registration of title, so it is often difficult to distinguish professionally accredited and nonaccredited degrees in official government statistics. The most recent official ABS data (Australian Bureau of Statistics, 1997) indicate that there were 9,111 persons calling themselves social workers. This was a 27% increase between 1996 and 2001, with the substantial part of this increase occurring in the nongovernment sector (52%) as opposed to the government sector (12%). The biggest sector increases were in the category of welfare workers (without professional qualification), which grew 45%, from 6,204 to 8,987, in same period. Community workers are the numerically largest group in the community services sector, with a total of 17,101 workers in 2001 (Healy, 2004; AIHW, 2001).

Work with the aged has historically been a traditional area of social work practice in Australia, particularly during the period when the situation of the aged was more synonymous with poverty than it is today (Harding, King, & Kelly, 2002). In more recent decades the emergence of specializations in health, mental health, and child welfare has to some degree stolen the limelight, though with shifting demographics a focus on the aged is reemerging.

There is very little accurate information on the proportion of social workers who identify their primary field of practice as work with older persons. Relatively few members of the Australian Association of Social Workers (AASW) identify gerontology as their primary field of practice. However, it is estimated that approximately one third of clients in health and welfare agencies are 65 years and over, so that people over 65 constitute a significant focus for most social work practitioners.

THE PLACE OF AGING IN THE SOCIAL WORK CURRICULUM

The primary qualification for accreditation by the AASW is the bachelor of social work, which is a 2-year degree following completion of a first degree in the behavioral and social sciences. The master's qualification in Australia is primarily taken as an advanced practice coursework degree or as a research thesis. The Ph.D. is primarily a research qualification. There are 22 schools of social work in Australia, which graduate approximately 700 students annually.

Despite social work's historical commitment to the aged, specialization in aging has been slow to develop in social work courses (Ozanne, 1989; Heycox, 1989; Hugman, 2000; Wiles, 2001), with only approximately 50% of social work schools offering aged-specific content and electives. Those schools, however, that have had a long commitment to aging studies have integrated material on aging across their curriculum, as well as offering a number of elective studies at the bachelor's and master's levels (Rosenman, 1988; Lubben, Damron-Rodriguez, & Beck, 1992). Several have also developed research centers on gerontology or are affiliated with multidisciplinary university centers, for example, Melbourne, Queensland, and Curtin Universities.

In the last half decade, external pressures on the tertiary education sector from government and national research councils to address population aging as a national priority have led to the development of university-wide gerontological consortia in which social work schools have variously participated. The sectors that employ the majority of workers in aged care are health, mental health, and community care services across the federal, state, and local government and nongovernment sectors (AIHW 2001).

Since the late 1980s there have been several special editions of the journal *Australian Social Work* published on aged care and several editorials calling on social workers to respond to the challenge of population aging (Jacques, 1989; Rosenman, 1988; Ozanne, 1998; Squires, 1998), the last occurring in the International Year of Older Persons. Social workers have also contributed to the *Australasian Journal on Ageing,* a publication of the Australian Association of Gerontology (Tilse, Wilson, & Setterlund, 2003; Hugman, 2001) and to international journals and collections on social work practice with the elderly (Setterlund, Tilse, Worrall, Wilson, & Hickson, 2002; Brennan, 1988; George, 1997).

WORKFORCE ANALYSIS IN RELATION TO POPULATION AGING

There is still a failure in Australia to identify the social and relational impact of an aging society. Workforce issues so far have been defined fairly narrowly as primarily health related, with a focus on nursing and personal care or direct care issues. An increasing number of reports, however, have been commissioned by government at various levels. Similarly, different industry sectors, philanthropic funds, and some nongovernment organizations have addressed various subpopulations of the aged care workforce. These include studies of residential care workers (Richardson & Martin, 2004), personal care workers (Angley & Newman, 2002), nurses (Australian Health Ministers' Conference, 2004), and community care workers (Healy, 2004), as well as the aged care workforce more generally (Wheeler, 2002).

There has been virtually no explicit work done in Australia on likely future demand of an aging population for human service professionals in general or social workers in particular, though several research theses are under way in this area. There is, however, evidence of a considerable shortfall emerging in case manager and policy planning positions in aged-related work in community care services, health and mental health, and family services, based on the present difficulty in filling these positions with suitably qualified persons. These professional workforce issues have yet to be seriously addressed.

CORE TASKS AND COMPETENCIES IN SOCIAL WORK PRACTICE WITH OLDER ADULTS

The debate about core competencies in relation to practice with an older population in Australia has been informed by several government statements about basic training competencies in aged care for various levels in the community services sector (Health, 2002), as well as more recent statements from the National Strategy for an Ageing Australia (Bishop, 2000) in terms of how the country might achieve "world-class" aged care practice standards. The AASW special portfolio group on aging has recently released for comment on their national Web site a three-page statement of Competent Practice for Professional Social Workers Working in Aged Care (2004; *http://www.aasw.asn.au*).

THE CONTEXT AND SETTINGS FOR SOCIAL WORK PRACTICE WITH OLDER ADULTS

The primary fields in which social workers work with older adults in Australia are health, mental health, community care, and family support services. The majority of social workers tend to be involved in direct service delivery as caseworkers or care managers, with approximately one third in program management or more senior policy and planning roles (AIHW, 2001).

Individual counseling family and intergenerational casework occurs primarily in family support services, community health and mental health centers, local government services, postacute rehabilitation services, and nongovernment aged and disability services and in private practice. Intergenerational family casework and group work are also practiced in these settings.

There has been a major expansion of community care services in Australia since the mid-1980s, from a small and fairly basic set of home support–type services to a broad mix of service types and a range of more and less intensive home support packages requiring active brokering and care coordination. Under new Extended Care at Home Packages (EACH), older persons can now be maintained at home even with very high levels of disability. Local governments employ social workers as assessment officers, care managers, and directors of aged and disability services. Social workers are also part of core staff groups in not-for-profit intensive home care agencies as care managers.

The most common form of social work practice with older adults is in acute and postacute care in hospitals and rehabilitation centers as program coordinators, discharge planners, case managers, and direct care workers. Social workers are key members of aged care assessment teams, which serve as gatekeepers to long-term care facilities and have a strategic role in relation to family support in interdisciplinary acute and postacute rehabilitation teams.

Social workers have key roles in psychogeriatric assessment teams and services, such as the Cognitive Dementia Assessment and Management Services (CADMS), which are focused on early diagnosis of dementia and appropriate referral for family members. They are also active in Alzheimer's advocacy organizations across Australia and in running the Living With Dementia group work program nationally.

Social work roles in long-term residential care are less well developed in Australia than in some other countries where social workers take more key roles in managing long-term care facilities. Managers of these facilities in Australia tend to be nurses (if they have qualifications at all), and social workers are employed primarily in direct care manager and service delivery roles in public high-level care facilities as caseworkers, family workers, group workers, and discharge planners.

Social work has had a long-term commitment to end-of-life care across a range of settings from the acute hospital to hospice to coronial services. There has been a major review and restructuring of end-of-life services over recent decades to keep pace with the demands of population aging and to ensure a timely, high, and equitable standard of response across all service types. Social workers, in partnership with other professional groups, have taken a strategic role in several of these developments.

Case management has seen steady development as a mode of practice in Australia over the last couple of decades in health, mental health, child welfare, vocational rehabilitation disability, and gerontology (Ozanne, 1996). The National Case Management Society, which was formed in Australia in 1998, holds an annual conference and produces a quarterly journal. Social workers have been active in this development both in broadening the approach to case management from a primarily health to more psychosocially focused activity and in introducing a diversity of practice populations. Two texts on case management practice in Australia have been published by social workers in concert with others (Gursansky, Harvey, & Kennedy, 2003; Ozanne, Howe, & Selby-Smith, 1990).

Australia has a universal health care system, Medicare, funded from taxation and a small population co-payment. Health care is thus still largely a public system, and Australia has so far not seen the development of large-scale managed care providers. New forms of public regional coordinated and integrated health care delivery systems are, however, being trialed, and these schemes increasingly mandate some form of case or care management as the preferred mode of practice (Fine, 1999; O'Looney, 1993; Silagy et al., 1999; Scotton, 1998; Lubben & Damron-Rodriquez, 2003).

Increasingly, private practice social workers have encountered the impact of population aging on individuals and families. Private practitioners are involved in intergenerational family counseling in nuclear and reconstituted families. In addition, social workers in private practice have encountered increased instances of having to assist families in a much longer-lived society with major life course transitions around divorce, widowhood, retrenchment, and retirement.

In the last decade numerous new social work roles have been created in the aged and community care service system as existing services have expanded and new service types have been created. Social workers have taken up new roles on guardianship and administration tribunals, as members, investigators, and guardians. They have assumed roles as complaints officers and ombudsmen in new quality assurance arrangements in health care. They have also become key players in aged care assessment teams, cognitive assessment and dementia management services, and care coordinators in rapidly expanding home care services implementing a range of new flexible and innovative home care packages.

WORK WITH UNDERSERVED AT-RISK POPULATIONS

In the Australian context, older populations identified as at particular risk are Aboriginal and Torres Strait Islanders, culturally and linguistically diverse populations, dementia sufferers and their caretakers, low-income and homeless aged, and rural and remote dwellers. Social workers are active in the targeted delivery of services to these groups, which are explicitly recognized in current government policy and program initiatives. There are also several underrecognized and underserved populations, for instance, older gay, lesbian, intersex, and transgender populations, the older disabled and older prisoners. Individual social workers have highlighted the plight of these populations and advocated for more explicit attention to their needs (Harrison, 1999; Bigby, Gordon, & Ozanne, 2002).

AGED ADVOCACY AND THE POLITICS OF AGING IN AUSTRALIA

Social workers have taken a prominent role in heading up some of the major aged advocacy organizations and peak bodies in Australia in both CEO and policy officer positions. Through these activities, several have also taken leadership positions in the International Federation of Ageing and regional Asia Pacific aged policy forums (George, 1997). Social workers have been active in the establishment of various self-help and advocacy organizations, like the Alzheimer's Society and the Carers Association, and hold roles as policy officers and researchers in these organizations.

As government has taken a more proactive role in the last decade in restructuring the service system in relation to an older population, so also key aged advocacy bodies and national councils have formed new coalitions and engaged in partnering discussions and mergers to increase their power and influence on government. Social workers have been active in these negotiations and in many instances have taken a leading role in pressing both industry and consumer claims (National Aged Care Alliance, 2004; Ozanne & Keogh, 2003).

VISIONING THE FUTURE

Recently in Australia the Myer Foundation, a philanthropic fund, sponsored the 2020 Vision project (Myer Foundation, 2003) to take an independent look at the present and future impact of population aging on health, income security, community services, housing, technology, and workforce development. Several reports were commissioned and forums held around the country, many in partnership with government and other interest groups, to promote debate on population aging and to push various contemporary campaigns related to aged housing, caregiver support, and expansion of community care (*www.agedcare.org.au/coalition/*). A recent independent evaluation of the project (Muller, 2004) concluded that it had had a major impact on promoting debate and acted as a significant stimulus to both government and the sector to engage in more proactive leadership in relation to population aging. The principal project officer driving this project was a social worker with a long history in aged care.

AN AGENDA FOR FUTURE ACTION

It is timely for social work in Australia to move ahead on a number of fronts:

1. *Defining the social work contribution to the quality of life of older persons:* There is perhaps a need in Australian social work circles and beyond to define more explicitly the social work contribution by ratifying a core national statement of knowledge, values and skills and articulating more explicitly to external publics what is unique about social work's focus in this area of practice.
2. *Mobilizing more effectively existing practitioner resources:* Frontline workers are presently mediating demands from aging baby boomers, often without specific training in gerontology or any continuing and further education backup from their professional organization or social work schools. There needs to be a two-way process whereby their frontline experience is mined (Epstein & Blumenfield, 2001) but also supported by appropriate developmental opportunities so practitioners might hone their skills in advanced provider sectors and research with older persons.
3. *Development of innovative field practicums:* Service reform has been an active part of govern-

ment restructuring in Australian aged services over the last decade and a half. In this period quite a lot of new service settings and practice models have been developed, pioneered by on-the-ground practitioners working collaboratively with other disciplines. These services are often also a part of larger regional service systems and networks. They represent the front line of change and are valuable primary training sites for social work students. Designing, supporting, and resourcing innovative field units in these settings is critical for the future training of students.

4. *National training institutes for faculty/postgraduate students:* Achieving funding support from some of the government aging workforce initiatives or a philanthropic body to support national social work training institutes for faculty and/or postgraduate students in gerontology would be one way to foster and develop teaching and research capacity in schools of social work. This might also be undertaken collaboratively with the new national Healthy Ageing Research Network.

5. *Emerging researcher forums:* Given the relatively small critical mass of gerontologists and social workers around the country, support for this type of event would appear essential to reinforce emergent research capacity.

6. *Funding for postgraduate scholarships:* There has virtually been no development of dedicated gerontological social work scholarships in Australia. The only scholarships presently available for master's, doctoral, and postdoctoral studies rely on individual faculty building in such scholarships to their individual grant applications. Philanthropic and government funding of dedicated scholarships is an option that would be timely to explore.

7. *Collaborating on joint research projects:* In order to increase their strike rate in gerontological research, social workers probably need to take maximum advantage of the ARC/MHNRC Ageing Well Research Network initiative to partner with colleagues from other disciplines on topics relevant to social work's core concerns website is *www.ageingwell.edu.av*. International collaborative research with Pacific Rim countries and gerontological centers in the United States, the United Kingdom, and Europe would help further this agenda.

8. *Visiting scholars exchange program:* Social work should perhaps take more advantage than it presently does of the R.M. Gibson Traveling Scholarship in Gerontology sponsored by the Australian Association of Gerontology in bringing key overseas social work gerontologists to Australia. Australian faculty would also greatly benefit from the opportunity for exchange with some of the key gerontological centers in the United States and Europe.

REFERENCES

Angley, P., & Newman, B. (2002). *Who will care? The recruitment and retention of community care (aged and disability) workers.* Brotherhood of St. Laurence, Melbourne, Australia.

Australian Association of Social Workers. (2004). *Communication with membership officer.* Retrieved from *http://www.aasw.asn.au*

Australian Bureau of Statistics. (1997). *Australian standard classification of occupations* (2nd ed.). Canberra, Australia: Author.

Australian Health Ministers' Conference. (2004). *National Health Workforce strategic framework.* Sydney, Australia: National Health Workforce Secretariat.

Australian Institute of Health and Welfare. (2001). *Health and community services labour force 1996* (National Health Labour Force Series No. 19). Canberra, Australia: Author.

Australian Institute of Health and Welfare. (2004). Ageing and aged care. In *Australia's welfare 2003* (pp. 215–329). Canberra, Australia: Author.

Bigby, C., Gordon, M., & Ozanne, E. (2002). Facilitating transition: Elements of successful case management practice for older parents of adults with intellectual disability. *Journal of Gerontological Social Work, 37*(3/4), 25–44.

Bishop, B. (2000). *National strategy for an ageing Australia* (World Class Care Discussion Paper). Canberra, Australia: Commonwealth of Australia.

Bishop, Hon J. (2004a). *Investing in Australia's aged care: More places, better care.* Canberra, Australia: Commonwealth of Australia, Australian Government Department of Health and Ageing.

Bishop, Hon J. (2004b). The way forward: A new strategy for community care. Canberra, Australia: Commonwealth of Australia, Australian Government Department of Health and Ageing.

Borowski, A., Encel, S., & Ozanne, E. (1997). *Ageing and social policy in Australia.* Melbourne: Cambridge University Press.

Brennan, Ann. (1988). Perspectives on Australian social Service delivery and social work practice in gerontology. In Merl C. Hokenstad & Katherine A. Kendall (Eds.), *Gerontological social work: International perspectives* (pp. 17–40). New York: Haworth Press.

Commonwealth Department of Health, Housing and Community Services. (1991). Aged care reform strategy mid-Term review 1990–91. Canberra, Australia: Australian Government Publishing Service.

Costello, The Hon P. (2002). *Intergenerational Report 2002–3* (Budget Paper No. 5). Canberra: Treasurer of the Commonwealth of Australia.

Costello, The Hon Peter. (2004, February 24). *Australia's demographic challenges.* Speech given by the Treasurer of the Commonwealth of Australia, Sydney.

Fine, M. D. (1999). Coordinating health, extended care and community support services: Reforming aged care, Australia. *Journal of Aging and Social Policy, 11,* 67–90.

George, Janet. (1997). Global graying: What role for social work? In M. C. Hokenstad & James Midgley (Eds.), *Issues in international social work: Global challenges for a new century* (pp. 57–73). Washington, D.C.: NASW Press.

Gibson, D. (1998). *Aged care: Old policies, new problems.* Cambridge, England: Cambridge University Press.

Gursansky, D., Harvey, J., & Kennedy, R. (2003). *Case management: Policy, practice and professional business.* Crows Nest, Australia: Allen and Unwin.

Harding, Ann, King, A., & Kelly, S. (2002). Incomes and assets of older Australians: Trends and policy implications. *Agenda, 9*(1), 3–18.

Harrison, J. (1999). A lavender pink grey power: Gay and lesbian gerontology in Australia. *Australasian Journal on Ageing, 18*(1), 32–47.

Healy, Karen. (2004). Social workers in the new human services marketplace: Trends, challenges and responses. *Australian Social Work, 57*(2), 103–114.

Heycox, Karen. (1989). Self-imposed limitations: Social work with the elderly. *Australian Social Work, 42*(3), 17–23.

Hogan, W. P. (2004). *Review of pricing arrangements in residential aged care.* Canberra, Australia: Commonwealth of Australia.

Hugman, R. (2000). Older people and their families: Rethinking the social work task? *Australian Social Work, 53*(1), 3–8.

Hugman, R. (2001). Ageing in space. *Australasian Journal on Ageing, 20*(3), 57–65.

Jacques, Anne. (1989). Special issues on ageing [Editorial]. *Australian Social Work, 42*(3), 1–2.

Kendig, H., & Duckett, S. (2001). *Australian directions in aged care: The generation of policies for generations of older people* (Australian Health Policy Institute, Commissioned Paper Series). Sydney, Australia: Australian Health Policy Institute, University of Sydney.

Lubben, J. E., & Damron-Rodriguez, J. (2003). An international approach to community health care for older adults. *Family and Community Health, 26,* 338–349.

Lubben, J., Damron-Rodriguez, J., & Beck, J. C. (1992). A national survey of aging curriculum in schools of social work. *Journal of Gerontological Social Work, 18,* 157–171.

Muller, Dennis. (2004). Evaluation of 2020: A Vision for Aged Care in Australia. Melbourne: Saulwick Muller Research.

Myer Foundation. (2003). *2020: A vision for aged care in Australia.* Melbourne, Australia: Myer Foundation.

National Aged Care Alliance. (2004). *Capital creation in residential aged care facilities.* Retrieved from http://www.naca.asn.au

National Commission of Audit. (1996, June). *Report to the commonwealth government.* Canberra, Australia: Australian Government Publishing Service.

O'Looney, J. (1993). Beyond privatization and service integration: Organizational models for service delivery. *Social Service Review, 68,* 501–534.

Ozanne, E. (1989). Ageing in the social work curriculum at Melbourne University, *Australian Journal on Ageing, 8*(2), 12–15.

Ozanne, E. (1998). 1999 International Year of Older Persons: Towards a society for all ages [Editorial]. *Australian Social Work, 51*(4), 2–3.

Ozanne, E. (2000). Constructing and reconstructing old age: The evolution of aged policy in Australia. In A. McMahon, J. Thomson, & C. Williams (Eds.), *Understanding the Australian welfare state: Key documents and themes* (pp. 185–198). Croydon, England: Tertiary Press.

Ozanne, E. (2001). Aged care in the new millennium: Retrospect and prospect. In Theresa Cluning (Ed.), *Ageing at home: Practical approaches to community care* (pp. 3–18). Melbourne, Australia: Ausmed Publications.

Ozanne, E., Howe, A., & Selby-Smith, C. (Eds.). (1990). *Community care policy and practice: New directions for Australia.* Melbourne, Australia: Faculty of Economics and Commerce, Monash University.

Ozanne, E., & Keogh, B. (2003). Interlinking theory and method in an analysis of an aged advocacy group. *Australian and New Zealand Third Sector Review, 8*(3), 107–120.

Richardson, S., & Martin, B. (2004). *The care of older Australians: A picture of the residential aged care workforce.* Adelaide, Australia: National Institute of Labour Studies, Flinders University.

Rosenman, L. (1988). Social work and the aged in Australia [Editorial]. *Australian Social Work, 41*(1), 2–3.

Scotton, Richard. (1999). Managed competition. In G. Mooney & R. Scotten (Eds.), *Economics and Australian health policy* (pp. 214–231). Sydney: Allen and Unwin.

Setterlund, D., Tilse, C., Worrall, L., Wilson, J., & Hickson, L. (2002). Participation and older people: Meaning, theory and practice. *Asia Pacific Journal of Social Work, 12,* 44–59.

Silagy, C., Pekarsky, B., Leigh, J., Fagg, B., Quigley, R., Masters, G., et al. (1999). *The Australian Coordinated Care Trials: Interim national evaluation summary.* Canberra: Department of Health and Aged Care.

Squires, Barbara. (1998). Aged care reforms [Editorial]. *Australian Social Work, 51*(1), 2.

Tilse, C., Wilson, J., & Setterlund, D. (2003). The mismanagement of the assets of older people: The concerns and actions of aged care practitioners in Queensland. *Australasian Journal on Ageing, 22*(1), 9–14.

Wheeler, Lorraine. (2002). *Resisting the quick fix: Workforce planning to deliver services to older Australians 2020.* Paper commissioned for 2020: A Vision for Aged Care in Australia. Melbourne, Australia: Myer Foundation.

Wiles, David. (2001). Gerontological social work. In Margaret Allston & Jennifer McKinnon (Eds.), *Social work fields of practice* (pp. 154–167). South Melbourne: Oxford University Press.

KEY WEB SITE ADDRESSES: AGING/AUSTRALIA

Government Agencies

Aged Care Standards and Accreditation Agency: *http://www.accreditation.aust.com*

Ageing Research Online: *http://www.aro.gov.au*

Australian Bureau of Statistics: *http://www.abs.gov.au*

Australian Federal Government: *http://www.fed.gov.au*

Australian Institute of Health and Welfare: *http://www.aihw.gov.au*

Carelink Centres: http://commcarelink.health.gov.au/

Department of Employment and Workplace Relations: *http://www.dewr.gov.au*

Department of Family and Community Services: *http://www.facs.gov.au*

Department of Health and Ageing: *http://www.health.gov.au*

Department of Veterans' Affairs: *http://www.dva.gov.au*

Health Insurance Commission: *http://www.hic.gov.au*

Minister for Ageing, Julie Bishop MP: *http://www.aph.gov.au/house/members/member*

Minister for Employment and Workplace Relations, Kevin Andrews MP: *http://www.aph.gov.au/house/members/member*

Minister for Health, Tony Abbott MP: *http://www.aph.gov.au/senate/senators*

National Centre for Social and Economic Modeling: *http://www.natsem.canberra.edu.au*

National Health and Medical Research Council: *http://www.nhmrc.health.gov.au/index.htm*

Office of the Commissioner for Complaints: *http://www.cfc.health.gov.au*

Office of Older Australians: *http://www.olderaustralians.gov.au*

Productivity Commission: *http://www.pc.gov.au*

Treasurer, Commonwealth of Australia, the Hon Peter Costello MP *http://www.treasurer.gov.au/tsr*

Professional Associations/Alliances

Australian Association of Gerontology: *http://www.aag.asn.au*

Australian Association of Social Workers: *http://www.aasw.asn.au*

Australian Geriatrics Society: *http://www.ags.asn.au*

Case Management Society of Australia: *www.cmsa.org.au*

Special-Interest Groups

Alzheimer's Association Australia Inc: *http://www.alzheimers.org.au*

Carer's Australia: http://www.carers.asn.au

Industry Bodies

Aged and Community Services Australia: *http://www.agedcare.org.au*

Council on the Ageing/National Seniors: *http://www.cota.org.au*

National Aged Care Alliance: *http://www.naca.asn.au*

Philanthropic Funds Interested in Aging

Myer Foundation: *http://www.myerfoundation.org.au*

Research Network

Australian Research Council/National Health and Medical Research Council Research Network on Ageing Well: *http://www.ageingwell.edu.au*

IRIS CHI

Older Adults in China

China, the world's most populous country, has been experiencing continued low fertility since adopting its one-child policy in 1979. All demographic indicators suggest that China is already an aging society. More than 10% of the total population is aged 60 years and older (China Population Information and Research Center, 2003). According to China's fifth national census in 2000, the nation has a population of nearly 1.3 billion, with an annual growth rate of 1.07% (National Bureau of Statistics of China, 2001). In addition, the population aged 60 and over was increasing at an annual rate of 3%, and the oldest elderly population (aged 80 and above) was increasing at an annual rate of 5% (National Bureau of Statistics of China, 2001). By the year 2040, a predicted 397 million people, or more than 28% of China's population, will be aged 60 or over (United Nations, 2003), more than the current population of France, Germany, Italy, Japan, and the United Kingdom combined (Jackson & Howe, 2004). China's total fertility rate dropped from about 7.5 in 1963 (Poston & Duan, 2000) to 1.8 in 2002 (China Population Information and Research Center, 2003). This rapid transition from a relatively young to a relatively old population is unprecedented.

Chinese population experts believe there will be four periods of population aging, beginning with an initial acceleration around 2000, a rapid increase in 2010, a peak in 2040, and a slowdown that will finally stabilize around 2060. Population aging can affect the broader socioeconomic system. In China, the total dependency ratio, which is a ratio of the nonworking population (people under age 15 and those 65 and over) to the working population (people aged 15 to 64), will increase from 59 per 100 in 2000 to 77 per 100 in 2050 (China Population Information and Research Center, 2003). The general trend is for the youth dependency ratio to decrease while the old-age dependency ratio rapidly increases. Projections show that by 2025, an average of 14 Chinese elderly will have to be supported by every 100 working-age people, compared with only 6 in 1990. This rapid increase in the number of elderly may hinder future economic growth as expenditures related to social security and other related social services experience parallel increases (Jackson & Howe, 2004; Zhang, 2002). This demographic change will affect not only the labor supply but also retirement policies and social norms.

The emerging issue of who will care for the elderly in China has attracted considerable attention from common people, demographers, and government officials. No clear solution to these problems has yet been found. It is both urgent and necessary for China to find the solutions to meet the challenges of its aging population. Some economists and sociologists believe that the way to deal with the negative effects of an aging population is to maintain a high rate of economic growth (Zhang, 2002). The relationship between the two is extremely complex, however, warranting much continued study. Whether China could find a strategic move to simultaneously solve the emerging aging issue and maintain economic growth is a question of great interest for gerontologists all over the world.

SOCIAL WORK IN CHINA

Social work has experienced three stages in China since the 1920s: introduction, abolishment, and reinstatement (Xia & Guo, 2002). Social work was introduced to China in 1922 by missionaries. Various types of social services were developed by religious organizations for disadvantaged people such as poor, sick, and disabled groups. Only a few faith-based universities and colleges located in east coast cities had teaching programs at that time to train a handful of social workers, for instance, Jinan University in Shandong and Ginling Women's College in Nanjing. Like many other universities, these colleges were forced to either close their programs or move to western or southern villages during a series of wars: the Japanese Invasion/World War II and civil war. After the Communist Party seized governmental control in 1949, both social work education and missionary activities were prohibited. Not until 40 years later, in 1988, was the first social work education meeting held in Beijing. The Chinese Association of Social Work Education was established in 1994 with only 20 social work programs. Nonetheless, currently there are more than 150 registered programs teaching social work in various Chinese universities and colleges. On average, these programs train more than 4,000 social work graduates per year. These graduates may or may not work in social work practice settings or social service programs.

Most of the social services in mainland China are subsumed under government organizations such as the Ministry of Civil Affairs, Youth League, Women's Federation, work units, street organizations, and the Rehabilitative Federation. These organizations used to hire individuals without social work training, usually high school or college graduates, to deliver services to their clients. Some of these organizations have their own training institutes, which provide both pre-service and in-service training to their staff members. In mid-1970s, the concept of social work and its prac-

tice were introduced to China from Hong Kong and other countries. Many of these training institutes began to develop social work programs in the late 1970s for their cadres.

In more recent years, the Chinese government has adopted a different approach in delivering welfare services. Instead of being a service provider, the government now focuses more on policy and planning, specifically on establishing the social security system under the market economy. Current policy encourages civil society and nongovernment organizations (NGOs) to take up the role of providing direct services. The work units now operate under the market economy, which requires self-sufficiency or making a profit. Many of these work units, which used to provide welfare services to their employees, are no longer taking up this responsibility. Therefore, more and more NGOs are being developed in various parts of mainland China and are now running various social services, ranging from child welfare to care for the aged. Therefore, social work in China has a tremendous market in the public, nonprofit, and private sectors. As with the development of the social security system, institutional social work in China is expected to make great progress in the near future (Xia & Guo, 2002).

On the other hand, social work professional development in Chinese societies outside mainland China, such as Hong Kong, Macau, Singapore, and Taiwan, has followed a different path. For instance, Hong Kong was a colony of Britian until 1997, and social work there has followed a British model. Five out of seven publicly funded universities and one private college provide social work training at various levels, including diploma, bachelor, master's, and doctorate, and more than 500 NGOs provide various kinds of social services. The Hong Kong government has been the primary funding source for both social work training and social service programs. In recent years, due to the aging population, the government has devoted more attention and resources to developing elderly programs. Taiwan, Singapore, and Macau have followed different social work development paths from that in Hong Kong. Nonetheless, there is an increasing emphasis on old-age social policies and program development in the last decade in these places, all of which are facing the challenges of a rapidly aging population.

FILIAL PIETY, FAMILY, AND CAREGIVING

In comparison with other cultures, more gerontology papers about Chinese older adults are related to family and filial piety (Chow, 1999; Chi & Chui, 1999), mainly because of the strong family influences on the quality of later life for Chinese older adults (Chou & Chi, 2001; Zimmer, 2002). Chinese family structures traditionally cluster around relatives who assist one another, and blood tie relationships are very important within each family. According to Chinese tradition, old age is a golden time of life, when one can harvest the rewards of lifelong efforts at establishing a family (Cooney & Shi, 1999). Successful aging in China is often measured by how well one's family is doing rather than by one's own achievements. A yardstick used to measure successful aging among the Chinese is whether one can enjoy filial treatment from one's offspring (Ho, 1994; Woo, Ho, & Lau, 1998). Over the past 2,000 years, virtually every dynasty has adopted Confucian philosophy as state orthodoxy. As such, the virtue of filial piety became the cornerstone of Chinese social structure (Chai & Chai, 1965). Confucius believed there was no greater crime than failing to practice filial piety. This social norm has been deeply rooted in Chinese societies, with most adult children and grandchildren still practicing some degree of filial piety (Holroyd, 2003; Patterson & Semple, 1998; Shyu & Chen, 2004; Zhan, 2001). Therefore, many policy debates surrounding this topic try to determine if the state should take up aged care responsibility (Pei & Pillai, 1999; Chi & Chui, 1999). Many Chinese policymakers believe that the state should not intervene in old-age issues because this will discourage families from supporting and caring for older family members. It is not uncommon to find family law or legislation on family care of older parents in Chinese societies such as mainland China and Singapore (Leung & Lam, 2000).

Riley and Riley (1995) linked individual aging with changes in social structure and suggested that structural lags occur when people's lives change dramatically and social norms, institutions, and laws fail to keep pace. For instance, the one-child policy has been enforced throughout China for the past 26 years and has greatly changed Chinese family structure. Old kinship patterns have diminished, and the 4-2-1 (four grandparents, two parents, and one child) family structure has emerged as the new dominant form. The "sandwich generation" of one-child couples will face the reality of having to care for four parents and their own child as well. In recent years, some researchers have suggested revisiting the concept of filial piety and its acceptable behaviors in contemporary society (Cheng, 1988; Li & Rogers, 1999; Sun, 2002; Yeh & Bedford, 2003). This is very important because without a new understanding of this concept, adult children who are no longer able to support their parents will have many guilt feelings and may be reluctant to seek professional help (Ng, Phillips, & Lee, 2002). At the same time, some older Chinese adults are extremely disappointed or unhappy and even have a strong sense of failure if their offspring cannot support or care for them (Lee, 1999; Lee, Woo, & MacKenzie 2002).

PHYSICAL AND MENTAL HEALTH

Nowhere is the mental and physical well-being of an aging society a more pressing issue than in China. China will have nearly 400 million elders at a time when its one-child policy will play havoc with traditional caregiving practices (Jackson & Howe, 2004). The impending intersection of increasing longevity, coupled with few social and economic supports for elders, suggests that maintaining independence in late life through good mental and physical health is imperative. This presents unusual challenges to the coping and adaptive skills of Chinese elders who have lived the majority of their lives immersed in, and adhering to, traditions that formed their worldview and ways of coping. Most of the current cohort of Chinese elders has no or little educational attainment, and many of them are illiterate. Without retirement pension schemes, Chinese elders have fewer resources than young people and thus are less able to live a dignified life in the rapidly changing market economic society (Raymo & Xie, 2000; Chi & Chui, 1999). They are aging in a society that is transitioning from an ancient culture, and as China becomes more industrialized and open to external cultural influences, they are losing their traditional ways and familiar supports (Chow, 1999; Kleinman & Kleinman, 1999; Li, 2002). This situation represents a major loss and can contribute to a variety of negative consequences.

Although almost all objective health indicators show that older Chinese adults are as healthy as their Western counterparts, subjective measures indicate otherwise (Lai, Lee, & Lee, 2000; Tang, Wang, Meng, Wu, Ericsson, Winblad, et al. 1999; Nevitt et al. 2002; Ho et al., 1997; Berkanovic, Chi, Lubben, & Kitano, 1994). In addition, older Chinese adults seem to have less sense of control over their physical health and functional capabilities (Chi & Lee, 1991). Social workers could play a significant role in Chinese health care settings if social work training were to adopt a focus on healthy, active aging. More emphasis should be placed on developing proactive and innovative health promotion and disease prevention programs and activities for Chinese older adults, who have special needs such as illiteracy, lack of financial resources, and different health beliefs and practices (Ma & Chi, 1995; Chi & Leung, 1999; Foreman et al., 1998; Cheng, Chi, Boey, Ko, & Chou, 2002). Numerous scientific papers have been published on the effectiveness of health intervention that adopts Chinese medicine, diets, and exercises, such as acupressure, Qigong, and Tai Chi (Chen, Lin, Wu, & Lin, 1999; Ng & Tan, 2004; Tsang et al., 2003; Bent et al., 2003; Chou et al., 2005).

Studies of the prevalence of depression in Chinese elders in China and Hong Kong (Chen, Copeland, & Wei, 1999; Chi et al., 2005) reported finding a low pooled prevalence of depression and depressive mood. The analysis also revealed patterns of risk factors that were similar to those in Western countries. Nonetheless, somatization is a particular concern for Chinese elders. For some time, it has been suggested that Chinese are more likely to somaticize depression and to manifest physical complaints and health problems (Kleinman, 1982). In an extensive review of the literature on depression among the Chinese, Parker, Gladstone, and Chee (2001) conclude that the existing evidence supports the hypothesis that the Chinese tend to deny depression or express it somatically. This presents a scenario in which misdiagnosis is probable, with little hope for improvement. Untreated depression creates ongoing hardship for the affected individual and is of concern to a society that is struggling to provide care to an ever-increasing number of elders. There is some relatively new evidence on the far-reaching effects of depression. One such example is reported by Chi and Chou (2000) in their study of Chinese elders in Hong Kong in which depression at baseline was negatively associated with cognitive functioning 3 years later, even after controlling for health, social support, exercise, education, and finances.

Suicide, on the other hand, is a major public health problem in China. It is the fifth-leading cause of death overall, and the elderly suicide rate is three times higher than the average rate (Yip, Chi, & Yu, 1998). China, in contrast to Western countries, experiences much higher rates of suicide among women, as well as rates in rural regions and among elders that far exceed those in the United States and other countries. The reasons for such striking epidemiological contrasts are insufficiently studied. Unlike among women in the United States, where suicide declines in the latter half of life, it rises sharply with aging for women in China, similar to the rise in rates for elder men living in rural China and in other parts of the world. It has been pointed out that indigenized social work practice with Chinese women should pay special attention to their self-concept and attitudes toward death (Cheung & Liu, 2004; Chong & Lang, 1998).

Social workers have taken strong advocate roles in developing research, policies, and services for the most disadvantaged older persons in Chinese societies, such as suicide prevention initiatives in Hong Kong. The Hong Kong government first recognized that elder suicide was a serious problem in 1998 after the first suicide study was published (Chi, Yip, & Yu, 1997); the Working Group on Elderly Suicide was established in 1999 to examine the causes of the problem and to recommend potential solutions. One of this group's recommendations was that more local research studies were needed to understand the factors associated with elderly suicide in Hong Kong. With government support, a series of elderly suicide research studies were commissioned by the government to carry out an elderly suicide, including a psychoautopsy study of elders, a community study to examine suicidal ideation in elder women, and epidemiological studies. This work has led to a number of publications (Yip, Chi, Chiu, & Kwan, 2003; Chiu et al., 2004; Chi et al., 2005), and ultimately these projects spawned the development of new aging and mental health services for elders and consequently these projects seemed to have an effect on lower suicide rates in recent years in Hong Kong.

CONCLUSION

Gerontological social work is urgently needed in China and other Chinese societies, and social workers should practice in a variety of settings along the aging wellness and long-term care continuum in order to make an impact on these rapidly aging societies. The role of social worker in these settings is often unique because social work's primary focus is the psychosocial well-being of elders and their families, which are directly related among older Chinese adults. Social workers should review their own attitudes toward social norms, including family and filial piety, sharpen their skills in family work, and increase their knowledge of indigenous evidence-based interventions. Furthermore, social workers understand the interaction between elders' needs and how to change the environment to meet those needs. According to the 2000 census in China, only 1% of the Chinese elderly population was living in institutions (National Bureau of Statistics, 2001), and most social workers were working in community-based settings such as senior centers, senior housing, day care centers, health clinics, and home care programs. It is anticipated that many social workers in China would practice in nontraditional settings. This may be a healthier trend or solution for the challenges of the aging population in China because older adults would be less excluded from society. To achieve this objective, an interdisciplinary training approach for Chinese gerontological social workers is crucial. After all, physically or psychologically healthy Chinese elders can be resources rather than a burden to each other, to the family, and to the community.

REFERENCES

Bent, S., Xu, L., Lui, L. Y., Nevitt, M., Schneider, E., Tian, G. Q, et al., (2003). A randomized controlled trial of a Chinese herbal remedy to increase energy, memory, sexual function, and quality of life in elderly adults in Beijing, China. *American Journal of Medicine, 115,* 441–447.

Berkanovic, E., Chi, I., Lubben, J. E., & Kitano, H. H. L. (1994). The physical, mental and social health status of older Chinese: A cross-national study. *Journal of Aging and Social Policy, 6,* 73–87.

Chai, C. U., Chai, W., Confucious & Mencius. (Eds.). (1965). *The sacred books of Confucius and other Confucian classics.* New Hyde Park, NY: University Books.

Chen, M. L., Lin, L. C., et al. (1999). The effectiveness of acupressure in improving the quality of sleep of institutionalized residents. *Journals of Gerontology Series A. Biological Sciences and Medical Sciences, 54,* M389–M394.

Chen, R., Copeland, J. R., & Wei, L. (1999). A meta-analysis of epidemiological studies in depression in older people in the People's Republic of China. *International Journal of Geriatric Psychiatry, 14,* 821–830.

Cheng, Z. Y. (1988). On Confucian filial piety and its modernization: Duties, rights, and moral conduct. *Chinese Studies in Philosophy, 20,* 48–88.

Cheng, Y. H., Chi, I., Boey, K. W., Ko, L. S. F. & Chou, K. L. (2002). Self-rated economic condition and the health of elderly persons in Hong Kong. *Social Science and Medicine, 55,* 1415–1424.

Cheung, M., & Liu, M. (2004). The self-concept of Chinese women and the indigenization of social work in China. *International Social Work, 47,* 109–115.

Chi, I., & Chou, K. L. (2000). Depression predicts cognitive decline in Hong Kong Chinese older adults. *Aging and Mental Health, 4,* 148–157.

Chi, I., & Chui, E. (1999). Ageing in Hong Kong. *Australasian Journal on Ageing, 18,* 66–71.

Chi, I., & Lee, J. J. (1991). Health education for the elderly in Hong Kong. *Educational Gerontology, 17,* 507–516.

Chi, I., & Leung, M. F. (1999). Health promotion for the elderly persons in Hong Kong. *Journal of Health and Social Policy, 10,* 37–51.

Chi, I., Yip, P. S. F., Chiu, H. F. K., Chou, K. L., Chan, K. S., Kwan, C. W., et al. (2005). Prevalence of depression and its correlates in Hong Kong Chinese older adults. *American Journal of Geriatric Psychiatry.*

Chi, I., Yip, P., & Yu, K. K. (1997). *Elderly suicides in Hong Kong.* Hong Kong: Befrienders International.

China Population Information and Research Center. (2003). *Four periods of populations aging forecast in China.* Retrieved April 28, 2003, from *http://www.cpirc.org.cn/e-aging2.htm.*

Chiu, H. F. K., Yip, P. S. F., Chi, I., Chan, S., Tsoh, J., Kwan, C. W., et al. (2004). Elderly suicide in Hong Kong: A case controlled psychological autopsy study. *Acta Psychiatrica Scandinavica, 109,* 299–305.

Chong, M. L. A., & Lang, G. S. (1998). Attitudes of Chinese elderly people towards death: Practical implications for social workers. *Asia Pacific Journal of Social Work, 8,* 50–63.

Chou, K. L., & Chi, I. (2001). Social support exchange among elderly Chinese people and their family members in Hong Kong: A longitudinal study. *International Journal of Aging and Human Development, 53,* 329–346.

Chou, K. L., Lee, P. W. H., Yu, E. C. S., Macfarlane, D., Cheng, Y. H., Chan, S. S. C., et al. (in press). Effect of Tai Chi on depressive symptoms amongst Chinese older patients with depression: A randomized clinical trial. *International Journal of Geriatric Psychiatry.*

Chow, N. W. S. (1999). Aging in China. *Journal of Sociology and Social Welfare, 26,* 25–50.

Cooney, R. S., & Shi, J. (1999). Household extension of the elderly in China, 1987. *Population Research and Policy Review, 18,* 451–471.

Foreman, S. E., Yu, L. C., et al. (1998). Use of health services by Chinese elderly in Beijing. *Medical Care, 36,* 1265–1282.

Ho, D. Y. F. (1994). Filial piety, authoritarian moralism, and cognitive conservatism in Chinese societies. *Genetic Social and General Psychology Monographs, 120,* 349–365.

Ho, S. C., Woo, J., et al. (1997). Predictors of mobility decline: The Hong Kong old-old study. *Journals of Gerontology Series A. Biological Sciences and Medical Sciences, 52,* M356–M362.

Holroyd, E. E. (2003). Chinese family obligations toward chronically ill elderly members: Comparing caregivers in Beijing and Hong Kong. *Qualitative Health Research, 13,* 302–318.

Jackson, R., & Howe, N. (2004). *The graying of the middle kingdom: The demographics and economics of re-*

tirement policy in China. Washington, DC: Center for Strategic and International Studies.

Kleinman, A. (1982). Neurasthenia and depression: A study of somatization and culture in China. *Cultural, Medicine and Psychiatry, 6,* 117–190.

Kleinman, A., & Kleinman, J. (1999). The transformation of everyday social experience: What a mental and social health perspective reveals about Chinese communities under global and local change. *Culture, Medicine and Psychiatry, 23,* 7–24.

Lai, D. J., Lee, L. M, et al. (2000). Effects of handicap on life expectancy: The case of China. *Public Health, 114,* 330–335.

Lee, D. T. F. (1999). Transition to residential care: Experiences of elderly Chinese people in Hong Kong. *Journal of Advanced Nursing, 30,* 1118–1126.

Lee, D. T. F., Woo, J., et al. (2002). A review of older people's experiences with residential care placement. *Journal of Advanced Nursing, 37,* 19–27.

Leung, J. C. B., & Lam, J. C. B. (2000). Enforcing family care obligations for the elderly in China through mediation. *Asia Pacific Journal of Social Work, 10,* 77–89.

Li, W. G. (2002). The cultural interaction between fashion and customs: The folk customs analysis of the grand triangle structure of Chinese culture among Beijing, Shanghai, and Henan. *Journal of An Yang Normal University, 86,* 70–71.

Li, Y. S., & Rogers, G. (1999). The graying of American and Chinese societies: Young adults' attitudes toward the care of their elderly parents. *Geriatric Nursing, 20,* 45–47.

Ma, S., & Chi, I. (1995). Health counseling for the older people in Hong Kong. *Educational Gerontology, 21,* 515–528.

National Bureau of Statistics of China. (2001). *China statistical yearbook.* Beijing, China: Author.

Nevitt, M. C., Xu, L., et al. (2002). Very low prevalence of hip osteoarthritis among Chinese elderly in Beijing, China, compared with whites in the United States: The Beijing osteoarthritis study. *Arthritis and Rheumatism, 46,* 1773–1779.

Ng, A. C. Y., Phillips, D. R., & Lee, W. K. M. (2002). Persistence and challenges to filial piety and informal support of older persons in a modern Chinese society: A case study in Tuen Mun, Hong Kong. *Journal of Aging Studies, 16,* 135–153.

Parker, G., Gladstone, G., & Chee, K. T. (2001). Depression in the planet's largest ethnic group: The Chinese. *American Journal of Psychiatry, 158,* 857–864.

Patterson, T. L., Semple, S. J., et al. (1998). The cultural context of caregiving: A comparison of Alzheimer's caregivers in Shanghai, China and San Diego, California. *Psychological Medicine, 28,* 1071–1084.

Pei, X. M., & Pillai, V. K. (1999). Old age support in China: The role of the state and the family. *International Journal of Aging and Human Development, 49,* 197–212.

Poston, D. L., & Duan, C. C. (2000). The current and projected distribution of the elderly and eldercare in the People's Republic of China. *Journal of Family Issues, 21,* 714–732.

Raymo, J. M., & Xie, Y. (2000). Income of the urban elderly in postreform China: Political capital, human capital, and the state. *Social Science Research, 29,* 1–24.

Riley, M. W., & Riley, J. W. (1995). Structural lag: Past and future. In M. Riley, R. Kahn, & A. Foner (Eds.), *Age and structural lag.* New York: Wiley.

Shyu, Y. I. L., Chen, M. C., et al. (2004). Caregiver's needs as predictors of hospital readmission for the elderly in Taiwan. *Social Science and Medicine, 58,* 1395–1403.

Sun, R. J. (2002). Old age support in contemporary urban China from both parents' and children's perspectives. *Research on Aging, 24,* 337–359.

Tang, Z., Wang, H. X., et al. (1999). The prevalence of functional disability in activities of daily living and instrumental activities of daily living among elderly Beijing Chinese. *Archives of Gerontology and Geriatrics, 29,* 115–125.

United Nations. (2003). *World population prospects: The 2002 revision.* United Nations Population Division.

Woo, J., Ho, S. C., et al. (1998). Care of the older Hong Kong Chinese population. *Age and Ageing, 27,* 423–426.

Xia, X., & Guo, J. (2002). Historical development and characteristics of social work in today's China. *International Journal of Social Welfare, 11,* 254–262.

Yeh, K. H., & Bedford, W. (2003). A test of the dual filial piety model. *Asian Journal of Social Psychology, 6,* 215–228.

Yip, P., Chi, I., Chiu, H., & Kwan, C. W. (2003). A prevalence study of suicide ideation among elderly in Hong Kong SAR. *International Journal of Geriatric Psychiatry,* 1056–1062.

Yip, P., Chi, I., & Yu, K. K. (1998). An epidemiological profile of elderly suicide in Hong Kong. *International Journal of Geriatric Psychiatry, 13,* 631–637.

Zhan, H. Y. J. (2001). The culture of filial piety: Explaining Chinese caregivers' task performance and reward. *Gerontologist, 41,* 88–89.

Zhang, B. (2002). *Aging population requires new action.* Retrieved April 16, 2002, from *http://www.cpirc.org.cn/enews20020329.htm.*

Zimmer, Z. (2002). Elderly Chinese in Pacific Rim countries: Social support and integration. *Population and Development Review, 28,* 156–157.

JUDITH PHILLIPS

Older Adults in Europe

An analysis of social work with older adults in Europe raises a number of definitional and conceptual problems. Difficulties arise when we consider what can be defined as "Europe." Shardlow and Walliss (2003) argue it is less a geographic location (such as that bounded by European Union [EU] member states) than an "ever-shifting idea or ideal" (p. 922) that is continually in a state of flux, socially, economically, and culturally. Additionally, there is no universal understanding of what constitutes "social work" in Europe, and the term is often used synonymously with "social services," "social care," "care management" (United Kingdom), and "social professions" or "social pedagogy" (Denmark, France). The boundaries of social work are also unclear, with different professions in different countries carrying out social work functions, based on history, culture, influence of occupational groups, and the role of the state (Shardlow & Payne, 1998). The definition of older adults also varies between European states, with "old age" being determined by state legislation on retirement age and pension entitlement, for example, in the United Kingdom, or linked with a "loss of power" in some European cultures (Bosnia) rather than being based on chronological age or external appearance (Vincent, 2003). Such diversity and the associated difficulties of researchers from "outside" studying another culture have led to a dearth of comparative empirical work on social work with older people across Europe. In a European study by Shardlow and Cooper (2000), no empirical studies were found in the topic area of social work with older people. Most literature reviews consider the wider social policy context, the organization of social services and health and social care systems, with little commentary on the role, function, and approaches of social work.

Despite not being able to compare "like with like," together with a lack of consensus regarding what should be included in a definition, social work in Europe can be defined by its diversity, in terms of policy and conceptual frameworks as well as practice traditions. This chapter will explore such diversity, drawing examples from countries illustrating different social policy traditions and welfare responses to older people.

Demographic factors are a unifying factor across Europe and have led to older people being recognized in the EU agenda for action. In responding to the challenges of an aging society across Europe, there have been a number of similar policy responses, such as the move from institutional to community care, changes in the management of care with the growth of managerialism in services, and the integration of health and social care. In addition, there have been a number of common ongoing difficulties, for example, the funding of long-term care, the reconciliation of work and family life, and the supply of social care workers to care for older people.

The consequences of an increasing older population provide the context and purpose for social work intervention, with the focus on increasing dependency needs of people in late old age and the concomitant support required, through intergenerational caregiving issues and through transitions in later life such as bereavement and loss of social support. Viewing older people as "dependent" and "in need," however, narrowly concentrates the social work response on practical and social support (Hugman, 1994). Focusing on what older people can contribute in terms of skills, knowledge, and experience will be of increasing importance. The social policy framework is changing across Europe, and further challenges are emerging. Consequently, new areas of social work are opening up, based on citizenship and social inclusion—a greater focus being placed on ethnic elders and asylum seekers and on challenging ageism and racism—emerging issues that will impact on social work with older adults in the future.

THE SOCIAL POLICY CONTEXT

There are a number of ways of defining "Europe." This analysis will focus mainly on welfare states in the EU, including recent states such as Greece and Poland, and will also include Israel. Because it is impossible to do justice to all countries falling within this definition, the concentration will be on states that typically illustrate the "welfare state regime" developed by Esping-Andersen (1990, 1999), who suggested three distinct clusters based on social protection systems. Social care and social work approaches can also be added to this typology (Lorenz, 1994), although caution must be exercised in taking the typology further because it does not address gender, race, and age, which do affect how people experience social welfare. The Esping-Andersen models include the following:

1. *The market liberal (residual) welfare state:* The United Kingdom is an example of this model. Social insurance plans predominate; benefits are targeted on the poor; families and charities have a primary role. Social work tends to concentrate on the poor and deviant. The social worker is a rationer and a gatekeeper of resources.

2. *The conservative corporatist state:* Germany is an example of this model. The state is predominant, with the market having only a marginal role; the church has an important role in shaping such regimes, and the emphasis is on family care. For example, German families are obliged to support their elderly relatives, and social services have a residual role.

3. *The social democratic welfare state:* The Scandinavian countries are examples of this model. The welfare state hinges on principles of equity, and the state pursues services of the highest standard. Benefits are high. The market has little role. The state takes direct responsibility for dependents, women are supported in their choice to be in paid work or in the household, and the home help service is the mainstay of care for older people. Social workers, employed by state agencies, enjoy a high status in society.

The Esping-Andersen framework does not adequately describe all European countries. Indeed, it might be appropriate to suggest an additional model when considering countries such as Spain and Israel. Thus, we identify a *Mediterranean welfare state* model in which there is a high level of public pensions but underdevelopment of family support. Social work is a recent development since World War II in most states that fall within this type. Church-run establishments are prominent, along with the Red Cross; in Greece, for example, social workers are involved in assessment and direct service provision to older people and their caregivers; they are also involved in the administration of public assistance and self-help organizations (Cannan, Berry, & Lyons, 1992).

Further developments in the conceptualization of "care" are also leading to changes in policies for older people in each of the preceding typologies. For example, in the Scandinavian countries there is increasing emphasis on the marketization of public provision and private social work (Denmark); the United Kingdom is undergoing reorganization of community care programs, and in Germany there is reform of long-term care insurance to establish more integrated care (Lowenstein & Ogg, 2003). The spread of democratic liberal governments across Europe has led to the enlargement of the EU, resulting in harmonization of civic and legal frameworks (Warnes, Friedrich, Kellaher, & Torres, 2004).

DEMOGRAPHIC CHALLENGES

Older people have moved to center stage on the European social policy and social work agendas in all welfare states through demographic, attitudinal, and legislative changes (Phillipson, 2002) and also through "grassroots" action by users and caregivers groups, such as the European Older People's Platform. In 2001 there were 62 million elderly people aged 65 and over in the EU, representing 16% of the total population. By 2010, the number of very old people aged 80 and over will rise by almost 50% (European Commission, 2003), with countries such as Belgium, Greece, Luxembourg, France, and Italy expecting to experience the largest increases in the next decade (Anderson, 2003). Coupled with an aging population are low fertility trends and increasing divorce, meaning smaller families with fewer members in the family available to care for older people. Many older people, particularly older women, also live alone. Increases in female labor market participation and the difficulties of juggling work and care add to the issue of who provides care and the costs of so doing.

At the EU level the debate has focused on the economic pressures of an aging Europe—intergenerational equity and the social and economic integration of nonworking populations, the main emphasis being on pension provision. The emphasis in the debate on the sustainability of current levels of economic, health, and social care provision has cast the aging agenda in a negative light, failing to acknowledge the rich potential older people bring to all aspects of life (Langebaek, 2003).

FAMILY CARE

"The family is the cornerstone for care in Europe" (Anderson, 2003, p. 4). The changing nature of the family in all states, however, has implications for the care for older people. One of the key issues is whether there is a legal obligation to give economic support to older members of the family. The guiding principle behind many states (particularly the conservative corporatist) is "subsidiarity," meaning that social action should be taken at the lowest level, that is, at the level of the individual or the family before the state is asked to intervene (Austria, Germany, Greece, and Luxembourg). Thus families have a legal responsibility to pay for the care of their elderly members. Mediterranean countries place a legal obligation on relatives to pay for the care of their elderly member, and in

Italy even in-laws and half siblings are obliged to provide support in proportion to income (Hantrais, 2000). It is in such countries that coresident care is common, with only around 4% of care provided to older people outside the household (Anderson, 2003). However, even in countries wedded to this principle, there is some mellowing as other ways of funding care, such as long-term care insurance, are introduced and there is evidence that older citizens are willing to shoulder the costs of care themselves (Krieger, 2004). However, social work in Germany, for example, can only be understood in the context of "subsidiarity," with little activity at the national level (Giarchi, 1996).

Filial norms and preferences for care also do not necessarily conform to the Esping-Anderson typology presented here. In a five-country study, Daatland and Herlofson (2003) highlight the north-south dimension in the support for filial norms, with the highest in Spain and Israel and the lowest support in Norway, England, and Germany. However, they note that "filial solidarity is not incompatible with generous welfare state arrangements, nor do filial obligations necessarily imply that the family is seen as the 'natural care provider' " (p. 537). Additionally, in all countries there was a call for more state responsibility. However, the role of the state is that of complementing rather than substituting between services and families, with the role of services not discouraging family help (Lowenstein & Ogg, 2003). In the same study of five countries (Norway, Germany, England, Spain, and Israel), services represented a source of autonomy and independence for both older and younger family members (Lowenstein & Ogg, 2003).

SOCIAL WORK AND OLDER PEOPLE

Only a minority of older people and their caregivers, even those who draw on social services, will encounter a social worker. Apart from Greece, Portugal, and Luxembourg, the 1992 Eurobarometer study indicated that fewer than 30% of older people received care, and fewer came in touch with a social worker. The role and function of social workers across Europe differ. In some countries they are state agents (Finland, Norway, Sweden, the United Kingdom, and Ireland) and in others they are nongovernmental (the Netherlands), although these organizations may be state funded; yet in no European state has social work become entirely a state service. Private social work as an alternative has not emerged as a trend. Social work in such contexts has elements of social control (particularly in Italy) as well as advocacy (the United Kingdom). In some countries a generic service is offered, whereas other states operate more specialist provision, with social workers specializing in work with adults and older people. In the Netherlands, for example, social work operates generically, and bureaus are open to all citizens without the need to be defined in a particular age category. Information and advice, material help, mediation and advocacy, as well as counselling and group work, are offered (Munday, 1996).

Apart from ideological differences in the organization of the welfare state and consequently social work, there are also differing academic discourses across Europe. In some countries (Germany, France, and Italy) the notion of "social pedagogy" is apparent. This is education and lifelong learning in its broadest sense aimed to help the poor in society "to realise their full potential and active membership of a society" (Lorenz, 2000, 92). In relation to older people the emphasis has been on providing people with means to manage their own lives and make changes in their circumstances (Hamalainen, 1989). There are some arguments that social work and social pedagogy in this sense are "unified in the modern concept of social work" (Hamalainen, 2003, p. 76).

Many commentators have noted the trend toward convergence in European social care systems with increasing welfare pluralism (Munday, 1996; Giarchi, 1996). Consequently, there are a number of common issues in social work practice across Europe. For example, there is consensus that community care is the best policy for older people.

Increasingly the agenda across Europe has been to develop community care, enabling older people to remain at home for as long as possible, preventing and deferring their entry to residential and nursing care. Support for community care is widespread across Europe and among different age-groups (Walker & Maltby, 1997). One of the primary roles of the social worker is to enable people to live at home, with the focus on home care. Coordinating care for older people and their caregivers in the community, however, is complex because different countries have distinctions between health and social care (apart from Denmark, the Netherlands and Italy). In addition, there are a multiplicity of providers—both for-profit and nonprofit private sector suppliers, as in the United Kingdom, voluntary nonprofit sectors such as in Germany and Belgium, and a range of religious and voluntary organizations in countries such as Greece, Portugal, and Spain (Walker & Maltby, 1997).

In the pursuit of community care in the United Kingdom and Sweden, the social worker has become a care manager increasingly taking on a managerialist and purchasing/assessing function and having less direct contact with service users providing a social work/counselling service (Weinberg, Williamson, Challis, & Hughes, 2003; Giarchi, 1996). Shortages of qualified social workers and social care workers have meant that in many situations social workers are unable to realize their full potential in their attempts to prevent dependency and are forced to take a reactionary rather than a preventative role, with increased targeting and rationing (Pijl, 1991). The United Kingdom fits this description, despite its emphasis on person-centered care (one of the standards of the National Service Framework for Older People developed by the Department of Health in 2001), whereas other countries, such as the Netherlands, as mentioned earlier, attempt a more preventative approach.

A further role for social workers in many countries is to coordinate care between formal and informal sectors and hence to support caregivers. This role is much more developed in some states, such as the United Kingdom, than in others, such as Greece, where there is less infrastructure of service provision to fully realize this aim (Walker & Maltby, 1997). The demand for residential care appears to be increasing across Europe as demography, family mobility, and long-term health care needs increase. Social workers may have a vital role to play in such a transition (European Foundation, 2004a).

A second common issue is the fragmentation of health and social care. Coordinating community care services, particularly between health, social care, and housing, for the benefit of users and caregivers is a problem throughout Europe (Jani–Le Bris, 1993; Walker, 1996). In Germany the institutional structures and funding arrangements that characterize health and social care systems contradict policy emphasis on community care (Scharf, 1998).

On a more positive note, however, more integrated and interprofessional approaches are being developed, with social workers acting with other professionals in the health care field, for example, psychiatric nurses, or in the housing arena in the promotion of the strengths and position of older people. Such an example can be found in a number of countries such as the Netherlands (Klein Beernink, 1994), where generalist social work is practiced (concentrating mainly on a therapeutic approach), or France, where social workers work in holistic and multidisciplinary teams and there is little division between social and health services (Munday, 1996), with many social workers based in sociomedical centers (Tester, 1996). Israel partially overcame service fragmentation through lower caseloads and adequate training and supervision (Lowenstein, 2000). In Greece, services for older people are concentrated mainly in hospitals, with little social work activity in the community other than indirect social services provided by the Greek Orthodox Church and the Red Cross, although families have primary responsibility to care for older members as in most Mediterranean states. Health and social care services are provided by voluntary centers (KAPIs), which form an important part of the community care system providing health and social care.

In Italy social work has located a "new occupational space" (Shardlow & Payne, 1998, p. 65) in relation to "integrated domiciliary care, covering health and social care needs through the provision of domiciliary hospital care; day care fostering for isolated older people; new forms of residential health care; group living; day centers; self-help groups and various other forms of voluntary help" (p. 65).

A multiprofessional first-contact team conducts assessment, and it is the social worker's role to transform that assessment into the planning, delivery, and coordination of care. One of the interesting aspects of the role in Italy is the support to active older people, as well as those who are frail, through the encouragement of activity with younger generations and assistance with initiating self-help groups, in an attempt at harnessing them as a resource. In Denmark, illustrating the Scandinavian liberal model, domiciliary care has high priority in the attempt to promote community care, with an emphasis on quality of life of both service users and caregivers (Cannan et al., 1992), and social care is seen as a right equal to medical care.

Despite the introduction of cash for care incentives introduced, for example, in the United Kingdom, Austria, Germany, Finland, the Netherlands, and Italy, the role of the family remains key to the whole development of community care, particularly in rural areas (Evers & Leichsenring, 1994), where there is little service provision. Regional inequality is another issue to be tackled in all countries.

Another common issue facing social workers in Europe is tackling ageism and racism. One of the major areas of social work practice in Europe in the 21st century is the focus on different ethnic groups with heterogeneous cultural and spiritual backgrounds. The challenge to social work is to address the values, norms, and traditions of such diverse groups (Guttmann & Lowenstein, 1991). New social challenges in relation to

this issue can be found in Israel. In Germany large private welfare organizations have taken on this role; in Italy special social services take on this role.

The in-migration of non-Europeans (from former colonies and asylum seekers) will grow in importance for the cultural diversity of older people within the coming decades in Europe. These immigrants are concentrated in the main metropolitan centers in Europe and are among the most deprived and vulnerable to social segregation and social exclusion (Phillipson, Bernard, Phillips, & Ogg, 2001; Scharf, Phillipson, Smith, & Kingston, 2002). Most countries (Netherlands, Spain, Greece, Italy, Denmark, Germany, France, Israel, and the United Kingdom) have services in place, with an emergency response and also more developed services, although many of these do not accommodate for older people to the same extent as younger people and suffer from institutional racism. The rise in the number of illegal immigrants and asylum seekers from within as well as outside the EU has led to unsympathetic responses. One of the difficulties is the lack of knowledge and experience transfer between countries on the role of social work with older people in this respect.

A further consequence of migration is that many areas are left depleted of a younger population, and population decline has disadvantaged older people who have remained and "aged in place." A related area is the welfare of increasing numbers of migrants who move from northern Europe, Scandinavia, Britain, and Germany, for example, to Spain and Portugal. Problems in health and social care develop particularly for those who cannot speak the language and where services are less well developed (King, Warnes, & Williams, 2000). Retirement migration into relatively isolated rural settlements can also be a source of problems requiring social work assistance, particularly if family support is at a distance.

A fourth common issue is working with users and caregivers. Increasingly social workers work with people who are physically disabled and cognitively frail or who have dementia and often a multiplicity of problems. Working with individuals who care for such older people also forms a major part of social work. Across Europe it is estimated that 1 in 10 Europeans over the age of 15 provide care (as a result of long-term illness, disability, or old age) within the household, and 1 in 7 do so outside the household (Walker, 1999); the majority of these caregivers are women. The empowerment and participation of users and caregivers is a primary objective of the social worker. Many caretakers juggle work with family life, which includes looking after children and older parents (Fagan, 2001; Phillips, Bernard, & Chittenden, 2002), with workers with elder care responsibilities more numerous in Greece, Italy, Portugal, and Spain than in Denmark, the Netherlands, and the United Kingdom (Anderson, 2003). The stress of these demands may lead to social work assessment and help, yet in only a few countries, for example, the United Kingdom, is there a right to a caregiver's assessment. This is an increasingly recognized issue due to the demographic impact on employment (fewer younger people in the workforce to replace those retiring), and the reconciliation of work and family life is a high priority on the European agenda.

How should social work in Europe respond to the care of older people? Should there be an aim for a consensus/convergence approach to strengthen the profession and lift its status? There can be no definitive interpretation of social work in Europe. Although it would be difficult to envisage a common model for practice across Europe, elements of knowledge-based best practice form a basis; among them are engaging with service users and caregivers on a more equal and effective footing. Social workers will have to engage with the notion of citizenship, even in areas where they have to evoke authority through legislation. Rights around citizenship are more common in Scandinavian countries (Munday, 1996). Empowerment and advocacy based on these principles have led some analysts to suggest that social workers act as ethnographers, searching for multiple views and narratives of the problem (Schindler, 1999).

Based on the preceding commentary, there is a case to be made for the development of a critical gerontological social work perspective across Europe. Ray and Phillips (forthcoming) argue that there is a lack of synergy between knowledge derived from critical gerontological research and social work knowledge and practice; they propose a model of critical gerontological practice that draws on key elements from the field of critical gerontology, the existing social work knowledge base, and critical practice theories. In Israel, gerontology has become much more professionalized and linked to social work (Lowenstein, 2001).

ROLE OF THE EUROPEAN UNION

The European Commission has been granted competence in areas of good practice in care for older people. This has mainly focused on transfer of knowledge through research programs and training programs. New states joining the EU, such as Romania, will increase the diversity of European social work because such states have nonexistent services for older people outside of major urban centers, yet issues around the social exclusion of ethnic groups such as travelers will be of increasing importance for all European states as labor market opportunities allow transnational migration. A future challenge will be to develop social work in states that have scant resources and no social security systems yet that place themselves in a European context. Bosnia-Herzegovina, for example, cannot offer local-based care to those who need residential or nursing care. The significant material gaps between new and potential member states and the 15 existing states in the EU are a challenge across Europe (European Foundation, 2004b).

CONCLUSION

Since the early 1990s, the emphasis across Europe has been on the costs and associated long-term funding of care of an increasing aging population. Cost containment and efficiency have been the overriding trends in policy and practice. A process of "substitution" has taken place between community and institution in the location of care. Community home-based care rather than institutional care has been favored as one response; another has been to broaden the welfare mix. Private markets were introduced in social and health service and housing provision. Social work, however, has remained within the state remit in all countries in Europe. Consequently, social work has shifted its focus from an emphasis on interpersonal skills, methods, and processes of social work to the role of a state agent in rationing and prioritizing care. New opportunities are provided to all states through the role of older people as caregivers across the generations, and their resources are being harnessed in self-help groups and volunteering. The notions of citizenship, empowerment, and participation even for dependent older people are at the forefront of European social work development, in both practice and training. Yet some states are more advanced than others, with the Esping-Anderson typology providing a convenient framework to look at this. Aging is characterized by its diversity, and this factor must not be ignored in our discussion. Not only structural and cultural diversity through age, race, ethnicity, and gender but also differences among older people with particular problems such as dementia, learning disability, and mental illness have to be acknowledged. Such older people face stigma and ageism in extreme ways. The trend is to place importance on person-centered care, which necessitates good communication between agencies. Consequently, the boundaries of social work are becoming increasingly blurred. Social work values and practices are widespread across Europe but they are "outside" of the social work profession as interagency working increases. Social work therefore has to grapple with its core identity across Europe in a time of uncertainty of future social policy provision.

REFERENCES

Anderson, R. (2003, June). *Health risks and resources in the life course and in different living arrangements.* Paper presented at the conference The Family in the Health System: A Cost-Raising or Cost-Reducing Factor, organized by the European Observatory on the Social Situation, Demography and the Family, Tutzing, Germany.

Cannan, C., Berry, L., & Lyons, K. (1992). *Social work and Europe.* London: Macmillan.

Cavallone, A. M., & Ferrario, F. (1998). Social work in Italy. In S. Shardlow & M. Payne (Eds.), *Contemporary issues in social work: Western Europe* (pp. 57–76). Aldershot, England: Ashgate.

Daatland, S., & Herlofson, K. (2003). "Lost solidarity" or "changed solidarity": A comparative European view of normative family solidarity. *Ageing and Society, 23,* 537–560.

Esping-Andersen, G. (1990). *The three worlds of welfare capitalism.* Princeton, NJ: Princeton University Press.

Esping-Andersen, G. (1999). *Social foundations of post industrial economies.* Oxford, England: Oxford University Press.

European Commission. (2003). *The social situation in the European Union 2003.* Brussels, Belgium: European Commission.

European Foundation. (2004a). *www.eurofound.eu.int/ living/family.htm.*

European Foundation. (2004b). *www.eurofound.eu.int/ living/qual_life/eb_findings.htm.*

Evers, A., & Leichsenring, K. (1994, March). Paying for informal care. *Ageing International,* 29–41.

Fagan, C. (2001). *Gender, employment and working time preferences in Europe.* Dublin, Ireland: European Foundation for the Improvement of Living and Working Conditions.

Giarchi, G. (1996). *Caring for older Europeans.* Aldershot, England: Arena.

Guttmann, D., & Lowenstein, A. (1991). Demographic changes in Israel and their implications for professional education in aging for the 21st century. *Journal of Aging and Judaism, 5,* 215–226.

Hamalainen, J. (1989). Social pedagogy as a metatheory of social work education. *International Social Work, 32,* 17–128.

Hamalainen, J. (2003). The concept of social pedagogy in the field of social work. *Journal of Social Work, 3,* 69–80.

Hantrais, L. (2000). *Social policy in the European Union* (2nd ed.). London: Macmillan.

Hugman, R. (1994). *Ageing and the care of older people in Europe.* London: Macmillan.

Jani–Le Bris, H. (1993). *Family care of dependent older people in the European Community.* Dublin, Ireland: European Foundation for the Improvement of Living and Working Conditions.

King, R., Warnes, T., & Williams, A. (2000). *Sunset lives.* Oxford, England: Berg.

Klein Beernink, L. (1994). Social work with the elderly: A new perspective. In K. Hesser & W. Koole (Eds.), *Social work in the Netherlands: Current developments.* Amsterdam: SWP.

Krieger, H. (2004, May). *Family life in Europe: Results of recent surveys on quality of life in Europe.* Paper presented at the Irish Presidency Conference, Families, Change and Social Policy in Europe. Dublin, Ireland.

Langebaek, S. (2003). Ageing in Europe [Guest editorial]. *Generations Review, 13*(4), 3.

Lorenz, W. (1994). *Social work in a changing Europe.* London: Routledge.

Lorenz, W. (2000). European perspectives on social work. In M. Davies (Ed.), *The Blackwell encyclopaedia of social work* (pp. 119–121). Oxford, England: Blackwell.

Lowenstein, A. (2000). Case management demonstration project for the frail elderly in Israel. *Care Management Journal, 2,* 5–14.

Lowenstein, A. (2001). Multidimensionality of education, research and training in social gerontology: The Israeli experience. *Educational Gerontology, 27,* 493–506.

Lowenstein, A., & Ogg, J. (Eds.). (2003). *Old age and autonomy: The role of service systems and intergenerational family solidarity.* Final report of the OASIS project, University of Haifa.

Munday, B. (1996). Definitions and comparisons in European social care. In B. Munday & P. Ely (Eds.), *Social care in Europe* (pp. 1–20). Hertfordshire, England: Prentice Hall and Harvester.

Phillips, J., Bernard, M., & Chittenden, M. (2002). *Juggling work and family life.* Bristol, England: Policy Press.

Phillipson, C. (2002). The frailty of old age. In M. Davies (Ed.), *The Blackwell companion to social work* (pp. 58–64). Oxford, England: Blackwell.

Phillipson, C., Bernard, M., Phillips, J., & Ogg, J. (2001). *The family and community life of older people.* London: Routledge.

Pijl, M. (1991). Netherlands. In A. Evers & I. Svetlik (Eds.), *New welfare mixes in care for the elderly* (vol. 2). Vienna: European Centre for Social Welfare Policy and Research.

Ray, M., & Phillips, J. (forthcoming). *Critical gerontological social work.* Basingstoke: Palgrave.

Scharf, T. (1998). *Ageing and ageing policy in Germany.* Oxford, England: Berg.

Scharf, T, Phillipson, C., Smith, A., & Kingston, P. (2002). *Growing older in socially deprived areas: Social exclusion in later life.* London: Help the Aged.

Schindler, R. (1999). Empowering the aged: A postmodern approach. *International Journal of Aging and Human Development, 49,* 165–177.

Shardlow, S., & Cooper, S. (2000). *A bibliography of European studies in social work.* Lyme Regis, England: Russell House.

Shardlow, S., & Payne, M. (1998). Finding social work in Europe. In S. Shardlow & M. Payne (Eds.), *Contemporary issues in social work: Western Europe* (pp. 151–160). Aldershot, England: Ashgate.

Shardlow, S., & Walliss, J. (2003). Mapping comparative empirical studies of European social work. *British Journal of Social Work, 33,* 921–942.

Tester, S. (1996). *Community care for older people: A comparative perspective.* London: Macmillan.

Vincent, J. (2003). *Old age.* London: Routledge.

Walker, A. (1996). Social services for older people in Europe. In R. Bland (Ed.), *Developing services for older people and their families* (pp. 58–78). London: Jessica Kingsley Press.

Walker, A. (1999). *Attitudes to population ageing in Europe: A comparison of the 1992 and 1999 Eurobarometer surveys.* University of Sheffield. Retrieved from *http://www.sheffield.ac.uk/uni/academic/R-Z/socst.*

Walker, A., & Maltby, T. (1997). *Ageing Europe.* Buckingham, England: Open University Press.

Warnes, A., Friedrich, K., Kellaher, L., & Torres, S. (2004). The diversity and welfare of older migrants in Europe. *Ageing and Society, 24,* 307–326.

Weinberg, A., Williamson, J., Challis, D., & Hughes, J. (2003). What do care managers do? A study of working practice in older peoples services. *British Journal of Social Work, 33,* 901–920. Retrieved from *www.bjsw.oupjournals.org.*

Population aging has emerged as one of the most significant demographic processes of the 21st century. The phenomenon is progressing rapidly in both developed and developing countries. Due to the impact of population aging, the elderly population in developing countries has outpaced those in the developed world. Current estimates are that more than 248 million of the roughly 418 million persons aged 65 and older in the world (59%) are living in the developing world. The projected population data demonstrate similar trends; a growing proportion of elderly persons are predicted to live in developing countries, 67% by 2020.

In Africa, for example, it is projected that the elderly population will increase from 3.3% in 2000 to 6.9% in 2050. Within the African continent, the southern region has the highest percentage of older inhabitants; 6.2% of the population in 1997 was estimated to be 60 years of age or older, slightly more than in the northern African region (Kinsella & Ferreira, 1997). The northern region follows closely with an estimated elderly population (60 and over) of 5.9%, compared with 4.6% in eastern Africa and 4.4% in western Africa during the same period (United Nations, 1980). Even though the variation in the elderly population may not be substantial, it has implications for contemporary welfare policies and programs for older persons. In Latin America and the Caribbean, the increase is from 5.4% in 2000 to 16.9% in 2050, higher than the current European average.

Asia is estimated to have the greatest number of elderly persons: 217 million, with China alone having about 87 million persons (6.8% of its population) aged 65 and older. This figure is projected to increase to 167 million (11.5%) by 2020. Also, India's elderly population is projected to increase from 51 million (5.0%) to 93 million (7.3%) by 2020.

OSEI DARKWA

Older Adults in Developing Nations

GENDER

As in the developed world, women are overrepresented among the elderly population in the developing world, a phenomenon that demographers describe as the feminization of the aged. According to the U.S. Bureau of the Census (1997), by 2010, of a population of 820 million African people, 14.2 million will be females aged 65 and older; 10.8 million will be elderly males. In the 75 and older age-group, there will be 4.3 million females and 3.1 million males. For example, by 2020, the total population of the sub-Saharan region will be just over 1 billion, with 19 million females aged 65 and older and 13.5 million males within the

91

same age-group. By 2025 this population will increase to 21.8 million females and 15.3 million males aged 6y years and older. In the same year there will be more than 4 million women aged and 4.6 million men aged 75 years and older (U.S. Bureau of the Census, 1997).

The population structure of specific African countries depicts a similar trend. For example, in Kenya women who reach 60 years are expected to live another 17 years, whereas men of the same age can look forward to an additional 15.5 years of life (Kinsella, 1992). In Zimbabwe, women will outnumber men in all age-groups by year 2005, and, as in most parts of the world, the rate of widowhood among women will increase (U.S. Department of Commerce, 1990). In Ghana, population indicators show that the elderly male population will rise from 262,000 in 1996 to 293,000 by 2000, and the elderly female population from 287,000 to 328,000 over the same period (Adlakha, 1996). In Morocco, the elderly male population was 554,000 in 1992 and is estimated to be 680,000 by 2000; the elderly female population was 570,000 in 1992 and is estimated to be 794,000 by 2000.

In addition to the gender difference in life expectancy, other gender differences have been documented in social roles and economic and health status (Pratt & Kethley, 1988). In most parts of Africa and Asia, consistent with cultural expectations, older women are likely to provide caregiving to their husbands, which may cause additional strains in their social functioning.

The economic status of women in developing nations is generally more negatively affected in old age than that of men. Even though both older men and older women continue to work well beyond official retirement age, older men tend to have more opportunities to earn income than older women. Retired older African males, due to their greater prior attachment to the formal labor market, tend to have greater access to statutory insurance schemes (e.g., social security) than do older women. Because older women in the developing world tend to operate within the informal sector, they generally have no retirement insurance in old age. Some women engage in petty trading to supplement income from farming activities, but they are less likely then men to have many opportunities to generate income. Additionally, older men tend to exercise control over valuable community resources (such as land), serve as spiritual leaders, and perform numerous community rituals. Some receive income (in the form of cash, in-kind, or token compensation) for their services, thus enhancing their economic position.

Accordingly, the feminization of the older adult population and significant gender differences in social and economic status present a special challenge in developing nations. Gender-specific policies and programs will have to be enacted. It is also worth noting that women live longer than men, and they tend to spend more of their older years in a disabled state (Colvez, 1996). Life expectancy of women is now about 10% greater than that of men. Any insurance programs targeting the needs of elderly women should take this factor into consideration. The implications of this gender imbalance for social support and public planning can be great, since older women are more likely to be widowed.

HEALTH CARE ISSUES

Most developing countries have a pluralistic medical system, with traditional and Western healers operating side by side. Because most elderly persons reside in rural areas, they tend to rely on traditional medicine to meet their health care needs. Empirical evidence on access to health services in a number of developing countries indicates that rural dwellers have less access than their urban counterparts (Apt, 1992; Banga, 1992, 1993). This is due to the limited number of health providers in rural areas and the disproportionate amount of public funds allocated to urban health care (Ebrahim, 1993). Since practicing in urban areas is more financially and professionally rewarding than operating in a rural environment, most doctors work in urban settings. A major barrier to obtaining access to health care is poverty, with most elderly people unable to afford the most basic health care (World Bank, 1993). In general, resource constraints have prevented health policymakers from extending health care services to rural areas equivalent to those in urban areas. Thus, access to health care for elderly rural people is more problematic than for elderly urban dwellers. The lack of guaranteed health care for older persons has contributed to poor access and utilization of formal health services, and poor older persons in the developing world continue to bear the greatest burden. The challenge today is to develop a health care system that offers equitable access to all elderly people on the continent. Suggestions in this regard are made later in the chapter.

One factor that is likely to affect population aging in the developing world is the incidence and prevalence of AIDS/HIV. Without question, the world in general and the developing world in particular have been severely impacted by the AIDS pandemic, with men, women, and children suffering equally. For example, although Africa's sub-Saharan regions contain only 12% of the global adult population, the vast majority of people living with AIDS or HIV infection are located in Africa. Of the 33.4 million adults and children estimated to be living with HIV or AIDS at the end of 1998, 22.5 million are in sub-Saharan Africa (UNAIDS, 1999). Further, in 1998, of the 2.5 million deaths from AIDS-related illnesses worldwide, 2 million of the casualties were in sub-Saharan Africa (UN-AIDS, 1996).

Even though most of the attention on the continent is focused on younger populations (commercial sex workers, pregnant women, young girls, etc.), the HIV/AIDS problem should be of great concern to the older adult population as well. The United Nations AIDS Programme (2004) fact sheet notes that many girls are getting infected through sex with older men because older men provide the girls with gifts, money, or other favors. What is more, condom use among older men may be lower than in the population in general.

AIDS/HIV is expected to affect life expectancy the world over, as a result of increases in mortality in the young and adult ages. For example, in East Africa and southern Africa, the regions most affected by the AIDS pandemic in Africa, infant mortality rates are nearly 70% higher than what they might have been without AIDS (World Population Profile, 1998). The impact of the HIV/AIDS epidemic raises a number of critical social questions regarding social work practice with older people in the developing world. With many people dying at a younger age, many older persons are left without family caregivers. Some governments in the developing world are increasingly showing sensitivity to these problems, but there is more to be done to address the multiple challenges posed by the problem.

Although family ties are strong and the family remains the primary source of support for older Africans, modern social changes (e.g., industrialization, urbanization) are changing the traditional family structure and its ability to support its elderly family members (Ingstad, Bruun, Sandberg, & Tlou, 1992). Some older persons no longer receive adequate physical and social support due to out-migration (Peil, Bamisaiye, & Ekpenyong, 1989). Whereas the industrialized countries of Europe and North America have provided statutory insurance programs such as social security, health care, education, and a number of state-mandated social services, very limited statutory programs have been enacted in most developing countries to address the challenges of population aging.

IMPLICATIONS OF POPULATION AGING

The rapid increase projected in the number of older persons globally has significant implications for many areas such as health care, financing of social services, social protection, housing, and the role of the elderly population in a rapidly changing and urbanizing society. Social insurance programs are needed to address emerging challenges created by population aging. It is feared that, as the population ages, the economically active age-groups will not be able to support the dependent age-groups, mainly children and older persons who are traditionally cared for by the family.

The incidence of disease and disability also increases with advancing age. Moreover, there are special problems of diagnosis, assessment, management, and care of people in the older age-groups. In many countries, governments have accepted the responsibility of supporting the needs of older persons. Therefore, in cases like Ghana, where the present supply of human resources and facilities for health care is inadequate, these services will be even further strained.

It is clear that the increasing numbers and proportion of older persons will mean that more facilities and services will be required to meet their specific needs. In response, it is necessary for governments in developing countries to instigate appropriate policies.

IMPLICATIONS FOR SOCIAL WORK PRACTICE

A number of institutional and community-based services have been developed to meet the changing needs of older adults. Among these are multipurpose senior centers, adult day care, respite care services, congregate living, and assisted living centers. Such programs provide a setting for older people to socialize, reduce the effect of isolation, and offer an opportunity to partake in life-enhancing activities. As much as programs of this nature contribute to the quality of life of seniors, they are limited in that they provide few avenues for seniors to use their talents to benefit other people who may need their services and expertise. One challenge confronting an aging society is how to utilize the talents and experience of older adults to help other age cohorts that might need their services.

FAMILY CAREGIVING

In most parts of the developing world today, the demographic transition is negatively affecting the social fabric and communal arrangements that made it a joyful moral obligation to care for older persons (Apt & Grieco, 1994; Peil et al., 1989). One important consequence of fertility decline is a progressive reduction in the availability of kin to whom future generations of older persons may turn for support. This process may have a significant impact on the well-being of older persons, especially in the less developed regions, where social support for the older person is largely provided by the immediate family (Hoyert, 1991; Wolf, 1994). At the same time, improved chances of surviving to the oldest ages are likely to spur efforts to improve the health status of the older population and lead to reforms in the pension and health systems.

Today, the family is undergoing changes in terms of form, proximity, roles and functions, relationships, power, and decision-making hierarchies. Given the demands placed on members of the family who could sell their labor within the new economic system, the traditional role of caring for older persons has been affected in both rural and urban Africa. Families are no longer in a position to fulfill the economic, cultural, and social functions that they did before colonization and industrialization. Today, due to the change in the social role of women (the traditional caregivers) and increased migration of youth from rural to urban centers, the family is undergoing a very rapid transformation (Peil, 1991). For example, an increasing number of women work outside the home for pay, and this new role has affected their ability to provide informal caregiving. The increasing migration of the youth to urban centers in search of a better life deprives older individuals of the physical support and services that they may need from them (Peil, 1989). In spite of these changes, policies should be geared toward supporting and encouraging family members to enable them to continue their caregiving role. Ultimately, professional effort will be needed to complement family caregiving.

STATUTORY PROGRAMS IN THE DEVELOPING WORLD

As more people live longer, retirement, pensions, and other social benefits tend to extend over longer periods of time, making it necessary for social security systems to change substantially to remain effective (Creedy,

1998; Bravo, 1999). But the features and scope of statutory programs in developing countries vary in terms of the programs provided, the basis of eligibility, and funding and administrative mechanisms. Social security appears to be the primary statutory program provided in most countries. It operates as either a provident fund (e.g., Nigeria and Kenya) or a pension scheme (e.g., Ghana and Cote d'Ivoire; Kludze, 1988). Some countries (e.g., Botswana, Malawi, Sierra Leone, and Somalia) provide only workers' compensation. Others (e.g., Algeria, Cape Verde, Egypt, Guinea, Morocco, South Africa, and Tunisia) provide four statutory programs (e.g., unemployment benefits, workers' compensation, social security, and family allowance). In the majority of the countries (e.g., Benin, Central Africa Republic, Ethiopia, Gambia, Ghana, Kenya, Libya, Madagascar, Nigeria, Sudan, Zambia, Zimbabwe), about 68% of the population have at least two types of social insurance programs.

In contrast to the Africa situation, there is largely universal coverage of the populations in most Asian countries. For example, the pension and provident fund systems of countries such as Korea, Malaysia, Singapore, and Taiwan Province of China have near-universal coverage. However, in other countries, coverage is very limited to those in the formal sector (Heller, 1998). The social insurance programs in most countries do not have universal coverage. Persons who are not part of the formal labor force or not employed in the civil service sector are not included. Also, most rural populations are excluded, since most workers are involved in the informal labor market. Social security systems, like the Beveridge model, were designed around a traditional male working life concerned with a man's ability to earn and provide (Pascall, 1986).

NONSTATUTORY INSURANCE PROGRAMS

Informal welfare programs exist in most developing countries, to provide protection against the unforeseen contingencies of life. Prior to the advent of modern social insurance programs in most developing countries, such informal structures were based on family and an elaborate network of filial obligation. The structures provided social protection to address the needs of people within the informal sectors. In spite of the advent of the modern welfare state in some developing countries, nonstatutory welfare programs continue to be the only source of security to a sizable percentage of older people in such countries.

Cultural and religious societies, rotating credit societies, funeral societies, and informal saving societies exist throughout the continent (Midgley, 1997).

An Array of Social Services

A fair mix of government and community-based social services could be created to meet the needs of older persons. Core services such as health care, social housing, food and nutrition, and transportation could be addressed under a comprehensive service model for older persons. For example, a percentage of social security funds could be invested in low-income social housing programs for older persons with prior attachment to the labor market and who have earned sufficient social security credit. The balance could be paid under a flexible social loan program over a period of time. Also, transportation services could be provided under contract with private social service agencies to transport older people to meet specific needs. For example, reduced fares could be offered to older consumers on all government-operated transportation services. Another service is adult day care centers. They would offer an avenue for elderly persons to meet their peers to exchange notes and engage in life-enhancing activities. South Africa is one of the few countries beginning to experiment with this idea.

Reinforcing Traditional Security/Welfare Programs

It is necessary to reexamine traditional forms of social protection with the view to strengthening them. A double-decker social insurance system, one for those in the rural areas operating in the informal sector and another for those in urban areas operating in the formal sector, may be the best way to address the needs of both rural and urban elderly persons (Darkwa, 1997). Non-waged-based protective programs such as crop and animal insurance may be needed to provide additional protection to the sizable majority of elderly persons who rely on these sources for their livelihood.

Redistribution of Caregiving

In additional to state-sponsored insurance programs, the private sector should play an instrumental role in providing welfare services to address the needs of older persons. Religious organizations and business groups should consider a comprehensive array of church-based and employee assistance programs (fringe benefits, adult day care services, etc.) to supplement the limited governmental effort. This will go a long way toward relieving employees from the caregiving tasks during working hours. To date, businesses are beginning to respond in sharing in elder caregiving, but there is still much to be done, given changing demographics. A matching fund program could be instituted by religious organizations and business groups. Under a scheme of this nature, churches and businesses could match financial resources raised by community groups in support of elderly services. Given the magnitude of resources controlled by businesses and religious institutions, their involvement in the provision of social services to older persons will be a fine and befitting gesture.

CONCLUSION

Older persons in the developing world are being affected to varying degrees by the demographic transition. With an increase in the elderly population, the need to provide pre- and postretirement social protection programs is greater than ever before. Migration, urbanization, education, and wage labor are the main factors bringing about changes in the structure and support systems of the family. Thus, any policies, programs, and services that are enacted to address the needs of older persons should take those factors into consideration. Furthermore, an array of social services should address issues such as caregiving, postretirement adjustment, generational equity, health care, housing, and institutional and community-based social services. Addressing the needs of older persons should be a shared responsibility among governments, family members, nonprofit organizations, religious and faith communities, and the business community. Such a redistribution of responsibilities would ensure that identifiable sectors of the society are involved in addressing the needs of older persons. In sum, we need to redesign our social insurance and welfare system to fit the realities of our current situation. As times change, we should be able to adopt the current scheme to new realities and emerging changes.

REFERENCES

Adlakha, A. (1996, July). *International brief population trends: Ghana.* U.S. Department of Commerce, Economics and Statistics, IB/96-1.

Aging trends. (1990). *U.S. Department of Commerce. Bureau of the Census.* Center for International Research.

Apt, N. (1992). (Ed.). Ageing in Ghana. In *Effective response to ageing in Africa by the year 2000.* African Gerontological Society.

Apt, N. (1997). *Ageing in Africa.* Geneva, Switzerland: World Health Organization Ageing and Health Programme.

Apt, N., & Grieco, M. (1994). Urbanization, caring for the elderly people and the changing African family: The challenge to social policy. *International Social Security Review,* 111–121.

Darkwa. O. K. (1997). Retirement policies and economic security for older people in Africa. *Southern African Journal of Gerontology, 6*(2), 32–36.

Ebrahim, G. J. (1993). The Bamako initiative. *Journal of Tropical Pediatrics, 39,* 66–67.

Heller, P. (1998). Aging in the Asian Tiger Economics, 35(2), 1–8.

Heuveline (2003). Aging of population. In P. Demeny and G. McNicoll (Eds.), *The encyclopedia of population.* New York: Macmillan Reference USA.

Ingstad, B., Bruun, F., Sandberg, E., & Tlou, S. (1992). *Journal of Cross-Cultural Gerontology, 7,* 379–398.

Kinsella, K. (1992). Aging trends: Kenya. *Journal of Cross-Cultural Gerontology, 7,* 259–268.

Kinsella, K., & Ferreira, M. (1997, August). *International brief: Aging trends:* South Africa. U.S. Department of Commerce, Economics and Statistics Administration, IB/92-2.

Kinsella, K., & Taeuber, C. M. (1993). *An aging world II* (International Population Report P95/92-3). U.S. Department of Commerce, Bureau of the Census.

Kludze, A. K. P. (1988). Formal and informal social security in Ghana. In Benda-Beckmann, Benda-Beckman, E. Casino, F. Hirtz, G. R. Woodman, & H. F. Zacher (Eds.), *Between kinship and the state: Social security and law in developing countries* (pp. 187–209). Holland: Foris Publications.

Midgley, J. (1997). *Social welfare in global context.* Thousand Oaks, CA: Sage.

Otunba, T. O. (1997, October). *Social Security for the ageing.* Paper presented at the Third Global Conference on Ageing in Durban.

Pascall, G. (1986). *Social policy: A feminist analysis.* London: Tavistock.

Peil, M. (1991). Family support for the Nigerian elderly. *Journal of Comparative Family Studies, 12,* 85–89.

Peil, M., Bamisaiye, P., & Ekpenyong S. (1989). Health and physical support for the elderly in Nigeria. *Journal of Cross-Cultural Gerontology, 4,* 89–106.

United Nations AIDS Programme. (2004). *Epidemiology in Sub-Saharan Africa.* Retrieved from *http://www.unaids.org/unaids/fact/factfr.html.*

U.S. Bureau of the Census. (1997). International Program Center, International Data Base.

World Bank. (1993). *World development report. Investing in health.* Oxford, England: Oxford University Press.

MARTHA N. OZAWA
SHINGO NAKAYAMA

Long-Term Care Insurance in Japan

92

At the U.S.-Japan Conference on the National and International Implications of Population Aging in Oiso, Japan, in 1986, Henry Aaron, a prominent scholar of social security, stated that Japan and the United States would have to reckon with the looming public spending on long-term care for their seniors (Conference on the Societal Impact of Population Aging in the United States and Japan, 1986). That prediction has become a reality. Starting in the early 1990s, the Japanese government opened the debate on long-term care, which led to the passage of the Long-Term Care Insurance Law of 1997, which went into effect in April 2000. Because of the comprehensiveness of its coverage and provisions, the act has been hailed as the most important legislation since the National Pension Law (Kokumin nenkin ho) of 1961. The total expenditures for the Long-Term Care Insurance program, including administrative costs but excluding co-payments, for fiscal year 2003 (ended March 31, 2003) are estimated to be ¥5.4 trillion (or $45 billion [dollar equivalents of yen values are calculated on the basis of the $1 = ¥120 exchange rate]; Dai 1 kai shakaihosho shingikai kaigo hoken bukai, 2003) and are projected to increase as the program is fully implemented and the aging of the population accelerates (Ministry of Health and Welfare, 1995). It is estimated that the expenditures for this program will reach ¥20 trillion (or $167 billion) in 2025 ("Kaigo hoken," 2003). Japan's Long-Term Care Insurance program was the third program in the world that took the social insurance approach; the first was implemented in the Netherlands in 1967, and the second in Germany in 1995 (Ikegami, 1997).

This chapter examines the following questions: What were the forces that led Japan to establish a long-term care program for elderly people? What are the law's provisions? Finally, what are the aspects of policymaking in developing this program that are unique to Japan?

FORCES BEHIND THE LEGISLATION

Multiple forces led the Japanese government to develop a public program for long-term care for the elderly: demographic imperatives, changing public attitudes toward the care of elderly people, misuse of hospitals for nonmedical purposes, and the obsolescence of the previous long-term care system. In addition to these forces, a new ideology of "socialization of care of the elderly" emerged that changed the tenet of Japan's welfare state. We will discuss each force in turn.

Demographic Imperatives

Japan's population is aging rapidly. In 2000, life expectancy at birth was 84.62 years for women and 77.64 years for men. The proportion of the elderly (aged 65 and older), 17.4% in 2000, is projected to reach 28.7% in 2025 and 35.7% in 2050 (National Institute of Population and Social Security Research, 2002, Table 1, p. 12). These demographic changes will take place in the context of a shrinking population: Japan's population is projected to decline from 128 million in 2007 to 101 million in 2050 (National Institute of Population and Social Security Research, 2002, Table 1, p. 12).

Because of these demographic changes, the living arrangements of the elderly have changed dramatically. From 1980 to 1992, the proportion of the elderly who lived alone increased from 8.5% to 11.7%, and the proportion of the elderly who lived only with their spouses increased from 19.6% to 27.6%. Conversely, the elderly who lived with their adult children declined from 69.0% to 57.1% during the same period (Ministry of Health and Welfare, 1995, p. 81).

Even if elderly people live with their adult children, the availability of women (the traditional caregivers) who can care for elderly relatives has declined, because of their increasing rate of labor force participation. From 1975 to 1992, the percentage of married women who worked increased from 42.6% to 52.2%, and the percentage of married women who worked outside their homes increased from 8.1% to 35.5%. Despite these changes, women still constitute 85.9% of the caregivers, and 54.2% of the caregivers are aged 50 to 69 (Ministry of Health and Welfare, 1995, pp. 59–60).

In the meantime, the number of elderly people who are in need of care has been increasing at a relentless speed. In 2000, a total of 1.5 million elderly people were bedridden, excluding those with dementia; 200,000 had dementia; and 1.2 million were frail. Thus, 2.8 million elderly people (or 12.7% of the elderly population) were bedridden, suffering from dementia, or frail (Ministry of Health, Labor, and Welfare, 2002b, p. 7; National Institute of Population and Social Security Research, 2002, p. 12).

It is projected that by 2025, a total of 5.2 million elderly people (or 15.0% of the projected elderly population) will be at risk of needing long-term care, of whom 2.8 million will be bedridden, 400,000 will have dementia, and 2 million will be frail (Ministry of Health, Labor, and Welfare, 2002b, p. 7; National Institute of Population and Social Security Research, 2002, p. 12). The probability of being bedridden and/or suffering from dementia increases from 1.5% for those

aged 65 to 69, to 3.5% for those aged 70 to 74, to 6.3% for those aged 75 to 79, to 11.5% for those aged 80 to 84, and to 33.5% for those aged 85 and older (Ministry of Health, Labor, and Welfare, 2002b, p. 58). It is estimated that 50% of those aged 65 and over will need long-term care in their lifetimes (Katsunuma Cho Yakuba, 2003). Furthermore, the time that the elderly need long-term care has increased because these elderly people live longer. In 1992, 47.3 % of bedridden people were in that condition for more than 3 years (Ministry of Health and Welfare, 1995, pp. 58–59).

Changing Public Attitudes

In spite of the Japanese traditional value that compels adult children to care for their ailing parents, more and more Japanese have come to accept the need to provide support and care for elderly people through a publicly provided long-term care program. Public opinion polls, conducted from 1994 to 1996 by three major newspapers, indicated that between 60% and 87% of the respondents favored some type of publicly financed and publicly provided long-term care system (Nagase, 2001; Ministry of Health and Welfare, 1995). A 1995 government survey indicated that 82% of the public supported long-term care insurance based on a social insurance scheme (see Masuda, 2001). In addition, the younger generations support publicly provided long-term care for their own parents more strongly than do the parents themselves. The Survey on Long-Term Care and Health Care in Old Age, conducted by the Ministry of Health and Welfare (1992), asked the respondents aged 45 to 64 where they want their parents to receive long-term care and asked respondents aged 65 or older where they wanted to be cared for. Only 31.3% of the younger generation versus 43.3% of the older generation stated that home was the desirable place to be cared for. Nonetheless, these figures indicate that a sizable proportion of both young and old generations accept the fact that the majority of the elderly should be cared for outside their homes.

Increasing Health Care Spending and Its Misuse

As in the United States, Japan's total health care expenditures have been increasing at a faster rate than the growth of its economy. It is expected that Japan's national expenditures for health care will increase at an annual rate of 5.6%, from ¥27 trillion ($225 billion) in 1995 to ¥54 trillion ($450 billion) in 2010, and at annual rate of 4.5%, from ¥54 trillion in 2010 to ¥104 trillion ($866 billion) in 2025, all in constant yen. For each period, the rate of increase in health care expenditures for the elderly is expected to be even greater. As a result, the share of national health care expenditures for the elderly is expected to grow from 39% in 1995, to 42% in 2010, and to 54% in 2025. These numbers indicate that at least in the aggregate, the health care expenditures for the elderly will grow disproportionately, relative to the increase in total health care expenditures in Japan. As of 1999, per capita health care expenditures for the elderly population were ¥782,000 (or $6,409), 2.8 times the amount for nonelderly people (Ministry of Health and Welfare, 1999a).

To confound the health care financing problem, many elderly people are hospitalized in general hospitals not because they need medical care but because they have no place to go—a phenomenon the Japanese call "social hospitalization." In 1999, 25% of hospitalized patients aged 75 and older could have been discharged if they had places to go (Ministry of Health and Welfare, 1999b). To decrease health care expenditures, policymakers were convinced that they had to provide long-term care to those who do not need to be hospitalized, under a separate long-term care program, because it would be more economically efficient to do so.

Macroeconomic Issue

Japanese policymakers recognized that without a comprehensive long-term care program, many prime-age women would be forced to curtail, or even terminate, their employment to care for their aging parents or in-laws. It is estimated that for each 10 persons who need long-term care, 1 person terminates his or her employment to care for an elderly person (Iwamoto, 2001). The result, policymakers believed, would be slower economic growth. Moreover, because policymakers wanted to see faster growth in the service-related and high-tech industries, maintaining well-educated women in the labor force was critical. Furthermore, they wanted the elderly—who were saving money at twice the rate of the non-aged and had a median of ¥6,500,000 (or $54,200) in bank savings accounts—to spend money for current consumption (Yusei Shou, 1999). The elderly were saving this much money because they were afraid of becoming in need of long-term care (Kyogoku, 1998).

Obsolescence of the Income-Tested Program

The previous long-term care program, which was instituted under the Social Welfare Law for the Elderly in 1963, became obsolete, both ideologically and programmatically, for meeting the long-term care needs of current and future generations. That program was generally targeted to low-income elderly people and those without other family members at home and was subsidized by the three levels of governments (national, prefectural, and municipal). Thus, high-income elderly people who live with other family members are effectively excluded. Under this program, a low-income elderly person pays almost nothing to stay in a nursing home, whereas a high-income elderly person, if admitted to a nursing home, pays as much as ¥240,000 ($2,000) a month. Those who did not meet the eligibility criteria had to find services in the marketplace and purchase both home-based and institutional care services and pay for them out of their own pocket.

Such a selection process created dissatisfaction among the public; even if elderly people who needed care lived with other family members, it had become difficult for family members to provide adequate care. Moreover, unreasonably high payments that were imposed on high-income residents of nursing homes were another source of contention (Ito, 2000).

Furthermore, the health and welfare systems were uncoordinated, so that elderly people had to apply to government agencies to receive home care or institutional care and deal separately with health providers (physicians and nurses) to receive medical care (Masuda, 2001). In spite of all these difficulties in the previous system and a relatively limited number of elderly people who were eligible for nursing home care because of stringent eligibility criteria, there were waiting lists for nursing home placements of 2 to 3 years in many localities (Ito, 2000).

A New Ideology in Japan's Welfare State

Perhaps more influential than any other force that led Japan to launch comprehensive long-term care insurance was the emergence of an ideology that adopted the notion of socialized care for the elderly. Since the end of World War II, the Japanese government concentrated, first, on the amelioration and prevention of poverty; second, on income security for retired workers, disabled workers, survivors of deceased workers, and dependents of retired or disabled workers; and, third, on the perfecting of universal health care insurance. In the 1980s, policymakers and the public started addressing the public provision of care services for the elderly. This new initiative represented a departure from the earlier assumption that only families were to be responsible for providing care for the elderly. Such an initiative signified the public acceptance of the governmental responsibility to finance and provide care services for the elderly. The public responsibility in this area was the start of a new ideology in Japan's welfare state, under which the central focus was to ensure adequate and effective support and care for elderly people so that they could continue to be productive members of society with the maximum possible vigor. Government leadership in developing such a new ideology is characteristic of Japan's policy making because the Japanese public has a high level of trust in and reliance on government.

Several pieces of legislation that ensued are the manifestation of the new ideology. The 1989 Gold Plan (formally called the Ten-Year Strategy to Promote Health and Welfare for the Aged) was the manifestation of this new ideology. It set specific targets for doubling the number of nursing home beds, tripling the number of home helpers, and achieving 10 times the number of adult day care centers, as well as establishing local agencies whose job was to coordinate home-based care services for the elderly (Ministry of Health and Welfare, 1996). Under the 1990 amendments to the Social Welfare Law for the Elderly, municipal governments were made legally responsible for developing a variety of home-based and institutional long-term care services. In 1994, in a governmental document entitled *21st Century Social Welfare Vision: Toward Establishing Shoshi-Korei Society*, the national government changed the weight of public social welfare expenditures from 5:4:1 (pensions, health, and social services) to 5:3:2 as a goal (Health and Welfare Statistics Association, 2001b, p. 190). The 1994 Gold Plan (which basically was the upgraded version of the 1989 Gold Plan) raised the already ambitious targets set in the 1989 Gold Plan on all fronts (Campbell, 2000; Campbell & Ikegami, 2000). In this way, Japan's welfare state started to make support and care for the elderly its centerpiece.

After the enactment of the Long-Term Care Insurance Law, the quest to develop infrastructures for long-term care provisions continued unabated. The Gold Plan 21st Century accelerated the quantitative targets for personnel, services, facilities, and manage-

ment technologies, as well as the development of a movement to improve the image of the elderly, the encouragement of independent living with dignity, and the establishment of mutually supportive local communities (Masuda, 2001; Ministry of Health, Labor, and Welfare, 2002b).

In summary, the Long-Term Care Insurance program was developed because of various external forces, such as demographic imperatives, changing public attitudes toward the care of elderly people, the misuse of hospitals for nonmedical purposes, and the obsolescence of the previous long-term care system. But the primary catalyst for establishing such insurance was the new ideology in Japan's welfare state. Anticipating the accelerating changes in demographics, family structure, and living arrangements of the elderly, the Japanese government and the public responded to the need for long-term care of the elderly aggressively and positively, however costly this program may be.

BASIC PROVISIONS OF LONG-TERM CARE INSURANCE

From the beginning of the policy debate in the mid-1990s, the planners of long-term care insurance set forth clear goals. Furthermore, they decided that the municipal governments were to be the insurers. Their goals were as follows:

- To spread the burden for paying for long-term care for the elderly throughout the society;
- To establish a clear link between contributions and benefits and to clarify the sources of funding for the program;
- To introduce a system under which health care services and long-term care services are integrated but funded separately;
- To adopt a social insurance scheme in developing a long-term care program; and
- To eliminate hospitalization for social purposes (Ministry of Health, Labor, and Welfare, 2002b).

The decision to designate municipal governments as the insurers came naturally (although some mayors resisted the idea; Ito, 1998) because, as provided under the 1990 Amendments to the Social Welfare Law for the Elderly and amendments to seven other laws related to social welfare (Kyogoku, 1998), municipal governments had played the primary role in developing various types of social welfare services, as well as "community plans" for health and social services for the elderly. That is, the planners of the Long-Term Care Insurance program conceived of long-term care as an extension of social welfare services, instead of an extension of health care services, and thought that municipal governments had enough experience to become the insurers of the Long-Term Care Insurance program (Kyogoku, 1998); moreover, municipal governments had been the insurers for the national health insurance plan for self-employed and nonemployed persons.

The consensus on adopting a social insurance scheme for a long-term care program was developed early in the policy debate—around 1994—and specific policies were developed later. The planners of the program dealt with basic principles in the following areas:

- The share of aggregate expenditures to be met by the national, prefectural, and municipal governments and the insured;
- Certification and classification of recipients of long-term care;
- Separate treatment of two age-groups of the insured with regard to contributions and eligibility to receive care;
- Types of benefits provided, the maximum payments to be met by the insurance, and the co-payments that are to be paid by the insured;
- Special, financial protection for low-income insured people; and
- Permission for for-profit organizations to participate in the insurance program as providers of home-based services (Ministry of Health, Labor, and Welfare, 2002b).

Shares of the Financial Burden

An extensive infusion of general revenue is involved in financing the Long-Term Care Insurance program. This is reflected by the proportion of the financial burden to be met by the three levels of government and the insured: 25% by the national government, 12.5% by the prefectural governments, 12.5% by the municipal governments, 17% (changed to 18% in 2003) by the insured aged 65 and over, and 33% (changed to 32% in 2003) by the insured aged 40 to 64.

Of the national government's contributions, 5 percentage points are to be set aside to assist municipalities that are facing financial difficulties because they have a high proportion of low-income elderly people, a large proportion of those aged 75 and older who are at high risk of becoming bedridden or having dementia, or many waivers of premiums because of

natural disasters experienced by insured people (insured people who encounter natural disasters do not have to pay premiums). In addition, the national government is to pay 50% of the administrative costs incurred by municipal governments.

The proportions of the financial burden placed on people aged 65 and over (17%, changed to 18% in 2003) and on people aged 40 to 65 (33%, changed to 32% in 2003) are directly related to the ratios of the populations in these age-groups: There are about twice as many people aged 40 to 64 (43 million) as people aged 65 and over (22 million; Nagase, 2001). Thus, the program was designed to impose the same financial burden on the two age-groups.

Premiums Levied on Two Age-Groups

People Aged 65 and Over

The premiums to be paid by elderly people depend on their incomes. For calculating premiums, elderly people are categorized into five groups according to five economic conditions: (a) elderly individuals who receive public assistance or old-age pensions and whose other household members do not pay municipal taxes; (b) elderly individuals in households in which no members pay municipal taxes; (c) elderly individuals who do not pay municipal taxes but whose other household members do; (d) elderly individuals who have annual incomes of less than ¥2,000,000 ($16,667); and (e) elderly individuals who have annual incomes of ¥2,000,000 or more, as of April 2003.

The program considers Group 3 the baseline group and requires people in that group to pay a set premium. Premiums for Groups 1, 2, 4, and 5 are derived from the baseline premium that is paid by Group 3. Table 92.1, which applies to the city of Aioi (2003), illustrates the point. Elderly individuals in Group 3 pay premiums of ¥34,800 (or $290) a year, Group 2 pays 25% less, Group 1 pays 50% less, Group 4 pays 25% more, and Group 5 pays 50% more. It is estimated that 72% of the elderly belong to Groups 2 or 3 (Ministry of Health, Labor, and Welfare, 2002b). The national average annual premium in 2003 is ¥39,516 ($329; "Kaigo hoken ryo," 2003). The baseline premium is set by municipal governments and can be changed every 3 years.

Premiums from elderly individuals are collected in two ways. For those who receive social security benefits of ¥180,000 ($1,500) or more a year (about 80% of the elderly), their contributions are deducted from

TABLE 92.1 Annual Premiums for Elderly Persons Aged 65 and Over, by Level of Income Status 2003–2005: The Case of Aioi City

Economic Status	Relative Premiums	Absolute Premiums
Group 1	0.50	¥17,400 (US$145)
Group 2	0.75	¥26,100 (US$218)
Group 3	1.00	¥34,800 (US$290)
Group 4	1.25	¥43,500 (US$363)
Group 5	1.50	¥52,200 (US$435)

Note: Group 1 = those who are on public assistance or receive old-age pensions; Group 2 = elderly people who do not pay municipal taxes, and neither does the rest of their household; Group 3 = elderly people who do not pay municipal taxes, but some of their household members do; Group 4 = elderly people with annual income less than ¥2,000,000; Group 5 = elderly people with annual income more than ¥2,000,000.

From City of Aioi, *Kaogo hoken ryo ni tsuite* (Aioi City: Author, 2003), retrieved from *http://www.city.aioi.hyogo.jp/sections/c/if/if_about.html.*

their social security benefits and sent to the municipal governments. Those whose social security benefits are less than ¥180,000 a year send their premiums directly to their municipal governments (Ministry of Health, Labor, and Welfare, 2002b; Nagase, 2001). In the aggregate, the contributions by those aged 65 and over are supposed to meet 18% (in 2003) of the total benefit expenditures in particular municipalities.

People Aged 40 to 64

Employed persons in this age-group must be insured for health care to be insured for the Long-Term Care Insurance program. (Ostensibly, the objective of not covering persons without health care insurance coverage is to prevent the use of long-term care insurance for meeting the cost of medical care.) Employed persons become insured by paying a premium in the form of payroll taxes on top of payroll taxes for health care insurance. The payroll tax rate for health insurance is 8.2% (in 2003), and the payroll tax rate for the Long-Term Care Insurance program is 0.89%. Because employers pay half the payroll taxes, the tax rate levied on employees for the Long-Term Care Insurance program is 0.445% of taxable earnings. For health care insurance and the Long-Term Insurance combined, employees pay 4.549% of their taxable earnings up to ¥11,760,000 ($98,000; Mitsui Seimei, 1998). The rates of payroll taxes for the two programs

can be changed annually. The payroll taxes for the Long-Term Care Insurance program are transferred to the Long-Term Care Insurance Trust Fund.

Self-employed or nonemployed persons, who also must be covered by health insurance before they can be covered by the Long-Term Care Insurance program, pay their premiums for both types of insurance directly to their municipal governments. Their premiums are based primarily on household income, with half the premiums paid by the national government. The premiums for the Long-Term Care Insurance paid by these persons are transferred to the Long-Term Care Insurance Trust Fund.

The Long-Term Care Insurance Trust Fund, which collects and pools the contributions from those aged 40 to 64 nationwide, transfers to each municipal government the amount equal to 32% (as of 2003) of the total benefits expenditures incurred by that municipal government. This proportion reflects the program design under which this age-group is to bear 32% of the total benefit expenditures.

The collection and distribution, by the Trust Fund, of premiums paid by those aged 40 to 64 has a built-in redistributive function. That is, because the distribution of funds reflects the budgetary needs—32% (as of 2003) of the total benefit expenditures in particular municipalities—and the collection of premiums reflects the economic capabilities of workers in such municipalities, some municipalities with greater financial needs will receive more from the Trust Fund than the premiums that are sent to the fund, and vice versa.

Certification and Classification of People in Need of Long-Term Care

The Long-Term Care Insurance program has an elaborate system for classifying insured people according to the level of care they need and certifying the existence of such need. This system is intended to treat insured people uniformly, fairly, and efficiently and to avoid fraud and abuse of the program. The law requires each municipal government to develop a Board for Certifying the Need for Long-Term Care composed of people with proper credentials in the fields of medicine, nursing, and social welfare. (If desired, two or more municipal governments are allowed to establish such a board together.) The first step in certifying the need for care involves a home visit by a municipal government official, who investigates an applicant's physical (i.e., functional) and mental conditions using an 85-item questionnaire that was developed by the national government and is used throughout the country. Indicators of physical and mental conditions are processed by computer to arrive at the overall scores. The investigator brings the computerized results to the board, which, together with input from the family physician, certifies the applicant's need for and level of care.

Applicants for long-term care are then notified whether they need just *support* or *care*. Those who are certified as in need of support receive only home-based care services. Applicants who are certified as in need of care are classified into five groups, depending on the level of care needed. The level of need is measured by the number of minutes per day of care and services that applicants need for daily living (Health and Welfare Statistics Association, 2001b, p. 188). Those certified in need of care are eligible to receive both home-based and institutional care.

After certification by the Board for Certifying the Need for Long-Term Care and final authorization by the municipal government, applicants are ready to receive services. The insurance program encourages them to hire professionals to develop a "care plan"—a package of services that they can receive most effectively and efficiently. To be a professional in this field, a person must pass a national examination that assesses one's knowledge about long-term care. Upon passing the exam, the person must complete a practicum of specified duration. After the successful completion of the practicum, the applicant receives a certificate, which enables him or her to be a care planner and/or care manager (see Kizaki, Masuda, Inagawa, & Hirata, 2001, p. 95).

Fees for care planners are paid for outside the maximum payment constraints (explained later) by the insurance program. The insured may establish their own care plans within the budgetary constraints. The insured can choose not to have a care plan, but, in that case, they must pay the entire cost of services and then claim reimbursements from the insurance program, which is impractical in most cases. Thus, the thrust of the law is to encourage the insured to hire professionals to develop care plans.

In addition, a professional "care manager" can be hired to monitor and coordinate the services that the insured will receive. Again, the cost of hiring such a professional will be paid for by the Long-Term Care Insurance program in the same way that the cost of hiring a professional to develop a care plan is paid. The care plan developer and the care manager can come from a qualified, service-provider organization that participates in the Long-Term Care Insurance program.

To be eligible for any type of services, those aged 40 to 64 must prove that their incapacities are the result of 1 of 15 recognized age-related diseases and illnesses, such as nervous disorders caused by diabetes, stroke, or Parkinson's disease. Thus, if one's incapacity was caused by an auto accident, for example, he or she is deemed ineligible. Other than this restriction, insured people aged 40 to 64 are treated the same as insured people aged 65 and over.

Those who successfully complete the certification are required to repeat the assessment every 6 months thereafter (Shakai Hoken Techo Henshubu, 2002).

Types of Services Provided and Co-payments

The insurance program provides two types of services: (a) home-based services and (b) institutional services. The insurance program recognizes 15 types of home-based provisions and 3 types of long-term care institutions in which insured persons can be placed. The maximum payments that the insurance program provides differ depending on the level of care needed, the type of facility, and the index of value of long-term care services (explained later).

Home-based care services include home helpers, bathing and toileting services, nursing services, rehabilitation services, and counseling on home care management. Under the law, short stays in various types of facilities and services provided in group homes (especially for people with dementia) are defined as home-based services. The provision of home-based care also includes the cost of renting or buying special devices and equipment. The program also pays for the cost of renovating homes, which is authorized by the Board for Certifying the Need for Long-Term Care, on a case-by-case basis.

Three types of institutions are recognized: (a) nursing homes for people who do not have severe medical or mental problems, (b) skilled nursing homes for people who need medical attention), and (c) sanatorium-type nursing homes for people with dementia and other chronic illnesses).

The amount of services (valued in yen) that the insured will receive depends on whether they need support or care; among those who need care, the amount of services depends on the degree of care needed, on whether they need home-based services or institutional services, and the type of nursing homes they are placed in. The monthly maximum payment allowed for home-based services for those who just need support is ¥61,500 (or $513) in 2003. Table 92.2 shows the maximum payments for home-based and institutional services in the same year for those who need *care* according to the classification of the insured, just described, and according to the types of nursing homes they are placed in. These payments are sent directly to the service providers, and the municipal government collect co-payments and other payments from the insured (explained later).

As Table 92.2 indicates, the maximum spending for home-based services is not necessarily low. For example, the level of maximum spending for home-based services for people in Group 5 is higher than for those in comparable groups who are placed in general nursing homes or skilled nursing homes. These standards reflect the high priority that is placed on home-based services to prevent institutionalization (Kyogoku, 1998).

The Ministry of Health, Labor, and Welfare evaluates the value of specific services on the basis of complexity and duration, using a unit system. For example, as of 2003, a physical care service for less than 30 minutes is valued as 210 units; the same service for .5 to 1 hour is valued as 402 units. A home-making service up to 1 hour is valued as 208 units; the same service between 1 and 1.5 hours is valued as 291 units (see Ministry of Health, Labor, and Welfare, 2003). Then, the sum of the units derived from various kinds of services for specific amounts of time is multiplied by ¥10. The product of the total units and ¥10 is the amount of maximum payments. In arriving at the maximum payments, the ministry took into account nine types of services that the insured who need support are assumed to need for daily living at home and the types of care that the insured in Groups 1, 2, 3, 4, and 5 (who all need care) are assumed to need at home or in a particular type of institution. The authority to change the yen value of a unit of service rests with the national government.

The co-payment by the insured is uniformly set at 10% of the cost of services received. In addition, while being institutionalized, the insured will pay a flat amount for meals and meet the cost of incidentals. However, a lower flat amount for meals will be charged to those in lower economic statuses, namely, Groups 1 and 2 (see Table 92.1). Specifically, the insured in Group 1 pay ¥300 per day, those in Group 2 pay ¥500/day, and the rest pay the normal rate of ¥780 per day ($6.50; Ministry of Health, Labor, and Welfare, 2002b). Generally, out-of-pocket expenditures equal a 10% co-payment and, for those who are institutionalized, charges for meals and incidentals.

TABLE 92.2 Maximum Monthly Payments for Home-Based Services and Institutional Services, by Type of Facility and Level of Need, 2003

Level of Care Needed	Maximum Payments Per Month
Home-Based Services	
Group 1	¥165,800 (US$1,381)
Group 2	¥194,800 (US$1,623)
Group 3	¥267,500 (US$2,229)
Group 4	¥306,000 (US$2,550)
Group 5 (high)	¥358,300 (US$2,986)
Institutional Services	
General nursing homes	
Group 1	¥205,808 (US$1,715)
Group 2	¥227,392 (US$1,895)
Group 3	¥248,672 (US$2,072)
Group 4	¥270,256 (US$2,252)
Group 5 (high)	¥291,536 (US$2,429)
Nursing homes for those needing medical care	
Group 1	¥248,976 (US$2,075)
Group 2	¥263,872 (US$2,199)
Group 3	¥279,984 (US$2,333)
Group 4	¥296,400 (US$2,470)
Group 5 (high)	¥312,512 (US$2,604)
Nursing homes for those with dementia and other chronic illnesses	
Group 1	¥249,280 (US$2,077)
Group 2	¥282,270 (US$2,356)
Group 3	¥355,072 (US$2,959)
Group 4	¥385,776 (US$3,215)
Group 5 (high)	¥413,440 (US$3,445)

From Health and Welfare Statistics Association, *Kokumin no fukushi no doko* (Tokyo: Author 2001b), Table 7, p. 190; Ministry of Health, Labor, and Welfare, *Zenkoku kaigo hosyu zigyo unei kijun tantosha kaigi siryo* (Tokyo: Author, 2003).

Protection Against Financial Hardship

The Long-Term Care Insurance program has a safety net to protect low-income people from undue financial hardship. First, the insurer (municipal governments) can waive the 10% co-payment. Second, the cost of meals provided in nursing homes and the insurance premium can be paid for by the public assistance program, which is financed entirely by the national government. The municipal governments make the determination on these matters on a case-by-case basis (Nagase, 2001).

Participation of For-Profit Organizations

The Long-Term Care Insurance program allows for-profit organizations to participate as providers of home-based services as long as the prefectural governments certify them. To receive certification, these organizations must meet the minimum standards for staffing and credentials of staff. The objectives of allowing for-profit organizations to participate in the program are to create competition, innovation, and, as a result, higher quality, and to ensure that enough services are available in the community to meet the need for services (Nagase, 2001). It is estimated that 45% of the total expenditures for home visits in 2003 was attributable to the services provided by for-profit organizations ("Kenshou kaigo hoken 3 nen," 2003).

DISCUSSION

Several aspects of the Long-Term Care Insurance program are unique to Japan's policy development.

Infusion of General Revenues

The first aspect is the heavy infusion of general revenue in this program. As was mentioned earlier, this program is financed 50% by general revenues of the three levels of government. However, such a practice is not unusual in Japan because other social insurance programs are financed in a similar way. For example, general revenues are used to finance half the spending on fist-tier social security benefits (the Japanese social security program uses a two-tier approach to calculating benefits). As a result, general revenues finance about one third of the entire social security expenditures (Ozawa, 1985).

Japan's use of general revenues for financing social insurance programs, such as the Long-Term Care Insurance program and the social security program, reflects the country's collectivist orientation for financing such programs. One effect of this orienta-

tion is that the financing side of these programs becomes more progressive than it would if the programs relied solely on payroll taxes. Another effect is that decision making tends to be shared more broadly by the old and the young populations, and, as a result, relatively radical changes in a social insurance program become possible.

Coverage of Those Aged 40 to 64

The second aspect is the inclusion of people aged 40 to 64. The Ministry of Health, Labor, and Welfare (2002a) reported that in 2001, only 0.2% of those aged 40 to 64 were certified as being eligible to receive support or care under the new Long-Term Care Insurance program, which indicates that the probability of this age-group receiving any type of long-term care services is small. Thus, the primary objective of covering this age-group was to transfer financial resources from this group to the elderly population. Policymakers knew that without contributions by this age-group, it would be difficult to develop an adequate system of long-term care for the elderly. In addition, from the beginning the Japanese government publicized that the entire society would bear the financial burden of providing long-term care for the elderly.

Coverage of the Entire Elderly Population

The third aspect is that all elderly people—rich or poor, Japanese citizens or foreigners—are covered (Kyogoku, 1998). This policy objective is reflected in the Japanese government's attempt to collect premiums from the elderly according to economic class and to subsidize the out-of-pocket expenses of low-income elderly persons, as discussed earlier. The inclusion of all elderly people in this program reflects Japan's way of policy making in general. In Japan's social security program, for example, policymakers made it possible for those who were too old to establish eligibility for social security benefits to receive flat-amount "old-age pensions," thus obviating the need for a program like Supplemental Security Income in the United States.

Japanese Version of Income Testing

The fourth aspect is how an income test is used in the program. As was shown earlier, to arrive at the premium amount, the Long-Term Care Insurance program classifies elderly people into five economic groups, such as those on welfare or receiving old-age pensions and those who do not pay any municipal taxes, and then develops the premium for each economic class; this is called *bracket income testing* or *categorical income testing*. Likewise, lower meal charges are used in nursing homes for lower economic groups. In both cases, the program does not use an income test that reduces benefits at a specified rate, as income level goes up, as is widely practiced in the United States with programs such as Temporary Assistance to Needy Families (TANF) and food stamps. Also, a similar bracket income test is used in the administration of Japan's children's allowances program (Ozawa, 1991). At any rate, Japan's method of income testing results in a simpler administration of income testing, as well as in less stigma.

American policy analysts may argue that the Japanese way of income testing creates a notch problem (i.e., at certain points of income, a one-dollar increase in income results in more than a one-dollar decline in net income). In the case of the Long-Term Care Insurance premiums, at some points of income levels, a one-yen increase in income results in more than a one-yen increase in premiums. Such an income test may create not only unfairness but also pervasive work disincentives. The Japanese public seems unconcerned about such a notch problem (Ozawa, 1991). Here, we see a clear cultural difference.

In the eyes of Japan's policymakers, the Long-Term Insurance program is not a finished product. The expenditures may grow faster than expected. The issue of transforming the program from the age-based one to a disability-based one is already being debated among policymakers. Given the flexible attitudes that Japan's policymakers have in developing a social insurance program, we believe they will face these challenges successfully and make changes in the Long-Term Care Insurance program as economic and demographic conditions change.

REFERENCES

Campbell, J. C. (2000). Changing meaning of frail old people and the Japanese welfare state. In S. O. Long (Ed.), *Caring for the elderly in Japan and the U.S.: Practices and policies* (pp. 84–99). London: Routledge.

City of Aioi. (2003). Kaogo hoken ryo ni tsuite. Aioi City: Author. Retrieved from *http://www.city.aioi.hyogo.jp/sections/c/if/if_about.html.*

Conference on the Societal Impact of Population Aging in the United States and Japan. (1986, February). Opening session on population aging, Oiso, Japan. Sponsored by the Carnegie Corporation of New York, the Association of Former Members of Congress, and the Japan Center for International Exchange.

Health and Welfare Association Statistics. (2001a). *Hoken to nenkin no doko.* Tokyo: Author.

Health and Welfare Statistics Association. (2001b). *Kokumin no fukushi no doko.* Tokyo: Author.

Ikegami, N. (1997). Public long-term care insurance in Japan. *Journal of American Medical Association, 278,* 1310–1314.

Ikegami, N., Campbell, J., & Masuda, M. (2001). Shinsyun zadankai: Kaigohoken no shido to 21 seiki no shakai hosho. *Shakai Hoken Junpo, 2084,* 28–37.

Ito, S. (1998). *Kaigo hoken: Sono jitsujo to mondai ten.* Tokyo: Aoki Press.

Ito, S. (2000). *Kaigo hoken to shakai fukushi.* Kyoto: Minerva Shobo.

Iwamoto, Y. (2001). *Shakai fukushi to kazoku to keisaigaku.* Tokyo: Tokyo Keizai Shinpo Sha.

Japan Medical Association, Department of Policy Research. (1997). *Kaigo hiken no donyu seisaku seikei katei.* Tokyo: Author.

Kaigo hoken, bappon kaikaku start (2003, May 28). *Yomiuri Shinbun.*

Kaigo hoken ryo: Zenkoku heikin de 13.15 up getsugaku 3,293 yen (2003, May 26). *Mainichi Shinbun.*

Katsunuma Cho Yakuba. (2003). *Korei shakai no genjo, 2003.* Katsunuma City, Japan: Author.

Kenshou kaigo hoken 3 nen: Kaigo business kencho, hoken gai wa kusen (2003, March 18). *Yomiuri Shinbun.*

Kizaki, N., Masuda, M., Inagawa, H., & Hirata, N. (2001). *Kaigo hoken keyword jiten.* Tokyo: Chuohoki.

Kokuho kanyusha no kaigo 2-go hokenryo (2000, February 16). *Mainichi Shinbun.*

Kyogoku, T. (1998). *Kaigo hoken no senryaku: 21 seiki gata shakai hosho no arikata* (2nd ed.). Tokyo: Chuo Hoki.

Masuda, M. (2001). Kango hoken seido no seisaku keisei katei no tokuchou to kadai. *Shakai Hoshou Kenkyu, 37*(1), 44–58.

Ministry of Health and Welfare. (1992). Long-term care and health care in old age. *Survey on Health and Welfare.* Tokyo: Author.

Ministry of Health and Welfare. (1995). *Aratana koreisha kaigo system no kochiku o mezashite.* Tokyo: Gyosei.

Ministry of Health and Welfare. (1996). *Trends in the nation's welfare.* Tokyo: Japan Kousei Tokei Kyokai.

Ministry of Health and Welfare. (1998). *Yuryo rojin home to no arikata ni kansuru kentokai hokokusho.* Tokyo: Author.

Ministry of Health and Welfare. (1999a). *Annual report on health and welfare 1999* (Vol. 1, Pt. 2). Tokyo: Author.

Ministry of Health and Welfare. (1999b). *Kanja chosa no gaikyo.* Tokyo: Author.

Ministry of Health, Labor, and Welfare. (2002a). *Kaigo hoken jigyo jokyo hokoku: Geppo.* Tokyo: Author. Retrieved from *http://www.mhlw.go.jp/topics/0103/tp0329-1.html.*

Ministry of Health, Labor, and Welfare. (2002b). *Long-term care insurance in Japan.* Tokyo: Author. Retrieved from *http://www.mhlw.go.jp/english/topics/elderly/care/index.html.*

Ministry of Health, Labor, and Welfare. (2003). *Zenkoku kaigo hosyu jigyo unei kizyun tantousha kaigi shiryo.* Tokyo: Author.

Minkan rojin home no ryokin: Down (1999, January 25). *Yomiuri Shinbun.*

Mitsui Seimei. (1998). *Standardized salary.* Tokyo: Author.

Nagase, F. (2001). *Kaigo hoken ho no kaisetsu* (Rev. ed.). Tokyo: Hitotsubashi Press.

National Institute of Population and Social Security Research. (1997). *The trends in populations: Japan and the world.* Tokyo: Author.

National Institute of Population and Social Security Research. (2002). *Population projections for Japan: 2001–2050.* Tokyo: Author.

Ozawa, M. N. (1985). Social security reform in Japan. *Social Service Review, 59,* 476–495.

Ozawa, M. N. (1991). Child welfare programs in Japan. *Social Service Review, 65,* 1–21.

Shakai Hoken Techo Henshubu. (2002). *Shakai hoken techo, 2003.* Tokyo: Kosei Shuppansha.

65 sai ijo kaigo hoken ryo: 6 dankai eno henkou o (2002, September 5). *Yomiuri Shinbun.*

Van de Water, P. (1981, June). *An overview of issues in social security.* Paper presented at the conference sponsored by the American Enterprise Institute for Public Policy Research, Washington, DC.

Yusei Shou. (1999). *Katei ni okeru kinyushisan sentaku ni kansuru chosa.*

BARBARA BERKMAN,
SECTION EDITOR

Social Work Research in Aging

OVERVIEW

New significant trends impacting access to and use of health and mental health services find social workers taking on new roles and new models of practice. Social work's biopsychosocial and multidisciplinary approach to care positions practitioners to have important responsibilities within emerging health delivery systems. As earlier chapters in this volume attest, social workers are critical in maintaining older individuals in their communities and reducing the cost of health services. Similarly, in collaborative work with other disciplines on behavioral and psychosocial processes, social work researchers are addressing the emerging issues in gerontology. Interdisciplinary research in behavioral and psychosocial processes is fundamental to the understanding of disease etiology, as well as to the promotion of health and well-being.

The incredible growth and diversity of this older population pose both opportunities and challenges for gerontological research. Social and behavioral research will have the opportunity to help improve health and functioning and contribute to reduced rates of disability for older people. But there is also a challenge. In the years to come, unprecedented numbers of elders will face risks of frailty and loss of independence. Social work research is challenged to understand and study issues related to practice with older adults and their caregivers. We need a strong social work research agenda in aging that can help improve the quality of life for older people and their caregivers. This part of the *Handbook* focuses on issues that social workers face in conducting research in aging; it concludes with a report on the current status of social work research and suggests future directions for our research agenda.

Amy Horowitz, in chapter 93, offers a comprehensive review of significant methodological issues in conducting research with older adults. There are research issues applicable to all age-groups, but this chapter raises the special considerations that apply to research in aging in general and focuses on many of the complicated areas in which social workers conduct research. The chapter covers many of these areas, such as design problems in cross-sectional and longitudinal research and interventions studies. In addition, sampling, recruitment, and retention of participants, data collection, and measurement problems are addressed. Horowitz pays attention to qualitative and quantitative methods and is particularly sensitive to the special issues in research with minority and other special populations. In addition, she addresses the complex informed consent and ethical concerns that frequently must be considered in human subjects research with older adults and their families.

Terry Lum, in chapter 94, challenges us to understand the value of research utilizing secondary analysis, introducing researchers to the rapidly expanding resource of public large data sets. During the last two decades, this resource has become increasingly accessible to geriatric social work researchers. This chapter elucidates the benefits and limitations of utilizing data sets, as well as offering valuable technical advice.

Chang-ming Hsieh and Elizabeth Essex, in chapter 95, present the critical program evaluation issues in measuring client satisfaction with care. Although client satisfaction is only one aspect of quality of care, it is an important indicator of service quality. The authors propose a clear methodological approach that can be readily adapted for agency use in assessing client satisfaction with services. Social work evaluators can follow the steps outlined to develop client satisfaction measures that directly relate to the goals of the specific agency.

In the final chapter of this part, Denise Burnette and Nancy Morrow-Howell provide an overview of the state of social work research in aging and offer directions for the future. They note that social work researchers in aging are beginning to establish a national presence in social work schools, but the extent to which they are conducting research is not yet clear. Furthermore, they find that social work researchers are contributing to the multidisciplinary knowledge base in aging but "barely have a foothold in federally funded research." However, the authors include findings from their studies on a social work gerontological research agenda, and they conclude with their belief that social work is "well positioned to . . . assume a true leadership role in research on aging."

This chapter addresses issues in social work research in aging. The intent is not to provide a methodological discourse or tutorial. Rather, the primary purpose is to introduce the reader to the major issues that need to be considered in designing and/or evaluating research in aging. Obviously, all aspects of the scientific method that are relevant to any age-group are also relevant to research on older adults. However, there are special considerations that apply to research in aging in general, and social work research in aging in particular, that are the focus of this chapter. These include issues relevant to design, informed consent and ethical considerations, sample recruitment and retention (especially in terms of ethnic elders), and data collection and measurement, including the use of proxy data. The chapter will conclude with a brief discussion of the current and future role of the social work profession in contributing to the knowledge base in gerontology.

GENERAL DESIGN CONSIDERATIONS

Cross-Sectional Versus Longitudinal Designs

Gerontological research has significantly broadened its reach over the past several decades, going beyond a relatively narrow focus on the study of older people to the study of the processes of aging. As follows, the study of *change* has become the hallmark of gerontological research, and longitudinal designs the preferred means to reach the objective. Whereas cross-sectional designs can and do continue to make important contributions to the field in several ways (e.g., identifying key processes for further study, examining rare populations, highlighting cross-cultural and cross-national comparisons), they remain limited by their inability to separate *age effects* (i.e., the actual effects of chronological aging), *period or time of measurement effects* (i.e., the effects of the environment at the time the data are collected), and *cohort effects* (i.e., the consequences of being born at a particular point in history in terms of subsequent life experiences; Ferraro & Kelley-Moore, 2003). In contrast, longitudinal data allow the investigator to examine dynamic processes, to make inferences about the cause and consequences of those processes (Alwin & Campbell, 2001), and to address the primary question underlying most aging research, that is, why and how do individuals change (or not) as they age (Hertzog & Nesselroade, 2003)?

AMY HOROWITZ

Issues in Conducting Social Work Research in Aging

There are several types of longitudinal designs. Longitudinal panel designs are the most common and follow a single group of individuals (typically a single cohort) over time. In cohort sequential designs, several cohorts are followed during an identical time period (Collins, 1996), adding to the ability to distinguish between age changes and age differences, but also adding significantly to the cost of the research. Both, however, are subject to the primary limitation of longitudinal designs, that is, bias due to nonrandom attrition. Attrition is a problem in longitudinal research with any age-group, but differential attrition is especially problematic in aging research due to selective mortality, morbidity, cognitive decline, and institutionalization (Ferraro & Kelley-Moore, 2003). Drawing conclusions based solely on the hearty individuals who survive in a longitudinal study can lead to seriously biased findings, especially since much of the research in aging, as well as research of special interest to social workers, focuses on the physical and mental health and well-being of aging individuals. An alternative approach is the cross-sequential design, which involves the collection of cross-sectional data from two independent samples of the same cohort at different points in time. Although this design results in assessment of change within an identified cohort, rather than individual change, it does avoid the problem of attrition (Collins, 1996). Fortunately, recent advances in statistical methods for the analyses of longitudinal data offer techniques that can account for nonrandom attrition (i.e., multiple imputation, full-information maximum likelihood methods, and multigroup estimation), as well as ones that can examine intraindividual change and interindividual trajectories. The interested reader is encouraged to explore the numerous resources, both print and instructional, that are now available (see, for review, Ferraro & Kelley-Moore, 2003; Hertzog & Nesselroade, 2003).

Use of Secondary Data

The increasing availability of longitudinal data sets for secondary analyses has been a major development in the field and one that has advanced, as well as benefited from the advances in, statistical methods for longitudinal data (Cutler, 1995; George, 1995). These data sets are often available on the Web and include, to name just a few, the National Health and Nutrition Examination Survey (HANES) I—Epidemiologic Follow-up (*http://www.cdc.gov/nchs/*

about/major/nhanes/datalink.htm); the Established Populations for Epidemiologic Studies of the Elderly (EPESE; *www.icpsr.umich.edu/NACDA/archive.html*); the Longitudinal Study on Aging (LSOA; *www.cdc. gov/nchs/lsoa.htm*); the National Long-Term Care Surveys (NLTCS; *http://nltcs.cds.duke.edu/data.htm*); the Assets and Health Dynamics of the Oldest Old (AHEAD; *http://www.pop.psu.edu/dataarchive/daman/ ahead1.htm*); and the Health and Retirement Study (*www.umich.edu/~hrswww*). They offer the researcher a range of rich and cost-effective options to explore research questions related to the health and well-being of aging individuals. In addition to serving as the primary data resource, public data sets are often used to provide external comparison groups for a study sample (e.g., comparing health status of a locally recruited older sample with representative national samples) or can also be used to provide outcome data for study participants (e.g., health care utilization data from Medicare and Medicaid records or mortality data from the National Death Index; Fredman, Hawkes, Zimmerman, Hebel, & Magaziner, 2001). However, Kasl (1995) warns against reliance on these data sets for "opportunistic analyses" to answer more complex questions regarding the social and psychological influences on the health of older adults. He argues that these data are seldom collected with the purposes of new investigators' questions in mind and that measurement of key variables is often limited because of the original broad scope of these studies. Both the advantages and the disadvantages of using available data sets further highlight that good research of any type is that in which the research question drives the research method.

Intervention Research

Of special relevance to social workers is the significant increase over the past decade in intervention research focusing on aging issues. Social workers are traditional change agents, and much of our research interest calls for the evaluation of treatment programs that are intended to assist consumers of social work services. Intervention research can be defined as involving "actions that alter, or are intended to alter, relationships between observable phenomena" (Schulz & Martire, 1999, p. 2). Intervention research may utilize observational or quasi-experimental designs, but the design of choice is the randomized clinical trial. When participants are randomly assigned to treatment and control conditions, one can assume (but should always verify) that characteristics that might influence outcomes, or interact with treatment, will be equally represented in each group. Thus, the only difference should be the planned intervention. However, intervention studies in the health and human services seldom take place in laboratories. It is often unrealistic to expect that participants in the no-treatment group will not seek alternate services. Therefore, it is critical that measurement of related services be incorporated in the design (Arean, Cook, et al., 2003).

Intervention studies are also subject to bias due to attrition. As with longitudinal surveys, participants with the poorest physical and mental health status are overrepresented among the dropouts. However, there is also treatment-related participant attrition (Schulz & Martire, 1998), that is, participants dropping out because of the nature of the treatment (e.g., too burdensome, or not receiving the desired treatment). Thus, to address this bias resulting from retention of the most committed participants, most randomized intervention studies base their analyses on the principle of "intent to treat"—that is, including all original participants assigned to treatment in the analysis regardless of how much or for how long service was actually received. Newer approaches such as mixed-effects modeling and survival models are also being used to identify treatment effects (Lebowitz, 2004).

There are numerous other considerations in the design of intervention research. Most important, there must be a conceptual link between the treatment and the outcome (Arean, Cook, et al., 2003). This means that the treatment should be reasonably expected to affect the outcome, and to manifest this effect within the time frame of the study. Further, although seemingly an obvious consideration, the target population must evidence need for the treatment. To provide an example of how these conditions were not met, one can consider the early caregiver intervention studies, most of which failed to report significant treatment effects for social support or psychoeducational group programs with the short-term outcome of reducing caregiver stress and depression. However, these programs were often not targeted to depressed or stressed caregivers (Toseland & McCallion, 1997) and, in fact, recruited volunteers who were likely to be more effective problem solvers. Thus, there was little room for improvement in stated outcomes. Similarly, the early case management interventions were supposedly designed to reduce institutionalization. However, even if they were successful, the follow-up period was typically insufficient for program effects on placement rates to emerge among populations that were not initially on the path to nursing home placement. Thus, working with clearly defined target populations and distinguishing between primary and secondary outcomes, as well as between short-term and long-term outcomes, is critical in intervention research. Further, as Shulz and colleagues have stressed (Schulz et al., 2002), the challenge to intervention researchers is to produce outcomes that are clinically meaningful, as well as statistically significant.

Qualitative Versus Quantitative Research: The Nondebate

We have hopefully gone beyond the stage where proponents of qualitative or quantitative research methodology advocate the virtues of one method to the exclusion of the other. As noted earlier, the research question must drive the methodology, not the reverse. Qualitative methods are being used more frequently, and more fruitfully, in gerontological research, as their contributions are being better understood and their methodologies for data collection and analyses have become more sophisticated. Qualitative research can offer an in-depth view of complex social processes associated with aging and can be defined as an "approach to the study of human behavior that relies on the analysis of narrative data to create an interpretation of the meaning of these behaviors from the perspective of the participants themselves, with their own social context" (Cobb & Forbes, 2002, p. M197). Qualitative research in gerontology can be especially useful, for example, when the research question addresses a phenomenon that is not well understood, to identify key variables for study, to generate research questions or hypotheses for future study, or to collect information that is needed for the development of quantitative measures. Qualitative methods, however, are not always a precursor to quantitative research. These methods can also be especially useful in identifying explanations for unexpected or anomalous findings (Barbour, 1999), as would be the case, for example, in examining why caregiver intervention studies often fail to produce significant quantitative treatment effects although caregivers typically self-report receiving many benefits of these programs. More recently, there has been an emphasis on combining qualitative and quantitative methods within studies, using "mixed-methods" approaches (Morgan, 1998), which offers opportunities to integrate the inherent strengths of both while minimizing their limitations (Bechtel, Davidhizar, & Bunting, 2000). The interested reader is referred to the many excellent textbooks available on qualitative sampling, data collection, and analyses (see, for example, Denzin & Lincoln, 2000; Gubrium & Sankar, 1993; Padgett, 1998, 2004).

RESEARCH ETHICS/INFORMED CONSENT

Research in aging presents ethical challenges, some of which are unique to the study of older adults and some of which are not (AGS Ethics and Research Committees, 2001). At the heart of any discussion of ethics in research is the process of securing informed consent from potential participants and/or their surrogates. The basic elements of consent are that it is voluntary, informed, and provided by someone who is competent to provide consent and who comprehends what he or she is consenting to (High, 1992). Being an older adult does not, in and of itself, constitute vulnerability in terms of research participation. However, even where participants are fully cognitively capable of providing informed consent, there are still issues to consider in securing informed consent from older adults. In general, older adults may need more time to understand the information completely (AGS Ethics and Research Committees, 2001). Sensory impairments are common among older adults and may interfere with the consent process. Large print and clear color contrast in informed consent documents are helpful even for those who are simply experiencing normal aging vision changes. For participants with vision problems, the informed consent should be read aloud by the researcher. For older adults with hearing problems, communication regarding questions about the study can be facilitated by the use of assistive listening devices, which consist of a microphone and headset and are easily available in retail stores to help with two-person conversations. Ironically, because of these special considerations for older adults with vision and/or hearing impairments, they are often excluded from general research studies, which, in turn, creates an ethical issue in terms of limiting their rights to research participation and underrepresenting their perspectives in research findings.

Another problem in securing consent is that older adults, although fully informed and willing to participate in a study, are often reluctant to sign documents at all, or would like someone in their family to review the consent before they sign it (Berkman, Leipzig,

Greenberg, & Inouye, 2001; Boult, Boult, Morishita, & Pirie, 1998; Cohen-Mansfield, 2003). In these cases, accommodations can be made for verbal consent, which is then independently witnessed, and adaptations made to the consent process so that it proceeds in two stages.

Conducting research with older adults with dementia and other cognitive impairments can raise questions about the appropriateness of proxy consent and whether such individuals should be participants in research studies even when there is no possible immediate benefit for them. However, the Alzheimer's Association has affirmed that persons with Alzheimer's disease should not be deprived of the potential benefits of participating in research, and U.S. federal regulations have endorsed proxy consent, as long as extra attention is given to monitoring the participant in terms of potential harm or discomfort (Post, 2003). Many older adults in the early stages of Alzheimer's disease and/or with mild cognitive impairment can contribute to the decision-making process (Sachs et al., 1994). Interestingly, a study of proxy decision making found that proxies commonly reported that the decisions were shared with the older patient, although whether this was true shared decision making or the proxy's attempt to involve the older adult was unclear (Sugarman, Cain, Wallace, & Welsh-Bohmer, 2001). In addition, Sugarman et al. (2001) found that caregivers often felt the "burden" of making the decision for the older person with dementia, suggesting that researchers need to be sensitive to this concern when soliciting consent. Some have argued that regardless of proxy consent, ethical standards would call for the participant themselves to show willingness to participate (Good, 2001). However, there is currently no requirement in federal regulations that assent be obtained from patients with dementia.

Another ethical consideration, especially for social workers, involves the sometimes dual roles of the practitioner-scientist (AGS Ethics and Research Committees, 2001). A clear conflict of interest can arise, or be perceived, if the social worker as researcher is also involved in the treatment of the research participant (Good, 2001). Even recruitment efforts by the social work or medical professional who is treating the older adult can be perceived as coercive (Cohen-Mansfield, 2003). At the very least, special care must be taken in the informed consent process so that expectations of the two roles are not confused by the research participant. However, the better solution is to avoid these situations entirely.

As is the case for all research studies, regardless of age-group, approval and monitoring of all human subject concerns, including recruitment and consent procedures, are the responsibility of the organization's institutional review board (IRB). IRBs can differ somewhat in their requirements from institution to institution, but they all follow the Code of Federal Regulations, known as the Common Rule. These regulations clearly spell out the required elements of the informed consent document (e.g., risks and benefits; how data will be stored and used; limits, if any, to confidentiality), as well as other aspects of human subject recruitment and protection. Detailed information on required procedures can be accessed through the Office of Human Research Protections (OHRP; *http://www.hhs.gov/ohrp/*). Furthermore, the Health Insurance Portability and Accountability Act (HIPAA) of 1996 included regulations about the use and confidentiality of individually identifiable patient health data known as the Privacy Rule and applies to covered entities, including health care providers as individuals or organizations. This is a complex set of rules that can apply when the social worker is conducting research within a covered entity in which he or she is employed or is seeking data from a covered entity. Additional patient authorizations may be required to release information, data may have to be de-identified before release, and/or the researcher may have to enter into a business associate agreement. Many IRBs now require documentation of compliance with HIPAA regulations. The final HIPAA Privacy Rule is available at *http://www.hhs.gov/ocr/hipaa*. Furthermore, most government agencies have developed educational materials for researchers about the Privacy Rule; see *http://privacyruleandresearch.nih.gov* for a series of helpful booklets for researchers and IRBs.

RECRUITMENT AND RETENTION OF RESEARCH PARTICIPANTS

The time, effort, and cost of recruiting and retaining participants in research studies should not be underestimated, and building in strategies for recruitment and retention is a key component of any research design. In this section, general issues and strategies for recruitment and retention will be reviewed, followed by a more detailed discussion of one of the critical problems in aging research today—the recruitment of ethnic minority elders in research studies.

Recruitment methods for nonprobability samples and intervention research vary significantly across studies and can include radio ads, newspaper ads, referrals by social and health care professionals, referrals by current research participants, presentations at public forums or senior organizations, mailings, flyers, and, more recently, notices on Web sites. As in all aspects of the research design, the nature of the study and the nature of the population drive the recruitment process (Cassidy, Baird, & Sheikh, 2001).

Understanding why older adults and their family members do or do not agree to participate in research is important in addressing concerns and developing strategies to maximize recruitment and retention. On the one hand, older people often report wanting to help others or wanting to share their story as reasons for research participation. Participation in clinical trials is often motivated by the desire for the treatment, receiving feedback about their current status, and receiving support from research staff (Connell, Shaw, Holmes, & Foster, 2001).

On the other hand, barriers to research participation include a distrust of research, preferences for treatment rather than randomization in clinical trials, problems with transportation, lack of time, and problems understanding the informed consent (Connell et al., 2001; Lovato, Hill, Hertert, Hunninghake, & Probstfield, 1997; Stahl & Vasquez, 2004). When research is conducted in residential centers, concerns about privacy and lack of perceived benefits, as well as problems with fatigue, can affect recruitment (Cohn-Mansfield, 2003).

Most studies, if possible, try to compare participants with nonparticipants on some key characteristics to identify potential biases. Common characteristics associated with refusal to participate in research include older age, lower education, and poorer health status (Ganguli, Mendelsohn, Lytle, & Dodge, 1998; Norton, Breitner, Welsh, & Wyse, 1994). However, one study found that even though refusers and participants had similar ages and health status at baseline, 3-year follow-up data indicated that the former had a significantly higher risk of nursing home placement and mortality than did the latter (Minder, Muller, Gillmann, Beck, & Stuck, 2002). This finding underscores the truism that research participants will always be different than those who choose not to participate, but we can never totally be sure in what ways.

In selecting recruitment strategies for any study, there are often trade-offs between cost and effectiveness. Patrick, Pruchno, and Rose (1998) compared five recruitment strategies for a study of older parents of disabled adults: agency referrals, support groups, participant referrals, media, and mass mailings. Overall, they found that the least time- and resource-intensive strategies were those that involved existing groups (i.e., agencies, support groups, and referrals from participants). Yet these strategies consistently underrepresented minorities, those with low incomes, and those who are more socially isolated.

There have been many suggested strategies to maximize recruitment that have varying levels of success depending on the target population. These include enclosing an incentive or gift (e.g., a dollar bill or a pen) in mailed questionnaires and including local newspaper articles or press releases about the study to support its legitimacy (Boult et al., 1998). All printed recruitment materials should be written in clear, nontechnical, and jargon-free language and composed at no more than an eighth-grade reading level (Warren-Findlow, Prohaska, & Freedman, 2003). Researchers will need to deal with the logistic barriers to research participation, which may involve providing or covering the cost of transportation, as well as providing respite care if the potential participant is responsible for the care of another family member. Providing access to a research staff on a regular basis and providing periodic feedback via written materials such as study newsletters (that will not bias future data collection) have been recommended to maximize retention (Connell et al., 2001), as has providing incentives in terms of small monetary payments for each session or interview (Cassidy et al., 2001). I have used techniques such as sending a thank-you letter after each interview with a reminder about the next wave, as well as reminder letters a few weeks before the next interview to maximize retention. Interestingly, a randomized trial of advance notice letters, versus no letters, mailed 2 weeks before a mailed survey found that the letter increased participation by Whites but not by African Americans (Napoles-Springer, Fongwa, Stewart, Gildengorin, & Perez-Stable, 2004). In a study of bereavement-related depression, one of the successful strategies, in addition to media announcements, was writing personal letters to bereaved spouses found through newspaper obituaries (Schlernitzauer et al., 1998), which again underscores that recruitment strategies need to be study specific.

The serious underrepresentation of ethnic minority elders in survey and clinical research has been given increased attention in recent years, with three journals devoting special issues to the subject (*Gerontologist*, 2003, 43(1); *Journal of Aging and Health,* 2004, 16(Suppl. 5); and *Journal of Mental Health and Aging,* 2000, 6(1)). Although the National Institutes of

Health Revitalization Act of 1993 mandates the inclusion of ethnic minorities in research, problems with recruitment of ethnic minority elders persist. However, recent federal initiatives, such as the creation of Resource Centers on Minority Aging by the National Institute on Aging (Stahl & Vasquez, 2004), have contributed to a growing knowledge base about issues and strategies relevant to the recruitment of ethnic minorities in research studies.

In addition to the numerous attitudinal and logistic barriers to research participation noted earlier, additional forces are at play when addressing ethnic older populations. The mistrust of medical research and the scientific community, based on a history of mistreatment, is cited consistently as the primary barrier to recruiting older African Americans for research studies, even those studies that address psychosocial rather than medical issues or treatments (Connell et al., 2001; Curry & Jackson, 2003; Moreno-John et al., 2004; Stahl & Vasquez, 2004). Furthermore, the stigma regarding mental illness and help seeking is a particularly strong force that deters involvement in clinical research by Latinos (Gallagher-Thompson, Solano, Coon, & Arean, 2003), as well as by Chinese elders and their families (Guo, Ley, Hinton, Weitzman, & Levkoff, 2000). On the other hand, it has also been suggested that failure to involve family members can also hinder recruitment of Latinos (Arean & Gallagher-Thompson, 1996). At the same time, the sense of fatalism regarding chronic illness in general that is prevalent in ethnic communities (Connell et al., 2001) and the belief that the health problem is a private issue for the family to deal with (Curry & Jackson, 2003) also contribute to lower participation rates among minority elders. The complexity of forms and procedures is often a barrier to those with low literacy (Curry & Jackson, 2003), and the lack of culturally sensitive protocols often leads to high dropout rates (Connell et al., 2001). Finally, failure to communicate the relevance of the research to the community has been a major factor in decreasing acceptance (Curry & Jackson, 2003).

Specific strategies have been suggested to increase recruitment of ethnic elders. In one study of African American caregivers, they themselves recommended that future research participants be contacted by those currently involved in the research (Connell et al., 2001). Dilworth-Anderson and Williams (2004) found that assigning the same interviewer to interview participants in a study of African American caregivers was a successful strategy. However, given the logistics of data collection and staff turnover, this is not always possible in a longitudinal study. Some researchers have recommended having interviewers ethnically matched with participants (Arean, Alvidrez, et al., 2003; Armstrong, Crum, Rieger, Bennett, & Edward, 1999). Curry and Jackson (2003), however, note that the data on matching research interviewer to participant on race are still very mixed, but still emphasize the importance of ethnic and racial minority researchers at all levels of research staff.

Regardless of the specific strategies, involving members of the ethnic community in the research process and forming research partnerships with them through a participatory research process has clearly emerged as the primary recommendation for increasing participation in research by ethnic elders (Arean, Alvidrez, et al., 2003; Burnette, 1998; Curry & Jackson, 2003; Gallagher-Thompson et al., 2004; Olin, Dagerman, Fox, Bowers, & Schneider, 2002; Reed, Foley, Hatch, & Mutran, 2003; Vesey, 2003). Targeting community opinion leaders and church leaders and partnering with local physicians represent important strategies for community involvement (Curry & Jackson, 2003). Levkoff and Sanchez (2003) also emphasize the importance of understanding the history between the academic or health institutions sponsoring the research and the community because this will affect initial relationships.

Although the importance of community involvement at all levels and phases of the research process cannot be overstated, it must also be recognized that community- and consumer-oriented approaches require additional staff, money, and time (Arean, Alvidrez, et al., 2003; Curry & Jackson, 2003). In addition, each culture and community will have its own unique history and concerns about research participation, and there is no one set of rules that will apply to all communities (Burnette, 1998; Stahl & Vasquez, 2004). Still, given the social and health disparities that permeate our society, the imperative to include ethnic minority older adults in research studies that can help address these disparities has never been stronger.

DATA COLLECTION

General Considerations

The primary methods of direct data collection with individuals include observations, self-administered questionnaires, telephone interviews, and in-person interviews, all of which have been successfully used with older adults. Each has its benefits and drawbacks.

Some suggest that there is a greater likelihood of answering sensitive questions on a self-administered questionnaire, but that the response rates are generally lower, and "don't know" responses are higher than for either telephone or in-person interviews (Pruchno & Hayden, 2000). Telephone interviews are less costly than in-person interviews and also have the advantage of increased interviewer safety and decreased interviewer effects. However, telephone interviews often elicit less-detailed responses to open-ended questions than do in-person interviews and have greater missing values (Wilson & Roe, 1998). Telephone interview are also more likely to recruit healthier older adults (Carter, Elward, Malmgren, Martin, & Larson, 1991).

The unique issues faced in collecting data directly from older adults have mostly to do with the effects of normal aging changes and age-related diseases on the ability to understand the questions and respond to them. More time may be required for the questionnaire or interview to be completed due to normal age changes in cognition. Some conditions, such as Parkinson's disease and stroke, can seriously affect both oral and written communication ability. As noted earlier, vision and hearing impairments can also affect the way data are collected. Self-administered questionnaires will be impossible for the many older adults with age-related vision impairments and can be difficult even for those with normal aging vision unless print is large and legible and has good contrast. In-person interviews often depend on visual aids, such as response category cue cards. These cannot be used with visually impaired elders, and alternatives, such as unfolding techniques when asking Likert-type scales, can be used without compromising the validity of the data. Obviously, persons with serious hearing impairments will have difficulty with either interview format, although some with mild or moderate impairments can function better face-to-face than they can on the telephone. Again, assistive listening devices should be part of every interviewer's supplies. When interviewing the very old, fatigue can be a factor. Thus, flexibility in scheduling and procedures to conduct the interview in multiple sessions need to be in place. Interviews of older adults are often conducted in the home, but this brings with it the potential for distractions from phone calls and household members, as well as concerns about privacy (Reed et al., 2003). Often family members or formal caregivers will want to stay in the room when the interview is taking place either because of curiosity or out of safety concerns. Our research group has found that a firm statement in the beginning about the importance of confidentiality is often required and successful. When it is not, the family member often leaves after only a few minutes. In any case, it is important to document the presence of another person during the interview and the perceived effect on the participant's responses so that the validity of interview can be assessed.

Use of Proxies

When an older adult cannot directly participate in a research study because of cognitive impairments or other health problems, a family member or other significant individual is often called upon to act as a proxy respondent. This raises the question of proxy reliability, that is, the extent to which a proxy can accurately report the elder's status. A great deal of research has addressed this question, much of it focused on assessing congruence in assessments of functional ability (i.e., activities of daily living [ADL]). Most studies find relatively good agreement among elders and caregivers in terms of ADL capability but also find that the family members tend to assess the elder as more disabled than does the elder him- or herself (Lyons, Zarit, Sayer, & Whitlatch, 2002; Magaziner, Bassett, Hebel, & Gruber-Baldini, 1996; Matthew, Adamek, & Dunkle, 1993; Neumann, Araki, & Gutterman, 2000; Todorov & Kirchner, 2000; Yip, Wilber, Myrtle, & Grazman, 2001; Zanetti, Geroldi, Frisoni, Bianchetti, & Trabucchi, 1999). There is less overall agreement between elders and caregivers when assessing mental health (Neumann et al., 2000). The direction of difference, however, is similar, with caregivers reporting the elder as experiencing significantly greater depression and poorer psychological well-being than do elders in their self-ratings (Bassett, Magaziner, & Hebel, 1990; Burke et al., 1990). Given this known bias in how proxies evaluate their older relatives, it is very important to interpret findings based on proxy respondents accordingly. This bias can be more problematic in research where both proxies and older adults are respondents. In these cases, proxy status is often incorporated in the analyses as a covariate.

MEASUREMENT

Aging research, as an interdisciplinary field, encompasses measurement in a number of domains, including, but not limited to, health, functional ability,

cognitive functioning, mental health, social relationships and social support, leisure and activity participation, personality, life events, psychosocial well-being, and caregiver functioning and well-being. There has been a great deal of psychometric work over the past several decades in the development of measures specifically for older adults and in the validation of existing measures for use with older people. As a result, there is an increasing potential for comparability across studies using similar measures (Cutler, 1995). There is, however, much more work to be done in determining the appropriateness of many existing measures for use with various ethnic minorities. This is a critical need, since many concepts that we measure (e.g., family, depression, pain) have culture-specific meanings. In fact, Burnette (1998) cautions against making cross-cultural comparisons based on participants' self-ratings, since these are made in the context of their own reference group, which will differ across cultures.

Twenty years ago, the first resource for measures in aging was published (Mangen & Peterson, 1982). Today, the researcher in aging has a number of excellent resources available, which present and discuss various options for measurement in domains of interest and their psychometric properties relative to application in various groups of older adults (see, e.g., Andersen, Rothenberg, & Zimmer, 1997; Lawton & Teresi, 1994; Lichtenberg, 1999; Skinner, Teresi, Holmes, Stahl, & Stewart, 2002; Teresi, Lawton, Holmes, & Ory, 1997).

CONCLUSION

Gerontology has traditionally been a multidisciplinary field, with a growing emphasis on using this strength to build interdisciplinary research collaborations. There has also been a tradition in gerontology of communication and collaboration between the scientific and practice communities, although in practice there is still much work to be done to translate research findings into applications that will benefit older adults (Pillemer, Czaja, Schulz, & Stahl, 2003). To facilitate this connection, the National Institute on Aging has funded an initiative to establish the Edward R. Roybal Centers in Applied Gerontology. The goal of these centers is to improve the process of applying findings from behavioral and social science research to programs that directly affect older adults.

Within this scientific environment, the social work perspective, with its dual emphasis on theory and service and its expertise in the health and social services, has much to offer the study of aging. A study of research priorities in social work research in aging identified several high-priority topics that were consistent with the current federal research agenda (Burnette, Morrow-Howell, & Chen, 2003). These included, for example, improving outcomes for ethnically diverse elders and intervention research that directly informs practice and policy. Yet a recent review of the research literature found that social workers are not well represented as contributors to the knowledge base in aging (Morrow-Howell & Burnette, 2001). Further, these investigators estimate that only 4% of all social work faculty have an interest in aging. Clearly, there is important work to be done in the field to develop the potential of social work researchers to contribute their unique perspective to the field of aging. To facilitate this process, the John A. Hartford Foundation has implemented a major initiative to increase the research capacity of the social work profession, through support and research training provided to both social work faculty and doctoral candidates in aging. This initiative has been a significant force in the field, as more than 50 faculty scholars have already been in the program. The impact of this program, along with other federal initiatives, can be expected to increase the contribution of social work to the research literature in aging.

REFERENCES

AGS Ethics and Research Committees. (2001). The responsible conduct of research. *Journal of the American Geriatrics Society, 49,* 1120–1122.

Alwin, D. F., & Campbell, R. T. (2001). Quantitative approaches: Longitudinal methods in the study of human development and aging. In R. H. Binstock & L. K. George (Eds.), *Handbook of aging and the social sciences* (pp. 22–43). San Diego, CA: Academic Press.

Andersen, E., Rothenberg, B., & Zimmer, J. G. (1997). *Assessing the health status of older adults.* New York: Springer.

Arean, P. A., Alvidrez, J., Nery, R., Estes, C., & Linkins, K. (2003). Recruitment and retention of older minorities in mental health services research. *Gerontologist, 43,* 36–44.

Arean, P. A., Cook, B. L., Gallagher-Thompson, D., Hegel, M. T., Schulberg, H. C., & Schulz, R. (2003). Guidelines for conducting geropsychotherapy research. *American Journal of Geriatric Psychiatry, 11*(1), 9–16.

Arean, P. A., & Gallagher-Thompson, D. (1996). Issues and recommendations for the recruitment and retention of older ethnic minority adults into clinical research. *Journal of Consulting and Clinical Psychology, 64,* 875–880.

Armstrong, T. D., Crum, L. D., Rieger, R. H., Bennett, T. A., & Edward, L. J. (1999). Attitudes of African Americans toward participation in medical research. *Journal of Applied Social Psychology, 29,* 552–574.

Barbour, R. S. (1999). The case for combining qualitative and quantitative approaches in health services research. *Journal of Health Services Research and Policy, 4,* 39–43.

Bassett, S. S., Magaziner, J., & Hebel, J. R. (1990). Reliability of proxy response on mental health indices for aged, community dwelling women. *Psychology and Aging, 5,* 127–132.

Bechtel, G. A., Davidhizar, R., & Bunting, S. (2000). Triangulation research among culturally diverse populations. *Journal of Allied Health, 29,* 61–63.

Berkman, C. S., Leipzig, R. M., Greenberg, S. A., & Inouye, S. K. (2001). Methodologic issues in conducting research on hospitalized older people. *Journal of the American Geriatrics Society, 49,* 172–178.

Boult, C., Boult, L., Morishita, L., & Pirie, P. (1998). Soliciting defined populations to recruit samples of high-risk older adults. *Journals of Gerontology: Series A, Biological Sciences and Medical Sciences, 53,* M379–M384.

Burke, W. J., Roccaforte, W. H., Wengel, S. P., McArthur-Miller, D., Folks, D. G., & Potter, J. F. (1998). Disagreement in the reporting of depressive symptoms between patients with dementia of the Alzheimer type and their collateral sources. *American Journal of Geriatric Psychiatry, 6,* 308–319.

Burnette, D. (1998). Conceptual and methodological considerations in research with non-white ethnic elders. In M. Potocky & A. Y. Rogers-Farmer (Eds.) *Social work research with minority and oppressed populations* (pp. 71–91). New York: Haworth.

Burnette, D., Morrow-Howell, N., & Chen, L. M. (2003). Setting priorities for gerontological social work research: A national Delphi study. *Gerontologist, 43,* 828–838.

Carter, W. B., Elward, K., Malmgren, J., Martin, M. L., & Larson, E. (1991). Participation of older adults in health programs and research: A critical review of the literature. *Gerontologist, 31,* 584–592.

Cassidy, E. L., Baird, E., & Sheikh, J. I. (2001). Recruitment and retention of elderly patients in clinical trials: Issues and strategies. *American Journal of Geriatric Psychiatry, 9,* 136–140.

Cobb, A. K., & Forbes, S. (2002). Qualitative research: What does it have to offer to the gerontologist? *Journals of Gerontology: Series A, Biological Sciences and Medical Sciences, 57,* M197–M202.

Cohen-Mansfield, J. (2003). Consent and refusal in dementia research: Conceptual and practical considerations. *Alzheimer Disease and Associated Disorders, 17*(Suppl. 1), S17–S25.

Collins, L. M. (1996). Research design and methods. In J. E. Birren (Ed.), *Encyclopedia of gerontology: Age, aging, and the aged* (Vol. 2, pp. 419–429). San Diego, CA: Academic Press.

Connell, C. M., Shaw, B. A., Holmes, S. B., & Foster, N. L. (2001). Caregivers' attitudes toward their family members' participation in Alzheimer disease research: Implications for recruitment and retention. *Alzheimer Disease and Associated Disorders, 15,* 137–145.

Curry, L., & Jackson, J. (2003). The science of including older ethnic and racial group participants in health-related research. *Gerontologist, 43,* 15–17.

Cutler, S. J. (1995). The methodology of social scientific research in gerontology: Progress and issues. *Journals of Gerontology: Series B, Psychological Sciences and Social Sciences, 50B,* S63–S64.

Denzin, N. K., & Lincoln, Y. S. (2000). *The handbook of qualitative research* (2nd ed.). Thousand Oaks, CA: Sage.

Dilworth-Anderson, P., & Williams, S. W. (2004). Recruitment and retention strategies for longitudinal African American caregiving research: The Family Caregiving Project. *Journal of Aging and Health, 16*(Suppl. 5), 137S–156S.

Ferraro, K. F., & Kelley-Moore, J. A. (2003). A half century of longitudinal methods in social gerontology: Evidence of change in the journal. *Journals of Gerontology: Series B, Psychological Sciences and Social Sciences, 58,* S264–S270.

Fredman, L., Hawkes, W., Zimmerman, S. I., Hebel, J. R., & Magaziner, J. (2001). Extending gerontological research through linking investigators' studies to public-use datasets. *Gerontologist, 41,* 15–22.

Gallagher-Thompson, D., Singer, L. S., Depp, C., Mausbach, B. T., Cardenas, V., & Coon, D. W. (2004). Effective recruitment strategies for Latino and Caucasian dementia family caregivers in intervention research. *American Journal of Geriatric Psychiatry, 12,* 484–490.

Gallagher-Thompson, D., Solano, N., Coon, D., & Arean, P. (2003). Recruitment and retention of Latino dementia family caregivers in intervention research: Issues to face, lessons to learn. *Gerontologist, 43,* 45–51.

Ganguli, M., Mendelsohn, A., Lytle, M., & Dodge, H. (1998). A follow-up comparison of study participants and refusers within a rural elderly population. *Journals of Gerontology: Series A, Biological Sciences and Medical Sciences, 53A,* M465–M470.

George, L. K. (1995). The last half-century of aging research—and thoughts for the future. *Journals of Gerontology: Series B, Psychological Sciences and Social Sciences, 50B,* S1–S3.

Good, G. A. (2001). Ethics in research with older, disabled individuals. *International Journal of Rehabilitation Research, 24,* 165–170.

Gubrium, J. F., & Sankar, A. (1993). *Qualitative methods in aging research.* Thousand Oaks, CA: Sage.

Guo, Z., Levy, B., Hinton, W. L., Weitzman, P. F., & Levkoff, S. E. (2000). The power of labels: Recruiting dementia-affected Chinese American elders and their caregivers. *Journal of Mental Health and Aging, 6,* 103–111.

Hertzog, C., & Nesselroade, J. R. (2003). Assessing psychological change in adulthood: An overview of methodological issues. *Psychology and Aging, 18,* 639–657.

High, D. M. (1992). Research with Alzheimer's disease subjects: Informed consent and proxy decision making. *Journal of the American Geriatrics Society, 40,* 950–957.

Kasl, S. V. (1995). Strategies in research on health and aging: Looking beyond secondary data analysis. *Journals of Gerontology: Series B, Psychological Sciences and Social Sciences, 50B,* S191–S193.

Lawton, M. P., & Teresi, J. A. (1994). *Annual Review of Gerontology and Geriatrics, Focus on Assessment Techniques* (Vol. 14). New York: Springer.

Lebowitz, B. D. (2004). Clinical trials in late life: New science in old paradigms. *Gerontologist, 44,* 452–458.

Levkoff, S., & Sanchez, H. (2003). Lessons learned about minority recruitment and retention from the Centers on Minority Aging and Health Promotion. *Gerontologist, 43,* 18–26.

Lichtenberg, P. A. (1999). *Handbook of assessment in clinical gerontology.* New York: Wiley.

Lovato, L. C., Hill, K., Hertert, S., Hunninghake, D. B., & Probstfield, J. L. (1997). Recruitment for controlled clinical trials: Literature summary and annotated bibliography. *Controlled Clinical Trials, 18,* 328–352.

Lyons, K. S., Zarit, S. H., Sayer, A. G., & Whitlatch, C. J. (2002). Caregiving as a dyadic process: Perspectives from caregiver and receiver. *Journals of Gerontology: Series B, Psychological Sciences and Social Sciences, 57,* 195–204.

Magaziner, J., Bassett, S. S., Hebel, J. R., & Gruber-Baldini, A. (1996). Use of proxies to measure health and functional status in epidemiologic studies of community-dwelling women age 65 years and older. *American Journal of Epidemiology, 143,* 283–292.

Mangen, D. J., & Peterson, W. A. (1982). *Research instruments in social gerontology.* Minneapolis: University of Minnesota Press.

Matthew, S. H., Adamek, M. E., & Dunkle, R. E. (1993). Research on older families when more than one member responds: Producing and interpreting findings. *Journal of Aging Studies, 7,* 215–228.

Minder, C. E., Muller, T., Gillmann, G., Beck, J. C., & Stuck, A. E. (2002). Subgroups of refusers in a disability prevention trial in older adults: Baseline and follow-up analysis. *American Journal of Public Health, 92,* 445–450.

Moreno-John, G., Gachie, A., Fleming, C. M., Napoles-Springer, A., Mutran, E., Manson, S. M., et al. (2004). Ethnic minority older adults participating in clinical research: Developing trust. *Journal of Aging and Health, 16*(Suppl. 5), 93S–123S.

Morgan, D. L. (1998). Practical strategies for combining qualitative and quantitative methods: Applications to health research. *Qualitative Health Research, 8,* 362–376.

Morrow-Howell, N., & Burnette, D. (2001). Gerontological social work research: Current status and future directions. *Journal of Gerontological Social Work, 36,* 67–79.

Napoles-Springer, A. M., Fongwa, M. N., Stewart, A. L., Gildengorin, G., & Perez-Stable, E. J. (2004). The effectiveness of an advance notice letter on the recruitment of African Americans and Whites for a mailed patient satisfaction survey. *Journal of Aging and Health, 16*(Suppl. 5), 124S–136S.

Neumann, P. J., Araki, S. S., & Gutterman, E. M. (2000). The use of proxy respondents in studies of older adults: Lessons, challenges, and opportunities. *Journal of the American Geriatrics Society, 48,* 1646–1654.

Norton, M. C., Breitner, J. C., Welsh, K. A., & Wyse, B. W. (1994). Characteristics of nonresponders in a community survey of the elderly. *Journal of the American Geriatrics Society, 42,* 1252–1256.

Olin, J. T., Dagerman, K. S., Fox, L. S., Bowers, B., & Schneider, L. S. (2002). Increasing ethnic minority participation in Alzheimer disease research. *Alzheimer Disease and Associated Disorders, 16*(Suppl. 2), S82–S85.

Padgett, D. (1998). *Qualitative methods in social work research.* Thousand Oaks, CA: Sage.

Padgett, D. K. (2004). *The qualitative research experience.* Belmont, MA: Wadsworth/Thomson Learning.

Patrick, J. H., Pruchno, R. A., & Rose, M. S. (1998). Recruiting research participants: A comparison of the costs and effectiveness of five recruitment strategies. *Gerontologist, 38,* 295–302.

Pillemer, K., Czaja, S., Schulz, R., & Stahl, S. M. (2003). Finding the best ways to help: Opportunities and challenges of intervention research on aging. *Gerontologist, 43,* 5–8.

Post, S. G. (2003). Full-spectrum proxy consent for research participation when persons with Alzheimer disease lose decisional capacities: Research ethics and the common good. *Alzheimer Disease and Associated Disorders, 17*(Suppl. 1), S3–S11.

Pruchno, R. A., & Hayden, J. M. (2000). Interview modality: Effects on costs and data quality in a sample of older women. *Journal of Aging and Health, 12,* 3–24.

Reed, P. S., Foley, K. L., Hatch, J., & Mutran, E. J. (2003). Recruitment of older African Americans for survey research: A process evaluation of the community and church-based strategy in the Durham Elders Project. *Gerontologist, 43,* 52–61.

Sachs, G. A., Stocking, C. B., Stern, R., Cox, D. M., Hougham, G., & Sachs, R. S. (1994). Ethical aspects of dementia research: Informed consent and proxy consent. *Clinical Research, 42,* 403–412.

Schlernitzauer, M., Bierhals, A. J., Geary, M. D., Prigerson, H. G., Stack, J. A., Miller, M. D., et al. (1998). Recruitment methods for intervention research in bereavement-related depression: Five years' experience. *Journal of the American Geriatrics Society, 6,* 67–74.

Schulz, R., Maddox, G., & Lawton, M. P. (Eds.). (1998). *Annual review of gerontology and geriatrics: Focus on interventions research with adults* (Vol. 18). New York: Springer.

Schulz, R., & Martire, L. M. (1998). Intervention research with older adults: Introduction, overview, and future directions. In R. Schulz, G. Maddox, & M. P. Lawton (Eds.), *Annual review of gerontology and geriatrics: Focus on intervention research with adults.* (Vol. 18, pp. 1–16). New York: Springer.

Schulz, R., O'Brien, A., Czaja, S., Ory, M., Norris, R., Martire, L. M., et al. (2002). Dementia caregiver intervention research: In search of clinical significance. *Gerontologist, 42,* 589–602.

Skinner, J. H., Teresi, J. A., Holmes, D., Stahl, S. M., & Stewart, A. L. (2002). *Multicultural measurement in older populations.* New York: Springer.

Stahl, S. M., & Vasquez, L. (2004). Approaches to improving recruitment and retention of minority elders participating in research: Examples from selected research groups including the National Institute on Aging's Resource Centers for Minority Aging Research. *Journal of Aging and Health, 16*(Suppl. 5), 9S–17S.

Sugarman, J., Cain, C., Wallace, R., & Welsh-Bohmer, K. A. (2001). How proxies make decisions about research for patients with Alzheimer's disease. *Journal of the American Geriatrics Society, 49,* 1110–1119.

Teresi, J. A., Lawton, M. P., Holmes, D., & Ory, M. (1997). *Measurement in elderly chronic care populations.* New York: Springer.

Todorov, A., & Kirchner, C. (2000). Bias in proxies' reports of disability: Data from the National Health Interview Survey on Disability. *American Journal of Public Health, 90,* 1248–1253.

Toseland, R. W., & McCallion, P. (1997). Trends in caregiving intervention research. *Social Work Research, 21,* 154–165.

Vesey, G. A. (2003). Recruitment and retention of minority elders in health-related research: A community-based approach. In L. Curry & J. Jackson (Eds.), *The science of inclusion: Recruiting and retaining racial and ethnic elders in health research* (pp. 82–89). Washington, DC: Gerontological Society of America.

Warren-Findlow, J., Prohaska, T. R., & Freedman, D. (2003). Challenges and opportunities in recruiting and retaining underrepresented populations into health promotion research. *Gerontologist, 43,* 37–46.

Wilson, K., & Roe, B. (1998). Interviewing older people by telephone following initial contact by postal survey. *Journal of Advanced Nursing, 27,* 575–581.

Yip, J. Y., Wilber, K. H., Myrtle, R. C., & Grazman, D. N. (2001). Comparison of older adult subject and proxy responses on the SF-36 health-related quality of life instrument. *Aging and Mental Health, 5,* 136–142.

Zanetii, O., Geroldi, D., Frisoni, G. B., Bianchetti, A., & Trabucchi, M. (1999). Contrasting results between caregiver's report and direct assessment of activities of daily living in patients affected by mild and very mild dementia: The contribution of the caregiver's personal characteristics. *Journal of the American Geriatrics Society, 47,* 196–202.

TERRY LUM

Using Large Datasets for Research on Older Adults and Families

94

Researchers in the fields of health and social sciences are increasingly interested in using large survey data sets for their research. Collecting data from thousands of respondents is expensive and time consuming, but researchers now have many opportunities to conduct research through secondary analysis of large data sets that they were not involved in collecting. *Secondary analysis* refers to "any further analysis of survey or social dataset that presents interpretations, conclusions or knowledge additional to, or different from, those presented in the first report on the inquiry as a whole and its main results" (Hakim, 1982, 12). The trend toward using secondary analysis of existing data sets in research on older adults and their families has been fueled by the increasing availability of public-use survey data containing information collected from older adults and their families, advancement in computer technology that allows researchers to analyze very large data sets on personal computers, the availability of commercial statistical software that can account for potential biases from complex sampling designs, and the Internet and data archives that make these existing data sets more accessible.

The use of secondary data analysis in the field of social work is still relatively uncommon for several reasons. First, many social work researchers do not have the skills to understand complex survey designs, complete preliminary data processing, and carry out the advanced statistical techniques required to take advantage of these available resources. Many social work doctoral programs do not teach secondary analysis of large data sets in their research curriculum. Further, some social work researchers still see secondary analysis of existing data sets as an inferior cousin to primary data collection. The goals of this chapter are to introduce geriatric social work researchers to the rapidly expanding resource of public-use large data sets and to describe the steps that geriatric social work researchers should take to benefit from these resources. Throughout the chapter, I will use the Study of Assets and Health Dynamics Among the Oldest Old (AHEAD) as an example to illustrate my discussion.

Study of Assets and Health Dynamics Among the Oldest Old (AHEAD)

■ The AHEAD is an ongoing longitudinal study of the joint dynamics among health (physical, cognitive, and functional), dementia, economic and family resources, and care arrangements. It provides data to address a broad range of scientific questions focused on the interplay of resources and late-life health transitions. The population of AHEAD includes all adults in the contiguous United States who were born in 1923 or earlier and reside in households. More detailed information about the AHEAD data can be obtained from its Web site at *http://hrsonline.isr.umich.edu/.* ▧

BENEFITS AND LIMITATIONS OF USING LARGE SURVEY DATA SETS IN RESEARCH

Large survey data are collected to provide information for funding and policy decisions, to monitor program or policy implementation, or to address specific social and scientific research questions. Federal government agencies in the United States, such as the U.S. Census Bureau and the National Center for Health Statistics, routinely collect large amounts of survey data from nationally representative samples to meet the information needs of the government. Examples of these national surveys include the U.S. Census, the Current Population Survey (CPS), the National Health Interview Survey (NHIS), and the Survey of Income and Program Participation (SIPP). Many of these survey data sets contain information on demographics, socioeconomic status, living arrangements, health, mental health, physical and cognitive functioning, and program participation from thousands of older people and their families. Federal governmental agencies regularly report aggregated data from these surveys, but the potential of these data for further analytical study is immense. Researchers can analyze individual-level information from these survey data sets to shed new light on many aspects of the health and well-being of older people and their families.

Many researchers outside of the government also collect survey data to address specific research questions. Examples of these surveys include the National Long-Term Care Survey (NLTC), the Americans' Changing Lives (ACL) Survey, and the Health and Retirement Study (HRS). Many of these survey data sets are not fully analyzed and may have potential utility beyond the specific research questions for which a particular study was designed. They provide an opportunity for testing specific hypotheses that have not yet been examined.

There are many benefits of using large existing survey data sets in researching issues related to older adults and families. First, it is an expeditious means of answering some types of research questions. Primary data collection is time consuming; using data sets collected by the government, services providers, or other researchers is a time-saving alternative. Second, secondary analysis of existing data makes economic sense in the current tight budget environment. Most of these data sets can be obtained free of charge, whereas primary data collection is very costly. Third, users of large survey data may benefit from the work of experts who are involved in survey design and data collection. Fourth, many of these large survey data files are collected from a nationally representative sample, thus allowing researchers to generalize their findings to a national level, an ability that is particularly important for policy research and program development. Fifth, many large surveys oversample certain subgroups of the population. This allows researchers to estimate reliable population parameters for some specific subpopulations, such as older people of color, lower-income older people and families, or the oldest old (Korn & Graubard, 1999). Sixth, the large sample sizes also give researchers enough statistical power to estimate the existence of weak to moderate associations between variables of interest, which is not possible using smaller sample sizes (Korn & Graubard, 1999). Finally, since researchers using existing survey data are not involved in research design and data collection, the concern of reactivity in the data is eliminated.

There are also some serious limitations in using existing data sets for research on older adults and families. First, secondary analysis of large survey data sets is not appropriate for answering all types of research questions. Some questions may require collection of preliminary data to test specific hypotheses or to get more in-depth responses from subjects. Other types of research questions may require an experimental design. Second, researchers may not be able to find any existing survey data sets that have variables and samples that are needed to answer their research questions. Third, even though they may find an existing data set that has variables related to their research questions, these variables may not be the most appropriate measurements for their constructs of interest. Since secondary researchers were not involved in deciding which measures were included in the original research, they can only use what is available. Fourth, researchers have no control over the survey design and data collection, and therefore no control over the quality of the data. Fifth, the learning curve of using large data sets can be very steep, and inexperienced researchers usually require extensive work and time to learn survey designs, primary data processing, and specific statistical methods needed to conduct data analyses. Many social work researchers find these tasks formidable.

Despite these potential limitations, with some training and education, most geriatric social work researchers would be able to expand their research capability by learning how to conduct secondary analysis of the rapidly expanding library of existing survey data.

UNDERSTANDING LARGE SURVEY DATA SETS

The main difference between survey and nonsurvey data (such as clinical and administrative data) is in sampling. Sampling lets researchers collect information from a relatively small number of individuals to provide accurate information about a much larger population. Most large survey data are collected from respondents selected through a complex sampling design that involves multistage sampling, stratification, clustering, and differential selection probabilities (i.e., weighting). In multistage sampling, individuals are first organized into small groups or clusters, such as geographic areas, counties, or city blocks. These clusters are sampled in the first stage of sampling. Individuals within the selected clusters are sampled in the subsequent stage. Several stages of cluster sampling (e.g., from counties to city blocks and then to households) may also be conducted before individuals are sampled. The first cluster to be sampled is known as the primary sampling unit (PSU). Cluster sampling is mainly used to improve logistics and to reduce the travel costs of data collection as interviewers only need to travel to a smaller number of clusters (e.g., counties) instead of traveling all over the country to collect data. Cluster sampling may lead to a correlation among sample units because individuals within the same cluster, such as household and neighborhood, are more homogeneous than individuals in different clusters. This correlation violates the assumption of independent observations in most statistical procedures and, if unaccounted for, leads to losses in precision in population estimates. Statistical analysis that does not take into account this potential correlation would potentially underestimate the standard errors of population estimates (Korn & Graubard, 1999; Lee, Forthofer, & Lorimor, 1989).

Stratification is the process of organizing individuals in the population into relatively homogeneous subgroups before sampling. The population may be stratified by income, race, geographic area, or other factors that are crucial to the analysis. Once these strata have been defined, sampling can be conducted independently within each stratum. For example, if the population is stratified by race, individuals in the population are first organized into Whites, Blacks, and other racial groups. Random sampling may then be conducted independently within each stratum. Individuals in different strata can have different probabilities of being selected into the sample. Unlike clusters, strata themselves are not being sampled in multistage sampling, and all strata are used in the sampling process. Stratification and cluster sampling can both be used at the same time in multistage sampling. Because individuals within a stratum are more homogeneous than individuals across strata, stratification may produce smaller estimates of variance and thus underestimate the standard errors of population estimates (Korn & Graubard, 1999; Lee et al., 1989). Researchers need to account for the effects of stratification in analysis of large survey data.

AHEAD Sampling Design

▓ AHEAD is based on a stratified multistage area probability sampling design with dual sampling frames. AHEAD households were assigned to one of two groups (those who were born after 1913 and those who were born prior to 1914) based on the age of the oldest person in the household. Households in the "born after 1913" group were selected exclusively from the area probability frame component. Households in the "born prior to 1914" group were selected using roughly a 50% sample from the areas probability frame and the remaining 50% through a stratified sampling from a list frame of Medicare enrollees. Households were organized into clusters of metropolitan statistical areas (MSAs), single large non-MSA counties, or groups of small non-MSA counties. Detailed information of sampling in AHEAD can be found in Soldo, Hurd, Rodgers, and Wallace (1997) and on the AHEAD Web site. Sample design variables were created in the public use data files for AHEAD users to adjust for features of the complex multiage design. ▓

In many large surveys, members of certain subgroups of the population, such as people of color or the oldest old, are sampled at higher rates relative to members in other subgroups of the population. Oversampling produces a larger sample size sufficient to allow separate inferences to be made for each of the subpopulations (Korn & Graubard, 1999). If uncompensated, however, oversampling may lead to bias in population estimates as the oversampled subpopulation has a greater influence on population estimates than it should have in the population. Many large survey data sets provide oversampling data in a base weight variable, which equals the inverse of the probability of selection into the sample. This base weight variable is used in statistical analysis to account for the differential probabilities of sample selection.

Nonresponse is another concern in analysis of large survey data, especially when the response rates differ across subgroups of the population. To account for the potential bias of differential response rates across subgroups of the population, researchers incorporate a nonresponse adjustment weight into the final analytical weight. The PSU and the sample subgroup are cross-classified to create weighting adjustment cells, and response rates in these cells are calculated. The nonresponse adjustment weights equal the inverse of the sample response rate within each of these cells. The analytical weight appropriate for estimating population characteristics is the product of the nonresponse adjustment weight and the base weight.

In spite of adjustments for differential sample selection rates and differential response rates, the weighted sample distributions of major demographic and geographic characteristics may still not correspond exactly to those for the population that are available from a source external to the survey data. The problem arises from the inherent inadequacies of the sample frame—individuals who should have been selected into the sample are not selected because they are not in the sample frame. To bring weighted sample distributions for important demographic and geographic subgroups in line with corresponding known population totals, researchers incorporate a small poststratification factor to analyze weights. They create poststratification adjustment cells by cross-classified sampling strata and the subgroups. The sum of the provisional sample weights (before poststratification adjustment) of all sampled individuals in each cell is calculated and is compared with a known census figure for the same cell. Assuming that the census figures are more accurate, the provision

sample weights are multiplied by a constant factor so that the sum exactly matches the census figures. These constants are used for poststratification adjustment (Korn & Graubard, 1999).

Oversampling and Weights Adjustment for AHEAD

▨ AHEAD oversamples Hispanics, Blacks, and households in the state of Florida. Household selection weight (i.e., base weight) is created to account for unequal selection probabilities of the three subpopulations. Weights are also created to adjust for geographic and race group differences in response rates and for the subsampling of households in a small number of locked buildings or dangerous areas. Poststratification adjustments are made at both the household and the person level to control sample demographic distributions to known 1990 census totals. Weights are also created for household analysis, as well as for individual analysis. ▨

SECONDARY ANALYSIS OF LARGE SURVEY DATA

Similar to other types of research, secondary analysis of large survey data starts with research questions and hypotheses. Once researchers have specified their questions and hypotheses, the next step is to find a data set that may contain the needed data to test the hypotheses. Several major data archives preserve and make available existing survey data for public use. Among them, the National Archive of Computerized Data on Aging (NACDA) is the best starting place for researchers who are interested in exploring the possibility of using secondary analysis of existing survey data for research of older adults and families. NACDA is funded by the National Institute on Aging and is located in the Inter-University Consortium for Political and Social Research (ICPSR). Since its inception about 25 years ago, the NACDA has preserved and made available the largest library of electronic data on aging in the United States. As of 2004, it had approximately 2,500 unique studies on aging and health with approximately 20,000 files (data, codebooks, documentation, and data definition statements). Researchers can search the library by keywords, specific variables, or subjects. Once they have identified one or more data sets that may be used to answer their research questions, they can download the codebooks and other documents of these data sets from the site. Researchers can also download most data sets directly from NACDA or through the official ICPSR representatives in their institutes. Table 94.1 shows some examples of large survey data sets that contain information related to geriatric social work. Researchers should evaluate all possible data sets by the quality of the measurements available, as well as by the sampling frame. The key question to answer is whether the survey data contain the needed information and sample at a reasonable quality to answer the research questions.

It is very important that researchers obtain and carefully read the codebooks and other documents of data sets before conducting any data analysis. These documents usually give researchers information about the sampling frame, sampling designs, oversampling, and response rates, as well as preliminary data processing such as coding for missing data, imputation, and creation of composite variables. They also give detailed information about the format of the data, the variable names, and the location. Many large data sets are stored in several smaller data files. These documents also provide detailed information about the content of each data file, the system of identification numbers, and how they can be merged. Some codebooks even give basic descriptive statistics, such as frequency and mean, for each variable in the data set.

SELECTION OF VARIABLES AND OBSERVATIONS INTO AN ANALYTICAL DATA FILE

Researchers typically use only a small group of variables in a large survey data set in their research. It is a good idea for researchers to select only those variables and observations that are relevant to their research questions into a new analytical data set. Recoding and other data manipulations should be performed on this analytical data set rather than on the original data set obtained from data archive. Most large data sets are in American Standard Code for Information Interchange (ASCII) data format and have a rectangular shape (sample units arranged in rows and variables arranged in columns). Researchers need to use their database or statistical software, such as SPSS or SAS, to extract variables from data files using column numbers and to save the extracted variables in a data format for their statistical program. Some newer data sets, such as AHEAD, come with computer programs that can convert their ASCII rectangular data files into specific statistical data files (such as SPSS or SAS data files), and researchers can directly extract variables using their statistical software.

Researchers may also find that only a subset of sample units, such as the oldest old or the working poor, is relevant to their study. It is therefore essential that researchers develop clear and objective criteria for case selection and exclusion. For survey data, case selection and exclusion affects the number of observations available across PSUs, and researchers must pay attention to the effects of case selection and exclusion on sampling designs.

PRELIMINARY DATA ANALYSIS

Prior to any substantive analysis, researchers should obtain unweighted tabulations on the distribution of sample units across PSUs to check whether enough sample units are available in each PSU to allow for meaningful analysis. If there are too few sample units in a particular PSU, researchers should consider combining it with adjacent PSUs in the same strata.

The second step of preliminary data analysis is exploring the univariate distribution of each variable used in the study. Recoding, such as log transformation, may be needed for variables that violate basic statistical assumptions. Recoding may also be needed to combine categories of variables or to change the ways that responses were coded. For example, in the AHEAD data, most negative responses are coded by the number 5, and positive responses are coded by the number 1. Researchers need to recode the negative responses from 5 to 0 to create indicator variables for further data analysis. Very often, researchers may need to create their own scales or indexes from existing variables in the data set. For example, the HRS survey asked each respondent several questions on education, including the number of years the respondent had attended school and the highest diploma achieved. Researchers may need to use this information to create their own variables for education.

The third step of preliminary data analysis is to decide how to incorporate the sample weights and account for stratification and clustering in the analysis. The decision to use weighted or unweighted estimators in survey data analysis is not always straightforward. Because use of weights in data analysis

TABLE 94.1 Examples of Large Survey Data Sets That Can Be Used by Geriatric Social Work Researchers for Secondary Data Analysis

Data name	Sample size and sampling	Survey design	Oversample	Remarks
Assets and Health Dynamics Among the Oldest Old (AHEAD)	8,222 respondents who were born before 1923. Multistage area probability sampling design with two sampling frames.	Ongoing longitudinal household interview survey.	Blacks, Hispanics, and residents of Florida.	Ongoing longitudinal survey. First wave of interview in 1993.
Americans' Changing Lives	3,617 respondents in first wave from a multistage stratified area probability sample.	Longitudinal study. Data were collected in 1986, 1989, and 1994.	Blacks and those 60 years of age and older.	
Census public use microdata files	1% or 5% of total U.S. population in 2000. Stratified systematic sample.	Cross-sectional self-administered questionnaire survey.	No	These data are from the national censuses taken every 10 years.
Current Population Survey	Ongoing monthly survey of civilian noninstitutionalized U.S. population aged 15 years and older. Sample size is about 60,000 households.	Ongoing rotation panel design. New households panel are brought into the sample every month. New households are interviewed monthly for 4 months, skipped for 8 months, and then interviewed for 4 months before being removed from the survey.	No	Ongoing survey since 1937.
Health and Retirement Study (HRS)	12,521 respondents in the 1931–1941 birth cohort from a multistage area probability sampling design.	Ongoing longitudinal survey. First wave of interviews was conducted in 1992.	Blacks, Hispanics, and residents of Florida.	The HRS and AHEAD were merged into one survey in 1998 with additional birth cohorts added to the sample.
Longitudinal Study on Aging	7,541 individuals who participated in Supplement on Aging to the 1984 NHIS and who were 70 years of age or older at that time.	Longitudinal study of a cohort of older people who were 70 years of age or older in 1984. They were reinterviewed by telephone in 1986, 1988, and 1990.	No	
National Health Interview Survey	Approximately 43,000 households including about 106,000 persons. Multistage area probability sample design.	Cross-sectional household interview survey.	No	An ongoing annual survey since 1957.
National Long-Term Care Survey, 1982–1989	6,393 persons who were disabled and community-dwelling in 1982 and their informal caregivers; a multistage probability sample.	Longitudinal study. Data were collected in 1982, 1984, and 1989.	No	

produces approximately unbiased population estimators, researchers should use weights, stratum identifiers, and sampling unit identifiers in their descriptive statistics to account for the effects of oversampling, nonresponse, clustering, and stratification (Korn & Graubard, 1999; Lee et al., 1989; Lepkowski & Bowles, 1996). However, use of sample weights when unnecessary may lead to larger standard errors and thus statistical inefficiency. Therefore, researchers should first check for the degree of inefficiency before any analytical statistical procedures are conducted. The degree of inefficiency is given by the following equation (Korn & Graubard, 1999):

$$\text{Inefficiency} = \left(1 - \left(\text{Variance of unweighted estimators} / \text{variance of weighted estimators}\right)\right)$$

If the inefficiency is small relative to the estimator, sample weights should also be used in completing analytical statistics, such as regression analysis. However, if the inefficiency is relatively large compared with the estimators, researchers should augment the weighted model with unweighted models or other alternative approaches that incorporate the design variables into the model (Korn & Graubard, 1999).

VARIANCE ESTIMATES IN LARGE SURVEY DATA

Many researchers are surprised to learn that the standard statistical software (such as SPSS) does not account for this lost precision due to complex sample designs (Brogan, 1998; Carlson, 1998; Lepkowski & Bowles, 1996). A number of statistical programs that implement these complex sample variance estimation methods are available to analyze large survey data. Two common approaches for estimating correct variance from survey data with complex sampling design are the replication approach and the Taylor series linearization approach (Brogan, 1998; Carlson, 1998; Korn & Graubard, 1999; Lee et al., 1989; Lepkowski & Bowles, 1996). The replication approaches, such as Balanced Repeated Replication, Jackknife Repeated Replication, and Bootstrap methods, use repeated subsamples from the whole sample to calculate the point estimates of the population parameters. The standard errors are then obtained using the variability of these subsample statistics. The linearization approach rewrites the population estimates in the form of a Taylor's series expansion with the assumption that all higher-order terms are negligible. The standard errors are obtained by applying a standard formula for the mean-square error to the first-order portion of the expanded estimates (Brogan, 1998; Carlson, 1998; Korn & Graubard, 1999; Lee et al., 1989; Lepkowski & Bowles, 1996; StataCorp, 2001). The detailed techniques of these two approaches are beyond the scope of this chapter. Table 94.2 summarizes several major statistical programs that can account for the imprecision from sampling designs. Researchers should learn to use one of these programs for secondary analysis of large survey data.

TABLE 94.2   Summary of Statistical Program for Survey Data Analysis

Program	Account for sampling design effect	Statistical procedures	Ease of use
Stata	Can handle most sampling designs, except two-state cluster sampling, probability-proportional-to-size sampling, poststratification, and certainty PSUs.	Has the most statistical procedures for survey data.	Relatively easy to use.
SUDAAN	Can handle all sampling designs.	Limited statistical procedure.	More difficult to use.
WesVar	Can handle all sampling designs except two-state cluster sampling.	Limited statistical procedure.	Easy to use.
SAS	Can handle all sampling designs except poststratification and two-stage cluster sampling.	Very limited statistical procedure.	Difficult to use.

From Survey Data Analysis Portal at UCLA, retrieved from *http://statcomp.ats.ucla.edu/survey/default.htm.*

CONCLUSION

Large existing survey data sets are valuable resources for researchers in the fields of social and health sciences. During the last two decades, these resources have become increasingly accessible to geriatric social work researchers. However, most geriatric social work researchers are challenged by the complex sampling designs and specific statistical techniques that are required to take advantage of these data sets. Some researchers who are already using large survey data sets do so incorrectly by ignoring the need to adjust for the complex sampling designs. This chapter addresses the benefits and limitations of using secondary analysis of existing large survey data in research on older adults and families. It shows steps that geriatric social work researchers should take to start using these data sets to answer some of their research questions. More and more resources are available either in print or on the Internet that geriatric social work researchers should consult to develop their expertise in secondary analysis of survey data.

REFERENCES

Brogan, D. J. (1998). Pitfalls of using standard statistical software packages for sampling survey data. In P. Armitage & T. Colton (Eds.), *Encyclopedia of biostatistics* (pp. 4167–4174). New York: Wiley.

Carlson, B. L. (1998). Software for statistical analysis of sample survey data. In P. Armitage & T. Colton (Eds.), *Encyclopedia of biostatistics* (pp. 4160–4167). New York: Wiley.

Hakim, C. (1982). *Secondary analysis in social research: A guide to data sources and methods with examples.* London: Allen and Unwin.

Korn, E. L., & Graubard, B. I. (1999). *Analysis of health surveys.* New York: Wiley.

Lee, E. S., Forthofer, R. N., & Lorimor, R. J. (1989). *Analyzing complex survey data.* Newbury Park, CA: Sage.

Lepkowski, J., & Bowles, J. (1996). Sampling error software for personal computers. *Survey Statistician, 35,* 10–17.

StataCorp. (2001). *Stata statistical software 7.0 user's guide.* College Station, TX: Stata Corporation.

USEFUL INTERNET RESOURCES

National Archive of Computerized Data on Aging: *http://www.icpsr.umich.edu/NACDA/*

The Inter-University Consortium for Political and Social Research: *http://www.icpsr.umich.edu/*

HRS and AHEAD Web site: *http://hrsonline.isr.umich.edu/*

Survey Data Analysis Portal at UCLA: *http://statcomp.ats.ucla.edu/survey/default.htm*

Software for Analysis of Surveys Information Page at Harvard University: *http://www.fas.harvard.edu/~stats/survey-soft/*

CHANG-MING HSIEH
ELIZABETH ESSEX

Measuring Client Satisfaction Among Older Adults and Families

Client satisfaction has long been an important part of program evaluation (e.g., Eckert, 1994; Kane, Bartlett, & Potthoff, 1995; Rossi, Freeman, & Lipsey, 1999; Royse, Thyer, Padgett, & Logan, 2001). Although the quality of care or services cannot be represented by client satisfaction alone, client satisfaction is generally accepted as an important indicator of care or service quality (Ingram & Chung, 1997; Royse et al., 2001). In measuring satisfaction with care or services for older adults, the clients may be the older adults themselves and/or caregiving family members (e.g., Atherly, Kane, & Smith, 2004; Tornatore & Grant, 2004).

There are, however, a number of limitations regarding client satisfaction studies. First, such studies have been criticized for using measures that are not contextually specific (Schneider, 1991). Popular generic satisfaction instruments, such as the Client Satisfaction Questionnaire (CSQ-8; Nguyen, Attkisson & Stegner, 1983) and the Reid-Gundlach Social Service Satisfaction Scale (R-GSSSS; Reid & Gundlach, 1983), may not provide helpful information for care or service providers because different settings usually have different service components (Chou, Boldy, & Lee, 2001).

Second, in general, most respondents of client satisfaction surveys indicate satisfaction with services received (e.g., Ingram & Chung, 1997; Royse et al., 2001). Older adults are particularly likely to indicate satisfaction with services, perhaps because of their dependence on service provision and fear of repercussions if they give negative responses. Or perhaps they have low expectations related to their own health outcomes (Atherly et al., 2004). Given the predominantly positive responses from client satisfaction studies, it is difficult for service providers to make sense of the data without comparing the results with other agencies or conducting multiple surveys longitudinally (Ingram & Chung, 1997).

Third, researchers have long argued that client satisfaction is multidimensional (e.g., Ruggeri & Greenfield, 1995). Although many published client satisfaction instruments provide information on various domains or dimensions of the instruments, these domains or dimensions are usually obtained through factor analysis and are often too abstract to make direct inferences for service provision. Users of these instruments generally end up obtaining only global/overall satisfaction scores.

Finally, many studies measure satisfaction by summing or averaging satisfaction scores across survey items to represent client satisfaction, assuming that all survey items carry equal weights (e.g., Chou et al., 2001; Kruzich, Clinton, & Kelber, 1992). This assumption is somewhat problematic because individual clients may perceive certain survey items to be more important, or to carry more weight, than others (Chou et al., 2001).

In this chapter, we propose an approach to measuring client satisfaction that can overcome the limitations just outlined. We first describe the main steps that go into this approach and provide a concrete example, using a community-based case management program for older adults. Readers can follow these steps and apply the approach to their own care or service settings. We then provide a theoretical perspective for this approach and discuss methodological issues of validity, reliability, and scoring.

PROPOSED MEASUREMENT APPROACH

Our approach to measuring client satisfaction can be applied to client satisfaction surveys in all service settings. For those who are interested in developing survey questionnaires that are administered by interviewers, the approach involves four major steps outlined in the following. For those who are interested in developing self-administered survey questionnaires, step 3 can be skipped, and therefore only three steps (1, 2, and 4) are required.

1. *Identify major aspects of care or services provided within the specific setting.* This step directly addresses the issue of contextual relevance. Major service aspects can be identified through combining literature review and discussions with care or service providers and clients. We recommend that these aspects be concrete so service providers can make sense of the results. We also suggest that the number of aspects not be too large to avoid a lengthy instrument that can be difficult for older adults to complete. It is also important to make sure that clients can easily recognize and distinguish between service aspects.

2. *Construct a Likert-type satisfaction rating item for each of the service aspects.* A typical item can be phrased "how satisfied are you," with each of the respective service aspects identified in step 1. We recommend the use of either a 5-point or 7-point response format, ranging from "completely satisfied" to "completely dissatisfied," to be consistent with most existing satisfaction measures.

3. *Construct a Likert-type importance rating item for each of the service aspects.* Clients are asked to in-

dicate the importance of each of the major service aspects to themselves, using a 5-point response format (e.g., 1 = "Extremely important" to 5 = "Not at all important"). This information will be used in step 4. For self-administered questionnaires, it is most straightforward to skip this step.

4. *Construct a mechanism to obtain an importance hierarchy for the service aspects.* The limitation in step 3, used for interviewer-administered questionnaires, is that clients may give two or more service aspects the same importance rating. To further distinguish the importance of service aspects to the clients, interviewers should, in this final step, ask respondents to rank order in importance those items for which they gave the same rating so a hierarchy of importance can be obtained. For self-administered survey questions, simply have the respondents provide the rank ordering of importance. The resulting importance hierarchy is used to calculate weighted satisfaction scores.

To illustrate the major steps, we now describe their use in developing a measure for client satisfaction with services provided by a community-based case management program for frail older adults. The program, located in a large midwestern city, provides case management services to about 4,000 adults 60 years of age and older. The case management agency wants to collect client satisfaction data and use the data to help improve its services. However, using popular generic instruments, such as the CSQ-8 (Nguyen et al., 1983) and the R-GSSSS (Reid & Gundlach, 1983), may not fit the purpose of the survey because these instruments are not specific to case management settings. Other instruments, like the Home Care Satisfaction Measure: Case Management Service (HCSM-CM13; Geron et al., 2000), are designed specifically for case management settings. The primary limitation with this type of instrument, however, is that it only produces global satisfaction scores. Without collecting the data longitudinally or comparing the data with that from other agencies, service providers often have difficulty interpreting the results.

To overcome these limitations, we follow the four major steps described earlier to develop an interviewer-administered client satisfaction measure for this case management service setting. We decided against a self-administered survey because of the population the agency serves. Many of the clients had very little education and therefore have minimal literacy skills. In addition, a number of clients have visual impairments. Although our intention is to illustrate the four major steps to develop an interviewer-administered survey questionnaire, we also provide sample wording for a self-administered survey questionnaire (in Appendix C) for those who are interested. Our steps in questionnaire development include the following:

1. From a review of the literature on elderly case management services (e.g., Geron et al., 2000; Robinson, 2000; White, 1986) and discussions with service providers and clients, five major aspects of service provision are identified: assessment of clients' needs, plan of care development, case manager's knowledge regarding available services, case manager's ability to get services for clients, and case manager's availability.

2. A Likert-type satisfaction rating item for each of the five major service aspects is constructed (see Appendix A, S1–S5).

3. A Likert-type importance rating item for each of the five major service aspects is constructed (see Appendix A, I1–I5).

4. We construct a two-step procedure to obtain the importance hierarchy. Interviewers are instructed to (a) rank the importance based on the results from the importance rating in step 3, and then (b) ask the respondent to rank order those items for which he or she gave the same ratings (see Appendix B).

THEORETICAL PERSPECTIVE

The theoretical perspective underlying our proposed approach is an extension of the first author's earlier work on life satisfaction (Hsieh, 2003, 2004). There are a number of similarities between client satisfaction and life satisfaction regarding measurement and conceptualization. First, client satisfaction, like life satisfaction, involves subjective evaluations of objective conditions (e.g., Reid & Gundlach, 1983). Second, client satisfaction is a multidimensional construct (Chou et al., 2001; Ruggeri & Greenfield, 1995), and so is life satisfaction (e.g., Cummins, 1995, 1996; Diener, 1984). Third, client satisfaction, like life satisfaction, can be measured by either a single-item global satisfaction or a composite of satisfactions with various domains (e.g., Nguyen et al., 1983). Given these similarities, the theoretical perspective that has been used

to address the measurement and conceptualization issues in life satisfaction literature can serve as a foundation to study client satisfaction.

Reflective Approach Versus Formative Approach

Besides using single-item global satisfaction measures, researchers who construct multi-item measurements of life satisfaction generally follow either a "top-down" or a "bottom-up" approach (Diener, 1984). The top-down approach assumes that global life satisfaction is a predispositional trait or personality that influences one's evaluation of satisfaction in multiple domains, whereas the bottom-up approach maintains that global life satisfaction can be regarded as the composite of satisfaction in various domains (Diener, 1984). Similar to the case of client satisfaction, the multidimensional nature of life satisfaction limits the utility of single-item global life satisfaction measures, since an individual can be satisfied with his or her overall life but dissatisfied with certain aspects of life (Cummins, 1996). In fact, the use of top-down and bottom-up approaches to measuring life satisfaction coincides with the use of reflective indicators (or effect variables) versus formative indicators (or causal variables) in measurement in general (e.g., Bollen & Lennox, 1991; Chin & Newsted, 1999; Cohen, Cohen, Teresi, Marchi, & Velez, 1990; Fayers & Hand, 1997; Fayers & Machin, 2000). In a formative indicators model, indicators are viewed as determining or causing the latent construct, which is similar to the bottom-up approach. In a reflective indicators model, indicators are viewed as determined by the latent construct, which is similar to a top-down approach (Bollen & Lennox, 1991; Chin & Newsted, 1999; Cohen et al., 1991).

Since the landmark study by Campbell, Converse, and Rogers (1976), it has become common to measure global life satisfaction by simply summing across satisfactions in various discrete life domains, such as health, finance, and friendships (e.g., Beatty & Tuch, 1997; Mookherjee, 1992). This so-called bottom-up approach (Diener, 1984) to measuring global life satisfaction can be applied to the measurement of global client satisfaction. That is, Campbell et al.'s (1976) conceptual model of life satisfaction can be adapted for client satisfaction (Figure 95.1). As portrayed in Figure 95.1, global client satisfaction is determined by satisfactions with various service aspects.

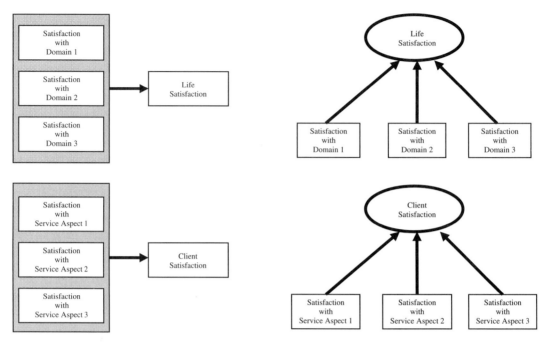

FIGURE 95.1 Parallel between Life Satisfaction and Client Satisfaction.

Weighting by Perceived Importance of Various Service Aspects

As many have observed (e.g., Cummins, 1995, 1996; Diener, Lucas, Oishi, & Suh, 2002; Diener, Napa Scollon, Oishi, Dzokoto, & Suh, 2000; Hsieh, 2003; Oishi & Diener, 2001), the correlation between the global life satisfaction outcomes produced by the different approaches (top-down vs. bottom-up) is usually not very high. A factor that might contribute to the low correlation is the possibility that individual satisfaction items do not carry equal weights (Hsieh, 2003, 2004). That is, simply summing satisfaction scores across various items, without considering the potential unequal weights of these items, may not provide a good indication of an individual's global satisfaction. In fact, researchers (e.g., Campbell et al., 1976; Inglehart, 1978) have long noted the possibility of unequally weighted individual life domains in the overall picture of life satisfaction. Despite different terms used to discuss this (e.g., domain importance by Campbell et al. in 1976; value priority by Inglehart in 1978; and psychological centrality by Ryff and Essex in 1992), researchers generally agree that global life satisfaction is a weighted composite, not a simple sum, of domain satisfactions, and the relative importance of each discrete life domain should act as a weighting mechanism.

Based on the findings in life satisfaction literature, it is very likely that simply summing client satisfaction scores across various service aspects may not be a good indication of a client's global satisfaction. Instead, client satisfaction measures can incorporate clients' perceived importance of service aspects as a weighting mechanism, linking satisfaction with various service aspects to global satisfaction.

METHODOLOGICAL ISSUES

As shown in the conceptual model (see Figure 95.1), we define and conceptualize client satisfaction as the client's sense of service quality that stems from satisfaction or dissatisfaction with the service aspects that are important to him or her.

Validity

Although our approach to measuring client satisfaction appears to have face validity, we recommend that any new measures using this approach still be cross-validated with existing measures to obtain concurrent validity. This can be done by using a correlation analysis between total scores (see later explanation of scoring for calculating total scores) for the new measure and those of existing measures. Using the example we provided, we suggest the new case management client satisfaction measure be validated with both generic client satisfaction measures, such as the CSQ-8 (Nguyen et al., 1983), and contextually specific measures, such as the HCSM-CM13 (Geron et al., 2000). In addition, a single-item global satisfaction measure can be included (see Appendix A, S6) as an existing measure to serve the purpose of cross-validation (see Hsieh, 2003, for an example).

Reliability

It should be noted that given the formative indicators model this proposed client satisfaction measure is based on, applying conventional guidelines for measurement construction may not be adequate. As Bollen and Lennox (1991) suggested, the concept of reliability based on internal consistency is only appropriate for a reflective indicators model. In other words, for a formative indicators model, using internal consistency as an indication of reliability is problematic (Bollen & Lennox, 1991). Therefore, reliability of the measures constructed using our proposed approach should be assessed through the test-retest method.

Scoring

Because we propose to construct measures using Likert-type rating items, it is unlikely that ratio level measurement data can be obtained. It is therefore difficult to justify why the assigned values of a 7-point scale should take 1 to 7 and not 2 to 8 or some other range of values. In fact, the issue of scoring is further confounded by the lack of conceptual or theoretical development regarding how importance should be incorporated into client satisfaction measures. It seems reasonable to assume that more important service aspects should weigh more. Without guidance from any conceptual framework, however, it is not clear if satisfaction with a service aspect that is "not important at all" should carry zero weight in one's global satisfaction, nor is it clear how much more weight should be given for each 1-point increase in a 5-point (or 7-point) importance rating scale.

The issue of weighting also exists in life satisfaction literature (Hsieh, 2004). A common way of obtaining weighted score is to use multiplicative scores:

multiplying satisfaction and importance ratings (e.g., Ferrans & Powers, 1985). As Trauer and Mackinnon (2001) pointed out, multiplicative scores can be problematic. The primary drawback of multiplicative scores is the difficulty in interpreting the meaning of the score, given that the same score can be obtained by the combination of a high satisfaction rating with a low importance rating or a low satisfaction rating with a high importance rating (Trauer & Mackinnon, 2001). To overcome the conceptual ambiguity produced by multiplicative scores, we suggest the use of the following general formula to produce weighted global client satisfaction scores (see Hsieh, 2003, 2004):

$$\sum \left(S_i \times I_i \right) / \sum I_i$$

where S_i is the satisfaction score for service aspect i, and I_i is the importance score for service aspect i. In other words, an individual's weighted global satisfaction score is calculated by summing the products of the satisfaction score and the importance score across all service aspects and then dividing by the sum of importance scores.

As pointed out by Trauer and Mackinnon (2001), multiplying two scores (satisfaction and importance) that do not have ratio level measurement properties is problematic. As a beginning step to deal with the issue of measurement properties, sensitivity analysis can be employed to check the dependence of the results on the score choices made in weighting schemes (e.g., Agresti & Finlay, 1997). Following Hsieh's earlier work on life satisfaction (2003), a few sensible score choices can be employed to see if any pattern emerges from the results. In addition to assuming that the weight of importance increases or decreases as a linear function, weighting mechanisms can be constructed on the assumption that the weight follows nonlinear functions, taking into account the nature of an ordinal scale (see Hsieh, 2003, for a more detailed discussion).

Unlike multiplicative scores, which may be difficult to interpret, the score obtained by our proposed weighting scheme clearly indicates an individual's weighted (by importance of various service aspects) satisfactions. A hypothetical example can be used to illustrate the case. An instrument obtains satisfaction scores and importance scores for two service aspects. Person A has a low satisfaction score of 1 and a high importance score of 5 for one service aspect and has a low satisfaction score of 2 and high importance score of 5 for the other aspect. To calculate person A's multiplicative score, which is 15, we multiply the satisfaction score by the importance score for each service aspect ($1 \times 5 = 5$, and $2 \times 5 = 10$) and then take the sum of these products ($5 + 10 = 15$). It will be impossible to distinguish person A from person B, who has a high satisfaction score of 5 for both service aspects and a low importance score of 1 for one service aspect and a low importance score of 2 for the other aspect, if a multiplicative score approach is used, since person B's multiplicative score will be 15 ($5 \times 1 + 5 \times 2 = 15$) as well. However, there will be a clear difference in the scores for person A and for person B using the weighting formula proposed here. To calculate each person's weighted global satisfaction score, the multiplicative score (15) is divided by the sum of the importance scores, resulting in a score of 1.5 (15/10) for person A and 5 (15/3) for person B. Table 95.1 shows these score values.

Another issue is the way importance should be measured. A common approach to measuring domain importance in life satisfaction literature is to ask respondents to rate the importance of each individual domain (e.g., Campbell et al., 1976; Ferrans & Powers, 1985). This approach is limited because it cannot provide direct comparisons across domains. For example, if both domains receive the same importance rating, can we conclude that they have equal importance? Building on the first author's earlier work (Hsieh, 2003), different service aspects can be ranked by asking the respondents to place these major service aspects into a hierarchy, based on their perceived importance of the service aspects. Using ranking is advantageous for two reasons. First, it not only shows the importance of each service aspect but also provides direct comparisons of importance across service aspects. Second, findings in life satisfaction literature

TABLE 95.1 Score Values for Two-Person Hypothetical Example

	Person A	Person B
Domain 1 score		
Satisfaction	1	5
Importance	5	1
Domain 2 score		
Satisfaction	2	5
Importance	5	2
Weighted global score		
Multiplicative weighting	15	15
Proposed weighting	1.5	5

suggest that the weighted composite (using ranking) of various satisfaction items is a better indicator of global life satisfaction than the simple sum of satisfaction items (Hsieh, 2003).

Proposed Scoring Method

To illustrate how to obtain a client's weighted satisfaction score, we again use the case management example. Assume a client gives respective satisfaction ratings of 3, 5, 5, 7, and 6 for the five satisfaction items in Appendix A (S_1–S_5); the client's importance hierarchy corresponding to the items (from first to last) in Appendix B is 3, 5, 4, 1, and 2. We first reverse the rank number of the importance hierarchy to give more important items higher numbers (weights). Thus, the most important item (ranked number 1) will become 5, and what ranked number 2 will become 4, and so on. Next, we follow the scoring formula to obtain the weighted global satisfaction score. For each service aspect, the satisfaction score is multiplied by the importance score, and these products are summed ($3 \times 3 + 5 \times 1 + 5 \times 2 + 7 \times 5 + 6 \times 4 = 83$). We then divide this number (83) by the sum of the importance rankings ($3 + 1 + 2 + 5 + 4 = 15$), resulting in a weighted global satisfaction score of 5.53. We recommend the use of this straightforward weighting method. For those who are interested in other types of scoring, see Hsieh (2003) for a discussion.

CONCLUSION

The method of measuring client satisfaction proposed here is designed to overcome the limitations of past client satisfaction studies. By asking the clients to rate their satisfaction with all major service aspects within a specific care or service setting, our approach addresses the issues of contextual relevance and the multidimensional nature of client satisfaction. In addition, this measurement approach addresses the possibility of unequal weights among the different service aspects by incorporating perceived importance into the measurement of client satisfaction. That is, the measure takes into account the potential interpersonal differences in perceived importance of various service elements. It is, therefore, a true client-centered satisfaction measure. Our example of this client-centered method of measuring client satisfaction can be easily adapted by other case management service agencies. Gerontological social workers in other practice settings can also follow the steps outlined in this chapter to develop client satisfaction measures that can pinpoint the exact sources of clients' satisfaction and dissatisfaction. Service providers can continue to maintain the service elements with high client satisfaction scores and make improvements on the sources of dissatisfaction. In addition, because most gerontological social workers face the issue of limited resources, this approach can help them set priorities for service improvement based on clients' perceived importance and ultimately benefit their clients.

APPENDIX 95.A

Satisfaction Items

The following questions ask how satisfied you are with different services provided by the Central West Case Management. Please use a number from 1 to 7 to indicate your satisfaction where 7 means "Completely satisfied" and 1 means "Completely dissatisfied." If you are neither completely satisfied nor completely dissatisfied, you would put yourself somewhere from 2 to 6; for example, 4 means neutral, or just as satisfied as dissatisfied.

S1. How satisfied are you with your case manager's assessment of your needs?   _____
S2. How satisfied are you with the plan of care your case manager developed?   _____
S3. How satisfied are you with your case manager's knowledge regarding the services that are available?   _____
S4. How satisfied are you with your case manager's ability to get services for you?   _____
S5. How satisfied are you with the availability of your case manager?   _____
S6. All together, how satisfied are you with the services you receive from the Central West Case Management?   _____

Importance Items

Some people may feel some areas of the case management services are more important than others. What areas of case management services do you consider extremely important or not at all important to you? Please use a number to indicate the importance of the services from 1 through 5, where 5 means "Extremely important" and 1 means "Not at all important."

I1. Case manager's assessment of your needs
         _____
I2. Your plan of care   _____
I3. Case manager's knowledge regarding available services   _____
I4. Case manager's ability to get services for you
         _____
I5. Availability of your case manager   _____

APPENDIX 95.B

Constructing the Importance Hierarchy

Directions to interviewer:

Based on responses to the importance items, please rank the five areas of case management services from 1 (the most important) to 5 (the least important) below. For items with same importance ratings, ask the respondent to rank order their importance. Use the same ranking number for any areas the respondent believes are equally important.

_____ Case manager's assessment of your needs
_____ Your plan of care
_____ Case manager's knowledge regarding available services
_____ Case manager's ability to get services for you
_____ Availability of your case manager

APPENDIX 95.C

Constructing the Importance Hierarchy

(Sample wording for self-administered survey questionnaire)

Based on importance, please rank the following five areas of case management services from 1 (the most important) to 5 (the least important). Use the same number for any areas you believe are equally important.

_____ Case manager's assessment of your needs
_____ Your plan of care
_____ Case manager's knowledge regarding available services
_____ Case manager's ability to get services for you
_____ Availability of your case manager

Partial support for this project was provided by the Hartford Geriatric Social Work Faculty Scholars

Program (supported by a grant to the Gerontological Society of America from the John A. Hartford Foundation).

REFERENCES

Agresti, A., & Finlay, B. (1997). *Statistical methods for the social sciences* (3rd ed.). Upper Saddle River, NJ: Prentice Hall.

Atherly, A., Kane, R. L., & Smith, M. A. (2004). Older adults' satisfaction with integrated capitated health and long-term care. *Gerontologist, 44,* 348–357.

Beatty, P., & Tuch, S. A. (1997). Race and life satisfaction in the middle class. *Sociological Spectrum, 17,* 71–90.

Bollen, K., & Lennox, R. (1991). Conventional wisdom on measurement: A structural equation perspective. *Psychological Bulletin, 110,* 305–314.

Campbell, A., Converse, P. E., & Rogers, W. L. (1976). *The quality of American life: Perceptions, evaluations, and satisfactions.* New York: Russell Sage.

Chin, W. W., & Newsted, P. R. (1999). Structural equation modeling analysis with small samples using partial least squares. In R. H. Hole (Ed.), *Statistical strategies for small sample research* (pp. 307–341). Thousand Oaks, CA: Sage.

Chou, S. C., Boldy, D. P., & Lee, A. H. (2001). Measuring resident satisfaction in residential aged care. *Gerontologist, 41,* 623–631.

Cohen, P., Cohen, J., Teresi, J., Marchi, M., & Velez, C. N. (1990). Problems in the measurement of latent variables in structural equations causal models. *Applied Psychological Measurement, 14,* 183–196.

Cummins, R. A. (1995). On the tale of gold standard for life satisfaction. *Social Indicators Research, 35,* 179–200.

Cummins, R. A. (1996). The domains of life satisfaction: An attempt to order chaos. *Social Indicators Research, 38,* 303–328.

Diener, E. (1984). Subjective well-being. *Psychological Bulletin, 95,* 542–575.

Diener, E., Lucas, R., Oishi, S., & Suh, E. M. (2002). Looking up and down: Weighting good and bad information in life satisfaction judgments. *Personality and Social Psychology Bulletin, 28,* 437–445.

Diener, E., Napa Scollon, C. N., Oishi, S., Dzokoto, V., & Suh, E. M. (2000). Positivity and the construction of life satisfaction judgments: Global happiness is not the sum of its parts. *Journal of Happiness Studies, 1,* 159–176.

Eckert, P. A. (1994). Cost control through quality improvement: The new challenge for psychology. *Professional Psychology: Research and Practice, 25,* 3–8.

Fayers, P. M., & Hand, D. J. (1997). Factor analysis, causal indicators and quality of life. *Quality of Life Research, 6,* 139–150.

Fayers, P. M., & Machin, D. (Eds.). (2000). *Quality of life: Design, analysis and interpretation.* New York: Wiley.

Ferrans, C. E., & Powers, M. J. (1985). Quality of life index: Development and psychometric properties. *Advances in Nursing Science, 8*(1), 15–24.

Geron, S. M., Smith, K., Tennstedt, S., Jette, A., Chassler, D., & Kasten, L. (2000). The Home Care Satisfaction Measure: A client-centered approach to assessing the satisfaction of frail older adults with home care services. *Journals of Gerontology: Psychological Sciences and Social Sciences, 55B,* S259–S270.

Hsieh, C. M. (2003). Counting importance: The case of life satisfaction and relative domain importance. *Social Indicators Research, 61,* 227–240.

Hsieh, C. M. (2004). To weight or not to weight: The role of domain importance in quality of life measurement. *Social Indicators Research, 68,* 163–174.

Inglehart, R. (1978). Value priorities, life satisfaction, and political dissatisfaction among Western publics. *Comparative Studies in Sociology, 1,* 173–202.

Ingram, B. L., & Chung, R. S. (1997). Client satisfaction data and quality improvement in managed mental health care organizations. *Health Care Management Review, 22,* 40–52.

Kane, R. J., Bartlett, J., & Potthoff, S. (1995). Building an empirically based outcomes information system for managed mental health care. *Psychiatric Services, 46,* 459–461.

Kruzich, J. M., Clinton, J. F., & Kelber, S. T. (1992). Personal and environmental influences on nursing home satisfaction. *Gerontologist, 32,* 342–350.

Mookherjee, H. N. (1992). Perceptions of well-being by metropolitan and nonmetropolitan populations in the United States. *Journal of Social Psychology, 132,* 513–524.

Nguyen, T. D., Attkisson, C. C., & Stegner, B. L. (1983). Assessment of patient satisfaction: Development and refinement of a service evaluation questionnaire. *Evaluation and Program Planning, 16,* 109–118.

Oishi, S., & Diener, E. (2001). Re-examining the general positivity model of subjective well-being: The discrepancy between specific and global domain satisfaction. *Journal of Personality, 69,* 641–666.

Reid, P. H., & Gundlach, J. H. (1983). A scale for the measurement of consumer satisfaction with social services. *Journal of Social Service Research, 7,* 37–54.

Robinson, M. M. (2000). Case management for gerontological social workers. In R. L. Schneider, N. P. Kropf, & A. J. Kisor (Eds.), *Gerontological social work* (2nd ed., pp. 136–164). Belmont, CA: Wadsworth.

Rossi, P. H., Freeman, H. E., & Lipsey, M. W. (1999). *Evaluation: A systematic approach* (6th ed.). Newbury Park, CA: Sage.

Royse, D., Thyer, B. A., Padgett, D. K., & Logan, T. K. (2001). *Program evaluation: An introduction* (3rd ed.). Belmont, CA: Wadsworth.

Ruggeri, M., & Greenfield, T. K. (1995). The Italian version of the Service Satisfaction Scale (SSS-30) adapted for community-based psychiatric patients: Development, factor analysis and application. *Evaluation and Program Planning, 18,* 191–202.

Ryff, C. D., & Essex, M. J. (1992). The interpretation of life experience and well-being: The sample case of re-location. *Psychology and Aging, 7,* 507–517.

Schneider, B. (1991). Service quality and profits: Can you have your cake and eat it too? *Human Resource Planning, 14,* 151–157.

Tornatore, J. B., & Grant, L. A. (2004). Family caregiver satisfaction with the nursing home after placement of a relative with dementia. *Journal of Gerontology: Social Sciences, 59B,* S80–S88.

Trauer, T., & Mackinnon, A. (2001). Why are we weighting? The role of importance ratings in quality of life measurement. *Quality of Life Research, 10,* 579–585.

White, M. (1986). Case management. In G. L. Maddox (Ed.), *The encyclopedia of aging* (pp. 92–96). New York: Springer.

All societies, political or academic, must choose;
these choices can be good, or bad. The worst choice
may be looking for answers before there is consensus,
or at least a debate, on what the real questions
should be. (Munger, 2000, p. 1)

In advocating for an integrated social science research
agenda, political scientist Michael Munger observes
that academic research has become diffuse, and the
enterprise of accumulating social science knowledge
unfocused. Current scholarship, he argues, is busily
coming up with answers, yet most have lost sight of
the questions. Increasingly, research agendas built on
some form of consensus provide both a vehicle and a
focus for taming the unruly process of determining
important questions and establishing guidelines for
the development, dissemination, and use of new
knowledge about these questions. The National Institutes of Health, for example, routinely use mechanisms such as expert consensus conferences and lay
consumer panels to inform the development of research agendas and to encourage and legitimate the
appropriation of resources to act on established priorities.

The National Institute of Mental Health (NIMH)
Task Force on Social Work Research (1991) provided
a critical impetus for refining the focus of social work
research. By the mid-1990s, research agendas began to
appear, for example, in social welfare (Coulton, 1996),
health care (Ell, 1996; Jansson & Dodd, 1998), and social work organizations (Auslander, 1996). As chair of
the NIMH Task Force, David Austin (1998) spurred
these efforts in calling for a strategic approach to social work research that is based on specific domains of
expertise. He recommended that each domain assess
the state of its own knowledge, identify critical knowledge gaps, and establish research needs and priorities
to address these gaps.

Drawing on multiple data sources and using several critical indicators, several years ago we initiated
an assessment of the current status of social work research in the field of aging. In the next section, we
highlight findings from that review. In addition, findings from a national Delphi project we conducted to
further articulate research priorities for gerontological social work are discussed. Finally, in light of this
review of social work research in aging to date and
findings from the Delphi study, we consider future research directions for the field of gerontological social
work.

DENISE BURNETTE
NANCY MORROW-HOWELL

Current Status of Social Work Research in Aging and Future Directions

CURRENT STATUS OF SOCIAL WORK RESEARCH IN AGING

In an effort to assess the current status of gerontological social work research (Morrow-Howell & Burnette, 2001), we used reports from professional associations, that is, the Association for Gerontology Education in Social Work (AGE-SW), the Council on Social Work Education (CSWE); published reports on research (Austin, 1998); public and private funding databases; and our own surveys of published literature to explore four specific questions: To what extent are social work faculty members identifying research interests in gerontology? To what extent are social work researchers contributing to the multidisciplinary knowledge base of gerontology? What topics are gerontological social workers investigating? To what extent are social workers being funded for their research?

Based on membership in AGE-SW and the Strengthening Aging and Gerontology Education for Social Work (SAGE-SW) interest list, we estimated that 296 social work faculty nationwide (4% of all social work faculty enumerated by CSWE) have a significant interest in aging. It is important to note that not all these individuals are actively engaged in research. Compared with faculty interest in other social work domains, gerontology ranked fourth as a domain of current or future research interest, after children, mental health, and health, respectively (Austin, 1998). These data suggest that a relatively small proportion of the nation's social work faculty is interested in gerontology, particularly as compared with interest in other substantive domains. Necessary first steps in advancing the field are thus to increase the number of social work faculty interested in aging, and then to increase the subset of these faculty who actively engage in research.

We next assessed social workers' contributions as lead authors or coauthors of articles published in the *Gerontologist* from 1995 through 2001. Social workers were lead authors of 12% ($n = 50$) of the 415 articles reviewed and coauthors of another 8% ($n = 38$). Twenty percent of articles published in the *Gerontologist* during this period thus involved social work. We interpreted this as a moderately successful achievement, although it is certainly underrepresentative of the level of involvement of social workers in gerontological practice.

In our review of topics of social work–authored articles in the *Gerontologist*, the largest category of interest was family caregiving, constituting nearly one third of all articles. Fourteen percent of articles focused on ethnicity, addressing such topics as ethnicity and disability, ethnic elders' participation in research protocols and Alzheimer's disease centers, and ethnicity as it relates to grandparenting, postacute care, depressive symptoms, and issues of morbidity and comorbidity. Another 12% of articles addressed formal service use, comparing users and nonusers and examining high users, extended users, and formal and informal care mixes.

In a parallel review of the *Journal of Gerontological Social Work* during the same 5-year period, about 17% of articles focused on caregiving and about 10% addressed ethnicity. Most articles on ethnicity described the service needs of subgroups of ethnic elders, and a few focused on service use and ethnic-sensitive practice. Another 7% of articles examined international aging and addressed issues in countries such as China, Hong Kong, Israel, Sweden, Britain, Canada, Japan, and Puerto Rico. About one quarter of articles (6% each) addressed four broad topics—adjustment to new settings or situations; volunteerism and work; professional gerontological social work training; and changing families. About 5% focused on development and testing of psychosocial interventions, including strengths-based approaches, solution-focused treatment for problem behaviors, a personal advocacy model, and a model of community-based mental health services. Other topics that received limited attention were formal service use and delivery, income and insurance, elder maltreatment, end-of-life care, mental health, and interdisciplinary practice. It is important to note here that social workers may be publishing on these topics in interdisciplinary or more specialized journals.

Our review of publications in these two major journals over a 5-year period suggests that social work researchers are indeed investigating a broad range of critical issues in our field. However, nearly 40% of the articles reviewed in the *Gerontologist* and 30% of those in the *Journal of Gerontological Social Work* focused on family caregiving or ethnic diversity. Although these are core topics for professional social work, other important topics appeared to be neglected. There was very little attention, for example, to developing and testing interventions that could directly inform the development of guidelines for practice and policy.

Finally, we sought information on the number of gerontological social worker researchers supported by external funding. Reliable estimates of these counts are not readily available, so we offer tentative findings.

We found that social workers are grossly underrepresented among funded investigators funded by the National Institute on Aging (NIA). Based on a review of several key private funding agencies, we concluded that social workers fare better with foundation funding but are still underrepresented.

To summarize the data we examined, social work researchers in aging appear to have established a small national presence in social work schools, but the extent to which they are conducting research is unclear. Social work researchers are contributing to the multidisciplinary knowledge base in aging, as indicated by manuscripts in the *Gerontologist,* but contributions to this literature are incommensurate with involvement in interdisciplinary practice. And, although gerontological social workers are investigating topics that are important to their field, attention to these topics varies, and a number of critical areas remain underexamined. Finally, social workers barely have a foothold in federally funded research in aging but seem to be faring better with some, but not all, private foundations.

We have thus made progress on some fronts, but we still have far to go. The absence of a disciplined, integrated research agenda has impeded our work, and continued advancement will depend on decisions about substantive priorities in social work and in gerontology, and on the multiple, mutable contexts in which social science research occurs. We will return to issues of context momentarily. With respect to substantive priorities, gerontological social workers must identify the most pressing gaps in basic and applied knowledge on older adults, their families, and communities. They should take an independent lead in developing social work research agendas that can be used to guide rigorous, systematic investigations on these topics. In addition, they should assume a key collaborative role in developing and participating in interdisciplinary agendas.

IDENTIFYING SUBSTANTIVE TOPICS: HIGHLIGHTS FROM A NATIONAL DELPHI STUDY

Based on our assessment of the status of social work research in aging, we initiated an effort to identify key substantive priorities for gerontological social work research through a national Delphi study (see Adler & Ziglio, 1996, for a review of Delphi methodology) of two expert gerontological panels—one of 46 academic social work researchers (Burnette, Morrow-

Howell, & Chen, 2003) and another of 52 social work practitioners (Morrow-Howell, Burnette, & Chen, under review). Each panel completed three successive questionnaires that were designed to ultimately delimit a set of high-priority, high-consensus research topics for the field.

To be included, a topic had to achieve a threshold of priority and consensus ratings (see Burnette et al., 2003, for details on calculations of these ratings). Coincidentally, each panel identified 16 top research priorities. Table 96.1 presents these data, with correspondent topics listed opposite each other to facilitate comparison. In some cases, topics that are conceptually similar, though not identical, are grouped under the same broad rubric. There is considerable overlap in substantive topics identified as priorities by the researcher and practitioner panels, but each panel also identified unique topics.

The academic researcher panel's top priority was developing and testing psychosocial interventions across specific populations and conditions, and they identified three other priority topics on intervention. The practitioner panel identified three of the same intervention topics as priorities: family interventions, ethnic-sensitive interventions, and management of dementia. The two panels also agreed on the need for research on workforce issues for an aging society. The researchers called for knowledge development on recruitment and retention of professionals more generally, whereas practitioners saw gerontological social work education as a top priority. Both panels also identified family caregiving, mental health problems, and transitions in living arrangements as high-priority areas for knowledge development.

Differences in these two stakeholder groups are also noteworthy. The researcher panel endorsed the need for research on interventions and on the service delivery system with greater specificity and breadth. They endorsed four topics related to use, coordination, and quality of services, plus a separate topic on services to family caregivers. Practitioners named only one topic on service delivery—outreach and service delivery to underserved populations. Other priorities unique to the researcher panel included psychosocial outcome measures, housing and living arrangements, and chronic physical health conditions and health-related quality of life.

The practitioner panel endorsed seven unique topics. Two topics, income security and long-term care policy, concern social policy, an area in which social work has yet to establish itself (Morrow-

TABLE 96.1 Comparison of Priorities of Researcher and Practitioner Panels

Researcher panel	*Practitioner panel*
Intervention research	
1. Developing and testing psychosocial interventions across populations and conditions	1. Family interventions
2. Developing and testing ethnic-sensitive assessment and interventions	2. Ethnic-sensitive interventions
3. Developing psychosocial outcome measures	
4. Developing/testing psychosocial and ecological interventions for cognitive and mental disorders	3. Management of dementia
Housing and living arrangements	
5. Maximizing housing/living arrangement options for aging in place	
6. Transitions and adjustments across care settings and environments	4. Transitions in living environments
Service delivery	
7. Coordination and integration of health, mental health, and social service systems	
8. Utilization and barriers to health, mental health, and social services	
9. Interface between informal and formal care	
10. Service use by ethnic elders	
	5. Outreach and service planning/delivery for underserved elders
Detection and assessment	
11. Determining needs of ethnically diverse elders	
Family caregiving	
12. Effective services to family caregivers	
13. Understanding specific caregiver population	6. Family caregiving, including grandparent caregiving and caregiving to developmentally disabled
Health/mental health	
14. Chronic illness, disability, and rehabilitation: Quality of life and psychosocial well-being	7. Quality of life in long-term care
15. Detection, assessment, and treatment of late-life depression	8. Depression assessment and treatment
	9. Mental health assessment and treatment
Workforce	
16. Recruitment and education of professional workforce for an aging population	10. Gerontology education in social work
Social policy	
	11. Income security
	12. Long-term care policy
Capacity building	
	13. Self-determination, decision making, and autonomy
	14. Empowerment strategies
	15. Planning for later life: Individuals and families
	16. Normal and successful aging

Howell & Burnette, 2001). Four other unique topics, which we term *capacity building,* concern issues practitioners typically encounter in their daily work: ethical issues of self-determination, decision making, and autonomy; client empowerment strategies; long-range planning with individuals and families for later life; and issues of normal and successful aging.

The research priorities identified by these expert panelists represent critical knowledge needs for social work in aging. Moreover, they overlap and complement the current research agendas of the NIA Strategic Plan (2001–2005) and the National Research Council's (NRC) report on the NIH Committee on Future Directions for Behavioral and Social Science Research (Singer & Ryff, 2001; see Burnette et al., 2003, for a discussion of this overlap). As such, these priorities can serve as a useful guide for the development and prioritization of social work and interdisciplinary research to improve professional practices and public policies that affect the well-being of older adults.

Finally, after comparing topics identified by the two expert panels and establishing their fit with major national research agendas, we suggest that these priorities be further organized in a tighter framework. We propose a combination of the four core substantive topics (housing and transitions in living arrangements; family caregiving; health and mental health; and workforce for an aging society) with four crosscutting themes (intervention research, social policy, service delivery, and capacity building). A first step in a refined agenda would then be to review and summarize the current state of knowledge on each of 16 topics in a hypothetical four-by-four grid. Such reviews would help highlight critical knowledge gaps, inform the development of key research questions, and eventually lead to a body of evidence-based knowledge and guidelines for gerontological social work practice and policy.

CONTEXTS OF SOCIAL WORK RESEARCH IN AGING

The process of assessing the state of research, identifying substantive priorities, and organizing topics in a theoretically meaningful and practically useful framework is necessary but not sufficient to ensure successful implementation of a research agenda. Research priorities are fundamentally context-dependent, meaning that social, political, and economic forces constantly influence preferences, options, and outcomes. To build and sustain a viable infrastructure for a program of research, gerontological social workers must garner sufficient professional and public awareness, create new and enhance existing opportunities for educating and cultivating potential funding sources, and credibly conduct, disseminate, and apply our knowledge and skills within and beyond social work.

Increasing Awareness and Support

Gerontological social workers must work actively to increase the level of awareness and understanding among colleagues in social work and other disciplines and the general public about the social, health, and economic needs of older adults and aging societies. With respect to gerontological associations and interest groups, who already understand the needs of our aging society, educational efforts should focus on the social work profession's vital role in meeting those needs. Within and beyond these organizations, gerontological social workers must educate widely about the role of social work research in addressing these needs. They should collaborate with professional organizations whose mission is to advance social work research to effectively convey this message to public media and to advocate for funding for basic and applied research on high-priority interventions, services, and policies.

Gerontological social workers currently have several strong venues through which to organize and promote their research. Founded in 1993, the Institute for the Advancement of Social Work Research (IASWR) aims

> to advance the scientific knowledge base of social work practice by enhancing the research capacity of the profession; to promote use of research to improve practice, program development and policy; and to strengthen the voice of the profession in public education and public policy determinations by ensuring that social work is represented within the national scientific community. (Institute for the Advancement of Social Work Research [IASWR], 2001, at *http://www.iaswresearch.org*)

Gerontologists are highly visible among IASWR leadership. In 2000, the organization sponsored an invitational meeting with NIA staff to discuss strategies to forge stronger links with social work researchers. The IASWR listserve also regularly distributes information on aging-related conferences and funding opportunities to its membership.

Other important resources are the Society for Social Work and Research (SSWR) and the Association for Gerontological Education in Social Work (AGE-SW). SSWR, a strong force in evidence-based practice, was established in 1994 to create a network for social workers involved in research, encourage social workers to engage in research, and advocate for research funding and research training programs. Gerontological social workers are also prominent among SSWR membership, leadership, and conference participants. Plans to establish a special aging interest group within SSWR are under discussion.

AGE-SW has existed in a variety of forms for several decades, and its membership has grown steadily in recent years. The group sponsors a number of research activities, including a gerontology symposium at the CSWE annual program meeting, initiated in the mid-1990s, and a mentoring program to assist junior faculty and doctoral students with research and teaching in aging. AGE-SW also has a long-standing research committee, but its organization and activities have vacillated over the years. Rejuvenation of this committee could provide a useful forum for advancing a unified gerontological social work research agenda.

Developing and Leveraging Funding Sources

The John A. Hartford Foundation's Faculty Scholars and Doctoral Fellows programs offer an unprecedented opportunity to increase the number and reach of geriatric social work researchers (Berkman, Silverstone, Simmons, Volland, & Howe, 2000; Lubben & Harootyan, 2002). To ensure that scholars supported by these initiatives realize their long-term potential, parallel investments in institutional infrastructure for social work research in aging are needed. As we have noted (Morrow-Howell & Burnette, 2001), such programs might focus exclusively on aging, or they could build gerontological research into existing programs and structures. The latter approach might include nesting aging research within existing program initiatives such as the Social Work Research Development Centers funded by the NIMH during the 1990s, those currently funded by the National Institute on Drug

Abuse, and other existing centers and projects. This strategy could help maximize resources, increase awareness of aging issues and the number of social work faculty involved in aging research, and promote knowledge development on aging across substantive areas within the profession.

In addition to building on existing institutional resources, the long-range impact of current initiatives that aim to focus and advance the field will depend on social workers' ability to successfully develop new and strengthen existing links to federal, state, and local funding agencies, philanthropic foundations, and other internal resources of academic institutions. As noted, social work ties with the NIA have been tenuous. Improving this linkage could have a major impact on research funding, interdisciplinary collaboration, and training and career development for social work researchers. The recent NIA-funded Institute on Aging and Social Work (Berkman & Mehrotra, 2003) is an example of what is possible. Efforts to strengthen ties with the NIMH should also be stepped up, particularly given the surgeon general's report on mental health (U.S. Department of Health and Human Services, 1999) and the institute's recent initiative to expand its research portfolio relating to aging (National Institute of Mental Health, 2001).

Also at the federal level, we would do well to explore opportunities for collaborative research with the Office of the Assistant Secretary for Aging, Administration on Aging, Center for Medicare and Medicaid Services, Social Security Administration, Agency for Healthcare Research and Quality, Department of Veterans Affairs, and Substance Abuse and Mental Health Services Administration (see Austin, 1998, p. 36; Council on Social Work Education [CSWE], 2001, p. 5).

Private monies also offer opportunities for expanding and enhancing gerontological social work research. An example is the recently established Institute for Geriatric Social Work (IGSW), funded by Atlantic Philanthropies and located at Boston University School of Social Work (Geron, 2002). IGSW is dedicated to improving the workforce of social workers to serve our aging society by offering continuing education to BSW and MSW practitioners. IGSW recognizes the need to document the effectiveness of social work interventions to support the expansion of reimbursement options for social work practitioners. Thus, a priority of the institute is promoting intervention research that builds an evidence base for geriatric social work practice.

FUTURE DIRECTIONS FOR SOCIAL WORK RESEARCH IN AGING

Nearly a decade ago, Ewalt (1996) noted that an ongoing decline in federal responsibility for social work–related problems has heightened the imperative for the profession to proactively establish directions for its practice, policy, and research agendas. The urgency of this mandate continues to grow, even as the aging of U.S. and other world populations becomes a more visible social and economic force in the 21st century. This demographic shift alone should ensure a topmost place for aging in any social research agenda. But gerontological social workers must use their collective experience, knowledge, and influence to systematically define and advance their own priorities. We conclude this chapter with a brief discussion of key areas of inquiry for social work researchers in aging and some of the changing contexts in which that research will likely take place.

Establishing a research agenda may help focus gerontological social work researchers' attention on important neglected areas of the profession. Three particularly critical areas of deficiency are social policy, psychosocial interventions and outcomes, and services research. Our review of social work–authored publications showed scant attention to policy development or policy analysis. Social workers' firsthand experience with the impact of social policy on older clients and their families should enable social workers to play a major role in the formulation, implementation, and evaluation of policy (Fahey, 1996), yet a seeming lack of interest and/or expertise has largely excluded them from public policy dialogue. Rigorous investigations of all phases of public policy processes are needed, and social work researchers should bring this knowledge to public debates through skillfully planned, coordinated dissemination activities.

There is also a clear need for increased attention to developing psychosocial outcomes measures, testing psychosocial interventions, and improving services at all levels of practice. These deficiencies are particularly troubling given the increased emphasis on research that directly informs practice. As Austin (1998) notes, "The most important issue for the immediate future is to bring the practice effectiveness concerns of social work practitioners together with the resources represented by social work researchers" (p. 27). Likewise, the SAGE-SW blueprint for improving quality of life for older adults and their families recommends two foci for gerontological social work research—increased opportunities and support for research and increased emphasis on practice-based, measurable research (CSWE, 2001, pp. 4–5). This report further calls for researchers to develop strategic outreach and incentives to faculty and field supervisors to conduct practice-based research and to assist in developing practice protocols.

Finally, with respect to the contexts of future research, there is a growing appreciation of the complexities of generating and applying knowledge in real-world settings. Social work's commitment to intervention and services research, including evidence-based practice, practice guidelines, and service effectiveness, will doubtless continue (Proctor, 2002; Rosen & Proctor, 2003). These lines of inquiry will require the development of measurable outcomes—a process that will entail concerted efforts over time (see Kane, 2003). Meanwhile, novel priorities will arise, along with new contingencies and resources, including more sophisticated methodologies, innovative technologies, changing values, and evolving political and economic climates.

It will be important to maintain sufficient focus while remaining vigilant to developing social, economic, and political contexts of social work research. Research agendas will need to be reviewed and revised periodically, and an effective balance preserved between long-range investments in high-priority areas with shorter-range and evolving issues. The latter tend to be initially localized and typically receive widespread attention only after a period of accumulating evidence. Social work researchers should thus remain in close touch with practitioners, whose work provides a peerless window into the world of newly developing issues. Similarly, the research process should be informed by the views of a variety of stakeholders. In addition to practitioners, the perspectives and interests of policymakers, consumers, and social work researchers in substantive areas such as health, mental health, disabilities, and families will also be valuable.

Interdisciplinary approaches to knowledge development and dissemination are also on the rise. The collaboration of biological and environmental scientists and social scientists on issues of aging, for example, permits the expansion of research questions and findings beyond a single social, biological, or physical issue. Research that informs practice guidelines and social policies may thus need to address a wider range of aging experiences and incorporate multiple sources of knowledge within and beyond conventional disciplinary and geographic boundaries. Collaborations with researchers in other domains of social work, other disciplines, and various stakeholder groups should enrich the experience, outcomes, and application of research about and with older adults. Important first steps will be to determine which topics are appropriate, which disciplines are key, which stakeholders are essential, and which funding sources are available.

It is also important to note that neither consensus nor resources guarantee the effective implementation of even the most carefully articulated research agenda. Focus and commitment are also essential. To maximize our ability to effectively address the psychosocial needs of older people and aging societies, social work must increase the production and dissemination of scientifically sound practice- and policy-relevant research. More highly skilled gerontological social work researchers will be needed to accomplish this goal, and their investigations of high-priority topics will require adequate short-term and long-range support. We are well positioned to create and take advantage of existing opportunities to assume a true leadership role in research on aging—to make unique, significant contributions to national research agendas, interdisciplinary research teams, and the profession's own knowledge base.

REFERENCES

Adler, M., & Ziglio, E. (Eds.). (1996). *Gazing into the oracle: The Delphi method and its application to social policy and public health.* London: Kingsley.

Auslander, G. K. (1996). Outcome evaluation in host organizations: A research agenda. *Administration in Social Work, 20*(2), 15–20.

Austin, D. M. (1998). *A report on progress in the development of research resources in social work.* Washington, DC: Institute for the Advancement of Social Work Research.

Berkman, B., & Mehrotra, C. (2003). Institute on Aging and Social Work. Grant proposal funded by NIA. Retrieved from *http://www.css.edu/programs/iasw/*

Berkman, B., Silverstone, B., Simmons, J., Volland, P., & Howe, J. (2000). Social work gerontological practice: The need for faculty development in the new millennium. *Journal of Gerontological Social Work, 34*, 1–23.

Burnette, D., Morrow-Howell, N., & Chen, L. M. (2003). Setting priorities for gerontological social work research: A national Delphi study. *Gerontologist, 43*, 828–839.

Coulton, C. J. (1996). Poverty, work and community: A research agenda for an era of diminishing federal responsibility. *Social Work, 41*, 509–520.

Council on Social Work Education. (2001). *Strengthening the impact of social work to improve the quality of life for older adults and the families: Blueprint for the new millennium.* Washington, DC: Author.

Ell, K. (1996), Social work and health care practice and policy: A psychosocial research agenda. *Social Work, 41*, 583–593.

Ewalt, P. L. (1996). Social work in an era of diminishing federal responsibility: Setting the practice, policy and research agenda. *Social Work, 41*, 439–441.

Fahey, C. (1996). Social work education and the field of aging. *Gerontologist, 36*, 36–41.

Geron, S. (2002). Institute for Geriatric Social Work. Grant proposal funded by the Atlantic Philanthropies. Retrieved from *http://www.bu.edu/igsw*

Institute for the Advancement of Social Work Research. (2001). *Strategic Plan 2001–2003.* Washington, DC: Author. Retrieved from *http://www.iaswresearch.org.*

Jansson, B. S., & Dodd, S. J. (1998). Developing a social work research agenda on ethics in health care. *Health and Social Work, 23*, 17–23.

Kane, R. A. (2003). Definition, measurement, and correlates of quality of life in nursing homes: Toward a reasonable practice, research and policy agenda. *Gerontologist, 43*, 28–36.

Lubben, J., & Harooytan, L. K. (2002). Strengthening geriatric social work through a doctoral fellowship program. *Journal of Gerontological Social Work, 39*, 145–156.

Morrow-Howell, N., & Burnette, D. (2001). Gerontological social work research: Current status and future directions. *Journal of Gerontological Social Work, 36*, 63–79.

Morrow-Howell, N., Burnette, D., & Chen, L. (under review). Setting research priorities for gerontological social work: Perspectives of a national practitioner panel. *Social Work Research.*

Munger, M. C. (2000). Five questions: An integrated research agenda for Public Choice. *Public Choice, 103*, 1–12.

National Institute of Mental Health. (2001). Late-life mental illness research at the National Institute of Mental Health: An analysis of fiscal year 2000 grants, contracts, and intramural research program projects. Department of Health and Human Services. Retrieved from *http://www.nimh.nih.gov/aging/aging reportFY2000.pdf.*

National Institute of Mental Health Task Force on Social Work Research. (1991). *Building social work knowledge for effective services and policies: A plan for research development.* Austin: School of Social Work, University of Texas at Austin.

Proctor, E. K. (2002). Quality of care and social work research [Editorial]. *Social Work Research, 26,* 195–197.

Rosen, A., & Proctor, E. K. (Eds.). (2003). *Developing practice guidelines for social work intervention: Issues, methods, and research agenda.* New York: Columbia University Press.

Singer, B. H., & Ryff, C. D. (2001). *New horizons in health: An integrative approach.* National Research Council Commission on Behavioral and Social Sciences and Education. Washington, DC: National Academy Press.

U.S. Department of Health and Human Services. (1999). *Mental health: A report of the surgeon general.* Rockville, MD: U.S. Department of Health and Human Services, Substance Abuse and Mental Health Services Administration, Center for Mental Health Services, National Institutes of Health, National Institute of Mental Health.

NANCY R. HOOYMAN,
SECTION EDITOR

Social Work Education and Careers in Aging

OVERVIEW

The four chapters in this closing section, *Social Work Education and Careers in Aging,* signal the dramatic progress in gerontological social work education that has occurred since the first stage of the gerontological social work movement (1965–1994), which JoAnn Damron-Rodriguez describes in her chapter. In the second stage (1995–2004), highly visible national leadership and external support replaced concerns about student disinterest and faculty resistance to gerontological social work; for example, the Bureau of Health Professions 1995 recommendations for geriatric social work education, the Geriatric Social Work Initiative funded by the John A. Hartford Foundation, the National Association of Deans and Directors 2002 report, *Promoting Social Work for All Ages,* and the annual National Conference for Gerontological Social Work in conjunction with the Council on Social Work Education's (CSWE) annual program meeting all were initiated during the second stage. Building on these two stages, gerontological social work education appears to be moving into a third stage, illustrated in part by these four chapters.

As identified by James R. Reinardy and Sara Zoff and Nancy L. Wilson, greater recognition now exists that organizational and curricular changes are needed to embed and sustain gerontological content within social work education programs. Accordingly, the dissemination of high-quality teaching resources is a necessary but not sufficient condition for curriculum transformation. Instead, the time-consuming, sometimes incremental process of change—assessing organizational barriers and enablers; obtaining the buy-in of faculty, student, and community stakeholders, and collaboration and partnerships—is essential to ensure that such teaching materials are utilized and institutionalized within social work curricula, not gathering dust on office shelves. Both Reinardy and Zoff and Wilson provide the reader with guidelines for sustainable curricular and organizational change, primarily oriented to the infusion of gerontological content in foundation curricula, but also to the development of advanced or specialized practicum options. Strikingly, their recommendations draw largely on the accomplishments of social work programs throughout the country—large/small, BSW/MSW, urban/rural—rather than on national directives or expert white papers.

Because of the national leadership and funding that characterized the second stage, the exciting work of the third stage is occurring at the program level, sometimes without external funding, among faculty, practitioners, and students committed to disseminating their lessons learned and best practices. The national geriatric social work movement is no longer abstract, distant, or confined to only resource-rich programs; instead, it is a campaign of relationship building, collaboration, and partnership at the local level. Hundreds of social work educators are not only drawing on models stimulated by foundation funding, such as Geriatric Enrichment in Social Work Education (GeroRich), Strengthening Aging and Gerontology Education for Social Work (SAGE-SW), and the Practicum Partnership Program, but are also generating their own transformative approaches, congruent with their programs' distinctive mission and goals. Perhaps the third stage will come to an end when gerontological social work education is no longer regarded as a new way of doing things, but as the way we do things, the rule rather than the exception (Bland et al., 2002).

Another distinguishing characteristic of the third stage is the development, implementation, and evaluation of gerontological social work competencies. Social work education has long struggled with whether and how to define competencies that can be measured. As documented by JoAnn Damron-Rodriguez, both the CSWE/SAGE- SW project and the Practicum Partnership Program have contributed to the field through their development of geriatric social competencies. In addition, some GeroRich projects drew on the generalist SAGE-SW competencies. Although further refinement and testing of generalist versus advanced competencies are needed, the groundwork has been laid for competency-based gerontological social work education and identification of best practices. Classroom- and agency-based educators must continue to address the challenge of evaluating the outcomes of a competency-based approach.

As suggested by Wilson, greater attention needs to be given in the third stage to improving the public image of gerontological social work and clarifying the geriatric social worker's distinctive roles and contributions, particularly on multidisciplinary teams. Continuing education and credentialing, which are congruent with the specialization model referred to by Wilson, are related to both of these goals. Robyn Golden and Monica White highlight social work's strengths in working with older adults and clarify the rationale for and benefits of credentialing for social work case managers in aging. Social workers are central to case management with older adults but are often less visible than other professions in the medical and rehabilitation fields. Certifying the knowledge and skills distinctive to social work case management with elders may enhance public and multidisciplinary awareness of geriatric social work.

In sum, these chapters document educational changes at the local level that are preparing graduates for working effectively with older adults, although not necessarily as a career in the sense of advanced specialization in gerontological skills. For those who do choose to specialize, however, the issue of credentialing and improving the public image of gerontological social work is critical not only to their careers but to the quality of services to older adults and their families.

REFERENCE

Bland, C. J., Starnaman, S., Wersal, L., Moorhead-Rosenberg, L., Zonia, S., & Henry, R. (2000). Curricular change in medical schools: How to succeed. *Academic Medicine, 75*(6), 575–594.

This chapter addresses the comprehensive strategies that are needed to implement sustainable gerontological curricular change on a program level. What steps, actions, and considerations do social work programs need to make to develop a curriculum that prepares students to meet the growing challenges of an aging society? We begin with a brief review of select literature on organizational and curricular change, including strategies for changing gerontological curricula. Then, after drawing from the literature on principles for change, we outline and illustrate the major considerations that should inform the change process: planning, implementing, and institutionalizing an aging-rich curriculum.

ORGANIZATIONAL AND CURRICULAR CHANGE

The major steps that typically make up the organizational change process are determining the need, developing and communicating a vision, identifying barriers, building a consensus, creating the change strategy, and then implementing and evaluating the change (Knorr, 1993). This process has its roots in the pioneering work of Kurt Lewin (1957), whose notion of force field analysis was grounded in systems theory and who depicted organizational change as a process of unfreezing, changing, and then refreezing. The key was to introduce a state of disequilibrium into the system where driving forces overcame restraining forces. In this view, often applied to business, top management must be strongly committed to the process. There is often a change champion with a compelling and consistent vision. Teams are involved in the process, attempts are made to reach all corners of the organization, and, especially important, organizations must modify their policies and procedures if change is to be sustained (refrozen) (McNamara, 1999).

A second arm of change literature, while incorporating much of the above, places more emphasis on elements such as cultural change, vision, power, and social control. Less emphasis is on top-down leadership and more on visionary leadership and bottom-up strategies (Wons, 2002). This approach is evident in the work of Nichols-Casebolt, Figueria-McDonough, and Netting (2000), who propose change strategies to integrate women's knowledge into social work curricula. They argue that a major transformation is needed given the marginalization of such content. Their analysis includes the type of

JAMES R. REINARDY
SARA ZOFF

Strategies for Implementing and Sustaining Gerontological Curricular Change in Social Work Education

97

culture characterizing the school, the kind of leaders available, opportunities for effective leadership, and other organizational characteristics that affect choice of strategy. Bottom-up change is also a theme in Brager and Holloway's (1983) classic model for changing organizations from within. They propose a detailed framework of questions, beginning with initial assessment (e.g., What are the forces for and against? Does the change represent the agency's values?) and preinitiation (e.g., How do you develop legitimacy? Increase agency stress?) through initiation (strategies of who, what, when) and institutionalization (building the change into policies and procedures).

Although these principles of organizational change apply to educational institutions, change leaders have to balance and build on the tensions specific to each university's threefold cultural mix of scholarship, teaching, and service (Hanley, 2001). Given tenure and the university reward system, faculty buy-in also becomes essential. Hagner and Schneebeck (2001) emphasize the need, when seeking faculty engagement, to assess the mix of the faculty and the different rewards to which each of its members will respond. Building on constituencies' and stakeholders' interests becomes even more imperative for achieving change as universities and colleges increasingly become open systems and respond to learning as both a social and a market-driven good (Graves, 2001).

Successful approaches to curricular change need to be comprehensive, multifaceted, and systems-based. This is demonstrated by Bland and colleagues (2000) in a recent review of the literature to determine the major strategies needed for curricular reform in medical schools. They identified reappearing themes that suggested 13 characteristics of successful curricular change: leadership, the institution's mission and history of change, politics (internal networking, resource allocation, external relations), organizational structure, need for change, complexity of change, cooperative climate, participation, communication, human resource development, rewards, performance dip, and evaluation.

GERONTOLOGICAL CURRICULAR CHANGE IN THE SOCIAL WORK LITERATURE

Most of the published social work literature in gerontological education addresses curricular frameworks, educational models, and pedagogy. Other articles

have investigated conditions affecting curricular change, such as barriers and enablers. Barriers include ageist attitudes, lack of organizational commitment, lack of training, few incentives, limited resources, and faculty and student disinterest (Browne, Braun, Mokuau, & McLaughlin, 2002; Kropf, 2002; Rosen, Levy, & Singer, 2002; Scharlach, Damron-Rodriguez, Robinson, & Feldman, 2000. Examples of enablers are linkages to a gerontology center, a multidisciplinary approach, and the presence of a medical school (Damron-Rodriguez & Lubben, 1994; Damron-Rodriguez, Villa, Tseng, & Lubben, 1997). A few authors, however, have described comprehensive change projects or models. Meredith and Watt (1994) present a comprehensive change project that links faculty professional growth with institutional development and curriculum development. Beginning with the social work dictum "Start where the client is," they conclude that *curriculum shift* and *sustainability* depend on the benefit perceived by faculty members. They were able to tailor seed grants, film discussions, resource kits, and conference opportunities to individual faculty member's perceived needs. They credited the success of curricular change to the involvement of those affected by the change as well as to a focus on enriching rather than replacing the curriculum.

A second project of interest applies Lewin's (1957) normative change model to integrating gerontology into the curriculum (O'Reilly & Kazanowski, 1993). Although applied to a nursing program, the principles transfer to social work education programs. The authors discarded a rational change model (i.e., that a group will change when given convincing information about the need for change, etc.) as not taking into account the emotions, culture, needs, attitudes, and values of the target system. Employing a respected champion, the project emphasized planning, group work, and consensus building in the change process. In the beginning, the leaders assessed both the driving forces (e.g., grant availability, employment opportunities, accreditation standards, demographic changes, patient needs) and restraining forces (time constraints, lack of interest and/or knowledge about gerontology, full curricula, few opportunities for publishing) that worked for and against the plan. In Lewin's model, part of the process of unfreezing involves introducing discomfort (e.g., leaders focus on a school/department's performance gap, or faculty are led to discover that they have ageist attitudes) and safety (group support, reward opportunities) at the same time. This change process placed emphasis on group work and consensus building and applied many of the strategies used by Meredith and Watt (1994). The authors emphasize that the process takes time—up to 2 years to integrate content into the curriculum—and that toward the end, at the refreeze phase, change energies tend to decline (a performance dip). Leadership and motivation are important at this point to maintain the process, and evaluation should be ongoing.

In addition to the literature cited, there are a handful of articles on specific strategies, such as student recruitment and collaborative field projects. These are incorporated in the following section, which applies change strategies to gerontological curricular change. Project reports and lessons learned from the Geriatric Enrichment in Social Work Education (GeroRich) Program (Hooyman & St. Peter, in press) are also applied. The program completed its third and final year on June 30, 2004, and surely will add much to the literature on aging and curricular change (see Hartford Geriatric Enrichment Social Work Program, n.d.).

GERONTOLOGICAL CHANGE STRATEGIES IN THE SOCIAL WORK CURRICULUM

As the models described earlier illustrate, curricular change entails multiple efforts to achieve faculty buy-in. But the curriculum is embedded within a program, which in turn is embedded in a department/school, university/college, and community. Thus, strategies for lasting change not only address the faculty but, as the organizational literature suggests, must target in a comprehensive, multidimensional manner all internal and external stakeholders that make up the system. They incorporate into the change process the mission, nature, and culture of the school/department, and they recognize that change is a transformative process that includes recognition of need, tension, vision and leadership, communication and consensus, a plan to follow, ongoing support and development, and rewards.

Change as Vision and Sustainability

Sustainability happens not only at the end or institutionalization phase of the change process, where changes are incorporated into program objectives and syllabi. It is just as important that it be related to vision, which guides the change process prior to its

inception and throughout. A key question is: To what extent and how will gerontological content be incorporated into the curriculum? Is the curriculum envisioned as a specialization, or as being integrated and infused with aging content (Singer, 2000)? Is it seen as transformed (Hooyman & St. Peter, in press)? Integration adds content to the curriculum, albeit in strategic places; specialization, at least at a minimum, adds a series of courses at the advanced level. Infusion attempts to fill the curriculum throughout with content related to aging across foundation courses: in exercises and assignments and course objectives. The more profound the vision, the more sustainable (if accomplished!) in that it will not only call for the addition of a course or an objective here and there, but will challenge the faculty and school to rethink the curriculum, the program's organizational goals, and its supports and linkages with the community. Hooyman and St. Peter encourage programs to work toward a curricular transformation to achieve long-term change.

Given these alternatives, change agents need to assess at the point of planning prior to initiation what is feasible in their program, including factors such as the program's mission, history of change, culture, resources on aging (in both the faculty and the community), possible resources for faculty development, and potential allies and pressures for change/resistance from within and outside of the program. Of all of the options, integration of content guarantees little sustainability. Content is easily lost with changes in personnel. More important, the faculty as a whole has not grappled with the question of how the educational experience leads to desired outcomes for their graduates.

Vision is of critical importance because it drives the change process. It requires that faculty members have both private and public conversations about the program's goals and values and about what they see as the learning outcomes for their students. This takes hold when leaders frame questions to enlarge debate, avoid premature closures, and act as proponents, not judges (Brown & Jackson, 2001). A central challenge to enlarging the debate is developing an integrating theme that builds on faculty interests as well as transforms the curriculum. The strategy is not simply to add on content, for several reasons. Infusion or transformation will not be achieved. Faculty members will grumble at having to add content to an already full curriculum. In addition, not only is there a natural resistance to change, but change often entails a loss (Bridges, 1991). Faculty members have worked hard to develop course and curricular content—they are going to be much more open to the transformation of their work rather than its replacement. Examples of crosscutting themes include use of the notion of aging across the life span to organize courses, the organizing theme of multigenerational practice, and the incorporation of aging as a dimension in a strengths-based perspective. The University at Albany, for example, has adopted an integrated framework of intergenerational and multicultural practice to incorporate into its curriculum both multiple generations and racial, ethnic, and gender identities. The University of Washington uses a multigenerational perspective to infuse content on aging. The curriculum incorporates interactions among generations, not only between them (see www.gerorich.org).

As discussed in the sections that follow, making the vision a reality involves a collaborative, multifaceted approach. It requires the involvement of faculty, administration, students, and stakeholders from the community, and it should draw from several potential process tools. These include design teams, curricular audits and assessments, individual interviews, focus groups, task forces, alumni partnerships, practitioner advisory boards, and faculty retreats. The vision also must respect the mission of the social work program and university. Although university and program missions appear all-encompassing, they take on a specific life in reality, and social work programs are more and more becoming open systems, responsive to a competitive environment where strategic planning is important (Mudrick, Steiner, & Pollard, 1992). If a program does engage in strategic planning, change leaders have an important opportunity to move the faculty to adopt a vision on aging content. Council on Social Work Education (CSWE) reaffirmation may also present such an opportunity, although the focus of the change effort can be lost in the complexities of the reaffirmation process.

Change as Collaborative Effort

Accomplished change leaders perceive all stakeholders to be both targets and advocates/forces for change. For example, students who are moved to embrace a career in social work with older persons also become advocates who seek change in the curriculum. A practitioner advisory board that begins recommending practice competencies to the curriculum committee

also becomes a gentle pressure on the faculty to undertake curricular reform. Potential stakeholders that are both targets and forces for change include faculty and staff, students, field instructors and practitioners in the community, gerontology centers, faculty and departments of related disciplines, professional associations, and other schools or departments of social work.

Faculty members, both as individuals and as forming the program's policy body, are a central focus of the change effort. Obtaining their buy-in and collaboration in a transformative change process demands a thoughtful assessment of their needs, motivations, and reasons for resistance to change. Hagner and Schneebeck (2001) recommend that change leaders assess the mix of their faculty. Some faculty members tend to be *entrepreneurs* or *lone rangers*. They are quick to take a project and run with it on their own. They have a high level of commitment but may require more attention to engage in a collaborative effort. Others are *reward seekers* whose motivational structures are closely tied to the university's reward system. Others are *risk aversives*. They are committed to quality learning but may be afraid that their current success in teaching and service may be jeopardized by the new vision. Risk aversives may need significant levels of institutional support; they may also profit from success stories told by peers who have incorporated aging content into their pedagogy.

The mix of change strategies depends on the type of faculty and culture of the department or school. Change leaders in a large program with a heavy research agenda may place more emphasis on individual faculty consultations and mini-grants for syllabi changes, whereas those in a smaller program may build more group processes into their change effort. Regardless of the number of strategies employed— brown-bags, focus groups, one-to-one meetings, faculty development workshops, faculty retreats, strategic planning, outside consultants, funded travel to workshops and institutes—the faculty as a whole must, in the end, own the new curriculum. This requires dialogue and decision making in faculty meetings and throughout formal policymaking bodies, such as curriculum committees. It also necessitates opportunities for faculty members to examine attitudes toward aging, their own as well as those of others. Videos, presentations to the faculty by outside consultants and older persons on life's challenges and rewards may be helpful. Many faculty members, often senior members in leadership positions, find themselves in the role of caregiver for their parents. This may be an opportunity to begin a dialogue.

Studies show that the number of students interested in working specifically with older adults is very low, around 5% (Kosberg & Kaufman, 2002; Kropf, Schneider, & Stahllman, 1993). Although this is a concern, it is easy to forget that a vision for transforming the curriculum must include all students, regardless of their career interests. A brown-bag on geriatric social work in the marketplace or the development of a gerontological student interest group will provide supports for students interested in aging careers. A brown-bag on end-of-life issues, on the other hand, or a presentation on kinship care may attract entirely different groups, helping these students link aging issues to their lives and careers. Nevertheless, a strong contingent of students interested in geriatric social work will be a force for change as well as a model to other students for interest in aging issues.

The GeroRich Web site provides examples of numerous strategies used by projects to recruit as well as stimulate and maintain students' interests in aging. These include focus groups and surveys to assess reasons for student disinterest as well as programs in service learning, stipends, simulation games, brown-bags, special conferences and job fairs, alumni mentors, and student interest groups. As an example, the University of Minnesota–Twin Cities sponsored an all-day workshop for its students in the field. The planners chose legislation on vulnerable adults and presented it as relevant to many practice settings, not just those serving older persons. Another strategy, one that directly feeds into the curricular change process, is to appoint students with interests in aging to key curricular and events committees.

Collaboration with stakeholders outside of the school, particularly in the community, is an especially important dimension of curricular change. Social work programs prepare their graduates for work in the community, and much of the learning experience takes place in the community through the practicum. An advisory committee made up of key stakeholders, including geriatric practitioners, field instructors, and older persons, can be of immeasurable help to the change effort, providing expertise in the development of the curriculum. For example, change agents may lead the advisory board in a series of structured group processes to develop and recommend knowledge and skill competencies for the curriculum. By building communication channels between the board and the faculty though

newsletters, a Web site, e-mail, and representative positions on important committees such as curriculum policy, the board may also exert a political influence on the transformation. Finally, advisory boards can help bring the change vision to the community, where the development of practice opportunities in working with older adults is critical. The GeroRich Web site highlights several strategies that build linkages with the community. Suggestions include a speaker's bureau of experts on aging available for guest lectures and role-plays, a Web site to feature alumni who are working with older adults, community focus groups for input into the curriculum, and mentor programs to link students with practitioners (*www.gerorich.org*).

The literature demonstrates the value of collaboration with other academic units. There is an association, for example, between aging content in the curriculum and multidisciplinary approaches to research and teaching. Also, the presence of a gerontological center at the university is associated with aging content (Damron-Rodriguez & Lubben, 1994; Damron-Rodriguez et al., 1997). Browne and colleagues (2002) at the University of Hawaii describe how a university-community collaboration formed and maintained two councils for guidance: an advisory council of community leaders and a consortium council of practicum instructors. With their guidance, the change project standardized competencies for the curriculum, initiated a "train the trainers" project to provide training in cultural competence and interdisciplinary practice for community practicum supervisors, developed a formative summative strategy to evaluate the curriculum, and implemented student recruitment strategies.

Change as a Multifaceted Campaign

Netting and colleagues (Netting, Hash, & Miller, 2002) describe the development of their Geriatric Rotational Education and Training Project as a collaboration *and* a campaign. Both characteristics speak to the multifaceted nature of change. Collaborative strategies involve working with stakeholders as allies in a change effort; campaign strategies are used to persuade. Both imply multiple processes at multiple levels to develop and implement a shared vision. Two important characteristics of this multifaceted approach are the importance of staging (Brager & Holloway, 1983) and the quality of leadership (Bland et al., 2000).

Although phases or stages of an organizational change effort run together, it is helpful for planning and organizing purposes to view the process in phases. Meredith and Watt (1994) describe their Gerontology Development Project in three phases: baseline curriculum needs assessment, resource development, and evaluation. The phases that are typically identified in the change literature are planning, initiation/implementation, and institutionalization (Glaser, Abelson, & Garrison, 1983). Planning involves an initial assessment of who the key stakeholders are and whether they will support or resist the change. Who are the allies on the faculty who will promote the infusion of aging into the curriculum? Change agents need to assess the change effort in terms of the school/department's values, the amount of resources required, and the complexity of the change. Also, what is the culture of the social work program? Constructive cultures are those that encourage achievement and self-actualization of faculty and students and that nurture teamwork; defensive cultures are associated with authoritarian administration (Nichols-Casebolt et al., 2000). A defensive culture, for example, will require a change effort that is closely tied to the dean's or director's support.

At the planning stage, change agents assess the feasibility of the vision, as discussed earlier. Will the vision engage the stakeholders? How can the change process spread that vision beyond a core group to all stakeholders? Faculty members with an interest in aging are a given, but what about those with other teaching and research interests? How can the project attract junior members who are pressured to prepare for promotion and tenure? What positive driving forces can be used to overcome resistance? In preparing to initiate or implement the change, it is also important to understand that lasting change comes from a process of building relationships (Simmons, 2003). Relationship building takes time: The literature suggests that a curricular change effort will take at least 2 years, preceded by several months planning. When should implementation begin? Projects that begin in the middle of the academic year risk losing momentum during the summer.

Because campaigns are about persuasion and persuasion requires several avenues to the heart and mind, the change initiative will need to implement several of the strategies discussed earlier. A major challenge throughout the campaign will be to link stakeholders together and to communicate the vision and the change process in a consistent, compelling manner. GeroRich Projects used multiple strategies to communicate their message, including Web sites, focus groups, newsletters, weekly dialogues, videos, and bimonthly curriculum development dinners. Leaders need to monitor and assess progress throughout the project and be willing to adopt new strategies when current ones are not working. The final phase, institutionalization, sometimes called refreezing, is the time when stakeholders no longer refer to curricular changes as *new ways of doing things* but as *the way we do things* (Bland et al., 2000. The change has been incorporated in the objectives of curriculum and syllabi and in the program's policies and evaluation standards. Most important, the teaching and values of faculty members reflect in their habits and actions the new but sustainable vision.

If there is to be sustainable change, particular attention must be given to the selection of the change leader, as his or her activities are vital to successful innovation (Fullan & Stiegelbauer, 1991). Although much of the change literature describes single leaders and change champions, leaders need not work alone; two of the models described in this chapter were based on a team or coleader approach (Meredith & Watt, 1994: O'Reilly & Kazanowski, 1993). Indeed, one of the first tasks for the leader of the change process is to build allies and form an innovation nucleus (Nichols-Casebolt et al., 2000). Many of the projects described in the GeroRich Program describe leaders who formed teams or boards or constituent bodies with which to work. Depending on the program's culture, administrative or senior status in a leader may be important (i.e., in a defensive culture); in other schools, the administration may welcome bottom-up initiatives. Several other characteristics are essential for the leader or champion. In their review of curricular change process, Bland and colleagues (2000) found that a key characteristic associated with success was the leader's ability to remain a leader throughout the project, communicating a consistent and engaging vision of change. Other characteristics include the leader's effectiveness in using organizational authority, building coalitions or empowering others to build coalitions, actively seeking input and participation from stakeholders, and articulating stories and symbols that represent the underlying mission of the organization. In keeping with earlier comments on engendering a sustainable vision, the most successful leaders use participative and value-influencing behaviors more than organizational power (Bland et al., 2000).

CONCLUSION

Sustainable gerontological curricular change requires far more than the notion of a faculty committee reviewing the curriculum and recommending additional content on aging. Sustainable change is transformative; it requires a comprehensive, multifaceted, and systems-based effort. In sum, it is a process—nurtured through leadership, campaign, and collaboration—whereby the stakeholders of a social work program become their vision.

REFERENCES

Bland, C. J., Starnaman, S., Wersal, L., Moorhead-Rosenberg, L., Zonia, S., & Henry, R. (2000). Curricular change in medical schools: How to succeed. *Academic Medicine, 75*(6), 575–594.

Brager, G., & Holloway, S. (1983). A process model for changing organizations from within. In R. M. Kramer & H. Specht (Eds.), *Readings in community organization practice* (3rd ed. pp. 198–208). Englewood Cliffs, NJ: Prentice-Hall.

Bridges, W. (1991). *Managing transitions: Making the most of change.* Reading, MA: Addison Wesley.

Brown, D. G., & Jackson, S. (2001). Creating a context for consensus. In C. Barone & P. Hagner (Eds.), *Technology-enhanced teaching and learning* (pp. 13–24). San Francisco: Jossey-Bass.

Browne, C. V., Braun, K. L., Mokuau, N., & McLaughlin, L. (2002). Developing and maintaining a multi-site project in geriatric and/or gerontological education with emphasis in interdisciplinary practice and cultural competence. *The Gerontologist 42*(5), 698–704.

Damron-Rodriguez, J., & Lubben, J. E. (1994). Multidisciplinary factors in gerontological curriculum adoption in schools of social work. *Gerontology and Geriatrics, 14*(4), 39–52.

Damron-Rodriguez, J., Villa, V., Tseng, T., & Lubben, J. E. (1997). Demographic and organizational influences on the development of gerontological social work curriculum. *Gerontology and Geriatrics, 17*(3), 3–18.

Fullan, M., & Stiegelbauer, S. (1991). *The new meaning of educational change.* New York: Teachers College Press.

Glaser, E. M., Abelson, H. H., & Garrison, K. N. (1983). *Putting knowledge to use: Facilitating the diffusion of knowledge and the implementation of planned change.* San Francisco: Jossey-Bass.

Graves, W. H. (2001). Transforming traditional faculty roles. In C. Barone & P. Hagner (Eds.), *Technology-enhanced teaching and learning* (pp. 325–44). San Francisco: Jossey-Bass.

Hagner, P. R., & Schneebeck, C. A. (2001). Engaging the faculty. In C. Barone & P. Hagner (Eds.), *Technology-enhanced teaching and learning* (pp. 1–12). San Francisco: Jossey-Bass.

Hanley, G. L. (2001). Designing and delivering instructional technology: A team approach. In C. Barone & P. Hagner (Eds.), *Technology-enhanced teaching and learning* (pp. 57–64). San Francisco: Jossey-Bass.

Hartford Geriatric Enrichment Social Work Education Program, (n.d.). Curricular change strategies. Retrieved June 30, 2004, from *http://depts.washington.edu/gerorich/change.shtml.*

Hooyman, N., & St. Peter, S. (in press). Creating aging-enriched social work education: A process of curricular and organizational change. *Journal of Gerontological Social Work Education.*

Knorr, R. O. (1993). A strategy for communicating change. *Journal of Business Strategy, 14*(4), 18–20.

Kosberg, J. I., & Kaufman, A. V. (2002). Gerontological social work: Issues and imperatives for education and practice. *Electronic Journal of Social Work, 1*(1), 1–15. Retrieved May 10, 2004, from *http://www.ejsw.net/Issue/Vol1/Num1/Artile9.pdf.*

Kropf, N. P. (2002). Strategies to increase student interest in aging. *Journal of Gerontological Social Work, 39*(1/2), 57–68.

Kropf, N. P., Schneider, R. L., & Stahllman, S. D. (1993). Status of gerontology in baccalaureate social work education. *Educational Gerontology, 19*(7), 623–634.

Lewin, K. (1957). *Field theory in social sciences.* New York: Harper & Row.

McNamara, C. (1999). Overview of organizational change. In *Free Management Library, n.p.* Minneapolis: Authenticity Consulting. Retrieved June 18, 2004, from *http://www.managementhelp.org/org_chng/org_chng.htm.*

Meredith, S. D., & Watt, S. (1994). The Gerontology Development Project: Infusing gerontology into social work curriculum. *Gerontology and Geriatrics Education, 15*(2), 91–100.

Mudrick, N. R., Steiner, J. R., & Pollard, W. L. (1992). Strategic planning for schools of social work. *Journal of Social Work Education, 28*(3), 278–290.

Netting, E. F., Hash, K., & Miller, J. (2002). Challenges in developing geriatric field education in social work. *Journal of Gerontological Social Work, 37*(1), 89–110.

Nichols-Casebolt, A., Figueria-McDonough, J., & Netting, F. E. (2000). Change strategies for integrating women's knowledge into social work curricula. *Journal of Social Work Education, 36*(1), 65–84.

O'Reilly, M. M., & Kazanowski, M. (1993). Using change theory as a model to integrate gerontology into the nursing curriculum. *Gerontology and Geriatrics, 13*(3), 55–66.

Rosen, A. L., Levy, J. L., & Singer, T. (2002). Basic gerontological competence for all social workers: The need to "gerontologize." *Journal of Gerontological Social Work, 39*(1/2), 25–36.

Scharlach, A., Damron-Rodriguez, J., Robinson, B., & Feldman, R. (2000). Educating social workers for an aging society: A vision for the 21st century. *Journal of Social Work Education, 36*(3), 521–538.

Simmons, J. (2003, February). *Sustainability: Making lasting change.* Paper presented at GeroRich Regional Directors Conference, San Diego.

Singer, T. L. (2000). *Structuring education to promote understanding of issues of aging.* SAGE-SW. Retrieved June 20, 2004, from *http://www.cswe.org/sage-sw/resrep/understandaging.htm.*

Wons, E. (2002). *Organizational change: An ethical, means-based approach.* Minnetonka, MN: JPC Training and Consulting. Retrieved June 18, 2004, from *http://www.jpc-training.com/change/.*

This chapter has three primary aims: (1) to review the need for a knowledgeable cadre of social workers prepared to fulfill many roles in a rapidly aging society, (2) to present alternative models and approaches to the education of "aging-savvy" social workers, and (3) to highlight best practices and resources to support educational innovation focused on improving the quality of life for aging individuals, families, and communities.

Academic leaders in gerontological social work have endorsed important principles in social work education to address the global challenges of population aging. The Task Force on Aging (Keigher et al., 2002) of the National Association of Deans and Directors authored a 2002 report: *Promoting Social Work for All Ages in Social Work Education: A Guide for Deans and Directors.* Recommending an approach to aging based on "human development across the lifespan," the report urges use of the "United Nations Principles for Older Persons" addressed in the United Nations (1991) statement *Toward a Society for All Ages: Independence, Participation, Care, Self-Fulfillment, and Dignity.* These principles, highlighted in Table 98.1, underscore "the importance, challenge, and vitality of the latter half of life, and the exciting intergenerational learning opportunities that lie ahead for the social work profession and academic community" (Keigher et al., 2002, p. 10). Given the broad, multidimensional mission of social work as a profession and the aging of the population, social workers in a wide range of settings are likely to have one or more practice roles that require education for effective practice across the life span.

NANCY L. WILSON

Educating Social Workers for an Aging Society: Needs and Approaches

ROLES FOR SOCIAL WORKERS IN AGING

There are consistent indications of a growing need for social workers capable of working with older adults and family members. An estimate by the National Institute on Aging in 1997 projected a need for 60,000 to 70,000 social workers by 2010 (Council on Social Work Education Strengthening Aging in Gerontology Education Program [CSWE/SAGE-SW], 2001, p. 1). Career forecasts published by *US News and World Report* as well as the Bureau of Labor Statistics (BLS) identify geriatric social work as a field of growing demand, with the BLS predicting particularly rapid job growth among gerontological social workers (21% to 35% between 2002 and 2012; Avery & Charski, 1998; U.S. Department of Labor, 2004). For decades, publications outlining the need for a gerontologically pre-

TABLE 98.1. Guiding Principles in the Design and Delivery of Social Work and Aging Education

---

Independence: People have a right to remain independent in later life. To be independent, people need access to the basic resources vital to living decently, including nutritional food, clean water, adequate housing, income, and health care. Older people need opportunities to earn money, to sustain a decent standard of living, to retire when they feel ready, to receive training, and to remain a vital part of the fabric of society. They need to live in safe environments that can adapt to their changing needs so that they may age without becoming unable to meet other needs.

Settings where social workers address independence: employee assistance, workplace, housing, community education, home modification programs.

Participation: Older people must be empowered to maintain vital social roles, to make contributions to society, and to have their contributions valued. This principle highlights the importance of social inclusion, seeing retirees as volunteers providing services and organizing social movements, but also their interpersonal strengths as familial agents whose connectedness with others promotes interdependence and social cohesion and builds social capital.

Settings where social workers support participation: family service agencies, neighborhood centers, community ministries, volunteer programs.

Care: Elders have a right to be cared for. Care includes health and social care, as well as elders' legal rights to receive and control how care is delivered. Social work involves advocating social justice and fairness in the allocation of services, providing competent, culturally appropriate social services, and facilitating the delivery of appropriately expert health or mental health care.

Settings where social workers ensure that care is provided: child welfare or aging service programs, home health agencies/clinics, hospitals, hospice programs, long-term care facilities.

Self-Fulfillment: Even with physical limitations, older people still need stimulation, challenges, and opportunities to enjoy the growth, caring, and sharing that enrich life. Social workers are concerned with the caring work done by many elders, and although it is unevenly distributed across demographic characteristics, it is full of meaning and power to those doing it. Additionally, learning from and teaching younger people is important.

Settings where social workers support self-fulfillment: case management, respite, support groups, counseling, and community support.

Dignity: People have a right to dignity in old age and in death. Older people should be able to live free from abuse, to be respected and treated fairly, and to be allowed control and dignity in dying. Regardless of impairments, people should have choices in where they live and how to structure their daily lives and should be helped to remain in familiar surroundings if they so choose. Elders are entitled to privacy and property, medical care, and medical decision making.

Settings where social workers enable dignity: health care, residential long-term care, protective services, and hospice.

Source: Abbreviated from Keigher et al. (2002).

---

pared workforce have identified several central roles for social workers: (1) serving as leaders in the creation of health, housing, human service, and economic policies responsive to population aging; (2) contributing to the health and well-being of older adults through leadership, scholarship, and advocacy; (3) providing high-quality direct services to older adults and families through outreach, preventive education, clinical practice, and case management; (4) developing and managing health and social service programs; and (5) serving as effective members and, as appropriate, leaders of interdisciplinary teams (Berkman, Damron-Rodriguez, Dobrof, & Harry, 1996; Berkman& Harootyan, 2003; Scharlach, Simon, & Dal Santo, 2000; Takamura, 2001).

Social work professionals and educators alike recognize that although specialists identified as geriatric or gerontological social workers will fulfill some of these roles, it is critical for all social workers to acquire

fundamental gerontological knowledge and skills (Berkman, et al., 1996; CSWE/SAGE-SW, 2001; Hooyman & St. Peter, in press; Rosen & Zlotnik, 2001; Scharlach, Damron-Rodriguez, Robinson, & Feldman, 2000). Proponents of quality care for older adults advocate that social workers prepared as geriatric or gerontological social workers work in the settings and systems identified in Table 98.2. This Older Adult Service Matrix is organized along two dimensions: service delivery systems and functional level of older adults.

There are other settings that are not identified in Table 98.2, however, where social workers with older clients could utilize the "United Nations Principles for Older Persons." A recent study of the public's understanding of the social work profession reported that 90% of the respondents envisioned a social worker's primary role as helping children and families (LeCroy & Stinson, 2004); accordingly, many so-

TABLE 98.2. Older Adult Service Matrix: Service Delivery Systems

	Wellness/ prevention	Social, Community, & Spiritual Engagement	Housing	Mental Health Care	Health Care	Legal System	Planning/Advocacy
Well Older Adults	-Exercise programs -Congregate meals • Nutritional services • Health clubs/ wellness programs • Health fairs & education programs • Abuse prevention services • Retirement planning services	• Recreation programs • Congregate meal programs • Information & referral services • Volunteer opportunities: RSVP, Senior Companions, foster grandparents, tutoring • Educational programs • Employment opportunities • Spiritual opportunities • Pastoral care services	• Home repair services • Independent senior housing • Retirement communities/ homes • Home sharing services • Transportation services	*See social and health* • Support groups • Psychoeducational groups • Retirement adjustment programs • Later-life transition programs	• Home emergency response programs • Primary medical care • Vision/hearing services • Emergency room services • Home health care • Acute in-hospital medical services	• Elder law services (estate planning, designation of POA, representative payee, health proxy, will, living will) • Crime prevention awareness programs	• Needs assessment • Public hearings • Lobbying • Program planning • Legislative advocacy -AARP

(continued)

TABLE 98.2. (*continued*)

	Wellness/ prevention	Social, Community, & Spiritual Engagement	Housing	Mental Health Care	Health Care	Legal System	Planning/Advocacy
Functionally Impaired Older Adults	*See above* • Caregiver support services	*See above* • Homemaker and chores services • Caregiver support groups • Case management, including money management • Adult Protective Services • Respite care • Adult day care • Nursing home • Ombudsman services	*See above* • In-home supportive services • Board and care homes • Shelters for abused, homeless • Assisted living • Continuous care communities	*See above* • Outpatient treatment services • Outpatient mental health rehabilitation • Support groups • Peer counseling • Psychiatric day hospital • Inpatient treatment • Residential dementia care • Substance abuse services	*See above* • In-home nutritional services • Acute hospitals • Outpatient rehabilitation services • Outpatient dialysis unit • Medical day care • Nursing homes	*See above* • Guardianship/ conservatorship	*See above*
End of Life	*See above*	*See above* • Caregiver support services, including hospice	*See health and mental health*	*See above* • Hospice: home • Bereavement services • Support groups	*See above* • Hospice: home • Palliative care • Hospice: inpatient or residential	*See above*	*See above*

Source: New Academy of Medicine (2004).

cial work students plan to work with children and families (CSWE/SAGE-SW, 2001). Both the popular media and many prospective social workers fail to recognize that practice with children and families often involves work with older individuals. For example, given the dramatic rise in the number of grandparents raising grandchildren, future social work graduates will more frequently encounter older adults in schools, pediatric clinics, substance abuse programs, public child welfare agencies, the juvenile justice system, and family service agencies (Kropf & Wilks, 2003). Likewise, younger family caregivers, often an employed daughter who is also a partner/wife and mother, provide the majority of care for older adults with disabilities. Caregiver stress may manifest in the workplace and produce health or mental health problems requiring social work services through an agency, clinic, or faith-based program. Furthermore, many of the problems being addressed in the systems noted in Table 98.2 are strongly linked to an older person's economic status and personal circumstances across the life course, which calls for social work intervention earlier in the life span of older individuals or within the systems structuring their lives.

Several independent surveys corroborate the importance of preparing all social workers to work effectively with older adults and their families. In a survey of the members of the National Association of Social Workers (NASW), over 60% of respondents, regardless of specialty, reported that they needed knowledge about aging (Peterson & Wendt, 1990). In a recent study of 138 MSW program graduates, a majority (77.2%) of those not employed in aging-related work noted that they had contact with older adults, and 63.4% reported a need for gerontological knowledge. A national survey conducted by the CSWE/SAGE-SW (2001) asked practitioners and academics (regardless of their interest in gerontology) to identify competencies needed in social work practice. Of the 65 age-related competencies included in the survey, respondents indicated that over half were needed by all social workers, not just those individuals specializing in aging.

However, most social work students are not prepared with such competencies, in part because of the lack of specialized aging content in their coursework at the BSW or MSW level (CSWE/SAGE-SW, 2001; Damron-Rodriguez & Lubben, 1997). In 1996, only 3% of all MSW graduates identified an aging or gerontology specialization, and only 2% of all MSW students not in an aging concentration had taken any graduate courses in aging (Scharlach et al., 2000).

Furthermore, a recent survey of accredited graduate programs in social work by Cummings and DeCoster (2003) reports that only 40 MSW programs (27%) currently offer specialized aging training (i.e., a gerontological concentration, specialization, or certificate program). Although growing numbers of social workers with aging training are needed, only a small number of current students complete specialized training in aging. As a result, many social workers enter work in aging after graduation (CSWE, 2003; Greene, 1988; Peterson & Wendt, 1990). The existing barriers to successful training of an adequate supply of social workers prepared to work across the spectrum of settings with aging issues are well documented. A summary of key barriers, along with some of the responses proposed to address these barriers, is included in Table 98.3 (CSWE/SAGE-SW, 2001; Damron-Rodriguez & Lubben, 1997; Kropf, 2002; Kropf, Schneider, & Stahlman, 1993; Rosen & Zlotnik, 2001; Scharlach et al., 2000).

LEADERSHIP, RESOURCES, AND MODELS FOR AGING IN SOCIAL WORK EDUCATION

Many of the barriers identified in Table 98.3, as well as some of the suggested solutions, are not new or unique to social work. The most important need in "gerontologizing" the field is to produce a cadre of faculty who have basic gerontological competencies. As described by Reinardy and Zoff (this volume), leaders and champions are needed to institute change within social work programs. To ensure the adequate gerontological preparation of social work students, two types of faculty expertise are needed: foundation gerontological knowledge and skills for effectively teaching life span content and skills across all areas of foundation curriculum and specialized gerontological knowledge and skills for teaching in the advanced curriculum, scholarship that informs practice and policy, and academic leadership to advance the field. Due to the investment of the John A. Hartford Foundation and the committed leadership of the Association for Gerontological Education for Social Work (AGE-SW; http://www.agesocialwork.org/), a number of faculty development models have been implemented to begin addressing this need.

In 1998, the John A. Hartford Foundation began funding a multifaceted Geriatric Social Work Initiative (GSWI), and as of September 2004, it has provided $35.52 million in support of five distinct programs headquartered at leadership organizations

TABLE 98.3. Barriers to Adequate Preparation and Programmatic Responses

Barriers to Training of Social Workers in Aging	Programmatic Responses
Lack of faculty with gerontological expertise to provide academic leadership and mentoring to prepare future leaders, scholars, and practitioners in gerontological social work.	• Faculty development • Academic mentoring • Financial support for development
Inadequate preparation and engagement of BSW and MSW faculty responsible for foundation courses, advanced courses in other fields of practice.	• Faculty development • Academic mentoring • Institutional leadership • Curriculum resources
Negative views and limited understanding of students, faculty, and broader society toward older adults.	• Increased exposure to diverse populations, range of positions, and settings available for work in aging • Financial aid, such as scholarships, stipends, or loan forgiveness
Lack of adequately compensated positions in aging services.	• Advocacy for legislation • Public education
Limited institutional resources and time for special curricula in aging	• Leverage resources of other disciplines • Partnerships across departments, agencies, and institutions

in aging and social work (consult the programwide Web site, *http://www.gswi.org/*, for further information and links to resources from each program). The GSWI has developed a clear framework for the professional education of BSW and MSW students of the future. Along with generating additional leaders and expanding faculty expertise, the framework involves the production of needed curricular resources, defined competencies in aging, models for field education, teaching resources, and evaluation tools. The mission of each major GSWI component is as follows:

1. Faculty Scholars Program: To support the career development and research of talented faculty.
2. Doctoral Fellows Program: To provide dissertation funding for promising doctoral students committed to gerontology.
3. Practicum Partnership Program: To develop and test innovative aging-rich field experiences for graduate students that connect communities and schools of social work.
4. Faculty Development Program: To strengthen social work faculty's ability to develop, integrate, and teach aging content in BSW and MSW foundation courses via training, resource exchange, and dissemination.
5. Geriatric Enrichment Program: To expand the number and quality of courses and learning experiences focused on aging at both the undergraduate and graduate levels.

As of July 1, 2004, the Faculty Development and Geriatric Enrichment Programs are no longer funded, but they provide the foundation for a new CSWE National Center for Gerontological Social Work Education.

ALTERNATIVE MODELS

Leaders and faculty in any social work program must choose a vision for incorporating gerontological content into the curriculum. They must also evaluate the institution's mission, resources, and educational culture to determine the optimum approach to curriculum change: integration, infusion, specialization, or transformation (Hooyman & St. Peter, in press; Reinardy & Zoff, this volume; Singer, 2000). Two decades ago, Lowy (1983), a pioneer in social work and aging, proposed five major organizational models for the inclusion of aging content in social work curriculum. These models addressed the ongoing debate of specialization versus foundation curriculum and the best strategies for specialization, either within social work or through a multidisciplinary gerontology certificate program/dual degree program with another discipline. To meet workforce needs and prepare for the future, increased understanding has been developed about the relationships between the foundation and advanced curriculum approaches. For example, a recent study of factors that predict MSW employment in aging produced findings supportive of what many gerontological educators have claimed for years: More contact with older adults and more rewarding interactions with older clients were the most significant predictors of aging-related work among program graduates (Cummings & Galambos, 2003). Furthermore, there is increased appreciation for the role of continuing education for social work graduates, which enables the large numbers of currently practicing BSW and MSW social workers without prior geriatric training to acquire skills and tools to meet the needs of older adults and their family members (*www.igsw.bu.edu*).

PROGRAM EXAMPLES: MODELS IN ACTION

The remainder of this chapter describes two programs of the GSWI that have generated significant resources and lessons for organizational approaches to social work education in aging: the Geriatric Enrichment in Social Work Education Program (GeroRich), which emphasizes foundation competencies, and the Practicum Partnership Program, which focuses on specialization. Examples from these two GSWI components illustrate all that is possible in the field.

GeroRich: Foundation Competencies

The GeroRich framework requires that social work programs and their community partners engage in a process of curricular and organizational change to incorporate gerontological learning experiences into the preparation of all BSW and MSW students (Hooyman & St. Peter, in press; Reinardy & Zoff, this volume). Some of the 67 social work programs (BSW, MSW, and joint BSW/MSW) involved in GeroRich have relied on close collaborations with other departments or disciplines within a broader university environment, such as gerontology centers or service learning programs (Dorfman, Murty, Ingram, & Evans, 2002). Other programs have formed strong partnerships with community agencies and created classroom assignments and field practicum experiences, which provide students the real-world contact with older adults that is often lacking in their personal lives or learning experiences. Each GeroRich program determined how to involve and support foundation faculty (most of whom are nonspecialists) in addressing aging competencies as learning outcomes in required courses in human behavior, policy, values, and ethics in practice. Extensive information from these programs—including materials to support aging-related instruction in classroom, practicum/field, and service learning—is available through the GeroRich Program Web site (*www.gerorich.org*) and also through CSWE-SAGE Social Work Toolkits (*http://www.cswe.org/sage-sw/index.htm*).

We turn now to a few examples of the infusion approach. As illustrated by Kropf and Wilks (2003), the issue of custodial parenting by grandparents is one example of the many intergenerational practice and policy issues that can be raised in different foundation classes. The infusion efforts of several GeroRich programs used an intergenerational framework and included one or more of the following themes within foundation courses: custodial grandparents as a social culture (culture diversity), kinship care and diversity of family forms (human behavior and social environment), and income maintenance for alternative families (social policy). Programs may begin with infusion of these issues into some courses and then expand to include others with further faculty development. For example, BSW students at George Mason University, who are required to complete an Intergenerational Advocacy Project, have addressed topics such as "Women and Social Security Across the Life Span" and "Grandparent Caregiving." The infusion approach at the Fordham University Graduate School of Social Work also illustrates a model for placing aging issues into the larger contexts of families and communities, which parallels the practice environment encountered by most social workers. Fordham GeroRich leaders worked with foundation faculty in each of the three first-year practice courses to produce a casebook of carefully crafted cases, avoiding negative stereotypes of older adults and incorporating "generalist competencies viewed from a gerontological lens" (Gutheil & Chernesky, 2003). For example, students learned care management, crisis intervention, and community assessment skills by working with the different cases, including an aging family and a community emergency care system.

In addition to preparing students to work effectively with older persons in all practice settings, the infusion approaches have other benefits reported by GeroRich programs. Having the opportunity for students to connect content on aging with their other interests in children, women, mental health, or substance abuse is an effective means of generating interest in gerontological social work as well (Hooyman & St. Peter, in press). In general, the emphasis in GeroRich has been not to

> view older adults as a 'specialized interest group' needing curriculum time because of their many problems, but rather to use a life course perspective throughout foundation courses and consider how race, class, gender, age and sexual orientation can be discussed in the broader contexts of person-environment, the strengths perspective and empowerment. (Hooyman & St. Peter, in press)

Models and Resources for Specialization

Another component of the Hartford GSWI, the Practicum Partnership Program (PPP), has been coordinated by the New York Academy of Medicine (*www.nyam.org*). It focused on field education and specialization at the graduate level. Developed and refined through six demonstration projects (comprising 11 MSW programs) over a 4-year period (1999–2003),

the model is composed of five essential elements, which are identified in Table 98.4. All six of the PPP projects focused on training social workers who would ultimately pursue careers in aging, either in practice or academia, to use leadership and practice skills in the settings identified in Table 98.2. By way of illustrating the model, Table 98.4 also provides further background about how one of the projects, the Geriatric Social Work Education Consortium (GSWEC), has individualized the PPP program to fit the learning environment, culture, and resources of the greater Los Angeles metropolitan area. Some of the PPP elements described in Table 98.4, in particular those addressing student recruitment and formalizing community partnerships, were also identified as important factors for success and sustainability in the GeroRich program.

The evaluated outcomes of this model have been highly favorable, and program support has come from other foundations to sustain the stipends provided to students as well as support for the expanded field instructor roles. Program graduates report a high degree of confidence in their skills as well as strong commitment to the field (see *http://www.gswi.org/programs_services/Ripples_2.htm*).

TABLE 98.4. Essential Elements of Geriatric Social Work Practicum Partnership Program, as Implemented by the Geriatric Social Work Education Consortium

---

University-Community Partnerships
Administered by the Partners in Care Foundation, four graduate social work programs worked with 21 agencies to develop, deliver, and evaluate training to 32 second-year students in geriatric social work with an emphasis on leadership for the students and the agencies and experiences across the continuum of care.

Competency-Driven Education for Geriatric Social Work
GSWEC used the Social Work in Aging Skill Competency Scale (Damron-Rodriguez, this volume) to organize student-directed classroom and field learning and to measure students' skills before and after completion of fieldwork experiences in two or more GSWEC agencies.

Integrated Field Education Across Multiple Programs, Populations, Interventions, and Disciplines Through Rotations
Four agencies have served as Centers of Excellence for training students using a *biopsychosocial model* and *adult learning theory* with a focus on *diversity* issues and *leadership* skills. In addition to their site rotations in these four multiservice centers, student interns participate in task rotations in other settings that take into account the broader roles social workers play in their agencies in team building and in interdisciplinary practice.

Expanded Field Instructor Role
In each Center of Excellence a GSWEC field instruction coordinator had expanded duties beyond the traditional roles of student orientation and supervision, mentoring, modeling, and evaluation. They coordinated additional instruction for students across settings or agencies, served as teachers in seminars or classrooms, and participated on GSWEC committees.

Focused Recruitment of Students to Geriatric Social Work
GSWEC academic and field agency partners were all engaged in increasing first-year student awareness of the range, diversity, and creativity of opportunities to work with older adults as well as the rewards of geriatric social work. Other recognition and support strategies used were stipends, employment listings, and preferential career support at Centers of Excellence.

Source: Abbreviated from New York Academy of Medicine and Partners in Care Foundation (2004). *www.geriatricsocialwork.org*.

CONCLUSION

Regardless of their field of practice or work setting, social workers have important roles to fulfill so that, as life expectancy is extended, life quality is not compromised. Social work educators and practitioners must collaborate in providing current and future social workers with the basic gerontological knowledge and skills needed in all sectors of an aging society, including government, industry, business, health care, education, housing, and human services. As the demand for social workers with specialized knowledge and expertise in aging will only grow, the need to educate all students in all fields is of paramount importance. Although many barriers to gerontologizing social work education remain, there are now a growing number of knowledgeable faculty leaders, curriculum models, and teaching resources. Through undergoing a curriculum transformation process, social work programs can hope to produce graduates who have had opportunities to learn about enabling independence, participation, care, self-fulfillment, and dignity throughout the life span of all individuals of our increasingly diverse society.

REFERENCES

Avery, D., & Charski, M. (1998, October 26). Twenty hot job tracks: Social work. *U.S. News and World Report*, p. 90.

Berkman, B., Damron-Rodriguez, J., Dobrof, R., & Harry, L. (1996). Social work. In S. Klein (Ed.), *A national agenda for geriatric education: White papers.* (pp. 220–246). Rockville, MD: Health Resources and Services Administration.

Berkman, B., & Harootyan, L. (Eds.). (2003). *Social work and health care in an aging society: Education, policy, practice, and research.* New York: Springer.

Council on Social Work Education Strengthening Aging in Gerontology Education Program. (2001). *Strengthening the impact of social work to improve the quality of life for older adults and their families: A blueprint for the new millennium.* Council on Social Work Education [online]. Available on August 23, 2004, at *http://www.cswe.org/sage-sw/resrep/blueprint.pdf.*

Cummings, S. M., & De Coster, V. A (2003). The status of specialized gerontological training in graduate social work education. *Journal of Educational Gerontology, 29,* 235–259.

Cummings, S. M., & Galambos, C. (2003). Predictors of graduate social work students' interest in aging-related work. *Journal of Gerontological Social Work, 39,* 77–94.

Damron-Rodriguez, J. A., Lawrence, F. P., Barnett, D., & Simmons, J. (in press). Developing geriatric social work competencies for field education. *Journal of Gerontological Social Work.*

Damron-Rodriguez, J., & Lubben, J. (1997). The 1995 WHCoA: An agenda for social work education and training. *Journal of Gerontological Social Work, 27*(3), 65–77.

Dorfman, L. T., Murty, S., Ingram, J. G., & Evans, R. J. (2002). Incorporating intergenerational service learning into an introductory gerontology course. *Journal of Gerontological Social Work, 39*(1/2), 219–240.

Greene, R. R. (1988). *Continuing education for gerontological careers.* Washington, DC: Council on Social Work Education.

Gutheil, I., & Chernesky, R. (2003, November). *Use of case studies to debunk MSW students' stereotypes about older adults.* Paper presented at the 56th annual scientific meeting of the Gerontological Society of America, San Diego.

Hooyman, N. R. (2004). *The value of funding programs to enhance older adults' independence and productivity.* Hartford Geriatric Enrichment in Social Work Education [online]. Available at *http://www.gerorich.org.*

Hooyman, N., & St. Peter, S. (in press). Creating aging-enriched social work education: A process of curricular and organizational change. *Journal of Gerontological Social Work.*

Keigher, S., Hook, M. V., Tebb, S., Langston, E., Briar-Lawson, K., Rosen, A., et al. (2002). *Promoting social work for all ages in social work education.* National Association of Deans and Directors, Council on Social Work Education [online]. Available on August 23, 2004, at *http://www.cswe.org/sage-sw/resrep/nadd reports_promoting.pdf.*

Kropf, N. P. (2002). Strategies to increase student interest in aging. *Journal of Gerontological Social Work, 39*(1/2), 57–67.

Kropf, N. P., Schneider, R. L., & Stahlman, S. D. (1993). Status of gerontology in baccalaureate social work education. *Educational Gerontology, 19*(7), 623–634.

Kropf, N. P., & Wilks, S. (2003). Grandparents raising grandchildren. In B. Berkman & L. Harootyan (Eds.), *Social work and health care in an aging society: Education, policy, practice, and research* (pp. 73–96). New York: Springer.

LeCroy, C. W., & Stinson, E. L. (2004). The public's perception of social work: Is it what we think it is? *Social Work, 49,* 164–174.

Lowy, L. (1983). Incorporation and specialization of content on aging in the social work curriculum. *Journal of Gerontological Social Work, 5*(4), 37–54.

New Academy of Medicine. (2004). *Educating for competent geriatric social work practice: A guide for implementing the Practicum Partnership Program* (draft). New York: John A. Hartford Foundation.

Partners in Care Foundation. (2004). *Geriatric Social Work Education Consortium.* Accessed on August 23, 2004, at *www.geriatricsocialwork.org.*

Peterson, D. A., & Wendt, P. F. (1990). Employment in the field of aging: A survey of professionals in four fields. *Gerontologist, 30,* 679–684.

Rosen, A. L., & Zlotnik, J. L. (2001). Demographics and reality: The "disconnect" in social work education. *Journal of Gerontological Social Work, 36,* 81–97.

Scharlach, A., Damron-Rodriguez, J., Robinson, B., & Feldman, R. (2000). Educating social workers for an aging society: A vision for the 21st century. *Journal of Social Work Education, 36,* 521–538.

Scharlach, A., Simon, J., & Dal Santo, T. (2002). Who is providing social services to today's older adults? Implications of a survey of aging services personnel. *Journal of Gerontological Social Work, 38,* 5–17.

Singer, T. (2000). *Structuring education to promote understanding of issues of aging.* Council on Social Work Education [online]. Retrieved June 4, 2004, from *http:// www.cswe.org/sage-sw/resrep/understandaging.*

Takamura, J. C. (2001). Towards a new era in aging and social work. *Journal of Gerontological Social Work, 36,* 1–11.

United Nations General Assembly. (1991). United Nations Principles for Older Persons Resolution 46/91 in Towards a society for all ages: Independence, participation, care, self-fulfillment and dignity. Accessed on September 23, 2005, at *http://www.un.org/esa/socder/ iycp/iycppcp.*

U.S. Department of Labor. (2004). Occupational outlook handbook, 2004–05 edition. Available on August 23, 2004, at *http://www.bls.gov/k12/html/edu_ sci.htm.*

BACKGROUND OF MOVEMENT TO GERIATRIC SOCIAL WORK

Recognizing the Need for Movement

By the mid-21st century, 1 in 5 persons will be over 65 years of age, creating a shift in demand for social work service to older persons and their families. Yet the need for gerontological social workers goes beyond meeting the demographic imperative. Although many professions are called to respond to the growing aging population (Hudson, 2003), the demand for gerontologically prepared social workers is grounded in the conviction that the profession's values, theoretical perspectives, and skills are essential to enhancing the well-being of older adults and their families (Berkman, Dobrof, Harry, & Damron-Rodriguez, 1997). The diversity of the older population in race/ethnicity, functional level, and cognitive capacity requires psychosocial assessment and intervention planning (Torres-Gil & Bikson-Moga, 2001). The profession is also garnering evidence of the value added by social work interventions to older adults' quality of life (Grimier & Gorey, 1998; Morrow-Howell & Burnette, 2001). Further, the development of gerontological social work acknowledges a burgeoning body of knowledge in the field of aging directly relevant to social work practice. The profession is moving toward the identification of social work competencies for effectively serving older persons (Damron-Rodriguez, Lawrence, Barnette, & Simmons, n.d.; Greene & Galambos, 2002).

Gerontological Social Work Movement Stage 1 (1965–1994)

Recognition of the need for specific gerontological or geriatric knowledge and skill was not present until the mid-20th century. Early leaders such as Louis Lowy (1979, p. 9) acknowledged, "Prior to 1945, not much had been happening in social work with the aging." In fact, older persons were not a targeted population in social work until the late 1960s and early 1970s, when many professions began to recognize that specialized knowledge and training were required to serve older persons.

From 1965 to 1980, federally funded educational programs in aging supported gerontological and geriatric education for a variety of professions, including social work (Berkman et al., 1997; Hudson, Gonyea, & Curley, 2003). These included the Administration on Aging (AoA) Title IV of the Older American's Act; Veterans Health Administration (VHA) Geriatric Research Education Clinical Centers (GRECC); and

JOANN DAMRON-RODRIGUEZ

Moving Forward: Developing Geriatric Social Work Competencies

Health Resources and Services Administration, Bureau of Health Professions Geriatric Education Centers (GEC). The GRECCs and GECs have grown in number and continue to support geriatric education, with the VHA providing the longest continuous stipend support for social work students. In contrast, AoA support for education has dwindled. The National Institute of Mental Health (NIMH) has not targeted older persons but has aimed to increase social work research through the establishment in 1991 of the NIMH Task Force on Social Work Research. The National Institute on Aging (NIA) support for aging research has not specifically targeted social work studies.

In the 1980s, the social work profession began to examine the relationship of its curricula to the longevity revolution. Early national surveys emphasized the need to increase aging content (Schneider, 1984). In 1988, the California GEC first surveyed all baccalaureate and graduate social work programs; they found practically no course work at the baccalaureate level and that only 3% of graduate students took an aging class (Damron-Rodriguez & Lubben, 1994; Lubben, Damron-Rodriguez, & Beck, 1992).

Gerontological Social Work Movement Stage 2 (1995–2005)

From 1995 to 2005, the profession moved forward with an agenda for social work in the field of aging. The Bureau of Health Professions (BHPr) in 1995 held a National Forum for Geriatric Education, which developed 12 recommendations for the social work profession and identified actions and responsible stakeholders, public and private, to accomplish the goals (Table 99.1). The BHPr is measuring accomplishment of these goals over the past decade. Several of these goals relate to the need to specify and develop geriatric social work skills or competencies.

In the late 1990s, the John A. Hartford Foundation, whose goal is to improve the care of older persons by strengthening geriatrics in the health professions, focused attention on social work. Through forums with social work leaders and a series of White Papers (Berkman, Dobrof, Harry, & Damron-Rodriguez, 1997; Scharlach, Damron-Rodriguez, Robinson, & Feldman, 2000), the Geriatric Social Work Initiative (*www.jhartfound.org*) was crafted. The long-range and multifaceted Hartford Initiative has had a major impact on the field, as described in other chapters of this volume (see also Robbins & Rieder, 2002).

Other private foundations have joined this effort, including Atlantic Philanthropies for the Institute for

TABLE 99.1. A Decade for Change: Social Work Recommendations from the National Agenda of Geriatric Education, 1995

1. Comprehensive integration of aging into social work curricula
2. Recruitment of minority faculty
3. Adoption of a life span matrix for social work education
4. Creation of Centers of Excellence in geriatric social work education
5. Preparation of social workers for interdisciplinary team practice
6. Aging education for individual/family, organizational and policy practice
7. Geriatric social work stipends and fellowships
8. Opportunities for postgraduate social work education in aging
9. Continuous quality improvement in practice and education
10. Establishment of standards for education for geriatric social work positions
11. Inclusion of aging content in social work licensure board examinations
12. Emphasis of social work commitment to public agencies and meeting needs of underserved

Source: Berkman et al. (1997).

Gerontological Social Work at Boston University. State and regional foundations, such as the Archstone Foundation in California, have also provided support. Thus, in the second stage of the social work movement, the major shift toward a geriatric-prepared workforce resulted from private foundations targeting social work, joining existing federal support that was not specifically social work–focused.

Stage 3: Working From a Multidimensional Definition of Social Work in Aging

Central to this next stage of geriatric workforce preparation is the delineation of competencies, beginning with a definition of the field of social work and aging. The BHPr White Paper definition of geriatric social work is based on the generic description of the field in the NASW (1981) *Standards for the Classification of Social Work Practice*. Terms for professional practice with older adults are "gerontological" (knowledge of the aging process) and "geriatric" (interventions with older persons with health-related issues), sometimes used interchangeably. Although the following definition was originally developed for geriatric social work, it is related here to social work practice broadly in the field of aging. Social work in the field of aging is professionally responsible intervention to:

1. Enhance the developmental, problem solving, and coping capacities of older people and their families.
2. Promote the effective and humane operating of systems that provide resources and services to older people and their families.
3. Link older people with systems that provide them with resources, services, and opportunities.
4. Contribute to the development and improvement of social policies that support persons throughout the life span. (Berkman et al., 1997)

This definition encompasses both direct or micro practice with older adults and their families and macro interventions involving programs and policies. It also acknowledges that social work is a strengths-based approach, identifying personal resources as well as problems (Chapin & Cox, 2001). The social work perspective is oriented toward family, social and community-based models of care, and public policy (Chapin & Cox, 2001). The major theoretical perspectives for gerontological social work bring a distinctive contribution to interdisciplinary geriatrics (Damron-Rodriguez & Corley, 2002; see Table 99.2).

DELINEATING COMPETENCIES

Competency-Based (Education) Evaluation

Competency-based education and evaluation (CBE) is an approach to producing a skilled workforce and ensuring that graduates can perform expected behaviors at a professionally acceptable level (Hackett, 2001). The evaluation of education inherent in CBE consists of two components (Bogo, Regehr, Hughes, Power, & Globerman, 2002): identification and development of educational goals in clear, measurable terms with indicators to judge varying levels of performance, and assessment of student skill acquisition measured through evidence-based criteria.

Graduates and employers recognize the field practicum as the primary locus for skill acquisition in social work (Fortune, 1994). Accordingly, Bogo, Regehr, and colleagues (2002) urge field educators to

TABLE 99.2. Theoretical Perspectives for Gerontological Social Work

1) *Life cycle developmental approach* with a focus on normal or healthy growth, development, and adaptation in late life
2) *Biopsychosocial framework* with an emphasis on persons-in-sociocultural-context as they relate to transitions in the life course, physical functioning, and illness
3) *Family systems approach* for intervention, recognizing the interdependence of family members
4) *Life course perspective*, which recognizes the impact of sociohistorical context on cohorts and individuals based on class, race/ethnicity, and gender

Source: CSWE/SAGE-SW (1999).

move toward direct measures of competence from direct practice observation.

Social work entered the dialogue around issues related to CBE in the 1970s (Arkava & Brennan, 1976). Proponents argued that CBE offered an objective, comprehensive approach to hold universities accountable for producing social workers that were adequately skilled. Other educators cautioned that reductionism is inherent in this model (Field, 2000) and that some important professional competencies are more difficult to measure, such as critical thinking and interpersonal skills for patient interactions (Carraccio, Wolfsthal, Englander, Ferentz, & Martin, 2002). Two decades of social work literature reflect the need for clear descriptions of required competencies and standardized measures for skill outcomes in social work (Bogo, Raskin, & Wayne, 2002).

The measurement of competence is to demonstrate the effectiveness not only of education but, more importantly, of interventions in improving the lives of older people. As examples, geriatric social work practice has been found to be effective in reducing the risk of institutionalization and caregiver burden (Mittelman et al., 1993), minimizing risk factors through multidisciplinary home evaluations (Stuck et al., 2002), and improving care through geriatric clinical care management (Rizzo & Rowe, 2005).

Competencies in Aging for Other Professionals

Competencies for work with older adults have been identified generally (Bennet[[AU: Bennett in refs; pls correct throughout]] & Sneed, 1999) and for specific professions: medicine (American Geriatrics Society, 2000); nursing (American Association of Colleges of Nursing and the John A. Hartford Foundation Institute for Geriatric Nursing, 2000); and mental health professionals (Molinari, Kier, & Kunik, 2002). Medical and other health professional education uses standardized patients and objective structured clinical evaluations. Age-specific assessment and intervention is an element in evaluation of health care systems by the Joint Commission on Accreditation in Healthcare Organizations (JCAHO, 2001).

Social Work Competencies

The identification of both micro and macro social work skills is ongoing (Dore, Epstein, & Herrerias, 1992; O'Hare & Collins, 1997; Vass, 1996). The Council on Social Work Education (CSWE) developed a competency-based generalist curriculum for baccalaureate social work (Gardella, 1997), and Dalton and Wright (1999) identified knowledge, skills, and attitudes most desired in social work graduates.

The Hartford-funded CSWE Strengthening Aging and Gerontological Education in Social Work (CSWE/SAGE-SW, 2000) initiated identification of aging-specific social work competencies. Phase I of this project included identifying competencies through the gerontological social work literature and consultation with national experts. This generated 65 competencies, which were organized into three major competency domains: knowledge about older people and their families, professional skills, and professional practice (Rosen, Zlotnik, Curl, & Green, 2000). In Phase II, a survey of the identified skills was mailed to 945 practitioners and faculty, asking them to rate 10 competencies related to generalist practice or 10 skills related to aging needed for all social workers and specialist practice in aging (Rosen, Zlotnik, & Singer, 2002).

The Geriatric Social Work Education Consortium (GSWEC), one of the Hartford Practicum Partnership Programs (PPP), conducted focus groups of employers and recent social work graduates in the field of aging and older persons and their caregivers (Partners in Care Foundation, 2000). Both employers and graduates identified the most important geriatric social work competencies to be conducting geriatric assessments, demonstrating self-awareness, practicing cultural competence, and recognizing the special needs of older adults and their families. Both groups also mentioned, albeit less frequently, skills in communication, networking, and providing emotional support and

competencies involving knowledge about the impact of ageism (Naito-Chan, Damron-Rodriguez, & Simmons, 2004).

GSWEC utilized the Geriatric Social Work White Papers, focus groups, and the pioneering work of the SAGE-SW Comprehensive Competency Survey (Rosen et al., 2000, 2002). In developing competencies to be used nationally for the field education project, a systematic effort was made to cross-reference all competencies identified separately and collaboratively with the SAGE-SW competencies. PPP focuses on specialty practice in aging; thus, the advanced practice competencies identified by SAGE-SW were included in the PPP skill scale.

Evaluation and Measurement of Competencies

Evaluation and measurement is another dimension of competency development. Studies have investigated the valid assessment of research competencies utilizing self-efficacy theory (Holden, Meenaghan, Anastas, & Metry, 2002) and of student field performance has been examined (Bogo, Regehr, Hughes, Power, & Globerman, 2002). Specialty-specific competency tools have also been developed to assess, for example, social work students' interviewing skills (Koroloff & Rhyne, 1989). Further, the reliability and validity of a measure to evaluate social work student performance has been examined (Bogo, Regehr, Hughes, Power, & Globerman, 2002). Competency standard development has been conducted in other professions to evaluate practitioners in nursing and medicine (Gordon, 1991; McKinley, Fraser, & Baker, 2000). In the health field, however, the focus on measuring student competencies tends to be on professional competencies, a focus primarily motivated by professional associations and licensure requirements and standards (JCAHO, 2001).

Self-Efficacy in Measuring Competence

Self-efficacy is defined by Bandura (1997) as the "belief in one's capabilities to perform actions required to produce given attainments." Self-efficacy has been established as a reliable and valid construct for predicting behavior and performance variation in a variety of health disciplines. Self-efficacy is thought to be task- or domain-specific and is concerned not with the number of skills acquired, but with the level of confidence felt necessary to meet specific goals. It entails having the confidence to organize many subskills including ones that are cognitive, social, emotional, and behavioral to meet specific goal-directed outcomes (Bandura, 1997). A positive and significant relationship was found among self-efficacy beliefs, academic performance, and persistence outcomes across subjects and designs in Multon, Brown, and Lent's (1991) meta-analysis.

However, few studies utilize the construct to evaluate the efficacy of an intervention to increase social work competency (Cuzzi, Holden, Chernack, Rutter, & Rossenberg, 1997; Holden, Meenaghan, Anastas, & Metrey, 2002), and none addresses geriatric social work student competency based on self-efficacy theory.

MEASURING GERIATRIC SOCIAL WORK COMPETENCIES

Practicum Partnership Program Description

The Hartford PPP's primary goal was to increase the number of master's-level social workers well qualified to work with older adults and their families by developing aging-rich field practicum sites. In 2000, 3-year implementation grants were awarded through a competitive grant process to six demonstration sites (11 graduate social work education programs/academic institutions). Four sites developed programs for their second-year MSW students, and two sites developed 2-year programs. Each PPP encompassed the following elements: a university-community partnership or consortium; competency-driven field education; rotations for experience across multiple programs, populations, interventions, and disciplines; an expanded role for field instructors; and focused recruitment to geriatric social work. The use of a competency-driven educational process was central to the PPP, as field education by its very nature is skill-based (Fortune, 1994). Demonstration sites based their programs on skill competencies for working with older adults and their families at multiple intervention levels (Hadden, Damron-Rodriguez, Lawrence, Dankkle, & Barnett, n.d.; Fortune, 2002).

Evaluation Design: A Focus on Competency

The New York Academy of Medicine Coordinating Center for the PPP provided leadership in collabora-

tively evaluating outcomes across the six demonstration sites. The items are based largely on sets of professional competencies for social work practice in aging developed simultaneously by GSWEC and the CSWE through different consensus-building processes. These sets were reviewed and synthesized for content relevant to the PPP's educational design. They were then matched against sets of competencies developed by the five other PPP sites, and additional competencies were identified; all were converted into statements of skills. These skill statements and new items with macro-, interdisciplinary, and research and evaluation content were then grouped into domains. Members of the PPP Evaluation Committee, who are experts in social work and aging, then reviewed items for clarity and validity. As a result of these reviews and pilot testing, some items were modified, others deleted, and new items developed to form the Social Work with Aging Skill Competency Scale.

The scale measures respondents' perceptions of their perceived level of self-assessed skill in aging practice as compared to a competent MSW geriatric social worker. Respondents rate each item on a 0 to 10 scale (0 = not skilled at all; 10 = very skilled). Students were asked to compare their skill with that of an effective geriatric social worker in practice. Each domain may be subscored by adding responses of individual items. A section for respondents to comment on their skill in each domain provides the opportunity to clarify their ratings, as some items are complex.

The remainder of this chapter describes one component of the collaborative PPP evaluation research that focused on competency self-assessment before and after the PPP field experience. Other aspects of the evaluation concentrated on measuring outcomes in student's knowledge, career paths, and institutional-level changes in aging programs at each site. Students completed a pre- and postsurvey of knowledge, career interest, and assessment of competency using the instrument described earlier.

Practicum Partnership Program Student Sample

As presented in Table 99.3, no significant differences were found on the demographic and academic characteristics of PPP students in different years of the program, except in age; the YR3 cohort represented a broader age range with more younger and older students. The average or mean age over the three years was 32.9. Approximately half of the PPP participants were students of color.

Most PPP programs target second-year students; the majority of these students had been social work majors and were in the enhanced field education for 1 year even though 80% of the programs offered a 2-year experience (see Table 99.4).

Table 99.5 presents the significant difference between pre- and posttests of student competencies, with the improvement highly significant in each domain ($p = <.000$). Each domain and each item received a wide range of responses, with significantly higher responses postintervention (PPP), and Values and Ethics having the highest scores (7.1 and 8.6, respectively) and Evaluation and Research the lowest (4.3 and 7, respectively). The combined means for all domains pretest (5.4) and posttest (7.9) are displayed in Figure 99.1.

The Competency Scale has a different number of items in each domain; the possible score (10 on each item within a domain) is converted to a percentage of the maximum. Table 99.6 provides another view of the high and low competency areas as well as the improvement before and after training.

Age, gender, enrollment status, current concentration, and prior employment with older adults were not significantly related to skill competency at pre- or posttest. However, educational level at pretest was significantly related to skill competency ($p = .002$) at pretest, with second-year MSW students scoring

TABLE 99.3. Demographic Descriptors of PPP Students (N = 323)

	Number of Students	Percentage of Total
Age		
21–29	165	51.4
30–39	86	26.6
40 and over	72	22.3
Range	21–69	
Mean	32.9	
SD	9.8	
Gender		
Male	53	16.5
Female	270	83.5
Ethnicity		
African American	59	18.4
Caucasian	162	50
Asian American	38	11.9
Hispanic/Latino	48	14.8
Other	16	5

TABLE 99.4. Academic Descriptors of PPP Students (N = 323)

	Number of Students	Percentage of Total
Educational Level		
BSW	19	5.8
MSW first year	93	28.7
MSW second year	207	64
Advanced standing	5	1.6
Enrollment Status		
Full time	287	89.0
Part time	36	11.0
Took Previous Courses on Aging		
Yes	168	52.1
No	155	47.9
If Yes, Number of Courses		
1 Course	98	30.2
2 Courses	75	23.3
3 Courses	45	13.8
4 Courses	106	32.8
If Yes, Level of Aging Course Taken		
Undergraduate	154	47.7
Graduate	83	25.7
Both	86	26.6
Age		
30–39	6	14.6
40–49	17	41.5
50–59	12	29.3
60 and over		
Gender		
Male	5	12.2
Female	36	87.8
Ethnicity		
African American	2	5.4
Caucasian	29	78.4
Asian American	3	7.3
Hispanic/Latino	2	4.9
Other	1	2.4

higher on skill competencies than students at earlier points in their educational program. Students who took classes in aging had higher skill competencies.

The first version of the competency instrument proved useful in student's self-assessment of their geriatric skills. It provided a eudiometric tool for learning

TABLE 99.5. Competency of PPP Students (N = 226)

Domains	Pretest	Posttest	Significant Difference
I. Values and Ethics			
Range	1.6–10.0	5–10	
Mean	7.1	8.6	0.000***
Standard Deviation	1.6	0.9	
II. Assessment			
A. Individual and Family			
Range	0.3–9.8	4.1–10.0	
Mean	5.5	8.0	0.000***
Standard Deviation	2.0	1.2	
B. Aging Services, Programs, and Policies			
Range	0–10	3.5–10.0	
Mean	5.1	7.9	0.000***
Standard Deviation	2.3	1.2	
III. Practice Intervention			
A. Theory and Knowledge			
Range	0–10	4.2–10.0	
Mean	5.1	7.9	0.000***
Standard Deviation	2.1	1.1	
B. Individual and Family			
Range	0–10	4.1–10.0	
Mean	5.6	8.2	0.000***
Standard Deviation	2.0	1.0	
C. Aging Services, Programs, and Policies			
Range	0–0	3.3–10.0	
Mean	4.5	7.4	0.000***
Standard Deviation	2.3	1.4	
IV. Interdisciplinary Collaboration			
Range	0–10	1.3–10.0	
Mean	5.4	8.2	0.000***
Standard Deviation	2.4	1.3	
V. Evaluation and Research			
Range	0–10	0–10	
Mean	4.3	7.0	0.000***
Standard Deviation	2.5	2.0	
Total Competency			
Range	0.3–9.9	4.5–10.0	
Mean	5.4	7.9	0.000***
Standard Deviation	1.9	1.0	

***$p \leq .001$

contracts with students and for assessing changes based on self-efficacy evaluations. The first version was revised because of length and problems in item construction (i.e., double-barreled and/or ambiguous questions).

GERIATRIC SOCIAL WORK COMPETENCY SCALE, VERSION II

The revision process consisted of several steps. First, the descriptive statistics of each of the original 58 item were examined. Those items with very small range and very high mode and mean ratings at pretest were examined for similar items that displayed a greater dispersion of ratings. Similarly, items that evoked little differences in skill were examined. The Cronbach alpha, a measure of internal consistency, was used to assess the degree to which the item related to the do-

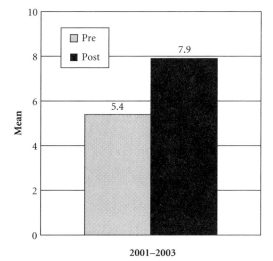

FIGURE 99.1 Mean Competencies

TABLE 99.6. Percentage of Possible Points on Competency Scores Translated to Percentage

Domains	Pretest	Posttest
I. VALUES AND ETHICS	71%	86%
II. ASSESSMENT		
A. Individual and Family	55%	79%
B. Aging Services, Programs, and Policies	51%	78%
III. PRACTICE INTERVENTION		
A. Theory and Knowledge	51%	79%
B. Individual and Family	56%	82%
C. Aging Services, Programs, and Policies	45%	74%
IV. INTERDISCIPLINARY COLLABORATION	54%	82%
V. EVALUATION AND RESEARCH	43%	70%
TOTAL COMPETENCY	53%	78%

main and the overall measurement of geriatric social work competency as defined by the scale as a whole. Items with low Cronbach alpha (under .70) were identified and scrutinized for more consistent measures.

The original instrument was then given to a small, nonrandom group of expert clinicians in the field of aging, the GSWEC field instruction coordinators, who rated themselves and provided feedback on each item's clarity. The tracking of their suggestions plus revision based on the statistical analysis was sent to the Principal Investigators of the Hartford PPPs for consensus. A statistician specializing in instrument design for geriatric competency development provided further technical assistance.

The resulting revised version of the instrument, PPP Geriatric Social Work (GSW) Competency Scale, has 38 items versus 58 items. Four domains have approximately equal numbers of items, in contrast to Version I, which had five domains with vastly different numbers of items in each (range from 33 to 4 items). The request to evaluate oneself against the standard of a "competent geriatric social worker" is replaced with a more detailed description of the skill level rating. The time in completing the self-assessment was reduced by half.

The new instrument was piloted with a convenience sample from social workers taking continuing education unit seminars with the Boston University Institute for Geriatric Social Work. See Tables 99.7

and 99.8 for the demographic and academic descriptors of the pilot sample.

As shown in Table 99.9, the mean overall competency score is high (3.2 on a scale from 1 to 5): "This skill is done with confidence and is an integral part of my practice." There was not a ceiling effect; few items were rated with a 4 or expert skill even for practitioners with aging experience. The high (Values, Ethics, and Theoretical Perspectives) and the low (Aging Services, Programs, and Policies) domains of skills for the practicing social workers were the same as for the students. Table 99.10 converts the ratings into percentages and by doing this conveys the low overall skill assessment of practitioners participating in the training.

When the scores were converted to possible points in each domain, there was no ceiling effect and the relative highs and lows were the same as for the previous scale. The research and evaluation questions were incorporated into domain IV. The instrument is provided as Appendix 99.1; this second version of the PPP Geriatric Social Work Competency Scale is identical to the version piloted except for two changes: (1) The scale was reduced to a 0 to 4 instead of a 1 to 5 measurement, with 0 (previously 1) described as "Not skilled at all"; (2) the second change came from a review of the PPP Geriatric Social Work Competency Scale in relationship to the CSWE SAGE-SW competencies by the National Center for Gerontological Social Work Education, resulting in the addition of two competencies and a 40-item instrument.

TABLE 99.7. Demographic Descriptors of Pilot Sample (N = 41)

	Number of Students	Percentage
Age		
30–39	6	14.6
40–49	17	41.5
50–59	12	29.3
60 and over		
Gender		
Male	5	12.2
Female	36	87.8
Ethnicity		
African American	2	5.4
Caucasian	29	78.4
Asian American	3	7.3
Hispanic/Latino	2	4.9
Other	1	2.4

TABLE 99.8. Academic Descriptors of Pilot Sample (N = 41)

	Number of Students	Percentage
Social Worker		
Yes	30	73.2
No	11	26.8
Field of Practice Gerontology		
Yes	26	63.4
No	15	36.6
Years of Professional Practice		
Less than 1 year	3	7.3
1–3 years	3	7.3
4–9 years	8	19.5
10 or more years	27	65.9
Took Aging Classes		
Yes	23	56.1
No	16	39.0
Have Training in Aging		
Yes	24	58.5
No	16	39.0

TABLE 99.9 Pilot GSW Competency Scale (N = 41)

I. *Values and Theoretical Perspectives*
Range	1.8–5.0
Mean	3.5
Standard Deviation	0.8

II. *Assessment: Individual and Family*
Range	1.0–5.0
Mean	3.2
Standard Deviation	1.0

III. *Intervention: Individual and Family*
Range	1.0–5.0
Mean	3.4
Standard Deviation	1.0

IV. *Aging Services, Programs, and Policies*
Range	1.0–5.0
Mean	2.6
Standard Deviation	1.1

Total Competency
Range	1.2–5.0
Mean	3.2
Standard Deviation	0.8

DISCUSSION AND IMPLICATIONS

Competency-based evaluation of educational outcomes is one aspect of the movement toward best practices in geriatrics. CSWE/SAGE-SW identified competencies that have been related to social work curricula (Greene & Galambos, 2002; Rosen, Zlotnik, & Singer, 2002). PPP has measured self-efficacy with regard to specific geriatric social work skills relevant to the field (Damron-Rodriguez et al., n.d.). The PPP Geriatric Social Work Competency Scale was designed as a pre-posttest to measure the effect of the PPP's innovative field education on the skills of graduate students who specialize in aging. It can also be used for educational planning after pretest administration for setting educational goals and has been adopted by the National Center for Gerontological Social Work Education for this purpose. Both scales are able to reflect variation in skill level.

A limitation of this CBE research is the small sample size, even for a pooled national evaluation. In addition, the evaluation was of graduate students with a stated interest in aging and in an enriched field placement. Use of the instrument with a group of students at different educational levels or generalist versus specialist in orientation has not been systematically studied. However, some sites in the CSWE Geriatric Enrichment in Social Work Education project have used the instrument for measuring outcomes from aging infusion projects (Browne, Braun, Mokuau, & McLaughlin, 2002). They found a significantly positive relationship between taking courses in aging and skill level.

In terms of next steps, collaboration with and learning from other professions as they move toward geriatric competency measurement will be beneficial (American Geriatrics Society, 2000). In addition to developing more behaviorally oriented competence measurement methods (Bogo, 2002), future work

TABLE 99.10. Pilot GSW Competency Scale Converted to Percentages (N = 41)

	Percentage
I. VALUES AND THEORETICAL PERSPECTIVES	71
II. ASSESSMENT: Individual and Family	64
III. INTERVENTION: Individual and Family	68
IV. AGING SERVICES, PROGRAMS, AND POLICIES	52
Total Competency	64

will involve linking knowledge, conceptual thinking, and theory from the classroom with skill development in the field and in practice (Reishch & Jarman-Rhode, 2000).

APPENDIX

HARTFORD PRACTICUM PARTNERSHIP PROGRAM GERIATRIC SOCIAL WORK COMPETENCY SCALE

The following is a listing of *skills* recognized by gerontological social workers as important to MSW graduates effectively working with and on behalf of older adults and their families. Please use the scale below to thoughtfully rate your current skill:

0 = Not skilled at all (I have no experience with this skill)

1 = Beginning skill (I have to consciously work at this skill)

2 = Moderate skill (This skill is becoming more integrated in my practice)

3 = Advanced skill (This skill is done with confidence and is an integral part of my practice)

4 = Expert skill (I complete this skill with sufficient mastery to teach others)

0	1	2	3	4
Not skilled at all	Beginning skill	Moderate skill	Advanced skill	Expert skill

Please add any comments and/or suggestions regarding the skills in each section.

NOTE

Research and program models described in this chapter were funded by a grant from The John A. Hartford Foundation of New York City. The author wishes to acknowl-

I. Values, Ethics, and Theoretical Perspectives (Knowledge and value base, which is applied through skills/competencies)	*Skill Level (0–4)*
1. Assess and address values and biases regarding aging.	_____
2. Respect and promote older adult clients' right to dignity and self-determination.	_____
3. Apply ethical principles to *decisions* on behalf of all older clients with special attention to those who have limited decisional capacity.	_____
4. Respect diversity among older adult clients, families, and professionals (e.g., class, race, ethnicity, gender, and sexual orientation).	_____
5. Address the cultural, spiritual, and ethnic values and beliefs of older adults and families.	_____
6. Relate concepts and theories of aging to social work practice (e.g., cohorts, normal aging, life course perspective).	_____
7. Relate social work perspectives and related theories to practice with older adults (e.g., person-in-environment, social justice).	_____
8. Identify issues related to losses, changes, and transitions over their life cycle in designing interventions.	_____
9. Support persons and families dealing with end-of-life issues related to dying, death, and bereavement.	_____
10. Understand the perspective and values of social work in relation to working effectively with other disciplines in geriatric interdisciplinary practice.	_____

Comments_____

_____

_____

(continued)

II. Assessment   *Skill Level (0–4)*

1. Use empathy and sensitive interviewing skills to engage older clients in identifying their
   strengths and problems.   _____

2. Adapt interviewing methods to potential sensory, language, and cognitive limitations of the
   older adult.   _____

3. Conduct a comprehensive geriatric assessment (biopsychosocial evaluation).   _____

4. Ascertain health status and assess physical functioning (e.g., ADLs and IADLs) of older clients.   _____

5. Assess cognitive functioning and mental health status of older clients (e.g., depression, dementia).   _____

6. Assess social functioning (e.g., social skills, social activity level) and social support of older clients.   _____

7. Assess caregivers' needs and level of stress.   _____

8. Administer and interpret standardized assessment and diagnostic tools that are appropriate for
   use with older adults (e.g., depression scale, Mini-Mental Status Exam).   _____

9. Develop clear, timely, and appropriate service plans with measurable objectives for older adults.   _____

10. Reevaluate and adjust service plans for older adults on a continuing basis.   _____

Comments_____
_____
_____

III. Intervention   *Skill Level (0–4)*

1. Establish rapport and maintain an effective working relationship with older adults and
   family members.   _____

2. Enhance the coping capacities and mental health of older persons through a variety of
   therapy modalities (e.g., supportive, psychodynamic).   _____

3. Utilize group interventions with older adults and their families (e.g., bereavement groups,
   reminiscence groups).   _____

4. Mediate situations with angry or hostile older adults and/or family members.   _____

5. Assist caregivers to reduce their stress levels and maintain their own mental and physical health.   _____

6. Provide social work case management to link elders and their families to resources and services.   _____

7. Use educational strategies to provide older persons and their families with information related
   to wellness and disease management (e.g., Alzheimer's disease, end-of-life care).   _____

8. Apply skills in termination in work with older adults and their families.   _____

9. Advocate on behalf of clients with agencies and other professionals to help elders obtain
   quality services.   _____

10. Adhere to laws and public policies related to older adults (e.g., elder abuse reporting, legal
    guardianship, advance directives).   _____

Comments_____
_____
_____

IV. Aging Services, Programs, and Policies   *Skill Level (0–4)*

1. Provide outreach to older adults and their families to ensure appropriate use of the
   service continuum.   _____

2. Adapt organizational policy, procedures, and resources to facilitate the provision of services to
   diverse older adults and their family caregivers.   _____

3. Identify and develop strategies to address service gaps, fragmentation, discrimination, and
   barriers that impact older persons.   _____

(continued)

IV. Aging Services, Programs, and Policies (continued)   *Skill Level (0–4)*

4. Include older adults in planning and designing programs.   _____

5. Develop program budgets that take into account diverse sources of financial support for the   _____
   older population.

6. Evaluate the effectiveness of practice and programs in achieving intended outcomes for   _____
   older adults.

7. Apply evaluation and research findings to improve practice and program outcomes.   _____

8. Advocate and organize with the service providers, community organizations, policymakers, and   _____
   the public to meet the needs and issues of a growing aging population.

9. Identify the availability of resources and resource systems for older adults and their families.   _____

10. Assess and address any negative impacts of social and health care policies on practice with   _____
    historically disadvantaged populations.

Comments_____

_____

_____

NRH1/24/05

edge the contributions of Patricia J. Volland, MSW, MBA, principle investigator of the Practicum Partnership Program (PPP) and vice president, New York Academy of Medicine; Frances P. Lawrance, Social Work Program officer, PPP Coordinating Center, New York Academy of Medicine; and the principle investigators of the PPP demonstration sites: Hunter College/Brookdale Center on Aging: Joann Ivry, PhD, and Rose Dobrof, DSW; University at Albany, State University of New York: Anne E. Fortune, PhD; University of California at Berkeley: Andrew Scharlach, PhD, and Barrie Robinson, MSSW; University of Houston: Virginia Cooke Robbins, MSW; University of Michigan: Ruth Dunkle, PhD, and Lily Jarman-Reisch, MSW; Partners in Care Foundation: June Simmons, LCSW, and JoAnn Damron-Rodriguez, PhD. The author also wishes to acknowledge Nadine P. Gartrell, PhD, Coordinating Center program officer, New York Academy of Medicine.

REFERENCES

American Association of Colleges of Nursing and the John A. Hartford Foundation Institute for Geriatric Nursing. (2000). *Older adults: Recommended baccalaureate competencies and curricular guidelines for geriatric nursing care.* New York: Hartford Institute and the American Association of Colleges of Nursing (AACN).

American Geriatrics Society. (2000). Core competencies for the care of older patients: Recommendations of the American Geriatrics Society. *Academic Medicine, 75*(3), 252–255.

Arkava, M. L., & Brennan, E. C. (Eds.). (1976). *Competency-based education for social work: Evaluation and curriculum issues.* New York: Council on Social Work Education.

Bandura, A. (1997). *Self-efficacy: The exercise of control.* New York: Freeman Press.

Bennett, J. M., & Sneed, J. (1999). Practice competencies for entry-level professionals in the field of aging. *Educational Gerontology, 25,* 305–315.

Berkman, B., Dobrof, R., Harry, L., & Damron-Rodriguez, J. (1997). Social work. In S. M. Klein (Ed.), *A national agenda for geriatric education: White papers* (pp. 53–85). New York: Springer.

Bogo, M., Raskin, M., & Wayne, J. (2002). *Thinking out of the box: Developing new approaches for field education.* New York: Field Consortium.

Browne, C. V., Braun, K. L., Mokuau, N., & McLaughlin, L. (2002). Developing a multisite project in geriatric and/or gerontological education with emphases in interdisciplinary practice and cultural competence. *The Gerontologist, 42*(5) 698–704.

Carraccio, C., Wolfsthal, S. D., Englander, R., Ferentz, K., & Martin, C. (2002). Shifting paradigms: From Flexner to competencies. *Academic Medicine, 77*(5), 361–367.

Chapin, R., & Cox, E. O. (2001). Changing the paradigm: Strengths-based and empowerment-oriented social work with frail elders. *Journal of Gerontological Social Work, 34*(3/4) 165–181.

Cuzzi, L. C., Holden, G., Chernack, P., Rutter, S., & Rosenberg, G. (1997). *Research in Social Work Practice, 7,* 404–414.

Dalton, B., & Wright, L. (1999). Using community input for the curriculum review process. *Journal of Social Work Education, 35*(2), 275–288.

Damron-Rodriguez, J. A., Lawrance, F. P., Barnett, D., & Simmons, J. (n.d.) Developing geriatric social work competencies for field education. *Journal of Gerontological Social Work.*

Damron-Rodriguez, J. A., & Lubben, J. (1994). Multidisciplinary factors in gerontological curriculum adoption in schools of social work. *Gerontology and Geriatric Education, 14*(4), 39–52.

Dore, M., Epstein, B., & Herrerias, C. (1992). Evaluating students' micro practice field performance: Do universal learning objectives exist? *Journal of Social Work Education, 28,* 353–362.

Dorfman, L. T., Holmes, C. A., & Berlin, K. L. (1996). Wife caregivers of frail elderly veterans: Correlates of caregiver satisfaction and caregiver strain. *Family Relations, 45,* 46–55.

Field, L. (2000). Organizational learning: Basic concepts. In G. Foley (Ed.), *Understanding adult education and training* (pp. 159–173). Sydney, Australia: Allen & Unwin.

Fortune, A. E. (1994). Field education. In F. J. Reamer (Ed.), *The foundations of social work knowledge* (pp. 151–194). New York: Columbia University Press.

Fortune, A. E. (2002). *Model for Geriatric Social Work Practicum Partnership Program.* New York: New York Academy of Medicine.

Gardella, L. G. (1997). Baccalaureate social workers. In R. L. Edwards (Ed.), *Encyclopedia of social work* (19th ed., Vol. 1997, Supplement, pp. 37–46). Washington, DC: NASW Press.

Greene, R., & Galambos, C. (2002). *Social work's pursuit of a common professional framework: Have we reached a milestone? Advancing gerontological social work education.* New York: Haworth Press.

Grimier, A., & Gorey, K. (1998). The effectiveness of social work with older people: A meta-analysis of conference proceedings. *Social Work Research, 22*(1), 60–64.

Hackett, S. (2001). Educating for competency and reflective practice: Fostering a conjoint approach in education and training. *Journal of Workplace Learning, 13*(3), 103–112.

Holden, G., Meenaghan, T., Anastas, J., & Metrey, G. (2002). Outcomes of social work education: The case for social work self-efficacy. *Journal of Social Work Education, 38*(1), 115.

Hudson, R. B. (2003). Emerging crisis: The geriatric care workforce. *Public Policy and Aging Report, 13*(2), 1–2.

Hudson, R. B., Gonyea, J. G., & Curley, A. (2003). The geriatric social work labor force: Challenges and opportunities. *Public Policy and Aging Report, 13*(2), 12–14.

Joint Commission on Accreditation in Healthcare Organizations. (2001). *Comprehensive JCAHO accreditation manual for hospitals: The official handbook.* Oakbrook Terrace, IL.

Koroloff, N. M., & Rhyne, C. (1989). Assessing student performance in field instruction. *Journal of Teaching in Social Work, 3*(2), 3–16.

Lowy, L. (1979). Social work with the aging: The challenge and promise of the later years. New York: Harper & Row.

Lubben, J., Damron-Rodriguez, J. A., & Beck, J. (1992). A national survey of aging curriculum in schools of social work. In J. Mellor & R. Solomon (Eds.), *Geriatric social work education* (pp. 157–171). New York: Haworth Press.

McKinley, R. K., Fraser, R. C., & Baker, R. (2000). Model for directly assessing and improving clinical competence and performance in revalidation of clinicians. *British Medical Journal, 322,* 712–715.

Molinari, V., Kier, F. J., & Kunik, M. E. (2002). Obtaining age-related mental health competency: What is needed? *Educational Gerontology, 28,* 73–82.

Morrow-Howell, N., & Burnette, D. (2001). Gerontological social work research: Current status and future directions. *Journal of Gerontological Social Work, 36*(3/4), 63–81.

Multon, K. D., Brown, S. D., & Lent, R. W. (1991). Relation of self-efficacy beliefs to academic outcomes: A meta-analytic investigation. *Journal of Counseling Psychology, 38,* 53–63.

Naito-Chan, E., Damron-Rodriguez, J., & Simmons, W. J. (2004). *Identifying competencies for geriatric social work practice. Journal of Counseling Psychology, 43*(4), 59–78.

National Association of Social Workers. (1981). *NASW standards for the classification of social work practice* (Policy statement 4). Silver Spring, MD.

O'Hare, T., & Collins, P. (1997). Development and validation of a scale for measuring social work practice skills. *Research on Social Work Practice, 7,* 228–238.

Partners in Care Foundation. (2000). *The Southern California Geriatric Social Work Education Consortium: Executive summary.* Burbank, CA: Author.

Reishch, M., & Jarman-Rohde, L. (2000). The future of social work in the United States: Implications for field education. *Journal of Social Work Education, 36*(2), 201.

Rizzo, V. M., & Rowe, J. (2005). Studies of the efficacy and cost-effectiveness of social work services in aging: A report commissioned by the National Leadership Council [online]. Available on September 1, 2005 at *http://socialwork.nyam.org/pdf/EfficacyFinal_Report.pdf.*

Robbins, L. A., & Rieder, C. H. (2002). The John A. Harford Foundation Geriatric Social Work Initiative. *Journal of Gerontological Social Work, 39,* 71–90.

Rosen, A. L., Zlotnik, J. L., Curl, A. L., & Green, R. G. (2000). *The CSWE/SAGE-SW National Aging Competencies Survey report.* Alexandria, VA: Council on Social Work Education.

Rosen, A. L., Zlotnik, J. L., & Singer, T. (2002). Basic gerontological competence for all social workers: The need to "gerontologize" social work education. *Journal of Gerontological Social Work, 39,* 25–36.

Scharlach, A., Damron-Rodriguez, J., Robinson, B., & Feldman, R. (2000). Educating social workers for an aging society: A vision for the 21st century. *Journal of Social Work Education, 36*(3), 521–538.

Schneider, R. (Ed.). (1984). *Gerontology in social work education: Faculty development and continuing education.* Alexandria, VA: Council on Social Work Education.

Torres-Gil, F., & Bikson Moga, K. (2001). Multiculturalism, social policy and the new aging. *Journal of Gerontological Social Work, 36*(3/4), 13–33.

Vass, A. A. (Ed.). (1996). *Social work competence, knowledge, values and skills.* London: Sage.

ROBYN GOLDEN
MONIKA WHITE

Credentialing Opportunities for Social Workers in Aging

100

This chapter discusses credentialing for social workers with older adults, with an emphasis on care management, as it is the only possible current credentialing opportunity addressing social work with older adults and their families. Following an overview of credentialing is a discussion of the case management knowledge and skills needed to provide services for a growing number of older persons and their families. Social work with older adults, especially with those who are frail and at risk, has become more complex in recent years because of fragmented health and social welfare policies, programs, and services, problematic legal and financial structures, and shrinking public resources. Given this, effective case management skills are critical.

Social workers who work with older adults are present in virtually every long-term care and human services setting and sector and often act as, or call themselves, case or care managers. There is no universal consensus about the definition or distinction between these terms. Many variations and models have evolved over the years to target specific purposes, groups, and settings utilizing the core tasks of case management: assessment care planning, implementation, and monitoring. It is because of the variations in practice and the imprecise use of the terms and their meanings that the question of credentialing surfaces.

Outside of the public sector, social work and nursing are the predominant disciplines among professional case managers working with older adults, yet many who hold these positions have little or no training related to either aging or case management. Accordingly, social workers with training, experience, and certification in case management with older adults are at a premium. Given the generalist training and perspective provided by social work education, a question addressed in this chapter is whether social workers need to be specifically trained and certified to serve the aging population.

CREDENTIALING

Credentialing of human services professionals through licensing or certification is not new. Laws regulating licensing, registration, or statutory credentialing for social work practice have existed since 1964 in every state in the United States as well as the District of Columbia, Puerto Rico, and the U.S. Virgin Islands. These laws control who can practice social work, what services social workers can provide, and which titles social workers can present to the public. A credential is evidence that a practitioner has met minimum standards to provide services to the public.

Another type of credentialing in social work is not a regulation established by law but voluntary certification programs developed by professional organizations. They typically require the applicant to meet the legal regulation requirements of the state as a condition of certification in a specialty area of social work. Licensing or registration establishes the minimum criteria for entry into professional practice, whereas voluntary certification regulates specialty areas of practice.

The development of licensing and other forms of credentialing is relatively recent in social work compared to other professions. At the same time that legal regulation for social work was being debated in California and other states, the newly formed National Association for Social Work (NASW; *http://www.naswdc.org/credentials/specialty/c-swcm.asp*) proposed a certification program for social work practice called the Academy of Certified Social Workers (ACSW). Adopted in 1960, the ACSW became the benchmark of practice certification for practitioners with a master's degree in social work.

NASW SPECIALTY CERTIFICATION

In 1998, NASW conducted a survey of its membership on the subject of certification. Respondents clearly identified the need for—and a strong level of interest in—the establishment of a national certification program in areas of social work specialization. The implementation of NASW's certification program is based on the assumption that certification provides the following benefits for members in today's competitive workplace:

- Enhanced professional and public recognition.
- Increased visibility as specialized social workers.
- Association with a select group of specialized social workers who have attained national distinction.

NASW's credentialing center has more than 20 years of experience developing credentials and certifications for social workers. Its specialty certifications, available to degreed social workers only, provide a vehicle for recognizing social workers who have met national standards and have specialized knowledge, skills, and experience. The NASW is committed to assisting with the process of certifying social workers and working to emphasize the importance of em-

ploying social workers who have specialized training and experience. Although these specialty certifications provide recognition to those who have met national standards for higher levels of experience and knowledge, they are not substitutes for state licenses.

Over the years, the number of credentials to certify specializations has increased and focus on a particular population or a specific type of practice approach or program. Certifications currently available through NASW are in health care; children, youth, and family; alcohol, tobacco, and drugs; school; and case management. The case manager certification, designated C-SWCM (Certified Social Work Case Manager), is of special interest to this chapter. NASW also offers an advanced certificate in case management, the C-ASWCM. To acquire the C-SWCM, social workers must provide evidence of the following:

- Current NASW membership.
- A BSW degree from an institution accredited by the Council on Social Work Education.
- One year and 1,500 hours of paid, supervised, post-BSW work experience.
- An evaluation from an approved supervisor.
- A reference from a BSW or MSW colleague.
- A current BSW-level license or credential.

In addition, candidates must agree to adhere to the NASW Code of Ethics, the NASW Standards for Social Work Case Management, and the NASW Standards for Continuing Professional Education, which are subject to the NASW adjudication process.

Why did NASW create a certification in case management when other sources of certification already exist? NASW members report that many social workers are being required by their employers to become certified in case management by a national professional association. Various settings that are establishing these requirements include large hospital systems, branches of the military, and managed care companies. Because a number of the case management tasks and functions have historically been at the core of social work practice, many NASW members prefer to hold a certification from their own national professional social work association instead of applying for a multidisciplinary case management certification that is not based in social work.

SOCIAL WORK CASE MANAGEMENT

As early as 1992, NASW developed standards for social work case management. As part of the standards, the following definition of social work case management was formulated:

> Social work case management is defined as a method of providing services whereby a professional social worker assesses the needs of the client and the client's family when appropriate. The case manager arranges, coordinates, monitors, evaluates, and advocates for a package of multiple services to meet the specific client's complex needs. Distinct from other forms of case management, social work case management addresses the individual client's biopsychosocial status as well as the program or system in which case management operates. Intervention occurs at both the client and systems levels. (NASW, 1992, p. 5)

Social work case management requires the social worker to develop and maintain a multifaceted relationship with the client. This may include linking the client with systems that provide him or her with needed services, resources, and opportunities and providing the emotional support to enable and facilitate utilization of these services. The social work case manager has the ability to coordinate these different needs with solutions, provide the therapeutic environment to facilitate acceptance of support and assistance, and follow up with monitoring and reassessment activities. Social work case management services may be located in a single agency or across several agencies and settings.

Social work training is especially well suited to case management. The understanding of relationships, family dynamics, human growth and development, as well as broader policy and service systems is fundamental to social work tasks and activities. The combination of macro and micro perspectives distinctive to social work education also supports a case management orientation. Austin and McClelland (1996, p. 258) note the compatibility of social work and case management, stating that "the roles and skills represented in case management clearly represent the *in vivo* application of many long-standing conceptualizations of social work practice: the person-in-environment perspective, the social-interactionist orientation, the systems basis of generalist practice and the social ecological framework."

To date, case management is not considered a profession; it is, instead, a method or approach that is utilized throughout the entire continuum of care, crossing settings, disciplines, populations, providers, communities, and funding streams. Not surprisingly,

every human services profession claims a role in inventing it (White, 2005, p. 202). Social workers often argue that they have been "doing case management" for more than 100 years. Although many of the tasks are, indeed, similar to social work, there are a few distinguishing characteristics. These include an emphasis on coordinating rather than providing direct services and, as noted by Dill (2001, p. 5), "the focus on service episodes and changes in client needs." Dill also points to the multiple objectives case managers attempt to achieve for both the client and the service system (pp. 5–6). Woodside and McClam (2003, p. 293) discuss the themes and challenges case managers face, including "large caseloads, clients with multiple needs, and scarce resources. In addition, they often work with clients who are silent, reluctant, or resistant in a bureaucracy that requires detailed documentation for each interaction."

Case managers must also attend to administrative goals such as utilization and costs of services (Scharlach, Guinta, & Mills-Dick, 2001, p. 8). They often work in restrictive circumstances, without adequate information or resources. To this point, Weissert, Hirth, Chernew, Diwan, and Kim (2003, p. 803) state, "Case managers face a daunting task: They . . . must make up for all the failing of the policies and systems within which they work. They must compensate for inadequate information and work within a variety of limitations."

OTHER CASE MANAGEMENT CERTIFICATION OPTIONS

In addition to the NASW Social Work Case Management Certification, credentialing can be obtained through some 20 other professional case management sources. This section highlights the development of two such opportunities, through the National Academy of Certified Case Managers and the Commission for Case Manager Certification.

An important project set the stage for development of a certification effort and the establishment of the National Academy of Certified Care Managers. This was an attempt to develop national standards for case management. Instead, the 1-year project, funded by a Robert Wood John Foundation grant, resulted in *Guidelines for Case Management Practice Across the Long-Term Care Continuum* (Geron & Chassler, 1994). The guidelines were formulated by a group of 11 case management experts, including social workers, nurses, and researchers. Although now more than 10 years old, the *Guidelines* continue to serve as a foundation for practice, training, and service development in community-based and long-term care case management. Five principles of case management serve as a framework for the development of these guidelines. It is important to note their compatibility and congruence with social work tenets and practice:

1. Respects consumers' rights, values, and preferences.
2. Coordinates all and any type of assistance to meet identified consumer needs.
3. Requires clinical skills and competencies.
4. Promotes the quality of services provided.
5. Strives to use resources efficiently.

The same year these principles were published, the newly established National Academy of Certified Care Managers (NACCM; *www.naccm.net*) utilized them as the foundation for the development of a certification exam that focused on the primary functions of case management as testing domains:

- Assess and identify consumer strengths, needs, concerns, and preferences.
- Establish goals and a plan of care.
- Coordinate and link formal and informal services and resources.
- Manage and monitor the ongoing provision of and need for care.
- Attend to legal, professional, and ethical issues.

The exam was developed under a strict process that involved several hundred professional case managers across the country and a professional testing company. The exam has since been administered to hundreds of experienced case managers from various disciplines, including social workers. NACCM's founding board consisted primarily of social workers and nurses working with older adults. Although not strictly geriatric, the emphasis of the exam questions is on older adults.

The establishment of NACCM was based on several felt needs (Bartelstone, 1999):

- Consumer protection: With the rapid proliferation of case managers, certification can assist consumers and service providers in making a choice when seeking qualified practitioners.
- Multiple parent professions: Case management is not a profession and is performed by individuals from many disciplines. Certification of experience

in, and knowledge of, core functions, tasks, and activities define the case manager.
- Need to establish standards: Exam development for certification purposes requires agreement on tasks, activities, and competency that form at least minimal standards.
- Advance the approach: As more individuals become interested in credentialing, the need for a body of knowledge, education and training, and research will increase.
- Self-regulation: There is no licensing or regulation of case management practice outside of specific professions (e.g., licensed clinical social worker). Certification promotes accountability and provides validation.
- Insurance and liability issues: An increasing number of insurance companies now require some form of case management credentialing for professional liability coverage.

Although a number of case management credentials were already available in the 1990s, they were heavily focused on licensed medical and health care professionals. Both social workers and nurses working with older adults in community-based and long-term care settings recognized the need for certification for professionals with a biopsychosocial background. NASW had not yet developed its case management credential; thus, NACCM offered an opportunity for this type of credential. NACCM offers the Care Manager Certified (CMC) to those qualified individuals who pass the examination. Eligibility requirements include a bachelor's or master's degree with 2 or 4 years, respectively, of full-time supervised care management work as defined by the Academy. This certification validates the core knowledge and skills of the experienced care manager (see *www.naccm.net*). Individuals from a variety of disciplines and settings have earned their CMC and work in diverse community-based, long-term care, and private practice settings.

COMMISSION FOR CASE MANAGER CERTIFICATION

The Commission for Case Manager Certification (CCMC; *http://www.ccmcertification.org/download/Application.pdf*) oversees the administration of the CCM designation to individuals who meet their requirements and pass their examination. The CCMC has the largest number of certified case managers in the country, primarily in nursing, rehabilitation, and health care but also in social work. According to the Commission's Web site, an applicant must be able to perform all six essential activities of case management: assessment, coordination, planning, monitoring, implementation, and evaluation in multiple environments in five of six core components:

1. Processes and relationships.
2. Health care management.
3. Community resources and support.
4. Services delivery.
5. Psychosocial interventions.
6. Rehabilitation case management.

Candidates must have a master's degree, be licensed in their area of educational specialization, and meet practice standards (see *www.ccmcertification.org*; Table 100.1). CCMs work in a variety of settings and serve all populations. The certification is increasingly recognized and preferred by health care and rehabilitation organizations.

CASE MANAGEMENT WITH OLDER ADULTS

In the early 1990s, a number of professional associations and organizations developed standards for the practice of case management specifically in health and aging. These include the American Nursing Association, the National Council on Aging, the National Association for Professional Geriatric Care Managers, and the NASW (Bartelstone & White, 2001). As noted, efforts to hold case managers to those standards through a variety of credentialing activities and organizations emerged, including the Case Management Society of America and the NACCM. In the late 1990s, NASW established its own case management credential for social workers. To date, more than 20 organi-

zations confer certification in case management, most of them in the medical and rehabilitation fields.

Case management, a formal, systematic approach to serving older adults, encompasses identifying problems, developing plans to address them, coordinating the planned services, and following up to ensure effectiveness. It became popular in the late 1970s with the rise of publicly funded, community-based programs for older adults and other populations with long-term disabilities. This movement was not unique to the United States; case management models were developing in other parts of the world as well (Geron, 2000).

In the United States, case management with elders grew dramatically during the 1980s when, in an effort to decrease nursing home costs, states were given the opportunity to apply for waivers from Medicaid to provide alternatives to institutionalization for low-income individuals 65 and over eligible for placement. The private practice and nonprofit sectors broadened the scope of case management by providing the service for a set fee or on a sliding-scale basis.

Credentialing of Social Work Case Management With Older Adults

The authors contend that social workers should have special expertise to perform specific functions such as case management with older adults. The fact that social workers are typically educated to work with the continuum of individual life stages, family dynamics, community organizations, and larger systems may or may not qualify them as geriatric care/case managers. Hackstaff, Davis, and Katz (2004), in their description of a Kaiser Permanente project that integrates behavior change theory into their care management program, emphasize both the level and importance of social work skills in working with a geriatric popula-

TABLE 100.1. Examples of Minimum Requirements for Case Management Certification

Minimum Requirements	NASW	CCMC	NACCM
Bachelor's Degree	BSW	No	Yes
Master's Degree	No	Yes	No
Professional License	No	Yes	No
Experience	1 yr/1,500 hrs	Not stated	4 yrs full-time
Case Management Focus	Social work rehabilitation	Health/medical/ long-term care	Community

tion, especially frail, at-risk elders. The theoretical grounding of social work combined with the broader case management functions has proven to be particularly effective in developing an intervention with this vulnerable patient group (Hackstaff et al., 2004).

On the other hand, an AARP study found that "many [care managers] are licensed . . . social workers, but these licenses do not necessarily guarantee an ability to address a client's financial or legal questions or provide comprehensive knowledge of all service options" (Stone, 2002, n.p.). As the number and proportion of older adults explodes, many social workers are finding themselves without adequate training to deal effectively and professionally with an aging society. Scharlach, Damron-Rodriguez, Robinson, and Feldman (2000, p. 525) have described the need for social workers with gerontological knowledge and skills as "desperate." The need for specialized geriatric training is not unique to social work. A recent study of psychologists whose practice includes at least some older adults found that fewer than 30% had any training in geropsychology and fewer than 20% had participated in an internship or practicum including older adults (American Psychological Association, 2004).

Several other indicators point to the importance of knowledge specific to working with the geriatric population. The California Board of Behavioral Science Examiners, for instance, now requires aging content for continuing education credits. The University of Florida has developed an online geriatric case management program. Other universities are considering similar offerings. Opportunities for dual degrees between programs in social work and gerontology are increasing. Sessions on case management are featured at most health, aging, and social work national meetings and conferences. NASW has also developed an Aging Specialty Practice Section designed to provide content expertise and inform members about current trends and policy issues that impact social work practice and service delivery in the field of aging.

Given these developments, the authors conclude that there is a case for social work certification with an aging emphasis, especially utilizing case management process and functions with the most vulnerable segment of the older population. There are a number of reasons that credentialing as an aging specialist is beneficial:

- The complexity of issues for aging individuals, family, and other caregivers.
- A growing preference by employers.
- Consumer demand.

- Insurance company liability requirements.
- Competition with other disciplines.

Two case examples are used to illustrate social work's case management role in addressing complex client situations.

A case manager in a community senior services settings is working with Mrs. M.

▓ Mrs. M is an 83-year-old, widowed female who lives alone. At the suggestion of Mrs. M's doctor, her daughter contacted me. Mrs. M has early-stage dementia. The physician has notified the Department of Motor Vehicles, so Mrs. M is no longer driving.

The physician and the daughter were concerned about Mrs. M's ability to care for herself. The daughter arranged for Mrs. M to move to an assisted living facility near her, but the day of the move, Mrs. M refused to go. Mrs. M's daughter visited her mother weekly to provide marketing, meal preparation, transportation, and house cleaning, but this arrangement was clearly overwhelming and the daughter's upcoming surgery would make her unavailable to her mother.

It became clear that Mrs. M was not taking her medication and was not eating regularly. After several failed attempts to schedule an in-home visit with Mrs. M, I contacted Adult Protective Service to intervene. Working closely with the APS worker and the daughter, I developed an intervention. The APS worker notified Mrs. M that she was not safe living alone and needed to move to a designated assisted living facility for a 1-week period and would then be reassessed. Mrs. M reluctantly agreed to the temporary move and her daughter transported her that day. In a follow-up telephone call to the daughter, Mrs. M had made a remarkable adjustment to the facility. She is involved in a number of activities and, according to her daughter, is "a new woman." (From J. Rosenblum, Center for Healthy Aging, Santa Monica, CA) ▓

Another example comes from a social work case manager in a physician's office:

▓ The phone rings and Mr. D wants to see me immediately. When he arrives, he gives me a stack of medical bills and explanation of benefits and says, "Help. What do I do with all these bills?" Mr. D's wife, who had been the one that managed the household and the bills, died 1 year ago. Now Mr. D must try to figure out the medical bills for his mentally disabled daughter, and he is struggling. He became so upset that he cancelled her supplemental insurance and is now not sure he should have done so.

We go through the bills one by one and I divide them up. When he leaves, he will need to call the providers of the service and give them the correct insurance information. I talk to him about having help paying the bills and dealing with the insurance. He is agreeable. I make a referral to get him the help and to get together some financial information to see if his daughter might qualify for QMB (a federal program that pays his daughter's Medicare premium and also functions as supplemental insurance). In the interval, I suggest he try to get his daughter back on the HMO he just cancelled. (From R. Felder, Council for Jewish Elderly, Chicago) ▪

Both cases illustrate the need for a wide range of skills and knowledge, including working with family members, physicians, and other providers such as adult protective services; understanding dementia and associated issues of care, insurance, and medical issues; knowledge of local resources such as residential facilities and money management services; and support for and problem solving with family members.

Based on interest, aging will be the next certification to be developed by NASW. This will occur by convening a national work group of seven experts from across the country who will look at criteria that the group feels is essential. They will send these recommendations to the NASW Competence and Certification Commission, which will then develop written criteria for eligibility.

CONCLUSION

Social workers with training and expertise working with older adults and their families are critical in institutional, health care, and home- and community-based settings. Empirical evidence from the social work literature shows that social workers who practice along the continuum of care are effective in ad-

dressing many problems related to aging, such as relieving depression and stress, increasing well-being and effective coping, and coordinating or providing support networks for both older adults and caregivers. In addition, there is some indication that interventions by social workers help delay or prevent nursing home admissions and reduce health care costs (Rizzo, 2003).

As the population ages, the demand for social workers who have the knowledge and skills to serve older adults effectively will increase. Credentialing and/or certification will be a critical factor in demonstrating the viability of social work's role in service delivery and quality of care. It is not a simple solution or conclusion, but like everything else in this complicated yet meaningful arena of social work and aging, credentialing and certification need to be reevaluated over time. The authors look forward to the profession's attempt to address these issues.

REFERENCES

American Psychological Association. (2004). Guidelines for psychological practice with older adults. *American Psychologist, 59*(4), 236–260.

Austin, C. D., & McClelland, R. W. (1996). *Perspectives on case management practice.* Milwaukee, WI: Families International.

Bartelstone, R. S. (1999, November). Working with credentialed geriatric care managers. *Society of Certified Senior Advisors Journal, 5,* 8–11.

Bartelstone, R., & White, M. (2001). Care management credentialing. In C. Cress (Ed.), *Handbook of geriatric care management* (pp. 131–146). Gaithersburg, MD: Aspen.

Dill, A. E. P. (2001). *Managing to care: Case management and service system reform.* Hawthorne, NY: Aldine De Gruyter.

Geron, S. M. (2000). Care management in the United States. In R. Applebaum & M. White (Eds), *Key issues in case management around the globe* (pp. 10–21). San Francisco: American Society on Aging.

Geron, S. M., & Chassler, D. (1994). *Guidelines for case management practice across the long-term care continuum.* Bristol, CT: Connecticut Community Care.

Hackstaff, L., Davis, C., & Katz, L. (2004). The case for integrating behavior change, client-centered practice and other evidence-based models into geriatric care management. *Social Work in Health Care, 38*(3), 1–19.

National Association of Social Workers. (1992). *NASW standards for social work case management.* Washington, DC: Author.

Rizzo, V. R. (2003). *Studies of the efficacy and cost-effectiveness of social work in aging: A report commissioned by the National Leadership Coalition.* New York: New York Academy of Medicine.

Scharlach, A., Damron-Rodriguez, J. A., Robinson, B., & Feldman, R. (2000). Educating social workers for an aging society: A vision for the twenty-first century. *Journal of Social Work Education, 36*(3), 521–538.

Scharlach, A. E., Guinta, N., & Mills-Dick, K. (2001). *Case management in long-term care integration: An overview of current programs and evaluations.* Report for the California Center for Long-term Care Integration. University of California, Berkeley, Center for the Advanced Study of Aging Services.

Stone, R. I. (2002). Geriatric care managers: A profile of an emerging profession. *PPI Data Digest, 82.*

Weissert, W. G., Hirth, R. A., Chernew, M. E., Diwan, S., & Kim, J. (2003). Case management: Effects of improved risk and value information. *The Gerontologist, 43*(6), 797–805.

White, M., & Gundrum, G. (2001). Case management. In C. J. Evashwick (Ed.), *The continuum of long-term care* (3rd ed., pp. 201–214). Albany, NY: Delmar-Thomson Learning.

Woodside, M., & McClam, T. (2003). *Generalist case management: A method of human service delivery.* Pacific Grove, CA: Brooks/Cole-Thomson Learning.

Index

AA. *See* Alcoholics Anonymous
AAAs. *See* Area Agencies on Aging
AAHSA. *See* American Association of Homes and Services for the Aging
Aaron, Henry, 973
AARP. *See* American Association of Retired Persons
AARP Foundation, 834
AARP-NRTA. *See* American Association of Retired Persons and National Retired Teachers Association
Abbeyfield Houses, 687
ABCDE approach, 267
aborigines, Australian, 945–46, 949
abuse, 437–38. *See also specific types of abuse*
academic medical centers, 414
Academy of Certified Social Workers, 522–23, 1066
accessory apartments, 887
accreditation. *See* credentialing
Accreditation Commission for Home Care, Inc. (ACHC), 428
ACL Survey. *See* Americans' Changing Lives Survey
ACMA. *See* American Case Management Association, Inc.
ACS. *See* American Cancer Society
ACSW. *See* Academy of Certified Social Workers
Action for Mental Health (report), 469
active listening, 267, 319
active neglect, 220
activities of daily living, 250, 523, 540, 560, 915
    arthritis sufferers and, 42
    cancer patients and, 11, 13
    cardiovascular disease patients and, 20, 24
    caregiver networks and, 198–99, 200
    colostomy maintenance and, 11
    congregate housing residents and, 696–97
    dementia patients and, 118, 119, 347
    falls and, 43, 44
    fractures and, 44–45

    functional status measures fpr, 742
    geriatric care management and, 448
    home as site of, 84
    home health care and, 424
    instrumental. *See* instrumental activities of daily living
    long–term care and, 870
    the oldest old and, 196, 197
    personal. *See* personal activities of daily living
Activity Card Sort, 83
actual ability, 564
actual disability, 196–97
acupuncture, 210, 261
acute care, 6
    hospitals and, 413–15, 417–18
    postacute care units, 593, 852
    post-event case management, 522
ADA. *See* American Diabetes Association; Americans with Disabilities Act
Adamek, Margaret E., 103, 149–58
Adams, B., 375
Adams, R., 809
Adams, W. L., 512
ADAPs. *See* AIDS Drugs Assistance Programs
Aday, Ronald H., 165–66, 231–40
ADC. *See* adult day care
Addams, Jane, 809, 816
ADEA. *See* Age Discrimination in Employment Act of 1967
adenocarcinoma, 9
adenomatous polyps, 11
ADHC. *See* adult day health care
ADL. *See* activities of daily living
Adler, I., 479
Administration on Aging
    adult protective services and, 553, 555
    as advocacy agency, 820
    aging services vertical integration and, 496, 879